ENCYCLOPEDIA
of CONTEMPORARY
CHRISTIAN
MUSIC

Mark Allan Powell

HENDRICKSON PUBLISHERS

© 2002 by Mark Allan Powell
Hendrickson Publishers, Inc.
P. O. Box 3473
Peabody, Massachusetts 01961–3473

ISBN 1-56563-679-1

Printed in the United States of America

First Printing — August 2002

Library of Congress Cataloging-in-Publication Data

Powell, Mark Allan, 1953–
    Encyclopedia of contemporary Christian music   /   by Mark Allan Powell.
       p. cm.
    Includes bibliographical references (p.   ).
    ISBN 1-56563-679-1 (alk. paper)
    1. Contemporary Christian musicians—Biography—Dictionaries.   I. Title.
    ML102.C66 P68 2002
    782.25—dc21
                        2002008473

For Melissa

"Preach the gospel. Use words only as necessary."
St. Francis of Assisi

"That which is too silly to say can always be sung."
Voltaire

"Why should the devil have all the good music?"
Martin Luther

"The purpose of all music is to glorify God."
J. S. Bach

"The medium is the message."
Marshall McLuhan

"Make something religious, and you make it irrelevant."
Bob Dylan

"I learned more from a three-minute record than I ever did in school."
Bruce Springsteen

"We weren't really sure what to do, but we figured it would be good
to stop cussing in our songs and to sing about God."
Daniel Davison (of the hardcore band Luti-Kriss,
after the entire group got saved at an Assemblies of God church meeting)

"I understand that the kind of music we do isn't going to hit huge. That's okay.
This is what we like, and we don't want to change it."
Myk Porter (of Six Feet Deep)

"It's not like these albums are meant to be theological treatises. They're meant to be fun."
Michael Roe (of The Seventy Sevens)

"Rock and roll is ridiculous, if you think about it."
Tony Palacios (of Guardian)

"Just gimmie a guitar, three chords, and the truth."
Bono (of U2)

Preface

I thought about being a rock star. In fact, at one point there were only two things standing between me and success: 1) looks; and 2) talent. I figure if I had *either* I could have made it. Lacking both, I went into theology and landed a less exotic career as a professor. The one good thing about being a professor is that you slave for six years and then get something special called a sabbatical. It's like the Jacob and Laban deal in the Bible, except they don't let you sleep with two women. Instead, they give you a year off to pursue a special research project.

So one could say that this whole thing started as a bit of a scam, by which I figured out how I could get my school to *pay* me to sit around and listen to rock and roll for a year. Yeah, and it worked, too! Except that, eventually, I did have to write the thing. Or one could view it as a legitimate research project. Perhaps I'm just buying my own hype, but I see this book as making a worthy contribution in two areas: a) the history of popular music; and b) the history of Christianity.

My school probably has little interest in the first, but I have. Let's face it—rock and roll (and by that I mean the whole enterprise, not just Christian rock) has done a lot more for the good of humanity in the last thirty-plus years than all the theologians on the planet. This music has brought so much joy into so many people's lives, while also challenging, stimulating, involving, and inspiring them in undefinable and remarkable ways. Martin Luther thought music was the second best of all God's gifts, behind theology—but then he'd never heard the Beatles. All I'm saying is, rock and roll is a beautiful thing, and it is my contention that the history of rock cannot be understood without consideration of the square pegs and misfits who inhabit the pages of this book. They have made far more significant contributions than is generally acknowledged. And, at times, they have made some really, really fine music.

As for the second point, I actually do view this book as a work of church history. I doubt it will ever get catalogued in that section of any library, but it should. The whole phenomenon that has given birth to an identifiable Christian music subculture/industry/empire is noteworthy. I think it is one of the more intriguing aspects of late-twentieth-century American Christianity, and yet it remains largely unexamined. About five years ago, I wandered into a large Christian bookstore and was struck by the fact that almost a quarter of the floor space was given to music (cassettes/CDs/etc.). Intrigued, I asked the manager where their books on contemporary Christian music were. Books? I thought there would be a section, or a shelf. No. Not a single volume. My professional instincts as a scholar were aroused—if this stuff is so big, why isn't anyone writing about it? Of course, there are testimony type books sometimes written by the artists themselves, but why aren't the church's theological leaders more invested in what seems to have captured the attention of its people?

Ah, now we hit upon what really draws me to this subject, more so even than the points above. I think what clinched it for me was a letter from the head of one of this country's largest theological publishing companies. I had suggested a book on the phenomenon of contemporary Christian music (not necessarily to be written by me) and submitted a summary and outline of what such a volume could entail. In his reply, he indicated this seemed a waste of theological time and talent, and said, "Frankly, I do not understand how you can think that people like Amy Grant and Andraé Crouch are so important when I have never even heard of them." Well, here's my response to that: first, it is somewhat shocking that a major religious publishing house can be run by someone so out of touch as to have never even heard the names of two such prominent religious figures. But, second, it is simply astonishing that such a person would assume something cannot possibly be important if she or he does not know about it.

I *hate* that kind of elitism. I regard the persons in this book as amateur theologians whose perspectives and insights on life and faith are every bit as valid as those of any Harvard professor or Rhodes scholar. That, I hope they realize, is why I approach their work in a critical vein. It is because I take them seriously. These are real people, attempting to articulate their experiences in the church and in the world, often with a vulnerability that scholars are trained to conceal. They offer no feigned neutrality, no illusion of dispassionate inquiry. And it does not bother me that these poets lack the proper nuances of reflection or expression taught within the guild. Jesus was a carpenter, and Peter, a fisherman. Only Paul was a scholar, and he is generally the most boring of the three.

I write as an outsider, with whatever benefits and deficits that brings. I don't actually know any of the people mentioned in this book. I am not part of the contemporary Christian music academy in any explicit way. I've approached the book as a theologically-informed researcher and reporter—as a journalist, really. The folks at *CCM* and *HM* magazines were kind enough to open their libraries to me and to allow me access to a wealth of materials. Erick Nelson and Doug Van Pelt read portions of the manuscript and offered valuable corrections and comments. Most of all, Hendrickson Publishers deserves the praise of both church and society for having the insight to believe in a costly project like this and the commitment to see it through. To personify that acknowledgment, Shirley Decker-Lucke is really the one who got the job done. She is an excellent editor and just seems to be a good person. Oh, and of course I should thank the good people at Trinity Lutheran Seminary who granted me the sabbatical and who do in fact support and even encourage my unconventional instincts—apparently out of a strong faith that God will ultimately keep me in line and bring something useful out of the odd meanderings.

Why write a book like this? Because when people do splendid things, their deeds ought to be remembered. And, sometimes, when people do ridiculous things, those things should be remembered as well. The categories are not mutually exclusive, of course, and there is plenty of the splendid and the ridiculous in the pages that follow. So, this book is my tribute to some people I don't know who have made life more meaningful and more pleasant for me. A lot of people could have done it better than I, but I did the best I could and here it is. Everyone I know thinks this was some kind of fluke or midlife prove-you're-still-hip project for me, and they hope I will get back to doing something respectable soon. Hmmm. . . . Well, no doubt it *was* what they suspect, but I still regard it as the most important thing I've ever done. I've waited sixteen books to dedicate a volume to the most important person in my life, hoping I'd produce one worthy of the inscription. This isn't quite that, but I'm getting older and I figure it's the best I'll ever do. So I dedicate this volume to my wife, Melissa, for whom my love and devotion is overwhelming, if not idolatrous. It's just you and Jesus, dear: with all my heart, and all my soul, and all my mind—forever.

Introduction

This book provides alphabetical listings of artists associated with contemporary Christian music. For the first time anywhere, an attempt is being made to present such data as personnel lists and discographies for these artists, along with essays that provide biographical information and critical summaries of their work. The book is fairly exhaustive in its treatment of performers associated with contemporary Christian music and, as such, provides a comprehensive treatment of the phenomenon itself.

They're all here: the saints, the pilgrims, the pious, the outcasts, the hypocrites, the prophets, the heretics, and the martyrs; they're all here in their earthly and spiritual glory. You'll read about miracles and scandals, about incredible sacrifices and greedy exploitation. You can trace the early gospel influences on some of rock and roll's biggest stars or explore the (sometimes temporary) midcareer detours of spiritual converts. You can find out what happened to a lot of folk now regarded as has-beens in the world at large, and you can also read about the incredible productivity of an impressive number of never-weres, folk who have labored in obscurity for decades, producing an impressive and occasionally brilliant body of little-known material.

Rolling Stone magazine refers to contemporary Christian music as "a parallel universe." That label rightly indicates that we are talking about a distinct world analogous to the realm of popular music in general. Thus, contemporary Christian music encompasses a wide variety of styles and genres. There is Christian rock, but there is also Christian country, Christian folk, Christian new wave, Christian punk, Christian death metal, Christian gangsta rap, and everything else imaginable. But one should not think that these styles simply mirror the general market or that the Christian artists are just creating Christian versions of whatever is hot in the world at large. In general, the Christian music world has an integrity of its own. Some artists are more creative and original than others, but the stylistic varieties tend to develop in a manner that is more *parallel* to the general market than simply reflective of it. In a few instances (a capella groups, third wave ska, rapcore) the Christian artists have even been in the forefront, with knowledgeable general market performers copping from them. *Rolling Stone* agrees: "The top Christian-pop artists aren't any more derivative than, say, 30 artists randomly selected from *Billboard*'s Top 100 in a given week."

If there is one great misconception regarding contemporary Christian music—aside from the idea that it is limited to a particular style or is necessarily derivative—it may be that the music is definitively religious. The perception is understandable, but it does not hold true: the divide between what gets called Christian music and popular music in general is not drawn with regard to what is religious and what is secular. As it turns out, a great deal of contemporary Christian music is completely secular and, of course, a fair amount of general market popular music is at least tangentially religious. Christian music artists do not just sing about God and church and Jesus and the Bible. They also write and sing songs about romance and the day their dog died and how cool their new car is. In quite a few instances (perhaps about 25%), the material labeled contemporary Christian and that labeled general market would be indistinguishable—if the tapes got mixed up or sent to the wrong radio stations, no one would ever know the difference. This, of course, begs the question as to why there should be a parallel universe in the first place.

What Is Contemporary Christian Music?

Joe Bob Briggs (America's self-proclaimed Drive-In Movie Critic) once defined contemporary Christian music as "bad songs written about God by white people." We're going to adopt a somewhat broader definition in this book, which can be understood only in light of the phenomenon's historical development.

Contemporary Christian music came into existence as a recognizable entity during the Jesus movement revival of the late '60s and early '70s. Artists like **Children of the Day, Andraé Crouch and the Disciples, Phil Keaggy, Love Song, Barry McGuire, Larry Norman,** and **2nd Chapter of Acts** began singing songs about Jesus that reflected the character of that revival and of their own transformed lives. The music was called Jesus music back then and, critically, it is probably more appreciated now than at the time. The simplicity and, indeed, naiveté of the songs can be charming, and the zeal with which they are delivered is inspiring. One would be hard-pressed to find another instance in popular music in which the performers *cared* as much about what they were doing as these young Jesus freaks. Of course, the production standards were terrible and the native talent of the artists sometimes left something to be desired, . . . but these people really did believe their records were going to change the world, and *that* is something difficult to capture in a studio. And, for hundreds of thousands of people, their records *did* change the world—a fact seldom noticed in either musical or ecclesiastical histories.

Contemporary Christian music, then, did not develop out of traditional or southern gospel. The Jesus music pioneers were for the most part completely ignorant of those forms (Crouch is an obvious exception). Rather, it developed out of rock and roll, as young musicians who were excited about Christ began writing faith songs in the only musical idiom available to them. But why did these Jesus music stars form their own network, separate from the popular music industry? I can think of three reasons: 1) there were simply too many of them. The revival produced hundreds of Jesus music bands. A few token Jesus songs made their way into the Top Forty, but DJs were prepared only to sample the onslaught, not to give it full control. This is understandable apart from any prejudice against Christianity. If, following James Brown's "Say It Loud, I'm Black and I'm Proud," hundreds of African American artists had all begun recording songs about how wonderful it is to be black, mainstream radio stations would not have played very many of them—not because they were racist, but because in the *general* market, songs that celebrate the special interests of a particular subgroup are by definition exceptional. 2) For all its joy and festivity, the Jesus movement revival had a dark side, an apocalyptic spirit that encouraged isolationism and mistrust. The Jesus people didn't want to sign contracts with unbelievers, lest they find themselves in the employ of the Antichrist. 3) Most of the music lacked widespread appeal apart from appreciation of its ideology. In this regard, the strength of Jesus music (and of much contemporary Christian music to follow) was also its weakness. Precisely because the music connected so well with its target audience, it failed to garner much appreciation from those on the outside. For those who were "into" Jesus, the Christian music from this period remains some of the greatest music of all time; but for those who weren't, it just doesn't do the trick.

By the '80s, the special-interest network that Jesus music had spawned had developed into a multimillion-dollar industry. Contemporary Christian music had its own magazines, radio stations, and award shows. The Jesus movement revival was over: some say it morphed into the Religious Right; others (including this author) contend that it was devoured (destroyed) by that aggressor. In any case, the world of Christian music was now less beleaguered. Big budgets and high production standards came into play, and artists like **DeGarmo and Key, Amy Grant, Petra,** and

Stryper came to define Christian music in radically different terms. The whole point, now, seemed to be that the music *was* just as good as anything the world could churn out and, indeed, *could* be appreciated on its own merits apart from any particular belief system. Often, these claims were true, and yet the music still did not get much airplay within the general market. Why not? The constant contention of the Christian artists was that this was due to a censorship born of ideological bigotry: Christian artists were persecuted for their faith by being blacklisted from general market radio stations and record racks. Many artists found they could not get past this impasse even when they recorded completely nonreligious songs (Grant is an obvious exception).

It is certain that such censorship sometimes did (and still does) occur. Music industry personnel and station programmers confirm (always off the record) that some radio stations had (and sometimes still have) unofficial policies against playing music by "any artist known to be a Christian." I asked one such programmer the rationale for such a policy. The reply: "Christianity is not cool. If people hear a Christian singer on our station, they will think we're not cool. It's as simple as that." Such an attitude goes a long way toward explaining the continued existence of contemporary Christian music as a parallel universe, as an entity that needs to exist to grant a forum for artists who are otherwise denied participation in the music business for reasons having nothing to do with the quality of their work.

But there is more to this censorship thing, and I think much (probably most) of the time, the bias is not against Christianity per se but, more legitimately, against any attempt to co-opt the music field for promotional purposes. A lot of Christian music is perceived (rightly or wrongly) as propaganda—as an attempt by a special interest group to gain free advertising for their cause. It is perceived this way not only by radio station programmers and music critics but also by the great majority of music fans (to whom the programmers and critics are accountable). Let us imagine for a moment that the Goodrubber Tire Company were to put together a rock band to promote their products—and let us assume that the band turned out to be one of the tightest, most competent, and indeed creative groups on the scene. My guess is that if they made a whole album of songs glorifying Goodrubber tires, they would get very little airplay on most radio stations, even if the songs were very good songs and even if they were played exceptionally well. But what if they made an album of secular party songs and love ballads, with only one tire song at the very end? Wouldn't their non-tire songs get some airplay? Maybe—but probably not. Once news about the band got around, there would be a critical and commercial backlash against the sneaky tire salesmen that would overshadow any appreciation of the music on its own terms.

In the '90s, things got a lot more complicated. With the growth of alternative rock and the viability of marketing through independent labels, many Christian artists rebelled against the stereotypes of their industry. Of course, there had been radicals and rebels all along **(T Bone Burnett, The Choir, Daniel Amos, LSU,** the **Seventy Sevens),** but now these increased exponentially until it became commonplace to hear a group say, "We are just Christians in a band—we're not *a Christian band.*" What they usually meant was that they did not want to be confined to the parallel universe of the Christian music subculture (or *ghetto* as it was increasingly called). In a few cases this seemed to work, but in far more it didn't, and the we're-not-a-Christian-band groups ended up with few fans outside the Christian music scene. By the turn of the millennium, a distinction was often made between Christian performers who pursue their music as *ministry* and those who view it as *art.* The distinction is of course arbitrary and flawed (the two need not be mutually exclusive), but discussion of the labels and categories helped some Christian music stars grapple with their identity crisis. Quite a few artists in this book make it clear that they view music as a means to an end. They view themselves primarily as ministers who merely use music as a medium for conveying evangelistic or edifying messages to the world. Many others, however, insist that they do not set out to create Christian music at all. They are simply artists creating music that is true to who they are, but, because they are Christians, the songs that are most true to who they are sometimes do end up revealing the faith that informs their lives.

It is usually with regard to the latter artists that the whole parallel universe scheme comes off as unnecessary and somewhat tragic. Artists like **Adam Again, Mark Heard,** the **Lost Dogs, Starflyer 59,** and the **Vigilantes of Love** do not at all fit the tire salesmen paradigm described above, but they have often suffered from a sort of guilt by association that stereotypes of Christian music foist upon them. Indeed, when someone does manage to gain a foothold in each world, he or she often gets pegged as a crossover artist: **Jars of Clay, MxPx, P.O.D.,** and **Sixpence None the Richer** are viewed as Christian artists who have crossed over into the general market, while **Creed** and **Collective Soul** are considered to be general market artists who have crossed over into the Christian realm. But in either case, *overlap* would be a better word than *crossover.* Some artists simply have a broad enough appeal to earn and maintain fans on both sides of the artificial divide.

So matters of definition are difficult and confused. Still, in putting together this book, I had to decide (with apologies to Bob Seger) "who to leave in, who to leave out." Which artists qualify as performers of contemporary Christian music?

First, as for the word *contemporary:* the term *contemporary* Christian music was coined as a euphemism for Christian *rock* music back in the days when many Christians could not bring themselves to admit that they were listening to the supposedly demonic sounds of rock and roll. Thus, by definition, the genre is distinct from traditional gospel (the politically correct term for what most people still call black gospel) and southern gospel. Books the size of this one could (and probably should) be developed for those genres as well, but only a smattering of traditional or southern gospel artists appear here (cited mainly for their role as influences). Likewise, there is no discussion of Charlotte Church's operatic renditions or of Paul Manz's organ fugues, though these would certainly have to be considered examples of contemporary Christian music in any literal sense of the phrase. We're talking about Christian pop music, loosely defined.

The harder question is how one considers whether the music is Christian. The problem has vexed the Christian music industry for some time as it grapples with such questions as "what records should be sold in Christian bookstores?"; "what songs should be eligible for Christian Dove awards?"; and so on. Two approaches to this problem have been proposed, neither of which works. I follow a third proposal (my own), which does.

The first proposal is that Christian music be defined in terms of *content,* as music that deals in an obvious way with matters explicitly related to Christianity. This is pretty much the official position of the Gospel Music Association, which in the late '90s adopted the following definition for gospel music: "music in any style whose lyric is substantially based upon historically orthodox Christian truth contained in or derived from the Holy Bible; and/or an expression of worship of God or praise for his works; and/or testimony of relationship with God through Christ; and/or obviously prompted and informed by a Christian worldview." Such a definition is fraught with difficulties. For one thing, it pretty much eliminates the possibility of there being such a thing as Christian instrumental music, wiping out a rather large subgenre of the field. It further encourages endless theological disputation as to what might or might not fit the grade: Why, exactly, does a song about a woman regretting an abortion qualify as Christian when a song about a woman wanting her husband to kiss her does not? Worst of all, a *content* definition (this one or any other) necessarily presents Christianity as merely a facet of one's life, as a compartmentalized religious or spiritual aspect of who one is. But one of the central claims of Christianity is that the faith is holistic, transforming the entire being and affecting every thought and action. Christians who actually believe what Christianity teaches will claim that everything they do (including every song they write or sing) reflects who they are as Christians and, accordingly, will be insulted by the notion that only the overtly religious songs reflect this. As rock critic Steve Turner puts it, "I am a Christian when I sleep or enjoy a bath, pull faces, eat dinner, and all the other things that humans do. Jesus wasn't more the Son of God when he was on the cross than when he ate and drank with his friends. He didn't have thirty years of a secular life and then turn into someone spiritual." Of course, many pundits would also note that the Gospel Music Association has never actually followed any standard similar to that which their stated definition was intended to describe. The Doobie Brothers and the Rolling Stones were never nominated for Dove awards for stellar material that would have met the criteria; other artists were presented with awards for songs that probably didn't (e.g., **Michael W. Smith**'s "A Place in This World").

A second suggestion is artist- or author-defined and holds simply that Christian music is music made by Christians. Of course, this would broaden things considerably, since a great many artists in the general market who are in no way associated with the Christian music scene may actually be Christians. And a problem immediately arises as to whether it is the faith of the performer or of the composer that is to be determinative. If Michael McDonald, who is known to be a Christian, writes a nonreligious song like "You Belong to Me" and Carly Simon sings it, is her version of the song now to be considered an example of Christian music—apart from any knowledge of her own faith stance? In any case, such a potentially broad definition may also run aground over quibbles as to just what qualifies an artist (or composer) as Christian. Anyone who has been baptized and who hasn't formally renounced the faith? Or only those who go to church regularly, or who show evidence of a vibrant relationship with Christ, or who espouse orthodox doctrine? And just who gets to make *those* determinations? Quite a few fundamentalists claim that Roman Catholics are not Christians, but a book on contemporary Christian music that excludes **John Michael Talbot** is pretty unthinkable. And then Harold Bloom, in his history of religion in America, claims that all the fundamentalists (including Southern Baptists and Pentecostals) have actually separated themselves from historic Christianity and should be viewed as adherents of another (gnostic) religion. Personally, I think such distinctions are ludicrous, but they just go to show the problematic character of ever defining Christian music as "any music that is written or performed by Christians."

What I propose is that we define contemporary Christian music exactly the same way we define all other genres. Such labels are always audience-driven and are based unapologetically on perception, not content or intent. If I were writing a book on punk rock, I would find out what people who call themselves fans of punk rock like to listen to. There would no doubt be squabbles among such fans as to who did or didn't deserve the label, but if large numbers of punk rock fans told me they considered a group to be punk, I wouldn't really care if someone else—even members of the band itself—insisted that they weren't. The thing with labels is, we never get to choose them for ourselves. And such labels never describe everything that a person or group is—they only indicate some aspect of what some people see.

If I had been hired by the Gospel Music Association to come up with a definition for contemporary Christian music, I would have proposed the following:

> Contemporary Christian music is music that appeals to self-identified fans of contemporary Christian music on account of a perceived connection to what they regard as Christianity.

So far, that agency hasn't employed my services. But for the purposes of this book, I include in my consideration of contemporary Christian music whatever large numbers of self-identified fans of contemporary Christian music consider to fit the genre. In actual fact, such perceptions seem to be based either on professions of Christian faith by the artist or on perceived Christian content in the music itself. I know of no instance where at least one of those two factors is not present, and in the majority of cases, both may be. But most self-identified contemporary Christian music fans seem to think that material by Christian artists like **Bruce Cockburn** or **Cliff Richard** qualifies as belonging to the genre even when the lyrics to the songs are not overtly religious or spiritual. They also tend to put into the genre music by artists whose personal faith convictions remain unknown **(Sounds of Blackness, Simple Minds)** when the songs themselves consistently seem to deal with faith-oriented topics. There are, of course, many questionable cases, and artists who claim that they don't want to be known as Christian bands **(Collective Soul, Creed)** sometimes get put into the mix regardless. On borderline cases, where I'm not sure what to do, I have followed the example of *The New Rolling Stone Encyclopedia of Rock and Roll,* which faced a similar dilemma in deciding which artists qualify as legitimate rock and roll acts. Those editors decided that "it is in the nature of rock and roll to err on the side of inclusion." I submit that it is in the nature of Christianity to do the same.

That said, space limitations prevent consideration of all but a smattering of minor artists and independent releases. I have tried to include enough of these to provide a representative sampling of what the Christian music field has to offer, but for the most part only those artists who have received considerable media exposure receive listings.

How This Book Was Written

This volume is the result of about seven years of research, including a year and a half of full-time work during which I took a sabbatical from my regular job and employed a number of student assistants. The first thing we did was gather an enormous data bank of material from media associated with Christian music. Every article, interview, review, or news reference from all issues of the following periodicals was copied and filed by artist name:

- *CCM* (formerly *Contemporary Christian Music*), began publishing 1978.
- *The CCM Update,* began publishing 1987.
- *Cornerstone,* began publishing 1971.
- *Harmony,* began publishing 1975; ceased 1977.
- *HM* (formerly *Heaven's Metal*), began publishing 1985.
- *Release,* began publishing 1990.
- *7ball,* began publishing 1995.
- *Shout,* began publishing 1995; ceased 1996.
- *True Tunes News,* began publishing 1989; switched to electronic format 1995.
- *Visions of Gray,* began publishing 1996; ceased 2001.

Other periodicals and underground newspapers (including *The Activist, Cutting Edge, Harvest Rock Syndicate, Hollywood Free Paper, Notebored, Renaissance, Right On!,* and *The Truth*) were accessed to the extent that copies could be obtained.

The archives of the following electronic publications were also plundered mercilessly, with every page of the on-line materials being printed and added to the files:

- *Bandoppler* (www.bandoppler.com). No longer active.
- *Christian Music* (www.christianmusic.com)
- *Christian Music* at *about.com* (http://christianmusic.about.com)
- *Christian Music Review Headquarters* (www.christianmusic.org)
- *CMCentral* (www.cmcentral.com)
- *Gospel City* (www.gospelcity.com)
- *Gospel Flava* (www.gospelflava.com)
- *Jesus Freak Hideout* (www.jesusfreakhideout.com)
- *Jesus Music* (www.one-way.org/jesusmusic)
- *The Lighthouse Electronic Magazine* (www.tlem.org). No longer active.
- *Musicforce* (www.musicforce.com)
- *The Phantom Tollbooth* (www.tollbooth.org)
- *Real Magazine* (www.realmagazine.com)
- *Solid Rock Radio* (www.solidrockradio.com)
- *True Tunes* (www.truetunes.com)
- *TSRocks* (www.tsrocks.com)

To these were added printouts from individual artist or label websites.

The entries for the volume are based largely on material drawn from these sources, in addition to information provided in the packaging of the recordings themselves (e.g., liner notes, album covers), information provided by record companies and artist management firms (e.g., press releases), and in some cases information provided through direct contact with the artists or with persons close to them. Information for the discographies and personnel lists was typically obtained the old-fashioned way, by sifting through enormous piles of records, tapes, and CDs and copying the data on an item-by-item basis. Both *HM* and *CCM* magazines made their music libraries available to me for this purpose. Information for the critical essays tended to be drawn from the files of periodical literature, though it is important to note that I have personally listened to about eighty-five percent of the albums discussed in this book.

Some of these sources, of course, are more reliable than others. I have had to make judgment calls with regard to conflicting reports. Where I have erred, I would like to be corrected. At times, all of my sources have failed me, and significant information is lacking. While it is embarrassing to admit to such ignorance, it seems better to include incomplete entries than to omit completely those artists for whom my knowledge is less than satisfying. Again, I would appreciate hearing from readers who are able to fill such gaps.

Key to the Entries

The listings may include the following elements, in order:

• Name

Artists are of two types: soloists and groups. Soloists are alphabetized by the first letter of their last name (Geoff Moore under *M*). Groups are alphabetized by the first letter of the first key word in their name (The Waiting under *W*). When the name of an individual and a group are combined, the listing is usually found under the last name of the individual (Andraé Crouch and the Disciples under *C*). Numerals are treated as though they were spelled out (4 Him under *F-O-U-R*).

• Personnel

For groups, a list of personnel is offered, indicating names of members and their primary roles in the band. Et al. will indicate additional contributors who are not named. The following abbreviations are used: *acc.*—accordion; *bgv.*—background vocals; *DJ*—disc jockey; *dulc.*—dulcimer; *elec.*—electronics; *gtr.*—guitar; *harm.*—harmonica; *kybrd.*—keyboards; *mand.*—mandolin; *perc.*—percussion; *prog.*—programming; *sax.*—saxophone; *synth.*—synthesizers; *tromb.*—trombone; *trump.*—trumpet; *voc.*—vocals. The original lineup of the group (on their first release) is given first, followed by a double slash (//). After the double slash, changes in personnel are noted in chronological order. Parenthetical dates indicate additions (+) and departures (-). N.B.: departure and addition dates are geared to the discography, indicating which personnel perform as official group members on which projects (ignoring compilations of previously released material and other such anomalies). If a group released albums in 1983, 1984, and 1985 and one member left in 1983 after the first album was released, the notation will not read *(- 1983)*—the actual date of departure—but *(- 1984)*—the date of the first release on which the person is no longer listed as a member.

• Discography

A relatively complete discography of the artist's significant recordings usually follows. The label on which the listed products were released can be assumed to remain the same until a new label is given. For some overlap artists who are known primarily for contributions in the general market (Glen Campbell, Aretha Franklin), a more selective discography lists only those works that have been of most interest to contemporary Christian music fans.

• Website

When available, the link to the artist's website is provided. Only official or endorsed sites are indicated. Such sites, of course, become outdated quickly.

- **Essay**

The essay that accompanies each entry is usually biographical and critical. Biographical details are often sketchy in keeping with available data and the relevance of that data for an appreciation of the artist's work. The essay normally focuses on a description of the artist's most significant work and attempts to summarize critical evaluations of specific or overall contributions. In a few cases, comments are also made regarding the theological perspective of the artist; such critique is never intended to promote or disparage anyone's religious beliefs, but to indicate what might be regarded as laudable or as problematic within the Christian music subculture, or within Christianity as a whole. **Boldfaced** names in the essay indicate that there is a separate entry for the artist named.

- **Chart Hits**

A list of the artist's charted Christian Radio Hits, if any, follows each essay. This information is based on charts kept by SoundScan and published weekly in *The CCM Update*. Only information from the CHR (Christian Hit Radio) chart (or its predecessors) is included. This chart is intended to provide the most mainstream data for Christian pop music, analogous to *Billboard*'s Hot 100 chart in the general market. In fact, the chart betrays a rather strong bias toward light pop and adult contemporary material. Data is available only for the years 1978–2001.

- **Awards**

A list of Dove awards and/or Grammy awards received by the artist is also included. The Dove award is presented annually by the Gospel Music Association. The Grammy is given by the National Academy of Recording Arts and Sciences.

A Word about Comparisons

Many of the entries attempt to describe the musical style of an artist by naming other artists who sometimes display a style that is similar at least some of the time or in certain respects. I recognize that many of the artists discussed will be unhappy with this portion of the book because, in my experience, most artists quite understandably do not like their work to be understood with reference to anyone else's. This dissatisfaction seems to be magnified in the Christian music subculture because Christian music sometimes bears the stereotype of being derivative of music in the general market (see above). Indeed, the matter has become a touchy one in the Christian music subculture, and many reviewers for Christian magazines refrain from comparisons altogether or offer them only with the utmost sensitivity, cushioned by caveats and apologies.

Well, I offer lots of comparisons without any apologies at all. Merely to point out an artist's influences, much less to indicate sonic analogies that their work evokes in the minds of certain listeners, in no way implies that the artist's music is derivative or uninspired. If early reviewers had said that the Beatles betrayed the influence of Chuck Berry or that they sounded kind of like Buddy Holly and the Crickets or Gerry and the Pacemakers, that would have been informative and correct without in any way indicating that the band was lacking in talent or creativity. There is a very simple test according to which my readers will be able to tell when my offer of a comparison is intended to imply that an artist lacks creativity. When I wish to suggest that, I do not imply it but state it outright. Search long enough and you will find a sentence similar to this one in the pages that follow: "GROUP XXX copied their style directly from GROUP YYY." And this one: "The song AAA follows GROUP X's song BBB so closely in sound as to amount to artistic if not legal plagiarism" (I leave out the names *here* to avoid the inequity of double condemnation for single offenses). When I say an artist sounds like another artist, I don't mean anything more than the two artists have a similar sound.

A Theological Postscript

It is important to note that the Christian music scene is a subculture not only with regard to popular music in general but also in some respects with regard to Christianity. Though this would begin to change in the '90s, the roots of contemporary Christian music lie within fundamentalism, and a large number of the primary participants continue to be drawn from sects representing Christianity's more conservative factions—and, in particular, from those churches that have their historical origins in America (Baptists, Nazarenes, Pentecostals, Free Methodists, and various nondenominational groups) rather than from those with origins in Europe (Episcopalians, Lutherans, Mennonites, United Methodists, Presbyterians, Roman Catholics). Thus, the image of Christianity expressed in most contemporary Christian music differs from that of historic and global Christianity in key ways. This is evident above all in an emphasis on a personalized, private relationship with Jesus as opposed to a concept of incorporation into a community that relates to Christ corporately. A more literalistic reading of the Bible also attends much of the contemporary Christian music culture, along with the notion that God may speak directly to the individual through Scripture (or other means). Likewise, the pursuit of holiness generally (though not always) stresses matters of personal morality over concern for social justice, and meaningful worship tends to focus on sentiment and piety rather than on liturgical heritage or sacramental experience. These observations are offered descriptively, without judgment, simply to acknowledge that those who know Christianity in alternative forms may find their faith expressions underrepresented in a field that lays claim to the very broad label *Christian*.

Bibliography

The body of literature on contemporary Christian music is sparse. Aside from personal testimonies and other devotional writings by the artists themselves (cited in the individual listings), only a handful of serious studies on the subject have been written. The following list includes the most excellent.

- Brothers, Jeffrey L. *Hot Hits: Christian Hit Radio: 20 Years of Charts, Artist Bios, and More.* Nashville: CCM Books, 1999.

- Di Sabatino, David. *The Jesus People Movement: An Annotated Bibliography and General Resource.* Westport, Conn.: Greenwood, 1999.

- Granger, Thom. *The 100 Greatest Albums in Christian Music.* Nashville: CCM Books, 2001.

- Howard, Jay R. and John M. Streck. *Apostles of Rock: The Splintered World of Contemporary Christian Music.* Lexington: The University of Kentucky Press, 1999.

- Joseph, Mark. *The Rock and Roll Rebellion: Why People of Faith Abandoned Rock Music—And Why They're Coming Back.* Nashville: Broadman & Holman, 1999.

- Thompson, John J. *Raised By Wolves: The Story of Christian Rock and Roll.* Toronto: ECW Press, 2000.

- Turner, Steve. *Hungry for Heaven: Rock 'n' Roll and the Search for Redemption.* Rev. ed. Downers Grove, Ill.: InterVarsity, 1995.

Updates

This book is a historical reference work and, as such, does not intend to compete with resources that are able to offer up-to-the-minute information on the newest works by the latest artist. The goal was to be as complete as possible regarding contemporary Christian music through the year 2001. Depending on reception, updates or subsequent editions may be published. In anticipation of such a likelihood, artists and publicity agents are invited to send materials regarding ongoing or future work to the address at the end of this entry.

In the meantime, readers should be cognizant of the following resources:

- The two best print resources for keeping informed with regard to contemporary Christian music are *CCM* magazine (online at www.ccmmagazine.com) and *HM* magazine (online at www.hmmagazine.com). In general, *CCM* has a more adult-oriented focus on the softer and more mainstream material, while *HM* pursues a youth-oriented take on the harder and edgier material.

- The two best Internet resources have been *True Tunes* (www.truetunes.com) and *The Phantom Tollbooth* (www.tollbooth.org).

Additions, Corrections, and Other Comments

may be directed to mapowell@trinitylutheranseminary.edu
or mailed to:
Mark Allan Powell
Trinity Lutheran Seminary
2199 E. Main Street
Columbus, OH 43209-2334

A

Aaron Jeoffrey (also **Aaron Benward** and **Jeoffrey Benward**)

Aaron Benward, voc.; Jeoffrey Benward, voc. By Aaron Jeoffrey: 1994—
Aaron Jeoffrey (StarSong); 1996—*After the Rain;* 1997—*The Climb.* By
Aaron Benward: 2000—*Imagine* (Sparrow). By Jeoffrey Benward: 1985—
Jeoff Benward (Communication); 1988—*The Redeemer* (ForeFront); 1990—
Set It into Motion; 2000—*Jeoffrey Benward* (Ministry).

A father and son duo formed in 1992, Aaron Jeoffrey craft albums of pleasing pop music replete with traditional evangelical themes. Jeoffrey is a classically trained musician who has worked in Christian music since the '70s. He harmonizes with his adult son Aaron to create a sound that reminds some critics of the Proclaimers or the Rembrandts (or, in Christian music circles, of **Phillips, Craig, and Dean,** for whom the elder Benward has written songs). Their song "He Is" has the almost unique distinction of mentioning by name every one of the sixty-six books of the Bible (cf. "The Statement" by **Transformation Crusade**). The hit "I Go to the Rock" was written by **Dottie Rambo.** Aside from their commitment to specifically Christian evangelism, Aaron Jeoffrey view their ministry goal as being to "show a positive parent/child relationship." The band has participated in events sponsored by Focus on the Family and Promise Keepers. Of their three albums, *The Climb* has a somewhat rougher, more spontaneous feel to it and has generally been the best received by critics.

In 2000, both father and son released solo albums. Aaron's *Imagine* showcases the younger Benward's songwriting skills with soft rock tunes focusing on the general theme of recogniz-ing what is possible through Christ (Philippians 4:13). He was perhaps affected by an event in 1999 in which he, his wife, and their children were unharmed by an accident that caused their truck to flip over four times. Jeoffrey's solo projects fit solidly into the adult contemporary genre, setting tried-and-true notions to familiar light pop sounds. Devotion to God, family, and country are all extolled in a confident baritone that is itself an inspiration. Both Benwards reside in Franklin, Tennessee.

Christian radio hits: By Aaron Jeoffrey: "One Million Reasons" (# 25 in 1994); "I Go to the Rock" (# 19 in 1995); "We All Need" (# 2 in 1996). By Aaron Benward: "Captured" (# 16 in 2000).

Jimmy Abegg (a.k.a. **Jimmy A**)

1991—*Entertaining Angels* (Sparrow); 1994—*Secrets.*

www.jimmyabegg.com

A musician's musician, Jimmy Abegg (b. 1954) from Alliance, Nebraska, was a member of the seminal Christian rock band **Vector,** and he continues to show up on albums by a variety of artists who persuade him to add his trademark swirling guitars to their projects. He has been a member of both **Rich Mullins' Ragamuffin Band** and **Charlie Peacock**'s Acoustic Trio. The solo albums listed above were actually released under the trade name "Jimmy A." Both are stellar presentations of jazz-tinged soft rock, reminiscent at times of Lindsey Buckingham. *CCM* called *Entertaining Angels* "one of the most musically exciting and creative albums of 1991," while also noting, "nothing here even remotely resembles the bulk of (Abegg's) work with Vector and Peacock." The song "Thin But Strong Cord" features both Peacock and **Vince Ebo** on shared vocals. *Secrets,* however, is the more focused and accessible of the two solo projects. Lyrically, Abegg's songs offer not direct statements of faith so much as reflections on life as viewed through Christian eyes. They often come across as simple exhibitions of a man who is in love (with his family, his world, his God, and life in general). Yet he is aware of paradox: "In a perfect world, time would surely linger / like the dawning of the day / and love would last forever"; so begins a song that has as its chorus, "This ain't no perfect world." On another tune, Abegg sings that "love is longing." But at the end of the day, he claims, "I am a simple man / I love my wife, my best friend / Don't need a lot to live / Don't want more than I can give / I believe in what Jesus said / how he dies . . . how he lives." As a composer, Abegg has written or cowritten hit songs for **Susan Ashton** ("Remember Not") and **Ji Lim** ("Full of Wonder").

For trivia buffs: Abegg is also a gifted photographer and painter. His pictures have been featured as cover art on albums by such artists as **Phil Keaggy, Michael W. Smith,** and **Chris Taylor.** He collaborated with **Kevin Max** to produce *At the Foot of Heaven* (StarSong, 1995), a visual collection of illustrated poems. He has also compiled a book of prayers called *Ragamuffin Prayers* (Harvest House, 2000).

Christian radio hits: "Thin But Strong Cord" (# 2 in 1991).

Able Cain

Greg Asher, voc.; Leo Gunther, drums; Matt McCabe, gtr.; Eric Schrepel, kybrd. 1994—*Able Cain* [EP] (Marathon).

www.finleysound.com/ablecain

Noted for a progressive '80s sound similar to The Fixx or **Simple Minds,** Able Cain produced only one five-song EP but drew considerable acclaim from critics. Two of the songs, "Fire Flower" and "Charlatan's Song," were featured on alternative Christian radio stations. Matt McCabe has since gone on to produce a solo project called *King Never* and to record with his wife Kristy McCabe under the name Clover.

Acappella

Keith Lancaster; Rodney Britt (−1991) // Gary Moyers (+ 1991); Duane Adams (+ 1991, −1991); George Pendergrass (+ 1991, −1996); Wayburn Dean (+ 1991, − 1995); Robert Guy (+ 1995, − 1999); Steve Reischl (+ 1996, −1999); Kevin Shaffer (+ 1996); Ken McAlpin (+ 1997); Barry Wilson (+ 1997). 1984—*Travelin' Shoes* (The Acappella Company); 1985—*Conquerors*; 1987—*Better Than Life*; 1989—*Sweet Fellowship*; 1990—*Growing Up in the Lord*; 1991—*Rescue*; 1992—*We Have Seen His Glory*; *Acappella Christmas*; 1993—*Set Me Free*; *Acappella Español*; 1994—*Gold*; *Platinum*; 1995—*Hymns for All the World*; 1996—*Beyond a Doubt*; 1997—*Act of God*; 1998—*The Collection*; 1999—*All That I Need.*

www.acappella.org

An all-male vocal group, Acappella has produced more than a decade's worth of Christian albums notable for their surprising diversity. The group has defied the apparent limitations of its chosen genre to create a style that *Release* magazine calls "part jazz, part street-corner doo-wop, part praise and worship, and completely captivating." With sales of more than three million albums and a touring schedule of more than 150 concerts a year, the band has built a substantial international audience. Their album *Hymns for All the World* appeals to this global constituency by featuring vocals in Russian, Portuguese, French, and Spanish.

The group was founded in 1982 by Keith Lancaster, who for some years was not only the lead singer but also producer, manager, songwriter, and head of the band's independent label. The personnel list above may be incomplete or inaccurate. Acappella has billed itself as a quartet, but on the first three albums only Lancaster and Rodney Britt were listed as members, and on the next two, no credits at all were given. Lancaster apparently retired to a solo career in 1988, but he has retained connections as Acappella's producer and creative force. By 1991, the group had stabilized somewhat as a quartet consisting of Duane Adams, Wayburn Dean, Gary Moyers, and George Pendergrass. Someone named Steve Maxwell is also said to have sung with Acappella at some undesignated point. In 1988, a spin-off group called **AVB** (or Acappella Vocal Band) was formed from former backup singers.

The album *Conquerors* includes a version of the gospel standard "John the Revelator" (cf. **Phil Keaggy**) in addition to "More Than Conquerors" by **Janny Grein** and "We Will Glorify" by **Twila Paris.** On *Better Than Life,* Lancaster and company offer **Michael W. Smith**'s "How Majestic Is Your Name," **Ray Boltz**'s "What Was I Supposed To Be," and several originals. By 1991, Lancaster was writing virtually all of the group's material, and by 1999 the bulk of the material was contributed by the individual singers. Besides earning recognition in the Christian market, Acappella has gained a reputation among fans of world music and of a capella singing in general. The song "When You're There" from *Beyond a Doubt* was chosen Best Gospel/Contemporary Christian Song by the Contemporary A Capella Recording Association. Acappella has also done uncredited commercials, including a popular spot for Sony Camcorders.

Lancaster made two solo albums for his Acappella Company label, *Prime Time* (1991) and *The Reason* (1994). He should not be confused with another Keith Lancaster, who led the bands **Bash, Bash-N-the-Code,** and **Found Free.**

Acappella Vocal Band

See **AVB.**

According to John

Ed Bunton, bass, voc.; John Waller, gtr., voc.; Jeff Billes; drums (–2002); Jason Hoard, gtr. (–2002) // Matt Adkins, gtr., voc. (+ 2002); John Fisher, drums (+ 2002). 1998—*A2J* (KMG); 2002—*Beyond What I See* (No Box).

www.accordingtojohn.com

An alternative pop band from Atlanta, According to John delivers a sound reminiscent of Toad the Wet Sprocket or **Smalltown Poets.** The group got its start as part of Big House, a youth outreach of First Baptist Church in Woodstock, Georgia, named after an **Audio Adrenaline** song. The ten songs on their debut album are all inspired in some sense by the Gospel of John, and they are all cowritten by lead singer John Waller. Perspectives of the latter John merge with those of the fourth Evangelist to produce an optimistic album with bouncing melodies and hope-filled lyrics. As second-generation Christian music artists, the members of According to John were all raised on **Steven Curtis Chapman** and **Russ Taff,** and their music shows these influences. Critical acclaim has focused especially on songwriting. "Justified" delights in the promise that Christians may live as forgiven sinners, while "Everlasting" celebrates the hope of life beyond death. The song "Nothing Back" was chosen by the family of Columbine shooting victim Cassie Bernall for a tribute video in her honor. After four years, the group resurfaced with the worship-oriented *Beyond What I See.* Lyrics, again, often focus on Scripture. "Standing Ovation" relates the story of the martyrdom of Stephen in Acts 7. "Song of Jabez" is based on the prayer in 1 Chronicles 4:9–10, which had been the subject of a very popular book by Bruce Wilkerson encouraging Christians to use prayer as a means of getting God to provide them with affluent and trouble-free lives.

Christian radio hits: "Justified" (# 9 in 1998); "Remedy" (# 14 in 1999).

Ace Troubleshooter

Josh Abbott, drums; Isaac Deaton, gtr.; Cody Oaks, bass; John Warne, voc. 2000—*Ace Troubleshooter* (BEC).

Ace Troubleshooter is a power-punk band from Minnesota that got its big break when they won a national battle of the bands competition sponsored by the Sam Goody record store chain in 1998. The group has the same sound as **MxPx** and dozens of other Green Day wannabes but is generally more hard-hitting. Their songs feature strong hooks that mollify the usual punk problem of everything sounding alike. Songs with obvious evangelical lyrics mix with more overtly secular material. "1 Corinthians 13" paraphrases the biblical chapter and "Phoenix" describes the process of spiritual rebirth. Complaints about girl problems are also prevalent. "Don't Trust That Girl" is sort of a modern version of Herman's Hermits' "A Must To Avoid." As *CCM* would note, however, "Yoko" crosses a line, and its warnings against someone who will "nag you to death" just come off as sexist and mean-spirited.

Acoustic Shack

Laura Misiuk, voc.; Michael Misiuk, gtr. 1991—*Acoustic Shack* (Blonde Vinyl); 1993—*Fret Buzz* (Broken); 1998—*A Distant Bell* (Red Moon); 2001—*Redeeming the Time.*

www.deara19.com

The Southern California duo known as Acoustic Shack (formed in Lake Forest, California, in 1991) has enjoyed more critical acclaim than commercial success. Their debut album produced only one minor hit in the Christian market, and the follow-up went unnoticed in the sales charts—while ranking number eight on *Billboard* magazine's Critics Choice for top records of the year. Lyrically, most of the songs focused on biblical themes, with some incursions from fundamentalist doctrine (e.g., references to the rapture). *Fret Buzz* moves away from simplistic theology to deal with more life-in-general issues. The second album also demonstrates a musical shift toward a more electric alternative rock sound that would render the group's name somewhat misleading. *True Tunes* likened the new sound to groups like Sugar or Psychedelic Furs. But there is diversity: "Radio Play" sounds like it could be an R.E.M. song, and Laura pretends she's Chrissie Hynde on "No Place Like Home." Highlights of *Fret Buzz* include the opening, "On the Wayside," and an intriguing cover of Creedence Clearwater Revival's "Bad Moon Rising." The group's third album continues to feature more distorted guitar and heavier percussion. Laura also takes over as principal songwriter on *A Distant Bell,* delivering lyrics expressive of desperation and yearning, set to tunes that start out sparse and gradually build with increased tempo and added layers. *Redeeming the Time* is a collection of classic hymns ("How Great Thou Art," "Just a Closer Walk," "I Have Decided," "Away in a Manger") mixed with a few modern numbers (**Andraé Crouch**'s "Soon and Very Soon") and a handful of faith-filled originals, the best of which is "Gloria." Michael Misuik is also a member of the band **The Kreepdowns.**

For trivia buffs: Laura Misuik's brother is Michael Pritzl, lead singer for **The Violet Burning.**

Christian radio hits: "It's Good to Know" (# 22 in 1992).

Acquire the Fire

Personnel list unavailable. 2000—*Live God Loud* (Pamplin).

Acquire the Fire is not so much a band as an event. The album *Live God Loud* is a live recording of a teen-oriented worship celebration sponsored by Teen Mania. The founder of that group, Ron Luce, serves as worship leader with metal meister **David Zaffiro** playing guitar and producing the album. Songs include **Lincoln Brewster**'s "All I Need" and **Darrell Evans**' "Whom Shall I Fear?" in addition to remodeled versions of the hymns "Just As I Am" and "I Have Decided to Follow Jesus."

A Cross Between

S. Luke Brown; Brishan Hatcher; Aaron Herman. 1999—*A Cross Between* (Benson).

A Cross Between is a contemporary pop trio formed from members of **AVB** (Acappella Vocal Band) who decided to add instruments for a more traditional pop sound. They drew immediate comparisons to general market acts like *NSYNC and the Backstreet Boys. The standout track on their debut album is a cover of the classic rock song "I Just Want to Celebrate," which was a Top 10 hit for Rare Earth in 1971 (cf. **Kim Boyce**). Another song, "Nicole Hadley's Heart" (cowritten by ex-**Allies** Randy Thomas), relates how the organs of a girl killed in Paducah, Kentucky, enabled five other people to live. Other songwriters contributing to the project include Regie Hamm, **Steve Hindalong** (of **The Choir**) and Dan Mukala (of **Mukala**). *Youthworker* magazine described the album as "an interesting blend of harmony-drenched, Beatlesque pop and groove-oriented rock."

A.D.

See **Kerry Livgren**.

Adam Again

Gene Eugene, voc., gtr.; Greg Lawless, gtr.; Riki Michele, voc.; Paul Valadez, bass // John Knox, drums (+ 1990). 1986—*In a New World of Time* (Dark Angel); 1988—*Ten Songs* (Broken); 1990—*Homeboys*; 1992—*Dig* (Brainstorm); 1995—*Perfecta*; 1999—*Worldwide Favourites* (KMG); 2000—*Live at Cornerstone 2000: Gene Eugene/Adam Again Tribute* (M8); 2001—*Remembering Gene* (Marathon).

www.afn.org/~afn45496/a_again

On March 20, 2000, Gene Andrusco died in his sleep at the age of thirty-eight. That untimely death (from an undiagnosed brain aneurism) was a great loss to the Christian music industry, since the man known as Gene Eugene was a consummate producer (200–300 albums by artists ranging from **Crystal Lewis** to **The Prayer Chain** to **Starflyer 59**), the cofounder of Brainstorm Records, and a member of three of Christian music's most innovative groups: Adam Again, the **Lost Dogs**, and **The Swirling Eddies**. The first of these three bands produced five pioneering albums that provide a lasting showcase for Eugene's most distinctive contributions.

With the able assistance of his wife **Riki Michele** and a stable rhythm section, Eugene shaped Adam Again into a band that prioritized musical excellence and lyrical depth over commercial appeal or even accessibility. Reviewers typically described their songs as "introspective," "transcendent," or "cathartic," but rarely used words like "upbeat" or "fun" (for the latter, see **The Swirling Eddies** or the **Lost Dogs**). Eugene's vocal stylings bore such remarkable similarities to those of Michael Stipe that comparisons with R.E.M. were inevitable, yet Adam Again's music had a darker edge and evinced a certain sadness that set them apart from the latter band. Critics praised the group for its intensity, passion, and honesty, yet, as one reviewer put it, "I haven't seen Adam Again play once when I did not feel the urge to cry." Eugene was comfortable appealing to a select constituency. "I'm not looking for **Amy Grant**'s audience," he joked to a reporter in 1992. "I want everything on this album *(Dig)* to be a little more difficult than usual." The group believed their faith to be a matter of record and was content to write and sing from that declared perspective without feeling the need to declare it anew on every album (or in every song). They rarely sang about Christ or God, but about life and human relationships, about the hardships of life and the pain of human relationships. What made the songs Christian was no more (and no less) than the fact that self-declared Christians wrote and sang them.

The first album, now long out of print and rare, contains the group's confession of faith and is the only one of the oeuvre that would be recognizable as a Christian record on its own. On "You Can Fall in Love," Eugene sings of Christ, "He was God and nothing less / He came to fill your emptiness." *Ten Songs* is known as Adam Again's "dance record" because of its roots in '60s funk. It contains the memorable "Eyes Wide Open," which warns against a myopic worldview. "Treehouse" likewise critiques the exclusive clubhouse-in-the-sky mentality that some Christians seem to adopt. "I've Seen Dominoes" addresses families and relationships that are falling down. The clearest faith statement comes in the concluding "The Tenth Song," which shares a prayer of thanks for forgiveness in Christ. *Ten Songs* was the only Adam Again album included (at Number Fifty-five) on a 2001 critics' poll of "The 100 Greatest Albums in Christian Music" sponsored by *CCM* magazine. *Homeboys* is less funky in style but more urban in content, featuring a number of songs dealing with the trials of life in the city ("Bad News on the Radio," "Homeboys"). "Save Me" is a cry for mercy and forgiveness written by Michele, and "Hide Away" is a sad song about distance between married lovers, with lyrics by **Steve Hindalong**. Also noteworthy on this third outing are covers of **Marvin Gaye**'s "Inner City Blues" and **Terry Scott Taylor**'s "Occam's Razor." *Dig* continues to explore the theme of "Eyes Wide Open" in songs like "It is What It Is (What It Is)." Overall, *Dig* has a harder edge to it than previous projects and is perhaps the group's finest album. It closes with "River on Fire," which Eugene considered their best song, and also features "Worldwide," which became their best-known song. Eugene would later comment, "when we were approached about putting together a collection of our hits, 'Worldwide' was the only one we could come up with." The song contains a reference to Headman Shambalala, a singer in **Ladysmith Black Mambazo** who was murdered, and asks the rhetorical questions, "Does anyone care about justice?" and "Why should anybody bother?" Its most memorable lines are, "Don't think I'll ever understand it / Don't think it matters if I do / Three billion people in the world / And I only know a few." *Perfecta* is the group's most cohesive recording, with a vibe that seems to hold from beginning to end. The album has a ragged, dynamic feel to it—the project was recorded live in the studio with feedback and noises between songs being left on the disc. Eugene described the process behind *Perfecta* as a "three-year jam session" during which the entire group created material out of their musical and spiritual experiences together. The latter comment is intriguing to the voyeuristic since it was during that time (1994) that Eugene and Michele divorced, though the two would remain close and continue to work together. The song "Stone" broaches the subject of a broken relationship specifically, while "Dogjam" and "All Right" seem to speak more obliquely of the issues involved.

For an artist so intimate and vulnerable in his songwriting, Eugene was reticent in interviews and private about his personal life. In the opening words to his favorite Adam Again song he sang, "What would you say if you knew what I was thinking? / Maybe you do, but you know not to dig too deep" ("River of Fire"). He likewise responded defensively to Christian critiques of the group as unnecessarily vague or cryptic: "I kind of revel in the uncertainty of spiritual things and in the mystery of them."

Michele's father, Pentecostal minister Johnny Bunch, officiated at Eugene's funeral, and she eulogized him to the press: "He was caring, sweet, funny, and most of all, just an incredible talent. He's my favorite songwriter." In 2000, M8 Distribution released a three-CD tribute to Eugene and Adam Again. It features one disc of songs performed live by the group with vocals by such artists as **Michael Knott** and **Michael Roe** and two discs of concert material from previous years. A year later, Marathon came out with a different tribute set featuring two discs of Eugene's songs being performed by various artists (**The Altar Boys, The Prayer Chain, The Violet Burning, Starflyer 59,** and others).

For trivia buffs: Gene Eugene had a pre-Adam Again career as a child actor. At age ten he starred as "Young Darren Stevens" in an episode of the TV show *Bewitched* ("Out of the Mouths of Babes"). The next year, he supplied the voice of Rogger Barkley in the animated series *The Barkleys* (they were dogs) and the voice of Flip in the animated series, *The Amazing Chan and the Chan Clan,* which ran for three seasons. Also at eleven, he played Vince Blaine in the movie "Gidget Gets Married" and Justin in an episode of the TV show *Cannon* ("The Rip Off").

Oleta Adams

1990—*Circle of One* (Fontana); 1993—*Evolution;* 1995—*Moving On;* 1997—*Come Walk with Me* (Harmony); 1998—*The Very Best of Oleta Adams* (Chronicles).

www.oletaadams.com

Oleta Adams is viewed as a soul singer with gospel roots in the general market and as a gospel singer with secular appeal in Christian circles. She grew up in Yakima, Washington, the daughter of a Baptist minister, singing in church and directing four choirs. As an adult, she ended up in Kansas City, where she recorded two unsuccessful self-funded albums and took to singing cabaret in the rotating Hyatt lounge. Her life changed when the latter establishment was visited by Roland Orzabel and Curt Smith of the alternative rock group **Tears for Fears.** They invited her to sing on two tracks ("Woman in Chains," "Badman's Song") on their definitive album, *The Seeds of Love* (1987). She joined the group for their tour and was sometimes listed as their third member. Orzabel subsequently produced her album *Circle of One,* which produced two hit singles: "Rhythm of Life" and "Get Here." The latter tune, a Brenda Russell song, hit Number Five on *Billboard*'s Top 40 charts and became something of an anthem for the Gulf War going on at the time. The album went platinum and Adams toured nationally with Michael Bolton. She has not repeated that level of commercial success but has continued to record in the pop market and, in 1995, contributed vocals to another Tears for Fears song, "Me and My Big Ideas," on their album *Raoul and the Kings of Spain.* With *Come Walk with Me* Adams dove headlong into the contemporary Christian market, serving up an album of songs that testify to faith in Christ.

Circle of One contains Adams' best-known songs and evinces strong gospel roots throughout. *Evolution* is mostly big pop ballads, such as James Taylor's "Don't Let Me Be Lonely Tonight" (featuring David Sanborn) and Billy Joel's "New York State of Mind." *Moving On* picks up the tempo with more funky, dance-oriented numbers. *Come Walk with Me* mixes traditional numbers with Adams' own compositions. Standout cuts include the title track, the soulful "This Love Won't Fail You," and "I Will Love You," which features backing by a **Take 6**-style vocal group called Special Gift. Notably, the 1998 collection album ignored these and other faith songs, selecting only tunes from the first three albums and other side projects. It does include one of Adams' best songs, a moving rendition of Elton John's

"Don't Let the Sun Go Down on Me," originally found on the *Two Rooms* tribute album for that artist (Mercury, 1991).

Adams rejects any clear distinction between her sacred and secular careers. She speaks rather of songs that testify directly to the message of Christ through their lyrics and of other songs—soulful ones—that tenderize the heart in ways that allow the Spirit to do its work. She tries to mention her faith in every interview, whatever the forum, and she does a gospel set complete with personal testimony as a part of every concert: "I tell them, don't get scared and run away . . . you won't get saved tonight if you don't want to."

Adams has been nominated for three Grammy awards, including one for Best Pop Vocal Performance—Female ("Get Here") and one for Best R&B Vocal Performance—Female ("Don't Let the Sun Go Down on Me").

Yolanda Adams

1987—*Just As I Am* (Sound of Gospel); 1991—*Through the Storm* (Benson); 1993—*Save the World* (Tribute); 1995—*More Than a Melody*; 1996—*Yolanda . . . Live in Washington*; 1998—*Songs from the Heart* (Verity); 1999—*Best of Yolanda Adams*; 1999—*Mountain High . . . Valley Low* (Elektra); 2000—*Christmas with Yolanda Adams*; 2001—*The Divas of Gospel* [with Albertina Walker] (Uni); *The Experience* (Elektra); 2002—*Believe*.

www.yolandaadams.org

With a voice that is often compared to that of Whitney Houston, Yolanda Adams grew up in Houston, Texas, to become first one of America's most promising young gospel singers and then a *contemporary* gospel singer with crossover appeal to fans of R&B. Before being discovered by gospel magnate Thomas Whitfield, she was an elementary school teacher who wanted to break into modeling. Her statuesque 6'1" frame and stunning appearance won her a number of jobs in the latter field, but it was her avocation of singing with the Southeast Inspirational Choir that brought the invitation to bid adieu to those first and second graders.

Whitfield guided Adams' first album of traditional spirituals. Follow-up records in the early '90s established her as a gospel staple, garnering several Stellar awards (traditional gospel's version of the Dove or Grammy). *Through the Storm* features her own composition "You Know That I Know," and *Save the World* includes "The Battle Is the Lord's" and "Let Us Worship Him." Then, with *More Than a Melody*, Adams changed gears, adopting a more contemporary, soulful sound. Reaction was mixed. In addition to predictable complaints from gospel fans who think "spiritual" and "worldly" are a twain that should never meet, musical objections were leveled by critics who felt Adams had gone from being something special to sounding like every other adult contemporary songstress. Her cover of the Steve Miller Band's "Fly Like an Eagle" suffered particular abuse. Still, the album was nominated for a Grammy and

earned Adams a spot on "Soul Train." The best tracks include "The Good Shepherd" and **BeBe Winans**' "What about the Children?" *Live in Washington* put Adams back in the good graces of the critics, earned another nomination from the Grammys, and snagged yet another Stellar award. That album opens with an impressive seven-minute number, "The Only Way," that showcases the incredible range and versatility of Adams' voice. The next album, *Songs from the Heart,* presented traditional hymns and worship songs sung in a diversity of styles. Then Adams switched to the general market label Elektra to broaden her appeal and audience. Her platinum-selling first album for that company *(Mountain High . . . Valley Low)* secured her identification as "the CCM Whitney Houston" (CCM being short for contemporary Christian music). It mixes beat-driven numbers like "Time to Change" with pop balladry ("Fragile Heart"). *The Experience* is a concert album recorded live in Washington, D.C. *Believe* includes an excursion into hip-hop ("I'm Thankful") and a duet with Karen Clark-Sheard of **The Clark Sisters** ("Fo' Sho' ") that recalls the work of Destiny's Child.

Adams' songs bear witness to the power of faith and prayer to sustain the faithful in the midst of personal struggles. She speaks openly of her own travails. The eldest of six children, she was especially close to her father who died tragically when she was thirteen, and to her grandfather who died a few years later. An abusive marriage ended in divorce shortly after her career as a gospel singer began. She dedicates one song, "In the Midst of it All" (from *Mountain High*), to "the mothers of the church," saying, "I know you are going through a hard time, but don't give up . . . I made it out." She is devoted to numerous children's charities, including Operation Rebound, which addresses the concerns of inner city children. "My music has evolved with the times," Adams grants, "but the truth is still the truth, and Jesus Christ is the center of everything I do."

Dove Awards: 1992 Traditional Gospel Album *(Through the Storm)*; 1992 Traditional Gospel Song ("Through the Storm"); 1999 Traditional Gospel Song ("Is Your All on the Altar?").

Grammy Awards: 2001 Contemporary Soul Gospel Album *(The Experience).*

The Advocates

Personnel list unavailable. 1973—*The Advocates* (Dovetail); 1975—*Here I Rest My Case.*

A British pop band in the grand tradition of the Beatles, The Advocates performed hook-laden songs with obvious melodies and lots of organ, a bit like the Grass Roots. Their first album features horns and is more rock and roll than the tamer follow-up. Each record includes an a capella song: "Rebel's Song" on the first, and the hymn "Man of Sorrows" on the second. *Jesus Music* describes the second outing as "a concept album, presenting the claims and evidences of the Christian faith through song."

Aeturnus

John Gibson, voc., gtr.; Matt Miller, bass; Josh Murray, drums. 1995—*From Blackest Darkness* (Cranial Captivity).

Not to be confused with the doom metal band Solitude Aeturnus, this Christian group played hard, fast, death-core music of the same genre but with evangelistic intent. *From Blackest Darkness* begins with a metal version of the Imperial Death March from the movie *Star Wars*. The gospel is seldom evident in the band's lyrics. One song, "Carnage," expresses the perspective of a serial murderer ("I kill to live, I live to kill"). Another, "Knee Deep in the Dead," describes the plight of that individual as he suffers the consequences of hell. Aeturnus liked to play in bars and clubs where they could reach unbelievers with an invitation to receive Christ. "Our lyrics are dark and we address dark issues," Gibson told *HM* magazine. "We try to convey that a life without Christ is unfulfilled." After the group broke up, Gibson continued to make music with a group called Dirge.

A Few Loose Screws

Dave Lantz, bass; Del Sauder, voc., gtr.; Matt West, drums. 1996—*Four-O-Five* (Alarma).

The single album by the punk-rock trio A Few Loose Screws was produced by Gene Eugene (of **Adam Again**). Their sound takes its cues from the Ramones or, in Christian circles, **The Altar Boys** or **The Huntingtons.** Thematically, one major topic is girls: appreciating them ("Rule the World"), wanting them ("Matt's Song"), controlling them ("Girl in My Pocket"). But an even more dominant theme is spiritual longing, expressed primarily through songs that bemoan the potential emptiness of life and extol the need for change. Standout tracks include "How I Feel" and "Rule the World" (the two most upbeat songs, lyrically) and a cover of **Resurrection Band**'s "Can't Stop Lov'n You." The album was re-released in 2001 by KMG, packaged unfortunately as part of a two-disc set with a questionable work by **Rainy Days.**

After the Fire (a.k.a. ATF)

Peter "Memory" Banks, kybrd.; Andy Piercy, gtr., bass; Nick Battle, bass (–1978); Ivor Twidell, drums (–1979) // John Russell, gtr. (+ 1978); Peter King, drums (+ 1980). 1978—*Signs of Change* (CBS); 1979—*LaserLove*; 1979—*80-f* (Epic); 1981—*Batteries Not Included*; 1982—*Der Kommissar* (CBS).

www.friends.afterthefire.co.uk

After the Fire was one of the first overtly Christian bands to achieve considerable success in the secular market. Still, they have been largely ignored by the Christian music community in the United States. This may be because their one hit in the American market ("Der Kommissar," # 5 in 1983) was a cover tune void of obvious spiritual content. The band recorded that song (which had already been a hit by Falco in Germany) only as a concession to their record company. Ironically, the song initially flopped in their native UK, and the group disbanded in frustration shortly before it became a worldwide smash everywhere else. ATF seems destined to be remembered in America as a one-hit wonder. Yet they *are* remembered, as "Der Kommissar" continues to show up on countless soundtracks and compilations of '80s music. The best-selling album named for that song was actually a greatest hits retrospective of their entire career.

After The Fire was founded by Peter Banks, who took the band's name from 1 Kings 19:12: "After the fire, came a still small voice." The group officially shortened its name to ATF in 1981 but continued to be known by both monikers; Banks also changed his first name from "Peter" to "Memory" (with similar inconsistency) to avoid confusion with a guitarist for Yes. In any case, the members of ATF had roots deep in the British Jesus movement. Banks and John Russell had played together in **Narnia,** who recorded a self-titled album for Myrrh in 1974. Andy Piercy was half of the Christian folk duo **Ishmael and Andy.** His partner in that endeavor, Ian Smale, later recorded albums of praise and worship music under the name **Ishmael,** with ATF providing uncredited backup.

The first ATF album was independently produced and enjoyed limited release, but today is regarded by some as a fine instance of the sort of progressive rock also being performed by groups like Yes or Genesis at the time. Every song ranges from seven to ten minutes in length with extended instrumental segues. The change in musical direction evident on their next record reveals that someone in the group had been listening to new-wave. The title *80-f* is a clever phonetic variation on their abbreviated name. *Laser Love* was one of the first albums anywhere to feature the synthesizer-driven sound that was to define '80s club music. It produced a Top 30 hit in the UK ("One Rule for You") and brought the band to the attention of the general market. The next two albums were produced by Mack, known for his work with ELO and Queen. ATF toured as the opening act for both of those bands and then opened for Van Halen's 1982 American tour, inspiring the latter group to adopt the more synthesizer-driven sound evident on their 1984 hit "Jump." In general, critics praised ATF for playing carefully crafted pop songs with precision and skill, but faulted them for having a predictable, programmed sound that lacked innovation. One critic credited them with having "a large following among those for whom street credibility comes a long way behind enjoyment."

The group was always forthright about their faith convictions, even if the lyrics to their songs were not as specific as some fans of Christian music would have wanted. They played the *Greenbelt* Christian music festival (a UK equivalent to *Cornerstone*) several times, interacting with such artists as **Larry Norman** and **Chuck Girard.** The British press regularly referred to them as "a Christian rock band," sometimes snidely. Indeed, the group's first hit, "One Rule for You" was written by Piercy as a rebuff to critics who dismissed the band as part of a religious subculture without attending seriously to its music. But ATF also suffered vilification from Christian critics who found them too worldly. Their management once issued a statement affirming the band's conviction that "entertainment is one of God's many gifts," and so defending the production of good music as a godly goal in its own right. After a seventeen-year hiatus, the band began performing sporadic reunion shows in 2000, and these included praise and worship songs in the repertoire.

While ATF was together, Ivor Twidell released solo albums under the name Iva Twydell: *Waiting for the Sun* (Tunesmith, 1978); *Secret Service* (Red Sky, 1981); *Duel* (Red Sky, 1982). Only the last of these was released in America (on Tunesmith); it has a sound similar to ATF and early Genesis recordings. Piercy continues to be a force in Christian music through producing, helming projects by **Matt Redman** and **Kim Hill.** A book about After the Fire called *Dancing in the Shadows* has been written by Julian Barr and is available at their website.

For trivia buffs: Andy Piercy once reviewed the (now classic) live album *How the West Was One* by Christian artists **Phil Keaggy** and **2nd Chapter of Acts** for a British music magazine (*Buzz,* August 1979). He didn't think much of it, and the review drew a flurry of letters from angry Christian readers. Piercy also drew a regular comic strip for *Buzz* called "Lost and Found."

Dennis Agajanian

1971—*Come to the Rock* (custom); 1981—*Rebel to the Wrong* (Light); 1986—*Friendly Fire* (Word); 1987—*Where Are the Heroes* (Sparrow); 1992—*Out of the Wilderness* (Asaph); 1993—*There Is a Road*; date unknown—*Just As I Am* (Asaph); *Best Picks; Empty Hearts; Outlaw, He Will Roll Away Your Stone; Pure Acoustic Bluegrass; Best Picks 2.*

www.dennisagajanian.com

In 1970, Dennis Agajanian was amazing teenagers at Lutheran Youth Alive congresses with his unbelievable flat pickin' guitar, rollicking wit, and tearful testimonies of God's grace. Thirty years later, having done both Vegas and *The 700 Club,* he remained a survivor—one of the few veterans of the Jesus movement to be still recording at the turn of the millennium. But unlike "The Pilgrim" venerated in a Kris Kristofferson song, Agajanian would remain an enthusiastic Christian soldier, not just some worn-out warrior who "prays to make it through another day." A veteran of modern country, Agajanian has worked with such talents as Ricky Scaggs and **Johnny Cash.** At one point, he was listed in the *Guinness Book of World Records* as the "World's Fastest Flat Picking Guitarist." Agajanian was born in California and raised on a small farm just north of Los Angeles. Early on, he often performed with his brothers, especially Danny Agajanian, and he has continued to do this from time to time. He also performed with Kentucky Faith, along with future members of **Brush Arbor.** Agajanian describes his sound as "outlaw music," referencing the Nashville-cum-Austin-based movement of country artists who in the late '70s became disenchanted with Nashville vogue, but also indicating the counter-cultural tendency of the Christian gospel. "I'm an outlaw for Jesus," he says.

CCM described *Rebel to the Wrong* as an album "full of knee slappin' tunes and sorrowful laments about those who find out the hard way." *Where Are the Heroes* was produced by **Terry Talbot** and the title song was written by **Steve Camp.** The song "She's a Servant" (written with Talbot) takes up a theme uncommon in Christian music, describing the life of a successful and fulfilled woman who chooses to remain single. *Just As I Am* is an instrumental collection that presents classical, bluegrass, flamenco, and country guitar versions of famous pieces like Bach's "Jesu, Joy of Man's Desiring" and Handel's "Hallelujah Chorus." *Out of the Wilderness* includes the Ken Munds song "Come To the Rock" (the title track from Agajanian's first custom record). The album *Outlaw, He Will Roll Away Your Stone* was recorded with a full six-piece band that took Agajanian to new heights musically. Alongside new versions of "Where Are the Heroes?" and "Via Dolorosa" (originally on the *Heroes* album), *Outlaw* offers **Charlie Daniels'** "Long-Haired Country Boy" and a number of songs that address various struggles of life. "Saigon" spoke powerfully to Vietnam veterans. Over the years, Agajanian has become known for a number of patriotic songs ("Lord, Give Us America") and for his frequent appearances at Promise Keepers rallies and Franklin Graham crusades. He travels on behalf of Samaritan's Purse, the humanitarian organization of which Graham is president. In 1986, he published an article in *CCM* magazine about his travels to Lebanon, El Salvador, Nicaragua, and Thailand.

For trivia buffs: Agajanian is a stock car race enthusiast, and he has sponsored cars in the Indianapolis 500. He composed the race theme song "Indianapolis 500 Dream" and has served as an unofficial chaplain for many races throughout the country. He says he is known to many of the drivers as "Dennis the Christian."

Agape

Fred Caban, gtr., voc.; Mike Jungkman, drums; Jason Peckhart, bass (–1971) // Richard Greenburg, bass (+ 1972); Jim Hess, kybrd. (+ 1972). 1971—*Gospel Hard Rock* (Mark); 1972—*Victims of Tradition* (Renrut); 1996—*The Problem Is Sin: Live and Unreleased* (Hidden Vision).

With a sound roughly analogous to early Grand Funk Railroad, Agape was one of the world's first Christian bands to play hard rock music. They released limited quantities of two albums now treasured by collectors. Fred Caban founded the group in 1968 after being converted at a Light Club Coffeehouse (associated with what was to become the Children of God cult) in Huntington Beach, California. The band made its home in Azusa, California, and played regularly at the Salt Company Christian coffeehouse (sponsored by Don Williams' Hollywood Presbyterian Church), where they supposedly inspired **Larry Norman** to play more religiously oriented music. The band's following formed the nucleus for what was ultimately to become the International Agape Ministries (first known as Covina Church in the Park). The original lineup included Lonnie Campbell as female bass player, but she was replaced by Jason Peckhart before the recording of the first album. Jim Hess, who joined for the second album, died of cancer shortly after the band broke up. Richard Greenburg (the *third* bass player) later recorded under the name The Rapid Richard Group, releasing what was essentially a solo album (*Did I See What I Thought I Saw? An Album of Parables,* Homespun, 1977).

The first Agape album, *Gospel Hard Rock,* features a number of songs with one-word titles ("Rejoice," "Freedom," "Happy") that remind historian/critic David Di Sabatino not only of GFR but of Hendrix and Cream. Those analogies at least describe the band's influences and aspirations, if exaggerating their abilities. The music is not actually "hard rock," but more of a blues-based midtempo style that is more rock-oriented than the folk groups associated with Calvary Chapel's Maranatha label. The second album, Di Sabatino continues, is "a more complex blend of blues-rock with jazz-fusion undertones." On both records, the group exhibits an evangelistic fervor in keeping with the revival spirit of the time. "I'm in love with somebody I can't even see," Caban sings in the debut album's opening lyric. "He loved me so much he died on Calvary" ("Blind"). Lyrical profundity, then, is not the band's strength: "I'm so happy / Do you want to know the reason why? / I'm so happy / 'Cause I'm not afraid to die" ("Happy"). Still, Jesus movement historian Frank Edmonson has said that Agape represents "Jesus rock at its crustiest, music which cuts through the thickest defenses of the non-Christian rock fan."

Agape Force

See **Candle.**

Age of Faith

Jimi Ray, voc.; Rick Harwell, gtr. (–1996) // Steven Blair, drums (+ 1996); Drue Bachmann, bass (+ 1996, –1998); Daniel Polydores, gtr. (+ 1996, –1998); David Buchannan, gtr. (+ 1998); Zack Plemmons, bass (+ 1998). 1990—*Age of Faith* (Benson); 1992—*Heart of the Young;* 1996—*Embrace* (Gray Dot); 1998—*The Truth;* 1999—*Still* (Songs of Restoration).

As the personnel list above indicates, Age of Faith has basically consisted of singer/writer Jimi Ray and whoever is playing with him at the time. The group has assumed a number of distinct incarnations since its formation in 1990. It began as a power-pop duo that fashioned itself as a Christian version of Bon Jovi and produced two albums aimed at evangelizing the young with arena anthems. *Age of Faith* is noted for its galloping version of **Donna Summer**'s "Unconditional Love" (cf. **The Altar Boys**); the second outing features more diverse styles, more ballads, and guest appearances by the likes of **Rick Elias** and **Bob Carlisle.** Neither record sold particularly well, and the group was dropped from the Benson roster. Back in 1996 with a new label and a new lineup, Ray and company now evinced a more rootsy unplugged sound reminiscent of Hootie and the Blowfish or Counting Crows. Mac Powell (from **Third Day**) sings on the premier single from *Embrace,* "The Love of Jesus." The album also features an impressive cover of Crowded House's "Something So Strong." Two years later, another new lineup released *The Truth,* a more electric album laden with Gin Blossoms hooks. The standout track, "Red Carpet," presents God as offering a royal welcome to the penitent. Continuing their tradition of unpredictable covers, the band also presents its take on **Lone Justice**'s "Shelter." On their 1999 offering, *Still,* the group opts for a worship-oriented approach, covering a number of standard songs including **Keith Green**'s "Make My Life a Prayer to You" and **Rich Mullins**' "I See You." Age of Faith has toured with numerous general market acts, including Gin Blossoms, Hootie and the Blowfish, and Toad the Wet Sprocket. Grace and forgiveness are the most prominent recurring themes in the Age of Faith repertoire. "I grew up believing God was mad at me all the time," Ray reflects. "We strive to have a grace-oriented ministry."

Christian radio hits: "For Heaven's Sake" (# 25 in 1991); "The Way That You Trust Me" (# 23 in 1992); "The Love of Jesus" (# 3 in 1997).

Angie Alan

1990—*Angie Alan* (Frontline); 1991—*The Bottom Line.*

Angie Alan (b. 1966 in Miami) mixes light soul ballads and dance-pop tunes in the tradition of the L.A. sound associated with such producers as Babyface or the team of Jimmy Jam and Terry Lewis. She began singing Christian music while a student at Dallas Baptist College and toured for six months as part of the Continental Singers. Her albums have been produced by **Tim Miner** (for whom she once sang background vocals) in collaboration with her husband, David Ebensberger. Her self-titled debut record includes "Sunny Side," a funky dance track, and "Today," which calls on hearers to pay attention to the needs of the homeless. *CCM* described the songs on *The Bottom Line* as "simple affirmations of faith and reliance on Jesus, peppered with calls to Christian action and social conscience." The song "Until We Meet Again" is a tribute to murdered rapper **D-Boy**.

Christian radio hits: "Sunny Side" (# 16 in 1990); "The Bottom Line" (# 12 in 1991); "Never Givin' Up" (# 16 in 1992).

The Alarm

Eddie McDonald, bass; Mike Peters, voc., gtr.; Dave Sharp, gtr., voc.; Nigel Twist, drums. 1983—*The Alarm* [EP] (I.R.S.); 1984—*Declaration*; 1985—*Strength*; 1987—*Eye of the Hurricane*; 1988—*Electric Folklore Live*; 1989—*Change*; 1990—*Standards*; 1991—*Raw*.

www.thealarm.com

Like **U2** (the Irish band with whom they are most often compared), The Alarm is not generally considered to be a Christian band. This may be because their songs tended to be more political than (overtly) spiritual or because only one member of the group (Mike Peters) was explicit about his faith. Nevertheless, there are many fans of contemporary Christian music who claim the band as one of theirs. **Geoff Moore and The Distance** had a Christian radio hit with their song, "Rescue Me." The Alarm's debut full-length album, *Declaration,* earned the band a review in *CCM* because—alongside anthems extolling pacifism—it offers a song of hope called "We Are the Light" and one of resistance addressed to "The Deceiver" ("You are not welcome in my life"). But on the follow-up, *Strength,* Peters declares, "I ain't gonna preach, no I ain't gonna teach / I'm just gonna sing about the things I need."

The Welsh quartet came together in the late '70s as an expansion of the Toilets (Eddie MacDonald and Peters) and first toured under the name Seventeen. They came to the attention of American audiences when they opened (as The Alarm) for **U2**'s 1983 arena tour. The group had a punk, Sex Pistols-inspired sound not unlike that of their headliners, save that Peters and Dave Sharp eschewed electric instruments in favor of amplified acoustic guitars. *CCM* once described their sound as evocative of "the Byrds playing punk-rock." Over the years, The Alarm scored only minor radio hits ("Strength," # 61 in 1985; "Rain in the Summertime," # 71 in 1987; Presence of Love," # 77 in 1988; "Sold Me Down the River," # 50 in 1989), but often received considerable airplay on college-oriented stations.

The Alarm were known in part for their covers of such songs as Neil Young's "Rocking in the Free World," **Bob Dylan**'s "Knockin' on Heaven's Door," and John Lennon's "Working Class Hero." In addition, however, Peters, Sharp, and MacDonald all contributed original songs, and some of these feature lyrics that lend themselves easily to religious interpretation: "The rock, the rock, the rock, will never let you down," Peters sings on *Change* ("The Rock"). "Declare Yourself an Unsafe Building" is about making a life-changing commitment to live with integrity. "The Stand" (inspired by the Stephen King book of that title) could have been used for altar calls ("Come on down and meet your Maker / Come on down and make the stand"), but The Alarm never gave altar calls or identified themselves in any other obvious way as the Christian band that some of their fans wanted them to be.

In 1991, both Peters and Sharp embarked on solo careers. The former put together a new act, Poets of Justice, which released a handful of albums: *Breathe* (Crai, 1994), *Feel Free* (Select, 1996), *Rise* (VelVel, 1998), and *Flesh and Blood* (21st Century, 2001). These records sometimes evinced a generic spirituality but only the first displayed any direct connection to matters of faith. A couple of the songs on *Rise* display what Doug Van Pelt (no prude) would denounce as "gratuitous cuss words" in his review for *HM* magazine. Peters then joined Coloursound (with Billy Duffy of The Cult and Craig Adams of The Mission), which released a self-titled album on 21st Century Records in 1999. Sharp, meanwhile, released a Dylan-esque romp, *Hard Travellin'* (I.R.S.) in 1991 that garnered more attention and acclaim than any of Peters' post-Alarm projects; it was followed by *Downtown America* (Dinosaur, 1996). Then in 2000 Peters put together a new group that he called The Alarm 2000 and toured extensively playing the band's old hits. At this time, Peters granted an interview with *HM* during which he clarified some of his spiritual beliefs and commitments: "Jesus Christ is someone I know, but I think that everyone has to formulate their own relationship with him. . . . He's much bigger than any dogma. He's much bigger than any religion. . . . I don't think the Bible has captured his greatness. He's much bigger than all of that. And I have a relationship with him that is mine, but I'm sure it is nowhere near the relationship that others have with him."

Ric Alba

1991—*Holes in the Floor of Heaven* (GlassHouse).

The former bassist for **The Altar Boys** surprised the Christian music market when he produced a cathartic album of songs only vaguely reminiscent of his work with that seminal Christian punk band. The material itself was distinctive, featuring songs that Alba had written after checking himself into a hospital for an extended period of psychological help. The opening lyric, "Scream 'til the monsters go away," sets the tone for the entire piece, in which Alba reflects on life as an adult through the eyes of a child. "Don't make me sleep in the dark," he sings in "Laughter"; "Don't say you know how I feel / Then leave me there to cry alone," he pleads in "Hold My Hand." Rich in metaphor (the title is a poetic description of stars), the album won acclaim from such notable critics as *CCM*'s Brian Quincy Newcomb, while remaining predictably unsuccessful commercially.

Albrecht and Roley (and Moore)

Mike Albrecht, voc., gtr.; Scott Roley, voc., gtr. // Alan Moore, voc., gtr. (+ 1977). 1975—*Albrecht and Roley* (Airborn); 1977—*Gently Flowing Feeling* (White Horse); 1979—*Starlighter* (Spirit); 1980—*Take It to the People*.

An acoustic folk duo/trio from Georgia, the group known as Albrecht, Roley, and eventually Moore was an extension of **Aslan,** with first Albrecht replacing Roley's brother Jeff, and then producer **Ron Moore**'s brother Alan being added to the titular lineup. The practice of using the member's surnames as the group's official designation may have been inspired by Crosby, Stills and Nash (and Young), whose lighter styles Albrecht, Roley, and Moore seemed to fancy. The first album has an appealing raw quality. *Jesus Music* says, "picture an unorchestrated Jim Croce or perhaps a demo tape by America and you'll get the idea." *Goldmine* magazine (for record collectors—not a Christian publication) misinterprets the source of inspiration and lists this album as one that "has a good stoned feel to it." In any case, the boys garnered enough respect for stars Bob Hartman (of **Petra**), **John Michael Talbot,** and **Al Perkins** to put in guest appearances on their second outing. The final two releases found the group mellowing out in the direction of adult contemporary Christian radio. **Scott Roley** went on to form a group called City Limits and then to a solo career.

Christian radio hits: "Eyes on the Clouds" (# 22 in 1979).

Aleixa (a.k.a. Sorrow of Seven)

Kevin 131, gtr., kybrd.; Laurel Snapper, voc. // April Lassiter, voc. (+ 1996, −1999). By Sorrow of Seven: 1992—*Red* (Flying Tart); 1993—*Teal*; 1994—*Amber*. By Aleixa: 1996—*Honey Lake* (Liquid Disc); 1999—*Disfigured* (BulletProof).

Aleixa's debut album of industrial techno dance music left mostly pleased reviewers scrambling for mixed metaphors to describe the heterogenous sound. The angelic female vocals summoned tonal images of Sinead O'Connor, the Cranberries, Missing Persons, or Yaz. But *beneath* those vocals (and sometimes on top of them) were the Trent Reznor-style guitars and programmed synthesizers of audio engineer Kevin 131. "Abba

on acid," *7ball* magazine suggested. "Debbie Gibson in a blender," Kevin himself offered.

Even more noteworthy than the sound were the dark reaches of the lyrics. "I could murder, I could kill / There's something inside of me," one song insists ("I Could Murder"). "I've got a knife that wants to have some fun," another reciprocates ("Spark"). This is dance music? *Christian* dance music? Occasionally, the specifically Christian content does come to the fore, but even then the images are violent. "In Adam we die / through Christ I am born," the song "Non-self" proclaims, before reflecting, "funny that blood could be so sweet / forgiving what once was mine to keep."

Kevin 131, who has also played guitar for **Deitiphobia** and **Argyle Park,** fronted an independent group called Sorrow of Seven with whom he made three demo EPs for Flying Tart records: *Red, Teal,* and *Amber.* The last of these features an infamous cover of the Shirley Temple song, "On the Good Ship Lollipop." Laurel Snapper's powerful vocals are featured on all three discs, which contain early versions of songs that would later surface on Aleixa's official debut album ("Non-self," "I Could Murder"). April Lassiter was recruited for vocal chores on *Honey Lake* only. Otherwise, Sorrow of Seven/Aleixa (pronounced *ah-lee-kah*) has always been a duo. Radio attention for the first album tended to focus on the single "Unloved," an anxious cry of self-discovery set to an incongruously celebrative beat. The album also features a bonus, alternative mix of that song by **The Echoing Green.** Aleixa's sophomore release, *Disfigured,* demonstrates musical growth and further experimentation, including the use of horns and saxophone (on "Black and Blue") and guest screaming by Sara Merritt of Pink Daffodils. Snapper's voice also appears modified, with inflections that reveal eastern influence. The title track is a prayer to be "made brand new inside." *Disfigured* features a cover of Duran Duran's "The Reflex."

Snapper, who writes most of the band's lyrics, also works as a staff member for a conservative Republican congressman from Texas. She claims that all of her lyrics are autobiographical, expressive of genuine if deplorable feelings that she and probably everyone must sometimes explore. The Christian witness, she insists, is subtle but real. Rather than presenting people with the gospel upfront, she prefers to raise questions that lead to fruitful dialogue. "My reaction when people shove stuff in my face is to turn away," she told *7ball.* "When people can relate to what they're hearing, it opens doors for discussion."

Allen and Allen

Bruce Allen, kybrd.; Allen T. D. Wiggins, sax. 1994—*Allen and Allen* (CGI); 1995—*A Blazing Grace*; 1996—*Come Sunday*; 1998—*A New Beginning*; 2001—*Love Sweet Love* (Allen and Allen).

The instrumental duo of Allen and Allen produces urban jazz music with a contemporary gospel spin. Their albums often feature guest vocalists and other performers. For instance, on the third outing Daryl Coley sings the Duke Ellington classic "Come Sunday," and Albertina Walker sings "You Don't Know What the Lord Has Done for Me." In general, the albums have become progressively eclectic and more appealing to a younger, hipper audience. *Allen and Allen* is fairly straightforward modern jazz. The later records add funkier beats and even a dose of rap. *Love Sweet Love* takes its title from a cover of the Bacharach/David standard, "What the World Needs Now," and includes guest vocals from members of **Take 6** on the song "Jesus, the Mention of Your Name."

Allies

Bob Carlisle, gtr., voc.; Randy Thomas, voc., gtr.; Matt Chapman, bass (–1992); Jim Erikson, drums (–1992); Sam Scott, kybrd. (–1987) // Brian Fullen, drums (+ 1992); Mark Hill, bass (+ 1992); Scott Sherriff, kybrd. (+ 1992). 1985—*Allies* (Light); 1986—*Virtues*; 1987—*Shoulder to Shoulder* (DaySpring); 1989—*Long Way from Paradise*; 1990—*The River*; 1992—*Man with a Mission*; 1995—*The Light Years* (Light).

Remembered primarily as the first successful pairing of **Bob Carlisle** and Randy Thomas, the Allies produced classic rock-pop albums that were generally ahead of their time for the Christian market in the late '80s. Before the Allies, Thomas was already well known in Christian circles for his role in the highly influential group, **Sweet Comfort Band** (which also included **Bryan Duncan**). The demise of that seminal act led him to contact old friends for a reunion of ex's from two previous outings: he had played with Carlisle and Jim Erikson in **Psalm 150** (which also included future members of **Andraé Crouch**'s Disciples, Damn Yankees, and Night Ranger) and with Sam Scott and Matt Chapman in a group called Sonrise. Thus in 1984 the Allies were born in San Bernardino, California. In later years, Chapman would turn up playing bass in **Clash of Symbols,** and Carlisle would earn fame for his sentimental ballad "Butterfly Kisses," written with Thomas. Besides penning that song, Carlisle and Thomas wrote "Why'd You Come in Here Looking Like That?" for Dolly Parton. Thomas would also become a member of **Identical Strangers.**

The first two Allies albums demonstrate a tendency to deal with social issues from a spiritual perspective: "Pardon Me" from the first album encourages children to forgive parents for the inadequacies of their upbringing, while "Prayer for the Children" on the second record addresses the issue of child abuse. Also on the sophomore release, "Jacque Remembers" relates Bob's gratitude for his wife's love, and "Let's Fall in Love (All Over Again") seeks to jar the conscience of those who might be considering divorce. The family orientation of such songs was to become a Carlisle/Thomas hallmark—years

before "Butterfly Kisses." Both albums were hurt by image-marketing that tried to capitalize on a current spiritual warfare fad (cf. **Petra, Matthew Ward**) by presenting the group in paramilitary outfits. *CCM* said these made them look like neo-Nazis and suggested a sound more in keeping with metal than pop. The group's third album, *Shoulder to Shoulder,* was self-produced in the band's own studio and was more successful commercially. The album emphasizes melody and hooks and capitalizes on the strength of Carlisle's voice on such pop anthems as "You're All I Needed" and "Looking on the Outside," as well as on the oddly paired "It's Never Easy" and "Easy as 1, 2, 3." *Long Way from Paradise* captured the attention of critics by displaying more of a garage-band sound. It closes with a cover of the **Elvis Presley** hit "Crying in the Chapel," and also includes a send-up of Muddy Waters' "Mannish Boy" entitled "Christian Man." *CCM* critic Thom Granger regards *Long Way from Paradise* as the Allies' masterpiece. It was the group's only album to make a list of "The 100 Greatest Albums in Christian Music" (at Number Sixty-nine) prepared by *CCM* in 2001. *The River* continues in this vein, though less successfully, with the soulful "Take Me to the River" (not an **Al Green** cover) and '50s style "Carried Away." The group goes for hard rock (à la Van Halen) on "Rock 'n' Roll Angel" and offers a plodding epic with the ten-minute "Can't Stop the River." *Man with a Mission* finds a re-formed group mostly returning to the mellow pop sounds of the earlier material. "In My Life" (not a Beatles cover) is an infectious sing-along piece. "I'm Crying" is Carlisle's testimony regarding the death of his father.

Throughout their career, the Allies struggled to find a musical identity and were sometimes overwhelmed by the eclecticism that could also be their strength. Songs like "Take Me Back" and "Crying" are gorgeous pop ballads; title tracks "Man with a Mission" and "Long Way from Paradise" are bluesy rockers. Also mixed into the stew are Journeyesque anthems ("All Day, All Night"), '60s bubblegum pop, and mellow numbers that certain critics would describe as pablum. Lyrically, the Allies tended to promote Jesus as the answer to personal and social problems, sometimes in a more simplistic way than Carlisle or Thomas would advocate in later years. In 1989, Thomas told *CCM* magazine, "As Christian songwriters, Bob and I always feel the pressure to 'redeem' the song or resolve it in a way that people have come to expect."

Christian radio hits: "Surrender" (# 3 in 1985); "Don't Run Away" (# 9 in 1985); "If You Believe" (# 6 in 1987); "How Much Love" (# 2 in 1988); "It's Never Easy" (# 7 in 1988); "Shoulder to Shoulder" (# 12 in 1988); "Take Me Back" (# 12 in 1989); "All Day, All Night" (# 14 in 1989); "Cryin' in the Chapel" (# 7 in 1989); "Trust in God" (# 4 in 1989); "I Wanna Be Like You" (# 22 in 1990); "Someone to Turn To" (# 11 in 1991); "Take Me to the River" (# 20 in 1991); "Grand Facade" (# 21 in 1992); "In My Life" (# 13 in 1992).

All Saved Freak Band

Mike Berkey, voc.; Ed Darkest, gtr.; Tom Eritano, drums; Rob Galbreath, kybrd., gtr.; Larry Hill, voc., kybrd.; Tom Hill, drums, bass; Morgan King, bass; Joe Markko, voc., gtr.; Randy Markko, bass (d. 1971); Kim Massmann, violin; Pam Massmann, cello; Tom Miller, voc. (d. 1971); Glenn Schwartz, gtr.; et al. 1973—*My Poor Generation* (Rock the World); 1976—*Brainwashed;* 1976—*For Christians, Elves, and Lovers;* 1980—*Sower* (War Again).

One of the most original bands in the history of contemporary Christian music sprang from an Ohio commune of Jesus freaks whose future would prove bizarre and tragic. The All Saved Freak Band was the musical outreach of Larry Hill's Church of the Risen Christ, and various members of the community's transient population performed with the group at different times. Tom Miller and Randy Markko died in a car accident in 1971 and so may or may not have contributed to recordings (Miller was a leader of the SDS and one of the Kent 25, the group of students who instituted the riots that preceded the shootings at Kent State University in 1970). **Phil Keaggy** supposedly played with the group before joining **Glass Harp,** but he does not seem to appear on any of the recordings. Still, the list of those who definitely did participate contains some impressive names: the Massmann sisters (Kim and Pam) are daughters of Dr. Richard Massmann, prestigious conductor of the Minnesota University Orchestra. Glenn Schwartz is the fabled guitarist who fronted the James Gang and **Pacific Gas and Electric.** In the late '60s Schwartz was considered one of the finest blues guitarists in the world. His work with James Gang was legendary, though he actually left that group (replaced by Joe Walsh) before they made any of their recordings. Around 1968, he got saved at the most famous of all Christian coffeehouses, **Arthur Blessitt**'s His Place on Sunset Strip. He founded **Pacific Gas and Electric** (later called PG&E, when the real Pacific Gas and Electric Company threatened to sue) and recorded what was to be their only major hit ("Are You Ready?" # 14 in 1971). While a member of this band, he played an instrumental role in the conversion of Rick Coghill, who later played with the group **Lamb.** Apparently Schwartz's family had him committed to an insane asylum, but after being released he joined the Ohio commune.

One-time Assemblies of God minister Larry Hill had founded the Church of the Risen Christ (first called Harper's Field Community Bible Church) in the late '60s. It was a Christian commune overseen by Hill and his right-hand prophetess Diane Sullivan. Initially, they focused on street witnessing to lost souls out and about in Cleveland or to students at Kent State. The musical group was used only to attract crowds. After Schwartz and the talented Massmanns joined, however, the emphasis changed to focus primarily on the band. The community moved to a farm near Orwell, Ohio, where everyone worked to support the band's ministry. Hill kept total control over all finances. ASFB toured extensively and was even named the official 1971 Mardi Gras band in New Orleans, designated to play the Mayor's Ball at City Hall. Meanwhile, Larry Hill had visions of the end of the world, which he published and declared the equivalent of Scripture. He determined that when redemption came, only members of his select group would be saved and so insisted that any who left the community's "Arc of Safety" would be damned for all eternity. The community began to stockpile weapons and to train in martial arts. Then Hill designated all women in the group to be his inner circle and sexual servants. Men were relegated to living in a barn and were periodically whipped or humiliated for various infractions. Eventually, government agencies intervened amid allegations of child abuse, and Sullivan voluntarily incriminated herself on all accounts. Hill reportedly fled the state to avoid prosecution.

The four albums by ASFB fluctuate between songs driven by Schwartz's guitar licks and ones that showcase the sweet vocals and baroque strings of the Massmann sisters. Hard rock and folk tunes intertwine, with flourishes of classical influence. The first album, *My Poor Generation,* capitalizes on Schwartz's firepower on only a couple of songs ("Great Victory," "Daughter of Zion"), but these feature harder edged Christian music than almost anyone else was considering at the time (but cf. **Agape**). The album opens with a folk-rock protest song ("Elder White") in the tradition of **Bob Dylan**'s "Ballad of Hollis Brown." The title track is a melodic pop song that seems intended as a response to Pete Townsend's "My Generation," lamenting the loss of youth to drugs and profligacy. Kim Massmann contributes a lovely rendition of the 23rd Psalm, and two otherwise unknown members, Carole and Morgan King, sing a duet that memorializes their lost colleague, "Tom Miller." The latter song is so remarkably reminiscent of Peter, Paul, and Mary that one may have to listen twice to be sure the Freaks didn't somehow obtain a Peter, Paul, and Mary outtake. But then they depart from the folk tradition completely with a slow blues number, "Ancient of Days." *My Poor Generation* also features "There Is Still Hope in Jesus," written in 1969 by Joe Markko as a theme song for Hill's aborted radio show and augmented now by spoken word testimonies and a brief sermon typical of the evangelical preaching that marked Jesus movement revivals. The album closes with another beautiful Massmann number, "Flowers of Time," which takes its inspiration from the concluding words of Romans 8. Hill sings lead on many of the songs on this debut ASFB album, and he does so quite admirably. *Jesus Music* lists *My Poor Generation* as a "totally essential Jesus rock album."

The most focused ASFB album is *For Christians, Elves, and Lovers.* Released simultaneously with *Brainwashed,* this record is loosely based on the works of J. R. R. Tolkien, which the group interprets in light of Christian spirituality and symbolism. Schwartz contributes two new rockers, "Waterstreet" and "Old Man Daniel," which have little to do with the theme. The Massmanns and Hill offer appropriately light and magical songs with titles like "Elfin Chimes," "By the Fire," and "Merry Go Round." A brooding "Theme of the Fellowship of the Ring" opens the second side. Interspersed with these Middle Earth fantasies are musical reflections on Scripture: "The 100th Psalm" is performed in what *Jesus Music* calls "a slow boogie style mixing fuzz bass with plucked strings and deep hums—just the kind of thing Tolkien's dwarves might have concocted."

If *For Christians* was intended as edification for the church, its companion *Brainwashed* seems to be directed to the unsaved. Mike Berkey calls on those who want peace and love to "Wake Up to Jesus" in the album's hand clappin', foot stompin' opener, "Peace Lovin' Rock 'n Roll." Schwartz humorously delivers his testimony amidst inspiring blues licks in "Messed Up" and in "Ode to Glenn Schwartz." Other tunes like "Seek Him" and "Don't Look Back" feature a psychedelic boogie sound that Canned Heat might have been proud to own. The song "Frog Alley" is a musical wonder but, directed at lower-income blacks who lived near the community, displays startling racial insensitivity. With Schwartz in the foreground, the Massmann sisters have a much more subdued role on this record, but they manage to provide warmth and mystery here and there ("Our Answer"). "Lonely" is perhaps their most melodic, happy song. Reviewing the album in 1976, *Harmony* magazine noted, "the ASFB seems to be particularly adept at composing haunting (if not eerie) songs." Indeed, that word *eerie* turns up in quite a few reviews of their work.

By the time *Sower* was released, the community had degenerated into infamy and the band was no more. Nevertheless, the album presents what many critics consider to be their best work, with Joe Markko dominating the vocals and other members exercised by an apocalyptic fervor that seems to ratchet everything up a few notches. The usually reserved Massmanns explode with the inflammatory but impassioned "Prince of the International Kaleidoscope" (apparently a rant against the papacy, though the Rockefellers, the Jesuits, and the John Birch Society all get a few whacks as well). Schwartz pulls out all stops on "All Across the Nation," which features a main riff borrowed from Mountain's "Mississippi Queen." The band's constant producer, Rob Galbraith, delivers his own version of "The Old Rugged Cross" as an appropriate finale. At least some of the material on *Sower* dates from 1971.

An announcement for a fifth ASFB album (called *Vow*) appeared in *Harmony* magazine in 1980, but such a record does not appear to have been released. As of 2000, Hill, the Massmanns, and Laura Markko (Randy and Joe's sister) continued to live together on an Ohio farm. Schwartz retired to Cleveland where he lives quietly with his brother and does not perform. Joe Markko became a minister with the Assemblies of God.

All Star United

Christian Crowe, drums; Ian Eskelin, voc.; Patrick McCallum, kybrd.; Brian Whitman, gtr. (−1997); Gary Miller, bass (−1998) // Dave Clo, gtr. (+ 1998); Adrian Walther, bass (+ 1999). 1997—*All Star United* (Reunion); 1999—*International Anthems for the Human Race*; 2000—*Smash Hits* (Essential); 2002—*Revolution* (Furious).

All Star United burst on to the scene of late '90s Christian music about the same time that ska groups (**The Supertones, Five Iron Frenzy**) were making an impression and **DC Talk** was ruling the airwaves. Formed in Nashville in 1996, they were immediately identified as part of a new trend toward "fun music," a label they well deserved. An ASU concert was first and foremost a party (or as reviewers were fond of saying, a "circus"). Blowing bubbles, leading the audience in the twist, donning ridiculous costumes, dashing frantically about on stage—this band would do whatever it took to be sure a good time was had by all. Their basic sound (described as a " '90s update of the Turtles" or "Oasis meets the Monkees") was so happy-go-lucky as to inspire amusement, and this was augmented through comical, tongue-in-cheek lyrics. The group initiated a retro-pop turn in Christian music that would soon be taken up in secular circles when bands like Smash Mouth mimicked them in content and style. Indeed, the latter group's biggest hit ("All Star") almost seems to have been written in tribute to their Christian forebears.

Singer/songwriter **Ian Eskelin** is clearly the group's leader. Formerly with **Code of Ethics**, he also enjoyed some success as a solo artist. In fact, the band originated as backing artists for what was intended to be a solo project. Patrick McCallum was recruited from the group **The Echoing Green.**

The first album features the song "Smash Hit," an irresistible Beatles-style ditty that pokes fun at the shallow consumerism of the Christian marketplace: "Join his name to any cause / Drop his name to get applause / This Jesus thing / It's a smash hit." The fact that the song became one of the year's most requested rock singles produced an irony not lost on its performers. But the song is only one of several bright spots on the debut album. The record opens with "La La Land," a hilarious send-up of Christians who think their faith guarantees them various temporal rewards: the Bible quoter who relies on "five happy verses," the evangelist who promises "a claim on power and wealth," and the fool who hopes his Jesus decal will save him from speeding tickets. All these are contrasted with saints and martyrs who surely would have demanded a better deal "if only they'd known their rights." The next song, "Bright Red Carpet," uses the image of entrance to an Oscars-like awards show to question whether the status-conscious will stroll the carpet at the most important opening of all, the kingdom of heaven. Other standout songs include the worshipful "Savior of My Universe," the sweet "Tenderness," and the bubbly "Beautiful Thing." Another song, "Torn," provides a brief departure from the album's light tone to take a poignant look at the sort of Christian struggle described by the Apostle Paul in Romans 7: "I'm torn in two / By what I should / Or should not do / Will you wait for me / If I run from you?"

International Anthems shows progression musically from the retro '60s sound to more of a retro '80s style—influences of Abba, Elton John, and Blondie are noticeable. The album was produced by Neill King (Green Day, Elvis Costello, Madness) who Eskelin says (gratefully) "didn't have a clue how Christian records ought to sound." From "Big Rock Show" (the opening, crunching rocker) through "Theme from Summer" (a happy nod to the Beach Boys) to "Thank You, Goodnight" (the appropriate prayerful closing song—though two hidden tracks follow), the album engages a diversity of styles with occasional flourishes of horns or strings. "Hurricane Baby" (one of the hidden tracks) is actually performed twice, once as a cabaret and then again the way Stray Cats-era Brian Setzer would have done it. Despite the variety of sound, Eskelin's penchant for humor and sarcasm remains constant: "Worldwide Socialites Unite" exhorts the status-conscious (his favorite target) to "keep the light in socialite"; "If We Were Lovers" plays on the double entendre of its title, using seductive language to invite Christians to become lovers of all people; "Popular Americans" pokes fun at airs of superiority stereotypically evidenced by Americans (and Christians); "Superstar" ridicules a culture of hero worship. Despite universally favorable reviews, *Anthems* lacked the novelty of ASU's first record and did not capture the attention (or dollars) of listeners to the same degree. A year after its release, a seemingly premature collection of hits was replacing it in the racks. That album *(Smash Hits)* does include two new relationship-themed songs ("Hang On," "Baby Come Back") that are quite worthy, but its exclusion of "La La Land" is inexplicable.

The 2002 album *Revolution* includes "Kings and Queens," a song that Eskelin says is about "the idea that we are all future royalty waiting to receive our crowns." "Sweet Jesus" is a personal worshipful tune, and "Global Breakdown" is a song that Eskelin says he wrote on September 11, 2001, while watching the events of that day unfold on CNN.

Christian radio hits: "Saviour of My Universe" (# 2 in 1997); "Tenderness" (# 6 in 1997); "Beautiful Thing" (# 13 in 1997); "Superstar" (# 4 in 1999); "Thank You, Goodnight" (# 4 in 1999).

All Together Separate

Dex Alexander, voc., kybrd.; Ben Rayls, drums; Charles Rumahlewang, bass, kybrd.; Andrew Shirley, gtr. 1999—*All Together Separate* (Ardent); 2001—*Ardent Worship: All Together Separate Live.*

www.alltogetherseparate.com

The group All Together Separate formed at California Baptist Bible College and cut its musical teeth performing for camps and various student conferences. The band's debut album consists of original material played in a mainstream style of R&B-inflected rock; it was nominated for the 2000 Dove award for Best Rock Album. A critic for *Christian Music* thought, "ATS is perhaps the closest thing to an Earth, Wind, and Fire-type sound that Christian music has ever produced." The Earth, Wind, and Fire connection is especially noticeable on "No Condemnation," but other tracks ("Face to Face") have a layered, textured sound more reminiscent of the Dave Matthews Band. The opening track, "On and On," is probably the best song musically, an all-out rock number with the bass defining its distinctive groove. All Together Separate is a ministry band and all four group members testify to their faith in language representative of their denominational heritage, speaking forthrightly of a "personal acceptance of Christ" as the ideal turning point of each individual's life. A primary theme of their album, however, is praise and worship. The song "Paradigm" is noteworthy: it begins softly and builds to a passionate conclusion, with the dreadlocked Dex Alexander screaming, "I give my life to you, so I may gain it back again." The multiracial composition of All Together Separate also gives them opportunity to testify to the inclusive nature of God's kingdom. Alexander says he hopes the group can "play a small part in showing the hope of Christ to our generation, to help them see themselves the way God sees them." In 2001, the band released a live worship album as part of a series of projects from their label (cf. **Satellite Soul, Skillet**). Recorded at their home church (Harvest Christian Fellowship in Riverside, California), the latter album features such modern worship songs as **Delirious?**'s "Did You Feel the Mountains Tremble?" and **Amy Grant**'s "We Believe in God." **Ta'ta Vega** provides guest vocals on "My Soul Finds Rest in You Alone."

The Alpha Band

T Bone Burnett, voc., gtr.; David Mansfield, gtr.; Steven Soles, gtr., voc.; David Jackson, bass (–1977); Matt Beton, drums (–1977) // Bill Maxwell, drums (+ 1978); David Miner, bass (+ 1978). 1976—*The Alpha Band* (Arista); 1977—*Spark in the Dark*; 1978—*Statue Makers of Hollywood*; 1994—*Interviews* (Edsel).

www.tmtm.com/sam

The Alpha Band was an outgrowth of **Bob Dylan**'s communal 1976 Rolling Thunder Revue. Dylan had assembled some of the finest country and blues musicians he could find for the long, successful tour. **T Bone Burnett,** David Mansfield, and **Steven Soles** were all alumni of the tour, and they stayed together to play their own Dylanesque music. The group released three albums (*Interviews* is a compilation) that were more critically acclaimed than commercially successful. The trio of guitarists gave the band a distinctively eclectic sound, which may have been as much a weakness as a strength. At times, they produced a retro-Beatles sound like that of Fleetwood Mac; other times the more predictable Americana sound of other Dylan protégés (e.g., The Band, Grateful Dead) came through. *Spark in the Dark* includes a cover of Dylan's "You Angel You" and features Ringo Starr on drums for two tracks. *The Statue Makers of Hollywood* is a sarcastic project that mocks the superficial esteem associated with celebrity. Bill Maxwell of **Andraé Crouch and the Disciples** joined the band for this third album, and Crouch arranged the background vocals.

All of the members of The Alpha Band were Christians, but they did not create records for the Christian music subculture, nor did they view their art in any primary sense as a vehicle for communicating their faith. Still, all three of The Alpha Band's albums contain some songs that touch explicitly on matters of faith and others that express a general worldview that challenges the dominant values of materialism. By the final project, some secular reviewers would complain that Burnett's "moralizing has become a bit strident." For some, The Alpha Band's albums represent an early entry of Christian music into the general marketplace. Historically, The Alpha Band is also significant for the influence they reportedly had on Dylan's 1979 conversion and for helping to launch Burnett's solo career. **Steven Soles** recorded a couple of solo projects also, in addition to producing albums for the **Seventy Sevens** and other Christian artists associated with the artistic Exit label; he then became manager for **Peter Case.**

The Altar Boys

Ric Alba, bass, kybrd.; Jeff Crandall, drums; Mike Stand, voc., gtr.; Steve Panier, gtr. (– 1984, + 1989); 1984—*Altar Boys* (M.R.C.); 1985—*When You're a Rebel* (Broken); 1986—*Gut Level Music* (Frontline); 1987—*Against the Grain;* 1989—*Forever Mercy* (Alarma); 1991—*The Collection;* 2000—*Live at Cornerstone 2000* (M8); *Mercy Thoughts.*

www.altarboys.com

As a seminal punk-rock trio, The Altar Boys gave Christian music a decade of unabashedly evangelical lyrics set to high energy riffs. They were founded in 1982 by **Mike Stand,** who has since gone on to pursue a solo career and to front the group **Clash of Symbols. Ric Alba** has also released a solo project. Stand's brother Kevin Lee (Annis) played with **Lifesavors** and **LSU.** Producer **Terry Taylor** has said of The Altar Boys, "One would be hard pressed to find another rock 'n' roll band in contemporary Christian music for whom the word 'passionate' is more fitting."

The first two albums did not see wide release. Radical for their time (in Christian circles at least), they demonstrate promising musicianship, though the several songs all tend to exhibit a singular plan of attack: a Ramones-inspired fast drive that made one critic say they sounded "like 33 1/3 LPs being played at 45 RPM." Most noteworthy, however, is the way The Altar Boys translate brash punk attitude into brazen profession of faith. Songs like "I'm into God" (which actually turns up on both of their first two records) evinces an audacity that is remarkable for a time when many Christian artists were looking for subtle or sneaky ways to talk about spiritual matters. The Altar Boys were into God and into Jesus, and they didn't much care whom that offended. In this regard, they did for one generation what **DC Talk** ("I'm not into hiding") did for another.

Gut Level Music brought the band national attention. Produced by **Terry Taylor** of **Daniel Amos** and featuring a cover of **Donna Summer**'s "Unconditional Love" (cf. **Age of Faith**), the group now embodied a sound more likely to be compared to the Clash or even to Bruce Springsteen than to the Ramones. The record opens with what was to become the group's best-known song, Stand's "You Are Loved," an anthemic rallying cry of affirmation. It also contains "You Found Me," which would be covered a decade later by **MxPx.** In a rather different vein, Alba's "Life Begins at the Cross" displays theological depth, inspiring critic Brian Quincy Newcomb to muse, "it's practically a Lenten hymn, worth publication in a postmodern hymnal." Still, the band retains their punk credentials through songs with an anti-institutional edge ("I'm Not Talkin' about Religion," "I Question It"). *Against the Grain,* also produced by Taylor, continues the development toward Springsteen-inflected working man's rock. Most noteworthy, perhaps, is the more pronounced empathy with troubled souls and the concern for a broader social ethic. Whereas *Gut Level Music* opened with the reassuring "You Are Loved," this album kicks off with "Fallen World" and continues with "Kids Are on the Run," "Hearts Lost in Nowhere," and "Broken." The album seeks to establish a common base between Christians and humanity in general. "Is the human sound just a scream?" an Alba composition asks ("Human Sound"). The title song provides something of an answer, with retrospective allusion to an earlier album title: "Love is what we need / It goes against the grain / If you want to be a rebel, maybe now's the time."

The olive branch that the Boys offered the general market with *Against the Grain* was accepted, and some doors opened for them to play in secular clubs. They even opened for the ironically named but very secular band, Jesus and Mary Chain. Still, the Boys' career was winding down. Stand recorded his first solo album in 1988 (enigmatically titled *Do I Stand Alone?*), then collaborated with the group one more time for

Forever Mercy. Produced by Steve Griffith of **Vector**—who also cowrote several songs—the album was a suitable finale, foreshadowing the new directions Stand and Alba would pursue while retaining a basic Altar Boys' crunch. Steve Pannier, an original Altar Boy who had left to form Fourth Watch, returned to add bluesy guitar on such standout tracks as "Ride This Train." The group reunited for a concert in 2000 that was released by M8 Distribution. That same year, Mike Stand put out *Mercy Thoughts,* a collection of twenty live cuts from his concerts (both with the Boys and as a solo artist) culled over an eight-year period. As of 2001, Stand was teaching music full time at an elementary school and playing worship music (with his brother Kevin Lee) for a youth group on Wednesday and Sunday nights.

For trivia buffs: Before hooking up with Stand and Alba, Crandall had a brief stint as a member of **Children of the Day** (about 180 degrees from The Altar Boys in musical style).

The Altered

Chuck Ash, voc., gtr.; Jeremy Ash, drums; Justin Bickers, gtr.; Buck Weiss, bass. 1997—*Yours Truly* (1997).

A small-town quartet from Illinois called The Altered produced a debut album of Midwest rock. Youth pastor Chuck Ash formed the group with his brother Jeremy, cousin Buck Weiss, and friend Justin Bickers. The band's name was taken from the William Hurt movie *Altered States.* The group was discovered in some sense by Peter King of **Dakoda Motor Co.,** who directed several videos that helped them to get noticed. Matt Slocum of **Love Coma** and **Sixpence None the Richer** adds cello and guitar on the album. Chuck Ash said he understood the band's vocation as "a ministry" in the broad sense, but he did not seek to be overtly evangelistic in his lyrics or stage shows. The ministry takes place as people notice "something different and have to attribute that difference to something." The song "Low" (not a Cracker cover) was nominated for a 1998 Dove award (Modern Rock/Alternative Song of the Year). Taking its cue from Ecclesiastes, it translates that book's philosophical musings about life without God into the simple confession, "I'm wasted without you." Another song, "Forty-Two," adapts the psalm of that number into a simple rock ballad, and "Ooh, Where Are You?" laments the loss of a friend who strayed from the narrow road. The title song is nicely reprised in an acoustic version as a hidden bonus track. The Altered disbanded after recording only one album, and Chuck and Jeremy Ash reemerged as a duo called **Ash Mundae.**

Rick Altizer

1998—*Blue Plate Special* (KMG); 1999—*Neon Fixation;* 2001—*Go Nova* (True Tunes).

www.rickaltizer.com

Although he is a licensed Nazarene minister who oversees worship at a church in a Nashville suburb, Rick Altizer defies whatever expectations those aspects of his résumé might conjure. "I won't do Christian fluff," he vowed to KMG executives before signing with that label, and indeed he hasn't. The singer/songwriter has collaborated with ex-King Crimson guitarist Adrian Belew on alternative-pop albums that travel in the same stream as The Cars or Elvis Costello, but are really too innovative for easy comparison. The title song from his first album expresses revulsion at what is advertised as "special" but is in fact only "yesterday's chicken . . . the same thing with cole slaw." Altizer has been determined not to serve up such musical mediocrities.

Aside from Belew's guitar, Altizer plays all the instruments on *Blue Plate Special,* but he credits these to various fictitious incarnations of himself whose photos are displayed in the packaging—an indication of the somewhat wacky humor that attends the project. The songs themselves also seem to arise from various incarnations. The disparity between the rocking opener "Make a Monkey" (which ends its verses with almost-quotes from Beatle songs) and the appropriately atmospheric "Oxygen Tank" recalls aural juxtaposition of Billy Idol's "Rebel Yell" and "Eyes Without a Face." Is this really the same artist performing both tunes? Then, on "In L.A." (an indictment of big-city indifference), Altizer does a credible Tom Petty imitation. But Altizer wears each guise authentically, grounding every mutation in solid song construction that is definitively his own. The album's first single, "How Many," muses on the greatness of God ("How many broken hearts have you mended? How many prayers have you heard?") and smallness of humans ("How many fears do I hold on to? How many sins . . .?"). "River of Grace" is a soulful worship song on which Belew's guitar seems literally to flow. Altizer's best received songs, however, have been the ones on which he goes Dylan: "Jan the Best" (an ode to his wife) and "When You Walked up That Hill" (a "Were You There?"-type spiritual about the crucifixion).

Neon Fixation continues in the same vein as the first album, with an overall theme stated in the title song: the human tendency to be attracted by artificial light as opposed to the light of God. Comparing the sophomore project to the debut, *Musicforce* notes, "the unforgettable hooks, the rapier wit, and the spiritually potent lyrics are (again) in evidence." Songs like "Disco Ball," "TV Preacher," and "Ray Guns and Plastic Flash" betray the sort of punchy pop and good humor associated with **All Star United,** while others ("Let It Go," "Surrender to You," "Untitled") continue in the folk-rock tradition of the first album's best material. Belew produces six of the eleven tracks. The centerpiece of the album is the somewhat unfortunate "I'll

Say Yes," Altizer's tribute to Cassie Bernall, a victim of the Columbine shootings in Littleton, Colorado. The song was written for evangelistic campaigns conducted by Dawson McAllister and, as such, is easily given to uses that capitalize on the teenager's death in exploitative ways. The song itself, however, avoids the extravagance of **Michael W. Smith**'s "This is Your Time" by focusing more on Altizer's own reaction to the news of Bernall's confession than on the incident itself. As such, it offers a call for personal affirmation of faith in the face of evil (*"I'll* say yes").

On *Go Nova* Altizer embraces a retro sound that often puts him in the company of **Randy Stonehill** or **Terry Scott Taylor** (whose "I Love You # 19" he covers). "CM Superstar" is a sort of "Uncle Rand" (cf. Stonehill) sarcastic song that mocks banality in the Christian music industry. Altizer also offers his own version of "Gold Coast" and "Last Day of Summer," which were covered by **Rebecca St. James** and **Skillet,** respectively, on Taylor's *Surfonic Water Revival* album (KMG, 1998).

Altizer's sometime producer and collaborator Adrian Belew has had an interesting career in his own right. He did not play with Robert Fripp on King Crimson's classic albums of the '60s and '70s (e.g., *In the Court of the Crimson King*), but was guitarist in a new version of that band assembled by Fripp in the early '80s. He also played guitar for David Bowie and then entered the Christian music scene as the producer responsible for twin masterpieces ("Liquid," "Flood") on **Jars of Clay**'s first album.

Christian radio hits: "How Many?" (# 16 in 1998); "I'll Say Yes (She Said Yes)" (# 11 in 1999).

Jason Alvarez

1981—*Just Give Me Jesus* (Light).

Cuban refugee Jason Alvarez grew up on the streets of Newark, New Jersey, and became a recognized composer in the general market before releasing a Christian album in 1981. Alvarez and his mother fled war-torn Cuba with the help of the American Embassy in 1961 (just before the Bay of Pigs invasion). After a rough adolescence, his musical gifts allowed him to transcend the poverty of tenement-house living, and he went on to compose songs for such artists as The Duprees, Chuck Jackson, The Moments, and Charlie Rich. His huge hit came early with "Shame, Shame, Shame," a Number One R&B song for Shirley and Co. in 1975, a song that would eventually sell three-and-a-half million records. Unfortunately, Alvarez had signed away all royalties to that tune in a bad contract negotiation. Alvarez was led to embrace Christianity in the early '80s through the witness of his estranged wife, Gail. His album *Just Give Me Jesus* features original songs in both English and Spanish. The style is disco-inflected R&B with heavy Latin leanings. The album did not do well commercially, arriving

about two years too late for the disco phenomenon and about nineteen years too soon for the Latin invasion that would afford success to similar-sounding artists like Ricky Martin.

Maia Amada

1993—*Maia Amada* (DaySpring); 1994—*Faith Remains* (Intersound).

A classically trained singer of Spanish descent, Maia Amada from Scarsdale, New York, brings a powerful voice to R&B flavored songs written by her husband Alan Pugielli. Involved in music since childhood, she performed in a Broadway show (*The Me Nobody Knows*) at age fourteen and a year later toured as a singer in the Alan Pugielli Band, eventually marrying the bandleader. She dreamed of being a "big emotional singer" in the tradition of Sarah Vaughan, Shirley Bassey (her favorite), or Billie Holiday. In 1980, a religious experience caused her and her husband to put their lives "in God's hands." Amada's two Christian albums feature a mix of upbeat, lively tunes and soulful ballads. *CCM* notes that her songs do not typically feature distinctive "Christian buzzwords" but celebrate love and other fruits of the spirit in ways that instill potential crossover general market appeal. The debut album scores with the adult dance numbers "There's a Place" and "Soul Deep" (not a Box Tops cover).

Christian radio hits: "Love Never Fails" (# 15 in 1992); "Love Is for Always" (# 1 for 3 weeks in 1993); "There's a Place" (# 5 in 1993); "Second Chances" (# 9 in 1995); "Love's the Key" (# 3 in 1995).

Amarachi (and Gail Moore)

Gail Moore, voc.; et al. As Amarachi: 1991—*Keep On Singin': Gospel Reggae, Vol. 1*. As Gail Moore: date unknown—*Faithfully* (Moore Ministries).

www.mooreministries.com

Amarachi is noteworthy for being the first Christian band to release an album of reggae music, thus prefiguring the work of **Christafari** and **Temple Yard.** The group was founded in Nigeria as the outreach of the local Calvary Chapel church, pastored by Austen Ezenwa. It became a showcase for the vocal talents of Gail Moore, a former backup singer to Phil Collins who has also worked with Michael Jackson and **Donna Summer.** The name "Amarachi" means "grace of God" in a Nigerian dialect. *Keep on Singin'* includes reggae versions of **Bob Bennett**'s "You're Welcome Here" and "Blessed Jesus." There does not appear to have been a Gospel Reggae, Vol. 2, but Moore's solo album is also a collection of Christian reggae songs. It includes a version of **Van Morrison**'s "Have I Told You Lately That I Love You."

For trivia buffs: Gail Moore is married to Art Moore, former NFL tackle with the New England Patriots. Together, they founded Moore Ministries in 1979 to "reach the youth of America with the positive life-changing message of Christ."

Amaziah

Paul Loader, bass; Dave Steel, kybrd.; Phil Williams, drums; Derek Elliot, voc. (–1979); Jez Strode, gtr. (–1979). 1979—*Straight Shooter* (Sonrise).

Amaziah was a hard rock British band featuring aggressive guitars and powerful synthesizers. Their album includes one power ballad ("All Is Peace") and one song that features a more progressive "modern rock sound" ("Way, Truth, Life"). Otherwise, it is what *Jesus Music* magazine calls "homemade, heavy, monster rock." That same publication calls Derek Elliott's vocals "an acquired taste." Amaziah's songs feature blatantly Christian lyrics—as do those of most '70s Christian rock bands. Their album was later remixed and reissued on red vinyl by a Canadian label (Tunesmith). This edition, which became much better known, features a new cover, containing a picture of the band—except that it *isn't* the band. Elliott and Jez Strode had left. Dave Steel's brother Kev stood in for the photo and everyone dressed up as punk-rockers—which they certainly were not. A copy of Amaziah's album with its original cover can sell for up to $1500.

Ambient Theology

Stefan Nelson; Greg Young. 1995—*Ambient Theology* (N'Soul).

Stefan Nelson and Greg Young, who also create techno music under the names **Bubblebaby,** Resolution, and **Virus,** produced one of the first albums of ambient music to gain much recognition in the Christian market. Adopting the name Ambient Theology, they crafted a concept piece dealing with creation and the interface of nature and spirit. The opening track, "Formless," combines the sounds of bubbling water with eerie synthesizers to suggest a world that is indeed "without form and void." Then the Spirit moves "Over the Face of the Deep." Several pieces deal with virtues of forgiveness, sacrifice, "Hope," and "Love." Of course, all of these pieces are instrumentals, and the ambient sounds are at best suggestive. Accordingly, a devotional booklet accompanies the album (cf. **Tom Howard**'s *The Hidden Passage*), providing meditations for each piece. When one uses the album as suggested—as background music for reading this accompanying book—one discovers that all the devotions are related to the life and teaching of Christ. Thus, "Formless" turns out to be about humanity, not just the primordial earth, and what seemed at first suggestive of creation is reapplied to redemption. Such polyvalence is definitive of the ambient music genre.

American Made

Aaron Brown, drums; Chris Brown, gtr.; Danneal Castillo, voc.; Eric Keeler, bass. 1999—*Against the Flow* (KMG).

American Made attempts to combine punk and rap music in a unique and diverse way. "We're probably the only rap/punk band ever to exist," lead vocalist Danneal Castillo told *HM.* "The rest of the band grew up listening to bands like Rancid and the Ramones. . . . I grew up on L.L. Cool J." Some critics would compare the band's debut album to the rap songs of **DC Talk** or **Reality Check.** A closer comparison would actually be **The Huntingtons,** as the group's punk drive tends to overshadow the pop and rap aspects. Strong cuts include the title track (a straightforward punk song) and their cover of The Corbins' "Kick It," which takes them into the '90s party rock sound of Sugar Ray. "That Thing I Do" is not the **Rick** and **Linda Elias** song that served as the title track for the Tom Hanks movie *(That Thing You Do),* but it is almost as catchy and melodic. Another tune, "Nintendo," exhibits the group's penchant for carefree lyrics: "I was thinking just today . . . of all the fun and joy Nintendo's given me . . . but Nintendo can't set you free." Critic Josh Spencer describes the band's sound as teetering on the brink between "overproduced-commercial" and "gritty authentic." *HM* magazine is less ambiguous: "It's hard not to totally fall in love with this band."

Among Thorns

Dave Childress, bass; Brandon Eller, drums; Matt Gilder, kybrd.; Jason Harrison, voc.; Gary Ishee, gtr.; Darin Sasser, gtr. 1999—*Among Thorns* (Worship Extreme); 2001—*Desperate* (Here to Him).

www.sirrealrecords.com

Billed as a "praise and worship band," Among Thorns is composed of a group of young men from Texas who met at a college Bible study and began performing for church youth groups and then started working with evangelist Ken Freeman. They have been especially popular at programs sponsored by Baptist churches. The songs on their first album are almost all addressed to God, heartfelt appeals set to acoustic pop melodies. "Call To You" celebrates the ability to call upon God in any time of need; "Embrace This Place" communicates the security of finding closeness to God in an environment of serene worship. *Desperate* offers more original songs, all with the "intense youth group feel" of a Midwest version of **Delirious?** The opening "No Rock" is straightforward praise, with reference to Luke 19:40. "Lay It Down" is a powerful modern hymn of consecration. "Wind of God" celebrates and invokes the Spirit, and the title track is a song of adoration: "What a beautiful God you are / Nothing I have seen compares to you."

Amplified Version

1975 Lineup: Michael Beaman, gtr.; Darryl Carter, kybrd.; Fred Llapitan, drums; Shirley Monroe, voc.; Carol Morgan, voc.; Paul Morgan, voc.; Billy Morgette, bass; Marty Powell, voc. Date unknown—*One in the Son*

(New World); *He's My Brother* (New Life); 1975—*Whatcha' Gonna Do?* (NewPax); 1979—*Alive* (Chrism).

This early Jesus movement band is remembered for its album *Whatcha Gonna Do?* which revealed their indebtedness to producer **Gary S. Paxton.** Their sound was distinctive in its use of brass (seven horns), recalling such early-'70s outfits as Chicago or Blood, Sweat, and Tears. Two Paxton songs received a lot of attention: "Jesus Is My Lawyer in Heaven" and "Jesus Keeps Takin' Me Higher and Higher." These and the title song constitute the album's high-energy numbers. Another Paxton song, "Gadget Man," is noteworthy for its complex and original structure. Rohn Bailey (kybrd.), **Bruce Hibbard** (voc., gtr.), Jorge Marsal (perc.), and Shirley Marsal (voc.) were also members of the group at some point.

Michael Anderson

1988—*Sound Alarm* (A&M); 1990—*Michael Anderson;* 1993—*Saints and Sinners* (ForeFront); 1996—*Love Is the Hard Part.*

www.michaelanderson.com

A prolific songwriter whose song "Promise Man" won the 1996 Dove award for Hard Rock Song of the Year for **Holy Soldier,** Michael Anderson is better associated in some circles with country and bluegrass music. Anderson's career has crossed boundaries between sacred and secular music as well. A Michigan native who moved to Los Angeles in 1977, Anderson was first signed as a rock singer to A&M, and the title track from his debut album for that label received considerable airplay on album-oriented stations (the lyrics were based on the prophetic oracle in Joel 2). Anderson also wrote "No Loving You" for John Fogerty and "Maybe It Was Memphis" for country singer Pam Tillis, which earned him a Song of the Year Award from the Country Music Association. At the same time, he was making his mark in Christian music, penning hits for artists as diverse as **Russ Taff** ("I Need You") and **Rhythm House.** In recent years, he has written or cowritten such Christian market hits as "Sticks and Stones" for **Code of Ethics** and "Go and Sin No More" for **Rebecca St. James.** He collaborated with **Michael Omartian** on his *The Race,* cowriting the hits "Faithful Forever" and "Let My Heart Be the First To Know."

Sound Alarm bewildered executives at A&M who weren't sure how to market a rock album with such high spiritual content. The eponymous follow-up, produced by Omartian, was more polished and less direct in its religious references, but did not do well commercially. Nevertheless, these first two records established Anderson as a singer who was impassioned about addressing life's problems from a perspective of faith. "Soweto Soul" looks at the tragedy of apartheid in South Africa, with one eye on the racial riots surrounding the Rodney King trial in Los Angeles. "I Think It's Time to Go Home" is a deeply per-

sonal statement about Anderson's reconciliation with his father after eighteen years of noncommunication. "I Know That You Can Stand" is a testimony to the power of faith to overcome fear and adversity.

Saints and Sinners was effectively Anderson's Christian market debut. The record pairs him with producer **Eddie DeGarmo** and showcases his soulful voice and acoustic guitar on country-inflected pop tunes. The Jordanaires provide background vocals, and **Ashley Cleveland** and **Bob Carlisle** also put in guest appearances. In several songs ("God's Been Good to Me," "I Keep Comin' Back to Jesus," "Man from Galilee") the gospel content is explicit. The album also includes a bluesy remake of "Sound Alarm" (with fiddle and dobro). The song "What You Gonna Do About Jesus?" features the provocative line, "He don't give a damn about your religion" (the *he* being Jesus).

The next album, *Love is the Hard Part,* defied expectations again as Anderson adopted a more Peter Gabriel-style eclecticism. He covers **Larry Norman**'s "Shot Down," offers some acoustic pop ("I Know It's Not the Rain"), and then churns out some funky Memphis-soul numbers ("Soul Man Myself," "No Easy Way"). The title track seems to be equally inspired by 1 Corinthians 13 and John Lennon's "Love." It reflects poignantly on the difficulty of fulfilling every Christian's prime directive: "Love's a river, love's a fire / Love is every heart's desire / Love is knowing only time will tell / Love is heaven, love is hell."

Anderson sees himself as a songwriter first and a performer second. Although he seems to have found his niche in the contemporary Christian market, he maintains that he never sets out to write "Christian songs." Rather, his songs are Christian because he is a Christian and the songs come from within him. "I don't know how *not* to do it," he avers, while remaining critical of the Christian music industry when it attempts to devise standards for defining whether a song is adequately "Christian" or not.

For trivia buffs: Anderson is also the author of the Civil War novel *Shiloh,* and he wrote the corresponding screenplay, *Shiloh: A Confederate Love Story.*

Christian radio hits: "Saints and Sinners" (# 8 in 1993); "I Know It's Not the Rain" (# 8 in 1996).

Scott Anderson

1988—*Somebody Loves You* (Pan Trax); 1992—*Somethin' Different* (Mercy).

Scott Anderson is regularly described as bearing an uncanny resemblance to **Larry Norman** in both musical style and personality. Silly songs are mixed with gritty ones in a bluesy blend that does not take itself too seriously but points quickly to Jesus Christ as the answer to problems large and small. His album *Somethin' Different* features old-fashioned folk-rock songs with titles like "Still Holding On to the Good News" and "Love Your Neighbor Kind of Stuff." Anderson also presents a straightforward message reminiscent of songs from the Jesus movement revival two decades before. He sings "There's a love I've found in Jesus" ("There's a Love") and suggests, "When you're feeling down and out / Take your heart to heaven for a while" ("Take Your Heart to Heaven").

Andrus, Blackwood, and Co.

Sherman Andrus, voc.; Terry Blackwood, voc., Bill Egtlin, kybrd., voc.; Rocky Laughlin, bass; Tim Marsh, drums; Bob Villareal, kybrd., voc.; Karen Voegtlin, voc. 1977—*Grand Opening* (Greentree); 1978—*Following You*; 1980—*Live*; 1981—*Soldiers of the Light*; 1982—*Step Out of the Night*; 1984—*Best of; Holiday* (Nissi).

The group (essentially duo) Andrus, Blackwood, and Co. was a spin-off from the highly successful vocal ensemble **The Imperials,** though both Andrus and Blackwood had musical pedigrees that preceded their involvement with that group. **Sherman Andrus** had been a founding member of **Andraé Crouch and the Disciples. Terry Blackwood** was the son of Doyle Blackwood, founder of one of the most successful gospel quartets of all time, the Blackwood Brothers. After bringing **The Imperials** to the attention of a younger audience, Andrus and Blackwood sought to find their own niche in the burgeoning contemporary Christian market. Andrus, Blackwood, and Co. was formed in 1977. The two were not songwriters, but their popular recordings helped to establish the careers of such composers as **Bruce Hibbard,** Hadley Hockensmith, Phil Johnson, and Tim Sheppard. Their music incorporated jazzy influences ("Step Out of the Night") and even Alan Parsons-style synthesizers ("No You May Not"), with more traditional songs reflecting their southern gospel roots ("God-Made Man," "The Other Side"). *Following You* is an ambitious two-record set with a gatefold cover and includes songs by Johnson and Sheppard, as well as by **Reba Rambo** and **Dony McGuire.** The *Live* album brings out some of the humor of the group's shows, as when Andrus offers a tongue-in-cheek '50s version of "Jesus You're So Wonderful." Andrus and Blackwood were a racially integrated duo (Andrus is black and Blackwood, white), a rarity in the music industry, religious or secular. At the height of their career, they dominated their genre in an unprecedented way. Indeed, in 1981, there were only nine weeks when the Number One song on Christian radio stations was *not* by Andrus, Blackwood, and Co. Both artists also pursued solo careers, as did background singer **Karen Voegtlin.**

Christian radio hits: "Following You" (# 10 in 1979); "You're So Good to Me" (# 9 in 1979); "Jesus You're So Wonderful" (# 1 for 20 weeks in 1981); "Soldier of the Light" (# 1 for 23 weeks in 1981); "Step Out of the Night" (# 1 in 1983); "Stone's Throw Away" (# 7 in 1983); "No You May Not" (# 29 in 1983); "Amen Again" (# 8 in 1985).

Sherman Andrus

1974—*I've Got Confidence* (Impact); 1976—*Soon Coming* (Shalom); 1978—*How the Years Go By*; 1982—*Revisited* (Christian World); *Caution to the Wind* (Amethyst).

Sherman Andrus was a founding member of **Andraé Crouch and the Disciples** and then, from 1971 to 1976, helped to give **The Imperials** (mainstays of southern gospel) credibility with a new, younger audience. During the latter period he released his first solo album, featuring his take on Crouch's "I've Got Confidence." Andrus also performed with Terry Blackwood in **Andrus, Blackwood, and Co.** He was, with Crouch, one of the first black singers to break into the contemporary Christian market. He humorously recalls his mission as being "to boldly go where no black man had gone before." Andrus attended Southern University in Baton Rouge, Louisiana. He also lived in Los Angeles and Oklahoma City.

Angela

1998—*Heaven Knows Me* (Solace).

Angela Crimi is a Roman Catholic pop singer who recorded her first album under her first name only at age twenty-two, just four years after being miraculously delivered through a Catholic healing evangelist from what she calls "a sinful life." At age eighteen, she was singing in her boyfriend's rock band, taking drugs, and suffering from anorexia and bulimia. When the evangelist placed his hands on her head and prayed for her—against her will—she maintains that the power of God came into her and changed everything. Angela is somewhat distinctive in the contemporary Christian scene for her devotion to Roman Catholic piety. Alongside her witness to the redemptive power of Jesus, she speaks forthrightly (in Catholic settings at least) of her devotion to the rosary and adoration of Mary: "Our Lady really brought me closer to her Son, especially through the Eucharist and the Mass. I always ask her for advice. She's our mother, why not go to her?" Angela cohosts a TV show called *Focus,* which uses popular music as a venue for talking about issues of importance to youth.

A different artist (an African American woman) named Angela recorded an album of Christian music called *Faithful and True* in 2000.

Angeldust

See **Circle of Dust.**

Angelica

Dennis Cameron, gtr.; Andy Lyon, voc. (– 1990) // Jerome Mazza, voc. (+ 1990, –1991); Robert Pallen, bass (+ 1990); Drew Baca, voc. (+ 1991); Bobby Lawrence, drums (+ 1991). 1989—*Angelica* (Intense); 1990—

Walkin' in Faith; 1991—Rock, Stock, and Barrel; 1992—Time Is All It Takes; 1993—Greatest Hits; 1998—Classic Archives (KMG).

The hard rocking Christian band Angelica was basically a showcase for the guitar histrionics of Dennis Cameron from Renfrew, Ontario. The rhythm section was uncharacteristically subdued for hard rock, and the band went through three different singers. It was Cameron's guitar that attracted all the attention, prompting somewhat exaggerated comparisons to Eddie Van Halen. *HM* proclaimed the debut record "the sleeper metal album of the year" and called special attention to the song "Are You Satisfied?" which deals with the spiritual status of a fallen friend. "Shine on Me" is a stadium screamer from that album, and the opening track, "There's Only One Hero," a midtempo power-pop song similar to something **Petra** might have done. Guest vocals on the first project were provided by Rob Rock of **Joshua** (and later **Impellitteri**). *Walkin' in Faith* was a bit of a sophomore slump commercially, but includes the very Van Halen-ish "Time and Time Again." The song "Harvest" is an instrumental that shows off some of Cameron's hottest licks, and the title track is an escalating number that explodes into a Bon Jovi-like arena anthem after more than a minute of instrumental build-up. For their last two albums, Angelica featured vocals by Drew Baca that seemed uncharacteristically clean and smooth for metal (*HM* called them "candy-coated"). This gave the group a modicum of pop appeal that set them apart from some of their peers. *Rock, Stock, and Barrel* displays a more blues-influenced hard rock approach à la Aerosmith. "Cover Me," "Home Sweet Heaven," "Keep Pushing On," and "Rhyme and Reason" are highlights, and an affectionate instrumental cover of "Oh Canada" closes the project. *Time Is All it Takes* is best remembered for the standout song, "Don't Stop" (not a Fleetwood Mac cover); the tune begins with a picking-and-strumming introduction and builds into an anthem with a guitar solo midway through. Its lyrics draw from Jesus' parable about building a house on rock or sand (Matthew 7:24–27). "Open Your Mind" is a particularly stellar Van Halen clone and "Gotta Get Ready" is another Aerosmith-like track urging preparation for the apocalypse. "Second Chance" is an atypical power ballad, a format that (unlike many Christian metal bands) Angelica avoided running into the ground.

Angelo and Veronica

Angelo Petrucci, voc.; Veronica Petrucci, voc. 1992—*Higher Place* (Benson); 1993—*A & V*; 1995—*Give Your Life*; 1996—*Not Enough*; 1999—*Change* (Harmony).

The husband and wife duo of Angelo and Veronica deliver urban R&B-flavored gospel music of the sort usually associated with African American artists. Actually, Angelo is Italian and Veronica is Puerto Rican, and the ethnic confusion has caused problems over the years. The group complained to *CCM* in 1994 that some white churches wouldn't book them because they thought they were black, and that some black fans had rejected them when they learned that they weren't. The couple comes by its sound honestly, having been introduced to Christian music through **Commissioned's Fred Hammond,** who has sometimes served as their producer. Angelo's smooth tenor reminds many listeners of **BeBe Winans,** while Veronica's belting howls recall Chaka Kahn. The couple met at the Berklee School of Music in Boston, married in 1992, and moved to Nashville.

The first record staked out a claim in urban sounds with fierce club tunes like "I Know" and "I'll Be There." It garnered the duo a 1993 Dove nomination for Best New Artist. *A & V* moves more into the adult contemporary market, featuring an exceptional remake of Carole King's "You've Got a Friend." The hit song "No Doubt About It" was cowritten by Michael Bolton. *Give Your Life* (released internationally as *Da Tu Vida*) returns the group to the R&B fold, but with more of a Latin feel on some songs. "Emotional" is the hot track on that album, and "Miracles," the pop ballad with a nice sax solo. By *Not Enough,* critics had grown tired of the Petruccis' disco-for-the-'90's sound and began to complain that they needed to show some innovation. Benson let their contract run out, but after a three-year hiatus the group returned with *Change* on an independent label run by ordained minister Raina Bundy. This release was the less-programmed product critics had desired. Two songs ("I've Been Thinking," "Make Up Your Mind") introduce rap, while "Praise the Lord" evinces a fully Latin sound complete with Spanish lyrics. Angelo covers the **Fred Hammond** hit that had introduced him to Christian music years earlier ("Running Back to You"), and the duo revamps Bill Withers' "Just the Two of Us." Unfortunately, the album ends with a spoken-word altar call that detracts musically and gives the project a sectarian cast.

Angelo and Veronica enjoyed slight secular success when one of their songs, "I Love You More," was featured on the CBS soap opera *As the World Turns.* Nevertheless, they claim to be "ministers first and musicians second." The lyrics to their songs are often strongly evangelical, with an emphasis on praise and worship. Their concerts can take on the air of revival meetings, peppered with shouts (from the stage and from the audience) of "amen," "praise the Lord," and "thank you, Jesus."

Christian radio hits: "Knocking on Your Door" (# 4 in 1993); "I Know" (# 6 in 1993); "I'll Be There" (# 17 in 1993); "You Loved Me When" (# 18 in 1994); "No Doubt About It" (# 19 in 1994); "Emotional" (# 16 in 1995).

Dove Awards: 1995 Contemporary Gospel Song ("God Knows"); 1996 Urban Album (*Give Your Life*).

Angie and Debbie

See **Angie and Debbie Winans.**

Anguish Unsaid

Brian Faucett, gtr.; John Edwards, voc.; John Ross, gtr.; Justin Thomas, bass; Shannon Tuttle, drums // John Jensen, kybrd. (+ 2000). 1999—*Wanting . . . Waiting* (Bettie Rocket); 2000—*The Chronicles of the Restoration of the Church*.

Anguish Unsaid is a hardcore band from Sacramento, California, whose sound is described by guitarist Brian Faucett as "kind of like Fugazi meets Black Flag meets Keith Green in a fist-fight in an alley." Their songs are notably more lengthy than those of many punk outfits and convey explicit gospel themes. The group has played a number of secular venues in spite of their evangelical orientation. "Most people can't understand the words to hardcore anyway," says lead singer and lyricist John Edwards, "but we talk in between songs." The group also hands out lyric sheets at its shows, for those who are interested. The debut album *Wanting . . . Waiting* deals with the theme of yearning for Christ's return. The sophomore project, *The Chronicles of the Restoration of the Church,* moves more in the direction of what *HM* would style as art-rock. Both albums feature songs with titles that seem to advertise theological treatises: "Confession in Times of Tribulation" from the first and "Key Factors the Devil Overlooked" from the second. The band says they took their name from the reluctance of people to talk about Christ's anguish on the cross: "people want to portray him always smiling or like he just took a shower, but nothing really portrays what took place."

Annie

Joel Bordeaux, kybrd., trump.; Patrick McNeely, bass; David Morton, drums; Stephen Nichols, voc., gtr.; Jeff Wickes, gtr. 1999—*Sci-fi Canon Blue(s)* (BulletProof).

With a sound reminiscent of Radiohead, psychedelic pop band Annie debuted with an album that met with universal raves from the alternative Christian music press. The quintet from Cleveland, Tennessee, presents eight songs laden with Beatles-style harmonies, ethereal guitar arrangements, and appropriate helpings of piano, trumpet, and strings. "Artsy but not pretentious," *The Lighthouse* said. The song "Shoot First, Leap Second" is bouncy light-hearted pop, while "Censer Silence" features more melodramatic crooning and existentialist lyrics ("When all things pass away / We will still remain / Through the supple lift of enormity"). "The Ice Storm" features Jeff Wickes's guitar and more accessible poetry redolent with Christmas imagery: "Late one night in a Middle East explosion / An eternal notion to save the world / To redeem the spirit of forgiving / The reason we are living has been unfurled."

While the members of the group are Christians and their songs have spiritual themes, they have resisted identification with the Christian market, claiming to have signed with the Christian label BulletProof only as a last resort. "There's so much in the Christian market that's belittling, I think, to the musicians, and quite frankly to God and Jesus Christ," says guitarist Wickes. "I think that the Christian market is based around taking a half-ass song, putting the right words on it, and selling a million copies . . . hence, a band like **DC Talk** that's really not all that good are millionaires."

Anointed

Steve Crawford, voc.; Da'dra Crawford Greathouse, voc.; Nee-C Walls, voc. (– 2001); Mary Tiller, voc. (– 1995). 1993—*Spiritual Love Affair* (Word); 1995—*The Call* (Myrrh); 1996—*Under the Influence*; 1999—*Anointed*; 2001—*If We Pray*.

The African American vocal group known as Anointed hails from Columbus, Ohio, where they formed in 1988 and were later discovered by producer Gene Eugene (of **Adam Again**). In 1992, they backed **Vickie Winans** on her album *The Lady*. The band combines hard-driving urban contemporary dance music with smooth-flowing ballads, most of which are written by the group members themselves. Steve Crawford and Da'dra Crawford Greathouse are siblings. The group began as a quartet with an unusual gender balance (one man, three women) and continued as a trio when Tiller dropped out, alleging sexual harassment on the part of Anointed's manager and suing the group for breach of contract related to their reluctance to fire that person (the other members of Anointed maintain that Tiller did not inform them fully of the problems and that the conflict had appeared to them to be a personal issue). By 2001, Anointed had shrunk to a sibling duo.

The debut album, *Spiritual Love Affair,* won Anointed an audience among fans of upbeat R&B and earned the group a Stellar award for Best New Artist. "God's Personality" opens the album with a swingbeat sound. "The Other Side" is a particularly funky number, with aural allusions to Mary J. Blige. The title track is an adult contemporary ballad disguising a worship song with double entendres that allow it to be heard as a paean to romantic bliss. With *The Call,* Anointed turned down the volume to the disappointment of some, and dug deeper theologically, to the delight of others. The album does feature the jazzy house-party song, "If I Labor," but also includes "Send Out a Prayer," which recalls the acoustic folk songs of Tracy Chapman. Its standout cut is "It's in God's Hands Now," which *CCM* magazine describes as "a painful confessional about letting go of a spouse who doesn't want to stay in a relationship." By dealing so effectively with a topic (divorce) that affects many Christians but is rarely mentioned in Christian music, Anointed scored points for daring and sensitivity. The song also enjoyed some mainstream success, charting on *Billboard*'s Top 40 R&B list. The next album, *Under the Influence,* continues the group's journey from urban to pop. "Waiting in the Wings" was compared to Christopher Cross's "Sailing" on account of its backdrop of waterfall guitars. The title track ("Under the Influence") opens and closes the album with diverse acoustic and upbeat mixes. It employs the strained but biblical (Acts 2:13; Ephesians 5:18) metaphor of drunkenness to describe life in the Spirit. Other tracks include "Get Ready," a funky/bluesy call to prepare for the Lord's return, and a beautiful, soulful rendition of "Take Me Back." The self-titled fourth album does take the group back to the more urban sound with which they began. Their vocals are backed with more contemporary electronic sounds. The appropriately rousing "Revive Us" received immediate attention, though greater depth can be found in "Something Was Missing" and "Love by Grace," songs that deal with life's disappointments. "Head above Water" and "It's All Good" offer encouragement to the frustrated and perplexed. *If We Pray* is a concept album focusing on the theme of daily prayer, which is encouraged in the Latin-pop of its opening title track. "Nothing Can Stop You from Loving Me" is a funky party song celebrating God's amazing grace. "Rejoice" and "One Fine Day" (not the Carole King song) are also strong upbeat numbers. The album's clear standout is "Things I Wish," a soulful ballad by **Tommy Sims** that showcases Steve Crawford's buttery vocals. The intended radio hit, "You'll Never Thirst," is a typical adult contemporary ballad with strong lyrics inspired by the story of Jesus and the woman at the well (John 4).

The members of Anointed all came from single-parent households and, when the group first recorded, ranged in age from nineteen to twenty-three. As such, they considered it part of their ministry to set positive role models for young people, especially young urban blacks. Notably, they all pursued college educations while recording, proclaiming a "stay in school" message alongside their more evangelistic exhortations. They have also striven to overcome racial barriers in Christian music, however, telling *CCM* in 1999 that they try to bring three diverse audiences together: young, conservative whites who like Christian pop; young, liberal African Americans who like urban music; and older, moderate African Americans who like gospel.

Christian radio hits: "God's Personality" (# 23 in 1993); "Send Out a Prayer" (# 2 in 1995); "The Call" (# 8 in 1995); "Under the Influence" (# 3 in 1996); "Waiting in the Wings" (# 2 in 1997); "Adore You" (# 3 in 1997); "Revive Us" (# 5 in 1999); "Godspot" (# 16 in 1999).

Dove Awards: 1996 Contemporary Gospel Album *(The Call)*; 1996 Contemporary Gospel Song ("The Call"); 1996 Urban Song ("It's in God's Hands Now"); 1997 Urban Song ("Under the Influence"); 2000 Contemporary Gospel Album *(Anointed)*; 2000 Urban Song ("Anything Is Possible").

Antestor

Armoth, drums; Gard, bass; Martyr, voc.; Vermod, gtr., kybrd. 1997—*The Return of the Black Death* (Cacophonous); 2000—*Martyrium* (SWE).

Antestor is a death- or black-metal band from Norway. Their sound is ominous and brooding, though the group testifies to their faith with unambiguous lyrics. The albums listed above were recorded in the opposite order of their release. *Martyrium* was actually recorded in 1994 and three of the songs were featured on a metal compilation album called *Northern Lights* (Rowe), but the full project's release was held up by legal complications. The song "Have Mercy" is based on Psalm 51. The group underwent a change of style for their second recording *(The Return of the Black Death),* slowing down the usually super-rapid pace and adding more atmospheric keyboards. They coined the term "sorrow metal" to describe what they took to be their own distinctive genre. Notably, the label on which *Return of the Black Death* was released (Cacophonous) is one especially known for artists associated with occult and overtly satanic music. That company's official press release for Antestor indicates that "lyrically, the band steers away from the well-worn paths of occultism and violence, concentrating more on . . . death and what happens hereafter." The song "Bridge of Death" proclaims, "Satan says he'll set me free, but he's a loser just like me." "Battlefield" exhorts, "Rejoice in the Lord, for him we'll fight." A song titled "Depressed" quotes directly from Psalm 51: "Create in me a clean heart O God / Give me a new and steadfast spirit / Do not drive me from thy presence." The most powerful song on the album, "A Sovereign Fortress," is based on Psalm 46 (as is Martin Luther's "A Mighty Fortress is Our God"). *Martyrium* is entirely in English, but the lyrics to some of the songs on *Return of the Black Death* are in Norwegian.

Antidote

Jorge Goyco, electronics; Leigh Goyco, voc. 1998—*What Mountain?* (N'Soul); 1999—*Fight or Flight*; 2000—*Forget Yourself.*

Antidote offers the following self-description of their sound: "electronic dance trip-hop funky acid trance." *The Lighthouse* just describes it as "experimental and out there." The husband and wife duo from Austin, Texas, present instrumental and vocal tracks directed to the rave scene of club dancers. The instrumentals tend to recall such general market artists as Tricky, Crystal Method, or Prodigy, while the vocal numbers are more reminiscent of Björk or Portishead. The third album exhibits a more focused sound than is evident on the first two. On all of the records, however, the lyrics on the vocal numbers are blatantly religious. The song "Love" from the first album is almost an instrumental, but with an electronic voice repeating the words "God is love" over and over again. "Everywhere I Go" from *Forget Yourself* is about taking a Bible wherever one goes. Another recurrent theme is renunciation of belief in alien life forms. Jorge Goyco thinks the "aliens" involved in so-called extra-terrestrial sightings (or abductions) are actually demonic manifestations sent to trick humans into believing that they are not a special creation of God. He further says the mission of Antidote is twofold: "One part is to tell unsaved ravers that God loves them . . . second is to encourage Christians into a deeper relationship with God." Then he adds what could be a third purpose, "to supply sanctified dance music for God's people."

Any Given Day

Personnel varies (see below). 1999—*Passionate Worship for the Soul* (BEC); 2001—*Earth to Heaven*.

Any Given Day is not exactly a group but a marketing label employed in a confusing and potentially deceptive manner. At first, BEC announced the formation of a new "praise and worship band" called Any Given Day, formed by two members of **The Supertones** (Jason Carson, drums; Tony Terusa, bass). The pair linked up with worship leader Andrew Bray and recorded a debut album of praise songs similar to what were traditionally featured in the worship segments of concerts by the Christian ska band. The debut album, *Passionate Worship for the Soul,* presents songs performed in a style popular with many collegiate Bible study/prayer groups. The sound, in other words, is *not* ska as **The Supertones** connection might have suggested (cf. the *Skalleluia* praise albums by **The Insyderz**), but, rather, features heartfelt singing to a basic guitar and piano accompaniment. Emphasis in song selection is on modern classics like "Lord, I Lift Your Name on High" and "I Stand in Awe." Any Given Day was featured as "a new artist" in various Christian publications and gave interviews in which they presented themselves as such. The second Any Given Day album *(Earth to Heaven),* however, was not by the group that had previously been called Any Given Day but was by a completely different band—in fact it was by the novice Christian group **Cadet.** A credible project on its own terms, its merits were spoiled by this apparent marketing attempt to trick fans of the defunct Any Given Day into buying an album by **Cadet** without knowing it. Even *CCM*'s Brian Quincy Newcomb (Christian rock's best critic) fell for the ploy and reviewed the album unknowingly as a second effort from **The Supertones**-spin-off band. Artist representation explained that BEC had decided to use "Any Given Day" as a logo for a series of worship albums, all of which would be by different groups. For information on the *Earth to Heaven* album, see the listing for **Cadet.**

A-1 Swift

Alisha Tyler, voc.; Christ Tyler, voc. 1994—*Turn Yourself Around* (Gospo-Centric); 1996—*Tales from the Swift.*

The husband and wife team of A-1 Swift is a male-female rap duo (a rarity even in the general market) that seeks to min-

ister to young people attracted to hard-edged gangsta rap. Chris Tyler was previously in a vocal/dance troupe called Cold Premiere (featured as rappers in the Kid and Play movie, *Class Act*). He converted his wife Alisha from the Catholicism in which she was raised (but from which she had strayed in any case) to a form of Christianity oriented toward a more individualistic understanding of salvation. Together, the two of them now express the message of this personal salvation through music that, according to Chris, sounds "like Ice Cube or A Tribe Called Quest." The group also seeks to address social issues, "such as guns, violence, and the image of being a gangster or drug dealer." The duo originally chose their name just because they liked the sound (inspired by a bottle of steak sauce) but they later decided that "Swift" could be an acronym for "Salvation Will Indeed Feel Terrific."

Apocalypse

Kirk Miller, voc.; Jamerson Smith, voc. 1991—*Holiness or Hell* (Frontline).

The members of the African American rap duo Apocalypse go by the stage names "Notorious K" and "Al Capone of the Microphone." *True Tunes* likens their style to Public Enemy, calling it "big time hard street rap." Apocalypse favors intense, confrontational lyrics that challenge Christians to be strong in their faith and to get tough with the devil and his allies. "Apocalypse Hot Mix" deals with racial strife through a message addressed primarily to black Americans, denouncing prejudice (against whites) disguised as black pride and lamenting, "because of slavery, servanthood is embarrassing." In "Crucifix," the group calls on the listener to "get your blessed assurance up off the church pew" and get involved in society.

Apologetix

J. John Jackson, voc., gtr.; Karl Messner, gtr. // Stan Haynie, bass (+ 1995); Fred Behenna, drums (+ 1999). 1994—*Radical History Tour* (independent); 1997—*Ticked!*; 1998—*Jesus Christ Morningstar*; 1999—*Biblical Graffiti*.

www.apologetix.com

Most Christian bands resent being regarded as the Christian counterpart to some artist in the general market, but Apologetix boldly announces that they are "a Christian version of Weird Al Yankovic." They put somewhat goofy biblical or inspirational lyrics to well-known rock songs. For instance, the Beatles' "Twist and Shout" becomes "Twins Came Out" (the story of Jacob and Esau); the Hollies' "Long Cool Woman in a Black Dress" turns into "Lawful Woman in a Bad Place" (the story of Rahab); the Beach Boys' "Fun, Fun, Fun" is now "John 1:1"; Aerosmith's "Walk This Way" becomes "Walk His Way." The first album applied such shenanigans to twenty rock classics like "Bohemian Rhapsody," "Maggie May," and "Cat Scratch Fever." The next took on twenty-two more, now including alternative/grunge hits like "No Apologies," "Lump," and "You Oughta Know." *Jesus Christ Morningstar* returned to the classics with eighteen parodies of songs like "Lucy in the Sky," "Pinball Wizard," and "American Pie." *Biblical Graffiti* mixed genres, lampooning the Monkees ("Pleasant Valley Sunday"), Smash Mouth ("Walking on the Sun"), and Metallica ("Enter Sandman").

The name Apologetix derives from a creative spelling of apologetics, the science of explaining or defending the truth of Christianity to skeptics (1 Peter 3:15). The seriousness of the name belies any notion that the group's parodies are all meant to be humorous. Apologetix mixes the silly with the serious. For instance, their remake of Beck's "Loser" as a worship song ("I want you to save me, so why don't you fill me?") aims to be inspiring, not funny. The band is a popular act on the Bible college circuit and repeatedly earns marks for their dead-on musical imitations of diverse pop genres. They recently received the endorsement of Weird Al's drummer, Jon "Bermuda" Schwarz, who sat in for seven tracks on *Biblical Graffiti*. Schwarz said, "Your material is quite good, and the message is . . . accessible . . . not every track is a sermon—a lot of listeners will appreciate that."

Apoptygma Berserk

Personnel list unavailable. 1993—*Soli Deo Gloria* (Tatra); 1996—*7*; 1998—*The Apocalyptic Manifesto* (Metropolis); 2000—*Welcome to Earth*.

Very little information is available about Apoptygma Berserk—from their label or anywhere else. The group is apparently a Norwegian trio that has been making Christian electronic music since 1989. Male vocals are provided by a Stephen Grothesk. The music is described as a blend of a driving, quick-pulse style of electronic music and more traditional synthpop. *Soli Deo Gloria* (i.e., "to God alone be glory") was their first full-length release, and the album *7* is generally regarded as the group's best work. It includes two songs that were successful club hits in Europe ("Non-Stop Violence," "Deep Red") and was re-released for American audiences on Metropolis in 1998. The *Manifesto* album on Metropolis is a collection of singles from the group's nine-year European career. *Welcome to Earth* is permeated with a futuristic sci-fi vibe and includes a cover of Metallica's "Fade to Black." Apoptygma Berserk's lyrics are often sparse and vague, making explicit Christian content less accessible than in, say, the dance music of **Scott Blackwell** or **Disco Saints.** The album *7* includes a song on which sampled voices describe Christ as a rebel for breaking with tradition ("Rebel"). *Soli Deo Gloria* and *Manifesto* both include a song called "Burning Heretic" about Christian persecution of other Christians (e.g., the Inquisition). Both of those albums also contain a song with the offensive title "Bitch" about broken relationships.

Applehead

Greg Minier, voc., gtr., bass, drums, kybrd. 1993—*Meaning* (Ocean).

www.crucifyd.com

Applehead is a solo project by **Greg Minier** of the hybrid-hardcore band **The Crucified.** On this side project, Minier goes for a basic Nirvana-grunge sound. The title track has a slow, ethereal '60s feel, and "Intermittent You" recalls elements of The Stone Roses. "Monkey on My Back" is the most energetic number. More interesting lyrically are "Six Feet Under," which reflects on death, and "Crutch," which accepts the accusation that Christians rely on Christ as a crutch, admitting that they (and all people) are crippled without him.

Appleseed Cast

Christopher Crisci, voc., gtr.; Aaron Pillar, gtr., voc.; Louie Ruiz, drums (– 2001); Jason Wickersheim, bass (– 2001) // Josh Baruth, drums (+ 2001); Marc Young, bass (+ 2001). 1998—*The End of the Ring Wars* (Deep Elm); 2000—*Mare Vitalis*; 2001—*Low Level Owl, Vol. 1*; *Low Level Owl, Vol. 2*.

www.theappleseedcast.com

Although they maintain they are "not a Christian band," Appleseed Cast from Lawrence, Kansas, has a following among Christian music fans who have sometimes thought of them as a Christian band nonetheless. Lead singer Christopher Crisci explains how he believes the "misconception" got started: "I'm a Christian and I have a few friends who are in Christian bands and we have done a few things with them." The band played the *Cornerstone* festival in 1998 and 1999 and has toured with other Christian artists, playing for primarily Christian audiences. A number of Christian music magazines *(HM, Cornerstone, True Tunes)* have profiled the band and run reviews of its albums. By 2001, however, the situation had changed and the group was distancing itself from the Christian music subculture.

Musically, Appleseed Cast plays what is called post-hard-core emo music. *Pillowfight* says "Appleseed Cast is all about feeling." *Bandoppler* describes their sound as "the shimmering tears of honest men." *Phantom Tollbooth* notes their potential for appeal to "the wounded of heart (or the chronically whiny, depending on your perspective)." The first album does not appear to draw from Tolkien's tales, as its title might suggest, but traces the story of a broken relationship (probably a marriage, given the titular "ring") and the consequent struggle to overcome lingering sorrow. The sound is often layered and unpredictable: "Portrait" features loud, driving feedback and discord; "Stars" introduces piano and a mellow saxophone. The second record, *Mare Vitalis* (Latin for "living sea"), was viewed as a major step forward, as a rare album that truly sounds unique. After a dark, brooding prelude, the sound suddenly takes flight with a stunning number called "Fishing the Sky." The finale to the album, "Storms," has also drawn special acclaim for its surprising beauty. Appleseed Cast also placed three songs on a special split-artist CD released by Deep Elm in 1999 (featuring their work and that of two other bands, Planes Mistaken for Stars and Race Car Riot). One of these, "Tale of the Aftermath," is apparently intended as an epilogue to the saga of *The Ring Wars*. In 2001, the group issued a two-volume twenty-six-song work, *Low Level Owl*. Volume One of this project begins with several songs reminiscent of the *Mare Vitalis* material (a tad too reminiscent for some critics) but then shifts into what *HM* would call a more "earthy" sound midway through. That same magazine describes *Volume 2* as continuing that "aesthetic revolution" with songs that "shiver your bones with probing melodies, wet whispers, itchy bridges, and misty harmonies." About half the tracks on each *Owl* volume are instrumental.

There is little in the lyrics to Appleseed Cast's songs to suggest specific connections to Christianity, but Christian fans do claim to find spiritual enlightenment and inspiration in the band's songs. Crisci says, "We write music that reflects how we feel, and sometimes that has something spiritual in it. I am happy that people can make that connection and that it means something to them. That's the way it should be." Still, the band certainly does not offer the sort of solutions to life's problems that are sometimes expected from Christian artists. "Remedios the Beautiful," from the split-artist CD, closes out that album with pretty guitars and soft voices singing, "Pain by the pound / I want to help you / But I don't know how."

In 2001, Crisci would tell *HM* magazine that he was the "only remaining Christian in the group" (Aaron Pillar is Jewish), and although they enjoyed the fanbase among the Christian culture, they did not think there was any integrity in trying to maintain that sort of connection. Specifically, he said the group had decided not to play *Cornerstone* any more, nor to support the festival. "I have really mixed feelings about Cornerstone," Crisci said. "It has the best and worst of Christianity. The best is the display of faith and community and access to a lot of music and artists, but at the same time there's that greed system at work . . . all these CDs, shirts, hats, visors, posters, jewelry, all with Christ's name or image being sold for profit. It's the 'Brood of Vipers' thing."

Other purveyors of emo popular among Christian music fans include **Dear Ephesus**, Mineral, **Pedro the Lion**, and **Sunny Day Real Estate**.

Apt. Core

Will Hunt; et al. 2001—*Rhythms of Remembrance* (Rocketown).

Producer Will Hunt put together a project he called Apt. Core that *CCM* would designate "one of the most left-field re-

cordings to come out of Christian music." *HM* described it as "a techno-influenced project that bursts out of Nashville like a bad boy out of the penalty box." Basically, Hunt weds Scripture recitation (both spoken and sung) to ambient, electronic music. The sound of *Rhythms of Remembrance* is often tame, but sometimes bursts into Chemical Brothers-inspired industrial music. The record's opening track, "Creed," features pulsating percussion and a Middle-Eastern-sitar backed reading of the Apostles' Creed. "The Way" focuses on John 14:6, sung by a melodic chorus. A version of **U2**'s "40" is included as the album's only accessible, melodic track. **Ginny Owens** and other singers contribute vocals on the album.

Christian radio hits: "40" [with **Ginny Owens**] (# 18 in 2001).

AP2

Buka; Level. 2000—*Suspension of Disbelief* (Tooth and Nail).

The figures in AP2's name stand for "Argyle Park Two." The group considers itself to be "the next generation" of the seminal Christian industrial band **Argyle Park,** whose story should perhaps be read prior to this one. In this version, **Level** (i.e., Dan Levler, who released a solo album in 1998) replaces Klay Scott (a.k.a. Scott Albert). The new album continues in the vein of the first by bringing together diverse sounds. Although the basic core is industrial rock, heavy influences of techno music and thrash metal are stirred into the mix, along with surprising moments of tribal chants and meditative acoustic guitars. The appeal of such amalgamation is heightened once more by the appearance of numerous guest stars, including vocals by Joel Bell of **Ghoti Hook,** Daren Diolosa of **Klank** and **Circle of Dust,** and Mark Salomon of **Stavesacre** and **The Crucified.** Scott returns to offer guest vocals on "Resurrection of the Ravens," and he produces two tracks that he also cowrote. The songs on *Suspension of Disbelief* continue in the angry spirit of those that made **Argyle Park** infamous, but this time the bitterness is directed against social injustices and worldly evils ("Heroin Hate") rather than against the bandmate's personal enemies.

Arcade

See **Heather and Kirsten.**

Iain Archer

1994—*Playing Dead* (Sticky Music); 1996—*Crazy Bird*; 1997—*Revelation Bell*; 2001—*For What Feels Like Forever.*

A folk-influenced singer/songwriter from Belfast, Iain Archer is often described as an Irish version of **Bruce Cockburn.** The singer is noted for his laid-back performances at Christian festivals where he chats casually with his audience between songs. Bill Mallonee of the **Vigilantes of Love** once said of his voice, "When that man *talks,* it's musical!" Archer's first album contains the single "Wishing," which has been described as "infuriatingly memorable," and the ballad "Papa Burns," which describes a chance meeting between two old school friends. *Crazy Bird* features Archer with no backing band. Accompanied by a lone guitar, he sings songs of love, loneliness, and quiet faith. The title track has a Celtic melody and has become a favorite of Archer's fans. *Revelation Bell* is a short album of seven songs with a darker, more electric tone. The lyrics, too, tend to be imaginative and impenetrable, somewhat confusing for his traditional audience. *For What Feels Like Forever* is an EP of just four songs, mixing acoustic and electric genres in a brew that reminds some reviewers of Neil Young. It includes "Mirrorball Moon," which *Phantom Tollbooth* called "Archer's best song to date."

Steve Archer

1982—*Solo* (Home Sweet Home); 1984—*Through His Eyes of Love* (Myrrh); 1985—*Action* (Home Sweet Home); 1987—*Off the Page*; 1988— *Steve Archer Hits*; 1994—*Christian Contemporary Classics with Steve Archer* (Diadem); 1998—*Stay Right Here* (Kle-Toi).

Californian Steve Archer (b. 1954) began singing professionally at the age of nine, and by nineteen was recording with the family group **The Archers.** After a decade with the family, he decided to apply his familiar voice to solo material, producing a debut album of adult contemporary, inspirational tunes. His second album (which includes an unpredictable rendition of **Mark Heard**'s "Eye of the Storm") rose to Number One on contemporary Christian Music charts. In 1985, he remade one of the songs from that album as a duet with **Marilyn McCoo** of Fifth Dimension fame. The resulting single, "Safe," was to be Archer's biggest adult contemporary hit, drawing attention to his third album *Action.* His next album, *Off the Page,* includes a cover of the Staples Singers' "If You're Ready (Come Go with Me)" as well as the funky "Jump" (with sizzling saxophone) and the toe-tapping opener, "S.O.S." Twelve years later, *Stay Right Here* would continue the formula of combining such bouncy tracks with worshipful blue-eyed soul ballads. By then, a reviewer for *The Lighthouse* couldn't decide "whether Archer has a retro feel or just sounds dated." At any rate, the music continues to appeal to those who like the sound of Hall and Oates or Mike and the Mechanics. Steve Archer was divorced in 1981 (just before his first solo album appeared) and then again in 1991. Those break-ups, however, did not bring upon him the sort of disdain that has sometimes come to Christian artists whose marriages fail.

Christian radio hits: "But You Didn't" (# 9 in 1982); "Treasure" (# 13 in 1983); "Through His Eyes of Love" (# 15 in 1984).

The Archers

Steve Archer, voc.; Tim Archer, voc.; Nancy Short, voc. (–1976) // Janice Archer, voc. (+ 1976). 1971—*Put On Jesus* (Charisma); 1972—*Any Day Now*; 1972—*Life in Jesus* (Benson); 1973—*The Archers* [= reissue of *Any Day Now*] (Impact); 1974—*Keep Singin' That Love Song* (Benson); 1974— *The Archers' Golden Classics* (Light); 1975—*Things We Feel Deeply*; 1975— *In the Beginning*; 1977—*Fresh Surrender*; 1978—*Stand Up*; 1979—*Celebrate (Live)*; 1981—*Spreadin' Like Wildfire* (Songbird); 1982—*The Archers at Their Very Best* (Light); 1984—*All Systems Are Go*; *Golden Classics*; 1991—*Colors of Your Love* (Reunion); *Second Time Around*.

A northern California singing family with roots deep in the Jesus movement, The Archers produced stellar albums of MOR pop and launched the solo career of **Steve Archer.** Just like Donny Osmond and Michael Jackson, Steve began singing with his brothers (Tim, Gary, and Ron) when he was only nine (in 1965). Gary and Ron both went on to be pastors (in California and the Netherlands, respectively), and in 1969, the duo of Tim and Steve took second place in a national competition. For six more years they continued to perform as The Archer Brothers before deciding to add a female vocalist, amend their name, and begin a recording career as the trio listed above. They would go on to produce several Number One songs on Christian radio (before charts were published), including "Jesus Is the Answer" (written by **Andraé Crouch**). In 1972, they sang before 250,000 enthusiastic Jesus people at *Explo '72* (dubbed "the Christian Woodstock" by *Life* magazine). In 1979, The Archers were invited to the White House to play for the Carters. In 1980, they won a Grammy Award for their contribution to *The Lord's Prayer* (Light), a musical by **Reba Rambo** and **Dony McGuire.** The Archers' sound featured tight, blended harmonies with members trading leads—similar to '70s-era **The Imperials,** but with the addition of female vocals. They won praise from *Billboard* magazine, which once wrote, "The Archers have too much going for them to miss." Rock guitarist Billy Masters played with The Archers from 1971 to 1976 and wrote some of their songs. The group also helped to launch the career of keyboard player Phil Kristianson, who went on to play for **Amy Grant**'s band and then to work as a band leader for Promise Keepers. Sister Janice (who officially joined when she finished high school, but had toured and sung with the group earlier) eventually married John Cruse of **The Cruse Family.** The Archers took a hiatus from recording in the mid '80s but returned in 1991 with *The Colors of Your Love.* The song "Be Our Guest" from that album is an invitation for the Holy Spirit to dwell in the lives of believers. Both *The Colors of Your Love* and its follow-up *(Second Time Around)* reveal a group striving to stay up-to-date with harder edged sounds, synthesizers, and more soulful vocals. Christian musician **Erick Nelson** has summarized The Archers' role in the development of contemporary Christian music as representing one-half of a convergence: traditional vocal groups like The Archers got hipper while the hippie rock groups (like the Maranatha bands) got more mellow—eventually both evinced the polished, commercial sound that would be identified as stereotypical contemporary Christian music.

Christian radio hits: "Fresh Surrender" (# 7 in 1978); "Pickin' Up the Pieces" (# 11 in 1979); "Stand Up" (# 9 in 1980); "Spreadin' Like Wildfire" (# 10 in 1982); "Heaven in Your Eyes" (# 2 in 1985); "Be Our Guest" (# 19 in 1991).

Carolyn Arends

1995—*I Can Hear You* (Reunion); 1997—*Feel Free*; 1999—*This Much I Understand*; 2000—*Seize the Day and Other Stories.*

www.carolynarends.com

A native of Vancouver, British Columbia, Carolyn Arends (b. 1968) has charted two general market Top 10 hits in her homeland ("This Is the Stuff," "I Can Hear You"). In the United States, she was pigeon-holed early as a Christian singer but within that more limited market racked up enough songs to fill a greatest hits package after only five years of recording. Arends composes most of her own songs and, in fact, was first signed to her label as a staff songwriter. Before recording her own material, she penned the Dove award-winning "Love Will" for **Michael James Murphy,** as well as other songs for **4 Him, Susan Ashton, Lisa Bevill** ("Place in the Sun") and **Kim Boyce.** As a performer, she has progressed stylistically with each of her albums, as though trying out different persona. On *I Can Hear You,* she comes across as a modern (upbeat) folk singer in the tradition of Shawn Colvin or Suzanne Vega. On *Feel Free,* she fronts a country-rock band and the comparisons shift to Bonnie Raitt. Finally, she moves to something "in between," to cite the title of a standout song on her third album. The best mainstream comparison for her full body of work might be to Sheryl Crow, who has also performed convincingly in a number of styles.

The song "Seize the Day" from Arends' first record relates successive stories of individuals who do or don't make the most of the time God has given them. The title track from that album, "I Can Hear You," is addressed to God, expressing Arends' recognition of the divine presence in everyday sounds (church bells, birdsong, laughter). She has identified the writings of Frederick Buechner as influential in shaping these thoughts. "This is the Stuff" offers the commonsense observation that the essence of life is found in everyday moments: "The smallest moments / This is the stuff I need to notice." The album's softest moment comes with "Reaching," a tender ballad of yearning and searching. "Altar of Ego" is a confessional song of commitment to the principle of self-denial. "Love Is Always There" is one of the most straightforward

evangelical numbers, proclaiming the abiding and constant presence of God's love. "The Power of Love" is not a Huey Lewis (or a **T Bone Burnett**) cover, but a song that cleverly contrasts the phenomenon named in its overused title with an even-more popular "love of power."

Feel Free kicks off with the Beatlesque "Do What You Do," which Arends maintains was inspired by the Dr. Seuss book *Oh, the Places You'll Go.* The album then moves on to "New Year's Day." This is not the **U2** song (though Arends did include a slow, passionate cover of that group's "Where the Streets Have No Name" in her tour to support the album), but an original composition focusing humorously on the failure of resolutions ("I buy a lot of diaries / Fill them full of good intentions"). "Father Thy Will Be Done" is a prayer of surrender built around the famous line from the Lord's Prayer. Arends would later reveal that she wrote the song in anticipation of a funeral for the husband of one of her friends. "There You Are" revisits the theme of finding God's presence in little and surprising aspects of everyday life. "This I Know" is one of Arends' most aggressive country-rock tracks, listing a few certainties in life—the title derives from a line of the children's song "Jesus Loves Me."

This Much I Understand opens with a song called "Happy," which sets the tone for what one reviewer called an "angst-free approach" ("You can call me a child / But I will not lie down . . . I will dare to dream / I will dare to believe"). On the same record, "Surprised Within Joy" displays a traditional gospel jubilance. Still, the overall mood of *This Much I Understand* is more contemplative and introspective than the first two records, reflecting perhaps Arends' grief over the death of her close friend **Rich Mullins.** "We've Been Waiting for You" is a touching reflection on the birth of the artist's first child set against a simple piano accompaniment. The retrospective hits package *(Seize the Day)* includes live versions of five songs (featuring guest performances by **Phil Keaggy** and Mac Powell of **Third Day**) and a new version of the traditional youth group song, "They'll Know We Are Christians by Our Love."

Arends' songs are typically perceptive—she holds a degree in psychology, as well as ones in English and music—and her lyrics betray the sort of personal intimacy found in **Amy Grant**'s best work (e.g., *Behind the Eyes*). "Lyrics that softly startle," *CCM* magazine said, as early as 1995. The song "In Between" relates, "We remember the highs / We can't forget the lows / We live most of our lives / Somewhere in between." Then, with an honest ambiguity that recalls **Sam Phillips,** it continues, "We are heroes, we are villains / We are lovers, we are leavers / We are skeptics or believers / We are everything in between." In 2000, Arends published a vulnerable and articulate autobiography called *Living the Questions* (Harvest House).

For trivia buffs: one of the guitars heard behind Arends on *This Much I Understand* belongs to Randy Bachman (of The Guess Who and Bachman Turner Overdrive). The album was recorded at a Vancouver studio owned by Bachman, and he sat in on certain numbers, especially "Even the Wallflowers."

Christian radio hits: "The Power of Love" (# 10 in 1996); "I Can Hear You" (# 13 in 1996); "New Year's Day" (# 12 in 1997); "Do What You Do" (# 3 in 1997); "Big Deal" (# 13 in 1997); "Father, Thy Will Be Done" (# 14 in 1998).

Argyle Park

Buka; Klay Scott. 1995—*Misguided* (R.E.X.).

The saga of Argyle Park is one of the more curious and potentially confusing stories in the annals of Christian metal music. Often hailed as "the greatest Christian industrial band ever," the group (or duo) made but one album, disbanded, and then reappeared (sort of) as **AP2**. An unusual amount of disinformation was dispensed with regard to Argyle Park, sometimes delightedly by the band itself, and then even more so by fans who were either confused or just joining in the fun of confounding reporters trying to write books like this one.

First, the personnel. The album credits list three group members: Buka, Deathwish, and Dred. Buka is the professional name for a performer who claims to have been a child of missionary parents and to have become enamored of percussion and "worldbeat" sounds while growing up in Africa. Dred and Deathwish, however, are both just aliases for Klay Scott, who used to go by the name Scott Albert and under that name gained renown for his work in **Circle of Dust.** Later, he would record with **Angeldust** and decide to change his name to both Klayton and Celldweller. In addition to the official members (Buka and Scott), Argyle Park included a plethora of guest performers, especially vocalists. The participation of members of **Chatterbox** (Jeff Bellew), **The Crucified** (Mark Salomon), **Focused** (Dirk Lemmenes), Foetus (Jim Thirwell), **Klank** (Daren Diolosa), **Mortal/Fold Zandura** (Jyro), and the **Vigilantes of Love** (Chris Donohue) has been confirmed, in addition to Tommy Victor of the secular band Prong.

Next, the lyrics. For a Christian album, the record evinces a surprisingly negative perspective, musing relentlessly on the pain of life, often from a position of bitterness, with no hint of hope or redemption. Supposedly, R.E.X. refused to print the lyrics for the album's liner notes in the false hope that they would prove unrecognizable; a spoken word conclusion to the song "Doomsayer" was removed at the insistence of label executives but then sneakily reinserted by the band as a hidden track. A wave of speculation at the Argyle Park website focused on the object of the group's hostility. Were they angry at the church? Or at God? Eventually, the group answered these queries with the following statement: "The album was against a person that we looked up to and trusted immensely. He betrayed our trust and led us down a path that brought us much pain and confusion."

The sound of Argyle Park was an amalgam of various styles competing for attention in metal music at the time. Buka told *HM* magazine that the whole concept was to make something "that has never been heard before." He described the process as one in which "we took all the styles we like and mixed them into one album." Thus, the record sways between sounds reminiscent of groups like Enigma and Nine Inch Nails. Throughout the entire record, however, the trademarks of industrial music can be heard: aggressive guitars, pummeling drum machines, and powerful, inhumanly distorted vocals. "Doomsayer" is industrial rap. In addition to their one album, Argyle Park recorded the **Steve Taylor** song "Drive, He Said" and the **Stryper** tune "Lonely" for tribute albums honoring those artists.

For trivia buffs: Tommy Victor liked the music to the song "Doomsayer" and supposedly recorded it with rewritten lyrics and a new name for a Prong album.

'Ark

James Kehn, voc., drums; Dave Kelley, voc., gtr.; Derek Jeffery, voc., gtr.; David MacKay, bass; Al Perkins, steel gtr. 1979—*The Angels Come* (Spirit).

Criminally unsuccessful, the pop band 'Ark was composed of country-rock star **Al Perkins** and four guys from the United Kingdom. They made one album of likable, melodic songs with a sound that suggested a merger between the Hollies and the Byrds (think, Crosby-Nash). At their best, they were able to find that line between aggressive pop and melodic rock that groups like the Rolling Stones demonstrate so well on "Out of Time" or "Ruby Tuesday." The opening track, "Hold Me Tonight," is but one of the pop gems ready to delight the ear and the soul with its jangly guitars, sweet British harmonies, and simple but evangelical lyrics ("Oh, Lord, a miracle is changing my life"). 'Ark's one-and-only album is long out of print and is not even sought by collectors—but it should be. **Dave Kelley** later released a solo album.

A different Christian group named Ark (with no apostrophe) released an album named *Voyages* independently in 1978. This band was from South Carolina.

Christian radio hits: "Standin' at the Door" (# 24 in 1979).

ArkAngel (a.k.a. Redemption) and Radiohalo

Richard Conine, kybrd.; Bekah Crabb, voc.; Kemper Crabb, voc., gtr.; Dave Marshall, gtr.; Randy Sanchez, drums. By Redemption: 1975—*Look Up* (Evan Comm). By ArkAngel: 1980—*Warrior* (Joyeuse Garde). By Radiohalo: 1992—*Illuminations* (Urgent).

www.kempercrabb.com/Pages/Home.html

Best remembered as the birthing ground of **Kemper Crabb,** ArkAngel released one of the most innovative and significant albums in the history of Christian rock. *Warrior* set new standards for artistic quality and innovation; at a time when many Christian artists were blatantly trying to imitate the sounds of successful secular performers, ArkAngel came out with a rock masterpiece that sounded nothing like anything that anyone had ever heard before—in either arena.

The group effectively began as an acoustic group associated with Castle Hills Baptist Church in San Antonio. Called Redemption, they released one album titled *Look Up* in 1973 (lineup: Richard Conine, Bekah and Kemper Crabb, with Ken Freeman also on vocals). Only 1000 copies of the record were pressed, and it would become one of the most sought-after collector's items in Christian music. With songs like "Anti-Satan Boogie" and the psychy "New Jerusalem," it bears no resemblance sonically to the progressive art-rock for which ArkAngel would be known. Evincing what *Jesus Music* calls "homespun charm" and "delicate murmuring," the album also includes covers of some classic Jesus music songs: **Blessed Hope**'s "Something More"; **Love Song**'s "Front Seat, Back Seat"; **Jamie Owens (Collins)**'s "May I Introduce You to a Friend."

Redemption relocated to Houston, became ArkAngel, and recorded *Warrior* with the lineup listed above. Though the group was signed to StarSong, the album was released on an independent label named after Lancelot's castle in *Le Mort d'Arthur.* One song off the record, "Dwelling Place," was a significant regional hit in the general market, reaching Number One on some Houston radio stations. Musically, *Warrior* comes closest to the sound of such progressive art-rock groups as Pink Floyd or Yes, but its utilization of medieval instruments and textures puts it in a class of its own. Many years later, some of those influences would filter into the popularity of Celtic music, but by any standard, ArkAngel was ahead of the game. The song "Praises in the Old Tongue" (sung here by Bekah) is an ancient poem written by the seventh-century herdsman Caedmon (from whom **Caedmon's Call** takes its name) that Kemper Crabb transcribed and set to music. The title track, "Warrior," reads like something out of the book of Psalms, but is an original composition inspired by Revelation 19:11–12. "The Lord is a Warrior," sings Crabb, "The Lord is mighty in battle . . . He gives strength unto His people . . . The angel of the Lord camps around the ones who fear Him." The album was praised by *CCM* as "excellent, innovative, and varied," though the reviewer clearly didn't get the medieval fascination—and wasn't too sure about all the fantasy images, either. The record-buying public didn't really get it either; *Warrior* would require another decade to come into its own as a classic of Christian rock. In the meantime, **Kemper Crabb** went on

to a solo career, recording a worship album called *The Vigil* that is often considered (alongside *Warrior*) to be one of the most creative and musically adept pieces in the contemporary Christian music genre.

In the early '90s, members of ArkAngel (the Crabbs, Dave Marshall, and Randy Sanchez) toured under the name Radiohalo. An album by Radiohalo called *Illumination* was released in 1992; it includes some new material recorded by just Marshall and the Crabbs as well as tracks recorded by ArkAngel members between 1984 and 1991. Despite the latter inclusions, however, Radiohalo should really be thought of as a separate entity and not just as ArkAngel under another name. Their sound is more in line with the world-beat style of Talking Heads or Peter Gabriel than with the art-rock of *Warrior,* though the latter influences surface on "Persistence of Vision" and the title track. The song "Sea of Blood" is a hyperbolic antiabortion song that would be popular with some pro-life groups. Toward the end of the '90s, Kemper and Bekah Crabb divorced; he played with **Caedmon's Call** for a brief spell and then joined **Atomic Opera.** An ordained Anglican priest, he is regarded as an intellectual within the contemporary Christian music community and is often looked to as a senior statesman for commentary on various issues. He writes a regular column "The Christian and the Arts" for *HM* magazine. **Caedmon's Call** covered the song "Warrior" on their worship album in 2001.

Armageddon Experience

Personnel list unavailable. 1970—*Armageddon Experience* (M/M).

Little is known of the Jesus movement group Armageddon Experience except that it showcased the early writing talents of **Michael Omartian.** The band was officially sponsored by Campus Crusade for Christ, which assembled several such ministry teams from their recruits to reach youth with a now sound and message (others included The Forerunners, Great Commission Co., and The New Folk). Creativity was a low priority and—from the perspective of rock and roll at least—the groups were hilariously trite. Much about Armageddon Experience seems camp, from the photo of eight (unidentified) clean-cut kids in their Sunday best to the way words like *groovy* get sprinkled into the mix just to show how hip they are. The group played at the *Explo '72* rock festival (the Jesus movement's answer to Woodstock) and gained a coveted spot on the soundtrack album from that festival, which provided many young Americans with their first introduction to contemporary Christian music (almost 200,000 copies were distributed free through a TV campaign). Nestled between songs by **Johnny Cash** and **Randy Matthews** was AG's tune "One Way," proclaiming the slogan of the Jesus movement. Turns out, it's a great song, well performed, with a solid rock beat. The group performed four Omartian songs on their self-titled album ("I've Got the Love," "People in Motion," "Revolution Now," "God Leads a Sheltered Life") along with **Noel Paul Stookey**'s "I Believe in You." The song "I've Got the Love" would later appear on the compilation album *Beginnings* (Sonrise, 1994) and both that song and "God Leads a Sheltered Life" can be found on *The Rock Revival: Original Music from the Jesus Movement* (Sonrise, 1994).

Armageddon Holocaust

Chaotik Armageddon; Destruktiv Armageddon; Dark Doktor; Dark Thriller. 2000—*Into Total Destruction* (THT Productions).

Armageddon Holocaust may be listed as one example of numerous independent bands that occupy a very dark Christian underground. The liner notes for *Into Total Destruction* lists the band members' fake names without any indication of what instruments they play. The album appears to employ a drum machine and features massive overlays of loud guitars playing very brutal rhythms. The vocals are not merely screamed but screeched, and what lyrics are recognizable prophesy death and destruction against God's enemies. Thus, the title track: "Time to die! Time to suffer! . . . Burn! Burn! Burn! / Hell awaits! / Burn! Burn! Burn! / Hell awaits!" Needless to say, this all comes off a bit cultic and more than a little disturbing in comparison to most contemporary Christian music.

Riley Armstrong

2000—*Riley Armstrong* (Flicker).

www.rileyarmstrong.com

Folk-beat singer/songwriter/producer Riley Armstrong comes from the remote farm town of Dapp, Alberta. Discovered by **Audio Adrenaline,** he recorded his first album for that group's start-up label at age twenty-three, shortly after earning a college degree in sound engineering. His self-produced music features simple vocals and acoustic guitars against a backdrop of all sorts of interesting sounds (banjos, oboes, synthesizers, drum machines). Armstrong reminds most reviewers of Beck, with two caveats: a) his voice is noticeably smoother, reminiscent of **Steven Curtis Chapman;** and b) he doesn't sing about being a loser who wants to die. His album produced an immediate hit with the song "Greater Than," which marvels at the wonders of creation and muses that its Creator must be more marvelous still. Another song, "The Table," reflects on warm, family gatherings. "Sleep" is a humorous, catchy number reminiscent of James Taylor's "Traffic Jam"; the lyrics deal with a topic with which many can identify: "By 9 a.m. my brain and body finally decide to meet / and we come to the same conclusion as yesterday . . . I never get enough sleep." The album also includes a cover of Paul Simon's "Bridge over Troubled Water."

Vanessa Bell Armstrong

Selected: 1987—*Vanessa Bell Armstrong* (Verity); 1989—*Wonderful One;* 1990—*Greatest Hits* (Muscle Shoals); 1993—*Something on the Inside* (Verity); 1995—*The Secret Is Out;* 1997—*The Truth about Christmas;* 1998—*Desire of My Heart: Live in Detroit;* 1999—*The Best of Vanessa Bell Armstrong* (Verity).

Vanessa Bell Armstrong is a gospel singer whose career has often answered the question, "What if **Aretha Franklin** had not left gospel for soul back in the '60s?" Over the years, Armstrong's powerful Aretha-like voice has been put to marvelous use singing the spirituals and hymns of traditional gospel music. A sampling of her many albums in that genre is found on the *Greatest Hits* package listed above. But just as Aretha occasionally ventures back into gospel, so Armstrong experiments now and then in the opposite direction. With her self-titled album, she tried out the Atlantic sound that made Aretha a star, belting out what she calls "message songs" (with lyrics informed by a Christian stance, but lacking specific religious references) to a strong R&B beat. The song "You Bring Out the Best in Me" was a hit on *Billboard's* Black Music charts. Then Armstrong collaborated with energetic producer John P. Kee to produce an album of passionate jazzy songs with unambiguous lyrics for fans of contemporary gospel. The result was *The Secret Is Out.* Kee performs with her on the title track. The album also includes a rousing version of the hymn "Love Lifted Me."

Christian radio hits: "Greater Than" (# 9 in 2000).

Ash Mundae

Chuck Ash, voc., gtr.; Jeremy Ash, drums. 2000—*Model Citizen* (Red Hill).

Ash Mundae is a retro-'80s pop band composed of two brothers who previously formed the nucleus of a Christian group called **The Altered.** The Illinois duo come from a musical family: their father served as a professional drummer in numerous bands, and their mother sang with a '50s group featured on the Ted Mack Amateur Hour. Ash Mundae moves away from the Midwest rock sound of **The Altered** to embrace a style that bears strong influence of Duran Duran, The Cars, and Human League. "In God's Eyes" is a standout track, with lyrics that remind the listeners of their worth in God's eyes. The title track and "Broke" evince some good-natured and tongue-in-cheek humor. "Hope" and "Heaven Waits" are more serious and poetic offerings, which the brothers say were inspired by the tragic adventures of Jean Valjean recounted in the novel *Les Misérables* by Victor Hugo.

Susan Ashton

1991—*Wakened by the Wind* (Sparrow); 1992—*Angels of Mercy*; 1993—
Susan Ashton; 1995—*So Far: The Best of Susan Ashton, Vol. 1*; 1996—*A Distant Call*; 1999—*Closer* (Capitol).

www.capitol-nashville.com

Almost from the start, Christian music critics claimed that
Susan Ashton (b. 1967) had what it takes to make a mark in
the world of mainstream country music, and they expressed
puzzlement as to why she did not capitalize more on what was
clearly her forté. The redhead from Houston, whose personality is described in her Capitol press release as "bubbly and fun
and flirty," did eventually do so and was soon opening tours for
Garth Brooks and singing backup on songs she had previously
recorded herself, now done by Brooks ("You Move Me") or
Martina McBride ("Here in My Heart"). She has also partnered
with **Glen Campbell** ("What's Going Without Saying") and
Patty Loveless ("To Have You Back Again").

Ashton's coming-to-faith testimony provides a tribute to
youth-to-youth evangelism programs. Raised as a member of
Houston's Evangelical Temple, she says she attended only because her parents made her and lacked any true devotion to
spiritual matters. She likewise attended the church's youth
night one time after striking a bargain with her parents that if
she didn't like it she would never have to go back. She *didn't*
like it and would never have returned if one of the members
had not called her that week to tell her how glad the group was
that she had come. "It blew me away that someone had actually noticed me," she would later relate, and the phone call inspired her to return and ultimately become a devout member
of the group. After high school, Ashton was committed to
using her life to "sing for the Lord," and she took on a number
of session projects, notably singing with **Wayne Watson** on
his hit song "Watercolor Ponies," and working with **Dallas
Holm.**

Ashton's first three albums were all produced by veteran
Wayne Kirkpatrick, who also wrote much of the material.
The debut album *Wakened by the Wind* was well received but established her as just one more competent female vocalist in the
crowded adult contemporary market. *CCM* likened her style to
"that of **Kim Hill** or the softer side of **Margaret Becker,**" citing also the inevitable Shawn Colvin comparison that seemed
to be applied to most Christian female vocalists at the time.
The songs themselves, however, plunge much deeper than
stereotypical Christian pop. In "No One Knows My Heart"
(written with Kirkpatrick and **Billy Sprague**) she declares,
"There's an agony in living / But there's a comfort in the
truth." Ashton herself cowrote the album's best song, "Beyond
Justice to Mercy" (with Sprague again, and Paula Carpenter).
Kirkpatrick's "Down on My Knees" describes the necessity of
prayer, and his "Benediction" becomes Ashton's request for di-

vine blessing on the path she has chosen. A couple of tracks
("Land of Nod," "Ball and Chain") hint at the country sound
that would come to fruition later. As it turned out, *Wakened by
the Wind* was the debut album of the year, spawning four
Christian radio hits and setting new sales records for first albums by Christian soloists.

The follow-up album, *Angels of Mercy,* mostly continues in
the same vein but exhibits a switch to crossover country as its
songlist progresses. It opens with a rock song ("Here in My
Heart") that places Ashton in brief competition with the
harder side of **Margaret Becker.** "Grand Canyon" is one of
Kirkpatrick's best songs, but in general the album's later songs
(the country ones—"Innocence Lost," "When Are You Coming
Back?" "Walk On By") were the most praised. Still, reviewers
were referring to Ashton as "the female **Steven Curtis Chapman**" (ultimately, the female **Gary Chapman** would prove
more appropriate). Her third eponymous album presents "more
of the same," as most reviews heralded—many as good news,
some as a complaint. It opens somewhat daringly with a
seven-and-a-half minute slow song called "Summer Solstice,"
which is probably its strongest track. "Remember Not" deals
with forgiveness and "Call of the Wild" with a marriage gone
awry due to a spouse's restless wanderings. "Waiting for Your
Love to Come" reminded a *CCM* reviewer of The Eagles' "Best
of My Love." *A Distant Call* actually has Ashton working with
three different producers (Kirkpatrick, **Brown Bannister,** and
Michael Omartian). Seventies-style rockers ("Crooked Man")
mix with down-home country ("Love Profound," with Allison
Krauss and Union Station) and tender love songs ("Spinning
Like a Wheel") in an eclectic mix that fans had come to expect
and critics to regret.

It was Ashton's first album for Capitol that cemented her
identity as a country singer. The opening song, "Come On Out
of the Rain," encourages a brokenhearted guy to give romance
another try. "You're Lucky I Love You" reminds a sweetheart
that he's got it good. "Breathless" expresses some welcome sensuality that may never have been allowed on an officially
Christian release ("He's got me learnin' and burnin' and tossin'
and turnin' and yearnin' for him all night"). "I Ain't Gonna Fall
for Love Again" features a duet vocal with Vince Gill and has a
classic country sound that makes it one of the album's strongest offerings. Two songs, "Shot for the Moon" and "Can't Cry
Hard Enough," are especially heart-wrenching. The latter expresses the overwhelming grief of losing a loved one to death.

Two of Ashton's greatest strengths have been song selection—an important attribute for a singer who is not primarily
a songwriter—and interpretation (Gordon Kennedy says, "A
song is safe when Susan sings it"). Estrangement is a familiar
theme in her songs. "Grand Canyon" describes the spiritual
chasm experienced by people who feel far from God; "Summer

Solstice" (by **Wayne Kirkpatrick**) reflects on the recognition that love or faith has grown cold ("what I thought to be maturity / was just neglect that I tried to vindicate"). In the hauntingly beautiful "Lonely River," her voice flows alongside lush piano and gentle strings to express the forlorn hope that God is working in ways unseen. "Innocence Lost" (by Karey and **Wayne Kirkpatrick**) expresses a longing for what philosopher Paul Ricoeur calls "the second naivete": "Milton lost his paradise / Dorothy lost her way / Vincent lost his sanity / Thomas lost his faith / Hoover lost the second time / Sigmund lost his friend / Me, I lost my innocence / And I want it back again."

Ashton has also contributed her soothing soprano to a number of various artist projects, notably dueting with country crooner **Collin Raye** on the title tune for a **Jim Brickman** Christmas release called *The Gift* (Windham Hill, 1997). That song would become a crossover hit, charting at Number Sixty-five on *Billboard*'s mainstream Top 40 chart, but doing significantly better in both country and adult contemporary markets. Ashton has also sung duets with Billy Dean on "In the Garden" for *Amazing Grace: A Country Salute to Gospel* (Sparrow, 1995) and with **Gary Chapman** on John Lennon's "In My Life" for the Omartian-produced *Come Together: America Salutes the Beatles* (Capitol, 1995). She sang "Summer Snow" on a **Keith Green** tribute project (*No Compromise,* Sparrow, 1992) and joined several other women artists on *Listen to Our Hearts* (Sparrow, 1998). She also constitutes one-third of the trio, **Ashton, Becker, and Denté.**

For trivia buffs: Susan Ashton's given name was Susan Hill. She adopted the professional name to avoid being confused with Christian singer **Kim Hill.**

Christian radio hits: "Down on My Knees" (# 2 in 1991); "Benediction" (# 4 in 1991); "In Amazing Grace Land" (# 3 in 1992); "Ball and Chain" (# 18 in 1992); "Here in My Heart" (# 3 in 1992); "Grand Canyon" (# 17 in 1992); "Hunger and Thirst" (# 20 in 1993); "Walk On By" (# 6 in 1993); "Waiting for Your Love to Come" (# 24 in 1994); "Remember Not" (# 3 in 1994); "All Kinds of People" (# 5 in 1996).

Ashton, Becker, and Denté

Susan Ashton, voc.; Margaret Becker, voc.; and Christian Denté, voc. 1994—*Along the Road* (Sparrow).

Three of the most popular female vocalists in Christian music—**Susan Ashton, Margaret Becker,** and Christine Denté (of **Out of the Grey**)—combined their talents for a single album and supporting tour in 1994. The record was produced by **Wayne Kirkpatrick** (responsible for most of Ashton's work), who also served as chief songwriter. In general, the artists take turns on lead vocals, such that the album amounts to a compilation of tunes by each of the three with the other two providing harmony and backup. There is, however, an overall feel of synchrony, as rhythmic, acoustic guitar

serves as the primary accompaniment on most tracks. The title tune was written by Dan Fogelberg and expresses a basic perspective on life as a work-in-progress.

Christian radio hits: "Oh Me of Little Faith" (# 19 in 1994); "Walk On" (# 9 in 1995).

Samuel Brinsley Ashworth

2000—*Sauté* (independent).

Samuel Brinsley Ashworth is regarded in Christian music circles as one to watch. He is the son of superstar **Charlie Peacock.** Aware that he will have to suffer that burden of fame, the talented youth has sought to enter the Christian music scene gently—for example, by doing backing vocals on projects his father produces. By age sixteen, however, he had composed the song "I Won't Stay Long," which was recorded by **Sixpence None the Richer.** He also cowrote "Seasons Always Change" with **Sarah Masen.** He then privately released a debut of his own work. Of course, the comparisons were inevitable: his voice sounds like Dad's and the music has the same Beatlesque quality. Still, *True Tunes* announced to the world: "he's good."

As If

Phil Goss, voc., gtr., kybrd.; Phil Heard, drums; Steve Rothwell, bass. 1996—*Forget Me Not* (New Dawn); 1999—*Strange Blue Thing*.

The UK trio that goes by the minimalist title As If performs techno dance music with straightforward evangelistic lyrics. Their sound can be located somewhere on the spectrum between New Order and Depeche Mode, with some creative twists, such as the eastern-inflected introduction to the song "Backwards" on their second album. The song "Area 51," also from that record, features apocalyptic you've-been-left-behind lyrics: "I don't know what's happening / I see my friends and loved ones ascend in the clouds."

Asight Unseen

Derek Bell, gtr.; Jason Lohrke, voc.; Mike Longridge, gtr.; John Oliveira, bass; Bert Sanchez, drums. 1991—*Circus of Shame* (New Breed); 1993—*Hollywood Proverbs* (MetroOne).

Asight Unseen was an alternative Christian band that created a hard-grunge sound in the same ballpark as **Collective Soul,** whose graphic style was copied for their debut CD's cover design. Associated with the Vineyard churches, they viewed themselves as a ministry band. "We're very upfront," Lohrke told *HM* magazine. "Our purpose is evangelism." They often performed in churches and concluded concerts with altar calls and appeals to the Lord for healing and deliverance. Fans of hard-rocking guitar music may have been attracted to those concerts by the group's two well-received albums. The debut opens with "Road to Bonos," which features a heavy smattering of horns. It also includes the infectious title track (with an INXS groove) and "Electric Angel Blues," which seems influenced by early **U2** and *Let It Bleed*-era Rolling Stones. The latter song winds down with an electrified version of the Lord's Prayer. *Hollywood Proverbs* contains "The Chant," a psychedelic tune that spells out the group's favorite theme: holiness, or being totally sold-out to God. The same theme is picked up in "Dave," a colloquial song about biblical King David. "The Big Watusi" is simply a fun, very upbeat tune that Lohrke says can "refer to whatever you want it to." The group liked to cover Lenny Kravitz's "Rosemary" in concert. After Asight Unseen disbanded, Jason Lohrke and John Oliveira went on to record an independent, self-titled album with a group called Bionic Jodi in 1998.

As I Lay Dying

Noah Chase, bass; Tim Lambesis, voc.; Jordan Mancino, drums; Evan White, gtr. 2001—*Beneath the Encasing of Ashes* (Pluto).

As I Lay Dying is a hybrid punk-metal act that has a brutal sound often likened to that of **Zao.** The group initially formed in San Diego in the late '90s, broke up while lead singer Tim Lambesis worked with the Texas band Society's Finest, then re-formed with a new lineup (in San Diego again) in 2001. Their debut album *Beneath the Encasing of Ashes* is unrelenting in its intensity, mixing fast hard songs with slow heavy numbers. As the group's name suggests, mortality is a frequent lyrical theme. On "Forced to Die," Lambesis invites the divine discipline that brings self-denial: "If this is what it takes to bring me to my knees / Then feed me pain until I realize I am but a slave." The song "When This World Fades" is a memorial tribute to the mother of guitarist Evan White.

Aslan (Airborn)

Greg Buick, kybrd.; Ted Kallman, gtr., voc.; Linda Kendall, voc.; Jeff Roley, gtr., voc.; Scott Roley, gtr., voc.; Martin Vipond, bass. 1972—*Aslan* (Airborn).

At least four different Christian groups have called themselves Aslan, after the lion who serves as a Christ figure in C. S. Lewis's Narnia tales. The one that recorded for Airborn featured nice blends of male and female harmonies. Their only album was produced by **Ron Moore,** who later had a career in Christian music himself. **Scott Roley** went on to sing on Moore's albums and to form the group **Albrecht and Roley (and Moore)** before launching a solo career. One of the group's better songs, "Further Up and Further In," turns up not only here but on the first *two* **Albrecht and Roley (and Moore)** albums. To avoid confusion with the Maranatha

band, this Aslan changed its name to Stillwaters in 1974 and toured for a while under that name.

Aslan (Maranatha)

Jim Abdo, voc., gtr., kybrd.; Rick Conklin, voc., bass; Johnnie Graves, drums; Mike Holmes, voc., gtr., bass; Bill Hoppe, kybrd.; Toni McWilliams, voc., violin. No albums.

http://hometown.aol.com/crparavel/index.html

Not to be confused with the group(s) listed above or below, the Aslan that worked with Maranatha was active in California from 1972 to 1978. The group began as In His Name but then decided the name of the Narnia lion had more of a ring to it. They were harder rocking than many of the Maranatha folk groups, and Toni McWilliams' violin also gave them a somewhat distinctive sound for Jesus music at the time. In general, they had a progressive, art-rock sound with ambitious harmonies, fitting into the same ballpark as acts like **Kansas** or ELO. The band was noted for its musicianship, performing music that was carefully orchestrated and meticulously rehearsed. The members were also well known for their humor, for being a wacky group that could almost be counted on to hit the stage in monkey masks, perform a song with kazoos, or pull some other bizarre and as-yet-untried stunt. Wendy Carter Fremin of **Children of the Day** once called Aslan "the best Maranatha band without an album" and **Erick Nelson** says they were the first group he knows of to receive a standing ovation at Calvary Chapel (which just wasn't done). Aslan toured extensively, opening for Nelson and other Maranatha artists, but they never recorded an album. They did place one song, "Who Loves the Lonely?" on the compilation disc *Maranatha Six: A Family Portrait.* That song has the feel of Elton John's *Goodbye Yellow Brick Road* material. Opening with a majestic church organ, it moves quickly into a building, piano-driven song about God's compassion for the disaffected and dispossessed denizens of urban America. When the guitars arrive, they soar for a moment that is too brief, but indicative of what Aslan was apparently capable of delivering. Aslan also recorded their one-time signature song "In His Name" for *Maranatha Five* (1976), but it was pulled for not fitting in with the rest of the songs (= being too rocky). Bill Hoppe played synthesizers (uncredited) on **Daniel Amos'** classic *Shotgun Angel* album. As of 2001, Abdo, Rick Conklin, and Hoppe were said to be recording together under the name Broken Works.

Aslan (UK)

Personnel list unavailable. 1976—*Paws for Thought* (Profile); 1977—*Second Helpings.*

The Narnia lion Aslan gave its name to at least three American Jesus music groups (see above and below) but was also claimed by a progressive folk band in the homeland of its creator. The group featured the same combination of layered vocals and acoustic Renaissance instruments (autoharp, recorder, glockenspiel) that groups like **Caedmon's Call** would bring to the fore two decades later. The first album features some traditional songs and cover tunes (including covers of **Parchment** songs); the second record is mostly original material. "Beauty" is simply a poem about creation recited (not sung) over acoustic guitar. "The King" is performed a capella. Other standout cuts include "Earthbound," "Song of the Seasons," and "The Ballad of Thomas Cook."

Aslan (Young Life)

Mike Bizanovich, gtr.; Mike Coates, kybrd.; Tony Congi, voc., gtr.; Bill McCoy, voc., gtr.; Brian O'Konski, voc., bass (–1997) // Dan Sewell, bass (+ 1997). 1997—*It's Amazing* (custom).

Yet another Christian group called Aslan worked with the organization Young Life in the '70s and '80s. A folk-rock group with a slight country air, the group played at camps and conferences throughout the country and attracted a strong following among Young Life members. They were apparently based in Ohio and recorded an album of eleven songs in the early '80s, about which no information is available. In the late '90s, members of the group reunited to record five new songs for inclusion on an expanded edition of this early album on compact disc. Aslan specialized in ballads but was also competent for the occasional bluegrass romp ("Why Cry?"). Perhaps their most popular tune is the footstomping **Larry Norman**esque "Jesus is the Rock and He Rolls My Blues Away." The songs understandably (and appropriately) focus on typical youth group themes. "Born out of His Love" features a campfire sing-along chorus expressing the thought of its title. "Waiting for the Captain" finds the group experimenting with a little more complexity, trying out some spacey synth effects and art-rock inferences.

ATF

See **After the Fire.**

Atomic Opera

Frank Hart, voc.; Len Sonnier, bass (– 1992); Jonathan Marshall, gtr. (–1996); Mark Poindexter, drums (–1997) // Jonas Velasco, bass (+ 1992, – 1996); Kemper Crabb, voc., mandolin (+ 1996); Ryan Birsinger, bass (+ 1997); John Simmons, drums (+ 1997). 1994—*For Madmen Only* (Collision); 1997—*Penguin Dust* (independent); 1999—*Alpha and Oranges*; 2000—*Gospel Cola* (Metal Blade).

www.atomicopera.com

Crossover Christian artists Atomic Opera had made an impressive splash in the general market even before legend **Kemper Crabb** joined the band. Under the leadership of Frank Hart, who grew up listening to Crabb's seminal Jesus movement band **ArkAngel,** the Houston group placed a single ("Justice") on MTV and metal radio stations and earned a spot as opening act for the very worldly group Dio. When Crabb signed on, all bets were off. He is featured on *Penguin Dust* and *Gospel Cola.* The group continues to be better known in the general market than in the Christian subculture, despite the obvious signs of their faith.

The first album was well received by fans of heavy Christian music, with the group being compared to **King's X** and **Galactic Cowboys** (both of whom also come from Houston). The hit "Justice" features the lyric, "When I pray 'Have mercy,' I will never ask for justice." Another song, "Blackness," proclaims, "We all want to change the world / But we don't want to change our mind." Unfortunately, the Collision label dissolved, leaving Atomic Opera to distribute their next two albums privately—selling them at concerts or through the mail. *Penguin Dust* is notable for speaking against what Hart calls the "tide of cynical disregard" in our society. "Make a God" is about humanity's propensity to fashion an image of God that reflects their own ideals. "Spirit of the Age" offers a litany of things that everybody knows, with the caveat that "most of the things that everybody knows are not true" (actually a quote from Batman). Samples of such bits of questionable conventional wisdom include the propositions "you should only love someone who cares for you" and "you should believe in yourself for the truth." The song most sure to grab attention on *Penguin Dust,* however, is "God of Hate," which lists things that the Bible says God hates (e.g., rebellion, greed, violence, death). Hart claims he wrote the lyrics—inspired by Reformed theology—as a counterpoint against "the smarmy God of Hallmark." A number of other songs also portray the group's religious leanings: "Thirst" draws its lyrics from the psalms; "Watergrave" is a remake of an old song by **The Imperials.** The next album, *Alpha and Oranges,* was a collection of early songs recorded between 1989 and 1993 with the band's original lineup, before they found their distinctive sound.

Gospel Cola is the group's first major label release with the definitive lineup (Hart, Crabb, Ryan Birsinger, John Simmons). Crabb brings an infusion of progressive art-rock that blends into the band's already established heavy metal sound. The result is something unique, a "weirdness that works," as *Phantom Tollbooth* said. Not many heavy metal bands display a strong penchant for vocal harmony, and very few feature such instruments as dulcimer, bouzouki, ocarina, or recorder (though Jethro Tull did do some amazing things with a flute). *Christian Music* began their review with the affirmation, "This ain't your daddy's heavy metal." The song "Malediction" (an anti-abortion anthem) begins with medieval and acoustic sounds that are eventually overwhelmed by a tidal wave of electric guitars. Lyrically, the song has a poetic quality that lifts it above typical sentimental or sensationalist (cf. **Grammatrain**'s "Execution") treatments of the topic: "Torn from their mother's womb / Denied the sky, denied a tomb / Conceived in lust to their own ruin." "Silence" is a reminder that God communicates through silences as effectively as through words. "Muse" laments the dismal state of true art in the (post)modern world ("too many singers, not enough music"). "Winterland" takes its cue from C. S. Lewis's Narnia tales, which describe a place that is "always winter but never Christmas." The song "Jesus Junk" ridicules those who, in Hart's words, are "so wrapped up in their little Christian subculture or ghetto that they need to de-secularize everything in their life," searching for Christian music, Christian belt buckles and, of course . . . Gospel Cola. The album packaging for *Gospel Cola* includes liner notes with numerous quips such as "Warning: Traces of Neo Platonism and Pietism may lead to chronic stupidity."

Atomic Opera is almost the stereotypical band of Christians that does not want to be known as a Christian band. In their case, however, the reluctance to accept such a label is not motivated just by the desire to avoid ignorant stereotypes on the part of those who think Christian music means **Amy Grant** and **DC Talk.** Rather, the aversion to such labeling arises from outright hostility against the Christian music industry and its philosophies. Hart describes that industry as interested in producing not art, but propaganda "designed to make their philosophical position look good." Such an approach does not sit well with the group that *HM* magazine describes as "a band of satirists and spiritual intellectuals." Hart continues, "We are not supposed to make art in order to draw people to Christ. We should make art because we are driven to make art and reflect Truth." Hart further insists that he does not want Atomic Opera to be known as a Christian band because, while he is not ashamed of Jesus Christ or of the gospel, he *is* "ashamed of what Christianity and the church mean to most people in our culture."

For trivia buffs: Atomic Opera's original bassist Jonathan Marshall is the son of another legendary guitarist, Dave Marshall, who once played with Crabb in **ArkAngel.**

Audio Adrenaline

Will McGinniss, bass; Mark Stuart, voc.; Bob Herdman, kybrd. (−2001); Barry Blair, gtr., voc. (−1998) // Tyler Burkum, gtr. (+ 1998); Ben Cissel, drums (+ 1998). 1992—Audio Adrenaline (ForeFront); 1993—Don't Censor Me; 1995—Live Bootleg; 1996—Bloom; 1998—Some Kind of Zombie; 1999—Underdog; 2001—Hit Parade; Lift.

www.audioadrenaline.com

Eclectic musical styles and high energy stage shows propelled Audio Adrenaline to fame and allowed them to domi-nate Christian rock charts as one of the top Christian bands of the '90s. At the beginning of that decade, Barry Blair, Bob Herdman, and Mark Stuart were students at Kentucky Christian College playing in a rock group called A180. Will McGinniss brought a song that he had written ("My God") to their attention, a tape of the song fell into the hands of **Toby McKeehan** (of **DC Talk**), and ForeFront proffered a contract. Audio Adrenaline was officially formed in 1992.

The first album was none too impressive, but "P.D.A." (the only standout cut besides "My God") does reveal a slightly irreverent sense of humor that would gradually disappear as the group gained in significance. At many Christian schools public displays of affection are forbidden. With a Bible college chic worthy of **Terry Taylor,** AA uses the phrase for that prohibited behavior as a descriptive moniker for Christ's life and death (a public display of God's affection for humanity). "My God" displays similar wit through its raucous examples of politically incorrect interreligious dialogue ("Buddha was a fat man"). Success came with the second album (more than 300,000 units sold), largely due to "Big House," the most amiable Christian pop song of the decade. Ready-made for singing by church youth groups, "Big House" was catchy, ecumenical, and just a little bit silly. Hand motions were added and the song entered the repertoire of camp counselors quicker than one could say "Kum Ba Ya." Still, Audio Adrenaline found that they now had a signature song that sounded nothing like most of the music they played. "Big House" was a long way from the rap-metal music with which they had begun or from the alternative dance music they now preferred. The title track to *Don't Censor Me* offers a strong statement to radio stations that will play songs containing all sorts of profanity but *won't* play anything that testifies positively to faith in Jesus Christ. "Jesus and the California Kid" is an uncharacteristic Beach Boys-type song. "Rest Easy" is a very fine hymnic ballad that would go all but unnoticed in the group's oeuvre until someone wisely chose to include it on their "greatest hits" compilation in 2001 (where it is misidentified as coming from *Bloom*). Audio Adrenaline would later dismiss their first two albums as filled with cheerleader songs, but the edgy "We're a Band" and the blues-tinged "Scum Sweetheart" from the second outing remain examples of their all-time best material.

John Hampton, known for his work with Gin Blossoms, stepped in to produce much of the appropriately titled *Bloom.* The suddenly mature and decisive sound took critics by surprise and earned AA respect to match their celebrity. Most reviewers agree that this is the no-filler album—not a bad track on it—but songs that especially stand out include "Secret," "Good People," "I'm Not the King," and "I Hear Jesus Calling." The first of these, "Secret," opens the album on a strong rocking note and declares the group's intention not to be coy about their beliefs. "I'm Not the King" has a strong Lenny Kravitz sound to it and features quirky-but-meaningful lyrics that somehow work Jim Morrison and Elvis references into a self-effacing tribute to Christ as the only King of Kings. "Good People" is a tribute to folk the band has met in its travels; musically it sounds a lot like **Geoff Moore and The Distance,** though it would have been the best song that band ever did. "I Hear Jesus Calling" is another of Audio Adrenaline's blues masterpieces, a bit like "Scum Sweetheart" with more edifying lyrics. "Walk on Water" and "Never Gonna Be As Big As Jesus" would become worthy Christian radio hits.

The band survived the subsequent departure of guitarist Barry Blair by adding the then eighteen-year-old Tyler Burkum (nephew to Jason Burkum of **Believable Picnic**) and finished out the '90s with two more albums that continue in the same vein as *Bloom* while demonstrating innovation and growth. *Some Kind of Zombie* is more funk-rock and less pop than previous AA albums. It scored big with "Blitz" (with guest horns from **The Supertones**), with "Chevette," and with a song influenced by southern gospel, "The Lighthouse." The title track is a powerful rock song with odd lyrics inspired by Mark Stuart's observations of voodoo-worship in Haiti, where he was raised as the son of missionaries. It has something to do with being "dead to sin," though the words don't work quite as well as the beat. "People Like Me" is a wonderful pop song with some of the group's best lyrics: "What do you think when you see / Continuous losers—the people like me / I hope you never believe / Just for a moment you're better than me." *Underdog* (the first truly self-produced album) features the foot-stomping "DC-10," an old song written by Herdman before he joined the group. The words bring back that old AA wit, reminding listeners that they could meet their Maker at any time ("A 747 fell out of heaven / Crashed through the roof of a 7–11 / You're working on a slurpee / Things get hazy / Reach for a twinkie / Now you're pushing up daisies"). This, on the same package with a worshipful version of the classic hymn "It Is Well," performed with **Jennifer Knapp.** "Get Down," the ultra-funky first single from *Underdog,* was one of the best rock songs of the year. Stuart says, "It's about becoming humble so God can be glorified." "Mighty Good Leader" would provide a strong follow-up as another extremely moshable track with pretty straightforward lyrics. The title track to *Underdog* quotes from KC and the Sunshine Band ("That's the way, uh-huh, we like it") in a very un-disco ode to the humble. "Jesus Movement" is sort of acoustic hip-hop with a Latino twist, a bit like Sugar Ray's "Every Morning." Unfortunately *Underdog* concludes with a dumb, drawn-out bonus track ("Houseplant") that might be humorous *once* but that nobody would ever want to hear a second time.

In 2001 Audio Adrenaline compiled some crowd favorites for a greatest hits album *Hit Parade.* Every critic would mourn omissions ("Don't Censor Me"? "Scum Sweetheart"?), but the album does reveal a repertoire of seventeen sensational songs. Two of these are previously unreleased numbers that are among the band's best. "Will Not Fade" is a hard-rocking song (almost like a **U2** anthem) that boldly proclaims the group's persistent allegiance to the gospel. "One Like You" sets worshipful lyrics to a more pop beat that reveals the boys in AA had not lost their "Big House" sensibilities completely. Later in 2001, Audio Adrenaline (now a quartet) released *Lift,* a record that advertising hype presented as "a return to the stylings of *Bloom*" (clearly the group's zenith). Less a party album than *Zombie* or *Underdog,* the record places more potential youth group anthems ("Rejoice," "Summertime") alongside worship songs with a more vertical orientation ("Glory," "Lift," "Tremble"). But the album also starts strong with two tracks ("You Still Amaze Me," "I'm Alive") that deliver the dynamic high-energy fix the band's fans crave. *Lift's* first single "Beautiful" (built on a melodic line copped from Lou Reed's "Walk on the Wild Side") would likewise provide a ready-for-the-mosh-pit celebration of rockin' 'n' rollin' for Jesus. "Ocean Floor" proclaims the removal of sin to the bottom of the sea.

As indicated, the later AA albums all offer a potpourri of styles, drawing from a variety of influences (country, blues, metal). But these are all filtered through a distinctive Audio Adrenaline blend of alternative rock and hip-hop. Almost every album features one or two power ballads ("Rest Easy," "Lighthouse," "Speak To Me") as well as at least one pure pop song so catchy one might swear it was left over from the '60s ("Good People," "People Like Me," "Ocean Floor"). And then there are the cover songs—dynamite versions of Edgar Winter's "Free Ride" and Pete Townsend's "Let My Love Open the Door," always performed better than the originals. Still, the core of each album consists of songs like "Beautiful," "Blitz," "Chevette," "Get Down," "Secret," and "Some Kind of Zombie": funky tunes that might remind one of the Red Hot Chili Peppers covering Three Dog Night but don't really sound like *anything* that anyone is likely to have heard before.

Audio Adrenaline also owes its success to relentless touring and to fulfilling on stage the promise of vigor and stamina that their name implies. They deliver a basic garage band show dressed up with all the sound, lighting, and stage effects that one would expect from a big-name general market act. Comic relief often arrives in the form of ludicrous covers: a barely recognizable, thrasher version of the Sunday school classic, "If You're Happy and You Know It"; a frighteningly precise reading of the Veggie Tales' "Hairbrush Song."

Diverse ventures have increased the group's profile. Members of the band coauthored the book *Some Kind of Journey: On the Road with Audio Adrenaline.* Herdman, McGinniss, and Stuart founded a recording company, Flicker Records, and signed **Riley Armstrong** as its debut artist. The band also sponsors a race car driven by Nashville driver "Barn" Dixon. The group describes its recording and performing as a ministry, focused primarily on communicating within the Christian subculture rather than (primarily) on converting outsiders. "Blitz" is about a road trip taken by "fourteen kids in an old church van." "Never Gonna Be As Big As Jesus" is the group's response to John Lennon's infamous comment about the Beatles. "Chevette" is the musings of a preacher's kid (Stuart) who understands his father's purchase of a not-so-impressive new car in light of commitments to more important matters. "Hands and Feet" (from *Underdog*) is a prayer to be used by God in doing Christ's work ("Let me be your hands / Let me be your feet"). "Man of God" (from *Bloom*) offers the grateful confession of one who realizes that *sometimes* he is the person God wants him to be. Devotion to boldness is a recurring theme in AA's lyrics and interviews. "Christian music is offensive to most of the world," Stuart told *Details* magazine in 1996. Blair agreed: "Christianity is one of the few things it's okay to be bigoted against. . . . We *want* to be known as a Christian band."

For trivia buffs: Stuart is married to the sister of **Toby McKeehan** of **DC Talk.**

Christian radio hits: "Who Do You Love" (# 13 in 1992); "Audio World" (# 16 in 1993); "My World View" (# 3 in 1994); "Big House" (# 12 in 1994); "Can't Take God Away" (# 12 in 1994); "Rest Easy" (# 10 in 1994); "A.K.A. Public School" (# 14 in 1995); "Never Gonna Be As Big As Jesus" (# 3 in 1996); "Walk on Water" (# 14 in 1996); "Good People" (# 3 in 1996); "Free Ride" (# 9 in 1997); "Man of God" (# 2 in 1997); "People Like Me" (# 2 in 1998); "God-Shaped Hole" (# 17 in 1998); "New Body" (# 11 in 1999); "Get Down" (# 1 for 4 weeks in 1999); "Good Life" (# 3 in 2000); "Hands and Feet" (# 1 for 2 weeks in 2000); "One Like You" (# 5 in 2001); "Beautiful" (# 1 for 6 weeks in 2001).

Dove Awards: 1998 Alternative/Modern Rock Song ("Some Kind of Zombie"); 2000 Rock Song ("Get Down").

Audio Paradox

Josh Pyle, voc.; et al. 1999—*The Iniquity of Time* (Flaming Fish).

The heavy industrial rock band Audio Paradox plays hard gothic music similar to that of **Autovoice** or general market band Kraftwerk. The band is essentially a truncated version of the group **Spy Glass Blue** (minus Alan Aguirre). Before recording their own album, they also served as the backing band for **Eva O.** Their music displays a somewhat lighter touch than most industrial rock, including moments of humor or at least sarcasm in songs like "Heart-Burning Transplant" and "Prosperkiller." A few lines from the latter tune also reveal their penchant for spiritual warfare: "You foul, rotten stinkin' devil / I'm gonna beat you up, you devil / I'm gonna cut you up in the name of Jesus!"

Aunt Bettys

Andrew Carter, gtr.; Chuck Cummings, drums; Brian Doidge, bass; Michael Knott, voc., gtr. 1996—*Aunt Bettys* (Elektra); 1998—*Ford Supersonic* (Marathon).

www.michaelknott.com

One of the more controversial bands on the Christian scene, the Aunt Bettys were in one sense just a secular version of **LSU.** All band members had played with that quintessential alternative Christian group at one time or another. Chuck Cummings was also a member of **Common Bond** and **Dakoda Motor Co.** Like **LSU,** however, the Aunt Bettys were essentially a projection of singer, writer, and sometimes solo-artist **Michael Knott.** Knott took up the project when the failure of his Blonde Vinyl label left him with enormous financial debts and he hoped that a release in the general market would help him to recoup those losses. Knott also admits, however, that he appreciated being able to record an album freed from the expectations of specifically Christian venues. "It felt good to cuss!" he told *True Tunes,* referring to the moment when he repeatedly yells "S**t!" on the Aunty Bettys' remake of Knott's "Rocket and a Bomb." *True Tunes* actually refused to carry the album in their catalogue, noting it was the first time in their history to refuse a project by a known Christian artist.

The Aunt Bettys enjoyed a fair amount of success in the general market, touring with such acts as Fastball and the Kenny Wayne Shepard Band. Notably, Knott never tried to justify his worldly side project as anything other than just that. He did not view the Aunt Bettys as a means for sneaking into the general market so that he could deliver the Christian goods later. He did not explicate the group's function in terms of ministry at all. It was just a fun experiment and a way to make some money. While Knott did not think that anything on the Aunt Bettys albums (or in their concerts) compromised his convictions as a Christian, he was forthright about saying the records were not Christian albums and should not be marketed through Christian stores. At the same time, Knott appeared to many (though he denies this) to have gone out of his way to offend the pious. The debut album's opening song and first single was actually called "Jesus." It presented the curious prayer of a drunk loser ("Come on, Jesus, give me one more drink . . ."). The CD's accompanying cover art depicted a stained-glass Jesus tending bar. But if Christians suspected Knott of ridiculing their Lord and Savior, the secular press tended to view the same song as "reverent" and "spiritual."

The mixed motives of catharsis and commercialism combined to make the Aunty Bettys' debut album an appealing slice of rock and roll. Musically, the group displays the sort of punk Americana sound of bands like Cracker, Spacehog, or Tom Petty and the Heartbreakers. Lyrically, the songs describe the lives of various outlandish characters Knott has met in Los Angeles. Knott claims the songs are at least based on true stories and the album is loosely structured as a tour of a seedy apartment building where all these folk supposedly live. "Lush" tells of a tattooed woman who seduces a man into coming back to her room, then ties him up and beats him; "Feel" presents an obsessed man who considers a sex change because he is in love with a woman who is a lesbian; "Star Baby" describes a woman convinced of the reality of alien abductions; "Kitty Courtesy" (a remake of an **LSU** song) portrays an even scarier woman, suspected of cannibalizing her late husband. Those looking for messages do not find the Bettys have much to offer, though some songs do convey an undercurrent of antidrug sentiment ("Addict"; "Little Fighter"). Others evince Knott's trademark perception into the human psyche. For instance, one verse of "Double" (another old **LSU** tune) tells, from a man's perspective, what happens when he and his wife learn their minister is getting a divorce. The wife's reaction to this news is not what the man would have expected: she is not concerned about what this will mean for the pastor, or for his wife, or for their children, or for the congregation; instead, she asks, if *his* marriage is over . . . how will *ours* survive?"

Such moments give any listener pause. But the overall mood of the Aunt Bettys' first album is no more (or less) than a roller-coaster ride through the traditional three-tiered theme park of sex, drugs, and rock and roll. With regard to the latter, "Skinny-Bones Jones" takes a poke at aging dinosaur bands (Knott explains it as "a little broke artist making fun of the Rolling Stones"), and the closing song presents "Rock and Roll" as the solution to an otherwise humdrum life: the verses present a litany of trials (you've got this problem, I've got that one), each leading to the refrain "Let's rock and roll." It's sort of a secular take on the old Jesus people slogan, "Praise the Lord (Anyway)!"

The second Aunty Bettys album is actually a collection of demos, outtakes, and live tracks: leftovers to provide fans of the first record with a second helping. *Ford Supersonic* contains less material that would be controversial for Christian audiences. Several of the songs are known to **Michael Knott** fans through other outlets: "Rock Stars on H" (in studio and live versions here) is an **LSU** song. "Getting Normal" and "Rikki Racer" are Knott songs that were performed by other artists on the eclectic **Browbeats** project. Another standout track, "Movie Star," has a more pop sound than most of the Bettys' work.

For trivia buffs: The Aunt Bettys originally organized and toured under the name Aunt Betty's Ford, but had to shorten

their name under threat of lawsuits from both an unamused Ford Motor Co. and an equally uptight Betty Ford Clinic.

Aurora

Lauren Smith, voc.; Rachel Smith, voc.; Raquel Smith, voc. 2000—*Aurora* (Red Hill); 2001—*Bigger Than Us* (Pamplin).

Aurora is a sister act intended to offer a Christian alternative to the girl-power music that was aimed at preteens and early teens around the turn of the millennium (cf. **ShineMK, V*enna, Whisper Loud, Zoe Girl**). At the time of their debut, Lauren Smith was twenty-one and her twin sisters Rachel and Raquel were twenty. The three young women were raised in a Christian home in Georgia, and they say they hope their music will enable younger women to deal with the temptations and difficulties of growing up in a non-Christian world. The sisters have been singing harmonies together since childhood and first learned synchronized choreography when they were all members of the same cheerleading squad. The first two songs on their self-titled album were produced by **John** and Dino **Elefante** and are its strongest tracks: "Out of This World" sounds very much like a Britney Spears song, and the Latin-inflected "Loving Me Like You Do" sounds quite a bit like Jennifer Lopez. Tony Palacios of **Guardian** plays guitar on the record. Jeff Deyo of **Sonicflood** adds guest vocals to the worshipful "Before the Throne." The album's closing song "Different Drum" (not a Linda Ronstadt cover) seems to sum up its central theme: in Rachel's words, "kids can stay away from some of the things their friends may be doing and still have fun." *Bigger Than Us* continues to focus the group mainly on their target teen-pop audience but allows for a little more stylistic diversity. On "Just the Way You Are" (not a Billy Joel song) and "Go On," they try out a more urban style. "Rekindle the Flame" is a worship song.

Christian radio hits: "A World with You" (# 12 in 2001).

John Austin

1992—*The Embarrassing Young* (Glasshouse); 1994—*Authorized Unauthorized Bootleg* (independent); 1996—*Byzantium*; 1998—*If I Was a Latin King* (Weathervane).

John Austin is a singer/songwriter in the mold of John Hiatt or Jackson Browne. He has won praise (and assistance) from many Christian artists who have enjoyed more commercial success than has come to him. A minister's son who attended Moody Bible Institute, Austin honed his craft singing in Chicago subways for change tossed by appreciative passersby. Somehow, a tape made it into the hands of Christian music legend **Mark Heard,** who produced Austin's first album. The title track from that record offers social commentary on a society that "doesn't believe in God or heaven, and has no room for the sick and the meek." Critics regarded the project as promising, but then in one year, Heard died, Austin's label went bankrupt, and the uninsured singer was assaulted by a gang of Hispanics in Chicago, leaving him with a badly broken arm and thousands of dollars in unpaid medical bills.

It was five years before he could produce another album for a major label. During the interim, however, Austin turned out two disparate private releases, both produced by Newton Carter of the **Vigilantes of Love.** The appropriately titled *Authorized Unauthorized Bootleg* is unplugged: Austin's voice, an acoustic guitar, and a harmonica are the only sounds to be heard on a batch of original songs, plus one cover of Heard's "Go Ask the Dead Man." *Byzantium* has a much more electric sound, with Austin fronting a full band made up of guests from the **Vigilantes,** Better Than Ezra, and Billy Pilgrim. The album takes its name from the Christian empire that succeeded Rome; to Austin, this is a metaphor for "a place to go after your whole world crumbles." A standout song is "Leave the Light On," about finding one's way in darkness.

If I Was a Latin King was produced by Bill Campbell of **The Throes** and **Poole.** The title reveals Austin to be struggling with the psychological aftermath of his assault (the Latin Kings are a street gang in Chicago) but also references his new Hispanic sound, replete with flamenco guitar, maracas, and cymbals. Overall, the theme of the album is one of hope and forgiveness, though numerous songs address harsh realities of modern life; the title track sets the tone with its reference to a world "where the violent and the beautiful go running hand in hand." The song "Be True To Your School" takes off on the old Beach Boys tune with creepy reference to school shootings. The most noticed song on the album has been "In Your Mama's Dreamz," a catchy tune (with Austin's wife Erin Echo sharing the vocals) about poverty, urban violence, teenage pregnancy, and the prayers that mothers say for their children.

Matt Auten

1995—*Where Loss and Gain Began* (independent); 2000—*New Found Land* (Silent Planet).

www.silentplanetrecords.com

Matt Auten is an unabashed folksinger, influenced by such artists as Joni Mitchell and **David Wilcox.** His music focuses on acoustic instrumentation, especially guitar. *New Found Land* (produced by **Tim Miner**) contains three instrumentals along with eleven vocal tracks. In his songwriting, Auten strives for what he calls "poetic storytelling" and "a touch of melancholy, but with a lyric that points toward hope." His style and lyrics have been compared to those of **Fernando Ortega** and **Pierce Pettis,** with whom he has toured.

Autovoice

Stephen Shoe, voc., elec.; Johnny Space-Echo, voc., elec. 1995—*00000011* (Mere); 1997—*A Living Death* (Flaming Fish).

www.yesic.com/~johnnys/autovoice

The Canadian industrial band Autovoice produces gothic electronic music that seeks to mimic the mechanical sounds of industry. Comparable groups in the general market would be Kraftwerk or Bauhaus, or, in the Christian market, early **Deitiphobia.** The music consists of fully manipulated and synthesized sounds, laced with ample feedback and distortion. Thus, the band opts for the keyboard-only type of industrial music that was favored by the genre's early pioneers, as opposed to the guitar-laced sounds employed by later innovators. The vocals are not understandable, but lyrics can be obtained through the band's website. Those who do obtain them will learn that they have been listening to songs describing dehumanization, decrying inhumanity, and proclaiming the need for a transcendent relationship with God.

Tom Autry

1974—*Tom Autry* (StarSong); 1978—*Blood of the Lamb*; 1980—*Better Days.*

Tom Autry is best known as author of the country hit, "A Mama and a Papa," first made popular by Ray Stevens. With a voice that has been compared to Richie Havens, he recorded early Christian albums of varied types. His first, abounding with pedal steel guitar (by **Al Perkins**), has a distinct country flavor. The second features keyboards and is more of a worship album. *Jesus Music* describes it as "art rock," noting that songs like "Blood of the Lamb," "I Want To Set You Free," and the instrumental "Sacrifice" convey a moody atmospheric sound that prefigures what would later be called New Age music. *Better Days* tries for a soulful balance of styles, as Autry covers Bill Withers' "Lean on Me" (with help from **Dallas Holm**) and **Mighty Clouds of Joy**'s "Master Plan." After these three albums, Autry delved into the easy listening market, recording independent albums for private release. He refers to himself as "a psalmist and a musicianary" and he travels extensively, leading worship at Pentecostal revival meetings. His wife Janie Autry sometimes sings with him.

Avalon

Jody McBrayer, voc.; Michael Passons, voc.; Janna Potter Long, voc.; Nikki Hassman, voc. (− 1997) // Cheri Paliotta (+ 1997). 1996—*Avalon* (Sparrow); 1997—*A Maze of Grace;* 1999—*In a Different Light;* 2000—*Joy;* 2001—*Oxygen* (Word).

www.avalonlive.com

Formed in 1995, the pop madrigal choir known as Avalon (after a medieval metaphor for heaven) scored nine consecutive Number One singles in the adult contemporary Christian market in the first three years of their existence. The group was assembled by Norman Miller and corporate executives at Sparrow who hoped to create another **Point of Grace** or **4 Him** (or, more accurately, a blend of the two, with gender balance). An early version of the group with a somewhat different lineup toured with the 1995 Young Messiah musical production, but the four members who formed the original recording group all had history in contemporary Christian music. Jody McBray and Janna Potter had both been in **Truth,** Nikki Hassman had sung backup for **Clay Crosse,** and Michael Passons had performed as a praise and worship leader. Songwriters were recruited and a self-titled album was commissioned with veteran producer **Charlie Peacock** at the helm. Hassman left the group after the debut album to pursue a mainstream career; she placed a song called "Any Lucky Penny" on the soundtrack for the TV series *Dawson's Creek* and signed a seven-album contract with Sony.

The first four tracks on *Avalon* received the most airplay, but the record's most impressive songs may be its final three: an a capella version of the hymn "My Jesus I Love Thee"; "Saviour Love," cowritten by group members; and a rendition of the **Andraé Crouch** song "Jesus is Lord." Also remarkable is "Give It Up," another song cowritten by group members that summons its listeners to give their lives as a sacrifice to Christ. *A Maze of Grace* opens with "Testify To Love," an anthemic number that features overlapping vocals and a determined melody line. The song would prove to be the longest running hit single of the decade on Christian adult contemporary charts. In general, Avalon's sophomore project features more up-tempo songs than the first record, successfully matching the vocal harmonies with dance music. The title track and a turbo-charged "Speed of Light" exemplify this approach best, though, again, the laid-back and beautiful "Adonai" is perhaps the album's showstopper. A hit titled "Knockin' on Heaven's Door" (not the **Bob Dylan** song) urges the persistence of prayer. The title of the third album, *In a Different Light,* seems to suggest a change of direction, but that is misleading. In spite of a new producer **(Brown Bannister)**, the group continues to churn out uplifting pop music ("Take You at Your Word") and tender worship songs ("I'm Speechless," "Let Your Love") just like those on the first two projects. The overall focus of the album is dependence upon God who remains ever faithful ("Can't Live a Day," "Always Has, Always Will"). The first hit from the album, "In Not Of" describes the relationship of Christians to an as-yet-unredeemed world. "Can't Live a Day" almost rivaled "Testify To Love" in radio popularity. "Always Has, Always Will" has an appealing, uncharacteristic style—

cowritten by **Toby McKeehan** of **DC Talk,** it almost sounds like a *Jesus Freak* outtake. After recording a Christmas album *(Joy),* Avalon came back with *Oxygen,* which was billed as a more musically progressive project. Indeed, *Oxygen* opens with a rock track ("Wonder Why"), and "Make It Last Forever" features some sizzling guitar work, but most of the project continues in a familiar vein guaranteed to please longtime fans without attracting many new ones. The clear standout song is "The Glory," a majestic choral number with lyrics celebrating Christ's sacrifice. The title track is addressed to God ("You are my oxygen") and was cowritten for the group by Richard Page of **Mr. Mister.**

CCM magazine describes Avalon as "hitting the bullseye on what is currently popular in the genre: straightforward, conclusive lyrics and music that is brimming with vim, vigor, and vitality." Naysayers complain that such an overt appeal to a targeted audience exemplifies "corporate rock" and belies the creativity and authenticity that should be integral to popular music. Peacock defends Avalon as "building on the foundation of what vocal groups have been in the past." Notably, gospel music has a long tradition of assembled vocal groups **(The Imperials, Truth)**, as does mainstream rock (from The Four Seasons and The Supremes to the Backstreet Boys and the Spice Girls).

For trivia buffs: Avalon's Janna Potter is married to Christian singer **Greg Long.**

Christian radio hits: "Give It Up" (# 13 in 1996); "This Love" (# 14 in 1997); "Testify To Love" (# 7 in 1998); "Knockin' on Heaven's Door" (# 15 in 1998); "In Not Of" (# 4 in 1999); "Take You at Your Word" (# 10 in 1999); "Always Have, Always Will" (# 5 in 2000); "Fly To You" (# 17 in 2000); "Make It Last Forever" (# 1 for 2 weeks in 2001); "Wonder Why" (# 11 in 2001).

Dove Awards: 1998 New Artist; 1999 Inspirational Song ("Adonai"); 1999 Pop/Contemporary Song ("Testify To Love").

AVB (a.k.a. **Acappella Vocal Band**)

Wes McKinzie (–1996); Terry Cheatham (–1991); Danny Elliott (–1991); Jay Smith (– 1991); Bret Testerman (– 1991) // Max Plaster (+ 1991, –1996); George Gee (+ 1991, –1992); Jarel Smith (+ 1991, –1992); John Green (+ 1992, – 1996); Brishan Hatcher (+ 1992, – 1999); Brian Randolph (+ 1992, –1993); Steve Reischl (+ 1993, –1996); Josh Harrison (+ 1996, – 1999); Aaron Herman (+ 1996, – 1999); Andrew McNeil (+ 1996, – 1999); Chris Bahr (+ 1999); Tony Brown (+ 1999); Todd Dunaway (+ 1999); Chris Lindsey (+ 1999); Jeremy Swindle (+ 1999). 1990—*Song in My Soul* (Acappella Company); 1991—*What's Your Tag Say?*; 1992—*Celebrate and Party*; 1993—*U and Me and God Make 5*; 1994—*Caminando en la Luz*; 1995—*The Road*; 1996—*Way of Life*; 1999— *Real.*

www.acappella.org

AVB developed as a spin-off of **Acappella** when it was decided that the latter group would pursue more traditional adult-oriented material and the former would stake out a claim on the younger audience. The separate band formed in 1988, some years before the appearance of Boyz II Men, when appealing to youth with a capella singing seemed to be a radical idea. The group's producer is Keith Lancaster, who is also responsible for the adult group's sound. Denominationally, AVB has its background in a branch of the Church of Christ that forbids the use of musical instruments in churches. McKinzie once explained in an interview that group members do not necessarily share this conviction, but their heritage has instilled in them a rich appreciation (and talent) for a capella singing. AVB's mission statement describes the group as "dedicated to stirring young people to a godly commitment, through cutting-edge vocal music."

Musically, AVB has not usually favored the soulful balladry associated with Boyz II Men but has opted for faster-paced, more rhythmic songs. Incorporation of jazz stylings has made comparisons to **Take 6** inevitable. On their early albums, the tendency was toward novelty: numerous short choruses often performed with a touch of humor. This was augmented in concert performances where it was revealed that the numerous electronic and percussive sounds heard accompanying the singers were actually produced anatomically. The title track to *What's Your Tag Say?* and "It's Not Enuff" from the same album display rap/hip-hop underpinnings reminiscent of Tony! Tone! Toni! These elements develop further on *Celebrate and Party,* as the racially integrated group embraces more of a doo-wop sound while still incorporating hip-hop rhythms. *The Road* is essentially a retrospective of previously recorded material, except that all songs were re-recorded in updated versions. One of these was their crowd-pleasing version of "Kyrie," a Number One general market hit for **Mr. Mister** in 1985.

Christian radio hits: "Kyrie" (# 23 in 1994).

The Awakening

Andrew Horrocks, gtr.; Allan Powell, bass; Mike Powell, drums; Ian Tanner, voc., kybrd. 1986—*Two Worlds* (independent); 1987—*Sanctified* (Reunion); 1988—*Into Thy Hands.*

Formed in 1985, the Canadian band The Awakening fashioned themselves as a Christian version of Yes, with some influence perhaps from Peter Gabriel-led Genesis. Tanner and Horrocks went on to form **One Hundred Days.** The Awakening produced progressive, synthesizer-heavy rock that aimed for transcendence. *Sanctified* mainly repeats songs from the custom debut, with two additions ("My Only Hope," "Distant Light"), which exhibit a marked improvement over the other material in terms of technical quality or commercial polish.

The Awakening actually covered Chris Squire's "Onward" on their final album, and the song "Don't Wait for Me" could have passed for an outtake from Yes's *90125.* Despite the limitations inherent in such imitative efforts, the group avoided the bombastic pretentiousness of their secular forebears and thus often produced accessible pop-oriented songs. They were also frequently compared to **Elim Hall** (in part due to a Canadian connection).

Note: a South African Christian band also called The Awakening has released at least three independent albums of brooding, gothic music similar in sound to **Dead Artist Syndrome** or **Type O Negative:** *Risen,* which features a cover of Simon and Garfunkel's "Sounds of Silence"; *Request,* which similarly covers Men Without Hats' "Safety Dance"; and *Ethereal Menace.*

Christian radio hits: "Give It Up" (# 13 in 1996); "This Love" (# 14 in 1997).

Bob Ayala

1976—*Joy by Surprise* (Pure Joy); 1978—*Wood between the Worlds* (Myrrh); 1980—*Journey*; 1985—*Rescued* (Pretty Good).

A native of Los Angeles and a child of the Jesus movement, Bob Ayala was voted "Best New Artist of the Year" by readers of *CCM* magazine in 1976. Ayala actually began his music ministry in 1969 by performing regularly at a famous Christian coffeehouse in Los Angeles called the Salt Company. He later became involved with Texas-based Last Days Ministries after the death of that organization's founder, **Keith Green,** performing Keith Green Memorial concerts and, taking up one of LDM's pet-concerns, antiabortion rallies. In the '90s, Ayala signed on as a songwriter with Integrity Music. Ayala is blind as a result of a genetic eye disease (retinitis pigmentosa). Ayala began his Christian music ministry in 1969 (long before his first album), and during the days of the Jesus movement, he toured constantly with his wife Pam, who was a strong partner in his ministry. At that time, he was noted for being one of the only short-haired clean-shaven Christian singers in an otherwise hippie environment. He was also known for his sense of humor, though most of his songs are in a serious vein. Ayala's musical style is best described as pastoral folk in the tradition of Dan Fogelberg and Harry Chapin; he has also been compared to Jose Feliciano. His first album, *Joy by Surprise,* was recorded with Buddy King at the latter's Huntington Beach house. It takes its title from the autobiography of C. S. Lewis, a wellspring of inspiration whose works Ayala would often tap (cf. "That Hideous Strength," on *Wood between the Worlds*). The album *Rescued* features guitar work by Hadley Hockensmith and saxophone by Justo Almario, both of **Koinonia.**

Ayala's theological maturity shows on songs like "Positive Confessions," which counters prosperity gospel teachings, and his sensitivity comes through on "Dear God," which suggests a priority of family time over church activities. Ayala wrote a number of songs that seem directed to individuals ("Anna," "Vanya," "Valerie," "Pamela," "Heidi"). In "Pamela," he expresses this touching thought: "God could work a miracle and make me see / But you know, if God would give me just one more miracle / I'd pray that God would give me a love as deep as yours."

Azitis

Don Lower, voc.; bass; Steve Nelson, voc., drums; Dennis Sullivan, kybrd.; Michael Welch, gtr., flute. 1970—*Help* (Elco).

www.geocities.com/Area51/Keep/3879/AZITIS.htm

Regarded by some as the world's first Christian rock band, Azitis produced one album of psychedelic art rock similar in sound to such mainstream artists as Fever Tree or the 13th Floor Elevators. The group preferred to call their music metaphysical rock. Founded by the rhythm section of Don Lower and Steve Nelson, the band first went by the name Help and released a single under that name with Capitol Records ("Questions Why" and "Life Worth Living"). When they signed with Elco, they changed their name to Azitis (supposedly from the phrase "on earth *azitis* in heaven") and used *Help* as the name of the album instead. That record is something of a rock opera, telling the story of Creation to Fall to Redemption to Judgment in songs that are meant to flow continuously one to the other. Vocals are subdued, with the accent on swirling organ sounds reminiscent of Iron Butterfly's "In-a-Gadda-Da-Vida." More ecumenical than most Christian musical groups, Azitis said their message was, "all religions give us hope and faith in our fellow man." Nevertheless, the album cover depicts a large cross emerging out of a globe, symbolizing "the invention of Christian faith, overshadowing the other philosophies of mankind." A second rock-opera by Azitis, *Window into It,* was performed at the University of Sacramento in 1975 and recorded but never released. In 2000, Lower said it dealt with "a blending of all religions" and may finally become available.

Philip Bailey

1983—*Continuation* (Columbia); 1984—*The Wonders of His Love* (Myrrh); *Chinese Wall* (Columbia); 1986—*Triumph* (Myrrh); *Inside Out* (Columbia); 1991—*Family Affair* (Word); *The Best of Philip Bailey: A Gospel Collection*; 1994—*Dance Tracks* (Zoo); 1997—*Avatar* (Avex); *Life and Love* (AMW); 1999—*Dreams* (Heads Up).

http://philipbailey.com

Blessed with an incredible four-octave voice, Philip Bailey (b. 1951) is known to millions for the lead falsetto vocals he supplied for Earth, Wind, and Fire on such hits as "Shining Star" (# 1 in 1975), "Sing a Song" (# 5 in 1975), and "After the Love Is Gone" (# 2 in 1979). That's Bailey crooning the classic EWF ballad "Reasons" and that's Bailey supplying those unforgettable Ba-Dee-Ya's in "September" (# 8 in 1978). One of the most successful rock/soul/funk bands of the '70s, EWF recorded numerous gold and platinum records, won six Grammy awards, and was inducted into the Rock and Roll Hall of Fame. A high profile member of the band almost from its inception, Bailey was also a devout Christian, outspoken about his faith. During and after his tenure with EWF, he recorded several solo albums of contemporary R&B and gospel music. As a solo artist, he had a major general market hit with the song "Easy Lover" (# 2 in 1984), which he performed as a duet with Phil Collins.

Born and raised in Denver, Colorado, Bailey was originally interested in percussion, especially as related to jazz music. He was working as a drummer when Maurice White (also a former session drummer) recruited his voice for the EWF ensemble.

That group was notable for its proud display of African culture, evident in the costuming and stage designs for its concerts. They were also known for their interest in mysticism and spirituality, though for White this was played out more with regard to astrology (hence the group's name) and Egyptian religion than orthodox Christianity. In 1975 the group opened for Santana on a European tour, and that group's singer **Leon Patillo** led Bailey and two other searchers in Bible studies that solidified their commitments to Christ. It would still be a full decade before Bailey released his first album of Christian music *(Wonders of His Love)* and began sharing his testimony widely in the press. Bailey has said such postponement was wise, because as soon as a famous person's conversion becomes public, that individual is subjected to scrutiny he or she is not ready to bear: "You just say, 'I'm a Christian,' and people want to know what color underwear you wear." Indeed his song "Easy Lover"—out the same year as his gospel record but on the Columbia album *Chinese Wall*—caused a stir in the Christian community among people who apparently did not listen to the lyrics. They thought he was extolling the accessible love of a loose woman rather than warning his (male) audience to shun this (à la Proverbs 7). Bailey's response to the minor scandal: "Man, people are stupid."

Altogether, Bailey released three albums aimed at the contemporary Christian market, plus a "best of" compilation, which drew from all three of these. *The Wonders of His Love* features "I Will No Wise Cast You Out," which has a definite EWF sound to it, and "I Am Gold," a funky song with an extended a capella introduction inspired by James 1:2–4 and 1 Peter 1:6–7. The title track was cowritten by Bailey with **Teri DeSario** and is reminiscent of **Seawind**'s jazz-fusion sound. *Triumph* offers nine songs (six of which would end up on the compilation) by nine different songwriters, sampling a variety of styles. "The Other Side" features a calypso beat. "The Love of God" is a soaring emotional ballad. The title song is a rousing number, closer to traditional gospel. *Family Affair* opens with a cover of **Charlie Peacock**'s "This Is How the Work Gets Done" but otherwise seems to waste Bailey's talent on mediocre adult contemporary fare.

Not to be ignored are the other albums listed above, mainstream R&B products performed by a Christian man who finds divine inspiration in the everyday stuff of life. Love songs predominate. *Continuation* contains guest appearances by **Deniece Williams,** Jeffrey Osborne, and Sister Sledge. Because of Bailey's well-known faith commitments, the album was reviewed in *CCM* magazine, which groused, "it contains nothing geared toward the Christian audience" (assuming that Christians want to listen only to music that is overtly religious). "Anything Is Possible" from *Life and Love* is inspirational. Bailey came full circle with the album *Dreams,* returning to his roots in jazz. That album features assistance from an all-star team of contemporary jazz musicians (people like Pat Metheny and Grover Washington Jr.) and allows Bailey to display his talents on jazz standards ("The Masquerade Is Over") and on jazzed-up versions of pop classics like **Van Morrison**'s "Moondance," Bread's "Make It with You," and Earth, Wind, and Fire's "Sail Away."

Christian radio hits: "I Will No Wise Cast You Out" (# 4 in 1985); "Wonders of His Love" (# 14 in 1985); "I Want To Know You" (# 11 in 1985); "Thank You" (# 14 in 1987); "All Soldiers" (# 7 in 1987); "Marvelous" (# 7 in 1988); "Lonely, Broken Hearted People" (# 12 in 1990).

Grammy Awards: 1986 Best Gospel Performance, Male *(Triumph).*

Tammy Sue Bakker

1987—*Sixteen* (Refuge).

Tammy Sue Bakker is the daughter of disgraced TV evangelists Jim and Tammy Fay Bakker. Long before her parents' empire was doomed by sex scandals and financial fraud—but not before it had come into disrepute among nonfundamentalists for promoting greed through a success-oriented theology—Tammy Sue made an album of contemporary Christian music produced by **Tim Miner.** She was only sixteen at the time, hence the project's title. Musically, the album moves decidedly away from the southern gospel melodrama evident in her mother's songs to embrace more of the R&B sound associated with Miner. *CCM* recognized potential in a few tracks ("Free," "Still in His Hand," "Higher") but couldn't help but note that

others were stained with the same thinking for which her parents were famous. "It'll Be Alright" directly contradicts Jesus (Matthew 10:16–22) by advising Christians to just "lay back" and realize that everything will be okay.

Tammy Sue's brother Jay Bakker would become a significant promoter of Christian music at the turn of the millennium. He is author of the book *Son of a Preacher Man* (HarperSanFrancisco, 2000).

Balance of Power

Chris Dale, bass; Lionel Hicks, drums; Bill Yates, gtr.; Paul Curtis, gtr.; (–1997); Tony Ritchie, voc. (–1997); Ivan Gunn, kybrd. (–1999) // Pete Southern, gtr. (+ 1997); Lance King, voc. (+ 1997). 1997—*When the World Falls Down* (Point); 1999—*Book of Secrets* (Nightmare); 2000—*Ten More Tales of Grand Illusion*; 2001—*Perfect Balance.*

Balance of Power is a British hard rock band known for their melodic, progressive style. They are often compared to general market groups like Queensryche and Dream Theater. Their first album was released only in Europe and Japan, and the lead vocalist and guitarist (Tony Ritchie) then departed—he formed another band called USM or United States of Mind and yet also continued on as key songwriter for Balance of Power. *Book of Secrets* features the more distinctive vocals of Lance King, which *Rad Rockers* has described as "plaintively mournful and wailing, like the last warnings of an Old Testament prophet before judgment falls on a civilization drenched in denial." The latter album takes its concept from *The Bible Code,* a best-selling book that tries to ascribe occult significance to scriptural texts. Its lyrics, however, are overtly Christian and explicitly biblical. "When Heaven Calls Your Name" proclaims, "He will wipe out every tear from their eyes and death will be no more" (cf. Revelation 21:4). The second album has a heavier sound and a more subtle lyrical approach: "There's a place that's soft and warm / It's a shelter from the storm" ("Blind Man"). *Perfect Balance* features "Shelter Me" and "Fire Dance," songs about which *HM*'s Doug Van Pelt would say, "hooks and melody reign supreme."

Trace Balin

1988—*Champions* (DaySpring); 1989—*Here and Now*; 1991—*Out of the Blue*; date unknown—*Glory Road* (label unknown); *Trace Balin, Past and Present*; *Heavenly Hits.*

A native of Beeville, Texas, Trace Balin grew up the daughter of a history professor in an intellectual environment. She claims to have been an atheist until her husband prompted her to see the movie *The Late Great Planet Earth* based on the book by Hal Lindsey. Transformed by eschatological hope, she turned her musical talents to a ministry of exhortation and encouragement of other Christians. A bout with pneumonia in

1986 damaged Balin's vocal chords, leaving her with a raspy voice similar to Kim Carnes or Tina Turner. Her debut album for DaySpring appears to have been an answer to the Queen anthem of 1977. The song "Who Are the Champions?" denies that real heroes are those persons the world is likely to idolize but rather are those who have been born of God and so have overcome the world. *Here and Now* offers the strong rocker "I Don't Have Love" and the moving ballad "Well Done," on which Balin evinces a more mature attitude toward the parousia than is usually associated with Lindsey-fanaticism: "I'm not looking for the rapture, but I want to live like the time has come." She also sings a rendition of the hymn, "All Hail the Power of Jesus' Name." *Out of the Blue* features three stellar songs: "Stranger," a poetic description of the Christian's journey through this life, and two blues-oriented tunes (the title track and "Changes"). The later album *Heavenly Hits* is something of a novelty record consisting of rock and roll oldies rewritten with religious lyrics: "Leader of the Pack" becomes "Preacher of the Pact" (cf. **Apologetix**). Balin is well known for her work with Crisis Pregnancy Centers. A cancer survivor, she is also able to testify to the role that her faith has played in facing that affliction.

Christian radio hits: "Only for You" (# 5 in 1988); "We Are an Army" (# 9 in 1989); "We Need Each Other" (# 9 in 1989); "All I Want To Do" (# 6 in 1989); "Well Done" (# 2 in 1989); "Never Let it Be Said" (# 14 in 1990); "This Is Where" (# 19 in 1991).

Ballydowse

Dave Baumgartner, violin; Brian Grover, bass; Craig Holland, gtr.; Dan Kool, voc.; Andrew Mandell, voc.; Robina Mandell, voc.; Nate Peters, voc., gtr.; Chris White, drums. 1998—*The Land, the Bread, and the People* (Grrr); 2000—*Out of the Fertile Crescent.*

A punk band with world music influences, Ballydowse crowds a stage with eight full-time players and such diverse instruments as bagpipe, didgeridoo, whirligig, bodhran, bullroarer, and moohran (in addition to the more traditional items listed above). The electric guitars, however, are aggressive, which is no surprise considering the group's roots. Andrew Mandell and Brian Glover were (are) members of **Crashdog,** and they founded Ballydowse with other members of Chicago's Jesus People U.S.A. commune while that group takes an extended sabbatical. JPUSA is the four hundred-member socially active community that also gave Christian music **Resurrection Band** and many other artists. Though all the members sing, the upfront vocal sound of Ballydowse is provided by an intertwining of Andrew Mandell's trademark yelps and shouts with the more fluid singing of Robina, his wife. The music is wildly eclectic, but Celtic influences are especially notable. Lyrically, the group favors social concerns. "Song for Elie" is a tribute to Holocaust victim Elie Wiesel. "Lucrece" broaches the

topic of sexual abuse. "Bud Morris" urges Christians to boycott alcohol and tobacco, not because these products are intrinsically evil but because their purchase puts money in the pockets of corporations that prey upon the vulnerable: "Indulgence can be freedom / Moderation liberty / But the freedom for the weakest / Is the one that is for me." *Out of the Fertile Crescent* deals especially with international issues, such as United States policies in Guatemala and child prostitution in Thailand.

The band became somewhat noted for its concern over the plight of Iraqis suffering under what they considered to be unfair economic sanctions imposed by the United States and other nations. The topic is addressed in sound clips and in some of the songs on *Out of the Fertile Crescent.* Prior to that album's release, Andrew Mandell defied the sanctions by visiting Iraq with (illegal) gifts of textbooks and medicine. On September 22, 2000, he and Dan Kool were audience members for the Oprah Winfrey show on the day she interviewed presidential candidate George W. Bush. Oprah had them removed from the studio during a commercial break after they asked Bush what she thought was an inappropriate question (i.e., "Would you continue the Democrats' policy of sanctions that kill 5,000 children a month in Iraq?").

Bam Crawford's Purpose

See **Beverly Crawford.**

Brown Bannister

1981—*Talk to One Another* (NewPax).

Texan Brown Bannister got his start in Christian music through collaborations with a college buddy, **Chris Christian,** and went on to become one of the industry's most prestigious producers. He has guided projects by a varied roster of stars including **Carolyn Arends, Debby Boone, Steven Curtis Chapman, Twila Paris, Charlie Peacock, Petra, Kenny Rogers, Kathy Troccoli,** and **White Heart,** but will forever be best remembered as the man who discovered **Amy Grant,** that is, as the producer who first brought her music to prominence. He has also been a prolific songwriter, penning such songs as "Angels" and "In a Little While" for Grant, and cowriting "Praise the Lord" for **The Imperials**—which the Gospel Music Association chose as the 1981 Song of the Year. In the early '80s Bannister recorded one album of solo material, which had a light-rock, adult contemporary sound. *CCM* called the album "a masterful blend of gentle love-with-a-capital-L-songs." Indeed, the record includes a trilogy of three such songs, a medley of "Love Waits for You" (by **Michael W. Smith** and **Billy Sprague**), "The Nature of Love," and a Christianized version of Leslie Duncan's "Love Song" (i.e., the song made popular by Elton John on his *Tumbleweed Connection* album).

The title track for *Talk to One Another* was cowritten by Bob Farrell of **Farrell and Farrell**; "Honesty" is a collaboration by Bannister with **Gary Chapman.**

In addition to those songs listed above, Bannister has written or cowritten Christian radio hits for **Farrell and Farrell** ("All You Need"); **Amy Grant** ("Old Man's Rubble," "Faith Walkin' People," "Look What Has Happened To Me"), **David Meece** ("And You Know It's Right"), and **Kathy Troccoli** ("Stubborn Love," "Holy, Holy").

Christian radio hits: "Carry On" (# 4 in 1982); "Talk To One Another" (# 11 in 1982).

Dove Awards: 1998 Producer of the Year; 2000 Producer of the Year; 2001 Producer of the Year.

John and Anne Barbour

1996—*Real Love* (Metro One).

The Barbours are a married couple who have worked for years as session singers in the Los Angeles area. Original members of the Maranatha Praise Band, they recorded an album of inspirational adult contemporary songs. The theme of the album is based on 1 John 4:20–21 and seeks to explicate the responsibility Christians have to "treat those around us the way God wants us to."

Valeri Barinov

1985—*The Trumpet Call* (I Care).

Valeri Barinov was a Christian musician in Russia who was sent to a Soviet gulag for seeking to propagate Christianity in ways that violated government restrictions. While imprisoned in the camp, he wrote and recorded a rock opera called *The Trumpet Call.* A tape of the musical was smuggled out of the camp, and a more professional recording was subsequently made by the **Dave Markee Band,** released on Fortress Records in 1985. Markee was a veteran English musician who had been a regular member of **Eric Clapton**'s band. Barinov's original tape of the musical was also released on the independent I Care label (sold through mail-orders only). Musically, *The Trumpet Call* recalls Pink Floyd at moments ("You Killed Him") while also venturing into techno-pop ("Golgotha"). Barinov was in the news again in 1988 when, released from prison, he staged a demonstration outside the Kazan Cathedral in St. Petersburg (then Leningrad). The Cathedral at that time had been transformed by the Soviet government into a museum of atheism. Barinov stood in the colonnade of the museum and preached about Christ for two hours while Soviet soldiers stood by. Perhaps due to a media focus on the demonstration, he was not arrested.

Barnabas

Kris Klingensmith, drums; Gary Mann, bass; Nancy Jo Mann, voc.; Monte Cooley, gtr. (– 1980) // Mick Donner, gtr. (+ 1981, – 1983); Kris Brauninger, kybrd., gtr. (+ 1981, – 1983); Brian Belew, gtr. (+ 1983). 1980—*Hear the Light* (Tunesmith); 1981—*Find Your Heart a Home*; 1983—*Approaching Light Speed* (Light); 1984—*Feel the Fire*; 1986—*Little Foxes*; 2000—*Artifacts and Relics* (M8).

http://leconte.com/barnabas

Barnabas was one of the first Christian hard rock bands. The group's sound was called "smashmouth music," a description that has nothing to do with the '90s rock band Smash Mouth but rather referred to an in-your-face hard sound produced by some of the more aggressive new-wave acts. The first two Barnabas albums displayed the group in formative stages, musically, geographically, and with regard to personnel. The band formed in Los Angeles, moved for a time to Illinois where they stayed with the Jesus People U.S.A. commune (cf. **Resurrection Band**), then landed in Des Moines, Iowa. Monte Cooley, who had founded the group in 1977, played on the first album only, then left to form another Christian band called the Bethlehem White Sox. Kris Brauninger and Mick Donner were present only for the second record. The classic lineup of Gary and Nancy Jo Mann, Brian Belew, and Kris Klingensmith made the three albums for which Barnabas is best known. Of these, the first two (*Approaching Light Speed, Feel the Fire*) feature a number of songs that would come to be regarded as big fish in the small pond of Christian metal: "Breathless Wonderment," "Northern Lights," "Stormclouds," and a brief epic, "Suite for the Souls of Our Enemies (Part One)." Then the group moved again, to Oklahoma, where the final album (*Little Foxes*) would be recorded as they were in the process of breaking up.

Barnabas emulated the hard rock stylings of what many Christians of the day considered to be overtly worldly music. Belew provided Van Halen-style guitar riffs while the rhythm section took its cues from bottom heavy bands like Rush. The sound of a heavy group with a female vocalist struck some as a novelty, though this was not unique (cf. **Resurrection Band, Servant**). As indicated, they took three albums to find their style, with a gradual evolution from punk to hard rock to metal. *CCM* called the first album (*Hear the Light*) a collection of "nine new-wave tunes and a folk song," but their review of *Find Your Heart a Home* would describe Barnabas as playing "straight ahead rock 'n' boogie." Then, when the third album (*Approaching Light Speed*) appeared, *CCM* said the group "tends to sound a little like an ultra-conservative Christian Black Sabbath."

Musically, Barnabas' albums hold up quite well. "There's a New World Coming" and "Little Faith" from *Hear the Light* feature memorable hooks and choruses, with guitars that simply soar. "Directory Assistance" from that same album points in the metal direction. The title track to *Find Your Heart a Home* is another hook-filled anthem; other standout tracks from the sophomore set include "The Conflict of Desire," which illustrates the war between spirit and flesh with interplay of flashy guitars, and "Southern Woman," a more pop-oriented rock ballad. *Approaching Light Speed* includes "Waiting for the Aliens," a little ditty about those left behind by the rapture rejoicing that visitors from outer space have apparently cleansed the earth of Christians. "Stormclouds" is an angry rant about the world's evils ("unborn children murdered by the millions") with a plea to the unsaved to join those waiting for redemption. The third album also includes Belew's "Warrior" and Gary Mann's "Crucifixion," but Klingensmith generally served as principal lyricist for all albums but the first. He could be quite poetic, as is evident in the three masterpieces from *Feel the Fire:* "Suite for the Souls of Our Enemies," "Northern Lights," and "Breathless Wonderment" (to sample from the latter: "From the dreadful crags of Zion, and the lowly Bethlehem / The mighty heart of God is pierced as nail pierces hand / The Spirit broods in silence as He did when time was young / The Father turns away from His beloved, tortured Son"). *Little Foxes* is perhaps the band's heaviest record, musically and lyrically (the song "Auschwitz 87" actually opens with samples of Adolf Hitler). Lyrically, the final album seems startlingly harsh, with an overwhelming theme of judgment about to fall on sinners of various stripes (e.g., Nazis, dopers, and whores). The title tune features the line, "Satan laughs, 'Your ass is mine, kiss it goodbye, kiss it goodbye!' " In 1997, when Klingensmith supplied the lyrics to this album for the band's new website, he appended a note: "My worldview has grown quite a bit since those strange, tumultuous days with Barnabas, and if I were to write a set of lyrics for yet another Barnabas project, they would be nothing like these."

In any case, the group fought with the Christian music industry throughout much of its tenure. They endured searing criticism from preachers like Bill Gothard, Bob Larson, and Jimmy Swaggart, who could not distinguish style from substance or bring themselves to heed **Bob Dylan**'s admonition, "don't criticize what you don't understand." In seven years, Barnabas played fewer than fifty concerts, and even with five albums, they made slim profits. Such struggles and disappointments took an emotional toll, and soon after the band's dissolution the Manns divorced, as did Klingensmith. Nancy Jo Mann went on to found and head an organization called Women Exploited by Abortion. In the year 2001, plans were underway for all five Barnabas albums to be released on CD, and there was discussion of a possible reunion tour. The *Artifacts and Relics* CD from M8 productions contains a couple of old Bethlehem White Sox songs, a trio of solos by Nancy Jo

Mann, and three poor recordings of live tracks from 1982; it is obviously intended for mega-fans only.

David Baroni

1982—*From the Heart* (LifeStream); 1983—*All for the Glory of God;* 1985—*Carry the Torch;* 1986—*Pressing Toward the Prize;* 1987—*The Heart Matters; Take Time: Songs of Worship;* 1989—*Perfect Love;* 1990—*Set Free* (by David and Rita Baroni); 1991—*The Other Side* (Diadem); *Seek My Face* (label unknown); 1992—*The Song of the Lord;* 1993—*The Bondslave, the Bride, and the Battle;* 1997—*In This Holy Place; Promised Land;* 1998—*Holy Desperation;* 1999—*A New Anointing for a New Day.*

David Baroni is a worship leader from Natchez, Mississippi, who writes spiritual songs and hymns with a focus on personal devotion and congregational praise. He has also been a prolific composer, writing "Soldier of the Light" for **Andrus, Blackwood, and Co.** and "Keep the Flame Burning" for **Debby Boone** and **Phil Driscoll.** In the mid '80s Baroni recorded a few Christian pop albums, two of which were reviewed by *CCM.* The album *Pressing Toward the Prize* includes the reggae-flavored song "You Are the Potter" and the guilt-inducing "Song to the Sleeping," on which he proclaims, "The Devil is invading our families / And instead of praying we just watch TV." *The Heart Matters* similarly takes on worldly penchants for designer clothing in "Passion for Fashion" alongside a tribute to his newborn twin daughters "Charity and Celeste." After moving more into the praise and worship genre, Baroni tended to emphasize a prophetic or charismatic leading of the Spirit in music (and in life), which for him seems to be antithetical to human endeavor. For instance, he maintains that the entire album *The Song of the Lord* was written by sitting down at a piano with a tape recorder and playing all of the songs straight through as God gave them to him. The album *The Other Side* features vocals by **Susan Ashton, Kelly Willard,** and **Chris Rodriguez.**

Christian radio hits: "We Need To Meet Them There" (# 24 in 1982); "Move On Up the Mountain" (# 34 in 1984).

Barren Cross

Mike Lee, voc., gtr.; Ray Paris, gtr.; Jim LaVerde, bass; Steve Whitaker, drums. 1985—*Believe* [EP] (Erika); 1986—*Rock for the King* (StarSong); 1988—*Atomic Arena* (Enigma); 1989—*State of Control;* 1990—*Hotter Than Hell!* (Medusa); 1994—*Rattle Your Cage* (Rugged).

Founded in 1983, Barren Cross was one of Christian music's first true heavy metal bands. They followed close on the heels of **Stryper** but had a heavier sound, akin to Dio or Iron Maiden. The first three albums were produced by **John** and Dino **Elefante** and featured Christian metal classics like "Out of Time," "Stage of Intensity," and "It's All Come True for You." A couple of songs from the Enigma albums ("Imaginary

Music," "Cryin' For You") saw some airplay on MTV. In 1989 the group appeared along with members of Kiss and Anthrax on *The Morton Downey Show* (a televised tabloid talk show) to discuss the topic of groupies in the rock scene. The band fell apart around 1990 with Mike Lee's departure to front what he called "a secular group" named Bare Bones. Different versions of Barren Cross with varying personnel continued to tour, but the live album *Hotter Than Hell!* and the reunion disc *Rattle Your Cage* both feature the original lineup.

Barren Cross always viewed their albums and concerts as expressions of a "mission to tell the world of the love of Jesus Christ through heavy music." Numerous songs address personal problems (dating, heartbreak) and social issues from the perspective of a Christian worldview. *Atomic Arena* features "Killers of the Unborn" (about abortion), "In the Eye of the Fire" (about suicide), and "Terrorist Child" (about the threat of terrorism). *State of Control* includes "Bigotry Man," which denounces prejudice. The power ballad "Let It Go, Let It Die" encourages forgiveness of wrongs suffered ("Jesus said, 'Let it go and let it die / I paid for that brother's wrongs with my life'"). Lyrics could also be boldly evangelistic. "Two Thousand Years" quotes almost precisely from Romans 10:9 ("If you confess with your mouth that Jesus is Lord / And believe in your heart God raised him from the dead / Then you will be saved and forgiven"). *Rattle Your Cage* is pure nostalgia, recapturing the '80s metal sound with intentional dismissal of whatever challenges the '90s might have been offering.

For trivia buffs: Steve Whitaker's mother wrote a book about being a mom to a rock star. See *The "Calling" of a Rock Star: A Christian Mother's Story* by Beth Whitaker (Hawthorne, 1988). After his rock star days, Steve became a police officer.

Brian Barrett

1993—Brian Barrett (StarSong); 1995—Nailed in Stone.

Singer/songwriter Brian Barrett was in the forefront of the '90s' Christian country movement. Emulating the new country sound made popular by such stars as Garth Brooks and Vince Gill, Barrett made albums that seemed to offer the Christian community a slightly more countryfied version of **Steven Curtis Chapman**. The son of gospel singer Barton Barrett, Brian was raised in Tennessee, starting bands in high school and later at Hardin Simmons University in Texas, where he earned a degree in theater/radio and television. He won the 1992 Gospel Music Association's New Artist Showcase. His first album produced the hit, "A Wing and a Prayer." *Nailed in Stone* attracted more attention with an even less confined-to-country sound but with traditional down-home country themes. "One Prayer Away" presents the final prayer of a mother for her wayward son. "Jimmy Got Saved" relates what

happens to a tattooed, knife-toting biker who "likes wild women and drinks cheap whiskey." The song "In Time" is basically Barrett's appeal for God to find him a spouse (a petition since granted). Guest appearances by **Al Perkins** give the album authenticity and flair.

Barry G

1995—Rugged Witness (Grapetree).

Raised in the rough Oak Cliff neighborhood west of Dallas, the rapper who calls himself Barry G targets his ministry at urban youth who seem destined to become hoodlums like he was before turning his life over to the Lord. Barry G founded the successful Christian rap group **P.I.D.** but left to become a youth pastor when he felt that group became more focused on entertainment than ministry. His solo album was one of the earlier releases on the seminal Grapetree label, and it include the singles, "Ain't Nuthin' . . ." and "Paper Ladies."

Bash-N-The Code (a.k.a. **Bash;** originally **Found Free)**

Found Free lineup (undocumented changes occurred): Bish Alverson, drums; David Michael Ed, kybrd., voc.; Rebecca Ed, voc.; Jack Faulkner, bass; Wayne Farley, gtr.; Keith Lancaster, voc.; Catherine MacCallum, voc. Bash-N-The Code: Keith Lancaster, voc.; Chris Kearney, drums; Mark Townsend, gtr., voc. (−1989); Scott Carmichael, kybrd., gtr., voc. (−1987); Trent Dean, kybrd., voc. (−1987); Greg Sparks, voc., bass (−1987); Rebecca Ed Sparks, voc. (−1987) // Jamie Kearney, voc. (+1987); Gary Williams, kybrd., voc. (+1987); Kirk Eberhard, bass (+1987, −1989); Scott Beck, gtr. (+1989); John Fett, bass (+1989). Bash: Keith Lancaster, voc.; Chris Mitchell, voc.; Kevin Stokes, voc. As Found Free: 1975—*Found Free* (Olde Towne); 1976—*Transformation*; 1978—*Closer Than Ever* (Greentree); 1980—*Specially Priced, Individually Wrapped* (Sparkal). As Bash-N-The Code: 1986—*Bash-N-The Code*; 1987—*Big Mouth*; 1989—*More Than Enough*. As Bash: 1991—*Holiday*.

Pennsylvania preacher's kid Keith Lancaster (not to be confused with the leader of **Acappella** and **AVB**) founded the song-and-dance ensemble Found Free in 1971 and remained with the group through its name changes to the very end. Otherwise, the group had a revolving membership (often undocumented) with at least twenty-three individuals taking part at various times. Keith's relatives David, Ed, and Michael were all members at the start but appear to have billed themselves as one person (David Michael Ed). **Rebecca and Gregg Sparks** were with Found Free on some projects and performed on the first Bash-N-The Code release. Indeed, they met as members (Rebecca went by the name Rebecca Ed, apparently because she was David's or Michael's or maybe Ed's sister), marrying in 1985. As Found Free, the group failed to win over critics. *Harmony* magazine noted that *Transformation* reveals material that "ranges from attempts at rock and roll to mellow worship choruses seasoned with jazz harmonies" and indicated that only the latter were successful. *CCM* thought *Specially Purchased* was outdated: "Found Free wants us to believe that they are a new-wave pop group when they are actually closer to a church group in the early '70s doing a musical."

As Bash-N-The Code, the group dropped any supposed pretensions of being a rock group. They performed Up-With-People style dance numbers augmented with skits and stories intended to convey the basic message "It's *fun* to be a Christian!" Costumed in nouveau attire, they hopped about stages and chancels in a way that prefigured the ministry of **World Wide Message Tribe.** *CCM*'s Brian Quincy Newcomb praised *Bash-N-The Code* as "a barnstormer of a dance album," singling out guitarist Mark Townsend and departing vocalist Rebecca Sparks as the major talents. The album includes "Testify," a duet between Rebecca and guest **Mylon LeFevre,** along with such joy-of-salvation rave-ups as "Power Praise," "I Will Win This Fight," and "Fanatic." Loss of the Sparks was a blow from which the group would never quite recover. The album *Big Mouth* begins with a hip-hop version of the Sunday school song, "The B-I-B-L-E," but also includes worship tunes like "We Magnify Your Name" and **Andraé Crouch**'s "Soon and Very Soon." The group also led cruises, though the title song for *Holiday* took its cue from the notion that "the ultimate vacation is finding rest in God." Performances were always geared to evangelism. "When you come to see us," Kearney said in 1987, "you're gonna be assaulted with the gospel—visually, audibly, in comedy—whatever we can think of." Bash-N-The Code's music and shows were actually quite tame, but nevertheless seemed outlandish (dancing in the sanctuary!) to uptight Christians who, it seems, are seldom in short supply. The last incarnation of the group, known simply as Bash, was an all-male trio.

Christian radio hits: As Bash-N-The Code: "Diamond" (# 4 in 1986); "Testify" (# 13 in 1986); "He Says" (# 5 in 1988); "More Than Enough" (# 8 in 1989); "Now" (# 10 in 1990); "Surprised Within God" (# 21 in 1990). As Bash: "There Stands the Cross" (# 18 in 1992); "You Can Have My Heart" (# 9 in 1992); "Gonna Take a Holiday" (# 25 in 1992).

Basix

Nancy Andell, voc.; Tom Larson, voc.; Shelli Marsh, voc.; Steve Manning, voc.; Alex Navarro, voc.; Jason Rosenquist, voc.; Jud Shelton, voc. 2000—*Believe* (Spring Hill).

www.basixministries.org

A vocal group with a sound similar to **Truth,** Basix began as a local congregational ministry at Yorba Linda Friends Church in Southern California. Two albums *(Today* and *Live)* were produced independently before the group was granted national distribution through Spring Hill. Most of the members are students or alumni of either Azusa Pacific or Biola Universities. **Scott Krippayne** and **Pam Thum** are among the impressive roster of songwriters who contributed material for the group's national debut.

Fontella Bass

1995—*No Way Tired* (Nonesuch).

Fontella Bass was pretty much a one-hit wonder in the '60s—but what a hit it was! In 1965 her song "Rescue Me" went to Number Four on the charts and became something of an anthem for soldiers in Vietnam. Today the song, which she also cowrote, is regarded as one of the greatest soul songs of all time. Still, Bass made few profits from the record and was in fact denied songwriting royalties for more than twenty-five years. As recently as 1993, she was obliged to sue American Express, who apparently forgot to get her permission before using the song prominently in an ad campaign. Such experiences instilled a basic disgust with aspects of the music industry that accounts for the low profile she maintained for three decades. A mother of four—divorced from a marriage to trumpet player Lester Bowie—she experienced inequities of status first hand. "It's no secret," she recalls, "that blacks, particularly black females, were taken advantage of in the music business."

When she did return, it was with a solid, critically acclaimed gospel album. Backed by a crack team of session players (including David Sanborn on saxophone), Bass delivers hymns like "The Light of the World" and "I Surrender All" alongside spiritual pop songs like Bill Withers' "Lean on Me" and the Bacharach/David hit, "What the World Needs Now." The title song to *No Way Tired* was composed by gospel meister James Cleveland and is performed here with rousing urgency. *People* magazine commented, "Just because she's gone holy doesn't mean she has lowered the flame. This collection *rocks.*" Bass was simply coming full circle. Her mother had been a gospel singer and she herself had toured and sung with gospel groups as a child. "Gospel is something I ran away from, because I was raised on it," she says. Actually, she did make a gospel album with her mother and brother called *A Family Portrait* in 1990, but it was *No Way Tired* that finally brought her home to where she hoped to stay. Since that album, Bass has been identified primarily as a gospel singer. She was the featured singer on jazz saxophonist David Murray's 1999 album *Speaking in Tongues* (Justin Time), providing vocals for gospel standards such as "How I Got Over" and "Just a Closer Walk with Thee."

For trivia buffs: Background vocals on "Rescue Me" are provided by Minnie Ripperton, whose own version of "Lovin' You" would be a Number One hit ten years later. The drummer for the band accompanying Bass is Maurice White, founder of Earth, Wind, and Fire.

Billy Batstone

1985—*One by One* [with Tom Howard] (A&S); 1991—*A Little Broken Bread* (Maranatha); 1999—*While the Door Is Open* (Pamplin).

A veteran of the Jesus movement, Billy Batstone played in the early band **Rebirth** and was a founding member of **Good News.** Later, he was a member of **Richie Furay**'s first Christian band and even wrote the title song for that group's first album *I Still Have Dreams.* He attended a Bible college in Culver City.

Batstone has sung and played on literally hundreds of Christian albums but probably made his biggest mark working with Maranatha's series of praise albums. He was an original member of the Maranatha Praise Band and a long-term staff songwriter for Maranatha Music. He and Tom Howard created the popular *Psalms Alive* series for that company. "Psalm 148," written by Batstone and Howard and performed by the Calvary Chapel Worship Community (including Batstone, Howard, **Richie Furay, Kelly Willard,** and **John Mehler**), reached Number Eight on the Christian radio charts in 1983. Batstone and Howard also recorded an album of worshipful songs called *One by One* in 1985. Batstone would become a staple of the Maranatha worship catalogue, contributing such memorable songs as "I Waited for the Lord," "Psalm 150," and "To Every Generation."

As a solo performer, Batstone provides bright, thoughtful pop songs that recall the tones and textures of the Jesus movement. His *A Little Broken Bread* album includes the song "Walking on the Water," a powerful retelling of Peter's adventure in Matthew 14:22–33. That song would be reprised in 2001 for a *Maranatha Anthology* collection. *CCM* magazine regarded *While the Door Is Open* as "adult pop at its graceful best." The opening song "Awaken Me" is certainly equal to **Steven Curtis Chapman** at his best. "Good Shepherd" is based on John 10 and "You Reached Down" takes its cue from Matthew 14:31. Batstone was also a member of the **Arcade** worship project, along with **Heather and Kirsten.** He has cowritten Christian radio hits for **John Mehler** ("Bow and Arrow"), **Kelly Willard** ("Silver and Gold"), and **Ta'ta Vega** ("In Your Light").

Battered Fish

Jeremy Bennett, bass; Matthew Gray, drums; Caleb James, voc., gtr. 1993—*Bent* [EP] (independent); 1994—*Lure*; 1996—*Megawhat?* (MRA); 1998—*Modern* (Toupee).

www.batteredfish.com

The Australian modern rock combo Battered Fish has a large following in their native land but is yet to find much of an audience in the United States. The group's overall sound is similar to that of moody intellectual groups of the early '90s

(The Cure, The Smiths). Some critics compare them to The Verve. An Australian edition of *Rolling Stone* described James' vocals as "oh-so-lazy but seductive." A distinctive style change occurred between the mostly acoustic *Lure* and fully electric *Megawhat?* That new style was continued and diversified on *Modern,* the only album released internationally. "Wish," the opening song on that project, begins with swirling guitars that reminded a *Phantom Tollbooth* reviewer of **Starflyer 59** or **The Prayer Chain.** But other elements are integrated into the mix: on "Sometimes" a cello creates the mood of sadness that the song looks to overcome; on "The Taste" a xylophone tinkles above violins to suggest hope in the face of doubt. Both of these songs reflect what is the record's most prominent theme, the conquest of melancholy through realistic confrontation. "Set-Up" denounces simplistic solutions, but "Sometimes" talks about a happiness that has "broken through the ground." Less gloomy than The Cure, these boys believe there is "Amazing Light" in the modern world. In their homeland, *Modern* won the Sunnie Award (Australia's Grammy) for Alternative Album of the Year, and James won "Songwriter of the Year" for "Amazing Light."

Battlecry

Dave Chumchal, voc., kybrd.; Robert Giverink, gtr.; Bret Kik, kybrd.; Mariko Martinez, kybrd.; Doug Morris, voc., gtr.; Ronald Simmons, bass. 1985—*Red, White, and Blue* (USA).

Battlecry was a Christian rock band from Hawaii whose only release is now regarded as classic album-oriented rock among fans of general market '80s music. Indeed, the group is better known in the general market than in Christian circles, despite the overtly confessional nature of their lyrics (e.g., "Life with the Lord" and "When the Lord Comes Back"). *Red, White, and Blue* contained only six songs, qualifying perhaps as more of an EP than a full album (though it was marketed as the latter). The overall sound was that of moderately hard, keyboard-driven rock similar to **Kansas** or Journey. The best songs on the record are generally held to be the high-powered opening title cut and the closing, midtempo "You've Got To Know."

Helen Baylor

1990—*Highly Recommended* (Word); 1991—*Look a Little Closer*; 1993—*Start All Over*; 1994—*The Live Experience*; 1996—*Love Brought Me Back*; 1999—*Greatest Hits* (Sony); *Helen Baylor . . . Live* (Verity); 2002—*My Everything* (Diadem).

www.helenbaylor.com

Helen Baylor was born in Tulsa and raised in Los Angeles. Although she has placed several songs on the charts of contemporary Christian and traditional gospel radio stations, her biggest hit to date has been "Helen's Testimony," the simple, spoken account of her conversion that she offered on 1994's breakthrough live album. As she relates in that captivating segment, she had enjoyed some success in the music business, working with Chaka Chan, **Aretha Franklin,** and Stevie Wonder, but seduced by the glamour of it all, she fell into a life of promiscuity and drug addiction. The prayers of her grandmother and the mercy of God combined to change her life and to propel her into a new career as an ordained minister and a husky-voiced gospel singer.

Baylor's first two albums established her as an artist with appeal to fans of both traditional gospel and more pop-oriented Christian music. *Highly Recommended* includes several dance tracks, in addition to the ballad "Can You Reach My Friend" (by **Billy Sprague**), which was once a Christian radio hit for **Debby Boone.** The title song to *Look a Little Closer* relates the experience of running into friends from her pre-Christian past and explaining the evident difference they now see in her. The third record, *Start All Over,* was produced by Bill Maxwell and includes a duet with singer/trumpeter **Phil Driscoll** ("Mount Zion"). The concert for *The Live Experience* was intended simply as a benefit project for a children's ministry, but the album took off and stayed at the top of gospel charts for months. It included her hits, plus a new Caribbean version of the Doxology, and the stirring testimony mentioned above. The title song for *Love Brought Me Back* was actually a slightly revised version of an R&B song that was a hit for D. J. Rogers in the '70s. That album introduces light jazz influences not evident before. Guest performers include **Andraé Crouch** and **Billy Preston,** with whom Baylor sings a duet on "Amazing Grace." The second live album (on Verity) does not reprise her hits but presents all new songs, most with a distinct worship focus. Testimony aspects of the latter album focus on the trials that Baylor and her husband of seventeen years had to overcome to keep their marriage together. "Still Here" is a song of confidence born of struggle. On *My Everything,* she covers **Marvin Gaye**'s "How Sweet It Is (To Be Loved By You)" and offers duets with **Bob Carlisle** ("Harambee") and Marvin Winans ("My Everything").

In 1993, Baylor was ordained as a minister at Crenshaw Christian Center in Los Angeles, California. In 1994, she was awarded an honorary doctorate in Sacred Music from Friends International Christian University. She has served on the board of St. Domenics, a facility for unwed mothers in Tulsa, Oklahoma.

For trivia buffs: At age seventeen, the pre-Christian Helen Baylor was the youngest cast member in the road company of the Broadway musical *Hair.*

Christian radio hits: "There Is No Greater Love" (# 4 in 1990); "Victory" (# 19 in 1990).

Dove Awards: 1994 Contemporary Gospel Album *(Start All Over)*; 1994 Contemporary Gospel Song ("Sold Out").

Beanbag

Phillip "Hirvey" Hirvela, bass; Michael Mullins, gtr.; Hunz Van Vliet, voc.; Phil Usher, drums. 1999—*Free Signal* (InPop); 2001—*Welladjusted.*

http://inpop.com/beanbag

A rapcore band from Australia, Beanbag entered the new millennium as one of a handful of Christian groups with the basic sound that was the most popular genre in rock at that moment. Like **P.O.D.,** they fit into the general category of music represented by such artists as Rage Against the Machine, Kid Rock, Korn, and Limp Bizkit—a genre that basically began with the Christian act **Every Day Life.** Beanbag's music is more melodic (less hard) than that of Rage or Korn, however, and Van Vliet's strong Australian accent helps to give the group a distinct sound. The opening words on their debut album are "Jesus Will Never Let You Go," and this theme is then expounded through intense hip-hop rapping in the song "Whiplash." Van Vliet has described the *Free Signal* album as being "about knowing God's will for Christian life." This is clear in "Face I Paint," which describes how bad habits can divert one's attention from the things of God. The song "Stale" is a particularly melodic number focusing on creation and addressing the issue of laziness. Otherwise, the typical structure for a Beanbag song involves a mellow beginning, subsequently engulfed by waves of distortion and whining guitars. "Obliviant," which deals with drinking and peer pressure, is described by *Musicforce* as a song that "attacks the listener with a chanted chorus and hip-hop overtones that will strike an appealing chord for every Beastie Boys' fan." *Free Signal*'s first single, "Desire of the Son of the Morning," is a lament sung from the perspective of Satan. "Taste Test" would be featured on an episode of the TV program *Dawson's Creek,* and both "Taste Test" and "Whiplash" would be played on ESPN's *Extreme Games.* Notably, Beanbag's debut album was the first release on the InPop label, a company founded by Peter Furler of **The Newsboys** in order to give international acts greater exposure in the American market. Phil Usher also sings lead for the very different band **Tonjip.**

The follow-up to *Free Signal* took the Christian music world by surprise. The opening track on *Welladjusted* reveals a band that appeared to have reinvented themselves. "Limit of Shunt" dispenses with the rapcore sound entirely for more of an Alice in Chains, grunge-alternative style. The opener is the album's best song, but *Welladjusted* remains interesting throughout. On track two ("Chubb") the group reverts to the growing-tiresome-by-2001 sound of its first record, but from then on, they mix the two styles (often in a single song) for a schizophrenic effect that seems appropriate for lyrics that speak of "selling my peace for anarchy" ("These Stains"). "Army of Me" is sustained by a clanking rhythm throughout, and "There Is More" features rapped vocals accompanying what almost sounds like a literal chainsaw.

Paul Beasley

See **Mighty Clouds of Joy.**

Beauty for Ashes

Edward Avila, bass; John Citarelli, gtr., kybrd.; Joseph Cuozzo, voc., kybrd.; John Hummel, drums. 1998—*Black Fades* (independent) [EP]; 1999—*Beauty for Ashes.*

www.beautyforashes.com

A regional band from Metropolitan New York City, Beauty for Ashes has crafted a unique sound that leaves critics mixing their metaphors in strained descriptions: "sort of like Cowboy Junkies meets The Cure on a jousting field" *(Phantom Tollbooth).* Others have suggested a darker, more melancholy version of **U2.** The musical potpourri results from an ample augmentation of traditional rock/funk with spooky bassoon solos, mournful cello, and abundant layers of accordions, tambourines, and xylophones. The group also features both male and female vocals, the former being not rock's usual tenor but a deep bass/baritone reminiscent perhaps of Crash Test Dummies. The main point on which all critics agree is that "none of the group's songs sound alike." They switch from goth to folk to boogie woogie with an ease that will delight those with eclectic tastes and probably disappoint anyone else. Lyrically, the songs are often based directly on Scripture, particularly the Old Testament. The group's name is taken from Isaiah 61:3.

Brian Becker

1984—*Home Again* (Rolling Shoals); 1987—*Getting in Shape;* 1989—*Daring 2 Be Different;* 1992—*No Longer the Wayward Son* (Benson).

www.tonionio.com

Brian Becker began as a sound engineer and helped to pioneer midi technology within the Christian concert scene. Becker was born and raised in Williamsville, Missouri. He graduated from the University of Missouri-Columbia in 1985 with electrical and computer engineering degrees. His recordings reflect his expertise with the developing new technology, and the latter two records feature duet vocals with his wife Toni Becker, who has also recorded an album of children's lullabies (StarSong, 1997). The Beckers actually met while Brian was recording *Daring 2 Be Different,* when Toni was brought in to sing a duet with him on the ballad "He Knows"; she had previously recorded a similar duet (as Toni Raider) with **Wayne Watson** on the song "Every Now and Again." *Daring 2 Be Different* also

features the pop-rock songs "Love Keeps Holding On" and "His Name Is Jesus" and the Motown-ish "Tender Touch." Becker's first three albums were all custom jobs, but Benson picked up the artist for *No Longer the Wayward Son,* allowing him to work with a bigger production budget. Overall, the album has a more aggressive feel, targeting adolescents with hook-filled pop songs. "Children of the Image" encourages conformity to Christ's example; "Prove It To You" similarly urges demonstration of faith in daily action. Brian Becker would go on to become the owner and operator of a computer Internet company in Poplar Bluffs, Missouri.

Christian radio hits: "Children of the Image" (# 3 in 1991).

Margaret Becker

1987—*Never for Nothing* (Sparrow); 1988—*The Reckoning;* 1989—*Immigrant's Daughter;* 1991—*Simple House;* 1992—*Steps of Faith (1987–1991);* 1993—*Soul;* 1995—*Fiel a Ti;* 1995—*Grace;* 1996—*Margaret Becker: The Early Years;* 1998—*Falling Forward;* 1999—*What Kind of Love;* 2002—*New Irish Hymns* [with Máire Brennan and Joanne Hogg] (Worship Together).

www.maggieb.com

Margaret Becker hails from Bayshore, New York. She attended James Madison University and got her start in Christian music singing backup vocals for **Rick Cua** on his *Wear Your Colors* tour and singing a duet with **Steve Camp** on the title track to his *One on One* album. In fact, Becker was originally signed to Sparrow Records as a staff songwriter, and in that capacity she cowrote a handful of Camp's songs including "One on One." *Billboard* magazine has referred to Margaret Becker as "the Christian music equivalent of Mary Chapin Carpenter," but that comparison is misleading if one thinks "country." Stylistically, Becker began as a Christian version of Pat Benatar and moved gradually to embrace a sound that resembles the smooth rock style of Annie Lennox. It is the deeply personal character of her songs rather than her voice that suggests the country tradition. "Margaret Becker has forged music of graceful strength," says *CCM* magazine, "never veering too far in the direction of either pop fluff or metallic thunder."

Becker's *Never for Nothing* was an immediately impressive debut, establishing her as an Irish/German rocker who wasn't afraid to let out the kind of yelps one usually heard from Benatar or from Ann Wilson of Heart. The latter artist provided the comparison of choice for most critics largely because (unlike Benatar) Becker not only sang but also played a mean electric guitar; of course it was actually *Nancy* Wilson who played the guitar for Heart but such details didn't matter. In any event, standout rockers on *Never for Nothing* include "Love Was Waiting" (cowritten by producer Billy Smiley of **White Heart** and **Chris Rodriguez**) and "Giants Will Fall" (by **Dave Perkins**); the opening "Fight For God" was a concert crowd pleaser but is spoiled by easily misunderstood militant lyrics. The debut record's best song is its somewhat atypical title track (cowritten with **Ric Blair**), a classic rock ballad that seeks to reassure the unrequited ("It's never for nothing / when you love with no return"). *The Reckoning* continues in the same mode with original songs whose lyrics seem to arise from a personal devotional life: "Who Am I?" from meditation on Psalm 8 ("Who am I Lord, that you call me by name?") and the bouncy "Streets of Innocence" from soul-cleansing confession. "Find Me" is another ballad, with a sad touch of country blues that offers the simple prayer, "Find me, find me / I'll wait for you." Elsewhere, Becker wails on "Take Me Away," slinks on "Pico Boulevard," and whoops it up on "Start the Fire," demonstrating a range of emotion rarely heard from female vocalists in the Christian market.

Becker's next four albums were made with producer **Charlie Peacock.** Highlights of *Immigrant's Daughter* include a stirring cover of **Curtis Mayfield**'s "People Get Ready" and a tune cowritten with Peacock, "The Hunger Stays," which effectively expresses the insatiable human desire to know God. The album's title track traces such a quest back to the determination and "simple faith" of the artist's grandmother, whose devotion to her new country and eventual offspring continue to inspire: "She married America / And she scrubbed it on her knees / Fiercely devoted / To who was yet to be." The song "This Is My Passion" defines the object of the quest more specifically: "This is my passion / Holiness, holiness / This is my cry / Mercy, mercy." Two songs, "Honesty" and "Just Come In," work together to encourage vulnerability before God. In 2001, a poll of critics sponsored by *CCM* magazine selected *Immigrant's Daughter* (at Number Forty-six) for their list of "The 100 Greatest Albums in Christian Music." At the time of the record's release, however, *CCM* complained that *Immigrant's Daughter* "runs out of energy toward the end." It doesn't do that; rather, the ballad-heavy project reflects a career change for the artist: for better or worse, Becker was leaving behind the gritty rock queen stylings of her first two records to embrace more of an aggressive pop sound. This far-from-mellow new sound is unveiled supremely on *Simple House,* an album that takes Becker into Peacockesque funk-pop with a flair not too far removed from styles sometimes employed by Cher, Madonna, and Diana Ross. The opening title track gurgles to a post-disco techno beat; "Talk About Love" is a Motown-ish number that sounds like a Supremes outtake. Both of these songs are Becker/Peacock compositions, as is "Look Me in the Eye," a prayer to recapture the urgent faith that the author had detected in reading a journal from her early days as a Christian. Basically, *Simple House* sounds like a female version of Peacock's own masterpiece *Strange Language* (from 1996); as with that album, every song seems to have its own integrity, with a style

of its own and an arrangement appropriate to its theme. "All I Ever Wanted" is an adult contemporary ballad sung with **Chris Eaton.** "I Will Not Lay Down" recalls Don Henley's "I Will Not Go Quietly." More rock stylings inform "Scatter These Thieves" and "The Strangest Things," both of which find the artist wailing and growling out lyrics about the glory of spiritual obsession and the desire to keep those passions. *Steps of Faith* compiles hits from Becker's first four albums with one new song (1996's *Early Years* is a truncated version of this collection that Sparrow released later—with two songs missing). Overall, the songs from this stage of Becker's career tend to be melancholy reflections on the struggles of living as a person of faith. She wrote as one who openly confessed her failures and disappointments, yet persevered—and invited her audience to witness the relationship with God that she found to be worth it all.

The album *Soul* evinces a more keyboard-based sound with increased R&B influence. It has also been described as Becker's first "happy album," reflecting inner peace and contentment rather than struggles of conscience. Indeed, every song focuses directly on her relationship with God. "The Flame" pledges undying devotion not with desperation but with bold confidence ("I will never leave your side / And this flame will never die"); "This I Know" confesses assurance that such commitment is more than mutual ("Only this I know / That your love never changes"). Musically, the project matches midtempo ballads with catchy, upbeat pop songs. "Soul Tattoo" would bring the Annie Lennox comparisons to the fore in a way that would make analogies with all those lesser talents soon forgotten. *Soul* also features "Say the Name," an especially beautiful worship song, and "Keeping Watch," a duet with **Bob Carlisle.** Its centerpiece is "The World I See in You," a song that describes the world as Christ intends it to be—merciful and accepting; on this number, Becker actually tries a little white-woman rapping in the same vein as (i.e., no more successful than) Deborah Harry on "Rapture." As a follow-up to *Soul,* the album *Grace* would allow the mature, content Becker to put in a second appearance. The songs "Noonday Sun" and "My Heaven" display an Ace-of-Base/Roxette dance club groove. The overall theme of the album is confident faith in God's immeasurable love, and this is announced in upbeat, funky songs like "Grace" ("Oh my my, could it be / The best things in life are free") and the self-explanatory "I Trust in You." The album's opener, "Deep Calling Deep," is another wonderful Becker and Peacock collaboration that sets a simple invitation to "deeper love and higher truth" to a funky beat and an unforgettable, celebrative melody. "My Heaven" offers a joyful description of her personal vision of paradise. Such songs helped to establish Becker as the new queen of thoughtful Christian pop. Some reviewers, however, complained that the sophisticated sheen of *Soul* and *Grace* was obtained at a loss of passion and realism.

After a hiatus of three years, *Falling Forward* would recapture a more raw guitar-driven sound, with several tracks being recorded live in the studio. Becker's voice is breathy, her guitar squeaks—the little distinguishing marks of rock and roll are not edited out. The album's theme of being persons "in process" is declared in lyrics like these: "I am clay and I am water / Falling forward in this order / While the world spins round so fast / Slowly I'm becoming who I am" ("Clay and Water"). As such, *Falling Forward* strikes a middle ground between the melancholy and happy poles of the singer's career to present what *CCM* would call "a picture of life with all of its colors." "Deliver Me" and "Irish Sea" are reverent; "Coins and Promises" is hopeful; "I Don't Know How" and "Take Me In" express honest but serene surrender; "Cave It In" and the wonderfully titled "Crawl" rock with the passion of one yearning to be free. Two back-to-back tracks illuminate the partners in the Becker-God relationship: on "Deliver Me" she looks into her own soul and identifies herself as her own worst enemy; on "Any Kind of Light" (a light jazz number), she scrutinizes God as a multi-faceted ever-stunning jewel.

What Kind of Love finds Becker removed once more from the musically raw sound, singing mostly catchy songs with assistance from the likes of Lynn Nichols of **Chagall Guevara/Passafist** and Peter Furler of **The Newsboys.** Thematically, however, the record continues to explore what it means to celebrate God in difficult situations. "I Won't Be Persuaded" deals frankly with theodicy, with the inability to understand why God does not remove suffering from the world. "Friend for Life" (cowritten with **Chris Eaton**), "Feel It All," and "Love By Your Side" all have the feel of contemporary pop radio singles. Becker also remakes the Staples Singers' "Hope in a Hopeless World," offers the beautifully melodic "Worlds Apart," and closes the album with the mournful yet worshipful "Poor in Paradise."

Although Becker was raised Roman Catholic, *CCM* magazine said in 1989, "her own salvation came through the ministerings of a friend while she was in college." In interviews surrounding the release of *Simple House,* however, the artist spoke frankly about her dissatisfactions with the fundamentalist Pentecostal Christianity in which she had once claimed to have found a true relationship with Christ. "I got tired of people telling me whether or not I was 'anointed'," Becker told *CCM* in 1991. "I got tired of people not carrying my record in their bookstore because it had a song about my grandmother (who was a Catholic), people telling me I had a sensual demon because I move on stage or dress differently than they do. . . . The clutter of what I should and shouldn't do had run me ragged." Two years later, she let it be known that she herself had

begun attending the neighborhood Catholic parish where "all the prayers I learned during my childhood confirmation fell into place and there was this beautiful sense of liturgy." As a result of her seeming endorsement of Catholicism, some of her concerts were picketed by protesters who claimed that she now represented the Antichrist. Moody Bible Institute, a fundamentalist school that publishes *Moody* magazine, dropped her from their network of Christian musicians.

Becker has contributed songs to numerous special projects, especially those devoted to presenting the voices of Christian women: *Sisters* (Warner, 1994), *Listen to Our Hearts* (Sparrow, 1998); *Heaven and Earth* (Sparrow, 1999). She has been a strong supporter of Habitat for Humanity and World Vision. Her album *Fiel a Ti* features several of her hits sung in Spanish. Becker is also one-third of the trio **Ashton, Becker, and Denté.** As a songwriter, she has written or cowritten Christian radio hits performed by **Steve Camp** ("One on One") and **Bob Carlisle** ("Bridge between Two Hearts"). *New Irish Hymns* is a special project in which she joins with some friends in popularizing Celtic songs written by Keith Getty.

For trivia buffs: Becker is a well-published author. She often writes youth-oriented columns for *Campus Life* magazine and contributes articles to women's magazines. She has published two books with Harvest House: *With New Eyes,* a collection of essays about real life experiences, and *Growing Up Together,* which features sibling stories.

Christian radio hits: "Never for Nothing" (# 3 in 1987); "For the Love of You" (# 7 in 1987); "Sacred Fire" (# 2 in 1988); "Find Me" (# 14 in 1988); "Who Am I" (# 3 in 1988); "Streets of Innocence" (# 2 in 1989); "The Hunger Stays" (# 12 in 1989); "Commit" (# 2 in 1990); "Solomon's Shoes" (# 9 in 1990); "This Is My Passion" (# 18 in 1990); "People Get Ready" (# 15 in 1990); "Simple House" (# 5 in 1991); "All I Ever Wanted" (# 12 in 1991); "Look Me in the Eye" (# 12 in 1991); "Talk about Love" (# 2 in 1991); "This Love" (# 2 in 1992); "This I Know" (# 15 in 1993); "Keep My Mind" (# 12 in 1993); "Say the Name" (# 5 in 1994); "Will Be with You" (# 2 in 1994); "How Long" (# 2 in 1994); "Deep Calling Deep" (# 1 in 1995); "True Devotion" (# 1 in 1995); "Only Your Love" (# 12 in 1995); "I Trust in You" (# 3 in 1996); "My Heaven" (# 5 in 1996); "Clay and Water" (# 10 in 1998); "Horses" (# 16 in 1999); "Friend for Life" (# 18 in 2000).

Dove Awards: 1992—Rock Album *(Simple House);* 1992—Rock Song ("Simple House").

William Becton (and Friends)

1995—*Broken* (Intersound); 1997—*Heart of a Love Song* (CGI); 2000—*B2K: Prophetic Songs of Promise.*

William Becton leads a small choir that sings contemporary gospel songs, most of which he writes and arranges with a definite urban flair. The group is sometimes billed as "William Becton and Friends" and seems founded on an obvious analogy to **Kirk Franklin.** Becton is an ordained minister and serves as radio announcer for the ABC-Rejoice network in Washington, D.C. His first album enjoyed some success when the song "Be Encouraged" was selected for mainstream airplay following the Oklahoma City bombing. The song reached the Top 40 on *Billboard's* R&B chart, and the album was subsequently nominated for a Dove award. The second album takes as its theme the centrality of God's love as a remedy for the brokenhearted. *B2K* is organized around the more questionable notion that God promises prosperity, good health, and an abundance of temporal blessings to those who uphold God's principles. The latter album includes "Still Encouraged," an apparent sequel to the former hit that features vocal trade-offs between Becton, former Temptation Ali Woodson, and a vocorder (electronic "talk-box"). Becton and friends also offer a Christianized cover of the Isley Brothers' "Harvest for the Word."

Beehive

John Graham, drums; Guy Houchen, gtr., voc.; Kay Lewis, voc.; Paul Lancaster, bass; Rob May, kybrd. 1997—*Brand New Day* (Word [UK]).

The British club band Beehive used to be known as The Funky Beehive. They won a MOBO award (i.e., Music of Black Origin) in their homeland for Best Gospel Act in 1997. Their debut album incorporates the guest talents of numerous Christian musicians in the United Kingdom, including **Terl Bryant** of **Iona.** The basic sound is jazzy funk with flourishes of brass. Beehive's lyrics are often clearly Christian, with appeals to universal human themes: "We're all looking for the answers / To the questions in our minds / For truth and understanding / In a world that's so unkind" ("Answer To Prayer"). As a result of ambiguous graphics on the CD's cover, retailers have sometimes misidentified the group's name as Brand New Day and assumed the album to be titled Beehive (rather than the other way around).

Dave Beegle

1999—*Clear the Tracks* (Hapi Skratch); 1999—*A Year Closer.*

www.davebeegle.com

Guitar hero Dave Beegle fronts the instrumental band **Fourth Estate** and also plays in several other outfits: a) the Beegle-Olson-Quist trio is a collaboration that puts him and **Fourth Estate** bassist Michael Olson at the service of vocalist Beth Quist, who has a fondness for Middle Eastern melodies; b) Artifact Symphony is a progressive techno/art band with a heavy flavoring of world beat music; c) Blindog Smokin' is a down-and-dirty blues rock band; d) the Jurasicastors is a classic-rock covers band that performs songs by Dire Straits, Jimi Hendrix, and Stevie Ray Vaughan. Most of these groups have produced independent releases, and Beegle's album *Clear*

the Tracks compiles selections from projects by the first three, plus a few songs by **Fourth Estate** and a couple of previews from his solo acoustic album *A Year Closer.* The latter album showcases not only Beegle's virtuosity but also the eclectic range of his stylistic influences. He moves easily from flamenco to jazz to classical to folk to blues and bluegrass. If it can be played on the guitar, he can play it. The Spanish instrumental "Malagueña"—once a staple of **Dennis Agajanian's** flat-pickin' repertoire—comes alive here, as does a sterling rendition of Bach's "Jesu, Joy of Man's Desiring." On "All the King's Men" Beegle clones himself via multi-tracking to play four different guitars at once and produces a Middle Eastern sound reminiscent of latter-day Robert Plant/Jimmy Page collaborations. "Rose's Garden" and "A Simple Prayer" are original melodies that seem just waiting for some lyricist to turn them into hymns. Beegle's talents have been repeatedly heralded in journals dedicated to musicianship (*Guitar Nine* magazine called him "the most criminally undiscovered guitarist in the instrumental rock genre"). A devout Christian, he takes seriously Bach's credo that the purpose of all music is to glorify God. He seeks to do this by attending to his art, producing the most technically proficient and stylistically innovative music he can, and then publicly testifying to the source of his inspiration in interviews and concerts.

Michael Been

1994—*On the Verge of a Nervous Breakthrough* (Warner).

Michael Been is founder and lead singer/songwriter/bassist for **The Call.** He recorded one solo album while that band was on hiatus. The record was a commercial failure and received little attention in the Christian market, despite critical acclaim and deeply spiritual, family-oriented lyrics. In general, the songs on *Nervous Breakthrough* are less anthemic than **The Call's** best-known works, though they feature a somewhat heavier guitar sound. Hammering rockers like "In My Head" and "This World" mix with moody, atmospheric numbers ("This Way," "Luminous"). The standout track, however, is the album's opener, "Us." This song, which received considerable airplay on college rock stations, is a joyous testimony to commitment. The verses list various things that Been doesn't care about: "phony affection," the "pursuit of perfection," etc. The refrain proclaims, "But I care about love / And I care about truth / And I care about trust / And I care about you / And I care about us." The album also includes a rocking version of The Yardbirds' "For Your Love," which extols a similar theme.

For trivia buffs: Been also wrote and performed the soundtrack for the Paul Schrader film *Light Sleepers* (1992), which was released as an EP in Britain. He also had a minor role as an actor in Martin Scorcese's 1988 film, *The Last Temptation of Christ* (see entry for **The Call**).

Believable Picnic

Jason Burkum, bass, drums; Jade Hanson, voc., gtr.; Jeff Bridges, drums (– 1999) // Nick Ayres, kybrd. (+ 1999). 1996—*Believable Picnic* (Absolute); 1999—*Welcome to the Future.*

Believable Picnic often gets compared to **PFR,** for no other reason than that main man Jade Hanson is the older brother of that group's leader, Joel Hanson. A more natural musical equivalent would be **All Star United,** though the Picnic puts a bit more bubblegum in their '60s blend of Beatlesque tunes. Still, like the All Stars, they season their sounds with humor. "We're modern rock with a spicing of Monty Python," says Hanson.

The self-titled first release shines with Hanson's shimmering, psychedelic guitar wrapped tightly around a capable rhythm section. The song "Big Fat Nothing" features big, fat harmonies reminiscent of Queen. "Shangri-La" (a poetic description of heaven) and "Spaceman" recall the Lemon Pipers' jangly "Green Tambourine." On the second album the group leaves their metaphorical garage to produce a more polished record, marked in part by the addition of keyboards. "Rollercoaster" is bouncy, enjoyable pop; "Ride the Wave" sounds like **Daniel Amos** performing a Beach Boys outtake; "Flowers" is exceptionally Beatlesque hippie music; "Easy Chair" starts off with a choral intro and segues into predisco '70s funk; "Hollywood Appeal" brings the album to a brooding close with a softer Simon and Garfunkel tone. Of the two albums, the second project has a more mature sound, but many listeners seemed to prefer the edgier debut.

Lyrically, Believable Picnic seeks to meet youth where they are with specific religious or spiritual messages. "Goodbye Girl" rehashes biblical warnings against pursuing ungodly women; "Easy Chair" is directed against self-righteous sideline quarterbacks who criticize those who step out in leaps of faith. "Spaceman" tries to address the adolescent feeling of not belonging by saying that it is all right for Christians to feel estranged from the world: "Feel like I've come from outer space / I don't belong here / I'm only visiting this place." Likewise, "Big Fat Nothing" rejects the adolescent tendency to ground self-esteem in peer evaluation: "I think, you think, I'm a big fat nothing / And I think that's just fine!" The problem with such lyrics is that they can become trite (as they do on "Mr. Good Intentions") or just plain hokey (as they do on "Wasted"—a straightforward-but-hip approach to sexual temptation that comes off like a parent's "I was young once" speech). There is some improvement on the second album. "Rollercoaster" effectively likens life to a scary ride, and "Sugar" recalls All Star United's "La La Land" in its humorous depiction of people who want to hear only what is appealing.

Believer

Kurt Bachman, voc., gtr.; Joey Daub, drums; Howe Kroft, bass (–1991); David Boddorf, gtr. (–1993) // Wyatt Robertson, bass (+ 1991, –1993); Scot Laird, violin (+ 1993); Jim Winters, bass (1993). 1989—*Extraction from Mortality* (R.E.X.); 1991—*Sanity Obscure;* 1993—*Dimensions.*

A Pennsylvania quartet that emulated the speed metal sound of early Metallica, Believer took a cue from that band and worked to expand the limitations of the genre. Their first album is speed metal all the way, with lyrics that have something to do with hope in Christ being screamed too fast for most human ears to receive. Given that, the standout cut is probably "Vile Hypocrisy," a fairly complex number on which the band gets everything just right. The title track, by the same token, suggests a potential for creativity by opening with a surprising violin/viola solo (by Scott Laird). On *Sanity Obscure,* the group "avoids becoming a parody of themselves" as *HM* magazine put it, by "stretching the boundaries of its genre a little bit." The song "Dies Irae" (i.e., Day of Wrath) begins with an operatic aria and then introduces strings—for no apparent reason except "to build something for Believer to destroy, which they do, crashing and thrashing into the classical arrangement like some child kicking over a sand castle." The album also includes the antidrug anthem, "Stop the Madness," and closes with a barely recognizable cover of **U2**'s "Like a Song." By the next album, *Dimensions,* Laird had become a full-fledged member of the group, and his violin is used to great effect on slower, ethereal numbers like "What Is Cannot Be." The project stays true to the thrash metal form, with lots of fast and furious delivery, but it is also undeniably ambitious. The entire second side consists of a "Trilogy of Knowledge" concept piece, marking a comeback for the operatic feel of "Dies Irae." The Trilogy consists of "The Lie," recounting the fall of humanity, "The Truth," focusing on Jesus' temptation in the wilderness, and "The Key," which encourages the redeemed to pursue a godly life.

The members of Believer were explicit about their Christian faith, both in the lyrics to their songs and in their comments in interviews. Bachman made it clear that witnessing to non-Christians was a prime directive for the group. The band had plenty of opportunities to do so since, besides playing *Cornerstone* and other Christian venues, they toured with mainstream acts like the death metal group Bolt Thrower. The group's sense of humor comes out on *Home Video,* a documentary they released of their European tour. Viewers get to see the group sprinting across the Autobahn and are treated to recurring footage of international bathrooms, indicating how different these are from ones in the States. Joey Daub later played drums on an album by **Fountain of Tears.**

Bell Jar

Charlotte Ayrton, gtr.; Duncan Forrester, drums; Paul Northrup, voc., gtr.; Stephen Whitfield, kybrd.; Mark Wijesinghe, bass. 1999—*Secret Volcanoes* (independent); 2001—*Flying Low* [EP] (Madan).

www.belljar.f9.co.uk

Formed in 1998, Bell Jar is a new musical incarnation for Paul Northrup and Charlotte Ayrton who once led the Christian band **Eden Burning.** The group seems to want to avoid any direct connection to the Christian subculture and refrains from offering explicit statements of faith on their recordings. Hastily produced in two weekends, the debut album evinces the sort of simplicity that Northrup sings about in its most memorable song: "Small is beautiful / Keep it that way / If you let it get big / You can't give it away" ("Small is Beautiful"). The song "Second Time Around" provides an autobiographical account of the group's origins (à la the Mamas and the Papas' "Creeque Alley"). The group's website describes their sound as *sort of* like "Nick Cave meets the Ben Folds Five." What that probably means is that the mixture of acoustic and electric guitars (and keyboards) gives them an eclectic jazzy sound, yet there is a distinct tendency for things to turn morose (hence the Nick Cave reference). The *Flying Low* EP was released as a prelude to an announced album tentatively titled *Under the Radar.* It includes the song "It Hurts," which features the refrain "Feel so ungodly, it hurts." The name Bell Jar derives from the title of a Sylvia Plath novel.

Margaret Bell

1991—*Over and Over* (Warner).

Margaret Bell is the younger sister of acclaimed gospel singer **Vanessa Bell Armstrong.** Her album *Over and Over* draws on her traditional gospel roots but is (in her words) "aimed at the tastes of young people." Her voice is similar to that of her sister; her musical stylings emulate those of Whitney Houston. The record features a few inspirational ballads but tends to be most impressive on the more upbeat, rollicking tracks like "What You Do" and the opening song, "Any Day Any Minute Now" (about anticipating the Lord's return). Bell is from Detroit; she attended Oral Roberts University on a music scholarship.

For trivia buffs: Margaret Bell is married to Philadelphia Eagles running back Keith Byars.

Christian radio hits: "Any Day Any Minute Now" (# 3 in 1991); "What You Do" (# 9 in 1992).

Steve Bell

1989—*Comfort My People* (Signpost); 1992—*Deep Calls to Deep;* 1994—*Burning Ember;* 1995—*The Feast: Songs for Advent, Nativity, Epiphany;* 1997—*Romantics and Mystics;* 1999—*Beyond a Shadow; Steve Bell Band: Live in Concert;* 2001—*Simple Songs.*

www.steve-bell.com

A Canadian singer/songwriter who is often compared to **Bruce Cockburn** or **Michael Card,** Steve Bell has sold 100,000 CDs in his native land but is not well known south of the border (in the United States). *Billboard* magazine describes him as "a Canadian musical treasure," and Brian Quincy Newcomb says his music is "intelligent, evocative, and emotionally moving." His voice bears strong similarities to that of Dan Fogelberg. The son of a prison chaplain, Bell traveled with his family as a child singing in a gospel band, then developed a solo style that inured him to the nightclub scene. Many of his songs use Scripture as their lyrical base: His first studio album opens with "Psalm 90" and closes with "The Lord's Prayer." *Deep Calls to Deep* was inspired by a trip to India and introduces sounds inspired by the Far East. *Burning Ember* opens with a song inspired by a Native American hymn ("Dakota Hymn") and also includes two more psalms ("Psalm 40," "Psalm 32") along with a song of appreciation for the artist's wife ("She's in Love with Me") and a hymn of eschatological yearning ("Even So Lord Jesus Come"). Bell's music often reveals a greater awareness of Christianity's liturgical heritage than is usually found in contemporary Christian music. The album *The Feast* is a collection of what are usually called "Christmas carols," but these are organized to reflect the *three* seasons that comprise the Christmas cycle (Advent, Nativity, Epiphany). Likewise, "Dark Night of the Soul," which opens *Romantics and Mystics,* is an adaptation of a poem written in 1528 by St. John of the Cross. "This is Love" from *Romantics and Mystics* derives from Jesus' prayer for his followers in John 17. That same album features a cover of Cockburn's "Can I Go with You" and two stellar original tracks about romantic relationships. "All for a Loveless Night" bemoans the devastation produced by a single act of infidelity. "Alone Tonight" evokes the sweet anticipation of a man returning home from a trip, imagining what sort of reunion his wife has prepared: "Lord, I pray there's only one smile at the door / If my friends are all there with her, oh the night will never end / Will we be all alone tonight? / Lord, I hope she has planned it that way." *Romantics and Mystics* won a Juno award (Canada's Grammy) for 1998 Gospel Album.

Beyond a Shadow was the first Steve Bell album released in the United States (on the Rhythm House label). A compilation project, it collects a number of the artist's spiritual songs the company thought would hold the most appeal for fans of contemporary Christian music. Rhythm House also released a United States version of Bell's subsequent *Live in Concert* album, though they retitled it *Each Rare Moment.* The 2001 project *Simple Songs* is an unplugged affair featuring just Bell, guitar, and an occasional mandolin performing songs in a living room setting. He covers two more Cockburn songs ("All the Diamonds in the World" and "Fox Glove," an instrumental) and offers three more adaptations of biblical psalms: "God Our Protector" (Psalm 84); "Fresh and Green" (Psalm 92) and "High above the Fray" (Psalm 113).

Bendixon

Chris Cleaver, bass, voc.; Mark Cleaver, gtr., voc.; Chris Erlandson, drums. 1999—*Bendixon* (Flaming Rodd); 2000—*The Slaying of the Dragon* (Rodd.net).

Bendixon is a light-hearted band who cites **All Star United,** The Rentals, and especially Weezer as among their musical influences. Their first effort emphasizes fun songs that are at least witty, if not completely off-the-wall. "Headgear" reminisces on the joys of orthodontia. "The State Fish of Hawaii" seems to exist simply because the band finds it amusing to sing the titular animal's name (the Hurnu Hurnu Nuku Nuku Apuaa). The song "Please Help Me Tonight," however, is serious and prayerful. With only eight tracks, the album is brief, hardly more than an EP. It was produced by Todd Gruener of **The W's.** The second album, a full-length CD, was produced by Ashley Stubbert, who has worked with Pearl Jam. The standout song, "The Laser is Mightier than the Sword," is a Weezer-ish college radio song in which Cleaver expresses his desire to get laser surgery that would rid him of contact lenses. Also noteworthy are "Deep Seeing Eyes" and "Humans Only Live So Long" (with a drum solo!). The song "Mulholland Ali" tells the tale of a young man who tries to woo a girl by quoting Cassius Clay, strikes out, then crashes his car into a much nicer car on Mulholland Drive.

Benjamin

Larry Babb, drums; Beth Fox, voc.; Benjy Gaither, voc.; Jon Arnold, gtr. (–1995); Scott Diertle, bass (–1995); Jeanne Stafford, voc. (–1995) // Tiffany Arbuckle, voc. (+ 1995); Scott Harper, bass (+ 1995); John Piscotta, gtr. (+ 1995); Ty Smith (+ 1995). 1994—*Benjamin* (StarSong); 1995—*As You Wish.*

Benjy Gaither is the son of **Bill and Gloria Gaither,** staples of the southern gospel and praise and worship circuits. Benjy founded the group Benjamin with an original lineup of friends and alumni from Anderson University. Arbuckle, who joined in for the second album, later became lead singer for **Plumb.** Babb went on to play with **Michael English,** and Beth Fox recorded a solo album for an indie label. Benjamin has performed songs that are either worship or ministry oriented, but with a decidedly more rock sound than the MOR choruses and hymns that made the elder Gaithers famous. On the first album, "Rain Down a Fire" (cowritten with his sister Suzanne) and "Tonight" (cowritten with his mother Gloria) are rock and roll

hymns, steeped in the R&B legacy of traditional gospel. "Shelter of His Love" is a catchy country song similar to The Traveling Wilburys' "End of the Line." The songs "Makin' My Way Back Home" and "Open the Gates" have the sound of tried-and-true adult contemporary ballads. The second outing offers a similar buffet, with a somewhat tighter, more focused sound. "You Can't Get To Heaven" is an entertaining bluesy song that recalls and refutes the Ozark Mountain Daredevils hit "If You Want To Get To Heaven (You Have To Raise a Little Hell)." The title tune is another stripped-down ballad.

Gaither says the group's "biggest goal is to disciple Christian kids . . . to encourage young people to seek God personally, to make a commitment, and to live out their faith." These sentiments are well expressed in the energetic opening songs on both albums. *Benjamin* begins with "Don't Tell Him You Love Him," which summons its audience to count the cost of being a follower of Christ, and *As You Wish* kicks off with "The Narrow Road," which calls for a clear (daily) decision to follow the difficult way of God. Less heavy-handed is the second album's closing song, "Against the Grain," which looks back to identify obstacles in life as gracious occasions for growth.

For trivia buffs: Benjy Gaither's piano teacher as a child was **Sandi Patty.**

Christian radio hits: "Rain Down a Fire" (# 5 in 1994); "Don't Tell Him You Love Him" (# 5 in 1994); "Until We Turn" (# 2 in 1995); "The Narrow Road" (# 3 in 1996); "On the Inside" (# 10 in 1996).

The Benjamin Gate

Costa Balamatsias, bass; Adrienne Liesching, voc.; Brett Palmer, drums; Marc Paultz, gtr.; Chris Poisat, gtr. 2001—*Untitled* (ForeFront).

The Benjamin Gate is a modern rock band from Port Elizabeth, South Africa. Their name derives from a reference in Jeremiah 20:2; the group was inspired by a sermon on that passage that identified the gate in Jerusalem's walls as being one through which shepherds would guide their sheep in and out to pasture. Critics identify the band's prime attraction as the passionate and aggressive vocals of nineteen-year-old Adrienne Liesching, who has been compared to Fleming McWilliams (of **Fleming and John**) or Delores O'Riordan (of The Cranberries). The group's debut album opens with "How Long," an eschatological anthem, and also includes "Nightglow" and "Blow My Mind," which have more of a Euro-dance club feel. "Rush" and "Scream" are thrashing guitar rock songs. "Halo" has a more laid-back, haunting sound reminiscent of Dido. Most of the album's songs have explicitly Christian lyrics that are both worshipful and introspective.

Christian radio hits: "All Over Me" (# 4 in 2001).

Bob Bennett

1979—*First Things First* (Maranatha); 1981—*Matters of the Heart* (CBS); 1985—*Non-Fiction* (StarSong); 1989—*Lord of the Past: A Compilation* (Urgent); 1991—*Songs from Bright Avenue*; 1997—*Small Graces* (Covenant).

http://home.hiwaay.net/~jrinkel/bob

Singer/songwriter Bob Bennett (b. 1955 in Downey, California) crafts songs that deal not only with the joys and victories of life, but also with its disappointments and failures. In the words of his biographer Joan Brasher, "His acoustic folk-style recordings have honestly confronted the messy side of human existence, sometimes making members of the Christian music industry a bit uncomfortable." Songs like "Madness Dancing" and "A Song about Baseball" would establish him as one of Christian music's most intelligent and sensitive songwriters, while displaying alternative pop styles *CCM* would call "ahead of tastes and trends in the '80s." Bennett's skill as a guitarist is impressive, and he is also famous for his disarming humor. Still, he describes himself with some candor as "critically acceptable but commercially mediocre." He did open concerts for **Carman** and **Amy Grant** (the *Unguarded* tour), and he headlined tours with **Michael Card** and **Rich Mullins,** but he never quite achieved the sort of status that most pundits thought his talent deserved. **Card** has described him as "one of the best songwriters I know, period" and points to Bennett's commercial standing as exemplary of what is wrong with the image-conscious Christian music industry and culture: "No one will sign Bob because he's not a celebrity and he doesn't want to be a celebrity."

Bennett's first album on Maranatha features acoustic folk songs presented in stirring jazzy arrangements. Standout tracks include "You're Welcome Here" and "Carpenter Gone Bad?" Historian David Di Sabatino singles out the album as exemplary for its honest appreciation of struggle and paradox, qualities often lacking in debut works by young Christians. The second album, *Matters of the Heart,* shows even more progression in Bennett's songwriting skills as, in his words, he realized he was "free to contemplate life in all its fullness and complexity." *CCM* Magazine chose *Matters of the Heart* as its 1982 Album of the Year, over **Amy Grant'**s *Age to Age* (which was Number Two). Six years later, they selected it as one of the "Top 20 Contemporary Christian Albums of All Time" and by 2001 they still put it at Number Sixty-five on a list of what critics regarded as "The 100 Greatest Albums in Christian Music." The record opens with its title cut "Matters of the Heart" and then closes with a number called "The Heart of the Matter." The songs reflect various aspects of life. "A Song about Baseball" would become a favorite among Christian music fans, despite its seemingly secular subject matter. "Come and See" is more overtly spiritual. Other particularly stellar songs include "Falling Stars," "1951," and "Together All Alone." The

follow-up album, *Non-Fiction,* deals with social issues, especially world hunger and poverty. The song "When Shadows Fall Like Rain" offers a powerful description of the loss of dignity associated with unemployment ("Family man in the welfare line / His pride dies slow, one check at a time").

After a five-year break, Bennett returned to Christian music with a compilation album *(Lord of the Past)* that includes four new songs. One of the new tracks, "Man of the Tombs," is a masterpiece built around the story of the Gadarene demoniac in Mark 5. The very idea of giving voice to the demon-possessed man is creative, and the song itself is especially well crafted. It is generally regarded as Bennett's most sophisticated song. Bennett next recorded *Songs from Bright Avenue,* a brilliant collection of songs that arose out of the turmoil surrounding the dissolution of his marriage. The song "No Such Thing as Divorce" garnered national attention with its refrain "There is no such thing as divorce / Between a father and his son / Between a daddy and his daughter / No matter what has happened / No matter what will be / There is no such thing as divorce / Between you and me." Media personality Dr. Laura Schlesinger began to feature it on her syndicated radio show, and it was also used in the NBC soap opera *Another World.* The songs "The Place I'm Bound" and "I'm Still Alive Tonight" also arose out of the pain of Bennett's personal situation and desire to rebuild a shattered life. On a lighter note, the album includes the humorous song, "Our Co-Dependent Love," sung in a nightclub-parody style. Bennett's wit is evident again on the album *Small Graces,* which features two songs ("The Better Part of Me," "Lone Star State") that deal with a romantic relationship with a Texas woman that began with a blind date but didn't work out so well (for him). But the main theme of the album is announced in its title (and title song): noticing the small things in life, which Bennett says "may seem insignificant but have an underpinning of hope." The song "The Only Risk Worth Taking" reveals that (divorce and bad dates aside) he still believes in romance.

As a lyricist, Bennett is both incisive and vulnerable. Thus his song "No Such Thing as Divorce" is directed to his children as both affirmation and confession: "Oh my dear children / How I love you with my life / And that will never change / Though your mom is not my wife / It's true I promised you / That this would never come to be / Please forgive me." And then: "Sometimes I cry over the things I can't undo / And the words I never should have said in front of you / But I pray the good will somehow overcome the bad / And where I failed as a husband / I'll succeed as your dad." The song "Here on Bright Avenue" identifies the source of his undying hope: "I'm walking toward a promise that frees this convict heart / The Lord will never lose me / And he can finish what he starts."

In the late '90s, Bennett would find acceptance as a mainstream folk singer in Southern California music clubs. He says, "My approach to ministry is a little different than some people's in that I regard the ministry as a secondary goal of what I'm doing. My primary goal is to communicate truthfully with people. If I can communicate the life of the Spirit and the always accompanying struggle along the way, then ministry happens as a natural result of that." **Erick Nelson** has said, "If I were to bring a non-Christian friend to anybody's concert, it would be Bob's. I could be assured that he would satisfy musically, that he wouldn't say anything stupid, and that he would communicate real truth in a powerful way."

For trivia buffs: Bennett was the college roommate of Dan Rupple, who would later make up half of the Christian comedy duo Isaac Air Freight. They both experienced spiritual renaissances at about the same time. The two later cohosted a morning talk show for Radio station KBRT.

Christian radio hits: "The Best" (# 17 in 1980); "Come and See" (# 6 in 1982); "Mountain Cathedrals" (# 20 in 1982); "Still Rolls the Stone" (# 9 in 1986); "Yours Alone" (# 21 in 1990).

David Benson

1995—*Holy Psychotherapy* (Viva); 1996—*Purpose of the Cross* (ATG).

David Benson bills himself as "a Christian Ozzy Osbourne," and indeed he does manage to feign an uncanny resemblance to that well-known heavy metal screamer. The song "America Wake Up" even seems to take its main riffs from Black Sabbath's "War Pigs." Lyrics, however, are explicitly Christian, even worshipful on "One More Chance." Benson is critical of bands that try to speak about spiritual matters in ambiguous ways. The title song to his first album is unashamed to name the Name: "Holy psychotherapy, redemption of your soul / Holy psychotherapy, let Jesus make you whole." "I really want to see people's lives changed through what I do," Benson says. Still, *HM* magazine panned the debut album as derivative and dismissed it as a novelty record. The very worldly *Scream* magazine, by contrast, gave *Purpose of the Cross* 4 screams out of 5; they thought the idea of a Christian Ozzy was "pretty cool." In 2000, it was reported that Benson was joining with Mick Rowe of **Midnight Orchestra** to create a new version of the Christian metal band **Tempest** and release an album titled *Crushing the Dark Cathedral.* Benson said it would "address and attack the very core beliefs of Satanism and its feeble practices."

Aaron Benward

See **Aaron Jeoffrey** (under "A").

Jeoffrey Benward

See **Aaron Jeoffrey** (under "A").

The Deven Berryhill Band

Deven Berryhill, voc., gtr.; Ken Burton, bass; Jeff Herman, kybrd.; Keith Sansone, drums; John Hendrickson, trump. (– 1994). 1992—*The Deven Berryhill Band* (Rolltop); 1994—*Danger! High Voltage Above.*

The Deven Berryhill Band played electric surf music with a strong "live" feel to it. Songs like "Landslide" (not a Fleetwood Mac cover) and "Peace Child" are funky and guitar laden; the band also does an edited and revamped version of **Bob Dylan**'s "Gotta Serve Somebody." The group's lyrics are bold and direct, often consisting of Scripture set to music. *HM* magazine thought the *High Voltage* album could make "a great tract for searching souls on beachfront property."

Bethlehem

Danny Daniels, voc., gtr.; John Falcone, bass, voc.; Dom Franco, steel gtr., voc.; Dan McCleery, drums, voc.; Randy Rigby, kybrd., voc. 1978—*Bethlehem* (1978).

The country-rock quintet known as Bethlehem had a sound similar to that of the early Eagles and to that of the debut album by **Daniel Amos,** but they came by it honestly. Dom Franco had played steel guitar in clubs for years, and that instrument became the group's distinctive hook. Danny Daniels led the group with a laid-back country vibe that evinced unusual tenderness and humility. Their sole album was produced by **Al Perkins** and **Tom Stipe.** Some reports hold that this album, and in particular the song "Dead Reckoning," had a part in changing the mind of evangelist Bob Larson, who crusaded against Christian rock for years. John Falcone would also play bass for **The Road Home.**

According to Daniels, the group Bethlehem was formed in 1974 by friends who all had known each other and played together prior to finding salvation: "A bunch of us lived together for a time, broke up, and then all got saved in different places over a four month period. After a time, we all got back together to visit and evangelize one another. What a joy to find out there was no need!" The group originally went by the name Bethlehem Steel to call attention to their trademark (then rare) steel guitar sound, but the moniker was shortened to prevent any ire from multinational corporations that might get fussy about trademark infringements. For a time Bethlehem was the house band at the Palomino Club in north Hollywood. But then in keeping with their name, they decided that their ministry should be to small, rural towns that other groups and artists seldom visited. By 1979 they had found a home in Boulder, Colorado.

Bethlehem also placed two songs on the important Maranatha compilation albums. "Bright and Shining Sea" (on *Maranatha Five,* 1976) is a worshipful, thank-you-Jesus piece similar in sound to many of the songs on **The Way**'s debut album. "Desert Song" (on *Maranatha Six,* 1977) is a traveling song, likening the journey of life to Israel's guidance through the wilderness to the Promised Land. Daniels released a solo album for Maranatha called *Sons of Thunder* in 1982. He then became one of John Wimber's closest allies in the formation of the Vineyard Church Fellowship (a group that split off from Calvary Chapel to become a new denomination). He and Rigby continued to write worship songs for Vineyard music (e.g., "Heart of Love" in 1988). Daniels has recorded several albums of worship music including *Hearts on Fire* (Bluestone, 1991), *Praise Collection* (Bluestone, 1994), *Another Shade of Blue* (Vineyard, 1995), and *Northern Light* (Third Day, 2001). He has been a staff pastor and worship leader at Vineyard churches in California and Aurora, Colorado.

Betrayal

Marcus Colon, gtr.; Chris Ackerman, voc. (– 1999); Jeff Lain, bass; Matt Maners, gtr. (–1993, + 1999); Brian Meuse, drums (–1993) // Bob McCue, gtr. (+ 1993, –1999); Jeff Mason, drums (+ 1993, –1999). 1991—*Renaissance by Death* (Wonderland); 1993—*The Passing;* 1999—*Leaving Nevermore* (Black and White).

www.listentothis.com/artists/betrayal

A forerunner of technical speed metal music, the Christian band Betrayal was founded by members of the group Martyr in 1989. After releasing two classic albums of that genre, the group disbanded in 1993. Marc Colon enlisted Matt Maners to help him put out a new release in 1999, then recruited a number of other musicians for touring and production of an anticipated fourth album.

Martyr had been composed of Colon, Maners, Brian Meuse, and Dave Prado. As an '80s' metal band, they specialized in the super-fast sound that would ultimately get labeled "thrash" or "speed metal." Possibly ahead of their time, they released a handful of albums with titles like *Death Is Dead, Frantic,* and *Imminent Warfare,* but never really caught on. The group's sense of humor made it somewhat distinctive within the Christian metal genre. The Anthrax-like punk anthem "Fall on Your Face" closes with an a capella rendition of "Heartbreak Hotel." The song "Get Drunk" features these lyrics: "Hey, stupid punk, why won't you get drunk? / Maybe then all the girls will think you're a hunk." Ultimately, the success of Betrayal sparked new interest in Martyr, leading to the release of a retrospective album called *Wickenstraut* (Tisch and Christo, 1993).

Betrayal's first record, *Renaissance by Death,* set a standard for thrash metal played with raw fury. The restrained "under-produced" sound pleased many, including one reviewer who said "it sounds like the band is attacking the listener" (this was a compliment). The title tune features the haunting sounds of a harpsichord. "Mortal Flesh" is an instrumental with an industrial edge. The most noticed song on the album, however, was "Escaping the Altar," a tragic tale about Satanic ritual abuse. At this time, Betrayal was vowing to devote its ministry to confronting, exposing, and challenging the "epidemic of Satanism" in America. Colon had been involved in Satanism himself before his conversion (instigated by seeing **Darrell Mansfield** on TV), and indeed the group's name reflected the paradoxical character of this turnabout (he had become a traitor to the kingdom of Satan). Still, the second album would reveal a broader focus, dealing with such issues as racism and the political prospects of America under what looked to the artists to be unrighteous rule (the Clinton presidency). The group also decided to balance songs like "Carnival of Horrors," "Feast of Madness," and "Race of Hypocrisy" with tunes that offer the positive message of Christianity. "Strength of the Innocent" recalls the biblical massacres of infants under Pharaoh and Herod. Musically, *The Passing* shows progression and variety, spicing the industrial hardcore delivery with jazzy interludes, speed-note riffs, and occasional melodious passages. Shortly after *The Passing*'s release, the band was involved in an automobile accident in which one occupant of the other vehicle was killed and another left paralyzed. In media interviews band members discussed their struggles to deal with this tragedy, which may have contributed to the group's demise.

A second incarnation of Betrayal arose a few years later. This group was almost a one-man band, with Colon now providing guitar, vocals, bass, keyboard, and drums. The album *Leaving Nevermore* evinces a gothic, modern rock sound. Colon's melodic vocal delivery is startlingly different from heavy metal screaming. Acoustic touches and surreal keyboards are added here and there. Overall, the songs on *Leaving Nevermore* portray a more positive outlook on life than Betrayal's previous material. "To Follow" is worshipful and "The Window," reassuring. Still there is ambiguity: "Has evil removed itself / Or the same party with new masks / You'll never know, until you're known / And I will never, in this place called home" ("A Place Called Home"). By 2000, Colon had assembled a new group that included Rigo Heute (bass, kybrd.), Brian Poindexter (drums), and Sean Silas (gtr.).

Between Thieves (a.k.a. **Judah**)

Jason Davis, drums; Jason Wesson, voc.; Jesse Reeves, bass (– 1997); Jimmy Varner, gtr., voc. (– 1997); Aron Vaughan, kybrd. (– 1997) //Josh Watkins, gtr. (+ 1998); James Yourman, bass (+ 1998). As Judah: 1994—*Simplistic* (independent); 1996—*Lay It Down.* As Between Thieves: 1997—*Between Thieves* (Tattoo); 1998—*Water.*

The pop-rock band Judah (formed in Texas in 1990) was described by one reviewer as "an unrefined **Newsboys.**" If that be true, then the group Between Thieves that emerged when Judah got a contract would have to be compared to **The Newsboys,** period. The refinement is there, on two albums that rock out with Beatles-inspired melodic tunes featuring hook-laden choruses, snappy harmonies, and happy beats. BT's self-titled debut reprises eight songs from the former group's *Lay It Down,* re-recorded to take advantage of the new production levels their label's budget could afford. The opening tune, "Despite the Rain"—their best song so far—went to Number One on Christian Rock charts. The next album, *Water,* was produced by **Steve Hindalong** (of **The Choir**) and features a more soulful, guitar-oriented sound.

The Dallas-based group identifies itself unabashedly as "a ministry band." They conclude concerts with altar calls, which limits their ecumenical appeal, but they succeed lyrically in writing songs that are both personal and universal in their application. "Despite the Rain" affirms the possibility of accepting oneself as forgiven and transformed by Christ's love. "Kindle" deals effectively with the topic of personal purity. "Carried Away" expresses the rapture of worship. "Simple Truth" proclaims the unfailing faithfulness of God.

Christian radio hits: "Kindle" (# 11 in 1997).

Lisa Bevill

1992—*My Freedom* (Vireo); 1994—*All Because of You* (Sparrow); 1996—*Love of Heaven*; 2000—*Lisa Bevill* (Ministry).

www.lisabevill.com

A pop-rock singer with the musical stylings of Madonna or Paula Abdul, Lisa Bevill (b. 1968 in North Carolina) is known for singing danceable tunes and emotional ballads that focus on issues of family and growing up. She draws on her own painful experiences of dealing with the illnesses of her parents. Her mother, diagnosed early with terminal cancer, was sick throughout her adolescence; her father died in her arms of rheumatoid arthritis when she was only nineteen. Bevill struggled for years with the grief, depression, and anger these losses brought, but after reading the Frank Peretti novel *This Present Darkness* began to direct that anger at Satan. Her understanding of life as spiritual warfare has motivated her to help young people to see their lives in these terms also. In particular, she focuses on encouraging teenage girls to accept themselves as creations of God and to see the hand of God in shaping their lives.

Bevill's first album is bubblegum pop of the variety Britney Spears would produce a few years later. A major theme is chastity, along the lines of Janet Jackson's "Let's Wait Awhile," though more specific (i.e., Let's Wait till after We're Married).

The opening song, "Chaperone," reminds teens that God goes with them on every date and watches what they do. "It's Gonna Be Worth It" offers the titular promise to those who preserve their virginity. Bevill became the first female spokesperson for "True Love Waits," a national campaign to encourage sexual abstinence. She was invited to Washington, D.C., to sing for Vice President Al Gore and his family on National Parent's Day.

All Because of You deals with themes that are a bit more substantial theologically and shows musical maturity as well. It continues to be regarded as Bevill's best work. The hip-hop sounding "Sunshine and Joy" (which contrasts the comfort of knowing Christ with the lonely feeling of "having the blues") quotes Philippians 4; "Hold On" draws from Isaiah 40; "No Condemnation" celebrates the promise of Romans 8:1; "Trouble the Waters" alludes to the story in John 5 (or, specifically, to a later addition to that story found in v. 4 of some English Bibles). The title song proclaims the ability to see oneself and to accept oneself because of Christ: "Out of the dark I come / Into the light, into the blazing sun / Scars on my soul for the world to see / But I'm standing here, all because of you." The next album, *Love of Heaven,* shows a retreat from the rock-inflected sound of Bevill's first two outings into the tamer arena of adult contemporary ballads. Bevill began to emerge as a songwriter, contributing to four of the tracks. Finally, after a four-year hiatus, her self-titled album would find her writing or cowriting half of the songs, including those generally acknowledged to be the best. "No Turning Back" is a powerful reaffirmation of faith; "How Strong He Is" draws on urban gospel influences and celebrates the majesty of God. Musically, this last album moves back again toward a more upbeat rock sound and reveals Bevill singing with conviction and maturity.

In 1993 Bevill wrote an article for *Brio* magazine about her struggles as an adolescent girl with "supermodel images" that led her to such insecurity and depression that she contemplated suicide. The article produced such a response from teenage girls around the country that Bevill made such concerns a focal point in her ministry. From 1995 to 1998, she ran "Place in the Sun" retreats (named for an upbeat song on her first album) for adolescent girls, at which no one (including her) was allowed to wear makeup or to cover up their feelings while discussing such topics as boys, weight, beauty, dating, and parents. Several of Bevill's songs address the special vulnerabilities of teenage girls, including "Tender Reed": "Although you're so fragile / Although you've been bruised / The gentle hand that grew you from a seed / Will be all the strength you need" (cf. Isaiah 42:3).

Christian radio hits: "Place in the Sun" (# 1 in 1992); "Chaperone" (# 6 in 1992); "Falling off the Face of the Earth" (# 4 in 1992); "I Took a Tumble" (# 4 in 1993); "It's Gonna Be Worth It" (# 24 in 1993); "No Condemnation" (# 2 in 1994); "Make It Better" (# 4 in 1995); "Sunshine and Joy" (# 2 in 1995); "Hold On" (# 3 in 1995); "Turn and Love" (# 21 in 1996); "Changed" (# 19 in 1996).

Beyond the Blue

Marty Funderburk, voc.; Richard Kelly, voc.; Steve Smith, voc. 1996—*Beyond the Blue* (Word).

The vocal harmony group Beyond the Blue released their first album about two years before groups like *NSYNC, 98 Degrees, and the Backstreet Boys would make their style of music the most popular in the land. No one doubted the abilities of the hyper-talented trio, but some had to wonder if there was an audience for this kind of music. There was—or at least there would be two years later. Stylistically, the songs teetered between R&B numbers and more polished pop songs. Numbers like "What a World" and "Reason for the Rain" showcase their vocal strengths. "For the Sake of My Heart" is a straightforward pop ballad that could have been done by **4 Him.** The album also includes a faithful rendition of the O'Jays' hit "Love Train" (# 1 in 1973). Beyond the Blue identified the focus of its ministry as being "encouragement within the church." They said they hoped to be role models for young men, showing them "something to stand for and someone to relate to." The group's name derived from the belief that life is a dress rehearsal for what is to come beyond the blue. They disbanded, and Funderburk became involved with the southern gospel label Daywind Records, doing production, vocal coaching, background vocals, songwriting, and arranging for their stable of artists.

Bi-Faith

Shana Gage, voc.; Larissa Straker, voc. 1996—*Bi-Faith* (Versatile).

Bi-Faith is a female duo that makes hip-hop music in the same vein as general market artists like Brandy or TLC. Their stated purpose is "to minister to heads in the street, to show them that Christianity is not wack, it's cool." When their first album was recorded, Gage was sixteen and Straker, thirteen. The opening song, "Never Alone," pits a slow rap against a swing style beat in a manner reminiscent of Toni Braxton. The songs "A God like You" and "My Jesus" also offer slow jams that glorify the Lord. *Godzhouse* electronic magazine (www.godzhous.com) reported in 1998 that Gage was leaving the group to be a premed student and would be replaced by Cheronda Montoute.

Big Dog Small Fence

Joel Catalan, sax., kybrd.; Greg Kawai, drums, perc.; Frank Loaiza, voc., gtr., bass; Dale Ovalle, drums; Missy Sortino, voc.; Pablo Tovar, bass, voc.; tromb.; Patrick Wright, trump.; Sammy Wright, gtr., kybrd. 1998—*Big Dog Small Fence* (Eclectica).

A Southern California ska band, Big Dog Small Fence fits loosely into the category of Christian bands that includes **The Supertones, The Insyderz,** and **Five Iron Frenzy,** but an upfront blend of female (Sortino) and male (Tovar) vocals gives them a distinct sound. A racially mixed group, Big Dog Small Fence also plays ska with more of a Motown groove than the other bands listed above. Their sound is closer to the original ska of groups like Madness and The Specials. Big Dog Small Fence songs deal more with life issues than with matters specific to the Christian faith, and coping with human weakness seems to be a dominant theme. The group nevertheless views itself very much as a ministry band and is in fact constituted as an outreach of the Mosaic Church in east Los Angeles. Pablo Tovar and Missy Sortino share songwriting duties. The former tends to focus on the gritty reality of life in the streets. His song "L.A." tells of a real-life experience in which he watched a friend be taken away for a twenty-five-year prison sentence and wondered what might have been done to prevent this. Sortino, a pastor's wife and mother of three, contributes the woman's perspective. "Impossible" presents the view of a wife and kid waiting at home for a man who likes to roam: "They want him there, but not the way he's been lately."

Big Face Grace

Timothy Gillespie, gtr., voc.; Jason Hutchinson, gtr., bass; Roy Ice, drums; Michael Knecht, gtr.; Sam Leonor, bass. 1996—*Face the World* (AD 27); 1997—*Big Face Grace* [EP]; 2000—*Smile* (True Tunes).

www.bigfacegrace.com

Big Face Grace offers a variety of evangelistic and worship songs performed through their own blend of mainline rock styles. Originally called Electric Fishermen, the group formed while its members were in college. Four of them have since earned Master of Divinity degrees and serve as youth pastors. While ecumenical in their ministry and outreach, the group has been closely associated with the Seventh-day Adventist Church, especially with that denomination's John Hancock Center for Youth Ministry at LaSierra University (Riverside, Calif.). Their contract with True Tunes, however, has brought them to the attention of a wider audience. MTV featured two of their songs (the soulful ballad "Floored" and a club remix of "The Way") on its popular *Road Rules* program, and ABC TV used two other songs ("Halo" and "It's Not Enough") on a series called *Making the Band* (cf. **O-Town**). Standout songs on *Smile* include the disco-inflected opener "TeleVision" and the energetic "Nothing Can." The latter song affirms the biblical promise that nothing can separate people from the love of God (Romans 8:39).

Big Tent Revival

Spence Smith, drums; Steve Wiggins, voc., gtr.; Randy Williams, gtr. // Rick Heil, bass (+ 1996; −1999); David Alan, kybrd (+ 1997); Steve Dale, bass (+ 1999). 1995—*Big Tent Revival* (Ardent); 1996—*Open All Nite*; 1997—*Amplifier*; 1999—*Choose Life*; 2001—*Live*.

Founded in 1994 by three boys from Memphis, Big Tent Revival spent the last half of the '90s churning out songs that draw heavily on the equally American traditions of Memphis blues and Baptist theology. Front man **Steve Wiggins** had begun as a solo artist, releasing an album in 1991.

The group's self-titled debut album features Claptonesque rockers ("Thief in the Night"), country songs ("Count On You," "Jesus Is Your Friend"), and a soulful remake of the Staples Singers' "Respect Yourself." It is best remembered, however, for the acoustic parable "Two Sets of Joneses," which has a sound similar to Billy Joel's "Piano Man." The lyrics of "Two Sets of Jonses" recount the separate lives of a rich couple who doesn't know Jesus and a poor couple who does. The rich folks end up divorced and miserable, the poor folks happy and trouble-free. Simplistic and a tad judgmental—a recurrent problem for BTR—it is nevertheless a great folk song, a classic of its genre.

Open All Nite was produced by John Hampton, known for his work with Gin Blossoms and Spin Doctors. It includes "Personal Judgment Day," which is not only the band's best song but one of the best Christian rock songs of all time. In fact, it probably defines rock and roll in the Memphis blues tradition as well as any song by any artist. Blazing guitar licks (think Dicky Betts or Duane Allman) soar over a shuffling rhythm as Wiggins testifies in a voice borrowed from Mellencamp but infused with Springsteen's urgency: "Accepted Jesus at forty-five / Said, 'Man, I'm glad to be alive / All my friends are dead you see / One bad trip and it could've been me'." The song is very simplistic and more than a tad judgmental ("Tell me, brother, when it's all through / Do you know Jesus and does he know you?"), yet there is not a thought in it that is not completely scriptural (the Bible itself can be pretty simple and judgmental at times). "Personal Judgment Day" is one of those rare perfect songs—not a single note, beat, or word could be changed without detracting from its quality and impact.

Open All Nite also features the songs "Mend Me" and "Famine or Feast." The former is a solid rock song, appealing to God for spiritual healing. The latter revisits the theme of "Two Sets of Jonses," as though Wiggins had rethought the cut-and-dried sentiments of his most famous song. This time, a poor man and a rich man worship God side by side, both cognizant of the (different) blessings they receive and the (different) struggles they endure. Another tune, "If Loving God Was a Crime," is a simple blue-collar ballad proclaiming Wiggins' willingness to bear persecution for his faith, if necessary.

The next two albums continued to deliver slices of Americana-roots rock and hook-filled pop songs. Unfortunately, *Amplifier* was pigeonholed as the album containing the adult contemporary ballad "What Would Jesus Do?" (which promoted the WWJD bracelet craze). Aside from that song, the album rocks harder than the band's previous releases. Songs like "Still Breathing" and "Wouldn't It Be Cool" recall the classic rock sounds of bands like Bad Company, the scorching "Rivalry" outdoes anything that group ever did, and with "God Made Heaven" the band even becomes worthy of comparison with Creedence Clearwater Revival. "Lovely Mausoleum" is also a great song, well written, tightly performed, with a completely unique sound (maybe if Counting Crows were to cover a Queen song?). BTR's fourth release, *Choose Life,* disappointed some critics, as it seemed the group wanted to capitalize on the success of "What Would Jesus Do?" by churning out radio-friendly hits. The album's songs are more catchy and more acoustic-based than previous products, but they are also more formulaic. The opening song, "Livin' Off Your Love," recalls Huey Lewis and the News with its "doo-de-do-do-do" chorus. The title track is a gorgeous ballad that reinterprets the antiabortion motto as an evangelistic slogan ("Choose *eternal* life"). "Fill Me with Your Spirit" and "I Worship You" are worship songs. "The Word of God" sounds uncannily like **Phil Keaggy.** "Will You Be Mine?" is a raucous Valentine to Wiggins' wife. Half of the songs on *Choose Life* were cowritten with **Billy Batstone.**

Big Tent Revival lives up to their name by viewing their career as an evangelistic ministry. They sincerely hope that people will get saved at their concerts and they try to foster such salvation by inviting audience members to make a decision to accept Christ as their personal Lord and Savior. The group has also worked tirelessly on behalf of the world hunger organization Compassion International. They publish an electronic newsletter called Canvas Life, in which a wacky sense of humor not apparent on their recordings comes to the fore. For a while Wiggins decided to spell his first name "Stev5," because "if you can have silent letters, why not silent numbers?"

For trivia buffs: In the "always a bridesmaid . . ." tradition, Big Tent Revival was (as of 2000) the only major Christian band to have been *nominated* for a Grammy award for every album they had made, without ever actually winning one.

Christian radio hits: "Two Sets of Jonses" (# 2 in 1995); "Faith of a Little Seed" (# 10 in 1995); "Thief in the Night" (# 5 in 1996); "Somethin' about Jesus" (# 10 in 1996); "Here with Me" (# 1 in 1996); "If Loving God Was a Crime" (# 1 in 1996); "Mend Me" (# 14 in 1997); "Famine or Feast" (# 3 in 1997); "The Best Thing" (# 13 in 1997); "What Would Jesus Do?" (# 12 in 1998); "Star in the Book of Life" (# 1 in 1998); "God Made Heaven" (# 3 in 1998); "Lovely Mausoleum" (# 14 in 1998); "Livin' Off Your Love" (# 1 in 1999); "Choose Life" (# 8 in 2000); "Fill Me with Your Spirit" (# 13 in 2000).

Charles Billingsley

1992—*Choice of a Lifetime* (Crest); 1993—*A Collection of Hymns: Until Then*; 1997—*Change* (Crest); *Charles Live!*; 1999—*Between Now and Then* (Pamplin); 2000—*Marks of the Mission*.

www.charlesbillingsley.com

Charles Billingsley attended Samford University (Birmingham, Alabama) as a religion major and went on to work as a self-described "musical missionary" in Atlanta. From 1994 to 1996 he sang with the popular Christian group **NewSong**. As a soloist, he performs primarily for church groups. He strives to sing songs that "leave absolutely no question" about his faith, yet ones that incorporate a variety of styles to appeal to different age groups. *Between Now and Then* was his first major label release. It includes the up-tempo song "Some Things Will Never Change," the worship anthem, "Within the Veil," and a deeply personal ballad, "Golden Streets." The latter song, which Billingsley wrote after losing several loved ones to death in a single year, offers comfort to the grieving by emphasizing the joys of heaven. The title song to *Marks of the Mission* reflects both on the scars of Jesus (as marks of his earthly mission) and on the lives of believers (who are marks of his ongoing mission today).

Birtles and Goble

Beeb Birtles; Graham Goble. 1980—*The Last Romance* (Capitol).

www.birtles.com

Birtles and Goble were a duo composed of two-fifths of the popular Australian pop group Little River Band. The latter group formed in Melbourne in 1975 with Graham Goble as its only native Aussie member. Both Goble and Beeb Birtles played guitar with the group. The band released three platinum and two gold albums between 1975 and 1981, scoring their biggest hits with "Reminiscing" (# 3 in 1978), "Lady" (# 10 in 1979), "Lonesome Loser" (# 6 in 1979); "Cool Change" (# 10 in 1979); "The Night Owls" (# 6 in 1981), and "Take It Easy on Me" (# 10 in 1981). Little River Band sometimes came off as a cheap version of Crosby, Stills, Nash and Young ("Happy Anniversary," # 16 in 1977), but they made a genuine impression on critics when they tapped into their jazz roots on songs like "It's a Long Way There" (# 28 in 1976) and "Reminiscing." After 1981, the group fell into a spate of constant personnel changes but continued to tour and record with minimal success (Birtles left in 1985 and Goble in 1992). Birtles and Goble were Christians, Goble having been raised a believer from childhood and Birtles experiencing a conversion to Christ shortly after the formation of Little River Band (as a result of seeing the film *The Road to Armageddon*). In 1980 they decided to express their faith on a side project that did not involve leaving the band itself. Birtles would describe *Last Romance* not as a Christian album

per se but as "a contemporary album with some Christian songs on it." The focus of the record, which *CCM* classed as "positive pop," is a presentation of selfless love as the basis for life and romance. A few tracks do contain very specific Christian lyrics. **The Imperials** would record the song "Into My Life" (written by Birtles) in 1980. **Illustrator** and **Rebecca St. James** have both recorded Little River Band songs. Birtles has continued to record solo material, his most recent project being *Driven By Dreams* (Sonic Sorbet, 1999). His biography and catalogue are posted at www.birtles.com.

For trivia buffs: The late '70s appear to have been a time of religious fervor for Little River Band. *Harmony* magazine reports that the group's bass player George McArdale left in 1979 to pursue a closer relationship with Christ. According to *Rolling Stone*, McArdale gave away all of his money and moved to Australia's Blue Mountains where he studied the Bible for three years.

Black Carnation

Craig Hoeve, drums; Jeff Seaver, gtr., voc.; Kendall Thomas, bass. 1992—*It Remains the Same* (Blonde Vinyl).

Black Carnation was a modern rock trio from Grand Rapids, Michigan, with a Morrissey-influenced sound similar to that of **Luxury** or **The Throes**. Completely ignored by the Christian media, their debut album on **Michael Knott**'s Blonde Vinyl label presents songs of anguish regarding life in a fallen world. "Black World" decries the legacy of racism from which Jeff Seaver sings, "I pray all day that I will go free." Nothing in the band's lyrics mark them as overtly Christian, though an air of spirituality informs much of the material. "Today I Danced upon a Fallen Tree" evinces a naive flower-child sentiment, and elsewhere Seaver hears the wind speak "of love and laughter" as Sister Freedom beckons him to come away with her ("On the Wind").

Black Cherry Soda

Dave Calamaro, bass; Dan Rauter, voc.; Tim Rauter, drums; Scott Tyson, gtr. 1995—*Grin* (Swirle); 1998—*Back on the Map* (BulletProof).

Philadelphia-based Black Cherry Soda describe the motivation for their hard pop-punk music as being a combination of "a love for life with a love for people and a desire to spread the joy of being a Christian." The group fuses the energy of hardcore punk music with more singable melodies in a blend similar to that made popular by Green Day and **MxPx**. They are also willing to slow down the usual rapid-fire delivery of punk to let their lyrics be enunciated and heard. Not preachy but positive, the members of Black Cherry Soda are known within the punk scene as exemplars of what they call the "straight-edge stance," a position that advocates substance-free living, acceptance of all races, and monogamous relationships. The most catchy, melodic song from the first album, "Friend," is about a friend in an unhealthy relationship. "If I Could Only" from *Back on the Map* also has a sing-along feel and expresses a spiritual quest: "If I could find an answer, if I could only see / If I could find a reason for me to believe."

Black Happy

Jim Bruce, drums; Jay Carkhuff, tromb.; Daryl Elmore, sax.; Mike Hassaveries, tromb.; Paul Hemenway, voc., gtr.; Mark Hemenway, bass; Greg Hjort, gtr.; Scott Jessick, drums. 1991—*Friendly Dog Salad* (Pacific Inland); 1993—*Peghead* (Macola); 1995—*The Last Polka* (Capricorn).

Black Happy had a curious mix of dance-funk and heavy metal. They began as a metal band named Sacramen, but they switched styles and names when a novelty funk song in their repertoire became the hands-down crowd pleaser. The group enjoyed a fair amount of success in the Northwest United States but disbanded in 1994 with Paul and Mark Hemenway reorganizing to form a band called Shoveljerk, named after one of their more popular songs. Capricorn released a post-breakup collection of outtakes and live songs. Lyrically, Black Happy's songs range all over the map, from silly concepts like "Garlic" ("Garlic makes my feet stink") to introspective ruminations like "Spirit" ("Don't we ever think about the other side? / My soul and I are just looking for some time"). A tune called "The F-Word" objects to the label applied to the band's music ("Don't label me FUNK!").

Steve Black

1997—*Time Passes* (Good Taste); 1998—*You Get What You Pay For;* 1999—*Going Home* (Silent Planet).

www.fortissimo.org/artists/black

A singer/songwriter from the Philadelphia area, Steve Black mixes influences of folk, Americana, and blues into personal songs about family, friends, and the meaning of life. For his first release with Silent Planet, he was backed by a band called Thompson's Station. The album *Going Home* includes four songs that he wrote for his father, as well as four remixed songs from each of his two previous records.

Blackball

Tom Barber, bass; Lorenzo Mauro, drums; Chris Scott, voc.; David Bishop, gtr. (– 1997) // Rocco Sigona, gtr. (+ 1997). 1996—*Superheavy-dreamscape* (Metro One); 1997—*Hope.*

Chris Scott, front man for the metal band **Precious Death,** founded Blackball and invited fellow PD alum David Bishop to play guitar as a guest member on the first album. With Black-ball, Scott has exchanged the clichés of metal for a basic hard

rock or even hard punk sound. More heavy than dreamy, *Superheavydreamscape* focuses on themes of resignation and lament (Scott was a college student, seeking a major in philosophy at the time). It opens with a burst of denial: "I don't even want to know / I don't even want to hear / Everything's o.k. / Doesn't matter anyway" ("Doesn't Matter"). "Get Outta Here" continues to insist, "You don't need to waste your time / Making lists of all my faults so you can read them to me." The song also contains the great line, "I can't pretend that I'm somebody you'd like better." In "There Goes the One" Scott continues, "You send your message with all the finesse of a letter bomb." But interspersed with all this resistance are acknowledgments of regret (the gloriously crunchy "Not the Way I Want It To Be") and admissions of need ("Wither," in which Scott asks, "Can I lean on you to keep from falling down?"). Scott has said that the album *Superheavydreamscape* was inspired by his reading of the book *He Is There and He Is Not Silent* by popular Christian author Francis Schaeffer.

Hope sounds like it was recorded by a completely different group. Suddenly there are horns and keyboards (courtesy of producer Gene Eugene of **Adam Again**), and the entire album has a funky, buoyant sound, reminiscent at times of 311 or the Red Hot Chili Peppers. The standout "All God's Children" is a made-for-radio dance song that draws on the tradition of whoop-it-up traditional gospel numbers. "Everybody Wants To Get Over It" is a Motown-like number with choral vocals. "Funk for Breakfast" and the opener "Downtown" evoke the '70s sounds of Sly Stone. Lyrically, the second album demonstrates a complete change of pace as well. The overall mood is one of promise and affirmation, with no hesitation to name the source of such inspiration. Scott explained the change in direction: "If we can't focus on the hope that we've found through our relationship with God, then how are we going to share it? That's the focus of the songs." And he continued, "so as not to bum anybody out, they're fun songs."

Black-Eyed Sceva

Brad McCarter, bass, voc.; Brent Nims, drums; Jeremy Post, voc., gtr. 1995—*Way Before the Flood* (5 Min. Walk); 1996—*5 Years, 50,000 Miles Davis.*

Black-Eyed Sceva was Jeremy Post's first band before he formed **Model Engine.** They made one album and a four-song EP, which was then extended to album length through the addition of live versions of songs from the debut and a cover of The Police's "Invisible Sun."

Critics often compared BES's college-alt sound to groups like Third Eye Blind and Matchbox 20, but Post's gruff style of singing and writing actually gave the group a more raw sound than those comparisons might imply. There is a definite Pearl Jam injection. Both albums were produced by Bruce Winter, bass player for Toad the Wet Sprocket. BES songs like "Justified" and "Nail Holes" (reflecting on John 20:25) deal with traditional matters of Christian faith. "Twain" and "Comte's Perspective" draw on Post's college studies in religion and philosophy, while "Ryan's Driveway" recalls arguments with skeptical friends. "Cleverness" contrasts the rhetorical ability to score points in such arguments with the sincere desire to discover what is true. Other songs engage various life issues. "Mudhouse" poignantly describes the instant (and long-lasting) regret that accompanies a lack of sexual restraint: "Gazes down between shivering legs / Nine months from now I could be a father . . . I wish that I would have waited." The song "Adrien James" bristles with unresolved anger over the pain of parental abandonment ("When Adrien James left Marie and son / one third of the whole was gone / Did you miss the part / Bout till death do us part?"). "Handshake" presents the act of shaking hands with a gay man who has AIDS as a bold act of compassion and faith, which unfortunately is how it might have been regarded in some of the circles this band apparently frequented. Reviewers found the song "daring," though Post would insist that he completely accepts conservative interpretations of Scripture that regard homosexuality as "one hundred percent sinful" and was interested only in "furthering Christian outreach to gays."

Both albums include a more controversial song, "Confirmation Day," which is laden with anti-Catholic polemic. Post himself was raised Roman Catholic, then later "became a Christian" through contact with the evangelistic group Young Life. Post maintains the song, which belittles the Catholic ritual of Confirmation, is *not* anti-Catholic, but an expression of disappointments specific to his personal experience. Post dropped out of Confirmation class as a youth, then entered into an adult program led by a priest who was irresponsible and ended up being sent to prison. The song, however, appears to generalize, inferring that the "twenty-five white-robed students" getting confirmed one Easter Sunday don't know the difference between "going to church and being saved." Watching the spectacle, Post actually concludes, "We are not all serving the same God." Such lyrics are all the more sad coming from a man who also wrote "Ecumenical," a song that advances the creed, "Unity in what is essential, liberty in nonessentials, and in all things charity."

For trivia buffs: Black-Eyed Sceva took its name from the minor biblical character mentioned in Acts 19:14. The group repeatedly indicated that the correct pronunciation of the last name was *see-vah* (not *skee-vah*) and even toyed with the idea of titling their last album *The Sea is Silent* (get it?).

Blackhouse

Ivo Cutler, voice, sampler, radio, chair, effects; Sterling Cross, voice, sound module, perc. 1984—*Pro-Life* (Ladd-Frith); *Hope Like a Candle;*

1985—*Hope* (RRR); 1986—*Five Minutes After I Die* (Lad-Frith); 1987—*Holy War* (RRR); 1989—*Stairway to Heaven* (Ladd-Frith); 1990—*We Will Fight Back;* 1991—*Material World; The Father, the Son, and the Holy Ghost;* 1990—*The Gospel according to the Men in Black* (Minus Habens); 1991—*Hidden Beneath the Metal* (Ladd-Frith); 1994—*Stairway to the Gospel World* (Discordia); 1995—*Shock the Nation;* 1998—*Shades of Black* (Blacklight); *Lawnmower Man* (NoWhere Arts); 1999—*Sex, Sex, Sex* (Dark Vinyl); 2000—*Dreams Like These.*

www.humboldt1.com/~lfmusic/blackhouse

Blackhouse was the first Christian industrial band and indeed is regarded as one of the forerunners of industrial music, period. Personnel for the group is somewhat vague. Most sources list the two names above, but at some point "Blackhouse" began issuing statements in the first-person, which may or may not mean that Blackhouse had become a solo act: "There is no 'This Guy'. There is no 'That guy'. To put names and faces on a Spirit seems so wrong to me now. Blackhouse is who I am" (1999). Many albums also list Brian Ladd as playing "untuned guitars" or tape recorders, though it is unclear whether this means he was ever thought of as a member of the band.

As the list of instruments above may indicate, Blackhouse's music defies easy conceptualization. *Phantom Tollbooth* describes the sound of Blackhouse's industrial music as consisting of "clinks, clanks, sounds of sledgehammers and steam, synthesizers in pain, power-drill guitar samples, off-kilter beats, distant and disembodied vocals . . . and music imitating the cold, impersonal rhythms and sounds of factories." The albums differ drastically in what sounds they choose to incorporate. *Pro-Life* features a good deal of screaming against a background of hard white noise. *Hope Like a Candle* favors pounding, banging rhythms propelled by a distorted beatbox. *Five Minutes After I Die* is described by the group as taking the listener "through the klanging and banging sinews of shredded scrap metal to an eerily calm bed of tinkling bells and humming machinery." The title song to *Stairway to Heaven* (not a Led Zeppelin cover) features plodding electronic footsteps punctuated by piano stabs and backmasked vocals. *Father, Son, and Holy Ghost* actually features sitars on one number ("Men in Black") and includes a twenty-eight-minute opus called "The Holy Ghost." The sound of *Hidden Beneath the Metal* was described by one reviewer as akin to "rolling around a glass factory in a barrel." *Shock the Nation* introduces hip-hop sounds and clips from rock hits (AC/DC/Zeppelin/Hendrix) superimposed on the sound of a house sliding down a hill and exploding. Finally, *Dreams Like These* attempts to portray "the pure ambient atmospheric" sounds of "the dark landscape of the not so distant future of planet earth," such that an advertisement could promise, "you will hear the sounds of mother earth puking up the insides of lost mankind into your stereo."

Lyrics are few and far between, but some of the later Blackhouse works include rapping. Thus, on *Shades of Black,* we get this exhortation: "When you're feelin' real fly, and when you're feelin' real dapper / Remember clothes don't make the man—they're just the wrapper." Blackhouse also favors postmodern Derrida wordplays: "Sex, Sex, Sex, it sells, sells, sells / Sex, sex, sex, it's cells, cells, cells." Indeed, the group's name is a pun, presenting both the political antithesis to American power structures (located in the White House) and providing a positive alternative to the music of a mainstream industrial band named Whitehouse.

In the world at large, hardcore industrial music (and to a lesser extent the tamer version popularized by artists like Nine Inch Nails) is associated with negative themes: nihilism, pornography, sadomasochism, and a rampant drug culture. "We took the body of Industrial," Blackhouse claims in an official statement, "shook it up, dusted it off, and brought out the good in it. Or, perhaps, we injected good into a movement based on self-destruction. We helped to resuscitate it and propel it into a new direction." According to *HM* magazine, Blackhouse was forced early on to be a studio-only band because their concerts drew violent protests both from non-Christians (who opposed the religious content) and from Christians (who opposed the style). But the controversies did not end there. The Blackhouse album *We Will Fight Back* originally featured as cover art a picture of a crucified rabbit—an idea first advanced by Larry Flynt as the cover for his pornographic magazine *Hustler* after his (short-term) conversion to Christianity. The idea behind such an obscenely gruesome picture was to shock viewers into considering the real meaning of Easter (Did a bunny die for your sins?). Still, a public outcry led to the cover being withdrawn. The members of Blackhouse maintain they never had any say in its selection. Later the Blackhouse track "Word" (in the version that appeared on *Stairway to the Gospel World*) was featured in the X-rated fetish film *Swelter in Vogue* (which, incidentally, starred Mark Arm of the rock group Mudhoney). Still later, Blackhouse presented the album titled *Sex, Sex, Sex* with a note saying, "I dedicate this CD to all the Warriors. Don't let them die in vain: Always use a condom and practice safe sex!"

Later Christian industrial bands would include **Deitiphobia** and **Saviour Machine,** both of whom avoided Blackhouse's excesses and attracted wider followings. Perhaps the last word on Blackhouse should be spoken not by a Christian reviewer but by a critic for *Industrial Music* electronic magazine: "I'm sure there must be an audience out there somewhere that would appreciate this avant garde style of electronic music, but I'm afraid it would be a rather small, elite group of individuals."

Scott Blackwell

1992—*Walk on the Wild Side* (Myx); *1800 Seconds of Motion, A Myx'd Christmas;* 1993—*A Myx'd Trip to a Gospel House; A Myx'd Trip to a Gospel*

House II; Once Upon a Time; 1994—*The Real Thing;* 1997—*Clubhouse* (N'Soul); 1999—*In the Beginning: Greatest Hits 1991–1995* (KMG).

Scott Blackwell is the king of Christian disco (or "dance music," to use the euphemism currently in vogue). He has spun his fingers in all the subcategories of that genre, including techno, house, and rave. Blackwell began as a DJ, playing songs in New York dance clubs (including Studio 54), and he parlayed his abilities into a ministry that provides soundtracks for Christian-based clubs where youth can dance to inspiring and godly lyrics. He began to work as a mixmaster (the album *Clubhouse* is actually a compilation of twenty tunes by a variety of artists, mixed by Blackwell) and then finally started to write and record his own music. Eventually, he founded the company N'Soul to foster projects by other Christian artists interested in dance. As a producer, he has been responsible for a series of albums called the *Nitro Praise* project.

Blackwell's early albums often feature the vocal talents of Sandra Stephens and Allegra Parks. *Walk on the Wild Side* includes a rollicking original composition, "Not Going Back" and a cover of Evelyn King's "Love Come Down." The *Gospel House* albums attempt to bridge dance music with traditional gospel by presenting house versions of songs by **Edwin Hawkins** ("O Happy Day") and **Andraé Crouch** ("Take Me Back," "All the Way," "Holding On"). *Once Upon a Time* features songs that are intended to challenge young believers to be more faithful to Christ. The chorus to the title track insists, "This ain't no fairy tale and there ain't no happy ending, unless you let Jesus in your heart." The verses, meanwhile, touch on a wide variety of problems illustrating what's wrong with the world today, from racism to sexual promiscuity ("it's meant for a lifetime, not hit-and-run time"). The album *The Real Thing,* on which Blackwell collaborated with Zarc Porter of **World Wide Message Tribe,** presents mostly instrumental tracks intended for celebration.

The Bible encourages dancing, and the great majority of Christians in the world have no problem with it. The theological slant of Blackwell's ministry, however, tends to put him in league with a fundamentalist minority for whom the legitimacy of dancing is questionable. Thus, he has been a controversial figure within his chosen circle and has had to be an apologist for Christian dancing. As such, he is cautious: "I don't endorse dancing for every Christian. If it's an area where someone has a problem, then they shouldn't do it."

Christian radio hits: "Not Goin' Back" (# 14 in 1992).

Terry Blackwood

1975—*All Things Work Together* (Word); date unknown—*Keep Holding On* (Bread and Honey).

Terry Blackwood (b. 1945) was born into gospel music as the son of Doyle Blackwood, founder of the Blackwood

Brothers Quartet. He earned a Business Administration degree from Memphis State University, sang with J. D. Sumner and the Stamps, and then joined **The Imperials.** In 1976 he and **Sherman Andrus** left that group to form **Andrus, Blackwood, and Co.** Blackwood's two solo albums feature inspirational songs in the vein of what would come to define adult contemporary music. Terry Blackwood married **Cheryl Prewitt,** who was Miss America 1980. They divorced a few years later.

Blah

Alex Rosas, voc.; Jacob Garza, bass (– 1998); Darrell Leach (– 1998) // Jameson Becker, drums (+ 1998); Jeremy Carlson, gtr. (+ 1998); James Jenkins, bass (+ 1998). 1996—*Born Lost and Helpless* (Rescue); 1998—*Blah* (BulletProof).

Blah plays mostly simple, fast punk-rock songs on the order of groups like **MxPx** or Green Day. They chose their name as an acronym for the title of an early album. The project titled simply *Blah* features seventeen tracks which have an average length of less than two minutes per song. The group boldly proclaims its convictions in songs like "Gangster Punk" ("Christ is why we exist") and "The Coop" (a basic conversion-from-drinking-and-drugs testimony). Rosas refers to his sinful self as "a rotten stinkin' jerk" on "Not My Own." The antidrug song "Stop Shooting Up" borrows from Neil Young's "The Needle and the Damage Done." A few songs break the predictable punk mold, as in "Stone Me," which introduces some touches of ska, and "Eye 2," an instrumental with elements of surf music. The song "145," based on the Psalm of that number, incorporates some southern blues with a rockabilly edge.

Ric Blair

1997—*Always by My Side* (Graceland); 2000—*Break the Walls* (KMG).

Ric Blair is a Celtic folk-rock singer with an impressive résumé. An actual descendant of John Blair (personal chaplain to *Braveheart* hero William Wallace), he was a member of an early Christian group called The Willoughby Wilson Band, then took to writing film scores for Hollywood motion pictures and cable network movies. He also cowrote the song, "Never for Nothing," which became **Margaret Becker**'s first hit record. Blair's voice is often compared to that of James Taylor, but he sings to the accompaniment of such Celtic instruments as Irish fiddle, tin whistle, uilleann pipes, and djembre. His first album includes the song "The Red Sea," which rehearses the Exodus story with a call to "never doubt God's mighty hand." Other standout songs include "Author of Love," addressing the theme of loneliness, and "Don't Close Your Eyes," a plea to be attentive to those in need.

For trivia buffs: Ric Blair was once Sheryl Crow's guitar teacher.

Blame Lucy

Doug Meacham, voc., bass; Ryan Smith, gtr.; Matt Blair, gtr.; Mike Niklaus, drums. 1998—*Gong Show* (Gray Dot).

www.blamelucy.com

Blame Lucy was described by *The Lighthouse* electronic magazine as playing "straight-ahead rock and roll music with bold Christian statements." The central Ohio group was founded by Doug Meacham, who formerly fronted a Christian heavy metal group called Legacy and became assistant pastor of Grace Chapel Community Church in Westerville, Ohio. The name was chosen by listeners in a contest sponsored by the local radio station; it is short for "Blame Lucifer." Meacham clarifies, "We don't blame Lucifer for causing us to sin, but for tempting us to fall." The group strives for a post-grunge modern rock sound somewhere in the area of that achieved by Matchbox 20 or **Common Children.** They have a trademark for creative lyrics. The song "Waikiki" compares heaven to a day at the beach. The title track to *Gong Show* takes 1 Corinthians 13:1 as its chorus while evoking images of the old TV show. The album's strongest cut, "Saturate," is about (in Meacham's words) "fully drenching one's life in God's amazing love."

The Blamed

Bryan Gray, voc., gtr.; Jim Chaffin, drums (– 2000); Eric Churchill, bass, voc. (–1995); Jake Landau, gtr., voc. (–1995) // Gary Ottosi, bass (+ 1995, –1998); Jeremy Moffett, voc. (+ 1995, –1998); John Hansen, bass (+ 1998, – 1999); Jeff Locke, gtr., bass (+ 1999, – 2000); Matt Switaj, gtr., voc. (+ 1999); Christopher Witala, bass (+ 2000); Trevor Witala, voc. (+ 2000). 1994—*21* (Tooth and Nail); 1995—*Frail*; 1998—*Again* (Grrr); 1999—*Forever*; 2000—*Germany* [EP]; 2001—*Isolated Incident.*

www.theblamed.com

The ever-changing hardcore punk band The Blamed has produced four albums, each with a different lead vocalist and a distinct sound. Constant member Bryan Gray has also worked with other bands, including **Rainbow Rider, The Echoing Green, Joy Electric, Mortal,** and **Six Feet Deep;** the spelling of his first (a.k.a. Brian) and last (a.k.a. Grey) name varies with almost every project. Drummer Jim Chaffin was in **The Crucified.** Vocalist Jeremy Moffet was once drummer for **Deliverance** and later for **Stavesacre.** Landau left The Blamed to play with **Chatterbox.** The Witala twins (Christopher and Trevor) both played with **Left Out** and **Sheesh,** Matt Switaj and Bryan Gray had also played with **Left Out,** making the 1999+ incarnation of The Blamed virtually indistinguishable from that (also constantly changing) band.

The debut record takes its name from the fact that it was recorded in twenty-one hours. Its sound is proudly described as old school punk along the lines of Minor Threat or Black Flag. It features numerous guest appearances: Mark Salomon (**The Crucified, Stavesacre**), Jeff Bellew (**Chatterbox, Stavesacre**), Daren Diolosa (**Klank**), Scott Silletta (**PlankEye, Fanmail**), as well as members of **P.O.D.** and **Circle of Dust.** Ronnie Martin of **Joy Electric** produced the album and wrote one song. *Frail* earned much praise for Moffet's vocals and also for the variety of material represented: melodic tunes like "Breeze" alongside thrashing hardcore songs like "Declaration Dead" and a crunchy cover of **The Crucified**'s "Guy in a Suit and the Pope."

In the interim between their second and third projects, the group not only changed labels but also associated with Jesus People U.S.A., the socially active Christian community in Chicago with which **Ballydowse, Cauzin' Efekt, Crashdog, The Crossing, Headnoise, Resurrection Band, Seeds, Sheesh,** and **Unwed Sailor** have all been associated. Not surprisingly, *Again* evinces more of a social conscience ("Live by Truth," "Covered"), earning The Blamed points in the lyrical department. The song "Do Sin Grate" is a cry for healing from self-inflicted wounds. Musically, however, the record introduces metal touches in ways that did not inspire critical acclaim. To be sure, *HM* magazine loved it, but elsewhere reviewers bemoaned Moffett's departure (to join **Stavesacre** as drummer) and noted that the vocals on *Again* are screamed in a strained and hardly intelligible voice. "God Has Mercy" was singled out as a song on which the style worked ("portraying a scream of anguish from a soul that is suffering"). "Deny" was similarly praised for its innovation (e.g., the use of a children's choir). Such creativity is even more in evidence on *Forever*. Here, Chaffin is joined by drummer Lance Garvin of **Living Sacrifice** on several cuts to produce a double-team tribal pounding. Hidle Bialchi of **The Crossing** provides what *Phantom Tollbooth* called "cool Celtic chick vocals" on the song "4/20/99." The song "Pistol Whipped" from *Forever* chides the gay-bashing that resulted in the murder of Matthew Shepard ("You made a martyr from a broken man . . . violence is a coward's tool"). Another song from the same album, "Beyond Your Passion Is His Passion," is written in opposition to the death penalty. The title track to *Forever* shouts the Christian gospel to a speed metal chorus: "Forever! Forgiven! Sanctified! / By the blood of Christ / Set apart to give God the glory / And love one another."

The band re-formed with the Witala brothers in 1999 and changed their style again, this time moving away from metal to fuse more classic rock influences into their basic format. *The Phantom Tollbooth* called the new sound of *Forever* "a more innovative form of hardcore." *HM* called it "manic rock 'n' roll." Matt Switaj would admit to the influences of groups like The

Who and Led Zeppelin. "This Moment" and "Social Calls" exemplify the catchy combination of melodic hooks and killer guitar riffs. "At Least We Have Each Other" and "The Piano Is Playing Our Song" provide softer moments with lyrical encouragement to let emotion overcome pride in struggling relationships: "Don't walk away, don't say a word / Embrace her like you'll never see her again" ("At Least We Have Each Other"). *Isolated Incident* continues in the new direction, inspiring some comparisons to Fugazi.

The Blamed are quick to identify themselves as "a ministry band." On one level, they say that they were inspired by the amount of violence and anger in the punk scene to "provide good punk music without motivating people to hurt each other." But beyond that, evangelism is a first priority: "We want to reach unsaved kids." The final track on *Germany* states, "To give hope to those who have no hope / We will reveal ourselves."

Michael Kelly Blanchard

1973—*Canticle* (Koinonia); 1977—*Quail* (Gotz); 1980—*Love Lives On*; 1983—*A Common Thread*; 1985—*Michael Kelly Blanchard in Concert*; 1986—*The Attic Tapes*; 1988—*The Holy Land of the Broken Heart*; 1989—*Be Ye Glad* (Diadem); 1991—*Mercy in the Maze*; 1994—*A View out the Window*; 1996—*Imago Dei/Image of God* (Goliard); 1998—*Car Tunes: The Lighter Side of Michael Kelly Blanchard*; 1999—*In From the Cold.*

www.m-k-blanchard.org

A singer/songwriter in the tradition of Gordon Lightfoot, Michael Kelly Blanchard has been performing Christian folk songs on guitar and piano for close to three decades now. He often performs with longtime friend **Noel Paul Stookey,** and he wrote one of the latter's best songs, an introspective biblical meditation called "Then the Quail Came." His wife Greta sometimes sings with him. Blanchard's songs have been performed by such artists as **Acappella, Debby Boone, Steve Green,** and Peter, Paul, and Mary, with his biggest hit being the song "Be Ye Glad," which became something of a signature tune for the group **Glad.** The album *Be Ye Glad* features his own version of that song, as well as "Danny's Downs," a track that both Stookey and Peter, Paul, and Mary would perform about a boy born with Down's Syndrome. Blanchard has also written two musical dramas *(Gamaliel, Heart Guard)* and a book of poetry and prose *(Unsung Heroes).*

Blaster the Rocketman (a.k.a. **Blaster the Rocketboy**)

Personnel list unavailable. As Blaster the Rocketboy: 1995—*Disasteroid* (Boot to Head); 1996—*Succulent Space Food for Teething Vampires.* As Blaster the Rocketman: 2000—*The Monster Who Ate Jesus* (Jackson Rubio).

The Indianapolis-based Blaster the Rocketboy/man is one of the more original acts in contemporary Christian music. In terms of musical style, think Dead Kennedys, but in terms of lyrics, They Might Be Giants. Otto Jack describes their music as "surfpopcowdeathforgirls," which may not help much, but does reveal something about their penchant for thinking outside of boxes. Actually, the sound is just basic punk with some influence from '60s surf music and '50s rockabilly. It is the aforementioned lyrics that take them completely to left field. On that score, Jack also describes Blaster as famous for G.A.G. ("Girls Are Gross") songs, because they don't sing about love or romance. What they *do* sing about is science fiction, often with some kind of Christian twist. The songlist for *Succulent Space Food,* for instance, includes "American Werewolf," "Ghouls of the Night," "Man-Eating Plants," and "The First in a Long Line of Cute Robots." The Christian connections are often rather strained (e.g., comparing a vampire's lust for blood to our need for the blood of Christ). The song "Wolverine" from *Disasteroid* appears to be about a character from the *X-Men* comic book, but for some reason features the line, "Jesus is our milk and he does a body good." *The Monster Who Ate Jesus* draws heavily on C. S. Lewis's trilogy of science fiction novels, especially *That Hideous Strength.* Most of the songs relate in some way to modern science's attempts to remove God from human equations (hence the titular monster).

Bleach

Sam Barnhart, gtr.; Davy Baysinger, voc.; Matt Gingerich, drums; Bradley Ford, gtr., kybrd. (– 1999); Todd Kirby, bass (– 1999) // Russ Fox, bass (+ 1999). 1996—*Space* (ForeFront); 1998—*Static*; 1999—*Bleach.*

www.bleached.com

Bleach was formed by five students at Kentucky Christian College, the same school that gave the world **Audio Adrenaline** a few years before. They burst on to the Christian music scene with a critically acclaimed debut album and quickly became one of the most popular alternative rock bands in the Christian subculture (neck and neck with **Skillet,** who debuted the same year). Bleach has crafted catchy, garage-pop songs that feature emotive nasal vocals layered over fuzzy guitars. Their name was chosen to symbolize the cleansing effect of the blood of Christ.

The first album, *Space,* was produced by Barry Blair of **Audio Adrenaline.** It scores with "Epidermis Girl," a Weezer-ish tune about desiring love that is more than skin deep, and with "Cold and Turning Blue," a haunting song about the spiritual status of one's unsaved friends. Other standouts include the somewhat precious "Perfect Family" and "Cannonball," which sounds very much like the Smashing Pumpkins doing a worship song. *Static* took Bleach to even greater heights, reinvent-

ing the group as a pop band. Everything on the album bounces, as melodic songs ("Code of the Road" and "Rundown Town") mix in with pull-out-the-stops rockers. Notable in the latter category are "Hurricane" (complete with musical atmospheric effects) and "Rock and Roll" (featuring Davy Baysinger's best Mick Jagger). Both the title track to *Static* and "Super Good Feeling" were played on episodes of TV's *Dawson's Creek,* and the band played the latter song live on *The Jenny Jones Show* when they became the first Christian band ever to perform on the tabloid-talk program. True to its name, "Super Good Feeling" is a joyful, boisterous song that belies Bleach's retail classification as hard rock—rather, on *Static,* they tend to play a somewhat harder version of the new fun rock made popular by **All Star United.** The song "Drive" is a tongue-in-cheek number worthy of ASU's chic; it is about witnessing to the neighborhood by playing Christian rock *very* loud on the car stereo. Repeated production assistance by Blair also gave the band the sound of an underclass **Audio Adrenaline** at times (note the whoop-it-up chorus of "Warp Factor Five"). For the third album, Bleach recruited Russ Fox from **Seven Day Jesus.** *Bleach* is distinctive in its inclusion of several songs that evoke a psalm-like attitude of worship ("You," "You Are Good," "All To You"). Otherwise, "Once Again Here We Are" revisits the ultra-catchy feel of *Static,* while "Straight Shooter" is just basic, solid rock and roll. "Breathe" evokes renewed comparisons to Weezer, while "All That's Sweet" and "Good" are more in the R.E.M./Radiohead vein of modern rock. *Musicforce* chose the hard-rocking tracks "Race" and "Sun Stands Still" as the album's highlights.

The KCC boys maintained from the first that their band was just an alternative route to what brought them to the Bible college in the first place: ministry. They write and perform songs that they hope will drive home spiritual messages, mostly aimed at edifying or convicting the Christians who make up most of their audience. The packaging, however, is winsome and effective. "I don't want to be your priest / I just want to be your friend," Baysinger sings on the title song to *Space.*

Note: The group Bleach described here is in no way related to the mainstream band of that name—a British quartet led by Nick and Neil Singleton who released a self-titled debut in 1991 and an album called *Killing Time* in 1992.

Christian radio hits: "Super Good Feeling" (# 1 in 1998); "Code of the Road" (# 9 in 1998).

Dove Awards: 1997 Alternative/Modern Rock Song ("Epidermis Girl").

The Bleed

Nick Nack, gtr., voc., bass, drums; Odd Job, gtr., voc. 1996—*Ouch!* (Rugged).

The names above are obviously fake—no one knows for certain who The Bleed really was. The mystery band delivered one hard alternative album. Their guitar-driven sound was compared to Stone Temple Pilots, while the duet vocals summoned images of Alice in Chains. Lyrics focused on the greatness of God ("Love Over All") and the smallness of humanity ("Stay the Same"). Rumors flew about that the members were well-known Christian rockers who wanted to make some new music incognito. **Rex Carroll** (also of Fierce Heart, **Whitecross,** and **King James**) has been recognized, and he now even lists the album on the discography posted at his personal website, with this intriguing tag: "A curious piece whereby management chose to dis-allow named credits." Oh, so it was those suits in management that kept everything mysterious. Well, at any rate, The Bleed should not be confused with the Swedish death metal band that is called simply Bleed.

Blenderhead

Ed Carrigan, gtr.; Matt Johnson, drums; Bill Power, voc., bass; Eben Haase, gtr. (−1995); Paul Henry, bass (−1995) // Tyler Vander Ploeg, gtr. (+ 1998). 1994—*Prime Candidate for Burnout* (Tooth and Nail); 1995—*Muchacho Vivo*; 2000—*Figureheads on the Forefront of Pop Culture*.

Blenderhead is a Christian punk-rock band from Seattle. The band is fronted by Bill Power, who in high school days led a Southern California punk band called Point Blank. Blenderhead's lineup for their first album also included three members of the defunct Christian band **Don't Know** (Ed Carrigan, Paul Henry, and Matt Johnson); Johnson would go on to be a member of **Roadside Monument, Ninety Pound Wuss,** and **Raft of Dead Monkeys**.

The debut Blenderhead release contains a dozen songs that Power describes as "angst-ridden angry emo-punk." It makes no reference to God or to Christ or to any obvious tenets of the Christian faith, but features songs with hard-hitting lyrics that expose the hypocrisies of a superficial life. "Alcohol House" deals with the denials of addiction: the song opens with the words, "When I come home tonight / You will tremble with fear / And even though I hurt you / I really love you dear." It continues in that vein, against a chorus of phrases like "We will get along," "I can quit anytime," and "Do not speak a word about this." Similar themes are found in the hard-rock "Soapbox," with its refrain of "I'll try to get it right this time," and in the more melodic, plodding "Internalize." Blenderhead's sophomore effort, *Muchacho Vivo,* showcases a more pop sound, leading *Slug* magazine to comment, "the songs vary from choppy down-stroke Gang of Four guitar to manic strumming over aggressive power pop songs." It includes a cover of the Talking Heads' "Once in a Lifetime." Blenderhead broke up in 1995 when Power put on a (metaphorical) suit and became Vice President of Operations at Tooth and Nail. They resurfaced with a new album five years later. *Figureheads on the Forefront of Pop Culture* displays more of an alternative rock sound than the first two projects, with expansion beyond simple punk screaming on tracks like "Versatile Solutions for Modern Living" and "Emerald City Indie Queen." That latter song is a sarcastic jibe at a female poser ("you'll have to climb real high to get over yourself"). Several other songs testify to love gone bad with lyrics that become somewhat monotonously misogynist ("I Gave Her My Heart, She Gave Me a Pen"; "You Know Who You Are").

For trivia buffs: a very early lineup of Blenderhead included Bryan Gray of **The Blamed** on bass. They recorded one single, "Invasion of the Body Snatchers," which turns up now and then on compilation discs.

Blessed Hope

David Rios, gtr., voc.; Jim Golden, voc.; David Burgin, gtr., voc. // Bill Bradford, kybrd., voc.; Pat Patton, bass, voc.; Don Kobayashi, drums; Doug Krupinski, gtr. No albums.

Blessed Hope was one of the many influential folk-pop bands of the early Jesus movement. The group was founded by Dave Burgin, who had been a member of the seminal country rock band **Joy.** Blessed Hope never recorded an album but did place some songs on compilation records, including one song on the record that remains the most historically significant Christian album of all time. The song, "Something More" (written by Burgin and David Rios), appeared on Maranatha's *The Everlastin' Living Jesus Music Concert* (1971). The words echo familiar themes of the Jesus people: "We've got something more than just salvation / We've got something more than just religion." At that time, the group appears to have been just a trio. Burgin eventually left the group for health reasons, and others joined, though it is difficult to tell who plays and sings on which successive songs. The addition of Bill Bradford would radically alter the band's sound, as he was a Leon Russell-style piano player with amazing keyboard skills.

A Blessed Hope song written by Jim Golden called "Never Knew the New Day" appears on *Maranatha Two* (1972) but is nothing special. *Maranatha Three: Rejoice in the Lord* (1974) offers "Never Be Lonely" (also by Golden), which is far more interesting and a total change of pace: a rollicking blues shuffle complete with lots of rinky-tink piano and near-falsetto vocals. But "So Much" (by Bill Bradford) represents the group's highpoint. The latter song appears on *Maranatha Four* (1974), the best of the Maranatha compilation albums, and though it moves toward adult contemporary balladry it avoids the formulaic song structures that would eventually mar that genre. Thematically, it moves from soulful expression of thanksgiving ("You have given me so much, my Lord"), to inquisition of the audience ("Where are you going tonight my good friend?") and then concludes with a fabulous saxophone solo. Maranatha! Music's concert library contains a cassette tape (catalog number CLC-1) featuring thirteen songs by Blessed Hope.

Arthur Blessitt and the Eternal Rush

1972—Soul Session at His Place.

Arthur Blessitt is not a musician, nor was he a member of the band Eternal Rush (which did include Jim McPheeters, brother of **Charlie McPheeters,** and O. J. Peterson). Rather, Blessitt is a Southern Baptist evangelist who supplied mostly spoken-word vocals on the above album. To be more specific, Blessitt was the exotic hippie preacher who ministered to the street people in Hollywood in the late '60s and early '70s. He founded the famous His Place nightclub on Sunset Strip, which offered an alternative to the scores of bars and strip joints and became the grand exemplar for the Christian coffeehouses that seemed to spring up everywhere in the early '70s. His Place was open all night, offering free food, drinks (coffee and Kool Aid), clothing, and, of course, music. At midnight, Blessitt would preach messages heavily laden with '60s slang to a congregation composed of (in his words) "acid heads, speed freaks, bikers, prostitutes, hippies, pushers, Hell's Angels, and Black Panthers." A number of semi-celebrity conversions ensued, including Glenn Schwartz of James Gang, PG&E, and finally the **All Saved Freak Band.** Blessitt had a flair for sensationalism to match that of certain Old Testament prophets. His preaching had all the subtlety of a circus barker. He would call out lines like, "What will make you feel better than booze . . . chicks . . . anything in the world?" with the well-trained audience shouting "Jesus!" in response to each entreaty. He conducted public "toilet services" where converts would dispose of their drugs, he picketed pornographic bookstores, and—when his lease was threatened—he chained himself to a twelve-foot cross and initiated a Ghandi-style starvation fast. Eventually, Blessitt decided that God had told him to carry that cross on a hike that would take him to every country on earth. He has been fulfilling that commission ever since, with 281 nations traversed at last count. He is now listed in the Guinness Book of World Records as having undertaken "the World's Longest Walk." Blessitt also wrote several books about the Jesus movement, the most important of which were *Life's Greatest Trip* (Word, 1970) and *Turned On to Jesus* (Hawthorn, 1971).

The album *Soul Session at His Place* has three parts. First Blessitt delivers a sixteen-minute sermon. Then the band Eternal Rush offers three songs of basic garage rock with Christian lyrics. Finally, as the main event, Blessitt offers what he calls a "Soul Session," in which he offers another message, this time delivered in a sing-song voice against the backdrop of gospel piano, with the band singing "Je-e-e-sus" mournfully in the background: "Let me tell you this, brother, if you really want to get turned on, I mean, where the trip's headed, just pray to Jesus, and he'll give you a high that will keep you for eternity." *Jesus Music* describes the album as an "oddball relic from another time." The "Soul Session" song is also available on *The Rock Revival: Original Music from the Jesus Movement* (Sonrise, 1994).

For trivia buffs: On *Soul Session* Blessitt describes his vision for a transformed Hollywood in which the Whiskey-a-Go-Go would become the Jesus-a-Go-Go and the Classy Cat would become the Saved Cat. That didn't happen, but the building that was His Place did become the even more famous (rebuilt) House of Blues, owned by Dan Aykroyd.

Blindside

Marcus Dahlstrom, drums; Simon Grenehed, gtr.; Christian Lindskog, voc.; Tomas Noslund, bass. 1997—*Blindside* (Solid State); 2000—*A Thought Crushed My Mind.*

www.algonet.se/~blndside/index.htm

Blindside hails from Stockholm, Sweden, but unlike Abba, Ace of Base, or the Cardigans, the band is not a showcase for attractive blonde female singers. Instead, Blindside is a hardcore rap group offering the Christian music scene an international version of the sound associated with bands like **P.O.D., Every Day Life,** and **Project 86.** First organized under the name Underfree, the group has been playing together since 1994. Unaware of American groups like Korn and Limp Bizkit, they created their sound without any imitative intention. Still, as *7ball* magazine puts it, "Christian Lindskog raps, sings, and screams at a fever pitch matched only by Korn's Jonathan Davies." Simon Grenehed describes the "main focus" of Blindside as being "to have fun together and dedicate our music to Jesus Christ."

The first album kicks into high gear with its energetic opener, "Invert," as Lindskog belts out, "Start the motor, let the engine spin / Give it fuel so it can't stop within." As it progresses, the song turns out to be a prayer to God to be bolder in life and witness. "Teddybear" deals with the tendency to grasp on to God for security and comfort, only to cast God aside when seeming maturity lends the illusion that all is well. The sophomore album, *A Thought Crushed My Mind,* also garnered praise from critics (Christian and otherwise) for its incorporation of (some) melodic singing into the chaotic aggression. Violins are featured on several tracks. The song "Nothing But Skin" alternates back and forth between choral singing (with violins) and chaotic hardcore guitar. The overall sound of the album diverges from the Korn-ish rapcore of the first release toward more of the hardcore European metal associated with groups like **Selfmindead** (also from Sweden, actually, but no pretty blonde women there either). The song "King of the Closet" made it into mainstream markets overseas, being featured on Swedish radio and European MTV. It offers confession of an unhealthy penchant for withdrawal into what appear to be safe arenas of privacy: "The heart pounds for love; pride says no." Another standout song, "Nara," has lyrics in Swedish.

Bliss Bliss

Lang Bliss, voc.; Reneé García, voc. 1995—*Bliss Bliss* (R.E.X.).

Bliss Bliss is a husband and wife duo composed of successful solo artist **Reneé García** and the man whose last name she took in 1986. The latter was a respected Christian musician in his own right, having performed as a session drummer for many artists, including a stint as a tour-band member of **Geoff Moore and The Distance.** García's Motown style and Bliss' preference for progressive rock are both evident in the musical mating that yielded their single album. The result is an R&B inflected Euro-pop sound similar to that associated with the Eurythmics or Peter Gabriel. Lyrical themes focus not only on the singers' relationship with God, but also on lessons for human relationship garnered from their marriage. "Love and Devotion" is a love song to humanity in the voice of God. "Building Bridges" stresses the need for love and cooperation to make it through life. "Fight for Peace" uses the ironic imagery of its title to express the idea that peace of mind can sometimes be found only by those with the nerve to make radical changes in their life.

Christian radio hits: "Fight for Peace" (# 12 in 1995); "When the World's Asleep" (# 11 in 1995); "Building Bridges" (# 13 in 1995).

Blood Brotherz

Andrew G., voc.; Connie T., voc. 1996—*Excellent* (Good Newz); 1999—*The Second Coming.*

The Blood Brotherz are a Jamaican duo composed of two relatively anonymous men who may or may not be actual blood brothers. Though both were apparently born and raised in Jamaica, the group is now located in Boston and makes albums of reggae music with a strong dancehall sound. The songs typically feature overt biblical lyrics, and Andrew G. describes their focus as being to "reach the unsaved." The band has toured with numerous mainstream reggae acts, as well as opening Christian tours for artists like **Fred Hammond** and **Kirk Franklin.**

Bloodgood

Michael Bloodgood, bass; Les Carlsen, voc.; Mark Welling, drums (−1989); David Zaffiro, gtr. (−1989) // Paul Jackson, gtr. (+ 1989); Kevin Whisler, drums (+ 1989, − 1991); Tom Heintz, kybrd. (+ 1993); David Huff, drums (+ 1993); David McKay, kybrd. (+ 1993); Paul Rorabeck, drums (+ 1993). 1986—*Bloodgood* (Frontline); 1987—*Detonation;* 1988—*Rock in a Hard Place;* 1989—*Out of the Darkness* (Intense); 1991—*The Collection; All Stand Together* (Broken Again); 1993—*To Germany with Love;* 1998—*Classic Archives.*

www.christianmusic.org/cmp/artists/index.cgi?command=Display_Detail&artist_id=272

Along with **Barren Cross, Stryper,** and **Resurrection Band,** the Seattle-based Bloodgood (formed in 1985) pioneered the sounds of Christian hard rock with a success that bands like **Agape** and **Barnabas** had only hinted at achieving. A typical '80s hair band in many respects, the group dressed in spandex and churned out loud, heavy metal music on the order of Twisted Sister, Ratt, or Quiet Riot, but employed more theatrics in their performances, such as were typical of **Alice Cooper** (lead singer Les Carlsen had a pre-Christian career as an actor-singer in a touring company of *Hair!*). Bloodgood produced five studio albums and several concert recordings. Mark Welling actually became a Christian after joining the band. **David Zaffiro** went on to become a successful producer, songwriter, and solo artist. Michael Bloodgood was also influential in the origins of **Grammatrain,** in which Paul Rorabeck was a member.

The band's first two albums are generally regarded as the Bloodgood "classics" (and both have been re-released on a single disc by KMG). The self-titled debut, produced by **Darrell Mansfield,** sets an apocalyptic tone with its warning to "Awake!" to the coming darkness. The album opens with a gang-vocal anthem called "Accept the Lamb" that immediately establishes the group as having the '80s-metal sound down pat. While that sound was already overworked and Bloodgood's debut was undeniably imitative, the group at least managed to pull off the Christian metal thing with more technical mastery and competence than many other groups would display. Most of the songs on *Bloodgood* ("Black Snake," "Demon on the Run," "Killing the Beast") draw on the imagery of Armageddon that was popular in '80s metal, but the summons is now for Christians to oppose whatever is against Christ through vigilant spiritual warfare ("Stand in the Light," "Soldier of Peace"). Assurance of victory and triumph are dominant themes.

Detonation is the group's legitimate masterpiece. The sophomore album shows a band developing its own recognizable sound. Lyrically, the band personalizes its spiritual warfare themes, such that the enemy might be seen as lurking within one's self ("Self-Destruction," "The Battle of the Flesh"). Along with this theological maturity comes a surprising liturgical turn: "Eat the Flesh" looks at the Lord's Supper, and the album's centerpiece is a pair of songs ("Crucify," "The Messiah") based on the events of Passion Week. It was in the tour to support *Detonation* that Bloodgood began to develop its theatric potential. During the songs "Crucify" and "Messiah," Carlsen would assume first the guise of Pilate and then, of Christ in dramatic portrayals. Ten years later, Doug Van Pelt of *HM* magazine could still describe the performance: "aided by strobe lights, guitarist David Zaffiro and bassist Michael Bloodgood would 'whip' Carlsen with their guitar headstocks, sending him writhing to the ground . . . he plays the part, making the audience wince in pain . . . the band immediately follows this with the passionate weeping song about the followers that took Jesus' dead body and prepared it for burial . . . it was a perfect marriage of visuals and sonics, truly a benchmark in the history of live Christian rock."

On *Rock in a Hard Place,* Bloodgood would allow a few pop sensibilities to creep in, prompting *CCM* magazine to suggest that they now sometimes sounded like a more intense, distorted version of Journey. That connection is especially evident on the songs "Never Be the Same" and "What Have I Done?" which almost sound like Journey outtakes. The song "She's Gone" came to be featured in another theatrical concert performance dramatizing the tragedy of suicide. Against a backdrop that portrayed an urban street scene with faux-brick wall, graffiti, and trash cans, Carlsen would offer impassioned pleas to a female dancer (played by his wife) via *Detonation*'s "Alone in Suicide" and then carry her seemingly lifeless body to the edge of the stage while singing "She's Gone." With major personnel changes, the group would revert to heavy metal on *Out of the Darkness,* which includes the Van Halen sound-alike "Hey! You" and a title track that is a crunchy and speedy paean to spiritual liberation. "America" is a typical conservative-Christian rant that laments the United States' decline from some holier state that it is supposed to have once occupied. Bloodgood's final studio release, *All Stand Together,* picks up where *Rock and a Hard Place* left off, moving away from speed metal toward modern hard rock sounds. The title song continues to expound the now-familiar theme of spiritual warfare, however, drawing on Gulf War imagery to describe the coalition of godly forces that occurs when the body of Christ acts as a unity. The album also revels in that metal-band staple, the power ballad, offering three instances of the genre: "Say Goodbye" is a sentimental tune about an elderly man losing his life partner; "Help Me" expresses the anguish of divorce; "I Want To Live in Your Heart" seems to borrow from Foreigner's "I Want To Know What Love Is" to assert the desire of Christ regarding every individual.

Like **Saviour Machine,** Bloodgood was more popular in Europe than in their homeland, so it is appropriate that their definitive live album *To Germany with Love* was recorded there. Here, the group's no-nonsense approach to evangelism becomes apparent. After performing the song "Crucify," front man Michael Bloodgood speaks to the crowd and leads them in

a sinner's prayer requesting Jesus to come into each person's heart to be his or her personal Lord and Savior. Then the band breaks into "Messiah" with its jubilant chorus: "Go! Go into the world and tell / Tell all creation He lives / He lives in the hearts of man / He's the Messiah!"

Christian radio hits: "I Want To Live in Your Heart" (# 9 in 1992).

Selena Bloom

1994—*Selena* (independent); 1995—*You're All I Need* (Free Rain); 1999—*Falling in Love* (Audience).

With a voice and style that begs comparison to Mariah Carey, Selena Bloom spent the latter half of the '90s touring relentlessly with messages of evangelistic and social concern. She shares openly about her life as a suicidal college student and her struggles to overcome eating disorders. She speaks and sings of the peace she has now found in Christ, and she serves as spokesperson for such social agencies as Food for the Hungry and American Leprosy Missions. Bloom had trouble finding a stable record company to harness her talents, but her third release, *Falling in Love,* finds her working with a crack band of Nashville's best musicians and with seasoned producers Jimmy Collins and **Peter Penrose** (who also contributed generously to the songwriting). It balances the danceable "Your Love Found a Way" and the funky rock tune "God's Love Remains" with adult contemporary ballads like "Whenever You Love Somebody."

For trivia buffs: In September of 1999, Selena Bloom was in the running to be a contestant on the popular TV show, "Who Wants to Be a Millionaire?" hosted by Regis Philbin. She made it to the final qualifying round for potential contestants but lost out on the round that would have actually placed her on the show.

Bloomsday

Mike Bravine, drums; Steve Leslie, bass; Blake Westcott, voc., gtr. 1996—*The Day the Colors Died* (Brainstorm); 1998—*Bloomsday* [EP] (Velvet Blue).

Few Christian bands ever got the alternative rock sound of the late '90s down better than Bloomsday, which is to say that the group had its own distinctive sound not quite like anything on commercial radio. The basic genre is the fluid, melodic-but-melancholic sound exemplified (sometimes) by groups like Blind Melon or Mazzy Starr. Like those bands, Bloomsday's creative time together would be short and their product meager—but substantial. *The Day the Colors Died* features two songs (the title track and "Just the Same") that could have been hits on mainstream college radio stations had the group not been pigeonholed as a Christian band. The lilting melodies of these tunes, however, are not characteristic of the album overall. "Blue Poetry" plods along for more than seven minutes of acoustic strumming, while "Song of Five" moves ominously through an array of haunting chords. The closing song, "Weight," drones on for more than twelve minutes in a hypnotic way that for some reason never quite gets boring. The album was produced by **Aaron Sprinkle** of **Poor Old Lu** and evinces his respect for musical subtlety and imagination. The lyrics are similarly subtle and intelligent, yet ripe with spiritual meaning for those with ears to hear. When the group broke up, an early indie EP was released as a parting souvenir. Westcott formed the general market band Saline with drummer Paul Mumaw of **Soulfood 76** and Ken Stringfellow of The Posies.

The Blues Apostles

Brother Robb, voc.; Kevin Dimmett [a.k.a. Boomer], bass; Jim Gumns [a.k.a. Bootch], drums; Alan Harvey [a.k.a. Large Al], gtr. 2000—*Blues to Soothe Your Soul* (independent).

Christian blues is a pretty small subset of the already not-very-large contemporary Christian music market, and underground (Christian) blues is tinier still. But that is where The Blues Apostles belong and that is where they reign: kings of the Christian blues underground. Located in Michigan City, Indiana, a stone's throw from Chicago, the band is fronted by Brother Robb, a pipefitter by day and a harp blowin' blues singin' evangelist by night. Their musical influences are not so much Christian artists like **Glenn Kaiser** and **Darrell Mansfield** as blues mainstays Muddy Waters, Little Walter, the Rev. Gary Dixon, and Mississippi John Hurt. The group's website proclaims their vision as being "to spread the simple truth of Jesus Christ to all people in real street language through our music and testimony with love and grace." They do this with unusually direct songs like "See the Light or Feel the Heat" and "Don't Let the Devil Ride." Brother Robb testifies to the drama of his own conversion in "Sledge Hammer Song": "Boozin' and losin' and fighting everything / Wimmin and sinnin and gettin' high as trees / Well the Lord took a hammer and man he let it swing / He let loose and knocked me to my knees." God is often referred to as "Big Daddy" as in the song "Big Daddy Shuffle." Many of the songs are up-tempo, but the slower ballad "Came and Bled and Died" seems to be a favorite among the group's fans.

BNB All Stars

Lenny Beh, drums, fiddle; Brad Davis, bass, voc.; Matt Davis, kybrd.; voc.; Nate Plante, trump.; Jeremiah Smith, gtr. 1999—*Man! These Cookies Rock!* (independent).

With an official motto of "Glorifying God through Nuttiness," the BNB All Stars from San Diego, California, combine elements of ska, polka, funk and '40s jazz into an unusual hybrid of sounds that they like to describe as "ice-cream truck music." There are occasional bits of disco and heavy metal in there now and then too. In 1998 the group participated in a local contest of some eight hundred groups to be chosen San Diego's "Best Independent Artist." The group originally tried calling itself the Bad News Bears but due to one of those pesky copyright infringement things had to opt for the acronym instead. Their album, like their live show, features mostly humorous songs with adolescent themes ("I Don't Play Basketball"; "PB&J: The Musical"). Every now and then a light message about being genuine or open-minded sneaks in ("Hypocrat," "Holy Monkey"). The group's website contains this "mission statement": "To bring one iota of joy into this cruel, dreary existence we call Life. . . . Also to break down negative stereotypes about Christian folk."

B.O.B.

Bob Bash, drums; Billybob Brown, voc.; Bobby Bogart, gtr.; Rob Cooper, trump.; Roberto Mondavi, sax.; Robert Slide, tromb.; Robbie Williams, bass; Roberta Wyte, kybrd., voc. 1999—*It's a Ska, Ska, Ska, Ska World* (KMG); *Ska-la-la-la-la.*

B.O.B. is a good-time Christian ska band that combines the looney fun of **Five Iron Frenzy** with the upfront piety of **The Supertones.** Their debut album features a good share of silly songs on the order of "(I Saw) Pastor Dancing," as well as a B-52s-like version of the old song of **The Newsboys,** "Not Ashamed." At the same time there is some fundamentalist chic, including a tribute to a "Homeschool Girl" (where the titular character is envied by a poor guy forced to learn he descended from monkeys) and a campy ode to virginity ("I'm Gonna Wait"). "Mission Trip To Mexico" rhymes "If I may say so" with the promise that salvation "won't cost you a peso." An occasionally serious song breaks through including the straightforward, creedal "What I Believe." Not to be outdone by **The Insyderz'** *Skalelluia* project, B.O.B. followed their debut album with a Christmas record that same year. It consists of a half dozen original songs (mostly silly ones about snowball fights, Christmas pageants, and putting lights on the doghouse) mixed in with ska versions of carols like "Deck the Halls" (which seems like it was always intended for a ska treatment) and "O Come, O Come Emmanuel" (which doesn't).

The letters in B.O.B.'s name stand for Bunch of Believers but the members obviously enjoy the playfulness of the acronym, as the phony first names given above attest. Unfortunately, their overnight success caused *another* Christian ska band named BOB to have to change its name (to Short for Robert).

Bob and Steve

Bob Houle, voc.; Steve Woodham, voc. No albums.

The duo known as Bob and Steve recorded only one song, a worshipful rendition of "Psalm 42" placed on one of Maranatha Music's influential compilation albums (*Maranatha Three: Rejoice in the Lord,* 1973). The song is significant not only because it is a piece of exceptional beauty but also because it marks one of a handful of early worship songs that would ultimately give rise to the modern praise and worship music movement that would transform the liturgies of most American churches by the end of the twentieth century. Steve Woodham, the composer of "Psalm 42," was involved in Calvary Chapel in Costa Mesa, California, in the early years of the Jesus movement. He teamed up with the otherwise unknown Bob Houle for the recording of "Psalm 42"; Houle sings the lead vocal, with Woodham on harmonies (and **Erick Nelson** playing an uncredited synthesizer). The pair toured with **Blessed Hope** and **Mustard Seed Faith.** Houle went on to get a Ph.D. in psychology. In 2000, Woodham (a barber in San Diego) would offer this remembrance: "In the late '70s I began to reexamine my beliefs and, being convinced the church was becoming too politically involved with right wing politics, antiabortion activities, antigay protests, and strong support for Ronald Reagan, I decided to focus more on secular music and living in a secular world." He admitted to still having "a warm and fuzzy feeling" about his days with Maranatha, and added, "I have the utmost respect for Pastor Chuck Smith (of Calvary Chapel); I just no longer accept all the doctrine I was taught." Erick Nelson regards another Woodham composition, "Caught on a Nail," as "perhaps the most memorable Maranatha song never recorded." Woodham continues to write and record on his own label.

Ray Boltz

1986—*Watch the Lamb* (Diadem); 1988—*Thank You*; 1989—*The Altar*; 1991—*Another Child to Hold*; 1992—*Moments for the Heart Collection*; *Seasons Change* (Word); 1994—*Allegiance*; 1995—*The Concert of a Lifetime* (Boltz); 1996—*No Greater Sacrifice*; 1997—*A Christmas Album*; 1998—*Honor and Glory*; 1999—*Moments for a Parent's Heart*; 2000—*The Classics.*

www.rayboltz.com

Ray Boltz wrote a little song called "Thank You" for his home pastor's appreciation day. It ended up propelling the singer from Muncie, Indiana, to unsought and unanticipated stardom, reaching Number One on Christian music's Inspirational chart. In 1990, "Thank You" was chosen Song of the Year by the Gospel Music Association. Boltz is an MOR singer who just writes and sings songs because it's what he "likes to do" and his freedom from all trappings of celebrity seems to be part of his appeal. *CCM* magazine once described his voice as having a "lived-in feel that sort of reminds you of how your next-door neighbor might sing."

Boltz's first album, *Watch the Lamb,* gained notice primarily for its title track and for an antiabortion song, "What Was I Supposed To Be?" The sophomore project was the one with the title song that hit big. "Thank You" remains one of Boltz's best-known songs, but that album also features tunes that bring out Boltz's humor ("Church Hop," sung in a doo-wop style). *The Altar* includes a title track that describes the gifts of God accessible through the sort of altar call prayers that are practiced in some denominations. "The Hammer" and "Feel the Nails" both focus on personalized application of Jesus' death on the cross. Boltz would continue to record mainly within the inspirational market, but in 1992 he offered an album (*Seasons Change*) that moved toward more radio-friendly adult contemporary pop. Two songs on that collection are especially notable for their upbeat messages about life: "Saving Grace" reflects on God's gracious guidance; "Seasons Change" promises that times of refreshment always lie ahead. With the album *Allegiance* Boltz experimented with a tougher sound and with tougher messages. "I Pledge Allegiance To the Lamb" suggests that violent persecution may be about to come to Christians in America. "The time is now," Boltz said in 1994, "when we could be arrested and even punished for our Christian values and beliefs." Many Christian music fans apparently drew inspiration from these projections, for the song became the biggest single ever on Christian music's Inspirational chart.

Boltz has excelled at writing worship songs ("Lion of Judah," "I Will Praise the Lord") and songs with the sort of story lyrics that often sustain country tunes. "Where I Met Jesus" tells of a woman who leads her husband to become a Christian before he dies. "What If I Give All?" relates the true story of a three-year-old boy who hears at a mission festival that a dime will buy a meal for the hungry. He pulls a dollar from his pocket and asks what that would buy. Told the answer, he then pulls out his other two dollars—all he has—and asks the question that gives the song its title. Notably, Boltz himself has a longtime association with Mission of Mercy, an organization that seeks to provide food and sponsorship for children in Calcutta. He has also worked with Teen Mania, an organization that sponsors mission trips for adolescents; his song "I Will Tell the World" was written on behalf of that group after Boltz saw how his own daughter benefitted from such a trip.

In all, Boltz has had twelve Number One songs on the Inspirational chart. He is never more effective than when he targets a particular audience: *Honor and Glory* is a tribute to Americans who have fought in service to their country (and to all who fight the good fight of faith); *Moments for a Parent's Heart* collects some of his most moving anthems to the grace and innocence of children, including "Another Child To Hold" and "What If I Give All?" In 2001, Boltz founded the label Spindust Records and defied stereotypes by signing the grunge/metal band **GS Megaphone** as the company's premiere act.

Christian radio hits: "What Was I Supposed To Be" (# 11 in 1986); "Saving Grace" (# 21 in 1992).

Dove Awards: 1995 Inspirational Song ("I Pledge Allegiance To the Lamb").

Bomb Bay Babies

Michael Knott, voc., gtr.; Jamie Makarczyk, bass, voc.; Neal Vorndran, drums, voc. 2000—*Bomb Baby Babies, Vol. 1* (Marathon).

Yet *another* **Michael Knott** project (cf. **Aunt Bettys, Browbeats, Cush, LSU, Strong Gurus**), the Bomb Bay Babies were no more or less than a 1987 sideline that took thirteen years to see the light of day. In between the **LSU** albums *Shaded Pain* and *Wakin' Up the Dead,* Knott decided to take a stab at mainstream success. Believing that '70s punk-rock was going to enjoy a revival, he put together a band that was first called Skinny Elvis and featured Brian Doidge (of **LSU, Aunt Bettys**). After Doidge left, they changed their name to Bomb Bay Babies and came up with a repertoire of original songs inspired musically by the New York Dolls and the Sex Pistols. The group enjoyed regional success, packing clubs like the Whiskey-a-Go-Go, and were signed to make an album. One thing led to another and . . . well, flash forward thirteen years. The album contains nineteen songs written by Knott—ten from the unreleased studio project and nine live tracks (including **LSU**'s "Waking Up the Dead"). On one live track, dedicated to any record company executives in the crowd, he sings the word "payola" over and over again to a tune reminiscent of the Kinks' "Lola." As with the **Aunt Bettys,** evidence of Christian faith is subtle at best.

Bon Voyage

Julie Martin, voc.; Jason Martin, gtr.; Travis, bass; Matt, drums; Gene, kybrd. 1998—*Bon Voyage* (BEC).

Ah, love. Jason Martin plays guitar for **Starflyer 59**—possibly the best Christian rock group of the '90s. Julie Martin sang background vocals for **Havalina Rail Co.** before she was a Martin. She took a job working for Tooth and Nail, Starflyer's record label. Jason and Julie met, she became a Martin, and together they produced an alterna-pop masterpiece. They had the help of three people with no last names (Gene is apparently Gene Eugene of **Adam Again** and Matt is possibly Matt McCartie of **The Throes** and **Driver**

Eight), but the album is mainly a duet: slick female vocals spread over Jason's incredible fuzz-tone guitar. Avid fans of **Starflyer 59** *love* Jason's hoarse whispered vocals, but the latter are admittedly an acquired taste, and less avid fans may sometimes wish he would just shut up and play the ax, or at least find someone who can sing for real. With Bon Voyage, they get their wish. Jason's guitar is still the big attraction here, but where that guitar is hard, Julie's voice is soft and smooth, giving Bon Voyage an imaginative leather and lace appeal—a bit like that achieved by the Jesus and Mary Chain when they asked Hope Sandoval to join them for a memorable tune. Lyrically, the album is mostly about being in love. It opens with a song called "Honeymoon" and it closes with Julie singing "La la la's." Along the way there is a sultry tune for which the pretty-much-only words are "Come on, baby, kiss my lips," and there is a gorgeous melodic ballad called "I Just Wanna Be with You." Other highlights include the surf-tinged "West Coast Friendship," the '80s sounding "You Got It, I Want It," and the straightforward "Together" and "You're Wonderful." BEC's official press release for the album stated that it just might "make you believe that the sweetness of new found love could last forever." That *is* the mood it evokes. Has there ever been another pop album made by two such talented people at the very moment they fell in love?

For trivia buffs: Julie Martin (before she was a Martin) played the title character in the video for **Starflyer 59**'s "A Housewife Love Song."

Booley (a.k.a. Booley House)

Peter Wilson, voc., kybrd.; Andrew Mitchell, gtr. (– 1999). As Booley House: 1997—*Lemonade* (Contraflow). As Booley: 1999—*Bathroom Floor* [EP] (Grassroots); 2000—*Bathroom Floor* (ICC).

www.benzineheadset.com

The duo known as Booley House became a solo act called simply Booley when Andrew Mitchell departed and Peter Wilson determined to carry on alone. Wilson, who shows the influence of Aimee Mann and Elvis Costello in his singing and songwriting, formerly fronted **dba,** one of the United Kingdom's better-known Christian bands. Alone, the Belfast artist has an acoustic singer/songwriter style, but he still sometimes performs with a full band, giving the material more pop-rock energy.

The first album by Booley House features the song "Time Is Right," which won an award for "Best Song for Peace" from the Northern Ireland Songwriter's Guild. The tune presents the contrasting feelings of two young people on either side of the unionist/nationalist split that divides that country. Wilson sings in English for the unionist side while guest vocalist

Cristiona Nic Shearraith sings in Gaelic for the nationalist side. The debut Booley House album also features guest vocals by **Joanna Hogg** (on "Take Me In" and "Pearl," an ambient instrumental with vocal effects but no lyrics) and by long-lost Barry Bynum of **Liberation Suite.**

Bathroom Floor was issued in two versions, as a seven-song EP by Grassroots, but also independently as a full-length eleven-track CD. Its title track is a song about hiding in a bathroom from relationship woes. "My Little Glory" recounts Wilson's testimony of how he once was lost but now is found. "Alright" is a socially conscious travelogue, recording disparities of justice observed on a train trip. "God on Your Side" is about a church leader involved in child abuse. "Let Me Bleed" is a curious prayer for God to allow the personal suffering that brings growth and long-term health.

Debby Boone

1977—*You Light Up My Life* (Curb); 1978—*Midstream*; 1979—*The Promise*; 1980—*Love Has No Reason*; *With My Song* (Lamb and Lion); 1983—*Surrender*; 1984—*Choose Life*; 1987—*Friends for Life*; 1988—*Reflections*; 1989—*Be Thou My Vision*; *Home for Christmas*; 1990—*The Best of Debby Boone* (Curb); 2000—*Greatest Hymns.*

For four years Debby Boone (b. 1956 in Hackensack, New Jersey) had the distinction of being the singer who had performed the most popular song to hit radio since **Elvis Presley**'s one-two punch of "Don't Be Cruel" and "Hound Dog" in 1956. Boone's version of "You Light Up My Life" occupied the # 1 spot on American radio charts for ten straight weeks. Presley had gone for eleven, but at least Boone prevented Rod Stewart's ode to deflowering virgins, "Tonight's the Night" (eight weeks) from becoming the most popular song of the '70s. "You Light Up My Life" won the Grammy for Song of the Year in 1977 (an award given to the songwriter Joe Brooks, not to Boone). On the strength of her performance of the song, Boone herself received a 1977 Grammy for New Artist of the Year.

Granddaughter of country music legend Red Foley and daughter of Shirley and **Pat Boone,** Debby had already recorded one contemporary Christian album with her sisters (see **The Boones**) before producer Mike Curb encouraged her toward a crossover solo career. Boone made a point of lifting her hands toward heaven when she sang her big hit, such that it became widely known that she was singing the words to God rather than simply to an earthly lover. As a result she became the butt of many jokes, the quintessential example of a goody-goody Christian who was out of her depth in the big bad world of rock and roll. Nevertheless, Boone was the first self-acknowledged contemporary Christian artist to cross into the mainstream market, and as such she deserves credit as the pioneer who proved it is possible for Christian singers to find success in the secular world without compromising or hiding their convictions. The album *You Light Up My Life* also includes the minor hit "California" (# 50 in 1978) and a cover of the **Keith Green**-Todd Fishkind-**Randy Stonehill** song "Your Love Broke Through." It also produced minor chart hits with "God Knows" (# 74 in 1978) and "Baby, I'm Yours" (# 74 in 1978). Boone solidified her G-rated status by singing the theme song for the motion picture "The Magic of Lassie" in 1978. That song, "When You're Loved," won the Academy Award for Best Song—as had "You Light Up My Life" a year earlier. Subsequent secular albums for Curb feature more adult contemporary pop to placate those who were already Debby Boone fans but contain nothing that got played on the radio. According to *The Rolling Stone Encyclopedia of Rock and Roll,* Boone played a role in influencing **Bob Dylan** to become a born-again Christian in 1979.

Boone would later indicate that her career in secular music was hampered both by her own attempts to introduce subtle faith expressions and by corporate pigeonholing of her as "this non-thinking, always-smile-on-your-face, naive daughter of **Pat Boone.**" With regard to the latter, she says, "They'd send me these sappy, nothing, songs . . . just nothing that it would take any talent to perform whatsoever." On the other hand, she would acknowledge by 1983 that she could understand how her attempts to incorporate a Christian witness into a secular performance came to be perceived as manipulative.

In 1980, Boone crossed back over to the Christian market with an album targeted for contemporary Christian music fans. *With My Song* is not what many would have expected (a collection of secular-sounding tunes with religious lyrics). Produced by **Brown Bannister,** the album has an integrity all its own: sacred songs sung in a reverent style. In many ways, it is a worship album, with Boone singing Christ's praises in a higher register than she usually uses. Standout cuts include the title track (written by gospel stalwarts **Reba Rambo** and **Dony McGuire**) and the beautifully prayerful "Morningstar." There is also "What Can I Do for You?" a previously unknown **Bob Dylan** song that would later end up on his album *Saved.* Boone first entered the Christian radio charts with "Keep the Flame Burning" from *Surrender,* a **David Baroni** song performed with **Phil Driscoll.** *Surrender* also includes her versions of **Rich Mullins'** "O Come All Ye Faithful," **Billy Sprague**'s "Can You Reach My Friend," **Pam Mark Hall**'s "Blessing," and **Harry Browning**'s "Keep Rollin' On." Boone's 1985 album, *Choose Life,* finds her teamed with **Michael and Stormie Omartian,** singing hook-laden songs written by that team. The record is more of a dance-music album than her other projects, with the title track and "Delight in Him" being especially upbeat and joyous paeans to life. *Friends for Life* opens with a stirring rendition of **Michael Kelly Blanchard**'s "Be Ye Glad" and features the Omartians' "To Every Generation," a song appropriate for weddings and commencement ceremonies. *Friends for Life* also finds Boone singing **Gary Chapman**'s "Sincerely Yours" and songs by **Billy Batstone** and **Chuck Girard.**

Boone wrote an early autobiography about her rebellious (?!) teenage years called *Debby Boone . . . So Far* (Thomas Nelson, 1981); she has since taken up writing children's books. In 1982, Boone married Gabriel Ferrer, son of movie actors Rosemary Clooney and Jose Ferrer. He has joined her in hosting occasional TV specials. Boone has also starred in a number of musicals, including *Seven Brides for Seven Brothers* (1982), *The Sound of Music* (1987, as Maria), *Meet Me in St. Louis* (1992), and *South Pacific* (1995). She also played a hired killer on an episode of the TV series *Baywatch Nights* and acted in two made-for-TV movies *(The Gift of the Magi* and *Sins of the Past),* but she never succeeded in breaking into feature films as she would have liked. In 1983 she told *CCM* that she had been shut out of Hollywood due to her reluctance to play roles that she would view as a compromise of her faith. Not quite the prude many would have expected, she made it clear that she made such determinations with a broad perspective. She even admitted that she would not be adverse to doing "some slight nudity" in a motion picture that supported her value system but indicated she would not play *any* part in a film that "uplifts things my whole life is against." This fact alone—or false perceptions of the star—appear to have kept her from receiving scripts.

For trivia buffs: Debby Boone's "You Light Up My Life" was *not* featured on the soundtrack to the movie of that name, also released in 1977. Joe Brooks chose Cissy Kasyck to sing it for the film instead. Her competing version peaked at # 80 on the charts.

Christian radio hits: "Keep the Flame Burning" (# 2 in 1984); "Can You Reach My Friend?" (# 8 in 1984); "O Come All Ye Faithful" (# 38 in 1984); "The Time is Now" (# 10 in 1985); "Choose Life" (# 10 in 1985).

Dove Awards: 1980 Album by a Secular Artist *(With My Song)*; 1983 Album by a Secular Artist *(Surrender).*

Grammy Awards: 1977 New Artist of the Year; 1980 Best Inspirational Performance ("With My Song I Will Praise Him"); 1984 Best Gospel Performance by a Duo or Group [with **Phil Driscoll**] ("Keep the Flame Burning").

Pat Boone (and **The Boone Family**)

As Pat Boone (selected): 1970—*Rapture* (Supreme); *Songs for Jesus Folk; Thank You Dear Lord;* 1972—*Pat Boone Sings Golden Hymns* (Lamb and Lion); *Pat Boone Sings the New Songs of the Jesus People* (Lamb and Lion); *Pat Boone and the First Nashville Jesus Band;* 1973—*Born Again; I Love You More and More Each Day* (MGM); 1974—*S-A-V-E-D* (Lamb and Lion); *Songs from the Inner Court;* 1975—*Hymns We Love* (Word); 1975—*Something Supernatural* (Lamb and Lion); 1977—*Miracle Merry Go Round;* 1979—*Just the Way I Am;* 1980—*The Time Has Come* (NALR); 1981—*Songmaker;*

1984—*What I Believe;* 1987—*Home* (Lamb and Lion); 1995—*Greatest Hymns* (Atlantic); 1997—*In a Metal Mood: No More Mr. Nice Guy* (Uni); 1998—*The Inspirational Collection* (Varese Sarabande); *Family Christmas* (Laserlight); 1999—*Golden Treasury of Hymns* (Gold Label); 1999—*Hymns We Love* (MCA). With The Boone Family: 1971—*The Pat Boone Family* (Word); 1973—*The Family Who Prays* (Lamb and Lion); 1973—*The Pat Boone Family in the Holy Land.*

As of 2001, Pat Boone was still listed as the tenth most popular artist in music history (behind **Elvis Presley,** the Beatles, Elton John, Stevie Wonder, James Brown, Madonna, the Rolling Stones, **Aretha Franklin,** and Michael Jackson). In the early '70s, when he entered the world of contemporary Christian music, he was behind only Elvis and the Beatles. A direct descendant of pioneer Daniel Boone, Pat (b. 1934 in Jacksonville, Fla.) is related to a number of famous people. His wife Shirley is daughter of country music legend Red Foley. His younger brother is Nick Todd, a Top 40 artist of the '50s best known for "At the Hop" (# 21 in 1958, unfortunately a version by Danny and the Juniors reached # 1 that same year). He is father to **Debby Boone,** and to three other daughters who would join her in **The Boones.** For that matter, he is also -father-in-law to **Harry Browning** and to Gabriel Ferrer (Debby's spouse), the son of Jose Ferrer and Rosemary Clooney. As a college student Boone won two highly significant talent shows, which gave him national exposure on TV programs hosted by Ted Mack and Arthur Godfrey. He made a few mildly successful records in Nashville and then hit it big with a white-bread cover version of Fats Domino's "Ain't That a Shame" (# 1 in 1955). Though it would come to sound very tame, that song topped the charts months before Elvis or **Little Richard** or Jerry Lee Lewis would make their first appearances. It was a milestone in the history of rock and roll. Boone would be in the Top Ten sixteen times in the next three years with songs like "I Almost Lost My Mind" (# 1 for 4 weeks in 1956), "April Love" (# 1 for 6 weeks in 1957), and "Love Letters in the Sand" (# 1 for 7 weeks in 1957). He also appeared in several motion pictures *(April Love, Bernadine, Journey to the Center of the Earth, State Fair)* and had his own TV show *(The Pat Boone-Chevy Showroom).* An icon for America's teens, he was as famous for his clean-cut living as he was for his trademark white bucks (basically, white leather sneakers, which Boone wore decades before there were Nikes or Adidas or Reeboks).

There are two schools of thought on Boone's success as an artist. On the one hand, many of his biggest hits were sanitized, tame versions of songs written and recorded by African American R&B performers. His versions of songs like Little Richards' "Tutti Frutti" and "Long Tall Sally" were like muzak; they seemed so obviously inferior to the original versions that critics wondered why anyone would prefer them, save for a predisposition against what was officially called "race music" (and unofficially something much worse). On the other hand,

Boone's white versions of black songs brought the music of many R&B artists (including not only Fats Domino and Little Richard but also El Dorado, the Five Keys, Ivory Joe Hunter, and Joe Turner) to a broader audience. In fact, in May of 1956, several southern churches banded together to sponsor Boone boycotts and record-burnings, claiming (seriously) that he was part of "a plot by the NAACP to destroy the moral fiber of white youth." Thus Boone can be viewed either as pillager or promoter; there is no question that he benefitted commercially from the racism of white music fans by getting hits with songs by people who couldn't get a hearing themselves, but there can also be little doubt that he did as much as anyone to deconstruct that racism. Indeed, one might say he worked to put himself out of business: he labored to teach white America to like the R&B music that he obviously loved, and to the extent that he succeeded at doing this, his fans found they no longer needed him. His last big hit was "Moody River" (# 1 in 1961), aside from the novelty song "Speedy Gonzales" (# 6 in 1962, with Mel Blanc as the voice of the titular cartoon character). Thus, Boone's career as a star really lasted only six years, but no one other than Elvis or the Beatles ever had six years like his.

Boone was always outspoken about his religious beliefs. He was fortunate enough to be making records at a time when an entertainer did not have to fear being banned from secular radio (i.e., labeled a "Christian singer") for telling a journalist he regularly attends church or believes in God. Thus the move toward recording gospel albums came naturally, and those records seemed compatible with his total oeuvre—more so, at least, than the gospel recordings of Presley. As early as 1959, Boone wrote a book *Twixt Twelve and Twenty* (Prentice Hall) in which he offers his clean-living advice to America's teens. Nevertheless, Boone did have a conversion experience of sorts in the late '60s, when he experienced the baptism of the Holy Spirit, began speaking in tongues, and became one of the country's best-known charismatic Christians. He details these experiences in an autobiography, *A New Song* (Creation House, 1970), and Shirley Boone covers much of the same ground from her perspective in *One Woman's Liberation* (Creation House, 1988). Influenced by evangelist George Otis, Boone embraced Pentecostal doctrine and experience to a degree that he was expelled from the Church of Christ, a denomination that believes supernatural manifestations of God's power ceased with the first century. In 1972, Boone starred as Pentecostal preacher David Wilkerson in the classic Christian drama *The Cross and the Switchblade* (with Erik Estrada as Nicky Cruz). In 1980, he published the book *Pray to Win: God Wants You to Succeed* (Putnam).

It was Boone's involvement with the charismatic renewal movement that brought him in touch with what is now called contemporary Christian music. Two of the albums listed above are especially significant for featuring the new style of rock-influenced gospel. On 1972's *Pat Boone Sings the New Songs of the Jesus People,* Boone croons his versions of songs by **Larry Norman** ("I Wish We'd All Been Ready"), **Love Song** ("Little Country Church"), and **Children of the Day** ("For Those Tears I Died"). Three years later, *Something Supernatural* offered the title track (a bluesy **Chuck Girard** song) in addition to Norman's "U.F.O." and songs by **Malcolm and Alwyn** ("Fool's Wisdom"), **Randy Matthews** ("Didn't He"), and **Mylon LeFevre** ("You Were on His Mind"). It also includes some lesser-known songs written by **Annie Herring** ("You'll Start Falling in Love," "Wing of Fire") and **Michael Omartian** ("Lord"). Taken together, these albums offer a compendium of some of the greatest hits of the Jesus movement, though of course the songs are all performed in Boone's decidedly un-hip style—a style not likely to appeal to stereotypical Jesus freaks.

Boone's Jesus music albums suffered and benefitted from the same ambiguity that had attended his renditions of R&B music. The Jesus people themselves did not know whether to feel insulted or complimented that he was turning their music into something their grandparents would like. He either ruined the music or legitimized it, depending on whom one asked. In the end, the latter perspective won out. Boone's endorsement of Jesus music made it respectable, and his arrangements proved the songs of the Jesus people had value that transcended any single appropriation. Notably, Boone was a significant early supporter of contemporary Christian music in other ways as well. He started a recording label, Lamb and Lion, to help artists get their material to the public. He even fronted the money ($3,000) for **Larry Norman** and **Randy Stonehill** to start another label (One Way Records) for the same purpose. Likewise, in 1980, Boone recorded an album of contemporary Roman Catholic songs (*The Time Has Come*) to help that church's North American Liturgy Resources gain greater recognition for worship materials by Catholic artists. He has also written and recorded music encouraging better Christian-Jewish relations and, in recognition of this, was named Christian Ambassador to Israel by the Israeli Tourism Department.

In the '90s, Boone came back with a surprising turn. He made an album called *In a Metal Mood: No More Mr. Nice Guy,* which features Big Band style cover versions of classic hard rock songs: Deep Purple's "Smoke on the Water"; Guns N' Roses' "Paradise City"; AC/DC's "It's a Long Way To the Top"; Metallica's "Enter Sandman"; Ozzy Osbourne's "Crazy Train"; Jimi Hendrix's "The Wind Cries Mary"; Led Zeppelin's "Stairway To Heaven"; and the title track from the pre-Christian **Alice Cooper.** As people who know these songs will recognize, there is nothing objectionable in their lyrical content. Boone agrees that he made the selections carefully, picking songs that did not compromise his faith in any way. He even made a few lyrical adjustments to Van Halen's "Panama" (an otherwise questionable line becomes "easing the seat back and fastening my seat belt"). Still, the album caused a flurry of controversy among Boone fans, who protested the project in ways that would demonstrate how far they had *not* come in the four decades since they had been shocked he would sing songs by "colored people." His variety show *Gospel America* was actually dropped from Paul and Jan Crouch's Trinity Broadcasting Network after he did a stint on TV to promote the album, wearing black leather and temporary tatoos.

Boone's motivation for the metal album seems to have been threefold. First, it was an act of penance, in which he took ownership for his past tendencies to judge people by the style of their music or clothing rather than by what they actually think or say. Second (and probably foremost), it was a joke: what could be more ridiculous than Pat Boone singing heavy metal? He hoped that by making fun of himself, he could give everyone a good laugh, especially those whom he might have hurt or ridiculed in the past. And finally, he wanted to demonstrate that he could be a good sport, and by doing so show the world that Christians are not the humorless narrowminded dunderheads that people often take them to be. In retrospect, he appears to have underestimated the number of Christians who actually *are* the humorless, narrow-minded dunderheads that people often take them to be. Sample the nonsense: "Pat Boone is now an instrument of the Devil. He has sold his soul for rock and roll, singing satanic songs on his new album. . . . The Bible *clearly states* that only sinners wear black leather [verse references suspiciously absent] and we all know that tattoos are sin." The Church lady on Saturday Night Live? No. Sister Rosetta, a self-described "longtime fan and personal friend of Pat Boone before his fall from grace." Boone responded to all this flack with seasoned verve: "I am willing and happy to take the heat. I deserve it, for I have been judgmental of others myself."

For trivia buffs: In the '70s Boone conducted evangelistic services at his Hollywood home, baptizing converts in the swimming pool. As it turned out, one small child he baptized was Andy Robbins, who later became lead singer for the hard rock Christian band **Holy Soldier.**

Christian radio hits: "Let Me Live" (# 40 in 1984).

The Boones (a.k.a. **The Boone Girls**)

Cherry Boone, voc.; Debby Boone, voc.; Laury Boone, voc.; Lindy Boone, voc. 1976—*Glass Castle* (Lamb and Lion); 1978—*First Class;* 1979—*Heavenly Love.*

Best remembered as the birthing ground of pop legend **Debby Boone,** the female quartet known as The Boones (or, on their first album, The Boone Girls) made some significant

contemporary Christian music in their own right. The Boones were the daughters of **Pat Boone** and hence granddaughters (via Shirley Boone) of country legend Rex Foley. The Dove award they won in 1977 for Best Christian Album by a Secular Artist is revealing. The Boones never were considered anything but a religious group; they made no impact (as a group) on secular music. The significance of their being regarded as "a secular act" (aside from providing testimony to the perpetually confused perspective of the Gospel Music Association on such matters) is that the musical *style* of The Boones' albums was indeed more like that of Debby's secular albums (albeit with Christian lyrics) than the latter's inspirational recordings. In other words, the sound was soft pop, prefiguring Wilson Phillips by more than a decade. The group debuted in 1970 by touring Japan with their father and The Osmonds. Their version of the Bacharach/David song "What The World Needs Now" was especially well received, such that *Variety* remarked that their act was "one of the most talked about shows of this or any other season." Their second album, *First Class,* brought them to Christian radio with the hits "You Took My Heart by Surprise" and "I'm a Believer" (not a cover of the Neil Diamond-penned Monkees song). "First Butterfly" was cowritten by Cherry Boone with **Annie Herring.**

The Boones had the distinction of gracing the premiere issue of *Contemporary Christian Music* (later *CCM*) magazine in 1978. Twenty years later, Debby still had a solo career, Lindy was singing with a '40s dance band called The Cordettes (in Laguna, Calif.), Laury was recording with her husband **Harry Browning,** and Cherry—a writer—lived in Seattle and worked with victims of anorexia nervosa. Cherry had in fact been the first public figure to be diagnosed with that eating disorder. Weighing only eighty pounds, she was hospitalized in 1977, a full five years before Karen Carpenter's death would bring the disorder widespread media coverage; indeed, Cherry played a significant role in Carpenter's battle for life and was often called upon to eulogize the latter singer once that battle was lost.

Christian radio hits: "You Took My Heart By Surprise" (# 7 in 1978); "I'm a Believer" (# 5 in 1978); "I Love You More (Than My Rock and Roll)" (# 20 in 1978); "First Butterfly" (# 8 in 1978); "Heavenly Love" (# 6 in 1980); "Rest in Me" (# 7 in 1981).

Dove Awards: 1977 Album by a Secular Artist *(First Class).*

Stephanie Booshada

1976—*Stephanie* (Celebration); 1979—*One in a Million* (Chrism); 1981—*I Know That I Know* (NewPax); 1984—*Sing the Glory* (Milk and Honey); 1998—*Collection* (independent).

www.stephanieboo.com

Oklahoma City native Stephanie Booshada is perhaps best known for her association with Pat Robertson's *700 Club,* for which she has sometimes served as cohost. As a student at Oral Roberts University, Booshada won the talent competition in the Miss Oklahoma beauty pageant, which opened doors to a recording career. In addition to making several adult contemporary inspirational albums, she has assisted her pastor-husband Wayne in the founding of several churches, including the Jubilee Christian Center, which they started in 1982. Booshada writes most of her own material; she also wrote "You Were There" for **Amy Grant** and has composed songs recorded by **Truth** and Billie Jo Spears. *CCM* described her album *I Know That I Know* as a "delightful surprise" that breaks with the MOR tradition of her previous work to offer "expressive, upbeat pop that boogies." *Sing the Glory* is a praise-oriented project filled with songs that "encourage Christians to enjoy praising the Lord for his power and his might."

Christian radio hits: "Comin' Home To You" (# 17 in 1980); "I Know That I Know" (# 2 in 1982); "Somewhere It's Snowing" (# 24 in 1984); "Sing the Glory (of His Name)" (# 11 in 1984); "Wanna Be Used Within You" (# 31 in 1984).

Born Blind

Nate Jarrell, gtr.; Kurt Love, drums; Judd Morgan, voc.; Chris Beckett, bass (−2000) // Billy, gtr. (+ 2000); Matt, bass (+ 2000). 1999—*Pressing On* (Facedown); 2000—*One for All* (Solid State).

www.facedownrecords.com

Born Blind describes themselves as an "old school hardcore band" out of San Diego, California. The group arose out of the ashes of **No Innocent Victim,** in which Chris Beckett, Kurt Love, and Judd Morgan were all members. Born Blind infuses the hard, fast pounding noise of hardcore music with catchy sing-along choruses, often featuring what *Bandoppler* calls a "proficient use of gang vocals." Morgan affirms the group's identity as "a ministry band." A recurrent theme in the group's songs, he continues, is a call for greater openness among Christians, for people to "respect the beliefs of others even if they don't agree with them."

BottleRockit

Johnny Crawford, voc., gtr.; Chris Finn, drums; Tim Walker, bass. 2000—*Angel on a Vespa* (independent).

A British three-piece band, BottleRockit combine "funky rock with some pop-punk attitude" *(Phantom Tollbooth),* with occasional Green Day inferences. Their debut album displays a penchant for switching tempos frequently, a trademark that even seems to be the topic of one song ("Speed Things Up"). Lyrically the album adopts a subtle approach that is far from preachy, though in the midst of good-time fun songs there is

muted concern to share their faith: "Hey come along won't you sing with me / To the man in the sky with the mic you can't see / And try / Try to believe" ("Duddle-a-duh"). The song "BottleRockit" offers a bit of the group's biography, thus far.

Brent Bourgeois

1990—*Brent Bourgeois* (Charisma); 1992—*A Matter of Feel* (Capitol); 1994—*Come Join the Living World* (Reunion).

A child prodigy at the piano, Dallas native Brent Bourgeois (pronounced *boo –jwah*) joined with his friend Larry Tagg in 1984 to form the musical group Bourgeois-Tagg in Sacramento, California. They scored a minor hit with "Mutual Surrender (What a Wonderful World)" (# 62 in 1986) and then left a more lasting impression on the charts with "I Don't Mind at All" (# 38 in 1987). Bourgeois embarked on a solo career in the early '90s and hit one more time with "Dare To Fall in Love" (# 32 in 1990). Suffering from addictions to drugs and alcohol, Bourgeois found redemption through the witness of his old drinking buddy **Charlie Peacock.** "Somewhere along the line, he got sober and saved," Bourgeois recalls, "and I started going to his church. I never looked back." Bourgeois gradually rediscovered the faith of his childhood—he had been raised Catholic and had served as an altar boy. He describes his album *A Matter of Feel* as sort of "a recovery album," made while he was struggling to overcome his addictions. In the song "Alcohol" he sings, "I thought you were my friend / But you let me down again." Peacock ended up producing Bourgeois' official Christian debut, *Come Join the Living World.* Stylistically the record recalls the Beatlesque pop sound of artists like Crowded House or Todd Rundgren (who produced Bourgeois-Tagg's second album, *Yo-Yo*). The album produced five Top 5 hits in the Christian market. Bourgeois went on to become a vice-president of Word Records, but he occasionally contributes to compilation or tribute albums.

As a songwriter, Bourgeois has written or cowritten Christian radio hits for **4 Him** ("Lay It All on the Line"), **Cindy Morgan** ("Moon Days"), **Jonathan Pierce** ("Rise Up"), **Michael W. Smith** ("Cry for Love," "Straight To the Heart," "Live the Life"), and **Tony Vincent** ("Must Be the Season," "Whole New Spin").

Christian radio hits: "One Love" (# 1 in 1994); "A Little More Like Jesus" (# 1 in 1995); "Restored" (# 1 in 1995); "Blessed Be the Name" (# 4 in 1995); "Perfect Harmony" (# 4 in 1996).

Joshua Bourke

1996—*Regenerated* [EP] (independent); *Restoration.*

Joshua Bourke produces "electrogoth music" in the area around San Diego, California. He has gained a significant international following with mp3.com songs available over the

Internet. He has also placed numerous songs on a variety of compilation discs. The sound of his music is described as experimental (in the mode of Fad Gadget) but with a commercial edge (Erasure, New Order). He weaves ambient synths with electronically produced rhythms and uses these as a backdrop for his relaxed vocals. The music is intended to feed the soul; lyrics are generally straightforward and expressive of spiritual themes. "Let it Go" urges listeners to trust matters to God and be free of anxiety. Bourke generally stays on the soft side of industrial music, though "Run" is a more experimental track with distorted vocals.

Kim Boyce

1986—*Kim Boyce* (Myrrh); 1988—*Time and Again*; 1989—*Love Is You to Me*; 1991—*This I Know*; 1993—*Facts of Love* (Warner); 1994—*By Faith*; 1997—*As I Am* (Diadem).

Beauty queen Kim Boyce from Winter Haven, Florida, has provided a decade of Christian music that has allowed her mostly female audience to age with her, many of them wishing they could *be* her. She began her music career singing disco pop songs for teenage girls and matured along with her fan base, eventually offering them sophisticated adult contemporary ballads. Along the way she has lived out many a young girl's fantasy, winning beauty contests, finding true love, and eventually becoming a devoted, proud mother. Boyce grew up singing gospel music with her family, then performed with her two sisters as The Melody Three Singers. A lifetime Christian, she has few hard-time stories to tell of profligate years or dramatic conversion. She was chosen Miss Florida in 1983 and entered the Miss America pageant. She landed a recording contract with a major label (Myrrh) and was successfully wooed by Gary Koreiba, a backup singer for **Russ Taff** on her first concert tour opening for that artist.

Boyce's first album features a collection of peppy danceable pop songs, including "Here" and a slightly rewritten cover of Alison Moyet's "Love Resurrection." She continued with more records in the same vein, scoring numerous radio hits and building a solid following among adolescent girls. *Time and Again* opens with a version of Rare Earth's 1971 hit, "I Just Want To Celebrate" (cf. **A Cross Between**). The song "Not for Me" on that same album is set to a tune similar to songs by '50s girl groups, a nostalgia theme enhanced by the album cover's portrait of Boyce made up in a chic Marilyn Monroe style seated in a '50s convertible. "Save Me" is a duet with Jimmie Lee Sloas of **The Imperials**. *Love Is You to Me* finds Boyce singing **Keith Green**'s "Oh, Lord You're Beautiful" and songs by Sloas, **BeBe Winans**, and **Tim Miner**. She married soon after that project, and her fourth album, *This I Know*, features the romantic song "True Love," sung as a duet with her husband Gary Koreiba. *This I Know* was produced by Miner and includes

several more of his compositions, in addition to "Right for Me" by **Amy Grant** and Tom Hemby.

A major shift in style begins with *Facts of Love*, on which Boyce moves away from dance-pop sounds in favor of ballads like "Everything" and "The Hurting People" (for those who suffer mental and physical abuse). Boyce completes this makeover on *By Faith*, such that *CCM* magazine would compare her evolution to that of Madonna in the general market: both artists demonstrated the desire and ability to escape the confinement of being labeled a dance queen icon. So *By Faith* finds Boyce singing about being a wife and mother: "What a Love" is a love song for her husband, and "Dreams I'm Dreamin' " is a tune inspired by the birth of their first son. *By Faith* also includes the song "Not Too Far from Here," which became something of a national phenomenon when **Mikaila Enriquez** sang it as a tribute to the victims of the 1995 bombing of the Arthur P. Murrah Federal Building in Oklahoma City. Boyce's next album, *As I Am*, continues the thoughtful progression, such that one critic called it the "opposite" of her early work, filled with "piano and string-laden songs that hew close to the middle of the musical road." Almost every reviewer selected two songs as especially noteworthy: "Remember Me (the Communion Song)," which is elegant, beautiful, and ready-made to be sung in church; and "The Sound of Your Voice," which has a velvety sound reminiscent of '40s ballroom "torch songs."

Boyce has also authored several books, including an early volume of beauty tips for young women and a whole series of devotional books such as *Dreams I'm Dreamin': Devotions for Mothers of Young Children*. She has served as the national spokesperson for Bee Alive nutritional products and has worked on behalf of Compassion International.

Christian radio hits: "Darkened Hearts" (# 3 in 1987); "Here" (# 7 in 1987); "Love Resurrection" (# 12 in 1987); "That's How You Touched My Heart" (# 5 in 1987); "Helpless" in 1987); "I Just Want To Celebrate" (# 2 in 1988); "Not for Me" (# 3 in 1988); "Save Me" (# 15 in 1988); "You're Always There" (# 15 in 1988); "Lovin' You" (# 8 in 1988); "For Every Lonely Heart" (# 16 in 1989); "Faith" (# 13 in 1989); "Tender Heart (Love)" (# 6 in 1990); "Love Is You To Me" (# 8 in 1990); "Good Enough" (# 2 in 1991); "Weapon of Good" (# 14 in 1991); "When Love Calls Your Name" (# 12 in 1992); "Facts of Love" (# 6 in 1993); "Love Has Made the Difference" (# 3 in 1993); "Dancin' To the Beat of Your Heart" (# 9 in 1993); "By Faith" (# 3 in 1995).

Terry Bradshaw

1980—*Until You* (Benson).

Super Bowl star quarterback Terry Bradshaw (Pittsburgh Steelers, 1970–1983) recorded a country gospel album in 1980. The record includes Bradshaw's rendition of gospel standards "Learning To Lean" and "This Ole House" in addition to some new songs. The standout tracks are "Dimestore Jesus" and "I'm Learning To Live for Jesus (for He Died for Me)." As all sports-trivia fans know, Bradshaw recorded some country songs for the general market as well; his version of Hank Williams' classic, "I'm So Lonesome I Could Cry" made it to # 91 on *Billboard*'s Top 100 chart in 1976. He kept his day job.

Brainchild

Scott Albert, gtr., voc., kybrd., samples; Doug Mann, drums. 1992—*Mindwarp* (R.E.X.).

The industrial band Brainchild is but one of several side projects for Scott Albert, best known for **Circle of Dust.** Doug Mann has worked (as producer) with **Believer** and **Living Sacrifice.** The sound of Brainchild is best described as heavy industrial music that you can dance to. To quote *HM* magazine, "the album captures the futuristic sounding appeal of industrial music with its rapidly programmed drum beats, eerie sound effects, and bombardment of musical and spoken word samples creating the sense that the listener is experiencing a multimedia musical event." Lyrically, the album displays the typical negative outlook associated with metal music in general (and industrial metal in particular). "Telltale Crime" reflects upon the American government's economic exploitation of its people, with samples from George Bush and other notables. Political issues—abortion, euthanasia, nuclear testing—are referenced in a number of songs and samples. "Prayers of a Dead Man" deals with guilt and shame as it offers a vivid look at a person about to commit suicide. Most interesting, perhaps, "Enshrined" takes its cue from *Foxe's Book of Martyrs*. The Brainchild song "Pale Reflections" was used by MTV as background music on an episode of *MTV Extreme Sports*. Albert later released a remixed version of this album as a **Circle of Dust** record: with a few alterations, *Mindwarp* by Brainchild became *Brainchild* by **Circle of Dust.**

Brainwash Projects

Pigeon John, voc.; B-Twice, voc. 1998—*The Rise and Fall of the Brainwash Projects* (Jackson Rubio).

The two rappers who now make up Brainwash Projects met almost twenty years ago and grew up together in Inglewood, California. The group was formed as a four-piece outfit in 1991 but has recorded only as a duo. They strive to rejuvenate rap by mixing elements of jazz, R&B, and classical into a basic hip-hop format. "When hip-hop started, it was about having fun," says B-Twice, lamenting the gangsta stereotypes that have become attached to the West Coast rap scene. Their debut album includes sixteen tracks that, indeed, present "fun" lyrics alongside spiritual messages. The song "Muchas Muchachas" is about the singers' favorite "girlies," while "Want for

Nada" is an affirmation that Christ has supplied all their needs. On "A Cold Day in Hell," B-Twice proclaims, "I rap for the hell of it / so you can feel the heat." The Drunk Kings provide guest vocals on "Speeding Porches."

Bonnie Bramlett (a.k.a. Bonnie Sheridan)

Selected: 1980—*Step by Step* (Refuge).

It is probably safe to say that Bonnie Bramlett is the only contemporary Christian singer who ever beat up Elvis Costello in a bar. At the time, she was traveling with Stephen Stills' band Manassas. One night in Columbus, Ohio, Costello happened into the same after-concert joint and began delivering soliloquies on the superiority of British to American music. Emboldened by alcohol, he had the audacity (and misfortune) to refer to Ray Charles as "a blind, ignorant nigger," at which point Ms. Bramlett punched his clock, so to speak.

Born in 1944 in Acton, Illinois, Bramlett rose to fame as one-half of the husband and wife duo Delaney and Bonnie. Before that, she had sung as one of the Ikettes (in a wig and blackface makeup) backing Ike and Tina Turner throughout the mid '60s. She met Delaney at a Los Angeles bowling alley in 1967 and the two married a week later. Somehow, the group lucked into the opening slot for the one and only tour by the legendary one-album band Blind Faith, featuring **Eric Clapton** and Steve Winwood. Clapton took a liking to them, riding in their tour bus which, reportedly, "turned into a rolling jam session." After the demise of Blind Faith, he actually accepted a humble role as the group's guitarist, recording and touring with them as an unannounced sideman. Word got out, and crowds flocked to see shows by Delaney and Bonnie with Friends. The "friends" sometimes also included such persons as Duane Allman, Rita Coolidge, George Harrison, Dave Mason, and Leon Russell. Eventually, however, these celebrities found other things to do and the novelty of supporting the hip couple wore off. Delaney and Bonnie had to cancel a 1970 United States tour when they discovered the crowds would not turn out in the same numbers to hear just them. Nevertheless, they made some memorable music, the best of which is found on a classic album, *On Tour with Eric Clapton* (Atlantic, 1970). *Rolling Stone* describes Delaney and Bonnie's sound as "a fusion of gospel, country, funk, and rock." Their absolute best song is a rendition of Dave Mason's "Only You Know and I Know" (# 20 in 1971), though some will remember them better for a novelty ditty called "Never Ending Song of Love" (# 13 in 1971). They also sang on a number of other projects, including Eric Clapton's first solo album—that's Bonnie wailing in the background on the original versions of "After Midnight" and "Blues Power." She also wrote Clapton's hit song "Let It Rain" and cowrote The Carpenters' smash "Superstar." Delaney and Bonnie were both members of John Lennon's Plastic Ono Band.

The couple divorced in 1972 and Bonnie went on to record several solo albums: *Sweet Bonnie Bramlett* (Columbia, 1973); *It's Time* (Capricorn, 1975); *Lady's Choice* (Capricorn, 1976); *Memories* (Capricorn, 1978). She also continued to sing on albums by Clapton and the Allman Brothers, being featured prominently on tours with the latter band. Then she joined Stills' band Manassas and the famous Costello incident occurred in 1979. It was around that time that Bramlett experienced a conversion to Christianity, the details of which are not known. She declared that she was a born-again Christian and recorded an album of Christian songs for the Refuge label. *Step by Step* features **Joe English** on drums and includes the song "Back Out on the Streets" by Bili Thedford, as well as a lovely rendition of the traditional "Whispering Hope." Bramlett herself cowrote "Sweet Rose of Sharon," which proclaims "My love is Christ—and He always will be." Bramlett would also turn up singing on a number of albums by other Christian artists, including English. She would also continue to turn up in unlikely places, singing with slacker punks Public Image Ltd. or on a tribute album to country star Dwight Yoakam.

In 1987, the now-remarried Bonnie Sheridan turned to acting, and in 1991 she had a small role in the Oliver Stone film *The Doors*. Throughout the early '90s, she had a recurring role on the TV series *Roseanne*. Meanwhile, her daughter Bekka Bramlett was pursuing a music career of her own and in 1993 would replace Stevie Nicks in Fleetwood Mac (she would also sing with Vince Gill and Billy Joel and record an album with Billy Burnette called *Bekka and Billy* in 1997). Somewhat ironically, *Rolling Stone* would report in a 1995 retrospective that the almost forgotten Delaney Bramlett had "overcome alcoholism, become a born-again Christian, and was making a living recording commercial jingles"; they betrayed no knowledge, however, of Bonnie's conversion or Christian music career.

Brandtson

Jared Jolley, voc., drums; Myk Porter, voc., gtr.; John Sayre, bass; Matt Traxler, gtr. 1998—*Letterbox* (Deep Elm); 1999—*Fallen Star Collection*; 2000—*Trying to Figure Each Other Out* [EP]; 2002—*Dial In Sounds*.

A hard rock/emo band from Ohio, Brandtson was formed by Myk Porter, front man for the widely followed Christian hardcore group **Six Feet Deep** after that band was laid to rest by disputes with their label. The decision to sign with a mainstream company reflected Brandtson's intention to distance themselves from "the entire Christian music industry," which Matt Traxler (also ex-**Six Feet Deep**) claims "left us with a really sour taste in our mouths, and we wanted nothing to do with it." Nevertheless, Brandtson has played at Christian music festivals and maintained a strong following among fans

of the previous band. The group has worked to forge its own identity, however, creating a distinctive sound based on the vocal harmonies of Porter and Jared Jolley. The first album retains the hard, driving feel of Porter's first group, but the harmonies are sufficiently melodic for critics to use the post-hardcore *emo* word to describe Brandtson's sound. A reviewer for *Jesus Freak Hideout* noted that "it is amazing that a guy can spend years screaming and growling in a hardcore band and come into a rock band and have one of the most beautiful and softest voices I have ever heard." The second album brings the harmonies to the fore and capitalizes on traditional emo elements for a more diverse overall package, such that *Phantom Tollbooth* said, "the stuff of *Fallen Star Collection* hardly sounds like the same band that recorded *Letterbox*." Specifically, the group adopted a more manic-depressive style, complementing introspective numbers with "a noticeable trend toward Weezer-ish pop songs." Smashing Pumpkins comparisons were also drawn, and the group would continue this trend on its *Trying to Figure Each Other Out* EP. The latter disc opens with "Sic Transit Gloria" (i.e., Glory Fades), which features an especially catchy melody line. *Dial In Sounds* continues the musical progression toward indie-pop with songs that focus on interpersonal relationships. "Cherokee Red" recalls wonderful moments of childhood friendships, while "With Friends Like You" reflects on the frailty of adult relationships.

Lyrically, Brandtson's songs tend to focus on the quest to find peace and understanding in a painful world—and this search is often internalized: "It's hard to see the truth sometimes, looking through these eyes, yet I try" ("Blindspot"). The song "Days End" is addressed to a fellow believer who has lost his faith: "Whatever happened to the reasons why we turned our lives around? / Are you pretending it was all for nothing and all just wasted time?" Power's potential for poetic artistry especially shines on "New Favorite Pastime," a classic description of depression: "Twenty-four more to go and it will be tomorrow / One more day older / One more day closer / To some sort of end . . . / Tell me what you meant / When you said everything would be o.k." The song "Things Look Brighter" tells of a lost girl who cannot find her way in life: "She looks to me to say 'I hope tomorrow doesn't feel this way' / She's heard about happiness / She's heard about Jesus / She's starving for the beautiful things / That people seem to believe in."

The Brave

Randy Roberts, drums, voc.; Stayce Roberts, gtr.; Freddie Tierra, gtr.; Malcolm Paris, bass (−1994); James Salters, voc. (−1994) // Steve Irwin, bass (+ 1994). 1992—*Battle Cries* (Pakaderm); 1994—*Trust*.

A hard rock "hair band" in the tradition of **Stryper**, The Brave formed in Lancaster, California, in 1989 and turned out two albums produced by **John** and Dino **Elefante**. As *CCM* magazine noted, the records are likely to please anyone who likes "memorable melodies along with crunching guitars and pounding drums." The debut opens with "All Together Now" (not a Beatles cover), which instantly attracts attention for its Boston or **Kansas** style background vocals (**John Elefante** *was* the lead singer for **Kansas** after all). Other standout songs include a power-rocker called "The Waiting" (not a Tom Petty cover) and "If That Ain't Love," about which *HM* magazine said, "If this song ain't enough to get you hooked on this band, you must be deaf." Drummer Randy Roberts takes over as lead vocalist for the sophomore album, though all the members continue to provide gang vocal harmonies. The title song for *Trust* reveals a slower Led Zeppelin approach, but *HM* praised the album primarily for "Dirty Water" (not a Standells cover) and "Down by the River" (not a Neil Young cover). Aside from the penchant for doing songs with famous titles, The Brave seeks to minister as Christians in a variety of ways. James Salters once suggested the group's motto could be, "We minister, we entertain, we dance, and we make mistakes." The group chose its name as a way of expressing the need for Christian youth to stand up for what they believe. Lyrically, the group's songs tend to express basic Christian principles such as redemption and repentance. "If That Ain't Love" proclaims, "He shed his blood for you and me / If that ain't love /Then I don't know what love is." "Tears of a Broken Heart" exhorts, "Turn from your wicked ways / You're playin' with fire."

Christian radio hits: "Just a Man" (# 24 in 1992), "Never Live without Your Love" (# 8 in 1993); "Tomorrow" (# 4 in 1994).

Brave Saint Saturn

Dennis Culp, gtr.; Keith Hoerig, bass; Reese Roper, voc., gtr. 2000—*So Far from Home* (5 Min. Walk).

www.bravesaintsaturn.com

Brave Saint Saturn is a supposedly one-time side project initiated by members of **Five Iron Frenzy.** Those familiar with that band, however, have been surprised to discover that there is no hint of ska. In terms of Christian music, the sound is more like that of **Shaded Red** or **Switchfoot**—basic '80s tinged guitar pop. The album *So Far from Home* is eclectic but is loosely held together by two themes. First, there is the obvious space theme suggested by the group's name and the CD's album art. Indeed, the group describes their music as "astrorock." The record opens with a "Prologue" of astronaut voices, and synthesizers offer spacey sounds (à la Steve Miller Band) throughout. One of the album's catchiest tracks is called "Space Robot Five." The second theme, however, is heartbreak. Reese Roper grieves over the death of his grandmother in "Two Twenty Nine" and mopes over a lost love in "Independence Day." Christ is invoked in both songs, albeit in diverse ways

that reveal the extent to which Roper's faith is integrated into his thought patterns. In "Independence Day," he mourns, "Waiting every day / Staring at the phone / Jesus Christ, I feel so empty and alone." Does he invoke that name as a curse or a prayer? Again, in "Gloria" he sings, "Too weak to wonder / Too tired to care / Jesus Christ, are you really there?" But in "Two Twenty Nine," there can be no doubt: "I said I loved her and she knew it / Whispered softly to the sky tonight / She is warm and safe in heaven / In the loving arms of Jesus Christ." *So Far from Home* also includes a cover of the **Michael W. Smith** song "Rocketown" and a humorous send-up of Christian rap ("Shadow of Def") featuring the owner of their record company as the guest rapper (memo: keep the day job). "Under Bridges" addresses Christ's identification with the poor by relating the story of a homeless man who looks like Jesus.

Breakfast with Amy

Caryn Parker Colbert, gtr., voc.; Christopher Colbert, gtr.; David Koval, voc., gtr.; Paul Pellegrin, drums; Edwin Wholer, bass. 1990—*Everything Was Beautiful . . . and Nothing Hurt* (Narrowpath); 1991—*Dad* (Blonde Vinyl); 1992—*Product # bvcd 3482 (love gift)*; 1995—*Live at the Hawleywood Bowl* (Flying Tart).

It is always impressive when an unsuccessful band retains an intensely loyal following ten years after the release of a flop album. In Christian circles Breakfast with Amy (or simply The Amys to their fans, a.k.a. Amyheads) has enjoyed the sort of cult celebrity attributed to Big Star in the mainstream market. Certainly, the band's talent far exceeded their commercial success, at least partly because their innovation did not lend itself to easy marketing. BWA owes their legend in part to stage shows (with new-wave/alternative covers of Pat Benatar, Iron Butterfly, and Jefferson Airplane) and to antics (Chris Colbert throwing his guitar in a swimming pool to see what it would sound like). But they also left behind some very fine music. After his work with BWA, Chris Colbert formed **Fluffy** (with Pellegrin), which then changed their name to **Duraluxe.** He also played with **Left Out** and became a successful producer of many bands.

The debut album (later re-released by Gray Dot with bonus tracks) is the classic. Side Two (the last five songs on the original release) were recorded first and distributed at concerts as a sort of EP cassette. These songs ("Funeral," "Everything," "Ferris Wheel," "Abandoned Houses," and "Social Studies") reveal a group very similar to the mainstream band Echo and the Bunnymen, which Chris Colbert admits was his main musical influence (especially the album *Ocean Rain*). But many Christian music fans had never heard Echo and the Bunnymen and to them BWA's combination of dissonant chords with plaintive guitar solos and melodic vocals was anything but derivative. To these five core songs were appended five more new productions that had a quite different sound and were destined to become signature tunes. The opening tracks "Icky" and "Power" are quirky guitar-driven numbers, equal parts **Violent Femmes** and Dinosaur Jr. Then there is "Cavewoman," a surprising piece of Christian bubblegum with a tune as catchy as that of **Audio Adrenaline**'s "Big House" and lyrics about being "born again." If it had been played on Christian radio, it no doubt would have gone straight to the top and inspired thousands of listeners to buy an album they would not have liked. "Cavewoman" is an incredibly pleasant song with an almost annoyingly memorable tune. Still, it is unlike anything else that the group ever did. Supposedly, everyone but David Koval hated it. Rounding out the now classic debut collection was an inspired cover of the traditional "This Train" (as in "This train don't carry no gamblers, etc.") and a kind of strange song about Mr. Ed (the talking horse?).

As indicated, the album didn't sell and the none-too-stable record company went under. **Michael Knott** tried to come to the rescue. A fine judge of unrecognized talent, he signed the Amys to his doomed Blonde Vinyl label. They produced one respectable follow-up that features a slightly psychedelic rendition of the Etta James' R&B classic "Tell Mama." There are serious songs on *Dad,* also, but these are overshadowed by tunes like "Sea Shanty of an Icelandic Midwife" and "The Short Life of Henrietta," which had critics comparing the band to **The Swirling Eddies.** Indeed, Brian Quincy Newcomb noted in *CCM* that the above-mentioned songs "shall heretofore define the term *out there* in all future reviews." As Blonde Vinyl was in the throes of bankruptcy, The Amys scraped together whatever they could find for what is sometimes referred to as their "worst-of" collection *(Product # bvcd 3482 [love gift]),* an assortment of previously unreleased material presented without any distinguishable conceptual focus. *Product # bvcd 3482* does offer some songs with strong pop sensibilities. "The Jello Wiggle" supposedly introduces a new dance craze and "Fashion Gal" gives voice to a basic slacker mentality: "I'm a product of pop psychology / I watch a lot of bad TV." But then there are also some spoken-word stream-of-consciousness meanderings, a hillbilly yee-haw folk song, and a good bit of Arabic chanting. After the band's demise, tapes of a concert surfaced *(Live at the Hawleywood Bowl),* which at least allow the uninitiated to hear some of those outlandish cover songs referenced above ("Hit Me with Your Best Shot," "In-A-Gadda-Da-Vida," "Somebody To Love"). The record was recorded at a bowling alley; the sounds of rolling balls and falling pins can be heard in the background of most tracks, and the audience is provided with updates on a tournament in progress between songs. Also on the bill is a muzak version of "Icky" and a revised Christmas carol called "Jesus Christ Is Coming to Town."

There is no such thing as a typical Breakfast with Amy song, but many songs focus lyrically on the confusions and ambiguities of life. "Ferris Wheel" likens life to a spinning amusement park ride of "surprise and doubt." The Christian content comes in the form of one-line affirmations or prayers. Thus, "Funeral" interrupts its description of a graveside ceremony to say, "I'm not gonna live there." And "Icky" affirms, "My life is simple / Yet complicated / A jigsaw puzzle / I'm so frustrated / I need your Spirit to pull me out of this mire." Perhaps the most profound summary of spiritual quest comes in "Your Name" from *Dad:* "You're the mystery of life / You're the mystery of love / Are you my friend / Or just my Lord?"

For trivia buffs: The photo on BWA's *Everything Was Beautiful* has become a legend in its own right. It is a magnificent picture of a little girl, sitting in front of what looks to be a pile of munitions, crying and clutching a handful of flowers. Actually, the photo was taken by Jack Smith at a military museum, where the unhappy child in question had just been told she had to get out of the exhibit and back on the other side of the rope.

Máire Brennan

1992—*Máire* (Atlantic); 1995—*Misty-Eyed Adventures;* 1998—*Perfect Time* (Word); 1999—*Whisper to the Wild Water;* 2002—*New Irish Hymns* [with Margaret Becker and Joanne Hogg] (Worship Together).

Máire Brennan, lead singer of Clannad, is one of the world's two most authentic interpreters of Celtic (specifically Gaelic) music. The other would be her sister Enya. With two solo albums and seventeen best-selling Clannad records commanding attention in the world music market, Brennan began making records targeted for the contemporary Christian community in the late '90s. Her two albums for Word make explicit the spiritual focus that is sometimes evident in her "secular" work. Raised a Catholic but married to a Protestant in war-torn Ireland, Brennan draws on the riches of her homeland's Christian traditions to espouse a message of faith that offers hope and peace. "Being Catholic or Protestant is not what's important," she told *CCM* magazine in 1998. "What's important is being a follower of Christ, loving God, and loving our neighbor."

The group Clannad is very much a family affair. Besides Brennan, the group includes her brother Cláran and two cousins, the twin brothers Noel and Padraig Duggan. Brother Paul and sister Enya were members once but left to pursue solo careers. The group began singing local folk songs in Gaelic at the neighborhood pub, which was owned by Máire's father Leo. They went on to research the history of the region's music, establishing official arrangements for hundreds of traditional songs that had been sung by milkmaids, field hands, children, or barflies for centuries. The music caught on, especially in Europe, and for some time what is now called "Celtic music" was actually better known as "Clannad music." In America, the group may be best known for two songs: 1) "The Theme from Harry's Game" (so-called because it was originally the theme for a British TV show), which was featured in the film *Patriot Games* and subsequently in a Volkswagen Passat commercial; and 2) "I Will Find You," which was used as the theme for the motion picture *The Last of the Mohicans.*

As a soloist, Máire (pronounced *Moya*) attracted attention for her 1986 duet with Bono, "In a Lifetime," and for her vocals on Robert Plant's *Fate of Nations* album. Her first two solo records reaped critical praise concomitant with that of the group's work, and *Misty-Eyed Adventures* even featured a couple of gospel songs. Still, the decision to produce a specifically Christian album came as a result of her own personal awakening and commitment to what had, in some sense, informed her life from infancy. "I lived the rock and roll life," she admits. "I drank too much. I thank God my parents did bring me up well, so I did know where to go to ask the Lord for help." She was also introduced to the Christian music subculture when **Iona** vocalist **Joanna Hogg** asked her for help in singing a Gaelic translation of "Be Thou My Vision" that Máire's grandfather had prepared.

Perfect Time features Máire's voice against lush orchestral arrangements with flutes, harps, and other Celtic instruments. The *Lighthouse* electronic magazine described it as "less a pop album than a classical one with some pop sensibilities." The album disappointed some Clannad fans musically in that it tried to reach traditional CCM audiences by "dumbing down" Máire's "foreign" sound with what *Phantom Tollbooth* called "**Point of Grace** inferences." Notably, though, only three of the album's ten tracks are entirely in English (two are instrumental, three in Gaelic, and two in both languages). "Ne Pástí" is essentially a Gaelic translation of the biblical account of Jesus blessing the children. The title track and "Heal This Land" are sung openly to God as pleas for personal and social renewal. *Whisper to the Wild Water* drew more favorable reviews with tighter arrangements and an authentic "family project" feel. On "I Lathair De (In God's Presence)," Máire sings a duet with her seventy-year-old mother Baba, who has conducted the choir at St. Mary's Catholic Church of Derryberg as long as anyone can remember. "Peacemaker" (a version of St. Francis of Assisi's famous prayer) features her five-year-old son Paul intoning in Gaelic. The album closes with Máire's own version of "Bi Thuise Mo Shuile," her grandfather's translation of "Be Thou My Vision" (the song recorded by **Iona**). *New Irish Hymns* is a special collection in which Brennan joins with **Margaret Becker** and **Joanna Hogg** to present songs by Celtic composer Keith Getty.

Máire objects to the usual classification of Clannad as New Age music. The music of her homeland is rooted in a spiritual-

ity that is not so generic as that label implies. An amateur student of Celtic Christian history, she maintains that those 1500 years of tradition have left a deep mark on the culture that can be recaptured. "At one time," she says, "ten percent of the Irish people were missionaries to the rest of the world." She now views herself as the heir of that tradition. "There are a lot of people out there who don't know about Jesus and His love, and what he can give. I just want to share that with people, and ask them, 'Do you know how wonderful it is to be a Christian?' " She has also contributed a stunning duet with former Doobie Brother Michael McDonald to a collection of Christian songs by female vocalists (*Streams,* Word, 1999). Brennan and McDonald sing Peter Gabriel's "Don't Give Up."

Lincoln Brewster

1999—*Lincoln Brewster* (Vertical); 2000—*Live to Worship.*

Guitar hero turned youth-oriented worship leader Lincoln Brewster is pushing the frontiers of what the contemporary Christian market usually regards as "praise and worship" music. An acclaimed studio guitarist, Brewster was selected by Steve Perry to accompany the former lead singer for Journey on his solo tour in 1994–1995 and to play on Perry's album *For the Love of Strange Medicine* (for which Brewster also cowrote several songs). Having recently been drawn into a closer relationship with God through the witness of his wife Laura, Brewster found the fame of being a rock star superficial and annoying. "There were nights I remember people grabbing at my legs while I'm out front playing a solo or something," he recalls. "I remember nights just looking up, going, 'God, I'm sorry. This is so silly.' " Afterwards, he helped evangelist Danny Chambers start the Oasis Church in Nashville, Tennessee, where he and Laura now serve as youth pastors and worship leaders. His first album of worship songs breaks with the traditional mix that places guitars in the background and puts the soaring solos right up front. These are electric guitars, too, with lots of pedal-to-the-metal, Hendrix/Van Halen influences. "Walk On" is not a Neil Young (or **U2**) cover but a beautiful acoustic treatment of how God's love overcomes fear and loneliness. The standout cut, however, is "Spin" with its high energy, arena rock chorus ("You make me want to jump up, spin around, get up, get down"). Other songs ensure diverse expressions for various moods: "Everybody Praise the Lord" is funky; "Broken" delves into the blues. Brewster was diagnosed with clinical depression prior to the recording of his second album, *Live to Worship,* and his cover of songs like "Lord I Lift Your Name on High" and **Darlene Zschech**'s "Shout To the Lord" represent his selection of songs that encouraged him during that trial. The project also includes an instrumental version of "Amazing Grace" similar in style to **Phil Keaggy**'s *The Wind and the*

Wheat material. Brewster wrote seven therapeutic original songs for the second album, including "The Power of Your Love," which he sings as a duet with Dan Haseltine of **Jars of Clay.**

Christian radio hits: "He's All I Need" (# 14 in 1999); "Take Me Higher" (# 17 in 2001); "Power of Your Love" (# 11 in 2001).

Jim Brickman

1994—*No Words* (Windham Hill); 1995—*By Heart;* 1997—*Picture This; The Gift;* 1998—*Visions of Love;* 1999—*Destiny; If You Believe;* 2001—*Simple Things.*

www. Jimbrickman.com

Jim Brickman, the almost undisputed king of easy listening, has a huge, loyal following in the mainstream market and has found subtle ways to introduce some of those fans (he calls them "Brickheads") to adult contemporary Christian singers. A native of Cleveland, Brickman is best known for his albums of romantic piano solos—the kind of music that (he says) is played in the background of massage therapy sessions and candlelit bubble baths. On his second album he decided to include one vocal performance, inviting Laura Creamer to sing the title track. The ploy was so successful that he continued on each album thereafter to employ occasional guest vocalists, including Janis Ian, Peabo Bryson, Kenny Loggins, Martina McBride, Pam Tillis, and Carly Simon. What is significant for Christian music is that he chose **Susan Ashton** and **Collin Raye** to sing the title track for his Christmas album, *The Gift.* The song and the album were huge hits on adult contemporary stations, helping Ashton to break out of the exclusively Christian ghetto. The same album also features **Point of Grace** on "Hope Is Born Again." Brickman would later invite **Michael W. Smith** to sing "Love of My Life" on the *Destiny* album. The upshot of such collaborations was *If You Believe,* a compilation of previously recorded songs marketed exclusively through Christian retail outfits. It contains the three just-mentioned songs with vocals by known Christian artists and a number of reflective instrumentals. In 1998, Brickman was chosen SESAC Songwriter of the Year for "The Gift."

For trivia buffs: Before Brickman found his niche in the Windham Hill New Age market, he worked as a composer of commercial jingles. He is the man responsible for "Food, Folks, and Fun" (McDonald's), "Just for the Taste of It" (Diet Coke), "10 Million Strong and Growing" (Flintstones Vitamins), and "We Bring Good Things To Light" (GE).

Dove Awards: 1998 Country Song ("The Gift").

Bride

Dale Thompson, voc.; Troy Thompson, gtr.; Scott Hall, bass (– 1988); Steve Osborne, gtr. (–1989); Stephan Rolland, drums (–1990) // Frank Partipillo, bass (+ 1988, –1990); Rick Foley, bass (+ 1990, –1995); Jerry McBroom, drums (+ 1990, – 1999); Steve Curtsinger, bass (+ 1995, –1998); Lawrence Bishop, bass (+ 1998, –1999); Andrew Wilkinson, bass (+ 1999, –2001); Lawrence Bishop, bass (+ 2001); Michael Loy, drums (+ 2001). 1986—*Show No Mercy* (Pure Metal); 1988—*Live to Die;* 1989—*Silence Is Madness;* 1990—*End of the Age;* 1991—*Kinetic Faith;* 1992—*Snakes in the Playground* (StarSong); 1994—*Scarecrow Messiah;* 1995—*Shotgun Wedding: 11 # 1 Hits and Mrs.; Drop* (Rugged); 1997—*The Jesus Experience* (Organic); 1998—*Oddities;* 1999—*Bride Live;* 2000—*The Best of Bride;* 2001—*Fistful of Bees* (Absolute).

www.bridepub.com

Bride might not be able to keep a bass player, but they have retained a sufficiently loyal fan base for enough years to become America's premier Christian hard rock band. The group that began as **Stryper** wannabes not only outlasted their mentors but also evolved into an act that would set new standards for Christian metal in the '90s. The Thompson brothers (not twins) became the Axl and Slash of the Christian world and, with more than a decade's worth of ear-splitting rock and roll to their credit, resisted all entreaties to cross over or back down. Blatantly evangelical, they seem to enjoy nothing so much as whooping a crowd into a frenzy and making a lot of noise in Jesus' name. "If it wasn't for Jesus Christ," says Dale Thompson, "we wouldn't be playing music." Dale has also released solo albums under the name **Dale Thompson and the Kentucky Cadillacs.** Stephan Rolland later played with **Killed by Cain.** Steve Curtsinger and Jerry McBroom formed **Zoo Babies.**

Dale and Troy Thompson hail from Kentucky, where they first fronted a group called Matrix (not related to the Ohio-based general market band of the same name). Matrix recorded two custom cassettes called *PG-13* and *Monkey See, Monkey Do;* these were later combined on a limited edition CD for Bride fanatics called *1983–1984.* The brothers formed Bride in Louisville in 1986. That group's first three albums evince the basic "glam metal" sound of the '80s. They excited fans while eliciting traditional complaints from critics: no melody, the songs all sound the same, the *bands* all sound the same, etc. The second album includes the song "Hell No," which featured a new take on an old chant: "Hell? No! We won't go!" *Silence Is Madness* does feature two songs ("Hot Down South Tonight" and "Rock Those Blues Away") that move away from the glam metal style toward more blues-oriented hard rock. It also opens with "Fool Me Once," a metal anthem with speedy guitars and high-pitched vocal wails sure to please fans of the '80s metal genre. "Until the End We Rock" sounds like AC/DC on speed and has few lyrics apart from the title. These early Bride albums were re-released (with lots of bonus tracks) in 2000 by M8 productions. Nostalgic fans were delighted and critics grudgingly decided to let them be—even the formulaic first album was described as "the perfect example of what glam metal *could* be."

End of the Age was a premature "best of" compilation from these moderately successful first albums, albeit one that included two new songs that also pointed prophetically to the band's future. Both of the new tunes, "Everybody Knows My Name" and "Same Ol' Sinner," display the more blues-inflected sound; when those two songs both soared to the top of the Christian Metal chart, the band and their new company (StarSong) took notice. With two Number One songs in their pocket, Bride went on to record three more albums that would rack up nine more consecutive chart-toppers. Dale Thompson cut his hair and the group hired Steve Griffith of **Vector** to produce *Kinetic Faith,* helping the band to obtain more of a '90s sound. Suddenly, critics liked this band. Bride was noisy, but they weren't just noise. There was a beat. There were blues riffs. There was even a melody. Dale Thompson, one magazine said, screams on-key better than anyone in Christian music. Comparisons shifted from Judas Priest to Guns N' Roses, and the band took this all in stride. They started performing GN'R's arrangement of "Knockin' on Heaven's Door" in concert, with Dale giving lessons on how to sound like Axl (it involves holding your nose). Meanwhile, however, the band complained that Griffith had mixed the *Kinetic Faith* album too smooth; they wanted a rawer sound and they got it on their next release.

Snakes in the Playground seeks to address diverse social ills and dangers that confront America's youth—drugs, alcohol, suicide, abortion. "Rattlesnake" kicks off the album with a raucous tone and a warning against evil that hides in little cracks and strikes the unsuspecting. "Dust through a Fan" is a sad song about groupies who sell their souls for sex. "I Miss the Rain" is a power ballad dealing with grief over the loss of a loved one. Theologically, *Snakes* contrasts New Age visions of Jesus as a happy hippy ("Psychedelic Super Jesus") with the commanding figure of the Bible who asks, "Would You Die for Me?" Musically, it continues to showcase Bride's growth as a legitimate rock and roll band. Dale Griffith of Kentucky Head Hunters adds country guitar to the song "Salt River Shuffle," and **The Newsboys** provide background vocals on two cuts. *Snakes* turned out to be Bride's most successful album, and "Rattlesnake" and "Psychedelic Super Jesus" won them Dove awards in separate categories. The next album, *Scarecrow Messiah,* was basically a continuation of *Snakes,* with similar innovation but a less hard sound overall. It takes its title from the provocative image of Christ on a cross, hanging alone in a field for the protection of humanity. Aside from the title track, the standout songs include the hard hitting opener, "Beast," the bouncy "Place," and the bluesy "Thorns." The first of these has odd lyrics possibly suggesting a variety of evil thoughts the devil places in people's heads (e.g., "let's go into the poor neighborhoods and machine gun them all"). By contrast "Thorns"

offers an empathetic description of a woman's experience of heartbreak and loneliness.

Changing labels again, Bride recorded the experimental *Drop,* featuring more of an alternative rock sound, complete with occasional banjoes and mandolins. The band was very pleased with the result, which was also well received critically, but traditional Bride fans thought things had gone too far. *The Jesus Experience* saw a partial return to the GN'R groove of their StarSong releases ("Till the End of the World" has an almost Led Zeppelin feel). In terms of both sound and quality, either of the album's two biggest hits—"I Love You" (a meditation on Matthew 25:31–46) and "The Worm" (a paraphrase of Psalm 22, now presenting the thoughts of the God-forsaken Christ on the cross)—would have fit securely between songs by **Creed** and Stabbing Westward on any hard rock radio station in America. "Human Race" shows strong Alice in Chains influences. The group followed this triumph with *Oddities,* not a collection of outtakes as the name may suggest, but a curious mix of new songs that makes for the most intense and yet diverse record of the band's career. The overall turn on *Oddities* seems to be back toward the metal music for which hardcore fans had been calling, but influences from the forays into modern rock remain: Dale's trademark screams are balanced with low, moody growls; Troy's guitars are crunchy and distorted when he wants them to be (most of the time), but soaring and ethereal when the moment seems right (the almost jazzy "Spirit"). "If I Told You It Was the End of the World" seems inspired by Aerosmith's "I Don't Want To Miss a Thing" but the overall mood of *Oddities* is aggressive and hard. Sweet and harsh styles get mixed together in a number of tracks, notably on "Closer To the Center of the Earth." For the first time in Bride's career, general market comparisons of their music began to invoke the name of the most revered band in heavy music, Metallica. The best tracks on *Oddities* are probably "Under the Blood" and "Die a Little Bit Every Day." The song "I Ain't Comin' Down" also offers a killer guitar riff and a rock chorus.

The group started the new millennium with *Fistful of Bees,* heralded in prerelease hype (as many of their albums have been) as another *Snakes in the Playground.* The record was produced by *Snakes* producer Pinky Giglio and deals, again, with such street-wise themes as the hardcore life of sinners and the desperation of the poor. Musically, however, it is a far cry from *Snakes,* revealing what *HM* would call "a band fighting for its survival." Most noticeable are Dale Thompson's decision to try out rap vocals on a number of tracks ("Too Tired," "Never Thought," "Do Your Own Time"). He comes off a bit too suburban for the intended Rage Against the Machine analogies to work. Better tracks include the frenetic "California Sunshine" and machine-gun boogie "Soul Winner." *HM* advised, "Stop trying to stay young, and just rock on."

Label changes have prevented the issue of any definitive Bride compilation. *Shotgun Wedding* builds on *End of the Age* with eleven songs from the mid '90s that reached Number One on the Christian Metal chart. *Best of Bride,* on the other hand, bears a potentially deceptive title, as it compiles only songs from *Jesus Experience* and *Oddities,* plus a couple of tunes from Thompson's solo projects.

Bride has been involved in two mini-controversies over the years, both involving the media. In 1992, it was publicly announced that Dale would leave Bride to replace **Michael Sweet** in **Stryper.** That didn't happen, and Thompson and **Stryper** related different versions as to what went wrong and why such an announcement had been made. Then in 1997 *CCM* magazine criticized the group for the lyrics to its song "The Worm," which suggest that the crucified Christ understands well the suicidal urges of those who wish that they could die ("Take my life before I take it myself"). The notion Bride expressed, however, is at least tenable on the basis of Scripture (Luke 12:50; Hebrews 4:15), as is the language of Christ taking his own life (John 10:17–18). In any case, the *CCM* reviewer's main point was that Bride should avoid any "propensity to romanticize or speculate" and strive rather to articulate (the reviewer's understanding of) "orthodox biblical theology." (Such remarks completely miss the point of what Bride and probably every other Christian artist in this book is about. Artistry necessarily differs from orthodoxy in that the latter explicitly lacks any appeal to emotion or imagination, seeking in its purest form, rote subscription. What could *any* artist ever accomplish if denied the properties of romanticism and speculation?)

Bride has stated that the targeted audience for their ministry is "the misfits of society," people who cannot be reached through conventional means. As such, Bride's approach to evangelism is ultra-basic and highly effective. The album *Drop* begins with a song, "Everyone Needs a Personal Savior." The tune "Place" (from *Scarecrow Messiah*) seeks to get under the skin of skeptics, prompting them to consider "What if there *is* a place called heaven . . . and a place called hell?" Basic and effective. The fact that Bride mostly plays to "Christian audiences" does not diminish for them the necessity of such a message. Says Thompson, "Just because a person goes to church doesn't mean they're saved."

Christian radio hits: "Goodbye" (# 18 in 1992); "I Miss the Rain" (# 17 in 1993).

Dove awards: 1992 Hard Music Song ("Everybody Knows My Name"); 1993 Hard Music Song ("Rattlesnake"); 1994 Hard Music Song ("Psychedelic Super Jesus"); 1995 Hard Music Album (*Scarecrow Messiah*).

Bridge (OK)

Personnel list unavailable. 1977—*Bridge* (Impact); *Peace in the Middle of the Storm;* 1978—*Live;* 1979—*Building.*

Not to be confused with the Jesus movement group listed below, Bridge was an Oklahoma band founded by Jim Van Hook. A group of six vocalists and eight musicians, their choral songs were augmented by guitars and brass. Bridge has been described (and dismissed) by *Jesus Music* magazine as a look-and-sound-alike imitation of Roger Breland's successful group **Truth.**

The Bridge (NC)

Personnel list unavailable. 1971—*Just for You* (CCSS); 1972—*Hallelujah;* 1973—*Unto the Lord;* 1977—*He Hath Done Great Things for Us* (Sword).

The Bridge was a large folk rock group from Greensboro, North Carolina, who are significant primarily for historical reasons. Their custom-produced albums gave the Jesus movement visibility in a part of the country where the influences of "hippie Christians" were otherwise sparse. Indeed, the first album contains nothing but cover versions of songs by such artists as **Love Song, The Way, Mylon LeFevre,** and **J.C. Power Outlet.** The next album, *Hallelujah,* contains original material that prompted *Jesus Music* magazine to describe the group as sounding like a plugged-in **Children of the Day.** The third endeavor evinces a tamer sound with less electric guitar and more flute accompaniment. One cover version is included, a slowed down rendition of the **Phil Keaggy**-Ted Sandquist song "Eternally Grateful." The group's fourth album (a two-record set) finds them abandoning folk-rock altogether to become just one more choral group singing adult contemporary ballads and praise choruses. Although The Bridge does not appear to have left the lasting impressions their counterparts in California did, their first three albums do convey some of the primitive excitement of the Jesus movement. Accompanied by guitars, maracas, banjos, cowbells, and an occasional kazoo, the group's spirited singing recalls that of hundreds of youth-oriented groups that infiltrated American churches in the early '70s. The exuberant naivete of the lyrics is also inspiring: "Jesus!" they sing, "He's the vibration that can get you in tune!" ("Jesus!").

Brighton

David Brighton, voc., gtr.; Steven Latanation, drums; Mark Robertson, bass. 1991—*Promise of Love* (Pakaderm).

The pop-rock trio Brighton released one album, produced by the seemingly omnipresent team of **John** and Dino **Elefante.** *CCM* magazine called it "great, summer fun." The group has a harder edge than most Christian pop bands, but memorable melodies and strong vocal harmonies give them a more accessible sound than that of '80s rock acts. Ahead of their time, perhaps, they just missed the post-metal craving for *songs* that would allow hard groups like **Guardian** (also on

Pakaderm at the time) to find an audience in the '90s. Crowd-pleasing songs on the album include the single "Wash Me in the Rain Again" and the uplifting cover of the Beatles' "Anytime at All." Mark Robertson went on to play with **Mark Pogue**'s band Fortress, and with the groups **Generation, The Stand, This Train, Under Midnight,** and **A Ragamuffin Band.**

Christian radio hits: "Wash Me in the Rain Again" (# 20 in 1991).

Luke Brindley

2000—*Luke Brindley* (Spring Song); 2001—*How Faint the Whisper.*

www.lukebrindley.com

Luke Brindley is a university-trained guitarist from New York City whose songs recall '70s-era **Bruce Cockburn.** His self-titled album is produced by his brother Daniel Brindley, who joins him on percussion, accordion, and keyboards. The album includes two instrumentals ("Threshold," "Dervish"), but the quality of Brindley's lyrics is the main attraction. His songs offer poetic observations on life, reality, and relationships: "I imagine a confrontation before every step / I only move, I only stir, when I forget / Don't want to lose you to the fire of roses" ("Fire of Roses"). *How Faint the Whisper* seems built around the metaphor of a rising sun, which features in several tracks ("Dawn," "Daybreak," "Darkness Done") and gives the album a strong sense of hope: "Pray for the dawn to come clear the mists of night / Now more than ever we need clear morning, clear sight" ("There is Nothing").

Broken Cedars

Johnny Bovee, voc.; Josiah Castellano, drums; Daved, bass. 2001—*Forever* (Screaming Giant).

Broken Cedars is a trio from San Bernardino, California, that *HM* magazine describes as having a "pretty punk" sound (their songs are "too melodic for punk; too fast for pop"). The group started out playing **MxPx** covers until they developed a repertoire of original songs, each of which they believe to be based on biblical passages. "Toast" offers thanksgiving for God's faithfulness; "Spush" is about realizing the extent of God's plan for one's life (with reference to Psalm 17:15).

Broken Heart

See **Mylon LeFevre.**

The Brooks

Personnel list unavailable. 1972—*Moving with the Brooks* (Light).

If there can be a Christian Ozzy Osbourne (cf. **David Benson**), then why not a Christian Partridge Family? The Brooks were a predictable attempt for Christian music to tap into "the wholesome family group" fad of the early '70s. The album cover of their sole release features graphics and smiling photos that make the four-member group look for all the world like a truncated Brady Bunch. The record itself is a collection of bubblegum pop songs with Christian lyrics. No lunch boxes were issued.

Dan Ryan Brooks

1995—*A Long Time Comin'* (Filadelfia).

http://danrbrooks.tripod.com

A product of the Jesus movement, Dan Ryan Brooks toured widely throughout the heyday of that revival but didn't get around to making an album until twenty-five years later. Hence, the title. Raised a Christian in a musical and devout Presbyterian home, he nevertheless experienced something of a conversion at a Billy Graham crusade in 1969—a call that brought him back from a typical adolescent time in which he "prioritized girls and team sports" over walking in the way of the Lord. Brooks worked with Calvary Chapel and other Jesus movement mainstays, opening concerts for **Karen Lafferty, Darrell Mansfield,** and **Parable.** He provided music for youth retreats and for functions of the Full Gospel Businessmen's Association, in addition to touring school assemblies with a show called "World of Illusion." For a while he joined with friend John Moffet in the country-rock Christian band Changing Heart. Brooks' songs were the sort of acoustic folk tunes that went over well in coffeehouses. He was also well known for his impressions—particularly Elvis and the Bee Gees. Finally, at age forty, working now as a school principal, Brooks recorded *A Long Time Comin',* which features some of the songs from those early years and a few new ones. Brooks continues to sing Jesus music in coffeehouses around his home in Riverside, California—almost as though the '80s, the '90s, and, for that matter, the '00s, never happened.

Lisa Page Brooks

As Lisa Page: 1997—*More Than You Will Ever Know* (CGI). As Lisa Page Brooks: 2001—*Lisa Page Brooks* (Atlanta International).

Lisa Page Brooks is a featured singer for the contemporary gospel group **Witness.** Her solo albums showcase her strong voice (likened to Anita Baker or Roberta Flack) on jazzy adult contemporary songs with an R&B flavor. "Do It Again," one of the more upbeat, urban numbers from the debut project, calls on backsliders to rededicate their lives to Christ. "Learn To Trust Him" is a reworking of Proverbs 3:5–6. Brooks is married to Michael Brooks, formerly of **Commissioned** and the producer responsible for putting **Witness** together.

Broomtree

Kylie Schlig, gtr., voc.; Nathan Westbeld, gtr.; Johnathan Batchelder, bass (–2000) // Scotty Yoder, drums (+ 1999); Glen Kimberlin, bass (+ 2000). 1997—*Sixty Cycle Hum* [EP] (Rustproof); 1998—*Broomtree*; 1999—*Transparent*; 2000—*Maybe This Time.*

Broomtree started out describing their sound as "hard and happy chick music," then adopted the (slightly) more politically correct phrase, "modern rock with a girl and a guitar." The Columbus, Ohio, combo has a sound similar to that of their state-mates The Breeders (who hail from Dayton, an hour down the Interstate). In Christian music, the closest comparisons would be **Morella's Forest** (also Dayton) and **Dakoda Motor Co.**: the former is hard, the latter happy; Broomtree (on their first album at least) is somehow both at once.

Broomtree is mainly Kylie Schlig with a backup band. The personnel list above (as always) is geared to their recordings; publicity photos and other information indicate other band members (Brian Scono, Rusty Scott) have come and gone in the group's short tenure. Schlig is the essential member, and she is a wonder. She is not only the lead singer, but she also plays a mean guitar and writes most of the songs. Few would suspect on the debut record that they are listening to a student from some little Christian high school in central Ohio. The group takes their name from the story in 1 Kings 19 where Elijah despairs of life as he sits under "a broomtree," but then is sustained by God who gives him strength to carry on. A good story for adolescents, Schlig says.

The first full-length album offers eleven songs, ten rockers and a midtempo pop tune ("Blue Skies") that falls just short of a ballad. The record kicks almost immediately into high gear with "Flower in Mud," a hard rocking pop song similar to the more energetic offerings of **Audio Adrenaline.** The pace does not slow down, but the rhythms and the hooks do surge and gush, swerving surprisingly and bouncing the listeners out of their comfortable seats. The album not only *rocks* but *rolls*—as though the band recorded it between youth-group trips to the Cedarpoint amusement park. Every song is a keeper, but "The Boy/Girl Song" is especially notable for its interesting tempo changes. "Save You," "Realize," and "Peace" are also catchy bits of ear candy. *Broomtree* was produced by Rick May of **The Walter Eugenes.** The follow-up album, *Transparent,* displays a less raucous and predictably more mature sound. Marc Byrd and Drew Powell of **Common Children** help out with writing and playing, Byrd produces, and the result is a record that fits a bit more easily with the conventions of contemporary Christian modern rock. Less guitar driven, with tighter arrangements, a number of the tracks ("For Dear Life," "Falling Over Me," "Human After All") could have been performed by No Doubt or **Sixpence None the Richer.** "Dollhouse" and "Shattered"

will please fans of the first album. "Away, Away" is gloriously catchy. Other standout cuts include the title track, which hit Number One on Christian rock charts, and "Beautiful," which features an especially haunting melody. A third album, *Maybe This Time,* shows the group incorporating more Brit-rock influences, with "Find Me" showcasing Schlig's vocal range and confidence.

Broomtree is blatant about their identity as Christians and their mission to "become individually and, as a band, servants for Christ." Virtually all of the songs have lyrics that deal directly with matters of faith. "Without You" expresses the impossibility of finding redemption or peace apart from Christ. "Save You" offers a Pelagian (or at least Arminian) statement of the doctrine of atonement: "He gave his life / Did all that He could do / Now it's up for you to ask / For Him to save you." "The Boy/Girl Song" delineates what Christ can do for relationship partners, whose problems are described in accord with gender stereotypes (*she* needs for Christ to take away her shame; *he* needs for Christ to break down his pride). "Beautiful" contrasts the ugliness of life without God with the beauty that God can create. Says Schlig, "Everything that I have experienced in life always came out O.K. when I had Jesus."

Brother Brother

Billy Plake, voc., gtr.; Carl Kelly, kybrd.; perc. 1993—*Young Warriors* (Giant); 1994—*Freedom.*

Brother Brother was a tight, clean-cut rock ensemble with a sound remarkably similar to that of **David and the Giants.** This was no accident, since David Huff actually served as the duo's producer, with his son Lance on drums. The principal theme of their music and ministry was encouragement for Christians to stand firm in their faith. As with **David and the Giants**, the lyrics were often simple to the point of being trite. "Jesus has already died / There's no need for suicide" ("No Need for Suicide"). The song "Somebody Prayed" encourages prayer for unborn children, indicating that sometimes when we see a child at play, "the only reason he's alive today is because somewhere, somebody prayed."

Brotherhood Lush

"Eye" Brown, gtr.; Dave Cullen, bass; Jeff De Arauo, drums; Ben McFall, voc. 1999—*Chinlifter* (independent).

The independent Australian band Brotherhood Lush is remarkable for their diversity of style. The album *Chinlifter* kicks off with a very aggressive song, "Sunflower"—with crunching guitars and rap vocals—before moving on to offer punk songs ("Superclean Mr. Clean" and "s>t>p"), an acoustic pop song ("Even If"), and a couple of numbers built around Hispanic classical guitars ("No One Else," "Mistaken"). Then the album closes with "Don't Go," a country/folk number. Spiritual themes are addressed, though subtly. "No One Else" speaks of the need to have a personal relationship with God and "Even If" describes God's love as unconditional. "Mind Your Head," a moshable head banger, warns against bad influences on the brain. The song "Mistaken" (which *Phantom Tollbooth* describes as having a somber tone, "like one of those songs you expect to hear in a Mexican restaurant") reveals particular lyrical strength, dwelling on the deception of love. "I'm so captured by this moment" McFall sings, "And I know, without discretion / This is precious / This is heaven / this is love." Sweet? Ah, but the song is called "Mistaken," and it continues, "Oh, I am a fool . . . There was nothing . . . nothing coming from you." The band also released a custom EP called *Milk* prior to the full-length *Chinlifter.*

The Brothers

Jacob Olds, Joshua Olds, Solomon Olds. 1995—*R.P.M.* (StarSong).

Jacob, Joshua, and Solomon Olds are the three teenage sons of southern gospel singer Jerome Olds. Their debut album targets young audiences with a variety of styles, ranging from a screaming cover of The Who's "Won't Get Fooled Again" to an MOR delivery of their father's "Saved." "Revolution" is a rap number reminiscent of early **DC Talk.** "Wake Up Everybody" is a Caribbean chant: "The world won't get no better / If we just let it be / The world won't get no better / If we don't change it, you and me." The record closes with three soft ballads that may display the group's best talents (i.e., Boyz II Men-style lullabies).

Brother's Keeper

Gabe Dunlap, voc.; Phillip Enzor, voc.; John Sanders, voc.; David Schrodt, voc. (−2002). 1999—*Brother's Keeper* (Ardent); 2002—*Cover Me.*

www.brotherskeeper.org

Although they sound like a Christian version of the Backstreet Boys, Brother's Keeper has been around long enough to quell any suspicion that they were put together in a quick attempt to cash in on the sudden (and probably fleeting) popularity of such boy bands. The four members met when they were all in high school and began singing a capella church-choir songs. They stayed together through college, moving musically through flirtations with **Take 6** jazz and swing to develop eventually the pop sound heard on their debut album. With help from Dana Key (of **DeGarmo and Key**), they crafted a self-titled record in the same vein as **4 Him** or **Phillips, Craig, and Dean**—that is, adult contemporary, but with more interesting hooks than that death-knell label can imply. The opening track, "Rain On," sets the tone with its charged rhythm and with lyrics that express confidence in God's overcoming

grace: "Rain on, I will not drown / I'm standing firm on higher ground." The song "Graceland" (not a cover of the Paul Simon song) dares to use Elvis' mansion as a metaphor for heaven, while "Heart of the Matter" sets a catchy motto ("The heart of the matter is the matter of the heart") to an equally catchy Latin beat. *Cover Me* opens with a title track that would have the group compared to **FFH,** and includes a couple of rap/rock experiments in the same vein as **Reality Check.** Brother's Keeper also placed a song on **Terry Taylor**'s compilation of Christian surf music (*Surfonic Water Revival,* KMG, 1998): the wonderfully fun "California Blue" sets their Beach Boys'-harmony vocals against a backdrop of **Phil Keaggy** guitars.

Christian radio hits: "I Saw Heaven" (# 16 in 1999); "Rain On" (# 16 in 1999); "Heart of the Matter" (# 5 in 2000).

Browbeats

1993—*Unplugged Alternative* (Alarma); 1998—*Wither Wing* (KMG).

Browbeats is not a group, but the name provides a convenient reference point to list two of the best Christian albums ever made. It is unclear whether the two are even related (the first is actually attributed to Brow Beat—two words and singular), except that some of the same artists (notably **Michael Knott** and Gene Eugene) were involved at the production level. The first of the records listed here, *Unplugged Alternative,* was really just a compilation disc featuring acoustic songs by several artists who had the potential to attract a following outside the ghetto of the Christian subculture. **The Choir** offers "Wilderness," **Poor Old Lu,** "Drenched Descent," **The Throes,** "Monday World," **Adam Again,** "Don't Cry." The **Lost Dogs** provide one of their best songs, the beautifully melodic "No Ship Coming In," which at the time of the album's release was the only song that could be found elsewhere. There is not a song on *Unplugged Alternative* that could not have made a major impression on '90s alternative college radio if only the programmers could have gotten past their "*Christian*? (snigger snigger)" prejudices and *listened* to it. Most likely Knott and Eugene hoped the disc would fall into the hands of some unwarned reviewer from *Spin* or *Rolling Stone* who would do just that. It didn't happen.

The next Browbeats project had more integrity. In the late '90s, having written more great songs than he could possibly record with his various projects (**Aunt Bettys, LSU, Bomb Bay Babies**), **Michael Knott** assembled an all-star studio band to back various vocalists in recording a few of them. Sort of like engineering your own tribute album—except that most of the songs were new and many cried out for a different voice and style than Knott would have given them. The result is an album that sounds like a compilation, but with more internal coherence than such projects generally have. Plus, again, most of these songs could not be found anywhere else. The album kicks off with "Stonergirl" sung (or rapped) by Ted Cookerly of **EDL** with a hip-hop intro by Dax. As such, the song sounds like nothing ever heard from Knott before; it might appeal to fans of the **P.O.D.**/Limp Bizkit sound but seems out of place on this particular album: barring broad tastes, those who favor "Stonergirl" will probably be disappointed by everything that follows—and vice versa. "Getting Normal" is an **Aunt Bettys** song (from *Ford Supersonic*) remade with vocals by Scott Silletta of **PlankEye** and **Fanmail.** Gene Eugene sings "Out of Time," which was written by Knott but now sounds like a long lost **Adam Again** outtake. Two versions of the **Aunt Bettys'** rollicking "Rikki Racer" follow, one by Knott himself, and another by a mystery female vocalist. **Terry Taylor** sings two songs; "Happy Old Man," which he cowrote with Knott, hearkens back to the glory days of **Daniel Amos** when they were recording tunes like "Ain't Gonna Fight It" and "Father's Arms" for Maranatha. "Just Wanna Be with You" is a great slow-rocker, played and sung by one of Christian music's best guitarists, Jason Martin of **Starflyer 59.** "Herb's Garage" is one of Knott's best ballads; it is sung here by an anonymous guest who sounds like David Lowery of Cracker (and Camper van Beethoven) but is probably Knott himself. Then, after a new rocking version of "Tattoo" that represents one of **LSU**'s finest recorded moments, Wayne Everett of **The Prayer Chain** sings the gorgeous lullaby that serves as the album's closing title track.

Both of these albums reveal the secular side of Christian alternative rock. The mood of the first, however, is serious and quietly spiritual. The second is more of a party album, with an upbeat, playful quality and narry a hint of religion.

Andy Brown

1991—*Pakajam* (Someone Up There); 1994—*Nice Moon.*

http://someone.co.nz

Presbyterian Andy Brown lives in Auckland, New Zealand, and makes acoustic-based pop records. Something of a sensation overseas and down under, he is yet to find much of an audience in the United States. Dubbed "Auckland's troubadour of the '90s" by one of Australia's leading music magazines *(Drum Media),* Brown's songs have a distinctly local feel to them (references to New Zealand place names abound). Off-putting to some, this feature can also be part of their charm, ensuring the authenticity of his personal investment and modest ambitions. Although forthright about his faith, Brown feels no need to sing about Jesus all the time. An artist cut from the same cloth as **Mark Heard** or **Bruce Cockburn,** he most often expresses his convictions through commitments to self-improvement and to social justice. The song "My Reflections" draws on his experiences of traveling through third-world countries. "Eddie Gilbert" tells the story of a local aboriginal cricket player in the 1930s: "On the field, he was a master / Off, he was a slave."

Jonathan David Brown

1997—*Sinners in the Hands of an Angry God* (Nazirite).

Jonathan David Brown (b. 1955) was a member of the early Christian group **Seth** and went on to become one of Christian music's top producers before a scandal threw his career off track. Brown is best known for helming all of the **Petra** albums from *Never Say Die* (1981) through *Captured in Time and Space* (1986), but he was also responsible for works by **Bob Bennett, Glen Campbell, Andraé Crouch, Daniel Amos, The Bill Gaither Trio, Mark Heard, Karen Lafferty, David Meece, Jamie Owens-Collins, Twila Paris, Russ Taff, Steve Taylor, Greg Volz, Kelly Willard,** and many others. In 1992, Brown was arrested and convicted of aiding a group of neo-Nazi skinheads involved in a drive-by shooting assault on a Jewish synagogue. Specifically, he was accused of helping the assailants paint a car, providing them with a new license plate and disguises, wiring them money while on the run, and lying to a federal grand jury about them. In the course of the trial it was revealed that Brown is a member of a sect called Christian Identity, which teaches that the white race (not Jews) are the true descendants of Abraham and that the so-called Jewish Holocaust of World War II never happened. Brown also admitted to being a member of the Ku Klux Klan (as a chaplain) and of a group called Aryan Nation, both of which he maintained do not advocate violence. Brown served two years in prison and his downfall led some within the Christian music business to question what sort of criteria (theological? spiritual?) ought to be applied to industry personnel. For his part, Brown continues to maintain that he was innocent of the main charges against him. He admits to holding some nontraditional views and allows that some of these (moral opposition to interracial marriage; concern that "multiculturalism" is oppressive to whites) provided points of contact with neo-Nazi groups. Still, he maintains that he was only trying to minister to those who were involved in such groups, leading a Bible study for "skinheads" that he hoped would steer them away from their more radical obsessions. He claims always to have opposed any form of violence and insists his religious views are not racist. He says he helped the youth in question without full awareness of what had actually transpired. A fairly lengthy account of the artist's position has been posted on the Internet at www.geocities.com/SunsetStrip/Palms/1331/JDB.

Brown has not continued to work within the contemporary Christian music industry, but in 1997 he released an independent solo album called *Sinners in the Hands of an Angry God.*

Taking its title from a famous sermon by Jonathan Edwards, the project consists of piano-based music similar to that of **Keith Green** or Bruce Hornsby. **Kelly Willard** sings on the album, which appears to be orthodox in its perspective, avoiding reference to any of Brown's more controversial ideas. Veteran Christian music critic Thom Granger says that "the lyrics remind believers of the value of the law in the New Covenant, of the righteous judgments of a holy God, and of the grace by which we stand."

Keith Brown

1993—*This Side of Heaven* (StarSong); 1995—*As Long as There Is Love* (Curb).

Keith Brown (b. 1965) is a Christian pop singer similar in style to Richard Marx or **Michael W. Smith.** Brown grew up in Christian music, starting a successful local band called Hearts of Fire when he was only fourteen. The band opened concerts for numerous acts that would come to venues in Brown's northern Kentucky locale (near Cincinnati). He graduated from Northern Kentucky University, and in the late '80s he appeared on the *Star Search* TV show. Professionally, Brown found a career as a songwriter for BMG Music, where he crafted tunes that were recorded by such artists as Anita Baker, Patti LaBelle, George Michael, and Jodi Watley. He has also contributed songs for Christian artists **Morgan Cryar, Billy Sprague,** and **The Imperials.** Brown was in the news in May of 1993 when he was beaten, stabbed, and robbed by two teenagers who assaulted him in a Nashville hotel. His first solo album was described by *The Lighthouse* as "a straight-out energetic pop album with soulful ballads." The song "Wind in the Fire" describes the Holy Spirit's penchant for stirring things up when faith gets bland. "Unto You" is a Christmas song and "Psalm 100," a pop hymn. The sophomore effort continues in the same vein but with more devotion to ballads.

Christian radio hits: "Wind in the Fire" (# 1 for 3 weeks in 1993); "Psalm 100" (# 9 in 1993); "What Kind of Man" (# 4 in 1993); "Reason Enough" (# 8 in 1994).

Ryan Brown

1999—*The Life and Times of Jesus Christ* (Worthless).

Phoenix-based acoustic artist Ryan Brown set out to write a Christmas song and ended up with a dozen tunes based on different aspects of Jesus' career. He organizes these chronologically on his debut record to form a sort of mini-musical on the life of Christ. As is often the case with such projects, a full half of the songs deal with the Passion Narrative (the events of Maundy Thursday through Easter). Brown is supported at times by a seven-piece acoustic ensemble that includes guitar, piano, cello, dobro, fretless bass, and various percussion instruments. "Emmanuel," the Christmas song that launched the project, received a fair amount of airplay on Christian radio in late 1999. Other songs present the perspectives of various biblical characters as they interact with Jesus. Brown strives as a lyricist to empathize with these figures and discern their thoughts and feelings. Peter and Mary Magdalene are the favorites. Three songs from the point of view of Jesus' lead disciple ("Where Else Could I Go?" "Reckless Abandon," and "Song of Peter's Denial") trace his doubts and fears as he resigns himself to following Jesus, tries to walk on water, and eventually fails the Master miserably. As with many retellings of the gospel, *Life and Times* presents Mary Magdalene as a fallen woman who looks to Christ with self-loathing and shame, a depiction that has no basis in Scripture (many scholars believe she was a successful business woman—not a prostitute—who helped to finance Jesus' ministry after he healed her of various diseases; cf. Luke 8:1–3). A song called "In You" works nonetheless, offering listeners an effective (if historically inaccurate) model for grappling with what Brown calls "feelings inspired by personal failure and dogma-induced guilt." Brown is part owner of Worthless Records and also serves as vocalist for the regional Arizona Wish Band.

Scott Wesley Brown

1974—*Scott Wesley Brown* (Georgetown); 1976—*I Am a Christian* (New-Pax); 1977—*I'm Not Religious, I Just Love the Lord* (Sparrow); 1978—*Songs and Stories (Live)* (Seven Locks); 1979—*One Step Closer* (Sparrow); 1981—*Signature*; 1982—*SWB*; 1983—*All My Best*; 1984—*Kingdom of Love*; 1985—*Somebody's Brother*; 1987—*The Language of Jesus Is Love*; 1988—*To the Ends of the Earth* (Word); 1990—*Living in the Comfort Zone*; 1991—*Passionate Pursuit*; 1995—*35 Favorite Songs* (Sparrow); 1996—*Mission of Praise* (Integrity); 1998—*More Like You* (Ministry); *Out of Africa* (Maranatha [South Africa]); 1999—*Let the Nations Rejoice* (Worship and Arts).

www.scottwesleybrown.com

A Christian music veteran of twenty-five years, Scott Wesley Brown began as a Gordon Lightfoot-style folk singer during the days of the Jesus movement. He persevered to become one of Christian music's foremost purveyors of easy listening ballads and worship songs. Especially noted for his compassion and social concern, Brown is the founder and director of I Care Ministries, and he has worked tirelessly on behalf of the poor and hungry of the world. Originally from Washington, D.C., he moved to Franklin, Tennessee, in 1981. In 1984 he compiled a project called *All the Church Is Singing* in support of Russian churches behind the Iron Curtain. Brown has also written songs for such artists as **Pat Boone, Bruce Carroll, Amy Grant, The Imperials, Sandi Patty,** and **Petra.** His song "My Treasure" was recorded by opera star Placido Domingo on the latter's million-selling *Perhaps Love* album in 1982. Brown authored a book titled *Keeping the Gospel in Gospel Music* (American Christian Writers, 1998).

Brown is backed by members of Sons of Thunder on his debut album, which opens with what would prove to be an uncharacteristic rock track, "Sing, Singing His Song." The second record (on **Gary Paxton**'s label) begins instead with "Rejoice," a pretty ballad carried mainly by strings, and concludes with "Love One Another," another pretty ballad consisting of mostly voice and piano. In between it displays some surprising diversity: Paxton's "Ride the Wild Horses" has a zany pop-rock feel, and "Excuses" had *Harmony* magazine comparing Brown to Tom Jones. The third album, *I'm Not Religious,* was to be Brown's first "classic." The title song and "I Wish You Jesus" became staples of late '70s Christian music, exemplifying the transformation of spontaneous-but-sloppy Jesus music into the polished-but programmed contemporary Christian sound. Brown now had his sound defined, and his career with Sparrow would establish him as a Christian musical equivalent of general market artists like Dan Hill or Michael Johnson. Lyrically, he sought to establish a straightforward Christian message in every song. The strong ministry component of his concerts is revealed on his 1978 live album, *Songs and Stories,* on which he is backed by the group **Glad.** He would release his next project, *One Step Closer,* amid self-confessed repentance from "the Jesus Star syndrome," consciously seeking to duck the spotlight and offer subdued, worshipful songs like "Jesus Is the Lord of My Life" and "Praise You in the Rain." *Signature* was produced by Dan Collins (husband of **Jamie Owens-Collins** and eventual head of Newport Records) and employs orchestral backing by the National Philharmonic of London. "He Will Carry You" would gain the most notice as a new inspirational standard. Collins also produced *SWB,* which gave Brown his most-acclaimed record since *I'm Not Religious.* Musically, *SWB* displays more of an orchestrated pop style reminiscent of artists like Neil Diamond. The project was voted one of the Top Five Christian releases of 1981 by editors of *Campus Life* magazine; *CCM* called it "a treasure chest of well-wrought MOR/inspirational songs arranged with high drama yet delivered with obvious and simple sincerity." Exceptional tracks include "This Little Child" (about the surprisingly humble manner of Christ's coming to the world) and a version of "The Lord's Prayer" that Brown had written for **Pat Boone** a decade earlier.

As years went by, Brown became a featured singer for such organizations as Promise Keepers, Campus Crusade for Christ, and Youth With a Mission. As indicated, however, missions and world hunger became pressing concerns. His album *Kingdom of Love* evinces a tougher sound and seems to draw upon his experiences in visiting countries in the Eastern bloc. The song "The Wall" is ostensibly based on Joshua's biblical victory over Jericho, but makes analogous political references to the Berlin Wall. "Peace By Peace" is a pacifist anthem declaring that lasting peace can never be accomplished through warfare. In 1987 Brown recorded an entire album of songs dedicated to the poor *(The Language of Jesus Is Love),* and in 1988 he recorded a similar concept album related to missions *(To the Ends of the Earth).* The first of these features a tribute to Mother Teresa and a title track sung as a duet with **Shirley Caesar.** The latter features "Please Don't Send Me To Africa," a satirical rendition of what Brown envisions to be the prayer of the American middle class: "Please don't send me to Africa / I don't think I've got what it takes / I'm just a man / I'm not Tarzan / I don't like lions or gorillas or snakes."

Brown entered the '90s with another adult contemporary pop record in the same vein as *SWB.* The album *Living in the Comfort Zone* has a definite international focus, incorporating touches of styles from around the world. Thematically, too, "This Is the Church" and "The Lord Who Loves Us All" encourage the listener to adopt a global faith perspective. Brown was back on Christian radio stations with the title track to the album and the song "Marvelous." *Passionate Pursuit* continues to seek a more up-do-date sound with a horn section on one song ("Let My People Go") and vocal duets with **Kelly Willard** ("Righteous and Holy") and **Ashley Cleveland** ("Tower of Pride"). The titular subject of *Passionate Pursuit* is evangelism, which is extolled so relentlessly that *CCM* would describe the album as "a high octane evangelical lecture." In the late '90s Brown focused on producing collections of worship songs, such as *Mission of Praise, More Like You,* and *Let the Nations Rejoice.* The album *Out of Africa* draws on his overseas experience to incorporate distinctively African musical styles.

Christian radio hits: "I Wish You Jesus" (# 12 in 1978); "I'm Not Religious" (# 16 in 1978); "One Step Closer" (# 3 in 1980); "This Little Child" (# 20 in 1981); "Learning To Live Like Jesus" (# 14 in 1981); "He Will Carry You" (# 19 in 1983); "It Is Finished" (# 21 in 1984); "Yeshua ha Mashiach" (# 14 in 1984); "Kingdom of Love" (# 29 in 1985); "Marvelous" (# 13 in 1990); "Living in the Comfort Zone" (# 13 in 1990).

Brown Bear Music

David Cocke, drums; Jon Kensington, bass; Ian Mizen, kybrd., samples, voc.; Andy Presdee, gtr., voc. 1992—*My Soul Thirsts for You* (Jax); 1994—*To Know You;* 1998—*Amazed* (Alliance).

Brown Bear Music is the music ministry of the Ichthus Christian Fellowship church, which meets at the Brown Bear Pub in southeast London. The group evolved out of Mizen and Presdee's worship leadership for that community. The general sound has been described by a British newspaper as "sanctified dance music" with lyrics that are "uncompromising but not cringeworthy." Strong influences of Radiohead may be detected, with occasional Led Zeppelin flourishes. Notably, the songs are not sing-alongs; Brown Bear apparently envisions worship as more of a performance than a participation rite. The third album, *Amazed,* seems to move away from the supposed worship genre altogether to present songs for private reflection. The song "Beyond the Fridge" (a Hilary Marshall poem) has drawn attention for its curious lyrics: "Perhaps if babies were born fully clothed for combat you would still be here" and "We prayed God would rescue you, clothe you for the ice cold combat here." Is it, perhaps, about fertility treatments and other prebirth ethical issues?

Harry Robert Browning and Laury Boone Browning

Harry Browning and Laury Boone: 1982—*Sweet Harmony* (Lamb and Lion); 1984—*Push Back the Darkness.* Harry Robert Browning (solo): 1980—*Things We Say and Do* (Dolybeck); 1986—*No Alibis* (Lamb and Lion). Laury Boone Browning (solo): 1988—*Thursday's Child* (Lamb and Lion); date unknown—*Prayers and Promises.*

Harry Browning married Laury Boone, daughter of **Pat Boone** and member of **The Boones,** and he and Laury made albums together and apart in the '80s. Harry's vocal style and delivery were compared to those of **Randy Stonehill** in one *CCM* review, while Laury's contributions bore closer resemblance to the country stylings of Nicolette Larson or Linda Ronstadt than to her well-known sister Debby. *Sweet Harmony* evinces a general bluegrass/mountain feel with a little departure into bayou rock on "Gospel Walkin' Shoes." In addition to Harry's original compositions, the duo covers **Kelly Willard**'s "Walk With Me" and **Roby Duke**'s "Earthen Vessels," as well as the traditional "Old Time Religion." *Push Back the Darkness,* produced by Duke, is more of an inspirational, worship record, with Harry taking the lead on most songs. The critics' favorite was the closing track, a warm emotional ballad called "In Time." For variety, "Help Me Put It in Your Hands" is more of a glossy pop song. Boone sings lead on two tunes, "Make Me a Vessel" and "When I Run To You." Harry's solo album *Things We Say and Do* has an easy country sound replete with rockabilly and bluegrass. Laury's *Thursday Child* includes the praise anthem "Come Lift Him Up" and a cover of James Taylor's "Shower the People," sung as a duet with **Bryan Duncan.**

Brush Arbor

Jim Rice, voc., gtr.; Joe Rice, mand.; gtr.; David Rose, bass (−1994); Dale Cooper, gtr. (−1979, + 1982, − 1989); Kevin Munds, voc. (−1979); Wayne Rice, banjo (−1979) // Kevin Watkins (+ 1982); Brad Carr, gtr. (+ 1989); Michael Wilson, voc., kybrd. (+ 1989, −1994); Gordon Jenewein, kybrd., voc.; Steve Wilkinson, bass, voc. 1973—*Brush Arbor* (Capitol); *Brush Arbor II;* 1976—*Page One* (Monument); 1977—*Straight;* 1979—*Hide Away* (Myrrh); 1982—*Hero;* 1983—*I Will Follow;* 1985—*Centerstage* (Light); 1989—*What Does It Take* (R&L); 1994—*Brush Arbor* (Benson); 1996—*The Way the River Runs;* date unknown—*Forgiven* (label unknown).

Jim Rice calls the music of Brush Arbor "West Coast Gospel"; his brother Joe prefers to call it "Southwest country." Whatever label is applied, the band has been producing Christian music with a strong country/bluegrass flavor for more than twenty-five years. The Rice brothers (Jim, Joe, and Wayne) all hail from Clarksville, Tennessee, but they put the group together in Southern California in the early '70s.

From the start Brush Arbor wrote and sang about the things that mattered to them, often with the same sort of faith perspective that could be heard on albums by The Byrds or Nitty Gritty Dirt Band. They won a number of country awards and played a large repertoire of secular-styled songs. *Brush Arbor II* includes covers of Gilbert O'Sullivan's "Alone Again (Naturally)," Gordon Lightfoot's "Cotton Jenny," and **Arlo Guthrie**'s "Washington County." Still the group was often identified as a Christian band. Their albums for Myrrh and Word did not fare well, Joe Rice says, because the sound was just "too country for Christian and too Christian for country." But that wasn't the only problem. *CCM* complained that *I Will Follow* was too much in the easy lisetening vein of John Denver, lacking the foot-stompin', finger-snappin' appeal of the band's live performances. Likewise, *Hero* (with two songs written by **Tim Sheppard**) was faulted for a lack of diversity. Recognition in the Christian market finally came with *The Way the River Runs,* which evinces a more accessible pop-friendly sound that had critics comparing the band to such groups as Diamond Rio and Poco. The record opens with the title track, which speaks metaphorically of a river that "no matter how far you've gone" will always take you back to Christ. It continues with a worshipful attitude with songs like "Come Unto Me" and the keyboard ballad, "My Song." "You're My Only Need" quotes from the Twenty-third Psalm. "Jesus the Son" and "Don't Look Back" are upbeat country rockers, while "Worthy Is the Lamb" gives the hymn from Revelation 5 a knee-slappin', banjo pluckin', bluegrass treatment.

Christian radio hits: "Only for the Love of the Lord" (# 16 in 1981); "I Will Follow" (# 29 in 1983).

Bruthaz Grimm

Silas Clark, voc.; Lee Boyd, voc.; Aric Wickliff, voc. 2000—*And Things Will Never Be the Same* (Grapetree).

The rap trio Bruthaz Grimm describe themselves as a family with a common vision and as warriors united against the dark forces of Satan. The group members all share personal testimonies of lives reborn from violence. Since coming together in 1993, they have used rap as a vehicle for proclaiming a fundamentalist theology of glory that emphasizes personal salvation and calls on individuals to "take authority over un-known unclean spirits" that would keep them from doing the will of God. Clark also records under the name **C.R.O.W.**

Terl Bryant

1995—*Psalm* (Alliance); 1997—*Beauty as Far as the Eye Can See* (ICC); 1999—*Timbrel* (Rhythm House).

Terl Bryant is drummer for the Celtic Christian band **Iona,** an integral part of the Celtic worship group **Eden's Bridge.** He has also founded an organization for Christian drummers called Psalm Drummers, which invites percussionists to meet together regularly for worship and mutual support. In 1999 Bryant toured as part of a band supporting John Paul Jones, formerly of Led Zeppelin.

The word *solo* may not actually be the best term to describe Bryant's side projects, since he has enlisted an abundance of supporting musicians for each of them. On *Psalm* he utilizes a number of different vocalists and other musicians (including **Iona** bandmates) to interpret his original compositions and ar-rangements of traditional material. The album features new versions of several classic hymns, including "The King of Love," "Come Holy Ghost," and "My Song Is Love Unknown." The album's most interesting song, however, is "The Battle Prayer," sung in English and Ibo by Ben Okafor. No guitars are used on the track, only walls of various percussive instruments welling up beneath Okafor's primitive yips and hollers. For his second album, Bryant called upon his wife Juliet (for vocals) and on a number of buddies in the Psalm Drummers group. The latter are especially evident in the thirteen-minute-long closing track, "Ten Drummers Drumming," which showcases the wide range of sounds obtainable through percussive instru-ments. Most of the songs, however, are in the Irish or British folk traditions associated with **Iona**'s albums. *Timbrel* is a com-pilation of songs from both albums, allowing them to be re-leased for the first time to the American market.

Bubblebaby (a.k.a. The Bubblebaby Experience)

Stefan Nelson; Greg Young. 1996—*The Bubblebaby Experience* (N'Soul).

www.nsoul.com/artists/bubblebaby

Nobody seems to be quite sure of this group's name: even in official literature from the recording company, the artist's name is variously listed as Bubblebaby, Bubble Baby, and The Bubblebaby Experience (which, at any rate, is the name of the album). In reality, they are the same group (if one can call it that) as **Virus** and **Ambient Theology.** In other words, *The Bubblebaby Experience* is a project of instrumental techno music programmed by a team of two producers, Stefan Nelson and

Greg Young. Their stated goal is "to create a pervasive atmo-sphere that is pleasing to God"; here that goal is pursued through what is called "trip hop," or perhaps, "acid house" music. Basically, Bubblebaby's music consists of futuristic disco sounds created by synthesizers; there is an emphasis on rhythm, and most of the tracks make much use of accumulated rhythms, beginning with a simple bass line and then adding layer after layer of multiple rhythms on top. *True Tunes* de-scribes the album as offering "free-form, postmodern club music, hell-bent on reinventing the genre." Comparable main-line artists would include the Chemical Brothers, Dr. Onion-skin, and Tricky.

Buck (and Buck Enterprises)

Mark Fahlstrom, tromb.; Rick Jacoby, bass; Dave Reynolds, trump.; Al Brown, cornet (−2000); Dan Reynolds, voc. (−2000); Josh Wheeler, gtr. (−2000) // Scott Mercer, voc. (+ 2000); Shawn Foster, gtr. (+ 2000); Bob Poole, drums (+ 2000). As Buck: 1998—*Buck* (Tatoo). As Buck Enter-prises: 2000—*Business as Usual* (Middle Class).

www.buckonline.com

Like **The Insyderz,** Buck is a Christian ska band from Michigan. The group has earned critical praise for striving to expand the somewhat limiting strictures of ska by incorporat-ing influences of swing, punk, and indeed classic big band music. Their debut album was produced by Mark Nash, drum-mer for **PFR,** who also plays drums on the project. The horns are upfront, dominating the sound to an extent that surpasses most other ska groups. The group identifies itself strongly as a ministry band and strives to perform songs that are either evangelistic or edifying. One tune that is just for fun, "Why Won't Josh Dance?" roasts their guitarist by suggesting a new meaning for the popular WWJD initials. The song "Next" elab-orates on the WWJD theme in a more serious vein, indicating that the next step after *asking* what Jesus would do is to go out and *do* it. Along the same lines, "Samaritan" retells one of Jesus' most famous parables. "Superman Soup" finds the group stray-ing into **Everybodyduck** territory, utilizing silly lyrics to drive home a potentially serious point; here, Jesus is presented as the one who has truly "come to save the day" (though, to be pre-cise, that line actually derives from Mighty Mouse, not Super-man). The band's name was supposed to be an acronym for Building Up Christ's Kingdom, but in 2000 they decided to change their name to Buck Enterprises. Personnel and genre changes attend the sophomore album as well, with the newly christened group rejecting ska in favor of a straight-up rock with horns sound (cf. **The Supertones**). The most notewor-thy song on *Business as Usual* is a cover of the Beatles' "Got To Get You into My Life" (apparently interpreted here as a song to Christ). "Barriers" displays a bit of the old ska/reggae influence on a song about breaking down the differences between religious denominations. "The Return" is a ballad inspired by the biblical story of the Prodigal Son.

Christian radio hits: "Next" (# 24 in 1999).

Jim Bullard

1997—*The Things We're Handed Down* (Genesis).

Jim Bullard is baritone vocalist and bass player for the popular Christian band **Glad.** Born and raised in Alton, Illinois, just across the Mississippi from St. Louis, he grew up a Christian in a church-going family and felt the call to Christian music when he heard **Andraé Crouch** perform as a teenager. After work as a session player with stints in several groups including the **Paul Clark** band, he found his home in **Glad.** In 1997, Bullard released a solo album. Highlights on that project include "Nothing Else," a duet with veteran singer **Kelly Willard,** and "The Mercy Seat," a surprisingly upbeat rock and roll tune. "The Man I Meant To Be" is a ballad with powerful lyrics about owning up to one's personal failures and disappointments.

Jon Buller

2000—*Sinner and the Saint* (True Tunes).

www.jonbuller.com

Singer/songwriter Jon Buller is from Winnipeg, Canada. He describes himself as "a worship leader and a story teller." After graduating from the University of Manitoba in 1993, he began singing in his local community and touring regionally. He made four custom CDs, one of which was picked up by True Tunes for distribution in the United States. The album was nominated for a Juno award (Canada's Grammy) for "Best Gospel Recording" and was listed by Toronto's *Christian Herald* as one of the ten best albums of 1999 (the record was released in Canada a year earlier than in the United States). A more secular reviewer grudgingly acknowledged in Toronto's *Perimeter* that "if you can get over the fact that Jon Buller is singing about Jesus, his newest CD is a pleasant sounding record." The album's sound is predominately acoustic, with guitars, keyboards, and an occasional infusion of other instruments (mandolin, violin, trumpet, tin whistle). On "Psalm 150" and "Benediction" Buller is accompanied by a choir. Other songs, like "Fundamental" and the title track, depart from the worship mode to present frank confessions of struggle in a time-honored folk-rock style.

Verne Bullock

1971—*Verne Sings* (independent); 1973—*Uriah* (Uriah).

Virtually unknown to most fans of contemporary Christian music, Verne Bullock deserves mention simply because he has one of the most beautiful voices yet to be heard in that subgenre. After being raised in a strict Mormon household, Bullock ended up on the streets of Los Angeles as a fairly stereotypical '60s hippie. He was swept up in the Jesus movement, finding salvation through the ministry of Don Williams' Hollywood First Presbyterian Church (as recounted in the latter's *Call to the Streets,* Augsburg, 1972). In the early '70s he toured widely, singing melodic folk songs in a voice that was unbelievably soft, sweet, clear, and convincing. His first record was sold only at concerts in limited quantities; it contains his version of Paul Simon's "Bridge over Troubled Water" along with several original compositions. The second album was recorded in Vancouver (British Columbia) and features a handful of original songs that are among the most beautiful of the Jesus movement era. The overall style is similar to that of debut albums by **The Way** or **Love Song,** but the production was stripped bare, presenting just Verne and a few acoustic instruments. Bullock's trademark style was to create songs of haunting simplicity, similar perhaps to John Denver's "Sunshine on My Shoulders." One such treasure is "Seagulls" (from *Uriah*), which instills musically the sense of calm that its lyrics promise can be found in Christ. Bullock's song "Jesus Is Coming Back To Stay" would be a Christian radio hit for **Barry McGuire** in 1980. Notably, Bullock found an audience among Lutherans (e.g., the ministries of Lutheran Youth Alive and Lutheran Youth Encounter), who despite the famous words of their founder ("Why should the devil have all the good music?") are generally out of the loop when it comes to contemporary Christian music (but see **Lost and Found, Jonathan Rundman,** and **John Ylvisaker,** in addition to The Jay Beech Band).

Bumblepuppy

Glenn Anderson, gtr.; Jason Erb, bass, kybrd.; Tim Forbes, drums; Jared Siebert, voc., gtr. 1998—*An Evening at the Feelies* (BulletProof).

www.cgocable.net/~bpuppy

Bumblepuppy makes intelligent mood-rock that inspires comparisons to Radiohead or The Verve. Jared Siebert and Jason Erb grew up together in a tiny, remote Canadian town (Zurich, Ontario). They met Glenn Anderson and Tim Forbes at a Bible college in Waterloo, and the band (based in Kingston, Ontario) formed in 1995. The Bumblepuppy website describes their music as a sound that "oscillates between dreamtime montage and wide-awake realism in an expansive melodic soundscape that embraces every part of the human experience." Can anyone say "Pink Floyd"? The group clearly draws influence from the latter band, but even more so from David Bowie, whom they quote in their opening song. Indeed, some newspapers have classified their sound as "glam rock," the style Bowie created during his Ziggy Stardust period.

Bumblepuppy's debut album scored rave reviews not only from the alternative Christian press *(True Tunes, HM, Phantom Tollbooth),* but also from secular reviewers, especially in Canada: "a surrealistic soundscape that has a very unique sound and is incredibly creative" *(Kingston This Week);* "The music is almost an unclassifiable meld of influences and styles, yet it is great art rock" *(The Critical Review).* Their lyrics contain frequent allusions to literature (à la Sting and "that book by Nabokov"). In general the references are to works no more obscure than *Lolita,* however, such that college grads will get a few of them, and English majors, the whole lot (Huxley, C. S. Lewis, Arthur C. Clarke, and Shakespeare are favorite inspirations). The band's name comes from *Brave New World.* Otherwise, the music works on its own terms, and the imagery is often captivating apart from any clear interpretation. Siebert has told Canadian newspapers that, although Bumblepuppy's songs are not directly religious, "Christianity is the key to unlocking the lyrics." Even obscure songs often contain obvious religious references. The first words of the first song present this couplet: "Just lie me on the floor / Luke 19:24" ("Earth Summit"; what that verse has to do with anything is unclear). And Bible readers shouldn't need Cliff's notes to appreciate the imagery of "Dead Room": "Broken and bloodied by the tireless room / Water flowed from his side / She lurched and she shook under his steady gaze / Her heart washed in the tide." Other intriguing songs include "Nancy Meets Nostrodamus" and "The Insane Protagonist."

At the time of the album's release, Siebert said, "We're just singing about some of the shock we had when we actually faced reality. We tried to find some real meaning in real life and how God fits into all that." Siebert would go on to pastor a church for generation-Xers called The NeXt Church. He describes his parish as being "a church for people who don't like church," and continues, "If a pastor is good, he's starting riots. . . . I don't see church as a peaceful place."

Burlap to Cashmere

Scott Barksdale, percussion; Steve Delopoulos, voc., gtr.; Michael Ernest, gtr.; Roby Guarnero, bass; Theodore Pagano, drums; John Philippidis, gtr.; Josh Zandman, kybrd. 1997—*Live at the Bitter End* [EP] (A&M); 1998—*Anybody Out There?* (Squint).

www.burlaptocashmere.com

Burlap to Cashmere was tentatively introduced to the Christian music market at the 1998 conference of the Gospel Music Association, where the band was treated to a thunderous standing ovation by media executives after performing only two songs. How come? The insiders knew they were hearing something rare in contemporary Christian music:

music that did not sound like anything that anyone had ever heard before. Perhaps if you blended the Grateful Dead with the Gypsy Kings? Or if Cat Stevens replaced Neil Young in CSNY? But, no . . . all comparisons failed.

The all-male combo began with cousins John Philippidis and Steve Delopoulos singing Simon and Garfunkel-style harmonies in New Jersey coffeehouses, accompanied by their own odd combinations of steel string and classical guitars. Friends from high school were added, Barksdale was recruited through a newspaper ad, and the group evolved into a folk-world music ensemble combining elements of flamenco guitar and Afro-Cuban rhythms with their own take on Greek bazouki music. They developed a strong grass roots following in the New York club scene before Christian rock-star-turned-producer-turned-CEO **Steve Taylor** came by to check them out. Although the band members knew next to nothing about "contemporary Christian music" as an industry or a subculture, they were all at least nominally Christians, and some of their songs, Taylor had noticed, contained biblical references and poignant spiritual lyrics. Signing the group to the fledgling Squint label was a bold move, as there were questions as to how well the band would fit in with the Christian market. Rumors flew around Nashville concerning lifestyle issues regarding certain members. The Christian focus of the group's songs seemed to stem primarily from Delopoulos's convictions. Was Burlap to Cashmere really a Christian band or just a secular band with a Christian songwriter? Taylor went slow with the group, allowing them to find out what they were getting into and challenging them to grow and mature as individual Christians. Eventually commitments (spiritual and commercial) were made, and Burlap to Cashmere became a reverse crossover group, an act with enormous potential in the general market that deliberately chose to focus their art within the Christian subculture instead.

Delopoulos cites persons like Paul Simon, Cat Stevens, and Harry Chapin as influences for his songwriting. The song "Divorce" does seem out of place on a Christian album, as it expresses a positive decision to end a relationship with an unloving partner ("See the people loving / As they're walking down the street / But you were never much like that / And now its time for me to leave"). But "Basic Instructions" is mainly Bible verses (John 3:16, Matthew 7:14) set to music, as "basic instructions before leaving earth." The title song to *Anybody Out There?* wrestles with humanity's apathetic response to Christ's incredible act: "Does anybody care? . . . Does anybody see . . . That he died upon a tree?" Several songs ("Treasures in Heaven," "Diggee Dime") express the hope of eternal life, while "Mansions" seeks the realized eschatology of heaven's internal dwelling here and now.

Anybody Out There?, the first studio album, demonstrates a wide range of diversity. "Digee Dime" is a boisterous Greek dance tune. "Scenes" is militant, with the tempo of a march. "Basic Instructions" brings Spanish flamenco elements to the fore, while "Divorce" contains unmistakably Arabic runs. "Good Man" betrays a few hints of country and "Treasures in Heaven" comes closest to the traditional Christian genre of a worshipful folk-ballad. Five songs featured on *Anybody Out There?* were performed live on the group's debut EP. The versions there are predictably less polished but, for that reason, more dramatic. The band rose to prominence on the strength of its live shows, and some of that spark was captured at the Bitter End. Burlap to Cashmere went on to tour as an opening act for **Jars of Clay** in 1998, and for Hootie and the Blowfish in 1999. They broke up in 2000.

Christian radio hits: "Basic Instructions" (# 3 in 1998); "Treasures in Heaven" (# 2 in 1999); "Anybody Out There" (# 2 in 1999); "Mansions" (# 16 in 2000).

Dove Awards: 1999 Rock Album *(Anybody Out There?).*

T Bone Burnett

As J. Henry Burnett: 1972—*The B-52 Band and the Fabulous Skylarks* (UNI). As T Bone Burnett: 1980—*Truth Decay* (Takoma); 1982—*Trap Door* [EP] (Warner); 1983—*Proof through the Night;* 1984—*Behind the Trap Door* [EP] (Demon [U.K.]); 1986—*T Bone Burnett* (Dot); 1988—*The Talking Animals* (Columbia); 1992—*The Criminal under My Hat.*

www.tmtm.com/sam

Among no-holds barred, blatantly Christian musicians, few are as well known or as highly regarded in the general market as rootsy singer/songwriter/producer T Bone Burnett. Friend of **Bob Dylan** and husband of **Sam Phillips,** Burnett is also one of the most sought-after producers in the business. His credits include some of the most highly acclaimed albums of the '80s and '90s: Counting Crows' *August and Everything After,* The Wallflowers' *Bringing Down the Horse;* Elvis Costello's *King of America;* Los Lobos' *How Will the Wolf Survive?* as well as records by The BoDeans, Jackson Browne, **The Call,** Marshall Crenshaw, **Bruce Cockburn,** Leo Kottke, **Tonio K.,** Delbert McClinton, **Maria Muldaur,** Nitty Gritty Dirt Band, Roy Orbison, and Gillian Welch. Some of Burnett's songs have been recorded by Phillips (as Leslie and as Sam), as well as by k. d. lang, Los Lobos, and **Arlo Guthrie.** He produced the highly acclaimed 1989 HBO concert film *Black and White Night,* in which many of rock's biggest stars paid tribute to Roy Orbison. He also has been in charge of the musical soundtracks for a number of Hollywood films, notably *Great Balls of Fire* (on the life of Jerry Lee Lewis), *Stealing Beauty, The Horse Whisperer,* and the Coen Brothers' movies, *The Big Lebowski* and *O Brother, Where Art Thou?* The latter record won the Grammy for Album

of the Year in 2001, and another of his projects, a compilation of songs by various artists called *Down from the Mountain,* won for Best Traditional Folk Album. Burnett himself was named Producer of the Year for his work on those projects. He has also recorded with Elvis Costello as The Coward Brothers.

T Bone was born Joseph Henry Burnett in 1948 in St. Louis, Missouri. Though he would come to live and work in Los Angeles, he was raised in Ft. Worth, Texas, and absorbed that area's distinctive Tex-Mex blend of country and blues. Playing with a number of local bands, he recorded his first album before acquiring the nickname that George Castanza (of *Seinfeld*) so earnestly sought. He toured with Delaney and Bonnie (i.e., **Bonnie Bramlett**) and then made contact with Dylan through mutual friend Bob Neuwirth. Burnett played guitar in Dylan's band for his triumphant (somewhat communal) Rolling Thunder Revue tour in 1976. He then formed **The Alpha Band** with fellow Rolling Thunder alums Dave Mansfield and **Steven Soles.** After that group's albums failed to sell, Burnett withdrew to pursue a smaller budget solo career. *Truth Decay* is considered to be one of his finest works, featuring cautionary parables and tales of personal struggle in the face of social injustice, untamed love, and greed. "Quicksand" is the opening track, setting the mood with a roots rock tone similar to **Johnny Cash**'s "Ring of Fire." It criticizes so-called technological advances that produce a culture marked by what Burnett calls "sensory fascism" and even takes on Disneyland as a prime example. Other songs on the album ("Talk, Talk, Talk, Talk, Talk," "House of Mirrors," "Madison Avenue") likewise challenge the substitution of illusions for reality in a consumer-driven society. *Truth Decay* also includes what would become Burnett's best-known song, "The Power of Love" (not the song done by Huey Lewis), and a tune called "I'm Comin' Home," which is something of a gospel number. *Trap Door* was included in *Rolling Stone*'s list of the Top 40 albums of 1982, with the reviewer for that magazine claiming that "T Bone Burnett is the best singer/songwriter in America right now." The song "A Ridiculous Man" from that record is based on a story by Fydor Dostoevsky. For *Proof through the Night,* Burnett seems to have called in all favors, as the album turns into a celebrity affair with guest appearances by Pete Townsend, Ry Cooder, and Richard Thompson. The song "Fatally Beautiful" (about Marilyn Monroe) deals with a favorite theme of Burnett, the tragedy of afflicted or exploited women. "Hefner and Disney" reveals what two seemingly dissimilar cultural icons have in common: a penchant for making money by fulfilling fantasies that ultimately destroy imagination and rob people of their dreams. Burnett himself would describe "The '60s" as "a really good song about the '80s"; it explores the loss of ideals on the part of a generation that somehow managed to "keep all the bad" and "destroy all the good." *CCM* selected *Proof through* *the Night* as one of its "Ten Best Christian Albums of 1983," placing it at Number Three behind works by **U2** and **Donna Summer** (?!). The self-titled follow-up album is comparatively scaled back, displaying Burnett's penchant for heartfelt country-folk songs. Outstanding tracks include a cover of Tom Wait's "Time" and the opening song, "River of Love"; the refrain of the latter tune seems to tie the two songs together: "There's a river of love that runs through all time"). "Little Daughter" is a touching lullaby that calls on God's angels to watch over the artist's child while he is away. Around this time Burnett produced *The Turning* for **Leslie "Sam" Phillips,** whom he would marry in 1990. But first he released his own *The Talking Animals* (a year after *The Turning* and the same year as Phillips' *The Indescribable Wow*). The album is more literary and less personal than previous projects. "The Wild Truth" quotes almost verbatim from Roman Catholic theologian Thomas Merton. "The Strange Case of Frank Cash" (cowritten with **Tonio K.**) is a postmodern experiment in poetry in which the character in the song rebels against the songwriter who has created him. "Purple Heart" is sung with Bono of **U2** (who cowrote it) and deals with the whole irony of persons reveling in acclaim for what were supposed to have been sacrificial acts.

Commercially, Burnett's work as a producer was far more successful than his own recording projects. He himself has described *Proof through the Night* and 1988's *The Talking Animals* as "calculated and pretentious." His wife Sam says, "When it comes to his own work, he is prone to shooting himself in the foot." For *The Criminal under My Hat* (which received a Grammy nomination), Burnett used Neuwirth as a coproducer and created a spartan, intimate sound that connected with audiences better than anything since *Truth Decay* and *Trap Door*). The album almost seems to have been released for his devoted cult following, without worrying about a wider sales market. The title song displays winsome self-incrimination, which is perhaps the album's theme. "Humans from Earth" offers trademark quirky lyrics, as the titular characters are portrayed as real-estate kingpins seeking to buy up the universe. "Over You" is a sad song about dealing with heartbreak ("Going to be a long time till I'm over you"). Political and philosophical views run through "I Can Explain Everything" and "Primitives."

Burnett was raised an Episcopalian and speaks of his confirmation at age eleven as a profound spiritual experience. In the late '70s, about the time he formed **The Alpha Band,** he experienced a deepening of his relationship with God. He is usually credited with having an influence on Dylan's adoption of evangelical Christianity in 1979. Spiritual matters are often addressed in Burnett's songs, though he relies on broad entry points of universal human experience to speak of such things in ways that will not alienate his mostly secular audience. As one mainstream reporter put it, the songs are "full of hope and love and faith but not sickening, mindless religion." The words to "The Power of Love" exemplify this: "The power of love can make a gangster cry / Make a loser try / Make a strong man weak / Make a bigot meek." Not too different from the Huey Lewis and the News song by the same name, but there *is* a twist: "The power of love can make a coward brave / Make a hero afraid / Make a miser give / Make a dead man live." Ever so gently, biblical imagery and gospel promises are introduced. What else can the power of love do? "Make a blind man see / Bring a man to his knees / Make a skeptic believe." Is this Christian music? Most of T Bone's fans probably don't think so, but they all know that he *is* a Christian and they allow him (even *expect* him) to speak of life within the framework of his own experience. Burnett once told *CCM* "my ministry is to make doubters out of unbelievers."

Comfortable being a Christian let loose in the world at large, Burnett has always seemed to be less than comfortable with the contemporary Christian music subculture (and especially its attendant industry). In the early '80s he wrote a series of guest editorials for *CCM* magazine, but his connections with the Christian music industry faded over time. As early as 1983, he allowed that he "personally dislikes much of today's Christian music" and complained about the attempts to turn spirituality into an industry. "People who want to know about Jesus don't want to hear it on the radio," he said. "They want to hear it from someone they know and trust. It's a very personal thing. I don't think the radio is the proper medium." He has been similarly critical of narrowly-defined, experiential born-again Christianity, which he describes as becoming "kind of like a cult," upholding instead the more historic traditions of churches that weren't born in America and have been less affected by the American personalization of the gospel: "The Episcopal Church, they give you the whole gospel every time you go in. You hear it all every Sunday."

In 1980, Burnett told *L.A. Weekly,* "If Jesus is the Light of the world, there are two kinds of songs you can write. You can write songs about the Light, or you can write songs about what you can see from the Light." This partially perceptive statement would become one of the most quoted comments in the contemporary Christian music field. Eventually Burnett (and his wife) would realize that one can even write songs about what they still can't see, even with the Light. But in any case Burnett has rarely drawn on his Christian faith to compose songs that are explicitly about Christ or God; instead he has sought to focus on how he (as a Christian) experiences life in this world. Some of his songs, at least, are not what one would expect to find on an album sold at Christian bookstores. "Pretty Girls" from *Truth Decay* states his somewhat lustful appreciation for Texas women. "Having a Wonderful Time, Wish You Were Her" (written with **U2's** Bono) offers a splendid parody on country western titles—but again not one most Christian artists would articulate. "I think it is dehumanizing to be called a Christian artist," Burnett once told *The Door* magazine. "A lot of 'Christian artists' make it seem as though all they do is read the Bible and go to church. They give the impression that they never go to a baseball game or play with the dog. That's demeaning." Burnett has described himself as "a less angry Bruce Cockburn." Occasionally the modifier becomes unnecessary, as on his song "I Can Explain Everything" (on *Criminal*), in which he despairs of politicians and media preachers, imploring his listeners to "throw all of these liars off television."

In 1997 Burnett wrote the music for a Sam Shepard play called *Tooth of Crime (Second Dance)*. It was reported by *Rolling Stone* in 2001 that he was planning to release a soundtrack album for this play, in addition to another solo album.

Grammy Awards: 2001 Producer of the Year.

Kim Burrell

1994—*Try Me Again* (Pearl); 1998—*Everlasting Life* (Tommy Boy).

www.kimburrell.com

Husky-voiced singer Kim Burrell bears well the legacy of traditional gospel from which she comes, but she has invigorated that tradition with jazz fusions that hearken back to Sarah Vaughan and Ella Fitzgerald. A proficient songwriter, she also composes most of her own material. Her first album was released on a small Texas label and did not see widespread distribution, but *Everlasting Life* became a national hit in the gospel market. "I Come to You More Than I Give" is a song about prayer and the human propensity to come to God most often when one wants to ask for something. *Gospel flava* magazine says Burrell possesses "one of the preeminent voices in gospel today" and predicts that her unique "jazz gospel" sound will make her "the first gospel diva of the new millennium."

Mike Burris

1996—*It's About Time* (Fisherman's Blues).

New England balladeer Mike Burris has released one independent album that attracted the attention of *The Lighthouse* electronic magazine. A 1994 graduate of the University of Vermont, Burris makes his home in that state and sings at colleges and coffeehouses around the country. His music consists of acoustic midtempo songs with an emphasis on storytelling. *The Lighthouse* describes his voice as a "gruff but pleasing tenor" and suggests his music may appeal to fans of **David Wilcox** or John Gorka. The song "Mrs. Wisdom" was written in appreciation of his mother and demonstrates his ability to "use candor and humor to convey the profound." Apparently, *this* Mike Burris bears no relationship to the evangelist of that name who

operates Mike Burris Ministries (and also sells CDs) out of Broken Arrow, Oklahoma.

Wendel Burton

1978—*Wendel* (Lamb and Lion); 1979—*Shinin' through the Rain*; 1983—*Closer*; 1985—*Heart of Eternity*.

Inspirational singer Wendell Burton was raised in Texas and Oklahoma, then moved to California where he attended Sonoma State and San Francisco State College. His talent for musical theater (lead roles in *Oh Dad, Poor Dad* and *You're a Good Man, Charlie Brown*) landed him a memorable role as the male lead opposite Liza Minnelli in the 1969 movie *The Sterile Cuckoo*. She won an Academy award and his part as "a naive young man" was also highly acclaimed. He followed this critical triumph by starring in the universally deplored exploitation film *Fortune and Man's Eyes,* about a naive young man who goes to prison and becomes the sexual slave of a convict to avoid being gang raped by everyone else. By the time the film was released, Burton had embarked on a spiritual quest that took him to India, a trek referenced in the song "Guru" from his first album. After sampling what various religions have to offer, he settled on just believing in Jesus Christ as his personal Lord and Savior. **Pat Boone**'s Lamb and Lion label was the perfect outlet for his Boone-ish Christian recordings. *Closer* breaks with the easy listening formula slightly to offer a couple of country tunes ("Just Like You," "Only Be Strong") and the jazz-tinged "Spreading All Over the World." *Heart of Eternity* offers "Lonely Boy in Kansas," a compelling autobiographical number, and "Benediction," a haunting praise song. In 1980, Burton returned to acting for a TV remake of the film *East of Eden* (based on the John Steinbeck novel, which is rich in biblical imagery). Other acting credits include movie roles in *The Red Badge of Courage, Go Ask Alice,* and *Journey from Darkness,* and TV appearances on *Dr. Kildare, Love American Style, The Rookies,* and *Medical Center.*

Christian radio hits: "Brand New Life" (# 14 in 1978); "It's Your Love" (# 22 in 1980); "Spreading All Over the World" (# 19 in 1984); "Who He Is" (# 40 in 1984).

Bushbaby

Kev. Bonnet, drums; Ben James, voc., gtr.; Matt Sims, voc., bass. 1999—*Medicine* (Massive Groove).

Bushbaby, a melodic metal band from the United Kingdom, was formerly known as Gethsemane Rose. They have *Bandoppler* magazine to thank for bringing their CD to the attention of American audiences (and M8 Distribution to thank for making it available to them). The album is billed as being by a "heavy groove band" similar to Creed or Days of the New. *Bandoppler* thinks the group is better than that, an immaculate

Euro-pop band that performs songs with "shimmering hooks, jubilant melodies, and smart lyrics." Admittedly, the basically pop songs have a grunge/metal undercurrent that erupts now and then in moments of uncontrolled distortion. Favorite selections include "Candlestick Cradle," "Coffee," "Heaven," "Monsters," "Space Corps 2000," and "Scotland Yard."

Chuck Butler

See **Country Faith.**

Barry Bynum

See **Liberation Suite.**

By the Tree

Aaron Blanton, drums; Chuck Dennie, voc., gtr.; Kevin Rhoads, voc., gtr., kybrd. 2001—*Invade My Soul* (Fervent).

By the Tree is a Christian modern rock band from Nashville that labored in indie obscurity for a time before producing a successful label release in 2001. The group has been stereotyped as a praise and worship band due to the vertical orientation of their lyrics, but they have a sound comparable to general market acts like Train and Tonic. *Invade My Soul* placed songs on Christian radio and found an audience despite the fact that it was generally ignored and unreviewed by the Christian media. Singer Chuck Dennie says, "I want to defeat the idea that Christian bands are inferior to mainstream bands."

Christian radio hits: "Reveal" (# 18 in 2001).

Patty Cabrera

1991—Patty Cabrera (DaySpring); 1996—Always and Forever (Curb).

Latin pop singer Patty Cabrera (b. 1968) is Christian music's answer to Gloria Estefan. A first-generation American of Puerto-Rican and Cuban descent, Cabrera was raised a Seventh-day Adventist and made her first album of Christian music while still a student at La Sierra University in Northern California (cf. **Big Face Grace**). She was discovered by a Word executive while singing in chapel and recorded a self-titled debut album that includes several pop ballads ("Until Now") along with the salsa-dance number "Get on Back to Love" and the traditional gospel-influenced "The River." Cabrera would later say that she had little to do with her debut album's production besides laying down the requested vocal tracks. Indeed, she would maintain that she did not really come into a close relationship with God until 1994, during the period between her two contemporary Christian releases. She was much more involved in the making of her second album, cowriting six of the ten tracks and giving the project a much more Hispanic feel stylistically. Jon Secada, a former member of Estefan's Miami Sound Machine, contributed the song "I Hear Love," and the entire album of mostly danceable pop tunes is augmented by that group's rhythm section and by Michael Jackson's horns. The song "Family" is notable for its inclusion of a Latin rap interlude. "Take It Away" is a heartfelt ballad presenting Jesus as one who takes away loneliness, pain, and despair. A remixed, extra-spicy version of *Always and Forever* titled *Siempre y Para Siempre* was also released by Curb to target the Hispanic market. In 1996 Cabrera was featured in *People* magazine as one of the "50 Most Beautiful People in the World." She is married to Haley Barbour, who was once the Chairman of the Republican National Committee. In 1996 she was invited to sing the national anthem at the Republican National Convention.

For trivia buffs: A successful basketball player, Cabrera is sufficiently gifted on the courts to have once been considered for a spot on the women's United States Olympic team.

Christian radio hits: "Until Now" (# 7 in 1991); "Way for the Wayward Child" (# 19 in 1991); "Get on Back to Love" (# 12 in 1992); "Always and Forever" (# 21 in 1996).

Cade

Jody Cade, voc.; Jonna Cade, voc. 1999—*Cade* (LaJolla).

The two sisters who make up the San Diego rock group Cade produced a self-titled independent project that their press release describes as "highly melodic, sometimes edgy." *Jesus Freak Hideout* thinks the group strives for the middle ground between **Point of Grace** and **Rachel Rachel.** Avoiding the sweetness of the former act, they strive to emphasize the latter half of the pop-rock label under which their album is marketed. Standout tracks include "Haven't I Seen You" and "Drowning."

Cadet

Chad Basom, drums; Jason Kennedy, bass; Ryan Smith, voc., gtr. 2001—*Cadet* (BEC).

Cadet is a Christian pop group that came together at Oregon State University, where Ryan Smith was a worship leader for the local chapter of Campus Crusade for Christ. The group's self-titled debut album has a sound similar to that of the general market band Weezer, with certain songs betraying strong influences of Teenage Fanclub ("The Girl," "Dream"). As with those groups, Cadet seeks to play modern rock with retro references (the Beatles on "Precious One"; the Beach Boys on "God-Man"). They even perform a punk version of Neil Diamond's "I'm a Believer" that bears little resemblance to the rendition made famous by The Monkees (or to the 2001 remake by Smash Mouth). Cadet has a penchant for naive lyrics that toe the line between quirky and dumb: "Jesus Is my Super Hero," Smith sings on "God-Man." But "Beyond" and "Land of the Living" are worship-oriented with a more serious stance. In 2001 the band recorded an entire album of praise and worship songs that BEC mismarketed under the name **Any Given Day.** It includes a cover of **Delirious?**'s "The Happy Song," some Vineyard classics ("I Will Lift up My Eyes," "Father of Lights"), and a handful of even more classic tunes from Maranatha's praise series ("Father I Adore You/More Precious Than Silver," "He Reigns," "As the Deer").

Caedmon's Call

Todd Bragg, drums; Garett Buell, perc.; Cliff Young, voc., gtr.; Danielle Glenn Young, voc.; Derek Webb, voc., gtr.; Aric Nitzberg, bass (–2000) // Randy Holsapple, kybrd. (+ 1999, –2000); Jeff Miller, bass (+ 2000); Josh Moore, kybrd. (+ 2000). 1995—*Just Don't Want Coffee* (independent); 1996—*My Calm/Your Storm*; 1997—*Caedmon's Call* (Warner); 1999—*40 Acres* (Essential); 2000—*Long Line of Leavers*; 2001—*In the Company of Angels: A Call to Worship*.

www.caedmons-call.com

The 1997 self-titled album by Caedmon's Call's was one of Christian music's most-anticipated debut releases in recent memory. The group had already sold 25,000 copies of their privately distributed independent albums. They had become a favorite on the college campus circuit, and *Musician Magazine* (a secular publication) had voted them one of America's Best Unsigned Bands in 1996. The record met all expectations commercially (with more than a quarter of a million sales) and was generally well received by critics (who often like to trash much-hyped bands). Like **Burlap to Cashmere** (whose debut with Squint both suffered and benefitted from similar propaganda), Caedmon's Call has a truly alternative eclectic sound that leaves reviewers scrambling for comparisons. All of the following acts have been referenced in analogies: America; Crosby, Stills and Nash; the Grateful Dead; New Riders of the Purple Sage; and, of course, **Burlap to Cashmere**. *Campus Life* magazine touted them as a humorless Barenaked Ladies (the "humorless" part was intended as a compliment). Though

based in Houston, Caedmon's Call was formed at Texas Christian University in Ft. Worth, Texas, in 1992. A good part of their distinctive sound derives from creative uses of percussion and from the employment of three different vocalists (two of whom eventually married). Aaron Tate serves as their principal songwriter and is something of an unofficial member. The group's name derives from an old church tradition about a seventh-century monk named Caedmon who was a prolific writer of religious poetry. Caedmon loved to sing, and according to one story, he heard God's voice one day calling for a song.

The group's eponymous album mixes some of the greatest hits from their independent releases with a handful of new songs. Early breakout tunes like "Look of Love," "Bus Driver," and "Stupid Kid" (with an R.E.M.-inspired electric vibe) were instant favorites, while many of the other songs are ones that take a bit longer to grow on listeners. "Center Aisle" explores the sadness and confusion that follows a teenage suicide. "This World" seems to discuss the paradox of living as "strangers and aliens" in a non-Christian environment (though notably Tate says he wrote it about "the world" of contemporary Christian music and its attendant subculture): "This world has nothing for me / And this world has everything / All that I could want / And nothing that I need." The album also features a cover of **Rich Mullins'** "Hope to Carry On." An enhanced CD-Rom called *Intimate Portrait* was released by Warner as a spin-off from this album, featuring two new songs, three alternative takes (a banjo version of "Bus Driver"), plus interviews and videos.

The next major label release, *40 Acres,* presents a more live sound, similar to that which the group had created in their concerts. This time they cover Shawn Colvin's "Climb On" and offer ten wholly original new songs. "There You Go" kicks things off with a delightful sound borrowed from '60s-era British pop and with lyrics extolling the surprising grace of God: "There you go, working good from my bad / There you go making robes from my rags." The next song, "Thankful," continues in the accessible vein with a catchy guitar-driven melody. But again, a number of the songs on *40 Acres* are ones that require close, careful, and probably repeated listening. "Petrified Heart" takes the biblical imagery of the Levite's concubine being cut for the twelve tribes of Israel (Judges 19) and applies it to Christ's body being broken. "Shifting Sand" expresses the difficulty of maintaining faith. With regard to the song, Tate says, "I wish that I found believing in God easy and that I woke up every morning believing in him completely . . . but when we're writing, we have to tell the truth." The song "Where I Began" deals with inability to escape God, with lyrical references to Jonah and to the parables of the lost coin and lost sheep (Luke 15).

Without straying too far from its trademark sound, Caedmon's Call tries out a few new tricks on *Long Line of Leavers:* the bouncy, opening song ("The Only One") is sustained by a horn section, and "Mistake of My Life" is an alterna-pop song more reminiscent of groups like Everclear than anything the group had done before. The album also includes a cover of **John Michael Talbot**'s "Prepare Ye the Way," one of Cliff Young's favorite songs from his youth group days. Most impressive, perhaps, is "Masquerade," a jazz-infused tune that Danielle Young sings in a new-found smoky voice as if it were a '40s torch ballad. Critics also singled out "What You Want," on which Webb adopts a raw vocal style, appropriate for caustic emotional lyrics that recall the sentiment of **Bob Dylan**'s "It Ain't Me, Babe." Otherwise, "Love Is Different" is a bit of a country shuffle and "Dance" is a jazz/country hybrid. "Ballad of San Francisco" is definitive Caedmon: happy or sappy, funky and fun, complete with whistling. In 2001 the group released a worship album, mixing original songs with traditional hymns by Isaac Watts ("I Boast No More," "Laden With Guilt"). The highlights of *In the Company of Angels* are the revival of two Kemper Crabb classics ("The Danse," "Warrior"). The group also offers a previously unreleased **Rich Mullins**' song ("Oh Lord Your Love").

Because of their early success in the college music scene, Caedmon's Call resisted identification as a contemporary Christian group for a time. They would eventually seem to make their peace with being a part of that industry and culture but would continue (in Nitzberg's words) "to share songs about everyday things—which is where the future of Christian music lies." Thus, "Daring Daylight Escape" is about ending a difficult relationship. "Somewhere North" expresses the longing for one who is absent. And "Bus Driver" is about a man who drives a bus.

Christian radio hits: "Lead of Love" (# 12 in 1997); "Hope to Carry On" (# 2 in 1997); "Coming Home" (# 1 in 1997); "This World" (# 2 in 1998); "There You Go" (# 1 for 2 weeks in 1999); "Thankful" (# 4 in 1999); "Where I Began" (# 18 in 2000); "The Only One" (# 17 in 2001); "Prove Me Wrong" (# 10 in 2001); "Who You Are" (# 8 in 2001).

Dove Awards: 1998 Modern Rock/Alternative Album *(Caedmon's Call).*

Shirley Caesar

Selected: 1966—*The Very Best of Shirley Caesar and the Caravans* (Savoy); 1977—*First Lady* (Hob); 1981—*Go* (Word); 1980—*Rejoice* (Myrrh); 1982—*Jesus, I Love Calling Your Name*; 1984—*Sailin'* (Myrrh); 1985—*Celebration* (Rejoice); 1986—*Christmasing* (Word); 1988—*Live in Chicago* (Rejoice); 1989—*I Remember Mama* (Word); 1993—*Stand Still* (Word); 1995—*He Will Come* (Word); 1996—*Just a Word* (Sony); 1997—*A Miracle in Harlem* (Word); 2000—*You Can Make It* (Myrrh); 2001—*Hymns.*

www.shirleycaesar.com

Widely known as "the First Lady of gospel," Shirley Caesar is prominently identified with traditional gospel music rather than with the contemporary Christian variety, but her prolific and distinctive contributions earn her at least a mention in a book dedicated to the latter. Born in North Carolina, Caesar began singing gospel professionally at the age of ten and in 1958 became lead singer for the gospel group The Caravans (from which Albertina Walker and James Cleveland also sprang). She embarked on a solo career in 1966 and became one of America's premier gospel singers. Caesar was the first black female gospel singer to win a Grammy award (in 1972 for her version of Ocean's 1971 hit, "Put Your Hand in the Hand"), and she has been instrumental in bringing the traditional gospel sound to broader, interracial audiences. A reviewer for *The Washington Post* once said, "Shirley Caesar is one of the greatest singers of our time. She can twist, compress, and enhance a lyric a dozen ways without abandoning her central message of affirmation." Caesar is especially noted for her vocal style, according to which she often shouts lyrics in order to emphasize particular aspects of a song's message. Caesar graduated from Shaw University in 1984 with a degree in Business Administration and has since become the pastor of a church in North Carolina.

Caesar's *Rejoice* album features a rendition of **Bob Dylan**'s "Gotta Serve Somebody" and a tune in honor of her mother called "I Love You, Momma." *Jesus, I Love Callin' Your Name* is an especially slick collection of songs that (to the disappointment of most critics) move away from traditional gospel toward adult pop-R&B sounds. *Sailin'* continues in that vein with more success. Alongside the Leon Huff/Kenny Gamble ballad "The Peace of God," Caesar sings **Leon Patillo**'s "Star of the Morning" and offers a memorable duet with **Al Green** on the album's title track. *Celebration* features **Steve Camp**'s "Martin" (a tribute to Martin Luther King Jr.) and **Russ Taff**'s "We Will Stand." After *Celebration,* Caesar moved back into the traditional gospel market where she has continued to make her biggest mark. *A Miracle in Harlem* was recorded live and includes her own composition, "You're Next in Line for a Miracle." *You Can Make It* (her thirty-fifth album) features the booming anthem "Reign, Jesus, Reign."

Caesar performed on Broadway, was featured on the Whitney Houston soundtrack for *The Preacher's Wife,* and had a role in the Hollywood film *Why Do Fools Fall in Love?* (with Halle Berry). With a voice that can be either gruff or mellow, she consistently sings songs that emphasize encouragement. Often boisterous and energetic, she views her music as a tool of God to encourage people suffering from the hardships or doldrums of life. She has published an autobiography titled *The Lady, the Melody, and the Word* (Thomas Nelson, 1998). "Everything I do has a spiritual purpose to it," she claims. "The Grammys, the albums, the videos, the book . . . they are all vehicles to touch people, change hearts and lead people to the Lord and motivate them to take up responsibilities to care for one another."

Dove Awards: 1981 Inspirational Black Gospel Album *(Rejoice)*; 1982 Traditional Gospel Album *(Go)*; 1985 Traditional Gospel Album *(Sailin')*; 1986 Traditional Gospel Album *(Celebration)*; 1987 Traditional Gospel Album *(Christmasing)*; 1989 Traditional Gospel Song ("Hold My Mule"); 1995 Traditional Gospel Song ("He's Working It Out for You"); 1996 Traditional Gospel Album *(He Will Come: Live)*; 1998 Traditional Gospel Album *(A Miracle in Harlem)*; 1999 Traditional Gospel Album *(Christmas with Shirley Caesar)*; 2001 Traditional Gospel Album *(You Can Make It)*.

Grammy Awards: 1971 Best Soul Gospel Performance ("Put Your Hand in the Hand"); 1980 Best Soul Gospel Performance *(Rejoice)*; 1984 Best Soul Gospel Performance *(Sailin')*; 1985 Best Soul Gospel Performance ("Martin"); 1992 Best Traditional Soul Gospel Performance *(He's Working It Out for You)*; 1993 Best Traditional Soul Gospel Album *(Stand Still)*; 1995 Best Traditional Soul Gospel Album *(Shirley Caesar Live . . . He Will Come)*; 1996 Best Gospel Album by a Choir or Chorus *(Just A Word)*; 1999 Best Traditional Soul Gospel Album *(Christmas with Shirley Caesar)*; 2000 Best Traditional Soul Gospel Album *(You Can Make It)*.

Patric Calfee

1974—DaySpring (Morning Star).

Patric Calfee was an Ohio representative of the Jesus movement. He released 1000 copies of a **Randy Matthews**-style album that incorporates both acoustic folk rock songs typical of the Jesus music genre and more electric songs that defy its conventions. "Joy Comes in the Morning" and "Eyes of the Lord" evince enough of a psychedelic style to have *Jesus Music* magazine compare their sound to **Glass Harp.** "Rock of Ages" likewise "boasts a crude electric blues riff with raw basement vibe and lengthy leads." The album closes with a hand-clapping, party version of "Down by the Riverside."

Calibretto 13

Joseph Whiteford, voc., gtr.; Aaron Richardson, bass, voc.; Chris Thomas, drums, voc. 2000—Enter the Danger Brigade (Tooth and Nail); 2002—Adventures in Tokyo.

Calibretto 13 is a group from Kokomo, Indiana, that describes their sound as "alternative folk-punk"; most critics notice similarities to Weezer and, especially, the **Violent Femmes.** The band is at its strongest when it sticks to novelty songs like "High Five," an undeniably fun tune that includes the lyric, "I think it's kinda funny that we're all a bunch of nerds." Another highlight of the debut album, *Enter the Danger Brigade,* comes in an enjoyable cover of Sweet's "Ballroom Blitz." Other songs appear to be finger-wagging serious. "Fall Away" describes someone who returns from a youth missions trip: "When he got back home he had such a fire / But just a month later he lost his desire." The band has complained that

Tooth and Nail censored their material, disallowing songs that "used words like *crap* and *whore.*" One song that made the cut would get the group into trouble. "Little Gay Man" ends with the group explicitly saying, "This is not a gay-bashing song!" but with lyrics like "Hey little gay man, you can like girls again . . . hey little gay man, drop that sin," it is at least condescending and uninformed. Those adjectives would also apply to "Uncle Sam," a predictable fundie-rant about how America has no values or morals. An unidentified band member tried to explain the latter song to *Bandoppler* and succeeded only in revealing that he should have paid more attention in Civics class: "We claim to be a Christian nation and we're not." In 2002 Whiteford acknowledged that some songs on the first album (he didn't say which ones) were "written when I was, like, fourteen or fifteen. . . . We come across as immature, because the songs were written by an immature kid. We'd take a different approach if we wrote them now."

The Calicoes

Rodney Demeglio, drums; Erich Jackson, gtr., voc.; Josh Yeats. 2000—*Custom Acceleration* (Velvet Blue).

The Calicoes are a hyperactive rockabilly band from Dallas/ Ft. Worth, Texas, whose sound betrays the influence of artists like The Reverend Horton Heat and The Stray Cats. Critics coin words like "punkabilly" and "psychobilly" to describe the blend of punk, country, and old time rock and roll. The group recorded its first album with the aid of Gene Eugene of **Adam Again** and Dennis Danell of the general market band Social Distortion. Five of the songs were composed by Eugene and Dannell, both of whom died before the album was finished (cf. **The Deluxtone Rockets, Value Pac**). The album also includes some rambunctious Ventures-style instrumentals ("Cosmic Thrill," "Rice Burner # 2"). In terms of theme, lead singer Erich Jackson says, "The whole message that God has put on my heart is really the same message that he gave **Keith Green,** and that is for the Christian community just to wake-up and not be so complacent, asleep in the light."

The Call

Michael Been, voc., gtr., bass; Tom Ferrier, gtr.; Scott Musick, drums; Greg Freeman, bass (−1984) // Jim Goodwin, kybrd. (+ 1984). 1982—*The Call* (Mercury); 1983—*Modern Romans*; 1984—*Scene beyond Dreams*; 1986—*Reconciled* (Elektra); 1987—*Into the Woods*; 1989—*Let the Day Begin* (MCA); 1990—*Red Moon*; 1991—*The Walls Came Down: The Mercury Years* (Mercury); 1997—*The Best of The Call* (Warner); 1998—*To Heaven and Back* (Cadence); 2000—*Live under the Red Moon* (Conspiracy).

Rick Clark describes The Call in the *All Music Guide* as "incorporating the fire of The Clash and the organic earthy soul of The Band to deliver spiritually rooted, socially aware themes."

The group's sound and spirit has been defined by the passionate singing and songwriting of **Michael Been.** Been grew up in Oklahoma (as recalled in a song on *Reconciled* named for that state) but formed the group with his friend Scott Musick in the California Bay area. Like **Jars of Clay,** The Call is an overtly Christian group that has enjoyed widespread success in the mainstream rock market. Unlike the former act, however, The Call is not regarded as a crossover group (a Christian act that somehow got the attention of the secular market). Rather, like John Wesley, they have always viewed the world (as opposed to the church) as their parish and from the outset have sought to make music for society at large rather than for some distinctive Christian subculture. In fact, the late '90s revealed The Call to be something of a reverse crossover act, as many fans of what gets labeled "Christian music" came to discover them for the first time. The Call is generally respected in the world of rock and roll, counting as their fans Bono (of **U2),** **Bruce Cockburn,** and Peter Gabriel, who once described them as "the future of American music." More recent artists such as Counting Crows and The Wallflowers list them as an important influence. *Rolling Stone* has referred to Been as "one of the best lyricists in rock today." In the contemporary Christian field, on the other hand, Been and his group have often been regarded with suspicion. Been's perspectives and priorities do not always match the approved politics or pieties of those who would control access to that market. Like many Christian singers, he is divorced, and, like many, he writes songs about a variety of life experiences without trying to incorporate blatant spiritual messages into every song. Beyond this, as an outsider to the Christian market (he had never heard of the *Cornerstone* festival before his band was asked to play there in 1997), he has nevertheless been critical of what he sees (and hears) there. The real problem, perhaps, may just be that Been's theological understandings are more advanced than those of many performers in the Christian industry, leading him to express his beliefs in language that strikes some as unnecessarily nuanced or complex.

The Call's first three albums for Mercury have never been released on CD. The debut is notable primarily because it features Garth Hudson of The Band on five tracks. *Scene beyond Dreams* is the group's least remarkable project, but *Modern Romans* delves into politics with an underlying theme of impending judgment. The album also spawned the group's first well-known song, "The Walls Came Down," which Been says he was inspired to write when he saw the idealism of the '60s give way to more materialistic and militaristic mindsets. Against a chorus recalling the biblical destruction of Jericho, Been sets lyrics like the following: "I don't think there are any Russians / And there ain't no Yanks / Just corporate criminals / Playing with tanks."

Reconciled is a more introspective project, with almost all the songs written in the first person, revealing what *CCM* magazine called "the story of a man who has unquestionably encountered a life-changing force and is struggling to come to grips with the alternative future available to him." This is particularly evident in the song "I Still Believe," a bold testimony to the perseverance of faith in the face of pain, grief, lies, and wars. The latter song was a Christian radio hit for The Call in 1986 and then again for **Russ Taff** in 1989; a version of the song by Tim Cappello appears on the soundtrack to the motion picture *The Lost Boys.* Other noteworthy songs on *Reconciled* include "Oklahoma" and "Everywhere I Go." Robbie Robertson of The Band plays guitar on "The Morning." *Into the Woods* explored more of the artist's dark side, opening with "I Don't Wanna," a song that lists all the things he is reluctant to do ("tell you how I feel," "listen when you speak," etc.). Then the group scored big with *Let the Day Begin.* The title song, a jubilant blessing, became one of college radio's most played songs and ensured The Call a permanent spot on any roster of alternative rock stars (the song went only to Number Fifty-one on *Billboard*'s pop chart but hit Number One on their Album Rock chart). From its opening line ("Here's to the babies in a brand new world") to its titular chorus, the song shines with a hope previously absent in Been's angst-ridden lyrics. Certainly one of Christian rock's best songs, "Let the Day Begin" remains the group's masterpiece and an almost quintessential statement of what Christian musicians have to offer the world: a wish or prayer for all humanity to know the "blessings from above" and the joy of life renewed. Other songs on *Let the Day Begin* also display gospel-informed lessons for life. "The truth can change a man in the wisdom of his days," Been sings. "It whispers soft but constantly, 'You cannot live this way'."

Rather than continue in the vein of their one and only commercial success, The Call chose to release the very different *Red Moon.* Eschewing anthemic or bombastic sounds, the band tried for a rootsier style. "With *Let the Day Begin,* we wanted to make an album that sounded like a live concert," Been explained. "But with this album we wanted it to sound like we came and set up in your living room and played just for you." Predictably, the record scored bigger with critics than consumers. The song "What's Happened to You?" recounts the pleasant surprise of an old friend beholding someone whose life has been changed for the better. "You Were There" offers testimony to the faithfulness of God, and on the album's title track Been sings (apparently to God), "I'd follow you to the ends of the earth." Though not released until 2000, the album *Live under the Red Moon* presents a concert taped ten years before, during the group's tour to support the *Red Moon* album.

The Call took an extended break after *Red Moon,* leading many to believe the group was permanently disbanded. The compilation album released in 1997 was truly a career retrospective, including songs from Been's solo project *On the Verge of a Nervous Breakthrough,* two new songs, and a dynamic cover of **Mark Heard**'s "We Know Too Much." Then the group suddenly returned with *To Heaven and Back,* a new collection of songs that *Phantom Tollbooth* called "thought provoking, faith inspiring, and emotionally riveting." The song "Think It Over" asks the big questions: "What do you live for? / What would you die for? / What do you stand for? / What are you made of?" A couple of songs ("Confession," "Compromise") seem to mourn a broken relationship. Others ("Soaring Bird," "Love Is Everywhere") express the same hope that made "Let the Day Begin" so appealing. Notably the album was the group's first to be released on a Christian label. It also reprises "Become America" and the **U2**-like "All You Hold On To," the two new tracks from the *Best of The Call* compilation.

Been seems to relish his role as a Christian musician who is an outsider to the Christian music scene. In actuality, his involvements have been greater than he sometimes lets on. In 1997 he told *7ball* magazine that his first encounter with Christian music was when he heard that **Russ Taff** was going to cover "I Still Believe" in 1988. But Been was involved with Christian music in the early days of the Jesus movement long before The Call. He played bass guitar on **2nd Chapter of Acts**' classic debut album, *With Footnotes,* and toured with that group as part of their original backing band (The Node Gang). He also played on **Jamie Owens (Collins)**'s album *Laughter in Your Soul.*

For trivia buffs: Michael Been played the role of John the Apostle in Martin Scorsese's 1988 film *The Last Temptation of Christ.* The movie, based on Nikos Kazantzakis's inspirational novel, was widely denounced by many conservative Christians (who perhaps did not understand its symbolism), and apparently Been was put on some sort of unofficial enemies list. As late as 1997, six of the nation's Top 10 Christian radio stations were still refusing to play any songs by The Call because of Been's prior involvement with what they considered to be a blasphemous movie.

Christian radio hits: "I Still Believe" (# 2 in 1986).

Michael Cameron

1995—*Healing Love* (New Dawn); 1997—*Hard on Your Heels*; 1998—*Fragile.*

Michael Cameron is one of Ireland's foremost Christian singer/songwriters. He has a fairly large following in the United Kingdom and is noted for performing songs that reflect his experience of good and bad times alike. The third album garnered attention in America, as producer Peter Wilson of **Booley House** gave Cameron a bit of a musical makeover. The familiar acoustic sound of his first two releases was rejuvenated through the incorporation of strings and electronics. A *Phantom Tollbooth* reviewer compared the new sound to that of Deacon Blue. Cameron sings in a high tenor voice, and American audiences are often charmed by his strong Irish accent. Lyrically, *Fragile* explores such themes as the inability to make a commitment in "Don't Ask Me How" ("My intentions are good, but I can't follow through") and anger against hypocrisy ("Name of the Father").

Steve Camp

1978—*Sayin' It with Love* (Myrrh); 1980—*Start Believin'*; 1981—*For Every Man*; 1983—*Fire and Ice* (Sparrow); *Only the Very Best*; 1984—*It's a Dying World*; 1985—*Shake Me to Wake Me*; 1986—*One on One*; 1987—*After God's Own Heart*; 1989—*Justice*; 1990—*Doing My Best*; 1991—*Consider the Cost*; *Doing My Best, Vol. 2*; *Compact Favorites*; 1993—*Taking Heaven by Storm* (Warner); 1994—*Mercy in the Wilderness*; 1995—*The Steve Camp Collection* (Sparrow); 1999—*Abandoned to God* (Ministry).

By the year 2002 Steve Camp had become best known for stirring up controversy in the Christian music industry in ways that could leave an unfortunate legacy, but Camp's long and distinguished tenure as a Christian singer prior to such frenzies should not be forgotten. Camp was born (1955) and raised in Wheaton, Illinois, where he became involved in Christian music at an early age. He started his own band while in the sixth grade, then sang with The Campus Life Singers in high school. He developed a close friendship with **Larry Norman** and contributed his talents to 1977 projects by **Petra** *(Come and Join Us)* and **Scott Wesley Brown** *(I'm Not Religious, I Just Love the Lord).*

Camp once described his early musical style as "a pop-Jamaican type of rock with a reggae kind of feel." He continued, "I try to make my songs middle-of-the-road, easy listening pop. I want my music to appeal to the young and the very old alike." A reviewer for *The Lighthouse* indicated that Camp's trademark '80s sound was "an up-tempo driving beat usually coupled with some incredible piano licks and by vocals that pour out of Camp as if he were a man possessed." Camp's first album, *Sayin' It with Love,* was inspired in part by the death of his father, an event that affected him deeply and moved him to compose songs reflective of his own inner feelings. This strong personal element comes through in "Let Not Your Heart Be Troubled" and "Song for Mom." **Larry Norman** wrote the song "Strong Love, Strange Peace, with Diamonds" and cowrote another tune with Camp ("If I Were a Singer"). Many reviewers noted similarities between the two artists, with Camp being either praised as a Norman protégé or dismissed as a Norman clone. Norman also cowrote a song for *Start Believin'* ("Under His Love"), but Camp would establish more of his own persona on the sophomore album, which features a bigger production and allows him to rock out in full dress. On *For Every Man,* he strips down the sound to allow the songs to stand on their own merits, less encumbered by a multitude of instruments. The album produced what was to be Camp's biggest hit, the militant "Run to the Battle." Camp wrote the song with new appreciation for the opposition Christians can face after a tour of Europe where he played to secular audiences that included persons who became upset when he so much as mentioned Jesus: "They would throw things at me on the stage in derision," he told *CCM.* "I came back bloody, battered, bewildered, perplexed, and broken."

Fire and Ice would be the first record on which Camp wrote or cowrote every song—including the confrontational "Living in Laodicea" and homiletical "Love's Not a Feeling" (sung as a mellow duet with **Michele Pillar**). The title track parodies Pat Benatar with a song similar to her hit that insists on the incompatibility of the two phenomena ("fire" and "ice") and whatever they are held to symbolize. "Where Are the Heroes?" is a rock version of Hebrews 11 and "Squeeze" is a Norman-esque tune that warns against the world's inherent tendency toward conformity: "it will tease you, seize you, squeeze you, until you're into its mold" (Romans 12:2). *It's a Dying World* was recorded virtually live with the Barratt Band while overseas and remains Camp's most raw and direct project. A tight, rock and roll number called "You Know What's Right" is a particular highlight, and "You Comfort Me" (written by **Mylon LeFevre** and **DeGarmo and Key**) offers a break from the preachy tone that affects many of Camp's own compositions—including "Light a Candle" from this project. As late as 2001 *True Tunes* would still call this album the artist's all-time best, and that same year a poll of critics sponsored by *CCM* chose it as the only Camp album to be included (at Number Ninety-six) on their list of "The 100 Greatest Albums in Christian Music."

A career nadir, *Shake Me to Wake Me,* piles the condemnation on thick with songs like "Lazy Jane," "Bad News for Modern Man," and "Stranger to Holiness." The first of these actually suggests that a Christian's faith "doesn't mean a thing" unless she (or he) participates in such activities as street witnessing and regular Bible reading. The album's few good moments come with the invitational "Surrender Your Heart" and the encouraging "Help Is on the Way." Camp's concern for righteousness would continue to be evident on *One on One,* but his theology got better. A centerpiece of that album is the song "Cheap Grace," inspired by the writings of Dietrich Bonhoeffer and cowritten by Camp with **Margaret Becker** and **Phil Madeira.** "Foolish Things" deals with the foibles of televangelists, but it takes an effective confessional and empathetic approach to such scandals: "It hurts me, it hurts you / All of the foolish things that we do." The ballad "He Covers Me" testifies to

God's mercy, and "He's All That You Need" almost sounds like a penitent rebuttal of the perspective previously extolled on "Lazy Jane." A duet with Becker on the title track provides one of *One on One's* finest musical moments.

After God's Own Heart retreats stylistically to the more inspirational and less edgy sound of *Start Believin'.* The album's only big hit, "Whatever You Ask," pledges faithfulness to God to a formulaic adult contemporary tune. *Justice* has a more '80s sound that caused veteran critic Thom Granger to compare Camp to Jackson Browne and Bruce Hornsby. The Browne comparisons are especially evident on the standout songs "I Believe in You" and "Playing Marbles with Diamonds." The latter album seeks, as it title implies, to address social issues. As such it sticks to such safe topics such as decrying abortion and racism and extolling compassion for AIDS victims, but it manages to be both challenging and accessible, compelling and memorable. The very Hornsby-ish "Living Dangerously in the Hands of God" states the overall theme that for Christians social action means not only confronting a system but also being conformed to Christ and his cross. The piano ballad "Don't Tell Them That Jesus Loves Them" is built around the chilling refrain, "Don't tell them that Jesus loves them / Till you're ready to love them too." The title track to *Justice* is a pounding guitar-driven rocker with some more choice words for exploitative televangelists. The album also includes a cover of **Larry Norman**'s politically charged "The Great American Novel." *Consider the Cost* continues to reveal the artist's growing theological depth with an album that focuses on "the gospel according to Jesus." The title song is a piano ballad very similar to some of **Keith Green**'s work, with lyrics that derive almost entirely from Scripture. The same is generally true of "Follow Me" (written as a tribute to Green) and "Guard the Trust." "For Every Time" is a lushly melodic song cowritten with **Steven Curtis Chapman** and **Rob Frazier** proclaiming the forgiveness that God offers for every sin, denial, and failing. "Carry Me" is a particularly moving account of a discovery many Christians have made: "I was told that trouble couldn't touch a child of God / So when the trials came furiously / They nearly sucked the life out of me."

Taking Heaven by Storm initiates a stylistic departure for Camp, as he slows down the tempo of his songs and (with the exception of the title track) adopts a softer, adult contemporary sound. Thematically the songs continue to exemplify his commitments to God ("I'm Not Ashamed") and to others ("I'm Committed to You," specifically written for his spouse). "There's not really a 'beat 'em up' song on this album," Camp told *CCM,* joking over his reputation for coming on strong with messages of rebuke. *Mercy in the Wilderness* presents an even more radical departure from the old angst-ridden, guttural Camp, offering what is essentially a worship album complete with high choir backups. It was at this time that Camp also published a well-written article titled "Kiss the Son" in *CCM* magazine (March 1995). The piece presented a biblical perspective on praise and worship and demonstrated a capacity for theological reflection beyond what can be conveyed through the media of songs. The new worship orientation would continue on *Abandoned to God,* an album of mellow, choir-girded devotional music. In 2000 Camp was reported to be working on an album that was based on the Psalms and tied in to the writings of C. H. Spurgeon.

Camp is an ordained minister who serves as pastor of Grace Community Church in Sun Valley, California, and is the author of numerous works on various topics. As indicated, he has always been a strong advocate of overt, uncompromising lyrics that confront church and world alike with Scripture's promise of redemption and call to repentance. His unquestionable role model has been **Keith Green,** whose "Asleep in the Light" and "I Pledge My Head to Heaven" he covers on *Shake Me to Wake Me* and *Abandoned to God,* respectively. Like Green, Camp has run the constant risk of coming off as self-righteous and judgmental, spewing out songs that offer harangues against sinners who don't measure up to his own high standards. But when Camp's work is taken as a whole, the dominant focus of the majority of his songs (as with Green's) is the grace and mercy of God. He *has* often been quick to offer rebukes, but he has also frequently pointed the finger of judgment at himself (cf. "Living in Laodicea," "Shake Me to Wake Me," and "Cheap Grace"). A more accurate critique of Camp's oeuvre would be that his relentless emphasis on separation from the world has utilized only one of several biblical models for church and society, one intended for times of abject persecution. A student of theology, Camp has favored puritanical, theocratic Calvinism to a degree that sometimes truncates the relevance of his message for those who adhere to other positions. Writing for *CCM* in 1989, Thom Granger commented that Camp's "rap has stayed the same: an emphasis on holy living balanced with the prevenient grace of God. What's missing? A discussion of the day-to-day issues of living in a fallen world and a cry for justice in an unjust society." In the decade following that review, Camp would do more to address the latter omission than the former.

Always the activist, Camp took a cue from Bob Geldof (who organized the Band Aid benefit project for famine relief in Africa) and organized a one-time gathering of Christian musicians called **CAUSE** (Christian Artists United to Save the Earth) for a similar purpose. Three years later, in 1988, he founded ACCT (AIDS Crisis and Christians Today) with Tony Campolo. His song "Do You Feel Their Pain?" (on *Justice*) encourages empathy with AIDS sufferers in a manner similar to **Marsha Stevens'** "The Body of Christ Has AIDS." Camp also

serves as an official representative of the organization Food for the Hungry. In 1998, however, he took what most would regard as a serious misstep by distributing 107 theses (on Reformation Day) titled "A Call for Reformation in the Contemporary Christian Music Industry." The document made some points that all would regard as valid (debunking commercialization and the use of the adjective *Christian* as a marketing label), but it also attacked several trends in modern Christian music: 1) songs that do not have explicitly spiritual, scriptural, and Christ-centered lyrics; 2) artists who view their vocation as entertainers rather than as ministers; 3) cover songs, by which Christian artists remake songs by secular performers ("a song written by an unsaved person does not espouse sanctified truth"); and 4) the signing of Christian artists to general market recording companies (which he dismissed as "unequal yoking" and "spiritual adultery"). Most biblical scholars and Christian theologians would regard Camp's arguments on all four of these points as certainly sectarian and probably unscriptural. At the heart of all concerns is an obvious personal conviction that what Camp has discerned as God's call on his life must be representative of God's will for all Christian musicians. At a deeper level, the objections are grounded in a gnostic-inspired, anti-incarnational theology that many whom Camp cites in support of his arguments would have rejected. Luther and Calvin, for instance, believed that God rules the entire world and is active in and through the (secular) world to support, edify, and even correct believers.

As a songwriter Camp has written or cowritten Christian radio hits performed by **Carman** ("Revive Us, O Lord"), **CAUSE** ("Do Something Now"), **4 Him** ("The Nature of Love"), **Rob Frazier** ("He's All You Need," "This Town," "Break My Heart"), and **Connie Scott** ("D.O.A.").

For trivia buffs: Steve Camp is associated with what Christian music historians cite as one of the "most memorable moments" in the history of *CCM* magazine. In the November 1986 issue of that magazine he actually used the word *bulls**t* and *CCM* printed it (without asterisks), precipitating a flurry of mail and a consequent change in editorial policy (the word was removed when the interview was reprinted in 1991). *CCM* had started out as a Christian version of *Billboard* but then for a while set its sights on being a Christian version of *Rolling Stone.* The Camp interview and its aftermath marks a turning point toward the magazine's becoming more of a Christian version of *Entertainment Weekly* instead. The context of Camp's remark was a response to the notion that some Christian artists might be called to provide entertainment rather than ministry.

Christian radio hits: "Gather in His Name" (# 9 in 1978); "Sayin' It with Love" (# 18 in 1978); "Run to the Battle" (# 1 for 16 weeks in 1981); "Love's Not a Feeling" [with **Michele Pillar**] (# 4 in 1984); "Living in Laodicea" (# 13 in 1984); "Lazy Jane" (# 10 in 1985); "On the Edge" (# 6 in 1986); "Surrender Your Heart" (# 14 in 1986); "He Covers Me" (# 3 in 1986); "Foolish Things" (# 4 in 1987); "One on One" (# 10 in 1987); "Whatever You Ask" (# 3 in 1987); "Come to the Lord" (# 3 in 1988); "After God's Own Heart" (# 9 in 1988); "The Church is All of You" (# 11 in 1988); "Do You Feel Their Pain?" (# 1 in 1989); "Living Dangerously in the Hands of God" (# 3 in 1989); "The Great American Novel" (# 21 in 1990); "Run to the Battle (new version)" (# 5 in 1990); "For Every Time" (# 3 in 1991); "Follow Me" (# 6 in 1991); "Guard the Trust" (# 8 in 1992); "Shade for the Children" (# 22 in 1992); "Taking Heaven by Storm" (# 3 in 1993); "I'm Not Ashamed" (# 18 in 1993); "I'm Committed to You" (# 1 for 5 weeks in 1994); "Give Me Some Time" (# 23 in 1994).

Glen Campbell

1985—*No More Night* (Word); 1989—*Favorite Hymns*; 1990—*Walkin' in the Sun* (Liberty); 1991—*Unconditional Love; Show Me Your Way* (New Haven); 1992—*Wings of Victory*; 1993—*Somebody Like That* (Liberty); 1994—*The Boy in Me* (New Haven); 1996—*Jesus and Me: The Collection* (New Haven).

www.glencampbellshow.com

Like Christian singers **Johnny Rivers** and **B. J. Thomas** (or, for that matter, **Bob Dylan**), country-pop icon Glen Campbell was singing about Jesus long before his official entry into the guild of contemporary Christian music. Born in 1936, Campbell was raised in Delight, Arkansas, and rose to fame in the late '60s as a permanent guest on the popular *Smothers Brothers* variety show and then as the host of his own *Glen Campbell Goodtime Hour.* He scored hits with the Jimmy Webb compositions "By the Time I Get to Phoenix" (# 26 in 1967), "Wichita Lineman" (# 3 in 1968), and "Galveston" (# 4 in 1969). In all, Campbell hit the Top 40 twenty-one times between 1967 and 1977, including two Number One hits in 1975, "Rhinestone Cowboy" and "Southern Nights." His success was the more remarkable because he was basically a country singer in the days when the pop charts were pretty much off-limits to country stars who were not named **Johnny Cash.** He is thus rightly attributed with having paved the way for such later crossover country artists as John Denver, Willie Nelson, and Garth Brooks. In 1967 Campbell made history by being the first singer ever to win the Grammy "Song of the Year" award in both country ("Gentle on My Mind") and pop ("By the Time I Get to Phoenix") categories. Campbell's happy-go-lucky attitude and commercial sheen did not always sit well with critics, but with the passage of time he has come to be regarded as a legendary talent and especially as a remarkable guitarist. His facility with that instrument, demonstrated in concert performances of Mason Williams' "Classical Gas" and of the main theme from Tchaikovsky's *1812 Overture,* earned him the apt description "a hillbilly Hendrix." Indeed, Campbell had been a well established and highly regarded studio musician years before he decided to sing, picking and strumming on records by

artists who could obviously afford the very best (Frank Sinatra, Nat King Cole, **Elvis Presley**). In addition to recording, Campbell has starred in the films, *True Grit* (of which he once said, "I was so bad it made John Wayne look good enough to get an Oscar"), *Norwich,* and *Strange Homecoming.* He also did the voice of Chanticleer the Rooster in 1992's *Rock-a-Doodle-Doo.* Since 1992, he has been headlining shows regularly at the Glen Campbell Goodtime Theater in Branson, Missouri. In 1994 he published an autobiography, *Rhinestone Cowboy* (Word, 1994), that recounts his abuse of cocaine and alcohol in the '70s, his torrid and abusive affair with Tanya Tucker, and ultimately his conversion and (fourth) marriage to a woman who he says literally saved his life.

As indicated, Campbell has deep roots in gospel music. His 1969 hit "Try a Little Kindness" was regarded as a folk-rock gospel song at the time and became a staple of youth group music at church summer camps. A year later Campbell released a country version of the **Edwin Hawkins Singers'** hit "O Happy Day." In 1973 he had a hit with the song "I Knew Jesus (Before He Was a Superstar)." Thus it may have surprised some Christians when Campbell announced in 1981 that he had (just) been baptized. Despite the divorces and rumors of fast-lane living, Campbell was often counted as a sheep who— straying and struggling—was basically within the fold. At any rate, his involvement with the distinctively Christian music scene increased dramatically at this time. Even musically, his *No More Night* album was a welcome release from the mainstream country ballad rut he had fallen into (a rut in which he had come to play second fiddle to **Kenny Rogers** anyway). The album opens with an up-tempo bluegrass-tinged number "When All of God's Singers Get Home," and includes a duet with **Johnny Cash** ("Suffer the Children"). "Trust in God" and the title track announce Campbell's convictions unambiguously. Campbell's albums with New Haven reunite him with songwriter Jimmy Webb on some tunes, as well as featuring songs by established Christian composers like **Bob Bennett** and **Phil Driscoll.** Likewise, these albums feature duets not only with country stars like Anne Murray (on "Show Me Your Way"), but also ones with **Russ Taff** ("The Greatest Gift of All") and **First Call.** *The Boy in Me* is a collection of Christian songs by Geoff Thurman and Lowell Alexander, plus an affectionate rendition of "Amazing Grace." A church choir is featured prominently on *Show Me Your Way,* and the Boys Choir of Harlem on *Wings of Victory.* The *Jesus and Me* collection showcases Campbell's songs from this period nicely. The title track (by Driscoll and Lari Goss) seems to present his personal testimony: "Taj Mahal to Paris, Galveston to Hollywood / I thought I'd done it all, then I met you / Now I'm singin' a new song / making music for Jesus my king."

For trivia buffs: Glen Campbell was once a member of the instrumental combo The Champs, which also featured James Seals and Dash Crofts (later, Seals and Crofts), though none of those three played on the group's only big hit, "Tequila" (# 1 for 5 weeks in 1958). Campbell was also a member of The Hondells, which included Gary Usher, Brian Wilson (of the Beach Boys), and **Chuck Girard** (of **Love Song**). The band scored a Top 10 smash with Wilson's song, "Little Honda," on which Girard sang lead. With Usher, Campbell was also a member of Sagittarius, which had a couple of minor hits in the '60s. He was even a touring member of the Beach Boys for a while—as was Toni Tenielle of the Captain and Tenielle.

Christian radio hits: "The Greatest Gift of All" (# 22 in 1991).

Dove awards: 1985 Album by a Secular Artist (No More Night); 1992 Southern Gospel Song ("Where Shadows Never Fall"); 2000 Country Album (A Glen Campbell Christmas).

Grammy Awards: 1967 Best Vocal Performance, Male ("By the Time I Get to Phoenix"); 1967 Best Country and Western Solo Vocal Performance, Male ("Gentle on My Mind"); 1967 Best Country and Western Recording ("Gentle on My Mind"); 1968 Album of the Year (By the Time I Get to Phoenix).

Kate Campbell

1994—Songs from the Levee (Large River); 1997—Moonpie Dreams (Compass); 1998—Visions of Plenty; 1999—Rosaryville; 2000—Wandering Strange (Large River).

www.katecampbell.com

Southern singer/songwriter Kate Campbell creates Americana music with a strong blend of country and folk and intelligent lyrics. Campbell holds a Masters in History from Auburn University and taught for a time at Belmont and Middle Tennessee State Universities. She was born in New Orleans and raised first in the Mississippi Delta, and then in Tennessee, as the daughter of a socially progressive (white) Southern Baptist minister who opposed segregation and opened his church to the Freedom Riders. Her memories of the civil rights movement remain formative influences on her songwriting, as do the writings of Flannery O'Connor. Campbell sought to pursue a career in Christian music early on but was encouraged by George King (later head of Reunion Records) to aim for the country market instead, as the Christian market was just not ready for her yet. That advice proved reliable, and her first few albums would gain acclaim among country-folk fans, who sometimes likened her to Mary Chapin Carpenter.

Called "one of the most innovative and fresh writers around" by Billboard magazine, Campbell also incorporates touches of humor into her work. The song "Galaxie 500" from Moonpie Dreams has been featured on the popular radio show "Car Talk." A tune called "Jesus and Tomatoes" (from Visions of Plenty) is about tomatoes that miraculously appear to look like Jesus. It was inspired by a sign she saw at a roadside market, "Jesus and Tomatoes Coming Soon." Musically, Campbell's songs take in a variety of southern influences. Moonpie Dreams includes an interesting Memphis blues song called "When Panthers Roamed in Arkansas," which features **Al Perkins** on dobro. Emmylou Harris appears as a guest vocalist on Visions of Plenty. Wandering Strange features backing from the Muscle Shoals musicians (sans horns). Campbell favors songs that tell stories, since "stories have universal themes that connect with people whose experiences differ." On Visions of Plenty, "Bus 109" recounts her positive experience of being bused as a teenager to a mostly black school in Nashville. On Rosaryville, "Who Will Pray for Junior?" tells the tale of a mother about to leave her child an orphan; "Ave Maria Grotto" is about a man who builds miniature versions of the world's architectural wonders in his backyard; "Rosa's Coronas" celebrates the dedication and pride a Cuban woman feels in her daily work of making cigars—she prays silently for the Pope's visits around the world while she rolls them. "In My Mother's House" is autobiographical reflection on Campbell's own upbringing and on how mother/daughter roles reverse in time; "Look Away" finds her still struggling to love the South in spite of its history of racial violence ("It's a long and slow surrender, retreating from the past"). Wandering Strange is Campbell's most overtly gospel album, featuring six hymns (from the 1956 Baptist Hymnal) and only four original songs, plus a cover of Gordon Lightfoot's "The House You Live In." One of the original tunes, "10,000 Lures," paints a picture in which the devil is fishing for souls with a tackle box full of tricks to catch them, but then concludes, "Before I end this song, before the music's through / I'd like to share a word or two: there's 10,000 angels watching over you."

Canaan

Bob Fraser, voc.; et al. 1974—Canaan (Dovetail); 1976—Out of the Wilderness (Myrrh).

A British country rock group that featured Bob Fraser on vocals, Canaan brought an English twist to the "Christian version of the Eagles" sound that so many mid '70s artists (including **Daniel Amos** and **Bethlehem**) sought to capture. According to Jesus Music magazine, the group had "really cookin' " guitars: on the first album, " 'Follow Me' and 'Lonely Man' both have loud acid guitar, while 'Mr. Jones' and 'Jesus Revolution' heavily utilize the reverb effect." The second record inspired comparisons to Jonathan Edwards (the singer, not the philosopher/preacher) and to Poco: "reflective, out in the country, sunny day stuff."

Candle (a.k.a. **Agape Force**)

Personnel list unavailable. As Candle: 1976—*To the Chief Musician* (Birdwing); 1977—*To the Chief Musician, Chapter 2*; 1977—*The Music Machine* (Sparrow); 1979—*Sir Oliver's Song* (Birdwing); 1978—*Nathaniel the Grublet*; 1979—*On the Street* (Sparrow); 1983—*The Music Machine 2* (Birdwing); date unknown—*The Birthday Party* (Sparrow). As Agape Force: 1971—*Unchoir* (Candle); *Potpourri*; 1974—*Favorites*; *Agapeland*; 1978—*Within the Gate* (Birdwing); *Bullfrogs and Butterflys* (=*Agapeland*).

Was Candle the name of a group or a company? The same people released several albums in the '70s, typically (but not always) calling themselves "Agape Force" when the albums were released on the Candle label, and "Candle" when the albums were released on some other label. Basically, Agape Force was an evangelistic ministry located first in California and then eventually in Lindale, Texas. Candle was the "Arts and Music Department" of the larger enterprise. To make matters a little bit more complicated, **Silverwind** was a still different music ministry under Agape Force, and Bulgarian refugee Georgian Banov, who headed up Silverwind, sometimes worked with Candle as well.

Albums produced by Candle or Agape Force were of two types. First there were worship albums similar to the successful Maranatha *Praise* series. The two *Chief Musician* albums are most representative of this genre, featuring soothing choral arrangements that *Harmony* magazine said "sound like the type of music that would be played in the background of a Bible bookstore." Second, Candle a.k.a. Agape Force released extremely successful children's albums that were the '70s equivalent of Veggie Tales. *The Music Machine* and *Bullfrogs and Butterflys* (featuring **Barry McGuire** on the title track) each sold more than three million copies, making them among the most successful Christian albums of all time. The success was well deserved. *Music Machine* teaches children about basic virtues (the biblical fruit of the Spirit, Galatians 5:22–23) with colorful and humorous anecdotes and fun songs that transcend specifics of Christian dogma. The result is a package with enormous crossover appeal, yet one that offers a gentle and appealing introduction to certain aspects of the Christian message. *Bullfrogs and Butterflys* is actually a reproduction by **Mike Deasy** of the earlier *Agapeland* album; it strives to teach a variety of lessons regarding the importance of prayer, the value of friendship, and the need for perseverance. The hit title track stresses what the titular metamorphed species have in common: "they've both been born again." *Sir Oliver's Song* teaches the Ten Commandments and fosters an ideal of inclusivity by sampling the music and languages of different cultures. *Nathanael the Grublet* warns against stealing and pride, while exalting Christ's command to "love one another." *The Birthday Party* is "a Christmas album for all year round" built around the idea that Christ can be born in the believer's heart each day.

Michael Card

1981—*First Light* (Milk and Honey); 1983—*Legacy; Known by the Scars* (Sparrow); 1985—*Scandalon*; 1987—*The Final Word*; 1988—*Present Reality; The Life*; 1989—*Sleep Sound in Jesus; The Beginning*; 1990—*The Way of Wisdom*; 1991—*The Promise: A Celebration of Christ's Birth*; 1992—*The Word: Recapturing the Imagination*; 1993—*Come to the Cradle; The Ancient Faith*; 1994—*Joy in the Journey: Ten Years of Greatest Hits; Poiema*; 1996—*The Early Years; Brother to Brother* [with John Michael Talbot] (Myrrh); *Close Your Eyes So You Can See*; 1997—*Unveiled Hope*; 1998—*Starkindler*; 2000—*Soul Anchor*.

www.michaelcard.com

Born in 1957 in Madison, Tennessee, Card is the son of a doctor and grandson of a Baptist minister (whom he extols in "For F.F.B." from *Poiēma*). He has earned undergraduate and masters degrees in biblical studies from Western Kentucky University, which gave him their Distinguished Alumni Award in 1997. While a student at WKU, Card began writing songs to accompany the sermons of his professor William L. Lane, a renowned biblical scholar. Card was a childhood friend of banjo player Randy Scruggs (son of the great Earl Scruggs), who encouraged him to record his music and produced his first album. That record, which features Card's first hit, "I Have Decided," evinces a sound very similar to Card's hero Dan Fogelberg, and some reviewers dismissed the new artist as no more than a Fogelberg clone. The next record, however, incorporates some piano tricks Card had learned from his new friend **Leon Patillo** and showcases a more original and developed sound. In the years to come, Card would become very much his own person and—far from being considered imitative—came to be regarded as an adult contemporary exemplar often imitated by others. Card's musical style favors meditative, simple acoustic arrangements (piano, guitar, some orchestration) such as is associated with traditional church music. Poetry is dominant, with a clear impetus toward worship or edification rather than entertainment. As years went by, the artist would also incorporate more diverse international sounds, drawing especially on his own Celtic heritage.

One of Card's early compositions, "El Shaddai," became a major hit on Christian radio for **Amy Grant** and nabbed Card a Dove award for Songwriter of the Year. The song reflects upon God's faithfulness from an Old Testament perspective, referencing, for instance, the compelling experience of Hagar: "To the outcast on her knees / You are a God who really sees" (Genesis 16:13). In 2001 Grant's version of the song was included on a list of "the 365 most significant songs of the twentieth-century" prepared by the Recording Industry Association of America (it was 326, right behind Elton John's "Candle in the Wind"). Card would include his own version of "El Shaddai" on his sophomore project, *Legacy*, which also features the stellar "Love Crucified Arose."

Card's albums have frequently provided musical reflections on scriptural themes and have sometimes been accompanied by books that explore those themes in more detail. *Legacy* presents Christ as the fulfillment of the Hebrew Scriptures. *Known by the Scars, Scandalon,* and *The Final Word* present a trilogy on the life of Christ, told in reverse order. *Known by the Scars* deals with the events of the Passion Narrative: the entry to Jerusalem, the cleansing of the temple, the Last Supper, and the crucifixion. *Scandalon* interprets the three-year ministry of Jesus, focusing on the biblical idea that God's coming to humanity in weakness is scandalous or offensive to human sensibilities. *The Final Word* is a more upbeat and joyous record dealing with the Incarnation and birth of Christ; it includes "Joy in the Journey" and the anthemic "Emmanuel." The latter three albums would later be repackaged as *The Life*.

The *Present Reality* album deals with the theological mystery of knowing God in the present moment. Card then embarked on another ambitious trilogy, this time based on the story of Israel in the Old Testament. *The Beginning* presents songs based on references in the Pentateuch (the first five books of the Bible), all of which are given christological interpretations: "A Face That Shone" deals with the unveiled face of Moses and "Lift Up the Suffering Symbol," with the healing serpent staff elevated in the wilderness. The standout song "Jubilee" is built on the emancipation of slaves and cancellation of debts announced in Leviticus 25:10. *The Way of Wisdom* draws its songs from Ecclesiastes, Proverbs, Psalms, and the Song of Solomon, with a four-song suite inspired by Job. *The Word: Recapturing the Imagination* tackles the difficult prophetic material, setting oracles to musically diverse tunes. "Valley of Dry Bones" has an Irish flavor, and "Why Will You Not Listen" is sung by a gospel quartet (featuring **Steve Green** and two other guests). The album's masterwork, however, is "I Will Bring You Home," a song for exiles that takes on universal meaning for all who long for heaven. Again, the three parts of this latter trilogy were eventually packed together as *The Ancient Faith*.

The Promise is less a Christmas album than a collection of original meditations on the events of Christ's birth. These events are considered from the perspectives of different biblical characters (Mary, Joseph, the shepherds, the magi). *Poiema* (from the New Testament Greek word for "masterpiece" or "poem") examines the theme of humanity as the crown of God's creation. *Unveiled Hope* sets to music songs taken from or inspired by the book of Revelation. On *Starkindler,* Card performs Irish songs of faith from the seventeenth, eighteenth, and nineteenth centuries, incorporating Renaissance and Celtic music into his sound. *Soul Anchor* draws on the letter to the Hebrews and features Dan Haseltine of **Jars of Clay** on the standout song "By Faith" (based on Hebrews 11). Although Card is known for writing songs with greater theological depth than is often found in contemporary Christian music, his best selling album is actually a collection of lullabies for children (*Sleep Sound in Jesus,* also accompanied by a book). This was followed by *Come to the Cradle,* which has been marketed as another children's album though Card says he wrote it "for parents."

All told, Card has authored or coauthored nine books, and he has sold more than four million albums. In 1987 he said, "The truth is too radical and foolish for the world to accept, and yet the church today presents Christ in a popular way that will make Christianity attractive to everyone. It sounds crazy, but I would like to present Jesus so accurately that ultimately some people, just as they did in Jesus' own time, would say no to him." Several years later, in 1995, he recalled how, when he first got started in Christian music, industry types offered to teach him "how to dress" and advised him not to "sing about the cross too much" in order to help him become a star. Disgusted with the Christian music business, he was advised by Lane (his professor), "Let the excellence of your work be your protest," a mandate he would always try to follow. In 2001 Card authored a book in memory of Lane recalling many such conversations he had with his mentor from his early days as a seminarian through the time of the latter's heart-wrenching death (*The Walk: A Moment in Time When Two Lives Intersect,* Thomas Nelson). Ultimately Card would describe the purpose of all of his books, concerts, and recordings as being "to focus in on and worship Christ" and "to assist in making Jesus Christ beautiful and believable to the world."

Different compilations of Card's songs are available, the best of which is *Joy in the Journey.* Sparrow's mistitled *The Early Years* offers a meager ten songs from *Scandalon* and *The Final Word,* ignoring Card's first three projects altogether. *Brother to Brother* is an innovative collection of songs by both Card and **John Michael Talbot,** with each artist interpreting the other's material. The album was heralded as an ecumenical effort, bringing together a Roman Catholic and a conservative Protestant who had long admired each other's work.

For trivia buffs: Michael Card is left-handed and, like Paul McCartney, plays the guitar upside down.

Christian radio hits: "I Have Decided" (# 8 in 1982); "Fan the Flame" (# 16 in 1982); "Jesus Loves Me" (# 8 in 1982); "Love Crucified Arose" (# 5 in 1983); "Abba Father" (# 4 in 1983); "Tell the World That Jesus Loves You" (# 32 in 1983); "This Must Be the Lamb" (# 14 in 1984); "Known by the Scars" (# 14 in 1985); "Scandalon" (# 3 in 1986); "The Final Word" (# 11 in 1987); "Celebrate the Child" (# 14 in 1987); "To the Mystery" (# 10 in 1988); "That's What Faith Must Be" (# 14 in 1988); "Know You in the Now" (# 6 in 1988); "Jubilee" (# 7 in 1990); "Lift Up the Suffering Symbol" (# 23 in 1990); "The Way of Wisdom" (# 15 in 1991); "How Long" (# 14 in 1991); "We Will Find Him" (# 16 in 1992).

Dove Awards: 1983 Songwriter of the Year; 1988 Praise and Worship Album *(The Final Word)*; 1994 Children's Music Album *(Come to the Cradle)*.

Bob Carlisle

1993—*Bob Carlisle* (Sparrow); 1994—*The Hope of a Man*; 1997—*Butterfly Kisses* [a.k.a. *Shades of Grace*] (Diadem); 1997—*Collection* (Sparrow); *The Ballads of Bob Carlisle* (Word); 1998—*Butterfly Kisses and Bedtime Prayers, Vol. 1* (Benson); *Butterfly Kisses and Bedtime Prayers, Vol. 2*; *Stories from the Heart* (Diadem); 2000—*Nothing But the Truth*.

www.bobcarlisle.com

Bob Carlisle will probably always be remembered for his sentimental 1997 hit, "Butterfly Kisses" (# 1 on *Billboard* adult contemporary charts; # 10 on the pop charts), but his career in Christian music stretches back to the early days of the Jesus movement and incorporates many non-Butterfly-related activities. Born in 1956 in Santa Ana, California, he joined the classic Jesus music group **Good News** (which also included **Billy Batstone, David Diggs,** and **Erick Nelson**) when he was only sixteen. Next he was in the lesser-known band **Psalm 150,** and then he and fellow Psalm 150 alum Randy Thomas formed the **Allies.** He and Thomas developed as a songwriting team and penned the song, "Why'd You Come in Here Lookin' Like That?" which became a Number One country hit for Dolly Parton. As a solo artist, Carlisle has carved out a niche in the soulful subset of the adult contemporary market, singing ballads that express his most heartfelt emotions. His voice and vocal stylings (on his solo projects) are often compared to those of Michael Bolton. Favorite themes are family and devotion to his Lord.

Carlisle's self-titled debut solo album features several songs that emphasize his willingness to be used as a servant of Christ ("Use Me," "Giving You the Rest of My Life," "Mind, Body, Heart, and Soul"). "Getting Stronger" is a powerful pop song with a strong hook and anti-machismo lyrics: "If you see me on my knees, it's not because I'm weak / I'm getting stronger / If you see me start to cry, you'll know the reason why / I'm getting stronger." The album closes with a touching remake of **Erick Nelson**'s "Going Home." *The Hope of a Man,* featuring four songs written with **Rick Elias,** was geared toward Carlisle's Promise Keepers audience, seeking to redefine masculinity away from the "macho standards" imposed by popular culture. The record opens with a pair of up-tempo R&B songs and closes with the traditional gospel sounds of "Last Train to Glory," but its main message is offered along the way through stirring ballads such as "When a Grown Man Cries." His next album was originally titled *Shades of Grace* but was renamed *Butterfly Kisses* and repackaged for distribution to the mainstream market after the song "Butterfly Kisses" became a crossover hit.

The song "Butterfly Kisses" was written by Carlisle and Thomas for Carlisle's daughter Brooke on her sixteenth birthday. It recounts the blessings of having been her father amidst memories of touching moments from her childhood (her first pony ride, the day she tried to bake him a cake). The chorus proclaims, "With all that I've done wrong / I must have done something right / To deserve a hug every morning / And butterfly kisses at night." The song came to the attention of Oprah Winfrey, among others, who featured it on a Father's Day special. *The Wall Street Journal* praised it in an editorial column as "the first tune in recent memory to use 'Jesus' as something other than an expletive" and identified its popularity as evidence of "the failed feminist campaign to turn women against their fathers." The most syrupy song to dominate radio since Bobby Goldboro's "Honey," the song was overplayed to an annoying extent but still remained effective. A Chicago shopkeeper told the *Tribune,* "I *hate* that song, but every time I hear it, I cry." Carlisle had intended the lyrics of the song as a private poem and only reluctantly included it on the album at the urging of his wife. He continues to wonder at the irony of the song's becoming a public phenomenon. (It is especially odd, he notes, to hear it sung by another artist.) He handled his sudden and temporary celebrity with modesty and charm, bearing up under the predictable goody two-shoes jokes that had been **Pat Boone**'s lot to endure two decades earlier (e.g., being asked on national TV what he'd say to the Spice Girls—at the height of their popularity—if he were *their* father). Notably, the song won Carlisle and Thomas a Grammy Award in the category of *Country* Song of the Year (as opposed to one of the *Gospel* categories to which songs that smack of Christianity are usually relegated). Incidentally, a "butterfly kiss" is "what happens when your baby's delicate eyelashes sweep across your cheek."

The album *Butterfly Kisses (Shades of Grace)* went platinum and became one of the best-selling Christian records of all time. Sparrow understandably rushed out a collection of songs from Carlisle's first two albums, and Word put together a compilation of Carlisle ballads. Two volumes of children's songs came out to capitalize on the moment of fame. A variety of books were issued. Carlisle's next album, *Stories from the Heart,* even featured a new sentimental Carlisle-Thomas song about the relationship of fathers and *sons* ("Father's Love"; the song was also featured on the soundtrack of the film *Jack Frost*). In other ways, too, the latter album seems programmed to push family values buttons with what *CCM* magazine called "heart-tugging ballads of domestic bliss." For the sake of inclusivity, a duet with Kathy Mattea ("Somewhere") reminds us that it's okay to be single too. The album's best moments come when Carlisle cuts the Butterfly-strings: the opener "We Fall Down" (with its memorable line "Saints are just sinners who fall down

. . . and get up"), "In the Hands of Jesus" (featuring **Fred Hammond** and the Radical for Christ Choir), and "Power of Love" (a rhythmic dance song propelled by a horn section). *Nothing But the Truth* features another potential tear-jerker, "River of Peace," which deals with the unanswerable questions people bring to God (e.g., why does their ten-year-old daughter die of cancer?). The song also lauds Vietnam veterans and the sacrifices they made for their country. Aside from the expected ballads, the album does offer a couple of surprises: "The Truth (La Verdad)" is a Santana-style Latin jam, and "Baby, Baby" is an unpredictably funky cover of the **Amy Grant** song.

Carlisle, for his part, dismisses criticism that he is trying too hard to recapture the success of "Butterfly Kisses." The reason he recorded "Father's Love," he explains, is that he does have a son (Evan) and he wanted to treat both children equally. He says he is completely at peace with the prospect of being a one-hit wonder (or as he puts it, being forever known as "Butterfly Boy"): "If you're gonna be known for just one song, what a nice one! It could have been 'The Macarena.' " In general, Carlisle's winsome self-deprecating humor has helped him to maintain good relations with both Christian stars who might envy his success and a secular media prone to religious stereotypes. His 1998 tour with **Bryan Duncan** featured a segment in which the two singers performed together as a duo called "The Self-Righteous Brothers."

For trivia buffs: Bob Carlisle was once a session singer for the heavy metal band Poison. Less surprisingly, he also worked as a session singer on albums by Barry Manilow, Pat Benatar, Juice Newton, and REO Speedwagon.

Christian radio hits: "I Am Not My Own" (# 19 in 1993); "Getting Stronger" (# 3 in 1993); "Giving You the Rest of My Life" (# 1 in 1993); "Mind, Body, Heart, and Soul" (# 7 in 1994); "Bridge between Two Hearts" (# 3 in 1994); "Use Me" (# 13 in 1994); "One Step Closer to Your Broken Heart" (# 4 in 1995); "Walkin' Up the Steps of Faith" (# 18 in 1995); "Mighty Love" (# 18 in 1996).

Dove Awards: 1997 Inspirational Song ("Butterfly Kisses").

Joanna Carlson

1995—*The Light of Home* (Reunion).

Soprano Joanna Carlson grew up as the daughter of northern California rice farmers who were also missionaries. She attended a Christian high school, became a music major at Portland Bible College, and garnered a record deal after winning a talent contest. She wrote the words and music to all of the songs on her debut album, which was produced by **Brent Bourgeois** and **Wayne Kirkpatrick.** The overall theme of the record is the promise of heaven that sustains us through this life. The song "Miracle" speaks of the freedom of being a new creature in Christ; "I Will Remember" promises God, "I will re-

member the love that set me free / I will remember the cross of Calvary."

Pete Carlson

1974—*Jesus, Your Name* (custom); 1976—*You Were There* (Tempo); 1977—*Hideaway* (Chrism); 1979—*Off the Beaten Path*; 1982—*Dreamer's Dream* (DaySpring); 1984—*Child of the Heavenly*; date unknown—*Living in the Name of Love* (label unknown).

A Christian songwriter from Bridgeport, Connecticut, Pete Carlson has written songs for **Sandi Patty** and is also responsible for the Christian musical *Follow Me.* His career in music started when he placed second in a national competition sponsored by Youth for Christ in 1968. Carlson sings in a soothing tenor and favors songs that seem to represent personal conversations between him and God.

Christian radio hits: "Dreamer's Dream" (# 3 in 1983); "One Last Goodbye" (# 23 in 1984).

Andrew Carlton and the Swing Doctors

1998—*It's a Swing Thing* (Rugged).

Andrew Carlton is a pop-oriented singer from Tennessee who first came to the attention of the Christian music community with a novelty swing album in 1998. At the time Carlton was serving as mascot for the Tennessee Volunteers for the University of Tennessee at Knoxville and working as a disc jockey at a Top 40 radio station. His album with (as) "the Swing Doctors" displays a sound similar to that of **The W's,** though *It's a Swing Thing* was actually recorded before that group's phenomenal debut appeared. Standout tracks include "Seeds" and "Hold Me Up." In 2000 Carlton announced that he was releasing a pure pop album that would have a style similar to that of the Backstreet Boys and *NSYNC.

Carman

1980—*God's Not Finished with Me* (Klesis); 1982—*Some-o-dat* [a.k.a. *Carman*] (Priority); 1983—*Sunday's on the Way*; 1984—*Comin' On Strong* (Myrrh); 1985—*The Champion*; 1986—*His Name Is Life* (Word); *A Long Time Ago in a Place Called Bethlehem* (Benson); 1988—*Carman Live . . . Radically Saved!*; 1989—*Revival in the Land*; 1991—*Shakin' the House . . . Live* [with Commissioned and the Christ Church Choir]; *Addicted to Jesus; High Praises I; High Praises II*; 1992—*Yo! Kidz: Heroes, Stories, and Songs from the Bible* (Word); 1993—*Lord of All: Songs of Carman; The Absolute Best* (Sparrow); *The Standard*; 1994—*Yo! Kidz 2: The Armor of God* (Word); 1995—*El Mejor* (Sparrow); *R.I.O.T. (Righteous Invasion of Truth)*; 1996—*I Surrender All: 30 Classic Hymns; Yo Kidz! The Hitz*; 1997—*The Best of the Early Years* (Sony); 1998—*The Best of the Early Years 2; Mission 3:16* (Sparrow); 1999—*Passion for Praise, Vol. 1*; 2000—*Heart of a Champion.*

www.carman.org

Carman is to contemporary Christian music what televangelists are to institutional Christianity. A penchant for over-the-top histrionics, a remarkable aptitude for media manipulation, and a frequent espousal of questionable theology have all conspired to marginalize him within the industry . . . yet his unqualified success and undeniable talent leave room for doubt as to whether *some* of the carping does not arise from old-fashioned jealousy. Five of Carman's albums have been certified gold, and one *(The Standard)* has gone platinum. *Billboard* magazine has twice named him "Contemporary Christian Artist of the Year" (1990, 1992). Still, struggling artists whom critics dub "authentic"—and the critics who so dub them—watch in bemusement as Carman draws 71,132 people to Dallas's Texas Stadium for the largest Christian concert in history. It is as though they are simple country parsons and he is the flamboyant faith healer setting up his tent on the edge of town. Of course, rock and roll has always been a bit of a circus—and in terms of showmanship, Carman probably has more in common with ringmasters like **Alice Cooper** or Ozzy Osbourne than he might be willing to acknowledge. He also has at least two things in common with performers like Ricky Martin and Antonio Banderas: a) he is considered to be extremely good-looking; and b) most of his fans are female.

The controversial singer was born Carmen Dominic Licciardello in Trenton, New Jersey, in 1956. As a child he played drums in his mother's band, then formed a teenage group called The Broken Hearts. Around the age of twenty he moved first to California and then to Las Vegas; once he began recording, he would operate out of first Tulsa, Oklahoma, and then Franklin, Tennessee. In 1976 he accepted Christ as his personal Savior at a Disneyland concert by **Andraé Crouch.** In 1980 he made a custom album and then in 1981 he was invited by Bill Gaither to tour with **The Bill Gaither Trio,** a turn of events that he maintains was "the biggest influence on my ministry." His first few records presented him to the world as a sort of Christian Elvis. *Some-o-dat* features a novelty title track but also includes "Bethlehem," which is a rock and roll wonder (and one of the artist's best songs). The much more successful *Sunday's on the Way* goes Vegas all the way with the artist singing '50s style rock and roll songs ("Temptation Boogie") and crooning MOR ballads ("His Name Is Life") in a mode copied from The King. The title track, "The Well" (a conceptual rip-off of **Honeytree**'s "Rattle Me, Shake Me"), and "God Don't Care (What the Circumstance)" are goofy tunes designed to work well in concert, but "We Have Come to Worship Him" reveals a kinder, gentler Carman with a voice as velvety as the sky he describes in the stirring Christmas carol. Switching to the more contemporary-oriented Myrrh label did not involve any immediately noticeable change in style or direction. The more popular tunes on *Comin' On Strong* would again be goofy

concert favorites ("Spirit-Filled Pizza," "Lazarus, Come Forth"). *The Champion* features the sensational "Revive Us, O Lord," written with **Steve Camp,** and the comforting ballad "Fear Not My Child." In 2001 when *CCM* sponsored a critics' poll to determine "The 100 Greatest Albums in Christian Music," *The Champion* would be the only Carman product to make the list (at Number Ninety-nine). *Radically Saved* takes full advantage of the live setting to offer the very energetic "Lord of All" and the '50s satire "Celebrating Jesus." It also offers "I Feel Jesus," an **Andraé Crouch**-like worship chorus sung by a female choir who are unfortunately interrupted by two minutes of unnecessary preaching.

Carman would not go down in music history as the little footnote that a Christian Elvis impersonator would certainly have been. As the years went by, he released increasingly sophisticated albums developed around conceptual (and even theatrical) themes. *Revival in the Land* includes "I Got the Joy" (an R&B gospel celebration), "Resurrection Rap" (the artist's first, but not last or best, attempt at hip-hop), and such joyous testimony songs as "Saved," "Jesus is the Light," and "God's Got an Army." *Addicted to Jesus* was unanimously regarded as a career nadir by critics, though it did generate hits with the title track and "Satan, Bite the Dust" (cowritten by **Toby McKeehan**). Its finest musical moment may be the somewhat mediocre inspirational hymn "Hunger for Holiness." *The Standard* shows marked improvement with such rave-ups as "Great God" and "Sunday School Rock," along with the now-effective hip-hop "Who's in the House?" and the sterling ballads "The River" and "Holdin' On" (sung with **Margaret Becker**). "Now's the Time" is a catchy little Caribbean praise ditty. *R.I.O.T.* features the contemporary gospel song "Whiter Than Snow" and the Huey Lewis-like "Step of Faith." Carman sets his testimony to a Latin beat on "My Story." The title track calls for a "righteous invasion of truth." Several songs on *R.I.O.T.* were cowritten with **Tommy Sims.** *Mission 3:16* is the artist's best rock album. It kicks off with a James Bond-inspired title track and moves quickly to a powerful number called "People of God." It also features a pretty midtempo number called "Never Be" (with **Out of Eden**), a Caribbean-inflected praise song ("Jesus Is the Lamb"), an emotional adult contemporary ballad ("We Are Not Ashamed"), and a couple of catchy sing-along pop songs ("The Prayer Anthem," "Do I Do"). Interspersed with these classic Carman albums have been numerous special projects and compilations. *Heart of a Champion* is a two-disc thirty-song anniversary package. It includes six new songs, including the radio-friendly "Faith Enough."

Musically Carman is perhaps the most versatile of any artist described in this book. He switches from hip-hop to calypso to rockabilly to adult contemporary to country to techno to big band. As *Shout!* magazine observes, however, he is *always* the Vegas showman at heart, trying on styles like they were costumes. They all seem like disguises, yet he wears them *so* convincingly. A writer for *Rolling Stone* reviewing a compilation of Christian songs was quite taken with Carman's "R.I.O.T." It may have been the only Carman song the reviewer knew. He wrote that "Carman should get a Grammy for best imitation of George Clinton by a white man." Carman a protégé of George Clinton? Hmmmm. Listen some more. But Carman has made one style his own: the trademark "talking song" in which he basically preaches or tells a story to musical accompaniment with occasional verses or choruses sung for emphasis. He didn't invent this style (African American gospel singers did) but he did perfect it, and it is an effective mode of presentation even if the content of what Carman presents sometimes leaves a bit to be desired. The early albums are filled with these ("Sunday's on the Way," "Lazarus, Come Forth," "The Champion," "Jericho: The Shout of Victory," "A Witches' Invitation"); later examples include "America Again" from *The Standard,* "There Is a God" from *R.I.O.T.,* and "Courtroom" from *Mission 3:16.* The last of these offers a seven-minute Perry Mason-styled drama in which a Christian is judged by God with Satan as the prosecutor and Jesus as his defense attorney. Such songs are obviously designed for live performance, where they work best. Carman has always maintained that he writes primarily for live performances, and virtually all of his albums have the feel of a live concert.

It should also be noted that Carman often integrates humor into these and other songs, almost to the point of blurring the line between singer and stand-up comic. For example, the talking song "Lazarus, Come Forth" (from *Comin' On Strong*) presents the deceased Lazarus in heaven with a collection of Old Testament saints, all talking about what God has done for them—rescued them from a fiery furnace or lion's den, etc. Carman adopts different voices for all the various persons and laces their descriptions with contemporary slang (Samson sounds like a big, dumb jock; Ezekiel like a hippie mystic). The climax comes, of course, when the discussion is interrupted by the voice of Jesus calling Lazarus to return to earth, raised from the dead. Carman also has a flair for twisting contemporary phrases or references in ways that are sometimes humorous, often corny, and occasionally irreverent. "The Champion" presents the apocalyptic contest between Jesus and Satan as a boxing match—an idea that worked better before it was taken up in a very different way in a famous episode of the irreverent animated TV series *South Park.* "Addicted to Jesus" is a take-off on Robert Palmer's "Addicted to Love" (stodgy critics questioned the appropriateness of describing devotion to Christ as an "addiction," though such metaphors were common in the Jesus movement revival that gave birth to

contemporary Christian music). In "Soap Song" (from *Live . . . Radically Saved*) Carman manages to work the titles of various afternoon TV dramas into an unfolding Christian narrative ("We must live for Jesus, the only Guiding Light / Not one but All the Days of Our Lives"). Only once has the comic sense really failed. His twist on the tagline of a beer commercial "This *Blood*'s for You" might have worked in a comical song, but he uses it in a deadly serious account of the crucifixion where the pun seems completely out of place ("This Blood" from *Revival in the Land*).

Lyrically Carman's songs almost all focus on one of three themes: praise to God, victory over the devil, or right-wing politics. There is certainly no problem with the first. Carman's praise albums *(High Praises I* and *II, Passion for Praise,* and especially *I Surrender All)* earn nothing but accolades from reviewers. There is no question that Carman has a gorgeous voice and that he is possessed with a passionate love for his Lord. Put those two qualities together and you have the makings of a very fine gospel singer. *Shakin' the House* is a live worship album that involves the listeners in three distinctly different styles of praise (courtesy of Carman, **Commissioned,** and the Christ Church Choir). Carman's Christmas album *(A Long Time Ago)* also fits into this worship music category. It features three traditional carols and seven striking original songs. Likewise, Carman's *Kidz* albums of children's songs are delightful, funky, and fun.

The "victory over the devil" songs are more problematic. Carman hit on this early with "Sunday's on the Way," a humorous talking song that relates a story from African American homiletic tradition about Satan and the demons in hell celebrating the execution of Jesus. They do this for three days before the latter busts loose from the bonds of death. The song was a justifiable crowd pleaser, and on subsequent albums Carman would follow it with more and more songs with a similar theme (e.g., "A Witch's Invitation," "God's Got an Army," "Get Outta My Life," "Revival in the Land"). On *Addicted to Jesus* no less than five out of nine cuts feature what John Styll, editor of *CCM* magazine, dubbed the "us-vs.-them-but-we-win" theme. The video for one of these ("Satan, Bite the Dust") actually shows Carman striding into a saloon and blasting away at demons like so many figures in a *Doom* video game. Styll called the song "ridiculous" and described the theme itself as "simplistic and tiresome." But neither Carman nor his fans tired of it, and after a brief respite from such tunes on *The Standard,* the prominence of spiritual warfare themes returned on *R.I.O.T.* ("No Monsters") and *Mission 3:16* ("Slam"). Both the exploitation of this theme and the objections to it may be revelatory of sectarian biases within Christendom. Triumphalist theology is part and parcel of American Pentecostalism and pops up in certain fundamentalist traditions, but it is rejected by almost all historic denominations. The more traditional Christian approach stresses personal responsibility for sin over the agency of the devil, obligations of service and sacrifice over promises of temporal success and glory, and acknowledgment of human weakness over acclamations of spiritual victory. Martin Luther, in particular, condemned the platter of ideas from which Carman feasts as an unscriptural "theology of glory," which he contrasted with a biblical "theology of the cross."

As for politics, Carman is certainly welcome to his opinions, but sometimes his views appear obtuse. His otherwise excellent album *The Standard* is spoiled by an inaccurate and uninformed spoken-word piece "America Again," on which the artist contrasts the supposedly moral and spiritual bankrupt status of modern America with the supposedly holy status that the country once had when it was founded as a Christian nation. Of course, America was *not* founded as a Christian nation but was explicitly founded as a non-Christian nation in radical discontinuity with the officially Christian countries from which the immigrants had come. Carman doesn't seem to get the principle of "separation of church and state" or to realize that many of the great Christian forefathers he cites in the song—George Washington, Thomas Jefferson—were actually non-Christian Deists. And does Carman really believe that legal allowance of abortion and the fact that homosexuals are coming out of the closet evidences a country decidedly worse than one that massacred Native Americans and enslaved Africans? "Our Turn Now" (from *Addicted to Jesus*) bemoans the loss of state-sponsored prayer in public schools. Would Carman really want the *government* to be in charge of his children's spiritual training? Would he want his kids praying to Mary or Buddha (if the prayers were teacher or pupil led)? Or to some generic "Great Spirit" (if the prayers were written by Congress)? Other issues are simply dealt with simplistically. Abortion, according to "Revival in the Land," is not so much *allowed* by persons who believe a fetus is not yet a human life as it is *urged* by bloodthirsty neo-Nazis who are controlled by demons. In short, Carman often articulates the stereotypical views of the religious right in ways that not only offend Christians who hold different positions but also embarrass Christians who would support his position, with more nuanced reasoning. Carman's response: "People who criticize what I do (politically) are just involved in dead, dry Christianity, willing to let the world go to pot all around them."

Carman is an extraordinarily *visual* performer. He does not so much craft albums as design musical shows, for which the albums are but souvenirs. Perhaps he is Christian music's Andrew Lloyd Webber. His concerts are filled with theatrics: dancers, special lighting effects, whatever it takes—and he himself sometimes dresses in outlandish costumes that make him an

easy target for parody by the likes of **Mark Lowry.** In addition to the awards listed below, he has won four Dove awards for *videos:* 1989 for *Radically Saved,* 1991 for *Revival in the Land* (the album); 1991 for "Revival in the Land" (the song); and 1993 for *Addicted to Jesus.* His every tour is an *event,* typically accompanied by devotional books and other paraphernalia designed to drive home the particular theme. The *Radically Saved* tour, for instance, was structured around a call for Christian service and included a contest by which church youth groups came up with plans for radical service to their communities through participating in various social programs. *Mission 3:16* was more evangelistically oriented as part of an announced plan to get one million people saved (i.e., to get one million responses to altar calls—at which persons are invited to access salvation in an individualist way). In 2001 Carman was busy working on a feature film called *The Champion,* based on a novel that he had written.

For all his excesses, Carman succeeds at garnering the support of other Christian artists. **DC Talk** duet with him on the "Satan, Bite the Dust" song, and **Petra** join in on "Our Turn Now." *Mission 3:16* features a host of guest musicians including **Phil Keaggy** doing a Ventures guitar and '60s vocal on "Surf Mission" and **Russ Taff** singing power-pop opposite Carman's Vanilla Ice rapping in "People of God." Tony Orlando and Boyz II Men sing along on a rendition of John 3:16 in "Legendary Mission." **Tammy Trent** joins him for "The Wedding Song," one of the new tracks on *Heart of a Champion.* Other albums feature collaborations with notables that run the gamut of the industry, from **Steve Taylor** to **CeCe Winans.**

So: reviled by critics, revered by fans, respected by peers. What is the bottom line for Carman and the Christian music camp? Contemporary Christian music has a primarily evangelical Protestant constituency. Nevertheless, if the subculture is able to stretch to include Roman Catholics like **John Michael Talbot,** then it should certainly be able to make room for Pentecostal fundamentalists like Carman. Actually, many contemporary Christian musicians are Pentecostal fundamentalists, though most have learned to keep the more idiosyncratic elements of their denominational faith out of the spotlight. Carman does on record what they might do in their home congregations. For all his posturing, he remains an ironically *authentic* representative of a major stream of American Christianity.

Christian radio hits: "Sunday's on the Way" (# 5 in 1984); "Lazarus, Come Forth" (# 13 in 1985); "The Champion" (# 1 for 4 weeks in 1986); "Revive Us, O Lord" (# 10 in 1986); "Abundance of Rain" (# 14 in 1986); "Jesus Is" (# 8 in 1986); "Radically Saved" (# 1 for 2 weeks in 1988); "Lord of All" (# 2 in 1988); "No Way, We Are Not Ashamed" (# 15 in 1988); "Jesus Is the Light" (# 3 in 1989); "The Same God" (# 8 in 1991); "Satan, Bite the Dust" (# 14 in 1991); "Addicted to Jesus" (# 16 in 1992);

"Come into This House" (# 18 in 1993); "Who's in the House" (# 23 in 1993); "Great God" (# 20 in 1994).

Dove Awards: 1993 Children's Album *(Yo! Kidz)*; 1995 Children's Album *(Yo Kidz 2)*; 1997 Rap/Hip Hop Song ("R.I.O.T.").

Ralph Carmichael

Selected: 1961—*How Big Is God* [by Gregory Loren and The Ralph Carmichael Orchestra]; *Carmichael Concert* (Word); 1963—*I'm Gonna Go Back* [by Jack Holcomb with The Ralph Carmichael Orchestra and Chorus]; 1965—*Old-Fashioned Sunday Evening*; 1966—*Christmas Spirit*; 1969—*City of the King: A Christmas Cantata* (Light); *I Looked for Love* [with The Young People]; 1970—*Tell It Like It Is: A Folk Musical About God* [with Kurt Kaiser]; *The Piano I Remember, Vol. 2*; *Electric Symphony*; *Sometimes I Just Feel This Way*; 1971—*Young* [with The Young People]; *Centurion*; *Old Gems/New Settings* [with World Action Singers]; *The Cross and the Switchblade*; *Miracle of Pentecost*; *My Little World*; *Natural High* [with Kurt Kaiser]; *Our Front Porch*; *Brass Choir*; 1972—*Have a Nice Day*; *Hymns at Sunset*; *Sunday A.M.*; 1973—*I'm Here, God's Here, Now We Can Start* [with Kurt Kaiser]; 1975—*The Savior Is Waiting*; *Old Quartet*; 1976—*Big Story*; *Christmas Joys*; *Rhapsody in Sacred Music* (Word); *102 Strings, Vol. 1*; *The Piano I Remember, Vol. 1*; *Garden of Prayer*; 1977—*102 Strings, Vol. 2*; *Portrait* (Light); 1979—*Easter Celebration*; 1981—*The Best of Ralph Carmichael*; *Garden of the Heart*; 1995—*Strike up the Band* (Brentwood); 1996—*Emmanuel* (Light); *Something Beautiful: Piano Duets* (label unknown); 1997—*Ralph Carmichael and Friends Live* [with Dave Boyer, Larnelle Harris, and Dave Boyer]; 1999—*Big Band Swing Classics* (Platinum); *Big Band Gospel Classics* (Intersound); *Big Band Christmas*.

If **Larry Norman** is the father of contemporary rock and **Marsha Stevens** is the mother of contemporary Christian music, Ralph Carmichael should probably be identified as the *grandfather* of both. In 1993 the founders of MUSICalifornia made him the first recipient of their now annual "Ray DeVries Church Ministry Award" and dubbed him "the Dean of contemporary Christian Music." But that sounds kind of boring. The grandfather idea is best. Carmichael's music is definitely *not* rock and roll (think Lawrence Welk), but at one point in time he probably did more than any other individual to legitimize Christian rock and to ensure that Christian music of diverse genres would be heard.

Ralph Carmichael was born in 1927 in Quincy, Illinois, though he spent most of his childhood in North Dakota before settling permanently in California in the late '30s. A preacher's son, he attended Southern California Bible College where, before flunking out, he gained recognition for his skill at arranging and conducting music of popular (big band/jazz) varieties. In fact, while still a student at the Bible school, he managed to put together a musical TV program *(The Christian Campus Hour)* that would air in Los Angeles (opposite Milton Berle) for seventy-six consecutive weeks. The show premiered in 1949 and in 1956 became the first Christian musical show on a commercial TV station to win an Emmy. Carmichael became min-

ister of music at Temple Baptist Church in downtown L.A., where he presented a major production of Handel's *Messiah* and wrote the evangelical hymn, "The Savior Is Waiting." But he also continued to enjoy considerable success in the general market. He worked on recordings by such artists as **Pat Boone,** Rosemary Clooney, Nat King Cole, Bing Crosby, Jimmy Durante, and Ella Fitzgerald. He had a steady job composing scene music for the *I Love Lucy* show. He collaborated with pianist Roger Williams on many projects, including the platinum-selling score for the film *Born Free.* But he also remained interested in Christian music, scoring films produced by Billy Graham's World Wide Pictures *(Mr. Texas, His Land, For Pete's Sake, The Restless Ones).* When the rock era hit, Carmichael was one of the first musicians to notice that there was nothing in church music even remotely similar to what his teenage daughter listened to at home. One of the first fruits of his labors was an influential folk-musical called *Good News,* first performed by a group of eighty youth (accompanied by guitars and bass) at a Baptist Conference in Glorieta, New Mexico, in 1966. The musical took off and was performed many more times in far more elaborate versions in a variety of venues. Just two years later, a cast and choir of 1300 performed it with a fifty-piece orchestra at the Southern Baptist national convention in Houston. Soon Carmichael and Kurt Kaiser began producing a steady stream of upbeat Christian musicals for the Light label: *Tell It Like It Is; Natural High; I'm Here, God's Here, Now We Can Start.* All of these musicals had more in common with Rodgers and Hammerstein than they did with *A Hard Day's Night,* but they did feature syncopated folk songs that sounded a lot like what was on the radio at the time (Peter, Paul, and Mary, The Seekers, The Fifth Dimension). *Tell It Like It Is* was the best of the bunch and was indeed revolutionary in introducing the Christian musical art form to the church; it features the classic songs "Master Designer," "That's for Me," and "Pass It On," all by Kaiser, in addition to the title track and "Love Is Surrender" by Carmichael. The Christian musical form was taken up by Carmichael protégées **Jimmy and Carol Owens** and reached its zenith with their *Come Together* (Light, 1972). But Carmichael wrote many more youth group songs himself, the best known of which is probably "He's Everything to Me" from *The Restless Ones.* Another Carmichael classic, "A Quiet Place," would be covered by **Take 6** in 1988. The proliferation of such songs within churches paralleled (and even predated) the development of Jesus music outside the churches. When the Jesus movement revival hit, Carmichael was one of the first leaders of the Christian music establishment to embrace the untethered phenomenon as a genuine movement of God. He founded Light records to provide a home for some of Christian rock's pioneers and so introduced the world to the music of

Andraé Crouch and the Disciples, Resurrection Band, and **Bryan Duncan.**

Carmichael himself made numerous albums, but unfortunately no authoritative discography is available (the albums released by Word in 1978–1979 may be re-releases of earlier works from some unknown label). Some of his projects were recorded by "Ralph Carmichael and the Young People," a sort of Up-With-People, positive-spirited group of singers that he directed. Others were made with The Ralph Carmichael Orchestra or The Ralph Carmichael Singers. He also released albums of piano music similar to those of Burt Bacharach. Perhaps his single most popular (and influential) work, aside from the musicals, was *I Looked for Love,* a collection of youth group songs that includes "Quiet Place" and "Love Is Surrender." Since 1990 Carmichael has served as musical director for The Young Messiah, a touring group that regularly incorporates many of contemporary Christian music's biggest stars in a dynamic Christmas production of Handel's classic. Toward the end of the decade, he returned to his love of big band music, releasing several albums of mostly instrumental, orchestrated versions of classic songs. His 1997 *Ralph Carmichael and Friends Live* album allows some of his classic songs to be sung by such stellar performers as **Larnelle Harris** and **Sharalee Lucas.**

Though he would ultimately be revered, Carmichael suffered from detractors throughout most of his pioneering career. He was called a heretic for putting gospel songs to a worldly big band beat in the '40s and worse things than that for letting *guitars* into sanctuaries in the '60s. "I don't think groups like **Jars of Clay** or **4 Him** feel the stigma I did growing up," Carmichael says with a glow of hope and a wince of pain. "It's wonderful that we have fought for and won the right to have this freedom of expression (within the church)."

Dove Awards: 1995 Instrumental Album (*Strike Up the Band*).

Bruce Carroll

1987—*Something Good Is Bound to Happen* (Word); 1988—*The Richest Man in Town;* 1990—*The Great Exchange;* 1991—*Sometimes Miracles Hide;* 1993—*Walk On;* 1995—*One Summer's Evening: Live;* 1996—*Speed of Light* (Benson); 1997—*For the Record* (Word); 1998—*Boomerang* (Benson).

Bruce Carroll was signed to Word Records as the premiere artist in a Christian country campaign, but his style is actually more inspirational pop than country. Reviewers often compare him with James Taylor or put him in the twang-less country camp of **Bob Carlisle** and **Steven Curtis Chapman.** He does have a penchant for ballads. Carroll was born in San Antonio, but he makes his home in Denver, Colorado, where he is worship leader at the New Community Christian Church. He spent a decade (1987–1997) in Nashville, where most of his recordings were made. An artist with a checkered past, he tells of his years as a drug addict, of the time he spent in jail, and of

how he lost all of his earthly possessions and came close to death before his persistent brother Milton finally succeeded in leading him to Christ.

Carroll's first album, *Something Good Is Bound to Happen,* features the song "Driving Nails," tracing Mary's perception of her son from manger to tomb. "Let Go, Let God" has a style reminiscent of Lee Greenwood and follows a country convention of setting a well-known cliché to a catchy melody. *The Richest Man in Town* includes a worship song, "Above and Beyond," extolling the extravagant love of God, and a driving blues tune called "Only You." *The Great Exchange* offers a title track that describes atonement with memorable imagery. "Who Will Be Jesus?" from the same album expresses a typical Carroll theme—the call for Christians to embody the presence of Christ on behalf of the needy in the world. A similar theme informs "If We Only Had the Heart" from *Sometimes Miracles Hide,* a song about loving AIDS victims. The title track to the latter album is a Carlisle-style tear jerker about a couple who decide to keep their baby when told the child will be retarded. They pray for the child to be normal, then come in time to appreciate the gift of that unanswered prayer. The antiabortion undercurrent of the song (another favorite theme for Carroll) comes up again in "Sometimes When We Love" (from *Walk On*), this time in a tale of an unwed young girl who heroically gives her child up for adoption. "Right at Home" and "What We Were Fighting For" extol the merit of home and hearth. *Speed of Light* contains songs that express the hope of release from addictive behaviors ("Someday I May Rise above It All") while honestly admitting that the road to recovery (or holiness) is a bumpy one ("Here I Go Again"). *Boomerang* has been hailed as Carroll's best album to date, with a more polished and full musical pop sound. The title track is a catchy expression of karma: basically, what goes around, comes around, you will reap what you sow. "The Room" is another of Carroll's touching domestic ballads, this time a moving description of the emptiness felt by a couple who cannot conceive a child. According to one report, Carroll released another album on a small label, Embassy Records, in 2000. The song "Angel's Chair" received some airplay on Christian radio.

Carroll's songs often focus on the everyday struggles and realities of life. He maintains that he was at first disappointed in Christian music because it seemed to lack this existential connection, but the music of **Bob Bennett** (another artist with whom Carroll can easily be compared) opened his mind to the possibility of down-to-earth contemporary Christian music, a genre that he has tried to expand. Carroll remains friends with country stars Ricky Scaggs and **Paul Overstreet,** who sometimes help out on his albums. He has written songs for a number of other artists, including "Back to Who I Am" and "Man of God" for **Paul Smith.**

Christian radio hits: "Fight to Be Weak" (# 11 in 1989).

Dove Awards: 1989 Country Album (Richest Man in Town); 1989 Country Song ("Above and Beyond"); 1991 Inspirational Song ("Who Will Be Jesus?"); 1992 Country Album (Sometimes Miracles Hide); 1992 Country Song ("Sometimes Miracles Hide"); 1993 Country Song ("If We Only Had the Heart"); 1994 Country Album (Walk On).

Grammy Awards: 1990 Best Southern Gospel Album (The Great Exchange); 1992 Best Southern Gospel Album (Sometimes Miracles Hide).

Rex Carroll

1995—The Rex Carroll Sessions (StarSong).

www.rexcarroll.com

Rex Carroll is the hard rock/metal guitarist from Chicago who has played with such Christian bands as **Whitecross, King James,** and (apparently) **The Bleed.** He has also played with a general market band called Fierce Heart, which released a self-titled album on Mirage in 1985. Carroll graduated from Northern Illinois University in 1982 with a degree in Classical Guitar Performance. Best known for bone-crunching metal riffs, Carroll slows down the tempo on his solo album and adds a healthy dose of country-blues flavor that summoned images of the Allman Brothers and Lynyrd Skynyrd for a *CCM* reviewer. The album has the primitive feel of a giant jam session with guests like **Jimmy Abegg** (bass) and **Phil Keaggy** (guitar) sitting in. Otherwise, the house band includes **Phil Madeira** on keyboards, Aaron Smith **(Vector/Seventy Sevens/A Ragamuffin Band)** on drums, and Jackie Street on bass. Carroll is not normally a vocalist; he sings a few songs here but lets **Dave Perkins** of **Chagall Guevara/Passafist** handle most of those chores. **Ashley Cleveland** sings the opening cut, "Do It for Love," in a predictably rousing fashion and later comes in again for "Invitational Blues." The song "Hands of God" invites listeners to trust in God's providential care. "I'm Gonna Be There" is Carroll's personal statement of commitment to his wife. "Anytime" extolls the constant faithfulness of God. The album also includes a cover of the R&B standard "I Just Want to Celebrate" (made famous in a 1971 version by Rare Earth). Carroll later commented in an undated interview posted on the Christian Metal Resources website (www.christianmetal.com/cmn/cmnmenu.htm) that this album was not the album he wanted to make: "It turned out being (coproducer) Phil Madeira's album. It goes back to doing something yourself, if you want it done according to your own vision." He said he is planning a second Rex Carroll's Sessions album.

Christian radio hits: "Hands of God" (# 5 in 1995); "Anytime" (# 20 in 1996).

Carl Cartee

1995—Be Quiet and Paint (Shelter); 1996—Break the Silence; 2001—Satisfied Soul (independent).

www.carlcarteecom

Carl Cartee is a singer/songwriter who leads worship at Christ Covenant Church in Shelby, North Carolina, but tours throughout America. He was born in Anchorage, Alaska, and attended Gardner-Webb University in his new hometown of Shelby. His acoustic musical style encompasses influences from jazz to bluegrass, with an emphasis on intimacy. His second album, *Break the Silence,* was recorded live at Bethel Baptist Church in Shelby and is a worship album in the truest sense, featuring congregational singing on most of the tracks. One song, "Pocket Full of Seeds," gained airplay on regional Christian stations. After a five-year hiatus Cartee returned with the more pop-oriented *Satisfied Soul.* "I Choose to Love You" is a wedding song, and "Life" has a particularly jazzy '70s pop sound. Most of the songs continue to be worship-oriented ("We Lift Your Name," "Shout Out Your Name," "Lost in You").

Peter Case

1986—Peter Case (Geffen); 1989—The Man with the Blue, Postmodern Fragmented Neo-traditionalist Guitar; 1992—Six Pack of Love; 1994—Peter Case Sings Like Hell (Vanguard); 1995—Torn Again; 1998—Full Service No Waiting; 2000—Flying Saucer Blues.

www.petercase.com

Born in 1954 in Hamburg, New York, Peter Case rose to fame as leader of The Plimsouls, a mid '80s Los Angeles rock quartet. The latter group, which took its name from British slang for "gym shoes," is best remembered for the song "A Million Miles Away," written by Case. Although it reached only Number Eighty-two on the national pop charts (in 1983), it was a much bigger hit on the West Coast, became a staple of college radio for a time, and even won the group a cameo appearance in the teen movie *Valley Girl.* The Plimsoul's California power-pop sound was at least a few thousand miles away from the Greenwich village folk music that Case really loved. Prior to his tenure with the group, Case had been hanging out with poet Allen Ginsberg and emulating Woody Guthrie. In 1984 Case announced that he had become "a born again Christian." He dissolved The Plimsouls and started playing the folk music dear to his heart, joining with revered Christian singer/songwriter **Victoria Williams** to form the Incredibly Strung Out Band. Case and Williams married in 1985 but divorced in 1989. **Steven Soles** of **The Alpha Band** has served as Case's manager.

Case's self-titled debut solo album was produced by **T Bone Burnett** and drew on the guest talents of John Hiatt and Roger McGuinn. It won high praise from critics for its slow and thoughtful songs and unabashed mellow sound. The song "Steel Strings" became a hit on many college radio stations. "Three Days Straight" is ostensibly about a coal-mining accident, but the metaphor of being trapped underground for three days lends itself easily to thoughts of sin and redemption. Case himself described his song "I Shook His Hand" as being about "the Kennedys and King, the idealism and the convictions by which they lived and then died." The second record *(Blue Postmodern . . . Guitar)* is regarded as something of a watershed, perfectly capturing what one reviewer refers to as Case's signature "train whistle harmonica and chugga chugga finger pickin' style." The artist would retreat temporarily from the shadow of Woody Guthrie that this description implies for *Six Pack of Love,* producing a more pop-oriented collection in the same musical vein as Squeeze or Crowded House. Case cowrote some of the songs for that project with **Tonio K.,** and *True Tunes* was able to find spiritual meaning in tracks like "Dream about You" and "It Don't Matter What People Say." On *Sings Like Hell,* Case goes all out for the unplugged folk sound, recording the entire record live on a two-track tape recorder set up in a friend's living room. The next three Case albums reveal a more solidified sound, recorded with a fairly consistent group of musicians, reflecting the "place where pop, country rock, and mountain music meet" *(Salon).* A generous dose of blues infuses his work as well, and *Flying Saucer Blues* pays musical homage to the Beatles' *Rubber Soul.*

As a Christian artist Case would have to be grouped with singers like **Bruce Cockburn** or **Mark Heard** (or the aforementioned Williams, Burnett, Hiatt, and McGuinn) who have felt no need to write or sing songs that completely express their faith in explicit (or specific) ways. Case is as at least as well known outside the Christian music subculture as he is within it—and he is probably *more* appreciated in secular circles. Thematically, he treats a wide variety of topics, sometimes with sensitivity, and often with a touch of humor: "I wish I woulda got a G.E.D. / You want fries with that BLT?" ("Coulda Shoulda Woulda"). He rarely talks about his faith in terms that would easily peg him as a Christian, leading to inevitable speculation that his conversion was temporary (cf. **Bob Dylan**). Still, magazines devoted to Christian music often review his albums, and many Christians appreciate his profound and intelligent songs all the more for the understated spirituality they think they find there. The song "Something Happens" may be a simple love song, but it reflects on love with such an appreciation of grace that even a nonreligious reviewer can describe it as "a paean to faith and fidelity": "When I look into your eyes / Shadows stir, I start to rise / Bright morning stars reappear / Something happens when you're near." Likewise, the song "A Little Wind Can Blow Me Away" describes the fragility of life with a surprising twist. Case unveils a story of a small girl trying to make it home through a woods filled with snakes and alligators as a terrible (even apocalyptic?) storm is brewing. Then he relates, "The stones kept right on rollin' / The sky was turnin' red / The little wind reached out his hand / And carried her home to bed." It is a surprise. The wind that seemed so threatening turns out to be her salvation. "I think *songs* can save lives," says Case. "You can create a place of refuge and comfort with a song."

For trivia buffs: Before The Plimsouls, Peter Case formed a West Coast punk band called The Nerves, which also included Paul Collins (later of The Beat). They recorded a rendition of the song "Hangin' on the Telephone" three years before Blondie released their definitive version of the song in 1980.

Johnny Cash

Selected: 1973—*The Gospel Road* (Columbia); 1979—*A Believer Sings the Truth* (Cachet); 1984—*I Believe* (Arrival); 1985—*Believe in Him* (Word); 1990—*Goin' by the Book* (Polygram); 1994—*American Recordings* (American); 1998—*Unchained* (Sony); 2000—*God Love Murder* (Sony); *American III: Solitary Man* (Columbia).

www.johnnycash.com

An icon of American country music, Johnny Cash came to faith early and hard and has struggled all his life with varying degrees of success to walk the line that he believes his confession of that faith should entail. Cash was born the grandson of a Baptist minister in 1932 in Kingsland, Arkansas, and he grew up listening to Pentecostal preachers at a church in Dyess where he says he was terrified by the prospects of hellfire and damnation. At the age of twelve he walked the aisle of the church while the choir sang "Just As I Am" and accepted Jesus as his Lord and Savior. But Cash got more from the church than a fear of God and hope for salvation: "I learned to sit through the scary sermons," he recounts, "just to hear the mandolins, fiddles, bass, banjo, and flattop guitars . . . the gospel, spiritual songs carried me above it all." As a young adult, Cash first auditioned his band (Johnny Cash and The Tennessee Two) for Sun Records as a gospel act. He was signed to that label by Sam Phillips (not the singer), who first suggested the group had to include some secular material if he was going to market them. The requisite secular songs were the ones that caught on, and the rest is history. Cash would become the most important crossover country artist ever. In addition to his numerous hits on country western stations, he hit the pop charts forty-eight times in the two decades after his debut in 1956. His biggest pop hit came with Shel Silverstein's novelty song "A Boy Named Sue" (# 2 in 1969), but he remains even better remembered for country-rock classics like "Folsom Prison Blues," "I Walk the Line," and "Ring of Fire" (cowritten by June Carter). Cash is a member of the Nashville Songwriter's Hall of Fame, the Country Music Hall of Fame, and the Rock and Roll Hall of

Fame. He is listed by *Billboard* magazine as one of the top three selling country artists of all time.

The '60s were a rough decade for Cash. At the height of his commercial success, he spent most of that decade in a blur of alcohol and drug abuse. He suffered from a serious automobile accident and a near fatal drug overdose; his wife divorced him; he was arrested and jailed for trying to smuggle amphetamines over the Mexican border. Around 1967, however, he cleaned up his act, crediting his redemption to the help of a good woman—singer/songwriter June Carter, whom he then married. She had not only gotten him clean and sober but had also reintroduced him to his spiritual roots, which he now embraced with a passion. In 1971 he went forward at an altar call at the Evangel Temple in Nashville and formally committed his life to Christ (again). He wrote an autobiography detailing his Christian testimony (*Man in Black,* Zondervan, 1975). Years later, Cash would relate that one significant element that led him to the rededication of his life to Christ came when he attempted to commit suicide by crawling aimlessly back into the dark tunnels of Tennessee's Nickajack Cave until he was hopelessly lost. As he reports in yet another autobiography (*Cash,* Harper, 1997), "Then, my mind started focusing on God . . . I became conscious of a very clear, simple idea: I was not in charge of my destiny." Overwhelmed with a sudden sense of inner peace—but still absent any sense of direction—he began crawling in the dark down one passage, toward God as it were, only to discover that he had haphazardly selected the only way out.

Cash headlined the all-important *Explo '72* Christian rock festival (the "Christian Woodstock"), which first brought contemporary Christian music widespread exposure in the national media. He joined with his new wife to make a movie on the life of Christ (*The Gospel Road,* 1973), filmed in the Holy Land and featuring a country music soundtrack. Curiously, Cash was not as maligned for his faith as **Bob Dylan** would be a decade later—possibly because his fans understood its roots and did not feel so "betrayed" by the conversion. Cash hosted a highly rated ABC TV variety show from 1969 to 1971 (*The Johnny Cash Show),* performed for President Nixon at the White House, and became a fixture at Billy Graham evangelistic crusades. He also dedicated himself to charities benefitting prisoners and Native Americans. He did not, however, become a major figure in the contemporary Christian music scene. In 1979 he recorded a superb gospel album called *A Believer Sings the Truth,* but it was ignored in the contemporary Christian market, being perhaps too country for white suburban tastes. The project includes some traditional songs along with some very fine original compositions ("Oh Come Angel Band," "The Greatest Cowboy of Them All"). It wasn't until 1986 that he finally did make a Christian album for the Christian market. In

1987 Cash published a novel based on biblical stories regarding the Apostle Paul called *Man in White* (Harper and Row). In 1991, perhaps as a joke, he joined the loud Christian punk band **One Bad Pig** in a deconstruction of his hit "Man in Black."

Something of an enigma to Christian music, Cash has always been more at home in secular than sacred environs. From the mid '80s to the mid '90s, he recorded off and on as The Highwaymen with Kris Kristofferson, Willie Nelson, and his old drug-buddy Waylon Jennings. In 1993 he sang a guest lead vocal on "The Wanderer" on **U2**'s *Zooropa* album. Thus it should be no surprise that Cash's best Christian work is found on what were never intended to be official Christian projects. The absolute best is found on *American Recordings* and *Unchained.* On both of these albums, Cash mixes songs of faith and songs about life in general into critically acclaimed masterpieces. He announced at the premiere celebration for *American Recordings,* "This album is about sin and redemption. Thank God for redemption. I wouldn't be here without it." Thus the album offers his version of Nick Lowe's "The Beast in Me" as a prelude to a rendition of Kristofferson's "Why Me Lord?" It presents his own composition, "Redemption" ("The blood was the price that set the captives free"), alongside a cover of "Thirteen" by self-professed satanist Glenn Danzig. *Unchained* ups the ante even more with the assistance of high-powered guests like Tom Petty and the Heartbreakers, Beck, and Chris Cornell of Soundgarden. Though virtually ignored by the Christian media, the record has been hailed in other circles as "a masterful statement of faith." On one especially tender track, "Meet Me in Heaven," Cash sings to the woman who by then had been his wife of thirty-four years, "We've seen the secret things revealed by God / And we've heard what the angels have to say / If you go first, or if you follow me / Will you meet me in heaven someday?"

In 2000 Cash released his magnum opus, a stellar three-CD set of forty-eight songs called *Love God Murder.* The three words in the title refer to themes: one disc is a compilation of love songs, another of God songs, and a third of songs about murder. Cash himself selected the songs, and he seems to have ignored all pressure to compile audience favorites or hits. Rather, these are the songs that he considers to be his best, the ones that he hopes will form a legacy by which he will be remembered. Songs like "Boy Named Sue" are noticeably absent while a few B-sides and other obscurities are included. Critics agreed with Cash's selections, noting that the hit-and-miss artist had here assembled a compilation that pays just tribute to his ultimate significance and undeniable gift. The three discs would eventually be released separately, allowing fans to select one theme apart from the others if so desired. All three discs are sensational collections, but *God* is one of the finest compilations of country gospel songs ever released. Granted that he had forty years of material from which to choose, there is not a mediocre cut on the album. "Redemption" from *American Recordings* is here, but so is "It Was Jesus" from a forgotten 1958 album (*Hymns by Johnny Cash,* Columbia). "The Kneeling Drunkard's Plea" from *Unchained* likewise sits alongside fairly traditional renderings of "Swing Low, Sweet Chariot" and "Were You There When They Crucified My Lord?" A few tunes from *A Believer Sings the Truth* turn up, but nothing from *The Gospel Road* or *Believe in Him.* Bono of **U2** wrote liner notes for the *God* album (June Carter Cash wrote them for *Love* and Quentin Tarantino for *Murder*), and he notes, "Grace and empathy are etched into (Cash's) voice. . . . Gospel music has a joy that in most hands comes off as sentimental, a sweetness so easily saccharine. . . . Johnny Cash doesn't sing to the damned; he sings with the damned, and sometimes you feel he might prefer their company." For his own part Cash describes the set as a chronicle of his own faith journey: "It's a sampling from over the years. At times, I'm a voice crying in the wilderness, but at times I'm right on the money and I know what I'm singing about."

In 1997 Cash was diagnosed with a degenerative nervous disorder called Shy-Drager Syndrome. In 1999 he was the subject of a TV tribute concert featuring **Bob Dylan,** Bruce Springsteen, and **U2.** The latter show was his first public appearance since the diagnosis—but by 2000 his health appeared to be improving, and there was some doubt as to whether the diagnosis had been accurate. He released another album in 2000, a collection of modern folk songs called *American III: Solitary Man.* It includes the (sub)title track by Neil Diamond, along with Tom Petty's near-Christian anthem "I Won't Back Down," **U2**'s "One," and the traditional hymn "Wayfaring Stranger."

Grammy Awards: 1967 Best Country and Western Performance by Duet, Trio, or Group [with June Carter] ("Jackson"); 1968 Best Country Vocal Performance, Male *(Folsom Prison Blues)*; 1969 Best Country Vocal Performance, Male ("A Boy Named Sue"); 1970 Best Country Vocal Performance by a Duo or Group [with June Carter] ("If I Were a Carpenter"); 1994 Best Contemporary Folk Album *(American Recordings)*; 1997 Best Country Album *(Unchained)*; 2000 Best Male Country Vocal Performance ("Solitary Man").

Rob Cassels (a.k.a. **Rob Castles**)

As Rob Cassels or Rob Cassels Band: 1979—*Evening Pastoral* (Sword); 1983—*Kamikaze Christian* (Morada); 1984—*Off the Wall.* As Rob Castles: 1988—*Straight Shot* (Dark).

Often compared to Leon Russell, Rob Cassels/Castles played piano-driven music with a southern boogie flair. The South Carolina musician says that he became a Christian in 1971 at the age of nineteen when he read one of Campus Crusade for Christ's *Four Spiritual Laws* tracts given to him by a

classmate. Prior to his conversion he had been heavily involved with drugs, and as a Christian performer he would sometimes haul a large ball and chain out on stage to testify about the shackles from which Christ had set him free. Cassels frequently played in clubs on the East Coast where he would sing down-home tunes in a broad southern accent: "Been a long week working like we should / Work's been hard but the Lord's been good." His first album, *Evening Pastoral,* features Steve Morse of The Dixie Dregs on guitar and includes the jazzy instrumental "Lunar Trot" along with such original stompers as "Darkness Is a Goner" and "Battles Won." The title track reveals a more mellow side of the performer. *Kamikaze Christian* was officially recorded by The Rob Cassels Band, which included Mark Edger, Dave Hosler, and Kent Redd (Morse played guest guitar again). Advertised as "southern boogie," the record opens with one of its strongest numbers, "You Think I'm Crazy," which celebrates the countercultural fool-for-Christ identification Christians often bear in modern society. "You Don't Know" is bluesy gospel with a touch of the Allman Brothers, and "Rebel Yell" (not the Billy Idol song) features some more of Cassel's ornery humor: "Trust in your riches / You're gonna lose your britches / In the next life." For *Off the Wall* the group updated their sound somewhat for the '80s with Cassels switching from piano to synthesizers. *Straight Shot* was rereviewed in *CCM* magazine as "an explosive round of high-caliber rock extolling love, faith, and the peace of God."

Catharsis and the Humdrum

M. G. Miller, bass; Jonathan Newby, drums; Kevin Thornton, voc. 1997— *Girl Takes Mercury (after All-Night Party)* (independent); 1999—*Death of Komarov* [EP].

A three-piece outfit from Anderson, Indiana, Catharsis and the Humdrum are described as an emo band by some. Rather than apply that overused label, *True Tunes* offers this description: "equal parts early '90s jangly guitar rock and noisy guitar fuzz fused with a sense of epic proportion that calls the likes of **The Violet Burning** to mind." If that isn't very clear, the group's lyrics are at least explicable, if not completely comforting. Their focus is on Thornton's spiritual questions and self-doubts. In "Jacob Are U Listening?" he asks the patriarch, "Was the blessing worth the pain in your hip?" Weighing spiritual rewards and temporal costs is indeed an obsessive concern. On "80 Different Ways" he describes a woman who is "contemptibly erotic," warning himself to stay away from her, even though he wants her in "eighty different ways." In "New World Order" this struggle between flesh and spirit is projected onto an apocalyptic canvas, and Thornton is frankly dubious as to whether he has what it takes: "When the apple drops and the computers crash / Will I receive the angels' kiss? The devil's lash?" Christians who want their music to be comforting should hit the pause button *fast,* before he continues, "I'll not refuse the mark of the beast when the new world order comes / I am without spine, and hunger scares me some." There *are* references to grace here and there ("The Great Divide," not a Neil Young cover), but *True Tunes* is no doubt correct in assuming that Catharsis and the Humdrum's penchant for honesty will relegate them to the underground of the Christian music subculture, to a sub-subculture, as it were.

Caul

1995—*Crucible* (Malignant); 1996—*The Sound of Faith* (Katyn); 1998—*Reliquary* (Eibon); 1999—*Light from Many Lamps* (Malignant).

http://caul.org

"Dark" and "elegant" are the two words most used to describe Caul's instrumental, ambient music. The official name for this music is *darkwave;* it doesn't have a big following, but those who do follow it are loyal. Caul is actually just one incarnation of Brett Smith, who also records under the names Blackmouth and Tertium Non Data (sometimes with collaborator John Bergin). He is the acknowledged master of the genre. *True Tunes* describes Caul's music as sounding like soundtracks for films that have never been made (except perhaps in Smith's head). Smith relies on a variety of sources, including found sounds (discovered in nature), synthesizers, and guitars to create sonic meditations on a variety of typically majestic themes. Notably, Caul's albums have displayed an increasing predilection for Middle Eastern sounds. There are no lyrics, but song titles are directly expressive of religious and Christian themes. *Light from Many Lamps* offers musical meditations on these themes: "Thine Is the Day, Thine Is the Night," "By the Breath of God," and "Crux Est Mundi Medicina" (i.e., "The Cross Is the World's Medicine"). *The Sound of Faith* opens with a low and lengthy "Kyrie" and continues with tracks titled "The Redeemer of Blood" and "Parousia." Even without such prompts, some listeners think the music conveys a sense of gravity and majesty, appropriate for reflection on the awesomeness of God. Knowledgeable audiences might even recognize that Smith has a knack for incorporating neoclassical sounds reflective of various international liturgical traditions.

CAUSE

The one-time assemblage of Christian artists known as CAUSE (for Christian Artists United to Save the Earth) was organized by **Steve Camp** as a specifically Christian parallel to the Band Aid project launched by Bob Geldof. The latter program brought artists in the United Kingdom together to sing the song "Do They Know It's Christmas?" as a benefit for victims of the ongoing famine in Ethiopia. A true media event, it inspired numerous such programs, the most famous of which

was USA for Africa, a collection of American artists who sang "We Are the World," written by Michael Jackson and Lionel Richie. The officially Christian version of this trend included ninety artists, and the proceeds from their song "Do Something Now" (written by Camp and **Phil Madeira**) went to the hunger organization Compassion International. The project was accorded the President's Merit Award. Members of CAUSE included **Dennis Agajanian, Sherman Andrus, Brown Bannister, Scott Wesley Brown, Kim Boyce,** Owen Brock (of **Servant**), **Shirley Caesar, Michael Card, Pete Carlson, Gary Chapman, Chris Christian, Billy Crockett, Robin Crow, Morgan Cryar, Rick Cua, Jessy Dixon, Bob Farrell, John Fischer, Rob Frazier, Bill and Gloria Gaither, Reneé García, Amy Grant, Steve Green, Tami Gunden, Pam Mark Hall, Candy Hemphill, Glenn Kaiser, Evie Karlsson, Phil Keaggy, Mylon LeFevre, Angie Lewis, Phil Madeira, Gary McSpadden, David Meece, Geoff Moore, Larry Norman, Sandi Patty, Michele Pillar, Connie Scott, Billy Sprague, Russ Taff, Steve Taylor, Kathy Troccoli, Sheila Walsh,** and **Lisa Whelchel,** as well as the groups **DeGarmo and Key, Found Free, Glad, 2nd Chapter of Acts,** and **Silverwind.**

Christian radio hits: "Do Something Now" (# 2 in 1985).

Cauzin' Efekt

Willie Kemp; Melvin Rich; Ron Thompson // Alpine (Noah Krough) (+ 1994); Samantha Bragg (+ 1994); Stacey Brown (+ 1994); Kamika Krough (+ 1994); Eve Tomlianovitch (+ 1994). 1991—*Listen to His Voice* (Grrr); 1994—*Famlee Affair.*

Cauzin' Efekt represented Jesus People U.S.A.'s entry into the rap/hip-hop genre. JPUSA is the socially conscious community of Christians who live and work together in Chicago and who sponsor several musical artists, including **Ballydowse, The Crossing, Crashdog, Headnoise, Resurrection Band, Seeds, Sheesh,** and **Unwed Sailor.** Willie Kemp joined JPUSA in 1984, after accepting Christ while in jail for gang-related activities. Ron Thompson found salvation through a drug rehabilitation program in 1987 and entered the community thereafter. Melvin Rich was actually bussed to the community in 1987 by a friend in a last ditch attempt to rescue his life after years of drug and alcohol abuse climaxed in a suicide attempt. A year later Rich was witnessing for Christ on the streets of Chicago and felt called by God to start the rap group with his brethren. The first album has a generally melodic, R&B feel to it and features fairly straightforward evangelical lyrics. It includes "Transformed," "Have a Good Time," and a number of cover songs. The group expands for the second record, adding songwriter Alpine and several female vocalists. The new sound is much closer to that of modern hip-hop, and direct religious references are toned down. *Famlee Affair* seeks to address the tough issues of living in the neighborhoods while offering the promise of God's salvation in creative ways. As the title implies, the importance of being part of a supportive family is a prominent theme. The group also rants against abortion ("Right 2 Be"), cookie-cutter Christianity ("Break Out Da Frame"), and secular music ("Kickin' Game").

Ceili Rain

Raymond Arias, gtr.; Lang Bliss, drums; Buddy Connolly, acc.; Bob Halligan Jr., voc., gtr.; Andrew Lamb, bass; Gretchen Priest, fiddle; Skip Cleavinger, bagpipes, whistles // Bob Harmon, bass (+ 2000); Burt Mitchell, whistle, pipes, flute (+ 2000). 1998—*Ceili Rain* (Punch); 2000—*Erasers on Pencils* (Cross Driven).

www.ceilirain.com

Founded in 1995 by Bob Halligan, Ceili (pronounced *KAY-lee*) Rain is a Celtic rock group that tries to combine the sounds of traditional Irish music (cf. **Máire Brennan, The Crossing, Iona**) with more accessible pop sounds. It's like "the Chieftains meet the Beatles," Halligan claims; critics more humbly suggest "the Chieftains meet the Lovin' Spoonful." In any case, the debut album attracted more attention in the mainstream market than in Christian circles, though many of the lyrics are explicitly religious. The song "Is That All the Lumber You Bought?" records a humorous conversation between St. Peter and an applicant at the gates of heaven. The song is about "tallying that ultimate balance sheet at the end of one's life," though Halligan admits it can apply more generally to accountability in any situation. Similarly, "I Don't Need a Picture (To See Your Face)" is primarily about believing in a God who has never been photographed, but the song is popular with people who simply apply the lyrics to a distant loved one. Halligan likes songs that have a slightly humorous or ironic edge. "Long Black Cadillac" is an upbeat, fun song that may take repeated hearings before one realizes it is about a man riding to his own funeral in a hearse. And anyone who has ever been miserable on a hot sweltering day may wince at the thought of what it would be like to live in "666 degrees" (which, as it turns out, is the constant temperature of hell). Some songs reveal a softer side. "I Wanna Be Different" exposes the adolescent ideal of "fitting in" as boring. "Call Home" is a plea to potential or actual runaways. The song "You Then Me Then You Then Me" explains the importance of yielding to others in a creative and humorous way. "Peace Has Broken Out" is a hopeful sing-along about war-torn Northern Ireland. Some of these songs were already familiar to Christian audiences, though perhaps with slightly different names: **Eli** recorded "The Lumber Song"; **Considering Lily** did "I Don't Need a Picture"; **Rebecca St. James** recorded "You Then Me." Country star Kathy Mattea made Ceili Rain's "Love Travels" the title track for her 1997 album.

Ceili Rain's sophomore album, *Erasers on Pencils,* is a celebration of the best things in life. The opening "Jigorous" urges the listener to get into the "swirling, whirling twirl of life around us." The same sentiment invigorates "Life Is a Polka," a well-named lively tune that invites hearers (lyrically and musically) to "Dance! Dance! Dance!" A song called "Thanks" expresses appreciation for many things, including life itself. There is a personal side to all this joy, as Halligan gives thanks to his wife and to God for a newly adopted son in the tender song, "God Done Good." Fatherhood also inspires the silly song, "It Only Tickles When You Do It." A bit more serious are the message songs "These Things Have a Way of Workin' Out" and the title track, both of which convey a "lighten up and don't stay mired in the past" attitude. "Junkyard" deals with a variety of things that can junk up one's heart or trash one's mind—things that are difficult to forget, whether a violent image, a pornographic photo, or a vicious rumor.

The group's musicianship is beyond reproach. Buddy Connolly has won the All-Ireland annual championship for accordion playing three times. Gretchen Priest has fiddled for Lyle Lovett. Lang Bliss is known to some as one-half of **Bliss Bliss.** Early incarnations of the band included **Rick Cua** (once of the Outlaws) or Lance Hoppen (once of Orleans) on bass. For a while, Cactus Moser of Highway 101 was Ceili Rain's drummer. The album was produced by Bob Halverson, famous for his work with Crosby, Stills and Nash. How are they able to attract such talent? Apparently Halligan's name has some pull. A native of Syracuse, New York, Bob Halligan Jr. had an interesting pre-Ceili career. In 1982 he collaborated with Rick Cua on the latter's first Christian release, *Koo-ah.* But Halligan soon found himself occupied outside the Christian market as his songs started to be performed by numerous mainstream artists. Curiously, heavy metal bands showed particular interest in Halligan compositions: Judas Priest recorded "Take These Chains" and "Some Heads Are Gonna Roll" (a warning about nuclear holocaust); Blue Oyster Cult did "Make Rock Not War" and "Beat 'Em Up" (a "battlecry to kids to do their own thing"). The all-but-forgotten hard rock combo Kix scored a Number Eleven hit with his "Don't Close Your Eyes." With amazing dexterity he wrote songs for Kiss, Joan Jett, Night Ranger—even Fabio. "Still in Love with You" (cowritten with Michael Bolton) sold four million copies for Cher. Halligan also worked the country circuit, writing songs with Patty Loveless. In 1985 alone twenty-seven of his songs were recorded by respected artists. In the Christian market, chart hits that he wrote or cowrote include songs performed by **Bliss Bliss** ("Fight for Peace"), and **Bob Carlisle** ("Giving You the Rest of My Life"), in addition to many of Cua's songs.

In 1991 Halligan recorded a solo album for Atco called *Window in the Wall* that he says was immediately "tossed in the dumpster." Ceili Rain represents his second attempt at performing. The group takes their name from an Irish word for "party," and they strive to be "a party band." The group plays most often for nonreligious audiences but also employs a separate publicist to book religious gigs. They are an especially popular act with Catholic youth groups.

Chagall Guevara

Wade Jaynes, bass; Mike Mead, drums; Lynn Nichols, gtr., voc.; Dave Perkins, gtr., voc.; Steve Taylor, voc. 1991—*Chagall Guevara* (MCA).

Chagall Guevara was Christian superstar **Steve Taylor**'s venture into the wild world of secular mainstream rock and roll. Lynn Nichols (formerly of **Dust**), Wade Jaynes, and Mike Mead had frequently played with **Phil Keaggy,** and Nichols had produced a number of Keaggy's classic albums. **Dave Perkins** had recorded a solo album and worked with a number of artists, including **Randy Stonehill.** Although Chagall Guevara's one and only album was generally acclaimed by critics, it was not commercially successful (Taylor says it sold "tens of copies"). Musically, they had a sound that incorporated elements of David Bowie, the Doors, the Replacements ("Violent Blue" is sustained by a riff that Paul Westerberg appears to have borrowed for his *14 Songs*), and Taylor's favorite, The Clash. In other words, basic rock and roll, with a harder edge than most of Taylor's solo material. The group's unusual name derives from a juxtaposition of the surnames of artist Marc Chagall and revolutionary Ché Guevara (hence, "revolutionary artists," get it? Must have seemed like a good idea at the time). *CCM* would describe the band's album as "more aggressive, more intentionally obtuse, more broad, and more populist," than Taylor's solo work, though the latter's song "Jim Morrison's Grave" comes pretty close to the Chagall Guevara sound. Most of the songs deal with societal ills and their impact on individuals. "Rub of Love" laments the growing trend for American fathers to abandon their children as unwanted burdens. "Candy Guru" warns against false prophets. "If It All Comes True" imagines what one's last act might be in the face of a nuclear holocaust.

Chagall Guevara is noted for its obscure lyrics, which the songwriters (Nichols, Perkins, and Taylor) refused to explain in interviews. Nevertheless, spiritual profundity awaits those who don't need everything spelled out for them. "Escher's World" uses the imagery of the famous artist's drawings to describe a world where "up's down, down is out, out is in." "Violent Blue" presents the same sort of challenge that Neil Young offers when he chastises those who have lost their faith in the "hippie dream": "We were headed for somewhere," Chagall Guevara reminds, "but that was before you traded in your peace sign for a finger." Or "don't you recall when the perfume of belief was all we needed?" Ah, but there are so many excuses

to explain the loss of innocence. They're not buying it: "I don't believe it's the way you were raised / Or the cards you were dealt / Or a poor self-image / I think you love yourself too much."

Chagall Guevara never toured, and that may help to account for their lack of commercial success. Having a name few people could pronounce was not an asset. The group's adventures in the general market would also become something of a paradigm for the sort of complications that Christian artists can encounter there. Taylor has often told the story of how executives at MCA cautioned him and the others not to express their views about subjects like abortion if interviewed by *Spin* or other such publications. He would say that the differences between the supposedly narrow and suspicious Christian industry and the supposedly broad-minded anything-goes secular market were actually more of kind than degree: "I just traded one set of restrictions for another."

Despite its poor sales, Chagall Guevara's album became a cult classic, and by 2002 used copies were selling for upwards of a hundred dollars. Three of the best songs ("Murder in the Big House," "Escher's World," and "Violent Blue") have been included on Taylor's *Now the Truth Can Be Told* compilation (Sparrow, 1994). Chagall Guevara also performs a high energy version of **Mark Heard**'s "Treasure of the Broken Land" as a highlight on the *Strong Hand of Love* tribute to that artist (Fingerprint, 1996). A lost Chagall Guevara song, "Tale o' the Twister," turned up on the soundtrack to the 1990 Christian Slater film *Pump up the Volume* (**Rick Cua,** who was the band's original bassist, plays on that song but was replaced by Nichols before the eponymous album was recorded). In 1994 Lynn Nichols and David Perkins would make a follow-up album of sorts under the name **Passafist.**

Greg Chaisson

1994—*It's About Time* (Graceland).

Texas blues guitarist Greg Chaisson is a veteran of the mainstream band Badlands. He played with Christian acts **Die Happy** and **Red Sea** before releasing a solo album of foot stompin' music in the tradition of ZZ Top and George Thorogood. The album gets off to a rip roarin' start with "Too Late to Pray," featuring the rather simple and straightforward lyric, "If I don't change, it'll be too late to pray." Another song, "My Dark Ride," is particularly dynamic, building to a bridge where everything stops and Chaisson speaks: "I could hear the voice as clear as if someone was standing in the room. The voice said to believe in him, and to pray, and not to judge all people by the few misguided ones I've been around lately."

The Lighthouse magazine once listed three prior albums in a discography for Greg Chaisson, without indicating the labels on which they were released: 1988—*In Difference;* 1991—*Off the End of the Pier Show;* 1992—*Fine Difference.*

Champion Birdwatchers

Mark Clatterbuck, bass; Eric Johnson, voc.; Nathan Johnson, gtr.; Ryan Johnson, drums; P. J. Paul, cello (–2000). 1998—*The Inconsolable Longing* (Redshift).

Champion Birdwatchers was formed by brothers Eric and Nathan and cousin Ryan in the mid '90s. The boys from Idaho's panhandle create an atmospheric, moody sound that *Phantom Tollbooth* called a "sprawling, improvisational mess of guitar, drums, percussion, bass, cello, and flute." That's a compliment. The group rejects conventional song structures and just allows their sounds to evolve naturally, drawing equally from classical influences and from post-'60s psychedelic jamming. Lyrically, the group favors brooding poetry influenced by the likes of C. S. Lewis: "Immanuel, the sunrise, I shall wait for you / Immanuel, my love, compose thy horizon and bring me into view" ("Resolution"). Eric Johnson says, "The whole goal of music should be effective communication. Our focus as a band is to write songs that share the truth that God is there and He loves us, and wants a relationship." So the creatively titled song "Keep a Constant Memory of the Future" reminds listeners of Christ's return. In addition to the above album, the band recorded a four-song EP called *Perhelion,* made available through mp3.com. Champion Birdwatchers' name was chosen for them when Nathan Johnson had a dream in which he saw a murky figure wearing a gold medallion with those words emblazoned on it.

Eric Champion

1990—*Eric Champion* (Home Sweet Home); 1991—*Revolution Time;* 1992—*Save the World* (Myrrh); *Hot Christmas;* 1994—*Vertical Reality;* 1995—*Soft Hits: Lover's Heart;* 1996—*Transformation* (Essential); 1998—*Natural.*

A prolific musician from central Florida, Eric Champion has actually had two careers in Christian music, first as a young prodigy dance-hall king and then as a remade alternative pop rocker. Champion was born in 1970 and traveled with his family's music ministry as a child. They eventually settled in Daytona, where his father founded and pastored the Victory Christian Center. Eric was integrally involved with the youth group in that congregation, and his music ministry emerged out of their experiments with creative approaches to worship and witness. He began composing music on a synthesizer, and when he was eighteen—a college student at Oral Roberts University, studying drama—his mother sent a tape of his music to veteran Christian producer **Chris Christian.** Calls were made and the college degree and acting career were put on hold.

Between 1990 and 1993 Champion was actually responsible for six albums—the four listed above, plus *One Big World* (Myrrh, 1991) with a group he started called Area Code, and *The B/W Project* recorded by a duo called B/W consisting of Champion and Rodney Taylor. The latter album features teenybopper/rap remakes of ditties by famous Christian performers like **Amy Grant, Rich Mullins,** and **Larry Norman;** it's something of a collector's item for its camp appeal. Champion's music at this time was of a mostly synthesized, disco-inflected, techno-dance style. Comparisons were often made to Prince or, on ballads, to Michael Jackson. The self-titled project opens with a pretty ballad called "Forever Love" and then goes for funk with "Brother, Brother." *Revolution Time* features "Generation of Right," an anthemic call for a rebellion of conservatives against societal ills perpetrated by a permissive society. His next two albums were released within a month of each other and continued the appeal to dance-floor aficionados. "Relivin' Life" from *Save the World* exemplifies well the infectious, dance club beat that could win over both audiences and critics. A funk/rap version of "Little Drummer Boy" from *Hot Christmas* also attracted quite a bit of attention. But Champion would become best known for more radio-friendly soft hits like "Peaceful" (from his self-titled album) and the flute-tinged "Smilin' " (from *Save the World*). Such numbers may have been intended as breaks to afford dancers a time to cool down, but they wear better than the disco tracks and would ultimately prove more satisfying.

In 1994 Champion released the most ambitious project from this stage of his career, a sort of *Mr. Roboto*-style pop musical called *Vertical Reality.* The concept piece (accompanied by videos and an elaborate stage show) was built around a science fiction theme in which some individuals in a future world ruled by computers manage to hack their way out of the system's memory and set out on a quest to find (as it turns out) the true God. Similarities to *The Matrix*—which *Vertical Reality* predates—are rather remarkable. Musically the album was Champion's most Prince-ly triumph, though the two songs that got most noticed were, again, the more subdued cuts. "Endless," a love song to humanity sung from the point of view of God, is a gorgeous masterpiece in the "soft hits" tradition. "Touch," a hook-laden pop song about feeling God's presence, features a female vocal that introduced the world to the talents of Fleming McWilliams of **Fleming and John.** Standouts among the ignored upbeat numbers include "N2 The Next Dimension" and "Dancin' in the Fire"; "My Life Is in Your Hands" is another fine ballad, with Champion's voice in top form. Around this time Champion cowrote the song "Here I Am" with **Rebecca St. James,** providing her with her first Christian radio hit.

One problem with Champion's techno whiz kid period was that it came during that interim when disco was being declared dead and rave had not quite caught on. He would later complain that he played "mostly for mothers in their 30s and 40s" rather than for people his own age. In any case, the album *Transformation* (note the name!) was announced with great fanfare as offering the "real" Eric Champion for the first time. The style is remarkably different, resembling in some respects that of **Charlie Peacock,** who produced the record. The album opens with "Dress Me Up," in which Champion declares, "I stink / I smell like dirt / I smell like myself and it won't come off," and then pleads for God to strip him bare and give him new attire. The upbeat ballad "Lifeform" insists that change is integral to life: "Yesterday I was not what I am today / I will not be tomorrow like I am right now / I'm an ever changing, re-arranging life form." Although Champion does not abandon the keyboard entirely on *Transformation,* guitars are much more in evidence, and hooks are emphasized over rhythm to give the still-bouncy songs more the feel of danceable pop than the straight-out disco assault of previous records. "What's in a Name" is particularly creative, built around an unusual mix of organ and banjo. "Temptannie" (warning against the wiles of a sexual temptress) is a fairly explosive grungy rocker, and "Higher" is just passionate enough to warrant comparison to the song of the same name that **Creed** would release a few years later. A sped-up punk-rock version of "Every Heartbeat"—the **Amy Grant** song that was actually written by producer Peacock—was included as a joke and can probably be enjoyed only if viewed as such.

Natural continues in the same vein as *Transformation,* with enough big squealing guitars to solidify Champion's modern rock credentials. At the same time, enough of the techno sound remains to mark Champion's style as a "fusion." Lyrically, the album repeatedly addresses the theme of narcissism or self-interest in modern society. The opening song ("Am I Looking Good?") again portrays the problem: "Well, your baby cheated on you / I'm so sorry to hear . . . / But enough about you / Let's talk about me a bit / You haven't said a thing about my new outfit." "Just Me" contains the great line, "My best friends are Jesus, I, myself, and me." The tune "I Am Nothing" offers the counterpoint: "Without your love, I am Nothing." "God Only Knows" (not a Beach Boys cover) recalls early work by **Steve Taylor** in sound. "Hacker's Prayer" (featuring the cute?/trite? lyric, "Let your love download on me") displays **Joy Electric** influence.

Overall, the new sound of both *Transformation* and *Natural* inspires more comparisons to Blur or Urge Overkill than to Prince or Michael Jackson. In 2001 Champion was teaching at a music school in Florida with no announced intention of recording again.

For trivia buffs: Champion's first band, Area Code, also included Leanza Cornett, who became Miss America 1993. The group charted one song on Christian radio, "Impossible Is Impossible" (# 30 in 1992).

Christian radio hits: "We Are the Young" (# 4 in 1990); "Forever Love" (# 21 in 1990); "Friends in High Places" (# 8 in 1990); "Peaceful" (# 24 in 1990); "Always Here" (# 15 in 1991); "Generation of Right" (# 23 in 1992); "What You're Looking For" (# 3 in 1992); "Save the World" (# 3 in 1992); "The Answer" (# 1 for 3 weeks in 1993); "Smilin' " (# 16 in 1993); "New Crusade" (# 7 in 1993); "Touch" (# 1 in 1994); "My Life" (# 21 in 1994); "Endless" (# 10 in 1994); "More about You" (# 2 in 1995); "Dress Me Up" (# 8 in 1996); "Life Form" (# 7 in 1996).

Change

Personnel list unavailable. 1996—*Change* (Freedom).

The five-man vocal ensemble Change would be the first Christian reggae group actually to come from Jamaica (cf. **Amarachi, Christafari, Temple Yard**). As such, one would expect authenticity of sound. If they do deliver that, American listeners are too ill informed to appreciate it. A writer for *The Lighthouse* (who apparently knew nothing of the group's origins) noted, "this album is to reggae what the '50s were to rock and roll—it is only the beginning of the evolution of the sound." Basically, Change strives for a gospel reggae sound influenced by doo-wop harmonies that might make the music more accessible to those who have never become fans of more hardcore varieties. Such an effort might indeed be more appealing to fans than to purist critics. The vocals are clear and smooth and especially rich in baritone—a trait that sets them apart from tenor-led American groups like Boyz II Men. Lyrically, the group is forthright in their evangelical witness to Christ. Standout songs include the opening track "We Have a Message" ("Tell it to the heathen / That Jesus the Savior reigns / Tell it to every nation / And let them burst their chains") and "Taste and See," with lyrics drawn from the Psalms.

The Channel Surfers

Tim Bushong, gtr., tromb.; Jon Hill, bass; Lance Hill, drums; Jason Brown, voc. (−1999) // Aaron Scantlen, voc. (+ 1999). 1997—*Tunnel Vision* (Organic); 1999—*Where I Wanna Be.*

Tim Bushong, guitarist for the hard rocking Christian band **Lovewar,** formed The Channel Surfers as a hybrid rap-funk-rock band affected by flourishes of pop and ska. Much tamer than groups like the Beastie Boys (with whom they are often compared), the band has a cleaner pop sound similar to that of **Reality Check** or 311. Bushong produced both of the band's albums, which feature two different lead vocalists. *Tunnel Vision* includes radio-friendly pop songs like "So Far Away" alongside songs such as "Like Job," which *Phantom Tollbooth* described as "louder than your average Dove nominee." Jason Brown affects a humorous James Brown imitation for the song "Lonely Guy," which lists famous lonely people such as Floyd the Barber (on *The Andy Griffith Show*) and Pee Wee Herman. "C.T.C." displays Beck influences on a mysterious song about growing up (the initials refer to Cerritos Town Center, a shopping mall in Long Beach, California). On *Where I Wanna Be* the group moves decidedly away from the rapcore feel of the first album toward slicker and sunnier sounds (*Tollbooth* wrote, "If you dig spic-and-span studio sheen, hop on. If edginess and real-life music sounds are your bag, run away"). Otherwise, the album repeats much of the first, even to the point of offering a sequel to "Lonely Guys" called "More Lonely Guys." The title track states the band's commitment *not* to withdraw from the world, since "Wherever God is, that's where I wanna be." One of three hidden tracks at the end offers a spoof of spandex metal with Tony Palacios of **Guardian** providing good-natured, self-incriminating vocals. The group has also done a faux-metal cover of the Veggie Tales' children's song "God Is Bigger."

The Channel Surfers are located in northern Indiana. They compose their songs as a band, jamming in the studio. A prominent theme of their work is the superficiality of modern culture and its alluring but ultimately unsatisfying relativism. The theological naivete that critics often detect in their lyrics is part of the charm, and indeed must be accepted as somewhat definitive of music by and for the young. More to the point, perhaps, is that the group does not appear to take itself (or its music) very seriously—a trait annoying to critics. On "Cheese Review," they mockingly accept but dismiss descriptions of their music as "cheesy": "Bands may come, reviews may go, but the cheese stands alone." Or again, on "Getting Away," Scantlen exults, "I like to wing it when I sing the Channel Surfers groove." Of course, the trait of not taking oneself too seriously can also have a certain charm, and it is a feature that—to the further annoyance of critics—Channel Surfer fans seem to appreciate. It is hard not to be amused when one of the group's comic songs baits a *CCM* critic into spending an entire review carping about how mean-spirited and immature the group is for making jokes about Ellen DeGeneres and Bill Clinton (public figures who, in fact, would probably have enjoyed the humor at their expense).

Chaos is the Poetry

Philip Bardowell, voc.; Lanny Cordola, gtr., voc.; Chuck Wright, bass. 1996—*Chaos is the Poetry* (Alarma).

www.pioneer-net.com/lanny/docs/chaos.htm

The trio of Bardowell, Cordola, and Wright also recorded as part of **Magdalen.** Their collaboration as Chaos is the Poetry

not only brought them together under what is probably the best *name* any Christian rock group has ever had but also produced an epic masterpiece of an album. Unfortunately, the record label folded just as the album was coming out, allowing it to slip into oblivion unnoticed by all but critics, other musicians, and intrepid collectors. Aided by several other musicians (notably Gregg Bissonette on drums and Chris Bleth on sax and a variety of woodwinds), the group creates jazz-inflected progressive rock that draws from a rich potpourri of influences. As with **Lanny Cordola**'s solo projects, the music is such a collage that it will appeal only to those with eclectic tastes, to people who like music *done well* whatever the style. The hard psychedelic opener "Why Buildings Fall Down" sounds a lot like the classic Arthur Lee-fronted '60s group Love and would become uncannily relevant five years later in the aftermath of September 11, 2001; Chaos also offers some pure pop funk in "Daisy Chain" and a slow jazz burn with "So Go I." Other songs worthy of note include the early rapcore experiment, "Longest Day in Mrs. Evers' Life," the acoustic-flamenco ballad, "Seashells," and especially the spooky, plaintive plea called "God's Empty Chair." Lyrically, the group presents songs that deal in one way or another with the intersection of religion and culture, touching on themes of racial violence and on efforts to relate the message of the gospel to the needs of society. The songs are rich in literary allusion and imagery in ways that may confound linear thinkers. They strive to draw on the affective strengths of poetry, while sacrificing the more direct and obvious referential values of prose. "God's Empty Chair" paints a picture of homeless persons huddled outside a downtown cathedral: "The lady with the Bible eases by the little hitlers / Her weary body trembles but her spirit is a general." What does *that* mean? It requires some reflection, at least. Cordola has also recorded with **Children of Zion, The Panorama Ramblers, Shack of Peasants,** and **Symbiotica;** Bardowell and Wright participated in some of these as well.

Gary Chapman

1981—*Sincerely Yours* (Lamb and Lion); 1982—*Happenin'*; 1987—*Everyday Man* (Reunion); 1994—*The Light Inside*; 1996—*Shelter; The Early Years* (Sparrow); 1997—*This Gift* (Reunion); 1999—*Outside*; 2002—*Circles and Seasons* (Crowne).

www.garychapman.com

Born in 1957 in Waukira, Oklahoma, Gary Chapman grew up in DeLeon, Texas, as the son of a Pentecostal minister. He attended the Assemblies of God College in Waxahachie, Texas, worked as a youth pastor in Ft. Worth, and then settled in Nashville where he played guitar for first **The Downings** and then **The Singing Rambos,** a famous southern gospel group that included **Reba Rambo.** He wrote the song "My Father's Eyes" for **Amy Grant** (# 3 in 1979) and recorded his first solo album amidst the unexpected excitement of winning the Dove award for Songwriter of the Year. Shortly after the release of *Sincerely Yours* he married Grant, and for sixteen years they were the most famous couple in Christian music. He wrote another Number Three hit for her in 1981, "Look What Has Happened to Me" (cowritten with **Brown Bannister**), and she returned the favor by penning what was to be his first Top 10 song, "Where Do I Go?" The two frequently toured together and supported each other on their respective albums. The marriage ended in 1999 amidst public reports that Grant had become involved with country singer Vince Gill, whom she soon married. Chapman went public with his bitterness over those events, telling *CCM* and other publications that Grant's relationship with Gill was the primary cause of the marriage's failure. "We had one 'irreconcilable difference'," he reported. "I wanted her to stay and she wanted to leave." Chapman remarried in July 2000.

In addition to his involvements with Christian music, Chapman has become something of a fixture in the Nashville country scene. He wrote the song "Finally" (# 1 on country charts in 1981) for T. G. Sheppard, and "I Prefer the Moonlight" (# 2 on country charts in 1988) for **Kenny Rogers,** in addition to songs for Alabama, Lee Greenwood, and Barbara Mandrell. He has opened concerts for mainstream artists like Bruce Hornsby and the Range (1987) and played the Grand Ole Opry (1996). Well known for his sense of humor, Chapman is frequently tapped for regional and national TV appearances. From 1995 to 1999 he hosted the popular TNN cable show *Primetime Country,* on which he interviewed numerous stars and legends of the industry. The Network even gave him a "Comedian of the Year" Award in 1998. He has also served as host of a nationally syndicated radio show, *The CCM Countdown,* which is basically a Christian version of Casey Kasem's famous Top 40 show. In 1995 he hosted the Dove Awards presentation.

In spite of his mainstream country-music associations, Chapman's own recordings would be more likely classified as "adult contemporary pop." His first three albums are competent productions but were only modestly received. *Sincerely Yours* includes the song "Open Up My Eyes" and a duet with Grant on "Anywhere." *Happenin'* was recorded live and includes Chapman's own rendition of "My Father's Eyes" in addition to "Treasure" and another duet with Grant called "Always." *Everyday Man* is a more developed country-pop affair with most of the songs dealing with relationships and romance. This time the requisite spousal duet is on a John Hiatt song, "Love Like Blood." The title track provides insight into the stress of celebrity marriages and expresses an autobiographical wish that life could be simpler. "When We're Together" is bouncy and affirming, as is "Love That Girl," an energetic track written with **Randy Stonehill.** The album

was regarded as a bit too passionate by some conservative Christians. In the title track Chapman sings, "Amy, she's a wild one / A rock 'n' roller / Tell you how she makes my heart so free / She can make me happy without tryin' / Unlock the thunder inside of me." The Hiatt song has some choice lyrics too.

Around the time of *Everyday Man's* release, Chapman admitted to instances of drug abuse. He all but disappeared from the Christian music scene for about seven years and then returned, rejuvenated, with a new pop style. He hit big with *The Light Inside,* which was produced by **Michael Omartian.** The opening song, "Where Are the Broken Hearts," urges compassion for hurting people in the world while the closing number, "Sweet Jesus," universalizes that hurt while moving beyond generic spirituality to name the ultimate source of compassion: "Sweet Jesus, please won't you hear us crying, we're all crying." The standout song (which gives the album its title) is "Sweet Glow of Mercy," which describes the permanent effect of experiencing God's grace: "I've been known to run, but I can't hide / I can't get away from the light inside." The record also includes two reprises of classic Chapman songs, "Finally" and "Treasures." It was a stirring success, bringing Chapman out from the shadow of his wife's career and earning him a Dove nomination for Artist of the Year. Emboldened, he followed quickly with *Shelter,* again produced by Omartian, and again continuing in the adult pop vein. More explicitly gospel than *Light Inside, Shelter* opens with an a capella version of the traditional hymn "Great Is Thy Faithfulness" and closes with a solid rendition of the standard "Gospel Ship" (in its famous **Mylon LeFevre** arrangement). The record also contains a rootsy rocker "Back Where I Started" and a tender duet with Grant on an eventually ironic ode to marital permanence, "One of Two." "Written in the Scars" testifies to the overwhelming effect of Christ's sacrifice. "If You Ever Need Me" features the sweet voice and viola of Allison Krauss. On the strength of *Shelter,* the artist would win what was fast becoming the Dove awards' dueling Chapmans competition (i.e., Gary or **Steven Curtis Chapman**—no relation) for Best Male Artist.

Chapman's next major release (*The Gift* was a Christmas album) came out the year of his divorce, and perhaps for that reason features fewer original songs. He wrote only two of the songs on *Outside,* most notably "Learning to Love" which tries to address the recent events in an "honest but nonjudgmental way." Still, Chapman said "the whole album is about forgiveness, healing, and moving on, which are pretty dominant themes in my life right now." The song "Hold On," for instance, offers a message of simple encouragement that Chapman thought was important for his children to hear at the stressful time. Musically, *Outside* has a different sound than its two successful predecessors, less of a rock orientation, and more of a slow, inspirational feel, similar to the music of

Bob Carlisle. Indeed, the most noticed song was the heart-wrenching Carlislesque ballad, "Daddy, Cut My Hair," a song written by **Michael Kelly Blanchard** about a father and son relationship. Chapman says, "I think it might be the best song I've ever heard. . . . It moves me every single time I sing it." *Circles and Seasons* would be a true solo project. Chapman not only wrote all of the songs for the very personal project but also played all instruments and produced the album in his own home studio. The record includes Chapman's version of "All I Ever Have to Be," a song **Amy Grant** recorded on her 1980 *Never Alone* record. The song "I Need Jesus" is a simple and straightforward testimony of faith; he calls it his "primal cry."

In addition to his major recordings, Chapman has contributed songs to numerous compilation and tribute albums, including the motion picture soundtracks for *Earnest Goes to Camp* ("Brave Hearts"), *The Apostle* ("I'll Fly Away," with Wynonna), and *The Prince of Egypt* ("You Are My Light"). He sang a duet with **Susan Ashton** on John Lennon's "In My Life" for the Omartian-produced *Come Together: America Salutes the Beatles* (Capitol, 1995). In 1997 he joined a bevy of country stars including Chet Atkins to make the award-winning album, *Hymns from the Ryman* (Word, 1997). As a songwriter Chapman has written or cowritten Christian radio hits performed by **Steve Camp** ("I'm Committed to You," "Give Me Some Time"); **Lesley Glassford** ("Soul Revival"); **Amy Grant** ("Father's Eyes," "Look What Has Happened to Me," "In a Little While," "Angels," "Love of Another Kind," "1974," "I Will Remember You"); **Wes King** ("Home inside of Me"); and **Kathy Troccoli** ("Stubborn Love").

For trivia buffs: Chapman is a private pilot with a preference for helicopters. He says, "It occupies both feet, both hands, and a big part of your brain. It's basically a pedal steel guitar that can kill you."

Christian radio hits: "Your Love Stays with Me" (# 14 in 1988); "Where Do I Go?" [with **Ashley Cleveland**] (# 4 in 1994); "Sweet Glow of Mercy" (# 15 in 1994); "Where Are the Broken Hearts" (# 2 in 1994); "Heal Me" (# 7 in 1995); "Floodgates of Love" (# 6 in 1995); "One of Two" (# 25 in 1996); "Back Where I Started" (# 9 in 1996); "Written in the Scars" (# 7 in 1996).

Dove Awards: 1981 Songwriter of the Year; 1996 Male Vocalist; 1996 Inspirational Song ("Man after Your Own Heart"); 1998 Country Album (*Hymns from the Ryman*).

Jerry Chapman

2000—*Making God Laugh* (Toxic Pop).

Formerly bassist for Two-Pound Planet, Jerry Chapman is now one-half of the folk rock combo **Life in General.** His first solo album on an independent album offers a handful of original songs alongside covers of diverse tunes originally performed by **The Choir, Daniel Amos,** Simon and Garfunkel,

and James Taylor. Chapman plays all of the instruments on the album and actually achieves a fuller sound than is evident in *Life in General*'s more stripped-back approach. His original songs are lyrically creative and stimulating. The opening song declares, "I'm passed out on Sunday in my very best clothes / And if I love Jesus, how come no one knows?" The closing song, "Basement," provides the line that gives the record its title: "Sometimes I get the feeling that I must be making God laugh."

Morris Chapman

Selected: 1979—*Jesus, I Put All My Trust in You* (Neotec); 1980—*The Lord Reigns* (Myrrh); 1983—*Longtime Friends* (Myrrh); 1984—*Lately*; 1985—*Voice of Praise* [with The Maranatha Singers] (Maranatha); 1986—*The Artist* (DaySpring); 1988—*Sunshine and Rain* (Birdsong); 1990—*Live Worship* [with The Maranatha Singers] (Maranatha); 1994—*The Best of Morris Chapman and the Maranatha Singers*; 1999—*Bethlehem Morning* [with The Maranatha Singers].

African American gospel singer Morris Chapman hails from Las Vegas and is best known in Christian music for his continuing work with the series of *Praise* albums for Maranatha music. Chapman's first two albums were described in *CCM* as vocally strong but "displaying no rock influence." *Longtime Friends* features one upbeat traditional gospel standard ("There'll Be a Fire One Day That Firemen Can't Put Out") and eight original compositions. The title track was equally upbeat, with the rest of the record devoted to more soulful piano ballads. Chapman's song "God Is About to Do" became a hit for Kenny Hinson (# 29 in 1983). Chapman went on to become a worship leader and to record several albums of praise and worship music with The Maranatha Singers.

Christian radio hits: "No More Night" (# 33 in 1984).

Steve and Annie Chapman

Selected: 1981—*Steve and Annie Chapman* (StarSong); 1982—*Second Honeymoon*; 1984—*Circle of Two*; 1986—*Times and Seasons; Bind Us Together*; 1987—*Guest of Honor*; 1988—*An Evening Together; Precious Moments*; 1989—*A Man and a Woman*.

Steve Chapman may be best known as the reason that **Steven Curtis Chapman** has to use his middle name, but he and his wife Annie have impacted Christian music in other ways as well. Both were once members of the seminal Jesus music group **Dogwood.** Indeed, they met and married while singing with **Dogwood** and then continued to record country folk albums as a couple after that group's demise. They are originally from West Virginia, but the couple's music ministry is now based in Nashville. They have worked closely with James Dobson's "Focus on the Family." Since leaving StarSong in 1989, they have released more than twenty independent recordings and have authored a number of books, focusing especially on family life. The Chapman's musical style has tended toward a soft MOR sound with country leanings. Songs frequently extol family values and prefeminist conceptions of family life. For example, the title song for *Circle of Two* expresses the need for a family to pray together, while "Goodnight Kiss" applauds the role of a mother who stays home with her children. "Where Did the Romance Go?" from *Second Honeymoon* offers some straight talk to men (inspired by Dobson's book *Straight Talk to Men and Their Wives*) about not expecting sex at night without romance in the evening. Annie Chapman also released a solo album for StarSong called *Celebration of Womanhood* (1990). Steve Chapman should not be confused with the syndicated newspaper columnist of the same name who writes for the *Chicago Tribune*. The latter should, perhaps, use a middle name, but he doesn't.

Christian radio hits: "As for Me and My House" (# 25 in 1983); "Circle of Two" (# 6 in 1985).

Dove Awards: 1988 Country Album (*An Evening Together*).

Steven Curtis Chapman

1987—*First Hand* (Sparrow); 1988—*Real Life Conversations*; 1989—*More to This Life*; 1990—*For the Sake of the Call*; 1992—*The Great Adventure*; 1993—*The Live Adventure*; 1994—*Heaven in the Real World*; 1995—*The Music of Christmas*; 1996—*Signs of Life*; *The Early Years*; 1997—*Greatest Hits*; 1999—*Speechless*; 2001—*Declaration*.

www.stevencurtischapman.com

Contemporary Christian music is a diverse genre, but in the '90s no artist represented the meat and potatoes of the field better than Steven Curtis Chapman. With more than forty Dove awards to his credit, he is clearly the industry darling, and yet critics like him too! Even metalheads and fans of alternative rock—people whose tastes generally run contrary to Chapman's power-pop, male-version-of-**Amy-Grant** style, will grudgingly admit he's "pretty good," more painless than, say, **Michael Card** or (Arggh!) **Michael W. Smith.** A writer for *The Lighthouse* magazine once observed, "I have *never* heard anyone say anything derogatory about Steven Curtis Chapman." What's the secret? He's warm, he's personable, and above all, he is just so *authentic.* No one ever doubts for a moment that SCC really does think and feel and believe everything that he expresses so clearly in his songs (and in all that homey stage patter that surrounds those songs at his concerts). Besides, he *is* pretty good—and then some.

Chapman was born in Paducah, Kentucky, in 1962. His musical gifts earned him a gig at Opryland, raising the hopes of his parents and community that the boy had a promising career in country music. But almost from the start Chapman felt "the call of God," and after seeing the movie *Chariots of Fire,* he was

able to identify the reason. Like Eric Liddell who claimed to "feel God's pleasure" when he ran, Chapman maintains that he feels God's pleasure in music. So he writes and performs songs that testify to that experience. He is also intentional about sharing testimonies to his family, which he obviously prizes as second only to God: his wife Mary Beth and their three children, Emily, Caleb, and Will Franklin. The former is the hero of many an SCC song; the latter a constant supply of humorous and inspirational anecdotes. Another notable attribute of Chapman's music is that, while most soloists get increasingly mellow with age, Chapman has gotten feistier. The general move through his discography has been from adult contemporary to pop to actual rock and roll—rather than the other way around.

Chapman's first two albums feature songs that all fit nicely into one of three categories: a) songs heavily influenced by Kenny Loggins ("First Hand," "Faithful, Too"); b) songs heavily influenced by Huey Lewis ("Run Away," "My Turn Now"); and c) MOR ballads ("Hiding Place," "His Eyes," "His Strength Is Perfect"). The third album, *More to This Life,* evinces some maturity and includes Chapman's first two great songs: the title tune came out of Chapman's reflections on mortality prompted by some unexpected funerals ("There's more to this life than just living and dying / More than just trying to make it through the day"); "I Will Be Here" is a painful pledge of commitment to Mary Beth, written in the shock of his parent's divorce after thirty years of marriage ("I will be here when the laughter turns to crying / Through the winning, losing, and trying / We will be together / I will be here"). Suddenly Chapman was a Christian superstar, sweeping the Dove awards for the first of many times. Then he read Dietrich Bonhoeffer's *The Cost of Discipleship,* a book from which few Christians escape unscathed. His response was "For the Sake of the Call," the title song from his fourth album which was to become a signature tune. The song expresses the essence of true Christian discipleship, of following Christ not for recognition or gain but simply in response to "a call." It has become especially meaningful to candidates for the ordained ministry or other church vocations, and it is printed (not always legally) on lots of inserts in lots of hymnals at lots of Bible schools and seminaries. Musically the song represents a stellar example of the recipe for a trademark Steven Curtis Chapman song: add killer hooks to acoustic underpinning and big vocals and let it all lead up to a big, big chorus (repeat several times). "What Kind of Joy" adds balance to the album with a nice, nonanthemic acoustic touch. *More to This Life* also includes "Busy Man" (about preoccupations that keep one from experiencing the "more" to life) and "No Better Place," a song of assurance about heaven. "Lost in the Shadow" sounds like Bonhoeffer again, with the lyric, "I want to get lost in the shadow of the cross."

With *The Great Adventure* Chapman reinvented himself with a grittier roots rock sound that would more quickly summon images of John Mellencamp than the Hip-to-Be-Square Huey Lewis. The title song (written with **Geoff Moore**) is a pop masterpiece, evoking Wild West imagery with a jubilant call to "saddle up your horses" and follow "our leader" into the great unknown. Chapman's country roots show up too, on "Don't Let the Fire Die," a song worthy of comparison to Pure Prairie League. Then, on "Got To B Tru," a song about authenticity, Chapman humorously demonstrates *in*authenticity by laying down what just might be the lamest white-boy rap in history (in a mock effort to impress guests **DC Talk**). He also offers a duet with **BeBe Winans** ("Still Called Today") and channels more of a heartland John Mellencamp sound on "Where We Belong" and "That's Paradise." *The Great Adventure* would be Chapman's first album to go gold (with sales of more than 500,000), and it would be his only one included (at Number Thirty-three) on a *CCM* critics' poll of "The 100 Greatest Albums in Christian Music" published in 2001. *Heaven in the Real World* continues to turn up the heat, presenting a whole spate of upbeat songs with a diversity of styles. Standouts include the title track, "Treasure of You," and the Caribbean-sounding "King of the Jungle." Even the ballads ("The Mountain," "Still Listening") feature some pretty unpredictable melodies. Then Chapman revisits his old Huey Lewis style on "Dancing with the Dinosaur," a song that is especially creative lyrically: the basic idea is that he is proud to be considered a dinosaur if that means being associated with such old-fashioned ideals as truth, conscience, and commitment. "Burn the Ships" is a rare misstep, taking a famous quote from the militant conqueror Cortez as representative of what Christ would say to us ("Burn the ships, we're here to stay / There's no way we could go back"). The intention is clear, but the song is still inappropriate, considering the original context of those words on the lips of a mass murderer.

With *Signs of Life* Chapman upped the ante and made an album that—while thoroughly religious—could easily compete with anything in the secular market. It is, first of all, a rock and roll record with guitars up front and a sometimes blistering band backing Chapman's strong vocals. Somewhere along the way he learned how to yelp, holler, and even squeal ("Rubber Meets the Road") like a rock star, though most of the time he just *sings* and lets the flourishes be no more than just that. The songs on *Signs of Life,* unlike previous projects, all have a musical quality that allows them to stand on their own even apart from the lyrics—they *sound* great regardless of whether one finds Chapman's sentiments inspiring. Hypothetically, non-Christians could have loved *Signs.* Indeed, it is virtually inconceivable that anyone who likes Don Henley or Billy Joel (or Kenny Loggins or Huey Lewis) would not like this

album. It rocks out for eight songs straight before finally offering three ballads among its four closing tracks. The rockers are also marked by an incredible diversity. The opener, "Lord of the Dance," is of course a dance song, but with a grunge edge. "Children of the Burning Heart" and the title track are arena anthems. "The Walk" is country rock, "Free" has a jazzy, Sting-influenced quality, and "Rubber Meets the Road" is straight-out blues. Through it all, Chapman emerges not only as a great, versatile singer, but also as a better guitarist than anyone had previously noticed. Likewise the ballads depart from the predictable mold described as "trademark Chapman" above. "Celebrate You" (a love song for Mary Beth) is a bouncy, midtempo number that is extremely melodic. "Hold On to Jesus" is a plaintive, personal hymn. "What I Would Say," featuring just Steven's voice against a piano and a few strings, is like something out of the prerock era, recalling perhaps the haunting torch songs of the '40s. Such a tune must be carried by its lyrics, and the lyrics here are strong. With raw vulnerability Chapman reflects on what he would like to say to a grandfather he never met—a man whose battle with alcoholism kept him from fulfilling responsibilities to his family.

Speechless was first and foremost the follow-up to *Signs of Life,* more of the same, and for that reason was received by critics as both "very good" and yet as "more of the same." The latter criticism is muted somewhat by the observation that, since the hallmark of *Signs* was musical diversity, an album that is "like it" is also, ironically, diverse. As one reviewer put it, everything that Chapman fans want and expect is here: "the touching love songs, the lush, orchestra-embellished, in-awe-of-God pieces, and the toe-tapping, heel-clicking, not-quite-head-banging guitar-driven rock songs." The record's opening track, "Dive," is certainly as good as or better than anything on *Signs.* An innovative rocker with just a sliver of techno-electronica added to the mix, the song exults in religious experience, portraying jubilantly the feeling of getting lost in the majesty of God, of diving headlong into that supernatural flow. Coincidentally, **DC Talk** released a song with the same title and the same theme about the same time. The title track to "Speechless" (written with **Geoff Moore**) is another of Chapman's anthems in the tradition of "For the Sake of the Call" or "The Great Adventure." "The Change" offers some killer guitar riffs on a very plugged-in call for Christians to show their faith by a changed life rather than by T-shirts and bumper stickers. "I Do Believe" actually evokes images of Aerosmith and **Collective Soul.** "Great Expectations" is a great acoustic pop song, and "Fingerprints of God" has one of the catchiest melodies Chapman has ever written. The latter song offers a poignant but tender word to his adolescent daughter ("I can see the tears . . . and I know where they're coming from. . . . The person in the mirror doesn't look like the magazine / Oh, but when I look at you,

It's clear to me: You're the masterpiece that all creation applauds, covered with the fingerprints of God"). Chapman and his pastor Scotty Smith coauthored a book titled *Speechless* to accompany this album (Zondervan, 2000).

Declaration opens with a brash Bryan Adams-like, wake-the-neighbors summons to live the Christian life openly and joyously ("Live Out Loud"). A couple of the other tracks ("See the Glory," "Bring It On") utilize the hardest electric guitars of any Chapman project thus far. "Jesus Is Life" qualifies as what Bob Seger would call "old time rock 'n' roll" and features sing-along youth-group ready lyrics. "This Day" and the creatively titled "Declaration of Dependence" are infectious pop tunes. The song "God Follower" was inspired by an incredible-but-true story of an Ecuadoran tribesman named Mincaye who, along with others, murdered five missionaries sent to them in 1956 but who, now converted, ministers alongside the son of one of the persons he killed. Mincaye himself chants on another song, "No Greater Love." The album also includes a tender piano ballad that Chapman wrote for his adopted daughter ("When Love Takes You In").

From time to time Steven Curtis Chapman has been in the news for reasons peripherally related to his main career. First, he was tapped by producer and actor Robert Duvall to provide songs for the highly acclaimed feature film *The Apostle*. Chapman wrote and sang "I Will Not Go Quietly" for the film's soundtrack, and Duvall appeared in the accompanying video. Second, a school shooting in Paducah, Kentucky, left three members of a prayer group dead at the same high school Chapman had once attended. He made several trips back to Paducah in attempts to minister to the grief-stricken community and was featured frequently on the national news covering the tragedy—including an appearance on *Larry King Live* the day after the shooting. He wrote the song "With Hope" (on *Speechless*) for one of the funerals: "We wait with hope / We ache with hope / we hold on with hope / We let go with hope." In 2001, Chapman was brought to Washington, D.C., to receive a Congressional award for his work in raising public awareness of adoption. Unfortunately, the day he was slated to receive the honor was September 11. Trapped in the city when simultaneous terrorist attacks were launched against the World Trade Center in New York City and the Pentagon, he had to forego all scheduled meetings with President Bush and various senators and embark on a surreal fourteen-hour drive back to Nashville with his wife, daughter, and a couple of business representatives. "We're shocked and stunned," he said in an interview from his car phone en route. "We're praying without even knowing how to pray."

Chapman is considered one of Christian music's best songwriters. He has won the Dove award for Songwriter of the Year several times, and even before entering Christian music as a performer he was penning songs for **Glen Campbell, Charlie Daniels, The Imperials,** and **Sandi Patty.** Country singer Billy Dean has recorded "I Will Be Here." If there is a dominant theme in Chapman's work it is that "God loves you and through that love, all things are possible" (cf. Philippians 4:13). A close second would be the theme of Christian responsibility, of "being all that we can be (for God)." Also strong is the affirmation that signs of life and of the rule of heaven are available all around us in the real world. Some have noted a paucity of songs that confess failure or address issues of social justice. In interviews, however, Chapman frequently does the former, and in his overall ministry he is attentive to the latter. He has worked especially closely with Prison Fellowship, Charles Colson's organization that ministers to the imprisoned and to their families. The song "Free" is about a death-row inmate who discovers the inner freedom of faith. As a songwriter Chapman has written or cowritten Christian radio hits performed by **Steve Camp** ("For Every Time") and **Geoff Moore** ("Simple Heart"; "A Friend Like U"; "Live to Tell"; "That's When I'll Know I'm Home").

Notably, every song on every Chapman album has a message to it, and a specifically religious message at that. This could be annoying—the Ned Flanders factor—but somehow Chapman pulls it off. He is just humble and (again) authentic enough that few people would mind having him as their goody-goody Christian neighbor. *Shout* magazine says, "He's nice, he's funny, he's a man of integrity, and he's good to his dog." He wears his success and popularity well. Even those with a more nuanced notion of faith might find something enviable about the confidence and security that sustains him. So the man never has a nonreligious thought? That is at least intriguing and at best inspiring. And there's the marriage/family thing: who wouldn't want to be (or have) a husband as good as he appears to be, with a wife as wonderful as the one he appears to have?

For trivia buffs: On January 4, 1999, *USA Today* ran a story with a photo announcing that Steven Curtis Chapman and his wife **Amy Grant** were getting a divorce. This was only one of the more spectacular instances of Chapman confusion. Steven is not related to **Gary Chapman** and he is not married to **Amy Grant** or to Beth Nielsen Chapman, the country singer/songwriter who has appeared on a number of Christian music projects. The "Beth Chapman" who Steven is married to is Mary Beth Chapman and she was actually named Mary Beth *Chapman* before they married. The identical last names resulted in their sharing a mailbox together at college, where one thing led to another. Steven Curtis Chapman is also not related to **Steve Chapman** or to **Annie Chapman** or to **Jerry Chapman** or to **Morris Chapman** (who is African American).

Christian radio hits: "Weak Days" (# 6 in 1987); "Tell Me" (# 14 in 1987); "Run Away" (# 8 in 1988); "His Eyes" (# 12 in 1988); "Faithful Too" (# 14 in 1988); "For He Who Really Is" (# 6 in 1988); "My Turn Now" (# 3 in 1989); "More to this Life" (# 2 in 1989); "I Will Be Here" (# 10 in 1990); "Love You with My Life" (# 5 in 1990); "Treasure Island" (# 5 in 1990); "For the Sake of the Call," (# 3 in 1991); "No Better Place" (# 1 for 2 weeks in 1991); "Busy Man" (# 3 in 1991); "What Kind of Joy" (# 11 in 1992); "You Know Better" (# 15 in 1992); "The Great Adventure" (# 3 in 1992); "Where We Belong" (# 6 in 1992); "Go There with You" (# 19 in 1993); "That's Paradise" (# 3 in 1993); "Still Called Today" (# 20 in 1993); "Heaven in the Real World" (# 1 for 5 weeks in 1994); "King of the Jungle" (# 1 for 3 weeks in 1994); "Dancing with the Dinosaur" (# 1 in 1995); "Heartbeat of Heaven" (# 19 in 1995); "Faithful Friend" [with **Twila Paris**] (# 22 in 1996); "Lord of the Dance" (# 2 in 1996); "Signs of Life" (# 2 in 1996); "Let Us Pray" (# 5 in 1997); "Free" (# 6 in 1997); "Not Home Yet" (# 9 in 1998); "I Will Not Go Quietly" (# 7 in 1998); "Speechless" (# 2 in 1999); "Dive" (# 1 for 3 weeks in 1999); "Whatever" (# 3 in 2000); "I Do Believe" (# 3 in 2000); "The Change" (# 4 in 2001); "Live Out Loud" (# 1 for 6 weeks in 2001).

Dove Awards: 1989 Songwriter of the Year; 1989 Pop/Contemporary Song ("His Eyes"); 1990 Artist of the Year; 1990 Male Vocalist; 1990 Songwriter of the Year; 1990 Inspirational Song ("His Strength Is Perfect"); 1991 Artist of the Year; 1991 Male Vocalist; 1991 Songwriter of the Year; 1992 Songwriter of the Year; 1992 Pop/Contemporary Album *(For the Sake of the Call)*; 1993 Artist of the Year; 1993 Songwriter of the Year; 1993 Pop/Contemporary Album *(The Great Adventure)*; 1993 Pop/Contemporary Song ("The Great Adventure"); 1994 Songwriter of the Year; 1994 Pop/Contemporary Song ("Go There with You"); 1995 Artist of the Year; 1995 Male Vocalist; 1995 Songwriter of the Year; 1995 Pop/Contemporary Album *(Heaven in the Real World)*; 1995 Pop/Contemporary Song ("Heaven in the Real World"); 1997 Artist of the Year; 1997 Male Vocalist; 1997 Songwriter of the Year; 1997 Pop/Contemporary Album *(Signs of Life)*; 1997 Pop/Contemporary Song ("Let Us Pray"); 1998 Male Vocalist; 1998 Songwriter of the Year; 1998 Pop/Contemporary Song ("Let Us Pray"); 2000 Artist of the Year; 2000 Male Vocalist; 2000 Pop/Contemporary Album *(Speechless)*; 2000 Pop/Contemporary Song ("Dive"); 2001 Male Vocalist.

Grammy Awards: 1991 Best Pop Gospel Album *(For the Sake of the Call)*; 1992 Best Pop Gospel Album *(The Great Adventure)*; 1993 Best Pop/Contemporary Gospel Album *(The Live Adventure)*; 1999 Best Pop/Contemporary Gospel Album *(Speechless)*.

Charisma

James Dudley, voc.; Marijean McCarty, voc.; et al. 1971—*Charisma Is Raptured* (Pinebrook); 1972—*Last Days* (Rite).

A teenage Jesus music group from Florida called Charisma (not to be confused with Charizma) was responsible for what *Jesus Music* magazine calls "the most low-budget rock recordings ever." Despite poor production quality, the albums exude some of the enthusiasm of the revival that spawned what is now called contemporary Christian music. The group's name suggests (but does not require) further association with the charismatic renewal movement that was at its height in the early '70s. The titles of the albums are indicative of the apocalyptic spirit of those times when both the Jesus people and the charismatics (who overlapped) expected their Lord to return very soon. Musically, the first Charisma album recalls the folk rock sounds of more successful West Coast bands like **Children of the Day,** though there are also some piano-based soft rock songs reminiscent of Elton John. The second record kicks off with a ten-minute version of Robert Johnson's "Crossroads," announcing that we have entered an entirely different sphere. "Jesus the Messiah" takes the group into what *Jesus Music* calls "prog-rock," and "Nowhere Blues" and "Blue Woman" are as moody and bluesy as their titles suggest. Thus, like Maranatha's **The Way,** Charisma showed sophomore signs of evolving from a folk ensemble into a genuine *rock* group, but then disappeared without the promise of what they might have become ever being fulfilled.

Charizma

Personnel list unavailable. 1985—*Rock the World* (United Rock); 1991—*Rockin' the World Together* (Melodiya); 1993—*The Ultimate Call* (United Rock); 1997—*To Be Continued . . .* (Asaph); 1999—*The Basics of Life.*

A hard rocking Christian band from Sweden, Charizma continues to be best known for their debut *(Rock the World),* which was re-released by M8 productions in 1999. The group is often likened to bands like **Stryper, Whitecross,** and **Jerusalem,** which is to say their music fits squarely in the genre of '80s melodic metal. They should not be confused with the '70s group **Charisma.**

Charlene

Selected: 1976—*Charlene* (Prodigy); 1977—*Songs of Love;* 1982—*Used to Be* (Motown); *The Sky's the Limit;* 1984—*Hit and Run Lover;* date unknown—*He* (independent).

www.geocities.com/motownscharlene

Charlene Duncan (née D'Angelo, b. 1950) had a huge mainstream hit with the song "I've Never Been to Me" (# 3 in 1982). Born in Hollywood, she had a somewhat difficult upbringing, dabbling with drugs and winding up married and pregnant by the age of sixteen. She divorced, with her ex-husband's parents taking custody of the child, and applied her musical gifts to singing commercials and the like. This led to an affiliation with Motown, where after five years she was tapped by Ron Miller to sing the song "I've Never Been to Me," which he had written with Ken Hirsch. An ode to self-discovery and positive self-esteem, it seemed the perfect anthem for what was subsequently dubbed "The Me Decade," but both the song and Charlene's debut album failed to chart. Some executives decided the problem might be that the spoken-word bridge was too "feminist" for the times, so that was omitted and a new edited version of the song came out on *Songs of Love,* a repackaged version of Charlene's first record. This time "I've Never Been to Me" made it all the way to Number Ninety-seven on the Top 100 Chart, then tanked. Meanwhile, Charlene had become a Christian and become involved with an Englishman she had met at her Los Angeles church. Determined to give up the music business for good, she married (becoming Charlene Oliver) and moved to England, where she took a job working in a candy shop. In 1982 a Florida DJ discovered the original version of "I've Never Been to Me" (with "feminist" bridge intact) and began playing the record. It became one of the year's biggest hits, and Motown sought to recall Charlene from her confections. She agreed to make an album supporting her big single if she could also make a gospel record expressive of her Christian faith. The deal was struck, and secular *(Used to Be)* and sacred *(The Sky's the Limit)* releases by Charlene came out almost simultaneously, both on the Motown label. Of those two, the supposedly secular project is the more interesting. The title track for *Used to Be* is a duet between Charlene and Stevie Wonder that deplores instances of injustice in the world, then concludes with the words, "Someone tried to say it / And we nailed him to a cross / I guess it's still the way it used to be." Several radio stations refused to play the song precisely because of these "controversial lyrics," but it went to Number Forty-six on the pop charts nevertheless. Like "I've Never Been to Me," the song "Used to Be" was written by Ron Miller, who also composed Wonder's "Heaven Help Us All." Charlene includes a version of the latter song on *Used to Be* as well, in addition to other spiritually charged secular songs: "Rainbows" is a love song (to God?); "You're Home" draws some of its imagery from Jesus' parable of the Prodigal Son. But this *is* the secular release. Alongside the aforementioned songs we find the self-affirming (as opposed to self-denying) "Never Been to Me" and also "If You Take Away the Pain until the Morning" (cowritten by Charlene and Miller), a sort of Help-Me-Make-It-through-the-Night paean for someone to sleep with. In the early '80s especially, self-affirmation and sexual (or even emotional) longing were not themes that most fans of Christian music wanted to hear expressed. *The Sky's the Limit* contained nothing even potentially offensive for Christian audiences but by the same token offered nothing to set it apart from the spate of inspirational albums by other female vocalists. *CCM* compared Charlene's voice to that of **Annie Herring** and singled out the opening title track and the closing "Cover Me" as the album's highlights. *The Sky's the Limit* also includes a cover of the Lionel Richie song, "Jesus Is Love," performed by the Commodores in 1980.

Charlene did not repeat the success she experienced in 1982. *Hit and Run Lover* was a dance pop album that failed to chart. Released from her contract with Motown, she has nevertheless continued to write songs and has released several self-produced albums. One of these, titled *He,* was a collection of more inspirational songs similar to those on *The Sky's the Limit.*

Chase

Virgil Burdick, gtr.; Ron Chase, bass; Jay Corey, drums; Scott Lowmaster, voc., gtr. 1993—*In Pursuit* (Salt).

The debut album from hard rocking Chase had the band being compared to **Idle Cure,** and hence to Def Leppard, whom that band so intentionally emulated. The album was actually produced by Bill Baumgart, who was also responsible for the early **Idle Cure** albums. The arena rock sound consists of hard, guitar-driven music with super-clean background vocals and big vocal choruses. This works especially well on songs like "Spectrum of Emotion." The ten tracks include eight such rockers and two power ballads (*HM* magazine notes that "I Am Living You" appears designed to give audiences a chance to get out their lighters). Lyrically, the songs focus positively on hope for reconciliation in human relationships: "So how can we live together / Knowing all that we've been through / Love should last forever / And Time will heal our wounds." The group should not be confused with the general market band named Chase, which scored a hit with the song "Get It On" (# 24 in 1971).

Chasing Furies

Joshua Meeker, gtr., voc.; Sarah Meeker, gtr., voc.; Rachel Meeker, kybrd., voc. 1999—*With Abandon* (Sparrow).

Chasing Furies is something of a **2nd Chapter of Acts** for the new millennium. One of the most-praised Christian acts of 1999, the Ft. Worth, Texas, group consists of three siblings who (like Annie, Nellie, and Matt) grew up singing together and have got those harmonies *down.* Their father and grandfather were both ministers of music at various churches in Texas and Colorado, and the Meekers moved around a bit. They also rebelled a little against the parochial expectations of preacher's kids. Indeed, they originally intended their ambiguously spiritual music for purely secular audiences but accepted an invitation in 1997 to attend a Christian Artists Seminar in Estes Park, Colorado. Their mere appearance (day-glo hair and multiple body piercings) caused something of a stir at that event, but the ultimate reception of their music allowed them to rethink their posture vis-à-vis the whole Christian music industry.

Chasing Furies is one of the few late '90s groups still deserving of the "alternative music" label. They were not overly familiar with contemporary Christian music at the time they were signed to Sparrow, and this may account, positively, for the distinctiveness of their sound, which a witty MTV correspondent described as "Radiohead meets Jonatha Brooke"

(Radiohead meets **Over the Rhine** would also work). The main components of that sound are Sarah's lush Sarah-MacLachlan vocals and Joshua's driving electric guitar. The songs themselves mostly sound like numbers that might have been performed by 10,000 Maniacs or the **Indigo Girls,** except that the aforementioned guitar takes them to an entirely different level. *With Abandon* features a couple of pretty songs ("Fair Night's Longing") and several numbers that sound like hard rock songs with pretty vocals. The songs also evince creative, unpredictable structures. One of the best, "Throw Me," starts and stops frequently like a roller coaster ride. "Thicker" (the album's opening track) starts with an acoustic piano solo, which is repeatedly assaulted by Joshua's distorted guitar before Sarah's clear and confident voice strides in and takes charge. It should also be noted that two of the eleven tracks depart from the formula altogether. Joshua takes lead vocals on "I Would Drown" and "Romance Me," and his voice is almost the opposite of his sister's: shaky, timid, and almost as distorted as his guitar. This is *not* a bad thing—the Joshua songs have an ethereal, haunting quality that allows them to work very effectively on their own very different terms.

Sarah and Joshua are the two songwriters, Sarah penning the lyrics for the songs she sings, and Joshua the words to his two contributions. Both rely heavily on poetic imagery and relish ambiguity. "Thicker" appears to liken the Christian effort to be spiritual to that of walking in and out of a fog. "Writhe for Healing" (a particularly good rocker) describes the Christian experience as one of constantly moving away from God, then back again. "I Would Drown" borrows Stevie Nicks' metaphor from the Fleetwood Mac song "Sara" ("the sea of love . . . where everyone would love to drown") and applies it to a prayer of devotion to God: "I would jump into your river / I would drown to be alive in you." The song "Throw Me," on the other hand, confesses fickle allegiance: "I don't look at you, when the light is shining." As many critics have noted, the lyrics to all these songs are sufficiently generic that there is no good reason why a group that sounds as good as Chasing Furies could not break into the mainstream market and enjoy widespread success. So far, however, they are one of the Christian subculture's secret treasures.

For trivia buffs: Sarah Meeker is married to Jonny MacIntosh of **Reality Check** and **Luna Halo.**

Christian radio hits: "Enchanted" (# 13 in 1999).

Chatterbox

Jeff Bellew, gtr., voc. 1994—*Despite* (Tooth and Nail).

Fans of Christian industrial music consider Chatterbox's one and only album to be a masterpiece of the genre. The group was not actually a band but a project of Jeff Bellew, who was part of the hard rock band **The Crucified.** Bellew's main partner is the almost omnipresent Scott Albert (**Circle of Dust, Argyle Park, AP2,** etc.), who serves as producer and helps program the drum machines to play things no human could ever play. A host of other musicians help out as well, including **The Crucified**'s Mark Salomon, who provides vocals on some tracks (notably "Epignosis"). Industrial music strives to go beyond heavy metal and traditional hard rock to create music out of pure noise. Bellew himself describes the Chatterbox album as "very heavy and dark . . . so filled with noise that there is not a single second of silence to be found from the beginning to the end." Lyrically, the album deals with two of the three traditional themes of such music, pain, and doubt—but not despair. Several songs are about pain and doubt, period. Bellew says, "I don't believe that every song has to deal with a problem *and its solution.* You're going to need the whole album to get the point." Thus the record begins with two songs, "Torque" and "Empty," that address the superficiality of people finding meaning in things that are not worthy. The song "Soulscum" insists the problem is internal: "Cleanse yourself of yourself." But as a centerpiece, "Fallen" offers the chorus that gives the record its title: "Despite our weakness / Despite our doubts / Despite our failings / Despite our sin / Forgiveness waits with arms outstretched / Return to Him." The album incidentally concludes its spate of very dark and heavy songs with an ironic cover of "You are my sunshine / My only sunshine." Bellew later formed **Stavesacre** with Mark Salomon.

Tami Cheré

See **Tami Cheré Gunden.**

Chevelle

Joe Loeffler, bass; Pete Loeffler, gtr., voc.; Sam Loeffler, drums. 1999—*Point # 1* (Squint).

The loudest band to emerge from **Steve Taylor**'s Squint Entertainment company, Chevelle features three home-schooled brothers from Chicago playing raw-but-not-sloppy hard rock music of the variety associated with Bush, Tool, or **Grammatrain.** Steve Albini, who helmed landmark releases by Nirvana and Bush, served as coproducer for their debut album (he has worked with a number of other Christian artists including **Ballydowse, Crashdog, Danielson Famile,** and **Ninety Pound Wuss**). The group has its own sound, however, with rhythm guitars and vocals more upfront than is often the case in hard music. Middle brother Pete has a voice reminiscent of Tool's Maynard James Keenan, and he uses it broadly, alternating between mellow whines and aggressive screams, between hushed whispers and warbled shouts. As *Phantom Tollbooth* notes, the entire album is caught up in a dynamic war between a heavily produced, technically proficient style and the pull of down-and-dirty grunge. It is tension that yields something distinctive. The first track, "Open," is an instrumental that serves really as an introduction to the title track, yielding a total of six-and-a-half minutes of accessible, ironically delicate hard rock. Then "Prove To You" destroys whatever mood might have been created with its massive grunge groove. And so the battle continues, back and forth throughout the disc. Pete also serves as chief songwriter, producing lyrics that he admits reflect "anger and disappointment at all the selfishness in this world." He does not avoid lyrics that are explicitly Christian, but he does shun clichés, preferring images that require some reflection. In "Mia" he sings, "Watch me heap up what I've sown / I'm made of peanuts not of shells," and again "God spares a quality of himself / Uniquely designed / But we can't help ourselves." The song "Dos" presents intriguing patterns of call-and-response: "Begging / Do you mean groveling? / Settling / It's not the same / Begging / Do we take what's left? / Settling / Don't take requests."

Dove Awards: 2000 Hard Music Album *(Point # 1)*; 2000 Hard Music Song ("Mia"); 2001 Hard Music Song ("Point # 1").

Children of the Consuming Fire

Eddie Arizemendi, gtr.; John Bestwick, gtr., kybrd.; Tim Curriel, drums; Marc Rivera, bass, voc. 1991—*Children of the Consuming Fire* (New Breed); 1993—*Come Home Phlubber (The Prodigal Son Epic)*.

The seldom-heard Christian rockers called Children of the Consuming Fire made melodic music far better than sales or recognition charts would indicate. Their early '90s sound is like a cross between **Galactic Cowboys** and **The Newsboys,** an odd combination. It's as though a hard rock band got handed the wrong playlist and spent their time in the studio doing pure pop songs instead of the head bangers one would expect. The opening song on the debut sets the tone perfectly. "I'm learning, I'm learning, how to be a good boy," Rivera sings repetitively in a bit of hard rock bubblegum that sticks firmly in the mind after just one listen. Calmer tunes like "Cry" and "Spirit of Love" (with some tasty flamenco guitar licks) sound a lot like **The Newsboys**. *True Tunes* picked "Pray for Rain" (which asks God for help in being a better witness) and "Saved By Grace" (a straightforward testimony to the gospel of Jesus Christ) as the album's standout tracks. *Come Home Phlubber* is not a mini-musical or rock opera as its subtitle might suggest, but a collection of rocking songs organized loosely around the theme of returning to God. Musically, the record is similar to the first, though there is more of an intentional leaning toward what was becoming known as "the Seattle sound" (= grunge). Rivera served as main songwriter for the Children, and he crafted songs with no-compromise Christian lyrics. "Speed Metal Mariachis" (which basically lives up to its name) pro-

claims, "If you die without Christ, you'll regret your birth"). Many of the songs draw explicitly on Scripture. "Father Take Me" (from *Come Home*) is a worshipful pledge of dedication: "Let me be your hands / Let me be your voice / Father take me."

Children of the Day

Marsha Carter Stevens, voc., gtr.; Wendy Carter Fremin, voc., gtr.; Russ Stevens, voc., bass; Peter Jacobs, gtr., kybrd., voc. (–1979) // Jeff Crandall, gtr., voc. (+ 1979). 1971—*Come to the Waters* (Maranatha); 1973—*With All Our Love*; 1975—*Where Else Would I Go*; *Christmas Album*; 1977—*Never Felt So Free* (Light); 1979—*Butterfly* (Light).

This is where it all started. Children of the Day should probably be viewed as the world's first contemporary Christian music group—except that it was called Jesus music back then. Of course any such assertion depends on how those genres are defined, but Children of the Day were the first of the numerous musical groups emerging out of the Jesus movement revival to record a well-known album of explicitly Christian music that sounded like the contemporary popular music of the day (as opposed to traditional gospel or church music). It was an album that *defined* the Jesus movement as well as any other album ever would, and it became a national phenomenon. As one historian puts it, "Children of the Day were first—and **Love Song** was about ten minutes behind." It is worth noting—since the Jesus people were widely dismissed by scoffers as just "kids going though another phase"—that all four members of Children of the Day remain devout Christians, actively involved in the church and in music to this day. **Marsha Stevens** has had a significant—if unconventional—career as a solo artist.

The thought that Christian music could sound like popular secular music was a radical innovation that would ultimately launch a revolution in liturgics unparalleled by anything since Reformers introduced congregational singing in the sixteenth century. But Children of the Day did not seem to know (or care) that they were innovators. They don't appear to have studied the works or thought of **Ralph Carmichael** or others who had tried for years to accomplish what they did in weeks. There was no intention or design. They weren't assembled by any record company or culled from the ranks of a gospel choir. They were just four kids (almost literally) who had been revived by personal encounters with Jesus and, like Peter in Acts, could not "keep from speaking of what [they] had seen and heard" (4:20). They could not help but speak of it, and since they could not help but sing of it. And—since they were teenagers—they could not help but sing and write songs in the musical idioms most readily available to them, the California sounds that they heard emanating from their transistor radios and eight-track tape players. The music seemed to bubble up from the depths of their souls and just spill out, as though they had very little to do with it themselves. Witnessing such a phenomenon inevitably touched the hearts of the curious and the questing, with profound results. Musically, they and their peers (especially **Love Song**) provided some of the single most authentic moments in American music of the early '70s. No one else in that post-Woodstock, predisco era *cared* as much about their music or performed it with as much conviction. No one else in the decade that followed the '60s really believed that their songs might—probably *would*—change the world. Indeed, no one (in Christian or secular music) seems to have thought so since.

All this is to say that there is a magic in Children of the Day's music that is still appreciable for those who were there but that may or may not come through on the records for those who were not. Some things just don't translate to vinyl or tape. The group's sound was tame by modern standards. In creating Christian music that sounds like secular music they chose to emulate acoustic folk-rock groups like Peter, Paul, and Mary or The Seekers rather than premetal monsters like Steppenwolf or Led Zeppelin (cf. **Agape, Wilson-McKinley**). This choice might eventually have been their undoing (had not other factors intruded), since by the end of the '70s Christian music was taking on a decidedly tougher edge. Perhaps not, for Children of the Day did show signs of musical growth, incorporating more and more elements drawn from their jazz and classical influences. But they are most associated with a sort of Hootenany folk style (stand-up bass, acoustic guitars, and untrained voices) that did not survive the decade. And they will always be best remembered for one incredible song: "For Those Tears I Died" (sometimes called "Come to the Waters"). An absolute masterpiece, written by a sixteen-year-old (**Marsha Stevens**), it expresses adolescent piety better than any other Christian song ever written—and yet does so in language that evokes imagery of baptism and liberation that even theologically mature adults (who may or not care for the sentimental qualities) can appreciate: "Jesus said, Come to the Waters / Stand by my side / I know you are thirsty / You won't be denied / I felt every teardrop / When in darkness you cried / And I strove to remind you / That for those tears I died."

Marsha and Wendy were still in high school when the group formed. Marsha was the first to discover the excitement of a personal relationship with Jesus, after attending an evangelistic service at the beach. She led her little sister Wendy (who was only fourteen) to the Lord as well, and then her friend Peter Jacobs, who at sixteen was already a professional musician. The Peter Jacobs Quartet, an instrumental jazz group that included Russ Stevens, had won the California State Battle of the Bands for their class. They had even made an album, giving Jacobs and Stevens a little early experience with the whole recording process. Almost inevitably, the duo

joined with Marsha and Wendy to form the foursome known as Children of the Day. The group took its name from 1 Thessalonians 5:5. A true ensemble, all four members wrote songs and all four sang and played. They were integrally related to the ministry of Costa Mesa's Calvary Chapel (ground zero for the Jesus movement) and, eventually, they all attended Azusa Pacific University, where they joined the choir and performed as a madrigal special attraction on tours. Marsha became a Stevens when she and Russ married shortly after the making of the first album. The marriage, however, did not last, and seven years later their divorce precipitated contemporary Christian music's first official scandal—augmented in the minds of many by Marsha's announcement that she was a lesbian and by her subsequent relationship with another woman.

Come to the Waters opens jubilantly with the exclamation, "I'm so glad you decided to turn your life over to Jesus!" The joy of that announcement carries throughout that first track, "New Life." It is a wonderful pop song that sounds like something that might have been released by Fifth Dimension or the Carpenters or Bread—all very big Top 40 groups at the time. It even has a bit of a Bacharach/David quality to it. At any rate, it sounds like popular music and the celebratory shout, "Old things have passed away!" now seems broadly prophetic. In the first thirty seconds of the first Children of the Day album, Peter Jacobs (who wrote the song) did succeed in changing *a* world—the world of Christian music, which would never again be even remotely the same. The second song, "As a Child," is a hauntingly beautiful composition by Jacobs and Wendy Carter, sung in that baroque tradition of songs that gradually work their way into the consciousness and lodge there permanently. The next tune, "Children of the Day," takes the opposite approach, a bouncy, country tune as catchy as anything that Hoyt Axton ever wrote (e.g., "Joy to the World" for Three Dog Night). The melody is instantly likable as well as unforgettable, and the lyrics serve (as the title implies) to proclaim the group's signature theme: "We're the children of the light and we're the children of the day / We need not always stumble in an ever-darker way." The song also features a one-line recipe for dealing with problems that, for a while, ended up on bumper stickers: "Don't try to drive the darkness out—just turn on the light." The song "The Search" likewise reflects the grace-filled orientation of the early Jesus people: "Jesus didn't come to give us laws / He died for our release / No, He didn't come to chain us down / He came to bring us peace." *Come to the Waters* also includes a madrigal version of "All Breathing Life" (by "Brother Bach," as Jacobs used to say) and a cover of Love Song's not-yet-released classic, "Two Hands." The highlight for most people, however, was the closing song, "For Those Tears I Died." Maranatha also included this track on their compilation record, *The Everlastin' Living*

Jesus Music Concert (1971), which remains to this day the most important album of Christian music (and one of the best) ever released. Maranatha actually held up release of *Come to the Waters* to let the compilation record come out first—and it sold a (then) phenomenal 25,000 copies in its first six months, largely on the strength of this song. *Come to the Waters* would eventually sell more than 150,000. The album, incidentally, was recorded for about $900, which Russ Stevens says they borrowed from Chuck Smith, pastor at Calvary Chapel. Buck Herring (eventual husband of **Annie Herring** of **2nd Chapter of Acts**) served as engineer at Abbey Sound in Hollywood, where the record was made. Stevens recalls that on one day they were unable to use the piano because a more histrionic artist recording the previous day had broken it. The guilty party? **Larry Norman.**

On *With All Our Love* the group is said to have perfected their sound. Often acclaimed as their best album musically, the record offers styles that range from haunting, somber odes ("Where Went the Days," "Under the Shadow of My Wings," "Be Ye Still"—all like "As a Child," only better) to bouncy country pop ("If You'll Take My Hand"—like "Children of the Day," only better) to folk-rock staples ("Can I Show You That I Love You?"—like "For Those Tears," and almost as good). "If You'll Take My Hand" is probably Jacobs' best pop song. Indeed, if one looks at a list of all the Number One pop songs of 1973 (Dawn's "Tie a Yellow Ribbon" for 4 weeks; Paul McCartney's "My Love" for 4 weeks), this one is so *obviously* better as to force a surprising conclusion: *some* of the time, at least, the much maligned Jesus freaks of the early '70s with their much maligned imitative, sanitized Jesus music were actually listening to *better* music than their haughty compatriots could access in the commercial pool of artists that the Christians were supposedly just mimicking. Thematically *With All Our Love* features two prominent themes. Side One addresses the problem of "backsliding," of friends and loved ones for whom Christianity did turn out to be just a phase. Compare the opening line of *Come to the Waters* to that of *With All Our Love*. The joyful shout "I'm so glad you decided to turn your life over to Jesus" is now replaced with the melancholy sound of a voice intoning, "Where went the days, you used to sing God's praise? / But now it's old, when did you grow so cold? . . . Where went the times, him always on your mind? / Now you're ashamed, yet now you feel the pain." It's a dark beginning. "Cry, you want to cry, you just don't know," the chorus continues. The next song asks more pointedly, "Did you really mean it when you gave your heart? / Did you really mean to make a brand new start? / Or did you come along just for the ride / Just pretending that you'd changed inside?" ("Just Pretending"). From there we move on to an epic account of "The Crucifixion" (featuring narration of the biblical story by Pastor Smith) and then to

"Can I Show You?" which identifies the real problem in loss of faith as getting over the stubborn wall of human pride. Side Two picks up a happier theme, the celebration of marital love. Marsha and Russ sing songs of love to each other. Her contribution ("Russ's Song," but since retitled "I'd Like to Write a Song for You") manages to exalt her earthly and heavenly bridegrooms simultaneously ("What I see and what I love is Jesus using you"). His song for her is simply one of the most beautiful Christian love songs that any contemporary Christian artist has ever recorded: "You're a gift from heaven above. . . . You were meant for me and I was meant for you." The lyrics need not be spoiled or compromised by knowledge of later developments—after all, lots of people continued to enjoy John Denver's "Annie's Song" long after it was someone other than Annie who was filling up his senses. Incidentally, "If You'll Take My Hand" is also a wedding-inspired love song, written by Jacobs for his wife.

On subsequent albums Children of the Day moved away from the folk rock style toward the mellow MOR sound associated with "adult contemporary." *Where Else Would I Go?* is more orchestrated than the first two albums and features studio assistance from a number of Maranatha stars: **Fred Field,** Alex MacDougall of **Daniel Amos, John Mehler** of **Love Song,** and John Wickham of **The Way.** Standout songs include the title track (which has a strong **2nd Chapter of Acts** feel) and the charismatic anthem, "The Holy Spirit." *Never Felt So Free* was the first album for Light and features a still fuller sound, made possible perhaps through a bigger budget. "Born Again" bounces with Christian radio potential and could no doubt be listed as one of the group's big hits if only charts had been kept back then. *Butterfly* came out as the group was coming apart but nevertheless contains some intriguing and creative moments, including instrumentals and a remake of "For Those Tears I Died" (with a fuller sound). Wendy Carter Fremin comes to the fore as a songwriter on this final product, composing six of the ten tracks. Overall this final product evinces a more jazz-influenced sound. Peter Jacobs' replacement on this album was Jeff Crandall—who would later obtain fame as drummer for the punk-rock band **The Altar Boys.**

Children of the Day was also the first contemporary Christian group to record a Christmas album, one that would hold up very well, with mostly traditional material performed in creative modern arrangements. The album is synthesizer based. To record it, Jacobs actually bought a keyboard, learned how to play it and recorded all the parts in one day, then returned it for a refund the next day. The group was also closely involved (as were many Calvary Chapel artists) in the making of *The Praise Album* (1974), a collection of contemporary worship songs that would serve to define a new genre of praise and worship music. All of the group members sing on the album, and Peter Jacobs did the important string arrangements. By all accounts Jacobs was one of the Jesus movement's early musical geniuses, excelling at keyboards and a variety of other instruments. Colleagues from the era believe that his role in Children of the Day (acoustic guitar and vocals) did not really allow his talents to be put to full advantage, but that he accepted his position with appropriate humility for the sake of the ministry.

Children of the Day were Christian music's definitive guitar-led folk combo, though they also sought to stretch the confines of that genre by incorporating innovative instrumentation (harpsichord, woodwinds, strings) and experimenting with a wide variety of styles. As *Jesus Music* magazine indicates, "They made it all work without sounding syrupy. The songwriting is exceptional, the arrangements are unique, and the harmonizing immaculate." At the end of the millennium, Peter Jacobs was leading a jazz group in California called the Wartime Radio Review Swing band. **Marsha Stevens** would remain one of the only artists from the Jesus movement (cf. **Phil Keaggy, Randy Stonehill**) to be still recording and performing contemporary Christian music full-time.

Children of Faith

Duane Clark; Terry Clark; Nancy Kent; David Ortega; two others. 1972—*The Children of Faith* (CoF).

Little is known of this early Christian group from south/central Texas, except that they formed the birthing ground for **Terry Clark,** who has had a solo career. Nancy Kent later became Nancy Clark (Terry's wife). Duane Clark is Terry's brother, and for a short time Terry and Duane joined the classic Christian band **Liberation Suite** (who were also from south/central Texas but moved to London and toured Europe for a while). Children of Faith's one custom album is dedicated to group member David Ortega, who drowned before the record came out.

Children of the Light

Randy Boldt; Bobby Chance; Greg Fraser; Dave Stanley; Steven Steffy. 1977—*Come On In* (Sparrow).

Children of the Light were one of several Christian groups to hop on the Eagles bandwagon and create an album of '70s country rock. As such, they represent Sparrow's entry into a submarket dominated by Maranatha (cf. **Bethlehem, Daniel Amos**). The group attains some credibility through the presence of producer **Al Perkins,** a member of such groups as Poco, the Flying Burrito Brothers, Manassas, and the Souther Furay Hillman Band, and a guiding light for many Christian acts. Perkins is generally considered to be the finest pedal steel guitar player in the business, and that instrument is put to good use here—along with conga, dobro, and other cowboy tools. As *Jesus Music* magazine indicates, however, the album has "frequent adult contemporary leanings" that no doubt account for its failure to connect with the country fans for whom it was targeted. Children of *the* Light should not be confused with a group called simply Children of Light, who recorded albums of schmaltzy sing-along choruses for Milk and Honey in the '70s.

Children of Zion

Philip Bardowell, bass, voc.; Rich Berkley, tromb.; Chris Bleth, sax.; Scott Breadman, perc.; Tony Chogren, perc.; Lanny Cordola, gtr.; Gary Griffin, kybrd.; Tony Guerrero, trump.; Sandra Stephens, voc.; Joel Taylor, drums; Greg Vail, sax.; Chuck Wright, bass. 1995—*Reggae Worship, Vol. 2* (Frontline).

The first *Reggae Worship* album was a **Christafari** project. The follow-up was organized as a **Lanny Cordola** project, featuring his cohorts from **Magdalen** and a number of other accomplished musicians. The album opens with an inspired version of **Rich Mullins**' "Awesome God." In addition to a few original Cordola compositions, the album includes reggae takes on **Keith Green**'s "Cut the Devil Down," the **Edwin Hawkins Singers**' hit "O Happy Day," Bob Marley's "Jammin'," and the traditional hymn, "Rock of Ages." Cordola has also recorded with **Chaos is the Poetry, The Panorama Ramblers, Shack of Peasants,** and **Symbiotica.**

Amy Choate

1998—*In His Light* (independent).

www.amychoate.com

Amy Choate is a classically trained singer who established herself securely in opera and musical theater before deciding, "for the rest of my life I want to sing and share God's amazing love and mercy." She holds a master's degree in Voice and is pursuing a doctorate at Cincinnati's Conservatory of Music. Perhaps her most notable triumph in mainstream music was taking on the role of "Christine" in the European premiere tour of *Phantom of the Opera,* a performance for which she received standing ovations and drew rave reviews. Her first gospel album is securely and predictably in the adult contemporary mode, featuring songs with explicit Christian lyrics sung in a style reminiscent of mainstream artists like Celine Dion. About half of the numbers are original compositions, written or cowritten by Choate herself, including the opening track, "My Heaven," a Celtic-tinged ballad. It is not necessarily music for rock fans. The critic for *Phantom Tollbooth* finds it "bland and derivative," but then he also admits that he places "listening to Celine Dion somewhere below having teeth pulled" on his personal list of life's pleasures. Choate's vocal training is very much in evidence throughout the album, and what other critics have described as her "silvery soprano voice . . . a vocal reincarnation of (Beverly) Sills" will no doubt be appreciated by audiences who prize sophistication and refinement as positive qualities in popular music. The album includes a cover of Minnie Ripperton's squeaky ballad, "Lovin' You," sung now to God—which admittedly seems a little odd given the sensual quality of the song.

The Choir (a.k.a. Youth Choir)

Derri Daugherty, voc., gtr.; Steve Hindalong, drums, perc.; Mike Sauerbrey, bass (−1986; + 1990; −1993) // Tim Chandler, bass (+ 1986; −1989; + 1993); Dan Michaels, sax, lyricon (+ 1986); Robin Spurs, bass, voc. (+ 1989; - 1993). As Youth Choir: 1985—*Voices in Shadows* (Broken); 1986—*Shades of Grey* (Shadow) [EP]. As The Choir: 1986—*Diamonds and Rain* (Myrrh); 1987—*Chase the Kangaroo*; 1989—*Wide-Eyed Wonder*; 1990—*Circle Slide*; 1993—*Kissers and Killers* (independent); 1994—*Speckled Bird*; 1995—*Love Songs and Prayers*; 1996—*Free Flying Soul* (Tattoo); 1997—*Let It Fly*; 2000—*Flap Your Wings* (independent); *Live at Cornerstone 2000* (Galaxy 21); 2001—*Never Say Never: The First 20 Years*.

www.thechoir.net/pages/fast_facts.html

The Choir were once described as sounding like "The Cure on Prozac," a reference that might apply best to their 1989 *Wide-Eyed Wonder* album. Otherwise, one should indicate parenthetically that the boys do tend to forget their meds. The word "morose" appears in many reviews (along with "atmospheric" and "visionary"), and their classic *Chase the Kangaroo* even takes Ecclesiastes 7:3 as its theme verse ("Sorrow is better than laughter"). Musically The Choir has a sound that suggests a blend of R.E.M. and The Police, and yet is sufficiently unique to justify their status as the premier '90s alternative rock band in Christian music. The *Los Angeles Times* has said they play "magical songs that combine strains of murky psychedelia with pure pop." *Billboard* lauds their "dark poetic leanings, effects-laden guitars, and strong melodic hooks." Ambiguity and metaphor are The Choir's trademark strengths. On the one hand this is achieved aurally through the combination of Derri Daugherty's melancholy guitar and Dan Michaels' lyricon, which seems to "float like a spectre above the melee," as one critic put it. On the other hand, it is the Daugherty-Hindalong connection that really makes The Choir work. Steve Hindalong is the main lyricist, and somehow Daugherty has managed with increasing skill to make the deeply personal songs his own. In addition to the albums listed above, Daugherty and Hindalong have been responsible for producing two worship albums (*At the Foot of the Cross, Volume One: Clouds, Rain, Fire* [Glasshouse, 1992]; *At the Foot of the Cross, Volume Two: Seven Last Words of Christ* [Myrrh, 1995]) and one Christmas record (*Noel* [Via, 1995]), which are officially "Various Artist" compilations but sound quite a bit like Choir albums with guest performers. Another Hindalong-produced

worship project, *City on a Hill* (Essential, 2000), also features The Choir rather prominently.

Founded in 1984 as a Police-style trio (Daugherty, Hindalong, Sauerbrey) called Youth Choir, the group soon expanded their sound (adding Michaels) and shortened their name (in a manner reminiscent of The *Young* Rascals in mainstream rock). The rotation of bass players indicated above is partly due to founding member Tim Chandler's other commitments, especially his comembership in **Daniel Amos**—and to Mike Sauerbrey's similar duties as a sometimes member of **LSU**. Robin Spurs was a member of the L.A. cult band The Toasters, and after her brief membership in The Choir she formed the Christian group **Rachel Rachel**. Similarly, Michaels has doubled as a member of **Adam Again** and Daugherty has had the **Lost Dogs** as an on-and-off side project. **Steve Hindalong** has recorded as a successful solo artist. Michaels also released a sax- and lyricon-heavy solo album called *Reveal* in 1991. Both Hindalong and Daugherty are heavily involved in producing albums for other Christian artists (e.g., **Between Thieves, Common Children, The Waiting**). The Choir began as a Southern California group but around 1994 moved to Nashville, where Daugherty now operates Neverland Studios.

The group basically had its trademark sound down from the first album on, though the debut reveals a need to work on distinctive song definition (i.e., the songs tend to sound alike). The album opens ("Someone's Calling") and closes ("A Million Years") with its best tracks. The latter is a worshipful song with lyrics addressed to God: "Looking forward to the day/ When this pain will go away." *Voices in Shadows* was widely praised by critics, and the band garnered further attention by touring with rulebreaker **Steve Taylor**. To capitalize on that coup, they rushed out an EP called *Shades of Grey* that would show marked improvement beyond the earlier full-length. All five songs are compelling (and distinctive). "Fade into You" (not the Mazzy Star song) has a midtempo new-wave feel with lyrics seeking mystical union with Christ. "15 Doors" seems to be inspired by Jesus' words in Matthew 25:31–46, but it has a staccato beat like some of The Police's early material. "More Than Words" is ethereal and "Tears Don't Fall" is set to a dance tune with a hot sax solo. "All Night Long" is definitive Choir, with words of worshipful yearning and longing. **Billy Batstone** played with the band on *Shades of Grey*. Both *Voices in Shadow* and *Shades of Gray* were released by M8 on a single disc in 2000.

The Choir became the first official alternative act to be signed to a major Christian label (Myrrh). *Diamonds and Rain* was produced by **Charlie Peacock**, who contributed the song "Kingston Road." The record was notable in the Christian market at that time for its use of subtlety and for its canvas of a broad range of issues: a Christian album—but every song wasn't about Jesus. Its standout track is probably "Render Love," an anthem to universal reconciliation that would have fit easily into **U2**'s late '80s repertoire: "Render love / Let there be peace in the land / Reconcile woman and man / Lay down your weapons and lift up your fear." That last word seems to reference the overall theme of the album: fear of God and fear of what God has made. "I Painted Mercy" presents the words of God expressing sorrow when humans do not appreciate creation ("I wanted to inspire you / It hurts me when you cry"). The group achieves a more distinctive sound on *Chase the Kangaroo,* still regarded as one of their best efforts. **U2** similarities are again evident in the instrumentation, but Daugherty's pinched vocals are so different from Bono's soaring wails as to prevent the similarities from becoming a distraction. "Consider" and "Children of Time" both belong to the anthemic tradition (with Edge-like guitars), but "Clouds" has a martial beat similar to that which undergirds Fleetwood Mac's "Tusk," with Daugherty's mother coming in at the end to sing a hymnic refrain. "Look Out" relates the story of an elderly man who died alone in an apartment and offers some compelling advice, encouraging people to care for their families: "Look out for your own / The world is a danger zone." The album's finest moment comes with the soaring "So Far Away," a missing-you-and-worrying-about-you song of separated lovers (similar in theme to Carole King's song by the same name). The CD version of *Chase the Kangaroo* also includes all of the songs from *Shades of Grey* as bonus tracks.

Wide-Eyed Wonder is best remembered as The Choir's happy record. Inspired by the recent birth of his daughter, Hindalong wrote an album's worth of upbeat, hopeful lyrics, and the group performed these with an almost commercial pop accessibility. The album bursts into full bloom with "Someone to Hold On To," an upbeat tune that is more quick-paced than anything else The Choir had ever done. "To Cover You" is a bold declaration of love comparable (in theme not style) to Bryan Adams' "Everything I Do": "I would do anything to cover you body and soul / I would torch everything to keep you warm / I would do anything to keep you from harm." The addition of female vocals gives a few songs a distinctive feel, though Spurs never really takes the lead. The group came close to scoring a hit with the atypical novelty tune, "Car, Etc.," which sounds a bit like something the Beach Boys might have done.

Circle Slide returns them to mopey form. The album opens with a seven-and-a-half minute opus that doesn't sound very happy but actually expresses a hopeful philosophy of life akin to (maybe even inspired by) James Taylor's "The Secret of Life." Like Taylor, The Choir likens the experience of life to a playground ride. But the song is immediately offset by the next tune, "If I Had a Yard," which reveals that the band members'

check-to-check existence does not yet afford them suburban circumstances that allow room for a swingset (or a circle slide). The rest of the disc is a mixture of what the group would later call (on their "best-of" compilation) "love songs and prayers." "Tear for Tear" is a love song, a statement of marital commitment ("Until by death we fade / I'll try to trade you / Grin for grin / and tear for tear"). "Restore My Soul" is a prayer, a plea to God ("I call to you / With one lung exploded / From breathing the dust of the earth"). "About Love" is both love song and prayer, with verses praising God for the gift of a woman who cares and a chorus that exults, "There's something wonderful about love." Always embarrassed by his own sentimentality, Hindalong admits an early version had the lyric as, "There's something *pitiful* about love."

Hard times beset The Choir in the early '90s. Frustrated by a lack of commercial acceptance in the Christian market, the group made an ill-fated bid for crossover mainstream success. "I'd just like to hear my songs on the radio," Hindalong said, but that never happened, and the band returned a little sheepishly to the Christian fold they had all but ignored for three years. *Kissers and Killers* was originally cut as a demo to shop around to secular labels. Clocking in at thirty-two minutes, it was little more than an EP, and seven of its eight songs were later incorporated onto *Speckled Bird.* That album is beloved by critics as one of Christian music's ironic high points, though the group came to regard it with some ambiguity. The song "Speckled Bird" captures well the paradox of success and burnout: "I'm already dying, already flying, it seems like I'm flying for the sun." The songs "Yellow Skies" and "Weather Girl" have a harder edge musically than most of The Choir's material. On the latter tune, Daugherty tries to copy Neil Young and ends up producing the best guitar sounds of his career. "Gripped" and "Like a Cloud" are classic Choir songs in a more typical vein, letting us know that Mr. and Mrs. Hindalong are *still* in love. The first goes, "I want to drink you like a flower drinks rain / I want to lift you up to heavenly places." The latter: "She grips my heart / Anytime she smiles / Anytime she cries." Still, the group has since expressed regret that the album has an overall depressed mood (the move to Nashville was hard on them), accentuated by unfortunate album art depicting a woman in chains. This is easily overstated: themes of transcendent faith, hope, and love abound, amidst the realization that "everyone travels in the wilderness" ("Wilderness").

In any case, the group tried to happy up again for *Free Flying Soul.* They didn't make another *Wide-Eyed Wonder,* but they did come up with a batch of songs that have a fairly overt spiritual focus. The album opens by asking, "Hey, isn't the light okay? Isn't the day all right?" ("Salamander"). "The Ocean" (a Beatlesque *Sgt. Peppers*-type tune) is practically a worship song, likening the Christian church to a sea that is continually purified by the tears of God. In general, the record celebrates the ability to find pleasure in little things, including a few things that aren't always on conservative Christianity's approved pleasures menu: a glass of wine at a wedding ("Away with the Swine") or a cigar with a neighbor who's just had a child ("Yellow-Haired Monkeys"). *Free Flying Soul* was supposed to be The Choir's last record, but a live souvenir called *Let It Fly* followed, with performances by an expanded Choir that now included Wayne Everett (of **The Prayer Chain** and **The Lassie Foundation**) and Bill Campbell (of **The Throes** and **Poole**). The album was actually an enhanced CD, including a number of interactive bonuses like videos and interviews for technologically advanced fans.

Then—always the pioneers—the group decided to release one more collection of all new material over the Internet. The result, *Flap Your Wings,* eventually made it to stores as well. A warm, relaxed, and generally gentle record, it revives their atmospheric tradition, with perhaps a little Radiohead influence showing around the edges. The title song opens the project with profoundly spiritual lyrics ("When the healer of hearts / touches your soul with holy hands / you sure should rise up / you sure should rise up from the dead") set around a gorgeous chorus ("Flap your wings . . . Fly!"). On a couple of tracks, the group sounds like **Daniel Amos;** "Shiny Floor" could easily be an outtake from that band's *Mr. Buechner's Dream.* The acoustic ballad "Mercy Lives Here" describes the presence of God in the midst of a pub's curious patrons and notably offers Daugherty's first lyrics. Hindalong wrote "A Moment in Time" about the first date he ever had with his wife, and he describes it as "the most sentimental song of all time." *Flap Your Wings* also offers a new worship song in "Flowing Over Me" and closes with "Beautiful Scandalous Night," a magnificent worship song that the group wrote for the first *At the Foot of the Cross* project mentioned above—it was sung there by **Bob Bennett** and **Julie Miller.** For many, though, the highlight of the album is sure to be "Hey Gene," a tribute to the late Gene Eugene of **Adam Again** and the **Lost Dogs.** As sentimental as any **Bob Carlisle** song, it recalls the mercy their friend always showed them, sheds a few tears over his absence, and then bids him adieu: "Give Jesus a kiss for us, hey Gene, flap your wings, flap your wings."

In 2001 a critics' poll sponsored by *CCM* magazine placed two records by The Choir on their list of "The 100 Greatest Albums in Christian Music": *Chase the Kangaroo* (at Number Fifty) and *Circle Slide* (at Number Fifty-three). That same year the group's music would be accorded rare box-set treatment. The *Never Say Never* collection is an eight-disc set that includes every song the group ever recorded through *Let It Fly,* in addition to four new songs, a batch of rarities and unreleased tracks, and a 170-page book chronicling the group's history.

Both Daugherty and Hindalong are Episcopalian, and the influence of Anglican tradition is evident in their songs. Notably, those songs reflect lifelong orientations in stark contrast to the quick-conversion mentality that marked contemporary Christian music's origins in the Jesus movement. Further, they display two qualities that are generally regarded as strong suits of Anglican theology: an appreciation for existentialist realism and an understanding of dialectical tensions. Hindalong admits that he writes many of the songs about relational experiences with his wife: "Sad Face" (*Chase the Kangaroo*) is about an early miscarriage; "Sentimental Song" (*Circle Slide*) stems from "the songwriter's fantasy to fix everything with a song": "Listen closely / I will sing for you / A sentimental song / And you will know how I love you." Furthermore, he tries to contradict himself enough to portray the sort of conflicts that typify life and especially Christianity. Thus "Render Love" calls for peace and nonviolence while "Rifleman" (*Chase the Kangaroo*) acknowledges a fascination with the undeniably violent figures our culture labels as heroes. The Choir's favorite contradiction, however, is the conflict between the real and the ideal; awareness of this anomaly seems to inform everything they do. *Shout* magazine maintains, "no other band in Christian music can so effectively package together hope and despair." Sometimes the paradoxes give way to complete ambiguity: it is not clear in "Away with the Swine" whether the titular pigs are exponents of debauchery or asceticism—or *both.* In any case, The Choir recommends a way of moderation, and they have asked that, barring true excesses, the usually uptight Christian music industry cut them (and everyone else) a little slack. The song "Wilderness" contains a straight-out complaint against those (concert promoters?) who "count the butts and bottles in the morning when we're gone."

Hindalong's poetic sensibilities are atypical for an industry with a decided tendency toward predictable expressions and themes. An example of the understated approach lies in the song "To Bid Farewell" from *Wide-Eyed Wonder.* As Hindalong (via Daugherty) leaves on another trip and says goodbye to his wife he notes, "Insurance policies are in the second drawer, love." That single line says so much, conjuring the usually unspoken realization that lies in the back of the mind each time lovers must travel part: something *could* happen, and this goodbye could be final. "We try to say things that have never been said," Hindalong explains. "I have never heard anyone say 'chase the kangaroo' before." He coined that line as an expression for perseverance, while working a day job as a ditch digger (on the presumption that, should he dig deep enough, he would come out—Bugs Bunny style—in Australia). "Yellow-haired monkeys" is an affectionate reference to a passel of blonde children at play. "Kissers and Killers" contains this juxtaposition: "Man of Sorrows hanging / Iscariot swinging / A curious polarity."

Despite their undeniable devotion to Christ and to the church, The Choir has always resisted any expectation that they view themselves vocationally as ministers, as pastors or evangelists who use their music merely as a means for spreading the gospel. As artists, they have sought to distance themselves not only from Christian music that tries to "paint by numbers" but also from that which seems designed as a marketing tool. "We're not trying to sell anybody anything," says Hindalong. True, Chandler and Daugherty did get their start playing in evangelist Dwight Thompson's TBN-TV band. And Michaels (the group's token Baptist) did get saved at a Calvary Chapel concert by **Resurrection Band.** But the members of The Choir feel called by God simply to be musicians. They try to fulfill that call by writing and performing music as honestly and as wonderfully as they can. Their connection with the Christian music industry began at a time when it was controversial for Christian groups to sing love songs, much less songs of despair or longing. Swimming upstream most of the time, enjoying almost unparalleled critical acclaim while enduring almost relentless commercial apathy, The Choir did as much as any other artist (cf. **Adam Again**) to broaden definitions of Christian music as inclusive of much that is not overtly religious. As *CCM* magazine put it, "their music tells of the complexity of human experience when encountered by God's all too amazing grace."

Christian radio hits: "When the Morning Comes" (# 7 in 1987); "Fear Only You" (# 17 in 1987); "Someone to Hold On To" (# 12 in 1989); "Wide-Eyed Wonder" (# 10 in 1989); "About Love" (# 25 in 1991); "The Ocean" (# 20 in 1996).

Dove Awards: 1997 Alternative/Modern Rock Album *(Free Flying Soul).*

Chosen

Unity Nkosis, voc.; Sitho Mbesa, voc.; Musa Motloba, voc.; Isaac Mthethwa, voc. 1996—*Abakhethwa* (Verity).

The members of Chosen were all born and raised in the impoverished township of Soweto, South Africa (just outside the opulent, white-ruled capital of Johannesburg), but they have been residents of the United States for several years now. Some critics have expressed disappointment that their debut album does not encompass more of an African sound (like **Ladysmith Black Mambazo** or King Sunny Ade), but that is unfair. The group can do whatever kind of music they like—and as it turns out their main influences are American R&B (Boyz II Men, Stevie Wonder, Luther Vandross), jazz **(Take 6)**, and gospel (James Cleveland, **Andraé Crouch**). The African influence *is* there, of course, and it comes through as an undercurrent—rather like the sound undergirding Paul Simon's *Graceland*

album. But the album is also decidedly American, described by the group as "accessible R&B flavored pop," intended to serve as an evangelistic tool in reaching the youth of America with the gospel of Christ. The group offers some a capella singing, but most of the tracks have accompaniment. "Easy Does It" exemplifies the straightforward R&B style. "Everything I Desire" is a worship song with a strong African (or is it reggae?) beat. "No More Pain" is a lush, moving ballad and "Keep Holding On," an instance of classy, smooth jazz. For those who do want African pop, "Sengiyohama" (sung in native tongue) will satisfy.

In Soweto, all four members of Chosen were children of pastors, and Unity Nkosis, Musa Motloba, and Sipho Mbesa all knew each other. They discovered their ability to harmonize while singing songs spontaneously as they walked home from Christian youth gatherings. Unity immigrated in the mid '80s, studied broadcasting, attended the Word of Life Bible Institute, and then founded Youth Vision Outreach Ministries in Atlanta, Georgia. He called on his childhood friends who were now students at Shelton College in Cape Bay, New Jersey, to join him in forming a musical magnet for the ministry, and they did, bringing along Isaac Mthethwa, a new acquaintance from the homeland, to fill out the sound. Motloba describes the message of Chosen as "hope, encouragement, and healing." Mthethwa adds that he wants only to bring "the joy of the Lord" to people's hearts. The lyrics to all of the songs are remarkably free of bitterness for persons who have suffered as victims of tyranny and apartheid. "We Can Live Together" is a plea for peace and reconciliation, with only a hint of the struggle that may be necessary to obtain those conditions: "It's time we come together / Let's pull the strongholds down / Through His eyes we can do it / We can turn this world around."

Christafari

Mark Mohr [a.k.a. Tansobach], voc.; James Pach, kybrd., voc. (– 1996); Erik Sundin, voc. (–1999) // Vanessa Mohr, voc. (+ 1996); Johnny Guerro, bass (+ 1996, – 1999); Bill Kaspar, gtr. (+ 1996, – 1999); Marky Rage, kybrd. (+ 1996, –1999); Ken Yarnes, drums (+ 1996, –1999). 1993—*Reggae Worship, Vol. I* (Frontline); 1994—*Soulfire* (Gotee); 1996—*Valley of Decision;* 1999—*WordSound&Power* (Lion of Judah); *Reggae Worship: The First Fruits of Christafari.*

www.christafari.com

Los Angeles-based Christafari was the first true reggae group in contemporary Christian music and, as such, had to endure the hostilities of shortsighted Christians who thought the sounds of reggae were somehow integrally and inextricably related to the beliefs of Rastafarianism. The latter movement is a Jamaican religion that worships former Ethiopian emperor Haile Selassie as the Messiah and smokes marijuana (ganja) as a sacrament. Actually, reggae originally came out of the Jamaican Christian church (Bob Marley, Peter Tosh, and Bunny Wailer all started their pioneering musical careers as Christians), but there is no denying that the sound has been largely coopted by Rastafarianism and, in Jamaica at least, a close connection between that music and that message does exist. Indeed in Jamaica Christafari is regarded as something of a traitor to the cause. The group's founder, Mark Mohr, an ordained minister with a theology degree from Biola University, has even written a book describing Rastafarianism as "a cult" (*Rastafari and the Bible*). Midway through the forty-six-city Sunsplash tour featuring several reggae bands, Buju Bunton, one of Jamaica's biggest artists, actually attacked Mohr with a knife in the lobby of a Cleveland hotel, slashing at him and punching him in the neck. Police detained the star—one of the tour's headliners—and threatened him with deportation, but Mohr declined to press charges, hoping to "demonstrate the forgiveness and grace that Christ offers."

Mohr himself was raised in a Christian home (in Los Angeles), but he flirted with Rastafarianism for a time (ganja and reggae being the main attractions) before dedicating his life to Christ and forming the band in 1989. It took five years, though, he says, to get the group he wanted: "people who love reggae music, can actually play it, and have the fire for Christ." The group's name—an intentional pun that rhymes with Rastafari—is derived from a Latin word for "Christ bearer." In their music and ministry, they utilize all of the typical accouterments of reggae. They wear their hair in dreadlocks and employ lyrics replete with patois (heavily accented slang). They regularly refer to God as "Jah" and have been known to indulge in a little toasting, the Jamaican equivalent of—or actually antecedent to—rapping. Toasting or chatting is a feature of a variety of reggae called "dancehall" music, and it tends to be much more varied and interesting than rap. For example, at times, several persons will rap together, either the same words in unison or different words in a confusing collage of sound.

The group's first album offers reggae versions of original and traditional worship songs. For most listeners, the highlights are the new twists put on familiar choruses, such as "Lord I Lift Your Name on High," which here features an abundance of horns and steel drums, or "The Blood of Jesus," written by Michael Pritzl of **The Violet Burning.** The album was re-released on a new label in 1999 with six additional tracks (see **Children of Zion** for information on another *Reggae Worship* album). *Soulfire* evidences smoother production and features the evangelistic anthem "Spirit City," a Marleyesque song that calls on listeners to submit completely to Christ. Other songs, such as "Listening," use strong male harmonies to capitalize on a shared feature of reggae and American R&B. *Valley of Decision* continues in the same vein, offering mostly joyful, upbeat

songs like "Best Friend" and "Jungle Inna Babylon" (an example of what some reggae aficionados call "jungle music," produced here by **Scott Blackwell**). The standout song on the album may be the title track, which takes a no-compromise position on the seriousness of discipleship: "This is no game / People have to die in his name." Another song, "Modern Day Pharisees," takes a swipe at people who judge others on the basis of their appearance (dreadlocks?) and musical tastes (reggae?).

In 1997 a dispute over the group's musical direction was resolved by Mohr's keeping the Christafari name and most of the other members leaving to form **Temple Yard.** Mohr recruited a host of other musicians to serve as a backing band called the "Soul Fire (or Soulfiya) Crew," and his wife Vanessa assumed a more visible role (she had been with Christafari in some capacity since 1992, marrying Mark in 1995). The new lineup's first album, *WordSound&Power*, displays less dance-pop influence than the previous works but continues to draw rave reviews from critics for its musical integrity and theological maturity. A full seventy-four minutes in length, the album includes twenty-four tracks—fourteen complete songs and a number of interludes tying tunes together with offerings of praise to God ("Jah"). Of particular note are "Why You Ago Look," a beautiful acoustic ballad; "Cry No More," a song of mourning for three people killed in Kingston in an act of senseless violence; "Food for the Hungry," an appeal to minister to the physical needs of others; and "Love of My Life," the first-ever Christafari love song, from Mark to Vanessa (and back again). The album title is based on a term in reggae culture: *WordSound&Power* (one word) is used as a synonym for reggae music, though of course for Christians it may summon other connotations. Christafari also offers a dub version of the *WordSound&Power* album over the Internet. *Dub* (short for "Drum and Bass") refers to a hardcore reggae sound in which virtually all vocals are stripped away, along with much of the instrumentation, to leave only an extremely rhythmic sound.

Christian radio hits: "Selah" (# 9 in 1995); "Give a Little Love" (# 13 in 1995); "Valley of Decision" (# 3 in 1996); "Can't Stop" (# 16 in 1996); "Surrender" (# 13 in 1997); "Keep on Looking Up" (# 16 in 1997).

Christ Fa Real

1999—*It's Personal* (Phat Boy).

Christ Fa Real is not a band, but a solo project featuring reggae singer/rapper Nakia Lunn. His debut album is noted for its stylistic diversity, straying from the reggae base now and then to explore strong R&B and hip-hop (dancehall) influences. An instance of the former would be the standout song "If You Love Him," which *Gospel flava* describes as "an infectious urban groove featuring a catchy hook and terribly tight harmonies." For the latter, "Rock the Show" and "Demon Killa" venture into the more hardcore world of urban rap. Fans of a more pure reggae style (i.e., Bob Marley) may prefer the album's gentler tunes ("My Love," "I Wanna Be Free"). Antonius and **Prime Minister** put in guest appearances on two songs ("Born Again," "This Is How We Do It"). Christ Fa Real offers songs with explicitly Christian lyrics, mostly directed toward an urban Christian audience. "If You Love Him" challenges Christians to be bold in their witness as ambassadors for Christ. "This Is How We Do It" appeals for reconciliation among (urban) people on the East and West Coasts.

Chris Christian

1976—*Chris Christian* (Myrrh); 1977—*Chance*; 1979—*With Your Love*; 1980—*The Best of Chris Christian*; 1981—*Just Sit Back* (Home Sweet Home); *Chris Christian* (Boardwalk); 1983—*Love Them While We Can* (Home Sweet Home); 1984—*Let the Music Start*; 1985—*Mirror of Your Heart*; 1986—*Live at Six Flags*; 1987—*Higher Ways*; 1988—*Thinking of You at Christmas*; 1988—*No Lyrics*; 1989—*Focus*; 1990—*Sketches*; 1991—*Fifteen Best of Fifteen Years*.

CCM Magazine once said that Chris Christian "practically invented the soft-pop/MOR sound in contemporary Christian music." Though best known to some for his syrupy sweet easy listening ballads and slightly bouncy pop songs, Christian's real mark on Christian music has been as an engineer and producer. He was instrumental in launching the careers of **Eric Champion, Amy Grant,** and **White Heart,** as well as the Christian music careers of **Marilyn McCoo, Dan Peek,** and **B. J. Thomas.** Christian was born in 1951 and was raised in Abilene, Texas, where he attended Abilene Christian College. He began his professional career as a performer in Nashville in 1974 and went on to achieve some success in the mainstream market. He performed at the Opryland theme park and later as part of Wayne Newton's Las Vegas stage show. While at college in Nashville, he was asked to produce the debut album for the group **Dogwood.** Having been brought up in the strict Church of Christ, which allows no musical instruments in worship, Christian says he had never heard any contemporary Christian music and so did not know what it was supposed to sound like. This proved providential for **Dogwood,** since the result was an album that sounded different from any other kind of Christian record at the time. "I was just trying to do music like I heard on the radio," Christian says. Soon after he was asked to produce **B. J. Thomas'** *Home Where I Belong,* which became one of Christian music's first gold records, and proved to be a pivotal point in Chris Christian's career as well as in the history of contemporary Christian music. Christian would also produce **Amy Grant**'s debut album and the influential *Sail On* for **The Imperials.**

He has written or cowritten songs recorded by **Steve Archer** ("But You Didn't"), **Pat Boone** ("Thank You"), The Carpenters ("Back in My Life Again"), Sheena Easton ("Telephone Lines"), **The Gaither Vocal Band** ("No Other Name But Jesus"), **Amy Grant** ("Mountain Top," "It's a Miracle," "Walking Away with You"), **The Imperials** ("Sail On"), **Marilyn McCoo** ("The Me Nobody Knows"), Olivia Newton-John ("Compassionate Man"), **Dan Peek** ("All Things Are Possible," "Ready for Love," "Your Father Loves You"), **Elvis Presley** ("Love Song of the Year"), **B. W. Stevenson** ("Headed Home"), **B. J. Thomas** ("Still the Lovin' Is Fun'," "Without a Doubt," "My Love," "Everything Always Works Out for the Best," "Odessa Beggarman"), and Dionne Warwick ("When the World Runs Out of Love"). In the mid '70s Christian worked with Jerry Reid and was part of a trio called Cotton, Lloyd, and Christian (with Daryl Cotton and Michael Lloyd), who had a minor hit with the song "I Go to Pieces" (# 65 in 1975). Although he began releasing albums of Christian music in 1976, Christian continued to experiment with sidelines in the mainstream market. His self-titled release for Boardwalk in 1981 was produced by Bob Gaudio of Four Seasons' fame and scored the Top 40 hit "I Want You, I Need You" (# 37 in 1981). A medley of the songs "Ain't Nothin' but the Real Thing/You're All I Need to Get By," performed with Amy Holland, also made it to the mainstream pop charts (# 88 in 1982).

Christian would score his first Christian radio hit in 1978 with "Now I See the Man," from *Chance,* on which he also offers his own version of "Sail On," his first song to be a big hit for another artist (**The Imperials**). Keeping pace with the latter group, he would also record **Brown Bannister**'s "Praise the Lord" for his next album *(With Your Love),* but **The Imperials'** version eclipsed his on the charts. *Just Sit Back* won special praise for its closing song, "New World." The album also contains some interesting collaborations: "Nobody," written with **Andraé Crouch,** and "Look How Far You've Come," written with **Jamie Owens-Collins.** Christian also sings Larry Gatlin's "Light at the End of the Darkness," and both Gatlin and Crouch appear on the album. *Love Them While We Can* features "Put Your Trust (in The Hands of Jesus)" and a cover of the R&B song "Sweet Destiny" (with reworked lyrics). The title track speaks of honoring one's parents. Christian took a break from songwriting on *Let the Music Start,* performing mostly songs written by Jeremy Dalton and Dwight Liles. The latter collection is praise-oriented, including such worship songs as "Lift Up His Name" and "O Magnify the Lord" (a duet with **White Heart**). By the late '80s Christian's soft-pop style would be out of vogue, but his albums continued to reach a more limited audience of adult contemporary fans. *Focus* opens with a song called "Focus on the Child," and four of its nine songs deal with parent/child relationships. "The Man behind the Man" is a tribute to Dallas football coach Tom Landry.

Christian founded Home Sweet Home Records and Gold Mine Studio in Nashville in 1981. Although he has since moved his base of operations to Dallas, Texas, he continues as CEO of the Home Sweet Home label. He is also involved in music publishing and operates a sound stage for TV, video, and film productions.

Christian radio hits: "Now I See the Man" (# 6 in 1978); "With Your Love" (# 25 in 1979); "Livin' for You" (# 5 in 1982); "Put Your Trust" (# 4 in 1983); "We Are an Offering" (# 32 in 1984); "Day Like Today" (# 14 in 1987).

Ulf Christiansson

1981—*In My Dreams* (Lamb and Lion); 1992—*The Lifestyle from Above* (Kingsway).

Ulf Christiansson was lead singer and guitarist for the seminal Swedish Christian metal band **Jerusalem.** His two solo albums, however, show a marked departure from that group's signature sound, showcasing melodic pop-oriented music. Christiansson's competence with the guitar, in particular, is more pronounced on these songs, which feature actual *strumming* as opposed to the repetitive sounds of power chords. *In My Dreams* features three songs that start as ballads and build into anthems ("He's Coming Like a Thief in the Night," "I Tell You Now in Honesty," "My Heart's Desire"). The second record evinces theological maturity. In a review of *The Lifestyle from Above,* *HM* magazine would note, "this isn't some teenager writing about how God can use rock music and how cool it is to headbang for the Lord" but rather "shows lots of thought and study of the Word." The song, "Your Clothes Are Whiter," is practically a worship tune: "The Bridegroom is coming / The wedding will soon begin / If you want to, you can come / I know that He will come / He is worthy, only He is worthy."

Church of Rhythm

Jason Gregory, voc.; Max Hsu, gtr., voc.; Nathan Clair, voc. (– 1995); Carlton Coleman, voc., kybrd. (–1995) // Matt Miller, drums (+ 1996); Paul Shamoun, voc., perc. (+ 1996); Dave Ghazarian, gtr. (+ 1996); Jerome Cunningham, bass (+ 1996). 1995—*Church of Rhythm* (Reunion); *Only the Funky: The Collective Remixes of Church of Rhythm;* 1996—*Not Perfect* (Pamplin).

Max Hsu (b. 1969) founded Church of Rhythm with three friends at Chicago's Willow Creek Community Church. The interracial group has tried out a wide variety of styles on its projects. Their debut album draws primarily on rap, hip-hop, and R&B influences, eliciting comparisons to Sounds of Blackness and Kool and the Gang. Vibrant, funky songs like "Take Back the Beat" and "Free" could be contrasted with such Boyz II Men style ballads as "Purity" and the group's a percapella (i.e., beats and voices only) rendition of the hymn "It Is Well With My Soul." The song "I Still Believe" testifies to the resilience of faith with a sound reminiscent of **Audio Adrenaline** (foreshadowing the group's later direction). The album *Only the Funky* features dancehall remixes of the debut's more up-tempo songs. Church of Rhythm's next album, however, all but dropped the rap and hip-hop stylings in favor of a modern pop sound. Sporting a mostly new lineup, the group put aggressive guitars upfront. The comparisons now would be drawn to acts like Deep Blue Something or **Between Thieves.** Indeed, the standout song "Matter of Time" features a melody similar to the former group's "Breakfast at Tiffany's" and is just as catchy a confection of pure pop joy. *Billboard* magazine praised the album's opening track, "Take My Hand" for "blurring the line between modern rock and funk with its fuzzy guitars and wriggling grooves." *Alternative Venue Press* likewise praised the entire album *(Not Perfect)* for the "sonic buzz" the group manages to create through a successful "combination of acoustic rock and grunge." Thematically, Church of Rhythm's songs frequently extol the need for personal faith, while also addressing social issues from a Christian perspective. "Life Is Worth Fighting For" is about teen suicide. Racial and ethnic harmony is also a prominent theme on both records, abetted no doubt by the group's composition (members hail from China, Korea, Canada, Lebanon, and the United States). Max Hsu went on to found the group **Superchick,** of which he is also a member.

For trivia buffs: Hsu and **Ian Eskelin** were students together at Wheaton College. They wrote a song together there, which has since been recorded by **The Echoing Green.**

Christian radio hits: "Free" (# 11 in 1995); "I Still Believe" (# 20 in 1996); "Matter of Time" (# 21 in 1997); "Not Perfect" (# 12 in 1997); "I Believe in God" (# 20 in 1997).

Dove awards: 1996 Rap/Hip Hop Album *(Church of Rhythm);* 1996 Rap/Hip Hop Song ("Take Back the Beat").

Circadian Rhythm

Paul Barber, bass; Dan Cuomo, drums; Aaron Paganini, gtr.; Will Pavone, voc.; Andy Zipf, gtr., voc. 2001—*Over Under Everything* (Gotee).

Circadian Rhythm formed at Jerry Falwell's Liberty Baptist University in Lynchburg, Virginia, the same fertile breeding ground that gave Christian music **DC Talk** and **Reality Check.** The group goes for a modern rock sound with notable **Delirious?** and **U2** influences. Their first album is a collection of worship songs, most of which are performed in a full-blown, rock-out style. The opening "Beautiful Savior" (not the traditional hymn) is a stellar example of the band at its best, as is "We Are Hungry," which features an instrumental track similar to **U2**'s "With or Without You." The group even covers the latter band's "Gloria," an excellent song that had become somewhat forgotten in their repertoire. "Raise" is a hook-laden pop song on which the British influences are less in evidence.

Christian radio hits: "Beautiful Savior (40)" (# 14 in 2001).

Circle of Dust

Klay Scott; et al. 1992—*Circle of Dust* (R.E.X.); 1994—*Brainchild*; 1995—*Circle of Dust* [2nd ed.]; 1998—*Disengage/Refractorchasm* (Flying Tart); 1998—*Jack of All Trades, Master of None* (independent).

www.dusted.com

Circle of Dust was the quintessential Christian industrial rock group. The only official, consistent member appears to have been Klay Scott, who also goes by such names and aliases as Scott Albert, Klayton, and Celldweller. Scott is a *wunderkind* of hard music, starring also in a side project known as **Argyle Park** and working as a major force in the production of albums by **AP2, Chatterbox,** and **Klank.** Scott's first group was known as **Brainchild,** and the second Circle of Dust album is actually just a remixed version of that group's sole recording (called *Mindwarp*). Two songs were re-recorded and others were just given a facelift. A bit of a perfectionist, Scott also released two editions of Circle of Dust's first eponymous album—three songs ("Exploration," "Technological Disguise," "Senseless Abandon") were dropped, four new ones were added, and the rest were all re-recorded for the 1995 version. Fans dispute which edition is better. The final album, *Disengage,* reflects the hardships, with some bitterness, that Scott had to endure when his label R.E.X. went bankrupt. It is split into two parts ("Disengage" and "Refractorchasm"), and some of the songs in the second part (drawn from a separately released EP) are actually remixes of tracks in the first. *Jack of All Trades* is billed as a Circle of Dust album, but it is actually a compilation disc from various projects that includes a few hard-to-find Circle of Dust tracks along with songs by **Argyle Park, Klank,** Prong, **Chatterbox,** and other artists with whose projects Scott has had some dealings.

The Circle of Dust sound is sometimes likened to the harder music of bands like Ministry or Nine Inch Nails (or to Prong, whose singer Tommy Victor is a friend and participates on some of the recordings). The emphasis is on noise, with loud, grinding guitars, echoing vocals, and walloping rhythms. What sets Circle of Dust apart from lesser industrial noise bands is what one magazine called "song structure and a warped sense of melody." In other words, it isn't *just* noise. Somewhere in the mix there are songs trying to get out. *Disengage* features a more heavily electronic sound (similar to Prodigy), with guitars absent altogether on portions of the second half. It also includes some purely instrumental tracks, including "Perelandra," named after a science-fiction novel by C. S. Lewis.

Lyrically, many of Circle of Dust's song lend themselves easily to Christian interpretation. One reviewer of the 1992

self-titled project writes: " 'Dissolve' is about how material wealth is meaningless in God's eyes. . . . 'Consequence' reminds the listener of the price of sin. . . . 'Nightfall' reminds the listener that Jesus is the only hope for salvation." The song "Refractor" from *Disengage* features the line, "I know now that it's easier to hate than to love" alongside the plea, "Oh, God, I long to feel the peace again and see the hate destroyed." Highly regarded outside the Christian market, Circle of Dust was sometimes described there as "the industrial band with a conscience." Songs like "Nothing Sacred" deplore the moral atrophy of American society; "Demoralize" specifically blames the media for creating a culture in which artists try to outdo each other in perversity. In an interview in *HM* magazine in 1992, Scott decried public nudity on beaches and the fact that "more people are for abortion than against it" as signs of depravity in our society. He stated his aim for Circle of Dust as to "hit people with the gospel, you know, hit them with the message and pray that some people will turn to the Lord because of us." Over the years, however, Scott became disillusioned with the Christian music industry and subculture. By 1994 he was telling *HM* that Circle of Dust was *not* a Christian band: "What is a 'Christian band'? What does that mean? I've never heard of a 'Christian' plumbing service or a 'Christian' architect firm. It seems a little bit ridiculous." Nevertheless, he continued to express his personal faith as "something I'm not afraid to talk about." He told *Visions of Gray* that he didn't like to call himself a Christian because that implies membership in some kind of organization, like a club: "I believe in God. I believe that Jesus Christ was a real person, and is a real person. I believe in the Bible as being the Word of God. But I don't believe in a church organization, like a specific denomination, or that kind of thing." After his work with Circle of Dust, Scott formed a general market band **Angeldust** (with Criss Angel), responsible for the independent release *Musical Conjurings from the World of Illusion* (1998). The music was intended to accompany Angel's theatrical magic shows. The sound, again, was industrial hard rock, though now with lyrics (e.g., repeated f-word) that seemed calculated to offend any fans who might have followed him over from the Christian marketplace.

City Limits
See **Scott Roley.**

Eric Clapton
Selected: 1969—*Blind Faith* [with Blind Faith] (Atco); 1975—*There's One in Every Crowd* (RSO); 1992—*Rush* [soundtrack] (Reprise); *Unplugged* (Warner Bros.); 1998—*Pilgrim* (Reprise); 1999—*The Best of Eric Clapton: Chronicle*; 2001—*Reptile.*

Although he is unquestionably one of the most significant artists in rock and roll history, Eric Clapton merits only a minor entry in this book, as his connections to Christian music have been slight, tentative, and mysterious. Noted for his work with the Yardbirds, Cream, Blind Faith, and Derek and the Dominoes, as well as for a stellar solo career, Clapton is best known as a superlative rock-and-blues guitarist, though he is also a competent singer and songwriter. In early 1969, while touring with the group Blind Faith (which also included rock legend Steve Winwood), Clapton let it be known that he had embraced Christianity. The lack of follow-through on this announcement would become a cause for speculation as to the sincerity or permanence of the commitments it seemed to imply. *The New Rolling Stone Encyclopedia of Rock and Roll* refers to Christianity as something that Clapton "has given up and reaffirmed periodically." But it may not be that simple. Clapton has never overtly renounced (or reaffirmed) his faith. Rather, the evidence of his faith is what seems to wax and wane, and recognition of such evidence is always very much subject to the mind of the beholder. From the start, Clapton's "embrace" of Christianity lacked the evangelistic fervor and the sort of complete-turnabout airs that accompanied **Bob Dylan**'s celebrated conversion a decade later. Coming as it did at the very start of the Jesus movement, Clapton's announcement naturally aroused excitement among those caught up in the throes of that revival. They had landed a big fish. Clapton, they thought (and said), is "one of us." But Clapton never was a Jesus freak, and he did not start putting out albums of Jesus music as had smaller fish like **Barry McGuire, Larry Norman,** and **Noel Paul Stookey.** The one musical testimony to his conversion—if it was that—is the song "Presence of the Lord," which he contributed to the Blind Faith album. This was indeed the first noninstrumental song that Clapton had written alone—and it is generally regarded as one of the two best tracks on that classic album (along with Winwood's "Can't Find My Way Home"). It is an undeniably great song, and its religious sentiment (unlike, say, the Doobie Brothers' "Jesus Is Just Alright") is unquestionably sincere: "I have finally found a way to live / Like I never could before . . . In the presence of the Lord." A live version of the song can be found on Clapton's *E.C. Was Here* album (RSO, 1975) with vocals by Yvonne Elliman (at that time famous for singing "I Don't Know How to Love Him" as Mary Magdalene in the rock-opera *Jesus Christ Superstar*). At one point Clapton dismissed the religious significance of the song by saying that it was about finding a quiet place in the country where the police couldn't catch him with his drug paraphernalia, but despite that oft-quoted denial, the song has continued to be regarded as a genuine testimony to at least a temporary surge of faith.

As the years went by, Clapton would sing more spiritual songs ("Motherless Children," Dylan's "Knockin' on Heaven's Door"), and his album *There's One in Every Crowd* particularly seemed to reflect a heartfelt embrace of Christianity—but he would also sing songs of sex ("Lay Down Sally"), violence (Bob Marley's "I Shot the Sheriff"), drugs (J. J. Cale's "Cocaine") and drunkenness ("Wonderful Tonight"). He seemed to live the stereotypical rock and roll lifestyle, marked by bouts with heroin addiction, alcoholism, and relationship scandals (e.g., publicly lusting for George Harrison's wife, eventually marrying and then divorcing her). Christians, of course, are not immune to such problems or failings, but Clapton's struggles combined with a lack of renewed and explicit testimony kept him from being viewed as a Christian in any public sense and kept his music—even the spiritual songs—from being viewed as Christian music.

Then in the '90s that seemed to change. In 1990 his agent and two of his band members were killed in the same helicopter crash that took the life of Stevie Ray Vaughan. Less than six months later, his four-year-old son Connor (by girlfriend Lori Del Santo) fell to his death through a window that a maintenance worker left open in a Manhattan apartment building. Asked to contribute a tune for the soundtrack of the movie *Rush,* Clapton delivered the spiritual and moving song, "Tears in Heaven," about being reunited with his son. The song became one of his biggest hits (# 2 in 1993) and won Grammy awards for "Record of the Year," "Song of the Year," and "Best Pop Performance, Male." **Dana Key** wrote a touching response to the song, titled "Dear Mr. Clapton." Four years later Clapton won another Grammy for "Record of the Year" for the song "Change the World," a deeply spiritual song written by three stalwarts of the contemporary Christian music industry: **Wayne Kirkpatrick** (producer and writer for **Susan Ashton, Amy Grant, Michael W. Smith,** and many others), and two alumni of **White Heart,** Gordon Kennedy and **Tommy Sims.** The mere fact that Clapton knew the song existed implied more familiarity with contemporary Christian music than can be credited to most general market performers (though actually he might have learned it from Wynonna, who recorded it first). In 1997 Clapton played on an album by **BeBe Winans.** Then in 1998 the album *Pilgrim* came out, which actually sounded more gospel than many of the records nominated for Dove awards that year. The hit song "My Father's Eyes" (# 16 in 1998) is practically a hymn, with background gospel choir vocals and lyrics that seems to express longing for heaven ("I'm like a bridge that was washed away / All my foundations were made of clay / And as my soul slides down to die . . . Bit by bit I realize / That he was here with me . . . I look into my father's eyes"). "Broken-Hearted" appears to reflect on Christ in Gethsemane, and the title song could almost be a synopsis of Bunyan's *Pilgrim's Progress.*

Grammy Awards: 1990 Best Rock Vocal Performance, Male ("Bad Love"); 1992 Album of the Year *(Unplugged)*; 1992 Record of the Year ("Tears in Heaven"); 1992 Best Rock Vocal Performance, Male *(Unplugged)*; 1992 Best Pop Vocal Performance, Male ("Tears in Heaven"); 1994 Best Traditional Blues Album *(From the Cradle)*; 1996 Record of the Year ("Change the World"); 1996 Best Male Pop Vocal Performance ("Change the World"); 1998 Best Male Pop Vocal Performance ("My Father's Eyes"); 2000 Best Traditional Blues Album [with B. B. King] *(Riding With the King)*; 2001 Best Pop Instrumental Performance ("Reptile").

Paul Clark

1971—*Songs from the Savior, Vol. 1* (Redeemer); 1973—*Songs from the Savior, Vol. 2* (Sonrise Mercantile); 1974—*Come into His Presence: Songs from the Savior, Vol. 3*; 1975—*Good to Be Home* (Seed); 1977—*Hand to the Plow*; 1978—*Change in the Wind*; 1980—*Aim for the Heart; Minstrel's Voyage*; 1981—*A New Horizon* (Myrrh); 1982—*Drawn to the Light*; 1984—*Out of the Shadow*; 1989—*Awakening from the Western Dream* (Seed); 1992—*When the Moon Is behind the Clouds* (Ministrel's Voyage); 1995—*Private World*; 1996—*Resonate.*

http://216.117.149.16

Paul Clark was one of the pioneers of the Jesus movement and during the early '70s assumed primary responsibility for representing Jesus music in John Denver's Colorado. He sang regularly at the Narrow Gate coffeehouse in Denver, reaching out to street people. Clark was born in Kansas City and was caught up in the hippie movement of the '60s before experiencing a dramatic conversion in May of 1970 (at which point he was lead singer/songwriter for a band called Rocky Mountain Goldrush). "I was an eighteen-year-old hippie, trying to find God," he recounts. While living with his band in a cabin commune in the Colorado Rockies, he received a box of books from his grandmother and read a volume that invited him to pray for Jesus to come into his life. In the eight days following this dramatic turning point, he wrote all of the songs featured on his first album, the title of which represents his belief that the songs were given to him by his newly discovered Savior. Clark began playing regularly at the Narrow Gate, and as he would later relate, a sixty-five-year-old man came in one day and asked if he had any recordings of his songs. He said "no," and the man wrote him a check for $3000 to get the songs recorded. That amount allowed a custom pressing of 1000 discs, 247 of which sold the first night they arrived at the coffeehouse. The album remains of historic importance, as it is one of contemporary Christian music's very first offerings, coming out before Maranatha's *The Everlastin' Living Jesus Music Concert,* which is usually credited with establishing the genre as a viable form. Eventually *Songs from the Savior Volume 1* would be re-released on Creative Sound, as well as on Clark's own Seed label.

Mostly ballads accompanied by piano and light orchestration, it is not Clark's best work musically, but it does effectively capture what historian David Di Sabatino calls "the emotional spirituality of the revival." The follow-up *(Songs from the Savior, Volume 2)* garnered far more attention (prompting people to ask, "Where can we get Volume 1?"), primarily because of the song "Climb the Hill Together." Sung as a duet with his wife Sharon, the tune became enormously popular as a Christian wedding song (second only to **Noel Paul Stookey**'s "Wedding Song"). The song and the album itself have a fuller folk rock sound than Clark's debut album—recalling at times Neil Young in his *Harvest* period.

Clark's next two albums show considerable expansion as an artist and are still regarded as his masterpieces. Officially credited to "Paul Clark and Friends," they feature Clark fronting a band of Jesus music stalwarts including **Phil Keaggy** on lead guitar and Jay Truax and **John Mehler** from **Love Song** on bass and drums respectively (also among his friends were Bill Speer and Mike Burhart). The result is a full rock sound which is applied to some of Clark's best material. Notable from *Come into His Presence* are the title song and "He'll Do the Same," and from *Good to Be Home,* "Holding On to You" (with Keaggy offering a **Glass Harp** sound) and "Which One Are You?" (a musical retelling of the Good Samaritan story). *Good to Be Home* is one album that would be included on any short list of Jesus music classics; it was a record that practically everyone connected to the Jesus movement knew and loved, and its soft-rock-with-country-undertones sound would still hold up surprisingly well on the twenty-fifth anniversary of its release at the end of the millennium.

Clark's subsequent albums lack the historical significance of the first four. They were little noticed among the flood of contemporary Christian music that began to appear. *Hand to the Plow, Change in the Wind,* and *Aim for the Heart* are notable nonetheless for Clark's experimentation with a more jazz-inflected aggressive sound. Piano is brought to the forefront, players such as Harlan Rodgers and Hadley Hockensmith of the jazz group **Koinonia** are introduced as new "friends," and a number of songs are provided with treatments that include brass, sax, synthesizer, and female backing vocals. *Jesus Music* magazine speculates that Clark's late '70s phase might have been inspired by artists like Steely Dan. *CCM* has called *Hand to the Plow* "the most radical record of its time," as the project was one of the first to break out of the folk rock rut into which Christian music had fallen. This is most evident on what was Side One; the second half of the project is dominated by adult contemporary ballads, including another wedding song, "Woman . . . The Man That I Love" (sung as a duet with **Kelly Willard**). The album *Change in the Wind* contains "Me in You" and "Come Back Home" in addition to its affecting title track.

Aim for the Heart displays the jazz-rock influences even further, while again preserving a hard side, light side arrangement. Standout tracks include "Death in the City/Opportunity," "Don't Be a Fool for Pride," and yet another wedding song, "Author of Love," also sung with **Kelly Willard.** *Minstrel's Voyage* is a compilation album featuring songs from 1970 to 1980.

Clark next made three albums on the Myrrh label, before opting out of his contract with the complaint that records on the Christian company did not reach non-Christian audiences. He told *Cornerstone* that even though his personal taste was for jazz-rock fusion sounds, he felt challenged by the Lord to play music of a commercial sort that would enable preaching of the gospel to as many people as possible. *A New Horizon* displayed this stylistic change but failed to garner any support commercially or critically. Clark would recover somewhat with *Drawn to the Light,* which opens with the jazzy "How Much More Can You Take?" reminiscent of the Doobie Brothers. "Good, Good Morning" is a praise psalm sung in a style more similar to **Bruce Cockburn.** The album also features an artsy eleven-minute suite called "Eye of the Storm" that instrumentally depicts periods of calm and turmoil in a song that conveys the message that peace can be found in the midst of trouble. *Out of the Shadow* features the song "The Minstrel's Voyage," which Clark seems to present as a signature tune for his career. The album opens with "Give Me Your Heart," sung from the perspective of Jesus to the seeking pilgrim. Songs of sadness ("I Need Your Love Again") balance with songs of hope for the future ("I Will Fly"). The song "Love of My Life" could well serve as yet another wedding song, this one for a ceremony set within the context of eucharistic worship.

Toward the end of the '80s Clark left the mainstream of contemporary Christian music behind and began releasing only self-produced albums on his custom label. *Awakening from the Western Dream* is a finely-crafted pop album that features two songs recorded with members of **Mr. Mister.** *CCM*'s Brian Quincy Newcomb called the album "thoughtful, perceptive, and satisfying." *When the Moon Is behind the Clouds* is a particularly vulnerable collection of songs seeking to express hope in the midst of discouragement. *Private World* offers raw unplugged versions of several old songs—and a few new ones. *Resonate* is a worship-oriented album stemming from Clark's ten years of experience as a worship leader at a local church in Kansas City. Stylistically the latter record includes a little of everything from rock to jazz to ballads to reggae. Although such latter releases have not garnered huge sales or recognition, Di Sabatino thinks they secure and confirm Clark's reputation as "one of the pre-eminent songwriters to emerge from the Jesus movement."

Early recordings of Clark performing "Listen Closely" (with Keaggy), "Song of Love," and "He'll Do the Same" (with Keaggy, Mehler, Truax, and Mike Burhart) are available on *The Rock Revival: Original Music from the Jesus Movement* (Sonrise, 1994) and on the compilation album *Beginnings* (Sonrise, 1994).

For trivia buffs: Paul Clark serves as chaplain to both the Kansas City Royals (baseball) and the Kansas City Chiefs (football).

Christian radio hits: "Tell Them All" (# 5 in 1982); "Drawn to the Light" (# 19 in 1983); "Give Me Your Heart" (# 39 in 1984).

The Clark Sisters

Jacky Clark-Chisolm, voc.; Dorinda Clark-Cole, voc.; Karen Clark-Sheard, voc.; Twinkie Clark-Terrell (– 1991). 1973—*Jesus Has a Lot to Give* (label unknown); 1974—*The Clark Sisters;* 1976—*Unworthy;* 1978—*Count It All Joy;* 1978—*New Dimensions of Christmas Carols;* 1979—*He Gave Me Nothing to Lose, But All to Gain;* 1980—*Is My Living in Vain?* (Sony); 1982—*You Brought Me the Sunshine* (label unknown); 1984—*Sincerely* (New Birth); 1986—*Heart and Soul* (Rejoice); 1988—*Conqueror;* 1991—*Bringing It Back Home, Live* (Word); 1994—*Miracle* (Sparrow).

Daughters of the legendary gospel singer Dr. Mattie Moss Clark, the four siblings known as The Clark Sisters recorded several gospel albums in the '70s and '80s that earned them a sturdy fan base and the respect of the industry. In 1981 *Record World* magazine named the group Best Female Group of the Year after their album *Is My Living in Vain?* occupied the Number One spot on their Spiritual (i.e., traditional gospel) chart for nine months straight. *You Brought Me the Sunshine* and *Sincerely* would also attract some notice in mainstream circles and opened the door for the group to sing on such televised programs as *The Joan Rivers Show* and *Soul Train.* The sisters recorded a commercial for Sunny Delight orange juice that received ample radio airplay. With *Heart and Soul* the group switched to the Word-owned Rejoice label and sought a broader audience. One song from that album, "Time Out," was remixed and issued in a more dance-oriented version for modern urban stations. Twinkie, the group's leader, songwriter, and producer, departed to pursue a solo career in 1991, and the trio that remained continued to pursue the more contemporary crossover sound. The album *Miracle* caught the attention of fans of contemporary Christian music more than any previous project, appealing to those who like **CeCe Winans** or the Pointer Sisters.

Dove Awards: 1987 Contemporary Gospel Album *(Heart and Soul).*

Terry Clark

1978—*Welcome* (Good News); 1980—*Melodies;* 1984—*Living Worship* (Firstfruits); 1986—*Let's Worship;* 1990—*Live Worship* (Maranatha); *Heaven Is Not That Far Away* (Asaph); *In the Secret Place;* 1992—*I Am Yours: Worship Collection;* 1993—*Ugadano* (Catalyst); 1996—*This Christmas* (Catalyst); 1998—*Love Heals;* 2000—*Only Believe.*

www.catalystcm.org

A bluesy vocalist from the Texas hill country, Terry Clark was a member of the early Jesus music band **Children of Faith.** In 1975 he and his brother Duane joined the San Marcos, Texas, band **Liberation Suite** for a year in London. Clark began making solo albums in the late '70s, and his career got a jump start with the popular song "Ugadano Thawanu Maija"—which is *not* an African worship song but a creative expression of a basic truth that becomes clear when the title is pronounced quickly out loud. The song appeared on Clark's debut album, *Welcome,* which was produced by his friend **Chuck Girard.** The sophomore album, *Melodies,* was praised by *Harmony* as even more interesting and diverse than the first, advocating a "go for it! Christianity" with its hand clapping, foot stomping songs. "Jesus is at the Wheel" is sung as a '40s style ditty. In time Clark would become best known as a worship leader, working often with the Maranatha Singers and with Promise Keepers. His voice has in fact been featured on numerous Maranatha *Praise* albums not listed above. Clark often travels and sings with his wife Nancy, who was also a member of **Children of Faith.** His album *Live Worship* is a classic of the genre and includes his stellar "God, You're So Good," a bluesy sing-along that gives some idea what might happen if George Thorogood should ever make a worship album. His last four albums have been produced by Roby Duke, with whom Clark has formed an especially effective partnership. *Ugadano* features songs with a strong R&B beat. *Love Heals* includes the song "O What Love Can Do," about the importance of reaching out to others. *Only Believe* celebrates the majesty of God's creation.

Christian radio hits: "Ugadano Thawanu Maija" (# 2 in 1979).

Clash of Symbols

Matthew Chapman, bass; Rob Goraieb, gtr., voc.; Steve Latanation, drums; Mike Stand, gtr., voc. 1994—*Sunday Is an Altogether Different Proposition* [EP] (Brainstorm); 1995—*Begging at the Temple Gate Called Beautiful.*

Mike Stand, famous for his work with **The Altar Boys,** formed Clash of Symbols in 1993. The group continued in the three-chord crunch tradition of the earlier punk band, with an updated-for-the-'90s grunge veneer. The debut EP includes seven songs including the Soundgarden-like "Please . . . Maybe," which features the lines "Please don't fall away" and "Maybe tomorrow" as its only lyrics. Their full-length album takes its title from the story in Acts 3:10 and features ten raucous, feedbacky songs with evangelical lyrics for those with ears to hear. "Portrait of a King" extols the need to behold something more substantial than what is offered through popular role models or bumper sticker faith. The song "Armistice Day" appears to be a plea for peace—Stand has said he meant it as a metaphor for coming to a truce with God, but "if some people

take it as an antiwar song, that's fine too." All told, the album offers what *Shout* magazine called a package of "hits squarely in the middle of the classic rock formula: big guitars, fast rhythms and simple sing-along choruses that offset more artistically weighted verses." Stand told *HM* magazine, "We can be both artists and have a ministry at the same time. Music is my art, not just a tool. But it's also a ministry. As a band, we're letting people know the good news of Jesus Christ." Stand has also made three solo albums. Matthew Chapman also played bass for the **Allies** and Steve Latanation drummed for **Brighton.** Rob Goraieb went on to form **Kosmos Express.**

Cynthia Clawson

1975—*In the Garden* (Triangle); 1976—*Bright New Wings;* 1977—*The Way I Feel;* 1978—*Angels;* 1979—*It Was His Love;* 1980—*You're Welcome Here;* 1981—*Finest Hour;* 1983—*Forever* (Priority); 1986—*Immortal* (DaySpring); 1988—*HymnSinger;* 1989—*CarolSinger;* 1990—*Words Will Never Do;* 1993—*Blessed Assurance* (Genevox); 1997—*River of Memories* (Chapel); 1998—*Prayer and Plainsong* (Civic); 1999—*Broken: Healing the Heart.*

www.kumbaya.com

Cynthia Clawson is an adult contemporary singer from Houston with a classically trained voice and a solid reputation in Christian music. Half Welsh and half Spanish, she began singing at the age of three in a Southern Baptist church where her father was pastor. She later graduated from Howard Payne University, where she studied opera and classical music. Also an actress, she was featured prominently in 1971's *CBS Newcomers,* a summer replacement for *The Carol Burnett Show* (though she herself would say she thought the show was "awful"). As a singer she emulated such artists as Petula Clark and Julie Andrews. Clawson has performed her inspirational songs at national gatherings of the Southern Baptist Convention and on such Christian TV programs as *The PTL Club* and *The 700 Club.* She is married to actor, playwright, and professor Ragan Courtney, with whom she cowrote the movie musical *Bright New Wings* and the children's musical *Angels.* Clawson was on the cover of *CCM* in 1983; the magazine described her as "a middle-of-the-road, gospel-singing, middle-American mama." Her *You're Welcome Here* album includes a rendition of **Honeytree**'s "The Pilgrim" and some MOR songs by **Bob Bennett.** But Clawson would sometimes complain that her record companies compromised her sound with prejudgments of what Christian audiences wanted to hear. Of the first several projects, she remained most pleased with *The Way I Feel* and *Forever.* The latter project reveals more of her predilection with jazz forms, especially on the standard "Hallelujah, Come On Get Happy." Clawson would become best known for singing hymns and traditional songs. Her version of "Softly and Tenderly" was featured in the movie *The Trip to Bountiful.* Her album *Prayer and Plainsong* was recorded a capella in an acoustically perfect two hundred-year-old mission in San Antonio. *Billboard* magazine once described Clawson as possessing "the most awesome voice in Christian music."

Christian radio hits: "Come Celebrate Jesus" (# 15 in 1983).

Dove awards: 1980 Female Vocalist; 1981 Female Vocalist; 1981 Inspirational Album *(You're Welcome Here).*

Clay House

Paul Dexter; David Snow. 1995—*Take Me* (N'Soul).

The Southern California duo Clay House recorded one album of pop Christian music reminiscent of groove-oriented European bands like Level 42. Melody driven, the songs nevertheless evince the strong "dance music" sound for which the N'Soul label is noted. "Still Life" is a slice of disco. "Master Painter" is a power ballad that extols the artwork of creation. The group has worked closely with Campus Crusade for Christ.

For trivia buffs: Clay House was originally known as "House of Clay," and the first 500 copies of their CD were actually pressed with this logo. The name change was made in midproduction to avoid confusion with another group, **Jars of Clay,** who were releasing a debut album about the same time.

Kevin Clay

1996—*Watch Me Fall* (Alarma); 2000—*Nashvegas: The Land of Milk and Money* (Fashion Pop); *Jesusville* (Reborn).

Jokes circulated around the contemporary Christian music subculture in 1995 about someone assembling a "Clay tour" featuring such artists as **Jars of Clay, Clay House,** and **Clay Crosse.** It is revealing that no one thought to include Kevin Clay on that mythical roster. The introspective artist who once fronted the band **My Little Dog China** was by then somewhat marginalized within the mainstream of Christian music. After his critically acclaimed work with the aforementioned band (1994), hard times befell Clay. In a chicken-or-the-egg scenario of cause and effect, he went through a nasty divorce while falling into alcohol abuse, and subsequently losing the right to see his stepson. His first solo album, produced by **Michael Knott,** was viewed by *7ball* magazine as an attempt "to document how a creative artist can fall away from God in such a public and pitiful manner, and yet still return to the peace and grace of the Almighty's love." It may have been that—but it was also an attempt to deal with the dearth of peace and grace that he had experienced in some circles while people were watching him fall. A couple of songs ("Shot Down," "Spacey Stacey") allude to his former wife's family. Even more at issue, however, was reference to a "theological conflict" in which Clay was involved at the church where he served as a youth minister. He was censored and dismissed by

the church's elders for counseling a youth that "it is natural and acceptable to have doubts and to investigate one's faith rather than just taking things blindly at face value." Two songs in particular—"Date Rape" and Coplandhagin" (combining the names of two evangelists famous for encouraging naive faith)—deal with Clay's disappointments with Christendom stemming from this incident. Other songs do offer strong testimonies to the hope and grace of God ("Rose of Sharon," "Come to Thee," "Squeaky Clean"). Still, *7ball* would issue a tongue-in-cheek warning to its readers that *Watch Me Fall* may be "too much like the Bible" in its accounting of sin and redemption for Christian music fans who "are content with cute bumper stickers set to music" to be comfortable with the project.

After a hiatus, Clay released two more albums revealing that whatever demons haunted him while making *Watch Me Fall* were not quite laid to rest. *Nashvegas* is actually a two-disc set dealing often with the hypocrisy and corruption Clay claims to have experienced within the Christian music industry. The first disc is subtitled "Rock 'n Roll Messiah" and kicks off with the line "I met a merchant selling Jesus" ("Call Me Black"). The musical tone here is more angular and electric than Clay's typical work, and the emotional tone, more angry. But, then, the second disc is subtitled "Modern Day Martyr of an Everyday Heresy" and features Clay in his more typically introverted mode. The songs on this second disc are all of the unplugged, acoustic variety, and are lyrically confessional, as Clay contemplates his own complicity in the system he has savaged. *Jesusville* is primarily an alternative version of *Nashvegas,* offering ten of the twenty-one songs from that package in slightly remixed and sometimes retitled form. He also appends eleven (!) bonus tracks, including live songs, demos from the *Watch Me Fall* sessions, and two interesting cover songs: the Sex Pistols' "Pretty Vacant" and **Michael Knott**'s "Rock Stars on H."

For trivia buffs: According to *True Tunes,* the songs on *Watch Me Fall* are presented in a different order than Clay intended. To hear the album as "a narrative" the tracks should be played in the following sequence: 3, 10, 7, 9, 6, 4, 8, 5, 1, 2, 11, 13, 12, 14.

Clear

Matt Berry, gtr., voc.; David Caton, bass; Nate Larson, gtr.; Alison Ogren, voc., kybrd.; Pete Sanders, drums. 1998—*Clear* (Ardent); 2000—*Follow the Narrow.*

An acoustic modern rock band with female vocals, the Minnesota-based band Clear is often compared to **Sixpence None the Richer** or to "**Jars of Clay** with a girl." A more accurate analogy—if one must go that route—would be "**Smalltown Poets** with **Sarah Masen** on lead vocals." The group shares the same manager as the Poets (Jesus movement veteran Mark Hollingsworth) and has toured extensively as their opening act. And Alison Ogren's voice is as emotional and melifluous as Masen's, though on certain songs ("Ready to Ride," "Clarity") she shapes it around Beatlesque stylings that recall **Sam Phillips.** Clear was formed in 1997 as a presumably one-shot entry in a talent competition which, as it turned out, featured Ardent President **Dana Key** as one of its judges. At the time Ogren was still in high school and "the four guys" were students at Bethel College. All five grew up in solid Christian homes, and their albums project musical and theological maturity uncharacteristic of artists so young. Such maturity is not always evident among reviewers, for whom Ogren's physical appearance sometimes becomes the focal point. In the secular press words like "babe," "megacutie," and "megababe" have all been generously applied. Christian reviewers tend to be less sexist (in this respect at least) and focus on her beautifully clear voice and seemingly intuitive gift for emotive stylings. Some allow that the quality of the *songs* has something to do with Clear's success, and in this regard the group really is a band, with four of the members providing original contributions. A critic for *The Dallas Morning News* chose *Clear* as Christian music's best album of 1998.

The debut album opens with Nate Larson's "Why?" a song that sounds immediately like a hit single, though on repeated listening the intelligent, probing lyrics almost seem to belie the light and breezy feel of the music: "Why am I afraid of living out the truth?" The next track is "Ready to Ride," a song that sounds like *Revolver*-era Beatles and expresses hope in the face of apparent abandonment. Matt Berry wrote the song, inspired by the plight of children who rode orphan trains between 1854 and 1929 in hopes of being adopted. David Caton contributes "Through My Window," which Ogren says is about "getting outside the comfort zones we build for ourselves as Christians." Ogren herself penned the album's closing track, "Chasing After," a Carole King-style piano ballad based on the book of Ecclesiastes' teachings on futility and vanity. Clear's sophomore album, *Follow the Narrow,* continues in the same musical vein of the first project but with more of a worship orientation. Typical of this new focus is "Blessed Are You," a modern hymn based on the Beatitudes. "Into Your Hands" is similarly worshipful but more upbeat. "Stand and Die" offers somber reflection on the Littleton, Colorado, murder of Cassie Bernall, while "Able and Willing" was inspired by Max Lucado's book *He Still Moves Stones.* "Travelers" is an appealing guitar instrumental.

Christian radio hits: "Ready to Ride" (# 5 in 1998); "What Your Grace Can Do" (# 9 in 1999); "Free" (# 12 in 1999).

Clearview

Danny McClendon, voc., bass; Steve Nichols, drums; one more. 1998—*Clearview* (independent).

Based in Dallas, Texas, the groove metal band Clearview performs hardcore songs with a slow to midtempo sound similar to Pantera. *Phantom Tollbooth* identifies singer Danny McClendon as the group's "secret weapon," providing "deep attitude-filled vocals that are better than those of many major-label bands." Steve Nichols was formerly drummer for Godfear, a Christian metal band known to some fans of the genre. Standout songs on Clearwater's first album include "2000 AD," "Broken," and "Fly." Thematically the group favors lyrics that describe the power of God's love to redeem bad circumstances. They should not be confused with a Minnesota-based female-fronted pop group on Ardent that is also called Clearview. The latter group, incidentally, sounds a bit like the Minnesota-based, female-fronted pop group on Ardent called **Clear** (a name change may be in the works).

The Clergy

Leon Goodenough, gtr.; Chris Simonatti, voc.; Jim Swanson; one more. 1993—*RUAMI* (Broken).

The Clergy were a hardcore Christian band that played what *HM* magazine describes as "loud 'n' raunchy punk music with melodic sense." *True Tunes* likened them to early Concrete Blonde or X, and their own press material said the band had a "psychedelic-thrash-garage-band sound." The distinctive factor in the band's sound was provided primarily by Chris Simonatti's female vocals. The band's one album bears a title that should be pronounced "are-you-am-I." The songs "Earthmaker" and "Purity" would be singled out as particularly feedback-friendly cuts. Touring with **Crashdog** and **Jesus Freaks** in 1994, Simonatti said, "God's really put it on my heart to encourage people who need encouraging." Leon Goodenough went on to form **Yum Yum Children.**

Ashley Cleveland

1991—*Big Town* (Atlantic); 1993—*Bus Named Desire* (Reunion); 1995—*Lesson of Love*; 1998—*You Are There.*

www.ashleycleveland.com

Pop-rock singer Ashley Cleveland never had any real intention of pursuing a career in contemporary Christian music until her 1991 mainstream release garnered the attention of Christian music fans surprised by the explicit spirituality of its lyrics. Cleveland was born in Knoxville, Tennessee, in 1957, but moved with her mother (following a divorce) to San Francisco, where she was brought up. In 1988 she moved to Nashville to pursue a music career and sang on projects by many general market artists (Joe Cocker, Shawn Colvin, Emmylou Harris, John Mellencamp, Patty Smyth, Steve Winwood) and by contemporary Christian singers **Amy Grant** and **Russ Taff.** A song that she wrote, "Threshing Floor," was recorded by **Steve**

Camp, and another, "Well Done," was a Christian radio hit for **Trace Balin.** Nevertheless, the record deal she sought and won (with help from John Hiatt) was with a mainstream company, and *Big Town* was intended as a purely secular release. The album, however, opens with a version of **Andraé Crouch**'s "Soon and Very Soon" and includes several other songs with gospel overtones. The title track is about heaven, and "Walk to the Well" is a tale of redemptive soul-searching inspired by the book *Inside Out* by Larry Crabb. *Big Town* was commercially unsuccessful, but news spread among fans of Christian music about this "secular singer" who had come from out of nowhere and was singing Andraé Crouch songs in a voice that defied all expectations. That voice—raw, gutsy, impassioned, and above all *powerful*—won over critics as well, and the unsuccessful *Big Time* was hailed by mainstream publications like *Billboard* as one of the year's "ten most overlooked albums." In 2001 a poll of critics sponsored by *CCM* magazine listed *Big Town* at Number Twenty-seven among the "100 Greatest Albums in Christian Music."

In any case, Cleveland was soon signed to a Christian label. Unfortunately, her first record in the new venue, *Bus Named Desire,* moves away from the bluesy big rock sound of *Big Time* and has more of a pop focus. Ironically, it also features less overtly spiritual lyrics than her general market release. As with many contemporary Christian releases, it deals mainly with songs about human relationships. The most wonderful of these is "Henry Doesn't Care," a song bemoaning her son's tendency to build walls to protect himself from the world. Some Christians, however, wanted explicit gospel songs and indeed reacted negatively to the sensuous "Skin Tight" ("Move a little closer / Take in the view / Lower the light / I want to be your lover"). Cleveland seemed surprised by the flack, stating simply, "sensuousness in my marriage is something for which I am grateful," and, "the fact that I feel value as a woman is something to celebrate." She did not realize, apparently, that the fan base of contemporary Christian music in America has been strongly influenced by the gnostic strains of Puritanism and does *not* typically regard even marital sex or sensuality as anything worth celebrating. Such artists as **Charlie Peacock, Amy Grant,** and the **Vigilantes of Love**—with the Bible on their side!—have all run up against the same persistent prudishness.

Lesson of Love did an about face, pushing for a gritty R&B sound and including a number of modern and classic hymns. The opening title track and the closing triumphant "I Know Who I Am" are Cleveland's own compositions. In between she remakes the classic hymn "Power in the Blood" as a bluesy shuffle, presents "Enter His Courts" as an arena-rock anthem, offers a sparse, soulful arrangement of "Holy, Holy, Holy," and serves up an appropriately reviving rendition of "Revive Us

Again." She covers **Phil Madeira**'s "Mighty Lord" (with Madeira on organ) and **Buddy Greene**'s "He Is." One of the album's lyrical highlights, however, is another of her own compositions, "You Are There," which updates the message of Psalm 139:7–12 for more intimate application ("When I cannot hold my tongue / You are there / When I have no prayer / You are there"). The latter song would become the title track for Cleveland's fourth album, a live recording that is often considered to be her best. In addition to providing "greatest hits live," it also includes a cover of Mick Jagger and Keith Richards' "Gimmie Shelter," originally recorded at a tribute concert for the Rolling Stones (the sponsors had wanted her to do "Brown Sugar," which probably would not have gone over with those fans who found "Skin Tight" to be threatening). Ashley Cleveland is married to musician Kenny Greenberg, who sometimes serves as her producer. They are the cofounders of 204 Records.

Christian radio hits: "Where Do I Go?" [with **Gary Chapman**] (# 4 in 1994); "Lesson of Love" (# 6 in 1995); "Enter His Courts" (# 17 in 1995); "Revive Us Again" (# 20 in 1996); "He Is" (# 1 in 1996).

Grammy Awards: 1995 Best Rock Gospel Album *(Lesson of Love)*; 1998 Best Rock Gospel Album *(You Are There)*.

Clockwise

Angelo Natalie, kybrd.; Mike Watson, bass; et al. 1978—*Anthem for His Majesty* (Mars Hill).

The group that came to be known as Clockwise originally formed under the name Jonah in Erie, Pennsylvania. A complete personnel list is unavailable, but *Jesus Music* magazine notes that songwriter Angelo Natalie's synthesizers were the key ingredient in creating their subtle art-rock sound. The one album, produced by Al Perkins, has an overall MOR sound with light jazz influences. *Jesus People* compared them generally to **Servant,** while *Cornerstone* thought they had an art-rock sound comparable to Yes. "Time to Dance" has an intriguingly complex sound with baroque stylings and poetic lyrics.

Closer

Larry Hampton, gtr.; Wade Varieur, drums; John Wyrosdick, voc., kybrd. 1992—*Rain* (New Breed).

Founded in 1986 as an outreach ministry of a church in Anaheim, California, Closer strove for a versatile sound that would appeal to different audiences. Their album has a general funk-pop-rock sound with a few ballads thrown in for balance. In concerts they sometimes evinced a harder, borderline metal sound. Closer had a strong ministry focus, with every song clearly serving one of three purposes: evangelism, edification, or worship. *Rain* opens with "Only You," which stresses the uniqueness of Christ. "Blood and Water" appears to offer a rebuttal of classic Christian doctrines of baptism: "Many claim to be saved by the water / But it's the blood that will see us through." A decade later a southern gospel group named Closer would form in St. Louis.

Cloud Merchants

Robert Evans, gtr.; Michael Van Elk, voc.; David Ybarro, bass; one more. 1995—*Release* (Salt).

The San Diego, California, band Cloud Merchants arose out of a group in that area that was originally known as O.N.E. They played both clubs and churches, striving to hold a ministry mindset with a wide breadth of vision. Musically the band strove to recapture the early '80s sound of groups like INXS or Tears for Fears. Vocalist Michael Van Elk received critical praise for crooning with both conviction and subtlety. *7ball* magazine called him "a veritable actor with broadly human, emotional range." *HM* thought the group had strong similarities to **The Choir** and lavished special praise on the melodic pop tune "Come Away" and classic rock song "Blind to It All."

Cloud 2 Ground

Jeremy Dawson; Chad Petee 1997—*E-Majn* (N'Soul); 2000—*The Gate* (Beautiful).

Producer Jeremy Dawson is the driving force behind Cloud 2 Ground, a techno group from Oklahoma City. He controls most of the samples and synthesizers that go into the musical stew, and the result is a sound that emulates techno meister **Moby** more than anyone else, though similarities to such acts as Prodigy, Chemical Brothers, Erasure, and New Order have also been noted. *E-Majn* opens and closes with different versions of "Raindown," the first an ambient piece featuring mainly piano and the last a very different, high energy dance track. Remixes by **A. J. Mora** and **Scott Blackwell** are also included on the album. *The Gate* displays more breadth, expanding beyond the signature backbeat sound and incorporating more vocalists. It features a track called "Boomerang Feat" that progresses through various styles throughout its almost twelve-minute run. As with most electronic music, lyrics—when they do occur—often take the form of simple repeated lines and phrases. For instance, "Emaj-n Green Lies" (from *The Gate*) is an unusually desolate tune in which the lyric, "Father, take this pain away" is repeated mournfully in the background.

The CMC's

Daddy Fre, voc.; Gizmo T., voc. 1996—*Everyday Death Sentence* (Holy Terra).

A gangsta rap duo from Carson, California, The CMC's were discovered by the **Gospel Gangstaz** and perform music with a similar style. Gizmo and Daddy (also called Miles) are

brothers from Samoa with a background of personal experience as gang members on the West Coast. Their music is explicitly directed to the gang members, drug addicts, and homeless youth they now target as the primary audience for their ministry. As is often the case with such music, spiritual warfare is a prominent theme, identifying Satan as the true enemy and directing passionate, gangsta-style threats against him.

Bruce Cockburn

1970—*Bruce Cockburn* (True North); 1971—*High Winds, White Sky*; 1972—*Sunwheel Dance*; 1973—*Night Vision*; 1974—*Salt, Sun, and Time*; 1975—*Joy Will Find a Way*; 1976—*In the Falling Dark* (Island); 1977—*Circles in the Stream*; 1978—*Further Adventures of*; 1979—*Dancing in the Dragon's Jaws* (Millennium); 1980—*Humans*; 1981—*Resumé; Mummy Dust* (True North); *Inner City Front* (Millennium); 1983—*The Trouble with Normal* (Gold Mountain); 1984—*Stealing Fire*; 1986—*World of Wonders* (MCA); 1987—*Waiting for a Miracle* (True North); 1989—*Big Circumstance; If a Tree Falls: A Collection of His Greatest Hits* (Liberation); 1990—*Live* (True North); 1991—*Nothing But a Burning Light* (Columbia); 1993—*Christmas*; 1994—*Dart to the Heart*; 1997—*Charity of Night* (True North); *You Pay Your Money and You Take Your Chance* [EP]; 1999—*Breakfast in New Orleans, Dinner in Timbuktu*.

Bruce Cockburn (pronounced Co-burn) is a well-known Christian singer/songwriter whose understated approach to spiritual issues and breadth of concern for engaging reality and social/political issues have won him a large following among people who are not usually fans of contemporary Christian music. He is especially popular in his native Canada, where he has won numerous Juno awards and racked up several gold and platinum albums. In the United States he has scored only one Top 40 radio hit, "Wondering Where the Lions Are" (# 21 in 1980), but has a loyal cult following. His 1988 song "If I Had a Rocket Launcher" received generous airplay on MTV, and 1994's "Listen for the Laugh" was played on many college radio stations. Cockburn is regarded by critics as a virtuoso guitarist and as a sensitive, compelling songwriter (*Rolling Stone* describes his music as "feverishly lovely"). A number of his songs have been recorded by other artists: Chet Atkins ("Together Alone"); Barenaked Ladies ("Lovers in a Dangerous Time"); Jimmy Buffett ("Pacing the Cage"); Dan Fogelberg ("Lovers in a Dangerous Time"); Jerry Garcia ("Waiting for a Miracle"); **Maria Muldaur** ("Southland of the Heart"); and Anne Murray ("One Day I Walk"), to name a few. He has also performed as a guest on recordings by artists as diverse as **The Call,** Rosanne Cash, and Todd Rundgren. Cockburn was born in Ottawa in 1945. In his late teens he traveled as a street musician throughout Europe, then attended the Berklee School of Music for a short time before dropping out to do his own thing. The school gave him an honorary doctorate in 1977.

Musically Cockburn began with a basic folk-rock style typical for singer/songwriters (cf. Canadian compatriots Joni

Mitchell and Gordon Lightfoot), but as the years went by he added flourishes of jazz, reggae, Latin, and Afropop to obtain an increasingly eclectic mix (cf. Joni Mitchell). The jazz-folk fusion was especially evident by the time of *In the Falling Dark* and the double live set, *Circles in the Stream.* Two albums offer career retrospectives of his first ten years (1969–1978): *Mummy Dust* and *Resumé,* marketed respectively for Canadian and American audiences. In terms of spiritual development, the details of Cockburn's journey of faith are not exactly clear. It is often reported that he became a Christian in 1974 after being heavily influenced by the writings of C. S. Lewis and George MacDonald. He told *Sojourner's* magazine in 1988, however, that his identification as a Christian can be traced in some way to an inexplicable mystical encounter with Christ that he experienced on his wedding day (in 1969). But this was only the beginning of a gradual and reluctant conversion, leading ultimately to a time when he could say unequivocally, "Okay, Jesus, I'm Yours." He has also indicated, "I made several albums before I became a Christian," and for those who press for a more definitive turning point, he indicates only that the song "All the Diamonds in the World" probably serves as such a marker. That song opens his 1974 album *Salt, Sun and Time.* From then on he would contribute numerous songs that provide poetic expressions of Christian faith: "A Life Story" from *Joy Will Find a Way,* and the title track from that same album, which became his constant concert-closer; "Lord of the Starfields" from *In the Falling Dark;* and "Can I Go With You?" from *The Further Adventures of. Circles in the Stream* is a live set that includes several faith-oriented songs. At this time *CCM* would describe the artist as one who "weds his music with his life experiences from a Christian world view." This, the magazine thought, seemed both nonconformist and promising.

The album *Dancing in the Dragon's Jaws* is lively and upbeat, extolling the virtue of remaining joyful in the face of everything. All seemed well with Cockburn's world at this point, and he even performed the breakout single "Wondering Where the Lions Are" with the Muppets on TV. But a year later (1980) his marriage ended in divorce. *Humans* digs deeply into reality, with an emphasis on global consciousness. He grapples with the problem of evil, on a personal and systemic scale, moving beyond simplistic answers to ask questions of ultimate purpose amid feelings of doubt and loss. The song "Rumours of Glory" expresses well the ambiguity of his hope. *Inner City Front* has a brooding, pensive tone, addressing the alienation of North American city dwellers. A series of politically oriented albums followed, voicing Cockburn's objections to the "fashionable fascism" that allows exploitation of others in the name of selfish national interests. The title song to *The Trouble with Normal* proclaims, "the trouble with normal is it always gets worse." Another song from that same album, "Civilization and

Its Discontents," seems to sum up Cockburn's personal state of mind at this juncture with the line, "Even though I know who loves me, I'm not that much less lost." *Stealing Fire* got some notice, not only for the semi-hit "If I Had a Rocket Launcher" but also for "Maybe the Poet," which was featured prominently on an episode of the TV series *Miami Vice.* "Nicaragua" and "Rocket Launcher" both deal with atrocities in Central America ignored or implemented by United States foreign policy. But *CCM* picked Cockburn's *Stealing Fire* as its Number Two Christian album of the year (behind only **U2**'s *The Unforgettable Fire*) on the assumption that the artist's concerns for justice and liberation are motivated by a distinctly Christian ethic. This seems to be the case—his thinking appears to be informed by the Third World liberation theology movement articulated, for instance, in the writings of Gustavo Gutiérrez. The song "Maybe the Poet" quotes from Galatians 3:28. In "Lovers in a Dangerous Time," Cockburn sings, "Sometimes you're made to feel as if your love's a crime / But nothing worth having comes without some kind of fight / Got to kick at the darkness till it bleeds daylight." Cockburn next offered *World of Wonders,* which includes "Call It Democracy" and "People See through You," both protests of American social policies. He finished out the '80s with *Big Circumstance,* which signaled something of a return to the stripped-bare folk style, with songs that continue to deal with social issues: "If a Tree Falls" would become an anthem for protectors of the world's forests; "Radium Rain" reflects on the Chernobyl nuclear accident. *Waiting for a Miracle* is another compilation album, this one a two-disc collection of thirty-three songs.

The '90s revealed a revitalized Cockburn with newly relevant songs. **T Bone Burnett** came in to produce *Nothing But a Burning Light,* with **Sam Phillips** and Jackson Browne providing background vocals and instrumentalists like Booker T. Jones (of Booker T. and the M.G.s) providing support. Political sentiments continue to be expressed—injustice to Native Americans in "Indian Wars" and United States imperialism in "Mighty Trucks of Midnight"—but the dour affections of the previous records give way to a hopeful eloquence ("A Dream Like Mine," "Child of the World," and "Great Big Love"). And suddenly a renewed spiritual zeal also comes to the fore. *CCM* described "Somebody Touched Me" as a flat-out love song to God. "Cry of a Tiny Babe" draws out the significance of Christmas for more than just a season: "Redemption rips through the surface of time / In the cry of a tiny babe." Inspired by the latter tune, perhaps, Cockburn leaned on Burnett and Phillips again to turn out a full album of Christmas songs, featuring traditional numbers alongside a Medieval carol, a Spanish hymn, and a Huron (Native American) song, all with deeply spiritual lyrics. *Dart to the Hart* opens with the pop masterpiece, "Listen for the Laugh," which seems to describe the divine perspective on human folly: "It's the wind in the wings of the diving dove / You better listen for the laugh of love." The song "Love Loves You Too" is also inspirational, and "Closer to the Light" seems to be a tribute to a friend or mentor who has died (possibly **Mark Heard**). On *The Charity of Night* Cockburn sounds like a biblical patriarch complaining about God's failed (delayed?) promises: "Oh, you been leading me beside strange waters . . . but where is my pastureland in these dark valleys?" ("Strange Waters"). Then on "Wake Up, Jonah" he resorts to apocalyptic imagery. The artist would end his third decade of music with his most playful album ever. *Breakfast in New Orleans, Dinner in Timbuktu* features a surprising, electric cover of "Blueberry Hill" and a sexually-charged parody of the famous forbidden-fruit-in-Eden story called "Mango" (featuring duet vocals with Margo Timmins of the Cowboy Junkies). Not to let go of political concerns, "The Embers of Eden" describes the human legacy in terms of the only two evidences of our species that are visible from space: the Great Wall of China and the scorched acres of land that were once rain forests.

In 1980, when *CCM* first discovered that Cockburn was a Christian, they did a major profile on the artist. He openly discussed his spiritual search, conversion, and (by then) decade-old faith. But he also said, "I'm not very good at being an evangelist. Of course, I hope people see that Christianity is an alternative for them as a result of hearing my music, but I am approaching it from a different place. I'm not trying to sell Christianity. I don't see myself as a missionary." Again in 1982 he told that same magazine that he does not consciously set out to write religious songs, but he cannot help but produce songs that reflect his life of faith. "I'm just reporting on one attempt—mine—to live a Christian life," he explained. "My whole approach is to tell about what I've been through and leave a trail as I go." Elsewhere he has insisted that his faith reflects how he sees things and so always affects his songwriting. But "I don't see the music as a way of selling that faith . . . that doesn't feel right to me." In 1987 he talked about his political commitments, telling *CCM,* "The increased social involvement of my songs has been the result of my commitment to Christianity. After visiting Central America, I realized there was a direct connection between loving your neighbor and political involvement." The real problem (as even *CCM* noted) was not Cockburn's political passions themselves, but the fact that he had joined what conservative American Christians thought was the wrong side: he supported Nicaragua's Sandinistas instead of the Religious Right/Republican party-favored revolutionaries.

In other ways, too, Cockburn defies stereotypes that often attend Christian musicians, especially in America. He occasionally uses vulgarities in his songs; he unabashedly smokes and drinks; he supports legality of abortion by performing at pro-choice benefits and insisting, "the state has no more right to say that people must be born than it does to say they must be put to death." Even his songs that feature the most obvious "Christian content" sometimes offer atypical twists on the familiar themes. In "Cry of a Tiny Babe," Mary responds to Joseph's suspicion that she has been with another man with the phrase, "What if I had been?" Cockburn says he decided to give her "a little bit of an attitude" to counteract the cliché that the Christmas story has become. Cockburn has always objected strenuously to the popular association of Christianity with right-wing political movements. On a 1982 concert tour he pointedly dedicated the song "Justice" (which decries self-righteous desires to see *others* get what they deserve) to Jerry Falwell and his ilk, saying "I'm inclined to be a religious person, but I want to make sure you know that I don't have to answer for those guys."

In 1993 Cockburn performed at President Clinton's inauguration. In 2001 a critics' poll sponsored by *CCM* magazine put two Cockburn albums on its list of "The 100 Greatest Albums in Christian Music": *Humans* (at Number Twenty-eight) and *Dancing in the Dragon's Jaws* (at Number Forty-two).

Code of Ethics

Barry Blaze, voc., gtr., kybrd.; Eric Switzer, kybrd. (–1992) // Rick Brainer (+ 1993, –1995), drums; Scott Kifer (+ 1993, –1995); Ted T., drums, bass (+ 1995; –1997); Steve Dale (+ 1997; –1999); Charles Garrett (+ 1997; –1999); Jerry Mowery (+ 1997; –1999). 1991—*Visual Paradox* (R.E.X.); 1993—*Code of Ethics* (ForeFront); 1995—*Arms Around the World;* 1997—*Soulbait;* 1999—*Blaze* (Word).

http://spring.eecs.umich.edu/jivey/code.html

Code of Ethics is one of Christianity's more successful electronic dance music bands. As the personnel list above testifies, the entity is really not a group, but a person—Barry Blaze, who hires on various musicians on a project-by-project basis. The liner notes to *Arms Around the World* and *Soulbait* list group members but indicate that Blaze played all instruments, leaving one to wonder just exactly what the other people did. *Blaze,* on the other hand, appears to be an official solo project (no other members pictured or listed), though instruments and voices are credited to a number of other artists. To complicate matters, Code of Ethics has also had varying incarnations as a touring band and has released various remix projects (not listed above). **Ian Eskelin** (later of **All Star United**) provides vocals and keyboards on one of these (*Mix,* R.E.X., 1992).

The son of a Baptist minister, Blaze (who spelled his name *Blazs* on the first album) was attracted to the club scene and became involved with drugs and other aspects of the subculture surrounding house music. He turned his life around with the help of a Christian counselor during his first year at Liberty University in Detroit, Michigan, where Eskelin was also a student. He formed Code of Ethics in Florida in 1988. With twin drummers and Eskelin as the original keyboardist, the group set out to be a Christian techno-house band. After some success in that arena, Blaze recorded *Virtual Paradox* with his friend Eric Switzer. The cassette-only release got the band immediately compared to Depeche Mode and New Order. A self-titled project two years later upped the ante with a number of radio-friendly songs. "Freedom" references the destruction of the Berlin Wall, while suggesting that true freedom is a matter of the spirit. "True Love" has a Human League sound and, like several songs on the album, is a love song to God. Such pop-style hooks portended genre-breaking possibilities, and these were finally fulfilled on the third album, where the two stand-out tracks were surprising cover versions of the Monkees' "Pleasant Valley Sunday" (written by Gerry Goffin and Carole King) and **Larry Norman**'s "Nothing Really Changes." Blaze broke free of the "Christian Depeche Mode" comparisons to demonstrate a capacity for power-pop similar to Smash Mouth or **The Newsboys.** Hard-core synth-pop fans were disappointed, but CoE found a new and larger audience, leaving groups like **dba, The Echoing Green,** and **Joy Electric** to serve the Christian synth-pop audience that they had largely created. *Soulbait* continues the reinvention with catchy, melody-driven songs set to danceable beats. In spots the album even moves into modern rock with what *CCM* called "a new emphasis on thick battalions of fuzzy guitars slathered generously over the tracks." General market comparisons shifted to Garbage. On *Blaze,* however, Code of Ethics does an about face to produce an electronic techno album of worship music. Especially noteworthy are the upbeat, synthesized version of the modern classic, "I Love You, Lord" and a Blaze-Eskelin original, "Hallelujah 2000."

Lyrically the songs on Code of Ethics' early albums take a subtle approach to proclamation of the gospel, often presenting a perspective from God's point of view. The song "Satellite Babies," for instance, declares, "Death is not the end for my satellite babies, if you put your trust in me." The explicit integration of Christian confession increases exponentially on the most recent worship-oriented album: "Even though we like it loud, we'll always be a Jesus crowd" ("Hallelujah 2000").

Christian radio hits: "Something Real" (# 1 for 3 weeks in 1993); "True Love" (# 3 in 1993); "Freedom" (# 13 in 1994); "Follow On" (# 21 in 1994); "Sticks and Stones" (# 1 in 1995); "Well Done" (# 2 in 1995); "Voice of Reason" (# 2 in 1996): "Take Control" (# 15 in 1996): "Pleasant Valley Sunday" (# 15 in 1996); "Soulbait" (# 23 in 1997); "Good Things" (# 25 in 1997).

Jim Cole

1976—*Complete in Him* (QCA); 1991—*Every Generation* (Impact); 1993—*Merciful God*; 1996—*Leap of Faith*; 1998—*Live in Cincinnati.*

Jim Cole is always called the "Christian James Taylor" since his natural voice and vocal stylings are remarkably similar to those of the famous mainstream performer. Cole insists the similarities are not affected—and he has recordings from very early years (before Taylor appeared) to prove it. But the comparison is hardly offensive, and Cole has learned to bear it. "Imagine how much *more* annoying it must be" he jokes, "for James to be told he sounds like *me.*" Cole's first album emerged from the Jesus movement and features both electric country rockers and moody rural ballads similar to those on **The Way**'s first album. As years went by he would make mostly acoustic music noted for its integrity and vulnerability. "I want to be as honest as I can about the things I've been through, good and bad," he explains. The title song from *Leap of Faith* relates the comfort of knowing that God is present in the midst of challenges and trials.

Daryl Coley

1985—*Just Daryl* (First Epistle); 1988—*I'll Be With You* (Light); 1990—*He's Right on Time: Live from L.A.* (Sparrow); 1992—*When the Music Stops*; 1994—*In My Dreams*; 1995—*The Collection: Twelve Best Loved Songs*; 1996—*Beyond the Veil: Live at the Bobby Jones Gospel Explosion*; 1997—*Live in Oakland: Home Again* (Light).

Daryl Coley is a jazz singer who also sings gospel music. His silky tenor voice can be heard on projects by many contemporary jazz artists, including **David Diggs,** Rodney Franklin, and Ramsey Lewis. In the '80s he sang a duet with Nancy Wilson (the jazz stylist, not the guitarist for Heart) on "Just the Two of Us," which was a hit on the adult contemporary charts. Known as a singer's singer, his albums are especially appreciated by aficionados of vocal artistry, of smooth, perfect-pitch singing applied to challenging arrangements. His albums tend to favor worship songs, traditional hymns, and gospel standards. On *Live in Oakland,* for instance, he duets with **Vanessa Bell Armstrong** on "Don't Give Up on Jesus," sings with a choir on "Jesus Saves" and "I Will Sing Glory," and demonstrates his jazz roots on a song called "Acapella Praise."

Dove Awards: 1993 Contemporary Gospel Song ("Real").

Collective Soul

Ross Childress, gtr.; Shane Evans, drums; Dean Roland, gtr.; Ed Roland, voc., gtr.; Will Turpin, bass. 1993—*Hints, Allegations, and Things Left Unsaid* (Atlantic); 1995—*Collective Soul*; 1997—*Disciplined Breakdown*; 1999—*Dosage*; 2000—*Blender.*

www.collectivesoul.com

Whether or not the mainstream giant Collective Soul is a Christian band depends very much on definition. The group, at any rate, has a strong following among Christian music fans who appreciate their spiritually uplifting and often biblical lyrics. They have played at some Christian music events, and their albums are often reviewed in the Christian press. Ed and Dean Roland are the sons of a prominent Baptist minister, and they grew up devoting a good four hours every Sunday morning to worship and Sunday school. They also sang (along with Turpin) in the church's youth choir, which their father directed. Indeed, all five members had strong religious upbringings—as either Baptists or Methodists—in the Stockbridge suburb of Atlanta, Georgia, the very buckle of the Bible belt, so to speak. The influence of such faith remains evident not only in their material (written primarily by Ed Roland) but also in their relatively sedate lifestyle. "Our bus driver has more groupies than we do," Roland joked, after *Playgirl* magazine named him one of America's "Ten Sexiest Rock Stars." The influence could extend to music as well. *True Tunes* indicated rather perceptively that the band's debut album sounds an awful lot like **Daniel Amos'** *Horrendous Disc;* the song "Sister Don't Cry" even sounds like the song "Horrendous Disc." Roland would eventually own up to being "very familiar" with the work of the latter band.

Collective Soul's first album was originally intended as no more than a demo to showcase Roland's songwriting skills. It ended up going triple platinum on the strength of the runaway hit single "Shine" (# 11), easily the most played song on college radio in the summer of 1994. Critics dismissed the group as a one-hit wonder novelty act who would still be singing "Shine" at county fairs and tractor pulls twenty years down the road. But the self-titled record that was supposed to be their sophomore slump produced three more hits: "Gel" (# 49), "December" (# 20), and "The World I Know" (# 19), all Number One songs on AAA charts. In fact, the second project (*Collective Soul*) would eclipse the debut album in sales. Beloved by the radio and *adored* by video networks (the *Playgirl* thing again—both Ed and Dean Roland, let it be said, are held to be attractive), Collective Soul did more than any other band to bring the sounds of grunge into middle-class living rooms. Of course this feat earned them no praise from grunge purists, who reacted as though the band had violated some sacred turf or thrown Seattle pearls into a pen of Georgia swine. Still, the hits kept coming: "Precious Declaration" (# 65 in 1997), "Heavy" (# 73 in 1999), and "Run" (# 76 in 1999) were all huge on college-oriented AAA stations. With their third, and especially their fourth albums, the band even won over most of the critics. *Dosage* reveals a mature rock band—not a grunge group or an R&B group, but a basic *rock* band that has created its own distinct sound, which it performs with vigor and verve. Collective Soul came to be regarded as not only one of the most popular American rock bands of the '90s, but also one of the best. *Blender* (which features "Perfect Day," performed with Elton John) was received favorably as what *Rolling Stone*

called an album "that simply shreds with unapologetic classic-rock energy."

Now as to content: The song "Shine" was so eminently danceable that perhaps not many of the flannel clad gen-Xers who flocked to hear the group perform it at Woodstock 94 realized they were moshing to . . . a *prayer.* But there it is: "Oh, Heaven, let your light shine down!" Generic, but spiritual, all the same. On "Goodnight Good Guy" Roland asks, "Who's going to straighten me up when I'm leaning? / Who's going to soothe my heart when it's burning?" Then, retiring without an answer, he responds, "I pray the Lord to keep / I pray the Lord to hold you tight." The album concludes with "All," which seems to offer an invitation from God: "Watch my world spin round, it stops for you . . . My kingdom is all yours to receive." Such themes continued to inform the next three albums: "Gel" is not about sex, as many seem to think, but about reconciliation, about people putting aside their differences and "gelling" into one body with a single purpose: the good of humanity. Also on *Collective Soul* is "Untitled," on which Roland proclaims, "I don't believe in the sorcerers or the preachers . . . the scholars or the wise men / I just believe in you." *Disciplined Breakdown* contains a song called "Forgiveness," which expresses with pain and subdued anger Roland's heartfelt desire to learn how to forgive a person he believes has wronged him. And on that album's standout cut, Roland writes and sings with the confidence of a preacher: "I believe all hope is dead no longer . . . I was blind but now I see / Salvation has discovered me" ("Precious Declaration"). The song "Listen" reads (or sounds) like a straight-out sermon, pleading with one who is "searching" and "hungering" for the truth to stop rationalizing away the answer to that quest: "No sign you see / Do you believe? / If only you could open up your heart / And listen." But then at other times he adopts the voice of the seeker himself: "No cure have I found / Guide me, save me, teach me" ("Everything"). On "Needs," he confesses, "I just need to learn the depth or doubt of faith to fall into." And perhaps most pointedly, in "Crown" (from *Dosage*) Roland asks, "Who's gonna be my Saviour now that I've learned to believe? . . . Who's gonna be the shepherd to lead this poor boy back home?"

The seemingly obvious Christian connotations of Collective Soul's songs sent off flurries of speculation as to whether they were a Christian band in disguise. Pundits in the often-biased, sometimes-bigoted world of secular rock wondered whether they weren't just a sneakier version of **Jars of Clay.** Many within the Christian subculture hoped that was what they were—and seemed delighted to imagine that the "wise as serpents, innocent as doves" approach had worked. By avoiding the conventional associations that officially label an act as "Christian," Collective Soul had managed to get past the censors and land several bona fide Christian rock songs on the radio. Indeed, there was a widespread rumor among Christian fans for a time that the group actually *was* **Daniel Amos,** performing under a pseudonym again (cf. **The Swirling Eddies**). As such speculation fueled Internet chat groups, Roland tried to set the matter straight in an interview with *Spin* magazine: "I'm not going to deny I'm spiritual, but I think it (the music) makes sense without me affiliating with any one religion. We're not a Christian rock band." That was not the end of the matter. Most Christian artists hope that their music will transcend specific applications within the Christian community, and many regret or even reject labels that would limit their relevance to that community. Thus many Christian music fans were prepared to regard Roland's distancing remarks as *Spin*-control, necessary to avoid blowing the group's cover. This interpretation was encouraged by the band's label, at least in conversation with Christian venues that were accounting for a substantial portion of the group's sales. Warner Resound executives told Christian retailers (in a semi-private sort of way) that the band didn't want to be saddled with the label "Christian" because that would inhibit their ability to reach the rest of the world, but that the group had confirmed to the label that they were all believers and wanted their albums to be sold in Christian bookstores.

But Roland said other things too, like that he's "not sure if he believes in sin anymore." What does that mean? Christians don't exactly "believe in" sin; they "believe in" God and in Jesus Christ. But of course sin (or evil) exists. Would Roland deny that? No one seems to know, but at most Roland seems to be entertaining doubts about the surety of certain Christian doctrines and the exclusivity of certain Christian claims. In "Crown" he says, "I hope I'm not lost, but I think that hope is now distancing." The *Blender* album, furthermore, seems less concerned with spiritual matters than previous projects, and the song "Vent" contains some rather startling profanity ("I love you cause you're such a prick"). Bottom line: Thinking Christians are still Christians. Questioning Christians are still Christians. Doubting Christians are still Christians. Even liberal, universalist, or profane Christians are still Christians. But then the Christian music club should not press too hard to make (or keep) Roland a member if he really doesn't want to be one.

A sneakier **Jars of Clay**? A tamer **U2** would be more accurate. The members of Collective Soul themselves (label execs aside) do not appear to have ever been sneaky about where they stand on anything—with either the mainstream or the Christian press. Like **U2**—or like **Creed** or **Simple Minds** or **Midnight Oil**—they are a decidedly secular band whose music, lyrics, lifestyle, and commitments are obviously influenced by the sometimes ambiguous beliefs of members who are at least tentatively Christian. *Campus Life* magazine, which runs a regular column warning Christian teens about dangerous music and suggesting safer Christian alternatives, considered the band and found them wanting. For one thing, it turns out the name "Collective Soul" itself comes from *The Fountainhead,* a novel by Ayn Rand, who is "known to be an atheist!" Despite the group's positive, uplifting lyrics, then, *Campus Life* readers were urged to find an unambiguously Christian substitute whose lyrics "clearly point to faith in Christ as the [simplistic?] answer to life's toughest questions." Not many Christian music fans have taken this advice; support for Collective Soul within the Christian music subculture remains high. Mark 9:40 applies.

Jamie Owens Collins

See **Jamie Owens-Collins.**

Color Theory

Brian Hazard, prog., voc. 1997—*Tuesday Song* (11th Records); 1999—*Sketches in Gray; Perfect Tears.*

Color Theory is yet another one-man band posing as a techno group (cf. **Cult of Jester, Ultrabeat**). As is often the case, the sound that Brian Hazard creates is often compared to that of Depeche Mode or Tori Amos, though some critics have found his more innovative moments to summon images of Ben Folds Five or Everything But the Girl. Hazard's strengths are sophisticated piano playing and heartfelt vocals that remove his albums from the cold and unemotional stereotypes that often attend electronic music. Hazard originally released *Sketches in Gray* as an independent demo in 1994; it was rereleased in an expanded version after *Tuesday Song* proved successful. The latter album has a mellow, retro sound often recalling the quiet songs of late '70s groups like Styx or Queen. "Outside Girl" is more of a disco song, and "My Gift to You" has a Christmas theme. Romance is the primary theme: "Entirely" offers the reflections of a man deciding whether to stay with his pregnant girlfriend; "The Perfect Song" was written by Hazard as a wedding proposal. The album has been described as "a perfect disc for people in love." *Sketches in Grey* has less of a retro feel but features emotional piano-driven ballads that one might associate with a romantic, candlelit supper. *Perfect Tears* branches out stylistically, employing more synthesizers and stronger drum and bass rhythms. "Acting Class" addresses the human tendency for people to pretend they are something that they are not. "For Good" promises enduring love to a mate, come what may.

Paul Colman Trio

Paul Colman, voc., gtr.; Phil Gaudion, drums; Grant Norsworthy, bass. 1999—*Serious Fun* (independent); 2000—*Turn.*

With a sound roughly analogous to the acoustic pop of **Steven Curtis Chapman,** the Paul Colman Trio rose to superstar status among indie acts in their native Australia, topping the Christian charts and selling out concerts despite the lack of backing from any major label. After a relatively successful solo album called *One Voice, One Guitar,* Colman teamed with Gaudion and Norsworthy. Their debut album features cover art presenting the group as a classic rock and roll trio similar to Buddy Holly and The Crickets. The upbeat, hook-driven songs focus lyrically on the love of God and the need for humans to appropriate this love in their lives. "The Killing Tree" demonstrates Colman's ability to fashion poetic lyrics with its reference to the cross of Christ ("Come away, come away, there's a sweet voice calling me / To the killing tree"). *The Phantom Tollbooth* describes the band's sophomore project *Turn* as the most hyped album of the year among Christian music fans in Australia. The album has a somewhat fuller sound, with more electric instrumentation, bigger bass, and louder drums. The title track became a major Christian radio hit in the homeland. A song called "The One" has a surf-rock sound and features a brief foray into rap. "The Sun, the Stars, and the Moon" is a worship ballad; "Same Mistakes" addresses the issue of premarital sex; "In the Middle" describes the dilemma of many Christian rock musicians who find their art is not accepted by either secular or traditional Christian venues (too Christian for the one, too rock for the other).

Bill Comeau

1970—*Some Beautiful Day: A Rock Celebration of the Life of a Dreamer Called Jesus* (Avant Garde).

Bill Comeau is a long-forgotten artist who released one long-forgotten album, a curious souvenir of pre-Jesus movement Christian rock. Nothing is known of Comeau, save that he made this album for a well-named independent New York City record company. It was released the same year as *Jesus Christ Superstar,* which was also the year George Harrison had a Number One hit with "My Sweet Lord" and **Norman Greenbaum** scored Number Three with "Spirit in the Sky." Comeau's contribution was more orthodox theologically, though probably more inventive musically than any of the above. Perhaps for those two reasons, it was also much less successful. Comeau appears to have been a Greenwich Village poet, a sort of Christian Allen Ginsberg. His poems are organized here as reflections on the life of Christ, set to music composed by Pete Levin. Comeau speaks and sings the lyrics with moods that vary from folk to jazz to blues to rock. The poems present Christ inventively as "a dreamer" whose dream is that humanity will want to be reconciled with God through him. It is a hippie Jesus, of course, appropriate to the age, but the analogies are not stretched. Some listings indicate that Comeau also

released an album curiously titled *Fragments of an Unknown Gospel* on Avant Garde in 1970—but no information about such a record is available.

Commissioned

Mitchell Jones, voc.; Karl Reid, voc.; Fred Hammond, voc., bass (– 1996); Michael Williams, voc., drums (– 1996); Michael Brooks, voc., kybrd. (–1990); Keith Staten, voc. (–1990) // Maxx Frank, voc. (+ 1991, –2000); Marvin Sapp, voc. (+ 1991, –2000); Eddie Howard, voc. (+ 1991, –1994); Montell Darrett, voc. (+ 1996, –2000); Marcus Cole, voc. (+ 2000); Chris Poole, voc. (+ 2000). 1985—*I'm Goin' On* (Light); 1986—*Go Tell Somebody;* 1987—*On the Winning Side;* 1988—*Will You Be Ready?;* 1989—*Ordinary Just Won't Do;* 1990—*State of Mind* (Benson); 1991—*Number 7; A Collection* (CGI); *Shakin' the House* [with Carman and the Christ Church Choir] (Benson); 1994—*Matters of the Heart;* 1995—*The Light Years* (Light); 1996—*Irreplaceable Love* (Benson); 1999—*Best of Commissioned* (Verity); 2000—*Time and Seasons.*

Commissioned is a Detroit R&B vocal group formed by producer **Fred Hammond,** who has also had a successful solo career. Mitchell Jones, Karl Reid, and Keith Staten had previously sung in a gospel group called Sounds of Joy, but they were tapped by Hammond for Commissioned in 1982. The group's first albums focused on tight harmonies and earned them frequent comparisons to another Detroit R&B gospel group, **The Winans.** *I'm Goin' On* features the fairly traditional " 'Tis So Sweet" and *Go Tell Somebody* includes one of the combo's best soul ballads, "Runnin' Back to You." By their third production, Commissioned was getting funkier, and they would eventually evolve into a '90s version of **Andraé Crouch and the Disciples,** playing unabashed gospel music set to a sound that seemed to be in step with the times. It took a few albums to really get this down, but *State of Mind* would be a significant breakthrough. "Let Me Tell It" is a vibrant dance track, and both "I Am Here" and "Everlasting Love" are smooth and sweet, revealing two sides of a group that could now be all things to all people. Modernization, of course, would demand experiments with hip-hop, and this came to the fore on the streetwise *Number 7* ("Second Chance," "King of Glory"). For *Matters of the Heart,* the group would even get **Run-D.M.C.** to join them for some rap on "You Can Always Come Home." But the signature Commissioned sound has remained that of velvety smooth ballads sung in soulful voices reminiscent of the mainstream group Boyz II Men. Somewhat ironically, it was Commissioned who influenced the Boyz rather than the other way around. "We're the originators of that sound," Hammond insists—and the Boyz freely acknowledge this. The sound is more than evident on *Matters of the Heart* on such songs as "Dare To Believe" and "When Love Calls You Home." The song "Love Is the Way" is bouncy and fun. The album also features two diverse covers: **Dottie Rambo**'s hymnic "We Shall Behold Him" and Phil Collins' "Another Day in Paradise."

Commissioned is well known among African American artists outside the gospel music scene, and Hammond (like **Andraé Crouch**) is recognized as having been influential for many acts that otherwise betray no noticeable interest in Christian music. Commissioned, nevertheless, has always maintained a strong ministry focus, with little overt interest in becoming a crossover act. The great majority of Commissioned's repertoire consists of material that is unambiguous in its testimony to Christ. Although Hammond was clearly the group's central figure, composing and arranging most of the songs, varying versions of Commissioned would continue to record after he left for a solo career. To some extent "Commissioned" then became simply a marketing logo associated with a trademark sound, but original members Mitchell Jones and Karl Reid did keep the vision alive. *Irreplaceable Love* features two songs written and produced by members of Boyz II Men ("Irreplaceable Love" by Shawn Stockman; "They Must Know" by Wanya Morris). The album also features more hip-hop with "Dominion" and includes the adult contemporary "More Than I," written and sung by short-term member **Montrel Darrett,** who would soon embark on a solo career. *Times and Seasons* is mainly worship songs, with "Testify" and "Glorious Praise" being noticeable standout songs. Commissioned also sings a setting of "Psalm 84" and remakes "Ordinary Just Won't Do" from the group's fifth album.

Keith Staten released two solo albums, *From the Heart* (Lection, 1990) and *No Greater Love* (Integrity, 1995). The latter record features his smooth voice on gospel standards like "I Bowed on My Knees" and "Great Is Thy Faithfulness." He then turned to worship-leadership and released two more collections of urban praise songs: *Worship in the House* (Integrity, 1996) and *Glory in the House* (Integrity, 1999). Christian rapper **Mike-E** is reported to have sung with Commissioned for a time.

Christian radio hits: "The Same God" [with **Carman**] (# 8 in 1991); "Love U with the Rest of My Life" (# 14 in 1992).

Dove Awards: 1990 Contemporary Gospel Album *(Will You Be Ready?).*

Common Bond

Chuck Cummings, drums; Steve Durham, gtr.; Ken Samuels, voc., bass. 1986—*Heaven Is Calling* (Broken); 1987—*Anger into Passion.*

Common Bond was a post-punk California band that developed a rock sound sometimes compared to Rush, primarily due to Ken Samuels' high-pitched Geddy Lee-styled vocals. The group's first album scored on the strength of its opening song, "Matter of Time," which solidified the classic rock sound with a justifiable hit. The second album, however, was much better

than the debut as an overall project. The group covers **Daniel Amos**'s "Walls of Doubt" and includes a couple of strong pop tunes, "Tarry" and "Face to Face." Thematically the group maintained that their first album was strongly influenced by the book *Addicted to Mediocrity* by Franky Schaeffer, the son of evangelical thinker Frank Schaeffer. Still, they would be best remembered for their sophomore project, which in the words of *Rad Rockers,* "reminded listeners that humans beings who choose to follow Christ must take the energies usually reserved for righteous indignation and turn them into a passion to show compassion." Chuck Cummings went on to play drums with a number of high profile Christian bands, including the **Aunt Bettys, Dakoda Motor Co., Fanmail,** and **LSU.**

Common Children

Mark Byrd, gtr., voc.; Drew Powell, bass, voc.; Hampton Eugene Taliaferro, drums, voc. 1996—*Skywire* (Tattoo); 1997—*Delicate Fade;* 2001—*The In-between Time* (Galaxy 21).

Among the hundreds of Christian alternative rock bands to emerge in the '90s, Common Children proved particularly successful at garnering acclaim from critics and maintaining a loyal fan base. The group formed at an Arkansas Bible college early in that decade and performed in coffeehouses and church basements up and down the East Coast. Combining the abandon of new punk with melodic sensitivity, they forged a sound fit for comparison with alternative mainstay Soundgarden—or even early Pearl Jam. Despite their Christian affinities, they were offered (and accepted) invitations to open for such general-market acts as Material Issue, Better Than Ezra, Dishwalla, and Cheap Trick. They were the first group signed to Tattoo, a new Christian alternative rock label, and **Steve Hindalong** of **The Choir** was brought in to produce their first two albums. The group never quite became the **Jars of Clay** crossover act that Tattoo envisioned, but they did receive some airplay on college radio. Dennis Rodman spun their songs on episodes of his MTV show, and the band opened for Bush at ESPN's "Xtreme Games." Still, their greatest success and acclaim was to be found in the Christian market.

Skywire was chosen one of the Top Five Albums of 1996 by *7ball magazine.* The song "Hate" probably attracted the most attention, though it is perhaps atypical (musically and lyrically) from most of the record. A hard-edged, almost metal song, it features Byrd screaming, "I hate myself" repeatedly (Byrd says the inspiration was the Apostle Paul's struggles documented in Romans 7). Also popular were "Drought" (another fairly hard-edged number) and "Treasures," which offers a much more exuberant, sing-along chorus ("Love is falling down like rain"). "Wishing Well" is also a bit of a sing-along, with a hook-filled melody line. "Last Time Out" is lush; "Dual Lens" is trippy; "Broken Smile" is melancholy and acoustic.

Delicate Fade proves that the debut record was no fluke, opening with the Pink Floyd/Radiohead inspired "Stains of Time," a masterpiece of modern rock that lets the group rise above any suspicion that they were just a Soundgarden clone. After a symphonic violin intro, Byrd intones over cello and plaintive guitar, "Will you show us all your glory / To soothe and erase the stains of time?" The album moves into post-grunge territory, which is not to say Common Children went soft. "Burned" and "Pulse" evince fiery and pounding sonics in keeping with their titles. Other standout cuts include the melodic "Eyes of God," the progressive British-sounding "Blue Raft," and the majestic pop song "Whisper" (featuring **Christine Glass**). After four years the almost-forgotten group returned with *The In-between Time,* an album that saw them moving still further away from hard sounds toward psychedelic space rock. "So Mysterious" is an upbeat song about a girl, and "Free" references **The Choir** musically and lyrically. "Crashing Down" is an atmospheric acoustic ballad that addresses sorrow: "This won't be the last time your heart comes crashing down . . . but one day, face to face, you will find your resting place."

Byrd cites G. K. Chesterton and C. S. Lewis as influences on his thinking. In the grand tradition of Job, Jeremiah, and Ecclesiastes, he seeks to write with "a gut-wrenching honesty that deals with real issues of life." He also views Common Children more as a vehicle for artistic expression than as a tool for evangelism. "Does a Christian artist only have to paint pictures of Jesus and hang them in churches?" he asks. "What if I want to paint a tree?" Like most Christian rock bands that show an interest in engaging (much less dialoging with) the world outside the Christian ghetto, Common Children have been criticized by Christians for being too vague in their testimonies or too overtly worldly in their approach. The song "Throw Me Over" (from *Skywire*) addresses this not-without-honor-except-in-one's-own-hometown syndrome: "Is this like the place called home?" Byrd asks the church, "Is this where the stones are thrown?" The group has also been involved with the ministry of Greencross, a group that presents Christian perspectives on environmental issues.

Christian radio hits: "Eyes of God" (# 5 in 1998).

The Company

Kristen Burns [a.k.a. The Diva]; Chili; Tadpole Lowenbad; Freaky O'Neill; Rockafeller; Rutheford. 2000—*The Company* (BEC).

Disco music isn't dead. The West Coast Christian band known as The Company embraces the sounds of the disco era unashamedly while alternately challenging or inspiring listeners with their lyrics. The group's members do not reveal their real names, but the lead female singer (The Diva) is actually Kristen Burns, and two of the other members are Brian Everett and Bradley Swanson. Everett was once a member of **Pep Squad,** and he and Burns alternate vocals to add interest to songs that might otherwise sound too much alike. "Will You Be There?" is a duet. The opening track, "Ooh, C'mon," calls on Christians to take a stand for their faith. "Boogie Machine" is a cleverly disguised praise song. *Bandoppler* magazine thinks "Will You Be There?" borrows rather noticeably from Irene Cara's "What a Feeling," while "In the Mix" would be right at home on a *Shaft* soundtrack with its "wocka wocka" guitars and hushed and breathy chorus. The album's best track, however, is probably the beach party dance number, "All Around the World," which invites everyone to stop the violence and just have fun. Production values on this album are especially high, with first-rate musicianship (strings are provided by the Portland Philharmonic).

Concrete Rubber Band

Duncan Long, kybrd., gtr.; et al. 1969—*Risen Savior* (American Artist).

Of historical significance only, Concrete Rubber Band made one album that could qualify as Christian rock music a full two years before the Jesus movement exploded in southwest California and a year before *Jesus Christ Superstar* would clutter the charts with what most regard as pseudo-Christian, pseudo-rock. It was the same year **Larry Norman** made what is usually called "the first Christian rock album." Of course, Concrete Rubber Band's record was a homemade project, produced on a very low budget, and fewer than five hundred copies were ever pressed, but still . . . the record has historical significance, and those fewer-than-five hundred discs are valuable to collectors. Notably, the main ingredient in CRB's sound is Duncan Long's synthesizer—a bit progressive for the late '60s. The music itself has a rather Iron Butterfly psychedelic twinge to it. Jesus music archivist Ken Scott describes the song "Wicked" as "Christian psychedelia at its most underground and extreme, with all the earmarks of a bad drug trip—which given the song's dark subject matter works just fine." The song "Christian" opens with a Bach fugue à la Walter/Wendy Carlos, and "What Shall We Do?" segues from a distorted guitar opening into a Pink Floyd-ish spooky ballad. The three members of Concrete Rubber Band were strict Baptists and as such refused to play at bars or dances. Since their style of music was hardly welcome at church events, they never got much of a chance to be heard.

An intriguing footnote to Concrete Rubber Band's non-career is that Duncan Long would go on to become an established writer of science fiction. He has also written extensively in three other areas (where one is tempted to say his interest in science fiction also remains evident): 1) religious studies, where the primary concern is apocalyptic topics (the Rapture, the Tribulation); 2) survivalism, where he is presented as an expert on such subjects as "getting food after a nuclear war" and "how to survive chemical weapons"; and 3) guns and ammo, for the love of which he writes prolifically against pacifism, wondering if it is only a coincidence that "all the genocides of the 20th century started with gun control?" Check it out at http://duncanlong.com.

Considering Lily (a.k.a. Serene and Pearl)

Pearl Barrett, voc., gtr.; Serene Campbell, voc. (– 1999) // Jeanette Herdman, voc. (+ 1999). As Serene and Pearl: 1995—*Crazy Stories* (Fore-Front). As Considering Lily: 1996—*Considering Lily* (ForeFront); 1999—*The Pieces Fit.*

Pearl Barrett and Serene Campbell are sisters, New Zealand immigrants whose father now pastors a church in Franklin, Tennessee. Their first album as the duo Serene and Pearl was recorded while Campbell was still in high school, and musically it represented a fairly flagrant attempt to copy the **Indigo Girls.** They then decided to record under the name Considering Lily (derived from Matthew 6:28, with intentional misspelling) and to drop the attempt to "sing American," allowing their native flair to be part of the charm (though the Indigo comparisons still held). Sometime after the release of the first Considering Lily album, Serene Campbell became Serene Allison and decided to quit recording. Thus the second Considering Lily album was not "Serene and Pearl" but "Jeannette and Pearl," Jeanette being the wife of **Audio Adrenaline**'s Bob Herdman. The group disbanded after recording *The Pieces Fit.*

Crazy Stories has an acoustic folk-pop sound. Its standout song is "Deep Water," which relates a childhood experience to the story of Jesus rescuing Peter from his ill-fated attempt to walk on water (Matthew 14:28–33). Two songs ("Wouldn't It Be Cool," "Everything") were written by **Steve Wiggins** of **Big Tent Revival,** and the duo also covers "Thief in the Night" by **Carolyn Arends.** The debut album from Considering Lily moves decidedly toward alternative rock. The opening track, "Pike's Peak," is a guitar-driven number that likens life without Christ to driving "down Pike's Peak at 90 miles an hour in the dark with the headlights off." The next track, "Beautiful You," asserts with some humor that all people are beautiful to God, no matter how nerdy or strange their distinctive features may be. "Consequences" is a bit of pop ear-candy on which the sisters sing, "You can't do anything, anytime, anywhere" to a '60s bubblegum tune. The album closes with two judicious covers: "Get Together," which was a Number Five hit for The Youngbloods in 1969 and became a stereotypical summary of what some regard as hippie naivete ("Come on, people now, smile on your brother . . ."), and Alex Chilton's "Jesus Christ Was Born

Today." The latter choice upped Considering Lily's hip credentials exponentially, as the song (first performed by the quintessentially alternative rock group Big Star) is virtually unknown to Christians but is well known in certain secular undergrounds. The album, *The Pieces Fit,* was produced by Michael Quinlan and by **Audio Adrenaline**'s Barry Blair. It features a lot of keyboards, with much more of an '80s rock sound than the previous project. Since Campbell had also been the principal songwriter, the songs on *The Pieces Fit* seem significantly different than those on *Serene and Pearl* and *Considering Lily.* The first two songs are big, bright, and cheery pop numbers: "Great Expectations" looks forward to whatever plans God might have for the singer; "Today" anticipates Christ's return, joyously proclaiming "I hope that Jesus comes today, hooray, hooray, today!" The song "Electric" seeks to portray the love of God as "electrifying," and "Put Me in the Picture" features a memorable melody and paints a vivid word picture. "I Want to Need to Know You" is a ballad that expresses spiritual longing in a provocative way. Critics tended to view *Pieces Fit* as "more sophisticated" than the previous projects, but also as "harder to get into." *CCM* complained about song quality, claiming that the numbers "sound like throwaway tracks from the last **Rebecca St. James** record."

For trivia buffs: Serene and Pearl have an older brother, Wesley Campbell, who managed a Christian rock band back in New Zealand that the girls referred to as "the shedboys," since they often lived in the family's garage. The latter group would eventually be known as **The Newsboys.**

Christian radio hits: By Serene and Pearl: "Crazy Stories" (# 14 in 1995); By Considering Lily: "Consequences" (# 5 in 1997); "Cup" (# 2 in 1997); "Real" (# 13 in 1997); "Great Expectations" (# 2 in 1999); "Whisper" (# 18 in 1999).

Sam Cooke

Selected: 1960—*I Thank God* (Keen); 1961—*Jesus Be a Fence around Me* [by The Soul Stirrers] (SAR); 1962—*Gospel Pearls; Encore* [by The Soul Stirrers]; 1964—*Soul Stirrers Featuring Sam Cooke* (Specialty); 1969—*The Gospel Soul of Sam Cooke with the Soul Stirrers, Vol. 1; 1971—The Gospel Soul of Sam Cooke with the Soul Stirrers, Vol. 2; The Original Soul Stirrers Featuring Sam Cooke; 1972—That's Heaven to Me* [with The Soul Stirrers]; 1991—*Sam Cooke with The Soul Stirrers; 1992—Jesus Gave Me Water; 1994—The Last Mile of the Way.*

Many of the early African American R&B singers began their career in gospel, but few experienced a crossover from sacred to secular as remarkable as that of Sam Cooke. Sometimes called "The Man Who Invented Soul," Cooke was an established and popular performer in traditional gospel before he lent his voice to crooning romantic odes like "You Send Me" (# 1 for 3 weeks in 1957), "Wonderful World" (# 12 in 1960), and "Cupid" (# 17 in 1961)—or dance hits like "Twistin' the

Night Away" (# 9 in 1962), "Another Saturday Night" (# 10 in 1963), and "Shake" (# 7 in 1965). In the '60s at least, gospel music fans were not too fond of romance or dancing, both of which were rumored to lead to sex, and Cooke was sometimes sharply vilified. He nevertheless remains one of the period's top R&B acts, with twenty-nine Top 40 hits between 1957 and 1965, including the earthy "Chain Gang" and the socially conscious "A Change Is Gonna Come," which he presumably wrote in response to **Bob Dylan**'s less hopeful "Blowin' in the Wind."

Cooke was born in Clarksdale, Mississippi, in 1931 and was raised in Chicago. The son of a Baptist minister, he sang in the church choir from the age of six and as a young teenager formed a gospel group called The Highway QC's with later R&B star Johnnie Taylor. The group had the opportunity of touring with The Soul Stirrers, the top gospel act in the country. The Soul Stirrers were led by Rebert H. Harris, who is credited with inventing many of the trademark techniques of gospel (and soul) music: delayed time signatures, melismas (a string of notes sung on a single syllable), antiphony (call and response singing), and falsetto leads. In 1950 Harris left The Soul Stirrers, concerned that gospel music was becoming more oriented toward show business than spiritual ministry, and Cooke was chosen to replace him. For six years he led the premiere gospel quartet of the day, recording a number of songs including the standards "Peace in the Valley" and "I'm Gonna Build on That Shore" and the gospel hits "Touch the Hem of His Garment" and "Jesus Gives Me Water." Cooke first began recording secular songs in 1956, persuaded by Robert "Bumps" Blackwell, the promoter who would also play an instrumental role in **Little Richard**'s career. His main inspiration for going secular, however, may have been Ray Charles, who (with no background in gospel music) was enjoying a good deal of commercial success by taking gospel songs and substituting a woman for God in the lyrics (e.g., "This Little Light of Mine" recast as "This Little Girl of Mine"). Cooke first tried this by re-recording The Soul Stirrers' hit "Wonderful" ("My God, He's so wonderful") as "Lovable" ("My girl, she's so lovable"). The song failed to chart and offended gospel fans, who were not fooled by the pseudonym (Dale Cook) under which he had released it. But then Cooke hit huge with the mellifluous "You Send Me," destined to become one of the top soul songs of all time. His 1957 appearance on *The Ed Sullivan Show* to sing the song caused a national scandal when the program ran out of time and cut him off—to many viewers, it looked liked racism.

As Cooke's hits continued to pile up, the previous music of The Soul Stirrers also attracted attention, and Cooke's recordings with them were packaged and repackaged in a variety of collections. Most music critics and historians allege that the gospel recordings supercede the secular records in quality,

evincing a passion that mainstream (white) pop audiences really did not want to associate with a black singer in the pre-Civil Rights era. The sensual potential of songs like "Only Sixteen" (# 28 in 1959) and "Having a Party" (# 17 in 1962) seems muted when compared to what Cooke's gospel performances prove he was capable of delivering (the grunts and groans in "Chain Gang" and the sad pallor of "Bring It On Home to Me" are a bit more revealing). Even Cooke's gospel recordings, furthermore, offer but a hint of what he is said to have been like fronting The Soul Stirrers live on stage. Jerry Wexler (producer for **Aretha Franklin, Bob Dylan,** and many others) says, "Nobody put more people in stretchers than Sam Cooke (with The Soul Stirrers). He's got to be the best singer that ever lived. The pop stuff never came close to making the fullest use of his talents. Most people don't realize how bad those records are." But Cooke did sometimes include gospel songs on his mainstream recordings, such as a rendition of "Nobody Knows the Trouble I've Seen" on *Night Beat* (RCA, 1963).

As indicated, there was predictable criticism of Cooke among gospel audiences for selling out, but this tends to be exaggerated. Rebert H. Harris has repeatedly told a story in Cooke documentaries about how, in 1958, Cooke found himself in Chicago at a time when The Soul Stirrers were performing and decided to pay his old buddies a surprise visit. He joined them on stage and was booed by the audience with cries of "Get that blues singer down. . . . This is a *Christian* program!" But Daniel Wolff, author of *You Send Me: The Life and Times of Sam Cooke* (Quill, 1995) claims this never happened—based on interviews with members of The Soul Stirrers and others who were supposedly present. Indeed, there is evidence that Cooke's secular success was sometimes genuinely appreciated by gospel fans who saw it as a sort of legitimation of their art form and as a rare instance of commercial success and critical acclaim being granted to an African American. In the latter regard, it is worth noting that Cooke became one of the most successful independent black businessmen in the country. He retained all of the rights and royalties to his music and started his own record label, music publishing company, and management firm.

On December 11, 1964, Cooke was shot to death by a female hotel manager named Bertha Franklin. According to the official police report, Cooke had abducted a twenty-two-year-old woman named Lisa Boyer and taken her to Franklin's motel, where he tried to rape her. Boyer escaped with his clothing and Cooke kicked in the door to Franklin's office looking for her. A coroner's inquest ruled the shooting an act of self-defense, but many questions remained regarding suspicious circumstances: Boyer was a prostitute (imprisoned some years later for killing her boyfriend); according to some reports, Franklin was also a former prostitute who may have been previously known to either or both parties; Cooke had registered at the motel with Boyer—with whom he had been seen on previous occasions—using his real name (odd behavior for a kidnapper); he was known to have had thousands of dollars in cash on him at the time, all of which vanished along with his credit cards and driver's license. The police investigation was severely compromised in that, even days later, the police admitted that they "did not know who Sam Cooke was" and had handled the incident as what they called "a routine, one-more-dead-Negro-in-a-sleazy-motel event." The crime scene, the body, and the witnesses had all been summarily dealt with before anyone realized the case's potential impact. The African American community was horrified, but their protests proved ineffective (Muhammad Ali said, "If this were Frank Sinatra, the FBI would be involved"). The general sentiment was that Cooke had been caught in some kind of con pulled off by one or both of the women, though a few more elaborate conspiracy theories would also be proposed. In any case, Cooke's image was permanently damaged by the ignominy of his demise, especially among religious fans of his gospel music. **Billy Preston** played the organ at Cooke's funeral, and Lou Rawls and Ray Charles sang hymns in his honor. A private investigation into the circumstances of his death was halted at the request of his widow, who married R&B singer Bobby Womack less than three months later.

Otis Redding, Rod Stewart, and **Al Green** have all named Cooke as the single greatest influence on their style, and an unacknowledged influence on Michael Jackson is also apparent to many. In 1986 Cooke was inducted into the Rock and Roll Hall of Fame, and in 1989 The Soul Stirrers were similarly inducted as a separate entity.

For trivia buffs: Sam Cooke's nephew is R. B. Greaves, the (half) Native American singer who had hits with "Take a Letter Maria" (# 2 in 1969) and "Always Something There to Remind Me" (# 27 in 1970).

Tommy Coomes

1981—*Love Is the Key* (Maranatha).

Tommy Coomes should probably be known as the father of contemporary worship music. He wrote the world's first modern praise and worship song, the wonderful "Holy, Holy, Holy," which closed out Side One of the most important Christian album ever made—*The Everlastin' Living Jesus Music Concert* (Maranatha, 1971). With that moment, he calmly introduced the world to a sound that within twenty-five years would become the dominant musical style of most nonliturgical Protestant churches in America. Very few of the successors to "Holy, Holy, Holy" would match that song in quality, but Coomes

can hardly be blamed for the dumbing down of liturgy that followed in its wake.

Coomes was also a founding member of **Love Song,** one of the most important—and best—Christian rock groups of all time. Though less visible than the group's putative leader, **Chuck Girard,** he brought a formidable influence to bear on the group's overall sound. Coomes played Harrison to Girard's McCartney (unfortunately, Love Song did not have a John Lennon), complementing the former's catchy melodies and sweet vocals with a harmonic sense tuned toward spirituality and choral worship. His best-known contributions to the group's material are "Let Us Be One," arguably the world's first *rock* worship song, and "Two Hands" (cowritten with Chuck Butler of **Country Faith**). Love Song's debut album was unquestionably the second most played record of the Jesus movement (right behind *The Everlastin' Living Jesus Music Concert*), and though the whole album seems spiritual, "Let Us Be One" is the only song that is actually addressed to God. The focus of the Jesus movement was more on evangelism than on worship—but Coomes was ahead of his peers in trying to incorporate both. Nowhere is this more evident than in the lyric to "Two Hands" ("With one reach out to Jesus / With the other, bring a friend"). At early Love Song concerts (before Girard wrote "Sometime Alleluia"), it was this song that had the Jesus people on their feet, hands raised above their heads *worshiping* the Lord. It was this song that segued not only into an altar call but also into a time of free prayer, with hippie Christians speaking in tongues, singing in the Spirit, and swaying to the music. After Love Song, Coomes joined **Wing and a Prayer.** His main contribution to that group, "Jesus is Standing Here," is also a worship song.

Coomes became an executive with Maranatha Music and predictably oversaw much of the production on their successful series of praise albums. He wrote "Light Our Way" on the *Praise Two* album and served as producer for several of the company's praise and worship projects. Along the way he stopped to make one solo album, filled with jazzy songs that feature infectious, sing-along choruses. *CCM* magazine praised the album for its lack of "hokeyness," that is, for its avoidance of phrases that might have played well in 1971 but would have been clichés a decade later. The main attraction for most listeners was "Singing Our Praises to Jesus," a surf-sounding worship song on which Coomes was joined by Love Song alums Girard and Jay Truax. The song was cowritten by Coomes and Girard and could almost be a Love Song outtake. Other standout cuts include the title track, "The Pleasure's Mine," and "Thinking of You."

Incidentally, Coomes also cowrote Love Song's "Front Seat, Back Seat" and "Book of Life" (both with Girard) and "The Cossack Song" (with **Country Faith**'s Tom Stipe). Those tunes all reveal a country-rock influence and a sense of humor that did not come to the fore in his other projects. He also cowrote the song "Our Love," which was a Christian radio hit performed by **Roby Duke** and **Kelly Willard.**

Alice Cooper

Selected: 1994—*The Last Temptation* (Epic); 2000—*Brutal Planet* (Spitfire); 2001—*Dragontown.*

www.alicecoopershow.com

Alice Cooper, the master of shock rock, quietly embraced Christianity sometime in the early '90s and subsequently made *The Last Temptation* as a testimony to his faith. Born Vincent Furnier in 1948 in Detroit, Michigan, Cooper was the son of Ether Moroni Furnier, a Baptist minister who, when the boy was thirteen, answered a call to become a missionary to the Apache Indians. He moved the family to Phoenix, where in two months' time the teenaged Furnier became violently ill. As it turned out, his appendix had ruptured a week before medical attention was sought; he was diagnosed with peritonitis, which had made its way throughout his digestive system. Doctors told his parents the situation was too far advanced and that he would die. He didn't, and even throughout his years as a renowned practitioner of the grotesque and the occult, he would always attribute his healing to a miracle of God. Indeed, in a 1976 autobiography called *Me, Alice,* Cooper wrote, "It was a miracle that I pulled through—thanks to Jesus, and the church, and the faith of everyone around me. Later, when my father would tell this story to people, they'd laugh and say, 'Why would the Lord save the life of Alice Cooper?'" To capitalize on the human interest angle of his preacher's-kid-gone-bad image, Cooper allowed his father to append a preface to that same autobiography. The minister bemoaned the fact that his son had "drifted away from church attendance" but clung to the hope that what had been sown in the young boy's heart would bear fruit at last. "Am I dreaming," he asked, "or suffering from wishful thinking—that after all this decadence there will emerge from this dynamic personality a servant of God?"

Cooper rose to fame in the '70s with outlandish metal-inflected hits like "Eighteen" (# 21 in 1971) and "School's Out" (# 7 in 1972). But he was best known for his stage shows, bizarre costume dramas that featured the performer draping himself with a large boa constrictor, chopping up baby dolls, and simulating executions on stage. Cooper seemed to flaunt occult and vulgar stylings likely to be offensive to the pious. He wore strange makeup (years before Kiss) and sometimes dressed in women's clothing. His press agents claimed that he adopted his stage name after a ouija board revealed that he was the reincarnation of a sixteenth-century witch by that name (something he would later deny). At the same time, Cooper al-

ways sent out strong signals that it was all just an act, a bit of surreal art that was not to be taken seriously. Indeed, in 1973 Salvador Dali crafted a holographic work of Cooper, dressed in diamond necklaces and a tiara, biting the head off of a replica of the Venus de Milo—an image *so* bizarre that it begged to be dismissed as camp. In 1975 Cooper did a prime time TV special (*Alice Cooper—The Nightmare*) that could have been a Halloween episode of *The Carol Burnett Show.* He put in several appearances on *Hollywood Squares* and hobnobbed (sans makeup) with the likes of conservative politician Barry Goldwater. He recorded a handful of ballads ("I Never Cry," # 12 in 1976; "You and Me," # 9 in 1977) that could have been done by Barry Manilow. In general Cooper came to be viewed as a mainstream entertainer for whom the fake occult/nightmare act had proved to be a successful novelty (cf. Michael Jackson's "Thriller"). Still, all was not well. In 1978 Cooper admitted himself to a psychiatric hospital for treatment of acute alcoholism. He chronicled the experience of getting sober on the album *From the Inside* (Warner Bros., 1978), which featured the hit "How You Gonna See Me Now?" (# 12 in 1978). In the late '80s he returned to form, capitalizing on the popularity of the heavy metal genre that he had helped to create. The album *Trash* (Epic, 1989) went platinum; the single "Poison" went to # 7 on mainstream pop charts. Cooper was featured prominently in the 1992 film *Wayne's World,* where he made fun of his persona: the big joke in the movie comes when Cooper's headbanging fans discover that their role model is actually a well-mannered, intellectual gentleman who only *pretends* to be a shockmeister when he is on stage (off-stage, he listens to classical music and reads philosophy). Likewise, in 2000–2001 he would deconstruct his bad boy image with a series of humorous television commercials for Residence Inn.

In 1994 Cooper released *The Last Temptation,* a concept album that seems to portray the story of a young man's conversion from satanism to Christianity. The opening song, "Sideshow," portrays a bored young man in search of a thrill. Then, in "Nothing's Free," he makes a deal with a ringmaster who, as it turns out, is the devil. The dark thrills he experiences as a result of this deal are detailed in a few songs that follow, but then in "My Temptation" the boy regrets what he has done and calls out for help: "And so I raise my voice to Heaven / Please hide me in some holy place . . . Mercy, please, I'm on my knees / You're my temptation." He continues this plea for forgiveness in the next song, "Stolen Prayer." But now the devil returns, challenging him in an "Unholy War" for his soul. In "Lullaby," the boy responds in Cooperesque language: "You can take your whiskey soaked, foaming at the mouth, toilet talking, pea soup spewing, sweating blood, demon breath out of my face!" But he need not battle Satan alone. The very next song is sung in the voice of Christ who has come to save him:

"What are you searching for? / I know you can find my door / I know you've sinned every sin / But I'll still take you in" ("It's Me"). And then the album concludes triumphantly with what any objective critic would have to acknowledge to be a Cooper masterpiece, the epic, "Cleansed by Fire." Even on its own— apart from the context of the entire album—this song offers a mini-opera (shades of Queen!) that is a magnificent testimony to a hard-won conversion. As the grand finale to *The Last Temptation* it is all the more revealing. The words, as befits Cooper, are addressed to Satan. One by one, he rejects the devil's offers, responding to claims of relativism with pointed rhetorical questions: "What about dark? What about light? What about wrong? What about right? . . . What about glory? What about Christ? What about love? What about faith in God above?" Finally, the concluding words of the song, and of the album: "It's over, you have no power / You're lost, and I'm found / And I'm heaven bound / Go back to where you belong, to where you fell / Go to hell." Musically, *The Last Temptation* rates among Cooper's best albums, adventurous but true to his typical style (subdued heavy music complemented by eerie vocals and strange sound effects). Although the imagery of telling Satan to "go to hell" was used by **Stryper** long ago and would seem a bit old-hat to Christian metal fans, the irony of presenting Christ as "the last temptation" for one who has tried everything else is novel and profound.

Cooper simply released *The Last Temptation* into the mainstream with no announcement of change in his personal life or views. As such, it was regarded as one more part of the act: Cooper engages the theme of redemption, with metaphorical but not necessarily autobiographical significance. Then, the artist began being spotted around town with such Christian celebrities as **Pat Boone** and **Glen Campbell.** Boone may have inadvertently outed him when defending his new friend against some mean-spirited invective. Cooper, who had never actually tried to hide his conversion anyway, quietly confirmed the rumors. In the early '90s he had returned to church, attending a small Baptist congregation in Phoenix with his wife and kids. They went every Sunday and participated regularly in a Tuesday Bible study. His faith was "deepening with every passing year." Asked if he was now a Christian rock star, Cooper immediately sought to distance himself from any such label, perhaps because he did not feel called to use rock music as a forum for promoting Christianity. He was not, he indicated, "a Christian rock artist like **Petra** or **DC Talk,**" but, he continued, "I am a rock singer, and, yes, I am a Christian." In 1997 he told a *Knight Ridder* reporter, "I'm not on stage preaching. I still do 'School's Out' and 'Eighteen.' I don't see why a Christian can't be a rock 'n' roller and have a really high energy show." He has since acknowledged, however, that a lot of material in his back catalogue has "gotten the axe." He refuses

to sing anything that encourages drinking, drug abuse, or casual sex.

Christian music fans had to wait six years to see whether Cooper's faith would stick. In 2000 he finally released *Brutal Planet,* which, as he had indicated, was *not* a Christian rock album in the mold of **Petra** or **DC Talk.** He does not use his music to proselytize or to promote the Christian faith, but critics quickly noted that the songs are free of debauchery and occult references. A song called "Sanctuary" decries the selfishness and materialism that gets attached to the American dream, and "Eat Some More" exposes the chasm that separates those who are well fed from the hungry poor. The title track describes the earth as a fallen world that was once "a holy garden": "Right here we stoned the prophets, built idols out of mud / Right here we fed the lions Christian flesh and Christian blood / Down here is where we hung him upon an ugly cross / Over here we filled the ovens, right here the holocaust." On a song called "Blow Me a Kiss," he urges his listener to think more deeply about life: "Take one in the eye (think about your soul) / Take one in the mouth (think about your savior)." *Dragontown* followed *Brutal Planet* rather quickly as the second installment in what the artist would term a trilogy. The album continues the exploration of the dark recesses of damned humanity, with specific reference to rock star excesses on "Disgraceland." The record's theme in a nutshell seems to be found in the song "It's Much Too Late": "The road to hell is littered with nice guys with good intentions / But once you're there, you're there / It's much too late."

In March of 2002, *HM* magazine published a lengthy interview with Cooper, in which the artist spoke candidly about his spiritual journey and faith development. "The most important thing that I know is dependence on Christ," he affirmed, while admitting that the previous decade had been a time of spiritual growth. "I think that I became a Christian, initially, more out of the fear of God," he said. "I did not want to go to hell. But when I started, you know, understanding Christianity, that's when I started becoming more in love with Christ. And *that* is an ongoing process. You learn to love him more all the time."

Simon Cooper

1999—*Hymns of the Ancient Fire* (independent).

A pop-jazz artist from the United Kingdom, Simon Cooper fashioned the unique album listed above as an example of what he calls "picture music." He combines the sounds of ambient synthesizers with choral voices (Peter Siedlaczek's Classical Choir, plus a boys' choir, plus a number of classical soprano soloists) to produce musical textures he hopes will evoke certain images and pictures in the mind's eye. A reviewer for *Phantom Tollbooth* saw images of cathedrals and landscapes, but Cooper's intent seems to have been more mythological. The liner notes suggest "gods, wizards, prophets, mythical beasts, fabled creatures, fairies, kings, warriors, and nature spirits." Is this Christian? For Cooper, it is. In the grand tradition of compatriots C. S. Lewis and J. R. R. Tolkien, he imagines such characters populating a story-world in which "God's creative and redemptive power" can be expressed.

The Corbans

Wade Myers, voc., gtr.; Aaron Kellar, bass (−2000); Sean Kellar, drums (−2000) // Tanya Myers (+ 2000). 1997—*Three* (Organic); 2000—*When the Godhead Speaks* (Micah).

Wade Myers founded the Arizona rock trio The Corbans in 1996 after the demise of Chlorine, a punk-rock band that consisted of Meyers and the two Kellars, plus Adam Bafaloukos. Chlorine released one independent album, *Monkeys with Car Keys,* in 1995. The Corbans took their name from a Hebrew word meaning "devoted to God" (though, ironically, the word is used by Jesus only with reference to a policy he denounces—Mark 7:11). Musically the group has a melodic, college rock sound similar to that of such successful mainstream acts as Matchbox 20. The tunes are often catchy, but with a rough edge, exposing glimpses of the Chlorine punk attitude. Notably, The Corbans' songs are often drawn closely from Scripture. "Focused" tells the story of Peter's denial, and "Paul" relates autobiographical reflections of the Apostle. "Numb and Senseless" (one of the best tracks on the debut album) expresses the overwhelming effects of sin. Other songs offer explicit testimonies to faith. "I'm called to serve my God / I'm called to serve my Lord," Myers sings in "Claim," the opening song on *Three.* "Anthem Song" from *When the Godhead Speaks* proclaims, "We stand firm on God's grace / Forever in his presence / With hands raised to the holy one."

Lanny Cordola

1991—*Electric Warrior, Acoustic Saint* (Intense); 1992—*Of Riffs and Symphonies* (ERG); 1998—*Salvation Medicine Show* (KMG).

Legendary guitarist Lanny Cordola has produced three solo albums in addition to his eclectic work with such bands as **Magdalen** (hard rock), **Shack of Peasants** (blues), **Children of Zion** (reggae), **The Panorama Ramblers** (bluegrass), **Chaos is the Poetry** (progressive rock), and **Symbiotica** (world music). A native of Southern California, Cordola earned an early reputation as a shredder (a guitarist who can play very fast), and he worked with numerous mainstream bands in the '80s, including a stage version of Vanilla Fudge and the moderately successful recording groups Giuffria and House of Lords. He played on the latter's first, self-titled album, which was produced by Gene Simmons of Kiss. In 1989, he started going

back to church, influenced by his student and friend **Ken Tamplin** and by the apocalyptic writings of persons like Hal Lindsey, Chuck Missler, and Grant Jeffries. His faith (which he says he had possessed all his life) was invigorated, and he determined to "get God involved in his life again." His first two solo albums came out around the same time as the first Magdallan record *(Big Bang).* Other experiments followed, with the third solo album eventually capping nearly a decade of involvement with Christian music.

Cordola's solo releases are marked by wildly eclectic offerings that demonstrate the full range of what he is able to do with a guitar. *Electric Warrior, Acoustic Saint* features more than twenty original songs and interludes (short selections) alongside some remarkable covers. He offers an extended version of Mozart's "The Marriage of Figaro" that somehow manages to mix elements of classical, heavy metal shred, and country music. Perhaps for the sheer novelty of the performance, it remains Cordola's most popular piece. The mostly instrumental album also includes Cordola's take on Gershwin's "Summertime," for which House of Lords' lead singer Jams Christian provides vocals. Jazz guitarist Joe Diorio joins Cordola for a presentation of the Hammerstein/Kern standard, "All the Things You Are," and the album concludes with a lovely acoustic version of "Amazing Grace." *Of Riffs and Symphonies* tries to cover all territories from hard rock ("The Obstinate Toy Soldier") to flamenco ("YV"), with lots of jazz and funk ("Nan," "Donna Lee"). Most of the pieces, again, are instrumentals, but four feature guest vocalists (**Jon Gibson** sings "Won't Be Long to Paradise"). *Salvation Medicine Show* is mainly acoustic and reveals a fascination with exotic instruments (calliopes, pump organs, bouzouki, ukuleles, toy pianos). A horn section gives the record a bluesy, jazz feel. And Cordola sings—in a grainy voice similar to that of **Eric Clapton** (who also refrained from singing on his first several projects). The song "God's Trombone" draws upon an African metaphor for describing someone who has gone to be with the Lord. "Living in Spin" takes a poke at the Clinton administration. "Confessions" is a country tune and "If I Ever Needed Someone," a **Van Morrison** cover.

Cordola has released other records as well, though they are not always clearly identified as his projects. In addition to side projects with the various groups listed above, he has been integrally connected with the following works: 1) *Blues for the Child* (Frontline, 1993)—an acoustic Christmas album (featuring *some* blues, but more folk and jazz) by an unnamed collection of artists led by Cordola and Gary Thomas Griffin; 2) *Shades of Blue* (Alarma, 1994)—a collection of mostly traditional songs and blues standards by a different unnamed band, led by Cordola and Griffin again, and showcasing Sandra Stephens on vocals; 3) *Jazz Trio—The Trinity Sessions* (Frontline, 1995)—a collection of traditional jazz songs performed by

Cordola on electric guitar, with Tony Guerro on trombone and Joel Hamilton on stand-up bass. As if this isn't enough to fill out the résumé, he has also been the driving force behind independent albums by keyboardist Teddy Andreas and by Pat Torpey, former drummer for Mr. Big. In both cases Cordola cowrote and played on most of their songs, and for Torpey he served also as coproducer. In addition, Cordola has been responsible for the soundtracks to certain feature films, including *Soundman* and *The Last Marshall.* In July of 2000 Cordola joined in a reunion of House of Lords that was to involve both concerts and some recordings.

For trivia buffs: Cordola has also done work in film and TV. He appeared in the 1988 movie *Tap* and made some fifteen appearances as a recurring character on the TV series *Full House.* He is good friends with *Full House* star John Stamos, who is also a musician, and he and Stamos have toured as members of the Beach Boys' backup band.

Cornerstone

Kent Franklin, voc., gtr.; Samuel Gustafsson, bass; Mattias Holm, gtr.; Fredric Käld, drums (−1998) // Mick Nordström, drums (+ 1998). 1993—*Dust* (Viva); 1995—*Flying Gasoline*; 1998—*Jesus Rides Harley Too* (Feedback).

The Swedish rock band Cornerstone bears no official connection to the Christian music festival or magazine that shares their name. Formed in 1989, the band has gone through unidentified personnel changes that may reflect their varying styles. The original group, which did not record, supposedly had a southern rock acoustic sound. The band that made *Dust,* however, had adopted a raw, powerblues sound. The album includes the song "Whiskey and Women," recorded on a cheap tape recorder at four o'clock one morning. *Flying Gasoline* was a much slicker production, featuring a generally heavier sound. By the third record, *Jesus Rides Harley Too,* Cornerstone had adopted a heavy sound that favored raw, unpolished rock. *HM* thought the album sounded a lot like early Kiss. The best track is probably the cover of Blind Willie Johnson's classic, "Jesus Is Coming Soon." Cornerstone has toured throughout Scandinavia and Russia and has played at Britain's *Greenbelt* festival.

Corpse

Sean Embert, bass; Jeff Hoskins, drums; Eric Masse, voc.; Jay Mattingly, gtr. 1998—*From the Grave* (Cling).

The appropriately named band Corpse plays what is known as death metal music, a subgenre of heavy metal that tends to favor guttural growling over high-pitched screaming. According to *The Rolling Stone Encyclopedia of Rock and Roll,* death metal is content-defined, a variation of thrash or speed metal that deals prolifically with the topic of death. Well-known examples in mainstream music might be Megadeath or Slayer,

and in Christian music, **Crimson Thorn** or **Mortification.** Corpse does not really pass the content test. They are classed as "Death Metal" because, as *Phantom Tollbooth* says, "they sound like they have a cadaver for a singer" (*Rad Rockers* says he sounds like "Lurch on 'ludes"), but the lyrics of their songs deal with overtly evangelical themes, such as facing temptation, overcoming doubt, and striving for unity. *HM* picked the song "The Will" as the album's musical standout.

Denny Correll

1979—*Standin' in the Light* (Maranatha!); 1980—*How Will They Know* (Myrrh); 1982—*Something I Believe In*; 1983—*Living Water: The Best of Denny Correll*; 1991—*Trust* (Maranatha).

Jesus music pioneer Denny Correll was an early member of one of the most important Christian rock group of all time—**Love Song.** Like Pete Best (of the Beatles), he toured with the band while they were still playing clubs (indeed, before the members had their definitive "born again" experiences), but he left before they made their first album. His influence lingers only as lyricist for the classic song "Changes." Indeed, by some accounts Correll was the first to witness to **Love Song**'s leader **Chuck Girard** at a time when the two were playing together in bands featured at the Pussy Cat a Go Go in Las Vegas. Correll was with a group called 5th Cavalry, and Girard with Six the Hard Way. One night, on a break, Correll is said to have gathered all the musicians together and told them they needed to find Jesus. His passion and conviction made a strong impression on Girard, who began reading the Bible and looking for God after his return to Los Angeles. Correll was also a member of Manna for a time, and he contributed several songs to **Darrell Mansfield**'s debut *Higher Power* album. He also sang with his brother Tim on *The Misfit* album recorded by **Erick Nelson** and **Michele Pillar** (Nelson called them "the Correll Chorale"). His solo albums feature his soulful, baritone voice on R&B songs with straightforward, evangelical lyrics. *Standin' in the Light* features the song "Living Water," which describes the street preaching of Correll's New Orleans grandfather and the lasting effect it had on him. *How Will They Know?* opens with two radio hits, "New Life in Me" and "He Set Me Free," both of which celebrate the artist's born-again transformation. He would ease up on the blatant testifying just a little for his third album, offering a simple wedding song called "Eternally" and an Eleanor Rigby-type song of empathy for the hungry and hurting people of the world ("Too Many Lonely People"). **Andraé Crouch** and some of his disciples sing background vocals on a few cuts, giving them the feel of hand-clapping traditional gospel.

For trivia buffs: Before **Love Song**, Correll was a member of the Tampa, Florida, quintet Blues Image, who scored a memorable hit with the song "Ride Captain Ride" (# 4 in 1970).

Christian radio hits: "He Set Me Free" (# 15 in 1981); "New Life in Me" (# 9 in 1981); "You Can Depend on Jesus" (# 7 in 1982).

Kim Costanza

1997—*Song of Solomon* (Clydesdale).

Kim Costanza strives, without apology, to be the Christian Kenny G. A mellow jazz saxophonist, he emulates that much-reviled mainstream performer by presenting easy listening, instrumental versions of Christian songs, mixed with appropriate popular songs by mainstream artists. His best-known album, *Song of Solomon* (said to be his fourth recording, though others cannot be found), explores marital sensuality by presenting classics like Jerome Kern's "All the Things You Are" and Lerner and Lowe's "Almost Like Being in Love" alongside **Steven Curtis Chapman**'s "I Will Be There." Two reviewers for *Phantom Tollbooth* split in their evaluations. One exudes, "this is the perfect album to listen to with your spouse, snuggled up in front of the fire on a cold winter night"; another warns, "if your standard for saxophone jazz is Coltrane and Parker, stay away." Compare **Sam Levine.**

Country Faith

Chuck Butler, gtr., voc.; Scott Lockwood, gtr.; Tom Stipe, gtr., voc. No albums.

Though they never recorded an album, Country Faith left an impressive legacy of songs that testify to their position as one of the pioneer Jesus music groups operating out of Calvary Chapel in Costa Mesa, California. The band is usually considered to be the first Christian country rock band, paving the way for **Bethlehem, Daniel Amos,** and **The Way**—but that honor should properly go to **Joy,** the band from which Country Faith sprang. **Joy** consisted of Scott Lockwood and Dave Burgin, who were playing their Christian pop songs up and down the West Coast even before there was a **Children of the Day** or **Love Song.** Eventually Burgin would form **Blessed Hope** with Dave Rios, and Lockwood would join with Chuck Butler and **Tom Stipe** to form Country Faith. Butler and Stipe were both significant figures in the Calvary Chapel music scene. Chuck Butler cowrote (with **Tommy Coomes**) the song "Two Hands," which for a time seemed to become the official theme song of the Jesus movement. Influential versions were recorded by both **Love Song** and **Children of the Day.** Stipe cowrote (also with Coomes) "The Cossack Song," which was also recorded by **Love Song.** In 1971 Country Faith (with **John Mehler** on drums) traveled to England to play before 80,000 people at the Festival of Light in Hyde Park and Trafalgar Square. Butler has been singled out as an especially good vocalist among the early Jesus music stars, who sometimes admittedly scored more points for their piety and sincerity that

for their musical excellence. Along with **Bob Carlisle, Denny Correll,** and **Bryan Duncan,** Butler is often mentioned as one of the early male vocalists who (piety aside) really was a very good singer.

Country Faith supposedly recorded a single featuring a song called "Stagecoach" for a general market label (possibly Capitol). Three other Country Faith songs made it to vinyl on the important Maranatha compilation discs. "Two Roads" is featured on *The Everlastin' Living Jesus Music Concert* (Maranatha, 1971)—often called *Maranatha One* for short. At 5:40 it is the longest of the ten tracks on that album and the closest thing to an epic among the otherwise simple camp songs and worship tunes. Written by Butler and Stipe, the song features an extended instrumental break and pre-Eagles harmonies on a chorus that, save for the date, would have gotten the band accused of copping the latter So-Cal group's sound. The lyrics are inspired by Jesus' words in Matthew 7:13–14, with just a touch of Robert Frost (cf. **Larry Norman**'s "One Way"), but they make an exegetical mistake that may or may not be revealing of the Jesus movement's more naive optimistic tendencies. "Two roads from which to choose," the song proclaims, "the rocky one or the Lord's new freeway / Choose before the Savior comes / The road to glory or the rocky one." The strong implication is that the way to salvation is easy and wide (a freeway), while the road to destruction is rocky and hard. This of course is the opposite of what Jesus says—and for that matter, the opposite of Frost's preference for "the road less travelled" as well.

Country Faith also placed two songs on *Maranatha Two* (Maranatha, 1972): the eschatological prayer, "Come, Quickly, Jesus," written by Stipe, and the challenging "Ballad of the Lukewarm," written by Butler. The first of these is a theologically sound song about the parousia—a rarity for Jesus music. It expresses a simple, heartfelt yearning for the Lord's return, combined with a realization that delay allows more time for others to find salvation. The "Ballad of the Lukewarm" is a little two-minute ditty that offers a typical Jesus people indictment of institutional religion, delivered with characteristic humor. The singer assumes the perspective of a middle-class American W.A.S.P. who claims to be a good family man and a fine upstanding citizen; he can't understand why his name isn't "written in the book of life." **Tom Stipe** would go on to record a wonderful solo song for *Maranatha Three: Rejoice in the Lord* (Maranatha, 1973) called "Big City Blues" and eighteen years later would issue one of the finest country albums ever recorded by any Christian artist. In between those efforts, he formed **Wing and a Prayer** with former Love Song members, **John Mehler** and Jay Truax; that group morphed into The **Richie Furay** Band when the big-name alum of Buffalo Springfield and Poco decided to join. Chuck Butler placed a throwaway song ("Nursery Rhyme") on the *Maranatha Three* album and performed the more worthy "Pearly Mansions" on *Maranatha Four* (Maranatha, 1974). His greatest contributions would be made later as a member of the band **Parable.** Some decades later, his son Chad Butler would become drummer for **Switchfoot.**

John Cox

1996—*Sunny Day* (Questar Mission); 2000—*80 Years* (independent).

www.coxrox.com

John Cox is a rock singer/songwriter/guitarist from Chico, Texas. After trying Memphis and Dallas, he moved to Nashville in 1991 and five years later released a critically acclaimed album on a minor label. Cox describes his music as acoustic hard rock. He establishes a heavy rhythm with acoustic guitar, bass, and drums, allowing the electric guitar to wander around over the top, adding flourishes here and there rather than just pounding out power chords. Most notable, though, is Cox's singing: soul-piercing, raw-edged vocals very similar to those of Robert Plant. In fact the Plant comparisons seemed so obvious that Cox's producer David Kerschenbaum (known for work with Tracy Chapman and Bryan Adams) actually tuned all the songs on *Sunny Day* a half-step lower than he had written them to make the singer sound a tad *less* like Led Zeppelin's famous wailer. The title track, indeed, is a charged-up rocker that recalls *Houses of the Holy,* but many of the songs seem more of the sort that John Mellencamp or Bruce Springsteen would record. Lyrically Cox focuses squarely on spiritual themes, explicitly detailing his devotion to Christ while avoiding the usual clichés of much Christian music. "Please don't look at me like I know all there is to know," he sings in "I Don't Know." The song "Hand I Hold" is a contemplative piece inspired by Psalm 8. "Tell Me," one of the only ballads, reflects on the endurance of Christ ("Jesus, tell me how you stood to wear the crown").

Cox has been singled out as a Christian artist with crossover appeal, one whose musical abilities could potentially attract a mainstream audience. His spiritual priorities, however, are such as to afford little interest in pursuing such success. "I'm afraid if I was opening for some major band," he says, "I'd have to stop in the middle of the concert and tell the audience, 'You don't need great music, you need a great Savior.' " His second album, *80 Years,* was at least initially made available only through his website. Top critic-pick songs include "Where I'm Going" and "Stone," which both celebrate the joy of salvation. "Live My Life" and "Perfect Part" are buoyant songs of worship.

Christian radio hits: "Sunny Day" (# 9 in 1997); "Tell Me" (# 18 in 1997).

Kemper Crabb

1982—*The Vigil* (StarSong); 1996—*A Medieval Christmas* (independent); *Live at Rivendell Café*; 2000—*Live at Cornerstone 2000* (M8); *Flotsam and Jetsam.*

www.kempercrabb.com

Raised in San Antonio as the son of two college professors, Kemper Crabb is a pioneer of contemporary Christian music who has never quite fit into any of the molds created by the Christian music industry. In addition to his contributions as a solo artist, he has been a member of the Christian rock bands **Redemption, ArkAngel, Caedmon's Call,** and **Atomic Opera.** An intellectual with an avid interest in science fiction and fantasy, Crabb is also an ordained Episcopalian priest. After serving for years with the Reformed Episcopal church, he switched denominational allegiance in the late '90s to the Communion of Evangelical Episcopal Churches. Both groups are small offshoots of Anglicanism that confess the Thirty-nine Articles, while combining Episcopalian liturgical and sacramental traditions with elements of evangelical and Reformed theology (especially as evidenced in America). All this is significant because Crabb often engages in theological disputation to a degree uncharacteristic of most contemporary Christian music artists. Still, Crabb allows that he is "not much into denominationalism," and he demonstrates his ability to transcend sectarian issues by writing a regular column for *HM* magazine called "The Christian and the Arts."

Raised Baptist, Crabb read the works of J. R. R. Tolkien while in the third grade and became fascinated with the imagery of the symbolic world created there. As a Christian teenager, he followed this fascination toward the symbolic world of liturgy. Reading avidly in the writings of the church fathers, he was drawn increasingly into the realm of medieval Christianity. At the same time he was developing his musical gifts, inspired by such early Jesus music stars as **Larry Norman** and **Love Song,** and especially the local San Antonio band **Hope of Glory.** Fueled by his fascination with all things medieval, he learned to play not only guitar but mountain dulcimer and other exotic instruments from the Middle Ages. The resulting music he made with **ArkAngel** was more innovative than anything that had been produced within the contemporary Christian music subculture. Indeed, the music was too out there for most Christian music fans, and **ArkAngel** garnered a bigger following in the general market than in the church.

In 1982 Crabb produced a solo album that is regarded as one of the great classics of contemporary Christian music. *The Vigil* is described by Crabb himself as a record of medieval music. It is at any rate a wholly original work of art. In recent years, Renaissance Fairs and the like have popularized the sounds that Crabb evokes on this record, but at the time it was recorded, there was simply nothing like it in Christian or secular markets. A concept piece, it incorporates three traditional hymns (including "Fairest Lord Jesus") and several of Crabb's own songs into a composition of progressive, classical (not classic) rock. A wide variety of acoustic instruments (mandolin, recorder, dulcimer, bagpipe, harp) are employed to supplement Crabb's sterling vocals on songs that recreate that symbolic world of knights and meadows and maidens fair. Lyrically, however, the focus is unabashedly spiritual, as Crabb uses the metaphor of a knight's unfailing allegiance to his king to speak of Christian devotion to the King Eternal. The album was criticized by some for glorifying the Crusades, which are assumed to have been a travesty born out of Christian greed. Crabb responds that, historically, "if it hadn't been for the Crusades, we'd all be Muslims now." At any rate the album is explicitly metaphorical, likening the vigil through which a knight prepared himself for combat or pilgrimage to the spiritual disciplines through which modern Christians might prepare themselves to do God's work in the world. Standout cuts include "The Danse" (covered by **Caedmon's Call** in 2001), "Thigpin's Wedding," and two versions (spoken and sung) of the title track. "They That Go Down to the Sea in Ships" is a Scripture chorus derived from Psalm 107:23–32.

In the years since *The Vigil,* Crabb has devoted himself to pastoring Christ Church in the Houston area. It is a congregation where, he estimates, eighty-five percent of the membership are musicians or artists. Divorced from his wife Bekah (a founding member of **ArkAngel**) in 1994, he took a leave of absence, went to school, and pursued what he calls "an almost monastic existence." Rejuvenated but still not comfortable as a front man, he returned to the music scene as a barely noticed member of **Caedmon's Call** for six months, playing his medieval instruments in a band that built its sound around a style he himself had pioneered a generation earlier. Then he joined **Atomic Opera,** fronted by one of his parishioners, Frank Hart. Along the way he released two more albums of medieval music. His Christmas album is a live disc, featuring exotic versions of traditional hymns (including an eleven-minute version of "God Rest Ye Merry Gentlemen"!) alongside lesser-known troubadour songs and a remake of *The Vigil's* "Doulos." The latter song relates an allegorical ballad of a slave who is given his freedom and then, as one who can no longer be bought or sold, pledges to continue serving his master voluntarily.

In 2000 Crabb appeared at the *Cornerstone* festival and also released a collection he called *Flotsam and Jetsam: Demos from the Nether Years.* The latter project presents rough takes on ten songs he had written and recorded at different points in the preceding two decades. Musically it offers a retro-tour of pre-'90s pop. "The Circle Is Closed" sounds like a long-lost '60s hit, like something The Zombies might have done. "Shattered Mirrors" has a more driving, '70s sound (think Golden Earring).

"The Heart Is a Rebel" is a country-pop romp that brings to mind some of those Crosby, Stills and Nash copy groups (like Firefall). It's possible Crabb had been listening to Kool and the Gang when he did "Passion Play," though the whompa-whompa beat and wo-oh choruses do get interrupted by some wailing electric guitar. Crabb also offers a slightly disco-fied cover of The Yardbirds' "For Your Love" and a reverent rendition of Danny Kaye's "Inchworm." Crabb has also recorded with **Radiohalo.**

For trivia buffs: Crabb's father, Kemper Crabb Sr. was once nominated for the Nobel Peace Prize for his work as a missionary in Nepal.

Cradle/Grave

Matt Aitchison; Warren Wheeler. 2000—*Saper Verdere* (Heartland).

The Australian duo Cradle/Grave (pronounced "Cradle to Grave") formed in 1996 and after several contributions to compilation albums, produced a full-length CD of ambient music that incorporates trip-hop beats uncharacteristic for that genre. The atmospheric music is generally dark and ominous, though this is broken occasionally by hauntingly beautiful piano passages. Mostly instrumental, the group does deliver some poetic lyrics, which are almost whispered over the music in a manner reminiscent of **Starflyer 59.** *True Tunes* praises the album as "a quality debut on all levels." *Cornerstone* calls it "a *must* for fans of dark, ambient electronic music." The song "Those Cold Nails," they say, "comes across like Peter Gabriel fronting Portishead."

Craig's Brother

Todd Bond, voc.; Scott Hrapoff, bass; Heath Konkel, drums; Adam Nigh, gtr., voc.; Andy Snyder, gtr., voc. 1998—*Homecoming* (Tooth and Nail); 2001—*Lost at Sea.*

www.craigsbrother.net

The Southern California combo Craig's Brother bowled over critics with a debut album that established them as a prominent punk band. *Bandoppler* said, "With words that cut like knives and songs that drive like stock cars, this band truly stands out and should be noticed." Classed primarily as hardcore punk, the group didn't quite fit that label. *The Lighthouse* noted that the "discriminating ear" will detect in their sound a "compelling strain of influences as diverse as the Beatles, Boston, and Metallica." The first of these is evident in the teenager-friendly melodic structure that many of their songs bear; the second in their fondness for employing three-party harmonies and double-guitar power chord onslaughts; the third (less often) in the heavily inflected riffs that shatter listeners out of the doldrums now and then. The group was formed by Andy Snyder in Santa Cruz in 1995, out of the ashes of a previous (heavy metal) band called Liquid Amber. They issued two EPs, *Craig's Brother* and *Keepin' It Real,* prior to the first full-length album.

Lyrically the songwriters in Craig's Brother have sought to express their Christian convictions with unflinching commitment to honesty and with an existentialist devotion to issues of life in the real world. Religious clichés and—for the most part—references to anything overtly spiritual are lacking. On "In Memory," Adam Nigh writes about the loss of a friend who died. "Lonely Girl" is Todd Bond's tribute to his mother, who raised him without a father. In "Going Blind," Bond deals with the usually taboo topic of masturbation, and of male lust in general. "One" (not a Three Dog Night cover) is about getting over a former relationship. Other highlights from *Homecoming* include "Nobody" (also not a Three Dog Night cover) and "Insult to Injury." The second album reveals a greater social consciousness. According to Bond, the "whole point" of the song "Prince of America" is that "the most powerful people in the world are Americans, yet we have no clue and we're completely apathetic." The song "Glory" deals with the United States' penchant for military interventions, with specific reference to events in Kosovo.

Bond has strong feelings about the Christian music industry's attempt to create a distinct subculture that is essentially a Christianized replicate of the secular world. "We've become 'of the world but not in the world,' " he said to *Bandoppler,* "and replaced Christ's command to 'Go into all the world' with an attempt to make the world come to us . . . we'll teach and spread the gospel, but only to those willing to join our culture." Bond further notes that Hrapoff (the group's bass player) is not a Christian and that his presence in the group keeps them all cognizant of how their lives are constantly perceived by those outside the church. Indeed, Bond insists that he does not want Craig's Brother to be known as a Christian band because "we don't want to be a part of the Christian culture." The mission of the group is simply "to make the best music we can possibly make" rather than "trying to be the Christian version of anything."

Crashdog

Brian Grover, bass; Andrew Mandell, voc., gtr.; Greg Jacques, drums (–1994); Spike Nard, voc. (–1995) // Greg Murphy, drums (+ 1994); Jason Burt, gtr. (+ 1995); Mike Perlmutter, gtr. (+ 1997). 1990—*Hard Knocks for Hard Heads* (Grrr); *Humane Society;* 1992—*Pursuit of Happiness;* 1994—*Mudangels;* 1995—*Cashists, Fascists, and Other Fungus;* 1997—*Outer Crust;* 1998—*90–97: 8 Years to Nowhere.*

www.grrrrecords.com

Crashdog was a hardcore Christian punk band with a strong political orientation. They were associated with Jesus People U.S.A., the socially conscious Christian community in Chicago that has also spawned such artists as **Resurrection Band** and **The Crossing** (as well as **Cauzin' Efekt, Seeds, Sheesh,** and **Unwed Sailor**). The group was founded by Spike Nard (née Tim Davis), a self-described runaway from Boulder, Colorado, who left home at fifteen and came to JPUSA for the free food. Transformed by the gospel, he started Crashdog as a vehicle for ministry within the inner city. After Nard's departure, Andrew Mandell took over as front man and lead singer. Musically Crashdog's sound is likened to general market bands like AC/DC, Dead Kennedys, or the Sex Pistols, or to lesser-known Christian groups like **One Bad Pig.** In the late '90s the group either broke up, went on an extended hiatus, or some would say morphed into **Ballydowse.** The name "Crashdog" has no hidden meaning; the band just thought it "described their sound" (the name "Spike Nard," on the other hand, comes from John 12:3 KJV).

HM magazine got Crashdog right with the following description of their music: "song after song of pounding speed-of-light rhythms, smash and burn guitar chords, and shouted vocals that spit out words in machine gun fashion dealing with not only an overt evangelistic message, but also social and political themes." The latter aspect allows the group to draw equally from the angry legacies of modern punkers and ancient prophets. Crashdog discerned their role as often being that of exposing sin, in the government and in the church. Such sentiments took them outside the mainstream of contemporary Christian music, which usually either ignores political issues altogether, covers them with a veneer of spirituality, or addresses them in terms that are defined by and inoffensive to the religious right. After **Barry McGuire** became a Christian in the early days of the Jesus movement, he would continue to sing his big secular hit "Eve of Destruction" only as a medley with a new song, "Don't Blame God." Crashdog covered the provocative political anthem on its *Cashists* album with no religious strings attached, leaving their audiences to wonder why a purely political protest song that didn't say anything about God would be on a *Christian* album. That same album, furthermore, opened by throwing these words in the face of the whole Moral Majority/Liberty Foundation/Christian Coalition alliance: "Vote Vote Vote the underclass / Kindly, gently down the drain / Christians and Republicans—Are these both the same?" ("G.O.P."). The significance of a contemporary Christian music group recording such a song must not be missed—since at the time the influence of the Religious Right was powerful enough to consign any Christian group that challenged them to the underground. Crashdog reveled in that consignment. Very much an underground band, they repudiated the notion of mainstream acceptance.

Cashists may have been Crashdog's best album, but every record they made was worthwhile, and several were stellar.

The earlier *Humane Society* opens with "Progress," a tongue-in-cheek number about how human progress consists of developing more effective means of destruction. Also on the album is "Bloodlane" (written by **Glenn Kaiser**), which adds Scottish bagpipes to the aural mix in a manner that prefigures **Ballydowse** by almost a decade. *Mudangels* was a major step forward musically, showing the group more relaxed, yet with a fuller, more unified sound. The song "Question Stupidity" from that album is a Crashdog classic. "Ichtheology" displays no particular religious or social agenda but is just a song about fishing—not metaphorically fishing for souls, but literally fishing for fish (Nard's favorite pastime—nice to know he isn't angry all the time). In addition to the songs named above, *Cashists, Fascists, and Other Fungus* includes "My God," a rant against Christian justifications for male domination of women and homophobia. *Outer Crust* was a do-it-yourself project in which the band tried to recapture a truly authentic garage punk sound, with songs addressing abortion, racial violence, and materialism. *90–97: 8 Years to Nowhere* is a retrospective with greatest (non)hits and live tracks.

Beverly "Bam" Crawford (and Bam Crawford's Purpose)

Selected: As Beverly Crawford: 1995—*Jesus, Precious King* (Warner Alliance); 1998—*Now That I'm Here.* As Bam Crawford's Purpose: 1997—*King Is Coming Any Day* (Harmony).

www.bamcrawfordministries.org

Dr. Beverly "Bam" Crawford is the pastor and founder of the Bible Enrichment Fellowship International Church in Inglewood, California. In her twenty-plus years of ministry there she has released numerous books and teaching tapes on a variety of subjects and has also recorded numerous albums of traditional gospel music. In 1997 she recorded a live worship album with her church choir, which goes by the name of "Purpose." Musically the album leans toward the contemporary gospel sounds of **Kirk Franklin**'s work with **God's Property**, though Crawford's group is less urban and probably less youth-oriented in its appeal. Notably, Sheila E., who is a member of Crawford's church, is a featured vocalist and percussionist on the project. Well-known worship leader **Ron Kenoly** sings lead vocals on two songs, including the title track. Abe Laboriel of the jazz groups **Koinonia** and Weather Report plays bass. The album strives to capture the spontaneity of Spirit-led worship. "During worship, songs are birthed," says Pastor Bam. Songs such as "Because of Jesus" and "It's All in the Worship" were in fact given by the Lord on the spot, she maintains, with the words coming first, then a line of melody, and the choir just improvising from there.

Michael Crawford

1998—*On Eagle's Wings* (Atlantic); 1999—*A Christmas Album.*

London-born Michael Crawford became an international star in the '90s as a result of his title role in the New York, Los Angeles, and London productions of Andrew Lloyd Webber's *The Phantom of the Opera*. Crawford's performance won him an American Tony Award and his second British Olivier Award (which he had won previously for his role in *Barnum*). The *Phantom* soundtrack album featuring his vocals sold more than twelve million copies. Since *Phantom*, Crawford has toured internationally, starred in the Las Vegas extravaganza *EFX*, and performed in a televised PBS special, *Michael Crawford in Concert*. A committed Christian, Crawford has recorded two albums of sacred songs, a traditional Christmas record and the inspirational *On Eagle's Wings*. The latter record mixes hymns ("Spirit of the Living God," "Ave Maria") with modern songs such as "Not Too Far from Here" (previously recorded by **Kim Boyce**). All are done in the bravura style of Broadway musicals, complete with horns, strings, and an occasional choir. The highlight of the album is probably Crawford's duet with **Máire Brennan** on "Amazing Grace," which is given a creative Celtic arrangement.

For trivia buffs: Crawford may seem to have come out of nowhere to become famous for his *Phantom* stint, but he has actually been around a while. It is possible to find him in numerous old movies. Most notable: as Cornelius Hackl in *Hello Dolly* (1969). Most fun: alongside John Lennon in *How I Won the War* (1967).

Creed

Scott Phillips, drums; Scott Stapp, voc.; Mark Tremonti, gtr.; Brian Marshall, bass (−2001) // Brett Hestla, bass (+ 2001). 1997—*My Own Prison* (Wind-up); 1999—*Human Clay*; 2001—*Weathered.*

www.creed.com

Creed insists rather defiantly that they are *not* a Christian rock band and, though this denial must be allowed to stand, it is hardly the end of the matter. The meaning of art never has been and never will be determined by assertions of the artist but always has been and always will be determined by perceptions of the audience. Furthermore, the denial seems based on a semantic that very few fans of Christian music would accept. Leader Scott Stapp says, at the group's website, "We are not a Christian band. A Christian band has an agenda to lead others to believe in their specific religious beliefs. We have no such agenda." But half the artists in this encyclopedia would probably not qualify to be called "Christian artists" if specific evangelistic or ministry intent was made the identifying criterion. Still, many of those groups openly admit that the band members are individually Christian, giving rise to the overworked and somewhat nonsensical cliché, "We are not a Christian band, but we are a band of Christians."

The issue is muddied for Creed by theological distinctions. At the band's website, Stapp responds to the question, "Are the members of Creed Christians?" by saying, "This is a very personal question, because the whole foundation of being a Christian is a personal relationship. I can say that all members believe in God, but we each differ on our methods to reach him. We are all still learning and growing and God can only answer this question because who are we to say that being a Christian is the only way to heaven." Of course, most nonfundamentalist, biblically literate Christians would agree that the mysteries of salvation cannot be narrowly defined. Still, Stapp—who perhaps still thinks of Christianity primarily in terms of the fundamentalism in which he was raised—seems intent on not misleading people by accepting a label that might imply things about him (or others in the group) that he is not sure hold. Still, in some instances Stapp has indicated unequivocally that he and the other members of Creed are Christians. In an interview with *Spin* in July 2000, he said that even though all the members of the group are believers, they do not want to be considered a Christian band because they want to create music for everyone. But again one would be hard pressed to find *any* artists who think that being a Christian band means creating music only for Christians. So let us say this: Creed does not *intend* to present itself as a Christian rock band. But then neither Jonathan Swift *(Gulliver's Travels)* nor Mark Twain *(Tom Sawyer)* ever intended to be authors of children's books. The fact is, Creed is a band composed of self-acknowledged Christians, and many fans of Christian music have found Creed's songs to be meaningful *as Christian songs.*

Creed was formed in Tallahassee, Florida, by Scott Stapp and Mark Tremonti. Stapp, the lead singer and—more important—songwriter, was raised in a strict and restrictive religious household. His father was a Pentecostal preacher who condemned all rock music as the work of the devil. After a brief stint at a fundamentalist Bible college, and strongly influenced by **U2**'s *The Joshua Tree* to see a spirituality in rock that his father had missed, Stapp became enamored of rock and roll. He was particularly infatuated with The Doors, whose influence can clearly be heard in Creed's music—especially in Stapp's vocal stylings. Other major influences and favorite bands (according to the website) are Led Zeppelin and—notably!—**King's X.** Stapp began keeping a journal in which he scribbled often rebellious thoughts about discovering freedom from his oppressive upbringing. A poem from that journal would become the title song to Creed's debut album: "I hear a thunder in the distance / See a vision of the cross / I feel the pain that was given / On that sad day of loss / A lion roars in the darkness / Only he holds the key / A light to free me from my bur-

den / And grant me life eternally." How can such words be heard as anything *other* than Christian? Ah, here is the great irony between internal and external understandings of evangelical Christianity in America. Most evangelical Christians view Christianity as a spiritual connection with God that frees them from the confining strictures of religion. Very few people outside the fold view it that way; more often, outsiders identify Christianity with the confining strictures of religion—Christianity is itself a religion, not a force that liberates from religion. Thus many Creed fans may identify *Christianity* as the burden from which Stapp had to be freed, as the prison from which he had to be released. But most fans of Christian music—many of whom have had experiences similar to Stapp's—read his trek as a (generic) discovery of what *real* Christianity (i.e., relational faith as opposed to just ritual religion) has to offer.

In any case, *My Own Prison* went quadruple platinum and became the best-selling hard rock debut album of all time. *Billboard* magazine named Creed the 1998 Rock Artist of the Year. The title track was not by a long shot the only song with strong spiritual themes. In "Unforgiven," Stapp sings, "Think I'm unforgiven / Step inside the light / And see the fear of God burn inside of me." Then he concludes "What This Life's For" with a lyric that seems both to blaspheme and exalt the Lord in a single breath: "Don't have to settle no goddam score / Cause we all live / Under the reign of one king." Creed's even-more successful sophomore album, *Human Clay,* continues to draw upon religious imagery and biblical allusions to present uplifting spiritual messages. In the album's runaway hit single, "Higher" (# 7 in 1999), Stapp sings, "Can you take me higher / To the place where blind men see? / Can you take me higher / To the place with golden streets?" On "Faceless Man" he describes an encounter in his mind with a spiritual force: "His yoke is easy and His burden is light / He looked me right in the eyes / Direct and concise to remind me / To always do what's right." A verse later he concludes with a decision of what he will do the next time they meet: "I'll say, I choose to live for always / So won't you come inside / And never go away." Who or what is this faceless man with whom he believes a personal relationship will bring him eternal life? The song itself never says, but the official Creed website identifies the spiritual force Stapp has encountered as "Conscience." The group's biggest song to date, "With Arms Wide Open" (# 1 in 2000), is a prayer of thanksgiving and devotion offered in recognition of impending parenthood. It won the 2000 Grammy Award for "Song of the Year." *Human Clay* sold well over six million copies, making it the best-selling hard rock album of all time. The group was (again) named Rock Artist of the Year by *Billboard* in 2000.

Possibly anxious about alienating the band's large fanbase among Christians, Stapp sought to prepare them for the group's *Weathered* album by stating (on the website and elsewhere) that the third project would not be as oriented toward spiritual matters as the first two. The religious lyrics, he explained, reflected "a time in my life when I was questioning how I was raised, and searching for where I stood . . . which is not to say I have abandoned those beliefs, but am just searching for where they fit into my life. Please do not limit this band to only dealing with spiritual issues. . . this band is not centrally focused around spiritual issues, so understand that not all of our songs in the future will deal with the same things." All the disclaimers turned out to be unnecessary, as *Weathered* again features songs that utilize Christian imagery and deal with theological concerns at least as deliberately as those of many self-identified Christian groups (e.g., **The Choir, Daniel Amos, Jars of Clay,** the **Seventy Sevens**). The first single from the album, "My Sacrifice," speaks of recovering faith and inner confidence that makes people feel like they can fly above all the ups and downs of life. The song was overtly touted as inspirational by all media outlets, who noted the special appropriateness of its message in the aftermath of the September 11 terrorist attacks on America (in spite of the uncanny relevance of lines like "how quickly life can turn around in an instant," the song was written prior to the assault). Similarly the album offers a biblical allusion to the fallen condition of humanity on "Who's Got My Back?": "The covenant has been broken by mankind." There are also references to prayer in the midst of doubt on "Don't Stop Dancing" and to the hope God offers in "One Last Breath": "Somewhere in His grace / I cried out to heaven to save me / But I'm down to one last breath." The latter song appears to be about turning back from suicide. "Freedom Fighter" might easily have been a **Petra** song, with its multiple Bible quotes and evangelistic commitment to proclaiming the truth to people whether they like it or not. Better is "Stand Here with Me," a song of appreciation to someone who Stapp says has reached out to him, helped him to believe, and shown him the right way to live. Musically *Weathered* is heavy and intense, staying true to the band's hard rock roots.

Even though Stapp does not want Creed to be known as a Christian band, he is sometimes solicitous and appreciative of those Christian music fans who continue to regard the band as such. In one note posted at the band's website, he all but apologizes to the group's Christian fans for using the word "goddam" in the song "What This Life's For," explaining, "there was never an intention of cursing God . . . it was strictly an emotional response to a tragic situation of losing two friends to suicide . . . it is a cry to the lost, put in a way that they could understand. . . . I know some of you live by the words of never taking the Lord's name in vain . . . some of you will never agree with my use of that word . . . I respect your convictions. I guess this is between God and me." Again, with reference to his ear-

lier comment that "being a Christian" might not be the "only way to heaven," he adds an empathetic footnote: "I know this might be hard to understand for all the Christians who follow the band—and trust me, I know where you are coming from—but let us continue to seek and we will find; if we continue to knock, the doors will be opened."

What do the critics say? Both *Rolling Stone* and *Spin* have suspected Creed of being some sneaky religious gospel group, and have accused them, as such, of employing rhetoric-filled lyrics that disguise (and thus ironically neuter) their affirmations of faith. *Bandoppler* minces no words in responding to such speculation: "Pure dribble, written by prejudicial bigots and ignorant posers, vying for self-glorification through their 'keen sleuth work,' throwing stones at windows they will not even try to look through themselves." On the other hand, self-appointed watchdogs of orthodoxy in the Christian media have attacked the group from another side. The usually perceptive *Christianity Today* maintains that evangelicals (by which they mean what I would call fundamentalists) are troubled by the fact that Creed has allowed their songs to be used on the soundtracks to horror films like *Halloween H20* and *Scream 3*. The often less-perceptive *Campus Life* dismisses the band, maintaining that Stapp's suggestion that "being a Christian" might not be the only way to heaven contradicts John 14:6 (it doesn't). Both publications were bothered by the fact that Stapp told *Spin* magazine his song "Higher" was inspired not only by the Christian Bible but also by some writings of Hindu monks that he had absorbed. *Phantom Tollbooth* hears Creed's music as "an honest exploration by one who knows God but still wrestles with him, like Jacob," and adds that "anyone who can't understand Stapp's struggles in the lyrics is just a little too close to the Pharisees." *Bandoppler* sums up the group's potential for Christian music fans this way: "Not for the narrow-minded or hard of heart, the music of Creed remains music that really can take you higher."

The group Creed discussed here has no connection to the overtly Christian band named Creed that released one album, *The Sign of Victory,* on both Pure Metal and StarSong in 1990.

Crimson Bridge

Steve Hornyack, drums; Gary Rand; et al. 1972—*Crimson Bridge* (Myrrh).

The liner notes for this band's sole album describe their music as having a "rock-jazz-Latin-progressive-blues-acid-folk sound." A simpler description would be, "the Christian equivalent of Blood, Sweat, and Tears." The lead singer has his David Clayton-Thomas impression down pat, and the jazz orchestrations of the horn-based songs summon immediate images of that band's distinctive arrangements. Aside from the imitative element, Crimson Bridge performs their music well, and the album is unusually progressive for what was generally being produced in the Christian music scene in 1972. One entire side is given to an ambitious number, "Suite in Three Parts." The latter is composed by **Gary Rand,** who would go on to record socially conscious solo albums and become known as a composer of worship choruses in the '80s. A *Time* magazine article on the Jesus movement (September 24, 1973) treated Crimson Bridge member Steve Hornyack as typical of the radical religious revival sweeping the nation. Hornyack is said to have "given up a $35,000 house, a Tornado (a car), and a career as a school band director when another Jesus musician challenged him to *go tell about Jesus.*" The group's album was not commercially successful, perhaps in part due to its hokey cover design and in part to the fact that Blood, Sweat, and Tears had peaked three years before and were no longer on the charts. Crimson Bridge had chosen to clone the sound of has-beens.

Crimson Thorn

Luke Renno, voc., bass; Kevin Sundberg, drums; Miles Sunde, gtr.; Paul Jongeward, gtr. (−1994) // Andy Kopesky, gtr. (+ 1997). 1993—*Plagued* (custom); 1994—*Unearthed* (Atomic); 1997—*Dissection* (Morphine).

Crimson Thorn is an unabashed Christian death metal or grindcore band from Minneapolis, Minnesota, with a musical style along the same lines as **Living Sacrifice.** The group released an early demo *(Plagued)* before losing their guitarist. They recorded their first major release *(Unearthed)* as a trio, then expanded to a quartet again for *Dissection.* As a genre, death metal arose from thrash metal, a blending of heavy metal and punk best exemplified by the fast *and* heavy sound of early Metallica (e.g., 1983's *Kill 'Em All*). *The Rolling Stone Encyclopedia of Rock and Roll* defines "death metal" as "thrash metal that incorporates graphic images of death and destruction in its lyrics" and defines "grindcore" as "death metal with industrial rhythms." With song titles like "Unearthed," "Your Carcass," "Asphyxiated," and "Comatose," Crimson Thorn certainly passes the content test for the former definition, and if critical descriptions of their sound are accepted, they probably qualify for the latter description as well. Notably, Crimson Thorn has not been fully comfortable with the labels death metal and grindcore because of connotations those terms carry. They prefer to identify their music as "gruntcore," which Miles Sunde then defines as "very brutal and very technical, but at the same time really fast and hard hitting." Not an acoustic guitar in sight.

The difference between Crimson Thorn and artists like Megadeath or Slayer is the use to which all those graphic images of death and destruction are put. Sunde describes the title track to *Unearthed* as a "kind of symbolic, coming-out-of-the-ground, coming-alive-to-Christ, dead-to-self kind of thing." The song "Your Carcass" is about the battle between flesh and

spirit. On songs like "Imminent Wrath," Crimson Thorn also likes to growl about judgment and the condemnation that awaits those who reject or ignore Christ. "Comatose" implies that those who do not know Christ are not truly alive (cf. 1 John 5:12). On "Malignant Masters," the group turns its ire toward liberal academics, or "self-appointed wise men" who are "infesting colleges and schools" though they are really "only fools." *Unearthed* was re-released with different artwork in 1995 by R.E.X. and again in 1997 by Morphine in an edition that includes bonus tracks from *Plagued*. The album *Dissection* did not attract much attention but is hailed by *Rad Rockers* as "the supreme perfection of Christian death metal." The group covers **Stryper**'s "Loud 'N' Clear" alongside the evangelical "Eternal Life" and obviously biblical "2nd Timothy 3."

Billy Crockett

1985—*Carrier* (Word); 1986—*Surprises in Disguises;* 1988—*Portraits;* 1989—*The Basic Stuff* (Urgent); 1991—*Any Starlight Night;* 1995—*Red Bird Blue Sky* (Walking Angel); 1997—*In These Days: Live;* 1998—*Watermarks;* 1999—*Simple Plans.*

www.walking-angel.com

Billy Crockett is a singer/songwriter from Dallas who founded his own label (Walking Angel Records) in that city in 1995. He holds a music degree from the University of Miami and has appeared on albums by numerous artists, including **Dion, 4 Him, Steve Green,** and **Cindy Morgan.** His stripped bare acoustic sound is often compared to that of performers like Mark Cohn, Don Henley, or Dan Fogelberg—or to Christian singer **Rich Mullins,** with whom he has worked (as a member of **A Ragamuffin Band**). Crockett's debut album offers an amicable collection of soft pop songs, including a duet with **Teri DeSario** ("The Way") and the Latin-flavored standout "Rhythm of God." The next album features the single "41 Lawnmowers," which pokes fun at the American urge to acquire possessions. *The Basic Stuff* features his praise song "Love Carrier" in addition to Crockett classics "Outta My Mind," "The Bottom of Life," and "Build a House." It was *Any Starlight Night,* however, that won Crockett acclaim as more than just a friendly voice and an accomplished guitarist. On this record (named for a painting by Georgia O'Keefe) he offers poetic word pictures of intense emotional power. Standout tracks include the haunting "Elena," the mystical "The Dance," and the whimsical "Bogart's Independence." *Red Bird Blue Sky* was recorded shortly after his marriage to Dodee (his "walking angel" and former ninth grade sweetheart) and reflects an overall spirit of joy and contentment. It remains his most popular outing, with the jubilant and popular songs "Song and Dance" and "Thankful Boys and Girls." Crockett's happiness on this record seems contagious; the invitational mood of the entire project is expressed well in these lines from "Come and See": "If there was a place that felt like home, would you go there? / If there was a chance that you could know love, would you try?" *Watermarks* attracted more critical praise for its theological depth. The title track draws on ancient baptismal liturgies to reflect the various ways that God has been in touch with people through water (the Red Sea, Jonah, Noah, Jesus washing his disciples' feet, and so on). "The Question Pool" rehearses various questions that have probably entered the minds of most people—believers or not—at one time or another. Of the latter song Crockett says, "I find that finding God is sometimes more about getting down to the right questions than it is about applying the answers." *Simple Plans* is an album Crockett made for the charitable organization Habitat for Humanity and is dedicated to that group's volunteers and to "kingdom builders everywhere." The song "It All Turns" acknowledges God in the passage of time. "Mark and Sammy" uses the careers of two of baseball's home-run leaders (Mark McGwire and Sammy Sosa) as a metaphor for the pursuit of excellence in life.

Crockett's songs convey a consistent introspective and theologically profound perspective on life and faith. He has cowritten most of them with friends or associates who help with the lyrics—early on with his former youth pastor Kenny Wood, later with friend Milton Brasher-Cunningham. *The Lighthouse* notes Crockett and company's consistent ability to "investigate the mystery of faith in the real world" and to "celebrate the wonder of love without over sentimentalizing it."

Christian radio hits: "Love Waiting" (# 13 in 1985); "41 Lawnmowers" (# 12 in 1987); "Love Carrier" (# 21 in 1990).

Barry Crompton

1978—*Harbinger* (Dove); 1979—*Ready to Fly* (Kingsway); 1981—*Hot in the Pot* (Marshalls); 1982—*Don't Look Down* (Pilgrim); 1985—*From Here to Eternity* (Shadow).

Despite a discography of five albums on five different labels—or perhaps *because* of that instability—Christian pop singer Barry Crompton has gone largely unnoticed in the Christian music market. Only his album *Don't Look Down* garnered much attention, when it was reviewed (favorably) by *CCM* magazine, who discovered it as a "small gem" when it was reissued in 1983 by a *sixth* label, Pilgrim America. The record is notable in part because Crompton is backed by the **Joe English Band,** which gives songs like "You're the One" a tight-edged rock sound to set them apart from the softer pop that would blend in with so much contemporary Christian music of the era. Crompton, for his part, offers passionate and competent vocals. The song "What Would Jesus Say?" predated the WWJD craze by more than a decade; "The Greatest of These" offers a paraphrase of 1 Corinthians 13; "Innocent Man" is sung from the perspective of Satan, owning up to the tactical error he might have made in taking Christ to the cross. *From*

Here to Eternity is consistent in style, with many of the same players. It opens with a worshipful song of trust ("I Will Call Your Name") and includes "Victim of Grace," which seems to be a response to The Eagles' "Victim of Love."

Crooked Smile

Jonathan Hart, gtr., voc.; Nathan Rudolf, bass; Brennan Simmons, drums; Matthew Whitley, gtr. 1997—*A Million Things to Say* (BulletProof).

Georgia-based band Crooked Smile offers thirteen slices of guitar-propelled progressive college rock on their critic-pleasing debut album. With songs in the four-to-seven-minute range, the group is clearly not going for radio hits, though they might have had one with a shorter version of the Spin Doctors rip-off, "Keep On Spilling." With the exception of that one song, the band's sound is as original as it is meditative, foregoing all the ska and hip-hop fads for their own version of the basic midtempo '90s rock sound associated with groups like Toad the Wet Sprocket or Gin Blossoms. The excellent opener, "Welcome to Our Dreamworld," and the equally compelling "Sometimes You Feel" might even recall a less atmospheric Moody Blues. Or, for Christian music fans, the overall sound might be compared to that of **Jars of Clay,** minus the latter's vibrato vocals. Hart is an especially expressive singer, with a smooth-as-butter tenor voice. He is also the group's songwriter, and he favors songs that raise existential questions about "finding one's place in this world." To do this, he adopts different personas, that of an abused woman in "Grow to Love" or of a heroin addict in "Subway Station." Notably, none of the songs mention God or Jesus by name; the Christian content must be read into them by listeners who are aware of the artists' orientations and are thus prompted to read the signs of hope that emerge here and there as pointers to something more specific. For instance, the final song, "Winter in My Soul," concludes, "There is a punishment for my crime I know I don't have to take." Hart posted an editorial on the group's website stating that there are two different types of "Christian bands": those that make provocative worship music for the heart and those that make intellectually stimulating music for the head. Straightforward, even simplistic lyrics may be appropriate for the former but can detract from the latter, in which context he hopes Crooked Smile's debut project will be understood.

Clay Crosse

1993—*My Place Is With You* (Reunion); 1995—*Time to Believe*; 1997— *Stained Glass*; 1999—*I Surrender All (The Clay Crosse Collection, Vol. 1)*; 2000—*A Different Man.*

www.claycrosse.com

Adult contemporary singer Clay Crosse was born Walter Clayton Crosnoe in Memphis in 1967. Raised in a Christian home and officially accepting Christ at age thirteen, he went on to sing at Memphis's Liberty Land theme park and filled in for **Mark Lowry** on a brief stint with **The Gaither Vocal Band** before being tapped for a solo career in Christian music by veteran producer **Gary McSpadden.** His debut album established Crosse as another **Michael English, Russ Taff,** or **Michael W. Smith,** and the potential for cloning any of those stars was enough to sway the industry into naming him the "New Artist of the Year." *My Place Is with You* opens with its title song, a beautiful ballad that affirms the identification of believers with Christ. "Give Him Roots" is a more jazzy song about child-rearing. The album also features a duet with **Kathy Troccoli** ("One Heart") and "If That's What It Takes," a song that expresses the extraordinary lengths to which God will go to provoke faith: "Do I have to push the sun into the sea to make you fall in love with me / If that's what it takes, then let it be." The most noticed song on *My Place Is with You,* however, would be "I Surrender All," a hymn of dedication that would become Crosse's signature song and would come to be regarded as one of contemporary Christian music's most beloved modern hymns. *Time to Believe* shows him branching out into a variety of styles: country, pop, and R&B, all performed under the adult contemporary umbrella. The record includes a remake of **Andraé Crouch**'s rousing "Just Like He Said He Would," complete with Motown horns and choir backing a very *white* lead vocal. The rousing "His Love Is Strong" is even better, with effective R&B/traditional gospel influence. "The Rock" is a building anthem, and *Time to Believe*'s title track is an atypical bluesy ballad. The third album, *Stained Glass,* shows progress musically, bringing Crosse into his own as "a premier vocalist in an industry full of talented singers" *(CCM).* Most critics agreed that it was his best project to date. Standout tracks include his renditions of Dan Mukala's "He Walked a Mile" (about how Jesus has walked in our shoes), Reggie Hamm's "Saving the World," and Russell and Scott's "He Ain't Heavy, He's My Brother" (the old Hollies' hit). The collection of Crosse's greatest hits that followed includes one remarkable new song: "I Will Follow Christ," sung in collaboration with **Bob Carlisle** and **BeBe Winans.**

Crosse now tells stories of crass moral degradation that had affected him throughout his career—until the life-changing year of 1998. Moral degradation? He has never tasted alcohol, and he is proud to relate that he and his wife were virgins when they married—following a six-year courtship. Still, Crosse admits with deep shame that he did sometimes watch questionable (R-rated) movies and comedians and that he occasionally allowed pornographic images and thoughts to enter his head. Brought to the brink of despair by these lapses, he finally broke down in 1998, confessing all to his wife and friends and totally rededicating his life to Christ. News of this trans-

formation played heavily into the marketing of *A Different Man* as the first album by Crosse on which he was *really* committed to Jesus. Such declarations had the unfortunate effect of implicitly trashing his previous work. Worse, the extreme concern with regard to what many—rightly or wrongly—perceive as peccadilloes made Crosse appear either too saintly or too prudish for the average Christian to relate to him. Of course, the continued quest for holiness is a noble endeavor, and Crosse was certainly sincere about his pledge—for him, at least, it was not just some marketing ploy. In any case, *A Different Man* turned out to be a pretty good record. The opener, "No Fear," sets a good tone with a touch of Caribbean flavor, and numbers such as "Till the End of the World" and "Memphis" have a pleasant R&B and Memphis rock edge. The first of these begins with an African vibe and segues into a choral tune with guest vocals from **Darwin Hobbs** and a number of other artists. "Memphis" offers a plea for racial reconciliation. The core of the album, though, is three testimonial songs reflecting on Crosse's transformation: "98," "Sinner's Prayer," and "Arms of Jesus." Of these the latter is by far the best, with an uncompromised message of grace and mercy. Notably, eight of the ten tracks on the album are cowritten by Crosse, who had previously sung mostly songs written by others.

Christian radio hits: "Sold Out Believer" (# 15 in 1998).

Dove Awards: 1995 New Artist of the Year; 2000 Inspirational Song ("I Will Follow Christ").

The Crossing

Mike Baznik, gtr., bouzouki, bass, dulcimer, kybrd.; Hilde Bialach, cello, piano, voc.; Mark Hall, flute, whistle, harp, dulcimer; Jennifer Igerson, fiddle; Tony Krogh, bagpipes, gtr., bouzouki, whistle, bodhran, didgeridoo, voc.; Pat Peterson, bodhran, whistle, bones. 1988—*Look Both Ways* (Bones and Wheat); 1990—*Rise and Go*; 1993—*Dancing at the Crossroads* (Grrr); 1997—*Dochás*; 1998—*The Court of a King: A Celtic Christmas Celebration.*

www.grrrrecords.com

The Crossing is dedicated to playing traditional Celtic music with intensity and integrity and to presenting a Christian worldview in songs that speak of joy and sorrow. The group is integrally related to the Jesus People U.S.A. community in Chicago, home also to **Ballydowse, Cauzin' Efekt, Crashdog, Headnoise, Resurrection Band, Seeds, Sheesh,** and **Unwed Sailor.** All group members also have full-time jobs in the community, which runs various social-service projects within the inner city and is responsible for producing *Cornerstone* magazine and the annual *Cornerstone* music festival. The group was founded by Krogh, who remains the main influence, though other members have assumed greater responsibility for songwriting and contributing to the overall sound. They are easily compared to another Christian Celtic band, **Iona,** but generally have a more traditional, acoustic-folk sound. Krogh admits that on the early recordings he was allowing the group to copy the styles of various Celtic artists (Jerry Read Smith, Ossian, the Tannahill Weavers), but he believes that with time they came to develop a sound all their own, on a par with Celtic acts in the general market. Critics agree, as the group has won recognition not only from Christian publications but from industry standards like *Billboard* and *Sing Out!* Indeed the group is one of very few United States bands to gain the respect of Irish purists for having effectively mastered the native instruments and applied them to original and traditional compositions. Not surprisingly, the group often performs songs that address social concerns—from inner city poverty to troubles in Ireland—in addition to ones that relate aspects of the life of Christ or paint metaphorical images of Christian experience. As an example of the former, "Rise Ye Up and Go" uses the image of medieval sentries in its portrayal of the call for Christians to be ready at any time to heed Christ's summons: "The watchman stands upon the hill / The piper on the wall / Waiting for the signal / To give the battle call." "Refugee," on the other hand, portrays the urgent distress of a homeless woman. The Christmas album *(The Court of a King)* is the most accessible package—especially for listeners not accustomed to the foreign sounds of world music. It mixes enough well-known carols in with the new songs and traditional tunes (including one in Norwegian) to keep the open-minded listening. Tony Krough says the band understands its ministry as pre-evangelism: "We play our music, we share our lives, and we invite people to talk with us."

Cross Movement

William "Duce" Branch [a.k.a. The Ambassador], voc.; Enoch, voc.; Brady Goodwin [a.k.a. Phanatik], voc.; Cleveland Foat Jr. [a.k.a. Earthquake], voc.; John Wells [a.k.a. The Tonic], voc.; Virgil Byrd [a.k.a. Tru-Life], voc. (–2000); Cruz Cordero, voc. (–2000). 1997—*Heaven's Mentality* (Cross Movement); 1998—*House of Representatives*; 1999—*Christology in Laymen's Terms*; 2000—*Human Emergency*.

www.crossmovementrecords.com

Cross Movement is a Philadelphia-based hip-hop community of rappers who function more or less as a group on albums released under the record company label. Most of the albums feature various members taking the lead on different songs, such that they really sound more like compilation discs than albums by a group as such. *Christology in Laymen's Terms* is sometimes construed as a solo album by William Branch (The Ambassador), as all of the songs feature him most prominently, with other rappers joining in as guests on various cuts. Apparently there were some minor scandals within the community around the turn of the millennium, since a note at the group's website indicates that Cruz Cordero and Tru-Life were

"released from the Cross Movement" as an act of discipline because "they made decisions that were not in line with our ministry standards."

In terms of overall concept, *Heaven's Mentality* seeks to shift the focus of audience perspective from secular humanism to divinity, and it challenges an understanding supposedly held within African American communities that, in Brady Goodwin's words, "makes the Black Man to be God." The latter point is not immediately obvious to all listeners, but the album leads off with "Blood Spilla," a testimony to the saving power of Christ that would become and remain the group's best-known song. The debut project is fairly typical East Coast rap in style. *House of Representatives* has a harder and heavier sound than the first album and compares earthly political realities with heavenly ones—its title track received some airplay on the MTV and BET video networks. John Wells (The Tonic) would also contrast the first two records this way: "*Heaven's Mentality* was about having the mind of Christ. Now we're coming with encouragement to live the life, to truly *represent* God." *Christology in Laymen's Terms* is sort of an urban version of *Mere Christianity* (by C. S. Lewis), an exercise in apologetics that seeks to present the gospel message of Christ in understandable idioms. *Human Emergency* addresses the fallen nature of the human race and its need for rescue work and ultimate salvation. It is built around the somewhat melodramatic concept that everyone who has not performed the ritual of accepting Christ is perishing and needs to do so *immediately* to avoid impending damnation. The first single, "Know Me (Huh What?)," features mile-a-minute rapping that spits out lyrics too fast for the untrained ear to comprehend.

Musically Cross Movement is regarded as one of the bright spots in Christian hip-hop, with records that really can compete with the best urban beats in the general market. Lyrically they are noted for reducing fundamentalist theology to bumper-sticker clichés and rhymes ("Test It" from *Heaven's Mentality*). This talent for rendering what is already simplistic more simplistic attracted the attention of *Time* magazine, which was amused by the following lyrics from the group's biggest hit, "Blood Spilla' ": "It's the 'Thrilla in Manila,' / Jesus Christ vs. every man's killa / Sin and death's got the world gettin' illa / So I praise God for the blood spilla." The group celebrated their appearance in *Time* on their website, perhaps not realizing they were being mocked—or perhaps just not caring, so long as their lyric was thereby enabled to witness to the world. "Know Me (Huh What?)" contrasts the orthodoxy of conservative Calvinist doctrine as compared with various heresies that understand God inadequately. Cross Movement (and especially Branch) demonstrate a penchant for unconventional evangelism and a talent for employing the odd or humorous turn of a phrase. "Blood Spilla' " goes on to refer to Christ as the one who is "gonna rise like a biscuit." On "Hold Your Ground" (from *Christology*), Branch says, "If you saw the measuring rod that God was holdin' / You'd know you fall shorter than Webster and Gary Coleman." On "One Two" (also from that album) he raps, "I'm in your area / I'm tellin' ya, Christ will marry ya / But you gotta switch, let him be your long distance carrier / No switching fee / And you'll get more than just some minutes free."

Andraé Crouch (and the Disciples)

Andraé Crouch, voc., kybrd.; Bili Thedford, voc.; Perry Morgan, voc. (–1971); Sherman Andrus, voc. (–1971); Ruben Fernandez, voc. (–1971) / / Sandra Crouch, voc. (+ 1971); Tramaine Davis, voc. (+ 1971, –1972); Bill Maxwell, drums (+ 1972); Danniebell Hall, voc. (+ 1973); Fletch Wiley, trump. (+ 1973, –1976); Bea Carr, voc. (+ 1976, –1978); Jimmie Davis, gtr. (+ 1976, –1978); Mike Escalante, kybrd. (+ 1976, –1978); James Felix, bass (+ 1976, –1978). As Andraé Crouch and the Disciples: 1968—*Take the Message Everywhere* (Light); 1971—*Keep on Singin'*; 1972—*Soulfully*; 1973—*Live at Carnegie Hall*; 1974—*Take Me Back*; 1976—*This Is Another Day*; 1978—*Live in London*. As Andraé Crouch: 1973—*Just Andraé* (Light); 1979—*I'll Be Thinking of You*; 1981—*Don't Give Up* (Warner); *More of the Best* (Light); 1982—*Finally*; 1984—*No Time to Lose*; 1994—*Mercy* (Warner); 1997—*Pray* (Light); 2000—*The Gift of Christmas* (Qwest). Mixed: 1974—*The Best of Andraé* (Light); 1986—*Autograph*; 1991—*Vol. I: The Classics* (CGI); *Vol. II: We Sing Praises* (Light); *Vol. III: The Contemporary Man*; 1995—*The Light Years*; 1999—*Gospel Music Hall of Fame* (CGI).

Andraé Crouch is easily the most important gospel singer of the modern era, possibly of all time. With no disrespect to gospel giants like James Cleveland, it was Crouch who changed the sound of gospel music forever such that, a hundred years from now, all gospel recordings from the twentieth century will be classified as pre- or post-Andraé. Crouch brought gospel into the '70s, infusing the genre with vital influences of R&B and rock and roll. Both of those fields had borrowed so much from gospel that a reverse transfusion might have seemed natural, even obvious. But it didn't. Crouch was not only the first to revolutionize gospel music in this way, but for quite some time he was the only one to do so. He changed the genre almost single-handedly, with little assistance and much opposition. The story of his early career is related in an autobiography: *Through It All* by Andraé Crouch with Nina Bell (Word, 1974).

Timing, of course, is everything. If the Jesus movement had not come along when it did, Crouch's experiments would no doubt have gone unheard. But just as he was tinkering with time-honored formulas in ways that gospel fans would repudiate, the Holy Spirit provided him with an audience of hundreds of thousands of Jesus freaks—right there in his California back yard—new hippie Christians who had no taste for traditional gospel but who were huge fans of R&B and rock and roll. Crouch is now honored as a great hero of traditional gospel, but at the time he made his greatest music his audience was mostly white kids—basically the same nonblack, nongospel crowd that made stars out of Sly and the Family Stone, a general market band with whom the Disciples can be loosely compared.

Crouch was raised in the Church of God in Christ, the largest Pentecostal denomination in America. His great-uncle, Bishop Samuel Crouch Sr., was the denomination's state overseer for California. His father, Benjamin Crouch, managed a family-owned dry cleaning business and restaurant, ministering to drug addicts, alcoholics, prison inmates, and hospital patients on evenings and weekends. Eventually, with a congregation of twelve that met in a garage, he began to explore the prospect of full-time ministry and started looking about for a music leader. Inspired one morning, so the story goes, he called eleven-year-old Andraé to the front of the congregation, laid hands on his head, and prayed, "God, if you've called me to preach, then give Andraé the gift of music." Three weeks later, he called the unsuspecting boy up front again and sat him down at the piano. Andraé recalls, "I had never sat at a piano before in my life, but he said to play, and I just started playing." So the father became a full-time preacher and his youngest son became the church's music leader, playing each week and writing songs for a choir he'd launched—all without the benefit of any formal musical training. To this day Crouch is unable to read music, but he says, "Every time I get on the piano, God gives me something . . . I just hear the song in my head." Whether the product of a miracle or simply a natural-born prodigy, the young Crouch's gifts were soon evident to all. He was afflicted with childhood stuttering—he says that until he was fourteen, when God healed him, he let his sister talk for him in public. Struggling with lifelong dyslexia, Andraé attended Valley Junior College and later Life Bible College, but his future was clearly with music. He formed an early gospel group called the COGICs (an acronym for his denomination's name), which included **Billy Preston** as a member. In 1965 he formed the Disciples with his twin sister Sandra (also a member of Janis Joplin's Full Tilt Boogie Band), and with Perry Morgan and Bili Thedford, two converts whom he had won to the Lord through his personal witnessing. At first the group performed only at his father's Christ Memorial COGIC church in the San Fernando Valley.

Ralph Carmichael was one of the first to recognize the Disciples' potential. Carmichael met Crouch in 1969 and encouraged him to record. An early single called "Christian People" on Liberty Records earned the group a Grammy nomination. That same year Carmichael signed the Disciples to his fledgling Light records and produced their first album, *Take the Message Everywhere*. If Carmichael had done nothing else—and he did plenty—this would be enough to ensure his legacy as the grandfather of Christian rock. The irony, in retrospect, is striking: Carmichael's Lawrence Welk-styled Big Band renditions of gospel standards are perhaps the *whitest* sounding Christian music ever put on record. Yet it was Carmichael who brought one of the most influential African American artists of the rock era to prominence. For that *is* what Crouch would prove to be—not simply the transformer of gospel music indicated above, but a major influence on secular music as well. Though he has never been profiled in *Rolling Stone* or any of the other staples of rock journalism, one would be hard pressed to find many African American performers—from Michael Jackson to Lenny Kravitz to George Clinton to Lauryn Hill—who do not cite Andraé Crouch as a major influence. But in 1968, when Crouch set out to change the worlds of traditional gospel *and* rock and roll, his main ally was an old white guy with no apparent connections to, experience with, or interest in, either.

In retrospect, *Take the Message Everywhere* was not terribly innovative. The group performs a version of Thomas Dorsey's "Precious Lord, Take My Hand," along with new arrangements of gospel standards like "No Not One" and "Wade in the Water." But the album also includes six original compositions, including "The Blood Will Never Lose Its Power," which has by now made its way into the hymnals of most Baptist, Pentecostal, and other conservative American-born denominations (the song was written by Crouch when he was fourteen years old).

Between 1971 and 1978, Andraé Crouch and the Disciples would release six albums that are each as significant to the history of contemporary Christian music as *What's Going On?* (by **Marvin Gaye**) or *Off the Wall* (by Michael Jackson) are to the history of mainstream rock.

From start to finish, *Keep On Singin'* is filled with Motown pop songs, making it the aural equivalent of any greatest hits package by Smokey Robinson, the Four Tops, or the Temptations. But at the time the album came out, these *weren't* greatest hits—they were all *new* songs, twelve potential blockbuster hit singles that, due to the ignorance or bigotry of general market radio, the Jesus people got to keep all to themselves. The wonderful bouncy title track and the ultimately classic "I've Got Confidence" were in keeping with the sort of Christian pop that Carmichael had aimed for with "He's Everything to Me," only better. "Take A Little Time," with its unforgettable "Thank You, Lord" chorus, is a soulful worship song, unlike anything that youth raised in white churches with funeral-dirge liturgies had ever heard before. Remarkably, one of the most ignored songs on the album when it was released was the less hooky closing song, a slowly building ballad called simply "My Tribute." Eventually that song would come to be listed in the Guiness Book of World Records as the most recorded gospel song in history (over 3000 versions). In more ways than one it

became Crouch's signature tune: "To God be the glory for the things he has done."

Soulfully, the well-named follow-up to *Keep On Singin',* shows tremendous musical growth for the Disciples, from a low-budget gospel group with great songs to a tight, well-produced band that could have held their own against any R&B act in the land. "You Don't Know What You're Missing" is another great pop song similar to the material on the predecessor record, but "Satisfied" is the Disciples' first full-bore rock song, with a beat every bit as driving as Steppenwolf's "Born to Be Wild." It would be one of the great highlights of Dallas' Explo '72 festival (the Christian equivalent of Woodstock), and a live version was featured on an album commemorating that event. "Oh, I Need Him" is as soulful as anything Otis Redding or **Sam Cooke** ever did. "It Won't Be Long" is a hauntingly beautiful number expressing undying, naive hope in the nearness of the Second Coming. And then there is "Through It All," Crouch's second signature song, the one that twenty years later would still seem to sum up his life better than any other: "I've had many tears and sorrows / I've had questions for tomorrow / There's been times I didn't know right from wrong . . . But through it all / I've learned to trust in Jesus / I've learned to trust in God."

Live at Carnegie Hall was the first live album to come out of the Jesus movement, and it would remain one of the two or three best (cf. **Barry McGuire** and **2nd Chapter of Acts**' *To the Bride*). It offers at least a glimpse of what (besides great songs) made Andraé Crouch and the Disciples an international phenomenon: electrifying live performances. The fact is—as a few non-Christian rock fans discovered—in the early '70s, Crouch and company were on a short list with The Who and The Rolling Stones for providing one of the best concert experiences to be had. Andraé called it "having church," and you couldn't get out without hearing a lot of preaching-to-the-beat music (a prelude, perhaps, to what would later be called *rapping*). On this record, the Disciples are backed by the band **Sonlight.** The most outstanding cuts among several gems are "Jesus Is the Answer" and "I Didn't Think It Could Be." The music is clearly *not* for those who belong to "the First Church of Frigidaire" as Andraé calls it. *Live at Carnegie Hall* was the first album released on a gospel label to receive a good bit of crossover attention in the general pop and R&B markets.

Take Me Back, Crouch's third classic studio album, includes the rousing "Just Like He Said He Would," an immediately noticeable song that seems like a surefire Top 10 hit on just one listen. Crouch was often at his enthusiastic best when writing about being filled with the Holy Ghost ("Satisfied") or about the certain (and probably imminent) Second Coming. "Just Like He Said He Would" falls into the latter camp, and it is usually thought to be one of Crouch's two best rock songs, the other being "It's Gonna Rain," a bonus track (about being filled with the Holy Ghost) on the *More of the Best* collection. On *this* album, however, the hymn-like "Take Me Back" and "Tell Them" (**Danniebelle Hall** at her best) will also melt their way into all but the hardest of hearts. "You Can Depend on Me" is lively and reassuring, and "It Ain't No New Thing" (about being filled with the Holy Ghost) is funky fun, featuring an interplay of old-time blues piano and clarinet. **Billy Preston** rejoined Crouch to play organ on this album.

The Disciples changed their style rather drastically on *This Is Another Day*. Disco was on the way, and its influence is felt on the upbeat title track. One can also hear the unmistakable voice of **Philip Bailey** Ba-Dee-Ya-ing on several cuts. In general, though, the album has a Caribbean sound, especially prominent on its standout cut, "Polynesian Praise Song." The opening track, "Perfect Peace," is also memorable, opening the album with a bit of *Shaft* nostalgia that segues into Danniebelle's lovely "My Peace I Leave with You." But by far the best-known track would turn out to be "Soon and Very Soon," an anthem about the imminent Second Coming. Because of its infectious melody and strong African rhythms, the latter song would find its way into the '90s hymnals of all the churches in America that wanted to be multicultural, whether they believed in an imminent Second Coming or not. It helps that the lyrics are completely scriptural ("Soon and very soon we are going to see the King / Hallelujah! Hallelujah! / We are going to see the King!") as, of course, is the idea of imminence—so long as one does not press for too specific a definition of *soon*. All told, *This Is Another Day* was probably the weakest of Crouch's six masterpieces; still, a poll of critics conducted by *CCM* magazine would place it at Number Twenty-four on their list of "The 100 Greatest Albums in Christian Music" published in 2001.

Live in London is a two-record set that offers live versions of many hits, plus a lot of preaching and some gems not to be found elsewhere: "You Don't Have to Jump No Pews" and "I Surrender All." Other highlights include the Disciples' take on the traditional hymns, "Revive Us Again" and "Power in the Blood."

The Disciples officially disbanded in 1978. Albums listed after that date in the above discography are either official solo releases by Crouch (as is 1973's *Just Andraé*) or collections of repackaged material. During its relatively brief tenure the band obtained a success unlike that of any other Christian group. They were the first contemporary gospel group to hit the one million mark in record sales, and they were the first to play such prestigious venues as Carnegie Hall and Royal Albert Hall. They toured as an opening act for Santana. They performed on *Saturday Night Live* (with Jesse Jackson hosting) and on Johnny Carson's *Tonight Show* (where Carson introduced the leader as "Andrew Crouch"). Paul Simon included the Crouch

song "Jesus Is the Answer" (performed by The **Jessy Dixon** Singers) on his best-selling *Live Rhymin' Simon* album (Columbia, 1974).

Crouch's solo albums have had less of a historical impact on Christian music but have always made impressive contributions to the milieu of adult contemporary, worship-oriented pop. On the early one, *Just Andraé*, he was backed again by **Sonlight** and was assisted vocally by a trio of female singers (Hall, Paula Clarin, and Phyllis Swisher). The praise song "Bless His Holy Name" (taken straight from Psalm 103) was the album's highlight, along with the profound, "If Heaven Never Was Promised to Me." *I'll Be Thinking of You* saw Crouch experimenting with a variety of styles, including disco ("I've Got the Best") and progressive jazz, in addition to the tried and true R&B and soft rock for which he had become famous. The title track (an adult contemporary ballad sung as a duet with an uncredited female jazz singer) and a hand-clapping traditional gospel number called "Jesus Is Lord" would hold up well as standout tracks. *Don't Give Up* was Crouch's first album for Warner, and it features some rare moves into social commentary. Taking on the issue of abortion, Crouch sings "I'll Be Good to You, Baby" from the perspective of God, promising divine care for those whom society rejects before they are even born. *Finally* is a worship-oriented project featuring the songs "We Need to Hear from You" and a new version of "My Tribute" featuring Crouch's own vocal (Thedford sang the original). The bouncy title track is another testimony song set to a pop beat ("Finally, finally, your love got through to me"). *No Time to Lose* continues in the slick production vein of the previous solo albums, offering a spine-tingling, zesty opening cut ("Got Me Some Angels") and "Livin' This Kind of Life," an up-to-date '80s piece with percolating synthesizers and an irresistible melody.

In 1982 a minor scandal threw Crouch's career completely off track. Stopped in Marina del Rey for a routine traffic violation (or, Crouch says, because he was a black man in a Mercedes), the singer was found to have a pipe bearing tiny traces of cocaine in the pocket of his sweatsuit. He was arrested and detained for more than ten hours. Even though all charges of drug possession were subsequently dropped, the police department rather irresponsibly leaked the story to the media, permanently damaging Crouch's reputation in some Christian circles. The artist maintains that the pipe belonged to some non-Christian friends who had stayed in his apartment while he was away, and that knowing full well what it was, he had been on his way to confront them with it and to protest their use of drugs under his roof when he was pulled over. Regardless of whether that account seems plausible, Crouch's closest associates (friends or not) all maintain that he has never been known to be a drug user and, certainly, his very public life in the two decades since the incident have revealed no hints of any connection to drugs. The true scandal appears to have concerned the actions of the Marina del Rey police department rather than those of Crouch himself. To many commentators, Crouch's *arrest* on charges that all agree would never have held up in court appears to have been motivated more by a zealous desire to besmirch a (black?) celebrity than by any genuine suspicion that an actual crime had been committed.

Although Crouch was not rejected by the church following his arrest, he was deeply humiliated and retreated from the spotlight of gospel music for ten years. *No Time to Lose* was already in the can, and when it came out in 1984 it won a Dove Award for the artist the next year. But despite such strong signs of support, Crouch stayed hidden and did not record again for more than a decade (*Autograph* is a compilation of previously released material). In 1993–1994 his mother and father both died of cancer, despite earnest prayers for their healing. Through struggling with his grief, Crouch came to a place of unusual peace with God. He returned to recording with the masterful *Mercy*. Employing once again a host of guest vocalists (including El Debarge), he offers up a slate of all-original compositions that dabble with traditional African rhythms, modern gospel, and jazz. The first two tracks showcase the talents of two of his associates who had appeared on most of his earlier solo projects: "Say-So" is a midtempo R&B number on which Kristle Murden's wailing vocal contrasts with Crouch's dry roar; "Give It All Back to Me" stars **Ta'ta Vega** on what *CCM* would call a "vaudeville show stopper," a zealous piano-rocker that calls on the listener to give all glory to God. Vega also trades vocals with Crouch on the hand-clapping title track, where they are supported by a gospel choir. DeBarge sings "The Lord Is My Light."

Within a year of *Mercy*'s release, Crouch's life was turned upside down again. His brother, Benjamin Jr., died of colon cancer, and in 1995 Crouch himself felt called by God to take over as Senior Pastor of Christ Memorial Church in Pacoima, California—the COGIC congregation Benjamin Jr. had led, the very same congregation developed by his father out of the twelve-people-in-a-garage nucleus years earlier. For Crouch, accepting that full-time position meant abandoning his plush West Valley mansion and moving into his parents' former two-bedroom home in the rough neighborhood around the church. He did that and also decided to forego a regular salary, living mostly on the royalties from his music but devoting himself almost full time to the needs of the now one thousand-member congregation. He would become actively involved in ministry to the inner city black and (mostly) Latino youth in the blocks around the church. He has found his celebrity status to be of little help in gaining an audience among such teens, he says, since most of them have never heard of him or of any of his

songs; for that matter, he says, they have never even heard of "Amazing Grace." But when Crouch was installed as pastor of the congregation, he changed the church's name to The *New* Christ Memorial Church, signaling a change in direction, which has included intense commitment to multicultural and gender-inclusive ministry. Amid widespread controversy, he ordained his sister Sandra to be the church's Assistant Pastor in 1998. Since accepting the pastorate, Crouch has also had health concerns related to those that took the life of his brother, requiring laser surgery to remove malignant tumors from his colon. Still, in 1997 he managed to release *Pray,* an album of worship-oriented urban pop and smooth ballads. "Come Closer to Me" actually sounds like it could have been a **Ralph Carmichael** song. The title track and "Distraction" have a more urban-contemporary sound. Other standout tracks include the salsa-flavored "Early in the Morning" and the closing track, "Until Jesus Comes." The latter is a shimmering ballad about "who we'll see in heaven"; as his church's choir testifies to hope eternal, Crouch calls out over the chorus, "My mother! . . . My father! . . . My brother!"

More than any other artist in Christian music, black or white, Crouch eventually crossed the barriers to appeal to a racially diverse audience. Notably, he indicates, his grandfather on his mother's side and his great grandfather on his father's side were both white and Jewish. He grew up with "a tremendous outlook on balance and with friends of all colors." Nevertheless, there were bumps in the road. At his first concert in Dallas, the crowd appeared shocked to discover that the man who had written "The Blood Will Never Lose Its Power" was black and, he says, "as we came on stage, the applause began to dwindle, and literally the first three rows got up and walked out." Undaunted, he launched into his song, "I Don't Know Why Jesus Loves Me." Crouch was generally cooperative but not always silent about his ironic role as the single biggest star in the white-oriented and white-dominated field that was coming to be called "contemporary Christian music." He told *CCM* in 1980, "I'm very racially conscious . . . yet, if I get up and say, 'I'm a black man,' I'm militant all of a sudden. People see that as a threat." Two decades later it is obvious that Crouch opened the door for a genuine influence of traditional gospel on contemporary Christian music. If not for Andraé Crouch, it is unlikely that contemporary Christian music fans would ever have heard of **BeBe Winans** or **Kirk Franklin,** to cite only the most obvious of his protégées.

Crouch also leaves a great legacy as a songwriter and arranger of contemporary music. Many of his hits have been covered by contemporary Christian artists—and even by mainstream artists (**Ashley Cleveland** opened her first, general market release with "Soon and Very Soon"). Even **Elvis Presley** recorded "I've Got Confidence." In 1986 Crouch performed with B. B. King in a tribute to the roots of gospel and blues. He has worked on the musical scores for major motion pictures, including *The Lion King, Once Upon a Forest, Free Willy,* and *The Color Purple,* and was nominated for an Oscar for his contributions to the latter film. He placed a new version of "Precious Lord, Take My Hand" on the soundtrack album for *A Time to Kill* (Atlantic, 1996). He composed the music for a TV presentation of Dr. Seuss's *Yertle the Turtle* (and voiced the title character). He has done arrangements for recordings by Whitney Houston, Michael Jackson, Diana Ross, Stevie Wonder, and Madonna. A revamped version of the Disciples called the Andraé Crouch Singers backed Jackson on "Man in the Mirror" (# 1 for 2 weeks in 1988) and Madonna on "Like a Prayer" (# 1 for 3 weeks in 1989). Yet incredibly Crouch has never been a crossover artist. Unlike Franklin and Winans, unlike **Amy Grant** or **DC Talk** or **Jars of Clay,** he has never written or sung anything that is even remotely generic or secular—no love songs, no songs about the value of friendship or the beauty of nature. Every song is about Jesus, and in some remarkable way it is the unflinching passion and conviction of his singular devotion that has won him long-term respect within the church and outside it as well. In 1993 Crouch received the Christian Artists' Seminars' Lifetime Achievement Award. In 1998 both Andraé Crouch (as a solo artist) and Andraé Crouch and the Disciples (as a group) were inducted into the Gospel Music Hall of Fame. As further testimony to his influence, a number of artists participated in a tribute album released by Warner in 1996. The roster of those performing his songs in his honor includes **Clay Crosse, Bryan Duncan, Twila Paris, Michael W. Smith,** and **Take 6.** In 1997 he was awarded an honorary doctorate from the Berklee College of Music in Boston. In 1998 a *CCM* poll of thirty critics chose "My Tribute (To God Be the Glory)" by Andraé Crouch and the Disciples as one of "the ten best contemporary Christian songs of all time."

Many of the Disciples went on to impressive careers. Bill Maxwell became a successful producer. Starting with *Take Me Back,* he produced many of Crouch's projects, as well as all of **Keith Green**'s albums; recently he has directed music for network TV shows, including *Martin* and *The Jamie Foxx Show.* **Sherman Andrus** sang with **The Imperials,** formed **Andrus, Blackwood, and Co.,** and then released solo albums. Tramaine Davis went on to a successful career as **Tramaine Hawkins.** Bili Thedford recorded two albums for Good News Records (*Music of My Second Birth,* 1977; *More Than Magic,* 1979) and had a Christian radio hit with the song "More Than Magic" (# 21 in 1979). Solo careers were also pursued by **Sandra Crouch, Danniebell Hall,** and **Fletch Wiley.** Before joining the Disciples, Mike Escalante and James Felix had formerly played with **Psalm 150.**

Christian radio hits: By Andraé Crouch and the Disciples: "You Don't Have to Jump No Pews" (# 25 in 1978). By Andraé Crouch: "I'll Be Thinking of You" (# 1 for 5 weeks in 1980); "It's Gonna Rain" (# 11 in 1981); "Sweet Communion" (# 12 in 1982); "No Time to Lose" (# 26 in 1984).

Dove Awards: 1977 Soul/Black Gospel Album *(This Is Another Day)*; 1978 Soul/Black Gospel Album *(Live in London)*; 1985 Contemporary Gospel Album *(No Time to Lose)*; 1998 Contemporary Gospel Album *(Pray)*.

Grammy Awards: 1975 Best Soul Gospel Performance *(Take Me Back)*; 1978 Best Soul Gospel Performance *(Live In London)*; 1979 Best Soul Gospel Performance *(I'll Be Thinking of You)*; 1981 Best Soul Gospel Performance *(Don't Give Up)*; 1984 Best Soul Gospel Performance *("Always Remember")*; 1994 Best Pop/Contemporary Gospel Album *(Mercy)*.

Sandra Crouch

1983—*We Sing Praises* (Light); 1985—*We're Waiting;* 1992—*With All of My Heart.*

Best known for her work as a member of her twin brother **Andraé Crouch**'s Disciples, Sandra Crouch released a number of solo albums after that group disbanded in 1978. An ordained minister, Sandra Crouch became the Assistant Pastor at Christ Memorial Church of God in Christ in 1998. This is the congregation in Pacoima, California, where brother Andraé is senior pastor and where her father and elder brother were previous senior pastors. Sandra and Andraé have always been unusually close. Andraé has never married, and Sandra was married for just five years in the early '90s, noting in retrospect, "I'm sure my closeness with Andraé played a part in my divorce." She has served as the latter's personal assistant for decades. Her ordination was a matter of some controversy since the Church of God in Christ has an official policy against the ordination of women. Andraé himself ordained her all the same, making her one of about fifty women pastors serving (not quite legally) in the five-and-a-half-million-member denomination. Sandra Crouch's solo albums bring her own compositional talents to the fore, as she has written most of the songs on each record. *We Sing Praises* also includes a version of the hymn "There Is Power in the Blood," and *We're Waiting* features "Nothing But the Blood." *With All of My Heart* is all original praise songs.

For trivia buffs: Sandra Crouch was a member of Janis Joplin's Full Tilt Boogie Band and is featured on that group's classic *Pearl* album. Joplin regularly referred to her as "the sanctified tambourine player."

Dove Awards: 1984 Traditional Gospel Album *(We Sing Praises)*; 1993 Traditional Gospel Album *(With All of My Heart)*.

C.R.O.W.

1999—*Operation K.A.P.* (Grapetree).

www.grapetreerecords.com

C.R.O.W. is a member of the Christian rap group **Bruthaz Grimm.** Converted to a passionate life for Christ through the ministry of Silas Clark, he now relates a testimony of leaving home at fifteen, living in the inner city, and eventually becoming a pimp. The songs on his solo album are all related to this testimony. He seeks to expose the ways men draw women into abusive relationships, exchanging emotional support for sexual favors or financial assistance. "Don't accept false love from a man because you feel no one loves you," he advises troubled women. "God loves you. You do have worth. Have a vision and a focused goal."

Robin Crow (and The Robin Band)

1982—*Legend of a Fool* (Sherwood); 1983—*Finish Line*; 1985—*Seven Seventy-Seven* (Fortress); 1986—*Creator*; 1988—*Windows to the World* [with Kerry Livgren]; 1992—*Electric Cinema* (Rendevous).

Robin Crow is a double-neck guitar hero known for creating moody, atmospheric, instrumental music. His first three projects included vocals, establishing him more overtly as a Christian artist, though none of the albums attracted much attention, critically or commercially. *CCM* thought *Finish Line* displayed a style "somewhere between Supertramp and Styx." *Seven Seventy-Seven* includes the worship track "Lift Up Your Voices," with lead vocal by **Michael Card.** Both of those albums included a couple of instrumentals mixed in with the vocal tracks, and Crow found these the most satisfying. With *Creator* he dedicated himself to a guitar-based instrumental style he has pursued ever since. When asked why, as a Christian musician, he makes only instrumental music, he answers simply, "It is what I do best . . . it's like an athlete at the Olympics finding the one area in which he can excel and then going for it." He has also become somewhat disillusioned with the evangelistic impact of vocal Christian music and with the notion that singers can win auditoriums full of people to the Lord with the words to their songs. "The world will be won to Christ one on one. . . . I've seen more fruit from being an instrumentalist than when playing Christian festivals or whatever." Crow cites progressive British artists like Emerson, Lake, and Palmer and Yes as primary influences, along with the more recent work of artists like Peter Gabriel and Sting. He also likes "Stravinsky, John Williams, Jerry Goldsmith, and people who do great movie soundtracks." Indeed, Crow's instrumental albums are often said to sound like scores for films no one has made yet, and something of that nature is implied by the title of *Electric Cinema.* On the latter disc Crow is accompanied by Mike Lawler, David Hungate, Larry Landin, and **Kerry Livgren.** The album includes a suite of three classic AOR staples: "Roundabout" (Yes), "I Still Haven't Found What I'm Looking For" **(U2)**, and "Another Brick in the Wall, Part II" (Pink Floyd). Crow has opened shows for Spyro Gyra, Peter Frampton, and **Kansas.**

Crowd of Faces

Mike Brandenstein, Chad Chapin, Steve Dintsch, Bill Randall, Brian White. 2000—*Talk Show Circuit* (Visual).

Crowd of Faces is a modern rock band whose debut release has all the markings of seasoned professionals. Their album was produced by Steve Griffith of **Vector.** Michael Tait of the bands **DC Talk** and **Tait** cowrote many of the songs and sings background vocals. The general sound is that of midtempo, guitar-oriented (but not dominated) rock. *7ball* found sonic similarities to Bon Jovi and **U2.** Crowd of Faces' debut album opens with "For So Long," which describes a longing for God amidst an ongoing struggle with sin. "Thin White Curtain" is a melodic and dreamy ballad dealing with the human attempt to veil sin from an all-seeing God. Now and then the group goes for a more aggressive sound: "Crawl" is set to an especially catchy tune, and "Testify" presents an urgent call for Christians to speak up about their faith.

The Crucified

Jim Chaffin, drums; Greg Minier, gtr.; Mark Cooksey, voc. (– 1987); Trevor Palmer, bass (–1987) // Mark Salomon, voc. (+ 1987); Mark Johnson, bass (+ 1987, –1991); Jeff Bellew, bass (+ 1991). 1987—*Take Up Your Cross* (independent); *Nailed* [EP]; 1989—*Live at the New Order* [EP]; *The Crucified* (Narrowpath); 1991—*The Pillars of Humanity* (Ocean).

The Crucified were a punk-metal band that formed in 1985, put out three demos on cassette only, then made two full-length CDs before disbanding in 1993. They are remembered as a classic Christian punk band, and their music has been sufficiently treasured to qualify for something rare in Christian music: reissue on a major label. Tooth and Nail re-released both of the full-length CDs and then in 1994 released a disc with both *Take Up Your Cross* and *Nailed.* Mark Cooksey sang only on the former demo tape; Mark Salomon is the primary vocalist associated with the band.

All of the early demos and the self-titled official debut album showcase a band that favors hardcore old-school punk with very fast vocal delivery of lyrics that seem to have been written in all-capital letters. Guitar riffs are tight and heavy. On *The Crucified,* the group comes off as hellfire and brimstone preachers who view Christ and Christianity primarily as ways to escape perdition ("The Pit," "Diehard"). The song "One Demon to Another" offers a narrative portrait of what happens to some poor guy who fails to make a decision for Christ in this life. "A Guy in a Suit and the Pope" lumps televangelists and the Roman pontiff together in way that is unfair to both and rants against them in a way that is at least unfair to the latter. *The Pillars of Humanity* secured the group's legendary status; *HM* magazine describes it as "three times more powerful than its predecessor." With low and chunky guitars and a pace slightly slower than the earlier material, the group found its niche. Musically at this point they could compete with any bands in the secular thrash scene, while lyrically they turned the punk intensity into furor against the ways of the world, the lusts of the flesh, and the wiles of the devil. "This world betrays," screams Salomon in one song, "This world, it feasts upon me." Thematically *The Pillars of Humanity* deals with a number of negative issues, including alcohol and drug abuse. **Greg Minier** would explain "Mind Bender" as being about "Americans being brainwashed by believing everything they see on TV and the media." On "Focus" the group states "we're here to do the Father's will."

The abrupt break-up of The Crucified took the Christian hard music scene by surprise, especially since songs from a never-to-be-released third album had been performed in concerts. The group indicated that their relationship with God was suffering and that the band itself had become more important to them than the Lord. Minier told *HM,* "basically what happened is that I was seeing a girl, and she got pregnant. I told the band, and I knew I had to quit." There was probably more to it than that, as all the other members confirmed, "the Lord was working with everyone in their personal lives and leading everyone to different things." Still, Minier thinks there is a lesson to be learned: "Just because someone is in a Christian band, that doesn't mean that fans should look up to them as spiritual." Bellew says simply, "The Lord told us He had something else in mind for us." The group officially disbanded in 1993 but played a farewell concert at *Cornerstone* in the summer of 1995, which they presented as an opportunity to "glorify God and to say thank you and goodbye." They ran through a set that concluded with a cover of **Rich Mullins'** "Awesome God." The crowd called out for more, someone from the group said, "We ain't got no more," and that was it.

Greg Minier would also release a solo album and go on to play with **Applehead.** Mark Salomon would sing for **Outer Circle** and **Native Son.** Jeff Bellew went on to form **Chatterbox.** Bellew and Salomon would be reunited in **Stavesacre.**

Crumbächer (and **Stephen Crumbächer** and **Crumbächer-Duke**)

Stephen Crumbächer, voc., kybrd.; Dawn Wisner-Johnson, voc., kybrd. (– 1989); Jimmy Wisner, drums (– 1989); Don Hohulin, gtr. (– 1987) // Christopher Duke, gtr. (+ 1987). By Crumbächer: 1985—*Incandescent* (Broken); 1986—*Escape from the Fallen Planet* (Frontline); 1987—*Thunder Beach*; 1989—*Tame the Volcano*; 1992—*Time After Time.* By Crumbächer-Duke: 1989—*Worlds Away* (Frontline). By Stephen Crumbächer: 1991—*Take It In* (Frontline); 1999—*Reinvention* (mp3.com).

Southern Californian Stephen Crumbächer formed the Christian group that bore his surname in 1983 with his high school friend Dawn Wisner (soon to be Wisner-Johnson) and her brother. The purpose was to evangelize teenagers, and the band attempted to do this with a keyboard-driven new-wave sound. The group never quite seemed to click, despite some memorable moments. *Incandescent* contains the first song Crumbächer ever wrote ("Jamie") and evinces the charm of a promising act by young amateurs. *CCM* announced the album as revealing "a new group on par with **Vector.**" The song "It Don't Matter" is a new-wave treat, carried by pneumatic synthesizers. "Jamie" is also quite good, dealing with concern for one who is getting lost in the bright lights of big city life. The sophomore release, *Escape from the Fallen Planet,* is a more developed, sci-fi concept album, but critics generally thought it promised more than it delivered. The idea is that Christians are aliens on this planet (cf. **Larry Norman's** *Only Visiting This Planet*). With *Thunder Beach* the band showed musical maturity and got national attention at last with the songs "Here Am I" and "Tough Act to Follow." Still, a reviewer for *CCM* panned the album, maintaining that "Here Am I" was adult contemporary not new-wave. Crumbächer added Christopher Duke as guitarist for their fourth and final group album. *Tame the Volcano* would be the band's best-crafted and most polished effort. "Waiting for You" and "Rainy Season" are hooky pop songs, and "Release Me" is fueled by Duke's guitar prowess. "Reckless Boys and Bad, Bad Girls" is a bouncy highlight, buoyed by a chorus of brass. The title track is a bit odd, trying to apply the image of Polynesian tribes sacrificing virgins to appease their volcano gods to the late '80s foibles of famous televangelists. *CCM* would note, "it's funnier than it was probably intended to be, done to wonderful excess, complete with monkeys and toucans." *Time After Time* is a retrospective compilation.

Stephen Crumbächer recorded two downsized albums without the Wisners—one with just Duke and then one on his own. *Worlds Away* offers a synthesizer-driven pop sound not too different from Electric Light Orchestra. "The Last Time" is an acoustic piano number. "Tears of Joy" and "Rock in a Heart Place" are also effective. The title track speaks of dreaming of heaven, with the refrain, "Heaven knows where my heart goes and wants to stay." *Take It In* is dramatically different from all of Crumbächer's earlier projects. He offers not only a softer, acoustic album but also a more poetic one, eschewing the tendency toward cute wordplay on earlier projects. "Autumn Life" deals with the dry spells that inevitably mark the journey of faith. "Over Me" describes the various ways different persons (the poet, the lover, the dreamer) live out their vocation before God. In 1999, Crumbächer put together a series of demos he had recorded in the last seven years and released it as *Reinvention,* an Internet album available only at mp3.com.

True to the *CCM* comment, Crumbächer achieved musical success only in the adult contemporary market. Their ministry, however, remained focused on struggling Christian youth. All the members had been raised in Christian homes, and they were effective at engaging Christians in conversation. "I get asked questions I never would have asked anyone," said Wisner-Johnson in 1988. "Maybe I would have thought about these things, but I never would have talked about them." Stephen Crumbächer cowrote the Christian radio hit "Lost Inside of You" for **Jon Gibson.**

Christian radio hits: By Crumbächer: "Here Am I" (# 12 in 1987); "Tough Act to Follow" (# 10 in 1987); "Waiting for You" (# 13 in 1989). By Stephen Crumbächer: "Rainy Season" (# 5 in 1989). By Crumbächer-Duke: "Worlds Away" (# 5 in 1990).

Crusade

Mano Hanes, voc.; Morris Holmes, voc.; Yolanda Holmes, voc.; Chanese Jackson, voc.; Charise Jackson, voc. 1994—*Crusade* (Warner).

Five African American youth from the San Francisco Bay area formed the group Crusade and released an album of vocal music blending jazz and R&B sounds on songs that were mostly worship-oriented ("I Praise Your Name," "Lord, You're Worthy to Be Praised"). The group developed out of the ministry of an organization called Young Followers of the Chief Cornerstone and sponsored a local weekly TV show called *Teen Task Force Forum.* They were profiled as "Faces to Watch" in the February 1994 issue of *CCM* magazine and then were never heard from again.

Crusaders

Personnel list unavailable. 1966—*Make a Joyful Noise with Drums and Guitars* (Tower).

Almost nothing is known of the Crusaders, whose only known album was discovered by Jesus music historian David Di Sabatino. The liner notes on the back indicate, "the Crusaders are five sincere young men . . . who have chosen the Big Beat as the means of expressing their religious faith. . . . Now, for the first time, God is praised in song through the most contemporary musical expression: The Beat!" The words "The Beat" and "The Big Beat" are apparently euphemisms for rock and roll, which is basically what the Crusaders offer, in their own campy mid '60s way. The album does exhibit excellent production values and was marketed through a subsidiary of Capitol Records. Di Sabatino notes that "this album is important in establishing that there were a handful of artists performing 'gospel rock' music well before **Larry Norman** or any of the other Jesus music artists emerged in the early 1970s." Indeed! The year the album came out songs by Petula Clark ("My Love") and Lou Christie ("Lightning Strikes") were still topping the charts.

The Cruse Family (and Cindy Cruse and Cruse)

Founding members of The Cruse Family: Joe Cruse, Nancy Cruse, Joe Cruse II, Karen Cruse, Janie Cruse, John Cruse, Cindy Cruse. By The Cruse Family (Selected): 1974—*Love Is Taking Over* (Superior); 1975—*The Cruse Family Album*; 1976—*Heaven Bound* (Canaan); 1977—*Faith*; 1978—*Transformation*; 1980—*Harmony* (Impact); 1981—*For Every Heart*; *The Best of the Cruse Family* (DaySpring); 1982—*The Cruse Family* (Priority); 1984—*Collection* (Impact); *Cruse* (Nissi). By Cindy Cruse (solo): date unknown—*Cindy* (Nissi); 1989—*The Edge*; 1991—*Small Town Girl* (Frontline). By Cruse: 1984—*Cruse 2* (Nissi); 1986—*Long Journey Home* (Greentree); 1988—*Cruse Praise*.

The Cruse Family began as a southern gospel singing family and slowly morphed into a (not very) contemporary pop group along the lines of **The Archers** and **The Boones.** The Cruse Family was formed in Jacksonville, Texas, in 1972 by ordained minister Joe Cruse, his wife Nancy Cruse, and their five children. Over the years new members were added, mostly through marriage. Though no authoritative list (with dates) is available, Karen married Jeff Adams, who became the group's sound engineer. Janice married Clark Stone, who joined as drummer. Joe II married Becky, who played piano; John married Janice Archer of **The Archers,** who switched her membership from the one family singing group to the other. Cindy Cruse, who was just nine when the family group formed, went on to a solo career.

Musically The Cruse Family was never even close to hip; at the height of their billing as a pop group (1978–1981), they had a sound similar to that of The Partridge Family or The Cowsills, who had peaked almost a decade earlier and who had been, at best, guilty pleasures even at the height of their careers. The Cruse Family performed mainly at revivalistic churches, doing evening services that would include a lot of hymns and a few "upbeat, modern songs for the kids." These inevitably sounded like the sort of music that '60s sitcom parents would have thought their teenagers *should* want to listen to. Still, this was the late '70s, and for those who longed for the *early* '70s—when the Waltons were on TV and "Billy, Don't Be a Hero" was on the radio—The Cruse Family sometimes did the trick. By their 1981 *For Every Heart* album, *CCM* was willing to admit that some of the songs had a sort of Fifth Dimension sound to them, while still warning readers that the outfit was too sedate for rock fans. *CCM* critic Thom Granger called their next album, *The Cruse Family* (1982), "a benchmark in their career . . . bright, punchy pop music as good as anything being played anywhere." Not surprisingly, Cindy and Janice are the featured performers. But the eponymous project was also their last . . . as a family. The next record (titled *Cruse* but officially issued by The Cruse Family) allowed for a segue into a new adult vocal group called simply Cruse.

Cruse was a trio formed out of The Cruse Family. Musically the group strove to continue in the pop direction of the family's final record, at times creating a sound similar to that of *Mansion Builder*-era **2nd Chapter of Acts.** *Cruse 2* features a song called "Rise and Fly" that is synthesizer-driven and energetic enough to qualify as rock. "The Sign of the Times" serves as something of a theme song for that project, on which most of the songs point to the sign of God's love revealed in Christ. The song "All the Hurting People" from *Long Journey Home* was written by Cindy with her husband **Tim Miner.**

Cindy Cruse launched her solo career in 1982. She met **Tim Miner** to record a duet with him on the song "Always," and the fateful session led to marriage—and naturally to future musical collaborations. The Christian radio hit "Colour Blind" from Cindy's third solo album was cowritten by the couple.

Christian radio hits: By The Cruse Family: "Power" (# 13 in 1980); "I Can Laugh Again" (# 11 in 1981); "Bless Your Name" (# 10 in 1983); "I Am the Mighty One" (# 4 in 1983); "Sing" (# 12 in 1983). By Cindy Cruse: "Always" [with **Tim Miner**] (# 5 in 1984); "Colour Blind" (# 6 in 1991). By Cruse: "A Sign of the Times" (# 13 in 1985); "All the Hurting People" (# 9 in 1987).

Dove Awards (The Cruse Family): 1978 Pop/Contemporary Album *(Transformation).*

Crux

Mike Boddington, drums; Greg Dimick, gtr.; Richard Phillips, voc.; Andy Wiseman, bass (−1997) // Bob Gosset, bass (+ 1997). 1994—*Crux* (Boot to Head); 1995—*Failure to Yield* (Tooth and Nail); 1997—*Cakewalk;* 1998—*How Does This Go?*

Founded in Portland, Oregon, in 1993, Crux was a Christian punk band with a hard metal edge. Lead singer (and songwriter) Richard Phillips has training in vocal jazz and brings to the mix an expressive technique uncharacteristic of punk-rock. He claimed to spend hours researching the often political topics of the band's songs. The self-titled album is a custom demo that opens with its best track, "Ingrown." Some of the songs would reappear on *Failure to Yield,* the only album to obtain widespread notice. "Tell Me" is based on Bill Bennett's index of cultural indicators, exposing the failures of recent social programs. "Price Check" wonders at the low value given to human life in a society that condones widespread abortion. "Agenda" takes an even harder tack on that subject, alleging that legalized abortion serves as a form of ethnic cleansing: "In third reich fashion / Empty the ghetto by scraping clean the uterus." The song "Wasted Day" deals with drug abuse. A humorous song called "Oh Krap (My Dad Was Right)" sometimes got official listing as "Good Golly (My Dad Was Right)." *Cakewalk* fea-

tures a few less outlandish songs, including one that exalts Christ in traditional language: "Thanks be to God / Who gave us victory through Christ / In order that what is mortal / May be swallowed up with life" ("Swallowed Up with Life"). Most Crux songs run for just two minutes or less, as is typical of old school punk. Andy Wiseman later formed the pop-punk band **Shorthanded.**

Morgan Cryar

1984—*Keep No Secrets* (StarSong); 1986—*Fuel on the Fire;* 1989—*Like a River* (Reunion); 1990—*Kingdom Upside Down;* 1995—*Love Over Gold* (UCA); 1998—*What Sin? The Best of Morgan Cryar* (Damascus Road).

Singer/songwriter Morgan Cryar was born in 1958 in Lake Charles, Louisiana. He studied for the ministry at Louisiana College in Piketon, graduating with a major in biblical studies. The plan to be a pastor, however, got sidetracked as his career in contemporary Christian music took off. Several members of the groups **King's X** and **Galactic Cowboys** first interned as members of Cryar's band. Cryar's debut album, *Keep No Secrets,* was an acoustic pop masterpiece that did well in the Christian market. It includes "A Few of My Old Friends" and "I Wanna Be Good" (a send-up of Chuck Berry's "Johnny B. Goode" written by Rick Crawford). It also features a duet with **Jayne Farrell** on "Holy Fire," a powerful song Cryar wrote with **Twila Paris.** *Secrets* was followed by the more rock-oriented *Fuel on the Fire,* which features "Pray in the U.S.A.," an anthemic take-off on Bruce Springsteen's "Born in the U.S.A." Cowritten with **Ty Tabor** of **King's X,** "Pray in the U.S.A." would become Cryar's best-known song. In the late '90s the song was remade with an accompanying video featuring a host of guest artists. Both Tabor and **Doug Pinnick** (also of **King's X**) wrote several other songs on *Fuel* as well. "Underneath Your Feet" and "I Gotta Know" are energetic rock songs; "Break the Chain" is a mellow ballad. The album would be Cryar's career triumph. *Like a River* mixes R&B and southern rock tunes in with a few lifeless ballads that, unfortunately, would prove popular with radio audiences. "The Voice of Experience" offers trite advice from an elder concerning the dangers of premarital sex. Much better is the let-'er-rip opening song "Holy Hands." Elsewhere Cryar invokes traditional gospel on "Name Above All Names" and Lynyrd Skynyrd on "I'm Still Dangerous." *Kingdom Upside Down* is best known for "See You on the Other Side," a song Cryar wrote and sang for victims of the 1995 Oklahoma City bombing. His self-produced *Love Over Gold* (not to be confused with the famous Dire Straits album) includes a cover of Tom Petty's song, "I Won't Back Down." Cryar has written Christian radio hits for **David Meece** ("Unknown Soldier") and **Bruce Carroll** ("Breaking the Law of Love").

Christian radio hits: "A Few of My Friends" (# 25 in 1985); "I Get Carried Away" (# 8 in 1985); "Made Up My Mind" (# 12 in 1985); "Pray in the U.S.A." (# 4 in 1986); "Sibling Rivalry" (# 9 in 1987); "The Voice of Experience" (# 4 in 1989); "Holy Hands" (# 3 in 1990); "Father" (# 2 in 1990); "Kingdom Upside Down" (# 18 in 1990); "I Ain't Got Nuthin' " (# 16 in 1991).

Crystavox

Fred Helm, drums; Loren Holmquist, gtr.; Adam Kemp, voc.; Tony Lopez, gtr. 1990—*Crystavox* (Regency); 1992—*The Bottom Line* (Ocean); date unknown—*Wear It Out* (label unknown).

The San Diego rock quartet Crystavox formed in 1986. The group's sound was described by *CCM* as "based largely on mid '80s metal, with pop melodies at the eye of the storm." Their first self-titled album garnered attention primarily for a hard-hitting song called "Sacrifice" and for an atypical power ballad, "Home Again." The sophomore project features a grittier, more earthy production and was praised by *HM* as a record that "completely blows the first one out of the water." Standout songs on the latter work include the freight-train rockers "Snakes in the Grass" and "Paradise," and a second "Home Again"-style ballad, "No Boundaries." The group's name is derived from Latin wording for "voice of Christ."

Christian radio hits: "Home Again" (# 7 in 1991).

Rick Cua

1982—*Koo-ah* (Refuge); 1983—*No Mystery*; 1985—*You're My Road* (Sparrow); 1986—*Wear Your Colors*; 1988—*Can't Stand Too Tall* (Reunion); 1989—*Midnight Sun*; 1991—*Within Reach*; 1992—*The Way Love Is*; 1993—*Songs to Live By* (UCA); 1995—*Times Ten*; 1997—*Like a Cool Drink* [with the Ah-Koo-Stiks].

A rock musician from Syracuse, New York, Rick Cua first played in a fairly successful regional group named CRAC (an acronym formed from the surnames of its members). Raised a faithful Roman Catholic, he got saved when he attended a nondenominational Pentecostal church in 1977. Still he continued to play in secular circles, knowing nothing about the Christian music scene and having no interest in pursuing that venue. "Those of us that got saved in New York at that time, we just got saved," he says. "We cleaned up our life, we loved the Lord, but we kept doing what we were doing career wise. We were professional musicians. We played music, and we went home." Thus in 1979 he joined the general market band The Outlaws (bass, voc.) for two albums. Subsequently introduced to the Christian music scene by **Joe English,** Cua began a solo career as a Christian artist while still a member of The Outlaws. But then leaving the group even before they disbanded in 1982, he found his niche to be in the Christian market after all, embracing it with commitment that led him to turn down offers to play in Spyro Gyra (in 1983) and a re-

formed Outlaws (in 1986). After eight solo albums he formed his own company (UCA) to release a compilation record *(Songs to Live By).* He also published a book offering personal testimonies and devotionals related to some of the songs *(Songs to Live By,* Honor Books, 1984). After one more album of new material *(Times Ten),* he joined Bob Halligan Jr.'s **Ceili Rain** in 1997, only to leave a year later to become Creative Director for EMI Christian Publishing Company. Two other Ceili alums (Emedin Rivera and Tony Hooper) formed a backing band called The Ah-Koo-Stiks to join him on *Like a Cool Drink.*

Cua's debut record is distinctive in that it features a host of general market guest musicians, including **Joe English,** Jimmy Hall and Mike Duke of Wet Willie, several members of The Outlaws, and Robbie Dupree—who had hits with "Steal Away" (# 6) and "Hot Rod Hearts" (# 15) in 1980. Dupree and Marty McCall (of **Fireworks** and **First Call**) sing background vocals on Cua's single, "Fly Me to Heaven" (written by Bob Halligan Jr.), which was released to the general market but failed to chart there. The album did take off in the contemporary Christian market, however, where Cua was accorded the status befitting a celebrity convert. But critical reception of the album was evenly divided, as was the musical content of the record itself: about half the songs (the ones the critics liked) evince the sort of guitar-army onslaught The Outlaws were noted for; the other half (the ones the critics didn't like) got called "typical Christian pop pablum." In general, Cua's producer John Rosasco got blamed for the latter batch, while Cua himself got credit for the former. The song "You Can Still Rock 'n' Roll" became a Joan Jett-like anthem promising youth that God and good music are not incompatible. In interviews Cua sought to assure his audience that he would always be a rocker. "Ten years from now," he promised (in 1981), "I will not be turning out love ballads with violins."

He kept his word, for the most part. The self-produced *No Mystery* opens with three hook-laden rock songs ("He Lives in Me," "One Way Out" and "Changed") and closes with the foot-stompin' "Help Me Out." Ian Bairnson, guitarist for the Alan Parsons Project, is featured throughout. *You're My Road* serves up the unabashed blues rock of "Don't Say Suicide." *Wear Your Colors* (produced by **Dave Perkins,** Cua's frequent guitarist) rocks even harder than the previous projects with the anthemic title track (about taking a bold stand for Christ) and another Halligan composition, "This Raging Fire." At this point (1986) Cua told *CCM,* "I'm rockin' out and that's the end of it. Where my heart's at is rock and roll—and I'm gonna do it!" That didn't happen—and both critics and audiences would hold the unfulfilled prophecies against him. Executives at his new label, Reunion, urged him to adopt a softer sound that "would attract more female listeners." *Can't Stand Too Tall* went straight for the radio-pleasing pop sound (no violins, though). It features the warm and melodic "Forever Yours," the encouraging "We Are All the Same," and an acoustic duet with Ron Hemby of **The Imperials** called "For the Love of God." *CCM* titled their feature article on the album "Cua Mellows Out: Rick Cua Hopes More Commercial Sound Means More Ministry." *Midnight Sun* comes halfway back toward the rock sound of earlier releases, but predictably the two least rocking songs on the album scored the biggest radio hits: "I'll Be Satisfied," a soulful Hall and Oates-style ballad and "Young Boy, Young Girl," a duet with **Rebecca Sparks** about exercising self-control until marriage. *Within Reach* seemed to reverse the trend, with both of its opening two rockers ("Message of Love," "Heaven Won't Stop the Rain") making the radio charts. But most of the album is mellow, and two of its best tracks are sentimental ballads dedicated to Cua's two daughters ("Fifteen," "Diamond Girl"). The trend proved permanent. *CCM* called Cua's style on *The Way Love Is* "white-bread power pop" like Toto or post-Peter Cetera Chicago. *Times Ten* offers mostly midtempo songs with just two songs recalling the heavier sounds of yore: the autobiographical rocker, "Italo Americano" (with a chorus in Italian) and "Bull by the Horns," a song of encouragement that could have been on *Wear Your Colors.*

Lyrically Cua has been primarily known for doing albums with youth-oriented songs about sticking up for the faith ("Wear Your Colors") or for tackling issues appropriate to teen culture ("Don't Say Suicide," "Young Boy, Young Girl"). *The Way Love Is* showed a maturity of perspective in which he dealt more with relationships, writing songs of romantic love and marital commitment that were informed by a Christian perspective without necessarily parading affirmations of faith explicitly. A trio of worship songs turn up on *Times Ten.* Cua often credits his wife Diana as the inspiration for his songs and cites her insights as guiding him throughout his career. At her prompting, he became one of the first Christian music artists to become involved with the charitable organization Compassion International, a relationship that has endured for more than a decade.

Christian radio hits: "You Can Still Rock and Roll" (# 1 for 5 weeks in 1982); "Fly Me to Heaven" (# 19 in 1982); "This Raging Fire" (# 11 in 1987); "Forever Yours" (# 5 in 1988); "For the Love of God" (# 2 in 1988); "I'll Be Satisfied" (# 7 in 1989); "Young Boy, Young Girl" (# 5 in 1989); "Dedicated" (# 4 in 1990); "Power of the Lord" (# 2 in 1991); "Message of Love" (# 2 in 1991); "Heaven Won't Stop the Rain" (# 19 in 1992); "What If?" (# 2 in 1992); "Be a Man" (# 16 in 1993).

Bob (and Joy) Cull

As Bob Cull: 1972—*Welcome to the Family* (Armchair); 1975—*Remember* (Maranatha); 1980—*Collection* (Chalace); 1991—*Whisper . . . Songs of Love* (Asaph). As Bob and Joy Cull: 1979—*Windborne* (Chalace); 1984—*Last Horizon.*

In 1976 inspirational singer/songwriter Bob Cull wrote "Open Our Eyes," one of the most beautiful and enduring worship songs to come out of the Jesus movement and surely the highlight of Maranatha's best selling *Praise Two* album, which Cull also orchestrated and arranged. Cull was a recent discovery, as just one year earlier Maranatha! had almost simultaneously released two albums by the unknown artist—a reissue of his privately produced *Welcome to the Family* and the brand new *Remember.* Both became classic examples of what would become the new inspirational music (previously that label had been used for traditional hymns sung by artists like George Beverly Shea). Cull also contributed "Wait on the Lord" to the *Praise Three* album (Maranatha, 1979).

Welcome to the Family was a self-arranged and orchestrated effort that Cull described as autobiographical, "reflecting his thoughts on his family, his audience, and his relationship with God" (Di Sabatino). The album features soft and melodious tunes with catchy choruses that *Harmony* said tend to "sneak up on you." Standout tracks include "Someone to Follow" and "All I Need Is You." On *Remember,* Cull was able to supplement his own keyboards and pleasant voice with the talent from Maranatha's fold: **Karen Lafferty, Lewis McVay,** Jay Truax of **Love Song,** and John Wickham of **The Way** and **Parable** all lend their voices and instruments to make it an easy listening family affair. The touching title track and "Love Is Pure" are especially memorable. A sample line from the latter is typical of Cull's lyrical finesse: "Love is not a fire, reaching out to consume / Love is winter fuel, offering itself to be used."

Bob Cull married Joy Strange of **Selah** and **Parable,** and the two of them released some inspirational worship-oriented projects together. These would feature the wedding song "Only the Beginning" on *Windborne* and a fitting follow-up, "Let's Keep Growing," on *Last Horizon.* The title song from the latter album has a country edge and builds on the metaphor of Christians adrift on the sea of life, heading for the last horizon of heaven. The Culls later divorced, and she remarried to become Joy Strange-Hutton.

Christian radio hits: As Bob and Joy Cull: "Last Horizon" (# 33 in 1984).

Cult of Jester

Ed Finkler, gtr., voc., kybrd. 1999—*Funkatron* (Flaming Fish).

www.funkatron.com

A one-man band, Ed Finkler attracted quite a bit of attention for some years before releasing Cult of Jester's *Funkatron* through numerous appearances on compilation albums and through the private release of demos that showcased his unique brand of futuristic techno, electro-goth music. His trademark sound involves swirling synthesizers and growled or whispered vocals mixed over highly danceable hip-hop beats. For those who follow that scene, *Funkatron* was almost like a greatest hits package of his best work, with a heavy inclination toward the industrial sounds of artists like Trent Reznor and Nine Inch Nails. The standout song on the album is probably his impressive cover of "Lucretia My Reflection," first performed by general market artists Sisters of Mercy. Other highlights include the opener, "Teenage Warhead," and two funkier tunes, "Retro O.G." and "Ripple N' Hookers." Nothing in the lyrics to any of the songs suggests specific Christian content, and indeed the album (marketed on a label associated with Christian music) contains a warning, "A few instances of mild profanity may offend easily offended listeners." The potentially offensive words actually occur in soundbites that are sampled here or there on the disc and involve nothing that is not said with regularity on network TV.

Finkler is sometimes associated with Christian music because of his label and because he testifies to his faith in interviews. Like techno master **Moby,** however, he is far better known in the general market, and he does not really fit into the contemporary Christian music scene culturally or theologically. He maintains that he does not listen to any bands that are not in the general market, and that, in any case, he objects to "the idea of grouping music based on the spiritual beliefs of the artist." In an interview with *Robotnik* electronic magazine (not a Christian publication), he volunteered this statement on his spiritual beliefs: "I definitely believe that Jesus was the Son of God, and that he died to redeem us . . . but I don't deny the validity of, say Buddhism or Hinduism. I don't necessarily accept every tenet of their faith, but I don't do that with traditional Christianity either. Basically, I think the most important thing a person can do is to constantly search for the Truth. As long as that is what they desire, I believe they will be saved." Finkler himself admits that his "attitude toward spirituality" does not have a lot in common with what he sees in the contemporary Christian music subculture.

Andrew Culverwell

1971—*Where is the Love?* (Polydor); 1973—*Andrew* (Manna); 1976—*This Is the Song*; 1978—*Take Another Look* (DaySpring); 1980—*Everyday*; 1982—*Alive Again*; 1984—*The Best of Andrew Culverwell.*

Not quite in sync with the rock era, English singer/songwriter Andrew Culverwell released several albums of Andy Williams style MOR ballads with an inspirational focus. At age seventeen Culverwell toured Great Britain with the Four Kingsmen. He later came to America to pursue a Christian music career at the urging of **Andraé Crouch.** He wrote the contemporary Christmas classic, "Come On Ring Those Bells," for **Evie.** He continues to record new material, which is available through his website.

Christian radio hits: "I've Seen Him" (# 15 in 1983).

Curious Fools

Troy Deaton, gtr.; Stephen Murray, voc.; Dave Frank, kybrd. (− 1996); Shane Atkinson, drums (−1998) // Tok, bass (+ 1996); Michael Feighan, drums (+ 1998). 1995—*Curious Fools* (VIA); 1996—*Read;* 1998—*Electric Soul* (Gotee).

Curious Fools came out of the gate as relatively seasoned professionals with experience in Christian music. All four members were brought up in Christian homes, and all landed in Nashville where they worked individually at studio and session work before finding each other (Shane Atkinson and Troy Deaton went to Belmont College; Deaton and Dave Frank had toured previously as members of **Margaret Becker**'s band, The Reckoning). The band got an early primo spot opening for the **Seventy Sevens** on their 1993 tour.

The debut *Curious Fools* was usually lauded, and occasionally chided, for the band's noticeable aural similarities to their heroes Led Zeppelin and **U2.** Stephen Murray's voice bears natural similarities to Robert Plant's, and he invests it with the forceful angst of Bono; Deaton seems to have Jimmy Page's familiar riffs and The Edge's angular chops down cold. With guests like **Jimmy A** and Wade Jaynes (of **Chagall Guevara**) and with production assistance from Steve Griffith (of **Vector**), the musicianship of the album was unquestioned. The lyrics, on the other hand, were so rich in metaphor and imagery as to leave many fans and critics wondering just what the songs were about. The least ambiguous song is a cover of the Janis Joplin hit "Piece of My Heart" (written by Erma Franklin, Aretha's sister), but even that left traditional Christian music fans wondering whether there was some hidden spiritual meaning to the song that they were missing. The next project was appropriately titled *Read,* and it explored themes of *mis*reading and ambiguity derived from the band's experiences with the first project. The **U2**/Zeppelin comparisons diminish as the band begins to forge its own guitar-driven modern rock sound, heavy on catchy choruses and memorable hooks. The group also ups their hip quotient way beyond Joplin by covering an obscure song by the underground '60s rock band Moby Grape ("Murder") as a hidden track. "Con Con" seems to poke fun at the superficiality of being a Christian star. "Se7en" might be about hope in apocalyptic circumstances. Unfortunately the album got little promotion due to VIA's financial woes. The next album, produced by **The Gotee Brothers** on their titular label, shows a third incarnation of the Curious Fools' sound: a much more direct melodic approach that drew comparisons to **Smalltown Poets** or **PFR** (though the Zeppelin influence was still in there somewhere). Murray and Deaton finally acceded to demands for more accessible lyrics, and on *Electric Soul* they craft songs that speak clearly of doubt, self-loathing, mercy, and reconciliation. On a lighter note,

Deaton, Murray, and Frank also formed the '80s-retro band **The Dell Griffiths** as a side project.

Johnny Curtis

Dates unknown—*Apache Country Gospel* (Canyon); *Leavin' This Reservation; With Apache Gospel Sounds; In Loving Memories; Spirit of God; In Loving Memories II; Live in Concert; Travelin' for Jesus; The Best of Johnny Curtis: 20 Years of Apache Gospel.*

www.canyonrecords.com/artcurtis.htm

Native American gospel singer Johnny Curtis was unknown to the world of contemporary Christian music at large until *True Tunes* magazine reviewed his career retrospective album in the late '90s. The recordings listed above were released between 1977 and 1991 and were not generally sold in stores. The production quality for many of the records was low budget, imparting a certain primitive quality to the albums that may or may not enhance their appeal. The general musical style is that of countrified rock, but over the years Curtis tried on a lot of musical hats. "Thank You, Jesus" is rockabilly; "Spirit of God" is an Eagles-style ballad; "Hold My Hand" features a chorus of children singing in Apache. Most of the songs speak explicitly and even evangelistically about the Christian faith. "Leavin' This Reservation," for example, offers a distinctive Apache look at the promise of heaven.

Cush

2000 Lineup: Eric Campuzano, bass; Wayne Everett, drums; Frank Lenz, drums; Andy Prickett, gtr.; Gene Eugene, kybrd.; Michael Knott, voc.; Doug Moss [a.k.a. Snowman], gtr., voc.; Jeff Schroeder, gtr.; Tim Taber, voc.; Blake Westcott, gtr.; Jyro Xhan, gtr. 2000—*New Sounds* (Northern); 2001—*Cush* [EP].

Cush was the ultimate Christian alternative rock supergroup. The lineup was incredible. For general market comparison, it would be as if Billy Corgan and Kurt Cobain had gotten together with Pearl Jam and half of Soundgarden to collaborate on a project that was then released shortly after Cobain's death. The band was supposed to be just a one-time experiment, though not in the sense of some thrown together all-star "We Are the World" jam. They really did gel as a group. A truncated version even played some festivals together. Here's how the credentials shake down: Eric Campuzano, Wayne Everett, Andy Prickett and Tim Taber had once made up **The Prayer Chain;** Gene Eugene was in **Adam Again** and the **Lost Dogs** (and died tragically just before Cush's first album came out); Frank Lenz and Jyro Xhan were in **Fold Zandura; Michael Knott** was in **LSU** and the **Aunt Bettys;** Jeff Schroeder was in **The Violet Burning;** Snowman (Doug Moss) was in **Honey;** Blake Westcott was in **Bloomsday.** Campuzano, Everett, and Schroeder were also in **The Lassie Foundation.** Popularly, Cush was viewed as a **Michael Knott** project, on which he was backed by a reunited **Prayer Chain** and assorted high profile guests.

Of course supergroups are notorious for making bad albums, but the verdict on Cush's main release is that the songs are all quite good. The overall sound is described by *Bandoppler* as reminiscent of mid '80s **U2.** Knott *is* the dominant influence, as he tends to be with any project in which he is involved, but elements of Radiohead mellow pop that are more associated with **The Prayer Chain** or **The Lassie Foundation** than with Knott are definitely evident. On the opening track, "Heaven Sent," Knott pleads with a child, "Tell your mother, don't give up on me." Hooks abound on songs like "The Touch," which features spacey nods to David Bowie and the Beatles. "Angelica" is a full-tilt rocker with Knott singing in a melodic falsetto voice. "Porpoise" is trip-hop jazz, with a curious trumpet line. "Crush Me" is an uncharacteristically confident love song. "The Smallest Part" has explicitly Christian Bonoesque lyrics ("For Christ to build my head / I'll do the smallest part").

The success of Cush may derive from the band members' commitment to being something of an anti-supergroup. Indeed *CCM* would say, "Cush is more of a musical concept than a band." The project was built around a "Cush manifesto" that had the members committing themselves to a variety of principles, including a willingness "to have anybody play any role, whoever is most suited for it at the time" and to making music "to be performed in any way, by any combination of people, in any setting." The name Cush is slang for "cushion," which relates to the Holy Spirit's designation (in some biblical translations) as "The Comforter" (John 14:16, 26; 15:26; 16:7). Knott said, "When you listen to this record, you're going to feel the Holy Spirit and know the Holy Spirit is moving. That's what Cush stands for."

Not to let a good thing die, a Cush remnant (with Knott noticeably missing but with at least Campuzano, Everett, Lenz, and Prickett participating) reunited to make another eight-song CD in 2001. The latter project has a totally different sound, more in line with British punk music of the '80s (Sex Pistols, Modern English). Most of the lyrics seem nonsensical ("Rabbits run where furs become the beating of hearts"), but a rambunctious song called "Rev It Up" includes the chorus, "Jesus! / Save our souls! / Jesus! / Rock and roll!"

Cyberhalo

Pashawkee; J. A. Ultra. 1999—*Cyberhalo* (Ionic); 2000—*Y3K.*

www.ionicrecords.com/cyberhalo.html

The anonymous electronic band Cyberhalo released a debut album that is unusually innovative for its chosen genre. Billed as "the first electronica/trance concept album," the record is an almost all-instrumental meditation on the book of Revelation. Cyberhalo incorporates expected synthesizer-driven pop and guitar thrashing industrial sounds but supplements these with surprising moments of world music (an Australian didgeridoo) and forays into eclectic styles (elements of swing). Vocal samples of sermons and Scripture readings enhance the theme.

Cybergrind

Mike Carlisle, gtr., voc.; Mike Forsberg, drums; Peter Sheils, bass. 2000—*Transcend* (Rowe).

Australian death metal/grindcore band Cybergrind was formed in 1995 by ex-**Mortification** guitarist Carlisle. Forsberg had played with Carlisle previously in a band called Ragewar. *Rad Rockers* describes them as offering "lightning fast double bass drumming, gutteral vocals shouted hoarsely, machine-gun guitar riffing, coupled with song titles and lyrics that must have been inspired by Ted Kirkpatrick (of **Tourniquet**)." *HM* notes that the group's vocals are "typical death metal" but that the diversity of guitar sounds keeps the group from sounding like every other metal band: "every song has a new riff, twist, or style to keep it from all sounding the same." The group themselves define their mission as being to "experiment with musical extremes with the intention of creating the most unearthly, brutal sound imaginable."

Cybershadow

Jess McIntyre, voc., gtr., kybrd. 1998—*The Birth of Future* (Flaming Fish).

One of Flaming Fish's one-man industrial bands (cf. **Cult of Jester**), Cybershadow (a.k.a. Jess McIntyre) released a debut album that is regarded as one of Christian music's darkest, yet most lyrically honest productions. The album, according to Flaming Fish, is intended as "a wake-up call" to a world that is "being slowly devoured by its vices." It is divided thematically into three trimesters, in accord with the metaphor of the title. The opening track, "Self Control," features McIntyre pleading, "Repetitive history . . . why this disgrace?" The next song, "Third World," deals with the horror of ethnic cleansing in the Balkans. Then "Civilian Tank Dept." offers a picture of menacing bureaucracy. The second trimester, however, moves from political to personal, with songs like "Shattered Trust," which deals with marital betrayal and spousal abuse. Though McIntyre presents himself as a Christian artist and a theme of hope does surface briefly on "Don't Fear Your Future," there is little in the content of *The Birth of Future* that points to any specific Christian ideas. The album displays industrial's typical fascination with science fiction in the theme song, "Universal Love," about a romance between an alien and a human. They kill themselves in *Romeo and Juliet* fashion.

D

Lisa Daggs (and Lisa Daggs-Charette)

As Lisa Daggs: 1991—*Who Are You* (LDM); 1993—*Angel in Your Eyes* (Pakaderm); 1996—*Love Is the Bottom Line* (Cheyenne). As Lisa Daggs-Charette: 1999—*The Only Truth I Know* (Serenity).

www.lisadaggs-charette.com

Christian country singer Lisa Daggs can relate a testimony of hard living prior to dedicating her life to Christ in early 1990. Born in Los Angeles, she was raised in Sacramento, California, by her mother. Her parents' divorce when she was ten hit her especially hard, and as a young adult she struggled with addictions to drugs and alcohol. With multiple arrests for cocaine possession, she was facing an extended prison term when she entered a recovery program and then two months later embraced Christianity with the fervor of a new convert. Clean and sober, and transformed within, she began singing and recording Christian music. Her style is basically that of the newer pop-country sound made popular by such artists as Trisha Yearwood and Mary Chapin-Carpenter. In 1993 Daggs would describe it as "country with a touch of rhythm and blues." The Christian Country Music Association named Daggs their Best New Artist in 1995 and a year later tagged her Entertainer of the Year. In 1995 she married Zach Charette and has continued to record under a hyphenated name.

Who Are You mixes ballads and worship songs with more upbeat tunes, including the opening title track. *Angel in Your Eyes* was produced by **John** and Dino **Elefante** and features more relationship-oriented songs than the first project. It also includes "My House," which Daggs describes as "a Christian re-covery song." Another song, "Leave Your Bags at the Door," expresses the invitation to come to Christ just as one is, "without baggage." But *Love Is the Bottom Line* was Daggs' breakthrough album. The songs "Be Like Noah," "Hands on the Plow," "You First Loved Me," "Cross It Out," and "Save It for a Rainy Day" were all chart toppers on the Christian country charts. *The Only Truth I Know* includes a cover of the old Grand Funk song, "Some Kind of Wonderful" (cf. **Mark Farner**), along with the ballad "He's Not a Baby Anymore" and the challenging single, "How Big Is Your Want To?"

Dakoda Motor Co.

Chuck Cummings, drums; Peter King, gtr., voc.; Derik Toy, bass; Davia Vallesillo, voc. (−1996) // Elliot Chenault, gtr. (+ 1994); Melissa Brewer, voc. (+ 1996). 1993—*Into the Son* (Myrrh); 1994—*Welcome Race Fans;* 1996—*Railroad* (Holiday).

Professional surfer Peter King formed Dakoda Motor Co. in La Jolla, California. The band first toured and gained a following under the name Dakoda but then had to adopt the longer name to avoid (legal) conflicts with the Pennsylvania group called Dakota. Showcasing King's pop sensibilities and Davia Vallesillo's incredible vocal talents, Dakoda Motor Co. remains one of the most highly regarded rock groups to come out of the Christian music scene. The group's sound is hard to categorize—a tribute to their originality. The strong female vocals fronting hard guitars had critics reaching for Belly or Concrete Blonde analogies, but on several songs the neo-hippie surf pop tone of King's songs are more suggestive of The-Bangles-meet-

R.E.M. King himself was a fixture on MTV, where he hosted both *Sandblast* and *Beach House,* and these connections helped the band to gain mainstream respect and exposure. The group also got an early chance to open for the general market band Mary's Danish, which included King's brother David as a member. Their song "Rockin' in the Mall" (from *Welcome Race Fans*) was used in an ad campaign for Chevrolet Camaro (in a new version called "Drivin' around the World"). *Billboard* magazine put the band on its 1993 Critic's Choice List, claiming "the sunny charm of this Southern California alternative Christian band can't be denied." After the group disbanded, Chuck Cummings (who had previously played with **Common Bond** and **LSU**) joined the **Aunt Bettys** and **Fanmail.** King went on to record with **The Surfers,** and Vallesillo sang on **Vector**'s *Temptation* album. As of 2002 she was married and living in California, writing praise and worship songs.

Into the Son won critics over immediately with a blend of jubilant rockers and acoustic based tracks like the first single, "Grey Skies," which looks for guidance in the midst of ambiguity: "Grey clouds in the sky, clutter up my mind / You are my light, guide me through the night." Other songs offer social commentary ("Wasteland," "All the Good Generals") and California praise ("Sing Hallelujah," "Son Dancer"). *Into the Son* also includes a remake of the **Bob Cull** song "Only the Beginning," rechristened as "Jesus Song." *Welcome Race Fans* continues in the same vein, serving up an entire platter of alternately warm, melodic, driving, and innovative tunes. "Stand Up" (the band's best song) and "Free" (with King on lead vocal) are especially noteworthy as fresh and fun songs, ready-made for car tape decks in the summertime. *Railroad* features a change of vocalists, a more overall electric assault, and a much more secular sound. Eschewing specific spiritual themes, the band (now on a division of Atlantic headed by David King) sings about topics like gossip ("Rattlesnake"), drug abuse ("Falling Down"), and relationships ("Sampled," "Tommy") from a Christian perspective without any overt allusions to faith. King (i.e., Peter) explained that the group did not want to "market its spirituality."

Indeed, as a group that straddles the distinctions between general and Christian markets, Dakoda Motor Co. was in the forefront of "crossover trends" and was often regarded as controversial for that reason. King allowed that he is all for evangelism and witness, but "I just don't see rock music as a powerful Christian ministry . . . Rock 'n' roll is just rock 'n' roll and I love it for what it is." Derik Toy agreed: "People don't become Christians because of something a band says from a stage." In fact, King alleged that much contemporary Christian music trivializes the gospel and does so for purely commercial reasons, using Jesus as a marketing ploy. He also became something of an apologist for the secular music industry, particularly MTV. He objected strenuously to the notion that the

video channel is biased against Christian music, claiming that it will "play anything they see as a potential hit, Christian or not."

For trivia buffs: Although Peter King is known in the Christian music subculture as a musician, he is actually better known in the world at large as a surfer. Having traveled with the World Professional Surfing Tour, he has been on the cover of *Surfing* magazine four times and has been a frequent poster boy for the California clothing company Billabong.

Christian radio hits: "Grey Clouds" (# 4 in 1993); "Freedom" (# 9 in 1994); "Truth" (# 14 in 1994).

Damascus Road

Pat Asher, bass; Dennis Byram, drums, voc.; Johnnie Helm, voc., gtr.; Tommie Helm, bgv.; Steve Schalchlin, kybrd. 1977—*A Glimpse of Freedom* (JesuSongs).

The Jacksonville, Texas, band known as Damascus Road was founded by evangelist Tommie Helm (twin brother of Johnnie) as an attention-getting vehicle for his revivals. Apparently they made two independent albums called *Spirit and Understanding* and *JesuSongs,* but *A Glimpse of Freedom* is the project for which they are remembered. It incorporates a wide varieties of styles, from country-blues rock to easy listening. *Jesus Music* magazine prefers the former and singles out "I'm Not Talkin' about Jesus" as a particularly impressive non-mellow number. Steve Schalchlin says the group began as a traditional southern gospel quartet but changed overnight after someone gave them a **Love Song** album. They toured Texas and Louisiana for five years in a van but never made any money. T. Helm drew up a hand-lettered Declaration of Dependence (upon God) document, fashioned to look like the Declaration of Independence, and had band members sign it. Eventually Schalchlin, who was the main songwriter, left the group when, as he puts it, he had "a crisis of faith and thought it would be hypocritical to continue." He later wrote a musical play, *The Last Session,* which gained some notice and popularity in New York City. It relates the story of a band reunion in a recording studio and "confronts issues of AIDS and homophobia."

Damask Rose

Bryan Linder, voc., drums; Steve Welfring, voc., gtr.; Matt Wineroth, voc., bass. 1999—*Point of View* (Planet).

Damask Rose formed in 1996 and is based out of San Jose, California. With a three-man lineup and hard rock trio vocals, the group seems to be going for a sound similar to **King's X.** *HM* magazine described their first major release *(Point of View)* as "what happens when a corporate rock band modernizes its sound." The record contains a strong collection of tunes with well-placed harmonies and a definite '90s feel. Standout songs include "Glory Train" and "I Am Waiting." The group's moniker comes from the name of a flower found in the Middle East and literally means "beauty ever new."

Damita

2000—*Damita* (Atlantic).

Damita is a first-name-only Christian R&B singer from Detroit. After being coached by Mattie Moss Clark (cf. **The Clark Sisters**) and singing backup for **Aretha Franklin,** she joined the gospel group Dettrick Haddon and the Voices of Truth, married the group's leader, and was then discovered by an Atlantic executive who called her voice "the best I've ever heard." Damita offers emotional ballads and hard-rocking street songs with straightforward gospel lyrics. She views her music as a ministry to youth, offering them a "new message" to counter "depression, abusive relationships, and despair." Her debut album features the midtempo "Why" and the more energetic "Hold On to Your Faith." It also includes a romantic duet with Haddon ("The Wedding Song") and a guest rap vocal from **Toby McKeehan** on "Truth," a rocker that recalls Janet Jackson.

Christian radio hits: "Spirit Inside" (# 7 in 2001).

Dana

1982—*Totally Yours* (Word); 1984—*Let There Be Love.*

A charismatic Irish Catholic woman by the name of Dana Scallon recorded at least two albums of Christian music in the early '80s. Dana was discovered by Kurt Kaiser (composer of the popular song, "Pass It On"), who produced her *Totally Yours* album. She was a native of strife-torn Ulster and offered a number of pastoral songs for healing and worship. An upbeat number called "Totus Tuus" (a Latin phrase meaning "totally yours") became a pop hit in her native land. "Mary's Song" (written by David Mullins) offers a tender treatment of the sorrows of Mary.

Dance House Children

Ronnie Martin, voc., kybrd.; Jason Martin, gtr. 1991—*Songs and Stories* (Blonde Vinyl); 1992—*Jesus.*

Dance House Children was a pioneering synth-pop/dance band founded by Ronnie Martin of **Rainbow Rider** and **Joy Electric** and his brother Jason of **Starflyer 59** fame. Jason is one of the best guitarists in Christian rock, but the Dance House Children were primarily a synthesizer band. Their two albums bear aural similarities to the Pet Shop Boys, especially on upbeat songs like "Grandfather Clock," "Spinning Wheel," and "Merry." Emotional midtempo numbers ("Held Up by Your Wishes"), romantic love songs ("Once Upon Your Lips"), and occasional excursions into house music ("Uncle Art") or techno ("The Locket Maker") add to the mix. Lyrically the songs are as cryptic as those on the Martin brothers' other projects, eschewing direct reference for poetic imagery. "Grandfather Clock" is about aging; the titular figure in "The Locket Maker" appears to be a symbol for God. Ronnie Martin would eventually tell *True Tunes,* "Dance House Children became incredibly boring and repetitive. I thought, 'I've got these synths; I've gotta see what I can do with them. I've gotta take everything to its utmost extreme.'"

Daniel Amos (a.k.a. **DA** and **da** and **dä**)

Terry Taylor, gtr., voc.; Jerry Chamberlain, gtr., voc. (– 1983, + 1993, –2001); Marty Dieckmeyer, bass (–1981); Steve Baxter, gtr., voc. (–1976) // Mark Cook, kybrd., voc. (+ 1977; – 1981); Ed McTaggart, drums (+ 1976); Alex MacDougall, perc. (+ 1981, –1981); Tim Chandler, bass (+ 1981); Greg Flesch, gtr. (+ 1986); Rob Watson, kybrd. (+ 1983, – 1987). 1976—*Daniel Amos* (Maranatha); 1977—*Shotgun Angel*; 1981—*Horrendous Disc* (Solid Rock); *Alarma!* (NewPax); 1983—*Doppelgänger* (Alarma!); 1984—*Vox Humana* (Refuge); 1986—*Fearful Symmetry* [as DA] (Frontline); *The Revelation*; 1987—*Darn Floor: Big Bite* [as da] 1990—*Live Bootleg '82* [as DA] (Stunt); 1991—*Kalhoun* [as dä] (Brainstorm); 1993—*Motor Cycle*; 1994—*Bibleland*; 1994—*Preachers from Outer Space: Live at the Anaheim Center, Easter Weekend 1978* (Stunt); 1995—*Songs of the Heart* (Brainstorm); 1998—*Our Personal Favorite World Famous Hits* (KMG); 2000—*The Alarma Chronicles Book Set* (Stunt); *Live at Cornerstone 2000* (M8); 2001—*Mr. Buechner's Dream* (Galaxy21).

www.danielamos.com

Prompted to decide who is "the greatest Christian rock band of all time," critics are generally pressed between naming Daniel Amos or the **Seventy Sevens** (depending on whether one prefers the Beatles or the Stones, respectively). The former got its start during the second phase of the Jesus movement and has been cranking out innovative and sometimes perplexing albums for more than twenty-five years. **Terry Taylor**'s gift for eclectic, melodic songwriting would enable the group to evolve rapidly from its country rock beginnings into a new-wave act that had potential to keep changing with the times. They have an intense following and are one of those rare acts (in Christian or general market music) that truly deserves the label "alternative"; in fact, Daniel Amos was playing alternative rock music for at least a decade before that genre officially existed. One critic has suggested that Daniel Amos has rarely played CCM ("contemporary Christian music") but FCM ("future Christian music"), indicating that they are the trend setters others seek to emulate. This has meant, of course, that their music has often been impossible to categorize and difficult to market. The discography above reveals that the band has had more than a little trouble sticking with a record company for any extended time—at least until they formed their own label(s), Stunt and Brainstorm. In the contemporary Christian music subculture, thinking that Daniel Amos is a person rather than a group is a faux pas tantamount to thinking Alice Cooper is a woman or Jethro Tull, a solo artist.

Daniel Amos is fronted by **Terry Scott Taylor,** who is also known as a solo artist, as a member of **The Swirling Eddies,** the **Lost Dogs,** and the **Rap'sures,** and as a consummate producer of other acts. **The Swirling Eddies**, in fact, include Taylor, Jerry Chamberlain, Rob Watson, Tim Chandler, and Greg Flesch, and so are sometimes regarded as simply Daniel Amos performing under another name. Prior to forming Daniel Amos, Taylor played in several other bands with more interesting names. While a sophomore at Los Gatos High School in San Jose, he formed The Scarlet Staircase. He left that act to join guitarist Tim Warner in The Cardboard Scheme, a cover band that opened for **Van Morrison** in 1966. A year later he reunited with Scarlet Staircase alums to form Copperplate Window, a group that (ironically, given later circumstances) tried to copy another local group called People by sporting two lead singers; one of People's lead singers was **Larry Norman.** Taylor completed high school in 1969 and joined a group called Pecos Bill (a.k.a. Down Home) where it is thought that he first learned the California country sound for which he would soon be famous. Then in 1971, just as the Jesus movement revival was breaking, Taylor (who had been brought up in the church) dedicated his life to Christ and soon learned that his old compatriot Tim Warner had done the same. Taylor and Warner formed one of the earliest Jesus music groups, an acoustic trio called Good Shepherd, which played all around northern California and was featured (along with **Larry Norman** and **Love Song**) in an early documentary film about the revival called *The Sonworshippers* (1971). Good Shepherd was set to record an album when Warner left for personal reasons. After a short-lived group called Judge Rainbow and the Prophetic Trumpets, Taylor formed another influential Jesus music group called Jubal's Last Stand (with Steve Baxter, Kenny Paxton, and Chuck Starnes). The group opened for **Love Song,** who encouraged them to move to Orange County and become part of the Calvary Chapel scene. With some comings and goings, Jubal's Last Stand (with the name shortened to just Jubal) morphed into the core of what would become Daniel Amos. The latter name was actually adopted on the spur of the moment when they signed up for a meeting of bands and discovered, somewhat incredibly, that there was already another Calvary Chapel group called Jubal (fronted by **Darrell Mansfield;** the group later became **Gentle Faith**). Since at that point Taylor thought they would be a country group, he just combined the names of two Old Testament prophets in an amalgam that he says reminded him of "an old country gentleman strumming on his front porch." For some reason—just out

of general weirdness, as near as anyone can tell—the group decided to change its name to either DA (pronounced *dee-ay*) or da (pronounced *dah*) for a few albums and to dä (pronounced *day*—perhaps?) for *Kalhoun.*

As for the other Daniel Amos members, Chandler has doubled as a member of **The Choir.** Ed McTaggart was previously a member of **The Road Home.** Alex MacDougall was also a member of **Selah, The Way** and **The Richie Furay Band.** He played with Daniel Amos on most of their early albums, though he is listed as an official member only on *Horrendous Disc.* Watson went on to join a late '80s version of The Surfaris, the '60s rock band whose original lineup scored enormous hits with "Wipe Out" and "Surfer Joe" (this version also included Jay Truax of **Love Song** and David Raven, also of **The Swirling Eddies**).

The self-titled *Daniel Amos* debut (produced by **Al Perkins**) was mostly—but not entirely—an Eagles rip-off. A number of Christian bands **(Bethlehem, Canaan, Children of the Light)** were trying to emulate that very popular group's made-for-gospel sound, but none did it so well as Daniel Amos. Song for song, and as a total package, *Daniel Amos* stands up to any of the albums the Eagles made prior to *Hotel California.* "Losers and Winners" and "Dusty Road" are every bit as compelling as "Tequila Sunrise." The song "Don't Light Your Own Fire" (with Baxter's gorgeous a capella "Servant's Prayer" prelude) is stunning. The album would sound dated on its twenty-fifth anniversary, but its sincere sentiments and sometimes awful theology are part of its enduring charm. Aging Jesus freaks fortunate enough to have one of the rare CD copies (which went for $100 in 1999) nod their heads and smile, "Yeah! We really did use to think like that!" The album opens and closes with songs that are as judgmental as they are hilarious. "Jesus Is Jehovah to Me" rips into the Jehovah's Witnesses ("If you're really 'Awake' / You'll make no mistake"). Then, for the record's closing, "Skeptic's Song," the boys abandon their cowboy garb completely and perform as The Maranatha Mood Makers, a vaudeville-styled Big Band outfit. The song itself cheerfully promises hellfire and brimstone to doubters: "Oh my! You'll fry, as we wave goodbye to you!" In 1991 Taylor himself said, "Those lines make me cringe." One *can* view it as "insensitive to the human condition" (Taylor's adult perspective) *or* one can view it as a variation on the Squirrel Nut Zippers' shtick—twenty-five years too soon. Other highlights from this debut project include "Abidin'," which also foregoes country-rock for light jazz, and "William," an ode to the Christian geek whom everyone made fun of in high school. The CD version of the album also includes two bonus songs, "Happily Married Man" and "Ain't Gonna Fight It." The latter is another of the group's Eagles-clone songs, but one of their absolute best. Originally placed on the *Maranatha Five* compilation album in 1976, the song features profoundly spiritual lyrics and perfect vocal harmonies. Forget "Tequila Sunrise." This one compares to "Best of My Love."

By 1977 *Daniel Amos* was already regarded as one of the three or four best Christian albums ever made. Pressure was enormous for a follow-up, and (in a manner that would prove typical) the group managed to surpass all of those expectations while simultaneously confounding critics and disappointing fans. *Shotgun Angel* is like two albums. Side One, admittedly, seems like *Daniel Amos, Part Two*. Three songs, "Days and Nights," "Praise Song" and the simply incredible "Father's Arms," are very much like the songs on the debut record, only better. But then there is "Black Gold Fever" and "Meal," country-rock gone . . . well, weird. And there is the album's bubblegum-country title track, written by **The Road Home**'s Bill Sprouse Jr. (who did write two of contemporary Christian music's best songs—"Since I Met Jesus" and "Psalm 5"—but also wrote this). It relates a "Convoy" story about Jesus talking to a trucker on his C.B. radio and sending an angel to drive the rig when the guy is too tired. Pretty stupid, actually, but Sprouse had just died, and perhaps Daniel Amos wanted to pay their respects. In any case, the album *Shotgun Angel* is famous for Side Two. Here the supposedly country rock group presents a neo-classical mini-opera that incorporates snatches of Queen, Pink Floyd, and *Abbey Road,* but that really sounds like nothing ever produced in contemporary music, Christian or otherwise. Thematically the epic was derived from the teachings of various prophets of dispensationalist premillenial eschatology, which unfortunately included the group's otherwise biblically-oriented pastor at Calvary Chapel, Chuck Smith. Beginning with an orchestral overture, the opus meanders through a series of songs based on ideas that are often derived from (or imposed on) the book of Revelation: the rapture, the tribulation, and the mark of the beast ("he's gonna do a number on you"). It all concludes with another glorious country song likening the returning Christ and his band of angels to "a posse in the sky." Side Two of *Shotgun Angel* was re-released in 1986 as a separate project called *The Revelation,* featuring interspersed narration by Chuck Smith and one new song ("Soon").

The Daniel Amos saga really heats up with *Horrendous Disc.* Forsaking the L.A. cowboy routine altogether, Taylor drew on his true influences, the Beatles and the Beach Boys, to produce an album that sounds like what the Fab Four might have come up with if they'd managed to hold it together for another decade. The title track is another little epic built on the creative metaphor of one's entire life being recorded (on a "horrendous disc") to be played on judgment day (see Matthew 12:36). Other classic, standout songs include "Hound of Heaven" (based on the famous nineteenth century poem by Francis Thompson) and the album's opener, "I Love You # 19." David

Di Sabatino calls *Horrendous Disc* "definitely one of the most unique Christian albums ever committed to vinyl." The record's production and release were accompanied by a good deal of controversy, much of which centered on disagreements between the band and Solid Rock president **Larry Norman.** Contractual disputes and quarrels over various legal and artistic matters kept the album in captivity for three years, while anxious fans waited and even mounted a campaign calling for its release. A reporter named Karen Platt wrote a lengthy article for *CCM* magazine laying the blame for the fiasco on Daniel Amos. The band's attorney responded with several quibbles. Platt later acknowledged she had been in "a relationship" with Norman at the time the article was written. The Norman/Daniel Amos feud would become something of a scandal within the contemporary Christian music community, often fueled by invective from the Norman camp. In early 1981 Norman released an album called *Barking at the Ants* (Phydeaux), which featured a cover photo of Taylor with claws drawn on his hands. In 1991 Norman's *Stranded in Babylon* album featured a song ("A Dangerous Place to Be") with the obscure lyric: "Falling down the Scarlet Staircase come Jubal's Last Band / They can't see the cross cause they're too busy listening to the clapping of one hand." The key to that first line is knowing that Scarlet Staircase and Jubal's Last Band were the names of Taylor's pre-Daniel Amos bands. The whole controversy was revisited when *Horrendous Disc* remained for several years the only Daniel Amos product unavailable on compact disc. It finally did come out on Solid Rock in 2000, albeit with lengthy liner notes by Norman, in which he gave his side of the story, claiming, for instance, an intimate involvement in the record's production that would ensure its eventual quality (Taylor says, "The truth is Norman had nothing to do with the recording of that record"). Norman also adorned the CD version of the album with two bonus tracks—not lost Daniel Amos songs or demos, but two different versions of Norman himself doing "Hound of Heaven." Thing is, they're both very good.

With three major successes in a row, the time seemed right for Daniel Amos to flub an album and nobody would have blamed them for a slump. But, no. On their fourth outing they produced what is, by most accounts, the masterpiece of their career. *Alarma!* took the Christian music world by storm with a completely different sound than the pop-oriented *Horrendous Disc* or the previous country-rock projects. Taylor had apparently listened to Elvis Costello or Talking Heads a lot during the *HD* captivity, and on the very heels of that record's eventual release, the result became evident: Daniel Amos had gone new-wave. But they had their own sound—a little bit like the Cars and the Police and Nick Lowe, but not really. Equally impressive was the new lyrical direction. Instead of trying to evangelize the unsaved masses (who seldom heard their music anyway), the group turned its attention to believers. The title song seeks to sound "the alarm" for complacent Christians who have become too comfortable, too ingrown, to deal with what is going on all about them. Additional songs tackle such issues as TV preachers ("Big Time/Big Deal"), isolationism ("My Room"), and world hunger ("Faces to the Window"). The church is accused of being judgmental ("Colored By") and of playing "Baby Games." In time, such issue songs would become run of the mill for contemporary Christian music, but they were not at all typical for a Christian band in 1981. In addition to the title track, the songs "Walls of Doubt" and "Ghost of the Heart" deserve mention as exemplars of the group's perfect blend of British new-wave and California surf music. In the former, Taylor goes retro (before it was cool), singing, "There's that look in your eyes / I know what you're thinking / It's just like the '60s to me / You paint it all black." And in "Ghost of the Heart," Taylor lays bare his own motives, the troubling of conscience as to whether he makes his music for Christ or for self: "The monster of vanity gets frightened by the ghost of the heart." Critics pulled out all the superlatives for this album: "the most exciting release of the year"; "brash, new, and intensely creative"; "possibly the most significant album in the genre of Christian rock."

As it turns out, *Alarma!* was just volume one of what would ultimately be a four-volume set. *Doppelgänger, Vox Humana,* and *Fearful Symmetry* followed as *The Alarma Chronicles* Volumes II, III, and IV. An unfolding story accompanied the releases, loosely tying their themes to a fantasy adventure epic with spiritual overtones (à la *Star Wars,* Tolkien, and so forth). Ultimately all four albums would be packaged into a three-disc set accompanied by an elaborate hardback book *(The Alarma Chronicles Book Set).* Musically the three records that succeeded *Alarma!* are all solid efforts. *Doppelgänger* and *Vox Humana* are more oriented toward Gary Numan/Thomas Dolby computer rock than the first in the series, and *Fearful Symmetry* brings it all to a grandiose conclusion with the group's sole venture into art rock. *Doppelgänger* is built around a rather ingenious concept, applying the science fiction notion of a ghostly double to the Apostle Paul's belief that humans live out their lives here on earth while, in some sense, they are simultaneously "seated with Christ in heaven" (cf. Ephesians 1:20). Taylor would later say he regarded "Youth with a Machine (YWAM)" as the centerpiece for *Doppelgänger* and perhaps of the whole project. The song warns of what Taylor would call "the siren call of technology," with its "whirlwind of commercialism and consumerism and blind eye to truth, compassion, and love." "Real Girls" is a response to Duran Duran's "Girls on Film," intended to protest the exploitation of women. "Angels Tuck You In" and "Big Cars" address questionable prosperity doctrines that are

taught in some fundamentalist branches of Christendom, and "Little Crosses" decries Christian fascination with trinkets and religious junk. The album also includes "Do Big Boys Cry?" and "Mall All over the World." The latter song presents the image of an omnipresent shopping mall as a tongue-in-cheek realization of the ultimate American ideal for global unity. *Vox Humana* offers "Home Permanent" (a melodic radio-friendly tune with subtle irony in the lyrics), "Sanctuary" (about entering into the peace of God), and the unforgettable "(It's the Eighties So Where's Our) Rocket Packs" (a clever song that wonders how progress ought to be measured). "When Worlds Collide" is an ambiguous love song (between man and woman or between God and humanity?). "The Incredible Shrinking Man" revisits the depersonalizing effect of technology, with further input from the growth of feminism and its likely effect on male roles and responsibilities. "Dance Stop" is a sarcastic, supposedly anti-antidance tune that would become a concert favorite. *Fearful Symmetry* is the series nadir (cf. *Phantom Menace* to the first three Star Wars films) but scores with one swirling opus of a song called "The Pool," a highlight of the eventual greatest hits package. Some fifteen years down the road, Christian rock's premier critic Brian Quincy Newcomb would remember the Alarma tetralogy as "the *Sgt. Pepper* and *Abbey Road* of Christian alternative," albums that were "entirely of and for their time," yet albums that remain "all the more relevant today."

In 1987 that same critic described *Darn Floor Big Bite* as the group's "best work to date, summarizing and expanding its strengths." *Harvest Rock Syndicate* called it "an exercise in discovery, a moody, magnificent album which defies easy description." The latter quality (defying easy description) seemed to be the whole point, as the theme of the album was that all human attempts to describe God fall short and fail. The title track derives from the phrase Koko the gorilla used to describe an earthquake (through sign language). *Darn Floor Big Bite* remains one of Daniel Amos' (or da's) stranger works, and it sold only 7,000 copies (their low point), but perhaps for those very reasons it remains one of the most treasured albums among their cult fans. In 1991 Taylor would say, "When I look back at all my records, I think I'm proudest of that one." *Kalhoun* followed four years later, during which time Taylor had been occupied with **The Swirling Eddies** and with producing records for the likes of **Jacob's Trouble** and **Scaterd Few.** The album includes "If You Want To," an arena rock love song, and "Father Explains," an uncharacteristically political song inspired by the Gulf War and by President Bush's talk of a "new world order." The song "Virgin Falls" offers angry commentary on the abuse of power; "I Will Return" affirms the promise of Christ's coming in the midst of a difficult present.

Motor Cycle was a bit of a Daniel Amos comeback album—as the second word in the title implies. With Chamberlain back in the fold and the band's full name restored, the group returned to the melodic '60s sound that had been evident in some of their early work *(Horrendous Disc, Shotgun Angel)*. Suddenly critics were comparing them to the Beatles (again), to The Who, or to the whole British Invasion in general. The album kicks off with "Banquet at the World's End" and continues through fourteen tracks that generally celebrate life in this world while simultaneously looking forward to improvement in the next. Mark Robertson wrote in *True Tunes,* "The overall feel of *Motor Cycle* is late '60s psychedelia but instead of drugs, sex, and alienation, we're treated to songs about mercy, grace, children, baseball, miracles, and a loving Father." He further described the project as that rare record that not only has "good songs and catchy melodies" but the capacity to "carry us away to another place and give us new insights to an old story." The unjaded quality of the album seems similar to that of **U2**'s *All That You Can't Leave Behind.* Great songs include "Hole in the World," "(What's Come) Over Me" (described by *CCM* as an " 'I Should Have Known Better' [Beatles] rewrite"), "Guilty," and "Grace Is the Smell of Rain."

Bibleland was a less cheerful production, but it does feature "I'll Get Over It," an optimistic number that is one of the group's all-time best pop songs. Overall, *Bibleland* has a gritty, "live" feel, and this is completely appropriate for its theme—struggling to maintain hope and to keep a positive outlook in what can be a depressing world. "I'll Get Over It" expresses that sentiment nicely, as does the title track. The song "Bibleland" is an ode to a run-down Bible-themed amusement park—a place that can be viewed cynically as superficial and tacky or, with a little humility, as a culmination of someone's dream, as a sincere (if unsophisticated) expression of hope and faith. Sure, the place features a leper as one of its tourist attractions, but Taylor seems to put himself in the same camp as those who come up with such campy schemes. And in "The Bubble Bursts" he addresses his would-be adoring fans directly: "I let you down, and I'll do it again."

With alternative rock finally becoming mainstream in the '90s, Daniel Amos apparently thought it necessary to move decidedly left of any accessible center with *Songs of the Heart.* A "concept album," it purports to relate the adventures of a fictitious middle-aged couple named Bud and Irma Akhendorf who embark on a vacation, visit a faith healer out of curiosity, reflect on the state of the world today, and interact with "a mysterious stranger." The album kicks off with an inspired cover of Frankie Valli's "Can't Take My Eyes Off of You," which is Bud and Irma's courtship song. All right. But then with songs like "Uneasy Lies the Head of the Confidence Man" and "Donna Nietzsche and Her Super-Race of Kickboxing Über-Parrots,"

the discerning listener may be excused for thinking he/she has picked up a **Swirling Eddies** album by mistake. Bud gets frisky in "Our Night to Howl, Time to Go Dancing" and serenades Irma with lines like, "The cows come home when I see you in your moo-moo / You're the apple of my strudel, the kit in my kaboodle." The Christian music market might have been ready for *Darn Floor Big Bite* by 1995, but they weren't ready for *Songs of the Heart.* But then as critic Newcomb once said, "Daniel Amos isn't ahead of its time; they are from an altogether different reality than most contemporary Christian music embraces." Even so, the two closing songs to *Songs of the Heart* are masterpieces and perfectly accessible to anyone who makes it that far. The penultimate tune, "When Everyone Wore Hats," is a delicate remembrance of simpler times. The closing song, "My Hand to God," is a sentimental song presenting Bud's last words as he looks into death's door and promises to wait for Irma on the other side.

Songs of the Heart wasn't very good (as a total project), and for six years there was no new material. Then out of nowhere Daniel Amos resurfaced with the best album of their career and one of the best alternative-pop albums of 2001 (Christian or otherwise). Again, beleaguered Christian music fans were left with the odd realization that market dynamics inspired by equal parts gnosticism (from the Christian side) and bigotry (from the general market) would prevent millions of people from ever hearing what might have been their favorite album of the year. "We've got them all to ourselves," John J. Thompson of *True Tunes* said, with a tear, not a smirk. A brilliant, shimmering two-disc collection of thirty-three songs, *Mr. Buechner's Dream* was quickly likened to the Beatles' "White Album" and to The Smashing Pumpkins' *Mellon Collie and the Infinite Sadness.* In other words, it joined that very small club of two-disc albums recorded by artists who actually had enough good material to justify the extravagance. The Christian music scene is not accustomed to such quality and, it is safe to say, was stunned. Periodicals were torn between headlining the album's release immediately as the story of the year and waiting to let it sink in, lest they be overcome by their own superlatives. *HM* wrote, "This sprawling double album is so unique, so full of life, so slobbered over with creativity, so packed with crazy good songs and new things to say, it's impossible to review adequately without sounding like a raving fanboy." Of course no reviewer wants to sound like that, especially not one for *HM,* which is supposed to be interested in hard music, not hook-laden, neo-Beatles toasts to a postmodern/post-metal millennium.

Musically *Mr. Buechner's Dream* offers a potpourri of up-to-the-minute '90s rock styles with roots firmly in the late '60s. There are strong influences of the quintessentially alternative pop band Big Star, headed by Alex Chilton in the early '70s.

Lindsey Buckingham and Lenny Kravitz are both in there somewhere, which is to say that generous contributions from Motown can be detected as well—and, of course, Brian Wilson's muse inhabits the melodies and harmonies. The song "This Is the One" is pretty and lush, a perfect (though ultimately ironic) introduction to an album that promises (in its title) to be dreamy. More pretty (and lush) songs like "I Get to Wondering," "Child on a Leash," "Flash in Your Eyes," and "Steal Away" are sprinkled throughout the project to bring the listener back to base for periodic safety breaks. "The Author of the Story" penetrates the stillness with sharp electric lines that pierce the eardrums with a cruelty suggested in its opening lyric: "She had one foot on the ground and one foot in the air / It seemed the world held her cold hand while the angels brushed her hair / But that's how it has to end on this side of glory / Some wounds will never mend, says the author of the story." The very next track, "Your Long Year," is one of two surefire radio hits; it starts with an innovative but extremely catchy melody and builds with an intensity that accents its most memorable lines ("How you been, in your beautiful skin?") in a way that super-glues them to the listener's consciousness regardless of whether he or she has any clue what the song's about (an address to a youth by an elder). Its surest companion is over on the second disc, a tribute to faith in hard times called "Pregnant Pause." Both of these tunes are irresistible; they summon images of what the Lemonheads might be recording if only they had turned out to be as good as they first seemed to be on *It's a Shame about Ray*. "Who's Who Here" is a sped-up rocker. "Ribbons and Bows" is bubblegum ear candy, as fits its theme of superficiality. "Ordinary Extraordinary Day" and "Joel" are both apocalyptic wonders, using swirling psychedelia and pulsating rhythms to great effect. "Faithful Street" recalls Frente's "Accidentally Kelly Street" for another touch of melodic sugar-pop. "The Lucky Ones" and "A Little Grace" savor a bit of garage rock. "Rice Paper Wings" is dainty. "Meanwhile" is plodding folk rock, delivering its lyric to a steady martial beat. "My Beautiful Martyr" is gorgeous in an ominous haunting way. "The Staggering Gods" is the rock masterpiece its name implies, creating aurally the image of drunken deities stumbling about the earth and disgracing themselves with final bouts of decadence. "Pretty Little Lies" sounds like one of Tom Petty's ballads. "Small Great Things" has a harsh sound that at first seems brittle but turns out to be only fragile, its bitterness dissolved by lyrics that enshrine those who move mountains with "fumbled prayers and bloodied knees." The song "She's a Hard Drink" is a creative carnival tune, with unexpected rhythm and tempo changes and *Sgt. Pepper* off-beat horns coming in at odd intervals. "So Far So Good" has an acoustic, otherworldly feel to it, like an '00s-cover of something The Zombies might have done a long, long

time ago. "Nobody Will" bangs and crashes like a noisy, stomping bunch of kids putting on a parade with pots and pans they swiped from the kitchen cupboard. "Fingertips" takes the psychedelic aura to heights untouched since Edgar Winter's "Frankenstein."

Conceptually the album is loosely constructed around a theme inspired by the writings of Frederick Buechner, especially *The Wizard's Tale*. The title track, reprised toward the end of Disc One, name-drops references to several other literary types, including G. K. Chesterton, C. S. Lewis, Flannery O'Connor, Charles Williams, T. S. Eliot, and Lewis Carroll. All these and more have apparently gathered for a mythical party (or, perhaps, Mr. Buechner is merely dreaming that they have), for an evening of story-telling and mirth-making. The songs that follow might be illustrative of the sort of musings that would then transpire, but the device is anything but constraining, and by the second disc seems to have been dropped altogether. Rather, Taylor deals with familiar themes albeit in often unfamiliar fashion. The coexistence of faith and doubt is prevalent as he wonders at the perseverance of his own confession. "Sometimes there seems to be no author of the story," he admits in the song of that name. "These thoughts occur to me on this side of glory." In a happier moment he allows, "It's a miracle we ever had faith . . . it's a miracle we ever got saved" ("Pregnant Pause"). The latter song is ostensibly about Abraham and Sarah, but one could be excused from wondering if Taylor isn't recalling his own Jesus-movement days when he sings it. "Child on a Leash" seems to be "a tale of grasping for God but finding him just beyond reach" (at least that's what a *Birmingham News* reviewer thought). As always, Taylor laments ("Nobody Will") and lampoons ("Faithful Street") the more stultifying aspects of modern religion. He exalts the liberating acknowledgment of paradox as never before in "Ribbons and Bows," a song that trifles with the minds and hearts of simplistically oriented linear thinkers: "Does everybody want it nicely, lined up in little neat rows? . . . I can hand it to you brightly, wrapped up in ribbons and bows." Aging is a big theme, as indicated by the aforementioned query that the fifty-one-year-old Taylor puts to some beautiful young man or woman: "Your long year ran right by here, just another short day to me / So how you been in your beautiful skin . . . did you solve all life's mysteries?" Elsewhere he's a real curmudgeon: "Jason and his Argonauts hanging out in parking lots / With teen twerps and some indie-ots and all the riff-raff / And strictly confidentially, what we've got here is essentially / A vulgar, vapid history of claptrap." And so it goes: humility and arrogance intertwine as paradoxically as faith and doubt. Daniel Amos ages gracefully, though perhaps not *graciously,* as they come out of hiding to show the twerps what thirty years of being an indie act has taught them. It's a little offensive but they pull it off. As of 2001 Daniel Amos was not only the best band in Christian music but were the *best that they had ever been*. How many artists from the early '70s can say that?

As the Buechner obsession suggests, Daniel Amos has always been a literate and intelligent group. The song "Doppelgänger" is inspired by Dostoevsky, and "Hollow Man" (also from the *Doppelgänger* album) by T. S. Eliot. *Vox Humana* contains "William Blake," a tribute to the British poet. Thomas Merton and the Polish poet Czeslaw Milosz have also been clearly recognizable influences on Taylor's lyrics. The song "Motor Cycle" proclaims, "We were still honest / Even when no one was looking," and that line could be an apt description of the band's career. "We've always tried to be real in what we expressed in our records," Taylor once said. "And part of being real is being truthful about doubts and fears and all those things that don't make for good radio." *True Tunes* says, "Daniel Amos has never dumbed it down, even when shooting for laughs." Or as one of Taylor's songs puts it, "There may not ever be anything new to say / But I'm fond of finding words that say it in a different way."

Our Personal Favorite World Famous Hits is a retrospective collection of pre-*Buechner* hits, with solid song selection—though no band in the history of Christian music would have been more deserving of a *two*-disc compilation. Two nostalgia-driven live recordings would also be released in the '90s. *Live Bootleg '82* records a concert from the *Alarma*-album tour with most of the songs deriving from that record. It concludes with a four-song "Surf Suite" featuring the Beach Boys' "Surfin' USA," The Surfaris' "Wipe Out," and the band's own "(near sighted girl with approaching) Tidal Wave" (from *Horrendous Disc*) and "Endless Summer" (from *Alarma!*). Similarly, *Preachers from Outer Space* presents a concert performed in Anaheim, California, one year after the initial release of *Shotgun Angel*. The band runs through songs from their first three albums, showcasing a wide variety of styles, and concludes with a new-wave cover of the Beach Boys' "I Get Around." In 2000 a two-disc concert from the *Cornerstone* festival was also released (with Chuck Cummings sitting in for Ed McTaggart on drums). *When Worlds Collide* is a tribute album that offers eighteen covers of Daniel Amos songs by various alternative and independent artists, including **Jimmy Abegg, Rick Altizer, Dead Artist Syndrome,** the **Seventy Sevens, Starflyer 59, Randy Stonehill,** and **The Throes.** The album was announced as a two-disc set, then released as a single one (minus advertised songs by **David Edwards, The Electrics, Scaterd Few,** and **The Wayside**). In 2001 a critics poll sponsored by *CCM* magazine put two Daniel Amos albums on its list of "The 100 Greatest Albums in Christian Music": *Alarma!* and *Horrendous Disc* (at Numbers Sixty-two and Sixty-three).

For trivia buffs: Daniel Amos has never been sufficiently successful for any of the members to quit their day jobs. Ed McTaggart is art director for Frontline Graphics. Greg Flesch is a rocket scientist. Really.

Christian radio hits: "I Love You # 19" (# 15 in 1981); "Soon" (# 18 in 1986).

Daniel Band

Bill Findlay, gtr., synth., voc.; Dan McCabe, voc., bass, kybrd.; Tony Rossi, gtr., voc.; Peter Cosman, drums (– 1983) // Matt DelDuca, drums (+ 1983). 1982—*On Rock* (Streetlight); 1983—*Straight Ahead*; 1984—*Run from the Darkness*; 1986—*Rise Up* (Refuge); 1987—*Running Out of Time*; 1993—*The Best of the Daniel Band.*

Canadian near-metal group Daniel Band offered Christian teenagers a sanctified alternative to Bon Jovi throughout the '80s and maintained a loyal fan base despite only moderate and grudging respect from critics. For a time the group toured as **Larry Norman**'s backing band. The group's sound remained consistent throughout their albums—a problem for some reviewers—built on a foundation of midtempo power chords and McCabe's Geddy Lee-style vocal scream. Rossi would sing lead occasionally ("Two Roads," "You Don't Need the Blues") for variety, and by the second album he had emerged as the group's principal songwriter. McCabe also contributed some original material, however, and the group's arena anthem "Reality" (from *Straight Ahead*) was a Findlay composition.

The debut *On Rock* album features "You Don't Need the Blues" as well as the standout rockers "Somebody Loves You" and "Never Again." The band immediately drew comparisons to other Canadian hard-rock units like April Wine and Triumph, though Rush would definitely emerge as the analogy of choice. For some reason, no songs from *On Rock* would be included on the group's career retrospective album *(Best of the Daniel Band),* but the album was re-released by M8 in 2000. In addition to "Reality," *Straight Ahead* offers the power ballad "In My Mind."

Run from the Darkness scores best with its title track and "Don't Give Up," which sounds like a less wimpy version of **Petra.** A song called "Walk on the Water" received generous airplay on MuchMusic, a Canadian video channel similar to MTV. *Rise Up* has a suitable-for-arenas title track and an air-guitar-head-banging screamer called "Bethel." *Running Out of Time* offers "Party in Heaven" and a synthesizer-heavy (cf. **Kansas**) exhortation to "Hold On." Lyrically, Daniel Band had a strong no-nonsense ministry-oriented approach. "Without the blood of Jesus, there ain't no hope for us all," they proclaim in "Reality." McCabe once told *Cornerstone,* "We are not musicians who preach; we are ministers who happen to be musicians, preachers with electric guitars." After the Daniel Band folded, Rossi recorded a blues-based album for R.E.X. in 1990 as TRB (Tony Rossi Band); a year later McCabe released an album with a group called **Dreamer.**

Charlie Daniels

Selected: 1994—*The Door* (Sparrow); 1996—*Steel Witness*; 1997—*By the Light of the Moon* (Sony); 1998—*Blues Hat* (Blue Hat); 1999—*Tailgate Party*; 2000—*Road Dogs*.

www.charliedaniels.com

Although country rock star Charlie Daniels may always be best known for his whimsical fiddle classic, "The Devil Went Down to Georgia" (# 3 in 1979), the long-haired country boy from Wilmington, North Carolina, has done battle with Ol' Scratch in more serious veins as well. When Daniels decided to enter the field of Christian music officially with twin releases in the mid '90s, he did so without the fanfare of any sudden conversion testimony—and indeed without turning his back on his previous and ongoing career in the general market. "I've always been a believer," he said in 1994 when his first official Christian album was released. "There has never been a time when I was not." Daniels also says that he has always performed gospel songs in his concerts and that his two albums for Sparrow are but an extension of that. Further, he indicates that none of his country music fans seem to resent him for performing contemporary Christian music and that he is somewhat baffled as to why his Christian music fans seem to resent that he still performs country music. "I don't do an 'all gospel show'," he explains, "but a clean, family show that people can bring their kids to. There's nothing wrong with being entertained."

After working in Nashville as a session player (for Leonard Cohen, **Bob Dylan,** Ringo Starr, and Pete Seeger), a songwriter (for **Elvis Presley** and Tammy Wynette), and a producer (for The Youngbloods), Daniels formed the Charlie Daniels Band in 1971. With a southern rock sound modeled after the Allman Brothers, the group hit the charts many times with three distinct types of songs: whimsical numbers like "Uneasy Rider" (# 9 in 1973), "Long-Haired Country Boy" (# 56 in 1975), and the famous Devil song; anthems like "The South's Gonna Do It Again" (# 29 in 1975) and "Texas" (# 91 in 1975, but *much* bigger in Texas); and political songs like "In America" (# 11 in 1980), inspired by the Iran hostage crisis, and "Still in Saigon" (# 22 in 1982), about the trials of Vietnam veterans. The political numbers sometimes went over the top for some people. The title song for Daniels' album *Simple Man* (Epic, 1990) suggested lynching drug dealers and abandoning rapists and child molesters in alligator-infested swamps. In any case, Daniels maintained a high profile by hosting sporadic "Volunteer Jam" concerts beginning in 1974 that attracted guest performers from Billy Joel to B. B. King to Garth Brooks. He also performed several benefit concerts on behalf of presidential candidate Jimmy Carter in 1976 and played at the latter's inauguration. In recent years (since 1995) he has regularly participated in Billy Graham crusades. In addition to the Christian albums listed above, Daniels has continued to record in the general market. *By the Light of the Moon* is a collection of old cowboy songs (e.g., "Back in the Saddle Again") and *Blues Hat* is a set of blues songs (e.g., "Hard Headed Woman"). *Tailgate Party* includes new versions of some of his old hits, along with copious covers of songs like the Allman Brothers' "Statesboro Blues," ZZ Top's "Sharp Dressed Man," and even Lynyrd Skynyrd's "Free Bird." His 2000 album, *Road Dogs,* features a song called "The Martyr" that was inspired by stories of Columbine victim Cassie Bernall's confession of faith.

The Door attracted immediate attention for its opening song, "The Business of Love," which Daniels cowrote with **Steven Curtis Chapman.** Another high point is "Sunday Morning," in which he relates a personal story of how he brought a friend to Jesus. "End of the World" sports the same interplay of singing and spoken-word vocals that made "Devil Went Down to Georgia" such a hit. The album closes with an elaborate fourteen-minute epic called "Jerusalem Trilogy." Overall *The Door* has a strong, celebrative tone, which is echoed in "Somebody Was Prayin' for Me" from *Steel Witness.* That song, with lots of fiddling and background vocals by the gospel group Fairfield Four, presents Daniels at his best. Otherwise *Steel Witness* has a more serious, apocalyptic tone. Several songs ("It's Happening Now," "Tribulation," "A Day in the Life") announce that the end is near. "New Pharisees" is a gleeful, sarcastic indictment of self-righteous Christians, and "Whose Side Are You On" calls for decision and boldness. "Payback Time" is another of Daniels' outlandish political statements, albeit with a religious twist: he lets the "hero in the big white house" and "the robots on the hill" know that they will have to answer to a supreme court of the universe, soon to be in session.

Daniels told *CCM* in 1994, "There may be some people who think I'm not the kind of person who should be doing gospel music. But anyone who knows anything about me knows I've professed Christianity all along. I've not always lived up to it by any means, but I've never made a secret of my beliefs. Still, there's a lot of Pharisees around who think if you don't do it the way they do it, you're not doing it right."

Christian radio hits: "Praying to the Wrong God" (# 23 in 1994).

Dove Awards: 1995 Country Album (*The Door*); 1997 Country Song ("Somebody Was Prayin' for Me").

Grammy Awards: 1979 Best Country Vocal Performance by a Duo or Group ("The Devil Went Down to Georgia").

Danielson (a.k.a. Danielson Famile)

Daniel Smith, voc.; with various instruments by Andrew Smith, David Smith, Megan Smith, Rachel Smith, and Chris Palladino. 1995—*A Prayer for Every Hour* (Tooth and Nail); 1997—*Tell Another Joke at the Ol' Choppin' Block*; 1998—*Tri Danielson!!!* (Alpha); 1999—*Tri-Danielson!!!* (Omega); 2001—*Fetch the Compass Kids* (Secretly Canadian).

New Jersey-based Danielson was started as a college project at Rutgers University by Daniel Smith, who coaxed his siblings and a cousin to become his postmodern "famile" and join him in making some convention-defying music. Darlings of critics in the contemporary music scene, the group is lauded for (as *Bandoppler* puts it) their "vulnerable ingenuity, musical daring, and endearing frivolity," in addition to a demonstrated capacity for "writing the wicked hook." Like **Daniel Amos,** the group has a cult following whose loyalty exceeds any estimate of the group's popularity that would be based on sales figures alone. Surprisingly the band has also made a splash in circles that are generally ignorant or dismissive of Christian music bands. *Spin* did a feature on the group, *CMJ Monthly* included a Danielson selection on one of their compilation CDs, and *Rolling Stone* published a review of *Tri-Danielson (Alpha)*. The group's musical forebears (though not necessarily influences) are weird geniuses like Frank Zappa, Captain Beefheart, and Todd Rundgren. The word most used in reviews and articles on their work is "interesting."

The debut album features more than seventy minutes of music, arranged into twenty-four short songs (one for every hour). The dominant theme may be described as "the joy of loving God," but the musical style highlights falsetto vocals over such instruments as whistles, tambourines, flutes, and out-of-tune guitars. Smith recorded the entire album on a small tape recorder set up in his home basement with his family backing him with whatever they could find. Mistakes, false starts, people talking or laughing in the background, missed notes, wrong notes . . . all become part of the mix. Releasing the album at a special discount price, Tooth and Nail acknowledged it was weird—and everyone agreed. But *7ball* found it "endearingly primitive," and *The Lighthouse* called it "one of the most original, creative, and honest pieces of work to appear in a long time."

Just before the release of the first album, Smith spent time living with the Jesus People U.S.A. community in Chicago (cf. **Ballydowse, Cauzin' Efekt, Crashdog, The Crossing, Headnoise, Glenn Kaiser, Resurrection Band, Seeds, Sheesh,** and **Unwed Sailor**) where he says he "just washed dishes and cleaned tables, humbling myself before the Lord and learning his ways." As indicated above, the debut album was made to fulfill a class requirement for a course Smith was taking at Rutgers. He and his family performed the whole affair on campus, dressed in matching name-tag T-shirts, wearing antennae decked with flowers ("feelers . . . to feel more"). He got an "A".

Somehow, avant garde New York musician Kramer (no relation to the *Seinfeld* character) heard Danielson's initial record and ended up producing their sophomore project. Unanimously regarded as a giant step beyond the debut, *Tell Another*

Joke at the Ol' Choppin' Block is no less quirky. In some basic sense it sounds like '90s hippie music, with banjo, lots of percussion, and various keyboards being played by "family members" ranging in age from 12 to 24. *Cornerstone* said, "the overall musical sound is a combination of a Middle Eastern orchestra conducted by Tom Waits." For other reviewers the project has the feel of retro-Jesus music, like something that might have been made by the **All Saved Freak Band** (minus Glenn Schwartz). But then there are those squeaky/shrill vocals and the unpredictable song structures. As *True Tunes* put it, Danielson takes a sledgehammer to the traditional verse-chorus-verse set-up: "It's as if the family had the sheet music to 3,000 different songs, randomly cut them up and pasted them back together, and decided to record the results." A track called "Smooth Death" comes closest to standard fare and provides a somewhat accessible entry point to the album. Lyrically songs address such subjects as monogamy, motherly love, and devotion to the Lord. The group said they were "intent on spreading good cheer, through silliness or encouragement." At this point they tended to perform live wearing medical garb (that people might visualize "the healing").

The *Tri-Danielson!!!* project was released in two volumes and features songs by three different incarnations of the basic Danielson entity. First, there is Brother Danielson, which consists of just Brother Daniel singing in his Mickey Mouse voice with an acoustic guitar. In concert, the Brother Danielson songs were sung from inside a nine-foot tall paper-mache tree. Next, there is Danielson Familie, the same entity from the first two albums, now singing what are called "hand clapping gospel songs" with the usual variety of instruments, albeit with more brass than previously. Finally, there is Danielsonship, Daniel and Chris joined by a miscellaneous collection of friends. The two albums are arranged in trios of songs, alternating the incarnations in a repeating ABC, ABC fashion. That's so "you won't get tired of the sound," Smith says. It all comes together at the end of *Omega,* when the song "Deeper Than My Gov't" is performed three times, by each "branch" of Danielson in succession. Subject matter ranges broadly over a wide arena: "Between the Lines of the Scout Signs" is about being friendly and kind (Smith is a proud Eagle Boy Scout); "Lord, Did You Hear Harrison?" inquires into the spiritual welfare of Beatle George; "Flesh" is an antiracism diatribe with lyrics that could have been written by Dr. Seuss; "A Meeting with Your Maker" unravels the perspective of a man reflecting on his imminent demise; "Idiot Boksen" laments the preoccupation of modern children with TV (the Smith household was raised without it). An album highlight is "Pottymouth," a hilarious discussion about cussing from the point of view of a girl who has never heard any of the words before (and so doesn't understand what they mean)—all to a tune reminiscent of The

Shangri-La's "Leader of the Pack." A hidden track on *Alpha* presents Smith singing "He's Got the Whole World in His Hands" with some distinctive lyrics ("He's Got the junkies and the flunkies in his hands . . . He's got your eyeballs at the beach in his hands").

Fetch the Compass Kids continues in the same general vein with guitars, bells, drums, flute, violin, banjo, bass, trombone, and organ all competing for attention but losing out to Smith's falsetto voice. The album was produced by Steve Albini, famous for his work with Nirvana, Bush, and Plant/Page but noted also for working with a handful of Christian bands (**Ballydowse, Chevelle, Crashdog, Ninety Pound Wuss**). Songs include bizarro trips like "Who the Hello" and "Good News for the Pus Pickers," along with such camp counselor fare as "Fathom the Nine Fruits Pie" (about the fruit of the Spirit in Galatians 5:22–23) and the title track (about focusing on Jesus). *CCM* said, "this music might best be described as the Little Rascals on speed" and they suggested that Smith's "beyond obtuse" lyrics bring to mind "what one might expect if Adam Sandler were to get saved." A sample: "We who have lips happy and sad gonna sing the wide and long and high and deep, oh Lord" ("Singers Go First"). *HM* found the fifth album a little closer to center, noting that the group comes "perilously close" to producing something that could be played on the radio with a couple of songs ("We Don't Say Shut-up," "Sing to the Singer").

Obviously Danielson owes a good deal to performance art. One critic called it "insane elfin experimental music" (a compliment). Another, "an exercise in free form expression." Another observed, "Danielson isn't just bizarre . . . Danielson forges a whole new kind of eccentricity." Part of the attraction is that they're not faking it. Smith is one hundred percent sincere, and he writes and sings without the slightest hint of sarcasm. He is as strong an advocate of honesty in art as he is of creativity—though the two are clearly related. He is also quite opposed to the idea of a Christian market and quite suspicious of a Christian music industry. "I can't believe that Christ wants to be in a market," he says. "Didn't he turn over those tables?" And again, "Danielson does not make Christian music. They make Christ-centered music. If the music affects people, Christian or not, it is because the Spirit uses it." *Rolling Stone* noted, "the alleged appeal (of Danielson) comes from their supposedly unbridled innocence." But then they continued, "the Family's off-key acoustic noise is too rhythmically inept to support apologists' claims that the Danielsons are reinventing bluegrass, and older brother Daniel's pseudodrawled squeals of tonsil terror are too painful to be charming." As Danielson has said from the first album on, "You either love it or you hate it, you get it or you don't."

For trivia buffs: The well-known contemporary worship song "Our God Reigns" was written by Daniel Smith's father, Lenny Smith. He released a new album *(Deep Calls to Deep)* on the family's private label (Secretly Canadian) in 2001.

Daniel's Window

Jesse Burhead, drums; Bill Coleman, bass; Heather Hershey, voc.; Caleb King, kybrd.; Alby Odum, gtr. 2000—*It's a Mystery* (True Tunes).

Daniel's Window released a radio-friendly debut album in 2000 that was more innovative musically than lyrically. John Gutierrez of **Buck** adds guest trumpet to the keyboard-heavy mix, which is also supplemented by occasional strings and a generous use of programming. Hershey's alto voice on top of all the electronica gives the group a sound that *Phantom Tollbooth* described as "quirky chick punk." The song "When You Hear the Sound" stands out, however, with an uncharacteristic male vocal. "Follow and Believe" has more of a pop feel in the mold of **All Star United.** Lyrically the album deals with straightforward Christian themes in familiar ways. The opening song, "Stay the Same," explicates the constancy of God. "I'm So Happy" deals with happiness in Jesus (cf. **Mustard Seed Faith, Hokus Pick**): "I'm so happy / Can't you see / Just what he has done for me."

Danniebelle

See **Danniebell Hall.**

The Darins

Heather Darin, voc.; Krista Darin, voc.; Rachelle Darin, voc.; Stacy Darin Zapeda, voc. 1999—*The Darins* (Pamplin); 2000—*Letting Go.*

www.thedarins.com

Sister act The Darins is composed of four siblings born and raised in Buena Park, California. The women cite the sounds of Motown as their primary musical influence, along with more recent divas like Whitney Houston and Mariah Carey. Hoping for another **Point of Grace,** Pamplin hired a team of top Christian songwriters (Regie Hamm, Jim Cooper, **Chris Eaton**) to provide material for a debut album, which was produced by **John** and Dino **Elefante.** According to The Darins' website, the result was "a project full of pop-oriented music with an underlying urban beat, reminiscent of En Vogue and the Spice Girls." The debut album opens with "All along the Road," a peppy song of encouragement based on Philippians 3:12–16. It also includes the ballad "Crosses and Crowns" and a strong R&B song called "Rejoice" (written by Chris Omartian, son of **Michael and Stormie Omartian**). *Letting Go* includes "Can't Stop," a pledge to be fervent in evangelism, and "Take Me," a modern hymn of consecration that showcases the sisters' harmonies at their best.

For trivia buffs: The pastor of the church in which the Darin sisters were raised is **Crystal Lewis**'s father.

Montrel Darrett

1999—*Chronicles of the Soul* (EMI).

Montrel Darrett is an urban contemporary Christian singer with deep roots in R&B and gospel music. His mother played piano for both **Shirley Caesar** and **Aretha Franklin,** and as a child he sang in a Darrett family group called the True Notes. Later he toured with gospel magnate John P. Kee and then had a brief stint as a featured vocalist and songwriter with **Commissioned.** In 1999 Darrett released a solo album that displays a variety of styles reflective of his upbringing, including classic soul, '70s funk (not disco), and the '80s Minneapolis Prince sound. "Tough Love" starts things off curiously with a song that sets lyrics about Christ's sacrifice on Calvary to a bluesy vamp. "Issues" deals with lingering racial prejudice in the church. "Shakedown" gets up-to-date with rap vocals and a hip-hop beat. "Oh! What a Friend" seems inspired by the sound of **Marvin Gaye**'s *What's Goin' On;* "Hold On" is equal parts Stevie Wonder and **Al Green.**

David and the Giants

David Huff, voc., gtr.; Rayborn Huff, voc., kybrd.; Clayborn Huff, voc., bass (– 1995) // Keith Thibodeaux, drums (+ 1979, – 1992); Dennon Dearman, bass, voc. (+ 1995); Lance Huff, drums (+ 1992). 1977—*Song of Songs* (Song of Songs); 1979—*This One's for You; Step in My Shoes*; 1980—*Almost Midnight*; 1981—*Heaven or Hell*; 1982—*David and the Giants* (Priority); 1983—*Riders in the Sky*; 1984—*Inhabitants of the Rock* (Myrrh); 1985—*Under Control*; 1987—*Magnificat*; 1988—*Strangers to the Night* (Giant); 1989—*R U Gonna Stand Up*; 1990—*Distant Journey*; 1992—*Long Time Comin'*; 1993—*Giant Hits*; 1995—*Angels Unaware*; 1996—*Dream*.

Despite their Sunday school name, David and the Giants was not originally a Christian band. The group formed as a general market act in 1969 in Forest, Mississippi. For eight years they toured, playing covers of artists like Yes and Jethro Tull. They were Christians, however, and in 1977 they did a reverse crossover and began releasing gospel-oriented albums for the Christian music market. The original lineup consisted of three Mississippi siblings (David Huff and his twin brothers Clayborn and Rayborn) plus the (barely) grown-up child actor Keith Thibodeaux. The latter had won the hearts of America playing Little Ricky on the *I Love Lucy* show from 1956 to 1959 and then starred as Johnny Paul (better known as "Opie's best friend") on *The Andy Griffith Show* from 1962 to 1966. Thibodeaux's eventual replacement, Lance Huff, is front man David Huff's son. From 1975 to 1977, Rayborn and Clayborn

were members of a mainstream group called Magic (while David pursued an unsuccessful solo career). David would also be a part of a parallel general market group called **Giant,** featuring another brother, Dann Huff (of **White Heart, The Front,** and **The Players**). David Huff was also a member of **White Heart** for a time.

David and the Giants have consistently turned out albums with a sound that critics describe as "classic" or "historic" rock. The music is simple and guitar driven, with little distortion, no synthesizers, and a generous influence of southern R&B. A reviewer for *The Lighthouse* once said, "they sound like your neighborhood basement band would sound if they played together for twenty years, got their craft down right, but never moved away from the roots of that basic rock and roll sound." To many, the lack of pretension is appealing; to others, the group just sounds dated and "resistant to growth."

The first five custom albums evince a relatively mellow pop-oriented sound, blending ballads with light rock. *Song of Songs* features "Roll On" (later covered by **Wayne Watson**) and "Glory Hallelujah," which the group had actually included on an earlier secular project. *This One's for You* offers the original studio version of "Noah," a concert favorite that has since appeared in varying renditions on a number of other albums; the song relates how various characters mock the ark builder—until it begins to rain. *This One's for You* also offers "He's Comin' Back," a five-minute southern rock number with a traditional gospel introduction. *Step in My Shoes* is the group's lightest album, featuring mostly love songs to Jesus, which David says are his personal favorites of all their songs. The group took on a harder sound in the '80s, evoking comparisons to general market bands like Foreigner or sometimes Hall and Oates. Their self-titled album for Priority in 1982 earned them their first notice in the Christian media, with *CCM* reviewing it as a debut project by a brand-new artist. It includes what would become the best-known recast of "Noah" along with the self-explanatory gripe "America (In God We Used to Trust)" and the more positive "God Is Love." *Inhabitants of the Rock* includes "I've Been Drinking," an ode to consumption of the living water referenced in John 4. *CCM* couldn't help but note that the song "I Can Depend on You" sounds a bit like Tommy James and the Shondells' "Crystal Blue Persuasion," and that "I Am Persuaded" seems built on the theme to the TV series *Hill Street Blues*. But a review of *Under Control* in *CCM* in 1985 referred to the group as "a perennially underrated rock band." From stadium arena-rock songs like "Rockin' for the Rock" to power ballads like "Here's My Heart," they said, the group consistently churns out basic crowd-pleasing material for those who aren't into heavy metal or new-wave or disco or rap. *Magnificat* was an experimental side-trip, a concept album built around the story of Christ's passion and designed for interpretation through liturgical dance. Thibodeaux's wife, an award-winning ballet dancer, helped to inspire the piece. *Strangers to the Night* includes "Perfect Love," a ballad sung by David Huff and his daughter **Kellye Huff.** *R U Gonna Stand Up* finds the group delving further into the soft mold of sunny-lite pop, as evidenced in the song "Here's My Heart." The title track and "Everybody Needs Love" have a little more rock energy behind them.

The '90s were not kind to David and the Giants, as the group is anything but alternative. The band pretty much fell off the radar screen of the contemporary Christian music scene, and their *Distant Journey* and *Long Time Comin'* albums were essentially ignored. They came to be associated with mellow light-rock, though their style—like **Big Tent Revival**—always retained a bit of blues-rock sizzle; *Distant Journey* opens with a solid rocker called "Never Had It So Good." *Angels Unaware* was good enough to demand attention. It also kicks off with a great rocker, "Can't Stop the Music," and concludes with a wonderful track that sounds like maybe Creedence Clearwater Revival hired Bob Seger to do vocals and Peter Frampton to play guitar ("The Beat Goes On"). *Dream* offers a song called "Love Everybody" that could almost be a Beatles outtake. Whatever the decade, demand always seems to exceed supply when it comes to basic rock, and David and Giant have been there to fill the gap.

The band's low profile in the Christian music industry is partly their own doing, as they released their first five albums on a private label and then, after achieving some notice with CBS-owned Priority and Word-owned Myrrh, decided to go back to the custom approach in 1988, starting their own independent Giant Records. "Major record companies don't impress us," David Huff said in 1988. "Before we were born again, we were with Capitol, MGM, and United Artists. When we came to the Lord, we didn't seek a recording contract, we sought the kingdom of God."

Lyrically David and the Giants display a penchant for unequivocal Christian messages: blatant statements of faith and evangelistic invitations. This, too, played better with critics in the '80s than in the '90s. A *CCM* reviewer for *Dream* complained that the "I-was-so-bad-off-until-I-got-saved-and-now-everything-is-better" theme has grown tiresome. The group has always enjoyed quoting from well-known pop songs. Numbers like "This One's for You," "Dream On," "Sweet Inspiration," and "You Ain't Seen Nothin' Yet" are not covers but original tunes that play on the titles and key phrases of the famous hits. Thus, in "The Beat Goes On," Huff echoes Sonny and Cher as he sings, "I gotta tell you, I'm not going through a phase / I got the Holy Ghost and the fire is a blaze / The beat goes on and on and on." This is all followed by a "na na na na" fade-out (called "Selah") that summons images of either Journey or Steam—depending on just how far back one's memories go.

Christian radio hits: "One Less Stone" (# 14 in 1982); "Highway to Heaven" (# 12 in 1982); "I Can Depend on You" (# 30 in 1985); "His Love Lifted Me Up" (# 13 in 1985); "Why" (# 4 in 1987); "Celebrate His Power" (# 7 in 1988); "Here's My Heart" (# 10 in 1989); "Everybody Needs Love" (# 19 in 1990); "Time on My Side" (# 28 in 1991); "Live and Learn" (# 16 in 1992); "Dream On" (# 18 in 1993).

Jody Davis

2001—*Jody Davis* (Pamplin).

Jody Davis is guitarist for **The Newsboys.** After a decade of hard touring, that band took a break in 2000 to allow Davis and **Phil Joel** to make solo albums. Davis chooses to pursue a '70s and '80s rock group sound that at times recalls early Chicago or such blue-collar groups as Huey Lewis and the News. His self-titled album opens with a crunchy rocker called "Believe" (not **The Newsboys'** song by that name) that confronts the listener with such lyrics as "Is there something you would die for? / That's your god / That's your faith." More retro-rock infuses "Velveteen," which appears to set a theme inspired by a children's book *(The Velveteen Rabbit)* to a tune inspired by Lenny Kravitz. "Satellite" is not a Dave Matthews Band cover but a driving pop song that one could easily imagine being performed by Davis's main band. The album closes with a cover of Todd Rundgren's "Love Is the Answer," which was a Number Ten hit for England Dan and John Ford Coley in 1979 (cf. **Tony Melendez, Cindy Morgan**).

Paul Davis

1970—*A Little Bit of Paul Davis* (Bang); 1974—*Ride 'Em, Cowboy*; 1976—*Southern Tracks*; 1977—*Singer of Songs, Teller of Tales*; 1980—*Paul Davis; Energizin' Love* (Spirit); 1981—*Cool Night* (Arista).

Pop star Paul Davis was born in 1942 in Meridian, Mississippi. He had early country hits with songs like "A Little Bit of Soap" (1970) and "Ride 'Em, Cowboy" (1974). Then he scored big on Top 40 pop radio with "I Go Crazy" (# 7 in 1977) and "Sweet Life" (# 17 in 1978). Though not primarily associated with Christian music, Davis did make explicit statements about his faith. His 1977 general market album includes two explicitly Christian songs, "Hallelujah, Thank You Jesus" and "I Never Heard the Song at All." In 1980 he released the song "Do Right" (encouraging adherence to a basic moral code) to both the Christian and general markets. The song, which Davis wrote, went to Number One on the Christian charts and also reached Number Twenty-three on the mainstream charts, making it the highest-rated crossover single ever (at that time). Davis, the son of a backwoods Mississippi Methodist preacher, said, "I've always been close to the Lord, but all of this contemporary Christian music thing is new to me, and sometimes what I run into when I talk to people scares me." Specifically, what scared him was an insistence from some radio programmers that he offer "proof" that he really was a Christian or relate some testimony as to when and where he had converted. Davis released the album *Energizin' Love* to the Christian market on a Christian label (Spirit), but *CCM* complained that its songs were a bit too easy listening to please anyone but adult contemporary fans. The album does include songs like "Lightshine," "You're the Father," and "Just around the Bend" that testify specifically to the artist's Christian faith. Davis continued to record for the general market, scoring another significant hit with " '65 Love Affair" (# 6 in 1982). He then returned to country music and continued to record throughout the '80s. On July 30, 1986, he was gunned down in Nashville but survived the shooting. In 1997 Davis joined James Ingram and Michael McDonald in singing on Terry McMillan's remake of the song "Do Right."

Christian radio hits: "Do Right" (# 1 for 4 weeks in 1980).

Dawkins and Dawkins

Anson Dawkins, voc.; Eric Dawkins, voc. 1993—*Dawkins and Dawkins* (Benson); 1994—*Necessary Measures*; 1998—*Focus* (Harmony).

Dawkins and Dawkins is a sibling group composed of two brothers dedicated to ministry through soul/urban gospel music. The Dawkins boys were born in Davenport, Iowa, and raised as the sons of a Pentecostal minister in Wintersville, Ohio. As children they performed in a trio with their mother, singing in church and at their father's revivals. Eventually they came under the influence of **Andraé Crouch, The Winans,** and especially **Commissioned.** Protégées of **Fred Hammond,** they were initially hired by him as musicians for **Commissioned** and were then groomed by him to make albums of their own. The self-titled project drew from R&B, rap, and urban gospel to present a very contemporary **Commissioned**-like sound. It earned the duo a Stellar award nomination for "Best New Artist." *CCM* magazine singled out the songs "Wonder Why" and "Watching over Me" as perfect for a "gospel skate night." The next record was less urban and more centered in the strong R&B sound that seems to be the duo's strength. The title song, "Necessary Measures," speaks of doing whatever is needed to win souls for the kingdom of God. *Focus* takes the group in another direction, an upbeat Boyz II Men style of worship music they like to call "Rhythm and Praise" (because "there are no blues when you are in the midst of praise"). "Wrapped Up" and "Your Joy" are songs of encouragement, presenting God as the answer to human sadness and despair. Eric Dawkins says, "We've got that kind of high that we won't come down off of. It's fun being saved. And we want all young people to know that it's not square to be saved. We have fun praising God and that's what our music brings across."

Tracy Dawn

1999—*Poetic Aftermath* (Atlantic).

Tracy Dawn is a female Christian rock singer who draws upon her experiences with the dark side of spirituality to emphasize transformation through Christ. Raised in Clay Center, Kansas, Dawson says she was raped as a teenager and experienced some sexual abuse but "didn't talk to anyone about it." She left home for Los Angeles to pursue a career in music but became involved in drugs and with the occult. Her conversion to Christ came about as the result of a dream in which Jesus rescued her from a demon. She then turned to reading her Bible and came to experience salvation and healing. In 1998 she began to seek a career in Christian music, opening concerts for **Michael W. Smith** and **Jars of Clay.** Dawn's debut album, *Poetic Aftermath,* was released to the Christian market on Atlantic in 1999 and to the general market on Warner Bros. in 2000. It opens with a hard-edged song called "Leave Me Alone" (addressed to Satan) that seems to promise a style akin to the tougher material of '80s rockers like Deborah Harry (Blondie) or Pat Benatar. That sound returns on the standout "All You Gotta Do," which features the line, "All you gotta do is say you're sorry (it's called repent)." Some of the other tracks display a quite different sound. "I'm a Junkie" is Bangles poppy and "Beloved" is typical adult contemporary Christian fare. "Mock" has a blues-rock sound to it that is effective. Lyrically, the song "Enter Savior" offers some of her autobiography, with no flinching on the ugly parts. "Revelation of Romance" takes a stab at explaining the classic problem of theodicy (why does God allow evil?), deciding that everything serves to purify the church to become a pure and prepared Bride for Christ.

Christian radio hits: "God in a Box" (# 13 in 1999).

dba (a.k.a. 65 dba)

Robbie Bronniman, voc., kybrd.; Shazz Sparks, voc.; Phil Ball, drums (– 1996); Danny Budd, gtr. (– 1996); Stu Robson, bass (– 1994). As 65 dba: 1992—*The Great Awakening* (Integrity); 1994—*Shout.* As dba: 1996—*Bubble* (Warner Alliance).

The British group that ultimately decided to be known as just dba (without the 65) is perhaps best described as Christian music's Human League. That description comes up in virtually every review of their work, if only because they play electronic music with back and forth male and female vocals. The group was formed in 1990 by producer Ray Goudie, with Robbie Bronniman and Shazz Sparks being supported by instrumentalists who would leave one by one until the group was just a duo. The original name (65 dba) was based on the decibel level restriction placed on the group at one of their early concerts. The debut album was advertised as Christian techno/rave music but failed to satisfy the expectations of critics familiar with that genre. The second effort came much closer to the mark. Sparks was praised for her stellar, clean vocals on tracks like "Peace" and "Without Your Love." Rapper Elis Nevitt contributed to some tracks, including a stirring break-beat ballad, "Crucified." It was *Bubble* that finally won the critics over and brought dba respect as a modern techno band. Standout tracks include "Universe" and a jazzy remake of the Bacharach/David classic, "I Say a Little Prayer." All of dba's albums have featured up-front Christ-centered lyrics that celebrate the joys of Christian living or move into the realm of praise and worship. Bronnimann and Sparks also record with Goudie under the name **Hydro.**

Christian radio hits: "Sea of Love" (# 4 in 1994).

D-Boy

1989—*Plantin' a Seed* (Frontline); 1990—*The Lyrical Strength of One Street Poet*; 1993—*Peace 2 the Poet.*

D-Boy was a Puerto-Rican Christian rap singer from Dallas, Texas. He was born Daniel Rodriguez in 1967. He worked as a counselor at Street Church Academy, an antigang ministry started by his parents, Cookie and Demi Rodriguez. The latter two had come to faith themselves through the ministry of David Wilkerson's Teen Challenge, and Cookie is one of the characters profiled in Wilkerson's best-selling book *The Cross and the Switchblade.* D-Boy made two albums of unequivocal Christian rap music, with an up-front emphasis on nonviolence. *Plantin' a Seed* was produced by **Tim Miner** and **Tommy Sims.** It celebrates dancing unto the Lord with "King David" and condemns use of crack in "It's a Disease." He reveals his sly humor on "Doggin the Devil" when he indicates that whenever Satan comes around, "I kick him a few rhymes and talk about his mama." But the main tenor of the first album is hope and encouragement, as reflected in the title track and "Pick Yourself Up." *The Lyrical Strength of One Street Poet* was reviewed as a major step forward qualitatively, as the artist honed his craft. Thematically the sophomore project is defined by "Cease for Peace," an anthemic protest of gang violence. D-Boy and his parents made national news in 1990 for offering Street Church Academy as a neutral meeting ground for rival street gangs to negotiate truces. On October 6, 1990, D-Boy was shot and killed by an unknown assailant in East Dallas, Texas. **Angie Alan** wrote and recorded the song "Until We Meet Again" as a tribute to him. D-Boy's sister Genie Rodriguez records under the name **MC Ge Gee.** *Peace 2 the Poet* compiles songs from D-Boy's two albums along with a tribute song to the artist by **MC Ge Gee.**

Christian radio hits: "Pick Yourself Up" (# 8 in 1990).

DC Talk

Toby McKeehan, voc.; Kevin Max (Smith), voc.; Michael Tait, voc. 1989—*DC Talk* (ForeFront); 1990—*Nu Thang*; 1992—*Free at Last*; 1995—*Jesus Freak*; 1997—*Welcome to the Freak Show*; 1998—*Supernatural*; 2000—*Intermission: The Greatest Hits*; 2001—*Solo* [EP].

www.dctalk.com/dctalk.html

DC Talk reinvented Christian music, almost single-handedly rescuing it from the contrived commercialism and derivative doldrums of the '80s. They demonstrated that—contrary to what any neutral observer of '80s Christian music would have concluded—one did not have to choose between performing music that was *good* **(The Choir, Daniel Amos,** the **Seventy Sevens)** and music that was *successful* (names charitably withheld). First they were to Christian music what **Run-D.M.C.** and the Beastie Boys *combined* were to the general market; then a few years later they were to Christian music what Nirvana and the Red Hot Chili Peppers *combined* were to the general market. Of *course* the Christian market was a few years behind the rest of the world in both instances—it always is. Still, DC Talk pulled off their twin revolutions with style, displaying a myriad of influences proudly, but never becoming mere copycats. They also did it with integrity: at a time when most Christian acts who had a shot at crossover success opted to sing songs with ambiguous lyrics, DC Talk assaulted mainstream radio with the question, "What will people do when they hear that I'm a Jesus freak?" and with the refrain, "Hey, you, I'm into Jesus." And—what was ultimately of the most significance for the industry—they pulled it off with commercial appeal. Two years from their founding, they were the most popular Christian act in the world, and three years later they had become the most popular overtly Christian act of all time. DC Talk wasn't the first Christian group to play rap or grunge, but they were the most successful—and they were one of the best. Critics who had waited a lifetime to use those two phrases ("the most successful" and "one of the best") in the same sentence could say only, "Praise God!"

Toby McKeehan, **Kevin Max** (or Smith—before he decided to use his middle name as a professional surname), and Michael **Tait** came together at Jerry Falwell's Liberty University in Lynchburg, Virginia, and then moved as a group to Nashville to pursue their recording career. Max and Tait are excellent vocalists, the former being oft compared to Bono and the latter to Seal. McKeehan would turn out to be one of Christian music's finest songwriters, but he was first recognized for his proclivity for rap. Derogatory comparisons of his style to Vanilla Ice are unfounded and frankly racist (both artists are *white,* and that's where the similarities end). Indeed, McKeehan is a good enough rapper that for three albums *his* vocal abilities would overshadow the obvious vocal gifts of his partners. It also should be noted that all three of the Talkers are considered to be physically attractive. McKeehan—with a Brad-Pitt-rebellious-bad-boy glint permanently fixed in his eye—has been gifted or cursed with the charisma to function as the most compelling front man in Christian music (unless, of course, **U2** is classed in that genre). McKeehan also records as a member of **The Gotee Brothers** and is a cofounder of Gotee Records. DC Talk's very tight backing band has recorded on its own under the name **Zilch**—a name derived from an old Monkees' song. The name DC Talk, incidentally, is short for "Decent Christian Talk," reflecting the trio's initial commitment to being a rap group. Originally it was McKeehan's moniker as a solo act, his second incarnation after a brief stint as Caucatalk. As such, the name was a bit of a pun since McKeehan, like Tait, was raised in Washington, D.C. (Max is from Grand Rapids, Michigan).

The group's first album wasn't very good and it *still* became the best selling Christian debut record of all time. Its opening track, "Heavenbound," received generous airplay on the BET video network, making it a notable crossover success for the time. "Gah Ta Be (Saved)" makes an effort at hip-hop/traditional gospel fusion, a trick the group would perfect on *Free at Last*. Still the album was universally panned by critics. *CCM* spent most of its short review of *DC Talk* making jokes about the band's name ("bust-it don't fili-bust it"; "good for your *constitution*")—a sure sign the reviewer didn't know what to say about the music (which he described as "Roxy Music gone hip-hop"). *True Tunes* groused that the group's debut "had all the muscle and integrity of New Kids on the Block." Why did the record sell? There was an almost total dearth of rap music in the Christian market at that time, and DC Talk offered kids a sanitized for your protection version of the dangerous new hip-hop sound that had become established in the world at large. Somewhat ironically, given the abuse the band would suffer from critics and from fans of real rap music, DC Talk did more to introduce Christian music fans to rap and hip-hop than any other artist. Their first album became something of a stepping stone to make the style accessible and to allow fans to move on to an appreciation of more authentic varieties. Analogies to the role **Pat Boone** played with regard to early African American rock and roll stars might apply.

Nu Thang was a much better product, combining rap and pop in a way that seemed inspired by **M.C. Hammer** but, in retrospect, was a harbinger of what was still to come. It features the group's first outstanding track, "I Luv Rap Music" (which actually has a bit of a dancehall reggae feel). The title track to *Nu Thang* would become one of the first rap songs to be a major hit on Christian radio. "Walls" has a hard, metal-influenced sound and addresses racism. "Children Can't Live (Without It)" is a down-tempo, antiabortion song with more than a touch of disco. Notably, nothing from the band's first two albums would rate inclusion on their eventual greatest

hits collection *(Intermission)*, and they would pretty much cease performing material from those albums after the release of *Jesus Freak* in 1995.

Free at Last would change the world of contemporary Christian music. With six huge hits that didn't even include what would ultimately become the album's best-known track (the opener, "Luv Is a Verb"), rap music went overnight from being practically nonexistent on Christian radio to ruling the airways. DC Talk hit upon a dubious but ingenious proposition: why not do rap music that isn't *boring*? But how? By supplementing rapped verses with sung choruses, perhaps, or even by creating hybrid styles that infuse the predictable hip-hop sound with inferences from pop, rock, and especially gospel. Though rap (or even hip-hop) purists might consider *Free at Last* blasphemous—or perhaps *because* of that—the album remains one of that genre's greatest triumphs inside or outside the Christian subcultures. It is, as one critic averred, one of those very few rap records you can put on the stereo for the first time without sensing that you have already heard it somewhere before. As noted, the album begins with "Luv Is a Verb," a bouncy and rhythmic plea to put love in action. The next track, "That Kinda Girl," is a rap tribute to a righteous Proverbs 31-type woman, with choruses sung in southern-California-meets-Motown harmonies. The sound is a little reminiscent of the Fat Boys' take on "Wipe Out" in 1987 and is just as infectious. It is also innocent enough not to be spoiled by the well intentioned but slightly chauvinistic lyrics ("I'll know how to treat her / By fulfilling all her needs"). Next up is the classic DC Talk remake of "Jesus Is Just Alright." They opt for the Doobies Brothers' version (as opposed to The Byrds' original) and in a stroke of genius manage to set the song against an instrumental backdrop sampled from Madonna's "Vogue." Suddenly it is a dance song, with super-charged hooks, DJ scratching, and new (rapped) lyrics. A sample from Snap!'s "The Power" turns up in there somewhere too. The album includes two other inspired covers: the great gospel/spiritual "Free at Last" is now a chorus sung by a choir and wailed by Veronica Petrucci (of **Angelo and Veronica**) as intermittent interruptions to McKeehan's new rapped lyrics; Bill Withers' classic "Lean on Me" lends itself to hip-hop so easily that the new version almost erases any thought that the song could ever have been anything else. Filling out *Free at Last* are rock songs prophetic of what was to come on later albums. "Time Is" recalls '60s rock with unmistakable similarities to The Chamber Brothers' "Time Has Come Today." "The Hard Way" (an ode to prison life) is the first of many DC Talk songs to summon images of **U2**, as Max croons well-crafted lyrics about being "the kind of guy who has to find out for myself." Even the album's low point ("I Don't Want It") isn't too low. It features some up-front and unconventional lyrics set to a slamming beat: "I don't want it /

Your sex for now / I don't want it / Till we take the vows." Thus it is a too-obvious and trite response to George Michael's "I Want Your Sex"; if they had listened to the latter song more carefully, they might have noticed that it, too, is actually an ode to monogamy. In 2001 *CCM* would choose *Free at Last* as one of the "Ten Greatest Albums in Christian Music," quite a distinction from a magazine that had dissed the band's first two records. *True Tunes* headlined their review of the third album: "DC Talk is Good at Last!"

Three years passed and then the world blew up. The world of contemporary Christian music, as transformed and invigorated by DC Talk, was completely blown apart at the seams with that group's release of a single song, "Jesus Freak." Somewhat ironically (or prophetically), the CD single featuring the song also included a live version of the group singing **Larry Norman**'s "I Wish We'd All Been Ready." Few were ready for "Jesus Freak," with its manic, searing guitars, speed rapped verses, confrontational lyrics, and some of the best riffs since Clapton played "Sunshine of Your Love" or "Layla." It wasn't that Christian music fans hadn't heard metal or grunge or rap or hooks before—they just hadn't heard them all in *one* song. Or, perhaps, more to the point, most Christian programmers (though they would never admit it) had just never heard a song *this* good come down the pike before. Whatever they said publicly, many persons whose *job* was promoting Christian music had trouble believing their own hype about it being "just as good" as the general market stuff. Now, they held in their trembling little hands what was unquestionably the best rock song of 1995, Christian or otherwise. And what about the poor DJ at the average (non-Christian) college radio station? The reaction across the nation was a bit like that of Archie Bunker (TV racist) when he got to meet his favorite singer—Sammy Davis Jr. Most college radio DJs and programmers *hate* Christian music, but what could they do when a very Christian song by a very Christian group turned out to be *unquestionably* the best rock song of the year? Some played it, fueled by requests from students who were less fixated on ideology and just wanted to rock; many, steeped in denial, just couldn't bring themselves to do so. *Rolling Stone* dismissed the song as "a knock-off of Nirvana's 'Smells Like Teen Spirit'." Come again? Parts of it might sound a little bit like Living Colour covering that song, with Arrested Development on guest vocals . . . but to say that is to wander a ways from "knock-off," isn't it? By 2000 it would become apparent that DC Talk's unreviewed and largely unplayed "Jesus Freak" had been the connecting link between grunge and rapcore, a song with significance for the history of *rock,* not just Christian rock.

The song "Jesus Freak" was not a rap song, but when the album *Jesus Freak* came out a couple of months later, it would turn out to be the closest thing to a rap song anywhere on the record. Rhythm and blues, grunge, soul, and straight on rock and roll were all in evidence, but nary a glimmer of rap—except on those verses of "Jesus Freak." There was some immediate disappointment that the boys who did "I Luv Rap Music" had jumped ship, but that was quickly ameliorated by the overwhelming quality of the new project. "Like It, Love It, Need It" is a creative modern rock song with a barely detectable '70s soul-rock groove poured into an unpredictable song structure. "So Help Me, God" is blistering funk; "Mind's Eye" and "In the Light" (a cover of **Charlie Peacock**'s song) are infectious softer tunes that stay edgy and stop short of mellow. "Colored People" comes pretty close to being a perfect melodic pop song. "Just Between You and Me" and "What If I Stumble" are soulful ballads with melodies worthy of comparison to **Al Green** and **Marvin Gaye.** "Just Between You and Me" actually did break through to reach Number Twenty-Nine on *Billboard*'s general market Top 40 chart. The group's drastically reworked version of "Day by Day" (the old *Godspell* song) is admittedly a stretch, but fits well with alternative rock's penchant for unpredictable covers. The album *Jesus Freak* went double platinum, selling more than two million copies. A book *Jesus Freaks* (Albury, 1999) was issued, relating the stories of saints and martyrs of the modern era. The 1997 *Welcome to the Freak Show* presents live versions of the album's main tracks in addition to favorites from *Free at Last* and very short covers of the Beatles' "Help" and R.E.M.'s "It's the End of the World as We Know It."

Supernatural was not a masterpiece on the same order as *Free at Last* and *Jesus Freak*—if only for reasons of historical sequence—but it was an excellent album in its own right, on a par with, say, the Chili Peppers' *Californication* or Pearl Jam's *Vs.* In other words, it was not groundbreaking but simply featured unsurprising, stellar examples of the group doing what they do best. Four tracks were among the best songs of the year (Christian or otherwise), another four were very good, and then—the only surprise—there was some filler. The four breathtakingly great songs are, a) "My Friend (So Long)"—the album's highlight. Even *Rolling Stone* fell for it, claiming, "if the sweet Raspberries-style harmonies (in the song) don't make these missionaries a few converts, then the rebel yelling at the hymn's end should." b) "Since I Met You"—the best surf song since 1969. The Talkers revisit and update Jan and Dean in the same way Billy Joel once did the Four Seasons ("Uptown Girl," "Tell Her about It"). c) "Into Jesus"—a beautiful, worshipful affirmation of faith, featuring one of the most memorable melodies in recent history. Anyone not into Jesus will hate this song if they hear it twice—and end up hypocritically singing it for days thereafter. d) "Supernatural"—a full-bore, all out-rocker with the intensity of Steppenwolf's "Born to Be Wild."

In addition to these four gems, *Supernatural* offers the more-than-worthy "It's Killing Me," "Consume Me," "Godsend," and

"Wanna Be Loved." The first of these opens the album with characteristic raunchy guitars and upbeat rhythms. It is effective but just a tad too similar to "So Help Me God" (the opening track on *Jesus Freak*). "Consume Me" is a soulful ballad, on a par with the "Marvin Gaye" songs on the previous record, but also, again, in a just-a-little-bit-too-similar vein. "Godsend" sounds like all the songs with which boy bands (Backstreet Boys, *NSYNC, 98 Degrees) were carpet bombing the airwaves soon after this album's release. Granted, it is a better song than most of the tunes by those groups, but it unfortunately still remains representative of one of the most overdone sounds in the history of popular music. "I Just Wanna Be Loved" is more fulfilling, featuring what *The Lighthouse* called "a funky, soulful, '60s groove that sounds like Prince singing a high-speed Stevie Wonder song." The rest of the album is fairly innocuous—nothing terrible or compelling. "The Truth," with its *X-Files* chorus ("The Truth is out there"), and "Red Letters," with its Bible marketing ploy assumptions (the words of Jesus printed in red), come off as kind of dumb (i.e., *not* tongue in cheek) even though they are apparently intended to be profound.

While DC Talk has not enjoyed the worldly success they might have found apart from their Christian connection and faith-inspired lyrics, the band has done extremely well. While *Jesus Freak* would remain the pinnacle of the group's commercial/crossover success, *Free at Last* and *Supernatural* both went platinum in sales, and even *Nu Thang* went gold. Indeed, *Supernatural* debuted at Number Four on *Billboard*'s "Top 200 Albums" chart (nestled between Marilyn Manson's *Mechanical Animals* and Kiss's *Psycho Circus*). What is ultimately most impressive is that, like **Andraé Crouch,** they have achieved their modicum of fame and respect without any subtlety regarding their convictions. Not getting this, *Rolling Stone* once said the group proffers "lyrics that, in the immortal tradition of **Amy Grant,** can be read as both sacred and secular." The reviewer probably meant **Debby Boone,** not Grant, but in any case, nothing could be further from the truth. DC Talk sings songs that are considered to be sacred, and songs that are considered to be secular, and songs that trash the artificial barrier between those labeled realms—but they have never sung any songs with lyrics that *appear* secular but don't *have* to be (e.g., love songs to an ambiguous "you"—Jesus or a girlfriend?). The title of the song "Jesus Freak" references the unabashed young Christians of the '70s Jesus movement—and, indeed, the members of DC Talk seem to embody the spirit that drove that movement more than most modern Christian music artists. They know that anyone who says "my best friend was born in a manger" will be viewed as an oddball—they just don't care. "I'm not into hiding," **Tait** sings on that most famous song. Even a weaker song like "The Truth" can be considered in this light: the group originally submitted it for inclusion on *The X-*

Files motion picture soundtrack. It was rejected because of the overtly Christian testimony woven into the lines. Surely the band is to be commended for their refusal to compromise on such matters, even when it costs them a high-profile shot at general market appeal. As McKeehan raps on *Free at Last,* "To the ones who think they heard / I did use that J word / I ain't too soft to say it / even if DJs don't play it." While they *don't* get much airplay in the general market, DC Talk do command a certain grudging respect that is only enhanced by their forthright attitude, tempered as it is with significant humility. *Spin* magazine picked up on this when they observed, "the band strikes a chord because their Godtalk is leavened with personal testimony . . . not giving answers, but sharing struggles." Beginning with "The Hard Way," the group has tended to be more self-deprecating than judgmental, and to be so in a manner that is convincing and sincere. Few Christian (or secular) singers have shown the vulnerability McKeehan displays in "What If I Stumble?": "What if I stumble? What if I fall? What if I go and make fools of us all?"

DC Talk also deserves special mention for their unprecedented efforts (in Christian music) to address the enduring problem of racism in American society generally and within Christian culture specifically. From the outset their position as a biracial rap group (**Tait** is African American) afforded them the opportunity to do this, and they have not allowed that opportunity to be missed. They have dealt with the topic on almost every album through humorous snippets like "Two Honks and a Negro" (from *Free at Last*) and more serious numbers like "Walls" (from *Nu Thang*), "Socially Unacceptable" (from *Free at Last*); and "Colored People" (from *Jesus Freak*). In 1997 McKeehan cofounded the E.R.A.C.E. foundation, a nonprofit organization devoted to promoting racial reconciliation (the acronym stands for Eliminating Racism And Creating Equality). The group headlined a special E.R.A.C.E. festival-tour that sought to expose their audience to the music of various ethnic artists including **God's Property, The Katinas, Grits,** and **Out of Eden.** Tait's great-grandfather was killed by the Ku Klux Klan, and the memory of that incident remained fresh in the family of **Tait**'s father, Nathel, who grew up as an African American in Alabama before and during the Civil Rights movement. **Tait** credits his father, nonetheless, with having bequeathed to him an example and a drive for loving all people without regard to race or color.

DC Talk has participated in numerous side projects. Their song "My Will" is the highlight of the modern worship compilation disc *Exodus* (Rocketown, 1998). They contributed the song "My Deliverer" to the *Prince of Egypt* motion picture soundtrack (Dreamworks, 1998) and a remake of **Norman Greenbaum**'s "Spirit in the Sky" to the soundtrack of the TV movie *Jesus* (Sparrow, 2000). The album *Intermission* is a lengthy greatest hits retrospective that suffers from poor song selection (especially from *Supernatural*). As a group, DC Talk was listed in 1996 as one of *Christianity Today's* "Top 50 Up and Coming Evangelical Leaders under the Age of 40." In 1999 they performed for Pope John Paul II at a "Light of the World" youth rally held in St. Louis in his honor. In 2001 all three members of DC Talk released solo albums under the names **Toby Mac, Kevin Max,** and **Tait**. The *Solo* EP includes tracks from each of those projects plus a truncated live version of the band covering **U2**'s "40."

Christian radio hits: "Nu Thang" (# 3 in 1990); "Talk It Out" (# 22 in 1991); "Jesus Is Just Alright" (# 2 in 1993); "Socially Acceptable" (# 1 in 1993); "Time Is" (# 12 in 1993); "Lean on Me" (# 1 for 5 weeks in 1994); "The Hard Way" (# 1 for 3 weeks in 1994); "Say the Words" (# 2 in 1994); "Luv Is a Verb" (# 15 in 1995); "Jesus Freak" (# 23 in 1995); "Mind's Eye" (# 1 for 7 weeks in 1996); "Just Between You and Me" (# 1 for 4 weeks in 1996); "In the Light" (# 1 for 3 weeks in 1996); "What If I Stumble?" (# 1 for 6 weeks in 1997); "Colored People" (# 1 for 5 weeks in 1997); "What Have We Become" (# 1 for 2 weeks in 1997); "Into Jesus" (# 1 for 2 weeks in 1998); "My Friend (So Long)" (# 1 for 5 weeks in 1998); "Consume Me" (# 1 for 3 weeks in 1999); "Wanna Be Loved" (# 1 in 1999); "Godsend" (# 1 for 2 weeks in 2000); "Dive" (# 4 in 2000); "Say the Words Now" (# 1 for 2 weeks in 2001).

Dove Awards: 1991 Rap/Hip Hop Album *(Nu Thang)*; 1992 Rap/Hip Hop Song ("I Luv Rap Music"); 1993 Rap/Hip Hop Song ("Can I Get a Witness?"); 1994 Rap/Hip Hop Song ("Socially Unacceptable"); 1994 Rock Song ("Jesus Is Just Alright"); 1995 Rap/Hip Hop Song ("Luv Is a Verb"); 1996 Artist of the Year; 1996 Rock Song ("Jesus Freak"); 1997 Pop/Contemporary Song ("Just Between You and Me"); 1997 Rock Album *(Jesus Freak)*; 1997 Rock Song ("Like It, Love It, Need It"); 2001 Modern Rock/Alternative Song ("Dive").

Grammy Awards: 1993 Best Rock Gospel Album *(Free at Last)*; 1996 Best Rock Gospel Album *(Jesus Freak)*; 1998 Best Rock Gospel Album *(Welcome to the Freak Show)*; 2001 Best Rock Gospel Album *(Solo)*.

D.D.C.

Jeff Adams, voc.; Aaron Weiderspahn, voc.; Scott Wilson, voc. 1995—*Plate Fulla Funk* (Grapetree).

D.D.C. is short for Direct Destination Confirmed. The alternative rap group was formed in 1991 by Wilson, a nightclub DJ who is also a regular contributor to *Heaven's Hip Hop* magazine. The group lays down often belligerent rhymes over unconventional sounds influenced by a heavy dose of pop and funk. Standout cuts include "Back to the Basics" (which features a sample of **DC Talk** and an odd Three Little Pigs-inspired bridge) and "Funky Style." The rappers also demonstrate they can sing on the minor key "Throw My Arms around You."

Dead Artist Syndrome

Brian Healy, voc.; prog.; et al. 1990—*Prints of Darkness* (Blonde Vinyl); 1992—*Devils, Angels, and Saints* (Eden); 1995—*Happy Hour* (Alarma); 2002—*Jesus Wants You to Buy This Record* (BCM).

Dead Artist Syndrome is sometimes credited with creating the first Christian goth music. Much controversy has ensued over whether Christians should play music of this sort, but Brian Healy's mission seems to have been to craft the style into a vehicle that deals with the typical themes (death and depression) from a Christian perspective and to provide a more positive alternative to the attitude of hopelessness than is associated with the goth music of some general market artists. Thus Dead Artist Syndrome mixes what are essentially worship songs into their repertoire of melancholy and often macabre musings: "Reach" (from *Prints of Darkness*), "With You" (from *Devils, Angels, and Saints*), and "Glory" (from *Happy Hour*). Later Christian goth bands would include **Saviour Machine** and **Wedding Party**. See also entries for **Eva O** and **Tara VanFlower**.

Although other musicians play on the albums, Dead Artists Syndrome seems actually to be just Healy, plus whatever crew he rounds up for any individual production. For *Prints of Darkness* the Dead Artists included **Michael Knott** along with Mike Sauerbrey (of **LSU** and **The Choir**) and both Gym Nicholson and Ojo Taylor of **Undercover**. For *Devils, Angels, and Saints* he snagged **Michael Roe** and **The Choir**'s **Steve Hindalong** and Derri Daugherty; Hindalong and Daugherty also produced the record. Roe returned for *Happy Hour*, along with fellow **Seventy Sevens** David Leonhardt and Mark Harmon. The musical tone of all three DAS albums is similar: mostly slow, melodic songs that capture sounds of sadness. *CCM* compared *Prints of Darkness* to the more somber work of Joy Division or New Order. The album opens with an atypical rocker called "Christmas," which is not a carol but an introspective examination of one who deigns to test the limits of grace. Apostasy and doubt are likewise explored in the songs "Red" and "Hope." *Devils, Angels, and Saints* is darker and better orchestrated, and it is generally considered to be the band's best work. "Angeline" takes Healy deeper into the goth tradition with a song that expresses grief for a lost loved one. Teenage immorality (a frequent theme) is the topic of "Obsexed." Salvation is also a pervasive concern, notably in a song called "Redemption" ("I pray for my redemption, grace and peace save my soul"). Indeed, the album opens with what could be a plea from Christ: "Won't you let me inside / The place in your heart / You go to hide" ("Hello"). This is answered in "Beautiful World" ("I'll take your hand, you lead me out of darkness"). *Devils, Angels, and Saints* also includes a rather creepy cover of the Mamas and the Papas' "California Dreaming." Healy is known for producing songs with wry and witty lyrics, and this is never more evident than on *Happy Hour*. The third album includes a song about Marilyn Monroe called "Y.S.D.," which stands for "young, sexy, and dead." An apparent response to songs like Elton John's "Candle in the Wind," it offers sarcastic bemusement as to why so many find the spectacle of a wasted life alluring. *Happy Hour* also includes a punk track called "Bride Song," on which Healy speaks of the church: "Jesus, I love you, but I can't understand your wife / She wears such funny make-up and she always wants to fight . . . In my world of black and grey, she argues shades of white." Musically, *Happy Hour* is relatively more upbeat, with some funky tunes ("Heaven," "Dance with You") that drop the goth posture altogether. *Jesus Wants You to Buy This Record* combines a few new songs with miscellaneious live takes and remixes.

The Deadlines

Jerry Attrick, gtr.; The Creature, drums; Shaun Coffin (née Shaun Sundholm), voc.; Joshua Griffith, bass. 2000—*The Death and Life of . . .* (Tooth and Nail); 2001—*Fashion over Function*.

The Deadlines are a Portland, Oregon, based punk band fashioned after The Misfits or The Ramones—with a twist. Dismissed by some as "a Halloween novelty act," the group began by singing virtually nothing but songs based on themes from campy sci-fi horror films. Sample titles from their first album include "Go-Go to the Graveyard," "Last Nail in the Coffin," and the band's biggest hit, "Vampires in Love." The group adds a Farfisa organ on many tracks, which creates an odd blend of punk and surf music. Like **Blaster the Rocketman,** with whom they must be compared, the lyrics touch on Christian themes, though sometimes obliquely. "Poison Tongue" references James 3 and "Dead Indeed" describes those who are "dead to sin, but alive in Christ" (Romans 6:10–11). "Horrible Night" begins, "It was a horrible night / It was a horrible sight / It was a horrible fright / The day I realized I had died." At first, the group clearly identified itself as Christian and played at *Cornerstone* and other Christian venues, but by 2002 they would be turning down such gigs, saying "Everyone in the band is a believer, but we've chosen not to be a Christian band." When touring behind their first album, band members dressed in zombie outfits and spit (fake) blood on the audience. In late 2001 The Deadlines released a second album that eschewed the horror shtick in favor of old-time garage rock (e.g., The Replacements).

Dead Pharisees

Personnel list unavailable. 1998—*Dead Pharisees* (independent).

Dead Pharisees is a heavy metal Christian band that strives to be in the same mold as **The Crucified, Mortification, Precious Death,** or **Tourniquet** (as acknowledged in their liner notes). The group's first album features sloppy thrash-punk songs that will appeal to metal fans who prefer a minimum of production gloss. Lyrical treats include this couplet from "Party in Hell": "Party in hell, party in hell / I thought this was a beer bash, but sulfur's all I smell." As the group's name indicates, there is also a bit of a grudge against religious authorities. The album's cover art features a design based on an M. C. Escher display that was inspired by Romans 3:13.

Dear Ephesus

Lu Defabrizio, bass; Jeff Irizarry, drums; Brett Levsen, gtr.; Ed Lamoso, gtr.; Aaron Wiederspahn, voc. 1997—*The Consolation of Pianissimo* (BulletProof); 1999—*The Absent Sounds of Me*.

The quintet from Orlando known as Dear Ephesus was one of the first Christian bands to be associated with emo music. Emo purists rather annoyingly insist that the band's music isn't *real* emo. In response, *Phantom Tollbooth* deigns to call them "not quite emo" and *The Lighthouse,* "somewhere on the border of emo." The group itself never labeled their sound "emo" or anything else and apparently didn't care what it got called. Their musical approach did feature the intermittent mellow-aggressive stylings of the emo genre, however, such that *7ball* says, "Dear Ephesus goes from calm to complete anarchy in the blink of an eye." Fast-paced songs like "Butter Never Bleeds" are somewhat reminiscent of the harder side of Smashing Pumpkins ("Bullet with Butterfly Wings"). Aaron Wiederspahn's voice bears similarities to Counting Crow's Adam Duritz. Also the band's lyricist, Wiederspahn said, "Everything I write is allegorical or metaphorical," which limits the accessibility of the songs for listeners inclined toward literalism. The band is not too interested in helping the latter out. For example, "Butter Never Bleeds" appears to employ an image for pride and superficiality, but Brett Levsen offered only this explanation: "If you want to know what it means, go down to the store and get some butter. Get a knife and cut that sucker in half. If it doesn't bleed, then you'll know." As for the group's mission statement, Levsen said, "So many people are trying to be rock stars and we're just not into that. We love music and we love Jesus and that's about it." The group broke up at the end of the '90s with three of the members re-forming as **Tenderfoot.**

The Consolation of Pianissimo includes "A Boy and His Kite" and "The Flight of Peter Pan." The latter tune appears to compare life without Christ to living in Never Never Land: "I never meant to spend years in your silly world," Wiederspahn sings to the titular character, "I've been ignorant, living in a fairy tale." Another song from *Pianissimo,* "The Drifter," will remind aging Jesus freaks of a common theme in early Jesus music (e.g., **Larry Norman**'s "The Outlaw"; **The Way**'s "Bearded Young Man")—the titular drifter is Jesus, only in this '90s update he's likened more to a homeless man than to a hippie. *The Absent Sounds of Me* demonstrates more melodic pop sensibilities on certain songs ("Big Brother," "Looked for in the First Place"). These tracks would get the band compared to Foo

Fighters, while slower, moodier numbers ("A Woe," "The Morning Sings") summoned comparisons to **Pedro the Lion.**

For trivia buffs: The group's name does not come from Paul's letter to the Ephesians, but rather from Revelation 2:2–7 where the risen Christ speaks a letter to the church in Ephesus.

Mike and Kathie Deasy

1976—*Wings of an Eagle* (Sparrow).

The husband and wife team Mike and Kathie Deasy were one of the first acts to record for Sparrow records. Prior to that Sparrow recording, however, Mike Deasy had released the solo albums *Friar Tuck and His Psychedelic Guitar* (Mercury, 1967) and *Letters to My Head* (Capitol, 1973) in the general market, where he was known as something of a guitar hero session player. His résumé includes work with such artists as Eddie Cochran, The Coasters, the Beach Boys, **Elvis Presley,** Billy Joel, and The Monkees; he also worked on film soundtracks, including *Dirty Harry.* Deasy accepted Christ at a Billy Graham crusade and was able to spice up a lot of early Christian music albums by providing more competent chops than recording budgets would have allowed. He can be heard on albums by **Andraé Crouch, Keith Green, Barry McGuire, 2nd Chapter of Acts,** and **John Michael Talbot,** as well as many others. *Wings of an Eagle* offers a collection of folk songs with a country flavor. **2nd Chapter of Acts** offer guest backing vocals on certain tracks and **Michael Omartian** helps out as well. "Humpty Dumpty" became the album's best-known song, partly because of its inclusion on certain sampler compilation packages. "Silver and Gold" is probably the best track. He also cowrote the song "Cosmic Cowboy" with **Barry McGuire,** which was a Number One Christian hit for an incredible thirty-five weeks in 1978–1979. He has also composed hits for **Phil Driscoll** ("World Overcomer," "Messiah"). He produced the Christian children's album *Bullfrogs and Butterflys* (Birdwing, 1978), which went platinum with sales of more than one million copies.

Decision-D

Stijn Bollinger, gtr.; Daniel Bootsma, gtr.; Gerard Vanderree, bass; Peter Zaal, drums; Christian Edwards, voc. (– 1995) // Edwin Ogenio, voc. (+ 1995). 1991—*Testimony on Stage* (custom); 1992—*Razon de la Muerte* (Crypta); 1993—*Moratoria*; 1995—*The Last Prostitute* (Bark Horse).

Decision-D is not a rap group from the Bronx as the name may suggest, but a progressive thrash metal band from Holland. Information on personnel is hard to come by, but Christian Edwards appears to have been the front man and vocalist for the first album and to have been replaced in those roles by Edwin Ogenio by the fourth record. (*HM* magazine offers contradictory reports as to whether Edwards or Ogenio was the

Moratoria vocalist). Other musicians listed above definitely played on *Last Prostitute*—if there were personnel changes from the first two records, these have not been reported. At any rate, the band first formed in 1986, and they brought some novelty to the staid thrash metal genre by introducing Latin and jazz elements. The debut album is a fairly straightforward aggressive speed-metal project in the same vein as American band **Believer,** albeit with more of a penchant for harmonic minor key sounds. *Moratoria* displays the group's creativity to greater advantage. It draws on the book of Revelation and on Old Testament prophets to present a disc devoted to apocalyptic themes from start to finish. A song called "Bastard" is directed to Satan and features such lines as, "I suffered all my life because of you / I hate you. I hate you." "Espiritu Santu" offers operatic falsetto vocals and Latin percussion on what is otherwise a basic death metal song. On *Last Prostitute,* the group adopts a slower, more melodic approach that takes them to a new level. *HM* had praised Decision-D's first two albums, but now claimed, "after two lackluster projects, this Dutch quintet has switched gears and run face-first into excellence." A standout song, "Smoke," again displays a heavy Latin influence. Other songs on *Last Prostitute* ("The Residence of Dishonor," "Searching for Identity in a House of Impurity") address controversies surrounding Ogenio's church God's Pleasure. The church and Ogenio himself (as its pastor) were featured in national news in Holland in 1994 when members who had been subjected to church discipline castigated the group as a cult.

Robert Deeble

1989—*Songs from the Sabbatical* [EP] (custom); 1995—*Days Like These* (Liberation); 1998—*Earthside Down* (Jackson Rubio).

Phantom Tollbooth may have scared away potential fans of L.A. singer/songwriter Robert Deeble when they characterized his music as "heaven for the patient connoisseur . . . but agonizing for the easily sleepy." It is true that Deeble's acoustic songs are relatively free of memorable hooks or catchy choruses; the attraction, rather, lies in discovering the multiple textures in songs that, at first, all seem possessed of the same somber consistency. Deeble arose out of the coffeehouse circuit where for some years he distributed cassettes of witty college-folk songs he had recorded himself. On his major releases he is accompanied by cello, bass, and occasional percussion, but the front-and-center attraction remains his plucked (never strummed) guitar and breathy baritone voice. *Days Like These* features **Victoria Williams** in a guest duet on "Rock a Bye." The album also includes "The Existential Lovesick Blues," which *Cornerstone* called "a great song that could have used some drums." *Earthside Down* strays from the formula on "Junkyard," with flourishes of flamenco guitar. Deeble's lyrical approach to the Christian faith is poetic and provocative, with lines like, "Jesus is your friend, when you're still a child." He writes often about social issues and personal relationships. The song "Two Statues" portrays the alienation between two people unwilling to compromise, while "Billboards" mocks the commercialization of modern culture.

Deezer D

1999—Livin' Up in a Down World (N'Soul).

Deezer D is the professional name used by actor Daron Thompson for his side projects as a Christian rap singer. Thompson is best known for his role as nurse Malik McGrath on the TV drama *ER*. He has also costarred with Chris Rock in the film *CB-4*, with Damon Wayans in *The Great White Hype*, and as one of "the Jam boys" in the gangsta rap spoof, *Fear of a Black Hat*. Critics regarded Deezer D's rap album as "average" and "competent" as a musical project, with the added element of lyrics that offer an insider's take on celebrity and stardom (from a Christian perspective). A consistent theme is the mistreatment Christians receive in our world today, predictably at the hands of a secularized media, but unfortunately also at the instigation of other Christians. The album includes a few especially melodic tracks ("Welcome Home," "Watcha Gonna Do") and an interview of the artist with Julie Smith. The uplifting theme suggested by the title comes through in "Come Back" with the line, "When you have a setback, don't take a step back."

Eddie DeGarmo

1988—Feels Good to Be Forgiven (ForeFront); *1990—Phase 2*.

Eddie DeGarmo is best known to Christian music fans as one-half of the highly successful duo **DeGarmo and Key,** and to industry insiders as the cofounder of ForeFront records, which he helped to run from 1987 to 1999. DeGarmo recorded two solo albums during his tenure with **DeGarmo and Key. Dana Key** did the same. Such ventures were regarded as side projects that allowed the artists to try out stylistic ventures different from what was most closely associated with the mother band. In DeGarmo's case, this meant exploring music that showed more overt influence of such soul masters as **Sam Cooke,** Otis Redding, and especially Booker T. and the MG's. DeGarmo's raspy voice, which is only rarely featured on D&G projects, gives his solo material a distinctive edge—one that is well suited to the material. The first album's standout track is "Picking Up the Pieces," which is not a cover of the well-known **Erick Nelson** song (cf. **Good News**) but a new testament to Christ's healing power cowritten with Key. *Phase 2* features "Fragile Heart," with background vocals by **Commissioned** and a gospel trio cover of **Bill and Gloria Gaither**'s "Something about That Name" performed with **Mark Farner**

and **Russ Taff.** "I Can't Stand Still" updates '60s Memphis rock in the same way Steve Winwood did with his general market hit "Roll with It." As a songwriter, DeGarmo has written Christian radio hits for **Code of Ethics** ("Sticks and Stones") and **Rebecca St. James** ("Side by Side"), in addition to numerous songs cowritten with Key.

Christian radio hits: "Picking Up the Pieces" (# 2 in 1989); "Fragile Heart" (# 7 in 1990); "Can't Stand Still" (# 5 in 1991).

DeGarmo and Key

Eddie DeGarmo, kybrd.; Dana Key, gtr., voc. *1977—This Time Thru* (Lamb and Lion); *1979—Straight On; 1980—This Ain't Hollywood; 1982—No Turning Back; 1983—Mission of Mercy* (Power Discs); *1984—Communication; 1985—Commander Sozo and the Charge of the Light Brigade; 1986—Streetlight; 1987—D&K; 1988—Rock Solid: Absolutely Live; 1989—The Pledge; 1991—Go to the Top* (Benson); *1992—Destined to Win: The Classic Rock Collection; 1993—Heat It Up; 1994—DeGarmo and Key's Greatest Hits, Vol. 1* (ForeFront); *To Extremes* (Benson).

DeGarmo and Key was a Christian pop duo composed of **Eddie DeGarmo** and **Dana Key,** both of whom also released solo albums. The two grew up as childhood friends in Memphis and formed their first band together (The Sound Corporation) while in sixth grade. When they were in high school (1972) the duo received a recording contract with Hi/London records for their current general market band Globe, though no product was ever released. The plans to be rock stars were sidetracked when DeGarmo answered an altar call at a **Dallas Holm** concert and then led his friend Key to accept Christ in a janitor's broom closet at school the next day. Initially abandoning rock music as inherently worldly, they worked as leaders with Youth for Christ for a few years and then formed the ministry-oriented combo DeGarmo and Key in 1977. The duo maintained a loyal following and enjoyed considerable commercial success (often in the face of critical apathy) for eighteen years. A groundbreaking act, they set new standards for technical excellence in the Christian market and were the first Christian rock group ever to be nominated for a Grammy award (for *This Ain't Hollywood*) or to place a song in rotation on MTV ("Six Six Six"—ironically, the network forced them to edit the video for excessive violence). They disbanded in 1995.

Musically DeGarmo and Key are often remembered as Christian music's Hall and Oates, though like any group with so long a tenure, they evolved through a variety of stylistic phases. They actually began with a wannabe stadium-rock sound (think Styx lite or, basically, Toto) and ended as a full bore classic rock band. These alpha and omega points are significant, as the group's first two and last two albums are generally regarded as their best. *This Time Thru* had an enormous impact on the Christian market, inspiring commentary that "it sounds as good as anything in the general market"—an unusual and perhaps unique feat for the time. DeGarmo's Keith Emerson-like keyboards lead the sound on cuts like "Emmanuel," while Key's somewhat bluesy guitar keeps things from getting too sterile or sappy. The sound is congruent with what was being played on late '70s FM radio at the time and is indeed of an equivalent quality from a technical and production standpoint. "Chasin' the Wind" sounds the tone, describing the futility of existence apart from Christ. The title track shows concern for the homeless and encourages the listener to make a difference in life; the same basic affirmation is sounded in the more anthemic "Sleeper." The album also includes a cover of the traditional "Wayfaring Stranger." *Straight On* remains the band's masterpiece. The Toto allusions are at an all-time high, but a) that group had only just appeared (first album in late 1978); and b) with the possible exception of "Hold the Line," Toto's songs (anyone remember "Georgy Porgy"?) were all inferior to D&K's. "Livin' on the Edge of Dyin' " has an extended synthesizer introduction worthy of **Kansas,** and "Go Tell Them" is a driving midtempo number with blues riffs worthy of the Allman Brothers. "Long Distance Runner" uses the biblical metaphor of 1 Corinthians 9:24–25 effectively in a song that captures (but does not copy) the sound of Atlanta Rhythm Section. *Straight On* would be the only DeGarmo and Key album included (at Number Ninety-five) on a *CCM* critics' poll of "The 100 Greatest Albums in Christian Music" published in 2001.

This Ain't Hollywood continues in the same vein as the first two albums, with a twinge of Doobie Brothers-style jazz rock and a noticeable move toward ballads ("You Gave Me All" and "Nobody Loves Me Like You," sung as a duet with **Amy Grant**). "Love Is All You Need" was written with **Mylon LeFevre.** "All Night" offers a stark portrait of a broken marriage. *No Turning Back* is a double live album summarizing the group's early career. Then the band fell into a creative slump, producing what are now best-forgotten exemplars of pop-pablum. Even at the time, critics recoiled at most of the albums from *Mission of Mercy* (1983) through *Go to the Top* (1991). Songs like "Hand in Hand," "Addey," "Casual Christian," and "I'm Accepted" all sound alike, and they all sound like that one mammoth power ballad that kept inundating the airwaves in slightly different incarnations for a good eight years after Journey did "Open Arms" (1982).

Mission of Mercy was DeGarmo and Key's first project with an '80s sound (not necessarily a good thing). It opens with a *Flashdance*-inspired song called "Ready or Not" and closes with a cover of **Billy Preston**'s "That's the Way God Planned It." *CCM* picked it as one of the Ten Best Christian albums of 1983, though that may say more about the contemporary state of Christian music and orientation of the magazine than about the record's enduring quality. *Communication* has a strong wor-

ship orientation ("Alleluia! Christ is Coming") and includes the aforementioned "Six Six Six." Apart from the latter highlight, however, the album was panned by *CCM* as "watered down" and "formulaic." *Commander Sozo and the Light Brigade* takes a different theme, employing the old guilt standby to motivate average believers into striving for excellence ("Casual Christian," "Apathy Alert"). Somewhat more inspiring is the anthemic "Destined to Win," which would be recycled by **E.T.W.** in 1991. "Charge of the Light Brigade" is a militant pop hymn.

The group tried to "return to rock" on *Streetlight* and *D&K,* but in a scary way. Granted that the albums have a more guitar dominated sound, the song "Rock Solid" sounds exactly like something from Foreigner's *Four* album, and *Streetlight*'s title song chucks and churns with riffs that had pretty obviously been invented by ZZ Top. Indeed, *Streetlight* opens with a song ("Don't Stop the Music") that features as its central line, "Kids wanna rock," the identical *lyric* to a very similar sounding song by Bryan Adams that was actually *titled* "Kids Wanna Rock." And then "Every Moment" is a near perfect imitation of Adams' "Summer of '69" (except now instead of being generically thankful for one great summer, D&K are grateful *to God* for every moment of their lives). *The Pledge* gave Christian music a Kiss-cum-**Petra** anthem, "Boycott Hell," which is a pretty good rock and roller. **Steve Taylor** would later make fun of the song's simplistic theme by rapping on a **Newsboys** record, "I agree we gotta boycott hell / But we gotta boycott dumb lyrics as well." Key himself would later characterize *Go to the Top* as "clinical, sterile, and predictable." It also revels in a simplistic and theologically questionable wartime spirituality with songs that try to rally Christians to militant victory in a most un-Jesus-like manner ("Stand, Fight, Win," "Victory," "March On").

Throughout their doldrums decade, D&K remained a commercially viable act, and for better or worse, were innovators responsible for defining the parallel universe of Christian music as an entity (or empire) in its own right. In one unique promotion, the first 100,000 copies of *D&K* included an extra free copy of the album on cassette tape for the buyer to give to "someone who needs to hear it." Then promotion for *The Pledge* introduced the whole notion of corporate sponsorship to Christian rock, with the group serving as spokespersons for the New International Version of the Bible ("Take the Pledge—Read the Word"). In 1991 the duo developed and published a *Go to the Top* Bible study curriculum to accompany their album of that name. Notably, DeGarmo cofounded ForeFront Records (which he helped run until 1999), and Key became an executive with Memphis-based Ardent Records. In retrospect, perhaps the best description of the group's music in the '80s would be, "the kind of rock music you would expect from company executives," i.e., careful and competent in execution, but very contrived. In time, the Christian music scene would come to resent the NutraSweet approach to rock represented by bands like DeGarmo and Key and **Petra** (*almost* as tasty as the real thing, and better for you!"). It should always be remembered, however, that before these two artists, Christian rock was famous for its inferior sound. The early Jesus music bands may have produced music with more heart, but what DeGarmo and Key lacked in creativity they made up for in competence. It would not be unfair to say that they changed the face of Christian music, setting new standards for excellence such that when the Christian alternative groups of the '90s sought to recapture the Jesus movement's vitality and integrity, they knew they had to do so without compromising on quality. Key even wrote a book defending the reputation of contemporary Christian music (*Don't Stop the Music,* Zondervan, 1989).

In any case, long after most had given up looking to DeGarmo and Key for anything of substance, the duo suddenly did the unexpected and made not one, but two good albums. *Heat It Up* and *To Extremes* represent another return to rock, but this time one grounded in a more generic classic rock influence. Hints of ZZ Top and Bad Company and tons of other bands show up, but these are all mixed into such an eclectic stew that no song really sounds immediately like anything or anyone else. *Heat It Up* opens hard with the tongue-in-cheek "God Good, Devil Bad," a bit of a self-deprecating joke regarding the group's infamous bumper sticker lyrics. Album standouts include the title track and "It's My Business," which counters popular prioritization of privacy over accountability: "It's my business to keep you between the lines / I'm just doin' what the Lord says to do / I hope your business is watchin' me too." The song "I Use the J Word" takes its title from a famous line in **DC Talk**'s cover of "Jesus Is Just Alright." The only real low point of *Heat it Up* comes with "Armed and Dangerous," the third in a series of songs by that name that presents Christians to the world as a united front whom people had better fear if they know what's good for them. **Matthew Ward** gets the blame for starting such nonsense with an album called *Armed and Dangerous* in 1986, on which he professes his intent to keep carrying on until the enemies of Christ all lie dead at his feet. **Petra** continued it with another song called "Armed and Dangerous" in 1990, capping off a Christians-can-beat-up-everybody-else theme that had marred much of their '80s material. DeGarmo and Key's song by the same worn-out title is the mildest of the three, but its use of militant imagery to present Christians as threatening the world with (spiritual?) violence remains inexcusable, especially in a nation where Christians wield political power as the dominant social group, and non-Christians (Jews, Moslems, etc.) actually do fear them. Musically though, the song rocks, with some especially impressive guitar leads.

To Extremes opens with three very strong tracks: the soaring rocker, "Stressed"; a bluesy, acoustic cover of The Rascals' "People Gotta Be Free"; and the Aerosmith-inspired "Hangin' by a Scarlet Thread." According to DeGarmo, the album's central song, "Rebel for God" (cf. **The Altar Boys**' "When You're a Rebel") tries to make constructive use of Generation X anger by turning that anger toward sin, which in this case means dirty books and pictures (nothing wrong with that, though ironically the unprompted anger of most secular Gen-Xers was *already* directed against such things as injustice, militancy, and materialism—all of which drew a lot more ire from Jesus than pornography). The song does feature some incredible woodshed fretting by Key, reminiscent of '70 era Stones. *True Tunes* praised the sound of *To Extremes* but continued to complain about lyrics that "confirm all the pre-conceived prejudices people have about Christian music"; the song "Hyperfaith," for instance, is a bit too TV-evangelist-friendly in its depiction of faith as a cure-all for life's woes. But Doug Van Pelt, editor of *HM* magazine, issued a surprising endorsement of *To Extremes.* "D&K got a little gnarly and nasty on this release," wrote Van Pelt. "This is the first album since *Straight On* that I've been able to say without feeling like a wimp, 'Here's a DeGarmo and Key album I like.' "

As indicated, DeGarmo and Key were always noted for straightforward lyrics that set out Christian messages in words that require little deciphering. This sound-byte approach has been criticized by those inclined toward poetic reflection or existentialism, but it clearly served the band's purpose of proclamation. "Ministry is the primary reason for the existence of D&K," Key said in 1993. "Our music is simply a vehicle to communicate a message." The group often employed altar calls at their concerts, at which persons were invited to access salvation in an individualistic way. This may have given their ministry an inevitable sectarian cast, but their dedication to blatant and unashamed testimony was noble and exemplary. At one point in their career, D&K was given the opportunity to open a tour for ZZ Top, provided they would not talk about Jesus from the stage. They didn't have to think twice about turning that one down. As such, D&K helped to define the genre known as contemporary Christian music as a world unto itself—for better and for worse. Music critic and historian Mark Joseph says in *The Rock and Roll Rebellion* that DeGarmo and Key "formed one of contemporary Christian music's first legitimate rock bands," meaning one of the first whose albums and concerts were of a quality comparable to what was being produced in the general market. Yet Joseph continues, "the duo are definitely to be counted among those who pursued an 'us vs. them' mentality that pervaded the contemporary Christian world and ensured its continued irrelevance to the wider culture." Indeed, Key attacked such secular bands as Spin Doctors and R.E.M. in his book *Can't Stop the Music* and noted in a 1993 interview, "ninety-nine percent of secular music" evinces a "fundamental Satanism." Thus Christians should not listen to secular music at all, but should listen only to Christian music as a godly alternative. By 1998, however, he indicated that DeGarmo and Key's calling to be part of a specifically Christian subculture should not necessarily be the norm: "I don't want anybody to follow in our footsteps. Our decisions are not to be applied to other artists."

Eddie DeGarmo and Dana Key have also served as producers for projects by many artists, including **Gary Chapman, Farrell and Farrell,** and **Jessy Dixon.** They have also written hits for **Jessy Dixon** ("Silent Prayer"), **Farrell and Farrell** ("Get Right or Get Left," "People in a Box," "American Man"), **The Gaither Vocal Band** ("Blessed Messiah"), **Look Up** ("It's Alright with Me"), and **White Heart** ("Jerusalem").

For trivia buffs: Dana Key is a direct descendant of Frances Scott Key (composer of "The Star Spangled Banner"), and Eddie DeGarmo is a direct descendant of Davy Crockett.

Christian radio hits: "Livin' on the Edge of Dyin' " (# 25 in 1979); "You Gave Me All" (# 19 in 1981); "Nobody Loves Me Like You" [with **Amy Grant**] (# 6 in 1981); "Let the Whole World Sing" (# 1 in 1984); "Ready or Not" (# 31 in 1984); "That's the Way God Planned It" (# 37 in 1984); "All the Losers Win" (# 28 in 1984); "Alleluia! Christ Is Coming" (# 4 in 1985); "Perfect Reflection" (# 25 in 1985); "Destined to Win" (# 2 in 1986); "Casual Christian" (# 9 in 1986); "Apathy Alert" (# 15 in 1986); "Every Moment" (# 1 for 6 weeks in 1986); "Inside Out" (# 12 in 1987); "When the Son Begins to Reign" (# 2 in 1988); "Stand" (# 6 in 1988); "If God Is for Us" (# 5 in 1989); "Hand in Hand" (# 7 in 1989); "I'm Accepted" (# 3 in 1990)"; "Who Will" (# 23 in 1990); "Against the Night" (# 6 in 1991); "Family Reunion" (# 8 in 1991); "I'll Come Out Fighting for You" (# 9 in 1993); "Talk to Me" (# 5 in 1993); "Soldiers of the Cross" (# 6 in 1993); "Never Look Back" (# 9 in 1994).

Deitiphobia (a.k.a. **Donderfliegen**) and Massivivid

Wally Shaw, voc.; kybrd.; Brent Stackhouse (−1994) // Sherri Shaw, voc. (+ 1994); Josh Plemon, gtr. (+ 1994, − 1999); Wil Foster, synthetics (+ 1998); Bob Carlton, bass (+ 1999, −2000); John Hogan, drums (+ 1999, −2000); Tom Wilson, gtr. (+ 1999, −2000). As Donderfliegen: 1991—*Digital Priests* (Slava). As Deitiphobia: 1991—*Fear of God* (Blonde Vinyl); 1992: *Digital Priest: The Remixes*; 1994—*Clean* (Myx); 1995—*Fear of the Digital Remix* (Myx); 2000—*Lo-Fi vs. Sci-fi* (Eclectica). As Massivivid: 1999—*Brightblur* (Tatoo); 2002—*Dressed to the Nines . . . Armed to the Teeth* (Accidental Sirens).

www.massivivid.com

Deitiphobia is a Christian industrial band with a heavy techno/dance orientation. Musically the sound is similar to that of general market bands like Nine Inch Nails and Skinny Puppy. The band is the brainchild of Wally Shaw, who says he became disillusioned with the church as a child after his father was repeatedly fired as a preacher at different congregations for rocking the boat. He later became involved with nondenominational fellowships and eventually served on the music team at the Willow Creek Community Church in Chicago. Shaw continues to criticize what he calls the white-tomb syndrome in many churches (cf. Matthew 23:27–28), according to which "things have to look really great, regardless of the pain that people who attend there are going through." Shaw is attracted to the theatrics of industrial music but tries to give the genre "an attitude adjustment from gloom and doom."

The group originated as a duo called Donderfliegen, which released 250 copies of a homemade tape called *Digital Priests* to the Christian market in 1991. That album, despite its slight circulation (on cassette tape only), is usually regarded as the first Christian industrial release and is prized by collectors and by fans of that genre. On the way to the 1991 *Cornerstone* festival, the duo decided to change their name to Deitiphobia ("fear of God") when someone told them the German sounding name had Nazi overtones. Deitiphobia's almost self-titled debut was to be the group's masterpiece. *True Tunes* says that here we find Shaw and Stackhouse "taking the basic elements of coldly synthetic European industrial culture and reworking them into an album of pristine beauty and near worship." A few years later the same journal would admit, "if ever there was a record an audience was not ready for, it was *Fear of God*" and would describe the project as sounding like "dance music for a German meat-packing plant." The tracks "Crucifixion of Will" and "Dancing Messiah" stand out as hard dance numbers, while "I Tore the Sky" is more ominous and majestic. Flaming Fish (a Christian industrial label) reissued the album in 1998 with three new tracks, including a funky collaboration between Deitiphobia and rapper MC White-E ("My Jesus Is Real"). As a sophomore project the group released a remixed version of the Donderfliegen *Digital Priests* album, with some new songs added. In general this album is regarded as every bit as good as *Fear of God* on a song-by-song basis, but lacking in the consistency that makes the latter project work as a whole. *Digital Priests: The Remixes* was also reissued by Flaming Fish with new tracks in 1998. The album titled *Fear of the Digital Remix* was a compilation of material from these first two projects, but of an odd sort. One critic called it "Deitiphobia meets an insane butcher." The butcher in question was **Michael Knott,** known for his solo work and for his albums with such bands as **LSU** and **Aunt Bettys,** and also former head of Blonde Vinyl records. He remixed the Deitiphobia tracks with radical alterations (spliced songs together, layering them on top of each other, adding samples, etc.) and even gave them all new titles. Some love it, some hate it, but most agree that it is almost more of a **Michael Knott** album than one by Deitiphobia.

After Stackhouse left (to record as **X-Propagation**), Wally Shaw continued to operate the group with his wife Sheri supplying KMFDM-styled female vocals now and then. Knott provides some guitar and vocals for *Clean*. That album is boldly evangelistic, dealing with issues of sin and redemption throughout. It is also, according to *True Tunes,* a "decidedly more dance-oriented affair" than previous albums, making it more accessible to general audiences. Then for some reason the band changed its name to Massivivid for an album. *Brightblur* evinces a much more guitar-driven industrial rock sound, similar to that of **Fold Zandura.** Lyrically the album struggles with the problems of technology—an appropriate subject for industrial music—relating the love-hate relationship of flesh and metal to that between flesh and spirit. The album's title derives from C. S. Lewis's *Letters to Malcolm,* and Lewis's influence is evident in several of the songs: the concept for "Deep Heaven" comes from the author's space trilogy; the song "Unmade" quotes from *Mere Christianity* ("fill me more and more with you, and make me less and less of me"). The band became Deitiphobia again for *Lo-Fi vs. Sci-Fi,* the most ambitious project to date. The latter album provides a soundtrack for an Internet comic book by Graeme Udd. The story deals ostensibly with class warfare in a futuristic technological society, but it moves toward an ultimate celebration of grace and mercy. Tracks include the bold "Humanifesto," a philosophical "Tripwire," and the unusually anthemic "Transmission." Another Massivivid album was announced for 2002.

Prior to her marriage to Wally Shaw and work with Deitiphobia, Sherri (then Sherri Swaback) led a synthesizer-based pop band called Hip Dream. They released one independent EP called *Jump to the Drum* in 1992. Brent Stackhouse's wife Heather also released a female industrial project called *Wigtop.* To help pay the bills, Wally Shaw has done musical soundtracks for video games, including *Summoner* for Playstation 2.

Dove Awards: 1999 Hard Music Album *(Brightblur).*

DeLeon

See DeLeon Richards.

Delirious? (a.k.a. **Deliriou5?**)

Stuart Garrard, gtr.; Tim Jupp, kybrd.; Martin Smith, voc.; Stewart Smith, drums; Jon Thatcher, bass. 1996—*Live and in the Can* (Furious?); 1997—*Cutting Edge; d-tour live album;* 1998—*King of Fools;* 1999—*Mezzamorphis;* 2000—*glo;* 2001—*Audio Lessonover; Deeper: The D:finitive Worship Experience.*

www.delirious.co.uk

Delirious? is frequently designated the "most popular British Christian band of all time." The accuracy of such description depends on how one regards such acts as **After the Fire** and **U2** (how do you define British? how do you define Christian?), but the band has certainly made an unusually big splash in the tiny pond of U.K. contemporary Christian music. The group began as a team of worship leaders at the Arun Community Church in Littlehampton, England. That team called itself the Cutting Edge Band, and it originally included Tim Jupp, Martin Smith, and Stewart Smith, who all had one thing in common: they were married to three daughters of one of the church's elders, a David Thatcher. Later that elder's son, Jon Thatcher, also joined, along with Stuart Garrard who is *not* a brother-in-law. Between 1993 and 1996, the Cutting Edge Band released four cassette tapes of worship music that are said to have had the same kind of effect on nonliturgical worship services in Britain that the music of the charismatic renewal movement had on nonliturgical American services two decades before. The songs swept the country, and to those within the low-church tradition at least, it seemed that *everyone* was suddenly singing them. In April 1996, following a car crash that brought Martin Smith and Jon Thatcher to reflect seriously on their priorities, the worship team decided to go full time and changed its name to Deliriou5? The use of a numeral 5 in place of an *s* was just a graphic gimmick with no real significance, and they eventually abandoned it. They do try to maintain the terminal *?,* however, as a reminder that the band's identity and direction must always remain uncertain, as they allow God to lead them one step at a time. As it turns out, such openness served them well, for an unexpected development met the band on the very day of its debut album's release. No one would have predicted that, of the music groups popular in Great Britain's evangelical Christian subculture, a praise and worship team would be the one most likely to find success in the *secular* market—but that is exactly what happened. The group's first full-length release, *King of Fools,* debuted at Number Thirteen on Britain's mainstream pop chart, and two singles from the album, "Deeper" and "Promise," each went to Number Twenty on the British charts. The BBC's Radio 1 network referred to the band as "pop's best-kept secret." Not surprisingly, the next major release, *Mezzamorphis,* took into account such possibilities and aimed for a more secular radio-friendly sound, albeit to no avail. In 1998, a journalist/fan named Craig Borlase published a book about the band's adventures titled *Purepop? The Delirious? Journey So Far* (Furious? Press). In 2001 the band toured Europe as the opening act for Bon Jovi and Matchbox 20.

In America the group's albums have been distributed by Sparrow in specifically Christian outlets and by Virgin in the general market. A two-disc compilation of the Cutting Edge worship tapes (called *Cutting Edge*) came out shortly before *King of Fools.* The first of these discs will be of historical interest only to most American music fans—the songs are nice (especially "Lord You Have My Heart," "Thank You for Saving Me," and "The Happy Song") but are not performed with any quality that would impress people familiar with all of the Maranatha and Vineyard compilations of praise choruses. The song "I Could Sing of Your Love Forever" would become a modern worship classic and seemed destined to remain Martin Smith's best-known and most beloved work. The second disc (comprising what was originally *Cutting Edge* 3 and 4) has an entirely different sound. Thatcher and Garrard were on board, and the worship team was beginning to sound like a fairly tight progressive rock band. One perceptive critic indicates that the group effectively reconceives worship leadership as a group function. In other words, the worship is led not by a singer backed by a band, but by the band itself, with the instrumental elements being as much a part of the worship experience as the vocals or lyrics. Never is this more evident than in the majestic anthem, "Did You Feel the Mountains Tremble?" which opens Disc Two with almost ten minutes of building, spiritual momentum. "Obsession" and the driving "Louder Than the Radio" are also remarkable. Brian Quincy Newcomb indicates that with this two-disc set, Delirious? has "not just written some little worship choruses, but has begun the arduous task of creating a modern hymnody for generations raised on rock and roll." Delirious? is also noted for being able to create spontaneous songs, spirit-led worship numbers invented on the spot. The liturgical equivalent of jamming, such expressions probably work well live but do not translate well on recordings. Seven such moments litter the *Live and in the Can* album, giving it an unfortunate "guess you had to be there" ambience. The *d-tour* album captures the group's live performance in a more enduring and accessible fashion.

King of Fools moves away from the praise and worship class to mainstream Christian rock. Musically the group creates a sound similar to that of **U2,** infused with elements of modern Brit bands like Oasis. The song "White Ribbon Day," a plea to end political violence in northern Ireland, bears more than just thematic similarities to U2's "Sunday Bloody Sunday," and "Sanctify" sounds a lot like U2's "One." *HM* jokingly reviewed the entire album as "the U2 album fans have been waiting for." But on "Promise" the group comes off as a first-rate, blistering rock and roll band in their own right. "Deeper" is the sort of infectious pop song that deserves to be a hit. "History Maker" starts off like an industrial track but evolves into another pop song with a sing-along chorus. "King or Cripple" is introspective and piano driven. *True Tunes* describes the record as a whole as "a good old-fashioned big budget pop album . . . with soaring vocals, swelling guitars, rhythm loops, and huge background vocals."

Anticipation was unrealistically high for *Mezzamorphis,* and sensing this perhaps, the group made an album that was defi-antly *not* some ultimate, grand consummation. It was only their sophomore effort, really, and they wanted the world to know that. The name itself is a hybrid of the words *mezzanine* (or "in between") and *metamorphosis* ("change"). Thus, Delirious? seemed to be announcing to their fans (and nonfans), "We are changing, and it is not yet apparent what we will become." Musically the album moves decidedly away from the **U2** comparisons (except on the standout "Beautiful Sun") and more in the direction of a Radiohead-type sound. "Heaven" (which again deals with northern Ireland's holy war) mixes hard and atmospheric guitar with electronic effects and strings. "Follow" is a melodic, slow rocker about following God that incorporates a bit of a hip-hop beat. "Gravity" and "Bliss" are stellar examples of aggressive rock and roll. While faith references are still present and obvious (with "Bliss" promising they won't "back down"), the album has more of a secular feel to it lyrically. The song "It's O.K." is about a young woman who looks like she's got it together but is hurting within. The ironic line "she's as pretty as hell" caused a flurry of controversy among the sort of Christians who get upset by such things. "Jesus Blood" is an explicitly faith-oriented ballad. "Kiss Your Feet" and "Love Falls Down" retain the band's worship orientation. Notably, the version of the album issued on Virgin records omits the obviously Christian tracks "Jesus Blood" and "Kiss Your Feet."

The *glo* album represents a decided return to praise and worship music. It opens with soft choral chanting in Latin (monks from Ampleforth Abbey singing Psalm 63) and then breaks into a Bonoesque anthem, "God, You Are My God." Love for God is beautifully expressed in "My Glorious," and God's persistent love for believers in "God's Romance." Musically the pop-oriented "Hang On to You" and the gentle ballad "What Would I Have Done?" are also highlights. In 2001 the band issued a collection of "best worship songs" called *Deeper: The D:finitive Worship Experience.* A two-disc, twenty-five-track collection, *Deeper* is unbalanced in song selection (thirteen songs from *Cutting Edge* and seven from *King of Fools*) but does include one new song ("Not Forgotten").

Delirious?'s *Audio Lessonover* album was produced by Chuck Zwicky, known for his work with Semisonic, Prince, and Madonna. The album was not well publicized and failed to make much of an impression on the British charts, indicating that the band's crossover-moment-in-the-sun might be past. *Audio Lessonover* features "Waiting for the Summer," a sunshiny pop song worthy of its name, and "Take Me Away," a power-melody track buoyed by the band's trademark euphoric choruses. Lyrically, both of these numbers are ambiguous love songs with lyrics like "You take me away to another place / Show a way to a higher place." Despite its title, "America" is a song of global consciousness, mentioning numerous nations with short tag lines ("America, you're too young too die . . . India, you're too hurt to cry"). After the terrorist assault on America on September 11, 2001, the song was released on mp3.com as a sort of tribute to the United States; a reissue of "White Ribbon Day" served in a similar capacity.

Christian radio hits: "Deeper" (# 1 for 4 weeks in 1998); "Gravity" (# 4 in 1999); "See the Star" (# 7 in 1999); "Love Falls Down" (# 7 in 2000); "Everything" (# 2 in 2000); "You Are My God" (# 9 in 2001).

Deliverance

Jimmy P. Brown, voc.; Chris Hyde, drums (–1991); Brian Khairullah, bass (–1991, + 1992a, –1992b, + 1993, –1994); Glenn Rogers, gtr. (–1990) // George Ochoa, gtr. (+ 1990, –1992); Kevin Lee, drums (+ 1991, –1994); Mike Gato, bass (+ 1991, – 1992); Mike Phillips, gtr. (+ 1992, –1995); Manny Morales, bass (+ 1994); Jeff Mason, drums (+ 1994); Mark Colon, gtr. (+ 1995). 1989—*Deliverance* (Intense); 1990—*Weapons of Our Warfare*; 1991—*What a Joke*; 1992—*Stay of Execution; Learn*; 1993—*Intense Live Series* [EP]; 1994—*River Disturbance* (Brainstorm); *A Decade of Deliverance* (Intense); 1995—*Camelot in Smithereens*; 2001—*Assimilation* (Indie Dream).

www.cs.ucsd.edu/users/bruss/Metal/groups/Deli.html

Deliverance may be the closest Christian equivalent to Metallica. Like that general market band, the group began as a basic speed metal act, but tiring of that somewhat limited genre ("just play it *fast* and *loud*"), they evolved into more of an alternative metal act, with a slower pace and more expressive vocals. The group formed in Los Angeles in 1985. Their first album was novel for the Christian marketplace, and though the group was immediately dubbed Metallica-clones, that appellation was sometimes meant as high praise. Solid sales afforded a bigger budget for *Weapons of Our Warfare*, which is still mentioned with hushed reverence among Christian metalheads as one of the best speed metal albums of all time. A video version of the title song became the first Christian metal song to gain airplay on MTV, and it placed among the top three on that network's weekly Headbanger's Ball countdown for twelve weeks in a row. Much later, in 1999 Lars Ulrich, drummer for the real Metallica, hosted a show in which he named Deliverance's "Weapons of Our Warfare" as one of his Top 10 metal videos of all time. That song and most of the *Weapons of Our Warfare* album deal with the tired theme of spiritual warfare, albeit with more theological integrity than metal bands would often muster. Many of the songs seem to be inspired by Frank Peretti's novel, *This Present Darkness* (Crossway, 1986). The group slows things down only once, for an almost-ballad based on the 23rd Psalm ("23").

Coming off of their career high, the group produced a transitional piece. *What a Joke* reveals a band coming apart at the seams, though a cover of Black Sabbath's "After Forever" remains a highlight, and an ironically noisy rendition of "Silent Night," a classic novelty. The tensions evident in *Joke* were resolved in *Stay of Execution* as front man Jimmy Brown now led a new lineup with a new sound that was often described as "David Bowie joins Metallica." The Bowie influence was indeed evident in Jimmy P. Brown's transformed vocals (more singing, less growling-screaming) and in the more experimental song structures. **Terry Taylor** of **Daniel Amos** produced the album (as he did the next three), and the group even covered the DA song, "Horrendous Disc." The metamorphosis was permanent, and on the subsequent albums *Learn, River Disturbance,* and *Camelot in Smithereens,* Metallica comparisons would give way to Queensryche analogies, except that Metallica themselves had abandoned the thrash metal scene about this time for more of a Queensryche sound as well. Deliverance's approach continued to be very heavy, but more brooding and reflective. *Learn* features another **Daniel Amos** cover, "Sanctuary." *River Disturbance* includes a collaboration with the rap group 12th Tribe ("A Little Sleep") that anticipates Korn by a few years. *Camelot* includes a cover of Bowie's "Beauty and the Beast" but becomes the best of the post-*Weapons* albums on the strength of fine original songs. "Not Too Good 4 Me" is infectiously hook-laden, and the introspective "Book Ends" is lyrically poignant. The independent *Assimilation* CD is a nostalgia trip, recorded after a six-year hiatus and displaying a decade-old early '90s sound.

Jimmy P. Brown has clearly been the band's central figure (and only permanent member). He has also been the chief songwriter, penning tunes that are often more relational than anthemic, and certainly more poetic than what is stereotypically associated with heavy metal. The song "Windows of the Soul" (from *Stay of Execution*) prays for the attitude of Christ with these words: "I'm tempted to judge every book by its cover / Fail to consider the spirit within / Give me the heart of the nail-torn lover / The bloodied and battered forgiver of sin." The tone of such lyrics set them far apart from Christian music's other premier metal band **Stryper** (whose "Surrender" Deliverance did cover as the opening track on their live-in-the-studio EP). Brown has since formed a band called Fearful Symmetry (after the title of a **Daniel Amos** album).

Hard rocking Deliverance should not be confused with the '70s contemporary gospel vocal group of the same name who recorded at least four albums: *To God Be the Glory* (Image, 1976); *Give It a Try* (New Pax, 1976); *Lasting Impressions* (Atlantic, 1978); *Tightrope* (Attic, 1979). The latter act had a smooth choral sound similar to **The Imperials.** In the late '80s an urban gospel group similar to **Commissioned** also recorded under the name Deliverance (*9 Teen 9D's,* Tyscot, 1991).

The Dell Griffiths

Troy Deaton, gtr.; Stephen Murray, voc.; Dave Frank, kybrd.; Roy, drums. 1995—*I . . . I Like Me* (Swirle).

The Dell Griffiths were a one-time "silly side project" (in Stephen Murray's words) by three members of the much more serious band **Curious Fools,** joined here by a friend named Roy. The goal was to create a retro-'80s sound nostalgically fashioned in the mold of groups like Missing Persons or a-ha. The Dell Griffiths got that sound down pat, complete with all the kooky synthesizer bleeps, pop hooks, and guitar energy. The title track offers the tongue-in-cheek reflections of a rock star who finally likes himself now that he's hip: "Once upon a time I wasn't this cool . . . I only thought about the wrongs in this world / Never the cut of my hair." Cover versions of Split Enz's "I Got You" and The Cars' "My Best Friend's Girl" are also included.

The Deluxtone Rockets

Johnny "Rocketti" Brown, voc., gtr.; Jimmy "Dean" Van Boxel, bass; Jakob Dykema, sax. (−2001); Richard Mittwede, tromb. (−2001); Jason Som, drums (−2001); Tim Tahoe, trump. (−2001) // Rodney Demeglio, drums (+ 2001); Lonnie, gtr. (+ 2001). 1999—*The Deluxtone Rockets* (Tooth and Nail); 2001—*Green Room Blues.*

The Deluxtone Rockets from Ypsilanti, Michigan, have had two distinct incarnations. They first came on the scene as a tight, first-rate Christian swing band, and then after a one-year hiatus, reappeared as a very different rockabilly duo. These style variations seem to match the advent and quick demise of the turn-of-the-millennium swing craze, but the group that appears on the band's debut album sounds like a band of experienced musicians who could have been playing the suddenly popular sound for years. Immediate comparisons were drawn to Christian music's best-known swing band, **The W's,** but The Deluxtone Rockets had a harder, bolder, and brasher sound than that equally competent act. Even then, elements of rockabilly were apparent, such that the sound bore more similarities to the Reverend Horton Heat than to The Cherry Poppin' Daddies. Johnny "Rocketti" Brown's voice is urgent and playful, often recalling the Mighty Mighty Bosstones' Dicky Barrett. But the best analogy for first edition Deluxtone Rockets would be found in the Brian Setzer Orchestra's harder '90s music (e.g., when they cover Setzer's old Stray Cats songs). The self-titled record immediately kicks into high gear with two driving up-tempo numbers, "Tijuana Jumping Bean" and "Green Eyed Cat." The song "Hi Fi Daddy" opens with a shouted chorus and then continues with an especially infectious bouncing horn line. "Rumble with the Devil" is almost a Setzer tribute, and one that allows specifically Christian content to come to the fore, albeit in a comical fashion. There is not a bad track on the album, but the band saves their best till last: "Kitten" closes the record out with a loud and gritty celebration of dancing and romancing. John Brown is lyricist for all of the songs.

The Deluxtone Rockets' first record was coproduced by Dennis Danell of Social Distortion and Gene Eugene of **Adam Again,** both of whom died during production for the follow-up (cf. **The Calicoes, Value Pac**); Chris Colbert (of **Breakfast with Amy** and **Duraluxe/Fluffy**) finished the job. The title of the sophomore album, *Green Room Blues,* reflects these tragic circumstances surrounding its production in Eugene's Green Room studio. Sans horns, the group's remaining members (Brown and bassist Jimmy "Dean" Boxell) hired a couple of temps (including **The Calicoes**' drummer Rodney Demeglio) to turn out a set of basic rockabilly songs that variously recall Buddy Holly and Johnny Cash. The disc opens with its most bouncy and pop-oriented track ("Broken Heart") and closes with "Judgment Day," a would-be swing tune on which the horns are rather noticeably absent. The Rockets also cover The Cure's "Love Song."

Denison Marrs

Jonathan Bucklew, drums; Joseph Bucklew, bass; Eric Collins, voc., gtr.; Daniel Day, gtr. 1999—*Holding Hands @ 35,000 Feet* (6x6); 2001—*Stavesacre/Denison Marrs* [EP] (Velvet Blue); *World Renown for Romance.*

Denison Marrs is a modern rock band with emo stylings from Florida. The group was formed in 1995 and gained a strong indie following for their emotional romantic music that seemed to draw on such influences as **The Prayer Chain,** Radiohead, **Starflyer 59,** and **Sunny Day Real Estate.** Songwriter Eric Collins is forthright about his Christian faith but does not typically use songs as vehicles for expressing religious beliefs. Because of his connection with the Christian music scene, some of his love songs have been taken as directed-to-God worship tunes. But at times such ambiguities are impossible: "I've been told by (Christian) interviewers that some of my lyrics are taken to be simply love songs between people. My reply is that some of them are that indeed. The thing is, wherever true love is found, God is prevalent." The debut album *Holding Hands @ 35,000 Feet* was released on 6x6, a label headed by Mike Lewis of **For Love Not Lisa** and **Puller.** *Stavesacre/Denison Marrs* is a split EP containing only three songs by Denison Marrs and three more by the band **Stavesacre.** Two of the DM contributions to the latter project are also on *World Renown for Romance,* the band's paean to girl-boy love as the greatest of all God's gifts. "Love and Its Grand Scheme" and "(I Have You) Memorized" seem appropriate for Gen-X candlelight dinners.

Al Denson

1985—*Stand Up* (Celebration); 1989—*Al Denson* (Benson); 1990—*Be the One;* 1992—*The Extra Mile;* 1993—*Reasons;* 1995—*Do You Know This*

Man?; 1997—*Take Me to the Cross*; 1998—*Tabula Rasa*; 2000—*From this Day On* (Spring Hill).

www.aldenson.com

Inspirational pop singer Al Denson has devoted his adult life to proselytizing teenagers for Christ. Born in Starkville, Mississippi, in 1960, Denson conducts his ministry out of Dallas, Texas. He has worked with Youth for Christ and he hosted their Youth Evangelism Congress in 1991 and 1994. He has also participated in the crusade ministries of Billy Graham, Franklin Graham, and Dawson McAllister. Since 1997 he has worked professionally as an evangelist himself, targeting high school students. To some this seems ironic, since his music is solidly adult contemporary, not rock or rap or whatever else youth supposedly like, but connections get made. He speaks regularly at high school assemblies, and as of 2000 had two well-received programs to offer: "Who Are You in the Dark?" (focusing on "the value of truth, honesty, and good character") and "When Tragedy Strikes" (dealing with school violence, untimely deaths, and life-threatening illnesses). These programs are specifically designed for presentation in public schools, but Denson invites all present to an evening concert at which he is no longer restrained by law from making a direct evangelistic appeal. Denson is also the author of several books for teenagers, including *Take Me to the Cross* (Tyndale, 1997), a devotional guide, and *I Gotta Know* (Tyndale, 1999), which offers "answers to tough questions students ask." In 1998 Denson pioneered the syndicated TV show *Studio 828*, and in 1999, *The Al Denson Show*. The latter program attempts to be something of a *700 Club* for teenagers and often features musical performances by Christian artists, while dealing with such issues as "The Fatherless Home," "Racism," and "Hollywood and the Media." In 1994 Denson was copiloting a small plane with his friend Grant Milner when the craft experienced engine failure on its approach for landing at the San Antonio airport. Milner was killed in the resulting crash and Denson suffered severe injuries.

Denson's first two albums were cassette-only releases. His self-titled project includes covers of songs by **DeGarmo and Key, Amy Grant,** and **Wayne Kirkpatrick,** with backing vocals by the group **Glad.** Denson's profile rose with *Be the One,* which features as its title track the theme song Denson had written for the 1991 Youth for Christ Evangelism Congress. *The Extra Mile* mixes a few more upbeat tunes in with the usual power-pop ballads and includes a song intended to help teenagers whose parents are divorcing ("That's What My Father Would Do"). *Reasons* is a concept album that offers "reasons for people to get to know Christ." The overtly evangelistic record includes a cover of Sly and the Family Stone's "Stand." *Do You Know This Man?,* the first album after the fateful plane crash, continues in the same vein with somewhat quieter songs over-

all, save for the rousing gospel number, "Church of Love." *Take Me to the Cross* is positive pop à la **Bryan Duncan,** with rock influences trying to creep in on songs like "Right about Now" and the Beatlesque "Rain Love." The standout song for *Tabula Rasa* (Latin for "clean slate") is a particularly energetic title track dealing with the theme of redemption. *From This Day On* offers "This Is Love (This Is Life)," an anthem to the dawn of a new relationship with Christ, and "He's Watching Me," a lump-in-the-throat story song dealing with grief and comfort in the face of death. "Until the Lights Go Out" is a sentimental ballad about a man's care for his dying wife.

Denson conducts his evangelistic ministry in accord with the conventions of those denominations that teach a personal decision theology and favor altar calls as the prime sacrament for accessing a relationship with the divine. His concerts always conclude with such rituals—indeed, they serve primarily as set-ups for the all-important sermon and invitation at the end. The approach appears to be highly effective within his chosen tradition (the website boasts that "Al has seen over 100,000 decisions for Christ since he started touring"), but of course renders those events aberrant if not offensive to Christians who belong to other traditions. Denson's song "One Brand of Truth" was a Christian radio hit for **Geoff Moore and The Distance** in 1991.

Christian radio hits: "Reckless Heart" (# 24 in 1990); "Nothing Can Separate Us" (# 22 in 1991); "Be the One" (# 12 in 1991); "Stand Up" (# 6 in 1992); "Living in the Heart of Your Love" (# 19 in 1994); "Say It with Love" (# 8 in 1994); "Reasons" (# 16 in 1994); "Do You Know This Man?" (# 25 in 1995).

Andy Denton

1999—*Midnight of Hope* (KMG).

A veteran of Christian music, Andy Denton took part in several projects before finally embarking on a solo career. In the late '80s he was lead vocalist for the hard rock Christian band **Ruscha** and wrote their hit "Come Home." After that group disbanded, he sang lead for **Legend Seven,** writing or cowriting all four of their chart songs as well. Then he formed **Identical Strangers** with Randy Thomas. His debut solo album reveals him to be a blue-eyed soul singer in the adult contemporary tradition of Thomas's other former partners, **Bob Carlisle** and **Bryan Duncan.** The strongest song on the album is its opening track, "On These Raging Streets," a compassionate plea for justice in a world that is not the way God intends. The next track, "What Kind of Church," sounds very much like a **Steven Curtis Chapman** song. Neither Denton nor Thomas cowrote either of those two standout cuts, but they do contribute to most of the remaining songs, which run the gamut from slow piano ballads ("Fifty Years from Now," "Midnight of Hope") to light pop tunes ("Why Do You Love

Me?" "At the Cross") to catchy, upbeat soft rock songs ("As Far As My Heart Can See," "Forgiveness"). There's even a "groovy" *Sgt. Peppers*-style parody of '20s jazz ("Plastic Paradise").

Will Derryberry (and The Derryberry Band)

The Derryberry Band: Will Derryberry, voc., gtr.; Ian Kilpatrick, bass; Baron Miller, drums. By Will Derryberry: 1994—*Mockingbird Won't Sing* (independent); 1998—*Learning Your Sky* (Fair Oaks). By The Derryberry Band: 2000—*Live August 31, 1999* (Fair Oaks).

www.willderryberry.com

Will Derryberry is a Christian singer/songwriter from northern California with an eclectic musical pedigree. Raised on Chicago and Delta blues, he took a detour as a teenager, playing in metal bands like Purple Haze and Pax Mortis. After becoming something of a metal legend in the northern California club circuit, he surprised everyone with an independent album of folk songs called *Mockingbird Won't Sing*. "It was very folky," Derryberry recalled in 2000. "It's embarrassing to listen to now. I'm not sure I'll ever live down that album." In any case, Derryberry recorded the acclaimed *Learning Your Sky* album four years later. The latter record is also rather folky, but with more of the blues influences showing through. *Release* would compare its sound to the retro-acoustic '70s style of other '90s artists like Layton Howerton and **Eli.** Those analogies are suggested by Derryberry's vocal similarity to Cat Stevens, but his intentions would become obvious when he rerecorded some of the same songs from *Learning Your Sky* live with a band. The resulting album by The Derryberry Band caught the attention of blues aficionados, and critics began comparing the artist to George Thorogood or Joe Cocker, and the band itself to Phish or Dave Matthews' outfit. In addition to songs from *Learning Your Sky* ("Got No Other," "I Can Count on You," "Hear My Cry," "I Saw an Angel"), *Live, August 31, 1999* includes the gospel-blues standards "Before You Accuse Me" and "This Train."

For trivia buffs: Ian Kilpatrick of The Derryberry band is the son of Bob Kilpatrick, a singer/songwriter who is also the owner of Fair Oaks Records.

Teri DeSario

Selected: 1983—*A Call to Us All* (DaySpring); 1985—*Voices in the Wind*.

Terri DeSario is a one-hit wonder in the world of popular music whose name comes up in trivia games as the answer to the question, "Who sang the duet vocals with KC and the Sunshine Band on their 1979 hit, 'Yes, I'm Ready' "? DeSario hails from Miami, and she actually had a semi-successful pre-KC career. Discovered by the Bee Gees' producer, she recorded her

first album on the Casablanca label and hit Number Forty-three on the pop chart with the song, "Ain't Nothing Gonna Keep Me Away from You" (written and produced by Barry Gibb). But then the duet with KC and company went all the way to Number Two, making her a household name for at least a few weeks. Struck by the emptiness of such fame, she entered a time of introspection and, as she puts it, "I cried out to the God of my youth." Two albums of faith songs followed, produced by her husband Bill Purse and featuring her own original compositions. Her songs are personal, without being necessarily autobiographical, and they speak poignantly of reflection and renewal. Both albums begin with songs encouraging praise ("Thank You," "Celebrate"), a sentiment that also fuels the catchy "Attitude of Gratitude." Other recurrent themes include testimony to God's design for the individual life ("I Dedicate All My Love to You," "Tapestry") and explication of internal struggles against temptation ("Battleline," "All Day Thursday"). The title track for *A Call to Us All* is a seven-and-a-half-minute opus that includes ethnic instrumentation intended to invoke major religious traditions of the world (Hinduism, Islam, Buddhism) along with words from the Latin mass for Holy Thursday and a prayer from the Jewish synagogue service. All of these ecumenical associations support the lyrical call to love all humanity and recognize persons of every race and religion as manifestations of the image of God. The first album also includes "Jesus Call Your Lambs," which calls on the Lord to heal broken marriages. *Voices in the Wind* displays unusual maturity with the song "I Don't Want to Be a Soldier," which repudiates the militant victor image of Christians being propagated by many contemporary Christian music artists at the time (cf. **DeGarmo and Key, Petra**). In 1985 DeSario told *CCM,* "I have felt the warm breath of God, and I know what it's like to be in the cold world without Him." In recent years DeSario has sung as a member of The Maranatha Singers. She cowrote the song "Wonders of His Love" with **Philip Bailey,** for whom it was a Christian radio hit.

Christian radio hits: "Battleline" (# 8 in 1984); "I Dedicate All My Love to You" (# 10 in 1984); "Tapestry" (# 5 in 1986); "Celebrate" (# 15 in 1986); "Attitude of Gratitude" (# 12 in 1986).

Detritus

Mark Broomhead, voc., gtr.; Andy Bright, drums; Earl Morris, gtr.; Andy Neal, gtr. 1990—*Perpetual Defiance* (Edge); 1993—*If But for One* (R.E.X.).

Detritus was a British thrash metal band led by Mark Broomhead, who also played bass for **Seventh Angel.** The group first came into being, with a slightly different lineup, as a collection of chums who grew up together in Nailsea, England. Though only Broomhead and Andy Neal were Christians, the band attended the *Greenbelt* Christian festival, where Andy Bright made a decision for Christ and Broomhead, inspired by the preaching of **Glenn Kaiser,** determined to clean house and reconstitute the band as a definitively Christian act. The uncommitted departed, Morris was recruited, and an album was made while all four group members were still in their teens. The British press dismissed Detritus as Metallica wannabes, and Broomhead later admitted that imitating Metallica was "what we did on purpose, because we wanted everyone to like us." The second album, however, was of a completely different order. Still metal headbangers, Broomhead and his pals introduced a number of creative textures and experimental effects. "Sailor's Farewell" is sort of a heavy metal sea shanty complete with jazz saxophone. "Masquerade" also features a jazzy acoustic introduction that provides the sort of accent **Lanny Cordola** might have suggested. "Feel" is a mostly acoustic song with building passion, and the title track incorporates generous blues riffs. *HM* magazine declared, "This album is a shocker . . . a knockout punch from England's best Christian metal import." Unfortunately the album was held up in production and did not actually get released until two years after Detritus had broken up.

Linford Detweiler

See **Over the Rhine.**

Deuteronomium

J.-J. Kontoniemi, drums; Manu Lechiten, bass; Kalle Paju, gtr.; Milka Partala, voc. 1997—*Tribal Eagle* [EP] (independent); 1998—*Street Corner Queen* (Little Rose); 1999—*Here to Stay.*

A Christian death metal band from Finland, Deuteronomium took the opposite course of most metal acts and first released an album that sought to break out of the predictable confines of the metal genre and then followed this with an album that fit those confines perfectly. The group's EP attracted some attention for its unusually melodic character (unusually melodic for death metal, that is) but the full-length debut, *Street Corner Queen,* really got the critics to sit up and take notice. The band offered a compendium of different hard styles, with every song different from the ones that preceded it. Two tracks, "Blue Moment" and "Northern Praise" (a worship tune), employ female vocals. The only serious misstep is an ill-fated excursion into rap and reggae ("Human Nature"). *True Tunes* described *Street Corner Queen* as "unquestionably one of the best Christian-made metal albums ever." The next record, then, was a disappointment, as the group simply presented thirteen death metal tracks (what they call "death and roll") that all pretty much sound alike. Death metal purists did not complain but everyone else did. *True Tunes* now moaned, "They've picked the easiest to play sound in their repertoire and slammed out a new album in less than a year." The group

disbanded soon after—or at least advertised for a new singer and drummer. Lyrically Deuteronomium's songs tended to be subtly evangelistic, focusing often on the bleakness of life without Christ. "Druglord" presents the words of a young addict, "I'm walking through my nightmare called life . . . Deep in my head I know the butcher." The title track to "Here to Stay" comes to the point: "I'm not here to stay forever / I gotta go and it won't take long / Just a bang and no me no more / But I have this moment and so have you / So what we gonna do?"

Dez Dickerson

1997—*Oneman* (Absolute).

In the '80s Dez Dickerson was lead guitarist for Prince's various bands, playing on that artist's classic (and best) albums, *Dirty Mind, 1999,* and *Purple Rain.* He even shared lead vocals with Prince on the song "1999," and he is featured prominently in the movie *Purple Rain* and in videos for such songs as "1999" and "Little Red Corvette." Dickerson had a dramatic conversion experience in 1980 but continued playing for Prince, as well as for Billy Idol, for some years thereafter. Finally in 1984 he quit the secular music scene, having been bothered for some time by what he considered to be graphic and lewd content of some songs. He went to work at StarSong (as President of Artists and Repertoire) and then founded his own company, Absolute Records. After producing albums for other artists, he finally decided to put out one of his own. Dickerson got assistance on *Oneman* from Phil Salem of The Rembrandts, Michael Bland of NPG, and Joel Hanson of **PFR.** The overall sound of the album is modern rock, with an eclectic range of styles from the Beatlesque pop of the title tune (which describes the unique status of Christ) to the heavy, guitar crunch of "Peacehopejoy." The record also features a couple of up-tempo funky numbers ("For You, For Me") but is otherwise heavy on ballads. "Fall into Me" is sung from the perspective of Christ: "If it hurts tonight, fall into me. Let it go." The album concludes with a spoken word message from Dickerson describing his devotion to Christ. Dickerson also cowrote the Christian radio hit "I (Surrender)" for **Paul Q-Pek,** whose album he produced. His son Jordan Dickerson fronts the teen-pop band **Squirt.**

Die Happy

Robyn Kyle Basauri, voc.; Larry Farkas, gtr.; Doug Thieme, gtr.; Glen Mancaruso, drums; Roger Martin, bass (– 1993) // Greg Chaisson, bass (+ 1993). 1992—*Die Happy* (Intense); 1993—*Intense Live Series, Vol. 4; Volume 2.*

Die Happy was essentially **Vengeance Rising** with a new vocalist. Indeed, Robyn Kyle Basauri was not even officially a member of the group on the first album, but as singer for a band called Jaguar, he was hired to lay down vocals on songs that were otherwise complete (Jaguar was fronted by Joshua Perahia of the band **Joshua,** and Perahia reportedly led Basauri to Christ). Basauri officially joined the band soon after the eponymous *Die Happy* was released, and Greg Chaisson came over from the general market band Badlands, where he had played with Ozzy Osbourne's lead guitarist Jake E. Lee. After *Die Happy*, Basauri dropped his surname and went on to form **Red Sea** as Robyn Kyle.

The group made two studio albums in addition to a live-in-the-studio project produced by **Terry Taylor.** The two main releases reveal steady progression from the thrash metal sounds of **Vengeance Rising.** The eponymous debut is more of a mainstream heavy metal project (as opposed to the speed-thrash variety) and *Volume 2* is hard classic rock in the tradition of Black Sabbath and Led Zeppelin. Standout songs on *Die Happy* include "Real," which was inspired by basketball star Magic Johnson's revelation that he had AIDS, and "Painted Truth," which reflects on how heroic legends about American pioneers obscure the facts regarding persecution and massacres of Indians. The title track and "Melrose" were mosh-pit manifestoes while "Bone Doctor" and "Cage" were just Metallica thrash attacks. The most surprising track on the album is "Celebration," a love song presented in a slow ballad style reminiscent of the Allman Brothers or Bad Company. As these examples suggest, *Die Happy* focused lyrically on a wide range of topics rather than simply repeating evangelical slogans. "Our beliefs haven't changed," Larry Farkas said, comparing the material to **Vengeance Rising**'s, "but we're trying to get people to think for themselves instead of just saying, 'This is what it is, and believe us'." Whereas Farkas and Doug Thieme wrote all the songs on the debut album, *Volume 2* was more of a community effort. "Sticks and Stones" is about inter-Christian rivalry and arises somewhat from Chaisson's experience as a loyal Roman Catholic playing in a field dominated by fundamentalist Protestants. "Justified" offers an affirmation of grace as a reminder to those who struggle each day with the weight of the world upon them.

David Diggs

1973—*First Flight* (label unknown); 1974—*Supercook* (Instant Joy); 1976—*Out on a Limb* (PBR Intn'l); 1978—*Elusion* (label unknown); 1985—*Streetshadows* (Palo Alto); 1986—*Right before Your Eyes* (TBA); 1989—*Nothing But the Truth* (label unknown); 1991—*Tell Me Again* (Artful Balance); Date Unknown—*Realworld* (Palo Alto); *The Artful Collection; Eye of the Storm; Westcoastal.*

www.daviddiggs.com

David Diggs is well known in the general market for his contributions to modern, synthesizer-led jazz. *Streetshadows* was on *Billboard*'s Top 10 Jazz chart for twenty-six weeks. Both *Billboard* and *Cashbox* ranked him as one of the top three Best

New Jazz Artists of 1985. Since that auspicious debut he has not only continued to make artful jazz records for the general public but has also done arranging, producing, and composing for numerous TV shows and films. A child prodigy, Diggs studied privately in Hollywood and was writing big band charts while still in his teens. He sold his charts worldwide to high schools and colleges and recorded two big band albums of original songs in 1974 and 1975. Diggs plays keyboards, drums, and guitars, along with a little of everything else as needed. He has produced albums for Irene Cara, Eric Gale, and The Brothers Johnson, in addition to doing the music for a Grammy-nominated comedy album by Jonathan Winters.

Less known are Diggs' early contributions to Jesus music and his continued participation in and support for the work of Christian artists. Diggs was a member of the very early group **Rebirth** and then became a founding member of the Jesus music group **Good News,** which also included **Billy Batstone, Bob Carlisle,** and **Erick Nelson.** For a short time he also joined **Mason Proffit,** led by **John** and **Terry Talbot.** He worked with **Richie Furay** on his early Christian albums and arranged strings for **Barry McGuire**'s Grammy-nominated *Cosmic Cowboy.* He was also the main man behind the *Love Songs Strings* project that compiled orchestrated, instrumental versions of songs by the classic Jesus music group **Love Song.** For many years, he worked with **Pat Boone** and **Debby Boone,** touring with them and arranging and producing their music. Diggs' daughter Rachel Diggs is also a recording artist with a style that has been compared to Joni Mitchell, Fiona Apple, and Sarah MacLachlan.

Dig Hay Zoose

Phil, voc.; Dave Anderson, gtr.; Bill Brown, bass; Jim Florez, drums. 1991—*Struggle Fish* (Brainstorm); 1993—*MagentaMantaLoveTree*; 1995—*Ascension 7: Rocketship to Heaven.*

Dig Hay Zoose was one of the first Christian bands to emerge in the alternative rock movement of the '90s, and they staked their claim to that territory before it became a marketing label applied so generously as to be virtually meaningless. The Kansas City, Missouri, quartet's basic sound involved a mix of metal, punk, and funk analogous (but not really similar) to that of the Red Hot Chili Peppers. The group's name might be just weird, or it might be an aural pun. If one says, "I dig hay zoose" aloud, it sounds like an affirmation of being "into Jesus," provided the latter's name is said in Spanish.

The debut album was produced by **Terry Taylor** and is impressive primarily for its creative, out-there sound, that is, for a degree of innovation rare in Christian music. Standout cuts include the title track, the opener, "Think about It" (which paraphrases Ecclesiastes: "Life is but a vapor"), and "Water's Way" (dealing with environmental concerns). "Zeptune" announces its inspiration proudly, while "Sunless Saturday" discretely clones the general market band Fishbone. The second record, coproduced by the band with Gene Eugene (of **Adam Again**), represents a major step forward. With samples ranging from The Doors to Mister Rogers, the album represents what *CCM* would call a "gloriously cacophonous mulligan's stew." "Dancing in Concert with the Infinite" is oddly poetic; "H8 Machine" expresses anger at the perpetuation of racism and hate in religious institutions; "Black-Eyed Pea" takes another stab at ecological awareness (comparing our dying planet to the titular vegetable); "Diggin' Away" describes guilt and self-loathing: "Wearing yesterday's sin like a raincoat / And your sky ain't nothin' but grey." The title track is a sort of hippie/ New Age love song: "I dreamt of a fountain-filled garden / I passed the pond / The water spoke / Embrace me it said / Reached down plunged under / A voice said she is your soulbride / Broke free from the surface in a field full of flowers / You were there." *Ascension 7* is a raw live recording of the band at the *Cornerstone* festival in 1994. Dan Michaels of **The Choir** and Allan Aguirre (of **Scaterd Few**) add sax and vocals, respectively, on some tracks.

After Dig Hay Zoose disbanded, Phil (no last name) went on to form a band called The Day Birds, which gained a strong regional following in the Kansas City area.

Justin Dillon and the Brilliantines

See **Dime Store Prophets.**

Susan Jane Dilts

1995—*The River Runs Deep* (Broken); 1998—*Rebuilding the Wall.*

www.justindillon.com

Susan Jane Dilts is a singer/songwriter from Kitchener, Ontario, who lends her almost-operatic soprano voice to modern hymns that reflect her personal triumphs over adversity. She was raised in the Scottish Presbyterian Church, her mother died of cancer when she was ten, and she and her sister Gail were alternately raised by grandparents and by an unstable, alcoholic father. The siblings became unusually close and began singing worship songs together. Later the adult Susan was confronted again with tragedy as Gail also died of cancer, followed shortly by the deaths of the grandparents who had raised her, and then by a difficult divorce. Dilts returned again to music and began writing songs of deliverance and hope. With more than 200 such songs to her credit, she took to recording. A reviewer for *Rebuilding the Wall* noted that the album reflects "a style that has a narrower following than the contemporary Christian music mainstream, but for those listeners grown on classical music or the hymns of the Reformation, it is an absolute gem."

Dime Store Prophets

Sam Hernandez, bass; Masaki Lui, gtr.; Justin Dillon Stevens, voc., gtr.; Phil Meads, drums (– 1997) // Joel Metzler, drums (+ 1997). 1995—*Love Is against the Grain* (5 Min. Walk); 1997—*Fantastic Distraction* (SaraBellum).

What if Bono joined the Gin Blossoms and they decided to do Bruce Springsteen songs? Some such strained analogy is necessary to describe the incredible sound of Dime Store Prophet's debut album, one of the best rock and roll records of 1995. The group formed in the San Francisco Bay area, where Justin Dillon Stevens and Masaki Lui had previously played in bands called Nine Red Roses and Radiation Ranch. Dime Store Prophets played what *The Lighthouse* called "rock music pulled from the ground, exposing its roots of folk and blues." Stevens wails and whispers passionately against a tight instrumental backdrop that is alternately jangly or gritty, as the mood requires. Lyrically the songs unfold stories of broken hearts and searching souls (hence the Springsteen element). "Baby's Got a Brand New Dress" and "Hobo's Jungle" treat themes like jealous love and homelessness with a poignancy Phil Collins could never muster. Musically the very best songs on an album filled with wonders are the anthemic "Feels Like Rain," the pensive "Hitler's Girlfriend," and the melodic "Love Song 58." *Fantastic Distractions* was not a bad album by any measure, but its title track—dealing with temporary-recovery programs ("twelve steps forward and thirteen steps back")—is only adequate: a pleasant, meaningful song, but one that fails to catch fire musically or to achieve any real intimacy lyrically. When a band introduces its second album with a lame first single, critics and fans immediately suspect the sophomore slump phenomenon is operative, and in this case, that suspicion prevented people from hearing more remarkable songs like "All About You," "Yeah, Sure, OK, Monet," and "Heavy As It Goes." There is also the interesting and ironic "King of the Tragic Ones," a song that sets uncharacteristic hooks against a funky '70s soundscape in an ode to one-hit wonders. But in general *Fantastic Distraction* sounds like a more subdued extension of the (better) first record.

Both of the Dime Store Prophets albums mix songs of pained desperation with evangelical promises of hope. The specifically Christian content is muted but clearly recognizable to any with ears to hear. In other words, the name "Jesus" does not pop up repeatedly in catchy choruses, but biblical imagery informs songs that consistently speak of redemption. "Ready for the Rain" is based on the parable of the wise and foolish builders in Matthew 7:24–27. "Heavy As It Goes" employs eucharistic imagery ("Bread crumbs, cheap wine / A feast to you / From my soiled hands").

The Dime Store Prophets disbanded soon after the release of *Fantastic Distraction*. Masaki turned to producing, helming projects for such artists as **The Electrics, Five Iron Frenzy,**

Seven Day Jesus, The Smiley Kids, and **The W's.** He returned to recording with **Rivulets and Violets.** Justin Dillon Stevens, as Justin Stevens, released an independent EP in 1998 called *Mello Dramatica;* then in 2000 he released a self-titled full-length indie project under the name Justin Dillon (no Stevens) and the Brilliantines. The latter album is worship oriented with an acid-folk sound similar to that of The Wallflowers.

The Dingees

Bean Hernandez, bass; Pegleg (Matt Roberts), voc.; Jeff Holms, gtr. (– 1999); Ethan Luck, drums (– 1999) // Justin Beradino, sax. (+ 1999); Dave Chevalier, sax., voc. (+ 1999); Steve Kravac, perc. (+ 1999); Ronnie King, kybrd. (+ 1999); Aaron Landers, gtr. (+ 1999); Frank Lenz, drums (+ 1999); Travis Larson, tromb. (+ 1999). 1998—*Armageddon Massive* (BEC); 1999—*Sundown to Midnight;* 2001—*The Crucial Conspiracy.*

www.jesusfreak.com/dingees

The Dingees have been variously described as "ska-core" and "white boy reggae," but they are basically a punk band at heart, forged in the grand tradition of The Clash and The Specials. They come by the ska elements honestly, however, since they originated as an almost spin-off of **The Supertones,** the granddaddy of all Christian ska (and of much secular ska, too, for that matter). Pegleg was a roadie for that band, and he originally formed The Dingees with two members of the group, Dave Chevalier and Tony Terusa. The idea was to play local concerts when **The Supertones** weren't touring, but as The Dingees caught on and recording contracts were offered, Chevalier and Terusa dropped out (unable to make the long-term commitment). Chevalier returned for the second album.

On their debut album The Dingees capture a sound similar to that of Sublime, who were at the height of their career at the time. The songs do not deal with explicitly Christian themes so much as with social issues, addressed from a Christian viewpoint. "It's no wonder they'll amount to nothing" Pegleg sings of troubled urban youth, "They've been told they're just a product of chance." The opening track, "Ghetto Box Smash," takes a poke at pop culture; "Rebel Youth" is an anti-aristocracy anthem. Other songs address racism, street violence, and drug abuse, all with an eye to the inner city. The album's best track, however, is an instrumental called "Betrayal." *Sundown to Midnight* drew a scathing review from *True Tunes* ("Inferior in every way to the debut") but got mixed reactions elsewhere. Basically, the band divided their styles by songs (1/3 punk, 1/3 ska, 1/3 reggae) rather than fusing the influences together into an eclectic whole. *Phantom Tollbooth* suggested that they had sold out punk for pop but still noted, "every song is super hooky and sing-along ready . . . and that bass sure thumps." The song "Dark Hollywood" is unlike anything else the group has attempted, a slow, beguiling number that is actually reminiscent of Sade. Depictions of urban violence ("Votes and Violence") and the potential of youth ("Leave the Kids Alone") are lyrical themes. *The Crucial Conspiracy* basically continues the fusion/confusion approach of stylistic exploration evident on *Sundown to Midnight.* The only traces of ska remaining are sultry horns here and there and reggae backbeats on a number of tracks. "Summertime" is an upbeat, old-school new-wave rocker. "Dear Sister, Dear Brother" is sing-along reggae with synthesizers and a wah-wah guitar solo. "Christina Fight Back" is an anthem against eating disorders and spiritual malaise. "We Rot the Voodoo" is a dark and mystical number dealing with spiritual warfare.

Dino

Selected: 1973—*Alleluia!* (Light); 1998—*Collector's Series* (Benson).

Classically trained pianist Dino Kartsonakis (b. 1942) is perhaps the antithesis of rock and roll, and his "Muzak" piano instrumentals have not been in fashion with adult contemporary pop fans for several decades either. The style—usually dismissed as "elevator music" or "doctor's office music"—has not been contemporary in chart terms since Henry Mancini played "Moon River" (# 11 in 1961) three years before the Beatles. Still, Dino has made dozens of instrumental albums in the last thirty years, and they sell to fans of contemporary Christian music who apparently regard them as guilty pleasures or as nice accompaniment for romantic dinners and other special occasions. Dino was born and raised in New York City and gained early recognition as a child prodigy. He studied formally at The King's College, the Julliard School of Music, and conservatories in Germany and France (with Arthur Rubinstein). For seven years he served as solo pianist for Pentecostal healing evangelist Kathryn Kuhlman. His album *Alleluia!* helped to popularize what was to become the most recognizable worship song of the charismatic renewal movement—a meditative mantra that simply repeated the word "Alleluia" over and over to a soft melody. In time Dino would become a Christian Liberace, performing stellar live shows on his nine-foot rhinestone piano. He has sometimes performed and recorded with his wife, singer Debby Kartsonakis; in the late '70s they hosted the *Dino and Debby Show* for religious TV. He has more than forty albums to his credit, some featuring piano renditions of show tunes and popular love songs in addition to the staple of hymns and spiritual songs. As of 2002, Dino was regularly performing Las Vegas style shows (with dancers and laser light effects) at a theater in Branson, Missouri.

Dove Awards: 1980 Instrumentalist; 1981 Instrumentalist; 1982 Instrumentalist; 1983 Instrumentalist; 1986 Instrumentalist; 1993 Instrumental Album (*Somewhere in Time*); 1996 Instrumental Album (*Classical Peace*).

Dion

Selected: 1980—*Inside Job* (DaySpring); 1981—*Only Jesus*; 1983—*I Put Away My Idols*; 1984—*Seasons*; 1985—*Kingdom in the Streets* (Myrrh); 1986—*Velvet and Steel* (DaySpring); 1989—*Yo Frankie!* (Arista); 1992—*Dream on Fire* (Vision); 1997—*Best of the Gospel Years* (Ace UK); 2000—*Déjà Nu* (Collectables).

www.diondimucci.com

Born Dion DiMuccci in 1939, the Bronx singer known simply as Dion was one of the more successful of the pre-Beatles rock and roll singers, a camp that would also include such stars as Buddy Holly and Roy Orbison. Dion fronted a group of neighborhood friends he referred to as "the Belmonts" (after Belmont Avenue, which ran through their Bronx territory). Between 1958 and 1960 they scored seven Top 40 hits, and then from 1960 to 1963 Dion had a dozen more Top 40 smashes as a solo artist. Some of his most memorable songs include "A Teenager in Love" (# 5 in 1959); "Runaround Sue" (# 1 for 2 weeks in 1961); "The Wanderer" (# 2 in 1961); and "Ruby Baby" (# 2 in 1963). Unfortunately Dion had acquired a heroin addiction as a teenager and so never fully enjoyed his success. Indeed, in 1959, when his biggest hit to date was near the top of the charts ("Where or When," # 3), he was in a detoxification hospital unaware of the accomplishment. It was not until 1968, after musical styles had changed and he was no longer selling records, that his wife Susan (the real-life "runaround Sue," whom he had married two years after warning the world to stay away from her) and her father finally managed to get him free of the drug habit. At the end of that year he had a comeback hit with the song "Abraham, Martin, and John" (# 4), a tribute to murdered leaders (Lincoln, King, and Kennedy) inspired by the assassination of Bobby Kennedy. He continued to record albums without great commercial success, releasing an antidrug single "Your Own Backyard" in 1970. In 1989 Dion was inducted into the Rock and Roll Hall of Fame. Billy Joel and Lou Reed both credit him as a major influence on their work.

Dion's conversion to Christianity—if it can be called that—is related in his autobiography, *The Wanderer: Dion's Story* (Beach Tree Books, 1989). He was brought up in a Catholic home, and as he relates in his book, he had a series of critical conversion experiences in which he turned his life over to God. Personal faith and commitment to God's care played a major role in his ultimate liberation from bondage to drugs. Still, it was not until a decade later that Dion says he had a personal encounter with Jesus. One morning while jogging, he beheld a vision of white light, and as he recounts, "I saw a figure, a man in front of me . . . his arms outstretched. And I heard him speak words of truth, not in my ear, but in my heart . . . 'I laid down my life for you. I'm here for you now'." In 1980 Dion began recording Christian music, and he turned out several albums of light rock songs expressive of personal faith. *Inside Job* made that faith a matter of public record with nine of his own compositions, including testimony songs like "I Believe (Sweet Lord Jesus)" and "Center of My Life." *Only Jesus* features more covers, including a stirring arrangement of the traditional gospel song "It's Gonna Rain" and "The Best," a Maranatha! praise song written by John Fowler (and featured also on **Bob Bennett**'s debut album). Dion would record a handful of other songs by Fowler and many more by Bob Smith over the span of his gospel career. *I Put Away My Idols* is a strong collection of songs that would be nominated for a Grammy award in the contemporary gospel category. "Here Is My Servant" has a '50s rock and roll sound to it. The title track lists those things that became idols for the artist while pursuing worldly success. The record closes with a beautiful Fowler song called "My Prayer for You." *Kingdom in the Streets* features another Dion testimony song in "Come to the Cross" ("The big city lights, they went straight to my head / I heard the music, never knew where it led . . ."). The album also includes a number of finger-snapping R&B songs like "Still in the Spirit," "Crazy Too," and the Ghostbusters-like "You Only Go 'Round Once." Most critics, however, think the artist's best Christian work is reflected in his sixth album, *Velvet and Steel,* which was recorded in Nashville. Here Dion contrasts his old passions with his current ones in the song "I Love Jesus Now." He duets with **Kelly Willard** on her "There in Your Heart." On "Simple Ironies" he describes the paradoxes of faith ("run to win, lose to gain"). Several songs feature a Belmont-like chorus of background singers composed of **Chris Rodriguez, Wayne Kirkpatrick, and Steven Curtis Chapman.**

The album *Yo Frankie* represents a return to mainstream pop to celebrate Dion's induction into the Rock and Roll Hall of Fame and to accompany the publication of his autobiography. Produced by Dave Edmunds, the record features guest appearances by a who's who of rock and roll, including Bryan Adams, Lou Reed, and Paul Simon. The single "And the Night Stood Still" features backing vocals by Edmunds and Patty Smyth. *Dream on Fire* continues in the same vein, with renditions of Bruce Springsteen's "If I Should Fall Behind," **Bob Dylan**'s "One Too Many Mornings," and Dave Edmunds' "I Knew the Bride (When She Used to Rock and Roll)." Eventually, *Déjà Nu* would present mostly original songs, with nostalgic sentiments. In interviews Dion made it clear that he had not abandoned his faith but had come to question his participation in a Christian music subculture that treats faith issues as distinct from concerns about life in general. "There's an intolerance to any kind of individual expression," Dion told *CCM* magazine in 1990. At first, he continued, he had been enthralled to write songs about God. Then, "I realized that (God) wants me to talk about myself too—my journey, my dreams, my growing, my humanity."

For trivia buffs: In February of 1959 Dion was part of a package tour of artists including Buddy Holly, the Big Bopper, and Ritchie Valens, all of whom were killed when their chartered plane crashed. Dion had passed on the chance to be on board the plane that particular night.

Christian radio hits: "I Believe (Sweet Lord Jesus)" (# 7 in 1981); "Center of My Life" (# 10 in 1981); "The Best" (# 2 in 1982); "Day of the Lord" (# 8 in 1983); "I Put Away My Idols" (# 12 in 1983); "Simple Ironies" (# 1 for 2 weeks in 1986).

Dirt

1999—*Plague* (Rescue); 2001—*A War to Restore* (Suntax).

Dirt is a hip-hop emcee who came to the attention of the contemporary Christian music subculture when he collaborated with producer Jesse Sprinkle (of **Poor Old Lu**) on a sophomore album. A previous record, *Plague,* had been recorded in 1997 and shelved for two years before it was released to no response. In frustration over the lack of opportunity street-wise artists have in Christian music, Dirt wrote a stirring piece called "Blunted Edge" that would become the standout track on *A War to Restore.* The song starkly articulates the artist's depression and rage, then segues creatively into words from a song by Courtney Love of Hole: "Go ahead and take everything / Take everything / I want you to" ("Violet"). *War to Restore* features a variety of styles, including jazz-lounge singing ("Essence"), funk ("Divine Lines"), and rap-rock ("Dirty Rotten").

Disciple

Tim Barrett, drums; Brad Noah, gtr., Kevin Young, voc. 1995—*What Was I Thinking* (independent); 1997—*My Daddy Can Whip Your Daddy* [EP] (Warner Resound); 1999—*This May Sting a Little* (Rugged); 2001—*By God.*

There have probably been many Christian groups called Disciple or Disciples (cf. **Andraé Crouch**) over the years, but the one that attracted the most attention in the late '90s was a grunge/metal trio from just outside of Nashville (cf. also **xDISCIPLEx,** a Pennsylvania metal band with whom the Nashville Disciple is sometimes confused). Disciple started out with a sound that was often compared to Soundgarden or Alice in Chains (on their indie debut), moved into Rage Against the Machine territory upon signing with Warner Resound, and then developed a Pantera-like metal sound.

Lyrically the group is message-oriented, and they don't mince words trying to be artsy or poetic. The song "Easter Bunny" (from *My Daddy Can Whip Your Daddy*) attacks social customs that surround Christian festivals, accusing the titular culprit of being a coconspirator with Santa Claus in a plot to rob Christ of glory. The title song to that EP is a tongue-in-cheek (one hopes!) attempt at interreligious dialogue, complete with lyrics like "God is good / God is good / He's so freaking awesome!" Such arguments—unlikely to convince intellectuals—carry over into the opening track on *This May Sting a Bit* as well: "I just know Jesus is the way . . . I just know Jesus is my God" ("I Just Know"). So apologetics are not their strong suit, but at least one knows where they stand. Such lack of encryption is also evident in "1–2 Conductor": "I don't give a rat's rear end what they say, as long as my God's happy." The song "Big Bad Wolf" is directed at Satan and comes complete with wolf growling noises. "Worship Conspiracy" attempts to shame Christians for the lack of devotion they display compared to those who "pray to Buddha everyday" or to "Moslems who fast for forty days." The song "Ten Minute Oil Change" likens God's work of salvation and redemption in a human life to a mechanic cleaning out a car's engine in a few moments of time. While such thoughts appall the theologically aware, Disciple's albums recall some of the naivete of early Jesus music and appeal to those who can identify with the basic piety behind their sentiments. The band's evangelistic zeal is also charming in a way that transcends the bumper sticker mentality and penchant for critiquing things that lie beyond their ken. The band includes a bonus three-song CD with *Sting* for the purchaser to give to "an unsaved friend." The latter album also concludes with a recorded "Altar Call" in which hearers are invited to pray a famous "Sinner's Prayer" in order to receive salvation and "be healed of the disease of sin."

Kevin Young previewed *By God* for *HM* by situating it between the other records and offered his own summation of the band's history: "On *What Was I Thinking,* we were really, I guess, grungy, you know—still kinda grooving, gettin' a little rappy . . . and by the time we got to *Sting* we were just real heavy, screaming a lot, no slow songs whatsoever." In contrast *By God* does contain a few slow songs, primarily ones that are worship oriented, but it also leaves the grunge scene behind for a resurrection of metal. "Metal rocks," Young says, "that's the bottom line. . . . And it's much better live. We just love to go nuts. I think the whole key to our success is, man, you come and watch us, you're gonna have a good time." The album includes "Not Rock Stars," which *HM* would describe as sounding "like *This Means War* era **Petra,** with way crunchier guitars." Other songs range from worshipful ("You Are Here," "A Thousand Times") to rather angry ("I Hate Your Guts"). "You Rock My Socks Off" is an ode to '80s metal.

Disciples of Christ (a.k.a. **D.O.C.**)

Absalom (Kelvin Harvey), voc.; Prophet (Michael Brown), voc.; Ben Reges (Alton Hood Jr.), voc.; The Warrior (Matt Stevens), drums 1991—*So, How Ya' Livin'?* (StarSong); 1993—*Pullin' No Punches;* 1994—*Righteous Funk.*

A trio of Pentecostals from Canton, Ohio, make up the rapping and singing group known to their fans as simply D.O.C. The origins of the group lie in the 1987 conversions of Harvey and Hood who at the time were students at Oberlin College involved with drugs and fascinated with the occult. As Harvey puts it, after a "supernatural act of the Holy Spirit" saved them and turned their lives around, they dedicated their talents at "beatboxing and rapping" to the Lord. About a year later they hooked up with Brown, a professional musician who was a member of their church, and the Disciples of Christ were born. Their first album gained notice for a track called "Deeper" (not the **Delirious?** song). The group does not want to be known as "a rap group" but as "a vocal hip-hop R&B band," and indeed their music, while making generous use of rap, transcends stereotypical limitations of that genre. *The Lighthouse* compared the styles displayed on their second album to **DC Talk** and Joey Lawrence. Though hip-hop dominates both of the first two albums, other styles are also in evidence: *So How Ya' Livin'?* includes a couple of urban ballads ("Thank You Lord," "Desire"); *Pullin' No Punches* includes a straightforward R&B ballad ("Old Tyme Way") and has guest artist **Bride** screaming vocals on the rap/metal song, "God Gave Rock N' Roll 2 You." The group really came into its own with *Righteous Funk,* which as its title suggests weds modern rap and hip-hop to the sounds of groups like Earth, Wind, and Fire, Heatwave, or Midnight Star. The record was coproduced by Bootsy Collins, former member of Parliament/Funkadelic and then Bootsy's Rubber Band. Collins, who also performed on the record, is said by Alton Hood to attend "a full-gospel, Holy Spirit anointed church." The album brings Michael Brown to the fore as a dynamic tenor and features more melodic harmonizing than previous projects, and, of course, more funk. Brown duets with Veronica Petrucci (of **Angelo and Veronica**) on the soulful ballad "Me 4 U." Around the time of this album's release, the group relocated to Tulsa, Oklahoma, where they wanted to study at the fundamentalist Rhema Bible Training Center founded by Kenneth Hagin. The trio has been clear that their music is primarily a ministry, that it is just a tool to assist them in evangelizing and exhorting young people in accord with the understandings of Pentecostal tradition.

Christian radio hits: "Innocent Warrior" (# 11 in 1993).

Disco Saints

Personnel list unavailable. 1995—*Dance House Praise* (Straightway); 1996—*Cosmic Cowboy.*

Disco Saints is an anonymous conglomeration of singers and dancers. Various persons called Julius, Paddy, Vicki, and others contribute to the projects, which have producer David Huff (of **David and the Giants**) creating the sort of hardcore Christian dance music for which **Scott Blackwell** is famous. Musical styles vary slightly from house to techno, but all of the material comes under the basic disco umbrella. The first album presents only one original tune ("The Power") alongside disco remakes of **Andraé Crouch**'s "Soon and Very Soon," **The Newsboys**' "Shine," and **U2**'s "40." The rest of the album is made up of familiar praise choruses ("They That Wait," "We Exalt Thee"). The second album is notable for its added use of guitar and for its innovative choice of covers: the title track is the all-but-forgotten song that was a *huge* Christian hit (# 1 for 35 weeks) for **Barry McGuire** in 1978–1979. Similarly, the group reaches back to pick up "The Devil Is a Liar," a hit for the jazz fusion group **Seawind** in the late '70s. They also cover **Bob Dylan**'s "Saved" and **The Road Home**'s "Psalm 5." Most out there, perhaps, is their version of "Time to Change," which was originally sung on the TV comedy *The Brady Bunch* in honor of Peter Brady's changing voice.

Christian radio hits: "40" (# 5 in 1995); "They That Wait" (# 23 in 1995).

Dissident Prophet

Andy Jennings, gtr.; John Large, drums; Tom Livemore, gtr., voc.; Simon Smith, bass. 1997—*We're Not Grasshoppers* (MGL Granite).

The British power-pop band Dissident Prophet released one album with a sound that could be likened to general market acts R.E.M. or Radiohead or to the alternative Christian band **The Choir.** The group put forth songs that are openly evangelistic, while clothed in language sensitive to the concerns of modern culture. In "Let It Go," Livemore sings, "You've been holding onto your life / Like it's something that you own . . . There's got to be much more / Than being stranded where you are." Or again in "Unconditional Love" (*not* a **Donna Summer** cover), he sings to Christ, "I asked how much you loved me / You cried out in pain / And then you died." The album did not sell, in part because the use of a swear word in "Watching All Alone" kept it out of the Christian marketplace, while overall content prevented much chance of acceptance within the general market. The group has disbanded.

Divine Regale

Chris Anderson, drums; Frank Couture, bass; Daniel Elliott, gtr.; Dwight Hill, voc.; Jason Keezer, kybrd.; Gary Leighton, gtr. 1994—*Horizons* [EP] (independent); 1997—*Ocean Mind* (Metal Blade).

Divine Regale is a progressive metal band from southeast New Hampshire. The group draws on such influences as Dream Theater and Queensryche to create hard music with intelligent, spiritually-focused lyrics. They were signed to Metal Blade after a homemade EP sold well in Germany, and the label marketed the band to *HM* as a Christian band without the members' knowledge or permission. A reviewer for that magazine subsequently chose the group's *Ocean Mind* as the "Christian album of the year." An interview with the band revealed that they had little awareness of the Christian music scene and did not really consider themselves to be a Christian band. Chris Anderson explained that three of the six members (himself, Dwight Hill, and Gary Leighton) were believers involved with churches, while Daniel Elliott professed no religious beliefs and Frank Couture was "closer to Buddhism." Early on, Leighton continued, he and Anderson were the only songwriters, which may account for the Christian orientation of their material's spirituality, but the group did not intend to present those songs as any kind of consensus statements. He also indicated that, in the future, such references would not be as blatant: "It can get stale after a while . . . and you don't necessarily have to talk about religion to hear faith through lyrics." The album *Ocean Mind* includes the song "Horizon," which Hill says is about "striving for your goals and yet reflecting on the past." A musical highlight is "No Part of This," which sustains lyrics about struggles with faith ("It's hard to go on believing") with power chords, climbing scales, and shouted vocals. "Cry to Heaven" expresses what some critics have taken to be doubt but could be theological maturity: "I used to believe that things happened for a reason / Now I'm not so sure anymore."

Jessy Dixon

Selected: 1977—*It's All Right Now* (Light); 1979—*You Bring the Son Out*; 1982—*Satisfied/Live*; 1983—*Sanctuary* (Power Discs); 1985—*Silent Partner*; 1987—*The Winning Side*; 1988—*Sold Out*; 1989—*I Know What Prayer Can Do* (Word); 1995—*My Brand New Home* (Chapel).

www.jessydixon.com

Jessy Dixon is well known as the leader of the Jessy Dixon Singers, the traditional gospel group that toured for eight years with Paul Simon and performed on several of his albums. Dixon was born and raised in San Antonio, and he attended St. Mary's College. A child prodigy, he was tapped at age twelve to come to Chicago as organist for the prestigious True Light Baptist Church. There he was noticed by gospel mainstay James Cleveland and ended up playing double keyboards with **Billy Preston** (Dixon on organ; Preston on piano) on albums under Cleveland's supervision. He formed a vocal group of his own, the Jessy Dixon Singers, which placed his voice alongside that of three women (Ethel Holloway, Elsa Harris, and Aldrea Lennox, later replaced by Charlotte Davis). In 1971 Dixon had something of a conversion experience and dedicated his life and music wholly to Christ. That same year the vocal group he had formed became the first gospel act ever invited to sing at the Newport Jazz Festival, where they were discovered by Paul Simon. The Jessy Dixon Singers did not simply open for Simon's concerts but were an integral part of the show, singing with him on such gospel-inflected numbers as "Mother and

Child Reunion," "Gone at Last," and "Loves Me Like a Rock" (for which Simon had employed the Dixie Hummingbirds on the original recording). Dixon himself sang Art Garfunkel's parts on certain classic Simon and Garfunkel tunes like "Bridge over Troubled Water." But the Jesse Dixon Singers were also given their own slot somewhere in the middle of the concert to perform gospel songs like "What Do You Call Him?" "Operator," and "You Bring the Son Out." Concerts would often conclude with Dixon and Simon singing "Amazing Grace."

The relationship between the black Christian gospel singer and the white Jewish folk star continued for years as an emblem of mutual respect and integrity. Dixon continues to praise Simon for being able to overcome prejudices against Christians and the gospel art form that are prevalent in the performing industry. Simon gave him complete control over selection of material for his portion of the show and respected Dixon's convictions with regard to the rest of the performance (e.g., he allowed Dixon and his group *not* to participate on the big hit, "50 Ways to Leave Your Lover," which they found offensive). Dixon says that Simon and his crew were even "careful not to cuss around us" and that Simon would sometimes ask him for prayer: "Paul believed in prayer and he believed that I was close to God, though he wasn't sure that he was close to God himself." The pinnacle of their collaboration probably came with the release of the concert album, *Live Rhymin'*, by Paul Simon and the Jessy Dixon Singers. The record, which included the group's rousing version of **Andraé Crouch**'s "Jesus Is the Answer," went gold, bringing the sounds of contemporary gospel to a previously untapped audience. Dixon was also featured in Simon's semi-autobiographical motion picture *One Trick Pony* (1980).

Dixon's own style of gospel represents a blend of the traditional gospel sounds he acquired from Cleveland with the jazz and blues he picked up while working as a young adult with persons like Willie Dixon, B. B. King, and Muddy Waters. He has numerous recordings to his credit, having made something like four albums a year for the gospel label Savoy in the years between 1967 and 1971. The better-known works, however, are the solo albums he made after beginning his work with Simon. The first of these was produced by **Andraé Crouch** and Bill Maxwell and presents the artist working with a variety of different vocal groups on different tracks, including a couple of different church choirs and various madrigals composed of members of Crouch's Disciples and other friends. *It's All Right Now* features "Born Again" and "Father Me" (written by Harlan Rogers) and introduces the song "I'm Satisfied" (different from the Crouch song of the same name), which would become a concert favorite. Crouch's Disciples all return to support Dixon on *You Bring the Son Out*, along with the horn section of Earth, Wind, and Fire. The album features a moving original song, "He Never Let Me Down Before." The high point of Dixon's solo albums, however, is probably the *Satisfied/Live* album from 1982. Here Dixon is backed by a full instrumental combo and eight vocalists, including the traditional Jessy Dixon singers and **Danniebelle Hall.** The concert was performed at Calvary Chapel in Costa Mesa, California, a decade after that church had served as ground zero for the Jesus movement. The exciting mix of new and aging Jesus freaks adds to the ambience and fuels Dixon and company to great heights on up-tempo numbers like the title track, "Jesus Is Alive and Well," and the showstopper, "Operator." *Sanctuary,* by contrast, is completely laid back, and while Dixon himself was not proud of it, it may appeal more to those who lean toward inspirational adult contemporary sounds. In 1985 Dixon began a close partnership with **DeGarmo and Key** and toured with them. The latter's influence is especially evident on the upbeat *Silent Partner* album. **DeGarmo and Key** wrote the title track (which deals with the invisible protection God provides through angels) and the hit "Silent Prayer." **Dana Key** produced the album and sings a duet with Dixon on yet another **DeGarmo and Key** composition, "Destined to Win." A number of other songwriters were employed for the project also, which in contrast to the early albums contains none of Dixon's own songs.

For trivia buffs: In 1979 a Jessy Dixon song, "That's What He's Looking For," was featured prominently in an episode of the *Laverne and Shirley* TV program.

Christian radio hits: "Silent Prayer" (# 4 in 1986).

DJ Maj

2000—*Waxmuseum: The Mix Tape* (Gotee); 2001—*Full Plates/Mixtape.002.*

The usual definition of recording artist must be stretched considerably to accommodate DJ Maj. The latter persona did not actually *record* any of the songs on the albums he has released. In a sense, the albums are simply compilations of songs by a variety of hip-hop artists, including **Out of Eden, Grits, The Katinas, Knowdaverbs,** and **Sup the Chemist.** What did DJ Maj do to justify releasing the songs under his own name? He selected them and, in some cases, remixed them to form sonic suites that work as concept pieces. The result in each case, as *CCM* puts it, is "a seamless flow of stylistically diverse tracks by different hip-hop artists that now sounds like an hour-long song."

D.O.C.

See **Disciples of Christ.**

Dodavahu

Jerry Baranski, gtr., voc.; Darrel Joseph Jesonis, bass, voc.; Matthew Keneske, gtr., voc.; Larry Larraga, drums. 1996—*steamroller.files* (Dwarf).

The heavy alternative band Dodavahu began to form in 1991 when Darrel Jesonis and Matthew Keneske forged an alliance with a shared vision of music and ministry. The group played together for some years and toured (with different drummers) with such acts as **LSU, Mortal,** and **Bride.** Their first full-length album would reveal them to have a "groove" not evident on previous contributions to metal compilation albums. Two singles from the album, "Mountain" and "Girls Girls Girls," reached the Top 10 on the alternative Christian Pure Rock Report, an accounting of airplay on certain Christian radio stations that do not follow the standard formats or industry standards of the Gospel Music Association. The song "Kick Agin' It" adds variety with gritty blues riffs and horns. Likewise, "Nebuchadnezzar" features infectious rap set against a churning chorus. The band's name is taken from a biblical character in 2 Chronicles and translates roughly as "the love of God."

Dog Named David

Andy Cloninger; John Wallace. 1999—*World Traveler* (Stell Sandal); 2000—*Acoustic Canine* (Awakening).

Dog Named David is an acoustic folk duo who create songs of faith and longing in the tradition of **Bruce Cockburn,** Mark Cohn, **Rich Mullins,** or **David Wilcox.** The main ingredients are simply acoustic guitars and voices, though *World Traveler* allows some percussion and strings to wander into the mix. Still, as *Phantom Tollbooth* observes, the boys manage to create a bigger sound than one might expect—more like **Caedmon's Call** than just two guys plucking guitars in some coffeehouse. The *Acoustic Canine* album was recorded live and proves they are able to create the same effect on the road as in the studio. Lyrics, of course, are especially significant in music this subdued, and in the grand folk tradition the lyrics of Dog Named David vary from humorous to profound. In "Pieces" they liken a relationship gone sour to the abuse of a Mr. Potato Head: "she sliced and diced me, she hashbrowned my head." One of their standout songs, "How Can I Believe?" deals with the big question: "How can I believe when all I see is hopelessness and lies?"

Dogs of Peace

Gordon Kennedy, voc., gtr.; Jimmie Lee Sloas, voc., bass, kybrd. 1996—*Speak* (Sparrow).

Gordon Kennedy and Jimmie Lee Sloas worked together for years in the Nashville area before finally adopting the moniker Dogs of Peace and recording an album of their own. Kennedy was once a member of the melodic metal band **White Heart** and subsequently earned renown as a session guitarist and a songwriter. He has penned tunes for numerous artists, including Martina McBride, Garth Brooks, Dakota Moon, Peter Frampton, **Kim Hill,** Allison Krauss, Patty Loveless, Kathy Mattea, **PFR, Collin Raye, Sierra,** Wynonna, and Trisha Yearwood. He won the Christian Hit Radio Song of the Year award in 1994 for "That Kind of Love," which was performed by **PFR.** Then in 1996 he took home the Song of the Year Grammy award for "Change the World," a song he cowrote with **Wayne Kirkpatrick** and **Tommy Sims** for **Eric Clapton.** Sloas was briefly one of **The Imperials** and then became a sought-after producer, responsible for all of the **PFR** albums and for projects by **Lisa Bevill, Geoff Moore and The Distance,** and **Whitecross.** As a songwriter he has cowritten Christian radio hits for **PFR** ("Great Lengths," "Forever"), **Geoff Moore and The Distance** ("New Americans," "The Vow," "More Than Gold") and **Whitecross** ("I Keep Prayin' ").

The Dogs of Peace album, *Speak,* is song-driven, with Kennedy and Sloas alternating vocals on Beatlesque pop songs performed in styles that seem to emulate various classic rock bands: Pink Floyd ("Do You Know"), Rush ("In the Event"), Mr. Mister ("Necessary Pain"), and The Eagles ("The Truth"). *CCM* calls "Thrown Away" a "better Paul McCartney tune than McCartney has released in years." The standout track, however, is the James Gang/Joe Walsh clone song, "I Wanna Know." Lyrically the album deals specifically with the main themes of Christian doctrine and discipleship: revelation, redemption, prayer, and submission. "Thrown Away," for example, describes the reality of forgiveness from the perspective of God: "Thrown away the records kept / They're swept from memory / When I gave my only Son / To set you free."

In 1998 Kennedy joined **Wayne Kirkpatrick** and **Tommy Sims** to write virtually all of the material for Garth Brooks' experimental album *The Life and Times of Chris Gaines* (Capitol, 2000). The idea of that album was to remake Brooks as the pop-rock singer he would portray in a film called *The Lamb* (Paramount), presenting what was supposedly a greatest hits retrospective of the fictional performer's career. The movie and the album were commercial failures. Kennedy has also contributed songs to a compilation album featuring prominent writers performing their own material (*Coming from Somewhere Else,* Rocketown, 2000). He offers his own rendition of "You Move Me," which had been recorded by **Susan Ashton,** Garth Brooks, and **Pierce Pettis** (with whom he cowrote it). He also joins cowriters **Wayne Kirkpatrick, Phil Madeira,** and **Billy Sprague** in performing the anthemic title track.

For trivia buffs: Gordon Kennedy is the son of Jerry Glenn Kennedy, a well-known Nashville guitarist who recorded an album with Chet Atkins at the age of ten and went on to become one of the area's most sought-after session musicians. That's Gordon's dad playing on Roy Orbison's "Oh, Pretty Woman," Tammy Wynette's "Stand by Your Man," and **Elvis Presley**'s "Good Luck Charm."

Dogwood (Nashville)

Ron Elder, gtr.; Steve Chapman, voc., gtr.; Annie Chapman, voc. (–1977). 1975—*After the Flood, Before the Fire* (Lamb and Lion); 1976—*Love Note;* 1977—*Out in the Open;* 1979—*Ordinary Man;* 1981—*Journey.*

There have been two prominent Christian recording artists named Dogwood in contemporary Christian music. The first was a late Jesus music country folk trio from Nashville; the second, a late '90s hardcore punk band from San Diego—confusion could easily result in customer dissatisfaction. The Nashville Dogwood consisted primarily of the duo Ron Elder and Steve Chapman (not **Steven *Curtis* Chapman**) playing and singing on songs that evince what *Jesus Music* calls "a warm, happy feel." Friends from childhood, Elder and Chapman grew up with similar backgrounds as the sons of ministers in West Virginia. The group's first album was produced by **Chris Christian** and represented his first time in the producer's chair. Christian has said that since he had never heard any contemporary Christian music at the time, he didn't know what the group was supposed to sound like and just went for a sound similar to what was popular on secular radio stations. This unconventional (at the time) approach provided the group with an album that sounded different from any other kind of Christian record. Acoustic guitars, banjos, and fiddles feature prominently in the sound. Annie Chapman (Steve's wife) sings background vocals on the first record, then assumes a more prominent role on *Love Note* to give that album more of a Peter, Paul, and Mary sound. *Free Love* magazine described *Love Note* as "an album that rises above the commonplace country gospel/Jesus music genre." On the last two records Dogwood became a male duo and adopted a more MOR sound. *Ordinary Man* includes a cover of **Randy Matthews**' "Miracle Man" in addition to several songs written by the Chapmans.

Pioneer Christian music critic Mark Hollingsworth described Dogwood's songs in *Harmony* magazine as "personal and descriptive about how they feel about Jesus and the life He brings." The standout track on the debut album, "Watergrave," is about baptism, a topic generally ignored in Christian music. Both **The Boones** and **The Imperials** would include Dogwood songs on their albums. Dogwood played regularly at Belmont Church's Koinonia Coffee House in Nashville. **Steve and Annie Chapman** went on to a fairly successful solo career, including work with James Dobson's Focus on the Family organization.

Christian radio hits: "If There Were Only Time for Our Love" (# 5 in 1980).

Dogwood (San Diego)

Russell Castillo, drums; Jason Harper, bass; Josh Kemble, voc.; Sean O'Donnell, gtr. 1996—*Good Ol' Daze* (Rescue); 1997—*Through Thick and Thin;* 1998—*Dogwood;* 1999—*More Than Conquerors* (Tooth and Nail); 2000—*Building a Better Me;* 2001—*Matt Aragon.*

www.christcore.com

Not to be confused with a former Nashville group of the same name, the San Diego-based Dogwood burst on the Christian punk scene in 1996 with an album of eighteen in-your-face songs featuring lyrics like, "Get off your rear end and get out the door / Make use of your time before we are no more" ("Billy Mahoney's Baby"). An independent production for the San Diego market, the album sold better regionally than the simultaneous release by hometowners Blink 182. *Through Thick and Thin* would serve up more issue-oriented songs dealing with such topics as abuse and abortion. Even aside from a few explicitly Christian numbers, the songs spoke of matters atypical for the punk genre ("Preschool Days" is about being raised in a single-parent home; "Tribute" deals with the loss of a loved one). Dogwood continued to solidify their sound, mixing elements of hardcore and rock into the basic surf-punk milieu, and eventually they garnered a contract with the prime label for Christian punk, Tooth and Nail.

The big label debut, *More Than Conquerors,* reveals an act that *Phantom Tollbooth* described as "more muscular in the vocals and guitars than the likes of (labelmates) **MxPx** and **Slick Shoes.**" In other words, they sound more like the Ramones than Green Day, while retaining some of the latter's pop sensibilities. As the title implies, *More Than Conquerors* is remarkably positive in outlook for a punk record. "Rest Assured" offers the words of a father to his son: "I'm already sorry for the hurt that is to come / I'm already thankful for the man that you'll become / So look up and laugh / We'll cross that finish line together." Other songs expressive of this hope-filled theme include the title track, "Never Die," "We Cry Victory," and "The Pain Is Gone" (which has an arena-breadth air to it similar to contemporary work by The Offspring). These are balanced with heavier songs ("Suffer," Confusion Zero") that keep things grounded in grim reality. *Building a Better Me* offers another package of tight and melodic songs that range from skate-punk praise ("Mycro") to serious social commentary: "The Good Times" is a sarcastically titled account of Josh Kemble's continuing resentment over growing up in a broken home ("Preschool," part two); "The Battle of Them vs. Them" goes global with its protest of international violence, exposing the effect of war on the innocent ("a small child sits and waits for his dad, hands clutching a brown telegram"). In late 2000 the group toured with **P.O.D.,** and the next year they released *Matt Aragon,* named for a friend of the group. This time the opening song was dedicated to 2001 high school graduates,

named for the year they were likely born ("1983"). "Nothing Is Everything" is the album's strongest rocker, but "Do or Die" and "Ballad of Hope" belong to the peculiar genre of punk worship songs.

Troy Donockley

See **Iona.**

Dan Donovan

1993—*Trashbone Thang* (Sticky); 1995—*Dust Shaker* (Mister M); 1999—*The Leaven Dell;* 2000—*The Hex the Ghears* (Magdan).

British singer/songwriter Dan Donovan (b. 1960) sometimes fronts the band **Tribe of Dan** and occasionally joins with Canadian artist Mr. Bennett to record under the name Swamp Cranks. Donovan also makes solo records that draw favorable comparisons stylistically to the music of Beatnik folk singer Tom Waits. His debut album, *Trashbone Thang,* was described by *Kerrang* magazine as sounding like it was recorded "under the influence of mulled wine and candlelight." *Dust Shaker* was described by *Mojo* as "funky, sinister, and impenetrable." *The Leaven Dell* is a completely acoustic affair, filled with slow, haunting songs that *Phantom Tollbooth* described as "sad stories full of mystery and poetry sung in a raspy, wheezy voice." For *The Hex the Ghears,* Donovan plugged in and recorded an album of electric songs that bear similarities to The Pixies.

The son of a Welsh preacher, Donovan writes and performs songs that draw on biblical and spiritual themes without overtly expressing uniquely Christian claims. On *Dust Shaker,* for instance, the song "Snakes Alive" is darkly apocalyptic ("Who's gonna make you fall? . . . Who's gonna make you crawl?"), while "Groovy Garden" appears to be about Eden. But his lyrics also sometimes employ what *True Tunes* calls "coarse language," and he has a penchant for what *Phantom Tollbooth* calls "pure metaphor madness," such that one often has no idea what a song might be about. "Shiny King" from *The Hex the Ghears* exclaims, "Drink a little punk juice / Frame a piece of rock moose / Shining on the inside / Holy shakin' so loose." *The Lighthouse* credits Donovan (in his more lucid moments) with "the rare ability to see the hope and beauty of the world without downplaying the harsh realities and brokenness both of himself and of those around him."

For trivia buffs: Dan Donovan is also a graphics artist. He has designed album sleeves for **The Electrics** and **Split Level.**

Don't Know

Ed Carrigan, gtr.; Dan Henry, voc.; Paul Henry, bass; Matt Johnson, drums. 1995—*Cooli P. Ramaswami Memorial Cheesecake* [EP] (Tooth and Nail).

Seattle quartet **Don't Know** was composed of three members of **Blenderhead** plus Dan Henry on vocals. The group recorded only enough songs for a single EP but was a sideshow attraction at numerous festivals and events around the Seattle area for a time. The band had actually formed prior to **Blenderhead** and so was not exactly a side project but—in Matt Johnson's words—was composed of "slackers with no real drive for success." Musically Don't Know favored funk over punk, adopting a style similar to that of early Red Hot Chili Peppers. Lyrically they went for whatever seemed zany, with no overt intention of being spiritual or edifying. The song "Cheese Whiz Craze," for instance, is no more (or less) than an ode to a microwavable dairy product. Johnson described the band's music as "geek core" or "nerd rock" and said they appeal mainly to "people who collect *Star Wars* trivia." When prompted to justify the band's participation in Christian music programs, he added, "God can bless people just by making them laugh." Johnson would go on to play with not only **Blenderhead** but also **Roadside Monument, Ninety Pound Wuss,** and **Raft of Dead Monkeys.**

Dove

Bob Landers; Randy Bugg (−1973); et al. // Bob Farrell (+ 1974); Sonny Lallerstedt (+ 1974). 1972—*Dove* (Myrrh); 1974—*Dove II* (Shalom).

Dove was an early soft rock Jesus music group that originally toured as part of Baptist evangelist Richard Hogue's SPIRENO (i.e., Spiritual Revolution Now) outreach ministry. The latter program was an official campaign of the Southern Baptist Convention that sought to harness the enthusiasm of the Jesus movement revival and shepherd newly converted youth into mainstream (preferably Baptist) churches. Hogue was a fire and brimstone preacher who also wrote books dealing with such topics as *Sex, Satan, and Jesus* (Broadman, 1973). A publicity photo (no date) for Dove reveals four men and one woman, though they are not identified. Bob Landers was the group's leader. Randy Bugg played on the first album, then left to join **Millennium.** For the second record, Bob Farrell and Sonny Lallerstedt came over *from* **Millennium.** Eventually **Pat Terry** would recruit Lallerstedt and Bugg (who must have rejoined) from Dove to join him in forming **The Pat Terry Group.** Farrell would record with his wife Jayne (who had also been in **Millennium**) as the duo **Farrell and Farrell.** The Farrells would become prolific songwriters and would see their songs recorded by Laura Branigan, **Eric Clapton, Michael English, Amy Grant,** Anne Murray, **Sandi Patty,** Diana Ross, **Rebecca St. James, Jaci Velasquez,** and others.

When not on the road with Hogue, Dove was based in Houston, Texas. The first Dove album features a cover with graphics almost identical to those which Myrrh would employ for the debut **Liberation Suite** album three years later. Mu-

sically the record contains cheerful folk-rock songs that are performed competently but are noticeably inferior (as songs) to what was being produced out west by **Children of the Day** and **The Way.** The second album, however, surpasses the debut considerably, incorporating synthesizers and mellotron to fill out the camp-counselor folk tunes with an air of progressive rock. "Bad News Blues" spends four minutes detailing the world's ills before quickening the pace dramatically to present Jesus as the answer. "Ugly Louise" offers the simple reminder that God loves the losers and ugly ducklings of the world. The album also includes covers of **Larry Norman**'s "The Outlaw" and **Pat Terry**'s "Seen It Now."

Linda Dove

See **Truth.**

Roma Downey

1999—*Healing Angel* (RCA).

Roma Downey is the star of the quasi-Christian TV series *Touched by an Angel.* She recorded a 1999 solo album on which she did not sing but offered readings against a backdrop of New Age music performed by Phil Coulter. The readings are all devotional and/or emotional in tone, and they vary widely in theme from joy at a wedding to grief over the loss of a parent to humble appreciation for the lives of children. Reviewers noted that while the individual readings might be meaningful for use on various occasions, the disparity of emotions prevents the album from working well as a whole.

Downhere

Jason Germaine; voc., kybrd., gtr.; Glenn Lavender, bass; Marc Martel, voc., gtr.; Jeremy Thiessen, drums. 2001—*Downhere* (Word).

Downhere is an electric folk-pop band that came on the scene late in 2001 with a debut album rich in vocal harmonies applied to appropriately melodic and hook-laden songs. "Larger Than Life" is a driving song that recommends reflection on the big questions of life—one's place in a vast creation and one's relationship with the Creator. "Free Me Up" is in the vein of a Dave Matthews Band song. "Raincoat" is '60s style pop with a wonderfully catchy tune and unfortunately trite lyrics (knowing God is like wearing a raincoat in a downpour). "Protest to Praise" is a harder edged song, indicating God's willingness to hear all manner of human cries. True to this sentiment, most of the album's songs are addressed to God, either as prayers, questions, or thanksgivings. The album's liner notes suggest a specific Bible verse for meditation on each song.

The Downings

Ann Downing, Paul Downing, Dony McGuire, Joy McGuire. 1974—*I Feel So Good About It* (Heatwarming); 1975—*Praise Him!*; 1976—*Spiritfest* (Impact); 1977—*Birthplace.*

The Downings were a southern gospel group along the lines of **The Cruse Family** or **The Singing Rambos.** The group is best remembered as the birthing ground for **Dony McGuire,** who pushed them to adopt a slightly more contemporary style in the mid '70s. Dony and Joy were also part of a short-lived post-Downings group called McGuire; after they divorced, they would both pursue solo careers. Eventually Dony would marry **Reba Rambo** and would write, produce, and record music with her. Ann Downing won the Dove award for Female Vocalist of the Year in 1970; she has continued to record solo gospel albums (e.g., *Ocean of Grace,* White Field, 1998).

Downpour

Andrew Adams, bass, voc.; Stephen J. Busch, kybrd., voc.; Brannon Hannock, voc., gtr.; Jason Scott Payton, drums. 2000—*The Real Me* (Rustproof).

Downpour evolved out of the Nashville rock band **Plaid,** with keyboardist Stephen Busch replacing that band's guitarist Andrew Salmon. The new group issued a debut album in 2000 that reveals a band straddling the line between mainstream contemporary Christian music and Christian alternative rock. On the one hand, certain songs ("Sometimes," "Lessons in Falling") employ enough industrial beats and synthesized vocals to convey a sound that is at least as off-center as **Bleach** or **Skillet.** On the other hand, "Hiding Place" seems like a **DC Talk** outtake and "Is It Me?" recalls **Jars of Clay.** Alternating between guitar-dominated rock ("Believe") and keyboard dance tunes ("In Love Forever"), the group provides a variety that bridges genres. The song "Sometimes" features a guest appearance from hip-hop artists **KJ-52.** Lyrically *The Real Me* is overt in its Christian confessions. Most of the songs are sung to God and are expressive of both human frailty and divine strength. On "Paradise," the first song to gain radio airplay, the group confesses, "If we believe in You, we will be in paradise."

O'Landa Draper (and The Associates)

1991—*Above and Beyond* (Myrrh); 1993—*All the Bases*; 1994—*Live . . . A Celebration of Praise*; 1996—*Gotta Feelin'* (Warner Alliance); 1998—*Reflections*; 1999—*Celebration of Life* (Myrrh).

O'Landa Draper was an innovative choir director who helped to blur the lines between traditional gospel music, contemporary gospel, and R&B. He was also noted for his work with other artists, including participation with Billy Joel on his "River of Time" song and video. Born in 1964 and raised in Memphis, Tennessee, Draper conducted choirs at Memphis' Overton High School and at Memphis State University before founding his sixty-voice ensemble called The Associates. He led the group in inspiring renditions of traditional and modern hymns that defied conventions and expectations of choral music. In reviewing the *Reflections* album, *CCM* magazine likened "God Will Provide" to a B. B. King "barn burnin' blues number" and "Give It Up" to late '60s Sly Stone funk. "In the sometimes inflexible world of choral gospel," the reviewer noted, "O'Landa Draper is still forging new paths." Two months after that review appeared, and a month before his wedding, Draper died suddenly of undiagnosed kidney problems. He was thirty-four years old.

Christian radio hits: "Wipe a Tear" [with **Russ Taff**] (# 17 in 1992).

Grammy Awards: 1998 Best Gospel Choir or Chorus Album *(Reflections)*.

Dreamer

Dan McCabe, voc., bass, kybrd.; Neil Charter, gtr.; Troy Cole, drums; Bill Davidson, bass; Daniel McAffee, gtr. 1991—*Full Metal Racket* (Image).

Dreamer was the second project organized by one of Christian music's metal pioneers, Dan McCabe. The latter singer fronted the well-received **Daniel Band** in the early '80s, and Dreamer has a sound similar to that group, updated with a sprinkling of Dokken and Scorpions reference points. "Cryin' " is a metal anthem expressing concern for the lost, and "Shake the Dust" is a screaming encouragement to "just let things go" sometimes. "Someone Cares for You" is a power ballad to comfort the broken-hearted. "Thank You, Lord" is nonmetal, acoustic praise.

Dream of Eden

Bret Pemelton; Diana Pemelton. 1993—*Wonderful Thing* (Essential); 1995—*Into the Here and Now.*

Dream of Eden is a husband-wife team, and so they are inevitably compared to **Out of the Grey.** Like Christine and Scott Denté, Bret and Diana Pemelton make acoustic-based pop records that fit comfortably into the mainstream of contemporary Christian music. Initially from Los Angeles, the couple moved to Nashville just before they started their recording career. The debut album offers the song "Blessed Are the Hungry," which addresses homelessness and unemployment with a directness unusual for Christian pop. Likewise, "Regina" focuses on the plight of a pregnant illegal alien. "This Is the Moment" is retro Jesus music, with a sound very similar to **Children of the Day.** "Under Your Sky" is a country-tinged ballad inspired by the prodigal son story (Luke 15:11–32), and "What Do You Want" is an atypical rock number, presenting

Diana in Pat Benatar mode. The sophomore project, *Into the Here and Now,* opens with the up-tempo "Real Love," then moves into a number of expressive and emotive songs ("How Lovely Is Your Face," "Psalm") that reveal the duo's greatest strengths.

Christian radio hits: "What Do You Want" (# 25 in 1994); "Right to the Heart" (# 15 in 1995).

Phil Driscoll

1970—*Blowin' a New Mind* (Word); 1972—*A Touch of Trumpet;* 1981—*Ten Years After* (Sparrow); 1982—*Sound the Trumpet; What Kind of Love;* 1983—*Covenant Children, I Exalt Thee; Songs of the Spirit, Vol. 1 and 2;* 1984—*Celebrate Freedom;* 1985—*Power of Praise;* 1986—*Amazing Grace and Other Favorites; Instrument of Praise* (Benson); *The Spirit of Christmas;* 1987—*Make Us One;* 1988—*Classic Hymns, Vol. 1;* 1990—*Warriors* (DaySpring); *Inner Man* (AB); 1991—*Classic Hymns, Vol. 2* (Benson); 1992—*The Picture Changes* (Word); 1993—*Heaven and Nature Swing* (Word); 1995—*In His Presence* (HeartCry); 1996—*A Different Man* (Word); 1997—*Live with Friends* (Word); 1999—*Plugged In!* (Phil Driscoll Music); *The Quiet.* Additional recordings listed at website.

www.phildriscoll.com

Renowned trumpeter Phil Driscoll (b. 1947) grew up in Cleveland, Tennessee, and began recording gospel music at the age of nineteen. His first two albums of gospel trumpet music were released by Word in the early '70s, portraying Driscoll as a sort of Christian Doc Severinsen. In the late '60s, however, Driscoll hired on with rock star Joe Cocker and played in his band for many years. He also worked with Blood, Sweat, and Tears and Stephen Stills. During this period of "secular success," he says that he abused drugs and then gave his life to Jesus in 1977. Driscoll returned to Christian music and remained prolific throughout the '80s and '90s, sometimes making two or three albums a year. In 1984 he shared a Best Gospel Performance Grammy with **Debby Boone** for the song "Keep the Fire Burning" from her *Surrender* album.

Driscoll's recordings feature a mix of vocal and instrumental tracks. He is an accomplished singer, and his voice is often compared to that of Cocker, which is to say that it is often compared to Ray Charles. Driscoll is best known, however, for his talent with the trumpet. *Sound the Trumpet* presents classic hymns ("My Jesus, I Love Thee") and contemporary praise songs ("Sing Hallelujah") along with covers of **Dottie Rambo**'s "We Shall Behold Him" and **Bill and Gloria Gaither**'s "Because He Lives." His next three projects, however, feature mainly original songs like "Will You Get to Heaven?" "Wings as Eagles," and "World Overcomer" with only the occasional cover (e.g., "Amazing Grace" and "El Shaddai" on *I Exalt Thee*). **Mike Deasy** often plays guitar on Driscoll's projects and sometimes contributes to the songwriting ("Awake My Cap-

tain"). Versatile and eclectic in his musical tastes, Driscoll has performed for CBS with the London Philharmonic Orchestra.

The emphasis of most of Driscoll's albums has been praise and worship. Reviewing *I Exalt Thee, CCM* said, "Driscoll has captured the true reverence and majesty of praise, which many traditional arrangers of hymns have missed." *Power of Praise* offers a slow, bluesy reading of "All Hail the Power of Jesus Name." *Instrument of Praise* features renditions of **Michael W. Smith**'s "Great Is the Lord" and **Leon Patillo**'s "Cornerstone." The two *Classic Hymns* albums allowed Driscoll to do what Wynton Marsalis was doing and record some bonafide "classical music" in a style free of Count Basie/Chuck Mangione-inspired histrionics. But on *Make Us One* he freely incorporates R&B and jazz references. *Heaven and Nature Swing* is a Christmas album, with holiday tunes performed in a Big Band style by Driscoll and **Ralph Carmichael**'s orchestra. *In His Presence* is notable for its variety of instrumentation: some songs have simple piano accompaniment, some feature Driscoll's traditional brass, and one ("New Sound") is even set against a dulcimer. **Mylon LeFevre** joins Driscoll on "Oh, Lord, How Majestic."

There is, however, another side to Phil Driscoll than "the trumpet wielding worship leader." The aptly titled album *The Picture Changes* departs from worship music altogether in favor of a more evangelistic presentation of soulful songs with spiritual messages. Notably, Driscoll uses his trumpet only sporadically on that album. Leon Russell—an old buddy from the Cocker days—plays piano on a cover of the latter's "A Song for You." Producer Bill Maxwell also convinced Driscoll to drop the Cocker imitation and sing in his "real voice," which as it turns out is reminiscent of Michael Bolton. Similarly, *A Different Man* is primarily a vocal production, in keeping with typical adult contemporary Christian music. Driscoll covers the Beatles' "The Long and Winding Road" and offers a number of R&B gospel songs ("The Lights of the City," "Road to Jerusalem"). *Plugged In* continues in the same vein with covers of **Eric Clapton**'s "My Father's Eyes," **Bob Dylan**'s "When He Returns," and Ray Charles' "Light out of Darkness," in addition to a song cowritten by Driscoll with **Billy Preston**, "Forever Ever Land." By contrast, *The Quiet* is easy listening, instrumental Muzak reminiscent of Yanni or **John Tesh.**

Driscoll is also known for his patriotism—*Celebrate Freedom* includes "The Star-Spangled Banner," "America the Beautiful," and "Battle Hymn of the Republic." He often performs at Democratic party conventions. In 1993 he said, "One of my highest priorities is to use my music to communicate to young people the hopelessness of drugs, the optimism of life, and the significant privilege of living in the land of the free." In 2000 Driscoll was invited to play at the annual "Pentagon Pops" held at Constitution Hall in Washington, D.C., on President's Day. He played "God Bless America."

For trivia buffs: When he was just starting out, Driscoll once won a CBS-TV talent show. He defeated The Carpenters.

Christian radio hits: "Keep the Flame Burning" (# 2 in 1984) [with **Debby Boone**]; "World Overcomer" (# 39 in 1984); "Messiah" (# 8 in 1985); "A Star Is Born" (# 16 in 1987).

Dove Awards: 1984 Instrumentalist; 1985 Instrumentalist; 1987 Instrumental Album *(Instrument of Praise)*.

Grammy Awards: 1984 Best Gospel Performance by a Duo or Group [with **Debby Boone**] ("Keep the Flame Burning").

Driver Eight

Andy Blunda, gtr.; Matt McCartie, voc., gtr., drums; Alex Parnell, bass. 1996—*Watermelon* (Tooth and Nail).

With a name taken from the lyric of an R.E.M. song, the band Driver Eight was one of Christian music's true alternative pop bands. Their songs bear similarities in style and structure to those of Buffalo Tom or Catherine Wheel, and Matt McCartie's voice is remarkably reminiscent of Billy Corgan's. He explained that similarity to *7ball,* "Like him, I can't really hold notes, so I end up doing things to deceive people into thinking I can sing." McCartie came by his alternative credentials honestly, having previously sat in as drummer with **The Throes** and **The Choir.** For the album *Watermelon,* he recruited two fellow students at Biola University, and recognizing his gifts, Tooth and Nail secured top-flight producer Armand Petri (known first for his work with Goo Goo Dolls and 10,000 Maniacs, then for assisting the breakthrough success of **Sixpence None the Richer**). The album is a solid debut, ultimately rising above its admittedly obvious influences ("Getting This Thing to Go" could be a Smashing Pumpkins' outtake, and the catchy "Waiting for Godot" sounds just like a **Throes** or **Choir** song). Lyrically McCartie tends to favor cynical reflection on what he considers to be non-Christian philosophies: postmodern relativism, existentialism, and the superficialities of intellectual psychobabble. An accompanying booklet offers one-line indications for the authorial intent of each song (e.g., "Cheers": "People hear truth, but don't want to listen"; "Carousel": "The things we chase to make us happy get us nowhere").

Dr. Onionskin

Shane Ries. 1996—*Split Pea Soup* (N'Soul).

CCM called Dr. Onionskin's *Split Pea Soup* "a novelty project with a little bit of everything" and speculated that the record might have been better named "Mulligan's Stew." The artist responsible for the album was Shane Ries, a DJ who, two years before, confused the Christian music industry with a

project released under a different alias, **Hymn Jim.** As the story goes, Ries went out for a cup of mocha one night and, standing on the street corner, heard a jazz trio playing in one ear and a car stereo pumping rap in the other. He thought it sounded so good he was inspired to create an album's worth of jazz/hip-hop fusion. That in itself might not be so novel, but Dr. Onionskin has a distinctive electronic take on the acid jazz genre. He did most of the playing, sampling, and programming himself, with some assistance from notables Aaron Delacruz on keyboards and Patrick Caro on bass. *Split Pea Soup* consists of seventeen tracks, most of which are instrumental, featuring horns, Spyro Gyra-type guitars, and keyboards, all laid down over a persistent hip-hop backbeat. Elements of disco ("Get into It"), lounge ("Shady Day"), and swing pop up here and there. What lyrics are present consist mainly of samples, though a beatnik poem is emphatically spoken in "Last of the Boheatniks." There are no explicit references to God, Jesus, or anything else that would smack of specific Christian content.

Dryve

Keith Andrew, drums.; Paul Donovan, gtr., voc.; David Pratschner, kybrd., sax.; Michael Pratschner, bass.; Steve Pratschner, gtr.; Cory Verner, voc., gtr. 1996—*Hum* (independent); 1997—*Thrifty Mr. Kickstar* (SaraBellum).

San Diego-based alternative band Dryve didn't endure, but they got their act together long enough to release one of the best college rock albums of 1997. They evolved out of a folk duo (Paul Donovan and Cory Verner) that merged with another such duo (Keith Andrew and Steve Pratschner) around 1993, then added Steve's two brothers to obtain a fuller sound. The group did not sound like any other band on the scene, but they did play the same sort of intelligent jangly rock music that artists like Counting Crows, Gin Blossoms, R.E.M., and the Wallflowers were performing at the time, music that sought to update the melodic and comfortable sounds of the Byrds or Poco. When they needed to, Dryve could pull out all the stops and rock hard ("Television"), but they never failed to deliver the hooks and riffs that had enabled rock and roll to conquer the world all those years ago. Three songs remain stellar examples of Christian rock at its best. "Nervous" is a near-perfect hit single, a magical song like something from *Out of Time*-era R.E.M. The title track is a rougher, roots rock tune that catapults its way into one's consciousness with simple (but effective) little tricks like stopping the music suddenly to begin the chorus with an a capella line. "Rain" is a gorgeous rock worship song that begins simply enough and builds into an overwhelming wall of music fueled by an extended instrumental jam. It is, as *The Lighthouse* put it, the kind of song that one can get lost in. On the strength of these tunes alone (not to mention "Television" and "Stay"), Dryve deserved crossover success in the general market as much as any Christian band ever did. "Nervous" did chart on some college stations, and the group became a club favorite in the local scene. Their debut demo, *Hum,* was nominated for Best Rock Album of 1995 in the regional San Diego Music Awards, and *Thrifty Mr. Kickstar* actually won Best Adult Alternative album in that competition two years later. Still the band was not able to break out of the Christian ghetto nationally. After a tour with **The Call** in late 1997, they decided to call it quits.

Lyrically Dryve's songs were intriguing and variously direct and curious. As *The Lighthouse* puts it, "They lament the loss of innocence, sing praises to God, and offer prayers and thoughts about people in their lives." On "It's My Fault" Verner sings, "I forgive me, and God forgives me, so when will you?" In "Stay," he addresses God with the enthusiasm of a new convert ("I junked my sex and my cassettes") while also revealing a certain desperation ("I need you under my skin / I need you at my throat / I wrote these songs about you."). As *True Tunes* noted, "it is this intensity of emotion" that lifts these lyrics out of the blasé milieu of Christian nice-boy rock and allows for faith to be expressed in "a way that neither insults the intelligence nor ignores the heart." Often the band's lyrics are cryptic and one cannot be sure what they are writing about; then, suddenly, statements of faith that would be uncommon for college radio come shining through: "Jesus, with arms wide open, he receives us when we ain't ready" ("She Ain't Ready"). "Rain," the praise song, starts out with heartfelt appreciation reminiscent of **Bob Dylan**'s wonderful "Every Grain of Sand": "When I wake, you're there / When I run, you run for me / When I call, you listen."

Christian radio hits: "Nervous" (# 22 in 1997).

Duckie

Eric, drums; Justin, gtr., voc.; Dan, bass. 1999—*Reservations Required* (independent).

Duckie is a trio from Maryland that plays basic youth group punk-rock in the style of a more overtly Christian **MxPx** or **Squad Five-O.** Alternately serious and silly, the band proclaims the reality of God's grace ("He Luvs Me Anyway") and testifies to the changes God has wrought in them ("Deep Inside"). The music seems targeted for a high school and younger crowd.

Keith Dudley

1994—*Talk about It* (Benson).

A native of China Grove, North Carolina, Keith Dudley was first inspired to pursue a career in Christian music by **Russ Taff**'s *Wall of Glass* album, which seemed to wed the sounds of Motown soul that Dudley loved with the southern gospel fla-

vor of music he always heard in church. A decade later Dudley landed a contract with Benson with the assistance of Mark Harris of **4 Him.** His album is indeed reminiscent of Taff's style and includes some songs written by Harris.

Roby Duke

1980—*Not the Same* (Firewind); 1984—*Come Let Us Reason* (Good News); 1986—*Blue-Eyed Soul;* 1989—*Down to Business;* 1994—*Bridge Divine.*

www.robyduke.com

Roby Duke (b. 1956) is a Christian pop-jazz singer whose contributions to music extend well beyond his own modest recordings. Duke grew up in the Mississippi Delta, playing bass in his father's band (The Delta Rhythm Boys) at the age of twelve. After recording one Christian album for MCA's Songbird label, he signed a contract to make five albums for the Word Records subsidiary Good News. Fulfilling that agreement became an onerous task, and Word eventually allowed him to count a re-release of *Not the Same* toward its completion. Duke had discovered many other musical interests that excited him more than being a recording artist, including producing, session work, and songwriting. Eventually he settled in Seattle, Washington, where he built his own studio, Red Door, and helped to develop the Arcade recording label. He took a job developing new products for Roland Instruments. An amateur musicologist, Duke began recording diverse a capella voices and became the first person ever to make a recording of Tuvan throat singing, an art form practiced by central Asian people who have learned a technique that enables one person to produce simultaneous multiple notes. Eventually Duke produced a Spectrasonics CD-Rom called *Symphony of Voices* that contains a multitude of diverse a capella vocal styles and has become a standard sound effects tool employed for the soundtracks of such motion pictures as *Titanic* and *Good Will Hunting.*

Duke's Christian albums all evince a pop orientation heavily influenced by his R&B roots. The first album features "Promised Land," a neo-spiritual that proclaims, "Someday we'll find an end / When we cross that river / Into a promised land / Where we'll never see a broken heart again." *CCM* proudly pegged him as "a Christian version of Boz Scaggs," in keeping with the thinking (c. 1982) that imitation of secular artists was a good thing. *Come Let Us Reason* is a less jazz-inflected but more up-tempo album. The title track is based on Isaiah 1:18, the passage that had inspired the well-known (but different) song "Come Let Us Reason Together" by **Ken Medema.** The album concludes with its only ballad, "There Is Just One Way," a touching memorial to Duke's father. *Down to Business* offers "I Shall See God," a song that captures the transcendent reality of eternity. Duke reflects on the temporal experience of sensing an invisible presence in the here and now ("It's almost as if someone is standing there") and muses about the almost incomprehensible experience of death: "As I go the way of the earth / As I step through the door / There where time is no more / I shall see God." In addition to his own recordings, he has produced albums for many artists, including **Pat Boone, The Boones, Terry Clark, Heather and Kirsten, The Katinas,** and **Deniece Williams.** Especially attracted to worship music, he sang on a number of worship albums by Maranatha and Vineyard in the '90s. As a songwriter, Duke has written or cowritten Christian radio hits performed by **Arcade** ("This Is Love"), **Bob Bennett** ("Yours Alone"), and **Heather and Kirsten** ("Betcha Didn't Know," "Shock-2-U").

Christian radio hits: "Our Love" (# 4 in 1984) [with **Kelly Willard**]; "Come, Let Us Reason" (# 11 in 1984); "Watching for You" (# 36 in 1985); "This Is Not a Game" (# 16 in 1986); "Down to Business" (# 3 in 1990).

Dumpster

Bradley Garnett, drums, voc.; Stephen Langella, bass, voc.; Grant Nelson, gtr., voc. 1998—*See through Me* (BulletProof).

www.powerup.com.au/~dumpster

The Australian modern rock band Dumpster formed in 1996 and has been very well received in their homeland, where they tour with both general market and Christian acts. Nelson maintains that when he first became a Christian, he tried to get into Christian music, but didn't know how, so he just formed a band for the club scene and, eventually, the Christian market took notice. The group's debut album has been praised by critics for its unpretentious, tasteful, and mature stylings, which *Phantom Tollbooth* likens to "a rare blend of Radiohead and *Mercury*-era **Prayer Chain,** mixed with a subtle hint of Live and Lemonheads." The song "Divine" moves back and forth between passionate rock and an acoustic chorus, heralding the lyric, "Hope is only / As what you put it in / Are you divine?" Such a "seeker mentality" informs much of the album, as the group prefers identifying with people's questions about God rather than trying to assert the answers. Still, "Set in Gold" concludes, "Now I'm part of that / Which won't part with me / Through everything / Christ is king."

Bryan Duncan

1985—*Have Yourself Committed* (Light); 1986—*Holy Rollin'*; 1987—*Now and Then; Whistlin' in the Dark* (Modern Art); 1989—*Strong Medicine;* 1990—*Anonymous Confessions of a Lunatic Friend* (Myrrh); 1992—*Mercy;* 1994—*Slow Revival;* 1995—*Unidos Por El; Christmas Is Jesus; The Light Years* (Light); 1996—*Quiet Prayers (My Utmost for His Highest)* (Myrrh); 1997— *Blue Skies;* 1998—*The Last Time I Was Here,* 1999—*Love Takes Time* (Myrrh); 2000—*Joyride* (Diadem).

www.placetobe.org/duncan

Christian superstar Bryan Duncan was born in 1953 in Ogden, Utah. The son of a pastor, he moved about during his formative years, settling eventually in North Carolina. He was barely out of his teens when he would gain renown as a member (with Randy Thomas) of the groundbreaking Christian rock band **Sweet Comfort Band.** Frustrated by that band's failure to achieve success appropriate to their abilities, Duncan decided to pursue a solo career in 1984. The move involved a scaled-down sound—more pop than rock—and enabled him to find his niche in the Christian market. Though critics often assume SCB was simply ahead of its time (in the Christian market, that is) and regard Duncan's solo work as less innovative, they also acknowledge that his post-SCB albums are masterpieces in their own right. They have, in fact, set the standard for "blue-eyed soul" music, offering up-tempo, danceable pop songs and heartfelt ballads that would become almost definitive of the Christian adult contemporary style. Duncan lives in Riverside, California.

On *Have Yourself Committed,* Duncan intentionally departs from the SCB sound in order to cut his ties and solidify his musical direction. The title song calls for commitment to Christ in a lighthearted manner; musically, it is joyful and vibrant, a '50s be-bop song fueled by Tower of Power horns. The same jubilant spirit imbues "Livin' on the Bright Side" and "Sweep Me Away." At the time the record was released, Duncan said, "I've rediscovered the joy of salvation." *Holy Rollin'* goes beyond the debut to offer what Duncan calls, "pew jumpin' music, straight ahead black gospel." Thematically, the album is also a bit more serious, dealing with the pursuit of holiness and the importance of obedience to God. The opening track, "Only Wanna Do What's Right," has more of those Tower of Power horns and is as jazzy as **Sweet Comfort Band**'s early (best) work. "Lead Me to the Water" is more sultry, with a saxophone replacing the brass. "Remember Me" sounds a lot like latter day SCB, while both "Your Everlasting Love" and "Hope of the Brokenhearted" are radio-ready adult contemporary ballads. The title track delivers the promised black gospel, with some Jerry Lee Lewis killer piano.

Duncan switched labels for *Whistlin' in the Dark,* but continued to present songs that were unapologetically optimistic. "Break Out of Chains" is an R&B celebration of how "the truth will set you free" (with female background singers). "Paradise" offers a bouncy description of the site Duncan has chosen for his final relocation. "You Can Rely on Me" sounds a lot like The Eagles' "Heartache Tonight," with much more hopeful lyrics. "I'm aware of all the social issues," Duncan told *CCM* in 1988, "but I don't write about that stuff. . . . Jesus is the only hope that I know of, and I think it's important to present that hope as plainly and as often as you can, without being boring." The latter caveat would become an issue, however, when Duncan's next album, *Strong Medicine,* seemed to be just more of the same. *CCM* critic Thom Granger complained that Duncan's consistency was wearing thin, though he did think the two jazzy tracks featuring **Take 6** pointed in a potentially promising new direction. To be fair, however, *Strong Medicine* does display new directions lyrically. Influenced by the book *Inside Out* by Larry Crabb (theology professor at Taylor University, where Duncan had performed), Duncan presents songs that are more introspective, songs that depart from the sunny appeal of his earlier efforts to deal honestly with aches, struggles, and desire for resolution. "I was getting a little tired of being the dancing bear," Duncan said in 1989. "The Lord wants us to get beyond, 'life's a party'." Fortunately, Duncan didn't allow that sentiment to sink in too deeply, and he next released some of the best dancin' bear party music of his career. *Anonymous Confessions of a Lunatic Friend* includes a remake of the **Sweet Comfort Band** hit, "Love You with My Life," but its real standout track is the upbeat "Ain't No Stoppin' Now," which brings back the horns and features a generous amount of sanctified whoopin' and hollerin'. "Sunday Go to Meetin'" also draws deeply from R&B/traditional gospel. "Leave Your Light on for Me" is one of Duncan's finer mature pop songs. "Lunatic Friend" and "Mr. Bailey's Daughter," are quirky novelty songs that break the more-of-the-same mold rather drastically but don't hold up to repeated listening. But the song "We All Need" has profound lyrics, in which Duncan admits to the ongoing consequences of his naive spiritual upbringing: "I was raised on the blessings in a victory speech / As I fought for the standards that I could not reach / And I hold my tongue when the pain is great / And I cover my tears as we celebrate."

The album *Mercy* marks Duncan's transition into a more mature adult-oriented brand of music. It is generally regarded as his finest solo project, as a "career album" that displays his talents at their absolute best; it would also yield his all-time biggest hit with the song "Love Takes Time." *Mercy* immediately kicks into high gear with the brass-tinged "Mercy Me," featuring gospel choir background vocals. "Into My Heart" has the sound of Motown soul with the prayerful lyric, "Gotta get you into my heart, out of my head." The song "Step by Step" has an R&B groove reminiscent of the 1986 hit "I Think It's Love" by Jermaine Jackson. "When It Comes to Love" is a wonderfully melodic and soulful song. "You Don't Leave Me Lonely" is a heart-tugging number sung from the perspective of a parent who has lost a child to death ("You don't leave me lonely / You leave me longing for you"). "I'll Not Forget You" is a biblical treatise on "waiting," based on the story of Abraham and Sarah. **Crystal Lewis** sings a duet with Duncan on "Five Smooth Stones," a song about a small shepherd boy who downs a giant (given an "inside joke" treatment through its performance by two artists who are famously short of stature).

Slow Revival is basically *Mercy 2,* but no one would complain about the new style getting at least one more outing. The album opens with its de facto title track, another blast of Philly soul called "A Heavenly Light." That sound also infuses "Your Love, My Saving Grace" and "Wheels of a Good Thing" (a rouser that also references early Chicago and some of Edgar Winter's gospel rave-ups). An ode to permanent romance, "United We Stand" recalls the song by that name made popular by Brotherhood of Man in 1970. "Traces of Heaven" (cowritten with **Michael Omartian**) is gloriously soulful, with an arcing vocal. The maturity of both *Mercy* and *Slow Revival* is not only evident in the music, but also in the lyrics. As Duncan said in 1994, "I've stopped trying to change the world, and I'm working on trying to change myself." As the titles of both albums imply, Duncan had come to realize that the Christian life is not a "quick change" but a grace-empowered struggle for continual growth. In "Traces of Heaven" (from *Slow Revival*), he sings, "I've learned a lesson and I've learned it well / Love don't get easier in the long run." The same theme had been sounded in "Love Takes Time" from *Mercy.*

This pair of classic albums was followed by a couple of side projects, a Christmas record and a collection of hymns *(Quiet Prayers)* recorded in tribute to Oswald Chambers' classic devotional book, *My Utmost for His Highest.* Then, Duncan returned with *Blue Skies,* which as its title implies backs off from the faith-born-of-struggle songs in favor of happier tunes reminiscent of his previous "sunny period." Backed by a stellar all-star band, Duncan recaptures the sounds of Philly, Memphis, and Motown soul on upbeat songs like the title track, "One Touch Away," and the truly outstanding "Joy Is a Singable Thing" (which features the lyric, "Don't want to lose it tryin' to figure it out"). "Turnin'" recaptures the midtempo white soul of '60s groups like The Rascals (e.g., "Groovin'"). "Dyin' to Meet You" is offered twice, once in a flamenco-flavored version and then again in a haunting reprise with minimal instrumentation. "After This Day Is Gone" is a tender ballad that opens with the famous intro to Tears for Fears' "Everybody Wants to Rule the World." The song "Take Another Look at Me" is one of Duncan's most beautiful adult contemporary ballads. *The Last Time I Was Here* gets funkier, with "Yes I Will" and "God Knows" invoking *Innervisions/Fulfillness*-era Stevie Wonder. Duncan also messes around with a little technology, using more synthesizers and even a Radiohead computer-generated voice at the beginning of the wonderful song "Strollin' on the Water." Strong mature-pop songs like "Once I've Arrived" manage to avoid the sappy or predictable pitfalls of much mellow adult-oriented music. "Sometimes in the Dark" is a slinky Atlanta Rhythm Section-type of song unlike anything Duncan has recorded before; "The Preachin' Is Easy" reveals that he is at least aware of hip-hop. Thematically, the album deals with temptation ("Yes I Will"), devotes several songs to the various ups and downs of the Christian life, and concludes with a song awaiting the "Glad Morning" when all struggles will be over.

On *Joyride* Duncan jettisons the adult contemporary stuff almost completely to deliver a full album of explosive pop-soul. He starts things off with "I'd Like to Thank You, Jesus," which sounds a lot like James Brown doing a '70s **Andraé Crouch** song (minus Disciples, Duncan is ably assisted by **Darwin Hobbs** and his thirty-voice choir). "It Gets Better" and "Everything in the Garden" (a humorous telling of the Eden episode from Adam's perspective) revisit the funk-boogie style the artist tried out on *Last Time I Was Here.* "Clap Your Hands" is a jubilant duet with **Ashley Cleveland,** joining the voices of what might be the two most powerful white singers in Christian music. "Where There's Love" is a duet about racial reconciliation sung with Donnie McClurkin; it's a *lot* better than "Ebony and Ivory," putting across the same basic message as the Stevie Wonder/Paul McCartney tune without inducing gagging in listeners. Elsewhere, Duncan actually does cover a McCartney song, but he has the wisdom to choose a good one ("Maybe I'm Amazed," spoiled somewhat by a too-obvious segue into a few bars from "Amazing Grace" at the end). "The Battle Is the Lord's" is old school traditional gospel hymnody and "I'll Always Have Jesus" is a slow jazz club number with tinkling piano.

Duncan's recording career has been summarized in two compilation albums: *The Light Years* collects songs from early albums, and *Love Takes Time* compiles favorites from *Anonymous Confessions* on (with a new recording of "Love Takes Time" featuring an uncredited duet with **Rebecca St. James**).

Duncan has one of the best voices in Christian music. Not only is he naturally gifted with a voice that is both powerful and pleasant, but he has learned to sing with attitude, to use his voice in ways that are unusually evocative and emotional. The voice itself is a bit like Stevie Wonder's, but the vocal stylings are more like those of James Brown, on the nonballads at least. As exciting as a Wonder-Brown hybrid may seem, however, the ballads are not to be dismissed. As plenteous as they are in Duncan's oeuvre, they are often stirring. It is hard to imagine a more beautiful song than "Bryan's Hymn (When I Turn to You)" from *Quiet Prayers.* Duncan's white-boy affection for soul and combination of bouncy "fun songs" with tender ballads has caused him to be labeled "the Billy Joel of Christian music"—but even taking into account the career diversities and evolutions of both artists, that comparison does not ultimately do either of them justice. If Duncan pales as a songwriter when compared to Joel, he is certainly a much better singer. Let the comparisons fall away, and replace them with *The Lighthouse*'s bottom line evaluation: "Bryan Duncan proves adult contemporary music doesn't have to be boring." Actually, *that* could be said of Billy Joel as well.

Christian radio hits: "Have Yourself Committed" (# 1 for 4 weeks in 1985); "Darkness Is Falling" (# 13 in 1986); "Hope of the Broken-Hearted" (# 8 in 1986); "Remember Me" (# 9 in 1986); "Your Everlasting Love" (# 16 in 1987); "Help Is on the Way" (# 3 in 1987); "Every Heart Has an Open Door" (# 4 in 1988); "Paradise" (# 8 in 1988); "Let Me Be Broken" (# 3 in 1989); "Don't Ya Wanna Reap?" (# 7 in 1989); "Stand in My Place" (# 5 in 1990); "Wonderful" (# 11 in 1990); "Ain't No Stoppin' Now" (# 1 for 4 weeks in 1990); "Puttin' in the Good Word" (# 19 in 1991); "Blessed Are the Tears" (# 30 in 1991); "I Love You with My Life" (# 30 in 1991); "Love Takes Time" (# 1 for 6 weeks in 1992–1993); "Into My Heart" (# 6 in 1993); "Step by Step" (# 4 in 1993); "When It Comes to Love" (# 5 in 1994); "Five Smooth Stones" (# 6 in 1994); "Traces of Heaven" (# 2 in 1994); "Things Are Gonna Change" (# 6 in 1994); "United We Stand" (# 14 in 1995); "Don't Look Away" (# 18 in 1995); "A Heart Like Mine" (# 24 in 1995); "Blue Skies" (# 4 in 1997); "After This Day Is Done" (# 25 in 1997).

Dove Awards: 1997 Inspirational Album *(Quiet Prayers [My Utmost for His Highest]).*

Gary Dunham

1980—*Happy Family* (NewPax); 1982—*The Pearl.*

Gary Dunham was a member of **Don Francisco**'s band who released two solo albums on **Gary Paxton**'s NewPax label. Born and raised in St. Joseph, Missouri, Dunham toured early on with a singer named Rosemary, whom he ended up marrying. The two had a rocky relationship, marked by repeated separations; during one of these they both gave their lives to the Lord and found a new basis for stability. The title song for Dunham's debut, *Happy Family,* relates this testimony and would become a major hit on Christian radio. It begins, "Thank you Lord, for giving her to me again / I thought it was the end / But you came and changed it." Successive verses deal with marriage and parenting, juxtaposed against the chorus, "A happy family is quite a thing to see nowadays." *CCM* chose *Happy Family* as one of the Ten Best Christian Albums of 1980. Dunham's follow-up project, *The Pearl,* features a title track that draws upon the parables of Matthew 13:44 to present Christ as "Eternity's Treasure" and as "The Pearl of Great Price." All songs on both albums were written by Gary and Rosemary Dunham.

Christian radio hits: "Happy Family" (# 1 in 1981); "The Pearl" (# 24 in 1983).

Brian Dunning

See **Jeff Johnson.**

Duraluxe (a.k.a. Fluffy)

Chris Colbert, gtr., voc.; Jeffrey Beans, bass (−2000); Nathan Pellegrin, voc. (−2000); Paul Pellegrin, drums (−2000) // Troy Daugherty, voc., gtr. (+ 2000); Fred McKay (+ 2000); Tommy Wedge (+ 2000). As Fluffy:

1991—*Fluffy Luvs You* (Blonde Vinyl); 1992—*Go, Fluffy, Go*; 1995—*Sugar Pistol* [= *Rock Music with Singing* by Duraluxe] (Flying Tart); 1996—*Fluffy vs. Phantasmic*. As Duraluxe: 1997—*Rock Music with Singing* [= *Sugar Pistol* by Fluffy] (Flying Tart); 2000—*Dolorosa* (Meddle).

http://duraluxe.com

Duraluxe was Chris Colbert's second experiment after the demise of his quirky but adored-by-a-few band, **Breakfast with Amy.** The group began as Fluffy and issued their three classic albums under that name before it came to their attention that a "girl group" in the UK already held the rights to the name and wanted to keep it that way. Thus, the band was rechristened Duraluxe. In a not-too-bright move, their most popular album *Sugar Pistol* was reissued with a new title *(Rock Music with Singing),* causing ill-informed fans to repurchase it under the impression that it was a new product (the suits at their record company reportedly thought "Sugar Pistol" sounded offensive). But any disappointment may have been short-lived. For some reason, Duraluxe dropped the song "Wayfaring Stranger" from the album and added an uncredited bonus track at the end that now serves as one of the album's highpoints.

Fluffy Luvs You offers an inauspicious beginning with none of the promise of BWA's creativity being fulfilled. The album has a basic L.A. punk sound, with ugly snarl vocals laid over a midtempo, driving rhythm section. Melodies, hooks, and riffs are sparse, and lyrics, undecipherable. *HM* magazine selected "Jello Soul," "Life through Death," and "My America" as standout tracks, but that is something of a misnomer since virtually all of the songs sound alike—indeed one must watch the digital counter on the CD player carefully with *Fluffy Luvs You* to know when one track has ended and another begun. In time, the album would come to sound like a tame preview of **Embodyment** and would continue to be treasured by the few and far between who like such fare. *Go, Fluffy, Go* is a different affair entirely. In the intervening year, Colbert had remembered how to sing and the group now delivered up *songs* as opposed to just sound effects. "Guitars, Guns, and Girls" reveals a group that just might amount to something, as does "Hulaville," "Crystal," and "White Trash." The snarling vocal returns on "Little Finger Eye," but is not inappropriate for a single track. As a special treat, Fluffy serves up a hard version of Rick Springfield's "Jessie's Girl."

Then the unexpected happened: Fluffy suddenly got good. *Sugar Pistol* is their masterpiece, the first draft of what would become one of Christian music's best bizarro-rock albums. The whole record is saturated with Colbert's trademark "wall of distortion" guitar playing. Guest stars like **Steve Hindalong** and **Riki Michele** abound. The opening track, "Shrimpy Brine," cooks up an ear buzz that begs to be played *loud.* "Dead Horse Grin" features a driving beat, an unforgettable melody,

and a guitar assault that even a reserved reviewer for *The Lighthouse* had to admit, "creates such an impenetrable exoskeleton of distortion, it can almost be labeled beautiful." Almost. "My Love" (not a Paul McCartney cover) takes a pretty song with female vocals and sets it against a propulsive groove that makes it (like most of these tracks) unlike anything that anyone is likely to have heard before. The album's guilty pleasure, "Chrissy Rides Fluffy Now," features a dumb almost-falsetto vocal that is unfortunately intoxicating. The album really only has one low point: its title track is just four-and-a-half minutes of filler (people talking, room noise, someone playing a kazoo). When someone said, "Let's put *this* on the album," it must have seemed like a great joke—but the humor wears thin for those who play the disc repeatedly. Still, the group does do a daring cover of David Bowie's "Moonage Daydream" that surpasses the original. And then, as indicated, the Duraluxe reissue of the album *(Rock Music with Singing)* saves the best till last: a live version of "Not Easy Being Me," a none-too-distinctive track from *Go, Fluffy, Go* transformed now into a spectacular jam that could shatter windows (or eardrums) but is so filled with hooks and tasty riffs as to make its enjoyment at high volume seem almost worth the cost. Almost. Why didn't someone remove the obnoxious "Sugar Pistol" from the reissue? Well, they almost did. On the new album cover, the song has been literally ripped out of the track listing, showing a hole where it used to occur and inspiring hope in those who had the first edition of the album that maybe the annoying garbage was now gone. But it just looks like it. It's really still there. Ha ha.

The album *Fluffy vs. Phantasmic* did not offer much new material but simply repackaged some classic Fluffy tunes (including "Sugar Pistol"!) on a disc that also includes five songs by the band **Phantasmic** and, for some unapparent reason, one by **Joe Christmas.** The novelty of the release was four songs by "Xtra Fluffy," a hybrid experiment of the two groups (Fluffy and **Phantasmic**) combining forces for a style that *7ball* would describe as "sanctified weirdness and melodic ambience." Then, after a four-year hiatus, Colbert assembled a new Duraluxe lineup that included Troy Daugherty of **Hoi Polloi.** Hindalong guested again on *Dolorosa,* and Sydney Rentz of **Morella's Forest** took over the occasional female vocals handled previously by **Riki Michele.** *True Tunes* described the new work as the band's "most linear and consistent to date," and went on to note the pros and cons of such a description. While offering more of "a look into Colbert's life and feelings," the album also "signals the end of the wild eclecticism and often bizarre unpredictability" for which the group was famous.

Thematically, albums by Fluffy/Duraluxe are a bit hard to figure. The lyrics are often unfathomable. What exactly does it mean to say that someone is "finger lickin' lonely and rooked" ("Bleach")? The insane punk song "Bakin' a Cake" is clear enough, but seems just to be about somebody baking a cake. *The Lighthouse* thinks that the group has consistently satirized "our society's inability to think for itself." Be that as it may, there isn't much that deals with specifically Christian content ("Chrissy Rides Fluffy" mentions someone who dreams about the rapture) or that seems to be intended to inspire, exhort, challenge, or rebuke the listeners. In short, Fluffy/Duraluxe are regarded as a Christian band not because of anything intrinsic to the music itself, but because the band members are Christians, they record for Christian labels, and they often play for Christian audiences. Colbert would later turn up playing for **Left Out,** and he became a major producer, eventually taking over the Green Room studio formerly run by Gene Eugene of **Adam Again.**

Allison Durham

Selected: 1993—*Walk into Freedom* (StarSong).

Southern gospel singer Allison Durham decided to try the contemporary Christian market with a single album in the mid '90s. Durham has worked with southern gospel mainstay Bill Gaither and is married to Brian Speer of The Speer Family, one of America's foremost southern gospel singing ensembles. She has released solo albums in the southern gospel genre herself. *Walk into Freedom* reveals a new pop orientation and would garner favorable reviews in the usual contemporary Christian media. *CCM*'s April Hefner singled out the title track, the praise chorus "They That Wait," and a piano ballad "When You Walk through the Water" as standout tracks. Durham has an expressive and dynamic voice, and *Walk into Freedom* fits well with Christian adult contemporary pop, but the album failed to sell. Durham returned to southern gospel and has continued to perform in that arena.

Christian radio hits: "Walk into Freedom" (# 12 in 1994).

Dust

Lynn Nichols; et al. 1972—*Dust* (Myrrh).

Very little is known of the early '70s Jesus music group Dust, but the electronic magazine *Jesus Music* records enough for their sole album to qualify as a novelty souvenir of another place and time. They lay down a few "psychy hard rock" songs ("Gone" and "Rich Man") and a couple of pleasant midtempo numbers ("My Song," "Stand by Now"). But then there is the main attraction: a seven-minute line-by-line exegesis of the Pledge of Allegiance spoken over a new rendition of The Hollies' song "He Ain't Heavy, He's My Brother." The hippie lead singer throws in a lot of "man's" and "dig it's" for effect. A typical line: "The government *is* the people, man!" Every middle-aged Christian who waxes nostalgic for **Love Song** and **Larry Norman** should be reminded that *this* was part of the Jesus movement too. Participants in that movement were not called Jesus *freaks* for nothing.

At the time Dust made this album, Lynn Nichols (the only known member) was a part of the famous Love Inn community in Freeville, New York. He had joined that Christian commune at the age of sixteen and its leader DJ-turned-minister Scott Ross served as his legal guardian. Nichols later became a producer and a member of the bands that backed **Phil Keaggy** on such legendary albums as *Emerging, Sunday's Child,* and *Crimson and Blue.* He produced the latter two albums—widely considered to be among the best Christian records ever made. He also served as the head of Myrrh records and then as vice-president in charge of A&R at Sparrow. In the '90s, he was a founding member of **Chagall Guevara** and **Passafist.**

This '70s hippie Dust should not be confused with a British '90s band of the same name. The latter group (a modern rock Christian band) released a four song EP called *See Red* on the independent KnewSense label in 1998.

Dust and Ashes

Jim Moors, gtr., voc.; Tom Page, gtr., voc.; John Duvall, bass (−1972) // Jim Sloan, gtr., voc. (+ 1972). 1970—*From Both Sides* (Custom Fidelity); 1972—*A Different Shade of Blue* (Avant Garde); *The Lives We Share.*

Dust and Ashes was a country folk group who didn't quite fit in with the changing times. As *Jesus Music* magazine indicates, they represented a second generation of Christian folk artists like **Ray Repp,** who wrote countless camp songs for youth groups to sing with guitar accompaniment. Dust and Ashes took that to the next level, plugging in as a full band that would actually perform concerts. But the Jesus movement was happening all around them, and they seemed at first unaware and then downright resistant to its influences. They repelled countless would-be fans with ill-timed anti-hippie rhetoric while sporting long hair and electric guitars that seemed to present them stereotypically as part of the hippie Christian revival themselves. The first album is the most acoustic and will be remembered by some former summer camp counselors as a classic of the youth group genre. It was on the second project that the group was transformed into an actual band, complete with a variety of instruments (electric guitars, drums, even violins), and fueled, apparently, by the professionalism of Jim Sloan. The third project became their most widely known. Songs like "The Windchimes" and "Peaceful River" showcase Sloan's talents. "The Lord's Vineyard," however, turns Isaiah 5:1–7 into an indictment against the institutional church, a theme that is further developed on "Our Church Has Got Religion Again" and "Someone's Locking the Doors (to the House of God)." The basis for the latter song's attack (if churches were truly spiritual, they wouldn't worry about theft or vandalism), seemed a bit unrealistic even at the time. And then there is "Talkin' Jesus Freak Blues," a basic anti-Jesus-movement diatribe parodying the evangelistic intents of the new enthusiastic hippie converts. The song could have been humorous and might have worked if done as self-deprecation from within the movement—it's the sort of thing **Tom Stipe** might have done well—but Dust and Ashes performed it with an "us and them" mentality that made the jokes seem meanspirited and unfair. If one wanted to be in a Christian rock band in 1972 and was opposed to *both* the organized church *and* the Jesus movement, there weren't a whole lot of places to go.

Some unconfirmed reports list an album titled *Lend Me a Sunrise* released by a group called Dust and Ashes in 1983 (no label specified). This may or may not be the same group.

Dust Eater Dogs

Harri Heikkanen, voc., gtr.; Benny Majapacka; Daniel Majapacka; Markus Majapacka. 1998—*Motor* (Day-Glo).

www.netti.fi/jrmeris

Dust Eater Dogs is a four-piece Christian rock band from Turku, Finland that describes its style as "a mixture of funk, hard core, and all kind of alternative crap." According to their website, they are known for their "highly aggressive live performance and very positive attitude." The Majapacka brothers (Benny, Daniel, Markus) say that they formed the group in 1994 under "the stupid name Chainflesh." After a procession of vocalists, the band morphed into Dust Eater Dogs (a nonstupid name?) around the time Harri Heikkanen was added. *Phantom Tollbooth* praised the debut album *Motor* as a "pop hardcore" record that puts American music to shame. Alternating between similarities to Rage Against the Machine and more melodic European funk artists, the group delivers songs that openly address Christian themes while avoiding the overworked clichés of Christianese. "Thunderleg" deals humorously with the theme of spiritual warfare, and "I Cannot Smile" offers an intentional parody of Korn. "Ultra" speaks against lifeless, cookie-cutter Christianity, while incorporating some ironic elements of ska. *Motor* was immaculately produced by Armand Petri, who was responsible for breakthrough projects by 10,000 Maniacs and the Goo Goo Dolls before jump-starting the career of **Sixpence None the Richer** (cf. **Driver Eight**). The album was released into both secular and Christian markets simultaneously, which, the band complains, necessitated some compromises. Some unspecified changes had to be made to the visual presentation in order for the record to be marketed to American Christian retailers, while a song called "Sex Belongs to Marriage" was cut as inappropriate for the general market.

The group's mission statement affirms the band's "main motive" as being "to play good music and transmit a positive picture of God and real Christianity through their songs and appearances." Daniel Majapacka threatened that, if *Motor* did not sell, the group would change its name (again) to the Dust Eater Boys and attempt a comeback as an *NSYNC/98 degrees/Backstreet Boys clone.

Bob Dylan

Selected: 1979—*Slow Train Coming* (Columbia); 1980—*Saved*; 1981—*Shot of Love*; 1983—*Infidels*; 1985—*Empire Burlesque*; *Biograph* [3 discs]; 1986—*Knocked Out Loaded*; 1988—*Down in the Groove*; 1989—*Oh Mercy*; 1990—*Under the Red Sky*; 1991—*The Bootleg Series* [3 discs]; 1994—*Bob Dylan's Greatest Hits, Vol. 3*; 1995—*MTV Unplugged*; 1997—*Time Out of Mind*; 2001—*Love and Theft* (Sony).

www.bobdylan.com

Bob Dylan (b. Robert Zimmerman in 1941) released three albums that he explicitly presented as Christian music after experiencing what was to be the most highly publicized conversion of the twentieth century. Then, he quietly withdrew from the Christian music scene without ever renouncing his loudly proclaimed faith or retracting the convictions he had so publicly professed. Twenty-some years later, Internet chat groups would still be devoted to the question of whether or not Dylan is *still* a Christian and whether his continued outpour of albums should continue to be regarded as Christian music. The dilemma was confounded by rumors as early as 1983 that he had in fact joined Brooklyn's Lubavitch sect of ultra-orthodox Hasidic Judaism; the rumor was both confirmed and denied in conflicting reports from prominent members of the sect. Dylan himself has been characteristically silent and ambiguous on the matter. As one who was accorded unsought mythic status before his time, he resents exaggerated estimates of his significance, repels idolatrous would-be disciples, and seems to enjoy being regarded as enigmatic.

Born in Duluth, Minnesota, Dylan moved with his family to Hibbing, Minnesota, when he was six. At nineteen, he took his stage name in honor of the poet Dylan Thomas and left for Greenwich Village where, in emulation of Woody Guthrie, he embraced the new style of American folk music that was emerging there. He soon became the leader of the movement, first popularizing the style of poet-artists like Guthrie, Pete Seeger, and Allen Ginsberg, then creating his own new variety of modern folk that would establish such artists as Joan Baez (with whom he had a relationship in 1963), the Kingston Trio, Peter, Paul, and Mary, and Simon and Garfunkel—all of whom recorded his songs. Ever evolving, he shocked the folk community by plugging in at the 1965 Newport Folk Festival and introducing yet another new genre, "folk rock." The latter style, adopted by such artists as The Byrds, the Band (who began as

Dylan's backup group), Buffalo Springfield, and the Grateful Dead, would become definitive of the late '60s and early '70s music scene. But Dylan himself moved on, eventually adopting and then adapting every style of music on the American horizon: country and western, blues, rock and roll, jazz, and, of course, gospel. Indeed, some musicologists even credit Dylan with inventing rap music, or at least with previewing it on 1964's "Subterranean Homesick Blues." With four decades of contributions, Dylan is generally acknowledged to be the most significant figure in twentieth-century popular music and is often regarded as the greatest American composer of all time. Such designations, of course, exclude classical music, which tends to exist at a remove from reality that renders temporal, spatial, or cultural placements less relevant. Dylan has only been interested in the moment, writing throwaway songs that were never intended to transcend their immediate contexts. Still, he has produced his classics. Songs like "Blowing in the Wind," "The Times They Are a-Changin'," and "I Shall Be Released" are likely to become as much a part of the American lexicon as "Down in the Valley" or "Swing Low, Sweet Chariot." Protest songs like "Masters of War" and "It's a Hard Rain's a-Gonna Fall" have already become historical archives revelatory of a turbulent time. Dylan's love songs ("Don't Think Twice," "Just Like a Woman," "Positively Fourth Street," "It Ain't Me, Babe")—if they can be called that—will be remembered for having set a new, harsh standard for lyrics expressive of betrayed romanticism. And many of his works will simply endure as long as they can as examples of perfect, wonderful pop songs: "Mr. Tambourine Man," "Shelter from the Storm," "Knockin' on Heaven's Door," "Lay, Lady, Lay," "Like a Rolling Stone," "Tangled Up in Blue," "All Along the Watchtower," and dozens more.

Dylan became *the* cultural icon of the Woodstock generation, though (more characteristically than ironically) he was one of the only American music stars of the '60s who refused to perform at the Woodstock festival—even though he actually *lived* in Woodstock, New York, at the time! Like a real-life Forrest Gump, he seems to have been everywhere, doing everything that mattered. He was in the forefront of the Civil Rights struggles and the Vietnam protests. He is reported to be the person who introduced the Beatles to marijuana. Lines from his songs pepper the memories of any who lived through those decades: "Let us not talk falsely now, the hour is getting late"; "He that ain't busy being born is busy dyin' "; "I gave her my heart, but she wanted my soul"; "Money doesn't talk, it swears"; "Even the President of the United States must sometimes stand naked." But in addition to crafting great songs and thinking up some memorable one-liners, Dylan could do something else. He had the heart of a poet, and he was able to put words together that created images of seemingly universal sig-

nificance: "Outside in the cold distance / A wildcat did growl / Two riders were approaching / The wind began to howl" ("All Along the Watchtower"). People would hear the words to his songs and say, "I don't know what he means, but I know exactly how he *feels*." Aside from Joni Mitchell, Dylan is probably the only rock star to have his compositions studied alongside the works of Auden or Eliot in college literature classes. **Van Morrison** says without blinking, "he is our greatest living poet."

Dylan suffered injuries from a major motorcycle accident in 1966 and struggled at about that same time with drug addiction. In 1970, he received an honorary degree in music from Princeton. That year he headlined a "Concert for Bangladesh" organized by George Harrison, the first major rock-festival benefit concert. In 1988, he was inducted into the Rock and Roll Hall of Fame. In 1990, he received France's highest cultural honor, being named a *Commandeur dans l'Ordre des Artes et des Lettres*. On May 25, 1997, he was hospitalized with histoplasmosis, a potentially fatal fungal infection surrounding his heart; released from the hospital, his only comment to the press was "I really thought I'd be seein' Elvis soon." Later that year, he performed for Pope John Paul II in Bologna, where he was reported to have greeted the Pontiff with the words, "So . . . you're the Pope, eh?" Dylan has been married only once, to model Sara Lowndes from 1965 to 1976. One of their children, Jakob Dylan, is leader of the successful rock group The Wallflowers.

In addition to releasing some forty albums, Dylan has had parts in three movies: *Pat Garrett and Billy the Kid* (1973); *Renaldo and Clara,* a concert film that he also directed (1978); and *Hearts of Fire* (1987). He has published two books: *Tarantula* (1971) and *Writings and Drawings by Bob Dylan* (1973). Neither the films nor the books met with any acclaim, though he did seem a natural for the walkthrough as a drifter named Alias in the *Pat Garrett* film. He has also recorded two albums as a member of the group Traveling Wilburys, which also included Tom Petty, Jeff Lynne, Roy Orbison, and George Harrison.

The announcement in 1979 that Dylan had become a "born-again Christian" was met with understandable surprise and then outright hostility. As Dylan toured for three years, sometimes singing *only* his new "Christian songs" and offering evangelistic testimonials from the stage, his legion of fans turned on him, regarding him as a sell-out and a traitor. When *Slow Train* came out, *Rolling Stone* editor Jann Wenner insisted on reviewing the album himself and, praising it musically, maintained that it didn't necessarily mean Dylan had really become a Christian—songs like "I Believe in You" and "When He Returns" didn't have to be about Jesus. Just two years later, when such denials were impossible, the reviewer for *Shot of Love* (Paul Nelson) completely ignored the album's music and attacked Dylan's faith with unconcealed hatred and bigotry;

indeed, he even decided that he was an amateur theologian and tried to critique the quality and content of Dylan's religious thoughts from an uninformed perspective that made him look ridiculous. Such strong reactions may have stemmed from the fact that Dylan was supposed to be "the voice" of his generation and he was now touting views that his generation did not espouse. He was accused of being "apocalyptic" and "judgmental," which of course he had always been. Still, it is one thing for a prophet to speak against his disciples' enemies and quite another to begin pronouncing oracles of woe and doom on those disciples themselves. Dylan discovered that he was now a prophet without honor among his own kin, and those who had followed him faithfully for almost two decades discovered that *they* were now in the uncomfortable position of one of his most famous characters, the confused "thin man" who didn't "get" whatever it was that motivated and energized the younger generation: "Something's happening here, but you don't know what it is, do you, Mr. Jones?" ("Ballad of a Thin Man").

Something *was* happening, but what? The details of Dylan's conversion remain shrouded in mystery. Every religious publisher coveted the rights to his "spiritual autobiography," but he never wrote it, or fully told it. "Jesus tapped me on the shoulder," he once related in a concert, "and said, 'Bob, why are you resisting me?' I said, 'I'm not resisting you.' He said, 'You gonna follow me?' I said, 'Well, I never thought about that before.'" But it wasn't just Bob and Jesus. Most observers speculate that the conversion had roots in the experiences of Dylan's famous 1975 tour, billed as the Rolling Thunder Revue, and featuring Bob Neuwirth, Rambling Jack Elliott, Roger McGuinn, **T Bone Burnett,** and what were later to be known as **The Alpha Band** as his supporting musicians. Burnett has commented, "I don't know what happened on that tour, but it is interesting that many people either became Christians or went back to church by the time it ended." While on that tour, Dylan took to performing a never-recorded original song called "What Will You Do When Jesus Comes?" that would have been right at home on *Slow Train Coming* four years later. *The New Rolling Stone Encyclopedia of Rock and Roll* reports that **Debby Boone** had a role in introducing Dylan to what they call "fundamentalist teachings." The more immediate influence, however, came through a congregation associated with the Vineyard movement (a group associated with Calvary Chapel that eventually became a separate denomination) in Malibu, California. The senior pastor of that church, **Kenn Gulliksen,** is known to Jesus music fans for his song "Charity" on the influential *Maranatha Two* compilation album (Maranatha, 1972). Dylan's girlfriend at the time, actress Mary Alice Artes, attended services there and requested that the pastors, Larry Myers and Paul Emond, pay a call on her boyfriend. The pastors had extensive and intelligent conversations with Dylan for several

days about Christ, the Bible, and other Christian teachings. According to Dylan, it was as an outgrowth of these conversations that he came to know Christ in a personal sense. "I truly had a born again experience, if you want to call it that" he told the *Los Angeles Times* in 1981. "I just sat up in bed at seven in the morning and I was compelled to get dressed and drive over to the Bible school. I couldn't believe I was there." He was baptized at the home of Vineyard pastor Bill Dwyer and subsequently enrolled in the Vineyard's school of discipleship, where he attended Bible and doctrine classes for five days a week for nearly four months. He was in a group of about twenty students, including housewives, an unemployed construction worker, and a few lay ministers. He chose, wisely, not to tell people of his new interest or of the commitment he had made until the course was completed. "By that time," he said, "I was into it. When I believe in something, I don't care what anybody else thinks."

Dylan embraced the faith with zeal and enthusiasm. He gave a series of benefit concerts in Los Angeles on behalf of World Vision, a Christian organization devoted to relieving global hunger. He became friends with **Keith** and Melody **Green,** whom he met at the Vineyard. He read several chapters from the Bible daily, worshiped regularly, and told the Greens that he loved to go out on the streets to witness to people or to "pick up hitchhikers in his beat-up old car and talk to them about the Lord without letting them know who he was" (see Melody Green, *No Compromise,* Sparrow, 1989). He gave few interviews but testified boldly to his faith from the stage. Some of the comments he made in concerts have been collected in a book called *Saved! The Gospel Speeches* (Hanuman Books, 1990). A constant theme is his embarrassing repetition of badly exegeted pretribulation millenialist theology, of how "the Bible teaches" that humans are living in the end times, that Russia is about to bring on Armageddon by attacking Israel, that the Antichrist is soon to arrive, and Jesus, soon to return. The specifics of these ideas derive from fundamentalist interpretations of Scripture, such as those popularized in the writings of Hal Lindsey (author of *The Late Great Planet Earth,* Zondervan, 1970). Dylan thought it would all come to pass in five or ten years, probably very soon. He often referred to the events of the day, Iran's holding of United States hostages or Russia's invasion of Afghanistan, as the fulfillment of biblical prophecies and as indicators that the apocalyptic moment was at hand. He was so sure of these realities that he was willing to put his credibility on the line: "I told you 'The Times They Are a-Changin' and they were; I told you the answer was 'Blowin in the Wind' and it was; I'm telling you now, Jesus is coming back and he is!" In certain respects, then, Dylan's eventual "disillusionment with Christianity" may have been a given, intrinsic to the brand of Christianity to which he had been introduced.

Pastor Gulliksen, however, had counseled Dylan not "to get into the Christian circuit" but to respect the platform the Lord had already provided him, to remain a general market performer rather than a stereotypical "Christian singer." Dylan took the advice, in part. He did not become a part of the Christian music subculture, as had previous converts like **Barry McGuire, Richie Furay,** and **Noel Paul Stookey.** But he didn't follow **T Bone Burnett**'s lead and simply allow his faith to inform his participation in what was still primarily a secular career. He was a big enough star to do anything he wanted, and what he wanted was to be a no-holds barred gospel singer in a nongospel marketplace. Thus, his concerts became evangelistic rallies at which Dylan proclaimed the good news of salvation:

> I believe in the God that can raise the dead. . . . When Jesus did go to the cross He did defeat the devil. We know this is true and believe it, and we stand on that faith. . . . You may never see me again, but sometime down the line you remember you heard it here, that Jesus is Lord! . . . Religion is another form of bondage that man invents to get himself to God. But that's why Christ came. . . . There's only one thing that can save you, only one person that went to the cross for you. . . . Nobody ever told me Jesus could save me. I never thought I needed to be saved. I thought I was doing just fine. . . . Jesus put his hand on me. It was a physical thing. I felt it. I felt it all over me. I felt my whole body tremble. The glory of God knocked me down and picked me up. . . . Eternal life is yours for the asking. . . . We're not talkin' about some dead man who had a bunch of good ideas. We're talkin' about a resurrected Christ who is Lord of your life. . . . This may be costing me a lot of fans. Maybe I'll have to start singing on street corners. Still, I'll give all praise and glory to God. (from *Saved: The Gospel Speeches*)

It didn't work. Christian music fans were characteristically suspicious of Dylan's failure to leave the world behind and become part of their little ghetto, and the world at large tired quickly of paying money to hear him talk and sing about religion. His demeanor also alienated critics and friends. A journalist by the name of Bryan Styble would later relate that Dylan asked him at the start of a brief interview, "Are you saved? Or are you a Jew? Or a heathen?" Mary Travers of Peter, Paul, and Mary complained that she found the Christian Dylan insufferable: "exasperatingly difficult and extremely self-indulgent." But Dylan felt *called* to do what he did. "You know when you are called or not," he said. "I know." In May of 1980, he de-

fended his preaching to hostile audiences, saying, "I know not too many people are gonna tell you about Jesus. I know Jackson Browne's not gonna do it, cause he's runnin' on empty. I know Bruce Springsteen, bless him, is not gonna do it, cause he's born to run, and he's *still* running. And Bob Seger's not gonna do it, cause he's runnin' against the wind. Somebody's gotta do it! Somebody's gotta tell you you're free!" The irony in all this was that for almost two decades Dylan had been playing the role of reluctant prophet, refusing to offer wouldbe disciples the advice they sought from him. For the first (and only time) in his career he decided he *did* have a message to proclaim, and the people who had been begging him to give it just wanted him to shut up. "You know I never did tell you to vote for anybody," he reminded angry Syracuse fans at a concert in 1980, "Never told you to follow no guru. Never endorsed no product for you. Never told you how to dress, how to wear your hair, what to eat or drink. Is that a fact? I really haven't told you anything. But I'm telling you now: Jesus is the way of salvation."

Less than a year later, Dylan told the *Los Angeles Times* he wouldn't be preaching anymore: "I don't feel compelled to do it. . . . I don't think it's necessary anymore." Others were better at preaching, he averred. He was an entertainer, paid to sing songs. "It's time for me do something else," he continued. "Jesus himself only preached for three years." Likewise, in a conversation he had in Worcester, Massachusetts, in 1981, he stated his new policy: "At first I felt compelled to say a lot of things. Now, I don't say anything unless the Lord tells me to." In keeping with that stance, Dylan continued to perform, mixing his "gospel songs" and "secular material" together without explanation and letting the songs speak for themselves. Now and then, a glimmer of the old evangelist would come through. "For those of you who don't believe there's a heaven and a hell," he mused at a concert years later, "just die—and find out!" Or, again, with reference to critics who review his albums, he once quipped, "you got to remember, a lot of reporters, they don't know God."

Two decades after Dylan officially swore off preaching, music encyclopedias and books on the artist would tend to gloss over his "Christian phase" as an unfortunate glitch in an otherwise stellar career and to dismiss his "religious albums" as horrible-but-now-forgivable missteps. *The Rough Guide to Rock* (1999) deals with the entire period in one sentence: "Being born again may have been good for Dylan's soul but it wrecked his muse, as a series of less than ecstatic evangelical albums were to prove." It is, however, grossly inaccurate to assume that Dylan's intense and passionate embrace of Christianity did not continue to affect and inform all of his subsequent work, and it is unfair to dismiss the three overtly Christian albums that he made as unworthy of his art. While not equal to his very best work *(Highway 61 Revisited, Blonde on Blonde, John Wesley Harding, Blood on the Tracks, Time Out of Mind)* the albums *Slow Train* and *Saved* certainly belong in the upper half of his repertoire; they have their low points ("Man Gave Names to All the Animals"!) but also contain some excellent material.

Slow Train Coming was recorded in Muscle Shoals, produced by R&B masters Jerry Wexler and Barry Beckett. If critical attention had not focused so singularly on the gospel lyrics, reviewers might have noted that the album marks Dylan's first real entry into soul music. With Mark Knopfler of Dire Straits adding his distinctive guitar throughout, *Slow Train* is tight and unusually competent in musicianship. Almost all reviewers agreed that *Slow Train* might just be the best *played* and the best *produced* album of Dylan's career. The question was whether the *songs* were any good. The opening track, "Gotta Serve Somebody," was pretty obviously a great song . . . but the others? As it turns out, many would improve with age. "I Believe in You" was almost ignored when the album came out, but came to be regarded as one of the artist's best love songs. Six years down the road, liner notes to *Biograph* would acknowledge the song to be "one of his most intimate and best" vocal performances, while indicating that it doesn't really matter whether the "the object of his feelings" was a woman or some higher power. In addition to those two standout tracks, "When You Gonna Wake Up?" and "Gonna Change My Way of Thinking" are splendid examples of Dylan getting funky, something that hasn't happened nearly enough. "Precious Angel" (with its "Shine the light, shine the light on me" chorus) and "When He Returns" are the album's purest gospel songs, and they are masterpieces of that genre. And then, of course, the bluesy, plodding title track is universally recognized as a triumph, lyrically and musically, whatever one thinks of its message. Dylan used to introduce the eschatological song by saying, "There's a slow train coming, but it's about to speed up." That only leaves a couple of downers. In 1998, a *CCM* poll of thirty critics chose *Slow Train Coming* as one of "the ten best contemporary Christian albums of all time" and "Gotta Serve Somebody" as one of "the ten best contemporary Christian songs of all time." Both **Maria Muldaur** and **Johnny Rivers** would later indicate that the album was instrumental in effecting their conversions to Christianity. In 2001, Bono of **U2** told *USA Today,* "This album was such a breakthrough. I was always annoyed that rock could cover any taboo—sexual, cultural, political—but nobody could be upfront about their spiritual life. Before Bob Dylan, no white people could sing about God. He opened me to these possibilities."

Saved has a "live" sound to it, as Dylan runs through a set of songs developed on tour, backed by the road band that had accompanied him. Wexler and Beckett are at the helm again, but they keep the production gritty this time. The album begins

rather embarrassingly with an uninspired cover of a traditional song ("A Satisfied Mind") but then kicks into high gear with the rollicking title track, fueled by gospel piano and "whoop it up" background singers. Prejudices aside, it is flat-out one of the best rock songs of Dylan's career. And so is "Solid Rock," ironically the hardest rocking song he has ever performed— ironic because many thought becoming a Christian would cause Dylan to "wimp out" and turn into some sort of adult contemporary caricature of himself. Both "Saved" and "Solid Rock" are remarkably energetic, *driven* songs that dare resistant malcontents to stay in their seats while the world about them is dancing. In that regard, they belong, curiously, to Dylan's tiny genre of "party songs," of which the best-known number is "Rainy Day Women # 12 and 35" (a.k.a. "Everybody Must Get Stoned"). A scorching cover version of "Saved" was performed by **Third Day** on their *Offerings* album (and a not-so-scorching version by the **Disco Saints** on *Cosmic Cowboy*). The rest of the album *Saved* is more subdued. "Covenant Woman" and "What Can I Do for You?" are excellent ballads. And then there is the heart of the album: four numbers that can only be described as "hymns": "Pressing On," "Are You Ready?" "Saving Grace," and "In the Garden." The inspiration for these songs (like "When He Returns") is not insipid Vineyard praise choruses but a rich tradition of African American hymnody. They are soulful, spiritual songs, and they are magnificent. Obviously, Dylan fans might be persons who simply don't like gospel hymns and their consequent disappointment with this album is understandable, but that disappointment is more a matter of taste on their part than execution on Dylan's. As the most gospel-sounding of Dylan's three so-called "gospel albums," *Saved* is generally the most despised. In retrospect, however, it appears to be the best of the batch, the one album on which he was so immersed in his experience of faith that he didn't care whether he was connecting with anyone or not; he was just praising the Lord. *Saved* is the most genuine, unaffected album of Dylan's career and remains one of the best Christian albums of all time.

Shot of Love, admittedly, takes a downward turn—with one incredible exception. The title track, "Trouble," "Watered-Down Love," and "Dead Man, Dead Man" all aim for a kind of catchy pop appeal that seems beneath the artist. In retrospect, they employ the same style that Dylan finally got down and used to great effect on "Tight Connection to My Heart" (from 1985's *Empire Burlesque*), but it wasn't working yet on *Shot of Love.* The good news on the album is that Dylan began to integrate faith and life such that *every* song didn't have to be about Jesus or the Bible. There is a straightforward love song ("Heart of Mine") and a surprising tribute to a famous social critic ("Lenny Bruce"). The *bad* news is that those songs pale in comparison to similar ones Dylan had done elsewhere. They might have been fine products from any other artist, but mediocre material from a genius is always disappointing. The same assessment probably applies to "Property of Jesus" as well, though it stands out as a worthy contribution. The raison d'etre of the album is the aforementioned "one incredible exception," namely the concluding song, "Every Grain of Sand." A simple testament to God's gracious care for humanity, the song features expressive, poetic lyrics set to a tune of mesmerizing beauty and power. Even the Christaphobic *Rolling Stone* reviewer who hated the album was awestruck by this song. "For a moment or two, he touches you, and the gates of heaven dissolve," he wrote with trembling reverence, quickly noting that this wasn't enough to "make you forget the creepy conservatism" of the overall project. More than one critic outside the Christian market has indicated that this just could be the best song Dylan has ever written, the crowning achievement of a truly incredible career. Notably, it is the only song he has ever written for which he refuses to take credit. In 1985, he revealed, "That was an inspired song that came to me. It wasn't really too difficult. I felt like I was just putting words down that were coming from somewhere else" (cf. **Noel Paul Stookey** and "Wedding Song").

Shot of Love might have had two such highlights—and the CD version of the album actually does. A song called "Groom's Still Waiting at the Altar" was left off the album because Dylan thought "it sounded okay, but it wasn't really the way I wanted to play it." The song, however, did get stuck on the B-side of a 45 R.P.M. single and critics quickly discovered it, hailing it as the best thing Dylan had done in years. The sound of the energetic song recalls his classic '60s period ("Like a Rolling Stone," "Stuck Inside of Mobile") while also pointing forward to the sound he would develop more fully on his acclaimed *Infidels* ("Jokerman"). Lyrically, it is a bit obtuse, but the imagery of a bride abandoning her groom is certainly suggestive of biblical imagery for the church neglecting Christ. The song was restored to *Shot of Love* when the album was released on compact disc.

More songs from this evangelical period of Dylan's work can be found on the *Bootleg* compilation of "rare and unreleased" tracks. Two otherwise unknown songs are especially notable: "Ye Shall Be Changed," a spirited outtake from *Slow Train*, and "You Changed My Life," an exuberant song of thanks that unfortunately didn't make the cut for *Shot of Love*.

Lyrically, Dylan's songs from this period deal especially with themes of apocalyptic judgment and persecution. His "Gotta Serve Somebody" remains one of Christian music's best examples of "just telling it like it is" in a manner that may not be politically correct, but is theologically sound: "You may own guns, you may even own tanks / You may be someone's landlord, you may even own banks / But you're gonna have to serve somebody / It may be the devil or it may be the Lord / But you're gonna have to serve somebody." Dylan's trademark knack for being provocative is in no wise muted on any of these songs. Even an ostensibly sweet song like "Precious Angel" slips in a reference to a time when "people will beg God to kill them but they won't be able to die." The song "Slow Train," few people seemed to notice, was not simply a religious song but a social-political one, promising eventual judgment that would fall upon "big-time negotiators, false healers and woman haters," as well as on "those who wear a cloak of decency . . . talking in the name of religion." The songs on *Saved*, notably, were less about judgment and much about perseverance and atonement, about justification and sanctification, all understood within a classic Christian purview of prevenient grace. But Dylan lost none of his poetic acumen in treating such potentially dull subjects. The title track opens with his rather original statement of original sin: "I was blinded by the devil / Born already ruined / Stone, cold dead / As I stepped out of the womb." Neither Wesley, Calvin, or Luther ever said it better.

If there is a lasting and legitimate critique of the evangelical trilogy, it is that Dylan eschews metaphor and ambiguity to deliver what Jonathan Cott called "preprogrammed, puritanical, and propagandizing" messages. In other words, he comes off as someone who thinks he knows all the answers, or at least the only answer that matters. Apart from "Every Grain of Sand" there is nothing on any of these albums that contains lines to match "circled by the circus sands / with all memory and fate / driven deep beneath the waves." But then the same could be said of songs like "Masters of War," "It's a Hard Rain's a-Gonna Fall" or "It's Alright Ma (I'm Only Bleeding)," all of which evince a fundamentalist surety of a different stripe. Heavy-handed propaganda was hardly unique to Dylan's so-called Christian period. The critiques of Dylan on this point are often stilted or hypocritical, as in Greil Marcus' allegation that the artist was suddenly trying to "sell a pre-packaged doctrine he's received from someone else" (conservatives might just as well have said the same thing about his earlier espousals of '60s activism—in fact, they did). The better point, as Steve Turner has said, is that on *Slow Train, Saved,* and *Shot of Love,* Dylan often seems so intent on getting the message across that he fails to engage his listeners' imagination.

As indicated above, it has become standard practice in rock journalism to regard Dylan's little detour into Christianity from 1979 to 1981 as a gaffe, a major downturn in a career that has had numerous ups and downs. Even the artist's *Greatest Hits, Volume 3* ignores all material from his overtly evangelical period except for "Gotta Serve Somebody," which was a Top 40 hit (# 24 in 1979). The better critics, however, lament these lapses and, a bit penitent of earlier dismissals, now acknowledge that Dylan's "Christian work" was actually pretty good. John Bauldie, who wrote the liner notes for the *Bootleg* compilation reflects thus on the *musical* quality of Dylan's evangelistic performances from this period: "The concerts bewildered many and dismayed a few, but such was the power and driving force behind them, and so inspired were Dylan's own performances, that they were some of the most impressive and memorable that he's ever given."

Dylan's so-called Christian phase is nowhere near as out-of-sync with his overall career as most of his fans seem wont to believe. For one thing, long before his explicit avowals of faith, the imagery and concerns of biblical teaching were unusually prevalent in his work. He was quoting Jesus already in "The Times They Are a-Changin'": "the first one now will later be last." Even before that, on his very first album, he had sung spirituals to and about Jesus: "I wore three links of chain / Every link was Jesus' name / Keep your hand on that plow, hold on" ("Gospel Plow" cf. "In My Time of Dyin'," "Fixin' to Die"). The title song to his classic *Highway 61 Revisited* (Columbia, 1965) opens with the words, "God said to Abraham, 'Kill me a son!'" The song "Father of Night" from *New Morning* (Columbia, 1970) is a pious prayer. Long before his official conversion, Dylan regularly referred to his stunning masterpiece *John Wesley Harding* as "the first biblical rock album"—while most people seemed to think it was about the Old West, practically every song is rife with religious imagery. This is pretty obvious in "I Dreamed I Saw St. Augustine," but how many fans realized that "The Wicked Messenger" was inspired by texts from Proverbs? Indeed it is startling now that people did not fully appreciate Dylan's biblical and often *New Testament* grounding all along. When Dylan sang, "I see my light come shining from the west unto the east / Any day now, any way now, I shall be released!" what exactly did people think he was singing *about*? (Cf. Matthew 24:27—actually Jesus said the light would shine from east to west, but that wouldn't have rhymed.) Like many other famous converts **(Barry McGuire, B. J. Thomas, Johnny Rivers)**, Dylan was singing and even *writing* gospel songs long before he was confessing personal allegiance to the gospel itself. In retrospect, Dylan's so-called Christian songs were of a piece with this material. In 1981, he claimed as much in an interview with New York DJ Dave Herman: "The music that I've always played is a healing kind of music, telling people, or hoping anyway, that whatever their sickness is, they can be healed." Notably, Dylan did not allow his art to be co-opted by the Religious Right; he did not sign with any Christian record company label; he did not publish any spiritual autobiography testimony books; and he did not drastically alter the values and commitments that had propelled him all along. He did not, for instance, write any antiabortion songs. He did not endorse gay-bashing or suddenly begin to rail against such

vices as drinking, smoking, and unmarried sex. Rather, the targets of his righteous indignation were what they had always been: materialism, militancy, pride, and injustice. His passions, in short, remained (as they had always been) more in line with the concerns of Christ than with the obsessions of modern-day Christians.

The other problem with regarding Dylan's three overtly Christian albums as part of a phase is that the so-called phase has never officially ended. In 1983, Dylan released *Infidels,* an album free of obviously evangelical songs. The contrast in content with the previous three records spurred rumors that Dylan had abandoned his faith, rumors abetted by the fact that he had recently traveled to Israel for his son's bar mitzvah and was known to have studied with the Lubavitch rabbis. But there was nothing on the album that conflicted with Christian teachings or morality. *Infidels* was, in that sense, just as Christian a record as anything ever made by **Bruce Cockburn** or **T Bone Burnett** *(CCM chose Infidels as one of their Ten Best Christian Albums of 1983, pairing it with Burnett's Proof through the Night and Cockburn's Trouble with Normal)*. As indicated above, Dylan had served notice in 1981 that he was through with *preaching,* but indicated (at that time) that this did *not* mean he had abandoned his faith. "This is no Maharishi trip with me," he told the *Los Angeles Times,* referring to the passing devotion paid to a famous guru by the Beatles and other celebrities, "Jesus is definitely not that to me."

The point, then, could simply be discernment of vocation or calling. Curiously, early in Dylan's career, he was often heralded as a prophet, a label he vehemently rejected. He preferred to be identified as an *entertainer.* "I'm just a song and dance man, really," he said at a famous press conference in 1967. When asked with what public figure he could most easily identify (Eldridge Cleaver? Abbie Hoffman? Bobby Kennedy?), he responded, "Dinah Shore." To many, therefore, it appears that after a brief stint of using his albums and concerts as pulpits for proselytizing, he concluded (correctly) that he was not meant to be an evangelist or a preacher, but, as always, an entertainer. Al Kasha, a Christian executive at Columbia records who, like Dylan, is ethnically Jewish, gave other reasons for Dylan backing off from his role as a singing evangelist. Kasha, who was close to Dylan and had become something of a spiritual mentor to him, told Mark Joseph (author of *The Rock and Roll Rebellion,* Broadman & Holman, 1999) that Dylan was concerned about being fair to his record company (Columbia) in light of the fact that his last two albums had not sold well. Further, Dylan had been disillusioned by the hypocrisy that he had witnessed on the part of certain evangelists who he had supported. As for the Lubavitch sect, Kasha said that he himself had studied there *as a Christian;* it was an intellectual group that provided good teaching on matters that Christians (particularly Christians of Jewish descent) would find enlightening.

In an interview with *Rolling Stone* in 1984, after *Infidels* came out, and in response to the rumors that he had converted from Christianity to Judaism, Dylan affirmed in no uncertain terms that he believed "the entire Bible literally." The reporter pressed him as to whether the Old and New Testaments are equally valid, and he said, "to me." Asked if he would try to convert Orthodox Jews to Christianity, he responded, "Well, yeah, if somebody asks me (about my beliefs), I'll tell 'em. But, I'm more about playing music, you know?" He then went on to talk at length about the book of Revelation and indicated that the song "Man of Peace" on *Infidels* is actually about the Antichrist who will come—though in contrast to his earlier predictions of "five or ten years," Dylan now said that he had no idea when it would be: "the end is at hand" but "it could be another 200 years." The *Bootleg* compilation also reveals that Dylan had recorded two very religious songs for *Infidels* that for some reason were not included. "Lord Protect My Child" is a father's prayer, expressing selfless concern for his child's future in a worrisome world. "Foot of Pride" is a powerful, prophetic song filled again with biblical imagery that promises judgment upon the proud and haughty (including, especially, evangelists who "build big universities" and "sing 'Amazing Grace' all the way to the Swiss banks"). Lou Reed did an inspired cover version of "Foot of Pride" for a tribute album celebrating Dylan's thirtieth year of recording (*The 30th Anniversary Concert,* Columbia, 1993).

In the years that have followed, Dylan watchers have been at a loss to determine the spiritual status of their idol. He told *Spin* magazine in 1986, "I'm not a believer in that born-again type thing," but that disclaimer struck most as a repudiation of a particular theological (and political) stance rather than an outright denial of the faith. His involvements with Judaism have evidently increased. He played for a Lubavitch telethon alongside his Torah observant son-in-law and wrote a blurb for a book one of the rabbis wrote on sexual modesty (Manis Friedman, *Doesn't Anyone Blush Anymore: Reclaiming Intimacy, Modesty, and Sexuality,* HarperSanFrancisco, 1990; Dylan's recommendation: "Anyone getting married should read this book"). He has often been spotted at temple services and, on at least one occasion, was invited to the front of the synagogue to open the ark. On the other hand, in 1997 he told a reporter from *Newsweek* that his "theology" could be found in songs like "Let Me Rest on a Peaceful Mountain," "Keep on the Sunny Side," and "I Saw the Light." "Here's the thing with me and the religious thing," he said, "I don't adhere to rabbis, preachers, evangelists, all of that. . . . I believe the songs." As many have noted, the three specific songs that he cited are gospel tunes, songs that speak of salvation in distinctively Christian terms. The

Hank Williams song he mentioned goes, "I wandered so aimless / life filled with sin, I wouldn't let my dear Savior in / Then Jesus came like a thief in the night . . . Praise the Lord, I saw the light."

What seems perfectly clear, contrary to popular perception, is that Dylan's devotion to biblical spirituality has remained a constant. Snippets of doubt arise here and there, such as in the line "I never could learn to drink that blood and call it wine" ("Tight Connection to My Heart")—whatever *that* means. But "When the Night Comes Falling from the Sky" from 1985's *Empire Burlesque* is an apocalyptic masterpiece that would have been right at home on any of the three officially Christian albums: "I'm asking for freedom / Freedom from a world that you deny / You'll give it to me now / Or I'll take it anyhow / When the night comes falling from the sky." It is followed by another judgmental song, "Something's Burning, Baby," which quotes Scripture left and right, warning the addressee that "You can't live by bread alone" (Deuteronomy 8:3) but promising that "charity is supplied to cover up a multitude of sins" (1 Peter 4:8). All this from what the rock press was celebrating as the "no-longer religious" Dylan. A little metaphor, a little parable, and only those with ears to hear will hear (Mark 4:10–12).

Also in 1985, when Columbia released Dylan's box set *Biograph,* the singer was asked to provide comments reflecting on the songs. He skipped some altogether, wrote just a line or two for others, but for "Every Grain of Sand" wrote an entire page of wandering thoughts on the state of society that seemed to be only loosely related to anything in the song. It was clear, however, that he had *not* renounced his faith, even if he chose to express it now in somewhat unconventional terms: "Make something religious and people don't have to deal with it, they can say it's irrelevant. 'Repent, the kingdom of God is at hand.' That scares the s**t out of people. . . . There comes a time, though, when you have to face facts and the truth is true whether you wanna believe it or not. . . . I like to keep my values scripturally straight—I like to stay a part of that stuff that don't change."

For the next fourteen years, Dylan sought to keep quiet about religion and most other things as well. Notably, he did continue to perform evangelical songs from his so-called Christian period in concerts, especially "Gotta Serve Somebody" and "In the Garden," sometimes announcing the latter song as being "about my hero." With the exception of *Oh Mercy* (Columbia, 1989), produced by **Daniel Lanois,** he spent the years from 1985 to 1999 in a creative slump. He put out compilation packages and a stellar live album (*MTV Unplugged*). He recorded albums of songs by other artists (*Good As I Been to You; World Gone Wrong*) and, in turn, inspired others to record his material for the grand *30th Anniversary Concert* tribute. He even opened his vaults and allowed spectacular and previously unreleased material to see the light of day *(Bootleg)*. All this kept him in the public consciousness, but more as a legend than as a player. The albums of new material, *Knocked Out Loaded, Down in the Groove,* and *Under the Red Sky,* were all critical and commercial disasters. In 1991, he was presented with a Lifetime Achievement Award at the Grammy celebration and passed on to the audience what he took to be the best advice his father ever gave him: "Son, it's possible to become so defiled in this world that your own mother and father will abandon you. And if this happens, God will always believe in your own ability to mend your ways."

In 1997, Dylan returned with *Time Out of Mind,* another **Daniel Lanois** production, and won his first Grammy since *Slow Train Coming.* The album was heralded, at first cautiously, then enthusiastically, as one of the very best records he had ever made and, surprisingly, it allowed some long-dormant sentiments to resurface. Lyrically, *Time Out of Mind* displays the perspective of one looking back on a life of faith. "I feel like I'm coming to the end of my way," Dylan sings, "but I know God is my shield and he won't lead me astray" ("Till I Fell in Love with You"). On another song, he speaks casually of something that happened as he "went to church on Sunday" and affirms that he knows "the mercy of God must be near" ("Standing in the Doorway"). And in considering his mortality, he asserts a bit tongue-in-cheek, "I'm just tryin' to get to heaven before they close the door" ("Tryin' to Get to Heaven").

Dylan seemed, to some, to be expressing explicit sentiments of faith again, minus the naivete and the pushiness from two decades back—but not necessarily minus the exuberance. When Dylan toured with Paul Simon in support of the album, the two folk legends opened their concert with a song called "Hallelujah! I'm Ready to Go!": "In the darkness of night not a star was in sight / on that highway that leads down below / then Jesus came in, and he saved my soul from sin / Hallelujah! I'm ready to go!" For Simon, who has never professed to be a Christian, the gospel song just seemed to be a musical adventure. But for Dylan, with his public and controversial Christian "past," and in light of his recent comments that his "theology is in the songs," the choice of *that* song as a concert opener was striking. On at least one occasion, Dylan also performed the hymn, "Rock of Ages" as part of his 1999 tour.

On the now infamous date of September 11, 2001, Dylan released his forty-third album at the age of sixty to more critical acclaim (a rare five-star review from *Rolling Stone*). *Love and Theft* has a distinctly different feel from *Time Out of Mind,* a more jubilant and traditionally melodic sound. Dylan samples a variety of styles, apparently intending a tour of American music (rockabilly, blues, cocktail lounge, saloon dance hall music). Dylan joked that the record is like "a greatest hits album but without the hits." Reviewers and fans alike noted

that the artist seemed to be enjoying himself and his music more than at any time in his career. Lyrically, the album is all over the place too—as Dylan himself put it, "it's about all the great themes—power, wealth, knowledge, and salvation." *Phantom Tollbooth* said, "he hits all the keys: life, death, love, women, faith, God, friendship, history, and heritage." Some of the songs inevitably seemed poignant in light of the national tragedies that marked the album's release. On "Mississippi," he sings about "sky full of fire, pain pourin' down." And in another song, he confesses, "I'm on the fringes of the night, fightin' back tears I can't control / Some people ain't human, they ain't got no heart or soul / But I'm a cryin' to the Lord, tryin' to be meek or mild / Yes, I cried for you, now it's your turn, you can cry a while" ("Cry a While").

In late 2001, Dylan gave a rare interview to *Rolling Stone*. At one point, he took off on a seemingly unprompted tangent and said, "You hear a lot about God these days: God the beneficent; God, the all-great; God, the Almighty; God, the most powerful; God, the giver of life; God, the creator of death . . . but if we know anything about God, God is *arbitrary*. So people better be able to deal with that, too."

The interviewer responded, "That's interesting, because so many people think that God is constant, you know, and unchanging."

"Oh, absolutely," Dylan said, apparently agreeing that God *is* constant and unchanging.

"But *arbitrary* would seem to imply a rather different view," the interviewer objected. "Is there something about the word *arbitrary* that perhaps I'm not understanding."

"No," said Dylan. "You can look it up in the dictionary."

What distinguishes Dylan from many (but not all) Christian artists is his refusal to identify himself with any particular manifestation of Christianity, be it a denomination (e.g., the Vineyard) or a community (e.g., JPUSA) or a movement (e.g., evangelicalism) or a subculture (contemporary Christian music). Like Bono (of **U2**) he appears to have some sort of a continuing relationship at least with God, and perhaps with Christ, while remaining aloof from Christianity and from Christendom. In his song "Solid Rock," he maintained, "I'm holding on to the solid rock / I won't let go / and I can't let go." He has never given any indication that this perspective has changed, but as a *Phantom Tollbooth* reviewer observes, "Dylan has always resented being labeled and he has always preferred to keep people guessing." T Bone Burnett simply says, "the whole story of Bob Dylan is one man's search for God. The turns and steps he takes to find God are his business." John J. Thompson of *True Tunes* says, "Whether or not Dylan is currently a Christian is a fascinating question that may say more about the bias of the fan than about the beliefs of the singer." In late 2001, Burning Rose Productions announced the recording of a tribute album tentatively titled *Pressing On: The Gospel Songs of Bob Dylan.* Artists slated for the album did not include rock or pop stars but traditional gospel singers like **Shirley Caesar** and **Mighty Clouds of Joy.** A book on the spiritual journey of Dylan was announced for publication in 2002 by a new Christian publisher: *Restless Pilgrim* by Scott Marshall (Relevant). Meanwhile, Simon & Schuster was also planning to issue a series of autobiographical volumes (tentatively called *Chronicles*) in which Dylan would offer his own reflections on his life and work.

For trivia buffs: In 1980, the Christian Broadcasting Network (headed by Pat Robertson and responsible for *The 700 Club*) unwittingly used an image of Bob Dylan in a design for a Bible cover. The picture was a publicity photo from Dylan's 1976 *Hard Rain* TV special. The CBN marketers did not recognize the photograph as a picture of Dylan; they used it because they thought the person "looked like Jesus."

Christian radio hits: "Gotta Serve Somebody" (# 4 in 1980); "I Believe in You" (# 18 in 1979); "Property of Jesus" (# 4 in 1982).

Dove Awards: 1978 Album by a Secular Artist *(Slow Train Coming).*

Grammy Awards: 1979 Best Rock Vocal Performance, Male ("Gotta Serve Somebody"); 1994 Best Traditional Folk Album *(World Gone Wrong);* 1997 Album of the Year *(Time Out of Mind);* 1997 Best Contemporary Folk Album *(Time Out of Mind);* 1997 Best Male Rock Vocal Performance ("Cold Irons Bound"); 2001 Best Contemporary Folk Album *(Love and Theft).*

Dynamic Twins

Noel Arthurton, voc.; Robbie Arthurton, voc. 1991—*Word 2 the Wise* (Broken); 1993—*No Room 2 Breathe* (Brainstorm); 1995—*40 Days in the Wilderness;* 1996—*Above the Ground* (Metro One).

The rap duo Dynamic Twins describe their hip-hop urban music loudly and proudly as "holy ghost funk." Noel and Robbie Arthurton actually are identical twins and they were raised in the Bronx before moving to California as teenagers. As their musical career took off, they worked first as dancers in New York's Dance System 10 and then later as rappers with JC and the Boyz and **SFC.** *Word 2 the Wise* was an early entry in Christian hip-hop. *CCM* noted that two tracks ("He's All I Need" and "We Need Love") sound forcibly radio-ready, but the other twelve have a toughness that would impress "the staunchest gangsta, were it not for the lyrics." *True Tunes* would hail *No Room 2 Breathe* as "a landmark in the Christian rap industry," in large part due to the use of "live instruments" (as opposed to programmed ones). The Twins established basic "stream of consciousness rap" as their trademark style, but by *40 Days in the Wilderness* they were integrating such West Coast elements as sung choruses into the mix. *Above the Ground* reveals what *CCM* called "a happy medium" between the New York roots and California influences. Like most rap artists in the late '90s, the Twins were constantly on the lookout for ways to rejuvenate their tired genre. "Dying to Live" features flamenco guitar and brassy industrial keyboards. Thematically, the group alternates between songs that offer encouragement in life's struggles and ones that promise judgment on the unrepentant. "The Blood Cries" exalts "brotherhood" or community; "Reap What You Sow" suggests that AIDS is divine punishment for immorality.

For trivia buffs: Robbie Arthurton played keyboards on an early record by 2 Live Crew.

e (a.k.a. e band)

See **Greg Volz**.

Eager

Patrick Andrew, bass, voc.; Paul Eckberg, drums; Mark Kloos, gtr.; Greg Pope, gtr., voc. 1997—*Eager* (Questar Mission).

Minnesota combo Eager was formed in 1997 by Patrick Andrew of **PFR** after that band's demise. As with **PFR,** Andrew shares lead vocals, this time with guitarist Greg Pope instead of with Joel Hanson. Pope formerly played with a band called Someday Soon, and Eckberg and Kloos were together in Apple Green. Eager's self-titled debut album was produced by Jimmie Lee Sloas of **The Imperials** and **Dogs of Peace.** The band has an edgier sound than **PFR,** though it continues to favor a similar blend of modern rock and pop. They seem to be strongly influenced by the Beatles (in a manner similar to Badfinger), and they also bear similarities to the '90s power-pop combo Jellyfish. The song "Crimson for Downey Flake" employs a new take on a biblical metaphor for forgiveness ("though your sins be as scarlet, they will be white as snow," Isaiah 1:18). "Touch" is a heavier guitar song about spiritual oppression ("I cannot touch what touches me"). "Decide for You" is a ballad expressing the need for personal commitment: "I've decided for me / But I can't decide for you." The group performed a cover of the Go-Go's "We've Got the Beat" on their 1997–1998 tour.

Christian radio hits: "Crimson for Downey Flake" (# 24 in 1997); "Decide for You" (# 17 in 1998).

Joni Eareckson (a.k.a. **Joni Eareckson Tada**)

As Joni Eareckson: 1981—*Joni's Song* (Word); 1982—*Spirit Wings*. As Joni Eareckson Tada: date unknown—*I Got Wheels* (Word); date unknown— *Let God Be God; Harps and Halos* (label unknown).

www.joniandfriends.org

Joni Eareckson was born in 1949 in Baltimore, Maryland, and at age seventeen became a quadriplegic as a result of a diving accident. Unable to use her hands, she subsequently learned to paint by holding a brush in her teeth and created numerous inspirational artworks, some of which have been sold as prints in Christian bookstores. Her autobiography, *Joni* (Zondervan, 1976), became a best-selling testimony of faith overcoming adversity and was made into a motion picture distributed by World Wide Pictures. She has subsequently written numerous devotional books and writes a regular column for *Moody Monthly* magazine. Her advocacy for disabled persons earned her a Presidential appointment to the National Council on Disability for three-and-a-half years. In 1993, she was named "Churchwoman of the Year" by the Religious Heritage Foundation. She was the first woman to be honored by the National Association of Evangelicals as their "Layperson of the Year" and, in 1998, she received an honorary Doctor of Humane Letters from Columbia University. She began recording albums of Christian music in 1981. Her debut *Joni's Song* attracted the most attention, with songs by **Honeytree** and Kurt Kaiser. She also covers **Larry Norman**'s "I Am a Servant" and **David Meece**'s "We Are the Reason." In 1982, she married Ken Tada and continued to write and record under the name Joni Eareckson Tada. Her albums contain inspiring songs in a basic MOR tradition. *Harps and Halos* is a collection of children's songs.

Christian radio hits: "Hosanna" (# 20 in 1983).

Earthsuit

David Hutchisen, drums; Adam LaClave, voc.; Paul Meany, kybrd.; Roy Mitchell, bass; Dave Rumsey, gtr. 2000—*Kaleidoscope Superior* (Sparrow).

www.earthsuit3d.com

New Orleans modern rock combo Earthsuit got its start in a Bourbon Street coffeehouse called Café Joel where Adam LaClave and Paul Meany played their songs for passersby and eventually attracted the additional musicians who now provide the band with a full, eclectic sound. The debut album was produced by David Leonard, who has previously been responsible for projects by the **Indigo Girls,** John Mellencamp, Oingo Boingo, Prince, and Toto. It has been variously described as "a musically innovative melting pot" and a "melange of electronica, reggae, jazz, and rock." The creative element in Earthsuit's approach is that rather than performing various songs in various styles, as do most eclectic bands, they try to pour diverse styles into every song. Thus, the opening track, "One Time," begins with a loping reggae groove, then moves into a metallic riff with a rapcore chorus. The band uses a similar approach to its lyrics. "Whitehorse" superimposes apocalyptic imagery on scenes of everyday life, such that one cannot be sure whether it is about Christ's return or abiding presence. "Said the Sun to the Shine" presents a dialogue between the sun and its light, apparently as exemplary of the relationship between God and God's creation. Meany says, "Our message is taking God out of the box." Again, he explains the band's take on ministry this way: "We're not trying to seem spiritual, but what motivates us is our desire to worship God. We just do what's in our hearts."

East to West

Neal Coomer; Jay DeMarcos. 1993—*East to West* (Benson); 1995—*North of the Sky.*

The pop duo East to West formed in 1993 at Lee College in Cleveland, Tennessee, where Neal Coomer and Jay DeMarcos were both students and members of a vocal ensemble called Danny Murray and New Harvest. Coomer (from Columbus, Ohio) and DeMarcos (from Louisville, Kentucky) had both attended regional high schools for the performing arts as teenagers. East to West had a sound that DeMarcos likened to general market bands Level 42 or Go West—very pop oriented with

"punchy horns, driving rhythms, and real hooky melodies." The group toured with **Al Denson** and **4 Him** before disbanding in 1997. *The Lighthouse* likened their sound to "a more jazzy version of **4 Him** with less harmonies." Both albums mix up-tempo songs and ballads, avoiding anything edgy, gritty, or "alternative." The debut album, which includes a cover of **Mr. Mister**'s "Kyrie," earned the group a Dove nomination for Best New Artist. Their Number One hit "Prince of Peace" was written by **Michael O'Brien.** Lyrically, East to West's songs focused on the love and mercy of God and on celebrating life in Christ.

Christian radio hits: "Welcome to the Next Level" (# 3 in 1994); "Prince of Peace" (# 1 in 1994); "Hungry for You" (# 3 in 1995); "Heart on the Line" (# 16 in 1995); "This Time Around" (# 5 in 1995); "Still in Love" (# 9 in 1995); "Live Like I'm Leaving" (# 19 in 1996); "Talk to Me" (# 15 in 1996).

East West

Mike "House" Housen, gtr.; James "JJ" Jenkins, bass; Mike Tubbs, voc., gtr.; Bobby Vegura, drums. 2001—*A Light in Guinevere's Garden* (Floodgate).

www.powerjams.com

East West is a diverse modern rock band that flirts with rapcore and a number of other contemporary styles. "We don't like to get pigeonholed," says lead singer and screamer, Mike Tubbs. Their debut album, *A Light in Guinevere's Garden,* opens with a track called "Wake" that bears some similarities to Korn, but other songs ("She Cries," "Superstar") would be more likely to summon images of Foo Fighters, with inferences from **U2.** The overall sound is hardcore, with lots of guitar banging and metal riffs. The common thread to the disparate material appears to be a passionate expression of heartfelt emotion. "We just write music that tries to inspire people, or that inspires us," says Tubbs, noting that the ballad "Let You Go" will "definitely make listeners sentimental in some way or another." A track called "Song X" was also included on the soundtrack to the motion picture *Extreme Days.* The group takes its name from Psalm 103:12.

Chris Eaton

1986—*Vision* (Reunion); 1995—*Wonderful World* (Sparrow); 1998—*What Kind of Love.*

www.chriseaton.com

British pop crooner Chris Eaton (b. 1958) is best known as a songwriter, whose compositions have been performed by Christian artists like **Susan Ashton, Bliss Bliss, Eric Champion, Michael English, The Imperials, Point of Grace, Billy Sprague, Russ Taff, Kathy Troccoli, Truth,** and **Wayne Watson**—and by other artists listed below. He has also written songs for mainstream stars Janet Jackson and Sheena Easton and, especially, for crossover Christian artists **Amy**

Grant, Cliff Richard, and **Donna Summer.** Raised in the West Midlands of England, Eaton performed in the '80s with the group Lyrix. Several of his songs were recorded by English sensation **Cliff Richard** ("Lost in a Lonely World," "Summer Rain," "Where Do We Go from Here," "Discovering"). He then formed a songwriting partnership with **Amy Grant,** contributing to two songs on her classic *Unguarded* album ("Stepping in Your Shoes," "Sharayah") before cutting his own debut album, *Vision,* a **Brown Bannister-**produced record that placed four songs on the Christian hit radio charts.

Eaton did not come out with an immediate follow-up to his debut album in the usual fashion of new Christian artists. Instead, he took nearly a decade off from recording and devoted his time to writing songs. He provided **Cliff Richard** with several more memorable tracks ("Under Your Spell," "Joanna," "All the Time You Need," "Saviour's Day"). He cowrote "Hats" with Grant for her *Heart in Motion* album, then wrote "Little Town" and collaborated with her on several more songs for her Christmas projects ("Emmanuel, God with Us," "A Christmas to Remember," "Christmas Lullabye"). Grant also wrote new lyrics to an Eaton song, "Breath of Heaven," turning it into a very popular contemporary Christmas carol that has since been recorded by Vince Gill, Melissa Manchester, and **Donna Summer.** When at last Eaton did return to recording, the result was an album that reflected deeply on the maintenance of faith in the midst of struggles. Eaton talked openly about the breakup of his marriage four years before and about the conflicting grace and shame that he had experienced while going through the divorce. In addition to his own version of "Breath of Heaven" (with Eaton's original, non-Christmas lyrics), *Wonderful World* features the song "Remember Me," which deals sensitively with the tearing apart of a relationship, and "Something New," which draws on Isaiah 43 to reflect on God's offer of renewal and hope. "Everlasting Love" is adult contemporary pop in the vein of **Michael W. Smith,** praising the surety and permanence of God's love. "Harvest Years" sounds like a Sting outtake.

Three years later, *What Kind of Love* would be a happier album, filled with what *CCM* called "finely crafted soul and R&B-influenced adult contemporary sounds." The title track is another Eaton-Grant collaboration, and "God So Loved the World" had been a Dove-nominated hit for **Jaci Velasquez.** Eaton sounds a bit like Sting again on "Old Friends," a song about being at peace with the world, with life, and with God. "Boat of Devotion" (written with Marty Magehee of **4 Him**) features a Celtic melody, enhanced by **Troy Donockley**'s flute. "That's What Faith is For" is a gospel-tinged anthem. *What Kind of Love* was released in Britain a year earlier with a different title (*Cruisin',* Alliance, 1997).

Eaton has also written or cowritten Christian radio hits for **Lisa Bevill** ("No Condemnation"), **4 Him** ("Lay It All on the Line"), **Reneé García** ("Living in the Vertical," "I See Love," "The Bounce," "Perfection"), **The Imperials** ("In the Promised Land"), **Tony Melendez** ("Ways of the Wise"); **Paul Smith** ("Under a Moonlit Night"), **Russ Taff** ("Believe in Love"), **Jaci Velasquez** ("Flower in the Rain"), and **Sheila Walsh** ("Surrendering" and "Heaven is Holding Us Now").

Christian radio hits: "It Was Love" (# 4 in 1986); "Love for the Common Man" (# 12 in 1986); "Don't Underestimate My Love" (# 1 for 2 weeks in 1987); "When My Heart Breaks" (# 8 in 1987); "Everlasting Love" (# 2 in 1995).

Vince Ebo

1992—Love Is the Better Way (Warner Alliance).

African American baritone Vince Ebo has become a tragic footnote in the history of contemporary Christian music. Born in Honolulu and raised in Sacramento, he pursued a career in music as a session singer with considerable success. He provided vocals for projects by Ben E. King and Todd Rundgren and sang jingles for such well-known companies as Wendy's hamburgers, Alamo rental cars, and J.C. Penney department stores. He served as lead vocalist for a number of Los Angeles based groups, including Visions, Sun Bear, and The Fit. At one point he joined **Charlie Peacock**'s band and, influenced by hearing Peacock's testimonies on stage, gave his life to Christ and determined to devote his gifts increasingly to Christian music. He supplied background vocals for **Jimmy Abegg, Margaret Becker, Maria Muldaur, Ron David Moore, Patsy Moore,** and **Michael W. Smith.** As an official member of the Charlie Peacock Acoustic Trio (with Peacock and Abegg), he is featured on their album *Live in the Netherlands,* which was not released until 1999. Ebo cowrote the song "Thin But Strong Cord" (with Abegg and Peacock), which was a Christian radio hit for Abegg in 1991. In 1992, Ebo recorded his own debut album of original songs. *Love Is the Better Way* was well received, offering what *CCM* called "an array of contemporary black pop forays" from '70s soul to modern R&B ballads. Lyrically, the album focuses strongly on positive themes of love (the title track) and forgiveness ("It's Over," "Forgiveness"). In interviews, Ebo highlighted these themes, emphasizing that Christianity is "a smiling type of event—a joyous thing." He contrasted the negative "repent or burn" preaching he had heard as a child with the witness he hoped to convey as a joy-filled child of God: "I've got God in my life and that's why I'm smiling. I want people to look at me and say, 'Hey, check this cat out!' " Unfortunately, Ebo had personal struggles the nature of which remain unknown. In December of 1993, he took his own life.

Christian radio hits: "Make It Work" (# 3 in 1992); "Forgiven" (# 4 in 1992); "(I Will Not Be) Shaken" (# 14 in 1993).

Echelon

Rob Carter, gtr.; Jon Grant, voc., gtr.; Steve Koning, kybrd.; Rob Lockey, bass; Chris Middleton, drums. 1996—*Shiver* (Liquid Disc).

Echelon was an art-rock group that released one album of Scripture-based melodic songs. The album *Shiver* was produced by Andrew Horrocks of **The Awakening** and **One Hundred Days.** The songs seem to be derived from psalms and prayers found in the Bible. The album opens with its strongest track, "Kneel," which shimmers with three-part harmonies suspended over energetic lyrics. "I Am Listening" sounds like an outtake from **The Choir.** "Crawl" has a more gritty sound appropriate to its lyric: "I could climb a mountain / But I would fall / To be in your presence / I'd rather crawl."

The group that released "Shiver" is not related to another Minneapolis band named Echelon that has released five independent albums (1995—*Some Assembly Required;* 1998—*Core;* 1999— *This Is Really Living;* 2000—*The Te Deum Sessions;* 2001—*Same Today*). For the latter band, see www.echelonministries.com.

Echo Hollow

Matthew Fallentine, bass; Gary Lenaire, gtr.; Guy Ritter, voc.; Matt Rosenblum, drums. 1999—*Diet of Worms* (independent).

www.echohollow.com

Echo Hollow is the project of two former members of the Christian metal band **Tourniquet** (Gary Lenaire and Guy Ritter). Their debut album offers a number of tracks that recall the old **Tourniquet** sound, but a few (e.g., the distortion-free finger-picking "Take My Shoes") that point in surprising new directions. The album's title has no culinary implications but refers to the council at which Martin Luther was excommunicated from the Catholic Church (a *Diet* is a Church governing board, and "Worms" is the city in Germany where the Diet met). The title track to the album celebrates Luther's courageous reliance on Scripture when he was condemned by church authorities at that council. The song "Thursday" addresses the spiritual dearth behind America's epidemic of school shootings with specific reference to the shooting at Thurston High School (in Springfield, Oregon), which both Lenaire and Ritter attended. Another song ("Sad") offers a plea for "Victor Ramirez and any other Christian who has lost his way" to return to God (*Phantom Tollbooth* confused the unknown Ramirez with former **Tourniquet** bassist Victor Macias and incorrectly reported that the song was addressed to him). Theologically, Echo Hollow stands firmly in the conservative Reformed tradition, emulating such popular theologians as Francis Schaeffer, R. C. Sproul, B. B. Warfield, and Charles Hodge. They post articles and notices at their website that refute silly and nonscriptural notions popular among some Christians (like the idea of an im-

pending rapture) while nevertheless revealing a tilt toward fundamentalism and political agendas of the Religious Right.

The Echoing Green

Joey Belville, prog., voc. // Dave Adams, drums; Jesse Dworak, kybrd.; Chrissy Franklin, voc. 1994—*Defend Your Joy* (Myx); 1995—*Aurora 7.2;* 1996—*Science Fiction;* 1997—*Hope Springs Eternal;* 1998—*The Echoing Green* (SaraBellum); *Electronica* (Different Drum); 1999—*Glimmer of Hope* (Flaming Fish); 2000—*Supernova* (Red Hill); 2001—*Music from the Ocean Picture* (Different Drum).

The Echoing Green has been one of Christian music's primary techno groups. The band is masterminded by Albuquerque, New Mexico, dance sage Joey Belville, who refers to the group's style as "aggressive smile-pop." It was officially started in 1992 by Belville and friend Aaron Bowman while both were in college. On early albums, The Echoing Green was simply a one-man band with various musicians working under Belville's direction, but he has told *Bandoppler* that around 1998 he bonded with three of his touring musicians such that they became "an actual band." Belville proudly lists Duran Duran as his biggest influence and says that he strives to write songs that, though computer driven, would stand on their own apart from all the blips and bleeps for which techno music is famous.

Defend Your Joy established the group as an energetic synth-pop band featuring Belville's powerful, melodic vocals. Songs are typically rhythmic, with strong hooks and soft female backing vocals lending what one critic described as a "relentlessly cheerful" tone. The album includes a buoyant title track with uncredited vocals by **Riki Michele** and an (also uncredited) cover of the song "Pray" by Prince. The group was immediately compared to general market act Erasure, though Belville objected to the comparison and told *The Lighthouse,* "With the next record, I will ditch that forever. I hate that. There's nothing that irritates me more than when people say, 'you sound like Erasure.' " *Aurora 7.2* offers only two new songs ("Aurora," "End of the Day") along with remixes of tracks from *Defend Your Joy* by such notables as **Scott Blackwell, Ian Eskelin,** and Greg Hobgood (of **Prodigal Sons**). *Science Fiction* includes a cover of **Joy Electric**'s "Candy Cane Carriage," but otherwise is mostly more remixes, including four different versions of "Aurora." One of these is by Kevin 131 of **Aleixa** and another one features just Belville on piano and Matt Slocum of **Sixpence None the Richer** on cello. The former prefigure what was to come on *Hope Springs Eternal,* an album of almost all new material on which Kevin 131 adds his industrial, crunchy guitar throughout. The song "Oxygen" (which Belville says "uses the air around us as a metaphor for how badly we need the breath of God"), was later picked up for use in a TV series called *First Wave* on the Sci-Fi cable channel ("unfortunately, the show's kind of lame," said Belville). As a whole, the album evinces what *Release* called "a bubbly blend of keyboard and electric-guitar pop akin to secular band Erasure."

On the self-titled *The Echoing Green,* Belville sought to broaden his horizons a bit. "All my other albums focused on healing and hope," he told *CCM,* "which is great—but after several albums, you're ready to write about other emotions." The song "Empath" speaks about not becoming desensitized to the world's pain. On "Supermodel Citizen," Belville adopts the point of view of a teenage girl who "thinks her self-worth is determined by her bra size." The album also includes a cover of Men without Hats' 1982 hit, "Safety Dance," and a worshipful overtly Christian song, "Redemption." The standout song "Hide" (written by Jyro Xhan of **Mortal/Fold Zandura**) features the simple chorus, "Let me hide myself in Jesus' care." Notably, *The Echoing Green* was recorded with no guitars. With the assistance of the mainstream band Deepsky, Belville crafted one-hundred-percent computer-generated songs that created Euro-pop soundscapes with strong melodic centers. The next album, *Electronica,* was an ad-hoc collection of odds and ends that Belville says he put together for the Christian synth/pop underground. In addition to remixes of previous material, the album offers Echoing Green's take on the Band Aid classic "Do They Know It's Christmas?" and on **Stryper**'s "You Won't Be Lonely." *Glimmer of Hope* is a live album recorded at the 1998 Tom-Fest festival. On *Supernova,* the group does at last seem like "an actual band," offering guitar-driven dance songs that have more of a Duran Duran feel than those on any of the previous albums. *Phantom Tollbooth* praised *Supernova* as Echoing Green's most mature project, musically and lyrically. Standout tracks include the opening title cut, and an uncommon ballad called "Waterfall." A song called "Liberation" expresses how God led Belville out of a period of depression and self-doubt. The record concludes with the poignant, "Nightfall and Splendor": "When the waters of my soul threaten to run dry / There your power holds . . . turning the tide." The band's 2001 release, *Music from the Ocean Picture,* was described by *HM* as sticking reverently to the "almost rigid standard of Euro-techno style" with a couple of edgier tracks ("Trip," "Noise"). Less edgy crowd pleasers include the sugary sweet "Goodbye" and "Beautiful," a synth love song. Belville released the album independently over the Internet and maintained that he intended it as a project for the general market. The song "Epiphany," he maintained, "is pretty much about our decision to say a quiet farewell to the Christian music industry—but that doesn't mean saying farewell to Christianity."

Eden Burning

Charlotte Ayrton; Charles Ingram; Mowf; Paul Northrup; Michael Simpson. 1990—*Thin Walls* (label unknown); 1991—*Much More Than Near* [EP]; 1992—*Vinegar and Brown Paper* (Storyville); 1993—*Smilingly Home;* 1994—*Mirth and Matter* (R.E.X.); *You Could Be the Meadow* [EP] (label unknown); 1995—*Be an Angel* [EP]; 1996—*Brink* (Alliance).

A progressive folk group from Gloucester, England, Eden Burning had a sound similar to a British version of **Caedmon's Call.** Their soft rock sound was driven by six- and twelve-string acoustic guitars, complemented by mandolin, harmonica, and woodwind whistles, and their songs were often upbeat, rhythmic numbers intended to produce toe-tapping. *True Tunes* described their sound as "Celtic-pop and alterna-jigs, like a happy, sober, well-adjusted version of The Pogues." The song "Much More Than Near" expresses the presence of God in creation. *Smilingly Home* is a live album, featuring concert versions of songs from the previous recordings as well as a cover of **The Waterboys**' "Medicine Bow." With *Mirth and Matter,* the band adopted somewhat tighter, more electric arrangements that brought their sound more in line with mainstream alternative acoustic rock. The group disbanded after an emotional farewell performance at England's 1996 *Greenbelt* Festival.

Eden's Bridge

David Bird, gtr.; Terl Bryant, drums, perc.; Richard Lacy, kybrd.; Sarah Lacy, voc.; Jon Large, bass. 1997—*Celtic Psalms* (Straightway); *Celtic Worship;* 1998—*Celtic Praise;* 1999—*Celtic Reflections on Hymns; Celtic Worship 2.*

Terl Bryant of **Iona** joined with other musicians interested in the revival of Celtic music to plumb the rich liturgical depths of that tradition. They released several albums of worship music under the name Eden's Bridge. The albums cover both traditional and original songs, played with the traditional native instruments of Ireland, Scotland, and Wales. Described by *Phantom Tollbooth* as "the place where MOR and Celtic meet," the albums are more Celtic in style than theme; i.e., the use of distinctively Celtic imagery is rare. The 1998 *Celtic Praise* album includes distinctive renditions of "Amazing Grace" and "Thy Word" (written by **Amy Grant**).

Edge of Forever

See **Final Judgement**

Edin-Ådahl

Frank Ådahl, voc., kybrd.; Simon Ådahl, bass, gtr., voc., kybrd.; Bertil Edin, bass, gtr., voc., kybrd.; Lasse Edin, voc., kybrd. 1983—*Alibi* (Refuge); 1984—*X-Factor;* 1987—*Signs* (Eagle One); *Miracle* (Edge); 1989—*Big Talk* (Refuge); 1990—*Into My Soul* (Alarma); 1991—*Revival;* 1992—*Edin-Ådahl.*

Two sets of multi-talented brothers made up the hardworking Swedish band Edin-Ådahl, which had a sound similar to that of the **Allies.** Critic Brian Quincy Newcomb would write in 1990 (seven years after the fact) that "when Edin-Ådahl released its 1983 record *Alibi,* they singlehandedly raised the standard for production values that we would expect from Christian artists." Like **DeGarmo and Key,** Edin-Ådahl created records that were comparable in musical competence and technical quality to anything being produced in the general market. They suffered from poor distribution, however, and for some years their albums evinced a more devastating problem: lousy lyrics. The group struggled to overcome language barriers, writing their lyrics in English, and though they managed to gain more airplay on Christian radio stations in America than most international acts, critics ripped their songs apart, pointing out clumsy and simplistic rhymes. For example, the aforementioned Newcomb, who thought so highly of *Alibi*'s production values, went on to say this: "Relying heavily on creedal stock-phrases and 'Christianese,' Edin-Ådahl offers a naive triumphalism that merely restates sterile truths, without the human emotion and flesh that make such truth applicable to real life situations." But by *Into My Soul, CCM* magazine was willing to declare the group had finally "arrived." They offered easy going R&B songs punctuated by crisp, Memphis-style horns. The sort of title track, "Heaven (Into My Soul)" would become their first big hit in America, followed quickly by "Like a Wind." In Sweden, the latter song won a national competition to become the country's 1990 entry in the annual European Song Fest. Notably, "Heaven" and "Like a Wind" are two of the more obvious spiritual-message songs on the album. Reversing his criticism of the group's predictable "Christianese," Newcomb would now observe that "those into direct Christian lyrics will find little on *Into My Soul* to meet their expectations, but those willing to dig a little deeper will find strong pop with insight into the human predicament." The same strengths are evident on *Revival,* which would bring the band unprecedented crossover success in their native land. The title track rose to Number Three on Sweden's general market charts (nestled between hits by Madonna and Michael Jackson). Other standout tracks on *Revival* include the Beatlesque ballad "Take Me through the Tears" and the hook-filled "Paradise." The song "Let It Shine" is an adult contemporary ballad. Simon Ådahl and Bertil Edin both also released solo albums for Refuge in 1985, titled *I'm in Touch* and *Cross the Border,* respectively. Lasse Edin formed a group called The Outsiders as a side project in 1990 and released *Unbounded Land* on Cantito.

Christian radio hits: "Your Heart Is in His Hands" (# 39 in 1984); "Yes, I Know" (# 14 in 1988); "Heaven (Into My Soul)" (# 1 for 2 weeks in 1990); "Like a Wind" (# 1 for 2 weeks in 1991); "This Fire" (# 1 for 2 weeks in 1991); "Revival" (# 5 in 1992); "Paradise" (# 16 in 1992).

EDL

See **Every Day Life.**

Rune Edvardsen

1998—*At Your Front Door* (Prima).

Swedish power-pop singer Rune Edvardsen is described by *True Tunes* as that country's "answer to '80s **Petra.**" With a voice similar to that of **John Schlitt,** Edvardsen mixes ballads and midtempo rock songs on *At Your Front Door* that seem like a time-warp back to *On Fire* or *This Means War.* His lyrics are also **Petra**esque in their simplicity ("Jesus come inside of me / Please won't you set me free") and are delivered with heartfelt if bombastic enthusiasm.

David Edwards

1980—*David Edwards* (Myrrh); 1983—*Get the Picture;* 1985—*Dreams, Tales and Lullabies* (Light); 2001—*Christmas Carols Old and New* (Jondeaux).

www.studioedwards.com

David Edwards was one of Christian music's first new-wave artists, arriving on the scene at a time when the overly commercial and contrived genre of contemporary Christian music needed an infusion of new life. With strong pop sensibilities and roots in Christian music that go back to the early Jesus movement revival, Edwards was nevertheless a bit too countercultural for the industry to market successfully. He would come to be best remembered for pioneering a style that was subsequently developed by bigger stars like **Steve Taylor** and **Sheila Walsh**—both of whom have named him as a prominent influence. He should not be confused with the David Edwards who fronts the Christian band **Sixteen Horsepower.**

Edwards was born in Belleville, Illinois, and brought up in Southern California. He was raised in a Christian home—his father a Nazarene minister of music and his mother, a choir director. He studied graphic arts and music theory at Pasadena City College (and, later, computer programming at Berkshire Community College in 1986). In 1973, he became bass player for **J.C. Power Outlet,** one of the most important non-Calvary Chapel bands associated with the Jesus movement. He left the group in 1975 to pursue a solo career, signing a contract with **Larry Norman**'s Solid Rock. This began a multi-year quest for what Norman called "ten great songs," a seemingly unattainable goal that proved both discouraging and inspiring to the artist. "We'll enter the studio as soon as you have ten great songs," Norman told Edwards year after year until the latter finally found another producer. Many of Norman's charges experienced similar frustrations, but years later Edwards would remember the imposed sabbatical with mixed emotions, admitting that it spared him "the lifelong embarrassment" of having some early songs recorded. Around 1977, Edwards also came to know **Keith Green** at a Bible study held in Norman's apartment, and the two enjoyed a fruitful personal/professional relationship of song-swapping, jamming, and theological argument.

In 1980, Edwards reentered the world of Christian music with a sound and an attitude incongruent with industry expectations. Nevertheless, his three '80s projects were issued on Myrrh and Light, two labels that were not particularly famous for experimental ventures. The self-titled debut album brought hyperbolic responses from critics, who were somewhat desperate for someone to break out of the formulaic doldrums into which Christian music had settled. *CCM* began their review of *David Edwards* by saying, "David Edwards' first album is some of the best rock ever recorded for any market—Christian or secular. It is also the best album ever produced by Buddy King." *Cornerstone* called it "an album that will please everyone from new-wave fans to children of the '60s." Fan-turned-critic Ed Rock would later reflect on the record as possessing the same kind of frenetic energy that was to be found on Devo's *Whip It,* while also incorporating the social conscience of a **Larry Norman** or **Randy Stonehill. Steve Taylor** would eventually call it "the first truly *contemporary* Christian music album." Musically, *David Edwards* evinces a full '80s sound but merges this with pop sensibilities straight out of the '60s. This is most evident on an inspired cover of "Kicks," an antidrug song that had been a major hit for Paul Revere and the Raiders (# 4 in 1966). Edwards updates the song with additional verses, but does not try to Christianize it by changing the original words. "Commercial Suicide" reflects on **Bob Dylan**'s conversion to Christianity and on the spiritual content of his lyrics on *Slow Train Coming* ("Watch how you say it / we'll never play it"). "Nagging Optimism" presents faith in God as the antidote for cynicism and features what *Cornerstone* would call "one of those little riffs that sticks with the hearer for weeks." The song "Not Gonna Fall Away" was later covered by Taylor and Walsh on their *Trans-Atlantic Re-mixes* project.

While *David Edwards* would sound tame in a few years, it was unlike anything else in the Christian market in 1980—a full year before **Daniel Amos**'s *Alarma!* At the time the record was released, Edwards was living with his family in a converted barn on a farm in California's upper Ojai Valley. He spoke to *CCM* about his music, saying that he hoped to provide "wholesome recreation" for listeners, a novel concept that went against the prevalent notion at the time that the raison d'etre for all Christian music was ministry (edifying believers or evangelizing the unsaved) as opposed to mere entertainment. Edwards seemed to think that providing "wholesome recreation" (i.e., entertainment) could *be* a form of ministry, an idea that had not yet taken root in the burgeoning contemporary Christian music industry. He also questioned the commercialism of the latter institution and raised troubling questions about its fundamental tendencies:

There are a lot of what I call false values being presented not just by the rock music medium, but by the whole entertainment industry. We in the Christian community don't always do so well in rejecting some of those values. We do all right when it comes to rejecting things like drug abuse or promiscuous sex, but we're a little shaky when it comes to the sins of vanity or idol worship or other misplaced priorities that are an outgrowth of our celebrity consciousness.

Get the Picture is a more accessible offering than Edwards' debut album with a more commercial and less raw sound that would disappoint some critics. Still, the songs evince intelligent, probing lyrics that almost belie the pop tunes to which they are set, leading more than one reviewer to compare Edwards to **Bruce Cockburn** and **Mark Heard.** Thematically, the sophomore album reflects on the universal longing for love and acceptance. "Girls Like You" is sort of a male version of Janis Ian's "At Seventeen," articulating the thoughts of an average guy who doesn't get why the really pretty, popular girls aren't interested in him. "Anything But Love" deconstructs the looking-for-Mister-Goodbar ethos of the era, suggesting that a better word than *love* should be found to describe shallow romances constructed to meet people's immediate psychological needs. "How Could You Throw It All Away?" addresses the person whose prayers for a companion have been answered, who has what so many people want, and then finds a way to destroy it. Between 1981 and 1984, Edwards toured extensively, alone and with **Randy Stonehill,** including the *Greenbelt* festival and other stops throughout Britain.

The 1985 album *Dreams, Tales, and Lullabies* is very different from Edwards' previous projects. *CCM* would note, "now that everyone is doing new-wave, Edwards returns with a classical children's album for adults." It isn't exactly a children's album, but *Dreams, Tales, and Lullabies* was inspired by the fantasy stories of George MacDonald. The songs are soft, melodic, and elfin, as Edwards sings in a sweet voice buoyed by symphonic arrangements. "Empty Pockets" is a poetic nursery rhyme in the tradition of Shel Silverstein's more serious works; Edwards likens the "pebbles in his pocket" to revealing aspects of his inner self: "joy and sorrow, faith and doubt." Other standout cuts include "The Son and the Angels" (a Christmas carol) and "When He Comes," one of Christian music's best songs of anticipation: "When he comes / We will see the last of winter / Watch as sorrow turns to light / Every wrong will be made right." Inspiration for the latter lyrics comes from C. S. Lewis's *The Lion, the Witch and the Wardrobe.*

All three Edwards albums were ultimately reissued on Blind Records and made available through his website. He has also posted a manuscript at that site titled *The Devout Masque,* a literate and theologically sound critique of the false dichotomy between sacred and secular dimensions that seems to be definitive of the contemporary Christian music subculture. Edwards argues that the terms *secular* and *sacred* are used in ways that contradict Scripture: "On the one extreme, Christians have distorted the meaning of the word *secular,* which if used at all, should convey the idea of neutrality. On the other extreme, we have adopted such a narrow definition of *sacred* that much of the Bible itself fails to conform to it."

While retired from the performing end of the music business, Edwards would continue to write songs, including "This Friend of Old," covered by **Randy Stonehill** on *Return to Paradise.* He also cowrote a number of songs with Stonehill, including "Old Clothes," "Little Rose," and "Everything You Know Is Incorrect"—all performed by the latter artist—and "Always in Your Heart," performed by **Common Bond.** In 2001, Edwards produced an album of mostly traditional Christmas carols that would serve, in part, as a benefit for Compassion International's post-September 11 relief fund for victims of the terrorist attacks on New York City and Washington, D.C. The project includes the original Edwards/Stonehill composition "The World Was in His Hands" and a cover of "Miriam" by **Pierce Pettis.**

Elder

Cat Albanese, perc.; Joe Albanese, gtr., voc.; Willie Dizon, bass; Chris Gildersleeve, drums; Bryan Whitfield, gtr. 1996—*Used to Be Adorable* (Liquid Disc); 1997—*Plagues and Woes* (BulletProof).

Elder is a heavy modern rock band based in Portsmouth, Virginia. Their sound evidences more than a little grunge influence, reminding one *HM* reviewer of **Scaterd Few.** Strong inferences from **Michael Knott** and **LSU** are also detectable. The band has its roots in a group called Four Living Creatures, which included front man Joe Albanese, his wife, Cat, and bassist, Willie Dizon (who at that time was going by the name Willie Cigon). Albanese is the principal songwriter, and he crafts lyrics that are straightforward but unpredictable. The band's debut album, *Used to Be Adorable,* includes the songs "Number Nine" and "Iron Lung," which focus on the power of God. "Red Earth" looks at abortion through the eyes of a regretful mother. An atypical acoustic track called "Number Nine" sounds very much like the Grateful Dead. The *Plagues and Woes* album received little publicity, being reviewed only by *HM.* It opens with a song called "Sugar Medicine," which that magazine describes as "funky tribal modern rock interrupted by a killer metal lead."

Rick Eldridge

1975—*Peace* (Herald); 1977—*Images* (Klesis).

Rick Eldridge was associated with the ministry Seeds, Inc. and released two albums of MOR Jesus music in the mid '70s. *Harmony* magazine described him as having a "smoky, mellow voice" and his songs as "down-tempo and moody." Standout tracks on the *Peace* album include "Reach for the Light," "Testimony," and the worshipful, "Thank You, Jesus, You're My Friend."

The Electrics

Paul Baird, gtr.; Sam Horner, bass; David McArthur, drums. 1991—*Visions and Dreams* (Nelson Word); 1993—*Unplug* (custom); *Big Silent World* (Pila); 1995—*The Whole Shebang;* 1997—*The Electrics* (SaraBellum); 1998—*Have a Jar on Me* (5 Min. Walk); *Livin' It Up When I Die* (SaraBellum); 2000—*Danger Live* (ICC).

With electric guitars and bagpipes dueling for control of rambunctious party songs, the Scottish-Irish band known as The Electrics have carved out a place all their own in Christian music. There is no other artist that sounds like them (in American markets at least), and yet their sound is infectious, exciting, and certain to be copied. The Electrics formed in 1976 at an independent community church in Dumbarton, Scotland. Sam Horner is Irish, having moved to Dumbarton from Belfast eight years earlier. He retains an interest in all things Celtic, adding uilleann pipes, accordion, mandolin, fiddle, and other native instruments to The Electrics' eclectic mix. Paul Baird's interests lean toward R&B, and David McArthur is an unabashed metalhead. Still, The Electrics began as a Scottish "folk-rock band" and played music somewhat reminiscent of that of The Pogues or The Proclaimers for their early British albums. Their self-titled 1997 album marked their United States debut, compiling favorite songs from their previous outings, all re-recorded now with Masaki (of **Dime Store Prophets**) serving as producer. Seven additional musicians back the trio on the various instruments mentioned above, and the result is an unusually tight and authentic-sounding blend of foot-tapping, head-bobbing tunes. "Pour Me a Pint" retells the story of Jesus' encounter with the woman at the well (John 4) in a pub setting (e.g., a thirsty man asks, "I don't know what you're drinkin' but pour me a pint"). "The Jig" is a self-explanatory instrumental. "The Blessing" offers some lovely lyrics set to a calmer tone: "As you make your way through this world of ours / As you see the beauty of the morning dew / As you smell the summer flowers / As you pass away the hours / May the saints and Saviour watch over you." *CCM* magazine noted the band "blends the charm of traditional jigs and ballads with the reckless energy of punk."

Livin' It Up When I Die, produced by **Phil Madeira,** jumps way beyond the eponymous project on the strength of a few songs that emphasizes the *rock* half of the band's "folk-rock" moniker. The album kicks off with a boisterous song called "Party Goin' On Upstairs." Based loosely on the parable of the

Great Banquet in Luke 14, the song tells of a tenement dweller viewing the strange goings-on in the apartment above him: "The blind were showin' up to see what's goin' on / And the hungry for a banquet fit for kings / The lame kept me awake with their dancin' all night long / And the ones who couldn't speak started to sing." Likewise, the album's title track offers an energetic, almost raucous foretaste of the great party in the sky that awaits those who believe. Horner trots out a series of humorous lyrics regarding the musician friends he expects will join him there: "When my flesh and bones decay, I'll hang out with **Jimmy A** (i.e., **Jimmy Abegg**) . . . I'll sing with Bud and **Julie Miller,** I'm not just some coffin filler. . . . I'll be playin' blues with Kaiser (i.e., **Glenn Kaiser**) cause I'm more than fertilizer. . . . I'll be livin' it up when I die!" Other highlights include "Hey Paddy" (which *HM* called "Celtic rockabilly"), "Rolling Home," a more traditional song reminiscent of the group's earlier style, and the concluding "Face," which features **Phil Keaggy** on scorching guest guitar. **Julie Miller** (who covered Horner's "Back of Your Head" on her *Invisible Girl* album) sings on "Come Back Down."

John Elefante

1995—*Windows of Heaven* (Word); 1997—*Corridors* (Pamplin); 1999—*Defying Gravity.*

www.johnelefante.com

New York native John Elefante was lead singer for the general market band **Kansas** from 1981 to 1985. As such, he replaced original vocalist Steve Walsh, whose voice is heard on the band's biggest hits ("Carry On My Wayward Son," "Dust in the Wind"). Walsh left the band when he became disgruntled over the strong Christian influence that founding members **Kerry Livgren** and David Hope were bringing to the group's projects. With the addition of Elefante, Kansas essentially became a Christian group for two years, releasing the moderately successful albums *Vinyl Confessions* (1982) and *Drastic Measures* (1983). Elefante sang on the minor hit singles from those projects, "Play the Game Tonight" (# 17 in 1982) and "Fight Fire with Fire" (# 58 in 1983). He wrote the latter song (which he says deals with "standing up for your faith") with his brother Dino. Elefante left Kansas in 1985 when record company executives began pressuring the band to tone down the spiritual content of their lyrics. At about the same time, he produced and performed a song ("Young and Innocent") for the soundtrack to the motion picture *St. Elmo's Fire.* After leaving Kansas, Elefante formed **Mastedon** with his brother and also recorded three solo albums. He is blessed with a powerful and melodious voice that lends itself to the power-pop of his solo work more effectively than it did to Kansas art-rock. Musical references to supergroups like Kansas and Supertramp remain evi-

dent on Elefante's albums, but the closest general market analogies would probably have to be drawn to Paul McCartney and Wings, due in large part to strong similarities between McCartney's and Elefante's natural voices and practiced stylings.

Windows of Heaven reveals Elefante to be solidly locked in the mid '80s. For better or worse—and critical opinions varied—the record sounds like it could have been recorded the day after he left Kansas, i.e., ten years earlier. Without apology, he serves up ten power-pop arena-anthems that testify boldly to the love and mercy of God. The title track could be a Genesis outtake. Standout songs include the power ballads "That's Why God Made the Moon" and "This Is What Love Is" (a reply to Foreigner's power ballad, "I Want to Know What Love Is"). "What If Our World" calls for a reexamination of priorities in the midst of routine daily hassles: "What if our world was without love and all the things that really matter?" The energetic "Hold Me in Your Arms" is based on the biblical story of the prodigal son. "No One's Ever Died for Me Before" is lyrically powerful and "Hello, My Good Friend" is innovative, addressing people from the perspective of Jesus: "Hello, my good friend, what have you been doing since I've gone?" The latter track is eminently Beatlesque (or at least Wings-ish).

Corridors continues in the same vein, with the title song asking for God's leadership "down the corridor that leads me to the cross." The song "Not Just Any Other Day" reflects poignantly on the historical significance of Christ's crucifixion: "The people of the town began their ordinary lives / Unsuspecting of a world about to change." Another song, "Where Does Our Love Go?" presents the thoughts of a couple looking for direction in their relationship, along the lines of Chicago's "Where Do We Go from Here?" The song "Treasures of Heaven" encourages trust in God and asks, "Do we really want to know all the answers?" On the song "Eyes of My Heart," Elefante sounds very much like **Phil Keaggy,** who also knows how to do the McCartney thing. "I Know You're There" showcases Elefante's soaring vocals on a powerful melodic line celebrating the presence of God that is recognizable in nature.

Elefante's next album, *Defying Gravity,* explores the theme of absolute surrender and devotion to God. The repetitive title track is the album's low point musically, but it employs an effective metaphor for resisting the "pull of the world" with regard to things that would separate believers from Christ. The same theme is brought out in the closing song, "Give It All Away." Musically, Elefante strives to broaden his repertoire of sounds on *Defying Gravity,* trying a bit of country swing on "Pass the Flame" (about continuing in a tradition of faith) and emulating the Eagles on "Home with a View." The song "Don't Leave the Band" revisits Chicago again, with affecting do-do-do harmonies. "The Stream" has classical influences, with a full orchestra accompanying the band. The best received songs, however, remain the more typical pop-rock numbers, "The Truth, the Life" and "The Way that You Loved Me." On the latter song, Elefante perfects his **Phil Keaggy** imitation to the point that it is unlikely very many fans of either artist would be able to tell the two apart. "Exit 39" is an interesting story-song that relates the tale of a man on a road trip who finds Jesus and salvation when he visits a church at a freeway exit.

The Elefante brothers founded Pakaderm Records and later opened a studio called The Sound Kitchen in Nashville, which has been used by numerous mainstream acts as well as Christian ones. Julio Iglesias, Allison Krauss, Barry Manilow, and Wynonna Judd are among their regular clients, in addition to **Gary Chapman** and **Point of Grace**. When John learned that Jill Sobule had recorded her poignant hit "I Kissed a Girl" at his studio, his embarrassingly homophobic response was published in *CCM* magazine: "Had I known she was recording that song at our studio, I probably would have thrown her out. When she was recording it though, I didn't get gay vibes."

As a producer, Elefante has helped to turn out classic albums by such artists as **Aurora, Barren Cross, The Brave, Bride, Brighton, Carman, Lisa Daggs, Guardian, Greg Long, Nouveaux, Petra, Jonathan Pierce,** and **Scott Springer.** As a songwriter, Elefante has written or cowritten Christian radio hits performed by **Kim Boyce** ("Helpless"), **The Brave** ("Never Live without Your Love," "Tomorrow"), **Guardian** ("I Found Love," "Never Say Goodbye"); **Halo** ("Saved within Grace," "Jacob's Dream," "Eye of the Storm," "Secret to Love"); **Troy Johnson** ("I'll Be There for You"), **Greg Long** ("Think about Jesus," "What a Friend," "Love the Lord"), **Petra** ("Thankful Heart," "King's Ransom," "First Love," "Hand on My Heart," "We Hold Out Our Hearts to You," "Enter In," "We Need Jesus"), **Mark Pogue** ("Love Is Just a Prayer Away," "Let It Go"), and **Scott Springer** ("Anytime," "Hello Forever," "Behold the Lamb," "On My Knees," "Promises"), and **Two or More** ("He's There," "Heaven Is Calling Your Name," "What Would I Say?"), in addition to numerous songs for **Barren Cross, The Brave, Rick Cua, Lisa Daggs, Fear Not, Nikki Leonti, Timothy James Meaney, Nouveaux,** and **Sweet Comfort Band.**

Christian radio hits: "Helpless" [with **Kim Boyce**] (# 6 in 1987); "This Is What Love Is" (# 2 in 1995); "No One's Ever Died for Me Before" (# 1 for 2 weeks in 1995); "What If Our World" (# 1 in 1996); "Hold Me in Your Arms" (# 3 in 1996); "Hello My Good Friend" (# 11 in 1996); "Eyes of My Heart" (# 14 in 1997); "Corridors" (# 12 in 1997); "Not Just Another Day" (# 7 in 1998); "Home with a View" (# 15 in 1999).

Element 101 (a.k.a. Element)

Nick Acocella, drums; Sal Ciaravino; Chris Mizzone, gtr.; Danny Papa, gtr.; Crissie Verhagen, voc. 2000—*Future Plans Undecided* (Tooth and Nail); 2001—*Stereo Girl*.

Composed of five Italian Americans from New Jersey, Element 101 was originally known as simply Element but had to change their name due to one of those pesky trademark disputes. Formed by Crissie Verhagen and Danny Papa in 1997, the group first released their debut album as Element on Burnt Toast Vinyl, but have since reissued it on Tooth and Nail. Verhagen describes the group as "a rock-n-roll band with pop punk influences and female vocals." The "love it or hate it" aspect of Element 101's sound seems to be Verhagen's sweet but nasal voice, which provokes divergent reactions from critics. The title of the debut album was taken from the 1999 film *Can't Hardly Wait*. Produced by Mike Herrera of **MxPx,** *Future Plans Undecided* offers catchy pop-punk songs about what the latter band would call "life in general." *Stereo Girl* reveals a more polished and practiced outfit, with a strong '80s Bangles-meets-The Cars sound. The standout track "Standing on the Edge of Night" describes a breakthrough moment, possibly in romantic perception but with a focus on divinity. Such ambiguities also run through the bouncy ditty "Today and Always" and the more droning "Twenty Years in the Making." Verhagen told *Bandoppler,* "Although we are all Christians, we don't really consider ourselves to be a *ministry* band. We don't preach from the stage or tell people how to live."

Elevator Division

Paul Buzan, bass; James Hoskins, voc., gtr.; Samuel Hoskins, drums; Joseph Hoskins, voc., kybrd. (– 2001). 1999—*Imaginary Days* (Ashland); 2001—*Movement* (independent).

www.elevatordivision.com

The Kansas City group known as Elevator Division creates ambient mood rock that couples introspective lyrics with dark musical tones that are often built around a single, echoing guitar. Their minimalist sound has been likened to *Mercury*-era **Prayer Chain.** Lyrically, the group tunes in with the human condition, or in the words of *Bandoppler,* "exploits every corner of our insecurity, loneliness, obsession, devotion, and tendency towards escapism." The group also likes to reshape songs of lost love as expressing God's feeling of being forsaken by humans. Thus in "Away" (from *Imaginary Days*), Hoskins sings wistfully about "those times when I held you in My arms, when you knew that you were Mine," before asking, "Have you seen my Son? . . . Have you seen my love? . . . When will you return?" In contemporary Christian music circles this tried but true theme tends to get dismissed by critics (who cynically label it the "God-is-my-girlfriend approach to lyrics"), but the imagery is at least as old as Hosea and, thus, thoroughly biblical. *Imaginary Days* also offers a nicely reworked liturgical song in the messianic, Hebraic "Christe Yeshue." After Joseph Hoskins left the band, his brother James took over as lead singer. The first album as a three-piece *Movement* has a more pop (albeit gloomy pop) feel to it. James Hoskins describes it as "about people trying to get from one point to another . . . trying to make progress, often at the expense of relationships and personal integrity." Standout songs include "Mute," "Alone," "Burning Bright," and "Tempo of Three." The latter offers remorseful reflection on the announced theme: "Business—it makes us all forget why we're even here, and who with."

Eleven

See **Industry Eleven.**

Eli (a.k.a. **Paul Falzone**)

As Paul Falzone: 1995—*Paul Falzone* (Rugged). As Eli: 1998—*Things I Prayed For* (ForeFront); 1999—*Second Hand Clothing*; 2001—*Now the News*.

www.forefrontrecords.com

Los Angeles native Eli is Christian music's Cat Stevens. His voice, stylings, and songs are all reminiscent of the blue-collar folk-pop music created by that singer in the early '70s. On his first album as Eli, he even recorded his own version of the Anglican hymn "Morning Has Broken," which Stevens also covered as a Number Six hit back in 1972. Born Paul Falzone, the singer who would come to be known as Eli came to faith hard, and his songs resonate with the honesty of one who maintains that faith without pretense. He turned to drugs at a young age, reacting against his parents' divorce, and eventually wound up living homeless on the streets of L.A. He found salvation at seventeen and three years later was given a guitar by a member of his church who told him that God had a plan for him. Indeed, he took to the instrument as if he had played it all his life. In 1995, he released a soon-to-be-forgotten album under his given name. It was not until adopting the pseudonym Eli that Falzone began crafting songs expressing common thoughts that not everyone knows how to put into words. For example, in his song "Captain," he addresses Christ with unveiled fear: "I wonder if this will be the time when you're not going to be there." In defense of that lyric, Eli told *Release*, "Biblical or not, that's how it is to be a Christian. Anybody who says they don't go though that is either deity or a liar." By the same token, Eli definitely views his singing as a ministry of some sort: "It is my desire to be someone who puts an album out that people will relate to, like I'm a friend. If I don't see lives being touched, I'm outta here, man. I'm gone."

Things I Prayed For is especially noteworthy for its title song, a simultaneously poignant and humorous reflection on how the artist's prayers have changed from when he was a child to the present. His rendition of "The Lumber Song" by **Ceili Rain** offers a similarly humorous look at the theme that

faith without works is dead. "Letters" is a more gritty expression of a person turning to God in desperation. "God Weeps Too" closes the album with a somber reminder that God shares in the pain of "all that we go through." *Second Hand Clothing* (produced by **David Zaffiro**) offers another collection of songs written from an unusually mature perspective. The title track deals with the notion of inherited tendencies, as Eli reflects bitterly on the dysfunctions bequeathed to him by his father: "I've spent a lifetime dancing with his demons / They're constantly comparing him with me / They tell their lies as they look me in the eyes / And say 'The apple doesn't fall far from the tree'." Yet another song with the same title ("Second Hand Clothing, part 2") celebrates the individuality of a young woman who eschews fashion-conscious materialism to shop at thrift stores; this too is allegorical, not of parents' sins being visited upon their young, but of God's grace that makes old things new. Grace is also the subject of "Unqualified," in which the artist relates some of the seamier aspects of his autobiography, and "Brother," in which he invites an ostracized sinner to return to the table where "our Father's been saving you your place." The songs "Valleys" and "I'll Stay Right Here" express the brokenness that Eli encountered in facing the break-up of his marriage, the death of his grandmother, and the loss of a good friend to cancer. Against that background, the song "Stand" (based on Ephesians 6) is all the more powerful and may serve as the album's theme song: "This is where my father tripped / This is the part my teacher skipped. . . . I tried to fight and be a man / When all I had to do was stand."

Now the News continues stylistically in the same vein with a collection of original songs inspired by newspaper clippings and biblical narratives. The musical selections are interspersed with snippets from "news room conversations" and spoken-word introductions that enhance the album's effectiveness as a concept-piece. "Beggars" takes its theme from Jesus' odd advice in Luke 14:12–14, and "Master's Feet" derives from Luke 7:36–50. "Never Knew You Looked Like That" seems to take its inspiration from Christ's prediction that he will go unrecognized in "the least of these" (Matthew 25:40). "Do What You Said" addresses the apathy of American Christians in the face of global poverty ("Take off your stupid bracelet / Unless you do what Jesus would"). "Better Days" closes the set with a hand-clapping song that anticipates a time when the ills of this life will be no more.

Christian radio hits: "Things I Prayed For" (# 5 in 1998); "King of the Hill" (# 4 in 1998); "Life on the Edge" (# 3 in 1998); "The Lumber Song" (# 24 in 1999); "God Weeps Too" (# 17 in 1999); "Stand" (# 2 in 1999); "Second Hand Clothing" (# 19 in 2000); "Unqualified" (# 14 in 2000).

Linda Elias

1991—*The Meaning of Love* (Wonderland).

Linda Elias is best known as a member of **Tuesday's Child,** the group she formed in 1995 with **Lesley Glassford.** She has also composed songs with and for her husband **Rick Elias** and **Margaret Becker.** In 1991, Linda Elias recorded a solo album of songs that she had written with her husband. To the surprise of many, the album evinces a generally sunny disposition in contrast to the painfully honest songs for which Rick was noted at the time. Linda's childlike voice often recalls the music of Frente (e.g., on "Miracle"), but layered background vocals cast several songs on *The Meaning of Love* into the style of groups like The Bangles, The Go-Go's, or Wilson Phillips. The title track is buoyant sugar-pop with humorous lyrics about how finding true love can transform a mundane existence. "Don't Take Your Love Away" has a '60s sound while "All I Can Do" is subdued '80s new-wave. "Yours and Mine" is a pop ballad sung as a duet with husband Rick. Linda later collaborated with Rick and with Scott Rogness to write the hit song "That Thing You Do," which served as the title track for the movie Tom Hanks made about a one-hit-wonder '60s band (called The Wonders). In real life, the supposedly Number One song made it to Number Forty-one on *Billboard*'s pop charts in a version performed by the fictitious band (composed of studio musicians, including **Rick Elias** on guitar). The song was also nominated for both Golden Globe and Academy Awards.

Christian radio hits: "The Meaning of Love" (# 3 in 1992).

Rick Elias

1990—Rick Elias and the Confessions (Alarma); *1991—Ten Stories; 1997—Blink* (Pamplin); *2000—Confessions of a Ragamuffin Man: The Best of Rick Elias* (KMG).

Roots rock singer Rick Elias hails from Tennessee, but he paid his dues for a decade on the Southern California club circuit before gaining critical acclaim in the early '90s with two albums cut from the same cloth as works by Tom Petty, John Mellencamp, and Bruce Springsteen. Fans of that style were drawn to what *7ball* called "his autobiographical songs of faith, his ragged rasp of a voice, and his fresh combination of poetic lyrics and soulfully played guitar." John J. Thompson of *True Tunes* said that his voice sounded "as if he had been gargling chipped glass and kerosene for ten years, yet it was melodically rich."

Thompson also described the debut album, *Rick Elias and the Confessions,* as "a gut-level expression of real-life faith amidst the wreckage of the western world." *CCM* went all-out and called it "one of the best debut recordings *ever* by a Christian artist"; ten years later, in 2000, they would place it at Number Fifty-eight on their list of the 100 Greatest Christian Albums of All Time. The songs "Confessions of Love," "Miles and Miles," and "The Word Is Love" are all built on strong guitar riffs, cementing the Springsteen connections. At his abso-

lute best (the opening of "Someday"), Elias was even able to summon images of *Zuma*-era Neil Young. "Without a Word" and "Stripped" are somber *Nebraska*-like meditations on soul-searching and relationships, respectively. His second album features the standout songs "I Wouldn't Need You (Like I Do)" and "When You Lose Someone You Love." The song "Steps" gallops along to an infectious tune, while "My Very Own Hero" and "Only Your Love" are especially Pettyesque.

Transcending a past fraught with physical and sexual abuse and having fought his way back from life-threatening drug addiction, Elias was able to relate story-songs with a ring of authenticity. "John Doe" (from *Ten Stories*) offers commentary on cycles of abuse that breed violence in society. No stranger to the tough streets of San Diego, Elias came to Christ only after a suicide attempt in 1985. Songs like "Streets of Rome" and "Stones" (both from his debut) deal with self-destructive behavior. All the characters in his songs, he told Brian Quincy Newcomb in 1991, share "a completely clueless aspect about their life," an inability to figure out "how to get from where they are to the better place they dream of." But despite a tour with **The Choir,** neither of Elias's two albums sold very well, and the artist all but disappeared from the main stage of contemporary Christian music. He continued to compose songs for other artists, however, and in 1996 cowrote five songs (with Scott Rogness and **Linda Elias**) for the Tom Hanks' film *That Thing You Do.* The title track was a minor hit for a fictitious band called The Wonders (# 41 in 1996) and was nominated for both Golden Globe and Academy Awards. Elias played guitar on the soundtrack album and had a cameo role in the film. He also resurfaced in the Christian market in the late '90s as a member of **Rich Mullins' A Ragamuffin Band,** which inspired KMG to release a collection of songs from his first two albums under the misleading title *Confessions of a Ragamuffin Man: The Best of Rick Elias.*

Ignored in the just-mentioned retrospective is a 1997 solo project called *Blink.* Elias described the latter project as "just a collection of demos," as personal, somewhat edgy songs that didn't seem right for any of the Christian artists who typically performed his material. Less gritty than the earlier albums, *Blink* also departs from the trademark story-song format to provide fare more typical of the contemporary Christian music market. Songs such as "Hole in My Heart" come off as just plain trite ("I need a hole in my heart like a hole in my head"), like something The Wonders might have done. "God, Inc.," however, puts a bouncy melody at the service of satirical lyrics lampooning Christian businesses that set out to market Christ for the masses. "Streets of Rome" is actually an update of a song from Elias's first album. Elias has never sounded more like Springsteen than on the moving ballads "Prayers of the Saints," which acknowledges the support of Christian community, and

"If You Believed," sung from the perspective of Christ. "Blink" reflects on the fleeting nature of life, and "The More Things Change" offers an elegant affirmation of God's steadfastness, set against a backdrop of piano and cello. Despite its concessions toward adult contemporary expectations, *Blink* retains the sober evaluation of Christian potential that endeared many fans to Elias's early work. "I hear people talking about 'the Christian walk' and I have to laugh," he once told *7ball*. "I never had a walk. It's always been a crawl."

At 6'4", Rick Elias is basketball-player tall. He is married to **Linda Elias,** who has played keyboards and sung backup vocals on his albums. In addition to his own recordings, he has worked as a producer for **Randy Stonehill, Chris Taylor, Tuesday's Child, Split Level, The Wayside,** and other artists. He also cowrote the Christian radio hit "Walkin' Up the Steps of Faith" for **Bob Carlisle.**

Christian radio hits: "Blink" (# 10 in 1998).

Elim Hall

Steve Marsh, drums (d. 1996); Glen Teeple, gtr., kybrd.; Ross Teeple, bass, voc. 1986—*Things Break* (Reunion); *Let It Thrive*.

Elim Hall was a progressive Canadian pop rock band that recorded two albums and toured North America as the opening act for **Michael W. Smith** in 1986. The group was composed of two brothers Glen and Ross Teeple and their cousin, Steve Marsh. They took their name from Elim Hall, a church built by their grandfathers. The band made two albums, which both came out on Reunion in the same year, though a custom version of *Things Break,* produced by **Gary Chapman,** had been available previously. The title track to the latter album is a meditation on mortality; "Let's Play 'Science Says' " is an indictment against the idolatrous equation of scientific fact with truth. Steve Marsh and Glen Teeple would join **One Hundred Days** for one of that group's albums, *Feels Like Love.* Marsh died of liver cancer the day that it was released.

Ellen B

Kenneth Eriksson, bass; Per Hedtjärn, drums; Lasse Olsson, gtr.; Lasse Nilsson Wihk, voc.; Robert Wirensjö, kybrd. 1989—*Prince of Peace* (Alarma).

Ellen B was not a female rapper but a Scandinavian power-pop band with a sound similar to that of **Petra.** No information regarding them remains available, but what appears to have been their only album was released on **Terry Taylor**'s Alarma Records, and the group thanks Charlie Norman (brother of **Larry Norman**) in their liner notes for help with translations. The opening track, "Don't End the Night," presents the thoughts of one who tosses and turns throughout a sleepless night, trying to sort out some basic questions of truth before

the distractions of a new day begin. The next song, "Real Man," juxtaposes the macho images of popular culture with one who "wept in His weakness / kept His word / Took care of the poor / And sat beside the whore." Such poignancy is typical of the project, which is certainly better than average musically as well.

The Elms

Chris Thomas, drums, voc.; Owen Thomas, gtr., voc.; James Thompson, gtr., voc. (−2001) // Thom Daugherty, gtr. (+ 2001); Keith Miller, bass (+ 2001). 2000—*The Elms* [EP] (Sparrow); 2001—*The Big Surprise*.

www.theelms.net

A modern pop band from Seymour, Indiana, The Elms were introduced by Sparrow on a five-song EP while they were still a trio in search of a bass player. For some years prior to this, Chris and Owen Thomas had led worship at their father's church under the name Just Visiting, and they recorded two independent albums under that name *(Gardenshow; Just Visiting).* They added James Thompson in 1997 and became The Elms in 1999. Sparrow seemed to think the group was too good to keep under wraps and wanted to generate buzz before the main album came out. It worked. The little sample revealed a group with memorable melodies, warm guitars, and big rock vocals, but most of all a group with at least five good songs in their repertoire. Official press materials compared The Elms to '90s superstars like Oasis and the Foo Fighters, but the better analogy would be to one-hit wonders like The Flying Machine ("Smile a Little Smile for Me," # 5 in 1969), Edison Lighthouse ("Love Grows Where My Rosemary Goes," # 5 in 1970) or Pilot ("Magic," # 5 in 1975). Like the first two of those bands, they even allow the catchiest of all their catchy songs to be about a girl named Rose. The exact point of "Goodnight, Rosa" is unclear, but it seems to present the concluding words of a guy who has witnessed to his date and now hopes she will *not* have a goodnight's sleep until she makes the choice he thinks she needs to make. Ample "la-da-dee-dah's" give the song a '70s bubblegum feel appropriate to the superficiality of its theme. The rest of the short album has a similarly retro sound that one critic described as **Jars of Clay** singing **Newsboys** songs. "Lifeboat" (not a **Steve Taylor** cover) is a radio-friendly worship song addressed to Christ. "You're Glowing" sounds almost like a children's song, with lyrics inspired by *Runaway Bunny* ("If you're down the tracks, I'll ride the train / If you're in the sky, I'll fly a plane"). Horns add an "All You Need Is Love" Beatlesque flourish. "You Think You Know a Guy" is a more serious Everclear-type ballad of unfulfilled needs. "Real Men Cry" (not the **Lost Dogs** song) is a moving description of Jesus as the ultimate role model for true masculinity.

After the debut EP, a rather different band with the Thomas brothers still at the core produced the full-length album *The Big Surprise*. Owen Thomas announced, "We abandoned the acoustic sound (of the EP) and made the disc for rock 'n' roll fans this time." No one else agreed with this assessment. Rather, *The Big Surprise* contains three songs from the debut and seven more equally sugary tunes that run the gamut from '70s power-pop to '60s bubblegum. The opening "Hey, Hey" reminded many listeners of The Bay City Rollers, with obvious influences from Toni Basil's "Mickey." The songs "Here's My Hand" and "You Get Me Every Time" are more lush, softer tunes. "The Buzzing Won't Stop" is sung in a soaring falsetto that recalls '60s pop.

Christian radio hits: "Lifeboat" (# 13 in 2000); "Hey, Hey" (# 5 in 2001).

Eloi

Jeff Gothard, drums; Bryan Hilliard, gtr.; Seth Poor, voc.; Stephen Smiley, bass. 1997—*Degrees of Freedom* (Hot Trax); 1999—*Mold* (Cross Rhythms).

Described as "a cross between Metallica and Ugly Kid Joe," the hard rock band Eloi offers a basic metal groove with what *Phantom Tollbooth* calls "just enough grunge to keep things interesting." The group comes out of Dallas, Texas, and takes its name from Jesus' cry of dereliction on the cross (Mark 15:34). The basic sound has been likened to Tool, Helmet, and Korn. Eloi's independent release *Degrees of Freedom* earned them the honor of being named *HM* Magazine's "favorite unsigned band" for 1997. That status was remedied for *Mold* with a resultant rise in production values. The title song to the album calls listeners to let go of their lives and let God change them. "Looking Christian" revisits a theme from the early Jesus movement contrasting the outward appearance of a man in a three-piece suit to a long-hair with tattoos ("I know Jesus takes me in / To him I'm looking Christian").

Elysian Skies

Ben Busch, kybrd.; John Feighey, gtr.; Keith Giles, voc.; Bill Schmid, drums; John Wahurmund, gtr., bass. 1998—*Exquisite Whisper* (Baby Angel).

Elysian Skies is an alternative modern rock band from Southern California remarkable for the big-name support they managed to pull in for their debut album. Gene Eugene of **Adam Again** as well as Wayne Everett and Andy Prickett of **The Prayer Chain** served as engineers and mixers to help executive producer J. J. Plasencio (of **Plumb** and **Sixpence None the Richer**) craft the band's sound in the studio. The result is a sound that *Phantom Tollbooth* said "suggests **The Waiting** with fewer frills." Elysian Skies has the modern rock swirling guitar sound down pat, but supplements it with folksy acoustic strumming. Giles' high pitched vocals also give the band a distinctive edge. The nine songs on their debut album all deal forthrightly with issues of faith, though sometimes in unexpectedly poetic ways. Dylanesque biblical imagery plays a role: "It rains on the unjust and righteous as well / The sound of the truth is louder than hell / A forgetful Samaritan passes away / His friends and his family have nothing to say." Proceeds from the sale of *Exquisite Whisper* were donated to "Feed the Children," an Oklahoma-based charity.

Embodyment

Andrew Goodwin, gtr.; Mark Garza, drums; Kevin Donnini, bass; James Lanigan, gtr.; Kris McCaddon, voc. (− 2000) // Sean Corbray, voc. (+ 2000). 1998—*Embrace the Eternal* (Solid State); 2000—*The Narrow Scope of Things*; 2001—*Hold Your Breath*.

www.embodymentcore.com

The Christian metal band from Arlington, Texas, called Embodyment has made two albums that sound like the work of two completely different bands. The group formed as early as 1993 as a straight death metal band akin to groups like **Crimson Thorn.** By the time of their first major release, however, they had leavened that sound with generous doses of punk hardcore. *Embrace the Eternal* is a very hard, rhythmic metal album with some similarity to the work of **Living Sacrifice.** The most distinctive element is the vocal style of Kris McCaddon, who somehow learned how to growl and scream at the same time. This excessively ugly sound is set against a pulsating rhythm section with virtually no relief in the form of guitar solos or anything else. The band was universally praised for their technical quality, while most reviews noted that all the songs sounded alike and none of them really sounded like *songs* as such; rather, the whole album had the feel of what *The Lighthouse* called "a collection of licks with vocals." Lyrics are not understandable, but when accessed through the accompanying liner notes reveal engagement with such issues as gossip ("20 Tongues"), lust ("Blinded"), and conscience ("Carnival Chair") from a distinctly Christian perspective and often in quite perceptive ways. The song "Breed" offers an explicit testimony to faith without apology: "Call me what you want / The truth remains the same / I am branded Christian . . . Falling to my knees / A servant unto Christ / In this world of disease." As Doug Van Pelt of *HM* noted, the band's assault style is particularly effective on the song "Prophesy," where the title is shouted repeatedly over a pounding double bass riff that recalls the beating of Jesus described in Luke 22:63–64.

Two years later, the band came back with an album closer to the emo-core sounds of The Deftones or **Stavesacre** than to anything in the death metal genre. McCaddon was gone (later to turn up in **Society's Finest**), and the new singer actually *sang,* often in a soft and beautiful voice. The songs had melodies, and guitars could be heard above the pummeling beat. Critics loved it, though die-hard death metal fans who still consider *Embrace the Eternal* to be a Christian classic complained noisily that the band should at least have changed their name if they were going to reinvent themselves so drastically. Point taken. Still, *The Narrow Scope of Things* remains the work of a metal band, or at least of a hard rock band with deep metal roots. The new vocalist, Sean Corbray, does his share of screaming and, as *Bandoppler* assured its readers, the songs "will make your ears bleed, even if there is some singing in them." Corbray also serves as lyricist for the group's new songs, and the word "poetic" was often used to describe his approach ("Naked trees are clawing for air"). The song "Assembly Line Humans" continues to reveal Embodyment's bone-crunching potential and "Like Cigarettes" comes close to recalling the Embodyment of yore. Still, "One Less Addiction" is actually offered as a ballad. That stellar song and "Killing the Me in Me" (which alternates internally between the very hard and more melodic styles) express the ongoing quest for holiness that surfaced frequently on the first album as well.

The third album, *Hold Your Breath,* merely completed the transformation evident on *Narrow Scope of Things.* Still hard rock, the music is completely melodic with no screaming whatsoever. Treble Bandoppler (writing for *HM*) indicated that concerts had revealed Corbray really wasn't a screamer but agreed that on *Hold Your Breath,* he had found his niche: soulful, powerful singing to accompany a heavy, brooding mass of undertones. Standout songs include "Heaven Is a Letter Bomb," "Belly Up," and "Yours Truly." With bands like Tool selling out amphitheaters and with Creed's records in chart-stratosphere, the radio-accessibility of melodic hard rock seemed to be at an all-time high. Embodyment indicated that they were ready and willing for a general market crossover.

emit ridge

Erik Doerksen, gtr.; Marty Gast, kybrd., bass; Derek Iddison, drums; Rob Lilley, gtr.; Mark Weise, voc. 1995—*Discretion* (Ridgerian); 1997—*Undivided Soul* (Light).

Toronto-based emit ridge (always lower case) emerged out of the Canadian club scene in the mid '90s as a low-key Christian band that sounded like a more pop version of Pearl Jam. The latter description immediately compares them to Atlanta's **Third Day,** an analogy that holds aurally but not lyrically. Although Gast says, "we really want people to see the hope through our music," the band is careful not to use explicitly religious language that would offend the secular audience they court. As Weise puts it, "you've got to be able to bring the culture truth and present it to them before they switch you off." Thus, songs that deal with relationships ("Pieces"; "She's Beyond") mix with ones that present the sort of muted spirituality one encounters with **Collective Soul.** "Now" is addressed to a presence that has always "been there" for the

singer and, he believes, for others through history. "Lazy Sunday" expresses disappointment that the easy faith he had as a child seems to have slipped away over the years. The group explains (or doesn't explain) their name with the following statement: "emit ridge is not a person, a place, a disease, or a name with a clever meaning."

Emmaus

Selected: 1989—*Come to Me;* 1991—*Walk into Grace;* 1996—*Five* [EP]; 1997—*All Over the World* [EP]; *Weight; Live at the Temple Bar Theatre Dublin;* 2000—*Closer Nearer.*

www.emmauscommunity.com/band/body.htm

Emmaus is the outreach ministry of the Emmaus Community Church in Dublin, Ireland. They have a history similar to that of Britain's **Delirious?** The group has a shifting membership of usually about eight members and is led by Ronan "Rojo" Johnston, a writer for MTV in England. Press reports often tout the group's ecumenicity in what appear to be exaggerated ways. Although it is reported that "band members include both Protestants and Catholics from both parts of the island," all of the members (regardless of their background or upbringing) appear to be members of the charismatic, nondenominational (and therefore Protestant) church that gives the group its name. The first two Emmaus albums consist simply of praise and worship choruses sung by members of the community. Two more lost albums followed, which are no longer listed in their discographies. With the EPs *Five* and *All Over the World,* they came into their own, shaping up as an actual pop band with a definitive rock/folk/country sound. *Weight* finally brought together a full album's worth of material, compiling favorite songs from the past projects along with some songs not previously available. The live album revisits many of these tracks again, albeit with a harder edge. *Closer Nearer,* the first album of all new material in years, represents a return to roots, with the group performing contemporary hymns and worship songs.

Musically, Emmaus presents an alternative rock sound (especially on its three 1997 albums) that is as heavily influenced by American funk and soul as by the Celtic sounds of its homeland. *Phantom Tollbooth* singles out "Peter" and "Voice in the Silence" as especially impressive tracks (both on the live album). The first of these offers a spoken word monologue over a funky bassline. The latter kicks in with distorted guitars and a pleading lyric: "Give me a voice in the silence / Give me a river in the desert / Give me some mercy with my justice / Give me love, love, love."

End Time Warriors

See **E.T.W.**

Priscilla Engle

1986—*Priscilla Engle* (Frontline); 1989—*Ageless Love* (Diadem); 1990—*Learning to Love.*

Christian pop singer and songwriter Priscilla Engle (b. 1959) is from Muncie, Indiana. Her debut self-titled album includes several original songs in addition to "Things Are Lookin' Up" by **Steve Chapman** and "Add Up the Wonders" by **Michael** and **Stormie Omartian;** likewise **Ray Boltz** would assist with songwriting on *Ageless Love,* a collection of light rock songs. *CCM* compared Engle's albums to contemporary works by **Sheila Walsh** and **Jamie Owens-Collins.**

Christian radio hits: "To Live Is Christ" (# 20 in 1986).

Joe English and The English Band

As Joe English: 1980—*Lights in the World* (Refuge); 1982—*Held Accountable;* 1983—*Press On* (Myrrh); 1984—*Live;* 1985—*The Best Is Yet to Come* (Refuge); 1988—*Back to Basics: English 101.* As The English Band: 1985—*What You Need* (Myrrh).

Drummer Joe English entered contemporary Christian music as a pop singer in 1980 after a stellar career in mainstream rock and a spectacular conversion to charismatic, miracle-oriented faith. Born in 1949 in Rochester, New York, English first began playing with the group Jam Factory at the age of eighteen and for six years toured with the group, opening for such acts as Jimi Hendrix, Janis Joplin, and the Allman Brothers. Jam Factory's 1970 album, *Sitting in the Trap,* was produced by Paul McCartney. For English, the years with Jam Factory were fraught with personal troubles, including a failed marriage. After he left the group, he worked as a session drummer, playing on over twenty albums that went gold or platinum. Then he was invited to join McCartney's band, Wings, with whom he played from 1974 to 1976. English was a member of Wings for the band's *Venus and Mars* and *Wings at the Speed of Sound* albums, and for the legendary tour that yielded the *Wings over America* live album. He left after three years, partly out of commitment to a relationship with a longtime girlfriend, Dayle, whom he would later marry. In 1977, English joined Sea Level, a group formed by three members of the Allman Brothers that is perhaps best remembered for their song "That's Your Secret" (# 50 in 1978). Shortly after this, Dayle crashed the couple's Porsche in an accident on a winding road one night that left her, following hospitalization, in constant pain and dependent on a walker. Although doctors had predicted a six-month recovery time, she returned home one night from a charismatic prayer group meeting claiming to be completely healed. Inspired by what he took to be a miracle, and driven for some time by an emptiness that neither money, fame, nor drugs had been able to fill, English gave himself over to God and joined a charismatic group in Indiana Springs,

Georgia, where the couple now lived. Saved and Spirit-filled, he continued to play with Sea Level until 1980, then went solo in order to have more opportunity to share the message and enthusiasm of his faith in ways that sitting behind a drum set did not afford.

English's debut album, *Lights in the World,* features background vocals by **Bonnie Bramlett** and evinces a level of production unusual for Christian music at the time. The sound is that of basic soft rock, and the lyrics emphasize English's interests in the Spirit-led life and in the end times. *CCM* magazine would pick the album, which yielded English's biggest hit, "Shine On," to be one of their "ten best records of 1980." *Cornerstone* described English's vocal style as "a cross between **Steve Camp** and **Matthew Ward.**" English would later complain that the debut album sounded like "it was recorded in a hospital zone—too clean and sanitized." *Held Accountable* was more of a band project, made with a group that had toured together. Its songs were split stylistically between light pop ("First Love," "My Strength Is in the Lord") and a rockier sound ("Wake Up," "The Best Is Yet to Come"). *Press On* continues in the same vein. Its title track alludes to English's past ("I walked away from fortune and fame / I count it all loss compared to Jesus' name"). The song "Royal Priesthood" has a hymnlike, worshipful quality. Most of the songs on English's first three albums were written by members of his band, especially keyboard player John Rossasco. Critical complaints that the albums were too bland may have prompted English to go for the tougher sound on *What You Need,* with official acknowledgment that the record was a group effort. The official lineup for "The English Band" included Paul Brannon on bass and George Cocchini on guitar. The title track to *What You Need* as well as "Children of the Light" are hook-filled rockers, while "I Will Follow You" (written by Cocchini with **Steve Camp**) is more of a pop classic in the typical English tradition. The album concludes with "Through the Veil," a synthesized hymn that seems out of place but is a treasure in its own right. *Back to Basics* returns to the soul-flavored pop of *Lights in the World* and includes a rewritten Christianized version of **Marvin Gaye**'s "How Sweet It Is" (cf. **Johnny Rivers, Take 6**). Better songs on that album are "Behold the Glory" and "Take Me Back" (not an **Andraé Crouch** cover).

In 1984, Joe English became a member of a band called **Forerunner.** The group is accorded a separate listing in this book because English's role in the band (on their only studio album) appears to have been limited to playing the drums. The *Live* album listed above, however, was also by this group, though it includes songs from English's previous albums (including three from *Lights*) with him on vocals.

English has continued to work as a session drummer on a number of projects. Mark Joseph (author of *The Rock and Roll*

Rebellion) credits him with "showing that an instrument such as the drums could not be intrinsically evil, a widespread misunderstanding in the Christian world." One hopes that such a misunderstanding has never been as widespread as Joseph implies. Not many in the Christian world at large have ever held to such a view, but it was prevalent for a while among certain fundamentalist Christians who liked to equate the rhythmic character of rock and roll with supposedly demonic jungle music from Africa. The racist connotations of such an idea were always obvious and the perspective was never taken seriously in responsible quarters.

Christian radio hits: "Shine On" (# 1 for 8 weeks in 1981); "Midnight Angel Choir" (# 4 in 1981); "Dyin' " (# 17 in 1981); "Praise Him" (# 5 in 1982); "First Love" (# 9 in 1983); "Stop" (# 18 in 1983); "Will Follow You" (# 14 in 1986); "The Master" (# 5 in 1986); "What You Need" (# 17 in 1986).

Michael English

1991—*Michael English* (Curb); 1993—*Hope;* 1995—*Healing;* 1996—*Freedom;* 1998—*Gospel;* 2000—*Heaven to Earth.*

In terms of musical style and ability, scandal-ridden gospel star Michael English has often been regarded as the Christian equivalent of Michael Bolton. Frequently dismissed by critics, he nevertheless managed to gain a loyal fan base and to achieve almost unprecedented "industry success" before revelations about his personal life in 1994 initiated what would become a pattern of ups and downs, marked by brief forays into the general market and by various comebacks as a chastened Christian star. English was raised in a strict Pentecostal church in Wallace, North Carolina, where, at the age of eight, he began singing with his family in a gospel group called The Singing Samaritans. After graduating from high school and briefly pursuing barber college with the notion of being a hairdresser, he became a professional gospel singer. His background, notably, is not in contemporary Christian music, but in the southern gospel world of quartets and family groups. He has sung with the Singing Americans (1980–1982, 1984–1985), the Happy Goodmans (1982–1983), the Couriers (1983–1984), and **The Bill Gaither Trio/The Gaither Vocal Band** (1985–present). Throughout the '80s, English was open with the press about the fact that he suffered from clinically diagnosed panic disorder, which made him susceptible to severe and inexplicable panic attacks. He testified in public to the help that he had received from his faith, from therapy, and especially from his wife, Lisa, in dealing with the disorder, and he led a campaign to educate people with regard to its oft-misunderstood nature and consequences.

In 1989, feeling more confident on stage, English decided to go solo and to move into the contemporary Christian market. His first, self-titled album was produced by **Brown Bannister** and featured a number of inspirational, adult contemporary songs like "Solid as the Rock," "Mary Did You Know," and its standout track, "In Christ Alone." The last named song was cited by Buffalo Bills' quarterback Frank Reich as providing him with the inspiration to lead his team in a historic NFL comeback against the Houston Oilers on January 3, 1993. The lyrics affirm, "In Christ alone will I glory / Though I could pride myself in battles won / For I've been blessed beyond measure / And by his strength alone, I overcome." In a review of English's debut project, *CCM* critic Kathleen Ervin wrote, "One can't help but think that an album like *Michael English* is what people had in mind when they originally thought of contemporary Christian music—an inspiring, rousing message infused with the best that music had to offer in its day." Very few critics agreed with that sentiment. Rather, as indicated above, English was typically regarded with the sort of disdain usually reserved for Michael Bolton. Like Bolton, English produced a sort of easy listening variety of soul music, the contrived nature of which was a sacrilege to rock purists and to lovers of real R&B. But, of course, there is nothing intrinsically wrong with creating new genres for new audiences, and (as with Bolton) critically negative reactions to English's work must be ascribed more to difference in taste than to legitimate assessment of execution. No one thought that English performed his brand of music poorly; many (critics) simply did not like the brand of music he performed. And those who appraise merit more on commercial potential than artistic integrity were extremely pleased. The Gospel Music Association named English "Best New Artist of the Year" even though, technically, he'd been recording for almost twenty years.

Two years later, the follow-up album, *Hope,* continued in the same vein with English delivering emotion-soaked adult contemporary ballads and rhythmic pop songs with a soulful passion. He pleads to be rescued in the breathy "Save Me." He belts out the hook-laden chorus to "There Is a Love" with convincing bravado, sustained by a dynamic choir. Equally upbeat is "Message of Mercy," while the theologically euphemistic "Love Moves in Mysterious Ways" is set to a simple piano arrangement. Lyrically, the album's titular theme is expressed in "Holding Out Hope" and "A Place Called Hope." The album secured English's reputation as the king of Christian MOR, and he headlined a national tour featuring **First Call, Angelo and Veronica,** and **Mark Lowry.**

In 1994, English received an incredible six Dove awards in a single evening, a new record for the most awards ever received at one time by any artist. Less than twenty-four hours later he called a press conference to announce what would soon become public knowledge: he had engaged in an extramarital affair with Marabeth Jordan, the (also married) singer for **First Call,** and she was now pregnant with his child (she subsequently lost the baby to a miscarriage). In crass irony, the affair had occurred during the aforementioned tour, which had served as benefit fundraiser for Mercy Ministries, an outreach to women facing unwanted pregnancies. English voluntarily returned all of his Dove awards, though the Gospel Music Association said he would continue to be listed in the record books as the recipient. Less graciously, Warner Alliance discontinued sales and promotion for both of his albums. English said he was retiring from gospel music, but in fact he continued to record with the **Gaither** group and, indeed, won another Dove award for his song with them ("I Bowed on My Knees") the very next year. In 1995, English was divorced from his wife. He continued to make tabloid news as he grew his hair long, dated a stripper, and made disparaging public remarks about the gospel music industry. In 1996, a twenty-year-old live-in girlfriend named Tina Wilmurth charged him with assault and theft after an incident in which he locked her out of their apartment and then chased her down an alley until he was restrained by security guards. Wilmurth later dropped the charges and told the press, "Every couple argues. Our argument just happened to be greatly exaggerated because of who Michael is in the music business."

In 1994, the same year that English swept the Dove awards and then returned his trophies, he recorded a duet with country star Wynonna that was featured in the Bruce Beresford film, *Silent Fall* (starring Richard Dreyfuss). The success of that song, "Healing," seemed to open the door for a possible career in mainstream music, leading English to release a couple of adult contemporary pop albums for the general market. The album *Healing* is actually a hasty compilation of some of the less-specifically Christian songs from *Michael English* and *Hope* plus the duet with Wynonna. *Freedom* is new material and includes "Your Love Amazes Me," which enjoyed considerable success on adult contemporary radio. English never left the gospel scene completely, though, as he continued to serve as producer on albums by such artists as Jeff and Sheri Easter (see **Heirloom**), **The Imperials,** J. D. Sumner and the Stamps, and **Russ Taff.** Even while touring as a mainstream artist, he often included a smattering of traditional gospel songs ("Blessed Assurance," "I Surrender All") in his concerts. The album *Gospel* was a collection of such songs, traditional hymns performed by English with his "secular" band. Standout songs include "John the Revelator," **Mylon LeFevre**'s "Gospel Ship," and Vince Gill's "Go Rest on That Mountain."

English's much heralded return to contemporary Christian music came with the album *Heaven to Earth* produced again by **Brown Bannister.** *CCM* and other media inaccurately reported that it was English's "first recording of Christian music in seven years." It was even announced as "the album he had intended to make in 1994," before all the troubles started.

Though far from a comeback to an industry he had never actually left, the record does serve up another feast for fans of inspirational adult contemporary. The songs "To Live On," "How Grace Feels," "I'll Believe in You," and "If You Only Knew" are all powerful examples of the form. Lyrically, forgiveness, faith, and the overcoming of affliction are prominent and appropriate themes. "Finally Free" seems like a potential autobiographical signature song: "I'm free to play the lesser role / Give up my need to have control . . . I'm finally free of me." Unfortunately, English's troubles were not behind him. No sooner had the album hit the shelves amid much hype and publicity regarding "our old friend who has finally gotten his life in order," then English checked himself into a rehabilitation center for an admitted addiction to prescription drugs. A police investigation ensued as to whether he had obtained the drugs illegally and the Christian music industry closed ranks against him, with several radio stations deleting the first single from his new album from their playlists. Typical of the "let's shoot our wounded" approach was the comment of Theresa Ross of Indianapolis' WXIR-FM radio, who said it was the station's policy not to play songs by any artists who "have gone through personal struggles" because the station "needs to hold to a higher standard." By contrast, Jerry Williams of Houston's WVFJ said, "If I pulled the song of every person who sinned, there would be no one left to play." English was eventually sentenced to three years of probation. He told *CCM,* "I don't know if I'll ever have a name for myself in this business again, but I don't feel like I would be doing the will of God if I gave up. I believe God has plans for me, but I keep screwing it up."

Christian radio hits: "Solid as the Rock" (# 1 for 2 weeks in 1991); "Mary Did You Know?" (# 28 in 1991); "Start a Party" (# 7 in 1992); "Love Won't Leave You" (# 4 in 1992); "Holding Out Hope to You" (# 14 in 1993); "Save Me" (# 4 in 1993); "There Is a Love" (# 6 in 1993); "Message of Mercy" (# 9 in 1994).

Dove Awards: 1992 New Artist of the Year; 1992 Male Vocalist; 1993 Male Vocalist; 1993 Inspirational Song ("In Christ Alone"); 1994 Artist of the Year; 1994 Male Vocalist; 1994 Inspirational Song ("Holding Out Hope to You"); 1994 Pop/Contemporary Album *(Hope).*

Engrave

Nathan Morris, kybrd. 1997—*Polaris* (Velvet Empire).

Engrave is the solo project of Nathan Morris, who uses synthesizers and drum machines to create dark ambient music for the Christian electronic scene. The album *Polaris* includes four tracks released on a 1996 cassette called *Benediction.* The music is entirely instrumental, with the exception of occasional samples. As with most ambient music, there is nothing intrinsic to the product that would identify it as Christian for most listeners, and there are no accompanying "texts for meditation" as with **Ambient Theology.** Engrave's instrumentals often have a sci-fi tone to them and are consistently described as "moody" and "captivating."

Jeremy Enigk

1998—*Return of the Frog Queen* (Sub Pop).

Jeremy Enigk was leader of the general market emo band **Sunny Day Real Estate.** The break-up of that group was a direct result of Enigk embracing the Christian faith of his youth, though he maintains there were other tensions that this only exacerbated. Eventually, **Sunny Day Real Estate** would regroup and make albums that many Christian music fans continue to regard as Christian records. During the group's hiatus, however, Enigk surprised everyone with a solo album featuring a twenty-one-piece orchestra backing his ethereal vocals on surreal songs that seemed to be derived from fairy tales. The title track and some of the other numbers have a *Sgt. Pepper* feel to them in that the orchestra not only accentuates but actually defines the song's structure and tone. None of the songs give overt expression to Enigk's faith, though in some ("Explain," "Shade and the Black Hat") there are pointers for those who already know him to be a believer. More often, the lyrics are simply obscure. *True Tunes* challenged its readers to make sense of lines like "moving through shallow water to spill there / crash a wave torn apart on its sail." Enigk continues to maintain a somewhat tenuous relationship with the contemporary Christian music subculture. In 2000, he told *HM* magazine that he does not necessarily see himself as a Christian in the same sense that many people want to apply the term (see the entry on **Sunny Day Real Estate**).

For trivia buffs: Jeremy Enigk also sang with the band **Poor Old Lu** when the other members of that group were still in seventh grade. He left before the band matured (literally and musically).

Mikaila Enriquez

1996—*This Little Light* (Unison).

Nine-year-old Mikaila Enriquez was a native of Oklahoma City in 1995 when a bomb planted at the Arthur P. Murrah Federal Building where her father worked killed 169 people. Enriquez' father was not there, due to the simple fluke of running late, but three of his close friends were killed. At her father's request, Enriquez began singing the song "Not Too Far from Here" from **Kim Boyce**'s *By Faith* album as a tribute to the victims of that terrorist act. News of the inspirational song spread and Enriquez was featured on the *McNeil-Lehrer News Hour, Good Morning America,* and other TV programs. Enriquez performed the song repeatedly, at a Walt Disney Children's Festival, at the 1996 Super Bowl Celebrity Gala, and at an Oklahoma City benefit concert on the one-year anniversary of the bombing. Eventually, she agreed to record it along with a collection of other songs on the *This Little Light* album, which was produced by Steve Siler, who cowrote "Not Too Far from Here" with Ty Lacy. Some of the proceeds from the project were designated for a Children's Support Fund on behalf of children who lost a parent in the bombing. Asked about her remarkably passionate performance of the song, Enriquez would later respond, "I had a reason to sing it."

Kathie and Michie Epstein

1977—*Friends* (Petra).

Kathie and Michie (pronounced *mish-ee*) Epstein were a sister act that remains of historical interest due to Kathie's later career. Two years after graduating from Oral Roberts University, the latter recorded a solo album *The Quiet Riot* for Petra Records, which was headed by the noted Christian producer, arranger, composer, and conductor **Paul Johnson.** That same year (1976), Kathie and Paul were married. She retained her maiden name for the project with her sister, an album of inspirational songs titled *Friends,* which was later re-released under the title *Celebration of His Love* on Bread and Honey records. The next year (1978), she recorded *Finders Keepers* as **Kathie Lee Johnson.** The Johnsons later divorced and Kathie married former NFL star Frank Gifford. She became famous as talk-show host Kathie Lee Gifford, coanchoring the popular morning show *Regis and Kathie Lee* with Regis Philbin.

Erinfall

Johann Fontamillas; Wilson Peraltla. 1997—*Breathe* (Velocity).

Erinfall mixes industrial rock with ambient techno music to offer diversity that appeals to those in the electronic scene who are not too obsessively committed to one or the other subgenre. The album *Breathe* begins with a *Twilight Zone* voice announcing the theme: "We live in an era when our cities are armed with steel and concrete. Computers and electronics barricade our minds." Most, but not all, of the album's tracks are instrumentals. On some, including the opening, "We Live in a World," the vocals are distorted. "No One's Listening" breaks down at one point to allow a female voice to say "God is speaking" (followed by a reverberating electronic bass sound that apparently conveys the sound of the Almighty's voice). Erinfall is often likened to **Mortal** in sound and style, with their harder, industrial numbers (including the title track) recalling that group's *Wake* album. The more danceable, techno numbers ("Land on Venus") are reminiscent of **Prodigal Sons.** Johann Fontamillas and Wilson Peraltla have also recorded under the names **Jyradelix** and Mindbender.

Craig Erickson

1993—*Roadhouse Stomp!* (Blues Bureau International); 1995—*Two Sides of the Blues;* 1994—*Retro Blues Express;* 1996—*Force Majeure;* 2001—*Shine* (Grooveyard).

Craig Erickson is a blues guitarist from Iowa. The son of a jazz guitarist and professional guitar teacher, Erickson grew up enamored of the blues rock tradition exemplified by Jimi Hendrix, Mike Bloomfield, **Eric Clapton,** and Carlos Santana. Later he delved into the roots of that music, discovering Buddy Guy, B. B. King, and Muddy Waters. His own recordings contain both instrumental and vocal tracks and have sometimes been compared to the work of Stevie Ray Vaughan. Though he does not try to use his music to promote Christianity in any overt way, Erickson is a believer who speaks and sometimes sings openly of his faith. In 1995, he told *HM,* "A big turning point came when I got married and I started working a more steady job—so I didn't have quite as much freedom to get into trouble. And then we started going to church more regularly, and it became clear to me, it's not something you can have one foot in each place and be a very happy person." *Two Sides of the Blues* displays different vibes reflective of Erickson's myriad influences—Hendrix on "Little Café," ZZ Top on "You Bring Me Up," **T Bone Burnett** on "Begg or a King." **Darrell Mansfield** offers some guest harmonica playing. *Shine* includes a cover of Hendrix's "Angel" and features vocals by Glenn Hughes of Deep Purple and Rob Lamothe of Riverdogs.

E-roc

1991—*Listen to the G.O.D.* (Reunion); 1995—*Jesus Smoke* (Pulse); 1998—*The Return* (Phat Boy); 1999—*Avalanche* (Grapetree).

The East Coast rapper known as E-roc was born in Vahalla, New York, and earned an academic scholarship to West Point. While studying there, he won a dance contest sponsored by a Dallas radio station that led eventually to his performance as a dancer with **M.C. Hammer** and, then, with Vanilla Ice. In 1990, after dancing with Ice on the American Music Awards show, he says that he became aware of "something missing" in his life and rededicated his life to Christ. He began making Christian rap records the next year and, according to his label, was the biggest seller in East Coast style Christian rap in the late '90s. His stage name was chosen as an acronym for Everett Relies On Christ. Critics regard *Listen to the G.O.D.* as a trial effort and *Jesus Smoke* as the artist's breakthrough project. *The Return* includes "Step to This" (which samples **Al Green**) and "Dead Man Walking" (with a '60s rock sound). *Avalanche* features guest performances by **Earthsuit, Sackcloth Fashion,** and numerous other artists. "Ear to the Tracks" and "Rockstars (Rock on Remix)" have been mentioned as standout tracks.

For trivia buffs: E-roc appears as a dancer/ninja warrior in the movie *Teenage Mutant Ninja Turtles II.*

Eschatos

Personnel list unavailable. 1974—*Eschatos* (Rain).

Little is known of the progressive Jesus-rock group called Eschatos who made one album on a custom label. The group did perform at the famous *Explo '72* festival (the "Christian Woodstock") sponsored by Campus Crusade for Christ in Dallas, Texas, in 1972. *Jesus Music* magazine describes their album as featuring unusually clean production and songs with creative compositional elements that are usually indicative of some formal musical training. The group incorporates jazz influences into their sound and uses horns on about half of their tracks. "Rubber Crutch Man" is described as featuring "some cool acid funk vibes and wah-wah guitar." The song "Lorelei Freedom" is more classic rock and roll in the tradition of Jerry Lee Lewis. "Benjamin" and "Have You Seen" feature dissonant chords, and "Nemo Whojew" has an echoey guitar solo. "White Cane Park" and "Hallelujah" are more typical ballads. The name Eschatos is derived from the Greek word for "last"; it is used in the New Testament to describe "last things" such as the end times or the final judgment, and in memorable sayings such as "the first will be last, and the last first" (Matthew 19:30).

Ian Eskelin (a.k.a. **Ian**)

As Ian Eskelin: 1993—*Brand New Language* (WAL). As Ian: 1994—*Supersonic Dream Day* (Reunion).

Ian Eskelin (b. 1970) eventually achieved fame in Christian music circles as the leader of **All Star United,** but prior to his work with that highly successful group, he released two not-so-successful electronic dance albums as a solo artist. Originally from North Carolina, Eskelin led a group called Business and Industry as a teenager, then moved to Chicago, where he attended Wheaton College. He was briefly a member of **Code of Ethics,** and he fronted the dance band Zero. Eskelin's solo projects emulate the style of **Scott Blackwell,** i.e., disco-influenced, techno-pop music with Christian lyrics like "He's gonna tame your heart in time to change your mind." The debut album *Brand New Language* includes the standout track "Destination Love" along with the radio-ready "Haven't You Heard" and the very catchy "Love to Be Loved." The title track for *Supersonic Dream Day* is about the great last day, which is set to arrive at a time when no one expects. "Come to Me" sets a bouncy invitation from Christ against verses in which the artist acknowledges the vanity and futility of trying to make it on his own. "To Be Free" has a slight reggae beat with understated horns. "Start Moving" is a disco exhortation to spiritual slackers not to be the weakest link in the body of Christ. Eskelin also founded International Concert Evangelism (ICE) Ministries.

Christian radio hits: "Haven't You Heard" (# 12 in 1994); "Come to Me" (# 2 in 1995); "To Be Free" (# 5 in 1995); "Start Moving" (# 19 in 1995).

Eso-Charis

Arthur Green, bass; Jayson Holmes, gtr.; Cory Putnam, voc., gtr.; Matt Putnam, drums. 1998—*Eso-Charis* (independent).

Eso-Charis is a four-piece hard rock band from Ft. Smith, Arkansas, whose name means "grace within" in Greek. Lead singer Cory Putnam has drawn attention for a vocal style that varies from intense high-pitched screaming to a clean, sometimes spoken style on particular tracks. Their self-titled album was produced by Bruce Fitzhugh of **Living Sacrifice.** The usually heavy music conveys urgency, as in the opening "Born with a Future," which has Putnam screaming "I love you" over and over again. "The Narrowing List" describes the diminution of Satan's list of damned souls as the band and others continue winning more disciples for Christ. Eso-Charis also released a seven-inch vinyl record featuring two songs, "The Absolute Progress of a Nothing Day" and "Home Left Empty." The death metal Christian magazine *Dead Zine* praised that record as sounding nothing like the debut album and complimented Putnam on developing a new style that offers "the closest vocals to sounding like Satan without being Satan" that they have ever heard.

Ester Drang

Bryce Chambers, voc., gtr.; James McAllister, gtr., kybrd.; David Motter, kybrd.; Sterling Williams, drums; Kyle Winner, bass. 1999—*That Is When He Turns Us Golden* (Red Crown); 2001—*Goldenwest* (Burnt Toast).

www.esterdrang.com

Ester Drang formed in Broken Arrow, Oklahoma, in 1996 as a trio composed of Bryce Chambers, James McAllister, and Kyle Winner. The eventual addition of David Motter and Sterling Williams gave the group a fuller sound, and they would earn a loyal following in the regional music scene in and around Tulsa. The local reviewer for *Tulsa World* described their debut album as filled with songs that "bristle with an otherworldly energy and seem held together by a physics more flexible than our own." The group has earned a national audience among Christian music fans primarily through their regular appearances at the *Cornerstone* festival in Bushnell, Illinois. With delicate melodies, hushed vocals, and walls of buzzing guitars, the group's sound is obviously fashioned after that of **Starflyer 59,** but the addition of keyboards adds diverse elements. At twenty-three minutes, the album *That Is When He Turns Us Golden* is barely more than an EP. It appears to be a concept piece with all nine tracks flowing together into what is almost a single song. The overall sound reminds a *Phantom Tollbooth* reviewer of a "lost in space" ambience in which the music seems to drift in from some place faraway, broken now and then by feedback or static and interrupted by various electronic beeps. Lyrical lines like "You're with me always," "I know I'll make it through with you," and "your love is all I need" offer hope to those who feel they are adrift among the stars. The *Goldenwest* album was produced by Chris Colbert of **Breakfast with Amy** and **Fluffy/Duraluxe;** it moves the band beyond Starflyer imitations into a realm of their own. The opening title track begins with a lone piano, then adds drums, and eventually builds into a full-band effort. "Words That Cure, Parts 1 and 2" have Beach Boy-like harmonies, and "How Good Is Good Enough" has touches of Radiohead. *Cornerstone* describes Ester Drang's concert performances (in Christian venues at least) as having "an atmosphere of worship" that is created less by the vocals or lyrics than through the feel of the instrumental soundscapes themselves.

Estis P@rc

Jared Ostrander, gtr.; Tim Stratton, bass; Magdely Waggoner, voc. 1998—*Sometimes Not* [EP] (Puddlegum); 1999—*And So It Begins*.

The trio known as Estis P@rc comes from Axtell, Nebraska. They combine '40s lounge singing with "wall of guitar" shoegazer rock for a sound reminiscent of **Starflyer 59** (or, even more, of the Starflyer spin-off **Bon Voyage**). After a debut at the 1998 *Cornerstone* festival's Best New Band Showcase, the group tested the waters with an EP and then issued a full-length release produced by Jesse Sprinkle of **Poor Old Lu.** Magdely Waggoner vocalizes in the style of "torch singers" of old. *Bandoppler* called her voice "wistful and haunting." *Phantom Tollbooth* was more candid: "She sings with a sultry seductiveness that is sexy in its execution." Nevertheless, the *Tollbooth* reviewer continues, "Underneath the flirtatious trappings lie very serious encouragements to follow God despite adversity and concerns about ministering to the lonely and downtrodden." Another reviewer dismissed the band as "a bad impersonation of **Starflyer 59** with a female vocalist," but the aforementioned lyrical underpinnings would make for an obvious point of distinction between Estis P@rc and their mentors in the modern lounge market. Whereas Starflyer's lyrics are seldom decipherable, the P@rc's songs have more obvious, if muted Christian intent. "While You're Away" appears at first to be simply a love song, but also works as a yearning for the parousia.

The Eternal Chapter

Thomas Woodrooffe, voc.; et al. 1998—*The Eternal Chapter* (independent).

The Eternal Chapter is a Christian goth band from South Africa, brought to the attention of American audiences by such publications as *True Tunes* and made available to them through distribution with Flaming Fish. With a sound similar to that of late '70s general market band Bauhaus, The Eternal Chapter preserves more of the morbidity of an original "pure goth" sound without the melodrama or shock appeal of '90s artists like Marilyn Manson. The record opens with an atmospheric instrumental called "Temptress," but most of the cuts feature Woodrooffe's deep and mournful vocals. "Death in the Water" features an unusual dance rhythm and is regarded by more than one critic as the album's standout track. "Here Comes the Man" is a cover of a song originally done by a group called Boom Boom Room.

Eternal Decision

Cory Boatright, gtr.; Kirk Campbell, drums; Joe Chambless, bass; Tommy Torres, gtr. 1993—*Miles from Nowhere* (independent); 1997—*Eternal Decision* (Cling); 1999—*Ghost in the Machine* (Godfather).

Christian metal band Eternal Decision began as a Metallica sound-alike group and then evolved to favor a sound more reminiscent of Seattle's Alice in Chains. Their self-titled label debut is a thrash metal classic for some because the Metallica imitation is so pat and the Christ-centered lyrics so blatant as to provide a good idea what the latter band might sound like if it suddenly got saved. On their sophomore release, Eternal Decision tries to be more than just a sound-alike artist but continues to draw on all of the trademark chugs and riffs that are familiar to fans of heavy music. *The Phantom Tollbooth* insulted more than just the group with its review: "This is completely unchallenging and uncreative and as a result most Christian metalheads should be happy with it." Lyrical themes on *Ghost in the Machine* deal mostly with addiction and with the constant struggle between spirit and flesh: "I need you now / To help me with this pain inside" ("Through the Pain"). Kirk Campbell subsequently founded Godfather Records and produced **Gears of Redemption**'s debut album.

Eternity Express

See **Illustrator.**

Ethereal Scourge

Asoka Gare, gtr.; Jared Murray, voc., perc.; Glenn Reseigh, drums; Greg Smith, bass. 1997—*Judgement and Restoration* (Rowe).

The band Ethereal Scourge is a heavy metal quartet from Adelaide, Australia, sometimes compared to Pantera, Sepultura, or **Mortification.** Vocals are of the growl variety, but not as dismal as death metal or grindcore. Asoka Gare dem-

onstrates unusual proficiency on his guitar, with classical influences (Mozart, Vivaldi) showing through. The band's debut album features the usual fast-tempo hard and heavy sounds of metal with more poetic lyrics than are generally associated with that genre. The opening track, "Through the Waters," begins, "To dwell in the light / Of the Ancient of Days / In bliss to see the glory / Of his awesome face / Drink the benediction / Divine endless grace / Emmanuel enthroned / By his side take your place." Such theological, even worshipful imagery is typical of the project. The track "Subconcious" is an acoustic instrumental played against the backdrop of a waterfall.

E.T.W. (a.k.a. **End Time Warriors**)

Elroy Forbes [a.k.a. MC El King], voc.; Mike Hill [a.k.a. Big Free], voc.; Johnny "Jam" Williams, voc. 1989—*End Time Warriors* (Graceland); 1991—*Stop! The Wild Hype* (ForeFront); 1993—*Let's Stay Together*; 1995—*Psychotheosocioghettopathic: The Escape*; 1997—*Ain't Nobody Dyin' but Us*.

The rap trio E.T.W. originally formed at Oral Roberts University in 1985 to compete in a local talent contest. Their debut release focused a bit too heavily on religious put-downs of the culture and tended to come off as judgmental and sloganeering. But *CCM* critic Jamie Lee Rake would describe *Stop! The Wild Hype* as "the most consciously danceable rap collection released on a Christian label yet." The album experiments with house music ("This Is the Life") and features a cover of **DeGarmo and Key**'s "Destined to Win." E.T.W. hit big with their third outing, which includes an inspired remake of **Al Green**'s "Let's Stay Together." The song broke through to mainstream charts, went into heavy rotation on the BET video network, and earned the band a new audience in the general market. In recognition of this, they reined in their testifying on the fourth project, which is considered to be their best. On *Psychotheosocioghettopathic,* songs with spiritual themes mix with simply positive hip-hop on a record that allows mainstream audiences to enjoy the music while sliding slowly into the message. "Yea Yea Yea" is a straight-up party song and "She's the One," a love song, while "Elevate Your Mind" and "Be a Man" offer the hope of the gospel as truth for tough times. "Abstract Reality" takes some sarcastic digs at contemporary ways of thinking (as reflected in the album's title) and "Momma's Prayers" gets sentimental in a way that just might touch the hearts of street-hardened urban youth. The standout track, however, is clearly the rant against black-on-black crime, "Ain't Nobody Dyin' but Us." The latter song was subsequently chosen as the 1997 theme song for Mother's Against Violence, and E.T.W. decided to use it as the title song for a compilation album two years later.

Christian radio hits: "This Is the Life" (# 29 in 1991); "Destined to Win" (# 10 in 1991).

Darrell Evans

1998—*You Are I Am* (Integrity); 1999—*Freedom* (Vertical).

Darrell Evans is a modern worship leader who writes and performs music in an uncluttered, guitar-driven style intended to appeal to congregations of members weaned on rock and roll. *CCM* says, "his songs are simple without being simplistic, repetitive without being redundant, and emotional without becoming maudlin." His album *Freedom* offers the upbeat confessional song "Trading My Sorrows," which features a joyous, affirmative chorus, and the more traditional "You Are My Portion," which relies on acoustic guitar, piano, and choral harmonies. The album's centerpiece is the almost eight-minute "I Am in Love with You," featuring an extended electric guitar solo by **Lincoln Brewster.** Evans says, "Once we get to heaven, all reservations about 'appropriate' methods of worship will drop off. We might as well get a jump-start on that now, and if that means being passionate about worship, or even being humiliated before God in front of people, so be it."

Eva O (a.k.a. **Eva O Halo Experience**)

Selected: As Eva O Halo Experience: 1994—*Demons Fall for an Angel Kiss* (Cleopatra). As Eva O: 1999—*Damnation: Ride the Madness* (MCM).

The goth and death metal underground strikes many as the musical environment least likely for Christian habitation, but there are in fact many Christian goth bands **(Dead Artists Syndrome, The Eternal Chapter, Midnight Orchestra, Saviour Machine,** and **Wedding Party).** At times, such artists appear to followers of true goth as mere posers who have adopted goth styles and fashions in some pitiful attempt to evangelize lost souls. Be that as it may, no one could or would ever question the authenticity of Eva O, who participated in the very invention of goth music at ground level before her dramatic conversion to Christ (cf. **Tara VanFlower**). In the late '70s, Eva O played and sang in the L.A. band Speed Queens, which for a time also included Jill Emery, later of Hole. The group functioned as a sort of sister band to Christian Death, which was fronted by Rozz Williams, often playing the same venues together and trading members. Christian Death, which despite its name was decidedly *not* a Christian band, is often credited by rock historians as being the first American goth band. Eva O often played with Christian Death in their club shows, as well as on many of their albums, and is sometimes listed as a member of the group. She herself says that she was not a member of the quintessential band but prefers to be thought of as "a friend who was there when Rozz needed me." After Speed Queens broke up, Eva O started a female trio called Super Heroines, who recorded several underground albums and became a mainstay of the goth scene. Williams eventually left Christian Death and joined with Eva O in forming another goth band, Shadow Project, which also recorded several albums considered to be pioneering classics of the goth genre. Throughout this period (1977–1993), Eva O and her cohorts were thoroughly immersed in a scene that glorified death and the occult. Acclaimed by the goth subculture as "the Queen of Darkness," she was a self-avowed Satanist, was heavily involved with drugs, and—in her own words—"hated humanity." She had a long-term relationship with Williams. The two of them moved to San Francisco together and for a while they were apparently married. She also had a close relationship with Richard Ramirez, the so-called Night Stalker later convicted of thirteen rape/murders in the Los Angeles area, and was in love with him. "Richard was my life," she has written at her website. "I was in love with Death and the Demonic world. Rozz was the first to pull me away from Richard and it hurt to move so far from Richard. We still talked every day and I still had the hope that I would see him when he moved to San Francisco to go to trial for the murders he had committed there."

Sometime in the early '90s, Eva O experienced a spiritual rebirth. She told *Cornerstone* that while she was making an album she intended to call *Angels Fall for a Demon's Kiss* she read the book *Angels* by Billy Graham as research, to learn about God's angels in opposition to the demons she favored. "I began to realize how important we are to God," she said. "After reading the book I accepted the Lord." The album was retitled *Demons Fall for an Angel's Kiss* and was released by the artist under the name Eva O Halo Experience. It ended up taking a very different tack than she (or her record company) had originally envisioned. The songs are explicitly Christian, to the point that critics complained about them being preachy. Certain tracks, including "Unveil" and "Take a Jesus," are actually worship songs, while "Angel of Death" offers a no-holds-barred warning against the temptations that Satan sets before people to entice them into sin. As the album title implies, angels are a dominant theme, figuring prominently in the songs "Angel of Earth," "Angel on Fire," and "For the Angels." The album's sound is basically that of '80s goth rock with heavy punk influence, though Eva O admits to having pursued "a lighter touch" to accompany the transformed theme than she had employed on previous projects. Her next project, however, would be as dark and heavy as anything she had ever produced. *Damnation: Ride the Madness* was billed as Part One of a two-part set, the second half to be titled *Salvation: Are You Ready to Die?* On its own, the *Damnation* album offers a bleak and eerie portrait of judgment and certain condemnation. Eva O combines dark-wave ambient keyboards with world beat percussion and industrial metal guitars to support a voice that speaks authoritatively of harsh and ugly things. Only at the very end, on the last track, does she declare, "I stand before his light. . . . Nothing is hidden, it's all exposed / He endures the pain and carries all the load / In his light I became broken. . . . Jesus is the King of Kings. . . . He will cleanse you from your sins." It is a triumphant conclusion, but many lack the fortitude to get that far, as she discovered performing the concept piece at the Christian *Cornerstone* festival in 1999. She now has a notice posted at her website: "Warning! *Damnation* is not for everyone!" with an explanation and a hint of what is still to come. The album was produced by Eric Clayton of **Saviour Machine** and also features Josh Pyle of **Audio Paradox.** In 2001, Eva O previewed *Salvation* in a profile for *HM* indicating that her theology was improving even as she prepared the project: "I no longer believe in the rapture," she said in reference to a nonbiblical doctrine popular among some fundamentalists. "And with the story found in *Salvation,* there came a point where the rapture happened, so I had to go through and change a few things."

As one of Christian music's converts from "the other side," Eva O has defied some expectations by not cutting off all contact with the culture from which she sprang. She continues to perform music of the goth/death metal variety and to dress in the black leather/negligee fashions associated with that scene. She speaks kindly and even fondly of many of the musicians with whom she has shared adventures in the past. She remained friends with Rozz Williams, who was named by Trent Reznor of Nine Inch Nails as well as by Marilyn Manson as "an influence of idolatrous proportion." In 1998, Williams committed suicide and, that same year, Eva O released a final, unplugged Shadow Project album (*From the Heart,* Triple X) as a memorial tribute to him. Eva O is married to another Christian goth musician, Alan Clayton, who plays with a band called The Wounded and has released independent solo albums (*Gorgitation of the Pure; The Wounded*).

Everdown

Eric Bureau, voc.; Ryan Leach, bass; Nate Shumaker, gtr.; Chris Wible, drums; Chris Allain, gtr. (−1996) // John Helmig, gtr. (+ 1996). 1995—*Sicken* (Tooth and Nail); 1996—*Straining.*

Everdown is a post-grunge metal band from New Hampshire that first established itself as a regional act in the Boston area and went on to enjoy some success as a club band in the general market. They have played with such groups as Stompbox, Sick of It All, and Fugazi. The group began performing under the name Dry Bones and released a limited distribution demo under that name. They changed their name to Crawlspace for a while until trademark problems arose (the California group by that name remains quite amused that there was once a *Christian* band that tried to use their name). The group's first album as Everdown impressed *HM* magazine, which liked the punk/metal blend (similar to **The Crucified**) and chose "Shelter," "Two," and the title tune as standout tracks. The group garnered much more attention with *Straining,* coming

into their own as a hard rock band with their own unique sound. *The Lighthouse* described their music as "grunge with intelligible lyrics"; *7ball* said the band was "certain to please fans of all things loud—especially those who think Soundgarden turned into a bunch of sissies." Lyrically, the group was more explicit about their faith on the first album, but demonstrated a knack for the poignant turn of phrase on both projects: "He seals his fate and his destiny without God / His shelter is sin" (from "Shelter"); "This will is gone / My smile is desire / In the suffering love of God" (from "Sweet"). Eric Bureau and Ryan Leach left the band soon after the release of *Straining.*

Evergreen

Ali Loader, voc.; et al. 1999—*Dalek Boy* (independent).

Evergreen is a British Christian rock band fronted by Ali Loader who previously led the band Infopop, a successful group in the British Christian music scene. Evergreen shows the grunge influence of the American Seattle sound, but fits best into the British tradition of groups like **Delirious?** and The Electric Revival that trace their dominant style back to **U2.** *Dalek Boy* is described by Loader as a worship-oriented record, though *Phantom Tollbooth* observes that most of the songs speak of life as informed by a faith perspective rather than evincing the addressed-to-God approach that a worship orientation usually implies. The title of the album derives from the popular science fiction series *Dr. Who,* on which the Daleks are a cyborg-like alien race that are the main character's mortal enemies.

Everybodyduck

Darin McWatters, voc.; Tim Brinkman, drums (−1998); Miranda Landers, voc. (− 1998); Tim Sovinec, gtr. (− 1998; + 1999); Mark Stafford, bass (−1998) // Mike Day, drums (+ 1998); Corey Knapp, bass (+ 1998); Josh Blanken, gtr. (+ 1998, −1999); Molly Jensen, voc. (+ 1998, −1999); Wendy Huckins, voc. (+ 1999). 1996—*Everybodyduck* (Rugged); 1998—*Still Know How to Groove;* 1999—*Seized by the Power of a Great Affection;* 2001—*Out of the Overflow: A Modern Worship Recording.*

Everybodyduck is a Christian bubblegum group initially formed in 1992 by five graduates of Southwestern Bible College in Phoenix, Arizona. Their musical style is reminiscent of that which carried Tony Orlando and Dawn to the top of the charts in the early '70s with ditties like "Knock Three Times" and "Tie a Yellow Ribbon 'round the Old Oak Tree." Of course, the latter group was no favorite of critics, and that has been the case with Everybodyduck as well. It is hard to find a review of their first album that does not use words like "trite," "cornball," or "cheesy." As *7ball* puts it, the songs all sound like "sermon illustrations rewritten to make them rhyme"; they feature "a miasma of clichés that youth pastors think are cool and kids routinely ignore." The song "Shags Has Hung Himself" tells what happened to a poor dog when he was given *too much leash* (get it?). "Suzy's Diet" is about a girl who despite good intentions fails to lose weight because she doesn't remove the foods that tempt her from her fridge. "The Happy Smiley Song" features these camp-counselor lyrics: "The grass is soft and cool and green / I think God's world is pretty keen."

On *Still Know How to Groove,* an almost entirely new group continues to do the same thing, though now they are better at it. Darin McWatters, the principal songwriter, serves up a new slate of silly tunes aimed squarely at the junior high school market. The song "8" is a story about a boy who celebrates his eighth birthday with a party at which he himself gets ignored. "Sunday Shoes" is probably the album's highlight, affirming (in an admittedly trite way) that it can be cool to be a Christian: "Jesus doesn't want me for a zombie / He's given me free will so I can choose / I've escaped this world's snare, but I don't have to be square / I've become a Christian but I still know how to groove." The song works because it deals with a theme appropriate to the preadolescent audience to whom Everybodyduck's music appeals. Indeed, harsh criticisms of this group's music hold only if one assumes that the music is intended for an adolescent or adult audience. As pre-teenybopper music, Everybodyduck works quite well. The only problem, then, is its penchant to have a lesson in every song. They miss the mark with their more serious songs like "Walk the Plank" (presenting a die-to-self theme). There is nothing wrong with the message per se; it is just not age appropriate for children under twelve, the only people likely to be listening to the album.

Seized by the Power of a Great Affection is a collection of worship songs, performed in an alternative-pop acoustic style. In addition to the classic hymn "My Jesus I Love Thee" and Melody Green's "There Is a Redeemer," the group performs several original songs written or cowritten by McWatters. Highlights include "Great Affection" and "Because You Are." These are compelling, beautiful, and profound songs, proving that McWatters and Everybodyduck are indeed capable of making adult or college-oriented music when they choose to do so. The group followed with *Out of the Overflow,* essentially a volume-two set of more worship songs. This time they cover **Delirious?**'s "Lord You Have My Heart" and **Darlene Zschech**'s "Shout to the Lord," as well as performing "You've Got the Right Words," best known by **Rich Young Ruler.** A standout original song, "You Are There," is sung by Molly Jensen, who appears to have returned after an absence.

Miranda Landers, who left Everybodyduck after their first album, became Miranda Richardson and recorded a solo album as simply **Miranda.** She and Tim Brinkman would also record as **Sparklepop.**

Every Day Life (a.k.a. **EDL**)

Tedd Cookerly, voc.; Carl Weaver, gtr., voc.; Eric Wilkins, drums, voc.; Oxx, bass (– 1999) // Jeff Elbel, bass, voc. (+ 1999). As Every Day Life: 1996—*Disgruntled* (Alarma); 1997—*American Standard.* As EDL: 1999—*Moment of Clarity* (KMG); 2001—*Every Day Life* (Fashionpop).

The Christian group Every Day Life should probably be credited with inventing rapcore, the musical style that would take over the world and briefly become the most popular (and despised) genre on the airwaves at the turn of the millennium. They are quick to share that credit with 311 and Rage Against the Machine, but they don't have to share it much more broadly than that. Every Day Life was performing rapcore (and calling it that) all around Southern California as early as 1992, a year before Rage Against the Machine released their first album and a year before Korn had even formed. Limp Bizkit wasn't even in the oven yet, though, to be fair, the Beastie Boys had been bashing about New York for over a decade, displaying all the ingredients that would eventually go into the rapcore stew. Still, it was EDL (as their fans call them) who first mixed these together and brought them to full boil. The fact that other bands *recorded* music of this type first is but a sad commentary on the Christian music industry, which is always wary of innovation and does not offer much support (much less contracts) to artists who do not sound like someone who has already achieved success in the general market.

The group's lineup went through some changes during its formative years, but Tedd Cookerly remained the front man and defining influence. Cookerly is quick to play down the band's historical significance, attributing the development of rapcore in various locations to the simultaneous evolution of musical ideas. Development of the EDL sound (angry, punk-seasoned rap vocals laid down over an intense metal bed of industrial noise), he says, "had more to do with providence and throwing down some freestyle jams than it did with becoming musical pioneers." He told *7ball,* "One of the ideas I had was to just kind of encompass everything that a person could hear on the radio at any given time—you know, pop, rap, R&B, hip-hop, rock-n-roll, heavy metal, the whole thing. We did the best we could with the instruments we had, but it took a while to gel." Cookerly also points to bands like Deprivation Chamber, Head, and Downset as influential on EDL's sound.

Disgruntled was produced by **Lanny Cordola.** The songs "E Coli," "Perseverance," and "Look" all enjoyed some crossover success on college radio stations in certain quarters. "Cry of the Lame" and "Bystander" (about divorce) also have a potent drive and menacing groove that *True Tunes* would say "jolts the system." The record, which had unimaginative critics calling the group "a Christian version of Rage Against the Machine," caused a bit of a stir in the Christian music subculture. Its cover shows a picture of the American flag with the band's name cut out of it, along with an aerial photo of the Reginald Deaton beating that occurred during the 1993 L.A. riots. The album itself features a rendition of a song called "Whitey on the Moon," originally written in the early '70s to protest government allocation of tax dollars for space exploration when millions of (minority) citizens were living in grinding poverty (cf. **Larry Norman**'s "The Great American Novel"). The racial sentiments in these aspects of EDL's work had some critics dismissing them as "angry black militants," a charge that was easier to sustain before it was learned that all four members were white.

The group came back with an even harder and heavier sound on *American Standard,* produced by **Michael Knott.** The title track suggests that selflessness rather than materialism ought to be the hallmark of a free society. "Ten Little Indians" deals with injustices perpetrated against Native Americans (often in the name of Christ). "Closure" addresses the destructive nature of church politics. "Electric Starter" reflects on the status of a society in which people say, "How Are You?" only as a greeting, without really wanting a reply. "Touched" deals with the subject of molestation or date rape, voicing the anger of the victim at his or her abuser. "Log Off" portrays an angry parent who thoughtlessly tells her child, "Kill yourself, kill yourself, why don't you just kill yourself!"

The album *Moment of Clarity* shows some evolution beyond the traditional rapcore sound, to the disappointment of some critics and fans. The band moves more toward hip-hop and commercially accessible pop à la Faith No More. Nevertheless, *HM* and *7ball* took the changes positively, as setting the band apart from what had become a barrage of sound-alikes. "Time to Change" actually sounds like an **Audio Adrenaline** song, with a pop anthem feel sandwiched between its straight-up rap lines. But *Moment* also contains several hard hitting numbers worthy of the EDL trademark: the opening "Let It Ride" (offering Cookerly's personal account of some past failings) and "Represent" (written for those who still want to fly a Confederate flag: "Let it burn down / Let it burn down to the ground / It doesn't represent me"). Jeff Elbel, the new bass player, had previously played with **Farewell to Juliet, LSU,** and **Sunny Day Roses.** KMG pushed *Moment of Clarity* as a crossover album for the general market, and it rose to Number Sixteen on CMJ's college music chart.

A couple of steps ahead of **Crashdog,** Every Day Life became the first group in Christian music to address political issues in a responsible manner. In reviewing *Disgruntled, True Tunes* said "never before has any Christian band really gone for the jugular, expressing intelligently and passionately any kind of dissatisfaction with the nation's political system." Predictably, such contributions were not always appreciated. The extremely pro-censorship Family Christian Bookstores (the largest Christian music retailer in America) refused to stock either of the first two albums. *Disgruntled* was ostensibly rejected out of noble racial sensitivity, since the song "Whitey on the Moon" uses the word "Nigga"; the word is actually uttered by a (black) guest rapper from **Gospel Gangstaz.** *American Standard* was rejected because the song "Ten Little Indians" was deemed "unpatriotic."

Every Man's Hero

Mike Heck, drums; Dillon McKnight, gtr.; Caleb Ralph, bass, voc. 2000—
No One Ever Said a Word (Bettie Rocket).

Every Man's Hero is a classic punk trio that melds old-school punk with hardcore rock. On their debut album, they deliver fifteen tracks played at a typical rapid-fire pace, inspiring comparison to Christian bands like **Ninety Pound Wuss.** Lyrics are not understandable, but the songs deal with such topics as racism, teenage runaways, and dating. *HM* notes that Caleb Ralph's abrasive shrieks and screams are effective on the angry songs ("Badlife") but sometimes seem inappropriate when spitting out lyrics like "Jesus, you save me. . . . I'm in love with you").

Evie

1974—*Evie* (Word); 1975—*Evie Again;* 1976—*Gentle Moments;* 1977—*Mirror; Come On Ring Those Bells;* 1978—*A Little Song of Joy for My Little Friends;* 1979—*Never the Same;* 1980—*Evie Favorites, Vol. I;* 1980—*Teach Us Your Way* [with Pelle Karlsson]; 1981—*Unfailing Love;* 1983—*Hymns; Restoration* [with Pelle Karlsson]; 1986—*When All Is Said and Done;* 1987—*Christmas Memories;* 1990—*Celebrate the Family* [by Evie and the Karlssons] (White Field); 1996—*Our Recollections* (Word); *Songs for His Family* [by Evie and the Karlssons] (label unknown).

The Norwegian singer best known as simply "Evie" was phenomenally popular in the '70s, when the Christian adult contemporary market was admittedly less crowded. Indeed, she deserves to be credited with starting or pioneering the distinctive subgenre of that style sometimes called "inspirational"—and few have ever performed it better. Evie produced numerous albums of sweet, inspiring music that offered Christian fans an alternative to the Christian rock movement. Musically, her sound recalled that of such light pop singers as Petula Clark or Peggy Lee. *Jesus Music* magazine says Evie was "definitely the sweetheart of easy listening contemporary Christian music" for a decade. She sang at the White House, played at venues like New York City's Carnegie Hall, and sold out far bigger arenas than almost any other Christian artist could have managed in the '70s. It should perhaps be noted that she was widely regarded as one of the most beautiful women in the world, and it is probably safe to assume that many twenty-something Jesus freaks thought they were in love with her. In 1979, she broke all their hearts by marrying Swedish pastor Pelle Karlsson, who had once been a pop star in his own land. Karlsson wrote a number of songs for Evie, including "Shine" and "Never the Same Again." The family eventually made their home in Florida.

Born Evie Tornquist (c. 1957) as the daughter of recent Norwegian immigrants, Evie became something of a child star in her parents' native land. She sang in programs there on the family's frequent trips back and forth across the Atlantic, recording an album and performing on national TV by age fourteen. For the next three years, she spent almost one week a month in Scandinavia and then, at age seventeen, recorded her first album for American audiences. The self-titled debut was a tremendous hit, featuring a range of songs from Ray Hildebrand's Vacation Bible School ditty "Say, I Do" to **Andraé Crouch**'s monumental "My Tribute." The album also includes Crouch's hymn, "The Blood Will Never Lose Its Power" and **Larry Norman**'s "Sweet Sweet Song of Salvation." On *Evie Again,* she covers "Clean before My Lord" by **Honeytree,** providing what many consider to be the definitive version of that song. On *Gentle Moments,* she turns Kurt Kaiser's campfire song "Pass It On" into a credible adult contemporary ballad and offers "Give Them All," one of her most beautiful and memorable songs. It was *Mirror,* however, that would become the ultimate Evie album, providing four out of eighteen songs for her eventual hits collection ("Mirror," "Born Again," "Praise You Just the Same," "Just Because I Asked"). Still, her biggest hit ever turned out to be the title track to a Christmas album. Evie's version of "Come On, Ring Those Bells" would become contemporary Christian music's first major contribution to a burgeoning catalogue of popular holiday songs. Over twenty years later, it was still receiving generous airplay every year at Christmas time and would remain the artist's best-known song.

In all, Evie recorded more than thirty albums, including several featuring songs in Scandinavian languages, two albums with her husband, and two more featuring the whole family (Pelle, Kris, and Jenny). *Teach Us Your Way* and *Restoration* are concept albums, the first a worship project and the latter a sustained musical treatise on the unity of the church. Both seem to be more intended for meditation and prayer than for casual listening or entertainment; both include a Pelle Karlsson song based on John 17 called "Jesus' Prayer." *Hymns* includes such standards as "The Old Rugged Cross," "All Hail the Power of Jesus' Name," and "How Great Thou Art." In 1981, Evie officially retired from performing. She remembers her fifteen years of constant touring with fondness and says she only hopes that the opening words of the song "Live for Jesus" will hold true: "Oh, I wanna be remembered / As the girl who sang her songs for Jesus Christ."

Christian radio hits: "Shine" (# 17 in 1979).

Dove Awards: 1977 Female Vocalist; 1978 Female Vocalist.

Exeter Flud

Jacob Dabbs, gtr.; Gabriel Howerton, drums; David Ott., gtr., voc., bass. 1998—*Exeter Flud* (BulletProof).

Exeter Flud was a short-lived Christian emo band that was hailed by some as "the next **Prayer Chain**" before their untimely demise. A trio from Georgia, the group was fronted by Ott who went on to play guitar with **Dear Ephesus.** The single album reveals a guitar-heavy sound with vocals reminiscent of **Bloomsday** and moody songs that recall **Champion Birdwatchers** or **The Violet Burning.** Standout tracks include the songs "Passion and Hesitation" and "You Decide," which *The Lighthouse* described as "just plain beautiful." Ott was also the group's songwriter, and he favored lyrics expressive of abstract emotion: "Time pushing against me / Through shadows always, always / Time was nothing to fail you" ("Darling D").

The Exkursions

See **Mike Johnson.**

Extol

Ole Børud, gtr., flute, voc.; Christer Espevoll, gtr.; Eystein Holm, bass; David Husvik, drums; Peter Espevoll, voc. (– 2001). 1999—*Burial* (Solid State); *Mesmerized* [EP]; 2000—*Undeceived*; 2001—*Paralysis* (End Times).

Extol is a Norwegian Christian death metal band with an insanely loyal following. Extol fans fill up Internet sites with ravings about the group as "surpassing every band in Christian music" and as being "one of the heaviest and most innovative death/black metal bands to ever grace the ears of mankind." Hyperbole, split infinitives, and archaic sexisms aside, the group does demonstrate unusual competence in their craft. Their sound is tight, with the fret-ripping guitars and frantic drumming all holding together at a breakneck pace, starting, stopping, twisting, and turning as a single entity. Such technical skill is uncommon in metal music, and Extol's legion of enthusiastic advocates have reason to be proud. The prime innovation, furthermore, is their employment of two lead singers: Peter Espevoll handles what are called grinding vocals, the morbid growls typical of death metal, while Ole Børud is officially charged with clean vocals, that is, normal and often melodic singing. Børud was formerly with the band **Schaliach.** Tor Magne Glidje, who fronts **Lengsel,** is sometimes listed as bass player for Extol. Emil Nikolaisen of **Royal** was also a member of Extol prior to the band's debut recording.

Burial features three songs in Norwegian, but otherwise the group performs all of its material in English, with moderate success ("Blessed is he who has got his sins forgiven"). The EP *Mesmerized* includes three new songs and three industrial remixes of tracks from *Burial,* prepared by techno industrial artists **Sanctum** and Raison D'Etre. The latter three tracks are of historical note, though Extol fans (who do not tend toward ecumenicity in their musical tastes) pretty much hated them. *Undeceived* moves more toward death metal, but features two instrumentals that are less aggressive and more melodic than the vocal tracks. Other tracks reveal classical and progressive influences, such as the use of violins or brief neo-Renaissance intros to ultimately heavy songs. "A Structure of Souls" is a showcase for the electric guitars, and both "Ember" and "Renewal" wed melodic metal with shrill, dark ambience for a contrast of extremes. The group is unabashedly Pentecostal, but tries to be ecumenical in their approach, extending their appeal at least to non-Pentecostal fundamentalists. "All of us believe in angels and demons and speaking in tongues, and that we're in a spiritual war where prayer is the most important weapon," says Espevoll. "But our mission is to see people get saved and receive Jesus in their hearts." On *Paralysis,* the band covers the song "Shadow of Death," originally performed by **Believer.**

Extreme (and Van Halen)

Pat Badger, bass; Nuno Bettencourt, gtr.; Gary Cherone, voc.; Paul Geary, drums. 1989—*Extreme* (A&M); 1990—*Extreme II: Pornograffitti;* 1992—*Three Sides to Every Story;* 1995—*Waiting for the Punchline.*

Extreme was not a Christian band as such, but rather a general market metal funk band led by a devout Christian (Gary Cherone). The group had nothing to do with the contemporary Christian music subculture and, though big in the world at large, was rarely noticed by media devoted to covering contemporary Christian music. The two major exceptions to this would be the attention given to Cherone and Extreme by *HM* magazine and by Mark Joseph in his book *The Rock and Roll Rebellion.* The band formed in Boston, Massachusetts, in 1985 when Cherone and Paul Geary, both of whom had been part of Boston-based Dream, connected with Portugese-born guitarist Nuno Bettencourt. The latter is noted as one of rock music's premier hard rock guitarists and provided Extreme with the metal edge their name implied. Ironically, however, the group became best known for two of its ballads, the memorable "More Than Words" (# 1 in 1991) and "Hole Hearted" (# 4 in 1991). On the basis of these two Top 10 hits, the second album *Pornograffitti* went double platinum, and the band toured triumphantly with ZZ Top.

Cherone was raised Roman Catholic. He left the church, but would later credit radio preacher Chuck Swindoll with reawakening him to a faith that he says he had ignored but never doubted. In interviews, Cherone talked openly about his belief in Christ "as the Son of God," while being careful not to implicate the rest of his band in a way that would get them labeled on account of him. As the group's chief songwriter, however, issues of faith did come to the fore. The self-titled debut album features an antiabortion song ("Rock a Bye Bye") and, more to the point, a song called "Watching, Waiting," which describes the crucifixion of Jesus. The words are intentionally a bit obscure, with the meaning only becoming clear when one reads the lyric sheet. The line that sounds like "I'm staring at the sun" is actually written "I'm staring at the Son." In a similar fashion, the hit song "Hole-Hearted" expresses a basic spiritual message in somewhat veiled terms. The song appears to be based on the classic dictum of Pascal to the effect that every human being is born with "a God-shaped hole" that must be filled before they can be complete. Yet the song is intentionally polyvalent. Cherone once explained that it is about a person looking for what he needs to make him happy, to give him peace. "It could be a girl, it could be God. I don't want to tell you what it is," he said, with artistic reticence, before adding, "to me, I'm looking for God." Other songs are less ambiguous. "Rise and Shine," from *Three Sides,* quotes the prophet Daniel and Jesus outright, while "God's Not Dead" offers a pretty aggressive spiritual statement. *Waiting for the Punchline* features a song with the tantalizing title, "There Is No God." It sets to music a line straight from Scripture, "The fool hath said in his heart / There is no god" (Psalm 14:1 or 53:1).

Aside from specific songs, Cherone's faith shaped the basic concepts for at least two of Extreme's albums. He has said that the underlying theme of the album *Pornograffitti* is the effect that pornography can have on a young mind and the struggle it produces later for issues related to morality, temptation, and sex. The character in the drama portrayed throughout that album is named Frances, but Cherone has openly admitted that the tale is autobiographical, "about some things that I had to go through." The album *Three Sides to Every Story,* which features ambitious stylings reminiscent of Queen, is a direct assault on modern notions of relativism. The titular three sides are my side, your side, and the truth, and the album is actually divided into three suites of songs dealing with these matters. Desire for change is expressed in "Who Cares?": "Tell me, Jesus, are you angry? . . . Am I ever gonna change?" The final suite, then, offers three songs (recorded at Abbey Road studios with a seventy-piece orchestra) expressive of eternal and ultimate truth. *Rolling Stone,* not normally an advocate of such ways of conceptualizing reality, praised the album as demonstrating Extreme's "eclecticism and willingness to experiment," singling out "the final three songs" as its highlights.

Being a Christian in one of America's premier heavy metal bands could not have been easy, and Cherone has been honest about expressing his successes and failures at toeing the line. A number of songs that he sang with the group used vulgar words that would not typically be heard within the Christian market. Asked about this by *HM* magazine, he seemed surprised that it was even an issue. He acknowledged, "It's just a lack of vocabulary, which I can be guilty of," but then continued a bit more defensively: "It's an emotion that's a part of me. I'm honest. I get emotional when I sing. . . . There are probably more important things that I would consider a compromise of my faith. . . . Who knows? Maybe it will get better. I know it won't get worse."

After Extreme broke up, Cherone was asked to replace Sammy Hagar (who had replaced David Lee Roth) as lead singer of Van Halen, one of the most popular metal bands of all time. Suddenly, in one of the most bizarre turnabouts in the history of rock and roll, the hard rocking party band that first broke into the airwaves with an anthem called "Runnin' with the Devil" was fronted by a devout Christian. More incredible,

perhaps, some of their songs were being written by a devout Christian. The partnership only lasted for a single album (the oddly titled *III*) in 1998, but two of the songs on that record make for peculiar Van Halen fare. "Fire in the Hole" deals with the damage that human beings inflict through their speech, and its lyrics seem drawn straight from the Bible: "Rudder of ship which sets the course / Does not the bit bridle the horse / Great is the forest set by a small flame / Like a tongue on fire no one can tame" (cf. James 3:3–5). The song "Once" offers a statement of the Christian doctrine of eternal security: "Once believed can't ever lose faith / Once shared can't ever be separate / Like the dawn of a brand new day / With the power of Deity, I can feel it inside of me / Can you feel it?" This is a long way from "Hot for Teacher," and Van Halen fans, for the most part, were not impressed. All the same, Cherone thanked the Christian author R. C. Sproul for inspiration in the album's liner notes.

Face Value

Steve Dresser, gtr.; Adam Long, drums; Brad Nagle, voc.; Pat Nagle, bass (−2000) // Nate Clay (+ 2000); Josh Keilman (+ 2000). 1999—*Never Stray* (Bettie Rocket); 2000—*There's Always the Radio.*

Face Value is a punk band from Detroit, Michigan, with a sound similar to that of **MxPx, Slick Shoes,** or early **Ghoti Hook** (see also **Craig's Brother, Dogwood, Hangnail, Noggin Toboggan, Shorthanded, Sick of Change, Twotimer, The Undecided,** and **Value Pac;** it's a crowded market). Their debut album, *Never Stray,* suffers from poor production, but deals with the overall theme of "making one's faith in God real and never straying from what one believes" (to quote front man Brad Nagle). The song "Habitual" emphasizes replacing bad habits with positive ones. *There's Always the Radio* has a cleaner, tighter sound. "Hatred" pays homage to **Stryper** with its opening riffs and presents an indictment of prejudice within the church: "Hatred now fills the halls where God's love should abound." A song called "2/14/00" offers some typical punk whining about romantic troubles. "On Valentine's Day I was listening to a bunch of nerds dedicate songs to their girlfriends, so I just wrote this song to outlet my frustrations," says the girlfriend-less composer, Adam Long.

Fade (solo artist)

1997—*The Debut* (Infiniti).

Fade is the name adopted by an African American solo artist who released one album of soulful ballads in 1997. The sound is similar to that of such general market artists as Babyface or Luther Vandross. The songs testify to the overwhelming and enduring character of God's love. "I just love the way you're guiding me through my life," Fade sings to Christ in "It's Alright." The album is a down-tempo affair, though on a few songs ("I Can't Be Stopped," "Dreams of a Better World") Fade's smooth vocals are supplemented by rapped interludes by guest artists Smartz and Spokesman.

Fade (group)

Personnel list unavailable. 1998—*Angel-Thieves* (North and South).

True Tunes and *Phantom Tollbooth* magazines are aware of a Christian duo with the same name as the R&B solo artist Fade. *True Tunes* praised the group as "the type of band you'll rarely if ever hear on the radio, simply because they're too difficult." *Tollbooth* pulls out all the stops and calls *Angel-Thieves* "one of the best independent CDs ever recorded." The duo produces a sound that "calls to mind the dark elegance of The Autumns or **The Violet Burning**" *(True Tunes)* or that suggests "a perfect melding of recent Radiohead with meditative **U2**" *(Tollbooth).* Their lyrics strive for haunting images steeped in ambiguity: "I found paradise in the lost and found / It came up from underground / And all the gods of this world are dying even now."

Scott Faircloff

1998—*Scott Faircloff* (Pamplin).

Born and raised in the Pacific Northwest, Scott Faircloff started playing piano when he was six, picked up guitar a bit later, and studied the songwriting styles of such heroes as the Beatles and Elton John. These influences show prominently in his debut album, produced by **John** and Dino **Elefante.** The project had numerous critics dubbing Faircloff "the Christian John Lennon" because on certain songs ("Pulling Me Closer," "Wrecking Ball Chain," "When God Whispers," "Under Your Wing"), Faircloff's vocal mannerisms and stylings seem to emulate that singer. Indeed, the songs themselves are reminiscent of Lennon's in structure and lyrical whimsy. On other tunes, Faircloff displays more of an American rock style **(Big Tent Revival, Jars of Clay)** that may represent his own emerging sound. The album's dominant theme is the spiritual journey of one who experiences a personal relationship with God. "Pulling Me Closer" focuses on the idea of God always drawing us nearer; "Under Your Wing" expresses peaceful confidence in being under God's protection. The song "Frog's Lament" departs briefly from the record's spiritual orientation to present the humorous thoughts of the fairy-tale frog who can't find a princess willing to give him that transforming kiss.

Christian radio hits: "Wrecking Ball Chain" (# 19 in 1998).

Faith Massive

Joey Davis, Jamey Wright [a.k.a. DJ Seven]. 1998—*Drum and Bass for the Masses* (N'Soul); 1999—*Visions.*

Faith Massive is composed of two DJs who compose and perform instrumental ambient music that varies in tone from meditative to head-bobbing. Their music may be compared to that of such mainstream electronic artists as Roni Size, Waverider, and Goldie. The debut album opens with a reading of Genesis 1:1. It features ethereal keyboards and generous doses of saxophone on several tracks that recall the slithering, sultry jazz sounds of Sade (minus the vocals). Other cuts favor a more avant-garde electronic style. The title of the album actually derives from the technical label applied to this musical genre and is not meant to imply that the group consists only of a rhythm section. *Visions* is a concept piece based on Acts 2:17. The infusion of jazz and even world music is more pronounced and, this time, a few of the tracks feature vocals. What lyrics are present are overtly Christian and often evangelistic. Sometimes, though, the spiritual application must be made by the listener, as on "Shelter," when jazz maven June April sings over mellow piano, "I really feel that I belong in the shelter of your love." *Musicforce* calls the album "romantic praise music." *7ball* says it is "the kind of stuff you could picture someone at a coffeehouse listening to, kicked back while drinking a cappuccino and writing some poetry."

Chris Falson

1992—*Chris Falson (Broken Again)*; 1995—*Live Worship with Chris Falson and the Amazing Stories* (Word); 1997—*A Tree by the Water* (Orchard); 1998—*For Dreamers Only*; 2000—*The Quiet.*

www.chrisfalson.com

Chris Falson is a worship leader, best known for his work with the Maranatha Promise Keepers Band. He has participated in numerous stadium conference events with that group. His self-titled album from 1992, however, reflected more of a laid-back coffeehouse approach, incorporating elements of acoustic rock, jazz, and blues into a mix that reminded some of early Dire Straits. "Wake Up" calls for Christian response to an ever-bleaker world. "Who Do You Love?" is not a cover of the Bo Diddley classic but a reflection on the choice between God and mammon. The album's standout attractions are "Ease the Pain," a description of everyone's quest for redemption and release, and the wonderful "Jammin' with the Angels," which offers a pretty good preview of what its title describes. *A Tree by the Water* also offers soulful ballads and bluesy rockers of the sort associated with James Taylor or **Van Morrison.** The other albums listed above are worship oriented. *For Dreamers Only* is an instrumental re-release of a project recorded in 1990.

Paul Falzone

See **Eli.**

Family of Love

Personnel list unavailable. 1977—*The Bible: A Rock Testament* (Polydor).

Whether or not Family of Love can be regarded as a Christian band would be a matter of controversy since the group was associated with the Children of God cult. The Children of God began as a countercultural parachurch group that was very much a part of the California Jesus movement but soon (long before 1977) grew into the definitive example of an extremist cult, accused of everything from heresy to brainwashing to prostitution (leader David Berg, a.k.a. Moses David, is reported to have interpreted Jesus' command to be "fishers of men" as meaning "hookers for Jesus" and so to have encouraged female followers to use sex as a lure for attracting new converts). The story of the movement is well known and has been recounted elsewhere (see bibliography in Di Sabatino's *The Jesus People Movement*). At any rate, Di Sabatino notes that *this* album "is completely orthodox, as well as being musically first-rate." The group rather ambitiously seeks to offer songs that cover the entire Bible from Genesis to Revelation (with an emphasis on the latter). Their penchant for finding sex in the Bible where others might not comes through on a love song that Ruth sings to Boaz after the two of them have supposedly consummated their relationship during their night on the threshing floor (cf. Ruth 3). For further consideration of whether an unorthodox group can produce orthodox and even inspiring music, compare the **All Saved Freak Band.** For more music from the Children of God, see **Jeremy Spencer.**

The Family Tree

Ian Smallwood, voc.; Ian Truscott, voc.; Phil Truscott, voc. 1975—*On Fire!* (Lamb and Lion); *If We Abide;* 1979—*Fine Love* (Milk and Honey).

The Family Tree was sort of a stripped-down Australian version of the Osmond Brothers, with only three instead of five male singers. Billed as "Australia's top harmony group," the outfit offered three albums filled with their white-bread versions of Jesus music songs. The first record, *On Fire!* features cover versions of **Parchment**'s "Light Up the Fire" and **Love Song**'s "Since I Opened Up the Door." Subsequent albums include more original material, including Ian Truscott's "Standing at the Door" on *If We Abide.* The trio sang with thick accents that some American fans found charming in a Herman's Hermits way. *Harmony* magazine complained that the group overused vocal harmonies rather than just allowing one or another singer to take the lead.

Fanmail

Scott Silletta, voc.; Chuck Cummings, drums (−2000); Nick Garrisi, gtr. (−2000); Erik Tokle, bass (−2000) // Jason Feldman, drums (+ 2000); Jason Fleetwood, bass (+ 2000); Dale Yob, gtr. (+ 2000). 1999—*Here Comes Fanmail* [EP] (Tooth and Nail); *The Latest Craze;* 2000—*Fanmail 2000.*

Fanmail was the second contemporary Christian outing for Scott Silletta, who first earned renown as the original singer and front man for the very popular **PlankEye.** Silletta gathered a bunch of his friends from other bands (Nick Garrisi from **Quayle,** Erik Tokle from **Rich Young Ruler,** Chuck Cummings from **Aunt Bettys**) to record some songs that he had written—those featured on the debut EP and first full-length album. He then had to assemble a different lineup when it appeared that the group might have some legs. Silletta told *Bandoppler* that Fanmail was avoiding the Christian band label that had relegated **PlankEye** to playing certain venues. The group toured with **MxPx,** playing bars and clubs.

The EP *Here Comes Fanmail* includes a cover of the song "Every Breath You Take" by The Police. *The Latest Craze* was described by *Phantom Tollbooth* as "a near-perfect summer album" and as "upbeat pop-punk, with catchy melodies throughout." The specter of **PlankEye**'s sound was definitely present, but the overall sound was much closer to **MxPx** than to Silletta's first band. "True Brand New" rather strongly recalls Tony Basil's '80s hit "Mickey." The song "Rock and Roll Star" borrows its theme from the old Byrds classic: "I wanna be in a rock and roll band / I wanna have lots of rock and roll fans. . . . It's not that hard, it's not that hard." On "Lame," Silletta turns a bit more introspective: "Have I gone too far / To receive blessings from above? . . . I've done things not the same / As I would have three years ago." *Fanmail 2000,* despite the different musicians, sounds the same as the first album, but the songs tend to be darker and more serious. An exception, however, is the just-for-fun sped-up punk version of the Backstreet Boys' song "I Want It That Way." The album closes with "The Other Side," a heartfelt tribute to Gene Eugene, the deceased **Adam Again** leader who as a producer, musician, and friend had an enormous impact on many musicians trying to find their place in the curious world of Christian rock: "Now I'm 27 and you were 38 / Thank you for all your time. . . . I know I bugged you sometimes / Thanks for loving me. . . . You taught me so much / Who will I go to?"

Farewell to Juliet

John Bretzlaff, gtr., bass; Jeff Elbel, gtr.; Brant Hansen, voc.; Jeff Schmale, drums (−1998) // Chad Dunn, drums (+ 1998); Stacey Krejci, bass, kybrd. (+ 1998). 1993—*Echoes of Laughter* (independent); 1998—*Grace and Dire Circumstances* (Marathon).

www.netads.com/arts/music

Chicago-based Farewell to Juliet is a critically acclaimed modern rock band with a unique sound that draws on a variety of influences. The group's name is derived from the title of a nihilistic poem by William Blount that, in Hansen's words, exposes "the bankruptcy of life without the promise of a hereafter." On their first album, *Echoes of Laughter,* the group displays a basic '80s prog-rock sound reminiscent of Rush and the Fixx, but with considerably more acoustic elements integrated into the mix. It includes the song "Endless Sky," a meditation on transience and transcendence that *True Tunes* would call a "perfect Christian alternative song." In addition, "Adam's Chain" addresses the deceptive allure of things that bring bondage, while "Mood Swing" deals humorously with people who get upset over insignificant matters. On *Grace and Dire Circumstances,* the prog-rock elements decrease in favor of sounds more closely associated with **Simple Minds** or The Church. In terms of Christian music, the group sometimes comes across as a mixture of **The Choir** and **Jars of Clay,** though when they want to, they can produce a much harder sound than either of those bands. They don't want to very often, but on *Grace's* "Thermostat" they do kick things into high gear. That song features a guest vocal by Rob Dickinson of Catherine Wheel and reflects on stardom in light of Kurt Cobain's suicide. *Grace* also includes a cover of **The Choir**'s "Chase the Kangaroo," and a number of other tracks that, to quote one critic, provide "lots of those swirly moments" that impressed college students in the '80s. "Browning's Pearl" even recalls the early work of **Sixpence None the**

Richer. Jeff Elbel has developed a reputation among guitar aficionados for his unconventional rhythm style, built around sweeping power chords, atmospheric solos, and lush sounds.

Lyrically, Farewell to Juliet presents songs that, as *True Tunes* puts it, "are balanced artfully between opaque, poetic references and obvious statements of faith." "Sorrow and Pride" from *Echoes* asks, "Are you ready? / Do you dare to cross the line? / Could be the old you / Is quite afraid to die." And on *Grace,* Elbel describes this dilemma: "I've found in my head a cynical thing / I've found in my heart a hopeful thing." Hansen indicates that the band is generally oriented toward the club scene rather than the specifically Christian market, but that "it is very important that audience members understand that we are followers of Christ." He views the music as establishing "a kind of friendly rapport with the listeners" but also wants to "let them know where these songs come from."

In addition to his work with Farewell to Juliet, John Bretzlaff has recorded with his wife, releasing the EP *Songs from the Orange Couch* by John and Kim (Marathon, 2000). Jeff Elbel has played on a number of projects by other artists, including the album *Hope* by **Blackball** and *Dogfish Jones* by **LSU.** He founded the indie band **Sunny Day Roses,** and in 1999 joined **Every Day Life.** In 2001, he formed a band called Ping and released an acoustic album (*No Outlet,* Marathon) to benefit Habitat for Humanity and a memorial fund for the late Gene Eugene (of **Adam Again**). As a writer/critic, Elbel is a regular contributor to *True Tunes* and *7ball,* as well as to an influential Internet magazine devoted to covering the indie rock scene, *The Big Takeover* (www.bigtakeover/playhear.com). The latter magazine is not devoted to Christian music, but Elbel makes sure that certain Christian artists get the attention they deserve.

Donna Fargo

Selected: 1980—*Brotherly Love* (MCA/Songbird).

www.donnafargo.com

Country-western singer Donna Fargo released one album of contemporary Christian music after a spiritual renewal that she attributed to her struggles with multiple sclerosis. Fargo (b. Yvonne Vaughn in 1949) grew up in Mt. Airy, North Carolina, a member of the local Baptist church, but has said that faith lost most of its meaning to her except as a system of moral rules. In 1972, she rose to the top of the charts with a song she had written called "The Happiest Girl in the Whole U.S.A." The song was Number One for weeks on the country charts and was also a crossover hit, making it to Number Eleven on *Billboard*'s pop charts. The album *The Happiest Girl in the Whole U.S.A.* went platinum, and the song was awarded the Country Music Association's "Song of the Year" award. It is the song for which she will always be most remembered, even though her

follow-up "Funny Face" was an even bigger hit (# 5 in 1972). The back-to-back million-selling singles established her briefly as a country superstar, and she was twice acclaimed the Best Selling Female Country Artist of the Year (1972, 1973). Fargo continued to have more country hits (with only minor crossover pop success), but then tragedy struck when she was diagnosed with MS in 1979. She was for some time completely debilitated by the disease, unable to dial a phone or cut her own food, and constantly racked by physical pain. It was at this time, through her conversations with a hospital chaplain, that she determined to "get serious about God." She recorded *Brotherly Love* at a time when the disease was in remission. The album contains traditional hymns ("Amazing Grace," "How Great Thou Art"), modern gospel songs ("Where You Lead," "I Knew Jesus Before He Was a Superstar"), and a few original songs, including "The Baptism of Jesse Taylor," which was a hit on some country stations. She also enjoyed a country hit with "Say I Do," which opens the album. Fargo has continued to record and to write, as able—the MS that afflicts her is the attack/remission variety as opposed to that which is systematically progressive. She has authored a collection of inspirational greeting cards and written a book of inspirational thoughts and poetry *(Trust in Yourself)*. She also composed and recorded the gospel song "Mighty Shield of Armor," which hit Number One on Christian country charts.

The Farm Beetles

Terry Taylor; et al. 1998—*Meat the Farm Beetles* (Stunt).

The Farm Beetles were a joke project for **Terry Scott Taylor** and a few of his anonymous cohorts—most likely fellow members of **The Swirling Eddies.** The group got together and performed hillbilly versions of classic Beatle songs complete with animal noises and revamped lyrics ("Yesterday / Love was such an easy game to play / Now I need a place to bale my hay / Oh, what the hey"). The group also slaughters "Helter Skelter," "Strawberry Fields Forever," "A Day in the Life," "Birthday," "Revolution # 9," "The End," and "Within You, Within You," as well as John Lennon's "Imagine"—which someone should have told them is not technically a Beatles song. The album was later combined with another joke record, **The Swirling Eddies**' *Swirling Mellow,* and released on a single CD. The Eddies' *Sacred Cows* would have made for a better pairing, but it's not like anyone is ever going to actually listen to any of the albums anyway.

Mark Farner

1988—*Just Another Injustice* (Frontline); 1989—*Wake Up . . . ;* 1991— *Some Kind of Wonderful;* 1992—*Closer to Home.*

www.markfarner.com

Mark Farner was the lead singer, guitarist, and principal songwriter for one of the '70s' biggest rock groups, Grand Funk (originally Grand Funk Railroad). He experienced a dramatic conversion to Christ in 1983 and later recorded three evangelical albums (*Closer to Home* is a "best of" compilation).

Farner was born in Flint, Michigan, in 1948. He began playing guitar at age fifteen when bad knees ended his prospects for a football career and he became a rock and roll professional after he was expelled from high school during his senior year. He got a job playing with a group called Terry Knight and the Pack, which scored a big regional and minor national hit with the song, "I (Who Have Nothing)" (# 46 in 1966). In 1969, the leader of that band retired from performing in favor of management and put Farner, drummer Don Brewer (also a member of the Pack), and bassist Mel Schacher (a former member of ? and the Mysterians) together as Grand Funk Railroad, a psychedelic blues/rock band fashioned after Cream or the Jimi Hendrix Experience. A mere two years later, the group had one gold and five platinum albums to their credit. In 1970, Grand Funk was the best-selling musical act in America, ahead of such artists as the Beatles, the Rolling Stones, Led Zeppelin, and Crosby, Stills and Nash. In 1971, they broke the Beatles' supposedly untouchable record for ticket sales at Shea Stadium. The group got into unfortunate contract disputes with Knight, who sued them for sixty million dollars. They settled the case by buying him out.

What is perhaps most amazing about Grand Funk Railroad's unparalleled success is that it came at a time when the band had produced only one minor Top 40 hit ("Closer to Home," # 22 in 1970) and was consistently ignored or maligned by critics. *Rolling Stone* would later reflect historically on this phenomenon, crediting Grand Funk with discovering an avenue to success that did not depend on radio airplay or favorable reviews: constant touring. Grand Funk became what *The New Rolling Stone Encyclopedia of Rock and Roll* calls "the prototypical people's band." It is unclear why critics and radio programmers hated them so much, except that the band seemed to exude an arrogance that belied their simplicity. Their bombastic stage shows were considered pretentious and their covers of classic rock songs (like the Rolling Stones' "Gimmie Shelter") were regarded as sacrilege (akin to Britney Spears doing "I Can't Get No Satisfaction" in 2000). But in any case, as ticket and album sales continued, first programmers, and eventually some critics realized that "the people had spoken," and Grand Funk acquired some grudging respect. One of the first to vocalize admiration for the band was rock legend Todd Rundgren, who produced two of their albums: *We're an American Band* (1973) and *Shinin' On* (1974). These brought the group into the second phase of their illustrious career. Suddenly, radio couldn't get enough of Grand Funk, and the band racked up hit after hit, including the Number One singles "We're an American Band" and "Loco-motion" and the Top 10 smashes, "Some Kind of Wonderful" and "Bad Time." As an odd quirk of rock history, Frank Zappa volunteered to produce their final album in 1976. Then Farner retired to a ranch in upper Michigan with his family and opened an alternative energy store. He made a couple of solo albums over the years (*Mark Farner* in 1977 and *No Frills* in 1978, both on Atlantic) and even reunited with Brewer to make a couple more Grand Funk albums in the early '80s, but the glory days were clearly over and these projects seemed more like hobbies than passions.

Farner had retired from the band to give his family the attention that living the life of a mega-rock star rarely affords. Thus, he was devastated in August of 1983 when his wife Lesia left him. Although he had not been raised in a religious household and had no real foundation for faith, he remembered something that had happened when he was a child of nine. At that time, shortly after his father had died, he had heard Billy Graham on TV, had prayed for Christ to come into his life, and found his pain to be eased. Looking for something similar, he wandered into a church in Onaway, Michigan, one Sunday morning. He was, to say the least, an unusual stranger amidst the elderly congregation of sixteen, and it was a pretty sure bet, he later averred, that the rather elderly preacher had never heard of Grand Funk Railroad and would not have had a clue who Mark Farner was if he had told them. Nevertheless, he says, when an altar call was given at the end of the service, "I went forward and prayed for God to forgive my sins and to bring my wife back to me." Unbeknownst to him, on that same morning some miles away, his wife had also attended a church, responded to a similar altar call, and accepted Christ as her Savior at approximately the same time. The two were reunited the next day and, recognizing that the miraculous power and mercy of God had taken hold of their lives, they became passionate in their faith, displaying evangelistic fervor. "I should have been locked up for a year," Farner later said. "I probably came on a little too strong." Initially, he also felt called to "give up music altogether" and put away his guitar with no intention of ever playing it again. He and Lesia joined an Assemblies of God church where they spent two-and-a-half years being discipled by the pastor, i.e., taught the Bible and basic ideas of Christian doctrine. Only then did Farner feel comfortable performing on stage as a Christian. At first he did not do so as a celebrity convert but quietly, as an almost unnoticed member of **Mylon LeFevre**'s band, Broken Heart.

Once Farner did go back out on the road he played mostly clubs or "oldies shows," often with a band he called the God Rockers. The group would do the old Grand Funk hits, with religious songs thrown in as well. Concerts often included unexpected evangelistic appeals. For instance, at a 1991 outdoor

Miller Beer festival in Detroit, Farner sang his classic, "Closer to Home" (unquestionably Grand Funk's best song), then proceeded to witness to the crowd: "When I wrote that song, I was crying out, searching for something, and now I have found what I was looking for . . . Jesus Christ!" Likewise, on a Super Seventies Fest tour that also featured Bachman Turner Overdrive, Dr. Hook, Rare Earth, and The Guess Who, Farner would testify to Jesus in his set and invite anyone interested to join him in Bible study and prayer after the show. He proudly related to *CCM* the numbers of people who got saved through this thoroughly secular series of shows—including members of the other bands. As time went by and news of Farner's proselytizing got out, some promoters and club owners would place a "gag order" in his contract, forbidding him to talk about certain matters during his shows. At the same time, many religious groups criticized him for playing at bars, nightclubs, and secular shows in the first place.

Farner's three albums display a musical style similar to that associated with Grand Funk, especially the band's lighter material. The songs are power-pop on the order of Christian groups like **Petra.** On the first album, *Just Another Injustice,* Farner delivers his testimony in the song, "Come to Jesus," which actually opens with a version of the Sunday school song, "Jesus Loves Me, This I Know." The song builds in power and in passion as Farner sings, "I told many stories, made many girls cry / I tried everything that money could buy. . . . I heard the voice of Jesus. . . . I know how it feels to give him control / I feel a revival down deep in my soul." That same album also features the hard rocking "Airborne Ranger" (with guitar by **Phil Keaggy**) and the appropriately titled, "Judgment Day Blues." Its highlight, however, is the softer toned "Isn't It Amazing," a spectacular tribute to God's grace by John Breland that affords Farner the best of all his postconversion performances. "Give Me the Works" and "Only You" are also nice power ballads, and "An Emotional Look at Love" is a melodic pop song about love being "more than just a physical feeling." All told, *Just Another Injustice* would come to be regarded as a classic of Christian rock, an album equal in quality to any of Grand Funk's secular works and, thus, of remarkable notice in the small pond of Christian music. *Wake Up* includes the anthemic title track, a stadium rocker that calls on people to "hear Jesus knockin' at the door" (Revelation 3:20) and respond appropriately. On the more midtempo pop number "If It Wasn't for Grace" he retells his testimony again, this time to a Caribbean beat. On "Come to Me," he assumes the point of view of Christ to address his audience with a traditional invitation: "Repent from all your sinful ways before the hour is due." Eventually, *Wake Up* came to be regarded as a "sophomore slump" album, lacking in direction and energy.

Some Kind of Wonderful contains the jazzy "Love from Above," which begins with a James Brown-style spoken-word rap. "Without You" is a gorgeous worshipful ballad, and "Not Yet" a bluesy accounting of excuses people give for ignoring what is essential. "Attitude of Gratitude" and "Conflict" are rollicking rock and roll after the fashion of **DeGarmo and Key**'s peppier material. Unfortunately, the album will always be remembered for the misstep of its title track, a new Christianized version of the old Grand Funk hit. The original song was an enthusiastic ode to monogamy that any Christian could sing proudly without alteration. In the new version, Farner sings the song about Jesus, with lyrics like, "Ooh when my Savior's huggin' me / My heart fills with desire / When he wraps his lovin' arms around me / It 'bout drives me out of my mind / Yeah, when my Savior's liftin' me / Chills run up and down my spine." Granted that the Bible does use sexual imagery to describe the relationship between Christ and the corporate church (Ephesians 5:31–32), the personal and detailed application here is a bit odd. Worse, the mere implication that Farner thought he had to salvage a song about romantic love by spiritualizing it seems to typify the gnostic attitudes so prevalent in American Christianity where—in defiance of Scripture (Genesis 1:31; John 1:3)—what is worldly is regarded as ungodly. This is unfortunate, because aside from this one slip, Farner does not seem to advocate such ideas and, in fact, has been more thoroughly committed to integrating spirituality with secularity than most Christian artists. Indeed, his decision to leave the Christian music subculture after the *Some Kind of Wonderful* album was motivated by an awareness that there was something not quite right about Christians having their own music, apparently designed to keep them apart from the rest of the world. "I feel compassion in my heart to go to the world," he told *CCM* in 1991, "cause I can identify with them. We can't just get in a church, close ourselves in, and point a finger at 'em."

Since recording his explicitly Christian albums, Farner has continued to work as a Christian in the general rock market. In 1996, he toured as a part of Ringo Starr's All Starr Band and in 1997 took part in a Grand Funk reunion tour. He revealed at that time that Mel Schacher had also "made a commitment to Christ" and, while keeping the concerts relatively free of testifying, Farner indicated that "we are accountable to God, and we're not having to compromise who we are as Christians." The reunited band released a two-disc live recording of a benefit concert for Bosnian orphans (*Bosnia,* Capitol, 1997). As of 2002, Farner was still playing with The God Rockers, doing Drug Free America programs for high schools.

Christian radio hits: "Isn't It Amazing?" (# 3 in 1988); "If It Wasn't for Grace" (# 12 in 1990); "Upright Man" (# 20 in 1990); "Some Kind of Wonderful" (# 3 in 1991); "Without You" (# 27 in 1991); "Not Yet" (# 8 in 1992).

Farrell and Farrell

Bob Farrell, voc.; Jayne Farrell, voc. 1978—*Farrell and Farrell* (NewPax); 1979—*A Portrait of Us All;* 1981—*Make Me Ready;* 1982—*Let the Whole World Know: Live;* 1984—*The Best of Farrell and Farrell; Choices* (StarSong); 1985—*Jump to Conclusions;* 1986—*Manifesto;* 1989—*Superpower; The Meek and the Mighty;* 1992—*The Early Works* (Benson).

http://members.fortunecity.com/ncognto/farrell.html

Farrell and Farrell were a husband and wife duo from Houston, Texas. As musical pioneers involved in the original Jesus movement revival, they sang together as a duo in the early '70s, touring with such legendary artists as **Randy Matthews** and **Love Song.** No recordings of the duo exist from this early period, but the two Farrells were also part of the group **Millennium,** which did record a self-titled album in 1973. That year, Jayne Farrell cut a solo album titled *Jayne* on Cam Records. A year later, Bob Farrell joined **Dove** and performed on their second album. In 1976, the couple moved to Edmond, Oklahoma, and began working as a duo again. They worked through the '80s, producing a number of pop albums that sold remarkably well (the first four alone sold over 200,000 total units, remarkable for Christian albums at that time). Bob eventually became well known as a songwriter, penning tunes for general market artists like John Berry, Laura Branigan, **Eric Clapton,** Anne Murray, and Diana Ross, in addition to many artists in the Christian market (see below).

According to *CCM,* Farrell and Farrell "had one of the most sophisticated early techno-pop shows on the road with heavy keyboard and electronic effects driving the musical sound." Live performance seemed to be their priority and the albums were produced for performance on the road. The debut record features the song "Lifesaver," which was later recorded by **Hope of Glory** and became one of their best-known songs. "Earthmaker" exalts God as Creator; "Homesick Soldier" uses the metaphor in its title to describe Christians as longing to be reunited with their Lord, while receiving love letters from him through Scripture. *A Portrait of Us All* provides the strongest collection of songs from the NewPax years, with no fewer than six of its eleven cuts later being favored for the *Early Years* compilation. "Jailhouse Rock" is not the song **Elvis Presley** made famous, but a clever reflection on the Apostle Paul's time in prison. "Boundless Love," "Fallen," and "All You Need" were written with **Brown Bannister,** who would become a frequent collaborator with the Farrells. *Make Me Ready* includes the instrumental "Sonata" and the tender songs "Old Friends" and "To Know That I'm Loved by You." The first of these is a reflection on the loneliness that senior citizens face in nursing homes (similar in sentiment to the Simon and Garfunkel song by the same name, coupled as it was with "Voices of Old People" on the album *Bookends*). "To Know That I'm Loved by

You" was written by Jayne Farrell with Bannister in response to the death of her father.

After the group switched to StarSong, they developed an increasingly sophisticated sound similar in many respects to that of **DeGarmo and Key.** Indeed, the latter duo sometimes served as part of the group's backing band, along with such artists as Mark Gershmehl (of **White Heart**), Stan Armor (of **Dogwood**) and **Twila Paris.** *Choices* was coproduced by DeGarmo, and its standout song may be the very clever and Beatlesque "Get Right or Get Left," cowritten by Farrell with **DeGarmo and Key.** Aside from that track, the record is essentially a worship album, filled with songs of praise like "Hosanna Gloria" and "He Reigns." *Jump to Conclusions* features what was to become one of the group's best-known songs, the infectious "People in a Box," a Thomas Dolby-type hit offering humorous commentary on TV culture. Such synthesizer-driven new-wave pop had become the group's norm, though *Jump to Conclusions* also includes a poignant ballad, "The Meek and the Mighty," as a tribute to the struggling church in Eastern Europe (the duo had been allowed to tour Poland, without their band, in early 1984). *Manifesto* would solidify their identity as a techno-pop band with the hit "Launch Window" sounding very much like a **Crumbächer** song. The closing track, "People All Over the World," offers prayerful recognition of what had been a recent outpouring of compassion songs (such as the famous "We Are the World" by the USA for Africa project). On *Superpower,* the group achieves their biggest sound ever, with the strongest cuts being the title track, "Eternity in Their Hearts," and "Heart of the Homeless."

As a songwriter, Bob Farrell has also written or cowritten Christian hits performed by **Bob Carlisle** ("I Am Not My Own," "Mind, Body, Heart, and Soul"), **Code of Ethics** ("Sticks and Stones"), **DeGarmo and Key** ("Let the Whole World Sing"), **Bryan Duncan** ("A Heart Like Mine"), **Hope of Glory** ("Lifesaver"), **The Imperials** ("Because of Who You Are"), **Michael W. Smith** ("I'll Be Around"), **The Pat Terry Group** ("Restored"), and **Jaci Velasquez** ("Un Lugar Celestial").

In 1996, Bob Farrell produced the musical *Saviour,* which won a Dove award. In 1996, he joined with Greg Nelson in writing *Emmanuel: A Musical Celebration of the Life of Christ.* In 1998, he coproduced a choral collection *Our Saviour . . . Emmanuel,* which also won a Dove award. Bob has retired from the road, but Jayne sometimes continues to perform, especially in Europe. She also writes country and pop songs. She is reported to have recorded an album of Celtic music.

Christian radio hits: "Earthmaker" (# 2 in 1978); "Heavensong" (# 23 in 1979); "Boundless Love" (# 13 in 1980); "All You Need" (# 3 in 1980); "Make Me Ready" (# 7 in 1982); "Let the Whole World Know" (# 25 in 1983); "Hosanna Gloria" (# 10 in 1984); "Give Me the Words" (# 4 in 1984); "Get Right or Get Left" (# 28 in 1984); "People in a Box" (# 4 in 1985); "American Man" (# 15 in 1986); "Launch Window" (# 13 in 1986);

"Manifesto" (# 9 in 1987); "Superpower" (# 15 in 1989); "Eternity in Their Hearts" (# 6 in 1989); "It's Gonna Take Love" (# 8 in 1989); "Heart of the Homeless" (# 11 in 1990).

Fasedown

Jim Chaffin, drums; John Hansen, bass; Mike Phillips, gtr.; Devin Schaeffer, voc. 2001—*Fasedown* (Rescue).

Fasedown is a hard rock band from Long Beach, California, that first attracted attention due to the pedigree of some of its performers. Drummer Jim Chaffin played with both **The Crucified** and **The Blamed,** bassist John Hansen was with the latter group, and guitarist Mike Phillips was a member of **Deliverance.** The group pounds out a groove on its debut album that *HM* describes as "bluntly and passionately numbing." On the song "Memoirs of a Modern Judas," singer/songwriter Devin Schaeffer asks, "Am I any different from those who do not believe?" In concerts, Schaeffer proclaims, "We are sinners saved by grace. We're no different, other than that we have the Lord in our lives."

Fatal Blast Whip

Personnel list unavailable. 2000—*Constellation* (Blacklight).

San Diego's Fatal Blast Whip is an electronic, industrial band noted for what *Phantom Tollbooth* calls "spooky dance music with a creepy edge." Inspiring comparisons to general market act Skinny Puppy, the group offers "icy beats that combine with eerie melodies to chill your soul." The anonymous band has been around for some years, placing songs on compilation discs, releasing a 1999 EP of material that is mostly on their debut album, and actually offering three more full-length albums to dedicated fans via mp3.com. *True Tunes* affirms them as providing "a positive alternative to the nihilistic world of Nine Inch Nails and Marilyn Manson."

Deborah Fatow

1998—*Submerged* (Rugged).

Deborah Fatow is the daughter of two ministers converted during the Jesus Movement revival. Her father, a converted Jew, pastors a church in Knoxville, Tennessee. Her mother, a former heroin addict who dated Noel Redding (of the Jimi Hendrix Experience), is involved in prison ministry. Fatow's first album, *Submerged,* finds her in a basic Alanis Morissette mode, albeit with a good deal of diversity in style. "My Wall" is a hard track dealing with the harsh effect that a lack of forgiveness has on a relationship. "You Are All I Need" is rock worship, with Fatow's vocals recalling the sounds of Ann Wilson (of Heart). "Make Me Stay" is another strong rocker, and "He Is Calling" is set to a martial drum beat. "I'm So Lost" is a delicate acoustic ballad more reminiscent of Shawn Colvin. Fatow composes her songs with Scotty Hoaglan of **Nailed;** he also plays guitar on her album. She is married to Chris Gaylon, drummer for **Nailed.**

Fear Not (a.k.a. **Love Life**)

Gary Hansen, drums; Rod Romero, bass; Larry Worley, voc.; Darin Eby, gtr. (–1993) // Michael Cutting, gtr. (+ 1993, –1993); Chris Howell, gtr. (+ 1993). As Love Life: 1991—*Goodbye Lady Jane* (Blonde Vinyl). As Fear Not: 1993—*Fear Not* (Pakaderm).

A metal blues-rock band from Houston, Texas, Fear Not was originally known as Love Life and released their first album under that name. With a sound reminiscent of Bon Jovi or Poison, the band took their place next to Christian giants like **Bride** and **Guardian** without ever achieving the success of those acts. Cutting, who played with the band for a short time, was also in **Holy Soldier.** The album *Fear Not* was hailed by *HM* as "a million times better than the Love Life album." Produced by **John** and Dino **Elefante,** the record nevertheless retains a gritty appeal that is often lacking in that duo's slick production jobs. *CCM* noted that this time "the Elefantes add just the right amount of polish to the band's blues-rock swagger," helping the album to rise above the crowded ranks of garage-sounding metal groups. It features head-banging anthems along with a couple of classic power ballads ("Suicide Sunshine," "Till the End of My Days"). Lyrics are generally simple and straightforward, dealing with the twin themes of how bad the world is and how good God is. The band was noted in concert for performing a roaring cover of the Beatles' "A Hard Day's Night." Larry Worley would later sing lead vocals on an album by **Robert Sweet;** Chris Howell joined **Red Sea.**

Another Christian band known as Fear Not operates out of Peace Lutheran Church in Poland, Ohio, and has released a custom CD. A folk-rock group best known for the song "Two Sets of Footprints," they have no connection to the heavy metal band.

Fear of Faith

See **Industry Eleven.**

James Felix

1980—*White as Snow* (Light).

James Felix recorded one album of light pop songs in the tradition of Michael McDonald or Christopher Cross. Produced by Bill Maxwell, the record offered ten songs displaying a strong influence of L.A. studio jazz. Most were original compositions, written from a first-person perspective expressive of faith-inspired love ("I Really Love You"), surrender ("I've Been Runnin' Too Long"), and hope ("He Is Coming Back Again").

Fell Venus

Mr. Venus, voc. 1995—@ (Via).

Critically acclaimed industrial band Fell Venus is the solo project of an artist who calls himself simply Mr. Venus and who employs various musicians to play under his direction to get the sounds that he wants. Thus, unlike much industrial music, more of the sounds are live instruments played in the studio by real people as opposed to merely synthesized sounds. Thus the record is something of an amalgamation between modern rock and techno/dance: songs like "Nice Guy," "Basket," and especially "Hate Disease" are guitar-driven numbers with electronic elements submerged in the background; "Shaped within Fear" and "Tie" are more traditional industrial dance tracks reminiscent of Nine Inch Nails. Mr. Venus often screams his vocals, sometimes with a Henry Rollins-type anger ("Penance"). In an interview with *The Lighthouse,* he said that he is from Vancouver, Canada, and that he has a degree in art design, with a minor in religion. He is a Christian but views his album more as the creation of an artwork than as a means to making some kind of representational statement that fans of Christian music might expect. Lyrically, most of the songs seem to deal with human frailty, giving expression to dissatisfaction with life as it is ("Hate Disease") and to a yearning for liberation ("Let Me Go"). Guest musicians on the album include Troy Daugherty of **Hoi Polloi** on guitar, and **Steve Hindalong** of **The Choir** on percussion. *Rad Rockers* recommends the album "for fans of **Mortal** and early Nine Inch Nails."

Becky Fender

1979—Becky Fender (Rainbow Sound); 1980—If You Need a Touch; 1982—Heaven's City Limits; 1984—I Give You Jesus (Good News); 1990—Bring on the Joy.

CCM began its review of Becky Fender's album *If You Need a Touch* by saying, "if her picture wasn't on the cover, you'd never know she wasn't black"—not a politically correct thing to say, but for readers in 1980, the point was "this is *soul* music, even *authentic* soul." Fender has made a series of adult contemporary albums that offer a mixture of up-tempo funk-rock songs and laid-back ballads. She is an occasional composer but has more often drawn on stalwart songwriters in the inspirational market such as **Stephanie Booshada.** Her album *I Give You Jesus* features three songs written by Reba Rambo and Dony McGuire.

Jeff Fenholt

1988—Jeff Fenholt Live (independent); 1990—Fenholt Hymns I; 1992—Fenholt Jesus 50's; 1993—Fenholt Christmas; 1994—Best of Praise; 1998—Celtic Glory.

Jeff Fenholt played the role of Jesus in the original broadway production of *Jesus Christ Superstar* and sang on a 1971 soundtrack album from that production (this was a different release from the better-known original cast *Jesus Christ Superstar* album released on MCA in 1970; Ian Gillan of Deep Purple sang the role of Jesus on that record). As a result, he appeared on the cover of *Time* magazine the week of October 25, 1971. Fenholt says, however, that he was not a Christian at that time. He lived the stereotypical life of a rock star and, indeed, a sex symbol, being featured as a pin-up centerfold in both *Cosmopolitan* and *Vogue* magazines. Sometime around 1980, he experienced a dramatic conversion, later recounted in a 1994 autobiography, *From Darkness to Light.* According to this book, Fenholt grew up in Ohio, a victim of child abuse and a frequent inhabitant of juvenile detention facilities. He attended Ohio State University on a voice scholarship and eventually married a woman named Reeni, a born-again Christian who persevered in prayer for his soul despite his abusive behavior that put her in the hospital. After his conversion, Fenholt toured with evangelist Nicky Cruz, the famous converted gang leader who is the subject of David Wilkerson's book *The Cross and the Switchblade.* Fenholt has recorded several independent albums of contemporary Christian music, working his way through a variety of styles: *Fenholt Live* is contemporary pop; *Hymns I* is traditional; *Jesus '50s* is rockabilly; *Celtic Glory* is old Irish and English hymns. He is said to be working on a southern gospel album, a heavy metal record, a contemporary rock album, and a jazz/blues project.

For trivia buffs: In 1984–1985, Fenholt replaced Ozzy Osbourne as the lead singer of Black Sabbath. He toured with the group and recorded songs for the album *Seventh Star.* All his material, however, was cut from that album before its release. A Christian at the time, he saw the opportunity of singing with the supposedly satanic group as a chance to be "a light in darkness." He later admitted, "It didn't work."

Few Left Standing

Jason Lancaster, gtr.; Chris Stafford, voc.; et al. 2000—Regeneration of Self (Takehold); 2001—Wormwood.

Few Left Standing is a Christian hard rock band from Memphis, Tennessee. Their sound bears the definite influence of **Living Sacrifice** with comparisons also being drawn to **NIV** and **Embodyment.** Bruce Fitzhugh of **Living Sacrifice** produced the group's first album, *Regeneration of Self,* which has a somewhat unpracticed sound to it. *Wormwood* takes its title not from the famous C. S. Lewis character (from *The Screwtape Letters*) but directly from the book of Revelation (which, of course, also inspired Lewis). The album is more progressive than the debut, with the songs "Give Credit Where Credit Is Due" and "No Apology" seeking to expand the group's repertoire somewhat beyond the hardcore genre. Leader Chris Stafford says, "I see a trend where bands say, 'We're not a Christian band, we're Christians in a band,' but whatever you call us, we're just out to raise some eyebrows about Jesus and spread what we know about Jesus to those who have an ear to hear."

FFH (a.k.a. **Far From Home**)

Jeromy Deibler, voc., gtr.; Jennifer Deibler, voc.; Brian Smith, voc., bass; Steve Croyle, voc., gtr. (– 2000) // Michael Boggs, voc., gtr. (+ 2000). 1998—*I Want to Be Like You* (Essential); 2000—*Found a Place*; 2001—*Have I Ever Told You.*

www.ffh.net

FFH formed in the early '90s as an a capella group but eventually developed a brand of vocal-based acoustic pop similar to **Smalltown Poets.** The group recorded indie records *(One of These Days, Called a Christian)* and toured regularly for six-and-a-half years before finally getting a contract for a major label debut. Their name at first was Four For Harmony (when they were an a capella quartet). They later shortened this to FFH, then expanded the acronym to Far From Home in reference both to their constant touring and to the distance that they, as Christians, feel from their heavenly home. But, as Jeromy Deibler says, "some group that had a lawyer was already using that name, so now we're just FFH again." Jeromy and Jennifer Deibler are siblings. The group is solidly committed to ministry. Jeromy says, "Our goal is to reach as many people as we can for Jesus as quickly as possible."

The album *I Want to Be Like You* was a reissue of songs from the indie projects. "One of These Days," "Take Me As I Am," and the album's title track are all classic folk-pop songs featuring trade-off vocals in the tradition of groups like Crosby, Stills and Nash. "Big Fish" is a clever and bouncy song reminiscent of **Caedmon's Call;** lyrically it describes the dilemma of those who resist God's call, with reference to a well-known Bible story: "Are you in the big fish? / Are you sitting in the belly of a world gone mad?" The song "I'm Alright" (not a Kenny Loggins cover) features Jennifer's vocals on a laid-back, slightly rockabilly song with a funky beat. *Found a Place* continues the tried and true formula with no recognizable change in style or sound. The opening track, "When I Praise," is a catchy, radio-friendly pop number enhanced by Jennifer's whispered off-beat background vocals. The jubilant song seems to establish a theme for the album, as several more songs also deal with the theme of worship ("Your Love Is Life to Me," "Because of Who

You Are," "Be My Glory," "Every Now and Then"). The creatively titled "Lord, Move, or Move Me" offers this prayer: "I feel a million miles away / And I don't know what to say / Can you hear me anyway?" This time out, Jennifer takes over the lead microphone for three songs, which tend to be album's most compelling cuts. *Musicforce* says, "There's a dusky quality to her voice that is quite compelling." *Have I Ever Told You* continues in the same general vein, but moves the group into the adult contemporary territory of vocal acts like **Avalon.** The album opens with "Watching Over Me," which features a Beatles-cum-**PFR** tune. It closes with a heart-tugging ballad "On My Cross," expressing the notion that Christ took upon himself the execution deserved by others ("Those were my nails . . . my thorns . . . you took my shame, my blame on my cross"). In between are more worship songs ("We Sing Alleluia," "You Write the Words") and another quirky fun song in the tradition of "Big Fish"—the song "Astronaut," which reflects on the greatness of God revealed in the heavens with lyrics like "I don't know that much about astronauts / But I know that Jesus cares a lot."

Christian radio hits: "Take Me As I Am" (# 14 in 1998); "Big Fish" (# 10 in 1998); "One of These Days" (# 3 in 1999); "I Want to Be Like You" (# 12 in 1999); "So Is His Love" (# 5 in 1999); "When I Praise" (# 4 in 2000); "Found a Place" (# 11 in 2000); "Because of Who You Are" (# 16 in 2001).

Fred Field

1976—*Fred Field and Friends* (Maranatha).

Fred Field is the Pete Best or Stu Sutcliffe of contemporary Christian music. He was an original member of the pioneering Jesus music group **Love Song** but, in a manner analogous to those former Beatles, left the group before they released the albums that would establish them as the most important Christian rock band of all time. Field had a lasting contribution to the group's music, however, for he cowrote (with **Chuck Girard**) five of their songs: "Since I Opened Up the Door," "A Brand New Song," "Joyous Lament," "Jesus Puts the Song in Our Hearts," and the quintessential "Little Country Church." Field and Girard also wrote the classic praise chorus "Bring My Body Closer," featured on the world's first modern worship album (*The Praise Album,* Maranatha, 1974).

Born in 1946 in Hollywood, California, Field grew up in the Los Angeles suburb of Downey. He began taking violin lessons at a very young age and was able to join the Downey symphony as a child prodigy at the age of seven. After graduating from high school, Field went into the army and spent eighteen months in Vietnam. After his discharge, he became part of a successful Salt Lake City rock band called Spirit of Creation, of which future **Love Song**ers Jay Truax and **John Mehler** were also a part. He then joined an early version of **Wing and a**

Prayer with **Tommy Coomes** and **Chuck Butler.** He ended up living in Laguna Beach with Coomes and Girard and was actually the first **Love Song** member to become a Christian, after reading a book given to him by a woman friend from the Salt Lake City days. Field played in **Love Song** for about a year and a half and then left to form a group in northern California called Noah (with Mehler for a time). Noah went to Europe for the Munich Olympics and spent two years in Europe, based in Amsterdam and Tel Aviv. They often played at United States military bases at the request of military chaplains and in support of drug prevention programs.

Eventually, Field would record his solo album with friends from **Love Song** and other Maranatha bands helping out. His violin—or, in this case, fiddle—became the featured instrument, and Field played it to great effect on tunes like "Country Life" and "He Lives." The latter song was used in the film *My Witnesses,* a documentary about the 1972 Munich Olympics. Field's song "When That Morning Finally Comes" is one of his best, looking forward to the consummation of life in a world beyond death. As of the year 2000, Field was pursuing a doctoral degree in linguistics.

For trivia buffs: It is not quite accurate to say that Fred Field does not play on any of **Love Song**'s recordings. He was part of the group when they recorded the version of "Little Country Church" that appears on Maranatha's classic compilation album *(The Everlastin' Living Jesus Music Concert)*. That version of the song is generally considered to be better than the version that appears on *Love Song,* and Field's guitar solo is often thought to be the highlight of the record.

Paul Field

1983—Restless Heart (Myrrh); 1984—Building Bridges.

Singer/songwriter Paul Field released two albums in the early '80s that had the basic sound of well-crafted '70s rock. He alternated between simple ballads reminiscent of James Taylor and power ballads like those of Journey, with occasional forays into more energetic material to rival Duran Duran. *Restless Heart* was built around a saying of St. Augustine (reflected in the title cut and in "Stranger in Your Eyes") to the effect that the heart will be forever restless until it finds its rest in Christ. *Building Bridges* scored with two powerful songs, "Return to Love" and "Sing a New Song" and with the traditional gospel-inspired "Keep Your Eyes on Jesus." Field was previously a member of the British folk group **Nutshell.**

Fighter

Billy Heller, gtr.; Sean Murphy, voc., drums; Mark Pence, kybrd.; Amy Wolter, voc.; Jim Wolter, bass. 1987—*Fighter* [EP] (custom); 1991—*The Waiting* (Wonderland); 1992—*Bang the Drum.*

Fighter was a Christian power-pop band cut from the same cloth as **Petra** and **White Heart,** though they never achieved the same success as those arena rockers. Based in Iowa, the group was led by Amy Wolter, who was also its principal songwriter. The bass player, Jim Wolter, was her husband. Jim and Amy had previously played together in a band called Sapphire, which recorded an album titled *Crystal Clear.* The distinctive element in Fighter's sound was the trade-off vocals between Wolter (who has been likened to Pat Benatar or to Patty Smyth of Scandal) and male singer Sean Murphy. *CCM* likened the style of the debut full-length album *The Waiting* to that of arena-rockers Journey, though they preferred the songs with female vocals (the title track, "Do What You Want Me To," and especially "Radio Man"). *Bang the Drum* offers some gritty blues rock on "Avalanche" and a bit of crunch guitar on "Try" and "So Much to Learn." The latter two songs, as well as the title track, deal with issues of legalism, encouraging Christians to follow Jesus' example of cutting people some slack, even when their lives don't measure up to what they should be. *The Lighthouse* described "Where Can Love Be Found" as "a touching and effective song about a runaway."

After Fighter disbanded, Amy Wolter would release a solo album, *Hit Me in the Heart* (WAL, 1994). A little more on the pop side, the project features a couple of rocking anthems ("There Won't Be a Next Time," "Be That Child") alongside dance pop ("The Promise," "Blue Skies") and a beautiful ballad ("We All Need").

Christian radio hits: "Star One" (# 7 in 1991); "Radio Man" (# 26 in 1991); "Do What You Want Me To" (# 18 in 1992); "Alone with You" (# 8 in 1993).

Filet of Soul

Adam Beadles, voc., sax.; Greg Beadles, gtr.; Randy Chester, bass; Cornelius Freeman, drums. 1998—*Incommunicado* (Shank).

www.filetofsoul.com

Filet of Soul is a funky folk-rock band from Athens, Georgia, that has been likened to the Dave Matthews Band or, in the words of *Phantom Tollbooth,* to a cross between Sly and the Family Stone and Toad the Wet Sprocket. *7ball* chose the group as one of America's top twenty-five indie bands in 1999. Their debut album includes songs that are variously melancholy ("Lower Me") and upbeat ("Copperpot"), but all with apparent pop appeal. Their Christian perspective is expressed most explicitly in "Broken Mirror," where Adam Beadle sings, "Here's my life, oh my God, make me in the image of your Son."

Final Destiny

Ronnie Evans, bass; Scott Hallman, gtr., kybrd.; Jeff Pope, voc.; Kelly Scercy, drums. 1996—*North of Hell* (Stepping Stone).

Final Destiny is a classic hard rock band on the order of Boston, Bon Jovi, or Kiss. Their album, *North of Hell,* includes a hard rock version of the worship song "I Surrender All." All of their songs are explicitly evangelical in the grand tradition of **Petra** or **White Heart.** *Phantom Tollbooth* especially liked "Just Walk Away," which conveys the same message as Phil Collins' "Just Another Day in Paradise," albeit to a very different tune.

Final Judgement

Jon Bodhan, gtr.; Derek Varner, drums; et al. 1994—*Desolation Sacrilege* (Anastasia).

Despite the British spelling of their name, the boys from Final Judgement came from Atlanta, Georgia. They were a solid metal band reminiscent at times of White Zombie. *HM* praised the group for its well-written lyrics while noting that they tend to be a bit preachy. "Prelife Vivisection" is a rant against abortion; "Habitual Sacrifice" accosts churchgoers whose relationship with God does not extend beyond Sunday morning. Jon Bodhan later formed Edge of Forever and released two albums through the Internet (members.aol.com/jonedge).

Fine China

Joshua Block, kybrd.; Greg Markov, bass, kybrd.; Thom Walsh, drums; Rob Withem, voc., gtr., kybrd. 1998—*Rialto Bridge* [EP] (Velvet Blue); 2000—*When the World Sings* (Tooth and Nail); 2002—*You Make Me Hate Music.*

Fine China is a moody alternative band from Phoenix, Arizona, that sounds like Psychedelic Furs or **Luxury** with female vocals. The singer, Rob Withem, is actually male but his soft alto voice floats above the keyboards and synthesizers with a fragility that would shield his gender identity from anyone missing the liner notes. The group recorded a four-track single for Velvet Blue in 1998 and then released their debut full-length album on Tooth and Nail two years later. Ronnie Martin (of **Joy Electric**) produced both projects, and the influence of '80s music is strong. *When the World Sings* opens with "We Rock Harder Than You Ever Knew," a catchy pop song that recasts words from the Beatitudes as a neo-hippie invitation to join the meek, the mild, and the poor of the world (who know the gentleness and hope of the Lord). On "They Will Love Us for Our Instruments," Withem sings in a lower register that makes Fine China sound a lot like the Pennsylvania band **The Ocean Blue.** The song "Give Us Treble" is possibly a tribute to Treble Bandoppler, publisher of *Bandoppler* electronic magazine. Fine China has played primarily the indie scene within the general market, and so is not well known within the Christian scene. Still, Withem says, "I want people to see the love of Christ in the way that we act and the songs that we sing. Music right now is at an all time low as far as the morality of the artists,

and the values portrayed through their songs. I want to prove that the life of a true Christian is pure and true joy, and I want to encourage people to throw off their baggage and hate and hostility, and to know Jesus." The band's 2002 album *You Make Me Hate Music* would be produced by Jason Martin (Ronnie's brother) of **Starflyer 59.**

Fireworks

Marty McCall, voc., kybrd.; Lance Avery, bass (– 1981); Chris Harris, drums (–1979); Gary Pigg, voc. (–1979); Cindy Lipford, voc. (–1979) // Jerry Gaston (+ 1979); Bob Sinkovic (+ 1979, –1981); Dave Curfman, gtr., bass (+ 1981); David Johnson, bass (+ 1981, –1982); Richard Cann, gtr. (+ 1982); Louie Weaver, drums (+ 1982). 1977—*Fireworks* (Myrrh); 1979—*Shatter the Darkness;* 1980—*Live Fireworks* (MCA); 1981—*Up;* 1982—*Sightseeing at Night.*

Fireworks was performing contemporary Christian music early enough for their rather tame style to be regarded as controversial in some churches. **Marty McCall,** a Southern Baptist with formal education in medieval and renaissance music, played an important role in bridging the gulf between secular and sacred musical worlds at a time when many in his church would have kept the two distinct. The group had its origin in a trio of studio backup singers (Marty McCall, Gary Pigg, and Gwen Moore) who worked under the direction of **Chris Christian** on such projects as **B. J. Thomas**'s *Home Where I Belong* and **Amy Grant**'s self-titled debut album. The trio was solicited by Word to become another **2nd Chapter of Acts,** and with Cindy Lipford replacing Moore and with the addition of a rhythm section, they became a band. McCall, who would later be part of the group **First Call,** was clearly the leader and would be the only member of the original lineup to stay with the group. Louie Weaver went on to play drums with **Petra.**

As personnel changed throughout the years, so did the Fireworks sound. Their debut album was in the vein of the 2nd Chapter clone the company had requested, though its piano-driven mellow pop numbers pale in comparison to that group's better works. The single "Don't Look Back" did get the group noticed. *Shatter the Darkness* showed remarkable improvement, with Fireworks developing a bigger sound. *Jesus Music* says, "McCall's highly emotive vocals are perfectly suited to slow intense rockers like 'Change My World' and the title cut." After the group moved to MCA, they adopted a more electric sound influenced by the new-wave phenomenon of the early '80s. Some of the music on their last two albums is more akin to the sound of **DeGarmo and Key** than to the vocal harmony style with which they began and to which McCall would return with **First Call.** *Up* is the most subdued of the four projects. It includes the songs "Adam," which laments the loss of Paradise, "Frontrunner," about John the Baptist, and "Maybe I'll Trust You Now," written by **James Vincent.** *Sightseeing at Night* moves back in the direction of rock and roll. "Broadway Mary" is a rollicking honky-tonk song about a woman "with pink platforms and purple hair" who gets saved at a revival and ends up becoming a "sidewalk missionary" in a sleazy part of town. "Don't Let the Sun Go Down" is a meditation on Ephesians 4:26.

Christian radio hits: "Don't Look Back" (# 7 in 1978); "Givin' It Up" (# 18 in 1982).

Firmament

Matthew Chinn, synth. 2000—*Open-Eyed Ascension* (Velvet Empire).

Matthew Chinn, who also records under the name **Frolic,** is a Christian New Age artist who produces contemplative ambient music intended for meditation. The debut Firmament album is completely instrumental and, in fact, has almost no drums, percussion, or other distinctively rhythmic instruments. Chinn's compositions also depart from traditional song structures, meandering about in unexpected ways. *True Tunes* calls it "perfect late night music." Firmament is similar in some respects to **Caul** or **Engrave.**

First Call

Marty McCall, voc.; Bonnie Keen, voc.; Mel Tunney, voc. (– 1989) // Marabeth Jordan (+ 1989, – 1995). 1985—*An Evening in December: A Christmas a Capella* (DaySpring); 1986—*Undivided*; 1987—*An Evening in December 2; Somethin' Takes Over*; 1989—*God Is Good* (Myrrh); 1992—*Human Song*; 1993—*Concert Melody; Sacred Journey*; 1995—*Beyond December* (Warner Alliance); *The Early Years* (Myrrh); 1996—*First Call* (Warner Alliance).

www.first-call.org

First Call was originally founded as a backing group for **Marty McCall**'s solo career after the demise of **Fireworks.** Mel Tunney is the wife of Dick Tunney; both she and her husband were members of **Truth** and would later record as **Dick and Melodie Tunney.** First Call's sound is that of a classic vocal ensemble with primary attention to jazz and pop arrangements. McCall is a classically trained singer who has performed opera and who has formally studied medieval and renaissance music. In 1985, he recorded an album called *The Messenger* (Fortress) with the group J.C. and Friends. Before recording on their own, the trio that composed First Call worked as studio singers on projects by a number of other artists. They got their first big break when invited to tour as backup singers for **Sandi Patty.** They went on to enjoy considerable success, appearing twice on the cover of *CCM* magazine. Their normative style was a clone of that originated by **2nd Chapter of Acts,** but they sometimes transcended this with a variety of other influences. First Call was briefly beset by scandal in 1994 when Marabeth Jordan confessed to having had an extramari-

tal affair with **Michael English,** with whom the group had recently toured. She subsequently left the group, and McCall and Keen continued as a duo.

The group has enjoyed its greatest success with its elaborate *Evening in December* Christmas projects. The first of these was nominated for a Grammy award and has become a holiday classic. The other early albums have a strong inspirational feel to them—on the easy listening side of adult contemporary with Manhattan Transfer appeal. Highlights on those albums were often the a capella numbers such as "Snap to It" on *Undivided* or "O Sifuni Mungu"—sung in Swahili—on *Somethin' Takes Over.* The former album also includes the very **2nd Chapter of Acts**-like "Messiah" and an appropriately synthesizer-heavy track called "The Future." The title track is an MOR anthem, and "God Is Greater," a typical adult contemporary ballad (that also sounds very much like **2nd Chapter of Acts**). *Somethin' Takes Over* was divided in two halves, Side One containing Manhatten Transfer-like jazz numbers ("Coming of the Lord," the title track) and Side Two focused on pop-rock hymns à la **2nd Chapter of Acts** such as "Lord of All." The group develops more of its own pop style on *God Is Good.* The standout song of that album is "Parable of the River," which betrays some traditional gospel influence. "Someday" and "Sweet Love" are also strong rock-oriented tracks. "Breaking Through" is a soulful midtempo song not too far removed from something that the Pointer Sisters might have done. "Legacy" is a nice ballad affirming the long-term consequences of positive actions and words. "True Love" is an energetic pop song propelled by a horn section.

God Is Good was a major advance over the previous albums, but in the opinion of most critics, First Call would really gel as an aggressive pop group on *Human Song.* Produced by **Michael Omartian,** the album includes covers of **Bob Dylan**'s "Ring Those Bells" and Stevie Wonder's "Don't You Worry 'bout a Thing." This record also evinces a thematic departure for the group with more of an emphasis on dealing with trials endemic to the human condition: divorce, abuse, and other real-life problems. Their self-produced *Sacred Journey* continues in the same vein with more of an unplugged and live-in-studio sound. The title of *Sacred Journey* was taken from a book by Presbyterian minister Frederick Buechner that stresses the sanctity of all of life. Freedom in Christ is the project's central theme, and this is expressed vividly in the song "Lazarus Unwound," which features a **Take 6** a capella vocal arrangement. The first post-scandal project for *First Call* was another Christmas record. On *Beyond December,* the duo of McCall and Keen combine their talents with high-profile guest performers (**Amy Grant, Russ Taff, Ashley Cleveland,** and, appropriately, **Dick and Melodie Tunney**). The album *First Call* opens with a new theme song, "Let the Healing Begin," which calls for forgiveness, learning from the past, and trusting God with the future. First Call has also released two albums in Spanish.

Christian radio hits: "The Future" (1986); "Messiah" (1987); "The Reason We Sing" (1988); "O Sifuni Mungu" (# 13 in 1988); "Sweet Love" (# 1 for 4 weeks in 1989); "Breaking Through" (# 4 in 1990); "Someday" (# 2 in 1990); "I'm Forgiven" (# 30 in 1991); "Broken Places" (# 21 in 1992); "I Will Always Come Back to You" (# 11 in 1992); "Don't You Worry 'bout a Thing" (# 7 in 1992); "Wanna Be" (# 15 in 1993); "Freedom" (# 21 in 1994).

Dove Awards: 1987 Group of the Year; 1988 Group of the Year.

First Gear

Larnelle Harris, voc.; et al. 1972—*First Gear* (Myrrh); 1974—*Caution! Steep Hill Use.*

The early Jesus movement group known as First Gear is remembered as a historical novelty because it featured inspirational crooner Larnelle Harris on lead vocals. The group had a soulful brassy sound like that of Earth, Wind, and Fire, led by electric guitars and accompanied by lots of horns. Both albums are more oriented toward offering positive entertainment than evangelistic proclamation—an anomaly that sets them apart from the Jesus music of the era and from Myrrh's normal releases. The first album, for instance, includes covers of Carole King's "I Feel the Earth Move," the Hollies' "He Ain't Heavy, He's My Brother," and Jerry Jeff Walkers' "Mr. Bojangles," while the creatively titled *Caution! Steep Hill Use* (with the group's name appearing beneath) serves up new renditions of two Seals and Crofts songs. A reviewer for *Jesus Music* listens to Harris screaming "yeah yeah yeah" throughout and wonders what he must think of the albums now. Or of the leisure suit he wears in publicity photos.

First Nashville Jesus Band

Personnel list unavailable. 1973—*Welcome to Nashville* (Lamb and Lion); 1974—*Peace in the Valley.*

The First Nashville Jesus Band was a small symphony that backed **Pat Boone** on a number of his releases. They also recorded two all-instrumental albums of their own, offering country-inflected versions of Jesus music tunes mixed with traditional hymns and a few inexplicable selections like "Daddy Sang Bass." *Jesus Music* says, try to imagine "the Tijuana Brass with steel guitars instead of horns."

John Fischer

1969—*The Cold Cathedral* (FEL); 1970—*Have You Seen Jesus My Lord?*; 1972—*Still Life* (Light); 1974—*The New Covenant*; 1976—*Naphtali*; 1977—*Inside*; 1979—*Johnny's Café*; 1982—*Dark Horse* (Myrrh); 1985—*Between the Answers*; 1986—*Casual Crimes*; 1992—*Wide Angle* (Urgent); 1999—*Some Folks' World* (Silent Planet).

www.fischtank.com

By the year 2002, John Fischer had become the undisputed senior statesman of contemporary Christian music, the master who had not only "been there" and "done that" but who was also able to reflect upon his thirty years in ministry and the industry with unusual candor and insight—a bit like Pete Townsend in the mainstream world of rock and roll. Born in 1947, Fischer graduated from Wheaton College in 1969 and toured with evangelist Leighton Ford. He eventually settled in Palo Alto, California, and formed the Arts Discovery Guild as a ministry of Peninsula Bible Church. Though he continued to perform music, he became better known over the years for his numerous books and for his role as a regular columnist in *CCM* magazine; some of the early essays were collected in *Real Christians Don't Dance* (Bethany House, 1988). A sought-after speaker, he also hosts the *Wide Angle Radio Show.*

Although they do not contain his best work, Fischer's first two albums are probably his most important. They are not Jesus music per se, for the Jesus movement had hardly gotten underway. Fischer was a prepioneer of that spiritual and musical revival, one of a handful of people who transformed American Christianity forever. In the '60s, before the Jesus movement revival, somber organ music was the order of the day—in white churches at least. Syncopation was said to be a perversion of God's natural order and guitars were rather obviously the instruments of the devil, being played by sex fiends (**Elvis Presley**), communists (Pete Seeger), and men with long hair (the Beatles). Anything "lively" was dismissed as irreverent. It was at such a time and in such a context that a few artists boldly brought the sounds of folk rock into the sanctuaries: **Ray Repp** in the Roman Catholic church, **John Ylvisaker** (a Lutheran) in mainline Protestant denominations, and—most important—such people as **Ralph Carmichael,** Kurt Kaiser, and **Jimmy and Carol Owens** among the conservative Protestants, whose ranks would swell when the Jesus movement swept the land. John Fischer belongs with the latter crowd. Notably, *The Cold Cathedral* and *Have You Seen Jesus My Lord?* were issued on Repp's FEL label, perhaps because the Roman Catholics were a bit ahead of the Baptists at this point in time (due to Repp himself, no doubt). On these two records, Fischer offered a collection of what were to become popular youth group songs, the kind of songs that the kids could sing at summer camp or Young Life meetings even if they weren't allowed to sing them at actual Sunday morning services. "Look All around You" from *Cold Cathedral* and the title track from *Have You Seen Jesus My Lord?* are special gems that stand the test of time. In the mold of the Kingston Trio or the New Christy Minstrels, such songs sound unbelievably tame by modern standards, but they opened the door, and once folks like Fischer got that door cracked, it would be impossible to keep folks like **Larry Norman, Marsha Stevens, Chuck Girard,** and

Barry McGuire from getting inside. The funeral dirges were doomed; the worst fears of those who worried over what this might lead to would all be confirmed (there couldn't have been a **Stryper** without a John Fischer; it just would not have happened). The first of Fischer's albums also features him doing a go-go version of "Got to Shout about It" (on organ) and the second offers a pedal steel guitar country rendition of "Trust and Obey."

Fischer's albums for Light would cease to be revolutionary, but would allow his own compositional skills to come to the fore, revealing him to be a thoughtful lyricist and gifted songwriter. Christian music's premier critic Brian Quincy Newcomb has said, "Albums like *Still Life* and *Johnny's Café* established Fischer as a singer/songwriter with a folk rock bias, and a tendency to write lyrics that sermonized his experiences into an obvious biblical truth." The album *Still Life* features the popular "All Day Song" with its "Love Him in the morning . . ." chorus—a throwback to the style of Fischer's first two albums. *The New Covenant* was actually a musical for children. *Naphtali* is probably Fischer's finest overall work: The title track takes the name of one of Jacob's sons, a word that means "a doe set free," and applies is as a metaphor for Christians, who may also fulfill the destiny of this son to be "one who gives beautiful words" (see Genesis 49:21).

As Fischer moved into the '80s he was able to accept the fact that his music was not only *not revolutionary,* but no longer even in vogue. With great humor, he would josh his audiences about "the old days of '60s radicalism," asking how many now worked at banks they once wanted to blow up, and claiming the concert had to end in time for everyone to drive their babysitters home. On the trio of albums he recorded for Myrrh, he evinces the mature folk stylings of a Gordon Lightfoot or a John B. Sebastian. The best of the three is *Dark Horse,* with a title track that urges Christians to be "dark horses" that stand out from the crowd, taking uncompromised stances for the truth. A decade later on *Wide Angle,* he would explore a different dimension of that theme, emphasizing now that the truth can have a broader compass than we realize. That album was produced by **Mark Heard** and featured an all-star band that included **Buddy** and **Julie Miller,** David and **Kate Miner,** and David Raven (of **The Swirling Eddies** and **Undercover**). The theme is stated well in the song "The Only Way": "Jesus is the only way, but there's more than one way to Jesus." Other highlights include "Cup of Cold Water" and "Where Did They Go?" both of which showcase **Julie Miller.** Unfortunately, *Wide Angle* did not reach the audience it deserved due to the bankruptcy of a distribution company. Fischer would later re-release the record on the Silent Planet label with three new songs and a new title, *Some Folks' World.*

The title track, one of the new songs, is a cover of a **Mark Heard** composition.

Fischer's books include the novels *Saint Ben* (1993) and *The Saints' and Angels' Song* (1994) and the manifesto, *Making Real What I Already Believe* (1991), all from Bethany House. Recently, he has written a number of devotional books for Servant Publishers, including *On a Hill Too Far Away* (1994), *Be Thou My Vision* (1995), and *What on Earth Are We Doing?* (1997).

Christian radio hits: "Johnny's Café" (# 14 in 1979); "Dark Horse" (# 3 in 1983).

Fish Co.

Steve Farnie, gtr., voc.; Steve Rowles, gtr., voc. // John Gordon, bass (+ 1978); John Hardwick, gtr. (+ 1978); Rowan O'Duffy, drums (+ 1978); Bev Sage, voc. (+ 1978). 1975—*Can't Be Bad* (Myrrh); 1978—*Beneath the Laughter* (Grapevine).

Sometimes it seems that a band could make it big if only they had the right *name.* As teenagers in Bristol, England, Farnie and Rowles formed a group called The Pink Hat Christianity Blues Band, but for some reason, that didn't do it. As Fish Co., they recorded a debut album of acoustic songs similar to those of their better-known compatriots **Malcolm and Alwyn.** Then in 1978 they produced an album with a full band and a much fuller sound. *Jesus Music* describes the songs on *Beneath the Laughter* as more introspective, especially the title track and the haunting "Sail Away." The year the album came out, however, the group changed its name again, this time to Writz. They pursued success in the general market with a single called "Night Nurse," but the latter failed to chart and the band broke up—sort of. Another incarnation of the group would appear in the early '80s, known first as Famous Names, and then as The Casual Tease. Farnie and Sage were later known to be performing together as a duo called The Techno Twins.

David Fitzgerald

1995—*Columcille* (ICC); 1997—*Lux Aeterna;* 1999—*The Eye of the Eagle* [with Dave Bainbridge and David Adam] (Kingsway); 2000—*Light Eternal* (Rhythm House) 2001—*Breath of Heaven* (ICC).

Saxophonist David Fitzgerald was a founding member of the group **Iona** but left that group to pursue a classical musical education. Shortly after earning his master's degree in music, he recorded his project *Columcille,* revealing his deep love for liturgical music that has come down through the ages. More of this would be seen on *Lux Aeterna,* which includes music used on a soundtrack for a BBC film, *Jesus—Then and Now.* Highlights of the album include Fitzgerald's instrumental version of the hymn "Steal Away" and the powerful epic "Golgotha," which conveys sonically the sense of pain and triumph associated with Christ's crucifixion. *Lux Aeterna* also includes a vocal track, "Only Jesus," with the vocals supplied by **Adrian Snell**, for whom Fitzgerald was once a backing musician. An American version of this album was reissued as *Light Eternal* with some variation in tracks. The American version also contains a seven-minute version of "O Come, O Come, Emmanuel" and a rendition of the hymn "When I Survey the Wondrous Cross." For *Eye of the Eagle,* Fitzgerald joins with fellow **Iona** alum Dave Bainbridge (gtr., kybrd.) to provide a meditative backdrop for the reading of poetry by Anglican Canon Dave Adam. The theme of Adam's work, rooted in Celtic spirituality, is awareness of God's presence in the mundane affairs of everyday life: "We need to keep a vision of this other world / Not as a place far away or set in another time / But a world that keeps breaking into our lives / Not a world that runs parallel to ours / But a world that is closely interwoven with ours." *Breath of Heaven* features modern hymns by such composers as **Chris Eaton** and **Graham Kendrick.**

Five Iron Frenzy

Dennis Culp, tromb.; Nathanael (Brad) Dunham, trump.; Keith Hoerig, bass; Jeff the Girl (Leanor Inez) Ortega, sax.; Micah Ortega, gtr.; Reese Roper, voc.; Andrew Verdecchio, drums; Scott Kerr, gtr. (– 1999) // Sonnie Johnston, gtr. (+ 1999). 1996—*Upbeats and Downbeats* (5 Min. Walk); 1997—*Our Newest Album Ever* (SaraBellum); 1998—*Quantity Is Job 1* [EP] (5 Min. Walk); 1999—*Live: Proof That the Youth Are Revolting;* 2000—*All the Hype That Money Can Buy; Electric Boogaloo.*

www.fiveironfrenzy.com

By the end of the '90s, ska would be one of the more crowded genres in the Christian market, but when the Denver, Colorado, band Five Iron Frenzy made their debut, they were only the second act known to be operating in that then-novel arena. Like their Orange County siblings **The Supertones,** they played neo-ska a few stages removed from the music of Madness or The Specials fifteen years earlier in Britain. For Five Iron Frenzy especially, the music had strong punk roots, such that *True Tunes* simply called them "a punk band with horns." Everyone agreed that, whatever FIF's music should be called, they played it with exceptional competence ("better than **The Supertones**" was a common response). Tight, harmonious horns, rapped vocals, punky guitars, and rapid rhythms cooperated to give the group one of the most recognizable and infectious sounds in Christian rock.

Upbeats and Downbeats features one near-perfect song: "A Flowery Song" conveys the joy of life better than anything since the Rascals' "It's a Beautiful Morning." The song begins on a similarly jubilant note: "Beautiful day / Wonderful feeling" and finally explodes into an up-tempo chorus of the classic doxology. FIF's debut also includes a punk take on "Everywhere I Go," the song made famous by **Amy Grant.** The group

also displays a penchant for social commentary in songs like "Third World Think Tank," "The Old West," and "Beautiful America." *Our Newest Album Ever* would score a major college radio hit with its ode to nerds, "Suckerpunch." The latter song features the memorable chorus, "They're all suckerpunching me / Get in line for a wedgie / All I want and all I need / Is someone who believes in me." The group took an ironic and humorous look at its own "stardom" in the songs "Superpowers" and "Handbook for the Sellout." Other standouts include "Blue Comb '78" and the eclectic "Fistful of Sand." The worshipful "Every New Day" became a hit on some Christian stations, but FIF also now enjoyed minimal general market attention and took part in a "Ska against Racism" tour alongside several mainstream bands.

Quantity Is Job 1 contains a cover of ELO's "Sweet Talkin' Woman" plus a groovy song called "Dandelions" likening a child's gift of flowers to his Mom to our worship of God. "Get Your Riot Gear" is a protest song regarding the Denver police department's use of excessive force following the 1988 Super Bowl. Supposedly an EP, *Quantity* actually includes an unlisted rock opera consisting of eight bonus tracks. Possibly titled "These Are Not My Pants," the mysterious epic explores how the titular pants have been worn by many people but are not in fact the singer's pants. The live album *(Proof That the Youth Are Revolting)* offers new versions of favorites plus a rendition of **Vengeance Rising**'s "Receive Him," a cover of Tom Jones' "It's Not Unusual," and a song called "Ugly Day" about Brad's breakup with his fiancé. The latter two songs also show up on *All the Hype That Money Can Buy,* which was billed as "a more rock record," but does not stray too far from the group's home turf. "Fahrenheit," from that album, offers a powerful, confessional indictment of homophobia, as Roper reflects on the uncaring reaction he had in middle school to the death of Freddy Mercury (leader of Queen) from AIDS. Sensing the impending death of ska, the band also expands their repertoire on *All the Hype* by trying out a few new styles: bossa nova on "Hurricanes" and calypso on "Solidarity" (with guest vocals by **Randy Stonehill**). The song "A New Hope" empathizes with the students of Columbine High School in Littleton, Colorado, returning to school after the massacre that occurred there (Micah Ortega's sister Amy was one of the students trapped inside the school during the shootings). "World without End" brings the group full circle (back to "A Flowery Song") with an ecstatic song of praise. *Electric Boogaloo* is the band's most consistently rock album. It opens with "Pre-Ex-Girlfriend," which offers a guy's pessimistic outlook on his ultimate chances with an object of his affection. "The Day We Killed" offers punk-rant social commentary on the American legacy of massacring its native population. "Blue Mix" targets questionable practices in the music business, where opening bands sometimes have to pay headline groups for the privilege of touring with them or where they sometimes actually have limits put on their sound mix to guarantee that the main group will sound better. "Spartan" and "Eulogy" are more explicitly Christian songs in which concerns are taken to the Lord in prayer.

For trivia buffs: The two Ortegas in Five Iron Frenzy (Micah and Jeff the Girl) are neither married nor siblings, but cousins.

Five O'Clock People

Kris Doty, bass; Drew Grow, gtr., voc.; Patrick Retreault, violin, mand., voc.; Andy Uppendahl, drums; Alex Walker, voc., gtr., kybrd. 1999—The Nothing Venture (Pamplin).

Five O'Clock People is a critically acclaimed alternative band from Portland, Oregon, with an eclectic folk sound similar to **Caedmon's Call.** They gained a sizeable following playing clubs and cafes in the Northwest for three years prior to their major-label release with Pamplin. An early lineup of the group consisted of Alex Walker and Patrick Retreault and two people named Brent and John. This incarnation released two privately distributed albums/EPs (Five O'Clock People in 1996 and Blame Taker in 1997); some tracks from these were subsequently remastered and released as Tripping the Spindley Distractive (2000). The Nothing Venture displays finely tuned songs played with the finesse of a group that has honed its craft. The record is entirely acoustic, and the songs offer sincere and sometimes fragile reflections on life, faith, and humanity. "I wonder, is doubt the way of faith" the group muses in "Lunar." Musically, "Remain" has a strong Dave Matthews Band vibe. "Living Water" is worshipful, with lyrics drawn from the Psalms. "Sorry" offers a revealing look at someone struggling to deal with a break-up: "The words that I would find to comfort me / Suddenly rebel at my questions / And I am resolved to love you / With whatever means are mine." The group also covers **LSU**'s "Blame." Five O'Clock People's name is derived from a reference in a parable Jesus tells in Matthew 20:1–16 about laborers who are hired at five o'clock in the evening and only work one hour but are paid the same as those who had "borne the heat of the day." The group intended the moniker as a self-deprecating response to all the hype that was being generated about them being "the next big thing."

Christian radio hits: "This Day" (# 12 in 2000).

Fleming and John

John Mark Painter, gtr.; Fleming McWilliams, voc.; Shawn McWilliams, drums; Stan Rawls, bass (– 1999). 1995—Delusions of Grandeur (R.E.X.); 1999—The Way We Are (Universal).

www.flemingandjohn.com

One of the best modern rock bands in the Christian music market, Fleming and John have a unique style and a mesmerizing sound that has captured the hearts of critics in the mainstream press as well. The group is fronted by singer Fleming McWilliams and guitarist John Painter, who are husband and wife. McWilliams is a distinctive and impressive vocalist. A soprano, her voice may recall Tori Amos in some respects, but she likes to sing with an overload of vibrato, more akin to Delores O'Riordan of The Cranberries. 7ball says, "She can shift from sounding frail and fragile to sounding psychotic and raging with no warning at all." The style is admittedly an acquired taste, and McWilliams' penchant for screeching makes the group a "love it or hate it" affair for some. Painter is a musical genius who has played just about everything (guitars, accordions, brass, keyboards, percussion, etc.) on albums for numerous artists in the Christian market, as well as for folks like Ben Folds Five and the **Indigo Girls.** He cowrote the Christian radio hit "Good Thing" for **Out of Eden.** He has served as engineer or producer and done string arrangements for countless projects as well. His primary contribution to Fleming and John is to cowrite the songs with his wife and to support her diva/rock goddess vocals with Led Zeppelin-inspired guitars. Delusions of Grandeur includes "A Place Called Love," a radio-friendly single that displays an intriguing Middle Eastern influence. The song appears to be about heaven and contains a quote from Revelation 22:17. It is the only obvious nod to anything spiritual or religious on the album. The song "Love Songs" also received some airplay on Christian stations. Another highlight is the album's aggressive opener, "I'm Not Afraid," which was sampled on an NBC commercial in 1997 touting the network's Saturday night lineup. Lyrically, the song contrasts occasions for fear with its titular affirmation: "I'm afraid of growing old / I'm afraid of staying young / Running out of fun . . . I'm afraid of multiple choice / When A and B and C and D are true . . . But I'm not afraid of you."

The Way We Are includes the group's most accessible and best song, "Ugly Girl," cowritten by the duo with Ben Folds, who also plays drums (!) on the album. On "Ugly Girl," McWilliams drops the vibrato and sings in a more traditional pretty voice. The very melodic song has humorous and profound lyrics. It presents the thoughts of a vain woman who has just met her ex-boyfriend's new paramour and discovered that the woman is physically unattractive. The chorus ("I can't believe you're leaving me for an ugly girl") and the verses decrying the new girl's imperfections reveal her own pettiness and superficiality with a delicious irony: she doesn't get why anyone would dump her for an ugly girl, but by the end of the song, the audience does. The album also includes "The Pearl," a song of searching officially inspired by John Steinbeck's novel, though the latter was itself based on Jesus' parable in Matthew 13:45–46.

Flick

Eve Hill, bass; Adam McGrath, drums; Oran Thornton, gtr.; Trevor Thornton, voc. 1998—*The Perfect Kellulight* (Columbia).

Flick is a modern rock band from Stockton, Missouri, that wears its influences (the Beatles, Pink Floyd) on its sleeve. All four members are in their teens or early twenties. Lead singer Trevor Thornton was thirteen when the debut album was recorded. The group favors the sort of neopsychedelic sounds suggested by its song titles: "Freezer Burnt" and "Electric Pear." They have that sound down well and offer a refreshing retro alternative to angst-driven '90s music.

Flick describes themselves as "a general market band with close connections to the Christian music industry." Although all four members are unapologetically believers, they do not bring faith issues into their songs or live performances in obvious ways. Oran Thornton, however, was a prominent member of **Johnny Q. Public** and wrote much of the material for that group's debut album. He is also married to Angie Thornton, who records as **Miss Angie** and has been heavily involved in writing and playing on her projects. Thus, the group has received considerable attention in the Christian press and has played some specifically Christian venues. While finding the very existence of a Christian music subculture to be regrettable, Thornton says the group will play wherever they are invited to play, but will no more put on Christian stylings for one audience than they will shy away from expressing their faith when it seems natural to do so in others: "We're who we are wherever we go."

Flight One Eighty (a.k.a. One Eighty and One Eighty, Inc.)

Jamin Boggs, drums; Josh Brisby, tromb.; Chris Tennberg, gtr.; Kim Tennberg, voc., trump.; John Anderson, sax. (–2001); Dave Desarmier, bass (–2001); Jerry Elekes, gtr. (–2001); Madelyn Mendoza, voc., perc. (–2001). As One Eighty: 1998—*Crackerjack* (BEC). As Flight One Eighty: 1999—*Lineup* (BEC); 2001—*Girls and Boys*.

www.flight180.net

Legal hassles caused the group originally known as One Eighty to change its name twice, first to One Eighty, Inc., and then to Flight One Eighty. The group formed on the campus of Southern California College in 1995 as a groundbreaking example of a female-fronted ska band. Their initial sound showcased the trade-off vocals of Madelyn Mendoza and Kim Tennberg, supported by an instrumental section that was tight and competent enough to meet the expectations of ska. From the first album, however, it was evident that the group's take

on ska was more influenced by pop than by punk, rap, or reggae—in fact the latter two ingredients were completely missing. Thus, the group sounds like the Go-Go's with horns, or, as one critic put it, a cross between the **Halo Friendlies** and **The W's**. *Crackerjack* even includes a cover of the Go-Go's hit "Vacation," along with standout tracks "Slacking" and "Lost in a Haze." Both of the latter songs reflect on the institutional apathy evident in churches that seem to be little more than social clubs. Overtly Christian themes feature prominently on several other tracks as well. "Sally" describes a troubled girl reaching out for love and reflects, "if only she knew Jesus. . . ." The song "Wait" promises those longing to find a life partner that everything is going according to God's plan and that the seeming delay may be "a blessing in disguise." A song called "When We First Dated" evinces a more mature perspective as a disillusioned spouse feels taken for granted ("I've learned to pray everyday that God will see us through"). Still, sentiment is generally more impressive than theology in Flight One Eighty's original compositions, and the band is at its best when it just offers good time music not too heavy on message. The latter forté is accentuated on their second album, which represents what was announced as a one-time detour for the group: an entire record of swing music that pays tribute to the classic Big Band sound of the '40s. In addition to a few originals and standards ("Get Happy," "Banana Split for My Baby"), *Lineup* offers new versions of **The W's**' "The Devil Is Bad," Brian Setzer's "Look at That Cadillac," and Rodgers and Hammerstein's "This Can't Be Love." They also perform the song "I Wanna Be Like You" from the Walt Disney movie *The Jungle Book*.

Shrunk to a quartet, the group took to describing their style as "chick rock" for their next project. *Girls and Boys* shuns most of the ska and swing influences while returning strong No Doubt references. Songs tend to focus on the dreams and fears of young teenage girls. The energetic opening song, "Prom Queen," reveals that the most popular girl in school is really "just your average insecure human being." The notion that God has specific plans for individuals' lives and brings things to pass with perfect timing informs several songs ("Little Girl," "I Want a Guy"). As before, the group is most profound when it reflects less on such mysteries of the universe and more on matters of the heart: the album's standout song, "I'm Sorry," offers a simple statement of regret following a fight. "Good Thing" cleverly piles up metaphors from pop culture ("a love that says you complete me" from the film *Jerry Maguire;* "a treasured map" from **Sixpence None the Richer**'s song "Kiss Me") as descriptions of an unnameable good thing that is available for free. The most obviously evangelical lyrics come in the ska-like "In the Midst," which offers an explicit prayer of repentance: "Jesus, have mercy on my soul / Cleanse me again and make me whole."

Derek Floyd

1983—*Arrival: Derek Floyd* (PTL); 1986—*Once Again;* 1991—*On the Horizon* (Diadem).

Singer/songwriter Derek Floyd established hip credentials with the younger generation early on when he wrote the hit "Reaching for the World" for Harold Melvin and the Blue Notes, which went to the Top 10 on the R&B charts in 1977. Around that time, he also toured with R&B artist Bobby Womack. It's been downhill from there, as he went on to become director of the youth choir for Jim and Tammy Bakker's *PTL Club*—not exactly a job that would endear him to rock and rollers. His albums consist of inspirational MOR songs performed with a sterling vibrato that reminds many reviewers of Johnny Mathis. Floyd does not sing rock music, or even pop—but he seems to have a certain unexpected appeal among some who just appreciate good songs and good voices. Remember when Tony Bennett suddenly became popular with the MTV crowd?

Fluffy

See **Duraluxe.**

Focal Point

Kyle Brown, bass; Ryan Clark, gtr.; Danny Dinh, gtr.; Robbie Imrisek, voc.; Robert Torres, drums. 1996—*Suffering of the Masses* (Tooth and Nail).

The metal-influenced hard rock band Focal Point released one album while all of its members were still high school students in the small town of Elk Grove, California, then broke up. They performed hard music with typically harsh vocals, though production quality gave their album a clean sound with minimal distortion. Most of the songs deal with social issues. "Homicide" offers a virulent attack on abortion clinics ("A beating heart treated like a worthless piece of trash / I hate what you're doing and I will not let it last"); "Neglected" deals with child abuse. "Broken Bonds" is confessional, bemoaning acts that have destroyed a friendship. Clark went on to be lead singer for the group **Training for Utopia.**

Focused

Dirk Lemmenes, bass; Tim Mann, voc.; Mike Merryman, gtr. // Chris Bowden, drums (+ 1995); Andrew Reizuch, gtr. (+ 1995). 1993—*Bow* (Tooth and Nail); 1995—*The Hope That Lies Within;* 1999—*The Wheels of Progress (1992–1996).*

Focused was a Southern California hardcore band often compared to **The Crucified.** Mann once described their music as "mood swing hardcore." He went on to explain, "It's not fast like **Crucified.** It has a lot of feel to it. It's aggressive, but it really swings." The album *Bow* opens with a passionate exhortation to the listener to "put your knee in the dirt and bow to the God that holds your blood red destiny in the palm of His awesome hands." The ten songs that follow offer what *HM* called "a slamfest" of intense proclamations, with a focus on calling attention to the grace and mercy of God. "Perfect Will" stands out as almost a hardcore worship song. The group changed little on *The Hope That Lies Within,* though the songs were noticeably more complex musically and more issue-oriented lyrically. "Killing Years" deals with rape and incest; "Consumer" offers an indictment of our materialistic society. Chris Bowden went on to form **The Merbabies,** and Dirk Lemmenes went on to play with former **Crucified** members Mark Salomon and Jeff Bellew in **Stavesacre.**

Fold Zandura

Jerome Fontamillas, bass, voc., elec.; Jyro Xhan, gtr., voc., elec.; Frank Lenz, drums. 1995—*Fold Zandura* (Xhan); 1997—*Return* (Sub-Lime); *Ultraforever* (BEC); 1999—*King Planet* [EP] (independent).

Fold Zandura began as a side project of **Mortal,** founded by that industrial band's main members (Jyro Xhan and Jerome Fontamillas). According to *CCM,* Fold Zandura "constructs a soundscape of thick, heavy guitars countered by dreamy electronics and samples." Xhan contrasted the group with its predecessor by saying that FZ does not endeavor to play industrial music but just "noisy pop songs." The band's custom debut contains their best songs, though these are remixed in better versions on the subsequent projects (in all, five of the nine songs from *Fold Zandura* end up on *Return* and two more surface on *Ultraforever*). *Return* opens with two midtempo pure pop numbers before toughening up a bit on the hard-edged "Ember"; the latter song is reprised comically as a bonus track at the end in a version that launched the recording career of **John Jonethis.** The song "Valgreen" recalls **The Throes** in its melodic tones. Similarly, *Ultraforever* offers "La Futura," "Mad Into," and "Tonight Forever" as catchy pop songs with memorable hooks, along with the potential hit single "Wencarla." After releasing two full-length albums in a single year, Fold Zandura took a break and then came back with the seven-track EP *King Planet,* which recalls the harder music of Mortal on "Avalanche" and on its title track. Strongly opposed to Christian/secular divisions in music, Fold Zandura likes to mix songs dealing with romantic frustrations with ones that offer confident affirmations of faith in God. "Forever Throw" is a splendid example of the latter: "It's You who sings the morning / And it's You who dreams the light." But, then, in "Never," FZ sounds like The Cure as Xhan sings, "The stars have lied / You and I / Were never meant to be." The song "Please Believe" pleads with a former lover not to look back in anger. "Jesus Eternal" offers what *True Tunes* called "a stream of consciousness meditation on the Lord's forgiveness toward an ignorant and damaged world." Xhan explains the meaning of their name as follows: the "Fold" part comes from John 10:16, where Jesus speaks of seeking out alienated people ("sheep not of my fold"). And Zandura? "I just thought it sounded cool."

Oden Fong

1979—*Come for the Children* (Asaph); 1986—*Invisible Man* (Frontline).

Oden Fong was a founding member of the Jesus music group **Mustard Seed Faith.** He recorded a classic solo album soon after the group disbanded. According to an Internet interview with *Jesus Music,* Fong grew up in Hollywood as the son of famous parents. His mother and father were both actors: May Lia appeared in *To the Ends of the Earth;* Benson Fong was in *Herbie the Love Bug* and *Girls, Girls, Girls* (with **Elvis Presley**) and played the recurring character "number one son" in the popular series of Charlie Chan movies. Fong attended Hollywood High along with Jeff and Beau Bridges and other celebrities' kids. He eventually landed in a Laguna Canyon commune headed by Timothy Leary. He practiced yoga, studied eastern religions, and took large doses of mind-altering drugs in search of spiritual enlightenment. He experienced miraculous deliverance from a near fatal LSD trip and had a vision of Jesus that foreshadowed his ultimate conversion and wholehearted embrace of Christianity. As leader of **Mustard Seed Faith** and as a solo artist, Fong became especially known for his prophetic boldness in proclaiming the gospel and for his dedication to street people, gang members, and other audiences that some might find a little scary.

Fong describes *Come for the Children* as "everything I wanted to do musically for many years." In 1999, historian David Di Sabatino would refer to it as "one of the most underrated Christian music releases of all time." The title track is the album's most remarkable contribution, a seven-minute powerful song that *Jesus Music* describes as "pretty serious rock 'n' roll, way heavier than anything on *Mustard Seed Faith.*" Also intriguing is "Crazy Voices," featuring an electronically modulated "chorus sound," and "The Mask," a fine example of Fong's atmospheric sonic portraits. About this time Fong also placed the song "He's Always There" on the *Maranatha Seven* compilation album (Maranatha!, 1980). It displays the slow, electric groove that typified much of the nonacoustic Jesus music and expresses simple confidence in God's abiding presence: "Though I could be anywhere / I bow my head / He's always there." *Invisible Man* addresses complacency in society and especially in the church, exposing Christians still ruled by the flesh ("Joker in the Age of Fools") and churches that don't put faith into action ("Faith/Action"). The song "Culture Shock" addresses a Christian subculture that was becoming increasingly ingrown, and on "So Long Ago" Fong owns up to his own preoccupations. Fong became pastor of Poiema Chapel in Huntington Beach, California, where he also oversees the Covering Wings homeless ministry and serves as chaplain to the police department.

Fono (a.k.a. Seven)

Ian Crawford, bass; Del Currie, gtr., voc.; Andy Ridley, drums. As Seven: 1996—*High and Wired* [EP] (label unknown); 1997—*Burn* [EP]. As Fono: 1999—*goesaroundcomesaround* (Big Deal).

www.fono.net

A high-energy modern rock band from the United Kingdom, Fono began their career as Seven—no relationship to the Christian band **Se7en** that records on Infiniti Records. As Seven, the band opened a tour for Bon Jovi and attracted a following in the general market. They have continued to build on that foundation as Fono, touring with both the Goo Goo Dolls and Robert Plant. Musically, Fono is often compared with the Goo Goo Dolls, but that analogy holds only for their softer material; the band has a harder overall sound. The band itself has suggested that their sound may represent "a cross between the Foo Fighters and The Who"; in Christian music circles this pop-meets-art-rock approach has also been employed effectively by **Fold Zandura** and **King's X.** Fono lead singer and songwriter Del Currie also performed with **Split Level** and **Tribe of Dan.** The effective debut *goesaroundcomesaround* took critics by storm, inspiring a *Phantom Tollbooth* reviewer to describe it as "one of the most surprising albums I've ever come across in Christian rock" and another to claim it was "probably the best radio-friendly alternative rock album by Christians ever." Indeed, every track on the album seems to have hit single potential. The opening track, "Collide," is a marvelous pop explosion, a fast-paced, hook-filled number with a memorable melody. "Alcatraz" is perhaps the album's most powerful track; it was inspired by the movie *Murder in the First* and uses imprisonment as a metaphor for emotional distress, with the line "I'll bend until you break" delivered repeatedly in an agitated rock star scream. By contrast, "Drift Away" is driven by acoustic guitar and shimmers with pop sensibility. "Under My Skin" pillages the lyric from an old Frank Sinatra (or Four Seasons) song with novel effect: "I've got you under my skin / Breathe you out, breathe you in." The object of this almost-worship song's affection is a female companion, not Jesus, but specifically Christian content is expressed in "Now She's 24," which relates the tale of a young woman's conversion. "Burn," a potential alternative rock hit if ever there was one, features the lyric, "Knock me down / I never wanted this pride / Tie my hands / So I can do no wrong." The album had been released on cassette a year earlier with slightly different songs (a nondescript number "All Falls Down" in place of "Round and Round," "Drift Away," and "Splendid").

Christian radio hits: "Now She's 24" (# 7 in 1999); "Drift Away" (# 16 in 2000).

Foreigner

See **Lou Gramm.**

Forerunner

Paul Brannon, gtr.; Joe English, drums; John Lawry, voc.; kybrd.; Tim Smith, bass. 1984—*a.k.a.* (Refuge); *Live.*

Forerunner was a one-time project fronted by **John Lawry,** who had also sung for **Petra.** The former drummer for Paul McCartney's Wings, **Joe English,** was also a member, as well as Paul Brannon, who had been a member of **The English Band.** The album packaging for the group's first album was confusing in that it listed the group's name as both "Forerunner" and as "The Joe English Band" (though English's participation seemed minimal). The songs are all explicitly Christian but vary in profundity. "Hard Times" relies heavily on cliché ("Hard times are just a way to grow"). "Nowhere to Run" presents Christ as the only sure refuge in a world torn apart by war. There are also two instrumentals and a powerful worship song written by Lawry ("Jesus Is Saviour"). The *Live* album released by Refuge in 1984 was officially credited to **Joe English** and Forerunner. It includes performances of a number of songs from English's solo albums.

Foreverafter

Jamey Lyons, voc.; Jennifer Lyons, voc.; Jay Lyons, acc.; Brent Milligan, bass; Alex Nifong, gtr. 1999—*Foreverafter* (Word).

www.foreverafter.net

Foreverafter is a labor of love for the husband and wife duo Jamey and Jennifer Lyons, who have spent some years ministering to youth groups, especially as worship leaders. Their debut album features simple pop songs targeted for church youth. Dan Mukala serves as coproducer and co-composer, and many of the songs recall the sound of his band **(Mukala).** Alex Nifong was also a member of **Mukala.** The opening track, "Who You Are" is typical: bouncy, repetitive, with a straightforward theme (loving Christ for who he is, and not simply what he does). The song "No" supports the True Love Waits campaign for sexual abstinence before marriage: "We'll wait together until we say forever." Most of the songs are worship ori-

ented with simple, youth-group lyrics: "Jesus, He's the King / He's the Lord of everything" ("The One for Me").

Forevertree

Geoff Breen, bass; Bob Gale, drums; Dwayne Jackson, voc.; Jeff Miller, gtr. 1998—*Turning* (BulletProof).

The Toronto-based quartet Forevertree belongs to the post-grunge genre of rock exemplified by bands like Live and **Creed.** They attempt to supplement, but not replace, Nirvana-style guitar histrionics with eclectic elements pinched from this or that alternative source. Thus, as *The Lighthouse* notes, their standout song "This Cage Me" features an impressive heavy guitar attack, but also a dissonant, haunting melody line that is chanted in a style reminiscent of Led Zeppelin. The group also moves beyond its staple domain on the songs "Six," a classic, three-chord pop number, and "Breathe," a masterpiece of understatement on which they allow unresolved musical tension to carry the song from start to close. Lyrically, Forevertree's songs address Christian themes like judgment and redemption with unmistakable clarity. On "Pure," the singer proclaims, "In Your will is where I want to be / In Your Word is where you'll find me / I'm pure in my mind."

For Love Not Lisa

Mike Lewis, voc., gtr.; Miles, gtr.; Clint McBay, bass; Aaron Preston, drums. 1993—*Merge* (Atlantic); 1995—*Information Superdriveway* (East West); 1999—*The Lost Elephant* (Tooth and Nail).

Although their name summoned retro images of flower power, For Love Not Lisa was a grunge band playing in the same ballpark as Nirvana, Foo Fighters, and Candlebox. They became best known for their song, "Slip Slide Melting," which was featured on the best-selling soundtrack for the motion picture *The Crow.* For Love Not Lisa was originally formed in Oklahoma by the mononymous Miles and a bass player named Matt Hilben. There were numerous undocumented personnel changes (including drummers Kent Ewing and Eric Myers and bass players Ahren Burns and Doug Carrion) but the eventual lineup included Aaron Preston and Clint McBay, both of whom had played with the band Chainsaw Kittens, and lead singer Mike Lewis, who became the identifiable front man. For Love Not Lisa was a moderately successful general market band and had nothing to do with the Christian music scene. After the group broke up, however, Mike Lewis and Miles formed the distinctively Christian group **Puller** and signed to Tooth and Nail, a company that is primarily associated with Christian music, though it also strives to break down barriers between so-called Christian and secular markets. The association of **Puller** with the label created something of a For Love Not Lisa revival among fans of Christian music who now sought out that group's records as well. **Puller** was clearly understood to be a Christian band by many Christian music fans and, by association, For Love Not Lisa came to be regarded as something of a quasi-Christian or proto-Christian group as well. In both cases, such labeling was based more on Lewis's external professions of faith than on recognizably evangelical content in song lyrics. Nevertheless, Tooth and Nail issued a final product by the defunct group, consisting of outtakes, songs from an out-of-print EP (called *Elephant*), and songs from an original demo the band had literally recorded in a basement. The primary interest in the latter album seems to have come from within the alternative Christian music community, though the album was distributed by the label to mainstream outlets only. It was withheld from Christian retail stores due to controversial artwork in the liner notes (in one photo McBay is playing a guitar that has a sticker on it reading, "Girls Kick Ass"). In 1998, Miles would join Lewis in **Puller,** essentially turning that band into For Love Not Lisa redux.

Forty Days

Brian Barth, drums; Chris Foster, gtr.; Drue Phillips, bass, voc.; Joel Warren, voc., gtr.; Mark Warren, voc. 2000—*Everyday* (Benson).

Forty Days is a basic acoustic rock band from Ft. Worth, Texas. Musically, they have the alterna-pop style of groups like Matchbox 20 and Third Eye Blind that became so big in the late '90s. Lyrically, their songs focus on worship, edification, and exhortation. In the Christian music scene, Forty Days would fit loosely into a genre represented by many other bands, including **According to John, Clear, FFH, PFR, Satellite Soul, Smalltown Poets, Sonicflood, Sundry,** and **The Waiting.** But Forty Days has a story to tell that made them the objects of sometimes unwanted media attention.

On September 15, 1999, while negotiations for what would be their debut album were still underway, the group played a See You at the Pole concert at Wedgewood Baptist Church in Ft. Worth, Texas (See You at the Pole is an annual event where young members of some religious denominations are encouraged to gather at their school's flagpole for a brief public display of faith and patriotism). About 450 people were present for the concert. Lead singer Mark Warren would later recall that in the middle of the worship song "I Will Call upon the Lord" he heard popping noises, but the music was loud and he assumed it to be a malfunction of the group's equipment. He continues, "Then I saw a disruption to the right of the stage, and I thought it was kids goofing off." The sanctuary was dark, except for a spotlight on the stage. "A couple of adults went over there, and I thought they were gonna handle it. But I still heard popping noises. Then I looked up and saw him in the aisle." A forty-seven-year-old man by the name of Larry Gene Ashbrook had entered the church with a gun and begun ran-

domly shooting members of the congregation, making his way toward the stage. The band scattered, ducking behind its equipment, except for guitarist Chris Foster who was frozen centerstage with nowhere to run. Cursing, Ashbrook fired at him repeatedly, but missed. Then he turned the gun on himself. Seven people besides the gunman were killed that day, with many more wounded. Over one hundred bullets were fired.

Reluctant to cash in on publicity surrounding this tragedy, Forty Days decided to hold up release of their album for over a year, when the story was no longer front-page news. The record *Everyday* is nevertheless dedicated to "all the people whose lives were forever changed at Wedgewood Baptist Church on September 15, 1999." The album was produced by Mac Powell of **Third Day** and includes a cover of the Beach Boys' "God Only Knows." The song "Long Way Home" is the album's most catchy and melodic number. "Remember" and "One Day" express a longing for heaven. "Everyday" and "I Run" were written soon after the 1999 shootings, inspired by the group's return to Wedgewood Baptist Church for another program there.

Christian radio hits: "Long Way Home" (# 18 in 2001).

Fountain of Tears

Joey Daub, drums; Anna DeRose, voc.; Mike DiDonato, gtr.; Jeff King, kybrd.; Erik Ney, bass. 1999—*Fountain of Tears* (custom).

www.fountainoftears.com

Pennsylvania-based Fountain of Tears is something of a Christian metal supergroup with a new female vocalist. Joey Daub was a member of **Believer,** Mike DiDonato and Erik Ney were both in **Sacrament,** and Jeff King played with **Sardonyx.** The group's independent debut album moves away from metal and into the realm of symphonic progressive rock, though the sound is still very hard. The album contains five songs, which are then repeated as instrumentals for a total of ten tracks. "The Sleeper" is a poem by Edgar Allan Poe narrated and set to music.

4–4–1

Glenn Holland, bass, kybrd.; John McNamara, voc.; John Giali, gtr. (– 1988); Steve Giali, drums (– 1988). 1985—*4–4–1* (Royal Commandment); 1986—*Mourning into Dancing* (Blue Collar); 1988—*Sacrifice* (Broken).

A mid '80s Christian pop band, 4–4–1 evinced an appreciation for Top 40 radio potential while also infusing their music with just enough new-wave sensibility to earn the respect of critics like Brian Quincy Newcomb, who praised both of their latter two albums in *CCM*. The first record, a custom release, has a strong '60s feel with the new-wave sound appearing on the standout track, "Show Me." *Mourning into Dancing,* as its name implies (cf. Psalm 30:11), emphasizes rhythmic and up-beat numbers. With the departure of the Giali brothers (John and Steve), the group released *Sacrifice* as a duo with a more acoustic and ambient sound. Newcomb compared the latter record to products by Crowded House and **Simple Minds.** Notably, *Mourning into Dancing* was produced by **John** and Dino **Elefante,** and *Sacrifice* by Gene Eugene (of **Adam Again**) and both albums exhibit the new professionalism that Christian music came to acquire in the '80s. Lyrically, 4-4-1 offers songs that communicate clear messages about life and relationships to Christians facing real-world situations. "Show Me" is not the song from *My Fair Lady,* but it does pick up the same theme as that hit: Don't just talk about what you believe, but "show me with your life what you're living for."

4 Him

Andy Chrisman, voc.; Mark Harris, voc.; Marty Magehee, voc.; Kris Sullivan, voc. 1990—*4 Him* (Benson); 1991—*Face the Nation;* 1992—*The Basics of Life;* 1993—*The Season of Love;* 1994—*The Ride;* 1996—*The Message;* 1998—*The Obvious;* 1999—*Best Ones;* 2000—*Hymns: A Place of Worship;* 2001—*Walk On* (Word).

www.4him.net

Based in Daphne, Alabama, 4 Him became the most popular male vocal group in Christian music in the '90s. The group was formed in 1990 by four members of the gospel group **Truth,** and it retains southern gospel roots while infusing the music with pop-rock instrumentation and enough of a beat to appeal to adults who were raised on rock and roll. The sound—similar to the less successful **NewSong** and, at least initially, to the legendary **Imperials**—is that of *slick* pop with an emphasis on vocal harmony. Each of the four singers is an accomplished soloist, and the constant trade-offs on lead vocals provide a strong element of diversity. Basically, 4 Him sounds like a more mature version of all those boy groups (Backstreet Boys, *NSYNC, 98 degrees) that conquered charts at the turn of the millennium. 4 Him albums tend to be heavily produced with nothing left to chance. The group's professionalism, musicianship, and packaged spirituality have all become definitive of a formula for success in the Christian music industry. The group traveled to Russia in 1994 to distribute Bibles as representatives of the American Bible Society. They have had more than twenty songs go to Number One on the Christian adult contemporary chart.

4 Him's debut album earned them a Dove award for Best New Artist, with the song "Where There Is Faith" attracting the most attention. Indeed, the album became (at that time) the second best-selling debut in the history of Christian music (behind **DC Talk**). The follow-up, *Face the Nation,* further established 4 Him as MOR superstars, on the strength of ballads like "He Never Changes" and "Why?" *The Basics of Life* offered

more of the same, but with a fine selection of songs held together by the theme of a return to traditional values. Notably, *The Basics of Life* would be the only 4 Him album included (at Number Sixty-six) on a *CCM* critics poll of "The 100 Greatest Albums in Christian Music" published in 2001. The song "Built on Amazing Grace" emphasizes the connection between the past and present of gospel music and features the members' fathers singing with them. The group's formula was set, and 4 Him seemed ready to deliver years of the no-surprises music adult contemporary fans wanted. But then *The Ride* would exhibit more kick than any of the previous projects, such that the group could now be more easily compared to **Steven Curtis Chapman** than to **The Imperials.** Indeed, the opening track, "Real Thing," sounds very much like a Chapman song and even echoes the lyrical theme of that artist's "Heaven in the Real World." The effective title track to *The Ride* (called "Ride of Life") compares the ups and downs of life to a roller coaster and utilizes cool sound effects to convey amusement park excitement. "For Future Generations" is a sort of Michael Jackson "Heal the World" anthem complete with the backing voices of a full choir. Mark Harris said of the album, "It's definitely not rock, just energetic pop." That description would also hold for *The Message,* which opens with the catchy, hook-filled "Lay It All on the Line" but also includes the very churchy-sounding title song. "Sacred Hideaway" stands out as something of a rarity—a track written by Mark Magehee with a subtle African flavor. The group described the album as "more edgy, more organic, more acoustic, and more guitar-driven" than their previous projects, and they admitted that the sound owed something to the gargantuan success of general market band Hootie and the Blowfish.

These stylistic influences would be far more noticeable on *The Obvious.* On all of their previous recordings, 4 Him had a distinctly religious sound. For better or worse (opinions differ), they did the sort of songs that one could immediately identify as *sounding like* Christian music even without hearing any of the lyrics. On their eighth release, the quartet finally evolved beyond its origins as a **Truth** spin-off and for the first time recorded modern pop similar *in sound* to what is actually played on mainstream radio. The opening track, "Let the Lion Run Free," has a particularly memorable melody, and "Signs and Wonders" even features a slightly nasal vocal supplemented by some tasty "Do Do Doo's" in the background. After their label (Benson) folded, 4 Him signed with Word Records for an album that continued in the same vein as *The Obvious,* albeit with more of a praise and worship focus. Vertical-orientation songs like "Psalm 112," "Surrender," and "Who Are You" pepper *Walk On,* but the album's best track is probably the soulful rock song "I Know You Now."

Lyrically, 4 Him's music is generally intended for the church, with messages that alternate between affirmation and challenge. Harris has developed as a songwriter over the years of the group's tenure and by *The Ride* was cowriting most of the material. "The Measure of a Man" affirms the personal worth of every individual: "You can doubt your worth and search for who you are and where you stand / But God made you in his image / when he formed you in his hands." "Great Awakening" promises a coming revival. Both "Center of the Mark" and "The Message" call on believers to fulfill the great commandments of loving God and loving people. The group has also made a Christmas album *(Season of Love)* and recorded an album of hymns.

Christian radio hits: "Couldn't We Stand" (# 21 in 1991); "A Man You Would Write About" (# 27 in 1991); "Freedom" (# 21 in 1993); "Wrecking Ball" (# 24 in 1994); "For Future Generations" (# 4 in 1994); "Wings" (# 1 in 1995); "Real Thing" (# 1 for 2 weeks in 1995); "Ride of Life" (# 4 in 1995); "The Nature of Love," (# 11 in 1996); "The Message" (# 12 in 1996); "Land of Mercy" (# 2 in 1996); "Measure of a Man" (# 16 in 1997); "Sacred Hideaway" (# 10 in 1997); "Lay It All on the Line" (# 13 in 1997); "Can't Get Past the Evidence" (# 8 in 1998); "The Only Thing I Need" (# 17 in 1999).

Dove Awards: 1991 New Artist of the Year; 1993 Group of the Year; 1994 Group of the Year; 1994 Inspirational Album *(The Season of Love)*; 1995 Group of the Year.

Found Free

See **Bash-N-the Code.**

Fourth Estate

Fred Babich, bass; Dave Beegle, gtr.; Jim Iltis, drums (– 1996) // Dave Spurr, drums (+ 1996). 1992—*Finesse and Fury* (Rubicon); 1996—*See What I See* (Hapi Skratch).

www.geocities.com/BourbonStreet/5078

Virtuoso band leader **Dave Beegle** describes the music of Fourth Estate as "ethno-alternative progressive instrumental rock." Beegle is a musician's musician; while not well known in the commercial market, he is regarded by professional guitarists as one of the world's great masters of that instrument. Magazines like *Guitar Player* and *Musician* regularly refer to him in the same category as Jimmy Page, Brian May, or Stevie Ray Vaughan. The group Fourth Estate, from Fort Collins, Colorado, is but one of his several projects. A generally hard rocking trio, Fourth Estate has been compared to Rush and **King's X,** but their music is more distinctive than such analogies allow. The overall sound is an eclectic blend of blues, rock, and jazz, and a unique quality is thrown into this mix via Beegle's choice of instruments: a computer assisted self-tuning guitar called the Transperformance DTS-01. The guitar was designed to be able to change to alternative tunings at the touch of a button. It does do this, allowing for such changes in the middle of a song, but—leave it to a rocker to figure this out—it also can be set to tune the guitar randomly in ways that produce completely unexpected experimental effects. Jimmy Page and Joe Perry have also played the Transperformance DTS-01 but Beegle is the acknowledged master, and Fourth Estate is the only group that has actually built songs around its capabilities.

Founded by Beegle in 1988, Fourth Estate produced three albums for private distribution *(Fourth Estate, Edge of the Shadows,* and *In Phase).* The album *Finesse and Fury* shocked critics with its diversity. The group performs a beautiful version of Bach's "Jesu, Joy of Man's Desiring," a countryfied stomp called "Mason Street Shuffle," and a raw all-out rocker called "Juggernaut." Beegle shows off his finger-picking finesse on the appropriately titled "Sorefinger Road." The song "Routier" from this album holds the distinction of being the first recording ever to feature a Transperformance guitar. *See What I See* exhibits a turn toward world music. The standout cut, "Kara Kum," is a three-part electric suite built on Bulgarian folk melodies and dance rhythms. "The Hammer Song" is a more traditional adrenaline rush of blues riffs. New drummer David Spurr (formerly with **Phil Keaggy**'s band) gets to shine on "Crazy Ivan." In 1999, Beegle released a compilation album called *Clear the Tracks,* which includes some songs from the Fourth Estate albums in addition to material he recorded with other groups.

Fourth Estate has performed at *Cornerstone* and in other ways identified themselves with the Christian music scene. Beegle is quick to identify himself as a Christian and he declares that his music—while lacking the explicit content that some songwriters provide through lyrics—is all written and performed to the glory of God. The most important things in life, he avers, are "inner peace, a relationship with Christ, friends, fellowship, and church." Words, he continues, can detract. "I find it offensive when people trivialize Christ in music, just throwing in the word Jesus." He hopes, rather, that his music in and of itself, will reflect what is genuine and true, testifying to who he is as a person in relationship with other people and with God.

Justin Fox Band

Chris Atchley, drums; Joe Servia, bass; Justin Fox, gtr., voc. 2000—*Angel Motel* (True Tunes).

http://justinfox.hypermart.net

Justin Fox grew up in Arcata, California, and recorded some independent releases (including *Stand* and *Matter of Soul*) with an earlier incarnation of his band. The group got noticed by the Christian press and *Angel Motel* was picked up by *True Tunes.*

"The groove is acoustic," said *CCM*, "the voice just raspy enough to bring you in like a warm embrace, and the songs are thoughtful, mature and show a lot of depth for a new artist." *Phantom Tollbooth* compared the band's sound to Counting Crows or a young Bruce Springsteen. Lyrically, *Angel Motel* depicts faith as a longing. Its opening words are "Well, I ain't perfect, I ain't even close" ("Take Me Over"). Later, Fox sings, "As the years go by like a bullet train / A silver blur in the driving rain / I want to be faithful."

Fraction

Jim Beach, voc.; Victor Hemme, bass; Robert Meinel, gtr.; Curt Swanson, perc.; Don Swanson, gtr. 1970—*Moonblood* (Angelus).

The very early Christian rock band Fraction released only one unsuccessful album that would acquire something of a cult following. The group's sound was reminiscent of The Doors due to Jim Beach's Morrison-like vocals. Curt Swanson excelled at guitar solos that seemed to be inspired by Ritchie Blackmore of Deep Purple. *Moonblood* features six long songs drenched in psychedelic effects. Lyrics are appropriately apocalyptic. The album cover (designed by Michael Hodges) featured a picture of the moon and was encased in red cellophane. According to one Internet site (www.angelfire.com), copies of the record with this cellophane still intact were valued at $3500 in the year 2002. *Jesus Music* warns against going over $2500. The album was re-released on the independent Rockaway label in 1999, with three bonus tracks.

Don Francisco

1976—*Brother of the Son* (NewPax); 1977—*Forgiven*; 1979—*Got to Tell Somebody*; 1981—*The Traveler*; 1982—*The Live Concert*; 1984—*Holiness*; 1985—*The Poet: A Collection of the Best*; *One Heart at a Time* (Myrrh); 1987—*The Power* (StarSong); 1988—*High Praise*; 1989—*Live in the U.K.* (Vision); 1991—*The Early Works* (Benson); *Vision of the Valley* (StarSong); 1992—*Come Away* (StarSong); 1994—*Songs of the Spirit, Vol. I: Genesis and Job*; 1997—*He's Alive* (Progressive); 1998—*Beautiful to Me* (Shelf Life); 1998—*Grace on Grace*.

www.donfrancisco.com

Christian folksinger Don Francisco (b. 1946) described himself to *CCM* in late 1998 as "a one-trick pony," alluding to Paul Simon's apt metaphor for an artist who gets pegged for a single song. Although Francisco has provided almost twenty-five years of steady contributions to contemporary Christian music, he seems destined always to be remembered for the song "He's Alive" from his sophomore album *Forgiven*. That song relates the discovery of Jesus' resurrection in simple narrative style, as told from the perspective of Peter. Closely following the biblical account, the song opens with Peter's thoughts of fear and despair, moves on to the report he hears from Mary Magda-

lene, traces his visit to the empty tomb, speculates on his discussion with other disciples as to what might have happened, touches on his shameful reminiscence of his denials, then suddenly breaks open in a surprising way that effectively conveys a climactic interruption: "Jesus stood before me with his arms held open wide / And I fell down on my knees and just clung to him and cried." Piano chords crash into the song, utterly destroying its structure and replacing the loping melody with a bombastic chorus, "He's alive! He's alive! / He's alive and I'm forgiven / Heaven's gates are open wide!" *Cashbox* magazine called the song "one of the best folk gospel ballads of all time." Over twenty years later, a bevy of critics for *CCM* selected it for the Top 10 on their list of the best songs in the history of contemporary Christian music. The song remains tied with **Dallas Holm**'s "Rise Again" as the longest running chart single in the history of Christian radio. It has been covered by many artists, including Dolly Parton in 1989.

The son of a Baptist minister and seminary professor, Francisco rebelled against his upbringing and left his home in Louisville, Kentucky, to become a hippie in Southern California. Eventually, he ended up in Decatur, Georgia, leading a rock and roll band. His life was turned around in 1974 when he says he heard the audible voice of God speak to him while he was meditating: "Don, this is Jesus. I love you. Why do you keep running from me?" Fifteen years later, he would still relate the significance of this miraculous occurrence: "It was a voice as clear as if someone had been in the room with me. In that instant, he showed me what he's really like and shattered all my religious preconceptions. I'd found everything I'd been searching for." Francisco went on to study music business at Belmont College and connected with **Gary Paxton** a short time later to make Christian albums for NewPax. In 1982, Francisco moved to Colorado. In 1985, he and his wife Karen went public regarding her struggle with alcoholism and a related suicide attempt.

The seven records Francisco made for NewPax (five plus a live set and a compilation) display the vocal style of a more laid-back Jim Croce on songs that favor storytelling. All of the records have a country flair, with doses of dobro, mandolin, banjo, and pedal steel guitar applied as necessary. In addition to "He's Alive," Francisco scored big with "Got to Tell Somebody," an ode to witnessing. The album for which that tune served as title track also includes "I'll Never Let Go of Your Hand," which Francisco would identify in 1998 as his personal favorite of all his songs. **Joe English** guested as drummer on *The Traveler*. Francisco's first four albums alone sold over half a million copies, making him one of the biggest stars in Christian music for that era. *Holiness* was produced by **Al Perkins** and reveals a turn away from the hippie folksinger persona with glimpses of a more settled posture reminiscent of **John**

Michael Talbot. *One Heart at a Time* came at a transitional time and offers a potpourri of various folk styles.

From 1987 to 1994, Francisco recorded with StarSong. He focused these albums on ministry in a way that *Holiness* had previewed, emphasizing worship songs and meditative pieces. His record *The Power*, in particular, reveals a man in charge of his craft, featuring the songs "Let the Waters Roll," "I'm Gonna Walk," and "One Thing I Ask." *High Praise* was his first self-produced project and contains both reflective pieces and a couple of handclappers. *Come Away* is built around a theme of retreat and refreshment. *Genesis and Job* offers story songs derived from those two books of the Bible and was intended as the first in a series of recordings that would feature "songs from every book of the Bible, God willing." But the StarSong years were difficult ones for Francisco. He was able to accept his decline in commercial success but struggled ideologically with a Christian music industry that seemed more interested in business than ministry. He also experienced marital difficulties and, indeed, released *Vision of the Valley* after a sabbatical on which he had struggled with family concerns. A vulnerable undertaking, that album offers a public witness to the personal inventory he had taken during that time and to his renewed commitment to God's priorities. Nevertheless, he and his wife divorced three years later. "People will understand or they won't understand," he related to *CCM.* "I'll leave it at that." In the years after his work with StarSong, Francisco has continued to perform and has made two independent albums that present new recordings of many of his classic songs, plus one record *(Grace on Grace)* of new material.

For trivia buffs: Francisco bought his first guitar at age fourteen with money he won in a poker game, when he and some other boys ditched Sunday school to gamble with dollars stolen out of the church's offering plate. "I didn't know what I was getting into," Francisco has reflected. "I got that guitar on God's time with his money—and he owned all the music that came out of me from then on."

Christian radio hits: "He's Alive" (# 1 for 14 weeks in 1978; the song was # 1 the week that the Christian Hit Radio chart debuted); "Adam, Where Are You?" (# 21 in 1978); "Got to Tell Somebody" (# 1 for 18 weeks in 1980); "Steeple Song" (# 16 in 1980); "Messengers from Heaven" (# 2 in 1982); "Holiness" (# 10 in 1984); "One Heart at a Time" (# 7 in 1985).

Dove Awards: 1980 Songwriter of the Year.

Aretha Franklin

Selected: 1956—*The Gospel Sound of Aretha Franklin* (Checker); 1972— *Amazing Grace* (Atlantic); 1987—*One Lord, One Faith, One Baptism* (Arista); 1999—*You Grow Closer* (Peacock); *Amazing Grace: The Complete Recordings* (Rhino).

Aretha Franklin (b. 1942) was born in Memphis, Tennessee, but grew up in Detroit, Michigan, where her father, the Rev. C. L. Franklin, was pastor of the 4500-member New Bethel Baptist Church. He was a famous preacher and also a well-known gospel singer, billed as "the Man with the Million Dollar Voice." Aretha's mother, Barbara, was also a gospel singer, but she left the family when Aretha was only six, and died four years later. Aretha says in her autobiography (*Aretha: From These Roots,* Villard, 1999), "I accepted Jesus Christ as my Lord and personal Savior and was baptized at the age of ten." She sang regularly in the church with her sisters Carolyn and Erma, and she recorded a gospel album at the age of fourteen. Several other songs recorded during this period (when she was sixteen) were released on the *You Grow Closer* album in 1999 (the standout track is a simple, live piano version of Thomas Dorsey's "Precious Lord"). Aretha maintains that the single greatest influence on her music was gospel singer Clara Ward, with whom she toured the gospel circuit. She also came to know such luminaries as James Cleveland, Mahalia Jackson (who stiffed her on what was supposed to be her first paid performance), and **Sam Cooke.** The latter encouraged her to cross over into R&B as he had done.

Between 1961 and 1967, Franklin made ten R&B albums for Columbia records that were only moderately successful. Then she signed with Atlantic and, in partnership with producer Jerry Wexler, came up with the distinctive sound that would become definitive of soul music. One of the most successful recording artists of all time, Franklin was a phenomenon in the late '60s, racking up nine Top 10 hits in 1967–1968 alone—hits on the mainstream pop charts, not just the R&B stations. Like Diana Ross and Stevie Wonder, she broke down color barriers and brought the sounds of black music to white audiences; in fact, she probably did so with less musical compromise than any other artist. A staple component of her sound was a gospel-inspired vocal arrangement that made use of call-and-response choruses.

Forever known as the "Queen of Soul," Franklin established herself as a remarkable interpreter of songs, able to rework well-known material into startling new classics. Her signature song remains her startling version of Otis Redding's "Respect" (# 1 for 2 weeks in 1967). Her versions of Carole King's "A Natural Woman" (# 8 in 1967), The Band's "The Weight" (# 19 in 1969), and Simon and Garfunkel's "Bridge over Troubled Water" (# 6 in 1971) sound nothing like the originals, yet are remarkable in their own right. Other unforgettable hits include "Baby I Love You" (# 4 in 1967), "Chain of Fools" (# 2 in 1967), and "Think" (# 7 in 1968). Franklin would remain a constant presence on the charts throughout the early '70s with hits like "Spanish Harlem" (# 2 in 1971) and "Until You Come Back to Me" (# 3 in 1973). The disco craze of the late '70s left her in a slump for a time, but she returned in the mid '80s with a powerful comeback and had eight more Top 40 hits, including

"Freeway of Love" (# 3 in 1985) and "I Knew You Were Waiting" (# 1 for 2 weeks in 1987; duet with George Michael).

Franklin's personal life has been marked by some turmoil and tragedy. Pregnant at thirteen, she would give birth to two sons before her seventeenth birthday. From 1961 to 1969, she was married to her manager, Ted White, a man who on one occasion struck her in public and on another shot her new production manager with a gun. She gave birth to another son out of wedlock in the early '70s. She was arrested in 1968 for reckless driving, and again in 1969 for disorderly conduct. In 1969, her father was arrested for possession of marijuana. He was also in the news that year for hosting a conference for black separatist groups that led to a violent confrontation with the Detroit police (one officer was killed). A decade later, he was shot by burglars and remained in a coma until his death in 1984. That same year, Aretha divorced her second husband, actor Glynn Turman, whom she had married in 1978. In 1988, her sister Carolyn died of cancer. Her brother (and manager) Cecil also died about this time. Perhaps because of these erratic and often painful experiences, Franklin has remained an enigmatic figure, generally refusing to give interviews or to discuss her personal life. Thus, she appears mysterious and often idiosyncratic in much the same way—though not to the same degree—as media-shy pop singer Michael Jackson. For instance, Franklin admits to a phobia about flying, which greatly curtails her ability to tour. Her stage shows and public appearances have often presented her in what many regard as bizarre or unseemly costume choices. She has a controversial penchant for wearing fur coats.

In 1972, Franklin recorded the highly acclaimed *Amazing Grace* album, which won her a Grammy and became her first gold record. A spectacular two-record set, the album was recorded live in Los Angeles with James Cleveland playing piano and conducting the choir. Produced by Wexler, the album includes many traditional gospel songs ("What a Friend We Have in Jesus," "Precious Lord"), as well as modern numbers like **Marvin Gaye**'s "Wholly Holy" and secular tunes that she recasts as gospel songs with new spiritual meaning ("You're All I Need to Get By," "You've Got a Friend"). Franklin also sings "Mary, Don't You Weep" and a couple of Clara Ward's songs ("How I Got Over," "Never Grow Old"), but the album's highlight may be her duet with Cleveland on "Precious Memories." The record came out when Franklin was a major star in top form and at a time when the Jesus movement was in full bloom. Unfortunately, fans of Jesus music regarded the album with suspicion, as Franklin did not offer any moving story of a conversion or indicate any intention of abandoning her worldly career. The inclusion of an instrumental version of George Harrison's "My Sweet Lord" didn't help, since many Jesus people considered that to be an almost anti-Christian

"Hare Krishna" song. The Jesus people—as youth caught up in the '70s Jesus movement revival were called—demanded absolute authenticity and sincerity, and they tended to define that quality in naive and judgmental ways. They weren't sure if Franklin was *really* an on-fire-for-Jesus Christian or just a soul singer drawing on her background to sing some Christian songs. If the latter, they didn't want anything to do with it—no matter how well done the songs might be. Jesus people didn't buy Judy Collins' version of "Amazing Grace" either—a Number Fifteen hit in 1970. They would rather listen to kids from Calvary Chapel warble little ditties than listen to stellar performances of masterpieces by divas who might not really mean what they were singing. That was the character of the Jesus movement, for better and for worse, and it is a legacy that has continued to define the contemporary Christian music subculture. In the case of Aretha Franklin, however, the suspicions seem silly. Franklin is a Christian with a lifetime of service in the church, though she apparently understands her primary vocational calling as being to provide wholesome entertainment for society rather than as being to evangelize sinners or edify saints. Very few (if any) of her "secular songs" have contained anything objectionable to Christians—unless of course the Christians in question are offended by such things as romantic love or sexual desire, aversions that do not properly derive from Christianity. For her part, Franklin would object to the advertising that presented *Amazing Grace* as her "return to gospel," maintaining that she never really left: "I never left church and I never will. Church is as much a part of me as the air I breathe. I have heard people say that one singer or another 'gave up gospel for pop' but that is not my case. I expanded, but I never abandoned." Although it has been largely ignored by fans of contemporary Christian music, *Amazing Grace* remains one of the great classics of the genre. In 1999, Rhino records released an expanded version of the album on CD, featuring several new tracks.

In 1987, Franklin offered up another remarkable gospel project, *One Lord, One Faith, One Baptism,* which once again would take the Grammy award for Best Soul Gospel Performance. The lengthy (ninety minutes) recording offers highlights from a three-day worship event at what had been her father's church. About a third of the album is taken up with spoken word messages, including a ten-minute speech by Jesse Jackson. The rest is music, featuring Aretha backed by an impressive choir and augmented by such guest stars as Mavis Staples of the Staples Singers. The selections are mostly traditional gospel numbers, including "Surely God Is Able," "Jesus Hears Every Prayer," and "Packin' Up, Gettin' Ready to Go." She also delivers a rousing version of "O Happy Day." In 1988, Franklin told *CCM* magazine, "God has been a rock for me. I'm not a theological student, but the gospel has been a constant in my life and in the Franklin family." In 1999, she wrote in her autobiography, "Gospel is and will always be an integral part of who I am. Gospel is all feeling and faith and about the life and teachings and miracles and trials and prophecies of Jesus, a music of unshakeable conviction and determination that things will get better. Its root is rock-solid optimism and the certain knowledge that God is real."

Franklin's significance for the history of American music, including gospel, has brought her numerous accolades. In 1968, she appeared on the cover of *Time* magazine and was presented with an award by Martin Luther King Jr. In 1976, she sang at the inauguration of President Jimmy Carter. In 1987, she became the first woman inducted into the Rock and Roll Hall of Fame. In 1994, she sang at the inauguration of President Bill Clinton.

For trivia buffs: Aretha Franklin coined the popular slang phrase, "Sock it to me," using it for the first time as an ad lib line in her version of "Respect" ("sock it to me, sock it to me, sock it to me").

Dove Awards: 1988 Traditional Gospel Album *(One Lord, One Faith, One Baptism)*.

Grammy Awards: 1967 Best R&B Recording ("Respect"); 1967 Best R&B Solo Vocal Performance, Female ("Respect"); 1968 Best R&B Vocal Performance, Female ("Chain of Fools"); 1969 Best R&B Vocal Performance, Female ("Share Your Love with Me"); 1970 Best R&B Vocal Performance, Female ("Don't Play That Song"); 1971 Best R&B Vocal Performance, Female ("Bridge over Troubled Water"); 1972 Best R&B Vocal Performance, Female *(Young, Gifted, and Black)*; 1972 Best Soul Gospel Performance *(Amazing Grace)*; 1973 Best R&B Vocal Performance, Female ("Master of Eyes"); 1974 Best R&B Vocal Performance, Female ("Ain't Nothing Like the Real Thing"); 1981 Best R&B Vocal Performance, Female ("Hold On, I'm Comin' "); 1985 Best R&B Vocal Performance, Female ("Freeway of Love"); 1987 Best R&B Performance by a Duo or Group [with George Michael] ("I Knew You Were Waiting"); 1987 Best R&B Vocal Performance, Female *(Aretha)*; 1988 Best Soul Gospel Performance, Female *(One Lord, One Faith, One Baptism)*.

Kirk Franklin (with **The Family, God's Property,** and **INC**)

By Kirk Franklin and The Family: 1993—*Kirk Franklin and The Family* (GospoCentric); 1995—*Christmas; Whatcha Lookin' 4.* By God's Property from Kirk Franklin's Nu Nation: 1997—*God's Property* (B-Rite). By Kirk Franklin: 1998—*The Nu Nation Project* (GospoCentric); 2002—*The Rebirth of Kirk Franklin.* By Kirk Franklin presents INC [a.k.a. One Nation Crew]: 2000—*One Nation Crew* (B-Rite).

www.nunation.com

Kirk Franklin was to the '90s what **Andraé Crouch** was to the '70s. If Crouch brought gospel music into the twentieth century (and he did), then Franklin got it ready for the twenty-first. Franklin was born to a fifteen-year-old mother in Ft.

Worth, Texas, around 1970—about the time Crouch began recording. He was raised in poverty by an elderly aunt (Gertrude Franklin) who collected cans on Saturday mornings to pay for his music lessons. A prodigy, he was singing and playing on the gospel circuit by the time he was out of kindergarten, and at age eleven was appointed minister of music at Mount Rose Baptist Church. He did sow some wild oats, fathering a child out of wedlock at age sixteen, but he was also regularly taunted as "Church Boy" and abused by the rougher elements in his neighborhood. He got more serious about his faith and his life when a teenaged friend was killed in an accidental, self-inflicted shooting. His first big break in gospel music came when industry legend Milton Bigham invited him to lead the Dallas/Fort Worth Mass Choir in a recording of a song that the young Franklin had written called "Every Day with Jesus."

As a young adult, Franklin created a new gospel sound by infusing the genre with strong elements of hip-hop and contemporary R&B. He initially performed his songs with a seventeen-member choir called The Family, and together they introduced the new sound to the world on a self-titled debut album. By some accounts (depending on the definition of "gospel"), *Kirk Franklin and the Family* became the first gospel album ever to sell a million copies—and it sold well over *two* million, changing the shape of gospel forever. The next album, *Whatcha Lookin' 4,* debuted at Number Twenty-three on *Billboard* magazine's mainstream pop charts. When *God's Property* debuted at Number Three on those same charts, *Rolling Stone,* the *Wall Street Journal,* and many other news agencies took note of the almost unprecedented occurrence. Gospel music had not made its presence felt in the general market since the **Edwin Hawkins Singers** did "O Happy Day" in 1969. By 1998, Franklin was responsible for having recorded the top four selling gospel albums of all time. Franklin's main talents lie in the areas of composing, arranging, and conducting; he is also a vocalist, but typically relies on other voices to do much of the actual singing on his projects. In addition to The Family and other acts listed on the album covers (God's Property, One Nation Crew), he employs a group of vocalists called Nu Nation on most projects.

Franklin's first album, *Kirk Franklin and the Family,* generated the hit "Why We Sing," a soulful reworking of the hymn "His Eye Is on the Sparrow." The album also contains the blissful ballads "Silver and Gold" and "Till We Meet Again." Aside from these quiet, prayerful songs, "He Can Handle It" introduces a little rap and "Speak to Me" has a tropical, calypso strain. *Whatcha Lookin' 4* features Franklin's moving tribute to the now-departed aunt who had raised him, "Mama's Song." The album had a number of other quiet moments as well, including the gentle worship song "Savior More Than Life," but the title song was the sort of rowdy gospel funk for which

Franklin was becoming famous. For his hugely influential *God's Property,* he employed the talents of a forty-five-voice Dallas choir called God's Property, founded by opera singer Linda Searight with students from an inner city high school for performing arts. In fact, there seemed to be some confusion as to whether the album was released by God's Property or by Kirk Franklin, though the latter was clearly the main attraction. Unhappy with her contract, Searight later filed a lawsuit. In any event, the album produced the megahit "Stomp," built around a sample of George Clinton's "One Nation Under a Groove" and featuring guest vocals from Cheryl "Salt" Jones of the hip-hop group Salt 'n Pepa. It became the first gospel song ever to be featured on MTV. Other highlights from *God's Property* include the slower R&B-influenced "Sweet Spirit" and the organ-driven "It's Rainin'," which actually sounds a lot like something **Andraé Crouch** might have done in the late '70s. *The Nu Nation Project* is most notable for its impressive single, "Lean on Me" (not the Bill Withers' song), which features vocals by Bono of **U2,** Mary J. Blige, R. Kelly, and **Crystal Lewis.** Lyrically, the song suggests that Christ is revealed to the world through acts of simple compassion. The follow-up single "Revolution" (not the Beatles' song) offers an electrifying call for revival via a staccato rap by Rodney Jenkins. The album also includes "Gonna Be a Lovely Day" (which actually *is* the Bill Withers' song "Lovely Day," with some new lyrics) and another hip-hop wonder, "Praise Joint." The album got reviewed by *Rolling Stone* (rare for Christian music), which said, *"Nu Nation* gets an amen for trashing musical boundaries, and it sure has a catchier beat than Marilyn Manson." For his next project, Franklin discovered or assembled yet another group, the ten-member multicultural vocal combo he christened One Nation Crew (or 1NC for short). The group performed their song "Nobody" on *Good Morning America.* "Be Like Him," from *One Nation Crew,* has an African a capella sound while "Unconditional" features Spanish rhythms and lyrics. "Breath Away" is a sweet piano-driven ode to Jesus; "It Could've Been Me" is Prince-inspired rock. "Donna" is a sweet/sad story of a young single mother who feels forgotten.

Franklin's worldly sound and commercial success proved controversial among some American fundamentalists. Realizing that he is on scriptural grounds, and with the support of the vast majority of the Christian community, Franklin has taken to lampooning and even baiting his opponents. *God's Property* opens with the words, "For those of you who think gospel music has gone too far . . . you ain't heard nothin' yet!" *The Nu Nation Project* similarly opens with someone asking him, "Is it not true that you are not a Christian artist but a secular artist posing as a Christian artist?" Franklin's success at bridging the gap between the gospel and general markets may be indicated by the fact that the General Mills' product Honey

Nut Cheerios was the official sponsor of Franklin's 1999 Nu Nation tour. Franklin and Christian artists **Trin-i-tee 5:7** and **CeCe Winans** were pictured on cereal boxes, which also advertised a sampler CD for special purchase through the food company (with a portion of the proceeds being donated to the National Council of Churches' fund to aid churches that had been victims of arson).

In 1996, Franklin suffered a near fatal accident when he fell into an uncovered pit while backstage for a concert in Memphis, Tennessee. That same year, he contributed two songs to motion picture soundtracks: "Joy" for *The Preacher's Wife* and "My Life Is in Your Hands" for Spike Lee's *Get on the Bus.* In 1998, he published an autobiography titled *Church Boy* (Word). Toward the end of 2000, he launched a clothing line called Praise Joint. In 2001, *CCM* magazine selected both *The Nu Nation Project* (Number Thirty-nine) and *Kirk Franklin and the Family* (Number Seventy-three) for its list of "The 100 Greatest Albums in Christian Music," curiously ignoring *God's Property,* the best and most significant of the artist's works. An album announced for release in 2002 *(The Re-birth of Kirk Franklin)* was said to feature a debut single "911," performed with spiritual-orator-turned-recording-artist T. D. Jakes.

Christian radio hits: By Kirk Franklin with God's Property: "Stomp," (# 9 in 1997); "You Are the Only One" (# 8 in 1998). By Kirk Franklin: "Lean on Me" (# 17 in 1998); "Revolution" (# 2 in 1999). By 1NC: "Could've Been Me" (# 17 in 2000).

Dove Awards: 1994 Traditional Gospel Album *(Kirk Franklin and the Family);* 1994 Traditional Gospel Song ("Why We Sing"); 1997 Contemporary Gospel Album *(Whatcha Lookin' 4);* 1998 Urban Song ("Stomp"); 1998 Urban Album *(God's Property);* 1999 Contemporary Gospel Album *(Nu Nation Project);* 1999 Urban Song ("Revolution").

Grammy Awards: 1996 Best Contemporary Soul Gospel Album *(Whatcha Lookin' 4);* 1997 Best Gospel Choir or Chorus Album *(God's Property);* 1998 Best Contemporary Soul Gospel Album *(The Nu Nation Project).*

Frank's Enemy

Alex A., drums; Marc Golob, bass, voc.; Julio Rey, gtr., voc. 1994—*Frank's Enemy* (Not Silent); 1997—*Neoblasphemies* (Cling); 1998—*Illumination.*

Frank's Enemy is a hardcore/heavy metal band fronted by Julio Rey. Prior to Frank's Enemy, Rey fronted a band called King James and the Concordances, then led a group known as **The Lead.** Frank's Enemy took their name from a famous quote of rock singer Frank Zappa identifying Christians as "the enemy." To be precise, Zappa spoke at a pro-choice rally and said, "Anytime you see a fish symbol on a car, you know that is the enemy"; he did not mean to identify all Christians as his enemies, but to indicate that the sort of Christians who put fish symbols on their cars will be likely to oppose those who desire abortion rights—and will be their enemy on that particular issue. Frank's Enemy sold three cassettes *(Qoheleth,*

Final Absolution, and *Atrocities)* through the mail, then cut a self-titled independent album that was well received in hard rock circles. *Neoblasphemies* features "In Answer to Your Questions," which the band describes as "an eight-minute doom metal song that spells out the plan of salvation." *Phantom Tollbooth* describes Frank's Enemy as "very fast, sloppy death metal with some hardcore vocals." The band favors brash lyrics that challenge relativism and proclaim the mercy of God: "The gate to your heaven so wide even Hitler can get in / because in your world there's no such thing as sin" ("You Are God").

The Frantics

John Gilbert, gtr.; Matthew Martin, bass; Chris Shandrow, voc.; Derek Sorrells, drums. 2000—*Meet the Frantics* (Organic).

As the title of their debut album implies, the midwest retro band known as The Frantics aspire to be like the Beatles, though their primary reference points seem to be '80s Beatles spoofs like The Knack and Cheap Trick. The band members, three of whom come from Madisonville, Kentucky, all grew up listening to Christian music, and so they also incorporate and build on the work of such artists as **Daniel Amos,** the **Seventy Sevens, PlankEye,** and **All Star United.** John Gilbert, Chris Shandrow, and Derek Sorrells all played together in **Miss Angie**'s backing band.

The album *Meet the Frantics* opens with "Not with a Bang," a song that proposes that global destruction is more likely to occur by attrition than by catastrophe, when "all our secrets eat us up inside." The tune "Little Bit Good" features a double-tracked solo reminiscent of Queen, and "What's Up with Your Homey?" touches on the subject of backbiting in a style borrowed from Weezer. "Into the Sun" deals with the pain of losing a friend due to issues related to faith, and features some impressive electric guitar work. "We're not ashamed to say that we're Christians and our faith is very real," says Shandrow, "but our lyrics are mostly about everyday life and the things that everyone goes through." The standout song "Kids of Summer" describes feelings of powerlessness or futility or, maybe, just laziness: "I don't wanna go to work again / Think it's the only place I've ever been. . . . My candle's burning and it's reached the end / But there's nothing I can say / To make a difference anyway."

Christian radio hits: "Let It Go" (# 18 in 2000).

Tom Franzak

1983—*Walk That Talk* (Myrrh); 1985—*Shadowboxing.*

Tom Franzak is a Roman Catholic singer/songwriter from Southern California whose two albums for Myrrh evince a driving rock style. Franzak's songs vary between what *CCM* called "stirring ballads, sparkling pop tunes, and punchy new-wave rockers." Franzak favored uncompromising and challenging lyrics, as in the title song to *Walk That Talk,* which calls on Christians to live in a manner that befits their confession of faith. "Theology 101," from *Shadowboxing,* urges Christians to go beyond the basics and enter deeper into the mystery of recognizing Christ's presence in their lives.

Christian radio hits: "Stuff" (# 11 in 1986).

R. K. Fraser

1985—*Heroes* (Bright Star).

Vietnam veteran R. K. Fraser recorded one album of original songs that addressed the plight of veterans, and especially called for America to embrace "the ideas and principles on which it was founded." These include devotion to school prayer and to such basic ideals as "faith in the providence and sovereignty of our Almighty God." Many of America's founding fathers were actually Deists not Christians, but Fraser had the support of many conservative American Christians in recasting the Deist ideals as Christian ones—which can usually be done with integrity. He was featured prominently in the March 1986 issue of *CCM.* Fraser is actively involved with an organization called ACTV (American Coalition of Traditional Values). His songs have been recorded by mainstream artists Eddie Arnold and Tom Jones.

Rob Frazier

1984—*Cut It Away* (Light); 1986—*This Town* (Sparrow); 1990—*Heartland* (Urgent); 1992—*Retrospect;* 1993—*The Long Run;* 1997—*The Things I Say* (Freedom); 1999—*Jammin' the Blues* (by Rob Frazier's Blues Farmers).

A singer/songwriter originally from Philadelphia, Rob Frazier was a member of **Petra** for three years (1978–1980) before launching a solo career in Christian music. He had already established himself as a songwriter, penning the general market hit for **Kansas** "Let's Play the Game Tonight" (# 17 in 1982). A frequent collaborator with **Steve Camp,** Frazier also wrote about half the songs on Camp's *Fire and Ice* album, and Camp contributed many tunes to Frazier's *Cut It Away.* Frazier's first few albums had a synthesizer-based style similar to **DeGarmo and Key.** On *Things I Say,* after a brief hiatus, he adopted more of a roots rock approach. *The Lighthouse* called that record "a wonderfully bouncy acoustic based pop/rock album" with songs that "often recall the Beatles in their memorability." Lyrically, Frazier frequently delivered issue-oriented songs that called for Christian activism. "The Silence" deals with abortion while "Train Up a Child" encourages responsible parenting. "Can an Angel Own a Gun" takes on gun control in similar fashion to Cracker's "Can I Take My Gun to Heaven?" The *Jammin' the Blues Album* includes Bob Marley's "One Love, People Get Ready." Frazier's songs have been recorded by such artists as **Margaret Becker, Rick Cua, John Fischer, Kenny Marks, Geoff Moore and The Distance, Connie Scott,** and **Dick Tunney.**

Christian radio hits: "He's All You Need" (# 21 in 1985); "Come On Elaine" (# 5 in 1985); "This Town" (# 3 in 1986); "Break My Heart" (# 12 in 1987); "Got Your Word on It" (# 22 in 1990); "The Heartland" (# 18 in 1991); "Go through Fire" (# 21 in 1991).

Freeto Boat

Dave Cohen, gtr.; Michael Hoppe, drums; Martin Jimenez, voc.; Corey Linstrum, bass; Mike Wright, gtr.; Logan Barnett, sax. (– 2000); Tyler Barnett, sax. (–2000); Andy Dollahite, trump. (–2000). 1998—*Hindsight 20/20* (Bettie Rocket); 2000—*End of the Beginning.*

Freeto Boat was a melodic punk/skacore band from Southern California. *HM* magazine appreciated the sometimes hardcore vocals of lead singer Martin Jimenez, whose voice they said was "honest and true" without trying for "that punk accent so often heard." The group's debut album, *Hindsight 20/20,* was the first record released by Bettie Rocket Records and was a somewhat hurried affair, rather indebted to the ska craze. On *End of the Beginning,* the band gets rid of the horns and goes for more straight-ahead punk. Mike Wright said, "We just try to reach out to people that are our age and be encouraging. . . . our songs are about people's attitudes, people judging each other and the struggle with telling people about God or not, and how to live your life for God just in every day life." In mid 2000, the group changed its name to Call of Elijah in a deliberate effort to distance themselves from any identification with the ska scene. Within a year, however, they would disband altogether.

Friction Bailey

See **Pushstart Wagon.**

Friends First

Steve McEwan; et al. 1986—*We See a New Africa* [EP] (StarSong); 1993—*Dumisani Ma-Afrika* (Myrrh).

Friends First was an interracial South African group led by pastor Malcolm du Plessis. The group was devoted to combating apartheid with messages of reconciliation in their home country and abroad. Many of their songs feature lyrics written by Nick Paton, the grandson of renowned author Alan Paton. Musically, the songs wed traditional South African rhythms to Western pop melodies in a manner reminiscent of Paul Simon's influential *Graceland* album. One member of the group, Steve McEwan, would go on to become a successful rock star in Great Britain, playing in the band World Party and then, in 2001, forming a group called Unamerican, which released a

self-titled album on Universal Records. McEwan also wrote the popular modern hymn "Great Is the Lord."

Christian radio hits: "Standing in the Fire of Love" (# 8 in 1987).

Fringe

Jason Clark, voc.; Shawn Harnish, gtr.; Eric Perry, drums; Kory Spencer, bass. 2000—*For the Vagabond Believer* (BulletProof).

Fringe is a hard modern rock quartet from upstate New York. *Real* magazine describes their sound as "a metal mix of Dave Matthews Band and Pearl Jam," and indicates that lead singer Jason Clark's vocals constitute an "almost supernatural combination of Dave Matthews and Eddie Vedder." Fringe's debut album, *For the Vagabond Believer,* features mostly riff-driven rockers like "Lightspeed" and "Down Dizzy." The group tries to transcend grunge and alternative clichés, experimenting with violins and saxophones here and there, and with unpredictable time signatures on a softer track called "Deeper." Lyrically, they avoid Christian-language clichés as well. None of the songs contain any overt references to God or Christ, though such divine topics as the character of grace are explored through **Creed**-like poetry and allusion: "When grace is received, it closes the distance / And we are one" ("Believe").

Frolic

Matthew Chinn, synth. 1999—*Permafrost* (Velvet Empire); 2001—*To Dream, Perchance to Sleep* (Projekt).

Christian ambient/new-wave artist Matthew Chinn records under the names Frolic and **Firmament.** The only noticeable difference between those entities is that albums by Frolic are not entirely instrumental but feature some singing by Chinn's wife Kelley. The music is intended to be relaxing and meditative, though its gloomy mood ascribes it to the darkwave genre (cf. Portishead, Lycia). Jon Beard adds some unsettling minor key guitar. Standout tracks on *Permafrost* include "Drift Away" and "Fields of Green." Some selections ("Reunion," "Sea") are atonal and off-key, apparently on purpose. *Cornerstone* recommends *To Dream, Perchance to Sleep* for rainy days; the opening track, "The Tides of March," actually combines the sounds of rain and thunder with Kelley's whispering vocals.

The Front (a.k.a. What If)

Tommy Funderburk, voc.; Larry Williams, kybrd.; Bob Wilson, drums; Dennis Bellfield, bass (–1987); Kevin Clark, gtr. (–1987); Dann Huff, gtr. (–1987). By The Front: 1984—*The Front* (Refuge). By What If: 1987—*What If* (RCA).

The Front paired Bob Wilson, founder of **Seawind,** with Tommy Funderburk, a studio singer who had worked with the general market band Boston. Larry Williams had also been a member of **Seawind,** and Dann Huff had played guitar for **White Heart** and would later be part of **Giant** and **The Players.** The Front's album was a modestly received R&B contribution. Several songs are almost creedal or hymnic in their overt statements of faith ("Holy Light," "King of Glory," "All under Him"). "The Promise" deals with the topic of abortion, and the album's liner notes declare in huge letters, "This album is dedicated to the 4000 children aborted in the United States everyday." The group was very vocal about that topic, declaring at one point that their Number One mission as a band was to "mobilize the church to halt abortion." Funderburk said, "The government has licensed the killing of children. We're starting to practice in America things we went to war with the Nazis over." Three years later a trio that had formed the core of The Front recorded an album for the general market under the name What If. The latter record includes a crunchy dance track called "She Rocked My World" in addition to a cover of **Tonio K.**'s "Perfect World." Funderburk later recorded in partnership with **Tim Miner** under the name Funderburk-Miner.

Christian radio hits: "Tonight" (# 15 in 1985).

Steve Fry

1983—*We Are Called* (Birdwing); 1986—*Steve Fry* (Sparrow); 1989—*Thy Kingdom Come* (Sparrow); 1996—*Higher Call* (Maranatha); 1998—*Fire in the Dark* (label unknown).

Steve Fry is an inspirational Christian singer who has presented well-orchestrated MOR albums similar in style to those of **Steve Green.** His album *We Are Called* is actually a musical that features performances by Green and **Silverwind.** *CCM* magazine called his *Thy Kingdom Come* album "surprisingly hip." Fry now serves as a worship leader in Nashville.

Christian radio hits: "I Want to Know You More" (# 25 in 1984).

Dave Fullen

1983—*I'll Keep an Eye on You* (Bread and Honey); 1984—*Hide and Seek* (Purpose).

Dave Fullen spent nine years performing the lead role in the contemporary musical passion play *Telestai* before recording two solo albums of adult contemporary music. Fullen's voice bears similarities to that of general market performer Michael McDonald. He drew into his work influences from R&B and jazz that reminded *CCM* of better-known projects by **Paul Clark** and **DeGarmo and Key.** Standout tracks on *Hide and Seek* include "Time after Time," a song about reconciliation; "Kay," a tribute to a severely handicapped woman; and "The Final Victory," which features a medieval melody reminiscent of **Kemper Crabb**'s work.

Richie Furay

1976—*I've Got a Reason* (Elektra); 1978—*Dance a Little Light* (Asylum); 1979—*I Still Have Dreams*; 1982—*Seasons of Change* (Myrrh); 1997—*In My Father's House* (Calvary Chapel).

One of the most underappreciated performers in mainstream rock, Richie Furay went on to become one of the most underappreciated artists in contemporary Christian music after a publicized conversion sometime around 1974. The founding member of Buffalo Springfield, Poco, and the Souther Hillman Furay Band was among a handful of artists to have his entry in the *Rolling Stone Encyclopedia of Rock and Roll* deleted as "no longer relevant" for the second edition (despite his induction into the Rock and Roll Hall of Fame two years after the new edition was published). As a Christian artist, he has recorded five albums, two of which rate among the most-acclaimed and yet least-heard albums in the history of contemporary Christian music. The first of these, *I've Got a Reason,* went somewhat unnoticed by Christian music fans because it was released on a secular label, and its lyrics were not overtly religious in a smarmy or predictable way. The second, *In My Father's House,* released more than twenty years later, was missed or dismissed by some Christian rock fans because it was released on a church label and its lyrics were *completely* religious.

Furay was born in 1944 in Yellow Springs, Ohio. He left home for New York at the age of twenty and entered the emerging folk scene as a member of a folk trio called The Monks, who tried to emulate Peter, Paul, and Mary and The Kingston Trio. Getting into the club scene, he became a member of a more successful folk group called The A-Go-Go Singers, of which Stephen Stills was also a member. After a brief hiatus, he joined Stills in California to form the now legendary Buffalo Springfield with Neil Young, Dewey Martin, Bruce Palmer, and eventually Jim Messina. The group is partly famous due to the future careers of Furay and other members—Stills and Young would go on to be half of Crosby, Stills, Nash and Young, and Messina, to be half of Loggins and Messina. But Buffalo Springfield won almost unprecedented acclaim as a band in its own right. Hailed by *Rolling Stone* as "the American Beatles," the group employed orchestral arrangements and four-part vocals way beyond the standards of its time, and it remains one of a few bands from the late '60s whose music is still regarded as vital three decades later (a box set of Buffalo Springfield recordings was released by Rhino in 2001). Furay himself has coauthored a biography of the band titled *There's Something Happening Here: The Story of Buffalo Springfield for What It's Worth* (Quarry Press, 1997).

While attention justly accrues to Stills and Young, the role Furay played in shaping Buffalo Springfield's sound should not be underestimated. He certainly had the best natural voice of the group's members, and he generally sang lead on all the "pretty songs." This is most evident on the group's first and best album (*Buffalo Springfield,* Atco, 1967) where it is Furay who gives life to the stunning "Flying on the Ground Is Wrong," who wrings pathos out of the potentially maudlin "Do I Have to Come Right Out and Say It?" and who gets all didactic on the rather bossy "Sit Down, I Think I Love You." He composed and sang three stellar songs for *Buffalo Springfield Again:* "A Child's Claim to Fame" (a country romp that sounds a good bit like Poco); "Good Time Boy" (a funk-soul James Brown imitation complete with horns and "sock-it-to-me" vocals); and "Sad Memory" (the most beautiful ballad the group would ever record). On the final Springfield classic, *Last Time Around,* Furay sings lead on what would become one of the group's best-known songs, "On the Way Home," in addition to offering another four of his own compositions. Of these, "It's So Hard to Wait" and "The Hour of Not Quite Rain" are a bit faux-artsy, but "Merry-Go-Round" is delightful pop, and "Kind Woman" is another stellar Poco preview. Buffalo Springfield is often regarded as the best American band of the '60s and (aside from Stills' "For What Its Worth") the group tends to be at its absolute best ("Flying on the Ground," "On the Way Home") on the tracks written by Young and sung by Furay.

Buffalo Springfield only lasted two years, and the band was falling apart most of that time. While Stills and Young tried to work through their ego crises, Furay and Messina formed another band called Poco (the group was actually called Pogo at first, but had to alter a letter after Walt Kelley, creator of the *Pogo* comic strip, served them some papers). Poco would also include Rusty Young, George Grantham, and two future Eagles: first Randy Meisner and, then, Timothy B. Schmidt. The group started in 1968, four years before the Eagles' first album appeared, and premiered the California country rock sound with which the latter group would have so much success in years to come. Why the Eagles made it so big while Poco labored in relative obscurity remains a mystery, but the dominant theory is that it was just a matter of timing. America wasn't quite ready for country rock in the Poco era, and then when the Eagles brought it on, they proceeded to raid Poco's members. Poco was nevertheless a perennial favorite of critics. During the years that Furay led the band, they cranked out six highly acclaimed albums without putting a single song into the Top 40. In 1973, Furay left the band that he had founded to try something else: a Crosby, Stills and Nash copy-cat group called Souther Hillman Furay Band. The union with country folk singer J. D. Souther and former Byrd Chris Hillman produced two decent albums but, again, no hits. Still, one nontitular member of the Souther Hillman Furay Band was **Al Perkins,** the Christian pedal steel guitarist who turns up on dozens of Jesus music records as performer and producer. According to Furay, Perkins led him to Christ. Shortly after this happened, Furay was asked

to write an article for *Crawdaddy* magazine on what it was like to be thirty years old. He accepted the assignment as an opportunity to proclaim his new faith in a very worldly forum. The article, "A Good Feeling to Know," was essentially a two-page testimony to the saving power of Jesus, complete with Scripture references. As a result, Furay became the butt of jokes and snide comments in the rock press, and reviewers seemed to be just waiting to mock his announced solo album when it appeared.

I've Got a Reason was, musically, the best work Furay had ever done and one of the best albums yet to appear in the emerging world of contemporary Christian music. Furay's voice has never sounded better than on the soaring opening track, "Look at the Sun." Other great rock numbers include "We'll See," "Gettin' Through," and "Still Rolling Stones." In retrospect, *Reason* was probably the first album to qualify as exemplary of a new genre of Christian rock as opposed to the simple-but-sincere Jesus music records that had preceded it. It was a post-Jesus movement album, recorded with full awareness that the revival was over or that it had at least worn out its welcome as far as American society was concerned. Yet the album had deep roots in that movement. It was officially recorded by The Richie Furay Band, which consisted of **Tom Stipe** of **Country Faith** along with **John Mehler** and Jay Truax of **Love Song**—Stipe, Mehler, and Truax had also all played together in **Wing and a Prayer.** Others involved included **Billy Batstone, David Diggs,** and Alex MacDougall (of **Selah, The Way,** and **Daniel Amos**). It was coproduced by **Michael Omartian.** Better Jesus music credentials would be hard to come by. Still, *I've Got a Reason* does not feature the sort of folk-rock love-songs-to-and-about-Jesus for which all of these artists had been noted. Indeed, it does not mention Jesus by name even once. Nor does it deliver the sort of Sunday school songs that critics in the secular press were poised to trash in the "has-been rock star turns into annoying Jesus freak" reviews they had outlined in their minds. Instead, it offers poignant glimpses into how a person of faith finds meaning in this damaged world. A recurrent theme is Furay's alienation from his spouse. "Mighty Maker" is his prayer for help in effecting a reconciliation (which, happily, did later occur). "Over and Over" refers obliquely to "living water" and to finding "the Answer," and "I've Got a Reason" offers something of a testimony: "Music was my life, finally took everything / Ain't it funny how you got it all and not a thing / Now I've got a reason for living each day." But Furay does not spell out "the Answer" or "the reason" he has found in so many words, relying perhaps on extrinsic announcements of his faith to fill in the blanks.

I've Got a Reason defied expectations in both sacred and secular camps and for that reason was largely ignored. Under considerable pressure from his record company to "tone down his convictions," Furay followed with two more purely pop albums for the general market that were not intended as anything but wholesome entertainment. *Dance a Little Light* features a cover of The Rascals' "Lonely Too Long." The title track to *I Still Have Dreams* charted as a minor hit (# 39 in 1979). In 1980, Furay recorded an original praise song "Glory to God" for inclusion on the *Maranatha Seven* compilation album (Maranatha). Then Furay put together another band called USR (for United States Rock). The idea was an innovative one: a general market band that was composed of all Christians but played "secular" music. Their witness would not be in their songs as such but in their *lives;* they would be "in the world but not of it." In addition to Furay, the group consisted of Virgil Beckham on guitar and vocals, **Billy Batstone** on bass, Hadley Hockensmith on guitar, and former Poco cohort George Grantham on drums. An album was recorded, but the company (Atlantic) balked at one song, "Yellow Moon Rising" (written by Furay and **Tom Stipe**), which they thought sounded too religious. Seeing red flags, Furay aborted the entire project and just recorded a flagrantly Christian album *(Seasons of Change)* on a Christian label (Myrrh) instead. The song "Yellow Moon Rising" is included on that project and is actually one of the least religious songs on the record, dealing not with faith as such but with the deception visited upon those who are easily seduced by cosmic portents. "Endless Flight" offers hope for renewal to those whose marriages are in trouble. "Seasons of Change" recalls Furay's testimony once more, of how he went from "big city lights" to being a citizen of heaven. "My Lord and My God" picks up on Thomas's acclamation in John 20:27–29 in a musical testimony to Christ's merits and benefits. The recurring theme on the album, however, is the second coming of Christ and the concomitant salvation and judgment that this will bring. "We are living in the days of our Lord's return," Furay wrote in the liner notes.

In 1982, Furay became an ordained minister and, since then, has served as pastor of a Calvary Chapel church in Boulder, Colorado. In 1989, he took a brief break to participate in a Poco reunion and finally scored two minor hits with that group: "Call It Love" (# 18) and "Nothin' to Hide" (# 39). The reunion album *Legacy* (RCA, 1989) also features his song "When It All Began" about their history. The nostalgia was short-lived, however, as he said that conflicts within the band quickly reminded him of why he had left it all behind. In 1997, he was inducted into the Rock and Roll Hall of Fame as a member of Buffalo Springfield. That same year, he released his second masterpiece, a collection of original praise and worship songs called *In My Father's House.* Musically, the album is steeped in the country-rock tradition, with generous bits of fiddle and snippets of bluegrass (especially on "Wake Up My

Soul"). The songs are not the repetitive jingles that one sometimes associates with modern praise albums. They are not just choruses but full songs. "Hallel" and "Give Thanks to the Lord" are roots rock, and the title track is a moving ballad, expressing confidence in God's permanent offer of a place for the troubled to find peace. "Peace That Passes Understanding" is not the **Debby Kerner** classic but a melodic new song also reflecting on the blessing in Philippians 4:7. As such, the record should not be filed too quickly under "Praise and Worship." It is either the finest collection of contemporary hymns yet to be released by a rock artist or, simply, a very fine country rock album with unusually religious lyrics.

In 2000, Neil Young publicly expressed his hope for a Buffalo Springfield reunion in his song, "Buffalo Springfield Again": "Like to see those guys again, give it a shot / Maybe now we can show the world just what we got / But I'd just like to play for the fun we had."

Christian radio hits: "My Lord and My God" (# 3 in 1982).

Furthermore

Daniel Fischer, voc.; Jason Jester, DJ, bgv; Lee Jester, bgv. 2000—*Fluorescent Jellyfish* (Tooth and Nail).

Furthermore is a hip-hop trio composed of three white kids from Salt Lake City, which is not exactly a hotbed of hip-hop activity. Nevertheless, *True Tunes* praised their debut album as "surprisingly good stuff," indeed as "one of the strongest hip-hop releases ever to hit the Christian market." The group displays strong influences from '80s rap groups such as Jazzy Jeff and the Fresh Prince and the Beastie Boys. Fischer's lyrics are identified as a strong suit, using word play and imagery to great effect. The lyrics are not religious, however, nor do they engage spiritual or moral themes in the manner that some would expect of Christian music. The band members simply identify themselves as Christians committed to making what they deem to be worthwhile music and to doing so in a way that is "nice, honest and trustworthy." They do not see themselves as professional ministers or evangelists. The song "Are You the Walrus?" plays on the Beatles' tune and relates a story of Fischer waiting in line behind a small girl who keeps asking him if he is the walrus. "Being a Ghost" is about a ghost who wants to be a human being. "Melted Vinyl" draws its themes and inspiration from the *X-Men* comic books.

Further Seems Forever

Chris Carraba, voc.; John Colbert, gtr.; Nick Dominiquez, gtr.; Steve Klesiath, drums; Chad Neptune, bass. 2001—*The Moon Is Down* (Tooth and Nail).

Further Seems Forever is a modern rock band that arose out of the ashes of the hardcore group **Strongarm.** The only member who was not part of that group, singer and songwriter Chris Carraba, quit the group before its first album was even released. Carraba seems to have largely defined the band's sound, making its future ominously uncertain. Like **Strong-arm,** the group is based in Miami, Florida. Musically, *The Moon Is Down* tended to be put in the emo genre due to the heart-and-soul passion of the band's songs. "New Year's Project" illustrates this tendency well, starting out calm before lurching into a driving, hard-hitting song with somber, heart-wrenching lyrics. "Snowbirds and Townies" and the title track are strongly melodic offerings. A few of the other tracks drew comparisons to Weezer.

Futrel

Janice Davis; Theresa Davis; Darlene Futrel; Evie Young-Nelson. 1989— *Worth the Wait* (Light); 1993—*Declarations* (Tribute).

Futrel is a Christian version of En Vogue, a quartet of sassy African American women who apply their immense vocal talents to R&B and its derivative, female funk. On *Declarations,* they offer a jazzy version of the Howard Arlen classic, "Get Happy," now retitled "Theme for Dorothy." They smooth things out with "Empty Promises," and jam with rapper/guitarist **Mike-E** on "Where Is the Love?" Cedric Dent of **Take 6** also puts in a guest appearance.

Billy and Sarah Gaines

1986—*Billy and Sarah Gaines* (Benson); 1988—*He'll Find a Way;* 1990—
Friends Indeed; 1991—*No One Loves Me Like You;* 1993—*Love's the Key;*
1995—*Through the Years;* 1996—*Come On Back* (SoundHouse).

Billy and Sarah Gaines are a husband-and-wife pop duo
best known for a funky R&B style of gospel that belongs in the
same ballpark as **Andraé Crouch and the Disciples.** Married
in 1977, they first performed with a group called Living Sacrifice (not the heavy metal group by that name), then moved to
Nashville in the early '80s, where Billy worked as a songwriter.
Due to the long and healthy tenure of their relationship, the
Gaineses are often featured in magazine articles dealing with
marriage and family life. The couple's debut album features a
much tamer MOR sound than their later work; the songs "He's
Risen in Me," "You Are Faithful," and "Come Drink at My
Table" all received airplay on some stations. Their next two albums elicited strong comparisons to the brother and sister duo
BeBe and CeCe Winans and it was these two records that
scored Billy and Sarah Gaines their moments on the Christian
Hit Radio charts. *He'll Find a Way* is an especially optimistic
album, with its theme of encouragement and restoration reflected in the standout song "Always Triumphant." Perhaps to
get out of the Winans' shadow, the couple developed a more
adventurous style on *No One Loves Me Like You* and broadened
their appeal. "Trust Me" and "If Only You Knew" are funkier
and more dance-oriented than the group's usual material.
Love's the Key continues to mix funky beat-driven songs ("I'll
Stand for You") with silky ballads ("At Jesus' Feet") and straight

gospel numbers ("The Same All the Time"). Several songs address Jesus' directive that "all the commandments" are fulfilled
by loving God and neighbor (Mark 12:30–31). Billy Gaines
founded SoundHouse records with **Michael Omartian,** and
Come on Back was that label's first release. Omartian produced
the album, which features a bevy of guest stars. The song
"Freedom" is an especially effective ode to aging gracefully and
with appreciation for the full work of God.

Christian radio hits: "While You Wait" (# 1 for 4 weeks in 1990), "He
Says" (# 11 in 1991), "Make Up Your Mind" (# 15 in 1991), "I Found
Someone" (# 8 in 1992), "No One Loves Me Like You" (# 25 in 1992).

The Gaither Vocal Band (and The New Gaither Vocal Band and The Bill Gaither Trio)

The Bill Gaither Trio: Bill Gaither, Gloria Gaither, Danny Gaither
(–1968) // Gary McSpadden (+ 1968, –1985); Michael English (+ 1985).
The New Gaither Vocal Band/Gaither Vocal Band: Bill Gaither; Gary
McSpadden (– 1990); Steve Green (–1984); Lee Young (– 1983) // Jon
Mohr (+ 1983, –1986); Larnelle Harris (+ 1984, –1988); Michael English
(+ 1986, –1996); Jim Murray (+ 1988, –1996); Mark Lowry (+ 1990); Guy
Penrod (+ 1995); Jonathan Pierce (+ 1996, – 1999); David Phelps
(+ 1998). As The New Gaither Vocal Band: 1981—*The New Gaither Vocal
Band* (DaySpring); 1983—*Passin' the Faith Along;* 1984—*New Point of View.*
As The Gaither Vocal Band: 1986—*One X 1* (Word); 1988—*Wings*
(StarSong); 1989—*The Best from the Beginning* (Word); 1990—*A Few Good
Men* (StarSong); 1992—*Homecoming;* 1993—*Peace of the Rock; Southern
Classics* (Benson); 1994—*I Bowed on My Knees* (Benson); *The King Is*

Coming; The Best of the Gaither Vocal Band: 16 All-Time Favorites (StarSong); *Reunion Precious Memories* (EMD); *Can't Stop Talkin' about Him; Testify* (Chapel); 1996—*Southern Classics, Vol. 2;* 1997—*Back Home in Indiana* (Spring House); *Lovin' God and Lovin' Each Other* (Spring Hill); *Joy to the World: Gaither Gospel Series; The Best from the Beginning* (Word); 1998— *Hawaiian Homecoming* (Spring House); 1998—*Still the Greatest Story Ever Told* (Spring Hill); *God Is Good;* 2000—*The Gaither Vocal Band, Vol. 1* (Verity); *The Gaither Vocal Band, Vol. 2; I Do Believe* (Chordant).

www.gaithernet.com

The Gaither Vocal Band developed out of The New Gaither Vocal Band, which had originally formed as an experiment in contemporary sound on the part of artists steeped in the southern gospel tradition. The template for both bands was The Bill Gaither Trio, which first formed in 1961 as a trio of siblings: Bill, Mary Ann, and Danny Gaither. A year later (prior to their first recording in 1964), Bill (b. 1936) would marry Gloria Sickel (b. 1942), who replaced Mary Ann in the lineup. Danny was then replaced by **Gary McSpadden,** who had sung with **The Imperials** and with the Oak Ridge Boys and who would also work as a solo artist. **Michael English,** who joined when McSpadden left, would also have a notable if controversial career as a solo artist. Over forty albums have been released by The Bill Gaither Trio or by some variation thereof— some are by Bill and Gloria Gaither, by The Gaithers, or by Gaither and Friends. All of these incarnations have served to introduce the world to songs written by Bill and Gloria Gaither, many of which have become classics of modern gospel: "He Touched Me," "The King Is Coming," "Because He Lives," "Something Beautiful," "Let's Just Praise the Lord," and "I Am a Promise." Gaither songs typically stress individual sentiment and they have tended to become best known in revivalistic churches, where Bill Gaither is regarded as a living legend. By contrast, they are seldom found in the songbooks of mainline denominations, where the Gaither name and music are virtually unknown. Musically, the Gaithers' relationship to contemporary Christian music would perhaps be comparable to Frank Sinatra's relationship to rock and roll. The Gaithers have never fit in with the sounds of the rock era, but they have managed to keep an old style relevant long after its tenure was officially up. They have occasionally waffled, as on 1979's *We Are Persuaded* (Word), where they decided to go disco, but in general their authentic commitment to a respectable sound has earned them the respect of their peers. Somewhat ironically, the Gaithers have often been revered by many Christian pop artists whose fans would quickly dismiss them. Their lasting influence on the development and diversification of styles in the modern gospel genre is undeniable. Bill Gaither has won the Dove Award for Songwriter of the Year an unprecedented eight times, with Gloria Gaither also winning that award once. Bill Gaither won a Grammy in 1973 for a solo performance, another one with the Trio in 1975, and a third with the duo of just Bill and Gloria in 1999. In 1982, Bill Gaither was inducted into the Gospel Music Hall of Fame. In 1996, he formed the alternative praise label 40 Records with **Toby McKeehan** of **DC Talk.**

The New Gaither Vocal Band was formed as a spin-off of the trio and tried to have a more contemporary sound in emulation of **The Imperials.** Members of the combo would include **Steve Green** and **Larnelle Harris,** both of whom went on to impressive careers as inspirational solo artists. The New Gaither Vocal Band's relationship to contemporary Christian music would perhaps be analogous to that of Andy Williams to rock and roll—certainly not the real thing, but close enough to allow some who were wary of rock to at least get their feet wet. The debut album was praised by none other than **Larry Norman** for representing an "enlightened conservatism" in MOR music. "I love to hear Scripture used intelligently, and praise music sung convincingly," wrote Norman, admitting that he was a fan of all the Gaithers' albums. This "wading pool for non-rock swimmers" approach could not endure the '80s, however, and Gaither began to revamp the group as a more traditional southern gospel quartet. In the mid '80s, the "New" was dropped from the group's name symbolizing a return to older, more traditional sounds.

The Gaither Vocal Band's first album, *One X 1,* featured a stellar cast, introducing **Michael English** alongside Harris, Gaither, and McSpadden. English and Harris soar on the opening "The Lord of Hosts," premiering a vocal tandem that unfortunately would not be heard again. Former **Imperial** Jim Murray replaced Harris on *Wings* and the GVB continued to serve as a training ground for artists who would pursue solo careers. **Jonathan Pierce, Buddy Greene,** and **Mark Lowry** all sang with the group. The Gaither Vocal Band has continued to record and has enjoyed considerable success in the southern gospel market. *Southern Classics* is one of their finest works. *Back Home in Indiana* (which opens with "John the Revelator") is also remarkable.

Christian radio hits: As The Bill Gaither Trio: "We Are Persuaded" (# 4 in 1980); "A Perfect Heart" (# 19 in 1982); "Fully Alive" (# 8 in 1984). As The New Gaither Vocal Band: "No Other Name But Jesus" (# 2 in 1983); "Majority" (# 6 in 1983); "Passin' the Faith Along" (# 37 in 1984); "Blessed Messiah" (# 4 in 1985). As The Gaither Vocal Band: "Can't Stop Talkin' about Him" (# 16 in 1987).

Dove Awards: For Bill Gaither: 1969 Songwriter of the Year; 1970 Songwriter of the Year; 1972 Songwriter of the Year; 1973 Songwriter of the Year; 1974 Songwriter of the Year; 1975 Songwriter of the Year; 1976 Songwriter of the Year; 1977 Songwriter of the Year; 1986 Praise and Worship Album (*I've Just Seen Jesus*). For Gloria Gaither: 1986 Songwriter of the Year. For The Bill Gaither Trio: 1976 Inspirational Album (*Jesus, We Just Want to Thank You*); 1978 Inspirational Album (*Pilgrim's Progress*); 1980 Mixed Group of the Year; 1993 Southern Gospel Album (*Reunion: A Gospel Homecoming Celebration* [by Bill and Gloria Gaither]). For The

Gaither Vocal Band: 1995 Southern Gospel Album *(Homecoming)*; 1994 Southern Gospel Album *(Southern Classics)*; 1994 Southern Gospel Song ("Satisfied"); 1995 Southern Gospel Song ("I Bowed on My Knees"); 1999 Southern Gospel Album *(Still the Greatest Story Ever Told)*; 1999 Southern Gospel Song ("I Believe in a Hill Called Mount Calvary"); 2000 Southern Gospel Album *(God Is Good)*; 2001 Southern Gospel Song ("God Is Good All the Time"); 2001 Southern Gospel Album *(I Do Believe)*.

Grammy Awards: For The Gaither Vocal Band: 1991 Best Southern Gospel Album *(Homecoming)*. For Bill and Gloria Gaither: 2001 Best Southern Gospel Album *(A Billy Graham Music Homecoming)*.

Galactic Cowboys

Monty Colvin, bass, voc., kybrd.; Ben Huggins, gtr., voc.; Dane Sonnier, gtr. (–1996); Alan Doss, drums, voc. (–2000) // Wally Farkas, gtr.; voc. (+ 1996). 1991—*Galactic Cowboys* (Geffen); 1993—*Space in Your Face*; 1996—*Machine Fish* (Metal Blade); *Feel the Rage*; 1997—*The Horse That Bud Bought*; 1998—*At the End of the Day*; 2000—*Let It Go.*

www.galacticcowboys.com

An art-metal quartet from Houston, Texas, the Galactic Cowboys were probably the most melodic metal band ever to exist in Christian or general markets. Their songs tended to exhibit pop structures and sing-along choruses that would have allowed them to be Top 40 fare if played with less fervor and at a lower volume. Vocals, furthermore, accentuated singing over screaming and even included a generous amount of harmony—sort of like a heavy metal version of Crosby, Stills, Nash and Young. Beginning with *Machine Fish,* drummer Alan Doss produced or coproduced all of the band's albums. The Galactic Cowboys were often compared with another Houston group, **King's X,** but the Cowboys tended to perform catchier songs. The group had a following within the general market and so, as is often the case, was uncomfortable about being labeled a Christian band, though they were never shy about stating their individual faith convictions. Lead singer Monty Colvin said they wanted their music to reflect their faith without "hyping" it. "We're musicians," he insisted. "Not preachers." The Galactic Cowboys disbanded in 2000.

Doug Van Pelt, editor of *HM* magazine, dubbed the Galactic Cowboys' self-titled debut album "the most exciting release of 1991," noting in particular the "massive vocal harmonies" and "great hooks" in songs like "I'm Not Amused" (with Spanish guitars and harmonica) and "Why Don't You Believe in Me?" (with an a capella chorus). *True Tunes* likewise heralded the release as the start of something big—a metal band capable of creating aural allusions to the Beatles ("Someone for Everyone") and Pink Floyd ("Speak to Me"). The rest of the world did not discover the group until *Space in Your Face,* a phenomenal offering that was head and shoulders above much of what the Christian music scene was producing. The group now displayed a tight aural delivery that previewed the pop-metal

sound that groups like **Creed** and Stabbing Westward would use to great effect later in the decade. The sophomore album opens with the title track, an unusually gruff number that lets the listener know this *is* hard music in case the power-pop sounds that follow should instill any confusion on that point. The next two numbers, "You Make Me Smile" and "I Do What I Do," are masterpieces of ear-candy that typify the Cowboy's love-it-or-hate-it trademark sound. An unimpressed reviewer for *Phantom Tollbooth* groused that "it sounds like Metallica hired the Beatles to sing for them"; *HM,* by contrast, fantasized that when (if?) Metallica hears the group they "will shake their heads and wonder, how can we compete with *that*?" The song "Circles in the Field" has an appropriately mysterious sound; "If I Were a Killer" relates its hypothetical story to memorable guitar riffs; "Blind" is particularly melodic; "About Mrs. Leslie" is propelled by the rhythm section.

By the time *Machine Fish* appeared, the world had taken note of the Galactic Cowboys, and the album was reviewed by numerous media outlets that usually ignore Christian music. The group had moved to a label that would promote them more worthily but still faced the daunting prospects of being a pre-**Creed** metal band in an alternative/grunge-dominated decade. Perhaps because of the addition of Willy Farkas, who favors "bone-crunching" guitar styles, *Machine Fish* was unquestionably the Cowboys' heaviest outing to date. If the "Metallica hires the Beatles" analogy mentioned above still held, it was at least clear that the Fab Four were by now *only* hired help, putting in an appearance now and then but exercising little creative control over the project as a whole. *Cornerstone* described Ben Huggins' vocals on "Stress" as "scraping across the ears with an intensity usually reserved for those being eaten alive by great white sharks." An atypical softer track, "The Lens" (about seeing through people's defenses), has the same sort of jangly neopsychedelic sound that carried Blind Melon's one and only hit ("No Rain"). Thematically, "Feel the Rage" calls for people to take a stand against systemic problems of greed and corruption in society, and "The Struggle" is about trying to do what's right on an everyday basis. Religious folly is also a focus, as "Psychotic Companion" is about phone-in psychic network lines, and "Ninth of June" refers to someone who had figured out the exact date of Jesus' return. An EP to promote the album, *Feel the Rage* also includes covers of songs originally done by Paul McCartney ("Junior's Farm") and Kiss ("I Want You").

The Horse That Bud Bought has a gentler sound overall, though this is broken by the energetic numbers "Buzz" and "Tilt-a-Whirl." Lyrics focus on cultural critique, such as the absurdities of political correctness and the duplicity of media bias. "Ribbon" lampoons the fad of celebrities wearing little lapel-bows to display their (selective) compassion. "Evil Twin" lambasts the blame-shifting tendencies of those caught in sin. "Tomorrow" attacks the music industry ("Pay no attention to quality / Turning out pap like a factory"). The title song from the album is based on an event in Colvin's upbringing: for a brief time his family lived in a religious commune in a farm in Oregon, which he says "became like a cult thing"; at one point, his father (Bud) bought him a horse, which evoked "a lot of jealousy, to the point that they said the horse was an abomination to God, and that was what triggered us to leave." *At the End of the Day* returns the group to their heavier style, such that a *CCM* reviewer would claim it made him want to get out his old Bon Jovi records. The song "Ants" is especially accessible and lively; Colvin describes it as being about "how people must look from where God is, way, way up there—not too profound, but cool"). The record includes a seven-song "Machine Fish Suite" that presents a somewhat harsh look at the music industry from the inside. The suite begins with a spoken word introduction: "At the end of the day, you've got to be able to look at yourself in the mirror and know that you have loved your neighbor and treated him right." By now, *HM* had noticed a major and apparently permanent departure from the art-metal style of the first two albums: "almost a different band, but cranking out another, brilliant musical formula."

On *Let It Go,* the group allows their humor full throttle with moments of silliness befitting a final project. The opening track offers a brief taste of their proposed new hip-hop sound (given their ten years of commercial nonsuccess with the hard rock variations). The closing track ("The Record Ends") is a long-drawn out ending that satirizes the inability of some metal bands (Galactic Cowboys included) to know when or how to end a song. "Hey Mr." is a musical highlight with a sound that hearkens back to the band's treasured first two projects. Thematically, the latter song offers a satirical look at the way in which politicians exaggerate their accomplishments: "Trees are greener now / Children laugh out loud / There is peace and harmony / No pain or poverty / Thanks to your politics." The song "Disney's Spinnin' " presents right-wing "fallen nation" ideology with reference to the creator of the children's entertainment empire: "I wonder what the forefathers would say / Land of the free, home of the depraved / I bet that Disney's spinnin' in his grave." Jerry Gaskill of **King's X** filled in as drummer on this final project.

The Galactic Cowboys were always critical about the existence of a separate market for so-called Christian music. "I think that the Christian music industry was developed by people who wanted to have a captive audience," Huggins once said. "So they could say, 'If you're a true Christian, you'll only buy from us.' " For this reason, the group refused to fit into the confines of that market or to service the Christian industry in expected ways. Nevertheless, Huggins maintained that "the

goal of the Galactic Cowboys is to write, record, and play great music to the glory of God," and he indicated that the unabashed Christian perspective of everyone in the group affected their songwriting, performance, and lifestyles in ways that were evident to all of their fans. Asked by *Bandoppler,* "Isn't it hard to be a Christian in the secular market?" Huggins replied, "Of course it is. It's supposed to be."

Danny Gans

2000—*Brand New Dreams* (Myrrh).

Full-time Las Vegas stage performer Danny Gans released a debut album of adult contemporary Christian music in 2000. Produced by **Michael Omartian,** *Brand New Dreams* contains some songs written by **Randy Stonehill,** in addition to a version of The Spiral Staircase's 1969 hit, "More Today Than Yesterday." Gans seems most in his element on "Best Stuff in the World Today Café," a whimsical allegory sung in a style similar to that of Harry Connick Jr. **Bob Carlisle** joins him in a duet on the ballad "As Far As You Can See."

Reneé García

1987—*Living in the Vertical* (Reunion); 1988—*A Different World.*

Renee García began her Christian music career as a backup singer for **David Meece** and then as a member of These Three, a group of backup singers for **Amy Grant.** A native of Ft. Wayne, Indiana, García married Lang Bliss in 1987 and the two of them eventually formed the group **Bliss Bliss.** García was especially known for performing in penitentiaries and juvenile detention centers. Her two solo albums have a distinct urban contemporary sound. On them, she performs many songs written by **Chris Eaton,** who also produced the projects. *A Different World* also includes some of her own compositions, including a title track written with Eaton and **Glenn Garrett.**

Christian radio hits: "Deepest Love" (# 4 in 1988), "Living in the Vertical" (# 3 in 1988), "I See Love" (# 14 in 1988), "The Bounce" (# 4 in 1988), "A Different World" (# 5 in 1988), "Perfection" (# 9 in 1988), "You Don't Need It" (# 10 in 1988).

Steve and Maria Gardner

1971—*He Loves You* (custom); 1972—*A Better Day* (Word); 1975—*Words of Hope* (Tempo); *We Belong;* 1976—*Mandy's Song;* 1977—*Give Them All to Jesus* (Word); 1985—*The Best Love Song* (Aslan).

Steve and Maria Gardner are a married couple who met while traveling and singing with The Spurlows in the '60s. Heavily involved with Youth for Christ, their family-oriented MOR songs were nevertheless a bit too hokey for the hippie Jesus movement converts who constituted the principal audience for youth-oriented Christian music in the '70s. The Gardners did better at finding their niche with their mid-'80s comeback, an unabashed adult contemporary album of easy listening Christian love songs called *The Best Love Song*. CCM referred to them as a Christian version of the Carpenters. The duo sang regularly for the *Words of Hope* radio program sponsored by their denomination, the Reformed Church in America.

Glenn Garrett

1975—*Signs of the Season* (custom); 1976—*Home Is Where You Are* (Jesus Folk); 1979—*Renewed Like an Eagle* (Cut Above); 1980—*It Is Written* (Greentree); 1982—*Nothing without You*; 1984—*Back Where Love Begins* (Zoe).

A singer/songwriter from Birmingham, Alabama, Glenn Garrett began recording Christian pop songs in the mid '70s but didn't really hit until 1980 when the ballad "I'm Born Again" from *It Is Written* sparked a chord for many listeners. Garrett toured extensively with his wife Kathy and emphasized the ministry component of Christian music. In December of 1982 he published an article in *CCM* magazine dealing with the importance of spiritual priorities of musicians who wish to be effective ministers. His songs were often of the story variety, similar to those of **Don Francisco.** "Stephen" articulates the viewpoint of that latter-day disciple (Acts 6–7) and "Widow's Mite" relates the tale from Mark 12:41–44. Stylistically, Garrett favored ballads, though "I've Had a Reason" from *It Is Written* exhibits a bit of new-wave inflection. Garrett is the founder of Zoe Records. He also cowrote the song "A Different World," which was a Christian radio hit for **Reneé García.**

Christian radio hits: "I'm Born Again" (# 4 in 1981); "You Are Jehovah" (# 5 in 1984).

Luke Garrett

1986—*Luke Garrett* (Home Sweet Home); 1987—*Ever Constant . . . Ever Sure*; 1989—*Fine Joy*; 1990—*Praise the Lord*; 1994—*Here and Now* (NewVision).

An MOR singer signed to **Chris Christian**'s label, Luke Garrett made a series of albums similar in style to those of **Larnelle Harris** or **Steve Green.** While a student at UCLA, Garrett won a prestigious Best Vocalist award given annually in honor of Frank Sinatra. He turned down offers for a general market recording career in order to serve as a music minister at First Baptist Church in Dallas, Texas, and to record albums of praise-oriented Christian songs. The records often showcase Garrett's incredible vocal range and aptitude for hitting high notes untouched by most tenors outside of the operatic genre. The songs themselves are typically either worshipful ballads or inspirational message songs. Reviewers believed Garrett improved with age and lauded successive albums over their predecessors.

Marvin Gaye

Selected: 1971—*What's Going On* (Tamla).

www.marvingaye.net

Marvin Gaye (b. Marvin Gay, 1939) was one of the most successful and enigmatic soul singers of the '60s and '70s. His commitment to Christianity seemed both nebulous and sincere—indeed, it was sometimes questionable precisely because of the sincerity that forced Gaye to distance himself from what he was unable to embrace as fully as he wished. Gaye's mellifluous tenor and three-octave range made him the perfect vehicle for romantic, sensual ballads that typified much of the black pop music of his era. He charted fifty-six pop hits in his two-decade career with many more songs scoring on specifically R&B charts. He may be best remembered for the enormous hit "I Heard It through the Grapevine" (# 1 for 7 weeks in 1968) and for such sexually charged numbers as "Let's Get It On" (# 1 for 2 weeks in 1973), "Got to Give It Up" (# 1 in 1977), and "Sexual Healing" (# 3 in 1982). Still, his most successful and most critically acclaimed album was *What's Going On,* a modern gospel record of Jesus music and songs of sociopolitical consciousness.

Gaye was known for being volatile and moody. He seldom gave interviews, preferred not to perform on TV, and even kept stage shows and touring to a minimum. His life was tumultuous even for a celebrity. In the late '60s, he recorded several duets with Tammi Terrell. The duo scored eight Top 40 hits together and they performed together on stage. At a concert in 1967 Terrell collapsed into his arms on stage, a victim of a brain tumor that took her life three years later. Gaye was deeply affected and troubled by her death. His fourteen-year marriage to Anna Gordy (sister to his boss, Motown head Berry Gordy) was publicly very rocky, and when in a divorce settlement he was ordered to make an album from which she would receive royalties, he responded with the bitter *Here, My Dear* (Tamla, 1978) that detailed matters of their relationship in ways intended to embarrass her. A second marriage to a woman literally half his age (he was thirty-four, she was seventeen; Anna by contrast was seventeen years his *senior*) also failed. In addition, Gaye had numerous feuds with the Internal Revenue Service, prompting him to move to Europe for two years. His most notorious quarrels, however, were with his father, a preacher who became insanely jealous of his son's financial success and disdainful of his worldly career. As biographer Steve Turner puts it, "The most painful thing for Marvin's father, must have been the realization that the son whom he had chastised had not only survived the humiliations but had gone on to supersede him in every area of life. It was Marvin, and not he, who had the huge congregations and whose opinions on spiritual matters were discussed in the media. And it was Marvin whose money had provided the family with a house." One Sunday morning—the day before Marvin's forty-fifth birthday—he and his father got into a typical shouting match, this time over insurance policies. Apparently, the young Marvin became physically abusive, intimidating the father who had once abused and humiliated him. The seventy-year-old Marvin Gay Sr. retreated to his room, only to return later with a gun. He shot his son at point blank range, killing him instantly.

Marvin Gay Sr. was an ordained minister in a Pentecostal denomination known as the House of God. He served as a bishop in that denomination and as a member of the national Executive Board, but retired from active ministry about the time that his son began his music career. Marvin Jr. had grown up in the strict church singing in his father's choir. He never renounced the denomination's beliefs or sought to join a different body, though he certainly ceased to be in good standing with the House of God. This sect teaches—contrary to most Christian groups—that followers of Christ are to keep all of the commandments of the Old Testament and that failure to live without sin means the loss of salvation. Gaye's personal life was marked by long bouts of cocaine abuse and by sexual extravagances for which he seemed to feel little remorse. As a result, and wishing to avoid duplicity, Gaye would identify himself throughout his career as a believer who loved God and Jesus Christ, but he sometimes hesitated to call himself a Christian.

Gaye had been working on an autobiography when he was murdered, which he had chosen to call *A Divided Soul.* The book was later finished by his collaborator David Ritz and published by De Capo Press in 1985. An even more incisive study of the artist, however, would be written by the British rock journalist Steve Turner: *Trouble Man: The Life and Death of Marvin Gaye* (Ecco, 1998). Both volumes document the bizarre circumstances of Gaye's upbringing. The elder Gay was strict with the children, savagely beating them for what seemed to be peccadilloes, while disregarding church rules in rather extreme ways himself. He was often given to bouts of drunkenness and had numerous flings with big-breasted women, some of which he would flaunt as trophies of his manliness. He was also widely known to be a transvestite, a situation that brought much ridicule upon the family within their neighborhood. Nevertheless, Gaye would tell Ritz shortly before his death that he appreciated what he regarded as a Christian upbringing, in spite of his father's legalism and hypocrisy: "I could see the truth, not in my father's example, but in the words he preached. He offered me Jesus. He made Jesus come

alive for me, and that's reason to be grateful to him for the rest of my life."

What's Going On remains Gaye's masterpiece and finest contribution to popular music. Gaye had to fight to see it released over Motown's objections, with Berry Gordy reportedly calling it "the worst record I've ever heard." It was one of rock's first concept albums, with all of the songs fitting together to present a single theme (basically, the need for social problems to be addressed at a personal and spiritual level). Even musically, the songs tie into each other so well that one seems simply to flow into the next without any interval of silence distinguishing one cut from another. *Time* magazine wrote, "Gaye weaves a vast, melodically deft symphonic pop suite in which Latin beats, soft soul, white pop, scat, and Hollywood schmaltz yield effortlessly to each other. He also praises God and Jesus, and blesses peace, love, children, and the poor." The album produced three major hits: "What's Going On" (# 2 in 1971), "Mercy Mercy Me" (# 4 in 1971), and "Inner City Blues" (# 9 in 1971). In keeping with the times, these and other songs protest the Vietnam war, pollution, and urban blight. "Flying High" exposes the "stupid-mindedness" of drug abuse while "Save the Children" (Gaye's personal favorite and arguably the album's high point) offers a sentimental appeal to work for a better tomorrow. "Right On" offers what Steve Turner would call "a funky version of the Sermon on the Mount," basically calling on all God's children to love one another. All of these songs arise out of a deeply spiritual perspective that comes to the fore in "God Is Love" and "Wholly Holy." The former exalts Jesus as "my friend," and as the one who "made everything," gave us this world, "forgives all our sins," and "loves us whether or not we know it." Then, on "Wholly Holy," Gaye proclaims that he "believes in Jesus" and in "the book he left us: In it we have a lot to learn." Gaye was also forthright about his faith in the liner notes to *What's Going On:* "Find God. We've got to find the Lord. Allow him to influence us. I mean, what other weapons have we to fight the forces of hatred and evil? And check out the Ten Commandments, too. You can't go too far wrong if you keep them, dig it. Just a personal contact with God will keep you more together. Love the Lord, be thankful, feel peace. Thanks for life and loved ones. Thank you Jesus."

At the time that *What's Going On* came out, the Jesus movement was in full bloom out in California and pop-religion was in the American air. *Jesus Christ Superstar* had sold millions of copies the year before, and *Godspell* would do the same the year following. Gaye's ambiguous spirituality fit more closely with the ideology of those projects than with the narrowly-defined evangelicalism of Calvary Chapel, but the Jesus people generally picked up on Gaye's vibe all the same. "Institutionalized religion is good for the masses but I have a special God who looks over me," Gaye said, echoing the Jesus movement's "personal relationship with Jesus" motto. "He is the same God that people worship institutionally, but I feel I have a special link." True, Gaye also talked about astrology and said he believed in reincarnation, but in 1971, a lot of the Jesus freaks hadn't sorted all that stuff out for themselves yet either. A decade later, such ideas would have gotten Gaye condemned as a heretic within the Christian music subculture, and self-identified Christian music fans may have wanted nothing to do with his project. But in 1971, he was viewed as a brother who was searching, and as one who knew enough of the truth to offer insight from which all could benefit. Gaye himself maintained that the album had been divinely inspired. He told Smokey Robinson that "God and I cowrote that album together." He told a journalist, "It was a very divine project and God guided me all the way. I don't even remember much about it. I was just an instrument. All the inspiration came from God Himself." Others seemed to agree. The NAACP honored Gaye with their Image award as "America's most socially significant entertainer," and Jesse Jackson said, "Marvin is as much a minister as any man in a pulpit." May 1, 1972 was proclaimed Marvin Gaye Day in Washington, D.C., where the artist was feted by a host of dignitaries and lauded as an ideal role model for American youth.

After such a sweeping masterpiece of spirituality, Gaye's audience was sent reeling by his next major project, *Let's Get It On* (Motown, 1973), an openly carnal tribute to the joys of illicit sex. He freely admitted to being inspired by his lust for an adolescent girlfriend, the enjoyment of whose pleasures he found in no way incompatible with his marriage vows. A follow-up album, *I Want You* (Motown, 1976), continued these obsessions and, now, instead of writing liner notes about keeping the Ten Commandments and loving Jesus, the artist appended a convoluted apologia for premarital, extramarital, and other forms of casual sex. By 1982's *Midnight Love,* he had somehow combined the two impulses, thanking "our Lord and Savior Jesus Christ" in the credits for a record that explicitly commends all varieties of kinky sex and cocaine-assisted orgies. The best-known song, "Sexual Healing," seems to promise salvation through orgasm, while the equally acclaimed "Joy" is a gospel song inspired by the preaching of Gaye's father and describing the delight he had found in worship as a child. *Dream of a Lifetime* (released after his death) pairs the ribald "Masochistic Baby" and "Savage in the Sack" with "Life's Opera," which closes with a moving version of the Lord's Prayer and an invitation to draw close to God. It also features the infamous "Sanctified Pussy" (listed as "Sanctified Lady" on the album cover), a pornographic ode that Gaye had described in interviews as a "very spiritual" and "deeply religious" song.

What was going on? Psychologically, Gaye's synthesis of sex and faith might be understood with reference to the repres-

sion and confusion that marked his upbringing, but *theologically,* such developments may be attributed to the paradoxes of gnosticism, which in lesser degrees affects much of the contemporary Christian music scene. Gnostic ideology is radically dualistic, setting whatever is material (the world, the human body, and its appetites) in opposition to that which is spiritual. From the second century on, the philosophy has found expression in two different forms: the dominant mode has been ascetic gnosticism, which sees denial of the flesh (fasting, celibacy, etc.) as the way to strengthen or free the spirit. But the same basic ideology also leads quite logically to a libertine gnosticism that views the body and the material world as simply irrelevant: those who are liberated in spirit may do as they please with their worthless bodies. Christianity has always officially regarded gnosticism (in both forms) as heretical, but the mindset persists at a popular level and among fringe groups, such as that in which Gaye was raised. Although his church would never have approved of his interpretations of their doctrine, he himself seems to have found his behavior consistent with a basic teaching that "God doesn't care about the body; the spirit is all that matters."

This aspect of Gaye's understanding is often missed. Biographer Davin Seay (author of *Stairway to Heaven*) expresses dismay that Gaye would "wear a thick rubber band around his wrist to remind him of the transitory nature of the material world" while at the same time evincing an unabashed affection for pornography. This is not incredible: realization that the flesh is only transitory seems to have been what justified Gaye's cavalier attitude toward such matters. Only the permanent reality of the spirit is what counts. But Gaye was of two minds on this, and at times he expressed guilt over not being able to live in accord with higher ideals. In 1981, during a temporary reversion to asceticism, he spoke with intolerance against anyone who used drugs or lived promiscuously. Such matters, he momentarily claimed, were not irrelevant to spiritual growth, but an impediment. "The problem is this stupid flesh that envelops our spirit," he said. "There are stupid pleasures and material interests and all kinds of things to stop us evolving toward eternity." Another of Gaye's associates remembers a time when the artist went berserk over someone lining up their cocaine on the cover of his Bible. "Get that s**t off the Bible!" he screamed, kicking over a table and raging about the room. Supposedly, he maintained that there was nothing wrong with snorting coke one minute and reading the Bible the next, but for some reason the two entities were not to be brought together.

To the end, Marvin Gaye seems to have believed (at least, sometimes) that his spirit was right with God, talking openly and reverently of his love for Jesus. In one interview, shortly before he died, he was asked if he considered himself to be a

Christian. He responded, "I consider myself to be a Christian because I believe in and love Jesus Christ. I'm not a fully evolved Christian at this point, but I'm working on it." But at almost the same time, he told another publication, "I don't believe I am a Christian. A Christian is a man who follows Christ and that is something I have been unable to do." Frank Wilson, a longtime producer of Gaye's albums, attributed such comments to false understandings of Christianity that had been pressed into Gaye's mind from infancy. Wilson (who later became a Baptist minister) had become a spiritual mentor and counselor to Gaye over the years, and at the time of the latter's death he told *CCM* magazine, "Marvin Gaye loved the Lord. His faith was in the Lord. He was saved."

For trivia buffs: The album cover to *What's Going On?* offers what would later read as a sad dedication: "Thanks to my parents, the Rev. and Mrs. Marvin P. Gay Sr., for conceiving, having, and loving me." Asked at his trial some years later if he had *ever* loved his son, Marvin Gay Sr. hesitated, then replied, "Let's just say that I didn't dislike him."

Grammy Awards: 1982 Best R&B Vocal Performance, Male ("Sexual Healing"); 1983 Best R&B Instrumental Performance ("Sexual Healing—Instrumental Version").

Gears of Redemption

Jeff Hester, gtr.; Jerry King, bass; Kevin Lindsay, voc.; Reese "Rizo" Logan, drums. 2000—*The War of Blood and Rust* (Godfather).

Gears of Redemption is an Oklahoma-based hard rock/ metal band. Their debut album was produced by Kirk Campbell, formerly of **Eternal Decision,** whose influence critics detect here. The song "Automatically" is an experiment in rapcore, while the rest of the album has more of a straightforward aggressive hard rock sound. Notably, the group's lyrics are blatantly and defiantly Christian. *Rad Rockers* says the band "will appeal to fans of Korn and Sevendust who, drawn by the raging music, won't be able to easily dismiss the Gearheads' attack on the futility of living without God in this increasingly wicked world."

MC Ge Gee

See under "M."

Generation

Bruce Franklin; Caesar Kalinowski; Randy Kerkman; Mark Robertson. 1993—*Brutal Reality* (Wonderland).

Generation was a one-time Christian project for Bruce Franklin, guitarist for the general market band Trouble. Without leaving his home band, Franklin got together with three other Christian musicians to record a metal album expressive of his faith. *Brutal Reality* has an angry metal sound similar to the music of Ministry or Prong. Industrial influences are felt throughout, and only six of the ten tracks have vocals. "Nothing to Give" recalls Led Zeppelin's "When the Levee Breaks" with its heavy guitar grooves and dominant drums. "I Live in Flesh" is more like a Van Halen party song, with ironic lyrics inspired by Romans 7: "I live in flesh / With the nature of sin / I live in flesh / It's a prison within." The song "Chemikill" is about substance abuse, satirically expressing the viewpoint of the addict who insists he is not hurting anyone but himself. "Still You Died" is a more traditional reflection on the atonement: "Born a King, you give up your throne / To pay for sins not your own . . . Here I am a man of hate / With words that burn and cause you pain / Still, you died / Still, you died." Mark Robertson has also been a member of **Brighton, The Stand, This Train, Under Midnight,** and **A Ragamuffin Band,** in addition to **Mark Pogue**'s band Fortress.

Generation Y

Rachel Gaines; Amanda Omartian; Christopher Omartian; Joey Richey; Akil Thompson; Kara Williamson. 1995—*Welcome to Youtopia* (Sparrow).

Generation Y was a Wilson Phillips-like amalgamation of the teenage children of Christian music stars. Chris Omartian, the son of **Michael and Stormie Omartian,** produced the album, while also playing drums and programming sequences. Rachel Gaines is the daughter of Billy and Sarah, and Akil Thompson is the son of session drummer Chester Thompson. Musically, the group presented a few original numbers but mostly concentrated on recasting Christian hits from the '80s in a more modern techno-pop style. **Keith Green**'s "Jesus Is Lord of All" gets this treatment with Joey Richey on vocals, and **Andraé Crouch**'s "Jesus Is the Answer" becomes a hip-hop song with Kara Williamson doing a rap. Other songs reinvented by Generation Y include **Cheri Keaggy**'s "We Have Come to Worship Him" and "You O Lord Are My Refuge" and **Michael W. Smith**'s "Emmanuel." As this list implies, praise and worship seems to provide the album's conceptual focus.

Gentle Faith

Paul Angers; Henry Cutrona; Don Gerber; Steve Kara; Darrell Mansfield. 1976—*Gentle Faith* (Maranatha).

An early version of the country-rock Jesus music band Gentle Faith recorded a song called "The Shepherd," which opened Side Two of Maranatha Music's *The Everlastin' Living Jesus Music Concert* (1971), the record with which the history of contemporary Christian music properly begins. That album was easily the most important of all the early Christian music records and served to introduce the world to what would become a genre, a market, and ultimately an industry. The song remains a classic Christian folk tune and, though not often re-membered, sounds as fresh and beautiful thirty years later as it did when first recorded. For "The Shepherd," however, Gentle Faith consisted of just Henry Cutrona with assistance from two otherwise unknown persons, Larry Needham and John Wilson. Unlike many of the bands featured on *The Everlastin' Living Jesus Music Concert,* Gentle Faith did not produce an album until six years later. Then, a self-titled project by a new incarnation of the band suddenly appeared. That album, too, is of historical interest in that it contains the earliest recordings of **Darrell Mansfield,** who would go on to gain fame as a solo artist and blues guitarist. Overall, though, *Gentle Faith* evinces a soft folk-pop style that has little in common with Mansfield's later work. The song "Jerusalem" is a particular standout and garnered the most airplay, though its slow rant against the Jewish people for not believing in Jesus sounded insensitive to many Christians even at the time. Mansfield also sings his own composition, "Home," in a voice that sounds a lot like **B. J. Thomas.** "Livin' in the Sunshine" and "It's So Good to Know" are also treats, full of the hopeful confidence that marked early Jesus music. Four songs from the album were later reprised on Mansfield's *Collection* album.

Ghoti Hook

Joel Bell, voc., gtr.; Adam Neubauer, drums; Jamie Tolosa, gtr., bass; Christian Ergueta, bass (– 2000); Conrad Tolosa, gtr. (– 1998) // Mark Lacasse, gtr. (+ 2000). 1994—*No Date* [EP] (independent); 1995—*Boca Grande* [EP]; *Sumo Surprise* (Tooth and Nail); 1997—*Banana Man;* 1998—*Songs We Didn't Write;* 2000—*Two Years to Never.*

www.ghotihook.com

The premier Christian punk band Ghoti Hook was formed in 1991 in the Washington, D.C., area. The group is especially noted for bringing a goofiness and humor to their material. In early years, they were somewhat infamous for performing a cover of the theme from "Fraggle Rock" in their live shows. *Sumo Surprise* was produced by Kevin 131 of **Aleixa.** The album includes seven tracks from the band's independent releases and another seven new songs. All fourteen numbers are played at a breakneck pace but feature strong melodies and stellar vocal harmony, making the critics scramble for ways to describe the ambiguous style. *HM* called it "skate rock"; *True Tunes* said the group was "a glam band trapped in a punk band's body"; *7ball* described them as a variety of "MTV punk," performing pop songs in a traditionally punk style but without the anger and angst that originally marked '80s punk-rock. "Body Juggler" takes a cynical look at dating, and "Tract Boy" relates a tale of street witnessing. "Samson and Me" draws on the famous biblical story to infer the politically incorrect moral that "girls are nothing but trouble."

The group was not happy with the mix for their album *Banana Man,* complaining that the "bottom end" of their sound was washed out in interests of obtaining a brighter style. The album displays a somewhat more serious tone than *Sumo* and is heavier musically. "Middle Ground" features shouted vocals reminiscent of The Offspring, and "Gimme a Chance" shows off the band's speed-punk style at its best. "Cowboy" is a standout track, with tight musicianship and background vocals. "My Bike" samples Pee Wee Herman on a song about how much someone likes his bicycle.

Songs We Didn't Write was a very wise choice for the band. With Kevin 131 still in the producer's chair, Ghoti Hook rips through cover versions of classic rock songs in a manner inspired by the Ramones' *Acid Eaters* and then taken up by **MxPx** with *On the Cover.* Fortunately, the Ghoti project has more in common with the former of these, giving new life to old songs and in some cases pumping life into tunes that never had it before. Songs they cover include Joan Jett's "I Love Rock and Roll," The Cars' "Just What I Needed," Katrina and the Waves' "Walking on Sunshine," and Willie Nelson's "On the Road Again." But along with these very well-known tunes, they also incorporate obscurities by the Dead Milkmen, the Pixies, and X, as well as two Christian chestnuts, **Michael W. Smith**'s "Friends" and **Stavesacre**'s "Acquiese." The result is one of the most fun albums to be produced in recent Christian music. With *Songs We Didn't Write,* Ghoti Hook managed simultaneously to broaden their appeal and to pay an appropriate tribute to God for the gift of music. Of course, not everyone got it. Someone wrote a letter to *CCM* magazine complaining that Ghoti Hook was "introducing kids to music of immense perversity." Ghoti Hook responded to the letter, saying, "Songs by believers and non-believers alike can be used to express musical qualities and glory to God."

On *Two Years to Never,* the group (minus Conrad Tolosa) grew up. The album is serious, poignant, and even sad from start to finish. The opening track, "One Step Away," presents the words of a man reflecting on his childhood and on the absent role of his father. Fans lamented the (inevitable?) maturity but critics hailed the album as the band's best work to date. The group also introduces new musical sounds that make the standard punk attack less repetitive. Flourishes of organ and acoustic piano turn up here and there, and the title track somehow incorporates a psychedelic solo and an arena chorus. "Next to Me" appeals to a loved one for patience. "Mach 3" cries out to God for protection. "Vs." addresses potential fans who would dismiss the band merely because its members are Christian.

For trivia buffs: The group's name, suggested by Adam Neubauer's father, is a phonetic spelling of "Fish Hook": The *gh* is pronounced as in *rough;* the *o* as in *women;* and the *ti* as in *nation.* But it's pronounced "Go-dee."

Nicholas Giaconia

1994—*Center of the Earth* (Storyville).

A singer/songwriter from central Ohio, Nicholas Giaconia has attracted a small following with songs in the tradition of artists like **T Bone Burnett, Bruce Cockburn,** and **Rich Mullins.** Though he has not enjoyed the success of those stars, his songs are every bit as poignant. Giaconia says that he became a Christian after a friend invited him to become involved in a Bible study group at Malone College: at the first meeting, everyone was invited to share their testimony, and he found himself having to make one up. With a voice that sometimes recalls Paul Simon, Giaconia sings with passion and spices his material with wit. The title track to *Center of the Earth* tells of a lost land where one can watch MTV with Elvis a few doors down from Jimmy Hoffa, a place divorced from reality where one is tempted to stay for more than just a spell. "Woman at the Well" relates the famous biblical story with the same sort of universal appeal that Peter, Paul, and Mary once evoked with their "Jesus Met the Woman at the Well." The closing song, "Psalm," offers worshipful reflection via a new set of beatitudes ("Blessed is he whose hate is forgotten"). A hidden track on the album ("The Amy Song") offers hilarious commentary on the mid '90s tendency for Christians to rag on **Amy Grant** for getting too worldly. The song borrows from Jesus' parable of the Pharisee and the Tax Collector (Luke 18:9–14) as Giaconia offers tongue-in-cheek thanks to God that he is more spiritual than she, and concludes with the lines, "When she dies, Lord, you can just relax / 'Cause I've already judged her / To take the burden off your back."

In his concerts, Giaconia often covers Matthew Sweet's "Evangeline" with some of the lyrics rewritten to make the song apply to his daughter who bears that name. He also sings a song that offers a very biblical response to those who think all Christian musicians should be ministers by vocation: "I'm not a preacher, a prophet, or a teacher / These things I do not desire / I'm just a guy with a guitar, a smile, and a song / And quite frankly, I'm for hire / 'Cause I got me a daughter and I got me a wife / I even got a dog and a cat / My ministry lies in providing for them / By singing my songs for the masses." Giaconia is an (almost) undiscovered treasure, one of Christian music's finest troubadours who is at once theologically perceptive and thoroughly entertaining.

Giant

Mike Brignardello, bass; Dann Huff, gtr., voc.; David Huff, drums; Alan Pasqua, kybrd. 1989—*Last of the Runaways* (A&M); 1991—*Time to Burn* (Epic).

General-market band Giant was led by Dann Huff of **White Heart.** Huff was well known in the Christian music world for his session playing; he had provided tasty rock and roll guitar on albums by numerous artists, including **Amy Grant** and **Russ Taff.** Later he would join **The Front** and be a part of a one-time project by a supergroup called **The Players.** His brother David was a similarly renowned session drummer and fronted the group **David and the Giants,** in addition to having been a member of **White Heart.** Mike Brignardello and Alan Pasqua were also established studio musicians. Giant had a pop-metal sound that *CCM* described as "heavier than Bon Jovi and lighter than **Bloodgood,**" though they also displayed a penchant for experimenting with a wide variety of styles on their two albums. Their songs did not contain blatantly Christian lyrics but sought to address the trials of life and romance in perceptive and appropriate ways. Most featured memorable choruses. Standout tracks include "I'm a Believer" (not the Monkees' song) and "Hold Back the Night" from the first album.

Jon Gibson

1983—*Standing on the One* (Constellation); 1986—*On the Run* (Frontline); 1988—*Change of Heart*; 1989—*Body and Soul*; 1990—*Jesus Loves Ya*; 1991—*The Hits*; 1992—*Jon Gibson: Forever Friends*; 1994—*Love Education* (Brainstorm); 1995—*Songs of Encouragement and Healing* (Frontline); 1999—*The Man Inside* (B-Rite); 2002—*Soulful Hymns* (Imagery).

www.jongibson.com

Jon Gibson (b. 1962) is popularly known in the music industry as "the white boy who sounds like Stevie Wonder." Early on, his manager would play his tapes for noted soul singers (and, once, for Mohammed Ali) and then win bets with them by proving that the voice not only was *not* Wonder's, but in fact belonged to a white kid from San Francisco. In time, Gibson became close friends with Wonder and he has joined the latter in concert, singing the Paul McCartney vocal on "Ebony and Ivory."

Gibson grew up hard on the mean streets of the Bay city; his parents abused alcohol and drugs and relocated the family eighteen times before divorcing when he was nine. Expelled from high school in the ninth grade, and following a few run-ins with the law and a frightful attack in which he was stabbed by a street gang, Gibson joined the army at the age of seventeen. When he returned home from a tour in Germany, he reconciled with his father, who had now become a Christian and who introduced him to the faith.

Gibson made his first appearance as a "guest lead singer" on the album *Wolf* by Bill Wolfer (Constellation, 1982). Wolfer was a member of Michael Jackson's band, responsible for the keyboards on that artist's *Off the Wall* and *Thriller* albums. Gibson sang lead on three songs for Wolfer, with Jackson on background vocals and Stevie Wonder on harmonica. Gibson's own debut album, *Standing on the One,* was produced by Wolfer. The record was issued on a general market label and sought to appeal to secular audiences, with subtle expression of religious themes. "Nation in Need" and "That Ain't No Way to Love" offer social commentary in keeping with a Christian perspective, and "Start It All Again" speaks of being born again. Five of the songs, including the title track, would be remixed for inclusion on *On the Run,* but it was a new song from that project, "God Loves a Broken Heart," that would give Gibson his big break into the contemporary Christian music scene. "Dreams" is also a notable keyboard-driven song from *On the Run,* and "Ain't It Pretty" combines rap and metal guitar in a manner similar to the **Run-D.M.C.**/Aerosmith collaboration "Walk This Way."

Gibson's next outing, *Change of Heart,* would be one of his biggest albums, producing four Christian radio hits. The song "Yah Mo B There" is a cover of a general market hit for James Ingram—its lyrics express the thought "God will be there" in Afrikaner dialect. "Friend in You" is a near-perfect pop song with strongly evangelical lyrics. *Change of Heart* also includes the innovative rock-rap number "The Wall," a racial reconciliation song that Gibson cowrote and performs with **M.C. Hammer.** *Body and Soul* features a remake of Stevie Wonder's "Have a Talk with God," with Wonder himself playing harmonica. The title track for *Jesus Loves Ya* sounds simplistic but is one of Gibson's most powerful, gospel-inflected numbers. That album also includes the infectious "Love Come Down"—not the song made popular by Evelyn King, but one that betrays a similar jazzy influence. Gibson invites MC Peace (a.k.a. **Peace 586**) to offer a rap break on an opening funk number called "Enough's Enough." The song "Forever Now" sounds like it was written for a traditional gospel choir, and the mellower "Watching All My Days Go By" invokes late-period Beatles. "Everlasting" is stellar as a soulful ballad, and "In Too Deep" offers a kitchen-sink mix of a melodic chorus with rapped verses, flamenco guitars, and a slightly reggae beat. *Jesus Loves Ya* was Gibson's strongest effort to date, but *Forever Friends* was stronger still and was voted "Album of the Year" by *CCM* magazine. MC Peace returns for that project and Gibson works with a crack studio band that includes **Lanny Cordola** on guitar and Rob Mullins of The New Crusaders on keyboards. The album opens with a wonderfully bouncy number called "You Are the One" and continues with a sweetly melodic midtempo ballad, "Can't Live without Jesus." The songs "Happy to Know Jesus" and "On My Way to Heaven" are hook-laden Top 40 fare. The group also covers Stevie Wonder's "Happier Than the Morning Sun" and **Edwin Hawkins'** "To My Father's House."

Love Education was a self-produced album on a new label, with songs sampling the styles of urban gospel, adult contemporary, and Caribbean reggae ("The Narrow Road," "Someday Paradise"). "So Blue" is a funky standout, though critics were beginning to complain about simplistic lyrics ("When I get so blue and I do / I think of how much that I love you"). Gibson

then disappeared for half a decade (*Songs of Encouragement* is simply a compilation project, a repackaged version of *The Hits* that the artist didn't even bother to list on his website's "Exhaustive Discography"). When he resurfaced with *The Man Inside,* he seemed "mellower and wiser," to quote one reviewer, but continued to deliver songs in his well-established R&B style. The title track for the project emphasizes the internal nature that humans of all races and persuasions share (a bit like Bob Seger's "Fire Down Below"). "There for You" (an ode to friendship) offers a soulful jam complete with '70s style horns and harmonies. "Layin' in the Streets" turns up the tempo to disguise a cautionary tale as a jazzy dance tune. "Who Are You Fooling?" encourages believers to develop a social conscience, and Gibson comes almost full circle with the gospel jam "God Will Find Ya," a remake of a song from *Body and Soul.* The album *Soulful Hymns* has a worship focus and was Gibson's first release on his own label, Imagery Records.

Christian radio hits: "God Loves a Broken Heart" (# 1 for 6 weeks in 1987); "Dreams" (# 15 in 1987); "Friend in You" (# 2 in 1987); "Yah Mo B There" (# 5 in 1988); "Lost Inside of You" (# 9 in 1988); "Technology Man" (# 6 in 1989); "Father, Father" (# 3 in 1989); "Have a Talk With God" (# 7 in 1989); "In the Name of the Lord" (# 2 in 1989); "God Will Find Ya" (# 5 in 1990); "Everybody Needs the Lord" (# 3 in 1990); "Jesus Loves Ya" (4 weeks at # 1 in 1991); "Love Come Down" (# 3 in 1991); "Happy to Know Jesus" (# 1 for 2 weeks in 1992); "You Are the One" (# 5 in 1992); "Happier Than the Morning Sun" (# 9 in 1993); "On My Way to Heaven" (# 15 in 1993); "Jesus" (# 4 in 1995); "Someday Paradise" (# 7 in 1995).

Gina

1995—*Eternity* (N'Soul); 1997—*It's All about Love.*

Gina Foglio (b. 1975) is an Italian American singer/songwriter from San Bernardino, California, who records under her first name only. She began her career in Christian music recording on the *Nitro Praise* projects produced by **Scott Blackwell.** She went on to perform with such bouncy musicians as **Kim Boyce, Jon Gibson,** and **Crystal Lewis** before making her own solo albums. *Eternity,* recorded when she was still technically a teenager, presents her as a vocal ringer for Lewis, performing songs that sound like outtakes from Madonna's early albums (albeit with obviously different lyrics). The album's highlight is probably Gina's high energy version of Kool and the Gang's "Celebration." She also delivers a cool acid jazz song, "For So Long," and a contemporary pop number, "Everybody." *It's All about Love* is less dance-oriented, opening with a cover of Stephanie Mills' "I Never Knew Love Like This Before." The song "Love Will Wait" offers Gina's testimony to the value of sexual abstinence.

Christian radio hits: "Everybody" (# 16 in 1995); "Way That You Love Me" (# 16 in 1996).

Chuck Girard

1975—*Chuck Girard* (Good News); 1976—*Glow in the Dark;* 1977—*Written on the Wind;* 1979—*Take It Easy;* 1980—*The Stand;* 1983—*All Those Years; The Name Above All Names* (Seven Thunders); 1991—*Fire and Light* (Frontline); 1996—*Voice of the Wind* (Newport).

www.chuck.org

Chuck Girard is without question one of the most important people in the history of contemporary Christian music. He fronted the group **Love Song,** which led the spiritual onslaught of the Jesus-movement revival and is often considered to be the most important Christian rock band of all time. His solo albums took up where **Love Song** left off and continued in the same vein, but, as musical styles changed and the doors that Girard himself had opened admitted waves of young, talented artists, his albums seemed increasingly dated and out-of-touch with the culture that grew up around contemporary Christian music. Ironically, the very person who was most responsible for introducing Christian rock music to the church (**Larry Norman** introduced it to the world) came to be classed as adult contemporary and to be ignored by a new generation that had grown up with AC/DC instead of the Beatles.

Although he was never billed as a famous convert (like Jesus music pioneers **Barry McGuire** and **Noel Paul Stookey**), Girard actually had a successful pre-Christian career in pop music. Born and raised in Santa Rosa, California, he formed The Castells while still a teenager. The group was influential in defining the early '60s "California sound" and put four songs on the national charts, including the Top 40 hits "Sacred" (# 20 in 1961) and "So This Is Love" (# 21 in 1962). This was still two years before the Beatles would arrive, at a time when **Pat Boone** was perhaps the most popular singer in America. Another of The Castells' songs was "Oh! What It Seemed to Be," a cover of a song that had been a Number One hit for both Frank Sinatra and Frankie Carle in 1942. After three years with The Castells, Girard and Joe Kelley left the group to form The Hondells, which also included Gary Usher, Brian Wilson (of the Beach Boys), and **Glen Campbell.** This supergroup had three national hits, including "Little Honda," an ode to a motorbike written by Brian Wilson and sung by Girard. The song went to Number Nine in 1964 and would remain a staple of oldies radio. In the latter half of the '60s, Girard became a fairly typical California hippie, searching for enlightenment through meditation and halucinogenics. Having rejected his Roman Catholic upbringing, he looked into eastern religions, tried vegetarianism, and even became enamored of Jesus as some sort of generic mystical figure. He moved to Hawaii for a time, where he says he sat on a big rock for five or six weeks and gradually "began to feel a sense of doing nothing for anybody." Back in the mainland, he was arrested twice for drug possession. Then he ended up at Costa Mesa's Calvary Chapel where he heard the gospel (as preached by Chuck Smith) and felt the Spirit. One of the original "Jesus people" (or "Jesus freaks" to some), Girard sought to spread the good news as a member of **Love Song** for three years and, then, as a solo artist. In 2000, his daughter Alisa Girard emerged as a member of the trio **Zoe Girl.**

Girard's first, self-titled album is clearly his masterpiece, a record that deserves to be set alongside the two **Love Song** projects as a flawless collection of pop songs with powerful evangelical themes. The opening track, "Rock and Roll Preacher," sets Girard's testimony to a rollicking beat and presents it with a dose of good humor: "Whoever thought I'd be a rock and roll preacher / Instead of just singin' the blues?" The song is justifiably a classic and would be played regularly on Christian music oldies shows if such things existed. Side two of *Chuck Girard* opens with another musically powerful number, the traditional gospel-inspired "Sea of Galilee," featuring female backup singers to great effect. There is not a weak track on the album, but "You Ask Me Why" and "Evermore" also rate as remarkable standouts, pop songs on a par with numerous Top 40 hits by groups like the Beach Boys and the Four Seasons. "Tinagera" is a melodic midtempo ballad about youth who have to face adult pressures before their time; the name is apparently short for "teenage era." Also of note are the album's concluding three songs: "Lay Your Burden Down" (a hymnic invitation to surrender all at the foot of the cross), "Slow Down" (a call for stressed-out people to just relax and trust God), and "Sometimes Alleluia" (a Jesus music worship song). All three display a laid-back calm tempo and, together, function as something of "a peaceful suite." While not his best song, "Sometimes Alleluia" would become Girard's best-known song, and its simple, swelling chorus of praise pointed in the direction his career and ministry would eventually take.

Girard's next few albums found him experimenting with styles, often setting worship songs, blues ballads, and surf pop tunes side by side. In the latter category, "Callin' You" from *Glow in the Dark* is especially wonderful, with a bouncy melody reminiscent of some of **Love Song**'s best work (e.g., "Changes"). Side two of that album opens with the song "Somethin' Supernatural," a straightforward blues-rock number that describes a new Christian from the perspective of a non-Christian friend. The song is once more leavened with Girard's trademark humor: "You don't read *Playboy* and you shun the liquor store / In many ways you're just no fun anymore." This ability to empathize with divergent points of view has been one of Girard's strong suits as a writer. He produced several personal ballad songs that describe an individual's life: "Tinagera" from *Chuck Girard,* "Old Dan Cotton" from *Glow in the Dark,* "Plain Ol Joe" from *Written on the Wind,* and the title song from *The Stand.* The Christian humor magazine *Wittenburg Door* (now simply *The Door*) once selected "Plain Ol Joe" as "the greatest Christian rock song ever written" because it defies expectations and does not tidy everything up with a happy Christian ending. It relates the tale of an ordinary person, a bit of a "loser" who lives an uneventful and unexciting life and eventually dies alone, unnoticed, and unmissed: "Everybody acted like you never lived / You're just a guy who never made the grade." This theme of the intrinsic worth of every human being would be expressed again in "Little People" from *Take It Easy*. Overall, that album (Girard's fourth) returns to the more rock-oriented sound of his debut (*Glow in the Dark* and *Written on the Wind* are more mellow). The opening track, "Take a Hand," kicks things into high gear almost immediately with a sound that most fans had missed since "Rock and Roll Preacher." *Take It Easy* also features a song called "Full Immersion Ocean Water Baptism by the Sea" about the early Jesus music days when hundreds of young adults would be baptized in the ocean at Corona del Mar beach.

Two other styles are especially important for considering Girard's contributions to contemporary Christian music. First, he has performed what might be described as "grand anthems," the best example of which might be "The Warrior" from *Written on the Wind*: heavily produced numbers with building, dramatic choruses and orchestration. And, second, he wrote and sang worship songs that express the joy of a life lived with Jesus: "So Thankful" from *Glow in the Dark* and "Hear the Angels Sing" from *Written on the Wind* would be on almost anyone's list of his very best material.

In 1981, Girard went through a time in his life that he now describes as "a time of correction and spiritual renewal," resulting in a commitment to refocus his music ministry on worship leadership. His latter three albums all reflect this new direction, providing the church with contemporary hymns and spiritual songs. *Name above All Names* focuses a bit more heavily than the other two on edification and prophetic challenge, for instance exhorting the church to care appropriately for its fallen members ("Don't Shoot the Wounded"). *Fire and Light* retains an up-tempo rock sound on about half of its songs; *Voice of the Wind* is completely mellow, filled with songs that are slow and intimate. Portions of *Voice of the Wind* were actually recorded in a live worship setting with a congregation.

For trivia buffs: Chuck Girard played and sang on '70s albums by the general market band Ambrosia (known for such hits as "Holding On to Yesterday," "How Much I Feel," and "Biggest Part of Me"). The same group accompanied him on his debut solo album.

Christian radio hits: "Take a Hand" (# 19 in 1979).

Glad

Ed Nalle; Chris Davis; Don Nalle (– 1987); Bob Kauflin (– 1985); Art Noble (–1988); John Bolles (–1982); Brad Currie (–1980) // Jim Gheen (+ 1980, –1982); Mark Baldwin (+ 1982, –1983); Tom Beard (+ 1985, –1990); John Gates (+ 1988); Mark Wilson (+ 1988, –1990); Rob Neal (+ 1989, –1993); Jim Bullard (+ 1990); Jeff Hamlin (+ 1993, –1995); Paul Langford (+ 1995, –1998); Don Pardoe (+ 1998). 1978—*Glad* (Myrrh); 1980—*Beyond a Star;* 1982—*Captured in Time* (Greentree); 1983—*No Less Than All;* 1984—*Live at Kennedy Center;* 1985—*Champion of Love;* 1987—*Who Do You Love?* 1988—*The A Capella Project;* 1989—*Romans;* 1990—*The A Capella Project 2* (Benson); 1991—*The Symphony Project; An A Capella Christmas;* 1992—*Floodgates;* 1993—*A Capella Hymns;* 1994—*The A Capella Collection;* 1995—*Color Outside the Lines* (Light); *A Capella Gershwin;* 1996—*The A Capella Project 3;* 1998—*The Collector's Series* (Benson); *A Capella Worship 1;* 1999—*A Capella Worship 2;* 2000—*Signature Songs* (label unknown); *Voices of Christmas.*

www.glad-pro.com

Glad is a progressive jazz vocal group that got its start at West Chester State University in Pennsylvania in the early '70s. Though best known for their a capella singing, they have also featured outstanding instrumentation. Art Noble was once named "Best Jazz-Rock Drummer" in America by the National Association of Jazz Educators.

The debut album *Glad* (still praised by *Jesus Music*) has a very different sound than that for which the group would become known. Basically, it sounds like it was recorded by a progressive rock group with jazz leanings. Comparisons were drawn to the general market '60s band The Association. A more choral style (quintet, quartet, or trio, depending on the album) would become evident on the next several projects. Each of these albums, however, features one song that was done a capella, beginning with "The Reason" on *Beyond a Star.* The best of these, "Be Ye Glad," became a well-known song of joyful praise sung by church choirs and madrigal groups across the country. Though it became their signature tune, "Be Ye Glad" was actually performed by Glad as a cover of a **Noel Paul Stookey** song, written by **Michael Kelly Blanchard.**

At first the a capella songs were just novelties and concert treats, but in 1988 Glad decided to do an entire album of such material, mixing traditional hymns ("A Mighty Fortress," "O For a Thousand Tongues") and original songs on *The A Capella Project.* This album was by far their biggest hit, selling over 400,000 copies, and the group responded to the obvious popularity with numerous follow-ups, including a Christmas project and a tribute album of a capella Gershwin songs. *The A Capella Project 2* includes **Keith Green**'s "You Put This Love in My Heart" alongside such traditional hymns as "Just As I Am" and "Crown Him with Many Crowns." For *The Symphony Project,* they sing to the accompaniment of The London Symphony Orchestra. Glad did keep their band, however, and every now and then would record with full instrumentation: *Floodgates* opens with a version of **2nd Chapter of Acts'** "Which Way the Wind Blows"; *Romans* is a concept album organized around themes from that letter of the Apostle Paul; *Color*

Outside the Lines (the best-received of the Glad-with-band projects) presents the group as a tamer version of **4 Him** on the title track and on "Faith Makes."

Christian radio hits: "All Things" (# 12 in 1979); "Take a Stand" (# 17 in 1980); "Maker of My Heart" (# 19 in 1984); "More Than Just a Little Bit" (# 33 in 1984); "There Is Hope" (# 22 in 1985); "Still on the Side of Love" (# 7 in 1986); "All the World Should Know" [with **Kathy Troccoli**] (# 3 in 1987); "Easter Song" (# 8 in 1988).

Christine Glass

1997—*Human* (Tatoo); 1999—*Love and Poverty* (Rustproof).

Christine Glass is an alternative rock singer/songwriter from Louisiana. She was raised in a fairly nonobservant Roman Catholic family but attended worship regularly at her Catholic school and was introduced both to a more evangelical type of faith and to contemporary Christian music when, as a teenager, she joined a Baptist youth choir. She majored in voice at Louisiana Tech University, training as an operatic singer. After graduation, she moved to Nashville where she worked first as a receptionist, then as an art director at Word Records while making music on the side. Glass is often compared with singers like P. J. Harvey and Suzanne Vega. As with those artists, her whispery vocals are often spread over experimental stylings, unusual harmonies, and unpredictable accompaniment. Glass's debut album, *Human,* attracted praise from a wide variety of critics. The songs themselves extol the virtues and lament the drawbacks of being a human being. "I'm dripping with humanity," she sings in "You Want." Elsewhere she affirms that "Time Doesn't Heal All Wounds" and proclaims, "Nothing's happening today / I see no miracles coming my way." Still she openly confesses her faith that "Jesus is coming and love will conquer all someday" ("I Believe"). "When Worlds Collide" (not the **Daniel Amos** song) concludes the album with a profound statement of the constant struggle between flesh and spirit that defines humanity. Glass's second project, *Love and Poverty,* has a generally laid-back vibe that pairs soft vocals with lush and dreamy guitars. This style is especially effective on "Poverty," a song expressing the "count everything as loss" attitude that constitutes blessed poverty of spirit. Also stunning is "Many Waters," an ethereal, liturgical chant taken from Daniel Pinkham's "Wedding Cantata" (inspired by Song of Songs 8:7).

Christian radio hits: "I Believe (Jesus Is Coming)" (# 15 in 1997).

Lesley Glassford

1985—*Heart's Desire* (Shiyrah); 1992—*Winds of Change* (Crossroads).

One half of **Tuesday's Child,** singer/songwriter Lesley Glassford recorded solo projects before forming that group with **Linda Elias** in 1995. An early album called *Heart's Desire* includes a couple of R&B-flavored tunes ("I Stand on Solid Rock," "We're Goin' Up"), in addition to a **Sandi Patty**-like anthem ("I Stand Here Amazed") and seven more songs that *CCM* would dismiss as "Christian fluff." The record did not gain much notice, and *Winds of Change* was presented as a debut recording, despite the fact that Glassford had been singing professionally for some twenty years. On that album, her mature voice and stylings bear close similarities to those of Olivia Newton-John. Lisa Glasgow and Marabeth Jordon of **First Call** sing with her on certain songs, creating a sound reminiscent of Wilson Phillips. The songs "Let It Go" and "Soul Revival" are dance-oriented (in the same mode as **Amy Grant**'s *Heart in Motion*) while "Where Love Runs Wild" is more somber. The album is notable lyrically, in that several of the songs touch on such difficult problems as Glassford's marital difficulties and describe rebellious episodes in her life when she had turned away from God. The overriding theme of the album is the possibility of God's love to renew and transform strained relationships.

For trivia buffs: Glassford is the principal cowriter for *Kurds 'n' Whay* children's projects.

Christian radio hits: "Soul Revival" (# 18 in 1993).

Glass Harp

Phil Keaggy, gtr., voc.; Dan Pecchio, bass, flute, bgv.; John Sferra, drums, bgv. 1970—*Glass Harp* (Decca); 1972—*Synergy*; 1972—*It Makes Me Glad*; 1977—*Song in the Air* (Star Song); 1997—*Live at Carnegie Hall* (Canis Major).

The Youngstown, Ohio, band Glass Harp is well known to Christian music fans as **Phil Keaggy**'s first group, but the band actually has significance for the history of rock and roll in general. An early wall-of-sound power trio in the mold of Cream or The Jimi Hendrix Experience, they played mesmerizing rock and roll that featured long instrumental jams and improvisational solos (flute, guitar, bass, or drum). Musically, they preferred blues-influenced rock and roll of a variety similar to Ohio compatriots James Gang, but they could also delve into Hendrix-inspired psychedelia or more progressive moody and atmospheric sounds. They were never considered to be a Christian group, though they were articulate about their faith, and the group did perform some of Keaggy's early Jesus music songs. The group had a strong, though regional, following in the general market, and they were able to count such notables as Ted Nugent and Jimi Hendrix among their fans. What national prominence they achieved came through touring; Glass Harp was the opening act for nationwide tours by Traffic, Yes, the Kinks, Humble Pie, **Alice Cooper,** Iron Butterfly, Ted Nugent, and Grand Funk Railroad. Reviews of their concerts and albums were almost invariably positive, dwelling especially on the lightning speed, precise technique, and highly lyrical style of guitarist Keaggy. The group has gotten together occasionally for brief reunion concerts (1981, 1987, 1993). In 1997, the group was honored with a special exhibit at the Rock and Roll Hall of Fame, and the trio played for a special concert at the opening ceremony.

Glass Harp formed in 1968, when Keaggy and John Sferra were both seventeen years old and still in high school. The group only made three albums, all for Decca in a relatively brief period. All three were produced by Lewis Merenstein, who *Rolling Stone* named Producer of the Year in 1970 for his work on **Van Morrison**'s *Astral Weeks* and *Moondance*. The self-titled debut album was recorded at Jimi Hendrix's Electric Ladyland studios; Hendrix died the day before it was completed. The album was a regional hit, selling 36,000 copies in Cleveland alone. A reviewer at the time noticed that no fewer than five of its ten songs mention "the sky" while three of the remaining ones talk about things like stars, rainbows, and the moon. This heavenly fixation may or may not have been evidence of the group's developing spirituality. Keaggy's mother, who managed the band's books, had died earlier that year, and her sudden loss sent the young man into a spiral of despair. While helping him through this time, his older sister led him to a spiritual conversion. The new perspective this transformation gave him is apparent on one of *Glass Harp*'s only Keaggy compositions, the opening song "Can You See Me?" (cowritten with Dan Pecchio). The number begins as a song of searching, typical for the Woodstock generation: "Can you see me, brother / Walking down the lonely road? / Can you see me, sister / Help me find which way to go." But then Keaggy answers his own question: "I know that it's hard to see / The way that we are meant to be / There's much that we can't see out there / But Jesus died for you and me / That we may live eternally / There is a peace we can share."

This evangelical spirit caused tension within the band, as Keaggy later recalled in a *CCM* interview: "We all knew there was a place for religion—being raised Catholic—but it was another thing to bring it to the stage." Keaggy did bring religion to the stage, regularly leading the group through a rousing version of the Sunday school classic "Do Lord" as a concert encore. Still, Sferra minimizes the notion of discord: "There was no such thing as a Christian band back then, yet Phil was speaking in bars to our audience about Christian doctrine, which Dan and I also believed. Sometimes the promoter or bar owner would flinch, but there would always be a full house. When you're successful, you can get away with a lot of things."

At any rate, the Jesus references did not decrease. On *Synergy* Keaggy sang, "The answer is Jesus / Believe me, he'll open the door" ("The Answer"), and on *It Makes Me Glad,* he put "Do Lord" on record alongside a song about "David and Goliath" and the evangelical "Song in the Air." Still, the group did not disband over Keaggy's faith; rather, he left the group persuaded that he should give up secular rock and roll for the Lord. He went to California and briefly joined **Love Song,** then relocated to upstate New York to work as a solo artist. His first solo album, the classic *What a Day,* appeared the same year as Glass Harp's swan song. John Sferra has also worked as a solo artist and has sometimes performed as a member of Keaggy's band, notably on the classic *Crimson and Blue* album. In 1996 he released an independent album called *Northbound* that has a classic rock sound hearkening back to Glass Harp in sound and diversity (Keaggy plays on the project). Dan Pecchio went on to play bass for the highly successful Michael Stanley Band and continues to be involved with music ministry at an evangelical church in the Cleveland area.

After Keaggy had gained a significant Christian audience as a solo artist, StarSong compiled the most "Christian sounding songs" (all written or cowritten by Keaggy) from Glass Harp's three albums and released these as *Song in the Air.* Twenty years later, a 1971 concert in which the group had opened for The Kinks at Carnegie Hall was released, again to capitalize on Keaggy's fame. That live album includes only five songs, one of which is a twenty-nine-minute version of "Can You See Me?" that will only appeal to those who think Iron Butterfly's "In-A-Gadda-Da-Vida" ends too soon (or who think *Wheels of Fire* records Cream's finest moments).

Keaggy has since reflected on his own immaturity as an adolescent "Jesus freak" in the wild world of rock and roll. In a 1989 *CCM* feature, he related with some embarrassment how Ted Nugent once asked him to show him how he played a particular lick on the guitar. Keaggy responded, "I'll show you how I do it . . . if you let me tell you about Jesus first!"

For trivia buffs: Glass Harp's name derives from a misappropriation of the name of the literary classic *The Grass Harp.*

Michael Gleason

1986—*Voices from the Old World* (Kerygma); 1990—*Children of Choices* (Pakaderm).

A friend of **Kerry Livgren,** Michael Gleason joined the general market band **Kansas** in 1983 and provided auxiliary keyboards and background vocals on that group's album *Drastic Measures* and on the supporting tour. This was part of Livgren's attempt to turn Kansas into a Christian band, and when that effort was thwarted Gleason joined Livgren and other Kansas alums in forming the group **A.D.** He left that group in 1986 to form his own production company and to record a solo album, about which no information is available. He later made *Children of Choices* with producer **John Elefante,** also a member of the ex-Kansas, ex-A.D. fraternity. Displaying a Kansas-like sound, the latter album features "True to Myself," an anthemic ode to integrity ("You can take me to the wall / But you can't make me live a lie") and "Front Page

News," a topical/political song that is lyrically similar to some of Don Henley's rants. By creating an album that was relatively free of overt religious language and "Christianese," Gleason hoped to provide a work accessible to those outside the Christian music community. "This is a great album to give to an unsaved friend," he told *CCM.* "It will get them to thinking about choices and issues." Gleason served as producer for **The Newsboys'** debut album.

Christian radio hits: "Children of Choices" (# 17 in 1990).

Glisten

Jason Petit, voc., gtr.; Adam Philips, drums; John Romero, bass; Travis Scott, gtr., bgv. 1999—*Starlight Wishlist* (KMG).

www.glisten.org

Formed in 1994, Glisten is a Dallas/Ft. Worth-based modern rock band with a sound that seems more British than Texan. On their debut album (produced by **Steve Hindalong** of **The Choir**), the group combines retro-'80s vocals reminiscent of Depeche Mode, Duran Duran, or The Cure with '90s guitars that sometimes stray into grunge. *CCM* praised the album: "Moody, spacey, and effected, *Starlight Wishlist* has a trippy instrumental feel, yet maintains a crisp song structure." Most of the songs feature lyrics with unambiguous Christian content, tending toward worship and praise ("Rejoice"). In 2000, Glisten's contract with KMG was dissolved, making the group an indie band again.

Global Wave System

Christian-E, voc., prog.; A. T. Matthew, voc., prog. (−1998); Christopher Buchholz, prog. (−1998) // Corey Diekman, gtr., voc. (+ 1998); Kevin Moore, drums (+ 1998). 1993—*Life Equals Death* (Intense); 1998—*HypercritEP* [EP] (Flaming Fish).

www.tenbyten.com/globalwavesystem

Global Wave System was one of Christian music's first industrial bands, and their debut album (produced by Brent Stackhouse of **Deitiphobia/X-Propagation**) is considered a classic by fans of that genre. The group formed in 1990 in Rock Island, Illinois, dissolved shortly after the first album was released, then reformed in 1996 and eventually relocated to Rochester, New York. They have placed numerous tracks on various compilation discs and have also made much of their music available through the Internet. On *Life Equals Death,* the group's sound was invariably compared to that of general market band Skinny Puppy. The music and lyrics have a characteristically dark tone, as the album relates the progression of a lost soul coming to Christ and subsequently struggling with the trials and temptations of this world. "Deathstroke to Youth" is a song about AIDS that rejects "the condom as the savior of our way of life" and reaches a somewhat melodramatic conclusion: "stay a virgin, marry one, stay faithful, or you will die." The song "CXLIII" presents a reading of Psalm 143 over a spooky, Skinny Puppy beat. On *HypercritEP,* the Skinny Puppy influence is less overt and a more original industrial sound emerges. "XLII" reprises the previous Roman numeral track, this time with a reading of Psalm 42. "Dissent" laments the tendency for Christian (fundamentalist) groups to argue over various millenial views of the book of Revelation. "Cardboard Box" satirizes human attempts to define or compartmentalize God. "Life and Works" and "Fountain" both draw their inspiration from C. S. Lewis's book, *The Great Divorce* (which is not about divorce, but about heaven and hell). Global Wave System's records have been well received outside the Christian market. A reviewer for *Sonic Boom* said of *Life Equals Death,* "Even being an agnostic, I found myself humming along to the catchy lyrics and enjoying the music." A different reviewer for the same publication said of *HypercitEP,* "The lyrics totally ruin the excellent programming and concise percussion; however, I will chalk that up to my own personal demons rather than blame the band."

Ben Glover

2001—*26 Letters* (Word).

Ben Glover (b. 1978) is an acoustic pop singer with a style very similar to that of **Steven Curtis Chapman.** Glover grew up in Loveland, Colorado, and set his sights early on a career in Christian music. His debut album, *26 Letters,* opens with the title track, a song cowritten by **Wayne Kirkpatrick** that declares the inadequacy of the English language to form words adequate for the praise of God. "Running after Me" expresses a basic "Hound of Heaven" theme of God pursuing the lost or straying sinner. "Stolen by Mercy" speaks cleverly of God as "the burglar of my soul" and begs God to "rob me of my shame." Less clever or profound is "Welcome to America," which repeats tired mantras of the Religious Right regarding how the United States has fallen from its former stature as a supposedly more God-honoring nation. But the latter song proves to be the only real low point. "All Comes Down" is a gorgeous adult contemporary ballad and "Hope Will Be My Song," an anthemic hymn that pledges perseverance in the face of hardship.

Godfear

Mark Bond, gtr.; Sean Vargas, voc.; et al. 1995—*The Empty* (independent); 1997—*Pound for Pound.*

The aggressive metal band Godfear gained national attention when their independent album was favorably reviewed by Doug Van Pelt in *HM* and that magazine subsequently did a feature article on the group. A Christian band from the Dallas/ Ft. Worth area, Godfear plays clubs with an eye to evangelistic ministry in secular environs. Musically, their sound draws on the influence of general market groups like Pantera or Korn.

Go Fish

Jason Folkmann, voc.; Andy Selness, voc.; Jamie Statema, voc. 2001—*Infectious* (InPop).

Go Fish is a trio from Minnesota that has a sound similar to groups like **FFH** and **Phillips, Craig, and Dean.** They sang a capella pop in their home state for a time, recording three independent albums. With the addition of acoustic instrumentation, they apparently hope to capitalize on the sudden and ironic popularity of adult contemporary music among young teens evidenced by all the boy bands dominating the charts in the first years of the third millennium. "Infectious" finds the group harmonizing like *NSYNC. Better stuff is found in the pretty melodies of "Until the Stars Fall" and "Cloverleaf Park." The sweet "You're My Little Girl" presents God's words to a young woman who might be struggling with issues of self-esteem. Almost the opposite effect is intended by "What Mary Didn't Know," a guilt-inducing song implying that teenagers might be held accountable before God if any of their friends die without having been told about Jesus—a terrible burden to place on a young person already traumatized by such a death. But "Silent Night" is a lovely **Take 6**-style rendition of the Christmas carol that gives a taste of what the indie a capella Go Fish sounded like.

God's Property

See **Kirk Franklin.**

Golgotha

Markus Kern, drums; Daniel Müller, bass; Martin Notz, kybrd.; Sven Wooster, gtr. 1996—*Merry Go Round* (Pila).

Golgotha is a Christian rock band from Germany, one of very few to receive notice in the United States. *Merry Go Round* displays a mostly hard rock sound that hearkens back to the '80s sounds of **Bloodgood** or **Guardian.** A few songs, such as "New Dawn Rising," have a softer, acoustic touch. All lyrics are in English and reflect overtly Christian themes.

Michael Gonzales

1980—*Fire in My Soul* (Sonrise).

Singer/songwriter Michael Gonzales made one album of light jazz/pop music, produced by **David Diggs,** who also played keyboards and guitar on the record. Most of the album's nine tunes were his own compositions, though one standout cut, "Wait for the Day," was cowritten by Diggs and **Erick Nelson.**

The Gonzalez Family

Personnel list unavailable. 1996—*No Better Way* (Light).

The Gonzalez Family is a seven-member Massachusetts-based family group (six men and a woman) who choose not to reveal their first names. They have recorded several Spanish language albums and produced one English album of Christian R&B songs in 1996. The record received very little notice, but displayed a sound that more closely recalls Stevie Wonder or Michael McDonald-era Doobie Brothers than the Gypsy Kings. While a Latin influence is evident in the percussion, the overall sound of *No Better Way* is timeless pop, funk, and groove. Standout tracks include "I'm Gonna Make It" and "Good Stuff."

Simon Goodall

1997—*Plugged In and Connected* [EP] (ICC); date unknown—*Stay with Me.*

Simon Goodall is a singer/songwriter from the United Kingdom whose voice often draws comparisons to **Cliff Richard.** Goodall's deceptively titled EP was actually completely unplugged acoustic songs, featuring two originals and selected songs by writers like **Paul Field** and **Wes King.** *Stay with Me* moves more solidly into mainstream pop and includes a cover of the **Delirious?** song, "Deeper." Lyrically, Goodall's songs are unambiguous in their affirmation of Christian themes and are often worshipful. In "All I Can Say," he sings, "Father, I lay down my life / In complete surrender to your will / May all my desires be founded in you / That I may bring glory and honour to you."

Brian Goodell

1992—*Simple Love* (Essential).

A singer/songwriter from Oakland, California, Brian Goodell is a son and grandson of ordained ministers who forsook his own plans to be a pastor and left Bible college to pursue a music ministry. He attended a Gospel Music Association convention and wound up with a record contract. Goodell sings keyboard-based songs somewhat in the tradition of **Keith Green,** with a healthy influence of traditional gospel and R&B. His radio hit "House of Love" is not the same song as that made popular by **Amy Grant** and Vince Gill.

Christian radio hits: "House of Love" (# 15 in 1994).

Grant Goodeye

1995—*The Wonder of It All* (Maranatha).

Actor Grant Goodeye has been a TV heartthrob twice, first as the oldest brother on the '70s family drama *Eight Is Enough,* and then again as Maggie's boyfriend on the quirky '90s hit, *Northern Exposure.* A full-time actor, Goodeye's avocation has been writing and singing songs for Christian churches, and as early as the mid '80s he began singing his original compositions in local congregations and sharing his testimony as a Christian at prayer breakfasts. *The Wonder of It All* collects some of his better-loved works, including "A Father's Love," an autobiographical tale about his unusually close relationship with his father.

Thomas Goodlunas and Panacea

Thomas Goodlunas, kybrd., gtr., voc.; et al. 1983—*Take Me Away* (Exit).

Thomas Goodlunas fronted an all-star backing band for a single album of his original compositions. Goodlunas brought a smoky, foghorn-strength voice to the project, with backing from such musicians as **Jimmy A** and **Michael Roe.** Goodlunas also plays piano, guitar, violin, and tympani on various tracks. The overall sound is a mixture of jazz, pop-rock, and folk, not unlike that which characterizes **Jimmy A**'s own first album *(Entertaining Angels).* The opening title track is perhaps the record's high point, a plea for paradise set against a tasteful saxophone (by Michael Butera): "Take me away to a land of shining sun / Where we're at peace with one another."

Tanya Goodman-Sykes

Selected: As Tanya Goodman: 1983—*More Than a Dream* (Word). As Tanya Goodman-Sykes: 1992—*Innocent Eyes* (Benson).

Tanya Goodman grew up as a member of one of southern gospel's premier singing families, The Happy Goodmans (later, just The Goodmans). She sometimes sang on family albums and is reported to have made three solo albums for Canaan/Word in the '80s, though information is available on only one of these. She also recorded a pair of children's albums, one of which won a Grammy award in a general market category. She became a part of the group **Heirloom** and then released *Innocent Eyes* under her married name Tanya Goodman-Sykes. The latter project was produced by her husband, Michael Sykes. Goodman is often compared vocally to **Susan Ashton,** though her career moves have been the opposite of that singer's, from country to adult contemporary rather than vice versa.

More Than a Dream is very much a Christian country album, and *CCM* hailed it as one of the best of the year. Coproduced by **Gary Chapman,** the album varies in style from Emmylou Harris-like Appalachian songs ("Who I Am") to more Linda Ronstadt-inspired country rock. "Love Shines" has a bluegrass feel and exalts the oft-unsung work of God's ministers ("When you save a soul, you don't make the evening news"). "Singin' for You" is a tribute to the artist's father, the legendary Rusty Goodman. As indicated, *Innocent Eyes* tones down the country influences decidedly and presents Goodman-Sykes as a sort of neo-**Kelly Willard,** who guests on two songs. Other guest artists include **Russ Taff** and **4 Him,** as well as Bonnie Keen and **Michael English,** who join Goodman-Sykes to produce a sort of **First Call** sound on "A Little Something." The song "For All of Us" presents a girl who has had an abortion and a homosexual dying of AIDS as examples of persons who need compassion rather than judgment from the Christian church.

Good News

Billy Batstone, bass, voc.; David Diggs, gtr., drums; Yvonne Lewis, voc.; Erick Nelson, kybrd, voc. (–1977) // Bob Carlisle, voc. (+ 1977); Keith Green, voc., kybrd. (+ 1977). 1975—*Good News* (Maranatha); 1977—*Good News 2* (Sonrise).

The early Jesus music group Good News was a band burgeoning with young talent, like some kind of Christian counterpart to Buffalo Springfield. An early version of the group featured **Billy Batstone, Bob Carlisle, David Diggs,** John Hernandez, Yvonne Lewis, and **Erick Nelson.** Batstone, Carlisle, Diggs, and Nelson all went on to play in other bands and to have successful and important solo careers. Hernandez went on to play with Oingo Boingo. Lewis was a former member of **Danny Lee and the Children of Truth.** The 1977 *Good News 2* album, furthermore, would feature a very young **Keith Green** on piano.

Good News is said to have begun as a backing group for Nelson and was initially just a trio featuring his piano and vocals supplemented by the rhythm section of Batstone and Diggs. Then a female vocalist (Lewis) was added, along with a sixteen-year-old Carlisle to give the group a fuller sound. Carlisle left to join **Psalm 150** midway through the recording of Good News' debut album and his voice is only heard sporadically; he is not even pictured on the album cover. The group disbanded after that first album was made, but in 1977 a reunion drew Carlisle back for a full album.

Good News got started when a friend of Diggs put up $3,000 for the band to do a record. Much of the money was spent on string players. Diggs did arrangements for the strings, which were a big part of the album, giving it a sophistication uncommon for many of the low-budget products turned out by Jesus music folk groups. Kurt Lofland played drums on the record. *Cornerstone* declared *Good News* to be "one of the best products to come out of Maranatha Music, . . . a sophisticated blend of acoustic and harder rock elements, producing an excellent overall sound." Nelson remembers that the song "Rock of Ages" was considered controversial because when Lewis sang that Jesus will "rock you in his arms and love you all life long" it sounded to some like she sang "all night long," which seemed weird. He also recalls that the album was slightly edited at the request of Calvary Chapel pastor Chuck Smith who insisted that they remove a sax solo by Tom Kubis because it sounded "too rocky." Jesus music historian David Di Sabatino notes, however, that "the song 'Tear Down the Walls' is an excellent rock and roll classic with Carlisle on lead vocals." The Nelson song "Going Home" would later be re-recorded by Carlisle on his first solo album. Another of Nelson's songs, "Jimmy," stands out lyrically and has been singled out for praise in that regard by **Randy Stonehill:** "Sunken eyes that staring, never see / A hunger rises deep within / But he has not the strength to turn the key." The most noteworthy song on *Good News,* however, is Nelson's "Picking Up the Pieces," a slow but building number reminiscent of Elton John's trademark ballads (e.g., "Don't Let the Sun Go Down on Me"). "Picking Up the Pieces" would become Good News' best-known song due in part to its inclusion on the important compilation album *Maranatha Four* (Maranatha, 1974).

The second Good News album *(Good News 2)* was a studio-only project by a nonexistent band that never really toured or performed together. The record opens with a Diggs/Nelson song ("Wait for the Day") and also features some early Carlisle ("Lord, We Feel Your Presence," "The Catch") and Batstone ("Ride Along Rider," "You Sure Have Been Good to Me") tunes. Batstone's "You Sure Have Been Good to Me" would become fairly well known, being covered by a number of artists including **Karen Lafferty.** Ultimately, the most notable track on *Good News 2,* however, would prove to be "Run to the End of the Highway," a bouncy pop song that introduced the world to the music of Keith Green. The album also includes another Keith and Melody Green composition, "Everybody's Talkin' 'bout Love," along with Diggs' "Singing Our Song" and a left-over Nelson tune, "Beside You."

A completely different band named Good News also released a self-titled album on CBS records in 1970 in the United Kingdom, with a follow-up called *New Life* in 1972. The group consisted of Michael Bacon and Larry Gold, but bears no relationship to the California-based band.

Goodnight Star

Rusty Arnold; Jesse Carrigan; George Kazaklis. 1999—*Goodnight Star* (Plastiq Musiq).

Goodnight Star is a trio of buddies who met at Bible college and decided to create programmed computer music on the same order as **Joy Electric.** Their debut album was produced by Ronnie Martin of that band on the label he founded as a subdivision of Tooth and Nail. The members of Goodnight Star emphasize that, musically, they try to create singable songs that are memorable in their own right—something that big-beat electronic bands like Prodigy tend to ignore. The group belongs, then, at the ultra-pop end of the electronica spectrum, creating Mario Brothers synthesized music that features sugary keyboards and a generous quotient of whistles, pops, and bleeps. Still, the group's sound is described as a tad more somber than **Joy Electric**'s, as "less bubbly" and with "more of a down tempo feel." Goodnight Star is outspoken about its faith, with virtually every song offering uplifting messages or, more often, direct praises to God. Carrigan says, "The band's foremost agenda is to promote God as Healer and Comforter and means to salvation through Jesus Christ." The band has often focused its ministry in ways that support Teen Challenge, an organization devoted to helping youth addicted to drugs and alcohol.

Go rin no sho

1999—*Inner Light* (Troupe).

Go rin no sho is an East Coast Christian rapper who places himself outside the circle of mainstream "Christian rap music" by incorporating vulgar expressions into his songs. He justifies this as a necessary adaptation, employing the "strong language of the streets," but the decision guarantees that his work is marginalized and generally ignored by the usual outlets for contemporary Christian music. Nevertheless, the more liberal *Bandoppler* calls *Inner Light* "an impressive and legitimate release" and singles out "The Game" as an especially strong track "with sassy female vocals and string-laden new jack swing."

Gospel Gangstaz (a.k.a. 2Gz)

Chille' Baby, voc.; Mr. Solo, voc.; Tik Tokk, voc.; D. J. Dove, voc. (–1999). 1994—*Gang Affiliated* (Myx); 1995—*Do or Die* (Holy Terra); 1999—*I Can See Clearly Now* (B-Rite); 2000—*All Mixed Up* (KMG).

Undoubtedly the most authentic-sounding of the West Coast Christian rap groups, the Gospel Gangstaz were probably the first Christian group to incorporate what are called gangster stylings into their hip-hop music. They have earned the praise of such general market artists as Coolio, Snoop Doggy Dogg, Salt 'n Pepa, and **Run-D.M.C.** The story of the group's origins reads like the script for a Hollywood film. Mr. Solo and Chille' Baby grew up in South Central Los Angeles, where they were members of the Crips street gang; Tik Tokk was a member of their arch-rival gang, the Bloods. All three had experienced the stereotypical abuses of ghetto life—poverty, absentee parenting, drug abuse, violence—and all three were involved in drug trafficking, theft, and other criminal activities. Mr. Solo was converted to Christ after being "blown away with a shotgun blast" in the midst of a streetfight. He miraculously survived his injuries, faced his mortality, and went to church with his mother. Through his influence, childhood friend and fellow gang member Chille' Babe was also won for the Lord. The two formed a Christian rap trio called U.T.A. (Under the Anointing) with Tik Tokk, who had been converted from a life of crime with his former gang, and they released one album with producer D. J. Dove (also of **SFC**), who then joined the trio to form Gospel Gangstaz (or Gangstas, as their name was spelled in the early years). The group made two albums that brought them a good deal of national attention. They also contributed two songs to the soundtrack of the John Singleton film *Higher Learning*. About this time, however, Tik Tokk's past caught up with him and he was sentenced to serve almost four years in a maximum security penitentiary for crimes committed before his conversion. "I'd been locked up before, but this time was different" he related. "I went this time as a saved individual, knowing the peace and the power of God." He maintains that he viewed his sentence as a "forced retreat" and spent the time in "prison ministry," sharing the Scriptures with other inmates and focusing on his own relationship with God. After his release, the group reconvened (without Dove) and recorded their most highly acclaimed album, *I Can See Clearly Now*. Again, the group was the focus of nationwide attention, including an appearance on *The Tonight Show* with **Kirk Franklin.** The fourth record listed above, *All Mixed Up,* is a compilation of mostly remixed songs from the first two albums; it was released without the group's authorization or endorsement.

Gang Affiliated no doubt has a certain novelty appeal (*Christian* gangsta rap?) but is impressive for its no-holds barred presentation of the gospel to ghetto audiences, for instance by depicting Jesus as a victim of gang violence. "We can't sugarcoat stuff," Dove said of the album's uncompromising message. "People need to know what Jesus went through for us, what he did willingly because he loves us." Tracks like "Tears of a Black Man" and "Y Cain't Da Homiez Hear Me?" not only proclaim Christ as the fulfillment of every person's need but also offer a valid (i.e., nonparty line) view of race relations from an inner city perspective. *True Tunes* warned that Young Republicans might be put off by the album's political (or sociological) stance, and in general it is as scripturally sound as such a warning implies. But most of the controversy surrounding *Gang Affiliated* stemmed from another matter. Many Christian music retailers refused to carry the album due to the group's abundant use of gang slang—particularly the word *nigga*— which was judged to be profanity. *Do or Die* exceeds the debut album in musical quality, yielding an especially impressive remix of "Y Cain't Da Homiez Hear Me?" But it was on *I Can See Clearly Now* that the Gangstaz would develop a mature,

first-rate sound equal in quality to any product by West Coast rap artists in the general market. The opening "Amazing Grace" is less a cover of the traditional hymn than it is a rapped reflection on it: "Amazing grace, to me it's the sweet sound / To catch a wretch like me, so let the beat pound / I once was lost to the cross, but now I'm found / I once was blind, but now I see." The title track which follows is not the Johnny Nash song, but a rapped testimony flowing out of the just quoted line of the "hymn." The song "Live It Up" counters the notion that Christianity takes the fun out of life. "I'll Be Good" is a rollicking head-bopping number with **Kirk Franklin**'s Nu Nation on board. "Whatcha' Gonna Do" features female rapper Alisha Tyler. "Let Us Pray" offers another instance of the group's simultaneously spiritually and socially conscious lyrics: "Ain't nothin' proper 'bout seein' my homies die / That's why I keep my faith and my head up / Hopin' one day we gone finally get fed up / God, I stand in the gap for the ghetto, give us this day / As we bow down our heads, repent, and pray."

The Gospel Gangstaz have toured California's correctional facilities and devote themselves especially to reaching juvenile offenders and gang members through their ministry. "By the grace of God," Tik Tokk told *Campus Life* magazine, "I'm now able to love. I'm able to feel when others hurt. I'm able to cry and show real emotion." Solo adds, "I gotta make the music for the homies. I understand their pain. I believe in bringing the church to the people, not just bringing the people to the church."

Gospel Seed

Gary Luttrell, gtr., voc.; Michael Moore, autoharp, voc. 1977—*Growing* (Myrrh).

Gospel Seed formed as a folk duo in 1974 and played the Christian coffeehouse circuit that had grown up during the Jesus movement. They also gave a nod to televangelism, appearing on both *The 700 Club* and *The PTL Club*. The group eagerly describes their music as a ministry: "The songs we write and sing tell a message of what Jesus Christ can do in a life." On *Growing,* the folk pop songs are orchestrated to the hilt with string accompaniments that led *Jesus Music* almost to dismiss it as "schmaltzy." The opening track, "The Singer's Song," is thematically very similar to **Larry Norman**'s "The Tune": a metaphorical account of a song that participates in the creation, fall, and redemption of humanity. "Top 10" was an ignorant attack on secular rock stars and their songs, most of which the artists clearly did not understand (e.g., the Rolling Stones' "Mother's Little Helper" is an antidrug song, not the pro-drug anthem they take it to be; *Jesus Christ Superstar* offers a *sympathetic* non-Christian perspective on Jesus, not one that mocks him, as they indicate; the line "Jeremiah was a bullfrog" has nothing to do with the biblical prophet who happened to bear that name, as they appear to assume; the Bible does not provide answers to the questions that **Bob Dylan** says are "blowing in the wind," as they claim, but agrees with Dylan that the answers are beyond human knowing; etc.).

Christian radio hits: "Top 10" (# 17 in 1978).

The Gotee Brothers

Todd Collins; Joey Elwood; Toby McKeehan. 1996—*ERACE* (Gotee).

In 1992 **Toby McKeehan** of **DC Talk** formed The Gotee Brothers with Collins and Elwood as a production company, with the original intention of launching a single act. A year later the trio founded Gotee Records and decided to record an album themselves. The result was a concept piece addressing the sin of racism (*ERACE* is an acronym for Eliminating Racism And Creating Equality). Musically, the album has the soulful feel of R&B rap groups like Arrested Development. In some respects it does not come off as the product of one cohesive group but does seem like a compilation album, with guest appearances by **Grits,** Lisa Kimmey (of **Out of Eden**), Mark Mohr (of **Christafari**), Kevin Smith (of **DC Talk**), and Mark Stuart (of **Audio Adrenaline**). Lyrically, the record often addresses the ills of racism from the autobiographical perspectives of Southerners struggling with their own roots and backgrounds. It includes a reggae version of the song "Why Can't We Be Friends," which was a Top 10 hit for the general market band War in 1975. *CCM* especially praised "New South (The Gotee Idyll)" as a "terminally grooveful" song, like "what Santana might have sounded like had they sprung from the Delta." Elsewhere, "Celia (Queen of the Senseless World)" exploits rap's potential for storytelling, and on "Wages of Sin," McKeehan reflects on his plight as a Caucasian involved with rap.

Christian radio hits: "New South (The Gotee Idyll)" (# 25 in 1996).

Dove Awards: 1997 Best Rap Hip Hop Album (*ERACE*).

Steve Grace

1986—*Young Australian Man* (independent); 1990—*Children of the Western World* (Triune).

www.stevegrace.com

Steve Grace was an Australian singer/songwriter who made a brief international impact on contemporary Christian music when his *Children of the Western World* album was picked up for release in the United States on Reunion Records. Grace was brought up at a Wycliffe Bible Translators mission station in New Guinea. He became involved with the Australian branch of Youth With a Mission and was encouraged in his musical career by John Smith, founder of the God's Squad motorcycle club. Grace sang his raspy blues and pop songs in Australian pubs as often as he did in churches, and in the late '80s he was reputed to be the country's best-known Christian artist. *Children of the Western World* was produced by Beeb Birtles of Little River Band and includes a bluesy meditation on "The Prodigal Son" in addition to punchy pop songs ("Big Dreams") and dreamy ballads ("Lessons of the Heart," "Song for Kerrie"). Grace told *CCM* in 1990, "I used to write some really deep, meaningful songs until I found that people responded to the really simple ones I thought were a bit corny. I began to see the effect a simple song could have on the right audience, very much in line with the parables Jesus told."

Ralph Graham and Day III

Ralph Graham, gtr., voc.; et al. 1996—*No Alternative* (Salt, Inc.).

Retro-rocker Ralph Graham belts out '80s-style arena anthems in a fashion that has caused some to designate him "the Christian Eddie Money." The songs that fill *No Alternative* are invariably melodic but powerful, with lyrics extolling the value of a personal relationship with Jesus Christ. "Cry of the Children" attracted some notice for its impassioned appeal for marital reconciliation: "Can somebody tell me what would happen if parents would fall to their knees? / And learn how to love, and just accept one another / Instead of demanding their right to be free?"

Lou Gramm

1987—*Ready or Not* (Atlantic); 1989—*Long Hard Look*.

www.foreigneronline.com

Lou Gramm (b. 1950) fronts the highly successful general market band Foreigner, of which he was a founding member in 1976. Gramm embraced Christianity wholeheartedly sometime in 1994 and discussed his spiritual life openly with *HM* editor Doug Van Pelt in the July/August 1996 issue of that magazine. Gramm has not made new recordings since this transformation; the solo albums listed above were recorded during a hiatus from Foreigner and do not necessarily reflect his new Christian orientation. Gramm does not, however, describe his spiritual awakening as a conversion; rather, he maintains that he had always acknowledged God's presence in his life, but not with the appropriate devotion. He describes the late '80s and early '90s as a time of "spiritual shopping."

Before Foreigner, Gramm sang in a group called Black Sheep, who performed cover versions of songs by bands like Free and Bad Company. He was invited to be lead singer in the group that would define his career by guitarist Mick Jones and keyboardist Ian McDonald (formerly of King Crimson). The group's debut album went quadruple platinum, with its sophomore effort doing even better. The band racked up ten Top 40 hits in five years, including such sexually charged lust anthems as "Feels Like the First Time" (# 4 in 1977), "Cold As Ice" (# 6 in 1977), "Hot Blooded" (# 3 in 1978), and "Urgent" (# 4 in 1981). Critics groused about the posturing, but admitted the group had classic rock competence and noted that certain songs ("Long Way from Home," "Double Vision") engaged the heart and head instead of just the libido. The potential evident in the latter style came suddenly to the fore on the band's biggest hit to date, "Waiting for a Girl Like You" (# 2 for 10 weeks in 1981). This tender love song, cowritten by Gramm and Jones, propelled the album *Foreigner 4* to almost unprecedented sales of over six million copies. The idea of a love ballad being performed by a hard rock group was still something of a novelty in 1981, and the term "power ballad" was coined to describe the phenomenon. To this day, "Waiting for a Girl Like You" probably remains the second best-known and most-loved example of the genre. The indisputable number one example, of course, would follow three years later when Foreigner's "I Want to Know What Love Is" soared to the top of the charts. For that song (written by Jones), the New Jersey Mass Choir was invited to accompany Gramm on the chorus. When the latter group gathered in the studio for the recording, the members all held hands in a circle and prayed the Lord's Prayer together before singing. According to Gramm, he and his bandmates were all dumbstruck by this simple act, realizing that the choir was singing the song with a conviction and an investment that the members of Foreigner themselves had not been prepared to offer. "We were just literally moved to tears that their performance was directed to our Lord," he told *HM.* "Anyone could feel that the song goes way beyond a love ballad." Even *Rolling Stone* would describe the single as "a gospel song," and Gramm remained profoundly moved by his experience of recording it.

Gramm also charted four hits as a solo artist, including the Top 10 smashes "Midnight Blue" (# 5 in 1987) and "Just between You and Me" (# 6 in 1989; *not* the same as the **DC Talk** song). Then in the early '90s he was invited by friends to attend a nondenominational church in his hometown of Rochester, New York. He spent some time there, studying the Scriptures and "really got into the book of Revelation." Eventually, he says, "I made the commitment and accepted Jesus as my Lord and my Savior instead of as just a part-time, get-me-out-of-trouble God." He began singing regularly in his home church, but did not feel any call to leave Foreigner or to pursue a career in the contemporary Christian music scene. He explains that his bandmates are "more curious than anything when they see me walking around with my Bible and devotionals and things like that, but they are certainly not disrespectful. . . . we're a secular band, but it's not like the guys I

play with are a bunch of crude heathens. We're all family men with morals and beliefs of our own."

Grammatrain

Dalton Roraback, bass; Paul Roraback, drums; Pete Stewart, gtr., voc. 1995—*Grammatrain* (independent); *Lonely House* (ForeFront); 1997—*Flying;* 2000—*Live 120798.*

Grammatrain was Christian music's premier example of "the Seattle sound," emerging out of that city around the same time as **MxPx,** but without the latter's Green Day neo-punk appeal. Grammatrain had drunk from the same well as Nirvana, Pearl Jam, Soundgarden, and Alice in Chains; they had the same general sound as all those groups but seemed no more derivative than any one of them would have been with reference to the others. They were not, in other words, just copying what was hot, à la Stone Temple Pilots. The group also showed considerable growth between its two major projects, and seemed to be a Christian band with a shot at finding respect in the general market. It ended too soon, but **Pete Stewart** did subsequently embark on a solo career and produce an impressive debut album.

The band had its origins in a Seattle Bible study group hosted by Michael Bloodgood, leader of the Christian band **Bloodgood,** in which Paul Roraback had been a member. The latter testifies that he continued to have a powerful drug addiction for three years after becoming a Christian, a period that he describes as "the loneliest time in my life": "The Christians wouldn't deal with me because I was still doing drugs. My stoner friends didn't want anything to do with me because I had become a Christian." The ambiguity and struggle reflected in such an experience were evident in Grammatrain's orientation and perspective on faith. They did not sing "happy in Jesus songs," but wrote and performed hard music for hard times. *Lonely House* became best known for songs like "Believe," an ironically titled song about doubt. "Jerky Love Song" is a somewhat moshable tune with traces of The Ramones that would become one of the group's most popular concert numbers. The song to attract the most attention, however, was "Execution," a rather grisly account of an abortion from the perspective of the fetus: "Suck me down your hose / Pieces of my fingers and toes / Use me to brew your rat stew / Dissolve my voice / For your woman's choice."

Critics and fans were surprised by *Flying,* which seized on new influences (the Beatles, R.E.M., Led Zeppelin, Pink Floyd), mixing these in with what remained hard, driving rock. The title song was the most disparate, a psychedelic fairy tale reminiscent of something from *Magical Mystery Tour.* The first single, "Jonah," however, retains the raw 'n' dirty grunge sound, presenting a Gen-X version of the titular character's desperate prayer (cf. Jonah 2). "Pain" is one of the group's trademark struggle songs: "I wish that I could say I am a perfect man / I wish sometimes that I would not be who I am / One day I decided I would think on this / Not knowing if faith and pain could coexist." The song "Peace" is a bit more mellow, featuring friendlier lyrics and jangly guitars; it got airplay on some stations that wouldn't have played the majority of Grammatrain's material. The band's farewell live album features favorites from the first two projects, plus a cover of **Larry Norman**'s "Six O'Clock News."

For trivia buffs: The group's name is a slurring of Gramma's Train and owes to a reference made by the Roraback's grandmother. She lived in a house where a train passed nearby and was fond of saying she was waiting for her train to come to take her to the better life.

Amy Grant

1977—Amy Grant (Myrrh); 1979—My Father's Eyes; 1980—Never Alone; 1981—In Concert; In Concert 2; 1982—Age to Age; 1983—A Christmas Album; 1984—Straight Ahead; 1985—Unguarded; 1986—The Collection; 1988—Lead Me On (A&M); 1991—Heart in Motion; 1992—Home for Christmas; 1993—Songs From the Loft [by Amy Grant and Other Various Artists]; 1994—House of Love; 1997—Behind the Eyes; 1999—A Christmas to Remember.

www.amygrant.com

Amy Grant (b. 1960) is the single most successful and popular artist in Christian music and, to date, is the only artist associated with the Christian music scene to become a major star in the general market. She is in that sense the reverse of **Bob Dylan**. Like that artist, she was one of the most highly respected figures in her field when she crossed over to the opposite camp and, as with Dylan, the move was regarded as a treasonous defection by narrow-minded critics and fans. Both Grant and Dylan also have this in common: neither intended or interpreted their participation in a wider sphere of culture as a "crossover," for neither acknowledged the legitimacy of defining "Christian music" as a distinct entity in the first place. In this regard—and in many others—Grant has been light years ahead of the so-called Christian music industry and subculture theologically, evincing a more mature understanding of music, industry, and culture than most of those around her. She has won five Grammy awards, all in the '80s and all in the category of "Best Gospel Performance." Musically, Grant has produced numerous pleasant but not particularly groundbreaking products. Twice, however, she has surprised with albums *(Lead Me On, Behind the Eyes)* that deserve to be called masterpieces—not only in Christian music but in the world of contemporary music in general.

Grant was born in Augusta, Georgia, but moved to Nashville as a child where she grew up in an affluent Christian home (her father is a radiologist; her grandparents were the owners of Burton Farms, a local landmark; her great-grandfather founded Life and Casualty Health Insurance). In the seventh grade, she was baptized in her home congregation, a conservative branch of the Church of Christ that forbade dancing and the use of musical instruments in worship. She experienced an awakening of faith in high school when invited to a Bible study at the Belmont Church, an inner city church that catered to what she calls "a remnant hippie group" of leftovers from the Jesus movement. There, she witnessed what was for her an unprecedented intimacy with God and came to experience God's presence in her own life in a new and vibrant way. At the age of fifteen, she began writing songs. A tape she made as a present for her parents fell into the hands of **Chris Christian** at his Home Sweet Home studio where she worked part time (sweeping floors), and she was offered a contract with Word Records when she was fifteen years old and still a junior in high school. Her first album came out a year later and sold a phenomenal 50,000 copies in its first year of release. As detailed in an unauthorized biography by Bob Millard (*Amy Grant: A Biography,* 1986), Grant's wealthy father was able to assist her in ways that most struggling Christian artists could never afford (e.g., hiring independent promotion for her first album). The luxury of not having to worry about making a living also allowed her to work at her music full time when she chose to do so. Still, according to Millard, there was some confusion in the young artist's mind when she was told that she could do her first concert for $300. She complained, "I only have $500 and I need it!"—not realizing that they would pay *her* instead of the other way around. Such naivete would soon vanish. For most of her career, Grant has been managed by her brother-in-law Dan Harrell and by her former youth pastor, Mike Blanton. Almost from the start, Harrell (backed financially by Grant's father) had a plan for her success: limit her concert appearances to increase demand, keep her out of fundamentalist churches, and search for the right pop material to put her on the mainstream charts. Her eventual impact on the world of contemporary Christian music might be indicated in a poll of thirty Christian music critics taken by *CCM* magazine in 1998. Those critics chose Grant's *Lead Me On* as the Number One Christian music album of all time. They also chose *Age to Age* as Number Three and picked five other Grant albums—*My Father's Eyes, A Christmas Album, Unguarded, Heart in Motion, Behind the Eyes*—among the Top 100. (A broader based, more up-to-date survey in 2000 kept *Lead Me On* at Number One, while kicking *Age to Age* down to a more reasonable Number Ninety-two; both lists underplayed the importance of *Behind the Eyes* and completely ignored Grant's third-best product, *Straight Ahead*).

As fame took an increasing hold on her life, Grant had to delay her studies, first at Furman University, then as an English major at Vanderbilt—where she remained twenty hours short of a degree in the year 2000 (but still planned to finish someday). During her student years, she complained that boys at Vanderbilt wouldn't date her because they thought of her as "a female Billy Graham." She hated the stereotype, stating publicly, "Hey, I can flirt. I can date. I will kiss." Her social life was redeemed somewhat as she toured intermittently with singer/songwriter **Gary Chapman;** the two did flirt—and fight—with some dating and kissing thrown in, for about three years. It was an off-and-on relationship, supposedly forbidden by her management team. Still, in 1982, Grant and Chapman married and for a time were Christian music's "cutest couple," repeatedly featured in profiles dealing with home and family life. But all was not well in their home, and stories of marital discord, of conflicting careers, of miscommunication, and of Chapman's struggles with substance abuse began to surface. For many more years, Chapman and Grant continued to be presented as the ideal Christian couple in a different sense: they were forthright about their marital troubles, about the value of marriage counseling, and about the need to work hard at maintaining a relationship. Few have ever worked harder than they did—or trusted more deeply in the sustaining power of God—yet in 1999 the marriage ended in divorce amidst widespread rumors that Grant had already become involved with the recently divorced country western singer Vince Gill, her neighbor and golf partner, with whom she had also sung duets. Grant later confirmed these rumors (*emotionally* involved, not sexually) and married Gill a few months after the divorce from Chapman was final. Tidbits of gossip fed scandal mongers and gave Grant more than a taste of another aspect of celebrity, becoming fodder for the tabloids. She handled it all with characteristic poise: "Divorce is not about good and bad people; it's about good and bad combinations." Her former husband was less tactful: "I don't think it's about either one. I believe it's about good and bad choices." Again, Grant would emphasize the long-term dysfunctions that had prevented their marriage from ever being what she thought it should be: "I tried at every turn to take the high road, and yet, my personal life kept just spiraling downward. . . . God provided marriage so that people could enjoy each other to the fullest. If you have two people who are not thriving healthily in a situation, I say remove the marriage." Chapman publicly blamed the divorce on Grant's relationship with Gill and said, "We had *one* irreconcilable difference: I wanted her to stay and she wanted to leave."

Grant's first set of albums for Myrrh were all produced by **Brown Bannister,** who had been the leader of her high school youth fellowship and had also worked at Home Sweet Home and established her as the definitive exemplar of typical Christian music: pop songs in the classic style of artists like Carole King, but with overt lyrics that communicated an obvious, specifically Christian message. The success of Grant's self-titled debut was fueled by the song "Mountain Top," a major Christian radio hit (though no charts were kept at that time). Eventually, the songs "Old Man's Rubble," "Beautiful Music," and "What a Difference You've Made in My Life" (the Archie Jordan song that was also a mainstream country hit for Ronnie Milsap) also gained popularity. This first album was originally issued with what came to be known as "the ugly cover"—a horrendous photo of Grant that was later withdrawn in favor of a more attractive picture. The second record features "My Father's Eyes," written by Chapman as a prayer to see the world and other people the way that God sees them—with compassion and wisdom. Her third project, *Never Alone,* would be chosen by *CCM* as one of the Top 10 Albums of 1980. Its best song is probably "Too Late," written by Grant with Bannister and **Chris Christian.** The artist also began to emerge as a songwriter on this project with "If I Have to Die." Around this time Grant recorded the duet "Nobody Loves Me Like You" with **DeGarmo and Key** and toured with that band, giving her a tougher image and helping her to transition from cute teen star to serious adult singer.

It was *Age to Age* that came to be regarded as Grant's first truly excellent album, a major step forward that was hailed early on as "a stunning collection of direct, mature, and inspiring material, delivered with emotion and skill" *(CCM).* The worshipful songs "Sing Your Praise to the Lord" (written by **Rich Mullins**) and "El Shaddai" (written by **Michael Card** and John Thompson) are now rightly regarded as Christian classics, and Grant's definitive renditions of the songs served to jump-start the careers of their composers—a feat she had already performed for Chapman and would soon also accomplish for **Michael W. Smith.** In 1998, Grant's version of "El Shaddai" was chosen in a *CCM* poll of thirty critics as the second-best "contemporary Christian song of all time" (behind Smith's "Friends"); in 2001, her version of the song was included on a list of "the 365 most significant songs of the twentieth-century" prepared by the Recording Industry Association of America (it was 326, right behind Elton John's "Candle in the Wind"). Also on *Age to Age,* the song "I Have Decided" reveals a rock edge that previews Grant's later *Unguarded* material. The best song on the album, however, is probably the simple ballad, "I Love a Lonely Day" (written by Chapman and Smith), which reveals how one who is seldom alone can covet the "down time" that others seek to avoid. *Age to Age* became the first album classed as Christian music to go "platinum"—sell a million copies—and by so doing it changed the shape of the Christian music industry overnight. Once those kinds of numbers (and dollars) were involved, a lot of people grew interested in the phenomenon who had never taken note of it before. On a more personal level, it changed Grant's life. Suddenly, she was doing *The Tonight Show* instead of *The 700 Club*—she was a genuine celebrity in the real world, as opposed to being just a big fish in a little pond.

Straight Ahead was even better than *Age to Age,* a stellar pop album completely free of the occasional embarrassments ("Giggle," "Grape, Grape Joy," "Fat Baby") that had marred previous projects. The record opens with the bombastic "Where Do You Hide Your Heart?" signaling immediately that Grant had thrown aside any MOR mantle that might have been cast upon her and turned into a full-throated singer of rock and roll. Carolyn Amedea would say in her *CCM* review of *Straight Ahead* that Grant "cuts like a sabre where she once would have slid, strikes like a cobra where she once would have drawled, and growls like a wildcat where she once would have squealed." Even the album's low points—the up-tempo "Angels" and bopping "Tomorrow" (which sounds very much like it should be a theme song for some TV game show)—are not very low; their weakness derives only from an excessive radio-friendly feel that would render them annoying over time. In a different vein is the understated beauty of **Rich Mullins'** "Doubly Good to You" (a simple, "count your blessings" song). And then there are the masterpieces, four of the best songs Grant has ever sung: 1) the title track, "Straight Ahead" (written by Grant with Chapman and Smith), applies a slow-burn impassioned vocal to an appropriately straightforward song about pressing on toward spiritual goals; 2) "It's Not a Song" (by Chapman and Robbie Buchanan) features Grant's voice at its gut-wrenching best, wringing every ounce of emotion out of the lyric "It's not a song till it touches your heart/ It's not a song till it tears you apart"; 3) "The Now and the Not Yet" (written by **Pam Mark Hall**) provides theologically profound reflection on both the anticipation of glory and the experience of its delay; 4) "Thy Word" (by Grant and Smith) is a hymn based on Psalm 119:105 that seems destined to be Grant's legacy, a song that will still be in hymnals decades or centuries after she is gone, though one cannot imagine it ever being sung better than it is right here.

Unguarded displays an unexpected turn that would establish Grant briefly as Christian music's first—and so far, only—sex star. Musically, the album was another solid pop outing filled with songs that were every bit as good (and indeed similar in style) to those of Madonna, mainstream's reigning queen of soft rock at the time. *CCM* would even offer a strained comparison to Tina Turner on the basis of such R&B rockers as "Fight" and "Wise Up." But the album's first three tracks ("Love of Another Kind," "Find a Way," "Everywhere I Go") are its most remarkable. "Find a Way" was so good that it actually found its way by popular demand onto mainstream radio stations, charting against all odds at Number Twenty-nine on *Billboard* magazine's Hot 100 and reaching Number Nine on the

adult contemporary chart. This was the first official invasion of the secular Top 40 from the parallel universe of Christian music. Songs about Jesus (e.g., the **Edwin Hawkins Singers'** "O Happy Day" or Ocean's "Put Your Hand in the Hand") had charted before, but that was before the development of Christian music as an identifiable entity with its own radio stations, record companies, and award shows. "Find a Way" (written by Grant and Smith, and featuring the lyric, "If God His Son not sparing came to rescue you / Is there any circumstance that He cannot see you through?") became the first Christian song by a Christian artist recorded on a Christian label (Myrrh) to gain exposure in the general market. A follow-up single, "Stay for Awhile," went to Number Nineteen on *Billboard*'s adult contemporary chart, and then Grant sang a duet with Peter Cetera on the secular song, "The Next Time I Fall in Love (It Will Be With You)," which went all the way to Number One. This was unbelievable. Conventional wisdom held that Christian singers would be ostracized from secular radio. That was, after all, the whole reason for the existence of contemporary Christian music as a genre and as an industry. Now, the premier Christian singer in America had the Number One song in the country, and had also scored a Top 40 hit with an explicitly Christian song. If such things were possible, why did there have to be separate Christian radio stations or charts or record companies? Perhaps the paranoia implicit in those questions had something to do with what happened next.

Grant was now even more of a celebrity than before, featured prominently in the media and appearing in *Life* and *Rolling Stone.* While the secular media focused on her talent and on her convictions, the Christian music industry seemed to become obsessed with only one thing: her image. Grant's stage show for *Unguarded* seemed consciously designed as a tamer version of what Madonna provided. Grant danced joyously (some would say provocatively) on stage, flirting with her husband as he played guitar. She showed up at the Grammy awards show barefoot, wearing the trademark (some would say sexy) leopard-skin print jacket that she also modeled in her album's cover photo. That cover (shot in four different versions) and other publicity photos presented Grant in chaste but highly attractive poses that seemed designed to capitalize on her physical appearance and innate sex appeal. Of course, many other Christian artists (male and female) did this as well (how many physically *unattractive* stars are there in Christian music?), but Grant broke the unwritten rules by *acknowledging* that she did so. She maintained that she saw no contradiction between being Christian and being sexy and claimed that she liked being both. Even the mainstream press was somewhat taken aback by this. Richard Harrington wrote in *The Washington Post* that Grant "is projecting a confusingly sexual image for an avowedly spiritual singer." Actually, Christianity teaches no dichotomy between what is sexual and spiritual, indeed insists that there are few things more spiritual than sexuality. But for some reason, contemporary Christian music gained its strongest appeal—at least throughout the '80s—among those branches of American Christianity most strongly influenced by Puritanism and fundamentalism—two movements that had been affected (ironically) by the anti-Christian teachings of gnosticism (a philosophical position that denigrates the physical world and the human body as evil rather than treasuring them as blessed creations of God).

Grant was no gnostic. As early as 1978, she had gotten in some trouble at a Florida concert when she looked out over a crowd of teens in beach attire and told them they all looked so good it made her feel "horny." Now, she managed simultaneously to support traditional Christian values and mores while also shocking and offending Christian fans with her frank and unembarrassed way of articulating them. In one interview, for example, she defended her decision to remain a virgin until marriage by saying, "I wouldn't want to compare Gary's moans with some other guy's." Then in June of 1985 Grant gave a frank and perceptive interview to *Rolling Stone* magazine in a feature that remains perhaps the single best treatment of a Christian artist ever to appear in a secular publication. She talked openly about Christianity, sexuality, and celebrity, telling the reporter, for instance, that she was comfortable with her body and enjoyed sunbathing nude in private locations. She also said "My hormones are just as on-key as any other twenty-four year old's. . . . I feel that a Christian woman in the '80s is very sexual." For the first time in history, *Rolling Stone* readers got a glimpse of a Christian artist who appeared to be a normal, healthy human being, imbued with love for God and the world—as opposed to the usual stereotypical image of some prudish misfit who had turned to religion as a way of dealing with their psychological dysfunctions. The magazine praised her as "hardly your stereotypical goody goody Christian singer" and urged its readers to transcend their prejudices and give Grant and her music a chance. Unfortunately, a backlash from within the Christian music subculture immediately swept away whatever good had been accomplished. When the *Rolling Stone* feature appeared, Christians who apparently had not read their Bibles enough to recognize a scripturally sound and theologically mature attitude toward sexuality screamed and hollered, prompting occasional boycotts of Grant's products and pressure from retailers for a retraction. Harrell (Grant's manager) claimed that the article had been edited in such a way as to make it "inflammatory" (which it certainly wasn't). Grant admitted that she had been naive and cavalier with her comments and that she had not realized how they would look in print. One hopes she was more sincere in the original statements than in the subsequent, politically necessary backpedaling.

In any case, those who doubted Grant's theological maturity would soon have to reconsider when, in 1988, she issued by far the best album she had ever made, *Lead Me On.* Notably, the record was also her first for a secular record company (A&M, though Myrrh would continue to distribute all of her records to specifically Christian outlets) and the first to demonstrate a breadth of vision beyond concern with matters that seem to be specifically religious. Grant later said that the content of her records for Word (Myrrh) was in some respects imposed upon her. "When I was fifteen and started writing songs I wrote about the whole spectrum of my life experience," she said in 1988. "When I signed a deal with a Christian record company, they knew that I wrote all kinds of songs, but they asked me to record only my gospel songs." Thus it was that Grant, who had become the paradigm for what is now called the propaganda approach to Christian music, was also to become the chief deconstructor of that paradigm in favor of a new "conversation model." She came to view the content of an album the way she might view a conversation with friends: they would not only talk about faith, but about all sorts of different topics, though she would feel free to allude to her faith and to state how it affects her perspective if and when that seemed appropriate. Furthermore, Grant would now maintain that, as a Christian, *everything* she said reflected her relationship with Jesus, since that relationship was "the defining reality and pulse" of her life as opposed to some compartmentalized orientation that affected only her ideas about religion. Thus, Grant's decision to sign with a secular label (A&M) and to broaden her range of topics was motivated primarily by a determination for her art to be a sincere and faithful representation of who she was. It was not primarily motivated by some simplistic evangelistic ploy (appeal to the unsaved and then hit 'em with the gospel when their guard is down). Nor was it a sell-out, motivated by a desire to sell more records and concert tickets—no more than **Bob Dylan**'s sincere desire to sing songs about his faith in Jesus when that was what most animated him could be interpreted as a sell-out to gain a Christian audience. In both cases (Dylan and Grant) the decision to be more true to one's self initially cost the artist more supporters than it gained. *Rolling Stone* has been perceptive in their recognition of this, noting in 1992 that Grant's "Myrrh albums are of a piece with her A&M releases—on both the Christian and the secular albums her songs make their point so subversively you don't always realize that her spiritual orientation informs every lyric."

Lead Me On became the first officially Christian album ever to ship gold, but it did not ultimately sell particularly well for an Amy Grant record. It remains, however, one of those albums that left critics pleasantly dumbfounded. Not even Grant's admirers had known she had this in her. The singing throughout was as empathetic and as impassioned as on her best work (the four songs from *Straight Ahead* mentioned above), but what was most striking now were the songs themselves, songs with poetic lyrics that rely on imagery, assume ambiguity, and trust in universal human experience to fill in the many blanks. The album also reveals a dark edge that had not been seen before. Grant had suffered, and it showed: public marital problems and a miscarriage, followed by a difficult pregnancy (early labor at six-and-a-half months) had taken their toll, and the carefree sweetheart of the early recordings was gone. Still, every song on *Lead Me On* is deeply spiritual. The opening track "1974" describes an experience of youth (probably her spiritual awakening): "Not a word / No one had to say that we had changed / Nothing else we lived through / Would ever be the same." But then the compelling song "Faithless Love" offers Grant's fans their first taste of a newfound brutal honesty that would surface again: "At times the woman deep inside me / Wanders far from home / And in my mind I live a life / That chills me to the bone." What are these fantasies that frighten her? Surely not *sexual* fantasies, her being a Christian and all! She gets a little more specific: "Who is the stranger my longing seeks? / I don't know / But it scares me through and through / Cause I've got a man at home who needs me to be true." This theme of temptation is also addressed in the chilling "Shadows," cowritten with Don and Karen Peris of **The Innocence Mission.** The album also picks up the theme of human suffering, questioning when and how it will be resolved ("Wait for the Healing," and "Lead Me On," which offers vivid portraits of people enduring slavery or persecution). Grant also takes a major step toward mainstream pop music by including two songs written by general market composers: "If These Walls Could Speak," by Jimmy Webb, and "What about the Love" cowritten by Janis Ian (the latter song, incidentally, holds the distinction of being the first—and, so far, the only—song written by an openly gay person to become the Number One Christian Radio Hit in America). The album concludes with "All Right," a minor-key, gospel ballad that offers hope and reassurance without trite resolution. As indicated above, *Lead Me On* has been repeatedly chosen by music critics as the best Christian album of all time. In a letter to that magazine following one such listing, a fan expressed an even greater tribute: "I would love for Amy to make another *Lead Me On* but I hope, for her sake, that she never has to."

Those who loved *Lead Me On* may have been disappointed by Grant's next two albums. Casting aside the seriousness, she made a pair of party records that basically celebrate the joy of living, with peppy, fun songs like those that kids used to listen to down at the beach on their transistor radios. *Heart in Motion*

was the blockbuster, ultimately selling close to six million copies and briefly making Grant a bigger star than Madonna had ever been. "Baby, Baby" (which she says she wrote as a literal ode to her six-week old daughter) was the first song to hit big and for the second time Grant had the Number One song in the nation. "Every Heartbeat" (written with **Wayne Kirkpatrick** and **Charlie Peacock**) soared to Number Two. "That's What Love Is For" (# 7), "Good For Me" (# 8), and "I Will Remember You" (# 20) all followed. Only the latter song has the poetic quality and heart-wrenching pathos that Grant displayed on *Lead Me On,* but considered on its own terms, *Heart in Motion* was for Amy Grant what *An Innocent Man* was for Billy Joel—not the artist at her/his most profound, but a remarkable collection of endearing fun songs. One might have thought that Christians would be delighted to have the secular airwaves suddenly filled with songs exalting love, understanding, and faithfulness, or to have a person known to be a Christian and articulate about her faith suddenly become a role model to millions of young people. No. Numerous Christians were not at all delighted at this but, rather, passed quick judgment on Grant, accusing her of abandoning or at least compromising her faith. When a video for the song "Baby, Baby" showed Grant in romantic (not sexual) scenes with a male actor, Christians who apparently did not understand the concept of *acting* called it adulterous. *House of Love* did nothing to quell accusations that Grant had "gone worldly." The album is basically *Heart in Motion, Part 2,* and it was similarly successful (though less so, selling closer to three million, which still made it one of the best selling albums of 1994). Grant had more radio hits with "Lucky One" (# 18 in 1994) and with her remake of Joni Mitchell's "Big Yellow Taxi" (# 67 in 1995). The title track, a compelling duet with friend Vince Gill, was subsequently featured in the soundtrack of the Michael Keaton-Geena Davis movie *Speechless.* The album's best song is probably the insanely infectious "Say You'll Be Mine."

Behind the Eyes was Grant's return to the form she had displayed on *Lead Me On.* Forsaking obvious commercial appeal, she simply poured her heart out in what may be the most painfully honest recording ever produced by any artist. The song "Takes a Little Time"—strongly reminiscent of Carole King at her best—was a surefire hit, a great song with a simple message (don't worry, have patience). "Somewhere Down the Road" is a song of promise, a new spiritual classic that Grant unfortunately had to sing at **Rich Mullins'** funeral and may be singing at other funerals for the rest of her life. But, as remarkable as those songs are, the core of *Behind the Eyes* may be found in its nakedly revealing songs that pick up where "Faithless Heart" left off. On "Like I Love You" Grant begins by asking, "Why do lovers drift apart and how does love fade away?" She then goes on to promise her husband that even though this may have happened, she will never leave him and they will not call it quits ("Ain't nobody gonna say goodbye / Ain't nobody gonna walk away"). She will stay and "learn how to love him." A few songs later ("Cry a River"), she addresses another person she has had to reject in order for that preceding promise to be fulfilled. She beings by lamenting the tragic irony of finding love at a place and time when it must be denied. She asks, "How do you live with a feeling in your bones / About what is and isn't meant to be?" And she answers, "Some things you just live with / And you never let it show / Like the pain / I felt the day I watched you leave." Her only hope now is that the forbidden and rejected lover will think of her now and then and join her in crying over "what might have been." Later, in another song, she does just that. She *regrets* her decision to do the right thing, without renouncing or revising it: "Missing you feels like a way of life," she sings seemingly to the person whose affection she felt called to renounce. "I'm living out the life that I've been given / But baby, I still wish that you were mine." And then in yet another song she seems finally to waver in her commitment: "I guess I'm letting go," she sings to her husband again. "I'm tired of stitching up my dreams with this thread of hope / A silly believer in two hearts and timeless love / And all I ever wanted was the feeling I had with us" ("The Feeling I Had").

Is this the saddest record ever made? Of course, not all of the songs have to be autobiographical (Grant says that "Missing You" was written from the perspective of her sister, whose son had gone away to college). Still, on the record, they fit together to relate a coherent but agonizing tale. Never before has any Christian artist so eloquently struggled with the commitment to be faithful when the life that one has "been given" is not the life that one would choose. The fact that Grant may have ultimately lost that struggle, was unable to maintain the commitment she had felt compelled to live with, only intensifies the record's ex post facto themes: the horror of divorce *and* the living hell that can sometimes become its only alternative. The project closes with the aforementioned "Somewhere Down the Road," in which Grant maintains that trusting God requires an act of faith that transcends experience: "So much pain and no good reason why. . . . And all that I can say is / Somewhere down the road there will be answers." *CCM* announced the album with this declaration: "Amy Grant—at considerable risk to her image—delivers a heart full of unadorned truth." *True Tunes* immediately dubbed it "the best album of her career," noting that in the midst of all the pain, "the overall tone is that of a deep-seated sense of peace and an undergirding of faith despite the worst of circumstances." To think that someone could hurt this much, indeed could accept such hurt as the cost of her commitments to faith and faithfulness . . . and *still* believe!

Ignored by critics in the general market, and perhaps beyond their ken, *Behind the Eyes* was generally recognized in the Christian media as one of the most thought-provoking and faith-inspiring albums ever made. The general reaction of most listeners was, "I haven't gone through half of what *she* has . . . if *she* still believes, then so can I." And, then, when the story behind the album became more fully known, the inspiration only intensified: Grant trusted God not only as one who had suffered, but as one who had *failed,* whose weaknesses had been exposed to the world in rather prominent and embarrassing ways. She seemed the ultimate fulfillment of what the Apostle Paul taught about witnessing for Christ two millennia ago, namely that the grace and power of God are more clearly revealed when humans acknowledge their weaknesses than when they testify to their accomplishments (2 Corinthians 12:9–10). But, of course, not everyone got it. *Christianity Today* ran an incredible two-page article on the album titled "Where's the Gospel?" in which the usually perceptive William D. Romanowski (professor at Calvin College) took Grant to task for being "discreet about her faith" and evincing a lack of "depth" in her lyrics! (one wonders what he would make of Psalm 22, much less the book of Ecclesiastes). To those with ears to hear, the depth of Grant's faith—a faith that does not just expect Jesus to fix things but is willing to sacrifice all and experience hell for his sake—has never been more evident or obvious than on her masterwork, *Behind the Eyes.*

More than any other artist associated with contemporary Christian music, Amy Grant has earned the respect of critics in the general market. *The Rolling Stone Album Guide* notes that "all of her albums have their virtues" and that "most everything she sings is good." They indicate that "her clear, dry voice projects a forceful personality, and her command of vocal dynamics is impressive." They further conclude that "Grant's success in the secular world is testimony to the power of her message, the persuasiveness of her performance, the quality of her songs, and the credibility of her stance."

Grant has also produced a handful of Christmas albums over the years that have been especially successful, and she has contributed a few original songs to the growing body of holiday carols ("Breath of Love," written with **Chris Eaton,** and "Tennessee Christmas," written with **Gary Chapman**). Many people are surprised to realize that Grant's *Home for Christmas* album (though inferior to 1983's *A Christmas Album*) has sold close to four million albums, making it the second-best-selling Christian album of all time (behind *Heart in Motion*) and putting it way ahead of most projects in the general market. Grant has often performed annual Christmas concerts or even tours, sometimes accompanied by symphony orchestras. In 1992, she sang songs from *A Christmas Album* at the White House for a nationally televised *Christmas in Washington* special. In 2001, she and husband Vince Gill toured together with a program of Christmas songs.

Grant has also participated in numerous other projects over the years. In 1984, she appeared as a Cinderella character in a made-for-TV movie, in which she sang the Doobie Brothers' "Listen to the Music." In 1989, she portrayed Mary to Art Garfunkel's Joseph in Jimmy Webb's *The Animal's Christmas* cantata. In 1992, she covered **Elvis Presley**'s "Love Me Tender" on the soundtrack for the film *Honeymoon in Vegas*. In 1995, she sang what was to become a prophetic cover of Carole King's "It's Too Late" on a tribute album for that artist (*Tapestry Revisited,* Atlantic) and a year later she covered 10cc's "The Things We Do For Love" on the soundtrack to an Ellen DeGeneres film called *Mr. Wrong*. Grant has served as a spokesperson for Habitat for Humanity and for the Sarah Cannon Cancer Research Center, named after the comedian whose stage name was Minnie Pearl (Pearl was a lifelong friend of Grant's, and Grant's daughter Sarah is named after her). She has also done commercial endorsements for Target department stores and for the National Dairy Council (one of those milk moustache ads). In 1995, Grant had surgery to repair a detached retina in her right eye.

As a songwriter, Grant has written or cowritten Christian radio hits performed by **Gary Chapman** and **Ashley Cleveland** ("Where Do I Go?"), **Michael W. Smith** ("How Long Will Be Too Long," "Give It Away"), and **Kathy Troccoli** ("Stubborn Love"). She also cowrote Smith's Top 40 general market hit, "Place in This World" (# 5 in 1991).

For trivia buffs: In 1990, an artist for Marvel Comics used Amy Grant's image for the figure of a sorceress on the cover of their March 15 issue of *Dr. Strange* comic book. Grant sued and settled out of court.

Christian radio hits: "Old Man's Rubble" (# 2 in 1978); "What a Difference You've Made in My Life" (# 5 in 1978); "Beautiful Music" (# 10 in 1978); "Father's Eyes" (# 3 in 1979); "Faith Walkin' People" (# 10 in 1979); "Look What Happened to Me" (# 3 in 1981); "Nobody Loves Me Like You" [with **DeGarmo and Key**] (# 6 in 1981); "Singing a Love Song" (# 5 in 1981); "I'm Gonna Fly" (# 4 in 1982); "Sing Your Praise to the Lord" (# 1 for 10 weeks in 1982); "El Shaddai" (# 2 in 1982); "In a Little While" (# 5 in 1983); "Ageless Medley" (# 3 in 1983); "Emmanuel" (# 20 in 1984); "Angels" (# 1 for 13 weeks in 1984); "Thy Word" (# 4 in 1984); "Jehovah" (# 2 in 1984); "The Now and Not Yet" (# 20 in 1985); "I Could Never Say Goodbye" [with **Randy Stonehill**] (# 4 in 1985); "Find a Way" (# 1 for 14 weeks in 1985); "Wise Up" (# 2 in 1985); "Everywhere I Go" (# 4 in 1986); "Sharayah" (# 2 in 1986); "Love of Another Kind" (# 12 in 1986); "Stay for a While" (# 1 for 4 weeks in 1986); "Love Can Do" (# 6 in 1987); "Saved by Love" (# 1 for 8 weeks in 1988); "Lead Me On" (# 1 for 6 weeks in 1988); "1974" (# 2 in 1988); "What about the Love" (# 1 for 4 weeks in 1989); "Say Once More" (# 2 in 1989); "Faithless Heart" (# 16 in 1990); "That's What Love Is For" (# 1 for 8 weeks in 1989); "Baby, Baby" (# 13 in 1991); "Every Heartbeat" (# 2 in 1991); "Hope Set High" (# 3 in 1991); "Ask Me" (# 3 in 1992); "I Will Remember You" (# 4 in 1992); "Children of the World" (# 1 in 1994); "Love Has a Hold on Me" (# 6 in 1995); "Helping Hand" (# 1 for 3 weeks in 1995); "Lover of My Soul" (# 4 in 1995); "Oh, How the Years Go By" (# 11 in 1995); "Takes a Little Time" (# 9 in 1997); "Nothing Is beyond You" [with **A Ragamuffin Band**] (# 24 in 1998).

Dove Awards: 1983 Pop/Contemporary Album (*Age to Age*); 1983 Artist of the Year; 1985 Pop/Contemporary Album (*Straight Ahead*); 1986 Artist of the Year; 1989 Pop/Contemporary Album (*Lead Me On*); 1989 Artist of the Year; 1990 Country Song (" 'Tis So Sweet to Trust in Jesus"); 1992 Artist of the Year; 1998 Pop/Contemporary Album (*Behind the Eyes*).

Grammy Awards: Best Contemporary Gospel Performance (*Age to Age*); 1983 Best Gospel Performance, Female ("Ageless Medley"); 1984 Best Gospel Performance, Female ("Angels"); 1985 Best Gospel Performance, Female (*Unguarded*); 1988 Best Gospel Performance, Female ("Lead Me On").

Natalie Grant

1999—*Natalie Grant* (Benson); 2001—*Stronger* (Pamplin).

www.nataliegrant.com

Natalie Grant looks like TV's Jenna Elfman and sounds like Top 40's Mariah Carey—a winning combination if ever there was one. The Seattle native grew up singing in church, and after attending Northwest Bible College in Kirkland, Washington, she spent two years (1994–1996) as a member of **Truth.** After relocating to Nashville, she remained an active member of the Strong Tower Bible church, an interracial congregation outside the city. Her self-titled debut album was coproduced by **Brown Bannister** and features mostly "big vocal" songs that showcase Grant's powerful yet willowy voice. Many of the soft pop songs ("Heavenly," "I Am Not Alone") betray the influence of traditional gospel in a way analogous to **Ashley Cleveland.** Others ("The Way It Is with Love") are typical adult contemporary ballads with a subtle spirituality that would allow them to sound right at home on mainstream radio stations. But Grant testifies to her faith in "There Is a God" and to her devotion in "At Your Feet" (a song inspired by the biblical story in Mark 14:3–9). "One Child" sounds like a hymn, and "We Are All the Same" is a soulful anthem to church unity. *Stronger* tries to present the singer as a Christian Celine Dion and Grant survives the comparisons. Album highlights include the strong pop songs "Keep On Shining" and "If the World Lost All Its Love." Grant follows in the tradition of Mariah and Britney by fronting a boy band in her duet with **Plus One** ("Whenever You Needed Someone") and brings the album to a close with a six-minute emotional epic cowritten with **Cindy Morgan** ("Finally Home").

Al Green

Selected: 1976—*Full of Fire* (Hi); 1977—*The Belle Album*; 1978—*Love Ritual*; 1979—*Truth and Time*; 1980—*The Lord Will Make a Way* (Myrrh);

1981—*Higher Plane;* 1982—*Precious Lord;* 1983—*I'll Rise Again; Al Green Sings the Gospel* (Motown); 1984—*Trust in God* (Myrrh); 1985—*He Is the Light* (A&M); 1987—*Soul Survivor;* 1989—*I Get Joy;* 1991—*One in a Million* (Word); 1992—*Love Is Reality;* 1993—*Gospel Soul* (Arrival); 1995—*Your Heart Is in Good Hands* (MCA); *Glory to His Name* (Capitol); 1997—*Anthology* (The Right Stuff); 1999—*Rock of Ages* (American Music); 2000—*Greatest Gospel Hits* (EMI); *Take Me to the River* (The Right Stuff).

www.algreen.com

One of the most successful soul singers of the '70s, Al Green has managed to move in and out of the world of contemporary gospel music without the sort of fanfare or controversy attached to other celebrities who have undergone conversions **(Bob Dylan)** or pursued crossover success **(Amy Grant)**. Perhaps due to an intrinsic relationship between gospel and soul music—or to the greater integration of faith and life that is often found within African American communities—Green has been able to retain his credentials in both fields and to be highly respected for both his sacred and secular offerings. Indeed, for Green there has always been a good deal of overlap between those categories, and throughout his career he has struggled with a recurring identity crisis regarding his commitments to one over against the other. Born Albert Greene in 1946 in Forrest City, Arkansas, the future star formed a gospel quartet called The Greene Brothers with his siblings when he was but nine years old. The quartet frequently toured the Midwest, but Al was expelled from the group by his father when he was caught listening to the "profane" music of Jackie Wilson.

Green's career as a soul singer took off in the early '70s when he was paired with producer Willie Mitchell and, together, they crafted a sound definitive of Memphis soul—heavy on backbeats with subdued horns and strings with Green's tenor-to-falsetto voice floating above it all. This sound was further supplemented by wildly spontaneous ecstatic cries and moans that owed a great deal to traditional gospel. Green would sell over twenty million records in the '70s, recording five gold albums and scoring six Number One R&B songs. His best remembered hits include some of the earliest ones, which also made an impression on the pop charts: "Tired of Being Alone" (# 11 in 1971), "Let's Stay Together" (# 1 in 1971), "Look What You Done For Me" (# 4 in 1972), "I'm Still in Love With You" (# 3 in 1972), and "You Ought to Be with Me" (# 3 in 1972). In 1974, a former girlfriend (Mrs. Mary Woodsen) poured boiling grits on him while he was bathing in his Memphis home, then killed herself with a gun. This incident seems to have triggered a spiritual crisis that had been building for some time, and Green, hospitalized with second degree burns, declared his intention to enter the clergy. In 1976, he was ordained a Baptist minister, pastor of Full Gospel Tabernacle in Memphis, about half a mile from **Elvis Presley**'s home at Graceland. At times, Green's church has been second only to

that latter establishment among Memphis tourist attractions. In the late '70s, a cover of his gospel song "Take Me to the River" (about baptism) would become one of The Talking Heads' best-known hits.

Green's new vocation did not alter his commitments as a soul singer, and he continued to perform, pastoring the church only when not touring. The same year that he was ordained he released *Full of Fire,* a deeply spiritual album that, despite inclusion of the hymns "Soon As I Get Home" and "I'll Fly Away," was still essentially an R&B record dealing with romance rather than religion. Green justified this by proclaiming, "I don't want to try and save the church folks." The same tendency continues on *The Belle Album,* which is generally considered to be Green's best post-ordination work. The song "Belle" is a romantic ballad addressed to a woman, but sung from the perspective of a Christian struggling with his devotion to God: "Belle, it's you that I want / But it's Him that I need." Like **Marvin Gaye**'s *What's Going On?,* the album was very well received in the general market despite its explicit Christian content. Greil Marcus wrote for *Rolling Stone* that it contained "a sense of liberation and purpose deep enough to make the sinner envy the saved." Ironically, the album was virtually ignored in the Christian market, perhaps because Green was still singing for a secular label. On *Truth and Time* he juxtaposes the driving gospel of the title track with inspired covers of "To Sir with Love" and "I Say a Little Prayer."

In 1980, however, Green signed with Word Records (Myrrh) and released a series of albums geared specifically to the contemporary Christian music subculture. His decision to do so appears to have been affected by an accident in 1979 in which he fell off the stage in a Cincinnati concert and narrowly escaped serious injuries. He apparently interpreted this as "a sign from God" that he should quit singing his secular hits and concentrate on spiritual songs full time. *The Lord Will Make a Way* offers the slinky "Too Close" and the roof-raising "Saved" alongside such standards as Thomas Dorsey's "The Lord Will Make a Way" and Fanny Crosby's "Pass Me Not." *Higher Plane* continues the treatment of modern classics (**Curtis Mayfield**'s "People Get Ready") and revival hymns ("Amazing Grace") but also offers some memorable original compositions. Green's "Where Love Rules" and "By My Side" are certainly more moving than his country version of "The Battle Hymn of the Republic." The most memorable song on *Precious Lord* is its title track (another Dorsey standard), but *I'll Rise Again* offers a funky, praise-filled song called "Ocean Blue" that recalls the Memphis soul sound that had made Green such a hit on '70s radios. But Green had committed himself during this period to recasting hymns of the church. *Precious Lord* also includes his take on "The Old Rugged Cross," and *I'll Rise Again* offers a version of "Leaning on the Everlasting Arms." He raids Dorsey's repertoire yet a third time to offer "No, Not One" on *Trust in God,* but the latter album also pulls him out of the traditional gospel rut with cover versions of uplifting, soulful, but not necessarily religious songs (Joe South's "Don't It Make You Want to Go Home," Frank Wilson's "Up the Ladder to the Roof," and Ashford and Simpson's "Ain't No Mountain High Enough"). The title track is an inspiring, original composition.

Green's tendency to mix sacred and secular would culminate in an eventual return to the general market with *He Is the Light,* an overtly Christian album on which Green was reunited with producer Willie Mitchell. The latter album opens with "Going Away" and features such standout cuts as "Power" and "You Brought the Sunshine" in addition to Green's rendition of the hymn "Nearer My God to Thee." The follow-up *Soul Survivor* is ostensibly a nongospel R&B comeback for Green, but it also features songs like "Jesus Will Fix It" and "Everything's Gonna Be Alright" (which proclaims "Don't let this world mislead you / Don't you ever go astray / Trust in God's word and believe it / 'Cause it will never pass away"). Green also offers a new version of "He Ain't Heavy (He's My Brother)" and sings a duet with **Billy Preston** on Carole King's "You've Got a Friend."

Green made another album for Word in the early '90s. *Love Is Reality* paired him with producer **Tim Miner** for an especially slick production. The album's more powerful songs include "I Can Feel It" (with accompanying horns) and "You Don't Know Me" (with wheezy organ and a relaxed swingbeat). *CCM* called "Just Can't Let You Go" the "best take on the old 'God is my girlfriend' tack in ages." *Love Is Reality* also offers the sounds of silky smooth soul on "I Like It" and gospel groove preaching on "Sure Feels Good."

In 1988, Green scored another Top 10 hit on the pop charts when he sang a duet with Annie Lennox of the Eurythmics on "Put a Little Love in Your Heart" (from the film *Scrooged*). In 1992, he appeared on Broadway opposite Patti LaBelle in the gospel musical, *Your Arm's Too Short to Box with God* (cf. **BeBe Winans**). In 1994, he won his first nongospel Grammy for a duet with Lyle Lovett on Willie Nelson's song "Funny How Time Slips Away" (for MCA's *Rhythm, Country, and Blues* compilation project). In 1995, Green was inducted into the Rock and Roll Hall of Fame. That same year, he released *Your Heart Is in Good Hands* (titled *Don't Look Back* in Europe), which mixes songs of faith with romantic odes. Seven of the tracks were produced by David Steele and Andy Cox of Fine Young Cannibals. At the beginning of the new millennium he was featured in a recurring role as a minor character on the TV series *Ally McBeal*.

A four-disc career retrospective of Al Green's work released in 1997 called *Anthology* contains some of his gospel recordings but none of the material recorded for Word or Myrrh. In the sixty-four-page liner notes, Green testifies to his faith and indicates that he had known from the start he was destined to sing

for God. He says he had prayed early on to be successful and that God had told him the prayer would be answered with one condition: "I will give you all of the things you want, but after you become successful, you must use all of the success and the things that you have gained in this life for the edification of the gospel of Jesus Christ." Green has also written an autobiography that contains a good deal of testifying: *Take Me to the River* (HarperEntertainment, 2000); a two-disc compilation album by the same name offers a collection of mostly nongospel radio hits (sort of a budget version of *Anthology*). Numerous compilations focusing on only his gospel recordings also exist, including *Gospel Soul* and *Greatest Gospel Hits.* The album *One in a Million* compiles songs from the five Myrrh albums only. *Glory to His Name* and *Rock of Ages* are collections of traditional hymns.

Christian radio hits: "Morning Star" (# 4 in 1982); "Everything's Gonna Be Alright" (# 6 in 1987); "Love Is Reality" (# 1 in 1992); "I Can Feel It" (# 16 in 1993).

Dove awards: 1983 Traditional Gospel Album *(Precious Lord).*

Grammy Awards: 1981 Best Traditional Soul Gospel Performance *(The Lord Will Make a Way);* 1982 Best Contemporary Soul Gospel Performance *(Higher Plane);* 1982 Best Traditional Soul Gospel Performance *(Precious Lord);* 1983 Best Soul Gospel Performance, Male *(I'll Rise Again);* 1984 Best Soul Gospel Performance by a Duo or Group [with **Shirley Caesar**] ("Sailin' on the Sea of Your Love"); 1986 Best Soul Gospel Performance, Male ("Going Away"); 1987 Best Soul Gospel Performance, Male ("Everything's Gonna Be Alright"); 1989 Best Soul Gospel Performance, Male ("As Long As We're Together"); 1994 Best Pop Vocal Collaboration [with Lyle Lovett] ("Funny How Time Slips Away").

Glenn Allen Green

1985—*A Living Fire* (Home Sweet Home); 1987—*Down This Avenue.*

A singer with a spectacular multi-octave voice, Glenn Allen Green recorded two albums for **Chris Christian**'s Home Sweet Home label but fared better with critics than consumers. His songs tend to feature the strong melodic power-pop of artists like **Petra.** The song "Run" is reminiscent of Journey, and "Beyond the Door" is techno-pop. Reviewing *A Living Fire, CCM* said, "Christian radio should jump all over the anthemic 'Mirror of My Heart' and the elegant ballad 'Forevermore.'" That didn't happen. *Down This Avenue* features stronger songs but weaker production. Standout tracks include the consciousness-raising "A Million Miles Away" and the somewhat comical "Living in Babylon."

Keith Green

1977—*For Him Who Has Ears to Hear* (Sparrow); 1978—*No Compromise;* 1980—*So You Wanna Go Back to Egypt* (Pretty Good); 1981—*The Keith Green Collection* (Sparrow); 1982—*Songs for the Shepherd* (Pretty Good); 1983—*The Prodigal Son; I Only Want to See You There* (Sparrow); 1984—

Jesus Commands Us to Go (Pretty Good); 1987—*The Ministry Years, Vol. 1, 1977–1979* (Sparrow); 1988—*The Ministry Years, Vol. 2, 1980–1982*; 1996—*Early Years; Keith Green Live (His Incredible Youth)* (Sonrise); 1998—*Oh Lord, You're So Beautiful: Songs of Worship* (Sparrow); *Make My Life a Prayer to You: Songs of Devotion; Because of You: Songs of Testimony; Here Am I Send Me: Songs of Evangelism.*

www.lastdaysministries.org

The untimely and tragic death of Keith Green (at age twenty-eight) on July 28, 1982 had an effect on the contemporary Christian music subculture analogous to that which the murder of John Lennon had on the mainstream rock and roll culture two years earlier. Green's status in Christian music was comparable to that of Lennon's in the general market and, though his actual significance can be overstated, his reputation has only grown with the passing years. By 2002, he was the closest thing to an icon in Christian music, revered by fans who had not even been born when he died. In 1989, Green's widow published a biography of her legendary husband (*No Compromise: The Story of Keith Green,* by Melody Green and David Hazard, Sparrow Press).

Green was born in 1953 in Sheepshead Bay, New York, but subsequently moved to San Fernando Valley, California. His father was a professional baseball player and his mother, a musician. He took to music early, starring in a theater production of Arthur Laurent's *The Time of the Cuckoo* when he was a child. The *Los Angeles Times* wrote that "roguish-looking, eight-year-old Keith Green gave a winning performance," one that "stole the show." Green also played the role of Kurt Von Trapp in a major production of *The Sound of Music* and began touring as a child performer in nightclubs. At the age of eleven, he became the youngest person ever signed to ASCAP (the American Society of Composers, Authors, and Publishers) when he published, recorded, and released an ironically titled song "The Way I Used to Be." With fifty more original songs in his repertoire, Green signed a five-year contract with Decca Records, who intended to make him a major teen idol. He was featured in teenybopper fanzines like *Teen Scene* and appeared on such national programs as *The Jack Benny Show, The Joey Bishop Show,* and Steve Allen's variety program. *Time* magazine hailed him as "a prepubescent dreamboat" and indicated that he "croons in a voice trembling with conviction." But Donny Osmond's rising star eclipsed whatever light was shining on little Keith, and his first few minutes of fame were brief.

Green entered a period of troubled adolescence, running away from home for the first of many times at the age of fifteen. He became immersed in the hippie culture, embracing recreational sex and mind-altering drugs, while studying various forms of eastern religion, astrology, and mysticism. His conversion to Christianity seems to have been somewhat gradual. In late 1972 and into 1973 he began identifying himself as having a personal relationship with Jesus, but he rejected "organized religion" and seems at first to have held syncretistic beliefs that, for instance, did not interfere with his penchant for dropping acid. But with the help of **Kenn Gulliksen** and others associated with Hollywood's Vineyard church fellowship, Green eventually came to an orthodox if somewhat dogmatic understanding of the faith. Because he was ethnically Jewish, Green sometimes referred to himself as "a Jewish Christian" in these early years. He exhibited an almost unprecedented zeal to live for the Lord and a seemingly relentless joy in God's presence. His partner in all of these adventures was Melody, a fellow-seeker and then partner-in-ministry whom he married in 1973. She cowrote many of his songs and was actually the sole composer of what might be his best-known song, "Make My Life a Prayer to You."

While the Greens were in California, they became friends with the newly converted **Bob Dylan,** who belonged to their church and reportedly sought their input on his songs for *Saved.* But Keith and Melody's commitment to ministry always went well beyond music. They began an outreach to street people in California, purchasing some seven homes to provide housing and care for prostitutes, drug addicts, and others who needed a place to stay. Eventually, they relocated to Linsdale, Texas, where they founded Last Days Ministries, which continued the social work, sponsored evangelistic crusades, operated an Intensive Christian Training Institute, and distributed literature commenting on various doctrinal and social concerns. Since Green's death, Melody Green (eventually remarried to Andy Sievright) has presided over LDM; in 1985 she also founded Americans Against Abortion and has served as its director. Under Melody's leadership, LDM has become an advocate for the role of women in ministry.

The tragedy of Green's death was both unnecessary and horrific. Green and eleven others were killed when their small and overloaded plane crashed on a sightseeing flight to show the Last Days Compound to visiting friends. Two of Green's children, three-year-old Josiah and two-year-old Bethany, perished in the crash. Also killed were the pilot, Don Burmeister, as well as the visiting pastors John and Dede Smalley and all six of their children. A tragedy of such proportions made the national news and even those who had never heard of Keith Green reeled at the incredible and senseless loss of life. The cause of death was obvious: the plane was found to have been 495 pounds overweight with twelve passengers crammed into its six seats. Unfortunately, many in the Christian community spoke of the incident in naive and insensitive ways, indicating, for instance that God liked Green's music so much that he just decided to bring him to heaven ahead of schedule (murdering little children and creating widows along the way). Melody Green, however, maintained dignity, composure, and perspective: she expressed anger at Keith (especially for having placed the children in such a dangerous situation), yet praised and protected his legacy in appropriate ways. Her public witness to her own struggles at moving through grief and denial to acceptance were instrumental in helping thousands deal with their sorrow and with the theological questions the tragedy had raised. **Kenn Gulliksen** also wrote an article for *CCM* at the time, dealing pastorally with some of the issues involved. As a nasty postscript to the whole tragedy, relatives of the Smalley family sued Last Days Ministries and won a quarter-of-a-million-dollar out-of-court settlement against the organization. In retrospect, Green's death presented the contemporary Christian community with its first, faltering experience at dealing with corporate grief. The community would fare better in dealing with subsequent losses **(D-Boy, Vince Ebo, Mark Heard, Rich Mullins,** Gene Eugene of **Adam Again)**.

Green was above all a person of conviction, and his unwavering commitments (evident in his motto of "no compromise") proved to be what would endear him to the generation of evangelicals that followed. Green had the personality of a Martin Luther, refusing to compromise on matters where virtually everyone would later say he was wrong—as well as on matters where most would later admit he was probably right. The latter instances were frequent enough to allow his persistence to be ultimately assessed as more virtue than vice. **Steve Camp** once referred to Green as "abrasive but anointed," and *CCM* commented that though he was "famous for his dogmatism, even those who may have disagreed with him never questioned his heart." Perhaps the most grievous instance of the dogmatism showed itself in a notorious tirade published as "The Catholic Chronicles," in which he offered an ill-informed and ill-advised assault on Roman Catholicism. He did not live long enough to repent of that misstep, but he *was* aware of his tendencies and often did make apologies. At one point when he apparently felt he had overstepped his bounds with his friend **Bob Dylan,** he wrote in his diary, "Tried to be the Holy Spirit to Bob Dylan today."

There were at least three major ways in which Green's stubborn convictions had ambiguous appeal but undeniable impact.

First, Green was perhaps the first and certainly the most prominent Jesus music artist to insist on greater theological depth in his material. The problem was that Green frequently lacked the maturity and training to pull it off. His lyrics are filled with theological errors, one example of which may be found in his popular story-song "The Sheep and the Goats." He interprets Matthew 25:31–46 as promising hell to Christians who ignore the needy, as though their faith in Christ counts for nothing; the biblical text actually presents a judgment of unbelieving nations in response to how they treated Christian "brothers" sent to them as missionaries (cf. Matthew 10:40–42). Green had a tendency to resist correction, publicly ridiculing those who sought advanced biblical understanding;

in his concerts, he sometimes mocked seminarians who thought they would understand the Bible better "by learning what it says in Greek." Nevertheless, his songs need to be compared to the often insipid jingles produced by most other Christian artists at the time. More than any other artist, Keith Green moved contemporary Christian music to adopt a more astute attitude that would require thought-out and thought-provoking lyrics rather than just cheerleading propaganda songs.

Second, Green identified his niche in Christian music as being that of a prophet (though he rejected the label) called to challenge Christians to greater holiness. His emphasis on good works and absolute devotion often took on such legalistic overtones that there were moments (in his late '70s concerts and on his *No Compromise* album) when he sounded like a man who desperately needed to hear the gospel. He certainly preferred the Old Testament prioritization of "obedience over sacrifice" (1 Samuel 15:22) to the Old and New Testament prioritization of "*mercy* over sacrifice" (Hosea 6:6; Matthew 9:13; 12:7). In a song titled "To Obey Is Better Than to Sacrifice" he even placed a shocking line on the lips of Jesus: "If you can't come to me everyday, then don't bother coming at all" (Melody Green says that she and producer Bill Maxwell both tried unsuccessfully to get him to change the line). Nevertheless, Green could also extol God's grace and, at his best, pressed Christian music fans to take the implicit demands of their faith more seriously. It is worth remembering that a large segment of those involved in the Jesus movement were novice Christians interested in "getting high on Jesus." Green challenged them to move beyond the spiritual rush of conversion and to "count the costs" of discipleship. All told, he did this more effectively than any other performer of his day. Melody Green has also noted (on the Last Days Ministries website) that Keith was able to repent of his excesses. As years went by, she writes, "Keith came into a deeper understanding of the sacrifice of Jesus on the cross. . . . it wasn't that Keith became less concerned with purity and holiness, but he was motivated more by love and less by fear."

Third, Green shook up the Christian music industry in 1979 with a new conviction. He was sure God had told him that it was wrong to sell the gospel. Thus he quit charging for his concerts and asked to be released from his contract with Sparrow, claiming that he could no longer charge money for his records. The Greens mortgaged their home so that they could privately finance the album *So You Wanna Go Back to Egypt?,* which they then offered at concerts and through the mail for "whatever you can afford." It was only a partial disaster. Early on, unscrupulous collectors helped themselves to arm-loads of the record (which featured **Bob Dylan** as a guest performer). A one-per-household rule was enacted but, eventually, the album had to be marketed through Sparrow anyway. Then, for a time, a label was placed on each copy telling the potential buyer that if he or she could not afford the record, one would be sent free of charge. In May of 1982, Green reported that he had shipped 210,000 units of the album under the "whatever you can afford" rubric, 61,000 of them at no charge whatsoever. Green's fourth album, *Songs for the Shepherd,* was released under similar terms. Such outlandish moves played gleeful havoc with all sorts of established procedures—for instance methods of charting an album's popularity based on its retail sales. Green was one of the Christian music industry's biggest stars at the time and his mess-with-the-establishment gesture inspired hundreds of other artists—not to mention executives and consumers—to reevaluate their commitments to materialistic and competitive aspects of the enterprise known as contemporary Christian music. None of them, however, started giving away records for "whatever you can afford."

In spite of the long discography above, Green really only made four albums, all of which were produced by Bill Maxwell of **Andraé Crouch and the Disciples** (the additional products are postmortem compilations). It should also be noted, however, that Green's debut in Christian music was not as a soloist. He played piano on a reunion album by **Good News** alongside such future stars as **Billy Batstone, Bob Carlisle,** and **David Diggs.** Though Green himself did not sing on the latter album, his song "Run to the End of Highway" would become the record's best-known track. In 1976, Green also performed on the *Firewind* album (Sparrow), a Christian musical written by **The Talbot Brothers** with **Jamie Owens (Collins).** The highlight of that album may be Green and **Barry McGuire**'s duet on **Terry Talbot**'s rollicking "Walk and Talk."

As with many Christian artists, Green began by attempting to clone a successful secular star. In this case, he sought to be "a Christian version of Elton John," and his first album, *For Him Who Has Ears to Hear,* frequently duplicates John's early honky-tonk piano style. It is at least a worthy imitation; one has to listen closely to "Because of You" to be sure that it *isn't* John. Other noticeable influences include "Piano Man"-era Billy Joel, **Bob Dylan,** and Joni Mitchell, whose singing style he later admitted to copying on "Song for My Parents (I Only Want to See You There)." The debut album opens with "You Put This Love in My Heart," one of Green's best songs, praising God as the cyclical source of the love that humans have to give (to God and others). Musically, that song and "Because of You" are foot-stompers that were always concert favorites. "Song for My Parents" is both apology and prayer: "I know it seems every time we try to talk, I try to make you see. . . . And I'm such a bad example, and so full of pride. . . . But it's only 'cause I care, I really want to see you there" (i.e., in heaven). The bluesy "He'll Take Care of the Rest" offers a touch of Green's off-beat humor ("He is de-vine and we are de-branches"). Humor is also the operative element in "No One Believes in Me Anymore," sung

from the perspective of the devil. "Trials Turned to Gold" was inspired by Hannah Hurnard's classic *Hinds Feet on High Places* (as was **Jars of Clay**'s *Much Afraid* album two decades later). *For Him Who Has Ears to Hear* also includes the amazing "Your Love Broke Through," cowritten by Green with Todd Fishkind and **Randy Stonehill** (the song had recently been covered by **Phil Keaggy** as the title song to his second album; it was later covered by **Debby Boone** on her best-selling *You Light Up My Life* album). "Your Love Broke Through" features a brilliant pop melody that renders its wordy lyrics infectious, sticking the following paragraph in the mind as firmly as any jingle for a burger chain: "Like a foolish dreamer trying to build a highway to the sky / all my hopes would come crumbling down and I never knew just why / Until today when you pulled away the clouds that hung like curtains on my eyes / I've been blind all these wasted years / And I thought I was so wise / Then you took my by surprise." As a bonus, Green closes the record with a fair rendition of **2nd Chapter of Acts**' "Easter Song," to which he appends an extra verse. Overall, *For Him Who Has Ears to Hear* is Green's best work, showcasing his most joyous themes and most brilliant piano playing. The album sold over 300,000 copies in its first few years, ten times the number that most Christian albums were selling at that point in time. In 1998, a *CCM* poll of thirty critics chose Green's version of "Your Love Broke Through" as one of "the ten best contemporary Christian songs of all time." They also selected the album *For Him Who Has Ears to Hear* as the Number Four "best contemporary Christian album of all time."

No Compromise is known as "the prophetic album" and tends to be favored or disparaged according to assessments of that part of Green's message. Musically, *No Compromise* is superior to the debut record, as the artist drops the silly Elton John impressions and finds his own style. Lyrically, it is generally his low point, as he embraces fundamentalist tendencies toward works righteousness and discovers the short-term motivational power of guilt. The album does, however, include "Make My Life a Prayer to You," a worshipful ballad that is easily its best song. "Dear John Letter (to the Devil)" is an all-out rocker, offering a humorous rejection of the evil one's wiles—almost a reply to "No One Believes in Me Anymore." There are also hook-laden pop masterpieces similar to those on the debut record ("You" and "Soften My Heart"). "I Don't Want to Fall Away from You" is a revealing ballad that derives power from its honest expression of self-incriminating anxiety. The song "Asleep in the Light" is a scathing but ultimately trite castigation of complacency (featuring lyrics like "Jesus rose from the dead / And you can't get out of bed"). "The Victor" is a theatrical number written by **Jamie Owens (Collins)** but performed here with just a little too much melodrama. Melody Green later allowed that on this album Keith had been heavily influenced by the writings of two preachers, nineteenth-century holiness revivalist Charles Finney and twentieth-century extremist Leonard Ravenhill—both of whom are generally more respected for their piety than their theology. On the other hand, "My Eyes Are Dry," "Make My Life a Prayer to You," and "I Don't Want to Fall Away from You" (three prayer songs) all sprang from a revival within the LDM camp, a time of reawakening that stressed personal responsibility for choices and actions.

The privately produced *So You Wanna Go Back to Egypt* displays no loss in quality; in fact it is the most sophisticated and has the most "expensive" sound of any of Green's releases. **Matthew Ward** and **Kelly Willard** sing background vocals throughout. The album's most-beloved track is probably the worship classic, "Oh, Lord, You're Beautiful." The song "Pledge My Head to Heaven" is also remarkable, though the famous harmonica solo by **Bob Dylan** is not really very impressive. Green wrote the song after a personal retreat to the mountains, where he pledged that he would give up everything and "count all things as loss" for the sake of the gospel. The title track to *So You Wanna Go Back to Egypt* is a kinda dumb jazzy blues shuffle relating the story of Israel's murmurings as they wander in the wilderness. Green continues his attacks on complacency with songs like "You Love the World (But You're Avoiding Me)," but balances these with "Grace by which I Stand." Grace is also the undergirding theme of "Romans VII," a self-incriminating meditation on that biblical chapter. "I Want to Be More Like Jesus" (written by Keith and Melody with **Kelly Willard**) is an introspective song of devotion. The latter songs inspired *CCM* to note that on this album Green comes off as "less of a preacher and more of a fellow struggler." The magazine chose the album as one of its "Ten Best of 1980."

Songs for the Shepherd is a collection of all worship songs, including the traditional hymn "Holy, Holy, Holy," musical settings for Psalms 8, 9, and 23, and "There Is a Redeemer" by Melody Green. *CCM* would pick the album as one of its "Ten Best of 1982," with critic Thom Granger saying, "What makes it work so well is the appropriateness of the musical vehicle to each respective set of lyrics." Green performs "Draw Me" in a country-rock style, "The Promise Song" as calypso, and "O God, Our Lord," with a generous dose of traditional gospel. *Songs for the Shepherd* came out the same month as Green's death and was his last official release. He was subsequently subjected to the Jimi Hendrix treatment, having his tapes scrounged for possible release of anything he had ever done and his legitimate recordings packaged and repackaged shamelessly in hopes of appealing to obsessive collectors or potential new audiences. As with Hendrix, however, there *was* some worthwhile material in the vaults. *The Prodigal Son* features "Melody's Song (Love with Me)" and "Josiah's Song," two unusually tender pieces that Green had intended for a possible

crossover album with pop appeal. "Only by Following Jesus" shows him trying out an **Andraé Crouch**-inspired urban beat. On the other hand, "The Prodigal Son Suite" is a thirteen-minute *too* long idea for a musical that comes off like Elton John performing one of **Carman**'s story songs. *Jesus Commands Us to Go* collects more unreleased songs, loosely organized under the rubric of missions. On "Thank You, Jesus" (apparently from the *Ears to Hear* sessions), the dead-on Elton John imitation resurfaces, this time with a couple of **Larry Norman** impressions thrown in for good measure. Green's own rendition of his **Good News** song, "Run to the End of the Highway" ends up here as well, and a graceful adaptation of Psalm 51 ("Create in Me a Clean Heart") is included, introduced by a four-minute-plus, spontaneous piano prelude. Years later, some slightly embarrassing Green songs would surface when his parents, Harvey and Char Green, released a live concert consisting of nine songs from his pre-Christian teen idol era. Green uses profanity on the record but plays a mean piano on songs about the environment ("Everybody's Rapin' Mother Nature"), vegetarianism ("Love All Your Animal Friends"), and long hair ("Haircut"). There is even a bitter adolescent rebellion song directed to his mother ("Letters to Mother [From the Road]"). Obviously the project's value is more historical than musical.

The Keith Green Collection was a premature "best of" album with songs from the first two albums only, further marred by inclusion of inferior previously unreleased tracks ("Scripture Song Medley," "The Sheep and the Goats"). *I Only Want to See You There* should have been called *The Keith Green Collection, Vol. 2;* it offers songs from the first four albums that had not been included on the previous compilation. The two volumes of *The Ministry Years* manage to compile virtually everything Green ever did onto four CDs, including numerous live tracks (mostly worship songs) and a few previously unreleased nuggets. There is a lot of filler, but the otherwise unavailable "Summer Snow" (a song Keith and Melody wrote for **Matthew Ward**'s debut solo album) is excellent. *Early Years* was a completely unnecessary compilation and the rationale behind all the 1998 projects (which reorganize songs thematically) seems thin. With the abundance of compilations, what is most needed remains unavailable: a single disc collection of well-selected best songs. In 1992, a number of artists joined together to create a tribute album in Green's honor: *No Compromise: Remembering the Music of Keith Green* (Sparrow). As a result, Green's songs were back on the radio. **Charlie Peacock** had a hit with "I Can't Believe It," **Petra,** with "I Don't Want to Fall Away from You," and **PFR** with "Trials Turned to Gold." Melody Green Sievright offers her own version of "Make My Life a Prayer to You." Since *No Compromise* featured only big-name established artists (including also **Susan Ashton, Margaret Becker, Michael Card, Steven Curtis Chapman, Glad, Steve Green, Rich**

Mullins, **Russ Taff,** and **Kelly Willard**), a second tribute project was organized by BEC Records to feature performances by newer, alternative acts. *Start Right Here: Remembering the Life of Keith Green* (BEC, 2001) includes songs by **Cadet** ("You Are the One"), **The Dingees** ("Dear John Letter to the Devil"), **Flight One Eighty** ("He'll Take Care of the Rest"), **Joy Electric** ("Make My Life a Prayer to You"), **MG the Visionary** ("My Eyes Are Dry"), and **MxPx** ("You Put This Love in My Heart"). In 2002, Sparrow Records released yet another tribute album *(Your Love Broke Through: The Worship Songs of Keith Green),* with performances by **Twila Paris, Michael W. Smith, Rebecca St. James, Michelle Tumes,** and **Darlene Zschech.**

Christianity Today summarized Green's controversial tendencies this way:

> His was a theological hybrid of Jesus movement millenialism and nineteenth-century holiness teachings. Green spoke out against "churchianity," Catholicism, counterfeit conversions, sin in the church, adding to and subtracting from God's Word, complacency and a lack of compassion, gospel preaching that says only "God loves you and has a wonderful plan for your life," worship of tradition, and the selling of "Jesus junk" and the commercialization of Christianity.

While this is all true, he certainly should not be remembered primarily for what he opposed. Green was also a passionate advocate for social justice, for the poor, for urban ministry, and for foreign and domestic missions. John Styll of *CCM* magazine maintains that Green was "easily the best Christian songwriter of his era," as well as "a man of remarkable integrity." **Twila Paris** has said, "Without qualification, more than any other Christian musician before or since, Keith Green influenced my life toward God." On November 27, 2001, Keith Green was posthumously inducted into the Gospel Music Hall of Fame.

For trivia buffs: Green and his friend Todd Fishkind once laid siege to Joni Mitchell's house, singing songs in her yard until she invited them in to serenade her more properly. That night he wrote in his journal, "She dug it, but we played too much for her to absorb. She gave us organic apple juice."

Christian radio hits: "Dear John Letter (to the Devil)" (# 8 in 1979); "Soften Your Heart" (# 7 in 1979); "Asleep in the Light" (# 11 in 1979); "So You Want to Go Back To Egypt" (# 8 in 1980); "Rushing Wind" (# 15 in 1981); "Dust to Dust" (# 33 in 1984); "Here Am I, Send Me" (# 14 in 1987).

Peter Green

Selected: 1970—*The End of the Game* (Reprise); 1979—*In the Skies* (PVK); 1980—*Little Dreamer;* 1981—*Watcha Gonna Do?* 1981—*Blue Guitar* (Creole); 1982—*White Sky* (Headline); 1983—*Kolors.*

www.petergreen.net

Peter Green was the founder of Fleetwood Mac and, for a time, one of the United Kingdom's biggest rock stars. His connection to Christian music is at least as tentative and ambiguous as that of compatriot **Eric Clapton** but deserves comment if only for the publicity he received. Born Peter Greenbaum in London in 1946, Green first came to prominence when he replaced Clapton as lead guitarist in the band John Mayall's Bluesbreakers. In the mid '60s, when one of the most common graffiti expressions in British subways was "Clapton Is God," many fans began scrawling an appended message, "Green Is Better Than God." As a result, the British press took to calling him The Green God, a label that would trouble him in more ways than one. In 1967, Green formed Fleetwood Mac with *wunderkind* slide guitarist **Jeremy Spencer.** In response to all the media hype concerning a band that would include these two guitar heroes, Green thought it a great joke to name the group after its unknown and insignificant rhythm section: Mick Fleetwood (drums) and John (Mac) McVie (bass). As it turns out, within a few years both Green and Spencer would leave the band for religious reasons, but the titular drum and bass players would stay with the group through multiple personnel changes until it finally became one of the most successful rock groups in history. In the early years, however, the group was actually billed as "Pete Green's Fleetwood Mac" and the others (especially McVie and Fleetwood) were generally considered to be little more than his backing band. Green made three albums with the group (*Fleetwood Mac,* 1968; *English Rose,* 1969; *Then Play On,* 1969) which were all very successful in England. At the time he left, the group was rated the third most popular act in the United Kingdom, behind only the Beatles and The Rolling Stones. The one Fleetwood Mac song from the Pete Green era that became well known in America was "Oh Well," which featured the memorable chorus, "Don't ask me what I think of you / I might not give the answer that you want me to." A cover of the song was later a Top 40 hit for The Rockets in 1979; it has also been covered by the Christian metal band **Tourniquet.**

Green's exodus from Fleetwood Mac was precipitated by his disaffection with a materialistic music industry. As early as 1968, he told the group that he "had given up girls" and lost all interest in being successful. In the summer of 1969, he suddenly declared that he had found Jesus and (being Jewish) was now "a messianic Christian." According to Mick Fleetwood, who wrote a biography of the band (*Fleetwood,* William Morrow and Co., 1990), this phase only lasted a few weeks, and Green would subsequently only speak of having "found God" without specific reference to any particular religion. He did take to wearing a very large crucifix around his neck, however, and he would give long, rambling talks about religion and generic spirituality to news magazines, which had a heydey mocking him for what often appeared to be outlandish, inconsistent, or simply bizarre ideas. He was heavily involved with drugs at the time, particularly LSD, and often seemed unstable in his perceptions. He was also deeply guilt ridden and developed an obsessive concern for the poor. According to Fleetwood, Green would sit in front of the TV almost nightly weeping and sobbing loudly as he watched documentaries on "starving children in Africa." He gave away tens of thousands of dollars—some suggest, his entire fortune—to the Christian charitable organization Save the Children. As a ploy to keep him in the band, Fleetwood suggested that the group "found an orphanage" and donate some of the proceeds of their next album to its maintenance. Green jumped at the idea but soon amended it, deciding that Fleetwood Mac would henceforth be "a non-profit, missionary band" that would donate one hundred percent of its earnings from sales and concerts to orphans. When told by bandmates and record company executives that this was not going to happen, he performed his last concert with the group on May 25, 1970 where, by most accounts, he was "crazed on acid" and tried to set the amplifiers on fire. One more belated single was released by Pete Green and Fleetwood Mac, a song called "The Green Manalishi," which described money as the manifestation of the devil. The term *manalishi* appears to be a reference to a demonic force, derived from Pacific Island mythology. As such, the song title seems to involve a play on words, not only referring to demonic green money, but also representing Green's castigation of himself in response to "The Green God" label he had worn for so long.

Green did release an early, nondescript solo album called *The End of the Game* but then settled into the life of a recluse in London. Almost a decade later, *In the Skies* appeared. It consisted of instrumentals as well as a couple of songs that seem to have explicitly Christian lyrics. The album was embraced by some Christian music fans as the work of a famous convert. Musically, however, the album is far from Green's best work. A widespread rumor (probably untrue) held that he did not even play guitar on it but only provided vocals for the non-instrumentals after the album had been basically completed by others. The songs, at any rate, were written by his brother Mike Green and, so, may or may not be reflective of Green's own faith development. A few more unimpressive solo albums followed, all of which lack the spiritual focus of *In the Skies*. *Blue Guitar* is a compilation of songs from earlier releases; *Kolors* is an embarrassing collection of outtakes. In 1984 Green dropped out of sight for over a decade. He was photographed in 1987 with fingernails grown so excessively long that it would be impossible for him to play the guitar. In 1996, however, an old friend took him in, cared for him and helped him to start playing music again. Supposedly, he had to learn to play the guitar all over again, as if from scratch. At any rate, he returned

to recording in 1997 with a blues band called The Splinter Group, which has released its albums on the Artisan label. There have been no further indications of Green's spiritual or religious views, and he has not sought to establish any further connection with Christianity or with the Christian music scene.

Lilly Green

1975—*Lilly* (Destiny); 1977—*Especially for You* (Myrrh); 1979—*I Am Blessed*.

An early singer of Jesus music, Lilly Green (née Crozier, b. 1951) was raised in Renfrew, Ontario, and grew up singing in churches. As a teenager, she moved to Michigan to continue her schooling at Spring Arbor College and toured Scandinavia with an organization called The Solid Rock Foundation. In 1972, she moved to California where she later became an office assistant for Duane Pederson's Jesus People organization and joined the Shekinah Fellowship, where her husband was minister of music (the latter group provided choral backup for artists, e.g., on **Chuck Girard**'s "Sometimes Alleluia"). Green's best-known contributions to contemporary Christian music are two songs ("I Believe in the Father," "Beautiful for Jesus") included on a compilation album called *Gospel Ship* distributed by Destiny around 1973. Her debut solo album contains another two songs that also attracted quite a bit of attention. "Satan, I Rebuke You" was a radio hit (before charts were kept), featuring the lines, "Greater is he who is in me / Than you who are in the world / So in the name of Jesus Christ, my Lord / Stay away from God's little girl." Another song, "God, a Woman, and a Man" became a very popular anthem for Christian weddings. Green was featured on the cover of *Harmony* magazine in 1975 and in the accompanying article told of her travails in recently giving birth to a stillborn child. Her next two albums ventured into the developing realm of adult contemporary music and helped to define that genre within the Christian market.

Steve Green

1984—*Steve Green* (Sparrow); 1985—*He Holds the Keys*; 1986—*For God and God Alone*; *A Mighty Fortress* (Birdwing); 1987—*Tienen Que Saber* (Sparrow); *Joy to the World*; 1988—*Find Us Faithful*; 1989—*The Mission*; 1990—*Toma La Cruz*; *Hide 'Em in Your Heart, Vol. 1*; *Hide 'Em in Your Heart, Vol. 2*; 1991—*We Believe*; 1992—*Hymns: A Portrait of Christ*; *Himnos: Un Retrato de Christo*; 1994—*15 Melodias Biblicas para Niños*; *En Vivo!*; *Where Mercy Begins*; *People Need the Lord*; *Steve Green: The Collection*; 1995—*The Early Years, Vol. 1*; 1996—*The First Noel*; *The Letter*; 1998—*The Faithful*; 1999—*Morning Light: Songs to Awaken the Dead*; announced for 2002—*Woven in Time*.

www.stevegreenministries.org

A mainstay of inspirational adult contemporary music, Steve Green (b. 1956) was raised in Argentina as the son of missionary parents. Due to his musical gifts and missionary background, he was invited as a prelaw college student to become a part of the group **Truth,** where he met his wife Marijean. He went on to sing with **The Gaither Vocal Band** and then became a founding member of **White Heart.** He maintains, however, that his heart was not right with God, that he was "a slave to lust" who "disobeyed the Lord in many areas" until 1983 when, confronted by his older brother Randy, he realized that he did not really "know or love God" and came to be truly born again. This personal revival inspired him (at the Gaithers' urging) to pursue a solo career. As of 2002, Green had sold over three million albums, including some children's projects (the *Hide 'Em in Your Heart* albums) and Spanish language recordings. Green perceives his music ministry as serving evangelistic purposes in line with traditional understandings of revivalistic churches. In other words, he leads altar calls and believes that individuals come to experience God's salvation when they accept Christ in a definitive and usually ritualistic way. Such understandings, while representative of only a minority of Christians historically or globally, are prevalent among the subculture most often associated with contemporary Christian music. Green has often sung for the Billy Graham Evangelistic Association and for Promise Keeper events. In addition to the evangelistic emphases, however, Green has become known as a worship leader, and has perhaps made his greatest mark musically with songs oriented toward praise and worship. The Greens make their home in Franklin, Tennessee.

CCM described Steve Green's self-titled debut album as "a pleasant work in search of an audience," noting that the presence of sprightly **Matthew Ward**-style pop tunes seem off-kilter with the main focus of the album: "beautifully arranged and orchestrated" MOR songs that showcase "the rich, operatic quality of Steve's tenor voice." Likewise, the same magazine noted with regard to *He Holds the Keys* that "only when Green dabbles in modern pop-oriented songs does the album falter." The title track of that album and the modern, piano-dominated hymn "When His Kingdom Comes" were singled out as instances of Green "in his element—the unabashed high church praise song." By this point, Green was regularly being referred to as "the male **Sandi Patty**"; the two artists shared the same producer (Greg Nelson).

For God and God Alone continues to mix relatively insignificant pop songs into what critic Mark Eischer would call "a musical event of great dignity and unprecedented scale, . . . the contemporary Christian music equivalent of Handel's *Messiah.*" Obvious exaggeration aside, the album was Green's most ambitious to date, recorded in large part with the London Philharmonic Orchestra with the backing of a full choir. The suc-

cess of that album, and of *A Mighty Fortress,* which followed, solidified Green's identification as an inspirational singer, making it easy to forget that he had once rocked and rolled with **White Heart.** In reviewing *Find Us Faithful* (which includes a stirring arrangement of "Joyful, Joyful We Adore Thee"), *CCM* would identify Green as one-third of "the MOR triumvirate, including **Sandi Patty** and **Larnelle Harris.**" On *The Mission,* an album devoted conceptually to ministry, he includes a rendition of **Jamie Owens'** song "The Victor" (cf. **Keith Green**).

Green hit a new highpoint with *We Believe,* the album that he would still describe as his favorite in 2000. Rousing anthems like the title track mix with more personal songs like "Hidden Valleys" (a duet with songwriter **Kelly Willard**). On *Where Mercy Begins,* Green goes for a more contemporary sound, recording songs by the likes of **Steven Curtis Chapman** but continuing for the most part in the praise and worship vein. The title track is a song based on the prodigal son story. *The Letter* is notable in that Green assumes an unprecedented role as co-composer on over half the songs, though the title track is a **Michael Card** song (not a Box Tops' cover) derived from the Apostle Paul's reference to Christians as "a letter from Christ" (1 Corinthians 3:2–3). The title track for *The Faithful* addresses a major theme for Green's ministry, the ongoing worldwide persecution of Christians. Green is affiliated with the organization Voice of the Martyrs, which seeks redress for such suffering. *Morning Light* is a devotional album, with a more intimate, meditative feel. It includes "All That You Say," a duet with **Twila Paris.** *People Need the Lord* is a compilation of hits, as are *Early Works* and *The Collection.*

Christian radio hits: "Proclaim the Glory of the Lord" (# 12 in 1984).

Dove Awards: 1985 Male Vocalist of the Year; 1987 Male Vocalist of the Year; 1987 Musical Album (*A Mighty Fortress*); 1990 Inspirational Album (*The Mission*); 1991 Children's Music Album (*Hide 'Em in Your Heart*); 1991 Choral Collection Album (*I Call You to Praise*).

Tom and Candy Green

1973—*Tom and Candy Green* (custom); 1974—*Born Again*; 1975—*Husband and Wife*; 1976—*Back Home*; *A Christmas Album*; 1977—*Learning to Rest*; 1978—*Becoming as Little Children*; 1980—*Nothing to Hide* (Elijah).

Since most of their albums have been independent, custom releases, not too much is known of the husband and wife duo Tom and Candy Green. *Harmony* magazine once described Candy's voice as having "a backwoods flavor" and Tom's as featuring a higher-pitched nasal style that "produces a sound like you'd expect to hear from a truckstop juke box." All this implies country and that is certainly the tone of *Husband and Wife,* which features abundant use of steel guitar and a seven-minute title track in which the two testify to how God saved their marriage. The debut album, however, is more in a folk vein, and *Born Again* displays a distinctively Hebraic sound (like that associated with Jewish folk songs).

Tom and Sherry Green

1975—*Testimony* (Big Rock).

Not to be confused with **Tom and *Candy* Green,** the husband and wife duo of Tom and Sherry Green produced one Jesus music album that consisted mainly of sweet folk songs directed to the Lord. Sherry was the principal songwriter, but Tom contributed two funky/bluesy songs that may be the album's highlights: "Thank You Lord Blues" and "Testimony." The latter tune contains the memorable line, "From pervert to convert, that's quite a change."

Norman Greenbaum

1969—*Spirit in the Sky* (Reprise); 1970—*Back Home Again*; 1972—*Petaluma*.

Norman Greenbaum is one of rock's definitive one-hit wonders. His psychedelic jug-band song, "Spirit in the Sky," hit Number Three and sold over two million copies in the summer of 1970. The song enjoyed a resurgence in 1995, rising to the top of the charts again when it was featured in the movie *Apollo 13*. It expresses simplistic devotion to and dependence upon Jesus, whom the singer claims is "gonna set me up with the Spirit in the sky . . . that's where I'm gonna go when I die." Christians tended to regard the song as mockery: its lyrics were heretical ("I've never sinned," cf. Romans 3:23) and its sentiments seemed tongue-in-cheek. Christian superstar **Larry Norman** lampooned the song on his 1978 album, *Streams of White Light into Dark Corners*. Without claiming to be a Christian himself, Greenbaum always insisted the song was sincere. He wrote it for a friend who was going through hard times, and he wanted the appeals to Jesus to be heard as evidentiary of a genuine (if somewhat generic) faith. In 1999, **DC Talk** covered the song with the heretical line amended ("We all have sinned"), giving the tune new credibility in the officially Christian arena.

Buddy Greene

Selected: 1986—*Praise You, Lord* (Fortress); 1987—*Quiet Harmonica Praise; So Far!* 1988—*Slice of Life*; 1990—*Sojourner's Song* (Word); 1992—*Buddy Greene and Friends Live* [label unknown]; 1994—*Grace for the Moment* [with Dr. Steve Brown]; 1995—*Minstrel of the Lord* (Fortress); 1996—*Simple Praise* (label unknown).

Christian country singer Buddy Greene came into his own with *Sojourner's Song*. Prior to that, Greene had performed with Jerry Reid and sung with **The Gaither Vocal Band,** but he remained best known for his prowess on the harmonica. He had

even released an entire album of harmonica praise songs that was regarded as something of a novelty within the industry. His *So Far!* album is a repackaging of his first two projects on one tape, collecting vocal and instrumental versions of traditional gospel songs and church hymns. *Slice of Life* has an essentially bluegrass style and includes a song called "Love Waits," which relates a cautionary traumatic tale of premarital sex. On *Sojourner's Song*, Greene moves into mainstream country and solicits help from such artists as **Ricky Skaggs, Ashley Cleveland, Phil Madeira,** and Pam Tillis. With the help of such friends, he performs songs by **Mark Heard** and **Gloria Gaither** in addition to his own compositions. "Suzanne's Song" is an especially sweet ballad, featuring a tasteful mandolin, and "How Long" delves into delta blues with enough harmonica intact to please die-hard fans.

Greene reached a new audience when he collaborated with **Mark Lowry** to compose the Christmas standard "Mary, Did You Know?"; the latter song has been recorded by Kathleen Battle, Billy Dean, Kathie Lee Gifford, Wynonna Judd, Kathy Mattea (who calls it her "favorite song of all time"), and **Kenny Rogers,** in addition to **Michael English** and numerous contemporary Christian stars. Greene offers his own rendition of the song on his 1992 live album, which also features **Bruce Carroll** on "Brother of Mine" and Tricia Walker singing a country version of "Moon River." Greene's song "Grace for the Moment" inspired TV preacher Steve Brown to construct a program built around its theme. The album *Grace for the Moment* intersperses musical tracks with Brown's messages. Greene seeks to duplicate the success of *Sojourner's Song* on *Minstrel of the Lord*. The latter album was produced by top Nashville producer Jerry Douglas, and it presents a collection of Greene's songs performed by a crack band of session players and guest vocalists (including **Ashley Cleveland, Julie Miller, Chris Rodriguez,** and **Kelly Willard**). *Simple Praise* is an instrumental follow-up to the *Praise Harmonica* album, on which Greene records fifteen well-known hymns and spiritual songs backed by piano and acoustic guitars.

Dove Awards: 1991 Country Album of the Year *(Sojourner's Song)*.

Jeanie Greene

1971—*Mary Called Jeanie Greene* (Elektra).

The contemporary Christian singer who recorded under the name Jeanie Greene once seemed poised to be Jesus music's first successful crossover artist. Greene's debut album derives its title from the fact that the singer's given name is not Jeanie but Mary. The record was recorded on Elektra, a general market label known at the time for such artists as The Doors, and it was primarily promoted through mainstream channels. Greene was a featured singer at the 1971 Concert for Bangladesh organized by George Harrison of the Beatles. The latter concert was a historic event that also included **Eric Clapton, Bob Dylan,** Leon Russell, and Ravi Shankar on the bill. A year later, Greene would perform at *Explo '72,* the "Christian Woodstock" event that brought the Jesus movement to the attention of the national media. Her album features mostly folk songs, sung in a voice that reminds some of Janis Joplin. She opens with a declaration of faith and empathy: "Hey all you sinners, I'm talkin' to you / I want you to listen because I am one too." Many of the songs are drawn from biblical stories. "Magdalene's Medley" presents the hymns "Oh How I Love Jesus" and "In the Garden" interwoven and sung from the biblical character's perspective.

Green Olive Tree

Justin Lane Alexander, drums; Jon Dodson, gtr., kybrd.; Brett Latimer, bass; Chris Latimer, voc., gtr. 2001—*Things I Tried to Be* (Syntax).

Green Olive Tree is a band whose members have their roots in worship leadership. Their debut showcases a diversity of styles with songs that are invariably faith-oriented. "Unassisted" has an Alice in Chains grunge feel to it, confessing to God an inability to meet life's struggles alone. "Red 13" (dealing with doubt and lack of direction) and "Pull" are more pop-punk songs, and "For Andy" is an melodic alternative-acoustic number. "Cacophony" features metal guitar riffs and an overall hardcore sound. The record's centerpiece comes with a mini-passion play called "Enter Golgotha, Vision of Tears."

Janny Grein (a.k.a. **Janny Grine)**

1976—*Free Indeed* [a.k.a. *Janny*] (Sparrow); 1977—*Covenant Woman;* 1978—*He Made Me Worthy;* 1979—*Think on These Things;* 1980—*The Best of Janny;* 1981—*Be Strong in the Lord* (Foundation); 1983—*Like the Wind* (Sparrow); 1988—*Stronger Than Before* (Mighty Wind); 1995—*Storm of Glory;* 1991—*Spiritual Freedom;* date unknown—*Signs and Wonders; Keys of the Kingdom; Anthology 1* (= *Free Indeed* + *Covenant Woman*); *Anthology 2* (= *He Made Me Worthy* + *Think on These Things*).

www.janny.com

Nashville singer/songwriter Janny Grein came into the contemporary Christian music scene in the latter stages of the Jesus movement, and her first two albums were received as Jesus music associated with that revival. At that time, she was one of a handful of female vocalists (cf. **Honeytree, Annie Herring**) in a field that would soon become crowded with them. Her name was (mis)spelled Janny Grine on her first few albums, but most of the time she was simply known as "Janny." Unlike most contemporary Christian singers—including those involved in the Jesus movement—Grein did not grow up in a Christian home, and she maintains she had virtually no knowledge of Jesus or of Christian teachings before she

watched the motion picture *King of Kings* on TV one night in 1975. Brought to faith, in part, through the witness of her husband Bill Grein—who also experienced a spiritual awakening at this time—the couple determined to devote their talents to the burgeoning contemporary Christian music community. Bill Grein is a photographer and he was responsible for producing album covers for a number of now-classic Christian records (**Honeytree**'s *Evergreen;* **Don Francisco**'s *Forgiven*). A native of Arkansas, Janny had already begun working as a singer and songwriter in the Nashville music scene, and so a debut in the Christian market was a natural transition.

Her first album was officially titled *Free Indeed,* though it was frequently just called *Janny.* It showcases her voice—a bit like that of Connie Francis and, especially, her songs, which tend toward the soulful folk sounds of artists like Janis Ian or Carole King. Other Sparrow artists (**The Talbot Brothers, Nelly** and **Matthew Ward** of **2nd Chapter of Acts**) lend audible support. "Glory Hallelujah" and "Call on Jesus" betray some traditional gospel influence. The title song, "Free Indeed," is probably the album's highlight, taking its cue from the Apostle Paul's bold words in Galatians 5:1. Grein's sophomore project, *Covenant Woman,* would be her greatest triumph. The song "Bread on the Water" and the title track quickly became favorites among aging Jesus freaks who were ready for Grein's mature and sensitive style. Both feature spirited sing-along melodies with strong gospel choruses. "Bread on the Water" collects scriptural promises of God's blessings (as does another popular Janny song called "Blessin's"). "Covenant Woman" opens with an unforgettable a capella verse that gives way to some serious testifying about the artist's intentions on how to live in the last days.

Perhaps the most notable feature of Grein's material is her strong reliance on Scripture. Her all-time best song is the powerful piano ballad "Eagle's Wings," which draws its words from Isaiah 40:27–31. Though she would remain best known for her two classic Jesus-music records, her subsequent albums would continue to present musical expositions of Scripture ("Psalm 20" on *He Made Me Worthy* and "Ninety-first Psalm" on *Think on These Things*). *He Made Me Worthy* produced three radio hits ("More Than Conquerors" is inspired by Romans 8:37 and "Count It All Joy," by James 1:2). The Greins also became involved in global missions and lead "Covenant Crusades" in Mexico, South Africa, and Eastern Europe. Janny Grein has authored a book titled *Called, Appointed, Anointed* (Harrison House, 1985) dealing with the ministry of music and worship leadership. In October 2001 she re-recorded a song called "Stronger Than Before" as a tribute to the emergency workers and others who lost their lives or their loved ones in the terrorist attacks on September 11, 2001.

Christian radio hits: "More Than Conquerors" (# 7 in 1978); "By His Word" (# 11 in 1979); "Count It All Joy" (# 25 in 1979).

Gretchen

Greg Godsey, bass; David Richards, gtr.; Mia Richards, voc.; Steve Robinson, drums. 2001—*Mouthful of Nails* (Rugged).

www.gretchenland.com

Gretchen is a female-fronted hard rock band from the Tri-Cities of eastern Tennessee. The group was founded by husband and wife David and Mia Richards as an acoustic duo and morphed into a band called Serenade, which *HM* described as "alterna-chick modern rock." Serenade released an independent album called *Fairy Tales,* which was heavy on acoustic guitars, background vocals, and ballads. Then Mia Richards braided her hair into dreadlocks, the band toughened up their sound and chose a new name inspired by the **King's X** album *Gretchen Goes to Nebraska.* The title of Gretchen's debut album, *Mouthful of Nails,* is intended to serve fair warning that sweetness is no longer a priority. *Phantom Tollbooth* says the album sounds like "what would happen if Leigh Nash (of **Sixpence None the Richer**) suddenly decided to perform heavy metal." They also describe the song "See Me, Hear Me" as "a Pat Benatar meets Rage Against the Machine rockfest." But the music is not all hard. Although Gretchen offers only one true ballad ("Inclined"), they sometimes go for more of the modern rock sound of artists like Veruca Salt ("Trophy") or Alanis Morissette ("Diamonds"). The group also covers Billy Idol's "White Wedding." Lyrically, the songs favor spiritual metaphors and vulnerability: "I'm just an ordinary girl / Trapped in a complicated world / Just like a crushed up soda can / Recycled, restored, to live again / For somebody else to use me up." Even "White Wedding" is presented as an allegory of Christ and the church.

Andy Griffith

1996—*I Love to Tell the Story: 25 Timeless Hymns* (Sparrow); 1998—*Just As I Am: 30 Favorite Old Time Hymns.*

There is absolutely nothing contemporary about TV personality Andy Griffith's albums of timeless and old-time hymns, but many fans of contemporary Christian music snatched them up all the same. *I Love to Tell the Story* won a Grammy and sold almost two million copies, making it one of the ten best-selling Christian albums of all time. Griffith was the star of the popular TV programs *The Andy Griffith Show* (in which he played lovable small-town sherif Andy Taylor) and *Matlock.* He does not have the voice of a trained or accomplished singer, but he brings his material to life by infusing the songs with the same sort of down-home sincerity that charac-terized his acting. Song selection on the albums strongly favors American compositions.

Grammy Awards: 1996 Best Southern Gospel, Country Gospel, or Bluegrass Gospel Album (*I Love to Tell the Story*).

Grits

Teron Carter [a.k.a. "Bonafide"]; Stacey Jones [a.k.a. "Coffee"]. 1995—*Mental Release* (Gotee); 1997—*Factors of the Seven;* 1999—*Grammatical Revolution.*

A Christian rap group from Nashville, Grits became one of the first acts signed to Gotee records, cofounded by **Toby McKeehan** of **DC Talk.** Their name derives from an acronym for "Grammatical Revolutions in the Spirit" (*grammatical* referring here to speech, i.e., rap). The group is composed of two former dancers for **DC Talk.** Such connections may have allowed the group to gain notice in the crowded genre of Christian rap, but their debut album, *Mental Release,* also revealed them as possessing native talent worthy of such attraction. Jazzy samples reminiscent of Digable Planets set Grits apart from any other hip-hop artist in the Christian scene at the time. The duo mixes urban poetry with acid jazz on tracks like "Cataclysmic Circles" and "Set Ya Mind" (which earned a Dove nomination for Rap Song of the Year). The follow-up *Factors of the Seven* further established the group as exemplars of creativity. Three years after its release, *7ball* would refer to the album as "an industry changer, now considered a benchmark project." The song "U.S. Open" is especially lively and danceable, with light-hearted lyrics. "Mirage" deals with hypocrisy in a thoughtful way. **Knowdaverbs** guests on the first of these two tracks, and **Out of Eden**'s Joy Danielle Kimmey adds vocals on the latter. *Grammatical Revolution* would turn out to be the best of the three albums. Along with a handful of fairly traditional songs, the group presents such innovative masterpieces as "Time Is Passing" and "It Takes Love," both of which featured Chic-style female vocals and Coltrane-inspired rhythms. **Knowdaverbs** shows up again on "C2K." The single "They All Fall Down" (featuring Latin-tinged guitar licks and lyrics urging listeners to make the right choices in life) gained some airplay on the video program *Yo! MTV Raps.*

As a group, Grits has been critical of the Christian music industry, alleging that it does not promote rap and hip-hop because the latter styles are so closely associated with sexual and violent imagery in the general market. Furthermore, they have publicly accused the Christian music community of racism due to the lack of exposure afforded music targeted for urban black youth (e.g., in a slam on "white-boy DJs" in the Grits song "Why"). On the one hand, this has sometimes come off as self-serving and illogical (**Tourniquet** does not complain that their songs don't get played in nursing homes and black gospel radio stations are seldom faulted for not playing **Pat Boone**). On the other hand, the claim that Christian radio stations need to serve their (mostly white) constituency has only begged the question as to why white Christian music fans should be more reluctant to embrace rap and hip-hop than their peers in the general market. In 1999, *Vibe* magazine reported that seventy-five percent of general market consumers who purchased rap albums were white. The percentage would have been much less in the Christian market, and Grits has been right to wonder why this is the case.

Dove Awards: 1999 Rap/Hip Hop Song ("Plagiarism"); 2000 Rap/Hip Hop Song ("They All Fall Down").

Groms

Hans Dalen, gtr.; Petter Gordon Jensen, drums; Haakon Johannessen, bass; Oyvind Johannessen, voc. 1994—*Ascension* (Arctic Serenades).

Groms billed themselves as "the first heavy doom/death metal band from Norway." The group's name was an acronym for "God Rules Over My Soul," and *Rad Rockers* identifies their debut album as "one of the most extremely brutal CDs ever to come on to the Christian market." With guttural vocals reminiscent of **Mortification** or **Crimson Thorn,** the group presents ten dark and grinding songs with overtly Christian lyrics. The album did much better than expected and went through three pressings, featuring two different cover designs.

Sara Groves

1998—*Past the Wishing* (independent); 1999—*Conversations.*

www.saragroves.com

Sara Groves (b. 1972) is a former high school English and history teacher from Minneapolis, Minnesota, who took to singing her songs of integrity and spirituality professionally in 1998. She graduated from Evangel College in 1994. Sara and her husband, Troy Groves, founded the independent company Past the Wishing and released two albums that met with positive critical reception. She was subsequently signed to INO Records and her *Conversations* album was reissued on that label in 2000. Musically, Groves' style is indistinguishable from that of dozens of other women with acoustic guitars, but like the best of her peers in that very crowded arena (Shawn Colvin, Sarah MacLachlan), her songwriting is sufficiently tender and vulnerable to get her noticed (cf. Emily Saliers of **Indigo Girls**). The opening title track to *Conversations* relates her uneasy, yet confident witness to friends who may regard the topic of religion as taboo. "Painting Pictures of Egypt" references the wandering Israelites' unrealistic memories of life in Egypt in a song about romanticizing the past.

Christian radio hits: "How Is It Between Us" (# 16 in 2001).

Shaun Groves

2001—*Invitation to Eavesdrop* (Rocketown).

Shaun Groves is a singer/songwriter cut from the same cloth as **Billy Crockett, Wes King, Wayne Kirkpatrick,** and **Chris Rice.** *Invitation to Eavesdrop* contains ten introspective songs worthy of its title. On "Should I Tell Them?" and "Two Cents" he balances awareness of his own human frailty and foibles against the realization that he is possessed of a great truth that can transform lives. Other tracks ("Abba Father," "After the Music Fades") are worship oriented. Musically, Groves goes for an acoustic pop sound that sometimes transcends the limitations of the male soloist genre for more of the alternative-rock stylings of combos like Matchbox 20 and Third Eye Blind.

Christian radio hits: "Welcome Home" (# 17 in 2001).

Gryp

Jeremy Davis, bass; Jonathan Deundian, drums; Jason Garcia, gtr.; Curtis Shamlin, voc. 1998—*Real* [EP] (independent); 1999—*Indecision* (Metro One); 2001—*Gryp* (independent).

www.gryp.net

A hardcore band from Fresno, California, Gryp has come to be associated with the rapcore fad of the new millennium, though their similarities to general market groups like Korn are only superficial. The overall style is unapologetically chaotic; *Phantom Tollbooth* says, "don't expect any radio-friendly songs or any kind of standard song structure." Curtis Shamlin's vocal style varies from whispers to screams, and the band's guitar-heavy instrumentation is supplemented by eerie electronic noises. The *Real* EP contains only five songs, four of which were re-recorded for *Indecision.* Lyrically, the band favors songs that first present "honest to God" questions, and then conclude with answers. For example, the song "You Were There" precedes its titular conclusion with these lines: "Where were you when my parents divorced? . . . You say you care / Where were you?" In another song Shamlin asks, "Why do I have to believe in some man who died for me? . . . Am I not good enough for you?" before concluding (now in the voice of Christ) that *no one* is good enough to "come to the Father but by me." The group takes its name from John 10:28, intending to convey the thought that "God loves us and He's not letting us go." The band's self-titled 2001 release includes a single called "Left Behind," which seeks to capitalize on publicity surrounding the sensationalist film *Left Behind.* Although it had no official connection to the film or to the novels by Tim LaHaye that inspired it, the song does deal with the notion of the rapture that was the topic of those media phenomena. Other songs on *Gryp* include "Can't Explain" (not a Who cover) and "Ungrateful" (a rant against former day job supervisors).

GS Megaphone

Chris Freeman, gtr.; Daniel Rosas, gtr.; Ben Shreve, bass; Randy Shreve, drums. 2001—*Out of My Mind* (Spindust).

GS Megaphone is a hard rock band from Arkansas that reflects a strong influence from Seattle grunge groups like Nirvana, Soundgarden, and Alice in Chains. *HM* notes that their "hair rock roots" (i.e., influence of '80s metal bands) show as well. Randy Shreve adds, "People say we sound like **Creed,** even though none of us are really big Creed fans." The group's debut album was released as the premiere product on the Spindust label, owned by none other than the decidedly nongrunge, nonmetal artist **Ray Boltz.** Defying all stereotypes, Boltz would identify himself as the group's biggest fan, partly due to an appreciation for their overtly Christian lyrics. Standout songs on *Out of My Mind* include the title track, which deals with taking on the mind of Christ, and "Use Me," a song of passionate consecration. "Prodigal Dad" puts a twist on the famous biblical parable, presenting the perspective of a son whose father has strayed from family and faith.

Guardian

David Bach, bass, voc.; Tony Palacios, gtr., voc.; Paul Cawley, voc., gtr. (−1990); Rikk Hart, drums (−1990) // Karl Ney, drums (+ 1990); Jamie Rowe, voc. (+ 1990). 1989—*First Watch* (Enigma); 1990—*Fire and Love* (Pakaderm); 1993—*Miracle Mile*; 1994—*Swang, Swang, Swung*; 1995—*Nunca Te Dire Adios* (Myrrh); 1995—*Buzz*; 1996—*Kingdom of Rock* (G-Man); *Delicious Bite-Sized Meat Pies* (Bootblack); 1997—*Promesa* (Myrrh); *Bottle Rocket*; 1998—*The Yellow and Black Attack Is Back* (G-Man); 1999—*Smashes* (Myrrh); 1999—*Live!* (G-Man); *Sunday Best.*

www.guard-dog.com/gd

Guardian was one of Christian music's premiere rock bands; along with **Bride** and **Resurrection Band,** they are generally regarded as one of the two or three best groups to have made the transition from '80s metal to modern postgrunge rock without losing their sense of style or integrity. Universally praised for excellent musicianship, the band also possessed the essential attitude of a rock and roll band—a penchant for ignoring expectations (even of their fans) and an uncanny ability not to take themselves too seriously. "We take our *faith* very seriously," Tony Palacios says, "and we work hard to be skilled musicians, but we never lose sight of the fact that we're in the business of rock and roll—and rock and roll is pretty ridiculous, if you think about it." Perhaps most important, Guardian has been a constantly evolving band, and though they started out strong, virtually every album has trumped the predecessors to be named "their best yet."

Guardian has its roots in a California band called Fusion formed by David Bach and Paul Cawley in 1982. The name changed in 1985 as other personnel came and went. *First Watch*

featured a preliminary lineup, but the standard quartet of Bach, Palacios, Karl Ney, and Jamie Rowe has held from the second album. The band eventually relocated from the Sunshine State to Music City (Nashville). Their career took off in 1992 when they were invited to tour with seminal metal band **Stryper,** and they entered a new circle of critical approval a year later when their album *Miracle Mile* set them apart from that band and its many imitators. The group disbanded in 1999, having recorded six major albums in addition to two Spanish records (to enhance their South American tours) and one novelty project—*The Yellow and Black Attack Is Back,* on which they cover an entire album by the band that gave them their big break. In 1998, Tony Palacios released an album of guitar instrumentals called *Epic Tales of Whoa!* (Cadence). One reviewer referred to it as "a monument to divinely inspired talent." Jamie Rowe has also released an EP of five songs (*The Beautiful EP,* Massive Groove, 1999) intended to preview a possible solo project. He then joined the melodic metal band Adrian Gale, which released an album in 2000 (*Feel the Fire,* Kievel).

First Watch and *Fire and Love* reveal a group that is more than competent at churning out the same sort of melodic metal for which **Stryper** was famous. "Livin' for the Promise" from the first album is a rock anthem extolling God's trustworthiness, and "One of a Kind" offers Christian music fans their own version of Van Halen party-rock, with more uplifting lyrics. *Fire and Love* has a very different sound, primarily due to the adoption of Rowe as new lead singer. The second album was also produced by **John** and Dino **Elefante** and presents a group able to hold its own in comparison to such contemporary arena acts as Warrant or Winger. It opens with another Van Halen-ish masterpiece, "Power of Love" (not the Huey Lewis song), and closes with an Aerosmith-like power ballad that got the group airplay on Christian radio ("Never Say Goodbye"). "The Rain" could easily be a Bon Jovi outtake. *Fire and Love's* title track is a typical anthemic screamer; "Send a Message" announces the group's unambiguous evangelical intent. "Forever and a Day" is a middisc power ballad that could have joined "Never Say Goodbye" on the Christian radio stations (or Aerosmith's "Angel" on general market ones).

As indicated above, it was *Miracle Mile* that first marked the exponential growth that would become Guardian's trademark. The primary distinction on this third outing is a greater influence of R&B, allowing the band to break out of the sonic confines of metal and just rock in creative ways analogous to (but completely different from) such bands as the Rolling Stones and Led Zeppelin. The sheer variety of the album is perhaps its most astounding feature—so many different styles, and all of them performed convincingly. "I Found Love" is a Tesla-type song with lots of big, jangly acoustic guitars and harmonic background vocals. "Curiosity Killed the Cat" is a high-energy screamer that takes off from a skat vocal of "ally ally oxen free" and features an extended electric guitar solo that surely *must* be a guest appearance by Eddie Van Halen (no, it isn't). "You and I" is the album's most catchy sing-along tune with a hook-filled melody and unexpected Beatlesque harmonies throughout. "Sweet Mystery" is another "let's get on the radio" acoustic ballad (with strings) about escaping from alcoholism. Lyrically, *Miracle Mile* features a number of songs that introduce interesting characters: "Dr. Jones and the Kings of Rhythm" (a sideshow evangelist) and "Shoeshine Johnny" (a humble man who loves to tell others about the Lord). The most remarkable song on the album, however, is the proto-feminist "Sister Wisdom," which draws on a theme in the book of Proverbs (1:20–21; 4:6–9; 7:4) to describe a female image of divinity that may rightly be the object of Christian prayers.

Swing, Swang, Swung took everyone by surprise. The group now severed all ties to metal and released a mostly unplugged blues album that remains one of the best Christian records ever made. The song "C'mon Everyone" alone is a rollicking praise chorus so infectious, so rocking, and so good that there is really no reason that it could not have been a major crossover hit in spite of its "lift the name of Jesus high" lyrics. It is one of those songs (like the Doobie Brothers' "Jesus Is Just Alright") that unbelievers might find to be so much fun they would hardly care about the words. "The Preacher and the Bear" is a hilarious traditional tune (a Dixieland jazz standard) done here with an innovative competence that lifts it beyond the novelty characterization. The rest of the album has a less commercial sound, but complements these obvious hits with deeply personal songs that reflect the diverse perspectives of the band's various members. The best of these is Palacios's "See You in Heaven," a sensitive ballad about the death of his mother: "The only thing that hurts more than losing you / Is all of the years living without you." Palacios also contributes the Beatlesque "Rich Man over the Line" and a grammatically dyslexic song called "The Way Home Back," which sounds like something he might sing in a rocking chair on a front porch: "Everybody's got something / They can give everyday / Make a little bit better / Help somebody find the way." Bach's "Endless Summer" is more of a rocker, with lyrics that proclaim an end of innocence and a waking up to reality: "It's said that money talks, and I'll not deny / I heard it once, it said goodbye." **Michael W. Smith** plays piano on "Like the Sun," a song that actually recalls the latter's pop style. *Swing, Swang, Swung* was mostly recorded in stripped-down sessions performed quite literally in producer **John Elefante**'s garage. Its diverse songs, like the diverse styles on *Miracle Mile,* somehow hold together through a recognizable but not quite definable chemistry that the band had developed through constant touring. *HM* magazine didn't

like the album (being at that point still a forum for metal) but their intended criticism highlighted its strength: "Rather than streetwise flash, this album has dirt-road sensibility."

On *Buzz* and on *Bottle Rocket,* the group returned to a harder sound, albeit one that was more in keeping with the edgier dynamics of mid '90s rock than with '80s metal. **Steve Taylor** produced both albums and contributed lyrics for five of the songs. The group's overall sound comes even closer to that associated with Aerosmith than on previous projects, as Rowe adds more bite and snarl to his singing and Palacios incorporates more blues licks into his heroic guitar solos. On *Buzz,* the song "This Old Man" starts things off with a pounding **King's X**-like tune that offers a twisted take on a familiar nursery rhyme. "Lion's Den" features some clever Taylor wordplay, comparing Daniel's experience with the beasts to the modern desire of people to be lionized by their peers. The melodic, Beatle-ish "Psychedelic Runaway" offers a lament for all the lost souls of the '60s. "Hand of the Father" goes for the grunge sound with references to Alice in Chains or Soundgarden. "State of Mine" features the "Love Sponge String Quartet" conducted by John Painter of **Fleming and John.** *True Tunes* would note the growing musical competence of the band as evident in their ability to impress even while showing restraint: on the midtempo ballad "Are You Gonna Keep Your Word?" Palacios eschews his Van Halen/Richie Sambora histrionics to "play only the notes that are necessary and let his guitar sing." *Bottle Rocket* has more of an alternative edge to it than *Buzz* but continues in the same modern rock vein. It opens with "Are We Feelin' Comfortable Yet?" a taunting, snarling, blues song with a theme reminiscent of Taylor's own "Easy Listening." The title track sounds exactly like an Aerosmith song, so much so that the latter group just might record the song if they were ever to hear it. Lyrically, it is a thinly disguised version of the Sunday school classic, "This Little Light of Mine." Many considered the standout track on *Bottle Rocket* to be "Coffee Can," a highly charged rocker with bizarro Taylor lyrics about the final judgment. The low point comes with "Queen Esther," a song that is similar in theme to Britney Spears' "Lucky" and about as profound. But *Release* would describe the *Bottle Rocket* album as a whole as "loud, raucous, and relevant," as "intelligent without being intellectual, relentless without being hopeless, accessible without being trite."

Numerous collections of Guardian songs are available. *Kingdom of Rock* compiles tracks from the pre-Rowe days, including a couple of Fusion songs. *Meat Pies* and *Live!* assemble concert tracks, and the latter record includes a cover of **U2**'s "Pride (In the Name of Love)." *Sunday Best* presents the band's own favorite selections of songs from *Fire and Love, Miracle Mile,* and *Swing, Swang, Swung* (some in alternative or live versions), plus an incredible bonus: live and studio versions of what is certainly one of the band's best songs: "Take Up Your Cross," a fabulous blues number that is similar to the material on *Swing, Swang, Swung,* but was previously unreleased. *Smashes* is yet another "best of" compilation with two songs from *Miracle Mile,* three from *Swing, Swang, Swung,* five from *Buzz,* five from *Bottle Rocket,* and three repetitive remixes.

Christian radio hits: "Never Say Goodbye" (# 14 in 1991); "Sweet Mystery" (# 9 in 1993); "I Found Love" (# 9 in 1993); "Like the Sun" (# 10 in 1995); "See You in Heaven" (# 17 in 1995); "C'mon Everyone" (# 12 in 1995).

The Gufs

Morgan Dawley, gtr.; Dejan Kralj, bass; Goran Kralj, voc., gtr., kybrd.; Scott Schwebel, drums; Brian Pettit, perc. (+ 1992; −1999). 1991—*Staring into the Sun* (Red Submarine); 1992—*Songs of Life;* 1993—*Circa '89;* 1995—*Collide;* 1996—*The Gufs* (Atlantic); 1999—*Holiday from You.*

www.atlantic-records.com

Although they are rarely associated with the Christian music scene, The Gufs have potential to raise the respectability of what is sometimes called contemporary Christian music, if that genre can be defined more broadly than ministry-oriented music associated with a particular (conservative) theological perspective. Formed in Milwaukee in 1990, The Gufs were one of the ensuing decade's finest alternative rock bands. Some of their songs had noticeable spiritual or religious themes, especially on the album *Circa '89* ("On Your Cross," "Out of Mind," "Tell the Man Upstairs"). As its title implies, *Circa '89* contained songs that the group had written and performed prior to its debut. Once The Gufs became established in the club scene, the religious songs became less prominent in their repertoire. Nevertheless, like **Collective Soul, The Ocean Blue,** or **Creed,** The Gufs attracted a following from fans of Christian music, which surged when the band toured with **Jars of Clay.** Their song "Sunday Driver" (from *The Gufs*) was played on some of the more progressive Christian radio stations: the song notes the role of paranoia and self-aggrandizement as factors in human ambition in a way that is compatible with Christian teaching. Musically, The Gufs have a jangly-guitar sound similar at times to such '90s bands as The BoDeans or the Dave Matthews Band and reminiscent of classic rock groups like The Byrds and Big Star. They first became known regionally for the song "Crash (Into Me)" which is *not* the song made famous by the Dave Matthews Band. In addition to that song, *Collide* contains "Smile" and "Listen to the Trees," an infectious bouncy number that remains their best song. *The Gufs* features new versions of the best songs from the group's independent albums, plus "Sunday Driver" and a few other new songs. *Holiday from You* is a painful album, reflecting on Goran Kralj's divorce. Produced by Arnold Lanni, who has worked with **King's X,** the album includes the song "Give Back Yourself,"

which features guest vocals by Rob Thomas of Matchbox 20. The song was written when a young friend and fan of the band was killed in an automobile accident.

Kenn Gulliksen

1975—*Charity* (Maranatha).

Kenn Gulliksen's enormous influence on contemporary Christian music would owe more to his pastoral gifts than his musical talents, though the latter were not altogether lacking. Gulliksen joined the staff of Calvary Chapel in Costa Mesa, California, during the early days of the Jesus movement. At that time, he wrote a song called "Charity," based on the "love chapter" of the Bible, 1 Corinthians 13. Gulliksen's version of the song ended up on Calvary Chapel's second compilation of Jesus music, *Maranatha Two* (1972), where his MOR vocals (which David Di Sabatino compares to Richard Carpenter) seemed out of place alongside folk-rock masterpieces by **Children of the Day, Country Faith,** and **The Way.** Nevertheless, the song itself is a wonder—if only **Marsha Stevens** or **Debby Kerner** had sung it, it might have been a masterpiece. The Jesus people picked up on this and Gulliksen's "Charity" became one of the most sung songs at Christian coffeehouses and prayer meetings for some years afterward.

In 1973, Gulliksen released an album of pleasant, mellow songs, but he was to remain Jesus music's definitive one-hit wonder. As a pastor, however, Gulliksen's Bible studies formed the nucleus for what would become the Vineyard Christian Fellowship. He is in some sense the founder of that denomination, though in 1982 he handed over the leadership to John Wimber. As pastor of the Hollywood Vineyard Church, Gulliksen played an instrumental role in the spiritual formation of both **Keith Green** and **Bob Dylan.**

Tami Cheré Gunden

As Tami Cheré: 1976—*Little Flowers* (custom); 1977—*Keep Singin' That Love Song* (Light); 1979—*He's Everything to Me.* As Tami Gunden: 1983—*Celebration;* 1987—*Written on My Heart* (Home Sweet Home); 1992—*Behind the Cover;* date unknown—*Best of Tami Gunden* (Small Globe); *The Songs I Love.*

www.tamigunden.com

Tami Cheré (b. 1964) from Bay Port, Michigan, is the niece of Danny Lee of the pioneering Christian group **Danny Lee and the Children of Truth.** Her uncle helped her get an early start in Christian music and she began recording at the age of ten. She made a big impression on **Ralph Carmichael,** who signed her as the youngest artist on his Light Records label. In 1978, she moved to Charlotte, North Carolina, and attended Central Piedmont Community College. With *Celebration* she matured from singing youth-group camp songs (Carmichael's

"He's Everything to Me") to adult pop in the mold of **Amy Grant**. *CCM* described her raspy voice as a cross between rock singer Bonnie Tyler and country star Emmylou Harris. **Michael W. Smith** wrote many of the songs on *Celebration* and also provided keyboards and background vocals for the project. The album's highlights include two non-Smith compositions, "Then He Comes" and the R&B-flavored "When You're Following Jesus (There's No Back of the Line)." Her second album as Tami Gunden would earn her a Christian radio hit with the title track, "Written on My Heart." On *Behind the Cover* she sings previously unrecorded songs by Smith and **Phil Keaggy** in an '80s pop style reminiscent of Belinda Carlisle or The Bangles.

Christian radio hits: "Written on My Heart" (# 13 in 1987).

Dann Gunn

See **Velocipede**.

Rhonda Gunn

1996—*Forgiveness* (Damascus Road); 1998—*I Wonder If . . . .*

Rhonda Gunn is a Christian country-pop singer from Arkansas. A successful songwriter, she has composed songs that have been recorded by Rita Coolidge, Barbara Mandrell, and Tanya Tucker. Although she is associated with country music in the general market, she cites such artists as Fleetwood Mac, Foreigner, and Ted Nugent as among her primary influences. *Forgiveness* presents Gunn to the Christian market as a rock singer not too dissimilar from Sheryl Crow. It includes the anthemic "No Turning Back" and a poignant song, "Autumn's Rain," which views faith development as a process of maturing through spiritual seasons. Country roots are all but invisible on *I Wonder If. . . .* Rather, the sophomore project revels in R&B sound on "Receive" and "Higher Faith" (a rousing hymn complete with gospel choir). The alleged Fleetwood Mac influences are also quite obvious on the opening song "Believe in Love." The title track is a more sedate reflection on the questions all people ask about God's ways. Other tracks present Gunn as a fairly typical adult contemporary singer. Billy Smiley of **White Heart** has worked as Gunn's producer.

Christian radio hits: "Without Love" (# 15 in 1997).

Arlo Guthrie

Selected: 1979—*Outlasting the Blues* (Warner Bros.); 1981—*Power of Love*; 1982—*Precious Friend* [with Pete Seeger]; 1986—*Someday* (Rising Son); 1991—*All over the World*; 1992—*Son of the Wind*; 1994—*More Together Again* [with Pete Seeger]; 1996—*Alice's Restaurant: The Massacree Revisited*; *Mystic Journey*.

www.arlo.net

Two years before **Bob Dylan** announced his very public conversion to Christianity, one of his most famous protégées—and the son of his mentor—underwent a similar but quieter transformation. Arlo Guthrie, perhaps the quintessential East Coast hippie (as distinct from the California variety) became a Roman Catholic.

Arlo Guthrie was born in 1947 in Coney Island, New York, the son of America's premier folksinger Woody Guthrie, the man responsible for "This Land Is Your Land" and numerous other ballads of the American frontier. Arlo grew up pickin' and grinnin' with the likes of Leadbelly and Pete Seeger. His father died when he was twenty, but by then he was already playing coffeehouses and touring with Judy Collins. The year of his father's death (1967), he released *Alice's Restaurant* (Reprise), the record for which he would always be best remembered. One of the definitive albums of the '60s, *Alice's Restaurant* succeeded on the strength of one oddball track, the eighteen-minute-plus, mostly spoken-word "song" he called "Alice's Restaurant Massacree." Here, Guthrie relates a hilarious tall tale about draft dodging and other aspects of '60s youth culture. The whole story begins with a yarn about converting Trinity Church in Great Barrington, Massachusetts, into a shelter for street people, a heavenly commune where hippies can gather for hassle-free enjoyment of a memorable Thanksgiving dinner prepared by the titular Alice. From there, the story's plot wanders a good bit, but by the time it reaches its end, the United States military has deemed Guthrie morally unfit to go to Vietnam and "murder women and babies" because he had once been arrested for littering. The epic played better in the late '60s than it ever would again, but at that time it established Guthrie as the country's most culturally relevant comedian, the missing link between Bill Cosby and Cheech and Chong. In 1969, the story was turned into a movie starring Guthrie. That summer, he performed at the Woodstock festival. His song "Comin' into Los Angeles" (a light-hearted song about dope smuggling) went over big there and subsequently turned out to be a highlight of both the film and the soundtrack album commemorating that event. In 1972, Guthrie scored his only Top 20 hit with a cover of Steve Goodman's "City of New Orleans."

The details of Guthrie's conversion are not known. He was raised Jewish by his mother but maintains that he was at best only a "humanitarian Jew" (accepting the basic moral code but without appreciating the theology that undergirds it). In 1977, he has said, he came to recognize Jesus Christ as his Messiah, accepted Catholic doctrine, and joined a lay fraternity or Catholic order called "the Franciscan Brothers of the Good News." He explained the transition to *Radix* magazine saying, "Catholicism comes directly into Judaism like a branch that is grafted on to a well-rooted vine. Jews don't covert to Catholicism but rather are fulfilled by it. They accept Jesus Christ because he was promised from the outset by his Father to be our Messiah, our Savior, and our friend. So I guess for lack of a better word, you could call me a Catholic-Jew." As for his choice to join the Franciscan order, Guthrie remarked to the *St. Anthony Messenger* that he admired Francis because of "his rebelliousness, a refusal to go along with fads of the time," and because of his "desire to pursue God at a deadly pace." The Franciscan order emphasizes prayer and service. In response to the latter, Guthrie began by sponsoring Vietnam refugees and bringing them to live on his farm in Washington, Massachusetts (where he lived with his wife Jackie and four children). He also continued to perform but regularly invited two of his Franciscan brothers to tour with him, and together they would visit hospitals in each town and sing and pray for the sick. Guthrie gradually incorporated modern and traditional gospel tunes into his concert sets, without eliminating the secular songs. He has often closed concerts with a double encore of "Will the Circle Be Unbroken?" and "Amazing Grace." In time, he began to tour regularly with Pete Seeger and became an activist for a variety of political causes, including antinuclear and ecological concerns. With life imitating art, he actually did purchase the Trinity Church featured in his most famous song and converted it into a recording studio (Rising Son records) and a home for his charitable service organization, the Guthrie Center. Still something of a comedian, Guthrie accepted the role of an aging hippie in a short-lived TV sitcom, *Byrds of Paradise* (1994).

Outlasting the Blues was Guthrie's most subtle but brilliant statement of faith. There was a bit of unintended irony in its appearance a few months after **Bob Dylan** released his first born-again manifesto, *Slow Train Coming*. Guthrie had been in Dylan's shadow throughout his entire career, dismissed as a less-profound version of the superstar genius. Now, it seemed, the latter had stolen his thunder again, heralding a far more dramatic conversion and issuing a much more bombastic testimony to his transformation just months before Guthrie allowed his quiet announcement of faith to appear. But, this time, critics unanimously recognized Guthrie's product (and even his faith) as the more genuine article. The first line of the first song on *Outlasting the Blues* ("Prologue") declares, "In the event of my demise, be sure to include this statement. . . ." The shroud of mortality that thus hung over the project was not born of paranoia. Guthrie's father and grandmother had both

died of Huntington's corea, and there was a fifty percent chance that the incurable degenerative disease would be passed on to him as well. If so, it would show itself within the next two years, and then he would die. Moved by such considerations, he delivers a mini-opus on Side One of *Outlasting the Blues* composed of five of the strongest songs of his career. After "Prologue" comes the powerful "Which Side Are You On?" The song describes the difficult trek of Moses in the wilderness, and then of Jesus to the cross as exemplars of persons willing to suffer for their commitments. Then it concludes, "Some men work for little things / And some men work for more / Some men work for anything / And some don't work at all / But me, myself, I'm satisfied / To sing for God's own Son / And ask you what I ask myself / Which side are you on?" The *New York Times* ran an article comparing the song with Dylan's "Gotta Serve Somebody" (from *Slow Train*). The critic praised Guthrie for his "unassuming humility" as opposed to Dylan's self-righteous stance, noting that, of the two converts, it was Guthrie who offered the more winsome and "consoling" view of Christianity, as opposed to Dylan's threatening vision of fire and brimstone. Continuing with this theme that the Christian faith instills peace, not rage, Guthrie next presents two tender and perfect love songs, not songs that articulate his faith as such but, rather, ones that express his new understanding of romance as informed by that faith. In "Wedding Song" he celebrates the gift of marriage, from that of Adam and Eve to Joseph and Mary to some unknown couple getting hitched down the street. "Let's go wish them well," he calls to his spouse. "It's been years since we've been married / I know we paid some dues / Now ain't it something just to lie here together / Me and you outlasting the blues." The side concludes with "Epilogue," a powerful statement of "no regrets" from a man who thought he might soon die. The *Rolling Stone Album Guide* rates *Outlasting the Blues* as Guthrie's best album. "It's popular music at its most honest," they exult. "A rigorous self-examination, spurred on by Guthrie's conversion to Catholicism, it meditates deeply on love, faith, and death." On subsequent albums, Guthrie's compositional skills were less in evidence. He covered **T Bone Burnett's** "Power of Love" for his 1981 release. He recorded a thirtieth anniversary version of *Alice's Restaurant* in 1996, along with a new studio album, coproduced by his son Abe. The latter project, *Mystic Journey,* includes the inspirational "Doors to Heaven" and a tribute to veterans, "When a Soldier Comes Home."

Deitrick Haddon (and Voices of Unity)

1995—*Come into This House* (Tyscot); 1997—*Live the Life;* 1998—*This Is My Story* (A&M); 1999—*Chainbreaker* (Tyscot); 2001—*Supernatural.*

Deitrick Haddon is an urban gospel singer and choir leader in the same mold as **Kirk Franklin.** Haddon has declared that he and his Detroit-based Voices of Unity have "a mission to destroy tradition," by which he means the destruction of religious rules that he believes limit the message of gospel music. Haddon serves as youth pastor and minister of music at Detroit's Unity Cathedral of Faith, a church that is pastored by his parents Bishop Clarence B. Haddon and Dr. Joyce Haddon. The artist's first three albums gained some notice in circles devoted to modern traditional gospel (with hits "Saved" and "Live the Life"), but Haddon first came to the attention of the broader contemporary Christian music market when his album *Chainbreaker* was reviewed by *CCM* magazine. The latter record mixes live tracks with studio recordings to offer a total of nineteen cuts running close to seventy minutes. "Totally Sold Out" has a guitar sound similar to Prince. Traditional gospel star John P. Kee joins Haddon for a duet on "Double Team." The *Supernatural* album is even more diverse with instances of R&B, hard rock, and reggae.

Michael Hakanson-Stacy

1991—*Shake the Dust* (Time and Strike); 1992—*Blues in the Belfry;* 1993— *Salted with Fire; Bottle on My Finger to the Blues on My Shoes;* 1994—*Lion's in the Den; News from the Cornerstore;* 1995—*Pearls and Stones;* 1996—*Sanctuary Blues;* 1999—*This Train.*

Michael Hakanson-Stacy is a blues singer and guitarist who specializes in a genre that he calls "gospel blues." Although he is far better known among aficionados of the blues in general than among fans of contemporary Christian music, he is famous for his creative adaptations of spirituals and hymns, as well as for original compositions in an old blues style. Hakanson-Stacy is best known as a purveyor of rootsy acoustic blues, favoring what are called resonator guitars and "bottleneck blues." He is also fond of playing East Coast folk music in a finger-picking style and sometimes alternates back and forth between the two genres on a single album. His debut album, *Shake the Dust,* was recorded with his friend **Brooks Williams,** and the songs betray the influence of such masters as Blind Willie Johnson and the Reverend Gary Davis. The album includes a rendition of the standard "John the Revelator," which many Christian music fans came to know when **Phil Keaggy** included it on his classic *Crimson and Blue* album. After *Shake the Dust,* Hakanson-Stacy would prove incredibly prolific, sometimes releasing albums six months apart. *True Tunes* and *Cornerstone* became the only Christian periodicals to give him any attention, with John Thompson of the former becoming a major supporter. *Salted with Fire* is all instrumental. *Bottle on My Finger to the Blues on My Shoes* includes a cover of **Larry Norman**'s "Watch What You're Doin'," with additional verses penned by Hakanson-Stacy. The album also has eighteen original songs, including "It Hurts Us So," about the pain of losing a loved one (the first verse focuses on **Mark Heard**). On *Lion's in the Den,* Hakanson-Stacy mixes in a few instrumentals and performs some traditional washboard blues numbers like "Slavery Chain" and Rev. Gary Davis's "I Belong to the Band." *Pearls and Stones* has a tribute to **Rev. Dan Smith** ("The Death of Rev. Dan"). The album *This Train* includes "Old Time Religion," "Leaning on the Everlasting Arms," "Old Gospel Ship," "I Shall Not Be Moved," and "What a Friend We Have in Jesus"—in addition to a more contemporary number called "Cakewalk to the Kingdom."

Halcyon Days

Gareth Black, gtr.; Jonathan Gibson, bass; Rick Johnston, voc.; Stephen Orr, drums. Date unknown—*Sometimes* (independent); 1998—*Alkaline Times* (Kingfisher).

Halcyon Days is a Christian band from Northern Ireland that *Phantom Tollbooth* thinks has a sound reminiscent of **Dime Store Prophets**—which is to say that (like many rock groups from Northern Ireland) they have a sound reminiscent of **U2.** The group's first album favors that band's arena-rock sound, while their second release incorporates more experimental keyboard effects (courtesy of Dave Lynch) to produce a sound more evocative of **U2**'s *Zooropa/Pop* period. Lyrically, Halcyon Days offers songs that avoid obvious Christian slogans but attempt to look at life with a spiritual orientation.

Danniebelle Hall

1974—*Danniebelle* (Light); *He Is King*; 1975—*This Moment*; 1977—*Let Me Have a Dream* (Sparrow); 1978—*Live in Sweden with Choralerna*; 1983—*Song of the Angels* (label unknown); *Unmistakably* (Onyx).

The world discovered the powerful voice of Danniebelle Hall on a now-classic album by **Andraé Crouch and the Disciples** when she sang the title track to *Take Me Back* and the unforgettable closing song, "Tell Them." Hall had just joined the group and her contributions were quickly recognized as the vocal highlights of what was to be the most significant Christian release of the year. She also sang on Crouch's *This Is Another Day,* notably performing the duet vocal on "Soon and Very Soon." Hall had originally sung with a Los Angeles group called The Danniebelles, which she founded in 1967. After gaining recognition for her work as a Disciple, she released several solo albums, which were clearly carried by the strength of her voice. *Danniebelle* emphasizes funky, big-production numbers like "Keep Holdin' On" and "Come On, Come On." *This Moment* features The Hawkins Family on backing vocals on mostly original songs written by the artist. "All of My Life" and "I'm Yours" are standouts. Danniebelle would adopt a more progressive, jazz-oriented approach on *Let Me Have a Dream,* which features "It's Freedom" and "I'll Be Right There." Her *Live in Sweden* project is a worship album recorded with a choir called Choralerna. Her Christian radio hit "I Go to the Rock" is

from this project. *Unmistakably* returns her to the style of the acclaimed *This Moment,* with a few R&B songs ("I Found Out," "God Will") included among the soulful ballads that feature the artist with simple piano accompaniment ("Precious Thought," "Hymn of Love," "Mary Had a Little Lamb").

Christian radio hits: "I Go to the Rock" (# 11 in 1978).

Pam Mark Hall (a.k.a. Pam Mark)

1976—*Flying* (Aslan); 1977—*This Is Not a Dream*; 1980—*Never Fades Away* (StarSong); 1984—*Supply and Demand* (Reunion); 1986—*Keeper*; 1993—*Paler Shade* (Storyville).

Pam Mark Hall was one of the more successful products of **John Fischer**'s Discovery Arts Guild program at the Peninsula Bible Church in Palo Alto, California. Fischer and his artistic community nurtured her native talents and assisted her with a debut album (recorded under the name Pam Mark). After two albums with the small Aslan label, she moved to Nashville where she worked as a songwriter and a freelance writer. She also hosted a Christian radio program and served as public relations director for the Nashville Salvation Army. Hall gained early recognition for the quality of her songs. Her contribution to **Amy Grant**'s 1984 *Straight Ahead,* "The Now and the Not Yet," was hailed as the theological highpoint of that album. She has also composed songs for **Debby Boone, First Call, The Imperials, Noel Paul Stookey, Russ Taff,** and **Kathy Troccoli,** and has written or cowritten Christian radio hits for **Rob Frazier** ("The Heartland"), **The Imperials** ("Holding On"), and **Geoff Moore** ("Heart to God, Hand to Man").

As a singer, Hall would evolve from acoustic folk roots through stages of more synthesized adult contemporary music. *Jesus Music* described her debut as reminiscent of Joni Mitchell's early work, but on *This Is Not a Dream,* she adds strings and replaces her guitar with piano as the most noticeable instrument. The latter album's centerpiece is "Not My Will," an emotional, semiclassical piece that reflects on Christ's prayer in Gethsemane. Critics referred to her as "the female **Michael Card.**" Hall covers **Bruce Cockburn**'s "Lord of the Starfields" on *Never Fades Away* and gained some airplay with her own "Little Miss Much Afraid," an ode to a woman who lives without miracles.

By *Supply and Demand,* Hall employed more rock-based pop styles similar to those of Grant and Taff. *CCM* praised the album when it came out but later referred to it as over-produced and "synthesizer laden" in comparison to *Keeper,* a more intimate collection of songs about a variety of life experiences. *Keeper* was produced by Wendy Waldman (a rare *female* producer) who was able to get the singer to capitalize on the emotional strengths of her songs. *Keeper* opens with the line, "I am hanging on, but just by a thread." The song "Jesus in the

Street" interprets Jesus' words about "the least of these" in a manner befitting one whose work with the Salvation Army has displayed much concern for the poor. On both *Keeper* and *Paler Shade,* musical comparisons for Hall's style shifted again to evoke such singers as Bonnie Raitt and **Ashley Cleveland.** She was singing with more power, and with a more throaty sound that lent credibility to lyrics that were not always sweet. *Paler Shade* (produced by **Dave Perkins**) features "Love's Possibility," an outstanding song (with Cleveland on guest vocals) that presents a woman's prayer to find a life partner: "I don't know if he's there or he'll ever be / God have mercy on a girl like me."

Hallelujah Joy Band

Bill Barlow; Bob Brennan; John Clay; Steven Glick; Dennis Krause. 1973—*Hallelujah Joy Band* (Creative Sound).

The Hallelujah Joy Band was one of the more authentic-sounding of the numerous country-rock Jesus music bands that appeared all over the country in the early '70s. The group was associated with the House of Agape community in Kansas City, Missouri, and they had a sound similar to that of the Grateful Dead. Their solo album features a handful of solid electric hippie tunes including "It's All Coming to an End" and "To All There Comes a Time." The standout track, "Jesus Broke the Wild Horse in My Heart," was later covered by the Flying Burrito Brothers (a Byrds spin-off that included Gram Parsons, Chris Hillman, and **Al Perkins** among its members).

Per-Erik Hallin

1983—*Better Late Than Never* (Refuge); 1989—*Per-Erik* (Royal).

Per-Erik Hallin plays keyboard-dominated pop similar to that of **Michael Omartian**'s early releases. He acquired a reputation for being "terminally happy" by writing and recording carefree songs that present faith as a wellspring of joy. *Better Late Than Never* opens with the declaration, "I don't have no doubt / I found the key to life" ("Let It Out").

Halo

Michael Graham, drums; Barry Graul, gtr.; Keith Mead, bass; Scott Springer, voc. 1990—*Halo* (Pakaderm); 1991—*Heaven Calling*.

The Alabama pop-rock band Halo formed in 1980 and played together for a decade before finally making two records and disbanding in 1993. **Scott Springer** pursued a solo career and guitarist Barry Graul joined first **Whitecross,** then **White Heart.** The group maintained that their name was an acronym for Heavenly Angelic Light Orchestra. The group's debut album had the impressive sound of practiced musicians but drew criticism from some for lyrical simplicity. This improved

on the follow-up, though most of the album continues to focus pointedly on the benefits of a personal relationship with Jesus. Both projects were produced by **John** and Dino **Elefante,** who not only produced but cowrote many of the songs. The band's own press release described them as "Pakaderm Power Pop" and compared them to Foreigner, Journey, and **Kansas.** Within the Christian market, they were commonly compared to **Petra** and **Mastedon** (also Elefante projects). Halo toured Guatemala in 1991.

Christian radio hits: "Saved by Grace" (# 2 in 1992); "Jacob's Dream" (# 5 in 1992); "Eye of the Storm" (# 13 in 1992); "Secret to Love" (# 15 in 1992).

Halo Friendlies

Natalie Bolonos, gtr., voc.; Deanna Moody, drums, voc.; Judita Wignall, gtr., voc.; Cheryl Hecht, gtr., voc. (– 1999) // Ginger Reyes, bass, voc. (+ 1999). 1998—*The Halo Friendlies* (Jackson Rubio); 1999—*Acid Wash* [EP].

www.halofriendlies.com

One of the few all-girl rock combos in Christian music (cf. **Rachel Rachel**), the Halo Friendlies are led by Judita Wignall, whose husband, Matt, heads Jackson Rubio records and serves as the band's producer (in addition to fronting **Havalina Rail Co.**). Alternating between similarities to the Go-Go's and The Breeders, the Long Island foursome makes pop punk music laden with oohs and ahhs. Lyrically, their songs occasionally touch on subjects spiritual and profound ("Cry of Job," "Falling Away") but more often address slumber-party themes such as "gossip hurts" ("Hush") or "boys are yucky" ("Let's Be Friends," "Jackie Chan," "Love Sick," and "Flake-o on my Scalp-o"). The group does not present itself as a ministry band, but hopes that as Christians they will be recognized as having something to say. "We don't want to come off as just being cute," Cheryl Hecht told *7ball* in 1998.

Hammer

See **M.C. Hammer.**

Fred Hammond (and **Radical for Christ**)

As Fred Hammond: 1991—*I Am Persuaded* (Benson); 1993—*Deliverance.* As Fred Hammond and Radical for Christ: 1995—*The Inner Court;* 1996—*Shakin' the House: Live in L.A.; The Spirit of David* (Benson); 1998—*Pages of Life, Chapters 1 and 2* (Verity); 2000—*Purpose by Design.*

Gospel innovator Fred Hammond has earned a spot in history alongside **Kirk Franklin** for bringing his chosen genre of music into the twenty-first century. If James Cleveland is responsible for defining traditional gospel's first generation and

Andraé Crouch its second, then Hammond and Franklin are the pioneers of stage three—what they call "Gospel music with an urban twist." Hammond grew up in the environs of Detroit. His father died when he was only nine and he was raised thereafter by a single mother who had a special talent for directing inner city choirs, in which Fred often sang. As a young adult, Hammond formed a modern gospel group called Saved, played bass for **The Winans,** and then in 1985 founded the groundbreaking group **Commissioned.** He recorded two solo albums while a member of that group, but then departed in 1994 to assemble the Radical for Christ choir, which would accompany him on succeeding projects. He has been instrumental in developing urban praise and worship music and in transforming liturgical traditions, especially within African American communities.

Hammond's debut solo album *I Am Persuaded* features "I Came to Jesus As I Was," with a Five Blind Boys sample. Hammond's gift for worship leadership becomes evident on *Deliverance*'s funk-driven title track and invitational "Drink and Be Satisfied." *The Inner Court* was nominated for a Stellar award. *The Spirit of David* is a concept album, presenting the rise, fall, and ultimate forgiveness of the biblical king. It also includes themes from the Psalms, but the easy highlight is the extra-funky "David's Dance," based on the incident in which the king threw aside all his inhibitions to frolic with joy before the Lord (2 Samuel 6:14–16). *Pages of Life* represents the most ambitious undertaking yet, a lengthy two-disc set combining one album of studio tracks with another of live takes (four of which are alternative versions of songs on the first disc). Hammond referred to the project as his *Songs in the Key of Life* (the career-defining work of Stevie Wonder). The album went platinum, placing Hammond into that rare stratosphere of gospel superstars. *Purpose by Design* scales back and evokes the mood of a congregational worship service, albeit one where the hymns are driven by a phenomenal rhythm section and fiery Earth, Wind, and Fire-style horns. Hammond's buttery vocals are even more in evidence on this work, particularly on "I Want My Destiny" and "Let Me Praise You Now." The album also includes a creative remake of **Sam Cooke**'s "Jesus Be a Fence around Me."

Dove Awards: 1999 Contemporary Gospel Song ("Let the Praise Begin"); 2000 Contemporary Gospel Song ("Power"); 2001 Contemporary Gospel Album of the Year *(Purpose by Design).*

Hangnail

Jacob Dosemagen, drums; Mike Middleton, bass, voc.; Nick Radovanic, gtr., voc.; Matt Wendt, gtr., voc. 1999—*Hangnail* (BEC); 2001—*Facing Changes.*

A competent pop-punk band from Wisconsin, Hangnail swims in the same stream as Christian artists **MxPx, Slick Shoes,** and **Value Pac,** all of whom owe a good deal to Green Day. The group lacks the rebel attitude associated with old-school punk (cf. **The Altar Boys**), preferring to accentuate the positive and to sing songs with inspirational messages. The band's debut album also features some occasional metal riffing that potentially sets them apart from the dozens of sound-alike groups in their crowded genre. "Friendly Advice" and "Don't Forget about Today" feature impressive guitar solos, and on a number of songs (notably, "Don't Let the Sun Go Down on Your Anger") the group incorporates vocal harmonies that are somewhat novel for a punk band. By *Facing Changes,* Hangnail would drop the harder riffs altogether and fall into the plethora of competent pop-punk groups whose sounds by then had become virtually indistinguishable (in the Christian market, see also **Craig's Brother, Dogwood, Face Value, Noggin Toboggan, Shorthanded, Sick of Change, Twotimer,** and **The Undecided**). Lyrically, Hangnail's songs emphasize ethical responsibility with special concern for the numbing of conscience ("Wrong Is Wrong," "Taken for Granted"). The group deals intelligently with life's struggles ("Facing Changes") without using explicitly religious or specifically Christian language. Still, Mike Middleton says, "Our number one purpose is to glorify God. . . . I would consider us to be a ministry band."

Larnelle Harris

1975—*Tell It to Jesus* (Word); 1977—*Larnelle . . . More;* 1978—*Free;* 1981—*Give Me More Love in My Heart* (Impact); 1982—*Touch Me, Lord; Best of Larnelle* (Word); 1985—*I've Just Seen Jesus* (Benson); 1986—*From a Servant's Heart;* 1987—*The Father Hath Provided;* 1988—*Larnelle . . . Christmas;* 1989—*I Can Begin Again;* 1990—*Larnelle Live . . . Psalms, Hymns, and Spiritual Songs;* 1991—*The Best of Ten Years, Vols. 1 and 2;* 1992—*I Choose Joy;* 1994—*Beyond All Limits;* 1995—*Unbelievable Love;* 1998—*First Love* (Brentwood); *Collector's Series* (Benson).

www.larnelle.com

Larnelle Harris is one of Christian music's premier inspirational singers, that is, a gospel performer whose style tends toward the easy listening end of the adult contemporary spectrum, roughly approximating mainstream artists like Johnny Mathis. Born in 1947, Harris grew up in Louisville, Kentucky, and graduated from Western Kentucky University. Before embarking on his solo career, he toured as a drummer with The Spurlows and also recorded two albums with **First Gear.** From 1984 to 1987, Harris also sang with **The Gaither Vocal Band.** As an African American artist who appeals primarily to white audiences, Harris has been in a position to address issues of racial tension within churches and to cross boundaries that still remain as a legacy of intentional segregation. Harris began to develop as a songwriter on *I've Just Seen Jesus,* and he scored a hit with his composition "I Miss My Time with You" on *From a Servant's Heart.* He also composed the title track and the standout song "I Give All My Life to You" for *The Father Hath*

Provided. Over the years, he has incorporated a variety of styles into his repertoire: big production numbers ("Let His Children Rejoice"); hymnic ballads ("There Stands the Cross," "No Wonder They Call Him Savior," "He Loved Me with a Cross"); and Motown pop ("I Look to You"). From *I Choose Joy* on, Harris has increasingly moved into the genre of R&B balladry, supplemented by the occasional dance track ("It Just Takes Time"). Lyrically, Harris consistently selects or composes songs that have explicit evangelical messages. Praise and worship are a common theme, along with songs that commend various virtues or values. "Blessing and Honor" opens *First Love* as a ready-made choir anthem with full orchestration and choral accompaniment. "The Other Woman" from *Beyond All Limits* is a sentimental ode to his now-grown daughter; "I'll Help You Cry" is about Christians relating to each other in tough times; "Teach Me to Love" deals with racial prejudice.

Christian radio hits: "How Excellent Is Thy Name" (# 7 in 1985); "I Miss My Time with You" (# 17 in 1987); "It Just Takes Time (Take the Time)" (# 23 in 1992).

Dove Awards: 1981 Contemporary Gospel Album *(Give Me More Love in My Heart)*; 1983 Inspirational Black Gospel Album *(Touch Me Lord)*; 1983 Male Vocalist; 1986 Male Vocalist; 1986 Inspirational Album *(I've Just Seen Jesus)*; 1988 Songwriter of the Year; 1988 Male Vocalist; 1988 Inspirational Album *(The Father Hath Provided)*; 1992 Inspirational Album *(Larnelle Live . . . Psalms, Hymns, and Spiritual Songs)*; 1996 Inspirational Album *(Unbelievable Love)*.

Grammy Awards: 1983 Best Gospel Performance by a Duo or Group [with **Sandi Patty**] ("More Than Wonderful"); 1985 Best Gospel Performance by a Duo or Group [with **Sandi Patty**] ("I've Just Seen Jesus"); 1985 Best Gospel Performance, Male ("How Excellent Is Thy Name"); 1987 Best Gospel Performance, Male *(The Father Hath Provided)*; 1988 Best Gospel Performance, Male *(Christmas)*.

Tracey Harris

1997—*Keep On Believin'* (Pamplin).

Tracey Harris first came to the attention of contemporary Christian music fans when she sang on a Grammy-nominated project called *Motown Comes Home*. *Keep On Believin'* mixes studio tracks with ones recorded live with the Greater Portland Workshop Choir. Harris' voice has been compared to both Whitney Houston and **Yolanda Adams.** "Dancin' in the Son" is an upbeat, cheerful song featuring sax and flute. "Celebrate" is a praise hymn with calypso/jazz influence. "The Wedding Song" and "Today" are mainstream pop ballads, the latter communicating a message against racial discrimination.

Pamela Deuel Hart

1977—*Pamela Hart* (Tempo); 1978—*An Unbroken Heart* (Hartsong); 1979—*Always Christmas* (Breeze); 1979—*Weary Child* (Spirit); 1990—*With Love We'll Survive* (label unknown).

Singer/songwriter Pamela Deuel Hart has emphasized ministry to Christian women throughout her career, making country rock albums that proclaim messages of edification and hope. Hart was the sister of TV actor Peter Deuel, who starred in the popular series "Alias Smith and Jones" but who committed suicide on December 31, 1971. She credits her spiritual rebirth to grappling with issues related to that tragedy. She subsequently married Tony Hart, president of Spirit Records, the third marriage for both of them, and together they sought to teach other couples lessons they had learned the hard way. Though trained as a jazz singer, Hart draws on southern gospel influences for her Christian albums. *An Unbroken Heart* contains covers of **Ken Medema**'s "Moses" and Archie Jordan's "What a Difference You've Made in My Life" (cf. **Amy Grant, B. J. Thomas**), along with a tribute to her brother called "Odin (Song for Peter)/An Unbroken Hart." *Weary Child* presents itself as a response to Linda Ronstadt's *Hasten Down the Wind,* recalling that album musically while offering songs that are intended to provide comfort by declaring the promise of God's unconditional love.

Sarah Hart

1997—*Goodbye Jane* (Sovereignty).

www.madbear.com/sarahhart

Sarah Hart is a classic country-folk singer in the tradition of James Taylor or Shawn Colvin. Born and raised in Lancaster, Ohio, she graduated from Ohio State University with a degree in music theory and composition, then moved to Nashville to pursue a career in contemporary Christian music. She sang on projects by **Michael Card, John Michael Talbot,** and **Kathy Troccoli,** and composed songs for **Christine Glass**'s *Human* album. *Goodbye Jane* includes nine original songs in addition to a rendition of the classic hymn "Be Thou My Vision" and a cover of Cyndi Lauper's "Time after Time." Her song "Marble and Moss" tells of a trip to a cemetery in which she was impressed by the certainty of death and the need to "make the most of these days." A Roman Catholic, Hart cites such writers as Flannery O'Connor, Thomas Merton, and Sylvia Plath as prominent influences on her thinking.

Harvest

Jerry Williams, voc., gtr.; Ed Kerr, voc., kybrd. (–1995); et al. 1979—*Harvest* (Everlasting Spring); 1981—*Morning Sun* (Milk and Honey); 1983—*Send Us to the World*; 1984—*Voices*; 1985—*The Best of Harvest*; 1986—*Only the Overcomers* (Greentree); 1987—*Give Them Back* (Benson); 1988—*Holy Fire*; 1990—*Carry On*; 1991—*The Early Works*; 1992—*Let's Fight for a Generation*; 1993—*Mighty River*; 1995—*41 Will Come*.

Based in Lindale, Texas, the vocal group Harvest produces contemporary Christian music with roots in southern gospel, similar to a stripped-down version of **The Imperials.** Harvest began as a duo, and Ed Kerr and Jerry Williams remain the core of the group, although additional musicians were added in the mid '80s after the switch to Benson. Bassist Tommy Hoeser (of **Hope of Glory**) has played with Harvest, in addition to Paul Wilbur (gtr., voc.), Ben Kelting (kybrd., voc.), and Wes Aarum (drums). Williams attended Oral Roberts University and was ordained as a Southern Baptist minister. Kerr (pronounced "car") is a classically trained musician with a masters degree from Indiana University. The group staked out their heavy evangelistic focus early on, insisting that "the primary message" of such albums as *Send Us to the World* and *Voices* was to make known the chilling fact that "not many American Christians will ever enter the kingdom of God." Theologically, then, the group has insisted on a personal life-transforming commitment as necessary for salvation, and their proselytizing typically focuses on those church members who they regard as "plastic, phony Christians" lacking this necessary devotion.

Musically, vocal harmony is the group's forté. In general, *CCM*'s critics have tended to prefer Harvest's more upbeat and rocking songs ("The Battle Is the Lord's") to their subdued piano or acoustic guitar ballads. *Only the Overcomers* left behind the country influence briefly for a foray into hook-laden pop. *Give Them Back* features "Rise Up," a prayer to God for deliverance and "What Are You Singing For?" on which the group's trademark guilt-inducing lyrics are at least rendered in a form of self-address. In 1995, a Kerr-less group that called itself Jerry Williams and Harvest issued the final album *41 Will Come.* The title track is a song of encouragement, promising that after a symbolic forty days of temptation (or struggle), relief will come at last. As of 2002, Kerr was working as a songwriter for Integrity Music and Wilbur was a worship leader, making praise albums for Hosanna! Music.

Another country rock group known as Harvest made two Christian albums in California: *Never Thirst Again* (Pure Joy, 1976); *New Season* (Shout, 1978). A hardcore band going by the name Harvest also emerged in the late '90s with two albums on the Trustkill label (*Living with a God Complex,* 1997; *Transitions,* 1998). The groups are not related.

Christian radio hits: "Because I Am" (# 8 in 1983); "The Wedding Day" (# 24 in 1983); "Behold God" (# 26 in 1983); "Army of the Lord" (# 1 for 4 weeks in 1984); "Blood of the Lamb" (# 8 in 1984); "If We Don't Believe" (# 12 in 1984); "On the Water" (# 21 in 1985); "Only the Overcomers" (# 16 in 1987); "All That Is in Me" (# 10 in 1987).

Harvest Flight

John Benas; Kerry Chester; Evan Williams, gtr., voc. 1971—*One Way* (Destiny).

Harvest Flight was a trio of Californians who produced one early Jesus music record notable for its hard, psychedelic sound. The group was led by Evan Williams, who also produced two albums for **Phoenix Sunshine.** Williams' fuzz tone guitar and breathy vocals are complemented by generous doses of swirling Hammond organ and occasional novelties, such as the harp that closes out the last track ("Epilogue"). The opening song, "Kingdom," is a hard rock standout, as is a surprising version of the popular chorus "One in the Spirit" (a.k.a. "They'll Know We Are Christians by Our Love"). Williams later released a solo album (*Minstrel for the King,* Destiny, 1978), which exemplified pop-jazz fusion with adult contemporary leanings.

Havalina Rail Co.

Mark Cole, perc.; Orlando Greenhill, bass; Eric Nieto, violin, drums; Matt Wignall, gtr., voc.; Jeff Suri, drums (−2001); Lori Suri, voc. (−2001); Nathan Jensen, sax. (−1999) // Mercedes [a.k.a. Starry Dynamo], gtr., voc. (+ 2001); Dave Maust, kybrd. (+ 2001). 1994—*Havalina Rail Co.* (Tooth and Nail); 1996—*The Diamond in the Fish;* 1997—*Russian Lullabies* (Jackson Rubio); 1999—*America;* 2001—*A Bullfighter's Guide to Space and Love* [EP] (Four Door).

www.havalinaland.com

One review of a Havalina Rail Co. album begins with the critic proclaiming, "I don't want to hear anymore bellyaching about the lack of originality in Christian music." The group's music may be an acquired taste, or even a hard-to-acquire taste for some, but it certainly does not lack originality. The band has succeeded in developing something rare in the music world—a sound that is utterly its own. The group is fronted by Matt Wignall, founder of Jackson Rubio records and husband to Judita Wignall of **Halo Friendlies.** Its debut album established them as weird and eclectic, presenting nineteen tracks that have a ragtime-jazz base but also borrow elements from folk, blues, rockabilly, country, and gospel. *CCM* noted, "You can only toss in everything but the kitchen sink for so long before you run the risk of confusing your audience." The follow-up, *Diamond in the Fish,* did little to redeem this potential problem. It features a blend of swing and lounge styles, with Wignall skat singing on a few takes.

Changing labels, the band finally found its groove on *Russian Lullabies,* an album that *True Tunes* describes as "a masterpiece of mood, music, texture, and emotion." Wignall wrote most of the material for *Lullabies* while traveling in Eastern Europe with his wife (who is from Lithuania), and the melodies and rhythms of that region become a controlling influence to provide focus for his disparate themes. *Russian Lullabies* does not attempt to emulate Eastern European music; rather it draws on the influences of composers like Stravinsky and Maurice Jarre to reconceive American pop in a way that transcends all traditional boundaries. "St. Petersburg" is upbeat and cheery and "Kalingrad," a vigorous march, but the bulk of the album evinces a moody and melancholy tone, emphasizing haunting melodies that alternately lurch and linger. Thematically, the album shows the influence of such writers as Dostoevsky, Pushkin, and Nabatov, extolling the existence of God alongside laments for the downtrodden and odes for lost love. "Total Depravity" is a meditation on the classic Calvinist doctrine.

Having earned the respect of critics, HRC determined to make an album of ethnic American music that could serve as a companion piece to *Russian Lullabies.* The result, *America,* visits surf rock, hip-hop, mexicali-blues, and Hawaiian tones—but not all at once—and so provides the listener with an ambitious tour of a diverse musical frontier. *True Tunes* proclaimed it their "most focused and best realized work." Lyrically, the album deals mainly with various portions of the country itself ("California," "Mississippi River," "Let's Not Forget Hawaii"). In late 2001, the band announced their next project would be an album called *Space, Love, and Bullfighting.* This was previewed by a five-song EP titled *A Bullfighter's Guide to Space and Love.* With organ as a common lead instrument, the new album has touches of Latin music but infects the latter with doses of pop (and indeed electronic Bowiesque space music) to create once again a novel entity. Wignall says, "We do have a habit of messing up the music we play and often unintentionally throwing it into the 'What the hell is *that?*' category." At the end of 2001, the band was also preparing a mock documentary on its own history titled *Havalina and the Creaky Old Bridge.*

For trivia buffs: After *7ball* magazine trashed *Diamond in the Fish* as containing "some of the lamest performances heard on any album to date," Judita Wignall wrote the reviewer calling him "a menace to every creative, innovative artist in this industry."

Haven

Kevin Ayers, voc.; Andy Bruner, gtr.; Tim Benton, drums (– 1996); Ed Bruner, bass // John Farrell, gtr. (+ 1996). 1990—*Your Dying Day* (R.E.X.); 1991—*Age of Darkness*; 1996—*Haven* (custom); 1997—*Straight from the Cutting Room Floor.*

Haven is a Christian metal band that operates out of the Lighthouse Tabernacle church in New Jersey. Their first two albums were well received by reviewers for *HM* magazine, which likened their sound to "the dramatic and melodic territory of Queensryche." As with many Christian metal bands, Haven often focused on the occult, with songs like "Seance" and "Witching Hour" aimed at warning Christian youth of the dangers inherent in various occult activities and pursuits.

Edwin Hawkins (and the Edwin Hawkins Singers)

1969—*Let Us Go into the House of the Lord* (Pavilion); *O Happy Day* (Buddha); *More Happy Days*; 1970—*Edwin Hawkins and the Hebrew Boys*;

1971—*Children (Get Together)*; 1972—*I'd Like to Teach the World to Sing*; 1973—*New World*; 1974—*Live*; 1976—*The Best of Edwin Hawkins*; *Wonderful* (Birthright); 1977—*The Comforter*; 1981—*Live with the Oakland Symphony* (Myrrh); 1982—*Imagine Heaven* (Lection); *Live with the Oakland Symphony Orchestra, Vol. 2* (Myrrh); 1983—*Mass Choir* (Mercury); 1984—*Angels Will Be Singing* (Birthright); 1990—*Music and Arts Seminar Chicago Mass Choir*; 1991—*Face to Face*; 1992—*O Happy Day Reunion* (Intersound); 1992—*Seminar '91* (Fixit); *Music and Arts Seminar Mass Choir: Los Angeles*; 1993—*If You Love Me* (Intersound); 1994—*Kings and Kingdoms*; 1997—*Music and Arts Seminar Mass Choir: Dallas* (Harmony); *The Best of the Edwin Hawkins Singers* (Capitol); 1998—*Tampa Music and Arts Seminar* (Harmony).

Edwin Hawkins will forever be remembered as the man whose choir scored a surprise hit with the hymn "O Happy Day" in the year of Woodstock, previewing the recovery of traditional spirituality that would erupt in the Jesus movement revival two years later. The genre of contemporary Christian music did not yet exist and there was nothing contemporary about "O Happy Day." It was a traditionally religious song (a gospel standard) performed in a typical fashion by one of the thousands of church choirs that sang such songs regularly every Sunday. Yet it sold over seven million records and remains the most successful gospel song of all time. The song charted Number Four on *Billboard* magazine's mainstream pop chart in 1969.

Edwin Hawkins was born in Oakland, California, in 1943 and at the age of five began playing piano for The Hawkins Family, a group that also included his brothers, Daniel Hawkins and **Walter Hawkins,** and his sister-in-law **Tramaine Hawkins.** While a student at Berkeley in 1967, he and an associate, Betsy Watson, organized a choir for their church, the Ephesian Church of God in Christ. The group was originally known as the Northern California State Youth Choir, and their album *Let Us Go into the House of the Lord* was recorded on a simple two-track stereo in a San Francisco church as a fundraising project. Five hundred copies were pressed, which the group hoped to sell locally to help finance a trip to Cleveland. When a DJ for a San Francisco station began playing the hymn "O Happy Day," however, the album and group were retitled for national distribution on the ironically named Buddha label. The song actually features the solo voice of Dorothy Morrison, who would later gain some prominence as a gospel singer. The lyrics are explicitly evangelical ("O Happy Day . . . when Jesus washed my sins away!") but did not seem to trouble secular audiences who appreciated the stirring, emotional power of the hymn. It provided many white audiences with their first real exposure to traditional (i.e., black) gospel music, a genre for which they had been primed by the recent popularity of R&B acts who drew heavily on gospel roots (e.g., **Sam Cooke, Aretha Franklin, Marvin Gaye, Al Green**). At the same time, the success of "O Happy Day" displayed the potential for gospel to connect with fans of R&B music and, as such, encouraged the development of the more contemporary gospel sound seen in work of artists like **Andraé Crouch.** The Edwin Hawkins Singers were almost immediately fractured by the success, with Watson continuing to lead a rival choir under the original name. It was Hawkins who had name recognition, however, and a year later, the Edwin Hawkins Singers scored a second Top 10 hit with "Lay Down (Candles in the Rain)," a song about the Woodstock festival on which they backed folksinger Melanie. The Edwin Hawkins Singers performed at Madison Square Garden and Caesar's Palace, made numerous TV appearances, and toured Europe for three years. In 1976, Edwin Hawkins joined Oakland's Love Center as choir director at the church pastored by his brother Walter. In 1978, he filmed the PBS special *Edwin Hawkins: Gospel at the Symphony* with the Oakland Symphony Orchestra. In 2001, "O Happy Day" by the Edwin Hawkins Singers was included in a list of the most significant songs of the twentieth century prepared by the Recording Industry Association of America.

Hawkins has continued to record, sometimes with a choir, sometimes on his own. *O Happy Day* remains the album that is most in demand, if only for nostalgic reasons. In addition to the big hit, the record's original title track ("Let Us Go into the House of the Lord") is a strong contribution. The record also includes an awful, cheesy version of Paul Anka's "My Way," with rewritten lyrics ("I Did it *His* way!"). *Angels Will Be Singing* (1984) has Hawkins directing the Music and Arts Seminar Mass Choir and features several family members (brother Walter, sister Lynette, cousin Shirley Miller) on a stellar collection of songs including Hawkins' own "This Day." *Imagine Heaven* (1982) melds gospel and pop into a fine collection of praise and worship songs geared for the R&B market.

Christian radio hits: "Still the Need Goes On" (# 26 in 1990).

Dove Awards: 1982 Inspirational Black Gospel album *(Live with the Oakland Symphony).*

Grammy Awards: 1969 Best Soul Gospel Performance ("Oh Happy Day"); 1970 Best Soul Gospel Performance ("Every Man Wants to Be Free"); 1977 Best Soul Gospel Performance *(Wonderful!);* 1992 Best Gospel Album by a Choir or Chorus *(Edwin Hawkins Music and Arts Seminar Mass Choir: Los Angeles).*

Tramaine Hawkins (a.k.a. **Tramaine**)

1981—*Tramaine* (Light); 1983—*Determined*; 1986—*The Search Is Over* (Rejoice); 1987—*Freedom*; 1988—*The Joy That Floods My Soul* (Sparrow); 1990—*Live*; 1994—*All My Best to You*; 1994—*To a Higher Place.*

Contemporary gospel diva Tramaine Hawkins (née Davis) grew up as a member of the Ephesian Church of God in Christ congregation in Oakland California, where the choir was directed by **Edwin Hawkins** and where, at the age of seven, she and Sly Stone's little sister formed a gospel girl group called

The Heavenly Tones. When Davis was twelve, the latter group made an album with James Cleveland, and when she graduated from high school she joined the Edwin Hawkins Singers and toured in support of their million-selling single, "O Happy Day." Then, she turned down an offer to join Sly's Family Stone, opting to become one of **Andraé Crouch**'s Disciples instead. She sang on that group's famous *Keep On Singin'* album, providing lead vocals on the song "I'm Coming Home." Then, at the age of nineteen, she married **Walter Hawkins** and came to be featured prominently on his popular *Love Alive* and other Hawkins Family projects. Walter Hawkins wrote and produced all of the songs for Tramaine's self-titled debut album, which has a traditional gospel sound. *Determined* brings ballads to the fore, with such standout tracks as "Greatest Lover" and "Rescue Me." The Hawkins' marriage ended in 1985, and on *The Search Is Over* Tramaine went for crossover appeal; the song "Fall Down (Spirit of Love)" became a Number One hit on *Billboard* magazine's Dance Music chart. *The Search Is Over* also includes a number of pure gospel tracks, however, and *CCM* would call it "a milestone in the commercial and aesthetic history of gospel music." On *To a Higher Place,* Hawkins sings a technologically enhanced "duet" with Mahalia Jackson on "I Found the Answer," a song Jackson recorded in 1959.

Dove Awards: 1991 Traditional Gospel Album *(Tramaine Hawkins)*; 1991 Traditional Gospel Song ("The Potter's House").

Grammy Awards: 1990 Best Traditional Soul Gospel Performance *(Tramaine Hawkins Live).*

Walter Hawkins (and **The Hawkins Family**)

1972—*Do Your Best* (Gospel Truth); 1976—*Love Alive* (Light); 1977—*Jesus Christ Is the Way*; 1978—*Love Alive 2*; 1980—*The Walter Hawkins Family*; 1982—*I Feel Like Singing*; 1984—*Love Alive 3*; 1987—*Love Alive Reunion*; 1990—*Love Alive 4* (Malaco); 1995—*The Light Years* (Light); *The Hawkins Family Collection* (CGI); 1997—*Ooh Wee* (Hot); 1998—*Love Alive 5: 25th Anniversary Reunion* (Gospo-Centric); *New Dawning* (Harmony); 2000—*Take Courage* (Bellmark).

Walter Hawkins is pastor of the Love Center Ministry in Oakland, California, which has become famous for the musical programs sponsored by Hawkins and his talented relatives. In the early '70s, Walter sang with his famous brother **Edwin Hawkins,** whose choir scored two major hits in the general market. At the same time, he pursued a call to ministry and was ordained a minister in the Church of God in Christ in 1972. That year, Hawkins released his own attempt at a crossover album, the ill-fated *Do Your Best.* In 1976, however, he released *Love Alive,* a traditional gospel album that would set new records for longevity, remaining on *Billboard's* music chart for over four years and selling an unprecedented 300,000 copies. That album set the standard for what would become the

Hawkins hallmark: live recordings featuring a congregation, a choir, and spirited singing by Hawkins himself, his wife **Tramaine Hawkins,** and other talented guests. *The Walter Hawkins Family* album from 1980 features performances by **Philip Bailey** and Maurice White of Earth, Wind, and Fire, supplemented by the famous Tower of Power Horns. Brothers Edwin and Donnie Hawkins, sister Lynette Hawkins Stephens, and cousin Shirley Miller—all of whom have recorded gospel albums of their own—also join in on many of the *Love Alive* and other family projects. Walter and Tramaine Hawkins divorced in 1985.

Dove Awards: 1980 Soul/Black Gospel Album *(Love Alive 2)*; 1982 Contemporary Gospel Album *(Walter Hawkins and Family Live)*.

Bryn Haworth

1974—*Let the Days Go By* (Island); 1976—*Sunny Side of the Street*; 1978—*The Grand Arrival* (A&M); 1979—*Keep the Ball Rolling*; 1980—*The Gap* (Chapel Lane); 1983—*Pass It On*; *Wings of the Morning*; 1985—*Mountain Mover* (Image 7); 1989—*Chronology* (Myrrh); 1989—*Blue and Gold* (Edge); 1991—*Take Our Lives* (Vineyard); 1992—*More Than a Singer* (Kingsway); 1993—*Live*; 1996—*Slide Don't Fret*; 1998—*The Finer Things in Life* [with Kevin Prosch]; 1999—*Songs and Hymns*.

http://members.aol.com/brynsongs

Bryn Haworth is a musician's musician, recognized within the guild as one of the finest slide (or "bottleneck") guitarists in the world. Slide guitar is a technique derived from blues that produces a distinctive sound of bending notes and chords; the technique was carried into rock and roll by such popular guitarists as Duane Allman and Lowell George. Haworth was already playing slide guitar in the late '60s as a member of the London band, Fleur de Lys. He moved briefly to California and played with the Jackie Lomax Band and with Wolfgang, opening for such acts as Led Zeppelin, Jefferson Airplane, and the Moody Blues. In 1973 he returned to England, where he has continued to record solo albums in addition to playing on projects by Joan Armatrading, Gerry Rafferty, and **Cliff Richard.** In 1974, Haworth became a Christian, and all of his albums from *Sunny Side of the Street* on have been reflective of his faith. The overall sound is that of mellow, blues-flavored rock, with an increasing interest in praise and worship music.

The Gap was Haworth's first record to be distributed widely in America and it is considered his classic project in the Christian market. StarSong released it two years after Chapel Lane with a new cover proclaiming "**Larry Norman** presents Bryn Haworth and the **Eric Clapton** band." Norman wrote liner notes for the project, and StarSong made much of the fact that Haworth's backing musicians (**Dave Markee,** Chris Stainton, Henry Spinetti, and Bruce Rowland) were indeed the same musicians who typically backed Clapton on his albums and tours. *The Gap* features "It Could of Been Me," which

CCM likened to the sound of Atlantic Rhythm Section, and "New Jerusalem," an acoustic mandolin ballad based on Revelation 21. The *CCM* reviewer for *Pass It On* complained that Haworth's lyrics resort to clichés and do not match the quality of his music. The *Live* album offers some of his better original songs in addition to **Curtis Mayfield**'s "People Get Ready." *Slide Don't Fret* mixes what *Renewal* magazine calls "the mean and moody 'Judgement Day' with the dance-friendly 'Cajun Song.' " On *The Finer Things in Life,* Haworth collaborates with Kevin Prosch to offer a collection of acoustic songs including "I Weep for You Now," a lament for those who will not withstand the soon-coming day of the Lord. The appropriately titled *Songs and Hymns* marks the twenty-fifth anniversary of Haworth's conversion and includes his versions of songs that have been meaningful to him throughout the years ("What a Friend We Have in Jesus," "Great Is Your Faithfulness," and an instrumental version of "How Great Thou Art"). Haworth's song "We're All One" was a Christian radio hit for **Sheila Walsh** in 1985.

Headnoise

Edie Goodman, voc.; Robert Goodwin, bass; Casey Logan, drums. 2001—*Dead to the World* (Grrr); *No Compromise*.

www.headnoise.org

Headnoise is an old-school punk band associated with the socially conscious Jesus People U.S.A. community in Chicago (cf. **Ballydowse, Cauzin' Efekt, Crashdog, The Crossing, Glenn Kaiser, Resurrection Band, Seeds, Sheesh,** and **Unwed Sailor**). The group's sound comes closer to that of The Ramones or Dead Kennedys than to the overworked pop-punk stylings of numerous other Christian bands (**Craig's Brother, MxPx, Slick Shoes,** and many more). The closest equivalent in the contemporary Christian music scene is probably **Officer Negative,** but even then lead female vocals give Headnoise a distinctive quality. The group began in Los Angeles and moved to the Chicago community after a tour of clubs in the southeastern United States. Lyrically, the band favors **Keith Green**-style confrontational lyrics dealing with holiness and corruption. "No Compromise" samples the latter performer and "War" concludes with a coda from Green's "Make My Life a Prayer to You." The song "MPG" attacks the triad of money, power, and greed and reminds the listener that no one can serve two masters. "Building a Better Mousetrap" deals with corporate concerns that sometimes drive church programs.

Brian Healy

See **Dead Artist Syndrome.**

Mark Heard (and Ideola)

1975—*Mark Heard* (Airborn); 1978—*On Turning to Dust* (AB); 1979—*Appalachian Melody* (Solid Rock); 1980—*Fingerprint* (Palmfrond); 1981—*Stop the Dominoes* (Home Sweet Home); 1982—*Victims of the Age*; 1983—*Eye of the Storm*; 1984—*Ashes and Light*; 1985—*Mosaics*; *Best of: Acoustic*; *Best of: Electric*; 1987—*Tribal Opera* [as Ideola] (What?); 1990—*Dry Bones Dance* (Fingerprint); 1991—*Second Hand*; 1992—*Satellite Sky*; 1993—*Reflections of a Former Life* (Home Sweet Home); *High Noon* (Myrrh); 2000—*Mystery Mind* (Fingerprint); *Millennium Archive Series* (Home Sweet Home); 2001—*The Final Performance* (Fingerprint).

Singer/songwriter Mark Heard is remembered as one of Christian music's most authentic and poignant artists and as one of its best-kept secrets. For fifteen years prior to his death in 1992 Heard produced music of a style and quality consistent with that of such artists as **T Bone Burnett, Bruce Cockburn, Sam Phillips,** and **Victoria Williams,** yet his name rarely appears on the short list of those and other Christian singers who are more appreciated in the general market than in the Christian music subculture. Heard remains virtually unknown to mainstream critics in spite of the fact that all the artists just listed—and many more—consistently name him as one of their favorite songwriters and performers. Among Christian critics, he is certainly one of the most highly regarded artists of all time, but that respect has not translated into sales or awards. *CCM* magazine reports, "Heard was never afraid to ask the hard questions . . . he was never one to let politics or commerce dictate his art." **John Fischer** twice devoted his monthly column in that magazine to discussions of Heard as the antithesis of (and antidote for) "shallow Christian music." **Bruce Cockburn** thinks he is perhaps America's "greatest contemporary songwriter." **Pierce Pettis** describes him as that rare artist who was "more concerned with telling the truth than selling the truth." **Ashley Cleveland** calls him "a man with the depth of a woman."

Heard was born in 1951 in Macon, Georgia. He formed a band in high school called Infinity Plus Three, which released an album of Christian music titled *Setting Yesterday Free* (custom, 1972). Only a few hundred copies of the record were pressed, and very few are known to still exist. Indeed, the album was regarded as mythical by historians for some time, but it is genuine and includes versions of the traditional song "All My Trials" and of **Eric Clapton**'s "Presence of the Lord," in addition to five Heard originals. Heard recorded a self-titled solo album three years later, but his career really got started after **Pat Terry** introduced him to **Larry Norman,** with whom he worked from 1975 to 1980. *On Turning to Dust* is actually a reissue of the *Mark Heard* album and was released on Norman's Solid Rock as well as on AB records. It has a "homegrown folk" (almost bluegrass) sound but remains of primary interest to collectors. Norman himself produced the classic *Appalachian Melody* disc, on which Heard matures and begins to develop the country-folk-rock sound for which he would be known. He seems to be emulating James Taylor on several tracks, and his songwriting skills come to the fore on "Jonah" and "Two Trusting Jesus." A childlike joy infuses many of these tracks, though *CCM*'s Brian Quincy Newcomb would opine in 1987 that the ballads ("Here I Am," "The Last Time," and the title track) would better stand the test of time. Heard next spent some time in Switzerland at Francis Schaeffer's L'Abri institute and recorded the album *Fingerprint* for distribution in that country only. A historical curiosity, the album reveals Heard during a period when he was, in the words of *Rad Rockers,* "just another bohemian folkie busker wandering throughout Europe and getting grounded in his faith." The dominant style, again, is one that emulates James Taylor's more upbeat numbers ("Nowadays," "Sleepless Dreamers," "Brown Eyed Sue"), but "I'm in Chains" is built around a Stones-inspired blues riff, and the chorus to "Negative Charge" shamelessly plagiarizes Steppenwolf's "Monster." The song "Remarks to Mr. McLuhan" was later covered by Ramona Silver.

Back in America, Heard entered what is called "the middle period" of his artistic career, recording several albums with more of a Springsteen-style rock and roll feel for **Chris Christian**'s Home Sweet Home label. Some lasting bitterness has attended this period of Heard's work as John J. Thompson (of *True Tunes*) and others maintain that Heard "got screwed" by the label and that "he never made any money from his Home Sweet Home albums." Apparently, Heard naively signed away his publishing rights and the label did not do as much to support his albums as some would expect. In any case, *Stop the Dominoes* did bring Heard to the attention of the Christian market with a review in *CCM* that raved about a "new artist" who sounds like Jackson Browne but writes lyrics "that reflect reality with irony, simplicity, and poignancy." The blues song "Stuck in the Middle" proclaims prophetically, "I'm too sacred for the sinners, and the saints wish I would leave." The album also includes a new version of "I'm in Chains" from *Fingerprint*. Otherwise, the first two songs, "One of the Dominoes" and "Stranded at the Station," have a McCartneyesque pop feel to them (hence those Jackson Browne comparisons) while "To See Your Face" closes the album with a hymnic psalm of worship.

Victims of the Age cemented Heard's position as a critic's choice. *CCM* chose it as one of their "Ten Best of 1982" and praised it as an incisive album that "transcends sugar-coated Christian pop and makes passage into a frontier where lyrical creativity and rock expression are effectively married into potent social comment." Conceptually, the album challenges the tendency toward isolationism in American ideology and

Christianity. "Some Folks' World" and "Faces in Cabs" describe the masses of people who populate an increasingly anonymous society. "Dancing at the Policeman's Ball" is a new-wavey tongue-in-cheek song worthy of **Steve Taylor.** "Nothing Is Bothering Me" (sung in a blues rap-style obviously learned from **Larry Norman**) and "Everybody Loves a Holy War" use satire to expose self-centered attitudes. "Heart of Hearts" (a stellar song of hope and faithfulness) features background vocals by a very young **Leslie Phillips,** who would later cover the song on her debut album.

Eye of the Storm detours back to the folk moorings of Heard's early work and features songs that had been written during an earlier period. The album even carried a disclaimer in its liner notes assuring audiences that it was only "a special one-time release of acoustic guitar-oriented material." This unplugged-before-it-was-cool approach would yield no radio hits but a handful of critical masterpieces, including "The Pain that Plagues Creation" and "In the Gaze of the Spotlight's Eye," which offers a vulnerable look at Christian concert audiences from the perspective of a solo performer. Two more songs from the European *Fingerprints* ("Well-Worn Pages," "Gimmie Mine") are reprised here. The title track offers a simple but bold faith statement: "Out in the eye of the storm / The friends of God suffer no permanent harm."

The real follow-up to *Victims of the Age* would be *Ashes and Light,* which presents serial tales of the downtrodden, such as the boy who "Can't See the Light" and the woman in "Age of the Broken Heart" who has "fought a war with callousness." The album opens with the chiming anthem "The Winds of Time," on which Heard sounds very much like **Michael Been** of **The Call.** The song "Threw It Away" (cowritten with **Pat Terry**) delves into the blues for an update on the Garden of Eden story. "I Know What It's Like to Be Loved" expresses the simple idea that those who have known forgiveness find it hard to hold grudges against others ("Hate is a swindler and often we know we've been had"). *Ashes and Light* was dedicated to the late Francis Schaeffer, and his influence is evident on the songs "We Believe So Well" and "Straw Men." *Mosaics* is Heard's most rocking project but finds him in something of a creative slump as the songs themselves are less distinctive; the standout track is his inspired cover of **T Bone Burnett**'s "The Power of Love" (cf. **Arlo Guthrie**). The best of the others include "All Is Not Lost," "It Will Not Be Like This Forever," and "Miracle." Heard's Home Sweet Home records were summarized on two compilation packages (*Acoustic* and *Electric*) and then, again, on 1993's meager twelve-song package, *Reflections of a Former Life.* The *Acoustic* and *Reflections* albums both contain a Heard cover of **Billy Batstone**'s "Family Name."

Heard took a break in the latter '80s but did release one experimental project under the name of the pseudo-group Ideola.

Tribal Opera is actually an excursion into techno new-wave with Heard functioning as a one-man band, engineering synthesizers, digital samples, and electronic drums. The closest general market comparisons would probably be to such solo artists as Lindsey Buckingham and Todd Rundgren with allusions to such acts as The The and XTC. It all works surprisingly well, on a par with similar projects produced by **Daniel Amos** at the time. Standout tracks include "Is It Any Wonder?" "Watching the Ships Go Down," and "How to Grow Up Big and Strong." The latter song, in Heard's own words, deals with "the evils of pragmatically getting something done in such a way that we forget humanity in the process." As a whole, however, the album is joy-oriented, with numbers like "Love Is Bigger Than Life" and "Go Ask the Dead Man" dealing with what Heard would call "the art of enjoying life."

Heard's most impressive output came in the last three years of his life, when he turned out a quick trio of albums that remain among the best records of the '90s by artists of any ideological persuasion. *Dry Bones Dance* mixes country and Cajun influences into the basic folk-rock brew and reveals a distinctive style that allowed Heard to rise above comparisons (Taylor, Browne, Springsteen, Buckingham) with a sound that was definitively his own. The songs themselves are remarkable. "Rise from the Ruins" accurately summarizes the human condition in its opening lines: "Nobody asks to be born / Nobody wishes to die." Disappointment (especially in relationships) is chronicled with haunting perception in "House of Broken Dreams" ("Penniless at the wishing well, memories will last") and "All She Wanted Was Love" ("She bears another kind of burden . . . a mind of her own"). On "Our Restless Hearts" Heard engages someone who he says likes to "smear the blame on me like cheap cosmetics" and on "Nobody's Looking" he sings slyly, "You can pray if you want to . . . nobody's looking but God." Thematically, *Dry Bones Dance* is all about resilience and renewal. The title track literally celebrates life's miraculous circumstances that bring about what the prophet Ezekiel envisioned in that valley of dry bones. "Mercy of the Flame" is an incredible paean to stubborn hope and stubborn love: "I know what I'm doing / I don't even feel the pain / Love ignites, and I have been so long / At the mercy of the flame." The song "Everything Is Alright" sounds very much like a lost Beatles track and would prove the perfect vehicle for a cover by **Phil Keaggy** on his Beatlesque *Sunday's Child* venture. Equally pop-oriented is "Strong Hand of Love," which carries a reassuring message as buoyant as its melody.

Second Hand offers a similarly strong collection, with "I Just Wanna Get Warm" as an especially noteworthy contribution. Heard also covers the Beatles' "I'm Looking through You" on this record, which has a generally mellow and acoustic feel to it. Conceptually, *Second Hand* deals with the passing of time and with the intermittent gratitude and regret that this brings. The record succeeds at being introspective without giving way to sentimentality. In the opening song, "Nod Over Coffee," Heard muses, "The dam of time cannot hold back the dust that will surely come of these bones / And I'm sure that I will not have loved enough / If we could see with wiser eyes what is good and what is sad and what is true / Still it would not be enough." On "Love Is Not the Only Thing," he offers some common-sense reflection on priorities: "Love is not the only thing / It's the best thing / Love is never everything / It's the best thing." In the same vein, "It's Not Your Fault" offers a simple acknowledgment of personal accountability that might form the foundation for any nondysfunctional relationship: "I get lonely sometimes / It's not your fault . . . I get helpless sometimes / It's not your fault." In 2001, a poll of critics (mostly from *CCM*) put *Second Hand* at Number Four on their list of "The 100 Greatest Albums in Christian Music."

Satellite Sky is typically regarded as Heard's finest work. The title track, "Tip of My Tongue," "We Know Too Much," "Treasure of the Broken Land," and "Orphans of God" are among his very best songs, and he performs these and others with newfound exuberance (on mandolin, with **Michael Been** of **The Call** on bass and **Sam Phillips** on backing vocals). The title track "Satellite Sky" contrasts the wonder Heard felt as a child when Sputnik was orbiting the earth with the disillusioned grim reality of modern youth. Likewise (but with varied application), "We Know Too Much" paints an apocalyptic portrait of a culture whose multitudinous discoveries have somehow not enriched the spirits of its denizens. Both "Freight Train to Nowhere" and "A Broken Man" also deal with the struggle to find meaning and value in a culture that discourages honest expression and seems to have lost its sense of dignity. Heard wrote "Treasure of the Broken Land" in grief over his father's death, though when he himself died a year later many fans would apply it to him: "Parched earth give up your captive ones / Waiting wind of Gabriel / Blow soon upon the hollow bones."

High Noon compiles classic songs from Heard's last three albums, adding a rendition of the hymn "I Know that My Redeemer Lives" and three previously unreleased tracks. Of these, "She's Not Afraid" is particularly meaningful, describing the inner fears of the outwardly strong: "She's not afraid of sticks and stones . . . of thunderstorms . . . of smartbombs blowing the world into little pieces / But she is afraid of a life alone / She is afraid of an empty home / She is afraid that her faith has flown / Afraid of losing memories." The collection is a far more fitting retrospective than the two posthumous releases *Mystery Mind* and *Millennium Archives,* both of which collect demos, live tracks, and other lost songs that Heard probably never intended to be released.

The Final Performance is a recording of a concert given by Heard at the *Cornerstone* festival on July 4, 1992. During the performance Heard said, "I think I'm having a heart attack." Known for his offbeat humor, everyone thought he was joking—but he wasn't. After the concert, which he completed, he was hospitalized and treated for what had been a mild cardiac infarction. Released a few days later, he suffered a major cardiac arrest while recovering at a nearby hotel. As his family would later report, he literally died laughing, cajoling at a story his sister had just told when the attack hit, sending him into a coma from which he never recovered. He was forty years old. Heard's death sent the Christian music community into mourning, the more so because so many fans of Christian music had only recently discovered his contributions. A motley assortment of artists soon cooperated to produce one of the most impressive "tribute albums" ever assembled in his honor. The project was initially released as *Strong Hand of Love* (Fingerprint, 1994) and then was expanded into a two-disc version called *Orphans of God* (Fingerprint, 1996). *Orphans* contains fourteen of *Strong Hand*'s seventeen tracks, plus twenty more for a total two-and-a-half hours of music. Most of the songs covered are ones from Heard's last three albums, but the contributing artists include not only predictable Christian stars **(Carolyn Arends, Ashley Cleveland, Bruce Cockburn, Phil Keaggy,** the **Vigilantes of Love)**, but also takes by several lesser-known artists and return visits from such almost-forgotten heroes as **Chagall Guevara, Tonio K.,** and **Pat Terry.** Artists who are not usually associated with the Christian market—Olivia Newton-John and Kate Taylor (James' sister)—pay their respects as well. The brilliantly diverse collection of talent and styles reflects well Heard's own disposition, as expressed in lines that could serve as his epitaph: "We are soot-covered urchins running wild and unshod / We will always be remembered as the orphans of God."

In addition to his recordings, Heard served as producer on projects by such artists as **John Austin, The Choir, John Fischer, Garth Hewitt, Jacob's Trouble, Pierce Pettis, Randy Stonehill, Pat Terry,** and the **Vigilantes of Love.**

Christian radio hits: "One of the Dominoes" (# 2 in 1982); "The Pain that Plagues Creation" (# 26 in 1983).

Lindy Hearne

1980—*Diamonds in the Rough* (Ariel); 1981—*Vessel of Love* (Voice Box).

Lindy Hearne made two albums of Memphis country rock in the early '80s that feature mostly original compositions. Hearne applied his strong voice to songs with minimal backup, highlighting lyrics that address struggles of the daily Christian life. The title tracks to both albums present the prayers of a Christian who understands the need for continual growth.

Hearne realizes he is still a "diamond in the rough" but asks God to make him a "vessel of love."

Heather and Kirsten (and **Arcade**)

Heather Ostrom; Kirsten Ostrom. By Arcade: 1989—*Arcade* (Maranatha). By Heather and Kirsten: 1990—*Betcha Didn't Know* (Arcade).

Heather and Kirsten Ostrom are sisters from Canada who recorded an album of bubbly Christian songs for teenage girls when they were fourteen and twelve, respectively. The girls' mother, Carolee Mayne Ostrom, is a known session singer in their homeland and helped them to land their first contract. Prior to their debut album, both girls were members of a corporate singing group called Arcade, which also included their mother and **Billy Batstone.** Arcade recorded a single self-titled album for Maranatha in 1989. Kirsten and Carolee Ostrom composed the songs for *Betcha Didn't Know,* with some assistance from producer **Roby Duke.** *CCM*'s Thom Granger allowed his fifteen-year-old daughter Kate to review the record for the magazine. She found the strongest tracks to be the title song, which encourages witnessing, and "Pouring Rain," a gentle ballad about leaning on the Lord. "If I Were to Say" is a tougher, four-minute song with jazzy accompaniment and growling vocals that belie the singers' age or innocence. The group toured in 1991 as the opening act for **DC Talk.**

For trivia buffs: Kirsten Ostrom was once featured on *Late Night with David Lettermen.* After discovering that his audience was unable to sing the Canadian national anthem, the talk show host brought teenaged Kirsten on a program to lead them in the song.

Christian radio hits: As Arcade: "Best Friend" (# 8 in 1990); "This Is Love" (# 4 in 1990). As Heather and Kirsten: "Betcha Didn't Know" (# 12 in 1991); "Shock-2-U" (# 19 in 1991).

Heirloom

Tanya Goodman-Sykes, voc.; Candy Hemphill (Christmas), voc.; Sheri Easter, voc. (– 1990; + 1995) // Barbara Fairchild, voc. (+ 1990). 1989—*Heirloom* (Benson); 1990—*Apples of Gold;* 1991—*Uncommon Love;* 1993—*The Best of Heirloom;* 1995—*Hymns That Last Forever;* 2000—*20 Favorites* (Budget).

Heirloom was a trio of country-oriented gospel singers put together as a deliberate imitation of the successful trio of Linda Ronstadt, Dolly Parton, and Emmylou Harris, whose collaboration bore commercial and critical fruit in the world of mainstream country. **Tanya Goodman-Sykes** is a member of the famous Goodman Family (a.k.a. The Happy Goodmans), one of southern gospel's most successful recording groups. **Candy Hemphill** also sang with a family group, The Hemphills [a.k.a. The Singing Hemphills], then recorded two solo albums in the early '80s; she married evangelist Kent Christmas in 1987 and

has continued to record as Candy Christmas. Sheri Easter has recorded successful southern gospel albums with her husband (as Jeff and Sheri Easter), including one *(A Work in Progress)* that won the Dove award for Country Album of the Year in 2000. A single from the first Heirloom album, "There's Still Power in the Blood," did well on southern gospel charts, but the group failed to attract the crossover audience of the contemporary Christian music market. Barbara Fairchild, who replaced Sheri Easter in 1990, had a Top 10 mainstream country hit with "Teddy Bear Song" in 1973.

Dove Awards: 1990 Country Album *(Heirloom).*

Heirship

David Boyd; Ron Elms; Michael Isble; Randy Phillips; Russ Obrey, drums; Wayne Smith; Ed Stiltz, voc. 1978—*Roadway to the Son* (Rainbow).

www.rancyland.net/heirship

A vocal group from the West Coast, Heirship made one progressive country rock album in the late '70s, which *Jesus Music* describes as having a sound reminiscent of America or **The Way.** The music featured vocal harmonies augmented by acoustic guitar, piano, and flute. In 1988, the members of Heirship participated in a "virtual reunion," sharing their thoughts about experiences with the band in documents later posted at their website. Ron Elms died of a heart attack on August 26, 2000.

Candy Hemphill (a.k.a. **Candy Christmas**)

1983—*Candy Hemphill* (Heartwarming); 1984—*Heart of Fire* (Impact); 1986—*Arms of Love* (Greentree).

www.candychristmas.com

Candy Christmas would become one of southern gospel's biggest stars in the '90s, but prior to the marriage that changed her name she made a brief foray into the contemporary Christian market. Born Carmel Hemphill in Bastrop, Louisiana, in 1961, Candy grew up as a member of the Singing Hemphills, a family group led by her father Joel that won the 1981 and 1986 Dove Awards for Southern Gospel Album of the Year *(Workin'; Excited).* Candy's debut solo album garnered a review in *CCM* but the magazine noted that, despite the attempt to bridge the gap between traditional and contemporary gospel, "*Candy Hemphill* may be best appreciated by southern gospel purists, not by listeners weaned on rock 'n' roll." The second outing was a greater success. *Heart of Fire* features a country rock band that *CCM* said "alternates between up-tempo and easy listening," while the blend of backing choir and soloist on the title track and "Can't Stop Reachin' " draws heavily on Hemphill's roots in a way that displays her greatest strengths. In the late

'80s, Hemphill became part of the trio **Heirloom,** which also tried to appeal to fans of a more contemporary sound. She married evangelist Kent Christmas in 1987 and began recording albums more solidly in the southern gospel tradition under her married name. In 2000, she worked as part of George W. Bush's presidential campaign, touring with the candidate and performing regularly at his rallies.

Christian radio hits: "In a Different Light" (# 28 in 1983); "Can't Stop Reachin' " (# 40 in 1984); "Take Us inside Your Love" (# 27 in 1985).

Kyle Henderson

1985—*More Than the Look of Love* (Kerygma).

Kyle Henderson is a classically trained musician who studied cello as a youth but then yielded to the lure of rock and roll to front an Atlanta combo called The Producers. The latter group had only one minor hit on the national charts ("What She Does to Me [The Diana Song]," # 61 in 1981) but regionally, they scored with both "What's He Got" and "She's Sheila." Videos for all three of these songs received attention on MTV. In 1984, Henderson experienced a conversion to Christianity and subsequently worked with **Kerry Livgren** on projects for **A.D.** and **Kansas,** as well as with **Benny Hester,** with whom he cowrote the song "Back to Basics." Henderson's solo album features a style remarkably similar to that of Bryan Adams, whose rough-but-melodic voice is comparable to Henderson's. Perhaps the most distinctive element of the record musically is the generous use of saxophone, supplied by Dennis Marcellino. As *CCM* noted, the combination of Marcellino's soulful sax and Henderson's raspy vocals creates an aura similar to that displayed by Bob Seger on his hits "Main Street" and "Turn the Page." Standout songs on *More Than the Look of Love* include the up-tempo rocker "Gift of Grace" and the more subdued "Fallen Angel."

Patrick Henderson

1983—*This Is Love* (Priority).

A soulful, African American singer from Dallas, Patrick Henderson has only recorded one album, but he has affected the Christian and general market music industries in other ways. In 1971, Henderson toured with Leon Russell and later played keyboards in Nils Lofgren's band. He formed a group called Black Glass for a while and then moved to Los Angeles where he connected with Michael McDonald of the Doobie Brothers. He and McDonald wrote the gospel-tinged songs "Open Your Eyes" and "Real Love," both of which were recorded by that group. Indeed, "Real Love" became one of the group's biggest hits (# 5 in 1980). Henderson also wrote or cowrote all of the songs on his own album, *This Is Love,* the most notable of which may be the rhythmic "I Believe" and the

moving ballad, "Charity," based on 1 Corinthians 13 (different from the **Kenn Gulliksen** song). Henderson's songs have a distinctly personal feel to them, and he sings them in a voice reminiscent of James Ingram, though with more of a rock orientation.

Christian radio hits: "Charity" (# 20 in 1982).

Kristy Hendley

1996—*Kristy Hendley* (Ransom).

Kristy Hendley moved from her hometown of Nashville, Georgia, to Nashville, Tennessee, to attend Belmont College and become a country western singer. A beauty contestant, she was second runner-up in the Miss Tennessee pageant (winning the talent competition) but would later reflect on the superficial and unhealthy aspects of a life obsessed with appearance. With her debut album, she entered the world of contemporary Christian music, singing country songs that extol the value of individual human beings as unique creations of God. She has targeted youth and college-aged women for her ministry, trying to help those who struggle with eating disorders and low self-esteem.

Kathy Herivel

1983—*Kathy Herivel and Runner* (Chalace).

Kathy Herivel is a jazz singer whose inspirational album with backing band Runner won praise from *CCM* for its variety and creativity. "Stay True," "Keep Me Livin' It," and "Smile" all have "an upbeat rocky feel," while "We'll Have Our Love," "I Need You," and "Peace" evoke "a deeper, more introspective mood." Herivel's lush voice is set against keyboard and guitar arrangements on original compositions.

Annie Herring

1976—*Through a Child's Eyes* (Sparrow); *Kids of the Kingdom* (Birdwing); 1978—*Kids of the Kingdom: Follow the Leader;* 1981—*Search Deep Inside* (Sparrow); 1989—*Flying Lessons* (Live Oak); 1990—*Waiting for My Ride to Come;* 1992—*There's a Stirring* (Sparrow); 1993—*All that I Am;* 1997—*Glimpses* (Spring Hill); 1998—*Wonder; Picture Frames.*

www.annieherring.com

Annie Herring is one of contemporary Christian music's greatest natural resources, an incredible talent who enjoyed (or endured) a few brief years of superstardom and then settled into a more comfortable existence as one of the dozens of female adult contemporary singers working in a field that had become an industry. In the early years of the Jesus movement (pre-**Amy Grant**), Herring was one of only three or four women in the limelight of spiritual and musical revival: **Marsha Stevens** was the sweet one; **Evie,** the beautiful child;

Honeytree was sort of whiny and introspective; and Annie Herring, she was the slugger who could belt a song out of the park every time she got up to bat. In 1977, Herring was named by *Record World* as the "Top New Gospel Female Vocalist." Herring remains best known for her work with **2nd Chapter of Acts,** the quintessential group she founded with sister Nelly and brother Matthew. From her work with that group, she became known not only for her powerhouse voice but also for her composing. She wrote or cowrote most of the group's songs, including such classics as "Easter Song" and "Mansion Builder." In the '70s, she was regarded alongside **Andraé Crouch, Keith Green,** and **Larry Norman** as one of Christian music's great new songwriters. Her song "Butterfly" was a hit for **The Boones,** and **Michael Omartian**'s song "Annie the Poet" (on his *Adam Again* album) is often thought to be a tribute to her.

Herring was born Annie Ward and raised as part of a large family in rural North Dakota. The family relocated to California in her later adolescence, where she sought to break into the popular music market. She was just on the verge of success, juggling promising offers, when her mother's death from a brain tumor (after a long, undiagnosed illness) in 1968 sent her into a spiritual crisis. This was resolved through a surprise reunion with her estranged boyfriend Buck Herring who had become "a born again Christian." He led her to embrace his newfound faith and they married in 1969. A year later, her father died of leukemia. Buck and Annie took in the two younger siblings Nelly (age fourteen) and Matthew (age twelve), which led to the genesis of **2nd Chapter of Acts.** Buck Herring served as the group's manager and engineer, accompanying them on tours and giving inspirational talks and conducting altar calls. Buck also would become a successful producer, not only of his wife's albums, but of projects by **Mike Deasy, Phil Keaggy, Barry McGuire, Michael** and **Stormie Omartian, Terry Talbot,** and **Matthew Ward.**

Herring's first solo album is a classic of Jesus music. Originally issued with a picture of the artist in a swing, the cover was later reshot with a close up of her face in a field of flowers. **Michael Omartian** plays keyboards and **Mike Deasy,** guitar. Her famous siblings add background vocals (along with Bili Thedford and **Stormie Omartian**), giving the album a feel very similar to the work of 2nd Chapter—particularly as evidenced on their later *Mansion Builder* project. The song "Grinding Stone" is an absolute masterpiece, one of Herring's best compositions and most powerful performances. Lyrically, it takes its cue from Matthew 24:41 but avoids the silly rapture theology that infected most Jesus music songs about the end times. This one sticks to what is actually in the Bible, albeit with personal emotional investment and evocative power: "I don't want to be the woman left at the grinding stone," Herring screams. "I don't want to be the woman left all alone."

Two other songs also demand attention: "Dance with You" is a moving upbeat number with a calypso twist, and "Liberty Bird" delves into disco at a time when no other Christian artist (and few secular ones) knew that genre existed.

After the stunning triumph of her debut, Herring took a break to record two albums of children's songs, an interest prefigured in such tracks as "Learn a Curtsey" and "Fly Away Little Burden" on the first record. Then she returned with the introspective, appropriately titled *Search Deep Inside,* a collection of often painful and poignant tracks. In "When You Come on My Mind," Herring addresses two children who she bore and gave up for adoption as a teenager: "I didn't want to leave you / The papers were hard to sign / But now I've found love / And pray about you / When you come on my mind." Juxtaposed with an antiabortion anthem, "Killing Thousands," the song's effect is all the more jarring. Then, beginning with *Flying Lessons,* she eased into the usual routine of adult contemporary pop, presenting melody-driven songs with a heavy emphasis on ballads or hymns. Her siblings join her on most of the projects, and **Phil Keaggy** provides guitar on *Wonder* and *Picture Frames.* Herring has increasingly tended toward the inspirational side of the adult contemporary spectrum, realizing her day of appealing to youth is past. *There's a Stirring* offers "Glory in the Highest," an original composition that begs to be sung by congregations in worship. *Glimpses* contains the modern hymns "My Redeemer" and "Glory, Glory, Glory" in addition to an unusually bouncy rendition of the Kyrie from the Latin mass. *Picture Frames,* too, is liturgical in its presentation of meditative, worshipful songs like "I Bow Down" and "To the King."

Benny Hester

1973—*Benny* (VMI); 1978—*Benny Hester* (Spirit) [reissued as *Be a Receiver* (Myrrh, 1983)]; 1981—*Nobody Knows Me Like You*; 1983—*Legacy*; 1985—*Benny from Here*; 1987—*Through the Window*; 1988—*Personal Best*; 1989—*Perfect* (Frontline); 1990—*United We Stand, Divided We Fall.*

A singer/songwriter from Waco, Texas, Benny Hester has attained his greatest commercial and critical success in a medium other than music. In the early '90s, he developed the children's program *Roundhouse* for Nickolodeon. The popular cable show, which featured Christian singer **Crystal Lewis** as a member of its cast, ran from 1993 to 1996 and was nominated for nine Cable Ace awards. Prior to this venture, however, Hester had a successful career in Christian music himself. He had been propelled into the Christian music industry after a failed career in the general market (which yielded the flop album, *Benny*). His first Christian release, originally titled *Benny Hester,* also failed to receive much attention until fans of the later music picked it up as a reissue (now called *Be a Receiver*). Hester would eventually become known as a high-voiced adult contemporary singer, but *Benny Hester/Be a Re-*

ceiver presents him in more of a hippie-styled, Supertramp mode, singing dreamy acoustic rock songs enhanced by flutes and other reed instruments. The album was produced by Brent Maher, who would later make his mark in country music as producer for The Judds.

Nobody Knows Me Like You was Hester's breakthrough album and remains one of his two best-known works. Produced by **Michael Omartian,** the album yielded a crossover hit when the title song made it to the Top 30 on *Billboard*'s general market adult contemporary chart. Partly due to the Omartian connection, Hester became established in the public mind as a Christian version of Christopher Cross (whose breakthrough album Omartian also produced). *Legacy* includes "Nobody's Listening," a hook-filled Toto-like song. Hailed as Hester's "best work yet" by *CCM,* the album nevertheless failed to catch fire. *Benny from Here* would return him to the top of the Christian marketplace. That album actually features a more rocking sound overall than the previous two projects, but somewhat ironically its intimate ballad "When God Ran" would become Hester's signature song, one of the biggest Christian hits of the decade. "Back to Basics," cowritten with **Kyle Henderson,** exemplifies the more catchy potential of Hester's pop style, but the success of "When God Ran" guarantees that he will always be best remembered as a balladeer. *Through the Window* is a deeply introspective album recorded at a time when Hester was going through a divorce. *Perfect* offers the two sides of Hester, with Side One featuring rock songs and Side Two, adult contemporary pop. *United We Stand, Divided We Fall* is a fairly upbeat, poppy album with several songs (including the standout "Rain, Rain, Rain") recalling Paul Simon's pre-*Graceland* material.

Hester has a degree in music from Texas Tech University. He has written numerous advertising jingles and continues to operate Rebel Entertainment with his wife in Hollywood Hills, California.

Christian radio hits: "Nobody Knows Me Like You" (# 3 in 1981); "Come Back" (# 16 in 1982); "One More Time" (# 19 in 1982); "Legacy" (# 5 in 1983); "Melody Man" (# 40 in 1984); "When God Ran" (# 1 for 13 weeks in 1985); "To Fill Our Empty Hearts" (# 6 in 1986); "Remember Me" (# 2 in 1987); "Perfect" (# 4 in 1989); "You Weren't Meant to Live Your Life Alone" (# 10 in 1989); "Before You Know It" (# 6 in 1990).

Garth Hewitt

1973—*The Lion and the Lamb* (Myrrh); 1974—*I Never Knew Life Was in Technicolor Till I Saw the Silver Screen;* 1976—*Love Song for the Earth;* 1978—*I'm Grateful;* 1979—*Did He Jump Or Was He Pushed?* (Patch); 1980—*The Best of Garth Hewitt* (Myrrh); 1982—*A Change in Me* (Pilgrim America); 1983—*The Road to Freedom* (Myrrh); 1985—*Alien Brain* [re-issued as *Broken Land* (DaySpring, 1985)]; 1988—*Scars* (DaySpring); 1991—*Lonesome Troubadour* (Word); 1992—*Memories;* 1994—*Stronger Than the Storm* (Myrrh); 1996—*Journeys with Garth Hewitt: Pray for the Peace: The Holy Land.*

Virtually unknown in the United States, Garth Hewitt has been one of the United Kingdom's biggest Christian stars for more than two decades. His dominant style is folk-rock with heavy emphasis on harmonica and hand-clapping, but over the years he has flirted with varieties of rural music, including country, bluegrass, calypso, and reggae. *Love Song for the Earth* is a classic, featuring ten original roots-rock compositions and guest guitar from **Bryn Haworth.** As a songwriter, Hewitt often employs humorous or inane phrasings (e.g., "It's Good to Have a Fat Friend When Times Are Wearing Thin," from *A Change in Me*), but his albums *Road to Freedom* and *Pray for the Peace* both document serious topics garnered from his travels. The first of these deals with the poverty and injustice he observed in India and Africa. The song "Nero's Watching Video" updates the cavalier attitude of the Roman emperor who supposedly fiddled while Rome burned, with modern reference to people in the West who seem obsessed with entertainment but deaf to the cries of the needy.

Bruce Hibbard

1977—*A Light Within* (Seed); 1980—*Never Turnin' Back* (Myrrh).

Pop singer/songwriter Bruce Hibbard was a member of the early Christian bands **Amplified Version** and **Sonlight.** He wrote the Christian radio hit "I'm Forgiven" for **The Imperials** and participated on some of **Kelly Willard**'s projects. Hibbard's two solo albums present smooth arrangements of somewhat jazzy pop songs, with Willard and some of Hibbard's **Koinonia** friends assisting. Hibbard was a self-confessed protégé of **Paul Clark,** and his albums are similar to that artist's work in style and content. Clark coproduced the album *A Light Within,* which includes the songs "All That I Want to Be" and "Given Myself Over." Hadley Hockensmith produced *Never Turnin' Back* and cowrote most of the songs for the sophomore project.

Christian radio hits: "Never Turnin' Back" (# 14 in 1980).

Ray Hildebrand

1967—*He's Everything to Me* (Word); 1971—*I Need You Every Hour;* 1973—*Special Kind of Man* (Myrrh); 1976—*Welcome Warrior* (Tempo).

Ray Hildebrand is a legend of early '60s rock, though his name remains unknown to all but the most arduous trivia hounds. Born in Joshua, Texas, in 1940, Hildebrand attended Howard Payne College in Brownsville, Texas, where he wrote a song called "Hey, Paula," a duet between two would-be lovers. Sensing hit potential, he set up a recording session to have the song performed by two studio singers, Jill Jackson and a male vocalist who failed to show up. In desperation, Hildebrand did the male vocal himself and the song was released by Jill and Ray in 1962. It tanked. Then Hildebrand re-released it as a song by Paul and Paula and that simple change made all the difference. "Hey Paula" by Paul and Paula was Number One for three weeks in 1963 and sold over three million copies. Later that year, Ray and Jill had two more Top 40 hits as Paul and Paula: "Young Lovers" (# 6) and "First Quarrel" (# 27). Hildebrand spent two years on the road, then experienced a reawakening of his childhood faith and determined that he wanted to sing and write Christian songs for the church. His first album, *He's Everything to Me,* brought the title song (written by **Ralph Carmichael**) to the attention of the Christian public. The record was widely distributed among churches looking for a contemporary way to reach young people; youth groups and camp counselors pillaged it for songs. Hildebrand's own song "Say, I Do" also became a favorite among Christian youth in the early '70s, taking a place alongside Carmichael's "He's Everything to Me" and Kurt Kaiser's "Pass It On." The song is sprightly and cheerful with a chorus that proclaims, "Anybody here want to live forever? Say 'I do' / Anybody here want to walk on golden streets? Say 'I do'!" It was performed by many early Christian singers, including **Evie.**

Hildebrand never capitalized on his celebrity and most people who knew and loved his songs never knew that he was the "Paul" of Paul and Paula, the man who had written and sung what was by then one of the most played oldies on their transistor radios. In contemporary Christian music Hildebrand's legacy is like that of Carmichael, Kaiser, **John Fischer, Jimmy and Carol Owens, Ray Repp,** and **John Ylvisaker.** He is one of the very few pioneers who created and popularized creative youth music for churches before the advent of the Jesus movement, music that prepared the way for Christian rock and its descendants.

Kim Hill

1988—*Kim Hill* (Reunion); 1989—*Talk about Life;* 1993—*Brave Heart;* 1994—*So Far, So Good;* 1995—*Testimony;* 1997—*The Fire Again* (StarSong); 1998—*Arms of Mercy; Renewing the Heart: Live Hymns and Songs of Worship;* 1999—*Signature Songs* (Greentree).

www.kimhillmusic.com

Kim Hill (b. 1963) possesses a mesmerizing alto voice that tends to cut through the clutter of female adult contemporary singers on Christian radio. Performing mainly ballads, often with a country accent, Hill nevertheless remains distinctive in her presentation and charm. Born in Starville, Mississippi, Hill was impressed early on by a spiritual revival that transformed her parents from mere churchgoers into persons who lived every moment with complete passion for the Lord: "They turned their whole circle of friends around," she says. "There

were these people who used to have parties at our house and now, suddenly, they were all holding hands and singing 'Praise the Lord.'" As a teenager, Hill attended Christian schools, was only allowed to listen to Christian music, and was very involved in such groups as Young Life and Fellowship of Christian Athletes. She was deeply affected by her participation in a Precept teen weekend, where she learned about spiritual devotions and a life oriented toward worship and holiness. She later attended Mississippi State University where she played in a band with Clarke Leake of **The Waiting.** After becoming one of Christian music's top female vocalists, Hill decided to cross over to mainstream country music in 1994 and enjoyed success with the song "Janie's Gone Fishin'," which reached Number One on both the CMT and VH-1 video networks. Hill returned to Christian music with a new passion in 1997, inspired in part by a **Twila Paris** concert she attended in Nashville. Since that time, she has served as worship leader for women's conferences sponsored by Focus on the Family. Her *Renewing the Heart* album was recorded live at one of these events held at Max Lucado's church in San Antonio, Texas.

Hill's debut album features "Psalm 1," a beautifully simple song that sets the biblical text to a single guitar accompaniment. Another track, "Unspoken Love," recalls Neil Diamond's "You Don't Bring Me Flowers," but is more poignant: "I wonder how many husbands and wives / Will cry themselves to sleep tonight / Wishing for the world / That they could just reach out across the bed / And hold each other the way they used to." The song was written by John Thompson (who also wrote "El Shaddai" with **Michael Card**) after he went through a divorce. Hill sings it with a wrenching pathos that makes it one of her most powerful and unforgettable songs. The debut album also includes "Faithful," "Change Your Heart," and "Refuge," all of which became major radio hits and set high expectations for Hill's role in the Christian music market. "Refuge" is stunning in its simplicity—straightforward lyrics ("I need a refuge") set to a memorable melody and beat that makes it one of Christian music's most perfect pop songs (Hill's repeat "echo" of the word "refuge" in the chorus is as brilliant a moment in Christian pop as, say, Randy Bachman's stuttering the lyric to "You Ain't Seen Nothin' Yet" is in the secular field). "Faithful" is a flowing song with a staccato chorus that emphasizes, again, the simple (unelaborated) sentiment of its lyric: "I want to be faithful." In all these respects, Kim Hill provides one of those rare instances in which *blatantly* Christian music fulfills its potential, succeeding *because* (rather than in spite of) the artist's (unapologetic) spirituality. An unnoticed song, "Black Shirts," celebrates the goodness of life in a way that is unfortunately almost atypical for Christian music: "I love wearing black shirts / And wearing them with my black Levis / Jump in my convertible and kick it into overdrive / I love good times." Hill was nominated for New Artist of the Year at the Dove awards (but lost to **Take 6**).

Talk about Life more than fulfilled all hopes generated by the promising debut. "Snake in the Grass" evinces a Melissa Etheridge-style roughness, while the title song is what *CCM* called "a cowpunk music track with a drawling speed-rap vocal laid over the top of it." The meat-and-potatoes of the album, however, are once again the poignant ballads. "Testimony" (written by **Wayne Kirkpatrick**) gets its subject matter exactly right by focusing on the sufficiency of God rather than on the transformed status of the convert: "You are my lifeline / You are my sanctuary / You are my torchlight / This is my testimony." The song "Secret Place" deals with the importance of having a quiet devotional time (something Hill discovered on the Precept teen weekend). On "Charm Is Deceitful" (cowritten with **Wes King**), she reflects insightfully on her reputed good looks: "I know that when He sees me / It won't be beauty that he longs to hold / It will be the love that he finds inside my heart / 'Cause charm is deceitful, beauty is vain / Flesh is unfaithful and is of no gain." On *Brave Heart,* Hill rocks out more than ever before, tearing things up on "Round and Round" and emulating the Beatles on "Words" and "Up in the Sky." Her country influence comes through on "Satisfied" (not the **Andraé Crouch** song), and she is at her soulful best on "Mysterious Ways" (not the **U2** song). Only "I Will Wait" recalls the soft folk sound of "Psalm 1," once again setting Scripture to an easy-to-strum guitar melody; Hill says she sang the song about "waiting on the Lord" with specific application to waiting for God to provide her with a husband. *Brave Heart* is widely regarded as Hill's best album, and the strong influence of her backing band (including **Phil Madeira** and former **White Heart** members Gordon Kennedy, Chris McHugh, and **Tommy Sims**) should be noted. Hill has joked that *Brave Heart* was essentially a **White Heart** album, with her serving as the group's lead singer. *Testimony* gathers ten of the best songs from Hill's first three albums for an appropriate (if unduly mellow) compilation. Unfortunately, the later *Signature Songs* compilation (also ten tracks) does not build on this collection, but simply repackages the same songs that were already available on *Testimony* (with "I Will Wait" replacing "Satisfied").

Hill's song "Snake in the Grass" was a crossover hit in parts of Europe, putting her on the radio alongside Madonna and Tracy Chapman. A tour of Sweden where she played secular venues gave her a taste of a different life, singing songs with spiritual themes for people whose interest in spiritual things was at least uncertain and perhaps untried. Hill decided to go into the general market full bore, and *So Far, So Good* was her entry into the country scene. Her ties with the Christian subculture remained firm, as her longtime producer **Wayne Kirkpatrick** continued to helm the project. In addition to the

hit "Janie's Gone Fishin'," the record features a song (written by Kirkpatrick and **Amy Grant**) with classic country lyrics: "You love to do the two-step / And you love the picture show / And you love to watch bull riders at the local rodeo. . . . Is there any love left for me?" The closing song on *So Far, So Good* is its only overt concession to religious themes. "When We're Home" is a bluesy number that looks forward to that day "a'comin' when we'll look up in the sky . . . hear that trumpet blow and kiss this world goodbye."

After a four-year absence, Hill returned to Christian music with a new sound. *The Fire Again* and *Arms of Mercy* both move away from country and away from the edgy pop of her early albums into a more predictable inspirational style. Hill embraces praise and worship music on both albums almost as much as on her live worship album. Breaking with Kirkpatrick, she used producers David Kershenbaum (known for his work with Bryan Adams and Tracy Chapman) and Andy Piercy (from **After the Fire**) on the two projects. While many fans would lament this transition, no one would question Hill's competence at the new genre. *Fire Again* opens with a medley of the traditional hymns "Nothing But the Blood" and "I Know a Fount." *Arms of Mercy* offers a version of **David Wilcox**'s "Show the Way" alongside the stunning "You Are Still Holy" (written by Rita Springer and featuring duet vocals from **Nichole Nordeman**). Another highlight of the latter project is "Committed to the Call," on which Hill is joined by **Ashley Cleveland.** Christian pop's loss was Christian adult contemporary's gain. Hill's incredibly rich and distinctive voice would establish her as the best adult contemporary singer in the Christian market, and as of 2002 she would remain *the* essential artist in that overpopulated field.

Hill is primarily an interpreter of songs, not a songwriter. Like **Susan Ashton,** she has demonstrated a good sense of selection, bringing material from such writers as **Brown Bannister,** Gordon Kennedy, **Wes King,** and **Wayne Kirkpatrick** to light—and, on her later worshipful records, songs by Rita Springer and **Kate Miner.**

Christian radio hits: "Faithful" (# 7 in 1988); "Change Your Heart" (# 13 in 1988); "Refuge" (# 6 in 1989); "Testimony" (# 1 for 2 weeks in 1989); "Inside of You" (# 3 in 1989); "Secret Place" (# 2 in 1990); "Snake in the Grass" (# 16 in 1990); "Stop, Watch, and Listen" (# 12 in 1990); "Mysterious Ways" (# 3 in 1991); "I Will Wait" (# 15 in 1992); "Satisfied" (# 1 for 2 weeks in 1992); "Words" (# 16 in 1992); "Like a Father Should Be" [with **Kenny Marks**] (# 22 in 1992).

Dove Awards: 1999 Praise and Worship Album *(Renewing the Heart: Live Hymns and Songs of Worship).*

Hillman, Leadon, Perkins, and Scheff

Chris Hillman; Bernie Leadon; Al Perkins; Jerry Scheff. 1993—*Down Home Praise* (independent).

The quartet known as Hillman, Leadon, Perkins and Scheff deserves special note due to the high profile stature of its members within the general music market. Though none of the four is a big star in his own right, all are justly famous among musicians and music critics in the rock world. All four are also outspoken Christians, though only Perkins has had any substantial involvement with the Christian music subculture. Chris Hillman was a founding member of The Byrds, one of America's most important country-folk-rock bands from the '60s (Roger McGuinn, leader of The Byrds, would also later become known for his Christian faith). Hillman was also a founding member of The Flying Burrito Brothers and was part of the Souther Furay Hillman band (along with **Richie Furay,** who would later record for the Christian market), and of Manassas (fronted by Stephen Stills). **Bernie Leadon** was a founding member of The Eagles, the country rock group that inherited The Byrds' mantle and, more than any other act, bridged the gap between country and rock that they had begun to close. **Al Perkins** is a master of the dobro, and is widely reputed to be one of the world's finest pedal steel guitar players. He has been at least a temporary member of many groups, including the Flying Burrito Brothers, Souther Furay Hillman, Manassas, and **Mason Proffit.** An early convert from the days of the Jesus movement, he has worked prodigiously in contemporary Christian music from its outset, producing numerous artists and playing on a wide spate of Christian albums. Jerry Scheff is simply famous as one of the most sought-after bass players in rock and roll, having played for everyone from **Elvis Presley** to **Bob Dylan** to The Doors. In late 1994, these four stars toured a number of midwestern clubs in a station wagon, playing gospel and country standards for lucky patrons at small venues. *Down Home Praise* is an equally humble collection of worship songs, performed in a folk-rock meets bluegrass style.

Steve Hindalong

1998—*Skinny* (Cadence).

Steve Hindalong is drummer for **The Choir,** one of Christian music's most acclaimed modern rock bands. More importantly, however, he is the chief songwriter for that group. Choir fans have long asserted that the secret to the group's success is the combination of Hindalong's songs with Derri Daugherty's emotive vocals. After one of **The Choir**'s supposed break-ups, Hindalong recorded a solo album on which for the first time he is heard singing his own material. The songs themselves all have the familiar Choir stylings, but the presentation is notably different from the lush and layered treatments of that group's albums. Instead, they are presented in understated and ragged fashion recalling the more acoustic

work of artists like Neil Young. Hindalong has worked as a producer in Christian music for years, helming projects by **John Austin, The Prayer Chain, The Throes,** and many others. His numerous connections in the industry are evident here as a plethora of stars add instrumental and vocal enhancements to *Skinny,* which Wayne Everett of **The Prayer Chain** produces. The songs themselves, however, are the real stars. The opening "Color Wheel" is classic pop; "Winniepesaukee" is fragile folk; "Diggin' Your Style" is an electrified rumble. Lyrically, the album does not offer the sort of overt testimony that many fans of Christian music expect from artists within their subculture. Hindalong sings about life and its troubles, employing imagery that is sometimes suggestive, sometimes obscure. Relationships and the struggle for love is a common theme: "When you don't feel for me the way that I feel for you, well what else can I do but try to make that untrue" ("Seven Colors").

Skinny is on all accounts a great album—one of the best Christian releases of 1998—but comparisons with **The Choir**'s albums are inevitable. Is it as good as the group's works, or even better? That judgment comes down to taste and to the relative prioritization a listener places on authenticity versus technical competence. Anyone who prefers Neil Young's *Comes a Time* or *Silver and Gold* to, say, The Police's *Synchonicity* will probably regard Hindalong's solo work as the superior project.

For trivia buffs: Hindalong's first solo appearance was actually on a **Stryper** tribute album (*Sweet Family Music,* Flying Tart, 1996), on which he sang "To Hell with the Devil." He accepted the project as a joke, telling *Release,* "I thought it would be fun to sing the worst lyric ever written."

Hip Dream

See **Deitiphobia.**

Darwin Hobbs

1999—*Mercy* (EMI); 2000—*Vertical.*

Soulful easy listening singer Darwin Hobbs is often compared to Luther Vandross, who actually contributed a song to Hobbs' sophomore project. A Cincinnati native, Hobbs began as a session singer and segued into gospel music by performing on albums by **Michael Card** and **Sarah Masen.** He also sang with the **Passion** One Day worship events alongside **Matt Redman** and other worship leaders. *Mercy* has a distinctly worship orientation, opening with the praise song "You're the One," and also featuring "I Can't Live without You." The album has a modern urban sound, however, with turntable scratching and funky synthesizer horns. Hobbs' sophomore project, *Vertical,* turns more toward traditional gospel and R&B. A number of high profile artists put in guest appearances, with Michael McDonald offering a duet on "Everyday" (written and produced by **Tommy Sims**), and **Donna Summer** joining the singer for "When I Look Up." Most of *Vertical* was produced by Cedric and Victor Caldwell (known for their work with **CeCe Winans** and Whitney Houston); several of the songs on the album were composed by Cedric Caldwell and his wife **Angie Winans.**

Joanna Hogg

See **Joanna.**

Höglund Band

See **Vincent.**

Hoi Polloi

Jenny Gullen, voc.; Andrew Horst, bass; David Ball, gtr. (–1995); J. Fityus, drums (– 1995); Troy Daugherty, gtr. (+ 1995); Scott Pearson, drums (+ 1995). 1992—*Hoi Polloi* (Reunion); 1993—*Spin Me* (Reunion); 1995—*Happy Ever After* (Via).

Originally from New Zealand, alternative garage rockers Hoi Polloi had a sound similar to such '90s bands as Veruca Salt or The Breeders, with roots deep in the Blondie tradition of aggressive female-fronted rock. Singer and songwriter Jenny Gullen was the centerpiece for the group, though guitar (by Ball, then Daugherty) was prominently featured. Gullen and Horst are married. **Glenn Kaiser** introduced the band to American audiences by bringing them to the 1990 *Cornerstone* festival, where they were a major sensation (though *CCM* would opine that this had more to do with the physical beauty and engaging personality of Gullen than with appreciation for the band's musical gifts). The group then relocated to Nashville and released a promising debut album that had *True Tunes* comparing them to Lone Justice and *CCM* to The Pretenders. "Justify Me" and "Come to Me" are especially catchy songs, and "The Other Name" (dealing with the anguish caused by marital infidelity) is both moving and meaningful. The sophomore project, *Spin Me,* was praised for its two lead-off tracks, "Dance" and "Love Shine Down" (which actually sounds like a Deborah Harry outtake). The latter album also contains a cover of Pete Seeger's "Turn! Turn! Turn!" *Happy Ever After* is the group's triumph on which, as *HM* observes, they don't seem to be afraid of "scaring people with their loud music or on-edge lyrics." The song "Tiptoe" (released as a single) proclaims, "I won't tiptoe through your world / Gonna stomp my feet down. . . . Gonna rattle your chains / And ring your bells." On "Falling Down" Gullen offers a painful look at child abuse that is considerably more poignant than Pat Benatar's "Hell Is for Children." Hoi Polloi came up through the club scene in their native land, where Christian and secular music are not so segregated as in the United States. As a result, *CCM* would note that they "don't carry all the baggage Americans bring to Christian music—notions like what it should sound like and where can it can or can't be played." Gullen has said, "As Christians, we can go into mainstream venues and play music that's going to affect people but not compromise our morality, our beliefs, or anything like that." *Happy Ever After* was added to playlists on over 150 college radio stations, gaining the band a hearing in outlets not traditionally connected to the Christian music scene. The name Hoi Polloi derives from the biblical Greek expression for "the masses" or "the common people." The group disbanded in 1996 and Scott Pearson formed a group called Form with **Sonicflood**'s Dean Rush.

Christian radio hits: "Come to Me" (# 20 in 1993).

Hokus Pick (and Hokus Pick Manouver)

Rick Colhoun, drums, voc.; Matt Pierrot, gtr., voc.; Russ Smith, voc., gtr.; Dave Strilchuk, bass, voc. As Hokus Pick Manouver: 1989—*The Independents* (Word Canada); 1992—*Pick It Up* (Via). As Hokus Pick: 1994—*Brothers from Different Mothers* (Vision); 1995—*Bookaboom* (Via); 1997—*Snappy* (Freedom); *The B-Sides;* 1999—*Greatest Picks* (Freedom); *Super Duper* (Freedom).

Canadian pop band Hokus Pick belongs to the genre of '90s "fun music" dominated in the Christian market by **All Star United** and exemplified in the mainstream by Smash Mouth or Sugar Ray. They are also frequently compared to The Monkees, due to the retro, catchy sound of their songs and the more-than-music package of video, drama, and stage antics that became intrinsic to their overall presentation. The group consciously makes what they call "happy feet music" and fill their concerts with what they call "lots of audience participation and stupid band tricks." One goal of a Hokus Pick concert, Russ Smith says, "is to make sure the audience has a very, very fun time. And the other is to tell them that Jesus loves them." The group came together in Vancouver, British Columbia, in 1989 when Rick Calhoun, Matt Pierrot, and Smith decided to form a Christian band. They wanted to include Dave Strilchuk, but he wasn't a believer. So, they took him to camp, prayed for him, and, according to Pierrot, "Voila! Two weeks later, he became a Christian and we had a band." The group played churches and coffeehouses and recorded regional albums. The big break came when **Steve Taylor** invited them to open his now famous Squinternational tour in 1994. The name Hokus Pick derives from a Canadian expression for surprise (similar to the American "Holy Cow!"). The band was originally called Hokus Pick Manouver but shortened the moniker after their first two releases.

Hokus Pick is widely known for their humor, for supplementing spiritual messages with sarcasm, satire, and general silliness. Concerts used to include an extended cover of REM's "The One I Love," presented in alternative country and disco versions. A song called "Gelatin" likens moshing fans to the jiggly dessert, while "Learn to Laugh" breaks down into a litany of what various stars most need: Sinead O'Connor needs to grow some hair, **Bob Dylan** needs to learn to sing, but **Michael W. Smith** doesn't need anything, he's perfect. Stickholz says, "God is supposed to be taken seriously and everything is readily laughed at and that's our approach: God is good and everything else is pretty funny." A problem sometimes arises with determining just what the band intends. Musically, their best song to date is one in which Smith repeatedly sings, "I hate this love stuff" ("Love Stuff" from *Brothers*). Thematically, the song seems to recall the J. Geils Band's "Love Stinks," except that at the very end, the singer whispers, "Just kidding." On the other hand, the song "I'm So Happy" from *Snappy* gives **The Newsboys**' "Breakfast" solid competition for recognition as the worst contemporary Christian music song of all time. Stupid lyrics ("I'm so happy / Feeling snappy / My life is rosy / I'm feeling comfy cozy") and an annoying melody combine to make the song a quintessential example of all the secular world's worst (and usually exaggerated) stereotypes about Christian music. The song is *so* bad that many critics speculate it is a satire, lampooning the simplistic and inane drivel that sometimes makes it onto Christian radio—but if that is the case, radio programmers failed to get the joke and "I'm So Happy" was put into embarrassingly heavy rotation on some stations throughout much of 1997.

Pick It Up was the group's United States debut and features even more of their wacky humor than later projects. Two of the songs are titled "I.G.Y.F.T.C.H." and "I B.I.J.I.T.O.F.W." (With key lines being "If God is your father, then call home" and "I believe in Jesus in the old-fashioned way"). "Love and Co." prizes romance over casual sex and "Sofa Logic" mocks the laziness that sometimes attends reflection on matters of eternal consequence. *Brothers* is noteworthy primarily for "Love Stuff" but also contains the more socially relevant "Safe Assumption" (which argues that "believing in ourselves" is not enough) and "No Conversation" (which deplores the rules of etiquette that suggest it is impolite to talk about religion). On *Bookaboom* producer Steve Murray adds enough distortion to the band's hook-filled mix to have *CCM* declare, "suddenly you've got a group that deserves the title 'alternative'." A cover of The Clash's "Train in Vain" is included. *Snappy* takes the group into ska on several tracks ("We Are the People," "Our God," "Comfort Song") and includes the praise ballad "Nothing More." Lyrically, "Our God" is an interesting song about two young adults meeting at a high school reunion and comparing

notes on their spiritual journeys. The album concludes with a fifteen-minute mock-radio drama called "An Appointment with Stupidity." *Super Duper* offers "I Know Better," a light-hearted look at people who seem obsessed with self-improvement, and "This Is Me," a sarcastic take on different Christian personalities. "Christianese" is about in-group language (like "baptized in the blood") that can easily be misunderstood by people outside the church; the song quotes musically from the youth group camp ditty "Children of the Lord" and from Gloria Estefan's song "Conga." *Best Picks* compiles songs from the band's pre-Freedom Records career. *The B-Sides* is a collection of lost songs, demos, and live tracks, including covers of **Petra**'s "Adonai" and Jose Feliciano's "Feliz Navidad."

Christian radio hits: "Safe Assumption" (# 20 in 1994).

Ken Holloway

1994—*Ken Holloway* (Ransom); 1995—*He Who Made the Rain*; 1997—*The Ordinary*; 1999—*Unplug the Jukebox*.

Christian country singer Ken Holloway spent years singing in Louisiana honky tonks before, as he puts it, "my wife and my mother prayed me into the kingdom." Since transferring his talents to Christian music, Holloway has retained the grit and grime of his preconversion sound, and he still prefers to sing for "the unsaved" when occasion allows. His self-titled debut album features "Runs in the Blood," which the Christian Country Music Association selected as Song of the Year for 1994. *He Who Made the Rain* includes "Not Enough Amazing Grace" (a mother's story of her wayward son who seems headed for an early grave) and "I'm Not Gonna Fall to Pieces," a duet with country songstress Lari White. *The Ordinary* opens with a soft spoken ballad, "We Gotta Do Some Talking," which admonishes Christians to refrain from being preachy and judgmental. Holloway is openly evangelistic in his performances, often concluding his concerts with altar calls. But he also recognizes a general potential for positive country music in a wider sense. There are a lot of country fans, he avers, "who just don't want to hear cheatin', drinkin' songs."

Dallas Holm

1970—*Dallas Holm* (Zondervan); 1971—*For Teens Only*; *Just the Way I Feel It*; 1972—*Looking Back* (Impact); 1973—*Didn't He Shine*; 1974—*Peace, Love and Joy*; 1975—*Nothing But Praise*; 1976—*Just Right* (Greentree); *Live*; 1978—*Tell 'Em Again*; 1979—*His Last Days*; *All That Matters*; 1980—*Looking Back at the Best of Dallas Holm*; *This Is My Song*; 1981—*Holm, Sheppard and Johnson* [with Tim Sheppard and Phil Johnson]; *I Saw the Lord*; 1983—*Signal*; 1985—*Classics*; *Change the World* (DaySpring); 1986—*Praise and Worship* (Greentree); *Against the Wind* (DaySpring); 1988—*Beyond the Curtain*; 1989—*Soldiers Again* [with Tim Sheppard and Phil Johnson]; 1990—*Through the Flame*; 1991—*The Early Works* (Benson); 1992—*Chain of Grace* (Benson); 1993—*Mesa* [with Dana Key and Jerry Williams]; *Com-*

pletely Taken In; 1994—Dallas Holm Live; Holm for Christmas (Diamante); 1995—Face of Mercy (Benson); 1999—Before Your Throne (Ministry); Signature Songs (Greentree).

www.dallasholm.org

Dallas Holm is a traditional MOR gospel singer whose thirty years in Christian music may parallel the career of an artist like Ed Ames in mainstream music. Holm incorporates touches of a modern sound that set him apart from a previous generation of hymn singers like George Beverly Shea, but for the most part he has remained out of touch with the lexicon of rock and roll. Still, Holm has produced a steady stream of inspirational albums that many Christian music fans respect for their religious sentiments and some appreciate for their classic MOR stylings. He will always be best known for the song "Rise Again," a Christian classic that remains tied with **Don Francisco**'s "He's Alive" as the longest-running chart single on Christian radio. Holm is the sort of singer that voice teachers point to as proper and practiced. While there is little that is "contemporary" about his songs or style, he enjoyed a period of stardom within what was ironically called contemporary Christian music during a time when that genre was suspicious of anything truly modern. Indeed, Holm was the only person in the '70s other than **Bill Gaither** to receive the Gospel Music Association's Dove award for Songwriter of the Year. His Live album was one of the first Christian records ever to be certified gold, with sales of more than 600,000 copies. His Last Days is the soundtrack for a Passion Play musical Holm wrote, one that would be turned into a full-length cinematic presentation.

Holm published a brief autobiography called This Is My Story (cowritten with Robert Paul Lamb) in 1980. Influenced by **Elvis Presley,** he first began singing with a rock band when he was in high school, prior to his Christian conversion at the age of sixteen. At some point in the late '60s he performed with a Christian group called the Tri-Tones and recorded an album titled I Saw the Light (Universal Audio Corp.). By the time the Jesus movement broke, however, he was already singing what would later be called adult contemporary songs. He toured widely with evangelist David Wilkerson, a hero of the Jesus people who became famous for his work with street gangs documented in the film The Cross and the Switchblade, though he was also a virulent opponent of "Christian rock." At this time Holm was officially the front man for a group called Praise, which also included Randy Adams, Rick Crawford, Phil Johnson, Tim Johnson, and Ric Norris. In a foreword to This Is My Story, Wilkerson describes Holm as "a dedicated young man who yielded his talent to Christ rather than squandering it in a rowdy rock world."

Every once in a while, Holm—like Ed Ames—has been known to take on an actual rock song. Among his early repertoire, Signal offers the Jamaican-inflected "You Rescued Me."

Then, beginning with the aptly titled Change the World on the DaySpring label, Holm seemed committed to updating his style with more pop-oriented tracks. "Prayer Warriors" from that album has an undeniable pop feel. Against the Wind ups the rock ante considerably with a title track that is not a Bob Seger cover but sounds like an acoustic ballad the latter performer might actually have done (sans synthesizers). CCM would call Beyond the Curtain the artist's "most contemporary project to date" and both that album and Completely Taken In present him more as a mature adult contemporary singer than as a traditional inspirational one. Chain of Grace offers the jangly "It's Time," which clearly recalls The Byrds (who Holm says was his favorite band in his pre-Christian days), and Face of Mercy features the Robert Palmer-like "I Will Fight for You." In 1992, Holm told CCM that he realized he had not been "diligent" in keeping up with musical trends and admitted to a sudden renaissance in that regard: "I have probably learned more about contemporary music in the last year than I have in the past 10, 15, or 20."

Still, Holm's pop forays have been limited and sporadic and they sometimes seem forced, as though the artist is trying to remake himself as a tamer version of **Carman.** As with the latter singer, Holm is at his best when he remains true to his nonhip preferred style, singing churchy hymns in a traditional but inspiring baritone. Holm's compositions and song selections tend to favor sentimental notions. "A Broken Heart," for instance, proclaims that Christ did not die from the nails and the cross but from a broken heart due to his unrequited love for humanity. At times, Holm has also expressed an asceticism atypical for the Christian music subculture (or with the generally world-affirming theology of historic Christianity); his song "I Just Don't Feel Like Dancing" (from Change the World) is an assault on Christian dance clubs. In defense of the latter attack, he asked CCM, "Where does a Christian young person get off with blowing their time and energy on some dance floor boogie-ing for Jesus when they don't have time to address the great issues of the day?" He would lighten up a bit in days to come, or at least turn the searchlight inward. Through the Flame features the introspective songs "A Better Man" and "Just What I Do" on which the artist examines his own motives for involvement in Christian music ministry. "I Still Love Jesus," from that same project, carries even greater conviction as a result.

Over the years, Holm has written and sung numerous classics of modern gospel music, but his signature song "Rise Again" is by no means his best. Instead of proclaiming Christ's resurrection with power and joy (cf. **2nd Chapter of Acts'** "Easter Song"), it adopts a subdued and jaundiced view, expressing the viewpoint of Jesus in Clint-Eastwood-Make-My-Day terms: "Go ahead, put the nails in my hands. . . . I'll rise again." A much more powerful song, theologically and musically, is "I Saw the Lord," based on the prophetic vision recounted in Isaiah 6. "Completely Taken In" is a splendid ballad of devotion. Holm also does a fine job on southern gospel songs like "Saved Saved Saved," "Love in My Heart," and "Hey, I'm a Believer." *Signature Songs* is the best collection of his material, containing most of the songs mentioned here.

Holm exemplifies the approach to Christian music that aims for edification beyond entertainment. "I don't think that every song has to quote John 3:16 or has to say Jesus," he asserts, "but the body of every Christian artist's work has to point to the cross." Evaluated by that standard, the quality of Holm's body of work would certainly exceed that of most contemporary Christian music artists.

For trivia buffs: Holm is a member of the Christian Motorcyclist Association and a longtime committed biker. His vehicle of choice is a Harley Davidson.

Christian radio hits: "Rise Again" (# 2 in 1979); "Tell 'em Again" (# 14 in 1978); "A Broken Heart" (# 6 in 1980); "All that Matters" (# 23 in 1980); "Saved Saved Saved" (# 7 in 1981); "No Other One" [with Debbie Amstutz] (# 6 in 1981); "Losing Game" (# 5 in 1984); "Hittin' the Road" (# 26 in 1984); "Prayer Warriors" (# 14 in 1986); "Against the Wind" (# 3 in 1987); "Be My Shelter" (# 9 in 1990).

Dove Awards: 1978 Songwriter of the Year; 1978 Male Vocalist; 1978 Mixed Group [Dallas Holm and Praise]; 1980 Male Vocalist; 1980 Pop/ Contemporary Album (*All That Matters*).

Holy Soldier

Andy Robbins, bass; Michael Cutting, gtr. (−1992, + 1995); Jamie Cramer, gtr. (−1995); Steven Patrick, voc. (−1995, + 1997); Terry Russell, drums (−1995) // Scott Soderstrom, gtr. (+ 1992); Eric Wayne, voc. (+ 1995); Jason Martin, drums (+ 1997). 1990—*Holy Soldier* (Myrrh); 1992—*Last Train*; 1995—*Promise Man* (ForeFront); 1997—*Encore* (Spaceport).

www.holysoldier.com

The hard rock Southern California band Holy Soldier has had two distinct incarnations, as the personnel changes listed above indicate. The most noticeable difference is the change in lead singers. The difference between the sound of the group with Steven Patrick and the sound with Eric Wayne is comparable to the difference between the Doobie Brothers with Tom Johnston versus with Michael McDonald. Holy Soldier formed as a **Stryper**-like glam metal band in 1985 in the Los Angeles area and was part of The Hiding Place church headed by Henry Cutrona. They established a strong following in the general market, playing the prestigious Gazzari's club where they held an attendance record second only to Van Halen.

The band was signed to Myrrh records as that label's first heavy metal act, and **David Zaffiro** was recruited to produce their albums. He would stick with the band through thick and thin in the years to follow. The self-titled debut includes the song "Stranger," which spent three months as the Number One song on Christian music's rock chart. Michael Cutting's guitar

is even more impressive on the ballad "Eyes of Innocence" and the rocking anthem "We Are Young, We Are Strong." *Last Train* features a cover of the Rolling Stones' "Gimmie Shelter" (cf. **Ashley Cleveland**) and includes a couple of nonreligious romantic songs ("Crazy," "Love Is on the Way") alongside the evangelical title track and "Hallow's Eve." The song "Tuesday Mourning" is hauntingly beautiful and deals with sorrow over the death of a loved one. Although both of the Myrrh metal albums (with Patrick on lead vocals) met with significant acclaim, they did not generate the kind of sales that Myrrh was accustomed to receiving with artists like **Amy Grant** and **Russ Taff.**

Dropped by the label, the band took a three-year hiatus and then returned (with a new singer) as a modern rock band with a sound suggestive of the Crash Test Dummies doing Soundgarden songs. The formula clicked and *Promise Man* broke the group to an entirely new audience, earning them even more critical acclaim. *Promise Man*'s best track is an inspired remake of **Larry Norman**'s "Why Don't You Look into Jesus?" a great song that Holy Soldier manages to update musically from its original hippie folk setting to a dark grunge ballad. Sonically, the whole record digs into the blues tradition of classic rock acts like the Doors and the Rolling Stones. Zaffiro is again at the helm and the songs are polished and melodic. The title track, "Rust," "My World," "Break It Down," and "Cover Me" are all amazing. "Mumbo Jumbo" is a hypnotically infectious song about the sleazy power of TV. "Love Conquers All" is the album's one true ballad, with overtones of Extreme. *CCM* called *Promise Man* "a brilliant record that ranks with the best of the year." It is easily that. The Christian equivalent of Soundgarden's *Superunknown*, it surpasses most of what was produced in the general market in 1995 and remains one of Christian music's all-time best hard rock projects. Incredibly, ForeFront dropped the band all the same, and Holy Soldier released the live retrospective/reunion album *Encore* on their own label, headed by Andy Robbins. Steven Patrick returned for this live "greatest hits" package, such that songs from both phases of the group's career could be included, with Patrick or Wayne singing, as appropriate. After Holy Soldier, Jason Martin (a different person than the **Starflyer 59** guitarist) would play drums for **Redline.**

For trivia buffs: Andy Robbins was baptized by **Pat Boone** in the latter's swimming pool.

Dove Awards: 1991 Hard Music Album (*Holy Soldier*); 1991 Hard Music Song ("Stranger"); 1996 Hard Music Album (*Promise Man*); 1996 Hard Music Song ("Promise Man").

Honey

Bill Dow, gtr.; Doug Moss, voc., gtr.; Roger Moss, drums; Paul Lagestee, bass (−1998). 1997—*Lovely* (SubLime); 1998—*Lost on You.*

The Chicago-area modern rock band Honey seems to have inherited the mantle of departing groups like **The Prayer Chain** and **The Choir.** They have connections with both of those bands via producers, and their combination of intelligent, abstract lyrics with a rhythmic sheets-of-guitar sound definitely places them in the same sonic ballpark. Produced by **Steve Hindalong** and Chris Colbert (of **Breakfast with Amy/Fluffy**), Honey's stunning debut, *Lovely,* suffers only from a certain sameness in the songs; individually, every track is mesmerizing, presenting midtempo, haunting melodies driven by guitar solos and melancholy vocals. The overall theme of the record is simply *love,* and any specifically Christian content is muted. Doug Moss's lyrics range from obscure ("maybe another 90, maybe a 43, 51st and fairplay," from "Blinder") to disturbing ("the sound is a knife, pleasing and scarring his nine-year-old frame," from "Still"). "Evergreen" and "Sipping Dust" are moody, ambient highlights. Eric Campuzano and Wayne Everett of **The Prayer Chain** produced the bulk of the band's second album, *Lost on You.* This time, the theme is *hope,* and the album is more recognizably Christian in presenting an intersection of art and worship, though for the most part this is only apparent from the liner notes. Moss appends explanations of his poetry; apart from these, songs like "I Am" and "Lost on You" might never be recognized as love songs to God. Musically, the record is, again, ethereal and dreamy, with even more memorable melodies. It opens with a new-agey instrumental that features lots of swirling guitars ("The First Vibration"). "My Heart Beats in This Time" employs free-floating harmonies and a heartbeat bass line that recalls the Beach Boys' *Pet Sounds.* A number of other touches on the album summon images of Radiohead's *The Bends.* Two songs—the title track and "I Am"—were produced by Dan Haseltine and Steve Mason of **Jars of Clay** and betray the influence of that band's sound, albeit in a transformed, more electric and Brit-influenced form. To cite so many references, of course, is to infer that Honey ultimately has a sound of their own. As provocative moodsmiths, they are in the forefront of Christian music's intelligent rock movement, crafting albums that slowly appeal to a variety of senses in understated and almost undetected ways. In 2001, *HM* reported that the group was working on a third, more rock-oriented project.

Honeytree

1973—*Honeytree* (Myrrh); 1974—*The Way I Feel;* 1975—*Evergreen;* 1977—*Me and My Old Guitar;* 1978—*The Melodies in Me;* 1979—*Maranatha Marathon;* 1981—*Growing Up: Honeytree's Best; Merry Christmas, Love Honeytree* (Sparrow); 1985—*Single Heart* (Benson); 1987—*Every Single Day* (Milk and Honey); 1989—*Best of Honeytree Classics;* 1994—*Pioneer: Twentieth Anniversary Recording* (Oak Table); *Dios Ha Abierto la Puerte.*

www.honeytree.org

Honeytree was the Jesus movement's counterpart to Judy Collins—a hippie chick folksinger who did the coffeehouse circuit but actually had a strong enough voice to make it (when times changed) in the adult contemporary market. Born Nancy Heningbaum in 1952, she adopted the English translation of her surname as her professional name—or, as she recalls, "Honeytree" was what her hippie friends had called her from adolescence anyway. She was raised in Davenport, Iowa, as part of a musical family and learned to play cello and guitar at an early age. Then, as a senior in high school, she was "led to Christ" by John Lloyd, founder of the influential Adam's Apple coffeehouse in Fort Wayne, Indiana, where she subsequently worked as secretary and began writing songs for Bible studies (the Adam's Apple coffeehouse is also credited with playing a big role in the spiritual and musical formation of **Jeoffrey Benward** and **Petra**). Honeytree would go on to become one of the most popular of the early Jesus music singers, especially in the Midwest where she and **Phil Keaggy** were the two biggest stars. She was featured on the cover of *Harmony* magazine and toured with Keaggy and with comedian **Mike Warnke.** During the '70s, Honeytree recorded several competent and memorable albums and one classic *(Evergreen).* In 1983, she was ordained as a minister by Calvary Temple church. She became involved in prison ministry, working closely with Charles Colson, and in a singles ministry directed to unmarried women. In the '90s, she decided to learn Spanish and to commit herself to mission work with Latin Americans, traveling to Mexico, Honduras, Peru, and Nicaragua. She married John Miller in 1990; five years later, their infant son died and they adopted a child. Still located in Ft. Wayne, Honeytree has continued to perform and occasionally record; most of her early music is being reissued on compact disc.

Honeytree's debut album was originally issued on a custom label (Superior) before being picked up for distribution by Myrrh (the Jesus music division of Word). It features "Treasures," a classic Christian love song that was sung at the weddings of many Jesus people, and "Clean Before My Lord," which many consider to be Honeytree's best song. The latter track expresses surprise and delight at the discovery of forgiveness and sets this notion to a simple but beautiful melody. Honeytree sang "Clean Before My Lord" as a folk song, but it was soon picked up by international phenomenon **Evie** whose more lush arrangement gave it widespread exposure beyond the bounds of Jesus movement coffeehouses. *The Way I Feel* continues in the folk tradition, adding some cello and classical guitar that previews the artist's easy listening disposition. The standout track, however, is "Heaven's Gonna Be a Blast," a joyous romp that casts the hope of eternal life in the lingua franca of the times (cf. **The Electrics'** "Livin' It Up When I Die"). *The Way I Feel* also includes the autobiographical "Honeytree" and two **Phil Keaggy** songs, "Precious Promises" and "I Believe in Heaven," with Keaggy playing guitar on both tracks.

Evergreen is Honeytree's masterpiece, her *Tapestry* or *Blue*. The two most remarkable songs are not her own compositions, but have become the definitive renderings of classic Jesus music tunes. These are **Phil Keaggy**'s "Lovely Jesus (Here I Am)" and **Larry Norman**'s "I Am a Servant." Both songs sparkle with an incredible beauty and piety that can only come out of the fires of spontaneous revival. Keaggy and Norman would record their own versions of the songs, but it is hard to imagine them ever being done better than here. *Evergreen* also features "Searchlight" and "Rattle Me, Shake Me." The former is the closest Honeytree would ever come to rock, an almost screeching plea for deliverance from self-deception ("when darkness comes in, turn your light on my sin"). "Rattle Me, Shake Me" is a silly novelty tune, but was probably *Evergreen*'s most popular song at the time of its release. It relates comical episodes in which the spiritual exuberance of a young convert is mistaken for chemically induced euphoria. Many hippie Christians who had discovered the sensation of "being high on Jesus" had experienced such reactions from the uptight: "Anyone as happy as you are must be doing something wrong." The song would later be covered by **David Meece**. Rounding out the *Evergreen* project are "Ruth" and "Mary and Martha," two songs based on stories of women in the Bible that deal specifically with women's issues that had not been addressed by any other artist at the time.

Me and My Old Guitar is a live album containing songs from the first three records. The somewhat overlooked *Melodies in Me* provided Honeytree with a segue away from the hippie folk scene into more traditional inspirational music. It opens with "The Broadmoor Song," a '40s-style torch song with heavy jazz influence. "Diamond in the Rough" deals with self-acceptance in recognition that life is a work in progress. Honeytree has since suggested that she had more artistic freedom on this album and that consequently it best represents who she is as a performer. *Maranatha Marathon* is an eclectic collection with styles ranging from the MOR sound of the title track to the '50s rock of "Go to Church." The album also moves into the praise and worship genre, featuring an orchestral interpretation of "Psalm 57" and the worshipful "Father Lift Me Up" and "Live for Jesus." The latter song was written specifically for **Evie;** around this time, Honeytree also wrote "Joni's Waltz" for **Joni Eareckson.**

The albums *Single Heart* and *Every Single Day* are directed to adult single women and present Nancy Honeytree (as she decided to call herself in the '80s) in a more sophisticated and feminine guise. Her faded blue jeans gave way to dresses and her trademark oversized spectacles to contact lenses. Even the long straight hair was cut and permed. The title song from her Twentieth Anniversary album *Pioneer* would sum up this "it's

okay to grow up and move on" attitude: "What you have done, others will do / Bigger, and better, and faster than you / But you can't look back / No, you gotta get keep pressing through."

Christian radio hits: "Making Melodies in My Heart" (# 14 in 1978); "Diamond in the Rough" (# 14 in 1979); "Maranatha Marathon" (# 3 in 1980).

Hope

Jim Coregart; Jeff Cozy; Dave Klug; Wayne McKibbin; Boyd Sibley. 1972—*Hope* (A&M).

A forgotten Jesus music band that never really made it, the Midwest group Hope nevertheless has a story that deserves to be told. As recalled by historian David Di Sabatino, the hard rocking mainstream band lived communally on a farm in Esofea, Wisconsin, where they sought to create "original music with spiritual overtones." They were converted to Christ after an encounter with a farmer who they had ridiculed for painting a Bible verse on the side of his truck. As a result, their first album on the general market label A&M ended up being a collection of evangelical songs. The group subsequently toured as the opening act for **Alice Cooper,** but their album flopped, a victim of a typical double whammy affecting Christian groups signed to secular labels at the time: it did not get distributed to the Christian bookstores where Jesus music fans might have discovered it, but, embarrassed by the record's contents, A&M did nothing to promote it in other outlets. According to some reports, the album was never officially released at all, but sent directly to cut-out bins. *Jesus Music* says Hope's music is mainly "mid-rocking stuff or backwoods rock and roll" with "some good blitzing guitar here and there." Hope should not be confused with the Texas band **The Hope** listed below.

Hope of Glory (a.k.a. **The Hope**)

Bubba Chambers; Gary Ingram, drums; Melvin Mar, gtr.; Rick Thigpen; Melody Shupp, voc. (−1974); Carol Wallace, voc. (−1975); Wayne Donowho (−1976) // Tim Wade, voc. (+ 1976); Mike Barnes (+ 1978, −1980); Rick Crawford (+ 1980); Paul Mills, kybrd. (+ 1980). As Hope of Glory: 1973—*Hope of Glory* (Shalom); 1974—*Under the Spout, Where the Glory Comes Out;* 1976—*Same Sweet Song* (Tempo); 1977—*Second Look* (Chrism); 1978—*Be Ready.* As The Hope: 1980—*Which Side Are You On?* (StarSong).

Hope of Glory was a fairly large Texas rock band founded in 1970 by bassist Tommy Hoeser who left before they made any recordings. The group was active in the San Antonio region and in the early '70s was one of the two best-known Jesus music groups in that area (along with **Liberation Suite**). Like many of the Jesus music groups, Hope of Glory was blatantly Pentecostal, celebrating the charismatic outpouring of God's Holy Spirit in their lives and ministry. Their name is derived from Colossians 1:27. They started out a bit sloppy in their music, but with practice and personnel changes tightened up to become a first-rate boogie band, playing southern rock with vocal arrangements that sometimes recalled southern gospel. Tim Wade, a fan who got recruited to join the group at a concert in Wayside, Georgia, proved to be a valuable addition. Wade took over singing the parts that had originally been written for the women, who quit as they married (Wallace to Chambers, actually). Eventually the group would become a backing band for singer Jim Moore.

Hope of Glory includes a cover of **Andraé Crouch**'s "I Didn't Think It Could Be" and an original song called "Jesus Never Broke My Heart," which was a Christian music hit in the Southwest. The second project (unofficially known as "the one with the stupid name") is a collection of praise choruses like "Father, I Adore You" and "Lift Jesus Higher." *Same Sweet Song* presents the group with a new sound, absent the female vocalists; it was also the first record to receive national attention, including a review and a feature article in *Harmony* magazine. Two songs on the record ("Two Different Worlds" and "One Man Band") were written by **Danny Taylor** and another two ("I've Been Wantin' To" and the title track) were composed by **Pat Terry**. The group also does a new version of a James Cleveland song ("Every Man Needs God") and some original selections by Rick Thigpen, Melvin Mar, Wayne Donowho, and Wade. *Second Look* was to be their last album of note. It features solid country rock songs like "Lifesaver" and "Kiss of Life," and some songs contributed by Bob Farrell (of **Farrell and Farrell**) and **Danny Taylor**. Things got a little embarrassing on *Be Ready*. Producer **Gary S. Paxton** treated the band as another version of **The Imperials,** that is, as a vocal group that no longer played its own instruments. The record itself, furthermore, is pressed in gold vinyl and packaged in a gatefold cover with a mirror ball back cover photo that looks like it was taken on the set of *Saturday Night Fever.* That's right! Hope of Glory had gone disco—or at least tried to jump on that bandwagon, experimenting with the new mod style on a few original songs in addition to Paxton's "Antiseptic Christians" and **Pat Terry**'s "Shelter in the Storm." By the last record, the remnants of the group were recording under a remnant of the name (as The Hope). The sound on *Which Side Are You On?* is purely mellow, but the song selection is eclectic and inspired: **Bruce Cockburn**'s "Hills of Morning," **Arlo Guthrie**'s "Which Side Are You On?" **Bryn Haworth**'s "Standing on the Rock," and **Pat Terry**'s "You Got Love."

Christian radio hits: "Heart of a King" (# 18 in 1978).

Horde

Anonymous; et al. 1994—*Heilig Usvart* (Nuclear Blast).

The Australian death metal band Horde was the project of a singer and songwriter who calls himself Anonymous. Their only album was a direct and pointed response to what was known as the black metal scene in faraway Norway. A number of metal bands in that country began playing very dark, fast, and heavy music in the early '90s as a part of a subculture that flaunted its admiration of violence through satanic rituals. The movement took an especially ugly turn when churches began to be vandalized and burned and devotees of different groups warred with each other. Eventually, the leader of one of the major bands—a singer who called himself Euronymous—was murdered. Another black metalist, Count Grishnacht, was arrested, accused of the murder and of three counts of arson. It was in response to these events that Horde released their album of material that emulates the black metal scene sonically but offers confrontational lyrics. Songs include "Invert the Inverted Cross" and "Release and Clothe the Virgin Sacrifice." *HM* magazine says of the music, "from now on, one will have to look back at this album as the new benchmark of extremeness" and "the vocals take the approach of grindcore, but instead of growling . . . hissing!" *Rad Rockers* calls *Heilig Usvart* "the most extreme metal CD we have ever had the privilege of offering. . . . the vocals will convince your parents that demons are coming out of the speakers." For what it's worth, the message of the record must have been received, as folks at the Nuclear Blast label (and at Rowe, who handled distribution in America) received death threats from Norwegians when it came out.

Hot Pink Turtle

Dave, gtr.; Jamin Rathbun, voc.; Dion, bass; Jay, drums. 1993—*Ticklewiggleigglepickle* (R.E.X.).

Hot Pink Turtle was, of course, a neopsychedelic band. Their debut national release sparkled with all sorts of sporadic experiments that broke conventions of rock and roll. The band formed in Kansas City in 1989 and at one time included Bill Brown of **Dig Hay Zoose** on bass. Like the lead singer of that group (Phil), the members of Hot Pink Turtle didn't have official last names, though Jamin's has been discovered. Asked to describe their music, the group called it "Anti Satan Disco Funk Metal." The musical base—to the extent that there is one—is Led Zeppelin funk and groove, but the band loves to mix things up by changing time signatures and tempos in the middle of songs. One never knows when a sonic boom might suddenly interrupt a peaceful quiet mood or, for that matter, when the singer might decide to start rapping (why not?). *HM* magazine describes "Guntistha Garden" as offering "a medley of the history of rock and roll." Heavy doses of the **Galactic Cowboys** influence tracks like "A Boat and His Boy" and touches of glam metal intrude on "Flourescent Funk." In general, the instrumentation is grungy and gritty but the vocals clean and clear. Melodies and harmonies are discernible amidst all the chaos, and evangelical lyrics can be clearly understood: "In God's eyes, I have no reason to hide / In God's eyes, I am beautiful inside" ("Myisci").

Jimmy Hotz

1980—*Beyond the Crystal Sea* (Vision).

Nothing is known of the artist named Jimmy Hotz except that he released one album that used mythic symbols of warriors, kings, and mountain lands to convey images of Christian spirituality with a heavy dose of '60s nostalgia. *CCM* described *Beyond the Crystal Sea* as "Christian space rock with heavy metal arrangements and angelic interludes."

House of Wires (a.k.a. **Pivot Clowj**)

Jon Sonnenberg, voc., synth., prog.; Rob Gutschow, synth., prog. By House of Wires: 1998—*You Are Obsolete* (Plastiq Musiq); 1999—*Monogamy*. By Pivot Clowj: 1994—*The Fish Who Could Swallow the Sea* (independent); 1999—*It's not as if it were the end of the world . . . that was yesterday* (Flaming Fish).

www.geocities.com/houseofwires

Anyone who has ever wondered what the Beatles would have sounded like had they made it to the '80s need only pick up on *You Are Obsolete* by Orange County's House of Wires. Of course, many think the answer to that hypothetical quandary is to be found in the music of The Cure, but the Cure-like House of Wires have got the Fab Four's melancholy sound down even better than their mentors. With modern technology only two musicians are now needed, though a host of other players-for-hire are brought in as needed. Aside from the Cure and the Beatles, noticeable aural references include Depeche Mode, Tears for Fears, and **Joy Electric.**

The two men who make up House of Wires also record as Pivot Clowj for Flaming Fish records. Although the reason for maintaining separate monikers is not clear, House of Wires appears to be the more officially Christian band. Ronnie Martin of **Joy Electric** signed House of Wires to Plastiq Musiq (a division of Tooth and Nail) and produced *You Are Obsolete* as that label's debut product. A creative and enjoyable record, the album is pure electronica with the expected moody vocals, but these are transcended by little surprises: dance rhythms in "Latency"; Latin-sounding horns in "Everything Lies in Ruins"; bouncy do-do-do-doo's in "Final Moment"; and a jungle cover of The Pixies' "Where Is My Mind?" The best track (and the most Beatlesque) is the opening "Busy." Specifically Christian content is muted but recognizable. "Born to die, but I don't mind / My life is eternal," Sonnenberg sings in "Death Is a Beginning." In "Final Moment" he affirms, "By your grace you set me free / It's with you I want to be." The follow-up album, *Monogamy,* is even more diverse, breaking out of the usual limitations of electronic music. The title track is, of course, an ode to monogamy minus the lust component of George Michael's take on the same topic ("I Want Your Sex"). "World of the Future" features jazzy drums and gangster movie horns from the roaring '20s. House of Wires also covers **Mad at the World**'s "The Door with 5,000 Locks" and does their best imitation of New Order on "Luxury." *Bandoppler* calls *Monogamy* "an adventure into a postmodern, slick—but raw—world of fusion experiments."

Pivot Clowj's official press release allows that the group's synthpop music is "darker and slower than most of their peers," and that "many traditional electronic pop fans will find them just a tad too weird for their tastes." The group is perhaps best considered an underground version of House of Wires that is even more given to experimentation. *True Tunes* describes their *It's not as if it were the end of the world* CD as "filled with a subtle sense of longing for something just out of reach that never quite lets go." *The Phantom Tollbooth* thought the album suffered from "a lack of passion" and from overly repetitive, mind-numbing loops.

Larry Howard

1986—*Sanctified Blues* (Refuge); 1988—*Shout!*; 1989—*Into the Light* (label unknown); 1991—*Redeemed* (ForeFront); 1992—*Cornerstone Blues Jam, Vol. I*; 1994—*Bright Side of the Blues*; 1995—*American Roots* (Active Arts).

www.hom.net/~lhblues

Larry Howard is a pioneer of Christian blues. He grew up listening to his father's bluegrass band, studied classical music, received trombone lessons from Count Basie's own Jazz Clinic Band and then turned to guitar. Throughout the '70s, he played with a country-blues band called Grinderswitch, touring with the Allman Brothers and with **Charlie Daniels.** When he began making Christian records in the '80s, the very notion of blues was so foreign to Christian music fans that the albums just disappeared into a commercial void. Eventually, he was joined by the more prominent **Glenn Kaiser** and **Darrell Mansfield,** whose albums attracted a bit more attention to the genre. Howard has recorded with both of these artists in various duo and trio combinations.

Sanctified Blues presents Howard backed by an ensemble of top-notch players including **Buddy Greene** and the Muscle Shoals horn section. He performs the Don Nix tune "Everybody Wants to Go to Heaven (But Nobody Wants to Die)" and a slightly refurbished "One Night without You." After *Sanctified Blues* and the follow-up *Shout!* failed to sell, Howard released an album titled *Into the Light* in Europe only. Then he came back with *Redeemed* on the major Christian music label ForeFront, a contract that he apparently won after performing on the song "There's Something about That Name" by one of that label's biggest stars, **Eddie DeGarmo.** *Redeemed* seems to strive for commercial acceptance, with only a couple of tracks ("Evangelistic Blues," "Seeds of Victory") really going for the down-and-dirty sound the artist is capable of delivering. Other tracks recall the rock sounds of Steve Winwood ("Dangerous Situation," "God's Word Will Renew Your Mind") or Stevie Ray Vaughan ("Holy Anger," with vocals by Michael **Tait** of **Tait** and **DC Talk**). *Cornerstone Blues Jam* is the recording of a live concert at the annual music festival featuring several gospel and contemporary Christian music stars. In addition to Howard's impressive treatment of "Nobody But You," the bill of fare includes **Margaret Becker** and **Mark Farner** singing "Some Kind of Wonderful," **Jessy Dixon** performing "Operator," and Kaiser and Mansfield joining Howard for a cover of **Eric Clapton**'s "Presence of the Lord." *Bright Side of the Blues* departs from the big horn Memphis orientation of Howard's previous albums for more of a Chicago sound. Produced by Kaiser, the album scores with the apocalyptic "11:59" and the Clapton-esque "I Found Out." On *American Roots,* Howard returns to his country-blues roots, backed on certain songs by the **Charlie Daniels** Band and by his old group Grinderswitch. "Bogey Man" opens the project with a ZZ Top swagger as Howard proclaims, "Me and Jesus ain't afraid of no bogey man." Howard has said that he views his career as a calling. "Blues music was born in the church," he insists, "but the people took this form of music into the world and made something ugly out of it. I suppose if I have a mission, it's to recapture this music and make something wholesome out of it again."

Tom Howard

1977—*View from the Bridge* (Solid Rock); 1981—*Danger in Loving You* (NewPax); 1985—*One by One* [with Billy Batstone] (A&S); *The Harvest* (Maranatha); 1986—*The Hidden Passage*; 1987—*Solo Piano*; 1991—*Bamboo in the Winter* (Myrrh); 1991—*Beyond the Barriers*; 1997—*Flight to Boston* (Ambient).

A pioneer of Christian New Age (or ambient) music, Tom Howard began his career in Christian music as a creator of soft rock albums similar to those of **Michael Omartian** or **Gary Paxton**. Before recording his famous instrumental albums, he made three more traditional albums (with vocals) for three different labels. Howard studied music theory and composition at the University of Minnesota, then joined **Larry Norman** and **Randy Stonehill** as part of the experimental Solid Rock record company run by Norman. *View from the Bridge* features the classic Jesus music songs, "One More Reason" and "All through the Day" but is characteristically mellow. Both Norman and Stonehill add acoustic guitars and harmony vocals throughout. Norman later re-recorded songs from this project and released them without Howard's approval in limited editions as *Labor of Love* and *Letter of the Law*. From Solid Rock, Howard moved on to Gary Paxton's NewPax label. *Danger in Loving You* is coproduced by **Terry Taylor** of **Daniel Amos** and contains another ten original songs. It opens with "Horizon," an instrumental that previews Howard's later work. *One*

by One is a joint project with **Billy Batstone,** an idea that should have worked. The two trade vocals and songwriting credits on a collection of songs that make up what *CCM* called "a decidedly melodic album" and "one of the year's real sleepers." The centerpiece is "Think on These Things," a sardonic take on Philippians 4:8. The lyrics run, "Whatsoever is cute / whatsoever is elating / whatsoever favors you with higher media ratings . . . think on these things." **Mark Heard** served as engineer for *One by One.* Howard and Batstone also created the *Psalms Alive* series for Maranatha, and their song, "Psalm 148," performed by the Calvary Chapel Worship Community (including Batstone, Howard, **Richie Furay, Kelly Willard,** and **John Mehler**) reached Number Eight on the Christian radio charts in 1983.

Howard came into his own when asked to contribute to Maranatha's "Colours" series, a set of instrumental albums intended to capitalize on the burgeoning craze for New Age music. Maranatha, of course, did not want to call it New Age music, since that label seemed to imply association with New Age religion, which is by and large incompatible with orthodox Christianity. Still, the Colours albums sounded like the records being produced by such New Age artists as George Winston, Vangelis, and Andreas Vollenweider—most of whom did not connect their music to any particular ideology but to generic moods such as *peace* and *calm. The Harvest* includes piano renditions of several original compositions in addition to versions of **Karen Lafferty**'s "Seek Ye First" and the classic hymn "For the Beauty of the Earth." *The Hidden Passage* features performances by an acoustic chamber orchestra called the Tom Howard Ensemble and includes a booklet explaining the thoughts behind each of the aural meditations (cf. **Ambient Theology**). The album closes with "Psalm 5," written by Bill Sprouse of **The Road Home**. Despite its title, *Solo Piano* is more digitalized, as Howard begins experimenting with various technological enhancements to his instrument of choice. These experiments would be significant for Howard's future, as he became more of a studio engineer, doing orchestral, piano, and string arrangements for such artists as **Bob Carlisle, The Choir,** and **Cindy Morgan.** He also does scores for TV and films and continues to record.

Doug Howell

1971—*Love's Lights* (Trinity); 1972—*Bluer Than It's Ever Been*; 1977—*I've Been Freed* (Eden).

Singer/songwriter Doug Howell reminded some critics of **Michael Omartian,** recording fairly mellow, keyboard-based '70s albums on which he did most of the engineering and played around with some synthesizers. What is most noteworthy—especially for the time period—is that he wrote songs that departed from the standard "I'm so happy in Jesus" vein and dealt with harsher realities of Christian living. This is most evident on *Bluer Than It's Ever Been.* The title track recalls Elton John's "Someone Saved My Life Tonight" musically, but portrays the need for Christians to stand firm in the face of trials that cause them to second-guess their commitments. *Harmony* magazine reassured its readers that Howell was not "backslidden." The artist, in their words, evinces uncommon honesty in describing "the *job* of being a Christian" as well as "the pain."

Layton Howerton

1998—*Boxing God* (Sparrow).

Layton Howerton is a rural singer/songwriter with a style similar to Marc Cohn or to an American version of Gordon Lightfoot. Raised by pioneer missionary parents in Appalachia, Howerton recovered from leukemia in a way that he believes to have been miraculous. He left for Nashville as a young adult to make his way into the music business. Despite some success as a songwriter, however, he felt a strong call to follow his father and grandfather into the ministry and, eventually, left Music City to pastor a Baptist congregation in Wyoming. There, he used his gifts to craft songs that would supplement his weekly sermons. As it turns out, the (Christian) music business found him, and Sparrow Records persuaded him to put a handful of his story-sermon songs on record. The result is a laid-back collection of earthy songs on which Howerton's voice is accompanied by little besides his strummed and plucked acoustic guitar. Songs like "Prayin', Sowin', Reapin' " and "International Harvester" (cf. Matthew 9:37–38) extract spiritual messages from images of rural life in the same way as Jesus' parables. The title track to *Boxing God* is an autobiographical reflection on the years when Howerton resisted God's call. "Larger Than Life" is a tribute to his father and begins, "As a boy I used to climb up on my daddy's knee / He had big bear paws and shoes size EEE." The closing song, "Samsonite," is a touching tale of faith amidst tragedy.

Katy Hudson

2000—*Katy Hudson* (Red Hill).

Fifteen-year-old Katy Hudson (b. 1984) was one of several Christian adolescent girls signed to recording labels in the late '90s, but unlike her peers she eschewed both the bubblegum stylings of Britney Spears (or **Nikki Leonti** or **Stacie Orrico**) and the manufactured adult contemporary antithesis to that style (cf. **Rachel Lampa**). A competent songwriter, the teenaged Hudson not only demonstrated more maturity than any of those other artists but, ironically, demonstrated more maturity than the adult producers and label executives that marketed them. She was fortunate enough to sign with a label that

allowed her freedom, and even then, she says, "I was a little pressured to be Christina Aguilera, and I was just like, there's not a lot of longevity in that. . . . and they thought that not all of my ten songs were radio playable, and I just said, 'Guys, I don't want them *all* to be radio-friendly.'" Hudson surprised the market with an album's worth of intelligent songs that had *CCM* comparing her to Fiona Apple. The opening cut, "Trust Me," *is* radio-friendly with rocking guitars and swooping strings. Lyrically, it addresses chronic worriers from God's perspective. "When There's Nothing Left" looks at that subject from the opposite point of view and with greater lyrical depth. "Last Call" recounts a suicidal phone call made to a help line and was, in fact, inspired by a crisis-line ministry sponsored by the church in Santa Barbara, California, where Hudson's father is a pastor. "Growing Pains" is not a remake of the old **Jamie Owens-Collins** song, but speaks similarly of moving through life from childhood to adult responsibility.

Lavine Hudson

1988—*Intervention* (Virgin); 1989—*Between Two Worlds.*

Lavine Hudson is a gospel diva in Britain, where she is much better known than in America.

Intervention was released in the United States by Reunion and *Between Two Worlds* by Sparrow (but not until 1991, and with two songs deleted). Born in south London, Hudson grew up the daughter of the local minister of the Pentecostal Church of God in Christ congregation. Like **Aretha Franklin** and other American soul singers, she learned R&B by singing in church—but there were fewer opportunities in the British scene for black singers and fewer still for those who wanted to perform gospel. Hudson came to America in 1983 and studied at the Berklee School of Music. She received some vocal training from Marvin Winans of **The Winans** and sang concerts with **The Clark Sisters.** Twinkie Clark helped to produce *Intervention,* which draws on R&B, soulful balladry, and hip-hop on a collection of mostly original songs. For *Between Two Worlds,* Hudson asked her friend Phil Collins for a song, and he contributed "All I Need" for the project. The latter album displays marked social concern in such tracks as "Turned Away," "Let's Build a World," and "Heartless Generation" (one of the songs deleted from the American release). **Philip Bailey** and the **Andraé Crouch** Choir also add vocal support on a record primed for crossover appeal to fans of African American pop.

Christian radio hits: "Intervention" (# 2 in 1989); "All I Need" (# 11 in 1992); "Keep Your Mind" (# 7 in 1992); "Tell Me Why" (# 3 in 1992).

Kellye Huff

1989—*In a Special Way* (Giant); 1990—*Faith to Faith*; 1992—*Life Changes*; 1998—*It's Not Over.*

Kellye Huff is the daughter of David Huff, famous for his work with **David and the Giants.** She began performing while still a teenager, touring as an opening act for Dad's band. The senior Huff has produced her albums, and he and his brothers have written or cowritten most of her songs. Still, it is Huff's husky alto voice (similar to that of **Kim Hill**) that is the main attraction, and that voice has gotten steadily better with each new project. Already on *Faith to Faith,* a reviewer for *CCM* was struck by how her voice had "blossomed" since the first record (which had been recorded while she was still in high school). Stylistically, Huff has gone for variety, singing pop songs with a rock edge, country inflected ballads, and a few tunes with an urban funk feel. **Phil Keaggy** puts in a few noteworthy guitar cameos on *Life Changes*. Huff finally arrives as a first-rate talent on *It's Not Over.* "Touched" is a scorching uptempo testimony to God's intervention in her life: "Touched by the hand of mercy / Touched by the hand of God." By contrast, "I Cherish Thee" is a gorgeous adult contemporary ballad on a par with anything that Hill has ever done. Lyrically, it expresses simple devotion to God: "Lord, I cherish thee . . . with all my heart and soul."

Human

Erick Garcia, drums; Randy Kinnet, voc.; Randy Sapp, gtr.; Vic Sapp, bass; Dean Martin Vanderwoude, gtr. 1998—*Out of the Dust* (Organic).

Human is a modern hard rock band similar in sound to Bush. The quintet hails from Houston, Texas (also home to **Atomic Opera, Galactic Cowboys,** and **King's X**), and their debut album was produced by Dino Elefante and by Billy Smiley of **White Heart.** The record opens with its strongest track, the **Bleach**-like "Read Your Mind," which reflects on what it would be like to know the thoughts of God. "I Can't Live" slows things down temporarily for a grunge ballad that passionately states the human need for a Savior. "Hand Me Down" starts out with Nirvana guitar riffs but segues into a singable tune that could almost have been on an **Audio Adrenaline** record. "Fat Man's Delicacy" takes a humorous look at temptation à la Proverbs 23:1–3. Halfway through *Out of the Dust* an unlisted cover of **U2**'s "Bullet the Blue Sky" turns up, a creative and pleasant surprise (cf. **P.O.D.**). Asked about their goals in Christian music, Kinnet has said, "We've been called to be disciples in our own lives, and to share with people that they are valuable and worthy to have a relationship with the living God."

Human Condition

Gary Egger, voc., gtr., kybrd. 1991—*Human Condition* (Image); 1993—*Impressions of Grace* (Broken).

Human Condition was essentially a one-man-band project by Gary Egger, who once played with the early Jesus music group **Servant** and later fronted a Christian new-wave band called Flock 14. Human Condition was perhaps the best of all the Christian groups that tried to sound like The Cure; indeed, they were so good at it that the self-titled debut album was criticized as the work of an imitative tribute band. But *True Tunes* would grant that on the sophomore *Impressions of Grace* Egger allows "influences to be influences and develops his own mode of Euro-alternative pop." Lyrically, the latter album is true to its name, offering glimpses of hope and beauty amidst a soundscape of "dark shades and haunting atmospheres."

The Huntingtons

Mike Holt, voc., bass; Cliff Powell, gtr., voc.; Mike Pierce, drums (–2000b, + 2001) // Brad Ber, gtr., voc. (+ 1997, – 1999); A. Jay, gtr. (+ 1999, –2000); C. J., gtr. (+ 2000a); Danny, drums (+ 2000b, –2001). 1996—*Sweet Sixteen* (Flying Tart); 1997—*Fun and Games; Rocket to Ramonia;* 1998—*High School Rock* (Tooth and Nail); 1999—*The Good, The Bad, and The Ugly; File under Ramones;* 2000—*Get Lost; Plastic Surgery;* 2001—*Songs in the Key of You.*

www.huntingtonsusa.com

The Huntingtons are Christian music's quintessential punk-rock band, inheriting the Ramones' mantle from **The Altar Boys** and wearing that mantle more authentically than that group ever did. The group initially formed in Delaware as a band named Cricket in 1993, and a few rare songs by them under that name can be found on obscure compilation discs. After a few personnel changes and a lesson in rock and roll history, they discovered that the name The Crickets was already taken (by Buddy Holly's still-existent backing band) and willingly abandoned the moniker, seeing how it was, as they put it, "a stupid name, anyway." They picked their new moniker, The Huntingtons, from a sign for a housing development because "it sounded cool." Guitarist Brad Ber was recruited from a mainstream band called Philibusters.

Two-thirds of the tracks on *Sweet Sixteen* deal with a subject of perennial interest to adolescent boys, namely adolescent girls (e.g., "She's So Uncool," "She's Alright," "She's Comin' to the Show," and "She's Probably Over Me"). The obsession continues on *Fun and Games,* where almost every track is about young love, exploring the many ways in which teenagers meet, split, and try to mend their broken hearts. The record began the group's association with producer Mass Giorgini, a fixture in the mainstream punk market. "Allison's the Bomb" is a highlight, written in praise of a girl who is, well, "the bomb." *Fun and Games* also includes a cover of "Come On Let's Go" by the world's first punk-rock band (Buddy Holly and The Crickets). *Rocket to Ramonia* is something of a novelty project, a collection of all-covers of Ramones songs. The band was not happy with their performance on the latter album and tried again two years later with the more satisfying *File under Ramones*.

High School Rock kicks off with its title track, the group's best song to date. An ode to good old-fashioned rock and roll music, the song is an anthem worthy of placement beside Joan Jett's "I Love Rock and Roll." Musically, the record moves away from the typical Ramones imitations and explores other dimensions of American rock and roll (*CCM* thought the band sounded "a lot like Buddy Holly and The Crickets"). "Jackie Is an Atheist" also offers a brief break from pubescent soap operas, hinting that at least *some* teenagers think about, you know, God and stuff. In the CD booklet for *High School Rock* the band members listed their names as Mikey Huntington, Cliffy Huntington, Mikee Huntington, and Bradley Huntington, faking out a number of critics and reviewers who had just discovered the band and thought they were all brothers. The group's live album *The Good, The Bad, and The Ugly* actually got reviewed in *Rolling Stone* magazine, which appeared to be completely unaware of any Christian music connection. The reviewer did appreciate the band's Ramones obsession: "The Huntingtons so love the Ramones that they all wear biker jackets, use the same stage surname, and zip through riff biscuits like the real thing, complete with 'One, two, three, four!' count-offs. Imitation? Yeah. Fun? Hell, yeah!"

Get Lost and *Plastic Surgery* display more of the band's humor, as they mock what was by now a famous Ramones-absorption. *Get Lost* contains a song called "What Would Joey Do?" a tongue in cheek confession that their own version of the WWJD bracelet craze involves imitation of Joey Ramone. *Plastic Surgery* similarly opens with "I Want to Be a Ramone." In another song from that project ("I'm Not Dangerous"), Cliff tries to convince a girl it's alright to go out with him: "Tell your mama and tell your papa / I'm gonna take you to a movie show where / there's no blood, there is no gore" and, after that, "we can sit down and read from Psalms." The band also experiments outside its formula a little with "Mutant Monster Beach Party," a surf-punk instrumental. With *Songs in the Key of You* the group finally issued what *HM* would term "a transitional record" that breaks out of the mold and demonstrates more pop aesthetics on songs like "80s Girl" and "If You Only Knew." The group's humor continues to show through on "That Guy Stole My Girl" and "Welcome Back," a song chronicling relational instability.

The Huntingtons' punk credentials are secure. The only question is whether and in what sense their albums qualify as Christian music. Few, if any, of their songs offer explicit faith statements but, as *Shout* magazine puts it, "they do deal with the spiritual consequences and frustrations of being a teenager." Group members attest that the greatest opportunities to share their faith occur off-stage, and they defend the legiti-macy of Christians making music that is simply "good, clean fun." In late 2001, the band suffered some major personnel shake-ups, including the departure of founding member Cliff Powell.

Hydro

Robbie Bronniman, voc., kybrd.; Roy Goudie, prog.; Shazz Sparks, voc. 1995—*Spiritualisation* (N'Soul); 1997—*Aborigination*.

Essentially a side project of the British techno group **dba**, Hydro provides an outlet for the programming duo of Robbie Bronnimann and Roy Goudie to exercise some of their more creative ideas. *Spiritualisation* is an album of ambient music, most notable for the track "Rawar." *Aborigination* is truly unique: the duo samples diverse forms of Christian worship from all over the globe and presents these in an extended techno mix. The title track features maori chants. African tribal rhythms and chants are heard on "Serengetti Storm," while "Liquid Prayers" incorporates operatic Russian vocals on segments from the Orthodox liturgy. "Jiggle" picks up Celtic themes. Musically, the album remains a dance project, despite all the multicultural excursions.

Hymn Jim

Shane Ries; et al. 1995—*Hymn Jim's Gospel Gems* (N'Soul).

Hymn Jim was a one-time project for Shane Ries, son of Calvary Chapel pastor Paul Ries. Since his only album contains no personnel list, it is impossible to know whether Hymn Jim was an actual group that also contained other members or simply a moniker for a personal studio outing. Ries appears to do most of the vocals and play most of the instruments, with occasional extras being employed. The album is a retro-'70s project in which worship songs are performed in styles varying from Lenny Kravitz-styled Hendrix to disco. There are a few original songs written by Ries, the best of which is the ballad "Someone." The bulk of the album, however, focuses on cover versions. The strongest track is easily "People Get Ready." Hymn Jim provides an unusually upbeat rendering of the **Curtis Mayfield** standard, which is typically sung in a somber tone. "O Happy Day" (cf. **Edwin Hawkins**) is done as a bouncy techno song complete with lots of synthesized bleeps and pops. **Graham Kendrick**'s popular college hymn "Shine, Jesus, Shine" gets a disco treatment. **Billy Batstone**'s "I Will Wait upon the Lord" is done in a fairly straightforward Euro-pop style. Betty Pulkingham's "There's a River of Life" (from Houston's charismatic Church of Redeemer) was always intended to be a fun, camp song, and that comes out in Hymn Jim's comical bluegrass arrangement. The record is similar in many respects to *The Joy Album,* a popular project released by Maranatha in 1975.

Ian

See **Ian Eskelin.**

Identical Strangers

Andy Denton, voc.; Randy Thomas, gtr. 1997—*Identical Strangers* (Damascus Road).

Identical Strangers came together as a group in the same way as Loggins and Messina. Rock-veteran-turned-producer Randy Thomas's involvement with what was originally to be a solo album for **Andy Denton** grew to such an extent that they just decided to credit him as a partner and present themselves as a group. Denton had sung previously with **Ruscha** and **Legend Seven,** and since Identical Strangers, he has pursued a solo career with some success. Thomas was a founding member of such bands as **Psalm 150,** Sonrise, the **Allies,** and **Sweet Comfort Band;** he is perhaps best known as the co-composer (with **Bob Carlisle**) of such major hits as "Why'd You Come in Here Looking Like That?" (performed by Dolly Parton) and "Butterfly Kisses" (performed by Carlisle). *Identical Strangers* presents Denton in classic pop form, singing hook-filled songs reminiscent of the '80s. "Lead On" opens the album as its most impressive rocker, an anthem of allegiance to God. "Julianna Wilson" is a story-song relating the tale of a fashion model who loses herself in a "city of sin."

For trivia buffs: The name "Identical Strangers" derives from a feature in *Mad* magazine that presents "Snappy Answers to Stupid Questions." The suggested response to someone who asks whether two obviously identical babies are twins is, "No, they're identical strangers."

Christian radio hits: "Extraordinary Love" (# 8 in 1997); "Julianna Wilson" (# 3 in 1997).

Idle Cure

Mark Ambrose, gtr.; Pete Lomakin, kybrd.; Steve Shannon, voc.; Chuck King, gtr. (– 1991) // Glenn Pearce, gtr. (+ 1991). 1986—*Idle Cure* (Frontline); 1988—*Tough Love*; 1990—*2nd Avenue*; 1991—*Inside Out*; 1992—*Breakaways*; 1994—*Eclipse* (Salt).

Idle Cure offers one of the best examples of what was a major trend for Christian music in the mid '80s: cloning the sound of a successful mainstream band so as to provide Christian youth with a Christian version of that artist. Many artists did this; in some sense, **Stryper** was a Christian version of Kiss and, for a brief time, **Amy Grant** tried to be a Christian version of Madonna. Idle Cure studied the hard, arena rock sound of groups like Foreigner and Def Leppard and got it down precisely. If they lacked originality, they at least had the competence to pull off the imitation and, in retrospect, they were probably no more derivative than such hot secular acts as Loverboy or Night Ranger. In the context of their time, Idle Cure represented a major step forward in the development of Christian music. Like **DeGarmo and Key,** they defied stereotypes that regarded Christian music as necessarily inferior to the general market in such areas as production values and technical competence. Brian Quincy Newcomb praised the debut record as holding up to the standards of mainstream rock's best. The group formed in Long Beach, California, when Mark Ambrose and Steve Shannon (who were playing with a group called Sojourn) hooked up with Chuck King from the Christian band Eden. King would also play with **Ken Tamplin** in **Shout.**

Idle Cure's first and last records are regarded as their best. The debut album features "Breakaway," their most famous and greatest song, a track that really could have fit on Def Leppard's *Pyromania* album without intrusion or embarrassment. The only notable distinction is the lyrics; the song deals with "leaving behind the old life" and daring to adopt values and commitments contrary to those of the world. The album also yielded a Christian radio hit with the bic-flicking power ballad "Take It." *Tough Love* was more of the same with bigger and punchier production. The band's third album, *2nd Avenue,* revealed a harder-edged quasi-metal group, and the band scored big again with "Pray," another stadium rocker with overtly religious lyrics. *Inside Out* also kicks off with a strong gang vocal track called "We've Lost Ground." Unfortunately, pablum intervened and the band often went for formulaic power ballads that made them sound like **Petra**-lite. Songs like "How Long" (from *Tough Love*), "Contend for Faith" (from *2nd Avenue*), and "High Mountain" all continue in the "Take It" vein of songs inoffensive enough to gain airplay on adult contemporary stations. *Breakaways* is a premature hits collection with songs from Idle Cure's first four albums only. Two years later, the group would release *Eclipse,* which *HM* magazine proudly declared to be "the best music of their career." Dann Huff (of **White Heart, Giant, The Front,** and **The Players**) adds guitar heroics and a number of other guest stars cooperate to give the group a sound similar to that of **White Heart.** "Bring Me through the Day" is a standout.

Christian radio hits: "Take It" (# 8 in 1987); "Come Back to Me" (# 4 in 1987); "How Long" (# 8 in 1988); "So Many Faces" (# 15 in 1989); "Contend for Faith" (# 8 in 1990); "Holy Mountain" (# 6 in 1992); "Living Water" (# 11 in 1994).

Ideola

See **Mark Heard.**

If Only

Ray Driscoll, drums; Matthew "Maff" Gaylord, bass; Sam Hargreaves, gtr., voc.; Nicola "Nic" O'Brien, voc. 1998—*It's All Gone Very Orange* (Meltdown).

If Only was a promising British modern rock band that earned critical acclaim with their debut indie album, then broke up. The group was formed in 1994 by members of the youth group at Cove Baptist Church. *HM* described them as a female-fronted version of **The Choir.** Their sound was especially influenced by Radiohead and The Cranberries—indeed they used to cover "The Bends" and "Zombie" in concert. Nic O'Brien's sweet soprano vocals are also a bit reminiscent of Leigh Nash of **Sixpence None the Richer.** All four members were aged between seventeen and twenty at the time *It's All Gone Very Orange* was recorded. *Phantom Tollbooth* especially pushed the group and praised its debut record. "Walking in the Clouds" is one of the best tracks.

Illustrator (a.k.a. **Eternity Express)**

Dan Gaub, gtr., perc., voc.; Dawndee Gaub, kybrd., voc.; Nathan Gaub, kybrd., voc.; Mark Matthews, voc., bass, sax.; Melody Gaub, perc., kybrd., voc. (−1987); Daryl Sutherland, drums, perc., voc. (−1987) // Kirk Allen, drums (+ 1987). As Eternity Express: 1977—*Good News! Good Music!* (Skylite); *Satisfied; Sometimes Only a Song Can Say It Right;* 1979—*Ken Gaub Presents Eternity Express* (New Born); 1985—*The Way Out* (Morock). As Illustrator: 1987—*Illustrator* (Ocean); 1989—*Somewhere in the World* (Ocean).

Eternity Express was a Christian rock band assembled by evangelist Ken Gaub to accompany him on his crusades and entice kids to come and get evangelized. Largely composed of members of the evangelist's family, the group was headed by Nathan Gaub, who summed things up pretty accurately when he told *CCM* in 1987 "the preconception of Eternity Express is that we're a bunch of lightweights in teeny-bop pop." Around that time, a major advertising campaign was launched to change the group's image. Rechristened Illustrator, a series of monthly ads in *CCM* challenged readers to guess the group's true identity. Finally revealed as a new, improved Eternity Express, Illustrator was heralded as a crossover band that would "get away from the cotton-candy Christian music mentality and reach a broader audience with the gospel of Jesus Christ." Reviewers described the debut album as evincing a style somewhere "between the Doobie Brothers and **Steve Camp**"— which is quite a gulf! Songs like "Lonely Hearts for Sale" and "Love's Not Your Enemy" reveal the group to have mastered mature pop stylings, while still being a long way from cutting-edge rock. *Somewhere in the World* includes a cover of Little River Band's "Help Is on the Way."

Imagine This

Tambri Hunt, kybrd., voc.; Ahmed Montgomery, bass; Rick Weiland, drums; Daryl Youngblood, voc., gtr.; Trey Herbert, voc., gtr. (−1995) // Eric Miller, gtr., voc. (+ 1995). 1993—*Imagine This* (Essential); 1995—*Love.*

Imagine This was a power-pop, retro-'70s band from Houston. Daryl Youngblood founded the group and wrote most of its material. The band had an eclectic sound, incorporating elements of funk and hard rock into their basic pop formula. Their multiracial and mixed-gender composition added to their potential for incorporating diversity. Ahmed Montgomery even adds some rap vocals on the debut album. As is often the case with such eclectic bands, Imagine This's best songs—the harder material—rarely gained airplay. With fifteen tracks, the self-titled debut offers a potpourri of sounds that are difficult to classify. *True Tunes* compared the group to **Extreme.** "Word to the World" sounds like much of **White Heart**'s tamer material. Better tracks are "Revolution" and "God," both of which emulate **King's X** with their metal-meets-the-Beatles harmonies. The same style (what Youngblood called GRIF for "groove intensive funk rock") is in more evidence on the vastly superior second album. Here, the liner notes even warn listeners that certain tracks are "extra spicy" and these are invariably the most inventive and memorable. "Feel" is their best song—a gritty rocker that starts with a sultry vocal hissing, "Do you like the way it feels? . . . Do you like that it's not real?" Then the guitars kick in and Youngblood howls over their crunching barrage, "God can see the way you feel." Another tough rocker, "Munky Jump," has dumb lyrics but really cooks. "Point of You" and "All the Answers" feature early Doobie Brothers-style vocals with lots of infectious wo-oh-ohs. As for the mild tracks, "Love" is a radio-friendly sing-along standout ("Your love is everywhere / Like a song in the air") and "As the Deer" (a cover of a traditional worship tune) would get them noticed by a few adult contemporary fans. Nice, but Imagine This was born to rock out and they never quite seemed to realize this. Youngblood and Rick Weinland went on to form **Lloyd.**

Christian radio hits: "Word to the World" (# 10 in 1994); "Love" (# 5 in 1995); "My Son" (# 5 in 1996); "As the Deer" (# 12 in 1996).

The Imitators

Richard Cabrera, drums; Barry Edge, voc., gtr.; Philip Mason, kybrd.; David Price, gtr., voc.; Robert Villegas, bass. 1984—*The Imitators* [EP] (Exile); 1985—*Once and for All* (Exile).

The Imitators were an '80s techno/dance band that drew on the basic new-wave sound that was in the air at the time. The group's influences ranged from the Psychedelic Furs ("The Kingdom of Heaven Is within You," "Idol") to The Cars ("Got to Feel the Fire," "I'll Keep Holding On"). The song "Children of the Lie" attracted some attention for what *CCM* called "adventurous lyrics." It describes two young people having sex in the back seat of a car: "They're into the Bible / She's using it for a pillow / He's moaning, Oh God."

Impellitteri

Chris Impellitteri, gtr., Rob Rock, voc.; James Pulli, bass; Ken Mary, drums (– 1998b) // Mark Bistong, drums (+ 1993, – 1994); Ed Roth, kybrd. (+ 1996); Glen Sabel, drums (+ 1998b). 1987—*Impellitteri* [EP] (Relativity); 1988—*Relativity*; 1992—*Grin and Bear It*; 1993—*Victim of the System* [EP] (JVC); 1994—*Answer to the Master*; 1996—*Screaming Symphony*;

1997—*Fuel for the Fire* [EP]; 1998—*Eye of the Hurricane; Live! Fast! Loud!* (N.E.M.E.); 1999—*Stand in Line* (Country Media); 2000—*Crunch* (JVC).

Though unknown in much of the contemporary Christian music subculture, the band Impellitteri is a metal band whose very name is spoken with hushed reverence by some fans of that genre. The group's core is composed of two of Christian metal's biggest stars. Chris Impellitteri is a slash-and-burn guitarist of mythic proportions, and Rob Rock has a stellar voice for melodic metal sung in a classic '80s style. Rock previously sang for the Los Angeles band **Joshua,** and the leader of that group, Joshua Perahia, reportedly led him to Christ. He also did guest vocals for **Angelica**'s debut album. *HM* magazine once proclaimed Impellitteri's *Screaming Symphony* "the album of the year." *Eye of the Hurricane* surprised fans with the group's first two ballads ("On and On," "Paradise") alongside more soaring, melodic metal songs. *Live! Fast! Loud!* is a collection of Japanese concert bootleg tracks, including a cover of Deep Purple's "Highway Star." *Crunch* is the group's heaviest album and represents enough of a departure from the usual style to alienate purists and yet win new fans. Impellitteri is one of the only Christian metal bands to be known and respected by metal artists in the general market. They are big in Japan, where it was only recently discovered that they are "a Christian band," inspiring stories about a conversion that, of course, never happened. They had been making the noise for Jesus all along. In 2001, Rob Rock released a solo album called *Rage of Creation* (Massacre) and guested as lead vocalist on an album by the heavy metal band Warrior (*The Code of Life,* Nuclear Blast).

The Imperials

Armond Morales, voc.; Jake Hess, voc. (– 1967); Gary McSpadden, voc. (–1967); Sherrill Nielson, voc. (–1966); Henry Slaughter, piano (–1966) // Jim Murray, voc. (+ 1966, –1987); Joe Moscheo, piano (+ 1966, –1987); Terry Blackwood, voc. (+ 1967, – 1976); Roger Wiles, voc. (+ 1967, – 1970); Greg Gordon, voc. (+ 1970, – 1971); Sherman Andrus, voc. (+ 1970, – 1971); Russ Taff, voc. (+ 1976, – 1982); David Will, voc. (+ 1977); Paul Smith, voc. (+ 1982, –1987); Ron Hemby, voc. (+ 1987, –1991); Jimmie Lee Sloas, voc. (+ 1987, –1990); David Robertson, voc. (+ 1990, – 1991); Jonathan Pierce, voc. (+ 1991, – 1995); Pam Morales, voc. (+ 1991, –1995); Jeff Walker, voc. (+ 1995, –1997); Steve Ferguson, voc. (+ 1995); Steve Shapiro, voc. (+ 1997, – 1998); Barry Weeks, voc. (+ 1998). Discography beginning with 1968: 1968—*New Dimensions* (Impact); 1969—*Love Is the Thing*; 1970—*Gospel's Alive and Well; Believe It*; 1971—*Time to Get It Together*; 1972—*Song of Love*; 1973—*A Thing Called Love; Live*; 1974—*Follow the Man with the Music*; 1975—*No Shortage*; 1976—*Just Because*; 1977—*The Collector's Series (1968–1972); The Best of the Imperials; Sail On* (DaySpring); 1978—*Imperials Live*; 1979—*Heed the Call; One More Song for You; The Imperials Featuring Terry and Sherman* (Impact); 1980—*Christmas with the Imperials* (Word); *Priority*; 1981—*Very Best of* (DaySpring); 1982—*Stand by the Power*; 1983—*Side by Side*; 1984—*Imperials Sing the Classics*; 1985—*Let the Wind Blow* (Myrrh); 1987—*This Year's Model*; 1988—*Feel the Fire*; 1990—*Love's Still Changing Hearts*

(StarSong); 1991—*Big God*; 1992—*Stir It Up*; 1994—*Treasures*; *Til He Comes* (Impact); 1996—*Legacy* (Word); 1997—*It's Still the Cross* (Big God); 1998—*Songs of Christmas*; *Hall of Fame Series* (Benson).

www.theimperials.org

The Imperials are more a name than a group. As indicated above, a continually revolving spate of artists have gone by that name over the years to produce contemporary gospel music that is rooted in the vocal quartets of traditional southern gospel (only founding member Armond Morales has remained the entire thirty-five plus years, a quarter century longer than anyone else). The group began as Jake Hess and The Imperials in 1964, and they recorded at least a dozen albums of hymns and traditional material not listed above (see website). With the arrival of the Jesus movement in the late '60s, however, the group shifted gears and went for a more contemporary sound. The most important singers at this time (besides Morales) were **Sherman Andrus** and **Terry Blackwood,** both of whom would later have solo careers after a post-Imperials run as **Andrus, Blackwood, and Co.** Andrus and Blackwood were not the only Imperials to make subsequent marks in Christian music. **Russ Taff,** who had a successful solo career in the '80s, fronted a classic lineup of the band. Imperial Jimmie Lee Sloas would become a renowned producer and sing with **Dogs of Peace. Jonathan Pierce** would go on to sing with **The Gaither Vocal Band** and would then pursue a solo career. **David Robertson** and **Paul Smith** also recorded solo albums.

In their early years, The Imperials sang, toured, and even recorded with Jimmy Dean and **Elvis Presley.** Like their contemporaries The Oak Ridge Boys, they garnered some attention as a gospel group in the general market, performing in Las Vegas, Reno, and Lake Tahoe. Unlike the former group, however, they did not capitalize on this opportunity by recording music with more secular content. They did win a Grammy award for their *No Shortage* album and were the first gospel act ever to perform at the Grammy awards ceremony. Like any group with such a long and varied history, The Imperials' songs (best sampled on the *Legacy* package) reveal a wide diversity of sound. They are probably at their most distinctive best when they stick closest to their roots. "Bread upon the Water" from *Sail On* and "The Old Gospel Ship" from *Imperials Live* closely approximate the gospel quartet genre, albeit with electric guitars and a backbeat.

Never is this more true than on the band's all-time best song, the title track from *No Shortage*—a danceable **Gary S. Paxton** number that balances southern gospel harmonies and modern funk perfectly. On tracks like "Stand by the Power" (from the album of that name) and "I'm Forgiven" (from *One More Song for You*) The Imperials turn into a legitimate rock and roll band in the vein of such groups as Hall and Oates. Inspira-

tional ballads like "All My Life" (from *One More Song for You*), "Because of Who You Are" (from *Stand by the Power*), and "You're the Only Jesus" (from *Side by Side*) are bland, surviving (if at all) on the strength of their content alone.

The Imperials often played a role in contemporary Christian music analogous to that played by **Pat Boone** in the history of rock and roll. The same ambiguity attends. On albums like *Time to Get It Together* and *Imperials Live* they performed tame versions of Jesus music songs (alongside **Bill Gaither** hymns), legitimating that music in skeptical churches while also robbing it of the worldly elements that gave it power. This trend would reach its culmination years later with *Imperials Sing the Classics,* which includes Imperialized versions of **Andraé Crouch**'s "Through It All," **Amy Grant**'s "El Shaddai," **2nd Chapter of Acts**' "Easter Song," and **B. J. Thomas**'s "Home Where I Belong." *No Shortage* and *Just Because,* however, were major breakthroughs, evincing modern pop with a winsome southern gospel twist; the quirkiness of the sound (prefiguring such acts as Huey Lewis and the News) became something of a guilty pleasure for rock fans. With *Sail On,* the band (headed by **Russ Taff**) moved even more strongly into contemporary pop. The title song, written by **Chris Christian,** sounds a lot like something the Beach Boys or **B. J. Thomas** might have recorded. *Heed the Call* took them over the top and established them as leisure-suited (white polyester) superstars on the strength of two enormous hits. "Oh Buddha" is a dumb novelty piece that some people must have thought was funny—though it seems unlikely that anyone could ever have wanted to hear it twice. It is basically just an attack on various world religions that doesn't even bother to get its fact straight (e.g., Mohammed did not direct anyone to trust in Hare Krishna). "Praise the Lord," by contrast, is a modern hymn with a certain Broadway musical flair. In 1998, a *CCM* poll of thirty critics chose The Imperials' version of "Praise the Lord" (written by **Brown Bannister** and Mike Hudson) as one of "the ten best contemporary Christian songs of all time."

Michael Omartian took over production on *One More Song for You* and *Priority* and the group functioned as a conduit for presenting his quirky, keyboard-based tunes to the public. *CCM* chose *One More Song for You* as one of its Ten Best Albums of 1980, and twenty years later chose it as Number Seventy-five on their list of "The 100 Greatest Christian Albums of All-Time" (the only Imperials product on that list). "Living without Your Love" (written by Tom Hemby) sounds like a Bee Gees song and is as good as some of that group's lesser material (e.g., "Too Much Heaven"); "Higher Power" is a powerful upbeat tune that displays the group's vocal strengths to full effect. "I'm Forgiven," one of six songs cowritten by Omartian, was the album's big hit. *Priority* features "Into My Life" (written by

Beeb Birtles of Little River Band), complete with an actual guitar solo. "Any Good Time at All" is an odd Omartian tune relating God's omnipresence to time travel—or something like that. "Trumpet of Jesus" strives a bit too obviously for anthemic status and the titular horns come off as more cheesy than rousing.

Minus Omartian and Taff, the group nevertheless scored big in the adult contemporary market with *Stand by the Power* on the strength of "Because of Who You Are" (written by **Bob Farrell**). Less predictably, the album also features a version of **Kerry Livgren**'s "How Can You Live." *Side by Side* was an experimental two-record set in which each of the four vocalists is featured for one entire side. The result is a collection of nondescript MOR pieces, with one historical novelty: "Make My Heart Your Home" sung by **Paul Smith** as a duet with Leslie Phillips, who would later become rock sensation **Sam Phillips.**

Producer **Brown Bannister** brought the group into the '80s on *Let the Wind Blow,* albeit with an emphasis on atmospheric worship tunes ("Not to Us, O Lord," "Let the Wind Blow"). "In the Promised Land" (written by **Chris Eaton**) is another of the combo's bouncy Hall and Oates-styled numbers. An abrupt shift marked *This Year's Model,* which features a heavy R&B sound, propelled by Jimmie Lee Sloas's gruff vocals. While "Wings of Love" is predictable radio fluff, "Power of God" is probably the band's most authentic rock song, and one of their finest tracks. This orientation would continue on *Free the Fire,* where the upbeat title track (an Omartian song) and the very soulful "Rest in Your Arms" recall the soft rock style of bands like Steely Dan and Pablo Cruise, with whom producer Bill Schnee had also worked. On *Love's Still Changing Hearts* the now Sloas-less band tries for a dance-pop style with the opening "Big Ball Turning," sounding a bit like Prince performing traditional gospel.

Initiating yet another new era, The Imperials added a woman (Armond's sister Pam) to the group in the '90s; female lead vocals are featured on "What Can I Do with This Love?" from *Big God.* For the most part, the '90s Imperials have been a predictable but tasteful adult contemporary vocal combo, but on *Stir It Up* they demonstrate a capacity for more pop-oriented R&B music. "Taking Your Love for Granted" is particularly radio-friendly and "Change the World" (written by Terry Esau) is strong lyrically ("If I wanted to change the world / I would start by loving you"). Armond Morales has summarized the group's long and varied career by saying, "The Imperials are a democracy. The identity of each of our records has come from who's in the group. We try to get the best out of the singers we have at any given time."

For trivia buffs: Country western singer Larry Gatlin was a member of The Imperials for one year (1971), though he did not sing on any of their recordings.

Christian radio hits: "Sail On" (# 3 in 1978); "Water Grave" (# 14 in 1979); "Praise the Lord" (# 2 in 1979); "Oh, Buddha" (# 1 for 8 weeks in 1979); "Overcomers" (# 15 in 1979); "What Can I Do for You?" (# 12 in 1980); "I'm Forgiven" (# 1 for 13 weeks in 1980); "One More Song for You" (# 10 in 1980); "I'd Rather Believe in You" (# 5 in 1981); "Finish What You Started" (# 2 in 1981); "The Trumpet of Jesus" (# 1 for 4 weeks in 1981); "Be Still My Soul" (# 19 in 1981); "Lord of the Harvest" (# 3 in 1983); "Somebody New" (# 9 in 1983); "Because of Who You Are" (# 37 in 1983); "Wait upon the Lord" (# 2 in 1984); "You're the Only Jesus" (# 20 in 1984); "Make My Heart Your Home" (# 13 in 1984); "Let the Wind Blow" (# 14 in 1985); "In the Promised Land" (# 9 in 1989); "Wings of Love" (# 2 in 1987); "How Do I Get to You?" (# 14 in 1987); "Get Ready" (# 10 in 1987); "Holding On" (# 3 in 1987); "Fallin' " (# 6 in 1988); "Free the Fire in Me" (# 14 in 1988); "The Boss" (# 16 in 1989); "You" (# 6 in 1989); "Big Ball Turning" (# 2 in 1990); "It's Gonna Be Alright" (# 4 in 1990); "Come into My Life" (# 12 in 1990); "Original Love" (# 13 in 1991); "Taking Your Love for Granted" (# 3 in 1993); "Change the World" (# 14 in 1993); "Standing on the Rock of Love" (# 9 in 1993); "Stir It Up" (# 4 in 1994).

Dove Awards: 1969 Male Group of the Year; 1975 Male Group of the Year; 1976 Male Group of the Year; 1976 Pop/Contemporary Album *(No Shortage)*; 1978 Male Group of the Year; 1980 Male Group of the Year; 1981 Artist of the Year; 1981 Group of the Year; 1981 Pop/Contemporary Album *(One More Song for You)*; 1982 Group of the Year; 1982 Pop/Contemporary Album *(Priority)*; 1983 Group of the Year; 1984 Pop/Contemporary Album *(Side By Side)*.

Grammy Awards: 1975 Best Gospel Performance, Other than Soul Gospel *(No Shortage)*; 1977 Best Gospel Performance, Contemporary or Inspirational *(Sail On)*; 1979 Best Gospel Performance, Contemporary or Inspirational *(Heed the Call)*; 1981 Best Gospel Performance, Contemporary or Inspirational *(Priority)*.

Indigo Girls

Amy Ray, voc., gtr.; Emily Saliers, voc., gtr. 1986—*Indigo Girls* [EP] (Indigo); 1987—*Strange Fire*; 1989—*Indigo Girls* (Epic); 1990—*Nomads Indians Saints*; 1991—*Back on the Bus, Y'all* [EP]; 1992—*Rites of Passage*; 1994—*Swamp Ophelia*; 1995—*1200 Curfews*; 4.5; 1997—*Shaming of the Sun*; 1999—*Come On Now Social*; 2002—*Become You.*

www.indigogirls.com

There seems to be little question that both Amy Ray and Emily Saliers are Christians—they have at times been outspoken and explicit about that. Still, the duo known as the Indigo Girls—one of the most successful modern folk groups in the general market—is rarely identified as a contemporary Christian group despite the obvious spiritual content of many of their songs. This anomaly has a political (and theological) explanation. The contemporary Christian music industry and subculture is composed of an inordinate number of Christians drawn from conservative segments of the church universal. Ray and Saliers publicly embrace liberal ideas and support causes that, while acceptable to millions of American Christians, tend not to be endorsed by the Religious Right mentality that informs much of the contemporary Christian music fan base. The Girls are open about their lesbian relationship, a matter that is anathema to many conservative Christians (cf. **Marsha Stevens**). They are also articulate feminists, support a pro-choice position on abortion, and in many other ways fail acid tests that would gain them approval within the official contemporary Christian music market. On the other hand, they are a favorite of many clergy in the liberal Protestant tradition from whence they sprang, and they have earned respect for their "spirituality" in a secular press that usually denounces such pietistic overtures.

Saliers and Ray were both raised in Atlanta and began singing together while in high school. Both women were brought up in the United Methodist Church, Saliers the daughter of a pastor. They adopted the moniker Indigo Girls while students at Emory University, where Saliers' father (Don Saliers) is a world-renowned Professor of Theology and Worship and where Ray majored in religion. Their independent releases attracted early attention and inspired such bands as R.E.M. and Hothouse Flowers to put in guest appearances on their Grammy-winning debut album for Epic. The latter record includes the song "Closer to Fine," which remains their best-known hit. Its lyrics speak of looking for faith in the midst of ambiguity with a postmodern awareness that would become fashionable in Christian music a decade later: "We go to the Bible / We go through the workout / We read up on revival and we stand up for the lookout / There's more than one answer to these questions / Pointing me in crooked line." At least two other songs on that album ("Prince of Darkness" and "Secure Yourself") also reflect on spiritual themes, as did "Strange Fire," the title song from their 1997 indie record. Around this time *CCM* magazine, perhaps unaware of the couple's potential for controversy, ran a two-page article on the new group, praising them as Christians making a difference in the mainstream. *Nomads Indians Saints* features a guest performance by Mary Chapin Carpenter and includes the song "Hammer and Nail," a hit on college radio. *Rites of Passage* brings in a host of guest stars (Jackson Browne, David Crosby) and experiments with more electric sounds. *Swamp Ophelia* goes even further in this direction with the Girls' first fully electric song, "Touch Me Fall." Likewise, *Shaming of the Sun* offers songs with tape loops and rock guitar leads, and *Come On Now Social* puts the girls in front of a full band (called Ghostland) with guest appearances by Lilith Fair friends Sheryl Crow, Joan Osborne, and Meshell Ndegéocello. The latter album includes the song "Karla Faye" about born-again Christian Karla Faye Tucker, who the state of Texas put to death in a controversial execution in 1998. The album *4.5* is a hits compilation and *1200 Curfews* is a live concert recording. *The Rough Guide to Rock* calls the Indigo Girls "the folkies that it's cool for intellectuals to like." The duo

often performs on behalf of such charities as Habitat for Humanity, Humanitas, and the Children's Health Fund. Both Saliers and Ray had acting roles in the film *Boys on the Side,* starring Whoopi Goldberg and Drew Barrymore. They also starred in a new version of the musical *Jesus Christ Superstar* (with Ray as Jesus and Saliers as Mary Magdalene).

Grammy Awards: 1990 Best Contemporary Folk Recording *(Indigo Girls).*

Industry Eleven (a.k.a. **Fear of Faith**)

Brent Otley, gtr., voc., synth., prog.; Geoff Grimstad, gtr., voc., synth., prog. As Fear of Faith: 1994—*Dredge* [EP] (Running Dog); *Tension* [EP]; 1995—*Blind* [EP]. As Industry Eleven: 1996—*Frustration* [EP] (independent); 1998—*The Days and Nights Surrounding Change.*

The industrial metal duo currently known as Industry Eleven began as Fear of Faith. They released two thrash/speed metal EPs almost simultaneously in lieu of a more traditional debut full-length album. With songs like "Guilt Hell" and "Demons of Bitterness" on the first and "The Killing" and "Rage" on the second, they established themselves as part of the dark metal Christian underground that dwells on death and destruction, albeit with samples of Scripture verses ("The Void") and little pointers toward the hope of Christ here and there. With *Blind,* the group shocked their fans by almost going unplugged with a selection of four melodic acoustic songs that pit harsh vocals against a mellow background. The EP recorded under the name Industry Eleven returns to the chainsaw guitar approach but with an attempt to integrate melody and what one critic called "a few moments of actual singing." *True Tunes* describes *The Days and Nights Surrounding Change* as an album cut from the same cloth as projects by **Klank** and **Circle of Dust**. Lyrics express the hopelessness of life in this world: "I always saw my death as the only way out of this pain and misery / I never thought there could be another way" ("Alone").

Infinity Plus Three

See **Mark Heard**.

Jason Ingram Band

Ron Fugelseth, perc.; Kevin Igarta, bass; Jason Ingram, voc.; Landon Schadel, gtr.; Matt West, drums. 1998—*JIB* (Audience); announced for 2002—*Jason Ingram* (Resonate).

The Jason Ingram Band from the San Francisco Bay area is an acoustic quintet fronted by singer/songwriter/guitarist Jason Ingram. The band has an acoustic sound that is generally similar to **Jars of Clay** with touches of such modern rock groups as the Dave Matthews Band. They are very direct lyrically, presenting unabashed songs about Jesus and those who follow him. Their debut album opens with "What's It Gonna

Be Like?" a song that looks forward to the second coming of Christ. "Because of Your Love" is a tribute to godly parents. Ingram's announced 2002 album appears to be a solo effort, produced with Rick Heil of **Sonicflood.**

Christian radio hits: "What's It Gonna Be Like?" (# 8 in 1999).

The Innocence Mission

Mike Bitts, bass; Don Peris, gtr., kybrd.; Karen Peris, voc., kybrd., gtr.; Steve Brown, drums (– 1999). 1986—*Tending the Rose Garden* [EP] (L List); 1989—*The Innocence Mission* (A&M); 1991—*Umbrella*; 1995—*Glow*; 1999—*Birds of My Neighborhood* (Kneeling Elephant); 2000—*Christ Is My Hope* (independent); 2001—*Small Planes* (What Are Artists).

www.theinnocencemission.com

The Innocence Mission is a college-oriented art-pop band from Pennsylvania with more connections in the general market than in the Christian music subculture. The group is led by the married couple Don and Karen Peris and is built around Karen's sultry soprano vocals and mystical, poetic songwriting. *7ball* describes her singing as "fraught with quiet passion and mildly self-conscious mutterings." Don Peris's guitar sound is particularly distinctive, featuring shimmering electric notes that *True Tunes* once said sound like the bells of a country church. The group's overall sound is often rightly compared to that of 10,000 Maniacs or The Sundays. *CCM* said that *The Innocence Mission* "seems almost a journal of someone's quest for faith ('Surreal') and attempt to live in faith ('Clear to You')." The Perises are Roman Catholic, and specific images of their faith appear frequently in their songs. "I so often leave You in churches" Karen sings to God on *Umbrella,* "and on my beads (i.e., rosary beads) . . . where I see You, I can feel You." Such a sentiment both extols and critiques the value of icons in a manner difficult for Protestants, much less non-Christians, to understand. *Glow* has a family history feel to it, as the songs introduce various characters and offer glimpses of their lives. The exceptional "Bright as Yellow" (with a subdued Stevie Nicks vibe) garnered some mainstream radio airplay. *Birds of My Neighborhood* is intimate and melancholy, dealing with various forms of loss. The band covers John Denver's "Follow Me" as a sad tribute to the lost artist and offers several original songs played in a style that *True Tunes* identifies as grounded in such classic projects as Simon and Garfunkel's *Sounds of Silence* and Neil Young's *Harvest.* Allusions and outright testimonies to faith are found in "You Are the Light" and "Birdless." A real treat for Christian music fans, *Christ Is My Hope* presents a collection of hymns and liturgical songs that the group recorded as a benefit project for the charitable organization Food for the Poor. Standards like "It Is Well With My Soul," "Beautiful Saviour," and "Were You There?" coincide with folk songs "Five Hundred Miles" and "Fare Thee Well." *Small Planes* collects unreleased outtakes and rarities from throughout the group's career.

Certainly one of the best artists on the Christian scene from a critical perspective, Innocence Mission also features some of the most artistic and perceptive lyrics in its songs. Two themes frequently recur in Peris's poetry. First, she displays a remarkable capacity for finding wonder in what is ordinary. In "The Lakes of Canada," she sings, "There's a sudden joy that's like / A fish, a moving light / I thought I saw it / Rowing on the lakes of Canada." Second, she expresses a hopeful realism, avoiding cynical resignation but with full awareness that simple answers are rarely complete. On "Brave" she sings, "You paint a tulip red with joy / You say the psalm, I will not fear / Somehow, knowing what you know / Still you tremble out and in."

The group enjoys some respect within the general market, especially in the folk scene. Karen and Don Peris sing harmony vocals on the Mila Drumke Band's critically acclaimed album *Illinois* ("Motorboat"); on Joni Mitchell's *Night Ride Home* ("Cherokee Louise"); on Natalie Merchant's *Ophelia* ("Frozen Charlotte," "When They Ring the Golden Bells"); on **Julie Miller**'s *Blue Pony* ("By Way of Sorrow"); on John Hiatt's *Bring the Family* ("Through Your Hands"); and on Peter Himmelman's *From Strength to Strength* ("No Running Away").

In Reach (a.k.a. **The Reach**)

Mike Bell, kybrd.; Scott Burrell, bass; Vince Grant, drums; Brett Williams, voc. As The Reach: 1988—*Under the Same Sky* (Image). As In Reach: 1992—*Waterline* (StarSong); 1993—*Power and Promise*; 1996—*Seven Days of Light* (Absolute).

The Seattle folk-pop band In Reach formed in 1986. They were first known as simply The Reach and released one album under that name (with a different lineup than that listed above) that portrayed them as sounding something like **White Heart.** They then retreated into a more authentic pop groove, recalling the jangly sounds of groups like Big Star or The Byrds. By their next album, they were calling themselves **Brett Williams** and In Reach, foreshadowing the vocalist's solo career. In Reach became best known for pop ballads typical of radio-oriented contemporary Christian music, but the group at times displayed a more creative and aggressive sound on songs like "Fire" and "Run," both from *Power and Promise.* The latter album is considered the band's best work. It also features "Best for Me," with vocals by **Julie Miller.**

Christian radio hits: "My Heart" (# 9 in 1992); "Faded Love" (# 7 in 1993); "Giving Me Reasons" (# 4 in 1993); "Best for Me" (# 11 in 1993); "Savannah" (# 12 in 1994).

The Insyderz

Beau McCarthy, bass; Nate Sjogren, drums; Kyle Wasil, gtr.; Joe Yerke, voc.; Mike Rowland, tromb. (–1998); Al Brown, coronet (–1997); Todd

Miesch, perc. (– 1997) // Bram Roberts, trump. (+ 1998); Sang Kim, tromb. (+ 1998). 1997—*Motor City Ska* (Gumshoe); 1998—*Skalleluia* (Squint); *Fight of My Life* (KMG); 1999—*Skalleluia Too.*

www.theinsyderz.com

The Insyderz are one of "the big three" among Christian ska bands (the others being **Five Iron Frenzy** and **The Supertones**). Their name is derived from a reference in Colossians 4:5 to non-Christians as outsiders, implying that those who do believe are the insiders. The group formed in Detroit in 1996 and traveled to the *Cornerstone* festival that summer where they were unable to get a gig on any of the stages. Unperturbed, they set up at their campsite and began to play, attracting a crowd and the consequent attention of record company executives. Eventually, Gene Eugene of **Adam Again** noticed them and got them their first album deal. Later, **Steve Taylor** signed them to his Squint label and helped them to make the all-important *Skalleluia* album. Most of the members come from a church background in the Salvation Army, which helps to explain their love of brass instruments as well as their overall commitment to service. The group takes a hiatus every November and December so that band members may participate in local bell and kettle fundraising activities during the holiday season. The Salvation Army, in general, has been a major supporter of the group and views them as one of its many outreach ministries.

Motor City Ska garnered favorable reviews for the band, with critics noting that their sound was more eclectic and generally "more bouncy" than that of **The Supertones** or **Five Iron Frenzy**. The song "Sacrifice" in particular features hardcore guitars and a Beastie Boys rap. But *Skalleluia* is the album that set The Insyderz apart from the pack. What could have been—indeed, what most critics thought would be—a novelty record turned out to be groundbreaking. As **Steve Taylor** noted, before *Skalleluia,* "most contemporary worship didn't really sound all that contemporary." The group performs a number of modern praise choruses and worship songs such as **Rich Mullins**' "Awesome God," **Twila Paris**'s "We Will Glorify," and **Keith Green**'s "Oh, Lord, You're Beautiful." As it turns out, the high energy of ska translates into either a slow burn passion or a raucous celebration that is entirely appropriate for the songs. Church worship bands all over the country were immediately requested to learn to play these songs The Insyderz' way. This comment assumes, of course, an informal setting with a worship band. All of the songs on *Skalleluia* are "modern classics" (none written before 1970) that would be unfamiliar to those who worship in churches with more formal liturgical traditions. This is too bad, because part of the fun of the album is hearing familiar songs performed in surprising ways—the trick does not work quite as well for those who do not know the songs in their previous incarnations. The

same can generally be said of *Skalleluia Too,* although that project includes a Dixieland version of "The Old Rugged Cross." On the second *Skalleluia* outing, the group also offers a couple of original songs plus new takes on **Delirious?'s** "I Could Sing of Your Love Forever" and **Darlene Zschech**'s "Shout to the Lord." The overall sound of *Skalleluia Too* is harder—more skacore than ska—than the first praise album. Liturgically, the accent is again more on performance than participation. Ultimately, both *Skalleluia* projects work better as worshipful entertainment than as exemplars for congregational praise. In 2000 a producer named Joe Ferry (who apparently knows nothing about The Insyderz) released an instrumental album titled *Skallelujah* (Electica). Despite the similar names, the projects are not related—Ferry's record focuses more on updated versions of classical pieces.

Fight of My Life was a radical departure from the *Skalleluia* projects, a record geared to a secular audience. The band previewed the material by touring clubs with general market ska bands. The songs on *Fight* convey a subdued but not muted approach to spiritual themes. "Paradise" celebrates the glory of creation. "Forgive and Forget" offers Yerke's heartfelt plea to a father who walked out on the family some years before. The sentiment of the piece is so sincere that the junior-high rhyme scheme actually contributes to its emotive power, evoking the pain of an abandoned child: "One thing I know and it's crystal clear / I love you Dad and I want you here / The times change and so do we / I still hope that you remember me." A well-chosen cover of The Cars' "Just What I Needed" provides a punchy distraction.

Christian radio hits: "Paradise" (# 20 in 1999).

Dove Awards: 1999 Hard Music Song ("Awesome God").

Iona

Dave Bainbridge, kybrd.; Joanna Hogg, voc.; David Fitzgerald, sax. (–1992) // Nick Beggs, bass (+ 1992, –1996); Terl Bryant, perc. (+ 1992, –2000); Mike Haughton, sax., voc. (+ 1992, –2000); Tim Harries, bass (+ 1996, – 1997); Troy Donockley, voc. (+ 1996); Phil Barker, bass (+ 1997); Frank Van Essen, perc. (+ 2000). 1988—*Iona* (ForeFront); 1992—*The Book of Kells;* 1993—*Beyond These Shores;* 1996—*Journey into the Morn; Treasures: The Very Best;* 1997—*Heaven's Bright Sun;* 2000— *Woven Cord;* 2001—*Open Sky.*

www.gospel.it/iona

Iona is Christian music's premier Celtic-music band, sort of a Christian version of Enya. Their sound incorporates many elements of progressive rock (Peter Gabriel, Yes, Pink Floyd, the Moody Blues) and their focus—uncharacteristic for contemporary Christian music—has been on recovering liturgical and historical traditions of the church. The name "Iona" is Gaelic for "Isle of Saints" and refers geographically to the actual island where St. Columba landed in 563 and introduced Christianity to Scotland. The group was founded in 1988 by Fitzgerald and Bainbridge. They recruited medical doctor **Joanna Hogg** after hearing her sing on a project by **Adrian Snell.** As indicated above, the group has gone through numerous personnel changes, though Hogg and Bainbridge have remained constants. Bassist Nick Beggs had been a member of the London synth-pop band Kajagoogoo, which scored a Top Five general market hit with the song "Too Shy" in 1983. Many members have also been involved in side projects. Hogg issued a solo album in 1999. **Terl Bryant** is also a member of **Eden's Bridge;** he is the founder of Psalm Drummers—a support group for Christian percussionists—and has recorded solo albums. Troy Donockley has also recorded a solo album of what he calls "Cumbrian folk music" (*The Unseen Stream,* Alliance, 1998). It includes a rendition of Sibelius' "Finlandia," and a fourteen-minute opus to a stream where Donockley played as a child ("The Yearl"). **David Fitzgerald** pursued a solo career after leaving the group.

Iona's albums typically display a high level of integral consistency. The debut, *Iona,* takes as its main theme the development of English Christendom, which is traced in songs related to the lives of three influential persons: St. Columba, St. Aidan, and St. Cuthbert. *The Book of Kells* is a carefully constructed concept album presenting songs related to a famous eighth-century manuscript by that name. The book contains lush illustrations of the Gospels and is considered to be a masterpiece of Celtic art, possibly developed at the monastery on the island of Iona. Each of the songs on *The Book of Kells* relates to one of the pictures in this book, and reproductions of the illustrations are included for accompanying reflection. The album is generally regarded as Iona's greatest work: four selections focus on traditional images for the four Gospels ("Matthew—The Man," "Mark—The Lion," "Luke—The Calf," "John—The Eagle"); a thirty-two-minute suite of instrumentals portrays Christ's temptation in the wilderness, arrest, and resurrection. *Beyond These Shores* tells the story of St. Brendan's divinely guided voyage to "a promised land," probably the Americas. The songs reflect on that figure's trust in God when venturing into the complete unknown. *Journey into the Morn* is not quite so tightly constructed around a single theme, but does depict stories about English clerics who engaged in missionary work to the rest of Europe. The group says that the entire album was inspired by the Gaelic hymn "Be Thou My Vision" and by a book of meditations on that hymn titled *The Eye of the Eagle.* The record opens with a version of the hymn sung in Gaelic. *Heaven's Bright Sun* is a double-disc album offering live versions of favorite songs, including a fifteen-minute version of the traditional hymn "When I Survey the Wondrous Cross." *Woven Cord* is also a live recording, this time featuring the group in performance with the All Saints Orchestra. *Open Sky* moves

the group away from the jazz stylings that Fitzgerald and Haughton had provided and toward the more traditional sax-free sound of a group like Clannad. The album's highlight is a three-song suite, "Song of the Ascent," based on a prayer of St. Columba. A full half of the album (including the nine-minute title track) is instrumental. Iona is clearly a critics' favorite. Few acts can touch their musicianship and their lyrics display a similar artistry that, as *CCM* puts it, "point to God in more poetic than dogmatic terms."

Christian radio hits: "Treasure" (# 10 in 1994).

Dove Awards: 1993 Inspirational Artist.

Isaac

Bob Buchanan, voc., kybrd.; Mike Cheney, bass, voc.; Kevin Josie, drums, voc.; Stan Majkut, trump.; Jim Mikles, strings; Bob Page, gtr., synth.; Shelton Parson, bass; Bob Roman, trump., voc.; Brian Scott, voc., gtr.; Alexander Walker, sax., flute. 1983—*City of Dreams* (Heavensong).

The rather large combo that called itself Isaac released a single album of big-band-influenced rock similar to that of Blood, Sweat, and Tears or **Liberation Suite.** Band members trade off on lead vocals, giving the project a diverse sound; the Blood, Sweat, and Tears analogy is especially prevalent on tracks where Brian Scott takes the lead ("Good Time Tonight," "Seasons," "Sower," "Crucifixion"). The opening song, "There's No Because in Your Love," is a testimony to grace with a jazzy rock flavor. The title track and "Good Time Tonight" both address the inevitable disillusionment that comes to those who set their hearts on worldly ambitions.

Ishmael United (a.k.a. **Ishmael and Andy** and **Ishmael**)

Ian Smale, voc., gtr.; et al. As Ishmael and Andy: 1973—*Ready Salted* (Myrrh UK). As Ishmael: 1975—*Charge of the Light Brigade* (Dovetail). As Ishmael United: 1980—*If You Can't Shout Saved! You'll Have to Face the Penalty* (Dove); 1981—*Land of Hope and Glories* (Kingsway); 1982—*Life Begins at 30.*

The many incarnations of Ishmael were all projects of the zany British rocker Ian Smale, who adopted that stage name in the early '70s. Ishmael and Andy were a duo consisting of Smale and Andy Piercy (who later fronted **After the Fire,** best known to Americans for their '80s hit "Der Kommissar"). Ishmael and Andy were a part of the British Jesus movement, working especially with the British Youth for Christ organization and performing in a folk style that was basically a more caustic version of **Malcolm and Alwyn.** The album *Ready Salted* is high energy acoustic rock with quirky lyrics: "You got a hallelujah sittin' way down inside of you. . . . Just give it a bit of air space." The song "Christian Schizophrenic" (about knowing Jesus as Savior but not as Lord) would reappear on *If*

You Can't Shout Saved! and become one of Ishmael United's best-known numbers. *Charge of the Light Brigade* finds Smale as an official solo artist, though he is in fact backed by **After the Fire.** He entertains his passion for the bizarre, banging on pots and pans and blowing what appears to be a duck horn on "Laodicean Church." Other cuts include "Mission to Seagulls" and the hard-rocking "I Am Just a Charismatic."

Five years later, the all-but-forgotten Smale would return with a band called Ishmael United. *If You Can't Shout Saved!* broke boundaries, especially in the United States (where it was released on StarSong). *CCM* regards it as "the first new-wave Christian record," prefiguring the work of **David Edwards, Steve Taylor,** and **Sheila Walsh.** The band takes a sarcastic look at smug Christian attitudes in songs delivered with raw power. Produced by Andy Piercy, the record was not well received in its homeland, however, where distinctions between Christian and secular music are less established. One critic titled his review "Christians 0, Lions 15" and savaged the album as the tepid work of a "second-rate **After the Fire.**" Ishmael United also embraced the sound of British ska (cf. Madness, The Specials), which preceded **The Supertones** by well over a decade. Smale launched another project in the '80s called Rev. Counta and the Speedoze; he later became involved in children's music and made many albums of praise and worship music for children, often recording under the name Ishmael and the Glory Co.

Israel

1996—*Whisper It Loud* (Cadence).

Israel is the professional name used by worship leader Israel Houghton (b. 1972), a singer and keyboardist from Oceanside, California. At the age of twenty, Houghton took over a struggling choir at a church in Scottsdale, Arizona, and transformed it into an impressive one hundred-voice ensemble with a twelve-piece band. He led worship for events sponsored by Champions for Christ, evangelist Danny Chambers, and Promise Keepers. His debut album *Whisper It Loud* is performed in a classic R&B style reminiscent of Babyface or Lionel Richie. A child of mixed race parentage, Houghton is dedicated to bridging gaps between blacks and whites, socially, spiritually, and musically. The song "Rescue" has a vintage Motown sound to it. "Solitude" is a praise song set to a jazzy R&B track. "Against the Stream" sets the lyrical theme for Israel's evangelistic summons, calling on youth to defy the conventions of mediocrity and make something epic of their lives.

Christian radio hits: "Against the Stream" (# 15 in 1997); "Something to Hold on To" (# 10 in 1997).

J

Becca Jackson

1997—It'll Sneak Up on You (Word).

Becca Jackson is a self-described "preacher's wife from southern Mississippi." She began singing in public at the age of four and performed at the World's Fair at fourteen. As an adult, she found work doing session singing in Nashville and performing at the Opryland theme park. Her first album for Word displays a style that *CCM* describes as "the pop-folk cocktail that has become the preferred center of the Christian music industry." Jackson's voice is distinctive, however, insofar as it has a rough quality similar to that of singers like Melissa Etheridge or Bonnie Raitt (whom she cites as her biggest influence). "Hands Tied" and the title track display her gutsy vocals to best effect.

Christian radio hits: "Hand's Tied" (# 12 in 1997).

Jackson Finch

Brian Finch, voc., kybrd.; Kevin Jackson, voc., gtr. 1993—*Beyond Complacency* (independent); 1996—*Experience* (Warner Alliance).

The duo known as Jackson Finch was formed in 1993 by two singers from Atlanta who met at Samford University in Birmingham, Alabama, where they led worship together for campus Bible studies. Their signature sound is what they call "new folk" influenced by Joni Mitchell, James Taylor, and especially Nanci Griffith. *Release* compares them favorably to **Extreme** with "less over-the-top vocals." *Beyond Complacency* varies between rhythmic, fast songs ("Sweet Salvation," "Lift My Eyes") and laid-back numbers ("Secret Hiding Place"). *Experience* opens with the **PFR**-like "Mile of Me" and a cover of Griffith's "It's a Hard Life" (a song dealing with racism). **Phil Keaggy** adds guitar riffs on the song "To Believe."

Christian radio hits: "To Believe" (# 15 in 1996); "Only You" (# 19 in 1996); "Mile of Me" (# 22 in 1996).

Nancey Jackson

1997—Free, Yes I'm Free (Harmony); *2000—Relationship*.

Nancey Jackson is an African American female vocalist from New Jersey who brings a powerful voice to songs similar in style to those performed by Whitney Houston or Patti LaBelle. Like many traditional gospel and R&B singers, Jackson grew up singing in church; in this instance, St. John's M.E.R. Church in Roselle, New Jersey, which her father pastored for forty years. Jackson's critically acclaimed debut album pairs her with producer Loris Holland, known for his work with LaBelle and Mariah Carey. Jackson and Holland cowrote many of the songs. Ballads like "Lead Me to the Rock" tend to showcase her tremolo vocal style best, while the African praise song "Sing Hallelujah" allows her to wail. "Set Time of the Hour" and the title track have a modern En Vogue vibe. "Just As You Are" is a duet with **Walter Hawkins.** *Relationship* takes Jackson simultaneously in different directions as she works with several writers and producers. Hip-hop influences are more pronounced, as the title track and "Don't Turn Your Back" includes some melodic rap. "You Don't Know" is an outstanding ballad that has Jackson skat singing over a bluesy arrangement.

Jacob's Dream

John Berry, gtr., kybrd.; James Evans, bass; Gary Holtzman, gtr.; David Taylor, voc.; Rick May, drums (–2001) // Billy Queen, drums (+ 2001). 2000—*Jacob's Dream* (Metal Blade); 2001—*Theater of War.*

www.truemetal.org/jacobsdream

Jacob's Dream is a metal band that (by their own admission) strives for a sound that owes equally to two great influences: Iron Maiden and Queensryche. *HM* thinks they mostly succeed, noting the pummeling guitar assault that links them to the first group and the slick production and ethereal keyboard atmospheres that introduce allusions to the latter. Rick May (of **The Walter Eugenes**) served as both drummer and producer for the group's first album. Their song "Crusade" compares examples of legalism in modern Christianity to forces that drove the scandalous eleventh-century expeditions. The title song to *Theater of War* casts Cain's slaying of Abel as the origin of all warfare. The group's sole ballad, "Sarah Williams," is written from the perspective of a penitent drunk driver.

Jacob's Trouble

Steve Atwell, bass; Jerry Davison, voc.; Mark Blackburn, gtr. (–1993) // Ron Cochran, drums (+ 1992); Keith Johnston, gtr. (+ 1992). 1988—*Jacob's Trouble* [EP] (custom); 1989—*Door into Summer* (Alarma); 1990—*Knock, Breathe, Shine*; 1992—*Let the Truth Run Wild*; 1993—*Jacob's Trouble* (Frontline); 1994—*Diggin' Up Bones* (Alarma); 1999—*Sampler Pack* (KMG).

The successful Christian pop band Jacob's Trouble was regarded as one of the most fun groups of the late '80s and early '90s. Their retro-'60s sound was eminently likable yet just quirky and eclectic enough to interest critics who would usually recoil at bands with such obvious commercial appeal. The group formed in Atlanta in 1988, beginning as a trio, swelling to a quintet for one album and then stabilizing as a quartet for their final and most successful project. The name was chosen from Jeremiah 30:7, a reference that the group members first heard in the movie *Image of the Beast,* one of many Christian exploitation films about the end times. On the Alarma albums they benefitted greatly from an association with **Terry Taylor,** who produced the projects and cowrote several of the best songs. Early Jacob's Trouble probably recalls The Monkees more than any other mainstream band, though strains of such artists as the Beatles, The Byrds, and Crosby, Stills and Nash are clearly detectable. Early **Daniel Amos** (Taylor's band) is also an obvious reference point. In fact, *CCM* critic Brian Quincy Newcomb once trivialized the group (after its first two full-length albums) as "a latter-day **Daniel Amos** tribute band."

The title track of *Door into Summer* is a cover of one of The Monkees' lesser-known songs (from their excellent *Pisces, Aquarius, Capricorn, and Jones* album) and the album also includes a remake of the Beatles' "Tell Me What You See." The record's most popular song was "Church of Do What You Want," a satirical folk-rock song that blatantly rips off Paul Revere and the Raiders' "Hungry." A much better song is "Wind and Wave," a rocking tune from the custom EP re-recorded here in a more countryfied version. "She Smiles at the Future" is a flower-power-pop song (think The Cowsills) about the "excellent wife" of Proverbs 31. *Knock, Breathe, Shine* demonstrates marked progression. It opens with a rollicking, **Daniel Amos** sound-alike, "Look at U Now," a very powerful, melodic, and hook-filled pop song. Another Taylor composition, "There Goes My Heart Again," offers what may be the band's finest recorded moment. A masterpiece of melody and harmony akin to *Pet Sounds*-era Beach Boys, the song uses romantic imagery to describe the experience of renewed devotion to Christ. "Beggars and Kings" rocks with a jangly guitar sound that hadn't been heard like this since The Byrds released their first *Greatest Hits* LP. "Dreammaker" is solid pop, composed by the band without Taylor's assistance, and "Little Red Words" likewise succeeds in spite of its dumb lyrics ("In the morning the first thing that I see / Are little red words in a big, black book"; cf. **DC Talk**'s equally dumb "Red Letters"). "Further Up and Further In" is a worshipful anthem based on a theme from C. S. Lewis's Narnia tales, reminiscent in sound to classic **Daniel Amos** tunes like "Praise Song" on *Shotgun Angel.* The group also covers **Bob Dylan**'s "I Believe in You" and offers the remarkable "Mr. Hitler," a track that evinces a **Steve Taylor** flair for tongue-in-cheek chic. It relates the musings of a disgruntled employee who wants to invite his boss and colleagues to dinner and "convince them right between their eyes" (i.e., with a firearm) that God is on his side.

Let the Truth Run Wild is a stronger album overall than *Knock, Breathe, Shine,* lacking anything comparable to the major embarrassments ("I'm a Little World," "About Sex, Part 2") that constitute unforgivable filler on that record. **Mark Heard** served as producer and his influence gives the project a consistency in quality despite a diversity of styles. This time, the masterpiece is Ron Cochran's song "Mornin' Light," a country pop tune that hearkens back to **Richie Furay**'s work with Buffalo Springfield and Poco. "Never Would Have Known," "Days That Passed Me By," and "Love Me Today," are all firmly embedded in that same tradition, and the band acquits itself well in adaptation to what seems to be a new and promising direction. But the real surprise comes toward the album's end: "Icicle Face" and "You Scare the Hell Out of Me" (a pragmatic meditation on what it means to "fear God") disregard the retro trend altogether and go for an up-to-date '90s rock sound that prefigures album number four with shades of INXS and **U2.** On a few other tracks ("Something Good Happens," "Just Like You," "Obligatory New Father Song"), the band tips its hat to more of a classic rockabilly sound. "Love Is the Reason We Live" offers a Bay City Rollers-inspired performance of a song that quotes liberally from the Beatles ("You say you want a revolution . . ."). One song that does not appear on *Let the Truth Run Wild* is "See Connie Naked," an ode to a stripper looking for redemption that Heard cut from the album due to perceived controversial content.

The Frontline self-titled album *Jacob's Trouble* seems to come from a completely different band than the group that made the three preceding projects. The sound is much more aggressive, capturing the energy of live performance in the studio. The disc kicks off with "Wild, Wild Ride," a galloping, guitar-driven number that leaves former Monkee comparisons in the dust. "Lovehouse" follows, insuring the band's new reputation as a first-rate rock and roll outfit on the same order as groups like Cheap Trick. "Desireé" is sung with strangely distorted vocals that must have seemed hip at the time. "This Moment" and "Tears of an Angel" demur from the new rock orientation in favor of smart pop. "Better Days" takes the group deep into **U2** territory, complete with anthemic Bono-esque vocals. "Lovin' Kindness" steals from Elton John's "Wrap Her Up" but does so with a flair that makes it one of the record's highlights. "Way of the Cross" is not terribly interesting musically but represents a high point theologically. Its lyrics (by Jerry Davison) relate numerous instances in which Jesus challenged convention ("He gave the keys of the kingdom to the meek and the mild / He told self-righteous grown-ups to act like a child").

Digging Up Bones offers all five songs from the band's original custom EP plus demo versions of other songs that will only interest major fans. *Sampler Pack* is a greatest hits collection spoiled by poor song selection and the inclusion of extended monologues from concerts that don't hold up to repeated listening. In 2000, Davison was playing in a band called Sideways8, which covered the **Daniel Amos** song "Hold Back the Wind, Donna" for a tribute album to that band (*When Worlds Collide,* Ferris Wheel, 2000).

JAG

John Allen Garies, voc., gtr.; et al. 1980—*The Longest Road* (Wave); 1991—*The Only World in Town* (Benson); 1992—*Fire in the Temple.*

The Christian rock band JAG took its name from the initials of its front man, John Allen Garies. The group's debut album was well received, albeit with complaints that JAG sounded very much like **White Heart.** Garies himself would later say the record is "best forgotten" with the exception of the song "Shake It Off," which brought him to the attention of producer Billy Smiley (of **White Heart**). JAG found more of its own sound on *The Only World in Town,* which features the Journeyesque arena rockers "Two Worlds Collide" and "Mastermind." *CCM* also identified "Hands in the Air" as "a sure-fire crowd pleaser, with splendid guitar hooks, nah-nah vocals, and an unforgettable chorus."

Jagged Doctrine

Gary Baker, voc., elec.; Rod Middleton, gtr., bass, voc. 1998—*I Wear the Mask* (Side A); 1999—*Welcome to the Playground* (mp3.com).

The definitively independent group known as Jagged Doctrine is made up of two anonymous musicians from Ohio. They play industrial metal music that has gotten them noticed in *Phantom Tollbooth* and other outlets. *I Wear the Mask* includes a cover of the **Dead Artist Syndrome** song, "Red," and in general, expresses angry sentiments that employ such atypical lyrics as "I hate you in Jesus' name." The song "Analogy" is about the spiritual dissatisfaction that led Kurt Cobain to commit suicide. *Welcome to the Playground* has a cleaner sound overall and features prominent use of guitars. "Skin Doctors" is reminiscent thematically of Paul Westerberg's "Mannequin Shop," a sarcastic commentary on cosmetic surgery ("Yeah, you might be looking good, but how's your soul and mind?"). "Prepared to Die" asks the simple question, "If this world goes under, am I prepared to die?" In early 1999, editors of *Rolling Stone* listed Jagged Doctrine as one of their "Top Five Unsigned Bands."

Sarah Jahn

1995—*Sarah Jahn* (independent); 1997—*Sparkle* (Warner Alliance).

Sarah Jahn is an alternative folk singer from Wood River, Illinois, and a living testimony that there must be something special about Greenville College. In 1994 a group of students from that college performing under the name **Jars of Clay** won the Gospel Music Association's Spotlight Competition, garnering immediate attention from record companies. Exactly one year later, Sarah Jahn—classmate and friend of the Jars boys at Greenville—won the 1995 GMA Spotlight Competition, again drawing industry attention that led to a contract. Jahn's style is often compared to such general market artists as Jewel or Sarah McLachlan and, as with those singers, the quality of her performance is largely driven by the songs themselves. Her debut album on Warner Alliance is noteworthy for featuring the most unflattering cover design of any record in the history of Christian music, surpassing even the famous "ugly cover" issued and then withdrawn for **Amy Grant**'s first release. The disc itself recapitulates five songs from an earlier independent album and adds five new ones. Jahn's husky voice fits the material like a glove. Three songs are particularly worthy of note. "Paradox" offers a biblical perspective on the positive role of doubt rarely evident in Christian music: "I can trust the Lord with all my might / In the light of what I know / But if I close the door on doubt I find / That the light can never grow." "Crucible" draws on the metaphor of a melting pot to speak of soul-cleansing: "Building a fire / To melt this heart of stone / With a love that burns the flesh / But chills me to the bone." The song "Chronic" describes the plight of Jahn's mother who has suffered from chronic fatigue syndrome for many years: "No more tears / No more prayers / I'm still living with the enemy / It's inside of me / I want to be healed." *Nashville Scene* magazine called *Sparkle* "one of the finest pop albums to come out of Nashville in 1997."

Christian radio hits: "Drinking Water" (# 6 in 1998).

Jai Anguish

2000—*Automata* (Blue Bunny).

The artist who calls himself Jai Anguish founded an independent paper called *Flygirl* around 1992 when he was a sophomore in high school and watched it grow into one of the more popular independent "zines" in the next few years. Soon, *Flygirl* was a sixty-four-page publication filled with Jai Anguish's critically lauded prose and deft photography. The general topic or theme was intersection of faith and the indie culture of art and music. Eventually *Flygirl* made the leap to the Internet. Anguish is, as *Bandoppler* says, "a postmodern renaissance man." In 2000, he released an album of "experimental noise" music, playing guitars, piano, toys, and drum machines, while singing softly about intimate and spiritual subjects. On "Jesus Song" he sings incessantly about having Jesus in his heart. *Phantom Tollbooth* comments, "The mainstream Christian culture will have a hard time relating to his repetitive tracks, . . . but the monotony is his genius. Rather than take you on a journey, Jai just lets you enjoy the place where you are."

Jake

Josh Penner; Marty Penner; Toby Penner. 2000—*Jake* (Reunion); announced for 2002—*Army of Love*.

A Canadian "boy band" with adult contemporary leanings, Jake is composed of three brothers (Marty and Josh Penner are twins). The music on their self-titled debut album is described as "hooky, pop-influenced stuff" that, despite the obvious Hanson comparisons, seems to aim more for the **4 Him** market. The song "Melt Me" offers a metaphor for Christian sanctification, with driving guitars and minor-key harmonies effectively creating an image appropriate to the title. "Waiting," which has a distinct **Jars of Clay** sound, is about prayer and patience. Many songs just deal with issues of concern to teenagers, such as dating and future dreams, with no explicit religious content. The song "Let Me Know" was a hit on Canadian radio, which does not segregate Christian and secular music in ways that are common in the United States.

Christian radio hits: "The Right Time" (# 11 in 2001); "The One" (# 12 in 2001).

Michael James (a.k.a. Michael James Murphy)

As Michael James Murphy: 1981—*Never Let Me Go* (Milk and Honey); 1983—*Surrender*; 1984—*Tender Heart*; 1986—*No Kidnap Today* (Home Sweet Home); 1990—*The Chisel* (Diadem). As Michael James: 1992—*Shoulder to the Wind* (Reunion); 1993—*Closer to the Fire*; 1995—*Where Love Runs Deep*.

Michael James is a honey-voiced "positive country" singer closely connected with the Promise Keepers organization. Born Michael James Murphy in 1959, the singer was raised in the ranching and farming community of Matador, Texas, in a family that prized the faith and brought him up to do the same. Professionally, he has had two incarnations. He began performing as a pop singer in the '80s, using his full name, Michael James Murphy, to distinguish himself from the popular general market artist Michael Murphy (who had a # 3 hit with "Wildfire" in 1975). This was, of course, insufficient and continuing confusions inspired the latter artist to start using *his* full name, Michael Martin Murphy, in 1984. That still wasn't enough and problems persisted until the Christian artist just gave it up and adopted the professional name Michael James in the '90s. The name change coincided with a transition to country music. James credits **Gary Chapman** with helping him come to a point of spiritual restoration that also refocused his energies toward family life. The overt theme of his three country albums is family values. *Closer to the Fire* features assistance from **Amy Grant, Susan Ashton, Michael Omartian,** and others. The song "Family Tree" looks at the beginning of a couple's relationship, and "Weather the Storm" examines the struggles they encounter later. *Tender Heart* offers a number of songs that focus on Christ's victory over evil ("Believers," "The Darker the Night," "I Have Returned") and has a strong worship orientation. The self-produced *Where Love Runs Deep* has been particularly well received. "A Promise to Keep" offers a pledge of commitment to marriage and family that could almost serve as the Promise Keepers' theme song. "Love Waits" is an ode to premarital celibacy, and "The Power of Forgiveness" extols the benefits of absolution and mercy. James has written songs for general market country artists Lee Greenwood and Highway 101.

Christian radio hits: As Michael James Murphy: "Surrender" (# 14 in 1983); "Every Single Step" (# 11 in 1984); "Believers" (# 2 in 1985).

Dove Awards: 1995 Country Song ("Love Will"); 1996 Country Album (*Where Love Runs Deep*).

Rick James

No Christian recordings.

www.rickjames.com

Funk superstar and all-around bad boy Rick James shocked the world with news of a conversion to Christ in 1987, though his subsequent music and behavior offered little in demonstration of this. In September 1987 James told *Rock and Soul* magazine that he had become "a Super Freak for Jesus." He explained that the conversion had come as the result of an extended telephone conversation with the mother of the girl about whom he had written the song "Seventeen and Sexy." He said, "One night when I was alone in my bedroom, after talking to her, I got on my knees and asked Jesus to come into my heart and into my life. I felt such an incredible feeling. I went to sleep and I remember waking up and I was just so happy. I felt the old Rick James was dead and there was a new Rick James, born of Jesus Christ."

James came to prominence in the '70s with songs that drew on the soul-funk traditions of Sly Stone and George Clinton (Funkadelic/Parliament). He only had two major hits on the pop charts ("You and I," # 13 in 1978; "Superfreak," # 16 in 1981), but was a major fixture on the R&B charts throughout the late '70s and into the mid '80s. James' influence was felt in other ways as well. In 1983, he presented the world with a group called the Mary Jane Girls, a trio of sexy women who sang songs that he wrote and produced for them. James also wrote and produced Eddie Murphy's hit single "Party All the Time" (# 2 in 1985). His song "Superfreak" enjoyed something of a comeback when rapper **M.C. Hammer** re-recorded it with new words as "U Can't Touch This" (# 8 in 1990).

James' music and stage shows were notable for their obsession with sexuality, debauchery, and violence. James seemed to work at cultivating his image as a bad boy but much of it came naturally. Born in 1948, he had been raised by a single mother who ran a numbers racket in Buffalo, New York. He was expelled from five different schools before finally quitting the system at the age of fifteen. In 1987, James declared, "Before I knew Jesus I was an employee of the fallen angel, Satan. I worked for him, and he literally had me, like he's had so many people. I accepted all of his gifts—drugs, alcohol, sexuality. He's the father of all lies and trickery." James did not make any new recordings subsequent to his conversion (though one album that was already in the can was released in 1988). He did not continue to talk about his new life, and in 1991 he was arrested on charges of sexual battery and assault. He and a female accomplice were accused of molesting and torturing two young women who had refused to engage in group sex with them. James admitted that he was a cocaine addict and that he had attacked the women while on a drug binge. Convicted, he was sentenced to five years in prison. In liner notes to a greatest hits compilation (*Bustin' Out: The Very Best of Rick James,* Motown, 1994) he said that he had been addicted to drugs for thirty-five years and indicated that the prison term was benefi-

cial in that it forced him into rehabilitation. There was, however, no more talk of Christianity. Soon after his release from prison, James recorded one more album (*Urban Rhapsody,* Mercury, 1997). In 1998, he suffered a stroke while performing on stage.

For trivia buffs: In 1966, James formed a band in Toronto called The Mynah Birds. At that time, he was AWOL from the Navy and living in Canada under the name Ricky Matthews. The Mynah Birds included James (Matthews), Bruce Palmer, Goldy McJohn, and a twenty-one-year-old Neil Young. Palmer would later play in Buffalo Springfield, McJohn would become a member of Steppenwolf, and Young would of course become a rock legend. The Mynah Birds did in fact record songs for Motown that, incredibly, have never been released.

Janny

See **Janny Grein.**

Jars of Clay

Dan Haseltine, voc.; Charlie Lowell, kybrd.; Steve Mason, gtr.; Matt Odmark, gtr., voc. 1994—*Frail* (independent); 1995—*Jars of Clay* (Essential); 1997—*Much Afraid;* 1999—*If I Left the Zoo;* 2002—*The Eleventh Hour* (Essential).

www.jarsofclay.com

Jars of Clay created a crisis for college radio stations in 1996 when their hot single "Flood" broke nationwide a few months before word got out that they were a Christian band. Embarrassed radio stations (some of which have unofficial policies against playing Christian music) were left to decide whether to pull the song or just treat it as some kind of a fluke. In at least one major city, the station that served as official sponsor for the group's concert did not even bother to send personnel to the show after a full-page newspaper article "outed" the band as Christians a few days earlier.

Jars of Clay is Christian music's undisputed best instance of an alternative rock band that fits loosely into the same category as groups like Gin Blossoms, Matchbox 20, and the Dave Matthews Band. The term "alterna-folk" was virtually coined to describe their self-titled album, to set it apart from associations of the "alternative" label with the Seattle grunge sound. The roots for their sound lie more in such "Americanized Beatles" bands as The Byrds, Big Star, Bread, and America. Dan Haseltine's Barry Gibb/Fine Young Cannibals vocals and poetic approach to composition often make the group sound like the Bee Gees doing R.E.M. songs—a frightening description of a phenomenon that actually does work. Put it this way: Jars combines the intelligent songwriting of R.E.M. at its best (think "Losing My Religion" not "What's the Frequency, Kenneth") with the Gibbs' vocal sensibilities at *their* best (think

"Words" not "Too Much Heaven"). By any objective standard, Jars of Clay would have to be regarded as one of the ten best alternative rock outfits in America during the late '90s, yet during that time *Rolling Stone* did not publish a single article or interview regarding them—not even a review of their work. The only exception to this shut-out would be brief mention of the group in an article on the 1996 Jesus Northwest Christian rock festival that a) referred to sixteen-year-old girls gushing over "the members of Jars of Clay, who could double as *Friends* stand-ins" and b) offered a stupid comment about "Flood," cited below. Otherwise, the group's double-platinum album *Jars of Clay* and sensational crossover success were completely ignored. *Rolling Stone* does tip its hat occasionally to such artists as **DC Talk** and **Kirk Franklin,** whose gospel-drenched hollerings are presented as something of a novelty. But Jars of Clay represent something far more disconcerting—a Christian group that does not primarily sing about Christ. Like the equally ignored **Sixpence None the Richer,** they seem to think of faith as something that applies to matters outside of church and Sunday morning—and the implications of *that* notion are terribly disturbing to the mindset that often underwrites the rock and roll industry and its media. Jars of Clay have less in common with **DC Talk** and **Kirk Franklin** than they do with **T Bone Burnett** and **Bruce Cockburn** with one very important qualification: they do not appear to espouse the liberal political pieties that endear those Christian exceptions to the mainstream rock journalists. Still, the group has resisted the obtuse fundamentalism and questionable Arminianism that infuses most of the contemporary Christian music scene; rather, they evince an informed grace-oriented perspective that is more in line with global and historic Christianity, particularly that of the Protestant Reformation. In late 1999, *Christianity Today* did a cover story on the band, dubbing them "a rock group that Luther and Calvin could love."

The group came together at Greenville College in Greenville, Illinois, where the four members met as students. The school actually has a contemporary Christian music *department* and sponsors a number of school groups in which the Jars members all played. Haseltine and Steve Mason first discovered their common musical bond when the latter wore a Toad the Wet Sprocket T-shirt to class. While students, the group gained local notoriety for a techno song called "Fade to Grey" (later on *Much Afraid*), for an unconventional version of "Little Drummer Boy" (released on two different singles in 1995 [Essential] and in 1997 [Silvertone]), and for a never-recorded version of "Rudolph the Red-Nosed Reindeer," which they had adapted to fit the tune of Nirvana's "Smells Like Teen Spirit." Their name derives from 2 Corinthians 4:7 and refers to the frailty of the human condition, which nevertheless contains the incredible treasure of life—the Apostle Paul says human beings are like earthen vessels (jars of clay) containing a precious treasure—the Spirit of God. While still at Greenville, the group recorded an independent demo album, *Frail,* that includes the original take of what remains their best song ("Frail," later on *Much Afraid*). Their performance of that song at the 1994 Gospel Music Association's Spotlight Competition for New Artists wowed industry executives in an unprecedented way. The group won the competition and came home with contract offers from a variety of labels. They chose Essential, which has distribution through Silvertone to general market outlets. College exams were ditched in favor of a life on the road, and the group soon became the most popular Christian band in the world. They have performed as the opening act for Sting and have toured with a number of other general market acts. A headlining tour with The Samples as *their* opening act did not work out so well—audience complaints about the latter group's use of profanity led to a midtour mutual decision to split the bill.

The song "Flood" was produced by Adrian Belew (of the classic rock band King Crimson—see listing on **Rick Altizer**) and is certainly one of Christian music's finest moments. The song itself is great and Belew manages to get the group's performance of it just right, adding tasteful strings and getting Matt Odmark to play that acoustic guitar like his life (as opposed to simply his career) depended on what he did in that particular moment. The song rocks with more passion than anything else the group has done. Its opening riff is now a classic and Haseltine's plaintive vocals at the midpoint are but a prelude to the sudden, shouted, counterpoint chorus that occupies the final sixty seconds before Odmark pummels his instrument into submission with merciless concluding fury. The song would eventually chart at Number Thirty-seven on *Billboard*'s general pop chart, but it went to Number Two on what is called the Triple A radio chart (Adult Album Alternative) for college stations. "Flood" was nominated for the Grammy award for best rock song (*not* "contemporary gospel song"—the category used later for the not-very-gospel track "Unforgetful You"). It was subsequently featured on the soundtrack for the film *Hard Rain* and was used in advertisements for Coca Cola. Lyrically, "Flood" describes the desperation of feeling out of control, of being overwhelmed spiritually and emotionally to the point that one cries out (to God or whoever is there) for ambiguous assistance: "Lift me up / Keep me from drowning." *Rolling Stone* trivialized the song's content by observing snidely that "before many programmers or listeners realized [the group was Christian], alternative rock's first nod to Noah and his ark had climbed into the Top 20." This comment is obtuse for at least two reasons: One, the very alternative **Violent Femmes** had done a song explicitly about Noah and his ark ("It's Gonna Rain") that was all over college radio a decade earlier. Two, the song "Flood" is not about Noah or his ark but merely alludes to the biblical tale in an off-hand way ("I can't swim after forty days"). Still, the journal's tacit admission that the song would never have gotten airplay if "programmers and listeners" had known the performers were Christians represents a rare and revealing moment of candor.

In addition to "Flood," the eponymous album contains the masterful "Liquid," also produced by Belew. The song opens with what may be rock music's most stirring violin solo followed by a cascading blend of percussion and vocal harmonies supplemented by samples of Benedictine chanting. Lyrically, "Liquid" treats the subject of Christ's crucifixion: "Blood stained brow / He wasn't broken for nothing / Arms nailed down / He didn't die for nothing." The next song, "Sinking," is a more subdued alterna-pop song in the style that Matchbox 20 would later use on hits like "3 A.M." and "Jumper" (Matchbox first toured as an opening act for Jars of Clay and was rather obviously influenced by the band's sound). The well-named "Love Song for a Savior" is a modern hippie-folk song expressing the desire to embrace the kind of simple piety that was evident during the Jesus movement. It is a beautiful song, sustained by a flowing melody and lots of appropriate la-la-las. The song "Like a Child" offers a similar sentiment (yearning for simple faith) couched in a rhythmic presentation propelled by mandolin, fiddle, and recorder. The song "He" takes an abrupt turn thematically to treat the dark subject of child abuse. "Worlds Apart" features the memorable lyric, "What I believe and what I need are worlds apart." All in all, *Jars of Clay* is a near-perfect album, a cohesive collection of strong material and stellar performances. There is not a mediocre song on it. In 2001, a critics' poll sponsored by *CCM* put *Jars of Clay* on their list of "The 100 Greatest Christian Music Albums of All Time." They placed the album at Number Twenty-two, a position that is certainly too low.

Providing a follow-up for such a triumph was a daunting prospect, and Jars wisely waited a full two years to let some of the hype die down. Belew was not associated with *Much Afraid,* and since he was largely credited with the critical and commercial success of the previous album's twin masterpieces ("Flood," "Liquid"), apprehension was high as to whether the Jars could pull it off on their own. For *Much Afraid,* they engaged Steve Lipson, known for his work with **Simple Minds,** Annie Lennox, and Whitney Houston. *Much Afraid* was not the commercial blockbuster that *Jars of Clay* was, but it did go platinum, selling over a million copies. The title of the album is taken from the name of a character in Hannah Hurnard's spiritual classic *Hinds' Feet on High Places,* which inspires the project's theme: total dependence on an unmerited grace that shatters the expectations of people whose lives are broken and frail. Musically, the album is slicker and more polished than its

predecessor, more adult pop in the vein of Sting or Seal than edgy, alternative rock. The songs tend to be quieter and more contemplative; while there is nothing with the commercial hit potential of the two tracks Belew produced for *Jars of Clay,* a number of songs are actually more worthy of extended listening. The aforementioned "Frail" is the album's centerpiece and highlight. Clocking in at almost seven minutes, it employs intriguing instrumentation (acoustic guitar notes and primal percussion fronting a chamber orchestra) in a way that is both captivating and beguiling. Haseltine's vocals are also more confident here (and throughout this album) than on prior work. *Much Afraid*'s concession to radio pop is the infectious "Crazy Times" (which was played on college radio stations but failed to register on mainstream pop charts). The Beatlesque "Overjoyed" has a similarly winsome quality. At the other end of the musical spectrum, "Tea and Sympathy" is more courtly than catchy, setting some of Haseltine's most evocative blank verse to a quiet melody. The song caught the attention of thoughtful critics for its sensitive, if obscure treatment of heartbreak; *True Tunes* thinks it seeks to "explore the emotional strings of marital infidelity," but no one really seems to know what it's about. "Fade to Black" employs eerie organ and a pulsating bass in a song about insecurity and doubt. "Five Candles" was originally written for the Jim Carey film, *Liar, Liar;* it offers a child's cry for his father's affection (the principal theme of that film). It was rejected for the movie, but turned up later on the soundtrack to *Jack Frost,* which actually had the same theme. The album closes with a lovely "Hymn" with lyrics that recall the poetry of another era: "Sweet Jesus, carry me away / From cold of night and dust of day / In ragged hour or salt worn eye / Be my desire, my well spring lye."

For their third major outing, Jars was determined to break with what was becoming a predictable sound for them and hired producer Dennis Herring (Counting Crows, Cracker) to help them "think outside the box." *If I Left the Zoo* evinces a more Deep South sound than the previous projects, with touches of blues and the influence of such southern artists as Wilco and Lucinda Williams popping up here and there. Ben Mize of Counting Crows plays drums on several tracks. The very title of the album (a play on the Dr. Seuss book *If I Ran the Zoo*) suggests the idea of release from a security that is also confining. True to this concept, the boys do take some risks. The opening song, "Goodbye, Goodnight" sounds like a *Sgt. Pepper's* outtake and features a mock sea shanty chorus. Lyrically, it expresses the supposed attitude of the *Titanic*'s string quartet that played on while the ship sank: "Strike up the band to play a song / And try hard not to cry / And fake a smile as we all say goodbye." This was sung with an eye to the Y2K hysteria that attended the turn of millennia. "Sad Clown" is set to a slightly out-of-tune saloon-dirge piano and has memorable do-do-do background vocals that make it an aural highlight. "Hand" recalls Mason's T-shirt band, Toad the Wet Sprocket, but is built lyrically on a quotation from Frederick Buechner. "Unforgetful You" is *Zoo's* "Crazy Times," a radio-friendly number that nevertheless doesn't sound quite like anything heard on the radio before. *Jesus Freak Hideout* styles it as "elevated alternative rock with quirky musical components." The song was featured on the soundtrack for the film *Drive Me Crazy.* "I'm Alright" is a soulful song that effectively employs a gospel choir in a rocking, satirical look at denial. "Collide" is the group's hardest rocking song to date, allowing Mason's considerable talents with an *electric* guitar to come to the fore. Lyrically, the song is about the seemingly eternal quest for the meaning of true love ("I collide with love as an elusive state of mine / I know there's something else it's supposed to be"). Again, the album closes with a quiet hymn: "River Constantine" is a prayer to the Holy Spirit to "come down, pour out on me." Critics were virtually unanimous in identifying *Zoo's* variations on the Jar's folk-rock sound as making it "their strongest effort to date" and even without a hit single, the album managed to go platinum. Somewhat ironically, *Playboy* magazine chose *If I Left the Zoo* as its recommended Album of the Month at the start of 2000, and for thirty days featured it right next to a topless Miss January on their website—complete with hyperlinks to *CCM* magazine.

The band's 2002 release *The Eleventh Hour* would be their first self-produced effort and, in general, it evokes the sound and spirit of an intimate coffeehouse setting. This is especially apparent on the worshipful ballad "I Need You," which features an acoustic melody line reminiscent of **Sixpence None the Richer.** But "Revolution" features abrasive guitars, tribal drumming, and an uncharacteristic vocal challenge for hearers to confront injustice and "be a revolution" in the world.

Jars of Clay has also recorded songs for a couple of various-artist compilation albums: "Headstrong" for *Roaring Lambs* (Squint, 2000) and "Everything in Between" for *The Prince of Egypt—Inspirational* (Dreamworks, 1998). The latter project paired them with producer Mark Hudson (of the '70s combo, The Hudson Brothers). The group also contributed the song "The Chair" to the soundtrack of the film *The Long Kiss Goodnight.* A few otherwise unavailable songs were released on a free *White Elephant Sessions* disc distributed through their fan club in 2000. They also released a song called "This Road" as a tribute to persecuted Christians worldwide in late 2000 and early the next year partnered with Amnesty International in a program to protect all forms of religious freedom. The band performed a free concert to celebrate Amnesty International's Fortieth Anniversary and issued a press statement declaring, "Whether Christian, Buddhist, Hindu, or Muslim, the persecution of those whose faith is different than others is one of the greatest forms of injustice."

For trivia buffs: When Jars of Clay first caught the wave of national exposure, the band members all agreed upon a no dating policy for two years during which everyone would concentrate completely on the band's success. This did not work out very well, and by the end of the period all four members were engaged or married.

Christian radio hits: "Flood" (# 4 in 1995); "Love Song for a Savior" (# 1 in 1995); "Like a Child" (# 2 in 1995); "Liquid" (# 1 in 1996); "Blind" (# 3 in 1996); "Crazy Times" (# 1 in 1997); "Five Candles (You Were There)" (# 1 in 1998); "Fade to Grey" (# 1 in 1998); "Overjoyed" (# 1 for 2 weeks in 1998); "Needful Hands" (# 4 in 1999); "Everything in Between" (# 4 in 1999); "Unforgetful You" (# 1 for 5 weeks in 1999); "Collide" (# 1 for 2 weeks in 2000); "I'm Alright" (# 2 in 2000); "Can't Erase It" (# 6 in 2001).

Dove Awards: 1996 New Artist of the Year; 1997 Group of the Year; 1998 Group of the Year; 2000 Alternative/Modern Rock Song ("Unforgetful You").

Grammy Awards: 1997 Best Pop/Contemporary Gospel Album *(Much Afraid)*; 2000 Best Pop/Contemporary Gospel Album *(If I Left the Zoo).*

Jason and the G-Men

Jason Harms, voc., gtr.; Isaac Harms, drums; Jesse Harms, bass; et al. (including at times Paul Babcock, drums; Jeff Brueske, gtr.; Rick Corliss, drums; Christopher Fashun, vibes; Dean Kleven, kybrd.; Don Stille, kybrd.). 1994—*Walkin' the Beat* (independent); 1996—*"G" as in Men* (Pauly); 1999—*Swing Hard, Swing Often* (True Tunes).

Jason and the G-Men may be Christian music's answer to Harry Connick Jr. Fronted by Jason Harms, the group seems intent on bringing about a revival of the dance-hall jazz sound once made popular by such artists as Frank Sinatra and Tony Bennett. The group's first album, *Walkin' the Beat,* includes a mixture of standards ("Count Your Blessings," "Jericho") and hymns ("Turn Your Radio On"), along with a few Harms originals (the standout "Hurry"). *True Tunes* notes that *"G" as in Men* represents "significant growth" for the band, though again all but two of the songs are standards. The album was recorded live to obtain an authentic lounge atmosphere complete with audience response. The same is true of *Swing Hard, Swing Often,* which *Phantom Tollbooth* chose as their "Pick of the Month" in April 1999. The latter album includes only one overtly Christian tune, the spiritual "Here's One" ("Talk about a man who do love Jesus, here's one"). Otherwise, the G-Men get down on show tunes like "Lida Rose" and "Surrey with the Fringe on Top," as well as with several original tunes and with traditional numbers like "Sixteen Tons."

B. B. Jay

2000—*Universal Condition* (Verity).

Christian rap artist B. B. Jay hails from Brooklyn and has a style comparable to that of another Brooklyn native, the late

Biggie Smalls. Jay seems to aim his music for the street culture rather than for the church, but his debut album *Universal Condition* finds him drawing on African American preaching traditions with lyrics that contrast the harsh reality of life apart from Christ with the perspective of faith. "For the Ladies" is something of an apology for the denigration of women that has been so prevalent in the rap music culture. The album's title track and "Out of Control" are more soulful R&B songs that provide momentary breaks from an otherwise incessant stream of old-school rapping.

J.C. and the Boyz

David "M.C. Scroller" Guzman, rap voc.; et al. 1989—*Never Give Up* (Broken); 1992—*Chill 4 Awhile* (Ocean).

A creative project of rapper David Guzman, J.C. and the Boyz is the rare rap group devoted to "blessing the bloods in the barrios," as *CCM* puts it. In other words, their music and ministry is focused on Latin American youth rather than on the urban blacks stereotypically associated with most rap music. The group nevertheless includes African American vocalists Sandra Stephens, Allegra Parks, and Teresa Williams. *CCM* regarded *Chill 4 Awhile* as a major improvement over the group's first album, classifying the musical style as "new-school freestyle" in the vein of general market performers like Lissette Melendez and Coro. The group covers the reggae tune "Try Jah Love," originally performed by Third World.

J.C. and Friends

See **First Call.**

J.C. Power Outlet (and **Pantano-Salsbury**)

John Pantano, gtr.; Ron Salsbury, gtr., voc.; Greg Prough, bass (−1977); Rick Frye, drums (−1974) // Bruce Neal, drums (+ 1974, −1977). By J.C. Power Outlet: 1972—*Ron Salsbury and the J.C. Power Outlet* (Myrrh); 1974—*Forgiven.* By Pantano-Salsbury: 1977—*Hit the Switch* (Solid Rock).

Pioneer Jesus music band J.C. Power Outlet was the first Christian group to gain widespread exposure for a (limited) hard rock sound. The band was not as cutting edge as groups like **Agape** or **Barnabas** but perhaps for that reason attracted a wider audience. A California outfit, their music often seemed quite radical compared to the Calvary Chapel sounds of **Love Song** or **Children of the Day.** The band was led by Ron Salsbury, who had some preconversion success with a general market band called Train (not to be confused with the group that performed "Meet Virginia" thirty years later). *Ron Salsbury and the J.C. Power Outlet* is notoriously sloppy, though, as some fans attest; that was and still is part of its charm. *Jesus Music*

calls it "raw, unpolished, high-energy rock-and-roll for Jesus . . . images of shaggy-haired Jesus freaks with big ol' goony grins are immediately conjured." Actually, the rocking numbers are only the most memorable moments—the album mixes these with a good number of acoustic ballads. The standout track is a righteous version of **Andraé Crouch**'s "Satisfied." *Forgiven* became famous for its album cover—featured on the cover of an early issue of *Harmony* magazine (vol. 1, no. 3). The picture is a simple photograph of an apple with a band-aid taping a bite that has been taken out of it back into place. This symbol of restoration struck a chord with many, regardless of whether they were fans of the band's music. Actually, the notion of atonement as a band-aid on sin is theologically limited, if not heretical—the Bible portrays Christ as "making all things new" (2 Corinthians 5:7) not just patching up what has been spoiled. Nevertheless, the music on *Forgiven* is noticeably tighter and more professional than the first album. Again, the record mixes hard rock with ballads. One of the latter, "I Choose to Follow You," became the group's best-known song due in part to its inclusion on a widely distributed compilation album called *Jubilation* (Myrrh, 1975). The song is a well-deserved hit, but "Peace and Power" and "My Sign" (an antiastrology anthem proclaiming "*my* sign is a blood-stained cross") should not be overlooked. "Don't Let Jesus Pass You By" also received a lot of attention among the Jesus people.

After recording the second album, **David Edwards** replaced Greg Prough on bass. Then in 1975, the group disbanded as Edwards and Bruce Neal left for other pursuits. Edwards would reappear a few years later as one of Christian music's first new-wave artists. Meanwhile, Pantano and Salsbury decided to continue as a duo. In what seems an incredibly naive stance, Pantano told *Harmony* magazine that the absence of a rhythm section shouldn't make much difference to their sound because "when people clap with us, they keep the beat and that's what the drums are all about." In any case, J.C. Power Outlet had attracted the attention of **Larry Norman** and he signed the remnant duo to his fledgling Solid Rock label. Their album, *Hit the Switch* features songs by Pantano, though "I'm Just a Record" was cowritten with Norman. Overall the mood is much more mellow, soft rock ("Soul Seeker," "Hold On") at its best and pablum pop at its worst.

For trivia buffs: Before forming J.C. Power Outlet, Pantano and Salsbury recorded a few songs with **Larry Norman** that later ended up on his classic *Bootleg* album.

Gordon Jensen

1976—*Gordon Jensen and Sunrise* (Rocketland); 1979—*Gordon Jensen* (Impact); 1980—*Gallery*; 1983—*Just in Time* (DaySpring); *Grace upon Grace*; 1984—*Fighting the Fight*; 1987—*Tuesdays and Thursdays* (Wordsong).

Gordon Jensen is an unabashed purveyor of MOR music, singing easy listening songs with subtle shadings of country, folk, or extremely soft rock. Critics have not been particularly kind to his out-of-vogue style. *CCM* calls one album "not adventurous or risky"; another, "pedestrian"; and a third, "trite and colloquial." Still, Jensen evinces the appeal of a bygone era, recalling the folk Christian stylings of **Ray Repp** and the vocal delivery of Roger Whittaker. *Just in Time* betrays a sense of humor with "I'll Break the Law of Gravity Someday." *Fighting the Fight* draws on buoyant southern gospel for "Joy in the Journey" and features a splendid ballad, "In the Beauty of Holiness." On *Tuesdays and Thursdays,* Jensen worked with producer David Hungate (formerly with the rock band Toto), who he says "coaxed him into some new territory." The album includes "You're the Only Jesus," a cover of one of **The Imperials**' weaker songs, and "Not Ashamed," a cheap shot at Christian singers who have a wholistic approach to life and ministry: "Singin' songs about love and freedom / It's Christian music, so they say / But I really wonder where it all is heading / When it seems I never hear His name." The notion that only songs that mention Christ by name should be considered Christian is theologically bankrupt, and the implication that Christians only sing about such things as love and freedom (or family or friends or anything else that might matter to them) because they are "ashamed of Jesus" is appalling.

Jerusalem

Ulf Christiansson, voc., gtr.; Dan Tibell, kybrd. (– 1994; + 1997); Klas Anderhell, drums (– 1984, + 1997); Anders Mossberg, bass (– 1982, + 1997) // Peter Carlsohn, bass (+ 1982, –1997); Michael Ulvsgärd, drums (+ 1984, – 1997); Reider Paulsen, kybrd. (+ 1994, – 1997). 1978—*Jerusalem* [a.k.a. *Vol. 1*] (Lamb and Lion); 1981—*Vol. 2*; 1982—*Warrior*; 1984—*Can't Stop Us Now*; 1985—*In His Majesty's Service (Live in U.S.A.)* (Refuge); 1988—*Dancing on the Head of the Serpent*; 1989—*Ten Years Later* (Pure Metal); 1994—*Prophet* (Viva); 1997—*Those Were the Days* (Alliance); 1998—*R.A.D.*

www.jerusalem.se/eng

Heroes of Christian metal, the Swedish hard rock band Jerusalem paved the way for heavier sounds in Christian music internationally in the same way that groups like **Resurrection Band** did in America. The band played more heavy rock than metal (think Deep Purple), but without Jerusalem, groups like **Stryper**—much less **Bride, Guardian,** or **Tourniquet**—seem unthinkable. **Ulf Christiansson** (b. 1949) founded the group in 1975 for the explicitly evangelistic purpose of reaching young people for Christ. Concerts often took on the air of fundamentalist revival meetings with Christiansson preaching between the songs, giving altar calls and even, sometimes, performing exorcisms. "I've been doing warfare with the music and getting demons out of young people," he told *HM* in 1992.

"If we can't learn to cast devils out of people, we will never, ever have the revival we're looking for." Still, the band was met with widespread resistance in its own land, where they were essentially the first Christian rock band. There, as in America, hard rock tended to be associated with drugs, violence, and Satanism. Jerusalem's ear-splitting songs were deemed inappropriate vehicles for the gospel and many Christian organizations tried to keep those songs from being heard.

Three years of touring and demon-fighting preceded the first album, originally released on the adventurous Swedish label Prism. It sold a phenomenal 20,000 copies within six months, opening the floodgates for what was to follow. After recording the follow-up *Volume 2,* the band toured European markets (Germany, France, Belgium) and then played the *Greenbelt* Christian festival in England. Musically, both of these first two albums suffer from poor production standards. Christiansson would later say that they made the records with a producer of traditional Christian music who didn't understand or appreciate rock. In addition, all of the songs were originally sung in Swedish, but for the American releases English vocals were somewhat artificially overdubbed. Christiansson also apologizes for the embarrassing quality of his translations, since at that time the group could not afford to hire a professional to advise them on such matters. *CCM* would still describe the music as "relentless and forceful," singling out such tracks as "Wake Up" and "Rock and Roll" from *Volume 2* for honorable mention.

Jerusalem's American debut came about through **Pat Boone,** who learned of the band through **Glenn Kaiser** and decided to release both of Jerusalem's initial albums on his own Lamb and Lion label, introducing the band to the considerable American market. Tours of the United States (with **Resurrection Band** and as **Larry Norman**'s backing band) followed, and the subsequent, acclaimed *Warrior* topped Christian sales charts. *Warrior* is often praised as the band's finest work. The title track calls Christians to "fight for God," knowing that the victory is already won. "Sodom" is a twelve-minute epic decrying worldly culture ("Sodom is Sweden / Sodom is Europe / Sodom is America"). In 2000, *True Tunes'* John J. Thompson would say, "*Warrior* stands as one of the finest Christian hard rock albums ever. The production was thick, the lyrics challenging, and the vocal and guitar work devastating." With *Can't Stop Us Now,* Jerusalem took a much more melodic turn, releasing a consumer-friendly album that in some respects previews Christiansson's solo work. The music is still guitar driven and riff heavy, but imbued with more sensibilities, some of which are reflected in a new use of synthesizers. The group's "enmity with the world" so evident on previous projects is also moderated somewhat in favor of a more congenial message of encouragement and hope. Standout songs are "Let's Go (Dancin')" and "Loves You More."

In 1985, the band took a break while the members enrolled in the Word of Life Bible school in Uppsala. After a year of studies, they made *Dancing on the Head of the Serpent,* a controversial album directed against the growing tide of occultism in Sweden. The cover of the album features a picture of a demonic creature being crushed beneath a large boot—though without close examination, it almost looks like the head of a child that is being squished. This image created no sensation in America but caused great consternation in Sweden, where the album was banned from Christian bookstores. *Dancing on the Head of the Serpent* betrays an about-face in the attitude department, featuring such less-than-winsome lyrics as "Why should I fear people / When God is on my side?" ("Come Higher"). Their spiritual weakness (arrogance) turns out to be a musical strength, however, as the brash, anthemic quality of the songs convey a passion appropriate to the genre. Featuring what *CCM* described as "gigantic choruses and arena-sized background vocals," the songs on *Dancing* move the group to another plane, closer to '80s pop metal than anything else the group would ever do. On "Plunder Hell and Populate Heaven" the band sounds like Kiss, which is to say they sound like **Stryper.**

Jerusalem then took a six-year hiatus, while Christiansson produced pop-oriented solo albums and traveled widely as a speaker at rallies and conferences. In 1992, the group suddenly reappeared with *Prophet,* which once again presented a change in style—elements of **U2**'s modern rock sound are integrated into the mix, which *HM* would describe as "a combination of alternative, art/progressive rock, and good old rock and roll." The hook-laden song "The Waiting Zone" (about AIDS) is one of the most memorable cuts musically, although its lyrics are a bit quick to condemn "safe sex" programs as encouraging sin. "Berlin 38 (Next Year in Jerusalem)" shows far more sensitivity, telling the tale of a Jewish family caught up in the holocaust: "We must never forget," Christiansson sings in the concluding line, "we must not forget it really did happen." *Ten Years Later* is a two-record set compiling hits from the previous projects. All six of the first albums were re-released on CD in 1996 on three discs titled *Classics 1, Classics 2, Classics 3.* Both *Those Were the Days* (sometimes called *Volume 3*) and *R.A.D.* (sometimes called *Volume 4*) present newly recorded versions of songs that were written prior to 1985—all performed by a reunion of the band's original lineup.

Jesse and the Rockers

Hero, voc., bass; Rocket, drums; Larry Rox, gtr.; Brian, gtr. (– 1999). 1998—*T.I.N.* (Screaming Giant); 1999—*Madison Road.*

Jesse and the Rockers are a Christian rock band that critics regard as promising. Their first album displays a sloppy pop punk sound with simplistic lyrics. "Great Tom" is about how great it is to be saved and "Abstain" encourages premarital celibacy. "Fired Up" urges the listener to accept Jesus as Lord. The band's lead singer (who calls himself Hero) would later describe *T.I.N.* as "just a tract." *Madison Road* is much tighter but, as *Bandoppler* says, is "still hampered with some overdone pop-punk, cheese, and redundancy." At the same time, the group displays "many elements of maturity and talent—excellent and strong vocals, well-played melodies, and scattered innovative riffs." Hero responds, "I don't really care what anybody thinks. . . . I love Jesus and I want to let people know what's up with that." In 2000, Larry Rox left the band and two new players were added.

Jesus Freaks

Eric Peterson, voc., bass; Lance Hahn, drums (–1996); Zach Martinez, gtr. (–1996) // Jeff Hutchinson, drums (+ 1996); Keith White, gtr. (+ 1996). 1993—*Socially Unacceptable* [EP] (Narrowpath); 1996—*Jesus Freaks.*

A heavy metal trio, Jesus Freaks issued one EP and then a debut full-length album before changing their name to Blind Eye Open. *HM* called *Socially Unacceptable* "a very credible thrash record" from a group that wore Metallica influences on its sleeve. Eric Peterson's voice and vocal stylings, in particular, seemed a studied imitation of James Hetfield's. Three years later, Peterson returned with an all-new band and released the full-length *Jesus Freaks.* The self-titled album suffers from poor production but nevertheless reveals a more than competent metal band playing songs that merge scriptural insight and emotional sensitivity. "Psalm 55" draws on the words of that biblical poem in describing the feeling of betrayal at the hands of a friend. "Testimony" presents a straightforward account of one person coming to faith in Jesus. Peterson described the Jesus Freaks as "a ministry band first, and a musical band second." He instituted a "no preach, no play" policy according to which they would only perform when allowed to proselytize the audience for converts: "These are the last days," Peterson said in 1993. "We need to share the gospel with whoever we can, so that more people will be prepared to go."

Jesus Music

Steve Morgan, voc.; Michelle Higgins, voc.; Mike Acevedo, gtr.; Sal Salvador, bass; Paul Asciutto III, drums (–1997); Jerry Mowery, drums (–1997) // Donna Morgan, voc. (+ 1997). 1996—*Flowers in the Storm* (4.4.1.); 1997—*Jesus Music* [a.k.a. *3-D*] (Organic).

The Hawaiian band called Jesus Music is usually regarded as the B-52s of Christian music. They do at times bear a remarkable resemblance to that quirky general market band, but the primary reference points for their music lie in the '60s, not the '80s. The group's debut album especially has a neo-psychedelic sound that hearkens back to the Summer of Love. Because of the group's name, many people seemed to assume they were trying to recapture the innocence of the Jesus movement—but *Flowers in the Storm* sounds nothing like the folk-rock sound that dominated that revival. Lyrically, the songs do have a certain naivete about them. The title track employs its metaphor as a potential description for Christians—"flowers in a storm." The self-titled album (often misidentified as *3-D* due to a cover graphic) moves away from psychedelic bubblegum to a more mature sound, and the B-52 comparisons are less dominating. The indisputable highlight of the sophomore project is a cover of "Born to Be Wild," a song that takes on new meaning in light of the group's definition of *wild* in another song ("Wild Child") as the opposite of *lukewarm*. Another standout is "Rain or Shine," a soulful organ-driven track with a certain Sir Doug Quintet feel to it. Lyrically, the song recognizes the difficulty of persistent love ("Wrong can be quick / Right takes a very long time") while also promising exactly that ("Rain or shine on me, I will love you").

Jet Circus

Ez Gomez, bass, kybrd.; Terry Haw, voc., gtr. 1991—*Step on It* (Wonderland).

With a proto-rapcore sound, Jet Circus was almost a decade ahead of its time. *HM* editor Doug Van Pelt described their first and only album in *CCM*, saying, "Jet Circus borrows influences from rap, metal, blues, and bass-heavy motorcycle rock to form a refreshing, new hybrid metal that should create a small revolution in Christian music." That didn't happen, but the band did seem to have a lot of fun, as evidenced by covers of "Let's Dance" (the David Bowie song) and "Be-Bop-A-Lu-Lu" (a Gene Vincent hit from 1956). "Victory Dance" includes the lyric, "You know, baby, we're happy to be born again / The vines of the Spirit are somethin' to be swingin' in." The song "Break the Jail" uses the age-old metaphor of a prisoner being set free to describe God's gift of justification. Gomez and Haw also played with the metal band **Leviticus.**

Jim and Jerome

1980—*Pauper in Paradise* (StarSong).

Jim and Jerome were a pair of brothers (last name unknown) who formed a folk duo that *CCM* described as reminiscent of "Peter and Paul, minus Mary." The group performed the type of music that had been popular a decade before, albeit with slightly more electric accompaniment. Standout songs on their *Pauper in Paradise* album include the title track and "Look Around." All of their songs feature evangelical lyrics, testifying to faith in Jesus.

Joanna

1999—*Looking into Light* (ForeFront); 2002—*New Irish Hymns* [with Margaret Becker and Máire Brennan] (Worship Together).

Joanna Hogg (sometimes rendered Hoagg) is best known as the lead singer for the Celtic Christian band **Iona.** In 1999 she was urged by her father (a Presbyterian minister) to record an album of traditional hymns and worship songs. In the grand tradition of Cher, Selena, and Enya, she released the project as a first-name-only solo artist. *Looking into Light* includes such classics as "My Song Is Love Unknown," "When I Survey the Wondrous Cross," and "Rock of Ages" (as well as the overdone Celtic masterpiece "Be Thou My Vision"), but its real highlights are a handful of songs unknown to most Americans. "Spacious Firmament" is a breathtaking adaptation of Psalm 19. "Almighty Father" and "I Ask No Dream" are also powerful. "Brightest and Best" features vocal harmonies between Joanna and three of her sisters (Helen, Doreen, and Muriel). *New Irish Hymns* is a special project on which Joanna joins **Margaret Becker** and **Máire Brennan** in singing songs by Celtic composer Keith Getty.

Joe Christmas

Zachary Gresham, voc., gtr.; Russell Holbrook, gtr.; Ryan, bass; Philip, drums. 1995—*Upstairs Overlooking* (Tooth and Nail); 1996—*North to the Future.*

Joe Christmas was one of the best of the '90s modern rock bands signed by premier label Tooth and Nail. No label had a higher hipness quotient during that decade, and the company that brought the world **The Supertones, MxPx,** and **Starflyer 59** also delivered Joe Christmas. The principal difference was that, in the latter instance, hardly anyone noticed. Well, reviewers did—and the praise was both overwhelming and unanimous—but it seems the Christian subculture was not ready for music of this quality yet. The group also had a knack for offending fundamentalists—smoking cigars in a sketch on stage and performing a song the mocked pseudo-Christian televangelist Robert Tilton.

The group was an alternative or modern rock quartet from Atlanta, Georgia, fronted by Zachary Gresham, who appears to have been its controlling influence. *7ball* magazine described Joe Christmas as a band that "rocks hard, but combs the depths of love songs in truly tender and romantic fashion, . . . that tells tales of love in well-rehearsed garage music, with burgeoning, thick guitar chords, strong melodies, and dark, unexpected chord changes." *Shout* describes their songs as "pure pop turned up just loud enough to sound dangerous" and insists that "the angst in their gawky teenage love songs is genuinely romantic, even if you're not sure which key the lead vocalist is trying to be in." As these descriptions suggest, Joe Christmas may come closer than any Christian artist since **Larry Norman** to recalling the work of Neil Young. Of course, the songs are not as good as Young's songs, and the guitars don't approach that star's blistering attacks—but still, the intent and aspiration is there, and the result is far from unflattering.

On *Upstairs Overlooking,* the group cuts loose twice, on "Bedroom Suite" and "Blue Rider," songs that seem to recall painful childhood memories and feature sloppy Crazy Horse instrumentation and appropriately strained vocals. "Couple Skate" is a more vibrant rock and roll number, with dopey lyrics about young summer love. Most of the songs on *North to the Future* are in the tradition of Young's subdued *After the Goldrush* or *Silver and Gold* material. "Tea Green and Fadey Mist" and "Dreaming for the Gold" are beautiful instances of progressive folk. "A Pretty Girl Never Lights Her Own Cigarette" has just a little of that infectious country flair. It opens with a picture of a boy being vulnerable with an actual or potential girlfriend ("So many things that I want to say / But I don't want to scare you away") and ends with him responding sardonically to her rejection ("I'm not that surprised / I can see through your eyes"). "I Ruined It" is one of those seemingly interminable ballads that just plods on and on, demanding much of its audience but yielding rich rewards for those who are patient. In terms of content, there is nothing on either of Joe Christmas's albums that would explicitly mark them as a Christian group. Nevertheless, the group recorded for a label that was primarily given to signing Christian artists, and they were largely perceived to be a Christian band and received as such by critics and consumers.

After playing with Joe Christmas, Zach Greshman formed a band called Summer Hymns, which released the album *Voice Brother and Sister* on Misra Records. Produced by Chris Colbert (of **Breakfast with Amy** and **Fluffy**), the album displays a more organic sound than Joe Christmas's work, with banjo and keyboards replacing the fuzzed-out electric guitars.

Joe Club

Danny Deane, voc., gtr.; Craig Lanquist, bass; Eddy Pow, drums; Bob Sheffield, gtr. 1997—*Leave It Up to You* (Temple); 2000—*Over the Moon* (label unknown).

www.joeclub.com

Joe Club is a straight-up rock and roll band with a sound that the group itself describes as "Gin Blossoms meets Hootie and the Blowfish meets Cheap Trick." The group originally formed as Right Mind in the '80s. Under that name, they opened concerts for such general market artists as Cheap Trick

and Joan Jett, in addition to Christian bands **Hokus Pick** and **PFR.** They even made an EP called *Hollywood* that was produced by Robin Zander of Cheap Trick. In a series of events in the late '80s, all four members experienced conversions or spiritual awakenings and they determined in 1990 that they ought to become a Christian band. At this point, they changed their name to Joe Club. The title song to *Leave It Up to You* is a testimony to God's grace. "Just No Question" is a father's grateful recognition that his children are blessings from God's hands. "Message" is a slice of rootsy country rock, in which the singer recalls his decision to break with convention and "take the road less traveled." Traces of John Mellencamp haunt "Miracle," which encourages the expectation that miraculous transformations of human lives and minds are possible.

Christian radio hits: "Just No Question" (# 25 in 1997).

Phil Joel

2000—*Watching over You* (InPop).

Phil Joel is bassist for **The Newsboys,** and his debut solo album was produced by bandmate Peter Furler. Joel says that he didn't want to create an album that sounded like "the Newsboys with the blonde guy singing," and he partly succeeded. *Watching over You* probably sounds more like **The Newsboys** than it does like any *other* contemporary Christian group, but the project has definite features that set it apart. Recording songs that could be reproduced live was not a major factor, and this freed Joel and Furler to play around with in-the-studio effects like overdubs and various enhancements. The result at times recalls Radiohead or **U2** during their *Zooropa* period. Lyrically, the songs are also much more autobiographical than those of **The Newsboys** and display a vulnerability seldom evident in the main band's repertoire. The song "Strangely Normal" was written in reflection on Joel's experience (as an adopted child) of meeting his birth mother. "Fragile" deals with a friend's terminal illness, and "Author of Life" expresses sincere doubts about God's presence in difficult circumstances. The album's title song "Watching over You" is an affirmation of God's providential care. "El Salvador" (not the **Noel Paul Stookey** song) is a simple statement of the impact that a visit to that war-torn land (in connection with the World Vision child sponsorship program) had on Joel. "My Generation" (not the Pete Townsend song) offers a sympathetic lament for "Gen-Xers" who can't find their way in this world. "Be Number One" is a prayer of simple commitment that Joel wrote when he was seventeen—one that he still prizes for its uncomplicated approach to spirituality ("I want you to be a part of everything I do / I want you to be Number One").

Christian radio hits: "Watching over You" (# 2 in 2000); "Strangely Normal" (# 5 in 2001).

Johnny Q. Public

Dan Fritz, voc.; Shawn Turner, gtr.; Ken Bassham, bass (−2000); Brian DuVall, drums (−2000); Oran Thornton, gtr. (−2000) // Brad Barnerd, gtr. (+ 2000); Nathan McCorkle, drums (+ 2000). 1995—*Extra*Ordinary* (Gotee); 2000—*Welcome to Earth* (Roadrunner).

Based in Springfield, Missouri, Johnny Q. Public is a primal rock and roll band, raw and natural in their approach, eclectic in their influences. They released one of the most impressive debut albums of 1995 and enjoyed some success as crossovers into the general market. The group is fronted by Dan Fritz, whose impassioned vocals run the gamut from plaintive to fervent to caustic. The guitar players, Oran Thornton and Shawn Turner, were fifteen and seventeen years old when the first album was released (Thornton later became a member of **Flick** and married Angie Turner, who records as **Miss Angie;** Shawn Turner is her brother). With regard to JQP's relative youth (the oldest member was twenty-three), *CCM* noted, "it's always fascinating to listen to musicians whose primary influences (Zeppelin, Cream) clearly date back to before they were born." But part of JQP's appeal was their ability to mix such classic sensibilities with clear inferences from the modern scene. The group was also insistent on its role as a ministry band, which due to their theological stance usually meant trying to get kids saved at concerts.

"Preacher's Kid" opens *Extra*Ordinary* with a sound akin to tougher Pearl Jam material, a sound that "rides that fine line between hard rock and alternative," as *Shout* magazine said. Lyrically, it reflects on an encounter Fritz once had with a child who was ignored by his father, a pastor preoccupied with affairs of the church. "Body Be" is the album's masterpiece, an original, rollicking song that breaks wide open in the middle for a surprising interlude of the classic guitar solo from Status Quo's "Pictures of Matchstick Men" (# 12 in 1968). The song takes its theme from 1 Corinthians 12 (If the whole body were an eye, or an ear, where would the body be?) but because the verses mention various body parts, it was apparently misunderstood by some executives at MTV who chose to play it as part of a show they did on fashion model (and famous body) Cindy Crawford. In any case, a video for the song was subsequently picked up by MTV and *Extra*Ordinary* was repackaged for general market distribution on the Elektra label. "Women of Zion" is a comical, acoustic treatment of the prophet Isaiah's threat that God would bring baldness (and worse) upon haughty women who do not repent of their ways (Isaiah 3:12–20): "Bald women! You should have been humble! / Bald women! You should have been smarter!" Fritz sings with a delight that is at least as politically incorrect as the attitude of the prophet. "Secret Trees" is another blistering rock attack paying deference to such modern artists as Dinosaur Jr., but with more pop appeal. The song challenges those who think

their sins are hidden to "think again" and know that all will be revealed. Johnny Q. Public also covers classic songs by **Bob Dylan** ("Gotta Serve Somebody") and **Larry Norman** ("Reader's Digest"). Fritz told *7ball* that no one in the group had ever heard either song before their producer brought them in and suggested that they do them. So much for the dominance of classic Christian rock influences.

In 1996, at least, a Johnny Q. Public concert was like some kind of bizarro fundie camp meeting. Mixed in with the undeniably energizing music were odd sermonic indictments of the audience: "Do you think you could take mud and rub in it some blind man's eyes and he would see? Do you have that power? You *do* have that power! You just don't have that faith. The reason you don't make a difference in this world is that you're too wimpy." The climax of the outdoor concerts would come with a ritual inspired by the band's song "Scream" (*Extra*Ordinary*'s low point). Fritz would badger everyone present to come down to a field near the stage and march in a huge circle while the group performed, telling them they were like the Israelite troops marching around Jericho (Joshua 6:3–5). Then, he would have them all scream as loudly as possible for perhaps five minutes straight, promising them that if they did, all the "walls" in their lives would come down. It was a weird combination of altar call, primal scream, and group therapy, all held together by some rather naive theology.

The group disappeared for four years and was all but forgotten. Then, suddenly, they were back with personnel changes (Nathan McCorkle was recruited from **Morella's Forest**). For some reason, *Welcome to Earth* includes remakes of "Preacher's Kid" and "Body Be," as though the first album were just a demo or never happened. "Silver" is a fast-paced, aggressive pop song, typical of what the band does best. "Already Gone" (not The Eagles song) is impressive in another vein—a dark and moody number that succeeds on its emotional strength. "Talk Show" is brilliantly catchy and hook-laden with lyrics that offer a sarcastic look at the modern media phenomenon referenced by its title. "What Am I?" is a **Newsboys**-like power-pop song expressing alienation ("How am I supposed to feel / When you just sit there, refusing to be real?"). "Hey Johnny" offers some pounding hard rock with churning guitars and gang vocals—a solid hard rock song with the melody that they had forgotten to include in "Scream."

Johnny Respect

Johnny Moustakas, voc., gtr.; Sammy Oginsky, gtr.; Mark Pulst, drums; Phil Smith, bass. 1998—*Blue Collar Moxy* (BulletProof); 1999—*Life Ain't What It Used to Be.*

Johnny Respect is a punk band from Detroit whose songs sometimes lean strongly toward a rockabilly style. They drew their name from a local newspaper article on Johnny Rotten (of The Sex Pistols) that asked, "Why doesn't Johnny respect the media?" The group has an especially impressive stage presence, but they suffer from the perennial problem of most punk bands—most of their songs sound alike and, for that matter, most of them sound like most of the songs by other punk bands. *Phantom Tollbooth* complained that on *Blue Collar Moxy* the group "sounds exactly like **MxPx.**" They only break this confinement when they go for the more rockabilly sound, as in "Ritchie" (about Ritchie Valens) and "One Day." The latter song has Frankie Lymon verses interspersed with an **MxPx** chorus. *Life Ain't What It Used to Be* shows maturity of sound. "Broken Homes" is an autobiographical song that poignantly expresses the pain that a child feels when parents divorce. "The Mind As a Hypocrite" and "Your Fear" also demonstrate a serious approach to lyrics.

Jeff Johnson (and **Brian Dunning** and **Sandy Simpson**)

As Jeff Johnson: 1977—*Anvil of God's Word* (Ark); 1978—*Please Forgive Us Lord*; 1980—*The Face of the Deep*; 1983—*Shadow Play*; 1984—*Icons*; 1985—*No Shadow of Turning* (Meadowlark); 1986—*Fallen Splendor* (Ark); 1987—*Born of Water*; 1989—*Pilgrimage*; 1990—*Similitudes*; *Centerpoint: Poetry and Music for Christmas*; 1991—*Great Romantics*; 1994—*Isle of Dreams*; 1996—*Psalmus*; 1997—*Navigato*; 1998—*Prayers of St. Brendan: The Journey Home* (Hearts of Space); 2000—*A Quiet Knowing: Canticles for the Heart* (Ark). As Jeff Johnson and Brian Dunning: 1992—*Songs from Albion 1*; 1993—*Songs from Albion 2*; 1994—*Songs from Albion 3*; 1997—*Music of Celtic Legends: The Bard and the Warrior* (Windham Hill); 2000—*Byzantium: The Book of Kells and St. Aidan's Journey* (Ark). As Jeff Johnson and Sandy Simpson: 1982—*Through the Door* (Ark); 1987—*The Awakening*; 1988—*Why Should the Heart Not Dance?*; *This Mystery I Pose.*

Jeff Johnson was an indie artist before it was cool, before indie was even a word. As early as 1977, he was making self-produced albums in a home studio in Portland, Oregon, and releasing them on his own label, Ark Records. Born in 1956, Johnson graduated from Portland State University. He has relocated to Camano Island, Washington. To help pay bills, he has composed music for Nike, Speedo Swimwear, and Mercedes Benz.

Although Johnson's music is varied and defies categorization, he is best known for producing albums of keyboard-dominated New Age music vaguely reminiscent of George Winston or **John Tesh.** The latter comparisons could be misleading, however, for Johnson is not an antirock adult contemporary performer; *True Tunes* once suggested (in a review of *Isle of Dreams*) that he has much in common with the more atmospheric material of Pink Floyd. Elements of jazz, classical, pop, folk, and rock all find their way into Johnson's musical meanderings, and inspirations from a number of literate sources (Blake, Milton, Tennyson, and the like) turn up in his lyrics.

Johnson's voice has been compared roughly to that of Al Stewart; many of his projects (especially in the '90s), however, are instrumental and some employ guest vocalists. *CCM* describes his career oeuvre as "music ranging from conventional contemplation to the wildly eccentric." *True Tunes* says, "He's always been ahead of everyone else." In addition to the albums listed above, Johnson has recorded three children's albums on his Ark label that feature a musical score accompanied by narration of a classic children's tale: *The Tale of Three Trees* (1990), *The Stormy Night* (1991), and *Calico Bear* (1992).

Johnson's first two albums are quite humble in contrast to the high-tech sonic textures for which he would eventually be noted. *Anvil* includes "Funeral for a Church," and *Please Forgive Us* features "Secret Agent Christian Spy" about a Christian who witnesses by leaving tracts on windshields. Such topics reflect concern over the failure of modern Christianity to engage its culture in meaningful ways. *Face of the Deep* was Johnson's first acknowledged masterpiece—years later he would refer to it as the first of his records that he could still listen to without cringing. The music is orchestral and impressionistic, with Johnson's keyboards and synthesizers creating soundscapes for his poetry. The breadth and profundity of the subject matter expands exponentially as he now offers social and artistic commentary on such basic themes as the human condition and the joy of romantic love. *Shadow Play* displays similar depth, exploring what *CCM* called "The dreams and shadows that follow each of us before and after conversion." The album includes songs that reflect on the thought of Vincent Van Gogh ("Borinage") and Albert Camus ("My Blue Camus"). *Icons* was initially released in a limited edition of 500 copies, though Sparrow and StarSong would eventually distribute it more widely. With a neoclassical sound, similar to that of Vangelis (the *Chariots of Fire* soundtrack), *Icons* was praised by *CCM* as "one of the most creative, high quality albums ever to be produced for the Christian market." Lyrics for the project are inspired by the writings of authors like Madeleine L'Engle and George MacDonald. *Fallen Splendor* opens with the overtly theological "Looking for God (Using a Spotlight)," which suggests the futility of spiritual quests that peer out rather than in. "Wind and Water" and "Sacrament" are particularly lovely compositions. *Pilgrimage* offers reflections on the theme of "finding splendor in the ordinary" and is said to be Johnson's most personal recording. He indicates that the project was born of his own realization that "part of the great grace of God and the working of God is through people." *Great Romantics* features an all-star cast of numerous jazz and rock musicians (including Deri Daugherty of **The Choir**) and includes an innovative cover of Don McLean's "Vincent." *Isle of Dreams* is a musical continuation of *Romantics,* with many of the same performers, but with songs related to the classic theme of longing that stems from faith in God.

Johnson also released several instrumental albums during the last half of the '80s, beginning with *No Shadow of Turning*. On *Born of Water* he is joined by jazz/New Age bassist Dave Friesen and saxophonist Dave Hagelganz. On *Why Should the Heart Not Dance?* he performs with guitarist Sandy Simpson and harpist/flutist Kathy McClatchey. *This Mystery I Pose* collects instrumental tracks from the earlier, mostly vocal albums—and also includes some pieces by Simpson. Two other collaborations with Simpson *(Through the Door* and *The Awakening)* include vocal tracks. *Similitudes* pairs Johnson with saxophonist Hagelganz again. One innovative track on the latter album ("Two Perspectives of Time") opens and closes with the sound of two clocks ticking in conflicting rhythms.

Psalmus is a masterful work of art based on the book of Psalms. Johnson offers a medieval score (Gregorian and Celtic) for classical vocalist Janet Chvatal to sing the Latin texts of several passages from the biblical writings. Johnson also sings English translations on some selections; Brian Dunning plays recorder and Daugherty, guitar. *7ball* calls it "a stylish adult alternative worship album with shades of light and dark." Dunning and Chvatal join him again for *Navigatio,* a collection of Celtic songs tracing the journey of St. Brendan to America, which becomes a metaphor for the mystery and fear of every human journey through life. Christian band **Iona** also recorded an album based on the story of St. Brendan's voyage. *Prayers of St. Brendan: The Journey Home* provides the logical follow-up to *Navigatio*—musically as well as conceptually. *A Quiet Knowing* offers twelve instrumental renditions of traditional and contemporary hymns, performed with strong Celtic and Appalachian inferences. Selections include "Be Thou My Vision," "Amazing Grace," "Love Divine," and "Children of the Heavenly Father," in addition to two of Johnson's original compositions.

Johnson has actually attained his greatest success with projects that he and Dunning have released as a duo. Paramount among these is the three-volume set *Songs from Albion,* in which the artists create soundtrack music for a trio of books by Stephen Lawhead, a collector of Celtic traditions. *Music from Celtic Legends* and *Byzantium* are also based on Lawhead writings. The content of these albums may not seem to be as explicitly Christian as some of Johnson's other works, but the songs (like the stories themselves) do presume a Christian worldview and treat legends commensurate with Christian history.

Kathie Lee Johnson

1978—*Lovin' You* (Bread 'N' Honey); 1979—*Finders Keepers* (Petra).

Kathie Lee Johnson is better known to the world as Kathie Lee Gifford, wife of former NFL star Frank Gifford, and coanchor (with Regis Philbin) for many years of the popular morning show *Live with Regis and Kathie Lee*. She was born Kathie Lee Epstein in 1954 in Paris, France, and grew up in Bowie, Maryland. At the age of fourteen she began singing with her sister Michie Mader as Pennsylvania Next Right. Her natural charm, talent, and wholesome appearance helped her to win several competitions, being named both Maryland's Junior Miss and Alabama's Junior Miss. She attended Oral Roberts University on a music scholarship arranged by Anita Bryant and upon graduation became one of ten singers featured regularly on Oral Roberts' TV show. In 1976, she and her sister recorded an album of Christian music as **Kathie and Michie Epstein.** That same year she married the record's producer, **Paul Alan Johnson,** and went on to make two solo albums under his direction. At that time, she also had a regular starring role as Nurse Callahan on the TV soap opera *Days of Our Lives* and was a featured singer on the TV show *Name That Tune.* The Johnsons divorced in 1983. Lee would marry Gifford three years later.

Most of the songs on Kathie Lee's solo albums are written by Paul Johnson, with a dominant lyrical focus on prayers for spiritual strength and psalms of thanksgiving. "Lovin' You" is a paraphrase of 1 Corinthians 13. *Finders Keepers* also includes the more traditional "Isn't That Just Like Jesus?" (by Ron Harris and Lela Gilbert). "You Make Me Feel Like a Woman," written by **Sharalee Lucas,** recasts the thought of Carole King's "(You Make Me Feel Like) A Natural Woman" into a spiritual ode addressed to Jesus.

Christian radio hits: "Finders Keepers" (# 21 in 1979).

Mike Johnson (and **The Exkursions** and Mike and Karen Johnson)

As The Exkursions: 1970—*The Exkursions* (custom); 2001—*21st Century Blazz.* As Mike Johnson: 1972—*Lord Doctor* (Freedom Light); *The Last Battle* (Creative Sound); 1973—*Velvet Prince* (Freedom Light); 1975—*Gentle Spirit* (CAM); 1976—*The Artist/The Riddle* (NewPax); 1977—*More Than Just an Act;* 2000—*The-X* (custom). As Mike and Karen Johnson: 1972—*Happy and Alive* (Freedom Light).

A pioneer of the Jesus movement, Mike Johnson made some of the world's very first Christian rock music. Born in Chicago in 1945, Johnson dropped out of high school to play music. After some trouble with juvenile authorities, he became an original member of the Mike Bloomfield Blues Band, and then went on to be lead guitarist for the now legendary groups Electric Flag and the Paul Butterfield Blues Band. In the days before his conversion to Christ, he also played with a popular Chicago group called Checkmate and accompanied Las Vegas entertainer Tony Bellus in his gigs at Chicago's Edgewater Beach Hotel. Experiments with drugs landed Johnson in a psychiatric ward at an early age. Looking for a way out, he sought the help of Teen Challenge, the Christian organization founded by David Wilkerson, and through that ministry came to faith. After becoming a Christian, Johnson attended a Pentecostal Bible college where he was taught that rock and roll was sinful and so took a brief respite from what had been his vocation and avocation. In 1968, however, he formed the group The Exkursions with Christian friends Phil Johnson (drums) and Leon "Spyder" Wilson (bass). The group's style represented a creative fusion of blues, rock, and jazz similar to the Bloomfield and Butterfield outfits, or to the soon-to-be-hot Blood, Sweat, and Tears (minus the horns). The Exkursions accompanied Anglican minister John Guest (a British folk singer in his own right) on evangelistic missions to college campuses and coffeehouses booked through InterVarsity Christian Fellowship. They had a unique strategy, playing nothing but mainstream music that would conclude with one (and only one) Christian song. Usually, this would be "Would You Believe?" an invitation to faith. Johnson would share his testimony and Guest would preach. More than thirty years later, Johnson would still insist that this low-key approach was the secret to their success. The band performed all over the Midwest and up and down the East Coast for a full two years before the Jesus movement became recognizable as a national revival. In 1969, they played for a Billy Graham crusade in New York City, marking one of that evangelist's earliest official collaborations with rock music. Johnson then released four solo albums on custom labels before scoring a major contract that allowed him to produce his three best-known releases for NewPax. After that, he was part of the good-idea-that-didn't-work combo of **Matthews, Taylor, and Johnson.** In 1978, Johnson became involved with the charitable world hunger organization Compassion International. He worked with the agency for many years, donating proceeds from concerts, and was instrumental in helping the fledgling operation to get off the ground. Some unfortunate hardships followed. Johnson hooked up with **Mike Warnke** and (like Matthews and Taylor) became a part of that entertainer's no-accountability, partying entourage. He declined into alcohol abuse and derailed his marriage by having an adulterous fling with one of Warnke's serial wives. These tragic aspects of Johnson's career are recounted in the book *Selling Satan: The Evangelical Media and the Mike Warnke Scandal* (Cornerstone, 1993). Johnson has also has written a book about his experiences titled *Jesus and the Music.*

The Exkursions has an aggressive, psychedelic sound similar to that associated with **Eric Clapton** bands like Cream and Derek and the Dominoes, with wild stereo separation that was a trip in those early days when headphones were a novelty. Johnson's guitar is the main attraction on tracks like "Baby You Lied" (a slow blues rocker) and "Third Eye." Their standard,

"Would You Believe?" is a soft jazz piece that is neither typical fare nor the album's highlight. "It's Been Set Down" is much better, evincing a fuzzy guitar buzz and some psychedelic blues worthy of Quicksilver Messenger Service or Cream. *Lord Doctor* is more mellow than the band's first album, but its title track (a penitent's prayer) would become a Johnson classic. "Pride" has a Moody Blues vibe to it. *The Last Battle* is almost a reissue of *Lord Doctor,* with one song ("Cause and Effect") deleted, "Pride" shortened, and two new songs added. The new title track is a rollicking blues-rock tune that takes its name from one of C. S. Lewis's Narnia tales and deals with the approaching cataclysm that some biblical literalists thought would soon bring the world to an end. "City City" is a prophetic oracle that sounds like something that might have been performed by Hot Tuna.

Johnson's next project was recorded with his wife Karen, but instead of the folk-duo collection of love songs one might expect, it actually recaptures the electric jazz of The Exkursions more effectively than any of his solo projects. "City!" (different from "City City") is raucous. "I'm High" has the sound of a hippie drug song, but the lyrics are about getting high on Jesus. Karen's lovely vocals are a treat. Owing to events mentioned above, their marriage would later end in a bitter divorce. Reminiscing in 1998, Johnson told *CCM,* "The failures were all mine, failures that later created years of guilt that was hard to overcome."

Velvet Prince reprises "Would You Believe?" and offers a "defy culture" anthem called "Dilemma." The song "Health Food" takes a satirical poke at nutrition fanatics: "Yogurt ain't got no saving power . . . kumquats can't set your soul free." This combination of social prophecy and humor recalls the late '60s albums of Country Joe and the Fish, as *Jesus Music* points out. *Gentle Spirit* moves decidedly into Johnson's quieter medium and should perhaps be regarded as one of the first praise and worship albums to be created within contemporary Christian music.

The Artist/The Riddle would bring Johnson into a bigger league with a better production budget. It is perhaps his finest moment. The polished album has two title tracks: "The Artist" has a country feel, while "The Riddle" goes for a renaissance sound enhanced by flute and recorder. "Lord Doctor" appears again. "The Wedding Song" uses a biblical metaphor to describe Christ coming to gather the church for an eternal consummation. "Little Boy" offers a moving tribute to the task and joy of parenting. *Harmony* magazine selected Johnson as "Artist of the Year" on the strength of this album. The follow-up, *More Than Just An Act,* continues to exemplify strong songwriting. A musical adaptation of Psalm 23 recalls the songs on *Gentle Spirit.*

As of 2002, Johnson was remarried, living in Nashville, working in real estate, and still singing for Jesus. The new millennium brought a new CD by him (called *The-X*) as well as a new CD by The Exkursions *(Twenty-first Century Blazz)*. He says he is delighted that when most people hear of him their first connection is not to Michael Bloomfield or even to The Exkursions, but to Compassion International. "Tremendous!" he exclaims. "Starting something that has helped so many kids is really a great way to be remembered." Two early Mike Johnson songs can also be found on compilation CDs: "City City" is on the *Ultima Thule* (Sonrise) compilation disc and "Your Friends Keep Calling" (a pleasant, James Taylor-styled bit of country folk) is on *Jesus Festival of Music* (Sonrise).

The Christian artist Mike Johnson should not be confused with the general market artist Michael Johnson who had Top 40 hits with the songs "Bluer Than Blue" and "This Night Won't Last Forever" in the late '70s, or with the singer named Mike Johnson who recorded several albums in the '90s (the latter performer is a baritone vocalist with a style similar to Lou Reed or Leonard Cohen; he also plays bass for the band Dinosaur Jr.).

Paul Johnson

Selected: 1973—*Paul Johnson Singers* (Tempo); 1974—*That the World May Know* (Word); *Here Comes the Son* (Word); 1975—*The Paul Johnson Voices Featuring Sharalee* (1975); 1976—*Choral Series* (Petra); 1978—*The Time of My Life* (Milk and Honey); 1980—*Believer* (Greentree); 1980—*Rise Again . . . He's Alive* (Songbird); 1986—*A Family Christmas Carol* (Word); 1988—*Majestic Praise* (Maranatha).

Paul Alan Johnson (not to be confused with the leader of The Packards) is a well-known composer, arranger, and producer of MOR and easy listening Christian music. First introduced to the scene by protégé **Ralph Carmichael,** he would go on to make dozens of albums featuring small choirs and chamber orchestras, sometimes recording as the Paul Johnson Singers or as the Paul Johnson Vocal Band. From 1976 to 1983 he was married to **Kathie Lee Johnson,** later to achieve fame as Kathie Lee Gifford, cohost with Regis Philbin of the TV program, *Live with Regis and Kathie Lee.* Some of Johnson's albums featured the voice of **Sharalee Lucas.** Johnson's albums are seldom noticed in contemporary Christian music circles, having a much more traditional choral or inspirational sound. *CCM* referred to *Rise Again* as "an unusual collection of contemporary hits sung a capella by an exceptional choir."

Paul Johnson and the Packards

Marc Burroughs, gtr.; Guy Hufferd, bass; Ray Huskey, drums; Paul Johnson, gtr. 1986—*Guitar Heaven* (Frontline); 1987—*California*.

The Paul Johnson who fronted the instrumental surf-rock combo called The Packards should not be confused with Paul (Alan) Johnson, the composer and producer of Christian easy listening music. Paul Johnson and the Packards made two albums of instrumental surf music comparable to the well-known '60s sound of The Ventures ("Hawaii Five-O"). Johnson was the real deal—in the late '50s, he had fronted a California band called The Bel-Airs who, along with such groups as the Ventures and the Surfaris, helped to create the genre known as surf music. The Bel-Airs' best-remembered song is a tune called "Mr. Moto," which never made the national charts but paved the way for many that did. The Packards' music is all instrumental, but many of the tunes bear religious titles such as "Those That Seek Me Early Shall Find Me" and "Let Us Go into the House of the Lord." The two Packards albums were later re-released on a single CD.

For trivia buffs: In 1962 Johnson was invited by Brian Wilson to join the Beach Boys when Al Jardine was drafted into the army. He declined.

Troy Johnson

1993—*Plain and Simple* (Word); 1994—*I Will*.

An R&B singer with a voice similar to that of Michael Jackson, Troy Johnson grew up in a single mother household and as a teenager took to the streets, where he became involved with gangs. His prospects took a turn for the better when an executive from Motown overheard him singing to himself in a rest room and invited him to meet with Leon Silvers, a producer for the label. Johnson cut an album for Motown and had a hit song nationwide on R&B stations ("It's You") in 1986. He says, however, that the increased money only made his life worse until he dedicated his life to Christ and subsequently shifted to a career in contemporary Christian music. The title song to his album *Plain and Simple* declares, "Plain and simple, simple and true / God loves you, yes really you." The album also features the hip-hop praise song, "Good (To Have the Lord in Your Shoes)," which was a hit at concerts when Johnson went on an interracial, cross-cultural tour with **Margaret Becker.** *I Will* is a more tightly focused album and includes a remake of **Marvin Gaye**'s "What's Going On."

Christian radio hits: "Good (To Have the Lord in Your Shoes)" (# 5 in 1993); "What Are Your Wants" (# 18 in 1994); "I'll Be There with You" (# 3 in 1995).

Jonathan

1994—*Shadowdance* (StarSong); 1996—*Push*.

Jonathan is the professional name used by Jonathan Pagano, who dropped the surname after he tired of people misspelling it. A singer and musician from New Jersey, Jonathan was the main man in the rock group **Novella,** but his solo records depart drastically from the sound of that band. Whereas Novella had a guitar-driven sound, Jonathan switched to keyboards for his solo material. The result is a sound similar to that of early Elton John or Billy Joel—and, no wonder, since Jonathan says he was aiming for a sound similar to **Keith Green,** who emulated those two artists. Green has inspired him in terms of ministry as well as music: "I want to bring back the passion that was so evident in the music of early contemporary Christian music pioneers." *CCM* called *Shadowdance* "unexpectedly excellent, rich with soul and blazing spirituality."

Christian radio hits: "He'll Never Leave You" (# 23 in 1996).

David Lynn Jones

1992—*Mixed Emotions* (Liberty).

Although David Lynn Jones is said to have made a couple of nondescript country albums prior to *Mixed Emotions,* it is the latter project that attracted the attention of Christian music critics. The record has ties to the Waylon Jennings "outlaw country" sound but it is also infused with a generous dose of Leon Russell blues and **Van Morrison** autobiography. Lyrically, the entire project is fraught with religious imagery, yet it remains ambiguous as to where the implied author of the songs might stand. "The Land of Allah" satirizes the ridiculous notion of holy war. "What Are We Livin' For" compares Christians positively to revolutionaries. But, then, on "Judgment Day," Jones seems to present his soul as the trophy in a war between God and Satan, without indicating who he thinks will win. In "Even One" he imagines himself locked in an eternal dialogue with the devil.

John Jonethis

1997—*Lounge Freak* (Essential); 1998—*The Ultimate Lounge Christmas.*

Nashville native John Jonethis is an authentic lounge singer in his hometown, the kind of guy comedian Bill Murray made fun of in his "lounge lizard" sketches on *Saturday Night Live.* Jonethis performs regularly at the Hermitage Hotel and the Wild Boar Restaurant, singing Frank Sinatra and Jack Jones standards and remaking current pop songs the way that Steve Lawrence might have done them. Jonethis is a Christian, and back in 1996 the rock group **Fold Zandura** thought it might be funny to have him sing a lounge version of their techno hit "Ember" as a hidden track on their *Return* album. A perennial good sport (he enjoys those Murray skits), Jonethis went along with the joke. He did similar favors for **Silage, Honey,** and **Kosmos Express.** Since it was becoming a fad, he put together an entire album of his own versions of Christian rock hits. It was marketed as a novelty, comparable to **The Swirling Eddies'** *Sacred Cows.* But the songs are done so authentically that, as *Christian Music* said, it "makes you wonder whether you're supposed to laugh or actually get into it." **Jars**

of Clay's "Flood" is a gem. Jonethis's rendition is so different from the original that it takes a couple of moments to realize just what song he is singing—yet his version is so captivating in its own right that no one will think for long that it is "just a joke." Other songs that work well are **MxPx**'s "Punk Rawk Show" and **Plumb**'s "Crazy." These obvious successes are the first three songs on the album. Songs that *don't* work are **Johnny Q. Public**'s "Body Be" and **The Newsboys**' "Take Me to Your Leader." **DC Talk**'s "Jesus Freak" is a disaster—Jonethis tries to speed up his vocals on what was originally the rap part and it just sounds silly. Still, Jonethis's take on **Audio Adrenaline's** "Never Gonna Be As Big As Jesus" (the *fourth* song on the album) is actually better than the original, which was never all that rocking in the first place—and *now* one can understand the words. Jonethis is the real thing. He knows that (most) people only want him to sing this way so they can laugh at him, but he perseveres and sometimes (at least four times), the laugh may be on them instead—when they find themselves, against all intent, actually liking what he does. Jonethis told *7ball,* "I know you can look at it as a novelty record. It's not. If you didn't know the song 'Flood' and you heard my lounge rendition of it, I would hope you would say, *This is a really good song.* That's my goal." A year later, Jonethis released a similar album of lounge version Christmas songs, though only one of these ("Silent Night") is a religious carol.

Brent Jones and the T.P. Mobb

2000—*Brent Jones and the T.P. Mobb* (Holy Roller).

Hip-hop choir leader Brent Jones comes from the same school as **Kirk Franklin** and **Fred Hammond,** but he takes his merger of modern urban-black music with traditional gospel in a different direction. Whereas Franklin and Hammond have typically emphasized the more upbeat and energetic aspects of urban music, which they find wholly compatible with gospel's celebratory spirit, Jones focuses on the more silky, soulful sound of hip-hop's midtempo music. Jones' Mobb is located in Los Angeles; the "T.P." in their name stands for "Total Praise." The song "Goodtimes" from Jones and Mobb's debut album recalls the '80s pop of Kool and the Gang ("Joanna," not "Ladies' Night"). *CCM* describes it as "a savory stew of wah-wah and talk-box guitars, rap bridges, female vocal counterpoints, and a punchy gospel chorus."

Jonny's in the Basement

Jonny Baker; Jim Birch. 1999—*Backbone* (independent).

The indie duo that calls itself Jonny's in the Basement attracted the attention of Christian 'zines like *Phantom Tollbooth* and *True Tunes* with a debut album that addressed the oppression of Palestinians in modern Israel. The group's name is taken from the opening line to the classic **Bob Dylan** song, "Subterranean Homesick Blues," but is a bit of a pun since the album was in fact recorded in Jonny Baker's basement. Musically, the duo employs a fusion of backbeat and ambient sounds, employing DJ scratching, Middle Eastern elements, and occasional industrial rhythms. Lyrically, the project is driven by a passion for justice that was infused in songwriter Baker on a visit to Israel where he witnessed gross violations of human rights firsthand. Baker cites Dylan and **Bruce Cockburn** as his primary influences.

Dawn Smith Jordan

1995—*Canopy* (Urban).

Dawn Smith Jordan is a Christian R&B singer whose soft voice is fit to songs that are appropriately sweet on her *Canopy* album. Jordan stays away from wailing, and sings almost timidly on "The Promise of Love" (a duet with Jerome Olds) and "Love that Leads to You" (a prayer that her daughter will find faith).

Cedric Joseph

1983—*Praise to Victory* (StarSong).

African American crooner Cedric Joseph made one Christian album in the early '80s focused on a specific theme: "preserving the institution of marriage." Joseph sang love songs and reminders of dedication in a somewhat naive attempt to reach couples in conflict and save their marriages by convincing them that "God hates divorce." Musically, Joseph travels in the same stream as Lionel Richie or Christopher Cross, with muted traditional gospel vocals in the background.

Martyn Joseph

Date unknown—*UnDRUGged* (independent); *Treasure the Questions* [with White Heart] (Ears and Eyes); *Ballads . . . In Quieter Moments*; 1983—*I'm Only Beginning*; 1984—*Nobody's Fool*; 1986—*Sold Out*; 1989—*Being There* (Sony); *An Aching and a Longing* (Myrrh UK); 1997—*Martyn Joseph* (Allia); 1999—*Full Colour Black and White* (Grapevine); 1998—*Tangled Souls*; 1999—*Far from Silent* (Pipe); 2000—*The Shirley Sessions* [EP]; 2001—*Thunder and Rainbows: Best We Could Find* (Piper); *Don't Talk about Love*.

Welshman Martyn Joseph has *The Phantom Tollbooth* to thank for bringing his material to the attention of American audiences—and they have only been interested in the last three projects. Apparently, Joseph has been recording albums of Christian music in his native land for over two decades. He regularly plays the *Greenbelt* festival in England and even released one album with powerhouse band **White Heart.** At one point he placed a song, "Dolphins Make Me Cry," in the British Top Thirty. But with *Tangled Souls,* an introspective yet passionate

Joseph came to the fore, and his songs began to take on the consistent poignancy of work by artists like **Bruce Cockburn, Mark Heard,** and **Van Morrison.** The song from which the title of that album is drawn was cowritten with Stewart Henderson of **Over the Rhine** and reflects on the "strange way to start a revolution" that God demonstrated in Jesus: "Strange dissident of meekness / And nurse of tangled souls / And so unlike the holy / To end up full of holes." The musical style of the record is mostly that of the traditional acoustic singer/songwriter, and this continues on *Far from Silent,* which *Tollbooth* chose as their "Pick of the Month" in December 1999. Here, Joseph mocks perceptions of his new identity in "Liberal Backslider": "People ask me how I'm doing / And I confirm all their fears / I'm swearing like a trooper / And drinking like a bum / I'm a liberal backslider / And it sure is a lot of fun." Otherwise, many of the songs are politically charged. "The Good in Me Is Dead" relates the tale of a Bosnian refugee waiting to see if his family has made it over the border of not. He muses Job-like about all he has experienced, about how absurd and obscene life must be if "there is no bigger picture," then concludes, "Ask me what I dread: that the good in me . . . is dead." *Far From Silent* also contains a cover of Joan Osborne's "One of Us?" The mood of *The Shirley Sessions* is completely different, the rumor being that the eight songs included on the project are ones that were judged too upbeat or happy for prior collections. Whatever the case, these are beautiful songs, mostly about beautiful things. "He's Mine" is indeed a song of faith. "Undiscovered Love" hints at promise and hope. "Kiss the World Beautiful" is a declaration of affection for this world and all its people. *Thunder and Rainbows* is a two-disc compilation of thirty-three songs spanning the artist's career (1988–2000). *Don't Talk about Love* is a live album, collecting songs from a decade of performances.

Joshua (Southwest)

Quincy Rogers; Shelby Rogers; Tony Sema. 1973—*Joshua* (Impact).

Almost nothing is known of the Southwest band Joshua that produced one of early Christian music's finest hard rock albums. For some reason, the record was released in England a year earlier than in the United States on the Key label, leading many to believe the band was British. The music fits into the same general category as **Agape** or **The Exkursions.** *Jesus Music* likens the album to **Petra**'s debut. A few Grateful Dead-style acoustic ballads mix with abrasive electric songs. Not too advanced in the humility department, the band proclaims in its liner notes that "this is one of the two or three best Jesus rock albums ever produced." Of course, in 1973 there hadn't been a whole lot more than two or three Jesus rock albums ever produced. But in any case, Jesus music historian David Di

Sabatino accepts the claim as valid and names "The Word," "Revelation," and "I Was Lonely" as standout tracks. The album also includes an impressive version of **Larry Norman**'s "I Wish We'd All Been Ready." Another hard rock Christian band named Joshua arose a decade later in Los Angeles.

Joshua (Los Angeles) (and **M Pire** a.k.a. **Joshua Perahia**)

Personnel for Joshua: Josh Perahia, gtr.; Stephen Fontaine, voc. (–1985) // Jeff Fenholt, voc. (+ 1985, –1988); Rob Rock, voc. (+ 1988). Personnel for M Pire [a.k.a. Joshua Perahia]; Josh Perahia, gtr.; Michael O'Mara, voc. (–2001); Joey Rochrich, bass; Eric Stoskopf, drums; Jerry Gabriel, voc. (+ 2001). By Joshua: 1982—*The Hand Is Quicker Than the Eye* (Enigma); 1985—*Surrender* (RCA); 1988—*Intense Defense* (RCA). By M Pire: 1995—*Chapter One* (Long Island). By Joshua Perahia: 2001—*Something to Say* (M&K).

Not to be confused with the early hard rock band Joshua that played the Southwest in the '70s, the Los Angeles group of the same name was founded by Joshua Perahia in 1980 and achieved its primary success in Japan, Europe, and South America. The group went through numerous personnel changes, totally disbanding two or three times, with Perahia recruiting a new batch of players and, notably, vocalists. In addition to the people listed above, Jim Wilkinson (later of Love/Hate) sang with the group at one point, though it is not apparent that he does vocals on any of the recordings. Another Joshua lineup included a trio of persons who would go on to form the nucleus of **Shout** (Joseph Galleta, Loren Robinson, and **Ken Tamplin**).

Although Perahia was brought up in the Greek Orthodox Church and was faithful to that tradition in beliefs and lifestyle, he maintains that he did not "get saved" until he attended a Bible study led by Hal Lindsey in 1983. His conversion, in other words, was not from paganism to Christianity, but from mainline Christianity to fundamentalism. In any case, the transformation did not sit well with his bandmates and they all departed—as did the entire eighteen-member road crew. "They thought I had turned into a loony," Perahia told *HM* in 1992. The band that recorded *The Hand Is Quicker Than the Eye* featured Stephen Fontaine, former lead singer for Uriah Heep. It includes "November Is Going Away," which would become the band's biggest international hit, going all the way to Number One in Japan. Perahia has said he does not regard this first Joshua album—released a full year before his conversion—as a Christian record, though it does reflect a basic faith in God on some tracks and contains nothing objectionable from the perspective of Christian values. Reissues have treated it as an integral part of the Joshua catalogue, even pairing it with *Surrender* on a single CD. In any case, *Surrender* and *Intense Defense* are metal albums with confrontational, evangelical lyrics. *Surrender* was recorded with lead singer **Jeff Fenholt**, famous for

having played the lead role in the Broadway production of the musical *Jesus Christ Superstar*. In between the recording of the Joshua albums *Surrender* and *Intense Defense,* Perahia put together a new version of the band that featured lead singer Rob Rock, later to achieve fame as lead vocalist for the Christian metal band **Impellitteri.** It was Perahia who reportedly led Rock to Christ. After the recording of *Intense Defense,* Perahia formed another (supposedly secular) band called Jaguar. Ever the evangelist, he also led the singer of that group—Robin Kyle Basauri—to Christ. Basauri went on to sing with the Christian bands **Die Happy** and **Red Sea.**

In 1995, Perahia resurfaced with a new band called M Pire. The group featured a lead singer named Michael O'Mara who *HM* described as having a confident, powerful voice reminiscent of Mickey Thomas (of Starship). M Pire made an album that was never distributed in the United States called *Chapter One* (Long Island, 1995). Six years later, M Pire was rechristened Joshua Perahia (according to M&K Records, Joshua Perahia is the name of the *band* not just its front man). Under that name, the band recorded *Something to Say,* produced by Keith Olsen (famous for Fleetwood Mac's *Rumours* and projects by Santana, Heart, and The Scorpions). Since new lead singer Jerry Gabriel (formerly with the bands Tower and Wasted Angel) was added during the recording process, Santana vocalist Alex Ligertwood originally sang on all tracks, and his vocals are retained on an alternative audio DVD version of the album. The project's title track and the song "The First and the Last" were featured in the motion picture *The Copper Scroll.* The M&K label also re-released all of the albums listed in the above discography as works by "Joshua Perahia" (the band not the person).

Joy

Dave Burgin; Jim Golden; Scott Lockwood // Bruce Cotton. No albums.

Joy was contemporary Christian music's first country rock band and, as such, pioneered a sound that would become extremely popular, especially in the early days of the Jesus movement (see **Bethlehem, Daniel Amos,** and **The Way**). Indeed, the group was one of the first Jesus music bands, playing up and down the San Bernardino valley even before there was a **Children of the Day** or a **Love Song.** Dave Burgin recalls a time when the *only* people doing Christian rock were "**Andraé Crouch, Larry Norman,** and us." He recalls a concert at Swing Auditorium in San Bernardino where the band opened for a very young Hal Lindsey, at that time just an unknown staff person working with Campus Crusade for Christ. Joy did not release any recordings, but some were made and can be accessed over the Internet at www.one-way.org/jesusmusic/joy.htm. Burgin and Jim Golden went on to form **Blessed**

Hope with Dave Rios. Scott Lockwood formed **Country Faith** with Chuck Butler and **Tom Stipe.**

Joy Electric

Ronnie Martin, voc., synth. // Jeff Cloud, synth. (+ 1997); Caleb Mannan, synth. (+ 1999). 1994—*Melody* (Tooth and Nail); 1995—*Five Stars for Failure* [EP]; 1996—*We Are the Music Makers; Old Wives' Tales* [EP]; 1997—*Robot Rock* (BEC); 1998—*Children of the Lord* [EP]; *The Land of Misfits* [EP]; 1999—*Christiansongs;* 2000—*Unelectric;* 2001—*The White Songbook Legacy, Vol. 1.*

www.joyelectric.com

Joy Electric is the most successful synth-pop band in Christian music. Basically a one-man outfit, it is a project of Southern California songwriter/producer Ronnie Martin. The closest comparison in the general market might be to the band Erasure, but Joy Electric is even synth-ier and pop-ier. Martin cranks out synthesized disco music that sounds like what is heard on the soundtracks to Atari or Nintendo video games. Much (but not all) of the music is definitively mechanical and lacking in depth or innovation. Still, it seems to be captivating to a subset of adolescents who apparently like to have those Mario Bros. blips and bleeps going off in their heads even when they're not making the little guys jump over lava pools to rescue princesses. Martin himself describes the group as sounding "maybe the way the inside of a clock would sound, with all the gears and everything moving at once." Martin started out with the groups **Rainbow Rider** and **Dance House Children** before hitting upon his winning formula. Joy Electric lacks the often beautiful orchestrations of the former group or the occasional guitar relief (courtesy of brother Jason Martin of **Starflyer 59**) of the latter. He sings in a high, silky voice with an affected British accent that even fans admit is "an acquired taste." Joy Electric has developed a tradition of alternating full-length albums with EPs that usually present alternative mixes of past or future songs. Lyrically, Joy Electric's material (with the exception of *Christiansongs*) has typically been ambiguous and nondescript, employing fantastic images (peppermint trolls, lollipop trees) or simply describing the music itself ("Notes go beep in perfect time"). In concert, however, Martin often assumes a challenging evangelistic stance, exhorting his Christian audience to abandon mediocrity and spiritual complacency.

Melody scored a hit with the self-explanatory "Drum Machine Joy." Much better is "The Dark Ages," a sonic fairytale that pushes the edge of the admittedly small envelope for progressive dance music. *True Tunes* would likewise note that, for those who make it through the album's first ten tracks, "Never Be a Star" and "Old at This Young" reveal a human center that seems to be ambiguously at odds with the electronic outer coating. *We Are the Music Makers* is held together by a medieval theme, which at least sets it apart from other projects. *7ball*

says it gives the listener an idea what music might have sounded like "if keyboards existed in the 1300s." *Robot Rock* suddenly took Martin out of his one-trick-pony-novelty-band mode. He crafted an album of genuine electronic techno music reminiscent of early '80s groups like Kraftwerk, Soft Cell, or Human League. The album opens with a bubblegum trifle ("Sugar Rush") but then proceeds to "Monosynth," an impressively moody piece that escapes the confines of bop-bop disco to demonstrate what a single synthesizer really can do. "Storybook Love" has a discernible melody, as do "Strawberry Heart" and "Forever Is a Place"—any of these might be considered a genuine pop song.

The pop attempt continued on the next project. *True Tunes* claimed, "Replace the synthesizers in any of the songs on *Christiansongs* and you've got a Beatles record." No way, but the album does have two good tracks. A cover of **Keith Green**'s "Make My Life a Prayer to You" is appropriately catchy and hopeful. The closing song, "Birds Will Sing Forever," needs to be set beside "Monosynth" as one of Joy Electric's two masterpieces, though the two songs sound nothing alike. "Birds" is a surprisingly pretty, melodic song that works completely on its own, apart from the backdrop of synthesized beeping. *Christiansongs'* opening number, "The Voice of the Young," copies its lyrical theme from a '60s anthem by The Association called "Enter the Young": "Here we are, here we come / We are the voice of the young." The plea not to be dismissed on account of youth is scriptural (1 Timothy 4:12) but struck many as a little odd on the lips of Martin, who was almost thirty at the time. The album also seems to launch verbal attacks at Christian musicians who are subtle in their expressions of faith. "Lift Up Your Hearts" asks, "Are they ashamed to bear the Name?" and "Children of the Lord" proclaims, "We don't want to hear the excuses / the doctrinal misuses / We just want to keep it pure / the Gospel must be heard." Again, all of this seems strange coming from an artist who had rarely, if ever, spoken openly of his faith on previous projects. Perhaps he meant it as a vow for the future: "We can't undo everything we've broken / But we will be outspoken." Martin next surprised everyone with *Unelectric,* a project on which eight of Joy Electric's old songs are re-presented without the dominant synthesizers. The prominent use of piano and acoustic guitar creates an entirely different atmosphere. The performance of "Monosynth" is obviously ironic, as Martin now extols the virtue of playing music on a synthesizer to an acoustic, piano accompaniment. Overall, the new arrangements tend to reveal previously hidden melodies, and several of Martin's compositions turn out to be pretty good songs after all.

The White Songbook Legacy, Volume One, is a labor of love that took Martin a year-and-a-half to perfect. It eschews rules and expectations to an unprecedented degree, allowing each song to develop on its own terms. Rather than three-minute sugar rushes, Martin offers a variety of more complex tunes, many of which are over five minutes in length. *HM* said, "it has been some time since a sterilized, synthetic work of catchy pop music has been so affectual, haunting, heavy, and downright moving." *CCM* singled out "The Boy Who Never Forgot," "The Heritage Bough," and "Shepherds from the Northern Pasture" as ranking among Joy Electric's "smartest songs." As the album's subtitle implies, it is intended to be the first in a series.

Martin has always insisted that he writes his songs on guitar and only adapts them for synthesizers later. "Melody is the number one thing," he told *7ball* in 1996. "At the end of the day, you're not going to be humming some stupid little blippity-bleep sound; you're going to be humming the chorus." He deserves credit for perseverance in what he calls a "tiny bubble within a small bubble," i.e., synth-pop within the Christian music scene. He appreciates that "the style of music is not one that many people will like" and yet experiences continued frustration at his ongoing lack of acceptance within the Christian music industry—especially when Joy Electric has garnered praise from general market publications like *Alternative Press*. "I feel like I've been fighting for so long," he told *Bandoppler* in 2000, "doing the music that's close to my heart in spite of whether it's a commercially viable style or not. . . . But the point is, do you believe, number one in the songs that you're writing, number two in the music you're doing, and number three in the message you're trying to convey. If you believe in those things strongly enough, then so be it."

For trivia buffs: Ronnie Martin wrote articles for *HM* magazine on such groups as **Mortification** and **MxPx**, even though the magazine—at that time—did not cover Joy Electric. "It's like the reverse thing with us," he said. "I don't like the bands in that magazine but that doesn't mean they're not legitimate."

The Juliana Theory

Chad Alan, gtr.; Brian Detar, gtr., voc.; Joshua Fiedler, bass; Neil Hebrank, drums; Jeremiah Momper, gtr. // Josh Koskar, gtr. (+ 2000). 1999—*Understand This Is a Dream* (Tooth and Nail); 2000—*Emotion Is Dead*; 2001—*Music from Another Room* [EP].

www.thejulianatheory.com

The Juliana Theory is a Pennsylvania pop-emo band formed by Brian Detar of the metal group **Zao**. The group initially formed in response to an invitation from a group of students (called The Julianna Group) at a Pittsburgh university who were conducting "a sociological experiment to study how people respond to what they are told and how people react to music." Detar says he is not at liberty to reveal any more about the experiment than that, indicating obliquely that "if I told you what they were trying to prove, I would basically disprove

it." The sound of Juliana Theory is radically different from that of Detar's metal outfit, although layers of heavy, chunky guitars continue to form the aural core of many songs. Detar's vocals, however, are smooth, and the pace of many of songs is slow to midtempo. Some critics draw comparisons to general market act Weezer. *Understand This Is a Dream* features songs of loss and longing. "For Evangeline" is a ballad that expresses a yearning for spiritual peace. "Music Box Superhero" addresses the issue of celebrity and band worship, to the tune of a beautiful atonal guitar. In any event, Brian Quincy Newcomb would praise the record in *CCM* as "bracketed in intelligent modern rock and guitar-driven power pop." Lyrics contend against materialism in "Show Me the Money," and celebrity obsession in "Music Box Superhero." *Emotion Is Dead* has a more focused, mature, and confident sound. A reviewer for *Phantom Tollbooth* said the songs "Into the Dark" and "Don't Push Love Away" are "two of the most beautiful songs I've ever heard." The group responds rather pointedly to critics in another song, "We knew you'd hate this before we wrote it / So listen up. We're telling you before you tell us. . . . You're an alias, an email address / We lay a lot more out than you do. . . . You're a paper fist, a faceless attack" ("To the Tune of 5,000 Screaming Children"). *Music from Another Room* offers a six-song farewell to fans on the Tooth and Nail label in anticipation of a 2002 debut for the general market on Epic. "Piano Song" evinces more commercial potential than much of the group's previous work, summoning images of slow songs by Ben Folds Five or Elton John.

The Julies

John Bada, bass; Greg Hohman, drums; Chris Newkirk, voc.; Alex Yost, gtr.; Patrick Zbysiewski, gtr. 1996—*Lovelife* [EP] (Flying Tart).

Christian pop band The Julies broke up before their only album—an EP—was released. The group from Eversham, New Jersey, only recorded six songs—but what a wonderful six songs they were! *True Tunes* calls them "the quintessential band that might have been" and begins their review of the album with the words, "Prepare for major frustration, because *Lovelife* is very, very good." The sound is basically that of modern British pop. "Drive Me Mad" and especially "Love Scene Seventeen" sound a lot like the British band James. Bill Campbell of **The Throes** produced the record and the Cure-affected sound of that band is referenced here as well. Still, The Julies had their own sound, and on *Lovelife* they went for quality rather than quantity: six stellar songs that most groups would require three albums to produce. Think of it as an honest greatest hits collection, with no filler. The album title appears to be a pun, for all six songs are about romantic love relationships, but they also espouse an attitude of love *for* life. The cover is deceptive of the album's depth, featuring a dopey cartoon of two google-eyed kids reminiscent of those trite Precious Moments pictures.

Jump5

Personnel list unavailable. 2001—*Jump5* (Sparrow).

Jump5 appeared toward the end of 2001 as Christian music's first entry in a genre that was beginning to be called preteen pop. Although the idea of dumbing down boy-band music was frightening to some, marketers had realized that there was an age gap between children enamored of Teletubbies and young teens in love with *NSYNC. Groups like A*Teens were created to provide a segue, and Nickelodeon and the Disney Channel provided ample after-school exposure for the new sound. Thus, Jump5 is a prepackaged quintet that performs highly choreographed, high energy songs with very simple melodies, sugary lyrics, and a repetitive beat. They acquit themselves well, coming off as every bit as competent as their general market counterparts. The emphasis in their songs, appropriately, is on good, clean fun ("Spinnin' Around," "Start Jumpin' "). Lyrics instill positive values and are spiritually devotional while remaining age appropriate. "The Meaning of Life," however, might be a bit much for an eight-year-old to ponder.

Christian radio hits: "Spinnin' Around" (# 13 in 2001).

Junko

1992—*No Secrets* (JuneCo); 1994—*I Live in Harmony*; 1997—*Joy*; 1999—*Eternal Treasure* (Rising Sun).

www.junko.com

Junko Cheng is an Asian-American inspirational singer who records under her given name and targets her bilingual ministry to other Asian Americans. Raised in Osaka, Japan, until the age of nine, she became a Christian as an adolescent. After graduating from the University of California with a degree in computer science, she devoted herself to full-time music ministry. In 1996, she was featured in a cover article in *Today's Christian Woman*. Her debut album contains the testimony song "Land of the Rising Sun" about leaving Japan and coming to America. The song won a 1993 award in the Gospel Music Association's New Artist Showcase. *Joy* is a Christmas album of carols and hymns. *Eternal Treasure* collects songs about family and friendship. "As for Me and My House" proclaims a parent's commitment to raise children in a God-centered home. "Yet I Will Praise You" is based on Habakkuk 3:17–18. "Love in Any Language" speaks of sharing God's love with people of all cultures.

Jupiter James

Angelo Esquibel, bass; Joseph Esquibel, drums; Travis Zimmerman, gtr., voc. 1996—*Called as Paul* (Velvet Blue).

Very little information is available about Jupiter James, whose album received virtually no publicity from their label or in the Christian media. *Called as Paul* was officially produced by Jason Martin of **Starflyer 59,** though he appears to have just set up some microphones in a studio and told them to have at it. This actually gives the album an appealing live feel. The individual songs evince a variety of styles. "John the Madman" and "Armored Car" are sludgy, heavy guitar anthems. "Sanctuary Island" is softer and more sensible, and "Nothin' Comes Easily" and "The Paper Song" are Beatlesque pop. "Sonshine" is propelled by a single guitar riff that recalls '60s groups like Iron Butterfly (minus the organ) or Mountain. "The Bomb" is similarly retro but goes for more of the slow, bluesy sound that characterized Quicksilver Messenger Service and, sometimes, Led Zeppelin. Lyrically, the album clearly reflects Christian ideas only here or there. The entire lyric to "Sonshine" goes, "I'm going to depend upon the son to show me the way back to it, cause he's going to give me new life." "John the Madman" is about John the Baptist. The opening line sort of makes sense ("I'm not from the '60s but I like my hair long and shaggy") but from there it just gets weird ("I like to drive rather swiftly / My ship's a trip it travels at warp 60," etc.).

Damien Jurado

1997—*Waters Ave South* (Sub Pop); 1998—*Gathered in Song* [EP] (Made in Mexico); 1999—*Rehearsals for Departure* (Sub Pop); 2000—*Postcards and Audio Letters* (Made in Mexico); *Ghost of David.*

www.damienjurado.com

Singer/songwriter and audio voyeur Damien Jurado has a bit in common with general market artist Beck: he is unpredictable, but seems to have a preference for lo-fi, folk stylings. A Seattle native, Jurado was once in a band called Coolidge, which placed a song on a compilation disc called *I'm Your Greatest Fan* (Tooth and Nail, 1996). *Waters Ave South* borders on emo, with mellow music that conveys a note of urgency. Ed Carrigan of **Blenderhead** plays guitar, bass, trumpet, and trombone on the disc; Paul Mumaw of **Soulfood 76** and **Rose Blossom Punch** plays drums. Jurado sings in a creaky voice with phrasings reminiscent of **Bob Dylan,** and most of the songs tell stories. "Yuma, AZ," for example, is about a girl whose mother is dyslexic, and "Treasures of Gold" about a woman who loses her husband to war. *Gathered in Song* is basically just a continuation of *Waters Ave,* though the songs are now more acoustic and less pop-oriented. On both projects, a Christian orientation is discernible but muted throughout. Sub Pop did not even bother to distribute *Rehearsals for Departure* to the Christian market, though its urban folk songs, again, are quite similar to those that are on Jurado's previous work. The opening track is the story of a girl making her way back to Ohio after being kidnapped by her estranged father.

Things don't get *really* weird till *Postcards and Audio Letters.* The latter album contains no music but is simply a collection of taped conversations that Jurado found on discarded cassettes while sorting through bins at flea markets and thrift stores. For instance, we get a long and rambling monologue left on some answering machine by a guy whose girlfriend has dumped him. The most disturbing piece records a domestic dispute between two parents, complete with screaming and cursing and what appears to be the sound of the father beating their child.

Jurado returned to music on *Ghost of David.* The origin of the album's name lies in a dream Jurado had that his friend David Bazan from **Pedro the Lion** had died, and the album touches often on themes of mortality. The title track is the song Jurado would have sung to Bazan's widow had he really died ("Forget him not, he still loves you / Life is short, but love is eternal"). There are more odd story songs: "Medication" is about a man having an affair with a cop's wife; "December" recounts how a man freezes to death in a car during a North Dakota winter. The song "Tonight I Will Retire" relates the thoughts of a suicidal man who thinks his revolver will deliver him "into the loving arms of my Savior." Jurado has also contributed a song to a Sub Pop tribute version of Bruce Springsteen's *Nebraska* album.

Justifide

Joey Avalos, gtr.; Jason Moncivaiz, voc., drums; Sambo Moncivaiz, bass. 2000—*Life outside the Toybox* (Ardent).

www.justifide.com

Justifide is an Arkansas rock band formed by three pious teenagers who say they devoted themselves to a period of fasting from TV, going out with friends, and video games while waiting on God to show them what to do with their lives. The album *Life outside the Toybox* was recorded when Jason and Sambo Moncivaiz were nineteen and Joey Avalos, eighteen. The group has a hard rock/rapcore style that fuses a variety of influences. Rock critic Brandon Curtis suggests they have a sound similar to Linkin Park or Disturbed. Lyrically, their songs are issue-oriented, dealing with such subjects as lust, teen

pregnancy, child abuse, and materialism. The album was produced by Billy Smiley of **White Heart** and includes one laid-back reggae tune ("Sweet New Found Joy"). Jason says, "God's given us the talent for music, and we look at that as art and give that our all. But at the same time, we're also doing this to reach people for Christ. It's one hundred percent of both."

Justus (a.k.a. Justus Three)

Danny Hackett, voc., bass, kybrd.; Kevin Pahl, voc., drums, kybrd.; Rod Pahl, voc., gtr.; kybrd. 1984—*Don't Turn Away* (Tunesmith); 1986—*Someone's Waiting* (StarSong).

A Canadian trio, the boys in Justus adopted that name as a pun after their Vancouver-based group went through multiple incarnations with many other musicians coming and going. The decision to be just a trio included a commitment to a stripped-down sound, favoring straight-ahead no-frills rock and roll. The songs on *Someone's Waiting* deal with basic Christian themes. "Rumor" addresses the destructive power of gossip; "That's Not for Me" is a rejection of the occult; "Give Us a Burden" and "Surrender" testify to faith in Christ.

Christian radio hits: "Take Me Home" (# 13 in 1987).

Jyradelix

Johann Fontamillas; Wilson Peraltla. 1992—*Invincible* (MYX).

The two artists who compose the techno band Jyradelix have also recorded under the names **Erinfall** and Mindbender. Their album *Invincible* is of interest to Christian music fans partly because their musical cousins Jerome and Jyro of the band **Fold Zandura** join them on the project. The music is classed as "old school rave," with swirling synthesizers, a constantly pulsing beat, and abundant use of samples and spoken phrases. "Take My Life" offers a prayer for spiritual cleansing, and "Mysteria" offers praise to God for triumphing over evil. Two songs, "Four 29–92" and "Repercussions," offer social (and spiritual) commentary on the 1992 race riots in Los Angeles. A bit of humor comes into play on "Ol' McRave," a techno version of the song, "Old MacDonald Had a Farm."

Justice

See **Brian White and Justice.**

K

Tonio K.

1979—*Life in the Foodchain* (Full Moon/Epic); 1980—*Amerika* (Arista); 1983—*La Bomba*; 1986—*Romeo Unchained* (What?); 1988—*Notes from the Lost Civilization* (What?/A&M); 1997—*Olé* (Gadfly); 1998—*Rodent Weekend '76–'96 (Approximately)*; 1999—*Yugoslavia*.

In a 1998 "Where Are They Now?" retrospective, *CCM* magazine would comment that "if ever a pop artist showed evidence of a true conversion, it was Steve Krikorian (a.k.a. Tonio K.)." The artist's works are regularly classified as preconversion (first three products) and postconversion (everything else with the exception of *Rodent Weekend,* which is mixed). The thing is, the artist himself tells no tale of any conversion. "I have always been a Christian," he insists, pointing to his upbringing in the Armenian church. Thus, he discounts all the reports in the Christian press that repeatedly claim that he got saved sometime between 1983 and 1986 as errant musings of a mindset foreign to his spiritual tradition. "In my teenage years I may have been more interested in James Brown (than Christ)," he avers. "But I always believed." What was apparent, at least, was a change in orientation, as the artist switched to making albums that were marketed through the Christian music industry with an eye to the Christian music subculture.

Krikorian was born in Palm Desert, California, in 1949. In 1972 he joined a version of The Crickets, fronting Buddy Holly's old backup band and singing the master's hits at oldies shows. He had a gift for songwriting, and in 1978, Irving Azoff (manager for The Eagles) decided to promote him as "the new

Bob Dylan." His professional name—which would later cause him to be mistaken for a rapper—was chosen from a character in a Thomas Mann short story named Tonio Kröger. Tonio K. turned out to be a critic's favorite, and a musician's musician, though Top 40 hits and commercial success eluded him. *The New Rolling Stone Encyclopedia of Rock and Roll* says that he distinguished himself with "sardonic self-consciously literate lyrics and high-velocity rock and roll." Another critic dubbed him "the angriest young man in rock," observing his penchant for rant-and-rave songs like "h-a-t-r-e-d." *Life in the Foodchain* was his masterwork featuring its powerful title track, "American Love Affair," and a couple of Lou Reed-inspired bizarro anthems with odd titles ("Willie and the Pigman," "The Ballad of the Night the Clocks All Quit"). Some critics turned on him when he released *Amerika,* which they took to be reeking with arrogance and intellectual conceit (e.g., lyrics in German and Greek). Krikorian insists that people didn't realize he "was just joking"—a recurrent problem for him. *La Bomba* would bring more jokes, including a new antiwar version of the Ritchie Valens' song that originally had been titled "La Bamba." All three of Tonio K.'s so-called pre-conversion albums feature profanity, crass descriptions, and misogynist lyrics that many fans of Christian music would find repugnant. Nevertheless, after *La Bomba* bombed and Tonio K. found himself without a contract, friends who knew he was a man of faith suggested he contact Myrrh Records and make an album for the contemporary Christian community. This seemingly unlikely scenario led to the production (on What? records, a Myrrh subsidiary) of what many regard as two highly significant contemporary Christian music albums.

Romeo Unchained seemed to just appear out of nowhere in 1986 and took the Christian music community completely by surprise. There was little celebrity-conversion hoopla surrounding the project since (unlike **B. J. Thomas, Mark Farner,** or **Bob Dylan**) Tonio K. was not a known quantity. Few fans of contemporary Christian music had ever heard of him or knew anything about his modest career in the secular realm. Critics knew him, however, and *Romeo Unchained* became one of those rare Christian albums that got notice in the mainstream press. Kurt Loder wrote a very positive review of it in *Rolling Stone.* Loder said the record was an arousing original" and "the best **Bob Dylan** album since Dylan lost interest in the pop-song form." The artist was also well known to musicians, and a stellar cast of performers like Tim Chandler **(The Choir, Daniel Amos)**, **Mark Heard,** David Miner, and Charlie Sexton all add their talents to the record, which was produced by **T Bone Burnett.** Musically, *Romeo Unchained* is a tad mellower than Tonio K.'s previous projects but it still evinces a post-punk new-wave sound not too dissimilar from that of **Steve Taylor.** Tonio K. has an Elvis-like voice and is able to reference Bowie in the same manner as Taylor when he decides to do so. But the Taylor comparisons are even more telling in his witty and satirical lyrics. One of the standout tracks on *Romeo Unchained* is "I Handle Snakes," which pokes fun at the bizarre worship practices of some Pentecostal groups. Thematically, though, the main focus of the record is human relationships. "Emotional War Games" and "You Belong with Me" explore the complexities of modern romance—a topic that seems to have been much on his mind (shortly after the album was released, Tonio married the photographer who shot the cover). Though his songs are informed by faith, Tonio K. remains a realist. "Perfect World" (like the later **Jimmy Abegg** song with the same name) is a lament that acknowledges love never works out quite the way it should. "Impressed" is an ode to great romances in fiction, noting a bit sardonically that the model they provide seems unrealistic. That song and "You Don't Belong Here" call to mind the work of Burnett or **Bruce Cockburn**—Christian artists who, like Tonio K., seem to function primarily as outsiders to the Christian music guild. "You Don't Belong Here" was covered by Charlie Sexton on his debut album *Pictures for Pleasure* (MCA, 1985). In 2001, a poll of critics sponsored by *CCM* magazine would select Tonio K.'s *Romeo Unchained* as one of "The 100 Greatest Albums in Christian Music"—they put it at Number Twelve, just ahead of **Randy Stonehill**'s *Welcome to Paradise* and **DC Talk**'s *Jesus Freak.*

Notes from the Lost Civilization dealt less with the foibles of modern romance than with socio-political issues, accenting the false hopes that culture offers. The album has a funky, R&B

flavored sound and was made with another all-star cast of players: Booker T. Jones (of Booker T and the MG's), **T Bone Burnett, Peter Case,** Jim Keltner, David Miner (who co-produced), and Charlie Sexton. *CCM* would distill the basic message as being "that faith, hope, freedom, and peace are acts of civil disobedience." The album opens with "Without Love," which sounds enough like Bruce Springsteen to confuse the latter's mother and takes its lyrical cue from 1 Corinthians 13:1–3. "I Can't Stop" has a touch of disco (just enough to be frightening), and "Where Is That Place?" (dealing with the demise of the American dream) seems like a Talking Heads song. A decade later, Krikorian would single out "The Executioner's Song" and "Children's Crusade" as what he still regarded as the *Notes from the Lost Civilization*'s outstanding tracks. At the time of the album's release, however, the song that drew the most attention was "What Women Want," in which Tonio K. offers a satirical perspective on women from the perspective of a chauvinistic male: "They want champagne and jewelry and German cars . . . they want roses by the dozen, wanna break your heart." But this was all satirical, as the final verses turn about to address such men (including himself) and indicate that perhaps what women *really* want is "love, someone they can trust, some affection, a little protection." In any case, executives at Myrrh figured that Christian music fans might be more obtuse than the general public and, so, decided that the album should be issued in two different editions: A version without the "controversial" song was released on What? and sent to Christian markets, while another version of the complete album was released through A&M and sold everywhere else. No big censorship controversy ensued and nothing of great substance was lost. Still, the decision to release different versions of *Notes from the Lost Civilization* would in later years assume symbolic value as exemplary of the Christian music industry's persistent disdain for its own clientele (cf. **Vigilantes of Love** and the "Love Cocoon" controversy).

Leaving the potential confines of the Christian label, Tonio K. recorded another album in 1990 for A&M only. Then, superstar Janet Jackson agreed to pose topless for her next album cover and A&M determined to cut all minor artists from their roster in order to put more money behind what they (rightly) assumed would be a bonanza. The completed Tonio K. album would collect dust in a vault somewhere for years, and for almost a decade the artist would be off the radar screen of public consciousness, though he continued to participate in the music scene through songwriting. His best-known composition from the period is probably "Love Is," a Grammy-winning duet by Vanessa Williams and Brian McKnight that would be declared "the most played song of 1993." He also wrote music for a number of TV shows *(Baywatch, Beverly Hills 90210,* and *Melrose Place)* and for motion picture soundtracks. **Al Green** recorded his "Nobody Lives without Love" for *Batman Forever* and sang his rave-up gospel song "Love God (and Everyone Else)" in *Michael*. He also composed songs recorded by **T Bone Burnett, Aaron Neville,** the Pointer Sisters, and Bonnie Raitt, and wrote or cowrote most of the material on Charlie Sexton's *Under the Wishing Tree*. That might have been the end of the matter, were it not for a fan with an idea. Sometime around 1996 a Tonio K. fan by the name of Mitch Cantor founded the small indie label Gadfly and took it upon himself to re-release the artist's complete catalogue. He also managed to obtain master tapes from A&M and finally released the 1990 record, which he titled *Olé,* in addition to an eclectic collection of other previously unreleased songs called *Rodent Weekend*. These endeavors all sparked new interest in Tonio K., primarily among a Christian music audience that now seemed more appreciative of his maverick approach. Inspired, the artist went back into the studio and offered Gadfly an album of all-new material called *Yugoslavia*.

Of the three Gadfly releases, *Olé* is clearly the most significant. Though it might lack the populist appeal to compete with Janet's (hand-covered) breasts, it is an impressive and mature work of art. Produced by **T Bone Burnett** and David Miner, the album features many of the same musicians who played on *Notes* (Jones, Case, Sexton), though this time David Hidalgo (of Los Lobos) and Paul Westerberg (of the Replacements) also lend a hand. Musically, though, the tone is more rootsy, evincing more the style of blues-influenced singer/songwriters than the new-wave pop of earlier albums. The Springsteen comparisons still hold, but with more homage to *Nebraska* than *Born in the U.S.A.* The album opens with a very strong cut, the almost rockabilly "Stop the Clock," which is followed by "Time Steps Aside," a fabulous pop song about a hippie girl in the '90s, an "outrageous" young woman who somehow transcends the decades to evince the values of '60s idealism ("peace, love, and free your mind") in a society that no longer appreciates such concepts. The artist's lyrical cynicism is still evident in songs like "Pardon Me for Living": "Where is that nation under God / With liberty and justice and blah, blah, blah? / It was a great idea on paper / But it hasn't actually happened yet." Yet in "Come with Me" the artist looks with hope to a celestial country where "acts of compassion are valued like pieces of art." Likewise, the song "What a Way to Live" is trademark Tonio, arrogantly dismissing an ex-girlfriend's attempt to slander him: "Anyone that knows me won't believe you / And anyone that doesn't, doesn't care / And anyone that spends a little time with you / Will soon realize the danger lurking there." But then "I'll Remember You" sounds like a gorgeous '60s pop ballad and fondly recalls an adolescent experience of young love. The album's most sensitive and moving song is "Hey Lady," a painfully biographical account of watch-

ing a woman in a store checkout line inflict emotional abuse on her children. As for *Rodent Weekend,* Krikorian admits in the liner notes that he doesn't understand why the songs are being released since he personally regards them all as rejects. Some of the tracks from his supposedly preconversion period contain shocking instances of profanity and expression of what many would regard as un-Christian ideas. The very album jacket jokingly lists a song called "F**k the Whales," though no such song actually appears. More offensive to some will be songs like "Don't Talk to Me" and "Everything, Including You, Disgusts Me," which once more reflect the artist's disturbing attitude toward women. Perhaps the most notable tracks are "I'm Supposed to Have Sex with You," a robotic ode that parodies the mechanical nature of sexuality in modern society, and "Too Cool to Be a Christian," which likewise lampoons that society's dismissive attitude toward religion; the latter track had once been intended to serve as the title track for the album *Notes from a Lost Civilization*. "Hey John" is addressed to the author of the biblical book of Revelation—the song was recorded but never released by **Johnny Rivers.**

The Phantom Tollbooth selected *Yugoslavia* as its "Pick of the Month" in December of 1999. Steve Stockman, chaplain at Queen's University in Belfast, called it "a benchmark for any Christian in the arts . . . as brilliant a lesson in how faith caresses and collides with real world as anything else this millennium." This *millennium*? Hyperbole aside, the album does return Tonio K. to *Olé* form, as he plays once more with the usual gang (Burnett, Case, Miner, Sexton) and actually allows his cohorts a bit more sway this time out. The artist says that he originally wrote "I Know a Place" and "Murder My Heart" as pieces he thought Tina Turner might record. The former is a tender-but-tough ballad about finding a "quiet corner of the heart" where there is inner peace; the latter relates an account of "the night someone I used to love tried to murder my heart." A song called "Student Interview (with the Third Richest Man in the World)" addresses the emptiness of materialism. "Home to You" is a sweety country love song. "Again" is a very Springsteenesque ballad of recurrent heartbreak. **Kate Miner** sings backing vocals on "Sure as Gravity." Krikorian offers some of his best world-weary reflections on a song titled "Life's Just Hard": "Nobody ever said that life was going to be easy / But no one ever told me about this / Sometimes I just hate it. . . . It's a fiery ordeal / You play your cards / And you say a prayer / And you look for love. . . . But it's just hard."

For trivia buffs: Tonio K. formed a short-lived band with Charlie Sexton in 1990 called Sixteen Tons of Monkeys. The group enjoyed quite a bit of regional success in the Austin area before Sexton decided to regroup Stevie Ray Vaughan's band to form Arc Angels.

Christian radio hits: "Perfect World" (# 8 in 1986); "True Confessions" (# 9 in 1986).

Glenn Kaiser (and Kaiser/Mansfield and Mansfield, Howard, and Kaiser)

As Glenn Kaiser: 1993—*All My Days: Songs of Worship* (Grrr); 1994— *Spontaneous Combustion;* 1997—*Throw Down Your Crowns;* 1998—*You Made the Difference in Me;* 1999—*Time Will Tell; Blues Heaven: The Best of Glenn Kaiser's Blues;* 2000—*Winter Sun* [by The Glenn Kaiser Band]; 2001—*Carolina Moon.* As Kaiser/Mansfield: 1990—*Trimmed and Burnin'* (Grrr); 1993—*Slow Burn.* As Mansfield, Howard, and Kaiser: 1995—*Into the Night* (Grrr); 1997—*Delta Blues.*

www.glennkaiser.com

Glenn Kaiser is best known as front man for the classic Christian rock group **Resurrection Band,** but he has also released a number of blues-oriented solo albums in addition to projects with his friends and musical soul mates **Darrell Mansfield** and Larry Howard. Kaiser was raised a nominal Lutheran but times were hard—the family was on and off welfare—and his life was completely shattered when his parents divorced while he was a teenager. He sought solace in music and became involved with drugs before becoming a born-again Christian. In 1994 he would recall, "Nothing else gave me so much happiness or sense of purpose until I asked Jesus Christ to come into my heart and become absolute Lord of my life." Kaiser hooked up with the Jesus People U.S.A. community (first based in Milwaukee), where he met his wife, Wendi. He and Wendi's brother, John Herrin Jr. would become elders in that community before they reached the age of twenty. Eventually, Kaiser would attend North Park Theological Seminary in Chicago and become an ordained minister in the Evangelical Covenant Church. JPUSA moved to Chicago and came to be noted for its socially conscious inner city ministry as well as for its musical outreaches. The community has produced numerous musical artists, including **Ballydowse, Cauzin' Efekt, Crashdog, The Crossing, Headnoise, Seeds, Sheesh,** and **Unwed Sailor.** JPUSA also publishes *Cornerstone* magazine (for which Kaiser is a frequent contributor) and sponsors the annual *Cornerstone* music festival, the granddaddy of all Christian music events. Kaiser is the author of *The Responsibility of the Christian Musician* (Cornerstone Press, 1994). As one of only a few contemporary Christian music artists with formal theological training—and as a pioneer who has been active in the field for almost thirty years—Kaiser has become something of a senior statesman in the guild, offering advice and wisdom to younger artists, promoters, and audiences. *True Tunes* has said that he is not only "the church's official blues man" but also "the Christian music industry's Town Crier," doing as much as anyone else to call people to integrity within the field. Similarly, *The Phantom Tollbooth* says that Kaiser not only has "one of the greatest voices in rock and roll," but also possesses a "nearly peerless" reputation for integrity both as a Christian and as a musical artist: "He remains a respected brother in the Lord willing to humble himself to God's call to ministry first, not someone who exploits his gifts for an easy buck and the praise of people."

As indicated, Kaiser's side projects have focused more on blues than on the more commercially viable but less satisfying metal music that has been the bread and butter of **Resurrection Band.** Thus, it is here, in his solo work, that he has earned the greatest respect from critics—a tougher audience than Rez' typical headbanger fans. Kaiser has often had to defend the idea of Christians playing "the blues"—a form of music that seems intrinsically connected to depression. "The biggest single category in the book of Psalms is the lament," he explained to *CCM* in 1994. "Who better than Christians to sing about pain and struggle and hurt?" And in response to those who call blues "the devil's music," he avers, "Well, the devil works and moves anywhere he's given ground—sometimes even in the Christian music industry."

The two projects as Kaiser/Mansfield are subdued, evincing raw production and a stripped-down, mostly acoustic approach: simple guitar lines supplemented by two ragged voices and an occasional harmonica. "Things I used to do, I don't do no more," Kaiser bellows on "Great Change" (from *Trimmed and Burnin'*). "The place you need to anchor is right on your bended knee," Mansfield advises in "Slidin' " (from *Slow Burn*). About half the songs from *Trimmed and Burnin'* are well-chosen covers; four are Blind Willie Johnson tunes, including the title track, which is based on a parable of Jesus in Matthew 25:1–13. Along with the Reverend Gary Davis's "I Belong to the Band" (which features the great lyric, "Talk about me just as much as you please / I'll talk about you down on my knees"), these songs demonstrate the roots that traditional blues shares with gospel. But if the somewhat nebulous genre of *modern* Christian blues can be said to have "classics," the title track from *Slow Burn* would be the top contender for that honor. It is not only authentic and gritty but also features sterling lyrics contrasting the temporal with the ultimate: "Earthly glory'll leave you cold / Live 'n' learn / It's like kissin' through a windowpane, pretending it's true love / Live 'n' learn / A love that'll last eternally / That's what I want / A slow burn!" Once Larry Howard was added to the mix, the sound grew more electric, with Kaiser and Howard typically trading guitar licks while Mansfield blows the harp. *Into the Night* was recorded live at the 1994 *Cornerstone* festival. Mansfield offers "Million Dollar Feelin', " and Howard, "I Found Out," but the album's highlight is Kaiser's reprise of a **Resurrection Band** song, "If I Leave This World Tomorrow," which finds him wailing to a slinky backbeat, "I've ha-a-a-ad my share of troubles, but God ain't failed me yet."

Of Kaiser's solo albums, *Spontaneous Combustion* is the only full-bore blues record and, this time, the style is more of a rousing Chicago-blues sound, complete with horns and an occasional choir. The title track shines, as does the incredible "Everybody Understands the Blues." *True Tunes* says "His voice sounds like its been breathing bar-room smoke and swillin' JD for 50 years (though we all know that isn't the case)." Lyrically the album moves back and forth between tales of a lamented wayward past and exhortations to get saved now and experience the power of the gospel. *Blues Heaven* is a fascinating compilation album in that it collects the best songs from all of the aforementioned projects plus several bluesy songs from **Resurrection Band** projects, revealing that the latter group actually had far more grounding in blues than typical associations would imply. As a bonus, the previously unreleased "Ain't Much Difference" is one of the best tracks on the album.

Four of Kaiser's albums are best described as blues-inflected rock. *You Made the Difference in Me* is a powerful R&B album, plumbing the influences of both Motown and Atlantic soul. It opens with the energetic "More and More," which features a gospel choir and rich horn arrangements. "Wind Me Up" has more of the gutsy brass bluster, this time in support of emotional praise lyrics. "Self-control" starts off with **Al Green**-style funk and finishes with a bit of Barry White low-bass growling. "Marry Me" is an ex post facto love song for Kaiser's longtime wife, Wendi. *Time Will Tell* is much more subdued, recalling the mellow sounds of such aging rockers as Rod Stewart or **Eric Clapton.** The songs "Good Hope and New Philadelphia" and "Deliver" recall John Mellencamp. Lyrically, the album explores a number of Kaiser's dissatisfactions. "Postmodern, Existentialist, Ivy League Blues" isn't really a blues song but it does note an objection to current trends in academia: "I heard the shot heard 'round the campus / It was the deification of humanity." Closer to home, "Ya Don't Say" notes the seeming reluctance of many new Christian artists to be explicit about their faith: "Perhaps just a little too young / Maybe just a bit afraid / Or maybe it's just a case of fantasy thrill / Maybe just wanna get paid." On *Winter Sun,* Kaiser fronts a trio that also includes bassist Ray Montroy (of **Resurrection Band**) and drummer Ed Bialach. The album rocks with a sound that sometimes recalls the classic blues-based power trio Cream or the more recent work of Kenny Wayne Shepherd. Songs speak variously of life's hardships ("Homesick Blues," "My Backyard") and ultimate hope ("Thief," "Three Below Zero"). "On My Dyin' Bed" brings the themes together with a testimony to the peace with which the artist regards his own inevitable death. Kaiser also covers the classic Blind Willie Johnson song "Nobody's Fault But Mine" (cf. **Darrell Mans-**

field, **Maria Muldaur, Seventy Sevens,** and Led Zeppelin). *Carolina Moon* features the Kaiser-Montroy-Bialach trio again and is similar to *Winter Sun* with the heat turned up several degrees. "This is one hot screaming rock album," declared a *Phantom Tollbooth* reviewer. The album opens with the well-titled "Torch," an attention-grabbing song thick with powerful guitar chords and drum beats. "Out Cold" presents a cautionary tale of a pill-popping "life in the fast lane" couple whose night on the town culminates with both of them dying in an almost-inevitable car wreck. "Mercy" is a touching song in which Kaiser personifies a quality of God as a woman; he extols Mercy in the same manner that Bono does "Grace" on **U2**'s *All That You Can't Leave Behind.*

Kaiser has also recorded two acoustic worship albums. *All My Days* is a folk-oriented piece with other JPUSA members (including **The Crossing**) playing along on some selections and the community's Grace and Glory choir adding harmony on others. It includes "In the Ocean of His Love," the first song Kaiser wrote after becoming part of the community, and the story-songs "Tapestry" and "Lord of All." John J. Thompson of *True Tunes* called the project "the best worship album that I've heard." *Throw Down Your Crowns* has more of a rustic, country feel. Especially noteworthy is the title track, which expresses the basic concept of ascribing all glory to God. "Cause My Heart" is also powerful lyrically: "Cause my heart to fear your name / Cause my life to reveal the same." In the liner notes to this album, Kaiser says, "I don't 'crank out' worship songs as a cottage industry. I worship God, personally and in accountable relationship with a solid, local church. If songs come, they come." The quality of both worship albums seems to demonstrate the validity of such a natural approach. The records seem less contrived (and less insipid) than the great majority of modern worship records; as with Kaiser's blues album, the songs seem born of authentic experience and, so, reflective of a holiness and joy that cannot just be concocted by design.

Mancy A'lan Kane

1998—*Mancy A'lan Kane* [EP]; (PMG); 1999—*Paper Moon.*

www.angelfire.com/ia/mancyalankane

Nashville native Mancy A'lan Kane came to the attention of most Christian music fans when she contributed female vocals for a **Jars of Clay** song ("Worlds Apart") on that group's multi-platinum debut album. The boys from Jars returned the favor by assisting Kane on her full-length album, providing both instrumental support and background vocals. Kane began writing poetry as a teenager, partly as therapy in dealing with her parents' divorce. Producer David Huff (of **David and the Giants**) heard her sing in church and put her on the fast track to a recording contract. She originally met **Jars of Clay** while working as a waitress at the Caffé Milano restaurant they frequented. Kane was just nineteen when she recorded *Paper Moon*. Her voice bears a striking similarity to that of general market artist Lisa Loeb, though Kane cites Natalie Merchant (of 10,000 Maniacs) as her primary influence. In any case, *Paper Moon* fits nicely into the female alt-folk genre defined by Loeb and Merchant, as well as by such artists as Shawn Colvin and Paula Cole. The title song, she says, is about "a moment of being over-dramatic about boys." In a more serious vein, "Taboo" deals with a third-hand account of incest and "After the Rain," with the pain of her parents' divorce: "After the pain and all the sorrow / When today turns to tomorrow / The sun will shine, after the rain."

Christian radio hits: "After the Rain" (# 19 in 1998).

Kansas

Phil Ehart, drums; Richard Williams, gtr.; Kerry Livgren, gtr., kybrd. (– 1984, + 2000); Robby Steinhardt, viol., voc. (– 1983; + 2000); Dave Hope, bass (–1984; + 2000); Steve Walsh, voc., kybrd. (–1982, + 1986) // John Elefante, voc., kybrd. (+ 1982, – 1984); Billy Greer, bass (+ 1986, – 2000); Steve Morse, gtr. (+ 1986, – 2000). 1974—*Kansas* (Kirshner); 1975—*Masque; Song for America;* 1976—*Leftoverture;* 1977—*Point of Know Return;* 1978—*Two for the Show;* 1979—*Monolith;* 1980—*AudioVisions;* 1982—*Vinyl Confessions;* 1983—*Drastic Measures* (CBS); 1984—*The Best of Kansas;* 1986—*Power* (MCA); 1988—*In the Spirit of Things;* 1994—*The Kansas Box Set* (Legacy); 1995—*Freaks of Nature* (InterSound); *Kansas* (Epic); 2000—*Somewhere to Elsewhere* (Magna Carta).

www.kansasband.com

Kansas was one of the most popular progressive-rock bands of the '70s, filling stadiums and selling millions of albums with a style of music indebted to the Moody Blues and Emerson, Lake, and Palmer. Often deemed pretentious by critics, the group nevertheless thrilled its audiences with over-the-top, effects-laden shows and created a cadre of fans who remain intensely loyal twenty-five years after the first albums appeared. The band scored only occasional hits on Top 40 radio but was a mainstay of album-oriented stations. The *Rolling Stone Album Guide* says that Kansas was "America's answer to Yes and King Crimson" while also noting that their version of the neoclassical art-rock sound was "more organic and less imperious than the British model." The band was formed in 1970 in Topeka and most of the members had been friends from high school days. After three competent albums, they finally hit big with the triple-platinum *Leftoverture,* which drew notice on the strength of its anthemic single, "Carry On, My Wayward Son" (# 11 in 1976). Similar success attended *Point of Know Return,* which features "Dust in the Wind" (# 6 in 1978). *Monolith* and *AudioVisions* would meet with more modest success, though both albums went gold and the songs "People of the South

Wind" (# 23 in 1979) and "Hold On" (# 40 in 1980) garnered some airplay.

But were they a Christian band? Even while the group was at the height of its popularity, speculation raged among fans of Christian music as to where Kansas stood with regard to the faith. Early on, the group had pledged in *Rolling Stone* that they would never do any songs about romantic love because "everything that could possibly be said about that topic has been said many times over." Instead, their songs focused on philosophical and spiritual themes, and Christian fans scoured the lyrics for double meanings and scriptural allusions. "Dust in the Wind" is a remarkable testament to mortality and the transience of life—the song's sentiment is quite compatible with the thought of such biblical writings as Job or Ecclesiastes. The song "Portrait," about a leader who "knew more than me or you," was widely thought to be about Jesus, though some thought it might just as well have been about Moses or Mohammed or the Buddha (composer **Kerry Livgren** has since revealed that he actually had Einstein in mind). In short, Kansas in the mid '70s was regarded in a manner analogous to **Creed** or **Collective Soul** in the late '90s. Christian music fans debated whether the group might be "a secret Christian band," keeping a low profile so as to get their music on the radio. Or perhaps they were just some ambiguously spiritual group whose ideas might even be heretical or dangerous. The reality, of course, was more complex than either of those scenarios. In fact, Kansas seems to have embodied at least three distinct ideological incarnations: the ambiguously religious band (1970–1979); the overtly Christian band (1979–1984); and the almost defiantly non-Christian band (1986–1995).

The group's spiritual identity has been determined primarily by their principal songwriter and de facto leader, **Kerry Livgren.** Livgren would later admit that, speculation aside, he was not a Christian during the band's tenure in the '70s, but was on a spiritual quest that led him to explore all the different religions of the world. It was these ecumenical ideas that found their way into his songs, vague references to spiritual principles and moral codes that almost all systems of faith and philosophy would recognize. An intellectual, Livgren was resistant to the idea of becoming a "born-again Christian" and wanted nothing to do with what he regarded as a simplistic, experiential, and narrow-minded approach to truth. Nevertheless, a series of events (see the Livgren entry) led him to a dramatic private conversion experience in an Indianapolis hotel room in 1979. He almost immediately recorded a solo album providing explicit testimony to his newfound faith, and he shared his story in magazines with the same enthusiasm that the born-again **Bob Dylan** was evincing at about the same time. The next Kansas album, *Audio-Visions,* contained songs that could be heard as espousing the same generic spirituality as previous projects but that spoke with specificity to any who knew of the composer's now very public faith: "A change has come upon me and I'm surely not the same . . . in a single timeless moment the old was cast away / the new was born into a world of simple joy" ("Relentless"). Some of the songs needed a little explanation, which Livgren was happy to provide. "Curtain of Iron" is not just about the political Iron Curtain, but about "the spiritual barrier between humanity and God." "No One Together" declares "the inability for people ever to get it together on this earth (apart from Christ)." The song "Hold On," a minor hit that encourages perseverance, is actually "addressed to any person who is on the brink of coming to Christ" (specifically, Livgren allowed that he wrote the song for his wife, at a time before she accepted Christ). What did the rest of the band make of all this? "They were well aware of what I was saying," Livgren would write in his autobiography, "but their tactic was to accept it for what it was and hope it would eventually go away."

It didn't go away, and three developments determined the next incarnation of the band. First, while the band was touring in support of *Audio Visions,* Dave Hope suddenly announced that he too had become a born-again Christian. Livgren was no longer alone. Next, lead singer Steve Walsh rebelled. He had indeed been patient for a time, singing the *Audio-Visions* material and even providing guest vocals on Livgren's Christian solo project, but when Livgren brought in a batch of explicitly Christian songs intended for the next Kansas release, he walked out and left the band. Notably, if any Christian singer were to leave a secular band at the height of its popularity, in effect sacrificing a chance to make a lot of money because he (or she) objected to the ideological content of the group's material, that singer would be praised for his or her integrity. Walsh, on the other hand, came in for a great deal of criticism from unappreciative Christians who claimed he just "couldn't handle the truth" or was too much of a coward to speak up for what was right. Livgren went with the former option: "Anytime you're singing about something that embodies the truth—that's a very uncomfortable situation," he told *CCM* in 1982. In any event, a third development significant for Kansas's future seemed almost providential. The band auditioned for a new singer and chose none other than **John Elefante** on the merits of his voice alone. The youthful Elefante was a devout evangelical who wanted to sing for a Christian band. He knew of Livgren's faith and auditioned for the Kansas spot without telling anyone involved about his beliefs or goals, praying that if God wanted Kansas to be a Christian band he would get the job. Shortly after he was hired, he surprised everyone by sharing this news and it became apparent to all that the Christians had taken over. Indeed, Elefante was also a songwriter, so Kansas now had two evangelicals writing their

songs (three, if one counts John's brother Dino Elefante). "The odds against this being coincidence are rather astronomical," Livgren exulted. "Imagine finding someone who could fill Steve Walsh's shoes both vocally and as a writer, and then learning that he was also a Christian. It was just incredible and it became obvious to me and to Dave Hope that *our* prayer had been answered in a very specific and dramatic way." The group hired yet another devout Christian, Warren Hamm, to tour with them, playing saxophone, flute, and harmonica.

Vinyl Confessions and *Drastic Measures* were both overtly Christian albums, sold in Christian bookstores and reviewed in Christian magazines. Kansas was now widely perceived to be a Christian band (with a few, almost invisible non-Christian members) and churches sent their youth groups by the busload to their concerts. Although the songs on these two albums were not as explicit in their proclamation of faith as records by bands like **Petra,** they previewed the more subtle approach to be taken by many Christian artists in the '90s. In that sense, at least, the group was ahead of its time, recording material that used enough poetry and imagery to allow the unconverted to appreciate the music on its own terms without having to feel like they were getting preached at on every cut. The overall theme of *Vinyl Confessions* is that there is good and evil in the world ("Borderline"), that one can choose between them ("Crossfire"), and that this choice has temporal and eternal consequences ("Diamonds and Pearls"). But the message goes beyond generic morality: "Deep within the hardest heart there is something there that knows / There's a hunger life can never fill 'till you face the One who rose." And on "Play On" Elefante sings what amounts to a song of praise to his "Morning Star," who lifts him up, leads him through life, and sets his heart on fire. "Chasing Shadows" challenges the listener to find such inspiration, too: "The truth will find us all someday / And the price is more than you can pay." The album's biggest hit, "Play the Game Tonight" (# 17 in 1982), is the only song not written by Livgren and/or Elefante—but there is a story behind it. The song that was originally given to the band by outside writers seemed a perfect match for the Kansas style but was called "Stay with Me Tonight" and seemed suggestive of a sexual liaison. Livgren, Elefante, and Hope vetoed it—but then got permission to change a few lyrics and turn it into a song about a *musical* one-night stand. The basic thought (Will you remember me after our night together?) is now expressed by a singer to his concert audience. *CCM* magazine selected *Vinyl Confessions* as one of their "Ten Best Albums of 1982," with reviewer Thom Granger describing it as "a stunning hybrid of Christian and secular music."

On *Drastic Measures,* the band pulled back from proselytizing a little bit, but not by much. "Life only comes from the one who made it," Livgren claims in "Incident on a Bridge." And in

"Don't Take Your Love Away," Elefante sings "You can have it all," pledging his riches, fame, dreams, and very existence in a song of dedication that would make little sense directed to a human partner. "Fight Fire with Fire," the song that received the most airplay from the album, deals with sticking up for one's faith. Most telling, "End of the Age" evokes all sorts of apocalyptic imagery drawn straight from Revelation to describe a final judgment "when the reign of man will end forevermore" and "the fools who believed in their empty ways / will be witness to a world that's set ablaze." Livgren would later maintain that he was in a writer's slump at this time, and that neither "End of the Age" nor "Incident on a Bridge" deserved to be on the album. He also admits that Kansas had "exhausted itself artistically" by this point, a sentiment echoed in the terrible reviews that *Drastic Measures* received in both the mainstream and Christian press. Writing for *CCM,* Brian Quincy Newcomb said the album "would appear to thwart the hope of many Christians that Kansas would become the first Christian supergroup in the secular market." Perhaps the best track on the album is Livgren's "Mainstream," which addresses the struggle that musicians face between the pull of artistic integrity and the drive for commercial viability. Newcomb and others found the song ironic on an album that, as a whole, failed to achieve either.

One might have thought that Elefante, Hope, and Livgren would be elated to have the platform that was every Christian band's dream. Their songs got played on mainstream radio and they retained a strong following within the general market in spite of the fact that they had been clear and articulate about their Christian faith. Audiences and critics either appreciated the faith, respected the band's convictions, or at least found the specifics of their ideology irrelevant so long as the music kept on rocking. But all was not well. The effort to make Kansas into "a Christian band operating outside the Christian subculture" did not sit well with the members who had not signed on to be part of some evangelical outreach, or with the record company executives who wondered whether to credit the sluggish sales of *Drastic Measures* to its ideological stance or admitted lack of musical innovation. As for the first point, reports surfaced in the media that the band had become so polarized that the Christian members no longer even sat with the non-Christians or had much of anything to do with them off-stage. Even if such rumors were exaggerated, the final straw came when Livgren presented his next batch of songs for what was to be the group's third faith-filled album. According to Elefante, executives at CBS drew a line in the sand and insisted that the band refrain from doing any more songs with "spiritually aggressive lyrics." They wanted us to "keep the rock sound in but take the Christian message out." This time, it was Livgren, Hope, and Elefante's turn to walk and Kansas came to

an end. Elefante, at least, has regretted that decision. In the late '90s, he told *Phantom Tollbooth,* "I look back in retrospect and think, man, if we could have just sat down and talked it out we could have survived the whole thing and stayed together." After the break-up, a re-formed version of the band fronted by Walsh played the has-been circuit and released a few unsuccessful albums, but many believed the *real* Kansas tradition was carried on in **A.D.,** a band that Livgren formed with Hope and a number of other alumni who had toured as extras with the group. **A.D.** made explicitly Christian albums targeted for the contemporary Christian music community. Elefante would similarly form **Mastedon** with his brother, and eventually the two of them (John and Dino Elefante) would become successful and sought-after producers in the Christian music industry. Livgren and Elefante would also make solo records. Hope became a youth leader at St. Andrews by the Sea, a charismatic Episcopalian church in Destin, Florida. Interestingly, the big *Kansas Box Set* completely omits all material from "the Christian period," in what amounts to a feigned denial of the very existence of *Vinyl Confessions* and *Drastic Measures.* Founding member Phil Ehart explains this lapse by saying the intent was to give the set focus by including only material by "the original band."

In 2000 a surprising reunion of the original Kansas lineup produced the album *Somewhere to Everywhere,* and the group toured with Yes. Livgren had already joined the band for a brief tour of Europe in the summer of 1990, an event that he says he viewed "foremost as an opportunity to reestablish some strained friendships." He also contributed a song ("Cold Grey Morning") to the 1995 *Freaks of Nature* album, without playing on it. Still, the 2000 reunion represents an even more visible and enduring reconciliation. Notably, Livgren wrote all ten songs on the album, and they are similar in sound and content to the generically spiritual songs of *Point of Know Return.* "Myriad" is actually an old song from 1970 that the band played but never recorded. "Distant Vision" is classic Kansas with majestic violins and soaring vocal harmonies. "Byzantium" incorporates Eastern influences. "Icarus II" is intended as a sequel to a hit off of the band's *Masque* album. For Livgren, at least, the return to general market music seemed to represent another swing of the pendulum, a different resolution of a paradox with which he has struggled for years. Even while pursuing his uncompromised career in the limited Christian market, he was able to see the ambiguity of that posture. "What good is music if nobody hears it?" he asked *CCM* magazine in 1989. Even then, furthermore, he could appreciate that the Lord works in mysterious ways: "More people have been led to Christ through 'Dust in the Wind' than through everything else I've written . . . and that song does not mention Jesus and I was not a Christian when I wrote it. It just tells the truth."

KarenLeigh

See **Truth.**

Karitsat

See **The Sheep.**

Tom Karlson

1980—*Living on the Edge* (StarSong).

Tom Karlson recorded one album of original pop songs with lyrics that are primarily evangelistic, directed toward nonbelievers. *Living on the Edge* was produced by **Benny Hester.** Karlson plays acoustic guitar on most tracks, but Hester provides the songs with additional electric instrumentation that gives them more power.

Evie Karlsson

See **Evie.**

Karthi

1993—*Karthi* (ForeFront).

Born in India, the R&B/pop singer known as Karthi immigrated to New York City as a child and then settled with her family in Joplin, Missouri. Growing up a young Hindu in the buckle of the Bible belt, she was surprised to learn that her mother had in fact been a Christian for over twenty years. "I couldn't believe that this was part of her that we had never known," the singer explains. "And when she spoke about Jesus she sounded like a woman in love." Eventually, Karthi came to embrace the Christian faith herself through the witness of a high school friend. Moving to Nashville, Karthi found work initially as a backup singer, working with **Morgan Cryar, Rick Cua, DC Talk, Cindy Morgan, Geoff Moore, The Newsboys,** and **Michael W. Smith.** Her debut album is a dance record of original R&B and hip-hop music that some would compare to the work of Christian artists **Lisa Bevill, Kim Boyce,** or **Angie Alan.** About half of the selections are produced by **The Gotee Brothers.** "Next to Ya" is a rave-up opener establishing the essential dance theme, but a number of other songs delve into deeper subjects lyrically than is usually thought necessary for dance music. "Are You There?" gives honest expression to the feeling of alienation from God, and "Air You Breathe" describes a cultural atmosphere that encourages people to define their worth in terms of performance and thus offers continual inducements to self-doubt and low self-esteem.

Christian radio hits: "Listen" (# 14 in 1993); "I Got the Joy" (# 8 in 1994); "We the People" (# 22 in 1994).

The Katinas (a.k.a. Katina Boyz)

James Katina, voc.; Jesse Katina, voc.; Joe Katina, voc.; John Katina, voc.; Sam Katina, voc. As Katina Boyz: 1991—*Katina Boyz* [a.k.a. *So Good*] (Arcade). As The Katinas: 1999—*The Katinas* (Gotee); 2001—*Destiny.*

www.thekatinas.com

A Polynesian R&B/pop group composed of five brothers, The Katinas have enjoyed two distinct periods of success in Christian music. The brothers moved to America from the island of Tutuila in Samoa in 1988 and eventually wound up in Nashville. *Katina Boyz* struck a chord with many fans of Christian dance music, and they toured with big name artists like **Andraé Crouch, Amy Grant,** and **BeBe and CeCe Winans.** The group changed its name to The Katinas in 1998 and scored again as part of the high-profile, multicultural E.R.A.C.E. tour led by **DC Talk.** Although that ill-fated tour surely failed to attain its goal of "eliminating racism and creating equality" (it started to unravel midseason due to representatives of **God's Property** squabbling over money), The Katinas came through it all unscathed and were able to gain a newer, larger audience.

Katina Boyz (sometimes titled *So Good*) was produced by **Roby Duke** and seeks to capitalize on the boys' natural propensity for harmonizing. On songs like "Wade in the Water" (a cover of the traditional song) they come off as an upbeat Boyz II Men, but on "Perfect Thing" their heritage shines though with a distinctive swingbeat and chanting in their native tongue. The song "So Good" is mild hip-hop with a rap interlude and a perky synth-pop backdrop. By the time the group made *The Katinas,* the so-called boy-group sound was all the rage, but their album was considerably better than the prefabricated fluff associated with such artists as the Backstreet Boys, *NSYNC, or 98 degrees. "Takin' Me Higher" is the opening, standout track—a **Toby McKeehan** song that could easily have been done by **DC Talk** but is owned quite competently by the Katina brothers. The theme of that song is essentially the same as that of Rita Coolidge's 1977 hit, "Your Love Has Lifted Me Higher and Higher" (also a gospel song, actually). "There You Are" is a lovely and poetic ballad about discerning the presence of God in nature. More urban, hip-hop influences come into play on "The Circle." The song "Nothin' But" has a classic Stevie Wonder vibe, and "Sing Me a Song" (another McKeehan composition) is appropriately melodic, recalling Earth, Wind, and Fire's "Singasong." A number of songs, "Mama," and "The Other Side," are touching tributes to the boys' departed mother, reminiscent of **Guardian**'s equally sweet "See You in Heaven." *Destiny* is a worthy successor to *The Katinas* and would be greeted as the group's sophomore project. Its most remarkable song, "You Are," finds the brothers pretending they're a madrigal choir on a song that swells into a soaring affirmation of hope in Christ alone ("You are my fortress when I'm not strong enough"). "My Samoa" taps into the Caribbean beat, and "Dance" offers a **Kirk Franklin**-styled funk celebration of God's mercy. "Who Do You Love?" is an especially melodic midtempo ballad probing the listener to consider a basic question about loyalties first posed by Jesus in the Sermon on the Mount (Matthew 6:24). Otherwise the album's songs have enough of the boy band sound to get noticed by fans of lesser groups and yet enough substance to introduce such fans gently to something less formulaic.

The Katinas' song "Writing a Letter" (from *The Katinas*) must be understood against a narrative of the brothers' upbringing and life. Their father, Moses Katina, returned from Vietnam an abusive alcoholic who, despite the fact that he became a pastor, beat his wife and children and ruled the household with fear. The brothers got out of the house early and had nothing more to do with him. Then they received notice that he had been forced into a veteran's rehabilitation center and as part of his treatment had asked to speak to the family. The boys all gathered around a speaker phone to hear his confession and request for their forgiveness. "I'm ashamed of a lot of the things I did in Vietnam," he related, "and there's been so much bitterness and anger and hate in my life that I've never given to God." After his release, Moses also wrote a three-page later to his deceased wife admitting to his shortcomings and asking for her forgiveness. The song "Writing a Letter" is based on this experience, and the senior Katina has sometimes shared his story in public in connection with its performance.

Christian radio hits: As Katina Boyz: "Come Back" (# 3 in 1991); "Perfect Thing" (# 11 in 1991); "So Good" (# 17 in 1992); "Draw Me Close" (# 20 in 1998); "Takin' Me Higher" (# 17 in 1999); "One More Time" (# 19 in 1999).

David Kauffman

1999—*Simple Truth* (Damascus Road).

www.davidkauffman.com

Roman Catholic singer/songwriter David Kauffman plays guitar pop songs similar to those of early Bryan Adams. He lives in San Antonio, Texas, and began performing in the late '80s. In 1989 his song "Come and See" was chosen as the theme for the National Catholic Youth Conference, and he ended up performing it for the Pope, in addition to singing it at numerous rallies and conferences. *Simple Truth* would score big with another tune, "I'm Sorry," which struck a responsive chord with thousands of sentimental listeners. The song is a simple attempt for Kauffman to find closure regarding a thoughtless act from his childhood. As he tells it, when he was eight years old he walked across the street to Sarah Banazsak's house and pushed her down because "making her feel small made me feel big." Remembering that day as an adult, Kauffman decided to track Ms. Banazsak down and apologize. The quest to find her

proved futile and he wrote "I'm Sorry" as a public declaration instead. Inspired by the song, people began sending him similar stories and he started a website at which people could say "I'm sorry" to those they could no longer locate to apologize for wrongs they had done. *Simple Truth* also includes the song "Don't Stop Looking," Kauffman's plea for others not to give up on him, and "Feed the Forgotten Soul," which expresses an insatiable need for God.

Cheri Keaggy

1994—*Child of the Father* (Sparrow); 1996—*My Faith Will Stay*; 1997—*What Matters Most*; 1999—*There Is Joy in the Lord: The Worship Songs of Cheri Keaggy*; 2001—*Let's Fly* (M2.0).

www.cherikeaggy.com

Cheri Keaggy (b. 1968) grew up in Southern California and received training in classical piano from childhood. She began her career in Christian music by working as a worship coordinator at her local church and occasionally writing songs to match the proposed sermons or themes of the day. She was discovered by **Charlie Peacock** when he heard her playing piano and singing in private before a concert at which her husband Eddie was to serve as audio engineer. As the story goes, Peacock called his record company the next day and said, "I've got two words for you: Cheri Keaggy." Peacock also produced her first two albums, both of which evince a basic adult contemporary sound. *Child of the Father* has a particularly vertical or worship orientation, while *My Faith Will Stay* focuses on the life of faith and on godly relationships. The first album spawned the hits "Open My Heart" and "Make My Life an Altar," earning Keaggy a Dove nomination for Best New Artist. The title song to *My Faith Will Stay* is a tribute to **Phil Keaggy**, her husband's uncle, and his longtime spouse Bernadette. "Lay It Down" from that album offers assurance that God is a source of help for every need. "Keep On Shinin' " was cowritten with **Randy Stonehill**, and "Heavenly Father" is a worship song that Keaggy says she composed while folding laundry in front of the TV. Throughout this album in particular, Cheri Keaggy often sounds remarkably like **Amy Grant** in her vocal phrasings and approach. For her third album, she switched producers to rely on the talents of Phil Naish who gave the record a more pop-oriented appeal. "What a Privilege," in particular, has a Beatlesque flair, in part because it pairs Cheri for the first time with uncle-in-law Phil. "Overture to Freedom" is an instrumental that she composed when she was fifteen. "Heaven's on My Mind" has a sort of spunky elegance that reminds some reviewers of **Susan Ashton**. *There Is Joy in the Lord* is a collection of mostly upbeat worship choruses, many of which had been featured on previous albums or else came from an even earlier period. They are performed with a backing choir and an emphasis on congregational praise. *Let's Fly* is another pop-oriented project with a few worship songs sprinkled into the mix. The title track (with guitar by Uncle Phil again) is noticeably catchy. The album's closing song, "Christ in Me," is also a heartfelt highlight.

Christian radio hits: "Open My Heart" (# 1 in 1994); "Make My Life an Altar" (# 12 in 1994).

Phil Keaggy

1973—*What a Day* (New Song); 1976—*Love Broke Thru*; 1977—*How the West Was One* (Live Oak); *Emerging* (New Song); 1978—*The Master and the Musician* (Myrrh); 1980—*Ph'lip Side* (Sparrow); 1981—*Town to Town*; 1982—*Play thru Me*; 1983—*Underground (Private Collection, Vol. 1)*; 1985—*Getting Closer* (Nissi); 1986—*Way Back Home* (Pan Pacific); 1987—*Prime Cuts* (Myrrh UK); *The Wind and the Wheat* (Maranatha); 1988—*Phil Keaggy and Sunday's Child* (Myrrh); 1989—*The Best of Keaggy/The Early Years 73–78* (Nissi); *Backroom Trax, Private Collection, Vol. 1* [= *Underground (Private Collection, Vol. 1)*] (PKC); *Backroom Trax, Private Collection, Vol. 2*; 1990—*Find Me in These Fields* (Sparrow); 1991—*Beyond Nature* (Myrrh); *Backroom Trax, Private Collection, Vol. 3* (PKC); 1992—*Backroom Trax, Private Collection, Vol. 4*; 1993—*Backroom Trax, Private Collection, Vol. 5*; *Revelator* [EP] (Myrrh); *Crimson and Blue*; 1994—*Blue* (Epic); *Backroom Trax, Private Collection, Vol. 6* (PKC); 1995—*Time* (Myrrh); *True Believer* (Sparrow); 1996—*220*; *Acoustic Sketches* (PKC); 1997—*On the Fly* (Canis Major); *A Christmas Gift* (Canis Major); *Phil Keaggy* (Myrrh); 1999—*Premium Jams* (Canis Major); *Majesty and Wonder: An Instrumental Christmas* (Word); *Music to Paint By: Brushstrokes* (Unison); *Music to Paint By: Splash*; *Music to Paint By: Electric Blue*; *Music to Paint By: Still Life*; 2000—*ReEmerging* (Canis Major); *Zion*; *Lights of Madrid* (WordArtisan); *Inseparable* (Canis Major); *Uncle Duke*.

www.philkeaggy.com

Next to the myth of "The Vanishing Hitchhiker," the single most popular urban legend making the rounds during the Jesus movement was that Jimi Hendrix was once referred to as the greatest guitar player in the world but he demurred, saying that the honor of that title should go to Phil Keaggy instead. Almost everybody knew someone who knew somebody else who had heard Hendrix (or sometimes **Eric Clapton**) say this. Exaggerations aside, Keaggy gave the Jesus people a legitimate source of pride. Musical taste was very much a part of self-identity in the early '70s and most Jesus music, despite its simplicity, beauty, and integrity, did not hold up to critical examination apart from devotion to the ideological content. Keaggy was one artist the Jesus people could point to and say, "This is what I like" without their unsaved friends laughing at them. He was never the greatest guitarist in the world, but in 1971 he may have been one of the top ten. Three decades later, when the number of guitar heroes had burgeoned exponentially, such a ranking would probably still hold, especially if by *guitar* one means more than simply "electric, rock and roll guitar." By 2002, Keaggy had established himself not just as one to be compared with Eddie Van Halen but also with acoustic maestros like Michael Hedges and John Renbourn. When he does rock out, he shows that he still possesses the chief identifying trait of any truly memorable rock guitarist. Like Hendrix, Clapton, and Van Halen—like Neil Young and Mark Knopfler—Keaggy possesses a readily identifiable style. Those who know it can hear a single riff or intro to a song and immediately claim, "That's Phil Keaggy!" The technical aspects of his virtuosity can probably only be understood by other guitar players—he has, for instance, developed a signature technique of slapping the guitar with two hands to create certain sonic effects, he has experimented effectively with alternative tunings, and he is the acknowledged master at using a device called the Jam Master that allows him to fix a certain riff and play it back with modifications. But what makes him most remarkable—indeed, unique—to the nonspecialist is his capacity to perform admirably in so many genres. Renbourn does not play rock, and Van Halen does not play "new acoustic"—but Keaggy plays both with impressive competence. As such, it is probably fair to say that Phil Keaggy is the most *versatile* guitarist who has ever lived, having taken on a wide variety of styles, mastering them all, and putting his own identifying stamp on them. It is easy to imagine both Jimi Hendrix and André Segovia smiling down on him, nodding their heads in approval, albeit with reference to completely different projects.

Phil Keaggy was born in 1951 in Youngstown, Ohio. He grew up on a farm just outside Hubbard, Ohio, as the ninth child (out of ten) in a family with a devout Catholic mother and a nonobservant Lutheran father. He first gained fame as lead guitarist for the now-legendary band **Glass Harp**. Even before that, however, he was in a band called The Squires, which recorded a single (Canadian Neil Young also started out in a band called The Squires over in Toronto at about the same time—but there is no connection). Then he played with The New Hudson Exit, who also recorded a single (Keaggy invited Joe Walsh to join New Hudson Exit, but the latter declined). He was only seventeen when he joined **Glass Harp** and quickly became the *wunderkind* star of that band. The group made three albums and toured with **Alice Cooper,** Grand Funk, Iron Butterfly, the Kinks, Traffic, Yes, and others. Ted Nugent was particularly taken with **Glass Harp**'s "kid guitarist" and has since said in public, "I don't know what ever happened to that Phil Keaggy guy. . . . Man, he could have saved the world with his guitar!" What happened is, instead of saving the world, Keaggy got saved himself. On Valentine's Day in 1970, shortly after **Glass Harp** first came together, Keaggy's mother was involved in a head-on traffic accident and died a week later. Phil's older sister Mary Ellen comforted the traumatized teenager, telling him about the personal relationship she had found with Jesus Christ and praying with him to bring

Jesus into his own heart. Keaggy reports that he came home from that encounter wanting to hear the song "Presence of the Lord" by Blind Faith. He took out the record and listened to Clapton's lyric over and over again ("I have finally found a way to live in the presence of the Lord"). He woke up feeling transformed and would soon be caught up in the Jesus movement revival that was already underway out on the West Coast and would soon sweep the nation. Later that same year (1970), he says he was "baptized in the Holy Spirit at a Kathryn Kuhlman service."

As part of **Glass Harp,** Keaggy testified powerfully to his faith in Jesus both on the albums and in the stage shows. Nevertheless, a number of ill-informed Christians advised Keaggy that, if he wanted to be "one hundred percent for the Lord" he should leave the world of rock behind. Thus, he left **Glass Harp** and determined that henceforth he would only make overtly Christian music for release on Christian labels, and that he would only play concerts sponsored by Christian organizations for primarily Christian audiences. That decision, many historians would say, is one of a few events that symbolically marks the beginning of the parallel universe now known as contemporary Christian music, the birth of an industry and a culture that—for better *and* for worse—coexists with the secular environment, with only occasional reference points between them. Keaggy became a touring member of the classic Christian band **Love Song** for a few months in 1973. Then he moved to Freeville, New York, where he became part of the Love Inn community headed by DJ-turned-evangelist Scott Ross (who, incidentally, is married to **Nedra Ross** of the Ronettes). He released his first album *What a Day* during the transition (before **Glass Harp**'s last album) and then submitted himself to the discipline of the Love Inn community, which he hoped would help to disciple him to be "a man of God." He has never doubted that it did that, but he has said since that the years at Love Inn were "a very hard time for me." For one thing, development of music was sometimes relegated beneath such menial chores as duplicating tapes of The Scott Ross Radio Show to fill mail orders. An invitation from **Paul Clark** brought him back into touch with the developing Christian music scene as he contributed noticeably to the latter's classic *Good to Be Home* album. Buck Herring also snagged him to play on **2nd Chapter of Acts**' *In the Volume of the Book.* Herring would produce *Love Broke Thru* for Keaggy, and Keaggy would also contribute to **Honeytree**'s *Evergreen,* making him a ubiquitous entry in the rather small early Jesus music catalog. He also toured, playing acoustic shows with Peter York, who would later become the head of Sparrow Records. Around this time, his wife, Bernadette, suffered a series of traumatic pregnancies. She miscarried in 1975 with a set of triplets. In 1976, an infant son named Ryan lived only for a few days. In 1977,

she suffered another miscarriage. Bernadette Keaggy later wrote a book about how God sustained the couple through these trials (*A Deeper Shade of Grace,* Sparrow, 1993). In 1979, the family moved to Leawood, Kansas (near Kansas City). Later they would relocate to Southern California, and eventually to Nashville.

Though it is difficult to imagine what contemporary Christian music would be like without Phil Keaggy, the artist has usually been somewhat aloof within that world. Most (but not all) of his albums have sounded more like records that *he* wanted to make than albums that record company executives thought he should make. In this regard, his career has been analogous to that of Neil Young in the general market—prolific, yet marked by curious experiments (some misguided, some brilliant), occasional sell-outs, frequent critical triumphs, and sporadic commercial success. But for Keaggy such aloofness is not just the quirk of an introvert but a spiritual principle. "You can't drum up anointing in a studio," Keaggy told *CCM* in 1980, and he has tried to live by that motto, striving almost always to make albums with a sincerity and an integrity that he believes is necessary for them to be vehicles of inspiration. At the same time, Keaggy has been featured many times in *Guitar Player* magazine, a mainstream publication that takes little interest in his spiritual motivations but does pay homage to his prowess. *Musician Magazine* also lists him as one of their "Top Guitarists of the 20th Century." In terms of guitar playing, Keaggy cites his early influences as The Ventures, Jeff Beck, George Harrison, Pat Metheny, and especially Mike Bloomfield. By 2000, he would also be praising the aforementioned Renbourn and Hedges. He has also recorded as part of the trio **Keaggy, King, and Denté.**

Almost half of Keaggy's recordings are instrumental projects. Indeed, for many years *The Master and the Musician*—contemporary Christian music's first instrumental project—was his best-selling album. But in general, the vocal offerings have been the best-known and most accessible works. Keaggy's voice is very similar to that of Paul McCartney. Over the years, Keaggy has responded to the inevitable, constant comparisons differently. At first he seemed flattered by them, admitting that he was a major Beatles fan and that he used to practice singing to McCartney records, trying to learn the singer's affectations. "I tried to fashion my vocal style like McCartney," he told *Harmony* in 1975. Later, he was annoyed by the comparisons and denied their substance. "Perhaps ears aren't discerning enough to realize there is a great difference," he told *CCM* in 1986. And, again in 1989: "You've got this 5'11" chap from Liverpool, and I'm this 5'4" guy from Ohio—we are *not* going to sound alike." Still later, he just accepted the comparisons with grace and humor, admitting with a laugh that his song "Love Divine" *was* "just a Beatles rip-off." In 2000, he said, "I sure don't mind the Beatles comparisons. They wrote the best songs of the rock era, period, and any comparison to them is a compliment." Of course, Keaggy's voice has its own quality and he has never been capable of hollering the way the early McCartney did. But then Keaggy is ten times the guitarist that either McCartney or his bandmates George Harrison and John Lennon ever were. He has also proved to be a more consistent songwriter than the post-Beatles McCartney, though he is sometimes plagued by the same problem as the latter artist— the perennial struggle of deciding (as Bob Seger once put it), "what to leave in, what to leave out." He resolves this by just releasing everything and letting his audience and critics decide what is worthy. And decide they do.

What a Day was one of Jesus music's first super albums—a phenomenal masterpiece that everyone (in the Jesus movement) owned and that no one would dare disparage. The story behind the record's production seems like an urban legend but is actually true: It was recorded at a cost of $1,800 in fewer than thirty-six dusk-to-dawn hours, and the songs so inspired producer-for-hire Gary Hedden, who was engineering the recording, that he became a Christian himself. In retrospect, the album only contains three really good songs, but none of it is embarrassing and, indeed, the whole project reflects the youthful exuberance of a new convert who is excited by his faith. Such naivete seemed inspiring in the '70s, but trite during the two decades that followed. By the end of the '90s, however, many adult Christians (including Keaggy himself) were developing what philosopher Paul Ricoeur calls "the second naivete"—a mature piety based on an informed rejection of cynicism rather than on simple ignorance of life's complexities. As such, *What a Day* and, indeed, much of the '70s Jesus music, began to sound refreshing once again. The record is James Taylor mellow, consisting of little more than Phil and his acoustic guitar in a studio. The three songs that hold up best are "Rejoice," a musical meditation on Luke 15:7 that features the album's finest guitar solo; "That Is What the Lord Will Do for You," a melodic and poetic statement of the promise of regeneration; and the title track, which looks forward to a reunion with the saints in heaven: "When I get home / I will see all / The holy men I read about / Peter and John / James, Luke and Paul / And brother Tom without a doubt."

Love Broke Thru broke all boundaries for what were then limits on the professional quality of Christian music. Keaggy was able to command first-rate production and he got it, turning out a lush album recorded with the very best session musicians (Leland Sklar, Jim Gordon, Larry Knechtel) and even a small orchestra backing him on some tracks. The album raised the bar for Christian music considerably and, in that regard, marks the dividing line between the simple days of Jesus music and the more competitive enterprise known as contemporary

Christian music. And if Keaggy's producer got saved during the making of *What a Day,* this time his background vocalist **Mylon LeFevre** would be so inspired by the *Love Broke Thru* sessions that he would later claim they marked the turning point in which he determined to give his life and career over to the Lord. Musically, *Love Broke Thru* is an album that could have held its own against most of what was produced in the general market that year. Mainstays **Michael Omartian** and Buck Herring (husband of **Annie Herring** and manager of **2nd Chapter of Acts**) served as coproducers. The title track (written by **Keith Green, Randy Stonehill,** and Todd Fishkind) is certainly a better pop song than most of what topped the secular charts that year (McCartney's "My Love"?; Helen Reddy's "Delta Dawn"?). It is, in fact, one of the best contemporary Christian songs ever written; it has been recorded many times by many artists, but Keaggy's version of it here is the best of them all. *Love Broke Thru*'s second highlight is "Time," an almost seven-minute electric rock track that presents a musically and lyrically powerful ode to mortality: "Well he hasn't always been around / And he won't always be. . . . his name is Time and he's coming to an end / His name is Time, where will you be my friend?" This song quickly became Keaggy's "Layla," his signature rock hit—it was still his most requested song twenty-five years later. In the Jesus movement days, Keaggy used to perform half-hour versions of it with long, searing jams that would break into a hard rock rendition of Grieg's "In the Hall of the Mountain King." *Love Broke Thru* surpasses *What a Day* with a few more excellent cuts. The C. S. Lewis poem "As the Ruin Falls" is set to a beautiful, haunting melody and the sometimes overlooked "Take Me Closer" is one of Keaggy's all-time best tunes, a vibrant pop song that bursts open at the seams as the artist joyously proclaims, "I love you, Lord!" Likewise, "Just the Same" (cowritten with Buck Herring) offers testimony to Christ's dependability in a powerhouse song that would have fit nicely on that Blind Faith album the adolescent Keaggy once treasured. On the other hand, the aforementioned problem of song inclusion does surface on this album. "Disappointment" is an awful song by any standard—predictable melody, hallmark card lyrics (*not* by Keaggy), and deplorable theology (when bad things happen it is because God appointed them). Many maturing Jesus freaks just shook their heads or cringed.

Songs from *What a Day* and *Love Broke Thru* are featured on the live album *How the West Was One,* an elaborate three-record box set that presents Keaggy in concert with the **2nd Chapter of Acts.** This was the one of the most important live albums of the Jesus movement, almost on a par with **Barry McGuire**'s collaboration with 2nd Chapter, *To the Bride,* or with **Andraé Crouch and the Disciples'** *Live at Carnegie Hall* in quality and importance. Keaggy's nine-minute version of "Time" is definitive, but the sixteen-minute take on "Rejoice" only offers a firm rebuttal to the adage that there can never be too much of a good thing.

Keaggy's third album, *Emerging,* has been his most neglected, though it is actually every bit as good as *What a Day* and *Love Broke Thru.* Part of the neglect is Keaggy's own doing, for he has never liked the record, calling it "a real let down." He especially complains about the record's production, which he says made his already high voice sound like "a choirboy." But he also says that difficult circumstances (the authoritative structure of Love Inn, his wife's miscarriages, and the death of his infant son) had left him "feeling broken." He told *CCM* in 1989, "It came across in the way I sang. I listen and I don't hear any emotion." Despite such disclaimers, the album holds up better than Keaggy thinks. It was officially released by The Phil Keaggy Band, a group that included **Phil Madeira** on vocals and keyboards and Lynn Nichols (of **Dust** and, later, **Chagall Guevara** and **Passafist**) on guitars, with Terry Andersen on drums and Dan Cunningham on bass. The opening "Theme" is a brief instrumental composed by Madeira that is one of the best pieces that artist has ever written. It sets the jazzy tone for the album and leads effectively into the wonderful "Where Is My Maker?" a sort of pop-jazz shuffle with lyrics from the book of Job and a unique sound. "Struck by the Light" is also a powerful song, and Madeira's lead vocal offers a break from the McCartneyisms. "Turned on the Light" and "Take a Look Around" are two of Keaggy's better rock songs, and the latter is especially poignant theologically. The message, "There's a kingdom emerging / And I find that very encouraging," summarizes the central message of Jesus' teaching (Mark 1:14–15) in a memorable way and establishes the titular theme of the album; the fabulous sax solo is an added bonus. "Ryan's Song" is Keaggy's "Tears in Heaven," a soft and touching elegy for his lost child. "Sorry" is a pop parable based on Matthew 25:1–13 and "Another Try" is a Beatlesque prayer for forgiveness. After more than a twenty-year wait, *Emerging* was finally released on compact disc as *ReEmerging* in 2000—with new songs added through a reunion of the original band, including Madeira's "Mighty Lord," which has also been recorded by a number of other artists. A sixteen-page booklet details the story of the band, their life at Love Inn ("in retrospect, somewhat cult-like," Madeira says), and the making of the classic album that Keaggy supposedly doesn't like.

After his trio of initial masterpieces Keaggy entered what he has called his "middle period," making albums of inconsistent quality. The triad of *Ph'lip Side, Town to Town,* and *Play thru Me* pales in comparison to the first three albums, but does offer a smattering of great songs. Of the three, *Ph'lip Side* is by far the best. The idea was to make a record with one side of acoustic songs like those on *What a Day* and one side of rock songs in

the tradition of "Time." What the project actually reveals is the disparity of quality between these two styles. The "hard side" features four of Keaggy's best songs, from the rollicking joy of "Just a Moment Away" (written with Doug Pinnick—not **Ty Tabor** as Di Sabatino reports—of **King's X**) to the heavy plodding of "Sunday School" to the driving beat of "Pulling Down" to the synthesizer-driven pop of "Royal Commandment." The "soft side," however, is just McCartneyesque fluff, akin to such lightweight excursions by the ex-Beatle as "Teddy Boy" or "Hi Hi Hi"—as good as those songs, but no better. The best of the bunch would be "A Child in Everyone's Heart," which offers a loving remembrance of childhood. The one soft song that did get considerable notice is "Little Ones," an antiabortion track with an affecting melody. While the song is cherished by some advocates of the pro-life movement, it resorts to melodrama that prevents it from having any appeal to those who are not already convinced of a rather extreme version of that doctrine. Presenting pro-choice advocates as baby killers whose "deliberate crimes" will bring the wrath of God upon the earth does not really advance the debate in any helpful way. For some, the song becomes more powerful by realizing the personal investment Keaggy must have had in this issue, having now lost four children to miscarriage and one to infant death. But perhaps that is the point—if he had written a *personal* song about how a couple that wants to have a child feels when confronted with the insult of widespread abortion—*that* might have been effective. Instead, "Little Ones" goes for the easy rhetoric and lacks any persuasive emotional power. It is, however, a much better song than "The Survivor" (from the *Underground* album), another antiabortion song Keaggy would write from the perspective of a fetus, who supposedly knows what is going on and wonders whether or not he will be murdered. This particular fetus, it turns out, is already a believer and prays to God for salvation (cf. **Kathy Troccoli**'s "A Baby's Prayer"). The song just makes abortion protestors look stupid and hurts the cause it intends to support.

Town to Town offers two very fine songs. The title track is a jazzy reflection on life on the road that recaptures the magic of *Emerging.* "Full Circle" is classic pop built around a catchy hook; the song had already been a Christian radio hit for **Nedra Ross** in 1978. In addition, "Let Everything Else Go" has a simple lyric that many have found to be inspirational. A version of the hymn, "Rise Up O Men of God" is spoiled by the sexist lyric—many denominations had altered the wording to "Rise Up O Saints of God" by 1981. *Play thru Me* offers a bevy of pleasant but nondescript soft rock songs typical of what one would expect from a lesser artist—say, **DeGarmo and Key.** The adult contemporary love ballads ("She Came to Stay") and children's songs ("Papa Song") failed to satisfy Keaggy fans who knew he was capable of more. The one exception may be

"Making a Change," on which he trots out some rock and roll licks reminiscent of **Glass Harp.** "Nobody's Playgirl Now" is a song about a converted *Playboy* model, set to a bouncy melody that seems inappropriate for the subject matter. Better tracks include "Happy," a mostly instrumental guitar extravaganza, and "Carefree," a little pop shuffle that lives up to its name. "Cherish the Moment" has especially nice lyrics: "We may never pass this way again, take nothing for granted."

About this time, Keaggy began releasing his "private collection" albums—six volumes of *Backroom Trax* (though Vol. 1 was originally called *Underground*) over the next decade. These lo-fi albums were all recorded in his basement and usually feature him playing all of the instruments. Like all the PKC releases listed above, they were originally made available only to his fan club, on cassette only, but were later given a broader distribution on CD. Of primary interest to collectors and megafans, they do not contain the artist's best work but they do reveal him in especially intimate and vulnerable modes. They are also testimony to his incredible stature as a composer. As with the "middle period" albums, the disappointments are keyed to the stature of the artist. With Keaggy, the throwaways and filler are often comparable to what lesser artists would count among their finest material.

In any case, the last half of the '80s would feature a triumphant return to form with two classic albums, *Getting Closer* and *Sunday's Child.* Sandwiched between these two magnificent albums was *Way Back Home,* a collection of quiet songs for family and friends that probably should have been part of the *Backroom Trax* series (*True Tunes* considers it "one of the truly great Christian albums of all time," but its intimate character handicaps appreciation by the general public). *Getting Closer* was hailed at the time (by *CCM* and others) as Keaggy's best work to date. The album opens with "Look Deep Inside," a worshipful paean to being "holy to the Lord" that is one of Keaggy's prettiest songs ever. Then he jumps immediately into the up-tempo "Where Has Our Love Gone?" a political song focusing on a perceived loss of compassion in modern America. "Movie" and "Sounds" are examples of what Keaggy probably does best: perfect pop songs, full of catchy hooks and soaring guitar solos. "Like an Island" is almost unbelievably sweet, and "I Will Be There" has a beguiling "You've Got a Friend" (James Taylor) feel to it. *CCM* called *Getting Closer* "the album on which Keaggy has finally hit full stride," and noted that Side Two (with "Sounds" and the scorching "Passport") recalls his classic work with **Glass Harp** more closely than any other solo project (to date; cf. *Crimson and Blue*). "Riverton" (written with **Richard Souther**) is also a standout track and has become something of a Keaggy classic.

On *Sunday's Child* Keaggy apparently decided to capitalize on all those McCartney comparisons and just make a Beatles album. He assembled an all-star band of Christian music's best—including **Rick Cua,** Derri Daugherty (of **The Choir**), **Mark Heard,** Lynn Nichols, **Randy Stonehill, Russ Taff, Steve Taylor,** and **Alwyn Wall**—and together they pulled it off. They made what has been called "the best album the Beatles never released." Blatantly imitative work is usually demeaning to both imitator and imitatee, but when it's the *Beatles* who are the prototype and when the execution is as flawless as it is here . . . respect must be paid. "Tell Me How You Feel" could have been on *Revolver* and "I Always Do" (written by Heard) on *Rubber Soul,* without any embarrassment. "I'm Gonna Get You Now" is built on the same riff as The Knack's "My Sharona" (which they stole from the Rolling Stones anyway) but gets more interesting as it progresses and even has Keaggy hollering like (latter day) McCartney by the end. Stonehill's "Ain't Got No" is also a screaming song, with the writer himself and **Russ Taff** helping out on the vocals. Stonehill sings lead on "Walk in Two Worlds" as well, a track that he and Keaggy wrote together about the necessary challenge of engaging society as a participant, not just an observer. On both of the preceding songs, Stonehill acts as effective Lennon to Keaggy's McCartney, adding a darker edge to the music in terms of both composition and vocals. "I've Just Begun (Again)" is a bright and sparkling track that is actually a refurbished **Glass Harp** tune from 1968. "Blessed Be the Ties" has a loping, understated melody that is remarkably compelling; the song also features especially poignant lyrics by **Steve Taylor** about the pros and cons of feeling tied down in a relationship. "Ever a pressure pressing / Ever an undertow / Why do the ties you've chosen / Slowly pull you low?" But then, commitment does offer benefits that might be missed: "I had a dream last night I was finally left alone / Nothing to tie me down / No one to kiss goodnight / Never again to feel your whisper pull me to your side." The band also turns in an incredible version of an old gospel standard, "Talk about Suffering," complete with jangly Byrds guitars and vocal harmonies by Heard and Jimmie Lee Sloas (cf. **Dogs of Peace**). The absolute highlight on what is by all accounts a stellar album, however, is the band's take on another Heard song, "Everything Is Alright" (available only on cassette and CD versions of the album). Produced by Nichols, the album also takes a more subtle approach to spirituality than most of Keaggy's work. With the exception of "Talk about Suffering," openly religious concepts are no more evident than on some of the Beatles' own records. Bottom line: anyone—Christian or not—who likes the Beatles and doesn't have *Phil Keaggy and Sunday's Child* has neglected what would probably be one of their favorite albums of the past twenty years.

The title song to *Find Me in These Fields* is a quiet prayer similar to what one would normally expect from an artist like

Michael Card or John Michael Talbot. It showcases cello by John Catchings. The album as a whole has a soft rock sound to it, but "Final Day" and "Carry On" pulse with an intensity that cries out for live performance. "Get Over It" is a six-minute opus with a touch of the blues vibe that Michael Roe brings to some of his Seventy Sevens projects. "Strong Tower" (based on Proverbs 18:10) and "Gentle and Strong" are fine pop songs, and "Be in My Heart" is a sweet worship song with a sing-along chorus. The *Find Me* album was recorded with a band that included Rick Cua and Phil Madeira along with Mike Mead and Lynn Nichols.

In 1993–1994, Keaggy pulled a Neil Young and established himself as a master of *three* decades. The album variously titled *Blue* and *Crimson and Blue*—the former for the general market and the latter for the Christian community—marks another zenith of his thirty-year career. Again, it is the use of a full band that makes all the difference. Keaggy reunites with Nichols and Madeira from the *Emerging/Find Me in These Fields* cast and that ensemble is augmented this time by drummer John Sferra of Glass Harp and bassist Wade Jaynes of Chagall Guevara. John Painter of Fleming and John plays mellotron and trumpet. *(Crimson and) Blue* is marked by the sort of joyous abandon evident on Keaggy's first two albums, and he maintains that every song was recorded in just two or three takes. It could almost be deemed his best work on the strength of two songs alone: a seven-and-a-half minute scorching rocker called "Doin' Nothin' " and an equally scorching seven-and-a-half minute version of the traditional gospel song "John the Revelator." The former has dumb, judgmental lyrics about the emptiness of Hollywood, but these are hidden beneath a magnificently overwhelming barrage of guitars. The latter sounds a great deal like Cream and is easily the best version of the song ever recorded by any artist, which is saying a lot. "John the Revelator" is a wonderful song on its own merits, though it was unknown to most fans of contemporary Christian music—not to mention most secular music lovers—before Keaggy introduced it in this, its definitive version. It really does deserve to be listed with "White Room" and "Sunshine of Your Love" as one of the best psychedelic blues rock songs ever put on vinyl. "Don't Pass Me By" (not the Beatles song) is another hard rock triumph, though the distorted vocals seem inappropriately trendy. The song deals with a basic theme of compassion, and was written with the charitable organization Compassion International in mind. "All There Is to Know" (written with Madeira) goes for more of a Tom Petty vibe, which is nice for variety. Another surprise is "Shouts of Joy," a remake of an old Ray Repp worship song, transformed now into an all-out rocker that recalls what Glass Harp once did with "Do Lord." In this case, the Scottish inflection and martial beat give the song a completely different feel than one would ever have

imagined for it. The band also covers (a bit slavishly) Van Morrison's "When Will I Ever Learn to Live in God" with Ashley Cleveland in the background. "Everywhere I Look" is another Keaggy-does-the-Beatles track and could have been an outtake from *Sunday's Child*. A Madeira composition, it's a very nice song, with a sprightly melody with meaningful lyrics expressive of the presence and availability of God ("Everywhere I look you are . . . Out beyond the farthest star / Even then, there you are"). "Stone Eyes" (cf. the Beatles' "Dr. Roberts") also seems like a *Sunday's Child* outtake. In 2001, a group of critics pulled together by *CCM* chose Keaggy's *Crimson and Blue* as Number Twenty in their list of the "100 Greatest Albums in Christian Music," indicating that, in their opinion, it is his best work (*Love Broke Thru* also appeared on the list at Number Sixty-four, and *How the West Was One* at Number Ninety-three).

Originally, the very title for *Crimson and Blue* was based on a *Ph'lip Side* concept: the record featured a "crimson" side of Beatlesque pop songs and another side of blues-oriented rock. Keaggy complained in interviews that the record company forced this concept upon him—he had wanted to do an entire album of "blue" material, and both fans and critics were unanimous in declaring the "blue" material to be superior. Still, the subsequently released *Blue* album is not really the less pop version of *Crimson and Blue* that its title implies. The two versions of the album only diverge with regard to a few selected tracks. *Crimson and Blue* contains a remake of "I Will Be There" in addition to a cover of the traditional gospel song "Nothing But the Blood" and two more shameless Beatles copies, "Love Divine" (cf. "All My Loving") and "Reunion of Friends" (cf. "Hello Goodbye" and "Strawberry Fields Forever"). Instead of these, *Blue* has a twelve-and-a-half-minute spontaneous instrumental jam between Keaggy and Sferra called "The Further Adventures of. . . ." Most critics would call it repetitive and indulgent. Keaggy himself calls it "the finest moment" on either of the two records. *Blue* also features a nice original Keaggy tune called "All Our Wishes" (very much a pop song) and a precise rendering of the song "Baby Blue"—a wonderful but little-known tune by the original Beatles clone band, Badfinger. Thus, *Blue* was no less a mixture of blues rock and Beatlesque pop; it was simply a slightly different mixture, targeted for general market release. It failed commercially in this regard, being tainted from the outset as "a crossover album by a gospel artist." Furthermore, as Keaggy admits, he was comfortable with his position as no more than a contemporary Christian artist, and he valued time with his family too much to do what Epic wanted him to do (tours, interviews, etc.) to break into the general market successfully.

After the critical triumph of *(Crimson and)Blue*, Keaggy succumbed at last to the conforming pressures of the contemporary

Christian music industry and for a time became just one more talented musician/singer cut from the same cloth as dozens of other artists. Fans were disappointed, but it did take longer for the machine to get him than it did to get most of the Jesus music refugees (**2nd Chapter of Acts** were the first to go; **Larry Norman,** at last check, had still escaped, though not exactly unscathed). *True Believer* is a slickly produced, lushly orchestrated album that presents Keaggy as a Christian pop singer doing songs that might just as well have been performed by **Steven Curtis Chapman** or **Michael W. Smith.** Good songs, in other words, done well, but not rock and roll—and not Phil Keaggy. The same thing, many critics noted, happened to general market artists like **Eric Clapton** and Rod Stewart. Keaggy is backed by Madeira and other capable performers, but everyone plays with a studied approach that gives the project a highly engineered studio sound. To add insult to injury, the album actually closes with "The Survivor"—the embarrassing antiabortion song that had previously gone almost unnoticed on the sparsely released *Underground* album. On the positive side, "Son of Man" does have an infectious melody and "Have Mercy Lord" does rock out with a certain bridled passion. The title track is also remarkable for what it is, a cheerleader song designed to be a hit on Christian radio. Still, the "look at us, aren't we wonderful" theme is beneath Keaggy, who didn't write the song, and his performance here is buried beneath several layers of unnecessary orchestration.

The artist would turn in some more nice but unexciting performances on his self-titled 1997 album. Without escaping from the contemporary Christian music industry and the confines of its expectations, he managed at least to make what could be regarded as one of the year's better adult contemporary Christian pop albums. *Phil Keaggy* is an eclectic production, sampling almost every style that the artist had tried over the years (with an emphasis on the mellow), and this time out the company allowed him to do his own material and to be a bit more in evidence on his own project. The album opens with its best song, "A Sign Came through a Window," an energetic, bluesy number that is built around a catchy bass groove. "Beneath the Blood-Stained Lintel" and "Above All Things" both incorporate Celtic influences. "Chase the Bad Away" and "My Unspoken Words" add some much-needed intensity, the former with an appealing moodiness. The soft ballad "Under the Grace" and the orchestral, very Beatlesque "Tender Love" articulate the album's overall theme of hope based in divine mercy. Indeed, *CCM* focused on *theme* as this album's strong point: "encouragement infuses every hook, line, and segue of this fine eleven-song effort." Keaggy says that "Above All Things" (a call for husbands to cherish and love their wives) was inspired by the writings of St. John Chrysostom. "Beneath the Blood-Stained Lintel" and "Quite Suddenly" draw from an old devo-

tional book by Henry A. Ironside *(The Continual Burnt Offering),* and "Tender Love" and "My Unspoken Words" have lyrics by Phil's sister Geri Bobeck.

As indicated above, Keaggy has also released numerous instrumental albums over the years, beginning with his best-selling *The Master and the Musician,* which builds on old English melodies and classical guitar stylings to present a soundtrack for a story related on the record sleeve. It features both acoustic and electric guitars and varies from soft folk melodies to more rock-influenced tracks. Way ahead of its time in 1978, the idea for the project was actually derived from early Genesis guitarist Anthony Phillips, who made a similar album called *The Geese and the Ghost.* Future instrumental projects would be less eclectic. *The Wind and the Wheat* and *Beyond Nature* are soft and beautiful. A work of quiet dignity, *The Wind and the Wheat* creates dreamy soundscapes such as "March of the Clouds," which Keaggy calls "one of the best recordings I have ever made." Thematically, the piece is based on Hebrews 12:1, which refers to departed saints as "a mighty cloud of witnesses"; Keaggy creatively expands the metaphor, imagining that the clouds which traverse the heavens are witness to all that transpires on earth. *Beyond Nature* is an all-acoustic album with a neoclassical, New Age feel. One highlight is a rare Keaggy performance of the second movement from Edvard Grieg's "Symphonic Dances." Another is "County Down," which is actually built on the same riff as "Like an Island" (from *Getting Closer*), set to an alternative tuning.

Acoustic Sketches incorporates elements of Spanish, folk, blues, jazz, and classical stylings into its panorama. It began as an intended *Backroom Trax* edition, but took on what Keaggy thought might be broader appeal. Keaggy describes *Sketches* as "a looser form of *Beyond Nature,*" with most of the album being cut in a single pass. By contrast, *220* is primarily an electric album of searing rock instrumentals. Songs like "Animal," "Stomp," and "The Great Escape" have enough visceral pyrotechnics to please most Hendrix fans. The first of these has a B. B. King/R&B feel, the second a bit of Lynyrd Skynyrd southern rock, and the third, a taste of Emerson, Lake, and Palmer. "Arrow" is another powerful rocker, with a British psychedelic sound. Along the same lines is the album *Premium Jams,* which features two discs full of in-the-studio jam sessions never intended for commercial release. Some of these come from the *Crimson and Blue* sessions and feature the crack band assembled for that album. Others are outtakes from *220.*

On the Fly is an eclectic collection of acoustic and electric pieces. Contrary to its title, the album features some of Keaggy's best developed works. "The Way of a Pilgrim" is a grand composition with six distinct movements. "The Sojourner" (nicknamed "I Never Met a Riff I Didn't Like" by Nichols) is a major opus that clocks in at over twenty-four minutes. "Praise Dance" features flamenco stylings and "Firewalker," a solid rock groove. "Homecoming" is an acoustic duet with Keaggy magically playing both guitars. The *Zion* album was recorded as a tribute to guitarmaker Ken Hoover of Zion Guitars and features full-on electric pieces with an emphasis on blues and Afro-Cuban influences. The *Music to Paint By* series offers four albums of background music to suit different moods (cf. **John Michael Talbot**'s *Pathways* series): *Sill Life* (soothing and evocative); *Brushstrokes* (gentle and inspiring); *Splash* (playfully enchanting); and *Electric Blue* (dynamic and stimulating). The *Lights of Madrid* album, finally, is a collection of acoustic instrumental pieces with a Latin feel. It is perhaps the closest thing to a purely "classical guitar" album that Keaggy has ever done. The songs, however, are all original compositions, except for a cover of "Canarios" by Gasper Sanz, a seventeenth-century Portugese artist.

Keaggy became unusually prolific at the end of the millennium, releasing ten albums of new material in 1999 and 2000 alone. The *Inseparable* album from Canis Major is a twenty-one-track, two-disc set of new material (Word also released an abbreviated single-disc version). It marks Keaggy's definitive escape from the contemporary Christian music empire, a full-blown defiant retreat into indie glory. Keaggy produced and engineered the album himself, making it for $1,500, or $300 less than the indie project *What a Day* almost thirty years before. Stylistically, the album hearkens back to that classic beginning, presenting beautiful folk songs in well-chosen arrangements that feature mostly Phil and his guitar (acoustic or mellow electric). Its overall theme seems to be captured in a line from the closing song ("Little Star"): "Few know how to measure the value of a peaceful, quiet mind." *Inseparable* is easily his best vocal album since *Blue* and, yet, is as distinct from that album as *220* is from *Acoustic Sketches*. The title track continues to convey the artist's Beatles fixation, and before the album is through, he even includes a cover of Paul McCartney's "Motor of Love." The ultimate indie album, *Uncle Duke*, falls into the novelty category, a collection of poems by Keaggy's seventy-four-year-old uncle Dave "Duke" Keaggy set to music and performed by the faithful nephew. Appreciation of the female sex seems to be a favorite topic in what comes off as a fairly secular production, in addition to quirky humorous meditations like "Duct Tape Universe" and "Double Your Pleasure" (a song about a two-headed duck). In an only slightly more serious vein, "Connie's Song" was written by Uncle Duke about how he met his wife (in a pool hall) some fifty-four years before.

In terms of compilation albums, the two-disc, thirty-five-song *Time* set contains few unworthy selections and manages to sample almost all of Keaggy's projects through *Crimson and Blue*. By contrast, Nissi's *Early Years* project does not cover a broad enough period to justify its existence, and *Prime Cuts* (re-leased in Britain) contains songs from *Ph'lip Side, Play thru Me, Town to Town,* and *Getting Closer* only. *Time* also includes some previously unreleased tracks and a few extraneous gems such as Keaggy's perfect version of "O God Our Help in Ages Past" from a collection of hymns by various artists. Keaggy has repeatedly said that he does not think any of the compilations contain what he personally considers to be his best work. In an interview with *Fingerstyle Guitar Magazine* in 2000, he said that the albums with which he personally remains most pleased are *Beyond Nature, The Wind and the Wheat, The Master and the Musician,* and *On the Fly* (all instrumental projects).

Besides performing at pro-life rallies, Keaggy has been an ardent supporter of Compassion International, a charitable organization devoted to easing world hunger. He has always viewed his music-making as a ministry. In 1975, when discussing his first album with *Harmony* magazine, Keaggy said, "When life goes into an album, life comes out. There is a lot of music that is fantastic technically, but it lacks life and spirit . . . then there's music that the Lord ministers through. He anoints it. . . . My goal is to really trust the Lord for all of it . . . it's all for the purpose of glorifying Him, to build up the Body, to bring news to the faint-hearted, and to set the captives free." In 2000, when discussing *Inseparable* with *CCM,* he said, "I want to be a blessing to people. I'm given the opportunity, the privilege, and the responsibility to share my walk. My listeners have grown old with me—hopefully with the years comes maturity, some wisdom, and humility. You can be proud of what you achieve, but let him who boasts, boast in the Lord."

For trivia buffs: Phil Keaggy is missing the middle finger of his right hand, which he lost in a farm accident when he was four years old. This does not seem to hinder his guitar picking, though he does use his thumb and little finger more than most.

Christian radio hits: "Where Is My Maker?" (# 15 in 1978); "Spend My Life with You" (# 12 in 1981); "Let Everything Else Go" (# 8 in 1982); "Morning Light" (# 6 in 1983); "Who Will Save the Children?" (# 11 in 1984); "I Will Be There" (# 19 in 1986); "Sunday's Child" (# 12 in 1988); "Talk about Suffering" (# 4 in 1989); "Tell Me How You Feel" (# 8 in 1989); "Be in My Heart" (# 5 in 1990); "When the Wind Blows" (# 15 in 1990); "This Side of Heaven" (# 2 in 1991); "Your Love Broke Through" [with **Russ Taff**] (# 22 in 1992); "Everywhere I Look" (# 25 in 1993); "Love Divine" (# 22 in 1993): "I Will Be There" (# 25 in 1993); "Reunion of Friends" (# 22 in 1994); "The True Believers" (# 4 in 1995).

Dove awards: 1988 Instrumental Album *(The Wind and the Wheat);* 1992 Instrumental Album *(Beyond Nature);* 1999 Instrumental Album *(Acoustic Sketches);* 2000 Instrumental Album *(Majesty and Wonder);* 2001 Instrumental Album *(Lights of Madrid).*

Keaggy, King, and Denté

Scott Denté, voc., gtr.; Phil Keaggy, voc., gtr.; Wes King, voc., gtr. 1997—*Invention* (Sparrow).

Three of Christian music's finest guitarists—Scott Denté (of **Out of the Grey), Wes King,** and the legendary **Phil Keaggy**—got together to record an album as the trio Keaggy, King, and Denté. The album is mostly instrumental with four vocal tracks—each artist takes one turn at the mic and then, on the closing song, "Something Somewhere," they all sing together in a Crosby, Stills and Nash sort of way. Forty different guitars (acoustic and electric) are employed, giving any true aficionado of that instrument a sampling of the different styles and sounds available. As for the instrumentals, "The Moors of Bellevue" is a rock jamfest, "Perspicuity" is jazzy, "Angel Treads" is mellow, and "The Quote Jester" is a quiet acoustic piece featuring only Keaggy. World music comes into play on the Celtic "Isle of Skye" and the Eastern European "Budapest Control." Keaggy and King's vocal offerings are Beatlesque pop songs. On "River of Life," Keaggy seems to flaunt the inevitable comparisons by kicking the tune off with a riff only slightly modified from "Day Tripper." Denté's "More to Be Revealed" has more of a **Collective Soul** feel to it, presenting the singer as a more competent vocalist than his day-job of playing and harmonizing behind his wife ever let on. All told, *Invention* is an outstanding pop album with appreciable variety for the open-minded.

Christian radio hits: "River of Life" (# 8 in 1997).

Dove awards: 1998 Instrumental Album (*Invention*).

John P. Kee (and The New Life Community Choir)

As John P. Kee: 1990—*Just Me This Time* (Verity); *There Is Hope* [by John P. Kee and friends]; 1994—*Colourblind.* As John P. Kee with The New Life Community Choir: 1987—*Yes, Lord!* (Verity); 1989—*Wait on Him* (Jive); 1991—*Wash Me*; 1991—*Surrender* (label unknown); 1992—*We Walk by Faith* (Tyscot); 1993—*Churchin'*; 1995—*Show Up!* (StarSong); 1996—*A Special Christmas Gift* (Verity); 1997—*Strength!*; 2000—*Not Guilty.*

www.johnpkee.com

John P. Kee (b. 1962) is a modern gospel choir leader whose work took a turn in the early '90s toward a contemporary sound similar to that associated with **Kirk Franklin** or **Hezekiah Walker.** Although Kee is not as well known as Franklin in the general market, he has long been something of a legend in traditional gospel music, where he is sometimes regarded as the heir apparent to James Cleveland. Kee grew up in North Carolina as the fifteenth child in a family that included ten girls and six boys. He studied voice and classical music at the North Carolina School of Arts in Winston-Salem and at Yuba College Conservatory School of Music in Marysville, California. What he calls "a time of corruption" followed during which he was involved in using and selling cocaine, but his life was turned around after he witnessed the slaying of a close

friend in a drug deal gone awry. Surrendering his life to Christ, he committed himself to conducting the New Life Community Choir at a community church in Charlotte, North Carolina.

Kee's early albums feature traditional gospel music such as might be performed in a church on Sunday morning. *Surrender* is actually a project of a female quartet from within the choir, directed by Kee. *We Walk by Faith* is notable in that it features **Vanessa Bell Armstrong,** whose solo album, *The Secret Is Out,* Kee would later produce. The album *Show Up!* evinces more of an urban groove, with an accent on excitement. Then, with *Strength!* Kee and company would come full-bore into **Kirk Franklin** territory. The title track actually recalls that artist's "Stomp" in some respects, though the employment of brass gives it a different feel. "Turn Around" and "Mighty God" blend in strong R&B influences. "Thursday Love" borrows from contemporary jazz. "Eastside/Westside" combines rap and choral singing for an urban anthem on gang violence. *Not Guilty* continues in the same vein as *Strength!,* offering an ambitious two-disc set of twenty-five original songs.

In addition to these projects, Kee has released a couple of solo albums. *Just Me This Time* is perhaps most notable for Kee's memorable tribute to his father ("I Miss You, Dad"). *There Is Hope,* released the same year as the debut solo album, was a special project in which Kee pulled together a number of singers and musicians to record songs addressing the problem of child abuse. The title track to *Colourblind* deals with racial prejudice and includes Kee's cover of the Stevie Wonder song, "Love's in Need of Love Today." Kee has also recorded a number of albums over the years with a group called the Victory in Praise Mass Choir, which forms at an annual Music and Arts Seminar (1991—*Never Shall Forget;* 1993—*Lily in the Valley;* 1996—*Stand!;* 1998—*Anyday*).

Lisa Keith

1993—*Walking in the Sun* (Perspective).

Lisa Keith is a prominent R&B singer/songwriter from Minneapolis who is probably better known in the general market than she is in contemporary Christian music. Keith says that she became a Christian around the age of twelve and has remained a person of faith ever since. Her introduction to the popular music industry came through her marriage to Spencer Bernard, who fronted a Top 40 band. In 1984, the couple began working with producers Terry Lewis and Jimmy Jam, and Keith ended up singing background vocals on projects by Johnny Gill, Human League, and Janet Jackson. She also did the lead vocal for three chart hits by Herb Alpert and the Tijuana Brass: "Keep Your Eye on Me" (# 46 in 1987), "Diamonds" (# 5 in 1987), and "Making Love in the Rain" (# 35 in 1987). Keith says that she considered a career in contemporary

Christian music but believed there were already a lot of singers like her in that field and thought she might better serve God by putting out music with positive lyrics "for the regular crowd." Her debut album netted the hit single "Better Than You" (# 36 in 1993; # 15 on R&B charts). It also includes a song called "Adonai" featuring the lyrics, "Adonai, Adonai / Every knee shall bow / Every tongue confess that Jesus Christ is Lord."

Kekal

Azhar, bass, voc.; Jeff, gtr., voc.; Leo, gtr.; Harry, voc. (–1999). 1998—*Beyond the Glimpse of Dreams* (Candlelight); 1999—*Embrace the Dead* (Fleshwalker); 2001—*The Painful Experience* (Clenchedfist).

http://thtunderground.tripod.com/kekal

Kekal is an indie death metal band from Jakarta, Indonesia. Their debut album inspired *Phantom Tollbooth* to claim that "death metal, despite its inherent ugliness, can be very beautiful, powerful, and moving music." The group takes its name from an Indonesian word meaning "eternal" or "immortal." Most of the band's songs are of the typical midtempo-to-fast, heavy, guitar-driven style, but the band does incorporate certain elements of variety into the sound. Vocals vary from normal singing to death growls to wailing screams, with the addition of what are called "sick vocals" by Harry on the first album. Both albums also make effective use of female vocals. None of the band members have public surnames, and drumming is credited to "The Black Box" (a machine). Both albums also begin and end with an atypical quiet song. "My Eternal Lover," which closes *Beyond the Glimpse of Dreams,* features piano, lightly picked guitars, and sweet female vocals singing worshipful lyrics. All of Kekal's songs are in (imperfect) English, and on the band's first two albums the songs testified to their Christian faith in an upfront way. On *The Painful Experience,* they pulled back somewhat from the overt approach that lead singer Jeff says tended to turn people against the band before they gave the music a chance. The group conducts its ministry in a context that is largely Muslim, and they maintain that three-fourths of their albums are purchased by non-Christians. *The Painful Experience* includes a couple of songs dealing with political situations and social life in Indonesia.

Nori (and Barbie) Kelley

As Nori Kelley: 1994—*Breaking Point* (Alliance). As Nori and Barbie Kelley: 1995—*Out of Egypt* (Heaven's Eyes); 1996—*Wind* (independent); 1997—*Worship*; 1998—*How Great Is Your Love.*

Singer/songwriter Nori Kelley is best known for his guitar work. He has, in fact, recorded instructional albums of guitar technique. *Breaking Point* has a folk rock quality reminiscent of The Byrds. *CCM* likened Kelley's voice to the Byrds' Roger McGuinn and his guitar style to Dire Straits' Mark Knopfler.

Kelley's next album was recorded with his wife, Barbie, and the two of them have continued to release independent, worship-oriented projects.

Lisa Kellogg

1996—*Rising Above* (Brainstorm).

Lisa Kellogg's debut was produced by Gene Eugene of **Adam Again,** and he gave the acoustic, soft rock material a slightly jazzy edge that sets it apart from many albums in this genre. As *CCM* indicates, the lyrics (written or cowritten by Lisa with her husband, Greg Kellogg) read like pages from someone's devotional journal. The songs are worshipful and edifying while retaining a strong sense of personal sentiment.

Dave Kelley

1980—*Crowning of a Simple Man* (Pilgrim America).

Dave Kelley was a member of the Christian pop band **'Ark,** one of the most overlooked Christian combos from the '70s. His solo album features straightforward acoustic rock and roll evocative of late '60s "British invasion" sound. The lyrics of songs like "God Knows" and "Turn Your Back" offer clear-but-calm Christian messages that don't overwhelm the listener with religious sentiment. "Ballad of J.C." is the most curious track, employing Scottish imagery of kings and castles, knights and dragons in a medieval parable of salvation.

Graham Kendrick

1971—*Footsteps on the Sea* (Key); 1972—*Bright Side Up*; 1974—*Paid on the Nail*; 1976—*Breaking of the Dawn* (Dovetail); 1978—*Fighter*; 1979—*Jesus Stand among Us*; 1980—*Triumph in the Air* (Glenmore); 1981—*Eighteen Classics* (Kingsway); *Cresta Run*; *The King Is among Us*; 1983—*Nightwatch*; 1984—*The Blame*; *Let God Arise*; 1985—*Magnificent Warrior*; 1986—*Make Way for the King of Kings: A Carnival of Praise*; 1988—*Make Way for Jesus: Shine, Jesus, Shine* (Make Way); *Make Way for Christmas: The Gift*; 1989—*Make Way for the Cross: Let the Flame Burn Brighter*; 1989—*We Believe* (StarSong); 1991—*Crown Him* (Integrity); 1992—*King of the Nations* (Word UK); *Crown Him: The Worship Musical*; 1993—*Spark to a Flame* (Megaphone); 1994—*Rumours of Angels*; 1995—*Is Anyone Thirsty?*; 1996—*Illuminations*; 1997—*No More Walls*; 1998—*No Scenes of Stately Majesty* [EP]; 2000—*The Millennium Chorus* (Millennium Chorus).

www.grahamkendrick.co.uk

British songwriter and worship leader Graham Kendrick was born in 1950, the son of a Baptist minister, in Northamptonshire. In his early twenties, he became a pioneer in the United Kingdom's Jesus movement and in the British version of Jesus music that accompanied the revival (in some respects, an American invasion). *Footsteps on the Sea* reveals him as a young acoustic troubadour not too different from the early **Bruce Cockburn,** but on his next few albums he developed a more British pop style analogous to **Malcolm and Alwyn.** Kendrick's music focused on worshipful ballads and on story-songs based on biblical accounts—like those of his American counterpart **Don Francisco.** He never became well known in the United States, but in the '80s he began writing contemporary hymns and assumed a role in his homeland analogous to that of **Ralph Carmichael** or Kurt Kaiser in the United States. He was, in other words, instrumental in bringing a more contemporary "secular" sound into the sanctuaries of mainline, liturgically-oriented churches. Although Kendrick has composed many songs that are well known in his homeland, he remains (like Kaiser) something of a one-hymn wonder in America. His song "Shine, Jesus, Shine" became the "Pass It On" of the '90s, making its way into the college songbooks and contemporary hymn collections of churches that rarely show any interest in pop-oriented music. In Great Britain, it was named the most popular modern hymn of the decade. Kendrick describes the song as "a prayer for revival," and he describes his mission as a hymn writer as being "to give people words to voice something that is already in their hearts." In light of the latter observation, he credits the popularity of "Shine, Jesus, Shine" to the fact that it "caught a moment when people were beginning to believe that an impact could be made."

Tom Kendzia

1980—*Light of the World* (North American Liturgical Resources).

Tom Kendzia is a Roman Catholic liturgical artist who in 1980 crafted an album of contemporary music for use in congregational worship. *Light of the World* features songs designed for use as processionals, recessionals, offertories and the like within the context of the Roman Catholic mass. The album was recorded with an eighty-voice choir and with traditional instruments (piano, organ) supplemented by a full rock accompaniment. Songs range in style from contemporary folk to at least one instance of full rock and roll ("The Lord of Love"). In many ways, the mere existence of *Light of the World* was more significant than the material on the album itself. Released by the Roman Catholic North American Liturgical Resources group, it marked that body's first official endorsement (fifteen years after **Ray Repp**'s experiments) of the use of rock-oriented music in the liturgy. *CCM* magazine dedicated its October 1980 issue to the new infusion of contemporary Christian music within the Catholic church. In that magazine, Kendzia said, "One of the joys of the Catholic church is that it is very open to all kinds and types of things."

Kenoly Brothers

Sam "Picasso" Kenoly; Ron "Bingo" Kenoly Jr. 1999—*All the Way* (NGMR).

The Kenoly Brothers is composed of two sons of premier praise and worship leader **Ron Kenoly.** Their debut album features mostly ballads, sung in an adult contemporary, light R&B style, with a few numbers shifting effortlessly into urban hip-hop beats. "Why I Love You" and "In the Midst" are directed to God as worship songs. "Hold On" and the title track are intended as edification for the congregation. "Come with Me" is one of the more lively tracks, a party song, urging listeners to join the brothers in praising the Lord. The Kenoly's have an Afro-Latino lineage, their mother being a native of Puerto Rico, and the brothers have indicated that they intend to include some songs in Spanish on their next record.

Ron Kenoly

1992—*Jesus Is Alive* (Integrity); 1993—*Lift Him Up*; 1994—*God Is Able*; 1995—*Sing Out with One Voice*; 1996—*Welcome Home*; 1997—*High Places: The Best of Ron Kenoly*; 1998—*Majesty*; 1999—*We Offer Praises*; 2001—*Dwell in the House.*

www.ronkenoly.org

Worship leader Ron Kenoly was born in 1944 in Coffeyville, Kansas. He grew up in a poor family, singing in church, and after a brief stint in the Air Force enjoyed a fairly successful career in mainstream music as a member of the Los Angeles-based R&B group Shades of Difference. He left this behind in the late '70s, troubled by the toll it was taking on his family life and, prompted at first by his wife's spiritual dedication, decided to commit his talent to the Lord. After completing a music degree at Alameda College in Oakland, California, Kenoly worked with evangelist Mario Marsillo and then became the worship leader at Jubilee Christian Center (led by pastor Dick Bernall) in San Jose. He would later earn a Master of Divinity degree from Faith Bible College and a Doctorate of Ministry in Sacred Music from Friends International Christian University. Kenoly's rich baritone is often compared with that of soul singer Lou Rawls. In 1997, *Release* magazine would credit him with "virtually reinventing contemporary praise and worship music," and his albums garnered sales phenomenal for the genre. *Lift Him Up*, in fact, became the fastest-selling worship album in history, and Kenoly's first four records alone accounted for some one-and-a half-million sales. His albums are recorded live and typically feature him leading an auditorium full of people in a musical worship service. Kenoly insists that he is not a performer, though his programs feature the same high standards for musicianship that would be expected of a Broadway show. For example, the program for *God Is Able* features the voice of **Matthew Ward,** in addition to participation from Justo Almario, Alex Acuña and other members of **Koinonia.** *Sing Out with One Voice* puts Kenoly in front of nine thousand worshipers whose voices become part of the production. An African children's choir and a full orchestra also contribute to that project, and the companion video reveals that the music on stage was accompanied by highly choreographed dance numbers. All of the pageantry serves to present a reenactment of the dedication of Solomon's temple, as recounted in 2 Chronicles. The album was named *Billboard* magazine's "Top Indie Contemporary Christian Album." *Welcome Home* draws its underlying inspiration from the parable of the Prodigal Son and focuses on the importance of family and, by extension, the local church. The song "Go Ahead" features the lyric, "If you catch hell, don't hold it / If you're going through hell, don't stop." *Majesty* and *We Offer Praises* return Kenoly to praise-oriented songs. On *Dwell in the House* he mixes the worship material with a few smatterings of R&B, including a cover of Bill Withers' "Grandma's Hands." Musically, Kenoly's projects tend to feature pop stylings reminiscent of an Andrew Lloyd Webber production, with a bit more influence from traditional gospel.

Christian radio hits: "Beauty for Ashes" [with **Crystal Lewis**] (# 5 in 1997).

Dove awards: 1997 Praise and Worship Album *(Welcome Home)*.

Keoni

1992—*Worldview* (Wonderland); 1994—*Keoni* (WAL).

The pop singer/songwriter who records under the name Keoni was born in Honolulu, Hawaii, and was adopted by an American couple who raised him in Colorado. Keoni studied music at Oklahoma Baptist University, then toured with the Continental Singers in 1987. He says that while "doing choir songs in front of about 6,000 bikers" he realized that the music was not connecting with the audience. He subsequently made two albums of soulful ballads and jazzy pop songs with confrontational, mission-oriented lyrics.

Debby Kerner (and Ernie Rettino)

As Debby Kerner: 1972—*Come Walk with Me* (Maranatha). As Debby Kerner and Ernie Rettino: 1974—*Friends* (Maranatha); 1975—*Joy in the Morning*; 1977—*More Than Friends*; 1978—*Changin'*; 1979—*The Best of Ernie Rettino and Debby Kerner.*

Debby Kerner was one of two sterling Christian folk singers (along with **Marsha Stevens**) to emerge out of the Calvary Chapel ministry in Costa Mesa, California, during the earliest years of the Jesus movement. Along with **Karen Lafferty,** she was eventually ordained by Calvary Chapel as a minister of music. With a lilting voice reminiscent of Joan Baez minus the excess vibrato, Kerner first came to the attention of the Jesus people with her song "Behold, I Stand at the Door," featured on Maranatha's *The Everlastin' Living Jesus Music Concert,* which remains the most influential album of contemporary Christian music ever recorded. That song, a sweet meditation on Revela-

tion 3:20, demonstrates her penchant and talent for melody, but it only whet the appetite for what was to come. Kerner's "The Peace That Passes Understanding" opened *Maranatha Two* (the 1972 follow-up to *Everlastin' Living Jesus Music Concert*) and along with **Children of the Day**'s "Can I Show You That I Love You?" was one of its twin highlights. Her best song, "Peace That Passes Understanding," is a gorgeous ballad that, in retrospect, deserves notice as contemporary Christian music's first adult contemporary standard. It is the type of song that would fill the albums of singers like **Susan Ashton** and **Kim Hill** two decades later, but it was recorded at a time when the genre seemed new and fresh. "Peace That Passes Understanding" fit into the musical lexicon of teenaged Jesus freaks as nicely as Baez' folk ballads fit with the eclectic celebrations of peace and love at Woodstock. In both cases, commitment to ideology and appreciation for what was simply good music triumphed over such individualistic concerns as personal taste. Both "Behold I Stand at the Door" and "Peace That Passes All Understanding" appear on Kerner's debut album, *Come Walk with Me.* It is a superb overall project, with much to delight fans of Peter, Paul, and Mary. The album features high concern with the end times ("Are You Ready?" "Hallelujah, Jesus Is Coming Back") but also displays a number of what should probably be called children's songs, foreshadowing the artist's later work.

Ernie Rettino placed a solo song called "I Will Never Leave You" on the *Maranatha Three* project (1973). A beautiful piano ballad, it really strains the definition of popular or contemporary music, essentially reprising the style of nightclub singers from several decades before the advent of rock and roll. In addition, the song has a traditional churchy sound that makes it stand out from the rock-and-blues-oriented *Maranatha Three.* It was perhaps the one cut on that album that the Jesus people were most likely to play for their worried parents or pastors to assure them that the Calvary Chapel crowd hadn't gone completely worldly.

In 1974 Ernie and Debbie suddenly came out with an album together. *Friends* seemed the perfect ode to the sort of platonic brother-and-sister-in-the-Lord relationships that many of the Jesus people found they could have with members of the opposite sex. Such relationships were indeed a major aspect of socialization for participants in the revival movement and, in some sense, a prime attraction of the community it engendered. There was perhaps nowhere else in America where young men and women could have such close nonsexual relationships with each other, relationships that could be vulnerable and intimate without the prospect of romantic involvement. It didn't always work, of course, but it often did, and in the days of the Jesus movement most young Christians had friends of the opposite sex with whom they would regularly bare their souls, friends with whom they could confess their sins, pray for guidance, weep over life's disappointments, and discuss hopes for the future. This all seemed strange to the outside world and, again, to worried parents and pastors who doubted that hormones could be sublimated quite so easily. Ernie and Debbie were the public example of such a relationship, and so many of the Jesus people greeted news of their marriage in 1976 with mixed emotions. There was an initial sense of betrayal—they were not supposed to be "more than friends"—but as time went by and divorces accumulated, the long and stable relationship of Ernie and Debbie became exemplary in another sense. The couple whose marriage was grounded in friendship, indeed, built on a base of singing and ministering together, was evidence of romance lived under the lordship of Christ.

The album *Friends* is the best of the four projects the couple did together. The album's highlight is the title track, a song that recalls **Marsha Stevens**' wedding song for her husband ("Russ's Song") on the second **Children of the Day** album: "I'd like to sing a song for you to tell you that I care / To tell you that I'm grateful for the times that we can share." Of equal quality is Kerner's "Promises," which features a sweet melody and lyrics drawn from Proverbs and the Sermon on the Mount. Rettino offers "Let Me See," another powerful ballad that offers a prayer for grace—one that could easily be heard as the human plea for which his earlier "I Will Never Leave You" supplies the divine response. Otherwise, the project offers what would become the couple's signature sounds: hootenany foot-stompers like Henry Cutrona's "Middle of the Day" and Rettino's "Written in the Word," and traditional spirituals like "Let Us Break Bread Together" and "Swing Low, Sweet Chariot." These styles are also in evidence on *Joy in the Morning,* which includes an updated version of "He's Got the Whole World in His Hands." That album also has "Mary Magdalene," another beautiful Rettino piano piece. The most noticed song on the project, however, was "The Wa Wa Song," which features a chorus of fourteen children singing and clapping to a happy tune. Both **Keith Green** and **Karen Lafferty** join the couple on *More Than Friends* and *Changin'.* After this, Debbie and Ernie moved into children's music, creating a character called Psalty the Singing Songbook, who was featured in several Psalty Kids albums for Maranatha. They also wrote the Christian musical *Hi Tops.*

Ernie and Debbie were both from a distinctive Judeo-Christian background and exemplified one controversial but noticeable element of the Jesus movement revival—the acceptance of Christianity by Jewish young people who saw the transition less as a conversion than as a fulfillment of their heritage. Kerner was the daughter of a Jewish Hollywood producer, while Rettino was born into an Italian Jewish-Catholic family. Both described themselves as "messianic Christians," who confessed Christ without renouncing their identification with Judaism (cf. **Lamb, The Liberated Wailing Wall**).

Dana Key

1990—*The Journey* (ForeFront); 1995—*Part of the Mystery.*

Dana Key is best known as one-half of the duo **DeGarmo and Key.** Like his partner **Eddie DeGarmo,** he has also recorded solo albums, though none have enjoyed the sort of success associated with the numerous group efforts. Key was born in Memphis in 1954 and he grew up a few blocks from Graceland, attending school with his friend DeGarmo and dreaming about being a rock star. As a junior in high school, he was actually invited to join the rock band Black Oak Arkansas as lead guitarist, but by then he and DeGarmo were already heavily involved in music ministry for Youth for Christ, and he shunned worldly aspirations and associations. Basically a blues guitarist, Key cites B. B. King, Jimi Hendrix, and Billy Gibbons (of ZZ Top) as his primary influences, affirming that he prefers "emotive guitar" to "frantic guitar."

The Journey suffered inevitable comparisons to DeGarmo's *Feels Good to Be Forgiven,* which came out at about the same time. As such, it may be called meditative or even literate since the work is more lyrically oriented than his partner's roadhouse rock. Key himself describes it as "a light rock album that was a teaching tool." Much of the album consists of a song cycle dealing with events in the life of Christ, and in this context it includes a version of the **Larry Norman** classic "The Outlaw." The song "Pray for Peace" was used during the Gulf War as part of a program called Operation Desert Prayer. *CCM* would describe the song as sounding like "Steely Dan doing black gospel." **DeGarmo and Key** had disbanded by the time Key released *Part of the Mystery,* and that album seems to provide either an inkling of new direction for the artist, or perhaps a farewell before immersing himself more heavily in the business aspects of the music business. The title track recalls the classic guitar sound of The Byrds. "By Divine Design" is also a musical treat, with lyrics expressive of a generic theistic philosophy. The most riveting song on the album, "Dear Mr. Clapton," is an open letter to **Eric Clapton** echoing the sentiment of the latter's "Tears in Heaven": "Thru Saturdays with no noise / Baseballs and untouched toys / They leave an empty feeling in your soul / He is in Heaven's care / There are no tears up there / For Jesus loves children more than we will ever know."

As a songwriter, Key cowrote the Christian radio hit "Thief in the Night," performed by **Big Tent Revival,** in addition to numerous songs for various artists referenced in the **DeGarmo and Key** entry. He serves as an executive with Ardent Records. He is the author of *Don't Stop the Music* (Zondervan, 1989) and *By Divine Design* (Broadman and Holman, 1995).

Christian radio hits: Up from the Dead" (# 8 in 1990); "The Outlaw" (# 3 in 1990); "Pray for Peace" (# 3 in 1991); "By Divine Design" (# 15 in 1996); "Dear Mr. Clapton" (# 25 in 1996).

The Keyhole

See **Fisherfolk.**

Khanyisa

Gio Fisher, voc.; Leon Jaftha, bass; Matthew Kennedy, voc.; Llewellyn Pearce, gtr.; Deon Plaatjies, voc.; Melony Shilliday, voc.; Andries Visser, drums; Rolf Weichardt, kybrd. 1997—*To Bring the Light* (independent); 2000—*Pictures* (Resolve).

Khanyisa is a multiracial, culturally diverse group of musicians from South Africa. The band was formed by Rolf Weichardt in 1991 and has developed into an international ministry bringing a Christian message of racial reconciliation and the struggle for justice. Their music lacks the distinctive African stylings that many would expect, evincing more influence of American pop. Standout songs on *Pictures* include the energetic numbers "Crazy Love" and "Jesus Is the Same." The group's name is derived from an African phrase meaning "to bring the light" in the Xhosa language and "church" in Swahili.

Kid Promise

Bradley Beckey, voc., gtr.; Quentin Gibson, gtr., voc. 1994—*My Generation* (StarSong).

Kid Promise was a radio-friendly hard pop band formed by two friends who were previously members of **Seraiah.** Tracie Ferrie and Kyle Dietz (both also of **Seraiah**) appear to have been somewhat unofficial members, though they were not pictured on the album cover. The band's name was taken from that of a boxer, but they put an evangelical spin on the term *promise.* The group's sound was similar to that of **The Newsboys,** though Beckey's voice is remarkably similar to Michael Jackson's. They would not enjoy the success of such megastars, however, in spite of a solid debut album. *My Generation* was produced by Steve Griffith of **Vector,** and the album represents an even more radical departure from the metal stylings of **Seraiah**'s debut than did that band's second album. The opening "Groove" is enhanced, as is the title track, by Steve Miller space effects. Lyrically, the album is subtle yet unflinching in its presentation of basic evangelical themes. "What Do We Call Love?" reflects on obvious discrepancies in what passes for love in contemporary culture while also proclaiming, "Love laid down his life for me." Both Gibson and Ferrie would also play with **Whitecross.**

Christian Radio Hits: "Two Hearts, One Love" (# 18 in 1994).

Killed by Cain

Tom Bowling, gtr.; Steve Curtsinger, bass; Stephan Rolland, drums; John Warren, voc. 1993—*Killed by Cain* (R.E.X.).

Killed by Cain was a Christian metal band that R.E.X. executive Tyler Bacon once described as sounding like Pantera covering Guns N' Roses tunes. The group began as Whiteray and issued half a dozen custom demos under that name before getting signed to the R.E.X. label. **Dale Thompson** of **Bride** produced their debut album and contributed lyrics to the song "Violence," which deals with prejudice. Stephen Rolland was once the drummer for **Bride.** Killed by Cain favored confrontational songs addressing apathy and sin—particularly sexual sins. "Walk the Line" is an AIDS-inspired call for chastity with a somewhat overstated "sex kills" message. "Sin City" deals with crimes of the mind: "I see visions in my mind / Took no action but committed the crime / It was in my heart, the damage was done." The provocatively titled "Burn the Church" draws on Jesus' words of judgment against the temple in his day to accost Christians who put their trust in religious practices or become embroiled in trivial disputes over doctrine.

Kindred Three

Lamar, voc.; Shone, voc.; Wenché, voc. 2001—*Kindred Three* (Pamplin).

Kindred Three appeared near the end of 2001 as Pamplin's version of a Christian boy band (cf. **Plus One, True Vibe**). The prime distinction for the group is their multiracial makeup: an African American, a Caucasian, and a Latin American. This diversity also affects their sound, which at times has a bit more Latin flavor than others in the genre (but cf. **The Katinas**). The group's first album was produced by **John** and Dino **Elefante.** "Sing a New Song" is a standout track, featuring a catchy chorus and lots of "shoo-be-doo" harmonies. "I Belong to Thee" is an a capella hymn similar in style to the work of Boyz II Men.

Christian radio hits: "Away" (# 18 in 2001).

Kindred

Christopher Donaldson; Walter Johnson Jr.; Tommy King; Greg O'Quin; James Wiley; one more. 1992—*The Quest for the City* (Word).

Kindred was an all-male urban gospel sextet that made one album of music similar in style to **Commissioned** with just a touch more of the doo-wop, hip-hop influence of hot-at-the-time artist Color Me Badd. Recalling the old Side A and Side B format of vinyl, *Quest for the City* is evenly divided between two styles. The first six songs are all dance tracks while the remainder are quiet, inspirational ballads. *Quest for the City* was produced by **Tim Miner.** Word Records did not bother to identify the group members in the album's liner notes, but names for five of the six have been determined and are listed above; **Greg O'Quin** went on to become an influential choir leader with the R&B gospel group Joyful Noize.

King James

Jim Bennett, voc.; Rex Carroll, gtr., voc.; et al. 1994—*King James* (StarSong); 1999—*The Fall* (Viva).

King James is a **Rex Carroll** project, one of several organized by the guitar hero best known for his work with **Whitecross.** Carroll recruited Jim Bennett from a Christian band from Atlanta called Sacred Fire. A number of other musicians play on their two albums, including **Stryper**'s **Robert Sweet** and Tim Gaines. The group has a basic '80s metal sound (Scorpions), updated somewhat on the second album with Seattle influences (Alice in Chains, Soundgarden). The debut features "Hard Road to Go," a song about Bennett's brother, who was arrested for dealing cocaine, and "Miracles," a song about his daughter, who he says was miraculously healed of a brain tumor. An acoustic remix of the latter song presents it in an alternative form, as a beautiful and emotional ballad.

Wes King

1990—*The Ultimate Underlying No Denying Motivation* (Reunion); 1991—*Sticks and Stones*; 1993—*The Robe*; 1995—*Common Creed*; 1997—*A Room Full of Stories* (Sparrow); 2001—*What Matters Most* (Artisan).

www.wesking.com

Singer/songwriter Wes King is noted for his guitar prowess and has played as a member of **Kim Hill**'s band. He wrote Hill's smash hit "Snake in the Grass" and cowrote her beautiful "Charm Is Deceitful." He has also recorded as part of the trio **Keaggy, King, and Denté.** King was born in 1967 and raised in Winder, Georgia. He experienced trauma as a child when his cousin was murdered and he had to be hospitalized for depression. Later, after attending Georgia's Covenant College, he moved to Nashville in 1986 and began his career in Christian music. He cites the '70s music and ministry of **Pat Terry** as a major influence on his decision to do this. Early on, King's style was described as "acoustic groove," guitar-based music that alternated soulful rockers with romantic ballads. His early songs were largely experiential but he soon moved into a more theological phase, writing and singing material with a strong didactic base. King is known in the contemporary Christian music scene for being an avid reader of theology; his major influences are Charles Spurgeon and J. C. Ryle, as well as Malcolm Muggeridge and Frederick Buechner. He is married to Shakespearean scholar Fran Harris. His songs often reflect on the pains of human striving and on the reciprocal mercy of God. "From Genesis to Revelation," says King, "the Bible is a racy,

tragic comedy about the foolishness of people and the love, wisdom, and power of God."

King's first two albums were coproduced by **Gary Chapman.** *The Ultimate Underlying No Denying Motivation* immediately inspired some comparisons to John Mellencamp. It kicks off with the energetic "Power in the Name" but is more memorable for stripped-down ballads like "Don't Say I Love You" and "Getting Used to the Light." By the time King made *Sticks and Stones,* comparisons had shifted to calling him an acoustic **Phil Keaggy,** as his expertise with the guitar came to the fore. "By His Wounds" presents a christological meditation on Isaiah 53, with poetic lyrics by King's literate spouse. "Another Man" is an especially tender bit of romance. The title track negates the adage that "words can never hurt me." Another highlight is King's cover of a song written by his mentor **Pat Terry,** the Byrds-inflected "Joseph's Troubles." On *The Robe,* King adopts a bit more electric sound and moves thematically to the overtly theological focus mentioned above. The album opens with "I Believe," a rocking song that is essentially a modern creed. "Martin Luther" pays appropriate homage to the father of the Reformation, and the title track derives from a sermon by one of his mentors, Charles Spurgeon. Though Luther would not have approved of much of Spurgeon's theology, he no doubt would have liked this message, which describes grace as a robe in which God clothes those who come to Christ naked and ashamed. *Common Creed* continues in this confessional vein, with its title song exalting Scripture as the common basis for faith of all Christians. *A Room Full of Stories* returns to the autobiographical, experiential tone of his early material. "Simplify" deals with the common habit of living a life filled with too many commitments, but it is presented here with reference to the lesson learned by Bilbo the hobbit, a character in J. R. R. Tolkien's famous novel. "Thought You'd Be Here" is an especially poignant and vulnerable song, expressing the pain of a couple seemingly unable to produce a child. King effectively avoids giving infertility the disease-of-the-month treatment and sings a simple lullaby to the child that he and his wife long to have (somewhat ironically, the couple had twins about the time the album was released). On "Remember," King recalls the day he answered an altar call. *What Matters Most* secures his position in the adult contemporary camp with what *CCM* calls "a simple, stirring and acoustically stellar collection of well-crafted—often just downright sweet—songs about life and love and faith." Songs focus on advice for Christian living, with emphasis on paradox: "Accept who you are, yet keep striving" ("What Matters Most"); "If you wish to find your life, you must give it away" ("There Is a God").

For trivia buffs: Even before he gained fame for his music, Wes King was noted for his skill at doing comic impressions, a number of which continue to surface in his concerts. He is especially known for his "Tim Conway" and his "Elvis."

Christian radio hits: "Power in the Name" (# 8 in 1990); "Break Away" (# 10 in 1991); "Motivation" (# 20 in 1991); "Home inside of Me" (# 12 in 1991); "Sticks and Stones" (# 11 in 1992); "The Robe" (# 21 in 1993); "I Believe" (# 1 for 2 weeks in 1993); "Second String" (# 9 in 1993); "Martin Luther" (# 4 in 1994); "Common Creed" (# 1 in 1995); "Remember" (# 10 in 1997); "Simplify" (# 12 in 1997).

King's Crew

MCDC, voc.; Mr. Ginsu, voc.; TR Rock, voc. 1990—*Kickin' That Beat* (Refuge); 1991—*Chillin' in the King's Castle* (Alternative); 1993—*This Ain't Make Believe* (Pulse); 1995—*Love Goes On* (label unknown).

King's Crew is a Christian rap group that has a bit more of the gangsta influence than the usual hip-hop orientated groups that dominate Christian rap. Though their sound falls short of the hardcore style of acts like **Gospel Gangstaz,** their pop sensibilities are held in check by an undercurrent of bass-heavy rhythm. The song "You're My Brother" from *This Ain't Make Believe* deals with the personal effects of racism. The same album features "Feel the Power," a standout house music dance track.

King's Road

Mark Intravia, gtr., voc.; Mike Peters, kybrd.; Bob Sale, drums; Eve Selis, voc.; John Khula, bass (−1996) // Jim Reeves, bass (+ 1996). 1994—*Where Angels Walk* (Broken); 1996—*Heaven and Earth* (WikiNaws).

King's Road is a San Diego-based Christian band that plays the sort of straight-ahead rock and roll that is usually associated with "the heartland." Their female-fronted sound has often been compared to that of **Margaret Becker**'s first two albums or to Bonnie Raitt's rockier side. The group is led by Intravia and Selis, who coauthor most of the songs. Sale and Khula once served as **Rick Elias**'s rhythm section; the Mike Peters who plays in King's Road is a different person from the Mike Peters who plays in **The Alarm.** *Where Angels Walk* includes the rocker "Brave New World," which speaks of liberation from a mundane existence. The song "Unholy Union" is about romantic involvements between Christians and unbelievers.

Christian radio hits: "Nothing without You" (# 13 in 1994).

King's X

Jerry Gaskill, drums; Doug Pinnick, voc., bass; Ty Tabor, gtr. 1988—*Out of the Silent Planet* (Megaforce); 1989—*Gretchen Goes to Nebraska*; 1990—*Faith, Hope, Love*; 1992—*King's X* (Atlantic); 1994—*Dogman*; 1996—*Ear Candy*; 1997—*Best of King's X*; 1998—*Tape Head* (Metal Blade); 2000—*Please Come Home, Mr. Bulbous*; 2001—*Manic Moonlight.*

www.kingsxonline.com

King's X is one of the most popular and most highly respected Christian bands in the world—though, like their spiritual soulmates in **U2,** the precise nature of their place in the contemporary Christian music subculture has often been tenuous and hard to define. Unlike generically spiritual bands like **Creed** or **Collective Soul,** the members of King's X have strong roots in the Christian music scene and have been explicit about their personal faith in Jesus Christ. Nevertheless, their devotion to the phenomenon known as Christianity has wavered over the years as they have struggled with the expectations that some Christians place upon them. Lead singer Doug Pinnick does not like for the group to be called "a Christian band" at all but prefers to identify King's X as "a secular band of Christians." As with the aforementioned bands (**U2,** Creed, Collective Soul), King's X is probably better known in the general market than in Christian circles. While they have not had many Top 40 radio hits, they have long been a staple of college radio stations and are regarded by many critics as one of the greatest hard rock outfits of all time.

Musically, King's X effectively melds the intensity of hard rock or metal music with the more progressive rock stylings of bands like **Kansas** or Genesis. The style has been described both as "Art-Metal" and as "Beatles-meet-Black Sabbath." The band is sometimes compared to the trio Rush—with whom they shared a manager for a time—but all agree that they have a distinctive sound unlike any other artist in the Christian or secular scenes. The group is also somewhat distinctive (but not unique—cf. The Jimi Hendrix Experience) in its biracial lineup, two white guys led by an African American (i.e., Pinnick). All three members contribute strong harmony vocals. Some would say that King's X almost singlehandedly rescued heavy metal, invigorating the tired genre with an unanticipated vitality that broadened its appeal from a cult of long-haired high school white boys to an audience including anyone who enjoys Steppenwolf or Led Zeppelin. For a group of Christians that has achieved such success and been accorded such accolades, King's X receives surprisingly little attention in the Christian media, for reasons that might become clear below. Still, they remain a favorite band among theologically discerning Christian rock fans (those whom *CCM* calls "thinking Christian headbangers") and also draw high praise from other Christian artists for the integrity, competence, and originality of their musicianship. Brian Quincy Newcomb notes that "King's X goes out of its way to share the intent of the gospel message, without religious trappings or proselytizing pressure. . . . never does King's X speak as if they have all the answers or offer any ultimatum; always, it is an invitation, shared with dignity, patience, and forethought." **Phil Keaggy** says, "Aside from Cream, they're the best trio group I've ever heard"—high praise from the man who headed the trio group **Glass Harp.**

Pinnick and Jerry Gaskill both played with **Petra** for a time and then in 1980 backed **Phil Keaggy** in support of his *Ph'lip Side* album. Pinnick cowrote the Keaggy classic "Just a Moment Away," from that album. While on tour, they met **Ty Tabor,** who was playing with Keaggy's opening act, a Christian group called The Tracy Zinn Band. Another version of their origin holds that all three met while attending college in Springfield, Missouri, where they formed a cover band called Sneak Preview (which supposedly recorded one independent album). In any case, they also formed a group that was initially called The Edge and, moving to Houston in 1985, they backed **Morgan Cryar** on his *Fuel on the Fire* album, for which they also wrote songs. Tabor, in fact, cowrote Cryar's big hit "Pray in the U.S.A." about the ultimate inefficacy of legal restrictions on school prayer ("Till they steal your heart away, you can still pray in the U.S.A.").

The decision to form King's X represented, in some sense, an intentional break with the Christian music industry. The name itself refers to a custom from medieval times, in which a king who sent a messenger to a foreign land would place a mark on the messenger signifying that the person was under his protection. In the same way, the members of King's X believed they were being sent by God into the world (though not necessarily as messengers) and that God would protect them from whatever dangers they encountered there. The group had actually been turned down by the Christian label Frontline before signing with a general market label. Tabor said they preferred the latter deal anyway because, "we wanted our music to be heard by everyone, not just played on Christian stations." In any case, the signing of King's X to Megaforce/Atlantic would be of momentous consequence for the history of Christian music and for rock and roll in general. Mark Joseph claims in his book *The Rock and Roll Rebellion,* "if Frontline had signed the band, the rock world would have been deprived of one of the greatest rock bands of all time." This is probably not an exaggeration. Even if King's X had made the same albums for Frontline that they made for Megaforce and Atlantic, the music would probably never have been heard by ninety percent of the band's current fans. As it turns out, King's X has toured the world with AC/DC, Living Colour, the Scorpions, and Pearl Jam. In 1995, they played at the Woodstock 95 concert, earning a favorable review from radio shock jock Howard Stern ("everybody sucked except for King's X"). *USA Today* also listed them as "the highlight of the evening" the day that they played. Despite an international following, King's X has also become the prime example of what is sometimes called "the Houston sound," typified also by such bands as **Galactic Cowboys** and **Atomic Opera. Ty Tabor** produces albums for many other artists, including **Resurrection Band.** Both he and Doug Pinnick have recorded solo albums.

The members of King's X talk openly in Christian magazines about their personal faith and about the effects (positive and negative) of the Christian orientation on their vocation and art. They have often objected to the confining aspects that the label *Christian* can carry. In 1993, Pinnick said that his "biggest problem with King's X" has been that "the world" perceives the band as one thing and "the Christians" as something else, while "neither one of them know what we are." King's X clearly does not understand itself to be "a ministry band." Pinnick says, "We never got together to minister. We got together to make music and to go out in the world and sing songs about the way we feel about life and faith." Before working with **Petra** or **Phil Keaggy,** Pinnick had been in a Christian band called **Servant,** in which he regularly preached and gave altar calls. A bit further along, he would admit that this was not his calling, and he believes it might be irresponsible to pursue it. "I try to keep my mouth shut as much as I can, cause I don't want to say the wrong thing and mislead people." He is quick to add that he rejoices in the letters he gets from people who claim to have found Christ through the group's music. Still, as early as 1989, he was saying, "I don't want Christians to start using us as this banner: 'Oh! We got another one! Listen to this band and they will change your life!' Forget that. Just let us do what we know how to do. If people expect more from us than rock and roll, they're going to be disappointed."

In a stronger vein, Pinnick (like Bono of **U2**) makes a distinction between faith in Christ and acceptance of Christianity: "I feel I need to be an example of truth, not an example of religion. . . . Jesus is the truth. The church, right now, is the scribes and Pharisees. . . . We've got so many rules and regulations that you can't even be yourself. What ever happened to just saying, 'I believe in Jesus Christ, and I believe He is everything He said He was.' " Likewise, Gaskill, Pinnick, and Tabor have all reacted strongly to the image of presumed holiness that many Christian music fans try to place on the group. The band has often received criticism for using profanity in their songs or stage shows, and the individual members' lives are sometimes scrutinized in ways that they consider to be invasive. "We're just normal human beings who do things that maybe the church looks down upon," Pinnick explained in 1993, pleading with Christian audiences to cut the band some slack: "Let us work through this in our own time and in our own faith. You tend to yours, and we can all make it together."

Like many contemporary Christian musicians, Pinnick seems to know Christianity primarily in the peculiar incarnation of American fundamentalism; his public comments reveal little awareness of the more biblical or gospel-oriented expressions of the faith that typify global and historic Christianity. This is perhaps never more clear than in his own account of his childhood in the band's biggest hit, "Over My Head." The song tells about the experience he had as a boy being raised by a grandmother who was always going to church, coming home, and playing gospel music in the room above his own. That music had a lasting effect on him, but so did the context in which he heard it. In concerts, Pinnick would often break with his own no-preaching policy during this song, delivering an extended rant against parents who abandon their children and speaking with tremendous emotion of his own trauma. In a version of this sermon recorded live at the Woodstock festival (and appearing on the *Best of King's X* album), he fumes like a TV evangelist:

> Late at night, she'd be in her room, singin' and dancin' and shoutin' and all that she used to do, and I'd be in my room feeling so alone, wondering why my mother left and my Daddy never came around . . . and my Grandma, she never said 'I love you,' she called herself a Christian and she never said I love you. She said, 'Nobody wants you, nobody needs you, nobody loves you.' And I grew up so confused. . . . If *you* plan on having kids, you make sure that your kids know that you love them more than anything in the whole wide world, no matter who they are, no matter what they look like or what they do, what kind of rock and roll they listen to or if they wear tattoos, cause if you don't show your children love, they will grow up *f**ked up*—and I know what I'm talking about!

The group's first three albums were made with producer Sam Taylor, known for his involvements with ZZ Top. *Out of the Silent Planet* immediately caught the attention of thinking Christian headbangers with a title lifted straight from a science fiction novel by C. S. Lewis. The record itself scored with three especially strong cuts: "King," "Goldilox," and "Shot of Love" (not the **Bob Dylan** song). The first of these became the band's traditional concert opener. It intersperses anthemic verses that proclaim "You are the one who causes me pain / You are the one who causes me grief" with a chorus that promises a king is coming. What is the song about? Are the verses addressed to the world? Or to the devil? Surely, the coming king is Jesus? King's X never explained these matters, leaving their fans to puzzle over the ambiguities. The fact that they began the song in concert with samples from recorded speeches by Martin Luther King Jr. didn't make things any more clear—perhaps he was the King who was coming.

The curiously titled *Gretchen Goes to Nebraska* brought the band their first big radio hit with the aforementioned "Over My Head." It also includes "Pleiades," the first song the band ever did as a group—indeed the song that inspired them to leave **Morgan Cryar** and strike out on their own. *Gretchen* opens with a song that one might think should have been on

the first album—"Out of the Silent Planet." Here Pinnick sings, "Father speaks / son becomes the story / essence of all truth." And in "The Mission" the band takes its first of many stabs at religious hypocrisy: "Who are these people behind the stained glass windows? / Have they forgotten what they came here for / Was it salvation, or are they just scared of hell?" Interestingly, Pinnick would say in an interview six years later (without any reference to this song), "I learned religion in a shaming way. Everything was from fear. My relationship with God has always been that I don't want to go to hell."

The third album takes its title straight from the Bible—*Faith, Hope, Love*. Throwing caution to the wind, they included the titular Scripture passage from 1 Corinthians 13 inside the CD booklet and decorated the front cover artwork with pictures of Christ's first and second comings. Two songs, "I'll Never Get Tired of You" and "Moanjam," are addressed directly to God. The group also followed the lead of **U2**'s *The Joshua Tree* by delving into politics—although unlike the latter group they took the somewhat safer route of extolling politics favored by the Religious Right with a strongly worded antiabortion song, "Legal Kill" (years later, producer Taylor would reveal that it was Tabor's song and only got on the album over Pinnick's and Gaskill's objections). The big hit from the project, however, was "It's Love," which is sort of a hard rock version of the Beatles classic "All You Need is Love." The hippie vibe of the lyrics ("It's love that holds it all together") is enhanced by sugary harmonies and spacey sound effects, but (and this is a significant *but*) the pounding rhythms and crunching guitars sound a lot more like Metallica than anything the Beatles ever dared to imagine. Another anthem, "We Are Finding Who We Are," offers the band's finest testimony to what Anselm called "faith seeking understanding": "We are finding who we are 'cause we can see forever / I know it's been said so many times before / I once was blind but now I see / And sometimes it just makes no sense / But I believe." In 1991, the group contributed the song "Junior's Gone Wild" to the soundtrack of *Bill and Ted's Bogus Journey*.

King's X marks a move toward a more alternative (some would say more commercial) sound. Tabor would later diss this album as "really sub-par," owing to pressure to make a certain type of record that was not representative of what the group wanted to do. The standout tracks and most-played songs from the album would be the hard rocking numbers "Black Flag" and "Lost in Germany." The first of these is confessional, giving heed to warning signs ("black flags") that one's life is not what it should be. The album cover for *King's X* features artwork portraying a small child picking up crumbs of bread beneath an altar table set for the sacrament of Communion. The album closes with "Silent Wind," a song that calls on

Christians to transcend denominational concerns and "listen to the silent wind" of God's Spirit.

The band would follow its two most overtly religious offerings *(Faith, Hope, Love* and *King's X)* with *Dogman,* on which they sound angry and resigned. "I don't care like I used to," Pinnick declares, "I don't care about you" ("Don't Care"). Again, ambiguity reigns supreme: do they mean to assert that they no longer worry about public opinion and trying to appease the world—or are they admitting to a loss of faith or lack of compassion? Other songs refer to love as just going through the motions ("Pretend") and confess, "I no longer know just what I'm saying / Is this how it's supposed to be?" ("Cigarettes"). "Black the Sky" is a powerhouse blues song relating a bitter tale of disillusionment. Reasons for the band's funk seem varied. The group had a bitter split with longtime producer Taylor, opting now to work with Brendan O'Brien. Pinnick admitted that he was seeking therapy for depression (from which he had suffered periodically for years) and alluded to sexual abuse he had endured as a child. Pinnick gave an interview to the Christian magazine *Visions of Gray* in which he shared his bitter feelings toward Taylor and his animosity regarding numerous things going on in Christian culture and in his home church. Instead of a prayer for understanding like "Silent Wind," the *Dogman* album closes with a cover of Jimi Hendrix's ode to confusion, "Manic Depression." *Dogman* also features a song called "Go to Hell," though the lyrics are less controversial than the title: "I don't wanna go to hell / Nobody in their right mind wants to."

Ear Candy would find the band more focused musically if not spiritually. Honesty had become their hallmark by this point: "Sometimes I want to live, sometimes I want to die / Sometimes I want to believe, sometimes I want to get high" ("Sometime"). In "Looking for Love," Pinnick claims, "Religion burns me at the stake / I questioned, I listened, I worshiped / How can I relate? . . . I guess I've lost my faith." In "Run," he alludes again to being brought up in a fire and brimstone tradition that he has had to flee in order to find God outside of the church. Another song, "Picture," derives from an experience Pinnick had as an adult when his family and relatives gathered to have a reunion photograph taken. While posing, he says, he realized that "this was the first time I had ever been in the same place as my parents, with my hands on both of them together at the same time." The album closes with "Life Going By," a testimony to the endurance of faith that suggests some of the demons from the past have been subdued if not quite expelled: "I've known a love forever, a Truth I couldn't sever. . . . I've stood on the mountain and drunk from the fountain / And poured it all out on the floor / Turned my back on glory . . . and come back to knock on your door." Through a retail agreement with Atlantic, *Ear Candy* actually became the first King's X

album to be distributed to Christian bookstores. Musically, the album is a bit funkier than previous projects, with "Sometime" recalling the early '70s sound of Sly and the Family Stone. "Fathers" has a strong '60s hippie vibe, "67" exhibits a tribal beat, and "American Cheese" is straight-ahead power-pop. "Mississippi Moon" is a ballad about lost youth written and sung by Tabor.

Changing record labels, the group produced its next two albums by itself. *Tape Head* would continue in the tradition of previous projects, with little variation in the trademark sound. If anything, critics noted that the band seemed to return to the more raw character of its early Megaforce releases on the Metal Blade albums. A few songs ("Groove Machine," "Fade") incorporate even more of the Sly and the Family Stone-inspired funk appeal previewed on the previous album. Lyrically, the album deals more openly with Christian themes than any other, though both the affirmations of the early works and the faith struggles of later ones are now replaced by an underlying Christian worldview that seems to inform every song. "Groove Thing" quotes an old hymn in what is pretty much its only lyric: "Lay down your burdens by the riverside / Take a deep breath and go for a ride." The song "Over and Over Again" is a power ballad that offers a heartfelt plea for forgiveness. "Ono" presents a series of ethical dilemmas ("Have you ever . . turned your head when someone's doing someone wrong? . . . lied to protect someone?"). "Higher Than God" attributes disappointment in a relationship to the idolatrous expectations that had been attached to it. Many of the songs also continue to reflect the hippie philosophy expressed in "It's Love"; this time, King's X advises their listeners to "put a little soul" in everything they do ("A Little Bit of Soul"), and to let the light within them shine ("Happy"). Such sentiments may be generic, but they are certainly not far removed from the teaching of Jesus in the Sermon on the Mount. At the same time, songs like "Hate You" appear to reflect the sort of self-loathing of the Apostle Paul (Romans 7). The bottom line, they maintain, is that while the world with all its troubles just keeps going round and round ("World"), faith, hope and love abide to carry us back home ("Ocean").

On *Please Come Home, Mr. Bulbous,* the group resolved the whole Beatles/Black Sabbath tension decidedly on the side of the Fab Four. While the album contains moments of unrepentant heaviness, it represents a radical departure from the sound of previous projects. Replete with psychedelic *Magical Mystery Tour* effects, the overall tone reflects a stronger pop-orientation with more emphasis on bluesy ballads and catchy hooks. Obvious Christian themes and imagery are less in evidence but not completely absent. "When You're Scared" gets at the source of much sin: "It's really easy to hate everyone when you're scared." The rather obscure "Smudge" is apparently about the devil, and the song contains a number of obtuse apocalyptic ("What's this mark upon my hand?") and religious ("I broke your rosary") references. The most overtly spiritual song, again, is the album's closer, a prayer to a God called "Keeper of Mysteries" to "move me and move me again" ("Move Me"). *Manic Moonlight* rocks hard but is pretty much devoid of spiritual themes save for one song, "Believe," which (at least on the surface) seems to counsel rejection of Jesus' demands: "If the cross you carry on your back makes it hard for you to move / In yourself believe / It's alright" (cf. Mark 8:34).

If King's X has a somewhat ambiguous status within the Christian music scene, it is largely because they refuse to inhabit a Christian rock ghetto that has so little to do with the real world in which most people (even Christians) live their lives. They also object to a perceived dearth of spirituality within the Christian music culture. "We all have gone through periods in the past where we have been very angry with the church—very angry with the Christian industry," Tabor told *CCM* in 1995. "The whole selling of Jesus like a cheap commercial just made me absolutely furious." Gaskill agreed, trying to explain why he is now reluctant even to call himself a Christian: "I believe Jesus is who He said He was, but I'm really tired of the whole 'Christian thing'—the culture, the industry, the market, the whole 'thing' that is defined as 'Christian'." Gaskill went through a difficult divorce during the recording of *Tape Head,* and a short time later an attempt on his life instigated a local police investigation. In 2001, Gaskill's two children, Jerrimy and Joy Gaskill, formed a band named Geek and toured as the opening act for **Poundhound.** As of the end of that year, Gaskill was planning to release a solo album.

Pinnick remains the most enigmatic of the trio. He prefers to emphasize the journey aspect of faith and wishes that Christian music fans would not expect him or the other band members to be people who have already arrived at some stagnant, conclusive goal. "I'm still trying to sort out who God is, who I am when it comes to my relationship with God and how to deal with that" he said in 1995. "If people are going to like King's X, they're gonna have to accept King's X as normal human beings—not as saints, not as spokesmen, not as role models." By the same token, he continued, the band's legion of fans in the general market get confronted with what to them may be the scandal of the band's unabashed faith: "Doug Pinnick is a Christian?! Yeah, I am. Deal with it!" In 1998 Pinnick released a solo album under the name **Poundhound.** On one song, "Darker," he again expressed doubts about his faith—though no more ominously than in *Ear Candy*'s "Sometime." In interviews accompanying the album, however, he indicated that if people want to say he's fallen away, he wouldn't argue. "Let them say it, there's nothing I can do." The issues with continuing to identify himself as a Christian, he said,

were practical and theological. First, he said that in touring the world he had seen all sorts of people with all different types of religions and noticed "how happy they are and how full their lives are," only to ask himself, "God, what's this? I'm miserable." Second, he was finally ready to admit that he was gay and that he had "struggled with homosexual feelings" for most of his life. This identification seemed to cause much consternation: "I've been raised to be homophobic," he said. "And there are verses in the Bible that I've been taught say God hates me, and that it's an abomination." Actually Christianity as a whole was sharply divided over the ethics of homosexuality at the turn of the millennium, but the fundamentalist and conservative churches that formed the base for the Christian music subculture would do little to quell the sort of fears and doubts that Pinnick expressed. Pinnick would also record an album with the group **Supershine.**

In late 2001, Tabor told *HM,* "I think we three, in the beginning, had more common ground between us in our beliefs. Over time, beliefs have changed, so there is no longer the connection of spiritual ideals that we used to share." Nevertheless, he affirmed, "There is still the connection of being truthful as human beings, and as artists."

For trivia buffs: In 1990, Doug Pinnick related his testimony of salvation to *HM* magazine; in retrospect, the tale seems oddly prophetic of the different path he would travel as a believer. He remembers answering an altar call, as expected within his denomination, at the age of twenty-one. But when the evangelist invited those who wished to accept Christ to come forward to the front of the church, Pinnick says he got up and went to the back instead—to the bathroom where he prayed in private, "OK, Jesus, forgive me of my sins and let's move on."

Wayne Kirkpatrick

2000—*The Maple Room* (Rocketown).

www.waynekirkpatrick.com

Wayne Kirkpatrick is one of the most successful and prolific songwriters in contemporary Christian music and is also one of the genre's most sought-after producers. A master of the crossover, his songs have also made quite an impression in the general market. He cowrote such *Billboard* Top 40 hits as "Every Heartbeat" (# 2 in 1991) and "Takes a Little Time" (# 27 in 1997) for **Amy Grant,** "A Place in This World" (# 6 in 1991) for **Michael W. Smith,** and "Change the World" for **Eric Clapton** (# 5 in 1996). The latter song even won him a Grammy for "Song of the Year" in 1997. Less laudable but still noteworthy, he cowrote most of the material for Garth Brooks' failed *The Life and Times of Chris Gaines* experiment, and he cowrote two songs with Peter Frampton ("You Had to Be There," "Hour of

Need") for inclusion on the *Almost Famous* motion picture soundtrack. Kirkpatrick has also written songs recorded by Joe Cocker ("Love to Lean On"), Faith Hill ("It Will Be Me"), Martina McBride ("Anything and Everything"), **Kenny Rogers** ("Now and Forever"), George Strait ("Remember the Alamo"), Wynonna ("Lead Me On"), and Trisha Yearwood ("Chance of a Lifetime").

Kirkpatrick was born in 1971 in Alexandria, Louisiana. He began writing songs as a young teenager, and when his father went into the ministry and moved the family to Baton Rouge, the congregation provided him with a ready audience for testing his material. He eventually attended Belmont College in Nashville, where he wrote "Wise Up" for **Amy Grant,** the star's first song to cross over to general market charts. After serving behind the scenes for so many years, Kirkpatrick finally decided to start the new millennium with an album of his own.

The Maple Room is what *CCM* calls "a spirited pop masterpiece similar in style to the works of **Phil Keaggy, Michael W. Smith,** or **Steven Curtis Chapman.**" The songs are all of the timeless pop variety that has sustained artists across the decades from the Beach Boys to Dan Fogelberg to the Goo Goo Dolls. As it turns out, Kirkpatrick has a decent voice, a warm tenor that is especially suitable for the mostly mellow songs he offers. The surprise on the album is "Wrapped Up in You," a rocking love song with a great lyric set to a Beatles-cum-Keaggy beat: "How do I love you? Well, let me see / I love you like a crooner loves a melody." In 2001, Garth Brooks would cover "Wrapped Up in You" and release it as the first single from his album *Scarecrow.* Lyrically, Kirkpatrick opts for an understated approach throughout *The Maple Room,* presenting songs about life and love as viewed from a Christian (or generically family-oriented) perspective rather than songs that are obviously religious. "It's Me Again" presents the thoughts of a man who yearns for the comfort of his spouse to ease his own self-doubt. "A Window in the Wall" describes an attempt to see through another's emotional defense network. "In Another Light" focuses on the conflicting role expectations of career and family. Such psychological, relationship-oriented songs (cf. "Blame It on Your Mother") appear to be Kirkpatrick's forté. The most overtly spiritual song is perhaps "Everywhere," which might be addressed to God ("I breathe you in like the air / You're everywhere") or might be an affirmation of the continuing presence of a lost loved one ("It's almost like you never went away"). The only clunker is "That's Not New Age." The song presents Kirkpatrick's defense against the criticisms of obtuse Christians who have tried to find ideas that smack of New Age philosophy in some of his more generically spiritual songs. Point taken, but some criticisms are perhaps too dumb to legitimate with a response. Besides, *some* New Age ideas are in fact derived from Christianity and are completely compatible with orthodox Christian teachings. Ironically, the aforementioned "Everywhere" could easily be a New Age song; it perfectly expresses a basic New Age tenet, albeit one that is also shared by Christianity. *The Maple Tree*'s best song is a hauntingly sweet (New Agey) ballad called "Kiss the Cheek of the Moon."

Kirkpatrick has also contributed songs to a compilation album featuring prominent writers performing their own material (*Coming from Somewhere Else,* Rocketown, 2000). He offers his own rendition of "Change the World" and "Place in this World" in addition to "Grand Canyon" (originally recorded by **Susan Ashton**). He also joins cowriters Gordon Kennedy, **Phil Madeira,** and **Billy Sprague** in performing the anthemic title track.

In 1996, **Gary Chapman** won the Dove award for Inspirational Song of the Year with his recording of Kirkpatrick's "Man after Your Own Heart" (cowritten with **Billy Sprague**). Kirkpatrick has also written or cowritten Christian radio hits for **Susan Ashton** ("Down on My Knees," "Benediction," "In Amazing Grace Land," "Walk On By"), **Rick Cua** ("For the Love of God"), **Michael English** ("Love Won't Leave You"), **Reneé García** ("Living in the Vertical"), **Amy Grant** ("Wise Up," "Love of Another Kind," "Stay for Awhile," "Love Can Do," "Lead Me On," "Children of the World"), **Kim Hill** ("Faithful," "Testimony," "Mysterious Ways," "I Will Wait," "Satisfied," "Words"), **Wes King** ("Simplify"), **Michael W. Smith** ("I Know," "Rocketown," "Wired for Sound," "Voices," "Old Enough to Know," "Emily," "Pray for Me," "Help You Find Your Way," "Hand of Providence," "Live and Learn," "On the Other Side," "I Hear Leesha," "Go West, Young Man," "How Long Will Be Too Long," "For You," "Seed to Sow," "Love Crusade," "Somebody Love Me," "Give It Away," "Kentucky Rose," "Cross of Gold," "Breakdown," "I'll Lead You Home," "Little Stronger Every Day," "Someday"), **Billy Sprague** ("Rock the Planet," "Love Has No Eyes," "What Goes Around Comes Around"), and **Kathy Troccoli** ("Talk It Out"), as well as numerous songs for **Margaret Becker, Lisa Bevill, Gary Chapman, Rich Mullins, Plumb, Sierra,** and **Jaci Velasquez.**

For trivia buffs: Kirkpatrick majored in landscape engineering in college but never pursued a career in that area. In 2001, a deck that he designed for his home in rural Nashville was chosen a National First Prize Winner and featured in *Garden, Deck, and Landscape* magazine.

Dove Awards: 1994 Producer of the Year.

KJ-52

2000—*7th Avenue* (Essential).

www.kj-52.com

KJ-52 is the professional name used by solo rap artist Jonah Sorrentino, who grew up in Ybor City, the ghetto area of Tampa, Florida. Sorrentino explains the name (pronounced KJ-five two, not fifty-two) as follows: the letters KJ are an acronym for the phrase "Knowledge is Justification" and the numbers five and two add up to seven which symbolizes completion. Numerology aside, the concept that knowledge leads to justification is more than a bit problematic theologically—one that all Christian groups would probably find heretical (Sorrentino cites Romans 10:9 as his basis for this assertion; that passage mentions neither knowledge nor justification, but Romans 3:25–26 links justification with faith and grace, which are certainly *not* the same thing as knowledge; cf. Matthew 11:25–26; 1 Corinthians 1:27; Ephesians 2:8).

Sorrentino describes his music as motivated by "a burden to reach the hip-hop community for Jesus." *7th Avenue* is named for the ghetto street on which the artist was raised. The album was produced by Todd Collins of **The Gotee Brothers,** and the songs are given an unusual variety for most hip-hop projects through numerous collaborations with such artists as Bonafide of **Grits,** Amani, **Knowdaverbs,** and Deuce and Phanatik from **Cross Movement.** On several tracks KJ-52 is accompanied by a crew that he calls simply "Sons of Intellect." He presents his testimony in an old-school rap number called "We Rock the Mic," and he also covers the **DC Talk** classic "The Hardway." Thematically, the songs are connected by several interludes that work together to present an unraveling story. The album opens with two urban kids talking about who the greatest emcee of all time is, and at the end it is revealed to be Jesus, though its hard to imagine any listener who wouldn't have had that mystery figured out from the get-go. Still, KJ-52 explains, "It's like I'm talking to this kid on the street about this emcee that had a crew 12 deep, and as the album progresses you figure out all of the metaphors. The guy I'm talking to asks, 'Who's this man you're talkin' about?' and that's when I present Christ. And then I have an altar call." *Real* and other magazines have weighed in with the opinion that this is just too corny to be effective. But *CCM*'s Brian Quincy Newcomb was more generous in recognizing the effort: "In all, KJ-52 offers up significant talent and a heart for communicating the gospel message in a way that it can be heard at street level."

Klank

Daren Diolosa, voc., gtr.; et al. 1996—*Still Suffering* (Tooth and Nail); 1997—*Downside* [EP]; 2000—*Numb* (Progressive Arts).

www.klank.net

Klank is one of Christian music's heaviest industrial death metal artists, churning out angry music comparable in sound to such mainstream acts as White Zombie and Fear Factory. As is typical for the genre, Klank tries to remain anonymous, offering no information on personnel in album liner notes. The truth—which is also often the case—is that Klank is not a band at all, but merely a moniker applied to products by a single artist: Daren Diolosa, who also played guitar and sang background vocals for **Circle of Dust.** The furtive tendency symbolizes in some respects the faceless character of the music itself, accenting the "industrial" notion of music in which machines dominate and subdue any human element. The audience is assaulted with walls of heavy guitars, pounding beats, and numerous electronic effects, which form a base for Diolosa's angry, growling vocals. All this is to say that Klank's albums sound very much like most heavy industrial metal albums by other artists, though *7ball* has aptly described the one feature that makes Klank distinct: "Diolosa eschews the typical industrial approach to delivering his provocative lyrics. Rather than bury the words under layers of distortion—a fairly standard practice for industrial music—Diolosa actually sings in a very intelligible growl that 'splits the difference between industrial and metal.'" One consequence of this is that listeners can actually understand the lyrics. The artist himself describes his music this way: "Klank is based heavily on the Groove factor—utilizing elements of dance, metal, electronics, heavy keyboards, and vocals that range from melodic to menacing to form a sound that we're trying to keep pretty unique."

Diolosa's relationship with the Christian music scene appears to be uncomfortable and imprecise, as is his relationship with Christianity in general. "I'm a Christian in the respect that I believe God exists and I try to be the best person I can be," the singer told *HM.* He admits that he is "not associated with any church" but also insists "I do not deny Jesus or his existence or his claim to be the Son of God." He has sometimes been noted for rock star antics that would be more stereotypically associated with artists in the general market. For instance, when asked to sign with Tooth and Nail, he sliced his hand open and signed the contract in blood ("I wanted to show them that I'm no joke"). In many respects, Diolosa's identification with the Christian music scene has come by way of association, as he maintains personal and professional contacts with a number of people who are more explicitly regarded as Christian artists (such as Michael Tait of **Tait** and **DC Talk**). It is at least fair to say that Diolosa does not view Klank as a band engaged in Christian ministry: "I am a Christian but I do not go out and talk to people about what I believe," he once told *HM.* "My religious beliefs, I think, should not really have any bearing on my music unless I decide to mention something about them in a song." Diolosa admits to having been brought up "in a strict household in which unless the music was 'boldly Christian' it wasn't allowed." He grants that this experience left him with negative impressions of "Christian music," which he thinks is often marketed on the basis of ideology despite an obviously inferior quality: "I wasted so much money in the past on bad music all in the name of, 'Well, it's Christian, so I kinda have to like it'."

Still Suffering was produced by "Celldweller," one of several aliases used by the annoyingly cryptic Klay Scott of **Argyle Park/Circle of Dust** fame. Lyrically, Diolosa presents his anger as "righteous wrath" against social evils like child abuse ("Disease") and against such personal sins as betrayal ("Deceived"). "Scarified" also deals with the frightening aspect of evil, and Diolosa says it was inspired by his personal encounters with child molesters in society and in the church. On "Animosity," however, his rage gets the better of him and he vents in a most un-Christian way, "I hate this world and all it has to offer / If I had a choice, I'd rather be dead." Such sentiments are perhaps redeemed in the closing track, the only overtly religious or spiritual song, "Woodensoul." Now, he sings, "My Savior bleeds / Calloused hands / With fury I need / To break my wooden soul." Likewise, "Burning" expresses soul-searching that reveals at least some aspect of faith: "Deep down inside my heart, I still believe / I know you exist, but where are you?"

Klank made *Numb* as an early follow-up to *Still Suffering,* but Tooth and Nail opted not to release it and custom copies were sold at concerts for a time prior to the eventual indie release. (*Downside* is a five-song EP featuring remixes of songs from *Numb.*) Diolosa produced the sophomore project himself and called the music "electro-groove metal." The overall sound, while not radically different, does evince more of the dance-funk stylings of Nine-Inch Nails or even Kid Rock in spots (notably on the title track and "Ghetto Dance Mix"). Apparently, Diolosa put together an actual band for this project, featuring such first-name only cohorts as Pat, John, and Ducci. Musically, *Numb* is more diverse than the first project, including not only the aforementioned dance beats but also a couple of somewhat softer songs, "God?" and "So Very Real." The first of these is especially honest and vulnerable: "I wonder if you do exist and what you mean to me / Sometimes I think you hate me." Unfortunately, the anger on *Numb* often seems to be directed at the artist's real or imagined personal enemies. "Bleed Me Dry" (with a chorus of "Suck! Suck! Suck!") appears to be addressed to fans, whom Klank seems to despise. "Don't Like" and "No Answers/No Reasons" assault the band's critics, with the latter song cynically concluding, "Why bother speaking when nobody gives a damn? What good are words when no one even tries to understand? / You want to know what I would do? / What makes you think I even have a clue?" Thus, Klank moved in the opposite direction than that which was evident in the transition from **Argyle Park** to **AP2** (from profound disgust to trivial tantrums, not the other way around).

This, again, is redeemed somewhat in the closing song, "So Very Real": "When I'm at my weakest you make me strong / You're the only reason I press on." But *Phantom Tollbooth* would conclude, "Klank's major lyrical problem is that they can't decide whether they want to write clichéd Christian lyrics or clichéd anti-Christian lyrics, . . . and the listener gets the impression that both sentiments are half-hearted and banal."

Kmax

See **Kevin Max.**

Jennifer Knapp

1996—*Wishing Well* (independent); 1997—*Kansas* (Gotee); 2000—*Lay It Down;* 2001—*The Way I Am.*

www.jenniferknapp.com

Singer/songwriter Jennifer Knapp (b. 1974) became the media darling of the contemporary Christian music world shortly after her debut album in 1997, generating more press (and hype) in three years than most artists accumulate in a decade. Knapp was quickly named the Best New Artist of the Year by the Gospel Music Association in 1998 and was then slated to play the very nongospel-oriented Lilith Fair in 1999. The Christian industry's affection for her no doubt owed to their perception that she could be the Christian version of Jewel or Joan Osborne or Natalie Merchant or Sarah MacLachlan or any one of the numerous other female alternative folk rock singers who dominated the charts for a few years before the millennial onslaught of boy bands and barely pubescent teenaged girls drove them into near oblivion. Stylistically, at least, Knapp is firmly grounded in the anti-Britney musical agenda of intelligent, adult-oriented feminist-folk.

Knapp grew up in Chanute, Kansas, where she says her childhood was marred by common traumas: a parents' divorce, family dysfunction, and low self-esteem. She says that she first learned to write cryptic poetry because, knowing that her parents read her journals, it gave her a way of reflecting on her life without them quite knowing what she was talking about. She spent some college years at Kansas's Pittsburgh State College (on a trumpet scholarship) "making horrible decisions," pursuing a self-indulgent and self-destructive lifestyle before finding what she calls "a peace within religious conviction." To be more specific, she yielded at last to a barrage of witnessing by Christian dorm mates, praying to accept Christ at three o'clock in the morning one night in a grocery store parking lot. Her conversion caused something of a sensation on campus, as she was known for her foul-mouthed demeanor and partying lifestyle. But before long she was using her poetry to explore the changes in her life and perspective. After writing a batch of deeply personal songs reflecting on what she calls "the seemingly ironic mixture of crushing realism and towering assurance," she toured coffeehouses and churches for three years and even made a custom album before landing the contract with Gotee. The contract seems ironic in itself, as the label is known for hip-hop and rock-oriented musicians, far removed from the "cerebral chick singer" or "girl with a guitar" tags that had been applied to Knapp. Indeed, her debut album's title, *Kansas,* is intended to play on such stereotypes, summoning images of plain, stark, white-bread realism, which she then proceeds to deconstruct. After the release of *Kansas,* Knapp continued to tour relentlessly, opening for such well-known Christian artists as **Audio Adrenaline, Big Tent Revival, DC Talk, Jars of Clay,** and **Third Day.** The album sold phenomenally well for a debut record in the limited contemporary Christian market, and was eventually certified gold with sales over 500,000. *Billboard* magazine profiled Knapp as a Christian artist who "stands poised for mainstream acceptance." In 1999, she performed for Pope John Paul II on his visit to St. Louis. She made the national news briefly when Jerry Falwell attacked her participation in the Lilith Fair, which he claimed was named after "a demonic figure from pagan legends" (it is actually named for a mythological character who figures in some folktales found in the Jewish Talmud). *Campus Life* magazine voted her "Female Artist of the Year" in their 2000 Reader's Poll. Knapp continues to be an avid supporter of numerous charities, doing benefit concerts for the Ronald McDonald House, Mercy Ministries, children's hospitals, and women's shelters. At the same time, she has done promotional endorsements for Tommy Hilfiger's Tommy Girl cosmetics and for Taylor guitars.

Kansas was produced by Mark Stuart of **Audio Adrenaline.** "In the Name" is an atypically energetic roots-rocker similar to something that **Big Tent Revival** or even the **Vigilantes of Love** might do. The two songs that garnered the most attention, however, are "Undo Me" and "Romans." The first of these is a prayer for God to meddle in her affairs. The latter is a confession of human frailty based on the Apostle Paul's words in Romans 7—with a peppy chorus derived from the triumphant conclusion to that dilemma recorded in Romans 8:1. All three of these songs are more the sort of gritty pop associated with female singers like Melissa Etheridge or Sheryl Crow than the acoustic folk stylings that otherwise dominate the album. "Martyrs and Thieves," for instance, is a much softer, slow number that must be carried entirely by its lyric. The album opens and closes with an especially beautiful a capella song, "Faithful to Me," an Enya-like carryover from Knapp's prior independent release.

Knapp joined Stuart in coproducing the follow-up, *Lay It Down,* and there is little variation in sound or style from the first project. Again, the thematic focus is on confessional songwriting with numerous songs expressing prayers to God for forgiveness ("A Little More") or intimacy ("Into You"). "A Little More" even quotes once more from Romans 7 ("what I do I don't want to do"), which seems to be the frailty-obsessed Knapp's favorite text. Even the worship song, "All Consuming Fire," begins with the lines, "I sit here and wonder why my God loves me / though I have never done a good thing, or a righteous deed." Never? One wonders. Not once? Perhaps she protests too much. Is there a hazy line somewhere between recognition of grace and melodramatic humility? Musically, *Lay It Down* again mixes styles. The title track is another catchy pop tune, not unlike "Undo Me," and "Into You" kicks the electric guitar into gear and really rocks. But again, softer fare predominates, with the prettiest of the pretty songs being "When Nothing Satisfies," which features a duet vocal by **Margaret Becker,** and the sweet closing song, "Peace." The album also includes Knapp's cover of Shawn Colvin's "Diamond in the Rough." *CCM* maintained that *Lay It Down* "raises the bar artistically over the well-received *Kansas.*"

The Way I Am is probably Knapp's best work to date. The album was produced by Tony McAnany, who has worked with Madonna and Missy Elliot. Her songs have an emotional, poetic, and somewhat dark edge to them. "In Two" seems almost like a Christian version of Fiona Apple's "Criminal," with the power-claim as more confession than boast: "Have mercy on me, I'm a girl. . . . I know how to break a man in two." The confession works well on this song, but on the title track she seems to wallow a bit too much (again) in lamenting her spoiled humanity. On "Say Won't You Say," Knapp complains, "Every morning I have a chance to rise and give my all / But every afternoon I have only wasted time." This constant I'm-a-big-disappointment-to-myself-and-everyone-else theme grows tiresome. One would think that after three albums focusing on the theme of grace, Knapp would learn to put more emphasis on the blessing itself rather than just belaboring listeners with accounts of her own undeserving. And then—she does! The song "Around Me" is not only her most beautiful composition musically but also a stunning exposition of the mystical experience of being caught up in God, surrounded by angels, enjoying immortal favor, and discovering that one's own best attributes are evolving. Musically, it almost sounds like Knapp had been listening to **Kim Hill**'s near-perfect first album. Theologically, she appears to have discovered, at least momentarily, what Bono of **U2** would call "elevation" as opposed to excavation ("like a mole / digging in a hole"). It is her finest work and it lifts her album to unprecedented heights. Similarly, "Charity" expresses wonder at finding God in unlikely places, and "Sing Mary Sing" is an excellent Christmas song. *The Way I Am* closes with another stellar song on which Knapp expresses her hope to be "Free from the worry / Free from the dark that lives in me / Free to embark on the passion / You've fashionably fashioned in me." The album's best moments show her beginning to fulfill that dream.

Christian radio hits: "Undo Me" (# 14 in 1998); "Whole Again" (# 3 in 1998); "Romans" (# 1 for 2 weeks in 1998); "Hold Me Now" (# 6 in 1998); "His Grace Is Sufficient" (# 11 in 1999); "In the Name" (# 8 in 1999); "A Little More" (# 1 for 6 weeks in 2000); "Into You" (# 3 in 2000); "Lay It Down" (# 1 in 2001); "Breathe on Me" (# 14 in 2001).

Dove Awards: 1999 New Artist of the Year; 1999 Rock Song ("Undo Me").

Gladys Knight

Selected: 1998—*Many Different Roads* (MCA); 2001—*At Last.*

Like **Aretha Franklin** and many other R&B singers, Gladys Knight got her start in gospel music. Born in 1944 in Atlanta, Georgia, she grew up singing with the Mount Moriah Baptist Church choir and at the age five toured several southern states as a featured vocalist with the Morris Brown choir. At the age of seven, Knight won a grand prize on the *Ted Mack Amateur Hour,* which brought her several TV appearances. She subsequently came to be featured as the leading member of a family group known as The Pips, after a nickname for one of the family members. The group scored its first big hit with "Every Beat of My Heart" in 1961 (# 6) and during the next two decades would rack up many more, the most memorable of which may be "I Heard It through the Grapevine" (# 2 in 1967); "If I Were Your Woman" (# 9 in 1970); "Neither One of Us (Wants to Be the First to Say Goodbye)" (# 2 in 1973), "Midnight Train to Georgia" (# 1 for 2 weeks in 1973), and "Best Thing That Ever Happened to Me" (# 3 in 1974). She won a Grammy in 1986 for the AIDS benefit song "That's What Friends Are For," recorded with Elton John, Dionne Warwick, and Stevie Wonder, and scored a 1996 hit with the song "Missing You" (# 25 pop; # 10 R&B), recorded with Brandy, Tamia, and Chaka Khan for the soundtrack to the film *Set It Off.*

In the late '90s, Knight was divorced from her third husband, motivational speaker Les Brown. It was then that she became a Mormon and returned to her gospel roots. In 1997, she published an autobiography, *Between Each Line of Pain and Glory: My Life Story* (Hyperion). She also released an album of hymns and spiritual songs titled *Many Different Roads.* The title song is a tribute to Princess Diana, Mother Teresa, and Knight's own mother. The record also features the modern praise hymn "Good Morning Heavenly Father" and the more traditional "Precious Lord," which features just Knight and piano. *At Last* focuses on more generically inspirational songs, such as Bill Withers' "Grandma's Hands." Knight offers her own tribute to her late mother and son in the touching "Something Blue." There has been resistance to distribution of her religious albums in some Christian markets since, as a Mormon, Knight

belongs to a non-Trinitarian sect that some do not recognize as Christian.

Grammy Awards (for Gladys Knight and The Pips, except as indicated): 1973 Best R&B Vocal Performance by a Duo, Group, or Chorus ("Midnight Train to Georgia"); 1973 Best Pop Vocal Performance by a Duo, Group, or Chorus ("Neither One of Us"); 1986 Best Pop Vocal Performance by a Duo or Group [with Dionne Warwick, Stevie Wonder, Elton John] ("That's What Friends Are For"); 1988 Best R&B Vocal Performance by a Duo or Group ("Love Overboard"); 2001 Best Traditional R&B Vocal Album *(At Last).*

Knights of the Lord's Table

Kevin Johnson; Joseph Ravitts. 1976—*Knights of the Lord's Table* (Holy Kiss).

Knights of the Lord's Table was a short-lived single-project duo that remains of historical interest due to their connections and originality. As for the first, the duo were the principal act on an experimental label started by Jesus music pioneer (and maverick) **Randy Matthews.** Matthews himself joins them on the song, "I Can Do No Wrong." The Knights were also highly original in that they sought to create an album of medieval music, with generous helpings of harpsichord and recorder—similar to the more masterful **ArkAngel** project, but preceding it by a good four years. Actually only about half of the tracks on *Knights* are faithful to the conceit, "The Fable of Young Roderick" and "Jesus Loves Young Men" being the finest of them. Other songs are more typical of country-folk contemporary Christian music.

Michael Knott

1992—*Screaming Brittle Siren* (Blonde Vinyl); 1994—*Rocket and a Bomb* (Brainstorm); 1995—*Strip Cycle* (Tooth and Nail); *Fluid* (Alarma); 1998—*The Definitive Collection* (KMG); 2000—*Live in Nash-Vegas* (Blonde Vinyl); *Things I've Done, Things to Come; Live at Cornerstone 2000* (M8); 2001—*The Life of David* (Metro One).

www.michaelknott.com

Innovative virtuoso artist Michael Knott is best known as the front man for a number of bands, including **LSU** and the **Aunt Bettys** (see also **Bomb Bay Babies, Browbeats, Cush,** and **Strong Gurus**). He has recorded a few solo albums, but there are no clear distinctions between what constitutes solo work and band projects; the same songs often show up in varied versions on albums by different Knott incarnations and the usual suspects often accompany him, whether as part of the band or as relatively uncredited backups. *The Definitive Collection* album compiles material from **LSU** along with songs from solo records without any designation of which were which. The absurd title of that compilation also prompted *True Tunes* to send this little public memo to KMG: "When an artist has more entries in their discography than there are tracks on a retrospective, *definitive* is a bad word to use." *Things I've Done, Things to Come* is an even more eclectic collection. Supposedly released as a Michael Knott album, it actually contains only three songs by Knott as a solo artist, preferring previously unreleased tracks that sample virtually all of his diverse endeavors. That leaves five legitimate solo projects and a couple of live albums.

In many ways, Michael Knott played a similar role vis-à-vis Christian music in the '90s to that played by **Larry Norman** in the '70s. An undeniable pioneer whose talent and vision far exceeds that of most of his peers, he has been sometimes solicitous of the Christian music subculture's approval while also making moves that seem almost designed to alienate himself from that culture and to define his role as an artist over against it. From his own perspective, Knott claims that he has also tried to keep a foot in each of two disparate worlds, creating both music for Christian audiences (**Browbeats, LSU,** his solo projects) while also maintaining side projects intended for the general market (**Bomb Bay Babies, Aunt Bettys, Strong Gurus**). But given the interconnectedness of all his work as mentioned above—not to mention the artificiality of defining Christian music and the general market as two distinct arenas—he has certainly succeeded in confusing actual and potential fans in both worlds. No one is ever quite sure what to expect of Michael Knott, and that unpredictability has become his most endearing (and ironically predictable) quality. *Bandoppler* refers to him as "an iconoclast, challenging all that is baseless or thoughtless in contemporary Christian music." *HM* calls him "the industry's most mysterious artist." Most accurate, perhaps, is the simple acknowledgment from one critic that Michael Knott represents one of Christian music's "most authentic rock stars." Simultaneously respected, reviled, critiqued, and admired, he seems driven by both an internal pursuit of art and an external passion for performance that forces him into an unresolvable love/hate relationship with his critics and fans.

Knott was raised Roman Catholic, and he says that in his junior year of high school he "started reading the Bible and developing a relationship with Jesus." He had friends who were "into the revival, born-again thing," though that never quite clicked with his own experience. "I had this friend who told me all I had to do was say this prayer to get saved. So I said the prayer and nothing happened. So I said it again, like 25 more times, and nothing happened. But I did come to realize that as you draw nearer to God, he draws near to you." Knott played in a secular rock band for a while but his growing spiritual sensibilities eventually led him to Costa Mesa's Calvary Chapel where he hooked up with a Jesus music band called Lifesavors (predecessor to **LSU** = Life Savers Underground). After record-

ing one album with that group, Knott formed a band called Idle Lovell and recorded an obscure six-song independent vinyl album called *Surge et Illuminare* (1983). Some Christian music historians would eventually call this "the first Christian goth album," though it may be best described as simply previewing that form with its droning melodies and minor key songs. Then Knott rejoined a new version of the other band (now called Lifesavers) and the true Knott seemed to emerge in 1987 with the **LSU** album *Shaded Pain*. A watershed in Christian music, that album shocked the industry with its gritty style and brutally honest lyrics. In 1990, Knott formed Blonde Vinyl records, one of Christian music's first true indie labels. Through that company, he was instrumental in bringing some offbeat music to the attention of a loyal fledgling audience— not only the music of **LSU** but also **Breakfast with Amy, Dance House Children, Deitiphobia,** and **Fluffy.** Then, he got burned badly when the label's distributor (Spectra) folded, ensuring that some 75,000 units would never reach their markets. Eight years later, Knott was still smarting (emotionally and financially) from this fiasco, which provided at least part of the motivation for his attempt at mainstream success with the **Aunt Bettys.** As *Bandoppler* puts it, "despite attaining much critical acclaim and decent commercial sales, Knott has never quite 'made it,' instead tottering on the brink of popularity for years." Nevertheless, over an eighteen-year period (1982–2000), he managed to produce over thirty albums with six bands on fourteen labels—and to engender as much creativity and controversy as any other artist in the business. Not bad for a happily married father of two whose personal life seems beyond reproach.

Screaming Brittle Siren took Knott musically into the postpunk sounds of groups like Jane's Addiction or Echo and the Bunnymen (also the principal inspiration for **Breakfast with Amy**). Like **LSU**'s *Shaded Pain,* the album deals frankly with temptation and human weakness. Some of the songs ("Hang Me High," "Draw the Line") seem to be confessional cries for deliverance. The self-explanatory "Crash and Burn" laments his personal realization of repetitive failure and need for redemption. But the artist pairs his self-deprecating "I'm Not the Christ" with a summons to evangelism, "Shine a Light." As Brian Quincy Newcomb said in *CCM,* Knott "concludes that we broken humans must still share what we know, the one thing we have that gives us any meaning at all." In "Shine a Light," Knott sings, "I'm not the Captain, just a reflection of the sea."

Such relatively traditional Christian sentiments would vanish with *Rocket and a Bomb,* which introduces audiences to various bizarre characters whom Knott met while living in a seedy apartment complex in Hollywood (the same apartment dwellers would later form the thematic basis for the *Aunt*

Bettys' first album, and two songs from *Rocket and a Bomb*—the title track and "Kitty"—would reappear there). "Jan the Weatherman" claims to be able to predict when it will rain and drops by Knott's room periodically "with a stick and a can" wanting to be his drummer. "John Barrymore Jr." is a loser down the hall who claims to be the illegitimate son of the famous actor. "Bubbles" is a young woman trapped in a cycle of drug addiction and prostitution. For Knott, these characters become metaphors of the challenges facing the church in modern and postmodern times. The title song to *Rocket and a Bomb* features some of Knott's typically profound-if-you-get-them lyrics: "Mr. God, is there a Mrs. God? / Can she help me find a job?" Biblically literate fans might recognize the reference to "Mrs. God" as an allusion to the church, which the New Testament often refers to as "the Bride of Christ." As such, the song becomes a prayer for God's people to make a real difference in the lives of the unemployed, and perhaps in the lives of social misfits like those who populate the album's other songs. Musically, *Rocket and a Bomb* is a departure from the sound of Knott's first solo project or of previous **LSU** works. *Shout!* would describe it as having more of a Lou Reed-ish surf-pop tone.

That same description would generally apply to *Strip Cycle*, except that this time Knott would experiment with using an alternative guitar tuning for the entire album that he discovered accidentally when his daughter Stormie messed with his instrument's tuning knobs. Thus, the record is technically acoustic but possesses an oddly buzzing sound that sets it apart from anything too folky. The album features two Knott classics: "Rock Stars on H," which has a rockabilly Tom Petty vibe, and "Tattoo," which would later be reproduced in an even better version on the second **Browbeats** project. Lyrically, many songs deal with the hardships of making it in life. "Bad Check" and "Am I Winnin' Something?" both describe a sort of desperate materialism that can be born of poverty or, perhaps, just a combination of misplaced values and poor stewardship. Knott's characteristically sardonic humor shows up on "Bad Check": "Wrote a bad check to the government / Wrote a bad check to my parents / Wrote a bad check to this cello player / She didn't know it at the time, 'cause I'm singin' it later." The closing song, appropriately called "Denial," describes the cynical last wish of a man who finds his only comfort in liquor: "One more drink and Heaven could be calling / And I don't care if the sky starts falling / Cause I feel free, with God and a bottle in me."

Fluid was intended by Knott as a musical experiment, one in which he explored the sonic textures of echo-delayed guitar, giving the album a flowing or liquid-type quality. Thematically, the album represents a fairly ambitious attempt at a rock opera similar to **LSU**'s *The Grape Prophet* or *Dogfish Jones*. It relates the story of a girl caught in a coma after a car accident while God and the devil both covet her soul. Somehow while actually in a comatose state she manages to try to pray to Jesus, which settles the debate. Jesus decides that in this instance trying to pray to him is close enough to count ("The Sky"). The overall message is that those who wait to say the prayer that instantly transforms their destiny risk being tortured by Satan for all eternity—though, sometimes, apparently, Jesus cuts questionable cases a little slack. Theologically, the suggestion that an individual's eternal salvation depends on whether or not that person performs a nonbiblical ritual ("accepting Christ" or "praying a sinner's prayer") is disturbing to say the least. But perhaps Knott means only to invoke the mythology of American fundamentalism in a manner that allows for some symbolic portrayal of a cosmic drama—good versus evil or commitment versus indecision. Perhaps he is playing with fundamentalist mythology on *Fluid* the way that Dante and Milton played with Roman Catholic mythology in their tomes. In any case, *Fluid* is Knott's nadir, musically as well as lyrically. The only good song on the album is the opening rocker, "Crash," which sets up the absurd little melodrama. Like The Who's "Pinball Wizard" (from *Tommy*), it works on its own—apart from the "opera" for which it was intended—and it is usually heard that way. The song tells of a girl who gets so angry with her boyfriend that she intentionally takes the one thing he loves most—his Cadillac—and crashes it. The last two lines find her telling him, "I'm gonna die, won't you kiss me once more / But I'll never be sorry 'bout your '64." Nothing very Christian about it, but it's great rock and roll.

In 2001, Knott released *The Life of David,* his most pious and overtly religious project. A concept album, the original songs are all inspired by meditations on the biblical figure of David, a passionate, flawed human being with whom Knott says he can identify. The focus is not on the supposed author of psalms, but on the character revealed through the historical narratives in the books of Samuel and Kings—the man "after God's own heart" who becomes an adulterer and a murderer yet persists in personal and professional godliness. Thus, most of the songs on *Life of David* deal with hope in God and acknowledgment of human frailty; most also transcend the immediate context to function apart from any particular story line. In "Chameleon," Knott sings about "loving all God's creatures / all but one," i.e., himself. On "Halo," he allows the voice of God to intone, "Hell, no, I don't care if your halo don't glow." On the closing "Hospital," he admits, "I think I need forgiveness / I think I need more than the rest."

Live at Cornerstone features acoustic versions of Knott's best-known songs, with little accompaniment besides a guitar and a violin. *Nash-Vegas* also takes the unplugged approach, as Knott is backed by **Steve Hindalong** on percussion. The latter set features mostly **LSU** and **Aunt Bettys** songs. Three songs from *Rocket and a Bomb* ("Jan the Weatherman," "John Barrymore Jr.," and "Kitty Courtesy") are related with appropriately humorous anecdotes.

Michael Knott is married to **Windy Lyre,** who has also recorded Christian music. In late 2001 Knott announced through his booking agent that he had entered a hospital detoxification program for treatment of alcoholism, to be followed by an intensive rehab program.

Knowdaverbs

Mike Boyer II, voc. 1999—*The Syllabus* (Gotee); 2000—*The Action Figure*.

www.knowdaverbs.com

Knowdaverbs is the professional name used by rap singer Mike Boyer II. Boyer was raised in Arizona and began rapping for the Lord at the age of twelve. The name Knowdaverbs is intended to summon an emphasis on knowing the word of God, with an emphasis on action words ("Know Da Verbs"). Knowdaverbs is part of a hip-hop community called Factors of Seven, which also includes members of **Grits** and mix masters DJ Max and DJ Form. The group meets together regularly for prayer and encouragement, and to hold each other accountable for spiritual and moral development. Musically, Knowdaverbs has been influenced by Mos Def and Common, though nonspecialists in the world of hip-hop may just notice similarities to **Run-D.M.C.** and to such early '90s acts as Arrested Development or De La Soul. Knowdaverbs gets help from such notables as **DC Talk, Grits, Out of Eden,** and **Temple Yard** on *The Syllabus*. The album takes its name from Boyer's intention to use Scripture to teach biblical principles. In actuality, however, he tends to focus more on experiential testimonies. "Good Measure" is a story about how God told him to put all his pocket money into the church offering plate even though he was strapped for cash—and then the next day he got his tax refund. *The Action Figure* is focused on a theme of mission and the title track features a "Mission Impossible" vibe. "God Is Big" proclaims the limitless power of God in a powerful opening track. "If I Were Mayor" is addressed to rappers who he hopes will realize they must someday give an account to God for every idle word they have spoken: "When you face Him at the seat, take your CD and play it for Him."

Koinonia

Alex Acuña, drums, perc.; Hadley Hockensmith, gtr.; Abraham Laboriel, bass; Bill Maxwell, drums, perc.; Harlan Rogers, kybrd.; Dean Parks, gtr. (−1984); John Phillips, gtr. (−1984) // Justo Almario, woodwinds (+ 1984). 1983—*More Than a Feeling*; 1984—*Celebration* (Sparrow); 1986—*Frontline*; 1989—*Compact Favorites*.

Koinonia was an instrumental jazz-rock fusion group that featured an all-star cast of session players who had played individually and corporately behind everyone from Dolly Parton to Weather Report. Hadley Hockensmith, Bill Maxwell, and Harlan Rogers all played with **Andraé Crouch.** Alex Acuña, Justo Almario, and Abe Laboriel were all a part of the Latin American All Stars jazz group that also included Ricardo Silveira of Brazil. The John Phillips who was in Koinonia is not the singer/songwriter who once made up one-fourth of the Mamas and the Papas.

The title track to *More Than a Feeling* is a fairly blatant Chuck Mangione rip-off. "Give Your Love" (featuring guest vocals by **Russ Taff**) likewise copies Herb Alpert's "Rise," but otherwise this album and the subsequent ones explore a number of styles that demonstrate the artists' versatility as musicians and creativity as composers. Similarities between Koinonia and other jazz-fusion groups like Spyro Gyra and Lee Ritenour's Friendship may also be noted but only as "in the same ball park" analogies. The last two albums emphasize more Latin and South American sounds (salsa, samba) on certain tracks. *Celebration* was recorded live while the group was on tour in Scandinavia.

One distinguishing characteristic of all Koinonia's albums was that (unlike Mangione or Alpert projects) the music was not built around a single star performer. The group played much more *as a group* than any other collaboration of session players on record. In this regard, they were true to their name, which is the word used in biblical Greek to describe Christian fellowship. Koinonia's most lasting contribution to Christian music—aside from their three very fine albums—remains their exaltation of instrumental music within the subculture. At the time they began recording, instrumental albums in contemporary Christian music usually consisted of orchestral renditions of well-known songs, such that the listener could easily hear the words in his or her head. The notion that music *without* words could be Christian was controversial in some quarters, and Koinonia (along with **Phil Driscoll, Phil Keaggy,** and **Fletch Wiley**) did much to legitimize the art form. Such legitimacy has far-reaching consequences, in that the question of what makes an instrumental Christian or secular exposes the ultimate inadequacy of such distinctions with regard to all music (or, indeed, to life in general). As Koinonia would repeatedly note, music is a gift of God and they wanted nothing more than to allow God to use them in conveying that gift to humans. The purpose of the music was not to evangelize or even (necessarily) to inspire, but simply to offer people something that God wanted to give them: sounds that enrich and ennoble life on earth. Of course, God does this through secular artists as well. So what's the difference? Not much—except, maybe, that Koinonia made a point of acknowledging the source of their charisms, in case the beneficiaries want to know who to thank.

Latin guitarist Abraham Laboriel would later play with the jazz band Weather Report. He released two solo albums in the

'90s, *Dear Friends* (Blue Moon, 1993) and *Guidum* (Integrity, 1995). He also joined his old Koinonia buddy to make *Abraham Laboriel and Justo Almario* for Integrity in 1995.

Kosmos Express

Beau Burchell, gtr.; Rob Goraieb, gtr.; G. J. Torres, bass; Ron Alayra, drums (–1998) // Mark Powell, drums (+ 1998). 1997—*Now* (SubLime); 1998—*Simulcast.*

Kosmos Express hails from California but presents itself as a Brit-pop band in the tradition of Oasis, Blur, or The Verve. As with those bands, the primary influence (besides the obvious Beatles) is actually Paul Weller, who once fronted The Jam and Style Council before going on to an illustrious solo career. The group even references Weller on a song from their sophomore CD ("In My Face"). Kosmos Express formed in 1996 around Rob Goraieb who once played with **Mike Stand**'s post-**Altar Boys**' band **Clash of Symbols** and who was hired by SubLime as a songwriter. The band's greatest strength probably lies in Goraieb's melodic sensibilities, which are not unlike those of the Lemonheads' Evan Dando. Both albums are filled with strong pop songs evincing catchy hooks, solid structure, and lyrical phrases that stand out as memorable lines even apart from the works as a whole. Even so, the first album is a slow burn. *True Tunes* reported that *Now* "doesn't seem like much the first time through, but Goraieb and Co. have the perfect pop formula for longevity." The best songs, perhaps, are "Beautiful" and "Little Tree," though these were also the most *Wonderwall*-ish rip-offs. The spiritual content of the songs is mostly muted; "Little Tree" is actually a reflection on the cross of Christ, albeit internalized: "O little tree that burns in me." For a somewhat different take, "Electric Eyes" and "Tangerine" have just enough punk influence (Oasis meets **MxPx**) to provide the album with versatility. By all accounts, *Simulcast* surpasses the debut exponentially. Gene Eugene of **Adam Again** produced the album and **Terry Taylor** and Rob Watson of **Daniel Amos** contribute their talents to the mix. The collaborations work well, giving Kosmos Express just enough edge to make them stand out amidst the increasingly crowded alternative rock scene. "On Top of the World" is particularly Beatlesque, and "Emotional" is a near-perfect alterna-pop song. "Lifetime" is in part a protest against the increased commercialization of Christian music: "I'm in love with Jesus Christ but I'm not selling him," Goraieb sings with overt and heartfelt piety. In "On the Top of the World" he continues, "You're lucky Jesus loves you / 'Cause sometimes I just don't."

The Kreepdowns

Ed Benrock, drums; Pat Guyton, bass; Howard Miller, gtr.; Michael Misiuk, voc. 1998—*Take a Spin* (BettieRocket).

The Kreepdowns began as a side project for Michael Misiuk of **Acoustic Shack.** For him, the group is just an indie side project with no particular agenda except to rock out in whatever direction their hearts tend to take them. Ed Benrock has also drummed with **LSU** and **Mortal.** Howard Miller's guitar work is of the finger-blistering variety, giving the band a fairly heavy sound. Nods to the Smashing Pumpkins show up here and there, and the music sometimes recalls that of **The Violet Burning,** with whom Misiuk has also played. Misiuk insists that The Kreepdowns are not a ministry band, yet he also says that he tries to represent Christ in everything that he does—including songwriting and performing. As such, many of their songs reflect spiritual themes, and he says he would not be surprised to see "God use The Kreepdowns as a vessel to lead souls to the kingdom of Christ." In the song "Go Now" (not a Moody Blues cover) the artist sounds like he just wants to get out of a bad situation, but Misiuk has said it is really about "hastening the rapture—being sick of the world and seeking God's return." A number called "Spiritual Beast" deals with televangelists, and "Red Ready" uses an oblique metaphor to speak of the "blood covering" that prepares one to meet God. Other standout tracks include "Select" and "Not Like That."

Scott Krippayne

1992—*What Matters* (custom); 1995—*Wild Imagination* (Word); 1997—*More*; 1999—*Bright Star, Blue Sky* (Spring Hill); 2001—*All of Me.*

www.scottkrippayne.com

Christian pop singer Scott Krippayne became known first for his songwriting and, indeed, in 1996, *American Songwriter* magazine named him Christian Artist of the Year. Born in 1969, Krippayne grew up in Puyallup, Washington, and attended the University of Washington before moving to Nashville in 1993. He wrote songs for **Aaron Jeoffrey, Avalon, Brian Barrett, Lisa Bevill, Kim Boyce, Glad, Sandi Patty, Point of Grace, Rebecca St. James,** and **Tuesday's Child** before signing with Word and releasing his own recordings. Krippayne has often worked with producer **Charlie Peacock** and his albums evince an MOR, clean-as-a-whistle style of radio-friendly pop. Krippayne's voice is not too dissimilar to that of **Brent Bourgeois** or **Steven Curtis Chapman.**

Wild Imagination features "Sometimes He Calms the Storm," a Number One inspirational hit which affirms that God allows trials to come into people's lives to make them stronger. Ironically, Krippayne did not write that song (or the album's title track, which is by **Kyle Matthews**), but he did turn out twenty-five other songs that were recorded by some fifteen artists in 1996. *Wild Imagination* also includes "Wish List," a song written with **Charlie Peacock** that in retrospect would seem like a Christianized counterpart to the Pearl Jam song with the same name. Krippayne's follow-up album, *More,* would demonstrate increased creative freedom and was accompanied by a devotional book titled *More Than a Story.* The album includes "Way Back Home"—not the **Phil Keaggy** song, but a similarly personal look at life on the road and the longing for family ties. The title song is a poignant, worshipful song, expressing a deep desire for a close relationship with the Lord: "You are more than a story written on a page / You are more than a Spirit spinning out in space." The song "Hands of Mercy" encourages Christians facing such issues as abortion and AIDS to respond with compassion rather than judgment: "The truth of love is in the hands of mercy." *Bright Star, Blue Sky* continues in a similar vein as the recordings for Word. Seven of the album's tracks are actually worship songs, including the vertically directed "I Wanna Sing" ("As long as I can sing, I wanna sing about You"). The title tracks expresses longing for "some light and joy" and was written on a cloudy day when Krippayne and his wife learned that her parents were separating. But one of *Bright Star*'s most noticed songs is a light-hearted pop tune called "The Coffee Song," an ode to America's favorite bean-induced wake-up call. "There's nothing spiritual about that song at all," says Krippayne, "but people can relate." *All of Me* offers a silky R&B ballad, "What Breaks Your Heart," and a jazzy tune called "Tell It Like It Is," written with **Kyle Matthews.** On the song "I'm Not Cool," Krippayne chants some basic Christian radio lyrics: "I'm not cool, but that's okay / My God loves me anyway."

Christian radio hits: "All My Days" (# 3 in 1995); "Sometimes He Calms the Storm" (# 25 in 1996); "Hope Has a Way" (# 17 in 1996); "Wild Imagination" (# 17 in 1996).

Jan Krist

1993—*Decapitated Society* (R.E.X.); 1994—*Wing and a Prayer;* 1996—*Curious* (Silent Planet); 1999—*Love Big, Us Small;* 2001—*Outpost of the Counter-Culture.*

www.jankrist.com

Detroit native Jan Krist was a part of the '90s "new folk revival" that brought a new wave of artists like Sarah MacLachlan and Tracy Chapman to the fore, but being somewhat pigeonholed in the Christian market she has never achieved commercial success to match the critical acclaim which her work has consistently received. *Billboard* magazine described *Decapitated Society* as "an incredibly powerful debut that is unreservedly recommended." They also gave *Wing and a Prayer* its highest rating, claiming "every song is a gem." In 1998, *CCM* Magazine chose *Curious* as one of its "Top 100 Christian Albums of All Time." Krist's voice is somewhat similar to that of Joni Mitchell, but her songwriting bears more similarities to **Bruce Cockburn,** and it is to the latter artist that she should

be compared when such analogies are necessary. Her songs are rarely evangelical in any obvious sense, but deal with social concerns and with matters of the heart (romance, relationships). She writes and sings, however, from an unabashed perspective of faith that becomes apparent to all who take the time to listen. A middle-aged woman with grown children, she says she used to be a bit more preachy in her younger years but has learned simply to describe alternatives, endorse empathy and kindness, and trust the Holy Spirit to convict the hearts that need convicting.

The strongest song from her first album is "Someone," which was thus reprised for wider distribution on *Curious.* The song was actually written out of Krist's experience of living in a poor, crime-ridden section of Detroit, and it reflects on the various guises and sources of evil: "So which one is really better / Wolves in sheep's clothing, or wolves who look like wolves?" Similarly, the title track to Krist's debut was inspired by an encounter she had in a doctor's office with a babysitter who had brought in a sick child: what kind of society, she wondered, finds it so easy for parents to operate at such a remove from their children that they can be unavailable even when the children are ill? *Decapitated Society* also features "Honey Moon," which reflects on the lifelong marriage of a couple in their later years. *A Wing and a Prayer* is a little more up-tempo but continues to reflect lyrically on poignant moments of life. The album opens with "Put Her to the Test," an account of a woman's struggle to survive that culminates with Krist drawing comparisons to her own life and insisting, "Maybe we're dysfunctional . . . but grace has come to me." The song "Crying Ice" describes a disintegrating relationship with the memorable metaphor of the subject's tears freezing on her cheeks. "Daisies in Your Bowl" provides a disturbing yet beautiful observation on loss, and "The Dishes" offers a sardonic look at household chores. On *Curious,* Krist works with a band and comes up with a fuller, more accessible sound. The band, in fact, included several members of **Vigilantes of Love** in addition to keyboardist Randall Bramlett, who has played with Traffic and Steve Winwood. In the title track, Krist wonders "If we send our sons and daughters off to fight our wars / Is there anything left at home worth fighting for?" And in the song "Time" she affirms, "Time changes everything but truth." The nicely titled *Love Big, Us Small* is mostly a compilation package, bringing most of the songs from the first two out-of-print albums together with four new cuts. *Outpost of the Counter-Culture* includes a cover of the Gershwin classic "Someone to Watch Over Me" and a jazz-influenced song called "Waiting for the Cosmic Shoe to Drop." The title track is built on a clever play on words, decrying how materialism (a culture defined by merchandise counters of department stores) dulls the senses to human suffering.

For trivia buffs: Jan Krist's daughter Amon was once lead singer for the rock band **Velour 100.**

Krush

Phil Castillo, gtr.; Dave Meriwether, voc.; Lou Tamagio, gtr.; J. D. Wetherford, bass; et al. 1997—*Lost* [EP] (custom); 1999—*Welcome to Paradise.*

www.geocities.com/masterkrush

San Diego-based Krush has garnered more attention than most indie bands with only do-it-yourself recordings to their credit. Not all of the attention, however, has been positive. Krush is a very hard glam-metal band that sounds like they are still in the '80s. This particular choice of retro drives most critics crazy, and the band has been almost universally panned for its archaic sensibilities. What no one doubts is that Krush plays '80s glam metal very well. The blistering guitars, the screaming vocals . . . they've got it down. But who wants it? the critics ask. Obviously some people do, and with defections by **Guardian** and **Bride,** Krush would be one of the only late '90s outfits to be still offering the nonalternative, un-updated, genuine article. The group is also explicit in their lyrical content, proclaiming the gospel in a manner designed to save the souls of their listeners as opposed to just commenting on their circumstances. The band calls its sound "hard music for hard times" and takes as its motto, "Shout it from the mountaintops, and if they can't hear you, use a really loud PA!" In 2000, Lou Tamagio and J. D. Wetherford left the group, replaced by Fred Helm (drums) and Stan Perl (bass).

The Kry

Jean-Luc Lajoi, voc., bass; Yves Lajoi, drums; Pete Nelson, gtr., kybrd. 1992—*I'll Find You There* (Asaph); 1994—*You* (Freedom); 1995—*Unplugged;* 1996—*What about Now?;* 1999—*La Compilation;* 2000—*Let Me Say.*

www.thekry.com

The Kry is an acoustic pop group that formed in Albuquerque, New Mexico, when Calvary Chapel youth pastor Pete Nelson recruited two newly converted brothers from Quebec to help him form a worship band. The French Canadian brothers Jean-Luc and Yves Lajoi had given up performing in bars in their homeland to make their way into the big time in Hollywood. Albuquerque was supposed to be a pit stop where they would spend a year with a friend and learn to speak English. During this time, however, both experienced religious conversions with the aid of media: Jean-Luc heard the gospel proclaimed over a radio station and Yves responded to the preaching of a TV evangelist.

As a group, The Kry's success has extended well beyond its humble beginnings, taking them on international tours and making them exemplars of Christian music's most commercial soft rock style. The group remains intensely committed to ministry, especially evangelism—which in their tradition means persuading young people to respond to an altar call. Such altar calls are typically a part of every concert, with the music serving as an extended introduction to requisite preaching. The Kry also describes the purpose of their albums as being "to provide believers with a tool to reach their unsaved friends."

The Kry's projects actually seem to reflect a higher view on the significance of music as art than such utilitarian descriptions indicate. Their debut album is a bit atypical in its youth group sound. Its most promising song is the title track, an adult contemporary ballad about discerning the presence of God. The album was re-released in 1995 with the addition of "Blind Man," a youth-meeting, camp-counselor standard that has never been performed better. With *You,* The Kry entered the world of radio-friendly contemporary Christian music with what one reviewer called "an album full of hits." With strong allusions to Bryan Adams, the group churns out song after song of heartland rock with obvious spiritual messages. "I Know Everything about You" testifies to God's unconditional love, while "Lay Down Your Gods" condemns modern idolatry. "He Won't Let You Go" is a quiet piano ballad similar in style and theme to **Ernie Rettino**'s "I Will Never Leave You." The group gets a little bit bluesy on a cover of Blind Willie Johnson's "Jesus Is Coming Soon." That song would be reworked as a medley with **Andraé Crouch**'s "Soon and Very Soon" on the live *Unplugged.* The latter album reprises a number of tracks from the first two projects with a gospel choir providing background vocals on a number of cuts.

What about Now actually had critics comparing individual songs to various mainstream rock (as opposed to pop) groups— "The Search" to **U2;** moments on "Paradise" to Smashing Pumpkins—but the overall sound of the album is more subdued than such references might imply. Lyrically, the album tends toward praise and worship. "Down at the Cross" is a gentle reminder that all persons are equal in their need for redemption. A musical presentation of Psalm 137:1 ("By the Rivers of Babylon") is offered in a '60s pop style that contrasts sharply with Boney M's version from 1978. *La Compilation* is a collection of six songs that the group recorded in French for their friends back home.

Let Me Say opens with what may be the group's best song to date—the title track, which finally moves the group sonically into the quasi-alternative mode of melodic college rock. Belonging now to the same general category as Third Eye Blind or Matchbox 20, The Kry offers its plaintive plea to be granted a hearing: "Let me say all I need to say / Life is so much more than what you think it is." The other song on the album to garner attention is "Cassie's Song," a poem written by Cassie Bernall two days before she was murdered in the Columbine shootings in Littleton, Colorado. Bernall's parents gave the poem to The Kry because they were the girl's favorite group; the group appended a chorus and set it all to music. **Rick Altizer, Clear, Charlie Daniels,** and **Michael W. Smith** have also performed Bernall tributes, but this one is perhaps the most personal and touching. *Let Me Say* also features the excellent pop songs "Get Away" and "Don't Turn Your Back."

The Kry has transcended the apparent limitations of their musical style and the sectarian aspects of their ministerial focus to develop broad-based appeal. Even the hard-rocking *HM* magazine notes that "While The Kry isn't out to make anyone forget **Mortification,** its sound contains enough of a rough edge to give metal fans something to chew on, while its penchant for melody and straightforward ministerial lyrics should open the eyes of more than a few 'rock and roll is always racket' fuddy-duddies." *CCM* adds that the quality of the group's music is consistently accompanied by a heart-on-the-sleeve devotion to God and to missions, and genuine love for people in pain.

Christian radio hits: "I'll Find You There" (# 4 in 1993); "In Your Eyes" (# 5 in 1993); "You're All I Need" (# 2 in 1994); "I Can't Stop Thinking about You" (# 5 in 1994); "Take My Hand" (# 3 in 1994); "Blind Man (Show Me the Way)" (# 3 in 1995); "I Waited for the Lord" [by Jean-Luc Lajoie with the Maranatha Praise Band] (# 10 in 1995); "He Won't Let You Go" (# 10 in 1995); "Everywhere" (# 1 for 2 weeks in 1995); "I Know Everything about You" (# 5 in 1996); "Little Love" (# 9 in 1996); "I Believe It" (# 8 in 1997); "Paradise" (# 19 in 1997).

K I I S

Kenneth Henderson [a.k.a. KaBac or K-Buc]; Donald Newman [a.k.a. D-Smooth]; Jennifer Newman. 1997—*Welcome to the New Era* (Metro One); 1999—*Better Dayz.*

K I I S is a ministry-oriented rap group whose name is shorthand for "Key to Salvation." The group appears to be primarily a duo, with Jennifer Newman (Donald's sister) offering occasional melodic vocal interludes. Kenneth Henderson and the Newmans were raised in Christian homes, and their message does not take the stereotypical approach of contrasting a preconversion street life with later bliss. On "Second Choice" (from *Welcome to the New Era*) the rap assumes the form of a divine call to worship: "I don't want to be your second choice / Lift up your hands and rejoice / If you hear this heavenly voice." The group's music is also kept interesting through various accompaniments. A choir is featured now and then on *New Era.* **Crystal Lewis** provides guest vocals for *Better Dayz* on a rewritten version of the Bee Gees' song, "How Deep Is Your Love," and **The Insyderz** perform on "Common Ground," a plea for Christian unity. On a side note, *Better Dayz* features keyboards by James Raymond, the son of rock star David Crosby.

The Hank Laake Band

Dan Brown, gtr.; Terry Fitzsimmons, gtr.; Hank Laake, drums, voc.; Dan Stokka, bass. 1982—*In the Spirit of the King* (Tunesmith); 1984—*Life and Death*; 1985—*How Laake Can You Get?*

The Hank Laake Band was a heavy Christian rock group of the early '80s that directed their evangelistic music toward alienated youth with a simple message of grace and a basic invitation to share in the joy of Christian community. Writing in 1984, Brian Quincy Newcomb compared the group's sound to that of early Jesus music—or at least to the early material by such Christian headbangers as **Petra** or **Resurrection Band.** The closest general market comparison to their style might be Sammy Hagar, who (in his solo material) also tended to copy heavy superstars from days gone by. Hank Laake came from Iowa, where he had once fronted a secular band called Red Pony. He came to know **Larry Norman** and recorded an early Christian album with that star that never saw release. *In the Spirit of the King* still betrays Norman's influence, partly in its organization: Side One is intended for evangelism and Side Two for worship and edification. The opening track, "Questions of the Seeker," is a blazing rock song that Laake actually adapted from his old Red Pony repertoire. According to Newcomb, The Hank Laake Band reveled in its "youthful energy, naivete, and evangelistic zeal" with the same unaffected motivation evinced by Jesus freaks a decade before. "Thankfully all Christian music is not as blatantly simplistic as *Life and Death*," he wrote in his review of that album, "but the Hank Laake Band does fill a niche."

Abraham Laboriel

See **Koinonia.**

Lads

Personnel list unavailable. 2000—*Lost @ Sea* (Driven); announced for 2002—*Marvel* (Cross Driven).

The Lads are one of New Zealand's top Christian pop bands, known almost as much for their comedy as their music. The group performs extravaganzas in their native land that feature stories, skits, and lots of songs all coming together for "a worship party." *Lost @ Sea* was produced by Malcolm Welsford, who in 1998 was named New Zealand's Producer of the Year. The sound is basic Brit-pop with lots of swirling keyboards and distorted guitars sustaining strong, bouncy melodies. The Lads bring to mind an amalgam of **All Star United** and **Delirious?** mixing "fun music" with a serious evocation of praise. Two songs from *Lost @ Sea* were featured on TV's *Dawson's Creek.*

Ladysmith Black Mambazo

Joseph Shabala; Jockey Shabala; Headman Shabala (d. 1991) // Jabulani Dubazana; Abednego Mazibuko, Albert Mazibuko; Geoffrey Mdletshe; Russell Mthembu; Inos Phungula; Ben Shabala. 1984—*Induku Zethu* (Shanachie); 1985—*Ulwandle Oluncgwele*; 1986—*Inala*; 1987—*Shaka Zulu* (Warner Bros.); 1988—*Journey of Dreams* (Warner Bros.); *Umthombo Wamanzi* (Shanachie); 1990—*Classic Tracks; Two Worlds, One Heart* (Warner Bros.); 1992—*Best of Ladysmith Black Mambazo* (Shanachie);

1994—*Liph' Iquiniso; Gift of the Tortoise* (Warner Bros.); *Inkanyezi Nezazi* (Flame Tree); 1997—*Heavenly;* 1998—*Vol. 2: Best of Ladysmith;* 1999—*In Harmony: Live at the Royal Albert Hall.*

www.mambazo.com

Like the **Jesse Dixon** Singers, South African choir Ladysmith Black Mambazo would never have been heard by most Americans if not for Paul Simon. Though the group had already achieved fame in its homeland, Simon "discovered" them and brought them to the attention of Western audiences. Joseph Shabala formed the group in the township of Ladysmith, South Africa with two of his brothers in 1964. Over time, other family members (the Mazibukos are Joseph's cousins) and friends were added. Ladysmith Black Mambazo sings a type of a capella Zulu music called *Isicathamiya,* which basically consists of R&B style call-and-response between a soloist and a backing choir. The music itself was born of apartheid, created by black workers in South Africa's diamond mines who would sing to each other to pass the time while separated from their families. Ladysmith Black Mambazo became masters of the form, winning several national contests and becoming the best-selling black musical group in South Africa even before Simon took them under his wing. In 1986, however, the group came to international prominence. After being featured on two tracks on Simon's acclaimed *Graceland* album ("Homeless," "Diamonds on the Soles of Her Shoes"), they toured the world with the singer and joined him in a number of TV appearances. A year later, Simon would produce *Shaka Zulu*—their first with songs in English—and they won a Grammy award. The group would go on to place songs on the soundtracks of major motion pictures like *A Dry White Season* and *Coming to America.* They collaborated with George Clinton on *Two Worlds, One Heart.* They appeared with Michael Jackson in his *Moonwalker* video and became frequent guests on *Sesame Street.* They also recorded two spoken-word albums of children's tales: *How the Leopard Got His Spots* (with narration by Danny Glover) and *Gift of the Tortoise* (both on Warner Brothers, 1989 and 1994). They recorded a popular (and award-winning) commercial for 7-Up and they performed as the chorus in a Broadway play, *The Song of Jacob Zulu.* A religious Christmas song called "The Star and the Wise Men" (from *Inkanyezi Nezazi*) was used by the Heinz corporation in 1997 for commercials marketing baked beans and spaghetti (perhaps as a result of such exposure, the song became a Top 20 hit in England).

Despite the group's acclaim—and its presentation to the world as a prime example of how things had supposedly changed in South Africa—an almost unbelievable tragedy struck in 1991. Headman Shabala, a founding member of LBM who had been with the group for over twenty-five years, was shot and killed along a highway near Durban, South Africa. A white security guard was convicted of manslaughter for the seemingly senseless crime. Apparently, Shabala had not been a target so much as just a black man in the wrong place at the wrong time—his assailant had not known the victim was famous, and obvious questions were raised as to whether the crime would ever have come to light if he had not been. The event is referenced in the song "Worldwide" by **Adam Again** as exemplary of the frustrating persistence of injustice in a world that likes to think it is getting better.

Ladysmith Black Mambazo is not often connected with Christian music and the exact tenor of the individual members' faiths may not be known. They have often recorded gospel songs, however, which they at least believe to embody a message of peace and hope that they want to share with society at large. Even *Rolling Stone* notes that the standout track on their *Journey of Dreams* album is a rendition of "Amazing Grace" arranged by Paul Simon. The highlight of the group's career for Christian music fans may be *Heavenly,* an album that is almost entirely devoted to gospel material. Alongside a few original tunes, the chorus presents innovative arrangements of such gospel standards as "Precious Lord, Take My Hand" and "O Happy Day." Some of their choices are interesting. Apparently, they think that **Bob Dylan**'s "Knockin' on Heaven's Door" is a gospel song, and there is no reason why, divorced from its original context as part of the film *Pat Garrett and Billy the Kid,* it can't be. As it turns out, Billy Joel's "River of Dreams" is a gospel song, too. Why not? Most intriguing, perhaps, is the group's decision to sing **Sam Cooke**'s "Chain Gang"—a song that is usually taken to be a crossover secular hit by the traditional gospel star, yet one that takes on new meaning when sung with the inflection of imprisoned mine workers. *Heavenly* is a first-rate production with guest appearances by Dolly Parton, Bonnie Raitt, Lou Rawls, and Phoebe Snow.

Karen Lafferty

1975—*Bird in a Golden Sky* (Maranatha); 1978—*Sweet Communion;* 1980—*Life Pages;* 1983—*Country to Country* (Asaph); 1989—*Land of No Goodbyes.*

Karen Lafferty was one of the very first female adult contemporary singers in Christian music and, as such, is a progenitor of **Susan Ashton, Margaret Becker, Amy Grant, Kim Hill, Crystal Lewis, Twila Paris, Pam Thum, Kathy Troccoli,** and many, many others. She released two classic albums of Jesus music in the mid '70s that foreshadowed the style of all those artists and then—despite a few more competent recordings—all but vanished from the scene as a result of her commitment to global missions. Lafferty will always be best-remembered as the composer of the simple Scripture chorus "Seek Ye First," which was first featured on Maranatha's extremely influential *The Praise Album* (1974). That song made its way into prayer groups all over the world and came to be sung in remote locations where Lafferty herself remains completely unknown.

Lafferty grew up in Alamagorda, New Mexico, and majored in music education at Eastern New Mexico State University. She committed her life to Jesus soon after graduating and tried out for one of Campus Crusade for Christ's musical teams. Unable to make the cut, she decided to pursue a career in secular entertainment and moved to Southern California, where she landed at Costa Mesa's Calvary Chapel where the Jesus movement revival was in full swing. Along with **Debby Kerner,** Lafferty would be one of two women ordained by Calvary Chapel's Maranatha label as a minister of music. In 1973, she went to Holland, opening for **Children of the Day,** and in 1978 she headlined a tour of Europe on the strength of her first two albums. While on this tour, she was struck by the enormous popularity of American music even in parts of the world where no general market acts ever toured. She asked missionaries whether it would be helpful to have Christian artists who performed in such popular styles come to their locales; the common response was that no matter how effective that might be, it was not a financially viable option. Lafferty returned with a determination to channel contemporary Christian music into not-for-profit missions. She founded Musicians for Missions in 1981 as an outreach of Youth with a Mission. The organization set up seminars to train Christian musicians for mission work and then sent them into the field where they would perform nonprofit concerts under the supervision of local mission organizations. She moved to Amsterdam to direct these operations, but continued to record occasional albums. She has been a featured singer on Maranatha's ongoing series of praise projects.

Musically, Lafferty's style fits with the soft rock typical of Maranatha's Jesus music artists, but she has less of the Mary Travers folksinger style that comes through in **Marsha Stevens**' and especially **Debby Kerner**'s work. *Bird in a Golden Sky* already possesses the sheen that would come to typify adult contemporary music a decade later. The album's songs were arranged by **Children of the Day**'s maestro Peter Jacobs, who tastefully applies horns and strings. The title track is Lafferty's most remarkable song, a gorgeous midtempo ballad with a soaring melody worthy of Joni Mitchell ("Help Me"). The song testifies to the freedom that one comes to experience in Christ, a prominent theme in pre-**Keith Green** Jesus music. It was excerpted to become one of several highlights on Maranatha's stunning compilation album *Maranatha Four* and so became her best-known song, aside from "Seek Ye First." The debut album also features "Grandma Stout," a tribute to Lafferty's pious grandmother, and "The Girl," a compassionate song about an adolescent who wants love but finds partners who are only interested in sex. *Harmony* magazine

touted *Bird in a Golden Sky* with some exaggeration as "the best album Maranatha has released." *Sweet Communion* attracted less attention but may actually surpass *Bird in a Golden Sky* in overall quality, evincing a bit more of a country feel on several songs. Produced by **Jonathan David Brown,** it featured the sterling song "Beautiful Day," in addition to "Father of Lights" and "Peace thru the Day." Another highlight from *Sweet Communion* is Lafferty's rendition of **Billy Batstone**'s "You Sure Have Been Good to Me" (which Batstone himself performs on the *Good News II* album, officially released as a project by **Good News**). *Life Pages* offers more of Lafferty's trademark autobiographical accounts of people and places she had come to know, though by 1980 the mellow MOR sound she had helped to popularize had become so prevalent in Christian music that she no longer stood out from the crowd. Still, the album includes the John Wytock song "Love of the Ages," which is one of the greatest pieces to come out of that first decade of Jesus music.

In 2001, Lafferty was still working with Musicians for Missions and was planning a 2002 release of a multiethnic recording tentatively titled *Multitudes: Sounds of Many Nations.* She was also working at putting the Maranatha albums out on CD along with some "Jesus movement mementos."

Christian radio hits: "Beautiful Day" (# 15 in 1978).

Lamb

Joel Chernoff, voc.; Rick "Levi" Coghill, voc., gtr. 1973—*Lamb* (Messianic); 1974—*Lamb II*; 1976—*Lamb III*; 1978—*Songs for the Flock*; 1980—*Lamb Favorites* (Sparrow); 1981—*Live*; *New Mix*; 1985—*The Year of Jubilee: An Offering of Messianic Praise* (Maranatha); 1988—*Dancin' in Jerusalem* (Messianic); 1991—*Seer*; 1993—*Come Let Us Celebrate*.

The Christian-Jewish folk duo Lamb is one of the very few early Jesus music groups that would still be making music as a consistent entity in the '90s. The group represents what for some must be a curious variation on that revival—the emergence of Jewish believers in Jesus who called themselves "messianic Jews" or "completed Jews" (a term that non-Christian Jews find especially offensive). The most famous organization of such believers is the group called Jews for Jesus, which sponsored the contemporary Christian music group **The Liberated Wailing Wall.** In general, Lamb kept a lower profile but was equally evangelical and inspired the same sorts of controversies that attended that group. Rick Coghill of Lamb produced some of **The Liberated Wailing Wall** albums.

Rick Coghill worked as a Nashville session musician and in his pre-Christian days played with James Brown. Then, in what he regards as his career nadir, he became a member of The Lemon Pipers, responsible for the psychedelic bubblegum hit "Green Tambourine" (# 1 in 1967), though he was not actually a part of the lineup that recorded that song. In any case,

Coghill told *Cornerstone* magazine that he felt he was "prostituting himself" as an artist and that he hated the music he was forced to play so much that he got heavily into drugs. Then, when the Lemon Pipers played American Bandstand, he saw another group named **Pacific Gas and Electric,** headed by Glenn Schwartz (once of James Gang and soon to join the **All Saved Freak Band**). Coghill recognized Schwartz as an old drug buddy and says, "I was really excited to see him again. He invited me back to his hotel room. I was looking for some real heavy drug experience and he hands me this little Bible and says, 'This is the best thing I could ever turn you on to.'" Schwartz witnessed to Coghill for hours that night. In the days that followed, more signs of what the media would eventually term "the Jesus movement revival" began cropping up: "The Episcopal minister of the church I'd been raised in got saved. Then the guy that sold me drugs got saved at one of those **Arthur Blessitt** rallies." Eventually Coghill prayed to accept Christ with a chaplain at a clinic where he had been hospitalized following a drug overdose.

Joel Chernoff is the son of Rabbi Martin Chernoff, who had come to believe in the gospel of Christ and ended up pastoring a church called Beth Messiah Congregation in Philadelphia. As a result Joel himself became a believer in Christ at the age of twelve, but it was his later experience of explaining that faith to Coghill that led him to take it all more seriously. Eventually, they both came to a literate and passionate understanding that "biblical Judaism" differs from the Gentile religion of Christianity but rightly includes faith in Jesus as God's true Messiah and as Savior of the world. With reference to the Apostle Paul's analogy of the olive trees in Romans 11, Chernoff would insist that it is Gentiles who must "convert" when they come to believe in Jesus and, so, are grafted into what is intrinsically a Jewish religion. By placing their faith in Jesus, he and Coghill were not converting from Judaism to (Gentile) Christianity but merely extending their faith in what seemed to them to be a scripturally consistent way. It should be noted that this understanding is rejected by most Jews who regard persons who call themselves "Christian Jews" pretty much the same way that evangelicals regard persons who claim to be "Christian Scientologists" (having moved on from Christianity—without abandoning it—to embrace more advanced, supposedly compatible views).

Musically, Lamb would draw often on the rich tradition of Jewish folk songs and liturgical music. Typically, Coghill has served as arranger and producer for the mostly independent albums, and Chernoff as the chief composer. Lamb's softer songs often take the form of laments or psalms; more upbeat numbers have an "Hava Nagila" folk dance flair to them. Acoustic guitar is the instrument of choice, especially on the early albums, but electric flourishes, flutes, harpsichord, and strings would all find their way into the mix eventually. In terms of content, the three classic Lamb albums (the first three) are directed toward evangelizing Jewish people with typical (though generally ineffective) appeals to Old Testament prophecies. As the duo matured theologically, they came to write scriptural songs that reveal a deeper understanding of the Hebrew Scriptures as significant in their own right. With *Songs for the Flock* they also move decidedly toward praise and worship music, crafting well-written folk music that has potential appeal for all who love the one they call Messiah. The rather atypical "Sh'ma" is essentially built on the same riff that Billy Squier would use for "Everybody Wants You" five years later; it seems unlikely that Squier had ever heard the Lamb song, but if "Sh'ma" had come out six years later, the duo would have been accused of plagiarism.

Those who were part of the Jesus movement will always remember Lamb's first three albums best—the ones on which Lamb sounds like a more-Jewish version of Simon and Garfunkel, like a couple of hippie fish-out-of-water Yeshua freaks who are making music that is so *necessary* it doesn't matter whether anyone ever actually buys it or not. Judged by that standard of purity (which seems inevitably linked to naivete), the absolute best Lamb songs would be "Baruch Hashem" and "The Sacrifice Lamb" from their first album. Close runners-up would be "Clap Your Hands" and "Clay" from *Lamb II,* and "Queen of Sheba" and "Rivers of Babylon" from *Lamb III.* If more sophisticated musical development is the standard, then a song like "Heal Me" from *New Mix* deserves special mention. Writing in *CCM,* Karen Marie Platt likened that song to something one would expect from the Moody Blues, "with billowing sound that rises and falls like the sea." And in 1991, Thom Granger (in the same magazine) said, "*Seer* is undoubtedly Lamb's best recording to date," noting that the duo had by now learned to combine their simple Hebrew folk song style with doses of world beat and modern pop. In 1999, Joel Chernoff released a solo worship album, *The Restoration of Israel* (Galilee of the Nations).

Christian radio hits: "He Is Messiah" (# 6 in 1991).

Brent Lamb

1984—*Tug of War* (Milk and Honey); 1986—*One Man* (Power Discs); 1988—*Outside These Walls* (Diadem); 1989—*Side by Side;* 1990—*Living Proof;* 1992—*To Be Like Jesus* (label unknown); 1994—*Drawing Pictures* (Genesis); 1996—*No Excuses, No Regrets* (Word); 1998—*Right Now, It's Raining* (Diamante).

www.brentlamb.com

Christian country singer Brent Lamb took a few albums to find his niche. Lamb was born in 1960 and grew up as a Christian musician in Nashville, playing as a teenager with local bands called Cornerstone and Love Note. After recording three independent albums, he made *Tug of War* for Milk and Honey, an unsuccessful pop album that remains notable for two songs. The upbeat "Waiting Is Worth It" was one of the first songs in contemporary Christian music to address the issue of premarital sex. The ballad "Quiet Please" challenges Christians who gossip about each other's difficulties by paraphrasing the simple advice of Thumper's father from the movie *Bambi*: "If you can't find something good to say, say nothing at all."

In 1985, Lamb was signed to Benson Records at the same time as **Steven Curtis Chapman** and the two became friends. Lamb's *One Man* (for Benson's Power Discs) attempted a more progressive pop sound, with several hard-driving tunes mixed in among the soul-searching ballads. It never took off, but he did find considerable success as a songwriter, composing "The Wedding Song" and "Army of the Lord" for the group **Harvest** and "My Turn Now" for Chapman. By the end of the '80s, he says his heart had changed "from youth-oriented lyrics to being a husband and a daddy." Along with the change in perspective came a stylistic shift toward country music, and it was there that Lamb would hit his stride. As a maker of adult-oriented, positive country music, he is often compared with Vince Gill. His album *No Excuses, No Regrets* features a light-hearted, danceable tune called "God Made You with Me in Mind." The title track offers common sense wisdom: "Real life is tough / But you can't forget / Tomorrow's worries ain't here yet / So live today like it's all you get / With no excuses and no regrets." In publicity materials for *Right Now, It's Raining,* he would describe his musical style as "adult contemporary with southern spice" and his thematic focus as "issues of hearth and holiness."

Lamb has shared in a number of magazines that he has suffered from a problem with stuttering throughout most of his life. As a child and as an adolescent, he was terrified to be in front of a group because, often, he was unable to read or speak aloud. In 1996, he told *Shout* that, still, "the only time I don't stutter is when I'm on stage . . . from a personal standpoint, I know it is God using me to give people hope." As a songwriter, Lamb also wrote "Household of Faith" for **Steve Green** and "Walk with the Wise" for **Steven Curtis Chapman.** His song "This Is America" was chosen by Walt Disney World to be the theme song of their patriotic extravaganza at Epcot Center.

Christian radio hits: "Quiet Please" (# 26 in 1985); "Another One Snatched Away" (# 14 in 1988); "One about Heaven" (# 20 in 1991).

Lament (a.k.a. **Beheaded**)

Abel Gomez, drums, voc.; Marco Perez, voc.; et al. 1997—*Tears of a Leper* (Rowe).

Lament is a Christian heavy metal band from Mexico City. The group began its career as Beheaded and performed under that name for many years. Drummer Abel Gomez serves as the band's spokesperson and chief composer, and he took over as lead singer after Marco Perez left the group in 2001. In 1997, Lament recorded the album *Tears of a Leper* with **Jeff Scheetz** serving as their producer. *HM* says that *Tears of a Leper* "ranges from moments of exquisite beauty to sheer brutality." Vocals are mainly growled in English and twin guitar leads demonstrate classic metal riffing on songs like "Lonely River."

La More

Anthony Latimore; Jacob Latimore; Jason Latimore; Nathan Latimore. 1995—*La More* (GospoCentric).

La More is an African American pop R&B group composed of four brothers whose sound is reminiscent of New Edition's music from a decade before. At least two of the Milwaukee-based quartet were still in high school at the time their self-titled debut album was made. The group offers personal love songs to Jesus ("Wanna Love You More," "You Are Everything to Me") and songs that testify to God's faithfulness in their lives. The song "This Is My Prayer" received attention on a number of gospel radio stations.

Rachel Lampa

2000—*Live for You* (Word); 2002—*Kaleidoscope*.

www.rachael-lampa.com

Fourteen-year-old Rachel Lampa was discovered by **Brent Bourgeois** and slated by him to become "a Christian version of Mariah Carey" (i.e., the next **Crystal Lewis**) in what would be an almost unprecedented campaign of hype and industry support. Naturally gifted with an incredible octave-spanning voice, Lampa is a native of Louisville, Colorado. She met Bourgeois in 1999 at a "Praise in the Rockies" program in Estes Park, Colorado (cf. **Stacie Orrico**). Apparently, some other companies noticed her as well, and she was immediately proffered a substantial and long-term contract. Bourgeois would later tell *Release,* "I more or less iced everyone else out. . . . A girl like this comes along once every twenty years—maybe!" Bourgeois then assembled a team of prolific and proven songwriters to meet together in his Franklin, Tennessee, house and produce songs specifically crafted for Lampa's undeniable talent. **Chris Eaton,** Da'dra Crawford Greathouse (of **Anointed**), **Cindy Morgan, Nicole C. Mullen, Ginny Owens, Jill Phillips, Chris Rodriguez, Michelle Tumes,** and Bourgeois himself all took part in the Lampa-fest, producing potential hits befitting a diva. An almost identical campaign had launched the career of **Jaci Velasquez** four years earlier and resulted in a debut album that went gold. Lampa's album was coproduced by Bourgeois and **Brown Bannister** with studio assistance from Dan Muckala of **Mukala** and a host of other Nashville greats.

Appearances on *The Tonight Show with Jay Leno, The View with Barbara Walters,* and the *Miss Teen U.S.A. Pageant* were secured to showcase Lampa's abilities.

The album was not quite the critical disappointment that so much industry involvement would lead one to expect. The no-margin-for-error production standards do seem to render any thought of reliance on spirit (human or holy) unnecessary, but the music is predictably stellar and competent, allowing *Live for You* to make a strong impression on fans of adult contemporary music. The opening track, "Day of Freedom," is enhanced by Middle Eastern instrumentation, and the title track has a quasi-Latin feel befitting Jennifer Lopez. "Hide Me" (by Morgan and **Bourgeois**) is one of the more beautiful ballads to appear in adult contemporary music (Christian or otherwise) in recent years. "Blessed" draws effectively on traditional gospel. The closing song, "My Father's Heart," borrows its tune from the Anglican "My Song Is Love Unknown," which Episcopalians and Lutherans have long known to have one of the loveliest melodies in their hymnals. *CCM* noted that "Lampa's debut is perhaps the best alternative Christian music has produced to such general market divas as Mariah Carey and Celine Dion"—and, indeed, it is difficult to imagine any Christian fan of those artists' equally contrived products who would not be thrilled with this album.

Kaleidoscope features a somewhat funkier sound and more of Lampa's own compositions. One of these, "Brand New Life," reflects how God has changed the way she views life and the world about her. The modern spiritual "Sanctuary" and ballad "Give Your Heart Away" continue to present Lampa in Mariahmode. *CCM* would say the album lacks depth but offers "a comfortable distraction and generally positive faith messages."

Christian radio hits: "Live for You" (# 1 in 2000); "God Loves You" (# 9 in 2000); "Shaken" (# 1 for 2 weeks in 2001); "You Lift Me Up" (# 4 in 2001).

Dove Awards: 2001 Inspirational Song ("Blessed").

Keith Lancaster

See **Acappella.**

Andy Landis

1993—*Stranger* (StarSong).

As the wife of producer Steve Buckingham, Andy Landis is one-half of a celebrity Nashville couple. Born in New Jersey, Landis moved to Los Angeles at the age of fourteen and subsequently enjoyed success as an actress, appearing on such TV programs as *Charlie's Angels, CHIPs, Dallas,* and *Twilight Zone.* She ran her own modeling agency for a time and also tried to break into the music business first as a solo artist and then with a short-lived rock band called Rockslide. Her spiritual quests, meanwhile, led her to a life-changing conversation with a friend in an L.A. restaurant where she says she came to understood the gospel for the first time and took the message to heart. In 1988, Landis moved to Nashville where she found new success as a songwriter, penning tunes for country artists like Sweethearts of the Rodeo. Her husband became one of Nashville's most sought-after producers, helming projects by Mary Chapin Carpenter, Dolly Parton, and Ricky Van Shelton. In 1993, the couple combined their talents and Buckingham produced Landis's *Stranger* album. Musically, the project has a pop-inflected modern country sound. Landis's voice bears similarities to Trisha Yearwood's and her talent is enhanced by guest appearances by numerous artists from the contemporary Christian and mainstream country communities: The Fairfield Four; **Twila Paris; Phillips, Craig, and Dean;** Dolly Parton; **Ricky Skaggs;** and Sweethearts of the Rodeo. The title song encourages compassion for immigrants in light of Matthew 25:38. A song simply titled "No" addresses the phenomenon of date rape with compelling realism. "Is She Still a Woman?" looks at the problems modern women face in juggling career and family. "She Stays" describes the resolve of a wife who doesn't ditch a marriage just because it has lost its spark: "In this day and age, she could walk away / No one would blame her, but she stays."

Christian radio hits: "He's Knocking" (# 23 in 1993).

Cristy Lane

Selected: 1978—*One Day at a Time* (label unknown); 1984—*Where I Belong* (Arrival); 1986—*One Day at a Time* (custom); 1987—*One Day at a Time* (Arrival); 1988—*All in His Hands* (Benson).

There is little justification for including inspirational singer Cristy Lane in a volume devoted to *contemporary* Christian music, save for the fact that her claim to have made the best-selling gospel album of all time merits consideration. Her story also reveals something—if only by contrast—of the ins and outs of the contemporary Christian music industry. Lane was born Eleanor Johnson in 1940 in Peoria, Illinois, and was raised in an economically depressed family in which she was the eighth of twelve children. In 1959 she married Lee Stoller who was determined to manage her career as a country western singer. She enjoyed modest success, placing five songs on the country charts from 1977 to 1979 ("Let Me Down Easy," "Shake Me, I Rattle," "I'm Gonna Love You Anyway," "Penny Arcade," and "I Just Can't Stay Married to You"). In 1979, she was named American Country Music's New Vocalist of the Year about the same time that her husband was jailed for financial irregularities. Then in 1980 the title song from her *One Day at a Time* album—a track written by recent convert Kris

Kristofferson—went to Number One on the country charts. The next year, she had her last chart hit, "Sweet Sexy Eyes."

The real brainstorm, however, was yet to come. When Stoller was released from prison, he had become imbued with the notion of media-marketing, having witnessed the incredible success of Slim Whitman, who had been a virtual unknown before his albums were hawked in a series of well-placed TV commercials. Thus, in 1986, a new version of the album *One Day at a Time*—"Not available in stores!"—sold a phenomenal five million copies through phone-in TV ads alone (a year later, a slightly different version of the album was made available in stores, in case a few buyers had been missed somewhere). In addition to its one and only hit, a song that was by now eight years old, the TV version of *One Day at a Time* featured traditional songs like "Just a Closer Walk with Thee," "In the Garden," and "Amazing Grace," in addition to more modern songs like "Rise Again" (by **Dallas Holm**) and "Give Them All to Jesus" (by Phil Johnson). *CCM* magazine would dismiss the album as "elevator music" in a scathing review; still, the incredible success of the record without any support from Christian radio or any involvement of the Christian music industry would leave pundits baffled and jealous. The latter sentiment showed itself, for instance, when the *CCM* reviewer insisted that the album would only have appeal "if the listener has not been exposed to some of Christian music's truly dynamic, expressive interpreters."

Lane and Stoller went on to package and repackage many more compilations of gospel songs and Lane became a regular performer in Branson, Missouri. An autobiography, also titled *One Day at a Time,* was produced. By the year 2000, the TV album was being advertised over the Internet, where it was listed as "the # 1 gospel album in the world," and Lane's autobiography was described as "perhaps the greatest success and life story ever told." Whether *One Day at a Time* remained the best-selling gospel album of all time in 2001 is open to question. **Amy Grant**'s *Heart in Motion* and **U2**'s *The Joshua Tree* both sold well over five million . . . but, are they *gospel* albums? In any case, the Internet ad claims that Lane's version of the album's title track is "the greatest song ever recorded in the history of music."

Robin Lane (and The Chartbusters)

1980—*Robin Lane and the Chartbusters* (Warner Bros.); *Five Live* [EP]; 1981—*Imitation Life*. As Robin Lane: 1984—*Heart Connection* [EP] (Recon).

Rock star Robin Lane worked exclusively within the general market where she seemed to defy all expectations regarding discrimination against Christians who are open about their faith. Indeed, the Christian music subculture did not learn of Lane's faith until *after* everyone else did. Stories and testimonies to the role of faith in her life and career were printed in the

mainstream press long before anything appeared in Christian media. The news trickled in and suddenly Christian music fans were saying, "Did you hear about Robin Lane? She said she was a Christian? What happened? Did she get saved?" In fact, Lane was simply a leader of a rock band who also happened to be a Christian—and she didn't care who knew it. She was, however, a little wary of stereotypes. "You've probably heard that I believe in Jesus," she said at the outset of an interview with *Rolling Stone,* as if to get *that* out of the way—or out in the open—right off the bat. Having nothing to do with the contemporary Christian music industry she objected to the whole commercial enterprise of selling Jesus like he was some kind of product. She also didn't want people putting all kinds of ascetic expectations on her. "I *really* do believe in Jesus," she said, "but I still smoke."

Lane has an interesting prehistory in music culture. There are numerous gaps in her biography, but she is known to have popped up here and there like some sort of female Forrest Gump. She is the daughter of Ken Lane, who worked for years as pianist for Dean Martin. A Los Angeles native, she also somehow ended up making friends in the '60s with Stephen Stills, Neil Young, and the members of the latter's band Crazy Horse. As most good rock and roll trivia buffs would know, she is the woman who sings the duet with Neil Young on "Round and Round (It Won't Be Long)" on that artist's classic 1969 album *Everybody Knows This Is Nowhere.* After a historical gap, she suddenly appeared again as the wife (for a time) of Andy Summers of The Police. That marriage didn't last, Lane went to live on a farm in Pennsylvania, and there is another gap before Robin Lane and The Chartbusters suddenly appear on the scene in Boston. What happened in the interim? Lane would only give out the short version: "I was going to be a psychiatrist, landed in the looney bin, took guitar lessons, found the Lord, and came to Boston—and everything's been fine since then."

Robin Lane and The Chartbusters had a basic rock and roll sound that drew on elements of punk and new-wave—a bit like early Blondie or a female-fronted Clash. They were too hip for Top 40 radio but were favorites on the college scene. Their best-known song was probably "When Things Go Wrong," which actually did make it to Number Eighty-seven on the charts in 1980. While she talked openly about being a Christian, she did not write songs that spoke directly or explicitly about faith. "When I first became a Christian, all my songs were about the Lord," she said. "But I eventually realized that I had to find a different approach." The song "Without You," on her debut album, was the closest she ever came to giving a testimony, and even then listeners would need extrinsic explanation to realize it was expressing dependence on God. Most of Lane's songs were about love and romance, and they often reflected on those topics with a deep appreciation for pain and hardship. In those days before **The Choir** or **LSU** this seemed strange to Christian music fans, and Lane was challenged by Christians as to why her lyrics had to be so depressing. "I don't know," she responded. "That's just me. I look at the world and I see one unhappy mess." Then she continued, "And Christianity is very much of the world." Lane's final solo album (or EP) did move away from the raw rock and roll of the Chartbusters CD and she seemed to nod toward the contemporary Christian music world by working with producer Dan Russell, known for his work in Christian concert promotion. Still, the disc consisted of four love songs (the standout being "Shot in the Dark"), all intended for the general public.

An accurate appraisal of Robin Lane's effectiveness at being a Christian in the world at large requires recognition of how she was perceived in that world (as opposed to simply within the Christian music scene, where she was generally ignored). Dave Marsh, premier rock critic for *Playboy* magazine wrote, "Lane's best songs about love are appropriately inextricable from her songs most steeped in Christianity. It's clear that her religion shapes her entire world view in terms of greater compassion and confidence."

Rick Lang

1992—*Big Dream* (Word).

Little is known of singer/songwriter Rick Lang, but his one album remains a lasting testament to timeless, finely crafted pop music. *Big Dream* was produced by Lang and **Charlie Peacock** after an independent cassette with early versions of nine of the tracks achieved acclaim two years before. The songs themselves have the same sort of classic structures and strong melody lines as material by Billy Joel or Elton John. Lang sings in a plaintive voice that can reference Joel or Michael Hutchence (of INXS) or even Bono (of **U2**), as the mood requires. The real treat, however, comes in the jazzy vitality provided by such guest musicians as **Jimmy A, Michael Roe,** and Aaron Smith (of **Vector/Seventy Sevens/A Ragamuffin Band**). Lyrically, Lang favors poetic observations for which specific referents remain obscure. None of the songs refer to God or Christ in any obvious way, but several reflect ideas from the Wisdom literature of the Bible (Psalms, Proverbs, the Sermon on the Mount). A recurring theme is the thought of recognizing the value of the present moment and not becoming distracted by concern for the future ("Bottom of It," "Big Dream," "Ragtop"). "What's Wrong" describes a strained and probably abusive relationship from a third-person perspective; "A Lifetime" asserts commitment to the permanency of marriage in a society of disposable relationships.

Daniel Lanois

1989—*Acadie* (Warner Bros.); 1993—*For the Beauty of Wynona*.

www.daniellanois.com

Daniel Lanois (b. 1951) is one of the most revered producers in modern rock, having worked with such high profile artists as **Bob Dylan,** Peter Gabriel, Emmylou Harris, Luscious Jackson, Willie Nelson, The Neville Brothers, Robbie Robertson, and **U2.** As those names suggest, Lanois is especially noted for working with persons whose work evinces a degree of spirituality, a factor that is no doubt abetted by his own deep embrace of Christianity. As *Rolling Stone* puts it, "Lanois was the single most important record producer to emerge in the '80s and is noted for stressing emotional vibrancy over the technical aspects of making albums." Indeed, it is generally believed that most of the artists he has produced have turned out the best work of their career under his guidance. For latter-day Dylan, that would be *Oh Mercy* and *Time Out of Mind;* for Gabriel it would be *Us;* for Emmylou Harris, *Wrecking Ball;* for The Neville Brothers, *Yellow Moon;* and for **U2,** *The Unforgettable Fire, The Joshua Tree, Achtung Baby,* and *All That You Can't Leave Behind.* Several of these were actually coproduced with Lanois' frequent studio partner Brian Eno.

Lanois was raised a French Catholic in Quebec, a child of musical parents. In 1963, he moved with his mother to Ontario (following a divorce), where he took up guitar and began to play with different Canadian artists. Lanois has recorded two solo albums that, despite their overt evocation of faith, have been completely ignored within the contemporary Christian music subculture. *Acadie* draws upon a link between the old Acadian culture with which Lanois is familiar and the descendant Cajun tradition of New Orleans. The songs offer narrative ballads populated with rural characters. Larry Mullen and Adam Clayton of **U2** play on the album, along with numerous other guests. "The Maker" is a hushed, propulsive prayer with **Aaron Neville** offering harmony vocals (Emmylou Harris would cover the song on her *Spyboy* album). The album closes with a rendition of "Amazing Grace." *For the Beauty of Wynona* features the standout songs "The Collection of Marie Claire" and "Rocky World." As *Rolling Stone* says, both of Lanois' albums were "received enthusiastically by critics" but "the quirky radiance of his songs haven't proved as accessible to pop fans as the work of his celebrated clients." Lanois was also responsible for the soundtracks to the motion pictures *Sling Blade* (which also includes "The Maker") and *All the Pretty Horses.* He played with Bono and Eno in the Million Dollar Hotel Band, which performed Bono's songs for the soundtrack to the film *The Million Dollar Hotel.* In 2000, a collection of independent artists (including **Phil Keaggy**) would record a tribute album of Lanois' songs titled *The Unbreakable Chain.*

Don Lanphere

Selected: 1982—*From Out of Nowhere* (Hep); 1983—*Into Somewhere*; 1984—*Don Loves Midge*; *Stop*; 1990—*Don Lanphere/Larry Coryell*; 1992—*Lopin'*; 1993—*Jazz Worship/A Closer Walk* (label unknown); 1996—*Get Happy*; 1997—*Don Still Loves Midge* (Hep); 1999—*Year Round Christmas* (label unknown).

Don Lanphere (b. 1928) is one of the premier saxophonists in jazz music and is widely known as an evangelical Christian. Lanphere was raised in Wenatchee, Wisconsin, but traveled to New York as a teenager in the '40s, where he played with such greats as Artie Shaw and Woody Herman, recording classic albums with trumpeter Fats Navarro. He succumbed to drug abuse and was arrested. For about thirty years after that unfortunate incident he all but vanished from the scene, working in a Seattle music store but no longer performing. Coaxed out of retirement in 1981, he revealed that in 1969 he had become a Christian and he shared this testimony in numerous magazines. Lanphere closed his 1982 comeback album with an instrumental version of "The Lord's Prayer," featuring just his sax and a grand piano. This selection became one of his best-known pieces, and he would regularly introduce it at concerts by saying, simply, "This is for my best friend." He would continue to place spirituals and hymns on his albums alongside traditional jazz or big band numbers and original compositions. *Don Loves Midge* closes with "There's a Sweet, Sweet Spirit in This Place." In 1993, he recorded a worship-oriented album. Lanphere says that about half of his concerts are given at Christian colleges, where he is also sometimes invited to speak, sharing his testimony and his views on Christianity and the arts. "Most Christian art is really bad," he maintains, but "we should be better—we got the Holy Spirit." He is also always on the lookout for opportunities to share his faith in the secular field. In December 1998, *All about Jazz* magazine ran a major interview with the artist, discussing his history of involvement with the twentieth-century art form. The interviewer concluded by asking him, "Is there anything else you would like to add?" and Lanphere responded, "The major thing would be my conversion to Christianity in 1969," and proceeded to elaborate on the life-changing effects of the experience thirty years earlier.

Ron Larson

1995—*Ron Larson* (New Light).

Acoustic inspirational singer Ron Larson used to sing for patients who were in recovery at a clinic in Arlington, Virginia, and his great strength as a songwriter seems to lie in conveying messages of hope. Larson has also served as resident songwriter for the group **Glad,** and two members of that ensemble (Chris Davis and Ed Nalle) produced his self-titled album of his own material. The musical style is easy listening, MOR music featuring Larson's lyrics and acoustic guitar. *CCM* magazine described him as "a prudent lyricist who writes compassionately about personal hope rising out of common brokenness." The song "Hope for the Hurting Heart" is exemplary of such empathy and perfectly suited to Larson's velvety vocals.

LaRue

Natalie LaRue, voc.; Philip LaRue, voc., gtr. 1999—*LaRue* (Reunion); 2000—*Transparent* (Reunion).

www.laruemusic.com

Natalie and Philip LaRue are siblings from Phoenix, Arizona, who released their first album of surprisingly pleasant acoustic pop when they were only fifteen and seventeen years old. The group was formed when Philip became ill with mononucleosis his freshman year of high school and had a long period of recovery at home. Natalie LaRue has a deep, resonant voice similar to that of LeAnn Rimes. She can carry a song completely on her own, and sometimes does, but the group's sound is diversified by the trade-off vocals and harmonizing of her older brother. The duo played together locally for three years before being offered a contract with Reunion, at which point the entire family picked up and moved to Nashville. LaRue was voted Favorite New Artist of 1999 by readers of *Release* magazine. They avoid the **Rachel Lampa** pitfalls by writing their own material and performing it in an appropriate adolescent pop-rock style (rather than adult contemporary). The songs deal with issues that teenagers face and whatever naivete attends them seems appropriate. The group has been active in sponsoring an "Abstinence Petition" according to which teenagers pledge to remain virgins until they are married. The words *la rue* are French for "the road," and though Natalie and Philip named their group after their given surname, they also tout the double entendre as referencing "the road we as Christians must walk on."

The duo used four different producers on their debut album. Its opening track, "Reasons," was produced by **Rick Elias** and is the strongest cut. Musically, it is Beatlesque pop with an edge, a sound that seems to draw on **Jars of Clay** as much as on the Fab Four. Lyrically, "Reasons" affirms that one can sense the presence of God ("You're all around me") while still having questions and doubts about life and religion. "Someday" is a near-perfect adolescent ballad in which Natalie expresses her wistful longing for a future, unknown life partner: "Someday we'll fall in love / You'll be mine and I'll be yours / Our hearts will be one / And our love will ever endure." The sophomore project *Transparent* features the lively "Wake Up," which addresses a generation of adolescents "lost in themselves." A piano ballad called "Brianna's Song" is about the LaRue's younger sister, who has cerebral palsy.

Christian radio hits: "Waiting Room" (# 10 in 1999); "Reason" (# 3 in 2000); "Someday" (# 4 in 2000); "Wake Up" (# 2 in 2001); "Fly" (# 2 in 2002).

The Lassie Foundation

Eric Campuzano, gtr.; Wayne Everett, voc. 1996—*California* (Blue Velvet); 1999—*Dive Bomber* [EP]; 2000—*Pacifico* (Shogun Sounds).

The Lassie Foundation represents a new incarnation of Eric Campuzano and Wayne Everett of **The Prayer Chain** fame. The two also played together in **Starflyer 59** and **Cush** and enjoy a somewhat legendary status among fans of progressive alternative Christian rock. The actual membership of the group is somewhat dubious; according to liner notes, Campuzano and Everett compose "Lassie" while "The Foundation" consists of a slightly changing cast of supporters: Jeff Schroeder and Jason 71, who have played with **The Violet Burning,** and Frank Lenz of **Fold Zandura,** and others. *True Tunes* would describe The Lassie Foundation's sound as "a tightly wound mixture of low-fi indie noise with just enough melody-consciousness to keep the songs accessible." This is kind. The band favors Sonic Youth-style background noise and sometimes likes to let it overwhelm melodies and everything else. Generous amounts of feedback are also solicited. Everett (who was drummer, not vocalist for **The Prayer Chain**) sings in a falsetto voice that evokes mixed reactions.

California evinces a lack of cohesion that had "side project" stamped all over it, though there were definite moments of brilliance for Campuzano/Everett fans. "Walking Spinning Backing Free" is similar to **The Prayer Chain**'s "Humb" with a similarly controversial lack of discernible melody. *Dive Bomber* merely reprises two songs from *California* (supposedly live) and previews three from the coming full-length album. *Pacifico,* then, is the product that counts, and it is here that the group begins to take itself more seriously. *True Tunes,* again, would note that "the songs seem to be written without the shadow of the **The Prayer Chain** looming behind," such that Lassie Foundation now sounds like a band in its own right. The songs are certainly as dreamy as they are noisy, with a fair amount of stylistic variety (one could dance to "I Got the Rock and Roll for You" or "Come On, Let Your Lime Light Shine"). Lyrically, the songs tend to evoke poetic images and romantic ideals. "Bomber's Moon" draws on a war metaphor to describe a full moon on a clear night. The only song that has any obvious spiritual overtones is "You Are Infinity," which describes the eternal aspects of God.

The Last Call of Shiloh

Diane Murray; John Murray; John Rosenberry; Rick Saylor; Jaimie Tsapatoris; Vicki Tsapatoris. 1969—*The Last Call of Shiloh* (Last Call).

Not much is known of the very early Christian band named The Last Call of Shiloh except that they were affiliated with a community in Sandpoint, Idaho, that bore the scary name Jesus People Army (cf. **Wilson-McKinley**). Their album features music that strives for a San Francisco hippie sound reminiscent of artists like Fever Tree, Jefferson Airplane, and Quicksilver Messenger Service. Eschatological themes are prominent. The group's name is derived from a biblical citation in Genesis 49:10 (KJV). The meaning of that verse is obscure, but for that very reason might have been taken as some sort of allusion to the first or second coming of Christ.

The Latinos

Richard Avalos; Brian Lucas; Harold Velasquez; Ronnie Velasquez; Phillip Wright. 1975—*We Believe in You* (Lamb and Lion); 1981—*It Must Be Love* (Word).

The Latinos were a hispanic gospel quintet that combined the sound of the Tijuana Brass with generous helpings of Motown soul. *CCM* called them "contemporary Christian music plus congas." Their tunes were generally danceable and their lyrics traditionally evangelical. In addition to "The Party's Over" (a basic eschatological summons), *It Must Be Love* features "Born Again" and "Santo," a psalm of praise.

Christian radio hits: "The Party's Over" (# 20 in 1982).

John Lawry

See **Petra.**

The Lead

Nina Llopis, voc.; Julio Rey, gtr., voc.; et al. // Andy Cole, gtr. (+ 1989). 1985—*The Lead* [EP] (Three Equals One); 1986—*Return Fire; Automoloch* [EP]; 1987—*The Past Behind;* 1989—*Burn This Record* (R.E.X.).

The Lead (pronounced with a long *e*) was a punk/thrash band that appealed primarily to the moshing crowd. Their first few albums were low-fi custom productions, *Return Fire* being issued on cassette only. *Automoloch* includes a version of **Resurrection Band**'s "Alienated." A compilation of indie tracks called *The Past Behind* led *CCM*'s Brian Quincy Newcomb to dub the band The God Pistols (with allusions to The Sex Pistols). Then R.E.X. released *Burn This Record,* which Doug Van Pelt (editor for *HM*) called "way rad." The Lead's songs tend to be of two types—dark, fast, and heavy numbers sung by Julio Rey, and lighter ones with more of a groove sung by Nina Llopis. Lyrically, the former focus on recognition and eradication of sin ("Internal Pain," "Oh, No, Not Again"). "Skate or Die," however, is just an anthem to the joy of skateboarding. Rey went on to form **Frank's Enemy** and Llopis released solo albums as **Nina.**

Leaderdogs for the Blind

Lyndon Perry, gtr. 1996—*Lemonade* (R.E.X.).

Leaderdogs for the Blind is officially a one-man band project of Flint, Michigan's Lyndon Perry, though vocalist Derek Cilibraise and guitarist Grant Mohrman seem to contribute enough to warrant inclusion in the group's official lineup. Perry refers to Leaderdogs' sound as "industry and melody." With help from the aforementioned cohorts, he produces what *7ball* refers to as "a sweet-n-sour mix of heavy grooves, heavy melodies, and heavy metal, all with industrial flair." *Shout!* described *Lemonade* as "a hybrid of introspective lyrics with a vocal delivery that offers growl and bite." Indeed, it is the vocals that cause Leaderdogs to be compared most often to White Zombie; otherwise, references to Filter or **King's X** would seem more appropriate. In any case, the album kicks off with a track called "The Yellow and Black Attack," an obvious nod to **Stryper,** though it is not a cover song. "Martin's Dream" focuses on racial tensions. "Sprout" (with vocals by Perry) is an ode to the artist's unborn son, and through the technology of sonogram features the latter on percussion. "Radiant Abyss" samples words from C. S. Lewis, read over a mass of beats and hums.

Bernie Leadon

No solo recordings.

Bernie Leadon (b. 1947) was a founding member of The Eagles, playing guitar and singing with the group from 1972 to 1975. He was with the group through the making of their first four classic albums, participating in all of the songs that would later be collected on *The Eagles' Greatest Hits*—the best-selling album of all time. He was replaced by Joe Walsh in 1975, and so did not play on the group's last two albums *(Hotel California, The Long Run)*. In 1979, Leadon and his girlfriend (later wife) Caroline experienced a powerful conversion to Christianity brought on by a series of dramatic events they later recounted to the *Los Angeles Herald Examiner*. First, Caroline attests that she was attacked by an invisible demon while alone in Hawaii one night. She felt a dark force—a "tangible presence"—get into her bed, crawl up her body, and exert strong pressure on her chest. The next day, Leadon (who had been raised Roman Catholic but was now intrigued by more exotic religions) suggested they contact a native "witch doctor" to drive away the evil spirit. As it turns out, the local "holy woman" who they contacted had recently been converted to Christianity; she exorcized the house in the name of Jesus, and no more malignant spirits were felt to abide there. A while later, Caroline, who was blind in her right eye, began to lose sight in the left eye also. Driven to mental despair, Leadon asked her to pray the Lord's Prayer with him, which he remembered from youth.

In the morning, he maintains, her left eye was completely healed and she had recovered partial sight in the right eye as well. A short time later, Leadon says that prayer likewise brought her through a difficult childbirth. Leadon interpreted these events as signs that God's hand was on them, and on Easter Sunday, 1980, he and Carolyn dedicated their lives to a new relationship with the Lord.

After his bold declaration of faith, Leadon would become peripherally involved in the Christian music scene. In 1983, he was profiled in *CCM* magazine and offered his criticisms of the mainstream music industry: "The bottom line is what's selling—sex, drugs, and rock n' roll—an anything goes lifestyle. . . . they're preaching escape from responsibility and the love of money. At the same time, they don't want to be promoting that there's this God who loves you, and He's also a holy God, a righteous God who expects something in return." In 1994, Leadon toured and played as part of the **Hillman, Leadon, Perkins, and Scheff** quartet and contributed to the album called *Down Home Praise* produced by **Al Perkins.**

Lenny LeBlanc

1976—*Hound Dog Man* (Big Tree); 1983—*Say a Prayer* (Heartland); 1984—*Person to Person*; 1991—*Prisoner of Love* (Maranatha); 1994—*All My Dreams* (Integrity); 1996—*The Bridge*; 1999—*Above All.*

www.lennyleblanc.com

In the mainstream music market, Lenny LeBlanc may be best remembered as one-half of the one-hit wonder outfit LeBlanc and Carr, who scored a hit with the song "Falling" (# 13 in 1978). He became a Christian in 1981 and has since devoted himself to making albums that fall somewhere between positive country and adult contemporary on the spectrum of styles. LeBlanc was born in 1951 in Leominster, Massachusetts. He first worked with Pete Carr as a session musician in Muscle Shoals, Alabama. LeBlanc wrote songs that were recorded by Joan Baez, Dobie Grey, Roy Orbison, and **Ricky Skaggs.** The title song from his pre-Christian *Hound Dog Man* album reached Number Fifty-eight on the pop charts, and "Something about You" (with Carr again) went to Number Forty-eight. It was "Falling," however, that made him a household name for a little while. He had another minor hit with "Somebody Sent My Baby Home" (# 55 in 1981). After LeBlanc embraced the Christian faith, **Michele Pillar** invited him to participate on her debut album, and he did so by writing some of the songs and singing on the project. With that introduction to contemporary Christian music, he went on to make two albums for Heartland, which were marketed as products of a mainstream artist in spite of their fairly overt spiritual themes. After an extended break, he returned to recording primarily as an artist associated with the various praise and worship projects sponsored by the Maranatha and Hosanna! music companies. He has also written songs for **Candy Hemphill** and **Kelly Willard.** LeBlanc's solo albums in the '90s were targeted for the contemporary Christian music subculture.

LeBlanc's voice is reminiscent of **Buddy Greene,** but his storyteller approach to songwriting most closely recalls **Bruce Carroll** or **Paul Overstreet.** Every song on *Say a Prayer* evokes a strong Christian message, though *CCM* names the poignant ballad "Preacher Man" and the hope-for-the-future anthem "New Tomorrow" as the album's highlights. *Person to Person* is slightly less sentimental with a more gritty taste of reality. Already, LeBlanc begins to shift audiences in favor of songs directed to the church, railing against hypocrisy ("Practice What We Preach"). The song "Desperado," however, is an evangelistic outreach to the title character of the Eagles' song by the same name ("Desperado—you need to call on the name of the Lord / and you won't need to run no more"). *Prisoner of Love* includes the ballad "Strong Arm," giving voice to God's personal concern for a troubled soul, *The Bridge* is a collection of gentle pop songs. "Message to You" addresses the feeling of abandonment by God; "Looking Up" and "When the Rain Comes" similarly encourage the listener to trust in Christ amidst life's many trials. *Above All* presents happy, upbeat songs of praise ("What a Wonder," "I Dance") recorded live at Harvest Church in Riverside, California.

Christian radio hits: "Say a Prayer" (# 9 in 1983); "He Is the One" (# 14 in 1985).

Ledfoot

Earl Wayne Davis, voc.; Matt Davis, bass; Larry Lee Dunbar, drums; Dennis Glasco, gtr. 1999—*Ledfoot* (Ninety Degrees).

Ledfoot is a blues-tinged heavy metal band that *The Phantom Tollbooth* says sounds a lot like "early **Guardian.**" Their debut album was produced by **Michael Roe,** guaranteeing immediate interest from his legion of fans. They consistently refer to Jesus as "the son of man" throughout the work's lyrics. The songs are mostly evangelistic, with words that, as *Rad Rockers* puts it, "warn the listener of the dangers of a pedal to the metal lifestyle on the highway to hell." The one exception is standout track "Unto the Church," which is addressed to pew-sitters who are called "twentieth-century hypocrites" and are raked over the coals for "scrutinizing and minimizing all the things the son of man would do."

Danny Lee and the Children of Truth

Danny Lee Stutzman, voc., kybrd.; et al. 1971—*One Way* (RCA); 1972— *Spread a Little Love Around;* 1974—*Essence* (Impact).

Danny Lee and the Children of Truth were one of the early "safe" Christian pop bands that drew on contemporary musical styles but presented a status quo image that was less likely to worry conservative parents and church leaders. They were favorites with Campus Crusade for Christ, and their one big song, "Spread a Little Love Around," ended up being included on the influential soundtrack album from the *Explo '72* festival sponsored by that organization. The group featured Danny Lee Stutzman on lead vocals with a chorus of female backup singers. Yvonne Lewis, lead singer for **Good News,** was a member of the group for a time, and **Erick Nelson** toured as their bass player. John Wytock, who later played in **The Road Home,** sometimes played guitar. The band's sound was rooted in southern gospel and prefigured the more pop sound that **The Imperials** would develop. Stutzman was an excellent gospel-style piano player as well as being a great singer; when he wanted to, he could get pretty funky. Interestingly, the band had a mainstream recording contract and their first two albums were released on RCA with distribution to the general market. *One Way* was propelled by its title song, the **Larry Norman** classic that became a theme song for the Jesus movement; indeed, Danny Lee and the Children of Truth deserve some credit for popularizing the song and bringing Norman to the attention of a wider, church-oriented audience. On *Essence* the group tried to get a little more worldly, both in appearance and sound, but by 1974, the Christian rock ship had sailed and worldly looking/sounding bands were in no short supply. Danny Lee helped to launch the careers of a number of other artists, including his niece **Tami Cheré Gunden.** He died in the '80s from a heart attack.

Laura Lee (with **Eternal Light**)

1984—*All Power* (Becket).

Laura Lee is an R&B singer who lent her smoky voice to an exciting album of gospel songs in 1984. Lee was born in Chicago in 1954 and began her career (along with Della Reese) as a member of the pioneering Meditation Singers gospel group. In the late '60s and early '70s, she had a number of R&B hits with titles like "Dirty Man," "Women's Love Rights," and "If You Can Beat Me Rockin' (You Can Have My Chair)." In 1973, she appeared in the low-brow movie *Detroit 9000.* In 1981, she began to get back in touch with her gospel roots by singing with **Al Green** on his *Higher Plane* album. On *All Power,* Lee fronts the gospel choir Eternal Light and comes off like a bluesy Mavis Staples. "Brand New Me" is a straight-out soul song, while "Just One Touch" has a more emotive Chicago-blues sound. The album also includes a rendition of "God Bless America," which seems strangely out of place.

Russ Lee

2000—*Words in Time* (Sparrow).

www.russlee.com

Russ Lee has been a featured singer with the Christian vocal groups **Truth** and **NewSong.** He recorded his first solo album at the turn of the millennium. Lee was born and raised in Cleveland, Tennessee, where, despite a happy childhood, trauma set in during his adolescent years as his father suffered from alcoholism and his mother grappled with mental illness. He says he turned to drugs and pornography and by the age of seventeen was not only playing in a bar band but also selling drugs out of his car. Distraught and unsatisfied with his life, he eventually accepted a friend's invitation to church and made the walk down front while the pastor was still preaching. On *Words in Time,* Lee applies his gritty voice to soulful pop songs that exhort the listener to a closer walk with God. Lee himself calls "Live What I Believe" a "rallying cry that throws down a gauntlet" for people to stand up for their faith. "Free Fall" describes faith as an act of "diving into the arms of Jesus and trusting that he will catch us." The dance song "Get Down" employs a double entendre similar to that which sustains the **Audio Adrenaline** song of the same name—but here the spiritual reference is to prayer (rather than humility). "Go There" derives from Lee's work with World Vision and encourages involvement in missions. He also covers "The Living Years," a 1989 hit by Mike and the Mechanics.

Mylon LeFevre (and **Broken Heart** and **Look Up**)

Personnel for Broken Heart/Look Up: Kenneth Bentley, bass, voc.; Ben Hewitt, drums, perc.; Stan Coates, kybrd. (– 1985) // Dean Harrington, gtr., voc. (+ 1983a, – 1985); Tim Huffman, gtr., voc. (+ 1983a, –1983b); Scott Allen, gtr., voc. (+ 1983b); Paul Joseph, kybrd., voc. (+ 1985); David Payton, gtr., voc. (+ 1985, – 1986); Michael Tyrell, gtr., voc. (+ 1986, – 1989); Trent Argante, gtr. (+ 1989). By Mylon LeFevre: 1970—*Mylon* [a.k.a. *We Believe*] (Cotillion); 1971—*Holy Smoke* (Columbia); 1972— *Over the Influence;* 1973—*On the Road to Freedom* [with Alvin Lee]; 1977—*Weak at the Knees* (Warner Bros.); 1978—*Love Rustler;* 1979— *Rock and Roll Resurrection* (Mercury). By Mylon LeFevre and Broken Heart: 1982—*Broken Heart* (MCA); *Brand New Start* (Myrrh); 1983—*More; Live Forever;* 1985—*Sheep in Wolves' Clothing;* 1987—*Crack the Sky;* 1988— *Greatest Hits; Face the Music* (StarSong); 1989—*Big World;* 1990—*Crank It Up;* 1991—*A Decade of Love.* By Mylon LeFevre with Friends: 1992—*Faith, Hope, and Love* (StarSong). By Look Up: 1986—*Look Up* (CBS).

www.mylon.org

Mylon LeFevre has been touted in Christian circles as "a major rock star who boldly confessed his faith in Christ throughout his impressive career, simultaneously impacting the worlds of mainstream and Christian rock in lasting ways." This is an overstatement, but LeFevre is important, not least because of factors that compel the exaggeration. In actuality, LeFevre has never been more than a footnote in the general history of rock and roll. He has never charted a song in the main-stream Top 100 and does not even merit a listing in the definitive *Rolling Stone Encyclopedia of Rock and Roll.* Even his work in contemporary Christian music is largely derivative and, though worthy in its own right, is hardly groundbreaking or trend-setting. Nevertheless LeFevre's story (told with particular acuity in Mark Joseph's *Rock and Roll Rebellion*) is an interesting one; he is perhaps the only artist in either the general or Christian markets to have *tried* to keep a profile in both worlds for a period of at least two decades, and both his limited success and the reasons behind his failures are revealing.

LeFevre was born around 1951 and as a child became a part of The Singing LeFevres, which was for many years one of the most successful and popular southern gospel groups in America (the family group was founded in 1921 by Mylon's parents Eva Mae and Urias LeFevre; it morphed into The Rex Nelon Singers after no LeFevres were active members, and finally became The Nelons after Rex Nelon's death; **Karen Peck** was a member from 1981 to 1990). Thus, Mylon grew up on the road, singing gospel songs on stage. In all, he recorded thirty-three albums with The Singing LeFevres and the equally popular Stamps Quartet before the age of seventeen. At that time he wrote the gospel song "Without Him," which would be recorded a year later by **Elvis Presley** and, subsequently, by hundreds of other artists including **Pat Boone,** Mahalia Jackson, and The Oak Ridge Boys. This early success did not thrust LeFevre into the limelight, but it did provide him with what seemed to be an inexhaustible supply of money (from royalties), which he did not quite know how to handle. Shortly thereafter he was expelled from the family group (and essentially from his family) for "smoking marijuana and growing sideburns." Thus, he began recording solo albums. He intended these records to be gospel albums, for that was the only field he knew, but by now he had come under the musical spell of rock and roll. Thus, his first self-titled project was rejected by Word Records for evincing an inappropriately worldly sound—the worst offence was a sitar solo, which was taken to imply endorsement of eastern religions. LeFevre shopped the disc to Cotillion (the general market label that had just scored big with the *Woodstock* soundtrack), and the album *Mylon* came out on that label as a rock-and-roll-for-Jesus record intended for the general market.

Mylon is sometimes credited with being "the world's first Christian rock album"; that honor would more properly go to **Larry Norman** for *Upon This Rock,* released a year earlier— though such accolades always depend on how one defines "Christian" **(Azitis),** how one defines "rock" **(Ralph Carmichael, John Fischer, Ray Hildebrand, Ray Repp)** and on how much distribution is necessary to be considered a contender (cf. **Concrete Rubber Band, Crusaders, The Excursions, Sons of Thunder, Wilson-McKinley**). In any case, none of LeFevre's solo albums sold very well. In the early years, there was no contemporary Christian music market, and despite flukes like the **Edwin Hawkins Singers**' "O Happy Day" (# 4 in 1969) or Ocean's "Put Your Hand in the Hand" (# 2 in 1971), there was no steady appetite for revved-up gospel songs in the secular realm. And, to be frank, apart from occasional songs like "Old Gospel Ship," LeFevre's albums were just not that good—especially when compared (as they were) to products in the big pool of mainstream releases. Christian fans and critics often aver that LeFevre should have been one of the biggest stars of the '70s, on a par with acts like The Doobie Brothers or Three Dog Night. Not so. In terms of the music of that decade, an objective appraisal of LeFevre's output would perhaps put him on a par with such minor artists as Black Oak Arkansas or The Outlaws.

Still, objective appraisals were not made, and it is accurate to say that LeFevre was discriminated against on account of his faith, and so cheated out of whatever modest stardom should rightly have been his. LeFevre's own management company was unhappy with his Jesus songs and treated him openly with disdain. They named the company that published his music "St. Lucifer Music" as a sort of cruel joke, and likewise rearranged his cover design for *Holy Smoke* so that a cross he had requested was displayed upside down as a satanic symbol. What was worse, though, was when major media outlets like *Rolling Stone* magazine functioned to support and convey an inexcusable bigotry. In one disgraceful display, *Rolling Stone* published a review of LeFevre's *Over the Influence* written by Nick Tosches. Ignoring the album's musical shortcomings, Tosches simply attacked the personal convictions of the artist. LeFevre, he said, is "part of the whole Jesus-creep movement and two-thirds of the songs on this album are totally devoid of any relation to the real world. No sex, no drugs, no booze, no cars, no worldly problems, no worldly happiness. Everything revolves around this f**king ghost Jesus." Such comments are not only fanatical in their religious intolerance, but implicitly racist as well. *Rolling Stone* would never have published a review that attacked **Al Green** or **Marvin Gaye** or **Aretha Franklin** for displaying gospel roots or references. The operating principle appears to have been that evidence of such commitments is tolerable only when an artist is black—presumably because Tosches (and *Rolling Stone*) assumed African Americans to be less advanced culturally or intellectually than white people and thus should be allowed to maintain their superstitions. Tosches continued his review of *Over the Influence* by asking in exasperation, "How can any human being possibly comprehend 'Blue Suede Shoes' and then turn around and warble stuff like 'Jesus is a waymaker / One day he made a way for me'?" Perhaps Tosches himself never comprehended "Blue Suede Shoes" or he might have known that both the person who

wrote that song (Carl Perkins) and the person who popularized it **(Elvis Presley)** were Christians steeped in gospel music who would have had no more trouble singing LeFevre's "Jesus Is a Waymaker" than they had warbling Hank Williams' "Praise the Lord, I Saw the Light."

But LeFevre didn't fit into the Christian culture either. Contrary to Tosches' assertion, LeFevre was never a part of the Jesus movement, and the "Jesus freaks" who participated in that revival did not buy his albums. The reason is not that the records had "a worldly sound" (cf. **Agape, Barnabas, Larry Norman, Wilson-McKinley**) but that they lacked the mysterious "anointing" that made projects appeal to the Jesus people. **Andraé Crouch, Phil Keaggy,** and **Love Song** all had it. There was never any question that they were motivated by a singular passion for the Lord and that the purpose of their albums was to glorify Jesus, bless his people, and spread his word. With LeFevre, it all seemed like a business. For the most part, the Jesus people had no more interest in his albums than they did in gospel records by **Elvis Presley** or **Aretha Franklin** (see listing). Thus LeFevre was marginalized by both anti-religious bigotry on the one hand and spiritual snobbery, on the other. This left him with a rather small target audience—basically, Baptist kids with liberal youth pastors—and there weren't nearly enough of them to go around.

LeFevre would later reveal that the Jesus people's apprehensions were more perceptive than they could ever have known. "I don't think I sang about Jesus because I loved him," he would recount in 1988. "I did it because it was my heritage." LeFevre became very much a part of the rock and roll culture, touring with The Who and hanging out with Duane Allman, **Eric Clapton,** George Harrison, and Billy Joel. "We were just a rock and roll band that happened to believe Jesus Christ was the Son of God," he explains. "Every night before we went on stage we would pray and smoke marijuana." Ironically, at the very time that *Rolling Stone* was criticizing LeFevre for lack of concern with "sex, drugs, and booze," the artist was in fact a heroin addict, a major user of cocaine, and an impresario of the partying lifestyle. In 1973, he recorded an album with Alvin Lee of Ten Years After. The record features guest appearances by George Harrison (listed as Harry Georgeson), Jim Capaldi and Steve Winwood (of Traffic), Ron Wood (of the Rolling Stones), Mick Fleetwood (of Fleetwood Mac), Box Burrell (of Bad Company), and Ian Wallace (of King Crimson and, later, Foreigner). LeFevre describes the making of the record as one huge party "during which we were getting so coked up that we were staying up seven or eight days and getting in George's Lear Jet and going to some strange places . . . when it's five in the morning and you got some blow that's got you so wired and you wonder what it's like in Mexico City, you can just go there! Why wonder? George would say, 'Hey, I'm gonna die before I spend all this. You got an idea we haven't tried before? Let's do it!' " LeFevre would later dismiss all of his '70s albums as not simply records made outside the sphere of gospel music, but also as products of an artist who didn't really appreciate the content of his own material. Nevertheless, his music proved to be an effective ministry in some quarters. **Dana Key** of **DeGarmo and Key** says that he was inspired to turn his life and career over to the Lord by his experience of a Mylon LeFevre concert in the mid '70s. In 1988, Alvin Lee would reveal that he had become a Christian due in large part to the way LeFevre had ministered to him during the time that they made the one album together. LeFevre himself shakes his head a bit incredulously at this, giving credit to the power of God's word that was cited in his songs and testimonies, "It's still the Word of God even if a donkey is telling it," he asserted in 1986. "It never returns void."

Musically, the 1970 album *Mylon* (a.k.a. *We Believe*) is deservedly a Christian classic, a raw example of down-home southern rock. A dominant organ, spicy guitars, and generous use of female background vocals give the project a funky-and-gritty combination of R&B soul and roots rock. The songs "Who Knows" and "You're Still on His Mind" testify to God's personal concern for every individual, the latter offering a sentimental take on the crucifixion story: "Think about that lonely day on cruel Calvary / Think about the way He suffered death for you and me / When you face reality I know that you will find / That you were on His mind." The album also contains such faith-based songs as "Sunday School Blues" and "Sweet Peace Within," but its undeniable highlight is "Old Gospel Ship," which would become LeFevre's best-known, signature song. Though he is often credited with writing the tune, it is actually a traditional number that he supplied with a definitive new arrangement, turning it into a passionate, R&B number that is guaranteed to have any audience shouting and singing along with the artist as he exults over "leaving this world behind." It is a justifiable masterpiece, a song that deserves to be placed in the same canon as Arthur Conley's "Sweet Soul Music" or Sam and Dave's "Hold On, I'm Coming." Not surprisingly, it has since been recorded at one time or another by most of the major southern and traditional (black) gospel groups—and, indeed, has been picked up by a few rock-oriented artists as well. As an interesting side note, the band of studio musicians that backed LeFevre on his debut album would later form the core for the Atlanta Rhythm Section. And the infamous sitar solo that caused Word to reject it was played by none other than Joe South.

LeFevre's later solo albums grew increasingly subdued in their spiritual references, mixing overt Christian songs with mainstream pop. LeFevre fronted a band for *Mylon* and *Holy Smoke* and actually toured with Black Sabbath and the Grateful Dead, singing songs like "Railroad Angels" with its admonition to "just try to keep Sweet Jesus on your mind." *Over the Influence,* the album that sent *Rolling Stones'* Tosches over the edge, did indeed contain a credible version of "Blue Suede Shoes" along with what was to end up being a favorite youth group summer camp song, "Waymaker." LeFevre also brought in **Little Richard** to duet with him on the latter's "He's Not Just a Soldier." *Weak at the Knees* includes an old gospel standard ("Old Ship of Zion") and the song "Understand It," in which LeFevre wails, "If I can't turn to you, Jesus, who can I turn to?" *Love Rustler* features no original songs, but LeFevre does do "Better Come Back," written by a pre-Chartbusters **Robin Lane,** "Another Slant," by a preconversion **Kerry Livgren,** and "Keep the Fire Burning," by Livgren's mentor, Jeff Pollard of LeRoux. On *Rock and Roll Resurrection,* LeFevre went almost completely secular, covering **Sam Cooke**'s "Shake" and the Isley Brothers' "Work to Do" alongside original compositions with sophomoric David Lee Roth-style lyrics: "Well, you're doing it to me baby and it feels so fine / I want you to do it to me all the time" ("Baby, Don't Hold Back Now"). Only on "Prisoner" does he reveal something of himself and his struggles: "Two thousand years, the story goes, what does this really mean? / It's been so hard, I must confess, My nose was not kept clean."

LeFevre's transformation into an artist who could be accepted by the contemporary Christian music community seems to have been brought on by a number of events. A drug overdose left him unconscious, and when he recovered, he was frightened by the realization that he had no assurance of where he would go if he died. Even more compelling was a change that he observed in the later years of his estranged father's life. LeFevre had known his father to be "a harsh and uncaring man," but in the late '70s, he became "a real kind, gentle, and caring man." The two reconciled, and when Mylon asked the elder LeFevre to account for what had happened to him, he replied, "It's just Jesus," with heartfelt sincerity that somehow transcended gospel music clichés. At the same time, LeFevre's desire to combine gospel and rock inevitably brought him into contact with key players in the burgeoning field of contemporary Christian music. He got to know **Phil Keaggy** and Buck Herring (cf. **2nd Chapter of Acts**) when doing background vocals for Keaggy's *Love Broke Thru* album and, as he would later indicate, he "saw something in their lives and wanted to be more like them." In 1979, LeFevre made a personal commitment to live for the Lord, and in 1980, at a **2nd Chapter of Acts** concert, he publicly responded to the altar call in a manner that he would later point to as the time when he was born again. After this, he decided he had to break his ties with the world of rock and roll completely. "I could not live for Jesus and be around rock and roll," he later explained, clarifying that this was due to his own frailty rather than to the supposed *intrinsic* incompatibility of religion and rock alleged by such strange bedfellows as Jimmy Swaggart and Neil Tosches. "I just didn't have the faith or the guts to do it." In a bold move, he sold off his publishing rights and in other ways decisively broke all ties with the industry. He worked as a janitor at the Mount Paran Church of God in Atlanta, submitting himself to the elders there for discipline and daily Bible study. Two years later, he would emerge as an ordained minister of that church, fronting a Christian band on a Christian label, making albums geared specifically to the Christian market. He had found his home and, for the most part, was content. In 1986 he would declare, "I want to live in such a way that God can enjoy me as much as I enjoy Him, because I have fallen in love with Jesus."

Ironically, no sooner had LeFevre embarked on what he considered to be a legitimate rock and roll *ministry* than certain well-known ministers singled him out as the prime example of a deluded soul who was playing "the devil's music." David Wilkerson, the heroic evangelist whose early career is recounted in *The Cross and The Switchblade,* and the much-less-heroic media manipulator Jimmy Swaggart joined forces to thwart LeFevre at every turn. Wilkerson had already disgraced himself a few years earlier by touting his own private visions and revelations as though they were Holy Scripture and Swaggart had been exposed repeatedly for bilking widows out of their Social Security checks under false pretenses (and claiming that "God used Adolf Hitler to punish the Jews")—but in the early to mid '80s both carried a lot of weight among the American fundamentalists who formed a sizeable chunk of LeFevre's potential audience. Ignoring lyrics, they publicly condemned his music as "demonic" on the basis of its intrinsic sound and with reference to the dazzling effects employed in performances—Wilkerson had attended a few minutes of a concert and witnessed a light show. LeFevre's repeated requests to meet with the evangelists were delayed or denied, but he managed to stick it out. In 1986, he told *CCM,* "Our music is rock 'n' roll. We don't even tell anybody it's contemporary Christian music. We are a rock 'n' roll band. We sound like one, we look like one, and at the end of the night, we smell like one."

By 1986 such claims might be legitimate, but when LeFevre and Broken Heart first appeared on the scene in 1982, they evinced a sound that was a radical departure from the earlier grit-rock the artist had been playing before he "got right with the Lord." *Broken Heart* and *Brand New Start* are reminiscent of mid '80s efforts by **DeGarmo and Key;** critics would also compare the group (a bit ironically) to Atlanta Rhythm Section. The title song to *Brand New Start* was the first song LeFevre wrote after his time of spiritual retreat, and it was originally intended for performance in jails where his church

conducted a prison ministry. That album includes "Stranger to Danger," which would become LeFevre's new signature song: "I'm no stranger to danger, but I'm brand new in love / And it's the last of the past that I'm finally free of." A video for the song, featuring the Holy Spirit on a motorcycle chasing down a furtive LeFevre, played on MTV. *Brand New Start* was selected as one of *CCM*'s "Ten Best of 1982," with historian/critic Paul Baker claiming that it "contains some of the most reverent and edifying compositions in recent contemporary Christian music. . . . every song is a standout in its own right." The basically mellow production also includes "Waitin' on Heaven," written for LeFevre by **Pat Terry,** and "You Comfort Me," contributed by **DeGarmo and Key.** *More* offers the power ballad "My Heart Belongs to Him" and concludes with a worship suite of "Praise Hymn" (with **Kerry Livgren** on synthesizers) and "The Gift" (with **Matthew Ward** on vocals). *Live Forever* is a live album with a tougher sound and a new rendition of **Annie Herring**'s "It's Alright," first sung by Ward (her brother) on his *Toward Eternity.* The album is unfortunately spoiled musically—and, for many, theologically—by the inclusion of a seven-and-a-half minute altar call.

Sheep in Wolves' Clothing not only bears the best title of all LeFevre's albums but also returns him to form with a new version of "Gospel Ship" and with the Allman Brothers-styled "Crucible of Love." The album features guest performances from the Christian rock elite (cf. *Faith, Hope, and Love* a decade later), including **Philip Bailey, Rick Cua, Joe English, Kerry Livgren, Larry Norman, Leon Patillo, Russ Taff,** and **Greg Volz** (of Petra). The big hit off the album would be "The Warrior," which is not the call to spiritual warfare that its title may suggest, but an invitation to rest ("Come on home, the battle's over, Christ has won"). On *Crack the Sky,* LeFevre retreats to what *CCM* called "the comfortable and safe niche of the adult contemporary to pop Christian radio format." It wasn't very good but, predictably, would produce his biggest hit ever with the extra poppy eschatological title track. *Face the Music,* by contrast, returns to the southern rock of the early Mylon years with songs that mimic ZZ Top ("Change of Heart") and Bruce Hornsby ("Praise the Lord All the Nations")—though numerous nods to Huey Lewis and the News can be detected as well. *Big World* opens with three sturdy rockers (the title track, "Love Comes Down," "Falling in Love"). Christian music's premier critic, Brian Quincy Newcomb, described it as "a solid rock and pop album that would fit into any FM format" and as the group's "best work to date." *Crank It Up* is known for its cover of James Taylor's "Shower the People," but also features "New Attitude," which displays a bit more of the boogie beat.

LeFevre did not completely abandon the idea of taking Christian rock outside the Christian ghetto. As early as 1980, he contributed a vocal for the song "Whiskey Seed" on **Kerry**

Livgren's general market (but subtly Christian) release, *Seeds of Change.* Then in 1986 he recorded an album with members of Broken Heart under the new band name Look Up. The eponymous project was released to the general market on CBS; it contained a mixture of purely secular pop songs and ones featuring subdued spiritual themes—including several tracks written with **Eddie DeGarmo** and **Dana Key.** Christian audiences didn't seem to know (or care) about the project and the targeted mainstream audience ignored it completely.

What the Look Up adventure did reveal was unresolved vocational issues, as LeFevre appeared now to be reconsidering his total retreat from the mainstream world. The pendulum, it would seem, had swung the other way, and he now found it necessary to justify rock and roll as a medium with legitimacy apart from any overt ministry focus. "Rock and roll is what I do," he told *CCM*'s John Styll in 1986. "I put on a good show. I entertain people. I have a good time with them. It is very frustrating to some people who are not very free for other people to have a good time." Besides, he continued, "I don't believe contemporary Christian music has ever changed anyone's life." But then the pendulum swung back the other way. LeFevre suffered a heart attack in 1991, and unable to continue with the rigors of touring, he subsequently disbanded Broken Heart. Shortly thereafter he declared, "Up until a few years ago, I was a Christian minister who preached a little, worshiped a little, and rocked a lot. Now I have become a minister who preaches and worships all the time." The result was *Faith, Hope, and Love,* an adult contemporary praise and worship album that includes a cast of Dove-award-winning extras. **Steven Curtis Chapman** and **Ricky Skaggs** join Mylon on "Invincible Love," **Carman** sings on "In the Name of the Lord," and **Michael English,** on "The Power of Love." English and **Michael W. Smith** join him on "Closer Than a Friend," and the boys from **4 Him** come in for "Give Thanks." As of 2002, LeFevre was living in Ft. Worth, Texas, preaching regularly and performing sporadically. In 1998 he was inducted into the Gospel Music Hall of Fame—not as a solo artist but as a child member of The Singing LeFevres.

For trivia buffs: Aside from all his celebrity contacts in the mainstream rock world and family connections in traditional gospel music, LeFevre also ended up being the father-in-law of **The Newsboys**' Peter Furler. Furler is married to LeFevre's daughter Summer.

Christian radio hits: As Mylon LeFevre and Broken Heart: "My Heart Belongs to Him" (# 10 in 1983); "The Warrior" (# 2 in 1985); "He Is Strong" (# 4 in 1985); "Trains Up in the Sky" (# 5 in 1986); "Crack the Sky" (# 1 for 6 weeks in 1987); "Closer Than a Heartbeat" (# 6 in 1987); "Let Me Be the One" (# 11 in 1988); "Won by One" (# 2 in 1988); "Sixteen" (# 12 in 1988); "Mercy Seat" (# 7 in 1988); "Jesus, It's You" (# 5 in 1989); "Love Comes Down" (# 1 for 4 weeks in 1990); "Give It Away"

(# 8 in 1990); "Shower the People" (# 4 in 1991); "Letter from the Front" (# 3 in 1991); "Secret Place" (# 13 in 1992).

As Look Up: "It's Alright with Me" (# 10 in 1986).

Dove Awards: 1988 Rock Album (*Crack the Sky*); 1989 Rock Song ("Won by One").

Grammy Awards: 1987 Best Gospel Performance by a Duo or Group, Choir, or Chorus (*Crack the Sky*).

Left Out

Bryan Gray, voc., bass; et al. 1996—*Pride Kills* (Flying Tart); 1997—*Serve Self;* 1999—*For the Working Class* (Grrr).

Left Out began as an all-star punk project formed at the Tom Fest Christian festival in 1995. Bryan Gray [a.k.a. Brian Gray, Bryan Grey, and Brian Grey—no one at his record companies or anywhere else knows how to spell his name] was a member of **The Blamed** and **Six Feet Deep.** For the first album he assembled a crew of friends that included Chris Colbert (famous for his work with bizarro cult bands **Breakfast with Amy** and **Duraluxe/Fluffy**), Daren Diolosa (a.k.a. **Klank**) and Jesse Smith (drummer for **Zao**). Jake Landrau and Myk Porter also played guitars, and all three of Gray's later cohorts in **The Blamed** (Matt Switaj, Christopher Witala, Trevor Witala) played with the band at some point. The group's mosh-punk sound is nonetheless determined by Gray's influence. *Pride Kills* evinces what *HM* would call a "deathy, near grind approach with hardcore backing." *Serve Self* went unreviewed and unadvertised, such that many of the band's fans did not even know it existed; *Cornerstone* would describe it as sounding like a collection of outtakes from **The Blamed**'s *21* album. For the third album, Gray would claim to have put together a group that sounds more like an actual band: Greg Jacques (from **Crashdog**), drums; Brent Kaping, bass; Jason Seiler, gtr. *For the Working Class,* recorded at Chicago's JPUSA, also features **Crashdog**'s Spike on "What the Song's About," which urges fans to pay attention to lyrics. "Hindsight or Clarity" successfully melds the old sound of early **Crucified** with more recent punk stylings of **MxPx** and Green Day. "Getting Away with Killing You and Everyone Else" is an antismoking anthem, encouraging teens not to be pawns of the tobacco industry. "Step Up to the Mic" is an intentional Beastie Boys parody on which Gray cries out against all kinds of things, including rivalry, propaganda, the goth scene, and vampire movies.

Legend (and Legend Seven)

Andy Denton, voc.; Mike Jacobs, gtr.; Randy Ray, bass, voc.; Billy Williams, drums. As Legend: 1992—*Legend* (Word). As Legend Seven: 1993—*Blind Faith* (Word).

The hard rock band Legend was formed in the early '90s by Andy Denton, Mike Jacobs, and Billy Williams, who had all been part of **Ruscha.** One of those pesky legal conflicts caused them to change their name (again) between albums. The group had what Denton called "a less angry sound" than **Ruscha,** with more of a blues-based emphasis. Critics often compared them to Bad Company, **Extreme,** and **Petra.** On the debut album, "Set This Place on Fire" is appropriately rousing and "Colours" reveals the group's metal roots, but the record is otherwise heavy on power ballads like "Carry Me," "Lead Me Back," and "Angela" (a Foreigner-type song about a young woman who yields too easily to peer pressure). "After the Fall" is about offering forgiveness within the Christian community, and "Friendly Fire" likewise draws on the Gulf War idiom to describe the phenomenon of judgmental Christians "shooting their wounded." The sophomore album has a more personal focus to it, with the most noticed songs again being spiritual ballads like "First Love" and "Call on Me." The title track, "Blind Faith," is perhaps the group's best upbeat song, featuring tasteful horns amidst a bluesy vibe. The group would perform Argent's "Hold Your Head Up" and Edgar Winter's "Free Ride" (cf. **Audio Adrenaline**) as crowd pleasers in concert. The band members all belonged to Bellevue Community Church in Nashville. The group disbanded in 1997 and Denton went on to form **Identical Strangers** with Randy Thomas.

Christian radio hits: "Carry Me" (# 4 in 1992); "Be Still" (# 1 for 2 weeks in 1994); "First Love" (# 10 in 1994); "Call on Me" (# 15 in 1994).

Lengsel

Tor Magne Glidje, gtr., voc.; John Robert Mjäland, bass; Ole Halvaard Sveen, drums. 2000—*Solace* (Solid State).

Lengsel is a Norwegian band that *True Tunes* describes as playing "impossibly tight, blistering fast, yet surprisingly melodic and emotive black metal." The group is fronted by Tor Glidje, who is sometimes also listed as bass player for the black metal band **Extol.** The name *Lengsel* means "longing," and the yearning that "citizens of heaven" have for their true home (Hebrews 11:13–16) is a prominent theme in the band's songs. "If man is sane, then I am not," Glidje sings in "Hours." *Phantom Tollbooth* admits that "to most music listeners the band will sound like untalented noise," yet they maintain that for the initiated (i.e., those who understand the genre of black metal), "it's very intricate, busy music with more musical precision in each song than most bands could dream of accomplishing." The album concludes with a standout track called "Avmakt," sung in Norwegian.

Nikki Leonti

1998—*Shelter Me* (Pamplin); 2001—*Nikki Leonti.*

www.nikkileonti.com

Nikki Leonti is one of several teenage singers who was discovered by the Christian music industry and vigorously marketed to adult contemporary stations in the late '90s. Leonti grew up in Corona, California, where she sang often in church. She was only sixteen when she recorded her debut album, which included one original composition ("One World") and nine songs written for her by hired guns. She was sent out on tour with adult contemporary stars **Greg Long** and **Sierra,** and the album faithfully generated a number of hits on Christian adult contemporary radio. *The Phantom Tollbooth* announced that "this young new artist is poised to make inroads into the mainstream pop music scene in much the same way as **Amy Grant,** and may well out-perform her." That seems unlikely, but Leonti does possess a powerful alto voice and a natural ken for interpretation similar to what could be found on the first albums by such teenage artists as **Crystal Lewis** and **Rebecca St. James.** The essential difference between Leonti and, say, **Rachel Lampa,** is that her music may also hold appeal to the preteen and barely-teen audience. On her debut album, Leonti is definitely more adult-oriented than Britney Spears (or **Stacie Orrico** or **Joy Williams**), but she comes closer to sounding like a young Mariah Carey than like an adult Celine Dion.

Shelter Me was produced by **John** and Dino **Elefante** and incorporates a variety of up-tempo pop songs, bright ballads, and rocking dance tracks. "Everlasting Place" and "Love One Another" (a duet with **John Elefante**) are attractive slow songs that showcase her vocal abilities. "It'll Be Alright" is sprightly pop, filled with hooks that seem to be just begging for Top 40 airplay; the song actually did appear on *Billboard's Top 200* mainstream chart, albeit at Number 179. "It'll Come to You" is an equally catchy midtempo number. "One World," the song Leonti wrote, calls on Christians to witness to their faith in Jesus. All the songs evince simple lyrics that rehearse basic evangelical themes and exude a "happy in Jesus" good feeling. Thematically, such songs seem entirely appropriate for adolescent radio—less so for adult contemporary. Leonti agreed that her songs "could appeal to a lot of high school and college kids as well as to my parents' generation." But she also was not really interested in record sales. "I've never dreamed of being some kind of big star, and I still don't," she said. "Jesus is the only reason I'm doing this."

In 1999, Leonti married Ryan Gingerich of the group **Scarecrow and Tinmen.** A minor scandal erupted when she disclosed a prenuptials pregnancy, especially since encouragement of premarital sexual abstinence had been a regular part of her concert performances. She ended up having to explain herself to an overly image-conscious Christian music subculture: "Before I started dating Ryan, I'd never kissed a guy or even held a guy's hand. I thought it was cool having my boyfriend on the road with me, but when you're staying in the same hotel, it's hard to keep everything in check." The second, self-titled album by the now twenty-year-old wife and mother continues in the same vein as her debut, with some noticeable vocal maturity. Leonti cowrote a half dozen of the songs, and somewhat deeper themes of dependence on God and the perseverance of God's mercy come to the fore. An album highlight is "Till I See You Again" written by **Billy Sprague** with Joe Beck.

Christian radio hits: "It'll Be Alright" (# 21 in 1998).

Level

Dan Levler, gtr., prog., voc. 1999—*Devil's Advocate* (Flaming Fish).

Level is the professional moniker under which industrial whiz kid Dan Levler likes to produce and record. Levler is well known in Christian industrial circles for his programming and remix work with bands like **Circle of Dust.** He was one-half of the combo **AP2.** *Devil's Advocate* was seven years in the making and much anticipated by fans of industrial metal. It delivers the goods with what *Phantom Tollbooth* calls "a collage of trance industrial programming, industrial metal guitars, and emotional vocals and lyrics." The album begins with a trilogy of songs called "She:Backslide," "She:Pay to Play," and "She: This Time." Monster guitar riffs are featured throughout all three, with the first being a particularly driving, intense song on which Levler screams, "Oh, God, she's trying to get me to backslide!" Other tracks are much more electronic in orientation, with subdued or nonexistent guitar. Betrayal is the primary theme throughout the album, with side reflections on sexual tension and hopelessness. The "Christian" part comes, perhaps, in Levler's plea for a better future, but his lyrics (like those quoted above) tend toward misogyny and disavowal of responsibility.

Mo Leverett

1993—*For the Benefit of Desire* (Storyville); 1995—*Sacred Desires.*

Mo Leverett is a football coach in the Desire housing project, an impoverished section of New Orleans. He writes and sings songs that reflect the violence, hardship, and despair of the people whose lives he shares. Leverett has a soulful, gutsy voice and his songs relate the gospel in insightful ways to real life experience. "Through the Streets of Mankind," for instance, describes Christ as one who "bandaged the wounds of harlots" and "tended the homes of orphans in dark city slums."

Sam Levine

2000—*Sax for the Spirit* (Spring Hill).

Saxophone player Sam Levine endeavors to be a Christian version of Kenny G, offering soulful instrumental versions of inspirational songs. His *Sax for the Spirit* albums includes

Steven Curtis Chapman's "For the Sake of the Call" and **Rich Mullins**' "Awesome God," alongside such mainstream fare as Paul Simon's "Bridge over Troubled Water" and James Taylor's "Shower the People." Compare **Kim Costanza.**

Leviticus

Kjell Anderson, drums; Bjorn Stigsson, gtr.; Ez Gomez, bass (– 1989); Terry Haw, voc. (+ 1989) // Niklas Franklin, bass (+ 1989); Peo, voc. (+ 1989). 1984—*I Shall Conquer* (Talking Music); 1984—*The Strongest Power* (Twilight); 1987—*Setting Fire to the Earth* (Royal); 1989—*Knights of Heaven* (Invasion); 1993—*Best of Leviticus* (Viva).

Leviticus was a Christian heavy metal band that came out of Sweden in the '80s and went over big in Europe. They attracted a smaller following among Christian headbangers in America who had to scramble to find their products. Over the years, the albums were released in the United States by a variety of labels, including Pure Metal, Refuge, Spectra, and Solid Rock, and as recently as 2000 some were reissued by M8. The group was led by melodic guitarist Bjorn Stiggson, and they began with the typical glam-metal sound associated with big hair and leather pants. Even *I Shall Conquer,* however, contains glimmers of other styles, as on the rock-oriented "Doubt" and the requisite power ballad "All Is Calm." *Setting Fire to the Earth* finally got the group noticed in North America as they toured the States for the first time in 1988, opening for **Larry Norman** and serving as his backing band. "Flames of Fire" and "Saved" are standout metal songs on that release, with "The Suffering Servant" being a particularly strong ballad (based on Isaiah 41 and 53). Then the group got completely Americanized, to the disappointment of most of their fans. *Knights of Heaven* was produced by **John** and Dino **Elefante** and exhibits a nonmetal rock sound remarkably like **Petra.** "Messiah" and "The World Goes Round" are strong contributions, representative of the group at this juncture. Gomez and Haw went on to form **Jet Circus.** Stiggson made a solo album called *Together with Friends* and then formed a new band called **XT.**

Grover Levy

1993—*Grover Levy* (Myrrh); 1997—*Wrestling Angels.*

Grover Levy is a folk-pop singer in the mold of Cat Stevens, Shawn Mullins, or Gerry Rafferty (minus the sax). Born in 1967 and raised in Nashville, he is a gym teacher at Cameron Middle School, but writes songs on the side and serves as a lay worship leader in his local church. His first album for Myrrh has a fairly subdued sound, but on the sophomore project he gained allowance to add electric guitars (courtesy of Gordon Kennedy of **Dogs of Peace**), giving the music some needed lift. The outstanding song from the debut is probably "There Is a Life," which deals with the struggle between flesh and spirit.

But Levy is most famous for "If You Want to Lead Me to Jesus" from *Wrestling Angels.* The lyrics seem to come straight out of the '60s but, apparently, continue to strike a chord with so-called Gen-X Christians, whom Levy claims to represent: "If you want to lead me to Jesus / you better find a better way / Cause your life is speaking so loud / I can't even hear a word you say." On the same album, Levy pleads with a young woman to give her heart to Jesus ("Marianne"), and on "Grace My Life" he extols how amazing indeed is the grace of God. The latter song features a repeated guitar line that is only slightly altered from Joan Osborne's "One of Us." Another outstanding (and more original) track is "Tell Us What We Want to Hear," on which Levy voices the perspective of those who prefer what is palatable to what is actually true: "Tell us we're the victims . . . tell us that we're blameless").

Christian radio hits: "Someday" (# 20 in 1995); "There Is a Life" (# 2 in 1996); "So in Love" (# 4 in 1996); "Fields of Wonder" (# 11 in 1996); "If You Want to Lead Me to Jesus" (# 1 for 4 weeks in 1997); "Part of Life" (# 3 in 1997); "Marianne" (# 9 in 1997).

Angie Lewis

1985—*Heart Dance* [EP] (Power Discs); 1986—*What's It Gonna Take.*

Angie Lewis is a musician from Fair Hope, Alabama, who made her way to Nashville convinced that God had told her to become a Christian singer. Lewis grew up singing in her grandfather's church and earned a degree in music from the University of South Alabama. Within three years of coming to Music City she did indeed get a contract to record an album of dance-pop music similar to that favored by **Leslie Phillips** at the time. The title song for her EP was written by **Steven Curtis Chapman** and **Geoff Moore.** Her full-length album was produced by Billy Smiley and features a duet with Moore, "Keep Holding On." The songs "Dancing around Each Other" and "Real Hero" are aggressive, while "The World Turns a Little Slower" is a reserved song with mournful lyrics about abortion.

Christian radio hits: "Heartdance" (# 7 in 1985); "What's It Gonna Take?" (# 16 in 1986).

Crystal Lewis

1987—*Beyond the Charade* (Frontline); 1989—*Joy;* 1990—*Let Love In;* 1991—*Simply the Best;* 1992—*Remember* (Metro One); 1993—*The Bride;* 1994—*The Remix Collection; Greatest Hits;* 1995—*Hymns: My Life; Wild Blue Yonder; Beauty for Ashes* (Myrrh); 1996—*Best of the Harvest* (Metro One); 1998—*Gold;* 1999—*Live at Woodlands;* 2000—*Fearless;* 2001—*More.*

www.crystallewis.com

Adult contemporary diva Crystal Lewis possesses a powerhouse voice that belies her five-foot, under-a-hundred-pounds frame. Lewis's sound is often likened to that of other R&B-inflected white women like Mariah Carey or Madonna—but her eclecticism is more worthy of comparison to Linda Ronstadt. Equally at home with soulful ballads, gospel spirituals, and disco dance hits, Lewis can also go Latin or belt out a Pat Benatar-styled rocker when she gets the urge. The media has not failed to notice her fashion-model good looks, which have improved with age and confidence (blonde hair and leather pants both served as wise career moves).

Lewis was born in 1969 in Norco, California, the daughter of a Nazarene minister. At the age of fifteen, she performed in the Christian musical *Hi Tops* (written by **Debby Kerner** and **Ernie Rettino**) and sang on the soundtrack album. She then balanced being a high school cheerleader with fronting the Christian band **Wild Blue Yonder** and, at seventeen, embarked on a contract for a solo career. She formed the label Metro One with her producer/songwriter husband, Brian Ray, in 1992. From 1993 to 1996 she also served as a cast regular on the children's program *Roundhouse* developed for Nickelodeon by **Benny Hester.** In 1993, she sang on two albums as a member of **Shack of Peasants.** In 1998 she sang with **Kirk Franklin** on his R&B hit "Lean on Me," and in 1999 she recorded an underground alternative album with the band **The Screamin' Rays.** Lewis has sung at evangelistic crusades sponsored by Harvest Crusades and Franklin Graham, and her song "Come Just As You Are" has replaced "Just As I Am" as the standard invitational hymn at their rallies, geared to a more contemporary audience. She is also a supporter of the Cross Seekers' student ministry program.

The album *Beyond the Charade* opens with "Frustrated," an up-tempo **Jon Gibson** song with a funky backbeat. The most noticed selection, however, would be Lewis's take on the Thomas Dorsey gospel standard "Precious Lord." Her interpretation of the hymn is completely traditional (and just a little rushed), but it would prove to be a surprising success, thrusting her into the contemporary Christian music limelight. On *Joy,* Lewis sings two songs produced by Gene Eugene of **Adam Again:** "Monday Comes," with a jazzy Anita Baker vocal, and "Come Together" (not the Beatles song), with a screaming lead guitar courtesy of boyfriend/husband-to-be Brian Ray. "Better Day" and "Bloodstained Pages" showcase some traditional gospel influences and let her display the sort of vocal histrionics that fans would come to expect and demand. That would also hold for her reworking of the standard "I Must Tell Jesus" on *Let Love In.* The title track to the latter album is a powerful upbeat pop song written by Brian Ray and performed with a choir singing "I believe that the world can be a better place to live" *ad infinitum* in the background. The album also includes a scorching hip-hop song called "Jump" and the blistering "Rock Solid," which features the Dynamic Twins on its rap bridge.

In her twenties with a fairly strong repertoire of hits, Lewis bleached her hair (like Madonna), formed her own label (ditto), and released *Remember*. The opening, "I Now Live," (another Ray song) is a howling piece of swamp rock with rapped background and interlude. One of Lewis's best tracks ever, it proclaims the simple message, "I now live because Christ died." The title track to *Remember* is a nice adult contemporary ballad with an unconventional Easter theme and implicit eucharistic associations (Luke 22:19). A cover of **Keith Green**'s "Grace by Which I Stand" exemplifies Lewis's ongoing venture into praise and worship music. *The Bride* takes its title from Isaiah 62:5 and emphasizes the great love that God has for humanity. The album features Lewis's most rocking song ever, "You'll Be Back for Me" (a screaming exultation in anticipation of Christ's return), and a jazz-lounge track called "Jesus Belongs in Your Heart," sung in the seductive style of a '20s torch singer. These are sung back to back with inspirational church songs, including traditional versions of the hymns "My Redeemer Lives" and "Amazing Grace." More of the latter would fill an entire album in 1995.

Beauty for Ashes is unanimously regarded as Lewis's finest work. When it came out, reviewers coined the term "dark worship" to describe its unique style—worshipful songs that seemed to transcend the usual superficiality of praise choruses to express faith borne of pain. This ironic mood is immediately established in the standout opening track, "The Beauty of the Cross." The album's title track is a rich and rousing number performed with worship leader extraordinaire **Ron Kenoly.** The song "People Get Ready . . . Jesus Is Comin' " is likewise propelled by a rollicking dance rhythm that would provide Lewis with the Number One adult contemporary hit of the year on Christian radio. "It's Heaven" and "God's Been Good to Me" have a similar lift to them, and "Over Me" (composed by **Maria McKee**) is an aggressive song with Middle Eastern guitar and a worldbeat chorus. This time, the quiet moments do not drive the album down but provide some of its strongest moments. "Healing Oil," written by Lewis's brother-in-law **Chris Lizotte,** closes the album with a song that sets the thoughts of a terminally ill person to a haunting, opaque tune.

Gold takes its title from Job 23:10 and reflects the theme that life's hardships can be ultimately redemptive. The title song to this album, again written by Lizotte, is sung in a nightclub torch singer style, offering comfort to "those who mourn"—in keeping with Jesus' beatitude (Matthew 5:4). Lewis and Ray's "Dyer Road" and "Not the Same" are rocking pop songs similar to what **Lone Justice** might have done. Lewis's own "Tomorrow" is an upbeat number that points up the problem with complacency and procrastination: "Tomorrow is much easier to deal with than today / But when tomorrow comes, I still don't want to change." As for ballads, her in-love-with-Jesus

take on Ray's "Be with Him" is especially sweet, and her rendition of Anne Barbour's "For Such a Time as This," profound.

The aforementioned leather pants come into play on *Fearless*. The album cover and ubiquitous print ads for the project depicted Lewis in what looked like a Calvin Klein ad, posing in ultra-skintight black leather pants and a sleeveless blouse, her head thrown back and screaming. The shot by noted photographer Sonya Koskoff was provocative artistically as well as sexually, and yet—Christian audiences being (a little) more mature than they were in the mid '80s—it did not precipitate the sort of scandal that previously attended **Amy Grant**'s leopard-skin outfit. It did illustrate the theme of the album with precious irony. A woman screaming can be a symbol of fear—but here is an over-thirty, conservative Christian woman who apparently likes the way her body looks and is not going to allow the values of the ignorant to take that away from her. The project's theme verse was 2 Timothy 1:7 ("God did not give us a spirit of timidity") and Koskoff's photo of screaming, leather-clad Lewis evokes anything but timidity. As for the music, *Fearless* puts Lewis more squarely in the mainstream pop vein than previous projects. "Reach Out" has a retro-'70s soul sound, and "Satisfied" owes more than a little to disco. "I Still Believe" was written and produced by **Kirk Franklin,** and "What a Fool I've Been" features guest rapping by **T-Bone** and J-Raw. "One Man" is the album's all-out rocker, a song that one critic would call a female counterpart to **DC Talk**'s "Supernatural." Lyrically, "One Man" identifies Christ as the only person who can truly change the world, and "Only Fools" skews materialism with pithy lines like "It is better to be poor than a liar." Musically, Jyro Xhan of **Fold Zandura** covers some tracks with swirling synthesizers, and Vinnie Colaiuta (a member of Sting's post-Police band) adds big electric guitars and manic drums. On the secular sound, Lewis would say, "I have a gift that appeals to people outside the church." As for the pants, she would maintain, "I've worn them for two-and-a-half years." And with regard to both, she concludes, "You can be fashionable and still live a very God-fearing, holy life."

Lewis has also recorded Spanish-language versions of her albums titled *Recuerdos, La Esposa, Himnos de Mi Vida, La Belleza de la Cruz,* and *Oro*. Compilations include three different collections of hits *(Simply the Best, Greatest Hits, More),* two live albums *(Best of the Harvest* and *Woodlands),* and a remix collection suitable for skating rinks or aerobic classes.

Christian radio hits: "Runnin' " (# 12 in 1988); "You Didn't Have to Do It" (# 3 in 1989); "It's Real" (# 14 in 1989); "God Is Somebody" (# 3 in 1990); "Rock Solid" (# 1 for 2 weeks in 1990); "Let Love In" (# 24 in 1991); "Jump" (# 13 in 1991); "Shine, Jesus, Shine" (# 13 in 1992); "I Now Live" (# 6 in 1992); "Lonely" (# 24 in 1993); "You'll Be Back for Me" (# 2 in 1994); "Little Jackie" (# 12 in 1994); "Joyful, Joyful" (# 7 in 1995); "People Get Ready . . . Jesus Is Coming" (# 1 for 3 weeks in 1995); "Beauty for Ashes" [with **Ron Kenoly**] (# 5 in 1997); "The Beauty of the

Cross" (# 14 in 1997); "God's Been Good to Me" (# 1 in 1997); "The Lion and the Lamb" (# 10 in 1997); "Not the Same" (# 5 in 1998); "Lord, I Believe" (# 13 in 1998); "Dyer Road" (# 30 in 1999).

Dove Awards: 1998 Female Vocalist; 1998 Spanish Language Album *(Le Belleza de la Cruz)*; 1999 Spanish Language Album *(Oro)*.

Liaison

Larry Melby, bass, voc.; Tim Melby, gtr.; et al. // Bill Baumgart, kybrd. (+ 1991, − 1992); Kelly Burns, bass (+ 1991, − 1992); Doug Matthews, drums (+ 1991, − 1992); Glenn Pierce, gtr. (+ 1991, − 1992). 1989—*Liaison* (Frontline); 1991—*Urgency*; 1992—*Hard Hitter*; 1996—*Cool Water* (Inundated).

Liaison was an arena rock band cast in the same mold as the **Allies** or **Idle Cure.** The latter reference is especially telling since the group was signed to Frontline by producer Bill Baumgart, who was also responsible for **Idle Cure**'s contract. Baumgart produced the band's albums and on *Urgency* was even listed as a member of the group, along with various session musicians. The real core of Liaison, however, were the Melby brothers (Larry and Tim), who grew up in a Christian home in Watford City, North Dakota, where they listened to **Phil Keaggy** and other contemporary Christian music acts throughout their childhood.

Critics were not always kind to Liaison's music. Brian Quincy Newcomb soundly thrashed the debut album in *CCM* as formulaic, but the song "You Are His Main Concern" does spice its metal guitar assault with a tasty sax solo. On their second project, the group attained a grittier sound. The song "Friend to the World" incorporates elements of the Beatles' "Eleanor Rigby." The Melbys attain their finest hour on *Hard Hitter,* on which they adopt the near-metal hard rock sound of bands like **Guardian.** Indeed, **Tony Palacios** plays guitar on the album, along with Oz Fox and **Lanny Cordola.** "Attitude" and "Violent Burning" encourage believers to remain strong and endure tests that come their way. As with many of Christian music's hard-rocking bands, however, the songs that usually landed on the radio were the power ballads ("Go and Sin No More," "Free Will"—not the Rush song—and "As Far As the East Is from the West"). After Liaison disbanded the Melby brothers continued to perform as a duo. Bill Baumgart released a solo album on Frontline, which produced the Christian radio hit "The Only Game in Town" (# 11 in 1988).

Christian radio hits: "Go and Sin No More" (# 9 in 1989); "The Way, The Truth, The Life" (# 5 in 1990); "Free Will" (# 9 in 1991); "Friend to the World" (# 14 in 1992); "Who Can Heal the Pain" (# 4 in 1993); "As Far As the East Is from the West" (# 16 in 1993).

The Liberated Wailing Wall

1973—*Hineni! Here I Am!* (Hineni); 1974—*I Am Not Ashamed* (Tempo); 1976—*We Were Like Dreamers* (Hineni); 1979—*Who Hath Believed Our Report;* 1980—*Favorites;* 1984—*Messianic Joy;* 1986—*Times and Seasons* (Jews for Jesus); 1990—*Let Us Exalt His Name Together;* 1991—*He Will Return;* date unknown—*David's Hope;* 2000—*This Is Jerusalem.*

The Liberated Wailing Wall is a musical outreach of the organization Jews for Jesus, which was founded in 1973 by Moishe Rosen. The group has roots in the Jesus movement, as many of the cause-oriented or countercultural young people embracing Christianity in that revival were of Jewish background. The organization became quite controversial because it targeted traditional Jews for evangelism and was, in some instances, highly effective at converting them to faith in Christ. Rosen claims the key to their effectiveness was attaining a degree of insulation against rejection and criticism. "We had to stop trying to avoid conflict," he explains. "Most workers in Jewish evangelism were well-meaning Gentile Christians who, above all, sought the goodwill of the Jewish community . . . as soon as missionary efforts began to be effective, Jewish leaders reacted with a show of displeasure and accused them of insensitive or offensive methods." The Jews for Jesus anticipated such displeasure while, at the same time, embracing cultural and even religious Judaism in ways that made charges of anti-Semitism difficult to sustain. The group has maintained, for instance, that there is no conflict between Jewish people accepting the cardinal doctrines of Christianity while continuing to celebrate such festivals as Passover and the Day of Atonement. Rosen led the group until 1996, at which point David Brickner took over as the new executive director.

Still active in the year 2001, The Liberated Wailing Wall takes the form of a choral ensemble with a constantly changing membership. They recruit members each year and travel about doing programs at churches. Of course, many Christian denominations, parachurch organizations, and even individual congregations sponsor similar music-and-witness teams. But in the '70s, The Liberated Wailing Wall was generally regarded as one more band performing Jesus music—and music of a distinctive style at that. The group began in 1971 as an informal group of singers who would perform on street corners in San Francisco. In 1972, they performed their first official concert at the All Lutheran Youth Gathering in Houston, Texas, and adopted the name Liberated Wailing Wall, suggested by member Benyonim Ellegant. Other influential members in the early years include Stuart Dauermann, Steffi Geiser, and Tuvya Zaretsky. The group traveled the country in a Dodge Ram Van, performing at churches and campuses and writing much of their now classic material in the van along the way. By the year 2002, some 180 different persons had been members of The Liberated Wailing Wall, and the group's modus operandus remained essentially the same, with the Dodge Ram being replaced by a converted thirty-four-foot bus with bunks and a galley on board.

The Liberated Wailing Wall's first two albums are particularly significant for the history of contemporary Christian music. Both were produced by Rick Coghill of **Lamb,** and the music is the same blend of upbeat folk songs and somber ballads associated with that group—except that the larger ensemble often provides for much more complex and dynamic arrangements. Rosen says that the style of the music was largely drawn from "Israeli folk dance music or from the borscht belt or from Yiddish theater." The group used electric guitars and a full rhythm section, but unlike most musical groups associated with the Jesus movement, they composed and performed songs that could easily be adapted for use in traditional congregations (e.g., sung by chancel choirs). The title song to *Hineni!* is an energetic Hebrew folk tune based on Isaiah 6:8; "I Am Not Ashamed," by contrast, begins with a solo voice intoning words from Romans 1:16, which are later picked up by a chorus and sung in multiple layers. Most of the group's songs were based on Scripture and, all told, The Liberated Wailing Wall can be cited alongside **2nd Chapter of Acts** and **John Michael Talbot** as providing some of the finest liturgical and worship music to come out of the Jesus movement.

Liberation Suite

Randy Hill, drums; Howard Lyon, tromb., voc.; David Bynum, bass, sax., voc. (−1980); Paul Lyon, trump., flute, voc. (−1980); Barry Bynum, voc., gtr., kybrd. (−1994) // Jim Hazel, gtr. (+ 1980); Fred Perez, bass (+ 1980, −1990); James Yager, kybrd., voc. (+ 1980). 1975—*Liberation Suite* (Myrrh UK); 1980—*Stride for Stride* (Chapel Lane); 1990—*Water and Blood* (Spark).

www.liberationsuite.com

Long before Christian ska, there was Liberation Suite, incorporating brass with hard-rocking Jesus music, first in the Texas hill country, and then in war-torn Northern Ireland and the British Isles. LibSuite, as they were usually called, was one of two important Christian groups to be part of the Texas Jesus movement. In the mid '70s—years before **ArkAngel,** much less **King's X,** were on the scene—it was just Liberation Suite and **Hope of Glory** in the Lone Star State. LibSuite's sound was likened to Chicago Transit Authority at the time (i.e., to the *rock* band that did "I'm a Man" and "Beginnings," not to the abbreviated adult contemporary remnant that later did all those "Hard for Me to Say I'm Sorry" pop songs). Indeed, Liberation Suite regularly performed "Where Do We Go from Here?" in their concerts, along with blistering versions of the Doobie Brothers' "Jesus Is Just Alright" and **Eric Clapton**'s "Presence of the Lord." Their first album remains one of the most important—and one of the best—contributions of the era.

The group formed in the small town of San Marcos, Texas, where all five members were part of the charismatic, nondenominational Hill Country Faith Ministries. The group consisted of two sets of brothers plus drummer Randy Hill, who would ultimately become the "keeper of the flame" in Mick

Fleetwood fashion, holding things together through numerous personnel changes. Barry Bynum led the band, for instance, and is featured on all three albums, though he would not continue to perform with the group after 1994. Bynum and Hill had met when they were just fourteen; in high school they hooked up with the Lyon brothers, who were sons of a band director, and LibSuite was born. The teenagers all had born-again, personal-salvation conversion experiences while still in high school, and LibSuite turned into one of the country's first Christian rock bands—they thought they were the *only* Christian rock band for some time, before heading west and learning about **Love Song** and **J.C. Power Outlet.** At first the band simply backed a choral group called Sound 70, but then, as Paul Lyon told *Harmony* magazine, they all got "baptized in the Holy Spirit" and began to realize their music served a greater purpose. Like true Jesus freaks, they joined a traveling tent ministry called "Christ Is the Answer" that moved from city to city putting on rallies every evening for the curious onlookers. LibSuite would play to draw a crowd and evangelist Bill Lowry would preach. Joe Greer, later guitarist for the band called **e,** was also a part of this Christian rock and roll circus. **Benny Hester** got saved at one of the rallies, as did Hill's future wife. Back in San Marcos, the group was told by a visiting preacher (Ray Barnett) that their music would go over well in Europe, and he offered them accommodations in his home, if they ever should feel led to visit. They did feel led, and the whole band flew to Northern Ireland without any clue as to what they would do when they arrived. They maintain that they did not even realize there was a war going on ("All I knew about Ireland was that it was really green and had a lot of sheep," Hill recalls), but they ended up staying for six months near Belfast during one of the bloodiest periods of the conflict. During that time, they would set up in downtown areas that had been blocked off due to car bombings, play their music to draw a crowd, and preach a message of Christ and reconciliation. In 1974, LibSuite played at the very first *Greenbelt* festival in England and subsequently became one of the top Christian bands in that country. For a time, **Terry Clark** (kybrd.), his brother Duane (bass), and keyboardist Stephen Houston were added to the group for an important tour of Europe with **Chuck Girard.**

Liberation Suite was produced by **John Pantry** and features a number of classic Jesus music songs. "Led to Roam" and "I Wanna Be with You" are Zeppelinesque, blues-rock numbers showcasing Bynum's guitar solos. "Run, Run, Lucifer" is progressive art-rock, drawing comparisons perhaps to Supertramp, **Kansas,** and Styx. The song starts out slow (like almost every Styx song) and then suddenly breaks into a fast smorgasbord of artsy influences and styles: Jethro Tull flute, a gang-vocal chorus, and even a Spanky-and-Our-Gang ba-de-ba-de-bah a capella interlude. In the early '70s it seemed incredibly cool to have so much going on in one song, and "Run, Run, Lucifer" was a rare example of Christian music that was more innovative than much of what was being produced in the general market. "Oh, Lord, You Know That I Feel So Fine" and "More Than a Matter" give the brass a chance to shine and sound very much like early Chicago songs. "My Lord Is a Remedy" is a kinda dumb (i.e., humorous) country rock song. "Reaching for the Sky" is a fabulous rock-ballad, a song like Chicago's "Colour My World" or Herb Alpert's "This Guy's in Love with You" that works precisely because of its simplicity. The standout cut on the album, however, and the one that would hold up the best twenty-five years later, is the simple acoustic song "Hearken."

As an artifact of the Jesus movement, *Liberation Suite* demonstrates both the passion and naivete of that revival. "More Than a Matter" proclaims that "the end is coming soon" and that salvation is "more than a matter of going to heaven or hell," two typical emphases of the movement. As historian David Di Sabatino points out, "Run, Run, Lucifer" exemplifies the "prevalent Jesus people belief that life is a contest between the cosmic forces of good and evil," while "My Lord Is a Remedy" typifies the "mindset of most adherents that Jesus is the answer to each and every problem." The latter song actually declares, "My Lord is a remedy for the common cold." In the early '70s, at least, the church in San Marcos from which the band sprang was a neo-Pentecostal assembly that did indeed teach that people of faith should not have to be troubled by such inconveniences as colds or dandruff or bad breath; Jesus would fix it all. The message of "Hearken," on the other hand, is direct and timeless: "Hearken to the Lord, O lost generation / After searching for so many years / It's written in the pages of the Good Book / The reasons for lying and dying and so many tears."

Stride for Stride moved the group more consistently toward the art-rock style of bands like Boston or **Kansas**—and comparisons to '80s Chicago would also apply. "Where My Home Is," a song about heaven, is easy California rock in the same vein as **Sweet Comfort Band**. "Heal the Broken Hearted" is a piano ballad calling on Christians to heed Jesus' example and become instruments of healing. *Water and Blood* was something of a disaster in that the record was poorly mixed and distributed without the group's consent. In 2000, a new, remastered edition was finally made available. The opening, "Talk to You," has the pop sound of Top 40 '70s radio and addresses the listener with a divine plea similar to those that would be posted on the numerous "message from God" billboards that became popular in the late '90s: "When you got time, I've got to talk to you." The same divine-quest-for-humanity theme informs "The Distance" (based on the prodigal son story). "All Things New" is a modern folk-hymn to God's victory over evil. "Emerald Isle" is more of a rock anthem closer to the sound of the band's classic debut, with Boston-like gang vocals and some

impressive guitar work. The album concludes with a new version of "Run, Run, Lucifer."

In an interview with *Jesus People* magazine in 2000, Randy Hill would continue to extol the basic passions of primitive Jesus music as opposed to what became the contemporary Christian music industry and empire: "The Jesus movement was quickly poisoned by Christian record labels, Christian music magazines, and media hype in general. . . . There doesn't seem to be much in the way of music evangelism anymore. It's either a bunch of preaching to the choir or bands crossing over to the secular arena and not saying much of anything at all." Barry Bynum has continued to pursue a solo career, working both in Northern Ireland and in San Marcos, Texas, where he became worship leader for Hill Country Faith Ministries. He has released two albums in Europe only: *Stickin' Your Neck Out* (1995) and *To You* (1998), which are available through his website (http://barrybynum.tripod.com/BarryBynum.html).

Lies Damned Lies

Steve Butler; Charles Irvine; Dot Reid. 1990—*Lies Damned Lies* (label unknown); 1991—*Flying Kites*; 1993—*The Human Dress*; 1995—*Release the Peace*; 1996—*Lamentations* (Sticky Music).

Lies Damned Lies is a progressive British outfit composed of musicians who are involved with the *Greenbelt* festival and with a modern worship program known as the Late Late Service. They also run the Sticky Music company. The music of Lies Damned Lies is moody, spacious, and complex, with male vocals reminiscent of Sting. Their albums have met with more critical acclaim than commercial success, particularly in America. *Lamentations* is based on the book of the Bible by that name and develops the theme that (as stated in the liner notes) "the lament is the song without which our claims to happiness turn to lies." The songs are often lyrically concise, featuring lines that strongly recall biblical passages: "Jerusalem, daughters of Jerusalem / What can I say to you? / How can I comfort you?" ("Lamentations I").

Lifehouse

Jason Wade, voc., gtr.; Sergio Andrade, bass; et al. 2000—*No Name Face* (DreamWorks).

www.lifehousemusic.com

Originally known as BLYSS, Lifehouse is a Los Angeles-based band founded by Jason Wade in 1996. Wade has roots in the Vineyard and both his parents are ministers. The group strives for a sound similar to that of general market band **Creed,** though with the exception of one song ("Quasimodo"), they do not come off quite so heavy. Their debut album opens with "Hanging by a Moment," a cry to God for help. "Sick Cycle Carousel" describes the dilemma of those trapped in addiction or other repetitive sinful behaviors. "Somebody Else's Song" describes the subliminal influence of music, by which songs can place unwanted thoughts in one's head. As with most Christian groups on general market labels, Lifehouse often crafts their songs such that the lyrics possess a certain built-in ambiguity, expressing more of a generic spirituality in a way that avoids specifically Christian language. This bothered a critic for *CCM* who noted that Wade has been alleged to espouse "a particularly humanist faith" and then spent the entire review wondering whether the group should qualify to be identified as *really* Christian. Memo from Theology 101: all Christians by definition espouse a humanist faith, since recognizing the image of God in all human beings (Genesis 1:26–27) is intrinsic to Christianity.

For trivia buffs: By the age of twenty, Jason Wade had earned a black belt in the martial art of Du Ye Chi Tao.

Life in General

Jerry Chapman; Jason LeVasseur. 1994—*Long Forgotten Toys* (Salem Mill); 1995—*Life in General* [EP]; 1996—*Gee*; 1997—*One Door Down*; 1998—*No Need to Be Lonely*; 1999—*So Long, True Love*; 2001—*The Lovely, Lovely Singing . . . .*

www.lifeingeneral.com

The acoustic duo Life in General is often described as a male version of the **Indigo Girls.** Their primary connection to Christian music lies in the fact that **Jerry Chapman** was once bassist for Two-Pound Planet and has also released a solo album with some spiritual implications. True to their name, however, Life in General does not limit its focus to the topics addressed by what is often considered to be Christian music. Chapman sings with a rich baritone while Jason LeVasseur has more of a bluesy, raspy voice. Both artists write songs and they take turns singing lead on their respective material. *No Need to Be Lonely* is a thirty-two-song, two-disc live set that includes covers of songs by Suzanne Vega and Wilco in addition to selections from the band's previous three records. On *So Long, True Love,* they produce a more polished set with some electric guitars, plus mandolins, dobros, pedal steel, and fiddles. The more enhanced sound recalls Uncle Tupelo in places. *The Lovely, Lovely Singing* offers ten covers of classic songs from the '60s, such as The Cyrkle's "Red Rubber Ball" and The Mamas and The Papas' "California Dreamin'." The duo also performs "If You Only Had the Time," originally performed by the '60s band Nova Local, of which Jason LeVasseur's father was a member.

Life of Riley

Timothy Clo, drums; Chris Dauphin, kybrd.; Bob Hutchins, gtr.; Kelly Hutchins, voc., gtr. 1999—*Life of Riley* (Rustproof).

Life of Riley is a brilliant pop band with female vocals hearkening back to pop's glory days of Jackie DeShannon, The Carpenters, and Petula Clark. They call their music "new stream pop." *Bandoppler* referred to them as the love child of Ben Folds Five and Dee-Lite and noted that songs like "The World's a Gonner" and "You Said" would be at home on any *Austin Powers* soundtrack. The albums opens with "Pillow for Your Soul," a bouncy bit of bubblegum that presents them as a Christian equivalent of Downey Mildew, with sassy vocals and retro grooves. The lyrics apparently refer vaguely to the "rest" that Christ offers to the weak and heavy laden (Matthew 11:21). The next song goes retro, reaching back to the swinging '20s for a jazzy beat while encouraging listeners to "smother the world with glee." The song "It's All Good" draws on Romans 8:28 for a good dose of positive thinking. From start to finish, *Life of Riley* is sheer delight, but the single best song is "I Want to Tell the World about Your Love," a midtempo ballad with a remarkably pretty melody.

For trivia buffs: Drummer Tim Clo is the brother of Dave Clo, guitarist for **All Star United.**

Lifesavors (a.k.a. **Lifesavers, Lifesavers Underground**)

See **LSU.**

The Lifters

Chris Brigandi, gtr., voc.; Brian Ray, drums, perc.; Kass Roll, bass. 1983—*The Lifters* (MRC); 1985—*What's Love All About.*

The Lifters are a Christian band that left a legacy of historical interest, at least. The California band was formed by three members of the **Lifesavors'** road crew. They were marketed on their pretty-boy good looks as though they were a Christian version of New Kids on the Block (though they actually preceded that group by a couple of years), but their sound was more like a Christian version of The Stray Cats. The rockabilly style was quite innovative for the Christian scene, and (along with **Undercover** and **Youth Choir**) The Lifters became part of Maranatha Music's second wave of innovation as acts on the MRC label (a subdivision of Maranatha) brought about a sort of minirevival recalling the golden years of the Jesus movement a decade before. The group's finest moment may be the title song to their second album; "What's Love All About" is a splendid rock and roll romp with an echo chorus: "You gotta be a servant like the Lord / Serve your brother forevermore / That's what love's all about." After two albums that didn't do as well as they deserved, Brigandi reformed the band, adding a fifteen-year-old pretty girl named **Crystal Lewis** to the mix (see **Wild Blue Yonder**). Lewis married Brian Ray, who wasn't in **Wild Blue Yonder** but who did turn out to be a very talented composer. She would later reunite with Chris Brigandi (who turned out to be a very talented guitarist and producer) in **The Screamin' Rays.**

Lightforce

See **Mortification.**

Like David

Patrick Fallon, bass; Marc Haley, voc., gtr.; Steven Mize, drums. 2000—*Beyond the Shifting Sand* (Bettie Rocket); 2001—*It Started with Twelve.*

Like David is a central California hardcore band that likes to describe itself as "a charismatic, Jewish Christian hard rock band." Musically, the band sounds a lot like The Deftones, and front man Marc Haley admits to strong influence of such Christian acts as **Focused, Overcome, Strongarm,** and **Unashamed.** The band is ministry-oriented and loves to play in bars and other secular establishments where they are sometimes able to engage audience members in conversations about their relationship with God. Their first album, *Beyond the Shifting Sand,* concludes with "A Time for New," a cathartic statement of God's intent to renew and restore humanity. In reviewing the second project *(It Started with Twelve),* HM observed somewhat sardonically that the band lacks originality musically and so "the prime justification for Like David's existence is as a Christian alternative for kids who can't or don't want to listen to bands that might stain their easily molded minds." But it is, of course, possible that some fans might find Like David's songs to be positively edifying or inspiring as opposed to simply nonperverting. A song called "Why Did Sarah Laugh?" encourages persistent faith in a manner that has specific significance for Pentecostal front man Marc Haley: his brother was paralyzed in an accident involving a trampoline and, he says, "God gave us a promise that he would walk again. . . . it's been six years now, but a promise from God never turns void. It takes faith to believe, to hold on."

Lil' Raskull

Date unknown—*Controverse All-Star* (Grapetree); 1997—*Cross Bearing;* 1998—*Glory 2 Glory;* 1999—*Certified Southern Hits; Because It Was Written* (Wine-O); 2000—*The Day After* (Grapetree).

One of Grapetree's family of rappers, Lil' Raskull is typical of those artists in that very little information is available concerning him—including his given name. According to the official press release, he grew up in the Fifth Ward, "one of Houston's worst ghettos," and turned to a life that involved gang violence, drug dealing, and prostitution before being convicted by the still, small voice of God to turn his life over to Jesus. He was then assisted by Christian rapper Nuwine who

brought him to church and prepared him for his new career. Apparently, Lil' Raskull made a preconversion mainstream rap album with Johnnie B. Walker (a.k.a. Tiger) for Dad Game Records in 1991. His trademark style involves an especially fast delivery in an authoritative voice. His first Christian album features the song, "Hell Ain't Fo Ya," which he says he wrote after heeding the advice of "a prophet" to stay in his house and fast and pray until God gave him something. Lyrically, Lil' Raskull's songs tend to focus on life on the streets. *The Day After* addresses the difficulties of living for Christ in the long haul, in the time following the initial "conversion rush" of salvation.

Ji Lim

1994—*Through Iron Walls* (Intersound).

Ji Lim is a native Korean, born in Jeonju, who studied classical music from childhood. After moving to Silver Bay, New York, he became a member of a string quartet while still a teen, and just after graduating from high school became a Christian through the influence of a friend who, he says, "lived Christ." Lim entered Temple University but eventually determined to enter the Christian music scene and transferred to Lancaster Bible College in Pennsylvania, where he got a degree in youth ministry. His album *Through Iron Walls* showcases mellow vocals against smooth guitar leads on a collection of original songs. *True Tunes* would liken the overall style to dance-pop groups like Erasure and Midge Ure. "If Only," "Full of Wonder," and "Walls" all have an upbeat, driving style, while "Without You with Me" is a more dreamy, midtempo number. The latter tune exemplifies Lim's poetic lyrics: "Without you with me, I can't fly, I can't dream/ Without you with me I am faith without love." Elsewhere, the song "Tonight" explores the paradoxes of faith (e.g., losing life to find it), and "Proud of Me" offers the plea of a son for parental acceptance even "when I can't fit your mold." A number of Christian artists assisted with *Through Iron Walls,* including **Jimmy A, Bob Carlisle,** and Scott Denté (of **Out of the Grey).** In the year 2002, Lim was serving as the assistant pastor of a church in Philadelphia and running Kurios Records, which caters to Korean Americans.

Christian radio hits: "Without You with Me" (# 1 in 1994); "Tonight" (# 2 in 1994); "Full of Wonder" (# 14 in 1994).

Limpic and Rayburn (and **Gerry Limpic**)

Gerry Limpic, voc., gtr.; Mark Rayburn, voc., gtr. As Limpic and Rayburn: 1976—*Limpic and Rayburn, with Dave Pollard* (Fanfare); 1978—*Caught in the Crossfire* (Myrrh). As Gerry Limpic: 1980—*Gentle Touch.*

Limpic and Rayburn was an acoustic duo that performed from 1974 to 1980, at which point Gerry Limpic embarked on a solo career. Limpic had previously been a member of the band Random Sample. *Caught in the Crossfire* is so definitively '70s that it actually portrays the artists in bell-bottomed leisure suits on the cover. Limpic was the principal songwriter, and he crafted lyrics with a vulnerability atypical for Christian music of the era. In the song "Crossfire" he confesses, "I'm a learner, learning slow / And the more I learn of You, the less I know." The same mood would continue on his solo album in songs like "Stranger" and "Alone," but there was also now a tone of judgment against a world gone crazy ("Ain't No Wonder," "America Babylon")—combined with an even stronger note of invitation for lonely people to "feel the gentle touch" of God's love ("Gentle Touch of Your Love"). "The God Who Is There" appears to be inspired by the writings of the popular philosopher Francis Schaeffer.

Christian radio hits: Gerry Limpic: "Gentle Touch of Your Love" (# 18 in 1980).

Lind

1994—*Stations* (Someone Up There).

Singer/songwriter Derek Lind comes straight out of the Woody Guthrie tradition with songs and inflections that recall early, pre-Newport, non-electric **Bob Dylan,** albeit with a voice closer to that of Gordon Lightfoot. His songs are written from an obviously Christian perspective ("This World Is Not My Home"), but are not at all preachy. Lind prefers social commentary and family themes. The standout track on *Stations* is the opening, "When the Bough Breaks," which reflects on his upbringing by caring, praying parents.

Little Anthony

1980—*Daylight* (MCA).

Little Anthony, born Jerome Anthony Gourdine in New York City in 1940, was the titular leader of the late-'50s doo-wop group Little Anthony and the Imperials. That group first hit big with "Tears on My Pillow" (# 4 in 1958). They later had hits with "Goin' Out of My Head" (# 6 in 1964) and "Hurt So Bad" (# 9 in 1965) and continued to record with moderate success throughout the '70s. Little Anthony's name owes to the fact that when the Imperials formed, he was only sixteen years old and only 5'4" in height; he soon grew to 5'10" but the name stuck. The all-black Imperials who backed Little Anthony are a completely different group than the mostly white **Imperials** in gospel music. In the late '70s, Little Anthony announced that he had become a born-again Christian and he made a solo album of gospel material produced by **B. J. Thomas.** "Reach Up" is regarded as the best song. It is also the only number that

Little Anthony wrote and the only one performed in his typical style. Otherwise, the album features traditional gospel songs ("Walk on Water," "Gospel Train") performed in an adult contemporary style that *CCM* would complain about sounding too "white." Little Anthony did not record any more gospel music. In 1992 he reformed the Imperials and took to the road playing oldies shows.

Little Richard

Selected: 1964—*Sings the Gospel* (Prime Cuts); 1979—*God's Beautiful City* (Word); 1986—*Lifetime Friend* (Warner Bros.); 1989—*It's Real* (Lection); 1999—*God Is Real* (Peacock).

www.kolumbus.fi/timrei/lre.htm

Little Richard is indisputably one of the most significant pioneers in the history of rock and roll and he is also famous for his Christianity. Nevertheless, he is not accorded much attention in the contemporary Christian music scene partly because he has made few recordings reflective of his faith and partly because his flamboyant and frequent bouts with what he calls "backsliding" have kept him at a distance from the more officially respectable contemporary Christian and traditional gospel artists. His eclectic theology and (reformed?) homosexuality haven't helped much either.

Born Richard Penniman in Macon, Georgia, in 1932, the man who would become Little Richard was brought up in a fairly devout Seventh-day Adventist family (his father was a bootlegger, but his grandfather and two uncles were preachers). He played piano and sang in church but at the age of thirteen was expelled from his family and home for his homosexual activities. His father told him, "My father had seven sons and I wanted seven sons. You've spoiled it, you're only half a son." Richard was taken in by a white couple (Ann and Johnny Johnson) who ran a local tavern, where he began performing. After playing with a number of bands and making a few unsuccessful recordings, he hooked up with Robert "Bumps" Blackwell, the same promoter, manager, and producer who had convinced **Sam Cooke** to leave gospel for a career in secular soul. Under Blackwell's guidance, Little Richard hit huge with "Tutti Frutti," one of the first songs to cross over from R&B into the emerging genre of rock and roll and one of the first to appeal to both black and white audiences. The song was originally a lewd ditty that Blackwell had discovered the artist performing just for fun in an unguarded, off-the-clock moment. It was Blackwell who had a lyricist clean up the song's words, got a recording, and released the raucous party song in place of the gospel numbers ("He's My Star," "Wonderin' ") that Little Richard had himself submitted. Although the song only went to Number Seventeen on *Billboard*'s official charts, the album featuring it sold a phenomenal three million copies. In the next few years, Little Richard had several more hits with songs like "Long Tall Sally" (# 6 in 1956); "Jenny, Jenny" (# 10 in 1957), "Keep a Knockin'" (# 8 in 1957), and "Good Golly Miss Molly" (# 10 in 1958). In 1957, he appeared with Jayne Mansfield in the film *The Girl Can't Help It,* delivering a salacious (musical) performance that defied all moral taboos regarding interracial sexuality. Throughout this time, he lived a life of debauchery and drug addiction, which he would later recount in the authorized biography, *The Life and Times of Little Richard* by Charles White (Harmony, 1984).

In 1957, Little Richard retired from rock and roll (for the first time), due to a series of spiritual experiences. First, he says that he had a dream in which he saw his own damnation. Next, he was on a plane that experienced engine trouble and he promised God that he would reform his life if spared. Shortly thereafter, another plane that he had been scheduled to board crashed. He also says that he saw the Russian Sputnik blinking across the sky while doing a concert in Sydney and the image caused him to recall a scene from an apocalyptic tract he'd seen as a child. Penniman interpreted all these events as divine signs, so he resigned from performing to find peace with God. Although accounts of this conversion testimony have conflicted over the years, it appears that a lay minister of the Church of God of the Ten Commandments by the name of Brother Wilbur Gulley also had something to do with Penniman's (first) awakening. Gulley was apparently knocking on the doors of random Los Angeles mansions in 1957 looking for spiritually-starved souls and he found in Little Richard an eager disciple. Gulley says, "Richard was ready, both spiritually and economically, to make a break with the world of show business. Misused, ripped-off, and cheated by racists, promoters, and record companies, he was also being hassled by the Internal Revenue Service." Such matters—dreams and visions aside—may have influenced his disenchantment with the rock and roll industry.

In any case, Penniman claims that the day after seeing Sputnik, he threw his jewelry into Sydney Bay and canceled the rest of his world tour. He entered Oakwood College in Huntsville, Alabama, where he eventually graduated. While a student there, however, he was also disciplined by the Board of Elders, who warned him to keep his hands off a young student (one of the deacons' sons). He married for a time, but divorce proceedings were instituted after he was arrested for engaging in public homosexual activity at a Trailways bus station. Penniman supposedly became an ordained Seventh-day Adventist minister, though even that is uncertain; he claimed that he was a minister for many years and he apparently officiated at a number of celebrity weddings, but by 2000 was denying that he had ever been ordained or served as a minister of any church. His music company, interestingly, continued to release

products and tried to keep his conversion a secret. According to some reports, Richard abetted this process by continuing to cut second-rate rock and roll tunes on the sly even while enrolled in Bible college. What is certain is that in 1959 he recorded a number of gospel songs, some of which would be released five years later by Prime Cuts *(Sings the Gospel).* The sessions do not reveal him as a particularly powerful gospel performer. He offers traditional hymns ("Just a Closer Walk with Thee," "Precious Lord") in a decidedly nonrock fashion that seems contrived as penance for his earlier rave-ups. An expanded set of these recordings would appear in 1999 on the Peacock label *(God Is Real).* Richard is also known to have recorded some better material, including "Joy, Joy, Joy," "Why Don't You Change Your Ways," and "He's Not Just a Soldier," but these may never have been made available on CD. In 1962 he reunited with his rock and roll backup band to record a rave-up gospel number, "He Got What He Wanted (But He Lost What He Had)."

Seven years after his first declared retirement, Little Richard would attempt a comeback, as he would continue to do now and then throughout the next three decades. He never again hit the Top 40, however, despite some stellar moments, such as his collaboration with Canned Heat on "Rockin' with the King" in 1972. Then in 1976 he "returned to the fold of the church" amidst much public repentance, including renunciation of all rock music and homosexuality. For a time, he began a career as a door-to-door Bible salesman, marketing the *Black Heritage Bible,* an edition published by a group claiming that many of the heroes of Scripture were actually black. He joined a little-known sect called the Universal Remnant Church in Riverside, California, proclaiming to the world, "If God can save me, he can save anybody." He claimed for a time to be "a non-denominational minister" in the church, though again he would later maintain that he had never been a minister in any church and would insist that he had never claimed to be one. In 1979, Little Richard attempted to enter the contemporary Christian music market with an album on Word called *God's Beautiful City;* the project tanked, not least because of the artist's lack of credibility with the Christian music subculture. The music, at any rate, is again nondescript, certainly not up to the standard of quality set by the star's rock and roll output.

Little Richard's career was rejuvenated briefly by his memorable role in the 1985 motion picture *Down and Out in Beverly Hills.* In a rare interview with *CCM* magazine that year, he talked openly about his devotion to Jesus while also referencing astrology to account for his personality quirks ("I'm a Sagittarius") and indicating it doesn't really matter whether one is a Buddhist or a Jehovah's Witness or whatever as long as their heart is right with God. Such sentiments would only alienate him further from the contemporary Christian music subculture. Around 1986, he announced that he had converted to Judaism. Shortly thereafter, however, he put out a gospel album, *Lifetime Friend,* on which every song expresses specific Christian convictions. The "lifetime friend" of the title track is clearly Jesus. The album's best song, musically, is "Great Gosh A-Mighty," cowritten by **Billy Preston.** Little Richard had earlier pounded out a part of the song in the *Down and Out in Beverly Hills* film; here, he offers a noneuphemistic version, singing the lyric as "Great God Almighty" in what *CCM* would call "a successful synthesis of rock and gospel stylings." Another gospel album, titled *It's Real,* in 1989 went unreviewed, failing to register on the radar screen of secular, gospel, or contemporary Christian music audiences.

Little Richard would continue to surface here and there, appreciated as much for his flaky demeanor as for his undeniable musical gift. In 1986, he was one of the first ten inductees for the newly established Rock and Roll Hall of Fame. He offered background vocals on **U2**'s "When Love Comes to Town" in 1989. In the '90s, he would do popular commercials for McDonald's and Taco Bell and perform on a series of children's albums including Disney's *Shake It All About* (1992) and The Muppets' *Kermit Unplugged* (1994). He sang the theme song for the PBS children's program *The Magic School Bus.* In 1992, he performed at Bill Clinton's presidential inauguration. He would also appear in a number of films, including *Last Action Hero* (1993), *Why Do Fools Fall in Love?* (1998), and *Mystery, Alaska* (1999). In 2000, he was the subject of a made-for-TV biographical movie starring the actor Leon.

Kerry Livgren (and A.D.)

Personnel for A.D. : Warren Ham, voc., kybrd., woodwinds; Kerry Livgren, gtr., kybrd. // Michael Gleason, voc., kybrd. (- 1988); Dennis Holt, drums, perc. (-1988); Dave Hope, bass (-1988). As Kerry Livgren: 1980—*Seeds of Change* (Kirschner); 1989—*One of Several Possible Musiks*; 1992—*Decade* (Sparrow); 1994—*When Things Get Electric* (Numavox); 2000—*Collector's Sedition, Vol. I*; 2001—*Collector's Sedition, Vol. 2*; *Cantata: The Resurrection of Lazarus.* As Kerry Livgren A.D.: 1984—*Time Line* (CBS); 1988—*Prime Mover* (Sparrow); 1997—*Reconstructions Reconstructed* (Numavox); 1998—*Prime Mover 2* (Numavox). As A.D.: 1985—*Art of the State* (Kerygma); 1986—*Reconstructions* (Sparrow); 1988—*Compact Favorites*; 1998—*Live* (Numavox).

www.numavox.com

Born in 1949 in Topeka, Kansas, Kerry Livgren would become famous as the leader of the progressive art-rock band that bore the name of his home state. He studied for three years at Washburn University and formed **Kansas** with friends from high school in 1970. Livgren was baptized and confirmed in the Lutheran Church in America (now part of the Evangelical Lutheran Church in America), but drifted from his roots and as a young adult became engaged in a spiritual quest that is often

evident in the lyrics to such classic **Kansas** songs as "Carry On, Wayward Son" and "Dust in the Wind," or in "Another Slant," written by Livgren but recorded by **Mylon LeFevre.** He sampled various world religions, including Buddhism and Hinduism, and tried out various systems of meditation and spirituality, finally becoming enamored of a modern gnostic philosophy called Urantia. He says he shunned "born-again Christianity" as unworthy of serious intellectual engagement; basically, he had "done" Christianity as a child, and was now more interested in the exotic faiths.

Eventually, Jeff Pollard, a friend from the Louisiana rock band Le Roux, began sharing his Christian faith with Livgren in a responsible and compelling way. Partly inspired by the book *The Liberation of Planet Earth* by Hal Lindsey, the artist came to a point of crisis in a hotel room in Indianapolis in July of 1979. There, at three o'clock in the morning, he prayed, "Lord, if Jesus Christ is your son, then I want to know him. If he really is the living God, my Redeemer, and my Lord, then I want to serve him with all my heart." He reports that he immediately felt transformed, a burden lifted from his soul. He awoke the next morning to be greeted by the song "Joy to the world, the Lord has come" blaring in the hotel restaurant—an oddity for the season, but part of a local "Christmas in July" celebration. His eyes filled with tears of joy at "understanding the words to that song for the first time," such that a waitress had to inquire if he was all right. Next, he raced over to a local Christian bookstore and bought everything that he thought would help him to grow in his new life. Back in his hotel room, he called his old Lutheran pastor from catechism class to tell him that "his labors had not been in vain."

Livgren's conversion took hold and changed his life and career. He continued to work with **Kansas** (see entry) for some years, but also produced solo albums that allowed him to testify more clearly to his faith. *Seeds of Change* opens with "Just One Way," a **Kansas**-like anthem that states what had once been the motto of the Jesus movement: "There's just one way from the dark to the light . . . there's one way home," the song proclaims, with allusions to Scripture ("when I found the truth, it set me free," cf. John 8:32). "How Can You Live?" expresses amazement that anyone can find satisfaction in life apart from a relationship with God. "To Live for the King" is a bold declaration of surrender and devotion to the Maker and Ruler of all. "Ground Zero" expresses hope in the second coming of Christ, with a word of warning to those who are not prepared ("Days are short and time so dear / So very much remains to be done / It's time to speak of one so near / 'Til all hearts have been won"). Perhaps the album's best track, however, is the heavy and ominous "Mask of the Great Deceiver," a song that uses a snarling heavy metal sound to describe Satan as an enemy to be avoided. The song works precisely because it at first sounds like just one more heavy metal song about the devil—but as the lyrics sink in, they offer slow realization that maybe all this fascination with the occult is not such a great idea. Ideology aside, the song is one of the best heavy metal songs about the devil ever written and there is a supreme irony that it is actually an anti-Satan number. In that sense, an analogy might be drawn to Steppenwolf's "The Pusher" (written by Hoyt Axton) or Neil Young's "The Needle and the Damage Done"—two of rock's best "drug songs," though a close listen reveals them actually to be antidrug songs.

For *Seeds of Change,* Livgren (who is not really a singer) drew upon several vocalists: **Mylon LeFevre,** Jeff Pollard, Steve Walsh of **Kansas,** David Pack of Ambrosia, and—most surprising—Ronnie James Dio of Black Sabbath. Neither Walsh nor Dio were Christians and their prominent inclusion on the album raised some eyebrows in Christian music circles. The selection of Dio was especially controversial since the music of Black Sabbath (as the group's very name implies) was often associated with the occult—but it is Dio's voice that gives "Mask of the Great Deceiver" credibility and makes it work. The metal maestro also sings "To Live for the King," pledging his life (unwittingly, as it turns out) to serving Jesus Christ as true Lord. Livgren seemed oblivious to the controversy. He knew almost nothing about the Christian music subculture at this point and saw the album as a release to the general market. He was obviously accustomed to working with non-Christians and thought the songs worked on their own terms. He says he selected each singer carefully, matching voice and style to the content of every tune. As for Dio, Livgren would only respond, "Ronnie is no Satanist, and his work on my album gave him an opportunity to sing lyrics diametrically opposed to what he does in Black Sabbath." Dio himself would later reminisce, "I didn't know that Kerry was a born-again Christian and I didn't realize that the song ('To Live for the King') was a Christian song. He told me afterwards." Nevertheless, the singer remained happy to have been a part of the project and he felt the two songs he did were of exceptional quality.

Livgren was already working on *Time Line* as a second solo project when his continuance as a member of **Kansas** became untenable. Besides Livgren, **John Elefante,** David Hope, and touring members Warren Ham and **Michael Gleason** were all evangelical Christians—but the remainder of the band was not committed to the group's increasingly spiritual profile. When executives at CBS advised the band to tone down the Christian content of its lyrics, the best solution seemed to be a split. The Christian members formed their own band, and allowed the others to continue operating under the **Kansas** name. Thus **A.D.** was born—a group that by all accounts was a more legitimate heir to the **Kansas** tradition than the remnant band (though, to be fair, the remnant did at least persuade original

singer Steve Walsh to join up with them). Livgren's albums with this group of mostly **Kansas** alums were sometimes released under the name **A.D.** and sometimes under the name Kerry Livgren **A.D.** (no conjunction); on the latter projects, the group tended to function as a backing band.

A.D. was an unusual experiment within the developing Christian music industry. Livgren and the others had never intended for the group to be relegated to the Christian market but viewed the band as a general market act whose music, though performed by Christians, would be aimed at a secular audience and would not be limited lyrically to exposition of spiritual themes. But a legal problem arose: the men who comprised **A.D.** were still contractually bound to CBS Records and the terms of their contracts forbade them from making music that could be perceived as competing with the music of **Kansas.** A compromise decision was reached whereby they were granted a waiver to make "religious records only." The exact interpretation of what such an agreement might mean was of course ambiguous, since even as of 2002 no one in either the National Academy of Recording Arts and Sciences or the Gospel Music Association had been able to determine what makes music "religious" or "secular." Livgren himself has responded, "I don't believe that any music, in and of itself, can be secular or spiritual. All good things come from God, and music is a good thing." But legal distinctions seldom hinge on theological perception. What the agreement meant, at least, was that **A.D.**'s products could be promoted only within the religious marketplace (regardless of sound or content or predictions regarding to whom they would most appeal). Almost overnight Livgren, who was accustomed to selling out arenas as one of the biggest rock stars in the world, found himself playing in church basements where he was expected "to preach" and give altar calls—despite his protests that God had not called him to be a preacher or blessed him with the gift of exhortation. "It's a shame we never really got a chance to be heard," he would reminisce some years later. "**A.D.** could have held its own anywhere."

Time Line was actually more of a Livgren solo piece with band support than a group effort. Aside from the title track, the best cuts are probably "Tonight" and "New Age Blues." **A.D.** did tour together from 1983 to 1985, however, and as a result *Art of the State* comes across as more of a band project. The album is unanimously considered to be Livgren's post-**Kansas** zenith. It opens with the hymnic "All Creation Sings" and contains mostly Livgren compositions with a few Michael Gleason tracks ("Heartland," "Games of Chance and Circumstance"). "The Fury" possesses near-metal bombastic power, speaking of the judgment to come. "Up from the Wasteland" sets Scripture from Romans 8 to a beautiful orchestral arrangement, while also invoking Ezekiel's vision of reconnected bones to describe the glory that follows desolation (with either apocalyptic or personal reference). "Zion" addresses the ancient promise of salvation to Israel and "The Only Way to Have a Friend" encourages personal witness in the world. *Reconstructions* was described by *CCM's* Brian Quincy Newcomb as "gracefully accessible yet not characterized by a commercial feel" and as "good, up-tempo, artistically interesting *progressing* progressive rock." By the latter comment, he means to indicate that Livgren departs from the trademark **Kansas** sound and explores new avenues of classically influenced artistic rock. Gleason contributes noticeably to the project, cowriting two of its best songs ("You Are the Distance," "All Fall Down"). Other standouts are "One Golden Thread" and "Exiles." The album was later remixed and remastered as *Reconstructions Reconstructed.* After *Reconstructions,* **A.D.** all but disintegrated and on *Prime Mover* the name referred to the duo of Livgren and Warren Ham (whose rock credentials go way back to 1971 when he was a member of Bloodrock, best known for their macabre hit "D.O.A."). The record, furthermore, moves back toward the **Kansas** style. In fact, most of the songs were originally written for that group several years earlier, and one ("Fair Exchange") is actually a cover of a **Kansas** song from *Vinyl Confessions.* Livgren has said since that *Prime Mover* wasn't really an **A.D.** album but was called that to "fulfill a contractual obligation." Never completely happy with how the album turned out, Livgren would later completely re-record the entire project (with five new tracks) and release it as *Prime Mover 2.*

One of Several Possible Musiks is a true solo project with Livgren playing all the instruments and making generous use of computer sequencing. He recorded the project at his home studio on a farm near Covington, Georgia, inspired by the music of Debussy and Mahler, which, he says, "brings glory to the Creator whether they realize it or not."

The album *Decade* is a repackaging of *Seeds of Change* and *Time Line,* with a few extra songs thrown in for good measure. *When Things Get Electric* was another home recording featuring an all new band of session musicians and singers auditioned by Livgren and dubbed the "Corps de Pneuma" (Army of Spirits). The Corps includes vocalists Jasone Beddoe and Darren Rogers and **Kansas** violinist David Ragsdale. The *Collector's Sedition* albums contain all new works.

Over the years, Livgren has contributed his talents to a number of other Christian music projects, playing on three albums by **2nd Chapter of Acts** and on David Pack's *Anywhere You Go.* He also wrote two songs for **Robin Crow**'s *Electric Cinema* and one ("Heart of Iron") for **Look Up,** and played on the albums by both of those artists. Livgren has written an autobiography, *Seeds of Change* (Sparrow Books, 1983; 2nd. ed., 1991) that details the story of his life, conversion, and subse-

quent ministry. In 1989, he suffered a case of tinnitis that left him with irreparable auditory nerve damage. In 1993, he dismantled his Georgia studio and built a new, improved one in native Kansas, where he founded the independent label Numavox. In 1997, Livgren provided the soundtrack music for a DVD video release by Sony called *Odyssey into the Mind's Eye.* The project, which features computer animation set to instrumental music, became the best-selling DVD in that company's history. In 2000, Livgren and Hope took part in a surprising **Kansas** reunion.

For trivia buffs: the song "Whiskey Seed" (about the dangerous allure of alcohol) is the only song in the Livgren/**A.D.**/**Kansas** catalog to feature the artist on lead vocals. Livgren jokingly refers to it as "my vocal debut and swansong."

Christian radio hits: As A.D.: "The Only Way to Have a Friend" (# 12 in 1985); "No Standing" (# 13 in 1986); "One More Song" (# 8 in 1989).

Dove Awards: 1990 Instrumental Album *(One of Several Possible Musiks).*

Living Sacrifice

Bruce Fitzhugh, gtr., voc.; Lance Garvin, drums; Dan (D.J.) Johnson, voc. (–1997); Jason Truby, gtr. (–2000) // Chris Truby, bass (+ 1995, –2000); Rocky Gray, gtr. (+ 2000); Arthur Green, bass (+ 2000); Matt Putman, perc. (+ 2000). 1991—*Living Sacrifice* (R.E.X.); 1992—*Non-Existent;* 1994—*Inhabit;* 1997—*Reborn* (Tooth and Nail); 2000—*The Hammering Process.*

www.livingsacrifice.com

Living Sacrifice began as a thrash metal band from Little Rock, Arkansas. Almost a decade after the release of their debut album, *Phantom Tollbooth* would still maintain that "no other Christian metal album has captured pounding, pure heavy thrash" as theirs did. At that time, all four members were still in their late teens. After three albums, D.J. Johnson left to attend Bible college and Bruce Fitzhugh took over as lead singer. Johnson had also been the band's primary composer, responsible for its trademark abstract, poetic lyrics. The group's name derives from Romans 12:2.

As indicated, the debut album is considered a classic of Christian thrash metal. Most critics and fans thought the band sounded similar to Slayer, the king of thrash in the general market. Living Sacrifice was touted as "the Christian alternative to Slayer" by metalheads who thought the latter band's blasphemous and violence-prone songs were inappropriate. Living Sacrifice imbues violent imagery with spiritual intent on "Phargx Imas," a song that describes the final judgment as a harvest of souls with reference to swinging sickles and vats overflowing with blood. On a lighter note, "Dealing with Ignorance" urges Christians to "exercise gentleness" toward those who shun believers because of their faith. On the sophomore effort, *Non-Existent,* the band begins to move toward death metal, with Johnson providing more of the growling, dark vocals associated with that subgenre. "Enthroned" is perhaps the first Christian death metal worship song. *Non-Existent* opens with a song written by Scott Albert of **Circle of Dust** ("Emerge"). Other songs deal with God's "plan of salvation" ("Atonement"), drug abuse ("Chemical Straight-Jacket"), and bigotry ("Without Distinction"). The first big change in the band's sound came with *Inhabit* after, as Johnson would explain to *HM,* he had time to practice the art of growling and get it down (*True Tunes* said, "Try to imagine if Freddie Krueger should decide to become a singer"). *Inhabit* became something of a breakthrough album commercially, bringing the band to the attention of a wider audience, who likened them now less to **Believer** or Slayer than to **Crucified** or Sepultura. Lyrically, the song "Not Beneath" stresses the Christian position of being "more than conquerors" through Christ (Romans 8:37). "Departure" is about adults coping with abuse from their childhood; "Darken" is an attack on liberalism inspired by Rush Limbaugh.

With Fitzhugh on vocals, *Reborn* seems almost to be by an entirely different group. All of the death metal references are replaced by a basic hard rock sound reminiscent of such mainstream groups as Sepultura, Tool, Helmet, or even nonrapping Korn. "Awakening" displays a particularly deep groove and the band surprises with an acoustic instrumental worship tune called "Presence of God." With even more personnel changes, the band goes for a straight-on metal sound on *The Hammering Process.* This album was praised by many critics as the group's best work to date, recapturing the speed metal glories of '80s bands. New guitarist Rocky Gray's blitzkrieg solos shine on the opening "Flatliner." Lyrically, Living Sacrifice continues to focus darkly on the dismal nature of life apart from God, though on "Altered Life" Fitzhugh screams more positively about the hope and peace that are attainable through faith. The group chose the title of *The Hammering Process* from a C. S. Lewis quote about God shaping people into God's image. Fitzhugh says, "It spoke to us personally in that, if you have a relationship with God, he never stops trying to instill his nature into us through his Word—it is a hammering process. Plus, it sounds metal."

Chris Lizotte

1991—*Free* (Frontline); 1992—*Chris Lizotte and Soul Motion* (New Breed); 1994—*Long Time Comin'* (Metro One); 1995—*Human Kind*; 1997—*Big Heavy World*; 2000—*Perfect Love*.

CCM magazine once said that "somebody upstairs gave Chris Lizotte a voice for the blues and a heart for praise." The Christian singer, who is a part of the Vineyard Fellowship in Anaheim, California, describes his diverse music as "steeped in the R&B tradition." For a few years, he was associated with the tiny genre of Christian blues (cf. **Glenn Kaiser, Darrell**

Mansfield). Lizotte's vocal delivery is often compared to that of Joe Cocker, and on his first two albums he performed with a band that included blues guitarist Ray MacDonald, who has also recorded under the name **Sleepy Ray.** He also sang on two blues albums in 1993 as a member of **Shack of Peasants.** Eventually, Lizotte signed with Metro One, the record company founded by his sister-in-law **Crystal Lewis** and her husband Brian Ray.

The blues influence is especially strong on Lizotte's sophomore project *(Chris Lizotte and Soul Motion),* the best known of his early works. *Long Time Comin'* takes a step toward praise and worship with its ballads and toward rock with a song ("Hold Me Up") that features duet vocals with **Maria McKee.** *HM* magazine extolled *Human Kind* as "chock full of those Midwestern tunes that are written too well not to like." Still, the blues licks are all but replaced on that album by folksy story songs ("The Sun Went Away") and, again, worshipful ballads ("Psalm 69"). As such, Lizotte's gift for composing becomes more evident, as his mostly autobiographical songs express thoughts about God and life with an intimacy that avoids cliché. In "I Got It All" he expresses profound gratitude for family, friends, and career. *Big Heavy World* sports the song "Gold," which was covered by **Crystal Lewis** as the title track for her 1998 album. "The Almighty" describes the greatness of God. "Breath of God" (also recorded by **Dicky Ochoa**) contains the lyric, "I don't wanna feel the breath of God / On the back of my neck anymore / I wanna feel it on my face." *Perfect Love* is a live recording of a praise festival at which Lizotte served as worship leader.

Lloyd

Eric Miller, gtr.; Rick Weinland, drums; Daryl Youngblood, voc., gtr. // Wade Wolf, bass (+ 1999). 1998—*Thoughts from a Driveway* (Pamplin).

Lloyd is the second Christian rock band to be organized by Daryl Youngblood and Rick Weinland, formerly of **Imagine This.** The band dissents from the previous group's retro-'70s and quasi-metal sound in favor of straightforward hard pop in line with what was being labeled "alternative" in the late '90s (Matchbox 20, Goo Goo Dolls). The closest references to their sound, however, would actually come from other Christian artists, combining elements of **All Star United, Seven Day Jesus,** and **Switchfoot.** The group's name is essentially meaningless, being taken from Eric Miller's pet goldfish (which died while they were on tour). The debut album title reflects the fact that the songs evolved lyrically from gab-fests the members held on Rick's or Daryl's front porch. *CCM* rightly notes that "where **Imagine This** aimed for anthemic songs of generalized feelings, Lloyd reflects a more personal viewpoint."

Driveway's lead-off song, "I Don't Wanna Know," is the most similar to **Imagine This** material, a joyful paean to blissful ignorance ("I don't wanna know all the answers on this earth / All I need to know is that You're always right there"). A similar attitude infuses the humility of "Human" ("Until we see the limits of our wits / We'll never see that we are only human"). The album's absolute standout is "Forever Song," a meaningful anticipation of eternal life set to a Gin Blossoms-like tune. Less profound are a knee-jerk response to blasphemer Marilyn Manson ("Mr. Warner"—after that artist's real name, Brian Warner) and the summary of a spiritual lesson learned from watching *The Mary Tyler Moore Show* ("Mary Tyler Moore"). The former song does contain one good line: "I bet it kills you to be forced to see you're no more a sinner than a man like me."

Christian radio hits: "Forever Song" (# 7 in 1998); "I Don't Wanna Know" (# 6 in 1999).

Lone Justice

See **Maria McKee.**

Greg Long

1994—*Cross My Heart* (Pakaderm); 1995—*Days of Grace* (Myrrh); 1998—*Jesus Saves*; 2001—*Now* (Word).

www.greglong.com

A singer/songwriter from South Dakota, Greg Long offers soulful interpretations of adult contemporary material in the same vein as **Clay Crosse** or **Bryan Duncan.** He has a distinctive voice, at times reminiscent of Barry Gibb, but never imitative of any other artist. Long grew up in a strict Christian home where he listened mainly to Christian music by artists like **Andraé Crouch, The Imperials,** and **Russ Taff,** though he admits to sometimes playing Hall and Oates or Kool and the Gang on the sly. His parents, in fact, had a traveling evangelistic ministry that he jokingly refers to as "sort-of a Christian Partridge family"; he traveled with the family as a child, and made his religious tradition's requisite "decision for Christ" at the age of four. A year later he was already singing and making recordings with the family group. After this tame upbringing—free from any "rebellious period"—Long attended Bible college, where he played football and founded a male vocal trio. He embarked on a career in Christian music upon graduation and received early assistance from producers **John** and Dino **Elefante.** Long is married to Janna Potter Long of the Christian group **Avalon.**

Cross My Heart includes a duet with **Margaret Becker** ("How Long"), which provided Long with his first hit on Christian radio stations. *Days of Grace* kicks off with an energetic song, "Love All Around the World." The same upbeat spirit infuses "Thankful," which the Elefantes provide with an art-rock **Kansas** sound, and "Love the Lord," which invokes '70s disco. *Jesus Saves* tones things down a bit, to present a collection of songs that are generally more MOR and less commercial pop. The title track is a funky exception, bearing strong traditional gospel inference but, otherwise, the standout tracks are ballads, such as the mellow, acoustic "Prove That by Me," the ethereal "More Like Jesus," and the closing Bee Gee-ish "I Saw an Angel Tonight." Long noticeably eschews metaphors and double entendres to make his piety explicit in songs like "We Love Jesus." *Now* offers what *CCM* would call "a versatile collection of adult contemporary pop songs." The best tracks come first: "Sufficiency of Grace" and "I Won't Take You for Granted" are melodic and commercial in the tradition of **Michael W. Smith.**

Christian radio hits: "How Long" (# 2 in 1994); "Think about Jesus" (# 9 in 1994); "What a Friend" (# 12 in 1995); "All Is Well" (# 23 in 1995); "Love the Lord" (# 5 in 1996); "Love All around the World" (# 24 in 1997); "Jesus Saves" (# 14 in 1998).

Look Up

See **Mylon LeFevre.**

Loose Goose

Carolyn Stilwell, voc.; et al. 1995—*Break over Me* (New Dawn); 1998—*Face Yourself.*

Virtually unknown in the United States, Loose Goose enjoys a popular following in the British Christian music scene. The group is actually a loose collection of musicians who play behind Celtic vocalist Carolyn Stilwell. Although their name sounds silly to American ears, it is intended to describe this free-spirited approach to performing (the goose is a Celtic symbol for the Holy Spirit). A ringleader of this motley crew is Sammy Horner of **The Electrics,** who serves as producer for Loose Goose projects. On *Face Yourself,* the backing musicians include members of **Delirious?, The Electrics,** Honey Thieves, and **Iona.** Stilwell sings Horner's "T-Hule Beannachd" (translated "With Every Blessing") and her own "Glastonbury Night," which reflects on the significance of Glastonbury, the site of an influential and famous monastery: "Glastonbury night is hung with every prayer that once was cried / In Him we're one and time has passed us by."

Lost and Found

George Baum, kybrd., voc.; Michael Bridges, gtr., voc. Date unknown—*Sikkibahm* (custom); *Speedwood 1; Speedwood 2; This; Christmas; Speedwood 3;* 2000—*Something* (Limb).

www.speedwood.com

Lost and Found is an acoustic duo that plays heavily interactive music that typically demands a degree of audience participation. The two musicians have been friends and musical partners since childhood. In 1986, they embarked on a year-long bicycle tour of America, riding from New York to St. Louis to Miami to San Diego to Seattle and back to New York in 340 days, playing some 270 concerts at churches and colleges along the way. Due to an unusually charismatic stage presence—propelled by a zany sense of humor—the duo has become famous for filling the role of M.C. at Christian music festivals, where they lead worship and keep the crowd entertained between events.

Lost and Found sometimes refers to its music as "speedwood" or "acoustic thrash," since it involves "a unique blend of folk and screaming." Others have simply referred to it as "summer camp music with an edge." Indeed Baum and Bridges got their start playing for church summer camps and the youth group roots show. Their best-known songs include the singalong "Lions" and the bluesy "Slide Girl." The latter is just a cool sounding tune with obscure lyrics (actually, it's about a girl whose picture was shown on a slide projector), but the former uses the image of first-century persecution as a metaphor for spiritual warfare in the modern age: "Oh them lions they can eat my body, but they can't swallow my soul / They keep on trying to crash my party, but they can't get control." The group also does the occasional ballad, offering songs like "Distant Land" and "Fruit We Bear" on *Something*. These latter songs are more typical of such worship-oriented artists as **Michael Card** or **John Michael Talbot.** Otherwise on *Something* the group offers a version of "Holy, Holy, Holy" that owes a bit to **Undercover,** and they go wacky on "These Days," expressing a perspective of life informed by what the Israelites might have thought while wandering in the wilderness: "These here days, they count for something / But I don't know what sometimes." Though their ministry is ecumenical, George Baum and Michael Bridges are both Lutherans and, as such, are rare representatives of what is probably the most under-represented denomination in contemporary Christian music (cf. The Jay Beech Band, **Jonathan Rundman, John Ylvisaker**). Indeed, Bridges has a degree in theology from Lutheran Theological Seminary in Chicago. Another of their better-known songs, "One Lord, One Faith, One Baptism," derives from Ephesians 4:5, and states a motto that became something of a slogan for the Protestant Reformation.

In the late '80s, there was a completely different Christian band named Lost and Found that recorded an independent album called *Welcome to the Real World.* This unrelated group was a six-piece outfit from California with a sound similar to **Petra** or the **Allies.**

Lost Dogs

Derri Daugherty, gtr., bass, voc.; Mike Roe, gtr., bass, voc.; Terry Taylor, gtr., voc.; Gene Eugene, gtr., bass, voc. (d. 2000). 1992—*Scenic Routes*

(Brainstorm); 1993—*Little Red Riding Hood* (WAL); 1996—*The Green Room Serenade, Vol. I* (Brainstorm); 1999—*Best of the Lost Dogs* (KMG); 2000—*Gift Horse* (BEC); 2001—*Real Men Cry.*

www2.thelostdogs.org/lostdogs

The Lost Dogs were intended to be a Christian version of The Traveling Wilburys (the band that brought **Bob Dylan,** George Harrison, Jeff Lynne, Roy Orbison, and Tom Petty together for two fine albums in 1988 and 1990). The four members of the Lost Dogs were the key figures in four bands that had attained legendary status in the Christian subculture: Derri Daugherty from **The Choir,** Gene Eugene from **Adam Again, Michael Roe** from the **Seventy Sevens,** and **Terry Taylor** from **Daniel Amos.** Daugherty, Roe, and Taylor have all released solo albums as well. Extra musicians Burleigh Drummond (drums, perc.) and Greg Kellogg (banjo, mand., pedal steel) were sometimes designated Deputy Dawgs and treated as members of the group. Kellogg has recorded as a member of **Mercy River.**

Artistically, the Lost Dogs were more successful than the Wilburys; they gelled as a group (by their second album) in a way that the secular, kind-of-a-joke side project never did. Everyone assumed that the Dogs (like the Wilburys, or for that matter, Crosby, Stills, Nash and Young) would make albums filled with good songs that showcased each of the members in turn with the others serving as more-than-competent backup. What happened is that they turned into an actual *band* in which the whole was more than the sum of its parts. One would like to think this is due to a dose of Christian humility that kept egos in check. Daugherty would eventually sing more than his share of the songs because, all things considered, he really does have the best voice—or, at least, the *prettiest* voice; Taylor would write more material because he is pretty obviously the best songwriter—or, at least, the most *consistent* songwriter. In any case, it soon became apparent that the Lost Dogs were not very much like the Traveling Wilburys at all. Whatever the inspiration of their origins might have been, the best general market analogy for the group would not be Dylan, Harrison, Lynn, Orbison, and Petty but Danko, Helm, Hudson, Manuel, and Robertson—a.k.a. The Band. The latter group enjoyed only modest success as a commercial outing but is universally recognized as one of the best artistic ensembles ever to record music. The same could be said of the Lost Dogs in the parallel universe of Christian rock. The sad thing is that the great majority of the people who would love their music have never heard of them.

The Lost Dogs made four albums before the sudden death of Gene Eugene in 2000, and then in 2001 produced a fifth album as a trio. All of the albums are good, and the group generally got better as they progressed (though quality of the songs themselves remained sporadic). *Best of the Lost Dogs* is a poor compilation, collecting songs almost exclusively from the first two albums while virtually ignoring the superior third project as well as the two forthcoming offerings.

Scenic Routes displays an acoustic country sound with more than a little influence from bluegrass. Its delightful title song is a restatement of the Grateful Dead's "Truckin'" (i.e., the song with the famous "what a long, strange trip it's been" line). "Bullet Train" is a song about gun violence that is a cross between Lynyrd Skynyrd's "Saturday Night Special" and The Jim Carroll Band's "People Who Died." There is also a nice little country tune by Eugene called "I Can't Say Goodbye," and the group covers both **Mark Heard**'s "Built for Glory" and **Bob Dylan**'s "Lord, Protect My Child." They do a hymnic version of Stephen Foster's "Hard Times, Come Again No More" and resurrect the old gospel-blues songs "You Gotta Move" made famous by the Rolling Stones on *Sticky Fingers*. The most obviously devout song, "Breathe Deep (the Breath of God)," closes the record with what was destined to become the Lost Dogs' best-known song. Musically, the song is Byrds-era folk rock with trade off vocals as each of the Dogs takes a verse. Lyrically, it is a simple invocation for "everybody everywhere" to breathe deep the breath of God, with the verses listing various heroes and villains, princes and paupers, winners and losers who are included in their prayer: "Gays and lesbians / demagogues and thespians . . . Meat eaters, wife beaters, judges and juries / Long hairs, no hairs, everybody everywhere / Breathe deep the breath of God." Despite such glorious moments, however, *Scenic Routes* has "experiment" stamped all over it; *CCM* would observe that the album as a whole sounds "like an idea that someone thought up at the end of a very long tour."

On *Little Red Riding Hood,* things came together. The record includes a cover of the classic Sam the Sham and the Pharaoh's song (as a hidden track)—partly as a tribute to the original artist who had become a Christian ("Sam ain't no sham no more," Taylor would say in concert); they also do the Beatles' "I'm a Loser" and an a capella gospel quartet version of the hymn "Precious Memories." Strange and eclectic stuff—but all part of the curious mix that can only be described as "Americana." *Riding Hood* opens with "No Ship Coming In," a masterpiece of a pop song reminiscent of *Pet Sounds* Beach Boys. It has such a pretty melody and the group sings it with such appropriately gorgeous harmonies that the listener will soon know all the words by heart, like them or not: "No money to spend / No ship comin' in / But we're gonna see it through together." The Southern California theme is carried a step further with "Jesus Loves You, Brian Wilson," Roe's sincere (but kind of silly) beatitude for the troubled genius who has brought the world so much joy. Along the same lines musically, *Riding Hood* officially closes with "Pray Where You Are," a little meditation on 1 Thessalonians 5:17. Perhaps intended to be another "Breathe

Deep," it follows a structure similar to the latter song, listing all the places that one can pray ("in the submarines and tanks, in the S&Ls and banks, in the cancer wards, the prisons, and the bars"). "Eleanor, It's Raining Now" is stellar modern rock with poetic lyrics filled with obscure but intriguing imagery. A second rocker, "Red, White, and Blue," details the devastation of the Vietnam War on an individual veteran's life, a worn-out theme treated here with new insight and dignity: "You can save your tears for the names on the wall / I'm a living example that pride comes before a fall." The song "You Satisfy" is a Mike Roe contribution that (as an exception to the general group coherence described above) could just as well have been on the **Seventy Sevens** *Tom Tom Blues* album; it is a good song, regardless. Unfortunately, the album also contains "Bad Indigestion," which is the only truly awful song the Lost Dogs ever recorded.

Riding Hood's lyrical masterpiece belongs to Eugene, a song called "Jimmy" about a friend who "died of a disease." It tells of the final conversation the two had together. What does one talk about with a friend who is dying? Well, this and that, games they played as kids, anything *except* mortality. Then the final verse: "Now I'm tied up / I'm busy / But I'll come over soon / We'll get some Chinese food / I'd like that wouldn't you?" And with that antepenultimate line, the listener suddenly realizes that the entire stilted conversation has apparently taken place *over the phone,* not in person. It is a chilling moment and Eugene's dispassionate Michael Stipe-like delivery makes it even colder. The effectiveness lies in the lack of any explicit moral. Eugene defers from any Cat's-in-the-Cradle sermonizing about lost opportunities and offers his audience a moment of grim reality—a photograph of a naked soul, as it were, and an invitation to empathize with his experience and draw whatever conclusions one may.

The Green Room Serenade features another handful of classic, truly great songs. *True Tunes* would proudly proclaim it "the best of the litter" and noted that "while they still dabble in country, blues, and folk, it seems the Dogs are snarling this time." The album as a whole has much more of a rock focus. Its opening track, "Up in the Morning," is a wonderful entry in the "pleasant little ditty" category, a more perfect vehicle for Daugherty's smiley voice than the morose songs that **Steve Hindalong** typically writes for him. Eugene sings "Cry Baby" and this time he sounds so much like Michael Stipe that uninformed listeners might easily mistake it for an R.E.M. tune—and one of their better ones at that. The ironic lyric, "I bet you never hear this song on the radio," offers a self-fulfilling prophecy. Eugene's "Mexico" propounds the same basic theme as the James Taylor song of that name but with rock and roll style: "I hear they throw some parties there / With people in their underwear." Taylor's "Sweet Work of Love" is the Lost Dogs' best rock song, an apocalyptic alt-rock number in the same vein as "Eleanor, It's Raining Now." The joke song this time (cf. "Bad Indigestion," "Little Red Riding Hood") is "Close, But No Cigar," which features Roe doing a sort of rockabilly-lounge singer impersonation. Along the same lines, "Hey, You Little Devil" sounds very much like The Fabulous Thunderbirds covering a Chuck Berry tune. This time the jokes work and the novelty songs hold up to repeated listening. In a more serious vein, "Reasonable Service" is a pop anthem with a spiritual theme derived from Romans 12:1, and "I Don't Love You" is a surprisingly sensitive blow-off song from Mike Roe, the same guy who wrote "Go with God . . . But Go!" for one of his solo projects. The group also covers Leonard Cohen's little-known song, "If It Be Your Will."

Gift Horse would return the group to its country-rock style, but with a more earthy and cohesive presence than they exhibited on the first two albums. Gone is the "smorgasbord" approach; this time, the Dogs come together so perfectly on such a cohesive mixture of songs that references to their other bands all but vanish. The reasons may be twofold. First, those other bands had all either broken up, gone into limbo, or indeed become the side projects for artists whose primary identification had become being a member of the Lost Dogs. And, second, Taylor wrote or cowrote all of the songs on *Gift Horse* (except for one cover), apparently crafting them to fit his bandmates' strengths. Once more there is a positive secular sound to most of the project that would allow at least half the songs to be right at home on country radio. "Honeysuckle Breeze" is a love song. "Ghost Train to Nowhere" is a "Hotel California"-type anthem about a metaphorical train that just runs in circles eternally. "If You Loved Here, You'd Be Home by Now" is a honky-tonk parody of "bumper sticker country" tunes built around clever titles. Still, the most noticeable aspect of *Gift Horse* is the deep draw from the well of southern gospel—not just musically, but thematically. "Blessing in Disguise" drives home a rather simple but profound message with reference to Scripture and respect for the paradoxes of real life: "Hold fast to the hope that's in you / Don't always trust your eyes / Sometimes it takes a long time to see it as / A blessing in disguise." Or, again, "Diamonds to Coal" presents the spiritual struggle of an outwardly successful man to be counted worthy in God's eyes: "I can't ignore the Savior King / I can't avoid the cross / I'll need the help his spirit brings / To count my gain as loss."

Southern gospel, of course, tends toward maudlin sentiments and melodramatic scenarios—and *Gift Horse* revels in such attributes. In many songs, the themes are a bit mawkish and overdrawn but such are the tales and truisms that touch human hearts. "A Vegas Story" relates the parable of an alcoholic gambler who trades his soul for "free drinks and a dream."

"Rebecca Go Home" presents the words of an elderly man who tries to give his lingering wife the permission and courage to die. But "Wall of Heaven" is the album's masterpiece, perhaps the Lost Dogs' finest song. With unabashed emotion, Taylor introduces us to a character who claims, "I've been a drunkard all my life / My drinkin' killed my darlin' wife / But there's never been a night she's left me alone." As it turns out, his widow comes to him in his dreams, not to haunt him but to whisper words of forgiveness and promise. There's just one thing that disturbs her: "There awaits a robe of diamonds and a crown for you to wear / But I've seen the wall of heaven and your name's not written there." For all their mawkishness, such songs work because, as *CCM*'s Brian Quincy Newcomb puts it, they relate stories "dripping with the human condition and longing for healing." Taylor tried this approach with limited success on *Riding Hood* with his teary "Rocky Mountain Mines." It worked there but it works much better here. Likewise, "Farther Along" reprises the same treatment given to "Precious Memories" on the sophomore album but, again, with improvement. It's a better hymn and their performance is top-notch—an easy appeal to the open-minded.

Real Men Cry follows in the same vein as *Gift Horse* with many fine songs but less consistent quality. Taylor again wrote almost all of the songs, which for the most part follow in the same unabashed goat-roper country style. Almost every reviewer would note the remarkable similarities in substance and style to Merle Haggard. The album opens with two of its strongest tracks. "A Certain Love" explodes with one of the group's all-time best retro-rock pop songs, a masterpiece that might easily have occupied the Number One spot somewhere between Neil Diamond's "Cracklin' Rosie" and George Harrison's "My Sweet Lord" back in 1970. "Gates of Eden" goes for a slightly countrified rock sound with a song that could have been penned by Robbie Robertson. "Three-Legged Dog" is the album's token dumb song, recalling Neil Young's "Old King" a little too closely (with a tip of the hat to Shel Silverstein). "The Great Divide" borrows only its title from Young (as "Gates of Eden" did from Dylan); the song itself is about death (not divorce) and is sung in a southern gospel ballad style. "Golden Dreams" is a pretty song in the tradition of **Daniel Amos**'s gorgeous oldies ("Ain't Gonna Fight It," "Don't Light Your Own Fire"). The stronger country influences come on the title track, the tear jerker "In the Distance" (about a man who loves a woman from afar), and the two non-Taylor songs: a hillbilly nugget by Roe ("Lovely Man") and another Dog cover of a traditional gospel song ("Dust on the Bible"). "No Shadow of Turning" offers a lullaby coda with Daugherty's vocals giving it the feel of a misplaced **Choir** gem.

The Lost Dogs recorded a *Green Room Serenade, Vol. 2* album at the same time as their third project, but as of 2002 it had not been released. A Christmas single featuring the Dogs performing "The Christmas Song" originally done by Alvin and the Chipmunks saw limited release in late 1999 and became a much sought-after collector's item.

Christian radio hits: "Pray Where You Are" (# 6 in 1994).

Loudflower

Mason Brazelle, drums; Wally Gates, gtr., kybrd.; Rob Groover, voc., bass; Loren Haefer, tromb.; Derrick Lee, trump. 1997—*Happy Now?* (Gray Dot).

One of the most creative bands in the Christian market, Loudflower blared out of Atlanta in the late '90s with a sound that no critic could quite describe. References to **Van Morrison** and The Waterboys were offered, but the closest analogy would require some kind of a cross between Counting Crows and Blood, Sweat, and Tears. The most obvious innovative element is the band's use of horns, not simply for flourish but as lyrical instruments that often carry the melody line. In 1997, brass was abundant in Christian music, but Loudflower did not play reggae or ska. The style of their songs—aside from the brass—was more folk rock, with more emphasis on *rock* than *folk*. The songs on *Happy Now?* are mostly upbeat numbers with a variety of fairly generic spiritual themes. The title track deals with the ephemeral nature of pleasure; "Can't Change Yesterday" addresses the futility of regret; "Saviour Business" describes the abusive fund-raising programs of big-money religion. The catchiest song on the album is "Crime of the Century," the meaning of which is obscure. Groover, who writes most of the material, says that he thinks of the group as more of a "spiritual night-time bar band" than as a Christian band per se. "To us, it's more an issue of how you live your life," he explains. "Everyone has a certain core belief—mine happens to be Christianity." The focus of the songs is not evangelistic in the usual sense but a message of "love, understanding, and tolerance."

Love Coma

Chris Dodds, drums; Jeff Duncan, bass, voc.; Chris Taylor, gtr.; Matt Slocum, gtr. (−1995) // Matt Mattingly, gtr. (+ 1995). 1992—*Soul Rash* (Etcetera); 1995—*Language of Fools* (R.E.X.).

Love Coma's ultimate legacy was to be the answer to a question in contemporary Christian music trivial pursuit: what band did **Chris Taylor** and Matt Slocum once play in? Both Taylor's solo career and Slocum's work in **Sixpence None the Richer** would exceed the San Antonio band in notoriety—but not necessarily in quality. For a brief time (one album, at least) Love Coma was one of the finest alternative Christian rock groups in the land. The group was founded by Taylor in 1991 and was originally called Windows. The album

released as *Soul Rash* was intended as simply a demo and its songs are promising but seem undeveloped (as, in fact, they were). *True Tunes* appreciated it nonetheless, comparing the band to Echo and the Bunnymen and The Church. The classic album *Language of Fools* was made after Slocum left. Produced by **Michael Roe,** it presents the group with a decidedly **U2**-influenced sound. Not surprisingly, given Roe's participation, several songs recall the **Seventy Sevens** as well. The songs themselves are a mixed bunch. Several deal with the emotions and experiences of life in a general way, but a few touch specifically on spiritual themes in an accessible manner that is, again, reminiscent of **U2**. Taylor's lyrics are invariably thoughtful and reflective. On "Summerwind" he sings, "Sense and reason are my enemies / You'll find me somewhere between glory and despair." On "Jigsaw Man," he references Psalm 61:2: "There's nobody left to rescue me / Lead me to the rock that is bigger than I." The absolute best song on the album, however, is a hidden (and thus untitled track), a midtempo tune with a haunting melody and equally haunting, poetic lyrics (it happens to be located on the disc as Track # 77—a little touch from producer Roe, no doubt). In concert, the band would perform **Bob Dylan**'s "All Along the Watchtower" as a curious medley with P. J. Harvey's "Down by the Water."

Darlene Love

1998—*Unconditional Love* (Harmony).

http://darlenelove.com

Darlene Love is an influential R&B singer who returned to her gospel roots in 1998 to record a contemporary Christian album. Born Darlene Wright in 1938 in Los Angeles, California, Love was given her stage name by Phil Spector, who managed her career as one of his many "girl group" singers in the early '60s. Love made a much greater impression than official charts reveal. Officially, she was lead singer for a group called The Blossoms, which never had any hits of their own but sang background vocals on records by Paul Anka, Bobby Darin, Duane Eddy, **Elvis Presley,** and many others. Then in 1962, Love recorded a song for Specter called "He's a Rebel," which the producer decided to use to promote another of his groups, The Crystals. Incredibly, he released Love's version of "He's a Rebel" under their name. The song went to Number One for two weeks, propelling The Crystals to fame even though they had absolutely nothing to do with the record. Specter then released another of Love's songs, "He's Sure the Boy I Love" as The Crystal's follow up song, and it went to Number Eleven. Later that year, Love did gain a Top 10 song as part of a trio called Bob E. Soxx and the Blue Jeans. They recorded a version of the song "Zip-a-Dee-Doo-Dah" from the Disney film *Song of the South*. The next year, she would have minor hits as a solo artist: "Today I Met the Boy I'm Gonna Marry" (# 39) and "Wait Till My Bobby Gets Home" (# 26). Love continued to sing with The Blossoms throughout the '60s, backing the Beach Boys, the Mamas and the Papas, and Tom Jones. From 1971 to 1981, she got a permanent gig as background singer for Dionne Warwick. Then she took an interest in acting and landed the role of the wife of Murtaugh (the character played by Danny Glover) in all four *Lethal Weapon* movies. She likewise starred in the Broadway production *Leader of the Pack.* In 1993, a show based on her life and career (called *Portrait of a Singer*) was created for her at New York City's Bottom Line club where she performed weekly. According to *The New Rolling Stone Encyclopedia of Rock and Roll,* Love has "long been respected as one of the top vocalists in pop music" by those familiar with her work. *Unconditional Love* was produced by gospel music giant **Edwin Hawkins.** It includes such standards as "It Is Well," "Because He Lives," and a "blood medley" of the hymns "There Is Power in the Blood," "Are You Washed in the Blood?" and "There Is a Fountain Filled with Blood."

For trivia buffs: Darlene Love's sister is Edna Wright, lead singer for Honey Cone, the band that charted a Number One hit in 1971 with "Want-Ads."

Love Life

See **Fear Not.**

Love Song

Tom Coomes, gtr., voc.; Chuck Girard, kybrd., voc.; Jay Truax, bass, voc.; Bob Wall, gtr., voc. (−1974); Fred Field, gtr., voc. (−1972) // John Mehler (+ 1974, − 1995). 1972—*Love Song* (Good News); 1974—*Final Touch*; 1977—*Feel the Love* (Word); 1995—*Welcome Back.*

www.one-way.org/lovesong

Love Song is usually considered the most important Christian rock band of all time. In the early '70s, they were known as "the Christian Beatles," and the impact of their work three decades later would prove that analogy to be no exaggeration. Love Song not only had a sound like the Beatles (more like America, Bread, or Crosby, Stills and Nash), but also demonstrated the sort of genre-breaking innovation of that band. They were instrumental in creating a new type of music— what would eventually be called "contemporary Christian music." Though there were forebears like **Mylon LeFevre** and **Larry Norman,** it was Love Song who defined the standards that would have to be either respected or resisted (but could not be ignored) by all who followed. Love Song was not the first contemporary Christian music group—they were at least ten minutes behind **Children of the Day**—but they were by far the most popular. If Christian music charts had been kept in 1972, the Top 10 songs for the year would have included

Children of the Day's "For Those Tears I Died," Norman's "I Wish We'd All Been Ready," and eight songs by Love Song. And just as the Beatles precipitated a global revival of youth culture, so Love Song more than any other human entity embodied and expedited the spiritual revolution that became known as the Jesus movement. After the group disbanded, Coomes, Mehler, and Truax would form **Wing and a Prayer** with **Tom Stipe** (of **Country Faith**) and **Al Perkins.** Still later, Mehler and Truax would become part of **Richie Furay**'s band. **Chuck Girard, Tommy Coomes,** and **John Mehler** would all record solo albums. Coomes became an executive at Maranatha music.

The Beatles analogy breaks down most noticeably in one regard—the group really only made one coherent album, followed by a *Let It Be*-like hodgepodge of unreleased material *(Final Touch),* a live concert recording *(Feel the Love),* and, much later, a novelty reunion package *(Welcome Back).* Still, that one album, the self-titled *Love Song,* remains the best Christian album ever recorded, on a par with *Sgt. Pepper's Lonely Hearts Club Band* not only musically but influentially. Like the latter record, its songs do not always hold up and its magic can be missed by latecomers. It is no masterpiece of production standards. It lacks the edge of **Daniel Amos** or **LSU** or the **Seventy Sevens.** It lacks the depth of **Adam Again** or **The Choir.** And the musicians, though competent, do not have the professional skill of the crack bands hired to back **DC Talk** or **Amy Grant** in the '90s. No matter. Love Song exceeds them all for two reasons. First, all of the just-named artists stand on Love Song's shoulders. Considered in context, with reference to the time and circumstances in which it was produced, *Love Song* is radically innovative and profound. Second, and most important, it is probably safe to say that no other album in the history of recorded music has ever evinced the artistic integrity or the purity of heart that is captured on this enchanted, charismatic disc. Like most of the Jesus people, the members of Love Song did not seem to care whether anybody ever bought their records or not, and so there is not a commercial note or beat anywhere on the self-titled masterpiece. They made the album not to sell records, but because they felt moved by the Spirit to do so—and it shows. The Jesus people spoke of this hard-to-define quality in terms of "anointing" and *Love Song* was and still is considered to be the most *anointed* record of all. Like many other Jesus music bands, the group used to list "the Holy Spirit" as their producer; in their case, the claim seems to ring true. Rarely, if ever, has any musical work sounded so *inspired*—though, of course, it might just come off insipid or lame to those who do not share the members' faith or theology.

To put it another way: there have been very few records ever made—possibly none—on which an artist connected so completely with their target audience as on *Love Song.*

Those who weren't there—who weren't part of the Jesus movement—will probably never be able to appreciate this aspect of the music's attraction. The Grateful Dead apparently could accomplish something comparable at times in concert, but never on disc. The *Love Song* album seemed capable of facilitating an experience that was deemed far more important than the music itself. One possible reason was that the "target audience" was not the tens of thousands of people who bought their records and came to their concerts. The real target audience was God, and on their first recording Love Song seemed to connect so completely with God that those who listened in on what was happening were able to partake as well. Similarly, Love Song concerts were sacramental experiences. The band did not exactly have fans. No one, it seemed, ever attended a Love Song concert and came away talking about how great the music was; the consistent response was an overwhelming impression of having been in the presence of the divine. Invariably, people left Love Song concerts talking about Jesus—claiming (often for the first time) that Jesus was real, present, someone to be known. Of course, there were plenty of scoffers and skeptics—especially ones who would ridicule (safely) from afar—but no journalist, theologian, or sociologist, and certainly no one among the band itself, could ever figure out just how it was done.

Love Song came together in Southern California in 1970. **Chuck Girard** (b. 1943), a professional musician who had enjoyed some success recording with The Castells and The Hondells, ended up living in a house in Laguna Beach with fellow hippie musicians Jay Truax, **Tommy Coomes,** and **Fred Field.** The four explored religion and philosophy together and one-by-one came to know Jesus as their "personal Lord and Savior." Field and Truax were the first converts, and for a time (according to the group's bio), there was "conflict in the house as the four became involved in complex arguments over doctrines they knew nothing about." Seeking counsel, they ended up going to a Bible study at Calvary Chapel in Costa Mesa where Girard (who had already been confronted with his "need to know Jesus" by **Denny Correll**) says he experienced a "feeling of love" unlike any he had ever experienced before. "God was obviously there and I felt like He was having a great time, too," Girard recalls. "I accepted Jesus that night as my only God, my total Lord." The trio (Field, Girard, and Truax) kept going to the Bible study and took to playing music there. They were asked to give a concert at the Orange County fairgrounds and invited Coomes to join them for a fuller sound. At that event, while on stage, Coomes says he personally experienced the love and power of God in the music. "During the song, 'Think about What Jesus Said'," he relates, "I broke down in tears, took off my guitar, and made my decision for Jesus."

As always, the personnel lists given above are geared to actual recordings. Love Song began as the quartet Coomes, Field, Girard, and Truax, with Mehler being added on drums within six months. Truax and Mehler had formerly played together in a band called Spirit of Creation in Salt Lake City, and the band signed Mehler after they played there and he dedicated his life to Christ at their concert. In the summer of 1971 (still before the first recording), Mehler and Field left the group to form a band called Noah, and Bob Wall was recruited as a new lead guitarist. Mehler later returned for the second album. Seminal member **Fred Field** is not featured on either of the albums (but he does play a memorable guitar solo on the version of "Little Country Church" found on *The Everlastin' Living Jesus Music Concert*). The same can be said of two other personnel anomalies. **Denny Correll,** the lead singer of Blues Image who had a Top 10 hit with "Ride, Captain, Ride" in 1970, was a member of what Girard calls "a pre-Christian" incarnation of Love Song, a version of the group that Girard assembled when he and others were spiritual questers. Correll would later also make Christian albums. Also, for a few months in the summer of 1973, Christian guitar hero **Phil Keaggy** joined Love Song and toured with the band.

With no models for their ministry, the members of Love Song were thrust into the limelight with little awareness of what was taking place. In the wild and wooly days of the early Jesus movement, principles of discipleship and accountability that would later become commonplace (and, ultimately, oppressive) in the contemporary Christian music industry were nonexistent. A personal connection with Jesus was deemed far more important than doctrinal orthodoxy or appropriate lifestyle. Thus, members of Love Song would reveal years later that they celebrated their baptisms by "going out and getting stoned." But the band did come under the auspices of Calvary Chapel and the members were discipled by that community's pastors, Chuck Smith and Lonnie Frisbee. Such leadership steered them under the general umbrella of orthodox Christianity, avoiding the excesses of the Children of God cult and the bizarre extremes that attended Ohio's **All Saved Freak Band.** Calvary Chapel was decidedly fundamentalist, however, and as such, Love Song along with most of the Jesus movement groups ended up embracing a piety and theology that distanced them from mainline Christianity. In their music and shows, they would espouse a number of ideas that marked them and their followers as a minority within the global or historic church. Paramount among these were 1) a conception of salvation as a private, individualized experience, linked to a definitive "decision" on the part of the recipient; 2) a hermeneutics of Scripture that regarded the Bible as capable of speaking directly to readers on matters of individual and immediate concern, with little regard for historical or literary context; 3) a notion of prophecy that would construe certain biblical passages as predicting that Jesus would return very soon, almost certainly before 1980; and 4) a gnostic-like evaluation of "the world" as a primarily evil realm distinct from the spiritual kingdom inhabited by believers. Such facets were key factors in the appeal of Love Song to those estranged from the church—to persons enamored of privatized spirituality and fascinated by apocalyptic speculation—but they also insured that the group would not gain much of a hearing within the church at large, especially within sacramental or liturgical denominations. However, Love Song's very appearance (long hair, beards, casual attire) probably would have ostracized them from many of the latter communities in any case, for churches of the status quo, while preserving doctrinal orthodoxy, have also tended to be much more infected by cultural bigotry.

Nevertheless, Love Song did find their audience. A concert scheduled for a two-thousand-seat arena at the Knott's Berry Farm amusement park drew an unanticipated twenty thousand guests, the largest single audience in the venue's fifty-three-year history. A year later, the group was slotted to play five shows a night there at a two-day Love Song Festival. The group was the most popular act at the *Explo '72* festival outside of Dallas, Texas, which brought the Jesus movement to the attention of the national media. They played nightly there for a week, in stadiums and amphitheaters, concluding before an audience of 250,000 at the International Freeway on the weekend. The next summer, they became a national sensation in the Philippines, playing a series of five stadium concerts in Manila. In that country, they were not simply a religious act, but the most popular group in the land—their song, "Love Song," was Number One on the mainstream radio stations and the group ultimately beat out the Beatles and the Rolling Stones to be voted the top band in the Philippines in 1973. Back in the States, Love Song was either ignored by the general market or treated as a novelty (like the Singing Nun a decade earlier). But they were the stars of the Jesus movement.

When the group first got the itch (i.e., felt led) to record, they met with MGM executive Freddie Piro at the Samuel Goldwyn studios in Hollywood. They played him two songs ("Two Hands" and "Welcome Back") and he ended up on his knees in the studio parking lot, praying with them to ask Jesus into his heart. Imbued with evangelical fervor, Piro left National General and established his own label, Good News Records, on which the two Love Song albums would appear. This apparently innocent move was, at least, symbolic of the development of contemporary Christian music as an entity distinct from the secular realm. The group's debut album remained the Number One selling gospel record in America for over a year and went on to sell a phenomenal 250,000 copies. Even if the Jesus freaks in the band didn't care about such transient

things, their commercial success did not go unnoticed by people who did.

Musically, *Love Song* takes *Sgt. Pepper* as its template, with celestial harmonies inspired by the Beach Boys' *Pet Sounds*. Thematically, it displays a careful arrangement of songs that lead from the simple invitation "Lend an ear to a love song" to testimonies ("I'm going through changes") to expressions of worship and commitment. The intention was to create on disc the same "experience of love" that had so overwhelmed first Girard and then Coomes (and Mehler and Piro) at live gatherings. It worked. Thousands of listeners, most of whom had never heard the band live, testified to a somewhat mystical experience through which they were able to "feel the love" just hearing the album. Certainly, no record in history has generated as many conversions to Christ or rededications to new faithfulness. Such success was only occasionally related to poignant lyrics of an individual song, but seemed to derive more often from the "feeling" that people claimed to experience from the work as a whole.

The titular theme, "Love Song," is appropriately brief but contains a melody as pretty as anything ever penned by Brian Wilson or Paul McCartney. "Changes" is the most perfect pop song on the record, with a bouncy, hook-filled testimony to the joyful transformations that Christ affects in human lives: "I'm doing what I want to and it's part of me / Keeping close to Jesus that's the way it's got to be." Notably, when the song was redone in 1995, Girard changed that just-cited lyric to say, "I'm doing what I can to follow faithfully," completely missing the point of his own song. The original message of "Changes" was compatible with the dictum of St. Augustine that the secret to the Christian life is to "love God and do as one pleases"—the point being that the one who truly loves God will *desire* to do what is godly. So, the early Jesus people embraced the Christian lifestyle not as something they should try to do in order to meet some external definition of faithfulness but as something they wanted to do because of the transformation that had occurred within. Girard changed other lines as well—references to "believing in the feeling that I know is right" and "knowing that this feeling will flow eternally" got deleted for not meeting some standard of theological correctness. But Love Song's appeal never had much to do with theology. The strength of the band's music was emotional and the *theme* of its classic album was *feeling* ("feel the love"), a dramatic realization that "the love of Christ" was not so much a doctrine to be believed in as it was a reality to be experienced. The original lyrics to "Changes" had actually been composed by Denny Correll, who was not happy with the later changes. Girard posted an apology of sorts on his website, indicating that he should not have made the changes without consulting Correll.

"Little Country Church," the next track on *Love Song,* was written by Girard and Field and became one of the band's biggest hits. Fueled by an infectious and wholly original tune, it describes a little fantasy of a typical rural congregation embracing people with the same open-minded attitude that the group members had experienced at Calvary Chapel: "long hairs, short hairs, some coats and ties / people finally coming around." **Pete Stewart** would cover the song on his solo album in 1999. Girard and Field also wrote "Brand New Song," one of contemporary Christian music's first praise songs. It draws appropriately on Psalm 96 to explore the biblical mandate for updating worship styles.

"Two Hands," covered also by **Children of the Day** on their debut album, remains a classic song of invitation. Tom Coomes and Chuck Butler (of **Country Faith**) wrote the song, which opens with the frank yet tolerant admission, "We're all gathered here because we all believe / If there's a doubter in the crowd, we ask you not to leave." It was this song more than any other that touched the hearts of seekers and turned them to the Lord. Coomes also contributes "Let Us Be One," the album's second worship song, and the only song on the album actually addressed to God. A prayer for unity and peace, it taps into the sentiments of the hippie culture by accenting concerns voiced also by the Jesus of the Gospels. It also features an incredible Santana-like rhythm and some very memorable ba-de-da-da-da's.

"Welcome Back" takes a slightly different but no less effective tack than "Two Hands." The song seems to be addressed to those who have wandered away but perhaps never really discarded the faith of their younger years (cf. **Children of the Day**'s "As a Child"). Theologically, it actually transcends the limitations of decision theology in favor of a much more congenial (and biblical) view of salvation as an ongoing process: "Welcome back to the things that you once believed in . . . Welcome back to what you knew was right from the start . . . Welcome back to the love that is in your heart").

Every song on *Love Song* is an indisputable classic, but Girard maintains that his personal favorite is the most overlooked song, "And the Wind Was Low," a slow-moving and beautiful tune that is in some respects similar to Neil Young's '90s pump-organ style. The thought is that the "wind is low" when God's Sprit comes near to earth. Girard says the song refers specifically to the day that he experienced his Pentecostal baptism in the Holy Spirit and spoke in tongues. "Front Seat, Back Seat"—the other big hit besides "Little Country Church"—is a humorous country rock number about letting the Lord be "the driver," that is, be in control of one's life. The song "Freedom" is a McCartneyesque suite (cf. "Band on the Run," "Uncle Albert") that merges ideas for at least two songs into an extended composition ending in a rousing call to "shout the joyful news

that Jesus is Lord." The album concludes with the beautiful, triumphant "Feel the Love," which describes the emotive power that summarizes the work's timeless appeal: "Save the sadness for another time. . . ." In retrospect, it was so prophetic. As the contemporary Christian music genre that Love Song created continued to develop, it would have to mature well beyond the "happy in Jesus" mood of the early Jesus people's songs. A time for addressing sadness—the difficulties and hardships of life—would come, but not yet. *Love Song* was, appropriately, about celebrating the initial joy of conversion and community.

Final Touch lacks the coherence of the first album. It is more a patchwork than a tapestry, but still includes a number of stellar songs. "Since I Opened Up the Door" is another great Girard/Field composition, a lively country song similar in mood to **The Road Home**'s fabulous "Since I Met Jesus." Another early song, "Think about What Jesus Said," is simple and unpretentious folk rock. "The Cossack Song" has dumbo lyrics based on fundamentalist teaching regarding supposed references to the Soviet Union in the book of Revelation, but it is at least rendered with a sense of humor. "Don't You Know" and "Joyous Lament" demonstrate directions Love Song might have taken had they held together long enough to develop. The first of these turns on electric guitars and rocks harder than anything else in their canon (with great pre-**King's X** gang vocals on the chorus). "Joyous Lament" has a darker tone to it, presaging more complexity musically and theologically than is typical of the group's oeuvre. "Living Water" (written by Girard and Truax) reprises the Neil Young feel of "And the Wind Was Low," with haunting chords and a bridge that Girard admits was inspired by the feel of Buffalo Springfield's "Expecting to Fly" (a Young song). The closing track, "Little Pilgrim," previews what fans could expect from Girard's successful solo career.

The band's live album is a disappointment, featuring mostly songs that also appear on the studio albums—and the studio versions are invariably better. Exceptions include a cover of Bill Sprouse's "Psalm 5," which was performed better by **The Road Home** on the *Maranatha Five* album, and an impressive drum solo by Mehler, which got cut from the CD version of the album. The reunion CD *Welcome Back* debuts one previously unreleased song, the bluesy "Take No Chances" (written by Girard and Field in 1970), but is otherwise unremarkable. **Phil Keaggy** plays guitar on the album and, to the surprise of many, jazz and classical performer John Patitucci plays bass (cf. **Tamarack**).

Love Song also placed a song called "Maranatha" on *The Everlastin' Living Jesus Music Concert* album from Maranatha in 1971. It features an unusual martial beat with a Hebraic undertone befitting the theme. Girard says the song was originally based on Luke 10:38–42 and said, "Mary Martha, Mary Martha, the Master's coming back," but once he learned that the word "Maranatha" means "The Lord is coming," the revised lyric seemed to work. Two little-known and uncredited Love Song tracks also appear on the Maranatha project titled *The Praise Album* (1974): the worship choruses "Bring My Body Closer" and "Praise the Lord." Love Song also puts in a cameo appearance on the song "Singing Our Praises to Jesus" on **Tommy Coomes**' solo album.

A few retrospectives of the band were taken in 1995 when members reunited for the *Welcome Back* album. At that time, Coomes was working as an executive at Maranatha! Records (he would later leave that position) and Girard was on staff at a Vineyard church. Bob Wall (who said he liked *Feel the Love* best of all the group's projects) was a computer expert and executive for a pest control corporation. Jay Truax reported hard times: "I've gone through a divorce after 16 years of marriage and lost everything—my business, my parents—but through it all I had a strong relationship with God, and that's what I held onto." He later became an architectural design consultant with some specialization in church architecture (Central Christian Church in Las Vegas is one of his designs).

Lovewar

Rick Armstrong, bass; Tim Bushong, voc., gtr.; Greg Purlee, drums. 1993—*Soak Your Brain* (Pakaderm).

Lovewar was a short-lived hard rock band founded by Tim Bushong in Indiana. Armstrong was drafted from **Whitecross.** The group's sound was definitely influenced by the Seattle grunge movement (Nirvana, Pearl Jam) but also showed unmistakable connections to the Houston sound of **King's X** and **Galactic Cowboys.** The latter influence is most obvious in their use of big harmony choruses on songs like "Welling Up." Lyrically, *Soak Your Brain* displays more interest in apologetics (defense of doctrine) than do most records in the Christian scene. Bushong claims to have been influenced by popular writers like Francis Schaeffer and C. S. Lewis and by discussions with college students who are given to syncretism and relativism. The title song invites the skeptical listener to "take a swim in the truth." The album was produced by **John** and Dino **Elefante.** Bushong went on to form **The Channel Surfers.**

Mark Lowry

1989—*For the First Time on Planet Earth* (Word); 1991—*This Is the Life* (Word); 1992—*The Last Word*; 1994—*Mouth in Motion*; 1996—*Remotely Controlled*; 1998—*But Seriously*; 1999—*Twenty Stories Tall*; 2000—*Just Singing . . . No Kidding.*

www.marklowry.com

Mark Lowry is better known as a comedian than as a musician, but he is both and actually began his career as a vocalist with strong connections to southern gospel. Lowry was born in 1958 in Houston, Texas, where his mother was a psychology professor and his father, a lawyer. At age nine, he landed a role in Houston Music Theater's *The Music Man,* produced by none other than Tommy Tune himself. Tune encouraged him to pursue a career in Broadway, but his parents balked. Instead, a year later, Lowry entered a gospel quartet contest in Nashville and at the age of eleven was granted a recording contract. He toured as the child star of a gospel group, singing at churches, camp and revival meetings and even recording an album titled *Introducing Mark Lowry.* Eventually, he attended Liberty University in Lynchburg, Virginia, and went on to sing with **The New Gaither Vocal Band.** Lowry cowrote the song "Mary, Did You Know?" (with **Buddy Greene**), which was a hit for **Michael English** and has also been recorded by Kathleen Battle, Billy Dean, Kathie Lee Gifford, Wynonna Judd, Kathy Mattea (who calls it her "favorite song of all time"), and **Kenny Rogers.**

From his childhood, Lowry exhibited signs of what would later be called ADHD (Attention Deficit Hyperactive Disorder). Although this caused problems for him in school and other formal settings, it also propelled him into developing his skills as an off-the-wall (albeit "clean") comic. Lowry began incorporating comic routines into his concerts with **The New Gaither Vocal Band** and eventually spun off a highly successful career as a stand-up comedian, working mostly in Christian venues. Knowing his audience, Lowry pokes fun at the foibles of the contemporary Christian music subculture, telling uproarious stories about his days as a child star and performing Weird Al Yankovic-styled parodies of Christian singers and songs. For example, he transforms **Steven Curtis Chapman**'s "The Great Adventure" into "The Date Adventure" (about blind dates) and **Michael W. Smith**'s "A Place in This World" into "A Face in This World" (about plastic surgery, with reference to Smith's perfect physical features). Lowry's chart hit, "Some Other Time, Some Other Place," is actually a parody of the song by that name originally sung by **Sandi Patty** and **Wayne Watson.** In 1993, he was honored by the Gospel Music Association as the recipient of their Grady Nutt Humor Award.

Most of Lowry's albums that are listed above contain mostly comedy routines and parodies, but they also include a smattering of serious songs. *Just Singing* is a compilation of the serious tracks from Lowry's first five albums. It includes his own version of "Mary, Did You Know?" *But Seriously* is a straightforward (noncomedy) project, on which Lowry is joined by a number of colleagues from the southern gospel world. Diva Vestal Goodman joins him on the song "I Can't Even Walk." **Michael English,** The Martins, and **The Gaither Vocal Band** also show up. *Twenty Stories Tall* is a compilation of favorite comedy sketches.

Christian radio hits: "Some Other Time, Some Other Place" [with **Sandi Patty**] (# 25 in 1994).

LSU (a.k.a. **Lifesavors, Lifesavers, Lifesavers Underground,** and **L.S. Underground**)

Personnel for Lifesavors: Kevin Annis, drums; Chris Wimber, bass; Michael Knott, gtr. (– 1983); Mark Krischak, voc., gtr. (– 1983) // Brian Goins, voc. (+ 1983); Kirk Heiner, gtr., kybrd (+ 1983). Personnel for all others: Michael Knott, voc., gtr., kybrd., perc.; Brian Doidge, bass, gtr. (– 1998); Kevin Lee (Annis), drums (– 1991) // Mike Sauerbrey, bass (+ 1989, –1993); Chuck Cummings, drums (+ 1992, –1993, + 1994); Ed Benrock, drums (+ 1993, –1994); Eric Coomes (+ 1993, –1994); et al. As Lifesavors: 1981—*Us Kids* (MRC); 1983—*Dream Life* (Refuge). As Lifesavers: 1986—*A Kiss of Life* (Frontline); 1991—*Poplife* (Blonde Vinyl); 1995—*Huntington Beach* (Brainstorm). As Lifesavers Underground: 1987—*Shaded Pain* (Frontline); 1989—*Wakin' Up the Dead* (Blonde Vinyl); 1991—*This Is the Healing;* 1992—*The Grape Prophet* [by L.S. Underground] (Blonde Vinyl). As LSU: 1993—*Cash in Chaos: World Tour* (Siren); 1994—*Grace Shaker* (Alarma); 1995—*Bring It Down Now* (Gray Dot); 1998—*Dogfish Jones* (Light); *Definitive Collection* [with Michael Knott (solo)] (KMG); 2000—*Live at Cornerstone '91 and '93, Vol. 1* (M8); *Live from Cornerstone '91 and '93, Vol. 2 + Wakin' Up the Dead; Live at Cornerstone 2000.*

Michael Knott is one of Christian music's creative geniuses, known not only for his solo work but also for his projects with **The Aunt Bettys, Bomb Bay Babies, Browbeats, Cush,** and **Strong Gurus.** But over the long haul Knott's major focus has been a band that had trouble deciding on a name, and would eventually end up being known as simply LSU. Being from California, they did not seem worried about being confused with Louisiana State University, which eventually furnished fans with an alternative source for purchasing what could pass for band T-shirts. Knott once explained the name distinctions to *True Tunes* as follows: "Lifesavers is extremely pop and kind of giddy; LSU would be more minor sounding and more vocals and guitars and stuff. The **Michael Knott** (i.e., solo) stuff would be a little bit more introspective." These differences, however, have not always been discernible to critics or fans.

Official personnel lists for the various Lifesavers/LSU combinations are ambiguous, but the core of the group was Knott, Brian Doidge, and Kevin Lee (sometimes listed as Kevin Lee Annis), with Chuck Cummings (of **Common Bond** and **Dakoda Motor Co.**) replacing Lee in 1992. Mike Sauerbrey of **The Choir** played bass on all albums from 1989 to 1991, though his status as a guest or band member is left to interpretation. The *Cash in Chaos: World Tour* album featured a one-time band consisting of Knott and Doidge, with Ed Benrock on drums and Erick Coomes on bass; *Grace Shaker* also features an anomalous rhythm section with Doidge switching back to bass

and Jeremy Wood on drums. **Aunt Bettys**' guitarist Andrew Carter plays guitar on *Grace Shaker* and *Dogfish Jones.* Cummings and Doidge would also become members of **The Aunt Bettys,** who were really just a secular (i.e., officially secular) version of LSU.

The Lifesavors debuted in 1981 with what *Rad Rockers* calls "the first Christian punk album," or an assortment of "California pop pogo-punk" songs, to be precise. Actually, it appeared almost simultaneously with **Undercover**'s self-titled debut, both on MRC, a sublabel connected with the pioneering Maranatha company. In 1999, M8 Productions would re-release *Us Kids* with a walloping ten bonus tracks. Although Lifesavors are remembered as "Knott's first band," Mark Krischak was the true leader and Knott was only the rhythm guitarist. Still, the group was banned from playing concerts at Calvary Chapel locations because the eighteen-year-old Knott danced while he played. *Dream Life* featured neither Knott nor Krishchak and took youthful naivete to an extreme: "Jesus, He's the One / He makes livin' so much fun / He takes care of my problems too / And if you want He can do the same for you" ("The One"). Kevin Annis (Lee) of Lifesavors is brother to **The Altar Boys'** Mike Stand. Chris Wimber is the son of John Wimber, the Calvary Chapel pastor who split from that group to found the Vineyard Christian Fellowship denomination with **Kenn Gulliksen** in 1982.

On *A Kiss of Life,* the band (now Lifesavers) broke with the punk/new-wave sound of Lifesavors and moved decidedly toward alternative progressive rock, prompting *CCM* to suggest similarities to The Psychedelic Furs. The songs still exhibit a blissful naivete, similar to early **Undercover** or early Jesus music. Knott and company exuberantly proclaim, "We Live for the Son!" and cover Pete Seeger's "Turn! Turn! Turn!" Liner notes to the *Definitive Collection* later described "She's on Fire" and the worship-driven "See Me Fall" as "happy, light songs about God."

Shaded Pain (now by Lifesavers Underground) is a radical departure and remains the most influential and acclaimed album of Knott's diverse career, the album that put LSU in league with the **Seventy Sevens, The Choir,** and **Daniel Amos.** With songs like "Die, Baby Die" (about dying to self) and "Plague of Flies," the mood is intensely dark but only superficially so, pointing to what *CCM* called "a hope that can stand the weight of grief and loss." On what would become the album's best-known song, Knott sings, "Bye, bye colour / Blue is my heart" ("Bye, Bye Colour"). On "Jordan River," he indicates that, like **U2,** he still hasn't found what he's looking for—and doesn't expect to do so in this life: "The Jordan river is chilly and cold / Jesus meet me in the air." *Shaded Pain* was produced by Chris Brigandi of **The Lifters** and **Wild Blue Yonder** (and eventually **The Screamin' Rays**). *Wakin' Up the*

Dead is similar musically, as the first release on Knott's ill-fated independent label (cf. listing for **Michael Knott**). Thematically, the album addresses the optimism of the new decade—the dawning of the '90s ("Revival Nineties"), while offering sober speculation that things would likely just stay the way they are ("Nineties Tease"). More often, the songs focus on traditional Christian themes (revival, judgment, resurrection, and a retelling of Bible stories) but without the traditional clichés. Lyrics are sufficiently shrouded in imagery as to demand some deciphering—a tendency that would become a Knott trademark and alienate him from the impatient. In keeping with its "indie" status, *Wakin' Up the Dead* was initially issued in a limited edition of only five hundred copies. It was remastered and given wider distribution in 1992, and then in 2000 was included in its entirety as a "bonus track" on M8's *Live from Cornerstone '91 and '93, Volume 2.*

In 1991, Knott released two albums almost simultaneously that supposedly represent two different incarnations of the Lifesavers phenomenon. Actually, Doidge did not play on either *Poplife* or *This Is the Healing* and most critics regard both as solo albums by Knott with a few session musicians. *Poplife* doesn't offer much beyond the self-explanatory "Surf with God," but *This Is the Healing* would become LSU's best-seller, offering hard-edged songs with incisive lyrics. "You've tried to philosophize your pain, but the hurt's in your heart, not in your brain" Knott sings in the title track. "You could be hit by the Spirit and made new." The song "Miracle" is about people praying for miracles that don't occur. "Not a Cuss Word" juxtaposes almost creedal lyrics ("Born of a virgin, baptized in the Jordan . . .") with the chorus, "My name is Jesus Christ / I'm not your cuss word, am I?" *HM* described the album with what they took to be rave compliments: "This is some of the coolest, weirdest Christian music out. It's *not* nice music. It's loud, angry, and very alternative."

The Grape Prophet is the first of Knott's "rock operas," deriving its theme from some goings on in the Vineyard denomination of which he had been a part. Some leaders in that charismatic church started a new movement called the Kansas City Prophets, getting a community of people to move with them to Kansas where, Knott says, "they did all kinds of weird stuff." For example, some members of the Kansas City Prophets adopted a practice of talking in obscure parables, which would then be interpreted by another supposedly divinely inspired member of the group. These little exchanges inspired the LSU song "English Interpreter of English." The Vineyard later condemned the movement as heretical, and Knott has been forthright about saying he does not want *The Grape Prophet* to be heard as an indictment of the Vineyard as a whole.

The *Cash in Chaos: World Tour* album constitutes a venture into progressive psychedelia, with ample allusions to Perry Farrell (of Jane's Addiction). The album is somewhat notable for dealing with a number of sexual themes (prostitution, sexual violence, masturbation) on such songs as "The Sell," "Pound of Flesh," and "Benny"). Other songs deal with hypocrisy in the church ("Radio Satan") and the duplicity of relationships ("Everything"). *Grace Shaker* is something of a departure in that it presents a fairly straightforward evangelical message in songs like "Blame" and "Christ Saves." *True Tunes* described the project as a whole as offering "a study in God's persistence in reaching out to self-destructive humans despite their pride and anger." The classic song on the album is "Double," a number that would be re-recorded many times in superior versions, the best of which is found on **The Aunt Bettys**' debut album (see that listing for discussion). The version here features Knott banging on pots and pans in lieu of traditional percussion. *Huntington Beach* was produced by Gene Eugene of **Adam Again** and represents something of a return to the punk sound with which Knott began. Perhaps that justifies use of the old Lifesavers name (sans Underground), though the music has little to do with *Kiss of Life* or *Pop Life*. It is actually more reminiscent of *Us Kids* (by Lifesavors), albeit with considerable updating. "Imagine a cross between Tom Petty and Joey Ramone," *Rad Rockers* would muse. There's even a song *called* "Joey Ramone," offering a paean to the patron saint of punk. "Huntington Beach Police" is about corrupt cops, and "When She's Gone" expresses Knott's disgust for a song that reminds him of an ex-girlfriend.

Like *Pop Life* and *This Is the Healing, Dogfish Jones* is more a Knott solo album than a band effort. An eclectic group of supporting musicians (including Cummings, Carter, Eugene, and Jeff Elbel of **Farewell to Juliet**—but not Doidge) back Knott on his second major "rock opera" (third, if one counts *Fluid,* released as an official solo project). The plot is quirky, involving a Homeric take on the Jonah tale, complete with killer mermaids, scurvy pirates, and a love affair between two characters named Barnacle Bob and Seashell Sally. The music is quirky too, with Irish drinking songs (sung by Knott's father) being woven into a tapestry that otherwise owes its inspiration to the psychedelic rock of The Who and Dave Bowie.

As befits a cult legend, everything that Knott has ever recorded is sought by collectors. In 2000 the M8 Distribution company began opening the vaults and releasing various concert recordings. *Bring It Down Now* and *Definitive Collection* are eclectic compilation albums.

Sharalee Lucas

1975—*Sharalee* (Word); 1976—*Jesus, You Are My Friend* (Petra); 1978—*Daughter of Music* (Greentree); 1980—*Finally Him, Finally Me.*

Sharalee Lucas was a Christian singer who achieved a fair amount of celebrity in the '70s. She was married to Jerry Lucas, the outspoken Christian basketball star who played for the New York Knicks. Sharalee sometimes recorded under her first name only and appeared on such TV programs as *The Tonight Show, Good Morning, America,* and *The Ed Sullivan Show.* She sang the title song for the motion picture *Love Minus One* and performed at the White House. In 1978, she served as host for the Dove awards. She is author of the book *Always Becoming* (Impact, 1978).

Sharalee's first three albums were decidedly MOR. On *Finally Him, Finally Me,* she branched out with a more rock (or at least pop) oriented sound. She brings her excellent voice to bear on **Denny Correll**'s "Lead Me Home" and **Gary Chapman**'s "Open Up My Eyes." She also delves into country with a song called "You Mean More to Me." Lucas also sang with the **Paul Johnson** singers.

Ron Luce

See **Acquire the Fire.**

Susie Luchsinger

1993—*Real Love* (Integrity); 1995—*Come As You Are;* 1996—*Inspirational Favorites* (Arrival); 1997—*Tender Road Home* (New Haven); 1999—*Raised on Faith;* 2001—*My Gospel Hymnal.*

Susie Luchsinger is a Christian country singer who has had an impact in the "positive country" movement that allows for more mainstream acceptance of religious songs than is usually experienced in the rock world. Born Susie McEntire, she is the sister of one of country music's biggest stars, Reba McEntire. Growing up in Oklahoma, Susie, Reba, and their brother Pate formed a group called The Singing McEntires, which performed at rodeos and fairs for some years before Reba launched out on her solo career. Luchsinger's debut album, *Real Love,* features a duet with **Paul Overstreet** called "I Don't Love You Like I Used To (I Love You More)," in addition to a song that calls Christians to live out their faith, "Walk Whatcha' Talk." *Come As You Are* evinces a strong family orientation with "Call the Family Together," an Annie Cunnigham song, with new lyrics that Luchsinger wrote to make it autobiographical. She also covers **Dottie Rambo**'s "God You Never Cried" (comparing a mother's grief to the Lord grieving for creation). Reba joins her for a duet on the adult contemporary ballad "If I Could Only Be Like You."

For trivia buffs: Luchsinger's husband Paul is a professional steer roper, an occupation shared by his father-in-law, who was once the world champion.

Luna Halo

Nathan Barlowe, voc., gtr.; Jonny MacIntosh, gtr., kybrd.; Brad Mino, bass; Jonathan Smith, drums. 2000—*Shimmer* (Sparrow).

www.lunahalo.com

Luna Halo was formed by a remnant of the **DC Talk**-clone band **Reality Check.** Nathan Barlowe and Jonny MacIntosh (who apparently joined **Reality Check** after that band recorded its only album) found a new rhythm section and rechristened the group. The name Luna Halo refers to the ring of light that can sometimes be seen around the moon at night—a symbol of light in darkness. The band does not continue in the post-rap **DC Talk** tradition, but takes after '90s Brit-pop bands like Oasis, Savage Garden, and Radiohead. Their music is moody and atmospheric but, above all, catchy and filled with hooks. In terms of the Christian scene, they fit into the same basic genre as **The Newsboys** and **PFR,** which is to say they draw heavily on the Beatles, albeit in an up-to-date fashion.

Shimmer is a stunning debut—one of the best modern rock products of 2000. The songs are hardly repetitive and yet each is memorable and appealing. Styles range from melodic mid-tempo ballads to hard, grungy rock (the Beatles are particularly invoked on "Carry Me," and Radiohead, on "Complacency"). Barlowe's voice recalls that of Al Stewart at times, but he handles the more rocking tracks with a confidence Stewart has seldom displayed. Lyrically, Barlowe trusts in metaphor and poetry but is seldom obscure. "Aliens" deals with the battle with foreign thoughts and impulses that remain a part of every Christian's sinful nature. On "Superman," Barlowe tells friends (and fans?) not to expect him to do for them what only God can do. "Forgiveness" describes God's grace as "falling like rain." The group also performs "Hang On to You," a song written by Martin Smith of **Delirious?** and later recorded by that band. Barlowe understands Luna Halo to be a ministry band with a distinctly evangelistic role: "Our purpose is not just to come and get the youth group excited but to make music for the person who would never set foot inside a church."

For trivia buffs: Jonny MacIntosh is married to Sarah Meeker of **Chasing Furies.**

Christian radio hits: "Superman" (# 17 in 2000); "Hang On to You" (# 20 in 2001).

Lust Control

Doug Van Pelt, voc.; Maury Millican, bass (−1989); Philip Owens, drums (−1989); Paul Q-Pek, gtr. (−1989) // Dan Poole, drums (+ 1989); Mitch Roberts, gtr. (+ 1989); John Wilson (+ 1989); Phil Borrero Jr. (+ 1992). 1988—*This Is a Condom Nation* (custom); 1989—*Dancing Naked;* 1991— *Fun, Fun Feeling* (Blonde Vinyl); 1992—*We Are Not Ashamed* (Enclave); 1994—*Feminazi;* 2000—*The Worst of Lust Control* (M8).

www.geocities.com/SunsetStrip/Lounge/4892/lust.html

Lust Control was basically a Christian version of Spinal Tap—a joke band that almost forgot they were supposed to be a joke and ended up becoming the real thing. Almost. The group was founded by Doug Van Pelt, editor of *HM* magazine. He convinced a hip pastor (Maury Millican) and two members of **One Bad Pig** (Philip Owens, **Paul Q-Pek**) to join him in putting together a band "as a lark." The group made a custom cassette with a provocative title *(This Is a Condom Nation)* and performed live at the 1989 *Cornerstone* festival wearing ski masks to shield their true identities. That would have been it, but Van Pelt was still having fun and had become convinced that Lust Control might fulfill a legitimate ministry. He reformed the band to make another custom cassette, and then selected the best songs from both to be re-recorded professionally as *We Are Not Ashamed*. The latter project was produced by Christian music legend **Kemper Crabb**. The reject songs (i.e., the ones not redone for *We Are Not Ashamed*) were remastered and released on CD as *Fun, Fun Feeling*. Eventually, all of the songs from three cassettes (the original two plus 1994's *Feminazi*) were released in their original versions on an album called *The Worst of Lust Control*—a limited edition release for collectors and fans; the title itself is a rip-off of Jefferson Airplane's original greatest hits collection. As bonus tracks, *The Worst of* includes a punk version of the hymn "There Is a Fountain" and a remake of **Steve Taylor**'s "I Blew Up the Clinic Real Good."

Musically, Lust Control was a thrash punk band on the same order as **One Bad Pig,** with angry rant lyrics screamed by Van Pelt—sometimes off-key. The group intentionally went over-the-top in ways that were variously perceived as humorous and disturbing. "Madolyn Murry O'Hair on Judgment Day" and "John Styll" are obvious jokes. The former describes the famous atheist (name intentionally misspelled) being labeled a "goat" at the final separation of humanity predicted in Matthew 25; the latter offers the editor of *CCM* magazine an ultimatum: "Put us on your cover, or you'll never see your mother again." A number of songs deal with sexual tension. "Mad at the Girls" features the line "I want to control my lust but my mind I cannot trust" and "The Big M" is what Van Pelt calls "the only song by any Christian band about masturbation." Abortion is the theme of "Planned Parenthood" and "Operation Rescue," songs that the band performed with **Alice Cooper** histrionics (chopping up dolls) that portrayed doctors as butchers and abortion supporters as murderers. Lyrically, the songs are a bit over the top as well: "You are pro-abortion / You are pro-gay rights / I know one thing you're against / You are anti-Christ" ("Planned Parenthood"). *We Are Not Ashamed* was packaged with five Bible studies on the topics of deliverance, grace, masturbation, virginity, and prayer.

Van Pelt maintains a good humor about the Lust Control experiment, and in 1999 *HM* magazine dubbed the group "The Worst Christian Band of the Decade" on one of its CD packages. In the next issue, a concerned but uninformed reader wrote in with several reasons for why this remark was inappropriate (e.g., it might have hurt the band members' feelings). Notably the reader did not actually *disagree* with the contention.

The most enduring benefit from Lust Control has probably been the first-hand insight that it afforded Van Pelt into the performance industry. In 1994, he wrote an article for *HM* (issue # 48) detailing some of the things he had learned from the experience.

Luti-Kriss

Daniel Davison, drums; Chris (Derr) Day, gtr.; Joshua Doolittle, bass; Scottie Henry, gtr., voc. 2001—*Throwing Myself* (Solid State).

Luti-Kriss is a hardcore band from Atlanta, Georgia, that incorporates flourishes of rap-metal, thrash, and even a dash of emo into their eclectic hard rock stew. The band has its origins in a group of high school students who were already playing together when Daniel Davison, who says he knew very little about religion, attended an Assemblies of God church and "was totally blown away and got saved that very night." On return trips, he brought his friends and bandmates with him and a local revival broke out. As for the band, Davison says, "we weren't really sure what to do, but we figured it would be good to stop cussing in our songs and to sing about God." With some personnel changes, the group eventually signed to Solid State and recorded their debut album, *Throwing Myself*. The songs feature lots of banging, smashing, and screaming, with homage to the group's heroes **Living Sacrifice, Travail,** and **Zao.** Lyrics are not understandable but the songs appear to deal with fairly straightforward evangelical themes.

Luxury

Glenn Black, drums; Jamey Bozeman, gtr.; Lee Bozeman, voc.; Chris Foley, bass. 1995—*Amazing and Thank You* (Tooth and Nail); 1997—*The Latest and the Greatest;* 1999—*Luxury* (BulletProof).

Hailing from just outside Atlanta, Georgia, Luxury plays an almost unique blend of music called "noise pop," which combines delicate lead vocals, celestial harmony, and hummable melodies with grunge-laden grinding guitars and a driving rhythm section. A distinctive tension is established between the singer (and composer) and the instrumentation, akin to that which is set up in an entirely different way by **Starflyer 59.** "I write these beautiful, nice songs, and then the band destroys them," says Lee Bozeman. At times, Luxury comes off as a harder variety of The Smiths (Bozeman's voice is similar to Morrissey's), The Jam, **The Throes,** or **The Choir** but no close analogy applies. Their debut was engineered by Chris Colbert of **Fluffy** fame (also **Duraluxe, Breakfast with**

Amy) and produced by **Steve Hindalong** of **The Choir.** *HM* magazine called it "a cross between alternative and melodic punk." The employment of such incongruities and the involvement of the aforementioned luminaries were early indications that something creative was going on. But then, on the way home from playing the *Cornerstone* festival in 1995, their van did two flips on the interstate and the band members spent six months recovering from injuries and contemplating mortality. The band's manager, Reid Davis, broke his neck, as did Glenn Black and Gabe Aldridge (lead singer for a band called Piltdown Man), who was traveling with the group. Lee Bozeman was the most seriously injured; pinned beneath the van, his chest was crushed, his lungs collapsed, and his neck, ribs, and pelvis were broken, in addition to other internal injuries. The group all but disbanded, but then arose phoenix-like in 1997 with the strongest album of its career.

Amazing and Thank You has a good sound as an overall project but the songs are not sufficiently differentiated to stand out from each other. The first two cuts, "Pink Revenge" and "South," are usually cited as the best. The post-accident work *The Latest and the Greatest* adds stylistic variance, offering surf music ("The Glory"), Brit-pop ("Not So Grand"), and straight-on rock and roll ("The Latest and the Greatest"). One song ("I Know Why the Caged Bird Sings") gives a nod to poet Maya Angelou. Lyrically, many of the songs seem to be tongue-in-cheek, extolling superficial values that the band would actually contest ("This is the good life, to be so young and to be so right!"). In "Metropolitan," Bozeman sings, "If this is the modern world, why do I feel so out of place." Yet the overall focus of *Latest* is peculiarly upbeat. "No, life is never fair, it owes me nothing," Bozeman sings, "But somehow God is good and God is loving." These sentiments did not go unnoticed in the mainstream press, which treated the album as an exceptionally good release by some "indie" band. *Bikini* magazine (a very secular publication) called it "a spirited and occasionally spiritual pop album" and went on to say that the band's ability to overcome their near-death experience and keep going would translate as "just a nice sentiment, if this weren't such a solid album—which, luckily, it is."

The band's self-titled album for BulletProof was also their first self-produced effort. *True Tunes,* at least, thought that this gave them the best sound yet, a more lush and even orchestral arrangement for their poetry. Critical comparisons switched from The Smiths to Radiohead. The lead-off track, "When Those That Are Not Become Those That Are," offers a series of twists on Jesus' proclamation that the first will become last and the last, first (Matthew 19:30): "calendar for the fat girl / nobel for retard . . . and crowns for the martyr who's been feathered and tarred." Obsessions with mortality (and immortality) continue, perhaps enhanced by the death of Foley's mother, to whom the project is dedicated. "To You Who Gave Me Hope and Were My Light" and "Robed in Light" both express a longing to be "made new" in a world beyond. When not fronting rock bands, Lee Bozeman is an English teacher, with particular interest in such authors as T. S. Eliot, Dante, and Gabriel García Márquez. His brother Jamey Bozeman also fronts a Christian band called Canary, which has released one independent album called *A Sound of Summer Raining* (2000).

Claire Lynch

1993—*Friends for a Lifetime* (Brentwood).

Claire Lynch is a bluegrass singer renowned in native Nashville for her work with Emmylou Harris, Kathy Mattea, and Dolly Parton. Lynch got her start as the lead singer of a bluegrass group called The Front Porch String Band, which also featured her husband Larry on mandolin. *Friends for a Lifetime* draws on both gospel and country traditions as she joins with a number of highly respected bluegrass musicians to perform original compositions with overtly spiritual, yet personal and introspective lyrics.

Windy Lyre

1991—*Windy Lyre* (Blonde Vinyl).

Windy Lyre is married to the ultra-prolific **Michael Knott** and is an intriguing alternative singer and songwriter in her own right. Her album for Blonde Vinyl applies her breathy voice to eight intimate songs in a way that makes them sound delicate if not fragile. "Blue" gives expression to an inner loneliness in what seems to be a prayer for comfort. "Ave" and "Drink" are both worshipful. *CCM* describes the album as "dark, yet hopeful, responding with questions and answers." Knott cowrote all of the songs and plays all the instruments on the album.

Beau MacDougall

1981—*This Side of Heaven* (Milk and Honey).

Pop singer and songwriter Beau MacDougall is the brother of Alex MacDougall, drummer for **Selah, The Way, Daniel Amos,** and The **Richie Furay** Band. His only album was self-produced with his brother, who also played on it, as did such session performers as **Tom Howard, Richard Souther,** and **Fletch Wiley.** Beau's voice and style bears similarity to early **Steve Camp** and his guitar playing shines on the song "Take Another Look." The album offers a variety of styles, including Beatlesque pop (the title track), jazz-rock ("Just Goes to Show"), and quiet ballads ("Virtuous Woman"). Beau had been a member of the early Jesus music group **Rebirth** and he went on to play with **Steve Camp.**

Judy MacKenzie

1970—*Judy* (Key); 1971—*Peace, Love, and Freedom;* 1974—*Thinking It Over* [with Dave Cooke] (EMI).

Judy MacKenzie was an influential part of the British Jesus movement, though she was virtually unknown to American audiences. *Jesus Music* magazine describes her debut album as having a "rough-edged garage approach." MacKenzie belts out upbeat blues rockers accompanied by James Brown-style horns, then switches to breathy vocals on dreamy, psychedelic songs. Her next album featured increased orchestration and an acoustic emphasis similar to that of **Honeytree.** After two albums of Christian music, MacKenzie crossed over to the Brit-ish mainstream, releasing a duet album of pop rock songs with general market artist Dave Cooke.

Mack the Coffee Man

See **Movies With Heroes.**

Bryan MacLean

1997—*Ifyoubelievein* (Sundazed); 2001—*Candy's Waltz.*

www.bryanmaclean.com

Bryan MacLean (1946–1998) was lead guitarist for Love, one of the most important underground rock bands of the '60s. Led by Arthur Lee, Love created a psychedelic fusion of classical, jazz, and folk music that had obvious influences on The Who (in their development of *Tommy*), the Moody Blues, and many others. The group was called "an underground band" because, despite a huge following, they did not normally release their songs for radio play and so had very few official hits. Formed in 1965, Love made three classic albums *(Love, De Capo,* and *Forever Changes),* then disbanded. Lee continued to tour and occasionally record with various new lineups until 1975, but the moment was past. The official reason for the group's demise, as reported in *Rolling Stone,* was that excessive drug use had driven the band apart. MacLean would later elaborate on this, saying that he nearly overdosed on heroin, joined a Christian community and suffered a nervous breakdown. In addition to his guitar playing, MacLean wrote four of the band's best-known songs: "Softly to Me," "Orange Skies," "Alone Again Or," and "Old Man."

In his day, MacLean was a far bigger rock star than **Rick Cua, Joe English,** or **John Elefante** ever were. Still, he successfully avoided the attention paid to celebrity conversions and kept a low profile while maintaining his faith over the next thirty years of his life. MacLean was the half-brother of **Maria McKee,** lead singer of Lone Justice, and a song written by him ("Don't Toss Us Away") appeared on that group's debut album. Patty Loveless later recorded the song and had a country hit with it in 1988. At the age of fifty, MacLean decided to get back into recording and made a collection of home demos called *Ifyoubelievein.* The project includes some songs from his days with Love and was not intended for widespread distribution. On Christmas Day in 1998, MacLean died of a heart attack at a Los Angeles restaurant where he was being interviewed by Kevin Delaney, a reporter writing a biography of the band Love. In an extended obituary, *Rolling Stone* noted that the performer had just finished recording his first album of Christian music for a major (unidentified) label. That album has not been released, but some of the songs intended for it may be included on *Candy's Waltz,* a posthumous collection of unreleased material and live tracks from the previous four decades.

For trivia buffs: Bryan MacLean grew up in Beverly Hills and his first girlfriend was Liza Minelli.

Toby Mac

2001—*Momentum* (ForeFront).

www.tobymac.com

Toby Mac is a stage name used by Toby McKeehan, front man for **DC Talk.** He decided to record a solo album under that name while his main band was on hiatus (cf. **Kevin Max, Tait**). McKeehan is also a member of **The Gotee Brothers** and co-owner of Gotee Records. He is well known in the Christian industry as a producer and songwriter. McKeehan started out as a rapper named Caucatalk, a name that he eventually dropped in favor of **DC Talk**—a pun derived from his location in Washington, D.C., and his intention to provide an antidote to artists like 2 Live Crew by offering the world "Decent Christian Talk." He joined up with **Kevin Max** and Michael **Tait** at Liberty University in Lynchburg, Virginia, and expanded his solo act into a full hip-hop band. But despite initial success with tracks like "I Luv Rap Music," **DC Talk** wouldn't become huge until they left the rapping behind and adopted a straight-forward modern rock sound (with generous doses of pop-R&B and just a pinch of grunge). Not surprisingly, McKeehan viewed *Momentum* as an opportunity to return to his first love, revisiting the rap/hip-hop sound of the early Talk albums. As many critics pointed out, *Momentum* offers a portrait of what **DC Talk** might have ended up sounding like if they had not veered off into modern rock with *Jesus Freak.* Several tracks are straightforward hip-hop: "Somebody's Watching," "Do You Know," "Wonderin' Why," "In the Air." But then another handful evince the up-to-the-minute sound of rapcore. The best of these, "Extreme Days," is a tune McKeehan initially recorded as the title track for the film *Extreme Days,* a movie about extreme sports. He was criticized by many reviewers for copping Limp Bizkit's sound, with hardly anyone noting how much the latter's hybrid of hip-hop and metal owed to "Jesus Freak." McKeehan also continues in the **DC Talk** tradition of radical hip-hop remakes ("Jesus Is Just Alright," "Day by Day") by working parts of Buffalo Springfield's "For What It's Worth" into "What's Goin' Down" and covering Diana Ross's hit "Do You Know? (Theme from Mahogany)" (# 1 in 1975). Likewise, "Somebody's Watching" is a radical makeover of Rockwell's hit ("Somebody's Watching Me," # 2 in 1984) with guest vocalist Joanna Valencia singing what's left of the tune while Toby Mac spins off new verses all around her. "J Train" is a funky duet with **Kirk Franklin.**

As a songwriter, McKeehan has written or cowritten Christian radio hits performed by **Audio Adrenaline** ("Can't Take God Away"), **Lisa Bevill** ("Chaperone," "It's Gonna Be Worth It"), **Carman** ("Addicted to Jesus"), and **Out of Eden** ("Good Thing").

Christian radio hits: "Somebody's Watching Me" (# 12 in 2001).

Mad at the World

Randy Rose, voc., perc., drums; Roger Rose, voc., kybrd., gtr., prog.; Mike Pendleton, gtr., bass, perc., voc. (– 1993) // Brent Gordon, gtr. (+ 1990, – 1993); Ben Jacobs, gtr. (+ 1993); Mike Link, bass (+ 1993). 1987—*Mad at the World* (Frontline); 1988—*Flowers in the Rain;* 1990—*Seasons of Love* (Alarma); 1991—*Boomerang;* 1992—*Through the Forest* (Frontline); 1993—*Ferris Wheel;* 1995—*The Dreamland Café* (Alarma); 1998—*World History* (KMG).

Mad at the World was a Christian pop-rock band that defied expectations, morphing through at least three distinct style changes and performing each convincingly. Founded by Randy and Roger Rose, the group began with a pair of albums that presented them as a keyboard-dominated new-wave band. Accurately described as "a sanctified Depeche Mode," they then switched genres and released several records in the underground hard rock style of bands like The Cult. Then, with some personnel shifts, they came back to offer two more servings of retro-'60s psychedelic folk rock. From 1991 to 1995, **Randy Rose** also recorded as **Rose,** turning out albums that had a very different, mostly metal sound.

Although they would come to sound very dated, Mad at the World's first two albums were cutting-edge experiments in

Christian music. Several years ahead of bands like **Code of Ethics, Painted Orange,** and **Dance House Children,** Mad at the World was the first successful synth-pop group on the Christian music scene. Songs like "No More Innocence," "Living Dead," and "Fearfully and Wonderfully" must be regarded as classics of that subgenre despite the obviously derivative Depeche Mode sound. Lyrically, both *Mad at the World* and *Flowers in the Rain* are dark, dealing with the condition of life in a fallen world. "No More Innocence" describes the loss of child-like faith; "In My Dreams" gives a first-person account of someone facing judgment day. "Taking the Easy Way Out" is an emotional antisuicide ballad and "Why?" poses age-old questions about the presence of evil and injustice.

The next three outings reflect the band's second phase. Gritty guitars rule, keyboards are all but banished, and real drums replace synthesized rhythm machines. Rose also tones down his faux British accent and acquires more of the vocal snarl of a Jim Morrison or Billy Idol. Standout songs from *Seasons* include "City of Anger" and "Promised Land" (about the deception of drugs). *Through the Forest* includes "That Lonesome Road." *Boomerang* offers the band's most controversial song, "Isn't Sex a Wonderful Thing?"—a sarcastic rant against abuses of sexuality in modern society. During this period, the group also took to recording new synthesizer-free versions of old hits ("No More Innocence" on *Boomerang;* "Mad at the World" on *Forest*). They also tried out a few acoustic ballads that had a greater chance of endearing them to Christian radio. The best of these is "I've Got a Heaven" from *Forest,* a simple piano song with excellent vocals.

Ferris Wheel and especially *The Dreamland Café* find MATW reaching all the way back to the Beatles for their primary influences, though reviewers chose Lenny Kravitz as the most likely analogy for the new sound. The lead-off track on *Ferris Wheel,* "Not the Same," rocks with a Kravitz intensity, but much of the album is more folk-oriented ("Eyes of Heaven," "Jesus Lead Me," "Losing Game"). *The Dreamland Café* is generally regarded as the group's best project. *HM* magazine described it as "very trippy" and "dreamy, dreamy, dreamy." The band successfully transcends its influences to create a truly original sound that can justifiably be called "alternative rock"; the closest analogy in the general market would be the Pennsylvania band The Greenberry Woods, who crafted a similar update of Byrds/Big Star pop. The opening cut, "On the Stage," explodes out of the speakers like the long-lost Top 10 follow-up hit that should have been performed by some one-hit wonder band like the Lemon Pipers or the Strawberry Alarm Clock. The title track is more like **Love Song**-era Jesus music, offering an idyllic picture of a Christian coffeehouse where Jesus' love for "broken-hearted castaways" becomes evident. While *The Dreamland Café* may be a tad ballad-heavy, "Living in the Shadows" draws

more from Golden Earring's brand of guitar-heavy bubblegum, and "This Is How We Get to Heaven" has the feel of '90s alternative rock.

World History is a not a legitimate compilation album. In lieu of the traditional "greatest hits" package, the band chose to select songs from all of their albums except their best (*Dreamland Café*) and re-record them, downplaying the guitars. The result is a tame, adult-contemporary package that is not representative of the group's actual contributions to Christian music. **Randy Rose** went on to found a group called Mothership, which also included his brother Danny and employed a space-synth sound similar to the more somber elements of Depeche Mode. The latter group released an independent album called *LP* on Plastiq Musiq in 1998.

For trivia buffs: Before becoming a rock star, Roger Rose was a mailman. Mad at the World got their first recording contract after he stuck a tape in a record company executive's mailbox.

Christian radio hits: "Dry Your Tears" (# 15 in 1987).

Phil Madeira

1986—*Citizen of Heaven* (Refuge); 1997—*Off Kilter* (Word UK); 1998—*Three Horseshoes* (Silent Planet).

http://philmadeira.com

Multitalented musician and producer Phil Madeira has been playing on Christian albums since the early days of Jesus music. He was a member of the **Phil Keaggy** band responsible for *Emerging,* which included his "Struck by the Light." He has also played with **Kathy Troccoli, Joe English, Rick Cua,** and the **Vigilantes of Love.** Madeira has written a number of songs, the best known of which may be the worshipful "Mighty Lord," which has been recorded by numerous artists. He cowrote "Do Something Now," made popular by **CAUSE** (a group of Christian artists organized in emulation of Band-Aid and U.S.A. for Africa). Musically, Madeira is best known for his skills on the Hammond organ, though he sometimes plays a number of other instruments as well. His solo albums have tended to be quiet little side projects. *Citizen of Heaven* is a jazzy pop album with an up-tempo feel; one funky song called "Don't Fix It" is basically an ode to the inerrancy of Scripture. On *Off Kilter* he plays virtually all the instruments, offering a collection of songs in the tradition of '70s singer/songwriters. "Jagged Heart" speaks of life as a process of refinement: "Not like I had a plan / Not like I saw the goal / You got to whittle down to nothing / Before you'll ever be made whole." *Three Horseshoes* continues in the same tradition, but this time Madeira brought in a host of guest musicians, including members of **The Choir** and **Dogs of Peace** as well as friends **Phil Keaggy, Al Perkins,** and **Terry Taylor.** The guest list is appropriate, for the theme of the album is friendship and camaraderie. Indeed, *Three Horseshoes* is named after a pub in Derbyshire, where the artist was impressed with British hospitality. Madeira has also contributed songs to a compilation album featuring prominent writers performing their own material (*Coming from Somewhere Else,* Rocketown, 2000). He offers his own rendition of "Everywhere I Look" (originally performed by Keaggy) and "Hunger and Thirst" (originally performed by **Susan Ashton**). He also joins cowriters Gordon Kennedy, **Wayne Kirkpatrick,** and **Billy Sprague** in performing the anthemic title track.

As a songwriter, Madeira has written or cowritten songs performed by **Susan Ashton** ("In Amazing Grace Land," "Ball and Chain," "Hunger and Thirst," "Walk On By," "Remember Not"), **Lisa Bevill** ("Make It Better," "Sunshine and Joy"), **Rex Carroll** ("Hands of God"), **CAUSE** ("Do Something Now"), **Ashley Cleveland** ("Enter His Courts"), **Michael English** ("Message of Mercy"), **Kim Hill** ("Like a Father Should Be"), **Kenny Marks** ("Heroes," "I'll Be a Friend," "The Next Time You See Johnny," "Like a Father Should Be"), and **Geoff Moore and The Distance** ("Evolution . . . Redefined").

Madelyniris

Carrie Munsell, voc.; Mark Munsell, gtr. 1999—*Madelyniris* (mp3.com); *Overflow with Tears.*

www.madelyniris.com

Madelyniris from Waterloo, Illinois, is the ultimate countercultural indie band. They refuse to release their albums on labels big or small, opting instead to make them available for free downloads on the Internet. Nevertheless, they have attained remarkable success, with well over a hundred thousand downloads of their self-titled debut. "If Word Records knocked on our door and laid out a million dollar record deal, we'd say, 'No'," Mark Munsell maintains. The group is composed of a husband and wife duo with strong musical backgrounds. Carrie Munsell is a classically trained vocalist with a music degree from Missouri State University. Mark has a history of playing with garage bands, including a Christian group called Missionary X. The two began writing songs as personal therapy during a difficult period when their infant daughter Madelyn Iris contracted Alopecia Areata, a rare skin disease causing permanent loss of her hair. They began casually posting the songs on mp3.com and one track, "New Day," was chosen by that website as its "Song of the Day," leading to three thousand downloads and numerous requests for more of their music.

Munsell once described the Madelyniris sound as "Sarah MacLachlan fronting **U2.**" Reviewers have noted general similarities to artistic pop groups like **Over the Rhine** and **Six-**pence None the Richer.** The Munsells do a cover of **U2**'s "Drowning Man" on their first album, with Bono himself introducing the song with a reading of William Yeats' poem, "Mother of God." Songs like "Scarlet," "I Want to Believe," and "Shadow of Your Love" are clearly written from a faith perspective, while retaining a nonpreachy poetic flair and a sincere sense of honesty. The second album would include the Celtic pop song "Strong" and a heavier rock number, "Blue Stained Veins."

Magdalen (a.k.a. Magdallan)

Lanny Cordola, gtr.; Ken Mary, drums (– 1994); Brian Bromberg, bass (–1993); Kim Bullard, kybrd. (–1993); Ken Tamplin, voc. (–1993) // Phil Bardowell, voc. (+ 1993); Chuck Wright, bass (+ 1993). As Magdallan: 1992—*Big Bang* (Intense). As Magdalen: 1993—*Revolution Mind* (ERG); 1994—*The Dirt* [EP] (Intense).

Except for the all-important connecting link of **Lanny Cordola,** Magdallan and Magdalen are two completely different bands, hence the change in spelling. Cordola is the legendary guitarist who played with the mainstream band House of Lords and who has also spearheaded such Christian projects as **Chaos is the Poetry, Children of Zion, The Panorama Ramblers, Shack of Peasants,** and **Symbiotica.** Magdallan was his debut venture in the contemporary Christian music market, undertaken with **Ken Tamplin,** a former guitar student. Tamplin, cousin to rock singer Sammy Hagar, played with the Christian band **Shout** and has recorded as a solo artist. The second incarnation of Cordola's band featured vocals by Phil Bardowell, a childhood friend. Ken Mary and Chuck Wright also played with House of Lords. Despite the odd spellings, the group's name was chosen as a tribute to Mary Magdalene, who Cordola mistakenly thought to be the central character in his "favorite Bible story" (the account of the woman caught in adultery in John 8:1–11).

Big Bang was originally slated to be a general market release and was recorded on a studio budget much bigger than most Christian music groups could ever afford. It belongs to the metal tradition of Def Leppard but showcases a wide variety of styles. The opening "End of the Ages" is a typical headbanger anthem and "Dome of the Rock," a warp-speed shredder, but "Shake" adds spice to the predictable mix with a heavy dose of Memphis blues and R&B shuffle. "Radio Bikini" features a Bon Jovi "wo-oh" chorus. The title track and "This One's 4 U" have strong jazz influences. "House of Dreams" and "Wounded Hearts" are the expected power ballads. Lyrically, the album is sparse in its religious references, attempting to blend them into a project that would have an overall secular appeal. Unfortunately, the messages that do occur are not positive statements of faith but lame attacks on the theory of evolution ("Big Bang," "End of the Ages"), which most nonfundamentalist

Christians do not find incompatible with biblical teaching. Thus, Magdallan earns their right to witness the hard way and then wastes it with sectarian and not very credible drivel that just makes them look foolish. "House of Dreams," however, offers a positive (though generic) vision of hope that contrasts with the despair and cynicism of much metal music.

The reconstituted Magdalen group brought a more blues-based sound to the fore, evoking comparisons to Led Zeppelin rather than to '80s arena rockers. A diversity of styles are again evident on *Revolution Mind,* as fast rockers ("White Rice") mix with ballads ("Soul Child"). The title track even features a gospel chorus. "Sad Sister Alchemy" sounds very similar to Rod Stewart's "Stay with Me" and "Samson and Delilah" is a cover of a Rev. Gary Davis tune. Lyrically, the album has a much more obvious Christian focus than the earlier project, though there is also a heavy socio-political direction to songs like "American Lament," "White Rice" (about poverty), and "Sad Sister Alchemy." The song "Waiting for the Son" points to Christ's return as the only ultimate resolution for the world's problems, and "Make It Through" promises that "in time justice will flow like a river." The EP *Dirt* is a mostly acoustic collection of six songs, including a cover of Black Sabbath's "War Pigs."

Christian radio hits: "House of Dreams" (# 11 in 1992).

Magnified Plaid

See **MxPx.**

Mahogany Rush

See **Frank Marino and Mahogany Rush.**

Malcolm and Alwyn

Alwyn Wall, voc., gtr.; Malcolm Wild, voc., autoharp. 1973—*Fool's Wisdom* (Grapevine); 1974—*WildWall* (Myrrh); 1981—*Live* (Ministry Resource Center).

Malcolm and Alwyn are probably best known as the subjects of a famous **Larry Norman** song, "Dear Malcolm, Dear Alwyn," in which he proclaims, "I'm your greatest fan." The group was one of the most popular acoustic folk duos of the Jesus movement, and they were certainly Britain's most noticed artists in the American version of that revival. Styled as a Christian version of Seals and Crofts, they actually had much more of a Crosby, Stills and Nash sound (or at least Crosby/Nash). The couple had first played together in a English band called The Zodiacs, when Wall was only fifteen. Out of that experience, they formed a folk duo to play the pubs and then, in 1969, both had spiritual conversion experiences within two days of each other.

Fool's Wisdom contains two songs on which the duo sounds very much like Simon and Garfunkel with mild British accents. These tunes—the title track and "Tomorrow's News"—are the most orchestrated songs on the record and would become two of its three best-known songs. The third would be another soft folk song, "The World Needs Jesus." But the opening "Say It Like Is" and "Heaven or Hell" already previewed a more rocking style, which would come to full bloom on *WildWall.* That album was simply ahead of its time. It seems tame by modern standards, but in 1974 it sounded too "worldly" to the band's church audiences, and the duo succeeded in alienating their already small fan base. "I Feel Fine" (not the Beatles song), "Spaceman," and "Buried Alive" all demonstrate that Malcolm and Alwyn had learned a lot from their fan Norman in the year between the two albums. "I'll Carry You Through" is extraordinarily Beatlesque, with guitar lines taken straight from George Harrison's *All Things Must Pass.* According to historian Di Sabatino, Davey Johnstone (Elton John's guitarist) and Johnny Gustafson, from the original cast of *Jesus Christ Superstar,* perform uncredited on the album.

Most of Malcolm and Alwyn's songs are either worshipful ("Always on my Mind," "Stay with Me") or message songs. "Seed of Corn" offers a modern agricultural parable similar to those in the Bible. "Things Are Getting Better" (another Simon and Garfunkel sound-alike) is a simple statement of the positive change that faith works in the singers' lives. "I'll Carry You Through" is sung as Christ's promise to flagging humanity. "Buried Alive" is about baptism. "I Love" seemed even at the time to be an obvious rip-off of the song "I Love" by Tom T. Hall. Both songs offer grateful acknowledgment of daily blessings. Like Hall (who loves "little baby ducks, country streams, and old pick up trucks"), Malcolm and Alwyn simply list lots of things that *they* love: "to see the moon when it's up and full . . . and when a fish gives my line a pull."

"Tomorrow's News" is an important if painful souvenir of the Jesus movement. The song describes in graphic detail what the newspaper will supposedly report the day after a so-called Rapture hits the earth and all the true Christians get zapped into the sky: cars are left without drivers, planes without pilots, and general chaos ensues. Such "Rapture" theology (more a product of fundamentalist fantasy than biblical scholarship) remains one of the more embarrassing aspects of the Jesus movement. It is touched on in many songs (**Larry Norman**'s "I Wish We'd All Been Ready," **Love Song**'s "The Cossack Song") but is never so blatantly extolled as in Malcolm and Alwyn's "Tomorrow's News." The song remains a significant reminder of how easily naive Christians can be duped by teachers who substitute charisma for a critical approach to Scripture.

Alongside the just-mentioned misstep must be set "The World Needs Jesus," which was regarded as Malcolm and Alwyn's best song when it first appeared and would still sound good three decades later. The tune is simple, the melody pretty, and the lyrics poignant. In successive verses, Malcolm and Alwyn sing about different sorts of troubles and conclude, first, "Ooooh, the world needs Jesus," then "the church needs Jesus," and finally, "I need Jesus."

Malcolm and Alwyn separated in 1976 but reunited in 1981 for a concert album. The latter project reveals more of their characteristic humor than is evident on the two studio records. In the interim, Malcolm Wild became a pastor at Calvary Chapel in Tampa, Florida, and recorded a solo album (*Broken Chains,* Grapevine, 1980) that has an early '70s folk sound reminiscent of Harry Nilsson. He would later record the album *Red Alert* with the temporary group Malcolm and the Mirrors (A&S, 1982). The latter project is a collection of apocalyptic songs that *CCM* would describe as "basic power pop with new-wave and heavy metal influences . . . one of the rockiest discs Maranatha Music has yet released." Alwyn Wall, meanwhile, had formed the critically acclaimed Alwyn Wall Band as early as 1977. The group consists of three members of a fairly well-known British Christian group called Mighty Flyers (Norman Barratt, gtr.; Nick Brotherhood, drums; Tony Hudson, bass), and Phil Holmes on keyboards. The Alwyn Wall Band released a self-titled debut album on Myrrh in 1977. *Jesus Music* magazine describes the project as "pretty much standard British rock of the era . . . with electric guitar work reminiscent of old **Larry Norman/Randy Stonehill**." Another album called *The Prize* was issued on Myrrh in 1978, and some sources list albums titled *Oasis* and *Midnight Fire* for the band that same year. In any event, Alwyn Wall would produce a solo album called *Invisible Warfare* on StarSong in 1982. The latter record was marketed as "**Larry Norman** presents Alwyn Wall," though it is not clear exactly what Norman had to do with the project. As of 1998, Wall was serving as a worship leader at Calvary Chapel Westminster in London. In 1999, Malcolm and Alwyn's song "Fool's Wisdom" was redone by British artist Mal Pope, who sings it as a duet with Martyn Joseph on his *Reunion of the Heart* (Kingsway) album.

Malcolm and the Mirrors

See **Malcolm and Alwyn.**

Barbara Mandrell

Selected: 1982—*He Set My Life to Music* (MCA).

www.barbara-mandrell.com

A great many mainstream country western singers have made a token gospel album at some point in their career, but

Barbara Mandrell approached her gospel project with an uncommon degree of public commitment and testimony. Born in 1948 in Houston, Texas, Mandrell was raised in Oceanside, California. She moved to Nashville in 1971 and became one of country music's biggest stars. A multitalented performer, she is not only a fine vocalist but also plays guitar, banjo, saxophone, and pedal steel guitar. Some of Mandrell's biggest hits were songs with strong sexual innuendo like "Woman to Woman" and "If Loving You Is Wrong, I Don't Want to Be Right." Indeed, her cover of the latter song (originally done by Luther Ingram) was not only her first Number One country hit but also her only song to make the Top 40 of the mainstream pop charts (# 31 in 1979). Mandrell would defend her decision as a Christian to record such songs by maintaining that their lyrics "speak the truth about things that go on in this world." From 1980 to 1982, she hosted a popular network TV program called *Barbara Mandrell and the Mandrell Sisters,* which became one of the only forums on network TV to feature contemporary Christian music artists. **Andraé Crouch** and **Jessy Dixon** both appeared on the program, in addition to such traditional gospel acts as The Blackwood Brothers. When Mandrell made her 1982 gospel album, *He Set My Life to Music,* she enlisted the help of many other Christian artists. She sings a duet with Crouch on his "Through It All," with **Dottie Rambo** on "I Will Glory in the Cross," and with **B. J. Thomas** on the hymn, "What a Friend We Have in Jesus." The album also includes "I'm Yours, Lord" by **Gary Chapman.** Mandrell appeared on the cover of *CCM* magazine in November 1982, relating in detail her life of constant faith. She indicates with some humor that, going against type, she was brought up Pentecostal but "got saved" in a Lutheran church that she visited at the age of ten. Two years after recording *He Set My Life to Music,* Mandrell was involved in a head-on collision with a reckless driver who was killed in the accident. She was severely injured but made a full recovery, as did her two children, who were in the car with her. She publicly testified to God's protective grace in saving them from harm and became a national spokesperson for the importance of seat belts.

Dove Awards: 1982 Album by a Secular Artist *(He Set My Life to Music).*

Grammy Awards: 1982 Best Inspirational Performance *(He Set My Life to Music);* 1983 Best Soul Gospel Performance by a Duo or Group [with Bobby Jones] ("I'm So Glad I'm Standing Here Today").

Bobby Jo Mann

1990—*Sending Out Signals* (Boy-O-Boy).

Almost nothing is known of the Christian pop singer Bobby Jo Mann, who released one independent album in 1990. *Sending Out Signals* was dedicated to the memory of Mann's mother and featured a collection of bright and upbeat songs with messages of hope ("Loved for Life," "Gotta Know Love," "Power to Forgive"). The album merited a rare indie review in *CCM* magazine, where Mann's music was described as warm and colorful, with a '60s tone recalling The Byrds or Fleetwood Mac.

Darrell Mansfield (and **Mansfield/ Turner**)

As Darrell Mansfield: 1979—*Higher Power* (Maranatha); 1980—*Get Ready* (Polydor); 1983—*Live* (Ministry Resource Center); *The Vision* (A&S); 1985—*Revelation* (Broken); 1989—*Darrell Mansfield Live* (Asaph); 1992— *Live at Flevo*; *Get Ready* (Ocean); 1993—*Give Him Your Blues* (Asaph); 1994—*The Collection* (Calvary Chapel); 1995—*Mansfield and Co.* (Ocean); 1996—*The Lord's House* (Tribute to Rev. Dan Smith); 1997—*Crossroads* (Son); *Delta Blues*; 1998—*Last Chance Boogie*; 1999—*Darrell Mansfield Band Live in Europe* (label unknown); 2000—*Soul'd Out* (custom); *Live on Tour* (Micah). As Mansfield/Turner: 1991—*Blues With a Feelin'* (Ocean).

www.darrellmansfield.com

Darrell Mansfield has become the world's best-known Christian blues singer, the undisputed king of what is admittedly a pretty small genre. Famous for his gravelly voice and stellar harmonica playing, he has resurrected such blues classics as "You've Got to Move" and "People Get Ready" for a new audience, reminding (or informing) his fans that "the blues" originated within the Christian church as a genre with close links to gospel and spirituals. Mansfield, who is a Calvary Chapel minister, further emphasizes that much of the Bible (the Psalms, Lamentations, the prophets) is expressive of the blues. Aside from the solo albums listed above—and the one project with guitarist Eric Turner—Mansfield has recorded as part of the group **Gentle Faith,** the duo **Kaiser/Mansfield** and the trio, **Mansfield, Howard, and Kaiser.** He also sang on two albums in 1993 as a part of the special blues project **Shack of Peasants.**

Mansfield's musical career began as a college student when he was overheard singing rock and roll songs while washing dishes in the school cafeteria and was invited to join a local band. A number of traumas (his parents' divorce, a failed romance) led him to attempt suicide, slitting his wrists on the altar of a church—where he was discovered and rushed to the hospital. Mansfield was first attracted to Christianity by the spirituality he observed in the mother of one of his friends. After attending a series of Bible studies and reading the autobiography of Jerome Hines (an opera singer who gave his life to God), Mansfield came to know Christ in a direct and personally fulfilling way. He joined the Calvary Chapel band **Gentle Faith** and later embarked on a solo career. Notably, his early music betrays little of the trademark sound for which he would become best known. On *Higher Power,* he sounds very much like **B. J. Thomas,** singing light pop songs. About half of

the songs on the album were written by **Denny Correll.** The brightest moments come with a guitar solo on Correll's "He Has Overcome" and a bit of harmonica playing on Mansfield's own "That's Alright." On *The Vision,* Mansfield reprises **Gentle Faith**'s "Jerusalem" and *Higher Power*'s "No More Blues," adding other songs that are mostly nondescript MOR pop. *CCM* trashed the album as mundane and impassive, though it is actually fine for what it is. The title track offers a lyrically powerful account of John's vision of Christ in the book of Revelation. The *Collection* album issued in 1994 should properly be called *The Non-Blues Collection,* since it draws almost exclusively from Mansfield's pop and adult contemporary repertoire.

The album that insures Mansfield's legacy in the history of Christian rock is *Get Ready.* Its release between *Higher Power* and *The Vision* explains the critical disdain for the latter work— and in fact for almost anything nonbluesy that Mansfield would ever do again. *Get Ready* took the world of contemporary Christian music by storm, assaulting the little subculture with sounds they had never heard before—certainly not within the kingdom. *CCM* selected it as one of the Ten Best Albums of 1980, describing it as a record that offers, "no strings, no horns, no ballads, and no holds barred . . . an album of solid, all-out rock 'n' roll." The "no ballads" comment is an exaggeration—"Flow Like a River" is another **B. J. Thomas** clone that would provide the *Collection* compilation with an excuse to include one song from Mansfield's best-known album, but overall *Get Ready* marks a transition from the Christian folk-pop of the '70s to the Christian hard rock and metal of the '80s. Notably, *Get Ready* was issued on Polydor records, a secular label, and was intended for the general market. Lyrically, Mansfield uses metaphors and generic euphemisms like "heaven" for referencing what he would normally attribute specifically to God or Jesus. *Revelation* (with Eric Turner on guitar and **Terl Bryant** on drums) revisits this territory, finding its finest moment on "Jesus Will Reign." The song "Bible Study" is a humorous boogie romp that describes young people gathering to study the Scriptures as though this were some kind of seditious activity. *Mansfield and Co.* presents the star in front of a crack band running through "Spoonful" and other blues-rock standards.

Mansfield's continued output of often privately released and hard-to-find albums reveals that he is frequently at his best when performing live. He also shines on standards, which occupy a good portion of the Mansfield/Turner album, *Blues with a Feelin'.* That record offers the duo's version of **Curtis Mayfield**'s "People Get Ready," Ben E. King's "Stand by Me," and Blind Willy Johnson's "Nobody's Fault But Mine" (made famous for rock fans by Led Zeppelin). *Soul'd Out* pairs Mansfield with Jaymes Felix on such songs as "Swing Low, Sweet Chariot," "Amazing Grace," and **Andraé Crouch**'s

"Soon and Very Soon." Mansfield has said, "I see myself more as an evangelist than a musician. Rock 'n' roll just happens to be my pulpit."

Christian radio hits: As Mansfield/Turner: "Stand by Me" (# 17 in 1991).

Mansfield, Howard, and Kaiser

See **Glenn Kaiser.**

Frank Marino and Mahogany Rush

Selected: 2000—*Eye of the Storm* (Justin Time).

Canadian Frank Marino (b. 1954) has led the cult metal band Mahogany Rush for some thirty years, forming the first incarnation of the group when he was only seventeen. An urban legend regarding the group's origins is an essential part of rock mythology. Supposedly, the young Marino was a nonmusician until the spirit of the recently departed Jimi Hendrix visited him while he was in a coma at a Montreal hospital; from that day on, he could play the guitar like Hendrix himself (well, almost). Marino did little at first to dissuade fans who swore this tale was true, but eventually he flatly denied that any such vision or unpracticed bestowal of gifts had ever occurred. He did, however, front a power trio (Jimmy Ayoub, drums; Paul Harwood, bass) similar to that of the Jimi Hendrix Experience and record an independent debut album *(Maxoom),* followed by seven more '70s albums on 20th Century Fox *(Child of the Novelty, Strange Universe, Mahogany Rush IV, World Anthem, Mahogany Rush Live, Tales of the Unexpected, What's Next).* As a pre-MTV metal band the group did not have any conventional hit songs but they did have a large and loyal fanbase. Marino continued to front various versions of the band throughout the '80s recording occasionally for small labels. He quit performing in 1992 but after an eight-year hiatus returned to form with a new album, *Eye of the Storm.* During the interim, he says that he grew in his understanding of theology and of grace. He repudiates all language of conversion stemming from what he calls the "born-again community," insisting that he is a lifetime member of the Eastern Orthodox Church and has always been a believer. Still, he acknowledges that in the '90s his associates in the music business came to view him "as a Jesus freak." For one thing, he began writing a series of spiritual tracts and mailing them out to friends or inquisitors. *Eye of the Storm* clearly reveals these new passions. *HM* called it "a whale of a faith-centered album, testifying to Christ and his sovereignty." On the song "Ordinary Man," Marino sings "I feel alive and know the truth is speaking / And the words pour out and they reach into my soul / I close my eyes and know the Lord is teaching." On "He's Calling," he offers these words: "To the lonely, the only way to go home / Is to go home / To the broken, He's spoken / Won't you come home?"

Pam Mark

See **Pam Mark Hall.**

Kenny Marks

1982—*Follow Him* (Myrrh); 1983—*Right Where You Are;* 1986—*Attitude* (DaySpring); 1987—*Make It Right;* 1989—*Another Friday Night;* 1992—*Fire of Forgiveness;* 1993—*Absolutely Positively;* 1995—*World Gone Mad* (Word).

A longtime veteran of Christian music, Kenny Marks performed with Billy Graham crusades for ten years before making his first album and then evolved into a sort of Christianized Kenny Loggins, that is, a musical chameleon capable of changing his style as new sounds came and went out of fashion. Over the years, critics would compare him to Bryan Adams, with shades of Tom Petty. Marks was on the cover of *CCM* magazine in August 1987 and was for a time one of Christian music's biggest pop stars. He is best remembered for helping to implement a style that he calls "horizontal music with a vertical connection": songs that may be informed by a spiritual orientation but are not overtly about spiritual things. Such a style would eventually carry the day in contemporary Christian music, but in the early '80s, Marks's songs about human relationships were somewhat anomalous in a field dominated by songs about worshiping God, following Jesus, resisting the devil, and reading the Bible. A stellar example of the Marks style is the so-called "Johnny and Jeannie" series of songs about a fictitious couple. In "Growing Up Too Fast" (from *Right Where You Are*) the two characters are introduced separately as two kids struggling with emotional surges and biological impulses. In "The Party's Over" (from *Attitude*), they meet in the backseat of Johnny's car and Jeannie ends up pregnant. In "Next Time You See Johnny" (from *Another Friday Night*) the listener learns that their hasty marriage didn't work out and the growing child is hurting over his father's absence from the home. A video version of this moralistic soap opera was commended by congressional groups and used in some Planned Parenthood programs. Marks described the series as "everything John Mellencamp didn't tell you about Jack and Diane." Later he added a fourth song to provide some resolution (the title track to *Fire of Forgiveness*).

Raised in Detroit, Marks is the son of Yugoslavian immigrants ("Marks" is an Anglicized, shortened form of Mrakovitch). He graduated from Messiah College in Philadelphia in 1971 and immediately went to work singing at crusades for Billy Graham and his associate Leighton Ford. *Follow Him* was his pop-oriented, hook-filled debut, but he didn't catch on with the Christian music public until *Right Where You Are,* which offers the jazzy "It's Incredible." The ballad "Single Minded Love" struck a nerve with many unmarried Christians who were waiting for God to provide them with a life partner.

Attitude offers several songs dealing with its titular theme, in addition to **Phil Madeira**'s "Heroes," an ode to the oft-unrecognized persons who work behind the scenes. The title song of *Make It Right* would provide Marks with his first super-hit; the song suggests that those who are looking for love need first to discover the source of love in God. Also on *Make It Right,* "White Dress" addresses the illegitimate guilt that haunts many children who feel responsible for their parents' marital problems. Another song, "Say a Prayer for Me Tonight," was inspired by an instance in which a person with whom Marks met for counseling after a concert committed suicide a few days later. *Another Friday Night* focuses on the theme of loneliness and offers a fine rock single in "Nobody Else But Jesus." *Fire of Forgiveness* takes a more mature, adult perspective on the same family-oriented issues Marks had been addressing for youth. Several songs deal with marital commitment ("Someone to Come Home To," "Promises to Keep," "Forever Love"). On a more personal level, Marks offers "1932," about his father's immigration to the United States, and "Like a Father Should Be," a tribute to the man, sung as a duet with **Kim Hill.** The title track to *World Gone Mad* was chosen by evangelist Josh McDowell as the theme song for his *Right from Wrong* campaign. Also on that album, "In My Mother's Eyes" is a touching song based on the twenty-five year reunion of Marks's wife with a daughter she had given up for adoption at the age of sixteen.

Overall, Marks's songs display an unusual degree of sensitivity to adolescent concerns. He is a gifted songwriter himself, though many of his songs are written or cowritten by his wife Pamela Marks and by **Phil Madeira.** Keith Thomas and **Paul Smith** also played key roles in developing his early material. Marks has often toured with a band he called The Remarkables, which included Madeira and wife Pamela.

Christian radio hits: "Right Where You Are" (# 12 in 1984); "Heroes" (# 14 in 1986); "Make It Right" (# 1 for 8 weeks in 1987); "Say a Prayer for Me Tonight" (# 5 in 1987); "White Dress" (# 11 in 1988); "I'll Be a Friend" (# 8 in 1989); "The Next Time You See Johnny" (# 3 in 1990); "Running on Love" (# 19 in 1991); "Don't Give Up" (# 3 in 1992); "Like a Father Should Be" [with **Kim Hill**] (# 22 in 1992); "Turn my World Around" (# 8 in 1992); "Absolutely, Positively Friends" (# 14 in 1993).

Dave Markee Band

See **Valeri Barinov.**

Mars Ill

Nate Corrona [a.k.a. DJ Dust], voc.; Greg Owens [a.k.a. Soulheir], voc. 2001—*Raw Material* (Uprok).

Mars Ill is an old-school hip-hop group fronted by a duo of artists who trade vocals **Run-D.M.C.** style with generous turntable scratching, instrumental breakdowns, and shout outs. The tone is generally laid-back with slow, thick grooves.

CCM calls the group's debut "a thinking person's hip-hop" record with intellectual lyrics that are more thought-provoking than confrontational. "Monotone" describes life without God as bland. "Love's Not" juxtaposes verses describing what love is with verses describing what it isn't. The group apparently likes the sound of old vinyl records, as a number of tracks sound like they are being played on a phonograph, complete with all the crackling noises that the nonexistent stylus is supposedly making in the nonexistent grooves (cf. **Wondergroove**).

Martha's Wake

Personnel for 1998: Drew Cullis, drums; Melody Nichols, bass; Jon Nichols, gtr., dulc.; J. W. Penzien, kybrd., gtr.; Lori Penzien, voc., trump., flute, perc. 1993—*Romans* (custom); 1995—*Sofia*; 1996—*Colouring China*; 1998—*Time and Elements* (Kingdom).

Martha's Wake is a progressive folk-rock band that was founded in 1988. Their name derives from the story of Jesus raising Lazarus from the dead (at a wake thrown by his sister Martha) in John 11. They have a diverse sound that *HM* describes as "elements of ethnic folk music, gothic rock, and new-wave combined with some pop elements." Jon Nichols describes the music as "atmospheric, driving, intelligent, emotional—and difficult to categorize." He further indicates that the band "has been a vehicle that lends itself to the spiritual growth of each member." In 1994, the group went to Bulgaria to participate in an International Festival of the Arts and to raise money for orphans. Expressions of faith in Martha's Wake material are sufficiently ambiguous to have aroused suspicion among some fans of Christian music regarding the group's orthodoxy (e.g., "There's a solitary God that watches me from beyond the Pleiades"). In response to some queries, the group attached a disclaimer to their liner notes for *Time and Elements* stating that the band "is in no way involved in New Age ideology." The latter album was the first to gain widespread notice in the Christian media. Produced by Dave Beegle of **Fourth Estate,** it features five instrumentals (dealing with the subjects "fire," "ether," "air," "earth," and "water"), written by each of the group members individually. Of the vocals, "Under My Skin" is an up-tempo tune drenched with emotion. "Razor-blade Girl" is about a suicidal young woman who is attracted to the occult. Nichols says that he wrote it out of his experience from working as a therapist for many years and that "the point of the song is the same point as the parable of the Good Samaritan—who is my neighbor and who are we, as Christians, called to reach?"

David Martin

1985—*Stronger Than the Weight* (Home Sweet Home); 1986—*Breath on the Windowpane* (Greentree).

Christian pop singer David Martin began his career in music as a professional songwriter. A native of Birmingham, Alabama, he moved to Nashville after completing college and worked as a songwriter for a general market pop-music firm. Raised a Baptist, Martin retained an interest in Christian music and eventually made contact with **Chris Christian** who hired him as a songwriter for his own production company. Martin composed "Let the Wind Blow," which was performed by **The Imperials** as the title song from their 1985 album. He also made two albums of his own. *Stronger Than the Weight* contains his own version of "Let the Wind Blow" and is described by Martin as "a thematic album on which all the songs deal with trusting God who generously gives His love, His blessings, and His strength."

Christian radio hits: "Eyes of a Child" (# 2 in 1986); "You're to Blame" (# 9 in 1987).

The Martins

Judy Martin Hess, voc.; Jonathan Martin, voc.; Joyce Martin McCullough, voc. Selected: 1995—*The Martins* (Spring Hill); 1996—*Wherever You Are*; 1997—*Light of the World*; 1998—*Dream Big*; 2000—*Windows*; 2001—*Glorify, Edify, Testify.*

www.the-martins.com

The Martins are a trio of siblings well known in the sphere of southern gospel music. Raised in rural Arkansas, they grew up in a cabin with no electricity or indoor plumbing. Deep faith and love for God enabled them to transcend such poverty and The Martins would end up touring Arkansas, Louisiana, Missouri, Tennessee, and Texas. They made a series of southern gospel cassette tapes and, then, began releasing albums on **Bill Gaither**'s Spring Hill label. In the mid '90s the trio started to adopt a more contemporary sound. The ballads "Timothy's Burden" and "Out of His Great Love" from their 1995 self-titled project first displayed this crossover potential. *Wherever You Are* was coproduced by **Michael English,** who imbued selections like "Well Water" and "Hazy Days" with an inspirational pop sound that earned the combo a favorable review in *CCM,* amidst frequent comparisons to The Judds.

The move into modern country continues on *Dream Big,* the album that really brought the group to the attention of the contemporary Christian music community. "He'll Be Holdin' His Own" offers a hint of blues and "Count Your Blessings" provides what might be the first bluegrass telling of the story of Job. "More Like a Whisper" (cowritten by **Scott Krippayne**) is an adult contemporary ballad reflecting on the "still, small voice of God." It is rendered here as a solo by Jonathan Martin. *Windows* employs more innovative backgrounds on "Mighty God" and "What God's Gonna Do," which feature horns, some jazz saxophone, and blues guitar licks. Again, it is the ballads—

"Your Ways Are Higher" and "Stars Below" (about life in heaven) that offer the connection between adult contemporary pop and southern gospel. Asked to describe their sound, Jonathan demurred: "It's not southern gospel . . . it's not pop . . . a little country . . . no rock 'n' roll. We can't place it anywhere. It's a little bit of everything, and it's working for us." *Light of the World* is a Christmas album. *Glorify, Edify, Testify* is a collection of hymns, with a southern gospel focus ("Pass Me Not," "Standing on the Promises").

Dove Awards: 1996 Southern Gospel Album *(The Martins);* 1996 Southern Gospel Song ("Out of His Great Love"); 1997 Southern Gospel Album *(Wherever You Are);* 1997 Southern Gospel Song ("Only God Knows"); 1998 Southern Gospel Album *(Light of the World);* 1999 Country song ("Count Your Blessings").

Martyr

See **Betrayal.**

Mary-Kathryn

1999—*Stream in the Desert* (Rhythm House); 2000—*One Spirit.*

Inspirational singer Mary-Kathryn (who goes by her first name only) combines elements of world music with an otherwise easy listening approach to worship-oriented Christian music. Describing herself as a psalmist, she applies a tender voice to soothing songs intended to invoke a sense of comfort and peace. She also incorporates tribal vocals into some of the material on *Streams in the Desert* and sings in three different languages. *One Spirit* opens with "Let Us Praise," which features Egyptian rhythms and a Middle Eastern sound. African influences surface on "Savior" and Hebraic effects add allure to "Taste and See."

Mary Mary

Erica Atkins, voc.; Tina Atkins, voc. 2000—*Thankful* (Word).

www.mary-mary.com

Mary Mary is an R&B duo composed of two sisters, neither of whom is actually named Mary. Erica and Tina Atkins were raised in Inglewood, California, in a strict family where no music other than gospel was allowed in the home. They sang in church with their five other sisters (and one brother), eventually landing a spot on the *Bobby Jones Gospel* program on the BET cable network. The duo then toured with two Michael Matthews gospel shows *(Mama, I'm Sorry* and *Sneaky)* and took to composing. A song called "Dance" was recorded by urban contemporary singer Robin S. for the soundtrack to the Eddie Murphy movie *Dr. Doolittle.* They recorded "Let Go and Let God" for the *Prince of Egypt (Inspirational)* soundtrack. The Las Vegas femme trio 702 recorded their "What More Can He

Do," and **Yolanda Adams** put "Time to Change" and "Yeah" on her *Mountain High . . . Valley Low* album. Mary Mary's debut offers a number of driving dance floor funk songs with praise-oriented lyrics. The song "Shackles" connects liberation and celebration in an especially meaningful way ("Take the shackles off my feet so I can dance . . . You broke my chains, now I can lift my hands / And I'm gonna praise you"). Other standout tracks include the guitar-driven "I Sings" and "I Got It." Slower tunes ("What a Friend," "Still My Child") focus on God's grace. Mainstream pop band Destiny's Child join the sisters for a remake of **Curtis Mayfield**'s "Good to Me," and a spirited version of the traditional song "Wade in the Water" closes out the project. The duo says they chose their name in honor of two of the several Marys in the Bible, specifically Mary Magdalene and Mary the mother of Jesus.

Christian radio hits: "Shackles" (# 5 in 2000).

Dove Awards: 2001 Urban Album of the Year *(Thankful)*; 2001 Urban Song of the Year ("Shackles").

Grammy Awards: 2000 Best Contemporary Soul Gospel Album *(Thankful)*.

Mary Said

Burke Gordon, bass; Justin Keough, drums; Dave McDonald, gtr.; Jared Summerell, voc., gtr. 1996—*Detergent* [EP] (Brainstorm).

A quartet associated with the Vineyard ministries, Mary Said created one six-song set of alterna-pop songs while the members were still in high school. The title song to *Detergent* deals with the subject of spiritual cleansing, while "Incline" describes the uphill struggle of Christian growth. With a humility atypical of budding rock stars, Jared Summerell told *7ball* magazine, "I don't know if we're ready to be a ministry type of band—I don't know if I'm mature enough to speak in front of crowds." The band was put on hold while its members attended college.

Sarah Masen

1995—*The Holding* (independent); 1996—*Sarah Masen* (re:think); 1998—*Carry Us Through*; 2001—*Dreamlife of Angels* (Word).

www.sarahmasen.com

Singer/songwriter Sarah Masen (b. 1975) appeared on the scene at the right time, entering the contemporary Christian music world just as a plethora of similar-sounding female singer/songwriters (Paula Cole, Lisa Loeb, Sarah MacLachlan, Sophie B. Hawkins) were making it big in the Lilith Fair-dominated general market. Masen sings in a flirtatious vocal style that alternates playfully between an affected falsetto and her more natural alto. She cites **Leslie/Sam Phillips** as her primary influence and describes her style as "metamodernfolk"—personal songs that are both philosophical and community-oriented.

For the most part, she has been on the edge of the contemporary Christian music industry, producing material that is unpredictable musically and, sometimes, lyrically poetic in ways that come across as vague or confusing. She accepts her borderline status with good humor, enduring the superficialities of the contemporary Christian music subculture with a wry smile (she once signed one of her posters at a Christian bookstore with the inscription, "We've gotta move this crap off the shelves"; she later said, "I got in trouble for that"). Masen has sometimes performed with a band she calls The Art Institute, which includes her brother on drums.

A native of Royal Oak, Michigan, she recorded an indie debut when she was but seventeen. Derri Daugherty of **The Choir** produced that project, which would be re-released in 2000 by BEC. A bit less complex than her later albums, *The Holding* offers alternative-tinged folk songs, including the melodic "Dear Friends" and the more upbeat "Mary."

Masen came to the attention of a wider audience with two albums produced by **Charlie Peacock** for his own re:think label. The self-titled album was recorded while Masen was a student at William Tyndale College in Michigan (her major in literature perhaps accounts for the allusions to Plato and John Donne). It opens with what justifiably became *the* big song of the summer on Christian radio, the very Beatlesque "All Fall Down." With lyrics that allude poetically to humility before God (as in the classic hymn line, "angels prostrate fall") and a bouncy tune that could sit without embarrassment between "Day Tripper" and "We Can Work It Out," the song is a pop masterpiece. "Break Hard the Wishbone" continues in a completely different vein, evoking images of Tori Amos or Sinead O'Connor (*True Tunes* would say it falls musically somewhere between Lou Reed's "Walk on the Wild Side" and Steely Dan's "Deacon Blues"). "Downtown" is an anthemic, metaphorical song that speaks of worship in times of doubt, and "Unveiled Faces" is a quirky, guitar-driven meditation on 2 Corinthians 3:18. Masen also covers **Victoria Williams**' "Love."

Some critics would complain that Masen lost her edge on *Carry Us Through,* opting for MOR lullaby-ballads that were almost devoid of pop or rock influences. Actually, the anti-pop orientation (cf. Ann DiFranco, P. J. Harvey) of *Carry Us Through* evinces a maturity of direction that presents Masen in a more innovative if less radio-friendly mode. Songs like "75 Grains of Sand" and "Jenni's Face" perfect her Lisa Loeb-like folk style in a simple way that brings their poetic lyrical strength to the fore. "Seasons Always Change" (the album's highlight) was written with **Samuel Brinsley Ashworth** (Peacock's son) and features a swaying melody similar to numerous Lenny Kravitz songs. The title song has a similar bluesy, gospel feel. "Wrap My Arms around Your Name" is a hauntingly beautiful song of worship.

The move away from familiar radio sounds continues on *Dreamlife of Angels,* which *Phantom Tollbooth* describes as "a stunning work of musical breathtake with catchy melodies and little brushes of musical accompaniment." Almost bereft of pop moments, the album eschews Masen's penchant for melody revealed on "All Fall Down" and "Downtown" in favor of quietly introspective and revealing songs. Some of the autobiographical pieces arise out of her recent marriage ("We Are a Beginning") and more recent motherhood ("Love Is Breathing"). Two songs, in her own words, tell "stories of women who need to get out of situations of oppression and fear, but fail to recognize quite what's happening." The song "Girl on Fire" points out "the inevitable deterioration of sanity when a mad kind of control creeps in between a woman and a man." The companion song, "She Stumbles through the Door," shows a girl "letting go of dysfunction in the hope that faith will meet her half way." Masen's curious but compelling lyrics are exemplified well by a song like "Hope": "We'll be taking off our clothes to sing / We'll be wearing our own skin / We'll be taking off a whole lot more / Just so we can sing." She also covers the Supertramp song "Give a Little Bit," which adds a little spice to the album halfway through.

Christian radio hits: "All Fall Down" (# 1 in 1996); "Downtown" (# 2 in 1996); "Unveiled Faces" (# 3 in 1997); "Come In" (# 9 in 1997); "Wrap My Arms around Your Name" (# 13 in 1998); "75 Grains of Sand" (# 2 in 1998).

Bill Mason Band

Personnel list unavailable. 1979—*No Sham!* (Kingsway).

Although they would not achieve the same success, The Bill Mason Band would precede **The Altar Boys** by a good five years with their album of Christian punk in the general tradition of The Ramones and The Clash. *Jesus Music* magazine indicates that *No Sham!*'s raw, neurotic guitars and bratty, adrenalin-paced vocals make it "the audio-equivalent of gulping twenty cups of coffee." The group declares that they are "checkin' out on Mr. G" (that would be God) and protests discrimination against Christian artists on "Radio." The song "Stand Up and Be Counted" would become something of a punk anthem for some young Christians.

Babbie Mason

1990—*With All My Heart* (Word); 1991—*Carry On;* 1992—*World of Difference; Comfort and Joy;* 1993—*Standing in the Gap;* 1996—*Heritage of Faith;* 1997—*Praise Celebration;* 1999—*No Better Place* (Spring Hill); 2001—*Timeless.*

Christian R&B/modern gospel singer Babbie Mason is native of Jackson, Michigan. Mason became the choir director of the Lily Missionary Baptist Church where her father was pastor and explored a brief secular career singing in nightclubs for a time. While a student at Michigan's Spring Arbor college, she became inspired by **Danniebelle Hall** and subsequently determined to devote her talents full time to Christian music. Relocating to Georgia in 1980, she recorded five independent albums before signing with Word in 1988. Her first few albums gained some notice for the songs "Carry On" (a humorous response of a pastor to someone complaining about the "carrying-ons" at his church), "Each One Reach One," and "World of Difference." *Standing in the Gap,* however, was the breakthrough album that gained her a wider audience. The title track to that record features guest vocalists **Cindy Morgan** and **Helen Baylor.** The song was written for those Christians who have suffered a public fall (i.e., scandal) and been ostracized from the Christian community as a result. On "So Close" Mason adopts a jazz style reminiscent of Anita Baker. On *Heritage of Faith,* Mason explores her roots in traditional gospel; the song "Stop by the Church" includes samples from one of her father's sermons and a duet vocal with Mom Wade. *Praise Celebration* is a live recording of a service in which **Trace Balin** and Terry McMillan also take part. *No Better Place* opens with a soulful celebration called "Holy Spirit, You Are Welcome Here." Other standouts include an anthem of commitment, "I Will Be the One" and the horn-infused rave-up "Show Some Sign."

Timeless points strongly toward the album Mason seems to have been born to make. Its first three tracks apply her smooth voice to long-neglected styles and mark the album as something very special. "Play It Again" is a wonderfully upbeat Big Band number with the singer backed by a small orchestra. "Timeless" is sung as a cabaret torch song. "Simply, I Love You" sounds like something from the Dean Martin catalogue, though the devotion of the lyrics seem appropriate only if applied to the Lord God: "I know your love is unfathomable / Your ways are unequivocal / Your ways are inscrutable / Your heart is undeniably true / But it's virtually impossible / To find the perfect syllable / To describe the indescribable You." These three treats brought the artist unprecedented praise from reviewers: "should go down in history as one of Christian music's greatest classics . . . one continually expects Nat King Cole or Ella Fitzgerald to join in on several songs." Unfortunately, Mason settles into a more formulaic adult contemporary style for much of what follows (including a cover of **Danniebelle Hall**'s "Theme on the 37th"). But she does get all slinky and sultry on "Black and Blue," and her take on the traditional "Wade in the Water" is a bonus. *Timeless* sets Mason apart from dozens of better-known singers in either gospel music or in the general market. It is her best work and establishes her as a talent of major proportion.

An accomplished songwriter, Mason composes most of her own material. She has written songs recorded by **Helen**

Baylor, **Michael English,** and **Larnelle Harris.** She has also written a musical for Word titled *Make Us One,* which deals with reconciliation and unity in the church.

Dove Awards: 1997 Traditional Gospel Song ("Stop by the Church"); 1997 Musical *(Make Us One).*

Mason Proffit

See **The Talbot Brothers.**

Mass

Personnel list unavailable. 1985—*New Birth* (RCA); 1988—*Take You Home* [EP] (Medusa); 1989—*Voices in the Night* (Enigma).

The heavy metal band Mass is best remembered for its *Voices in the Night* album, which was produced by **Stryper**'s **Michael Sweet** for Enigma records, a general market label that experimented with Christian metal in the late '80s (**Stryper** also signed with them for a time). The band tends toward the power-pop side of the metal continuum on songs like "Reach for the Sky," "Carry Your Heart," and "Miles Away" (about teenage runaways). The group mixes mainstream songs about romance with explicitly Christian tunes that speak of salvation and praise to God.

Massivivid

See **Deitiphobia.**

Mastedon

John Elefante; Dino Elefante; et al. 1989—*It's a Jungle Out There* (Regency); 1990—*Lofcaudio* (Pakaderm).

Mastedon was not really a band, but more of a collection (or two collections) of studio musicians assembled by the Elefante brothers as a side project to their work as producers. **John Elefante** was briefly a member of the art-rock band **Kansas** and he and his brother Dino have written numerous songs for various Christian artists. The Mastedon albums were a bit of a transition for John, being recorded after he left **Kansas** and before he embarked on his '90s career as a solo artist. Both albums feature a hard rock sound that has more near-metal bite than **Kansas**'s *Vinyl Confessions,* but they also display a lack of cohesion owing to the involvement of rotating players—and especially lead vocalists—from song to song. **Bob Carlisle** of the **Allies,** Bob Hartman of **Petra,** David Pack of Ambrosia, and Tony Palacios of **Guardian** are among the myriad of guests who become group members for a spell. Commercial hard rockers on the first record include the title track and "Get Up," but more airplay was given to the more subdued "Islands in the Sky" and "Shine On" (with vocals by Pack). The sophomore project opens with a worship song, "Holiest One";

the song "Life on the Line" encourages those who are hurting to make their pain known to God. The group's name is apparently a pun on the brothers' surname, as is the name of the company they founded (Pakaderm). "Stampede," an instrumental from *Lofcaudio,* runs the joke into the ground.

Rob Mathes

1992—*Heart of Hearts* (Night Music); 1995—*William the Angel* (Night Music); 1998—*Christmas Is Coming* (Mercury).

Although he is not well known to fans of contemporary Christian music, producer and musician Rob Mathes has been involved in the music business as a Christian for decades. Mathes began by playing guitar and keyboards for Chuck Mangione. He has gone on to work as an arranger, producer, and session player for numerous big name artists, including Babyface, Boyz II Men, Tracy Chapman, **Eric Clapton,** Natalie Cole, Sheryl Crow, Celine Dion, Elton John, Jon Bon Jovi, Michael McDonald, Joan Osborne, David Sanborn, Shania Twain, Vanessa Williams, Stevie Wonder, and Trisha Yearwood. On the officially Christian side of the street, he has also participated in projects by **Susan Ashton, Margaret Becker, Steve Green, B. J. Thomas,** and **Jaci Velasquez.** Mathes wrote the title songs for Kathy Mattea's Grammy-winning *Good News* and Vanessa Williams' *Star Bright* (both Christmas albums). He also contributed greatly to Luciano Pavarotti's *For War Child* album recorded as a benefit project for Bosnian relief efforts. Mathes performs an annual Christmas concert on PBS, which brings together many of his famous friends to benefit the organization Food for the Hungry. All three of Mathes's albums are Christmas projects, based on these shows (*Christmas Is Coming* is an edited version of the 1997 concert). The most intriguing is *William the Angel,* which includes a suite of songs about a chubby, bumbling angel who is given the mission of saving a single soul. *Phantom Tollbooth* writer Doug Wensey, who knew Mathes in high school, says the songs were inspired by an overweight Christian boy who endured relentless ridicule but maintained a positive witness of returning insults with blessings. As of 2002, Mathes lives in Greenwich, Connecticut, where he is involved in Young Life and assists with worship at his local church (the real William lost a lot of weight and is an Emergency Medical Technician with an ambulance company).

Matrix

See **Bride.**

Kyle Matthews

2000—*See for Yourself* (Benson).

Songwriter Kyle Matthews established himself as one of the most prolific composers in contemporary Christian music before finally recording an album of his own. Matthews grew up the son of a Baptist minister in Waco, Texas. He has frequently collaborated with **Scott Krippayne,** for whom he has written many songs (including the hit "Wild Imagination"). The same can be said of **Grover Levy,** with whom Matthews wrote "Marianne," the smash "If You Want to Lead Me to Jesus," and many others. He has also written or cowritten songs that have been recorded by **Bob Carlisle** ("We Fall Down"), **Gary Chapman** ("Outside"), **Glad** ("The One Who Loves Me Most"), **Larnelle Harris** ("I Want to Go"), **The Martins** ("Come to My Senses"), **Babbie Mason** ("What in the World"), **Ginny Owens** ("If You Want Me To," "Beneath the Symbol of a Lost Cause"), **Point of Grace** ("God Forbid"), and **CeCe Winans** ("One and the Same"). *See for Yourself* presents the artist in the mode of a '70s singer/songwriter like Billy Joel or Jackson Browne, offering up ten entirely new songs (as opposed to reprising ones that were hits by other artists). The overall theme of the album seems to be the reality of having first-hand experience of God. The title track presents the Christian life as an adventure with new developments revealed as one progresses on the path of discipleship. "Been through the Water" is a testimony to the sustaining power of baptism. "Billy Walks through Walls" (with possible apologies to **Julie Miller**) is a creative ode to a high school student who defies cliques and fashion trends.

Randy Matthews

1971—*I Wish We'd Been All Been Ready* (Word); 1972—*All I Am Is What You See* (Myrrh); 1973—*Son of Dust*; 1975—*Now Do You Understand?*; 1976—*Eyes to the Sky*; 1977—*The Best of Randy Matthews*; 1978—*Live in Australia* (Rhema); 1980—*Randy Matthews* (Spirit); 1981—*Plugged In*; 1987—*Streets of Mercy* (Refuge); 1990—*The Edge of Flight* (Wave).

One of the most important of the early Jesus music pioneers, Randy Matthews leaves a legacy equal to that of a number of artists whose names may remain better known **(Barry McGuire, Larry Norman, Randy Stonehill).** Matthews can be connected with a number of historic firsts in the development of contemporary Christian music, and at least two of his albums *(Son of Dust* and *Now Do You Understand?)* remain classics of the early genre. An exemplar of all the best attributes of the Jesus movement, he would also come to grief as a result of the narrow-minded fundamentalism that often served as that revival's dark underbelly. Though his betrayal at the hands of those he served may not have equalled that endured by **Marsha Stevens,** he did encounter a similar antigospel legalism—albeit for entirely different reasons.

Unlike many of the Jesus people who were converts (from paganism or staid, mainline religion) Matthews was raised in the tradition of revival-oriented gospel music. He is the son of Monty Matthews, one of the original Jordanaires who also performed with a successful gospel quartet called The Matthews Brothers; the latter group was, in fact, responsible for making the first musical (i.e., non-spoken word) recording for Word records. As a college student at Ozark Bible College, Randy himself joined a quartet called The Revelations, but while touring with that group he came to believe that the gospel could be communicated more effectively through music that had a more contemporary sound. "I sang that type of music," he would tell *CCM* in a retrospective years later, "because my minister had convinced me that this was the only style of music that God would honor." After moving on to Cincinnati Bible Seminary, Matthews began writing and singing folk songs on his acoustic guitar and in 1970 he contacted his father's record company about doing a recording. Matthews' *I Wish We'd All Been Ready* was the first nontraditional gospel record to be issued on any gospel label. It was produced by Billy Ray Hearn and featured a collection of very tame pop songs, with lots of piano and female backing vocals. In retrospect, the whole project sounds quite "churchy," along the same lines as early albums by **John Fischer** but, at the time, the very concept of doing Christian songs in a supposedly contemporary style was controversial. The liner notes for the record quote Isaac Watts as saying, "I just take the music of the people in the streets and put the message of Christ in it. . . . After all, why should the devil have all the good music?" The latter line—actually a quote by Watts from Martin Luther—was picked up by **Larry Norman** as the title of a song a year later and became something of a slogan throughout the Jesus movement revival. The title song for Matthews' *I Wish We'd All Been Ready* is, of course, a cover of Norman's most famous tune, though at the time Matthews had only found the song and knew nothing about the songwriter. The record also includes two songs written by Sonny Salsbury, brother of Ron Salsbury of **J.C. Power Outlet.** One of Matthews' own songs, "Hallelujah Brother," would be picked up by former Miss America **Vonda Kay Van Dyke** and recorded on an album by her for Word, giving Matthews a little official respectability.

The same year that *I Wish We'd All Been Ready* appeared (1971), Matthews joined with **Arthur Blessitt** in organizing a Spiritual Revolution Day in Cincinnati. The two of them carried large crosses around the downtown to attract media attention that would result in the founding of The Jesus House ministry center (fashioned loosely after Blessitt's His Place). Matthews thus became the principal figure associated with the Jesus movement in his area. A master communicator, he filled the bill of "head Jesus freak" nicely, sporting the outward appearance of a hippie but knowing the language of conservative church folk. His sincere piety won over many skeptical religious types and his wonderful, self-deprecating sense of humor endeared him to the secular press. Still, when he presented the tapes for his sophomore album, *All I Am Is What You See,* to Word, the project was initially rejected as too radical. It was Matthews who suggested the company create a subsidiary that could release such projects without tarnishing the parent company's name. This proposal led to the birth of the highly influential Myrrh records, with Billy Ray Hearn as president and *All I Am* as the debut project. Again, the record is actually quite tame, albeit with a few horns and guitar solos spicing up the sound here and there. The standout songs are two acoustic numbers—the title track and a wedding tune called "Flesh of My Flesh." The closing song, "Country Faith," is a fun tune that became a concert favorite.

Son of Dust is the album that would insure Matthews a place in the Jesus music Hall of Fame (if such a thing were to exist). He seems to have gone into the studio armed with the best songs of his career and, somehow, to have overcome all the industry restrictions that would have prevented him from playing them the way they were meant to be played. The sound is still folk rock, but its down-and-dirty, blues-inflected folk rock is reminiscent, perhaps, of *Everybody Knows This Is Nowhere*-era Neil Young. Matthews sings in a gruff and gritty voice that *Jesus Music* says makes the first two albums "sound like easy listening" by comparison. There is not a bad cut on the album, but "Holy Band" and "Didn't He" are the two classics that became Matthews' twin signature tunes. "Holy Band" is a roaring concert opener that uses the metaphor of being in a band as a descriptive image for becoming part of the people of God. Over two decades later, **Audio Adrenaline** would borrow this idea to great effect with their equally rousing "We're a Band." The song "Didn't He" is a slow, deeply emotional song about Christ's crucifixion ("Didn't he die . . . for you and me?"). When Matthews played it he would slam the box of his guitar with the heel of his hand to simulate the sound of nails being pounded through flesh and the reverberating echoes of those haunting tones never failed to reduce a crowd to silence, if not to tears. Matthews previewed the song at the *Explo '72* Jesus music festival the summer before *Son of Dust* appeared. There, in front of some 250,000 people, it became one of the defining moments of the festival, a moment that would later be broadcast on national TV and then captured on a widely distributed soundtrack album of music from the festival. Many other artists would record the song in the '70s, and in 1987 **Geoff Moore** resurrected it for a new generation on his album *The Distance.* Other highlights of *Son of Dust* include "Mighty Fine," "Brown Eyed Woman," "Pharaoh's Hand," and "It Ain't Easy" (which features the memorable lyric, "I wanna go to heaven, but I'm scared to die").

Now Do You Understand? is nowhere near the musical treat of its predecessor but remains an essential souvenir of the Jesus movement—such that one could hardly understand the historical phenomenon of that revival without it. It is a live album, a two-record set that preserves an apparently unedited concert featuring just Matthews' voice and guitar. The absence of a band makes for inferior presentations of numerous songs, but allows for absolute candor and intimacy. Much of the sixty-eight minutes is taken up with conversation, as Matthews tells funny stories (life on the road, his false start as a quartet singer, a childhood crush), talks to God, and wonders aloud whether Jesus ever ate a pastrami-on-rye sandwich. These musings of an unabashed hippie Christian (pictured on the cover with long, scraggly hair, John Lennon spectacles, and—for some reason—wearing a silver "space cowboy" suit) are ultimately more precious than the songs. One of the best live gospel albums ever made, *Now Do You Understand?* was recorded at Houghton College, where obtuse administrators were so repulsed by the "radical content" that they requested all mention of the school be deleted from the liner notes. Christian music's most important and best critic, Brian Quincy Newcomb, was actually in the audience as a student at the time. The project was probably never intended to hold up to repeated listenings, but it does provide an accurate aural representation of what a Jesus music concert was like. The album *Live in Australia,* released only in that country, functions as a supplementary disc, containing no duplication of material with the two-record American concert. On both projects, Matthews comes off as a consummate entertainer, which is how he used to describe himself. "God gives us each different gifts," he commented early on, with remarkable theological insight. "I sometimes wish he had given me another gift (e.g., ministry), but what I feel best about doing is entertaining both Christians and non-Christians." Challenged with regard to the potentially nonspiritual character of such a vocation, he responded, "The way I stay on track is to constantly picture Jesus sitting in the front row. That tends to keep me in line."

By the time *Now Do You Understand?* was released, Matthews' life had come undone. In 1974, he was offered the opportunity (based on the merits of *Son of Dust*) to tour as an opening act with the general market bands ZZ Top and Lynyrd Skynyrd. Excited by the prospect of bringing gospel rock to an audience unlikely to have attended *Explo '72,* he put together a crack band and toured bars and clubs, allowing them to learn their chops and become more sensitive to the dynamics of playing in non-Christian venues. He decided to break the news of the impending tour to the Christian community at the *Jesus '74* festival held in Pennsylvania. There he debuted his band, playing their electric style of music. In the middle of the third song, however, the concert organizers pulled the plug on his equipment, having decided that it was "demon music." What happened next is difficult to determine. Matthews and the band retreated from the stage in confusion, trying to find out what was happening. People were shouting that he was possessed by the devil. The crowd surged forward and, Matthews claims, he was chased by what he took to be hostile people. He tried to climb a fence but blacked out and has no memory of what then transpired. The next thing he knew, he told *Harmony* in what was to be that magazine's premiere issue, he woke up in a hotel room, his clothes ripped and clumps of hair missing from his chest. People associated with the concert, meanwhile, circulated rumors that Matthews had been "high on drugs" and most of his contracts for future performances were canceled. "That one situation wiped everything out for me," Matthews would tell *CCM* twenty-three years later. "People would actually come up to me and say, 'I pray that God takes away your voice and that you never write another song'."

Historically, the unplugging of Randy Matthews became an event in the annals of Christian music analogous to the booing of **Bob Dylan** at the 1965 Newport Folk Festival. In short order, the sort of electric rock Matthews had sought to introduce to the Pennsylvania crowd would carry the day and the people who thought God could honor only folk music would be lumped in the same category as those whose tiny little God could "only work through quartets." But the event symbolized a division within the Jesus movement analogous to that which developed in the early Christian Church: a schism between ultimately orthodox world-affirming Christians and ultimately sectarian separatists. Such divisions have in fact marked the history of Christianity in every time and place with a consistent result: the separatists win many battles, but always lose the war. *Jesus '74* was a battle they won; it was an ambush and they had the element of surprise. In time, they would lose the war, but Randy Matthews was all but slain on the field of battle. Unlike **Bob Dylan,** he did not recover.

Matthews' bitterness toward the culture that so easily judged him would come through on his next album, *Eyes to the Sky.* Produced by recent convert **Austin Roberts,** it approaches *Son of Dust* in quality with such stellar songs as "It Took a Carpenter," "Captain," and the hard-rocking "Four Horsemen" (the song that got him unplugged). The acoustic ballad "Oh My" would also become something of a classic with its parallels between world-affirming Jesus freaks and the ministry of Jesus ("I talked with junkies, I ate with whores / I stuck your stickers on bar room doors"). The most noticed song, however, was "Pennsylvania Weekend," a hastily written commentary on the recent assault: "You pulled the plug and drained my soul." *Harmony* criticized him for including the latter song: "The subject is much overworked and hackneyed. It was better left buried two years ago where it belonged." A pic-

ture on the cover of the album depicts Matthews as a modern-day Elijah being fed by ravens, an obvious reference to the story of the banished prophet for whom God provided when he had to flee from his oppressors (1 Kings 17).

The same year that *Eyes to the Sky* was released, Matthews recorded with the trio **Matthews, Taylor, and Johnson.** *Harmony* magazine and many others in the contemporary Christian music industry attempted to rehabilitate his image but everything he did seemed tainted with a shadow of suspicion and doomed to fail. Ironically, some of the stories circulated about him began to come true. In a 1986 "Whatever Happened To . . . ?" article in *CCM,* Matthews says he came to feel alienated from the Jesus people communities he had helped to establish. "I was sort of de-fellowshipped from the whole industry and the only people who would have anything to do with me were rock musicians." Like Taylor and Johnson, Matthews also hooked up with **Mike Warnke** who, while billing himself as a Christian entertainer, was almost openly pursuing a stereotypically decadent lifestyle. In any case, Matthews says that he took to "imbibing and toking" and "then slid downhill into the harder stuff—acid and mescaline."

Four years after *Eyes to the Sky,* Matthews attempted a comeback with two albums on the Spirit label. His self-titled album kicks off with a cover of **Arlo Guthrie**'s "Whose Side Are You On?" and *Plugged In* would afford him a minor hit with "Ball and Chain." After another hiatus, he released *Streets of Mercy,* an inconsistent album that despite its noble theme (compassion for the poor and hungry) Matthews would later admit is better off forgotten. *Edge of Flight* (his only product ever released on CD) brings in a host of guest stars **(Robin Crow,** Gordon Kennedy of **Dogs of Peace, Mike Johnson, Phil Madeira)** and offers a number of personal songs: "Defender of the Faith," about his grandfather, and "Sir," for his role-model Dad. "Ti Chapé" offers a touching chronicle of his work for Compassion International. Still, the album would be received as a nostalgia trip and it was purchased primarily by persons who would have preferred to buy the unavailable earlier records. The failure (as of year 2001) for any label to release those projects would remain perhaps the most telling testimony and the ultimate insult.

Matthews took part in a 1997 Jesus music reunion, performing "Didn't He" and "Ti Chapé" on the *First Love* album (and video) released by Newport in 1998. By that time, Matthews, who somewhere along the way had become an ordained Baptist minister, was living in Englewood, Florida, and running a store called "A Nouveau Native" that specializes in Native American-themed art. "Nobody here knows I made records," he confided. "I'm not very visible and I don't mind that a bit." Still, he finds the Christian music scene's low appreciation for history disconcerting: "I wish we could recognize our pioneers a little bit more. Even secular rock 'n' roll does that. It kind of hurts."

Christian radio hits: "Ball and Chain" (# 13 in 1982).

Matthews, Taylor, and Johnson

Michael Johnson, voc., gtr.; Randy Matthews, voc., gtr.; Danny Taylor, voc., gtr. 1976—*Matthews, Taylor, and Johnson* (NewPax).

The trio of Matthews, Taylor, and Johnson was a flagrant attempt to clone Crosby, Stills and Nash. Many such efforts were made in the secular music industry as well, all demonstrating that the success of the latter group was more fluke than paradigm. For some reason that no one has ever been able to figure out, the blending of Crosby, Stills and Nash's disparate voices and the combination of their very different styles made for a whole that was exponentially more than the sum of its parts. The almost magical appeal of that group is directly linked to the fact that such a mélange had never worked before and would never work again (except, of course with Crosby, Stills, Nash and Young). In this case, gritty folk rocker **Randy Matthews,** jazz/blues artist **Mike Johnson** and easy listening crooner **Danny Taylor** managed to put together an album with some fine songs ("Somethin' in Common," "This and That," "Second Coming Sunset"), but it contains nothing that could not just as easily have been on their solo albums. More a compilation disc than a true band effort, the project also served as something of a swan song for all three performers who, as part of **Mike Warnke**'s entourage, had yielded to the partying lifestyle exhibited by that entertainer; their careers came undone with his.

For trivia buffs: Matthews, Taylor, and Johnson had actually recorded together previously, as part of **Charles McPheeters'** Bible Belt Boogie Band.

Mayfair Laundry

Paul Dexter, bass; Frank Sandoval, gtr. (– 1999); Dave Snow, drums (–1999); Shannon Woolner, voc. (– 1999) // Steve Latanation (+ 1999); Kim Sipus, voc. (+ 1999); Mark Stills (+ 1999). 1997—*Scrub* (Organic); 1999—*New and Improved* (Planet).

www.mayfairlaundry.com

Mayfair Laundry plays ska-influenced pop similar to that of No Doubt or **Dakoda Motor Co.** Steeped in humor and a postmodern resistance to obvious or unilateral meaning, the band is playful and quirky but fairly direct in their statements of faith. Dexter chose the group's name when he saw the words on the side of a truck in a Beatles' concert video. "The name suits us," he quips, "because it shows we don't know who we are."

Produced by **John** and Dino **Elefante,** *Scrub* offers the bouncy, infectious "Lovely Feet" and the retro-'60s "Wavy Gravy" (named after a famous Woodstock cook turned concert M.C.). Punchy horns add power to "Bucket Brigade" and "Swing Your Partner" and the album concludes with a straight-on, shades-of-early-Blondie rocker, "My Dear Watson." The band seemed to delight in challenging listeners to get their oddball lyrics. Why does Woolner want lovely feet? See Isaiah 52:7. Likewise, "Bucket Brigade" is really a warning not to stifle the Holy Spirit, and "My Dear Watson" is a declaration that the basic message of the gospel really is "elementary." On *Scrub,* Mayfair Laundry was clearly Woolner's band; the media ignored everyone except "the very lovely Shannon Woolner" (as *Phantom Tollbooth* called her). *CCM* put the matter simply: "She was made for video." Another publication compared her to "a young Ann Margaret, who the camera follows like a lovesick puppy." Her departure seemed a definite death knell, but Dexter found another singer and got the group to squeeze out one more album on an independent label.

No one felt compelled to comment on Kim Sipus's video presence, but *Musicforce* did liken her high-pitched baby-doll voice to Fleming McWilliams of **Fleming and John.** Although *New and Improved* does not live up to its title, it does deliver a fairly satisfying blend of modern rock and bubblegum pop. Dexter's Beatles fixation comes into full view, as the group covers George Harrison's "Here Comes the Sun" and—as perceptive critics would point out—musical ideas if not entire lines from "Lucy in the Sky with Diamonds" and "A Day in the Life" get worked into the songs "You're Really" and "Spinning for You," respectively. *New and Improved* also drops the guitar-based sound of *Scrub* in favor of a more '80s blend of keyboards and drum machines.

Curtis Mayfield

Selected: 1999—*Gospel* (Rhino).

Like many African American R&B singers, Curtis Mayfield got his start in the world of gospel music and he drew heavily on that influence throughout his career. Mayfield wrote and originally performed the song "People Get Ready," which would come to be regarded as a gospel standard almost on the same level as Thomas Dorsey's "Precious Lord (Take My Hand)." Still, Mayfield's involvements with the contemporary Christian music culture—or with gospel music or, for that matter, Christian churches—have been practically nonexistent, with the result that his specific connection to the field and commitment to the faith remains undefined.

Born in Chicago in 1942, Mayfield grew up the son of a minister, singing with gospel groups associated with his grandmother's Traveling Soul Spiritualist Church. In 1957, he formed The Impressions with fellow gospel singer Jerry Butler, and the group would have thirty hits on the mainstream pop charts (many more on the R&B charts) before Mayfield left for a solo career in 1970. Two of their biggest songs were "It's All Right" (# 4 in 1963) and "Keep On Pushing" (# 10 in 1964). The most remarkable hits, however, came back-to-back in late 1964 and early 1965, at a time when the Beatles and The Supremes were alternating between control of the charts. "Amen" (# 7 in 1964) was a rousing gospel tune originally performed for the soundtrack of the Sidney Poitier film *Lilies of the Field*. Then, the group released the aforementioned "People Get Ready" (# 14 in 1965), a song that was covered hundreds of times, notably by Rod Stewart and Jeff Beck in 1985. The lyrics speak about a metaphorical "train to Jordan" and proclaim "all you need is faith . . . you don't need a ticket, you just thank the Lord." After Mayfield left The Impressions, he worked as a composer, producer, and performer, but would become best known for the soundtrack album to the black exploitation film *Superfly,* which *The New Rolling Stone Encyclopedia of Rock and Roll* calls "an eerie blend of Mayfield's knowing falsetto with Latin percussion and predisco rhythm guitars." On the strength of two gold singles ("Superfly"; "Freddie's Dead"), the album would sell an incredible five million copies. Mayfield's connections to gospel would surface only occasionally throughout his solo career on such songs as "A Prayer" and "Something to Believe In." Rhino records has collected all of these on their *Gospel* compilation album.

Despite the evangelical sentiment of songs like "Amen" and "People Get Ready," Mayfield's theology seemed generic and syncretistic. He imbued the spiritual songs with specific political implications, geared to his involvement in the Civil Rights movement. A song called "Jesus" seems to indicate that the central figure of the Christian faith can also be known by other names. "When We're Alone" appears to suggest that people find salvation by loving others in a romantic sense. Mayfield's first chart hit as a solo artist was called "Don't Worry—If There's a Hell Below, We're All Gonna Go." Questions as to whether such sentiments were sincere or playful, and as to whether they were meant as criticisms of Christianity or as expressions of a resilient (albeit liberal) Christian perspective have never been answered.

On August 14, 1990, while performing at an outdoor concert in Brooklyn, New York, a lighting rig fell on top of Mayfield, leaving him permanently paralyzed from the neck down. In 1994, he was inducted into the Rock and Roll Hall of Fame. In 1996, he recorded a final album *New World Order* (Warner) by singing one line at a time (a limitation caused by his paralyzed diaphragm). **Aretha Franklin** and Mavis Staples appear as guests on that project. Mayfield died in 1999. He was posthumously inducted into the Songwriters Hall of Fame in 2000. At least two tribute albums filled with cover versions of his songs have been released. Artists ranging from Prince to Bruce

Springsteen to **Charlie Peacock** cite him as a major influence on their musical style.

Kevin Max (a.k.a. **Kmax**)

2001—*Stereotype Be* (ForeFront).

www.kevinmax.com

Kevin Max is best known as a member of Christian music's all-time most popular band **DC Talk.** Born Kevin Max Smith, Max is the Bonoesque member of that trio, offering vocals that occasionally take the hip-hop oriented group into close **U2** proximity. The group tends, however, to be dominated by front man and main songwriter Toby McKeehan (cf. **Toby Mac**), and it is no secret that Max often desires a bit more room to exercise his own creative impulses. In 2000, at the end of the group's *Supernatural* tour, Max announced that he was quitting **DC Talk.** After further negotiations, he retracted the defection; rather, the band would take an eighteen month sabbatical, during which time Max would record a solo album. As it turned out, all three members recorded such projects (cf. **Toby Mac, Tait**), though Max's was received as the most experimental of the three. In October 2001, a thirty-one-city reunion tour by **DC Talk** (featuring the three artists' solo outings) was canceled at the last minute when Max requested "time off to attend to personal matters." The tour did resume in January 2002.

To no one's surprise, Max's *Stereotype Be* ended up sounding only a little like **DC Talk** but a lot like **U2.** The album opens with Middle Eastern droning that yields to the *Pop*-ish "Return of the Singer." The soaring anthem "Be" sounds enough like one of the Dublin band's midtempo ballads to leave even Mrs. Vox wondering, but on "Existence" the Bono impressions are offset by a haunting flute solo and interrupted by some rapping from Coffee of **Grits.** Both "Angel with No Wings" and "Dead End Moon" have more of a "Desert Rose"-era Sting quality, with diverse and unpredictable percussion. The artist tips his hat to the Beatles on "Shaping Space" with some *Sgt. Pepper* horns and Bono-cum-Lennon vocal inflections. Much of the album from that point is filled with glorious power-pop songs ("I Don't Belong," Blind," "On and On," "Her Game"), songs with big choruses, huge hooks, and enchanting melodies.

With production by Adrian Belew (once of King Crimson, cf. **Rick Altizer, Jars of Clay**), *Stereotype Be* is anything but formulaic. "Alycen and the Secret Circle" offers four minutes of melancholy strangeness worthy of Billy Corgan and his Smashing Pumpkins. Belew plays guitar (wonderfully) on the project and his old comrade in King Crimson Tony Levin plays bass, with Matt Chamberlain (drummer for Fiona Apple, Tori Amos, and The Wallflowers) completing the rhythm section. All told, despite the sometimes distracting **U2** pretensions (no worse than **Simple Minds, The Alarm,** or any number of other artists), *Stereotype Be* is an album of remarkable power and mystique, a surprisingly creative contribution that (like **DC Talk**'s best work, but in a very different way) deserves to be heard in a broader forum than the Christian market allows. Mincing few words, *HM* said, "This is the record that the stagnant, plasticine, cookie-cutter mainstream Christian music industry has for years needed so very badly." Lyrically, the album is not as overt in its proclamation of specifically Christian ideas as **DC Talk**'s projects. "Be" offers some pretty generic advice: "Be yourself . . . 'cause if you don't, then who is going to?" Romance and relationships are persistent themes. On "Angel with No Wings," Max flits back and forth between physical attraction ("I like the way you look outside") and deeper connections ("I wanna girl with a college mind . . . so come back when you can make some tea and read St. Augustine"). The song "Existence" pays homage to someone who is searching for truth (in this case, a "sad-eyed girl"). On "I Don't Belong" Max addresses his uneasiness with hero worship and with his own identity as a rock star in the music business. "Shaping Space" deals with preservation in a way that could apply equally to the eternal security of Christians or to confident hope in a particular relationship: "You and I were meant to be / Much more than they could see / You and I were meant to stay / As they waste away." Max authored a book called *Unfinished Work* (Thomas Nelson, 2001) that presents reflections on each song from *Stereotype Be,* mingled with a good deal of autobiographical accounts of his life and thought. He reveals something of what it was like growing up a nonconformist in a sheltered environment, relates a few, relatively tame stories of rebelling against expectations, and describes his psychological struggle with being an adopted child who eventually sought out his birth parents to discover more fully who he was.

Max is a well-regarded poet (which is different from being a lyricist). One book of his poetry, *At the Foot of Heaven* (Jubilee, 1998) features illustrative paintings by **Jimmy A.** Max also recorded an incredible version of the Beatles' "Birthday" for the album *Ten: The Birthday Album* (ForeFront, 1998) and sang **Mark Heard**'s "Lonely Moon" on the tribute album for that artist, *Strong Hand of Love* (Fingerprint, 1994).

Christian radio hits: "Be" (# 18 in 2001); "Existence" (# 12 in 2001).

Maximillian

1997—*Deeper Than Most* (N'Soul).

Maximillian is a solo artist who creates Christian dance music that draws on a funky base of R&B pop. *Deeper Than Most* features a number of instrumentals, in addition to songs that encourage listeners to "Be Free" or "Sing Amen." On the latter tracks, Maximillian combines silky vocals and rich harmonies with the usual pumped-up electronic beats to drive home simple messages and introduce a note of celebration into what remains primarily a mode of entertainment.

Marty McCall

1997—*Images of Faith* (Warner Alliance).

Marty McCall was the central figure in two influential Christian groups, **Fireworks** and **First Call.** A formally educated musician of Scotch-Irish descent, neither his roots nor his training in medieval and renaissance music seemed to find fruit in those projects. On *Images of Faith,* McCall delves into the rich heritage of the church's music in a manner not seen since **Kemper Crabb**'s amateur fascination produced the classic album *The Vigil.* McCall plays such medieval instruments as the ottavino, uilleann pipes, chimpta, and dumbek on songs that convey what *CCM* calls "an otherworldly sense of unity, awe, and reverence." The original compositions are flavored with Celtic spirituality and sustained by ancient liturgical traditions, while also influenced by modern eclectic trends that lead him, for instance, to wed African percussion with old English intonement.

Andy McCarroll (and Moral Support)

Moral Support: Jimmy Davis, gtr.; Alan Gillespie, bass; William Hilary, kybrd.; Andy McCarroll, voc.; Ian Sloan, drums. By Andy McCarroll: 1975—*Through Different Eyes* (D&A); 1978—*Epitaph for a Rebel* (Grapevine). By Andy McCarroll and Moral Support: 1980—*Zionic Bonds* (Pilgrim America).

Coming out of Northern Ireland, Andy McCarroll and Moral Support made a little splash with a new-wave Christian album in 1980. Well ahead of its time, *Zionic Bonds* draws on such influences as The Police and The Clash to present a sound that is both melodic and raw. "Living a Lie" is about prejudice, drawing specific inspiration from religious strife in the artist's homeland. "How the Kids Are Feeling" is a driving song about the confusion of adolescence, made more complicated by having "parents who need Jesus." Other topics include abortion ("I Am Human"—sung from the perspective of a fetus) and the hope for world peace ("20th Century"). McCaroll had recorded two little-noticed solo albums prior to his work with **Moral Support.** Neither album evinces the new-wave sound; according to *Jesus Music,* the first is "aggressive folksy rock and roll with a full band sound," while the second is more MOR. *Epitaph* contains a nine-minute Dylanesque protest song against the devil ("Tombstone"). Many years later, McCarroll would produce the debut album for the British rock group **Split Level.**

Debbie McClendon

1985—*I Can Hardly Wait* (Light); 1987—*Count It All Joy* (StarSong); 1989—*Morning Light* (Frontline); 1990—*Get a Grip*.

Christian R&B/pop singer Debbie McClendon has a voice and style similar to that of **Deniece Williams.** Her albums were produced by Scott V. Smith, who wrote many of the songs. *I Can Hardly Wait* is imbued with an aura of worship and a consciousness of how superficial life apart from God can be. It includes "When I Get in His Presence" and "When You've Got Nothing Left But God," both written by Mike Murdock. With *Count It All Joy,* critics started calling her "the black **Sandi Patty,**" in part due to her penchant for hitting crystal-shattering high notes. *Morning Light* focuses on the magnificence of God and on divine love. On *Get a Grip* McClendon delivers a tranquil treatment of **Larry Norman**'s "I Wish We'd All Been Ready" and begins to experiment with more hip-hop and urban contemporary influences.

Christian radio hits: "He Won't Let Me Down (Every Time I Call)" (# 12 in 1987); "In the Valley" (# 13 in 1989); "Fear Not" (# 19 in 1990).

Donnie McClurkin

1996—*Donnie McClurkin* (Warner Alliance); 1999—*The McClurkin Project* (GospoCentric); 2000—*Live in London and More* (Verity).

www.donniemcclurkin.com

Donnie McClurkin is a contemporary traditional gospel singer and choir leader who *Christian Music* once described as "a cross between **Andraé Crouch, Larnelle Harris,** and **Kirk Franklin.**" Born and raised in Amityville, New York, McClurkin grew up in a world characterized by violence, alcoholism, and abuse. He found a safe haven in his church, the Gospel Tabernacle Assemblies of God, where he accepted Christ at the age of nine. Two years later, he came to know contemporary gospel legend **Andraé Crouch** who became his mentor and role model, regularly sending him postcards while on tour. In 1979, McClurkin formed The McClurkin Singers with his siblings and friends; then, in 1987, he moved to Detroit where he would eventually become assistant pastor (to Marvin Winans) at Detroit's Perfecting Church. In 1989, he formed another musical group called The New York Restoration Choir, whose album *I Feel Well* attracted notice in the gospel music community. He also worked a stint with the New Jersey Mass Choir. McClurkin came to know Oprah Winfrey, who invited him to appear on her show several times and even sang with him at a special hour-long event she organized in Cape May, New Jersey. McClurkin would also place a song on the soundtrack album to the animated motion picture *The Prince of Egypt.* He has performed twice at the White House, for both President Bush and President Clinton.

McClurkin's self-titled solo debut applies his velvety baritone to ballads and worship songs, including the original composition "Stand" and the classic hymn "Holy, Holy, Holy." It also features a duet with **Andraé Crouch,** "We Expect You." Other guests include **Billy Preston** and members of **Take 6.** The album would go gold, propelling McClurkin into the spotlight. His next project, recorded with a sextet of sisters and female friends, offered a blend of easy listening ballads and uplifting worship anthems, including a version of Handel's "Hallelujah Chorus." McClurkin sings with **Tramaine Hawkins** on "Is There Any Way?" *Live in London* was recorded with a full choir and features "That's What I Believe," sustained by a rock-steady groove, and **Kyle Matthews**' worshipful ballad "We Fall Down." This time the singer offers a duet with pastor Winans on "Who Would've Thought."

Dove Awards: 2001 Traditional Gospel Song ("We Fall Down").

Marilyn McCoo

1991—*The Me Nobody Knows* (Warner Bros.).

www.mccoodavis.com

Marilyn McCoo (b. 1943 in Jersey City, New Jersey) and her husband Billy Davis Jr. were the lead singers of the very successful pop group Fifth Dimension. Early on, McCoo won the Grand Talent Award in the Miss Bronze California pageant. While working as a fashion model, she and her photographer Lamont McLemore decided to form a vocal group called The Hi-Fi's. The group toured as a part of Ray Charles' revue and then split, with McLemore and McCoo recruiting Davis (McLemore's cousin) and two others to form Fifth Dimension (the other members of The Hi Fi's regrouped as Friends of Distinction, best remembered for the late '60s hit "Grazing in the Grass"). Davis had a gospel background, having been a member of the Saint Gospel Singers. **Johnny Rivers** signed Fifth Dimension (first known as The Versatiles) to his fledgling Soul City label and the group went on to make seven gold albums and chart twenty Top 40 hits, including their medley of songs from the musical *Hair,* "Aquarius/Let the Sunshine In" (# 1 for 6 weeks in 1969). They were responsible for bringing songs of Jimmy Webb ("Up, Up, and Away") and Laura Nyro ("Stoned Soul Picnic," "Wedding Bell Blues," "Save the Country") to national prominence. McCoo's voice is prominently featured on such remarkable songs as "One Less Bell to Answer" and "(Last Night) I Didn't Get to Sleep at All." The group performed at the Nixon White House. In 1975, Davis and McCoo left as a couple and became hosts of a successful televised summer variety show. They had two major hits as a recording duo, "You Don't Have to Be a Star to Be in My Show" (# 1 in 1977) and "Your Love" (# 15 in 1977). McCoo then took over hosting the TV show *Solid Gold* (1981–1984). At some point in the late

'80s, McCoo says that she "accepted Christ" over the phone on one of many long conversations with Bunny Wilson, the wife of Motown producer Frank Wilson. Shortly after, Billy Davis Jr. also accepted Christ at a program called *Jesus at the Roxy* featuring **Philip Bailey** and **Deniece Williams.** McCoo decided not to leave her career in the general market, telling *CCM* magazine, "I'm a secular singer who is a Christian." She did, however, record a duet with **Steve Archer** ("Safe") for his *Action* album. She also recorded the contemporary gospel album *The Me Nobody Knows.* Produced by **Chris Christian,** the album features songs with Christian lyrics performed in a style similar to McCoo's secular work. The song "Warrior for the Lord" offers her personal statement of how she views her role in music and society: "No matter where I am, whether it be the secular field or the Christian field, I want to be a warrior for the Lord." In the '90s, McCoo would have a recurring role on the TV soap opera *Days of Our Lives.* She sang the title track for the soundtrack of the Disney movie, *Parent Trap II.*

Christian radio hits: "The Me Nobody Knows" (# 24 in 1991).

Howard McCrary (and The McCrarys)

Personnel list for The McCrarys: Alfred McCrary, voc.; Charity McCrary, voc.; Linda McCrary, voc.; Sam McCrary, voc.; Howard McCrary, voc. As The McCrarys (selected): 1972—*Sunshine Day* (Light). As Howard McCrary: 1985—*So Good* (Good News).

Christian R&B singer Howard McCrary grew up in Youngstown, Ohio, where he sang with a family group initially called The McCrary Five in a rather obvious nod to The Jackson Five. The group first sang gospel music and enjoyed some success, taking a second place on the *Ted Mack Amateur Hour* TV show. As The McCrarys, they made an early album of pop-soul songs that sounded like a cross between The Jacksons and **Andraé Crouch and the Disciples.** The album *Sunshine Day* produced one big hit on Christian radio (before charts were kept) with the song, "I Never Was So Happy." The McCrarys went on to pursue a general market career without brother Howard (who left in 1975) and they had an R&B hit with the song "You" (# 45 on pop charts in 1978). They opened for The Jacksons on their important 1979 tour. Howard, meanwhile, moved to Los Angeles where he did session singing, arranging, and producing for a number of big name artists (George Benson, The Pointer Sisters, Lionel Richie, Stevie Wonder). In 1985, he recorded his solo album *So Good* for the contemporary Christian market. *CCM* described his voice as unusually versatile, recalling **Al Green** on the title track and David Bowie on the song "Sold Out." The most noticed song on the album, "Hold Steady," offers counsel to those who might be contemplating suicide. In interviews, McCrary revealed that he had attempted suicide twice himself.

Michael McDermott

1991—*620 W. Surf* (Giant); 1993—*Gethsemane* (SBK); 1996—*Michael McDermott* (EMI); 1999—*Bourbon Blue* (Midwest); 2000—*Last Chance Lounge* (Koch).

www.michael-mcdermott.com

Acoustic singer/songwriter Michael McDermott would not normally be considered part of the contemporary Christian music subculture, though he has many fans there who are attracted by his songs that deal with spiritual hopes and struggles. Musically, McDermott fits into the general tradition of artists like Elvis Costello or *Nebraska*-era Bruce Springsteen, and Christian music fans often liken him to **Bruce Cockburn** or **T Bone Burnett.** Though McDermott's current faith status remains undefined, he was raised Roman Catholic and the imagery and piety of that upbringing figures in his songs. Growing up in Chicago, he actually considered being a priest but, on the advice of a priest who served as something of a mentor, decided to delay that vocation for a time to explore his artistic abilities and vision. McDermott struggles with life and faith with an honesty that might not be appreciated by all fans or gatekeepers within the Christian music industry. Even early on, when he was featured in Christian music magazines, he would talk frankly about such things as drinking too much or superficial sexual relationships that leave him feeling humiliated or ashamed.

Explicit faith statements seem to pepper his debut album, which was accordingly reviewed in *CCM*. In the title track, McDermott sings about going to church "just to pray" only to come back home feeling "the same way." When the song concludes "but I still believe," the audience cannot be sure whether such stubborn faith is irrational or resilient—or both. On the same album, McDermott indicates on one song that "the book of truth" does not contain answers to the questions he seeks, yet on another sings, "I will be free someday from these things that drag me down" ("Sacred Ground"). Elsewhere, he quotes the Sermon on the Mount and pleads with St. Jude (the patron saint of desperate causes). The *CCM* reviewer would conclude that "some listeners may be disturbed by the confessional nature of the album," but that the album could be reassuring for "those wrestling with the same issues and doubts." The song "A Wall I Must Climb" was featured prominently on MTV.

True Tunes' John J. Thompson also noticed McDermott from the very start and, unlike *CCM*, would continue to follow him throughout the ensuing decade. *Gethsemane* has a much harder rock edge to it musically, with songs that "present a feeling of desperately clinging to God." A standout track called "The Idler, The Prophet, and a Girl Called Rain" offers an eight-and-a-half minute Dylanesque narrative about three characters who in reality represent different aspects of the human psyche. "Whiskey and Water" is chilling—an acoustic ode to alcohol that was written by a friend of McClendon's shortly before being killed in a drunk driving accident. *Michael McDermott* takes the artist into ever darker territory with songs about different characters in various types of dysfunctions and dire straits. Most of the religious references serve mainly to illustrate how far the prodigals have traveled from their homes. Stephen King wrote the liner notes for the album.

McDermott released two more albums on minor labels that would be ignored in the Christian media and market. *Bourbon Blue* is a follow-up to the self-titled project, with more tales of desperate characters real or imagined. The set of introspective poems is broken by an Irish folk song, "When the Irish Were Kings of New York." *Last Chance Lounge* reprises a few songs from the unsuccessful *Bourbon Blue* along with some better material: "Annie and the Aztec Cross" is a moving ballad about a girl with AIDS; "Leave Her to Heaven" is a heart-breaker dealing with the sorrow of loss. "Unemployed" presents the none-too-convincing fete of a self-confessed loser: "Hallelujah, I'm overjoyed / Drunk again, and unemployed!"

Donna McElroy

1990—*Bigger World* (Warner Alliance).

African American pop singer Donna McElroy came to the attention of Christian music fans as a member of the trio These Three, who backed **Amy Grant** on her classic albums and tours of the late '80s. McElroy's solo album, *Bigger World,* demonstrates her capacity to handle a wide variety of material, including R&B, jazz, urban pop, and rap. The song "Take It Away" is perhaps the most noteworthy number, built on a strong R&B groove and possessed of what *CCM* would call "wonderful abandon." McElroy also covers Duke Ellington's "Come Sunday," complete with Ella Fitzgerald-styled skat singing.

Christian radio hits: "Unconditional Love" (# 16 in 1990).

Will McFarlane

1982—*Right from the Start* (Refuge); 1984—*A Colony of Heaven;* 1987—*Only the Heart;* 1990—*Hear the Voice;* 1998—*Axe to the Root* (Freedom).

Will McFarlane was born on a navy base in California and grew up to pursue a career as a session guitarist. McFarlane played for Jackson Browne and then became part of Bonnie Raitt's semi-permanent band from 1974 to 1978. In the late '70s, he moved to Florence, Alabama, where he would continue to work as part of the Muscle Shoals Rhythm Section. McFarlane became a Christian sometime around 1980 and **Ed Raetzloff** recorded two of McFarlane's songs on his 1981 *Drivin' Wheels* album. McFarlane released a series of light pop albums featuring mostly original songs. "You Call Me a Dreamer" from his debut project presents the words of a Chris-

tian to an acquaintance who tries to dismiss the substance or reality of the believer's faith. The song has a melody similar to that of Air Supply's "Lost in Love," which is characteristic of McFarlane's preferred soft-rock-to-inspirational approach. His sophomore album emphasizes the unity of the church as one body, a theme developed in the title song ("A Colony of Heaven") and in "One Body," which includes the lyric, "Lord, of course I love my brother . . . but do I have to hang out with him?" On *Axe to the Root,* McFarlane delves into the blues with a sound that features more of his trademark guitar playing, supplemented by snappy horns and organ riffs. "I Am Listening" reprises his love for the adult contemporary ballad, but "Be There in That Number" exhibits the Latin influence of Carlos Santana. The album also includes renditions of the traditional spirituals "Lay My Burden Down" and "Amazing Grace."

Christian radio hits: "You Call Me a Dreamer" (# 8 in 1983); "This Is the Message" (# 23 in 1983); "A Colony of Heaven" (# 12 in 1985).

MC Ge Gee

1990—*I'm For Real* (Frontline); 1991—*And Now the Mission Continues.*

Female rapper MC Ge Gee is the younger sister of Christian rapper **D-Boy,** who was murdered in 1990, shortly after her first album was released. That record attracted attention primarily for being the first release by a solo female rapper in contemporary Christian music. It evinces several eclectic variations on hip-hop, incorporating influences of salsa ("Latino Style"), jazz ("Jazzin' It Up"), reggae ("You Can Make a Difference"), and '70s funk ("Let's Fight Back"). Her second album, however, was better received by critics. The song "I Caught the Mic" gained special notice as a tribute to her brother (picking up on his song, "Drop the Mic"). Overall, MC Ge Gee prefers a harder mix of rock and funk than her brother did, and this comes to the fore on such tracks as "Love Is the Answer," "Soul Sister," and "Trust."

Barry McGuire

1973—*Seeds* (Myrrh); 1975—*Lighten Up; To the Bride* [with 2nd Chapter of Acts]; 1976—*C'mon Along* (Sparrow); *Anyone But Jesus* (Masterpiece); 1977—*Have You Heard* (Sparrow); 1978—*Cosmic Cowboy;* 1979—*Inside Out (Live);* 1980—*Best of Barry McGuire* 1981—*Finer Than Gold;* 1989—*Pilgrim* (Live Oak).

www.talbotmcguire.com

In the general market world of mainstream music, Barry McGuire is known as a one-hit wonder—or possibly as a two-hit wonder for those who are up on their rock and roll trivia. His best work, however, came almost a decade later when, as a passionate, evangelical Jesus freak, he blazed new trails in the burgeoning world of Jesus music, making three of the most important albums ever to be associated with the genre. In retrospect, it seems a bit ridiculous that he was regarded as a "celebrity convert" in the little pond that made up the Jesus people subculture, but in the days before **Bob Dylan** or even **B. J. Thomas** embraced the faith, McGuire and **Noel Paul Stookey** provided the closest thing to celebrity endorsement that the hippie Jesus people could find—unless, of course, they wanted to count **Pat Boone,** and they didn't. But what seems even more ridiculous is that, to the present day, millions of fans of folk-rock music remain completely oblivious to the existence of two of the best folk-rock albums ever made. Whether this is because they intentionally avoid "Christian music" for whatever stereotypes they erect concerning it, or because they have been disenfranchised by programmers and retailers who make such decisions for them, the fact remains that they have never even heard records that probably would have been among their favorite albums of the past thirty years. Bigotry has its price. Still, Christian music fans fall victim to another vice, the lethargy of an industry that persists in despising its own legacy. As of 2002, virtually all of McGuire's significant work remains unavailable on compact disc.

Born in 1935 in Oklahoma City, Barry McGuire became a founding member of The New Christy Minstrels, an unhip folk choir that sang regularly on the unhip *Andy Williams Show.* Other members of the group included actress Karen Black, future Byrd Gene Clark, Kim Carnes, John Denver, and Kenny Rogers—in addition to some members of The Association and Rogers' First Edition. They had their first and biggest hit with "Green, Green" (# 14 in 1963), a song written and sung by McGuire. In 1965, he left the group and recorded the quintessential protest song "Eve of Destruction." Contrary to widespread rumor and even supposedly authoritative reports, McGuire did not write the latter song. It is a composition of P. F. Sloan, who also wrote numerous hits recorded by The Turtles and The Grass Roots. The latter band actually backs McGuire on "Eve of Destruction," and the former recorded an alternative version of the song at almost the same time but held up its release as a single until their cover of **Bob Dylan**'s "It Ain't Me, Babe" cleared the charts. By then it was too late: McGuire's rendition had skyrocketed to Number One, despite (or perhaps because of) being banned by many radio stations as "anti-American" and "fatalistic." Comparing the two takes, it seems unlikely that The Turtles' sugary version could have had the kind of effect on the national conscience that McGuire's gruff roar induced.

In the years following his hit, McGuire was absent from the Top 40, but he remained a fixture in the counterculture. He followed his successful *Eve of Destruction* album (Dunhill, 1965)—which also included the folk songs "Child of Our Times" and "That's Exactly the Matter with Me"—with two more projects that failed to sell (*This Precious Time* in 1966 and *The World's Last Private Citizen* in 1968, both on Dunhill). But he also played a role in getting The Mamas and The Papas off the ground, as documented in the latter group's autobiographical song "Creeque Alley." He also landed the lead role in the Broadway cast of *Hair.* Then in 1971 he "met Jesus" and became one of the most visible exponents of the Jesus movement and a pioneer of the music it produced. The details of his conversion are typical for many of the era. McGuire had been on a spiritual and intellectual search for many years, reading in science, psychology, philosophy, and religion in quest of "the meaning of life." The hostile public reaction to his song "Eve of Destruction" further convinced him that "people don't want to know the truth." Then, as the Jesus movement exploded out on the West Coast, he began hearing about Christianity not as some dead religion practiced by an out-of-it generation, but as a phenomenon that seemed vibrant, fresh, and exciting: "Everywhere I went, I kept being confronted with the name of Jesus Christ." An encounter with a member of **Arthur Blessitt**'s outreach in Hollywood was particularly influential. And then one day McGuire picked up a copy of the book *Good News for Modern Man,* intrigued by the title. The volume was actually a paperback edition of the New Testament in an edition that the American Bible Society mass produced and sold for 25 cents in the early '70s. McGuire took the book home and read it. As he would later tell Paul Baker, "I was thirty-five years old and I had never read a New Testament in my life. It blew me away! I discovered the truth I'd been looking for so many years. It was Jesus!" McGuire says he prayed a simple doubter's prayer, "Jesus, are you really there?" and that Christ spoke words of assurance to him in his mind. Then, he continues, "Christ opened up my memory and showed me all the things that my selfishness had done to other people. All the lives that I'd ruined." He was baptized on Father's Day in 1971. McGuire emerged a totally transformed man and demonstrated a rare nondefensive ability for dealing with the ridicule that celebrity conversions usually bring. When someone said that he had been "brainwashed," he replied, "You're right! My brains were dirty and sick, man. They needed a scrub!" When a DJ said, "I hear you've jumped on the Jesus bandwagon," he responded, "That's right, man. I have jumped on the Jesus bandwagon, but let me tell you, his was the only bandwagon that was goin' anywhere. And I know because I've been on every wagon in the ballpark."

Seeds and *Lighten Up* are the two McGuire masterpieces on which his spiritual passions and musical talents combine in a spontaneous way that no artist or producer could ever contrive. Brimming with the zeal of a new convert, he tears through some of the best material he would ever write (or acquire), backed by such musicians as **Mike Deasy, Richard**

Souther, Michael Omartian, and **2nd Chapter of Acts.** Both albums sparkle with apocalyptic fervor as though the players had all assumed the Lord would return before the records hit the stores anyway and, so, just played for the sheer glory of the music itself.

This tone becomes immediately evident on *Seeds'* "Last Daze Waltz," an in-your-face challenge to those who think the day of recompense and/or salvation will never come: "and if you want to read about tomorrow, today, it's all there in God's word." Likewise, Side Two opens with McGuire's own "Lear Jets," a rousing rocker addressed to all those who turned their "backs so long ago on Jesus and his Dad," telling them, "you can live in the sunshine brother, step right out of the rain." The latter song melds seamlessly into "Father's Son," which makes the invitation more specific ("open up your heart my friend, and welcome in the Father's Son"). Three more songs are also incredibly good. "Love Is" (which juxtaposes Matthew 22:37–39 with 1 Corinthians 13:4–8) and "Peace" are powerful folk rock songs equal in quality (and similar in style) to the much later *Damn the Torpedoes*-era Tom Petty. "Shauna's Song" is a tender, personalized prodigal-son-type ballad that, in its day, had the power to soften the hearts and put tears in the eyes of many a street-hardened biker or runaway: "I just don't understand a man / Who'll stand and say, 'I forgive you' / Say 'I love you' / But don't you know / Now it's true / I love him too."

On *Lighten Up,* McGuire re-recorded "Eve of Destruction" as part of a trilogy that he had previewed in front of 250,000 people at the *Explo '72* festival two years earlier. The suite merges Sloan's protest lyric with two of McGuire's own songs, which insist that a) America's problems are not God's fault but the consequence of her own sin ("Don't Blame God") and b) God will in fact heal the country if people repent and pray ("II Chronicles 7:14"). This tidy bond has the unfortunate result of diluting the power of the original hit, almost implying that his critics had been right in deeming it inappropriate (without attachments). Sensing this perhaps, or maybe inspired by **Crashdog**'s unvarnished remake in 1995, McGuire would revert to performing "Eve of Destruction" without caveats in the '90s. Still, on their own terms, "Don't Blame God" and "II Chronicles 7:14" are fine songs. Historian David Di Sabatino notes that, along with **Larry Norman**'s "Reader's Digest," McGuire's "Don't Blame God" is one of the "few songs to turn the anti-institutional frustration of the counterculture against the established church." The lyric he probably has in mind runs, "We've got million dollar churches / But no one's on their knees / So many selfish people / Just doing what they please." This, of course, seems like a very heavy note on which to begin an album called *Lighten Up.* "Pay the Piper" also threatens divine judgment and "How Many Times" plays the guilt card in a

way that only the most heartless would be unaffected. Then on Side Two, McGuire does lighten up. "Hey World" is a raspy rocker that promises "It's time for the morning to come . . . darkness will die in the dawn." Then McGuire offers the rollicking good-time song "Happy Road," which would become his best-known piece from this period. The album closes with a joyous romp in which McGuire proclaims why he's not going to sing, shout, or talk about "anyone but Jee-ee-ee-ee-sus!" Perhaps the best of the best on *Lighten Up,* however, would be "Callin' Me Home," a gorgeous folk ballad that acquires a stunning sort of rough beauty when sung against type in McGuire's gravelly voice.

Both of McGuire's first two albums were produced by Buck Herring—as was the classic *To the Bride.* The latter project is probably the best live album ever made by a Christian artist— its only competitor for that title being **Andraé Crouch and the Disciples'** *Live at Carnegie Hall.* McGuire and **2nd Chapter of Acts** perform together and separately, backed by a group called "a band called David" (Rick Azim, gtr.; Jack Kelly, drums; Herb Melton, bass; Paul Offenbacher, gtr.; **Richard Souther,** kybrd.). The McGuire songs are almost exclusively ones from *Seeds* and *Lighten Up,* but the real treat becomes the dialogue between the songs, in which he introduces them with alternately amusing and moving stories. His rapport with the audience is palpable and his songs become more personable and affecting. Records like this may not hold up well to repeated listening (they are not intended to) but they do provide an important link to the artist that makes the studio releases more enjoyable. Along with **Randy Matthews'** *Now Do You Understand?,* McGuire's *To the Bride* offers an important and appealing historical portrait of what the Jesus movement was all about. It is also the only place that one can hear McGuire sing "Jesus People," a cute and playful song that anticipates the rapture by assuring those who find the Jesus people annoying that, if they just wait, "in a little while, they'll be gone."

Around this time, McGuire gave an extensive interview to *Harmony* magazine that offers a very different picture of him. He rambled on for many pages about politics and Mormons and extraterrestrials in ways that mix fundamentalist mythology and hippie paranoia into a bizarre concoction that makes him sound loony. He had gotten a hold of an anti-Semitic tract called the *Protocol of the Learned Elders of Zion* and, apparently unaware of its origins or intent, was exercised over a secret group of Jews who were conspiring to bankrupt the world's economy and bring the earth under Israeli (and, hence, satanic) rule. "Nixon was their man" and so was Kissinger, and all the space aliens and Lucifer and Moroni and Armageddon fit into the grand conspiracy one way or another. The interview is worthy of recall for historical purposes: it illustrates well the "latching on to every wind of doctrine" phenomenon that was a dangerous but inevitable part of the Jesus movement revival, a carefree openness to revelation that is perhaps intrinsic to all religious revivals. It should be noted, however, that McGuire and most of the Jesus people ultimately navigated these treacherous waters quite well.

Of course, the *Harmony* interview also serves as a reminder that the artistically talented are not necessarily theologically perceptive and that, indeed, the appeal of most Christian music (or for that matter, rock and roll) lies not primarily in the message itself but in the integrity with which the artist's concern is held and the passion with which it is delivered. As McGuire would say in a later interview, "Music is truly an expression of our spirit, of our deep inner being." This explains, he would continue, why so much secular music is better than Christian music. Ironically, the necessary accountability to which Christian artists are held works against their artistic merit: "Christians are afraid of being seen for what they really are. Secular artists don't care what anybody sees." The latter attitude might not make for responsible deportment, but it does make for good music: "Secular singers are more involved emotionally." That analysis explains, precisely, why McGuire's first three albums can compare in quality with the best of general market music. As the Christian music industry evolved, artists were expected to be more responsible theologically. The music also improved dramatically with regard to technical competence and production values. Still, few projects would display the carefree passion and level of emotional involvement that McGuire evinced in his wild and wooly Jesus freak days.

McGuire did not make another record of consistent quality with his first three Christian releases, but there would be songs here or there on which his great potential would be realized. "Clouds" from *C'mon Along* is a sweet and simple ballad about longing for the Lord's return. "Communion Song" from *Have You Heard* is probably the finest song he has ever recorded. It is also one of only a few contemporary Christian songs to deal with the very biblical subject of the eucharistic meal that is to be at the heart of Christian worship. The title song from *Cosmic Cowboy* would become the biggest hit on Christian radio for the year 1978. Cowritten with **Mike Deasy,** the song is rather obviously inspired by The Byrds' "Chestnut Mare," but *that* song is so innovative that anything inspired by it is likely to be more original than ninety percent of what is heard on Christian radio stations. *Inside Out* is a live album recorded on behalf of World Vision International, a hunger relief organization; its highlight is a cover of "Jesus Is Coming Back to Stay" by **Verne Bullock.** The album *Finer Than Gold* contains almost no original songs, relying instead on compositions by Becky Hernandez, Georgian Banov, and Mark Pendergrass; by contrast, *Pilgrim* is filled with highly personal songs that McGuire

wrote while touring for World Vision. Both are competent but unremarkable; on a par with a typical **Steven Curtis Chapman** project, they might have seemed stellar for an average artist but they pale in comparison to the legacy McGuire had established for himself with his early works. A song called "Heartbreaker" from *Finer Than Gold* is worth mention as a standout, as a straightforward call to repentance and an invitation to accept God's shelter from the evils of this world.

In 1978, McGuire had his biggest hit ever, composing and singing the title song on **Agape Force**'s children's musical *Bullfrogs and Butterflys.* The infectiously cute Sesame Street-style song about transformation ("Bullfrogs and butterflys / They've both been born again") would sell over three million copies (more than "Eve of Destruction" actually), opening doors for McGuire in terms of children's ministry. For a time, he put together a program called *Kids for Kids* that involved children's choirs doing programs to benefit children in need. In 1979, he performed at the White House. From 1984 to 1990 McGuire lived in New Zealand, working full time as an emissary for World Vision. He wrote a novel called *In the Midst of Wolves* (Crossway, 1990) about the leader of a motorcycle gang who becomes an evangelistic Christian. He became critical of the Christian music subculture, viewing it as a phenomenon that serves to insulate devotees from the world at large. For a time, McGuire quit recording because, he said, "I am tried of making generic records . . . they all have the same words . . . it's all 'Hallelujah, Praise the Lord,' which is wonderful in context, but there has got to be more. We have got to get out of just the Christian ear." In the early '90s he would become part of the duo **Talbot-McGuire,** and would close out the millennium singing both religious and secular songs intended for audiences that were not segregated by faith.

In addition to the albums listed in the discography above, McGuire sang the role of Peter in the musical *Firewind* (Sparrow, 1976) written by **Jamie Owens (Collins), John Michael Talbot,** and **Terry Talbot.**

For trivia buffs: Barry McGuire did one other thing that must remain only slightly less embarrassing than the *Harmony* interview or taking his clothes off on stage in *Hair.* In 1971, he starred in a movie called *Werewolves on Wheels* about bikers who, well . . . the title says it all. Unlike his albums, it is still available.

Christian radio hits: "Cosmic Cowboy" (# 1 for 35 weeks in 1978–1979); "Bullfrogs and Butterflys" (# 11 in 1980); "Jesus Is Coming Back to Stay" (# 13 in 1980).

Dony McGuire (and McGuire and Heaven's Connection)

Personnel for McGuire: Jeff Catron, bass; Dony McGuire, voc., kybrd.; Joy McGuire, voc.; Fred Newell, gtr.; Fred Satterfield, drums. By

McGuire: 1978—*Destined to Be Yours* (Greentree). By Dony McGuire's Heaven's Connection: 1979—*Get in Touch with the World* (NewPax). By Dony McGuire: 1981—*Inspiration* (Light).

www.rambomcguire.org

Christian pop singer Dony McGuire is probably best known as a songwriter, especially for the work he has produced with frequent collaborator and eventual wife **Reba Rambo.** McGuire began his career in Christian music as a member of **The Downings.** He formed McGuire with his wife Joy (also in The Downings—and winner of the 1976 Dove Award for Female Vocalist of the year) as a spin-off group with a more contemporary sound. Their one album featured eight of Dony's own compositions and a cover of Ashford and Simpson's "One Love in My Lifetime." The short-lived combo came to an abrupt end when Dony and Joy divorced. He briefly formed another vocal group called Heaven's Connection, which made one nondescript album, and then began writing songs with Rambo. In 1980 the duo completed a masterful musical called *The Lord's Prayer,* which features songs based on each petition of the prayer taught by Jesus. A variety of musicians were drafted to sing the songs and the production would win the Dove award for 1981 Praise and Worship Album. In 1980, McGuire and Rambo married. He began producing her albums, and also released an MOR solo record of inspirational songs that he had originally written for other artists. It includes "Because of Whose I Am" and "With My Song," both written with Rambo. The latter song was the title track for an album by **Debby Boone.** Also on *Inspiration* is McGuire's version of "We Are Persuaded," which he wrote with Bill and Gloria Gaither. McGuire and Rambo also wrote **The Bill Gaither Trio**'s hit "A Perfect Heart." They have continued to record albums as Rambo/McGuire.

M.C. Hammer (a.k.a. Hammer)

By M.C. Hammer: 1988—*Feel My Power* (Bust It); *Let's Get It Started* (Capitol); 1990—*Please Hammer Don't Hurt 'Em;* 1991—*2 Legit 2 Quit* [as Hammer] (Oaktown); 1994—*The Funky Headhunter* [as Hammer] (Giant); 1995—*V Inside Out;* 1996—*Greatest Hits* (Capitol); 1998—*Family Affair* (Oaktown); 2001—*Active Duty* (World Hit).

www.mchammer.com

The singer known as M.C. Hammer (née Stanley Kirk Burrell) became the top rap artist in America in the early '90s and brought that genre of music to a much broader audience (including more whites) than it had ever enjoyed before. M.C. Hammer was born in 1963 and he grew up in a rough neighborhood in Oakland, California. He was active in church and took part in a singing group called The Holy Ghost Boys. As an adolescent, he became the official bat boy and unofficial mascot of the Oakland A's baseball team. He frequently entertained the team with his song-and-dance routines and in fact received the "Hammer" nickname because some of the players thought he resembled Hank Aaron, who was known as "Hammerin' Hank." The singer tried to break into pro ball himself, but eventually a couple of the A's invested in a record company and financed his music career. His first homemade album, *Feel My Power,* produced a Number One regional hit ("Ring It"). It was then remade as the major-label release *Let's Get It Started,* which went double platinum with sales of over two million copies—a phenomenal level of success for a rap album. But *Please Hammer Don't Hurt 'Em* would sell over ten million copies, in spite of the fact that it had literally been recorded on the back of the artist's tour bus with a budget of less than $10,000. The biggest hits were "U Can't Touch This" (# 8 in 1990) and "Pray" (# 2 in 1990). The first of these was a recast version of **Rick James**' "Superfreak," with new rapped lyrics. But "Pray" was a gospel song (built on the rhythm track of Prince's "When Doves Cry") and its success marked the biggest intrusion of gospel on the mainstream pop charts since the **Edwin Hawkins Singers** did "Oh Happy Day" in 1969.

M.C. Hammer became a huge celebrity for a short period. A popular M.C. Hammer doll was sold in toy stores, and there was even a *Hammerman* TV show featuring him as a cartoon character on Saturday mornings. He had more hits with "Have You Seen Her?" (# 4 in 1990), "2 Legit 2 Quit" (# 5 in 1991) and "Addams Family Groove" (# 7 in 1991) from the motion picture *The Addams Family.* He was presented as something of a role model for African American youth with clean-cut "don't do drugs," "stay in school" messages, and he was also outspoken about his Christian faith. The *2 Legit 2 Quit* album featured another gospel song, "Do Not Pass Me By" (# 62 in 1992) which presented the traditional hymn sung by **Tramaine Hawkins** with Hammer providing rap breaks. In the liner notes to the latter album, Hammer wrote, "I have felt guilty about my success. I possess all of my material dreams and yet there is a void. God has shown me his mercy and reclaimed me. That brings me joy. But there is a hurt and a burden I feel. I need to help my people." Hammer also appeared on Christian albums by **Jon Gibson, Prime Minister,** and BeBe and CeCe Winans.

By the end of 1992, however, Hammer's moment in the sun was up. A backlash against the popular artist set in, fueled largely by rap artists with more street credibility who felt that he had diluted the hip-hop form by mixing it with commercial pop. Rick James sued him over the sampling of "Superfreak" in what would be a landmark royalties case regarding such borrowing. The artist fell off the charts and all but vanished from the public eye. He attempted an unsuccessful comeback with a new gangsta rap persona in 1994 (*The Funky Headhunter*) and filed for bankruptcy in 1997. In 2001, he released another album on his own label (World Hit).

Phill McHugh

1974—*Saviour* (Tri-Art); 1976—*All Glory to You* [= re-release of *Saviour*] (Jesus Folk); 1977—*Canvas for the Sun* (Lamb and Lion); 1980—*Reference Point* (New Born); 1986—*In Heaven's Eyes* (First Vision).

Folk troubadour Phill McHugh has his roots in '60s protest songs and claims that, as a Christian, he "keeps writing with the same attitude but with attention focused on the Lord and what He has done for the world." McHugh's voice reminds many critics of **Noel Paul Stookey** or Jim Croce, both of whom were his contemporaries in the early '70s. McHugh toured with **Phil Keaggy** and **Pam Mark Hall** and a number of his songs were recorded by other artists, notably "I Am Stone" by **Debby Boone** and "People Need the Lord" by **Steve Green.** *All Glory to You* is actually a retitled re-release of an earlier custom album. The title song offers what *Harmony* magazine would call "the most vivid description of the tragedy at Calvary in Jesus music." Subtle use of synthesizers gives *Canvas for the Sun* a more modern sound, reminiscent of **John Michael Talbot.** *CCM* described *Reference Point* as "mellow music to listen to on a rainy day." *In Heaven's Eyes* is a reassuring album, focusing on the generous and gracious evaluation of God. Its title song proclaims, "In heaven's eyes, there are no losers."

Maria McKee (and Lone Justice)

Personnel for Lone Justice: Ryan Hedgecock, gtr., voc.; Maria McKee, voc.; Martin Etzioni, bass (– 1986); Don Heffington, drums (– 1986) // Bruce Brody, kybrd. (+ 1986); Shayne Fontayne, gtr. (+ 1986); Rudy Richman, drums (+ 1986); George Sutton, bass (+ 1986). As Lone Justice: 1985—*Lone Justice* (Geffen); 1986—*Shelter*; 1999—*The World Is Not My Home*. As Maria McKee: 1989—*Maria McKee* (Geffen); 1993—*You Gotta Sin to Be Saved*; 1996—*Life Is Sweet*; 2000—*Ultimate Collection: This One Is for the Girl* (Uni).

www.mariamckee.com

Maria McKee is often referred to as "a female Bruce Springsteen" on account of the passion and verve that she brings to her blue-collar songs. She is also likened to Janis Joplin as a vocalist, although her songs are typically more Merle Haggard-country than Joplin-blues. Although McKee is far better known in the general market than in the contemporary Christian music scene, her Christianity has at times been prominent in her material, prompting many reviewers to comment on the contributions of her faith. Born in Los Angeles in 1964, McKee first hooked up with Ryan Hedgecock to form an acoustic duo playing clubs in the L.A. area. They eventually added a rhythm section and became Lone Justice, attracting almost unprecedented acclaim from local critics and making fans

of such musicians as Bono (of **U2**), **Bob Dylan,** Tom Petty, and Bruce Springsteen. The band was almost completely reconstituted for the sophomore project, with only McKee and Hedgecock remaining. After that, she simply performed as a solo artist with various backing musicians. On *Maria McKee,* these would include luminaries Robbie Robertson and Richard Thompson. For *You've Got to Sin to Be Saved,* she brought back the rhythm section from Lone Justice, supplemented by Gary Louris and Mark Olson from the Jayhawks.

The first Lone Justice album includes the song "You Are the Light," a straightforward modern gospel number with blatantly religious lyrics: "You are the light in my dark world / You are the fire that always will burn." McKee also wrote "After the Flood" and "Soap, Soup, and Salvation" for the album, which evince gospel influences musically and touch on spiritual and biblical themes. The former song applies lessons from the deluge to a modern-day tragedy in which a mudslide destroyed the singer's homestead ("A natural disaster can't hold nothin' on me . . . Life goes on after the flood"). The latter describes life at "a rescue mission." *Lone Justice* also includes "Ways to Be Wicked," a song donated to the group by Tom Petty, and "Don't Toss Us Away," written by McKee's half-brother **Bryan MacLean.** *Shelter* moves to a less rootsy, mainstream rock sound with songs that are even more obviously spiritual in their focus. The album's highpoint, perhaps, is "Inspiration," in which McKee sings, "How my spirit longs for your inspiration / Fill me up, fill me up, fill me up." The title track is a midtempo ballad with a "Bridge over Troubled Water" theme, and the opening "I Found Love" is a rousing testimony to spiritual awakening. *Shelter* was sufficiently "Christian" to earn Lone Justice a review in *CCM* magazine, which commented positively on "the depth of sentiment" McKee brings to her songs "whether concerning the Lord or interpersonal relationships." *The World Is Not My Home* is a compilation disc of songs from the previous two Lone Justice projects, with an additional ten previously unreleased tracks. These include a cover of Merle Haggard's "Working Man's Blues," a song recorded with **Bob Dylan** ("Go Away, Little Boy"), and an odd cover of Lou Reed's "Sweet Jane," performed as a duet with Bono. Both of the original Lone Justice albums were produced by Jimmy Iovine, known for his work with Petty and **U2**. The group opened for the latter band on its *Unforgettable Fire* tour.

McKee's first solo album includes the beautiful "Breathe," which would become one of her most beloved songs. It seems to many at least to be a prayer addressed to the Spirit of God: "I will let you breathe through me." Otherwise, most of the songs deal with romantic relationships—or, more often, the lack thereof. McKee becomes the veritable voice of loneliness: "Though I've never really been in love, I know what it means to miss someone," she wails. "Am I the Only One Who's Ever

Felt This Way?" she asks. "I've Forgotten What It Was in You That Put the Need in Me" she moans. She's pretty pitiful, alright, and she's willing to reveal just how pathetic it can get: "Your boyfriend's good-looking / He's got it all there / Looks like God made him with somethin' to spare . . . Has he got a friend? / Has he got a friend for me?" The album closes with "Drinkin' in My Sunday Dress," a country romp that expresses the sort of spirit-is-willing-but-flesh-is-weak ambiguity that marks much of McKee's music. The same can be said for the title song to *You Gotta Sin to Be Saved.* The song is equal parts Ozark Mountain Daredevils ("If You Want to Get to Heaven, You've Got to Raise a Little Hell") and pre-Christian St. Augustine ("Lord, make me holy . . . but not yet!"). Still, it does not ridicule Christian discipleship; it merely expresses an inability to walk that row—and a hope that the infirmity will not prove permanent. The *Sin to Be Saved* album opens with what is perhaps McKee's best song, the Motown influenced "I'm Gonna Soothe You," an inviting appeal for some world-weary lover to find comfort and succor in her arms: "Let me kiss your tears away . . . Lay your head on my breast / I'll do the rest." On a more spiritual note, "Why Wasn't I More Grateful When Life Was Sweet?" acknowledges the tendency to take blessings for granted, and "I Forgive You" draws musically on the rich tradition of gospel music in a song offering pardon to an errant mate. McKee also includes two **Van Morrison** covers ("Lonely, Sad Eyes"; "The Way Young Lovers Do") and a little-known Carole King-Gerry Goffin song ("I Can't Make It Alone"). McKee's career got a big boost when a song intended for *You Gotta Sin* ended up on the soundtrack for the motion picture *Pulp Fiction*—the haunting, spooky "If Love Is a Red Dress (Hang Me in Rags)." *Life Is Sweet* is a hit-and-miss ad-hoc collection of what *The Rough Guide to Rock* calls "post-Nirvana squall," that is, songs that travel in an alternative rock vein and betray little of the artist's formative influences—though the title track is on a par with the best of her work. She returned to form in 2001 with a rendition of "Wayfarin' Stranger" on the soundtrack for the film *Songcatcher.*

For trivia buffs: the cover photo for the *You Gotta Sin to Be Saved* album (a startlingly tough-but-vulnerable portrait of the artist) was taken by actor Dennis Hopper.

Toby McKeehan

See **Toby Mac.**

Charles McPheeters (and **The Bible Belt Boogie Band**)

By Charles McPheeters: 1971—*High on Life* (Landmark). By Charles McPheeters and The Bible Belt Boogie Band: 1979—*Faces* (Holy Ghost Repair Service).

Charles McPheeters was a radical street evangelist in the early days of the Jesus movement. He was not primarily known as a musician but, like **Arthur Blessitt,** he did have some musical talent and used it to further his ministries. McPheeters actually got his start in a little-known gospel folk group called Disciples Three, where he drew early opposition from church people for thinking acoustic folk guitars could be used to accompany godly music. He worked with a California branch of David Wilkerson's Teen Challenge and then became a regular performer at Blessitt's His Place coffeehouse on the Sunset Strip. One night while playing there, his brother Jim McPheeters turned up unawares in the audience. The latter had just finished a stint in Vietnam and did not even recognize the transformed Charles as the club performer. Jim experienced a conversion through his brother's ministry and became a member of Blessitt's band Eternal Rush. Around 1972, Charles McPheeters left His Place and stayed for a time with the Love Inn community in upstate New York (cf. **Dave Perkins, Phil Keaggy**). In 1969, he did a stint as a DJ for Pat Robertson's Christian Broadcasting Network. Finally, in 1972, he ended up in Denver, Colorado, where he founded a street ministry called The Holy Ghost Repair Service, which he later transplanted to north Hollywood. The ministry focused on the down-and-out, drug addicts, prostitutes, and the hordes of runaways who had left their homes to live on the streets.

McPheeters' first album, *High on Life,* is mostly a spoken word testimonial, in which he recounts his former life as a drug addict and his salvation through Christ in a humorous style that would later be picked up by **Mike Warnke.** Along the way, five songs are interspersed purportedly as illustrative of sermonic points, but also just to hold the listener's attention. McPheeters performs one of his own compositions, "Bad News Blues," and covers of four other songs: **The Exkursions'** "Would You Believe," **Noel Paul Stookey**'s "Hymn," Joe South's "Walk a Mile in My Shoes," and James Taylor's "Fire and Rain." The second album, *Faces,* is a Jesus music classic, if also something of a novelty. McPheeters' Bible Belt Boogie Band included **Mike Johnson** (who produced the album), **Randy Matthews,** and **Danny Taylor.** McPheeters knew that he was not a great musician and so wisely went for a fun, goof-ball approach, as is indicated by songs with titles like "Greasy Truth" and "First Church of the Frigid-Air." Every song on the album is done in a different style. The group samples doo-wop, cocktail jazz, mariachi, and rock and roll songs, with McPheeters doing an Elvis impression one minute and becoming a Perry Como-style lounge singer the next. Two songs off of the album gained a wide hearing and were later included on the compilation of Jesus music called *The Rock Revival* (Sonrise, 1994). "Practice What You Preach" is a rinky-tink Bo Diddley piano tune that warns Christian artists against adopting worldly motives. The style and sound of the song preview **Steve Taylor**'s much more sophisticated "Guilty by Association" by about five years. On "Ain't Got No Time," McPheeters parodies Creedence Clearwater Revival in a delightful romp about living in the last days. In the early '80s, McPheeters was diagnosed with stomach cancer that would ultimately take his life. **Barry McGuire, Terry Clark,** and other artists performed in a 1982 benefit concert to help defray his medical expenses.

Justin McRoberts

1999—*Reason for Living* (5 Min. Walk); 2000—*Father;* 2001—*Untitled EP* [EP].

www.justinmcroberts.com

Christian pop singer Justin McRoberts has worked closely with the youth organization Young Life, which trains teenagers and young adults to "earn the right" to share their faith with others by forming close and caring relationships with those outside the church. A native of the East San Francisco Bay area, McRoberts did not grow up a Christian but became involved in Young Life while in seventh grade. Attracted to the group for social reasons, McRoberts credits the efforts of one adult leader who stayed in touch with him for a period of six years for bringing him finally to embrace the faith in a personal and meaningful way. McRoberts went on to become a staff worker with Young Life in the Diablo Bay area of California. His father, who suffered from depression, committed suicide in May of 1998.

McRoberts' debut album evinces a bluesy sound on its title track and on "Jump Back" and "5th Wheel" (a song for adolescents about feeling out of place). He establishes identification with the pain of those who feel lost in this world in poignant ways on "Heaven Help Me" and "Michael's Hands." The song "The Story Stands Alone" is rather reminiscent of **Dime Store Prophets.** Although *Reason for Living* is a well-polished and slickly produced album, McRoberts gained some attention while touring for appearing on stage alone with his guitar. The stripped-down approach is captured more effectively on his second album, *Father,* on which a number of songs seem to touch on the grief surrounding his father's death and on his growth in faith related to this. "Always Deeper" expresses the belief that God's grace and love run deeper than any human need, a prominent theme throughout the album. "Waiting on Your Love" is sung as a duet with **Nichole Nordeman.** "At the Cross" identifies a meeting place for Christians who differ in their political or doctrinal views. *Untitled EP* is a collection of worship songs presented in a "sing around a campfire" setting featuring sparse arrangements and light production.

Gary McSpadden

1979—*Higher Purpose* (Paragon); 1981—*It Was Enough;* 1984—*Separate Journeys;* 1986—*One Song, One Voice* (Word); 1987—*The Best of Gary McSpadden* (Greentree); 1988—*Hymns from the Heart* (independent); 1989—*All Time Favorites;* 1991—*From My Soul;* 1993—*Highest Praise;* 1998—*Back Home Again.*

Gary McSpadden was a founding member of three of the most significant southern gospel groups of all time: The Oak Ridge Boys (who crossed over into mainstream country sometime after McSpadden's departure), **The Imperials,** and **The Bill Gaither Trio.** He has been inducted into the Gospel Music Hall of Fame twice as a member of the latter two groups (in 1998 and 1999, respectively). He also sang with **The New Gaither Vocal Band,** which had a slightly more contemporary sound. McSpadden was born in 1943 in Mangum, Oklahoma. He grew up in Texas wanting to be a member of a gospel quartet and at the age of eighteen joined The Statesmen as a temporary fill-in for gospel legend Jake Hess. The next year he and Hess did a similar stint as members of the original Oak Ridge Boys, and then in 1964, McSpadden and Hess became founding members of **The Imperials.** McSpadden left **The Imperials** in 1967 to join his father in founding a church in Ft. Worth, Texas. After more than a decade of serving as an associate pastor there, he returned to music as a member of **The Bill Gaither Trio.** While singing with the Gaither groups, McSpadden also made solo albums of MOR music that were similar in style and content to the groups' projects. His album *It Was Enough* features the song "He Is the King," which McSpadden wrote after an experience that drove home the temporal nature of all earthly authority—he was actually in the West Wing of the White House at the time when President Reagan was shot and, a witness to the panic that ensued, was struck by how easy it is for a nation to lose its leader. On *Separate Journeys,* McSpadden sought a more contemporary sound that included some more up-tempo songs than those with which the Gaithers were associated. Otherwise, he has been content to apply his rich baritone to hymns and inspirational ballads.

Christian radio hits: "He Is Risen" (# 24 in 1984).

Lewis McVay

1978—*Spirit of St. Lewis* (Maranatha); 1984—*Coming Attractions* (Heartland).

Lewis McVay was a member of the Jesus music group **Mustard Seed Faith,** and he wrote the title song to that band's classic album *Sail on Sailor.* Like his partner in MSF, **Oden Fong,** he made a couple of solo albums after the group disbanded. McVay has a highly melodic voice, and his *Spirit of St. Lewis* album features midtempo rock songs and folk ballads. Historian David Di Sabatino singles out "How Long?" and

"Time" as standout cuts. Christian music progressed considerably as a genre by the time McVay made *Coming Attractions,* and the sophomore project displays a much more aggressive sound. The opening and closing songs ("Moon Eyes," "Working Man") are solid power-pop songs in the '80s **Petra** tradition. "Can't Live without Your Love" was written by Loyd Boldeman of **Prodigal** and features a killer guitar solo courtesy of Jon Goin. The title track (and the album cover) announce Jesus' impending return as though it were an event at a local theater. For a time, McVay headed Calvary Chapel's Asaph record label. As of 1998, he was performing as the character Tigger at Anaheim's Disneyland.

Mitch McVicker

1998—*Mitch McVicker* (independent); 2001—*Chasing the Horizon.*

www.mitchmcvicker.com

Despite his own musical gifts and contributions, Mitch McVicker seems likely to be best remembered as "the other guy in the jeep," that is, as the friend and partner of **Rich Mullins** who narrowly survived the accident that took the latter's life. McVicker grew up in Topeka, Kansas, and met Mullins at Friends University. Prior to coming under Mullins' influence, McVicker regarded music only as a hobby, expecting to pursue a career as a basketball coach; he played guard on the college team. Soon, however, McVicker and Mullins were writing and performing together, and after McVicker graduated, the two of them moved to New Mexico where they lived and worked together. McVicker cowrote *Canticle of the Plains,* a musical on the life of St. Francis of Assisi produced by Mullins. He also sang some of the songs on that project, revealing a voice and style very much like Mullins' own. Mullins coproduced McVicker's debut album with Mark Robertson (of **Brighton, Generation, The Stand, Under Midnight, A Ragamuffin Band,** and **This Train**). In fact, Mullins and McVicker finished tracking on the album just hours before the accident. On their way from the recording studio to a benefit concert, their jeep was struck by a truck. It was initially reported that both Mullins and McVicker had been killed in the collision, but McVicker survived in a coma with massive head injuries, a collapsed lung, and crushed eye socket. His album was held up for release but ten months later, it came out on an independent label with a new song added—the artist's own rendition of "My Deliverer," a song he had written with Mullins and one that had just won the Dove Award for Song of the Year (based on the version sung by **Rick Elias** on Mullins' posthumous *The Jesus Record*). *Mitch McVicker* sold better than expected and was re-released on Rhythm House in 1999. Its robust opening track "Here and Now" invites people to join the singer in his pursuit of faith. "The Lemonade Song" is a silly ditty that had gained a good response when McVicker performed it at Mullins' concerts. "My Deliverer" is sung in an eerie, scratchy voice, recorded while McVicker's vocal chords were not yet healed. Two other songs ("Gospel Rain" and "New Mexico") were also cowritten with Mullins. In 2001, McVicker would release *Chasing the Horizon,* another album of new material recorded after the accident. It includes a cover of Mullins' song "When You Love," and features "Rich's Song," an emotional tribute to the artist's friend. "Upside Down" is a Tom Petty-like contemplation on how his beliefs and values seem to be the reverse of what passes as the norm in the world at large. McVicker's solo material has been compared to that of **Justin McRoberts** and **Bebo Norman.**

Timothy James Meaney

1993—*Be the Child* (Wise Man); 1995—*Life Again;* 1996—*The Big Chair* (Pamplin).

Timothy James Meaney grew up at a Bible camp near Bellevue, Washington, where he learned early on to play guitar and lead worship songs. In 1989, he started his own independent label, Wise Man Music, and released two albums of camp songs. *The Big Chair* includes new versions of four songs culled from these projects and marks Meaney's official debut for a broader audience. *CCM* noted strong influences of **Gary Chapman** and **Brian Barrett** on the more country-flavored songs, but suggested that Meaney is better at performing adult contemporary ballads ("Here's Everything," "Work of Art"). The title track to *The Big Chair* derives from Campus Crusade for Christ's famous *Four Spiritual Laws* tract, which asks every individual to consider who is on the throne ("big chair") of his or her life: Christ or self?

Ken Medema

1972—*Fork in the Road* (Word); 1974—*Sonshiny Day;* 1975—*People of the Son;* 1976—*Just Us Kids;* 1977—*Through the Eyes of Love;* 1980—*Looking Back;* 1981—*Kingdom in the Streets;* 1982—*Yesterday's a Sign;* 1984—*Flying Upside Down* (Briar Patch); 1985—*November Tomatoes;* 1992—*Just Kiddin' Around; One Good Tune Deserves Another;* 1994—*In the Dragon's Jaws;* 1995—*Someday: An Album of Hymns and Songs;* 1997—*25 to Life;* 1999— *All the Way to Bethlehem;* 2000—*Little Pictures;* 2001—*The Weaver.*

www.kenmedema.com

Blind from birth, Ken Medema is a classically trained musician who has produced several albums of inspirational, adult contemporary music, in addition to a number of Scripture-based collections of children's songs. He told the story of his early life and career in an autobiography: *Come and See,* by Ken Medema with Joyce Norman (Word, 1976).

Medema taught himself to play the piano by listening to tape recordings and by reading music in braille. He eventually earned a master's degree from Michigan State University. In the early '70s he worked as Director of Music and Creative Arts Therapies at the Essex County Hospital Center, a children's psychiatric facility in New Jersey. While there, he recorded *Fork in the Road* as a collection of songs written for the children. *Just Us Kids* and *Just Kiddin' Around* provided additional sets of children's songs. *People of the Son* was recorded live at a church in Waco, Texas, and brought him to the attention of the contemporary Christian music subculture that was just beginning to emerge from the Jesus movement. *Harmony* magazine reviewed *People of the Son* alongside **Chuck Girard**'s first solo album, noting that Medema "effectively bridges the gap between contemporary and traditional music." The album earned him a Jesus music hit with the fun song "Moses," a humorous retelling of the lawgiver's arguments with God. In a more serious vein, Medema would score a major inspirational hit (before charts were kept) with the piano ballad "Come Let Us Reason Together" from *Through the Eyes of Love;* the song had appeared in an earlier version on *Fork in the Road. Kingdom in the Streets* focuses on the Christian obligation to care for the needy, encouraging people to "wake up to the biblical call to justice so long neglected by the American church."

In 1985, Medema launched his own independent label, Briar Patch. *In the Dragon's Jaws* is a collection of contemporary pop songs addressed to people of faith. *Little Pictures* relates story-songs about people he has met over the years. *25 to Life* and *Yesterday's a Sign* offer collections of favorites. *Someday* is an album of hymns. *November's Tomatoes* and *One Good Tune* are instrumental albums. *All the Way to Bethlehem* is a live Christmas recording featuring soprano soloist Stacey Rigg and a full choir. At the turn of the millennium, Medema was still performing solo concerts at which he would appear alone on stage with a grand piano, two synthesizers, and an electronic percussion machine. One critic remarked, "If he had a full orchestra to back him, it would only be extra baggage." His shows feature a generous dose of comedic presentations as well as music. Thematically, he strives to convey an inclusive vision that challenges people of all persuasions to dream and work together for peace and justice. Not limited to churches, Medema frequently performs for school programs, state fairs, and corporate conventions.

Bill Medley

Selected: 1993—*Going Home* (Essential); 1997—*Almost Home* (Vesper Alley).

One of the most widely recognized crooners in the history of popular music, Bill Medley was once one-half of the duo known as the Righteous Brothers. Born in 1940 in Santa Ana, California, Medley was introduced (at the age of twenty-two) to fellow-Brother Bobby Hatfield by lounge singer John Wimber, who arranged the duo's first two hits ("Little Latin Lupe Lu" and "My Babe") and told them that God had "something special" planned for them. Wimber would later become the founder of the Vineyard Christian Fellowship churches. The Righteous Brothers went on to record "You've Lost That Loving Feeling" (# 1 for 2 weeks in 1964), "Unchained Melody" (# 4 in 1965), "You're My Soul and Inspiration" (# 1 for 3 weeks in 1966), and a number of other chart hits in the early '60s. The group regularly included a gospel song or two in their performances and they even had a Top 20 hit with the modern hymn "He" in 1966. The group disbanded in 1968 but reunited briefly to take "Rock and Roll Heaven" to Number Three on the charts in 1974 (the song was written by Alan O'Day, whose 1977 hit "Undercover Angel" put producer **Michael Omartian** into a quandary). Much later in 1990, the song "Unchained Melody" was featured in the motion picture *Ghost* and enjoyed a resurgence of popularity, becoming the number three song of the year in terms of radio airplay. In 2000, a national survey of Americans asked to name their "favorite song of all time" revealed the Righteous Brothers' "You've Lost That Loving Feeling" to be the top choice. Medley would also record several general market solo albums over the years.

In 1973, Medley lost his voice and was told that he could never sing again. At that time, as he would later relate to *CCM* magazine, a vocal coach by the name of Jack Coleman came into his life, claiming to have been sent by God to help him recover his vocal abilities. Coleman put him through a rigorous period of therapy and voice lessons, refusing to accept any compensation for his efforts, maintaining, "God told me to do this, and you don't charge a fee when God is giving the orders." The treatments were successful and Medley vowed to make a gospel album in appreciation. His life took a number of other turns before he was able to act on that promise. In 1976, his wife Karen was murdered, prompting him to retire completely from music for at least five years. In 1987 he suddenly was at the top of the charts again when he sang a duet with Jennifer Warnes on the song "(I've Had) The Time of My Life" for the motion picture *Dirty Dancing*. Then *Ghost* brought him and his old partner back into the limelight. Twenty years after the sessions with Coleman, Medley went into the studio and recorded *Going Home*. "I've known the Lord all my life," he told *CCM* in 1993. Still, he dedicated the project to the now-deceased Coleman who he said had instilled in him "the yearning for a personal relationship with Jesus Christ" and inspired him to surrender his life completely to the Lord. The album includes six of Medley's own compositions and remains the most personal statement of his career. A 1997 album called *Almost Home* includes gospel standards like "You'll Never Walk Alone" and "Precious Lord" and appears to be a reissue of the earlier project.

For trivia buffs: Medley is co-owner of a Las Vegas night-club called Kicks. His partner in that enterprise is musician Paul Revere (of Paul Revere and the Raiders).

Grammy Awards: 1987 Best Pop Vocal Performance by a Duo or Group [with Jennifer Warnes] ("[I've Had] The Time of My Life").

David Meece

1976—David (Myrrh); 1977—I Just Call on You; 1979—Everybody Needs a Little Help; 1980—Are You Ready?; 1982—Front Row; 1983—Count the Cost; 1985—7; 1986—Chronology; 1987—Candle in the Rain; 1989—Learning to Trust (StarSong); 1993—Once in a Lifetime; 1995—Odyssey.

www.david-meece.com

As the king of Christian MOR, gifted pianist and singer David Meece has often been referred to as "the Christian Barry Manilow." Meece has dominated adult contemporary charts and radio stations for a quarter of a century with inspirational pop songs that reflect his classical training. Over the years, however, he has grown as an artist (as did Manilow, actually) moving from the bubblegum pop with which he remains most associated to a less commercial but much deeper brand of introspective balladry. Meece grew up in Humble, Texas, where he was regarded a musical child prodigy. By the age of ten, he was giving solo piano recitals and performing with major symphony orchestras. At fourteen, he made his conducting debut with the Houston Symphony Orchestra, and at that same age, he wrote a Christmas song called "One Small Child" that continues to be recorded and performed. The next year he toured Europe as featured pianist with Youth for Christ. At sixteen, he played one of Mozart's piano concertos with the Houston Symphony Orchestra, which at that time was under the direction of André Previn. He attended Baltimore's prestigious Peabody Conservatory of Music and, while there, he had a spiritual conversion experience through which he says he "gave his heart to God and made the serious decision to follow Christ." He had been raised a churchgoer and, he says, never got into much trouble: "I was your basic right-wing good guy with short hair." Musically, his plans to be a concert pianist were somewhat derailed by an affinity for more contemporary sounds—not rock, he says, but prepsychedelic pop music such as that played by Gerry and the Pacemakers or Freddy and the Dreamers. Before graduating from Peabody, Meece composed a pop-opera based on the biblical story of the conversion of Paul.

Meece's first album had the effect of broadening the minds of a number of Jesus freaks. Fans of **Barry McGuire, Phil Keaggy,** and **Larry Norman** were understandably taken aback by this quasi-classical Christian Mancini. He was their age, but his music sounded like the stuff that their parents listened to—still, he was a brother in Christ, so they gave him a chance. The situation offered an ironic twist on an old theme: while conservative, middle-aged Christians struggled with the question of whether God could use rock and roll music, thousands of young hippie Christians listened to David Meece and wondered if God could really be glorified through what they would normally dismiss as "easy listening schmaltz." David was produced by Paul Baker, an eminent Christian DJ and author of the book Why Should the Devil Have All the Good Music? (Word, 1979). It features mostly piano ballads, including the love song "I'll Sing This Song for You" and the patriotic "Come Home, America."

Neither David nor I Just Call on You were commercial hits, but Meece found his niche with his next two projects (Everybody Needs a Little Help and Are You Ready?) and enjoyed almost unprecedented success as one of the Christian market's top artists. Furthermore, his light pop style appealed specifically to a new (post-psychedelic) generation of fourteen- through nineteen-year-olds who were grooving on Air Supply and Christopher Cross. Although Meece would never admit it, his youthful good looks also made him something of a heartthrob with teenage girls for a few years (though he had married a viola player back at the Peabody). Everybody seemed to perfect what would be a Meece trademark: love songs to God written in the second person such that the "You" references could also be interpreted in a secular/romantic sense ("I can't believe it's true / All the lovin' that I found when I found you"). On Are You Ready? Meece tones down what CCM had called his "imitation Bee Gees falsetto" and makes better use of his impressive three-octave range. The album includes a Christmas song, "We Are the Reason," which has since been recorded by over two hundred artists. Front Row was a successful and well-received live album. In addition to a sixteen-minute medley of modern and classical tunes related to the theme of Jesus' crucifixion, Meece covers **Honeytree**'s "Rattle Me, Shake Me" and performs a mini-musical called "Mother, Muffler, Mozart, and the Beatles," which includes snippets of Mozart's Sonata in A minor and "Sgt. Pepper's Lonely Hearts Club Band." Notably, Meece's concert performances are typically laced with humor and a spirit of good will that makes them enjoyable even to those for whom his style of music does not hold immediate appeal.

Count the Cost includes "Making My Life Brand New," an R&B-inflected love song to God, as well as the hit, "And You Know It's True," a song about the assurance of faith written by Meece with **Michael W. Smith** and **Brown Bannister** (who has produced most of Meece's albums). The title track was written by Randy Scruggs and John Thompson. Hints of techno-pop show up on Count the Cost also ("Gloria"), and such influences would only increase with 7, which produced a spate of radio hits. "You Can Go" (written with **Michael Card**) works a Bach invention into a synthesized pop song in a manner reminiscent of Manilow's classical-pop hit, "Could It Be Magic?" (built on a Chopin theme). "We Can Overcome It" is a powerful, militant anthem, powered by thundering percussion. Such commercial success continued with *Candle in the Rain,* made with several producers, including Brown Bannister, **Jonathan David Brown,** and, notably, Gino and Joe Vanelli.

In 1988, Meece was hospitalized for what was later diagnosed to be emotional and physical exhaustion. While in the hospital, a doctor asked him if there was any alcoholism in his family and he responded, saying the words aloud for the first time in his life, "My father is an alcoholic." A couple weeks later he related this story to *CCM* and then "lived in terror" (as he would later recount) for the intervening weeks before the magazine appeared. "I had broken the family silence," he explained. Meece took a break from recording to seek counseling and get help dealing with his past and with the dysfunctional life patterns that typify adult children of alcoholics (e.g., inferiority complexes, obsessive-compulsive behavior, denial, and even suicidal tendencies). He talked to *CCM* a second time and detailed harrowing stories of abuse and trauma: nights spent hiding in a closet, his drunk father waving a gun and threatening to kill the whole family, his parents' divorce when he was in high school, a brief meeting with the man at one of his concerts years later, and finally the funeral at which Meece says he remembers "feeling no emotion at all."

With *Learning to Trust,* Meece matured as an artist in a way that earned him the respect and admiration of former detractors. Writing in *CCM,* critic Bruce Brown said, "as one who thought Meece only capable of bouncy, one-dimensional pop froth, I am delighted to say that *Leaning to Trust* is a mature, well-crafted and seamlessly performed recording." The record is certainly his most personal and vulnerable offering. The song "When I Was Seventeen," addresses his adolescent traumas in an appropriate and meaningful way. Musically, the song is also more of a rocker than Meece's usual fare. "Somebody Calling Your Name" incorporates some slow, traditional gospel influence and "This Time" begins with a Chopin prelude. Four years later, *Once in a Lifetime* would be even more cathartic. The album's title track could serve as a theme song for twelve-step recovery programs, and its opening song, "Inside Out," derives from a book by the same name by Meece's therapist, Larry Crabb. Most poignant, perhaps, is the song "My Father's Chair," which expresses his feelings over discovering the vacant role of father in his life, a role that he now believes must be filled by God. He would dedicate his next album *Odyssey* to "those who are wearied by the doubts, loneliness, and pain of living in a world more adept at accepting evil than expecting good."

Christian radio hits: "I Can't Believe It's True" (# 2 in 1979); "Never Gonna Serve Anyone Else But You" (# 9 in 1979); "Follow You" (# 4 in 1980); "We Are the Reason" (# 14 in 1981); "Jesus" (# 13 in 1982); "And You Know It's Right" (# 3 in 1983); "I Don't Know What I'd Do without You" (# 20 in 1984); "You Can Go" (# 1 for 5 weeks in 1985); "Forgiven" (# 8 in 1985); "We Can Overcome It" (# 10 in 1986); "The Unknown Soldier" [with **Twila Paris**] (# 8 in 1986); "The Alien" (# 15 in 1986); "Seventy Times Seven" (# 2 in 1986); "Come That Day" (# 6 in 1986); "All Is God's Creation" (# 2 in 1987); "Candle in the Rain" (# 2 in 1987); "His Love Was Reaching" (# 10 in 1988); "Amor Conquesta Todo" (# 8 in 1988); "Higher Ground" (# 15 in 1988); "Man with the Nail Scars" (# 1 for 2 weeks in 1990); "When I Was Seventeen" (# 9 in 1990); "To Know Him" (# 6 in 1990); "Learning to Trust" (# 9 in 1990); "To the Glory of God" (# 2 in 1990); "This Time" (# 15 in 1990); "The Rest of My Life" (# 24 in 1991); "Once in a Lifetime" (# 16 in 1993); "Over You" (# 10 in 1993); "Inside Out" (# 9 in 1994); "Every Little Step" (# 19 in 1994).

John Mehler

1982—*Bow and Arrow* (A&S); 1987—*Back in Love* (Exile).

John Mehler is best known as the drummer for **Love Song,** a quintessential Christian rock group of the Jesus movement revival. Mehler's frantic drum solo was a part of almost every **Love Song** concert, as was the impassioned Jesus-freak testimony he would give all-out-of-breath afterwards. One such solo was recorded for the band's 1977 *Feel the Love* album but was unfortunately cut when that two-record set was compressed to fit onto a single CD. Mehler was born in Long Beach, California, and eventually became good friends with Jay Truax, who would also later be a part of **Love Song.** The two of them moved to Salt Lake City, Utah, and formed a successful band there called Spirit of Creation; **Fred Field** was also a part of the group for a time. Mehler stayed in Utah when Truax headed west to join the lineup for **Love Song**'s first album, but later, when that group did a concert in Salt Lake City, he committed his life to Christ and signed on with the band. After **Love Song** disbanded, Mehler played with numerous groups, including a reggae pop band called **Tamarack** that included Rob Watson of **Daniel Amos** and John Patitucci, who would eventually earn renown as the world's premier jazz and classical bass player. Mehler would join **Wing and a Prayer** and then **The Richie Furay Band.** He also toured as part of **Mark Heard**'s backing band. Mehler's *Bow and Arrow* was made in collaboration with **Billy Batstone,** who cowrote all of the songs—except for the appropriate cover of "Little Drummer Boy." The title song is a prayer for divine and eternal direction: "Keep me on the straight and narrow . . . You are the bow and I'm the arrow." *Back in Love,* also produced with Batstone, was designed as a mainstream rock album intended to "bring encouragement to those who have had a rough go of it for some time now." Mehler later recorded several jazz albums with Kenneth Nash: *Light the Night* (A&S, 1984); *Jazz Praise* (Maranatha, 1985); *Shine On* (Salt, 1993).

Christian radio hits: "Bow and Arrow" (# 10 in 1982).

Tony Melendez

1989—*Never Be the Same* (StarSong); 1990—*The Ways of the Wise* (StarSong); date unknown—*Hands in Heaven* (ToeJam).

www.tonymelendez.com

Tony Melendez came to national prominence as a symbol of courage and perseverance when he played his song "Never Be the Same" for Pope John Paul II on September 15, 1987. A "thalidomide baby," Melendez was born without arms in Nicaragua. Raised a devout Roman Catholic in Chino, California, he taught himself to play the guitar with his feet and ultimately proved to be a gifted composer and singer. At the time of the Pope's visit to America in 1987, Melendez was playing the guitar daily on a street corner in Laguna Park, in exchange for pocket change tossed into the case by passersby. Someone who knew about him passed his name on to the appropriate channels and he was suddenly invited to play for the Pope before a televised audience of ten million viewers. The Pope was visibly moved by his performance, rising and crossing several barricades to embrace Melendez and bestow a special blessing upon him. The singer became an immediate celebrity, appearing on numerous TV programs where he testified to his faith. He sang the national anthem at the 1989 World Series and performed at the Summer Olympics in Seoul, Korea. He would also publish an autobiography, *A Gift of Hope* (Harper and Row, 1989). In 1991, *The Tony Melendez Story* aired on NBC TV.

The album *Never Be the Same* features the original song that brought him such attention. Melendez has continued to sing and record in a variety of capacities. He made a Spanish-language album titled *El Muro Se Cayó* and sang a duet with Jodi Benson in an animated video, *Why Christmas Trees Aren't Perfect*. He has sung for the Pope three more times, including once at the Vatican, once in Poland, and again at the 1993 World Youth Day in Denver, Colorado. Melendez moved from California to reside in Texas, though he performs frequently in Branson, Missouri. Notably, his *Ways of the Wise* was reviewed by many critics who knew nothing of his handicap. Apart from the novelty or sympathy factor that such knowledge might contribute, the album was praised as an adult contemporary project in the style of singers like Dan Fogelberg. **Gary Chapman** and **Phil Keaggy** (who plays guitar with a much less severe disability) contribute their talents to the album, which includes the mellow worship song "You Are My God" and the more upbeat pop number "Heart of Stone." The title track was written by **Chris Eaton,** and the song "Bed by the Window" is based on a short story that once appeared in *Reader's Digest* magazine about roommates in a nursing home whose recollections of life provide a substitute for what might be viewed through an actual window to the outside world. *Hands in Heaven* includes a remake of Todd Rundgren's "Love Is the Answer" (made popular by England Dan and John Ford Coley, cf. **Jody Davis, Cindy Morgan**) and a touching love song that Melendez wrote for his wife called "I Wish I Could Hold You."

Christian radio hits: "Ways of the Wise" (# 5 in 1990).

The Merbabies

Lynn Barron, drums; Chris Bowden, voc.. gtr.; Brian Ure, bass. 1997—*The Merbabies* (Jackson Rubio); 1998—*Indio* [EP].

The Merbabies is a Laguna Beach "noise-rock" band formed by Chris Bowden, who was once drummer for **Focused.** The group takes after such underground general market acts as Dinosaur Jr. or Built to Spill, with a bit more of a country lean. Whiny vocals and early-Neil-Young-style sloppy guitar riffs provide them with a hip garage band sound for late-'90s aficionados of lo-fi music. Most of the group's songs (written by Bowden) focus on romantic relationships. Lyrically, "She Dreams of Me" from the first album is like a more religious version of the Linda Ronstadt/James Ingram "Somewhere out There," built on the hope that God will provide the singer with a significant other in time. The debut album also features some infectious surf instrumentals and the catchy song "Here We Go Again," which is based on Romans 7:7–25. "The Fix" from *Indio* is a lament for a friend who died of drugs. The overall theme of the album, *HM* suggests, is "take your lumps and get over the bumps."

Mercy

Lorraine Lewis, voc.; Erik Levy, bass; et al. 1993—*Mercy* (Broken).

Mercy was a fairly hard rocking band with an alternative edge fronted by Lorraine Lewis who had previously led the general market group Femme Fatale. The latter act was a metal band that capitalized on the image of being an all-male group with a "sex-bomb" female singer. They made one album that enjoyed a fair share of MTV success and then the group broke up mainly because Lewis wanted to pursue a more blues-oriented rootsy sound. Lewis, who was raised Roman Catholic, was drawn into a more personal connection with God through her manager, a woman who testified to receiving miraculous healing of brain cancer. "I turned my life over to the Lord on March 7, 1991," Lewis told *HM* magazine, and soon after that she met and married Erik Levy, who was in a punk band called Black-Eyed Susan. The two formed Mercy and released a single album on the Broken label. Standout tracks include "P.L.F.," an acoustic ode to peace, love, and faith, and the harder rocking "Mother's Lullaby," written by Lewis as an empathetic expression of Levy's late mother's affection for her son. *True Tunes* compared the group to latter-day (nonacoustic) **Acoustic Shack.**

Mercyme

Jim Bryson, kybrd.; Nathan Cochran, bass; Bart Millard, voc.; Mike Scheuchzer, gtr.; Robbie Shaffer, drums. 1999—*The Worship Project* (Mercyme); 2000—*The Need*; 2001—*Almost There* (INO).

Mercyme is an unabashed praise and worship band, albeit one that plays high-powered pop and alternative rock and roll. Eschewing the typical praise chorus, the group writes love songs addressed to God and performs them in a style that fits well with the sound of late '90s rock. *The Worship Project* leads off with the deceptively titled "Happy Little Love Song," a building Pearl Jam-type anthem fit for arenas. "It's My Joy" has more of a loping bluesy rhythm with '70s organ that segues into a sample of Bach's "Joyful, Joyful We Adore You" the way that Sly and the Family Stone might have done it. "Hearts Sing Louder" has noticeable aural references to Smash Mouth. When the group signed with INO for its first major-label release, press materials said they had six independent albums to their credit, though no information is available on anything beside the two just cited. In any case, *Almost There* features the sterling ballad "I Can Only Imagine," written by Brad Millard when his father died of cancer and focusing on what heaven might be like. **Amy Grant** expressed an intent to cover the song on an upcoming album.

Mercy Miles

Brad Coleman; Glenda Hoffman. 1993—*Mercy Miles* (Storyville).

Mercy Miles is an acoustic folk duo from Southern California. *CCM* likened the sound of their self-titled album to the Cowboy Junkies or to "a slightly less dour Neil Young." Glenda Hoffman provides the lead vocals on songs that speak of subjugating one's own desires in order to serve God ("This Heart of Sin") and of dealing honestly with the weakness of being human ("I Can't Help Myself").

Mercy River

Gregg Kellogg; Harold Wayne. 1992—*Coyote Moon* (Brainstorm).

Mercy River was a Christian country project that owed a good deal to **Terry Scott Taylor,** with whom Greg Kellogg had worked in the **Lost Dogs.** Taylor produced the group's one album and wrote or cowrote half of the songs. Thus, "Elvis Has Left the Building, Jesus Is Coming Soon" comes off like a **Swirling Eddies** song and "Shelf Life of Love" (cowritten with **Randy Stonehill**), like a missing **Lost Dogs** track.

Mercy Rule

Aaron Byrnes, gtr., voc.; et al. 1989—*Overruled* (R.E.X.).

Mercy Rule was a European metal band that garnered a rare review in *CCM* courtesy of Doug Van Pelt, editor of *HM* magazine. The group evinces a sound similar to that of The Scorpions, but their album suffered from production problems. The group reaches its potential, according to Van Pelt, on the classy ballad, "If You Knew."

The Mercy Seat

Gordon Gano, voc., gtr.; Zena Von Heppinstall, voc.; Patrice Moran, bass; Fernando Menendez, drums. 1987—*The Mercy Seat* (Slash).

The Mercy Seat was a one-time side project undertaken by Gordon Gano of **Violent Femmes.** Gano joined with female vocalist Zena Von Heppinstall to record a set of ten gospel songs, including four that she had written and six standards. The originals include "He Said," a slow bluesy number, and "Soul on Right," a finger-snapping tune with a loping bass line. The album opens with "Let Me Ride," a galloping number that features Von Heppinstall and Gano trading vocals in a "call and response" style typical of traditional gospel. *CCM* likened their medley of "Let the Church Roll On/I Won't Be Back" to "The Ramones in church with James Cleveland." The Mercy Seat toured in 1987, playing bars and clubs with an all-religious show that left many **Violent Femmes** fans dismayed.

Skatman Meredith

1990—*Way of Life* (independent); 1991—*Hope for Us*; 1997—*Skatman Meredith* (Dwarf); 1998—*The Garden* (Silent Planet); 2000—*Mercyside*.

www.skatman.com

Singer/songwriter David Meredith, who records under the professional name "Skatman," describes his music as "Intense Alternative Folk Rock." Critics compare him to **Bruce Cockburn, Life in General,** and the **Vigilantes of Love,** with *The Lighthouse* calling him "a male version of Tracy Chapman." For his first two releases, Meredith was unknown to all but *True Tunes,* who styled him as an underground artist who knew how to "integrate his salvation with life circumstances." A 1997 self-titled release garnered wider notice and attracted praise for the quality of its songs, presented in bare, folksy arrangements with little but Meredith's voice and acoustic guitar to sustain them. "Wise Move" reflects with knowing appreciation on his decision to be a person of faith, and "Bitter End" speaks explicitly of Jesus as the friend who will never let one down. "Strangest Places" (redivivus from *Hope for Us*) describes life at a rescue mission: "You can smell soup in the air and the hope amidst despair / You'll find love in the strangest places." The song "Sally Smith" incorporates a piano playing softly in the background and describes a young girl coming to grips with the reality of death. Meredith's first major-label album, *The Garden,* features a fuller sound and more advanced production.

The use of electric guitars on what remain jangly folk songs brought comparisons to R.E.M. and James Taylor, whose tuneful voice Meredith sometimes emulates. The title track is an atmospheric number with Indian influence. "Wrecking Ball" features a memorable melody and lyrics that challenge the ultimacy of evil in this world. "Remain in Me" offers a worshipful, closing benediction.

Messenger

Rick Riso, voc., gtr.; Si Simonson, kybrd; one more. 1976—*The New Has Come* (Light); 1978—*Bringin' the Message*.

Messenger was a disco lounge trio fronted by **Rick Riso.** The group made two albums, which *Jesus Music* describes as "equal parts George Benson, **Sweet Comfort Band, Seawind,** and Steve Lawrence." Songs such as "The New Has Come" and "Take My Yoke" feature cocktail-lounge crooning. Riso would go on to record numerous worship albums as a solo artist and in collaboration with his wife Cathy. Located in Los Angeles, he often works with Promise Keepers.

Christian radio hits: "Bringin' the Message" (# 22 in 1979).

Messiah Prophet

Charlie Clarke, voc.; Brian Nicarry, gtr.; Joe Shirk, bass; Andy Strauss, gtr.; David Thunder, drums. 1984—*Rock the Flock* (Morada); 1986—*Masters of the Metal* (Pure Metal).

Messiah Prophet was a classic Christian metal band of the '80s. *Masters of the Metal* is considered a classic of the genre and was re-released in 1997. The record got the band compared to Judas Priest stylistically; it features songs that praise Jesus ("Master of the Metal"), reject Satan ("Fear No Evil"), and urge compassion ("Hit and Run"). A year after *Masters of the Metal,* Clarke and four other musicians recorded a song called "Blinded" under the name Messiah Prophet for a popular compilation album (*Ultimate Metal;* StarSong, 1989). Clarke left the group soon after this and varying versions of Messiah Prophet (with no original members) continued to play together throughout the '90s. One edition recorded an album called *Colors* (U.C.A.N., 1997).

Metanoia

Lisa Bennett, bass; Steve Bennett, gtr., voc.; Justin Smith, voc. (– 1998); Dylan Speerstra, drums (– 1998) // Mark McCormack, gtr., drums (+ 1998); Yowie, voc. (+ 1998). 1995—*In Darkness or In Light* (Rowe); 1998—*Don't Walk Dead;* 1999—*Time to Die.*

http://members.tripod.com/metanoia_metal

Metanoia is a metal band from Australia. Formed by Lisa and Steve Bennett (husband and wife) in 1990, the group began playing thrash metal but says they were inspired by **Mortification** to adopt death metal vocals. The debut album features a song called "Enslavement," which deals with the oft-avoided subject of masturbation (which the band regards as immoral and addictive behavior). The title track is a bit of a novelty, an acoustic ballad with growling death metal vocals. *Don't Walk Dead* shows marked improvement in sonics and more incorporation of what band leader Steve Bennett would call "extreme metal" sounds. "Musically, we are a metal band that tries not to fall into a particular category," he told *HM.* "We try to be diverse, heavy, and interesting." *Time to Die* offers "Now Listen Up," with more of a funky groove à la **Tourniquet** or Pantera. "Offensive," "Corpse," and the anthemic "Feel the Fire" all evince more of a classic metal sound than material on previous albums. "Paradise" is an ironic statement about the Bennetts' homeland—which they say has one of the world's highest youth suicide rates. The group's name derives from the word used in the Greek New Testament for "repentance." Steve Bennett says, "Our goal as a band is to see individual people come to a point of repentance in their lives. To know Jesus has been the most ultimate experience in my life, and I want others to know Him as well."

Metropolis (a.k.a. Satellite Circle)

Alexander Corday, voc., kybrd.; Blake Osborne, drums; Texas, bass. By Satellite Circle: 1995—*Fade* [EP] (Steedog). By Metropolis: 2000—*International* (Absolute).

Metropolis is a Christian band from Orlando, Florida, with a retro-'80s sound recalling such acts as Depeche Mode, Echo and the Bunnymen, and the Psychedelic Furs. They formed in 1991 and first recorded an EP called *Fade* under the name Satellite Circle. Two songs from that outing ("Inside," "You") garnered airplay on progressive Christian radio stations. *International* mixes worship songs with romantic odes such that the singer seems to be always lost in love, sometimes with Jesus ("To Truly Love You"), sometimes with a woman ("Everything with You"). *HM* describes the project as suitable for an "art-film soundtrack."

MG the Visionary

2000—*Transparemcee* (Uprok); 2001—*Sinner's Prayer* (BEC).

The artist who calls himself MG the Visionary is one of the more authentic hip-hop acts in Christian music. A native of the Tacoma, Washington, area, he worked for about a decade in the underground scene (under the moniker 3nP for Third Nail Productions) before being contacted by Brandon Ebel of Tooth and Nail Records about establishing a hip-hop/rap-oriented sublabel. "I'm like, you guys don't know hip-hop. I do," he related to *Bandoppler.* "Just allow me to express my freedom." The label did pretty much that, setting up MG as the premiere act on its Uprok imprint. The resulting album, *Transparemcee,* is radically diverse, eschewing the copycat trend of most Christian rap music. MG's trademark style is mile-a-minute lyrics that *7ball* would liken to "trying to understand the plot of a movie while fast-forwarding through it." The song "U-Trip" issues its warning about the end of the world with machine-gunned rhymes. But then there are also songs that offer slow rap, rap with a Latin guitar, and even rap with bagpipes. "Let's Cruise" brings out the acoustic guitars for a soulful and intelligent love song. Critics who search for comparisons reference Arrested Development and Pharcyde but all agree that MG the Visionary is an original—and that he is "the real thing" as opposed to some record company's idea of what a Christian counterpart to some secular act should sound like. MG does not even like being called "a Christian rapper." Evoking a distinction that remains unclear to most, he insists, "I am not a Christian MC. I am a Christian who's been anointed to MC and that's what it is." His name, incidentally, came to be short for Man of God. As he puts it, "A kid came up to me after a concert and asked, 'Does MG stand for 'Man of God,' and I said 'From now on, it does'." *Sinner's Prayer* is a collection of favorite praise and worship choruses arranged and produced in a hip-hop style by MG.

MIC

Quintin Delport; George Mhondera; Stephen Rothquel; Gunther Schroeder. Date unknown—*Stories from a Dry Land* (label unknown); *Superhuman; Millenium: Gone and Beyond;* 1998—*Crazy World* (Word UK); 1999—*Acoustic* [EP] (GMI).

www.micweb.co.za

The Christian pop band MIC hails from Johannesburg, South Africa. They released at least three albums in their native land before coming to the attention of a broader audience when their album *Crazy World* was picked up for distribution in Great Britain. Sometimes called "a South African version of **DC Talk,**" the group performs lively dance pop songs. They are racially integrated (George Mhondera is black; the others, white), a fact that makes a strong statement in a country recovering from apartheid. The title track from *Superhuman* bears more than a passing similarity to **DC Talk**'s "Jesus Freak." *Stories from a Dry Land* features the R&B song "Round and Round," with rap vocals about a guy with superficial priorities ("he's not concerned with the state of his soul / as long as he's got his remote control"). *Crazy World* includes "Once," a song about a suicidal girl's failure to find Jesus. *Acoustic* offers unplugged versions of the three songs listed above, in addition to covers of Crowded House's "Weather with You," **Matt Redman**'s "I Will Offer," and a new rendition of the traditional camp song "Blind Man" (cf. **The Kry**).

Bobby Michaels

1985—*I Have a Reason* (Word); 1988—*Time.*

Bobby Michaels is an inspirational, adult contemporary singer along the same lines as **Steve Green.** Gifted with an impressive, multi-octave voice, Michaels attained more success in Europe than in America. *CCM* described his sound as "MOR that stops short of elevator music." Michaels' *I Have a Reason* includes a six-and-a-half minute opus called "You Are Most Blest," in which the artist provides a melancholy and chilling narrative of Christ's final hour.

Michelangelo and the Difference (and Michelangelo)

Eric Borgen, bass; Michelangelo Coggiano, voc., gtr.; Daniel Ortega, perc.; Jon Wiest, drums. By Michelangelo and the Difference: 1995—*Mercy Suite* (custom); 1998—*Under Rower* (Cadence). By Michelangelo: 2000—*Acoustic* [EP] (Worthless).

Michelangelo and the Difference is a progressive southern rock band from Phoenix, Arizona, whose sound is built around their namesake lead singer's rich vibrato vocals. Critics have noticed similarities in their sound to such groups as The Black Crowes, **Third Day,** and **Johnny Q. Public.** The band itself acknowledges **U2** and **The Prayer Chain** as notable influences. The title of their breakthrough album *Under Rower* is a roughly literal translation of the Greek word used in the New Testament to refer to a "servant" *(hypēretas)* in such passages as 1 Corinthians 4:1. "Through the Fire" is a steady rocking slow song (over six minutes) with pounding tribal drums and liturgical lyrics ("Agnus dei, Agnus dei . . ."). By contrast, "Ode to My Friends" has a bouncy, fun beat and simply expresses gratitude for friends. "The Firm" is rockabilly blues and "George" uses horns for a quasi-ska interlude. More lyrically poignant are songs like "Carry Your Mountain" and "Let Me See," both of which evince a deep, incarnational spiritual vision. *Under Rower* did not do as well as it deserved, in part because the Cadence label folded. The band continued playing together, though Michelangelo Coggiano cut an all-acoustic solo EP. The latter features "Precious Rose," a song dealing with the struggles of a faithless girl set to a tune reminiscent of **Extreme**'s ballads. Also included is a worship song called "Daddy" (a roughly literal translation of the Aramaic word "Abba," which Jesus used to address God).

Riki Michele

1989—*Big, Big Town* (Broken); 1993—*One Moment Please* (WAL); 2002—*Surround Me* (independent).

www.rikimichele.com

Riki Michele is best known as a member of the seminal Christian alternative band **Adam Again.** She provided female vocals for all of that group's albums, and garnered attention for her inspired and funky dancing that enlivened the songs in concert. For a time, Michele was married to **Adam Again**'s leader, Gene Eugene. They divorced in 1994 but continued to be friends and, in fact, to record together until Eugene's death in 2000. Michele's solo albums have been well received critically.

On *Big, Big Town,* produced by husband Eugene, Michele sings songs written by him and by such high-profile friends as **Terry Taylor** and **Steve Hindalong.** The more funk-oriented numbers ("Look at This, Look at That," "I Want to Talk about It Now," "A Little Grace," and the bluesy title track) seem like an extension of **Adam Again**'s *Homeboys* period, but with her voice brought to the fore. A more distinctive style comes through on the lullaby "Secrets," the acoustic "Ghost in the Rain," and the a capella "Spirit, Father, Son." Another pair of songs would be ironically prophetic: "Bride's Song 1984" describes the excitement of a newlywed and "Bride's Song 1989" looks at the hardships of keeping a marriage together in the modern world.

Michele was going through her divorce at the time *One Moment Please* was made and that album has a much more personal and vulnerable tone to it. Produced by Taylor, the project moves away from urban funk toward more of a Steely Dan-oriented jazz/pop sound. This time out, however, Michele writes or cowrites several of the songs herself, including the upbeat title track. She also covers the Steve Miller Band's "Fly Like an Eagle" and an especially melodic **Michael Roe** tune called "Mind to Mind." The title track, "Love You Now," and "In the Calling" (by Taylor and Eugene) both focus on the need for forgiveness and grace in human relationships. "Far, Far" is a gentle ballad written by **Randy Stonehill.** The most rocking song on the album is a Taylor composition called "Love, Life, and Dance," a tribute to three things Michele seems to value. She would call it "a light-hearted Neneh Cherry cross between **Rick James** and Sade."

After a nine-year hiatus, Michelle had a new solo album slated for release at the beginning of 2002.

Mickey and Becki

Becki Moore; Mickey Moore. 1976—*Everything Is under Control,* Wo-Wo (Maiden); 1977—*Studio and Live;* 1979—*Brand New;* 1981—*Love Song for Number Two.*

Though not a mainstay in contemporary Christian music, the husband and wife duo known as Mickey and Becki are a testimony to the value of persistence. In the late '70s and early '80s, Mickey Moore's day job was working as a graphic arts illustrator for InterVarsity Press (including four years as art edi-

tor for *HIS* magazine). Becki Moore worked as a fashion designer. On the side, she wrote songs, which the two of them performed. Sensing that they were destined to make a mark in the contemporary Christian music world, the duo auditioned with record company executives in Nashville, where they were told (somewhat rudely) that they had no future in gospel music. The day after that meeting, Mickey says, he awoke convinced that God had told him, "It's not over yet. Don't worry about the record companies. Start your own label." Together, Micky and Becki founded Maiden Music and created four albums. The fourth one hit with a song called "Love Song for Number Two," which Becki had written for her husband, promising him that he was more to her than anything but Jesus (who is Number One). The song became a major hit on adult contemporary stations, charting appropriately at Number Two for two weeks. The Moores shared their belief that the secret to keeping a marriage together was the priorities expressed in the song. "Christians are tired of hearing of another famous preacher, singer, or Christian writer getting a divorce and remarrying," Becki told *CCM.* "They know that this is wrong. They want to be told the truth and see it in the lives of those who preach it, sing about it, or write about it." The album *Love Song for Number Two* also contains a slightly rewritten version of **Mike Johnson**'s parenting song "Little Boy."

Christian radio hits: "We Get Lifted Up" (# 19 in 1983).

Midnight Oil

Peter Garrett, voc.; Rob Hirst, drums; Jim Mogine, gtr., kybrd.; Martin Rotsey, gtr.; Andrew James, bass // Peter Gifford, bass (+ 1980, −1990); Dwayne Hillman, bass (+ 1990). 1978—*Midnight Oil* (Powderworks); 1979—*Head Injuries;* 1980—*Bird Noises* [EP]; 1981—*Place without a Postcard;* 1983—*10, 9, 8, 7, 6, 5, 4, 3, 2, 1* (Columbia); 1984—*Red Sails in the Sunset;* 1985—*Species Deceases* [EP]; 1987—*Diesel and Dust;* 1990—*Blue Sky Mining;* 1992—*Scream in Blue Live;* 1993—*Earth and Sun and Moon;* 1996—*Breathe;* 1997—*20,000 Watt R.S.L.;* 1998—*Redneck Wonderland;* 2000—*The Real Thing* (Sony).

www.midnightoil.com

The general market Australian rock band Midnight Oil is fronted by Peter Garrett, a professing Christian who explicitly links the group's social and political concerns to his biblical faith. The band formed in Sydney, Australia, in 1976 and became a national sensation in its homeland. From the start, they were noted for songs dealing with controversial issues of social justice and ecological concern. In 1984, Garrett (who has a degree in law but has never practiced) ran unsuccessfully for a seat in the Australian senate on a Nuclear Disarmament platform. The band was hardly noticed in America until *Diesel and Dust* became one of the biggest college rock albums of the year, on the strength of its **U2**-styled hits "Dreamworld," "The Dead Heart," and "Beds Are Burning." The latter song would become a staple of college radio for years to come and even rose to Number Seventeen on *Billboard's* mainstream pop chart (at a time when that chart was otherwise dominated by Michael Jackson, Whitney Houston, and Gloria Estefan). The song is a radical and angry outcry on behalf of aboriginal land rights ("The time has come / A fact's a fact / It belongs to them / Let's give it back"). *Blue Sky Mining* would score another college hit with "Forgotten Years," a song protesting any military draft that robs young people of what could be the prime of their lives. The title song for that album expresses the thoughts of a blue-collar worker who fears the ecological havoc his company is wreaking upon the earth but doesn't know what he can do about it. *Scream in Blue Live* records a concert from the *Blue Sky Mining* tour. In 1991, Midnight Oil performed a live concert outside the Exxon Building in Manhattan to express its disgust over the *Valdez* oil spill. *Earth and Sun and Moon* includes "Truganini," a lament over the treatment of Australia's last full-blooded Tasmanian Aborigine, and "Tell Me the Truth," a rant against media deception. On *Breathe,* the concern for justice seems more intimate and personal than global or political. "We are so human, we're so small," Garrett observes, "We're always coming back for more / A second helping, third and fourth / It's gone" ("One Too Many Times"). Similar sentiments infuse "Sins of Omission" and "Time to Heal." The latter song finds Garrett musing, "Where is the hope of a clean tomorrow / Hope only offers when justice is coming / Now is the time to heal." *Redneck Wonderland* is directed against race-based politics in their native country. The song "White Skin, Black Heart" was banned from radio airplay in that country for its attacks on government policies. *20,000 Watt R.S.L.* is a compilation album of favorite songs throughout the band's history (including tracks from the then yet-to-be-released *Redneck Wonderland*). *The Real Thing* contains live and acoustic versions of ten Midnight Oil classics, plus three new songs.

Christian music publications usually feel obliged to point out that Midnight Oil is "not a Christian band" but simply a band that has a committed Christian as its leader. The distinction is artificial at best. Supposedly, the group is not "a Christian band" because they write and perform songs about social issues rather than about narrowly defined "spiritual matters." Their material, however, evinces signs that indicate the connection between Garrett's controversial views and religious faith is anything but superficial. "Forgotten Years" begins with a quotation of Exodus 34:7 ("The sins of the fathers are visited upon the sons"), and "Blue Sky Mining" features a chorus that repeats the question "Who's gonna save me?" in a mode reminiscent of many a gospel song. The fact that most fans of contemporary Christian music do not think of Midnight Oil as a faith-oriented band is revealing. If the group sang songs pro-testing abortion, denouncing homosexuality, or decrying premarital sex, there is no question but that they would be darlings of the contemporary Christian music scene regardless of whether they explicitly mentioned Jesus in those songs. The issues that the band does address are actually more grounded in biblical teaching than any of the above; what the Bible says about social justice outweighs what it says about personal morality a hundredfold, and Midnight Oil—or at least Garrett—is generally faithful to answering and voicing a prophetic call in tune with Scripture. The group has performed at the *Greenbelt* Christian music festival in Britain and they have given interviews to Christian music magazines in their homeland. Because of his unflagging commitment to ecological concerns, Garrett was elected president of the Australian Conservation Foundation in the late '90s and was subsequently declared an "Official Living Treasure" by the Australian National Trust. Midnight Oil performed at the closing ceremony for the Summer Olympic Games in Sydney in 2000.

Midnight Orchestra

Mick Rowe; et al. 1999—*Land of Nod* (Minuteman); 2000—*Digital Saviour* (Syntax).

Mick Rowe of the '80s metal band **Tempest** formed Midnight Orchestra to explore a darker sound closer to goth rock in genre. His brother Jamie Rowe of the band **Guardian** joined him on *Land of Nod,* which was produced by Tony Palacios of the same band. Palacios and Sherri and William Waters of **Wedding Party** appear on both Midnight Orchestra albums. *Land of Nod* has a more melodic-alternative feel to it than most goth projects (one critic called it "goth-lite") and the album ends with a woman giving a minute-and-a-half altar call prayer. *Rad Rockers* describes *Digital Saviour* as having "a dark sound blending aggro-metal, electronica, and rapcore." *HM,* however, gave the second record a rare, negative review: Midnight Orchestra moves away from goth on *Digital Saviour* and incorporates elements of hip-hop that are not quite convincing. The closest general market comparisons would be to Nine Inch Nails with a generous dose of Rage Against the Machine. In 2000 it was reported that Rowe was joining with **David Benson** to form a new version of **Tempest,** which would release an album titled *Crushing the Dark Cathedral.*

Mid South

Bobby Bowen, voc., bass; Darren Humphrey, drums; Kent Humphrey, voc.; Robby McGee, kybrd. 1992—*Lessons of Life* (Word); 1994—*Give What It Takes* (Warner Bros.); 1996—*Mid South* (Warner Alliance).

Mid South is a contemporary Christian country band that has roots deep in southern gospel. The group originated as the Mid South Boys in the late 1950s in central Arkansas and recorded several southern gospel albums. Around 1985, they began gradually incorporating a more mainstream country sound into their repertoire. *CCM* took note of the Mid South Boys in 1989 when their album *Down to Earth* (New Canaan) featured more progressive songs like "Broken Chains" and "He Didn't Lift Me Up to Let Me Down." After one more album (*Shoulder to Shoulder* in 1991), the group followed the biblical model of adopting an official name change to signal their conversion. They became simply Mid South and embraced an unabashed progressive country sound.

Lessons of Life presents three-part harmony versions of story-based songs by such writers as Robbie McGee, **Paul Overstreet,** and Aaron Wilburn. The group's breakthrough album, however, would be *Give What It Takes* (produced by **Al Perkins**), which netted them a crossover hit with the song, "Without You (I Haven't Got a Prayer)." Both spiritual and romantic, the song made it big on mainstream country radio and even hit the Top 20 of general market adult contemporary charts. Some pundits thought this might signal the next step in Mid South's evolution—from Christian country to plain old secular country, after the fashion of the Oak Ridge Boys. The next album, *Mid South,* tones down the overt religious content in favor of generic, positive songs about family, friends, and small-town security. "Love Still Does" traces the history of an elderly couple's enduring romance, and "Fall Reaching" offers good advice for life in general: "If you're gonna win, win graceful . . . and if you're gonna fall, fall reaching."

Dove Awards: 1996 Country Song ("Without You [I Haven't Got a Prayer]").

Mighty Clouds of Joy

Joe Ligon, voc.; Richard Wallace, voc.; Elmo Franklin, voc. (–c. 1999); Johnny Martin (d. 1987); Ermant Franklin, voc. (–c. 1977); David Walker, voc. (–c. 1977) // Paul Beasley (+ c. 1980, –1987); Johnny Valentine, voc. (+ c. 1980, –c. 1991, + c. 1999); Michael Cook, voc. (+ 1987, –1993); Wilbert Williams, voc. (+ 1993, –c. 1999); Michael McCowin, voc. (+ c. 1991); Ron Staples, voc. (+ 1999); Tim Woodson (+ 1999). 1961—*Family Circle* (Peacock); 1962—*Live at the Music Hall;* 1964—*Presenting: The Untouchables;* 1966—*Sing Songs of Rev. Julius Cheeks and the Nightingales;* 1968—*Live! At the Apollo;* 1972—*A Bright Side;* 1973—*Best of Mighty Clouds of Joy;* 1974—*It's Time* (ABC); 1975—*Kickin';* 1977—*Truth Is the Power;* 1978—*Live and Direct;* 1979—*Changing Times* (Epic); 1980—*Cloudburst* (Myrrh); 1982—*Request Line* (ABC); *Miracle Man* (Myrrh); *Mighty Clouds Alive;* 1983—*Sing and Shout;* 1987—*Catching On* (Word); 1989—*Night Song;* 1990—*Mighty Clouds of Joy Live* (MCA); 1991—*Pray for Me;* 1993—*Memory Lane: The Best of the Mighty Clouds of Joy; Best of the Mighty Clouds of Joy, Vol. 2;* 1994—*Faith, Mercy, Glory* (King); 1995—*Power* (Intersound); 1996—*Live in Charleston; Glory Hallelujah* (MCA); 1999—*It Was You* (CGI).

The Mighty Clouds of Joy are to traditional gospel what **The Imperials** are to southern gospel: the single best example of a group with a long tradition that successfully maneuvered

its way from traditional to contemporary sounds with most of its audience still intact. A significant difference, however, is that Mighty Clouds has enjoyed periods of respect and crossover success in the general market that would never come to **The Imperials.** No authoritative biography or discography for the group is available, such that what is presented here must be unfortunately sketchy. Worse, The Mighty Clouds of Joy almost never identify the members of the group that participate on individual albums, making personnel shifts virtually impossible to track. In addition to the persons listed above, Jimmy Jones was also a founding member of the group that formed in 1955 and Leon Polk joined around 1960, but both of these singers appear to have left before recording any of the albums listed. Johnny Martin died in 1987. Paul Beasley of The Gospel Keynotes joined for a time and later recorded a solo album of contemporary Christian songs in 1984 (*My Soul Is Free,* Myrrh). The officially anonymous quintet responsible for 1999's *It Was You* consisted of founding members Joe Ligon and Richard Wallace along with longtimer Johnny Valentine, and newcomers Ron Staples and Tim Woodson.

When the group formed, its founding members were still in high school in Los Angeles, California. Their earliest recording was the gospel song "Steal Away to Jesus" in 1960. Joe Ligon was enamored of the gritty, grunting sound of gospel singer Julius Cheeks, who also provided the inspiration for Wilson Pickett's style. The Mighty Clouds stayed with the Peacock label for a decade, recording what they would later call "traditional black songs." Toward the end of that period, they supplemented the imitation Cheeks sound with trademark high harmonies similar to those employed by **Curtis Mayfield** and the Impressions. The group would also become the first gospel group to add drums and bass to their instrumental accompaniment, causing them to be dubbed for a time "The Temptations of Gospel."

In the early '60s, black artists were primarily played on segregated black radio stations but by the end of that decade those stations had largely eliminated gospel groups from their playlists. In order to stay relevant, the Mighty Clouds embraced an increasingly modern R&B sound. Many traditional gospel artists (including **Sam Cooke, Aretha Franklin, Marvin Gaye, Al Green**) "went secular" at this time, partly out of a need to survive (and partly because they were simply attracted by the opportunity of singing about all aspects of life), but the Mighty Clouds of Joy kept their identity as a gospel group with more integrity than perhaps any other crossover act. The group signed with a general market label in the early '70s— about the time **Andraé Crouch and the Disciples** were opening a whole new field for black artists in the Christian market that might have made such a move unnecessary. At any rate, Mighty Clouds missed the Jesus movement entirely.

While Crouch and his crew were playing for hundreds of thousands of screaming (mostly white) Jesus freaks, Mighty Clouds were performing before sedate, mostly black unbelievers. Crouch's crew looked just like any band at Woodstock but they played in churches. Mighty Clouds looked like a church choir (matching polyester suits) but they played in clubs and concert halls. In 1974, the group had the Number Ten song on the secular R&B chart with "Time" from *It's Time,* an album produced by Kenny Gamble and Leon Huff that featured the group backed by the Philadelphia band MFSB (who had a Number One pop hit with the instrumental "TSOP" in 1974). Two years later, they scored another Top 10 R&B hit with the disco song "Mighty High" and they became the first gospel group ever to perform on TV's *Soul Train.* As the decade progressed, they opened concerts for Earth, Wind, and Fire and the Rolling Stones. A brief disco period would follow and the group would come to be widely recognized as a gospel band in touch with the times. Frank Wilson, known for his work with The Supremes and The Jackson Five, would produce the Grammy-winning album *Changing Times* (and later, *Night Song*). In 1993, Mighty Clouds of Joy were invited to open for Paul Simon during his month-long series of concerts in New York City.

The contemporary Christian music scene did not notice Mighty Clouds of Joy until they signed with Myrrh (an officially Christian label) in 1980, and even since then, the attention paid has been scant. *Cloudburst* was produced by Al McKay, guitarist for Earth, Wind, and Fire. At that time, the primary attraction was singer Paul Beasley, whose high falsetto voice was similar to Smokey Robinson's. *CCM* put the group on its cover and reviewed the album as "hand clappin', foot stompin', praisin' the Lord kind of music," noting such standout cuts as "Wings of Faith," "Praise the Lord," and "I Don't Feel as Noways Tired." A few years later, The Mighty Clouds would be noticed again for *Sing and Shout,* an album that highlights Ligon's gutsy lead vocals on songs like "Jesus Is Comin' Back." Beasley was still with the group, however, and his voice carries "God Is Always Standing By." Founding member Richard Wallace has a proud moment with his own composition, the Caribbean-flavored "God's Word." *Catching On* features more extensive strings and horns and includes a soulful Ligon take on **Sam Cooke**'s "A Change Is Gonna Come." *Power* would earn a favorable review in *Cornerstone.* Ligon is the main star of that album and he shines both on the soulful "In God's Will" and on jumpier numbers with titles like "I'm Ready" and "Power of the Holy Ghost." On *Power,* The Clouds also cover **Russ Taff**'s "We Can Stand" and **Van Morrison**'s "Have I Told You Lately?"—which they rewrite, transforming the sweet, sentimental song into a guilt-inducing and supposedly more spiritual number called "Have You Told Him Lately?"

Grammy Awards: 1978 Best Traditional Soul Gospel Performance *(Live and Direct);* 1979—Best Traditional Soul Gospel Performance *(Changing Times);* 1991—Best Traditional Soul Gospel Album *(Pray for Me).*

Mighty Flyers

Davie Rees, voc.; Mick Abrahams, gtr. (−1975); et al. 1974—*Low Flying Angels* (Myrrh UK); 1975—*Under New Management* (Trust); 1976—*What Kind of King.*

Mighty Flyers was a British Jesus movement quintet about which almost nothing is known, save that their lead singer was a baritone by the name of David Rees and that Mick Abrahams, former guitarist for Jethro Tull, played on their first album. The group performed a style of country rock that seemed to be inspired by "Americana" groups like The Band. *Low Flying Angels* includes a take on the traditional "Dark End of the Street" and an original song called "How Can a Poor Man Stand Such Times and Live?" The story-song "We Will Not Find You There" is sung to an unbeliever by a group of friends who fear that, in his case, the circle will be broken in the sky. *What Kind of King* presents the Gospels' Joseph as a truck driver in a song called "Thinking of Mary Tonight." More traditional songs include the worshipful "Love Like an Ocean" and the hope-filled "I Looked Down."

Mighty Sam McClain

Selected: 1993—*Give It Up to Love* (Audioquest); 1995—*Keep On Movin';* 1996—*Sledgehammer Soul and Down Home Blues;* 1998—*Journey; Joy and Pain: Live in Europe;* 1999—*Soul Survivor: The Best of Mighty Sam McClain* (Audioquest).

www.mightysam.com

The Phantom Tollbooth deserves primary credit for bringing Mighty Sam McClain to the attention of the contemporary Christian music community, though he is still much more acclaimed in the general market than in that little subculture. McClain's story is a fascinating one. Born a poor black in 1943 in rural Louisiana, he grew up literally picking cotton and hauling water in a life that differed from slavery more in terms of legal definition than practical reality. But McClain sang in his mother's gospel group and, gifted with a sensational voice for the blues, he was picked up by a number of bands and developed a taste for bright lights. Catching the early wave of soul music in the '60s, he provided lead vocals on recordings by Little Melvin Underwood and had a solo hit with a cover of Patsy Cline's "Sweet Dreams." He toured with Solomon Burke and **Gladys Knight** and played Harlem's legendary Apollo Theater. Then, as a result of a fluke here or there, his record company dropped him and denied him royalties from his own works (as was common in those days, especially with black artists). McClain ended up homeless. For fifteen long years (all of the '70s and half of the '80s), the singer says he was a drunkard, living on the streets, eating out of garbage cans, and sometimes mopping floors at a greasy-spoon restaurant. He was rediscovered at the latter establishment and almost miraculously (McClain would omit the almost) ended up singing again, as part of a blues and soul revival program in Japan. Back on his feet, he relocated to Boston, quit drinking, found love, married, and got a recording contract to produce what many blues magazines consider to be four of the finest albums of the twentieth century.

McClain's Audioquest recordings were all made in the '90s but they sound like the impassioned soul music of '60s stars like Otis Redding, with touches of B. B. King, **Marvin Gaye,** Bill Withers, and early Stevie Wonder. McClain wails and growls and whispers his way through original compositions and occasional standards, often pointing his audience to the Lord God who took mercy on him and redeemed him. "I've been there, I've lived it, I know the other side of the tracks," he sings on *Journey* in a song about his cotton-picking childhood ("The Other Side of the Tracks"). In "Hangin' on the Cross" he identifies his own pain with the Lord's crucifixion and his despair with the Savior's cry of dereliction. But there is joy as well as pain. "Here I Go Falling in Love Again" is an unbridled shout of awakened feeling. "Where You Been So Long?" celebrates his new bride. But God gets all the credit, as he declares in a simple song called "Thank You." On "Forgive and Forget" McClain gets beyond bitterness, pledging to his Lord that he'll show the same mercy to others that has been given him. "New Man in Town" proleptically announces the return of Christ as an electrifying fanfare that changes everything. *Soul Survivor* samples from all four albums, and includes the singer's cover of **Al Green**'s "Love Will Make a Way." *Joy and Pain* was recorded live in Germany and features concert versions of many of the favorite songs from McClain's Audioquest sessions. As a special treat on that album, he also includes the traditional "Long Train Running," which the rock and roll generation usually know only as a Doobie Brothers song.

Mike-E

1991—*Mike-E and the G-Rap Crew* (Reunion); 1992—*Good News for the Bad Timez;* 1995—*Pass It On* (Big Doggie).

The Christian rapper who goes by the name Mike-E was once described by *CCM* as "a thinner, godlier counterpart to Heavy D." Born Mike Wright, the artist was raised as the son of a pastor (and bishop) of a Black Pentecostal church in Detroit. His first musical experiences included classical training on the cello and membership in the Detroit Junior Symphony. Then he learned to play guitar and ended up accompanying such groups as **Commissioned, The Clark Sisters, BeBe and CeCe Winans,** and **Michael W. Smith.** Eventually these gigs led to a featured role in Smith's performances, where he would rap and sing as well as play. Mike-E's debut, *Mike-E and the G-Rap Crew* includes the autobiographical "I Got Straight," in which he shares his testimony of street-life as a warning to others (while estranged from church life, Mike-E fathered a child out of wedlock at the age of sixteen). On *Good News for the Bad Timez,* he runs through a fairly extreme song called "Hell? No!" (cf. **Bride**), complete with metal guitar riffing and organ interludes. The same album, however, features quieter songs like "I'll Do Anything," which employs **Take 6** on what amounts to a soulful adult contemporary ballad of atonement. *Pass It On* includes "Take a Ride" and some reminiscence of the artist's childhood in "Back in the Day." Mike-E has participated in a number of inner city street ministry programs, some in partnership with the professional football players Reggie White and Art Moore (cf. **Amarachi**).

Dove Awards: 1992 Rap/Hip Hop Album *(Mike-E and the G-Rap Crew);* 1993 Rap/Hip Hop Album *(Good News for the Bad Timez).*

Millennium

Baily Dickerson; Bob Farrell; Jayne Farrell; Larry Wallbreck. 1973—*Millennium* (Shekinah).

The progressive Jesus music band called Millennium is now best remembered as the first group to feature Bob and Jayne Farrell, who later joined **Dove** and then recorded as **Farrell and Farrell** (they were replaced in Millennium by Randy Bugg who had been a member of **Dove**). *Millennium* is much more in tune with '70s rock than **Farrell and Farrell** pop would be. Sonny Lallerstedt, guitarist for **The Pat Terry Group,** guests on the album and provides a sizzling solo on the song "Freedom." Other tunes ("Put Love in Your Life"; "Lullaby to a Lost Generation") feature a good share of '70s organ.

Buddy Miller

1995—*Your Love and Other Lies* (High Tone); 1998—*Poison Love;* 2000—*Cruel Moon;* 2001—*Buddy and Julie Miller* [with Julie Miller] (Hightone).

Buddy Miller is best known to fans of Christian music as the husband of **Julie Miller** and as the man who cowrites many of her songs, produces her albums, and both plays and sings on them. But Miller is known in his own right in country music circles, where he has produced albums by Emmylou Harris, Steve Earle, and other artists. He plays guitar as a part of Harris's band Spyboy and is respected as a behind-the-scenes contributor for numerous artists. Miller got his musical start playing in an '80s bar band in Austin, Texas, called The Buddy Miller Band. Shawn Colvin and the soon-to-be **Julie Miller** were both members of the group. Julie left on account of her conversion to Christianity and Buddy pursued her. Six months later, he became a Christian as well and they were married.

After many years of supporting her musical career, he would take to recording himself, bypassing the officially Christian marketplace in favor of a more mainstream but spiritually progressive country genre. His friends—Colvin, Earle, and Harris—and wife join him on all his albums, along with **Phil Madeira** on keyboards. Earle called *Your Love and Other Lies* "the country record of the decade." In 1999, the Nashville Music Awards chose Miller as Guitarist of the Year.

In terms of content, Buddy Miller's albums are not as overtly Christian as Julie's work has tended to be, though he strives to capture "the sound of conflict and contradiction" as *CCM* would put it, of "heartbreak wrestling with hope." There is always evidence of some core belief that justifies persistence in the face of overwhelming odds. *Cruel Moon* juxtaposes his own title song lament ("You shine as if there's nothing wrong / You shine on down like she's not gone") with a cover of Gene Pitney's optimistic "I'm Gonna Be Strong." The album's opening track is a classic Miller and Miller country composition called "Does My Ring Burn Your Finger?" Jesus music pioneer **Al Perkins** plays steel guitar on the record. Before any of the records listed above, Miller released a limited edition effort called *Man in the Moon* in Holland only (where both Millers have a huge following). In 2001, he released a project with his wife called *Buddy and Julie Miller.*

Heather Miller

1998—*Once upon a Time* (KMG); 2000—*Send Me an Angel*.

Perky pop singer Heather Miller (b. 1975) grew up in Lakeland, Florida, where she traveled and sang with her father, Assemblies of God evangelist Lemuel Miller. The highlight of *Once upon a Time* is a cover of the **Phil Keaggy** song "Lovely Jesus (Here I Am)," which was a staple of the Jesus movement in a version performed by **Honeytree**. Miller also shines on the upbeat "Do You Know Now" and the funky rocker "Go with Me," both written by producer Billy Smiley (the former with **Rhonda Gunn**). She also covers **Amy Grant**'s "Thy Word." *Send Me an Angel* demonstrates considerable growth, as Miller trades in the teenybopper pop for a rootsy, grittier, more rock-oriented sound. Critics, who pretty much ignored the first album, now strutted out comparisons to **Ashley Cleveland** and **Jennifer Knapp** as well as to Sheryl Crow (the closest analogy). The album was produced by Michael **Tait** of **DC Talk** and **Pete Stewart** of **Grammatrain.** Miller cowrote all of the songs (several with the producers), save for a cover of **Russ Taff**'s "Winds of Change." The opening song, "Angel," is a rocker that testifies to God's ever-present, invisible care. "We Will See Him" is a melodic, catchy worship song that was obviously intended to be a Christian radio hit. "Life to Me" is a shimmering, emotional ballad that even *Phantom Tollbooth* (not usually oriented toward adult contemporary ballads) would admit marks the highlight of the album. "On His Way Home" possesses an edgy tempo and enough driving guitars to make it qualify for legitimate "alternative rock" status. The lyrics are straightforward: "On His way home, he was crucified, and He died, all because He loved us."

Christian radio hits: "Lovely Jesus" (# 18 in 1998); "We Will See Him" (# 14 in 2000).

Jimmy Miller

1970—*Rhythm, Rap, and Laughter* (Mark); 1975—*Loving Him* (Pure Joy); 1984—*Sold* (Counselor).

Jimmy Miller made albums of pious adult contemporary music that struck a nerve with some of the Jesus people who would not normally have been attracted to such MOR sounds. His album *Loving Him* was well received as a worshipful production similar to the contributions of **Bob Cull.** An impressive cast of some twenty-five assistants join him on the album—including **Fred Field, Karen Lafferty, John Mehler** and Jay Truax of **Love Song, Al Perkins,** and Joy Strange of **Parable.** "Skipping on the Mountains" and "Because of Me" are hymnic, the former sustained by choral vocals and classical instrumentation (concertina, piano, flute, and piccolo). The song "Watchman Nee" is a tribute to the Chinese pietist whose writings became quite popular during the Jesus movement and later had a profound effect on Bono of **U2.**

Julie Miller

1990—*Meet Julie Miller* (Myrrh); 1991—*He Walks through Walls*; 1993—*Orphans and Angels*; 1994—*Invisible Girl* (Street Level); 1997—*Blue Pony* (High Tone); 1999—*Broken Things*; 2001—*Buddy and Julie Miller* [with Buddy Miller] (Hightone).

www.buddyandjulie.com

The alternative folk, pop, and country sound of Julie Miller fits into the same general category as that of her friends and frequent collaborators Shawn Colvin and Emmylou Harris, but Miller's career finds its closest parallel in that of **Leslie/Sam Phillips.** Early on, her voice was often compared to that of Phillips (though Cyndi Lauper would provide a closer match) and her intelligent, personal songwriting also evoked such analogies. More to the point, her penchant for honest introspection and taboo-busting lyrics made it increasingly obvious with each album that she would eventually have to leave the confines of the contemporary Christian music subculture behind. Like Phillips, Miller would go on to a less restricted and more widely appreciated career in the general market, but she would do so without prejudice, remaining on good terms with the audience that gave her a start.

Details of Miller's autobiography are not widely publicized—owing in part to some of the aspects revealed below—but she first came to prominence (before her last name was Miller) as lead singer of The Buddy Miller Band in Austin, Texas. The group was led by guitarist **Buddy Miller** and was a popular local bar band that opened for Bo Diddley, Willie Dixon, Albert King, and Muddy Waters. Shawn Colvin was also a member of the group. Miller would later describe the band as her escape from a life of confusion and pain. "My whole childhood was a mixture of church and insanity," she told *CCM* in 1990, "but when you're growing up you don't know it's weird." She was raised in the small town of Waxahachie, Texas, and when she was seven, she says, she asked Jesus into her heart at the church where her parents regularly taught Sunday school. But the dysfunctions of her family life left her disillusioned and seeking mental distance from everything associated with her upbringing. While singing in the Austin bars, she attempted suicide more than once, overdosing on sleeping pills and then slashing her wrists in a way that bought her three months in a mental institution. And then, one night before a club date, she says she heard the Lord speak to her, in a small whispering voice that she heard clearly in her mind. He said, "Julie, I never wanted your life to turn out this way. All I ever wanted was for us to be together." A short time later, when the band was doing some shows in New York, they were on their way to a movie one night and passed a church with a sign reading Conference on the Holy Spirit. She insisted that the group let her out there, which turned out to be her resignation from the band. An elderly man at the church took her to the altar and prayed with her, a couple took her to dinner, and she got on a plane and flew home to Texas without even returning to the hotel for her things—lest she change her mind. Devoted to a new life in Jesus, she left the band and all that she associated with it behind. By this time, however, she and Buddy Miller had become romantically involved and he pursued her. In an effort to understand her new commitments, he read the New Testament, and six months later, he became a Christian as well. They were later married and he became a successful producer, not only of her work but also of Shawn Colvin, Steve Earle, Emmylou Harris, and a number of other artists. He has also recorded a number of acclaimed solo albums and served as session guitarist on countless albums by a variety of artists.

For nine years after her spiritual transformation, Miller kept a low profile, accepting background roles that nevertheless brought her increasingly in contact with the Christian music scene. She sang on projects by **Benny Hester** and **Russ Taff** and worked extensively with the Christian children's ministry **Agape Force** from 1982 to 1988. Finally, in 1990 her debut solo album came out amidst much media hype presenting her as "the next big thing." The song "You Knew the Way to My Heart" typifies her college crowd appeal with its jangly guitars and catchy hook. The real surprise on *Meet Julie Miller,* however, was "What Would Jesus Do?" a powerful ballad written some years before the WWJD bracelet craze would run its titular theme into the ground. Miller's song has nothing to do with fads or fashions and is a hundred times better than the **Big Tent Revival** song by the same name that sought to capitalize on the craze. It is a call to pay attention to the "broken hearts and lonely faces" that populate this world—a theme that would play often in Miller's oeuvre. It also features background vocals by **Russ Taff** and **Amy Grant**—a development that also signaled a trend. Although Miller's "little girl" vocals are affecting, they do not always wear well over an extended collection of songs; sensing this, she would learn to supplement them with a generous supply of background singers and with outright duets—often featuring a roster of Christian and general market celebrities. Such stellar musicians as Derri Daugherty, **Steve Hindalong,** and **Phil Madeira** would also become mainstays on most of her albums—but her major support has come from husband/producer Buddy, who cowrites, sings, and plays his amazing guitar on every project.

Miller opened some new doors with her sophomore project, *He Walks through Walls.* She came out of the closet and told family secrets, revealing that the dysfunctions in her upbringing that she had alluded to in earlier interviews involved prolonged sexual abuse at the hands of her Sunday-school-teaching father. The songs on *He Walks through Walls* came off as the work of someone in recovery, as therapeutic exercises of a darker sort than would usually be found in Christian music. The stellar cut "Broken Things" is a prayer of both desperation and hope: "You can have my heart, if you don't mind broken things . . . I heard that you make all things new / So I give these pieces back to you." More Christian-radio oriented is the song "Never Gonna Give Up On You," a tribute to an unbelieving friend, who Miller is determined to pray into heaven. Shawn Colvin, **Mark Heard,** and Kelly Willard all appear on the album. Perhaps the most telling song for the project was her angry though ear-catching rant "Sick of Sex," on which she vents her disgust with a culture that desensitizes people to immorality and abuse: "I'm sick of sex being abused / I'm sick of sex being used and misused to sell me." Executives at Myrrh would not allow the song on the album—but it made the cut on Miller's next project, *Orphans and Angels,* where it actually seems out of place. Most of that album has a more traditional gospel focus, opening with "River Where Mercy Flows" and closing with the Appalachian styled "Praise to the Lord, Amen!" Miller also dusts off the old Jackie DeShannon chestnut "Put a Little Love in Your Heart" (cf. **Al Green**) and covers **Mark Heard**'s "Treasure of the Broken Land." **Wes King,** Shawn Colvin,

Valerie Carter, and **Victoria Williams** all put in appearances, but the finest moment may be a duet with Emmylou Harris on "All My Tears," a song Miller originally wrote for Heard. Harris also recorded the song on one of her albums, as did jazz vocalist Jimmy Scott.

After the three Myrrh projects, Miller would release one more album for the Christian market and then cross over into the secular field. *Invisible Girl* is notable for the song "Nobody's Child," which features the true-to-form lyric, "Come all of you ragged and unshod / Come be embraced and loved by God." Miller also sings two songs written by Marvin Etzioni of **Lone Justice** ("Weapons of the Spirit," "I Can't Cry Hard Enough"), performs "I Will Be with You" as a trio with **Charlie Peacock** and Valerie Carter, and fronts **The Electrics** on a Celtic shuffle called "Back of Your Head." The album was dedicated to abuse victims and derives its title from the idea that, as Miller would say, "the victim is invisible as a person to her attackers—like she's not even human." She told *True Tunes* that during the recording of *Invisible Girl* she struggled with the knowledge that her stepsister's daughter was being abused and molested, and a number of the songs ("When You Come Home," "In My Eyes") were written specifically for that child. In interviews and other forums, Miller made it clear that, as uncomfortable as the subject may be, she could not leave it alone, as though the revelations surrounding *Walks through Walls* had closed that chapter on her life. She talked positively of her many years in therapy and spoke candidly of the traumas that she continued to deal with on a daily basis. "When I first came to the Lord," she told *CCM* in 1994, "he did this instantaneous measure of healing that was necessary just to keep me alive. But there have been many more stages since then, each one part of an ongoing healing process." She also shared without elaboration that her father had "come to know the Lord before he died."

Miller officially left Christian music for her general market debut *Blue Pony,* but in actuality the album is hardly different from her previous contributions. Specific religious references are scaled back a bit but, as *CCM* would note, the album is in many ways "the most spiritual" work of her career. Musically, it has more of the Americana-country-funk sound that she had crafted with The Buddy Miller Band all those years ago. "Take Me Back" is a duet with her husband about watching a couple's marriage fall apart. She offers two Celtic songs as a nod to her Irish heritage, one a duet with Emmylou Harris ("Forever My Beloved") and another with Steve Earle (the Psalm-like "I Call on You"). She also sings "By the Way of Sorrow" with Karen Peris of **The Innocence Mission.** Along with the usual suspects (Hindalong, Madeira), Matt Slocum of **Sixpence None the Richer** and Bill Mallonee of the **Vigilantes of Love** contribute to the project, offering the general market a taste of talent that is largely unknown outside the Christian ghetto.

Entertainment Weekly would call *Blue Pony* "one of the year's most haunting surprises" and Christian music fans got a boost of confidence watching the mainstream press slather compliments all over the "debut album" by a "new artist" who some of them had followed for years. Much of the supporting cast would return for *Broken Things,* which reprised as its title track the song the world had missed on *Walks through Walls* (sung now as a duet with Emmylou Harris). "All My Tears" is resurrected here as well. "I Still Cry" (a duet with Patty Griffin) is a song of mourning over the loss of her friend Donald Lindley. "Strange Lover" is a song about cocaine addiction, sung here with Steve Earle, who had just gotten out of jail for offenses related to a drug addiction that almost took his life. "Orphan Train" pairs Miller with **Victoria Williams** on a fairly straightforward gospel song proclaiming that all people can be adopted by God and live as equals in God's eyes. "Maggie" relates the there-but-for-the grace-of-God-go-I saga of an abused child who grows into an abusive adult alcoholic. *Buddy and Julie Miller* is an official duet project with husband and wife performing some of their own songs and some well-chosen covers (**Bob Dylan**'s "Wallflower," Richard Thompson's "Keep Your Distance"). They form a trio with Emmylou Harris to sing "That's Just How She Cries," but the highlight of the set is a resurrection of Bruce "Utah" Phillips' stellar "Rock, Salt, and Nails" (best known, perhaps, from Joan Baez' classic *David's Album*).

Miller has often repeated an amusing story about her decision to cross over into the general market. While contemplating what to do, she misread a biblical passage from Isaiah 49:6, thinking it said, "Is it too small a thing for you to help restore the tribes of Israel?" Applying these words to her own situation, she took the rhetorical question as meaning that she should not despise her relatively low status as one whose focus was limited to building up the church (comparable to restoring the tribes of Israel). Later, when she checked the text, she saw that the passage was not a question but a direct statement: "It is too small a thing for you to help restore the tribes of Israel." As a result her proof text for justifying why she wanted to stay in the small but comfortable Christian environment was destroyed—it pointed, in fact, in the opposite direction. She decided, accordingly, that singing as a Christian for Christians was "too small a thing"; it had only been the beginning of what God wanted her to do.

A number of Miller's songs have been recorded by other artists. "My Love Will Follow You" was cut by Brooks and Dunn for their triple-platinum album *Borderline.* Both Julie and Buddy Miller are members of Emmylou Harris's touring and studio band, Spyboy.

Christian radio hits: "How Could You Say No" (1990); "What Would Jesus Do?" (# 21 in 1990); "Mystery Love" (# 16 in 1990); "Never Gonna

Give Up on You" (# 11 in 1991); "Put a Little Love in Your Heart" (# 15 in 1993); "Angels Dance" (# 15 in 1993); "Nobody's Child" (# 17 in 1995).

Millions and Millions

Mark Stitts, gtr.; kybrd.; Mike Stitts, voc., drums. 1992—*Millions and Millions* (DaySpring).

Millions and Millions was a duo composed of siblings who had worked for many years with **Tim Miner**'s Dallas-based Knightlight Studios, writing, arranging, and producing for **Al Green** ("Love Is Reality," "I Can Feel It") and other artists. For their own project they adopted a blend of Euro-pop, R&B, and dance music that may have been too diverse for fans to lock in on a defining style. *CCM*'s Bruce Brown noted that listening to successive songs brought to mind such disparate comparisons as Richard Marx, then Thomas Dolby, then Bruce Hornsby. "Way Back Home" is a retelling of the prodigal son story, and "Help Somebody" challenges Christians to make a difference in the world.

Christian radio hits: "Help Somebody" (# 5 in 1993).

Mindrage

John LeComp, voc., gtr.; Chad Wilburn, drums; Nick Williams, bass. 1999—*Sown in Weakness, Raised in Power* (BulletProof); 2000—*S/T* [EP with Nailed Promise] (Pluto).

Mindrage is a Christian metal band from Arizona that has been compared to **Embodyment** and **Selfmindead,** though *HM* would say they are "less hardcore sounding and more straight up growl metal." Drummer Chad Wilburn describes their debut album as "a total blessing and a lot of fun." The song "Destructive Patterns," he says, is about "lifestyles that we live that will eventually lead us to hell if we do not give them up and accept Jesus Christ as our Savior." The song "Voice of Disgust" is about "how the world wants us to tolerate sin and not voice our concerns or beliefs." The song "Lying Breed" concerns "false religions and cults and how Christianity is the only way to salvation." The band has also contributed four songs to a split EP recorded with the group **Nailed Promise.**

Kate Miner

1999—*Live Worship from the Strip* (Sovereign).

Kate Miner has an urgent, passionate vocal style that has been likened to **Ashley Cleveland** and **Maria McKee,** but she has been content for many years to work as a session and background singer in Christian (and sometimes mainstream) music rather than become a recording artist in her own right. She is married to David Miner, bass player for **The Alpha Band,**

Tonio K., and many others. Together, the two serve as worship leaders at the Vineyard Fellowship church in Malibu, California, and three of Kate's songs were recorded by **Kim Hill** on the latter's *The Fire Again* album. In 1997, Miner opened for **Delirious?** at that group's series of concerts at The Roxy theater on Hollywood's Sunset Strip. "I loved that night," she told *Release*, "because there were three bands and I was the only one who didn't have a record company, and I didn't want a record company. So, I got to do whatever I wanted, which was to worship God." Those concerts weren't recorded, but a producer in the audience was inspired to duplicate the experience later, and the resultant *Live Worship from the Strip* successfully captured the passion of a live rock show with the passion of uninhibited worship. Miner tears through mostly original songs, including the driving "Carry Me," and also covers **The Call**'s "I Still Believe" and **Matt Redman**'s "Better Is One Day."

Tim Miner

1984—*Tim Miner* (Nissi); 1988—*I Know You Think You Know* (Sparrow); 1990—*A True Story* (Frontline); 1992—*Tim Miner* (Motown).

Tim Miner is an R&B/pop singer who has played a major role in Christian music as a producer and songwriter in addition to his work as a solo performer. Born in 1964, Miner grew up in Oklahoma City where he formed the group Light while still in high school and earned his first record contract at the age of eighteen. He moved to Los Angeles briefly after graduating, but in 1984 moved to Dallas where he established Knightlight studios where many Christian and general market artists would record. Although Miner is white, his musical roots are deep in the African American traditions of soul and R&B; primary influences—especially for his early work—seem to include Michael Jackson, Lionel Richie, and Stevie Wonder. For his first self-titled album, Miner would offer the midtempo rocker "Love All the Hurt Away" and the heartfelt ballad "Always." The latter song is sung as a duet with **Cindy Cruse** and the pairing turned out to be more than musical; Miner and Cruse would marry, and she became a cowriter on many of his future songs. *I Know You Think You Know* offers more soulful ballads ("Cover Me," "Did I Forget to Say") and a youth-oriented antidrug song called "Smarter Than Crack."

On *A True Story*, Miner delves into more contemporary urban sounds, mixing R&B with hip-hop. "Forgive Me" is intimate and worshipful. "White Boy" provides a humorous look at his role as a racial minority in the field of urban music. Thematically, the album is built around mostly traumatic events in the artist's life. His father, an Assemblies of God minister, committed suicide when he was two years old. The song "Yesterday" began as the letter he now wished to write to his mother about that event. "Walked across My Heart" (with guest rapping by **D-Boy**) deals with the time in his life after his mother was remarried to a man who was abusive to her and the children. After the three albums targeted specifically for the Christian market, Miner signed with Motown, where he produced another, completely different self-titled album for the general market (with distribution to Christian retail outlets through Frontline). Some of Miner's old songs ("Love All the Hurt Away," "Yesterday," "Forgive Me") are reprised here, but most of the material is new. For the most part, Miner defies modern trends in black music and goes for a classic '80s sound. "Where Did They Go?" recalls Stevie Wonder's "Boogie On Reggae Woman." The opening "Come and Go with Me" has an Earth, Wind, and Fire swing to it, as Miner invites his audience to join him on the path to heaven. "Wouldn't Change a Thing" and "Promise of Love" are strong dance numbers and "Heart," a romantic ballad. Notably, Miner does not back off on the spiritual content of his songs, but mixes strong gospel proclamations with simple human love songs.

As a songwriter, Miner has written or cowritten songs performed by **Angie Alan** ("Sunny Side," "The Bottom Line," "Never Givin' Up"), **Kim Boyce** ("Here," "Tender Heart," "Good Enough," "Weapon of Good"), **Cruse** ("All the Hurting People"), **Cindy Cruse** ("Always," "Color Blind"), **D-Boy** ("Pick Yourself Up"), **Al Green** ("I Can Feel It"), **Leon Patillo** ("Isn't It Crazy"). His songs have also been recorded by Paula Abdul and **Gladys Knight.** He has produced numerous albums by both Christian and mainstream artists, including Paula Abdul and Brian McKnight.

Christian radio hits: "Always" [with **Cindy Cruse**] (# 5 in 1984); "Did I Forget to Say?" (# 2 in 1988); "Cover Me" (# 10 in 1988); "You Know I Love This Feeling" (# 8 in 1989); "Tell Me" (# 30 in 1990); "I Wouldn't Change a Thing" (# 25 in 1993).

Greg Minier

1990—*Minier* (R.E.X.).

Greg Minier is guitarist for **The Crucified** and **Applehead.** He released a solo album in between those two projects. A thrash-punk album in the same ballpark as early Nirvana, *Minier* features an angry artist screaming warnings about the reality of hell ("Do Not Be Deceived") and opposition to such things as abortion ("Killing the Innocent") and intellectualism ("Prophecy of Man"). On a somewhat more optimistic point, "Prophecy" announces the impending return of Christ—though that won't be good news for everyone either.

Kelly Minter

2001—*Good Day* (Word).

When Kelly Minter's debut album appeared in 2001, *CCM* magazine celebrated its appearance with a grand welcome to another singer who they thought fit the mold of **Ginny Owens, Nicole C. Mullen, Rebecca St. James, Jennifer Knapp,** and **Kendall Payne.** Actually, the last thing in the world that the contemporary Christian music market needed in 2001 was *another* female adult contemporary pop singer of the sort just named. But fortunately, Minter is better than any of those artists and doesn't really sound very much like them. More mature than St. James and less boring than Knapp, she actually belongs in a category with early **Kim Hill,** early **Margaret Becker,** and early **Ashley Cleveland.** *Good Day* reveals an artist with a healthy and husky voice suitable for rock and roll. Knowing her audience, Minter wastes that voice on a few formulaic songs but she also delivers a handful of tunes that reveal greater promise. The very best tracks open and close the album. "Any More Sure" is a guitar-soaked rocker that poses the hypothetical question whether actually witnessing biblical miracles would make faith any more certain or easier. "Whatever I Do" is a haunting, slightly country ballad about making every moment count for God.

Miranda

1998—*Miranda* (independent).

Miranda Richardson of **Everybodyduck** joins Cher and Selena as singers who choose to record under their first name only. Her independent solo album is more acoustic than the band's work, though most of the songs were written by **Everybodyduck**'s Tim Brinkman and display the same superficiality that typified most of that group's work. Things don't get much deeper than "I'm so happy since I found Jesus" ("I'm So Happy"), but Richardson apparently intends the songs for youth group and camp ministry, where they might be entirely appropriate. Critics have been understandably hard on her—and on her former group—but they tend to forget that most of the early Jesus music from which contemporary Christian music sprang was of a similar sort (cf. **Mustard Seed Faith**'s "I'm So Happy in Jesus"). Richardson and Brinkman would reprise some of the same songs in another indie project called **Sparklepop.**

The Miscellaneous

BoH, gtr.; Stef Loy, voc., gtr.; Magnus Sjölander, drums, gtr., voc.; Sooi Groeneveld van der Laan, voc. // Øyvind Eriksen, bass (+ 1997); Patrik Jonasson, kybrd. (+ 1997, – 1999). 1994—*She Walks alone With Me* (Megaphone); 1997—*All Good Weeds Grow Up* (Gray Dot); 1999—*Moth and Rust.*

The Miscellaneous is a peculiarly international band with a modern rock sound that favors an eclecticism worthy of its name. Led by American Stef Loy, the group also features female vocals by Sooi van der Laan of Holland; all of the other members are Swedes. The band actually got its start in Canada, where Loy, BoH, and Magnus Sjölander traveled under the name Perry and the Poor Boys and made one album that was produced by **Michael Roe** (*No Fear in Love,* Spark, 1992). Loy cites many of Christian music's premier alternative acts as his major influences—**Daniel Amos, LSU,** and **Steve Taylor,** but the band's sound is wholly unique. The core of each album consists of power-pop songs with catchy melodies and radio-friendly hooks (like **The Throes**), but lurking around the edges are more complex and darker compositions that are less immediately accessible (like **The Prayer Chain** or **The Violet Burning**). The group formed in 1994 and their first album was released that year in Europe only. One song, "Black Lips Saturday," made it on to the secular European radio stations and was a considerable hit. A reviewer in Sweden wrote, "It makes me long for summer nights and a beach. What a song! What a chorus! Thank you!" Eventually, the song would be placed on a compilation disc in the United States (*IRV2,* Blind Records, 1996) and was played on alternative Christian stations.

The title of the album *All Good Weeds Grow Up* is intended to reflect Loy's opinion that "God has made every person in the world to be beautiful." The album kicks off with "Bunker Pew," which sounds very much like **The Throes.** Its brightest and cheeriest moment comes with "Cando," a Beatlesque tune with layered harmonies that strays close to '60s bubblegum with its unforgettable melody and layered harmony vocals. At the opposite end of the spectrum is "Horizon Blue," which has almost no melody and features obscure lyrics offered in a very quiet, distorted voice. The song "me" is a beautiful hymn with church organ and choral, almost a capella vocals. About three-quarters through, it suddenly dissolves into a slow, electric rock song that is surprising and effective in its intensity. "Miracle" is another pop treat, similar in sound to the best songs of the all-too-neglected band Downey Mildew (cf. "Left Foot Down," "A Liar Needs a Good Memory"). *All Good Weeds* was produced by Armand Petri, known for his work with the Goo Goo Dolls, 10,000 Maniacs, and **Sixpence None the Richer.** *Moth and Rust* starts with a spacey rocker called "Bug" that makes fun of the Y2K paranoia that attended the changing of millennia. A similar theme informs the album's most radio-friendly song, "1929," which uses the stock market crash of that year as a metaphor for personal depression ("but you'll be fine, you'll pull through," Loy sings reassuringly). Groeneveld van der Laan takes the lead on "Surround Her," a Cranberries-like tune that asks God to protect her sister with angels. "Crumbs" is a tougher song that reminds the ambitious that "moth and rust" will have final dominion over all material things. Loy is the band's primary lyricist and he generally favors a metaphorical and poetic approach that avoids Christian clichés and obvious or simplistic conclusions. "I don't really

know how these things work," he says, "but I pray that this music will touch the listener as we endeavor to touch the heavens."

Miss Angie

1997—*100 Million Eyeballs* (Myrrh); 1999—*Triumphantine.*

Angie Thornton (b. Angie Turner in 1977) grew up in Christian music. Her father, who she describes as "a converted hippie," was always playing in local Christian rock bands and she sometimes tagged along and sang backup vocals. For a while there was a family group called The Turner Family, which she says was sort of a Christian Partridge Family. Her brother Shawn Turner later became guitarist for **Johnny Q. Public,** and she tagged along with them for a while also. Eventually, such tagging led to romance with that band's other guitarist Oran Thornton. In 1998, Oran and Angie married and, thereafter, her husband left JQP and formed **Flick** with his brother Trevor. Regardless of marital status, Angie Turner/Thornton has recorded under the name Miss Angie, and her albums evince a Blondie-inspired blend of crunchy guitars and happy pop tunes, sustained by her light, angelic voice. She describes her sound as "stardusty rock and roll with a girl singer." The title song to *100 Million Eyeballs* is taken from apocalyptic descriptions of weird creatures in the biblical books of Daniel, Ezekiel, and Revelation. Musically, the song recalls Blondie's "Rapture," with Thornton doing an almost spoken-word take on the verses. "Trampoline" is subdued modern rock with the basic message that life (including the Christian life) has its ups and downs. "Lift My Eyes Up" is standard (as opposed to alternative) rock and roll, with a straightforward theme of dependence on Christ. The album closes with a cover of **2nd Chapter of Acts**' "Which Way the Wind Blows," which lacks the power of the original, but reworks the song as an interesting, plodding commentary on the uncertainties of life. On *Triumphantine,* Miss Angie eschews grungy guitars for synthesizers and drum machines to produce an album filled with retro-electronica sounds. "Let's Get Together" and "I Love Light" have disco/glam underpinnings. On "Jesus Get Me" she offers a breathy, childlike prayer to be completely taken over by Christ. "Doom" is an acoustic ballad about the Rapture and "2222" is an upbeat guitar-driven song based on 2 Timothy 2:22. "Getcha" returns to the Blondie sound, with a Doors-era organ carrying its midtempo melody. More avant-garde and less accessible than her debut, *Triumphantine* never really rocks but does achieve a certain modern alternative update of psychedelia. Thornton writes most of her own material, often with her husband. She says that her songs are aimed at "church kids who don't have a clue about who God is."

Christian radio hits: "100 Million Eyeballs" (# 25 in 1997).

Mission of Mercy

Randy Keckman, gtr., voc.; Mark Schwarzburg, bass, voc.; Chris Wicklas, drums. 1994—*Yonder Boy* (Etcetera).

Mission of Mercy was a grunge trio from Chicago with a sound that sometimes recalled **King's X** but was even more similar to Soundgarden. Bruce Franklin of the Chicago band Trouble plays guitar on their song, "Candyland." One of *Yonder Boy*'s highlights is the song "Colors" about race relations. It features the line "God makes the color, but the color doesn't make you god," which Keckman saw on a T-shirt at the *Cornerstone* festival and didn't realize was already a line from **Resurrection Band**'s song "Afrikaans."

Mr. Mister

Steve George, kybrd.; Pat Mastelotto, drums; Richard Page, voc., bass; Steve Farris, gtr. (−2001) // Buzz Feiten, gtr. (+ 2001). 1984—*I Wear the Face* (RCA); 1985—*Welcome to the Real World*; 1987—*Go On*; 2001—*The Best of Mr. Mister* (Buddha).

The Los Angeles-based pop-rock quartet called Mr. Mister produced secular radio hits with explicit Christian content while trying to avoid any identification as "a Christian band." Although in terms of content, their music was more religious and even more specifically Christian than that of **Jars of Clay** a decade later, their attitude toward the Christian music scene was more in keeping with that of **Collective Soul** or **Creed**. Mr. Mister had their first minor hit with the song "Hunters of the Night" (# 54 in 1984). A year later, the group hit big with *Welcome to the Real World* with back-to-back smashes "Broken Wings" (# 1 for 2 weeks in 1985) and "Kyrie" (# 1 for 2 weeks in 1985). The former song appears to be a prayer, addressed to God, though it expresses a generic spirituality with imagery common to Christianity and a number of other religions. The latter, however, draws its lyrics directly from the liturgy of the Christian church. The word *kyrie* is Latin for "Lord" and is used in liturgical churches as a primary address for God (the phrase "kyrie eleison" used in the song translates, "Lord, have mercy"). The band also had a Top 10 hit with the song "Is It Love?" in 1986.

The spiritual content of Mr. Mister's lyrics set off a wave of speculation that a Christian band had somehow finagled their way into the secular market. Addressing this "concern" primarily in the mainstream press, the group's leader and lyricist Richard Page assured the media that he was not "a born again Christian" and that Mr. Mister was not "a Christian band." It is difficult to determine what was meant by such denials. In the late '80s most Christians in the world would probably have insisted that they were not "born again Christians" since at that time that label was being applied to one particular subset of Christians—namely, those who interpreted John 3:3 as im-

plying that one could not be "saved" without experiencing a definitive conversion as the result of one's own decision to accept Christ. Also in the late '80s (and even more in the '90s) a large number of groups functioning within the contemporary Christian music subculture would have insisted that they were not "Christian bands," meaning that although they themselves might be Christians they did not intend for their music to be played only for Christian audiences or used as some sort of propaganda tool for promoting the faith.

In any case, Mr. Mister's next album, *Go On*, features songs that are even more religious, spiritual, and specifically Christian than the first. The project's best track, "Healing Waters," offers allusions to baptism with Page singing lines like "Silent God, moving in my heart" with a gospel choir in the background. "Man of a Thousand Dances" describes a person being pursued by God, only to surrender eventually amidst a sea of "hallelujahs." The group hit the Top 40 again with "Something Real (Inside Me/Inside You)," a rather anthemic song encouraging humanitarian compassion. The song "Stand and Deliver" was used for the soundtrack of a motion picture by the same name.

In a 1987 interview with *CCM*, Page acknowledged that his own life was like the character in the song "Man of a Thousand Dances": "I don't really understand my own connection with God . . . but He just keeps following me." He indicated that he grew up in church, singing in a choir directed by his father, and that those influences were still a part of him musically and spiritually. He specified his reason for not wanting Mr. Mister to be known as a Christian band as being, "we don't just want to have Christian fans," and he indicated that his problem with most Christian music is that it tends to be removed from reality: "it's candy coating, about how we're all happy and we're all in love with God. We are—but we're not always like that."

Moby

1992—*Moby* (Instinct); 1993—*Early Underground; Move* (Elektra); 1995—*Everything Is Wrong*; 1996—*Rare: The Collected B Sides 1989–1993* (Instinct); *Animal Rights* (Elektra); 1997—*I Like to Score*; 1999—*Play* (V2); 2000—*Mobysongs 1993–1998* (Elektra).

www.moby.com

Richard Melville Hall (b. 1965) records techno/rave music under the moniker Moby, a nickname he acquired in his youth for being the great-grand nephew of Herman Melville, author of *Moby Dick*. Hall was born in New York but grew up in Darien, Connecticut, where he began studying classical guitar at the age of ten. As a teenager, he played with a punk band called Vatican Commandoes and briefly filled in as vocalist for the hardcore band Flipper while their usual singer was in jail. In the late '80s, Moby took up dee-jaying, entered the techno scene, and soon became its acknowledged master. *The New*

Rolling Stone Encyclopedia of Rock and Roll refers to him alternately as "the king of techno" and "the first face of techno." He first garnered widespread attention with a single called "Go," which was a radically reworked version of the theme from the *Twin Peaks* TV series set to a frantic dance beat. Such beats became the order of the day and at one point Moby was listed in the *Guinness Book of World Records* for having recorded "the world's fastest song" ("Thousand," at 1015 beats per minute). Moby is distinctive as a DJ in the techno/rave genre in that he allows his own personality to come out in recordings and performances. Indeed, the latter often feature him coming out from behind the banks of speakers and synthesizers to "surf" on his keyboards, stage-dive into the audience, and on occasion trash some of the equipment in a manner reminiscent of The Who. In addition to his own albums, he has done remixes for the B-52s, Depeche Mode, Brian Eno, Erasure, Michael Jackson, and the Pet Shop Boys.

Moby's album *Everything Is Wrong* is generally regarded as his breakthrough work. Experimental and innovative, it is no exaggeration to say with Brian Quincy Newcomb that the record singlehandedly "re-invented dance music as an expressive art-form that was not just for calisthenics." *Animal Rights* breaks with tradition, taking the artist into guitar-driven punk and hardcore. But Moby returned to dance music with *I Like to Score,* a creatively titled collection of instrumental pieces written for movie scores. His "James Bond Theme" from that album was used prominently in the skating competition of the winter Olympics of 1998. *Play* is the album that made him a household name, topping critic polls, garnering Grammy nominations, and going triple platinum with sales of over three million copies. The song "South Side," featuring No Doubt's Gwen Stefani, gave Moby his first major hit on the pop charts (# 14 in 2001). One of *Play*'s most innovative aspects is its mixture of old field recordings of blues and gospel chants with synthesized loops and beats. In late 1999, an expanded edition of the album was issued featuring an extra disc called *Play: The B Sides* and the artist's old label tried to capitalize on his new success by issuing a collection of old material called *Mobysongs 1993–1998.* Moby was now a celebrity and he even appeared in a series of Calvin Klein jeans commercials. Moby's music has appeared on soundtracks to the films *Any Given Sunday, The Next Best Thing, Whatever It Takes,* and *Play It to the Bone,* and it has been used in many TV programs including *The X-Files, Jack and Jill, Judging Amy, Party of Five,* and *Dawson's Creek.*

The *Rough Guide to Rock* rightly notes that Moby is "as well known for his environmentalism, antidrug declarations, and Christian faith as he is for his music." A strict vegan (that is, a person who does not eat or wear anything that comes from animals), he has placed an inscription on most of his singles that reads, "Animals are not for eating. Love to Jesus Christ." Songs

that are obviously faith-inspired on his albums include "God Moving over the Face of the Waters" on *Everything Is Wrong* and both "Natural Blues" and "Why Does My Heart Feel So Bad?" from *Play.* Nevertheless, his version of Christianity has been sufficiently unorthodox to keep him out of the contemporary Christian music subculture. On the one hand, Moby has often identified himself as "a born-again Christian" in secular publications, talking about how he accepted Christ at the age of twenty and about why he advocates and practices total abstinence from alcohol and drugs. On the other hand, he also talks rather openly about such things as his love for pornography and unabashed delight in masturbation. Much of his posturing is born of an anti-institutionalism that leads him to reject much of organized religion. Some of his ideas, however, have come through intellectual study of the faith that sometimes gives him a better understanding of certain matters than many Christian music fans are wont to possess. His pronouncements that "the Christian Coalition's political agenda is antithetical to the teachings of Christ" would not seem controversial to most mainline theologians. By the same token, however, Moby sometimes expresses his views rhetorically in ways that go beyond intellectual debate to become hyperbolic assaults. For instance, in his liner notes to *Animal Rights,* he offers a blistering attack on the Christian Coalition that concludes, "Masquerading pro-business, pro-greed, racist, sexist, homophobic bigotry under the banner of Christianity is disgusting." Most informed observers would take *those* characterizations as extreme and unfair.

In 1999, Moby talked to *CCM* about his views and how they had changed over the years. "In the past, I've defined things in very rigid terms," he said. "I looked down on people who took drugs, people who eat meat, people who aren't Christian, people who don't like dance music." As to his Christian faith and place in the Christian community, he continued, "Ultimately, the one thing I'm grounded in is that I love Christ. I love Christ's involvement in my life, I love the teachings of Christ, I love the character of Christ as revealed in the New Testament. I may (now) be uncomfortable calling myself a Christian, but I have no trouble calling myself a Christ lover."

Model Engine

Eric Herzog, drums; Brad McCarter, bass, voc.; Jeremy Post, voc., gtr.
1997—*The Lean Years Tradition* (SaraBellum).

Model Engine is simply **Black-Eyed Sceva** with a new drummer. There is little discernible difference between the sound of the two bands; Jeremy Post indicated the name change was due mainly to the fact that no one could pronounce or spell their previous moniker. *The Lean Years Tradition* continues in the same vein of raspy modern rock set by BES, with intelligent, sometimes quirky lyrics that have caused the group to be compared to XTC. Oriented toward college-rock audiences, Model Engine has little to offer contemporary Christian radio stations that favor what is comfortable and predictable. The opening track, "Hang You Upside Down," uses the crucifixion of Peter as imagery for describing persecution of those who seek truth in the modern day. "Reeperbahm" derives from Post's experience of being propositioned by prostitutes in Germany and the frustration of not knowing how a Christian should respond in such a situation (beyond rejecting the offer). "Scarred But Smarter" and "Walking Wounded" both speak of painful growth experiences, apparently connected to a failed romance.

Modern Mission

Iggy, voc.; Dave Newman, gtr.; Sugarbear, bass; Zac, drums. 1985—*Modern Mission* (Exile).

Modern Mission was a mid-'80s new-wave quartet featuring one member with a real name and three others who remain somewhat anonymous. The album sports hard-hitting music with direct and aggressive Christian lyrics. Brian Quincy Newcomb of *CCM* wrote that the band "may only do one thing, but they do it quite well." Songs like "Stick to Your Guns" and "Time to Fight" exemplify their militant take on theology.

Modest Attraction

Personnel list unavailable. 1992—*Modest Attraction* (custom); 1994—*The Truth in Your Face* (Viva); 1996—*Divine Luxury* (custom).

Modest Attraction is a melodic metal band from Sweden that has received some attention in the American Christian music scene due to reviews in *HM* and distribution through *Rad Rockers. The Truth in Your Face* offers "The Healing Touch," an invitational song with gang vocals on the chorus, and "Your Love Is True," a foray into soulful blues.

Monk

Ric Hordinski, gtr.; Brian Kelly, drums; et al. 1995—*A Rough Shaking* (independent); 1997—*Quiver;* 1998—*Hush* (Ether); 1999—*Blink.*

Monk is an acoustic trio led by Ric Hordinski, who was once guitarist for **Over the Rhine.** Their music tends to be ethereal, mixing acoustic and electric sounds into ambient jams similar to the work of **Daniel Lanois.** *Hush* varies in mood from pastoral ("Ring Out, Ye Crystal Spheres") to ominous ("Tattoo," "Coal Train"). *Blink* is a live recording that includes favorite numbers from previous projects, an improvisational track, and a rendition of **Over the Rhine**'s "Circle of Quiet."

Dorothy Moore

1986—*Givin' It to You Straight* (Rejoice).

Dorothy Moore (b. 1946) had one of the biggest R&B hits of the '70s with her remake of an old country song called "Misty Blue" (# 3 in 1976). Moore had grown up in Jackson, Mississippi, singing in church. She maintains that she had always wanted to be a gospel singer, but the doors did not open until after she achieved secular success. She attended Jackson State University as a voice major and became lead singer for The Poppies, who had a minor '60s hit with the song "Lullaby of Love" (# 56 in 1966), which set words to the tune of Brahm's lullaby. For a decade after that experience she worked as a session singer doing backup vocals before hitting the charts with "Misty Blue." One of the biggest international hits of 1976, that song would continue to be placed on compilation albums of classic soul twenty-five years later. "Misty Blue" was nominated for a Grammy award and in 1976 Moore was chosen by both *Billboard* and *Record World* magazines as the Best New Female Artist of the Year. She followed her biggest hit with two more R&B versions of country songs: Willie Nelson's "Funny How Time Slips Away" (# 58 in 1976) and the Addrisi Brothers' "I Believe You" (# 27 in 1977). The latter tune was also nominated for a Grammy award in 1977. A decade later, Moore would release *Givin' It to You Straight,* a collection of mostly MOR gospel standards, such as "Keep Your Eyes on Jesus" and "I'm So Glad I'm Standing Here Today." The album also includes the more contemporary sounding "Captain of My Ship" (with a reggae beat) and a cover of Lionel Richie's "Jesus Is Love."

Gail Moore

See **Amarachi.**

Geoff Moore and The Distance (and Geoff Moore)

Personnel for The Distance: Dale Oliver, gtr. (−1990); Arlin Troyer, bass (− 1990); Lang Bliss, drums (− 1989); Tom Reynolds, kybrd. (− 1989) // Geoff Barkley, kybrd. (+ 1989); Greg Herrington, drums (+ 1989, −1995); Roscoe Meek, gtr. (+ 1990, − 1997); Gary Mullett, bass (+ 1990); Chuck Conner, drums (+ 1995); Joel McCreight, gtr. (+ 1997). By Geoff Moore and The Distance: 1988—*A Place to Stand* (Sparrow); 1989—*Foundations;* 1990—*Pure and Simple* (ForeFront); 1992—*A Friend Like U;* 1993—*Evolution . . . Redefined;* 1995—*Home Run; Familiar Stranger: Early Works* (Sparrow); 1996—*Greatest Hits* (ForeFront); *The Early Years, Vol. I;* 1997—*Threads.* By Geoff Moore: 1984—*Where Are the Other Nine?* (Power Discs); 1985—*Over the Edge;* 1987—*The Distance;* 1988—*All the Good Music;* 1999—*Geoff Moore* (ForeFront).

The best general market analogy for pop singer Geoff Moore would be Bob Seger. Both artists hail from Michigan and have a similar sound (a mixture of old time rock and roll and meditative ballads). Moore grew up in Flint, Michigan, and attended Taylor University. He supposedly began performing on a college dare. In 1985, he moved to Nashville and embarked on a brief solo career that produced three albums. Then, from 1988 to 1998, Moore would record and tour with the band he called The Distance. In 1999, he returned to his solo career. Moore has often cowritten songs with **Steven Curtis Chapman,** including the latter's hits "Faithful Too," "For Who He Really Is," "The Great Adventure," and "That's Paradise." Chapman, in turn, has cowritten a number of Moore's hits, including "Simple Heart," "A Friend Like U," "Live to Tell," and "That's When I'll Know I'm Home."

Moore's earliest solo albums evince a pop-'80s sound less mature than his later work with the band. On *Over the Edge,* for instance, he covers **Larry Norman**'s "Why Should the Devil Have All the Good Music?" in a version that pales beside the remake that he would perform with The Distance on their *Evolution . . . Redefined* album. Highlights from the period include "Open Your Eyes," a **Petra**esque ballad about looking for the Second Coming of Christ, and "Over the Edge," which testifies to the thrill that taking a leap of faith can bring. "Inside Out" is a rocking treatment of the manner in which God transforms people (from the inside out) and "Never Wanna Go Back" presents commitment to Christ as a decision one can make without regret. Moore also introduced **Randy Matthews**' song "Didn't He" to a new generation on his album *The Distance.* Collections of songs from this period are compiled on the albums *All the Good Music* and *Familiar Stranger.*

Geoff Moore and The Distance recorded two albums for Sparrow that evince a tougher and tighter sound (the 1996 compilation album called *The Early Years* contains songs from these two albums). *A Place to Stand* finds them offering barrelhouse rockers like "Go to the Moon" (about Christian separatism) alongside commercial ballads like "Heart and Soul" (about stewardship). *Foundations* features a cover of **Lone Justice**'s "I Found Love" and solidifies the group's reputation as heartland rockers. The songs on the latter album are particularly direct and soul-baring. Eight years later, in separate reviews of what would be the group's last album, both *CCM* and *Release* looked back to *Foundations* as the band's most brilliant and best work.

After Moore and The Distance moved to the ForeFront label, their sound seemed to gel, albeit in more of a pop direction. This is less true of *Pure and Simple,* which most critics would place alongside *Foundations* as a benchmark for heartland rock in the Christian market. It includes a cover of **The Alarm**'s "Rescue Me" and takes its title from the song "Simple Heart," a Don Henley-style tune that offers the wisdom of a rural farmer who has learned the priorities of life. On *A Friend Like U* the new teen-pop orientation becomes apparent. The album features a catchy title track and one of Moore's best numbers, "Good to Be Alive." The latter song offers a celebration of remembrance as he looks back on his childhood, adolescence, and young adulthood, recognizing the changing blessings that each period of life seems to bring. "Listen to Our Hearts" from the same album is one of Moore's nicer ballads—expressing the thought that human words ultimately fail to convey the worship that is due to God. "House of Faith" (cowritten with **Charlie Peacock**) provides a bouncy, almost-disco affirmation of tolerance and unity within the church ("there can be no labels in the house of faith").

The next album *(Evolution)* offers "Life Together," which is another Moore masterpiece—a joyous, anthemic song about life in Christian community. Moore also covers Johnny Nash's "I Can See Clearly Now," as well as the aforementioned Norman classic ("Why Should the Devil . . . ?"). Unfortunately, *Evolution* is best remembered for its lame title track, cowritten with **Phil Madeira.** The song is built on a good idea—using the concept of evolution as a metaphor for spiritual growth—but Moore ruins it with a dumb first verse attacking the traditional concept of evolution with innuendo about college professors claiming "your uncle was a monkey" (**Mark Lowry** puts in a guest appearance as the voice of the professor). As such, the song only furthers the stereotype that Christians who are opposed to evolution (not all Christians are, of course) don't understand the basics of the theory they dismiss.

Home Run returns to the bubblegum pop that the band had flirted with on *A Friend Like U.* The title track comes off as a kind of dumb **Carman**esque song about Geoff and his team taking on the devil in "the ballgame of life." For those who know that Moore's father had a career in professional baseball, the song at least evokes a personal, autobiographical note. "New Americans," by contrast, is a brilliantly funky song calling on young citizens to defy the stereotypes of Generation X and rise up with a religious patriotism that will make their country great again. "Evidence of God" atones theologically for the "Evolution" fiasco with a strong statement that human beings are themselves the best evidence for the existence and intention of divinity. But then there is "The Vow," a ballad written with Jimmie Lee Sloas (of **The Imperials** and **Dogs of Peace**) that is theologically troubling. It presents the prayer of a Christian who has made promises of faithfulness to God before and failed at keeping them. Instead of suggesting (in accord with biblical teaching) that the person needs to trust in God's grace rather than in his own good intentions, the song suggests that he just needs to try harder—make another promise ("a vow") and, this time, really, really, *really* mean it.

After the *Home Run* nadir, Moore and the Distance made a triumphant return with *Threads,* the best album of their Fore-

Front years, if not of their career. New guitarist Joel McCreight was recruited from **My Friend Stephanie.** The album gets off to a roaring good start with a surprising cover of The Who's "I'm Free" (from *Tommy*). After that, ballads and rockers alternate in a presentation that was universally praised as a mature and solid effort to break out of the formulaic pop mold. "In Betweens" is a song about finding meaning in life in everyday moments. "Only a Fool" offers encouragement to ministers and missionaries who are regarded as foolish for making sacrifices and devoting their lives to others. "The Scattering" lambasts complacent Christianity and "Declaration" issues a bold evangelistic challenge to reach the current generation for Christ.

Moore's first solo album would continue the high note. A bit more acoustic than the band's efforts, but rootsier and grittier than pal Chapman's music, *Geoff Moore* offers what a self-titled album should: a compelling look at the artist who made it. Moore strips down the sound and also lays bare some of his own personality in ways that make him less a cheerleader and more a real person. "Out Here" draws on his love of camping to describe a place of retreat from the chaos of life where the refreshment of the Spirit can be found. "With You" is a tender and moving love song for his wife. "Thanks to You," sung as a duet with Chapman, is a song the two friends wrote together about their friendship. Moore also covers **Rich Mullins'** "Boy Like Me, Man Like You." The highlight of the collection, however, is "String around My Finger," which appears to present his penance for "The Vow": "You are faithful / I'm forgetful of the ways / You are always graceful."

In 1998, Moore endorsed curriculum for the Southern Baptist Church's *Christ for Native Youth* program. The same year, he hosted an antievolution video documentary titled *No Accident . . . No Apologies.* He has worked extensively with the charitable world hunger organization Compassion International. His *Greatest Hits* collection compiles only songs from *Pure and Simple* through *Home Run* (with two new tracks), missing the critical *Foundations* and *Threads* material. It does include a bonus disc of live tracks, but these are also versions of songs from the ForeFront sessions.

Christian radio hits: "Where Are the Other Nine?" (# 11 in 1985); "Obey" (# 5 in 1987); "Heart and Soul" (# 14 in 1988); "Tearin' Down the Walls" (# 2 in 1989); "Foundations" (# 9 in 1989); "Rescue Me" (# 11 in 1991); "Simple Heart" (# 10 in 1991); "One Brand of Truth" (# 16 in 1991); "Peace" (# 21 in 1991); "More Emotional" (# 25 in 1992); "A Friend Like U" (# 1 for 3 weeks in 1992); "House of Faith" (# 10 in 1992); "Reminders of You" (# 3 in 1993); "Good to Be Alive" (# 3 in 1993); "Evolution . . . Redefined" (# 1 for 2 weeks in 1993); "Live to Tell" (# 4 in 1994); "Life Together" (# 1 for 2 weeks in 1994); "That's When I'll Know When I'm Home" (# 9 in 1994); "Heart to God, Hand to Man" (# 7 in 1994); "Godgotaholdonme" (# 2 in 1995); "Home Run" (# 1 for 2 weeks in 1995); "New Americans" (# 9 in 1995); "The Vow" (# 1 in 1996);

"More Than Gold" (# 5 in 1996); "Only a Fool" (# 1 in 1997); "Threads" (# 2 in 1998); "In Betweens" (# 11 in 1998); "Declaration" (# 16 in 1998); "String around My Finger" (# 14 in 1999).

Mickey and Becki Moore

See **Mickey and Becki.**

Patsy Moore

1992—Regarding the Human Condition (Warner Bros.); *1994—The Flower Child's Guide to Love and Fashion.*

Patsy Moore (b. 1964) grew up a Southern Baptist on the island of Antigua. After earning a degree in broadcast journalism from the University of North Carolina, she took a job as a staff writer at a publisher in Nashville and wrote songs on the side for **Trace Balin** and **Kim Hill.** She later recorded two more-acclaimed-than-successful albums of her own material. An African American, Moore seems to favor the jazz-pop stylings of singers like Dionne Warwick over the R&B or hip-hop genres in which black singers are often expected to work. In fact, her greatest influences seem to be persons like Joni Mitchell, Paul Simon, and Peter Gabriel. Her sound is eclectic, with equal contributions of folk, '60s rock, jazz, and world beat. No two songs sound alike. *Regarding the Human Condition* features "Lies (That I Have Known)," a critique of pop psychology and pseudo-intellectualism. "I Remember," a ballad with piano and strings, looks back to a time when she suffered depression and engaged in suicidal fantasies. *The Flower Child's Guide to Love and Fashion* takes its intriguing name from two of its tracks. "Flower Child" uses the metaphor of a flower blooming to describe the regeneration of the human spirit. "How It Should Be (Love and Fashion)" describes a modern hippie's visit to a traditional church. The album also includes "Under the Sign of Love," a Fifth Dimension-type song that offers an alternative to astrological determinism ("I was born in liberty / Under the sign of love"), and "The State I'm In," a duet with **Phil Keaggy.** In 1992, Moore told *CCM,* "I think I have more the poet's soul than a minister's soul, in the sense that one is called specifically to a ministry. But I think art in and of itself has the ability to communicate ideas to people, and there is always the potential for someone to walk away from what you do feeling that they've been ministered to."

Christian radio hits: "A City on a Hill" (# 7 in 1992).

Ron Moore

1969—Lo and Behold [with Bill Moore]; *1971—Wilmore* (Airborn); *1973—Airborne; 1975—Silence Is Music; 1976—Live Studio Concert* [with The Angel Band]; *1978—Death Defying Leap; 1983—Dauntless; 1985— Champion* (Morada); *1990—Change the World; 1999—Mystery.*

Jesus music historian David Di Sabatino names Ron Moore as one of the most underrated contributors to the development of what became contemporary Christian music. The son of Methodist missionary parents, Moore was born in Seoul, Korea, but eventually ended up in Wilmore, Kentucky, home to Asbury College (and seminary). He and his brothers (Alan Moore was part of **Albrecht, Roley, and Moore**) were into Jesus music before it was called that, before the Jesus movement revival garnered enough attention for such labels to be invented. Ron and brother Bill recorded *Lo and Behold,* an album of acoustic folk rock in 1969—the same year that **Larry Norman**'s *Upon This Rock* came out. *Lo and Behold* features only four original songs, opting mainly for covers of mainstream hits with spiritual meanings: Jesse Colin Young's "Get Together"; **Noel Paul Stookey**'s "Hymn"; James Hendricks' "Look to Your Soul" (made popular by **Johnny Rivers**). By 1971, however, when things were just starting to heat up out on the West Coast (cf. **Children of the Day, Love Song**), Moore had already started his own independent label, Airborn, on which he would not only produce his own albums but also projects by **Aslan, Albrecht and Roley,** and **Mark Heard.** Always an innovator, Moore would later be responsible for the first direct-to-disc album in the Christian market, *The Live Studio Concert.* That project also reveals him as a performer whose wit is as compelling as his music. A noted humorist, Moore has blended music and comedy (funny stories and silly songs) into his performances for over thirty years.

Moore's style has grown and matured over the years but '60s acoustic rock (James Taylor, Crosby, Stills and Nash) seems always to be at the base. On *Wilmore,* he put together a trio with Doug Southworth and Roger Hughes and served up songs that remind some reviewers of early **Bruce Cockburn.** For *Airborne,* he formed a similar unofficial group with his wife, Kerry, Ed Kilbourne, and **Mark Heard.** Both *Wilmore* and *Airborne* would be reissued on Hartsong in 1979. *Silence Is Music* is appropriately quiet. Beginning with "Good Morning, Sunshine" and ending with "Song for Nightfall," it takes the listener through the day (cf. Moody Blues' *Days of Future Passed*) with songs of thanksgiving for the beauty of nature. *Death Defying Leap* heats up with a few more electric and peppier moments ("Surfin' All Day"), including remakes of some songs from *Silence.* Both **Pat Terry** and **Mark Heard** are among the supporting cast.

After the initial excitement of the Jesus movement revival subsided, Moore continued to produce for a variety of artists and to make barely noticed independent albums from time to time. *Champion* is actually an edited version of *Dauntless.* The indie Christian scene suddenly noticed him as "a new artist" when he released *Mystery.* The album was received as music in touch with the times. "Let's Go Shopping" offers a satirical look at the obsessions of American consumerism. "Mary" is a song of tribute for the person who—though usually ignored by Protestants—is the most godly character in the Bible aside from Jesus.

Ron David Moore

1991—*The Vision's Clear* (Warner Alliance); 1992—*My House* (Warner Alliance); 1994—*Shape of Your Heart;* 1998—*Way with Words* (Premiere).

Christian country singer Ron David Moore is well regarded as a prominent songwriter in mainstream country music. Moore, whose albums often get listed or filed with those of **Ron Moore** (or vice versa), grew up in a small town in South Carolina, where his first involvements with music were singing and playing pedal steel guitar for southern gospel groups. In 1979, he became a part of Jeannie C. Riley's touring band, and then in 1980 signed on with T. G. Sheppard. The pressures of the road got to him, however, and he would spend much of the '80s as a cocaine addict. He also sought throughout that decade to make it as a solo country artist, and though the career failed, his songs were picked up and recorded by such persons as Mickey Gilley, Alan Jackson, Johnny Lee, T. G. Sheppard, George Strait, Conway Twitty, and Tammy Wynette. In 1989, Moore got his life together after his brother, now a minister, came to pastor a church in the area and he "felt obliged" to attend. He felt particularly convicted one morning when his nine-year-old son answered an altar call to make the decision for Christ expected in his tradition, and he joined the boy at the altar in dedicating his own life to the Lord as well. Since then, Moore has made albums of "positive country" geared specifically for the Christian market. Moore's contemporary sound is not too dissimilar from the more country outings of **Steven Curtis Chapman.** His song "Spiritual Storm" (from *My House*) speaks of resting in the eye of God to survive the tempests of life. The title song to *Shape of Your Heart* seeks to offer healing for broken homes.

Christian radio hits: "Spiritual Storm" (# 12 in 1993).

A. J. Mora

1996—*Transformed* (N'Soul); 2000—*Soul of a DJ.*

A. J. Mora is a Christian DJ who began by placing a number of dance tracks on *Nitro Praise* compilation albums released by N'Soul. His full-length albums present music that appeals to fans of the hardcore rave scene—very beat-heavy, fast songs with a neodisco feel to them. Mora makes use of sampled vocals as well as inviting a number of guest vocalists to sing on the projects. Tracks like "He Is Love" and "Take Me Higher" feature overtly Christian lyrics that reconceive dance-house music as a subset of praise and worship.

Christian radio hits: "I Found Something Real" (# 24 in 1996).

Moral Support

See **Andy McCarroll.**

Morella's Forest

Shawn Johnson, gtr.; Christopher McCorkle, bass; Nate McCorkle, drums; Sydney Rentz, voc. 1990—*Morella's Forest* (Narrowpath); 1995—*Hang Out* [EP] (Tooth and Nail); 1995—*Superdeluxe*; 1996—*Ultraphonic Hiss*; 1998—*From Dayton with Love.*

Morella's Forest is an ultra-alternative female-fronted band similar in sound to Lush, Veruca Salt, or Mazzy Star. The signature style features subdued, almost bored vocals (no screaming) spread thinly over a mass of buzzing **Starflyer 59-**style guitars. The group comes from Dayton, Ohio, and might also be compared with such mainstream bands as Belly or The Breeders (which also have Dayton connections).

Morella's Forest released a few custom projects (a demo called *Bass* and an EP called *Bozur*), but did not garner much attention until they were picked up by Tooth and Nail. *Superdeluxe* was coproduced by Chris Colbert of **Breakfast with Amy** and **Fluffy** fame. A shoegazer affair, it includes the coffeehouse ballad "Oceana" and a song called "Fizzle Kiss," which features ethereal background vocals courtesy of **The Throes'** Bill Campbell. *Hang Out* features a cover of "Voices Carry" by 'Til Tuesday and some songs from the *Superdeluxe* sessions that emphasize the pop half of the noise-pop equation. In the same vein, on *Ultraphonic Hiss,* Morella's Forest tones down the static buzz that was part of the wall of sound Sydney Rentz had to sing over on previous projects. The result is a less innovative but more accessible album that takes a fairly straightforward approach to modern rock. "Pastel Straws" actually has a **Sixpence None the Richer** feel to it and "Butterscotch Boy" features particularly melodic guitar lines. The group then added some keyboards and spacey sci-fi effects ("Bounty Hunter") for *From Dayton with Love,* which includes the catchy pop song "Living on Takeout" and a clever cover of Kim Wilde's "Kids in America." In terms of content, Morella's Forest favor songs with obscure lyrics that sound sort of Christian to those who are on the lookout for such inferences. For instance, in "Gate Called Beautiful" (a possible reference to the story in Acts 3:1–10), Sydney sings, "finding such a gift / was not done on my own."

Nate McCorkle left the band to join **Johnny Q. Public.** The group separated from Tooth and Nail in 2000 but planned to continue recording as an independent act.

Cindy Morgan

1992—*Real Life* (Word); 1993—*A Reason to Live*; 1995—*Under the Waterfall*; 1996—*Listen*; 1998—*The Loving Kind*; 2000—*The Best So Far*; 2001—*Elementary.*

Cindy Morgan (b. 1968) grew up in Harrigate, Tennessee, and worked in shows at the Dollywood Theme Park before catching her break in Christian music. As a session singer in Knoxville, she also contributed vocals to projects by Michael Bolton, **Ray Boltz, Steve Camp, Carman, Wes King, Babbie Mason,** and **Point of Grace.** Then, after signing with Word, she released one of the most successful debut albums in the history of contemporary Christian music. *Real Life* produced three Number One songs—and another that went to Number Two. Still, the true measure of Morgan's career would be her ability to change with the times, adopting different musical styles on almost every album. With a voice often likened to Mariah Carey or Anita Baker, Morgan proved that, like those artists, she would not be tied down to a single format.

The first two projects were produced by Mark Hammond and they present Morgan as an R&B diva. "It's Gonna Be Heaven" and the title track from *Real Life* bounce along like Paula Abdul dance-pop songs, while "Let It Be Love" resembles one of Gloria Estefan's slow-but-rhythmic ballads. Much better is "How Could I Ask for More?" a soulful song of thanks that recalls classic **Andraé Crouch** and remains Morgan's all-time best song. *A Reason to Live* differs from the debut primarily in its lyrical content. Morgan eschews evangelistic anthems in favor of more personal yet equally rousing songs—cowriting eight of the tracks. The title track offers the simple advice, "You can make life all it can be, but you can't make it what it's not." Otherwise, the opening "Picture Me in Paradise" is basically "It's Gonna Be Heaven" redux, lyrically and musically. On *Under the Waterfall,* Morgan's style shifts rather abruptly toward the adult contemporary market. Songs like "Sweet Days of Grace" and "I Know You" offer a delicate assurance of faith. But then, just when many fans thought they had lost another artist to the adult contemporary glut, Morgan came roaring back with a modern-rock album in the same piano-driven genre as Tori Amos or Kate Bush. That program, *Listen,* is generally regarded as her finest product. The title track is as bouncy as anything on her debut but with reference to jazz rather than disco. On other tracks, as *CCM's* April Hefner put it, "Morgan lets loose with a verve and spirit that shakes foundations ("God Is Love") while also offering such vulnerability as to tingle any spine ("Need")." *Listen* was produced by **Brent Bourgeois** and Craig Hansen. *The Loving Kind* represents yet another diversion—a mostly worship album organized around the concept of Christ's last week on earth. "Take My Life" and "Praise the King" are hymns, one of dedication, the other of praise. Morgan sings a duet with **Wes King** on "The Last Supper." For her greatest hits collection, she would record a remake of Todd Rundgren's "Love Is the Answer" (made popular by England Dan and John Ford Coley, cf. **Jody Davis, Tony Melendez**). On *Elementary,* she explored a variety of genres, including Gershwin-like jazz and techno, in addition to her usual pop styles. The first single from that project, "Good Thing," flirts with an electronica sound. On the song "Believe" Morgan advises, "Take a ride / Take a long holiday / From the fear / That's been keeping you at bay." Morgan is author of the book *Barefoot on Barbed Wire* (Harvest House, 2001) and she is married to author Sigmund Brouwer. The couple maintain homes both in Nashville and in Red Deer, Alberta.

Christian radio hits: "Let It Be Love" (# 1 for 2 weeks in 1992); "It's Gonna Be Heaven" (# 1 for 4 weeks in 1992); "Real Life" (# 1 in 1993); "Love Can Break Your Fall" (# 2 in 1993); "A Reason to Live" (# 14 in 1993); "Storybook" (# 4 in 1994); "Picture Me in Paradise" (# 1 in 1994); "We Can Live Together" (# 1 for 3 weeks in 1994); "The Days of Innocence" (# 1 in 1994); "I'll Stand" (# 13 in 1995); "Sweet Days of Grace" (# 3 in 1995); "Reaching with His Love" (# 22 in 1995); "Painted a Rainbow" (# 10 in 1996); "Listen" (# 2 in 1997); "The Master's Hand" (# 9 in 1997); "Moon Days" (# 4 in 1997).

Dove Awards: 1993 New Artist of the Year.

Van Morrison

Selected: 1968—*Astral Weeks* (Warner Bros.); 1970—*Moondance; His Band and the Street Choir;* 1971—*Tupelo Honey;* 1972—*St. Dominic's Preview;* 1978—*Wavelength;* 1979—*Into the Music;* 1980—*Common One;* 1982—*Beautiful Vision;* 1983—*Inarticulate Speech of the Heart;* 1984—*A Sense of Wonder* (Mercury); 1986—*No Guru, No Method, No Teacher;* 1987—*Poetic Champions Compose;* 1989—*Avalon Sunset;* 1990—*Enlightenment; The Best of Van Morrison* (Polydor); 1991—*Hymns to the Silence;* 1993—*The Best of Van Morrison, Vol. 2; Too Long in Exile;* 1994—*A Night in San Francisco;* 1995—*Days Like These;* 1996—*How Long Has This Been Going On?; Songs of Mose Allison: Tell Me Something Good* (Polygram); 1997—*The Healing Game* (Polydor); 1998—*The Philosopher's Stone;* 1999—*Back on Top* (Pointblank); 2000—*The Skiffle Sessions: Live in Belfast, 1998.*

www.harbour.sfu.ca/~hayward/van

Universally regarded as one of the most important singers and songwriters in the history of rock and roll, Van Morrison is a self-described "Christian mystic" who is very private about all aspects of his life, including his faith. In 1985, rock journalist Steve Turner—who is also a Christian—interviewed Morrison for his book *Hungry for Heaven* and caught the artist at a moment when he was surprisingly candid. Nine years later, Turner published a biography of the artist titled *Van Morrison: Too Late to Stop Now* (Viking Press, 1994). Morrison threatened to sue Turner and even attempted to buy all copies of the book from the publisher to prevent its release. Exactly what aspects of Turner's book incensed him is unclear. The biography is positive in its portrait, though it does present Morrison as a notoriously private but ambiguously religious man, none of which is debatable. *CCM* opines that the objections stemmed from a general distaste for publicity according to which Morrison "hates to have *anything* written about him." Whether or not Morrison is to be regarded as "a Christian artist" depends very much on one's conception of Christianity. Morrison himself rejects such labels. Still, his songs have often portrayed a spirituality that makes them especially meaningful to fans of Christian music who sometimes regard some of his recordings as part of the genre.

Morrison was born in Belfast, Northern Ireland, in 1945. His father was an avid collector of blues recordings and his mother, a singer. He would later reveal that as a child he was subject to a number of "unprovoked mystical experiences" that he discussed with no one because "there was no way of talking about it." These experiences, whatever their nature, helped to propel his lifelong spiritual quests. They determined his affection for the poetry of William Blake and John Donne, who had similar "awakenings." In later songs, Morrison would frequently write and sing about his "angel" or muse that comes to him to bequeath inspiration, enlightenment, or just a "sense of wonder" (see, for example, "She Gives Me Religion," "Cypress Avenue," and "Madame George"). At any rate, Morrison became a professional musician by the age of fifteen and by the time he was twenty had formed and recorded with the classic band Them, a group that would compete with The Kinks and The Rolling Stones for mastery of the British rock scene. Their best-known song, for American audiences, remains "Gloria" (with its famous "G-L-O-R-I-A" chorus), in part because it was redone by The Shadows of Knight in 1966 and by Patti Smith in 1975. The band also had hits with "Here Comes the Night" and "Mystic Eyes." Frustrated with the music industry, Morrison disbanded the group (which actually was more of a rotating roster of session musicians—including Jimmy Page—anyway). He was coaxed into recording a few solo demos, one of which became a hit in the United States when it was released without his permission. That song, "Brown-Eyed Girl" (# 10 in 1967), remains one of the most recognizable songs from what would be dubbed "the summer of love."

Morrison would go on to make some of the most important albums in rock history. In 2000, when rock critics composed their lists of the "100 Best Albums of the Century," almost everyone included *Astral Weeks, Moondance, Tupelo Honey,* and *St. Dominic's Preview* on his or her list. *His Band and the Street Choir* from the same period includes the hits "Domino" (# 9 in 1970) and "Blue Money" (# 23 in 1971). "Wild Night" (# 28 in 1971) from *Tupelo Honey* would later be redone by John Mellencamp and Me'shell Ndegéocello. Other standout songs from this prolific period include "Into the Mystic," "Caravan," "Moondance," "Tupelo Honey," and "Jackie Wilson Said (I'm in Heaven When You Smile)."

Little is known of Morrison's personal life except that he married a woman whom he nicknamed Janet Planet in 1968 and that they divorced in 1973 (the former Mrs. Morrison, now a Los Angeles songwriter named Janet Morrison Minto should not be confused with the jazz singer who has tried to capitalize on the semi-famous name by recording as Janet Planet). Morrison has maintained that despite the somewhat spacey nature of his lyrics, he never used hallucinogenics: "I've always had experiences without drugs. Anything like that would impair it." But from *Astral Weeks* on, his albums have evinced spiritual yearning, amidst themes of personal transformation. Terms like "sense of wonder," "beautiful vision," "mystical ecstasy," and "rapture" pepper his poetry, pointing to some sort of connection with a world beyond what is experienced through the five senses.

On *Into the Music* the imagery suddenly became more specific, setting off a rash of speculation that the artist had become "a born-again Christian." But then in the liner notes to *Inarticulate Speech of the Heart* (his most panned project), Morrison offered thanks to L. Ron Hubbard, the founder of Scientology. Next, *A Sense of Wonder* would offer his most overtly religious statements to date, with songs drawing on Celtic and specifically Christian imagery once again ("Ancient of Days," "The Master's Eyes," "A New Kind of Man"). At this time, he explained to Steve Turner that childhood experiences and ongoing perception of mystical guidance had led him to study Buddhism, Christianity, and Hinduism, and indeed to enroll in Scientology courses. "All I was interested in," he said, "was somewhere to put my experiences. To find out what they were." Morrison also told Turner of a muse or guiding spirit that directs his life, claiming that he sometimes does not understand his own lyrics. "It's like I'm receiving some sort of inner direction," he explains. "There's something inside that directs me." When Turner asked him how he would describe himself, he replied, "as a Christian mystic." Earlier in the interview, however, Morrison had indicated that he was unable to accept that Jesus Christ was God. Accordingly, Turner asked him why he regarded his mysticism as "specifically Christian." He replied, "Because I'm not a Buddhist or a Hindu. I was born in a Christian environment in a Christian country, and I was born after the Christ event. So that makes me a Christian."

After this encounter, however, Morrison's musical "statements of faith" only seemed to increase. In 1986, he issued *No Guru, No Method, No Teacher,* an album that by its very title seems to suggest rejection of Hubbard, New Age, Scientology, and all other human systems of enlightenment. In the song, "In the Garden" (perhaps intentionally borrowing its title from a gospel hymn), Morrison declares his only needs: "No guru, no method, no teacher / Just you and I and nature / And the Father and the Son and the Holy Ghost / In the garden wet with rain." Christians (and others) understandably took this to represent some sort of a conclusion to his quest—a rejection of generic spirituality in favor of a relationship with the Holy Trinity. And *then* he released *Avalon Sunset,* his first album in

years to match the 1968–1972 oeuvre in quality and a record that is, by all accounts, an outright gospel album. The project opens boldly with "Whenever God Shines His Light," an overtly Christian song about living in the name of Jesus, sung as a duet with Great Britain's most famous contemporary Christian music star, **Cliff Richard.** The album continues with what has since become a gospel standard, "When Will I Ever Learn to Live in God?" and also includes "Have I Told You Lately?" a gorgeous song of praise to his lover and of thanksgiving to God "who gives us love." The latter song would become a major hit when covered by Rod Stewart (# 5 in 1993). Two years later, Morrison included literal hymns ("Just a Closer Walk with Thee," "Be Thou My Vision") on his *Hymns to the Silence* album. Spiritual themes would be less obvious, however, on the rest of his '90s output—which included a number of detours and side trips. *Too Long in Exile* revisits his early rock and roll years (with a remake of "Gloria"); *How Long Has This Been Going On?* collects jazz standards; *Days Like These* features a title track that would become a peace anthem in Northern Ireland; *The Healing Game* invokes the artist's Belfast childhood; *The Philosopher's Stone* compiles rarities.

In 1993, Morrison was inducted into the Rock and Roll Hall of Fame. In 1996, he received the title Order of the British Empire.

Grammy Awards: 1995 Best Pop Collaboration with Vocals [with The Chieftains] ("Have I Told You Lately?"); 1997 Best Pop Collaboration with Vocals [with John Lee Hooker] ("Don't Look Back").

Amy Morriss

1995—*I'm a Believer* (Myrrh); 1997—*Within the Sound of Your Voice.*

Pop singer Amy Morriss (b. 1969) has had two incarnations so far in Christian music, releasing two albums so distinct that they sound like they come from different artists. Morriss grew up a Southern Baptist in Tyler, Texas, where her father, Steve Morriss, played keyboards for **The Cruse Family.** Blessed with an incredible voice—often compared to that of Celine Dion—Morriss began singing at an early age, at first with her sisters in a general market trio called Ms. Adventures. That group had a Top 10 hit on the Dance charts with the song "Undeniable" in 1990. Morriss then signed with Myrrh and recorded the Christian R&B album *I'm a Believer.* Produced by Dennis Matosky, the album brought out similarities to artists she claims as her major influences, **Gladys Knight** and **Aretha Franklin.** The title track (not the Monkees' song) and equally upbeat "Givin' It Up" left audiences amazed that such powerful soulful sounds could come forth from Morriss, a blonde, white woman just a little over five feet tall. But on *Within the Sound of Your Voice,* producer Dennis Matosky redefined her as an adult rock singer more in the mold of Sheryl

Crow. The latter album's sound is driven by strong guitars and Morriss often sings in a lower register. Standout tracks include "In the Name of Jesus" and "Underneath All Stars."

Christian radio hits: "I'm a Believer" (# 18 in 1995); "Devotion" (# 25 in 1996).

Mortal

Jerome Fontamillas, bass, voc., elec.; Jyro Xhan, gtr., voc., elec. // Ed Benrock, gtr. (+ 1994, –1995); Troy Yahuda, drums (+ 1994, –1996). 1992—*Lusis* (Intense); 1993—*Fathom; Intense Live Series, Vol. 5;* 1994—*Wake;* 1995—*Pura;* 1996—*Mortal* (5 Min. Walk); 1998—*Godspeed* (KMG).

Mortal began as a Christian version of Skinny Puppy or Nine Inch Nails, though they showed enough originality from the very start to avoid being written off as a clone band. Combining elements of metal, pop, techno, and punk, the group participated in the crafting of a style that would eventually be called "industrial music." *HM* said (of the album *Lusis*), "it's got the energy and minor key discordant feel of metal and the bounce and rhythm of dance music." Christian music's premier critic Brian Quincy Newcomb went ape over Mortal's first album, declaring it "the strongest debut project to enter the alternative Christian market in years" and insisting that it "achieves the kind of innovation, integrity, and cutting edge timeliness that will make it relevant to all fans of the genre, whether they are Christian or not." Produced by alternative pioneer **Terry Taylor**, *Lusis* takes its name from the New Testament Greek word for "freedom." The album opens and closes with "Enfleshed," an industrial noise/dance hybrid similar in sound to Rob Zombie's "Dragula." Lyrically, the song presents the redemptive implications of Christ's *incarnation* (as opposed to crucifixion), an advanced theological point rarely touched on in contemporary Christian music. *Fathom* delivers more of the same sound on its energetic songs ("Electrify," "Godspeed," "Alive and Awake") while dragging a bit on the slow ones. Around this time, Mortal would also contribute the beautiful acoustic song "Bleeder" to the first **Browbeats** project.

Wake was announced as the band's final album, complete with a much-hyped "farewell tour." In reality, however, the group was simply pulling a Barbra Streisand (saying goodbye and then not leaving), as they would go on to record two more complete albums, not counting the compilation *Godspeed*. In any case, *Wake* reveals a very different side to the group, which had temporarily expanded into a live band (with Benrock recruited from **LSU**). On the one hand, Nirvana's influence is felt throughout, with grunge replacing dance on tracks like "Filter," "June First," and "Oceanful." On the other hand, the album is more mellow, with a number of ballads (including the standout "Fall") and songs with Beatlesque harmonies (including a cover of "Nowhere Man"). The Mortal duo of Jyro Xhan (who sometimes—but inconsistently—spells his first name

Gyro) and Jerome Fontamillas produced the album themselves and soon became established as producers for a number of other artists as well.

After the official disbanding of Mortal, Xhan and Fontamillas formed **Fold Zandura,** which most critics and fans regarded as Mortal recording under a different name. Then, to add to the confusion, **Fold Zandura**'s self-titled 1995 album was quickly followed by another 1995 album released by Mortal. *Pura* sounds almost nothing like anything previously released by either of the two groups. It is mainly a set of ambient, instrumental music played on synthesizers. *HM* described it as "what **Jeff Johnson** would sound like if he used a techno beat." Of the few songs with vocals, "Grip" revisits the old Mortal sound of the *Lusis* album and "Nightfall and Splendor" is an adult contemporary worship song sung by guest Holly Steinhilber. The next year would bring the self-titled *Mortal,* the group's debut and swan song for the 5 Min. Walk label. That album seems to bring the group full circle, delivering another package of industrial music with a dance groove. Three of the tracks were actually recorded under the **Fold Zandura** name, confirming everyone's suspicions concerning the artificiality of name distinctions.

The group has often incorporated guests into their projects. Mark Salomon of **The Crucified** and **Stavesacre** does vocals on "Godspeed" and "Neplusultra" from *Fathom.* Jeff Bellew (from **The Crucified, Chatterbox,** and **Stavesacre**) and Bryan Gray **(The Blamed, Six Feet Deep,** and **Left Out)** also lend a hand from time to time. Mark Rodriguez was often responsible for mixing the group's sound, a role so significant for this genre that by the last outing he was being listed as a member of the band.

Mortification

Steve Rowe, voc., bass; Michael Carlisle, gtr. (–1995); Jayson Sherlock, drums (–1994) // Phil Gibson, drums (+ 1994, –1995); Bill Rice, drums (+ 1995, –1996); Jason Campbell, gtr. (+ 1995, –1996); Keith Bannister, drums (+ 1996, –2000); Lincoln Bowen, gtr. (+ 1996); Adam Zaffarese, drums (+ 2000). 1991—*Mortification* [a.k.a. *Break the Curse*] (Intense); 1992—*Scrolls of the Megilloth;* 1993—*Post Momentary Affliction; Live Planetarium;* 1994—*Blood World;* 1995—*Primitive Rhythm Machine; The Best of Five Years;* 1996—*Live without Fear* (Rowe); *Envision Evangelene;* 1997—*Noah Sat Down and Listened to the Mortification Live CD While Having a Coffee;* 1998—*Triumph of Mercy;* 1999—*Hammer of God;* 2000—*Ten Years Live Not Dead; The Silver Cord Is Severed.*

In 2000 *Phantom Tollbooth* would refer to Mortification as a "living metal dinosaur," approaching the group with the same incredulous awe evinced by the paleontologists catching their first glimpse of Jurassic Park. The band that inspired such wonder was from Christian music's metal heydey, still pounding out the noise at the end of the millennium, and appreciation for such tenure could only be deepened by an awareness that front man Steve Rowe had struggled with leukemia throughout the last few years of the decade, his physical mortality as much in question as that of his chosen art form.

The group formed in Australia. They started out calling themselves Lightforce (with Cameron Hall rather than Michael Carlisle on guitar) and recorded an album called *Break the Curse* under that name in 1990. It was re-released after Mortification made it big, along with *The Best of Lightforce: Mortification's Beginnings,* which was not really a collection of that band's "best," but a compilation of *all* tracks from two Metal Blade EPs *(Battlezone; Mystical Thieves)* plus a few live takes from 1989.

On their first four albums (counting the live one), Mortification embodies the sound of a death metal band and betrays all the limitations of that genre. Vocals are growled, not sung; guitars and rhythm keep a plodding, unchanging tempo with virtually no melody. It was often pointed out (especially with regard to the first two projects) that all of the band's songs sounded alike and that they were all . . . well, ugly—but such facts were (and still are) of little consequence to the band's legion of fans who *like* ugly and tend to prefer familiarity to innovation. The group began to move away from grindcore toward power metal (with comparisons shifting from Slayer to Iron Maiden) on *Post Momentary Affliction,* but the real change would come when Rowe began screaming some of his vocals on *Blood World.* The last album for Intense *(Primitive Rhythm Machine)* regressed stylistically to more of the old grindcore sound again; Rowe has since said that it "wasn't really a band effort. . . . I had all these ideas that people just couldn't play."

Rowe has described the group's role at this time as "metal missionaries," allowing that their ministry may have been focused on "a small and segmented part of today's society that nevertheless needs to hear the gospel as much as anyone." Their message, typically, was an in-your-face-challenge to the devil worshipers who supposedly make up a large part of the fan base for death and power metal (the main lyric to "J.G.S.H." from *Blood World* is the repeated line, "Jesus grinds Satan's head"). The band also targeted Roman Catholics for evangelism in a rather disturbing way, claiming that "most people in the Roman Catholic Church are not born again" (apparently because they have never "accepted Christ" in an altar call ritual or because they do not usually describe their faith in the language of "a personal relationship with Jesus"). But the band was effective. Keith Bannister, who joined as drummer in 1996, had himself become a Christian at a Mortification concert. Memorable songs from Mortification's Intense period include "Bathed in Blood," "Brutal Warfare," "The Abyss," "Terminate Damnation," and "Grind Planetarium" (which mocks the rock star's desire to be worshiped). Predictably, the group had few

fans among critics. *7ball* suggested that *The Best of Mortification* should have been a blank CD.

Rowe formed his own label and, after another live album, released *Envision Evangelene* by a new version of Mortification that sported a seventeen-year-old shredder guitarist (Lincoln Bowen). The style was now firmly established as classic metal, especially as manifested in the British tradition. The opening, title track is an eighteen-minute opus with blazing lead guitar. *Triumph of Mercy* includes one of the band's all-time best songs, "Influence," which commissions the listener to serve God rather than seek human acclaim. The album also features a song that seems to testify to Rowe's miraculous healing from cancer ("Visited by an Angel"). The title track attributes this to the prayers of his fans: "Warrior upon warrior around our distant globe / Kept the vigil fight of prayer of power that can't be stopped / And as the folks cried out to God / He heard them and I live. . . ." After that album was recorded, however, Rowe again became very sick and came near death. But he didn't die, and a year later another album appeared. *Hammer of God* revisits the classic sounds of '80s metal (with conspicuous addition of keyboards), leaving most critics complaining that it sounded "dated." *HM* loved it, however, regarding it as "a true tribute to the classic metal sounds that influenced the band from the beginning." The songs "Lock Up the Night" and "Liberal Mediocrity" employ the brutal aural assault against those whom the band perceives to be enemies of God in the world and in the church. *Ten Years Live Not Dead* presents a 1999 concert from the group's homeland with a run-through of favorites from the past and one new song ("Dead Man Walking"). *The Silver Cord Is Severed* weds classic rock melodies with revived '80s metal in a style that somehow seems more modern than retro. *HM* would say, "They have somehow taken the old hairspray rock that was thrown away ten years ago and made it bearable to listen to again." The songs "Hardware" and "Bring the Joy" are standouts. The title to the album reflects Rowe's priorities and awareness of mortality via a reference to Ecclesiastes 12: "Remember God before the silver cord is broken."

Mothership

See **Mad at the World.**

Movies With Heroes (a.k.a. **Mack the Coffee Man**)

Jeremy Bentley, drums; Jeff Royer, bass; Keith Wilson, voc. // John Donohue, gtr. (+ 2000). By Mack the Coffee Man: 1998—*Every Blessing Tonight* [EP] (independent); 1999—*Light Pours through the Sun/The Sun Has Been Cut Out of the Sky* (Burnt Toast). By Movies With Heroes: 2000—*Movies With Heroes/Ran Away to Sea* [split EP]; 2001—*The Slate* [EP].

An indie band from Lancaster, Pennsylvania, Mack the Coffee Man was described by *True Tunes* as "**U2** and The Cure mixed together and run through an emo filter." In 2000, they tired of being asked "Which one of you is Mack?" and changed their name to Movies With Heroes. Fronted by Keith Wilson, the group alternates between hard and dreamy moods, performing songs with introspective and "journal musing" lyrics. On their debut EP, "Superpowers in the Four Corners" is about Wilson's separation from friends who have been influential on his life. "October's Anthem" meditates on what can be learned from both good and bad experiences in life. The long and strange title of the sophomore project owes to its origin as two separate EPs that ended up being released together (against the band's wishes) as a full-length project. The first half of the album (the "Light Pours Through" section) is raw and emotionally intense. On what would have been the title track to that first section, Wilson remembers how, as a child, when he saw rays of light pouring through the clouds, he thought each time that "Jesus was on his way." Then, he continues, "But we're all grown up now, aren't we? It's just chemistry of light and water, isn't it?" After adding another guitarist and changing their name, the band contributed three songs to an EP that also has tracks by the group Ran Away to Sea. A second EP of their own material *(The Slate)* opens with a song that compares Hurricane Floyd to shifting perceptions in the fashion world ("Hurricanes and Runways").

M Pire

See **Joshua** (Los Angeles).

Mukala

Jason Collum, drums; Dan Mukala, voc., kybrd.; Alex Nifong, gtr., voc. 1998—*Fiction* (Essential).

Nashville band Mukala (named after its leader, whose name is spelled Muckala on his birth certificate) produced one of the most solid pop albums of the late '90s, a record comparable in sound to Smash Mouth's *Astro Lounge* and Sugar Ray's *14:59*. A native of Minneapolis and a graduate of Belmont University (in Nashville), Dan Mukala has also written or cowritten Christian radio hits performed by **Benjamin** ("On the Inside"), **Clay Crosse** ("He Walked a Mile"), and others. Alex Nifong toured with **Zilch** and would go on to play with **Foreverafter,** whose songs were produced and mostly cowritten by Mukala. Mukala (the band)'s music is very danceable, but unlike many keyboard-driven techno projects, the songs are so well crafted that any one of them would be fetching on an acoustic guitar. The melodies are catchy and the choruses are filled with memorable hooks. As *CCM* indicated, there is not a bad—or even a mediocre—track on the album. "Soap" testifies to the

power of God's love to cleanse the human heart. "Skip to the End" directs the inquisitive to the book of Revelation if they want to know how the future will eventually resolve. "Regret" fosters a view of life as fraught with possibilities and second chances. "Original Sin" decries the so-called art of those who exploit society's seemingly insatiable appetite for anything shocking. "Jesus Shirt" addresses the superficiality of mistaking faith for a fashion statement. In "High," a pilot reflects on the grandeur of the earth and the enduring grace of God that holds everything together.

Christian radio hits: "Soap" (# 13 in 1998); "Skip to the End" (# 4 in 1999).

Maria Muldaur

Selected: 1980—*Gospel Nights* [with The Chamber Brothers] (Takoma); 1982—*There Is a Love* (Myrrh); 1983—*Sweet and Low* (Tudor); *Transbluecency* (Uptown); 1991—*On the Sunny Side* (Music for Little People); 1993—*Louisiana Love Call* (Black Top); 2000—*Maria Muldaur's Music for Lovers* (Telarc).

Maria Muldaur had one of the most memorable hits of the '70s with her sexy take on "Midnight at the Oasis" (# 6 in 1974). She announced that she was "a born again Christian" in 1980 and produced some music for the contemporary Christian music community. Born Maria d'Amato in 1945, the singer grew up in Greenwich Village and became part of the '60s folk scene where she sang with John Sebastian and Steve Katz in an early group called the Even Dozen Jug Band. She married folksinger Geoff Muldaur and the two of them released two albums together. After their divorce in 1972, both became acclaimed solo artists, though only Maria would see (brief) commercial success. Her second solo album (*Maria Muldaur,* Reprise, 1974) went gold on the basis of "Midnight at the Oasis" (# 6 in 1974). A follow-up (*Waitress in the Donut Shop,* Reprise, 1974) produced a second hit with the Lieber and Stoller standard "I'm a Woman" (# 12 in 1974). Three more albums failed to sell despite some critical acclaim.

The catalyst for Maria's conversion to Christianity was **Bob Dylan**'s *Slow Train Coming.* "I realized through the words of the songs on that album," she told *CCM* in 1981, "that my life had become not necessarily an evil life, but a very *sloppy* one." This thinking led her to a moment of decision when her daughter Jenni (who later also became a recording artist) was injured in a near-fatal traffic accident. Shortly thereafter, she accompanied an African American friend to a black Pentecostal church where she says, "They did a laying on of hands and I received the baptism in the Holy Spirit and started speaking in tongues." Muldaur would continue to perform her usual set—which had always included gospel songs anyway—but gave testimony to her faith in key ways. An early concert with The Chambers Brothers (famous for the 1968 hit "Time Has Come

Today") was recorded as *Gospel Nights*. The album features such sterling selections as "My Jesus Is All" (cf. **Glenn Kaiser**) and "Nobody's Fault But Mine" (cf. Kaiser, **Darrell Mansfield, Seventy Sevens**), but it disappointed contemporary Christian music fans in that the repertoire consisted of standards and hymns rather than new songs. Muldaur's 1982 album for Myrrh *(There Is a Love)* would deliver more of what they were looking for (adult contemporary Christian ballads) and spawned one hit for the Christian radio stations. The album features covers of **T Bone Burnett**'s "Keep My Eyes on You" and Stevie Wonder's "I Was Made to Love You." It concludes with a blues song, "Is My Living in Vain?" Both of Muldaur's first two albums were produced by **T Bone Burnett.**

In general, Muldaur has done best with albums geared for the general market. *Sweet and Low* is a smart collection of jazz songs and includes a number of tracks with spiritual themes ("Adam and Eve Had the Blues," "There's Going to Be the Devil to Pay," "Brother, Seek and Ye Shall Find"). *Transbluecency* is more jazz and was even better received critically. On *Louisiana Love Call,* Muldaur delves into New Orleans music (more jazz, of course), with guests like Dr. John and **Aaron Neville** helping her celebrate that city's musical heritage. *On the Sunny Side* is a children's album.

Christian radio hits: "Keep My Eyes on You" (# 20 in 1982).

David Mullen

1989—*Revival* (Myrrh); 1991—*Faded Blues*; 1994—*David Mullen* (Warner Alliance).

David Mullen became the first rock act ever to win the Gospel Music Association's Best New Artist Award. Born in 1964, he grew up in Cullman, Alabama. He testifies to a brief wayward period involving substance abuse, but credits his dedication to Christ primarily to Bible reading. At one point, a game of Trivial Pursuit with friends led to a discussion of biblical themes (prompted by some obscure question about Moses). Somewhat convicted, Mullen left town and sequestered himself for a full month, reading the entire Bible and meditating on its contents. This led him to an assurance of faith and, after graduating from the University of Florida with a degree in biology, he moved to Nashville to pursue a career in Christian music. Mullen toured with a band called One Blood, featuring guitarist Scott MacLeod and drummer Kevin Twit. He is married to recording artist **Nicole C. Mullen.** They are one of the only interracial couples in contemporary Christian music (David is white and Nicole is black).

Mullen's versatile voice has been compared to **Geoff Moore, Russ Taff,** and even to **U2**'s Bono when he sings in his lower register. His bluesy rock music is perhaps closer to John Mellencamp in general style. Though successful in the Christian market, Mullen was supposed to be a crossover act in the mainstream as well. He was signed to a dual contract with Myrrh and Warner Brothers with his projects being promoted by the respective labels in both fields. At the time, such an approach was experimental and industry insiders watched closely to see if it would work. It didn't. Mullen's "no compromise" Christian rock was embraced within the little contemporary Christian music scene but despite major label support his songs did not get airplay in the general market and singles failed to chart.

The title song for *Revival* is a celebrative gospel tune with lyrics that lend themselves to polyvalent interpretation. "Live So God Can Use You" is an optimistic anthem encouraging youth to make a difference in the world; it was inspired by a Muddy Waters song with a similar name ("Why Don't You Live So God Can Use You?") and it features a chorus reminiscent of "Will the Circle Be Unbroken?" The closing song, "Hang My Head and Cry," offers a lament of personal repentance. *Faded Blues* opens with its title track, a high-production rocker about coming to grips with the past. Mullen has said that the sophomore project is a concept album, built around the theme that "a person is known by their pain." Thus, the song "Alone" chronicles the artist's realization that he would rather taste death than be alone and devoid of God's presence. "Water into Wine" is built on a mixed metaphor that doesn't quite work: when one is drowning in a "sea of tears," Jesus turns the water into wine. The centerpiece of the self-titled project is a song called "Hero," which presents Jesus as the Christian's role model. *David Mullen* generally exhibits more stylistic variety than the first two albums, ranging from acoustic ballads to R&B. Since 1992, Mullen has concentrated on songwriting and has seen over a hundred of his songs recorded by other artists, including his wife.

Christian radio hits: "Somebody Say Amen" (# 7 in 1990); "Heavens to Betsy" (# 1 for 4 weeks in 1990); "Revival" (# 7 in 1990); "Water into Wine" (# 5 in 1991); "Under the Same Sun" (# 9 in 1992).

Dove Award: 1990 New Artist.

Nicole C. Mullen (a.k.a. **Nicole**)

By Nicole: 1991—*Don't Let Me Go* (Frontline); 1992—*Wish Me Love*. By Nicole C. Mullen: 2000—*Nicole C. Mullen* (Word); 2001—*Talk about It; Following His Hand: A Ten Year Journey* (KMG).

www.nicolecmullen.com

Nicole C. Mullen (b. 1967) met with only moderate success when she first tried to break into contemporary Christian music as a solo artist in the early '90s; her name at the time was Nicole Coleman, though she recorded as simply Nicole. In 2000, she came back big time with a much hailed album that benefitted from her wealth of experience (and connections) in the Christian music subculture. An African American woman from Cincinnati, Ohio, the artist grew up in a fairly poor, urban environment, but one sustained by faith (her grandparents were Pentecostal ministers). In 1984, she attended Bible college in Dallas, Texas, and sang with a group called Living Praise, where she caught the attention of Christian R&B artist/producer **Tim Miner**. For many years thereafter, Nicole Coleman would serve primarily in background roles—singing backup, dancing, and, notably, doing choreography for a number of major artists' tours **(Amy Grant, The Newsboys, Michael W. Smith)**. She met and married Christian rock artist **David Mullen**. In 1998, Nicole C. Mullen became the first African American woman ever to have a composition win the Dove award for Song of the Year; the song was "On My Knees," performed by **Jaci Velasquez** (who cowrote it).

Mullen's first album was produced by **Tim Miner** and it tried to present her as a female rap artist, which didn't really work, perhaps in part because there were few female rap artists in Christian music at the time. The song "Don't Let Me Go" is one funky offering from the project that did gain some notice, but otherwise it was the ballads that proved most endearing: "I Need to Know" and "My Everything" are adult contemporary and "Love Is Everything" and "Oh, Jesus Loves Me" (based on the children's song) are midtempo pop. The second album pigeon-holed her as "the Christian Janet Jackson," which was closer to the mark. "Mama Say No" is an upbeat dance tune that shares from personal experience the value of listening to maternal advice; the song touches upon the artist's involvement in a relationship that became physically abusive, a topic she also discussed in some interviews. "Miracles" gets the hip-hop vibe down right with some '70s funk vocal-distortion and an appearance by a guest male rapper. "Show Me" is an especially Janet-ish dance track that calls on God for assistance in godly living and thinking. "Wish Me Love" expresses a longing for love that is eternal.

Since Christian radio stations hardly ever play oldies, Mullen's hits had been forgotten by the end of the '90s, and her self-titled Word debut presented her as though she were a new artist. Drawing on such classic R&B influences as **Aretha Franklin** and Stevie Wonder, Mullen now drew comparisons to Lauryn Hill, especially on the standout tracks "Butterfly" and "Family Tree." A bluesy song, "Black, White, Tan," uses the racial composition of Mullen's family (white husband, mixed race children) to address themes of ethnic diversity and to tell everyone, "You are not a color." The song "Color" deals with a similar theme ("Color is skin deep, but true beauty lives on and on"). "Freedom" refers proudly to the civil rights movement: "We marched in 'Bama / We marched in Tennessee / Brown men and white men / Stood for equality." The album's high-

light is probably the gospel song "Redeemer," inspired by the declaration of Job, "I know that my Redeemer lives" (Job 19:25). Her second project for Word, *Talk about It,* provides what *CCM* called "a no-nonsense collection of soul-stomping grooves." The title track is an especially rhythmic dance number in celebration of the gospel. The album encourages believers to share their faith ("Witness," "Talk about It"). On "Let Me Go" Mullen departs from the adult contemporary mold to which she sometimes seems pressured to conform, and slinks through a sultry declaration of an exodus from fear. In late 2001, KMG released *Following His Hand,* which collects the best songs from Mullen's first two albums.

For trivia buffs: Nicole C. Mullen sings the well-known theme song for the Veggie Tales video *Larry Boy and the Fib from Outer Space,* which was written by her husband. The song has sold over five million copies. She is also the voice of Serena the Cat in the children's video series *Yo Kids!*

Christian radio hits: Don't Let Me Go" (# 6 in 1991); "Wish Me Love" (# 10 in 1992); "Show Me" (# 1 in 1992); "Miracles" (# 10 in 1993).

Dove Awards: 2001 Songwriter of the Year; 2001 Pop/Contemporary Song ("Redeemer").

Rich Mullins

1986—*Rich Mullins* (Reunion); 1987—*Pictures in the Sky;* 1988—*Winds of Heaven . . . Stuff of Earth;* 1989—*Never Picture Perfect;* 1991—*The World As Best As I Remember It, Vol. 1;* 1992—*The World As Best As I Remember It, Vol. 2;* 1993—*A Liturgy, a Legacy, and a Ragamuffin Band;* 1995—*Brother's Keeper;* 1996—*Songs;* 1997—*Canticle of the Plains* [with The Kid Brothers of St. Frank]; 1998—*The Jesus Record* (Myrrh); 1999—*Songs 2* (Reunion).

www.richmullins.com

At the time of his death in 1997, Rich Mullins was the most beloved troubadour in contemporary Christian music and probably came as close as anyone else in the field to being regarded as "a saint." Mullins was famous for his gentle demeanor, his simple lifestyle, his love for children, and his overwhelming compassion for the poor. Many of his songs, such as "Awesome God" and "Sing Your Praise to the Lord," had already become staples of modern hymnody.

Mullins was born in Richmond, Indiana, in 1955. He was raised as a Quaker (Society of Friends) with some connections to the independent Christian Church. Always ecumenical, he would come to work most closely within the Methodist tradition while becoming increasingly enamored of Roman Catholicism. Mullins attended Cincinnati Bible College (cf. **Randy Matthews**) and first came to prominence as a songwriter. An organization called Zion Ministries sponsored a recording of some of his songs in 1980, and in 1982 **Amy Grant** had a huge Christian radio hit with his "Sing Your Praise to the Lord" (# 1 for 10 weeks). It was another four years before he would finally begin recording his own material; in the meantime he served as a Methodist youth pastor in Ohio and as a music minister at a small church in Grand Rapids, Michigan. In 1989, Mullins formed a monk-like order called The Kid Brothers of Saint Frank, after St. Francis of Assisi. In 1993, he put together a loose confederation of musicians called **A Ragamuffin Band,** which at various times included **Jimmy Abegg, Billy Crockett, Rick Elias,** Mark Robertson (of **Brighton, Generation, The Stand, Under Midnight,** and **This Train**) and Aaron Smith (of **Vector** and the **Seventy Sevens**); the group would continue recording after Mullins' death. In 1995, Mullins received a degree in music education from Friends University in Kansas. Involved in social ministry to Native Americans, he moved to Window Rock, Arizona, and lived on a Navajo reservation where he taught music to children. He has often composed songs with a friend who is known only as "Beaker." Mullins performed numerous benefit concerts each year on behalf of Compassion International and other church groups and charitable organizations. It was while traveling to one such event with his close friend **Mitch McVicker** (to benefit a Methodist youth organization) that he lost control of his jeep for some unknown reason. The vehicle rolled on the freeway, ejecting its two passengers. Mullins was then struck by a tractor-trailer and died instantly; McVicker was severely injured. A tribute album with a number of Christian artists singing his songs was released the next year (*Awesome God: A Tribute to Rich Mullins,* Reunion, 1998). Mullins is also the author of a devotional book, *Home* (Voxcorps, 1998). A biography of his life was written by theology professor James Bryan Smith (*Rich Mullins: His Life and Legacy: An Arrow Pointing to Heaven,* Broadman and Holman, 2000).

Mullins' first few albums established him as a competent interpreter of his material. On his self-titled debut, he sets forth a theme that would govern his career: "You should be glad you're alive, and look forward to being dead" (cf. Philippians 1:21). Mullins' voice on this early material is equivalent to that of Dan Fogelberg: "although not a dazzling singer," *CCM* would say, "he seems to know just how far he can reach without overstepping his range." A standout track on the first album is "Save Me," in which Mullins lists a number of things from which he desires to be saved, including "any value I can put a price tag on" and "trendy religion that makes cheap clichés out of timeless truth." *Pictures in the Sky* takes a step backwards with the more dopey than funny "Screen Door," a song built on the already tired cliché of something making "about as much sense as a screen door on a submarine." The song "Verge of a Miracle" redeems the project somewhat. *Winds of Heaven . . . Stuff of Earth* is the artist's first consistently strong collection of songs. It includes his own version of "Awesome God" and also features both "The Other Side of the World" (encouraging a global perspective) and "If I Stand"

(stating an intention to trust in God, come what may). *Never Picture Perfect* was his second masterpiece. It opens with a beautiful a capella hymn, "I Will Sing" (performed by Mullins with **Ashley Cleveland** and Pam Tillis), and moves straight into the folk rock anthem "Hope to Carry On." The next song, "Why Do the Nations Rage?" is a strong ballad that updates Psalm 2 with specific christological references.

Mullins next released a two-volume cycle with the creative title *The World As Best As I Remember It.* The project displays maturity in musical presentation and in his vocal style, while the lyrical quality of the material remains strong. The second volume of the set, however, is noticeably better than the first, making *CCM*'s selection in 2001 of *Volume One* as one of the ten all time "Greatest Albums in Christian Music" the more perplexing. The highlight of the collection is the praise hymn "Step by Step" (written by Beaker) which actually occurs four times, twice under that name on *Volume One* and twice again as the new, improved "Sometimes by Step" on *Volume Two.* Other highlights include "Boy Like Me, Man Like You" on the first disc and "Hello Old Friends," "Everyman," and "All the Ways My Savior Leads Me" on the second one.

Mullins would follow the cycle with the best album of his career, *A Liturgy, a Legacy, and a Ragamuffin Band. CCM* chose this one as the Number *Three* best Christian album of all time. It certainly is not that, but sympathy votes aside, the album is a masterful and impressive project whose legitimate merits should not be dismissed by any backlash against hyperbole. The first official recording with the titular band, *A Liturgy, a Legacy, and a Ragamuffin Band* demonstrates that adult contemporary music does not have to be boring. The songs are strong, without exception, and they are presented in innovative pop styles that frequently draw on Celtic themes. "52:10" offers almost Hebraic chanting over an instrumental track that recalls "Tubular Bells" (the theme from *The Exorcist*). This segues into "The Color Green," built on creation metaphors, with a choir proclaiming the glory of God. "Hold Me Jesus" is a sweet and personal prayer that comes off sincere and inspiring. "Creed" is a musical adaptation of the Apostles' Creed, drawing on liturgical resources often ignored in contemporary Christian music. The Liturgy half of the disc ("Side One" in anachronistic terms) concludes appropriately with a communion hymn and benediction ("Peace"). The Legacy half features autobiographical songs of struggle ("Hard") and commitment ("I'll Carry On"), with Mullins drawing on immigrant imagery as a reliable metaphor for life in this world on the way to heaven ("Land of My Sojourn"). The disc also includes a surprising cover of **Ideola**'s "How to Grow Up Big and Strong." The follow-up album, *Brother's Keeper,* was also recorded with the Ragamuffins and is filled with songs dedicated to approaching all humanity with unconditional love and acceptance

("Brother's Keeper," "Let Mercy Lead"). The 1997 musical *Canticle of the Plains* was written by Mullins, Beaker, and Mitch McVicker. It offers songs inspired by the life of St. Francis with vocals by the writers and by Leigh Bingham of **Sixpence None the Richer** and Kevin Smith and Michael **Tait** of **DC Talk**. But Mullins was saving his very best till last. His *Songs* album, a compilation of hits, features the new track "We Are Not As Strong As We Think We Are," which is the single best written and best performed song of his oeuvre. On this track, finally, Mullins' voice appears to have attained such rich maturity that he actually sounds very much like Neil Diamond. The voice itself holds sufficient appeal that it might even carry weak material—and this song is anything but that. It offers a sober estimation of humanness, set to a beautiful and haunting melody: "We are frail / We are fearfully and wonderfully made / forged in the fires of human passion / Choking on the fumes of selfish rage . . . Oh, we are not as strong as we think we are."

Mullins died while making *The Jesus Record*. He had told members of his band that this was the record he had been put on earth to make—a concept album exploring the personality, ministry, and characteristics of Jesus from a real-life perspective. Just hours before driving to Wichita, he bought a cheap boom box and recorded his demo song ideas for the project. He would never return from that trip. The Ragamuffins decided to record the songs anyway, with Abegg, Elias, and Robertson doing many of the vocals and eager guests volunteering for others: **Amy Grant** on "Nothing Is Beyond You"; **Michael W. Smith** on "Heaven in His Eyes"; and **Ashley Cleveland** on "Jesus." This worked well, since with the exception of "We Are Not As Strong" the main appeal of Mullins' music had always been the songs themselves. Highlights of the album include "My Deliverer" sung by Elias and "All the Way to Kingdom Come," featuring guitar by **Phil Keaggy**. As a bonus, *The Jesus Record* also contains a second CD of Mullins' original demo—just him singing the songs into that home tape recorder with an acoustic guitar and a good bit of background noise. For many, that disc takes on a special, ethereal quality unmatched by the finished versions of the professionals.

In 1998, a *CCM* poll of thirty critics chose Mullins' version of "Awesome God" as one of "the ten best contemporary Christian songs of all time" (it was Number Three). As indicated, a similar poll in 2001 put *A Liturgy, a Legacy, and a Ragamuffin Band* at Number Three and *The World As Best As I Remember It, Volume 1* at Number Seven on a list of "The 100 Greatest Albums in Christian Music."

Mullins' songs have been performed by countless artists, including **Carolyn Arends, Debby Boone, Caedmon's Call, Eric Champion, Gary Chapman, Ashley Cleveland, Billy Crockett, The Crucified, Amy Grant, Benny Hester, The Insyderz, Jars of Clay, Geoff Moore and The Distance, Chris Rice, Michael W. Smith,** and **Billy Sprague**.

Christian radio hits: "A Few Good Men" (# 12 in 1986); "Verge of a Miracle" (# 5 in 1987); "Screen Door" (# 2 in 1987); "Pictures in the Sky" (# 4 in 1987); "Awesome God" (# 3 in 1988); "Other Side of the World" (# 13 in 1989); "If I Stand" (# 8 in 1989); "Such a Thing as Glory" (# 9 in 1989); "My One Thing" (# 1 for 6 weeks in 1990); "While the Nations Rage" (# 2 in 1990); "Alrightokuhhuhamen" (# 4 in 1990); "Somewhere" (# 8 in 1991); "Boy Like Me, Man Like You" (# 16 in 1991); "Where You Are" (# 3 in 1992); "Sometimes by Step" (# 19 in 1992); "Creed" (# 9 in 1994); "Hard" (# 21 in 1994); "Let Mercy Lead" (# 21 in 1995); "Sing Your Praise to the Lord" (# 20 in 1996); "My Deliverer" (# 13 in 1998).

Dove Awards: 1998 Artist of the Year; 1999 Songwriter of the Year.

Michael James Murphy

See **Michael James**.

Mustard Seed Faith

Pedro Buford, kybrd., flute, voc.; Oden Fong, voc., gtr.; Wade Link, gtr., voc. (−1975) // Lewis McVay, drums; voc. (+ 1975). 1975—*Sail on Sailor* (Maranatha); 1980—*Limited Edition* (custom).

Mustard Seed Faith was one of the most important of the "second wave" of Jesus music groups coming out of Calvary Chapel in the early '70s. The first wave of such bands included **Love Song, Children of the Day,** and **The Way,** groups that defined standards and styles in ways that would remain effective for years to come. The "second wave" included **Parable, Daniel Amos, Sweet Comfort Band,** and Mustard Seed Faith. If MSF and **Parable** would ultimately be less known than the other two, it is because both **Daniel Amos** and **Sweet Comfort Band** went on to record numerous additional projects after leaving Maranatha and spawned soloists who would record into the next millennium. **Parable** made only two albums with radically different lineups. Mustard Seed Faith made but one record—and it does not contain their best work. The band's most memorable songs are found instead on the very important compilation discs released by Maranatha in the early '70s. The historic *Maranatha Three* (1973) opens with the group's "Happy in Jesus," a five-and-a-half minute opus of a song that is far more progressive than almost anything else that had been produced by the Calvary Chapel bands at the time. Ironically, the very phrase "happy-in-Jesus-songs" would come to be used in a dismissive way by critics who faulted later Christian music for being out of touch with the hardships of life in the real world. MSF's song could be the quintessential example of such songs lyrically: "I'm so happy in Jesus / and the love He gives to me / He makes me feel like a bird on the wing / Or a sailboat out to sea." But the mood is perfectly appropriate for capturing the euphoria of the revival that produced it and, musically, the tune is far more complex than such wording might suggest. Progressing through mood changes reminiscent of Pink Floyd or the Moody Blues, it culminates finally in choruses of "Alleluia." *Maranatha Three* also showcases MSF's "Rest," a prayerful ballad written by Wade Link and carried by Pedro Buford's haunting flute. The second masterpiece, however, came with "All I Know" from *Maranatha Four* (1974), a gorgeous meditation on 1 Corinthians 2:2.

Needless to say, Mustard Seed Faith's debut album was eagerly anticipated and for the most part, it delivered. The album holds together with the same appealing atmospheric quality that made the earlier songs so popular. New member Lewis McVay composed the title song ("Sail on Sailor"), a pleasant country rock highlight with a sound that would have been right at home on Pure Prairie League's debut album released that same year. Otherwise, the songs are all by Oden Fong (who also wrote "Happy in Jesus" and "All I Know"). "Lighter Side of Darkness" is hand-clapping gospel, complete with rinky-tink piano and lyrics about "angels all around." Beauty is the operative word for most of the tracks, however: "More Than the Sunlight" uses trumpet enhancement in an effective manner that recalls Love's "You Set the Scene." The songs "The Question," "Once I Had a Dream," and "Back Home" are mellow '70s rock at its finest. The album cover for *Sail on Sailor* was designed by Rick Griffin and was later reprinted as one of "the fifty greatest album covers of all time" in a coffee-table book presenting *The Album Cover as Art;* it was the only contemporary Christian music album among the honorees. Mustard Seed Faith disbanded in 1977 due to being "burnt out" by the rigors of touring (60,000 miles on the road in one year, Fong says). **Oden Fong** and **Lewis McVay** both released solo projects. The group did reunite, however, for a custom album in 1980. McVay contributed a few more songs the second time around. Fong's "Sidney the Pirate" is a standout.

The Mustard Seeds

George Bernhardt, gtr., voc.; Matt Bissonette, voc., bass; Doug Bossi, gtr., voc.; Jorge Palacios, drums. 1996—*The Mustard Seeds* (Entourage); 1998—*Red* (Radio Mafia).

The Southern California indie band called The Mustard Seeds has been described by *CCM* as "a virtual power popper's dream." The group's songs are filled with "killer harmonies and contagious hooks" that sustain optimistic lyrics offering an alternative to the cynicism of life plagued by drugs, violence, and suicide. Front man Bissonette formerly played bass for David Lee Roth, and the whole group has served as a studio band behind a number of other general market artists. On their liner notes to their first CD they acknowledge a debt to **King's X,** and that influence is detectable in their sound, though the songs are not nearly so heavy (*Phantom Tollbooth* suggested more of a cross between **PFR** and **Extreme**). One song, "Cats

and Dogs," was picked up by *Rolling Stone* magazine for inclusion on their *New Voices, Volume 4* album. The group tightened their sound for *Red* and gained even more of an alternative edge that took them further from the hard rock/metal moorings of **King's X.** Lyrically, the group sings about themes that are of interest to Christians and that may have special meaning to a Christian audience, without becoming overtly religious. "Alabama Sings" is a tribute to Martin Luther King Jr.; "Coming Up Roses" is about a process of conversion.

MxPx (a.k.a. **Magnified Plaid**)

Mike Herrera, voc., bass; Yuri Ruley, drums; Andy Husted, gtr. (−1995) // Tom Wisnewski, gtr. (+ 1995). 1994—*Pokinatcha* (Tooth and Nail); 1995—*On the Cover* [EP]; *Teenage Politics*; 1996—*Move to Bremerton* [EP]; *Life in General;* 1998—*Slowly Going the Way of the Buffalo* (A&M); *Let It Happen* (Tooth and Nail); 1999—*At the Show;* 2000—*The Ever Passing Moment* (Atlantic); 2001—*The Renaissance EP* [EP] (Fat Wreck).

http//mxpx.com

MxPx is the most popular Christian punk band of all time, though both their Christian and their punk credentials have been challenged by would-be purists of both stripes. The group formed as a trio in Bremerton, Washington, when all of its members were still in high school. Their name is somehow short for Magnified Plaid and derives from a comment that one of Mike Herrera's girlfriends made about a shirt he was wearing (featuring a large plaid design). They caught the emerging "melodic punk" wave of which Green Day and The Offspring would prove to be major exponents. Indeed, some of MxPx's songs sound so much like Green Day it is questionable whether Billy Joe himself could tell the difference—but the band did develop and Herrera's uncanny knack for melody helped the group gain mainstream respect with favorable reviews in *Rolling Stone, Spin,* and *AP* magazines. In the beginning, MxPx was known locally as a bar band but nationally as a Christian act. Asked in 1997 if MxPx was "a ministry band," Herrera replied, "I guess we're ministers in the fact that God uses us in some way, but I don't consider myself a preacher or anything." By 2000, they had gained a prominent national reputation as a mainstream group with fading connections to the Christian music scene as such—though they continued to be upfront about their faith and even suffered some abuse on account of this. Over the years, they have toured with Bad Religion, Blink 182, Rancid, and a number of other artists not associated with the Christian market. Herrera's mother, Michelle, acts as the band's business manager.

Pokinatcha is the closest the group would ever come to raw Ramones-styled punk: twenty-one short, fast songs, many of which betray a kooky sense of humor ("Bad Hair Day," "Want-Ad"). The name for the album comes from an annoying Snickers bar commercial (in which the actor describes a craving that keeps "pokin' at 'cha"; the band decided the word sounded like a good name for a small town: Pokinatcha, Wisconsin). The songs on *Pokinatcha* appear on the surface to be about usual adolescent topics, but Herrera told *HM,* "Just about every song is talking about God" because "God is an everyday thing to me." *On the Cover* offers eight cover versions of wildly disparate songs: Bryan Adams' "Summer of '69"; Buddy Holly's "Oh Boy"; Joy Division's "Drum Machine Joy"; and a-ha's "Take on Me." Mixed in with these were some Christian classics unknown to the band's mostly secular audience: **Keith Green**'s "You Put This Love in My Heart" and **The Altar Boys**' "You Found Me."

Teenage Politics offers "Punk Rawk Show," easily the best song of the band's early years. Propelled by a joyous melody (atypical for punk), the song is simply a celebration of music: "We ain't got no place to go / Let's go to the punk-rock show / Darlin' take me by the hand / We're gonna see a punk-rock band." Also on *Teenage Politics* is "Delores," an ode to Delores O'Riordan of The Cranberries, for whom Herrera confesses a crush. In a possibly more serious vein, "Americanism" challenges political rhetoric ("They're lying when they tell us / This is the home of the brave and the land of the free"). On "Money Tree," he disses higher education as service to materialism: "Four more years ain't right for me . . . Won't let them teach me how to be a money tree." Then in "False Fiction" Herrera declares, "Unless you know Christ, you won't know how I feel." That being the case, the group was nevertheless attracting more of a following from among the masses, and specifically spiritual lyrics were altogether absent on *Life in General.* The very title of the project seems to indicate broader concerns than "just religion" and, in fact, the primary concern appears to be that staple fixation of adolescent boys: adolescent girls. The ultra-catchy pop song "Move to Bremerton" sought to persuade some girl (or maybe all girls) to move to the artist's hometown with hyperbolic promises of what life there could hold for her (them). The song "Chick Magnet" finally broke the group into the big time, gaining major airplay on college radio stations and on MTV. Although they now had three full-length albums to their credit, the college press delighted in making fun of the band's youth and they joined in the mirth themselves with such songs as "The Wonder Years" and "My Mom Still Cleans My Room."

In 1997, it was widely reported that MxPx had gone secular and left Tooth and Nail for A&M. This was only partly true, as Tooth and Nail retained distribution rights for the band's albums to Christian retail outlets. The label also put out a thirty-two song retrospective *(Let It Happen)* that includes many previously unreleased cuts and a live album *(At the Show).* The next major release, however, was *Slowly Going the Way of the Buffalo* and it was treated as a general market production all the

way. The brightest spot musically is the infectious "I'm O.K., You're O.K.," which is not a paean to the pop psychology of Thomas Harris but a positive statement about trusting one's partner (and oneself) when apart. Christian fans also took note of one line in the song "Tomorrow's Another Day": "God is faithful even if you don't have faith in yourself." For the most part, though, the album's spiritual content came through most loudly in its silences: songs about girls and romance that were almost devoid of sexual reference; songs about partying that did not mention alcohol or drugs. *The Ever Passing Moment* would find the band sporting a new Elvis Costello fashion, performing some of their best material yet. *Rolling Stone* praised "It's Undeniable" as "perfect punk pop." *CCM* noticed that the group's Christianity was starting to resurface, albeit defensively. "Educated Guess" and "One Step Closer to Life" refer pretty clearly to acts of faith, and "Buildings Tumble" relates the sadness of a wasted life. "Foolish" is an outright response to fans and critics who had chosen to ridicule the band on account of its faith. Herrera wrote in the liner notes, "We're not here to preach. We respect people for what they believe. Most bands in the music scene we're in are anti-religious and I understand that. But some people actually hate us. Grow up!"

At the end of 2001, the band was preparing another release and issued *The Renaissance EP* to give fans and critics a taste of what to expect. The self-produced indie project presents songs similar to their early material performed in the newer, more developed style. The song "Struggle" has clearly recognizable Christian content.

My Brother's Mother

Brian Eichler, drums; Jaime Eichler, voc.; Andy Prickett, gtr. 1995—*Deeper Than Skies* (5 Min. Walk).

My Brother's Mother was an apparently one-time effort by Andy Prickett of **The Prayer Chain,** supporting female vocals by Jaime Eichler, who had previously sung backup for **The Violet Burning.** Those vocals gave the group a sound similar to **Innocence Mission** or **Over the Rhine,** though as *Shout* magazine would note, the fetching and distinctive quality of the group's album lies in the "much needed sensuality" that Eichler brings to the material, a worshipful quality that regards Christ as not just Savior and Lord but as Lover as well. Such an emphasis is scriptural (e.g., Ephesians 5:25–32) but understandably ignored in most Christian music—contemporary or not. "Heart of Gold" (not the Neil Young song) sings of an angel with lips of wine that brings salvation. In "Be Still, My Love," she sings lyrics that could almost have come from the Song of Solomon: "Like a lover, your presence fills my room / As a fire that burns me through and through."

My Friend Stephanie

Drue Bachman, bass, voc.; Kevin Heuer, drums (−1999); Chris Ebert, gtr. (−1997); Joel McCreight, gtr. (−1997) // Jeff Apel, gtr. (+ 1997); Scott Bachman, kybrd. (+ 1997); Tim Watts, drums (+ 1999). 1996—*Makeover* (Innocent Media); 1997—*All the Pieces* (Grey Dot); 1999—*One of Those Days.*

Post-grunge alternative rock band My Friend Stephanie was formed by Drue Bachman as a reinvention of his first band **Sunday Blue.** In 1995, Bachman was involved in a near fatal accident while on tour with **Sunday Blue,** leaving him hospitalized for an extended period. That brush with mortality may have influenced his songwriting, which takes an intelligent look at faith amidst the struggles of life (romantic and otherwise). Bachman has said, "We don't really sing religious songs. We sing honest songs—but they are all from a Christian perspective." *7ball* noted that the band has two common themes, both of which are also typical of biblical poets: "hope in the midst of pain, and thanksgiving for what God has given us." Drummer Kevin Heuer would join the 2000 edition of Bill Mallonee's **Vigilantes of Love.**

Musically, the group's sound falls into the same "distorted power pop" genre as bands like James or Toad the Wet Sprocket. On some songs (the title track from *All the Pieces;* "Maria" from *One of Those Days*), they sound very much like Matthew Sweet. Bill Campbell of **The Throes** has served as the group's producer, and similarities to that group's sound sometimes come through as well. *Makeover* offers an unusually strong collection of songs from the confessional "Feel the Rain" to the lovely "Lullaby." Faith statements come through particularly in "Embrace," "Everything Has a Reason," and "In Light." Some reviewers thought the songs on *All the Pieces* were less consistent, though explicitly Christian convictions are expressed even more clearly in "You Are God" and "Time Heals."

Musically, "Love Again" is a particularly catchy **Throes**-like anthem, while "Journey" is innovative and displays a rock edge. The shift to more radio-friendly pop was completed on *One of Those Days,* with the title track and "Believe in You" being obvious potential hits. "1969" offers an interesting look at the year in which Bachman was born, complete with political analysis and references to **Larry Norman** and the Jesus movement. "Mom and Dad" and "Are You There" offer testaments to Bachman's parents, with gratitude for their support after his accident. The album closes with a stunning eight-and-a-half minute remake of "Lullaby" from the first album.

My Little Dog China

Mike Belfield, bass; Kevin Clay, voc., gtr.; Jason House, drums. 1994—*The Velvis Carnival* (Alarma).

My Little Dog China was the edgy but critically-acclaimed alternative rock band that introduced the controversial **Kevin Clay** to the contemporary Christian music scene. Clay is something of a **Michael Knott** protégé and My Little Dog China fits under the general stylistic umbrella of Knott's **LSU.** Their only album was produced by **Steve Hindalong,** with alternative credentials getting a boost from associations with Chris Colbert (of **Breakfast with Amy** and **Fluffy**). Thematically, *The Velvis Carnival* offers an assault on commercialized Christianity. In the liner notes, Clay writes that "the machine of the music industry, media, and church creates false images to sell their product and/or message to people." The song "Her Marching" declares, "It's the machine that turns blood to green."

Mylon

See **Mylon LeFevre.**

Nailed

Justin Bolli, voc.; Chris Gaylon, drums; Brandon DeVotie, bass; Scottie Haglan, gtr. 1996—*All Washed Up;* 1999—*Entity* (Rugged).

Nailed is a hard rock quartet from Knoxville, Tennessee, where they often share stages with their musical and spiritual soul mates, **Disciple.** The group has a sound similar to that of the general market band Mudhoney. *All Washed Up* opens with a screaming song full of power and passion ("Life") but also includes some fine ballads ("Soul Cryer," "Dig"). *Entity* was produced by **Dale Thompson** of **Bride** and is mainly driving, guitar rock with screamed lyrics like "My God loves you / But He hates your sin" ("M2"). The group occasionally ventures into Alice in Chains grunge territory on songs like "Broken."

Nailed Promise

Ryan Brown, bass; Travis Brown, voc., gtr.; Nathan Garcia, voc., gtr.; Matthew Miller, drums. 1999—*Realize* (Rescue); 2000—*S/T* [EP with Mindrage] (Pluto).

Nailed Promise is a southern hardcore band whose sound *HM* describes as "aggro-rock at its bone crushing best." The group formed around 1994 and played clubs for a few years before recording an album that was coproduced by Mario Curiel of **P.O.D.** Interestingly, the band secured corporate support from Red Bull, an "energy drink" produced in Austria that is very popular in Europe. Drummer Matt Miller, who does like the beverage, wrote the company and suggested that an "energetic rock band" could present a positive promo for their image. Red Bull was just beginning to import their drink to America and liked the idea, forging a relationship with the band despite its overt commitment to Christian ministry. Miller attributes the deal to his "God-given talent for figuring out how to get stuff for free." *Realize* features lyrics like "I will not waiver, I will not fail / God is the reason I stand up tall" being screamed over pummeling (if somewhat repetitive) guitar riffs. Christian rapper Dirt puts in a cameo appearance on the song "Inner Fire." In 2000, four more Nailed Promise songs would appear on a "split EP" recorded with the band **Mindrage.**

Narnia (Sweden)

Carljohan Grimmark, gtr.; Christian Liljegren, voc. // Martin Claesson, kybrd. (+ 1999); Andreas Johansson, drums (+ 1999); Jakob Persson, bass (+ 1999). 1997—*Awakening* (Nuclear Blast); 1999—*Long Live the King;* 2001—*Desert Land.*

www.narniaworld.com

The Swedish band Narnia makes metal music that sounds like it came straight out of the '80s. *Phantom Tollbooth* lists the essential ingredients: "clean, smooth guitars, epic keyboards, repetitive hooks, and echoing background vocals." *Rad Rockers* references bands like **Bride, Guardian,** and **Stryper** as Narnia's obvious influences, with the closest general market comparisons being Deep Purple and Uriah Heep. Narnia evolved out of a general market band called Modest Attraction in which Liljegren was lead vocalist. Prior to that he also sang with a band called Borderline, known to some fans of Scandinavian metal. The group sets itself apart from many metal wannabes by the high technical level of their musicianship. Grimmark is a top-flight shredder guitarist and Liljegren a vocalist in the Ronnie James Dio tradition. Their name (like that of the group listed below) is taken from the mythical land that serves as a setting for allegorical Christian fairy tales written by C. S. Lewis. This theme is referenced again in an instrumental from *Awakening* titled "The Return of Aslan." The debut album received good press in the general market with the British *Hard Roxx* magazine noting that "while songs like 'Time of Change' and 'Touch From You' have a Christian message, this is never overpowering and does not detract from the overall quality." In 1998, the band actually toured Europe as the opening act for Dio. *HM* regards *Desert Land* as a significant step forward, moving the group into "the memorable arena of radio-ability" lacking on their first two projects.

Narnia (UK)

Peter Banks, kybrd.; Pauline Filby, voc.; John Russell, gtr.; et al. 1974—*Aslan Is Not a Tame Lion* (Myrrh UK).

The magical land of Narnia forms the setting for a series of seven Christian fairy tales written by popular theologian C. S. Lewis. The main character of the stories is a lion named Aslan, who serves as a thinly veiled allegorical symbol for Christ. At least three Christian bands have recorded under the name Narnia, and another three under the name **Aslan.** The UK version of Narnia was a '70s progressive rock quintet fronted by female vocalist Pauline Filby, who had previously released a solo album of folk music called *Show Me a Rainbow.* Filby also composed all of the band's songs, except for a cover of Tom Paxton's "You Better Believe It." Banks and Russell went on to form **After the Fire,** best known to American audiences for their '80s hit, "Der Kommissar." The title of Narnia's album is drawn from one of the more famous lines of the first Narnia book *The Lion, the Witch and the Wardrobe.* A different, Canadian band named Narnia released an album called simply *Aslan* on Master's Collection in 1988.

Native Son and the Foundation

Mark Salomon; et al. 1992—*Life in the Grave* (Ocean).

Native Son and the Foundation was a one-time side project for Mark Salomon of **The Crucified** (and, later, **Stavesacre**). The singer, known for hard rock and metal, adopted an alter ego as a rapper backed by a conglomerate of percussion instruments (bongos, congas, etc.) played by an assortment of African American artists. *CCM* noted with some irony that the result was "the strongest hip-hop debut to come from the

church yet." Salomon recorded another very different side project under the name **Outer Circle.**

Neale and Webb

Michael Neale, voc.; Devin Webb, voc. 1995—*At the Cross* (Liquid Disc).

The pop duo Neale and Webb put together one critically acclaimed package of songs produced by **Vector**'s Steve Griffith. The duo has an interesting origin in that, as teenagers, each of the singers competed in Assemblies of God song festivals and were often rivals for the prize. In 1989, seventeen-year-old Neale faced thirteen-year-old Webb in the finals at an event in Florida. "I went after this really high note and I missed it," Neale would recall. "But Devin (Webb), his voice hadn't changed yet, and he nailed it. He won by two points." At a similar competition some time later in Indianapolis, one of the judges (Kirk Sullivan, later of **4 Him**) thought the two singers' voices would blend well together and suggested they quit competing with each other and form a team. *CCM* referred to *At the Cross* as "an irresistible collection of pop tunes that shouldn't be missed." The strength of the album lies in the songs themselves, most of which display such classic Beatles elements as captivating hooks, interesting chord progressions, and bridges that build into a climactic chorus. The title song is similar lyrically to **Chuck Girard**'s "Lay Your Burden Down," imploring Christians to let go of the past, trusting in Christ's forgiveness.

Necromanicide

Andre, gtr., voc.; Adrian, bass, voc.; Jeret Christopher, drums; Stefan, bass; Nick Lee, gtr. 1998—*Hate Regime* (Pony Canyon).

http://members.tripod.com/necromanicide

The Christian metal band Necromanicide is of interest mainly because of their setting. The group formed in 1995 in Malaysia, a strict Moslem country. According to a press release, all five members have experienced drastic conversions: "three were saved from Buddhism, one from Hinduism, and one from witchcraft." The group's sound is basic '90s thrash metal (with occasional death metal flourishes) similar in some respects to such American bands as **Betrayal** and **Mortification.** A trade-off between two lead singers provides some variety, and on one song, "Unwanted Killer," they try out some **Galactic Cowboys**-style harmonies. Lyrically, Necromanicide comes across as espousing fundamentalist rhetoric through songs that champion biblical truth and rail against evolution, godlessness (= other religions), and the evils of modern society.

Erick Nelson

1976—*Flow River Flow* (Maranatha); 1979—*The Misfit* [with Michele Pillar]; 1980—*Pickin' Up the Pieces: Decade in Review*.

http://ericknel.home.attbi.com

Erick Nelson was one of the Jesus music pioneers associated with Calvary Chapel in Costa Mesa, California. He was a member of the bands **Selah** and **Good News** and also played keyboards and bass guitar with many other groups. Nelson made one classic solo album and recorded another project as a short-lived duo he formed with **Michele Pillar.** Nelson has said that he felt like something of a "misfit" among the Calvary Chapel "Jesus freaks" since he did not come out of the hippie culture of street life and drug experimentation. He was raised a Lutheran in California and went to Pomona College where he majored in philosophy. He says that he had come to question the faith of his childhood and was no longer a believer, but came to a new experience of Christianity as a vibrant reality at the beginning of his sophomore year. His testimony includes reference to a mystical dream or vision that he had of Jesus on the cross in shining red and white, but the dominant factor in his "conversion" was the influence of an Episcopalian priest named Cameron Harriot. Nelson describes Harriot as "the first person I ever met who I was certain really *knew* God." Harriot also introduced him to such academic influences as C. S. Lewis and St. Francis of Assisi. Nelson had been part of a successful vocal group called Friends but his awakened spirituality led him to leave that group in order to sing about Jesus. This decision was at least in part influenced by visits to Calvary Chapel, where he was impressed by the ministry potential of **Love Song.** At any rate, he joined **Selah** for two years (1971–1973) and then formed **Good News** with **Billy Batstone, David Diggs,** Yvonne Lewis, and a sixteen-year-old **Bob Carlisle.** Nelson wrote and sang the best and best-known songs by both of those groups (**Selah**'s "He Lives"; **Good News**' "Pickin' Up the Pieces"). Around this time, Nelson also sang a solo version of "Set My Spirit Free" on *The Praise Album* (Maranatha, 1974), the record that was to initiate modern praise and worship music and change Christian liturgical practices in America forever. Most of the Jesus people did not know the song (a traditional spiritual); for them, it became closely associated with the man who introduced it to them, and for several years Nelson was misidentified by young pietists as "the man who wrote 'Set My Spirit Free.'" Even in 2002, his version of the song would remain the best-known rendition in contemporary Christian music. He later sang "Christ in Me" on the *Praise 2* album (Maranatha, 1976) and "Fairest Lord Jesus" (the hymn also known as "Beautiful Saviour") on a collection of hymns called *Hosanna* (Maranatha, 1979). For a time, he played bass and toured with **Danny Lee and the Children of Truth** and

with Harold Brinkley (who he would still describe thirty years later as "hands-down the best speaker I ever heard").

Nelson's solo album, *Flow River Flow,* is dedicated to a group of people called The Wheelchair Gang. The latter were a semi-community of disabled persons who shared an apartment complex, rescued persons like themselves from convalescent homes, and came as a group to many Calvary Chapel concerts and activities. Nelson's brother David was stricken with an undiagnosed degenerative disease that ultimately took his life in 1979. Before his death, David Nelson became something of a hero to many Christians, appearing on Robert Schuller's TV program and in other forums. Schuller devoted one chapter of a book about "amazing people" to telling his story and, some twenty years after his death, mentioned David Nelson in a sermon as "the best example he knew" of a person with a positive attitude. The title track of Nelson's solo album takes notice of such persons and calls upon Christians to remember those whom it is easy to forget. Likewise, "Moving On" offers a tribute to the late Bill Sprouse Jr. (of **The Road Home**), also something of "a misfit" on account of his physical bulk. The song "Something Happened to You" became the album's best-known number because it was also included on the popular compilation disc *Maranatha Five* (Maranatha, 1976). It has a rock feel with traditional gospel backup and soulful saxophone. Lyrically, it expresses wonderment at the spiritual transformation observable in a female friend ("Glory Hallelu-ya / somethin's happened to ya"). "He Gave Me Love," featured on *Maranatha Six* (Maranatha, 1977), is an adult contemporary piano ballad (with choral backing) testifying to the incomparable love of God. "Soldiers of the Cross" (featuring an introductory guest vocal by **Michele Pillar,** then Michele Takaoka) would receive some attention and later be included on a compilation CD (*Best of Maranatha, Vol. 2,* 1979). *Flow River Flow* was produced by Lenny Roberts, who had served as engineer on numerous hit singles by Sonny and Cher, Bobby Sherman, and **Johnny Rivers.** David Foster (later to become a legendary Grammy-winning producer in his own right) did the arrangements and played additional keyboards. In 2001, Nelson would recollect that Foster gave him "the greatest musical compliment I ever got" when (while recording "Something Happened to You") he said, "I can't play this Elton John (stuff)—let Erick do it!" The well-known title track to the album actually began as a Friends song written by two members of Nelson's former vocal band—Steve Berg and Don Stalker. Originally, the song conveyed the idea of "the river of success" flowing by a struggling artist. Nelson adapted the words and Berg and Stalker sang background vocals, as they did on much of the album.

In 1979, Nelson joined with friend **Michele Pillar** to record a concept album. *The Misfit* tells the story of a person who "doesn't fit in," of how he finds Christ, and of what happens to him thereafter. *CCM* chose the record as one of their Ten Best Albums of 1979 and, more than twenty years later, no less authority than **Bob Bennett** would relate, "*The Misfit* was an album way ahead of its time. The songs were challenging and sophisticated lyrically, in many ways open-ended as to interpretation. . . . in short, the album gave listeners a lot of credit for having brains and taste and the ability to sort through for themselves. Perhaps not novel today, but back in prehistoric 1979, it's a wonder the album even got made." The record has a pop-rock sound consistent in quality with products by male-female duos of the era (The Captain and Tennille, The Carpenters, Peaches and Herb). "Carry Me Along" is a gorgeous melodic ballad sung by Pillar about discovering guidance through the unpredictable ways of life. "Stand" is an upbeat rocker with lots of electric guitar. "Take Me to the Light" sounds like the sort of genetically engineered surprise that one might expect to result from a cross-fertilization of Elton John's "Grow Some Funk of Your Own" with **Larry Norman**'s "Shot Down"—a piano-based rocker that extols resilience and persistence in the face of trials and temptations. The album also has three two-song medleys that present tunes that are thematically linked: 1) "Sail On" and "Can't Find My Way Home" (not the Blind Faith song) seem to describe the loss of direction that can come upon those who plot their own course in life, seeking only freedom and independence. 2) "The Moon's a Harsh Mistress" and "He's Asleep" both have a certain (though perhaps ironic) lullaby quality. The first is one of the earliest recordings of what would ultimately become a classic Jimmy Webb song (voted one of "the ten most perfect songs of all time"). Nelson says that **Larry Norman** played Joe Cocker's rendition of the song for him at a Vineyard Bible study and suggested he do it. The second ("He's Asleep") was written by Nelson's cousin Alf Clausen, who would later achieve some fame doing music for the TV series *The Simpsons*. 3) "Love Hurts" and "He Gave Us Love" presents one of rock's classic statements about the pain of love (a Top 10 song by Nazareth in 1976) in tandem with an affirmation of Christ's sacrificial love for humanity. The album concludes with "The Martyr Song," an anthemic tribute to persecuted heroes throughout the ages that is musically reminiscent of **Bob Dylan**'s "Chimes of Freedom."

Nelson and Pillar played college settings rather than churches and met with reasonable success. *The Misfit* was actually released by Maranatha on their new A&S imprint with hope of generating some crossover sales in the general market. Though that did not happen, the project did not go unnoticed. At one point, The Carpenters expressed interest in covering the duo's "Moon's a Harsh Mistress/He's Asleep" medley (The Carpenters were very big on medleys), but they wanted to change a few words to the latter song and Clausen was reluctant to grant permission; negotiations were forestalled by Karen Carpenter's tragic death.

Nelson developed a strong interest in the field of apologetics (offering rational defense for Christian beliefs and doctrine) in the early '70s, and in 1978–1979 he wrote a year-long research paper for John Warwick Montgomery at the Melodyland School of Theology. He taught a semester course on "Critical Thinking" (a class in logic) at Simon Greenleaf Law School and gave many presentations on the topic "Why I Think Christianity Is True." For a time he hosted a radio series for station KYMS, interviewing college professors about why they thought Christianity was false and then offering his rebuttal. In the early '80s, Nelson attended Claremont Graduate School and earned an M.A. in philosophy. In 1983, he married and moved to Seattle, Washington, where he pursued a career as a computer programmer. He has written an Internet book titled *The Metaphorical Gospel Theory* (posted at his website), which offers insightful critique of certain trends in modern "historical Jesus" studies and New Testament interpretation. As of 2002, Nelson was serving as Systems Development Project Manager for Airborne Express, performing only occasionally on request. He has, however, been more intentional than most of the Jesus music pioneers in keeping alive the traditions of that revival and providing a personal history of what happened and why. Nelson has posted a lengthy personal account of his remembrances, with access from his website or from www.one-way.org/jesusmusic/interviews/nelson.

Neon Cross

David Reeves, voc.; Don Webster, gtr.; Michael Betts, drums (−1995); Ed Ott, bass (−1995) // Dave Stankey, bass (+ 1995); Troy Woody, drums (+ 1995). 1988—*Neon Cross* (Regency); 1995—*Torn* (Rugged); 1998—*The Best of Neon Cross* (custom).

Neon Cross began as a classic Christian metal band whose first album showcased the talents of screaming vocalist David Reeves and guitarist Dan Webster. *HM* described the self-titled debut as offering "ten, hot, nonstop metal songs that never let up." Standouts include "We Are the Children" and "Far Cry." The group broke up soon after the record's release, but five years later their drummer Michael Betts was president of Rugged Records and persuaded Reeves and Webster to get back together for another project. *Torn* is less the total metal onslaught, though it still falls into the basic hard rock genre. "Change" is an acoustic number in the tradition of Led Zeppelin's acoustic songs, and "Bitterness" is a hard grunge tune that Doug Van Pelt (of *HM*) says is built on "a riff identical to that in 'Outshined' by Soundgarden."

Nervous Passenger

Neil Alton; et al. 1998—*Taller Trees* (Room 3).

Nervous Passenger is an acoustic group from Edinburgh, Scotland, whose debut album had them immediately pegged as "the Christian version of Counting Crows." Lead singer and songwriter Neil Alton does indeed recall the latter band's Adam Duritz in both his vocal and compositional styles. As *Phantom Tollbooth* would note, however, the Counting Crows are not a bad band for more Christian artists to imitate, being known for intelligent lyrics and well-crafted music. Thus, Nervous Passenger joins such American Christian groups as **Caedmon's Call** and **Burlap to Cashmere** in offering songs that reveal "an introspective and artful elegance."

Aaron Neville

Selected: 2000—*Devotion* (EMI).

Adult contemporary crooner Aaron Neville (b. 1941) has been friendly to the contemporary Christian music world for years, letting it be known that he is a believer. In 2000, he finally recorded a contemporary gospel album that was marketed specifically to the contemporary Christian music subculture. Neville grew up in New Orleans where he and his family became musical legends at an early age. His brother Art Neville formed a band in high school called The Hawkettes and they had a major regional hit with the carnival favorite "Mardis Gras Mambo" in 1954. Aaron sang with The Hawkettes for a while, then went solo in 1958 when his brother went into the navy. Almost a decade later, he hit big with the national Top 40 hit "Tell It Like Is" (# 2 in 1966). He had a few other hits, too, especially on the R&B charts, but did not make another major impression until, another decade later, he joined Art and two other siblings in The Neville Brothers. That group issued an ill-fated disco album followed by the highly acclaimed *Fiyo on the Bayou* (A&M, 1981). Mick Jagger became a fan and invited the group to open for the Rolling Stones' 1982 American tour. Neville's biggest break, however, came when Linda Ronstadt asked him to duet with her on the song "Don't Know Much," which provided him with another major Top 40 smash (# 2 in 1989) some twenty-three years after "Tell It Like It Is." Neville would record more duets with Ronstadt, including "All My Life" (# 11 in 1990), and he has also enjoyed success as a solo artist ("Everybody Plays the Fool," # 8 in 1991). *The New Rolling Stone Encyclopedia of Rock and Roll* notes that part of the attraction has been "the incongruity of Neville's angelic falsetto voice emerging from his imposing, hugely muscled physique and rather intimidating, craggy visage."

The album *Devotion* includes a mixture of gospel standards ("Mary, Don't You Weep," "Banks of the River Jordan," "Were You There?") and contemporary pop songs with spiritual themes (Paul Simon's "Bridge over Troubled Water," **Bob Dylan**'s "I Shall Be Released," and the Anglican hymn "Morning Has Broken," made popular in 1972 by Cat Stevens). Neville also sings a duet with **Rachel Lampa** on a new song, "There Is Still a Dream," and **Avalon** joins him for "By Heart, By Soul." In 2001, it was announced that he was preparing a second gospel collection.

Grammy Awards: 1989 Best Vocal Pop Performance by a Duo or Group [with Linda Ronstadt] ("Don't Know Much"); 1990 Best Vocal Pop Performance by a Duo or Group [with Linda Ronstadt] ("All My Life"); 1994 Best Country Vocal Collaboration [with Trisha Yearwood] ("I Fall to Pieces").

New Direction

2000—*Get Your Praise On* (Myrrh).

New Direction is a forty-one-voice African American youth choir that fashions itself after such **Kirk Franklin** projects as The Family, **God's Property**, and **One Nation Crew**. The Chicago group was assembled by brothers Jeral and Percy Gray, and their worship-oriented album contains both live "worship experience" tracks and studio cuts. "Hold Out" is a seven-minute-plus opus that begins like a lullaby and builds to a crescendo of preaching and praise. "You Love Me" is an R&B tinged worship song. "Lighthouse" is soulful with a classic gospel sound, while "Worship Christ" is up-to-the-minute relevant with its rap/choir groove. The group covers "Lead Me On," written by **Michael W. Smith** and performed originally by **Amy Grant.**

New Faith

Charles Ewing; Malika Haki; Dennis McMillan; Victor Shears; Carl Smith; Ira Williams. 1992—*New Faith* (Warner Alliance).

New Faith was a one-time venture organized by producer Moses Dillard featuring inmates at the Tennessee State Penitentiary. The core of the group consisted of six members of the prison choir, with the lead vocalist being lifer Victor Shears. Musically, the *New Faith* album has a style similar to that associated with Sounds of Blackness. A few songs ("Let Me Hip You to the Streets," "Love Is the Bottom Line") are infused with dance club elements including rapped vocals and a rapid percussive beat. Dillard was somehow able to pull in some big talent to help with the project. Teddy Pendergrass sings a duet with Shears on "You Were Always There" and Sam Moore (of Sam and Dave) does likewise on "I Am Amazed."

New Identity

Greg Golden, Jon Golden, John Key, Eddie Luckey, Shannon Luckey, Albert Morton, Kashaan Stephens. 1997—*Cloud Eight* (StarSong).

New Identity is an African American vocal group similar to **Commissioned.** The Cincinnati group sang together for almost fifteen years before recording their first album. *Cloud Eight* spans formats from silky pop songs to edgy urban numbers. The title track implies that perfection and ultimate happiness is only possible through Christ. "We can make it to cloud eight," says Morton. "But cloud nine is right there and with Christ we can go all the way." The album closes with a fairly traditional gospel rendition of Vince Gill's "Go Rest High on That Mountain," which had just been selected as the Country Music Association's 1996 Song of the Year.

Christian radio hits: "If I Know God" (# 24 in 1997).

New Jerusalem

Personnel list unavailable. 1998—*New Jerusalem* (BulletProof).

New Jerusalem is a Christian hard rock band that seems to specialize in cloning such '70s and '80s groups as Led Zeppelin and AC/DC. The lead singer's voice bears an uncanny resemblance to that of Robert Plant, facilitating the imitative character of their music. Lyrically, the songs all deal with blatant Christian themes, presenting Christ as the only hope for salvation amidst threats of hell and promises of forgiveness. *The Phantom Tollbooth* was especially harsh on the band: "This album is like an Elvis impersonator. It's kind of fascinating to see how well done it is, but after a bit it all starts to seem pathetic." *Rad Rockers,* on the other hand, saw it as "a return of **Stryper**/Kiss rock that makes the death of grunge worth celebrating."

New Life

William Jett; et al. 1975—*Faith as a Grain of Mustard Seed* (Trinity).

New Life was a Christian band formed around William Jett who for a short time played guitar with the southern rock band Black Oak Arkansas. It is not clear what the extent of his involvement with that group actually was. Black Oak Arkansas was led by Jim Dandy Mangrum and went through numerous personnel changes; the original guitarist was Ricky Reynolds. In any case, the Jesus people were hungry for celebrity converts and when they heard the news that Black Oak Arkansas's lead guitarist had been saved, nobody pressed the matter too much. The New Life album turned out to be a disappointment in any case because Jett seemed intent on showing how much he had changed from BOA's raunchy music and turned in a set of MOR country rock. *Harmony* complained about the sameness of the songs, which all seemed to drag, then concluded, "If they can escape trying to convince people that they really are Christians, their next album should contain some surprising changes." But there was no next album.

The New Gaither Vocal Band

See **The Gaither Vocal Band.**

The Newsboys

Peter Furler, voc., drums; John James, voc. (– 1998); Sean Taylor, bass (– 1994) George Perdkis, gtr. (– 1990) // Jonathan Geange, gtr. (+ 1990, – 1991); Corey Pryor, kybrd. (+ 1991, – 1994); Vernon Bishop, gtr. (+ 1991, – 1992); Jody Davis, gtr. (+ 1994); Kevin Mills, bass (+ 1994, – 1996); Jeff Frankenstein, kybrd. (+ 1996); Duncan Phillips, perc. (+ 1996); Philip Urry, bass, voc. (+ 1996, –1998); Phil Joel, bass (+ 1998). 1988—*Read All about It* (Refuge); 1990—*Hell Is for Wimps* (StarSong); 1991—*Boys Will Be Boyz*; 1992—*Not Ashamed*; 1994—*Going Public*; 1996—*Take Me to Your Leader*; 1998—*Step Up to the Microphone*; 1999— *Love Liberty Disco* (Sparrow); 2000—*Shine: The Hits*; 2002—*Thrive.*

www.newsboys.com

The Newsboys may be Christian music's best pop band; they should at least be considered neck-and neck with **Audio Adrenaline** for that title. The band has had many personnel changes and more than its share of identity crises: they are not a rock band on the order of **Midnight Oil** with whom they were often compared in the early years—mainly because they were from Australia and their lead singer (James) had a shaved head. They are not really a techno-pop band, like they tried to be for a little while *(Boys Will Be Boyz),* and, although they could be a good disco group, they have probably figured out that no one wants them to be. They are a pop band in the classic, eclectic tradition of Abba, The Police, and Three Dog Night, and when they recognize this, they can be one of the finest pop bands in the world. Early on, band leader Peter Furler told *Shout* magazine, "If there is one thing I'm really proud of, it's that we don't sound like a Christian version of something." He was absolutely right. If there was a problem (and there was), it was that, at the time, they didn't sound like themselves either. But they got it together with a little help from some friends and left a major impression on the contemporary Christian music scene and, indeed, on American popular music in general.

The Newsboys officially formed in 1987 in West Orange, New Jersey. They would later move to Memphis, and then to Nashville. But the group's origins go back to Australia, where Aussie natives Furler and John James played in a band called The News. They immigrated along with their manager Wes Campbell (brother to **Serene and Pearl**), who would end up being pastor of a church in Franklin, Tennessee. Early on, the band was mostly noted for gimmicks: Furler would play his drums suspended upside down; the guitarist would throw his instrument high into the air and catch it; things would blow up on stage. For a time, they played mainly high schools, operating on a pattern perfected by **Al Denson:** do a public school assembly with a nonreligious antidrug message and invite everyone to an off-campus concert that night where an evangelistic message could be included.

Read All About It is sing-along dance music similar to what was produced by **The Lifters** or early **Undercover.** *Hell Is for Wimps* continues in the same vein with a bit more bite: energetic songs with in-your-face lyrics. *CCM* compared the sound to **Mylon LeFevre and Broken Heart,** an analogy that would seem ironic when Furler later married LeFevre's daughter Summer. The group tried a little foray into techno and rap with *Boys Will Be Boyz,* which includes the hook-filled "Taste and See"—the first song in the group's oeuvre that might have qualified for inclusion in their eventual "greatest hits collection" (though it didn't). In a few years, Furler was hoping everyone would just forget the band's first three albums. "You can tell we were young Christians," he told *Shout* in 1995. "There were things we sang about that were pretty silly, but that was just how we were and we were just being honest. We were a Christian band, but we were also a lousy band."

The group was rescued in a sense by **Steve Taylor,** who took them under his wing, helped with the songwriting and coproduced three albums of increasing quality. *Not Ashamed* found them temporarily without a guitarist, so **Dave Perkins** of **Chagall Guevara/Passafist** filled in. With mellotron by John Painter (of **Fleming and John**) and organ by **Phil Madeira,** Taylor made sure the boys had tight instrumental support. Their sound emulated secular acts EMF and Jesus Jones, but more to the point, they had good songs. The title track to *Not Ashamed* is especially strong, an energetic proclamation of the group's intention to ignore all the market research that suggests subtlety with the gospel as a formula for success: "Who we tryin' to please . . apologizin', like we're spreadin' some kind of disease?" The opening "I Cannot Get You out of My System" establishes a solid groove with effective use of sequencing. The band also covers **DeGarmo and Key**'s song "Boycott Hell" in a radically transformed, tongue-in-cheek version that includes a rap by Taylor: "I agree we gotta boycott hell / But we gotta boycott dumb lyrics as well." *Going Public* took another giant step forward, offering "Shine," the first of the band's perfect pop anthems. "Real Good Thing" and "Spirit Thing" are also hook-filled songs with pleasant, memorable melodies. The former reminds the listener that it is "a real good thing" when people *don't* get what they deserve; the latter tries to explain the Christian's sense of "inner guiding" to those oblivious to such experiences ("it's not a family trait / it's nothing that I ate"). "Let It Rain" is a ballad imagining the disciple Peter's reflections in the days after Easter as he waited for the promised Spirit to fall. "Truth and Consequences" addresses the phenomenon of wolves in sheep's clothing—especially those who prey on lonely women in church singles' groups. "Elle G." was inspired by the suicides of Kurt Cobain and **Vince**

Ebo. Keyboardist Corey Pryor left the band after *Going Public* and formed the dance band **Sozo** with his wife Danielle.

Take Me to Your Leader is the first of The Newsboys' two back-to-back masterpieces. It opens with one of the band's more blistering rock songs, "God Is Not a Secret." Thematically, the song makes the same point as the title songs to their two previous albums, but it makes it better, or at least makes the same point to better music. The next song, "Take Me to Your Leader," is one of the most original pop songs ever recorded by any group, a song that rates in the same one-of-a-kind category as Mungo Jerry's "In the Summertime," Chumbawamba's "Tub Thumping," or **Norman Greenbaum**'s "Spirit in the Sky." Lyrically quirky (converting space aliens to Jesus?), the song is built on spacey sound effects interrupted by driving guitar with stop-and-start vocals. No one in the music business—Christian or secular—would doubt that it would have been a Number One smash on the mainstream charts if it had seen general market release. *Rolling Stone,* usually oblivious of Christian music, caught wind of it and oohed and ahhed appropriately. Industry personnel at Virgin records heard it and declared, "This is not a 'Christian hit', this is a *hit*." A year later the album was actually re-released on Virgin accordingly but, it turns out, God *is* a secret to be kept on most general market radio stations, and The Newsboys were robbed of whatever treasure on earth they might have accumulated in a less prejudicial environment. Still, *Take Me to Your Leader* did not stop with two winners. "Breathe" is another big guitar song (keyboards take a back seat on this album), incorporating words from the classic hymn "Breathe on Me, Breath of God" into its alternating hard-soft-hard structure. "Reality" offers a funky retelling of the prodigal son story in which the wayward boy ends up shoveling elephant dung in a circus, writing his parents for money, and asking that they find a better picture for the milk carton. After four highlights in a row, the group can almost (but not quite) be forgiven for song number five, which remains one of the worst tracks ever performed by any contemporary Christian music artist. "Breakfast" sets much dumber lyrics than **DeGarmo and Key** ever wrote to an annoying bubblegum melody. Most critics assume the song was supposed to be a joke (or even an intentional parody of "a bad song"), but it got released as a single and played *ad infinitum* by programmers who didn't realize this. If **Steve Taylor** should somehow *fail* to boycott hell, he would no doubt be forced to listen to this song for all eternity.

By now, the (usually) unspoken perception of most critics and insiders was that Taylor was the force behind The Newsboys and that they would be nothing without him. That turned out to be hyperbole. At the very least, Furler had learned a few things from the master, for Taylor had nothing to do with the next project and—produced by Furler alone—it turned out to be the pinnacle of the band's career. This was all the more surprising since founding member and lead singer John James departed the group and returned to Australia and Furler took over as lead vocalist as well. Without Taylor or James, the very making of *Step Up to the Microphone* seemed like an act of desperation and many pundits braced themselves to see just how badly Furler would embarrass himself. It was not to be. *Step Up to the Microphone* comes off like a greatest hits collection by any other artist, delivering more stellar, potential Top 10 pop songs than any non-Beatles album by any group in memory. Overall, the album moves back toward Europop style with shades of INXS and *Pop*-era **U2**. Thematically, it is more pre-evangelistic than evangelistic, delivering sprightly tunes that might have the masses singing along with spiritual lyrics they don't quite get. Catchy choruses, interesting danceable rhythms, and hook-filled melodies are this album's strengths. The opening "Woo Hoo" is pretty dumb lyrically, but remains a great song all the same. The title track and "Entertaining Angels" are gloriously infectious, on a par with anything that Smash Mouth or Sugar Ray would serve up in the late '90s, and yet completely original; none of those first three songs ("Woo Hoo," "Step Up to the Microphone," "Entertaining Angels") sound like anything else on the radio, nor do they sound like each other. "Believe" follows as the obligatory ballad, but what a fine and soaring ballad it is! "Tuning In" is a ready-to-mosh song (with little flamenco flourishes) that sets a creative description of God's accessibility to its pogo beat. "Truth Be Known—Everybody Gets a Shot" has a chant quality to it that works (short-term) as effectively as Queen's "We Will Rock You" or The Offspring's "Why Don't You Get a Job." The song "Deep End" is the best of the best, a wonderfully catchy pop song that takes the secular description of a new convert as "going off the deep end" and runs with it. "Hallelujah" sounds like it came straight off of Michael Jackson's *Thriller* instrumentally, with vocals that suddenly recall Al Stewart. After eight solid keepers, the group finally expires in a heap and concludes with two "cool-down" but slightly boring ballads. Even the latter of these manages a resurrection three-fourths of the way through, concluding with a Bee Gees-like chorus that takes things out in style.

No one thought it would be a good idea for The Newsboys to follow their career triumph with a disco album, but they did so anyway and the project is not quite the fiasco that some critics suggested. In keeping with the pattern of their past four albums, they open *Love Liberty Disco* with what appear to be the strongest cuts. "Beautiful Sound" and "Good Stuff" (based on 1 Corinthians 13) are solid pop songs that could easily have fit on *Step Up to the Microphone*. The title track is the only pure '70s disco track on the album and it is actually the highlight.

Every bit as good as Kool and the Gang's best, it comes out of the speakers like some long-lost gem from another era, like a just-discovered but worthy outtake from the *Saturday Night Fever* soundtrack. Still, market research could have told the band that '70s disco was not hot in 1999, and the album was basically viewed as a failure ("Say You Need Love" and "I Would Give Everything" also have enough of a disco flavor to turn off the nondisco inclined). When compiling their career retrospective "best-of" album, the group chose to include the same number of cuts from *Love, Liberty, Disco* as they did from the first three albums: zero. *Shine: The Hits* does, however, include three new songs featuring **Steve Taylor** ("Praises," "Who?" "Joy") and a remake of "God Is Not a Secret" featuring **Toby McKeehan.** The 2002 release was announced as a return to the "jaunty rock" style of *Step Up to the Microphone.* "Cornelius" is fun and bouncy. "It Is You" presents itself as a radio-ready praise song. "John Woo" references the popular director of action films.

In 1996, The Newsboys made a movie with **Steve Taylor** called *Down under the Big Top.* In 1997, they drew an impressive crowd of 33,000 fans to the Houston Astrodome for a concert. That same year, they performed at Pope John Paul II's World Youth Day. In 2000, the group attempted an innovative tour in which they carted a large inflatable Airdome around with them, setting up in vacant fields. The next year, the group founded what is expected to be an annual Festival Con Dios tour, featuring several artists in a traveling all-day carnival/rock show. Peter Furler is founder of the InPop record label, which seeks to help unsung artists get exposure. **Beanbag** produced the label's premiere product in 1999, followed by a solo album from bassist **Phil Joel.** Guitarist **Jody Davis** also went solo in 2001. In 2000, The Newsboys' former bass player Kevin Mills was killed in a motorcycle accident.

Christian radio hits: "All I Can See" (# 22 in 1990); "Simple Man" (# 13 in 1991); "One Heart" (# 2 in 1991); "Stay with Me" (# 6 in 1992); "I'm Not Ashamed" (# 1 for 3 weeks in 1992); "Where You Belong/Turn Your Eyes on Jesus" (# 9 in 1993); "Upon This Rock" (# 4 in 1993); "Dear Shame" (# 11 in 1993); "Be Still" (# 2 in 1994); "Shine" (# 1 for 6 weeks in 1995); "Let It Rain" (# 7 in 1995); "Spirit Thing" (# 1 for 2 weeks in 1995); "Real Good Thing" (# 1 in 1995); "Truth and Consequences" (# 1 for 2 weeks in 1995); "Reality" (# 1 for 5 weeks in 1996); "Take Me to Your Leader" (# 1 for 4 weeks in 1996); "Let It Go" (# 1 for 2 weeks in 1996); "Breakfast" (# 4 in 1997); "Breathe (Benediction)" (# 2 in 1997); "It's All Who You Know" (# 6 in 1997); "Shine 2000" (# 4 in 2000); "Entertaining Angels" (# 1 in 1998); "Woo Hoo" (# 1 for 4 weeks in 1998); "Believe" (# 1 for 4 weeks in 1999); "Step Up to the Microphone" (# 1 in 1999); "Beautiful Sound" (# 1 for 2 weeks in 2000); "Good Stuff" (# 1 in 2000); "Mega-Mix" (# 17 in 2000); "Love Liberty Disco" (# 7 in 2001); "Joy" (# 1 for 5 weeks in 2001); "Who?" (# 1 for 4 weeks in 2001).

Dove Awards: 1995 Rock Song ("Shine"); 1995 Rock Album *(Going Public).*

NewSong

Eddie Carswell, voc., perc.; Billy Goodwin, voc., gtr.; Bobby Apon, voc. (– 1994); Eddie Middleton, voc. (– 1994) // Leonard Ahlstrom, voc., gtr. (+ 1994); Scotty Wilbanks, voc., sax., kybrd. (+ 1994, – 1999); Russ Lee, voc., gtr., trump. (+ 1994, – 1999); Charles Billingsley, voc. (+ 1994, – 1997); Matt Butler, kybrd. (+ 2001); Michael O'Brien, voc. (+ 2001); Steve Reitschl, voc., gtr. (+ 2001). 1982—*The Son in My Eyes* (Covenant); 1984—*The Word* (Canaan); 1986—*Trophies of Grace* (Word Nashville); 1987—*Say Yes!* (Word); 1988—*Say Yes! And Their Greatest Hits*; 1989—*Light Your World*; 1990—*Living Proof*; 1992—*One Heart at a Time*; 1993—*All around the World* (Benson); 1994—*People Get Ready*; 1997—*Love Revolution*; 1999—*Arise My Love: The Very Best of NewSong*; 2001—*Sheltering Tree*.

www.newsongonline.com

NewSong has actually been two different groups. The initial group was a southern gospel quartet from Atlanta, Georgia; they were remarkable simply for keeping the same membership for fifteen straight years. Even as a quartet, the group gradually introduced contemporary stylings into their songs in a manner similar to **The Imperials** or **The Bill Gaither Trio.** By *Say Yes!, CCM* magazine was still calling them "a more conservative" version of **The Imperials,** but by *Light Your World* that magazine was comparing them to **Glad.** Then, in an article on *Living Proof,* the magazine would note that "NewSong has evolved from an inspirational quartet into a contemporary pop group, which blends in a dash of modern country." **Michael Omartian** helped out with that album, which includes "Whole Hearted," a copy of Michael Bolton's "Soul Provider." The group would cover the Four Tops' "Reach Out (I'll Be There)" on *All around the World* and *CCM* compared them repeatedly to **4 Him.** The big change, however, came in 1994 when founding members Bobby Apon and Eddie Middleton left and four new singers and players were recruited. The latter were multitalented individuals who would help Eddie Carswell (the principal songwriter) and Billy Goodwin (the main lead singer) turn the group into an actual band, a pop-rock group on the order of **PFR** or **The Kry.** NewSong was retooled for the '90s. "No more wearing matching jackets and using microphones and pointing at stuff nobody can see," Russ Lee would say with a laugh. The transformation was successful as *People Get Ready* was the band's biggest hit and earned them unprecedented critical acclaim. The lead-off song is a very soulful cover of **Curtis Mayfield**'s hit, done with some respect for Rod Stewart and Jeff Beck's 1985 remake. They also cover their own hit from *Say Yes!,* providing a greatly improved version of the worshipful hymn "Arise, My Love." **Charles Billingsley** left the group after that album to pursue a solo career, and **Russ Lee** (who had previously sung with **Truth**) followed him to do the same after *Love Revolution.* The latter album features Lee as lead singer on a number of its more energetic songs, including the rousing ode to abundant life, "More Fun Than Sin." Goodwin continues to use his smoother, warmer tone for the inspirational ballad "Hold On to the Cross." *Love Revolution* also includes "Rhythm of the World," a funky innovative song with Spanish sounds, oriental tones, and a Swahili groove. In 2001, the group came back with three new members (Steve Reitschl was recruited from **Acappella**), and their sound returned to the less rock, more adult contemporary stylings of *All around the World.* The title track to *Sheltering Tree* was inspired by a piece from preacher Charles Swindoll; it focuses on how God can surround a person with friends when his or her life is going badly. NewSong appropriately called on numerous friends to join their voices to the anthemic song—including **Carolyn Arends, Natalie Grant, Fred Hammond, Charlie Peacock,** Mac Powell (from **Third Day**), and **Rebecca St. James.** The album also includes a heart-touching ballad called "The Christmas Shoes," about a young boy's quest to buy his sick mother a pair of shoes so that she can look beautiful when she meets Jesus.

Christian radio hits: "What Goes Around, Comes Around" (# 6 in 1988); "Light Your World" (# 7 in 1989); "Living Proof" (# 4 in 1991); "Whole Hearted" (# 20 in 1991); "My Heart's Already There" (# 13 in 1995); "When I'm with You" (# 9 in 1995); "Miracles" (# 10 in 1997); "Rhythm of the World" (# 5 in 1997); "Love Revolution" (# 25 in 1997).

Nicholas

Brenda Nicholas; Philip Nicholas; Lindy Laury Harold (–1985); Steve Jackson (– 1985); Dale Atkins (– 1983); Lathette Brooks (– 1983); Lonnie Nicholas (–1983) // Rodney Friend (+ 1983, –1985). 1981—*Tell the World* (Message); 1983—*Words Can't Express*; 1985—*Dedicated* (Command); 1987—*A Love Like This*; 1988—*Contemporary; Inspirational*; 1990—*More Than Music*; 1991—*Back to Basics* (Command).

Nicholas is a traditional gospel vocal group formed in West Chester, Pennsylvania, in 1971 by Philip Nicholas with his brother, Lonnie, and Steven Jackson. The group took a hiatus in 1977–1978 while Philip was a member of another group called Spirit. In 1981, the group re-formed with the lineup given above, now including Philip's new wife, Brenda Watson Nicholas. Personnel changes after 1983 were frequent and sometimes undocumented, but the essence of the group became the duo of Philip and Brenda. As a vocal group, Nicholas incorporates light jazz and R&B stylings into their material, crossing over from traditional gospel to touch on the contemporary Christian sound (*CCM* described their music as "black Christian MOR"). Their first album features the song "God's Woman" on which Brenda states her intention to be obedient enough "for all the world to see," and "Little Birdie," an upbeat waltz about the Holy Spirit. *Words Can't Express* includes a reworked version of the Roberta Flack/Donny Hathaway hit "The Closer I Get to You," which segues into **Andraé**

Crouch's "Thank You, Lord." Beginning with "A Love Like This," the group (duo?) would fashion a style that had critics comparing them to mainstream acts like Ashford and Simpson or Peaches and Herb. *CCM* regards *More Than Music* as their finest moment, with a variety of styles on display: "Excuse Me" is urban contemporary; "Holy Spirit," a beautiful ballad; and "I Do Promise to Love You," a soulful love song. Nicholas also performs Crouch's "It Won't Be Long" on *More Than Music.*

Christian radio hits: "How Long Can This Go On?" (# 12 in 1992).

Nicole

See **Nicole C. Mullen.**

Nina

1991—*No Shadow of Turning* (R.E.X.); 1997—*I'm Your Child* (Light).

Nina Llopis, lead singer for the Christian punk band **The Lead,** has released solo albums as simply Nina. After **The Lead** disbanded, Llopis worked for a time fronting a group called Out of Egypt. In her solo work she displays a style that has been likened to Juliana Hatfield and Sheryl Crow—an angst-driven voice with stripped-down accompaniment. *I'm Your Child* was produced by **Vector**'s Steve Griffith and features the standout tracks "Here's My Heart" and "His Love." Llopis was raised Jewish and majored in art at the University of Miami.

911

Kiko Campo, voc.; Cathi Denman, voc.; T-Bone Denman, gtr.; Brian Hicks, kybrd.; John Klingbiel, bass; Eric Stretz, drums; Kristi Stretz, voc. 1986—*Time Will Tell* (Exile).

911 was a sibling vocal trio similar to **2nd Chapter of Acts** with a four-person rhythm section. Kiko Campo and his two sisters, Cathi Denman and Kristi Stretz, harmonized on songs that sought to "answer the questions that both Christians and non-Christians struggle with in life." The group, which included the two sisters' spouses, was based in Las Vegas and played often on the West Coast. Their song "Where Are You Now?" garnered the most radio airplay.

Ninety Pound Wuss

Jeff Bettger [a.k.a. Jeff Suffering née Bettger], voc.; John Himmelberg, gtr. (– 1999); Marty Martinez, drums (– 1999); Matt Nelson, gtr. (– 1997) // John Spalding, gtr. (+ 1997); Dale Yob, bass (+ 1997, – 1999); Matt Johnson, drums (+ 1999); Brian Trimble, bass (+ 1999). 1995—*Ninety Pound Wuss* (Tooth and Nail); 1997—*Where Meager Die of Self-Interest*; 1999—*Short Hand Operation*; 2001—*Hierarchy of Snakes* (Live).

Ninety Pound Wuss is an anti-pop Christian punk band from Port Angeles, Washington. When they first appeared, the closest comparison many critics could offer for their sound was **MxPx,** but Ninety Pound Wuss lacks the melodic Green-Day appeal of that band. They opt instead for vocals shouted rapidly over repetitious guitar riffs with little concern for making one song sound distinct from another. The Dead Kennedys would make for a better analogy. Lyrically, the group addresses social problems and adolescent concerns with occasionally overt spiritual references. For example, the song "Red" (from their debut) is about racism, indicating that no matter the skin color, all people have the same red blood; then from out of nowhere it includes the line, "Purify me, Jesus, with the blood that you bled." Lest anyone think their name might be autobiographical, the group tries for a harder sound on their second album as lead singer Jeff Suffering (real name: Jeff Bettger) goes from shouting to screaming, often in a tortured voice. Suffering was in an angry mood for the sophomore project and both church and society get lambasted for their many failings. "Sick and You're Wrong" (from *Meager*) castigates the church for telling mentally retarded and physically handicapped people that "they have no faith" and "can't glorify the Lord"—leaving one to wonder just what sort of bizarre sect the artist had been attending. By the third project the group (with only Suffering remaining from the original lineup) had developed to the point that they could appreciate complexity and diversity. While maintaining the basic hard punk sound, they also explore a number of other avenues, adding industrial electronics, feedback, samples, and occasional pop flourishes, with enough variety in tempo and volume to create an emo effect. *Bandoppler* referred to *Short Hand Operation* as "one of the most innovative, dynamic albums ever produced." The song "Nostalgia" features a keyboard-pop introduction. "Torment in Tension" displays gorgeously complex layers of sound and "It Seems So Far" is an instrumental that evokes a mood worthy of its title.

In general, Ninety Pound Wuss adopts the clichéd position of maintaining they are "not a Christian band but rather, Christians who are in a band." They have never felt compelled to use their performances as vehicles for some type of ministry. "We felt pigeon-holed," Suffering said of their strained relationship with the Christian music industry, "We felt like there were all these expectations on us . . . and we're artists, not pastors." In the same way, he says that he does not intentionally write songs with "some contrived Christian message," but simply writes about whatever is "on his heart."

Band members Johnson, Spalding, and Suffering also formed the band **Raft of Dead Monkeys** with Doug Lorig of **Roadside Monument** (in which Johnson had also been a member). After that, Suffering formed another band called Suffering and the Hideous Thieves, which released an album in 2001 (*Real Panic Formed,* Velvet Blue). Before Ninety Pound Wuss, Johnson had played in **Don't Know** and **Blenderhead.**

Pat Nobody (a.k.a. **Nobody Special**)

1988—*Nobody Special* (Frontline).

Pat Nobody is the younger brother of Joey "Ojo" Taylor who fronted the important Christian band **Undercover.** In 1988, Nobody made a punk album that was quite a bit ahead of its time for the Christian music market. It was, according to *CCM*'s Brian Quincy Newcomb, the first hardcore punk released on a major Christian label (artists like **One Bad Pig** and **The Lead** had independent distribution). Nobody avoided the relative accessibility of **The Altar Boys,** going for an ultra-intensity that featured in-your-face (blatantly evangelistic) lyrics shouted over an often chaotic mix of noise. The album did not sell, but about ten years later, Alarma would re-release it as a self-titled work by an artist now identified as Nobody Special.

Noggin Toboggan

Jeffrey Newsome, voc., gtr.; Jeremy Wells, voc., bass; Mike Andersen, drums. 1999—*Snapcase* (Bettie Rocket); 2000—*Your Days Are Numbered*; 2002—*Pleased to Meet You.*

www.noggintoboggan.com

Noggin Toboggan is a punk trio from northern California noted for their humorous and idiosyncratic material. The group's basic sound is similar to that of **MxPx, Slick Shoes,** and Blink 182. The emphasis is on short, fast, fun songs. *Snapcase* offers "Kingdom Hall Crashers," a diss on Jehovah's Witnesses (cf. **Daniel Amos**' "Jesus Is Jehovah to Me") that includes the lines, "We're not tryin' to be jerks / But God saves by grace, not by works." *Your Days Are Numbered* features the explosive "Sometimes You Wonder" (47 seconds long) and "Random Christmas Song" a stream-of-consciousness meditation on things like Santa Claus and food.

No Innocent Victim (a.k.a. **NIV**)

Jason Moody, voc.; Corey Edelman, gtr. (– 2001); John Harbert, bass (–1997); Kurt Love, drums (–1997) // Jason Dunn, drums (+ 1997); Judd Morgan, bass (+ 1997); Tim Mason, gtr. (+ 2001). 1995—*Strength* (Rescue); 1997—*No Compromise*; 1999—*Flesh and Blood* (Victory); 2001—*Tipping the Scales* (Solid State).

No Innocent Victim formed in 1992 as a hardcore punk band with a strong ministry focus. Musically, the group has a heavy sound that offers a hybrid mixture of punk and metal, with vocals growled and shouted in a manner that is rarely intelligible. Lyrically, they are best known for harangues reflecting fundamentalist political agendas, but they do sometimes take up spiritual matters more intrinsic to the Christian faith. The shortened form of the group's name plays on the popular abbreviation for the New International Version translation of the Bible.

Strength contains a farcical rant against evolution called "Monkey Crap." *No Compromise* contains two antiabortion anthems, "Won't Back Down" and "Pro-Kill"; the latter song got them banned from one club in the more-permissive-than-tolerant town of Berkeley, California. After their first two albums, the group signed with the general market label Victory and toured with that company's well-known hardcore group Agnostic Front. *Flesh and Blood* continues to manifest the basic San-Diego-hardcore sound, but shows no backing off on the commitment to articulate convictions, as is evident in a song that is actually called "My Beliefs." Bruce Fitzhugh of **Living Sacrifice** provides guest vocals on the song "Tear Us Apart." *Tipping the Scales* features "Degeneration," inspired by President Clinton's involvement in sex scandals. The title track has a judgment theme: "Since the day you were born, you've been tipping the scales."

Noisy Little Sunbeams

Dale Bray, voc.; Troy Nilson, gtr., bass; Khena, drums. 1992—*Noisy Little Sunbeams* (Benson).

Noisy Little Sunbeams were an Australian trio that played a blend of fairly hard rock combined with elements of pop and rap. Overtly Christian, they nevertheless displayed little interest in proclaiming the gospel on their album for Benson, preferring to focus on condemnation of those whose ideologies they reject. The group even felt obliged to include a disclaimer in the liner notes indicating that they don't hate any of the people they condemn but are just "deeply saddened" by the destructive lives and views of those persons. Astrologers get blasted in "Bad Attitude"; Mormons are bitterly attacked (less for their beliefs than for their dress, lifestyle, and evangelistic zeal) in "They're Knockin' "; and pop singer Madonna has her musical abilities critiqued ("if only you could sing just a little in tune you wouldn't have to wear that bra") before being threatened with eternal damnation in "Turn or Burn." Musically, the latter song is classic '80s metal, as is "Money in Your Pocket," which condemns commercialization in the church, as demonstrated by celebrity evangelists and Christian music stars. On a somewhat brighter note, "Always in Heaven" is pure **Newsboys** pop; "Live Forever" (not the Oasis song) was cowritten with the latter band's Peter Furler. The Sunbeams also cover Bryan Adams' "Kids Wanna Rock," performed the way AC/DC might have done it.

Christian radio hits: "Always in Heaven" (# 2 in 1992).

Nonpoint (a.k.a. **Nonpoint Factor**)

Robert Rivera, drums; Alexis Benitez, bass; Kermit, voc.; Sam Mori, bass. As Nonpoint Factor: 1994—*Depression '94* (custom). As Nonpoint: 2000—*Statement* (MCA).

Nonpoint Factor was a popular Christian aggressive metal bands of the mid '90s. The group was formed by drummer Robert Rivera and made a five-song cassette dealing with the negative emotions the group had felt during the previous year. "1993 was a horrible year for me and the band," Rivera said. "We went through a lot of stuff together . . . so hopefully people will get that they're not the only ones with problems." The group disbanded before releasing anything else, although a CD titled *Anger through an Art Form* was announced and even reviewed in *HM* magazine. Progressive Arts would later re-release *Depression '94* on CD as part of their Millennium Edition Series. Then in 2001 Rivera surfaced with an entirely new band now called simply Nonpoint. The latter group functioned largely outside the Christian music scene, and their album for MCA even carried a Parental Advisory sticker for the use of profanity. Rivera told *HM* that only he and front man Elias Soriano were Christians, but that the two of them continued to be vocal about their faith whether fans like it or not. The band's songs are not overtly evangelical but try to convey what Rivera calls "a positive message." As for the profanity, Rivera says, "Sometimes you have to speak in harsh words for people who don't have their ear out, to turn their heads and listen, and when I do use any curse word, it's in context and, you know, it's not every other word. We're not 2 Live Crew." In 2001, all members but Rivera left the band and were replaced by Andrew Goldman (gtr.), KB (bass), and Elias Soriano (voc.)

Nichole Nordeman

1998—*Wide-Eyed* (StarSong); 2000—*This Mystery* (Sparrow).

www.nicholenordeman.com

Nichole Nordeman snuck quietly on to the Christian music scene in the late '90s with a debut album filled with intelligent, original songs performed without fanfare. Nordeman has a competent, unpretentious style, avoiding Whitneyisms that steal the spotlight from the songs themselves. Her movie-star good looks were seldom exploited in promotion and her personal life was not broadcast as some kind of inspirational biography. Critics and fans alike appreciated the lack of hype and the Gospel Music Academy nominated her for Best New Artist in 1999 and Best Female Artist in 2000. A native of Colorado Springs, Nordeman earned a college degree in psychology and then traveled to Hollywood where she worked as a waitress and tried to break into the music scene. Raised a Christian, she says she experienced some alienation from her upbringing when, at age eighteen, her parents' divorce met with ungracious responses from the legalistic church the family attended. She got over it, though, and subsequently earned her first contract by winning a contest sponsored by the Gospel Music Association. Nordeman's songs are almost all piano-based

numbers and her husky yet ethereal voice has invited comparisons to Sarah MacLachlan, **Kim Hill,** and **Jennifer Knapp.** Many critics compared her first two albums to the early works of **Cindy Morgan;** both were produced by Mark Hammond, responsible for Morgan's first three projects.

Wide-Eyed opens with "To Know You," a powerful pop ballad that speaks of a desire to know and love God in a way that transcends doubt. The title track confesses to a realization that all persons—even quirky and annoying ones—are created in the image of God and, so, ought not be casually dismissed. "Who You Are" is a building anthem of wonder expressing an ever-expanding awareness of God's grandeur. *This Mystery* was inspired by Madeline L'Engle's book *Walking on Water,* which deals with Christianity and the arts. The theme of the project seems to be that some mysteries of faith lie beyond understanding. "Small Enough" (sung with **Fernando Ortega**) affirms that God's greatness is ironically revealed in the divine ability to be "small enough" to be attentive to every individual concern. "Every Season" deals with the presence of God in all that life brings; the song was inspired by Nordeman's experience of singing at the wedding of a friend and then, four years later, at the funeral of the groom. "Tremble" resists cozy Jesus-is-my-buddy theology by giving voice to a reverent awe based in the biblical theme of godly fear. Another highlight is Nordeman's cover of Stevie Wonder's hit "As."

For trivia buffs: Just after Nordeman got her start in Christian music she was featured in an article in *U.S. News and World Report* (Oct. 26, 1998) on "jobs for the future." The magazine presented her as an example of the job "gospel performer," reporting her "entry level salary" as about $20,000 a year (less than waitressing).

Christian radio hits: "To Know You" (# 11 in 1998); "Who You Are" (# 7 in 1999).

The Normals

Mark Lockett, gtr.; Andrew Osenga, voc., gtr.; Clayton Daily, bass (−2000) // B. J. Aberle, bass, voc. (+ 2000); Cason Colley, kybrd. (+ 2000); Mike Taquino, drums (+ 2000). 1998—*Better Than This* (ForeFront); 2000—*Coming to Life;* 2002—*A Place Where You Belong.*

www.thenormals.com

The Normals are an acoustic pop group formed by Andrew Osenga and two high school friends from Normal, Illinois. All three of the original members were also students at Belmont University, where the group came together. The members all had strong backgrounds in the organization Young Life, having participated in the group, first as youth themselves and, then, as adult leaders. Their musical team came together naturally as part of this youth-oriented ministry. The overall style of both albums is melodic, acoustic pop that inspires comparisons to

Caedmon's Call, PFR, and especially **Jars of Clay.** *Better Than This* (produced by Billy Smiley of **White Heart**) was received as a competent-but-ordinary album, with lots of critics seizing on the group's name or the album's title to offer too-obvious-to-be-clever comments on the work's nonexceptional character. The most radio-friendly song is the catchy "Everything (Apron Full of Strings)," which tells of encounters with a disenchanted waitress and a homeless veteran and wonders how Christians can offer the fullness of Christ to such persons. Other tunes are more introspective and demanding. Leigh Nash of **Sixpence None the Richer** offers a duet vocal on "If Tomorrow Was Forever."

For *Coming to Life,* the expanded band worked with demanding producer Malcolm Burns, known for his work with such artists as Better Than Ezra, Emmylou Harris, and **U2.** Burns took them to New Orleans for a year and pushed them to develop what critics accepted as a greatly improved, refined sound that was consistent with the first project but more distinctive. *7ball* called it "one of the best modern pop albums of the year" and *True Tunes* praised it for exhibiting "depth, maturity, and passion." The opening song, "Every Moment," has an early **U2** quality to it. Equally strong and Bonoesque is "Full On (Don't Hold Back)." The song "Black Dress" is an eloquent meditation on the problem of male lust, but its reliance on the David and Bathsheba story as a vehicle for discussing the subject is anachronistic: given power differentials, the liaison between those two persons is better understood as an act of rape than as some sort of mutual extramarital affair (cf. 1 Kings 11:2–5). "We Are Beggars at the Foot of God's Door" is a sweet and thoughtful ballad extolling the grace of God. "Two Wrongs and a Right" features an especially catchy melody with reflection on the consequences of sin. "No Alibis" is a **Jars of Clay** sound-alike (cf. "Frail").

On *A Place Where You Belong,* The Normals display a diverse tapestry of sounds that reflects the influence of artists from Dire Straits ("Romeo on the Radio") to Tom Petty ("Less Than Love"). The song "Grace" deals with sexual purity in a subtle but effective manner. *CCM* calls the third album "contemplative and compelling."

Christian radio hits: "Everything" (# 2 in 1998); "Forgive" (# 7 in 1998); "Song and Dance" (# 13 in 1999); "The Best I Can" (# 12 in 2000).

Bebo Norman

1996—*The Fabric of Verse* (custom); 1999—*Ten Thousand Days* (Watershed); 2001—*Big Blue Sky.*

www.bebonorman.com

Bebo Norman is an unabashed folk singer from Columbus, Georgia. After earning a premed degree in biology, he decided to take one year off from school to explore his passion for music and created an independent album that sold an astonishing 35,000 copies without any recognizable public distribution. Cliff Young of **Caedmon's Call** took note and signed him to the new Watershed label that he had started. *Ten Thousand Days* repeats three songs from the custom album and infuses the mainly folk stylings with occasional pop elements (notably on "Stand" and "The Man Inside"). The closest general market analogies to Norman's music are provided by his acknowledged influences, Mark Cohn and **David Wilcox.** The overall mood is subdued: slow, quiet songs (like those of **Michael Card**) with thoughtful lyrics that reflect on the weakness of humanity and the wonder of God's grace; the aforementioned pop songs break the mood with moments that recall **Chris Rice.** Reviewing Norman's *Fabric* debut, *Performing Songwriter* (a secular publication) said, "Nowhere is his skill as a storyteller more evident than in the stunning ballad, 'The Hammer Holds'—if he never wrote another tune, this incredible fable of faith would make him a songwriter with a capital S." That number is included on *Ten Thousand Days.* "A Page Is Turned," written for his brother's wedding, testifies to the faithfulness of "the God of second chance." A piano ballad called "Deeper Still" offers a poignant look at the tragedy of divorce and relates how one woman discovered the strength of will and the power of God to finally bring thirty years of failed marriage to its appropriate conclusion. The closing song, "Rita," is an especially beautiful and haunting eulogy to a friend who died too young.

Norman's *Big Blue Sky* reinvents him as a pop-rock singer in the same vein as Billy Joel or **Stephen Curtis Chapman.** The jaunty opening beat of "I Am" affirms God's omnipresence: "I am in the fire / I am in the flood / I am in the marrow and the blood." The next song, "Cover Me," seems to be a lyrical mirror image of its predecessor, praying for God's presence to be realized in all of life. At times, Norman invokes Springsteen balladry, with songs like "Sons and Daughters" recalling the latter's "Secret Garden."

Larry Norman

1969—*Upon This Rock* (Capitol); *Street Level* (One Way); 1972—*Bootleg; Only Visiting This Planet* (MGM); 1973—*So Long Ago the Garden* (MGM); 1976—*In Another Land* (Solid Rock); 1977—*Streams of White Light into Darkened Corners* (AB); 1978—*Starstorm* (Starstorm); 1979—*Live at the Mac* (CS); 1980—*The Israel Tapes* [with People] (Phydeaux); 1980—*Roll Away the Stone* [with Mark Heard and Randy Stonehill]; 1981—*Something New under the Son* (Solid Rock); 1981—*The Tune* (Phydeaux); 1983—*Letter of the Law; 1983—Labor of Love; 1983—The Story of the Tune; Come As a Child* [with Barry McGuire]; 1983—*Quiet Night* [with The Young Lions]; 1984—*A Chronological History (1966–1984)* (Stress); *Stop This Flight* (Six Blue Lions); 1985—*Back to America* [EP]; 1986—*Rehearsal for Reality* (Royal); 1986—*Down Under But Not Out* (Phydeaux); 1988—*White Blossoms from Black Roots* (Solid Rock); 1989—*The Best of the Second Trilogy*

(Phydeaux); 1989—*Home at Last* (Solid Rock); 1989—*Live at Flevo* [with Q-Stone] (Spark); 1990—*The Best of Larry Norman* (Royal) [= *Confiscated* (Phydeaux)]; 1993—*Stranded in Babylon* (Spark); 1994—*Omega Europe* (Solid Rock); 1994—*Totally Unplugged: Alive and Kicking* (Street Level); *Children of Sorrow*; 1994—*Footprints in the Sand* (Street Level); *A Moment in Time*; 1996—*Re-Mixing This Planet* (N'Soul); 1998—*Gathered Moments: Somewhere in This Lifetime* (Howling Dog); 1998—*Shouting in the Storm* [with Beam] (Solid Rock); 1998—*Breathe In, Breathe Out* [with Beam]; *Copper Wires*; 1999—*Live at the Mac*; *We Wish You a Larry Christmas*; *The Vineyard*; *The Cottage Tapes, Book One: Where the Woodbine Twineth* [with Randy Stonehill]; 2000—*In the Beginning*; *Kiss the Blarney Stone*; *Sticks and Stones*; 2001—*Tourniquet*; *Rough Diamonds * Precious Jewels: The Belfast Bootlegs* (independent).

www.larrynorman.com

Larry Norman is usually referred to as "the father of Christian rock" and that title is well deserved. As **Randy Stonehill** once said, "If not for Larry Norman, we might all be doing Christian polka or something, but not Christian *rock.*" Norman is the single most important individual in the development of the genre and, though the scope of his influence would fade rather quickly, he would continue to provide the quintessential example of another course that history might have taken. General market artists as diverse as Frank Black, John Mellencamp, and three-fourths of **U2** (Bono, The Edge, and Larry Mullen Jr.) have all cited Norman as a prominent influence—and his unacknowledged influence on Gordon Gano of **Violent Femmes** is also unmistakable. The term "Jesus freak" was first coined to refer to him, and no other person in history has ever been more deserving of the appellation. In many ways, Norman's saga is a sad one, for by 1990, he would appear to be either marginalized or alienated from the contemporary Christian music subculture that grew out of what he had created. Yet, from a historical perspective, Norman had never wanted to have anything to do with what came to be called "contemporary Christian music" anyway. Norman was into rock and roll and, like **Michael Knott,** he would exhibit the qualities of a stereotypical "rock artist" personality—mysterious, dismissive, manipulative—but, above all, possessed with an undisputed genius that would consistently set him beyond the comprehension or reach of those who would offer (sometimes legitimate) criticisms of his life and his work. In many ways, he is Christian music's Neil Young.

Norman was born in Texas in 1947, but he grew up in a mostly black area of San Francisco. Unlike most pioneers of Jesus music, he did not have any "conversion experience" as a young adult but grew up an evangelistically minded Christian. He was raised in a conservative church, officially "accepting Christ" at the age of five and never really knowing a time when he was not a devout believer. If there was a "conversion" it was not *from* the hippie culture to the church, but the other way around. Norman came as a young Christian to embrace parts of the counter-cultural youth movement, while clearly rejecting other aspects of it. He never did drugs and he was not noted for protesting the Vietnam war or for supporting civil rights. He did, however, grow his hair down to his waist and learn to play "protest songs" of Dylanesque stature. He spoke in the idiom of the day (minus obscenities) and he espoused enough anti-institutionalism and showed sufficient disrespect for (selected) authorities to earn him a place in the hearts of America's hippie youth. Most of all, he embraced rock and roll, which was completely absent from the liturgies of virtually all churches. Norman later maintained that even as a child he wondered why they sang "ancient songs" in church with lines about "bulwarks never failing" instead of songs like those on the radio with words that he could clearly understand. He actually got in trouble with his parents as a child for writing and performing a "shocking" song called "Moses in the Wilderness" for a church picnic.

Norman moved to San Jose, California, and at the age of eighteen formed a band that he called People (as a response to all the groups with animal names—The Turtles, The Byrds, etc.). They recorded an album featuring a remake of a Zombies song, "I Love You." The song features a long, psychedelic instrumental introduction (reminiscent of Vanilla Fudge or Iron Butterfly) leading finally to Norman's climactic vocal, the line "I love you, but the words don't come—and I don't know what to sa-ay" sung in a high, nasal whine. The song took off, becoming Number One in many parts of the country and eventually reaching Number Fourteen on the national charts. Although the album containing the song was not particularly religious, Norman titled it *We Need a Whole Lot More of Jesus and a Lot Less Rock and Roll* and designed the cover to have an artistic representation of Jesus on the front. According to Norman, executives at Capitol nixed these ideas and without even contacting him changed the title to *I Love You* (Capitol, 1968) and placed a photo of the band on the cover. Norman says that the day the album came out and he saw what they had done, he quit the group. A slightly different version of this story related by historian David Di Sabatino holds that Norman was also at odds with the other group members over their beliefs in Scientology. In any case, People would go on to record two more nondescript albums without Norman: *Both Sides of People* (Capitol, 1969) and *There Are People and There Are People* (Paramount, 1970); actually Norman can be heard singing on some of *Both Sides'* tracks, which must be outtakes from the first project. The group People that Larry Norman founded was in no way related to the Christian glam-rock band named The People who recorded an indie album named *The Premise Is Sound* in 2000.

After leaving People, Norman wrote and staged two musicals. According to rock historian Wally Rasmussen, Pete

Townsend has acknowledged that one of these *(The Epic)* served as the inspiration for The Who's *Tommy,* providing him with both the basic idea of "rock opera" and also with an essential plot line (involving a misunderstood messianic leader). Norman was also offered the lead role in the Broadway cast of *Hair,* which he turned down (it was subsequently filled by **Barry McGuire**). Then in 1969 he recorded what would come to be regarded as the world's first Christian rock album.

In retrospect, *Upon This Rock* looks like a "greatest hits" compilation, for practically every song on it would become a Norman classic. Many of these, however, would become better known in alternative (and better) versions included on subsequent projects. The aforementioned "Moses in the Wilderness" is here in all its junior-high church camp glory. Norman retells the story from Exodus in a rambling song that recalls Bill Cosby's humorous monologue on the Noah tale: "Moses kept bugging the Pharaoh . . . he bugged him and bugged him . . . used real bugs too." That song along with "You Can't Take Away the Lord" and "Nothing Really Changes" are the main gems that would not turn up conspicuously elsewhere. "Walking Backwards down the Stairs" is a brilliant prophetic folk song in the tradition of *Another Side of Bob Dylan,* but it is done here in an overly slick version with too much orchestration; a better rendition appears on *Bootleg.* Three songs ("Ha Ha World," "The Last Supper," and "Forget Your Hexagram") feature a blend of apocalyptic imagery and psychedelic sound that make for a perfect match. The two most famous songs from *Upon This Rock,* however, are "Sweet, Sweet Song of Salvation" and "I Wish We'd All Been Already." The former is a fairly safe "camp song" that caught on in youth groups all around the country and was covered by many, many artists. "I Wish We'd All Been Ready" was even more widely covered, but is anything but "safe."

Perhaps the second most popular song of the Jesus movement (after **Children of the Day**'s "For Those Tears I Died"), "I Wish We'd All Been Ready" begins with the chilling lines, "Life was filled with guns and war and everyone got trampled on the floor," and then things *really* get bleak. The song's imagery is brilliantly poetic ("children died, the days grew cold, a piece of bread could buy a bag of gold") and mysterious ("two men walking up a hill, one disappears and one's left standing still"). On the basis of this one song, *Billboard* magazine introduced Larry Norman as "the poet laureate of the Jesus movement" and as "the most important songwriter since Paul Simon." Musically, "I Wish We'd All Been Ready" features a haunting melody to match its disturbing theme. Theologically, it is completely off base, but revelatory of some of the more cultic features of the Jesus movement. The song purports to describe the plight of people who remain on earth after faithful Christians have been "raptured into heaven." The idea of such a

scenario—of a rapture of the saints preliminary to the return of Christ—is a nonscriptural invention of politically motivated fundamentalist thought, but in the early days of the Jesus movement revival some teachers and preachers presented the doctrine as though it were straight out of the Bible, and the Jesus people lacked the theological acumen to evaluate such teachings. Norman's song quotes from Matthew 24:40–41, a text that clearly refers to the parousia of Christ (cf. 24:39) rather than to some preliminary rapture (plus, according to Matthew 13:49–50, when the great harvest does come, one wants to be left, not taken). All the same, it is worth noting that while most Christian music of the early '70s was of the light, I'm-so-happy-in-Jesus variety (cf. **Mustard Seed Faith**), Norman started things off on a much darker note. Most of the songs on *Upon This Rock* ("Ha Ha World," "Walking Backwards down the Stairs," "The Last Supper," "I Wish We'd All Been Ready") have an alternative edge to them that would not become prominent in Christian music for another fifteen to twenty years. As a trivia note, *Upon This Rock* features "background singing and thigh claps" by Matthew, Nelly, and Annie Ward—the trio of siblings who would later be known as **2nd Chapter of Acts.**

Street Level and *Bootleg* would follow *Upon This Rock* as hodgepodge collections of songs and song ideas, many of which would eventually end up on later concept albums. Norman recorded the albums with some money (about $3000) loaned to him by sympathetic entertainer **Pat Boone** (one of hundreds of artists to cover "I Wish We'd All Been Ready"). Norman actually made *three* albums with that loan. The third project was apparently the debut **Randy Stonehill** album *Born Twice*—though David Di Sabatino thinks a collection of songs and interviews with various artists called *The Son Worshippers* (One Way, 1972) was also produced with the Boone loan, making for a total of four projects. In any case, *Street Level* was issued in two different versions. Side One (in both cases) records a solo concert performed at Don Williams' Hollywood Presbyterian Church. Anti-institutionalism seems to be a prominent theme. Norman opens the concert with a poem by Nigel Goodwin called "First Day in Church" and also sings a song called "Right Here in America," which offers a scathing attack on the "dead Christianity" he saw in so many of the country's sanctuaries. Side Two of the first version of *Street Level* contains songs from one of Norman's musicals (a play called *Lion's Breath*), including the soon-to-be-classic, "Six O'Clock News"; Side Two of the better-known second version consists of songs performed with a group called White Light, which includes **Randy Stonehill** on second guitar and vocal harmony; they perform "Baby out of Wedlock" and "No More LSD for Me (I Met the Man from Galilee)."

Bootleg is one of the finest albums of Norman's career. It opens with one of his best songs, the bluesy Neil Young-like "I Think I Love You" (not the Partridge Family song), which would never turn up elsewhere (at least not conspicuously). The same is true for his "The Day That a Child Appeared" (featuring just Larry at his piano) and the country-flavored "A Song Won't Stop the World"—brilliant moments of stripped down folk-blues at its best. Better known, but more commercial are the eschatological ballads "Six Sixty Six" and "UFO," which play against type by setting the potentially dark subject of the world's end to pretty melodies that are sung in a lullaby sweet voice. Norman's best version of "Walking Backwards down the Stairs" is found here along with his ironic methinks-thou-dost-protest-too-much ballad, "I Don't Believe in Miracles." He performs "Ha, Ha World" the way that Jefferson Airplane would have done it. Other very special songs—and absolutely essential for any true Jesus freak—are "Even If You Don't Believe" and "Song for a Small Circle of Friends." And then there is the literal anthem of the Jesus movement, "One Way," which Norman wrote to accompany the practice of raising an index finger toward heaven as a sign of faith—a practice that he started. The more church-friendly **Danny Lee and the Children of Truth** used "One Way" as the title song for their debut album in 1971, bringing Norman to the attention of a wider audience.

One full side of *Bootleg* (a two-record set) features interviews and spoken monologues by Norman. These provide valuable and authentic documentation of the thinking that fueled the Jesus movement: paranoia and naivete are much in evidence but so are enthusiasm, unflinching commitment, and a generous amount of sardonic joy. Without such documents, it would be difficult for anyone in the twenty-first century to realize that in 1971 hundreds of thousands of young Christians in America really did believe that authorities (Nixon, the United Nations, and even the World Council of Churches) were going to start hunting them down and shooting them. It would be even more difficult to appreciate the fact that these young people fully expected this to happen very soon and that they welcomed the day when they would get to die for their Lord: "When they come, you just pray for them, and when they lead you away, sing glory to God. And when they shoot you, just smile."

Both *Street Level* and *Bootleg* contain versions of a rockabilly song, "Blue Shoes White," in which Norman puns about "getting our souls rehealed." Both also contain alternative versions of Norman's best song, "Why Don't You Look into Jesus?" (though on *Street Level* it is called "Jim Ware's Blues"). That one song alone could establish him as the ultimate Christian rocker, for never before or since has any artist presented an invitation to the gospel in an idiom so perfectly crafted to rock

and roll. "Drinkin' whisky from a paper cup / Drown your sorrows till you can't stand up" Norman sings, and it only gets rawer from there: "Gonorrhea on Valentines Day / Are you still lookin' for the perfect lay?" Norman indicated at one point that the song was written for Janis Joplin, who he wished to challenge with its all important conclusion: "Why don't you look into Jesus? He's got the answers." It would later be covered for the '90s by **Holy Soldier** (with the gonorrhea reference updated to HIV). Around this time, Norman also recorded a song called "Dear Malcolm, Dear Alwyn" (basically a musical fan letter to **Malcolm and Alwyn**) that would become one of his best-known songs due to its inclusion on an influential compilation album (*Jubilation,* Myrrh, 1975).

Norman's best-known output came in the form of a carefully conceived trilogy, or at least in the form of two-thirds of that trilogy. The first installment, *Only Visiting This Planet* (with arrangements by George Martin, known for his work with the Beatles), is universally regarded as his strongest work. In 1988, a poll of critics conducted by *CCM* magazine chose *Only Visiting This Planet* as the single best Christian album of all time. Ten years later, a similar poll would still place it at Number Two, behind **Amy Grant**'s inferior *Lead Me On.* Practically every song on the disc would still be regarded as a classic of Christian rock thirty years later, and the only two exceptions to this appraisal are two nonreligious songs that are, in fact, two of the album's finest tracks. One is the classically influenced and quite lovely "Pardon Me," a completely secular love song. The other is the opening cut, "I've Got to Learn Live without You," which is a plaintive piano ballad of lost love, inspired by Norman's marital problems—which would result in the divorce the song predicts, though not until 1980. In retrospect, it is staggering that one of the most popular and influential Christian albums of all time would open with a divorce song—and with a very secular divorce song at that (no mention of God or faith or Jesus).

As indicated, the eight non-secular songs on *Only Visiting This Planet* would all become standards. "The Outlaw" is a simple country folk song presenting Jesus as a counter-cultural figure who ran amuck of the legal and religious authorities of his day. "Righteous Rocker" offers a magnificent rock and roll interpretation of 1 Corinthians 13:2: "You can be a brilliant surgeon or a sweet young virgin . . . without love, you ain't nothin." There are also three Dylanesque songs in the vein of that artist's "Masters of War"/"Hard Rain" protest period. Many artists copied Dylan's technique on such matters, but aside from P. F. Sloan's one success (cf. **Barry McGuire**), none ever did so more effectively than Norman on this outing. "I Am the Six O'Clock News" rants against the media's indifference to suffering—a rare objection from any quarter in those days. "The Great American Novel" (which Norman would later play at the White House for President Carter in 1979) offers specifically Christian protests against American life, venting on matters that would soon become clichés (putting "In God We Trust" on money, which is itself the true basis for American confidence) or would be driven into the ground by the Religious Right. In 1972, such complaints at least sounded fresh, though, even then, many of the gripes were strained: the Supreme Court ruling that children cannot be pressured to pray in school hardly constitutes *forbidding* children from doing so. In such respects, "The Great American Novel" offers a forecast of the disastrous social agendas that would create a caricature of Christianity in the decades to come—presenting Christians as persons who whine about being persecuted in a society where faith brings privilege and who approach politics with a selfish lack of concern for citizens who do not share their beliefs. A much better song is "Readers' Digest," which comments on popular culture with lots of tongue-in-cheek humor, taking swipes at numerous celebrities ("I've been listening to Paul's records—I think he is dead") and public policies ("sent some people to the moon . . . they brought back a big bag of rocks, only cost 13 billion . . . must be nice rocks!"). Still, the highlight of *Only Visiting This Planet* for many is the anthemic "Why Should the Devil Have All the Good Music?" based on a saying of Martin Luther. A rollicking, good-time party song, it says all that needs to be said about the purpose of (and need for) Christian rock: "I ain't knockin' the hymns, Just give me a song that moves my feet / I don't like none of them funeral marches . . . I ain't dead yet!" All these songs are paired with what for most listeners would become the definitive versions of "Why Don't You Look into Jesus?" and "I Wish We'd All Been Ready." Only the latter song is out of place—since the supposed theme of the record is "the present," not the future, but it was Norman's best-known song at the time and apparently that justified breaking up what is an otherwise impeccable song order. *Only Visiting This Planet* would be Norman's only project to gain much attention outside the Christian music scene. Pop stars Petula Clark, Gene Cotton, and **Cliff Richard** all covered songs from the record on regular general market albums.

So Long Ago the Garden is part two of the trilogy, supposedly dealing with "the past." It is a very strong collection, but failed commercially. In general, it has a secular feel and appeal to it, which probably turned off the increasingly narrow-minded Jesus people who didn't want to waste their time or pollute their minds listening to songs that didn't specifically mention Jesus. Some of the songs, apparently, derive from Norman's pre-Jesus-movement involvement, perhaps from the two musicals that he wrote in 1969; MGM reportedly pulled some more spiritual songs off the project. "She's a Dancer" (originally from version one of *Street Level*) is a lovely, atmospheric song of

the sort that Neil Young occasionally contributed to Buffalo Springfield ("I Am a Child," "Expecting to Fly"). Several of the other songs seem to have been inspired at least indirectly by Norman's marital problems. "Baroquen Spirits" is a song about failed romance built around the lyric, "It must be hard to respect a man who needs you more than you need him." The song "Lonely by Myself" expresses the desire to find a suitable helpmeet, establishing an identification with the pre-Eve Adam who lives in what would otherwise be paradise. Another highlight, "The Same Old Story," is a beautiful pop song about falling in love with someone who "you know is going to break your heart." *Garden* also features "Christmastime," a song that would become better known when included on **Randy Stonehill**'s debut album with extra lyrics (who but Larry Norman would begin a Christmas song with the words, "Santa Claus is comin' and the kids are gettin' greedy")? "Nightmare #71" is a Norman rap, fashioned after **Bob Dylan**'s talking "dream" songs, but its stream-of-consciousness paranoid lyrics have never been understood. Aside from the seemingly nonedifying character of its songs, *So Long Ago the Garden* took a beating in the Christian marketplace for another, even dumber reason. The photo on the album cover shows a lion in a field of grass superimposed on Norman's torso; a few observers mistook some of the grass for pubic hair and rumors spread that Norman was naked on the cover (how likely would *that* have been?). Many stores refused to stock the album, and some did not carry it even after a new edition with a closely cropped cover had been released. The CD re-release of *So Long Ago the Garden* years later includes a demo of "Dear Malcolm, Dear Alwyn" as a bonus track.

In 1973, Norman came back strong with part three of the trilogy, his most commercially successful project ever. Partly because of its theme (the future), *In Another Land* features songs of faith from start to finish, including new, polished versions of "One Way," "UFO," "Six Sixty Six," and "Song for a Small Circle of Friends"—wonderful songs that most Christian music fans had not yet heard (given the low distribution of *Bootleg*). The album opens with "The Rock That Doesn't Roll," a rousing piece of R&B rock that sounds like *Sticky Fingers*-era Rolling Stones and deserves to be placed beside "Why Should the Devil Have All the Good Music?" in the canon of Norman's great rock and roll songs. It is followed by "I Love You"—not the original People song, but a new, catchy pop tune written by **Randy Stonehill** for the Billy Graham film *Time to Run*. The breathtakingly beautiful "Deja Vu (If God Is My Father)" is sung almost a capella. "I Am a Servant" offers a graceful and sincere statement of Christian humility. "Shot Down" is '50s rockabilly (à la **Elvis Presley** or Ricky Nelson) and provides a bold statement of persistence in the face of persecution: "I've been shot down, talked about . . . but like a moth drawn to a flame / Here I am, talkin' about Jesus just the same." Norman maintains that, in an ironic bout of reverse censorship, Word records insisted that he cut some "non-spiritual" songs from the album before they distribute it to the Christian retail market. Dudley Moore, who would later become a famous British actor, plays piano on parts of the album.

Norman also produced some rather esoteric projects during his first decade. *Streams of White Light into Darkened Corners* is a parody album on which he plays a number of quasi-spiritual songs by general market artists (**Norman Greenbaum**'s "Spirit in the Sky"; George Harrison's "My Sweet Lord"; Simon and Garfunkel's "Bridge over Troubled Water") lampooning their attempt to jump on the spiritual bandwagon. **Randy Stonehill** guests as a fast-talking DJ introducing the cuts with quips like "here's a trilogy of songs about faith, hope and royalties." *The Tune* was recorded in 1977, featuring Norman singing a few spirituals and a very long, narrative song that he made up on a concert stage in 1970. Mostly spoken word, the latter song (called "The Tune") relates an allegorical tale of people searching for "a tune" that they once knew (cf. The Moody Blues' *In Search of the Lost Chord*). Performance of this number would offer a popular break from music during Norman's concerts, though the song doesn't really hold up to repeated listening as a musical work. The albums *Letter of the Law, Labor of Love,* and *Quiet Night,* all feature Norman performing songs written mainly by **Tom Howard,** in the interest of establishing that artist as a songwriter. *CCM* would call *Quiet Night* the "most commercial album Norman has ever released, sounding right at home with the musical styles of **Amy Grant** and **Russ Taff.**" *Letter* and *Labor* had very limited distribution.

Something New under the Son is another Norman masterpiece, perhaps his most underappreciated work. Although released in 1981, the project was actually recorded in 1977. Dealing with the theme of alienation, it draws strongly on a blues tradition for a sound that Di Sabatino likens to the Rolling Stones' *Exile on Main Street.* Norman's oft-time guitarist John Linn especially shines on the album. "Hard Luck, Bad News" and "Born to Be Unlucky" are blues rock classics on the same order as Booker T. Jones' "Born under a Bad Sign." Sandwiched between those highlights are two slowed-down shuffles with the titles "Feeling So Bad" and "I Feel Like Dying." The first of these expresses the thoughts of a man wallowing in depression who interprets his lover's new relationship with the Lord as "cheating on him." A song called "Nightmare # 97" picks up where the last Nightmare song left off, with the same basic tune that "Bob Dylan's 115th Dream" borrowed from "Stagger Lee." The songs "Watch What You're Doin' " and "Leaving the Past Behind" are both remarkable. The former (covered by The Pixies) features lyrics worthy of **Victoria Williams**' best work: "Momma killed the chicken / Thought it

was a duck / Put it on the table with its legs stickin' up / Papa broke his glasses when he fell down drunk / Tried to drown the kitty cat, turned out to be a skunk / You gotta watch what you're doin'." The album's absolute standouts, however, are "Put Your Life into His Hands," which features a traditional gospel sound, and "Let the Tape Keep Rollin'," a sped-up Chuck Berry-style song. On both numbers, Norman sings like Mick Jagger with touches of **Van Morrison.**

After the triumphs of the '70s (to which *Something New* rightly belongs), Norman's career as a Christian music star was all but over. He would release many more albums—some very good and some pretty bad—but none caught the attention of the Christian music crowd (fans or critics) the way that *Only Visiting This Planet* and *In Another Land* did. The discography above appears lengthy, but there were only four albums of substantial, new material in the twenty-five years after *Something New Under the Son* was recorded.

Stop This Flight features a lovely, bittersweet song called "Looking for a Woman of God (Proverbs 31)," which revisits some of the same territory as "Lonely by Myself." *Flight* includes a number of songs regarding recovery from love gone bad: the desperate "Don't You Want to Talk about It?"; a funky, I'm-over-you song called "Out of My System" (which ironically demonstrates by its very existence that she isn't out of his system yet); and the very nice, confessional, looking-for-closure ballad "I Hope to See You in Heaven" ("I was wrong to let you go / I was a child and I did not know"). The song "What's Wrong with This Body?" preaches to the church and "Messiah" returns to Norman's favorite Second Coming theme. The album was recorded before a live audience but is of studio quality.

Home at Last deals with family issues and provided Norman with his first and only official Christian radio hit. "Somewhere out There" (not the Linda Ronstadt/James Ingram song) is about accepting responsibility for being a parent and even more about appreciating the joys of fatherhood. "We Three Twogether" is sort of a novelty song (sung in a "swingin' '20s" style) for Norman's son Michael. The "three of us" who Norman joyously proclaims are "now happy together" are the post-divorce family consisting of Larry, Michael, and their dog Phydeaux. "My Feet Are on the Rock" is a strong blues number in the tradition of *Something New.* "Country Church" celebrates the faith of rural people and was inspired by the rugged faith of Norman's grandparents. "Letters to the Church" offers a pointed critique of prosperity-oriented religion that fails to seek holiness. *Home at Last* was originally intended to be the first installment of "a second trilogy" that would also include *Behind the Curtain* and *Stranded in Babylon.* The middle part did not see release.

Stranded in Babylon renews much of the social-political commentary found on *Only Visiting This Planet*. It opens (after a moment of silliness) with a strong rocker, "God, Part III," which provides Norman's response to John Lennon's song "God" from his seminal *Plastic Ono Band* album ("God, Part II" was a similar but less overtly theistic response performed by **U2** on *Rattle and Hum*). "Step into the Madness" is a harangue against the evils of modern America, and specifically, against a system that sells "justice" for money. "Come Away" offers an invitation of repentance to a harlot who probably serves as a metaphor for modern America. "Hide His Heart" is a remarkably perceptive song about the man who finds himself unable to share his true feelings with the woman he loves. *Babylon's* highlight is "All the Way Home," a strong midtempo song affirming the sufficiency of God's love for making it through a life that can seem hard and long.

Norman continued to tour throughout the '80s, alternately using such hard rock groups as **Jerusalem, Daniel Band,** and **Leviticus** as his backing band. Still, by the end of that decade, he had become somewhat isolated and even alienated from the Christian music subculture. A number of problems set in. First, there were Norman's strained relations with other artists. *In Another Land* was the premiere release on Norman's own Solid Rock label, a company that also signed **Mark Heard, Tom Howard, Pantano-Salsbury, Randy Stonehill,** and **Daniel Amos.** Solid Rock was not a commercially successful venture. Years later, John Thompson, editor of *True Tunes,* maintained, "By releasing high-quality music by the best bands, Norman doomed his label to certain financial ruin—he was simply way ahead of the curve." In any event, the problems were not only financial but personal: both Stonehill and **Daniel Amos** ended up leaving the label with negative attitudes, complaining about how they had been mistreated (see listings). Next, there were problems with the Christian media. In 1989, *CCM* printed an interview with the artist in which he talked about his divorce, indicating that his wife had wanted out of the marriage two weeks after they wed, had run around on him, and had finally left to marry someone else. He also said that the strife with the Solid Rock artists was partly due to the fact that "all of the artists were leaving their wives" and that he had insisted they spend time getting their spiritual priorities in order (but none of the members of **Daniel Amos** have ever been divorced). Norman indicated, further, that they were all now in contact with each other and that there were no hard feelings. In the very next issue of *CCM,* however, the magazine published the following statement: "We have received letters and phone calls from some of the artists and others mentioned in the interview (including Norman's ex-wife) which very strongly counter several of Norman's statements . . . many of the people mentioned by Norman in the interview take strong

exception both to his recollection of their past dealings with him and his characterization of their present relationships." In response, Norman would publish what he called "the blue book" (printed in blue ink), which reprinted the *CCM* interview along with extended explanations of some of the comments. Similarly, as Norman would re-release his albums on compact disc, he often included long liner notes (or "linear notes" as he liked to call them) that commented on the songs and explained situations in his life. Thom Granger of *CCM* dismissed the notes to *In Another Land* as displaying the artist's "penchant for revisionist history, which is always entertaining, if nothing else." Norman responded in the notes to *So Long Ago the Garden* by referring to Granger and Harvest Rock Syndicate critic Brian Quincy Newcomb by name as examples of the "liberal journalists" who had formed some sort of conspiracy against him. Eventually, notes by Norman would be included in Solid Rock's release of **Daniel Amos's** *Horrendous Disc* presenting his version of the fiasco surrounding that project's initial release; notes included with *The Cottage Tapes* would likewise reflect extensively and one-sidedly on his relationship with **Randy Stonehill.** Such extravagances inevitably made the artist look bad to all but his most ardent supporters, but the roots of his bitterness against the press run deep and, whatever his own failings may be, his feeling of resentment is at least understandable. In 1995, *CCM* had published a piece titled "Troubled Troubadour" in which reporter Steve Rabey claimed, "Today, Norman is a black cloud. People who once worked closely with him say he has vanished from their lives and has turned away from his friends, his loved ones and the church. He has been divorced twice. Some say he has lost his creative juices, and possibly his mind." Norman's faxed response to the comments said simply, "I think you should have faith in your brothers and sisters instead of attacking them or gossiping about them. And you should sit back and let them make their music. Give them the time they need to elucidate their message."

Norman has also suffered from a variety of health problems. In 1989, he told *CCM* magazine that over a decade before (in 1978) he had suffered brain damage as the result of an airplane accident. By his account, the ceiling panel of a 747 in which he was a passenger collapsed on his head when the plane landed at the Los Angeles airport. As a result, he was unable to compose lyrics or to remember words to his songs for a ten-year period. A few journalists have wondered whether the story is exaggerated—partly because it was not reported for over ten years and then seemed to provide a convenient excuse for Norman's virtual absence from the music scene. Norman maintains that, although he was checked at the airport by paramedics, the extent of the damage was not readily apparent—he himself did not realize the cause of his disabilities until he was diagnosed many years later as having suffered a bipolar trauma. Then in 1992 Norman suffered what was reported as "a massive heart attack." In 1995, it was reported that he had suffered at least one more heart attack, in addition to two attacks of "sudden death syndrome." Some of his albums contained appeals for donations so that he could obtain a heart operation to receive a defibrillator implant. In 1994, a compilation album called *Footprints in the Sand* would include a new song inspired by such brushes with mortality. "Goodbye, Farewell" is one of Norman's all-time best songs. It offers what the artist thought should be his final words to his friends, recorded at a time when he thought his time on earth was up: "Goodbye, farewell, we'll meet again / Somewhere beyond the sky / I pray that you will walk with God / Goodbye, my friends, goodbye." On November 13, 2001 Norman suffered yet another major heart attack and, as a result, underwent a quadruple bypass.

For whatever reason, Norman moved completely out of the Christian music mainstream in the '90s and became a virtual unknown to most fans of Christian music. He would continue to record, however, and though his output could be spotty and eccentric, it would also be marked by moments of sheer brilliance. The good but strange year 1998 introduced half a dozen new classics that were unfortunately spread out over four discs. Midway through the live concert album *Shouting at the Storm* Norman unveils an essentially new song called "Let the Rain Fall Down" that is breathtakingly beautiful, hauntingly introspective, and terribly disturbing all at the same time. A studio version of this masterpiece had actually been previewed as a bonus track on the CD release of *Babylon,* but the rushed, toss-off delivery that it is accorded there disguises its power. The song begins with the words, "My woman left me / She left me for another man / You know it came as some surprise / It wasn't in my plan." It goes on to relate his feelings of betrayal with gut-wrenching pathos and yet with ultimate trust in the God who makes the rain to fall on the good and the bad alike. It is a magnificent song and its empathetic power suffers naught from the realization that it (obviously) reflects Norman's own biased perspective on his ended relationship(s)—nobody has ever cared what Carly Simon or Jon Bon Jovi's former paramours would have said in response to songs like "You're So Vain" or "You Give Love a Bad Name." The album *Copper Wires* has a low-tech demo sound and contains mostly covers (Pete Seeger's "Turn! Turn! Turn!" **Curtis Mayfield**'s "People Get Ready," **Bob Dylan**'s "When He Returns," and People's "I Love You"), but it also features four new songs. "Heaven Wants to Bless You" and "Oh, Little Sister" sound like classic Dylan songs—the first a beautiful affirmation of promise in the midst of pain, and the second, a confessional apology for wrongs unwittingly done. "Protect My Child" is no-holds-barred rock, giving voice to every parent's desperate plea. "In the Garden (How It Could Have Been)" reflects on lost paradise with a poi-

gnancy that makes it seem the artist was actually there. The same year, Norman released the strange *Breathe In, Breathe Out* album, a two-disc set of studio recordings made with the rock group Beam while on a break from a European tour. Much of the space is taken up with talking between songs, instrumental jams, remakes of classics songs ("I Wish We'd All Been Ready" and "Why Don't You Look into Jesus?"), and more covers (**DC Talk**'s "Jesus Freak," **Bob Dylan**'s "Like a Rolling Stone"). But there are new songs, including "Friendship's End," a hard rock song on the order of **Grammatrain** that seems (to voyeurs at least) to speak of Norman's broken relationship with people like **Randy Stonehill** and the members of **Daniel Amos** and to express some longing for reconciliation. "Goodbye, Farewell" occurs here also, in what may be its sterling, definitive version. Had the new songs from *Shouting, Copper,* and *Breathe In* all been placed on a single-disc album, Norman would have had another project of similar stature to *Only Visiting This Planet* or *Something New under the Son.* Even as it is, he probably had three of the twenty best Christian songs of the year for 1998.

In 2001, Norman staged a comeback with what was regarded as his first real album of new material since *Stranded in Babylon. Tourniquet* is a well-recorded studio effort that seems like a finished work, though *HM* would report that it is actually a prerelease version of what might eventually become the long-anticipated *Behind the Curtain* album (the missing link between *Home at Last* and *Stranded in Babylon*). Even as is, the record is a solid set of songs superior to eighty percent of what the contemporary Christian music empire would yield that year. *Tourniquet* opens with "Turn," which uses fire-and-brimstone revival rhetoric in service of Greenpeace agendas. After this ecological "Eve of Destruction," Norman bemoans his romantic misfortunes. First, he describes his ideal fantasy girl in "Woman of God," concluding "You're not a woman I've held and kissed / And in fact, you probably don't exist" ("Endless Life of Dreams"). This sentiment segues into the next song ("Center of My Heart"): "People talk about lasting love, but it never happened to me." But then the whining takes an unexpected turn and suddenly Norman is singing about his genuine appreciation for a love he has found that is certain and sure. Whether he found a satisfying human paramour at last or simply made his peace with Jesus over the matter is completely ambiguous. The most noticeable songs on *Tourniquet* are "Rock the Flock" and "Feed the Poor." The first of these offers a third-millennium update of Norman's previous I-love-rock-and-roll anthems ("Rock That Doesn't Roll," "Why Should the Devil Have All the Good Music?"). "Feed the Poor" (previewed in a thirty-second version on *Copper Wires*) is a full-blown rocker with an in-your-face challenge straight from Scripture ("When Jesus asks you, Did you feed the poor?' / What are you going to say?"). "It's All Right" is a powerful blues track similar to those on *Something New under the Son,* and "Father of All" offers a Stonesy prayer on which Norman pulls some of his old Mick Jagger inflections out of retirement. Norman performed at the *Cornerstone* festival in 2001 and even appeared together with **Randy Stonehill** in a surprise reunion that left fans shocked—since the two artists were thought to be famously estranged.

Norman has maintained an intense cult following throughout the years, a loyal core of collectors who want everything he has ever done. In the late '70s, he started his own custom label Phydeaux and sold products primarily through the mail, which helps to account for the eclectic scope (and length) of the discography above. Many of the albums are live recordings: *The Israel Tapes* is a reunion concert featuring Norman and his old band People (doing both the 1968 People song called I Love You" and **Randy Stonehill**'s 1971 song by that same name). *Roll Away the Stone* is a poorly recorded concert where the music is muffled by crowd noise. *The Story of the Tune* is a benefit concert for a Calcutta Mission featuring "The Tune" and four other songs. *Come As a Child* is another (poorly recorded) benefit concert for the same mission, featuring a guest appearance by **Barry McGuire.** The 1989 *Live at Flevo* album was recorded in Holland with a strong rock guitar sound (courtesy of the band Q-stone) and includes covers of "Shout" and "Twist and Shout." *Children of Sorrow* records a United States concert from 1991 and *Omega Europe,* a 1993 concert in Sweden. *Live at the Mac* is a bootleg recording of a concert taped on a smuggled-in cassette recorder—Norman himself says he thinks it is "horrible" but released it on CD to please collectors and to let people "know what a real bootleg sounds like." *The Vineyard* is a double-disc set with lots of talking between songs. *In the Beginning* is a two-disc set with three complete concerts from 2000. The independently released *Rough Diamonds * Precious Jewels* is a four-disc box set that contains material culled from years of concerts in Belfast; it reportedly contains at least one take of just about everything the artist has ever performed there.

There have also been many compilations of favorite Norman songs, none of them definitive. Both *Down Under But Not Out* and *White Blossoms from Black Roots* are eclectic, combining a handful of obvious choices with some lesser-known critical faves. *Starstorm* stands out for including "I've Got to Learn to Live without You" and a full version of "If God Is My Father" (greatly abbreviated on *In Another Land*). Embarrassingly awful is *Re-Mixing This Planet,* which offers disco-fied electronic bastardizations of several songs. Several collections of rarities are also available. *The Cottage Tapes* contains sixteen songs that Norman and Stonehill recorded together in 1970, but which did not see the light of day until almost thirty years later. Most are early takes on songs that would turn up elsewhere, but a few are otherwise unknown. *Rehearsal for Reality* is a Swedish

import album of studio tracks from the '80s. *A Moment in Time* is a rough mix collection of studio tracks from 1993 to 1994. *Gathered Moments* collects some nineteen songs (some studio, some live) that were not available previously. Similarly, *Blarney Stone* and *Sticks and Stones* compile songs that Larry and his brother Charley recorded with guitarist Jon Linn over a period of many years—and which are not found anywhere else. The latter two albums were released as a memorial tribute to Linn, who was killed in 2000 (struck by a car while crossing a street), and to his brother Jimmy (also a remarkable guitarist), who died of cancer one week before Linn's death.

Norman's songs have been recorded by over 300 different artists. "I Am a Servant" was a major Christian radio hit for **Honeytree** (before charts were kept). **Steve Camp** would have a chart hit with "The Great American Novel," and **Dana Key,** with "The Outlaw." In 1996, a number of artists produced a tribute album, offering their versions of some of his classic songs. Highlights include **DC Talk**'s take on "I Wish We'd All Been Ready" and **Holy Soldier**'s powerful rendering of "Why Don't You Look into Jesus?" **Michael Anderson** got a new start in his career through his soulful crooning of "Shot Down" and **Rebecca St. James** hit her career highpoint with a funky version of "Sweet, Sweet Song of Salvation." As the end of the second millennium approached, Norman's quaint apocalyptic images got a new reading. Tim LaHaye and Jerry Jenkins unloaded some twenty million *Left Behind* books on the gullible and fearful, and in 1998 an album called *People Get Ready: A Musical Collection Inspired by the Left Behind Series* included two Norman songs: "I Wish We'd All Been Ready" by **DC Talk** (again) and "UFO" by **Geoff Moore and The Distance.** In 1999, Frank Black (former leader of The Pixies) recorded "Six Sixty Six" (another of Norman's left-behind songs) for his *Frank Black and the Catholics* album. Black admits to having been raised on Norman's music and to emulating him to the point of once winning a Larry Norman Look-Alike Contest.

According to *CCM* some of the artists who took part in the 1996 tribute project did so cautiously, wanting to pay their respect for Norman's music without appearing to lend any endorsement to the artist himself. Such backhanded compliments seem to typify the grudging appreciation Norman is accorded within the dominant Christian music culture. Still, in 1998, *CCM* would drop all polemic to refer to him admirably in a gala issue celebrating the history of contemporary Christian music. It was reported there that Norman was "involved in foster care, prison ministry, and a campaign to end child pornography." On November 27, 2001 (about a week after his quadruple bypass), Larry Norman was officially inducted into the Gospel Music Hall of Fame.

Though Norman has the propensity to be a master spin doctor, there have been few artists over the years who have equalled his ability for cutting through hype and propaganda and describing things as they are. And, so, this entry closes with a brief compendium of Norman quotes on various matters:

On the Jesus movement: "The Jesus movement was misrepresented. It was 90 per cent comprised of nice, middle-class kids who had early exposure to Christ in churches and then when they became seventeen or eighteen, accepted him personally. The movement was not made up of ex-drug addicts and ex-Hell's Angels. The Jesus movement was not a street movement and it was wrong to portray it that way."

On his primary audience: "I was singing directly to the disenfranchised. . . . I felt that someone needed to fight for the dignity of the skeptic, to befriend him and recommend that he take a closer look at God."

On "celebrity conversions": "If Mick Jagger became a Christian, his fans wouldn't decide that he had made a wise decision and that his previous stature in their lives recommends that they look into Christianity themselves. No, they'd think he's flipped. They'd think that it's a bummer and that he's a turncoat."

On being a celebrity: "Autographs are like a status system. You only want the autograph of somebody above you. I don't want to be above you."

And again: "I'm a Christian. I'm a human. I'm a person. I'm not a commodity."

On ministry: "A lot of people have the right to get up and sing songs because they know pitch and they know how to sing, but they haven't got the right to tell anybody what God thinks. . . . I'm not really in a ministry. I'm not an evangelist. I'm a musician."

On persecution of Christian musicians in the secular scene: "Persecution is when they throw you in prison or break your bones for witnessing. I don't know any Christian artists in America who have been persecuted, including myself."

On being "the father of Christian rock": "I never invented Christian rock. The blacks invented it two hundred years ago."

For trivia buffs: Norman did institute the famous "one way" sign that became as definitive for the Jesus movement as the "peace symbol" was for the counterculture in general. He did so somewhat by accident, however. When people would applaud at his concerts he would raise his index finger toward heaven, meaning "give God the glory, not me." Someone decided he meant to indicate that Jesus is the "one way" (i.e., the only way) to finding peace, and the Jesus people began flashing the single finger one-way sign as an alternative to the popular two-finger peace sign.

Christian radio hits: "Somewhere out There" (# 12 in 1989).

Northbound

Bob Book, voc.; Tim Camp; Ron Gollner, voc.; Dave Workman; et al. 1983—*Northbound* (Myrrh).

Northbound was a Christian band from Oregon that played a variety of funk/rock touching on styles favored by such acts as Pablo Cruise, Steely Dan, and the early Doobie Brothers. The two lead vocalists would often swap melody lines and then come in together for climactic harmony on the chorus. According to *CCM* several of the members were ministers in Oregon. Standout songs include the energetic "Dancin' in the Aisles" and "You Got Me Singin' " (with some rinky-tink piano). "Evening Song" is a more moody contribution, carried by a seductive saxophone. A few songs ("Maybe Tonight," "When I Look in Your Eyes") have a secular appeal to them, without any obvious connection to religious themes.

Norway

Doug Huibregtse; Eric Melzer. 1999—*the essence of norway* (Plastiq Musiq).

The synth-pop duo known as Norway has nothing to do with that country. Doug Huibregtse and Eric Melzer come from northern California and were picked up by **Joy Electric**'s Ronnie Martin to make music for the label he heads. The music is rather similar to that of Martin's band, with recognizable traces of Erasure and the Pet Shop Boys. For the most part, the group's lyrics are not overtly or explicitly Christian in content, but Melzer says, "We are both Christians so a lot of the lyrics are from that perspective. For me to write a song about life or love, to me, still glorifies God, you know." The group offers a cover of **Undercover**'s "Jesus Girl."

Not the Joneses

Russell Bergum, bass; Mark Chaffee, voc., gtr.; Victor Consolo, drums; Doug Schoenbeck, gtr. 1999—*Not the Joneses* (True Tunes).

www.ntj.com

Not the Joneses is a Christian bar band from Chicago. The core of the group came together with the lineup listed above in 1995 and honed their craft in local honky tonks for four years before finally recording an independent album. The eponymous debut presents a basic classic rock style with some modern edges. *The Phantom Tollbooth* describes "Time Ain't No Reason" as sounding like "The Guess Who with some assistance from Soundgarden." A song called "God Is Dead" sets to narrative the very old joke about two pieces of graffiti, one reading "God is dead, signed Nietzsche," and another, "Nietzsche is dead, signed God." It is hard to imagine anyone who has been to college not already knowing the joke—but then Tony Orlando and Dawn's "Tie a Yellow Ribbon" found an audience in spite of the fact that the story it told had been run into the ground for two decades. "One Time Woman" is a catchy tune addressed to a would-be groupie, with essentially the same theme as Hall and Oates' "Family Man."

Nouveaux

Paul Alan, kybrd.; Steve Ashley, gtr.; Kurt Lehman, bass; K. C. Smothers, gtr.; Brad Angus, drums (– 1996) // Jeff Ausdemore, drums (+ 1996). 1994—*Beginnings* (Benson); 1996—*. . . And This Is How I Feel.*

Originally from Michigan, Nouveau was a pop vocal group whose 1996 album appeared just a few years too soon to catch the tidal wave of popularity accorded to similar-sounding general market groups like *NSYNC and the Backstreet Boys. The group actually began as a rock band with light metal leanings. They were an integral part of a Michigan public schools' antidrug program called Break Out. Thus, their repertoire consisted of positive-message, nonreligious songs that they would play for school assemblies, though they would sometimes also do more spiritually focused concerts at sponsoring churches in the evenings. Nouveaux's first album was reviewed in *HM,* and editor Doug Van Pelt likened Nouveau's harmonic style to that of Def Leppard. "United We Stand" is an antiracism song and "Some Things Never Change" affirms the unchanging love of God. The album closes, however, with a song ("Across the Miles") that sends a signal of what was to come, a tune that Van Pelt called "a dead ringer for **Michael W. Smith.**" Sure enough, on *And This Is How I Feel,* the group morphed into a soft rock/pop outfit. Produced by **John** and Dino **Elefante,** the sophomore album contains one song similar in sound to **Kansas** ("Chasing Shadows"), but is otherwise a collection of songs more reminiscent of Toad the Wet Sprocket. Vocal harmonies carry the opening track, "Maybe Tomorrow," which was universally praised as the album's finest moment. Thematically, the song belongs on a list with Linda Ronstadt's "Somewhere out There" and Rod Stewart's "Somebody Special"; it is a love song for someone yet to be met, an encouraging promise that somebody special *is* out there and that soon—maybe tomorrow—true love will be found. Composed of five bachelors, Nouveau became very active in the nationwide chastity-till-marriage campaign called True Love Waits, and "Maybe Tomorrow" became something of a theme song for that movement. Another highlight of *This Is How I Feel* is "If Only," which describes the implicit praise of God evident in all creation. The group disbanded and, in late 2001, Paul Alan released a solo album (*Falling Away,* Aluminum).

Christian radio hits: "Holding My Own" (# 17 in 1995); "A Time to Cry" (# 11 in 1995); "If Only" (# 2 in 1996); "Wonder" (# 21 in 1996); "Through Heaven's Fields" (# 3 in 1996); "Maybe Tomorrow" (# 5 in 1997); "Listen" (# 2 in 1997).

Novella

Adam Gibson, drums; Jonathan Pagano, voc., gtr., kybrd.; John Spinola, bass // Derek Jan, gtr. (+ 1992). 1991—*One Big Sky* (StarSong); 1992—*A Liquid Earth.*

Novella was a metal band from New Jersey led by Jonathan Pagano, who would later record solo albums as simply **Jonathan.** The band played melodic hard rock not unlike the style of general market act Journey, and analogies to the latter group were augmented by Pagano's vocal similarities to Steve Perry. Much was made of the classic "power trio" lineup for their first album and songs like "Running Home" and "Fire Eyes" attracted special attention, along with the ballad "Whispers in the Night." The group was on the cover of *HM* magazine in May-June of 1992. Their sophomore release has a generally softer tone to it, despite the addition of a second guitarist. *A Liquid Earth* favors ballads, including the two hits "Right in the Middle" and "Heaven's on My Mind." The latter song exemplifies the group's thematic focus, using euphemisms to express vaguely spiritual notions rather than the in-your-face, name-of-Jesus preaching style associated with most Christian metal bands. "I definitely think Novella has a ministry," Pagano told *CCM,* "but not in the classic definition of the term. We want people to think about what salvation is and what it means, instead of just laying it out on a platter for them."

Christian radio hits: "Right in the Middle" (# 16 in 1992); "Heaven's on My Mind" (# 18 in 1993).

The November Commandment

Jan Carleklev; Halkan Paullson; et al. 1988—*Complete Structure* (label unknown); 1991—*Dark Dawn* [EP]; 1993—*Exile Station* [EP]; 1999—*A Motorised Mind* (Flaming Fish).

The November Commandment is usually credited with being Christian music's first electro-industrial band. Based in Sweden, they produced one full-length album and two EPs for an international label—though according to some sources *Dark Dawn* was never actually released. In 1999, Flaming Fish compiled the tracks from all three of these releases (nineteen in all) on one CD called *A Motorised Mind.* The group's music has an industrial core sound (its name is derived from that of a factory slogan) with some Depeche Mode synth-pop stylings. The songs tend to have a sameness to them, but the group may be viewed as pioneers of a genre that was later explored by such diverse acts as **Mortal, Deitiphobia,** and **Circle of Dust.** Jon Carlekev and Halkan Paullson later formed the group **Sanctum.** Carlekev also recorded an album of ambient/industrial music under the name *Parca Pace* (Flaming Fish, 1999); that project consists of a single fifty-minute instrumental selection originally intended to serve as the soundtrack for a multimedia presentation about the closing of a factory and consequent effects on a small community.

Nutshell

Paul Field, voc.; Heather Barlowe, voc. (– 1978); Pam May Thiele, voc. (– 1978) // Annie McCaig, voc. (+ 1978); Mo McCafferty, voc. (+ 1978).

1976—*In Your Eyes* (Myrrh); 1977—*Flyaway;* 1978—*Begin Again;* 1979—*Believe It or Not.*

Nutshell was a British folk trio David Di Sabatino likens to an English version of **2nd Chapter of Acts,** featuring one male and two female vocalists. The group started out under the name Jesus Revolution, then made two albums as Nutshell before breaking up. Principal songwriter **Paul Field** put together another version of Nutshell for two more albums, and then went on to pursue a solo career.

Nu Colors

Lawrence Johnson, voc.; Faye Simpson, voc.; Mark Beswick, voc. (−1993); Nicky Brown, drums (− 1993); Neville Forbes, voc. (− 1993); Jenny Howard, voc. (−1993); Priscilla Jones, voc. (−1993); Bryan Powell, voc. (−1993); Wayne Michael Wilson, kybrd. (−1993) // Lain Gray (+ 1993); Pat Knight (+ 1993); Carol Riley (+ 1993). 1990—*Man Within* (Sparrow); 1991—*Forever Mine* (label unknown); 1993—*Everlasting Love.*

Nu Colors was an R&B vocal group formed in the late '80s by nine members of the London Community Gospel Choir. On *Man Within* the group performs a number of dance songs and soft jazz ballads along with the traditional hymn "On Christ the Solid Rock I Stand." The most remarkable song is "God Is Trying to Tell You Something," cowritten by **Andraé Crouch** with Bill Maxwell, Quincy Jones, and Dave Del Sario, and performed by Nu Colors in a traditional gospel style. The 1991 lineup is unknown, but only two original members (Lawrence Johnson and Faye Simpson) remained by 1993.

Christian radio hits: "Man Within" (# 15 in 1990); "Only You" (# 18 in 1990); "Say a Prayer" (# 20 in 1990).

Michael O'Brien

1995—*Michael O'Brien* (Benson); 1996—*Conviction*; 1998—*Godspeed.*

Michael O'Brien is a Christian pop singer whose music falls into the same general category as **Clay Crosse** and **Michael W. Smith.** O'Brien hails from Miami, Florida, where he sang with a group called the Heritage Singers. He moved to San Diego in 1989 and first garnered national attention in the Christian music scene when he wrote the song "Prince of Peace" recorded by the group East to West. O'Brien's debut album earned him a Dove award nomination for Best New Artist of the Year in 1996. The Benson label tried to market the work as a conversion piece with lots of bad-boy-gets-saved hype reflecting on O'Brien's abuse of alcohol and drugs during his college years. This all seemed more than a little exploitative and artificial since he had been connected with the church in some sense all along and had been clean for over six years. It was also foolish, in that his adult contemporary music was not really targeted for the sort of audience impressed by such tales.

All three of O'Brien's albums are filled with mainly upbeat, keyboard-based pop songs with solidly evangelical lyrics. He lists David Foster as his "musical hero," and that influence is especially evident on the sweeping ballad "Free Again" from his debut. Some of his material, especially on *Conviction,* also brings the piano arrangements of Bruce Hornsby to mind. "If I Said Nothing" from that album was written for O'Brien's father who, he told *CCM* in 1996, "doesn't know Jesus." The song describes his intention to quit talking to his parent about faith or religion and just live in such a way as to bring convic-

tion. O'Brien's third album, *Godspeed,* updates that saga with "Somebody Cares," patterned after something O'Brien's father said after "he came to know Christ." *Godspeed* opens with "Let There Be Light," which has a Celtic flair and also includes the instrumental "A Time to Dance." *CCM* has referred to O'Brien as "one of the most underrated pop vocalists in Christian music."

For trivia buffs: O'Brien is a skilled photographer, whose work has been featured on album covers by such artists as Buffalo Tom and Alex Chilton.

Christian radio hits: "Nothing's Gonna Turn Me Around" (# 1 in 1995); "Higher and Higher" (# 18 in 1995); "If I Said Nothing" (# 23 in 1996).

The Obvious

See **One Hundred Days.**

The Ocean Blue

Rob Minnig, drums; Bobby Mittan, bass; David Schelzel, voc., gtr.; Steve Lau, kybrd. (– 1996) // Oed Ronne, kybrd., gtr. (+ 1996). 1989—*The Ocean Blue* (Sire); 1991—*Cerulean;* 1993—*Beneath the Rhythm and the Sound;* 1996—*See* (Mercury); 2001—*Davy Jones' Locker.*

www.pianalto.com/tob

A college rock band from Hershey, Pennsylvania, The Ocean Blue is a general market group with loose connections to the Christian music scene. Both their debut album and *See* were reviewed in *CCM* and that magazine also printed a profile of the group in their May 1997 issue. Musically, The Ocean

Blue crafted a style that would become definitive of "alternative pop," a marriage of minimalist music and lofty lyrics that features jangly guitars and dreamy sweet vocals. Their hook-filled songs feature hummable melodies offset by moody, bittersweet tunes. The closest musical analogies may be found in such English bands as Echo and the Bunnymen, The Smiths, or the Cocteau Twins, though American fans are more likely to hear the band as a cross between The Byrds and **Jars of Clay.** Schelzel's voice lacks the alternately brooding and whiny characteristics of the British acts. He confesses to a fondness for early **U2,** and that influence can be heard in their music as well.

The band's debut garnered some well-deserved airplay with the songs "Between Something and Nothing" and "Drifting, Falling." The track "Love Song" quotes a few verbatim lines from 1 Corinthians 13. *Cerulean* is quite similar to the debut in sound, with "Breezing" its most memorable song. The title track (built around a word for heaven) offers a picture of looking to the sky (or heaven) for help. "The Planetarium Scene" references Psalm 8:3–4: "Stars above, stars below / And what is man?" *Beneath the Rhythm and the Sound* is a pop masterpiece; virtually every song on the album shimmers and shakes and cries out to be played repeatedly. The songs "Sublime" and "Don't Believe Everything You Hear" enjoyed heavy rotation on many college radio stations, and the album includes several additional gems: "Either/Or" and "Ice Skating at Night" are simply beautiful; "Listen, It's Gone" is hauntingly atmospheric; and both "Bliss Is Unaware" and "Crash" are catchy, bouncy, and instantly memorable. Lyrically, the recurrent theme again is to press for some serious thought about the meaning of life, which includes considering the possibility that there might be some absolutes among all the ambiguity. "Either /Or" seems to describe the person who doesn't know what or how to believe: "So far removed / So in between / So back and forth." *See* introduces a new dual guitar attack that gives many of the songs an edgier quality. "Whenever You're Around" and "Bitter" actually recall the punk-pop sound of The Cars.

The Ocean Blue first caught the attention of Christian audiences when they joined fellow Pennsylvanians **The Innocence Mission** in putting together a benefit album on behalf of a Christian radio station (WJTL in central Pennsylvania). The group members were all in high school at the time, and the project was actually their first recording experience. David Schelzel, who is the group's principal songwriter, emphasizes that he cannot speak for everyone in the band ("there's one guy who would disagree with about 90 percent of what I would say"), but indicates that he is a Christian and a churchgoer. He says he grew up listening to music by bands like the **Seventy Sevens** and **Daniel Amos,** and continues to have utmost respect for Don and Karen Peris (of **Innocence Mission**), whom he calls, "some of the most devout, genuine Christians that I have ever met." Lyrically, there is little in the content of the group's songs (aside from the occasional biblical allusion) that would identify them as "a Christian band" to outsiders. In the early days, the group performed the **Seventy Sevens**' "Renaissance Man" as an encore in their concerts. Still, Schelzel says The Ocean Blue is certainly not "a Christian band" in the sense of a group whose "primary focus is going to be ministering, evangelizing, or leading in worship."

Dicky Ochoa

2000—*Dicky Ochoa* (Metro One).

Soulful singer Dicky Ochoa got his start in Christian music participating in praise and worship projects sponsored by Maranatha and leading worship for three years at Promise Keepers rallies. Jyro Xhan of **Mortal/Fold Zandura** apparently saw a potential for something more and coproduced Ochoa's debut album for the Metro One label. It was perhaps the most shocking debut of the year, revealing the youthful Oregonian as a husky rock singer influenced by Bruce Springsteen and latter-day **U2.** Ochoa's coarse voice is perfectly suited for the rough songs he sings, songs of devotion that seem to arise out of a heart of worship without giving way to the otherworldly excesses that sometimes spoil albums in the praise and worship genre. Ochoa invites the listener to "Lose Yourself" in divine mystery and proclaims that he is "in love with God" on a song about "falling apart" in the arms of his Maker ("I Fall Apart"). But the gravel in his voice keeps such sentiments mired in an earthiness that renders them convincing. It is the same sort of spirituality evident in the work of **Van Morrison** and, indeed, one of the closest musical equivalents to Ochoa's sound would be the Morrison clone-band Counting Crows. Christian fans will notice similarities to **Third Day** as well (especially to the latter's *Offerings*). The singer's passion is well displayed on **Chris Lizotte**'s rocking "Breath of God" and his tenderness comes through on "Madi's Song," an acoustic number written for one of his daughters.

The O.C. Supertones

See **The Supertones.**

Erin O'Donnell

1996—*A Scrapbook of Sorts* (Cadence); 1998—*Scratching the Surface;* 2001—*No Place So Far* (Word).

www.erinodonnell.net

Adult contemporary pop singer Erin O'Donnell edged her way into the most crowded genre in Christian music in the late

'90s, taking her place alongside such stars as **Susan Ashton, Sarah Masen, Julie Miller, Twila Paris, Rebecca St. James,** and **Kathy Troccoli**—all of whom reviewers would cite as comparisons to her lilting style. The ability to get noticed at all in such a field is a testimony to her talent. O'Donnell has an especially pleasing, creamy voice and she applies it to introspective and slightly quirky songs written by her husband Brad O'Donnell. Born in 1971, Erin O'Donnell (née McDonald) grew up in Massachusetts. She earned a degree in jazz vocal performance from the University of Miami in Florida, from which Brad also graduated with a music degree. Although she was raised Roman Catholic and describes herself as "a lifetime churchgoer," O'Donnell came to experience a more personal dimension of faith while at college, primarily as a result of her discovery of contemporary Christian music. Attracted first by the musical stylings of artists like Ashton and **Out of the Grey,** she was compelled to think more closely about the faith to which these singers gave testimony and to reflect on her own faith life accordingly. In 1998 she told *CCM* that in her sophomore year she "finally caught on and became a Christian." *A Scrapbook of Sorts* offers some typical Christian radio fare with the catchy songs, "Didn't Even Know" and No Better Place," but the album also achieves some distinction through the obvious jazz influences that inform both singing and writing. Ethnic excursions add a little flair as well; a few songs employ Indian and Australian instruments and, here or there, O'Donnell seeks to invoke her Celtic roots. Lyrically, most of the songs are not about God or Christ, but about people, life, and relationships as viewed from a Christian perspective ("Things I Cannot Say" is especially sweet and romantic). "Be Still and Know" breaks this pattern, as a modern hymn with a melody more upbeat than its title implies. *Scratching the Surface* was produced by Alain Mallet, whose former wife Jonatha Brooke (lead singer of the general market band The Story) sings with O'Donnell on the standout cuts "Wide Open" and "All of This." The latter song opens with an orchestral selection lifted from The Verve's "Bittersweet Symphony" and moves the singer into a more appealing, slightly alternative venue than her first album. The ballad "Crazy" is also a highlight, testifying to the irrational character of God's overwhelming love, with supplementary vocals from Steve Mason of **Jars of Clay.** O'Donnell's third project, *No Place So Far,* includes "Damaged Goods," a song about salvaging hope from heartbreak, and "Hold On to Jesus," an encouragement to trust in God's grace.

For trivia buffs: O'Donnell first came into contact with the folks at the Cadence record label via an Internet chat room. She struck up e-mail conversations there with Randy Spencer, vice-president of Cadence, and ended up sending him a demo tape. The media has dubbed her "the first recording artist discovered on the Internet."

Christian radio hits: "No Better Place" (# 1 for 2 weeks in 1996); "Be Still and Know" (# 8 in 1997); "Even in My Youth" (# 13 in 1997); "Didn't Even Know" (# 9 in 1998); "All of This" (# 13 in 1998).

Officer Negative

Chad Wiggins, voc.; Casey Wisenbaker, bass; Michael Dragon, drums (–2000); Josh Handley, gtr. (–2000). 1997—*Dead to the World* (Screaming Giant); 1999—*Zombie Nation; Live at the Roxy;* 2000—*Split EP* (with Lugnut) [EP].

Officer Negative is an old-school punk band based in Ventura, California. The band has a strong commitment to Christian ministry, stating that "Officer Negative is not a *band;* it's a ministry. Our focus is spreading the love of Jesus." The group's name derives from use of the word *officer* as a verb in punk slang: to "officer the negative" means to control or restrict negative influences. That said, the group has an angry punk sound that has been likened to Rancid or Black Flag. Their second album, *Zombie Nation,* was the first to gain any notice in the Christian market; it has a decidedly political slant to it, with the usual rants identifying modern America as a godless nation that faces impending judgment. "American Dream" deals with the corruption of money and "Human Garbage Can" focuses on abortion as evidence of society's moral decay. A song called "New World Disorder" features talk-over vocals reminiscent of **The Crucified.** The title track, "Zombie Nation," is about (in the words of Chad Wiggins) "how unbelievers are kind of like zombies in the way they seek out wealth and an artificial way of living." The group had a dispute with their label (Screaming Giant) over the album because one song ("Failure to Submit") was cut from the record against their wishes for undisclosed reasons. "It is, by far, one of the best songs we've ever written," says Wiggins. After completing *Zombie Nation,* Officer Negative announced that they were breaking up and released a farewell concert album. Wiggins later retracted the announcement, claiming the band would continue with personnel changes. Josh Handley, the guitar player and principal songwriter, went on to record as **Zippy Josh and the Rag Tag Band.**

Off the Record

Keith Allen, voc.; Dan Atkinson, gtr.; Danny Hidalgo, drums; Chris Ozorio, bass; Ryan Schueller, gtr. 2000—*Remember When* (Tooth and Nail).

Off the Record is a Christian punk band whose debut release on Tooth and Nail drew mixed and contradictory reviews from the 'zines that are most attentive to that label's products. *The Phantom Tollbooth* regards the group's music as "an intriguing blend that is equal parts punk, skate, and heavy metal," while *Bandoppler* calls them "easily more legitimate than most of what is being passed off as punk-rock nowadays." The latter comment is not necessarily a compliment, as "legitimacy" in punk can be taken to mean "monotonous," with all songs exhibiting the same basic riffs and half-screech vocal style. The *Tollbooth* reviewer allows that the first three songs avoid this pitfall; after that, the group "loses a lot of steam." Lyrically, *Remember When* avoids clichés but is expressive of ideas compatible with the Christian faith. The title track deals with regret for past actions.

Oil

Matthew Joy, bass; Blake Nelson, gtr.; Ron Rinehart, voc.; Jason Vanderpal, drums. 2000—*Refine* (Kalubone).

The power metal band Oil was founded in Southern California in 1997 by Ron Rinehart, former lead singer for Dark Angel, a general market group that (as its name implies) focused heavily on occult themes. Rinehart left the group after a dramatic religious conversion at a Harvest Crusade. Oil's sound is predictably loud, fast, and angry, with shouted vocals over thumping rhythms and characteristically crunchy guitars. The band has a penchant for fire and brimstone lyrics, and almost all of the songs are written in the second person, addressing the listener directly with spiritual challenges: "The Son remains at the door to your heart / Will you answer?" ("Waiting There").

Ojo

Joey Taylor, kybrd. 1988—*Relative* (Broken).

Ojo was not actually a group, but a solo project produced by Joey Taylor of the band **Undercover.** (Ojo is Taylor's nickname; he is alternately identified as Ojo Taylor and as Joey Taylor on **Undercover** albums, causing some confusion among those who are not die-hard fans. Ojo and Joey Taylor are not brothers; they are the same person.) Following **Kerry Livgren**'s example, Taylor wrote the songs for his *Relative* album and employed a variety of vocalists to sing them, including **John Elefante, Michael Knott** of **LSU,** John McNamara of **4-4-1,** and **Terry Taylor** of **Daniel Amos.** A couple of tracks ("Box of Treasures," "Dance of the Secret People") are also rendered as instrumentals.

Ben Okafor

1985—*Children of the World* (Ears and Eyes); 1991—*Nkiru* (Edge); 1992—*Generation* (Plankton); 2001—*Coffee with Lazarus.*

Ben Okafor is a Nigerian Christian whose African pop and worldbeat-reggae music is much better known in Europe and on his home continent than in the United States. Okafor was raised a Christian and says he had everything he could ever want until the age of thirteen when the Nigerian-Biafran war forced him and his family into refugee camps. The horrors of that war and the experiences of living as a refugee would have a permanent impact on his developing social conscience. As a college student in England, he became increasingly aware of the effects of colonialism in his native land and became sensitized to racism. Back in Nigeria, he remained critical of the social inequalities symbolized by expensive churches in impoverished neighborhoods and by "priests who live in massive mansions and yet they have all these people in their congregations who can't pay their rent." He admits to becoming disillusioned with Christianity, but with the help of his brother, who fronted a Christian rock band, he found his way back, with no less of a critical posture toward Western Christianity and its often negative impact on Africa and other Third World communities. Okafor's first album shows heavy influence from Bob Marley; *Nkiru* moves into what *CCM* would call "the Johnny Clegg and Richie Havens-like musical territory of more Euro-based Afro-pop and gentle folkiness." *Generation* has a solid reggae feel, with catchy pop choruses; it eventually was re-released by R.E.X. and obtained wider distribution in traditional (Western) Christian music outlets. Then the artist surfaced again in 2001 with *Coffee with Lazarus,* which *Phantom Tollbooth* describes as "an example of reggae minimalism . . . almost reminiscent of Sting's most laid-back moments, but with a slight reggae accent." Lyrically, Okafor's material alternates between "horizontal" numbers dealing with political and social-justice issues and "vertical" songs of praise and worship. The title track to *Generation* deals with police-state injustice, while "Sanctify My Soul" is typical reggae praise. "Sweet Lady" offers a tribute to a loving mother who is always there for her son. *Coffee with Lazarus* features "So I Believe" as a testimony to faith, and "Deep Love" and "Give Food" as encouragements to good deeds.

Jerome Olds

1989—*No Disguise* (StarSong); 1990—*Eyes of a Common Man;* 1997—*I Belong to You* (Urgent); *There's a Change in Me* (label unknown).

Jerome Olds is a protégé of **Bill Gaither** whose roots are deep in southern gospel. In the late '80s, the Atlanta-based singer attempted a crossover to more contemporary pop-oriented music. *CCM* was not impressed with his ironically titled debut, noting that the songs all seem to copy styles of other successful artists: Bruce Hornsby ("Is It Right?"); Paul Simon ("Sing Out"); and **Mylon LeFevre** ("God Will Find a Way"). Olds at least came by the latter disguise honestly, having composed one of LeFevre's biggest hits ("Trains Up in the Sky").

Christian radio hits: "Is It Right?" (# 9 in 1989); "You Can Be the One" (# 23 in 1991).

Gary Oliver

1995—*Gary Oliver* (Benson); 2001—*More Than Enough* (Integrity).

Gary Oliver (b. 1957) is a native of Silsbee, Texas, but he became known to the Christian music scene as music director of Carlton Pearson's Higher Dimensions Church in Tulsa, Oklahoma—a position he acquired in the '90s after similar stints at churches in Ft. Worth, San Antonio, and Long Island. A couple of his praise choruses ("Celebrate Jesus" and "Hosanna") gained wide appeal and were sometimes recorded without his even knowing it. In 1992, the church's choir recorded two volumes of Oliver's songs under the title *High Praises* in a program sponsored by **Carman,** who was a member of the congregation. Oliver then moved to Nashville, landed a contract with Benson, and made an album of his own. Raised in the Pentecostal Holiness Church, Oliver played piano in many a storefront church while growing up, and the music of those (mostly black) congregations left its mark on his style. For a self-described "skinny, white guy," he possesses a funky, soulful tenor, comparable to that of Peabo Bryson or Jeffrey Osborne. His self-titled debut is similar in style to **Carman'**s more R&B influenced work and it features a number of worship-oriented cuts. The song "What It's All About" is addressed to the church, issuing a simple call for commitment and integrity: "What the world really needs to see / Is Jesus in you and me." *More Than Enough* records a live worship service at the New Birth Missionary Baptist Church in Decatur, Georgia, and includes Oliver's first recording of his song "Celebrate Jesus." A number called "As We Sing Holy (Brandon's Song)" was composed as a tribute to Oliver's eighteen-year-old son who was killed in an automobile accident in 1998.

Christian radio hits: "What It's All About" (# 21 in 1995).

Michael Omartian (and Stormie Omartian)

By Michael Omartian: 1974—*White Horse* (ABC); 1976—*Adam Again* [a.k.a. *Onward*] (Myrrh); 1986—*Conversations*; 1990—*The Race.* By Michael and Stormie Omartian: 1979—*Seasons of the Soul* (Myrrh); 1980—*The Builder*; 1981—*Odyssey*; 1982—*Mainstream*; 1983—*Together Live* [with 2nd Chapter of Acts]. By Stormie Omartian: 1982—*Exercise for Life* (Sparrow); 1984—*Exercise for Life 2.*

Michael Omartian is the quintessential example of a Christian artist who bridges the two worlds of Christian music and the general market. While he has made more of a mark (in both camps) as a producer than as a recording artist, he is nevertheless well known and highly respected in both religious and secular cultures. Omartian was born in 1945 and raised in Evanston, Illinois. He began playing piano at the age of four and grew up studying both classical and jazz music. He spent some time in a mental institution as a teenager, but as a college student became a Christian "on Christmas Day, 1965 at the age of 19." The catalyst for this conversion, he says, was the prompting of his cousin to turn his troubles "over to the Lord." It was just that simple, he told *Harmony.* "I said, 'I know I can't handle this myself. Jesus, you're gonna have to help me 'cause there's nowhere else I can go.' " After attending Tarkio College in Missouri and Northwestern University in Illinois, Omartian headed west to work on the staff of Campus Crusade for Christ. He led two of their ministry music teams, **Armageddon Experience** and New Folk, before moving to Los Angeles in 1969, where he got a job playing in a band called Gator Creek, which also included singer Kenny Loggins. As a spin-off of that group, the two hooked up with Jim Messina from Buffalo Springfield, and the duo Loggins and Messina was born. Omartian was a more or less permanent member of Loggins and Messina's band, playing on their important first three albums. He declined to tour with the group, however, preferring to stay put and work in the studio with a number of other musicians. The résumé of his session work is long and impressive: for instance, it is Omartian, not Joel, playing the piano on Billy Joel's "Piano Man" (1974), and it is also Omartian playing those famously perfect keyboards on Steely Dan's "Aja" (1977), as well as on tracks from that group's *Pretzel Logic* (1974) and *Katy Lied* (1975); other artists he's assisted include **Glen Campbell,** David Cassidy, **Eric Clapton,** Neil Diamond, Fifth Dimension, the Four Tops, Art Garfunkel, Michael Jackson, Al Jarreau, Ricky Lee Jones, B. B. King, **Gladys Knight,** Manhattan Transfer, Richard Marx, Dolly Parton, **Johnny Rivers, Austin Roberts,** Boz Scaggs, and Seals and Crofts.

Stormie Omartian (née Sherric) grew up an abused child, the daughter of a mother who beat her, locked her in closets, and forced her to watch favorite possessions being destroyed as punishment for usually imagined offenses. "I was always afraid she was going to kill me," Stormie recalled in 1980. "And I always wished her dead." The young girl attempted suicide twice before she was fourteen, but a few years later discovered that physical beauty could open doors that would take her away from home and on to the TV screen. As a child, she had a number of minor roles on various sit-coms, and as a young adult, she found herself playing the stereotypical "dumb blonde" in regular sketches on variety programs hosted by **Glen Campbell,** Mac Davis, and Dean Martin. Sometime in the late '60s, she found peace as a Christian and left acting to begin writing lyrics for Christian music, in partnership at first with Ron Harris. Michael and Stormie Omartian married in 1973, and she wrote the lyrics to all of the songs on *White Horse* and *Adam Again.*

Even before recording albums of his own, Michael became thoroughly involved in the fledgling Christian industry. His name appears in the liner notes of numerous early Jesus music albums, including ones by **Mike and Kathy Deasy, Richie Furay, Annie Herring, Phil Keaggy, Barry McGuire, Jamie Owens,** and **2nd Chapter of Acts.** His main connections, however, remained in the general market, and Christians often regarded him as a celebrity guest on their projects, bestowing a certain legitimacy on the music and giving the artists a boost in self-esteem.

As years went by, Michael Omartian discovered he had a knack for producing. His first forays into this area came through working up themes for TV shows that had potential for radio success. In the years before MTV, Omartian was one of the first in the music industry to realize the guaranteed airplay that such a program provided for a song (and, vice versa, the free publicity that a hit song could provide for a TV show). At that time, he has said, the music and TV industries were "two completely different businesses and people involved in the one did not know the people involved in the other." Following through on his idea, Omartian put together a group of studio musicians dubbed Rhythm Heritage and had them perform an instrumental disco track that served as the theme for the TV drama *S.W.A.T.* The resultant "Theme from S.W.A.T." became the Number One song in the country in 1975, and Omartian followed it with "Baretta's Theme (Keep Your Eye on the Sparrow)" (also by Rhythm Heritage; # 20 in 1976), and "Theme from Happy Days," which was a Number Five hit for his friends **Pratt/McClain** in 1976. His version of "Gonna Fly Now (Theme from *Rocky*)" tanked, but only because Bill Conti released an alternative version that went to # 1 in 1977. With such successes, Omartian gained access to big budgets and big stars and went on to become one of the industry's most successful and sought-after producers.

Omartian's production style is distinctively slick with an emphasis on synth-pop and rhythms. It is perhaps displayed most clearly in the work of an artist he all but created, Christopher Cross. Cross's debut album yielded the enormous hits "Ride Like the Wind" (# 2 in 1980) and "Sailing" (# 1 in 1980) and sold over nine million copies. Those familiar with Omartian's Christian releases did double-takes, as the music basically sounds like an Omartian album with different vocals. The familiar sound would also set Rod Stewart's *Camouflage* (1984) and **Donna Summer**'s *She Works Hard for the Money* (1983) apart from anything else that either of those artists had ever done. Omartian cowrote the title track for the Summer project and it turned out to be her biggest hit. He has also produced albums for **Michael Anderson, Susan Ashton,** Michael Bolton, **Debby Boone, Carman,** Peter Cetera, **Gary Chapman, First Call, Billy and Sarah Gaines, Amy Grant, Benny Hester,** Whitney Houston, **The Imperials, Sheila Walsh,** and **Wayne Watson.**

Omartian's decision to remain in both the Christian and general markets has been made advisedly, with full awareness of the distinctions that exist. Generally speaking, he recognizes that projects for Christian labels must be made on smaller budgets and, accordingly, he often cuts his own fees by at least half what he would normally earn for his involvement on a mainstream label. He has also frequently donated studio time and brought in high-powered session musicians for his pet Christian projects to insure that the quality of musicianship and production values are on a par with what would normally be expected of a much more expensive outing. In the '80s, Omartian was one of the persons most responsible (along with **John** and Dino **Elefante** and **DeGarmo and Key**) for bringing Christian music to a level of professionalism competitive with music in the mainstream. He is, of course, well known for his faith within the secular world, and while some musicians might refuse to work with him on that account, others have actually been drawn to him because of his convictions. **Donna Summer** is one obvious example, for she came to Omartian seeking a make-over from her sexpot "Bad Girls" image after experiencing a spiritual reawakening in her own life. Omartian says that when Peter Cetera first contacted him, the artist immediately wanted to know, "So what's this born-again Christian thing all about." Omartian laid out his beliefs in a nutshell, and Cetera responded, "Well, I don't know if I believe all that, but you sound like someone I can trust." No one is quite sure why Rod Stewart wanted to work with Omartian—perhaps just for a change of sound—but the producer has said that during the making of *Camouflage* Stewart was reading **Pat Boone**'s spiritual autobiography as well as books by Robert Schuller. And, he continues, "Rod and I had many opportunities throughout the project to talk about the Lord . . . there were two Christians in his band who drew strength from our conversations. I encouraged them toward getting back to church and reading their Bibles and praying."

There have been two infamous incidents in which Omartian's faith and vocation came into conflict. In 1977, he produced Alan O'Day's hit song "Undercover Angel" (# 1 in 1977). The song is filled with sexual innuendo raunchy enough for it to be banned from several radio stations. Omartian took some criticism from supporters of Christian music for having compromised his principles through involvement with the project, and he acknowledged a lack of discretion, saying it was a mistake that would never happen again. Then in 1984, when he was making *Camouflage* with Stewart, the latter artist brought in a song called "Bad For You" toward the end of the session that he wanted added to the album. Omartian objected to the song's lyrics and the two decided that it could only go on the album with a disclaimer. Thus, *Camouflage* carried a note that read, "The song 'Bad For You' does not represent the views of Michael Omartian, a born-again Christian." Both the religious and secular media jumped on this tidbit and exaggerated the significance of the "saint-and-sinner rift"—Stewart was often quoted as having described the album as "born-again Christian meets born-again drunk." Actually, Omartian says, "There was no yelling, screaming, or backstabbing. He told me that he respected me for my beliefs and for what I did, but that he had to do what he had to do, and I said that's okay." Some time later, Stewart told *Billboard,* "There was one time when Omartian wanted to change some lyrics to a song because he's a born-again Christian, but generally speaking, I would love to work with him again, even though we did have a few punch-ups."

As for Omartian's own recordings, *White Horse* is by far the most significant. Musically, the record was more high-tech than anything the limited Jesus music genre had produced, and in many ways it was ahead of its time for the secular scene as well. The sound is basically a softer version of what Toto would premiere four years later; in fact, the members of that group were all session musicians who were friends or associates of Omartian, and some of them have acknowledged *White Horse*'s influence on the development of their style (David Hungate actually plays on the album). *White Horse* opens with the bombastic "Jeremiah," which sets sound bytes from various Old Testament prophets to a synthesized rock beat. The next song, "Fat City," is also regarded as a standout, a funky tune about the ultimate inadequacies of mammon. "Silver Fish" is a midtempo jazzy rock song with poetic, metaphorical lyrics. Jazz stylings also feature prominently on the title track, which features especially impressive guitar work by Larry Carlton and a sax solo by Dean Parks. "Take Me Down" is about baptism, and "The Orphan" is a tender ballad of concern for the lonely and disenchanted people of the world. In 1988, a panel of *CCM* critics listed *White Horse* as Number Four on their list of what (at that time) were considered to be the best Christian albums of all time.

Adam Again suffers from being more of the same, with weaker songs. Not by any means a bad album, it mostly just lacks the surprise punch of a Christian album with mainstream sound. "Whatchersign" is a somewhat annoying bubblegum disco song that pokes fun at astrology. "Annie the Poet" seems to be a tribute to **Annie Herring.** The best material is gathered into a "Telos Suite" on Side Two: a four-song opus that concludes with "Here He Comes," about Jesus returning "through the smog." Neither *White Horse* nor *Adam Again* were as successful as they ought to have been. Omartian suffered the classic double whammy of making records that were "too Christian" for the general market, but "too secular-sounding" (or just too avante-garde) for Christian music fans.

In 1979, the Omartians recorded the first of several albums as a duo, *Seasons of the Soul.* With Stormie taking lead vocals on ballads, the duo moves decidedly away from the progressive rock of *White Horse* into safer pop territory not too different from **Farrell and Farrell.** Jazzy influences still affect some songs (with shades of Michael's Steely Dan connections) and **Phil Keaggy** provides tasty lead guitar. On all three of their albums as a duo (*Odyssey* is a "greatest hits" collection), the couple would be forthright about their troubled pasts and about the ongoing process of counseling and quest for healing related to such problems. Thus, on *Seasons,* the song "Ms. Past" deals with the continual effort not to be defined by one's history. Lyrically, that album's high point comes with "Where I Been," addressed to other Christians: "I may not be as far along as you, but I started way behind / While you were making choices, I was trying to survive / If you think compared with you, I don't hold up so well / Well, Jesus had a lot to do, when he brought me back from hell." *The Builder* was a career nadir, filled with trite and predictable songs like "Mr. Trashman" (about ridding one's life of spiritual garbage) and "Dr. Jesus" (about spiritual healing). Despite terrible reviews, it outsold all previous projects. *Mainstream* was something of a recovery, with the beautifully poetic "The Calling" (featuring a cameo by Christopher Cross) and the exciting inducement to worship "Praise His Name and Let It Happen." At the time, the Omartians were members of the Church on the Way in Van Nuys, California, and in 1983 they recorded a concert there with **2nd Chapter of Acts.** Being the third live set from the latter group (who offer thirteen of the eighteen songs)—and being inferior to both of the previous ones *(To the Bride; How the West Was One)*—the album *Together Live* was received as unnecessary. It remains of some value for the personal testimonies that tie songs together, including moments where both of the Omartians speak convincingly about how the power and love of God continues to work healing in their lives.

In the mid '80s, Stormie Omartian would make a pair of Christian aerobics albums with accompanying videotapes fashioned after the successful videos and records produced by Jane Fonda. She appeared on the cover of *CCM* in July 1984 touting a Christian approach to "health and fitness, God's way." In 1986, she published an autobiography titled *Stormie: Story of God's Restoration;* it was republished as *Stormie: A Story of Forgiveness and Healing* (Harvest House, 1997). She has also written many more spiritual and devotional books, including the following: *A Step in the Right Direction: Your Guide to Inner Happiness* (Thomas Nelson, 1991); *Greater Health God's Way* (Sparrow, 1993); *The Power of a Praying Parent* [with Christopher and Amanda Omartian] (Harvest House, 1995); *The Power of a Praying Wife* [with Michael Omartian] (Harvest House, 1997); *Finding Peace for Your Heart: A Woman's Guide to Emotional Health*

(Thomas Nelson, 1999); *Just Enough Light for the Step I'm On* (Harvest House, 1999); *Prayers of the Heart* (Harvest House, 1999); *Child of the Promise* (Harvest House, 2000); *Lord, I Want to Be Whole: The Power of Prayer and Scripture in Emotional Healing* (Thomas Nelson, 2001); *The Power of a Praying Husband* (Harvest House, 2001); *Praying God's Will for Your Life: A Prayerful Walk to Spiritual Well-Being* (Thomas Nelson, 2001).

Michael Omartian would eventually produce two more solo albums. *Conversations* was one of Christian music's first instrumental recordings. *CCM* would describe it as "an interesting mix of classical, jazz, and rock elements . . . that is equal parts Gershwin, Copland, and Elton John." Though most of the tracks feature synthesizers and orchestration, a song from *White Horse* called "Right from the Start" is reprised as a piano solo that brings out its previously overlooked melody. "The Feast" is a harpsichord Bach tribute in the tradition of Walter/Wendy Carlos's *Switched On Bach*. Five years later, *The Race* would give Omartian his first (and only) solo hits on Christian radio. He wrote his first lyrics on a song appropriately called "Alone," stating Christ's identification through the cross with different types of victims who appear to face injustice on their own. Most of the other songs have lyrics by **Michael Anderson**. The opening track, "Faithful Forever," is a bright and commercially appealing song with a catchy melody and uplifting lyrics. In 1995, Omartian would record an album with the trio **Omartian, Pratt, and McClain**. In 1996, he founded the recording label SoundHouse with **Billy Gaines.**

As a songwriter, Michael Omartian has written or cowritten Christian radio hits performed by **Steve Camp** ("Taking Heaven by Storm"), **Gary Chapman** ("Where Are the Broken Hearts," "Floodgates of Love"), **Bryan Duncan** ("Step by Step," "Traces of Heaven"), **Amy Grant** ("That's What Love Is For," "Lover of My Soul"), and **The Imperials** ("I'm Forgiven," "Finish What You Started"). Michael and Stormie have likewise written or cowritten Christian radio hits performed by **Debby Boone** ("The Time Is Now," "Choose Life"), **4 Him** ("The Nature of Love," "The Message"), and **The Imperials** ("What Can I Do for You?" "One More Song for You," "I'd Rather Believe in You," "The Trumpet of Jesus," "Free the Fire in Me").

For trivia buffs: Michael Omartian holds the distinction in the music industry of being the only producer who has had Number One records in three decades (the '70s, '80s, and '90s).

Christian radio hits: By Michael Omartian: "Faithful Forever" (# 11 in 1991); "Let My Heart Be the First to Know" (# 8 in 1992). By Michael and Stormie Omartian: "Ms. Past" (# 10 in 1979); "Heaven Will Wait for Me" (# 22 in 1979); "It Is Done" (# 23 in 1982); "Praise His Name and See It Happen" (# 10 in 1983).

Grammy Awards: 1980 Producer (*Christopher Cross*).

Omartian, Pratt and McClain

See **Pratt/McClain.**

Omega Sunrise

Personnel list unavailable. 1983—*Feel the Change* (New Jerusalem); 1985—*Run from the Night* (Morada).

Omega Sunrise was a band of nine young people (at least initially) fashioned as what seemed to be an alternative version of **Seawind.** Their first album was produced by **Seawind**'s saxophonist, Kim Hutchcroft, and the group's sound was remarkably similar to that of the popular jazz-fusion act. The principal difference lay in lyrical direction; whereas **Seawind** targeted mainstream audiences with their subtle-but-ultimately-evangelistic approach, Omega Sunrise sang to the church with songs intended to prick the consciences of believers by spotlighting habits and lifestyles in need of reform.

One

Brent Henderson, voc.; Brian McSee, voc.; Don Peslis, voc. 1988—*One* (custom); 1989—*Spirit to Spirit* (word); 1991—*Dare to Believe.*

One was an interracial vocal trio with a sound similar to that of **The Imperials.** The group formed at Anderson University in Indiana when Don Peslis asked two fellow students to help him with a youth program he was leading. Their debut for Word, *Spirit to Spirit,* includes songs written by **Steven Curtis Chapman** and Billy Smiley (of **White Heart**), with background vocals by **Sandi Patty.** Stylistically, the group sticks to mostly MOR ballads, with occasionally more catchy songs like "The Word Is Alive." Unfortunately, the group would be best remembered for matters having nothing to do with music: Don Peslis had an extra-marital affair with Patty when the group toured with the singer in 1991. Both Patty and Peslis later divorced their spouses and in 1995 married each other. News of the four-year-old affair was made public two weeks after the wedding in a *National Enquirer*-type investigation sponsored by the normally responsible *Christianity Today* magazine.

One Bad Pig

Philip Owens, drums, voc.; Paul Q-Pek, gtr., voc.; Daniel Tucek, bass, voc.; Carey "Kosher" Womack, voc. 1986—*A Christian Banned* [EP] (Porky's Demise); 1989—*Smash* (Pure Metal); 1990—*Swine Flew* (Myrrh); 1991—*I Scream Sunday*; 1992—*Live! Blow the House Down*; 1994—*The Quintessential One Bad Pig, Vol. 1* (StarSong); 2000—*Live at Cornerstone 2000* (M8).

www.onebadpig.com

One Bad Pig from Austin, Texas, got their start as the Christian equivalent of a general market band like Green Jellö—a novelty act that eventually transcended the limitations of their satirical orientation to achieve cult status as a legitimate band. Indeed, the group is quite possibly the most popular hard-punk act ever to arise within the Christian music scene. Although they became known as a "party band," as famous for their stage antics as for their music, the group had a very serious ultimate focus on ministry. Carey Womack was studying to be a Baptist minister (and eventually became one) and **Paul Q-Pek** once sang with the Continental Singers, a southern gospel choral group. One Bad Pig had its origins in street ministry conducted by the members outside hardcore punk clubs in downtown Austin. They would gather there on Saturday nights to "just stand outside and talk with the kids about life and Jesus." Eventually (on a dare?), they ended up playing a concert at one of the clubs and this evolved into a series of shows in which the group would perform often humorous songs that poked fun at various institutions, including punk-rock itself. The concerts always had a craziness to them, as band members would spray each other and the audience with silly string or bring in a plastic swimming pool filled with whipped cream—with predictable results. The group's name was derived from a logo for a radio station (St. Louis's K-She 93), an emblem of a pig in a leather jacket with a rock and roll sneer.

Their music was a cross between punk and heavy metal that some just called "pig music." With an AC/DC core and references as varied as Henry Rollins and Perry Farrell, their repertoire of hits ranged from wild metal excursions ("Smash the Guitar") to faux-punk anthems ("Hey, Dude") to serious meditations on Scripture ("Isaiah 6") to encouragements of sound theology ("Never Forget the Cross"). *Smash* finds them thrashing about with wild experimentation (including, for instance, polka on a song called "Looney Tunes"). "I'm Not Getting Any Older" is perhaps their first standout song. *Swine Flew* features a number of high-profile guests (**Phil Keaggy, Petra**'s Bob Hartman, Dann Huff, **Tommy Sims**). Songs include the Pig classic "We Want You" (which addresses the titular lyric to a number of female Christian rock stars) in addition to covers of **Larry Norman**'s "Christmas Time" and **Petra**'s "Judas Kiss." *CCM* was now calling the group "one of the most creative bands working in metal-oriented music." *I Scream Sunday* proved to be the masterpiece, however, with its title track and the mince-no-words challenge, "You're a Pagan." As an ultimate coup, the group somehow persuaded **Johnny Cash** to sing a duet with them on the latter's hit "Man in Black," now done in a style reminiscent of AC/DC's "Back in Black." The song "Cut Your Hair" sets a parental admonition to screaming metal music. "Up Your Nose" presents its antidrug rant with the lyric, "This is your brain on drugs . . . This is your brain *in hell!!*" Two hits collections were issued: the live set includes a

surprise cover of The Clash's "Rock the Kasbah," and the studio compilation offers five new songs (some from the early EP), including "I Am the Chief," which sets Paul's statement about being "chief of sinners" (1 Timothy 1:15) to an incongruous Native American beat. **Paul Q-Pek** tried to expand the group's sound in various directions ("Take a Look at Yourself" is **Adam Again-**style funk), and he would continue to explore such possibilities as a solo artist. He and Owens also joined *HM*'s Doug Van Pelt in putting together **Lust Control.** A One Bad Pig reunion concert was taped at the *Cornerstone* festival in 2000.

One Eighty

See **Flight One Eighty.**

One Hundred Days (a.k.a. **The Obvious)**

Andrew Horrocks, voc., gtr., perc.; Ian Tanner, voc., gtr., kybrd., perc. // Steve Marsh, drums (+ 1996, d. 1996); Glen Teeple, bass (+ 1996, –1999); Derek Lind, gtr. (+ 1999); Darryl McWaters, gtr. (+ 1999). By The Obvious: 1992—*Counting by Heads.* By One Hundred Days: 1995—*The Obvious* (Liquid Disc); 1996—*Counting by Heads* [= 1992 release]; *Feels Like Love;* 1999—*The Super Terrific Happy Hour* (Audio X).

Canadian pop duo One Hundred Days was formed in 1992 by two members of **The Awakening** who intended to call themselves The Obvious. Their first album, *Counting by Heads,* scored a Top 20 hit on mainstream radio in their homeland with the song "Beauty of the Night." The group then changed their name to One Hundred Days and titled their debut album (under that name) *The Obvious.* A year later, they re-released the real debut as a One Hundred Days album along with a third record of all new material *(Feels Like Love).* The duo has a strong Beatlesque sound, featuring hook-filled melodies and soaring harmonies. Critics often compare the artists to other Beatlesque groups like **PFR,** Squeeze, Crowded House, or the Rembrandts; on certain songs ("Trust," "After 'So Long' ") they sound almost indistinguishable from **Phil Keaggy.**

Counting by Heads is primarily notable for its hit ("Beauty of the Night"), but *The Obvious* scores with a number of pop masterpieces, especially "She's the Only Girl," which offers a tongue-in-cheek description of the perfect mate: a "cheap and simple socialite" who can serve as "a disposable piece of female wallpaper" to decorate a superficial life. *Feels Like Love,* however, was the first project to work as a cohesive whole. "Hard Man to Soup" touches on the harder edge of '60s psychedelia; "Darkest Day of the Year" is a moody meditation on the consequences of unfaithfulness to God. The tighter, tougher sound on *Feels Like Love* owes somewhat to the contributions of former **Elim Hall** members Steve Marsh and Glen Teeple, who joined the duo for this one album. Marsh died of liver cancer the day that the record was released. Another album, *Super Terrific Happy Hour,* was recorded in 1998, but not released until 2000. The group seems to throw caution to wind on the project, eschewing commercial accessibility to embrace their indie status in all its glory. *Super Terrific Happy Hour* has a raw guitar-dominated sound that is more like Matchbox 20 than Crowded House or **PFR.** A number of songs ("Sandals," "First Plane") feature the expected hooks, but others exhibit a degree of XTC quirkiness. "Mr. Lovely" deals with contestants on a TV disco dance program, and "Carpet Time" pokes fun at Pentecostal holy rollers. In 2001, the band was preparing to release a two-disc set consisting of previously unreleased outtakes and live material.

Christian radio hits: "Friends from a Distance" (# 15 in 1995); "Feels Like Love" (# 25 in 1996).

100 Portraits

See **Waterdeep.**

INC (a.k.a. **One Nation Crew**)

See **Kirk Franklin.**

One Truth

Bill Drago, drums; Floyd Butler, voc.; Randall Butler, voc., kybrd.; Terry Butler, voc., gtr.; Andy Osbrink, bass; Scotty Price, voc., kybrd., gtr. 1976—*One Truth* (Psalm); 1977—*Gospel Truth* (Greentree); 1980—*Playing for Keeps* (Greentree).

One Truth was a vocal group from Southern California with a style that ranged from soft rock to a country folk sound similar to **The Way.** Member Scotty Price, who did arrangements for the group's songs, continued to be active in contemporary Christian music, often in a behind-the-scenes capacity of arranging strings and horns. **Paul Johnson** produced the group's third album. In the late '90s a completely different band (a hardcore punk group) called One Truth would come out of Milano, Italy, and attract some attention from *Bandoppler.*

One 21

Kenny Klein, voc.; Kris Klein, gtr.; Tom Manns, bass; Vince Radcliffe, drums; Paul Sanders, gtr. (– 1999) // Adam Garbinski, gtr. (+ 1999). 1997—*In the Year King Uzziah Died* (Flying Tart); 1999—*When the Dragon Is Laid to Rest* (BulletProof).

One 21 is an old-school punk band from Philadelphia. The band emerged out of a group called Uzziah in 1995 and cites the Ramones and Rancid as primary influences. They count Cliffy Huntington of **The Huntingtons** as a friend and supporter. Guitarists Kris Klein and Adam Garbinski also play with **Squad Five-O.** The band specializes in two-minute wonders with lyrics that are, in their own words, "hardcore for

Christ." *When the Dragon Is Laid to Rest* includes "Morality," which seeks to dispel the notion that one can get to heaven by being good. It also contains a cover of the old Animals' hit "We Gotta Get Out of This Place."

Greg O'Quin (and **Joyful Noyze**)

1997—*try'n 2 make u see* (Word Gospel); 1998—*Conversations;* 2001—*Clichés* (World Wide Gospel).

Contemporary gospel worship leader Greg O'Quin was one of hundreds of choir conductors to jump on the **Kirk Franklin** bandwagon in the wake of that artist's unprecedented success in the late '90s. O'Quin is a Dallas native who graduated from the University of Texas in Arlington with a degree in Music and Communications. After college he served what he calls "an apprenticeship" with R&B/pop artist **Tim Miner,** working with the Miner's Dallas production company. He also worked with Bernard Wright, producer for **Commissioned** and **The Winans,** and for a time was a member of the Christian hip-hop, doo-wop vocal group **Kindred.** Eventually, he became the leader of a Dallas choir called Joyful Noyze. The two albums recorded by them fit broadly into the camp of R&B gospel favored by Franklin, William Becton, and Hezekiah Walker. Unlike their projects, however, O'Quin's albums are studio recordings—a feature that *CCM* thinks helps them to attain a more contemporary sound. O'Quin cites influences as varied as Babyface, David Foster, and **Fred Hammond.** The albums *tryin' 2 make u see* and *Conversations* offer a blend of ballads, hip-hop, funk, and occasional snatches of foot-stomping traditional gospel.

Ordained Fate

Marge Curtner, bass; Annette Cvengros, gtr.; Terry Cvengros, drums; Pam Scott, voc., gtr. 1992—*Gethsemane* (Wonderland); *Ordained Fate;* 1995—*Glimmer of Hope* (P.A.C.).

Ordained Fate is an Illinois-based, mostly female, heavy metal band. The drummer (and only male member) is guitarist Annette Cvengros's husband. The group actually formed in 1983 as a purely secular band and went through a decade of transformation as each member left and then rejoined after making a personal commitment to Christ. Finally, with the original lineup restored, they began to record as an evangelistic Christian group. The title song to *Gethsemane* seeks empathy with Christ in his hour of despair, while "Holy Wars" addresses unnecessary splits in the church. *Cornerstone* reviewed *Glimmer of Hope* with the acclamation that "Ordained Fate plays a metallic stomp à la (Black) Sabbath, injected with something rarely found these days: genuine atmosphere." "That's Entertainment" and "Gates of Faith" showcase Scott's female-metal vocals.

Oreon

1980—*Oreon* (P.C. Associates).

The female singer who went by the single name Oreon was one of many Christian artists associated with the Adam's Apple coffeehouse in Ft. Wayne, Indiana, which was very influential during the Jesus movement revival of the early '70s. A native of Van Wert, Ohio, Oreon went there in 1970 looking for a gig and, according to *Harmony,* ended up "accepting Jesus Christ as her personal Savior." She was twenty-one at the time, and for the next decade sang at the coffeehouse and at numerous Christian music festivals. Her developing style would show the influence of **Honeytree,** who was also associated with Adam's Apple and seems to have served as a mentor in some respects. Even more obvious though are stylistic influences of *Harvest*-era Neil Young and **Larry Norman.** Indeed, Oreon's voice often recalls that of Norman. Despite her musical abilities and spiritual gifts, Oreon was best known to the casual festival-goer as "that *really* tall girl." She is 6' 4" (the same height as **Rick Elias** actually). After a decade of performing, Oreon would record a single album which features guest assistance from **Honeytree, Joe English,** and **Albrecht, Roley, and Moore.** The self-titled work demonstrates an appreciation for humor and includes a cover of Lennon and McCartney's "Help."

Stacie Orrico

2000—*Genuine* (ForeFront); 2001—*Christmas Wish* [EP].

Fourteen-year-old Stacie Orrico from Denver, Colorado, got her start in Christian music at the age of twelve when she won a competition at the 1998 "Praise in the Rockies" seminar held in Estes Park, California (an annual event, won in 1999 by **Rachel Lampa**). Signed to ForeFront, she was teamed with a stellar cast of producers and songwriters. The ironically titled *Genuine* displays two styles: songs that sound like Britney Spears and those that sound like Christina Aguilera, with the latter style predominating. Even so, "Don't Look at Me" is a strong R&B-flavored tune better than ninety percent of anything by either of those mainstream mentors. Cowritten by Orrico, the song is also profound lyrically, suggesting that if one looks too closely at an artist's life and personality, disillusionment is bound to ensue. Another highlight, "Without Love" (written by **Eddie DeGarmo** and Tedd T.), recasts the thought of 1 Corinthians 13 in terms appropriate for adolescents. The album closes with a tender ballad, "Dear Friend," composed by Orrico for a friend suffering from anorexia. *The Phantom Tollbooth* praised the album as "incredibly strong from a musical, lyrical, and artistic standpoint," taking issue with what they regarded as unwarranted criticism of industry processes: "This project may have been well produced and well promoted, but it is not hype." Orrico's *Christmas Wish* EP was recorded as a benefit project for the Make-A-Wish foundation. She has also authored a book called *Genuine: Being Real in an Artificial World* (J. Countryman, 2001). Her music may be compared to that of Lampa, **Nikki Leonti,** and **Joy Williams.**

Christian radio hits: "Genuine" (# 1 for 2 weeks in 2001); "Without Love" (# 9 in 2001); "Don't Look at Me" (# 1 for 7 weeks in 2001); "Stay True" (# 16 in 2001).

Pete Orta

2001—*Born Again* (Word).

Pete Orta served as guitarist for **Petra** for a two-album period and then embarked on a solo career in 2001. His debut features what *CCM* describes as "guitar and keyboard-led, stadium-ready L.A. pop rock." With a voice reminiscent of Ricky Martin, Orta offers the soft rock song "Broken" and the acoustic ballads "Shine" and "Liberty." He also covers Desmond Child's "You Make Me Feel."

Fernando Ortega

1991—*In a Welcome Field* (independent); 1994—*Hymns and Meditations*; 1996—*Night of Your Return* (RPI); 1997—*This Bright Hour* (Myrrh); 1998—*The Breaking of the Dawn*; 2000—*Home*; 2002—*Storm* (Word).

www.fernandoortega.com

Fernando Ortega is an inspirational singer of worshipful adult contemporary music with elements similar to the work of **Michael Card** and **Rich Mullins.** A native of New Mexico, Ortega is a descendant of eight generations (and three centuries) of blanket weavers. He describes his classically influenced music as "a hybrid of church music and pop music." *CCM* praises his voice as "unusually engaging . . . steady and tranquil, yet full of passion." As a teenager, Ortega had a mixed bag of spiritual and religious experiences, joining the extremist Children of God cult led by Moses David Berg for a short time and then becoming involved in a Pentecostal fellowship called The Answer. Disillusioned, he says he turned away from the Christian faith completely, and entered the University of New Mexico as a music major. He was eventually reconnected with the church when he took a job as pianist at a Southern Baptist church, and then went on to serve on the staff of Campus Crusade for Christ for four years.

Ortega began recording in his early twenties but did not land a major label contract for sixteen years. What is reported to be his fifth independent album, *Night of Your Return,* earned him his first notice in *CCM* with its collection of five original songs and new arrangements of such classic hymns as "My Song Is Love Unknown" and "This Is My Father's World." Then, at forty, he recorded *This Bright Hour* for Myrrh and toured with **Michael Card,** coming at last to the appreciative attention of a widespread audience. *Bright Hour* features background and duet vocals with **Kelly Willard** and offers a Celtic interpretation of "All Creatures of Our God and King," a moving rendition of "Children of the Living God," and a rich interpretation of a Spanish classic, "Jehova, Señor de Los Cielos." An original song, "If You Were Mine," reflects on the heartbreak Ortega and his wife experienced after a failed attempt to adopt an infant daughter. On *The Breaking of the Dawn,* he continues to cover classic hymns ("Be Thou My Vision") but also sings a rather passionate love song for his wife, "Margee Ann," and offers a joyful ode to travel, "Road Song." The title track speaks of a longing for life as it once was. *Home* is a more cohesive project, presenting mainly songs dealing with both the literal hearth of earthly splendor ("This Good Day") and the spiritual resting place for which he longs ("Beyond the Sky"). It offers more original material than previous projects, along with versions of "Pass Me Not" and the African American spiritual "Give Me Jesus." *Storm* is a quiet album that *CCM* would call "a tranquil oasis." Standout songs include a duet with **Amy Grant** on "Come Ye Sinners, Poor and Needy" and a sparse arrangement of "Let All Mortal Flesh Keep Silent."

As indicated, Ortega typically juxtaposes hymns of the church with what he calls "hard songs" dealing with raw human emotions and, often, with life's disappointments and tragedies. On *Night of Your Return* he sings, "the world spins without meaning now that you're gone" ("Now That You're Gone"). In 1998, he said, "If our art is not grounded in the reality of the human condition, it will not ring true to anyone." Thus, "No One Else" from *Home* is what Ortega calls "a moody wilderness tune—a reminder that emotions fail us, understanding fails us, but God never fails us."

Dove Awards: 1998 Bluegrass Song ("Children of the Living God"); 2001 Inspirational Album (*Home*).

O-Town

Ashley Parker Angel, voc.; Erik-Michael Estrada, voc.; Dan Miller, voc.; Trevor Penick, voc.; Jacob Underwood, voc. 2000—*O-Town* (J Records).

www.o-town.com

The most sexually obsessed boy band making lascivious, pubescent music at the turn of the millennium was not the Backstreet Boys, *NSYNC, or 98 degrees. No, the most sexually obsessed boy band making that kind of music was, surprisingly, a Christian group called O-Town. One of the most peculiar anomalies ever to appear in the Christian music scene, O-Town was composed of five guys who sang gleefully about their libidos without the slightest clue (or concern) that some members of the Christian music subculture might find such a singular fascination confusing, or embarrassing, or even . . . offensive. O-Town is probably the first Christian group ever to record a song about wet dreams (much less a song that *delights* in such bodily functions) and that, at least, makes them unique.

The group had a unique origin as part of the ABC TV program *Making the Band.* The latter series traced the development of the group from its beginnings, insuring a general market audience. As the show unfolded, the five young musicians got together, publicly aired their frictions, gelled predictably, and honed their skills. There was little attention to spiritual matters—certainly ABC did not present them as "a Christian band"—but the group was also promoted separately and quietly within the Christian subculture, where it was "let out" that all five of the guys were believers. When they finally produced their debut album, it was guaranteed large sales in spite of obvious mediocrity. *O-Town* debuted at Number Five on *Billboard*'s pop charts and went on to sell over a million copies. The band appeared on *Good Morning America, Live With Regis and Kelly, The View,* and other high-profile TV shows. The album presents a group that sounds just like Backstreet Boys or *NSYNC wannabes, with a large dose of Michael Jackson influence. The problem—aside from copping a style that was already overdone—is that they simply don't have the material. There is only one song on the album ("All for Love") that has a tune worthy of their practiced harmonies; everything else pales in comparison to their mentor bands' weaker songs.

In the liner notes to *O-Town* each member of the band gives thanks to God for various concerns. Erik-Michael Estrada and Jacob Underwood praise their Savior Jesus Christ, express gratitude for role model Christians, and pray that they might fulfill God's plan for their lives and have an impact on people through their music. Underwood continues, "I also want to thank you for putting 'revival' in my life. . . . Thank you for groups like **Creed, DC Talk, P.O.D.** and so many others for staying true to the reason why music was created." The lyrics to O-Town's songs, however, are nothing like those on albums by the just-named groups. The album opens with what would be its first hit, a little number in which the boys all celebrate the fashion models and celebrities who cause them to have nocturnal emissions ("Liquid Dreams"). "Every Six Seconds" discloses how often they find themselves physically aroused (with numerous double entendres: "I can't keep it undercover"; "it's getting harder all the time"). The boys confess that they will be miserable "until you give me some," and subsequent songs tell a paramour that she is the "Sexiest Woman Alive" and that she needs to decide whether to give them what they want ("It's time for show and tell / Cause I want it all or nothing at all"). Even the relatively chaste ballads are littered with references to "the curve of your body" and "the feel of your skin" ("The Painter"). The album concludes with its second hit single, called "We Fit Together." In short, practically every song drips with adolescent lust; none of them disclose the sort of spiritual urgency or commitments implied by the liner notes. Nevertheless, *O-Town* was sold through various Christian music clubs.

Outer Circle

Matt Bailey, bass; Kevin Kribs, gtr.; Jesse Nason, drums; Mark Salomon, voc. 1998—*Outer Circle* (Tooth and Nail).

Outer Circle is basically a side project for Mark Salomon, who rose to fame in some Christian circles with his punk group, **The Crucified,** and then went on to even greater heights with the hard-rocking **Stavesacre.** Supposedly, Outer Circle was actually formed before the latter group and they recorded a single demo, which led Tooth and Nail to get interested in a full album project sometime after **Stavesacre** was already in full swing. The sound is basically a return to the "old school punk" of early Crucified and, indeed, of bands like Minor Threat and Social Distortion. This, in other words, is a far cry from the "pop punk" of Green Day or The Offspring. The self-titled album features no guitar solos, just bare-bones two-and-a-half minute punk songs. "Parasite" offers social commentary regarding abortion; "Manifesto" calls young people to quit talking and act on their beliefs; "Impostor" takes a shot at unoriginal bands that strive to imitate other acts. Salomon recorded another, very different side project with **Native Son.**

Out of Darkness

Tim Andersen; Tony Goodman; Carl Grant; Wray Powell. 1970—*Out of Darkness* (Key); 1993—*The Celebration Sessions* (Plankton).

Not much is known of the early hard rock band Out of Darkness, which appeared in London as part of the British Jesus movement in 1969. The quartet was interracial and, apparently, the two black members (Carl Grant, Wray Powell) had been part of a group called The Soul Seekers. Goodman previously played with The Pilgrims. The band is significant because their Hendrix-inspired psychedelic blues-rock was much harder than almost anything else in Christian music at the time (cf. **Agape, Glass Harp**). Their only album was a commercial failure but, years later, would become a much sought-after collector's item, bringing up to $300. In response, a tape of a 1972 concert was released on CD in 1993. Liner notes to the latter project indicate that the group would subsequently move toward an "afro-rock" sound with Powell taking over lead vocals and Bruce Duncan added on bass.

Out of Eden

Andrea Lynn Kimmey (Baca), voc.; Joy Danielle Kimmey, voc.; Lisa Nicole Kimmey, voc. 1994—*Lovin' the Day* (Gotee); 1996—*More Than You Know*; 1999—*No Turning Back*; 2002—*This Is Your Life.*

www.outofedenonline.com

Out of Eden is a Christian R&B group composed of three siblings from Richmond, Virginia. Musically, they fall into the same general category as TLC, En Vogue, or Destiny's Child, but the group is not overly imitative of any particular general market act. The girls began singing at a very young age as an opening act at concerts by their mother, singer and concert pianist DeLice Hall. In 1990, the family moved to Nashville where Mom became director of the Jubilee Singers and an instructor in music at Fisk University; the three siblings worked as dancers with **Angelo and Veronica, Karthi,** and **Michael Peace.** The big break came when **Toby McKeehan** of **DC Talk** discovered the sisters (all still teenagers) and signed them on for his group's *Free at Last* tour. McKeehan and his fellow **Gotee Brothers** Joey Ellwood and Todd Collins later produced their first album, which sparkles with what has been called "soulful fun-loving femme music." The song "Lovely Day" (a cover of the Bill Withers hit) crossed over to the general market and received airplay on the urban-oriented BET-TV video network. "Good Thing," written by the Gotees is a full-tilt disco number. In a more serious vein, the ballad "There Is a Love" offers a virginity-till-marriage theme. In 1996, the group sang on an episode of the TV show *Moesha,* starring pop singer Brandi, who confessed to being an Out of Eden fan.

By the time the group made their sophomore album, oldest sister Lisa had married producer Michael Bragg and the two of them took the helm. The focus on *More Than You Know* continues to be "positive pop," as the group avoids spiritually specific or obviously religious lyrics in favor of uplifting and morally responsible sentiments. "Greater Love" would be featured in the Eddie Murphy film *Doctor Doolittle.* In 1998, the group took part in the multicultural E.R.A.C.E. tour headlined by **DC Talk.** Around this time, the trio seems to have experienced a career makeover whereby someone decided that they should be presented as a Christian version of the Spice Girls, who were then at the pinnacle of their short career.

No Turning Back would prove the ambiguity of that decision and of an almost-too-late realization that sought to reverse the trend. The trio complained in interviews that their "white sound" and "black bodies" made for an ambiguity in marketing that hurt them commercially. The title track to *No Turning Back* is urban-oriented, with rap artists **Knowdaverbs** and **Grits** joining in, but the song that garnered the most attention was "River," an upbeat pop number that fit in well with the format of adult-oriented Christian pop radio. And a *Phantom Tollbooth* reviewer must have been looking at the group's picture on the cover when he drew a strong comparison between "Spirit Moves" and Lauryn Hill, since musically the song sounds much more like "Tell Me What You Want" than it does like "That Thing." Another highlight of *No Turning Back* is "Here's

My Heart," a love ballad featuring **The Katinas,** with lyrics subtly addressed to God.

The group sought to eschew the Spice Girls vibe for their 2002 project, *This Is Your Life.* "That really wasn't us," Danielle said. The album leads off with "Different Now," an up-tempo number that testifies to the transforming power of Christ in a believer's life. A number of other songs are supremely funky as well, but "Rolling Stone" stands out for its simple arrangement set against acoustic guitars, strings, and horns. "All You Need" dips into jazz and showcases the performers' layered harmonies. Lyrically, "Rolling Stone" addresses the problem of absentee parents (as in, "Papa was a . . ."), and "Showpiece" rejects the exploitation of attractive women as male "trophies."

In 1999, the members of Out of Eden became the first civilians allowed to perform in war-torn Kosovo and Bosnia when they were airlifted to a number of army bases for a series of USO shows.

Christian radio hits: "Lovely Day" (# 18 in 1994); "Good Thing" (# 9 in 1995); "Come and Take My Hand" (# 7 in 1995); "Show Me" (# 7 in 1995); "You Brought the Sunshine" (# 5 in 1997); "More Than You Know" (# 3 in 1997); "Greater Love" (# 7 in 1997); "It's Me" (# 6 in 1998); "Get to Heaven" (# 8 in 1998); "Can't Let Go" (# 6 in 1998); "If You Really Knew" (# 9 in 1999); "River" (# 1 for 3 weeks in 1999); "Window" (# 1 in 1999); "Here's My Heart" (# 16 in 2000); "Tomorrow" (# 8 in 2000).

Out of the Grey

Christine Denté, voc.; Scott Denté, gtr. 1991—*Out of the Grey* (Sparrow); 1992—*The Shape of Grace;* 1994—*Diamond Days;* 1995—*Gravity;* 1997— *See Inside;* 1998—*Remember This: The Out of the Grey Collection 1991–1998;* 2001—*6.1* (Rocketown).

www.outofthegrey.com

Out of the Grey is a wife-and-husband duo composed of two formally trained, professional musicians: vocalist Christine Denté and guitarist extraordinaire Scott Denté. The couple met at the Berklee School of Music where both were pursuing degrees in their relative areas of expertise (voice, guitar). Christine was going through a period of spiritual renewal at the same time that Scott was on a philosophical/religious quest. The former "witnessed" to the latter incessantly. Both were strongly influenced by the faith of **Amy Grant,** especially as reflected on her *Unguarded* album and in a concert performance that they attended. Eventually, they came together spiritually, musically, and romantically. They married in 1987 and moved to Nashville to pursue a career in Christian music. They made connections with **Charlie Peacock,** who was impressed by the exceptional quality of their musicianship. Peacock produced their first four albums, cowriting most of the songs with the couple. Musically, Out of the Grey is often compared to another husband/wife team, **The Innocence**

Mission, though the duo has defined a sound that is very much its own. Scott's guitar tends toward the jangly tradition of American pop that began with The Byrds. Christine's voice sometimes recalls Karen Peris (of **The Innocence Mission**) but is more often reminiscent of **Amy Grant**'s strong, pop stylings. The group's name was originally chosen as a rebuttal of relativism, an affirmation that there are absolutes in life (black and white, right and wrong). As such, the name did not serve them well, since the group has generally demonstrated a thoughtful appreciation for the ambiguities of life.

Out of the Grey's self-titled debut album has an alternative edge that later projects lacked, though lyrically it lacks the insight or depth the group would later develop. Several songs ("Wishes," "Time Will Tell," "The Only Moment") sound like outtakes from Grant's *Unguarded.* "Wishes" expresses the hope for a loved one to find eternal salvation, but spoils the sentiment by juxtaposing that concern as a higher priority than such lesser matters as respecting one another or living with honesty and integrity. "Write My Life" expresses a deterministic view of divine guidance and/or extreme predestination that most Christian groups would regard as borderline heretical. Much better are "Remember This" (a testimony to God's unfading love) and "He Is Not Silent" (a biblical reflection on what it means to listen to God). In 2001, a poll of critics sponsored by *CCM* chose *Out of the Grey* for their list of the "100 Greatest Albums in Christian Music," placing it at Number Forty-seven. It is, however, the duo's weakest album, less worthy of such acclaim than later projects.

Both *The Shape of Grace* and *Diamond Days* move decidedly in the direction of mainstream pop, the latter album especially having just a little too much sheen to it. But the songs themselves show marked improvement. "Bigger Than Life" is a broad anthem proclaiming that the wonder of Christ's love defies all human imagination. "Steady Me" is a catchy pop gem that summons sonic images of Sheryl Crow while offering a simple prayer for balance and stability. "To Keep Love Alive" is a song of commitment that realistically expresses the difficulties of maintaining romantic love. "Nothing's Gonna Keep Me from You" is a gorgeous statement of confidence in the mercy of God, with an echo effect on the chorus that is remarkable and unique. Pulling out all the stops, *CCM* would praise *The Shape of Grace* as an album on a par with the latest contributions from Sting and R.E.M., as "a smart brand of pop music that you can share with anyone, anywhere at anytime without reservation or apology." *Diamond Days* offers the very **Amy Grant**-like "If I Know You" and "All We Need" in addition to the imaginative ballad "The One I've Been Waiting For," which expresses the same thought that **2nd Chapter of Acts**' "Prince Song" conveyed almost two decades earlier (fairy tale dreams become reality through Christ).

On *Gravity,* the duo achieves a near-perfect balance between earthy realism and spiritual rapture. Melissa Riddle wrote in *CCM* that on *Gravity* the couple convey "the sound of vulnerability and release found in Christ, weighed in the day to day." The album's high point is "So We Never Got to Paris," which reflects on the value of prizing life's current blessings and realizing that "there's so much on the plate / Between the living and the learning / Some things must wait." *See Inside* represents a career high, recapturing the energy and intensity of the first album but with the benefit of a more mature theological perspective and more highly developed poetic sensibilities. Brown Bannister steps in as producer and his mix allows Scott's considerable skills to come to the fore more often than on previous outings. The lead song, "No Leaving," has an uncharacteristic rock edge to it and expresses the compelling quality of God's grace. The same theological principle is explored in "Not a Chance," which articulates the Reformed position that God chooses people for salvation and grants faith to them. "Disappear" is almost as aggressive as the opening song, describing the role of a Christian in terms similar to those once employed by John the Baptist (John 3:30). "Come Clean" praises God for the gift of holiness, and "Winter Sun" uses the image of its title to describe the inability of theological knowledge to warm the affections apart from a genuine experience of passion and love. All told, *See Inside* was Out of the Grey's first *rock* album, and the new posture fit them like a glove. *CCM* said, "it sounds like they got to make the record they wanted to make."

The compilation album *Remember This* includes three new tracks (including one instrumental). Dropped by their label, the couple took a three-year hiatus and then returned with the musically adventurous *6.1.* That album explores a variety of styles and even features lead vocals by Scott Denté on one track ("Out of the Ordinary," which recalls his buddy **Phil Keaggy**). "Waiting" has what *CCM* calls "a funky and murky" sound, with lyrics testifying to the experience of not knowing what to do and "waiting on God for a sign." The standout "Tell Your Story" encourages people to share their struggles and "secret sadness" with others.

Christine has also recorded as part of the trio **Ashton, Becker, and Denté.** Scott has recorded as part of the trio **Keaggy, King, and Denté.**

Christian radio hits: "Wishes" (# 1 for 2 weeks in 1991); "He Is Not Silent" (# 2 in 1992); "Write My Life" (# 8 in 1992); "Time Will Tell" (# 11 in 1992); "The Only Moment" (# 21 in 1992); "Nothing's Gonna Keep Me from You" (# 1 for 5 weeks in 1993); "The Door of Heaven" (# 2 in 1993); "Steady Me" (# 1 in 1993); "Feels Like Real Life" (# 4 in 1993); "One I've Been Waiting For" (# 3 in 1994); "If I Know You" (# 2 in 1994); "All We Need" (# 3 in 1994); "When Love Comes to Life" (# 4 in 1995); "Stay Close" (# 5 in 1995); "Hope in Sight" (# 8 in 1996); "Disappear" (# 1 in 1997); "Not a Chance" (# 1 for 2 weeks in 1997); "Come Clean" (# 7 in 1997); "Walk by Faith" (# 15 in 1999).

Overcome

Jason Stinson, voc.; Rob Krueler, bass (– 1999); Jason Obergfoll, gtr. (–1999); Reggie Shumay, gtr. (–1999); Ryan Hayes, drums (–1997) // Alex Woodford, drums (+ 1997, – 1999); Matt Brooks, bass (+ 1999); B. J. Ovsak, gtr. (+ 1999); Ethan Pajak, drums (+ 1999); Nick Westby, gtr. (+ 1999). 1995—*Blessed Are the Persecuted* (Tooth and Nail); 1997—*When Beauty Dies;* 1999—*The Life of Death* [EP] (Facedown); *Immortal until Their Work Is Done.*

Overcome is a self-described "spirit-filled hardcore band." The group released their first album while all five members were still in high school; only Jason Stinson would endure the personnel changes to still be part of their band after they switched labels four years later. Regarding *Blessed Are the Persecuted,* Doug Van Pelt of *HM* writes, "This outfit does nothing but slam for 12 songs" (a compliment). The music features all the main ingredients of hardcore: angry, in-your-face lyrics; disorienting, down-tuned guitars; plodding bass lines; gunning drumbeats; and intense emotion. Another reviewer says, "Stinson makes us think he's in pain for all twelve songs" (also a compliment), while *Phantom Tollbooth* calls attention to what they regarded as "absolutely atrocious production" (*not* a compliment). The song "Help" is not the Beatles tune but could be a response to it, indicating that it makes a difference where one looks for such help or from whom one receives it. "Priorities" insists that God should be the first priority in one's life rather than other causes (vegetarianism or whatever). The title track expresses the band's commitment to stand firm in their beliefs even if they face opposition or commercial ostracism within the hardcore scene. *When Beauty Dies* went unreviewed, but evinces the same basic sound as the debut record, with slightly more metallic riffs; its standout track is probably the opener, "A Case for Life." Then the band completely fell apart due to what Stinson calls "a total difference of opinion over what we wanted to do with the band." Still, the 1999 edition of Overcome has essentially the same sound as the first incarnation. Their first EP for Facedown features a song called "Thorns Compose" which treats the lyrics of Isaac Watts' classic hymn "When I Survey the Wondrous Cross" to a hardcore delivery. *Immortal until Their Work Is Done* departs from the stereotyped sound momentarily for "Reverence," a song with worshipful lyrics that are ironically screamed at God over a medley of clean guitars and piano.

Overland Stage

Personnel list unavailable. 1972—*Overland Stage* (Epic).

The saga of Overland Stage (recounted by David Di Sabatino) is of more interest than their product. The group was a completely secular bar band from South Dakota who landed a contract with the general market label Epic. Between the time that the papers were signed and the recording session conducted, however, the tidal wave known as the Jesus movement came careening in from the West Coast, sweeping over the band's presumably serene Lutheran/Catholic frontier state and leaving six rabid Jesus freaks in its wake. The transformed band entered the studio with a batch of hastily rewritten songs and cut an album of evangelistic material that Epic had no idea how to market. The back cover liner notes consist of a rant against the more worldly lyrical content of typical rock and roll. Because of its major label status, the album *Overland Stage* merited a review in *Rolling Stone*. The reviewer was predictably unpersuaded by their rhetoric and singularly unimpressed with their music. In the early '70s such a review (for an unknown band) was a commercial death knell, and what copies of the album had made it to stores were quickly thrown into cut-out bargain bins and forgotten. Twenty-five years later, Di Sabatino would write, "musically, the album is more astute and interesting than most of the music released in this genre . . . exceptional cuts are 'Salvation' and 'I'm Beginning to Feel It'."

Paul Overstreet

1986—*Lost and Found* (Necessity); 1989—*Sowin' Love* (Word); 1991—*Heroes* (RCA); 1992—*Love Is Strong*; 1994—*Best of Paul Overstreet*; 1996—*Time* (Scarlet Moon); 1999—*A Songwriter's Project, Vol. 1*; *Living by the Book*; 2000—*The Best of Paul Overstreet*.

www.pauloverstreet.com

Paul Overstreet is well known in modern country music—as a songwriter and as a Christian—though he remains somewhat obscure within the contemporary Christian music scene. *CCM* has published at least four profiles on the artist and reviewed every one of his albums, but he is yet to have a chart hit on Christian radio stations (that is, aside from Christian *country* stations, which are rather few and far between). Overstreet was born in rural Mississippi and raised as the youngest son of "a die-hard Southern Baptist preacher." His parents divorced when he was six and he says he spent the rest of his childhood being shuttled between warring parties in California and Mississippi. His mother's second marriage also ended badly when he was a young teenager. He headed for Nashville immediately after high school and spent a good decade singing in honky tonks and establishing a reputation as "a major boozehound." In 1984, he says, he got in a conversation with some people who didn't believe in God or Jesus and when he said that he did, they asked, Why? "I looked at them," he recalls, "and just said, 'I don't know.' I had to find out, so I went out and bought a Bible, and started stayin' home reading the Bible instead of honky-tonkin' and that was really the thing that brought me back around."

After going through a time of personal transformation, Overstreet set out to change the world of country music. He was disturbed by the genre's typically pessimistic outlook on life. "A lot of it is just self-pity," he says. "It's like, who can complain the most and get paid for it?" He read in the Bible that "as he thinketh in his heart, so is he" (Proverbs 23:7, KJV) and decided that his calling was to infuse his world (country music) with a more positive outlook. The idea that a virtually unknown country artist could have such an effect seemed ridiculous, and Overstreet admits to a degree of self-doubt. "I wasn't at all sure that country fans would go for songs that were moral or uplifting," he says. "And, the truth is, it's a lot harder to write positive songs than it is to write miserable, heartbreaking, cheating songs." But he went for it and soon country legend George Jones scored a respectable hit with his "Same Ole Me." Then in 1987 singer Randy Travis recorded his anti-adultery ode, "On the Other Hand," and wound up with the biggest country hit of the year. The very next year that success was repeated when Travis hit his career highpoint with Overstreet's "Forever and Ever, Amen," which would later also be a hit for George Strait. Overstreet was suddenly a country celebrity, having been named Songwriter of the Year by the Country Music Association two years in a row. Everyone wanted his songs, it seemed, and major country stars were recording them as fast as he could write them. Travis scored again with "Diggin' Up Bones," "No Place Like Home," and "Deeper Than the Holler." Tanya Tucker hit Number One with both "One Love at a Time" and "My Arms Stay Open All Night." The song "When You Say Nothing at All" was a hit first by Keith Whitley, then a Number One smash in a reworked version by Allison Krause, and then gained attention a third time when it became the featured song in the Julia Roberts/Hugh Grant movie *Notting Hill* (now performed by British rock star Ronan Keating). In all, Overstreet would see twenty-six of his songs hit the Top 10 performed by artists like The Forester Sisters ("You Again," "I Fell In Love Again Last Night"), The Judds ("Love Can Build a Bridge"), Michael Martin Murphey ("A Long Line of Love"), Marie Osmond ("You're Still New to Me"), Ronnie Milsap ("Houston Solution"), Kathy Mattea ("The Battle Hymn of Love"), Anne Murray ("When I Fall"), and Pam Tillis ("One of Those New Things").

Overstreet came to be viewed as the primary instigator of what has been called the "positive country" movement. By 1996, he had won six Grammy awards and was the only artist in history to be named BMI Songwriter of the Year five years in a row. Always articulate about his faith (thanking "my Lord and Savior Jesus Christ" from the podium for every award), he remains one of the best-known Christians in country music circles. The lack of attention to his work in contemporary Christian music circles stems in part from the low profile accorded to country artists and even more from the fact that Overstreet's songs deal more with issues of family life (as viewed from a Christian perspective) than with specifically religious or spiritual matters. It is also safe to assume that some Christian music fans would find his enthusiasm for certain aspects of married life to be a little unsettling: songs like "Let's Go to Bed Early" (with fairly obvious implications) and "Blackberry Cobbler" (figure it out) are not for the prudish. Still, in 1991, *CCM* would write, "Overstreet is salt and light in a beer and whiskey world . . . never preachy, always true, he has done what most Christian artists only dream of doing in terms of having a major influence in his field."

The first album that Overstreet cares to recall is *Lost and Found,* released on an independent label that he started himself (he did have at least one pre-Christian release called *The Wanderer* on an indie label in Arkansas in the early '70s). *Lost and Found* shows him struggling with his new identity and is more of a gospel project than later releases. *Sowin' Love* would be his only album on a specifically Christian label, marketed for the contemporary Christian music audience. The song "Love Helps Those (Who Cannot Help Themselves)" witnesses to the biblical offer of hope, while the title track and "Seein' My Father in Me" encourage responsible parenting. Those three songs all charted in the Top 10 on country radio stations, as did "All the Fun," which counters any notion that equates living a "straight life" with somber existence. Overstreet got **Brown Bannister** to coproduce his *Heroes* album, which also charted major country hits with its title track and with "Daddy's Come Around (To Momma's Way of Thinking)." The song "Billy Can't Read" became an anthem for the literacy movement and moved Overstreet's own mother to become a teacher. The title track to *Love Is Strong* is a creative rewrite of 1 Corinthians 13. "What Goes without Saying" offers encouragement to speak words of love aloud and features duet vocals by **Susan Ashton, Glen Campbell,** and **Kelly Willard.** "There But for the Grace of God Go I" encourages empathy with the downtrodden. "Still Out There Swinging" employs a staple of country lyrics, the pun, in a song about the ineffectiveness of tolerating a wayward spouse's indiscretions: "She gave him enough rope to hang himself / And he's still out there swingin'." A titular pun also sustains "Tonight, I'm Gonna Ring Her" (about an engagement proposal) from *Time.* A highlight of the latter album would be "We've Got to Go On Meeting Like This," a country-rock song that celebrates marriage as a lifelong romance. *The Songwriter's Project* allows Overstreet to sing his own versions of songs that he originally wrote for others. *Living by the Book* is a collection of specifically gospel songs.

Overstreet is intentional about giving his wife Julie the primary credit for his positive conception of marriage and family. When they married, he says, "I didn't know what a good marriage was supposed to look like. When we wed, I told her, 'We can try, and if it doesn't work out, we can go our separate

ways' and that just broke her heart, because for her there had to be commitment to the relationship." His change in outlook is perhaps documented in the aforementioned "Daddy's Come Around (To Momma's Way of Thinking)." In any case, the couple would raise six home-schooled children on a small farm outside of Nashville. Julie appears with her husband in the video for "We've Got to Go On Meeting Like This" and maintains, "We don't have the perfect marriage—but it's the perfect marriage for us." Overstreet has also authored a book (*Forever and Ever, Amen,* Destiny Image, 2001).

Grammy Awards: 1992 Country Song of the Year ("Love Can Build a Bridge"); 1998 Country Song of the Year ("Forever and Ever, Amen").

Dove Awards: 1991 Country Song of the Year ("Seein' My Father in Me"); 1993 Country Album of the Year (*Love Is Strong*); 1994 Country Song of the Year ("There But for the Grace of God Go I").

Over the Rhine

Karin Bergquist, voc.; Linford Detweiler, gtr., kybrd.; Ric Hordinski, gtr. (–2000); Brian Kelly, drums (–2000). 1991—*'Til We Have Faces* (Scampering Songs); 1992—*Patience* (I.R.S.); 1994—*Eve*; 1996—*Good Dog, Bad Dog* (Scampering Songs); *The Darkest Night of the Year*; 2000—*Amateur Shortwave Radio* (Grey Ghost); 2001—*Films for Radio* (Backporch).

www.overtherhine.com

Cincinnati-based Over the Rhine were darlings of the indie rock scene throughout the '90s, touring incessantly with the Cowboy Junkies, appearing on stage with such artists as **Bob Dylan** and Shawn Colvin, and building a cult following of intensely loyal fans that included a core of thoughtful Christians. The group's origins have some strained connections with Jesus music as Linford Detweiler, Ric Hordinski, and Brian Kelly first played with Owen and Sandie Brock in a rejuvenated version of **Servant.** In any case, Over the Rhine's sound has been defined primarily by the combination of Karin Bergquist's sensual, classically-trained vocals with multi-instrumentalist Detweiler's eclectic songwriting. The closest comparison might well be the Cowboy Junkies, though instances of Mazzy Starr, **The Innocence Mission,** and even **Sixpence None the Richer** intrude here or there. In terms of genre, Over the Rhine probably falls into the broad category of Americana, but they often favor more atmospheric effects than groups associated with that style (The Band, the **Lost Dogs, Vigilantes of Love**). Bergquist once described their sound (half-joking) as "Cocteau Twins meets **Johnny Cash,**" invoking the idea of "a meeting of opposites." In the late '90s, their songs would be featured on the TV shows *Felicity* and *Third Watch.* In 1996, Detweiler and Bergquist married, and in 1999 they actually joined The Cowboy Junkies as "honorary members," appearing as part of the group in TV performances (e.g., on *The Late Show with David Letterman*).

When Over the Rhine came together in the late '80s, they described themselves ideologically as "four individuals all concerned at some level with ideas of faith and truth and hope and mercy and justice and grace." The Christian media did not notice them until *Good Dog, Bad Dog,* their most acclaimed project to date. *'Til We Have Faces* (named for a C. S. Lewis novel) and *Patience* are coffeeshop music in an alterna-folk tradition. *Eve* is more rock, a bold, bluesy record with a searing electric sound; the song "My Love Is a Fever" would become an Over the Rhine standard. Ric Hordinski's guitar playing is much more in evidence on the first three albums than on the 1996 releases, at which point he was apparently in the process of leaving the band. At any rate, two songs on *Good Dog, Bad Dog* in particular sparked the attention of folks in the Christian music subculture. "A Gospel Number" is a bluesy shuffle in which Bergquist wonders what would happen if "a man named Jesus" were to look her in the eye. "Poughkeepsie" is a quiet song of transformation from suicidal despair to redemptive hope, sung to the bare accompaniment of a lone guitar. Neither song offers the kind of explicit Christian confession that some Christian music fans look for from their artists, but both invoke a subdued spirituality that is simultaneously affecting and challenging. Several of the other songs on *Good Dog* also display what *CCM* would call "some aspect of our need for grace in light of human frailty." The opening "Latter Days" speaks of the conclusion of a relationship—possibly a romance or, as many theorized, the band's less-than-blissful parting with the soon-to-be-defunct I.R.S. label. "All I Need Is Everything" is another highlight; *CCM* thought it was about "our need for God and sometime refusal to let Him in." And, intentionally or not, "Happy to Be So" alludes to a classic hymn as Bergquist breathes over a melancholy cello, "I know a love that will not let me go." That same song continues, "My heart is bound and gagged and on death row / It's so happy to be so."

By 1997, Over the Rhine was a duo who fronted an ever-changing lineup of different performers. As Detweiler put it in 2001, "Over the last few years, we've toured as a seven-piece, as a trio, a quartet, and sometimes just a duo. It's been great to dress the songs up in all those different guises." It would be five years before the group put together a major release of new material. A 1997 album called *Besides* was released through mail-order to members of the group's fan club. *Darkest Night of the Year,* released the same year as *Good Dog,* is a Christmas album, coming out of a longstanding tradition for the group to play Christmas concerts every year. A few original songs join well-known carols like "The First Noel," "O Little Town of Bethlehem," and two different versions of "Silent Night." *Amateur Shortwave Radio* was released to commemorate the group's ten-year anniversary. It features live performances of songs that provide a career retrospective, in addition to three new songs

and covers of the Rolling Stones' "Ruby Tuesday" and the Beatles' "Blackbird."

Films for Radio (coproduced with **Dave Perkins**) reveals another metamorphosis for the group as they incorporate loops, samples, and drum machines into a more experimental sound. The song "I Radio Heaven" finds the singer desperately manipulating an antenna and switching channels in an attempt to contact God. "The World Can Wait" opens the album with a paean to emotion and sensuality: "I want to feel and then some / I have five senses / I need thousands more at least." In the same vein, "The Body Is a Stairway of Skin" is a celebration of the flesh that combines spirituality and sexuality in a most non-gnostic way. The group also covers Dido's "Give Me Strength."

Detweiler is the son of a Christian minister and he says he grew up aware of some of the music in the contemporary Christian scene. He even says he thought about going into that field "for about five minutes," but that he decided to avoid the whole "Christian music industry thing" because he was "uncomfortable with the idea of marketing spirituality." There is something intrinsic to art, he says, that is compromised when it serves as a means for propaganda, no matter how noble the ideas that are being promoted. "I feel that the Christian music industry on some level is responsible for a lot of bad art because the premise is wrong," he says. "They're taking something that is very pure and trying to use it to market a way of thinking." Nevertheless, at **Steve Taylor**'s request, the group did contribute one song ("Goodbye," also on *Films for Radio*) to the *Roaring Lambs* album (Squint, 2000)—a project of songs by "Christian artists who are making a difference in the world." *True Tunes* describes Over the Rhine as "one of a few bands whose chief aim seems to be the communication of beauty . . . neither to rock the masses, nor to convert them, but merely to *move* them." Detweiler also told *Bandoppler* in 1999, "I think of the band as an extension of my prayer life, as a way for me to explore what I believe is true."

Over the Rhine has also placed songs on in-store compilation albums put together (and sold) by Pottery Barn and Starbucks. Their song "All I Want Is Everything" appears on the *Journeys* album (Virgin, 2000), alongside tunes by John Lennon, Don McLean, and Paul Simon. Linford Detweiler has released an album of solo piano music, *I Don't Think There's No Need to Bring Nuthin'* (Grey Ghost, 1999). The compositions are in the style of George Winston, and many bear titles that are at least playful and bear no obvious relationship to the music ("Weak in the Knees across the Sky," "OK As Long As You Don't Squeak or Bark or Make Other Animal Noises"). Ric Hordinski and Brian Kelly formed the group **Monk.**

For trivia buffs: Over the Rhine was honored in a special episode of *The X-Files* TV series when a fan of the group who is a writer for the show named two characters in one episode "Linford Detweiler" and "Karin Bergquist." On the show, Detweiler ended up getting a stake through the heart; Bergquist was slated to die in David Duchovny's arms (at the real Karin's request) but that got edited out and she wound up just dying alone instead.

Ginny Owens

1999—*Without Condition* (Rocketown); 2002—*Something More.*

www.ginnyowens.com

Adult contemporary singer Ginny Owens has a jazz-tinged piano-driven style that is often compared to Sarah MacLachlan or Fiona Apple. A native of Mississippi, Owens graduated cum laude with a music degree from Belmont University in Nashville before signing with **Michael W. Smith**'s Rocketown records and recording her debut *Without Condition.* Owens' delicate, pretty voice is invariably described as "celestial" or "angelic," though she is able to adopt a more bluesy, less ethereal tone when the mood suits her. Songs like "Land of the Grey," "Symbol of a Lost Cause," and "I Wanna Be Moved" from her debut album illustrate the latter tendency. The former comes through on a heavenly rendition of the hymn "Be Thou My Vision," a song that has special meaning for Owens, who lost her eyesight at age two due to a hereditary condition. The album's title track, "Without Condition," is a perceptive response to someone (reportedly, a Belmont professor) who struck Owens as a bit too secure in his/her beliefs ("You can't find the answers till you learn to question"). That song won her an appearance at the Nashville stop on the Lilith Fair in 1999. "If You Want Me To" was cowritten with **Kyle Matthews** and offers a simple song of submission to God's sanctifying processes ("I will go through the fire, if you want me to"). Owens would also place a duet with **Brent Bourgeois** on the *Roaring Lambs* theme album (Squint, 2000). Her songs have been featured on such TV shows as *Felicity, Charmed,* and *Roswell.* She has sung at the Sundance Film Festival. The 2002 album "Something More" was announced as featuring "some stylistic changes, including a more up-tempo sound and some urban influences." These are mainly evident in a handful of heavily synthesized tracks that *CCM* did not find appealing. The album's first single would be "I Am," which offers a personal and passionate retelling of Bible stories.

Christian radio hits: "Free" (# 5 in 1999); "Springs of Life" (# 13 in 2000); "If You Want Me To" (# 15 in 2000); "I Wanna Be Moved" (# 9 in 2000).

Dove Awards: 2000 New Artist of the Year.

Jamie Owens-Collins (a.k.a. **Jamie Owens**)

As Jamie Owens: 1973—*Laughter in Your Soul* (Light); 1975—*Growing Pains* (Light). As Jamie Owens-Collins: 1978—*Love Eyes*; 1980—*Straight Ahead* (Sparrow); 1985—*A Time for Courage* (Live Oak); 1987—*The Gift of Christmas*; 1999—*Seasons* (Newport).

Jamie Owens-Collins (b. 1954) is the daughter of **Jimmy and Carol Owens,** who, along with **Ralph Carmichael** and Kurt Kaiser, were responsible for turning out several influential Christian musicals performed in and by churches in the early '70s. Their best work was *Come Together* (Light, 1972), which was the best of *all* the musicals produced in this era, though *Show Me* (Impact, 1971) and *If My People* (Light, 1975) were also influential. A native of Oakland, California, Jamie's musical style evolved from an early Joni Mitchell-style singer/songwriter to that of an adult contemporary songstress with a strong worship orientation.

Jamie grew up surrounded by Jesus music pioneers and so became the most recognizable figure of the Jesus movement's mid '70s "second generation." At age fifteen, she sang the song "Long Distance Love" as a duet with **Randy Stonehill** on her parents' *Show Me* album. Two years later, she sang "May I Introduce You to a Friend?" as a solo on *Come Together.* The adolescent sweetness of her voice fit the latter song perfectly, and she sang it with such sincerity that it justifiably became one of the most popular tracks on the record. She was deluged with requests to sing on albums by other artists and, at age seventeen, released her first solo album, *Laughter in Your Soul*—a record that includes "May I Introduce You?" and two other songs that the artist wrote herself. It would go on to become the best-selling contemporary Christian album of 1975 in Great Britain. *Laughter in Your Soul* remains a Jesus music classic. It opens with an **Annie Herring** song, "You'll Start Falling in Love," which features Herring and the rest of **2nd Chapter of Acts** rather conspicuously in the background. Jamie also covers two songs that had already been made famous (among the Jesus People) by **Barry McGuire:** "Peace" and "Love Is." And she delivers the best recorded version of **Kenn Gulliksen**'s wonderful "Charity." The album is arranged such that three songs in a row exegete 1 Corinthians 13:4–8 ("I'm So Happy," "Charity," "Love Is"). *Growing Pains* demonstrates her growth as a songwriter and shows an unexpected maturity of perspective in dealing with songs about growth (as the title implies and "Hard Times," the opening track, indicates). In addition to several original songs, she sings "I'm Yours" by **Gary Chapman** and interprets the traditional hymn "My Jesus I Love Thee." The song "New Jerusalem" was cowritten with **Terry Talbot.** The centerpiece (and highlight) of *Growing Pains,* however, is Jamie's own "The Victor," which was later performed by **Keith Green.** The first two records are the only ones released under the name Jamie Owens. Subsequent recordings were attributed to Jamie Owens-Collins, reflecting her marriage to Dan Collins, an industry executive who worked with Sparrow and founded Live Oak, Aslan, and Newport Records. Following in her parents' footsteps, she cowrote the musical *Firewind* (Sparrow, 1976) with **The Talbot Brothers.**

Her albums *Love Eyes* and *Straight Ahead* presented her as the predecessor to **Amy Grant,** in whose shadow she would somewhat ironically be lost. *Love Eyes* gave her two Christian radio hits with the title track and "Pleasure Servin' You." *Straight Ahead* rocks harder than any of Owens-Collins' other albums on songs like "Liar on the Loose" and "Holy Fire," but the ballads ("Walkin' On," "Shine through Me") would prove to be most memorable. *A Time for Courage* offers the up-tempo songs "Shine Your Light" and "Never Turn Around." It concludes with one of her all-time best songs, the moving ballad "Hearts Courageous." Owens-Collins' commitment to praise and worship music would remain evident, as would her focus on ministry within the church. From 1989 to 1995 she and her husband were members of the Maranatha Praise Band, singing in support of crusades by such evangelists as Franklin Graham and Greg Laurie. In 1996, Dan and Jamie worked on a remake of the musical *If My People,* now titled *Heal My Land.* Over the years, Owens-Collins would establish herself as a prominent songwriter, penning well-known songs like "Look How Far You've Come," "You Have Broken the Chains," and "Jesus Christ Is the Risen Son." These and other worship songs are included on her 1999 album *Seasons.*

Still, Jesus movement veterans will always remember Jamie best as a teenager, popularizing songs like "Jesus People" (later recorded by **Barry McGuire** on *To the Bride*) and opening for acts like **Liberation Suite** or **Mason Proffit** (who she said "rocked her socks off") at primitive Jesus music festivals. As "Jamie Owens" she came into prominence at the very time that many of the Jesus people were becoming parents, and she represented what they all hoped their children would be like: an adolescent who was as "turned-on to Jesus" as they were.

Christian music hits: "Pleasure Servin' You" (# 13 in 1978); "Love Eyes" (# 6 in 1979); "I'm Yours" (# 2 in 1981).

Jimmy and Carol Owens

Selected: 1971—*Show Me!* (Impact); 1972—*Come Together* (Light); 1973—*Tell the World in '73*; 1975—*If My People*; 1978—*The Witness*; 1984—*Victor*; 1986—*Come Together Again* (Live Oak).

Jimmy and Carol Owens made their most significant mark in contemporary Christian music by composing Christian musicals that could be performed in churches. They also made many other albums with titles like *Turn On the World of Youth* (Word, 1968) that were intended to help youth pastors get hip with the kids, but the musicals would prove most effective and enduring. The template for all of these was the very secular hippies-on-Broadway production *Hair,* which embedded light rock numbers into a loose stream-of-consciousness narrative

that served mainly to set up the songs. Mimicking *Hair's* style and success, **Ralph Carmichael** and Kurt Kaiser composed a folk musical for churches in 1970 called *Tell It Like It Is.* The latter production gave the world such classic "youth group" songs as "Pass It On" and "Master Designer" and seems to have inspired the Owenses to come up with the similar-themed *Show Me!* Whereas the former piece sought to be primarily evangelistic, however, *Show Me!* directed its message to the church, unmasking attitudes and hypocrisies that stifle its witness to the current generation. A pompous church leader surveys the hairy denizens of Woodstock nation and surmises, "I think if only they were shaved / That then perhaps they could be saved." Notably, the album cast for this musical features a number of developing Christian stars, including **Sherman Andrus, Michael Omartian** (who delivers "Ode to My Disenchanted Friend"), and **Randy Stonehill.** Its highlight is probably the musical debut of the composers' daughter, **Jamie Owens (Collins),** who sings "Long Distance Love" as a duet with Stonehill.

Come Together was the Owens' highpoint, and by the year 2002 would remain the best contemporary Christian musical of all time, the benchmark for all other contributions to what became a major genre in its own right. Writing for *Jesus Music,* David Burgin has called the record "the very first (contemporary) praise album," and it may just be that. Released two years prior to Maranatha's *The Praise Album,* which is usually accorded that status, *Come Together* is indeed a collection of songs that serve well in informal congregational worship. Practically every song in the musical would be excerpted and sung at prayer meetings and in "free praise" sessions apart from any connection to the musical as such. The best of the best include the title track, "God So Loved the World," "Clap Your Hands," "Holy Holy," "Hallelujah! His Blood Avails for Me!" "May I Introduce You to a Friend" (by daughter Jamie), and "Freely, Freely." Again, an incredible roster of Jesus music pioneers participated in the recording of the album, including **Pat Boone, Barry McGuire,** the **2nd Chapter of Acts,** and many members of the various Maranatha groups. After this career triumph, the Owenses would produce *Tell the World in '73,* a somewhat nondescript work related to the nationwide "Key '73" evangelism campaign being conducted by many churches. *If My People* (prominently featuring **Pat Boone**) was a much better return to form, but its patriotic theme played too easily into the ambitions of the Religious Right, which was already quenching the spirit of the Jesus movement revival; in 1996, **Jamie Owens-Collins** and her husband Dan worked up a remake of *If My People,* now titled *Heal My Land.* By the time *The Witness* was released, the church musical genre that the Owens had helped to create had burgeoned to the point that it was hardly noticed among the multitudinous resources becoming available.

Even at the time they appeared, *Show Me* and *Come Together* were regarded as somewhat "hokey" by real aficionados of rock. They may have been a guilty pleasure for some of the more rock-oriented Jesus freaks, but more often they served as a safe transitional phase for those who had been taught that rock and roll was the devil's music and had no place within the church. As **Larry Norman** has rightly noted, the media's portrayal of the Jesus movement as a conversion of street people was grossly exaggerated. The great majority of youth involved in the Jesus movement were tame kids who had been raised in churches but who identified culturally with certain aspects of their generation's ethos. They grew their hair long, wore tie-dyed T-shirts, and listened to Jefferson Airplane without actually burning draft cards (or bras), renouncing parents, living on the streets, and dropping acid. The Owens' musicals appealed primarily to these faux-hippie church kids. As incredible as it might seem three decades later, the staging of a Jimmy and Carol Owens musical was once the sort of radical act that could cost a youth minister his or her job. But when the youth of a church did put on such a production, those who got to sing folk-rock and maybe even play guitar inside the sanctuary found a connection between faith and culture that reaffirmed the institutional church's relevance to their daily lives.

Pacific Gas and Electric (a.k.a. PG&E)

See **All Saved Freak Band.**

Lisa Page

See **Lisa Page Brooks.**

Paige Lewis

2001—*Paige* (Word).

Sixteen-year-old singer Paige Lewis released a debut album in mid 2001 that reveals a potentially mature singer in search of a style. The first half of *Paige* (what would have been called Side A in the old days) presents her as a cuter version of Alanis Morissette (or **Rebecca St. James**). The rest of the project (Side B) presents her as a cuter version of **Jennifer Knapp.** What prevents the record from being dismissed as one more clone-effort is the fact that Lewis wrote all of the songs herself and they reveal deeper insights than one would expect from a youth. In the opening trance-like "Hide Myself in You," she sings to Christ, "sometimes I think it'd be easier to die for you than to live for you." Elsewhere, she admits to her personal responsibility for the crucifixion and acknowledges her worthlessness apart from God. As *CCM* would note, such insights are *so* adult as to feel a bit disconcerting. Shouldn't she be a bit more self-obsessed, struggling with identity crises and wondering why God doesn't make all the boys like her? "It's so not about me," she sings, "It's all about You / Who You are, what You've done . . . Take this stupid spotlight off of me" ("So Not about Me"). At least in "True" she sings about being "madly in love" with God, an expression not found in most adult contemporary music.

Painted Orange

Craig Fain, gtr.; John Lovell, drums, kybrd.; Otto-M, voc., kybrd., prog. 1989—*Educate* (custom); 1990—*Painted Orange*; 1996—*Out of Egypt* (R.E.X.).

Painted Orange was a Christian synth-pop band from Oklahoma with a sound very similar to that of general market artists Depeche Mode and Erasure. The group did not gain widespread exposure until its second independent album was re-released on R.E.X. in 1991. Even then the self-titled project was trashed by *True Tunes* as "a lackluster record" that had "the rare distinction of being a techno record that was impossible to dance to." *CCM* just thought the sound was about four years behind what was happening in the secular scene. In retrospect, the group should at least be given credit for being one of the first bands in American Christian music to experiment with the euro-tech sound; they beat **Code of Ethics** to the punch and were a good four years *ahead* of **The Echoing Green** and **Joy Electric.** From the eponymous album, the song "Voyager" got the most notice, using the theme of God leading the Israelites as a metaphor for guidance through modern wildernesses. Five years later, the forgotten band would emerge again with *Out of Egypt,* which was much better received. The album kicks into gear with space-age keyboards on "After the Rain" and then melds easily into a highly melodic number called "Run to

You." Industrial touches enhance "Love Is," while "Invitation (96)" has a darker edge reminiscent of The Cure. Lyrically, the album is poetic while retaining a clear, explicitly Christian focus.

Tony Palacios

See **Guardian.**

Paloma

Chad Anderson; et al. 1999—*The Spooky Loop* (Dog Bone).

Paloma was a possibly one-time project initiated by progressive rock musician Chad Anderson who formerly fronted the East Coast band Dizzy Monk. Disillusioned by the compromises of the music industry, he headed to California after that band broke up hoping to work with **Terry Taylor.** Instead he wound up with Taylor's friend and sometimes bandmate Gene Eugene (of **Adam Again** and the **Lost Dogs**). They assembled a motley collection of musicians from the Christian and secular fields and recorded *The Spooky Loop* under the name Paloma. Jesse Sprinkle of **Poor Old Lu** and The World Within played drums and Madelyn Waggoner of **Estis p@rc** offered female vocals. The project has a nonderivative modern rock sound with touches of influence as diverse as Radiohead, The Pixies, **Annie,** and **Adam Again.** Thematically, *Spooky Loop* offers what *True Tunes* calls "a carefully crafted look at the spiritual decay and resounding shallowness of urban North America." Distributors for the album insisted on the removal of one song ("Sunday Morning") because of a lyric that they took to be sexually prurient: "I woke up in heaven / I woke up on you" (Anderson says the line is just poetry and he did not intend anything so specific or literal by it). That experience, and respect for artistic integrity in general, would produce a certain disaffection for the Christian music industry in the artist. Anderson told *Bandoppler* in 1999 that he was hopeful that his music would be "thought-provoking enough to make people consider the reality of Jesus Christ, and take their own lives into account," while also admitting that "the majority of what we consider to be the church doesn't go over with non-Christian people; it chases them away."

The Panorama Ramblers

Lanny Cordola; et al. 1995—*Return to Hamilton County* (Benson).

The Panorama Ramblers was a one-time side project for the very prolific **Lanny Cordola** (see also **Chaos is the Poetry, Children of Zion, Magdalen, Shack of Peasants, Symbiotica**). Cordola plays guitar, mandolin, and dobro with a crew of nine of his pals as they run through bluegrass versions of mostly traditional and cover songs. Hank Williams' "I Saw

the Light" is a natural choice; **Bob Dylan**'s "I Threw It All Away," a bit of a surprise. "Somebody Touched Me" recalls the definitive rendering given the tune by **Dennis Agajanian** twenty years earlier.

Pantano-Salsbury

See **J.C. Power Outlet.**

John Pantry

1978—*Empty Handed* (Dove); 1979—*Nothing Is Impossible* (Kingsway); 1980—*To Strangers and Friends*; 1981—*Hot Coals* [with Fresh Aire] (Marshalls); 1983—*Not Guilty* [= *Hot Coals*] (Pilgrim America); 1983—*It's For You* (Eyes and Ears); 1985—*Eighteen Classics* (Kingsway); *Discovery* (Eyes and Ears); 1986—*Simple Sailing for Beginners*; 1988—*Breaking New Ground* (Pulse); 1992—*The Church Invincible.*

John Pantry is a British artist whose synthesizer-based worship music has not gained much of a hearing in North America. Prior to recording, Pantry earned a **Michael Omartian**-like reputation in his homeland for production work on albums by The Bee Gees, The New Seekers, and The Who. Only Pantry's first album gained much notice in America, when it was released on Maranatha and promoted as a fairly mellow adult contemporary project consistent with much of their late '90s catalogue. A perky song called "He Will Take Care" was included on a Maranatha sampler album called *Maranatha Current* (1979) and subsequently became Pantry's best-known song west of the Atlantic. **Kelly Willard** is not credited as performing on *Empty Handed* but many fans swear they can hear her voice on several tracks ("Strong Love," "Empty Handed," "Will I Ever Get over This?"), and it is known that she and Pantry were friends. Pantry would also serve as producer for some classic Jesus music albums, including **Liberation Suite**'s self-titled debut, **Debby Kerner** and **Ernie Rettino**'s *Changin',* **Lewis McVay**'s *Spirit of St. Lewis,* and **Parchment**'s *Shamblejam.* Pantry's own *Hot Coals* [a.k.a. *Not Guilty*] was recorded live with the jazz vocal group Fresh Aire providing backing vocals.

Papa San

2000—*Victory* (B-Rite).

Reggae artist Tyrone Thompson, who goes by the professional name Papa San, is known in his homeland as "the fastest mouth in Jamaica." He practices a variety of reggae singing called toasting (or sometimes "chatting" or "DJ-ing"), which may sound like rap to the nonspecialist but actually served as a historical predecessor to the latter; indeed many pop-music historians trace American rap music's origins to Jamaican toasting. Papa San is known for his rapid-fire delivery of lyrics, and mainstream rapper Busta Rhymes cites him as the number one influence on the development of his similar style. A popular artist in his home country, Papa San was also the first reggae artist ever to have a Number One hit on *Billboard*'s Dance Music chart.

In 1997, the artist announced that he had given his life to Christ and would henceforth be singing for the Lord. In 1999, he provided vocals for an album by the Rev. Jackie McCullough released on the Gospo Centric label. A year later, he released his own Christian debut. *Victory* is blatant in its evangelical lyrics. "As a Christian" provides a do's-and-don't's list of appropriate behaviors, and "First Him" lays down a gauntlet in challenge to the often anti-Christian Rastafarian community. The artist also offers his own testimony in "Jesus Love" and reworks an old hymn in "Fly Away Home." "Over the years I have misled youth," Papa San told *Release* magazine. "It is my responsibility now as a Christian to go back and tell them about Jesus Christ."

Parachute Band

Mark de Jong, bass; Libby Huirua, voc.; Wayne Huirua, gtr.; et al. 1999—*You Alone (Here to Him)*; 2000—*Always and Forever*; 2001—*Love and Adore*; announced for 2002—*Amazing* (Parachute).

Parachute Band is a spiritually focused praise and worship group from New Zealand. The team of contemporary worship leaders has dedicated themselves to collecting praise choruses being sung in their native land and making these available to the global church. Their albums display a variety of styles, including American jazz, European pop, and Caribbean rhythms, all of which are popular in their homeland. "Our congregations are very mixed racially," De Jong explains, "and we don't really categorize styles the way they do in America." Libby and Wayne Huirua wrote some of the songs that appear on the projects, but many were simply collected from churches throughout the land. *You Alone* has the most low-budget feel, with somewhat contrived whoops and hollers added to the mix as a second thought. *Always and Forever* is more solid, with a number of high-energy praise tracks. *Love and Adore* is a two-disc set consisting of two albums that were originally released separately in the homeland (*Love* and *Adore,* the latter being a live production). In general, the group has turned up the volume as their albums have progressed chronologically, with *Love and Adore* featuring loud guitars on a few rock-oriented numbers.

Parable

Chuck Butler, voc., gtr.; Don Kobayashi, drums; Joy Strange, gtr., voc. (– 1977); Pat Patton, bass, voc. (– 1977) // Gary Arthur, bass, voc. (+ 1977); Alan DiCato, kybrd., voc. (+ 1977); Lisa Faye Irwin (Wickham), voc., perc. (+ 1977); John Wickham, gtr., voc. (+ 1977). 1975—*More Than Words* (Maranatha); 1977—*Illustrations.*

Along with **Mustard Seed Faith,** Parable is a quintessential example of the second wave of Maranatha groups that helped to define Jesus music in the days just before "contemporary Christian music" would develop into a recognizable genre (and industry) with all the benefits and deficits that such categorization would bring. The "first wave" of such bands **(Children of the Day, Love Song,** and **The Way)** changed the sound of Christian music forever. Parable and **Mustard Seed Faith** got their albums out just a couple of years too late to have that kind of effect, but the key players for the bands had actually been a part of the scene from the beginning. In the case of **Mustard Seed Faith, Oden Fong** and **Lewis McVay** had been tooling around Costa Mesa's Calvary Chapel playing with other groups before the official act came together. Likewise, Parable was received by most Christian music fans as the heir to **Country Faith,** a very popular band led by **Chuck Butler** that kept putting songs on the influential Maranatha sampler albums but never recorded an album of their own. The actual origins of the group lie in a folk trio that Butler put together with Pat Patton and with Joy Strange of **Selah.** The group had a countryfied Peter, Paul, and Mary type of sound and toured as Chuck, Pat, and Joy for a while, but once they added a drummer, they wisely chose to eschew all the first names and just call themselves Parable. Like many of the Maranatha groups **(Daniel Amos, Bethlehem),** Parable fashioned its sound after the lighter fare of The Eagles ("Best of My Love") with Strange's female vocals adding a degree of distinction.

Butler and Strange trade lead vocals on *More Than Words,* one of the sweetest and most melodic albums to come out of the Jesus movement. "Maybe" and "Peter, James and John" are pop gems that represent some of Butler's best material. Strange sings the title track (which she also wrote), a lovely song in the tradition of **Marsha Stevens**' contributions to **Children of the Day.** Lyrically, it offers a prayer for the Holy Spirit to reveal to loved ones the mystery that Christians experience but are never quite able to explain. Butler's "Sweet, Sweet Song" sounds a lot like a Peter Jacobs **Children of the Day** tune, which is to say it's very nice indeed.

The CoD comparisons would drop out with the next album, as the group underwent drastic personnel changes. Strange left to marry **Bob Cull,** and her **Marsha Stevens** voice was replaced by Lisa Irwin's throaty warble; Irwin's eventual husband John Wickham also came over from **The Way** to add lead guitar solos that gave the group a harder edge. Gary Arthur was a former member of **The Way** as well, giving the second incarnation of Parable a sort of Maranatha supergroup feel. Just about everyone sang and the songs often achieve the same level of quality (in composition and performance) as those of the numerous harmonic country-rock bands assaulting mainstream charts at the time. "The Plain Truth" (written by Butler and **Fred Field**) is good enough to have been on a Poco album. "There's a Reason" is a Gary Arthur tune that has the anthemic quality expected of a concert opener. "Come Untangled" has a call-and-response R&B gospel sound to it, not unlike the Allman Brothers' "Revival." The group also performs "Got to Decide" by **Joy Cull** and closes with Irwin singing one of John Wickham's quiet hymns, appropriately titled "A Prayer."

Paradox

Ralph Dix, voc., bass, kybrd.; Lissa, voc.; Steve, gtr., kybrd. 1999—*New Devotion* (Seeing Ear).

The somewhat anonymous synth-pop band Paradox comes from Perth, Australia, and displays a retro-'80s sound very similar to that of The Human League ("Don't You Want Me?") or Soft Cell ("Tainted Love"). The keyboard-oriented group turns out peppy, techno songs with male and female vocals proclaiming love for Jesus and hatred for Satan. "In My Dreams," their album's closing cut, paints apocalyptic images of Jesus' second coming. An unrelated Christian band named Paradox released two custom albums called *Ruler* (1987) and *Power and Glory* (1989).

Paramecium

Andrew Tompkins, voc., bass; Mosh, gtr. (−1994); Steve Palmer, drums (−1994) // Jason De Ron, gtr. (+ 1994, −1996); Jayson Sherlock, drums (+ 1994, −1996); Ian Arkley, drums (+ 1996); Mark Orr (+ 1996). 1991—*Silent Carnage* [EP] (custom); 1994—*Exhumed of the Earth* (R.E.X.); 1996—*Within the Ancient Forest* (independent); 1997—*Repentance*; 1999—*A Time to Mourn*.

Australian death metal band Paramecium has had at least three completely different incarnations, all built around singer Andrew Tompkins, whose vocals *HM* once proudly described as sounding like "a man with no tongue coughing up a hairball." The best-known version of the group is that which made *Exhumed of the Earth*. According to Tompkins, the guitarist on this album, Jason De Ron, had been "led to the Lord" by his predecessor (a man called Mosh) as a direct result of Paramecium's ministry. The band's drummer Jayson Sherlock previously played with **Mortification.** A concept album, *Exhumed* takes a storytelling approach to the Bible, relating the basic gospel message in a series of seven tracks based on the life of Jesus. The opening number, for instance, is over seventeen minutes long and is titled "The Unnatural Conception in Two Parts: The Birth and The Massacre of the Innocents." Musically, Paramecium integrates progressive art-rock elements into their basic doom metal sound, including **Kansas**-like violins. Such an approach would continue to be in evidence on

their later independent albums, *Within the Ancient Forest* and *A Time to Mourn*. The latter project features some soprano vocals provided by a guest from the world of classical music, Tracy Bourne. The *Repentance* album is a re-release of the original band's demo EP *(Silent Carnage),* with two additional songs.

Parca Pace

See **The November Commandment.**

Parchment

Sue McClellan; John Pac; Keith Rycroft (−1975) // Brian Smith (+ 1975). 1972—*Light Up the Fire* (Pye); 1973—*Hollywood Sunset;* 1975—*Shamblejam* (Myrrh); 1977—*Rehearsal for a Reunion.*

The progressive British folk group known as Parchment was a bit of an anomaly in the Jesus music scene, releasing only one unsuccessful album *(Shamblejam)* in America, a record that served only to confuse suspicious patrons of Christian music who thought the group had an "eastern" and therefore possibly occult sound. Parchment had been a part of the British Jesus movement almost from the start, releasing their first album in England the same year that **Love Song** debuted in California. Jesus music historian Ken Scott likens their sound to groups like Fairport Convention, in that they combined the traditional instruments of British folk music (guitar, mandolin, recorder, violin) with elements of modern rock. The first two albums were released on a general market label and the group enjoyed a minor mainstream hit with the title song from *Light Up the Fire.* The songs "Love Is Come Again" and "Son of God" bring out the eastern feel with a prominent use of sitar played by John Pac (real name, John Pacalabo). The group could also bring out a dobro for more footstomping numbers like "Better Than Yesterday" from the first album and "Get on the Road" from *Hollywood Sunset.* Myrrh Records took a chance with the group on *Shamblejam,* which features a more electric sound—perhaps out of deference to American audiences. The album was produced by **John Pantry,** and *Harmony* magazine would call attention to its able cast of backup musicians that supply the trio with a lot of muscle. The song "Light of the World" from this album would also be included on Myrrh's influential *Jubilation* compilation album (1975), allowing it to become the band's best-known cut and, for most, their defining moment. A truly great song, it impressed the open-minded as one of the most inventive cuts on *Jubilation*—a break from the predictably melodic numbers that filled that set at a time when most Christian groups were trying to sound like **Children of the Day.** "Light of the World" plods along with a psychedelic Seals-and-Crofts-on-acid feel. The album it was intended to showcase also includes a handful of bluesy numbers ("The Speaker's Corner," "Denomination Blues") that summon images of Jethro

Tull colliding with Canned Heat. Unfortunately, open minds were a limited commodity among Christian music fans in 1975, and *Shamblejam* didn't get much of a hearing. Parchment's fourth album shows the group experimenting with horns (including a rendition of the Dixieland classic "Jesus on the Mainline") and moving toward adult contemporary fare with a number of ballads.

Twila Paris

1980—Knowin' You're Around (Milk and Honey); 1982—Keepin' My Eyes on You; 1984—The Warrior Is a Child; 1985—The Best of Twila Paris; Kingdom Seekers (StarSong); 1987—Same Girl; 1988—For Every Heart; 1989—It's the Thought; 1990—Cry for the Desert; 1991—The Early Works (Benson); Sanctuary (StarSong); 1992—A Heart That Knows You; 1993—Beyond a Dream; 1995—The Time Is Now [EP]; 1996—Where I Stand (Sparrow); 1998—Perennial: Worship Songs for the Seasons of Life; 1999—True North; Twila: Collector's Series (Benson); 2001—Bedtime Prayers, Lullabies, and Peaceful Worship (Sparrow); Greatest Hits: Time and Again.

www.twilaparis.com

The October 1981 issue of *CCM* magazine introduced debut albums by five new MOR female vocalists with a single review. Complaining about a similarity in sound that marked all of these new contenders for attention in an already crowded field, the magazine nevertheless singled out twenty-one-year-old Twila Paris as the most promising of the group, which included **Sandi Patty**. Complaints of "sameness" would be the bane of Paris's career but, as in that proleptic introduction, she often proved able to rise above them. In time, she would come to be one of contemporary Christian music's most respected composers and performers of "modern hymns," of worshipful music that, as *CCM* would later say, "doesn't ruffle the feathers of preachers concerned about demonic syncopations."

Paris was born in 1959 in Fort Worth, Texas, but she grew up in Springdale, Arkansas, in a family with strong connections to the organization Youth With a Mission. Her father, Oren Paris, was head of the local branch of YWAM; his brother headed the branch in Tyler, Texas (the organization's national headquarters), and his cousin Loren Cunningham was one of the group's founders. Paris entered the group's discipleship program just out of high school and began her music career singing at YWAM programs. In 1983, she participated in a YWAM-sponsored tour of Guatemala. Paris is married to her manager, Jack Wright, who has struggled with health problems since the early '80s, having been diagnosed with Epstein-Barr disease (chronic fatigue syndrome) and Hepatitis C.

Paris worked with producer **Jonathan David Brown** for ten years and eight albums, before his career ended in disgrace. Her debut record *Knowin' You're Around* features the song "I'll See You Sunday," which displayed the young composer's talent for satirical humor: the singer tells a troubled friend who

wants to talk, "I'll see you Sunday morning . . . right now I haven't got the time," then, in a subsequent verse, repeats the same words to God in prayer. *Keepin' My Eyes on You* brought strong **Amy Grant** comparisons, especially as Brown's arrangements and production seemed styled after those used for Grant by **Brown Bannister.** The album opens with a praise song, "We Will Glorify," sung by Paris with **Jamie Owens-Collins** and her husband Dan Collins. The latter couple also joins her on the title track. A standout track, "Humility," features a fluent melody somewhat reminiscent of Janis Ian's "At Seventeen." *The Warrior Is a Child*, however, was the project destined to propel Paris to superstardom on the strength of its title track, which remained the Number One song on Christian radio for an incredible eighteen weeks. The song is less militant than its title implies, emphasizing rather that those who seem to be the Lord's mighty warriors in this world are only fragile children clothed in God's armor. The ironic metaphor for divine strength and human weakness is effective and expressive of a winsome quality that would mark much of Paris's work. Years later, in 1998, a *CCM* poll of thirty critics chose Paris's "The Warrior Is a Child" as one of "the ten best contemporary Christian songs of all time." The same album features the beautiful worship song, "We Bow Down." All three StarSong albums would continue to be regarded as Paris's classic works. Over the years, three different compilation albums *(The Best of Twila Paris, The Early Works,* and the two-disc *Twila: Collector's Series)* would be composed entirely of songs from these three albums.

Kingdom Seekers took the first of several detours from the mellow pop that had characterized Paris's first three albums to explore a sound that she would call "contemporary classical." The song "Release of the Spirit/He Is Exalted" is typical of the album's majestic grandeur; "Runner" is performed with **David Meece.** The highlight of the album, "Lamb of God," would become one of Paris's best-known hymns. "Faithful Men" is somewhat shocking for its lack of inclusive language, given that Paris intended it for congregational worship a good five years after most American denominations had purged their hymnals of such blatant sexism. By the time Paris had recorded *Same Girl* and *For Every Heart,* the seams were beginning to show, as each new album just delivered more songs that would please fans of her previous work without really taking them anywhere new. *Same Girl* offers the atypically rock-tinged "Prince of Peace," which would fit into the same genre as classic **Annie Herring/2nd Chapter of Acts** material. The latter group is also referenced by the album's opening song, "Holy Is the Lord," which features majestic strings, a church-bell opening and background vocals by **Matthew Ward.** "Let No Man Take Your Crown" pairs Paris with **Kelly Willard.** *CCM* complained again about **Amy Grant** cloning in its review of *For*

Every Heart, which they somewhat unfairly dismissed as a pale imitation of *Lead Me On.* The shining moments, they allowed, come with the worship songs: "All That I Need" and "For the Glory of the Lord." But there is also a lovely adult contemporary ballad, "Every Heart That Is Breaking," and what could be a great traditional gospel hymn, "Sweet Victory."

Cry for the Desert represents a safe break with tradition as Paris left producer Brown for the first time to work with the very similar **Brown Bannister.** Reviewers hardly noticed the change, remarking that "writing and composing" are the artist's forté such that each album may be appraised (positively) for the quality of the songs it offers, songs that may or may not turn up on Christian radio but seem destined in any case for congregational worship. In this case, the best such song would be "How Beautiful," a modern hymn that relates the image of the church as "the body of Christ" to the physical body of Jesus that served and suffered on its behalf. On *Sanctuary,* Paris seemed to realize what audiences most wanted from her and eschewed the pop star persona to serve as worship leader on an artistic record produced by instrumentalist **Richard Souther.** The latter keeps the keyboard orientation of most Paris projects but brings in a variety of Latin session players (including Abraham Laboriel of **Koinonia** and Weather Report) and even introduces Gaelic fiddle and some guitar work by **Phil Keaggy.** *Sanctuary* was intended as an aid for personal worship, offering what the artist called "calming, soothing music with a vertical focus." The album shimmers with the unpredictable, including three instrumental versions of Paris compositions and a new take on "He Is Exalted" featuring Brazilian rhythms and lyrics sung in Portugese. It also introduced two new praise choruses ("The Joy of the Lord," "Come Worship the Lord") to the repertoire of contemporary worship liturgies. *Beyond a Dream* moves in the opposite direction, reuniting Paris with Bannister for another stab at the pop-star thing. This time, Paris embraces a more aggressive approach and scored what many would call her first "rock hit" with the song "God Is in Control." *Beyond a Dream* also features "Watch and Pray," an upbeat song that enthusiastically anticipates the second coming of Christ. On "70 Years Ago," Paris reflects on the legacy of her ancestors; she had discovered while investigating her roots that her grandmother used to write songs for evangelistic camp meetings. The album *Where I Stand* features a duet between Paris and **Steven Curtis Chapman** on the song "Faithful Friend," which they wrote together. The song reflects on what it means to be a Christian friend to someone, in terms of being supportive and not judgmental. *True North* was produced by **Charlie Peacock** and includes the radio-friendly title track in addition to its confessional opener, "Run to You" and "I Choose Grace." *Bedtime Prayers, Lullabies, and Peaceful Worship* offers quiet songs for pre-

Sunday schoolers. The project celebrated the birth of a son to Paris and Wright after fifteen years of childlessness.

As an author of numerous hymns already being placed in modern hymnals, Paris has recorded two albums of church hymns that reflect on the church's rich liturgical traditions. *It's the Thought* is a Christmas record and *Perennial* collects praise hymns and spiritual songs. Both albums intersperse Paris's own material with such classics as Handel's "Hallelujah Chorus" and John Newton's "Amazing Grace." The album *A Heart That Knows You* is a partial career retrospective that supplements the collections listed above with a compilation of songs from the middle period *(Kingdom Seekers* through *Cry for the Desert).* It also includes two previously unrecorded songs, "A Heart That Knows You" and "Destiny," which are particularly stellar examples of her **Amy Grant**-like pop worship style. The later *Greatest Hits: Time and Again* includes fifteen classics and three new songs. Paris has coauthored a book on worship with Wheaton college professor Robert Webber called *In This Sanctuary* (StarSong Publishing, 1994).

In 2001, a poll of critics conducted by *CCM* magazine chose two of Paris's recordings to be among its "100 Greatest Albums in Christian Music": *Kingdom Seekers* (# 57) and *Sanctuary* (# 79).

Christian radio hits: "Humility" (# 16 in 1983); "Keepin' My Eyes on You" (# 12 in 1983); "I Commit My Love to You" (# 27 in 1983); "The Warrior Is a Child" (# 1 for 18 weeks in 1984); "Do I Trust You?" (# 2 in 1984); "We Bow Down" (# 32 in 1985); "Runner" [with **David Meece**] (# 7 in 1986); "The Unknown Soldier" (# 8 in 1986); "It All Comes Back" (# 9 in 1986); "Prince of Peace" (# 12 in 1987); "Every Heart That Is Breaking" (# 8 in 1988); "True Friend" (# 11 in 1989); "See You Standing" (# 8 in 1990); "Cry for the Desert" (# 9 in 1991); "Nothing But Love" (# 8 in 1991); "Undivided Heart" (# 12 in 1991); "God Is in Control" (# 14 in 1994); "Faithful Friend" [with **Steven Curtis Chapman**] (# 22 in 1996).

Dove Awards: 1992 Praise and Worship Album *(Sanctuary)*; 1993 Female Vocalist; 1994 Female Vocalist; 1995 Female Vocalist.

Parkway

Lance Black, voc., gtr.; Damian Horne, voc., gtr. 2000—*Glad You Made It* (Essential).

Parkway is an alternative power-pop band formed by the two front men of **Silage** after that group disbanded in 1999. The new group's debut retains some of the experimental elements of that band's sound while moving toward a generally more accessible and radio-friendly mainstream. *Musicforce* would describe *Glad You Made It* as "rather like a buffet," as the various songs seem to sample different musical expressions of the pop frontier. The most noticeable adventure comes five songs in with the hip-hop track "Need Someone," featuring guest rapper **KJ-52.** The song is a stark contrast to "Surround," which revels in its Top 40 sound complete with big, repetitive choruses and an extra-catchy melody. "Found Me Out" (about owning up to secret sin) comes closer to the Red Hot Chili Peppers with a mix of acoustic and electric guitars supplemented by turntable scratching, bass beats, and background rapping. "Your Love Surrounds Me" is a typical Christian radio worship song, with Dan Haseltine of **Jars of Clay** joining in the vocals. "Don't Do It" addresses Christians who tend to belittle people who don't share their faith. "Soothe Me" is a groove-laden prayer to God for inner peace. Two of the album's highlights come at the end: "Save Today" is reflective and features a haunting melody in the mode of Smashing Pumpkins' *Adore* songs. "All You Deserve" closes the project with what *Musicforce* calls "an alt rock slam dunk."

Stephen Mark Pasch

See **Three Crosses.**

Janet Paschal

1990—*Language of the Heart* (Word); 1991—*Simple Trust*; 1994—*I Give You Jesus* (Shiloh); *Journey of Grace* (Word); 1997—*The Good Road* (Spring Hill); 1998—*Sweet Life*; 1999—*Christmas*; *An Evening with Janet Paschal* (Shiloh); 2000—*Songs for a Lifetime* (Spring Hill).

Janet Paschal is an inspirational singer who often seems a generation removed from what is called contemporary Christian music but who sometimes crosses over from easy listening into the broadly defined adult contemporary camp. Often affiliated with events sponsored by **Bill and Gloria Gaither,** Paschal has compiled an impressive roster of "signature songs," most of which were composed by songwriter Dawn Thomas: "I Am Not Ashamed," "Washed in the Blood of the Lamb," "Take These Burdens," "Jesus You're Everything to Me," and "Written in Red" are all well known to fans of inspirational music, and are all found in newly recorded versions on Paschal's career retrospective *Songs for a Lifetime. Journey of Grace* and *The Good Road* merited reviews in *CCM,* who noted similarities between Paschal and such artists as **Babbie Mason** and **Pam Thum.** A singer's singer, Paschal's mezzo-soprano voice is always clear and on perfect pitch. Her songs often express a deeply personal piety that sees God at work in everything.

Passafist

Lynn Nichols; Dave Perkins. 1994—*Passafist* (R.E.X.).

The alternative-meets-industrial rock band Passafist arose out of the ashes of **Chagall Guevara** after that group's front man, **Steve Taylor,** returned to his solo career. The two men that composed Passafist, however, had long histories in Christian music. Lynn Nichols had once been a member of **Dust** and had actually been raised in the famous Christian community Love Inn (in Freeville, New York) with influential DJ Scott Ross as his legal guardian. It was there that he met **Phil Keaggy,** with whose band he would often play and whose albums (including *Sunday's Child* and *Crimson and Blue*) he would often produce. Eventually Nichols would serve as the head of Myrrh records and, then, as vice president in charge of A&R at Sparrow. **Dave Perkins** has recorded as a solo artist and sung with **Rex Carroll,** in addition to producing and playing for many other artists, including **Rick Cua, The Newsboys,** and **Randy Stonehill.** The idea for Passafist arose from a single song that Perkins was preparing for a film soundtrack. The song "Christ of the Nuclear Age" (imagining what might happen if Jesus were born in America today) so impressed Nichols that he wanted in on the project, and the post-Guevara duo was formed. That song especially reveals the influence of Nine Inch Nails' industrial stylings, though the latter is thoroughly meshed with enough guitars to create something eclectic and new. Likewise, the album's lead-off track, "Emmanuel Chant," combines industrial beats with Middle Eastern music and low, whispered vocals that are again reminiscent of Trent Reznor's early outings. "Love-900" satirizes the irony of porno-phone services that manage to make cheap sex expensive. "Glock" reflects on the absence of gun control and escalation of violence in modern society. "The Dr. Is In" offers more social commentary on the proliferation of nuclear weapons in a post-cold war environment; the song's title refers to the lead character in Stanley Kubrick's classic film *Dr. Strangelove,* which is sampled throughout the song. The socio-political bent of the project comes to a head with a stirring and creative cover of the Rolling Stones' "Street Fighting Man."

Passage

Richard Heath; Louis Johnson; Valerie Johnson. 1981—*Passages* (A&M).

Passage was a jazz-fusion group formed in Los Angeles by Louis Johnson of the mainstream Brothers Johnson group. Johnson is joined by his wife Valerie on vocals and by his friend Richard Heath, who served as percussionist for the Brothers Johnson. The trio recorded a number of mellow jazz tunes (called "pacific jazz" by aficionados) spiced with a few upbeat R&B tracks (including one hard disco number, "Power"). All of the songs feature evangelical lyrics typical of traditional gospel. The group covers **Jamie Owens-Collins'** "Lovin' Eyes" and **Amy Grant**'s "Faith Walking People."

A completely different group named Passage (associated with Promise Keepers) released a self-titled album of worship music on Maranatha Music in 1999.

Christian hit radio: "Open Up Your Heart" (# 12 in 1982).

Passion

1999—*Live Worship from the 268 Generation* (StarSong); *Better Is One Day* (label unknown); 2000—*The Road to One Day* (StarSong); *One Day Live* (Worship Together).

www.268generation.com

Passion is not a group, but a movement led by youth worship leaders Louie and Shelley Giglio. They sometimes also go by the label "268 Generation," derived from Isaiah 26:8. In the late '90s, the Giglios began sponsoring worship conferences (fashioned externally after the successful Promise Keeper events) devoted to the seemingly dubious proposition that "praise and worship music does not have to be boring." Numerous Christian music artists have taken part in the events, the most visible of whom have been **Matt Redman** and the members of **Waterdeep**. Essentially, the group has tried to duplicate for America the modern worship movement spearheaded by artists like **Delirious?** in Great Britain. The "big event" is an annual gathering called One Day, and most of the albums above are live recordings from those conferences: *Live Worship from the 268 Generation* from the 1998 conference in Houston, Texas; *Better Is One Day* from a 1999 conference; and *One Day Live* from the 2000 conference in Memphis, Tennessee. *The Road to One Day* is a studio recording of mostly new songs. In general, the Passion recordings move worship music light years beyond the modern worship movement that began with Maranatha's *The Praise Album* in 1974 but did not progress much beyond what was presented there for two decades. The style of choice is that of the **U2** arena anthem, which often seems better suited to congregational praise than the campfire folk choruses that the Jesus movement bequeathed to informal churches. A liturgical consciousness informs much of the music, *ad infinitum* repetitions are avoided, and the pious desire for intimacy with God is balanced by a reverent awe that respects the necessary distance intrinsic to any divine/human encounter.

Leon Patillo

1979—*Dance Children Dance* (Maranatha); 1981—*Don't Give In* (Myrrh); 1982—*I'll Never Stop Lovin' You*; 1983—*Live Experience*; 1984—*The Sky's the Limit*; 1985—*Love around the World*; 1986—*A Funny Thing Happened*; 1987—*Cornerstone: Leon Patillo's Best*; *Brand New* (Sparrow); 1989—*On the Way Up* (Ocean); 1992—*Hands of Praise* (label unknown); 1993—*Church Is on the Move* (Positive Pop); 1994—*Souly for Him* (Campus); 1996—*The Classics* (Positive Pop); 1999—*I Can*; *Breathe on Me*.

www.leonpatillo.org

When Leon Patillo began recording Christian music in the late '70s, the celebrity-hungry Christian music industry tried to capitalize on having hooked another big fish, i.e., the lead singer for the hugely popular general market rock band Santana. This might have impressed the gullible, but it only con-fused those who were in the know. As all true Santana fans would have realized, that group did not exactly have a lead singer, but utilized a wide variety of studio and session vocalists over the years. The *Rolling Stone Encyclopedia of Rock and Roll,* for instance, does not list Patillo as ever having been an official member of the band, and though he did sing on some of their projects, his vocals are not heard on any of the group's hits or well-known songs. The marketing strategy was misguided in any case since Patillo's albums were of a very different sort than those of the Latin rock band, and it is not likely that fans of the one would be drawn to the other. But the singer would recover from this false start. Once he was allowed to be simply Leon Patillo instead of some converted pseudo rock star, it was discovered that he could command an audience of his own. He went on to be one of the more successful contemporary gospel singers of the '80s.

Patillo was born and raised in San Francisco, the son of a taxi driver and a homemaker. He credits his start in music to a preschool teacher ("Miss Hughes") who noticed his interest in piano when he was four years old and persuaded his parents to let him take lessons. By the age of fourteen, Patillo was helping with the choir at his Methodist church, and then at eighteen he joined a group called the VIPs, which performed at dances in the area. After graduating from San Francisco City College, he formed the mid '60s rock band Creation in an effort to duplicate the commercial success attained by his friend Sly Stone. Creation did eventually cut an album for Atlantic and toured as the opening act for War. Moving to Los Angeles, Patillo did background vocals and arrangements for such acts as Funkadelic, Martha Reeves and the Vandellas, and the Pointer Sisters. Carlos Santana heard him singing on a demo tape of some songs he was trying to sell and recruited him for his group in 1973. "He said, we don't want the songs, but we'll take the singer," Patillo recalls. About the same time, in 1974, Patillo attended a Bible study, at which he would later report that he "became a Christian." Patillo toured and sang with Santana for four years, appearing on the albums *Barboletta* (1974), *Festival* (1976), and *Moonflower* (1977). This was during what would later be considered the nadir of the group's career (though two of the albums went gold and one platinum), but the lack of vitality had more to do with the leader's unfocused musical experimentations than with Patillo's undeniable talent. In any case, the singer was uncomfortable with the lyrics to many of the songs that he was given to perform and tensions developed between him and the band leader. At the end of a tour in 1977, he was fired, officially because Carlos Santana was unhappy with his vocal performances. Patillo maintains the real reason was that he was successfully evangelizing people on the tours and that "lots of people were becoming Christians, but nobody was becoming Buddhist." Patillo's most famous convert was **Philip Bailey** of Earth, Wind, and Fire, who accepted Christ and later pursued a career in Christian music as a result of Patillo's influence when the two bands toured together. Patillo also claims that Santana later regretted the decision to fire him and asked him to come back for another album—but by then he was already involved with the music ministry of Calvary Chapel in Costa Mesa, California (home to Maranatha records).

Dance Children Dance appeared at the height of the disco movement and was one of Christian music's first and liveliest dance albums. The title track and "Temple to the Sky" open the two sides of the record with upbeat songs that are short on lyrics ("Dance, children, dance" consists primarily of those three words repeated over and over) but long on rhythm. *Don't Give In* continues in the same vein (on a different label), with a cover of "Your Love Is Lifting Me Higher" thrown in for good measure. The sophomore album includes "Flesh of My Flesh," a wedding song that became one of Patillo's most enduring and popular numbers. *I'll Never Stop Lovin' You* would snag the artist a Dove award and give him the biggest Christian radio hit of the year with "Cornerstone"—the song that kept **Amy Grant**'s "El Shaddai" (and many other memorable songs) out of the Number One spot. The album also includes "River," a generically spiritual number written with Carlos Santana in 1977. Still, Patillo came to regard *The Sky's the Limit* as his personal pick for best album and most critics agreed. *CCM* chose it as one of their Ten Best of 1985, noting that "every cut on *The Sky is the Limit* is strong, both musically and lyrically." The album opens with "I Heard the Thunder," which dazzles with its interplay of keyboard wizardry and drumming downbeats. "Life Is What You Make It" has a Caribbean feel, and the rocking "J-E-S-U-S" is a hand-clapping gospel tune with classic call-and-response sequences between Patillo and a bevy of background singers. "God's People" seems to pick up on the *Star Wars* craze with lots of spacey sound effects.

In 1985, Patillo attempted to pull an **Amy Grant** and cross over into the mainstream market, while keeping his Christian audience intact. *Love around the World* was produced by general market jazzman George Duke and featured a number of romantic R&B tracks along with a couple of spiritual songs (including a musical setting for "The Lord's Prayer"). Patillo's tour to support the album was somewhat notorious in that he went out fronting an all-girl band of female dancers and vocalists. Years later, in 1998, he would recollect, "it really split my audience; about 60 percent liked it, and 40 percent hated it." But ten years earlier, he had offered what is probably a more realistic evaluation: "Many people perceived it as presenting lust and not the Lord. It was a mistake and I guess I didn't think it through enough." After that tour, Patillo took an official sabbatical year off, which turned into a career hiatus. After that,

his personal and professional history becomes a bit obscure. Patillo has said publicly and in print (most recently in *CCM* in 1998) that *Love around the World* was his "last record," but as the discography above indicates, this was certainly not the case.

In 1986, Patillo tried a slight career change and worked for a time as a stand-up comic. The album *A Funny Thing Happened* presents him in this mode, relating humorously paraphrased biblical stories that he had often told in concerts. A year later, a career retrospective was released, along with the comeback album *Brand New*, which spawned two Christian radio hits (including "Isn't It Crazy," written by **Tim Miner**) but failed to reestablish the artist as a mainstay in Christian music. *On the Way Up* in 1989 was self-produced as a "one-man show" with programmed drumming and Patillo playing all of the instruments himself. Despite an unconvincing venture into hip-hop ("Cold Turkey"), the album sounded "stale and mechanical" to *CCM*. At some time in the late '80s, Patillo and his wife divorced; a decade later he would blame the failure of his marriage on his own misplaced priorities, putting "ministry" ahead of health and family. In 1993, Patillo began hosting the show "Leon and Friends" for the religious Trinity Broadcasting Network. He started a church in Long Beach, California, and founded his own independent record label called Positive Pop. The album *Classics* on that label features reworked versions of Patillo's best-known songs. *Breathe on Me* offers a stripped down approach to praise and worship, intended to inspire prayer.

Christian radio hits: "Dance Children Dance" (# 12 in 1979); "Temple to the Sky" (# 7 in 1979); "Star of the Morning" (# 2 in 1981); "Don't Give In" (# 16 in 1981); "Have Faith" (# 9 in 1981); "Cornerstone" (# 1 for 16 weeks in 1982); "John 3:17" (# 15 in 1983); "I've Heard the Thunder" (# 4 in 1984); "J.E.S.U.S." (# 27 in 1984); "The Sky's the Limit" (# 37 in 1984); "One Thing Leads to Another" (# 2 in 1986); "Love around the World" (# 8 in 1986); "Isn't It Crazy" (# 8 in 1987); "I'm Brand New" (# 2 in 1988).

Dove Awards: 1983 Contemporary Gospel Album (*I'll Never Stop Loving You*).

Sandi Patty

1979—*Sandi's Song* (Milk and Honey); 1981—*Love Overflowing* (Impact); 1982—*Lift Up the Lord*; 1983—*Live . . . More Than Wonderful*; *The Gift Goes On*; 1984—*Songs from the Heart*; 1985—*Inspirational Favorites* (Christian Classics); 1985—*Just for You* (Benson); 1986—*Morning Like This* (Word); 1988—*Make His Praise Glorious*; 1989—*Sandi Patti* [sic] *and the Friendship Company*; 1989—*The Finest Moments*; 1990—*Another Time, Another Place*; 1991—*Open for Business* [with The Friendship Company]; 1992—*Celebrate Christmas 1992* (Hallmark); 1993—*Le Voyage* (Word); 1994—*Find It on the Wings*; 1995—*O Holy Night*; 1997—*Artist of My Soul*; 1999—*Together* [with Kathy Troccoli]; 2000—*These Days*; 2001—*All the Best: Live*.

www.sandipatty.com

Sandi Patty may have the most misspelled name in contemporary Christian music but she has heard it read aloud by presenters opening envelopes at the Dove Awards more often than any other artist. The most decorated singer in the field, she was actually chosen Female Vocalist of the Year *eleven* years in a row (1982–1992). Without casting any aspersions on her undeniable talent, such a run does reveal a bias within the supposedly contemporary Christian music industry. There is very little that is "contemporary" about Patty's music, especially that of the early years. Her style actually has more in common with Judy Garland or Connie Francis than with the mainstream artists with whom she is most often compared: pre-pop Barbra Streisand and post-rock Celine Dion. As such, she became the perfect icon for the terminally unhip Gospel Music Association, which seemingly wanted to present her to the world as a Christian performer of "today's sound" without realizing how ridiculous this made them look—a bit like the '60s parents who would buy an album of Lawrence Welk covering the Beatles to show their kids how "with it" they were. The fact that Patty was repeatedly chosen Female Vocalist of the Year over such performers as **Margaret Becker, Amy Grant,** and **Sheila Walsh** is revealing: as her other awards indicate, Patty probably was (and probably still is) the best *inspirational* singer of her generation, but the GMA apparently assumed for over a decade that inspirational singers are by definition better than rock, country, or R&B singers, such that the woman who makes the best inspirational album should almost automatically be proclaimed the best female singer, period. It took a sex scandal to put an end to Patty's eleven-year run; after that, though her vocal chords did not appear to have suffered, her talent would be held in less esteem.

Patty was born in 1956 in Oklahoma City. Her father was a Minister of Music at various congregations associated with the Church of God denomination and her mother taught her piano from an early age. After moving to Indiana, she sang in a family group led by her father, The Ron Patty Family. When she was in eighth grade, the family moved to San Diego, California. Patty attended San Diego State University for two years and then graduated from Indiana's Anderson College, a small Bible school associated with her denomination. She worked for a time as a session singer, doing jingles for some national advertisers (Juicy Fruit, Steak-and-Shake, Chick-Fil-A) and performed with a Christian group called New Creation. In 1978, she recorded a custom album appropriately titled *For My Friends.*

Patty's first few albums were nondescript MOR contributions that pleased fans of competent, easy listening music but did not overwhelm critics. Indeed, *Sandi's Song* went virtually unreviewed, and *CCM* would only mention *Love Overflowing* in a survey of products by five "MOR ladies" who the magazine complained all sounded too much alike (they found **Twila Paris** to be the most impressive of the pack, which also included Debbie Amstutz, Micki Fuhrman, and Kathie Sullivan). The first album does include Phil Johnson's "The Day He Wore My Crown." The second features **Dottie Rambo**'s "We Shall Behold Him" and a duet with **Russ Taff** called "The Home of the Lord." Patty's first big break came when she toured as a background singer for **The Bill Gaither Trio** in 1981–1982 and was featured as soloist for one or two songs during their concerts. In a review of one such concert, *CCM* could not resist referring to "the cute brunette in the flowing chiffon whose soprano highs soared above the usual listening range of the crowd." In short, she stole the show. Perhaps as a result of such exposure, her rendition of **Michael W. Smith**'s "How Majestic Is Your Name" would propel her third album, *Lift Up the Lord,* on to the charts and bring her an early flurry of Doves. A live album recorded at a church in Lakeland, Florida, brought more acclaim, with its title track, "More Than Wonderful," being performed as the first of what would be several career duets with **Larnelle Harris.** That album also includes a humorous presentation of "Jesus Loves Me," sung the way Barbra Streisand would supposedly perform it. *Songs from the Heart* includes the big praise hit "Sing to the Lord" as well as a surprise cover of **Scott Wesley Brown**'s "Wonderful Lord." It also features the Dove Award-winning "Via Dolorosa" (not the **Dennis Agajanian** song but a number cowritten by **Billy Sprague**), which tells of Christ's suffering on his way to the cross.

A big break came on July 4, 1986, when Patty's version of the national anthem was chosen for televised airplay during the festivities surrounding the dedication of the refurbished Statue of Liberty on Ellis island. Her stirring rendition of the patriotic song brought a national response of the same intensity accorded Rosanne Barr's performance of the song years later—though for completely opposite reasons. The phone lines at ABC TV literally jammed with calls from viewers wanting to know more about the singer. It was a defining moment in the history of contemporary Christian music: a singer completely unknown outside the little Christian music ghetto was suddenly thrust into the spotlight and celebrated as one of America's greatest treasures. Patty bore her fame well, testifying to Jesus and speaking on behalf of various social causes as she was shuttled about from *Regis and Kathie Lee* to *The Tonight Show* to all the various network news programs. She sang at the White House and for the Pan-American games. She became the paradigm of the talented, successful, religious, family-oriented, patriotic American woman, a symbol with which politicians and religious leaders wanted to be associated. She sang at presidential inaugurations and Billy Graham crusades. For many years thereafter, she would serve as the national spokesperson for the charitable hunger-relief organization World Vision.

While her success was appreciated within the Christian music community, there was also a somewhat growing concern that Patty was not really very representative of what modern Christian music could (and perhaps should) be. Even before Patty sang the national anthem, many Christian music fans had been annoyed that the world at large associated "Christian music" with **Amy Grant** rather than with **T Bone Burnett** or **Michael Knott** or **Daniel Amos.** Once Patty became the public, defining symbol of "contemporary Christian music," all hope of combating secular stereotypes of the genre as safe and predictable "inspirational songs" seemed lost. Say what you will about Patty's gift and devotion; no one ever dared to suggest that she had an edge. Indeed, shortly before coming into the national spotlight, she had defined her mission by saying, "My ministry is directed to the body of Christ. The assumption I make is that the people I'm singing for already know Jesus." How, then, some would wonder, did she end up being the primary ambassador of Christian music to the world at large?

The problem, in part, was that Patty's style became so predictable and formulaic. All of her albums seemed to have the same basic sound and many songs on each would display what became known as signature "Pattyisms." Arrangements often seem intended to show-off the soprano's four-octave range by having her leap an entire octave in a single crescendo. Or, again, numerous songs feature bombastic big endings, full of key modulation changes and stratospheric high notes. Johnny Carson called Patty "a belter." Her albums have always been slickly produced (many of them by Greg Nelson), with a very religious, churchy sound. Praise and worship songs predominate, which, while stirring, reveal little about the artist herself or about her struggles with faith and life—a tendency exacerbated by the fact that Patty herself is not a songwriter and has tended to rely on material cranked out by such industry composers as the Gaithers, **Bob Farrell, Dick and Melodie Tunney, Dottie Rambo,** and **Dony McGuire**—almost all of whom have their roots in traditional southern gospel (which tends to lack the reflective intimacy of modern rock). She typically sings against a symphonic backdrop of overly lush orchestration. Still, the single greatest impediment to her career—aside from the marital indiscretions discussed momentarily—stems from a marketing decision made at some point in the '80s. Someone decided that the orchestral backdrops to Patty's albums could be sold as instrumental accompaniment tapes for aspiring soloists to use when performing her songs in local settings. This was done with other artists as well, but never so abundantly as with Patty, whose songs were especially well suited for congregational settings. Thousands of copies of such tapes were sold and, as a result, millions of people who belong to congregations where such things as musical integrity or even good taste are not priorities would have to sit through countless anthems by Sandi-wannabes singing to a canned symphony that is about as inspiring as a laughtrack. The pervasive influence of such posers has lent an air of self-parody to Patty's most sincere performances, in the same way that Bill Murray's lounge singer routine on *Saturday Night Live* makes even the genuine article (cf. **John Jonethis**) seem like a novelty act.

Apparently aware that she was being pigeon-holed in ways that were not always flattering, Patty offered her most pop-oriented album to date with *Morning Like This.* Songs like "Hosanna," with synthesizers and vocal support from **2nd Chapter of Acts,** moved her into a sound more typical of Christian adult contemporary. "Face to Face" (sung with **First Call**) has a classy Manhattan Transfer appeal. Likewise, *Make His Praise Glorious* features a handful of pop-rock offerings, such as the guitar-drenched "Love Will Be Our Home." On *Another Time, Another Place,* Patty chooses such unlikely duet partners as **Amy Grant** (on "Unexpected Friends") and **Wayne Watson** (on the title track; she would later have another hit by singing a duet with **Mark Lowry** on a parody of the song called "Some Other Time, Some Other Place"). *CCM* observed that the *Another Time, Another Place* album was "the first step" in remaking the artist in ways that would transcend the rigid boundaries of modern inspirational music, a genre, ironically, she had done more than anyone else to define. It was actually the *second* or *third* step, but in any case, Patty seemed well on her way to a solid career as a '90s adult contemporary diva.

But 1990 was a year of tragedy. In April of that year, Patty's office and studio were set on fire and a spokesperson for an unknown terrorist group called Equal Religious Coalition claimed responsibility for the act. A caller to a local paper said, "We believe religion is not for sale. As a group, we vow to fight the likes of Mrs. Patty and we will continue to do so in our own way." The artist was afforded twenty-four-hour police protection for a time, though the alleged terrorism appears to have been a hoax. A year later, a man arrested for the crime confessed to starting the fire only to cover up a burglary, with no knowledge of who Patty was. But before 1990 was over, Patty announced—seemingly out of the blue—that she was filing for divorce from John Helvering, her college sweetheart, business manager, and husband of thirteen years. The frequently judgmental Christian music industry closed ranks against her, pulling her products from stores and her songs from radio playlists. The intensity of that response was somewhat staggering, since many other Christian artists had divorced without provoking such reactions; indeed many had done so in quiet and private ways that were not even reported in the press. In 1980 a report in *CCM* announcing the marriage of **Dony McGuire** and **Reba Rambo** caused a bit of a stir, since it was thought to be public knowledge that McGuire was married to Joy Downing of **The Downings,** their divorce never having been publicized. In part, the ungracious response to Patty's troubles was due to the fact that she had worked hard at cultivating a "family values" image. She regularly brought her husband and children out on stage during concerts, introducing them to the audience. In practically every interview (including those given within a year of the divorce) she talked glowingly about her husband, her marriage, and the importance of keeping family first in her life. By contrast, when **Amy Grant** and **Gary Chapman** announced their divorce some years later, there was disappointment, but little shock—the couple had been forthright for years about their ongoing marital problems. Something more insidious seems to have informed the anti-Patty crusade, however. Most retailers who pulled her products justified the action by saying it was because she would not "provide specific reasons for the cause of the separation." None ever bothered to indicate why such details would be any of their business, much less a concern of the general public. Still, the meddling curiosity was fueled by a thinly-veiled suspicion that Patty's request for privacy was meant to conceal some potential scandal. The voyeurs had to wait three years but eventually they got their story.

In the meantime, Patty revealed to *CCM* in 1993 that she had been sexually abused as a child by a woman who was a friend of her parents. The incidents occurred when she was only six years old and was left in the care of the offender for a week. The almost-buried memory had been recovered through therapy and became a dominant issue that helped explain a number of personal and relational dysfunctions. While struggling to deal with these, however, she admitted to becoming emotionally distant and, at the same time, emotionally needy and vulnerable. While taking care not to blame her divorce on the abuse, she did indicate (rightly) that such traumas have far-reaching consequences, making relationships built on trust and intimacy especially difficult to maintain. She also spoke eloquently of her concern and commitment for children who suffer from long term abuse: "Mine was just an isolated week, and from someone I did not have to love, someone I could hate . . . but for those people who have survived years of abuse, especially from a parent . . . my heart goes out to them." At this time, Patty recorded a distinctive album titled *Le Voyage,* a concept piece that tells an allegorical story similar to that of *Pilgrim's Progress.* The songs on *Le Voyage,* written mainly by Greg Nelson and **Bob Farrell,** present the tale of a person called Traveler who moves through various dilemmas—notably a "Forest of Fears"—with the constant guidance of a Companion that sustains her faith and proffers hope. Musically, the project is again much more pop-oriented than Patty's '80s albums. "Home Will Find You" pairs her with **John Elefante** on a **Kansas**-like power-pop song, emblazoned with lead guitar by

Dann Huff. *CCM* would compare "Long Look" to the R&B style of **Ashley Cleveland,** and "The Dilemma" to the adult contemporary rock of **Margaret Becker** or **Kim Hill.** The next year, *Find It on the Wings* would see a return to the old Patty style: "good news for those who didn't enjoy *Le Voyage,*" *CCM* announced, "bad news for those who did." Like its predecessor, the album did not chart any hits, as prejudices against the artist still lingered in the hearts of many station programmers. It did, however, include a stellar adult contemporary duet with mainstream star Peabo Bryson ("Make It Till Tomorrow") in addition to a new song cowritten by Burt Bacharach ("If I Want To"). Likewise, "Carry On" is a powerful song of praise contributed by Bob Farrell and **Michael W. Smith.**

In early 1995, Patty shocked the Christian music world again by suddenly canceling all dates of what was to be her big post-divorce comeback concert tour (with **4 Him**). The reason, she declared, was that she did not believe she could responsibly "take a place of spiritual leadership in ministry." She went on to say, "As I continue to grow daily in the Lord, the far-reaching effects of my wrong and sinful behaviors have become evident to me." Inquiring minds were left to wonder for another six months what that might mean. Then in September it was suddenly announced that Patty had married Don Peslis, a physical trainer who was also a member of **One,** the vocal group that served as backup singers for Patty on her *Another Time, Another Place* tour in 1991. Two weeks after the wedding, some investigative reporters (Doug Jolley and Timothy Morgan) published an article in *Christianity Today* magazine revealing that Patty and Peslis had engaged in an adulterous affair four years earlier, at a time when both of them were married. The article also informed the world that Patty had been involved in "an intimate physical relationship that did not result in sexual intercourse with yet another man earlier in her marriage." The Christian music world's response to such invasive journalism was mixed. *CCM* magazine picked up the story and reported it as news, but editor John Styll also authored an editorial saying that he had known about the affair—that Patty had confessed it to him—but that his staff chose not to reveal it in print on the conviction that "matters of confession, repentance, and discipline should happen on the church level rather than in the media." Patty herself admitted with shame that the story in *Christianity Today* was true: "I had an affair and that was wrong. I was not honest about it and that was also wrong." She also, for the first time, offered a number of defensive and uncharitable remarks about her former husband, claiming that he had been "emotionally abusive" to her and that he had repeatedly rejected her in ways that left her "emotionally vulnerable." She filed a suit to end their joint custody relationship, seeking to obtain sole custody of the four children.

The Sandi Patty Affair, as the whole debacle came to be called (probably with pun intended) offered the Christian music subculture one of its first experiences in dealing with scandal. Actually, the news came within a year of the **Michael English** adultery scandal, which perhaps contributed to the media frenzy (was it a trend?). By all accounts, the matter was badly bungled, with almost everyone except John Styll and Patty's local pastors disgracing themselves in one way or another. Her manager, Matt Baugher, also kept things in perspective, telling *CCM,* "Sandi, like every one of us, has made mistakes in her life. I would hope that we all would have the same courage to face these setbacks in a similar restorative process."

Patty's post-scandal albums have been received positively but without the same enthusiasm as in her heyday. "Remember the days when a new Sandi Patty album was an *event*?" a review of *These Days* in *Christian Music* magazine began. *Artist of My Soul* did put her back on the stage at the Dove Awards, as she garnered one more bird-trophy for Inspirational Album of the Year. It features a stirring rendition of the nineteenth-century hymn "I Will Sing the Wondrous Story" and convinced skeptical *CCM* reviewer Melissa Riddle that "the beautiful, powerful interpretive voice of the original, real Sandi Patty" could indeed make her forget all those wannabes singing to taped backups she'd grown up with. *These Days* locates Patty firmly in the admittedly crowded niche of adult contemporary pop. It opens with an actual rock song, the bouncy, hook-filled "Wouldn't Trade It for the World." A children's chorus gives the song "Shine" (written by Troccoli) a sound similar to that of The Carpenters' hit "Sing." Patty eschews the typical superstar duet to sing with Latin vocalist Miguel Guerra on a lovely Spanish ballad, "Solo el Amor (Only Love)."

Patty has recorded three Christmas albums over the years: *The Gift Goes On, Celebrate Christmas 1992,* and *O Holy Night.* The second of these was released by the Hallmark card company and contains only a half dozen Patty songs, interspersed with instrumentals and offerings from the Mormon Tabernacle Choir. Two compilation projects, *Inspirational Favorites* and *The Finest Moments,* present early material only and are far from definitive; the latter bears a deceptive title, being released by Word in 1989 but containing only pre-Word material with nothing later than 1985. She has also recorded two albums for children with a group called The Friendship Company. *Just for You* is a collection of hymns ("How Great Thou Art," "Amazing Grace," etc.). *Together* presents the artist (along with **Kathy Troccoli**) doing what she appears to have been born to do, singing a set of classic songs that were written by George Gershwin ("Summertime") and/or performed by Judy Garland ("Over the Rainbow"). *CCM* noted the only flaw as being the somewhat embarrassing juxtaposition of the two artists: "Patty overshadows Troccoli both musically and artistically."

An early biography of Patty titled *Sandi Patti* [sic]: *The Voice of Gospel* by Don Cusic (Dolphi, 1988) was written without the singer's cooperation and mainly summarizes what was generally available as public record to any reporter at the time. Patty herself has written *The Book of Words* (Hal Leonard Books, 1987) but it is less an autobiography than a series of devotional reflections on certain aspects of her life (with tributes to the artist from her father and from Gloria Gaither). In 1982, Patty said, "I try to bring a real positiveness to my messages and the songs that I sing so that maybe the people can leave the concert feeling very uplifted and positive about the Christian way of life, and know that Jesus loves them." That goal would seem to change little throughout all that the years would bring. Publicly, at least, she has born no ill will for her fall, a fall she would ultimately describe as being not from, but into, grace: "The past few years have been rough," she said in 1998, "but the struggles came through nobody's fault but my own."

For trivia buffs: The misspelling of Patty's name started with a typographical error that led to it being printed as "Sandi Patti" on her first album (and, thus, on several subsequent ones). The name is also sometimes rendered "Sandy Patty" or "Sandy Patti." The correct spelling is given above.

Christian radio hits: "How Majestic Is Your Name" (# 12 in 1982); "More Than Wonderful" [with **Larnelle Harris**] (# 2 in 1983); "Upon This Rock" (# 2 in 1983); "O Magnify the Lord" (# 6 in 1984); "Sing to the Lord" (# 1 for 4 weeks in 1984); "We Will See Him As He Is" (# 4 in 1985); "Was It a Morning Like This?" (# 4 in 1986); "Let There Be Praise" (# 9 in 1986); "Love in Any Language" (# 11 in 1986); "They Say" (# 1 for 2 weeks in 1987); "Make His Praise Glorious" (# 6 in 1988); "Another Time, Another Place" [with **Wayne Watson**] (# 8 in 1991); "I'll Give You Peace" (# 24 in 1991); "Some Other Time, Some Other Place" [with **Mark Lowry**] (# 25 in 1991).

Dove Awards: 1982 Artist of the Year; 1982 Female Vocalist; 1983 Female Vocalist; 1983 Inspirational Album (Lift Up the Lord); 1984 Artist of the Year; 1984 Female Vocalist; 1984 Inspirational Album (More Than Wonderful); 1985 Artist of the Year; 1985 Female Vocalist; 1985 Inspirational Album (Songs from the Heart); 1986 Female Vocalist; 1987 Artist of the Year; 1987 Female Vocalist; 1987 Inspirational Album (Morning Like This); 1988 Artist of the Year; 1988 Female Vocalist; 1989 Female Vocalist; 1989 Inspirational Album (Make His Praise Glorious); 1989 Inspirational Song ("In Heaven's Eyes"); 1989 Instrumental Album (A Symphony of Praise); 1990 Female Vocalist; 1990 Children's Album (Sandi Patti [sic] and the Friendship Company); 1991 Female Vocalist; 1991 Inspirational Album (Another Time, Another Place); 1991 Pop/Contemporary Song ("Another Time, Another Place"); 1992 Female Vocalist; 1992 Inspirational Song ("For All the World"); 1992 Children's Album (Open for Business); 1995 Inspirational Album (Find It on the Wings); 1998 Inspirational Album (Artist of My Soul); 1999 Spanish Language Album (Libertad de Mas).

Grammy Awards: 1983 Best Gospel Performance by a Duo or Group [with **Larnelle Harris**] ("More Than Wonderful"); 1985 Best Gospel

Performance by a Duo or Group [with **Larnelle Harris**] ("I've Just Seen Jesus"); 1986 Best Gospel Performance, Female *(Morning Like This)*; 1986 Best Gospel Performance by a Duo or Group [with **Deniece Williams**] ("They Say"); 1990 Best Pop Gospel Album *(Another Time, Another Place)*.

The Pattons

Dee Patton; Jim Patton. 1976—*Homesteading* (Candle Co.).

The Pattons were a wife-and-husband duo who were part of the **Candle**/**Agape Force** group responsible for making several successful children's albums in the late '70s. They also wrote some songs that were recorded by **Barry McGuire:** "To Know Love," "Railroad Man," and the rollicking "Last Days Waltz." Their only album as a duo features a number of folk-rock songs, including their own version of "Last Days Waltz."

Sara Paulson

1996—*Once and for All* (Pamplin); 1998—*Word to the World*.

Sara Paulson is an adult contemporary singer who offers well-produced, somewhat formulaic recordings of inspirational music with few surprises. In reviewing her first album *Shout!* magazine noted, "she follows in **Sandi Patty**'s footsteps, not only in her selection of mellow songs that end with a swell, but also in hitting those glass-shattering high notes." On *Word to the World,* Paulson would try a more pop-oriented style that reminded a *Phantom Tollbooth* reviewer of **Amy Grant**'s early records.

Pauper's Field

Personnel list unavailable. 1998—*Voice* (Cling).

Pauper's Field is a hard-rocking Christian band from Battle Creek, Michigan. Their sound has been compared to such groups as **Dig Hay Zoose** and **Hot Pink Turtle,** though they display more of a penchant for arena rock guitars than either of those outfits. Most of the songs on the group's debut are of the hyper power-riff variety, though "Radium" is more mystifying and relaxing, with sampled voices of a child's song adding an element of suspense before the driving rhythm kicks in. "Farewell My Friends" reveals a different side of the band, with a capella male and female vocals singing a cavernous hymn about being "bound for Canaan's land."

Gary S. Paxton

1976—*The Astonishing, Outrageous, Amazing, Incredible, Unbelievable, Different World of Gary S. Paxton* (NewPax); 1977—*More from the Astonishing, Outrageous, Amazing, Incredible, Unbelievable World of Gary S. Paxton*; 1978—*Anchored in the Rock of Ages* (Pax); *Terminally Weird But Godly Right*; 1979—*Gary Sanford Paxton*; *The Gospel According to Gary S. Paxton* [by The Gary Paxton Singers] (Paragon); 1980—*(Some of) The Best of Gary S. Paxton (So Far)* (NewPax); 1981—*Take Your Turf for Jesus* (Pax).

http://timeforjoy.com/gary

The avant-garde and somewhat zany gospel singer Gary S. Paxton has had an interesting but quirky connection to contemporary Christian music almost from its very start. Despite involvement with celebrities and murder mysteries, no major media outlet has ever produced a profile on the artist. His music was rarely reviewed, he has seldom been interviewed, and facts about his life are difficult to come by. Paxton was born and raised in Coffeyville, Kansas. He became involved with music in the late '50s. He recorded hit songs as one-half of the duo Skip and Flip (he was "Flip," partnered with a singer named Clyde Battin). Skip and Flip would have two significant hits: the million-selling single "It Was I" (# 11 in 1959), which was written by Paxton, and "Cherry Pie" (# 11 in 1960), a cover of a 1954 hit by the group Marvin and Johnny. Shortly thereafter Paxton stumbled upon his greatest success one night when his car ran out of gas in Southern California and he hiked to a desert filling station. The "two kids" working at the station that night recognized him from *Teen Beat* as "Skip" and insisted on playing him some songs they had written. One of the songs they played for Paxton was "Alley Oop," a comical, novelty song about a caveman who was a character in a popular comic strip. Paxton recorded the song "Alley Oop" with Sandy Nelson banging on garbage cans and doing caveman yelps in the background, then released it under the name The Hollywood Argyles. "Alley Oop" was a Number One hit in 1960 and would become a staple of oldies radio, enjoying a renaissance, for instance, when it was featured again in the 1978 film *Animal House*. The song remained Paxton's biggest hit in terms of songs on which he himself sings, but it was not in any sense his last or even his biggest commercial success.

With a mind for the music business, Paxton founded the Garpax music label and turned to producing. His first success came with the platinum single "Honey I Do" by the Innocents (# 28 in 1960). Then, inspired no doubt by his own success with "Alley Oop," he took a chance on the Halloween novelty song "Monster Mash" by Boris (actually Bobby Pickett) and The Crypt Kickers. As a bit of music trivia, it may be noted that Pickett's band, The Crypt Kickers, included not only Paxton but also superstar Leon Russell and lesser-known luminaries Johnny MacCrae (of Ronny and the Daytonas) and Rickie Page (of The Bermudas). As Paxton recalls, the song was turned down by every major label in the business: "No one else wanted it; they all laughed." The Number One hit went on to be the only single in history to be released three times (in 1962, 1967, and 1972) and to sell over a million copies each time. The first time, Paxton says he made a phenomenal $265,000 from the record, most of which "went to Las Vegas and liquor stores." Broke, and with severe liver trouble, he moved to Nashville and used his midas touch as a producer to mint gold records for Tommy Roe ("Sweet Pea," # 8 in 1966; "Hooray for Hazel," # 6 in 1966) and The Association ("Along Comes Mary," # 7 in 1966; "Cherish," # 1 for 3 weeks in 1966). Twice nominated for a Grammy, he was by 1967 considered to be among the most prominent hitmakers in the business. Nevertheless, for some reason, he decided to move out to Bakersfield, California, and get involved in a variety of other adventures. What he would later call his "Bakersfield empire" included a record label, a music store, two studios, a marina, a mountain hotel, twenty-six cabins, a radio show, and a house rental business. His connections with music at this time were more limited, but he did discover and bring to prominence a duo called The Lewis and Clark Expedition, which consisted of Michael Martin Murphy and Boomer Castleman—both of whom would later have solo hits as country artists. According to Paxton, the Bakersfield Empire collapsed as a result of "two much boogieing, i.e., sinful and self-indulgent activities of this world." Moving back to Nashville, he says he took a paycut from $10,000 a month to a $100 a week and worked as a contract songwriter. Then, he notes with no further detail that in September of 1971 he "got saved" and his "life transformed."

Paxton began writing gospel songs but, in the meantime, some of the country tunes he had composed took off: Don Gibson made "Woman, Sensuous Woman" the Number One country song in the nation, and Paxton was nominated for a Grammy for Song of the Year. Roy Clark had a Number One hit with "Honeymoon Feelin'" the following year (1974). Paxton would continue to work with mainstream country music even after getting involved with gospel and contemporary Christian music. His hit list as a songwriter includes "Travelin' Light" for George Hamilton IV; "One Day at a Time" for Don Gibson; "The Great Divide" for Roy Clark; "Don't Let the Good Times Fool You" for Melba Montgomery; "Pictures on Paper" for Jeris-Ross; and "If I'm Losing You" for Billy Walker.

In 1974, Paxton had his first success in gospel music when his song "L-O-V-E" won a Grammy award for the southern gospel group The Blackwood Brothers. More gospel hits would follow, as such traditional but big name artists as Doug Oldham, **The Bill Gaither Trio,** the Florida Boys, and the LeFevres recorded his songs. With his background in rock and roll, a crossover to more contemporary sounds seemed inevitable, and it came about appropriately through his work with the first major southern gospel group to enter contemporary Christian music, **The Imperials.** Their funky recording of his song "No Shortage" would provide them with the best song of their career and establish their credibility with a new audience; Paxton also produced the group's landmark album for which that song served as the title track.

Paxton's debut Christian album signaled a comical approach with its long-winded title and cover photo (depicting the artist poking his head out of a manhole). Side One, then, seemed a bit calm with fairly typical Christian country-folk ballads, the most notable of which would be "Love, It Comes in All Colors." Side Two, by contrast, took off with upbeat, zany rock songs (performed in a style similar to **Elvis Presley**) of the sort that might delight fans of **Larry Norman** or, later, **Steve Taylor.** The standout song "Sophisticated Savages" describes the insanity of modern civilization with references to an impending, apocalyptic and nuclear destruction. "Jesus Keeps Takin' Me Higher and Higher" picks up on the frequent (though somewhat questionable) analogy that the Jesus people often made between spiritual bliss and drug-induced euphoria. The antismoking anthem, "You Ain't Smokin' Them Cigarettes (Baby, They're Smokin' You)," is reminiscent of **Randy Stonehill**'s "Lung Cancer." The same point would be made again in a song from Paxton's sophomore album ("There Goes a Cigar Smoking a Man"), with broader application to other materialistic vices. *More of . . . Gary S. Paxton* also includes Paxton's own version of "No Shortage," plus such Paxton classics as "Jesus Is My Lawyer in Heaven" and "The World Didn't Give It to Me (And The World Can't Take It Away)." Less remembered but even stronger songs include "Hooked on a Good Thing" and "Nineveh Noose." The highlight of the second album, however, and for many the ultimate Gary Paxton song, is a little meditation on mortality called "When the Meat Wagon Comes for You." *Anchored in the Rock of Ages* produced a minor hit with its title track. On *Terminally Weird But Godly Right,* Paxton asks the musical question, "Will There Be Hippies in Heaven?" He also offers the provocative "Fat, Fat Christian" and an antiabortion rant called "The Big A = The Big M," along with a reading of the traditional hymn "Blessed Assurance." In 1979, Paxton produced twin surprises: *The Gospel According to Gary S. Paxton* features a choir singing medleys of his better-known songs; the self-titled *Gary Sanford Paxton* opens with a track called "Ain't Gonna Sing No Rock and Roll Song Tonight" and then features Paxton singing a number of classic hymns, including Thomas Dorsey's "Peace in the Valley" and "Precious Lord (Take My Hand)."

In late 1980, a bizarre occurrence would place Paxton in the news for reasons having little to do with his musical output. On December 29th of that year, two men came to his home and requested help with their automobile. Paxton later reported that "a strong word from the Lord" told him something was wrong, and he placed a pistol in his pocket before leaving the house. He would never get a chance to use it. Once inside Paxton's van (ostensibly so he could drive the men to their car), the pair attacked the singer, striking and choking him. He maintains that he shouted repeatedly, "In the name of Jesus, you cannot hurt me!" Nevertheless, his collarbone and shoulder were broken and his right eye split open, blinding him with blood. One of the assailants had a gun and shot him in the hand. Paxton then managed to turn that gun around and pull the trigger, shooting the man who held it. Escaping from the van, Paxton tried crawling for help but was shot twice more in the back. Neighbors secured aid and the assailant he had wounded was arrested. Police determined that the men had been "contract killers" hired by a third party to murder the artist. According to Paxton's publicist, the killers had in fact been hired by an unnamed country singer whose album Paxton was producing. Paxton recovered from his injuries but they took him out of recording for eight years and had some permanent physical and emotional effects.

In 1991, Paxton contracted Hepatitis C as the result of several blood transfusions. By 1996, he was divorced from his third wife, retaining custody of his only child. As of 2001, Paxton lived in Branson, Missouri, and continued to write numerous gospel songs, while declining interviews.

Christian radio hits: "Anchored in the Rock of Ages" (# 18 in 1979).

Grammy Awards: 1976 Best Inspirational Performance (The Astonishing, Outrageous, Amazing, Incredible, Unbelievable, Different World of Gary S. Paxton).

Pax 217

Josh Auer, bass; Jesse Craig, gtr.; Aaron "Skwid" Tosti, drums; David Tosti, voc. 2000—Two Seventeen (ForeFront).

Pax 217 is a band from Orange County, California, that most critics regard as a Christian version of Limp Bizkit or 311, assembled to cash in on the rapcore craze. The group has a bit more musical integrity than that. Although its roots go nowhere near as deep as **EDL** or **P.O.D.**, the youthful members seem to have come by their sound honestly—they are not so much Christians attempting to fabricate an imitation of a secular band as they are kids playing what was popular when they were in high school. At the time their first album was released, front man Dave Tosti was only twenty-one and his drumming brother was a mere sixteen. The two were admittedly Bizkit and Beastie Boys fans, but they say they also listened to **U2** and The Police. Discerning ears can certainly pick out those influences in their mix. As for their unusual name, *pax* means "peace" and 217 is a veiled reference to Ephesians 2:17, which says "(Christ) came and preached peace to you who were far off and peace to those who were near."

Pax 217's debut album was produced by Howard Benson, best known for his work with such general market acts as Ice T, Motorhead, and Sepultura. The group delivers songs born out of the traumatic experiences of their relatively short lives. The song "No Place Like Home" is a Bizkit-like rap number (cf. "Just One of Those Days") about a divorce that the Tostis' parents went through a couple of years before the album was cut. David raps, "Yeah, I grew up in a Christian house / Listenin' to Psalty and Charity Church Mouse / Never did I know and never did I guess / That 18 years later our home would be a mess." The next track, "Free to Be," has a very different feel, with a strong reggae beat. It was written a few hours after Tosti watched his house burn to the ground, an event that left him with a lasting impression of the ephemeral nature of material goods. In the song "Skwid," Tosti remembers when his younger brother was first born and was thought to be mentally handicapped.

In 2000, Pax 217 was part of the Extreme Days tour that combined certain Christian groups (rap and hard alternative) with proponents of extreme sports, playing skate parks where professional skateboarders demonstrated their skills between acts.

Christian radio hits: "Till the Sun" (# 18 in 2000).

Payable on Death

See **P.O.D.**

Kendall Payne

1999—Jordan's Sister (Capitol).

http://hollywoodandvine.com/kendallpayne

Kendall Payne was only fifteen years old when she recorded the demo tape for her debut album, a general market release. She named it *Jordan's Sister* as an ironic joke on her own quest for self-identity, having grown up in the shadow of an older sibling who she describes as "a beautiful, outgoing, perfect body ballerina." Payne's vocal style has been compared to such general market artists as Alanis Morissette and Juliana Hatfield and to such Christian stars as **Sarah Masen** and **Jennifer Knapp.** Though she is open about being a devout Christian, she has not sought a career within the Christian music industry. Signed to Capitol, she has for the most part avoided venues associated with the Christian music subculture, opting instead for tours with Seal, Jewel, Chris Isaac, and Natalie Cole. In 2000, she played the Lilith Fair. Fashion designer Tommy Hilfiger has named a lipstick after her. Still, she has received more coverage in the Christian press than in mainstream publications, and there is little question that Christian music fans account for the majority of her sales. Her Christian convictions come through most clearly in the songs "On My Bones" (which speaks of God's sustaining life and of the atoning "death on a cross") and "Never Leave" (a prayer of gratitude for God's ever present care). Both of those songs reflect a theological depth and maturity of perspective (not to mention a finely tuned poetic sensibility) that is staggering in one so young. Other songs are just remarkably perceptive slices of adolescent life. "Perfect by Thursday" describes a teenager's last-minute attempt to get in shape for an important date. In a more serious (and sentimental) vein, Payne offers the words she imagines a friend's deceased father would want to speak to his daughter: "Heaven's quite a sight to see / I'm sure you'll be here too / And though it's beautiful my dear / It can't compare to you."

Two other songs on *Jordan's Sister* are deserving of special note. "Supermodels" was chosen as the theme for the Warner Brothers TV program *Popular*. It is strong musically, but is unfortunately the only lyrically weak song on the album. Payne adopts all the stereotypes that portray models as unintelligent ("retarded") and assumes that anyone who is physically beautiful must have shallow values. It is difficult for her to protest a society that judges people by appearances when she is obviously doing exactly that herself. If she really wanted to parody the extremes of a beauty-obsessed culture, she should have just covered Paul Westerberg's "Mannequin Shop," which makes the point much more effectively and with good-natured humor. "It's Not the Time," on the other hand, is one of the two or three most powerful antiabortion songs yet to be performed by a Christian artist (the others being **Vector**'s "Who Were You?" and **The Wayside**'s "I Cry Myself to Sleep"). It avoids all the baby-killer nonsense that ruins so many songs on this subject (**Phil Keaggy**'s "The Survivor," **Grammatrain**'s "Execution") and goes right to the heart of the matter: a woman facing an unwanted pregnancy stands before a mirror and wonders "what is wrong and what is right"; she considers what everyone has said to her and admits "I am so confused . . . It's not a person yet" but, still, asks "Is it life? Can I deny it's life?" The haunting honesty of this meditation possesses a persuasive power that cruel rhetoric can never achieve.

Christian radio hits: "Closer to Myself" (# 9 in 2000).

Dove Awards: 2001 Modern Rock/Alternative Album (*Jordan's Sister*).

Peace 586

1996—*The Risen Son* (Uprok); 2001—*586*.

Rap singer Peace 586 adopted his trade name in honor of the month and year that he was saved, at which point he also started his career in Christian rap. He performed as one half of a rap duo called Freedom of Soul, who recorded an album called *Caught in a Land of Time* (Broken) in 1991. But whereas that group carried a big production sound that featured sing-along pop stylings, Peace 586 went for a minimalist approach on his debut solo outing, utilizing little more than a synthesizer, a drum machine, and a turntable. Lyrically, *The Risen Son* focuses on artistic poetry that expresses street-smart attitudes. "Lessons in Worship" lectures on spiritual matters, while "Just a Hip Hop Love Song" is more internally reflective. The artist

told *7ball* that his goal was "to reach the unsaved, non-Christian hip-hop fan." After a five-year hiatus, he returned with *586*, an album dedicated to the late producer Gene Eugene (of **Adam Again**). The song "You Here" features a guest appearance by **Sup the Chemist** and pays tribute to Eugene's faith and friendship.

Michael Peace

1987—*RRRock It Right* (Reunion); 1988—*Rappin' Bold*; 1989—*Vigilante of Hope*; 1990—*Loud-N-Clear*; 1991—*Threat to Society* (StarSong); 1994—*Outta Control*.

Michael Peace is one of the most significant of Christian music's pioneering rap artists. His *RRRock It Right* album is generally regarded as the first Christian rap album. As Brian Quincy Newcomb indicates, the *very* first Christian rap album was actually *Gospel Rap* by the **Rap'sures**, which **Terry Taylor** and crew released almost as a joke. Like many of Taylor's tongue-in-cheek efforts, however, it was done with sufficient competence to be taken seriously in many circles. Other early rap ventures in Christian music include a 1982 twelve-inch single by Pete McSweet called "Adam and Eve, the Gospel Beat" (Lection), two projects by **Stephen Wiley** (*Bible Break* and *Rappin' for Jesus),* and a 1987 indie release by white-skinned Roy Suthard creatively titled *Plain White Rapper.* Still, Peace's album was the first to demonstrate the commercial viability of rap in the Christian marketplace.

Peace grew up in what he calls "a tough section" of New York City but did not become politically aware of the root causes for the poverty and injustice he experienced until he majored in African American studies at Brockport State College in upstate New York. There, he became a self-described "black militant student activist." He was chosen president of the school's Black Student Union, but also engaged in what he would later call "acts of vandalism and terrorism" on behalf of what he saw as "the cause." While still a student, Peace says "I received Jesus as my Savior"; the conversion did not stifle his commitment to fighting racism and injustice but did affect his strategies for reconciliation. Basically, he told *CCM* in 1987, "I learned that it is a sin issue, not a skin issue—and that true Christianity means loving white folks, too."

RRRock It Right was in Peace's own reflective estimation "a timid album," lacking the gritty edge of rap projects in the general market. Still, the basic ingredients (beat-box rhythms, synthesizer bursts, samples, stereo panning) are all there and the record afforded sheltered denizens of the Christian music enclave their first opportunity to hear this dangerous new sound in a way that was not completely alienating. Peace even included a rap cover of **Amy Grant**'s "Wise Up" as "a way to appeal to a fresh audience with something that would be a little familiar." The song "In the Ghetto" (not the Mac Davis song) offers some autobiographical reflection on his upbringing. "Automatic Witness" describes a saintly Christian friend whose life he would like to emulate. *Rappin' Bold* comes much closer to the sound of the streets, so close, in fact, that a number of critics found it derivative. On *Vigilantes of Hope,* Peace teamed for the first time with Prince guitarist **Dez Dickerson** for a more groove-laden and original sound. Still, the artist suffered the plight of many pioneers, in that what he was trying to do often didn't connect with his potential audience. Newcomb expressed this well in his review of *Vigilantes:* "At times Peace sounds like those preachers on street corners . . . while one can agree with much of the content, the context and posture feel awkward and ineffective." Of course, such a comment says as much about the audience (and critic) as it does about the artist. *Loud-N-Clear* would provide something of a turning point for Peace. A live album on which he reworks much of his previous material, he now seems to deliver the songs in a more convincing manner—and with a dollop of humor lacking on the previous recordings. The '90s would bring an explosion of talent into the Christian rap market, and Peace's projects would be all but lost among the new offerings. In general, the '90s projects show increased influence of jazz stylings, similar to such acts as Arrested Development and Digable Planets. *Threat to Society* includes "They Call Me Crack," and *Outta Control,* "In the Ghetto"—both original, issue-oriented songs with a distinctly evangelical focus.

Throughout his career, Peace has demonstrated a consistent commitment to ministry. "I've never considered myself to be a Christian *artist,"* Peace said in 1987. "I'm a soul winner. Rapping just provides a forum for preaching the Word of God." In the '90s, he eschewed traditional tours and concerts in favor of what he called an "urban assault." According to this strategy, he and his entourage would go to an inner-city church without charge to the congregation for at least a two-week period, preparing the church and the community for a series of events that would include concerts and seminars. "Handing out flyers never works in urban areas," Peace told *CCM* in 1992. "You have to develop a personal relationship with people, going door-to-door and talking with them."

Charlie Peacock

1981—*Last Vestiges of Honor* [by The Charlie Peacock Group] (label unknown); 1984—*Lie Down in the Grass* (A&M/Exit); 1986—*Charlie Peacock* (Island); 1987—*West Coast Diaries, Vol. 1* (Jamz Ltd.); 1988—*West Coast Diaries, Vol. 2;* 1989—*West Coast Diaries, Vol. 3;* 1990—*The Secret of Time* (Sparrow); 1991—*Love Life;* 1994—*Everything That's on My Mind;* 1996—*Strange Language* (re:think); 1996—*In the Light: The Very Best of Charlie Peacock;* 1998—*Live in the Netherlands* [by The Charlie Peacock Trio]; 1999—*Kingdom Come.*

Charlie Peacock is one of the most talented producers and performers in Christian music. He has gained some notice in the general market despite few deliberate attempts at "crossover," and he has been unusually influential in the development of contemporary Christian music. Impossible to categorize, he has waxed and waned for two decades, defying critics and fans who always seemed to have opinions about what he should do next. Indeed, *7ball* once observed humorously that the "phases" contemporary Christian music went through in the '80s and '90s could be defined largely in terms of whether Charlie Peacock was cool or not. He started out very cool, as an experimental, alternative artist who was often compared to Brian Eno of Roxy Music or to David Byrne of The Talking Heads. He did controversial things that shook up the uptight squares in his audience and made the suits in Nashville tremble. Then in 1990, he moved to Nashville and in the minds of many became a sell-out. He *was* a suit, an industry man responsible for a good deal of the unchallenging pop music that alternative rock was supposed to be rebelling against. Peacock said in 1991, "I was put in the alternative camp without my permission. . . . I certainly never wanted to be alternative, and I don't consider myself to be an alternative artist." In any case, by the end of the decade, Peacock was cool again, rehabilitated and regarded as a crafter of many a fine and intelligent song. In retrospect, the stages of his reception seem to have had far more to do with what was going on in the minds and hearts of his listeners than with any drastic inconsistencies in his own persona or oeuvre. Peacock's output has varied in style and quality over the years but in retrospective evaluation it can all be seen as the work of an artist committed to pop music with strong R&B and jazz flavorings. The closest general market equivalents would be Sting, Peter Gabriel, or Paul Simon. Ironically, such artists have been only rarely mentioned in the twenty-plus years of criticism to which Peacock's work has been subjected, perhaps because his music does not sound like theirs in any immediately obvious way. The analogy is deeper: like Sting, Gabriel, and Simon, Peacock is a *thoughtful* pop artist who tries to create music that has both artistic integrity and potential for widespread commercial appeal. He has no compunction against going for "a hit" (cf. "De Do Do Do, De Da Da Da," "Sledgehammer," "Cecilia") but he is smart enough to know that *long-standing* commercial appeal attends work that is innovative and interesting. In the history of mainstream pop, Sting, Gabriel, and Simon were no less commercial than the Spice Girls—they were just more interesting.

Peacock was born Charles William Ashworth in 1956. He grew up in Yuba City, California, and at the age of twenty-one chose the stage name Charlie Peacock in honor of the jazz musician, Gary Peacock. News about his early life, career, and conversion is sketchy. He recorded an early secular album called

Last Vestiges of Honor in 1981 with The Charlie Peacock Group (Darius Babazadeh, sax.; Jim Casselli, drums; Mark Herzig, gtr.; Eric Klieven, bass); the project was re-released by CP Collectors' Series in 1999. According to an account that Peacock gave *CCM* in 1995, he experienced a conversion to Christianity in 1982. He said, "Christianity was what I was raised with as a child, but I was really the seed that fell on rocky ground. I started making choices that sent me in another direction. For about 10 years, I was out there floundering." Peacock married, but he says that he and his wife "got totally debased . . . we got totally in the gutter—our hearts were intent on evil . . . drugs, alcohol, violence . . . they all invaded our home and ripped our lives apart." Then, he continues, "One afternoon in my little music room on 56th Street in Sacramento, I got down on my knees, and I confessed that I was a sinner. I asked the God of the Bible through his Son Jesus Christ to take my sin away from me, forgive me." As a result, he would testify, "our entire lives have been transformed."

A year later, Peacock became part of an unusual "community of artists" located in Sacramento and associated with the Exit record label headed by Mary Neely. Peacock joined with **Jimmy Abegg, Brent Bourgeois, Michael Roe, Steve Scott,** and others who were committed to the vision of creating music as Christians that was not specifically designed for marketing within a Christian music subculture. Neely managed to set up commercial alliances between Exit and such companies as A&M and Island Records, guaranteeing distribution beyond Christian bookstores, a rarity for Christian artists at the time. The enterprise did not prove to be successful over the long haul, but it did launch some stellar careers. The most important of the Exit bands were Bourgeois-Tagg, the **Seventy Sevens,** and **Vector.** Peacock was very much in evidence with all of these: **Brent Bourgeois** and Larry Tagg (of Bourgeois-Tagg) had initially been members of The Charlie Peacock Band (though they did not record with him on *Last Vestiges of Honor*); the **Seventy Sevens**' seminal *All Fall Down* was produced by Peacock; and Peacock was actually a founding member of **Vector** (though he went solo after their first album).

After his impressive work on **Vector**'s *Mannequin Virtue,* Peacock would quietly release *Lie Down in the Grass,* an album that would come to be regarded as one of Christian music's great classics. The project was issued in two slightly different versions: the Exit release contains two songs called "Watching Eternity" and "Human Condition," where the A&M product has "Young in Heart" and "Love Doesn't Get Any Better." Musically, *Lie Down* fits in with the general scheme of sound being explored at the time by such artists as Thomas Dolby, the Eurythmics, and the Thompson Twins. The title track offers a creative but subtle invitation to accept the stress-relieving providence offered in Psalm 23:2. Peacock sometimes had to explain in interviews on the secular circuit that he wasn't referring to the kind of lying down "in the green grass behind the stadium with you" that **Van Morrison** had in mind in his hit "Brown-Eyed Girl." The song "Whole Lot Different (Whole Lot the Same)" speaks of the differences *and similarities* between Christian and non-Christian world views. *CCM* magazine chose *Lie Down in the Grass* as one of their Ten Best Albums of 1984, but the artist was being marketed primarily outside traditional Christian music circles, touring with The Fixx and General Public. His next Exit release, a self-titled album, almost slipped past the Christian market altogether, though it has some very nice and obviously spiritual songs. *Charlie Peacock,* an exclusively general market release on Island Records, opens with "Message Boy," in which the singer warns his audience that his songs are going to reflect his convictions: "There is nothing in this world that can stop me from my task / I'll respect you and your privacy, where and when is all I ask." A track called "Dizzy Dean Movie" reflects wistfully on his childhood, with the off-hand comment, "I only prayed on Sundays then." The highlight of the record comes with "Down in the Lowlands," a plea for divine mercy that draws heavily on traditional gospel.

Peacock's not-always-wanted and not-always-deserved indie/ alternative status is best experienced through a collection of three discs called *The West Coast Diaries* that he released in the late '80s. They all contain outtakes and live cuts, including a large number of songs not found anywhere else. The discs are not of equal quality. *Diaries 1* and 3 have their moments (Vol. 3 offers a pre-Lemonheads cover of Simon and Garfunkel's "Mrs. Robinson"), but *Diaries 2* is an especially intimate collection of tracks by Peacock, **Jimmy Abegg,** and **Vince Ebo** performing as The Charlie Peacock Trio. The takes are somewhat improvisational, revealing a vulnerability seldom found on more public offerings. "Unchain My Heart," "Down in the Lowlands," "The Way of Love" (also on Vol. 1) and "Psalm 51" are notable highlights. "No Place Closer to Heaven" was written for the dedication of a church building and has become something of a standard for such occasions. A similar sound informs The Charlie Peacock Trio's album *Live in the Netherlands,* which was not released until 1999, a decade after it was recorded.

The Secret of Time was the first of Peacock's Nashville albums. As if the geographical move were not enough to damage his hipness credentials, he chose to have the album produced by **Brown Bannister,** who was (somewhat unfairly) regarded as the quintessential example of industry-types responsible for churning out market-driven pop. *Time* would be Peacock's most stereotypically commercial outing to date, with half its tracks destined to end up on his *Very Best of . . .* CD six years later. Only a couple of those are truly among his best; *CCM*'s Brian Quincy Newcomb complained that "it just isn't the Charlie

Peacock we've learned to expect," which is hardly a salient point. Still, "Put the Love Back into Love" and "Dear Friend" stray into insipid adult contemporary territory. Of course, there are exceptions, as Newcomb acknowledged: the funky opening track, "Big Man's Hat," employs an effective image for "getting older without growing up." On "Almost Threw It Away," Peacock gives thanks to his wife for persevering in their marriage when he would have thrown in the towel, trading "truth for a lie, diamonds for clay." His high voice on the song sounds a lot like Smokey Robinson. *Secret's* closing song, "Experience," ends the album on a rousing note with a driving R&B groove that features the artist assuring his fans, "I ain't no company man / I ain't no company man." Doubts regarding that assertion would only increase, however, when the next year Peacock cowrote the song "Every Heartbeat" for **Amy Grant,** helping to provide that star with a huge Number Two hit on *Billboard*'s mainstream charts. An undeniable triumph for both Grant and Peacock, "Every Heartbeat" did little to sustain the fan base he had once shared with artists like **Michael Knott** and **Daniel Amos.** Later, **Eric Champion** would have a little fun with the fray by performing an angry-punk version of "Every Heartbeat" on his Peacock-produced *Natural* album.

Love Life was another commercial pop product in the same vein as *Secrets,* but it was a superior album in every way. It was hyped as a "controversial" recording perhaps in an attempt to restore Peacock's edge, but there was nothing even mildly scandalous about it. The nonissue concerned a song called "Kiss Me Like a Woman" in which Peacock celebrates the joys of physical affection and sexual love ("we can lie naked and unashamed, made one by divine connection . . . the intimate moment is beautiful in God's sight"). The very biblical song is one of Peacock's best, and it fits perfectly with the overall relational theme of the *Love Life* album. Other romantic odes include the Smokey Robinson-like "After Loving You" and the sweet "Another Woman in Tears," on which Peacock offers his public apology for being away from home too often. There are other highlights, too. "What's It Like in Your World" is a bouncy affirmation of empathy. "Forgiveness" is a soulful song that builds from a simple piano ballad to a fervent traditional gospel anthem. "I Would Go Crazy" dives into world beat with a Brazilian influence. And then there is the little South African pop number, "In the Light," that would prove to be Peacock's biggest Christian hit, and then would garner even more attention when covered by **DC Talk** on their *Jesus Freak* album. In 2001, a poll of critics sponsored by *CCM* magazine put *Love Life* at Number Fifteen on their list of "The 100 Greatest Albums in Christian Music." *The Secret of Time* (# 26) and *Lie Down in the Grass* (# 67) also made the list.

Though some media pundits tried to style Peacock's "Kiss Me Like a Woman" as a "daring" song for no other reason than

that it referred to sex, they invariably missed the potential that allowed it to achieve a status in some circles that might at least merit the word "controversial." The catalyst for a different interpretation arose from the final verse: "I heard a fool on the radio / Talking trash about the love we make." Peacock apparently intended the line as a reference to secular musicians who refer to sex in irreverent ways. Some listeners applied the lines to radio preachers and evangelists who disparage types of sex of which they don't approve. Add to that the ambiguity of the word *like* in the song's chorus ("kiss me *like* a woman" = "kiss me the way you would if you were a woman"), and the song became a favorite among gay Christians, who heard it as an affirmation of love between same-sex partners. Apparently, Peacock never intended this interpretation and may not even be aware of his featured stature among a select but beleaguered sub-subculture (gay Christian music fans).

After *Love Life,* Peacock took a three-year break from recording. During that time, he scored an almost accidental hit with a song he did for a **Keith Green** tribute album ("I Can't Believe It," written by Keith and Melody Green). He also got into producing more heavily and made a series of worship albums with songs by various artists called *Coram Deo* (Latin for "presence of God"). The albums attempt to break down artificial sacred/secular barriers by articulating how worship can be integrated into the affairs of daily life. Then Peacock returned to solo performing with *Everything That's on My Mind,* a more rock-oriented project that takes a step back from the too-slick sound he had adopted since leaving Sacramento. It did not start out well. The opening track, "One Man Gets Around," wastes a catchy melody on mediocre lyrics (expressing amazement over the fact that people in many different countries have heard of Jesus). But from there, things get a lot better. The best song is probably "Inside Out, Upside Down," a rocking testimony to human ignorance with background vocals by **Brent Bourgeois** and **Steve Taylor.** "Climb a Tree" starts out reminiscent of Simon and Garfunkel's "My Little Town" but then kicks into gear with distorted guitars by Jerry McPherson and some lyrical surprises that prove imaginative. "Monkeys at the Zoo" won a Dove award for Best Modern/Alternative Rock Song; it's not particularly "modern," it's certainly not "alternative," and it probably isn't even "rock," but it *is* a nice adult contemporary pop song appealing to the Spirit of God for internal cleansing. Likewise, "Slippery Pearls" offers sweet and soulful recognition of the ephemeral quality of so much that humans value; **Ashley Cleveland** adds some inspired wailing toward the end. "My Father's Crown" is a lovely piano ballad in which the artist reflects on his father's recent death ("So this is what it's like to be the child of a man who's dead and gone"); the rumination on loss and mortality would seem all the more poignant when Peacock's friend and oft-time colleague **Vince Ebo** committed suicide about the time that *Everything on My Mind* was released. Ebo had always credited Peacock with having "brought him to a saving knowledge of Jesus Christ." Three months after his death, Peacock could only say, "I'm pretty much in denial over it. . . . I'll just have to go to my grave knowing that I'll never know (why he did it)."

The best was yet to come. *Strange Language* represents the zenith of Peacock's impressive career. *CCM* announced it boldly as "an album as good as his first two," and as time went by few listeners would doubt that it was even better than those prized masterworks. The opening title track is a jazzy rock song on which the artist actually sounds a bit like Sting. Theologically, it's one of the strongest songs ever to appear in the contemporary Christian music market, using the image of glossolalia (1 Corinthians 14:23) to convey how a gospel message that makes familiar sense to believers can sound foreign in the ears of those who have few reference points for recognizing what it describes: "might filter from the lips of a criminal set free / might glimpse it in the sorrow of a man half mad with grief . . . might make you deadly nervous / might bring you some relief." Peacock goes on to insist with the Apostle Paul (1 Corinthians 1:18; 2:14) that the mysterious, foolish-sounding language of the gospel is all there is—there are no irrefutable arguments, absolute proofs, or guaranteed arguments to render radical faith unnecessary, just a strange language "haunted by an even stranger truth." The song "Insult Like the Truth" is a remarkably creative song, built on a riff that is almost like one of Led Zeppelin's Middle Eastern dirges. It is, again, both poignant and provocative lyrically, pointing up a series of philosophical ironies similar to that expressed in the title: "there's no strength like utter weakness, there's no insult like the truth." A much softer sound informs the beautifully melodic "Rocket" (with **Sarah Masen** on background vocals), in which Peacock describes his ambiguous feelings while watching a friend experience the predictable crash and burn consequences of the life he had been living. The concluding verse holds, "When I finish my little song / Maybe I'll love mercy more than being right." Critics also loved "Struck Blind," with its Peter-Gabriel-meets-industrial sound, and "Liquid Days," which starts out like a '60s guitar song and somehow segues into saxophone-driven jazz fusion toward the end. Every song on *Strange Language* is worthy of celebration, but two more are particularly notable and demonstrative of the incredible diversity of sounds that Peacock's eclectic genius is capable of producing. "The Harvest Is the End of the World" reflects on the ultimate end of mourning with jazz fusion and a generous influence of world music. "Lady Soul" is a tribute to **Aretha Franklin** and itself recaptures the joyful spirit of classic Atlantic soul. As an artist who is sufficiently grounded biblically to believe that "the secular world" is as much an expression of

God as the religious domain, Peacock can glory in Aretha's music for no other reason than that it reminds him "how wonderful it can feel to be human."

Kingdom Come is another masterpiece. Peacock seems here to be at peace with the realization that no matter how good (or how secular) his music might sound, it is not going to get played outside the strange little world of contemporary Christian music. Here, then, is a record for "that little pond" as he sometimes calls it. It is some of his best work and falls, along with certain products by artists like **Phil Keaggy** or **Daniel Amos,** into that category of "precious secrets": albums that are actually better than ninety-five percent of the products by similar sounding artists in the general market but which remain the property of only a select few. Musically, *Kingdom Come* diverges from the anything-goes sonic experimentation of *Strange Language* to provide a more straightforward collection of strong adult pop songs. "Is the Brightness Still in Me?" asks the question all aging rock stars must consider: "Can I hold my own like I did when I was young?" But here there is a twist—the question is not just one of remaining musically relevant, but also an honest inquiry into whether his mature, theologically informed faith can have the same appeal as the vibrant piety he displayed when he first believed. The album, indeed, is very strong theologically: "Wouldn't It Be Strange?" returns to some of the paradoxes of faith touched on in "Insult Like the Truth": "Wouldn't it be strange if power made you weak? . . . If victory came to those who turn the other cheek?" The song "Cheer Up Church" was written as a tribute to one of Peacock's spiritual mentors, Jack Miller, and contains similar lines ("It's just like God to make a hero from a sinner") with the concluding exhortation derived from Miller's own words: "Cheer up, Church, you're worse off than you think!" The album's title track reflects on the central paradox of New Testament doctrine—a theme that is curiously absent from most contemporary Christian music—namely, the presentation of God's kingdom as a future reality that is somehow, mysteriously already present. An especially fun ditty called "Don't Be Afraid" offers words of encouragement set to a Tom Petty-like tune. "The Night Won't Last Forever" speaks of ultimate hope. "Sacrifice of Love" offers a secret for dealing with conflict in marriage: "A superficial kiss won't be enough / the only bridge across our canyon / Is built upon the sacrifice of love." The album concludes with a song of ethereal beauty that leaves the listener with the thought "I will share the hope I hold in Christ / But only you can open up your heart" ("Only You").

As indicated, Peacock has probably had an even greater influence on contemporary Christian music through his work as a producer than as a recording artist. He has been responsible for many of the most significant albums in a variety of genres, helming products for such major stars as **Jimmy Abegg,**

Audio Adrenaline, Avalon, Margaret Becker, Lisa Bevill, Brent Bourgeois, Bob Carlisle, Eric Champion, The Choir, Vince Ebo, Al Green, Kim Hill, Cheri Keaggy, Phil Keaggy, Scott Krippayne, Rick Lang, Sarah Masen, Out of the Grey, Twila Paris, and the **Seventy Sevens.** In 1996, Peacock started Re:think, a Nashville-based multimedia company, a label that he said was dedicated to creating a place for artists to exercise their imaginations. Peacock is also the father of composer and recording artist **Samuel Brinsley Ashworth.**

Peacock is author of *At the Crossroads: An Insider's Look at the Past, Present, and Future of Contemporary Christian Music* (Nashville: Broadman and Holman, 1999). The book issues a call for repentance and creative reimagining within the Christian music industry, insisting that "the ideas that form the foundation for Christian music . . . do not accurately reflect a comprehensive kingdom perspective." In 2000–2001, Peacock took a sabbatical during which he attended Covenant Theological Seminary in St. Louis and recorded three improvisational jazz recordings: *The Exactness of Feel* (solo piano); *Arc of the Circle* (duets with saxophone); and a collaboration with jazz artists Ravi Coltrane and Kurt Rosenwinkel.

Peacock has written or cowritten Christian radio hits performed by **Audio Adrenaline** ("Good Life," "Hands and Feet"), **Margaret Becker** ("The Hunger Stays," "Solomon's Shoes," "Simple House," "Look Me in the Eye," "Talk about Love," "This Love," "Say the Name," "Will Be with You," "Deep Calling Deep," "True Devotion," "I Trust in You," "My Heaven"), **Bob Carlisle** ("Getting Stronger," "Bridge between Two Hearts"), **DC Talk** ("In the Light"), **Amy Grant** ("Every Heartbeat"), **Sarah Masen** ("Come In"), **Geoff Moore and The Distance** ("House of Faith"), **Russ Taff** ("Down in the Lowlands"), and **Tony Vincent** ("Simple Things," "Out of My Hands," "High").

Christian radio hits: "Big Man's Hat" (# 6 in 1990); "Dear Friend" (# 22 in 1990); "Almost Threw It All Away" (# 1 for 6 weeks at 1990); "One Thing" (# 17 in 1991); "In the Light" (# 1 for in 8 weeks in 1992); "Personal Revolution" (# 4 in 1992); "What's It Like in Your World" (# 4 in 1992); "I Would Go Crazy" (# 20 in 1992); "I Can't Believe It" (# 2 in 1993); "One Man Gets Around" (# 1 for 2 weeks in 1995); "Slippery Pearls" (# 2 in 1995); "Inside Out, Upside Down" (# 5 in 1995); "That's the Point" (# 4 in 1996); "Insult Like the Truth" (# 13 in 1996); "Sneakin' Up on Me" (# 5 in 1997).

Dove Awards: 1995 Producer of the Year; 1996 Producer of the Year; 1996 Modern/Alternative Rock Song ("Monkeys at the Zoo"); 1997 Producer of the Year.

Karen Peck and New River

Karen Peck, voc.; Susan Peck, voc.; David White, voc. (− 2000) // John Rowsey, voc. (+ 2000). Selected: 2000—*A Taste of Grace* (Spring Hill).

www.karenpeckandnewriver.com

Although she is hardly known in contemporary Christian music, Karen Peck is a big name in southern gospel. A readers' poll in *Singing News* magazine, southern gospel's leading trade publication, has chosen her female vocalist of the year fifteen times. Peck began her career in 1981 as a member of The Nelons (formerly The LeFevres, the family group that spawned **Mylon LeFevre**). After ten years, she formed the vocal trio New River with a male vocalist and her sister Susan. That group would release ten albums in the next decade, with an ever more contemporary sound. *Christian Music* compares New River to **The Martins** as a group that "is helping to bring southern gospel into the 21st century by making use of modern instrumentation, crisp harmonies, and just plain beautiful music." The first record to catch the ear of contemporary Christian music fans (and critics) was *A Taste of Grace*. Here, Peck delivers a strong ballad called "Four Days Late," which uses the biblical story of Lazarus's death (John 11) as an analogy for the despair that unnecessarily sets in when humans do not anticipate the power of God to transform their lives. "Like the Truth Is" showcases new vocalist John Rowsey on a song that bears strong traditional gospel influence. Sister Susan sings lead on a modern country number "His Love Runs Deep."

Pedro the Lion

David Bazan; et al. 1997—*Whole* [EP] (Tooth and Nail); 1998—*It's Hard to Find a Friend* (Made in Mexico); *The Only Reason I Feel Secure Is That I'm Validated by My Peers* [EP]; 2000—*Winners Never Quit* (Jade Tree); *Progress* (Suicide Squeeze).

www.pedrothelion.com

Pedro the Lion is one of Christian music's most outstanding and critically acclaimed indie bands. Their style is usually classed as emo, or sometimes as "indie folk rock" but the band is nothing if not distinctive. A typical Pedro album (if there is such a thing) features thoughtful story-songs related in the first person to haunting and mostly acoustic instrumental riffs. Words like "hypnotic" and "mesmerizing" occur frequently in reviews. *HM* has said, "Pedro the Lion's work, whether near silent and plaintive, or raucous and challenging, is some of the most haunted, meaningful, and reverent rock music made today. . . . The songs are filled with sharp parables about temptation and redemption."

The exact composition of the so-called band changes from album to album, but the constant link is singer, songwriter, and guitarist David Bazan. He began his music career as a young teenager playing in hardcore bands around Seattle; at fifteen, he was drummer for a group called The Guilty that was fronted by **Damien Jurado.** Pedro the Lion's first EP was released by Christian music's quintessential alternative label Tooth and Nail and so gained the band an early hearing. *HM* thought the title track ("Whole") had "a beautiful melody and honest, questioning lyrics." Thematically, *Whole* seems to describe an individual's struggle with drug addiction and discovery of salvation. The following year's full-length album would have more lyrical breadth. *It's Hard to Find a Friend* delves into the angst of adolescent existence with a note of Christian hope always in the background. *Spin* magazine, which is often hostile to Christian artists, named the project one of their "Ten Best Albums You Didn't Hear in 1998." The song "Of Minor Prophets and Their Prostitute Wives" puts a contemporary spin on the Hosea story, and "Secret of the Easy Yoke" expresses some disillusionment with a church in which Bazan feels called to serve "an unseen, distant Lord." An uncharacteristically catchy song, "Big Trucks" offers what *Phantom Tollbooth* would describe as "a dissertation on the Golden Rule." The song "When They Really Get to Know You They Will Run" expresses dismay at cosmetic appearances and superficial behaviors people adopt in the quest for peer acceptance. The same theme would inform a follow-up EP titled *The Only Reason I Feel Secure Is That I'm Validated by My Peers.* As that title implies, the artist now turns the prophetic gaze of the previous album inward and owns up to his own foibles. The opening track, "Criticism Is Inspiration," starts out by continuing his rant against superficiality of modern culture, with lyrics more graphic than are usually found in Christian music ("Then there's your girlfriend / She spreads her legs and gives your life meaning / Is that what you love her for?"). But at midpoint, the song turns the necessary self-deprecating corner: "It makes me feel so good to always tell you when you're wrong," Bazan sings, "It makes me look so good to always put you in your place / I could write it in a song but never say it to your face." Another intriguing number called "Letter from a Concerned Follower" addresses God or Jesus with the tongue-in-cheek suggestion that they need to keep up with the trends if they want to retain a following ("You won't survive the information age / Unless you plan to change the truth to accommodate the brilliance of men"). The five-track collection concludes with the hymn "Be Thou My Vision" sung as a private prayer.

Winners Never Quit is a concept album that relates the story of two brothers, one a drunkard who gets a second chance, the other a charismatic politician who ends up committing murder in his quest for power. The two-edged theme of falling into grace and opting out of it ties the songs together from the cynical opening line ("A good person is someone who hasn't been caught") to its open-ended conclusion. With lyrics that recall the morality plays of **T Bone Burnett** and a voice that sometimes echoes Counting Crow's Adam Duritz, Bazan meditates on hypocrisy and self-deceit in ways that continue to reveal his own struggling conscience. Musically, he also manages to transcend the moping, mellow style that characterized the previous projects, building his songs, at least some of the time,

into electric rock and roll pieces. The four-track *Progress* offered a handful of additional songs that apparently didn't fit with the story. "April 6, 2039" offers a glimpse into the future (à la "In the Year 2525") and reveals that despite technological advances, families are likely to remain dysfunctional.

At a point between *Hard to Find a Friend* and *Winners Never Quit,* Bazan commented on his own work as an artist: "Art is at its most vital when it's disorienting, indefinite. And I fail in this area a lot, because I grew up in a Christian culture that was pointed, concrete, necessarily definitive all the time." In his later work, however, Bazan seems bent on transcending that limitation, drawing less inspiration from the Christian religion (with its inherent need of orthodoxy) than from the Bible (with its intrinsic contradictions and embrace of disparate perspectives). When he signed with the general market label Jade Tree, he told *Bandoppler,* "I think that the pretense of Christian music, and the actualization of Christian music, is pretty much an abomination to God. . . . I actually think it would be immoral for me to sign with a Christian label because I think what the Christian labels do is antithetical to the gospel."

Dan Peek

1979—*All Things Are Possible* (Lamb and Lion); 1984—*Doer of the Word* (Home Sweet Home); 1986—*Electro Voice* (Greentree); 1987—*Crossover;* 1988—*The Best of Dan Peek.*

Dan Peek was a member of the trio America, which was one of the most popular Top 40 bands of the early '70s. He says that he left the group as part of "a covenant with God" and went on to a career in contemporary Christian music that offered only a shadow of the commercial success he had known, though, within the limited genre, he was still regarded as a major star. Peek was born in 1950 in Panama City, Florida. He met Dewey Bunnell and Gerry Beckley when the three of them attended high school together in London while their fathers (who were all in the military) were stationed overseas. They first formed a band called Daze in 1970, which they then reconfigured as America when they moved back to the States in 1972. The group recorded four gold and four platinum albums during the years that Peek was one of their lead singers. Their first, self-titled album would include their biggest hit, the Neil Young rip-off "A Horse with No Name" (# 1 for 3 weeks in 1972), in addition to the love song "I Need You" (# 9 in 1972), the underground classic "Sandman," and the Disneyesque "Muskrat Love," which would later become a Number Four hit for Captain and Tennille. In 1975, the group would record what is considered to be one of the best pop songs of all time, "Sister Golden Hair" (# 1 in 1975). Other hits would include "Ventura Highway" (# 8 in 1972) and "Tin Man" (# 4 in 1974). Less successful but better songs include the wonderful "Daisy

Jane" (# 20 in 1975) and the quirky gem "Woman Tonight" (# 44 in 1975). America had an image as squeaky clean as The Monkees and were noted for hopeful songs that portrayed a positive attitude toward life and love. Peek was not a primary composer, but he did contribute two songs to the group's repertoire that are especially significant: "Don't Cross the River" (# 35 in 1973) is a country rock tune that offers some basic good advice for living; in retrospect, it essentially puts Jesus' exhortation to "count the cost" to a catchy beat. More important, Peek's "Lonely People" (# 5 in 1974) would provide the band with one of its biggest hits through a song that sounded like much of what could be heard on Christian radio stations at the time. While avoiding specifically religious references, the song offers hope to lonely and hurting people, pointing them toward heaven: "Don't give up until you drink from the silver cup / And ride that highway to the sky."

Peek was raised in a strong Christian family, and he would later reveal that he prayed to God in early 1972, "If you will make me a success, I'll use that platform to spread the word about you." Within the year, he says, the prayer was answered, but for a time he found the allure of money and fame too strong to keep his end of the bargain. "After seven years I was miserable because I had wandered from the Lord," he told *CCM* in 1986, and he determined that leaving the band was the only way to fulfill his calling. Not surprisingly, his solo albums sought to duplicate the sound of America, but with more evangelical lyrics. *All Things Are Possible* was something of a crossover hit; its title song actually charted on *Billboard*'s mainstream Hot 100 (at # 78) and the album itself remained on the general market's adult contemporary chart for a record-setting thirty-four weeks. Both of Peek's first two solo projects were produced by **Chris Christian,** who also wrote many of the songs on the debut. By *Doers of the Word,* Peek was doing the bulk of the composing himself and the songs were becoming increasingly less generic and more explicit in terms of Christian content. On the title track (written by Jeremy Dalton), America alum Beckley joins Peek on vocals to produce a sound indistinguishable from that of the group's trademark hits. For *Electro Voice,* Peek would re-record "Lonely People" with slightly altered lyrics: "Don't give up until you drink from the silver cup / And give your heart to Jesus Christ." Thoroughly embedded now in contemporary Christian music subculture, the album also included an original composition based on Romans 8:28 ("All Things Work Together for Good") and another, unfortunate tune about "The Rapture." In 1993, Peek would reunite with America briefly for a tour on which the band opened for the Beach Boys. He also formed an independent acoustic group called Peace.

For trivia buffs: America would have only one more hit after Peek left. In 1982, after touring as a duo for a decade, they made a comeback with the Number Eight song "You Can Do Magic." Replacing Peek in the band (at that time) was Billy Mumy, who once played Will Robinson on the TV series *Lost in Space.*

Christian radio hits: "All Things Are Possible" (# 1 for 13 weeks in 1979); "Divine Lady" (# 25 in 1979); "Doer of the Word" (# 2 in 1984); "Redeemer" (# 26 in 1984); "Lonely People" (# 2 in 1986); "Electro Voice" (# 7 in 1986); "Crossover" (# 13 in 1987).

Pegtop

David Peightal, voc., gtr.; Terry Steinmeyer, drums // R. Matt Patrick, bass (+ 1997). 1995—*Just Us* (Dirt Road); 1997—*The Great Reverse; The Gift;* 1998—*Run, Run;* 1999—*Pegtop 5 Live.*

www.pegtop.com

A prolific indie band from Minneapolis, Pegtop is known locally for setting up on street corners with amplifiers powered by an old car battery and playing their quirky folk music for whoever passes by. On such occasions, their instrumentation usually consists of a single acoustic guitar, a bass, and a unique drumset made from a wooden box with a small snare drum attached. The group's songs are overtly religious numbers in the new-folk musical vein of Tracy Chapman or **David Wilcox.** Various reviewers have drawn comparisons to the musical styles of such groups as **The Alarm,** Barenaked Ladies, and Uncle Tupelo. *The Great Reverse* would introduce the sound of drummer Terry Steinmeyer's homemade percussion set (featuring a large cardboard barrel, five-gallon pails, a metal tackle box, a mini tambourine, and some small cymbals). The most polished production to date is *Run, Run,* which includes "Hit the Highway," an update on the Good Samaritan parable; "Nick," a song about the loss of a child to Sudden Death Syndrome; and the title track, which uses Philip's chasing after the Ethiopian eunuch's chariot (Acts 8) as an image for encouraging passionate evangelism. The band invests a good dose of humor in much of their material, as is evident in "Jerusalem," which offers commentary on Jesus' subversive act of table turning. "Big Cat" is apparently about Aslan, the Christ-figure lion who is a character in C. S. Lewis's Narnia tales. *The Gift* is a collection of Christmas songs. *Pegtop 5 Live* was recorded at a coffee shop in Falcon Heights, Minnesota, and contains mostly performances of songs from the early albums. The group's name mocks frequent mispronunciations of their leader's name. David Peightal is an ordained minister and the son of missionaries to the Takima Indians.

Ken Pennell (a.k.a. Kent LeRoy)

1981—*Love Is the Reason = Quiero Cantar del Amor* (Sparrow).

Ken Pennell was one of the first contemporary Christian music artists to draw on the resources of Latin American music and to orient his ministry specifically toward Hispanics. *Love Is the Reason* was issued by Sparrow in both English and Spanish versions, the latter under the stage name Kent LeRoy, which Pennell had been using with Spanish audiences. Even the English version features two songs with Spanish lyrics, including a translation of **John Fischer**'s "The Lord's Prayer." Pennell favored a melodious folk style similar to such artists as John Denver and Don McLean. In 1980, he was appointed head of a Spanish division of Sparrow records responsible for distribution of Spanish language albums in Central and South America. A 1980 album titled *Quiero Decirles Que Yo Soy Felix* saw limited release in the United States.

Peter Penrose

1997—*Peter Penrose* (Benson).

A former member of the vocal group **Truth,** Peter Penrose has worked extensively as a solo artist with Chuck Colson's Prison Fellowship ministry. He has also recorded one album of adult contemporary blue-eyed soul music. The self-titled record consists mostly of power ballads cut from the same cloth as those of **Clay Crosse** and **Russ Taff.** Regie Hamm produced the album and cowrote many of the songs. Standout tracks include "That's Where You Come In" and "I Feel" (an anthem that reminds a *CCM* reviewer of Stevie Wonder).

Pensive (and Seasons in the Field)

Pensive: Brian Deter, gtr.; Martin Lunn, bass; Chad Monticue, voc.; Joshua Walters, drums. Seasons in the Field: Russ Cogdell; Brian Deter, gtr.; Daniel Weyandt. By Pensive: 1997—*The Subtlety of Silence* (2 Jake Records). By Pensive/Seasons in the Field: 1998—*The Psalms of Ariana* (Akeldama).

Pensive and Seasons in the Field appear to have been evolutionary stages in the development of the hard rock band **Zao.** The Pennsylvania group known as Pensive was the first band signed to Grrr Records' subsidiary 2 Jake, which sought to compete with Tooth and Nail as a home for hard alternative acts. *The Subtlety of Silence* is notable primarily for Chad Monticue's vocals, which come in two styles: melodic singing and death metal screaming. The alternation of these two styles (sometimes in a single line) provides for a distinctive though somewhat jarring sound—a virtual combination of emo and metal. The album ends with fifteen minutes of beach noise (waves, seagulls, etc.). In 1998, the group recorded a split CD with half the songs by a new version of the band now called Seasons in the Field (featuring Brian Detar, Rick Cogdell, and Daniel Weyandt—all of whom would become members of **Zao**). Seasons in the Field showed less of the emo stylings and had a much harder metal sound very similar to that of **Zao.**

Pep Squad

Bryan Everett, voc., gtr., bass; Kim Hoskins, voc., gtr.; Evan Railton, drums; Brad Swanson, bass, gtr., voc. 1998—*No Doy!* (BEC); 1999—*Yreka Bakery* (Tooth and Nail).

Pep Squad has been described by *Bandoppler* as "one of the most under-rated and misunderstood bands out there." The West Coast group has a pop sheen and a name that seems to suggest **Everybodyduck-**style pop. They even had a cartoon drawing of a band majorette on their first album cover. But it's all a joke, *Bandoppler* insists, for Pep Squad turns out cheesegrater, anti-pop music that makes a facetious mockery of bands that seem bent on doing what is approved and expected. A close examination of that cover reveals that the majorette has just set fire to a lodge now burning in the background. Pep Squad's two albums have been produced by Chris Colbert of **Breakfast with Amy** and **Fluffy/Duraluxe** fame, with Gene Eugene of **Adam Again** helping out on the second project. Their sound actually bears a strong resemblance to that of BWA or, even more so, to such general market bands as Sonic Youth and Superchunk. *7ball* describes the sound as "an interesting mixture of breathy vocals and noisy feedback-laden guitars held together in a pop-song format."

No Doy! opens with a brooding but intriguing track called "Angel" and then moves rather quickly into catchier numbers that often sport memorable choruses. Bryan Everett sings lead on most songs with a slightly creaky, off-kilter voice. Kim Hoskins (his sister) lightens things up whenever she appears. The two trade vocal lines in an especially appealing way on the song "Supertrooper." Heavy instrumental distortion is juxtaposed with vocal bliss: ah-ahh's on "Never Netherlands" and ba-ba-bah's on "Barbapoppa." Occasionally ("Jamie's Kisses"), the group strays into bubblegum.

The sophomore album shows some maturity of sound in the direction, in retrospect, that the debut was certainly headed. The group described this sound as "the-Pixies-meet-Weezer," and those quirky fun-pop acts provide the best analogies for what is recorded on *Yreka Bakery* (the title is a palindrome). Yet the songs also betray a wild eclecticism of style selection. The album opens with a rumbling shuffle called "Wild Pack." "Freak Show" is a more Weezer-ish alternative pop outing. "On That Day" offers a curious break with a mostly acoustic, very pretty ballad. "The Floor" is a fabulously funky disco number that invokes images of Prince or **Donna Summer.** Along the same lines, the group delivers a surprising, updated-for-the-'90s cover of Adam Ant's "Friend or Foe." A track called "Black and Blue" does "Never Netherlands" one better and has no lyrics at all except for lots of ah-ahh's and a few de-do-do-do-de-doo's.

Pep Squad rarely sings about anything with specific Christian content. "Hot" is about a girl who Everett thinks is hot.

"The Fabulous Moolah" is about a grandmother who wrestles with the WWF. "Erik's Got a Girlfriend" is about a young man who likes Barbie dolls. On the first album in particular, lyrics sometimes vary from the poetically obscure to what many critics have euphemistically called "silly" or "goofy." On "Bug-Nut," Everett sings, "He's got a dragon on his back / And a knife between his toes / And he flies through the air." "On That Day," however, is a traditional contemporary Christian track with all of its lyrics drawn straight from Scripture (mostly regarding perseverance in times of apathy or tribulation). Everett, who credits the shoegazer group My Bloody Valentine as a major influence on his songwriting, says Pep Squad has no intention of doing evangelistic songs. "We're Christians, but we have to live in this world," he says of the mundane content of the band's songs. "And God is not some cheap plastic toy you play with. I think music and art should be much deeper than that."

Joshua Perahia

See **Joshua.**

Chuckie Perez (a.k.a. **Chuckie P**)

1990—*Do You Have a Problem with That?* (Arcade); 1993—*Universal* (Essential); 1996—*Rhythms of Tomorrow* (Diadem).

Chuckie Perez made two albums of '70s disco music that did not sell particularly well (it was the '90s) before switching to more adult-oriented pop. His first project, *Do you Have a Problem with That?* (recorded under the name Chuckie P), is particularly teen-oriented, with guest appearances by **Crystal Lewis** and **Jon Gibson.** *Universal* features a combination of Michael Jackson-like dance numbers ("Universal," "Losing Your Soul") and Kool and the Gang-style ballads ("You're Amazing"). "Mind Set on You" sounds like an outtake from *Saturday Night Fever* (imagine The Trammps singing a leftover Bee Gees song), but before the song is over Perez offers a rap break just to keep things current. "I'll Be Waiting" is Latin-pop, featuring flamenco guitars and a Spanish children's chorus. The sound of the latter song would prove to be the norm for *Rhythms of Tomorrow.* On that album, "The Church Moves On" offers encouragement for evangelism, and the upbeat "Power" reveals Perez' Pentecostal influences. The album also includes a cover of Foreigner's "I Want to Know What Love Is," with more flamenco guitars. Perez has a strong **Carman**-like penchant for imbuing his concerts with narrowly defined evangelistic intent; concerts typically include altar calls and seem to be intended to serve as occasions for converting audience members to fundamentalist Christianity.

Al Perkins

No recordings.

Al Perkins has never released an album of his own, but he is one of the most prolific sidemen in the history of rock and country music. Like **Michael Omartian,** his involvement with Christian music—especially in the early years—helped to infuse the genre with a professionalism and a quality it could not possibly have achieved without him. Perkins became known in the early '70s as a master of two instruments that were becoming popular in country-rock bands: the dobro and the pedal steel guitar. Eventually, the Gibson guitar company would label him "the world's most influential dobro player" and in 2001 chose him to endorse their "Al Perkins Signature" instrument in that line—a dobro designed and autographed by the artist. It was Perkins' pedal steel, however, that attracted the most attention, and along with Sneaky "Pete" Kleinow, he has generally been regarded as one of the two best performers ever to play the instrument. From 1970 on, if a musician wanted pedal steel on their album and if they could afford the very best, either Kleinow or Perkins would get the job. Thus, Al Perkins has worked with a wide variety of stars over the years, including Tori Amos, Garth Brooks, The Byrds, The Eagles, Wynonna Judd, Dolly Parton, Tommy Womack, and Yo La Tengo. He has been an actual member of several groups, including the Flying Burrito Brothers, Manassas (with Steve Stills), **Mason Proffit,** the Nash Ramblers (backing Emmylou Harris), Poco, and the Souther Hillman Furay Band.

Perkins has also been involved with Christian music from the very early days of the Jesus movement. He can be heard playing on early albums by such artists as **Albrecht, Roley, and Moore, Tom Autry, Jamie Owens-Collins, Jimmy Miller, Phoenix Sunshine, Salvation Air Force,** and **Shiloh.** He also emerged as a producer, and so was responsible for helming many of the most important albums of the decade, including projects by **Bethlehem, Daniel Amos, Don Francisco, Terry Talbot, The Pat Terry Group, Becky Ugartechea,** and **The Way.** In all cases, the fledgling artists benefitted from Perkins' generosity, as his contributions brought a level of competence far beyond what budgets at that time would have allowed. Thus, Perkins became the quintessential example of a Christian musician who straddled two worlds, moving equally in and out of "sacred" and "secular" realms without any regard for the artificial barriers being erected by gatekeepers in both camps. **Richie Furay,** with whom Perkins played in Poco and the Souther Furay Hillman band, would later credit Perkins with "leading him to Christ." Perkins was also a short-term member of two stellar Christian bands: **'Ark** and **Wing and a Prayer.**

Perkins would continue to show up on albums by a number of Christian artists throughout the '80s **(Phil Madeira)** and the '90s (**Brian Barrett, Sixpence None the Richer**). He produced projects by **Kate Campbell** and **Mid South.** In 1994, he took part in the **Hillman, Leadon, Perkins, and Scheff** adventure that yielded the independent album *Down Home Praise.*

Dave Perkins

1987—*The Innocence* (What?).

Dave Perkins established his credentials in Christian music as a producer for such artists as **Rick Cua, Servant,** and **Randy Stonehill.** He also worked in the secular market, backing such performers as Emmylou Harris, Carole King, and Jerry Jeff Walker. In the early '80s he played with **Ed Raetzloff** and wrote that artist's Christian radio hit, "Keep the Big Wheels Turning." For a time he fronted a Nashville-based group called The Dave Perkins Band, which commuted to play regular engagements in Greenwich Village and at a couple of New York City pubs. A *New York Times* critic described that group's sound as "acid country."

Perkins says he made *The Innocence* as an outlet for integrating his spiritual and socio-political beliefs. The album focuses on the problems facing America's cities and the implications that these have for the lives of often forgotten people. "I had to allow myself to become sensitized to the fact that there are people dying and starving, not only in Asia and Northern Africa, but on the streets of New York," he told *CCM.* "I put my children in the place of those children, and it made that anguish real to me for the first time." Musically, Perkins draws on the broad British background of guitar groups like The Animals, The Kinks, and The Yardbirds, though his more immediate influences seem to be modern students of The Byrds, like Tom Petty and R.E.M. The album's title track expresses dismay at the world's capacity to introduce fear into the lives of human beings at an early age. The album opener, "Revolution," connects social change and personal (spiritual) renewal. "You Can Make Me Feel" describes the awakening of a "heart of stone," and "Harvest Home" juxtaposes the biblical image for ultimate hope with the modern landscape of urban blight. "Every New Day" draws on Lamentations 3:23 to describe God's grace as a daily gift. Perkins also sings Pete Seeger's "Turn! Turn! Turn!" as a duet with **Steve Taylor.**

After his solo venture, Perkins went on to form **Chagall Guevara** with Lynn Nichols and **Steve Taylor.** His name would continue to pop up here and there throughout the '90s, playing with **The Newsboys** in 1992, fronting **Passafist** in 1994, and singing with **Rex Carroll** in 1995. As a songwriter, Perkins has also composed songs that were Christian radio hits for **Ed Raetzloff** ("Keep the Big Wheels Turning") and **Russ Taff** ("Walk Between the Lines").

Mike Peters

See **The Alarm.**

Andrew Peterson

2000—*Carried Along* (Watershed); 2001—*Clear to Venus.*

Andrew Peterson sings unhyphenated folk music in what the artist calls "a literal sense . . . music for the common people, that's not lofty, artsy, or hard to understand." In a story almost too good to be true, Peterson was discovered by **Caedmon's Call**'s Derek Woods, who read some of the artist's poems that were posted on the Internet and was so impressed that he invited the singer to play some concerts with the group. He ended up having Caedmon's Aaron Tate as his manager, with a contract to record for Watershed Records, which is headed up by Caedmon's Cliff Young. Peterson's style is quite similar to that of another Caedmon protégé, **Bebo Norman.** His songs tell "slice of life" stories and he sings in a voice vaguely reminiscent of **Bob Bennett** and James Taylor. *Carried Along* is not quite a solo production, as his wife Jamie and fellow guitarist Gabe Scott harmonize with him on several tracks. Many of Peterson's songs reflect on his relationship with God, which he says he began taking seriously as a young adult. A standout track, "Nothing to Say," reflects on the beauty of the Arizona countryside. "Faith to Be Strong" is a prayer for sustenance since "life is not long, but it is hard." Another prayer song, "Come, Lord Jesus," is offered with reference to personal failings and disillusionment with the church. *Clear to Venus* includes a cover of Mary Chapin Carpenter's "Why Walk When You Can Fly" and a previously unpublished poem of **Rich Mullins** that Peterson set to music ("Mary Picked the Roses"). The song "Loose Change" is about a penny languishing in a fountain. On "No More Faith," Peterson sings, "Have you wondered how He loves you / If He knows how dark you are inside?" Peterson attended Florida Christian College, just outside Orlando.

Michael Peterson

1986—*Michael Peterson* (Sparrow).

Michael Peterson attended Pacific Lutheran University in Tacoma, Washington, where he simultaneously pursued careers in music and athletics. He became involved with a group called Power Ministries that put on *That's Incredible*-style programs featuring musical selections and feats of skill or strength, woven together with personal testimonies from the presenters. Eventually, Peterson turned increasingly to songwriting, partly as catharsis for dealing with a number of painful experiences in his life: his parents divorced, his father was murdered, and his stepfather committed suicide. In 1985, Peterson would collaborate with **Deniece Williams** on two songs ("We're To-gether," "He Loves Me, He Loves Me Not") from her album *Hot on the Trail* (Columbia). The next year, he finally released an album of his own material. The music tends toward adult contemporary ballads ("Autumn Falls," "Beyond the Very Best") with songs like "Draw Me Near" giving way to R&B pop. On "Never Go Away," Peterson expresses the Christian doctrines of justification and sanctification in a succinct couplet: "I believe He accepts who I am today / But He loves me too much to leave me this way."

Petra

Bob Hartman, gtr., voc. (–1995, + 2001); John DeGroff, bass (–1979); Greg Hough, gtr. (–1979); Bill Glover, drums (–1977) // Rob Frazier, gtr., kybrd., voc. (+ 1979, – 1981); Mark Kelly, bass (+ 1981, – 1988); John Slick, kybrd. (+ 1981, –1985); Greg Volz, voc. (+ 1981; –1986); Louie Weaver, drums (+ 1982); John Lawry, kybrd, voc. (+ 1985, –1995); John Schlitt, voc. (+ 1986); Ronny Cates, bass (+ 1988, –1998); Jim Cooper, kybrd., voc. (+ 1995, –1998); David Lichens, gtr., voc. (+ 1995, –1998); Kevin Brandow, gtr. (+ 1998, – 2000); Lonnie Chapin, bass (+ 1998, – 2001); Pete Orta, gtr. (+ 1998, – 2001); Kevin Thomason, kybrd. (+ 2000, –2001). 1974—*Petra* (Myrrh); 1977—*Come and Join Us*; 1979—*Washes Whiter Than* (StarSong); 1981—*Never Say Die*; 1982—*More Power to Ya*; 1983—*Not of the World*; 1985—*Beat the System*; 1986—*Captured in Time and Space*; *Back to the Street*; 1987—*This Means War*; 1988—*On Fire!*; 1989—*Petra Means Rock*; *Petra Praise*; *The Rock Cries Out* (Word); 1990—*War and Remembrance: Fifteen Years of Rock* (StarSong); *Beyond Belief* (Word); 1991—*Unseen Power* (Word); 1991—*Petrafied: The Very Best of Petra* (StarSong); 1992—*Petraphonics*; 1993—*Wake-up Call* (Word); *Petra Power Praise* (StarSong); 1995—*The Rock Block*; 1995—*No Doubt* (Word); 1996—*The Early Years* (StarSong); 1997—*Petra Praise 2: We Need Jesus* (Word); 1998—*God Fixation*; 2000—*Double Take*; 2001—*Revival* (InPop).

Petra is generally regarded as Christian music's oldest and most successful rock band. The group's name derives from the Greek word used in the New Testament for "rock" in such theologically significant passages as Matthew 16:18. Petra was certainly not the first or the only group to be playing flat out rock and roll in the early days (cf. **Agape, Barnabas, Wilson-McKinley**) but they were easily the best known and—more to the point—were the only group to still be doing so on a regular basis five years later, much less *twenty-five* years later (**Resurrection Band,** a year older than Petra, would record pretty sporadically in the '90s). Reports of the band's persistence are easily exaggerated—given the numerous personnel changes throughout the years—and their highly publicized anniversary celebrations always seem a bit odd when, sometimes, not a single person at the party was actually in the band on the date being commemorated, but there has been a coherence to Petra's vision and style that belies the changing cast of characters listed above. In large part, that coherence owes to founder Bob Hartman, who continued to manage the group's affairs and

serve as their executive producer even after he gave up touring for family reasons and removed himself from the band's official roster. In a secondary sense, it owes to **John Schlitt,** who has served as lead vocalist for fifteen years. In 1997, Bob Hartman authored a devotional book titled *More Power to Ya,* which provides Bible studies and explains the messages behind a number of Petra songs. **Rob Frazier** and **Greg Volz** left Petra for solo careers, and **John Schlitt** also made successful solo albums on the side. In 1991, John Lawry also cut a solo album called *Media Alert* (StarSong), on which he was able to demonstrate his keyboard and programming skills to a degree not always evident in the band's guitar-based music. He later sang with **Forerunner.**

Petra has rarely been a favorite among critics. *HM* once said, "Petra sounds like Christian rock for kids whose parents don't let them listen to (real) rock," and *CCM* once referred to them as "the band that will not go away." Most, however, will at least, grudgingly, give the band its due. Part Def Leppard and part Air Supply, Petra is often regarded as a competent but not too original group of devoted overachievers—a work horse, not a race horse. Almost everyone will agree that they have churned out some pretty good stuff over the years, but just about everyone also thinks their output has been terribly inconsistent. Disagreements sometimes occur over *which* Petra period is to be preferred; the Volz or Schlitt argument largely parallels the Roth vs. Hagar debate among Van Halen fans. Ultimately, the group's staying power (and consequent significance for the world of contemporary Christian music) derives from two ironically compatible traits: a remarkable capacity to take abuse and an ability to compromise. The first trait helped them through the very difficult early years, when they were ridiculed outside the Christian community and maligned within it, especially in the early '80s when ever more radical bands like **Stryper** were arising that made Petra seem somewhat tame. Then something of a Petra backlash arose among critics who saw the group chart innumerable hits as one of the only "token rock bands" that Christian radio stations would play. So the abuse continued and now the group that had been despised for being "too hard" was trivialized as "not hard enough." They hung in there, and at least some of the hits were well deserved. In 1997, *Rolling Stone* magazine called Petra "one hell of a pop-metal band."

Bob Hartman was born in 1949 in Byron, Ohio. He attended Bowling Green University and then attended the Christian Training Academy in Ft. Wayne, Indiana. He formed Petra there with three fellow students. Hartman would later give CTA a lot of credit for supporting the band at a time when "Jesus-rock" was virtually unheard of and most conservative Bible schools were condemning rock and roll as intrinsically demonic. It helped, he said, that the members were all known to the staff as "people interested in communicating the gospel, not as simply a bunch of new Christians with a few wild ideas left over from days in 'the world'." The group played frequently at The Adam's Apple in Ft. Wayne—an important coffeehouse that was also headquarters for tamer artists like **Honeytree.** At this time, with the few exceptions mentioned above, most Christian groups played folk music or soft pop songs like **Love Song.** Unlike any of the exceptions, Petra somehow landed a contract with the premier Christian music label, Myrrh (a division of Word). Thus, they received potential nationwide distribution and received far more attention than any of the other Jesus rockers of the day. They were regarded (and in fact promoted) as the musical bad boys of Christian music, the dangerous avant garde who were pushing the new genre over the edge and into a new frontier.

The debut album, *Petra,* is a true classic of Christian rock in spite of the fact that, in retrospect, it isn't very good. The group would later admit that they hardly knew what they were doing and that their producer, Billy Ray Hearn, had never even tried to produce rock music before. The budget was slim and the band was especially weak in the vocal department (Hartman was de facto singer for the first and almost last time). The album produced only one truly memorable song ("Backslidin' Blues"), but at the time, it was unlike anything else that could be found in the Christian bookstores. *Petra* displays a southern rock sound more reminiscent of The Allman Brothers or Marshall Tucker Band than what would be heard on later projects. "Wake Up" features an extended electric guitar solo and became a major concert favorite when the group played the song with an extended jazz fusion introduction. "Walkin' in the Light" was another up-tempo guitar-driven concert favorite. "Get Back to the Bible" has a southern-fried boogie sound, with lyrics exposing the inefficacy of competing religions that vied for the attention of youth at the time (Hare Krishna, Satan worship). On several songs (especially "Gonna Fly Away" and "Mountains and Valleys") the group comes off as a **Larry Norman** rip-off band, a tendency accentuated by Hartman's pinched high vocals that sound quite similar to Norman's. The album only features one horrible embarrassment, the hillbilly novelty song "Lucas McGraw." But then there is "Backslidin' Blues," the first blues song in Christian rock and a strong example (for the time) of the genre. The song deserves special mention not only for its quality but because it would be selected from the album for inclusion on Myrrh's two-record *Jubilation* release (1975), a very important compilation set that introduced many people to contemporary Christian music. It was, perhaps, the only true rock song on that album, the one that many *Jubilation* owners would no doubt skip. But for others it held the strongest potential of anything in the collection. Years later, **Pete Stewart** of **Grammatrain**

would say, "My parents had this album of Christian music called *Jubilation* or something like that and it had this one song on it called 'Backslidin' Blues.'" The track was the only Petra song that many knew for at least five or six years, and it still remains one of their best.

Petra almost didn't get another chance. Poor promotion, ineffective marketing, and especially lack of opportunity for the band to tour insured that *Petra* would be a commercial failure. But three years later, Myrrh gave them another try, and they produced *Come and Join Us,* a far better album in every respect and, in the mind of some fans, the group's proudest moment. Louder and heavier than the debut, the record was intended by the band to serve as an evangelistic tool "to reach the unchurched and unsaved lover of rock music" (supposedly, it was going to get crossover distribution and airplay into the general market, but that never happened). Recognizing their weakness in the vocal department, the group recruited a number of different singers for their project (cf. **Kerry Livgren,** Santana). The guest singers include **Steve Camp, Austin Roberts** (who produced the album), and **Greg Volz,** who would eventually join the band. *Come and Join Us* opens with a cover of the song "God Gave Rock and Roll to You," an obscure track originally recorded by the one-hit-wonder band Argent (the British group led by ex-Zombies Rod Argent that took "Hold Your Head Up" to Number Five in 1972). It was written by Argent member Russ Ballard, a prolific rock songwriter who also penned Redbone's "Come and Get Your Love" (#5 in 1974) and numerous other hits for various artists. The glitz rock group Kiss would later make the song famous and many rock historians regard their definitive version as more a cover of Petra than of Argent. Volz sings that memorable song as well as another harder selection of *Come and Join Us,* "Woman Don't You Know," which features an instrumental jam and some inspired shouting and testifying. The entire album rocks with an intensity and an integrity that had never before appeared in any national Christian release. "Sally" asks why a person would want to "walk away from God and all His love." The song "Holy Ghost Power" could have been a Rare Earth-style anthem to the Pentecostal experience, but it is ruined by silly cartoon voices that turn it into another novelty track. The project also contains an altar-call ballad, "Ask Him In," sung by Hartman in his **Larry Norman** voice. But those are the only two downers. "Without You I Would Surely Die" displays well Hartman's rationale for why rock music is an appropriate medium for communicating the gospel. As he said at the time, "Rock music is *exciting* music, and there are very many things to be excited about in being a Christian."

Unfortunately, *Come and Join Us* did not sell particularly well either and Petra all but disbanded. "Those years were rough for us," Hartman would later recall, "There were times we literally didn't have any food to eat." Indeed, the group essentially *did* disband but Hartman put together a new version, recruiting Volz to join full time. Volz had formerly been a member of a seminal Christian rock group called simply **e** (or **e band**). He received the invitation to join Petra at approximately the same time that he was asked to take a position as lead vocalist for REO Speedwagon. A sacrificial commitment to ministry led him to turn down the obviously more lucrative offer in favor of fronting the new Petra. The group also signed to a new label and as part of the move agreed to a change in style that some Christian rock fans will forever cast as "the great sell-out." Convinced that real rock just wasn't going to make it in the Christian market, StarSong executives Darrell Harris and Wayne Donowho convinced Petra to morph into "a pop band" instead. "Some people accused us of selling out when we mellowed out," Hartman would say in 1982, "but there are no doubts in our mind that God was telling us to do so." Along with the stylistic change came a new vision. Hartman now saw the band's primary ministry as being to Christians. "We want to be an edification to the body of believers," he said. "We believe God has given us an ability to bring a release to people in their spirits and to free them to worship God in a new way." The group would continue to give altar calls and they encouraged fans to bring "unsaved friends" to concerts, but the focus shifted from an appeal for conversion to an affirmation of Christian self-esteem. "If those kids bring their friends," Volz told *HM*, "they're saying to us, 'Hey! Prove to my friends that it can be cool to be a Christian!' "

It is unlikely that many who liked the group's first two albums would find anything "cool" about the first StarSong release. Keyboards largely replace guitars and melodic vocal harmonies sustain the MOR project. *Washes Whiter Than* attracted some attention on the basis of a dopey easy listening single, "Why Would the Father Bother?" which the group admitted was recorded as a gratuitous ploy to get some radio airplay; it worked. That song, and others like "Yahweh Love" and "Taste and See," would have been right at home on the current **Imperials** project. This new image for the group was sealed with "The Coloring Song," the opening track on *Never Say Die*, which would unfortunately become one of Petra's biggest hits. A little ditty that sets nursery rhyme lyrics about the crucifixion ("red is the color of the blood that flowed") to a Sesame Street melody, "The Coloring Song" would only demonstrate for serious music lovers the extent to which Petra would denigrate themselves for a hit. *CCM* and other media extolled the song as the first song ever to become a major hit on the rock, adult contemporary, inspirational, and southern gospel charts, but that feat says far more about the state of Christian radio charts at the time than it does about the quality of the song (there is nothing even remotely "rock" about it). As if in pen-

ance, the group would follow it on the album with two power-pop songs ("Chameleon," "Angel of Light"), which traveled in the mode of bands like Journey or REO Speedwagon with progressive art-rock keyboards and some actual rock singing. Another track uses a creative lyric: "Killing My Old Man" is not an adolescent patricide fantasy but refers to the biblical notion of putting to death the "old" and sinful nature (Romans 6:6; Ephesians 4:22; Colossians 3:9). The closing song, "Praise Ye the Lord," previews the group's later interest in "power praise" (actually, both "Praise Ye the Lord" and "The Coloring Song" were old **e band** songs).

In 1981, the group hired Mark Hollingsworth to be their manager. John J. Thompson of *True Tunes* and others credit the young Hollingsworth with making all the difference in the band's career. A fan of Christian music from the early days and a former reviewer for *Harmony* magazine, Hollingsworth had also worked in general market radio. Soon, the band went from their hand-to-mouth existence to selling out huge arenas. Petra became Christian music's first "stadium-rock band" and, indeed, the genre's first "supergroup." The group put on a show just like that of Styx or **Kansas,** traveling with a stage set up that required three semi trucks and a crew of twenty (in fact, they actually bought **Kansas**'s light show after that group's *Audio Visions* tour and utilized the same equipment for their own productions). On their 1983 *More Power to Ya* tour, they also set a new paradigm for concert ministry by giving away free tickets for what was to be an evangelistic show. The band's next two albums would each sell over a million copies and, by extension, pull sales of their back-products up into the hundreds of thousands.

The music did get better, too. The sound of the new Petra would finally gel on *More Power to Ya,* an album of arena rock comparable in sound and quality to products produced by such acts as Foreigner, Journey, REO Speedwagon, Loverboy, 38 Special, or any number of other bands in the '80s. All of those groups were sometimes trashed by critics for being formulaic, and such complaints might have been leveled against Petra as well, but the Christian media was simply awed by the fact that this evangelical band was now cranking out music that was every bit as good (and no *more* uncreative) than what was arguably the most popular sound in America at the time. Tracks like "Second Wind," "Disciple," and "Stand Up" are powerful pop numbers that were just as infectious and hold up at least as well as "Any Way You Want It" (Journey), "Turn Me Loose" (Loverboy), or "Head Games" (Foreigner). Another rocker, "Judas' Kiss," laments lukewarm Christianity and hypocrisy as modern betrayals of the Lord. *CCM* called the album "a well-rounded product of exhortation, encouragement, and worship," selecting it as one of their Ten Best for the year. A year later, they bestowed the same honor on *Not of This World*. That album and *Beat the System* were both produced by **Jonathan David Brown** (who also did the next three projects). The band's sound did not change significantly on those two albums, except that synthesizers played an increasing role. More standout arena rock songs came in the form of "Grave Robber," "Bema Seat," and "Godpleaser" from *Not of This World,* and "Beat the System" and "Clean" from *Beat the System.* The latter album also features an *Alarma*-era **Daniel Amos** clone called "Computer Brains" in addition to a quirky new-wave remake of "God Gave Rock and Roll to You." Also worthy of mention is an excellent ballad addressing problems of world hunger called "Hollow Eyes"; Petra has been an early, constant, and strong supporter of the charitable organization Compassion International, to whom this song is dedicated. Throughout this period, Petra tended to score radio hits only with their softest and most atypical songs ("Not of This World," "Grave Robber").

Lyrics would not be a strength for the band at this stage of their career (Hartman is rarely empathetic or introspective), though they did show some improvement. The opening song on their debut had featured lines like, "Walkin' in the Light, every day and night / Livin' in the Spirit, really out of sight." By "Beat the System," even Hartman's cheerleader songs had a little more meat to them: "You can be more than a conqueror, you will never face defeat / You can dare to win by losing all, you can face the heat." A word should be said, however, about the band's penchant for militant imagery. Cover photos for both *Never Say Die* and *More Power to Ya* displayed the band destroying their enemies by firing upon them from guitar-shaped ships and space ships (respectively). The group sometimes wore camouflage-style fatigues or *Star Wars*-like space suits in their concerts. Lyrically, a great many of their songs present life as warfare and the world as a battleground. Of course, Petra interprets all of this in light of "spiritual warfare"—struggles against the world, the flesh, and the devil. Their reliance on such imagery is no more pronounced than that of equally apocalyptic Christian metal bands in the '80s, but it seems more disturbing due to the group's white-bread popularity. At the very time that Petra was making their classic '80s albums, most of America's major denominations were rethinking their use of such hymns as "Onward Christian Soldiers" or "The Battle Hymn of the Republic"—not because there is necessarily anything wrong with the hymns themselves (properly understood) but because the imagery appears to condone violence (at least violent thoughts) in the name of religion. Petra, like much of the contemporary Christian music culture, appeared completely oblivious to what was going on in the Christian church at large (witness the absence of inclusive language!). By 1980, most theologians and most church leaders had come to the conclusion that emphatic uses of militant imagery (and for that matter, dualistic rejections of the world) were antithetical

to the kingdom of God (cf. "Not of This World")—particularly in a society where violent persecution of Christians is virtually unknown (the biblical passages that use such language all derive from contexts where Christians experienced intense, violent rejection, not passive religious freedom). Indeed, in a context where Christians wield enormous social power and other religious groups—some of which Christians have persecuted—are in the minority, the triumphalist we-can-beat-up-everyone-else attitude comes off as inevitably threatening and terribly inappropriate, as future revelations regarding producer **Jonathan David Brown** would demonstrate. But for Hartman, it has always been a matter of us plus God vs. them. In terms of favorite Bible verses, he appears to prefer Matthew 12:30 to Mark 9:40.

In 1986, Volz left Petra, apparently as a result of personality clashes with Hartman, but also out of a desire to spend more time off the road with his family. In any case, a third phase of the band's career was born. Amidst many rumors of the band's breaking up, Hartman located and hired **John Schlitt,** former lead singer for the mainstream rock band Head East. The latter group was a quintet from St. Louis best known for their hit "Since You've Been Gone" (# 46 in 1978), which was ironically written by Russ Ballard. By the '80s Schlitt had become a Christian, left the band and, indeed, left music altogether—even to the point of no longer listening to the radio. He says he knew absolutely nothing about Christian music. But Hartman, who once had an extended conversation with Schlitt when the two had coincidentally been seated together on an airplane, heard of the man's conversion and tracked him down. The invitation to sing for a Christian band with a sound not too dissimilar from that of his former outfit struck Schlitt as a call from God—and a new version of Petra was born. Interestingly at the time, Schlitt knew practically nothing about the contemporary Christian music industry or subculture, and so harbored few expectations about what "Christian music" could or should sound like.

Schlitt's full and raspy voice convinced fans on *Back to the Street* that there may be life in the old Petra beast yet. The song "Shakin' the House" offers an especially good showcase for some rock shrieking beyond anything that Volz was ever able to deliver. *Back to the Street* was the group's first venture with producers **John** and Dino **Elefante,** famous for turning out slick products that critics often regard as over-produced but that have undeniable radio-friendly hit potential. The Elefantes cowrote the hits "Thankful Heart" (another adult contemporary worship ballad) and "King's Ransom" with Hartman, and they would continue to offer both production and compositional assistance on all of the group's remaining projects save one *(Wake-up Call).*

This Means War is a concept album focusing almost exclusively on the unfortunate militant themes mentioned above. But here, it gets even worse. The title song is a faux-metal anthem sung to the devil with a theme borrowed from **Carman**'s "Sunday's on the Way." The next track, "He Came, He Saw, He Conquered," applies the famous line uttered by Caesar to Jesus' triumph over death and hell. "Get on Your Knees and Fight Like a Man" promises similar victory to the one who is fervent in prayer. While any such song might be theologically orthodox as an isolated instance, an album full of them amounts to a denial of the cross—or at least a loss of perspective that treats the cross only as a mark of triumph and victory, but not as an emblem of suffering and shame. Petra seems to lose all contact with reality (and with Scripture) on *This Means War,* and any call to Christian humility, service, or sacrifice goes down the tubes. Instead, the dominant message is one of overcoming faith that will bulldoze anyone or anything that stands in its way. This is the ideology that fueled the Crusades and the Inquisition, and Christians who are keen to its abuses are suspicious when it is invoked. The fact that the band was involved in a **Carman**esque political campaign supporting a Constitutional amendment that would legislate prayer in public schools was a good indication that the band's enemies had shifted already from the world, the flesh, and the devil to include skeptics, liberals, and heretics. By *This Means War,* Petra's central message had become, "Look out, world! The (fundamentalist) Christians are coming and not only Moslems and Jews, but Roman Catholics, mainline Protestants, and average American citizens have good reason to fear them." Reflecting on this album and on similar themes in the music of **Russ Taff,** the **Allies,** and **DeGarmo and Key,** Christian music's senior statesman **John Fischer** wrote, "Mass self-righteousness is a terribly dangerous and powerful thing. Hitler built his regime on it. Cries of 'We're right and everyone else out there is wrong. We're gonna win! We're gonna be vindicated! God is on our side!' can create an emotional blind that masks an evil greater than if evil were personified."

After such a bad album, the group came back with *On Fire!,* a better production musically and theologically. The record that *CCM* would call "one of the best Petra albums to date" was also their hardest rocking experience (Schlitt would later complain that it had "gravitated too much toward metal"). "All Fired Up" and "Hit You Where You Live" are screaming masterpieces, and "Counsel of the Holy" is a strong Bon Jovi-type power-ballad (with more emphasis on power than ballad). Only one track ("Mine Fields") relies on the very tired "life is a battlefield" theme; "Homeless Few" is another compassionate song reminiscent of "Hollow Eyes," and "First Love" is actually confessional and personal. Petra changed labels after *On Fire,* recording with Word for the rest of their career. Over the next few years, StarSong would release no fewer than seven compilation albums repackaging songs from the nine records they had released with the label: *Petra Means Rock; War and Remembrance; Petrafied; Petraphonics; Petra Power Praise; The Rock Block; The Early Years.* The label perhaps deserves some sort of award for commercial chutzpah, especially considering that many of the projects were released without the band's permission and, indeed, over its objections. John Schlitt would say it best: "Every time we put out a new, legitimate Petra record, they put out a combination of songs, call it 'best of,' and ride on the momentum of our new record, which has done nothing but hurt us. It's a scam. It's ungodly, it's uncool, and we're embarrassed." That said, the best of the best-ofs would be *Petra Means Rock* or, if one prefers the mellow stuff, *Petraphonics.*

Petra entered the '90s with the strong likelihood of being regarded as an irrelevant dinosaur band but, like Aerosmith, they transcended those expectations and earned themselves a new lease on life. Indeed, their best decade still lay ahead of them. It did not start out well, however. *Beyond Belief* retreads the old themes and opens with yet another song that presents Christians as "armed and dangerous" warriors who the enemies of God had *better* fear, if they know what's good for them. While it may seem incredible that a Christian group would actually call a song about the Christian presence in the world "Armed and Dangerous," Petra was neither the first nor the last to do so. **Matthew Ward** had already trotted out an even worse song—and a whole album—by that name in 1987. And **DeGarmo and Key** decided it was worth a third go in 1993. But "Armed and Dangerous" is the only Christians-as-hate-group song on an otherwise solid album. "Creed" sets lyrics based loosely on The Apostles' Creed to a passionate tune in a way that helps to connect the band's ministry with mainline Christianity. "Underground" provides more driving arena rock, and "I Am on the Rock" captures the band's Def Leppard sound with shades of "Pour Some Sugar on Me." The song "Love" presents the words of 1 Corinthians 13 as an acoustic ballad, extolling all the qualities (patience, gentleness, humility) that were disregarded in the album's opener. "Prayer" is another quiet moment, offering appropriately humble thanksgiving for mercy undeserved. When a 2001 poll commissioned by *CCM* magazine selected the "100 Greatest Albums in Christian Music," *Beyond Belief* was one of only two Petra projects to make the list (at Number Seventy-one, with *More Power to Ya* at Number Ninety-eight).

Unseen Power would prove to be one of the band's most diverse and experimental outings. While maintaining their basic hard rock groove on almost-metal songs like "Destiny," "Ready, Willing, and Able," and "Dance," the group also added some R&B spice to their mix. "Who's on the Lord's Side?" (written by the Rev. Timothy Wright) finds Petra backed by what sounds like a full traditional gospel choir; it is one of the most exciting tunes the band has ever recorded. Likewise, the ballad "Hand on My Heart" sounds like something right out of the Smokey Robinson catalogue. "I Need to Hear from You" is a more conventional power-pop song, expressing the thoughts of one who is waiting on divine direction. *HM* declared *Unseen Power* "Petra's best to date" and even a non-Petra-loving, Elefante-bashing critic like Bruce Brown (for *CCM*) had to give the boys and their producers high marks for this effort.

For *Wake-up Call,* Petra broke with the Elefante tradition for one album only and switched to producer **Brown Bannister.** His influence or some other combination of factors (the passage of time) allowed the group to emerge with a more mature perspective that remains challenging without all the phony bravado. "Marks of the Cross" deserves special commendation in this regard; it combines a folk melody and a catchy chorus in a worshipful song about service and sacrifice. And on "He's Been in My Shoes," Hartman demonstrates that he has finally learned how to draw on his own brokenness for a more moving and persuasive message: "I am lonely, forsaken again," he begins in a song that almost appears to repudiate a lot of the band's previous material. "I'm wounded and left here to bleed, with no solace from a stranger or friend." Needless to say, this image of a fallen soldier crying for mercy and healing offers a far more effective medium for presenting the gospel of Christ than that of invincible, armor-clad warriors mowing down their enemies in the name of God. But discovering humility (or, perhaps, discovering the gospel) did not cause Petra to wimp out or lose its prophetic edge. The album title relates to the song "Sleeping Giant," which portrays the institutional church as a drowsy behemoth that needs to hear an alarm. "Midnight Oil" is another strong rock track based on the biblical story of the bridesmaids in Matthew 25:1–13. "Just Reach Out" is a closing power ballad written by John Schlitt.

It was after the triumph of *Wake-up Call* that Hartman, the founder and only charter member of Petra, decided it was time to quit. By this time, however, Schlitt had been with the band in a prominent way long enough that he was perhaps the member most responsible for defining the group's sound. Thus, the band determined to continue. Hartman wrote or cowrote almost all of the songs on *No Doubt* anyway, and he played lead guitar (as a guest) on the album. Indeed, some critics complained that if there was a problem with *No Doubt,* it was that the album sounded too much like Petra's other albums, continuing with a sound that had pretty much been run into the ground, whereas the personnel change might have afforded an opportunity to try something new. But the album would delight Petra fans. "Enter In" draws on the theology of the epistle to the Hebrews to describe Christ's atoning sacrifice as the basis for access to God. "No Doubt" sounds a lot like an old Styx ballad ("Babe," "Don't Let It End") and expresses well the need for people of little faith to place their hope in the faithfulness of God (what God will "no doubt" do). Similarly, the tough rocker "Right Place" describes "trusting God" as the right place to be even when the situation seems hopeless. "Sincerely Yours" and "We Hold Our Hearts to You" are soft worship songs of surrender and devotion.

God Fixation found Schlitt and senior member Louie Weaver (formerly of **Fireworks**) fronting an entirely new band (with Hartman still composing and playing guitar as a "non-member") that would only endure for two albums. Schlitt had fired two of the other members (Jim Cooper, David Lichens) and replaced them with two musicians he had used in his work as a solo artist (Kevin Brandow, Pete Orta). The result was a band with a modern rock sound so distinct from anything Petra had done before that *HM* had to question why the group hadn't just changed its name (Schlitt responded that, duh, the name "Petra" carries a pretty marketable recognition factor). In any case, the songs on *God Fixation* still show some signs of '80s arena rock: "Falling Up" and "Shadow of a Doubt" sound like Styx outtakes. But "A Matter of Time" features some growling guitars that draw from the **Collective Soul** well, and "Hello Again" features the distinctive neo-Beatles sound favored by such modern rockers as Oasis. With such up-to-date influences, *God Fixation* would prove to be one of the group's most innovative and strongest albums. Then, sensing correctly that people might say "Petra doesn't sound like Petra anymore," the group re-recorded a whole slew of their classic songs (ones they planned to play in concert) and released these as *Double Take.* The good news would be that most of the songs sounded better in the new style than in their original versions. The bad news, however, was that it was painfully apparent that several of the tracks the group dredged up from the past ("The Coloring Song," "He Came, He Saw," "This Means War") had never been any good to begin with. Hartman's abilities and, especially, his theology had so improved over the years that New Petra doing Old Petra sometimes cannot help but come off as a strong band with weak material. But *Double Take* also includes two new songs that are special treats ("Breathe In," written by Pete Orta, and "The Longing" by Joel Hanson of **PFR** fame). Shortly after *Double Take* was released, all of the new Petra members left (**Pete Orta** launched a solo career) and Petra was released from its longstanding contract. Schlitt and Weaver persuaded Hartman to come back on board (officially) and the trio recorded the excellent album *Revival* for InPop.

Revival is a worship album, following in some respects in the tradition of two other classic albums the band had recorded over the years. *Petra Praise* had set new standards for the genre of "praise and worship music" with strong rock versions of classic songs by **Keith Green, Rich Mullins, Michael W. Smith,** and **Billy Sprague;** the 1989 album outsold all previous Petra projects and earned the group its first gold record. On *Petra Praise 2* the band would be joined by such guest vocalists as **John Elefante** (formerly with **Kansas**) and **Lou Gramm** (formerly with Foreigner) to offer a funky southern rock version of Rick Founds' "Lord, I Lift Your Name on High." They also provide an innovative take on **Billy Batstone**'s "I Waited for the Lord on High," and they serve up several original numbers. As strong as those albums are, *Revival* is much better, truly transcending the "praise and worship" category with the sound of a straightforward modern rock album. In fact, Petra seems more up-to-date than ever, as though Hartman and company had been listening to a lot of **Newsboys** and **Audio Adrenaline** albums. The opening "Send Revival, Start with Me" (a remake of an old song) has an infectious and pleading quality to it that breaks at about the two-minute mark into a quirky choral rock song with overtones of Boston or Queen. "The Noise We Make" begins with Middle Eastern chanting and is built around some innovative and unpredictable percussion. The band also delivers what may be history's most rocking version of "Amazing Grace," and they cover **Matt Redman**'s "Better Is One Day."

In 1996, a number of contemporary Christian music's biggest stars put together a tribute album for Petra called *Never Say Dinosaur* (StarSong). The song selection was worthy but for some strange reason featured only pre-1984 songs from the group's pre-Schlitt incarnations. Nevertheless, many of the renditions were innovative and inspiring; highlights include **Audio Adrenaline**'s "Taste and See," **MxPx**'s "I Can Be Friends with You," **Jars of Clay**'s "Rose Colored Stained Glass Windows," **Sixpence None the Richer**'s "Road to Zion," **Grammatrain**'s "Wake Up," and **PlankEye**'s "All the King's Horses."

Petra deserves credit for opening the minds of fundamentalist and conservative Christians (not an easy task) with regard to the viability of rock music as a medium for Christian expression. Even after the early days of standing out like a throbbing thumb amongst the plethora of hippie Jesus music groups, they faced the bigotry of such big-name fundamentalist leaders as Bill Gothard, Jimmy Swaggart, and David Wilkerson. They persevered and eventually earned the vocal support of Josh McDowell, a semi-fundamentalist evangelist popular with youth organizations. Nevertheless, for many years, Petra was Christian music's best-selling band (selling over six million total units). As late as 1995, they set a new record as the first artist ever to have four albums on Christian music's Top 100 chart simultaneously (*No Doubt; Beyond Belief; Petra Praise; Wake-up Call*), a feat that is even more impressive since none of the four were compilations of previously released material. The group was the only Christian act invited to play at the historic Farm Aid Festival (1992), and they were the first Christian band to be enshrined in the Hard Rock Café. In 2000, in what amounted to an act of repentance on the part of the Gospel Music Association, the band became the first rock group ever to be inducted into the Gospel Music Hall of Fame. Petra has won four Grammy awards in addition to their numerous Doves and has charted more songs as Christian radio hits than any other artist classified as "rock."

Petra has also, always, kept a primary commitment to ministry and spoken of membership in the band as "a calling." In the '70s, Hartman said, "We are not musicians who happen to be Christians; we are Christians who happen to be musicians. *Ministry* is why we do what we do." In 1983, he would respond to charges that the band's style was too secular by saying, "We are missionaries, and missionaries must learn the language of the people they are trying to reach." In 1996, he would reveal that the band had turned down occasional offers for a crossover career: "We were told that we could do a lot more if we were less gospel and more just inspirational or positive. What that translates to is, 'Take the Jesus out. We can deal with God. We can deal with good times and good feelings and family and all that, but take Jesus out.' . . . No stinkin' way. Jesus stays in because He is everything. If I can't talk about Jesus, there is no sense in doing this."

Christian radio hits: "Why Should the Father Bother" (# 3 in 1979); "Yahweh Love" (# 20 in 1979); "The Coloring Song" (# 8 in 1981); "More Power to Ya" (# 13 in 1983); "Not of This World" (# 3 in 1984); "Grave Robber" (# 22 in 1984); "Hollow Eyes" (# 7 in 1985); "Beat the System" (# 2 in 1985); "Witch Hunt" (# 13 in 1985); "Voice in the Wind" (# 13 in 1986); "Back to the Street" (# 5 in 1986); "Thankful Heart" (# 3 in 1986); "Whole World" (# 13 in 1987); "King's Reunion" (# 13 in 1987); "Don't Let Your Heart Be Hardened" (# 1 for 4 weeks in 1987); "I Am Available" (# 8 in 1988); "Get on Your Knees and Fight Like a Man" (# 10 in 1988); "First Love" (# 1 for 6 weeks in 1989); "Homeless Few" (# 2 in 1989); "Open Book" (# 2 in 1989); "Onward Christian Soldiers" (# 14 in 1989); "We Exalt Thee" (# 8 in 1990); "Salvation Belongs to Our God" (# 23 in 1990); "Prayer" (# 1 for 2 weeks in 1990); "Love" (# 3 in 1991); "Beyond Belief" (# 3 in 1991); "I Need to Hear from You" (# 1 for 4 weeks in 1992); "Hand on My Heart" (# 1 for 2 weeks in 1992); "Who's on the Lord's Side" (# 23 in 1993); "I Don't Want to Fall Away from You" (# 11 in 1993); "Just Reach Out" (# 1 for 6 weeks in 1994); "Marks of the Cross" (# 1 for 3 weeks in 1994); "He's Been in My Shoes" (# 12 in 1994); "Praying Man" (# 9 in 1994); "No Doubt" (# 8 in 1995); "Sincerely Yours" (# 3 in 1996); "We Hold Out Our Hearts to You" (# 16 in 1996); "Enter In" (# 17 in 1996); "We Need Jesus" (# 6 in 1997); "The Holiest Name" (# 11 in 1997); "Lord, I Lift Your Name on High" (# 13 in 1997); "If I Had to Die for Someone" (# 11 in 1998).

Dove Awards: 1991 Group of the Year; 1991 Rock Album (*Beyond Belief*); 1991 Rock Song ("Beyond Belief"); 1993 Rock Song ("Destiny"); 1994 Rock Album (*Wake-up Call*); 1996 Rock Album (*No Doubt*); 1998 Praise and Worship Album (*Petra Praise 2: We Need Jesus*).

Grammy Awards: 1990 Best Rock/Contemporary Gospel Album (*Beyond Belief*); 1992 Best Rock/Contemporary Gospel Album (*Unseen Power*);

1994 Best Rock Gospel Album *(Wake-up Call)*; 2000 Best Rock Gospel Album *(Double Take).*

Pierce Pettis

1988—*While the Serpent Lies Sleeping* (High Street); 1991—*Tinseltown*; 1993—*Chase the Buffalo*; 1996—*Making Light of It* (Compass); 1998—*Everything Matters*; 2001—*State of Grace.*

Alabama folk singer Pierce Pettis is an artist who belongs to the same acoustic-based tradition as **T Bone Burnett, Bruce Cockburn,** and **Mark Heard.** He is better known within the general market than in the contemporary Christian music arena but, as a devout Christian, he frequently writes and sings material reflective of his faith. Pettis actually considered a career in Christian music briefly, and one of his earliest recorded songs was a track called "7 x 70" on a Christian sampler CD called *Twelve New Faces* (1988). Even before that, he had seen some of his songs recorded by such artists as Joan Baez, **Dion,** and **Randy Stonehill.** But then the general market label Windham Hill determined to create a subdivision called High Street for singer/songwriter types and Pettis was invited to be their premiere artist, an offer he felt he should not refuse. His debut album, *While the Serpent Lies Sleeping,* would feature "7 x 70" in addition to two songs that express a yearning for Christ to return and usher in the kingdom ("The Longing," "Come Home"). *Tinseltown* was produced by **Mark Heard** and includes an overtly religious song called "Swimming" (about the struggles of faith that often hide behind images). On *Chase the Buffalo,* Pettis covers Heard's "Nod over Coffee" and sings a song of compassion for AIDS victims called "Stickman." The third album also features "Lions in the Coliseum," which equates the beasts of Rome with greedy preachers or evangelists who seek to devour Christians (or at least their pocketbooks).

Pettis's faith-orientation would become increasingly noticeable on his Compass releases. He had the assistance of both Deri Daugherty and **Steve Hindalong** of **The Choir** on *Making Light of It.* That album opens with Heard's "Satellite Sky" and also includes a couple of biblical epics: "Miriam," about the young girl (a.k.a. Mary) who would bear the Savior of the world, and "Absalom, Absalom," which relates King David's lament over his murdered, rebellious son with appropriate empathy: "All the vanity, cruel arrogance, and greed / Absalom, you learned it all from me." In a song called "My Life of Crime," Pettis acknowledges the role that pursuit of his career played in the destruction of his marriage, and in "You Move Me" he recalls a time he felt the peace of God's presence after going through a gut-wrenching divorce. "It was my first Christmas alone," Pettis told *CCM,* "but the best I've ever had. I got up that morning and had a Pop Tart and a cup of coffee. There were no decorations and I was sitting in the kitchen, looking out the window." Written with Gordon Kennedy of

Dogs of Peace, the song would later be covered by both **Susan Ashton** and Garth Brooks. It includes the poignant lines, "Here's how life seems to me / Life is just therapy / Real expensive, and no guarantee." Another standout song, "Love's Gonna Carry Me Home," is a testimony to undeserved affection: "Amazing grace, big surprise / Hits you right between the eyes / Hits you hard, like a small flat stone / Slays your giants and leads you home." Kennedy produced his next album, *Everything Matters,* which includes "Love Will Find a Way," a beautiful love song to his (new) wife, and "My Little Girl," a song for his daughter. A creative song called "Just Like Jim Brown (She Is History)" draws a lesson for life from the career of the football player who retired while he was still in good form: "Jim knew something fools don't know / He knew when it was time to go." On "Hole in My Heart," Pettis sings about the frustration of praying continually with no clear sign of being heard. But then on "God Believes in You," he affirms a basic evangelical tenet: "When your light burns so dim / And you swear you don't believe in Him / God believes in you." Another song, "Kingdom Come," is about the life of St. Paul. The most poignant thought, however, comes in the song "Comet," on which Pettis discloses the mystery of how God ultimately works: "Doesn't God look out for children and for fools / Who can blindly stumble right into the truth / Till all the pieces fit into a grand design / A brilliant accident we had coming all the time." The album also includes a cover of Heard's "Tip of My Tongue." *State of Grace* includes two covers (Heard's "Rise from the Ruins" and **Bob Dylan'**s "Down in the Flood"). "Long Way Back Home" (cowritten with Gordon Kennedy, cf. **Dogs of Peace**) offers this observation: "The only difference 'tween the pilgrim and the prodigal son / Is the difference 'tween the dream and the thing you become."

The abundance of **Mark Heard** covers on Pettis's albums is deliberate. Pettis cites Heard as one of his greatest influences and counts his chance to work with the artist on *Tinseltown* as one of his great life experiences. Ironically, Pettis performed with Heard only once—at the famous 1992 *Cornerstone* concert at which Heard had a heart attack on stage. Heard died within a week, but Pettis continued to feel a personal loyalty to him and to his material. He has said that he always intends to include one song by Heard on each of his albums as a tribute to his friend and mentor, and also as a way of introducing audiences to Heard's incredible catalogue of largely unknown material: "This man was probably the best songwriter that this genre of music is ever going to produce," Pettis told *True Tunes* in 1998. "There are all these brilliant songs that nobody's heard."

As to whether Pettis considers himself to be "a Christian singer," he says that, while he is certainly a Christian, he does not write songs that are contrived to present the message of

Christianity. He thinks God has called him to be an artist, not a minister, and that he serves God best by creating songs that have artistic merit. "My purpose is not persuading people," he told *CCM* in 1997. "I would be delighted if someone would consider the gospel because of something I might have said, but that's something God does. He might use me, but then He might use someone who hates the gospel in a way that causes people to consider the alternative."

PFR (a.k.a. **Pray For Rain**)

Patrick Andrew, bass, voc.; Joel Hanson, voc., gtr.; Mark Nash, drums, voc. By Pray For Rain: 1992—*Pray For Rain* (Vireo). By PFR: 1993— *Goldie's Last Day* (Vireo); 1994—*Great Lengths*; 1996—*Them*; 1997—*The Late, Great PFR*; 2001—*Disappear* (Squint).

PFR was perhaps the most popular of the Christian neo-Beatles groups that rode the wave of alternative-retro appreciation for melody in the mid '90s. The group's origins were even more directly related to church summer camp youth ministry than is normally the case with such guitar-strumming pop bands. Hanson and Nash met at Camp Shamineau in Minnesota, where Hanson was music director and Nash was a counselor. They formed a two-piece and later recruited one of the youth (Andrew) to play bass. The group was first known as Inside Out and they did typical evangelism and worship programs for youth groups. Andrew himself "accepted Christ" at their second concert. Eventually they came to the attention of **Steve Camp,** who hooked them up with Jimmie Lee Sloas (of **The Imperials** and **Dogs of Peace**), who would produce all of their albums. They decided to record under a new name, Pray For Rain, which turned out to be an unfortunate choice as there was already another group with that moniker. Lawyers convinced them to shorten it to PFR. The group crafted a sound that was strongly influenced by the Beatles, but also by such artists as Dan Fogelberg, The Byrds, and R.E.M. Their albums are roughly comparable in sound and often in quality with works by Crowded House, the Rembrandts, and Toad the Wet Sprocket. They, in turn, were a primary influence on **Jars of Clay** and **Smalltown Poets.** In 1996, Mark Nash married Leigh Bingham (thus Leigh Nash) of **Sixpence None the Richer.** Joel Hanson is the brother of Jade Hanson of **Believable Picnic.** After PFR disbanded, Patrick Andrew formed **Eager,** but he joined the others for the 2001 reunion.

The self-titled debut album shows the group developing its sound. Standout tracks include "Let Go," which encourages listeners not to hang on to their problems, and the very catchy "Do You Want to Know Love?" The group was nominated for a Dove award for New Artist of the Year and took home the trophy for Rock Album of the Year. *Goldie's Last Day* takes its title from a song about the death of Andrew's dog—a bittersweet and, yet, sort of fun song that remains a bit of a novelty. Hits

like "That Kind of Love" are a bit too camp-counselor predictable in their acoustic sound and devout lyrics, but "I Don't Understand" reveals more of an edge. It is what Andrew would call "a question song" (as opposed to an answer song). "It's kind of like asking God, 'Why are these things happening to me?'," he told *CCM.* Other strong tracks include "Walk Away from Love," which has a bit of a **King's X** sound to it, and "Satisfied," which indicates (contra **Andraé Crouch**'s song by that name) that a Christian is never satisfied, but always growing, changing, and learning. "Spinnin' Round" was a Number One hit on Christian Rock charts. The album concludes with "Wait for the Sun," which segues into a cover of "Let the Sunshine In" from *Hair.*

Great Lengths opens with a title track that is a pop masterpiece, with beautiful harmonies that almost hide the pain of its confessional lyrics: "Why didn't I go to such great lengths to try to please you?" Almost as good is "The Grace of God," a pulsating, rhythmic track that extols its titular subject to a tune that could easily have been employed by Crowded House. The band's range of styles is further demonstrated in "Last Breath," which again evokes **King's X,** and "The Love I Know," which sounds just like Bread. "It's You Jesus" sounds a lot like **Jars of Clay** (or is that the other way around?). The group also covers **Keith Green**'s "Trials Turned to Gold" and performs two songs written by Gordon Kennedy of **Dogs of Peace** ("Life Goes On," "Merry Go Round"). *Them* is the album that could have made PFR competitive artistically in the general market. Its opening track, "Pour Me Out," had at least as much right to be a college radio hit as, say, Blind Melon's "No Rain" or Alice in Chains' "No Excuses." It has the same moody, psychedelic, ethereal quality—as does the album's title track (a rant against media). "Anything" and "Ordinary Day" are particularly Beatlesque, catchy, hook-filled pop songs with a happy-go-lucky sound that runs counterpoint to the hidden probing of their lyrics. "Garden" is a beautiful yet powerful ballad, and the song "Daddy Never Cried" displays deeply soul searching lyrics that reveal an unusually vulnerable side of the band. *The Late Great PFR* is a "greatest hits" collection with three new songs. PFR also contributed a song ("We Can Work It Out," played with **Phil Keaggy**) to the **Michael Omartian**-produced tribute album, *Come Together: America Salutes the Beatles* (Capitol, 1995).

In 2001, the band suddenly rose from the dead, reuniting four years after a much heralded farewell concert to produce another album for **Steve Taylor**'s Squint label. The reunion got a proleptic start with a one-song contribution ("Kingdom Come") to Squint's *Roaring Lambs* compilation album (2000). The ironically titled *Disappear* was the band's first post-Matchbox 20/Third Eye Blind album and so had the group compared to those acts. *HM* styled the songs "Gone" and "All

Ready" as tunes "that intrigue at first and then become addictive after just a few listens." Extreme Beatlesque moments come into play here and there ("Closer," "Even a Whisper"). "Missing Love" is a stellar rock ballad that showcases Andrew's voice. The closing track, "You," has a mysterious psychedelic-waltz quality that sets it apart from everything else. The record features songs that avoid obvious Christian slogans or religious language, while expressing an undeniable spirituality for those with ears to hear. Andrew explains that the opener, "Amsterdam," is about a time when he felt he had a greater sense of purpose in life and wanted to rekindle his passion for Christ.

Music historians such as Mark Joseph attribute significance to PFR's aforementioned song "Goldie's Last Day." Although it may seem odd to anyone not acquainted with the confining strictures of the contemporary Christian music culture, the tune sparked a good deal of controversy at the time it was released—not because there is anything controversial about the song but only because there is nothing *religious* about it. It is simply a song (as Joseph says) about "life in the real world, where dogs usually die long before their human friends." As such, there is no noticeable difference between "Goldie's Last Day" and songs that would be played on regular Top 40 radio. The question was, what makes it "a Christian song" and a candidate for airplay on Christian stations? The concern seems ridiculous, since one of the basic tenets of Christianity is that faith encompasses all of life, not just religious matters. But the question was raised nonetheless and PFR ended up serving as the forerunners to **Sixpence None the Richer** in challenging silly assumptions that undergird much of the contemporary Christian music industry's activities and (it must be admitted) sometimes serve as its raison d'etre. Joseph says that ultimately PFR's greatest contribution to contemporary Christian music (though certainly not their best song) was "their magical song about Goldie the pooch, which showed a generation of young contemporary Christian music fans that rock bands comprised of Christians could and would sing about anything—and that this was entirely proper in the eyes of God."

For trivia buffs: While attending the Grammy awards in Los Angeles in 1993, PFR had to rescue singer/satirist Weird Al Yankovic when his car broke down. They took him to a party and suggested that he do a parody of one of *their* songs. He didn't.

Christian radio hits: "Do You Want to Know Love?" (# 10 in 1992); "Pray for Rain" (# 8 in 1993); "Home Again" (# 13 in 1993); "That Kind of Love" (# 1 for 3 weeks in 1994); "Wait for the Sun" (# 2 in 1994); "Great Lengths" (# 1 in 1995); "The Love I Know" (# 4 in 1995); "The Grace of God" (# 1 for 2 weeks in 1995); "Blind Man, Deaf Boy" (# 16 in 1995); "Trials Turned to Gold" (# 16 in 1995); "Anything" (# 2 in 1996); "Line of Love" (# 5 in 1996); "Ordinary Day" (# 9 in 1997); "Forever" (# 5 in 1997); "Kingdom Love" (# 15 in 2000); "Missing Love" (# 2 in 2001).

Dove Awards: 1993 Rock Album *(Pray For Rain)*.

Phantasmic

Tess Wiley, voc., gtr., kybrd.; et al. 1996—*Fluffy Vs. Phantasmic* (Flying Tart); 1998—*I Light Up Your Life*.

Phantasmic was an almost novelty project fronted by Tess Wiley, one-time guitarist for **Sixpence None the Richer.** Wiley hooked up with bizarro producer Chris Colbert, front man for both **Breakfast with Amy** and **Fluffy** (a.k.a. **Duraluxe**) and in 1996 she recorded five of her songs with him, backed by various musicians (including Colbert and Fluffy/**Hoi Polloi** bassist Troy Daugherty). Instead of releasing an EP, Colbert put the songs out on a CD padded with five tracks from Fluffy's *Sugar Pistol* album (plus, for some reason, a bonus song from **Joe Christmas**). The five Phantasmic tracks reveal a basic '90s female-grunge sound not too dissimilar from Courtney Love or Liz Phair, but none of the songs is a standout ("Rainy Day Assembly" appears to be a misplaced Sixpence track with Wiley on lead vocals). In search of stronger material, Wiley next recorded an entire album of disparate cover songs called *I Light Up Your Life.* The famous **Debby Boone** track ("You Light Up My Life") is included along with Michael Jackson's "Say, Say, Say," Pat Benatar's "Love Is a Battlefield," The Misfits' "I Turned into a Martian," and Level 42's "Something about You." All of these are performed in an '80s Deborah Harry style with some flourishes of postmodern Colbertisms: Nazareth's "Love Hurts" is performed in a disembodied voice with the noise of a running film projector as a backdrop. Slight Christian content is introduced with a cover of another song called "Love Hurts," namely the one written by then-Christian pop star **Leslie Phillips.** Wiley released an independent solo album called *Rainy Day Assembly* at the end of 2001.

Phat Chance

Brandon Johnson, gtr., kybrd., voc.; Brent Lain, gtr.; Dallas Morgan, drums; Justin Keith Morgan, bass; Bryan Nance, voc., gtr. 2001—*Without You* (Flicker).

Phat Chance is a band of all-male teens from North Carolina, but their sound is much more similar to Smash Mouth than the expected *NSYNC—sugary harmonies are less prominent than power guitar chords and vibrant hook-filled melodies. The group's debut album was produced by Tony Palacios (of **Guardian**) and Jason Burkum (of **Believable Picnic**), and generous songwriting assistance was offered by Scotty Wilbanks, formerly of **NewSong.** The album's standout track is probably the opening "Sunshine Daylight," which is sort of a lyrical cross between Guardian's "Bottle Rocket" and *Hair!*'s "Let the Sunshine In." Lyrically, the album is strongly evangelical, with "Love Somebody" celebrating God's acceptance of the undeserving. "Just a Little" is worshipful, and "The One" pairs male and female vocals (courtesy of Dawn Chere) in an ode to premarital sexual abstinence.

Phatfish

Louise Fellingham, voc.; Luke Fellingham, bass; Nathan Fellingham, drums; Alan Rose, gtr.; Michael Sandemann, kybrd. 1999—*Purple through the Fishtank* (Pamplin).

Phatfist is neither an urban hip-hop band nor a Phish knock-off group as their name might imply, but a British praise and worship band with roots in acid-jazz and funk. They started out as Purple Phatfish and apparently recorded four independent albums in the United Kingdom (one titled *We Know the Story* was released on Survivor Records). *Purple through the Fishtank* was their first album to receive international distribution. On it, the group moves decidedly toward a mainstream pop sound, losing much of the jazz-funk sound in the process. *True Tunes* would say, "their new sound is stronger and more commercial, at the cost of the band's distinctive edge." All of the songs are praise oriented, but they are full rock songs (on the order of **Delirious?, Fono,** or **Matt Redman**) rather than simple choruses. Louise Fellingham's lead vocals were described by *Christian Music* as "a cross between **Out of the Grey**'s Christine Denté and **Chasing Furies**' Sarah Meeker."

Philadelphia

Brian Clark, bass, voc.; Ronn Flowers, gtr.; Brian Martini, drums; Phil Scholing, gtr. 1984—*Tell the Truth* (Patmos); 1985—*Search and Destroy*.

Philadelphia was an early Christian metal band who suffered the slings and arrows of fundamentalist bigotry when they tried to use the worldly genre of music for evangelical purposes. They actually came together in 1982, a year earlier than the more successful groundbreaker **Stryper.** The group was from Shreveport, Louisiana. They chose their name because Revelation 3:7–10 portrays the church in Philadelphia as "small in stature and not too powerful, but nevertheless, holding fast." *Tell the Truth* features a collection of "big hair" metal songs (think Poison, Quiet Riot, Twisted Sister, Winger) with challenging lyrics about the offer of salvation and the threat of impending judgment. "No Time for Honey" declares their resistance to the wiles of a wicked woman (named Honey) who walks the streets in the shadow of a churchyard. "Livin' in Love" equates religion with superstition in accord with the notion that "religion" as such is merely a human system of rules that does not involve a living relationship with God. The song "No Compromise" gained some Christian radio airplay. *Search and Destroy* is a high concept piece telling the story of a young man named Bobby who experiences such trials as child abuse, life as a runaway, and drug addiction before finally being re-

deemed in Jesus. Clark told *CCM* the intent was "to reach the secular audience, the people who need to be reached for Jesus." The album, however, required a full listen, as individual songs taken out of context did not necessarily convey any gospel message (cf. **Resurrection Band**'s *Lament*). This provided ammunition for preachers to condemn the band unjustly, and those most lacking in integrity took the opportunity to do so. In 2000, M8 Productions re-released both of Philadelphia's albums on CD for the cadre of collectors and fans who regarded them as classics. Bonus tracks were added (including some selections from a third, never-released project, *Warlord*). In a real coup, M8 persuaded the boys to reconvene and record two new tracks (for *Search and Destroy*). One of these, "Kids in America," is about school violence, written in response to the Columbine shootings.

Phil and John

Phil Baggley; John Hartley. Date unknown—*Lonely Dancer* (Word); 1989—*Don't Look Now, It's the Hallelujah Brothers*; 1997—*Providence* [with The Woodthieves] (Alliance).

Phil and John are a British duo with a longstanding act that is equal parts Simon and Garfunkel and Smothers Brothers. The two friends grew up together in Mansfield, England, in the same area as **Alwyn Wall.** They describe Wall's first band, **Malcolm and Alwyn,** as a dominant influence, saying, "They were our heroes." In 1982, they began performing with Youth for Christ in Derby and gained a reputation for live shows that were a blend of comedy sketches and folk-pop. They released a number of independent albums in Britain before signing with Word. *Lonely Dancer* was their first project distributed in the United States; it was produced by **Chris Eaton** and, indeed, has a sound rather similar to Eaton's own projects. Their second United States release, *Don't Look Now, It's the Hallelujah Brothers,* gained attention primarily because it was produced by **Steve Taylor** and Lynn Nichols of **Chagall Guevara.** Taylor and Nichols got the duo to "return to their roots" and deliver vocals that would recall the Everly Brothers on "Young at Heart" and jangly guitars reminiscent of The Byrds on "Please Tell Me Why." They also covered Nick Lowe's "(What's So Funny 'bout) Peace, Love, and Understanding?" After *Hallelujah Brothers,* Phil and John fell off the radar screen for contemporary Christian music (in America at least), but *Phantom Tollbooth* uncovered a new album called *Providence* released by them in the United Kingdom in 1997.

Phillips, Craig, and Dean

Shawn Craig, voc.; Dan Dean, voc.; Randy Phillips, voc. 1992—*Phillips, Craig and Dean* (StarSong); 1994—*Lifeline*; 1995—*Trust*; 1996—*Repeat the*

Sounding Joy; 1997—Where Strength Begins; 1998—Favorite Songs of All; 2000—Restoration (Sparrow).

www.pcdministries.com

Phillips, Craig, and Dean is a vocal trio of Pentecostal pastors who have background associations with southern gospel. Randy Phillips is an associate pastor in Austin, Texas; he wrote the hymn "Healer in the House," recorded by Christ Church Choir. Shawn Craig is a minister of music in St. Louis, Missouri; he has written songs recorded by **The Archers, Michael English** (the signature song "In Christ Alone"), **The Gaither Vocal Band,** and **Michele Wagner.** Dan Dean is an assistant pastor and music director in Irving, Texas; he has written songs for The Cathedrals, Janet Paschal, and Two Hearts. Early on, their adult contemporary pop sound was described as "a male version of Wilson Phillips." By the end of the '90s, the best description would probably be "an adult version of the Backstreet Boys." All three pastors write and all three sing.

The debut album sold over 100,000 copies on the strength of songs like "Turn Up the Radio" (a tribute to the healing power of music, written by Geoff Thurman) and "Midnight Oil" (a testimony to motherhood). Other songs include "This Is the Life," which celebrates the joy of abundant life in Christ, "Little Bit of Morning," which describes the new opportunities each day brings, and "Favorite Song of All," which draws on passages like Luke 15:7 to describe the celebration in heaven when a person on earth finds salvation. *Lifeline* features "The Concert of the Age," which presents the return of Christ as a main stage event with the angel Gabriel intoning, "We know you heard Beethoven / And the king of rock and roll / But on behalf of the Father / We give you the king of heart and soul." In a more adult contemporary vein, the southern gospel ballad "I Want to Be Just Like You" expresses a parent's motivation for seeking godliness: "I want to be just like you, because he wants to be like me." The group refined its super-slick style even more on *Trust,* which features the standout songs "Mercy Came Running" and "Crucified with Christ" (based on Galatians 2:20). Both of these songs are more theologically advanced than much contemporary Christian music, expressing biblical teachings on grace and consecration, both of which are understood in light of the cross. Unfortunately, *Trust* also includes a number called "Christian" (written by Geoff Thurman and Wayne Berry) that describes unbelievers as people with "no hope in their heart, no love in their eyes," whose lives are only wasted. Juxtaposed to this description is an arrogant boast ("But I'm proud that I'm a Christian") that makes Phillips, Craig, and Dean look a lot like the Pharisee in one of Jesus' more memorable parables (Luke 18:9–14). *Favorite Songs of All* collects songs from the first three albums along with three additional tunes. Twelve of the fourteen tracks had been Number One songs on the Christian adult contemporary chart.

Where Strength Begins showcases some vulnerable songs with provocative themes. "Pray Me Home" succeeds because of its lack of resolution: "It's no neatly tied up package," Dean would say of the song. "It just presents the problem and says, 'I need help'." Likewise, "The Blessing in the Thorn" is a challenging song written by Phillips for a member of his church suffering from a rare bone disease. It asks the probing questions, "When does the thorn become the blessing? / When does the pain become a friend? / When does my weakness make me stronger? / When does my faith make me whole again?" Another song, "Let the Blood Speak for Me," was cowritten by Dean with Joel Hanson of **PFR.** *Restoration* includes a remake of the **Benny Hester** classic "When God Ran" (which derives the image of its title from Luke 15:20). That song and the album's other strongest tracks ("Table of Grace," "A Place Called Grace") focus on the incomprehensible mercy of God. "Freedom's Never Free" is both patriotic and spiritual, reminding listeners of the blood shed by people who died to preserve their liberty and by Christ, who died to obtain their eternal salvation.

Phillips, Craig, and Dean have described their ministry goal as being "to affect and change hearts toward God." They also recognize that they are a group geared primarily toward the church, and indeed toward baby boomers rather than teenagers within the church. "We're not feeling called to evangelize in secular venues," Dean told *CCM* in 1997. "We're called to bring encouragement and strength and hope to Christians. Our goal is to bring people into a closer relationship with God." *Repeat the Sounding Joy* is a Christmas album. *Let My Words Be Few* is a worship album featuring the trio's rendition of songs by **Matt Redman** ("Let Everything That Hath Breath," "The Heart of Worship," and the title track) and other contemporary composers, including one apiece by each member of the group.

Christian radio hits: "Turn Up the Radio" (# 18 in 1992); "The Concert of the Age" (# 16 in 1994).

Jill Phillips

1999—*Jill Phillips* (Word); 2001—*God and Money* (St. Jerome).

www.jillphillips.com

Jill Phillips entered the crowded scene of Christian female singer/songwriters in the late '90s with a sound that got her immediately pegged as "the Christian Shawn Colvin." The similarities between her vocal style and Colvin's is remarkable enough to require a close listen at times to distinguish the two. Despite the drawbacks of such a comparison, the analogy indicates that Phillips sings unusually intelligent songs and does so in a crystal clear voice, augmented by tender, finger-picked guitar and occasional atmospheric piano. *Youthworker* magazine described her debut as "mature and road-tested, with

God-centered lyrics and nice poetry." *CCM* said that its songs "mix intimate coffeehouse folk and pure pop without leaning too far either way." A native of Chesapeake, Virginia, Phillips graduated from Belmont University in Nashville, Tennessee, in 1998. She is married to Andy Gullahorn, who has released an independent solo album titled *Old Hat*. Gullahorn plays guitar with her and writes some of her material. She cites Jonatha Brooke and **David Wilcox** as primary influences, as well as Lyle Lovett, who she says is "my hero because he's quirky and different." On her self-titled debut, the songs "Only One" and "All of Your Love" are catchy, sing-along numbers, while "Everything" and "Live by the Sword" reveal a quiet and more enchanting, indeed, mesmerizing sound. *God and Money* continues in the same vein, with a cover of **Pierce Pettis**'s "God Believes in You" and a title track echoing Matthew 6:24. "You Don't Belong Here" questions attitudes and policies that exclude certain people from Christian fellowship ("Hey, you with the rainbow flag / I can hear them say / You don't belong here / Not if you're gay").

Sam Phillips (a.k.a. Leslie Phillips)

By Leslie Phillips: 1983—*Beyond Saturday Night* (Myrrh); 1984—*Dancing with Danger*; 1985—*Black and White in a Grey World*; 1987—*The Turning; Recollection*. By Sam Phillips: 1988—*The Indescribable WOW* (Virgin); 1991—*Cruel Inventions*; 1994—*Martinis and Bikinis*; 1996—*Omnipop (It's Only a Flesh Wound, Lambchop)*; 1999—*Zero, Zero, Zero: The Best of Sam Phillips*; 2001—*Fan Dance* (Nonesuch).

www.tmtm.com/sam

Pop star Sam Phillips (b. 1962) began her career in music by recording several albums under her given name, Leslie Phillips, for the contemporary Christian music market. Her evolution from a teenage Christian phenomenon to an adult prophet critical of conservative Christianity and of the contemporary Christian music business is revealing. A vignette from Phillips's first career may help to illustrate the distinctive and therefore uncomfortable nature of the contribution she has made. Phillips wrote and performed a song called "Strength of My Life" for her *Dancing with Danger* album. It begins with an extended introduction describing mundane and burdensome aspects of daily life ("I open my eyes to the sound of morning news / And wish for ten more minutes of sleep . . ."). Then the song moves into a typical verse/chorus structure extolling God as "the hope I hold on to, the strength of my life." Mark Joseph, an analyst of Christian music, notes in his book *The Rock and Roll Rebellion* that the song was subsequently incorporated into numerous hymnbooks, without the introduction. "The way this song is used in church circles," Joseph claims, "is a metaphor for what is wrong with contemporary Christian music, where many prefer music that skips over life's difficulties and focuses on its rewards." But appreciation for real-life scenarios

would provide only an early warning sign that Phillips was a square peg in the contemporary Christian music scene. That element alone would not have necessitated a genre move, but would only have placed her on the edge—or even in the forefront of the trend toward more realistic songwriting in the '90s.

Phillips has said that she was not raised in a Christian home, by which she probably means a home where Christianity was a dominant focus or where personal piety was construed in terms of an experiential "personal relationship with Jesus" (the family was Presbyterian). In any case, she has said that her brother became a Christian in junior high school and, when she was ten, he took her to a performance of the **Jimmy and Carol Owens**' musical *Come Together*. In 1986, she told Steve Rabey, "I cried through the whole thing. Suddenly I knew that whatever life was all about, this was it—being a Christian." In eighth grade, she became involved with Jack Hayford's Church On the Way in Van Nuys, California, and was enthused (for at least a time) with the spirituality of the charismatic renewal movement. She also became part of a Christian subculture at her school where, she says, "My girlfriends and I used to say we would like to be the kind of girls **Randy Stonehill** would like." Other role models would include **Keith Green** and the **2nd Chapter of Acts** (who were also members of Hayford's church). At the same time, she admits to not always being impressed by contemporary Christian music. Living in Southern California, she was widely exposed to at least the second wave of Jesus music; she attended a concert by **The Way,** which she found impressive, but says "when I was exposed to a lot of the middle of the road music and half-done rock 'n' roll, I kind of went, 'Ugh'." In fact, she thought, even at fourteen, I could write better songs than that." And, before long, she did.

Phillips's debut in contemporary Christian music actually consisted of a song called "Bring Me Through" that Maranatha Music placed on a compilation album of various artists called *Back to the Rock* (1981). She was still a teenager when the song was released but, as Mark Joseph observes, it already demonstrated a certain character that ran against the grain of most contemporary Christian music at the time. Although it cloned the sound of Pat Benatar musically, the lyrics were striking. Phillips begins, "I've been in the basement / Groping for the light / But it just goes to show / That I walk by faith and not by sight." In fact, she says, "the dark is blacker than it's ever been." A portrait of depression—indeed of a depressed Christian—the song has far more in common with biblical psalms of lament than with the "happy in Jesus" songs that constituted the majority of Christian music in the early '80s. "Bring Me Through" offers no happy-ending resolution but concludes with a simple prayer, "You gotta bring me through / I'm leavin' it up to you." Almost as profound as Paul Craft's "You Keep Me from Blowing Away" (sung by Linda Ronstadt in 1974), "Bring Me Through" could not help but stand out amidst all the songs in contemporary Christian music that were more concerned with making orthodox statements than expressing genuine emotion.

The official debut, *Beyond Saturday Night,* includes "Bring Me Through" even though it was issued on Myrrh, not Maranatha. The album is impressive simply because it is filled with wailing electric guitars and because the twenty-one-year-old rocked harder than **Amy Grant** or **Margaret Becker** or any other Christian female singer outside of metal (e.g., **Resurrection Band**). The worshipful "I'm Finding" and adult contemporary piano ballad "Let Me Give" are atypical. Songs like "Hourglass," "Gina," and "He's Gonna Hear You Cryin' " continue to present Phillips as "the Christian Pat Benatar" (a fortunately short-lived aspiration), but elsewhere ("Beyond Saturday Night," "Heart of Hearts") her gravelly voice comes through in ways more reminiscent of "Edge of Seventeen"-era Stevie Nicks. The album only contains one instance of pure pablum ("Will They Love Him?" presenting the sentimental words of an angel watching Jesus leave heaven to be born on earth). **Mark Heard**'s "Heart of Hearts" (on the realities of urban life) is a perfectly chosen cover, and Phillips's other compositions reflect the same concern for real-life engagement that "Bring Me Through" suggested she was capable of delivering. The title track is especially strong lyrically, offering a serious though nonjudgmental response to the mentality of songs like Loverboy's "Working for the Weekend," suggesting that the gospel of Christ really does offer something more than escapism. "Gina" expresses the guilt that Phillips felt when a non-Christian friend died in a fiery car crash ("before I could tell her about Jesus," Phillips would write in the liner notes). "He's Gonna Hear You Cryin' " addresses suicide and suicidal thinking. "Put Your Heart in Me" is a **Keith Green-**like cry to become more faithful ("I want to feed the hungry / I want to fight for justice") from the inside out. In interviews, Phillips spoke forthrightly about wanting to address the "condemnation so many Christians feel because they are not living 'the victorious Christian life'." She told *CCM* "that's not what being a Christian is—you can go through hard times—you just have a different source of strength." She also said—in a terribly revealing way for 1983—that "this past year, I've been realizing a lot of flaws in the church and a lot of hypocrisy." She continued, "The tendency would be for me to write a very negative album, commenting and really slamming a lot of people in the church, or the church itself. I don't want to do that. I don't feel that is the way to get your message across. You have to do it gently and with love." *CCM* chose *Beyond Saturday Night* as one of its Ten Best Albums of 1983; in fact, it was chosen Num-

ber Five for the year, right behind *Proof through the Night* by **T Bone Burnett.**

Phillips quickly succumbed to the expectations of the contemporary Christian music culture and her next two albums were industry projects that lacked the edge she had begun to exhibit in her debut. They were nevertheless competent industry projects establishing Phillips as one who critics would dub "the brightest star in the contemporary Christian music pantheon" and as "the premier female Christian rock singer." A less hyperbolic estimate of her career would simply recognize that for four years she was the number three female contemporary gospel singer in America, behind **Amy Grant** and **Sandi Patty.** There is no easier and safer way for a young, single, female vocalist to ingratiate herself with the Gospel Music Association crowd than by singing an ode to sexual abstinence, which Phillips does on her inappropriately titled *Dancing with Danger* album ("Light of Love"). **Russ Taff, Greg Volz,** and **Matthew Ward** all supply background vocals on that album, and Ward duets with Phillips on the Scripture song "By My Spirit" (based on Zechariah 4:6). The most interesting song on the album lyrically is the title track (done in a new-wave style with a quirky instrumental break), which is addressed to the stereotypical prodigal child who rebels against his or her religious upbringing: "Raised with a Bible in your hand / You met your parents' strict demands / But now that sweet religious child / Is like a hurricane gone wild." Otherwise, the only song that cracks the mold of what one would expect to find on any album by any number of Christian artists is "Powder Room Politics," a bit of a take-off on Elvis Costello's "Girls Talk."

By the time *Black and White in a Grey World* appeared, Phillips seemed to be juxtaposing two different styles—envelope-pushing Christian rock in the tradition of **Amy Grant**'s *Unguarded* album and MOR praise songs in the tradition of almost every other well-known female singer in contemporary Christian music at the time. *CCM* would note, "There are dozens of songstresses out there crooning undistinguished tunes like 'Your Kindness' and 'You're the Same,' but precious few can pull off the dramatic rock 'n' roll of something like 'Tug of War' or 'Walls of Silence.' " This is not completely fair. "Your Kindness" is one of Phillips's best songs from her Leslie period, a paean to divine grace ("It's your kindness that leads us to repentance, O Lord") sung in a voice much like that which she would showcase later as Sam. She wrote the song after breaking off an engagement with a man she had dated for four years and its appreciation for spiritual blessings is grounded in an earthy awareness of unfulfilled hope: "The eyes of God have found my failures, found my pain." The song "Psalm 55" is also worthy of note as a praise anthem in the tradition of **U2**'s arena rockers. *Dancing with Danger* and *Black and White in a Grey World* hold their own against most of mid '80s contemporary

Christian music; they disappoint only when compared with Phillips's other projects.

What is intriguing in retrospect is that the title song to *Black and White in a Grey World* offers a simplistic rejection of ambiguity, embracing the tendency of fundamentalism to view truth and especially morality in absolute terms that ignore interpretative nuances of context. Even at the time, those listening to the song may have sensed that Phillips protested too much; the view she articulates (that issues should be viewed in terms of "black and white" without shades of grey) seems so obviously untenable that she almost confesses her discomfort even as she sings it: "I feel so out of place / Like I've landed on the moon," she admits, before quickly adding "But I don't mind being different / Cause I'm different for the truth." Of course, being "different" is one thing; being out of touch with reality ("on the moon") is another. On a number of her songs up to this point, Phillips had dealt honestly with the struggle of maintaining faith and faithfulness. In "I Won't Let It Come between Us," she had admitted, "You know wrong can look so good some times," and in "Tug of War" she had said, "You know I want to do what's right, but I'm so torn apart." But even in these instances, the assumption was that she knew full well what was good, right, and proper and only had to struggle with the temptation to do what she knew was bad, wrong, or improper. Phillips's commitment to intelligence and integrity determined from the outset that she would have to face greater struggles: questions of doubt and uncertainty that assault all believers who press on to theological maturity.

The seams began to show. A year after *Black and White* was released, Phillips admitted that she had been pressured to include some of the more "typical contemporary Christian songs" on her previous projects. "I let the pressure get the better of me," she told *CCM*'s Thom Granger. "Some of the songs were sell-outs. I didn't do what I knew I should do." At the same time, she said that she had come to question the whole idea of a teenager with a guitar being expected to provide answers to the deep questions of life: "Christian audiences expect you to teach them and to be this incredible example. I haven't been to seminary. . . . The pressure on Christian artists is incredible. We expect them to be our heroes, to exemplify Christianity, and to do what we can't do." Then in the spring of 1987, Phillips performed new material before an audience at Knott's Berry Farm in Southern California, and the Christian audience was so scandalized that she had to cancel the rest of her tour. Exactly *what* was offensive is difficult to determine— Phillips had dyed her blonde hair black and she wore a skirt short enough to set a few conservatives on edge. She sang a cover of **Bob Dylan**'s "It Ain't Me Babe." Whatever it was, stories spread quickly among traditionalists—many of whom were still reeling from the "scandal" of **Amy Grant** "going secular"—

that Phillips was now "too worldly." She would later tell Brian Quincy Newcomb that the controversy had less to do with spirituality than with "show biz." She allowed that it is "really frightening" how people in Christian music circles "confuse spiritual issues with show business and musical taste." In any case, Phillips soon announced that her next album, *The Turning,* would be her final release for "the Christian music market."

That album, as it turned out, was her masterpiece. Produced by **T Bone Burnett,** who Phillips would later marry, the record demonstrates the potential for what Christian music can sometimes deliver. In 2001, a poll of critics (sponsored by *CCM*) put *The Turning* at Number Eight on their list of "The 100 Greatest Albums in Christian Music." Its pieties are sufficiently subdued for it to appeal broadly to fans of Sam Phillips's music as well—in fact, it was later re-released on Virgin as a Sam Phillips product. The opening track is a beautiful, acoustic ballad written by Burnett and featuring Phillips's low register voice over a strummed guitar. She confesses her belief in the reality of love; it flows "through all times," undeterred by grief or lies. "Love Is Not Lost" makes the same point with narrative and possibly autobiographical detail. More upbeat in tempo, the latter song has a sound similar to some of Sam Phillips's later hits ("Baby, I Can't Please You," "Strawberry Road"). Phillips admits that her heart has been broken, her ideals shaken, yet, "love is not a lost cause." She even invokes a little Cartesian philosophy to back up her stubborn resilience ("if true love did not exist, how would we know its name?"). "Libera Me" gets to the heart of trusting faith with its confession. "I don't know all the truth from the lying, but I know that I need you." Likewise, in "Answers Don't Come Easy," Phillips recognizes that, like biblical Job, she may not get answers to some of her most pertinent questions yet she reconciles herself to saying, "I can wait." Many of these songs were received by the Christian community as prayers addressed to God, though their lyrics are (intentionally?) polyvalent enough to allow other interpretations. "Expectations" might just be about a failed romance, but many found its descriptions of unrealistic pressures apt for the artist's experiences in the Christian music scene. The only overtly religious song on *The Turning* is its closing track, "God Is Watching You," in which Phillips affirms the hidden presence of God at every stage of life and all it brings: "when you're a hero to us all . . . when you take that fated fall . . . God is watching you"). Harmony vocals on *The Turning* are provided by Burnett, **Peter Case,** and **Tonio K.**

Phillips's transition from Christian music to the general market was not a segue (à la **Amy Grant**) but a radical break. She not only changed labels but insisted on recording under a new name—Sam Phillips, which was not chosen in honor of the producer who jump-started the careers of **Elvis Presley** and **Johnny Cash,** but had in fact been her nickname from childhood. It seemed obvious to most that she did not just want to expand her market but to disassociate herself with the previous work, which she no longer performed in concerts. Her departure was viewed by some within the contemporary Christian music subculture as a betrayal. As *CCM* put it, "some accuse her of losing her faith, or deserting Christianity, or of having been brainwashed into theological liberalism by Burnett." Of those three alternatives, only the latter bore any semblance to the truth. Phillips had indeed been introduced to more nuanced theological perspectives by Burnett and others, to views that might seem "liberal" to fundamentalists, though for her this was less like brainwashing than deprogramming. "I started reading books (G. K. Chesterton, Thomas Merton, Flannery O'Connor) and meeting all kinds of people—and the fundamentalism I experienced in gospel music didn't hold up," she told Newcomb. Or, again, in 1988, when she reluctantly granted one more interview to *CCM* to respond to queries, she said, "I still have a deep faith, but I've had to start over with my faith, and go back to the question, 'What does love require?'." In that same interview, however, she spoke harshly about expressions of faith that she had come to regard as destructive: "I think the born-again movement in this country has about as little to do with real Christianity as a Xerox of a hundredth-generation print of the Mona Lisa," she said. "The born again movement is more about obsession and narrow-mindedness and repression—and true Christianity is about mercy and freedom and love."

Phillips's need to separate her "Christian" and "secular" careers so definitively may be viewed somewhat ironically as a continuation of her penchant for viewing things in "black and white" without shades of grey, a penchant she had come to renounce but had not completely transcended. **Amy Grant,** by contrast, has always been able to perceive a continuum between the Christian and secular markets and to slide back and forth on that scale. Notably, many (indeed, most) leaders in the contemporary Christian music movement have defended Phillips's transition to the general market and endorsed the music she has made there. *CCM* concluded their 1988 interview by editorializing, "Anyone who claims that Phillips' faith has lessened or become more shallow through this set of changes does not know her." Brian Quincy Newcomb wrote in his *Harvest Rock Syndicate* that the contemporary Christian music industry only had itself to blame for losing Phillips to the world at large (which he did not, in any case, consider to be a bad thing): "She was encouraged to produce propaganda that supported the status quo and promised to please the record buying public," Newcomb noted, indicating that Phillips was right to seek a different podium for expressing her views. *CCM* and other publications continued to review her albums and concerts (always favorably) and they encouraged their readers

to heed her insights, buy her products, and consider her challenges. Eventually, her continued harangues against the Christian music scene would begin to ring hollow, especially since she seldom took any personal responsibility for seeking to be a part of (indeed helping to define) the culture that she ultimately found confining. She seems, in fact, to have seized on the image of "Christian music's prodigal daughter" as a part of her defining persona, an element that sets her apart from a myriad of other pop stars and always gives her something interesting to talk about in interviews. Her complaints are legitimate and her (new) convictions are sincere, but she was an adult when she signed those contracts. And selling half a million albums by the age of twenty-five hardly qualifies one for victim status.

As Sam Phillips, the artist unveiled a new sound with her debut album, *The Indescribable Wow.* She called her style "acid-pop" and sang catchy songs with tunes reminiscent of the Beatles, a comparison fueled by the psychedelic "backwards guitar" accompaniment provided by her husband and producer (along with '60s sitar, organ, and harpsichord). Her voice acquired a high, nasal twang and a Stevie Nicks vibrato. Songs like "I Don't Want to Fall in Love" and "I Don't Know How to Say Goodbye to You" convey an introspective look at the unsure side of romance, while the standout track "Holding On to the Earth" offers a critique of the materialism of the yuppie culture. "Remorse" reflects on the story of a South American man who killed his mother. Elvis Costello would join the cast of characters playing on *Cruel Inventions,* a more complex album than *Wow.* "Where the Colors Don't Go" retains the same pop feel of the previous project, but the true standout tracks on *Cruel Inventions* ("Lying," "Hole in Time," and the title track) have a less immediately accessible and more experimental quality to them. Critics loved both *Wow* and *Cruel Inventions,* though neither was a commercial blockbuster. *Billboard* called Phillips "a compelling, often intoxicating writer whose lyrics are filled with imagery." *Rolling Stone* said, "Sam Phillips is a rarity—an artist who seduces and disturbs." *The New York Times* cited her work as "proof enough that the secular and the spiritual can intersect in strange and affecting ways." She would tour with the Counting Crows, Cowboy Junkies, Elvis Costello, and **Bruce Cockburn.**

Martinis and Bikinis was Phillips's breakthrough album in the general market, and the only product to achieve commercial success in addition to critical acclaim. The songs "I Need Love" and "Baby, I Can't Please You" were hits on college radio. The former song features the memorable lines, "I need love / Not some sentimental prison / I need God / Not the political church." In concerts, Phillips would dedicate "Baby, I Can't Please You" to conservative political commentator Rush Limbaugh, who had become her ideological archenemy. The song "Signposts" refers to a book by Walker Percy called *Signposts in a Strange Land;*

according to Phillips, Percy knew what it meant to be "saved from the answers by the questions." *Martinis and Bikinis* ended up on many critics' lists of the best albums of the year; *Rolling Stone* noted its return to the "acid pop" style of *Indescribable Wow* by saying, "If the stubborn spirit of John Lennon has whispered in anyone's ear this year, it's probably Sam Phillips'." The song "Strawberry Roads," based on a Native American legend that the road to heaven is lined with strawberries, is powerfully Beatlesque (though nothing like "Strawberry Fields"), and *Martinis* even concludes with an inspired cover of the neglected Lennon song "Gimme Some Truth." The album garnered Phillips a Grammy nomination for Best Female Rock Singer; she also took second place in *Rolling Stone*'s annual critics' poll for best female songwriter. In 1994, Phillips recorded the old Nancy Sinatra hit "These Boots Are Made for Walkin' " for the soundtrack of the motion picture *Pret-a-Porter.*

Her next album bore the bizarre title *Omnipop (It's Only a Flesh Wound, Lambchop)*. It presents an equally strange collection of songs that would strike many as a mishmash of diverse styles, from Tin Pan Alley to showtunes to industrial rock to lounge pop. "Entertainmen" and "Power World" come closest to exemplifying her familiar neo-Beatles style. "Zero, Zero, Zero" features a chorus played by horns reminiscent of the Tijuana Brass. "Animals on Wheels" has a quirky, circus calliope sound. "Slapstick Heart" was written out of an instrumental song idea R.E.M. had sent to Burnett ("I raped and pillaged their song," Phillips said). The album *Zero, Zero, Zero* collects favorite songs (though not the one by that title) along with a couple of new compositions and alternative mixes. In 2001, Phillips released her first album of new music in five years, *Fan Dance*. Both *Rolling Stone* and *HM* gushed over it, the former noting "it's really all about her voice—a torn-through-the-middle, slightly smoke damaged and rough thing of beauty." The latter noted vague references to God ("Below Surface") along with Lao-Tse ("Five Colors"). The best songs are probably "Wasting My Time" (with cellos), the sparsely accompanied "Say What You Mean," and the melancholy-but-peaceful "Love Is Everywhere I Go."

Phillips's move to the big leagues put her in the spotlight where, because of her background, she was often quizzed about her faith. In 1988, she told the *Los Angeles Times* that her three role models were Jesus, the Beatles, and Marilyn Monroe (the "sacrificial lamb of the feminist movement—and I can really identify with a lot of the insecurities, fears, and self-doubts she had"). In 1989, she told *The Georgia Straight* newspaper, "one of the reasons I got so fed up with religious music is that the audience wants you to be very one-dimensional. . . . I believe that Jesus was a very secular, life-embracing person. He didn't hang out with the church hierarchy of the day; he hung out with the street people and the rebels. A lot of Christians have lost that part of him." That same year, she told the *Chi-* *cago Tribune,* "my previous label (Myrrh) insisted that my art be propaganda and I wanted the freedom to write about whatever I'm going through, whatever I'm thinking at the moment, and not have any kind of restrictions on me." In 1991, she told *Entertainment Weekly,* "Fundamentalism is a horrible human disease; it has nothing to do with love," and *Rolling Stone,* "I'm very negative about the Christian media [music business] in general; I feel that it's exploiting somebody's faith, basically." In 1994, she explained her departure from the Christian music scene to *Newsweek* by saying, "People would say you were a heretic if you asked questions. . . . I wanted to write songs about spirituality, and I had thought that the church would be a good place to do that. I was very wrong." In 1996, she told *Goldmine,* "I think [fundamentalist Christians] are afraid of something—although I'm not exactly sure what. And I think they should just shut up. Everybody has heard it and everybody gets it. It's not as if there are very many people left in the world who don't know what Christianity is saying. I think they should just be quiet, and start being loving and serving their communities. . . . They seem basically narcissistic and a little crazy and a little needy." Then, as a seeming afterthought, she added, "But I don't think most church people are like that. Most people in the church are not that fanatical or stupid."

Ten years earlier, Thom Granger of *CCM* had asked Phillips in an uncomfortable interview if she had any parting words for the contemporary Christian music industry. She replied, "Think about what you're doing, how you're affecting people, and why you're doing this."

For trivia buffs: In 1995, Phillips made her acting debut in the popular movie *Die Hard with a Vengeance*. She turned in a remarkable performance as the sexy, mute wife of the Number One terrorist bad guy, played by Jeremy Irons. A knife-wielding assassin in her own right, she slices and dices an unfortunate bank guard in one memorable violent scene. As an inside joke—supposedly to help Phillips get into character—the director found an actor who was a Rush Limbaugh look-alike to play the part of the unfortunate guard.

Christian radio hits: "Heart of Hearts" (# 14 in 1983); "I'm Finding" (# 31 in 1983); "Make My Heart Your Home" [with **Paul Smith** and **The Imperials**]; "By My Spirit" (# 12 in 1984); "Here He Comes with My Heart" (# 6 in 1985); "Strength of My Life" (# 9 in 1985); "Dancing with Danger" (# 11 in 1985); "Your Kindness" (# 1 for 4 weeks in 1986); "The More I Know" (# 7 in 1986); "Psalm 55" (# 8 in 1986); "Libera Me" (# 2 in 1987); "Love Is Not Lost" (# 14 in 1987); "Answers Don't Come Easy" (# 11 in 1987); "No One But You" (# 11 in 1988).

Philmore

Justin Greiman, voc., gtr.; Kayle Greiman, bass; Brett Schoneman, drums. 2000—*Philmore* (5 Min. Walk).

www.planetphilmore.com

The band Philmore offers the musical equivalent of a shotgun wedding between the Hatfields and the McCoys: they merge '80s punk music with the glam metal sounds that such music was originally rebelling against and they do it under the banner of "it's all rock 'n' roll." The group organized in Iowa and then relocated to Tulsa, Oklahoma. Their debut album for 5 Min. Walk kicks off with a pair of songs ("Together," "Smile at Me") that sound just like all of the other Ramones clones, but then on track three, "Our Finest Hour," Philmore suddenly fires up some electric guitars and moves into a sound that might have Sid Vicious rolling in his grave but has wowed many an audience. "Our Finest Hour" is very much Philmore's finest moment, a triumphant rock and roll anthem that bears some similarities to **PlankEye,** perhaps owing to the album's production by Scott Silletta (and Chuck Cummings). They follow the song with a cover of Bon Jovi's "Livin' on a Prayer." From there it's mostly downhill, with silly ("In My Boat," "Fishy") and sentimental ("If You Only Knew," "Wish You Were Here") songs. The album concludes with a worship ballad, "As I Lift My Hands."

Philmore is blatantly Christian and message-oriented in their lyrics. "Our Finest Hour" celebrates an apocalyptic victory when Christians and angels storm the gates of hell to destroy the hosts of darkness. It seems to be inspired by Frank Peretti's novels (e.g., *This Present Darkness*) and suffers from the same theological problems that plagued **Petra**'s militant anthems of the '80s. "If You Only Knew" expresses God's love for sinners through words of extravagant affection placed on the lips of Christ: "If you only knew the love that's in my heart / I suffered and gave my life / I stretched out my arms and died / The tears ran down from my eyes / For you."

Phoenix Sunshine

Paul Amschler, gtr., voc.; Debbie Cowan, voc.; Gary Cowan, gtr. 1972—*Shinin' in the Light* (Destiny); 1975—*The Exodus.*

Phoenix Sunshine was one of the lesser-known country folk-rock bands associated with the Jesus movement. Their two albums were produced by Evan Williams of **Harvest Flight,** who plays guitar and keyboards on the projects. *Shinin' in the Light* is a low-budget project filled with what *Jesus Music* calls "handclappin' jangly folkrock tunes." Standout songs include "He Lives" and a progressive eight-minute composition, "Broken Wing." The second album is far more polished, but according to *Harmony,* "the songs are not as strong." The most interesting moment comes with the title track, which features a mix of Scottish bagpipes, Indian sitar, and numerous ethnic instruments (gaida, gadulka, tamboura, tapan, and kaval) played by the Pitu Gull Folk Orchestra of Bulgaria. **Al Perkins** also provides some beautiful steel guitar work on "God's Prologue." Another song is revealing of a certain sentiment of the era: "Pa-

perback Bible" extols the simple (even disposable) commodity that every hippie Christian treasured, with a sideways glance at the fashionable and expensive "designer Bibles" that many companies were trying to market at the time. In 1975, one could pick up a copy of the American Bible Society's *Good News for Modern Man* (paperback New Testament) for just twenty-five cents; a leather-bound Thompson's Chain Reference Study Bible (with often inaccurate "helps") was forty dollars.

P.I.D. (a.k.a. Preachas In Disguise and Preachas)

Barry Hogan, voc. (−1992); Fred Lynch [a.k.a. Doug Tray], voc. (−1992) // K-Mack, voc. (+ 1991); King Solomon J., voc. (+ 1992). As P.I.D.: 1988—*Here We Are* (Graceland); 1989—*Back to Back;* 1991—*The Chosen Ones* (Frontline); 1992—*Born with the Gift: John 3:16 Factor;* 1998—*The Very Best of P.I.D.* By Preachas: 1993—*Violent Playgrounds* (Myx).

P.I.D. was one of the earliest Christian rap groups. The duo of Barry Hogan and Fred Lynch rhymed lyrics that present the gospel in simple street language. When the group got its start, **D-Boy** and **Michael Peace** were among the only rap artists working in Christian music and the genre was still largely unappreciated. Their first album features seven tracks on Side A and then instrumental "def DJ Mixes" of the same seven tracks on Side B to encourage fans to construct their own raps. The sophomore project, *Back to Back,* demonstrated tremendous growth and would break the group as an act to be taken seriously. Two years later, Jamie Lee Rake would write in *CCM* that "P.I.D.'s *Back to Back* was the first authentic Christian hip-hop album . . . it was resolutely street smart while retaining church smarts by being informed with black gospel preaching and backbeats." The song "Bible Stories" samples the central chorus of Rufus's '70s hit, "Tell Me Something Good." Expanding to a trio, P.I.D. refined their sound in the direction of stylistic diversity for *The Chosen Ones,* a twenty-track manifesto that deals with a variety of issues. Numbers like "The Book" and "Get You a Bible" (remade from their first album) are straight-out exhortations to live by "the Word." "Victim of the System" offers a socio-political commentary on the hopelessness of ghetto life. The album is musically eclectic as well: "Grace" has a very jazzy, club-oriented sound; "Joy Like a River" features church organ and a gospel choir. Segments of various storefront preaching and, at one point, words from Louis Farrakhan, are sampled throughout. *Born with the Gift* was recorded by a trio consisting of K-Mack and two previous unknowns, King Solomon J. and Doug Tray. But according to the record company, only Barry Hogan had left (replaced by King Solomon), and Fred Lynch had simply decided to change his name (to Doug Tray). Such idiosyncracies aside, *CCM* would call the album the group's "most satisfying set to date," noting the combo's effective strategy of mingling "self-reference with culture bonding metaphors and gospel-jazz-funk invention." "What Love Won't Do" (with sampled Peabo Bryson vocals and female background singers) and "Tell Him" are especially pop-conscious and radio-friendly. "Sleeping with the Enemy" begins with words ("A brotha got cut . . .") that suggest it might refer to some internal group troubles that led to Hogan's departure. In 1993, the group changed their name to Preachas and released the album *Violent Playgrounds* on Myx.

Jonathan Pierce

1995—*One Love* (Curb); 1997—*Mission*; 2000—*Sanctuary*.

Jonathan Pierce (née Hildreth) grew up in Odessa, Texas. After moving to Nashville, he sang with the acclaimed Christ Church Choir, where he caught the attention of church member Naomi Judd, whose husband, Larry Strickland, would become his manager. Pierce got his big start in Christian music as a member of **The Imperials** (1991–1994). He also sang briefly with **The Gaither Vocal Band** (1994–1995) before going solo. Pierce infuses his adult contemporary songs with a soulful sound that draws on classic R&B pop in a manner sometimes reminiscent of such artists as **Michael English** or **Clay Crosse.** On *One Love,* he uses a variety of producers including **Michael Omartian, John** and Dino **Elefante,** and Guy Roche (known for his work with Michael Bolton and Celine Dion). The album includes the hit song "Rise Up" (written by **Brent Bourgeois**), a Stevie Wonder cover, the upbeat "Carry Me Through," and a song contributed by **Gary Chapman.** Pierce would continue to work with a variety of producers and songwriters on *Mission,* though he cowrote eight of the songs himself. Like the first project, that album offers an eclectic mix of styles, from the excellent ballad "Farther Than Your Grace Can Reach" to the disco-like "Hold Me in Your Arms." Pierce also remakes **Brown Bannister**'s song "Praise the Lord" (originally a hit for **The Imperials**) with Bannister producing. The most consistent criticism of Pierce's first two albums was that his use of multiple producers resulted in hodgepodge collections of songs that may be strong individually but do not make for coherent albums. For *Sanctuary,* Pierce worked exclusively with producer Phil Naish, and some of the same critics complained that "while the song quality is very nice, there is little variation to distinguish one from another." The title track and the song "All I Know Is That You Love" reveal a more vulnerable Pierce than was evident on previous projects. **The Katinas** add vocals to "I Hold in My Heart," a song that Pierce says he wrote after an exchange of letters with "a stripper" that resulted in the woman coming to one of his concerts with a testimony of her transformed life (and career).

In 1999, between his second and third solo albums, Pierce was given the opportunity to play the part of Angelus in the play *Les Misérables* on Broadway. He followed that with a turn as the lead character in a Nashville revival of *Joseph and the Amazing Technicolor Dreamcoat* (Andrew Lloyd Webber's first Bible-based epic before *Jesus Christ Superstar*). A fully secular production (staged for entertainment value, not inspiration), Pierce anticipated some backlash from the Christian community for his role, but racy costumes aside, the play is largely orthodox and all but the most myopic fan understood Pierce's involvement as an opportunity to introduce some worldly people to a biblical narrative and, possibly, to the gospel albums of the play's star.

Christian radio hits: "Rise Up" (# 6 in 1996); "Carry You with Me" (# 18 in 1996).

Pillar

Rob Beckley, voc.; Travis Jenkins, gtr.; Kalel, bass; Brad Noone, drums. 1999—*Metamorphosis* (independent); 2000—*Original Superman; Above* (Flicker).

The group Pillar from Hays, Kansas, emerged at the end of the twentieth century as one more 311-influenced rapcore group alongside **Pax 217** and **P.O.D.** Their independent albums garnered them an unusually large following, and the major label debut (on **Audio Adrenaline**-owned Flicker Records) had critics insisting that, despite obvious similarities to Rage Against the Machine and the groups just mentioned, "Pillar has their own vibe—a sound of their own." The group does not display the penchant for screaming demonstrated by Limp Bizkit or Korn, though they do bring in a guest (Kevin from **Disciple**) to handle those chores on one track ("All Day, Every Day"). **Knowdaverbs** also stop by to put down a rap on "Galactic Groove." The title track ("Above") showcases catchy guitar riffs with the primary lyric being the worshipful acclamation, "Everything to my God above / He's my one and only true love." A few songs ("Live for Him," "Open Your Eyes") juxtapose sung, melodic interludes with the monotone rap delivery that otherwise continues from start to finish, making the album a bit tiresome for those who aren't strong fans of the genre. Buried near the end of the album, "Reaching Out" is a more pop-oriented number that allows the by-then very familiar rap to segue into a sing-along chorus. The project also concludes with a completely traditional **Delirious?-**style worship-and-testimony song ("Father"). Lyrics are explicitly Christian with an emphasis on declarations of the band's own piety rather than assaults on the listeners' presumed inadequacies. "Original Superman" (repeated here from the sophomore indie album) compares Jesus with the comic book hero in a way that some may find a bit trite: "He's always there to save the day . . . Kryptonite can't slow him down. . . ." The group may have a certain fixation with this topic—its bass player likes to go by the name the comic book character was given at birth (Kal-el). Pillar took their name from 1 Timothy 3:15, which describes God's household as "the pillar and foundation of truth."

Dove Awards: 2001 Hard Music Album (Above).

Michele Pillar

1979—*The Misfit* [with Erick Nelson] (A&S); 1982—*Michele Pillar* (Sparrow); 1983—*Reign on Me*; 1984—*Look Who Loves You Now*; 1988—*Compact Favorites*; 1991—*Love Makes All the Difference* (Urgent).

Michele Pillar (née Zarges) is an adult contemporary female vocalist known for her association with groups like Focus on the Family. Raised in Long Beach, California, Pillar became associated with Calvary Chapel's Maranatha! Music program just after that label introduced a wave of Jesus music groups definitive of the Jesus movement revival in the early '70s. As part of the "next generation" of Maranatha, Pillar was part of the label's shift from evangelistic secular-sounding music toward praise and worship choruses intended for use in informal church settings. The first recording of her silky alto voice appears to be on the first verse of the classic worship song "Thou Art Worthy" from *Praise Two* (Maranatha, 1976). She then joined **Erick Nelson** as part of a short-lived duo and the two of them made a concept album called *The Misfit* (see listing for Nelson). Pillar would gain wide notice in the contemporary Christian music scene with three albums for Sparrow, the first two of which were recorded in Muscle Shoals, Alabama, with the producer/songwriter team J. L. Wallace and Lonnie Ledford. Wallace and Ledford wrote "Walk across Heaven" for her self-titled album, on which she also performs **Phil Keaggy**'s "You" and her own "More Than Just a Man," in addition to a couple of songs by **Lenny LeBlanc.** That tradition would continue with *Reign on Me.* Wallace and Ledford contribute the bluesy title track (featuring a sax intro by Muscle Shoals legend Ron Eades), a strong rock number, "My Heart Is a Stone," and another radio hit, "He Rolled Away the Stone." LeBlanc offers "Shout It from the Rooftop" and Pillar herself brings in the ballads "Don't Wait Too Late" and "When Love Draws Near." Pillar's biggest hit would come with the title track to her third album, *Look Who Loves You Now.* Written by Steve Stone, the song is a catchy pop tune with somewhat ambiguous lyrics (à la "You Light Up My Life") that could be sung either to God or to a human object of affection: "Wanting to touch you / Wanting to see you / I know there'll come a day / But, oh, Lord, if you could / Right now if you would / Cast a glimpse my way" (the "Lord" could be construed as an exclamation). Pillar also sings "To Worship You" as a duet with **Sheila Walsh.** *Look Who Loves You Now* was produced by Larry Carlton, the pop-jazz guitarist who was once a member of the Crusaders

(1972–1977) but who may be best known for his recording of the hit "Theme from Hill Street Blues" (# 10 in 1981)—though performance of the latter song is often unfairly credited to its producer and composer, Mike Post.

For a time, Pillar was widely known for her work in singles ministry. She began leading seminars for Christian singles when she was still Michele Zarges and singing with **Erick Nelson.** In 1979, she married Steve Pillar and continued to lead the seminars for another seven years, drawing on her marriage for examples and illustrations of a stable romantic relationship grounded in friendship and mutual respect. In March, 1985—after her three albums for Sparrow—she was on the cover of *CCM* magazine not for her music but in regard to a feature story about her marriage and her role in relationship counseling and singles ministry. This was an ironic swan song—she would not be heard from again for a few years and when she did resurface she was married to Larry Carlton. She sang on his Christmas album, *Christmas at My House,* in 1989. Two years later, she released one more album, *Love Makes All the Difference,* which was again produced by Carlton and features a number of hymn-like easy listening tunes, including "Some People's Lives" by Janis Ian and Kyle Fleming. In an accompanying article, she told *CCM* magazine, "I came from an alcoholic and broken home, and even after becoming a Christian, I still had no concept of the unconditional love of God. . . . It took six years of walking through the valley of the shadow of death, but the discovery of the healing that comes from brokenness and repentance is now my greatest treasure."

Pillar recorded the theme song for James Dobson's *Focus on the Family* radio show. She also wrote a children's book called *The Angel Tree* and has since become affiliated with Prison Fellowship's Angel Tree program. In 1988, Carlton was shot in a robbery attempt; he suffered near fatal injuries but eventually made a full recovery. He went on to become a member of the highly successful jazz quartet Fourplay. (A legendary guitarist, Carlton has played on countless pop albums over the years in addition to pursuing his main career in jazz; *Rolling Stone* lists his guitar riff on Steely Dan's "Kid Charlemagne" as the third best guitar lick of all time). Pillar also sang on Carlton's 1996 album, *The Gift.*

Christian radio hits: "Walk across Heaven" (# 4 in 1982); "More Than Just a Man" (# 11 in 1982); "Love's Not a Feeling" [with **Steve Camp**] (# 4 in 1984); "Reign on Me" (# 9 in 1984); "He Rolled Away the Stone" (# 4 in 1984); "Look Who Loves You Now" (# 1 for 13 weeks in 1985); "Each Day He Gives Me" (# 12 in 1985); "Love Makes All the Difference" (# 29 in 1991).

Doug Pinnick

See **Poundhound** and **Supershine.**

Pivot Clowj

See **House of Wires.**

Plaid

Andrew Adams, bass, voc.; Brannon Hancock, voc., gtr.; kybrd.; Jason Payton, drums; Allen Salmon, gtr., voc. 1997—*Plaid* (Boingy); 1998—*Understanding God* (Rustproof).

Plaid was a Christian rock quartet from Nashville that got its start playing at **Michael W. Smith**'s Rocketown nightclub. Their sound owed a generous debt to classic rock, especially Led Zeppelin—and to such other Zeppelin-inspired groups as Live and **The Prayer Chain.** The title track to *Understanding God,* however, is a rousing number sustained by jazz horns that gives it more of a Blood, Sweat, and Tears or early Chicago feel. The album's opener, "Pick Your Poison," is hard, guitar-driven modern rock with a searing solo and passionate vocals. "Beautiful" slows things down enough for what *7ball* would describe as "a bareback acoustic guitar ride through fields of accordion and Hammond organ." Lyrically, the album presents stories of everyday life with God. "Listen" challenges the audience to really hear the cries of hurting people. The title of the album, Hancock maintains, is a double entendre, intended to summon both the image of a sympathetic Creator and that of a human quest to know that Creator better. Derri Daugherty of **The Choir** assisted with the album's production. The group's earlier independent album (on Boingy) featured eight tracks, six of which were re-recorded for the official debut on Rustproof. In 2000, the band replaced guitarist Salmon with keyboardist Steve Busch and changed their name to **Downpour.**

PlankEye

Eric Balmer, gtr., voc.; Luis Garcia, bass, kybrd.; voc.; Adam Ferry, drums (– 1999); Scott Silletta, voc., gtr. (– 1999) // Kevin Polish, gtr. (+ 2001); Luis Ruiz, drums (+ 2001). 1993—*Spill* (Walk the Plank); 1995—*The Spark* (Tooth and Nail); 1996—*Commonwealth*; 1997—*The One and Only* (BEC); 1999—*Relocation*; 2001—*Strange Exchange.*

www.plankeye.com

Sometimes known as "the other band from Orange County, California," PlankEye arose in the Christian music scene in the shadow of their local labelmates **The Supertones.** PlankEye is no ska band, but at one time or another, they seem to have been almost everything else. *7ball* described the group's ever-changing sound as "an unlikely mixture of punk passion, hyperactive new-wave, and simple, straight ahead rock 'n' roll." *CCM* noted in 1997, "Part of what makes PlankEye so refreshing is that they don't easily fit into any one category of the increasingly splintered rock market. Refusing to copy a certain style of music, the band continues to create loud, noisy, energetic, and fun power-pop music, dressed up in modern rock clothes." The group formed just after front man Scott Silletta "got saved" in 1991 and, with progressively better albums, eventually became one of the most exciting groups in the Christian market. For a time, they were one of a handful of bands associated with the more progressive modern rock wing of contemporary Christian music that was also blatantly devoted to evangelical ministry. "We want to see people get saved," Silletta said in 1996. "Our first goal is to share Jesus with people." Eventually the entire group would identify themselves more specifically with the Reformed faith (bucking a silly tradition in the contemporary Christian music industry that encourages artists to be coy or evasive about their denominational heritage or specific theological preferences). "We are all staunch, pro-Calvinists," Silletta remarked without apology—and without any hint of the divisive or sectarian proselytizing that pundits wrongly assume must encounter such declarations. The group also quit giving altar calls at their concerts out of concern for accountability, i.e., "turning a handful of kids who respond to our invitation over to discipleship counseling conducted by people (concert sponsors) we know nothing about." PlankEye's concerts continued nevertheless to feature praise and testimony. "Welcome to the PlankEye show," Silletta would say at the start of some performances. "We invite you to worship with us this evening." The group's name apparently comes from Matthew 7:3.

PlankEye was sometimes called a punk band in their early days, but *HM* immediately clarified the description in their review of the debut *Spill,* indicating that the characterization only holds insofar as the original Orange County punk bands "were basically making raw pop music." *Spill* does have a certain garage band sound to it, but the group also demonstrates a strong sense of melody and a penchant for writing catchy hooks. Lyrically, the songs tend to be a tad superficial and predictable: the song "Power" begins, "Knock, knock, it's Jesus there / He's at the door of your heart." Still, the blatant expressions of faith marked the band as standing apart from most of the alternative groups in the Christian scene at the time: "I love you Lord, and I don't say it enough" ("Step Away"). *The Spark* took a big jump forward, with the song "Open House" garnering the most attention. Some critics compared the band to such groups as Green Day and Duran Duran, though PlankEye members protested the analogies.

Commonwealth is the masterpiece that would guarantee PlankEye a place in the annals of great Christian rock. Indeed, Silletta said that it was really the first real PlankEye *album,* the earlier projects being "just collections of songs we had been playing." Without exception, every review of *Commonwealth* praised the album for exhibiting growth far beyond the previous projects (which were no slouches). Relentless touring, coproduction by Luis Garcia and Gene Eugene (of **Adam**

Again), or some other combination of factors brought the group together with a progressive modern rock sound that actually drew allusions to The Moody Blues at some points, without abandoning the basic integrity of the garage sound (an unpretentious Moody Blues, perhaps?). Had the album been noticed by the general market, it might easily have rated among the Top 10 college albums of the year—assuming consumers could get past what they might regard as religious and spiritual imagery. Basically, PlankEye deepened their sound with more full and heavy guitar tones, distorted at times, ringing with melody at others. Silletta improved dramatically as a vocalist, both technically (overcoming a little pitch control problem on the previous projects) and emotionally. More important, the band simply had better songs—there is no filler on *Commonwealth* and at least five of the tracks are real gems—great pop songs, and terrific rock and roll. "B.C." and the title track are roller coaster songs, with churning guitars that carry the tunes up and down and around hairpin turns at breakneck speed. "Struck by the Chord" starts out at a slower pace but is filled with surprises that build, twist, and transform the song into something impossible to predict. "Placement" is an energetic, hard rock worship song in which the band either remembers some of their punk tricks or else cops them from old **Altar Boys** albums. "He" is a driving rocker, and "Beautiful" offers a midtempo break from the mostly hard rock with an atmospheric texture interrupted by occasional bursts of guitar firepower. The band also demonstrates considerable growth in the lyrics department on *Commonwealth.* Many of the tracks are addressed to God, some as praise, but all grounded in the realities of earthly existence. On "Whisper to Me" Silletta sings, "When I think you've left forever, I hear your voice whisper to me. . . ." On "Beautiful," he gives thanks for his beloved: "It's the little things she does that magnify your grace / And your grace resonates in my soul every time I see her face."

By the time *The One and Only* came out, PlankEye had become known as "the band that changes its sound every time out." The fourth disc would be no exception to what *Phantom Tollbooth* dubbed "the plank-rule." This time, they moved from the progressive classic rock of *Commonwealth* to embrace the post-punk, alterna-pop sound of groups like Foo Fighters. "Someday" and "Fall Down" have a bit of a Wallflowers feel, the former even featuring a harmonica. "It's Been So Very Long" sounds like it might have been written by Elvis Costello and played by Big Star. The group also continues to demonstrate theological and poetic depth in their songwriting. Silletta sings to God, "I guess it just takes this long to realize how much I don't know," and suggests, "If you keep opening doors, I promise that I'll keep testing the locks" ("How Much I Don't Know"). "Fall Down" seems to be inspired by Psalms 20 and 39. "Let's Try Again Tomorrow" was written about a fight

the band members had over where the group should be located. *The One and Only* was again produced by Eugene and Garcia. Though it lacked the surprising punch of *Commonwealth,* it was unanimously praised by critics. *7ball* said, "PlankEye is an oddity in that it retains its zesty youthful enthusiasm as it matures," and *CCM* dubbed the album, "Easily one of the most solid rock records out right now."

Then Silletta, who most people thought *was* PlankEye, left the band (and later formed **Fanmail**), along with drummer Adam Ferry, who went into full-time ministry. The group continued anyway, and like Genesis without Peter Gabriel, found a new sound that was probably no more of a radical transition than previous metamorphoses. BEC tried to hide the loss by not including any band pictures or list of band members in the liner notes to *Relocation,* but anyone who followed the Christian media knew that by now PlankEye was only a duo (Luis Garcia and Eric Balmer). Frank Lenz of **Fold Zandura** and **The Lassie Foundation** guested on drums, and producer Gene Eugene did the same on keyboards. In general, the group now displayed a pop-emo sound that would inspire references to Blur ("Break of Dawn") and Sting ("Break My Fall"). The project was received as the group's "most accessible album to date" and as "its most radio-oriented project," though few critics meant such comments as unqualified compliments. *Relocation* opens with the familiar sound of churning guitars (which they had not lost), introducing a bright, power-pop song with the dark title "Say Now That You're Sorry." Many would take the words as directed to Silletta: "Say now that you're sorry / I forgive you / I promise to restore now the order that we once had / Before all this came down." The album features more soft songs than previous projects, and almost everyone agreed that two of these represent the strongest cuts on the album. "Goodbye" is moody and melancholy, with a haunting, unforgettable melody. "Break My Fall" (the song that sounds like Sting) offers a vulnerable plea to either God or some human partner: "Break my fall today / I lack the strength it takes / To be invincible." As a bottom line, critics and fans who approached *Relocation* on its own terms praised it, while those who insisted on comparing it to previous PlankEye albums found it wanting. "There's nothing not to like here," wrote *True Tunes.* "An excellent find for fans of melodic modern rock!" On the other hand, *Phantom Tollbooth* couldn't resist quoting from what they regarded as the album's only truly great song ("Walk away / It's time to say Goodbye") and remarking that "the band needs to listen to their own lyrics."

By *Strange Exchange,* the band was a quartet again, with drummer Luiz Ruiz coming over from **Appleseed Cast.** Chris Colbert of **Fluffy/Duraluxe** coproduced the album and adds fuzzy feedback guitar to several tracks (notably, "Let Me Be Near You"). The opener, "This Is," is a power-pop song that sets the album's tone for straight-ahead emotional rock. "My Wife" comes as an acoustic cool-down halfway through the project. Most reviewers singled out an extended hidden track called "My Daughter" as a curious highlight—an eight-minute, sparse dirge dealing with the loss of a child.

Christian radio hits: "Compromise" (# 13 in 1998); "Fall Down" (# 22 in 1998).

J. J. Plasencio

2000—*J. J. Plasencio* (independent).

J. J. Plasencio was for some years the bass player for **Sixpence None the Richer,** leaving just before the band attained widespread commercial success. He became a pastor of music and arts at the Gateway Community Church in Austin, Texas, while playing bass for **Plumb** on their first album. In 2000, Plasencio recorded an independent album that features a number of guests from the above bands, as well as members of **Love Coma** and **PFR.** *Phantom Tollbooth* called the album "a refreshing piece of adult alternative music," and *True Tunes* described it as "a rewarding trip through the heart and soul of a true artist who has not left himself in the dust of narcissism and cynicism." The opening song "As Do I" is a particularly well-crafted and accessible number, relating Plasencio's testimony of finding God in art and creation. In "Little Boy" he recounts his feelings about having been abandoned by his birth mother as an infant. Another standout, "It's Alright," features lead vocals by **Plumb**'s Tiffany Arbuckle.

Platypus

See **Ty Tabor.**

The Players

Eric Darken, perc.; Mark Douthit, sax.; Tom Hemby, gtr.; Dann Huff, gtr.; Shane Keister, kybrd.; Terry McMillan, harmonica; Michael Omartian, kybrd.; Chris Rodriguez, gtr.; Tommy Sims, bass. 1996—*The Players* (Warner Alliance).

The Players was a one-time project put together by producer Bobby Blazier. Nine of Nashville's finest session musicians, all of whom have been involved with contemporary Christian music, were invited to contribute original songs (one apiece) and then gather to jam on each other's material. The mostly instrumental result was released as a benefit album for the Feed the Children hunger relief agency. All of the instrumentalists are well known for their contributions to albums by artists in the Christian and general markets. **Michael Omartian, Chris Rodriguez,** and **Tommy Sims** have also recorded as solo artists. Sims and Dann Huff had been members of **White Heart** (and Huff, of **Giant** and **The Front**). Sims,

who cowrote the Grammy award-winning song "Change the World" for **Eric Clapton,** once played bass for Bruce Springsteen. Many of the tracks have a spontaneous jam-in-the-studio feel to them, though a wide variety of styles is represented. Omartian offers a stripped-down piece with mainly acoustic piano and bass; Terry McMillan's "Soul Surfin" is a Latin-tinged number reminiscent of Santana or War.

Dove Awards: 1997 Instrumental Album *(The Players)*.

Plumb

Tiffany Arbuckle, voc.; Joe Porter, drums; Matt Stanfield, kybrd.; Stephen Leiweke, gtr.; J. J. Plasencio, bass (−1999) // B. J. Aberle, bass (+1999); Thad Beatty, gtr. (+1999). 1997—*Plumb* (Essential); 1999—*candycoatedwaterdrops*; 2000—*The Best of Plumb.*

The Nashville-based alternative rock band Plumb had inauspicious beginnings as their record label apparently wanted lead singer Tiffany Arbuckle to be "a Christian version of Alanis Morissette," but Arbuckle turned out to be too talented for such designs, and the group made some significant contributions that transcended the requisite clone songs. Arbuckle previously sang with the group **Benjamin.** The group's name was initially chosen from a song Arbuckle liked called "My Favorite Plum," by Suzanne Vega. She would later also relate it to the theme of a plumbline in the writings of certain biblical prophets (e.g., Amos 7:7, 8).

The debut album opens with the song that would gain the most radio airplay on progressive stations, "Sobering (Don't Turn Around)"—a song that sounds so much like everything on Morissette's *Jagged Little Pill* album as to be embarrassing. The same could also be said of "Who Am I?" the album's second and biggest hit (on college radio). Once the album got to track three, broader ranges of influence would appear. "Unforgivable" is more vaguely reminiscent of P. J. Harvey than of Morissette, and the very pretty "Endure" is closer to the female-fronted pop-rock of Garbage or No Doubt. The official closing song, "Send Angels," is a loop-filled, trance-like number reminiscent of Bjork. With so many images being invoked, the final effect is innovative and eclectic. *Phantom Tollbooth* praised the record for its "outstanding production values, powerful vocals, edgy guitars, and infectious rhythms." *HM* said, "This album's got everything that's cool: very strong female vocals, walls of distortion, the occasional techno sound popping its head up, and a few drop-a-cement-mixer-on-your-head industrial drums." The song "Crazy" is a standout track, a somewhat screechy tune that doesn't sound like anyone in the general market, though the Cranberries might provide the closest reference point if one were absolutely required. *Plumb* was coproduced by Dan Haseltine of **Jars of Clay** and that group's sometime producer, Matt Bronleewe. The album includes one old Jars song, the fairly hard rocking "Concrete," on which

Haseltine contributes vocals. The album is also worthy of note due to the dearth of female-fronted alternative rock bands in Christian music in the late '90s. Plumb and **Fleming and John** pretty much had that field to themselves. Lyrically, the album tends to be both issue-oriented and a bit quirky. Arbuckle describes "Crazy" as "a sarcastic song about people who look to celebrities or others as idols," though that is not necessarily evident otherwise. "Send Angels" deals with temptation with some poignancy, describing the lure of adultery for a man who feels he is not aging kindly. "Willow Tree" deals similarly with alcoholism and its consequences for a marriage. "Unforgivable" deals with the effort of a grown woman to relate to a cold and verbally abusive father who treated her like a burden throughout her childhood. As a hidden bonus track, Arbuckle sings "Pluto," a song she wrote with **Eric Champion** speculating on the possibility of extraterrestrial life.

On *candycoatedwaterdrops,* Plumb moved decidedly toward mainstream and predictable contemporary Christian music. That said, Arbuckle nevertheless delivers some fine songs in the relaxed tradition of artists like Suzanne Vega, Sarah MacLachlan, and especially Natalie Imbruglia. Arbuckle told *Release,* "Over the last year, I've been thinking, I'm not really the 'Crazy' type." The album starts strong with "Late, Great Planet Earth," a song about the end of the world that features some driving, crunchy guitars and a string section of the London Symphony Orchestra, as conducted by **Tom Howard.** The closing title track is also excellent and interesting, a slow, country number in a style reminiscent of **Over the Rhine.** Otherwise, the album is "neither derivative nor daring," as *CCM* would put it, delivering mostly adult contemporary pop numbers like "Stranded" that have little edge to them but possess an integrity of their own. Lyrically, the song "God-Shaped Hole" (written with **Wayne Kirkpatrick**) represents a cliché-ridden nadir, but "Drugstore Jesus" takes on demagogue preachers who offer a lower-case, trinket version of the Lord. "Late, Great Planet Earth" is actually profound and poetic in ways not at all like the book from which it apparently takes its name. Overall, the album has more of a thematic focus on man-woman relationships ("Worlds Collide," "Stranded," "Lie Low") than the debut project. *The Best of Plumb* is an unnecessary album that has "contractual obligation" written all over it. It came out about the same time that **All Star United** also left Essential, releasing a compilation of hits from all two of their recordings.

For trivia buffs: Essential Records originally signed Arbuckle to be a clone not of Alanis Morissette but teenybopper Debbie Gibson. Although the album (titled *Galaxy Girl*) was never made, one of the publicity shots portraying her in a pink wig and tu-tu was included as a bit of a joke in the *Plumb* CD booklet. "It was so stupid," she claims.

Christian radio hits: "Unforgivable" (# 19 in 1997); "Endure" (# 9 in 1997); "God-Shaped Hole" (# 1 in 1999); "Here with Me" (# 1 for 2 weeks in 1999); "Phobic" (# 18 in 2000).

Dove Awards: 2000 Alternative/Modern Rock Album *(candycoatedwaterdrops).*

Plush

Matt Camp, gtr., voc.; George Hoppenstedt, voc.; Tim Vaughn, gtr., voc.; Clint Walker, drums, voc. 1999—*Plush* (Absolute).

Plush is a Midwest Christian rock band that was a favorite of *HM* magazine critics and readers for a couple of years before they landed a major-label deal with Absolute. The group has a heartland rock, guitar-based sound not too dissimilar from Bruce Springsteen or John Mellencamp. "Desiree," a song about a young woman who hasn't been able to find her way in life, first attracted attention to the band. Cowritten by Tony Palacios of **Guardian,** the midtempo song features a memorable chorus ("Don't fade, Desiree / Kiss the Son, come out and play") and lyrics that struck a chord with a number of people when the band was still playing mostly secular venues. "We do outdoor shows where we get, probably fifty percent unsaved people just walking up and watching," group leader Vaughn told *HM.* After placing a couple of songs on that magazine's compilation discs, the group recorded their self-titled album, which was produced by Palacios, who cowrote most of the songs. "Desiree" is one of the more down-tempo numbers. "Forever" extols the eternal quality of God's forgiveness. "You Belong to Me" is sung from the perspective of Jesus to a Christian, explaining the reason for their trials ("If everything just turned up roses, you would never know the grace that I have for you").

Plus One

Nathan Cole, voc.; Gabriel Combs, voc.; Jeremy Mhire, voc.; Jason Perry, voc.; Nathan Walters, voc. 2000—*The Promise* (Atlantic); 2002—*Obvious.*

www.plusoneonline.com

Plus One was Christian music's first and most blatant attempt to get in on the "boy band" phenomenon. The group is as indistinguishable musically from the Backstreet Boys, *NSYNC, and 98 degrees as all of those general market groups are from each other. Five cute young men (aged eighteen to twenty) from Assemblies of God churches (Nathan Cole, Gabriel Combs, and Jason Perry are preacher's kids) were selected from nationwide auditions for an ensemble that specialized in vocal harmony and choreographed stage movements. Plus One was an enormous success. Their debut album and summer concert tour broke all kinds of sales records. The group was invited to sing at the Democratic National Convention with Stevie Wonder and Mary Chapin Carpenter and they appeared on an episode of the TV series *Days of Our Lives.* Wherever they would perform, hordes of barely pubescent girls would scream through every song and, after the show, line up for hours to meet their heartthrobs in person and give them stuffed animals, notes, and home phone numbers in exchange for pictures and autographs.

Musically, the only difference between Plus One and other boy bands is that in addition to singing sentimental songs above romantic love they also sing sentimental songs about God. Not that there's anything wrong with that, as Jerry Seinfeld would say—and, for what it's worth, they sing those songs exceptionally well. The familiar smooth, flowing harmonies and lyrical melodies allow no compromise in quality from what would be found on any of the releases by the general market bands listed above. *The Promise* was produced by David Foster, who has also produced albums for Boyz II Men, Brandy, and *NSYNC. "Written on My Heart" and "Last Flight Out" are chaste romantic songs that would be right at home on Casey Kasem's Top 40. "My Friend" is an ode to friendship. The Christian part comes on the album's title song, which describes God as constant and true ("You're never alone—that's His promise"). "God Is in This Place" offers a similar assurance of presence. The group's spirituality seems age-appropriate for their audience; they avoid preachy moralizing and threats of judgment and present the Christian experience and vision in appealing and heartwarming ways. "Soul Tattoo" and "My Life" are also standout tracks. *The Promise* went gold with sales of over 500,000. On their next album, the boys would reprise the high-energy pop songs ("Start to Fly") and passionate ballads ("Calling Down an Angel"), but also worked more aggressive rock songs ("Camouflage," Under the Influence") into the mix. Group members took on a larger share of the songwriting, and the sophomore project shows some development toward engaging spiritual themes at a deeper level. "Kick Me" challenges fair-weather friends (or Christians) who are quick to pass judgment and kick people when they're down.

Plus One is actually less an example of Christian music stealing *from* the secular arena than it is an instance of taking something *back*. All of the general market boy bands are basically just junior versions of **4 Him,** with roots that ultimately trace back to southern gospel quartets. Many critics have noted the irony of young teens and preteens becoming so enamored of what is essentially adult contemporary music. Just as *NSYNC and company tend to have a fan base of teenyboppers *and* their parents (but no one in between), so Plus One seems to cause gagging among college students while appealing both to those too young to know the band is not cool and to those too old to care.

Christian radio hits: "Written on My Heart" (# 1 for 7 weeks in 2000); "God Is in This Place" (# 2 in 2000); "My Life" (# 1 in 2001); "Soul Tattoo" (# 3 in 2001).

Dove Awards: 2001 New Artist of the Year.

Pocket Change

Charlie Arnold, bass; Timme Asimos, voc., gtr.; Brian Saunders, drums. 1997—*Steadfast* (Liquid Disc); 1999—*Wake Up* (RMC).

Pocket Change began as a melodic punk band from Virginia but moved toward a harder sound on their second outing. Many critics compared *Steadfast* to **MxPx,** even noting similarities between Timme Asimos's vocals and those of Mike Herrera. The worship song "My God" from that album gained some notice as the only track to feature a ska sound, complete with horns. The band also performs a punchy version of the classic youth group song "I Have Decided to Follow Jesus." *Wake Up* has a faster and heavier sound, while retaining melodic flavor. A number of tracks, including "Give It Up," feature the sort of "whoa-oh-oh" background vocals that added spice to **Imagine This**'s best album, *Love*. The band also delivers a metal version of "Amazing Grace," perhaps in hope of replicating the novelty success of "I Have Decided" (the most popular track on *Steadfast*).

Asimos says that Pocket Change did not begin as a Christian band and that they did not even know any Christian music until the entire group attended a concert by the band **Strongarm** and came to recognize that "the only reason to make music is to glorify God." After that, they would assume a strong ministry focus, performing songs with blatantly evangelical lyrics and concluding their concerts with altar calls.

P.O.D. (a.k.a. **Payable On Death**)

Noah "Wuv" Bernardo, drums; Marcos Curiel, gtr.; Traa Daniels, bass; Sonny Sandoval, voc. 1993—*Snuff the Punk* (Rescue); 1996—*Brown*; 1998—*Live at Tomfest*; 1999—*The Warriors* [EP] (Tooth and Nail); *The Fundamentals of Southtown* (Atlantic); 2001—*Satellite*.

www.payableondeath.com

Southern California's hard rapcore band P.O.D. has a success story similar to that of artists like **Jars of Clay** and **Amy Grant.** All three of those musically diverse artists belong to the small handful of Christian performers who have successfully crossed over to find acceptance within the general market. Unlike Grant, however, P.O.D. did so with material that did not represent a departure from their normal faith-filled repertoire. And unlike Jars, they did not just happen into mainstream success on their debut outing but only achieved it after some eight years of tooling away in church basements and parking lots. Indeed, the band's worldly sound and appearance prevented them from gaining much of an audience even in the Christian market before they hit big in the secular scene with *The Fundamentals of Southtown* in late 1999. That album went platinum and the group wound up in constant rotation on MTV. Suddenly, the Christian subculture woke up, discovered the group, and said, "Hey, they're one of ours!" To be fair, some Christian publications like *HM* and *7ball* had been stumping for the band all along, but both *Rolling Stone* and *Spin* did features on them before *CCM*. In January 2001, when P.O.D. was probably the most popular and best-known Christian band in the world, they were finally featured in a cover story for *CCM* and lead singer Sonny copped a bit of an attitude: *"Now* it's a little bit easier to like P.O.D. Everyone is like, 'Dude! P.O.D.! I'm down with ya!' . . . Man, why didn't you see it before? Why did you wait for the world to start embracing P.O.D.?"

The group formed in 1991 in Southtown, a small, mostly Hispanic area south of San Diego and close to the Mexican border that (before P.O.D.) was best known as the location of the McDonald's restaurant where a gunman killed 21 people in 1984. Sonny and Wuv (group members go by first names only) were cousins and next-door neighbors, growing up in a rough environment. "Our Dads were fifteen, sixteen, when they had us," Wuv told *Rolling Stone*. "They were still kids, still doing their partying. . . . People used to break in and put my Mom and Dad down, looking for drugs." Wuv's father was indeed a drug dealer, but he underwent a dramatic conversion to Christianity after attending a Christian music concert, demonstrating the power and reality of such faith for his son. Sonny's devotion to Christ was aroused when his mother died of cancer and his adolescent struggle with grief and mortality brought him to an epiphany of grace. The two formed the nucleus for P.O.D., recruiting neighbor Marcos and Cleveland native Traa to round out the group. The group's sound was a blend of reggae, rap, hard rock, and thrash metal that would ultimately have them compared to artists like Korn and, especially, the Korn-like Limp Bizkit. But P.O.D. was on the scene before Korn was making much of a splash; the primary influence for their sound would appear to be Rage Against the Machine, leavened, perhaps, with generous dollops of Santana. In 2000, Christian music fans (and magazines) would tend to lump P.O.D. in with Korn, Bizkit, and even Kid Rock as part of a new craze; the groups may sound alike to those who are not true rapcore fans, but they are actually quite distinct. P.O.D. has always brought a Latin-inflected variation to the genre that marks them as unique.

From the start, P.O.D. was unapologetically evangelical and at least in the early years they viewed themselves primarily as a ministry band. "Our first year together, we were totally different on stage than we are now," Marcos told *CCM* in 2001. "We were a little more to the right-extreme, you know what I'm saying? But that's all we knew at the time. We were being straight out, 'Jesus this . . . If you don't turn, man you're gonna burn.' " As the band's reputation preceded them, secular venues closed their doors and, since the group had little support from the Christian market either, they determined to tone down the rhetoric. "We had to reevaluate," says Marcos. "Over

the years, we've learned it takes love and it takes compassion and it takes wisdom." The group's rep would indeed change, but unlike **U2** or even **King's X,** they would always be strongly identified as "a Christian band—and proud of it!" *Rolling Stone* said, "Sonny gets krunk with Christ without stooping to overt Bible thumping." *The Chicago Tribune* ran a headline, "P.O.D. is into God, With Tact." When appearing on MTV's *Total Request Live,* Wuv responded to a question about whether the group takes any heat for being so open about their faith: "People might talk trash, but they're gonna know we're down for what we believe in—and that's all that matters." Host Carson Daly said, "That's about the dopest thing I've ever heard on this stage" [Ed. note to the un-hip: "dope" is good, like "cool" or "rad"].

Both *Snuff the Punk* and *Brown* would be remastered and re-released in greatly improved versions after *Southtown* hit it big. The first of these presents the group forging their style and serves less as a continuing musical legacy than as a historical testament to their role as pioneers in the rapcore field. *Brown* contains "Full Color" in which Sonny offers his testimony, focusing on his mother's struggle with leukemia, which took her life at the age of thirty-six. The six-minute-plus track starts slow and builds into a reggae/rock groove, with compelling lyrics ("Why, O why did my mommy have to die / Too many questions, no answers, confuses my mind / Like what did I do? what did she do? / Who's to blame?"). The song "Preach" blatantly states the band's intention of proclaiming their creed. "Live and Die" deals with the environment in which most of them grew up, amidst gangs, crime, and urban violence. "Breathe Babylon" and the slower paced "Selah" would also become favorites among fans. Many of these songs would reappear in live versions on *Live at Tomfest,* recorded at an annual Christian festival.

P.O.D.'s big break came in 1997 when Atlantic Records agreed to sign the band to a major label, general market deal (their previous "company," Rescue, was an independent label designed just for the band). While waiting to get the big album out, the band satisfied impatient fans with *The Warriors* EP, which contained a demo of the song "Southtown" and new versions of songs from *Brown*. Then *The Fundamentals of Southtown* was released. Produced by Howard Benson, who had also worked with such bands as Sepultura and Motorhead, the record seems likely to be the defining moment of the group's career. P.O.D. describes the project as "our hardest, fastest, and loudest album to date." More to the point, Traa would tell *HM,* "We've taken every element of every style of music we're into and put it all into one album . . . it's everything that we are!" Eventually, three songs on the album would burn up video channels and radio airwaves on stations devoted to hard music: the title track, which deals with life in the ghetto;

"Rock the Party," a dance manifesto that became the Number One request song on MTV for the entire summer of 2000; and a near-metal cover of **U2**'s "Bullet the Blue Sky," which segues into a recitation of Psalm 150 in Hebrew. "Hollywood" and "Outkast" are also furious songs, with lyrics that speak of taking a stand for God over against the expectations of a superficial society. "Set Your Eyes to Zion" is a slower, reggae song with a worshipful feel. "Follow Me" takes its lyrics from the words of Jesus: "What good is it for a man to gain the whole world yet lose or forfeit his very self? / He must deny himself and take up his cross daily and follow me."

Satellite sent the single "Alive" spinning into the stratosphere of general market charts with celebratory lyrics matched in the history of popular music only by The Rascals "Beautiful Morning" or **U2**'s "Beautiful Day." The song landed like a hand grenade on cynical post-grunge, I-hate-myself-and-the-entire-world radio stations, exploding with the lines "Everyday is a new day / I'm thankful for every breath I take / I won't take it for granted." Sonny sings unapologetically to God, "I feel so alive for the very first time . . . Now that I know you I could never turn my back away / Now that I see you I believe no matter what they say." Strong evangelical sentiments also inform "Without Jah, Nothin' " (a hardcore song that dissolves into a reggae jam session with repeated Sunday school lyrics of "Jesus loves you") and "Thinking about Forever" (a celestial rap ballad that presents Sonny's letter to his departed mother). The closing song, "Portrait," repeatedly lifts up Christ by name. On a broader scale, however, the recurrent theme of *Satellite* seems to be facing the reality of evil in the world. Somewhat ironically, the album was released on September 11, 2001, and some of its lyrics seemed relevant to the point of prophetic: "Who's to blame for the lives that tragedies claim / No matter what you say, it don't take away the pain" ("Youth of a Nation"). The just-quoted song actually reflects on the senselessness of Columbine-like violence among youth with a first verse that updates Neil Young's "Powderfinger" by presenting from-the-grave thoughts of a massacre victim ("Last day of the rest of my life, wish I would've known / 'Cause I didn't kiss my mama goodbye / I didn't tell her that I loved her and how much I cared / Or thank my pops for all the talks / And all the wisdom he shared"). Musically, *Satellite* is hardhitting and diverse, with guest appearances by reggae artist Eek-a-Mouse ("Ridiculous"), Christian Lindskog of **Blindside** ("Anything Right"), and H.R. of Bad Brains ("Without Jah, Nothin' "). Both "Alive" and the title track are performed in a new **DC Talk**-inspired style that weds rap with singing. "Boom," "Set It Off," and "Portrait" are built on moshable rhythms with enough loud screaming to appease fans of Bizkit, Korn, or *Southtown.*

P.O.D. placed songs on numerous film soundtracks, including *Any Given Sunday, Little Nicky,* and *Blair Witch 2.* In the summer of 2000, they played the prestigious Ozfest tour headlined by infamous Black Sabbath front man Ozzy Osbourne. In general, the group has not only met with respect for their convictions in the general market, but (with few exceptions) has won acclaim among Christian pundits for their uncompromising ability to remain faithful as sheep in the midst of wolves. They have met with criticism only from narrow-minded and anti-incarnational quarters (James Dobson's *Focus on the Family* attacked them for touring on the same bill with non-Christian bands). Curiously, the group has not only served as ambassadors of Christ to the world but also has sought to defend the secular scene against unwarranted biases that fans of Christian music often harbor. They have, for instance, given the lie to the common assumption that general market labels will not promote Christian bands unless they compromise on their lyrics. "At first, Atlantic didn't even bring up our faith," Sonny told *Release* magazine. "It was us who kept bringing it up to make sure it wasn't an issue. I was expecting them to tell us to tone down the preaching. I let them know we weren't going to change, and they said they didn't *want* us to change. They said, 'Everyone is preaching something, so why not preach God?' "

The commitment to Christian faith and spirituality is indeed a part of P.O.D.'s basic persona and one gets the impression that even their legions of non-Christian fans would be disappointed if they tried to hide it. *Rolling Stone* said (in its review of *Satellite*), "If P.O.D.'s religious devotion is what inspired them to turn out the most soulful hard rock record so far this year, then maybe more new-metalheads should get down with God." An analogy may lie with the music of Rastafarian Bob Marley—one of P.O.D.'s obvious influences. "Ninety-five percent of Bob Marley's lyrics are straight Scripture," says Sonny. Non-Rastafarians and even completely irreligious people not only enjoy Marley's music but enjoy it in part because of the religious devotion that informs it. In a similar way, no P.O.D. fan, Christian or otherwise, can miss the fact that this band is driven by something that imbues their music with meaning and power. "Every song might not say 'Jesus' in it," says Marcos, "but the passion and emotion behind it—I'm playing that to the higher power above, which is God, dude."

Christian radio hits: "Set Your Eyes to Zion" (# 19 in 2000).

Mark Pogue (and Fortress)

1991—*Restoration* (Pakaderm).

A notable session guitarist who had played with **Margaret Becker, Morgan Cryar, Rick Cua,** and **DeGarmo and Key,** Mark Pogue made one solo album for **John** and Dino **Elefante**'s Pakaderm label. His band, Fortress, included Dave Raven on drums and Mark Robertson (of **Brighton, Generation, A Ragamuffin Band, The Stand, Under Midnight,** and **This Train**) on bass. Pogue's raspy voice comes through best on blues-based songs like "Holy Man" and "Money Can't Buy." The song "Why Do I Believe?" reached Number Two on the Christian radio rock chart. The song that attracted the most attention was "Bride of Restoration" written out of an autobiographical experience. "Seven years ago, I came to the Lord while I was going through a divorce," Pogue told *CCM* in 1992. "Restoration was impossible at that point." But some three years later, Pogue's former wife "came to know the Lord after a concert that featured Pogue and Cryar," and their remarriage prompted the song: "Just like a tale told in a story book . . . he put hope in my heart / To heal a marriage that broke apart."

Christian radio hits: "Bride of Restoration" (# 9 in 1991); "Love Is Just a Prayer Away" (# 5 in 1992); "Let It Go" (# 13 in 1992).

Point of Grace

Heather Floyd (Payne), voc.; Denise Jones, voc.; Terry Lang (Jones), voc.; Shelly Phillips (Breen), voc. 1993—*Point of Grace* (Word); 1995—*The Whole Truth*; 1996—*Life, Love, and Other Mysteries*; 1998—*Steady On*; 2000—*Rarities and Remixes*; 2001—*Free to Fly*.

www.pointofgrace.net

Point of Grace are the undisputed superstars of '90s adult contemporary Christian music. The all-female vocal quartet charted some fifteen Number One songs on adult contemporary Christian radio in their first five years together. Those songs, all teeming with contagious melodies, tight harmonies, and a bright outlook on life would set the standard that groups like **Avalon** and **Sierra** strove to meet. Point of Grace is purely a vocal group—none of the members write or play instruments. They have drawn on a bevy of professional songwriters (including Grant Cunningham, Regie Hamm, and Geoff Thurman) for material. The four women have distinctive voices and they trade off singing lead. Unfortunately, no credits are provided on their albums to let the listener know who sings what.

Point of Grace was first introduced to the Christian market as a female version of **4 Him** and was often compared to Wilson Phillips. Neither analogy quite works, as at least two of the women have stronger voices than any of the men in **4 Him** (or any of the women in Wilson Phillips), making POG a much better musical group at least some of the time. To be more specific, the group scores best when it takes on R&B songs like their first hit, "I'll Be Believing." Otherwise, they tend to lapse into being just one of the dozens (hundreds?) of MOR adult contemporary madrigal groups, singing ballads that may inspire fans of that genre but are in no way distinctive. Of course, adult contemporary music is almost by definition indistinct, since fans of such music generally find a "heard it before" sound appealing. POG serves such interests well but also

pushes the edge of the envelope by challenging the "no surprises" preference of their fan base a few times on every outing. The combo began in 1991 as a trio called the Ouachitones, formed at Ouachita Baptist University in Arkadelphia, Arkansas, consisting of three friends who had grown up together as part of the same church in Norman, Oklahoma. With the addition of Shelley Phillips, who had come to the college from Little Rock, they became Say So (not to be confused with the Nashville duo **Say-So**) and then adopted the name Point of Grace after winning the grand prize at the Christian Artist Seminar in Estes Park, Colorado, in 1992.

The group's debut album was one of the most successful projects in Christian music history, selling over 200,000 copies and easily nabbing the group a Dove award for Best New Artist. Industry hype trumpeted a Guinness-like statistic: *Point of Grace* was the first album in the history of recorded music (any genre, any market) to produce six consecutive Number One radio singles. Of course, such accolades depend on *which* chart one is talking about, and who keeps the records—the Christian music industry keeps its own charts, which reflect ratings for a relatively small pond, and in this case, the Number Ones were all accumulated on a subchart for a sub-sub genre (Christian Music—Adult Contemporary). Still, the album did take the Christian music world by storm and also got the group noticed within the world at large. Write-ups on the group would appear in *U.S.A. Today, Ladies Home Journal,* and *Saturday Evening Post.* As time went by, the group would not only do *The 700 Club* but also *Live with Regis and Kathie Lee, CNN Showbiz, ABC World News Tonight,* and *CBS This Morning.* Their talent and charm never failed to endear them to hosts and audiences alike as they became real-life symbols of the vision that many held for white-bread America. "None of our parents are divorced," Denise Jones said, "and we all have remained sexually pure and drug-free." The wholesome, squeaky-clean image has been both a strength and weakness. A *New York Times* reporter who followed them around for a while noted, "They are among the nicest, most sincere people I have ever met . . . they are also quite possibly the blandest." Critics sometimes complain that their albums, while filled with songs that emanate commitment, faithfulness, and hope, betray little awareness of struggle, confusion, or mystery. *7ball* once observed that a POG song is much like a '60s era sitcom *(Father Knows Best, Ozzie and Harriet, Leave It to Beaver)* in that all problems are "summed up and neatly packaged" by the end in a feel-good way that assures the audience all is right with their world. A less cynical response might simply note that POG strives to communicate encouragement.

Point of Grace opens with the aforementioned "I'll Be Believing," professing a constancy of faith, come what may. "Faith, Hope and Love" is also in the R&B groove, tapping into traditional gospel for an effective a capella intro. "Living the Legacy" is another powerful song, extolling the benefits of holding to a faith that goes back three generations. On "This Day" POG sounds like **Matthew Ward**-less **2nd Chapter of Acts.** *The Whole Truth* has two highlights, the rousing opening song, "Gather at the River," and "The Great Divide," which uses an age-old image to depict the cross of Christ as a bridge crossing the canyon that sin has carved between humanity and God. *Life, Love, and Other Mysteries* received the weakest reviews of all the group's projects, with an ill-advised cover of Earth, Wind, and Fire's "Singasong" coming in for the most abuse. But by 2001, *CCM* critics chose this one alone of the group's albums for placement on its list of "The 100 Greatest Albums in Christian Music" (at Number Forty-three). By then, they liked the up-tempo "Keep the Candle Burning," the acoustic "Circle of Friends," and the piano ballad "God Forbid." *Steady On* was produced by **Brown Bannister** and, unfortunately, contains none of the R&B numbers that the group does best. The album does feature one stellar song: "Amazing" (cowritten by **David Zaffiro**), sung in a sultry style that almost recalls the incredible debut album of **Kim Hill.** There are other strong numbers. "Drawing Me Closer" begins with an intro on which the group sounds enough like Wilson Phillips to have fooled any of those girls' famous parents, and then morphs into a surprising upbeat song about the appealing shelter of God's grace and peace. "Saving Grace" and "Better Days" are classic pop, perfectly performed. "The Wonder of It All" (by **Brent Bourgeois** and **Michael W. Smith**) strives to be a Celine Dion-type anthem with hymnic lyrics. "The Song Is Alive" demonstrates that POG is not a rock group, something that most people probably could have told them without the evidence. *CCM* described *Free to Fly* as "the most progressive, energetic collection of Point of Grace's career," but the reasons for such a claim are hard to discern. Working with six different producers, the women present eleven Christian-version-of-Wilson-Phillips songs very similar to those on their previous projects, with a noticeable tilt toward the sound of teen-pop sensations like Britney Spears and Jennifer Lopez. "Begin with Me" and "Something So Good" (by far the best cut) do feature some rock guitar, and on "Free Indeed" one of the women tries out a slightly distorted Alanis Morissette vocal. The quality of the songs themselves, furthermore, is consistent and strong (given the musical limitations of the adult contemporary genre). "Praises Forevermore" is a worship song written by **Darlene Zschech.**

Point of Grace endorses and supports the charitable organization Mercy Ministries, which builds homes for unwed teenage mothers. Two of their songs ("The House That Mercy Built" from *Whole Truth* and "Circle of Friends" from *Life, Love, and Other Mysteries*) concern the work of that organization. In 2002, they launched a new organization, Girls of Grace, which sponsors conferences "to encourage young women to live their lives from the inside out, cultivating beauty within and experiencing the unconditional love of God." The group has also taken part in annual Young Messiah tours and recorded a Christmas album. Their *Rarities and Remixes* provides collectors with a few songs from an indie demo they recorded as Say So, as well as two songs recorded for various artist compilations and some new mixes of favorite hits. The women have also coauthored a book with Davin Seay that relates anecdotes from their daily lives and offers advice to teenage girls about such matters as dating and sexual purity (*Life, Love, and Other Mysteries,* Simon and Schuster, 1996).

Christian radio hits: "I'll Be Believing" (# 7 in 1993); "One More Broken Heart" (# 20 in 1994); "Faith, Hope and Love" (# 17 in 1994); "Dying to Reach You" (# 10 in 1995); "Gather at the River" (# 14 in 1995); "God Is with Us" (# 11 in 1996); "Love Like No Other" (# 14 in 1996); "Keep the Candle Burning" (# 7 in 1996); "You Are the Answer" (# 4 in 1997); "Circle of Friends" (# 20 in 1997); "Steady On" (# 10 in 1998); "The Song Is Alive" (# 14 in 2000).

Dove Awards: 1994 New Artist of the Year; 1996 Group of the Year; 1996 Pop/Contemporary Album *(The Whole Truth);* 1996 Pop/Contemporary Song ("The Great Divide").

Point of Recognition

Aaron, voc.; Michael; Jesse; Ryan; Jason, voc. (–2000). 1999—*Admiration of a Son* (316); 2000—*Refresh, Renew* (Facedown).

Hardcore punk band Point of Recognition from Marietta, California, makes music in an old-school style that delights fans of Christian groups like **Focused, Strongarm,** and **Unashamed.** The band has a hard metal edge but says they have avoided going into metal because "there are just so many groups doing that, and there's not enough old school." For their debut album, the group (whose members only have first names) employed twin vocalists, but one of these (Jason) damaged his vocal chords while making the album and had to drop out of the band when the CD was released. In their lyrics, Point of Recognition offers blatantly Christian statements that allow no doubt as to where they are coming from. "True purity is only from Jesus Christ," they declare on "Unlawful Burden": "Come to reality, open your eyes." They also embrace the bold militancy of punk: "Fight for Jesus, and no one will bring you down." Their sophomore album features the songs "No One Gets Out Alive" and "No Regrets."

Polarboy

Pol Buckingham, voc., gtr.; Matthew Loftis, drums; Joe Nawrocki, gtr.; Rob Wilson, bass // Greg Walton, kybrd. (+ 2000). 1998—*Back from Nowhere* (Rustproof); 2000—*4008.*

Polarboy is a Christian band from the heartland that plays basic rock and roll. The members all met while they were students at Lexington Baptist College in Kentucky and they formed the group without any immediate career or ministry goals. The debut album, particularly, showcases this "make music for the joy of it" motivation. Critics reached far and wide for general market comparisons (Counting Crows, Wallflowers, Matchbox 20) to describe the group's sound but nothing ever seemed to click. The best may be this: "Polarboy mixes electric and acoustic guitars, playing with an earnest energy that mixes punk passion with Dave Matthews Band-styled sensitivity." In some respects, the group resembles such Christian market acts as **Seven Day Jesus** and **The Waiting.** A wide range of influences is detectable in a punchy rock mix that never allows any one reference to dominate or become distracting. The debut opens with one of its two strongest songs, "I'll Try," a rhythmic track that bursts out of the gate with an a capella vocal chanting the intriguing line, "Run away my dove, run away my dove / Getting easier to push and easy to shove." Then the trap set kicks in, and the guitars, and it all just *rocks.* The lyrical theme, as it turns out, seems to be about seeking to remain in the will of God amidst all the temptations and allure of the music business. *Back from Nowhere* also includes one other triumph—the bouncy, infectious "In My Shoes," a relationship song about making painful decisions amidst heartbreak. On both tracks, and throughout the album, Polarboy scores mainly on the basis of Buckingham's clear and powerful vocals. The sophomore release increased the quotient of R.E.M.-like southern rock and even featured one banjo-driven yee-ha anthem ("Mountainmen"). The standout song "In the Name of" is a strong prayer that finds the group backed by a gospel choir. Polarboy's keyboard player, Greg Walton, released an independent album called *The Simple Truth* in 1999.

Poole

Harv Evans; Harry Evans; Jeff Booth (−1999); Combat Chuck (−1999) // William Campbell (+ 1999); Dean Nitz, bass (+ 1999). 1995—*Alaska Days* (spinART); 1999—*Among Whom We Shine.*

Poole was formed by two former members of **The Throes** and after some personnel changes morphed into a band composed of four members of that band, including **Throes** front man William Campbell. *Alaska Days* was a fine collection of pop songs by Harold "Bear" Evans but saw virtually no distribution, being sold mainly through the mail. *Among Whom We Shine* is essentially a **Throes** reunion album, though it is musically brighter in sound and attitude, lacking the darker elements of **Throes** material. *HM* describes it as "a jangly yet driving album full of bouncing beautiful pop harmonies."

Poor Old Lu

Nick Barber, bass; Scott Hunter, voc.; Aaron Sprinkle, gtr., kybrd.; Jesse Sprinkle, drums, perc. 1992—*Star Studded Super Step* (independent); 1993—*Mindsize* (Alarma); 1994—*Sin; Straight Six* [EP]; 1996—*A Picture of the Eighth Wonder;* 1998—*Chrono 1993–1998* (KMG); *In Their Final Performance.*

www.pooroldlu.com

Seattle band Poor Old Lu arose out of the '90s grunge scene with connections to that environment but with an almost anti-grunge melodic accessibility and hopefulness that also set them apart from other Christian Seattle bands like **Grammatrain** and **Sometime Sunday.** The group took its name from a central character of C. S. Lewis's Narnia tales, a girl named Lucy who sometimes gets called "Poor Old Lu" by her companions. The group was one of the most accomplished and creative Christian bands of the '90s. One of the few bands in Christian or secular music truly deserving of the "alternative rock" label, they crafted an original sound that sometimes sounded like a brighter Soundgarden or a livelier Smashing Pumpkins but always created more precedents than it followed. They often seemed influenced by late '60s psychedelia. One critic called them "a Seattle version of R.E.M.," noting the penchant for dry, sometimes jangly guitars, and for subdued, sometimes breathy, vocals set back in the mix. **Aaron Sprinkle,** who would pursue a solo career, became famous for his waves of guitar, but his brother Jesse was perhaps the band's standout talent—one of the finest drummers and percussionists in modern rock. **Jeremy Enigk** of **Sunny Day Real Estate** sang with the band in an early incarnation, but left before their first recording. In terms of composition, Poor Old Lu usually crafted intelligent and poetic songs that, to quote *7ball* "wed bright pop bounce with sudden, violent explosions of doubt and anger." The group disbanded in 1996, giving "their final performance" in a high school gymnasium. Barber and Aaron Sprinkle formed the short-lived **Rose Blossom Punch.** Jesse Sprinkle recorded with a band called The World Inside.

Pool Old Lu recorded an independent debut album called *Star Studded Super Step* when the members were aged sixteen to eighteen. Released on cassette only, the project has a muddy quality and all of its significant songs were later redone for subsequent albums. Once the group took off, however, *Super Step* became a collector's trophy, prompting Alarma to release it on CD in 1995 with fourteen bonus tracks (demos and fun-in-the studio bits of humor and half-songs). After the group disbanded, KMG released a 1998 abbreviated version of this CD with only four of the bonus tracks. *Mindsize* was **Poor Old Lu**'s breakthrough album, produced by **Terry Taylor** with assistance from Derri Daugherty. The album immediately caught the attention of critics and won the group a strong fan base. It is a surprisingly mature production, especially considering that all of the members were still in their teens. "All Pretty for TV" critiques middle-class materialism with an attitude typical of the '60s, but then "Cruciality" turns a gospel gaze on the ultimate bankruptcy of flower power as well. "This world needs the Son," Hunter concludes. *Sin* is something of a concept album insofar as almost every tracks deals with the titular subject, but the band is too intelligent to focus on excesses of the flesh or other mundane matters that often drive the obsessions of gnostic-influenced American Christianity. Rather, self-absorption is exposed as the root of all evils, as Hunter lays bare his own vulnerabilities and prods listeners to examine themselves just as honestly. If "I Am No Good" wallows a bit too greedily in Calvinist total depravity, "My World Falls Down" and "Sickly" expose the ultimate emptiness of life that revolves around one's own predilections. "Ring True" approaches worship with its chorus, "Love the Maker / Crown the King / Who gives us all / And makes me sing." The rocker "Sickly" reveals a tougher, almost **Black-Eyed Sceva** sound. A similar sound would inform the POL classic "For the Love of My Country," the standout track from their *Straight Six* EP; the latter song gives the lie to the old "America: Love It or Leave It" motto by pointing out how acts of rebellion and protest are expressions of patriotism. The EP closes with a cover of a song recorded in the late '80s by an obscure Christian band called The Swoon ("Speak Soft").

The best was still to come. *A Picture of the Eighth Wonder* is the group's finest album, with several strong tracks, including one that is head and shoulders above everything else. The remarkable "What If Uncle Ben Had Lived?" is one of those instant classic tunes destined to provide POL with a permanent legacy. A true original, it mixes subdued Iron Butterfly organ with a martial rhythmic beat and lilting, heavenly vocals to create a haunting effect never heard before in popular music. It is, indeed, one of those handful of Christian songs that could have become one of the most played songs on college radio—right up there with '90s nuggets like Alice in Chains' "No Excuses" and Red Hot Chili Peppers' "Under the Bridge"—if only the group had gotten a hearing outside the Christian ghetto. The song survives on the strength of its beauty and melody; its lyrics are obscure—though interesting in a weird, P. J. Harvey sort of way. Other very strong songs on the *Picture* album include the acoustic "Chance for the Chancers," with its (ironic or reassuring?) chorus "Everything is going to be okay." Most of the time, however, POL avoids the pop approach of the latter tune. *True Tunes* says, "Poor Old Lu avoids blatantly hooky songs in favor of layered songs that require repeated listenings." Thus, *Picture* opens with a lumbering seven-minute track called "Rail" that starts with the lyric "What do I do / When it seems I relate to Judas more than you?" and proceeds to explore the antitheses between confession and reality, inten-

tion and delivery. Thick and moody, with homage to The Cure, it is a truly fine song—a quest for peace, a paean for grace, and a prayer for lucidity amidst chaos—but as *7ball* would indicate "it's not how you open an album if you want to be pop stars." Yet the group brings in strings for "The Weeds That Grow around My Feet" and they end the album with a lullaby, "Closing Down." The *Chrono* compilation exhibits good song selection and includes the admirable "Drenched Descent," previously available only on the first **Browbeats** album. *In Their Final Performance* is just a souvenir for heartbroken fans. In predictable defiance of its title, the band reunited repeatedly for concerts at the summer *Cornerstone* festival and, by the end of 2001, was planning another album.

Robyn Pope

1983—*Always* (Rooftop); 1986—*Let Them Know* (Greentree).

Californian turned Floridian Robyn Pope struck some as an **Amy Grant** parallel when she recorded her first album, *Always,* at the age of seventeen. The project features all original songs, including a title track that *CCM* predicted would become another standard in the tradition of **Brown Bannister**'s "Praise the Lord" or **David Meece**'s "We Are the Reason." Other strong tracks include "Without Love" and the family-oriented "Bless This House." Pope continued the singer/songwriter tradition on her follow-up album, writing seven of its ten tracks.

Pop Unknown

Matt Breedlove, gtr.; Caspar Echols, bass; Joel Ganucheau, gtr.; Tim Lasater, voc., gtr.; Gabe Wiley, drums. 1999—*If Arsenic Fails, Try Algebra* (Deep Elm).

Pop Unknown is marketed as an emo band from Austin, though their songs are a bit more accessible and catchy than the emo label usually implies. *HM* magazine describes them as "too melodic to be called emo, but too creative to be called pop." The band was formed in 1997 by Lasater and Wiley (formerly of Mineral). The group recorded an EP *(Summer Season Kills)* and a few songs for compilation discs before finally hitting on a definitive lineup. The triple guitar onslaught gives them opportunity for a number of aural effects, but only the opening track of their debut album evinces a hard sound ("Head in the Sand"). Otherwise, most tracks begin with a lightly picked guitar and then unfold like aural light rock tapestries replete with passionate vocals and tear-jerking melodies. Although there is a general spiritual tone to some of Pop Unknown's lyrics, the group prefers not to be labeled a Christian band. Joel Ganucheau told *Bandoppler,* "Yes, most of us are Christians but we do not write about religion . . . we do not want people to think that we represent Christianity in general

. . . that's not what we're about." The group often plays Christian venues, Matt Breedlove explains, because "We just like supporting good things. We are always willing to play to a positive group of people . . . we just want to spread the good vibe."

Don Potter

1984—Free Yourself (Myrrh); 1987—First Love.

Don Potter is an acoustic singer/songwriter who wrote material for a number of artists including Chuck Mangione and The Judds before entering the contemporary Christian market with two albums for Myrrh. He served as both musical director and permanent guitarist for The Judds from that group's inception in 1983. By the end of the '80s, he also played guitar on projects by **Buddy Greene, Paul Overstreet,** and Bob Seger. Potter's roots are in jazz and nuances from that background enter into material on songs like "Free Yourself" and "So Good (Martha's Song)." He eventually came to be more closely associated with country music, however, and in 1990 was featured in a *CCM* article encouraging rock and pop fans to broaden their horizons and give "Christian country" a try. "Country music is real," he said, "and country songs have helped me take a long, hard look at who I really am as a human being and as a believer in Jesus Christ." Potter's vocal style has been compared to **Bob Bennett** and **Billy Crockett.** *Free Yourself* includes an original Christmas song ("It's the Messiah") and covers of **Bruce Cockburn**'s "I'm Gonna Fly Someday" and **Curtis Mayfield**'s "People Get Ready."

Poundhound

Doug Pinnick, gtr., bass, voc. 1998—Massive Grooves from the Electric Church of Psychofunkadelic Grungelism Rock Music (Metal Blade); 2001—Pineappleskunk.

Poundhound is not actually a group, but merely the name under which **King's X** front man Doug Pinnick chose to release a solo album. The record came out at about the same time that Pinnick scandalized some people in the Christian hard rock scene by admitting that he was gay and by indicating—perhaps as a corollary to that revelation—that he wasn't certain to what extent he should be identified as a Christian anymore. About this time, he also took to playing a guitar with a visible sticker on it that read, "F**k 'em if they can't take a toke." With all the hoopla, Poundhound's extravagantly titled debut contains little that would be either inspiring or offensive to Christian fans of **King's X.** He raises a few questions with individual lyrical lines such as "my world just got darker" ("Darker"), but as *HM* reports, "Doug may have some ideas and thoughts that challenge a believer's mind, but he doesn't really push the envelope here." Musically, Poundhound evinces a psychedelic funk that seems like a cross between Prince and

Hendrix. On the opening title track, he creates an aura of gospel, calling on listeners to "let your soul come taste the music" in a voice borrowed from an evangelistic preacher. "Soul" describes the goals of an angry man who is fed up with living in a city where everybody rips everyone off: "We're gonna buy ourselves a mountain / We're gonna find our way back home / We're gonna find a way of living / We're gonna free our soul." Elsewhere, "Psycholove" alludes to the pain of divorce, and "Friends" tells sobering accounts of people's pain-filled lives. Pinnick also recorded another post-**King's X** project under the name **Supershine.** A second Poundhound album came out late in 2001.

Steve Powell

See **Rainbow Promise.**

Power Alley

Chuck Bentley; Wayne Chasteen. 1985—Power Alley (Stronghold).

Power Alley was a short-lived pop-rock duo that seemed to be fashioned after the general market band Wham. They took their name from the baseball metaphor, which they applied to prayer as the "power alley of access to God." The duo wrote all of the songs for their sole album, which includes high-energy selections like "Come As You Are," "Jump Back," and the title track, in addition to a number of midtempo tunes and ballads.

Andy Pratt

Selected: 1978—Motives (CBS); 1982—Fun in the First World [EP] (Enzone); 1985—Not Just for Dancing (Aztec); 1990—Perfect Therapy (GMI).

Andy Pratt (b. 1947) was a general market artist from Boston who made several soft rock albums before experiencing a religious conversion around 1978 and switching over to the contemporary Christian scene. None of Pratt's secular albums were national hits, though he did place one song from the self-titled *Andy Pratt* (Columbia) on *Billboard*'s Hot 100 Chart: "Avenging Annie" peaked at #78 in 1973. Apparently, Pratt experienced his conversion while recording his sixth album, *Motives,* and that project turned into a general market release with overtly religious content. Songs like "Saviour" and "Cross on a Hill" are modern hymns set to a soft rock beat. The album did not sell particularly well, however, and Pratt's next project was an independent EP produced by Larry Radcliffe of **Robin Lane**'s Chartbusters. Touching on a new-wave style, that album features five songs with a subdued apocalyptic theme. The title track to *Fun in the First World* is not a celebration of life in the good world that God created but a more questionable critique of reckless desires for pleasure on the part of those who fail to realize that the next world is all that really counts. "Burn Up in the Fire" poses the question, "I know the world's a powderkeg, but how short is the fuse?" The song "Paper Money" unveils the inherent bankruptcy of a world controlled by purely arbitrary economic standards. "Israel" affirms the character of God's unshakable promises to the chosen people, and "Who Will Be My Friend?" presents the poignant plea of an orphan. Brian Quincy Newcomb noted similarities to **Larry Norman** and praised the artist for connecting matters of spiritual and political concern. The full-length *Not Just for Dancing* would later include the five tracks from *Fun in the First World* along with eight new songs and a cover of the Beatles' "I'm Only Sleeping."

For trivia buffs: Pratt is the great-grandson of the founder of Standard Oil.

Pratt/McClain (and Omartian, Pratt, and McClain)

Truett Pratt; Jerry McClain // Michael Omartian. By Pratt/McClain: 1974—*Pratt/McClain* (ABC). By Omartian, Pratt and McClain: 1995—*Like Brothers* [EP] (Sonrise).

Truett Pratt and Jerry McClain were cohorts of **Michael Omartian,** who became a superstar producer established in both Christian and general markets. They recorded an early self-titled album of Jesus music under the name Pratt/McClain in 1974 (the same year that Omartian's debut solo album appeared). Omartian produced *Pratt/McClain* and played on the album, making the sound indistinguishable from later work when the three recorded as an official trio. Music historian David Di Sabatino describes *Pratt/McClain* as a collection of "progressive pop songs." Perhaps the best-known track would be "Here I Am (The Antichrist Song)," which evinces the eschatological obsessions of the Jesus movement. The record also features a cover of Pete Seeger's "Turn! Turn! Turn!" Two years later, the duo (or trio) hit big when they recorded the theme song from the TV program *Happy Days* under the name Pratt and McClain. Omartian produced that recording and played on it as well, and the single went to Number Five on the general market's Top 40 charts in 1976. Twenty years later, Omartian, Pratt, and McClain (with the producer's now famous name officially added to the roster) released a four-song EP presenting the song "Like Brothers," which they had written for Promise Keepers and dedicated to Coach Bill McCartney for his work with that organization. The song is a basic adult contemporary ballad expressing "brotherly love" in a manner that is not intended to be gender exclusive but, rather, specifically applicable for a men's group. The EP also includes a version of "Turn! Turn! Turn!"

The Prayer Chain

Eric Campuzano, bass; Wayne Everett, drums; Andy Prickett, gtr.; Tim Taber, voc. // Jeremy Wood, perc. (+ 1996). 1991—*The Neverland Sessions* (Chatterbox); 1992—*Whirlpool* [EP] (Reunion); 1993—*Shawl* (Rode Dog); 1994—*Live*; 1995—*Mercury; Mercurios*; 1996—*Antartica* (Brainstorm).

The Southern Californian band The Prayer Chain became the epitome of Christian underground, attracting a strong cult following of fans and critics who regarded them as one of the most proficient and innovative rock bands of all time. The closest general market analogy in that sense—though not necessarily in terms of musical style—is probably Pink Floyd. Unfortunately, The Prayer Chain had a much shorter tenure than the latter act, but they did exhibit the same tendency to polarize audiences: Christian rock fans tended to either "get" Prayer Chain and regard them with hyperbolic affection or else dismiss them as hopelessly irrelevant. In retrospect, both reactions seem to have been grounded in different aspects of the truth: though their genius was exaggerated, Prayer Chain did make one indisputably great album *(Shawl),* and they at least managed to stir up a lot of creative controversy with their subsequent material.

The band formed in 1990. Musically, they had a sound that fit into the general scheme of grunge evinced by such artists as Alice in Chains, Nirvana, Red Hot Chili Peppers, Smashing Pumpkins, and Soundgarden, but they were as different from all of those groups as those bands are from each other. In early reviews, *CCM* actually described their sound as a conglomeration of "Jane's Addiction, Pearl Jam, and The Doors," and *HM* called it **"U2** meets Genesis." The very desperation of such descriptions reflects the breadth of the band's originality as well as its influences. The Doors reference is telling, as Taber's vocals do often recall Jim Morrison in his more unbridled moments (e.g., "The End"). Campuzano's poetry is also sometimes reminiscent of the Lizard King's musings.

In 1991 Prayer Chain released a custom CD called *The Neverland Sessions* from which six songs were later selected for their major-label debut EP on Reunion. *Whirlpool* reveals a band that has not quite discovered its style, but Prayer Chain scored two early hits with "I Believe" and "Shine Your Love on Me," both of which evince a simple and confident faith in stark contrast to the more brooding and questioning explorations with which they were later associated. Indeed, *HM* described *Whirlpool* as "upbeat" and "bouncy," two words that would never again appear in any Prayer Chain review.

Shawl has been best described as "Middle Eastern grunge." It opens with the "Ay-yi-yi-yi" Indian chant of the strong rock track "Crawl," which also proclaims "Shine is dead." This reference to their earlier hit reinforces the aural declaration that the band is no longer interested in pop appeal but intends to explore the dark recesses of the soul. On "Dig Dug," Taber admits to Christ, "I hold the doubts of Thomas as hard as I hold your promise," and concludes, "I'm just like the rest / Need to stick my finger in your wrist." The most Morrison-like track on the album is its anthemic "Never Enough," a six-and-a-half-minute opus that includes a grinding, distortion-soaked guitar solo and builds to a passionate climax that features Taber screaming, "I crawl to the blood of the healer" before dissolving into a long atmospheric fade of celestial voices that seem to be singing off in some faraway heaven. Aforementioned Middle Eastern elements are especially evident on tracks like "Wrounde." The unusual "Grin" starts off like a blazing punk-à-la-Clash song, wanders in the woods for a while, and eventually ends up deep in grunge territory. "Worm" seems to express the blow to self-esteem that meeting with rejection can bring, while "Psycho-flange" offers either a bolder or more defensive response to the same ("Don't tear me down / The contempt you feel is not worth your time"). *Shawl* became a classic—almost *the* classic—of counter-cultural Christian alternative rock, and many critics pinned their hopes on The Prayer Chain as the most likely Moses-figure to lead contemporary Christian music out of its captivity to formulaic impulses. The band could do no wrong. Then they released *Mercury.*

The ostensibly "sophomore album" was not a slump in the usual sense of the word; the group did not make the typical mistake of following a strong debut with a presentation of weaker material done in the same style. Rather, working with producer **Steve Hindalong,** they changed their style (again), going for an experimental tone that had more in common with Pink Floyd than with any of the Seattle groups named above. They did not want to repeat *Shawl,* they said, because other bands were now mining that field: "Smashing Pumpkins came out and got huge, and they do that style tons better than we do. So, we said, let's see if we can't mold our style." Still, the template here was less *Dark Side of the Moon* than *Ummagumma,* which is to say that, musically, *Mercury* muddies the line between innovative and just plain strange. As *True Tunes* noted, "time signatures change mid-song, vocals float in and out of the mix, and sometimes songs take their own sweet time in getting from point A to point B." The album opens with a five-and-a-half minute track called "Humb" that consists mainly of a one-chord Middle Eastern drone that buzzes exclusively for a while and then continues to buzz over the top of some barely perceptible vocals (intoning Psalm 136) before finally being subdued to buzzing in the background behind some ethereal chanting, rhythmic pounding, and Middle Eastern guitar lines. The group would attempt to explain the piece as an elaborate "worship offering." Campuzano says, "Andy had this nice drone that you can get lost in, and totally just meditate to, and then here comes this loud bass and drums to destroy any semblance of relaxation and peace. That's essentially what our

walk with God is like, and our lives are with each other in this band. To me, 'Humb' is a very crucial part of this record." It may be that, but what it *sounds* like is five-and-a-half minutes of electronic buzzing, not unlike what one can experience by simply turning up the volume on a receiver with a bad connection. *Mercury* does have moments of brilliance, but it is almost devoid of hooks or discernible, much less catchy, melodies. Sensing that the album contained no singles (i.e., nothing that would ever get played on the radio), the record company initially rejected the project, requiring the group to come up with five additional, more accessible songs. They did, but in a compromise solution, added only one of these to the original press for the album. That track ("Sky High") runs almost nine minutes in length, effectively negating its commercial potential.

Mercury met with a predictably controversial reception. Many critics rushed to a preemptive defense of their favorite band in ways that were insulting to the general public. *Shout* magazine said, "Most listeners will dismiss the record on the first listen as too weird, or over their heads." Actually, many dismissed it as too weird even after repeated listenings—and there are plenty of intelligent and musically literate people who simply do not enjoy listening to droning, buzzing noises quite apart from whether the performers' artistic intent is "over their heads" or not. *Mercury* was invariably described as "experimental" and "daring"; it was that, but it was also elitist, pretentious, and frequently boring. Still, it has its moments. "Sky High" is a powerful and moving exception, though it does come much closer to cloning the sound of the Stone Roses than any critic seemed to notice. "Waterdogs" is a feedback-laced rock track that could have been on *Shawl.* "Creole" (about a dying man who is first frightened, then comforted by visions of angels) also has a bit of the Stone Roses sound and features some blistering guitar work underpinning a haunting vocal performance—appropriate for lines like, "All the old ghosts will let you know just how far gone you are." The title track is a beautifully atmospheric song with obscure lyrics ("All your feelings are streaming down your leg"). But "Shiver" is boring; "Grylliade" (written from the perspective of a cricket who has been stepped on) is strange and boring; "Sun Stoned" is strange and long (almost nine minutes); "Manta Rae" is just . . . well, boring. Nevertheless, the album remained a much-revered masterpiece among a small cadre of supporters. In 2001, critic Anthony DeBarros would still regard it as "one of Christian music's most artful successes."

Members of Prayer Chain eventually revealed that the making of *Mercury* was not a harmonious process. "I couldn't listen to the album for three or four months after we recorded it," Everett told *7ball,* insisting that it was the result of an artistic feud between Taber and the rest of the band. Taber told the same magazine (in a separate interview) that "*Mercury* was mostly a vision of Everett's and Campuzano's." Campuzano admits, "We were sort of attacking each other through the music . . . and then, on top of that, we were taking out our frustrations on the Christian music scene. It was all very reactionary." The group did not survive these tensions and *Mercury* was to be their official swan song.

In 1995, Prayer Chain released a limited edition two-CD set called *Mercurios* that included both the *Mercury* album and thirteen additional tracks (including the other four "more accessible songs" the label had required of the band). The previous year, the group had fed collectors two different editions of a live EP (both titled *Live*), one with four songs, the other with eight. The 1996 collection, *Antartica,* contains no new material, but, rather, six songs from *Mercurios* (including those "more accessible songs") plus eight live numbers from what was supposed to be the group's final concert (December 30, 1995). *CCM* pointed to "Chalk" and "Loverboy" as songs that might have helped *Mercury* along, while noting that "Antartica" is built on grating guitars that "render it nearly unpleasant." Despite a split that was publicly acrimonious in a manner uncharacteristic of the Christian music scene, members of Prayer Chain reunited for a concert on October 4, 1997 and made 1000 copies of a custom album called *So Close . . . Yet So Far* (Chatterbox) available to attendees only. The instant collector's item is a two-disc set that includes all but two songs from *The Neverland Sessions,* two songs from the earlier limited edition live EP, and some rarities, including a cover of the Cheap Trick song "Surrender" played in the style of Kiss.

After the break-up of Prayer Chain, Andy Prickett formed **My Brother's Mother.** Campuzano and Everett joined **Starflyer 59** and then formed **The Lassie Foundation.** The four original members of Prayer Chain later played with **Cush.**

Pray For Rain

See **PFR.**

Preacha

1996—*Geography of a Journey* (Alliance UK).

Cameron Dante, known for his work as front man for **World Wide Message Tribe,** recorded one solo album under the pseudonym Preacha. Liner notes explain that the album is literally autobiographical with various songs relating to different phases of Dante's life: he served as a DJ in Spanish club resorts on the Mediterranean, had some general market hits in the United Kingdom as a member of the group Bizarre, Inc., and lived a notorious rock and roll lifestyle (sex, drugs, etc.) before becoming a Christian. Curiously, the songs on *Geography of a Journey* are not sequenced chronologically, so they must be played out of order in accord with instructions in the notes if the map of a life announced in the title is to be followed. Musically, *Geography* falls into the "house" subgenre of dance music. Numerous vocalists, especially female singers, are featured; Dante delves into the rap style for which he is best known only occasionally ("Inner Peace"). The album's lyrics evince the same refreshingly simple or annoyingly simplistic (depending on perspective) characteristics as **World Wide Message Tribe**'s material.

Preachas and Preachas In Disguise

See **P.I.D.**

Elvis Presley

Selected: 1960—*His Hand in Mine* (RCA); 1967—*How Great Thou Art;* 1972—*He Touched Me;* 1975—*Promised Land;* 1989—*Known Only to Him: Elvis Gospel, 1957–1971;* 2000—*Peace in the Valley: The Complete Gospel Recordings.*

www.elvis.com

The King of Rock and Roll is not primarily appreciated for his gospel music, and fans of contemporary Christian music have generally doubted the sincerity of his conviction to the form (as well as to Christ). Nevertheless, Elvis Presley's roots in gospel are indisputable and the influence of that music on everything else that he did is obvious and well known. His facility with gospel songs is also acknowledged, though he took a very traditional approach atypical of the creativity he would allow himself on other material. The antipathy toward Presley's gospel music in the contemporary Christian music subculture probably has a lot to do with that community's immaturity during the performer's lifetime. Even undeniably sincere works by artists like **Marvin Gaye** and **Aretha Franklin** were rejected by the Jesus people due to a prejudice against "compromised" artists who continued to perform within the general market. The fact that Presley's secular oeuvre and personal lifestyle often involved matters of offense to conservative Christians furthered the divide. Still, if Presley had lived, it is quite possible that Christian music fans would have come to view him in a manner analogous to **Johnny Cash** (or **Bob Dylan** or U2's Bono)—as a struggling believer whose faith statements do not need to be discounted just because they are part of a complex persona acquainted with doubt and sin as well.

Presley was born in East Tupelo, Missouri, in 1935, and he died in Memphis, Tennessee, in 1977. Decidedly blue-collar, his mother was a seamstress and his father, a truck driver, who spent time in prison for writing bad checks. Elvis was raised in the Assemblies of God, but was never baptized and, so, never officially joined the church. He heard a lot of southern gospel in church but according to his pastor, the Reverend James Hamill, he never sang or took part in any musical programs.

Thus Presley did not "cross over" from gospel music to rock, as did Franklin, **Sam Cooke,** and a number of other early R&B performers. He never performed as a gospel singer as such but, after graduating from high school, began his musical career as a semi-successful country singer under the tutelage of producer Sam Phillips. In 1956, his career and the future of popular music took an unanticipated turn when he hooked up with manager Colonel Thomas Parker and began to record what would be called "rock and roll" records in Nashville. His first hit was "Heartbreak Hotel" (# 1 for 8 weeks in 1956). This was followed by the double-sided single "Don't Be Cruel"/"Hound Dog," which occupied the Number One spot for an unprecedented eleven weeks (and only then was unseated by his own "Love Me Tender"). "Don't Be Cruel" was deemed the most popular song of all time, a record it would hold for almost forty years until Boyz II Men made "I'll Make Love to You" Number One for *fourteen* weeks (the record has been broken repeatedly almost every year since then, a development most pundits attribute to "low competition," i.e., a dearth of good songs). But Presley would establish himself as the most commercially successful artist in history, with ultimate record sales of over one billion worldwide and far more chart hits and gold/platinum recordings than anyone else. On such matters, his numbers were double those of the Beatles, who remained in second place in 2001.

Presley created controversy primarily on account of his sex appeal, which he exploited shamelessly in hip-swiveling performances and on screen in films geared to the adolescent market. But at the same time, he began releasing gospel records early on, almost in tandem with the sexually-charged libido numbers. His recording of the hymn "(There'll Be) Peace in the Valley" was a Top 40 hit (# 25 in 1957) sandwiched between "All Shook Up" (# 1 for 9 weeks in 1957) and "(Let Me Be Your) Teddy Bear" (# 1 for 7 weeks in 1957). He regularly performed even his secular songs with the gospel group J. D. Sumner and The Stamps providing backup. But as of 1961 Presley quit performing, and once the Beatles arrived on the scene (1964) he would be almost permanently excluded from the Top 10 on the pop charts—save for a quick revival in 1969–1970 when he began a series of Las Vegas shows that would ultimately render him a parody of his former self. Obese and addicted to prescription drugs, Presley's personal life became tabloid fodder and both his financial security and artistic integrity were destroyed by Parker's exploitative practices (e.g., selling off the singer's royalties and taking an unheard-of fifty percent commission on his profits). Nevertheless, as most biographers note, Presley remained deeply committed to spiritual values until the end. For instance, he did not drink alcohol or use any recreational drugs—apparently as a consequence of his religious beliefs. It is also noteworthy that despite Presley's overwhelming impor-

tance for the history of popular music, he only won three Grammy awards—all for gospel music. According to Sumner, at one point when he was singing in Las Vegas, Presley seriously considered doing gospel full time. He was discouraged in this regard by evangelist Rex Humbard, who told him that by performing "How Great Thou Art" at a Vegas show he was "tilling more soil" than he ever could by singing nothing but gospel.

Presley's gospel recordings consist mainly of hymns performed in an inspirational southern gospel style. In 2001, the Gospel Music Association decided to recognize Presley's contributions and in a better-late-than-never gesture inducted Presley into the Gospel Music Hall of Fame. Graceland's Todd Morgan spoke for the artist: "Elvis is already a member of the Rock and Roll Hall of Fame and the Country Music Hall of Fame, but this is one that would have meant a lot to him personally."

Grammy Awards: 1967 Best Sacred Performance *(How Great Thou Art)*; 1972 Best Inspirational Performance *(He Touched Me)*; 1974 Best Inspirational Performance (Non-Classical) ("How Great Thou Art").

Precious Death

David Bishop, gtr.; Chris Scott, voc.; Andy Koehler, bass; Roger Sampson, drums (−1996) // Lorenzo Mauro, drums (+ 1996). 1993—*Southpaw* (custom); 1994—*If You Must* (Metro One); 1996—*Precious Death*; 2000—*Hardest Hits.*

Precious Death was a Southern California group that *7ball* once described as "a retro hard rock band with a modern metal twist." The group alternated between songs with a clear and explicit Christian message and ones that were simply written by Christians about life in general. "If we write a song about anything that we do in our lives," Scott said, "that cannot be any less glorifying to God, because everything that we do is about our relationship with Him." After a demo creatively titled *Our Stinkin' Demo,* the group put out a one-step removed custom album called *Southpaw* that was later re-released by Metro One. *Southpaw* revels in its hardcore intensity while playing with the stereotypical formulas of that genre in creative ways. The title track features what *HM* called "attitude-saturated punk vocals, killer background vocals, a monster crunch, a beefy low-end, drum sonics, choice wah-wah leads, and sheer power." The song "Shine," however, showcases more of a heavy prog-rock sound with funkier radio viability. "King of Sian" recalls Rush, and the album ends with a ballad, showcasing the group's ability to embrace a variety of styles. Shades of hardcore would continue to show up on the next two projects, albeit with even more excursions into mood-altering, contemplative sounds and funk-metal. *If You Must* opens with another hard punk song, "You Can't Break Me," with chanted choruses reminiscent of **The Crucified.** "You're Gone, I'm Here" is a more melodic standout. "All Over Now" is an emotionally gripping song about the consequences of sin. Oddities include a song called "Oscillating Fullwave Bridge Rectifiers" and a number titled simply "E" (written in praise to something referenced by that letter).

In 1996, Scott and Bishop formed a new band with drummer Lorenzo Mauro called **Blackball.** The latter group had more potential commercial appeal than Precious Death, and would indeed prove more successful. **Blackball** released albums in 1996 and 1998, but in the interim Precious Death reconvened for a self-titled project. This eponymous album was essentially recorded by **Blackball** with a different bass player, and projected a sound somewhere between the two groups—more stripped down than previous PD projects but nowhere near as pop-oriented as **Blackball.** *True Tunes* pegged them as analogous to alternative act Pavement—this is especially evident on the standout closing track, "Psalm." The *Hardest Hits* compilation album contains no new songs but a fair selection of the best tracks from the previous three projects.

Billy Preston

Selected: 1965—*The Wildest Organ Ever* (Vee Jay); 1966—*The Most Exciting Organ Ever;* 1969—*That's the Way God Planned It* (Apple); 1978—*Behold* (Myrrh); 1980—*Universal Love;* 1995—*Minister of Music* (Pepperco Music Group); 1996—*Words and Music* (with Edna Tatum).

www.billypreston.net

Billy Preston seems to have lived at least three professional lives: one as perhaps the most famous sideman in the history of popular music; another as a brief but successful solo artist, and yet another as a contemporary gospel artist whose relationship to the contemporary Christian and gospel music scenes was always a bit tenuous. Preston was born in 1946 in Houston, Texas, and he moved at the age of two to Los Angeles. He gained renown for his skill with keyboards and at the age of sixteen was invited by none other than Little Richard (a *very* big star in 1962) to join the latter on a European tour. After being a part of Little Richard's entourage, Preston played with the house band for the TV show *Shindig* and then joined Ray Charles for three years as a permanent member of his band. It was in that capacity that he eventually came to the attention of George Harrison, who effectively asked him to "join the Beatles." Preston played on a number of the Beatles' latter-day projects (notably the *Let It Be* album) and, although he never actually became an official Beatle, he was frequently photographed with the quartet as though he were part of the group and was regularly referred to in publicity materials as "the fifth Beatle." Such inclusion no doubt served political purposes, helping the lily-white foursome maintain a hip image with their late '60s liberal fanbase. From a marketing standpoint, "Black Power" was in, and Preston was a large African American man who dressed in hippie African garb and sported a huge Afro hairdoo. For this reason alone, there can be little doubt

that John, Paul, George, and Ringo benefitted almost as much from having Preston in their photos as he did from having them in his. Nevertheless, his pounding piano and swirling organ did make a distinctive contribution and—as all Beatles-trivia maniacs know—the group's Number One hit "Get Back" was actually released as a single by "the Beatles with Billy Preston," making it the only official collaboration song the group would ever record. He later performed the song solo in the notoriously awful *Sgt. Peppers' Lonely Hearts Club Band* film, in which he also appeared (as Sgt. Pepper himself, no less). Preston also made prominent contributions to George Harrison's *All Things Must Pass* and played the trademark funky organ that can be heard on almost all of the late '60s and early '70s hits by Sly and the Family Stone. Then, as if all this were not enough, he went on to become a sort of unofficial member of The Rolling Stones. For many years, he would play on most of that band's classic albums *(Sticky Fingers, Exile on Main Street, Goat's Head Soup, It's Only Rock and Roll, Black and Blue)* and tour with the group internationally.

In 1969, Preston emerged as a solo artist when he took part in the benefit concert for Bangladesh organized by George Harrison and featuring appearances by Ravi Shankar and **Bob Dylan.** In the early '70s, Harrison produced two albums of solo material for him, the acclaimed *That's the Way God Planned It* and a forgettable follow-up called *Encouraging Words.*

The artist then signed with A&M and beginning in 1971 released an album a year for the next seven years *(I Wrote a Simple Song, Music Is My Life, Everybody Likes Some Kind of Music, The Kids and Me, It's My Pleasure, Billy Preston, A Whole New Thing).* These records showcased a funky R&B style similar to that of Sly Stone and they earned Preston a spate of gold records. In all, they produced eleven chart hits, including four Top 10 smashes: the instrumentals "Outta Space" (# 2 in 1972) and "Space Race" (# 4 in 1973), and the vocal smashes "Will It Go Round In Circles" (# 1 for 2 weeks in 1973) and "Nothing from Nothing" (# 1 in 1974). Ironically, Preston's most famous song would be "You Are So Beautiful," a romantic ballad that he wrote and included on an album but did not release as a single; Joe Cocker found it and scored a hit with a version of the song that would remain one of the most played golden oldies on late-night radio decades after funk was out of fashion. With a sideways glance at what might have been, Preston wrote a similar sounding song a few years later and recorded "With You I'm Born Again" for the soundtrack of the very forgettable motion picture *Fastbreak* (starring Gabe Kaplan of *Welcome Back Kotter).* Preston performed the song as a duet with Syreeta Wright, who was at that time married to Stevie Wonder. It went to Number Five in 1979 and was followed by another, less successful duet ("One More Time for Love," # 52 in 1980).

Little is known and less has been documented regarding Preston's connections with gospel music, though these go back to his childhood. A prodigy, he began playing piano for his church at the age of three and when he was six began directing the one hundred-voice choir at Victory Baptist Church in Los Angeles. At the age of ten, long before hooking up with Little Richard or other celebrities, he was playing keyboards on recordings by gospel maven Mahalia Jackson. Preston became a founding member of the COGICs, the singing group that included **Andraé** and **Sandra Crouch** (along with Gloria Jones, Frankie Springs, and Edna Wright) and would eventually evolve into **Andraé Crouch and the Disciples.** In the mid '60s, Preston recorded two instrumental gospel albums, consisting of what he called "wild" versions of hymns played on the organ as only he could play them. At that time he is also said to have made several albums with gospel godfather James Cleveland, including ones that featured "double keyboards" by Preston (on piano) and **Jessy Dixon** (on organ). He also toured with **Aretha Franklin** when she was known exclusively as a gospel singer. In the '70s, when the Jesus movement introduced new forms of Christian music, Preston—who was by now known in rock circles—naturally come to be associated with the emerging genre of contemporary Christian music, but his involvements were far more subdued than other "celebrity Jesus freaks." At the very time when performers like **Larry Norman** and **Barry McGuire** were abandoning the secular scene to make rock and roll for Jesus, Preston was moving out of gospel into the general market with "Will It Go Round in Circles." Still, the Jesus people tended to regard him as one of their own. He maintained that his involvements in "the world" had evangelistic potential. "I think the Lord put me in this environment just to be an example and to witness to people," he claimed. Preston played on Andraé Crouch's classic *Take Me Back* album. "That's the Way God Planned It" was received as a gospel song by the emerging Christian music subculture despite its somewhat generic lyrics; years later, it would be a Christian radio hit for **DeGarmo and Key.** In any case, the artist would sign with Myrrh records in the late '70s and record two albums of MOR material specifically for the contemporary Christian music community. Both records feature explicit testimony songs like "I'm Giving My Life to Christ" and "Jesus" (both written by Preston) in addition to new arrangements of songs like "He Brought Me Out," "Motherless Child," "Amazing Grace," and "All to Jesus I Surrender." The musical quality of these projects, however, was generally thought to be inferior to Preston's secular work. The albums received little promotion and they went all but unnoticed in the Christian media. They also suffered from the fact that "With You I'm Born Again" came out in 1979. The latter song is simply a romantic ballad, and many fans of Christian music were offended by Preston using a popular metaphor for spiritual transformation to describe a sensual encounter ("lying here within your arms, I'm born again"). *Behold* featured another original song called "Born Again" that came out at almost the same time with a more traditional interpretation ("I've been born again with God's Spirit deep within"), but Christian music fans (who are seldom noted for their appreciation of polyvalence) were not able to make the leap. Still, the artist wrote on the cover of *Behold,* "I want to be used by God and as long as God gives me the opportunity I will try not to fail the Lord." *Universal Love* is a bass-heavy, dance-oriented album that concludes with a soft cool-down version of "Amazing Grace." *CCM* said, "While not theologically profound or especially creative, the songs [on *Universal Love*] express an unbridled joy in salvation."

After a long hiatus, Preston would return to contemporary gospel music in the '90s, but his ability to connect with the Christian music subculture was hampered by his personal problems and run-ins with the law. In 1992, Preston was arrested on charges of assault and possession of cocaine. He pled no contest and was sentenced to a brief prison term, followed by house arrest and probation. He admitted publicly that he had been addicted to alcohol and to crack cocaine for over thirty years. Then in 1995 he reemerged as a gospel musician playing alongside **Andraé Crouch** on albums by **Helen Baylor** and **Donnie McClurkin.** He also released two more gospel albums of his own—his first in fifteen years. On *Words and Music,* he mainly just plays organ to accompany readings by gospel orator Edna Tatum. But in 1997 Preston was arrested again for cocaine possession and was sentenced to three years in prison. While serving the sentence, he was indicted for insurance fraud and accepted a plea bargain by which he pled guilty and testified against the other defendants (including his former manager) in exchange for no further jail time. Preston has resumed performing since his release. In 2001, he played on **Eric Clapton**'s *Reptile* album.

For trivia buffs: At the age of twelve, Preston had a small role in the motion picture *St. Louis Blues,* a film starring Nat King Cole, Pearl Bailey, and Eartha Kitt about the life of composer W. C. Handy. Preston played Handy as a child.

Grammy Awards: 1972 Best Pop Instrumental Performance ("Outta Space").

Cheryl Prewitt (and Cheryl Prewitt-Blackwood)

As Cheryl Prewitt-Blackwood: 1983—*Desires of My Heart* (Impact). As Cheryl Prewitt: 1985—*Choose to Be Happy* (Love Song).

www.salemfamilyministries.org

Cheryl Prewitt (b. 1958) was crowned Miss America 1980, testifying on national TV and in newspapers to her faith in the miraculous power of God. Growing up in Ackerman, Mississippi, Prewitt had her left leg crushed in a near-fatal car accident when she was eleven years old. Doctors reportedly said she "would never walk again," but she maintains that on October 21, 1974, she was miraculously healed: the bone in her leg grew two inches instantaneously when a man at a revival meeting prayed for her. Prewitt graduated from Mississippi State University and then entered the Miss America pageant in 1979.

Cheryl had performed as a child with her siblings in a singing group called The Prewitts. In 1981, she married gospel singer **Terry Blackwood** and recorded an album under the name Cheryl Prewitt-Blackwood. *Desires of My Heart* consists of mostly worship songs and includes numbers sung as duets with her husband ("Together in Love," "We'll Be Together," written by **Stephanie Booshada**). *CCM* magazine picked "Wherever You Are Is Holy Ground" as the album's standout track. She recorded the album *Choose to Be Happy* as Cheryl Prewitt (following a divorce). *CCM* praised it as her "best music to date," singling out the soaring anthem "I Will Lift Thee Up." Prewitt also published an autobiography titled *A Bright Shining Place: The Story of a Miracle* (Doubleday, 1981).

Prewitt later married Harry Salem, Vice-President of Operations for Oral Roberts Ministries and, in 1987, she published the book *Health and Beauty Secrets* by Cheryl Prewitt-Salem (Harrison House). She and her husband founded Salem Family Ministries, which they say is dedicated to "the unity of family, personal relationships, financial goals, and parenting." She has authored or coauthored at least sixteen additional books for Harrison House, including *The Mommy Book* (1995); *A Royal Child* (1996); *An Angel's Touch: The Presence and Purpose of Supernatural Messengers in Your Life* (1997); *Being # 1 at Being # 2* (1998); and *Mourning to Morning* (2001). The latter volume deals with the loss of their daughter Gabrielle, who died of a brain tumor in 1999.

Christian radio hits: "I Will Sing" (# 28 in 1983).

Priesthood

J-Raw, voc.; Papa Semm, voc.; Swift, voc. 1999—*Sprinkle Me Luv* (Metro One); 2001—*Keepin' It Real*.

The talented hip-hop group Priesthood differs from many artists in their genre through an embrace of classic soul. The group formed in 1994 as a duo composed of the front men from what had been separate gospel rap groups: J-Raw from Prophets of Peace, and Papa Semm from Next of Kin. Two years later, Swift was added and the group began working on more complex harmonies. Priesthood's approach follows the mellow tradition of such West Coast artists as Tupac Shakur and Bone Thugs-N-Harmony; indeed both *7ball* and *True Tunes* would identify them as a blend of those two artists with an implicit critique that they tend to be a bit too imitative. The opening title track to *Sprinkle Me Luv* is a gorgeous flashback to the golden age of black music with harmonies worthy of comparison to the softer side of The O'Jays or Harold Melvin and the Blue Notes. For three-and-a-half minutes, it is as though disco, much less hip-hop and gangsta rap, never happened. The rest of the songs give the kids their rhythm fix in a thoroughly modern way, but always against an R&B backdrop. The song "Sunshine" is a joyful affirmation of hope. "You Can't Hide Love" presents J-Raw's affectionate tributes to his son, his wife, and his friends. "Highlife" and several other songs testify overtly to the experience of life in Christ; "If Luv Is a Crime" lays out the doctrine of Christian atonement. *Sprinkle Me Luv* was produced by Jyro Xhan of **Mortal**/**Fold Zandura** fame. *Keepin' It Real* offers "Luv for My Thugs" (a tune about life on the streets) and "Mama Dearest" (a tribute to the singer's mother). "Tonight" looks forward to the parousia of Christ. On "All about You," the group departs from hip-hop for a full-fledged R&B song with sung vocals.

Prime Minister

2000—*Inside Out* (Grapetree).

Prime Minister is one of several anonymous Christian rap artists recording on the Grapetree label. He has a typical testimony of being delivered out of a gang lifestyle to find new life in Christ. His musical style is sometimes compared with that of Tupac Shakur, though he varies his rhythm styles in ways that span the spectrum from mellow to dance tracks. **M.C. Hammer** provides guest vocals on *Inside Out*. **Out of Eden** also spices up the song "When I Feel" with some funky guest harmonies.

Prism

1984—*First Things First* (Reunion); 1986—*Blue*; 1987—*Yellow*; 1988—*Red*; *Green: The Christmas Collection*; 1989—*The Hits*.

Prism was not a band, but a series of children's albums conceived by record company executives and helmed by songwriters Mark Heimermann and Chris Harris. Various Reunion artists including **Gary Chapman, Amy Grant,** and **Chris Rodriguez** were employed to sing worship choruses and Sunday school songs. A few of the tracks made it on to the airways of Christian radio.

Christian radio hits: "This Little Light of Mine" (# 11 in 1987); "Pass It On" (# 9 in 1987); "Sweet, Sweet Spirit" (# 14 in 1988); "Seek Ye First" (# 12 in 1988).

Prodigal

Loyd Boldman, kybrd., voc.; Rick Fields, gtr., voc.; Mike Wilson, bass; Dave Workman, drums, voc. 1982—*Prodigal* (Heartland); 1984—*Electric Eye*; 1985—*Just Like Real Life*.

A quartet from Cincinnati, Prodigal was in tune with the sounds and spirit of the early '80s. Fronted by keyboard whiz Loyd Boldman, the group fit in with the technology-driven sounds of bands like Styx (or **DeGarmo and Key**), while writing songs that expanded the boundaries of the worship or evangelism fare that typified contemporary Christian music at the time. Boldman and Dave Workman contribute about equally to the songwriting, and Rick Fields and Boldman trade off lead vocals in a way that provides variety. The self-titled debut album features a mix of rock songs and ballads. The opening "Invisible Man" speaks on behalf of forgotten people, rejected by society. A standout track called "I Don't Know Who You Are" expresses the thoughts of a bewildered seeker. "Sleepwalker" focuses on pleasure seekers who go through life without acknowledging their need for something more substantial. *CCM* selected Prodigal's sophomore project as one of its Ten Best Albums of 1984. *Cornerstone* described it as "a mix of stadium rock energy and new music technology" that addresses a variety of social issues from a discernibly Christian perspective. And *Visions of Gray* would single it out ten years later as a "Hall of Fame" album that desperately needed to be reissued. The title track, "Electric Eye," addresses the spiritual impoverishment of a society that is increasingly defined by its technology. "Emerald City" uses a *Wizard of Oz* motif to express the human longing for paradise. "Shout It Out" is a strong cut that departs from the album's overall focus, exhorting Christians to be bold in their evangelistic efforts. "Neon" draws upon a theme presented in the sci-fi film *Blade Runner* to present one possible outcome of such a development: a hellish world that has become completely driven by its own technological accomplishments. *Just Like Real Life* features more of the melodic synthesized rock for which the group was famous, with one "rough and raw cut"—the well-titled "Burn It Up." A dramatic power ballad, "Under the Gun" is the most overtly Christian song on the record. In March of 1983, Boldman (who also worked as a graphic artist and served as pastor of Calvary Chapel in Cincinnati) published an article in *CCM* defending Christian artists who play "secular venues" in order to minister to those outside the church.

Prodigal Sons

J. R. Barbee, M.C.; Greg Hobgood, kybrd.; Chris White, sampling, scratching. 1993—*Texno Theology* (Metro One); *Return*; 1997—*Fast And A . . .* (N'Soul); 2000—*Reignite*.

Prodigal Sons is an "old-school" techno band that records instrumental albums that sound like the soundtracks to old Nintendo and Sega games: very little melody, no harmony, just lots of computers bleeps enhanced by filter sweeps and sequenced arpeggios. "Apricot Tree" from *Return* even appears to feature vocals from one of the Mario Brothers chirping "Okey Dokey" now and then. The group is actually following the staple for such music set by early **Moby,** but even on their 2000 *Reignite* album they demonstrate no interest in moving beyond the style that informed their first project. *Phantom Tollbooth* introduced its review of *Reignite* with the line, "The Prodigal Sons have returned and they're ready to party like it's 1993!" Christian content is introduced via samples. Two minutes into "Ravival" (from *Return*), this conversation is suddenly overheard, as though spoken by two dancers who are moving to the beat: "You're a Christian?" "Yeah" "And you're a raver?" "Yeah" "You don't do drugs?" "No" "You don't do anything immoral?" "No." The same album offers "Firebrand," with some subdued chants of "all praise be to God" popping up for a moment in the mix. Likewise, a track called "Ephesians 5:19" on *Reignite* features vocal samples of prayers and preaching; that album also concludes with a "hidden track" featuring a child singing a worship song. *Fast* is distinctive in that it uses much more soothing, ambient sounds with traditional piano to produce what *True Tunes* called "a peaceful, underwater effect." Barbee said, "We wrote that album near the time of the Oklahoma bombing. Our hearts went out to the children and the parents and the music described what our hearts felt at the time."

Project 86

Alex Albert, drums; Steven Dail, bass; Andrew Schwab, voc.; Randy Torres, gtr., kybrd., voc. 1998—*Project 86* (BEC); 2000—*Drawing Black Lines*.

www.project86.com

Project 86 came on the scene with a sound very much like **P.O.D.,** causing them to be classed with "Christian rapcore" artists who took after such general market bands as Korn and Rage Against the Machine. The group resented the rapcore label and sought to distinguish themselves from the other acts. "There is a bit of rapping in our music," Schwab told *HM,* "but it's not a hip-hop influence. You take some heavy music with groove, melody, some rap, screaming, and weird stuff, and mix it all together, and that's Project 86." At the turn of the millennium, the band became one of the very few Christian acts to gain exposure in the general market.

Despite disclaimers, Project 86's self-titled debut album would strike most listeners as solid rapcore, with an emphasis on the harder end of that spectrum. The songs tend to feature cryptic, down-tuned guitars, grooves are heavy and plodding, and vocals are half-spoken, half rapped. Most of the songs move at a relaxed tempo and some reviewers complained that they sound too much alike. *7ball* said "the album oozes with a strong sense of mental claustrophobia," with songs like "When Darkness Reigns" exemplifying a mostly gloomy lyrical perspective. "Stalemate" addresses the inertia of attempting to live a compromised life. For *Drawing Black Lines,* the group scored a coup by enlisting the services of producer GGGarth, who has made albums for Rage Against the Machine, Kiss, and the Red Hot Chili Peppers (as well as **The Supertones**). As a package deal, GGGarth comes with his own programmer, Fu, notable for his work on albums by such artists as Marilyn Manson and Orgy. Such contacts not only insured a first-class production equal to anything in the general market but also allowed the band access to venues that are not often open to Christian bands. The song "P.S." ended up being played in the motion picture *Blair Witch 2* and is included on that film's soundtrack album in addition to appearing on *Drawing Black Lines.* The track's lyrics deal with the exploitative aspects of pornography; it also displays a fascination with Asian culture that surfaces in much of the group's material by including a bridge in which a woman speaks softly in Japanese. Another song, "One-Armed Man," gained wide airplay on MTV. It features **King's X**-style harmonies with lyrics that describe the modern world as a spiritual wasteland, with specific reference to alcohol abuse. Musically, *Drawing* exhibits more variety than the group's first project, sometimes going for the thrashy rapcore sound, but often demonstrating a heavy emotional style reminiscent of **Stavesacre.** "Set Me Up" seems to be addressed to critics and enemies; *CCM* says it "attacks the cliquish nature of the Christian music industry and its stars with a healthy (and overdue) dose of righteous indignation." The opening track, "Chapter 2," speaks obliquely of spiritual rebirth ("breathe on me for my new beginning"). "A Toast to My Former Self" treats a similar theme.

Schwab has described Project 86's mission as being "creatively and artistically presenting the gospel of Christ to today's post-Christian youth culture. Most people have heard the gospel before, so it must be presented in a new way. That's why we as a band do what we do."

Promise

2000—*Tell Me What You See* (Kalubone).

Promise is a fairly typical Christian rap artist whose hip-hop album *Tell Me What You See* is distinguished mainly by the forthright but fundamentalist orientation of its lyrics. The artist has a commonplace conversion testimony of being rescued from a street life filled with violence, sex, and drugs. He attempts to avoid glossing over issues out of a concern for

what is "proper" and speaks his mind in straightforward and sometimes shocking ways. The song "Lustful" addresses sexual promiscuity head-on in a way that might make some Christians blush. "Father, Mother, Child" describes the emotional pain of child abuse; perhaps the album's strongest cut, the track touches on the range of emotions from sorrow to grief to anger and emphasizes the long-term effects of such abuse. "Killers," on the other hand, is an irresponsible antiabortion song that portrays his ideological opponents as bloodthirsty murderers. His songs also include frequent references to supposed fulfillment of biblical prophecies and to an impending "rapture of the church."

Prosper

Joel Boone, bass; Gregg Eilers, voc.; Chad Pippen, gtr.; Andrew Platt, drums. 2000—*Brevity of Man's Days* (Bettie Rocket).

Prosper is a melodic hardcore rock band from Modesto, California. With a style equally influenced by Helmet and **Stavesacre,** they favor music that tends to be both heavy and slow. *HM* says that their debut album "revels in dynamic swings between noise, power, and melody." Standout tracks include the rocker "Davenport" and the more catchy "First Timothy." Prosper takes a strong stand as "a ministry band," explicitly proclaiming their faith in the lyrics to their songs and in testimonies from the stage. "There is nothing lamer than a band on a Christian label that doesn't say anything or preach the gospel," Pippen told *Bandoppler.* "We have a desire to see people come to know the one true Living God. It is by this standard that our success is measured."

Psalmistry

Personnel list unavailable. 1998—*Double Edged* (independent); 1999—*Armchair Rebellion* (N'Soul); 2000—*All This Noise.*

Psalmistry is a generally hard-edged techno-dance group from the United Kingdom. Their early independent work got them compared (sometimes favorably) to **World Wide Message Tribe.** The group does not list personnel as such and, perhaps, is not exactly a band in the usual sense. *Armchair Rebellion* features Edi as M.C., with samples and engineering by Matt, Ben, and Toby, and vocals by Lucy and Helen. That album—the first to be released in America—reveals a style more similar to Prodigy and Chemical Brothers than to **World Wide Message Tribe.** The title track, however, is an acoustic-driven number that reflects lyrically on the tendency for some "spoon-fed" Christians to accept whatever is told them without thought or exploration. The album also features the Tori Amos-like "Fireworks" and the ambient "By Your Side," which opens with a capella female vocals singing the refrain, "Lord, be my guide / Draw me nearer to your side." *All This Noise* would move Psalmistry in a pop direction, which they indicated was due to the influence of Fatboy Slim. A track called "Knucklehead" showcases sampled guitar riffs and strong synths similar to **The Echoing Green.** One of the album's most pleasant tracks, however, is another acoustic outing: the song "Fall Free" with a single guitar and male vocals by Ed Johnston.

Psalm 150

Bob Anglin, gtr.; Greg Eckler, trump., perc., voc.; Jimmy Ericson, perc., voc.; Mike Escalante, kybrd., voc.; James Felix, bass, gtr., voc.; Allen Gregory, trump. 1974—*Make Up Your Mind* (Manna).

A curiosity in the annals of Christian music, Psalm 150 remains best known for its early *non-recording* lineup. The personnel list above is for the jazz-funk group that made a 1974 indie album, *Make Up Your Mind.* In an earlier incarnation, Psalm 150 included Jack Blades (bass), **Bob Carlisle** (gtr., voc.), Sam Scott (keyboards), and Randy Thomas (gtr., voc.), with Jimmy Ericson on drums. Blades later played in the successful mainstream band Night Ranger ("Sister Christian," "Sentimental Street"), and then would join Ted Nugent in Damn Yankees ("High Enough," "Where You Goin' Now?"). Carlisle, Scott, Thomas, and Ericson formed the **Allies,** which was essentially a Psalm 150 reunion—albeit with a very different sound. Prior to his involvement with Psalm 150, Carlisle had played in **Good News;** after the **Allies,** he became a successful solo artist, best known for the 1997 Number One adult contemporary hit "Butterfly Kisses." Thomas would actually make his greatest mark on Christian music in the interim between Psalm 150 and the **Allies,** when he joined **Bryan Duncan** as a founding member of the seminal Christian rock group **Sweet Comfort Band.** He cowrote "Butterfly Kisses" with Carlisle, and the two of them also wrote the country hit "Why'd You Come in Here Looking Like That?" for Dolly Parton. According to Carlisle, Psalm 150 toured up and down the West Coast, playing for "love offerings." As he says, "There was a lot of love, but not a lot of offerings." The classic lineup did not record, but the popular worship song "I Want to Praise You, Lord" (Maranatha Music) appears to have been written by Scott and Thomas while they were in Psalm 150 (though the two had also been together in an earlier group called Sonrise). The group that recorded *Make Up Your Mind* had a soul-plus-brass sound reminiscent of Tower of Power. *Harmony* magazine also compared some of the more upbeat tracks to Chicago and Average White Band. Tight horn arrangements are in evidence throughout, and funky keyboards (notably clavinet) typical of the '70s come to the fore on about half of the tracks. Another notable feature of the album are the traditional gospel background vocals that add spice to several of the songs. *Make Up Your Mind* opens with a strong cut, "God Be Magnified." Other highlights include "Live in Me" and the predisco "Get Yourself

Together." A second Psalm 150 album was produced by **Andraé Crouch** but never released. Escalante and Felix became members of Crouch's Disciples.

Psalters

Scott Krueger; et al. 1999—*Prayers to Be* (Burnt Toast Vinyl); 2000—*Sya a Ku.*

Psalters is not a band but, according to its lead thinker Scott Krueger, "an attitude, an artistic expression, a refining movement, a community, a style of worship, a social consciousness, or even a social conscience." It is also the epitome of indie music. For the first Psalters project, Krueger gathered a motley collection of eclectic musicians to play ethnic instruments on a variety of modern psalms expressing various attitudes toward God (with laments in greatest evidence). The music is mostly Middle Eastern in style, though Native American, African, and other expressions sometimes wind their way into the mix. "I'm Free" is a new song but seems directly derived from the African American Spiritual tradition of slave days. **Michael Knott** contributes the song "Fattened Frothing Swine," which seems out of place insofar as it offers third-person commentary on modern lifestyles, whereas everything else is couched in second-person address to God. The second Psalters project is titled *Sya a Ku,* which means "Cries from the Cave." It continues in the same tradition as the first album with a notable exception. Whereas on *Prayers to Be* the various musicians took turns playing their instruments one at a time or on separate tracks, on *Sya a Ku* they tend to jam all at once. This makes for a sound that *Phantom Tollbooth* describes as both more community-oriented and more confusing "for those who need a few moments of quiet amidst the chaos."

PSPAZZ

Mason Bundschuh, gtr.; Kyle Maligro, voc., gtr.; Robin Ryder, drums; Zach Wilhelm, bass. 1995—*Missile Toe* (Brainstorm).

PSPAZZ was a Christian youth band from Kauai, Hawaii, who sought to make fun music with a healthy emphasis on nonsense. Indeed, the group's name is intended to be nonsensical; it doesn't mean or stand for anything. The same postmodern embrace informs the opening, title song for their *Missile Toe* album: it consists of several unrelated phrases joined together and set to a catchy beat as a deliberate foil to obsessive-types who scrutinize song lyrics for messages. Musically, the group plays a pop-punk style of music that also shows such strong influence as '60s beach music and those masters of postmodern fun, The Monkees. Several songs are goofy, with adolescent-humor lyrics like "Kyle's got B.O. 'cause he didn't put deodorant on." But a few songs actually have messages. "Mask" is about a girl who puts on the cosmetics and wears designer clothes but is still ugly on the inside. "Mayor" satirizes political advertisements. "Roller Coaster" is about emotional ups and downs. Specifically Christian content comes in around the edges and is most evident in the songs "Freak Who Loves God" and the uncharacteristically cliché-ridden "Let Go and Let God." Robin Ryder is also drummer for PSPAZZ's "brother band," **Spooky Tuesday,** which is also from Kauai.

For trivia buffs: Kyle Maligro is a world champion body-surfer, a sport that involves surfing on a foam "bodyboard" rather than a traditional surfboard.

Puller

Mike Lewis, voc., gtr.; Geoff Riley, drums; Corey French, gtr. (– 1998); Ryan Jewel, bass (– 1998) // Dustin Holt, bass (+ 1998); Miles, gtr. (+ 1998). 1996—*Sugarless* (Tooth and Nail); 1998—*Closer Than You Think;* 2000—*What's Mine at Twilight.*

The mostly Christian rock band Puller was formed in Oklahoma by Mike Lewis, former front man for the general market group **For Love Not Lisa.** "I was the only Christian in that band," Lewis says of FLNL's demise, "and I was just tired of touring with those guys and I was tired of going through the motions. The music industry kind of trashed us and turned us out. When we broke up, no one really liked each other." Nevertheless, Lewis put Puller together as a group that was dedicated from the start to being a general market band, to playing "clubs not churches." Indeed, he told *HM* early on that "one of the four members of Puller is not a Christian," but he "totally accepts the whole thing." Lewis critiqued the whole notion of "building up a little Christian community outside the world" as "not very biblical." He also would indicate a couple of years later that "we are getting frustrated with the whole Christian market because it's generated around youth kids who don't really listen to music . . . they just come to be silly." Puller, in his estimation, was a college rock band with a mature sound and with thought-provoking lyrics that deserved to be taken seriously. As for "message," Lewis would also fault "the Christian marketplace" as just expecting artists "to quote the Bible" and "give little speeches." He indicated that neither was his style, though that did not mean Puller did not have something to say: "I'm not here to entertain. I want people to be affected and changed by what they're hearing, or else what's the point?"

Sugarless is a hard-rocking piece distinct from the two later albums. The sound is driven by crunchy sheets of guitar and traditional rock riffs. The opening "Shut Off" (a song about alienation) features jagged shifts in tempo giving it a start/stop feel similar to some songs by such modern rock outfits as Filter or Poster Children. Another track, "6x6," saw some significant exposure on MTV. "# 1 Fan" makes fun of celebrity adulation

and its T-shirt-buying masses. Stylistic and personnel changes would mark the sophomore project, *Closer Than You Think.* The group relocated to Los Angeles and Lewis allowed that Radiohead's *O.K. Computer* had been a primary influence on his artistic development. One of Lewis's old cohorts from For Love Not Lisa (the guitarist known simply as Miles) joined the band. *Closer* features a number of slower and more melodic songs, leading the media to characterize it as the work of "a kinder, gentler Puller." Lyrically, however, the album has a darker and more introspective tone, owing to a divorce that Lewis was going through at the time. "That album is really just me going through the mire," he told *Bandoppler.* "The other guys in the band go, 'Man, it sure made for a good record but . . . your life sucked!' " A song called "Wishing" is particularly world-weary with its recollection of a time when the artist would say, "This is all the damage I care to take." Lewis empathizes with the woman at the well in John 4 in the song "Am I Samaritan?" and the track "Bring Me In" seems to be a prayer for healing. "If I Had These Things" is a beautifully strummed acoustic song expressing a hesitant willingness to make a change—with reference to the biblical story of Peter walking on the water (Matthew 14:28–37). On the heavier side, "She" rocks with a punk-like intensity and "Out of My Head" has a strong Pearl Jam sound, complete with Eddie Vedder vocals and sledgehammer guitar riffs. *What's Mine at Twilight* continues in the same vein as the second album with melodic songs and a sound that *HM* would describe as "like the Foo Fighters without all the sugary pop frosting." Standout cuts include the opening "Hold On to Me" and the closer, "If She's the One." On "These Days," Lewis confesses, "I want to live like Paul, but I think like Thomas, and I'm more like Judas—these days." And, he avers, "If Jesus loves His people / He'll tear down every steeple in this town." Guitarist Miles recorded a side project album under the name Sequoyah called *Good Night Evening Star* (6x6 Records).

Pushstart Wagon

Benjamin Eggehorn, drums, perc.; Jonathan Elliott, gtr., voc.; Stephen Guiles, gtr., voc.; Eric Shouse, bass. 1996—*Squeaky Clean* (Brainstorm).

Pushstart Wagon was an alternative pop band from south of Los Angeles with a sound similar to The Lemonheads or The Rembrandts (with louder guitars). Discovered by Scott Silletta of **PlankEye,** they made one album that was produced by Andy Prickett of **The Prayer Chain** and was an instant favorite of critics. The group's unabashed penchant for singable catchy songs rarely went unnoticed in reviews. "They write fun songs packed to the gills with catchy hooks and then they play them loud," *Cornerstone* said. "They simply play hook after hook with all the energy and vivacity they've got," *True Tunes* chimed in. Identification with the contemporary Christian music scene may have hurt the band commercially, as their album *Squeaky Clean* was sufficiently subdued in its spirituality to have made an impact on regular college radio but was perhaps too subtle to win over suspicious Christian programmers. "Our music isn't highly evangelistic," Guiles admitted to *7ball*. "It's just about our relationships with each other, how we relate to God and how we relate to our world." One of the strongest tracks is "A Different Hue," a bit of ear candy that offers praise, probably to God, for brightening the songwriter's life. "I Take You Everywhere I Go" is a pop-punk anthem in the tradition of **The Altar Boys,** but with obscure meaning (who or what does he take everywhere he goes?). "Surf's Up On 64th" is indeed a surf song. "Tightrope Boy" is done in Euro-pop tradition and employs the fairly obvious circus metaphor for apprehension that its title suggests. "Open" offers a pledge of vulnerability; "I Will (Run for Cover)" is about giving to street beggars; "Affection" describes the plight of a girl who keeps getting used by guys who say, "I'm not in love with her, but she'll never know." Pushstart Wagon did not record a sophomore album, but Steve Guiles recorded with his wife Joy under the name Friction Bailey. Their independent 2000 album *Tango Yellow Petal* offers a batch of songs dealing with family issues and romantic love, sung in a '70s folk-pop sound rich with harmony. "I'm a Sucker (For Your Love)" is a special treat.

Paul Q-Pek

1996—*Touch the Ground* (Absolute).

Paul Q-Pek was the bandana-wearing, guitar-smashing hero of the wild Christian punk band **One Bad Pig.** Five years after that group's demise, he reappeared as a polite adult-pop solo artist. The cover photo for *Touch the Ground* shows him dressed for Sunday morning in a suit with his hands nicely folded and eyes closed in prayer. The album is a shocking departure from his previous porker rock. "Bring Jesus to Me" is a nice adult contemporary ballad in the same vein as **Bob Carlisle.** Most of the album, however, sounds more like Peter Gabriel, so much so on some songs (the title track, "I [Surrender]," "Sea Creatures") as to seem annoyingly imitative. "All over You" is better, drawing on rich R&B tradition with female background vocals supporting a testimony to "the witness of the Spirit." Likewise, "If I Were President" gets funky with political satire in a way that recalls Don Henley ("Dirty Laundry," "All She Wants to Do Is Dance") and offers a break from the album's dominant style. *Touch the Ground* is more imaginative lyrically than musically. Its title track declares, "I know that we should watch and pray / That is something we must never lose / But all I see is people wanting to escape / Instead of doing what he told us to do." Another song, however, is a tad troubling: "Capitol Hill" seems intended to ridicule homeless, unemployed, and hungry people for looking to the government to help them rather than simply trusting in God. If that really is the point, the message clearly contradicts the thought of "Touch the Ground," not to mention the Bible. The album's greatest contribution comes with

Pat Terry's "Open the Door," which introduces a new generation to a selection from the Jesus music pioneer's oft-ignored repertoire. "Things Can Only Get Better" is a cover of the 1985 hit by English pop singer Howard Jones. The album was produced by Absolute president and former Prince guitarist **Dez Dickerson** with Tedd T.

Christian radio hits: "Touch the Ground" (# 10 in 1995); "I (Surrender)" (# 6 in 1996); "Things Can Only Get Better" (# 10 in 1996).

Quayle

William Coker, bass; Nick Garrisi, voc., gtr., kybrd.; Javier Hernandez, gtr.; Kevin Pollard, drums. 1997—*Quayle* (SubLime).

The Southern California group that went by the name Quayle began as Spud Puddle and played pop-punk for a while under that name before deciding it was time for a change. They insisted the new moniker had nothing to do with the former Vice President, though their album cover rather obviously tried to capitalize on the associations with a red, white, and blue/stars-and-stripes design that looked like a political campaign poster. The album was produced by **Michael Knott,** but the group did not quite attain the alternative credentials that such an association might suggest. Rather, they moved in the same vein as fairly traditional melodic rock groups like **Common Children** or Foo Fighters. The mellifluent closing song, "Superman Sun," may be the best track, with introspective lyrics set to an acoustic backdrop. "Leaving the Lights On" has a harder edge and seeks to offer comfort to the fearful. "Rockstar

Romeo" holds up the mirror to a celebrity's girlfriend who is really only one step removed from being a groupie. "The Pretender" voices the frustration of a phony who has become so caught up in his deceptions that he can no longer find himself amidst all the illusions. The group tried to enact its Christian vocation by offering thought-provoking messages rather than through explicitly evangelistic or worship-oriented songs. "We strive to reach kids with real problems by sharing that we go through them too," Coker said.

Quickflight

Ric DeGroot, kybrd., voc.; Dale Dirksen, bass, voc., kybrd.; Greg Johnson, gtr.; Pete Cordalis, voc. (–1983); Gary Hendricks, drums (–1983); Mike King, gtr. (–1983). 1980—*Breakaway* (Tunesmith); 1983—*Decent Beat* (StarSong).

Quickflight was a heavy electronic band from Canada. Their first album, *Breakaway,* presented them as the up-and-coming next big thing on the order of synthesizer-driven arena rockers like Styx, albeit with slightly more of a new-wave edge. Their concerts were major productions for the time with lots of *Star Wars*-era sound and light effects. An affectionate profile in *CCM* announced that each one of the band members was a solo artist in his own right. The group was also said to have played together for four years and to have a sound that was "incredibly tight." *Breakaway* includes one regional (Canadian) radio hit, "Pink Shirts," in addition to the energetic title track, the MOR "Simple Way," and the reggae-inflected "To the Way." A track called "Modern Romans" (sung by King) addresses the contemporary Iranian "hostage crisis" with reference to the failed rescue mission ordered by President Carter. More explicitly Christian

fare can be found in the confrontational "Atheist" and the theological "The Cross Is Crazy (To the People of the World)." By the second album, the group was down to a trio, but *True Tunes* declared *Decent Beat* to be "miles ahead of its time in both writing and production." A style shift reveals the influence of British synthesizer bands like Human League, Soft Cell, and especially **After the Fire.** Lyrics on this project are mostly opaque, "articulating the questions of urban youth and pointing in the direction where the answer can be found," to quote *CCM.* The clearest such pointer comes in "Fade to Glory," which appears to be addressed to Christ, who is referenced as Agnus Deo Son: "Give me all You've got to give . . . Loose these chains and let me live."

Quiet City

Monty Andersen, bass; Michael Reiser, kybrd., voc.; Brandon Sensintaffar, drums; Sparquis, gtr. 1995—*Quiet City* (Salt).

Quiet City was a one-time project put together by Michael Reiser of Tulsa, Oklahoma. He and his cohorts offer a thematic exploration of theodicy, that is, of the questions concerning the relationship of pain and suffering in the world to the belief in a good and powerful God. The concept was inspired by a 1940 Irwin Shaw play (for which Aaron Copland wrote incidental music) in which characters reveal their thoughts about the distress of urban society. Reiser's music is appropriately moody, moving from lush atmospheric pieces (the opening "Killing Fields") to hard rock. "Touch Tomorrow" quotes from Psalm 30:5 ("weeping may endure for the night, but joy comes in the morning"). "Believing" explores the thesis that "trust is the hardest step toward revelation."

R

Rachel Rachel

Brynn Beltran, kybrd.; Cheryl Jewel, voc.; Jennifer Sparks, drums; Heli Sterner, gtr., voc.; Jennifer York, bass (– 1993) // Robin Spurs, bass (+ 1993). 1991—*Way to My Heart* (DaySpring); 1993—*You Oughta Know by Now*.

Rachel Rachel was consistently billed as the world's first "all-girl Christian rock band," and on the basis of the gender factor alone their sound was compared to The Bangles, Wilson Phillips, the Go-Go's, and Heart. In actuality, they sounded much more like labelmates the **Allies** or **White Heart,** with whom they often toured (Brynn Beltran eventually married Mark Gersmehl of the latter band). The group was inevitably promoted as a novelty act but managed to earn modest acclaim and grudging respect from critics for their legitimate musical contributions. Resistance to the "cute factor" in marketing was abetted by the fact that all of the girls (as they are invariably called in every known article or review) were in fact women in their midthirties—almost old enough to be the mothers of the adolescent boys who made up their target audience. The group was formed in 1991 at the instigation of Jennifer York. The future bass player was working at a Christian radio station in New York when, she says, she received a prophecy from the Lord (based on Isaiah 42:6–10) telling her to drop everything, go to California, and form an all-girl band called Traeh (which is "heart" spelled backwards). Apparently, York did not play an instrument at the time, but in obedience to the vision she moved to Los Angeles, enrolled in music school, and shared her idea with a management company that agreed to follow through on the idea. As it turns out, a recent Christian convert named Cheryl Jewel was working as a secretary at that company and felt the call to become the band's lead singer. Auditions were held to fill the remaining spots, and after a few gigs Traeh decided to become the more marketable Rachel Rachel. York would leave the band in 1993 (though she appears to have played on the second album) to pursue a career as a network news reporter for an L.A. TV station. She was replaced by Robin Spurs, who had once fronted a Los Angeles cult band called The Toasters and had also played with **The Choir.**

Billy Smiley of **White Heart** produced both of Rachel Rachel's albums. The big surprise on *Way to My Heart* is an effective cover of the **Kansas** song "Carry On, Wayward Son." The track showcases the group's vocal strengths and a turn-it-up-loud toughness that would convince skeptics they could rock. The first album also features another rocker, "Long Lost Love" (about not giving up on a relationship), the acoustic "Outside Looking In," and a slick pop song, "I Will Stand by You." Though all of these styles are performed with competence, some critics complained about the inconsistency—just as they did with **White Heart.** In general, critics preferred Rachel Rachel's rock-oriented sound, but the group scored its biggest hits with tamer fare. Thus, in reviewing the sophomore project, *CCM* praised the Heart-like "Dust to Diamonds" and the show-stopping "Lay Down Your Head" while regarding the destined-for-Number-One sweet pop tune "You'll Never Know" as a faux pas. The group's biggest hit, "Only Heaven

Knows," is also its prettiest song, an unplugged number featuring mandolin and gentle percussion, with lyrics that speak of Christ's empathy with those who suffer hurt or sorrow.

Christian radio hits: "I Will Stand by You" (# 4 in 1991); "There Ain't Enough Love" (# 13 in 1992); "Only Heaven Knows" (# 1 for 2 weeks in 1993); "You'll Never Know" (# 1 in 1993); "You Are Always There" (# 11 in 1993).

Rackets and Drapes

Charlotte; Kalliapi; Kandy Kane; Larvae. 1998—*Candyland* (Fifty 280); 1999—*Trick or Treat* (MCM); announced for 2002—*Love Letters from Hell.*

www.racketsanddrapes.com

Rackets and Drapes was a faux-controversial Christian band that got marketed as "the first Christian shock-rock band" and, specifically, as "a Christian version of Marilyn Manson." Formed in 1994, the group was composed of four men who went by fake feminine names and who often performed wearing dresses or skirts, with faces lathered in Mansonesque makeup. Their musical style was a form of industrial metal with gothic overtones. *HM* described it as "dark, doomy mood music with shock shrieks for the masses." At its best, the group could lay claim to performing a genre of music usually ignored by explicitly Christian artists, delving into the dark side of Halloween without losing sight of the fun or freedom that confident faith provides. The latter tendency is best illustrated by their standout track "Scary Go Round" from *Trick or Treat*. The problem is that, aside from superficialities that could only offend unthinking traditionalists, the group was not really very radical. Lyrically, they often came off as pawns of an ultra-conservative Religious Right, espousing what appeared to be the party line of a defensive cult that had replaced reason with rhetoric and no longer cared about communicating with the world at large. Thus, on "Baby Killer" they scream about "homicide" and "genocide" in ways that would embarrass most opponents of abortion (i.e., those who understand the issue to be a bit more complicated than such aspersions imply). Another track, "Burning Your Witches," uses remembrance of a bygone era when Christians used to torture and murder young women suspected of practicing the occult as a *positive* image for taking an uncompromising stand against sin that should be adopted in the present day (in a more metaphorical vein—perhaps). Thus, at their worst, Rackets and Drapes was able to make Christians look stupid *and* vicious. On the other hand, *Candyland,* which features both of the above-named tracks, also includes powerful statements about child abuse: the song "Love with a Fist" addresses physical abuse in a manner reminiscent of Pat Benatar's "Hell Is for Children," and "Ball and Chain" goes even deeper to offer a glimpse of the sort of emotional damage uncaring parents inflict upon an unwanted child.

Candyland was re-released by MCM in 1999, but most critics regard the sophomore project *Trick or Treat* as a vast improvement. Here, the group does an innovative cover of Depeche Mode's "Personal Jesus" and they return to the topic of child abuse with the opening "Mommie Dearest." Their penchant for condemning sin (particularly sexual transgressions) continues on the songs "Trick or Treat," "Virgin in the Midst," "Rotten Apples," and "On Your Knees." The latter track makes an effective (potentially shocking) use of S&M imagery to describe the "bondage" of unrepentant sin. "Beat the Devil" carries forward the **Stryper** and **Carman** tradition of victory-over-Satan songs ("Hallelujah! Praise the Lord! / I beat the devil / I beat him down!"). The same sort of fundamentalist orientation informs "Plastic Jesus," an outsider's attack on religious iconography and jewelry that fails to discern the meaning such items actually possess for those who prize them. The album concludes with a "hidden track" in which the band's pastor preaches an evangelistic sermon and invites the listener to pray a prayer for personal salvation. Rackets and Drapes called it quits in 2001 and Kandi Kane offered some last words to the group's detractors in *HM* magazine: "R&D is no longer, but not because you prayed so hard against us, or protested when we passed through your city. It is over because God has shown me that we have arrived at a dead end on a one-way street."

Radiohalo
See **ArkAngel.**

Ed Raetzloff

1981—*It Took a Long Time to Get to You* (NewPax); 1982—*Drivin' Wheels.*

Christian roots rocker Ed Raetzloff fronted the general market band Blue Jug for many years before his conversion to Christianity in the fall of 1978. Although Blue Jug did not have much success at achieving radio airplay or chart hits, they were an acclaimed bar band, and the rock press called attention to the "character and sensitivity" evident in Raetzloff's songwriting. After becoming a Christian, Raetzloff made two solo albums, employing **Dave Perkins** as lead guitarist for the first and Randy Scruggs for the second. He continued to perform for a time with a band called Jericho.

It Took a Long Time to Get to You features a testimony tune called "Praise Him" that documents Raetzloff's reasons for quitting Blue Jug to play Christian music. Songs like "It's So Easy to Be Free" and "I Know the King" rock harder than what was deemed acceptable for most Christian concert venues at the time, leaving Raetzloff to continue playing primarily in clubs and college auditoriums. As his debut album faltered in sales, he would complain to *CCM* that "everything is so lackadaisical in this business," indicating that the general market was more adept at promoting products and supporting artists than the Christian industry. *Drivin' Wheels* was produced by Turley Richards and features a couple of Richards' songs ("Going Home," "Holy Holy") in addition to covers of **Curtis Mayfield**'s "People Get Ready" and **Tim Sheppard**'s "Hey There Stranger." The album also introduces the newly converted **Will McFarlane** to Christian audiences by giving exposure to two McFarlane songs ("This New Love," "You'll Have It All") before that artist would embark on his own career in Christian music. The hit "Keep the Big Wheels Turning" was actually written by **Dave Perkins,** apparently as a leftover from the first project. *Group* magazine described *Drivin' Wheels* as "blending hefty southern rock with the Good News for twentieth-century prodigals."

Christian radio hits: "Keep the Big Wheels Turning" (# 7 in 1982).

Raft of Dead Monkeys

Matt Johnson, voc.; Doug Lorig, gtr.; John Spalding, gtr.; Jeff Suffering, voc. 2001—*Thoroughlev* (Burnout).

Raft of Dead Monkeys was started in Seattle as a novelty or parody band by persons associated with Christian music. Matt Johnson and Doug Lorig were once members of **Roadside Monument;** John Spalding and Jeff Suffering (and Johnson briefly) had been in **Ninety Pound Wuss.** The group was not set up as a Christian band and from the start behaved in ways certain to alienate traditional Christian audiences. The group viewed its concerts as "performance art" and made a conscious decision to use a good deal of profanity in its music. Johnson told *Bandoppler,* "the lyrics were deliberate to show how ridiculous rock culture can be. We over-personified a kind of rebellious stage presence. By using profanity you don't communicate anything—that was the point! That's what rock culture is about." The band obtained a following in the club scene in Seattle and became something of the house band at a bar called The Breakroom. "As far as Christian fans go," Johnson told *Bandoppler,* "I would have to say that they generally don't 'get it'—and I would not expect them to." Indeed, Johnson eventually left the group, saying he had "ethical problems" with the controversy that was involved. He indicated that, although he understood what the others were trying to do, he was also conscious of Paul's words about not being an offense to another (1 Corinthians 8:9) and did not personally feel that he could "offer anything positive to people through playing in that band." In 2001, the group released an album *Thoroughlev,* with liner notes that offered no lyric sheet or personnel list. That same year, Suffering would also release an album called *Real Panic Formed* (Velvet Blue) by a group called Suffering and the Hideous Thieves.

A Ragamuffin Band

Jimmy Abegg, voc., gtr.; Rick Elias, voc., gtr., kybrd.; Mark Robertson, voc., bass, gtr.; Aaron Smith, drums. 1999—*Prayers of a Ragamuffin* (Word).

www.aragamuffinband.com

In a sense, the group that goes by the tag A Ragamuffin Band is a Christian supergroup composed of four individuals, each of whom has been highly regarded for his contributions in other areas. **Jimmy Abegg** was a founding member of **Vector** and of **Charlie Peacock**'s Acoustic Trio, and he has recorded two highly acclaimed albums as a solo artist. **Rick Elias** has also been a critics' favorite as a rootsy solo artist and producer; he enjoyed a few minutes of fame in 1996 when four of his songs were used in the motion picture *That Thing You Do;* the title track charted at Number Forty-one in a version performed by a fictitious band called The Wonders. Mark Robertson has been a member of **Brighton, Generation, The Stand, Under Midnight,** and **This Train.** Aaron Smith played with **Vector** and then became drummer for the **Seventy Sevens.** All four of the Ragamuffins also played as the backing band for **Rich Mullins,** who bestowed on them their name. In another sense, however, the notion of the Ragamuffins as "a supergroup" is most ironic, for the whole idea of the group is a uniting of those who recognize themselves to be misfits, square pegs, or, frankly, "not good enough" in popular estimation to be celebrities or stars. The Ragamuffin Band was first organized by Mullins as an anticelebrity vehicle for certain counter-cultural Christian musicians to exercise their art and piety without concern for meeting expectations that supposedly determine commercial or critical success. The term *ragamuffin* actually comes from a book by Brennan Manning *(Ragamuffin Gospel),* which defines ragamuffins as "the burdened, the wobbly and weak-kneed, the inconsistent, unsteady disciples . . . the smart people who know they are stupid . . . the honest disciples who admit they are scalawags." Mullins recruited folks who embraced that description to play with him on his acclaimed 1993 album, *A Liturgy, a Legacy, and a Ragamuffin Band.* With some personnel shifts, the unofficial group was set to back him on *The Jesus Record* as well when, shortly before production began, Mullins was killed in a highway accident. Abegg, Elias, Robertson, and Smith made the difficult decision to record the album anyway, with guest vocalists. That record could easily be deemed A Ragamuffin Band's debut outing, though it is usually listed as Mullins' final product instead (a separate disc of him singing demos for all of the songs is included). In any case, the trio recruited Smith and toured *The Jesus Record,* performing a series of emotional concerts that kept Mullins' vision and music alive. "On the road, we became a true band, a separate entity," Elias told *Prism* magazine, explaining a convergence that would lead the quartet to make another album of their own.

Prayers of a Ragamuffin is a thematic concept album, presenting ten songs that all deal in some sense with the topic of spiritual devotion or prayer. Musically, however, the work has the hodgepodge feel of a Crosby, Stills and Nash album—songs in at least three wildly different styles, each of which reflects the predilections of one of the rotating front men. Elias comes off sounding very much like Bruce Springsteen on the radio-friendly "Faith, Hope, and Love" and "Shout"; indeed the latter song is a knock-off that (aside from its "Praise the Lord" lyrics) could have fit unobtrusively between "Cadillac Ranch" and "I'm a Rocker" on *The River*. "God Grant Me the Tears" is more original than those songs and may be the album's strongest track. Robertson's "Bouncing off the Ceiling" is a humorous country rock song (about seemingly unanswered prayers) that might have been included on either of **This Train**'s quirky, fun albums. Abegg departs most noticeably from his trademark solo sound, with songs that seem strongly influenced by Mullins. The title of "Brother Sun, Sister Moon" comes from Mullins' favorite movie, a Zeffirelli biography of St. Francis of Assisi. (The film, incidentally, features a different, also beautiful song called "Brother Sun, Sister Moon" written and sung by hippie folk singer Donovan.) The St. Francis connection is also expressed in what became *Prayers of a Ragamuffin*'s most famous song, an Elias composition titled "Make Me an Instrument." It takes its lyric from a well-known prayer of the famous saint, with an addendum from the breastplate of St. Patrick ("Christ within me / Christ before me / Christ behind me / Christ above me . . ."). Reminiscent of Mullins' "Creed," the song was chosen by Pope John Paul II to be the official theme song for the International Catholic Youth Day, and the band was invited to sing a multi-lingual version of it in front of some two million youth. *Prayers* concludes with yet another Abegg song, "We'll Be Together Again," sung to Mullins by friends who miss him.

A book that might serve as a companion volume to the album was compiled by Abegg and published as *Ragamuffin Prayers* (CCM Books, 2000). It collects prayers and devotional writings from a number of poets including many contemporary Christian songwriters **(Carolyn Arends, Ashley Cleveland, Phil Keaggy, Sarah Masen, Kevin Max, Charlie Peacock, Michael W. Smith)** with photographs and illustrations by Abegg.

Rage of Angels

John Fowler, drums; Dale Gilfort, bass; Frank KiCostanzo, gtr.; Greg Kurtzman, gtr.; Don Mariano, voc. 1989—*Rage of Angels* (Regency).

A melodic metal band from Connecticut, Rage of Angels did not stick around long enough to gain much of a following, and their only album slipped into obscurity, only to become a collector's item among ex post facto fans who elevated the

group to a "hall of fame" status once they were no longer around. The band exhibits a double guitar assault on nine tracks, including "Do You Still Believe in Love" and the reassuring "Leave You Nor Forsake You." *Rad Rockers* compared them to **Stryper, Whitecross,** and **Impellitteri.**

Raiderz of the Lost

Personnel list unavailable. 1999—*Prepare 4 tha Spillage* (CMN).

Raiderz of the Lost is a hip-hop artist that features rap vocals by someone called Messenger. The album *Prepare 4 tha Spillage* has a military theme throughout, opening with the militant "Raiderz Anthem," which *CCM* describes as "featuring an army of MCs who are gonna march into the enemy's camp and straight rip it up." Another track, "Frontline Soldier," is basically a battle hymn with possible inspiration from 2 Timothy 2:3. "Code of Honor" likewise draws upon traditions of military conduct to find parallels for Christian morality. Such imagery has undeniable roots in Scripture but when taken to an extreme, as here, tends to present Christians to the world as self-obsessed triumphalists, rather than as peacemakers who are more concerned with loving their enemies than with defeating them.

Rainbow Promise

Steve Powell, gtr.; et al. 1972—*Rainbow Promise* (New Wine).

Almost nothing is known about the psychedelic Jesus music quintet Rainbow Promise except that guitarist Steve Powell was a member. The group's custom album has a more scorching, guitar onslaught sound than was typical for the folk-oriented era. It begins with a trio of rockers, "Get Ready," "Someone You Need," and "Do You Hear?" and then completely falls apart with two cornball summer camp songs, "Romans 8:28" and "Joy of the Lord." Side Two includes a cover of **Love Song**'s "Little Country Church." Copies of *Rainbow Promise* became extremely rare and sold among collectors at high prices. More than a decade later, Steve Powell released a more laid-back solo album called *Revelation . . . The Party's Over* (Sine Skin, 1983).

Rainbow Rider

Ronnie Martin; et al. 1993—*Beautiful Dazzling Music No. 1* (Siren).

Rainbow Rider was an intermediate project for synthesizer whiz Ronnie Martin, recorded in between his two albums with **Dance House Children** and numerous takes with **Joy Electric.** With an emphasis on orchestration, the one-time project is generally considered to be his best work, catching the artist in his prime, before he hit on the formulaic sounds with which he was destined to be most associated. *Beautiful*

Dazzling Music was recorded on one of **Michael Knott**'s labels and was intended to be the first in a series that was unfortunately never continued. The label folded and *True Tunes* panned the album, limiting interest among what would already have been a fairly small pool of potential fans. Working without his brother Jason (of **Dance House Children** and **Starflyer 59**) for the first time, Martin did get some assistance from his sister Amy and from friends Tom Danielson and Jeff Cloud. The album features two poetic tracks about the Second Coming ("Resurrection Railway," "Rapture Day Bliss") and two praise songs ("Sing It from the Mountain," "Majesty 1700"), in addition to a few romantic love songs. In 2000 it was re-released on Velvet Blue Music and a repentant *True Tunes* declared it "the best synth pop record ever released to the Christian market . . . pure pop music from another planet . . . it shows just how far ahead of his time Martin was."

Rainy Days

Jason Feltman, drums; Jason Fleetwood, gtr.; Jeff Jacquay, bass; Sean McCulley, voc.; Shawn Stopnik, gtr. 1996—*Homecoming* (Alarma).

Rainy Days was a punk-rockabilly band that made one album of high energy songs dealing with aspects of teenage life and presenting legalistic messages that they apparently thought had something to do with Christianity. Lyrics vary from simply trite to curiously quirky to extremely disturbing. In "Aubrey's Fall," McCulley comes very close to sounding like Ned Flanders from *The Simpsons:* "I think I understand your frown / Put that gosh darn glass down." In a song called "Cha-Cha-Cha," God answers the prayer of a kid who hates his life by letting him get hit by a bus, then telling him, "I'll give you another chance, but this time enjoy it." A frighteningly bizarre song called "The Gunslinger" appears to use a Columbine-style massacre as an image for the final judgment: a man who appears to be a Christ figure enters a town on "the last day" and calmly and mercilessly guns down "39 men, 14 women, and 5 children" who had been followers of "a man in black." They try to get away, but there is no escaping his bloodthirsty wrath. The track would be alarming enough on its own; as it is, Rainy Days couples it with another song ("WAJO") in which they identify themselves as "the Lord's soldiers" whom he has appointed to fight on his behalf, taking down his enemies. Why a Christian label like Alarma would release such a work remains a mystery but, then, KMG actually re-released it in 2001 as part of a double-disc set that would also include the completely unrelated project *Four 'o Five* by **A Few Loose Screws.**

Buck and Dottie Rambo

See **The Singing Rambos.**

Reba Rambo (a.k.a. **Reba**) (and **Dony McGuire**)

By Reba or Reba Rambo: Date unknown—*Reality* (Impact); *Songs My Mother Taught Me;* 1972—*Resurrection;* 1977—*Lady* (Greentree); 1978—*The Lady Is a Child;* 1979—*The Prodigal According to Reba;* 1980—*Dreamin';* *Confessions* (Light); 1981—*Remembering* (Greentree); 1982—*Lady Live* (Light). By Reba Rambo and Dony McGuire: 1980—*The Lord's Prayer* (Light); 1982—*Messiah, Bright Morning Star;* 1984—*Special Moments from the Bride* (Impact); 1986—*Plain and Simple Truth* (New Kingdom); 1990—*Mission Possible;* 1991—*Live in the Combat Zone* (RMR).

www.rambomcguire.org

Reba Rambo is the daughter of southern gospel superstars Buck and Dottie Rambo and first sang with them as part of the family group **The Singing Rambos.** She also began recording solo as a teenager, and when the Jesus movement revival broke out in the early '70s she became something of a bridge figure enabling some of the participants in that revival to discover the legacy of southern gospel. Reba was about the same age as the hippie Jesus freaks but her churchy music and proper demeanor was the antithesis of their countercultural style. Still, she toured with **Andraé Crouch and the Disciples** and at the age of nineteen sang at the influential *Explo '72* festival (a Christian version of Woodstock). John Styll of *CCM* magazine called her "one of the best singers I've ever heard."

Rambo's first big album was *Lady,* recorded under her first name only. It established her as the premier "adult contemporary singer" in Christian music. With a powerful voice similar to that of Barbra Streisand, Rambo would be to the '70s what **Sandi Patty** would be to the '80s. *Lady* leads off with one of her most popular songs, "The Land of Oohs and Ah's," which uses imagery from *The Wizard of Oz* as descriptions for heaven and spiritual transformation. It segues into a stellar performance of "Somewhere over the Rainbow." *The Lady Is a Child* brought Rambo more radio exposure with another song about heaven, "All Day Dinner," and "Sunshine Saturday," a generic "you've made my life wonderful" song that could be addressed to God or a human lover. "Child of the Music Maker" is a joyful celebration of music that acknowledges it as a gift of God.

1980 was a banner year for Rambo, seeing the release of three albums. *Dreamin'* followed in the style of earlier productions and closed out the Greentree phase of her career (for which 1981's *Remembering* would provide a retrospective compilation). The most unusual track on *Dreamin'* is an eleven-minute "Dressing Room Sketch" that presents a mini-drama of music and dialogue, recording the singer's conversations with God (voiced here by Don Butler) about her insecurities as a performer. *Confessions* would take Rambo in a new direction on a new label. Embracing the sounds of the moment, she comes off as a Christian **Donna Summer,** singing soulful R&B ballads and upbeat dance songs with equal tinges of disco and traditional gospel. In the meantime, Rambo had also collaborated with **Dony McGuire** on a musical called *The Lord's Prayer*. A concept album, *The Lord's Prayer* features individual songs addressing each line of the famous prayer (e.g., "Lead Us Not into Temptation"), with further reflection on the subject of prayer in general. A cast of singers including **The Archers, Cynthia Clawson, Andraé Crouch, Walter** and **Tramaine Hawkins,** and **B. J. Thomas** all participated in the recording, which won both Grammy and Dove Awards.

Rambo and McGuire's partnership turned to friendship and then to romance in a natural way that avoided controversy even within the hypersensitive subculture of contemporary Christian music. Both were well-known gospel singers (McGuire had sung with **The Downings,** McGuire, and Heaven's Connection) and both went through quiet divorces in the late '70s. Indeed, the announcement of their marriage in the fall of 1980 took some by surprise, as news of the previous divorces had not even been published. Nevertheless, they encountered none of the hostility that would later be visited upon such stars as **Sandi Patty** and **Amy Grant.** The differences might be attributed to timing and circumstance, but also seems to reflect a more supportive environment within the world of southern gospel (cf. **Steve Archer**), which had been dealing with such matters for decades. In any event, the solo careers of both Rambo and McGuire would now merge into a husband and wife team that was still producing worship-oriented albums in the year 2001. *Messiah, Bright Morning Star* reassembles the cast of *The Lord's Prayer* for a series of songs on the life of Christ, from birth to resurrection, with a final plea for his return ("Take Us Home"). *Plain and Simple Truth* features eight original tunes by the couple, plus a rendition of **Sharalee Lucas**'s "I See Jesus in You" and the romantic "Flesh of My Flesh, Bone of My Bone," one of many songs that McGuire has written with his mother-in-law.

In addition to their own recordings, Rambo and McGuire have written numerous songs for other artists, including "With My Song," the title track for an album by **Debby Boone,** and "A Perfect Heart," which became a Christian radio hit for **The Bill Gaither Trio.**

Christian radio hits: By Reba or Reba Rambo: "Child of the Music Maker" (# 13 in 1978); "All Day Dinner" (# 3 in 1978); "Sunshine Saturday" (# 18 in 1978); "Never Ending Love" (# 20 in 1979). By Reba Rambo and Dony McGuire: "Ready for Battle" (# 32 in 1984).

Dove Awards: For Reba Rambo: 1977 Pop/Contemporary Album of the Year *(Lady)*; 1982 Songwriter of the Year. For Reba Rambo and Dony McGuire: 1981 Praise and Worship Album of the Year *(The Lord's Prayer)*.

Grammy Awards: For Reba Rambo and Dony McGuire: 1981 Best Gospel Performance, Contemporary or Inspirational *(The Lord's Prayer)*.

Gary Rand

1981—*Break That Ground* (Milk and Honey); 1983—*Caught by Surprise*.

Singer/songwriter Gary Rand was a member of the Blood, Sweat, and Tears imitators **Crimson Bridge** in the '70s but he exceeded that note on his résumé with two albums of socially conscious songs in the early '80s. The sound of Rand's solo material was much less ambitious than Crimson Bridge, allowing the songs themselves to take center stage. Rand played and sang in a folk-pop style that reminded some of Jackson Browne. *Break That Ground* features the call to social action, "Let Justice Roll Down," and the liturgical "Communion Song," which is one of a surprisingly few offerings in contemporary Christian music to reflect upon the eucharistic meal that is at the center of most Christian worship services (cf. **Barry McGuire, John Michael Talbot**). *Caught by Surprise* offers "Turnaround," a denunciation of apathy, and "Kindness," an encouragement to practice a neglected virtue. "So Hard to Live," with its Christlike prioritization of concern for the poor over self-preservation, moves decidedly away from the political agenda of the Religious Right: "Tonight . . . mountains of weapons, but children with nothing to eat."

Ransom

Lisa Faxon, voc.; Michael Preciado, bass; Dave Holman, drums (–1991); Tony Dierden, gtr. (–1992) // Tony Ortiz, gtr. (+ 1992). 1989—*Once and for All* (custom); 1991—*Ransom* (Intense); 1992—*Soul Asylum*.

Ransom was a female-fronted Christian metal band from California. The group was organized by bass player Michael Preciado and first placed a song called "Sin Kills" on an influential compilation album, *California Metal,* in 1988. Lead singer Faxon gave the group a sound like that of a harder version of Heart. Ransom's self-titled, major-label debut includes a track called "When I Die" that features the lyric, "When I die / And if I find it was all a story / I would not change a thing / Knowing how You've changed me." The group used a studio drummer for their sophomore release (Joseph Galletta of **Shout**) and also got assistance from **Lanny Cordola,** Oz Fox (from **Stryper**), and Larry Melby (from **Liaison**). The album includes "Soul Hymn" and "Watching over Me," a song about God's faithfulness that features a children's choir.

In 1999, a completely different Christian band named Ransom released an independent album called *Dead No More*. That group has a **Petra**esque sound and is fronted by singer Richard Czypinski.

Rap'sures

Doug Doyle, Terry Scott Taylor, Rob Watson. 1985—*Gospel Rap* (StarSong); 1987—*OT Rap*; 1990—*Loud and Proud and Born Again*.

The Rap'sures were a project of **Terry Scott Taylor,** best known for his work with **Daniel Amos, The Swirling Eddies,** and the **Lost Dogs.** The albums were kind of a joke, but they ended up selling much better than expected. The albums have a "camp" quality to them, presenting Bible stories and simple evangelical slogans ("Two Commandments," "In Everything Give Thanks") in a repetitive but memorable style. *Gospel Rap* actually has the distinction of being the first Christian rap album released on a major label. *OT Rap* retells Old Testament stories like "David and Goliath" and "Moses and the Burning Bush" in a manner that might have been used for a hip Vacation Bible School program. *Loud, Proud, and Born Again* breaks with the biblical tradition and goes for humorous reflections on everyday life: "Bless This Mess" is a prayer for (yuck!) cafeteria food. "Freddie's Dead, Jesus Lives" picks up on a theme from what was then the latest *Nightmare on Elm Street* installment. Taylor says, "There wasn't any rap on the Christian labels. We did it as a kids' thing. We saw it as appealing to 7 to 9 year olds. No one was doing it. We just brainstormed a little bit and we did it, and then didn't think that much about it, and it was successful. Don't ask me why." Asked about the authenticity of the project, Taylor readily admits that he was not really very familiar with rap and could never pull off a genuine rap project. "We thought, no one will take this seriously, we're just doing it for kids."

The same year that *Gospel Rap* came out, **Stephen Wiley** also released a Christian rap album—possibly the first in the genre. Another singer named Pete McSweet had released a twelve-inch single called "Adam and Eve, the Gospel Beat" on Lection as early as 1982, but McSweet never followed this up with a full album. **Michael Peace** released a commercially successful Christian rap album in 1987, but the genre didn't really take off until it was picked up by **DC Talk.**

Raspberry Jam

Wes Faulk, drums; Flames, gtr.; Herb Grimaud, bass; Philip Kim, voc., gtr.; Angel Short, voc. (−1995) // Destiny, voc. (+ 1995). 1991—*Raspberry Jam* [EP] (independent); 1993—*Buzz* [EP]; *Chi-Rho* (Metro One); 1995—*Oceanic.*

Raspberry Jam is a Southern California group that experimented with a few different sounds before eventually deciding on the neo-hippie atmospherics their name had suggested all along. *Chi-Rho,* the group's official debut (after two indie projects), was titled after the two letters in the Greek alphabet that are often used as a symbol for the name of Christ in religious iconography. Musically, *Chi-Rho* is a funky, dance-oriented album that includes a cover of a Prince song ("The Cross"). The album garnered attention primarily by association, as Gene Eugene of **Adam Again, Steve Hindalong** of **The Choir,** and Michael Pritzl of **The Violet Burning** all played on it as supporting cast members. Dismissing *Chi-Rho* as unremarkable, critics later announced *Oceanic* as "the surprise of the year." "It doesn't even sound like the same band," *Shout* observed, noting

the shift to a "psychedelic wash of guitar feedback and melodic moodiness." The band had truly hit upon a unique and alternative sound, close in some respects to general market groups like Lush but with a generous dose of edgy musicianship along the lines of **The Prayer Chain**'s controversial *Mercury* (with hat tips to Pink Floyd and The Moody Blues). The album also introduces a new female singer, Destiny, whose soft vocals (like Aimee Mann of 'Til Tuesday or a subdued Madonna) complement those of Philip Kim. *Oceanic* sports three songwriters, each of whom contributes material of a different style. Destiny's songs ("Surrender") tend to be mystical, focusing on a personal relationship with God. Kim's are expressive of wonder and amazement ("The Wonders of Love" and "Oceanic," in which he likens God to an ocean and God's love to the rain). Herb Grimaud's poetry, however, is darker, introducing questioning and troublesome thoughts on "Now Watch the Man" (a meditation on death) and "Burns Like Fire." The song "Easter" is introduced by a reading of the 1633 George Herbert poem of the same name, offering a comparison of culture and concept. Grimaud has also played as a member of **The Violet Burning.**

Raven

2000—*24K A.D.* (Metro One).

Raven is the recording name used by a northern California rap singer whose vocal style has been likened to that of **T-Bone** and Cypress Hill. His testimony is that of the typical Christian rap star: good kid (PK) joins a street gang, gets involved with drugs and violence, then dedicates his life to Christ. The one point of interest in his version of that familiar story is that he actually performed as a hip-hop singer prior to his conversion, rapping under the name The Grim Creeper. The new name was chosen with reference to Genesis 8:7: just as the raven was sent out by Noah to go to-and-fro until the waters of the Great Flood receded, so Raven feels sent by God to go to-and-fro preaching to a lost generation until the waters of time recede and the Lord Jesus Christ comes back. Tracks include "The Dawning," "Cosmic Cowboys," and "Bird's Eye View."

Marty Raybon

1995—*Marty Raybon* (Sparrow).

Country singer Marty Raybon is lead vocalist for the successful general market group Shenandoah. That band has often been noted for performing family-oriented hits: "Sunday in the South" relates the story of a church picnic; "I Want to Be Loved Like That" is about love and faithfulness; "The Moon over Georgia" tells of a woman who chooses true love over riches; "The Church on Cumberland Road" weds gospel imagery with rural sentimentality. Raybon was brought up in a Christian home but says he strayed and developed a drinking problem in the late '80s. Sometime around 1990 he rededicated his life to Christ and gained notoriety for his evangelical fervor. His self-titled 1995 album was his first official solo release (though all the members of Shenandoah play with him on it). It also marks his first offering to the contemporary Christian music community. Coproduced by Raybon and featuring several of his own compositions, the album offers a more personal look at the artist than any of his group's projects. Stylistically, however, it resembles Shenandoah's oeuvre, especially on story songs like "Daddy Talks to Jesus" and "Drive Another Nail." The latter track strives to convict the persistent sinner by indicating that each unrepented sin "drives another nail in the Savior's hand." The up-tempo tracks "When He Reigns" and "Get Up in Jesus' Name" sound just like rollicking dance-floor numbers with choral background vocals adding spice. "Harvest Wind" is a tender ballad that uses a farm metaphor to describe the final peace awaiting Christians at life's end. Raybon began singing some of his solo gospel songs in Shenandoah concerts. He told *Shout* magazine, "I believe in the saving grace of Christ, my Savior. The thing that needs to be realized by those who don't know that grace is that their destiny is elsewhere, in the chambers of hell. I'm going to do all I possibly can to change their destination. They don't have to accept me, but they have to accept Christ."

Collin Raye

Selected: 1997—*Direct Hits: The Best of Collin Raye* (Word Nashville).

www.collinraye.com

Collin Raye is not a contemporary Christian music artist per se but a Christian who has enjoyed a highly successful career as a multi-platinum-selling country artist. He is not a songwriter but throughout his recording career (which began in 1991 with the debut *All I Can Be*) has tried to select songs that he believes are at least compatible with if not outright expressive of his faith. Raye was born in Arkansas in 1967. He married Connie Parker in 1980, and the couple had two children, one of whom was born with cerebral palsy. In 1983, while living in Portland, Oregon, he converted from his Baptist upbringing to Roman Catholicism. "I felt a presence of Christ there like I had never felt before," Raye told *CCM* of the Catholic Church. "I liked the humility of it. When I was growing up, Christianity was like a badge. In the Catholic church, I saw everybody on their knees." From 1985 to 1990, he commuted to Las Vegas, working as a cabaret singer in what became a grueling and unsatisfying life. "The only good that came of it was perfecting my craft," he says. "It was the hardest time in my life without question." During that time, his marriage ended, though he would later maintain that he and his former wife

were good friends; he bought her a house thirty feet from his own so she could be near their children, who continued to live with him. Once Raye found his niche in country music, he would chart numerous hits with spiritual themes. "Little Rock" deals sensitively with the destructive power of alcoholism, and "I Think about You" addresses sexism. More blatantly, his "What If Jesus Comes Back Like That?" (written by Pat Bunch and Doug Johnson) takes on judgmental and apathetic attitudes within the church, reminding Christians that Christ said he would be found in "the least" of all. One verse, for instance, looks for him in a drug-addicted baby: "What if Jesus comes back like that? / Two months early and hooked on crack? / Will we let Him in or turn our back?" A later song, "The Eleventh Commandment," likewise uses biblical themes to address the issue of child abuse. In 1997, Raye was invited to sing a duet with **Susan Ashton** on the title song for a **Jim Brickman** Christmas project called *The Gift* (Windham Hill). That song would receive some attention in the mainstream pop market (# 65 in 1997) in addition to being a chart-topper on country and adult contemporary stations. The duet with Ashton also brought Raye to the attention of contemporary Christian music fans who might have missed his previous work. Thus, when Epic records released a compilation of Raye's "greatest hits" they allowed for an alternative version of that album to be released on a Christian label. Epic sent one version of *Direct Hits* to general market outlets and Word Nashville sent a slightly different, more religious version to Christian bookstores. Both editions include "The Gift" and "What If Jesus Came Back Like That?"

Dove Awards: 1998 Country Song ("The Gift").

Raze

Ja'Marc Davis, voc.; Donnie Lewis, voc.; Mizzie Logan, voc.; J. D., voc. (−2000) // Todd, voc. (+ 2000). 1998—*That's the Way* [EP] (ForeFront); 1999—*Power*; 2000—*The Plan*.

Raze practically exploded on to the scene of teen-oriented Christian pop in the late '90s and expired in infamy three years later in a manner sure to provoke debate for years to come regarding standards of accountability within the Christian music industry. The group was assembled by its front man Ja'Marc Davis, who began dancing with the Christian rap group **E.T.W.** when he was sixteen and then became a dancer on tour with **Carman** before determining that a more youth-oriented variety of the latter's theatrical shows could be effective with the middle school and high school crowd. Davis recruited two female friends, Mizzie Logan, who he had known since seventh grade, and Donnie Lewis, who he had met in a youth group when she was just fifteen. Auditions were held for the fourth "revolving door" position, which was occupied on tour by a number of singers, and on record by two persons who didn't use surnames.

Visually, the group presented a balanced mix of gender and race: two men and two women; two blacks (Ja'Marc and Donnie) and two whites (Mizzie and J.D./Todd). Musically, they perfected a sound often described as a hip-hop version of *NSYNC. The closest general market comparisons might be to C and C Music Factory. The influence of **World Wide Message Tribe** was also obvious, with Zarc Potter of **World Wide Message Tribe** cowriting several songs and producing the first full-length recording; Donnie Lewis is the daughter of **World Wide Message Tribe**'s Deronda Lewis. The music was obviously geared to a young audience and college-to-adult-oriented critics lodged all of the usual complaints about repetitive sounds and simplistic lyrics. They might as well have criticized Disney movies for flat characterization and tidy plot resolution. Raze connected well with their target audience and made some of the best teenybopper music of their era. When they were at their best, the group's songs could surpass those of their influences in quality. Their stage shows were dynamic entertainment extravaganzas with exceptional choreography. The group performed primarily at schools and youth conferences, often staying in one location for up to a week, performing music, teaching dance steps and conveying positive messages. They were perhaps best known for their presentations on sexual abstinence, fueled in part by the courageous testimony of Lewis, who was a teenage mother with a son born outside of marriage. The group also followed the ministry strategy perfected by **Al Denson,** doing nonreligious programs for public schools during the day and inviting the youth to an off-campus evening program that could be explicitly evangelistic.

Raze's debut EP *That's the Way* showcases their various styles with five songs and three remixes. The title track and "In the Name" are both bouncy and catchy tunes with trade-off vocals, a little rapping, and sing-along choruses. Their kitchen-sink, everything-in-the-mix feel suggests a merger of The Temptations' "Ball of Confusion" with The Spice Girls' "Tell Me What You Want." Another track, "Always and Forever" (not the Heatwave song), is a sugary piece of girl-group fluff seasoned with a few moments of subdued Ja'Marc rap between the verses. Both "In the Name" and "Always and Forever" would reappear on *Power* as two of the stronger tracks on that album. Nothing on the full-length debut comes up to the quirky energy of "That's the Way," though "Shoulder Shake" offers a trippy, syncopated celebration of dance. Otherwise, *Power* consists mainly of midtempo Europop tunes and ballads that never quite kick into gear. "Brighter Day" sounds as though it were supposed to be another Spice Girls-meet-The Temptations number—except that the latter act never shows up. *The Plan* recaptures the party atmosphere (and, frankly, the

power) that *Power* was missing. This is especially evident in the group's cover of Kool and the Gang's "Celebration." Likewise, the title track is propelled by tight harmonies and lots of those Moog synth bleeps that kids raised on video games seem to find so pleasing. "Follow Your Dreams" is a generic positive song with Davis offering a growling lead vocal reminiscent of Stevie Wonder's "Boogie on Reggae Woman." The group also covers the **Delirious?** worship song, "Did You Feel the Mountains Tremble?" and submerges itself completely in a sea of **Avalon**-like adult contemporary balladry with the string-accompanied "I Will Go." The album concludes with a spoken affirmation of God's love and an invitation to prayer. This is done sensitively, but nevertheless limits the album's appeal to Christian sects that favor altar calls and understand salvation as a consequence of personal commitment.

After winning the 1999 Dove award for Best Rap/Hip Hop/Dance album, Raze was scheduled to headline a widely publicized national tour that would also feature **Tammy Trent, Whisper Loud,** and **Aurora.** The tour kicked off with a concert in Davis' hometown, Tulsa, Oklahoma, but immediately after the performance, police were waiting offstage to take Davis into custody on five counts of lewd molestation, three counts of rape by instrumentation, and three counts of forcible sodomy. The arrest affidavit reported that three years earlier, at the age of twenty-two, Davis had commenced an eighteen-month-long sexual relationship with a thirteen-year-old girl who traveled with Raze as a backup dancer. During the same time period, the affidavit stated, Davis had also had sexual relationships with two sixteen-year-old girls, but legal charges stemming from these encounters could not be pressed in Oklahoma where the legal age of consent is 16. Further investigation revealed that Davis had confessed to these transgressions up to two years before his arrest, seeking spiritual counsel and "a need for restoration." Apparently, his pastor, his manager, and executives at his record label (ForeFront) had been made aware of the issues and he had been "pulled off the road for a six-month sabbatical" in the summer of 1999. Legal authorities did not find this sufficient and sentenced him to five years in prison.

Christian radio hits: "That's the Way" (# 4 in 1999); "Always and Forever" (# 1 for 2 weeks in 1999); "Place in My Heart" (# 3 in 1999); "All around the World" (# 6 in 2000); "More Than a Dream" (# 1 in 2001).

Dove Awards: 2000 Rap/Hip Hop Album (*Power*); 2001 Rap/Hip Hop/Dance Song ("All around the World"); 2001 Rap/Hip Hop/Dance Album (*The Plan*).

The Reach

See **In Reach.**

Reality Check

Nathan Barlowe, voc., gtr.; Chris Blaney, voc.; Dave Muckel, horns, voc.; Rod Shuler, voc. 1997—*Reality Check* (StarSong).

Reality Check was a short-lived, ever-morphing group with a youth-oriented sound similar to that of **The Newsboys** or **DC Talk** (on numbers that incorporate rap). In fact, the group first came into existence as a trio (Barlowe, Blaney, and Shuler) at Liberty University in Lynchburg, Virginia, where **DC Talk** had formed a few years previously. Muckel was officially added to the lineup for their sole recording, and other musicians (Yinka Jolaoso, perc.; Jody Waldrop, drums; Dave Wyatt, bass) were sometimes listed as members. Johnny MacIntosh (husband of **Chasing Furies**' Sarah Meeker) joined to play guitar and keyboard. Described in their own press materials as "a hyperactive octet," the group did high energy shows enhanced by choreography (Muckel was famous for on-stage back flips). They maintained a strong ministry focus, concluding most shows with evangelistic preaching and altar calls. Prior to the release of their debut album, Reality Check won the Gospel Music Association's Spotlight Best New Artist award for 1996. Their album sold well and earned favorable reviews, but the group disbanded in 1998. Barlowe and MacIntosh formed **Luna Halo.**

The self-titled album presents a buffet of well-crafted pop/rock-and-rap songs, touching on influences as varied as the Beatles and the Beastie Boys. The best tracks are "Plastic," "Know You Better," and "Speak to Me." The first of these has a very secular sound (a high nasal voice singing lead over a rock beat with rap vocals in the breaks) and lyrics about the unreliability of artificial friends. "Know You Better" is a ballad with a sound reminiscent of **Jars of Clay;** it is a worship song, once again emphasizing that true spirituality lies in getting beyond the self with its pretensions and delusions ("to get to know you better / to love you more than myself"). "Speak to Me" is a rap song with a soaring rock chorus. At the opposite end of the spectrum, "Carousel" (not The Hollies' song) is a dippy bubble-gum number with clichéd lyrics about being on a "sin-carousel" and wanting off. "Midnight Confessions" (not The Grass Roots' song) is a talk-rap meditation on the quest for holiness, especially with regard to sexual purity.

Christian radio hits: "Know You Better" (# 2 in 1997); "Carousel" (# 13 in 1998).

Reba

See **Reba Rambo.**

Rebirth

Billy Batstone, voc., bass; David Diggs, kybrd.; Paul Johnson, drums; Alex MacDougall, perc.; Beau MacDougall, gtr.; Nick Nichols, voc.; John Wickham, gtr. No recordings.

Rebirth was an early Southern California Christian band that (like **Psalm 150** or **Seth**) brought together many artists who would later play in better-known groups. The group was independent of Calvary Chapel but played in the same geographical area (around Costa Mesa) where groups associated with that ministry **(Love Song, Children of the Day)** were most active. Their chosen venues were primarily high school dances, where they would nevertheless witness for Christ between songs. They enjoyed a reputation for musical excellence. **Billy Batstone** and **David Diggs** would become founding members of **Good News** (along with **Erick Nelson** and, later, **Bob Carlisle**) and then go on to impressive but very different solo careers. Diggs was also noted for his work with **Pat** and **Debby Boone,** as well as many other artists. Alex MacDougall played with **Selah, The Way,** and **Daniel Amos.** Notably, Batstone, Diggs, and (Alex) MacDougall were all part of **Richie Furay**'s band. Alex's brother **Beau MacDougall** recorded a solo album and played with **Steve Camp.** John Wickham became a guitarist of legendary status in early Christian music, playing with both **The Way** and **Parable.** The Paul Johnson who was a member of Rebirth is not the same Paul Johnson who led the Packards or the Paul Johnson who formed the Paul Johnson Singers.

Recess

Tony Bobalik, kybrd.; Dave Carlson, sax; Jerry Gassie, gtr.; Mike Kondourajian, drums; Tim McGuire, voc.; David Quinones, bass; Dianne Songer (Gadberry), voc. 1989—*Recess* (Reunion); 1990—*Discipline of the Groove.*

Recess was a pop-funk band formed by Tim McGuire in 1980 at Mt. Olivet Nazarene College. The group went through a variety of stylistic and personnel changes but by the end of the decade had adopted a dance-oriented sound greatly assisted by the addition of bassist David Quinones, who had made numerous Hispanic Christian albums on his own. Both of their albums for Reunion were produced by Morris "Butch" Stewart, best known for his work with Earth, Wind, and Fire and The Pointer Sisters. The debut was basically a renovated version of an earlier demo with two new tracks, "Search Me" and "Nothing I Wouldn't Do." The latter songs were the album's strongest, with a sound similar to Wham-era George Michael. *Discipline of the Groove* is a superior project with the fetching "My Own Way," which *CCM* compared to the S.O.S. Band's "Take Your Time (Do It Right)" in sound, and "Hands That Made the World," which showcases Diane Songer Gadberry on lead vocals. The album also includes the strong ballad "I Found Love." In 1991, the Chicago-based group took part in an unusual project involving Haven Middle School in Evanston, Illinois. Four members (Tony Bobalik, Dave Carlson, Tim McGuire, and Dianne Gadberry) worked with producer Stewart for four months putting together an extravagant talent show featuring the middle school youth. Working with a production budget over $100,000, they developed a musical composed of songs written by the students. When the project was finally staged, it received coverage on all of the Chicago-area TV stations.

Christian radio hits: "Are We Wasting Time?" (# 13 in 1987); "Search Me" (# 8 in 1989); "Nothin' I Wouldn't Do" (# 15 in 1989); "In That Number" (# 4 in 1990); "That's the Way He Planned It" (# 5 in 1991); "Discipline of the Groove" (# 16 in 1991); "My Own Way" (# 21 in 1992).

Recon

Personnel list unavailable. 1990—*Beyond Enemy Lines* (Intense).

Recon was a Christian metal band that *HM*'s Doug Van Pelt described as "sounding like Sacred Warrior's twin brother." The group made one album of songs with the same commercial appeal as that Queensryche-style progressive metal act. "Choose This Day" and "Dreams" are standout tracks; "Holy Is the Lord" is metal praise.

Redemption

Jude Hulteen; et al. 1974—*Gone Fishing* (Triumphonic).

Two Christian bands named Redemption entered the field of Jesus music at about the same time in the mid '70s. For the group based in San Antonio, Texas, that released the album *Look Up!* see the listing on **ArkAngel**. The band that may have prompted them to change their name was an eight-piece outfit from New York City with a contemporary sound vaguely reminiscent of groups like Lighthouse, the Ides of March, and Blood, Sweat, and Tears. The lineup included a female lead singer, Jude Hulteen, backed by brass and other instruments. *Gone Fishing* offers a mix of original songs and renovated hymns. It is of interest primarily as a souvenir of squabbles within the Salvation Army at the time. As Paul Baker documents in his book *Why Should the Devil Have All the Good Music?*, the founder of the Salvation Army, General Booth, put brass bands on street corners because, at the time, brass bands were the equivalent of rock and roll, the "hottest, most popular form of music" of the day, especially among the young. When Christian rock first began to emerge out of the Jesus movement revival, progressive elements in that organization sought to capitalize on the trend and quite a few local Salvation Army rock bands were formed. Disgruntled traditionalists objected and a bit of a brouhaha ensued, with some "questioning the merits of using rock music in the salvation of souls" and others maintaining that "it's not the type of music but the saving of souls that's important." Redemption seems to represent a moderate compromise, a tame pop band whose album *Harmony* described as "very tasteful and not too loud," while not-

ing that "the arrangements sound a little dated." The Salvation Army has also contributed **Pam Mark Hall, Michele Pillar,** and **The Insyderz** to the world of contemporary Christian music.

Redline

David Mast, voc.; Adam Redding, gtr.; Jason Martin, drums; Jo, bass (– 2000) // Elisa Lee, bass (+ 2000). 1998—*Clearer* (Freedom); 2000—*Supernova.*

Redline is a Christian grunge (a.k.a. "modern rock") band from Nashville. The group was founded by sixteen-year-old guitarist Adam Redding, who recruited his brother David Mast to sing. Their debut album garnered a favorable review in *HM* with indication that the band could range in style from the "the vocal-heavy and happy sound of Weezer to the quirky bass-driven riffs of Nirvana (see "Should I Never Be") to the dirty guitar rock of Collective Soul (see "Confusion")." *Supernova* was viewed as a vast improvement, however, with the band moving into an emo-influenced heavier sound that drew primary comparisons to Stone Temple Pilots. "Asleep before Midnight" stands out as a potential hit single. Lyrically, Redline addresses personal plights and failings with reference to God's expectations and mercy. Jason Martin (who formerly played with **Holy Soldier**) cites his college theological studies as a growth experience in which he was encouraged to take ownership of his own beliefs rather than just accepting whatever he had been programmed to think: "That's what I like to think we do," he told *Release.* "We encourage teens to question their beliefs and find the truth."

Matt Redman

1998—*The Friendship and the Fear* (StarSong); 1999—*Heart of Worship;* 2000—*The Father's Song* (Sparrow).

Matt Redman is a worship leader from the United Kingdom who, in his early twenties, became the premier composer of praise and worship music for charismatic and nondenominational fellowships throughout his native land. His music is similar in style to the worship songs of **Delirious?,** with whom he often works, and is in the basic tradition of the American contemporary worship movement that began with a series of praise albums issued by Maranatha in the '70s and continued with copycat versions from the Vineyard churches that were issued throughout the '90s. In its simplest form, such music tends to replace the classical underpinnings of traditional liturgy with instantly memorable tunes reminiscent of commercial advertising jingles. The bane of liturgical purists, the songs are undeniably affecting and popular. Redman and others (cf. **Graham Kendrick**) have attempted to take such popular worship music to the next level, fashioning songs of dignity and reverence that nevertheless retain the simplicity that accounts for the genre's appeal. Many of Redman's songs ("Better Is One Day," "Once Again," "O Sacred King") have become standards in churches that favor informal worship styles.

Redman comes out of a British movement called Soul Survivor that grew out of a popular charismatic conference called New Wine. Eventually Soul Survivor established its own youth-oriented church (in Waterford, near London), sponsoring celebration events, a magazine, and a record label (Survivor, an imprint of the British Kingsway label). Andy Piercy of **After the Fire** and Martin Smith of **Delirious?** did a lot of the production work on his early recordings. The discography above lists Redman's American releases, which differ somewhat from his British ones. *The Friendship and the Fear,* as issued on StarSong, compiles songs from an album by the same name on Survivor as well as some from an earlier British project called *Passion for Your Name.* The latter album offers "Better Is One Day" (cf. **Passion**) and "It's Rising Up," a prediction of imminent revival cowritten by Redman with Martin Smith. Newer songs include "Once Again" and "The Friendship and the Fear." The first of these is a powerful track with heartfelt lyrics ("Many times I've wondered at your gift of life / And I'm in that place once again"). The latter is especially poetic, capturing the intimacy and majesty of God that draws worshipers into the divine presence with a cautious sense of awe: "There is one thing you have spoken / There are two things I have found / You O Lord are ever loving / You O Lord are ever strong." *Heart of Worship* was issued as *Intimacy* in the United Kingdom (and *Phantom Tollbooth* reports that the British edition was "the most hotly anticipated Christian music release of the year" in Redman's homeland). The song "Heart of Worship" is a vocal duet featuring Redman and Martin Smith (whose voices are very similar). "Everything That Has Breath" features **Terl Bryant**'s Psalm Drummers on a prominent, spontaneous instrumental break. "Now to Live the Life" is more experimental, with a trip-hop beat and slightly distorted vocals. *Father's Song* offers "Justice and Mercy" as a beautiful congregational song based on several Scripture passages (Isaiah 58; Psalm 40:3; James 1:27). "Let My Words Be Few" is a melodic paean of unabashed piety: "I'll stand in awe of you / And I'll let my words be few / Jesus, I am so in love with you." It is set to an especially lovely melody and is probably Redman's finest work. It was later recorded as the title track for a 2001 album by **Phillips, Craig, and Dean.** The title track to *Father's Song* is a rare worship tune that could serve as a radio pop song in its own right, an adult contemporary ballad that is performed here as a solo reflecting on the Bible's sole reference to God singing (Zeph. 3:17).

Musically, Redman's projects are largely acoustic, supplemented by occasionally edgy, electric guitars. They rock, wail, and dance from time to time, but always return to the quiet and reflective moments that seem to be their bedrock. As with **Delirious?,** early **U2** provides the basic reference point for Redman's sound, though *Father's Song* would begin to move away from the anthemic approach this comparison suggests. Adoration and commitment to holiness are the principal themes of Redman's songs. "When I get up, it's never to perform," he says. "It's always to worship the Lord and hope that other people will follow. If people end up focusing on me, then I've actually failed in my job."

Matt Redman is married to Beth (Vickers) Redman, who formerly sang for **World Wide Message Tribe.** Both of them have been involved in the public-schools ministry of the evangelistic group **Storm.**

Red Sea

Greg Chaisson, bass; Chris Howell, gtr.; Paul Huesman, drums; Robyn Kyle, voc. 1994—*Blood* (Rugged).

Robyn Kyle formed the hard blues-rock band Red Sea after the demise of **Die Happy,** where he sang as Robyn Basauri. Chris Howell was formerly lead guitarist for **Fear Not,** and Greg Chaisson of Die Happy and Badlands played bass on Red Sea's only album. Kyle described Red Sea's music as " '70s based rock with kind of a '90s edge," likening the groove of many songs to Deep Purple, Led Zeppelin, or Bad Company. *HM* called *Blood* "a searing, serious outbreak of pure rock 'n' roll power." The songs "Wolves at the Door" and "Hellbound Train" display the band's no-holds barred approach, expounding on the wages of sin and the reality of hell that awaits the unrepentant. "Tears of Joy" is a heartfelt gospel number, complete with female background vocals.

Linnae Reeves

1996—*Linnae Reeves* (StarSong).

Seattle native Linnae Reeves took a break from her studies toward being a physician's assistant to record an album of adult contemporary Christian pop music. She wrote or cowrote all ten songs on the project, which was produced by David Kershenbaum, known for his work with Bryan Adams, Tracy Chapman, and Kenny Loggins. Reeves has a soft, childlike voice that has often been compared to that of Lisa Loeb. A constant theme in her songs seems to be encouragement, assuring those who are going through rough times that God is in charge and will make all things right. "Phil. 4:6" calls on listeners to cast their cares on Christ; "Lord My Maker" is a devotional ballad inspired by Revelation 19:7–8.

Reflescent Tide

Jon-Paul LeClair, drums; Brian Oates, bass; Jeff Weiss, gtr., voc.; Todd Lehrman, gtr. (– 1998). 1995—*Reflescent Tide* (Rugged); 1998—*Spring Catalog*.

Reflescent Tide formed in Oshkosh, Wisconsin, where two members (Oates and Weiss) were students at the University of Wisconsin. They explained their unusual name as coming from a mispronunciation of the word *flourescent:* "When we were in grade school, flourescent colors were popular and kids mispronounced the word," says Weiss. "And we came up with *Tide* because we like our music to wash over you." The band adopted a solid grunge sound similar to Soundgarden, Stone Temple Pilots and, in retrospect, to **Creed**—though that group was not yet known when Reflescent Tide debuted. "Wasted Me" is the powerful opening track for their debut album and a song that represents their style well. The album's highlight, however, is the worshipful ballad "Distant," a beautiful song of longing that is at once expressive and inspiring. When *Spring Catalog* appeared, Reflescent Tide had stripped down to a power trio and the band described the new project as "twelve times better than our debut." Weiss told *HM* that he now viewed the first album as "an orchestra tuning their instruments" compared to the full symphony of their self-produced sophomore work. The songs "Callous" and "Harvest" are **King's X**-style rockers, and the opening "Butterfly Wings" has a chunky guitar groove like that of "Wasted Me." These are balanced, again, with a number of more mellow and acoustic turns. "We do really heavy stuff and lighter stuff," Weiss told *HM,* "because in your life you don't always feel real aggressive." Lyrically, Reflescent Tide favors a literate approach to what they hope will be "engaging contemplations and concerns." The song "Avendesora" was inspired by Robert Jordan's Celtic fantasy *Wheel of Time,* and "Unmaking of Me," by C. S. Lewis's myth *Till We Have Faces.* "Butterfly Wings" is an homage to Oswald Chambers (not Smashing Pumpkins), and "Leaving" draws on the teaching of Max Lucado.

The Reign

Harold Bloemendahl, voc.; Doug Dorr, drums; Curtis Holtzen, bass; Greg Kemble, gtr.; Travis Sheets, kybrd. 1989—*Back from Euphoria* (Jondo).

The Reign released one album of alternative indie rock produced by Gene Eugene of **Adam Again.** The record was re-released a year later on Image, bringing the band to the attention of a slightly larger audience. *Back from Euphoria* contains tunes in the southern rock vein of melodic pop acts like The Connells and, at times, the group seems to strive toward the sound of Christian alterna-pop superstars **The Choir.** "Trouble on My Mind" is an acoustic blues number with

Darrell Mansfield sitting in on harmonica. "In Another Room" confronts the issue of suicide while "Looking for You (on Christmas Day)" explores the feeling of heightened loneliness that can attend the holiday season.

Reigning Mercy

Maribeth Garels, voc.; Jalann Marshall, voc.; Shari Rowe, voc. 2001—*Reigning Mercy* (Q Records).

Reigning Mercy is a female vocal harmony group with a sound similar to **The Darins** or **Sierra.** Garels and Rowe are sisters and Marshall is their sister-in-law. The group signed to Q Records as the first Christian act on that subsidiary of the QVC shopping network. *Christian Music* picked "I Hope You Dance" and "Freedom Found in You" as being among the trio's standout cuts.

Kelli Reisen

1993—*Dream of a Lifetime* (Pakaderm); 1995—*Someday*.

Kelli Reisen is an adult contemporary Christian singer from Cincinnati, Ohio. She graduated from Olivet Nazarene University in Illinois and then signed with **John** and Dino **Elefante**'s Pakaderm records. The Elefante brothers, best noted for slick stadium rock, produced both of her albums, which represented something of a new direction for them and their company. Reisen's voice and style has been compared to that of Celine Dion, and *CCM* says that she sings with an urgency "as if each breath is dependent upon her delivery of the next phrase." Reisen draws from a number of composers, including songs by Lanny Wolfe ("My House Is Full") and **Rick Cua** ("I Believe") on her debut album. "The Wind Blows" offers a twist on Jesus' parable of the two builders (Matthew 7:24–27), placing them in the same domicile: "I built on stone, he built on sand . . . We built a house and not a home." The songs on *Someday* tend toward the inspirational side of the adult contemporary spectrum, conveying assurances that God's promises are true ("Someday," "You Always Do") and offering encouragement to the faltering ("When You Haven't Got a Prayer").

For trivia buffs: Reisen sang the theme song for ABC TV's *Afterschool Special* series.

Christian radio hits: "After the Hurricane" (# 7 in 1993).

Relient K

Steve Cushman, drums, voc.; Matt Hoopes, gtr., voc.; Brian Pittman, bass; Matt Thiessen, gtr., voc. 2000—*Relient K* (Gotee); 2001—*The Anatomy of the Tongue and Cheek*.

www.relientk.com

Relient K is a Christian pop-punk band that formed at Malone College in Canton, Ohio. They have a sound very similar to that of Blink 182 or **MxPx** with a penchant for wacky lyrics that recalls Weezer or Barenaked Ladies. At the time their debut album appeared all four members were nineteen. The most noticeable attribute of their self-titled debut project is its use of images from pop culture. The opening track, "Hello, McFly," draws on the popular *Back to the Future* motion picture series to make a semi-serious point about wishing one could go back and erase previous mistakes. "My Girlfriend" is a song about a Christian girl who lost her faith after becoming involved in the goth movement; it compares the anti-Christian music star Marilyn Manson to the devil image of 1 Peter 5:8: "Marilyn Manson ate my girlfriend / She used to believe in truth, now she believes in sin." Likewise, "17 Magazine" takes on the artificial notion of beauty perpetuated by *Seventeen,* and "Balloon Ride" offers a testimony of personal repentance and prayer. On a less serious note, the group covers the theme song for the TV show *Charles in Charge* and offers a love song of adolescent pining for the fictional juvenile sleuth Nancy Drew. Relient K seems to get its quirky tendencies under control on their sophomore outing, without extinguishing them altogether. One of the best tracks on *The Anatomy of the Tongue and Cheek* is "Pressing On," a more-or-less straightforward proclamation of growing faith that nevertheless concludes with lyrics swiped from *The Mary Tyler Moore Show* theme ("We're gonna make it after all"). "Sadie Hawkins Dance" is just about trying to impress girls, but the very melodic "Maybe It's Maybelline" effectively satirizes affinities for finger-pointing. "Breakdown" is about a car that keeps breaking down, and "Lion-O" takes its cue from the animated series *Thundercats.* The group also denounces racism ("Failure to Excommunicate"), judgmental attitudes ("Down in Flames"), backsliding ("What Have You Been Doing Lately?"), and spiritual apathy ("My Way or the Highway"). Perhaps the strongest songs lyrically are those that eschew both wacky and prophetic tendencies in favor of heartfelt worship ("Those Words Are Not Enough," "For the Moment I Feel Faint," "Less Is More"). In 2001, the group was offered a deal with youth-oriented clothing stores Abercrombie and Fitch, insuring a chance to bring Christian music into a very secular environment. They withdrew from the contract, however, after Focus on the Family and other famously narrow-minded groups complained (apparently because they consider some Abercrombie and Fitch ads to be too racy).

Ray Repp

1966—*Mass for Young Americans* (FEL); *Allelu;* 1967—*Come Alive;* 1968—*Sing Praise;* 1969—*The Time Has Not Come True;* 1972—*Hear the Cryin'* (Myrrh); 1975—*Give Us Peace* (Agape); 1978—*Benedicamus* (Joral); 1980—*Sunrise, In the Dead of Winter* (K&R).

Ray Repp is the earliest of all the pioneers of contemporary Christian music. To quote *Jesus Music* magazine, he can be considered as "the guy who started it all." The history of contemporary Christian music usually traces the genre to the Jesus movement revival of the early '70s, which is when it emerged as a recognizable entity outside the church. Half a decade earlier, however, Repp and a handful of others **(Ralph Carmichael, John Fischer,** Kurt Kaiser, and **John Ylvisaker)** were creating youth-oriented music within the church that would pave the way for acceptance of the secular-sounding Jesus music when the revival hit. Of these forerunners, Repp was easily the most significant within America's mainline denominations, especially those churches that had their historical origins in Europe (Roman Catholic, Episcopalian, Lutheran, Presbyterian, and some Methodists). It is unlikely that any single artist has ever had the monopoly of influence that he either enjoyed or endured for the four years spanning 1966–1969. If a survey of Christian youth had been taken at any time during that period, the ten favorite "Christian songs" of American young people probably would have included "Kum Ba Ya" plus "They'll Know We Are Christians by Our Love" (by Peter Scholtes), "He's Everything to Me" (by Carmichael), "Pass It On" (by Kaiser), a rewritten Shaker hymn ("Tis a Gift to Be Simple") called "Lord of the Dance," and about five songs by Ray Repp. Of course, once **Love Song, Larry Norman,** and **Children of the Day** arrived on the scene, it was all over. Repp fell into obscurity and his songs were pretty much forgotten, at least among Protestants. He remains the John the Baptist of the movement and that prophet's sentiments, as expressed in John 3:30, apply as vividly to him as to any other.

Repp's significance for the development of contemporary Christian music is somewhat ironic given the sparse number of Roman Catholic artists who would ultimately end up being included in a book like this one (cf. **Margaret Becker, Angela Crimi, Tom Franzak, Arlo Guthrie, Sarah Hart, Innocence Mission, David Kauffman, Tom Kendzia, Tony Melendez, Collin Raye,** and **John Michael Talbot**). His work really began with the revolutionary encouragement of the Vatican II Council for Roman Catholic churches to develop liturgical materials relevant to their cultural settings. Repp became affiliated early on with the FEL publishing company founded in 1963 by David Fitzpatrick. That company's first release was a 1964 folk recording called *Glory Bound* by a Catholic artist named Paul Quinlan. A year later Repp released his *Mass for Young Americans* while he was still a seminarian. That album provided an alternative setting for a full worship service, set to folk music tunes not too different from the sound of popular artists like Peter, Paul, and Mary or The Kingston Trio. The following year's *Allelu* was a collection of original folk hymns. Together these projects gave the church such songs as "Clap Your

Hands" (based on Psalm 47), "Here We Are," "Allelu," "Hear, O Lord," "Shout from the Highest Mountain," and "Come Away," and they prompted FEL to release its *Hymnal for Young Christians,* the first youth-oriented songbook for mainline churches.

A year later, *Come Alive* would introduce the song that might be Repp's best-known and most enduring classic, "I Am the Resurrection," a tune with a rock edge that continued to be played and sung by numerous Jesus music groups well into the next decade (**Undercover** would do a punk version of it for the '80s). *Sing Praise* includes electric reinterpretations of several of his better-known songs. *The Time Has Not Come True* reveals what *Jesus Music* calls "a softer folk and pop mixture." Notably, these early albums were not marketed to youth themselves, nor did anyone seem to buy them to listen to them at home in lieu of the New Christy Minstrels or some other worldly equivalent. Rather, they were sold to youth pastors and camp counselors who wanted to learn the songs to play with their church youth groups. The focus was entirely on group singing, not performance or entertainment. Since the albums were basically just teaching tools, there was no substantial commitment to production standards. *Mass for Young Americans* and *Allelu* sound like someone taped a youth service led by a few guys with guitars. By later standards, Repp's music would also seem ridiculously tame, but the radical nature of his approach may perhaps be grasped by realizing that the name of his just-formed recording company (FEL) was in fact an acronym for Friends of the English Liturgy. Seminary student Repp was transforming his church's liturgy at a time when the very idea of singing in English (as opposed to Latin) was controversial—much less singing folk-rock to the accompaniment of guitars! **John Fischer** (a Baptist) released his first two albums on the FEL label also.

As the Jesus movement revival swept America, contemporary Christian music became the norm for many informal worship fellowships, and Repp's "church songs" no longer sounded very worldly. The focus shifted to music played outside of sanctuaries for purposes of evangelism, edification, or entertainment. Then Maranatha released its 1974 *The Praise Album,* which initiated a contemporary worship movement among Protestants that would have an ironically sectarian non-denominational feel to it. The liturgical sensibilities of Repp's music were lost on most purveyors of this music, which almost by definition aimed for a generic lowest-common-denominator spirituality that was not dependent upon (or sensitive to) the historical legacies of any particular tradition. Repp's day was over, though he did continue to record. *Hear the Cryin'* actually came out on Myrrh, the premier Jesus music label, but failed to attract much attention. *CCM* speculated that it was ignored in part because of references expressing opposition to the Vietnam War. *Benedicamus* is a collection of liturgical pieces for gui-

tar and piano. *Sunrise, In the Dead of Winter* continues to move in a liturgical direction, with some songs derived from the tradition of Gregorian chants. It also features Repp's version of "Lord of the Dance."

Resurrection Band (a.k.a. **Rez** and **Rez Band**)

Glenn Kaiser, voc., gtr.; Wendi Kaiser, voc.; John Herrin, drums; Stu Heiss, gtr., kybrd.; Tom Cameron, harmonica (−1980); Jim Denton, bass (−1988) // Roger Heiss, perc. (+ 1979, −1980); Steve Eisen, sax. (+ 1982, −1984); Roy Montroy, bass (+ 1988). By Resurrection Band: 1974—*Music to Raise the Dead* (custom); *All Your Life;* 1978—*Awaiting Your Reply* (StarSong); 1979—*Rainbow's End;* 1980—*Colours* (Light); 1981—*Mommy Don't Love Daddy Anymore;* 1982—*D.M.Z.;* 1984—*Best of Rez* [as Rez]; *Live Bootleg* (Sparrow) [as Rez Band]; *Hostage* [as Rez Band]; 1985—*Between Heaven and Hell* [as Rez]; 1988—*Compact Favorites* [as Rez]; *Silence Screams* [as Rez] (Grrr); 1989—*Innocent Blood* [as Rez]; 1991—*Civil Rites* [as Rez]; 1992—*20 Years* [as Rez]; 1993—*Reach of Love* [as Rez]; 1995—*Lament; The Light Years* (Light); 1997—*Ampendectomy* (Grrr).

www.resurrectionband.com

Resurrection Band is one of Christian music's two dinosaur rock bands, groups that cheated extinction to survive against all odds from the primordial days when Christian rock first oozed out of the Jesus movement. No museum exhibit or lumbering brontosaur, they have remained a living, breathing testimony to the authenticity of their name, continuing to stomp, roar, and tear up scenery like some *Jurassic Park* T-Rex long after their kind was supposed to have vanished from the earth. The other dinosaur band, of course, is **Petra,** who started recording at the same time (1974), but whereas that band would finish the '90s with no original members, Resurrection Band had basically just traded in a bass player—and even the new guy (Roy Montroy) had actually been with them, uncredited, from the start. **Petra** has consistently out-sold Resurrection Band, but in terms of quality the latter group is many times better. **Petra** may have done some memorable power-pop songs, but Resurrection Band is a world-class, innovative rock band that has had a transforming effect on their genre. It is hard to imagine what Christian rock music would sound like without them. Furthermore, Resurrection Band has not wasted their talents on cheerleader songs about victory over the devil but has consistently dealt with gritty real-life issues in artistic and theologically responsible ways. Their twenty-five-year career has rarely seen a slump or a misstep; virtually every album was a masterful work of its time and the great majority of them would still sound good at the turn of the millennium. Resurrection Band offers the very definition of Christian music's "classic rock." As of 2001, the band's status was on hold in a manner analogous to that quintessential general market dinosaur The Rolling Stones, but (as in that instance) no one was counting them out.

The origins of the band are closely connected with those of the Jesus People U.S.A. community. That group began with a team of about seven persons led by Jim and Sue Palosaari, who set up the Milwaukee Discipleship Training Center community in Wisconsin. They grew to about 150 and bought a hospital building before amicably splitting into smaller groups in order to evangelize more effectively. Music was often a part of such witnessing. The Palosaaris formed the group **The Sheep,** which went to Europe for a while, then landed in the Pacific Northwest (two different bands named **Servant** are loosely related to this group in a somewhat complicated way). Another of the Milwaukee spin-off communities was headed by John Herrin Sr. and featured a folk band called Charity composed of his son John Herrin Jr., his daughter Wendi, her husband Glenn Kaiser, and a few other hippie Jesus freaks. In 1972, Charity would morph into Resurrection Band, adopting a decidedly tougher sound ("hard music for hard hearts," Kaiser would say); John Herrin Jr. reportedly had to learn to play the drums after the band was already formed. At any rate, Charity/Resurrection Band initially just functioned as an attention-getting device for attracting a crowd. The community (sixteen at the time they left Milwaukee) drove about the country in a painted school bus staging ad hoc revivals in small towns. Jon Trott, who would become a noted evangelical theologian, was a part of the group and, while only peripherally involved with the music ministry, remained a major advocate for Resurrection Band's approach. "We were sort of the ragtags, the mutts of the Milwaukee community," Trott would reminisce years later. The nomadic evangelists traveled to Florida in 1972, then settled in Chicago for reasons that are not completely clear ("It's where the bus broke down," says Trott; "we came for a one-week revival," claims Kaiser, "but at the end of the week, the revival continued, so we decided to stay as long at it lasted and . . . well, we're still here"). The group adopted the name Jesus People U.S.A. At some point, John Herrin Sr. left and much of the leadership fell to his wife Dawn Herrin (called "the heart and head of JPUSA" by *CCM*). John Jr. and Glenn Kaiser became elders at an ironically young age. Jim Denton, Resurrection Band's bassist, sought theological training at nearby North Park Theological Seminary, which led, eventually, to the entire community becoming affiliated with that school's sponsoring denomination, the Evangelical Covenant Church. Glenn Kaiser and others would become ordained ministers within that denomination. Church leaders like North Park professor Klyne Snodgrass—one of the most highly respected biblical scholars in America—would sometimes serve as advisers to the community and to the band.

The JPUSA community (pronounced *juh-poo-zuh* by members) is well known and highly regarded for its work among the poor and for its effective approach to Christian discipleship (which includes voluntary acceptance of accountability to a community of believers). Members of the community live in several inner city buildings (including an old hotel on North Malden Avenue noted for its Friendly Towers sign) and many hold jobs at community-owned businesses (JP Roofing, JP Carpentry, JP Moving, JP Graphics, and so on); membership numbers vary, but in 1986, there were 350 adults and 125 children. All earnings go into a common purse with personal needs of members being provided in a manner inspired by Acts 2:44–45 and 4:32–37. The common purse also buys daily meals for hundreds of homeless and street people, necessitating a meager lifestyle for all involved. "We live very close to the poverty level," Kaiser explains. "We maintain a standard of living and life-style that will continue to validate the gospel we are preaching to the poor." Such an approach, he maintains, is necessary to overcome the "hypocrisies" that give people reason to reject the church and its message as irrelevant: "Two kinds of people drive Cadillacs in the ghetto," Kaiser told *CCM* in 1983, "pimps and preachers." All profits from Resurrection Band's albums and concerts go into the common purse to sustain the JPUSA community and to help feed the urban poor. JPUSA also publishes *Cornerstone* magazine and sponsors the annual *Cornerstone* Christian music festival in Bushnell, Illinois. The community has sometimes presented a formidable political presence within its district, being credited with insuring the election of certain aldermen who would support its demand for increased low-income housing and other issues of social justice. Trott, who has been heavily involved in mayoral elections and other political campaigns, once reported that the community "goes to the polls as a block" and that its visible endorsement of candidates carries recognizable weight within the neighborhood.

JPUSA was attacked in a controversial book by anticult sociologist Ronald Enroth (*Recovering from Churches That Abuse,* Zondervan, 1994). Enroth maintains that, in spite of the group's commendable ministry within the inner city, the community is cult-like in its internal operations. He interviewed some forty former members of the community, including former Resurrection Band bassist Jim Denton, who had gone on to serve as a Covenant pastor in Virginia. Enroth maintains on the basis of their testimonies that JPUSA is authoritarian and ostracizes departing members. These allegations and Enroth's methods of research have been sharply challenged (with regard to JPUSA as well as with regard to other religious groups that he dismisses as "cults") but, in any case, even Enroth singled out the music ministry of Resurrection Band as an instance in which "the community has a positive impact on the Christian world."

The JPUSA community has always encouraged involvement in the arts and has produced or strongly influenced many contemporary Christian groups, including **Ballydowse, Barnabas, The Blamed, Cauzin' Efekt, Crashdog, The Crossing, Danielson, Seeds, Headnoise, Sheesh,** and **Unwed Sailor.** But it was the original house band that would provide its most enduring contributions in this area. After two custom albums, Resurrection Band traveled to Pasadena, Texas, and, at about the same time John Travolta and Debra Winger were filming a movie *(Urban Cowboy)* lampooning the supposedly backwards country culture of that sizable town, they recorded two blistering hard rock albums that surpassed anything the Christian music culture had yet produced. The one-two punch of *Awaiting Your Reply* and *Rainbow's End* on Pasadena's StarSong left Christian music fans dazed and confused. As *True Tunes'* John Thompson would report, these were world-class rock efforts, easily on a par with albums of the same era by Aerosmith or Blue Oyster Cult. In them, Christian music had its own wholly original and fully competent hard blues-rock band. The Christian kids who discovered them could play them for friends without embarrassment; this was no watered-down imitation of the real thing; this *was* the real thing and, Christian or not, no serious rock fan could doubt it.

Still, the music was much harder than what constituted the great majority of Christian music at the time (but see **Agape, Barnabas, Jerusalem, Wilson-McKinley**). Resurrection Band was perhaps the quintessential example of a Christian rock band that was "too Christian" to get played on rock radio and "too rock" to get played on Christian radio. Without airplay, their albums languished. Furthermore, as Christian music's premier hard rock group, they became a special target of the narrow-minded. Early on, Jacob Preus (the president of the Lutheran Church—Missouri Synod who split his denomination and all but destroyed its flagship seminary with McCarthy-like witch-hunts against those he regarded as "heretics") had attacked Kaiser and crew for their sound, driving the young Christian out of the Lutheran Church. In the early '80s, Bob Larson (who later repented), Jimmy Swaggart, and David Wilkerson (who changed his mind, then changed it back again) castigated the group publicly for using "the devil's music," sometimes publicly burning Resurrection Band albums in demonstration against this creeping scourge that they assumed must offend the Lord's tastes as much as it did their own. John Thompson reports in his book, *Raised by Wolves,* "at one seminar, a clip from a concept video that the band had made was presented as the band advocating a raucous lifestyle full of violence and money. The teacher didn't relate that the clip was taken out of context, or reveal that the band was part of a (pac-

ifist, ascetic) Christian community, that the band members didn't even own cars or houses of their own." Still, the seminar reached about 20,000 people in one day, more than Rez Band could play for in a year.

Resurrection Band's first two albums, *Music to Raise the Dead* and *All Your Life,* were cassette-only releases of homemade recordings that are of historical interest only. The first reveals the blues roots of hot guitarist Kaiser, while the second moves in more of an acoustic-folk direction atypical for what would become the band's trademark sound. *Music to Raise the Dead* includes original songs "Down Baby" and "Growin' Stronger." Liner notes indicate that it was recorded on a four-track machine in Gary Rotta's basement and "mixed entirely with headphones 'cuz Mrs. Rotta was trying to sleep." *Awaiting Your Reply* introduces the band to the world with characteristic humor. The album opens with the voice of a radio DJ announcing that the song "Sugar Sugar" by The Archies has just ended and "next up, we have Resurrection Band. . . ." Guitars riff, Wendi screams, and some very un-bubblegum-like sounds come hurling out of the speakers. The song is "Waves," one of the group's best and a tune that in reality would never be played on any radio station back-to-back with "Sugar Sugar." Intense rock and roll, it rips through all namby-pamby perceptions of Christian rock that auditors might have harbored, leaving memories of Maranatha Music far behind. It is the Christian music equivalent of John Belushi smashing Stephen Bishop's guitar in *Animal House;* **Love Song** almost sounds like The Archies compared to this. Glenn growls, Wendi wails, and there is nary a sweet harmony in sight. Even the lyrics to "Waves" signal a change from the "I'm So Happy in Jesus" songs of Southern California: "We see wave after wave of people in the street / Playing their songs, but missing the beat." This is city music: concrete, dirty, noisy, and real. The next track, "Awaiting Your Reply," is also a masterpiece, featuring Wendi in Grace Slick mode, a style that would sometimes get the band compared to a cross between Led Zeppelin and Jefferson Airplane. "Broken Promises" is a strong blues track; "Lightshine" kicks out the jams with an extended electric guitar intro; and "Irish Garden" is a suite that lulls the listener into a false sense of security with over a minute of acoustic flute and dulcimer before turning into another full-bore rocker and then coming home again. "The Return" offers a perfect coda with soulful saxophone as Glenn sings in his most plaintive voice, "I know it won't be lo-o-ong / Until the Savior co-o-omes." In 2001, a poll of critics sponsored by *CCM* magazine chose *Awaiting Your Reply* as one of the only hard rock recordings to be included on their list of "The 100 Greatest Albums in Christian Music."

Rainbow's End lacked the element of surprise but in the minds of many would surpass *Awaiting Your Reply* in its intensity of sound and thought. The most remarkable track is "Afrikaans," a protest against apartheid in South Africa that marks Resurrection Band as one of the first rock groups ever to address that issue. The classic line, "God makes the color, but the color doesn't make you God" would still be printed on T-shirts years later (cf. **Mission of Mercy**). "The Wolfsong" is especially Zeppelinesque. Wendi shines on "Sacrifice of Love" and the title track, which presents Christ as the goal of every dreamer's idyllic quest. "Paint a Picture" is an unusually melodic song with a strong vocal, offering conflicting images of bondage and release. "Concert for a Queen" is a pretty acoustic number with a slightly medieval sound similar to "Irish Garden" or **ArkAngel.** "Every Time It Rains" is a powerful blues ballad foreshadowing Kaiser's later solo work.

The Light years (summarized in a compilation album by that name) showcase Resurrection Band during their most memorable period; though the sound remains consistent with the first two StarSong releases, many of the songs became better known, partly as a result of the compilation. *Colours* begins with the powerful "Autograph," which opens with a full two minutes of exciting guitar riffs before Wendi weighs in with her Grace Slick vocals. The album's title track is an offering of cosmic worship that concludes with the poetic refrain, "Whatever one could ask of faith, obedience will give / Together all express the love in hearts where Jesus lives." "N.Y.C." describes the harsh urban life in the mean streets of Chicago's big sister city, but "Amazing" expresses wonder at the hope and help God offers those who are metaphorically or literally homeless. "City Streets" and "Beggar in the Alleyway" continue the social consciousness, an attribute of Resurrection Band's albums almost totally absent from other mainstays of Christian music at the time. "American Dream" predicts an apocalyptic nuclear holocaust: "It will happen / Just don't think about it!" The group's most poignant song, however, would be the more personal title track to their next album, *Mommy Don't Love Daddy Anymore.* It offers social commentary (on the American culture of divorce), but it does so on an immediate level, by describing one child's description of his family's dysfunction: "Mommy says, She don't love Daddy anymore / Daddy says, Mommy's walkin' out the door / Sister says, she's getting married to escape / Brother says, he thinks enlisting sounds just great / And me—I don't know who to believe . . . how to maintain the world that used to be / Cause everyone is leaving me." Powerful enough as it is, the song becomes more chilling to anyone who learns **Glenn Kaiser**'s life story (see entry) and realizes how autobiographical this detailed scenario is for him. *Mommy Don't Love Daddy Anymore* is largely an album about relationships, with "Little Children" addressing child abuse and "The Crossing" describing the self-denial necessary to achieve emotional peace of mind. "The

Chair" offers a troubling statement of how a person with physical disabilities responds to being a target for social pity. Critic Mark Hollingsworth would say, "I can't recall ever hearing lyrics like these from a socially relevant folkie, let alone a group of lava-riding rockers." Two songs on *Mommy Don't Love Daddy Anymore* ("Can't Get You Out of My Mind," "Lovin' You") are hook-filled love songs that seem radio-friendly and require a close listen to pick up on any specific religious or spiritual implications. *D.M.Z.* offers some of Resurrection Band's most powerful musical testaments: "Military Man" is a blistering opening track sung by Glenn about the loss of a soldier's humanity in the struggle to survive. "White Noise" features Wendi's all-time best raw vocal on a song about the rhetoric of a culture that prioritizes stockpiling arms over feeding children. It begins with a ninety-second feedback-drenched guitar solo by Stu Heiss that is Resurrection Band's answer to Van Halen's "Eruption" and is generally considered to constitute the single greatest non-**Phil Keaggy** guitar moment in Christian rock. "Area 312" (named for Chicago's area code) is a teenager's lament about the loneliness of the inner city. "No Alibi" is a confessional anthem in the sonic mode of **U2.**

The band's short stint on Sparrow represents what some purist fans consider their nadir. They shortened their name to Rez Band (and, then, simply to Rez) and exhibited other signs of a midcareer identity crisis. The half-mistitled *Live Bootleg* album was recorded over two nights at The Odeum in Chicago (where **Steve Taylor** was the opening act). The concerts were specifically set up for a professional recording and there is nothing "bootleg" about the project. Its sound steps away from the band's hard rock roots with synthesizers and drum machines being introduced to give the band a solid '80s sound, especially on the new tracks "Gameroom" and "Playground." *Hostage* continues in that tradition with a new set of studio recordings. The lead-off track is a techno-pop tune called "S.O.S." that would nab the band its first official Christian radio hit. Still, a year later, the group told *CCM,* "we were enticed into the realm of keyboards and drum machines, which seemed like nice little toys to play with, but I don't think we felt that comfortable with them." Rez' last album for Sparrow, *Between Heaven and Hell,* marks a return to more of the metal sound, with a twist. The album was supposed to be a vehicle for crossing over to the general market. The group quit doing altar calls in their concerts, scaled back explicit talk about "the Lord," and created an album of issue-oriented songs (not too different from what they had been doing anyway) in a drive to break into the secular AOR format. A video for their song "Love Comes Down" went into mild rotation on MTV (as had "Crimes" from *Hostage*) but the group was never widely noticed outside the little Christian pond. *Between Heaven and Hell* rocks hard and honest all the same. It kicks off with a stadium rock number called "The Main Event" and features at least one more suitable-for-arenas number: "Shadows" starts off like a requisite power ballad and turns into a Bon Jovi shouter that is one of the group's best songs. "Zuid Afrikan" takes another look at apartheid (six years after *Rainbow's End*) and "Walk On" updates the story of the Good Samaritan.

After a hiatus, Rez did a 180-degree turn and came home to their much beloved blues-rock sound, with albums aimed at the Christian market (the altar calls and concert preaching returned also, to the distress of Christian fans from churches with less revivalistic understandings of salvation). Indeed, *Silence Screams* debuted on the band's own label, the Kaiser-founded Grrr Records. At least some pundits think the name was intended to rhyme with Myrrh Records, the very tame Christian label best known for producing **Amy Grant**'s pop albums. Grrr would be anything but tame (cf. **Crashdog**), and *Silence Screams* comes across appropriately loud and dangerous. The two highlights may be the group's cover of **Eric Clapton**'s "Presence of the Lord" and a blues-based song called "Rain Dance" written by new bassist Roy Montroy and theologian Jon Trott. "You Got Me Rockin' " is a good-time "party for Jesus" song. "You Get What You Choose" addresses the current spate of televangelist scandals, and "Someone Sleeps" is about the awful toll of war and terrorism.

As the '80s turned into the '90s, Rez just kept on, churning out three more stellar albums in the same vein. *Innocent Blood* offers another Zeppelin-like tune with "80,000 Underground," about a cemetery discovered under a Chicago subdivision and the implicit lack of respect for the dead this revealed. "Right on Time" resummons the familiar Jefferson Airplane (or by now, Starship) analogies. The album also features another competent cover (The Who's "Bargain," which works surprisingly well as a hymn to God). "Child of the Blues" and "Rooster Crow" draw on earthy Delta blues traditions, and "Great God in Heaven" is a stripped-down worship classic. The band would impress fans and critics even more with *Civil Rites,* one of Christian rock's finest collections of original songs. The opening "Lovespeak" and the very solid "Mission Bells" are intense rock equal to anything Guns N' Roses or, again, Aerosmith was putting out at the time. And after twenty years of being compared to Grace Slick, Wendi Kaiser decided to just go for it and deliver a scorching rendition of "Somebody to Love," introducing a new generation (most of whom were born after 1967) to one of rock's great songs. *Civil Rites'* finest moments, however, come with "Footprints" and "In My Room," bluesy numbers in which, as Brian Quincy Newcomb said, "Kaiser's distinctive, wailing voice has room to breathe in the mix, and Stu Heiss's guitars wrap around the searing heart-rending melodies." Notably, Montroy wrote all of the music for the new songs on *Civil Rites* and he would do the same for

Reach of Love. That album's opening track, "Heart's Desire," is a blazing, shout-it-from-the-rooftops announcement of devotion and thanksgiving ("You are my heart's desire / You set my soul on fire / You're all I need"). Other songs continue to reflect upon the band's two-decade tenure in the inner city: "Numbers" is about a disillusioned vet; "Empty Hearts" tells of a tragic death that occurred just outside the community's apartment building; "Dead to the World" celebrates the transformation of a junkie prostitute who found redemption. "Chaos reigns without a tear," Kaiser sings in one of the album's most poignant songs, "Upon unburied treasure here / They find no profit, just neglect / In the land of stolen breath" ("Land of Stolen Breath"). *Twenty* is a two-disc live collection, featuring one song from each previous album, plus a glorious rendition of the gospel hymn "My Jesus Is All" sung with Willie Kemp of **Cauzin' Efekt** and the JPUSA gospel choir, Grace and Glory.

In the late '90s, Resurrection Band reclaimed their old name and experienced a career renaissance. They only made two albums, both drastically different from anything they had done before and both undeniable works of art. For over two decades, the group had regularly been compared with the Rolling Stones, Led Zeppelin, and Aerosmith, but despite the "Bargain" cover, no one had noticed how much they had in common with The Who. This changed overnight with *Lament,* a concept album that was almost a mini-rock opera. Several of the songs ("Across These Fields," "Song and Dance") sound like they could actually have been on *Tommy* or *Quadrophenia,* though Kaiser's voice and the band's stylings provide them with a distinctive Rezzy character. The album was produced by **Ty Tabor** and relates a young prodigal's journey through life. It opens with the words, "I don't believe / Not in you / Nor in us / Nor in this place"—an odd way to start "a Christian album." Of course, the boy will find his way to God by the album's end, but Kaiser avoids the clichés. There are no songs here of descent into wretched excess and debauchery only to find the Lord at the end of one's rope. Instead, the unbeliever sings a beautiful song about his elation at facing the life that lies before him with all its possibilities and pleasure ("Across These Fields"). Still, there is loneliness ("Summerthrow") and realization that "the fullness of life" is itself pretty empty ("Song and Dance"). Midway through the project, he speculates as to whether he doesn't need something, but concludes, "In change could be the admission of regret / And I don't know if I'm ready for that yet." Disillusionment leads to cynicism and to an apparent acceptance that life is just a "Dark Carnival," with rides that initially thrill but grow old. When grace enters the picture it comes unexpectedly ("Surprised"). A reprise of "Across These Fields" recasts the initial excitement over life in this world as the perspective of one born again, looking to life here and beyond as an adventure in eternity. Musically, *Lament* is innovative, exploring a variety of styles, including progressive art-rock, acoustic folk music, and blues. Much of the music is heavy, but very little ("Mirror" perhaps) sounds like the trademark hard rock for which the band is best known. One song, "Richest One," is practically a Kaiser solo, featuring the main man strumming and singing a Harry Chapin-type folk song that doesn't quite fit in with the album as a whole but serves as a nice distraction or bonus track.

Ampendectomy was more predictable, given the onslaught of "unplugged" projects from numerous general market bands. Kaiser and crew went into the studio and recut acoustic versions of many classic songs. "Irish Garden" and "Across These Fields" seem like they were intended for such treatment all along; "Lovespeak" comes off more bluesy than ever; some original rockers ("Colours") and techno experiments ("2000") are thoroughly refurbished.

With the exception of *Lament,* all of Resurrection Band's albums have been self-produced, often in collaboration with the harmonica-playing Tom Cameron, who was listed as a group member on one record *(Colours).* Many were recorded in their own studio, Tone Zone, built in the JPUSA Chicago neighborhood. The early records especially are noted for featuring album covers with some of the best graphic design of the rock era. At the twenty-year point in Resurrection Band's career, Glenn Kaiser told *HM* magazine, "As far as what we've tried to accomplish, it's been real simple: win people to Jesus, disciple people who are already Christians, and really challenge people to care about those who are disabled, who are oppressed, who are poor." From an artistic standpoint, however, he would admit, "I don't think it's accurate to say that the band is simply an excuse to minister. We really do take the music seriously in its own right. We're a rock and roll band, and we like playing rock and roll music. I can't say in all honesty that it's *just* a way of sharing the gospel—but we do that too and without apology." It is also worth noting that Glenn and Wendi Kaiser's marriage is often cited as that rare example of a celebrity union that seems to have worked. Celebrating their thirtieth anniversary in 2002, the couple appears to have overcome whatever peculiar stresses apply when two rock stars wed, in addition to the inherited baggage of their backgrounds—what Wendi calls, "really broken relational situations with a lot of destructive lifestyle problems and dysfunctional family systems." Glenn says, "Wendi is my best friend, and she's the most beautiful person I have ever known."

Christian radio hits: "S.O.S." (# 14 in 1985); "Rain Dance" (# 14 in 1989).

Ernie Rettino

See **Debby Kerner.**

John Reuben

2000—*Are We There Yet?* (Gotee).

www.johnreuben.com

A Christian version of Eminem? John Reuben (b. John Zappin) is a white Christian hip-hop artist from Columbus, Ohio, whose outward style resembles that of the ultra-controversial, mother-hating, gay-bashing general market superstar but whose lyrics celebrate various aspects of life in Christ. Reuben has the upbeat rap sound down pat, varying his approach between rapid speech and a relaxed conversational style, with some outright singing. *Christian Music* says, "Reuben's vocals don't come across as the typical lazy rapper sound; he actually puts some personality into it." Supplemental female vocals are even introduced, Dido-style, on "Do Not." No mere copycat, Reuben comes by his sound honestly. He began performing at the age of fifteen, the same time that his parents divorced and he dropped out of school to help his mother pay bills. After earning a G.E.D. and working the fast-food scene, he made his way to Los Angeles, where he made a splash mixing sounds at local record stores and clubs. His debut album is unusually likable, featuring at least three dance party tracks ("Gather In," "Him Her He She," and "Hello Ego"). The lead track, "Divine Inspiration," features a whole crew rapping, singing, and whistling their way through an invitation to "let Christ increase" as they decrease. **Toby McKeehan** joins Reuben on "God Is Love," the album's most melodic track. "Do Not" offers a typical glimpse at the sort of confident-but-spiritual lyrical direction of the project: "All you ever been told is that you walk this way / You talk this way / You front this way / You pose this way / You act this way / Nah, nah, that ain't me / I got to be who God created me to be."

Christian radio hits: "God Is Love" (# 13 in 2000).

The Revolutionary Army of the Infant Jesus

Personnel list unavailable. 1987—*The Gift of Tears* (Probe Plus); 1991—*Mirror;* 1996—*Paradis* [EP] (Apocalyptic Vision).

The Revolutionary Army of the Infant Jesus is regularly described by critics who notice them as "one of the most original bands in the world." Virtually no information about the group itself is available, though it seems from the sound of the albums to be quite an ensemble. Musically, the Revolutionary Army goes for eclecticism with an emphasis on multicultural affections—but they are probably more closely related to industrial music than to world beat. The albums have all been issued in Germany, primarily on a label that specializes in goth music (Apocalyptic Vision, which reissued *The Gift of Tears* and *Mirror* along with an EP called *La Liturgie pour la Fin du Temps* on a two-disc set in 1994). But the group itself is based in England (Liverpool, no less—though their sound bears very little resemblance to that town's most famous musical sons). On any one of their albums the listener can hear Celtic folk singing, Gregorian chants, madrigals, tribal percussion, insanely distorted heavy metal guitars, beautiful childlike vocals, singing in three different languages, and samples from foreign films and radio broadcasts. The music, furthermore, has a strong religious orientation. *The Gift of Tears* opens with a piece called "Come, Holy Spirit," that is at least in part an offering of praise and worship. But later, "De Profundis" seems like an exercise in experimental noise, carried along by what appears to be random banging and clanging of, possibly, pots and pans. "Lament (Ashes in the Water)" is a dark ambient piece. *Mirror* mixes techno dance tracks ("Hymn to Dionysus," "Le Monde du Silence") with a male/female duet singing "Joy of the Cross." *Paradis* includes a Bolero-like piece called "She Moves through the Fair," which recounts a ghost story of betrothed lovers not quite separated by death set to a chilling martial tune.

Rev. Run

See **Run-D.M.C.**

Darren Rhodes

1988—*Darren* (Frontline).

Blue-eyed soul singer Darren Rhodes made one album of Christian music for Frontline Records. The album *Darren* was produced by Scott V. Smith who, *CCM* says, "couples Rhodes' crystal clear tenor with infectious R&B music that goes for the jugular and doesn't let go." Rhodes' voice is similar to that of crooner Tommy Funderburk and, not surprisingly, he is most impressive on emotional ballads.

Rhubarb

Steve Drinkall, voc.; et al. 2000—*Kamikaze* (InPop).

Although very little information was available about Australian band Rhubarb by the end of 2001, the group had apparently been together for five years in their native land where they enjoyed quite a following. They signed to InPop Records, the label headed by Peter Furler of **The Newsboys** (cf. **Phil Joel, Tree 63**) and their debut album was produced by Caleb James of **Battered Fish**. It won the hearts of critics: *The Phantom Tollbooth* gushed, "Seldom does a debut album impress so much." *CCM* said, "If there's any justice in the world, Rhubarb will be a big force in 2001" (they weren't). The group's sound is an eclectic mix of melodic Beatlesque pop (reminiscent of **The Newsboys** actually) with an edgier, punk-influenced sound. Songs range from the instantly catchy and radio-friendly "En-

ergizer" to more moody and melancholy tunes. Spiritual themes are subdued, appearing only vaguely and sporadically on cuts like "Lead Me" and "Waiting for Me." Otherwise, "Nice Girls" is a two-minute pop-punk salute to the opposite sex and "Zero" (not the Smashing Pumpkins song) offers some obscure you-figure-them-out lyrics: "Nothing changes after zero / Everyday is my tomorrow."

Rhythm House

Keith Emerson, bass; Charlie Hueni, kybrd.; Dave Innes, kybrd.; Jeff Pummill, voc.; Marvin Sims, drums; Kevin Sowers, gtr. 1991—*Rhythm House* (Myrrh).

Rhythm House was not a dance band as their name seemed to suggest but a multiracial combo that seasoned commercial pop with accents from a funk rhythm section and rock guitar. Formed in 1988 in northern Indiana, the group won a recording contract at a "battle of the bands" competition a year later at Greenville College in Illinois. Critical comparisons ranged from references to Richard Marx (on their ballad "The Promise") to Jimmie Lee-era **Imperials,** though groups like **White Heart** and **Petra** would seem to offer more promising analogies, allowing for a touch of jazz fusion to round things out. "Keep On Runnin' " is a power-pop tune superior to the songs that received airplay.

Christian radio hits: "I Believe" (# 1 for 2 weeks in 1992); "Make It Right" (# 14 in 1992); "One by One" (# 16 in 1992).

Rhythm Saints

Lee-Jane Nixon; Stephen Nixon; et al. 1994—*deep sustained booming sounds* (N'Soul); 1995—*Golden*; 1996—*Continuum: The Remix Project.*

Rhythm Saints is a British dance band headed by wife and husband duo Lee-Jane and Stephen Nixon, who often speak openly about their Christian faith. The group makes popular house and club music that draws on both the Europop and New York styles of electronic dance-oriented sounds. Lyrically, their songs deal primarily with interpersonal relationships and only rarely touch on overtly spiritual themes. Stephen maintains that people in secular culture are turned off by Christian musicians who think they have to push their faith on everybody all the time. Suzanne Vega, he points out, is a Buddhist and all of her fans know this but they respect her (and Buddhism) the more because she isn't always trying to convert everybody. "Many Christians don't have the confidence in God to just chill," he told *7ball*. Lee-Jane adds, "We don't evangelize because we ain't very good at it. Our music is about life."

Chris Rice

1997—*Deep Enough to Dream* (Rocketown); 1998—*Past the Edges;* 2000—*Smell the Color 9; The Living Room Sessions.*

www.chrisrice.com

Chris Rice took the Christian music scene by surprise in 1997, releasing a debut album that got him nominated for six Dove awards including Best New Artist and Best Male Vocalist. Though he didn't take home any of those birds, all the market analysts were left pondering just what the attraction of the unassuming new troubadour might be. Rice is an acoustic singer/songwriter with an Art Garfunkel voice and a James Taylor style that Melissa Riddle of *CCM* describes as "soothing, yet never tiring, a welcome friend for days both sunny and overcast." But singer/songwriters are in no short supply in Christian music and Rice has drawn a following that seems out of proportion to that accorded many practitioners of the overworked genre. His recordings are also sometimes compared to the sound of **David Wilcox.**

Rice grew up in Clinton, Maryland, just outside the nation's capital. He is the son of Christian bookstore owners and says he has been surrounded by contemporary Christian music all his life. He did not begin recording until the age of thirty-four, however, having worked as a camp counselor for twelve years before signing to **Michael W. Smith**'s Rocketown record company. He had gained some notice already as a songwriter, with "Go Light Your World" being nominated for a Dove award after it was recorded by **Kathy Troccoli.** Even after he became "the next big thing," however, he continued his camp work, eschewing the regular concert circuit to continue performing for youth retreats. Indeed, Rice indicated that he had been reluctant to enter the music business professionally for fear it would interfere with what he took to be his calling and first priority. "I have no question that I am alive to be involved personally in the lives of students," he said. Though most of his music has a seriousness to it, Rice's concert and ministry personna retains the typical camp counselor looniness. The week after the 1997 Dove awards, he led a crowd in an "0-for-6" chant to commemorate his nonvictories and displayed a coveted Parrot Award that he had been given by friends instead. All kidding aside, he really would win the Dove for Male Vocalist a year later, beating out big boys like Smith and **Steven Curtis Chapman.**

Deep Enough to Dream draws on Rice's years of working with youth to present some of the most eloquent and effective songs he had written over that time. *CCM* called it "one of the best acoustic folk/pop debuts of 1997." "Welcome to Our World" offers an anthem to the Christ child sung against a simple piano. Most of the tracks, however, feature Rice's well-played acoustic guitar buoying up his lively, crystal-clear voice. Highlights include "Prone to Wander" (describing the "spirit is willing, flesh is weak" character of the human condition), the worshipful "Hallelujahs," and the radio-friendly "Clumsy." "Sometimes Love" takes Christ as the model for sacrificial love ("Sometimes love drives a nail in its own hand"). *Past the Edges*

opens with "Smelling the Coffee," an upbeat song with some horns and crunchy guitars, but then moves quickly back into the folk tradition with a series of songs based on questions that students ask about God and "the meaning of it all." The strength of the material lies in Rice's ability to frame the questions without neatly answering them, to give voice to the fears, doubts, and desires of youth in ways that are themselves poignant and telling. The hope for resolution is aroused while the prospect of finding any denouement apart from transcendence is negated. The theme of the project is well stated in "Big Enough," a song on which he sounds very much like James Taylor singing some lyrics a tad more philosophical than the real Sweet Baby James ever attempted: "When I imagine the size of the universe / And I wonder what's out past the edges / Then I discover inside me a space as big / And believe that I'm meant to be filled up / With more than just questions." The song "Live By Faith" offers the only solution for honest doubters. "And Your Praise Goes On" offers worship inspired by the wonders of life and nature. Rice goes camp counselor on a hidden track at the end of the album that wonders what would happen "if cartoons got saved" and replicates the various ways that the Flintstones, the Smurfs, Scooby Doo, Bullwinkle, and many others would sing the word "Hallelujah." That sort of nuttiness is in more evidence on *Smell the Number 9,* which features a handful of experimental songs departing from the usual folk style. The title track is a bit of a cliché reminiscent of the old line that "talking about love is like dancing about architecture"; this time, Rice maintains that trying to find God is like "trying to smell the number 9." So also the album's opening track features lots of circus noises and carnival effects (borrowing, it would seem, from the Beatles' "Being for the Benefit of Mr. Kite") on a song that lists wacky questions he would like to ask God someday ("Questions for God"). Such tracks work better live and in youth group settings than on an album marketed for adult contemporary listening, but *Smell* does offer a few more traditional songs for Rice's mellow fans. The best of the bunch is "Life Means So Much," a prayer for recognition of the truth that Louie Armstrong once confessed in his "What a Wonderful World": "Teach us to count the days / Teach us to make the days count . . . Life means so much." *The Living Room Sessions* is an instrumental album on which Rice plays well-known hymns in simple piano arrangements ("Savior, Like a Shepherd Lead Us," "This Is My Father's World," "Fairest Lord Jesus").

Christian radio hits: "Clumsy" (# 17 in 1997); "The Power of a Moment" (# 20 in 1999); "Smellin' Coffee" (# 9 in 1999).

Dove Awards: 1999 Male Vocalist.

Cliff Richard

Selected: 1967—*Good News* (Word); 1970—*His Land* (Light); *Two a Penny; About That Man* (EMI); 1974—*Help It Along;* 1978—*Small Corners;*

1982—*Now You See Me, Now You Don't;* 1984—*Walking in the Light* (Myrrh); 1988—*Carols* (Word); 1989—*Songs of Life: Mission '89.*

www.cliffrichard.org

Although he is only a minor star in the United States, Cliff Richard is the most popular singer in history in his native England. With a career spanning more than forty years, he has had more chart hits than any other artist, including **Elvis Presley** or the Beatles. As of 1995, when *The New Rolling Stone Encyclopedia of Rock and Roll* was published, he had hit the British Top 40 107 times, with sixty-one songs in the Top 10 and thirteen Number Ones. He is also well known for his Christian faith, having first announced his conversion at a Billy Graham rally in London in 1966 and consistently reaffirmed his devotion to Christ ever since. Although his contributions to what is generally called contemporary Christian music have been minor, he is quite possibly the most famous and best-selling Christian popular musician in the world (depending on how one classifies **U2, Bob Dylan,** and a few other anomalies). In a mid '90s survey, Richard was listed in first place as the "best-known Christian figure in Great Britain" (ahead of the Archbishop of Canterbury at Number Two and the Pope at Number Three). An early biography of the artist relates the story of his upbringing and conversion: *New Singer, New Song: The Cliff Richard Story* by David Winter (Word, 1967).

Richard was born Harry Rodger Webb in 1940 in Lucknow, India, where his parents were second-generation British nationals. His career in music started in 1958 when he formed a group in London called The Shadows (first known as The Drifters, not to be confused with the American doo-wop group by that name). Their first song, "Move It," went to Number Two and was immediately followed by back-to-back Number One hits ("Living Doll," "Travellin' Light"). In the days when the United Kingdom was reeling from an "American invasion" of stars like **Elvis Presley,** Ricky Nelson, and Bobby Darin, Richard became the first local boy to play the new sound and he will always be remembered as Britain's first homegrown rock star. His significance for the '60s in the UK, Australia, Germany, and much of Europe would be difficult to exaggerate. He had some twenty-five Top 10 hits in a five-year period and appeared in five motion pictures *(A Serious Charge, Expresso Bongo, The Young Ones, Summer Holiday,* and *Wonderful Life).* In 1963, he was named an officer of the Order of the British Empire. The definitive teen idol, Richard would be at the height of his popularity when he suddenly appeared on stage with Billy Graham on that fateful day in 1966 and declared, "It is a great privilege to be able to tell so many people that I am a Christian. I can only say to people who are not Christians that, until you have taken the step of asking Christ into your life, your life is not worthwhile." In time, he would learn to soften the sentiment of that latter remark, but his confession of faith would always retain the enthusiasm of a new convert.

Like every other musician of the day, Richard's professional career was all but blown off course by the sudden explosion of British talent in the mid '60s that brought artists like the Beatles and The Rolling Stones to the fore. Still, he would be one of a small handful of performers to survive that onslaught. In 1968, for instance, when the Beatles were singing "Hey Jude" and the Stones were doing "Jumping Jack Flash," Richard released "Congratulations," which *Rolling Stone* reports was the Number One song "almost everywhere in the world, except the United States." To make a long story short, the hits kept coming. Almost two decades later, Richard finished 1987 with the Number One song, the Number One album, and the Number One video of the year in his homeland. In 1989, an album called *Stronger* became the best-selling record of his career, though it was not even released in America. In 1993, a project called simply *The Album* would debut at Number One the week it was released, though it too would never be made available to American markets.

Why Cliff Richard never caught on in America is something of a mystery. In the early years, before the Beatles, there appears to have been corporate resistance to promoting music by foreign artists; later, when the time may have been right, Richard chose not to tour in the United States (he did no concerts in America between 1965 and 1979). It is also possible, though by no means certain, that his public religious convictions held him back from becoming a major star in the United States—certainly the American "separation of church and state" (and, especially, misunderstandings of that doctrine) make it more difficult for those who are perceived as being "Christian performers" to gain a fair hearing in the secular marketplace than would be the case in countries where the church enjoys official recognition. For a brief period during the late '70s, however, Richard did make an impact on the American charts. In 1976, his song "Devil Woman" soared to Number Six, introducing American listeners to what they regarded as a new artist with a style similar to Hall and Oates. A bit ironically, the song caused some controversy among American fundamentalists who got all upset when they heard a professed Christian singing about a woman who was a witch or some sort of spiritual medium. Not bothering to listen to the lyrics, they apparently did not realize that the song actually warns listeners to beware of such involvements (cf. the equally ludicrous hubbub over **Philip Bailey**'s "Easy Lover"). A few more hits followed: "We Don't Talk Anymore" (# 7 in 1979), "Carrie" (# 34 in 1980), "Dreaming" (# 10 in 1980), and "A Little in Love" (# 17 in 1980). Richard also sang a duet with Olivia Newton-John for the movie *Xanadu* ("Suddenly," # 20 in 1980) and charted a cover version of the old Shep and the Limelites' hit, "Daddy's Home" (# 23 in 1982).

British rock historian Steve Turner says, "Prior to the **Bob Dylan** of *Slow Train Coming,* there was only one notable precedent for a Christian in pop or rock, and that was Cliff Richard." Richard's stance was not perceived as terribly radical since, for one thing, his musical style generally remained within the safe confines of tame pop music, avoiding the more worldly sounds of dangerous rock and roll. Furthermore, as Turner indicates, "Richard was not a songwriter, he didn't see his music as a means of self-exploration, and he was by nature a comfortable, nice person." Thus, Richard seems to have filled a role in England analogous to that of **Pat Boone** in America. He was viewed as a Christian celebrity, but his expressions of faith seldom raised questions about the anomalous combination of religion and rock. This was also, in part, because he appeared to keep the "secular" and "spiritual" spheres separate. Unlike the Jesus music performers of the early '70s (and most contemporary Christian music stars ever since), Richard did not view his professional career as a ministry and he did not perform songs for the purpose of evangelism, edification, or worship. He did make some contemporary gospel albums, but these were presented as side projects for a more select audience. For the most part, he simply worked as a pop singer like anyone else in the field, with the obvious caveat that he would only sing material that he felt comfortable performing as a Christian. In this way, he may have prefigured the '90s career of **Amy Grant.** In a 1970 book called *Questions* (Hodder and Stroughton), he wrote, "I'm a professional entertainer. That's my job. As I see it, my responsibility is to do that job to the best of my ability and to the glory of God until He calls me to leave it and do something else. It does not seem to me any 'worldlier' than being a bank manager or shopkeeper. There is nothing especially immoral or sordid about the job itself."

But in spite of his relaxed approach to proselytizing, Richards sometimes experienced the hostility toward Christianity that is so prevalent in the rock media. Turner notes that Richard "suffered ceaseless personal ridicule for his faith" (in this regard, of course, he also resembles both Boone and Grant). To take a curious analogy, in the early '80s many homophobic American journalists found it necessary to offer crass comments about pop singer Boy George's personal life while also praising his albums as masterful works of art. In a similar way, the British press seemed ever-ready to display snide bigotry regarding Cliff Richard's chosen lifestyle and espoused values while simultaneously commending his products to the record-buying public. Richard has never been combative about such matters. "Surely, as a Christian living in a non-Christian world, I should expect pressure and learn to cope with it," he wrote in 1970. "This would be just as true if I were working in a factory." Fifteen years later, however, the abuse had grown tiresome and he actually filed a libel suit against Britain's *New Musical Express* when they published a review of a concert that he thought crossed the line. The event was actually a nonprofit benefit performance that Richard did on behalf of an African relief organization; it had been advertised in churches and billed as a gospel performance. A reviewer for the mainstream publication, however, was horrified at the content of Richard's overtly Christian songs and proceeded to attack his faith and that exhibited by audience members. She called the performer "a little Hitler" and ended the review by telling the artist's fans, "If the bomb drops, I hope it drops right on you."

Aside from making occasional inspirational albums, Richard has sought to express his faith through comments in interviews and by using his celebrity status to endorse what he regards as appropriate causes. He has often appeared at crusades sponsored by Billy Graham and other evangelists, offering a brief testimony and singing a handful of spiritual songs. Early on, in the late '60s, he began a tradition of releasing an annual Christmas song, and many of these would become staples of the season in the UK. Indeed, his "Mistletoe and Wine" became the best-selling single of the year in that country in 1988, and two years later the more explicitly religious "Saviour's Day" would also be a Number One hit on mainstream radio. Similarly, Richard has kept a longtime tradition of doing an annual "gospel concert," which (to the chagrin of the *New Musical Express*) has become something of an institution in his homeland. He has also done numerous benefit concerts for a variety of charities and has served as a public spokesperson in campaigns intended to promote sexual abstinence and drug-free living. An autobiography titled *Which One's Cliff?* published in 1981 caused a bit of a stir when the unmarried star maintained that he had not had sexual relations with a woman for more than sixteen years. He also forcibly denied that he was a homosexual, a common rumor that seems to feed on nothing more than his lack of public romantic involvements with women.

The discography above lists only a small sampling of Richard's enormous output, naming albums that have featured his most obvious excursions into gospel territory. Some of these are inspirational collections of hymns similar to Elvis's gospel releases, and several *(About That Man, Help It Along, Small Corners)* were never released in the United States. *His Land* and *Two a Penny* are actually movie soundtracks for religious films. Of particular interest to contemporary Christian music fans is *Small Corners,* on which Richard pays homage to the Jesus movement by singing songs written by **Annie Herring, Malcolm and Alwyn, Larry Norman,** and **Randy Stonehill.** While appreciating the thought, *Jesus Music* magazine questions the execution. Given the abundance of great songs by those and other artists, they wonder why Richard would pick a dumb tune like Malcolm and Alwyn's "I Love" (which was just a Tom T. Hall rip-off anyway) or Stonehill's less than spectacular "I've Got News for You." At the other end of the spectrum, Norman's "Why Should the Devil Have All the Good Music?" requires a more rebellious stance than an artist like Richard is able to provide. The best song on *Small Corners* is the only noncover, a tune called "Yes, He Lives" written by Richard's own guitarist, Terry Britten. By contrast, 1982's *Now You See Me, Now You Don't* is a well-produced album that features mostly gospel-oriented songs including "Thief in the Night," a song that became a hit single in the UK, and it remains one of Richard's best-known "religious tracks." Written by Paul Field, "Thief" looks to the final day with biblical imagery: "He will come in glory, a rider in the sky / The lion and the lamb rest side by side." Richard actually included one or two such songs on many of his projects, and *Walking in the Light* draws several of these together as a compilation of his gospel hits. The title song and "You Got Me Wondering" were written by Terry Britten; two others ("Lost in a Lonely World," "Summer Rain") are **Chris Eaton** compositions, and there are also a couple of rare songs written by Richard himself ("You, Me, and Jesus," "Love and a Helping Hand").

Richard remains largely a stranger to the contemporary Christian music subculture. He did produce a Christian album on Myrrh for David Pope and he served as coproducer and performer on some of **Sheila Walsh**'s releases but, for the most part, he has seemed to be more at home in the "real world" that creates popular music for the general market. He often works with mainstream performers. Besides the aforementioned song with Olivia Newton-John, Richard has sung duets with Phil Everly ("She Means Nothing to Me") and Janet Jackson ("Two to the Power of Love"). His most notable collaboration, however, is "Whenever God Shines His Light," a moving spiritual song that Richard sang with **Van Morrison** on the latter's *Avalon Sunset* album.

Though, as indicated above, Richard may appear to Christian music fans to keep his "secular" and "spiritual" spheres separate, he actually sees no real distinction between them. While recognizing that, in terms of content, a special-interest project might be labeled "a gospel album" in the same way that a collection of carols is called "a Christmas album," he does not understand why Christian music is supposed to have overtly religious lyrics. Using a broader definition of Christian music than does America's Gospel Music Association, Richard says, "I am a Christian, so nothing I ever do is secular. Even when I sing a pop song that doesn't mention Jesus, it's still a Christian song because I am presenting it. If my record is played on a mainstream radio station, they are playing a Christian record whether they know it or not."

In 1995, Richard was knighted in recognition of his service to charity. In 1999, he had yet another Number One song in Britain with the inspirational "Millennium Prayer." That same year, he sold out Royal Albert Hall for thirty-two nights straight for what was billed as his "40th Anniversary Concert."

DeLeon Richards (a.k.a. DeLeon)

1984—*DeLeon* (Myrrh); 1987—*Don't Follow the Crowd* (Rejoice); 1989—*We Need to Hear from You* (Word); 1992—*New Direction* (label unknown); 1996—*My Life* (Intersound); 2001—*Straight from the Heart* (Tommy Boy).

DeLeon Richards, who sometimes records under her first name only, is a child-star of traditional gospel music who would begin to cross over into more of a **CeCe Winans** adult contemporary style in the late '90s. Richards was propelled to fame when her mother somehow got her a spot on a national gospel spotlight show in Chicago at the age of five. The show was held at Chicago stadium in 1981, and five-year-old Richards reportedly stole the show in front of twenty thousand people, including representatives from every major gospel label in the country. That same year, she sang for President Reagan and then, at the age of seven, she toured with **Mighty Clouds of Joy** under the moniker "God's Little Helper." She recorded her first gospel album at nine and became the youngest person ever nominated for a Grammy award (barely edging out Michael Jackson). *DeLeon* would remain her most memorable album, in part for the novelty factor of hearing gospel standards sung powerfully in a child's voice. Richards continued to record as a teenager, but *CCM* would regard her adolescent albums as having a "bubblegum R&B" sound that failed to convince. *My Life* was hailed as a comeback, her first adult project. Recorded while she was a student at Illinois' Lake Forest College, *My Life* is filled with praise songs that sound like R&B-inflected love songs for the Lord (cf. "Dear Jesus, I Love You," "I'm Yours"). "Fountain Filled with Mercy" gained a wide hearing with its catchy beat and lyrical invitation to bathe in Christ's forgiveness. *CCM* said, "like **CeCe Winans** and **Crystal Lewis**, DeLeon Richards manages the iffy proposition of navigating through deep gospel roots and R&B modernity to make music approachable to fans of both genres." *Straight from the Heart* presents the artist in fairly predictable adult contemporary form. "Faith Is" (based on Hebrews 11:1) and "Stop" continue to display dance-oriented rhythms, but the album is ballad-dominated. The lyrics to "Stop" seek to identify freedom of religion in American society (i.e., prohibitions against teacher-led prayers in public schools) as the cause of moral and social degeneration. DeLeon sings with her mother on a praise and worship medley that includes **Bill and Gloria Gaither**'s "Because He Lives."

Cindy Richardson

1984—*Crusader* (Heartland).

Cindy Richardson is a pop singer from Muscle Shoals, Alabama, with strong country roots. She has done a good deal of session work there, singing jingles for companies like McDonald's and contributing to albums for America, Crystal Gayle, **Barbara Mandrell,** and **Michele Pillar.** Her greatest claim to fame is cowriting the song "Almost over You," which was a major hit for Sheena Easton in 1983. Richardson recorded one album of country-flavored Christian pop songs. Titled *Crusader,* it includes a mix of ballads and rollicking numbers on which she is backed by the famous Muscle Shoals Rhythm Section. Songs of the latter type include a rocking track called "Celebrate the Son," a bluegrass version of the standard "I Dreamed I Searched Heaven," and a camp-meeting take on the hymn "Love Lifted Me." The song "Safe in the Harbor" displays her finest vocal prowess on a powerful plea from a person who's grown apart from the Lord.

Christian radio hits: "Safe in the Harbor" (# 20 in 1985).

Rich Young Ruler

Jennifer Bender, voc.; Rob Bender, voc., gtr.; Mead (Chesbro), voc., gtr.; Ron Mukai, perc., drums; Erik Tokle, bass; Mark Bornsteirn, cello (–1998); Scott Silletta, drums (–1998) // Garrett Burrow, recorder, perc. (+ 1998). 1995—*Storytime* (Brainstorm); 1998—*Rich Young Ruler* (Benson).

When critics wrote their rave reviews of Rich Young Ruler's sophomore album they compared the group's sound to America, Bread, the Byrds, the Beach Boys, the Carpenters, Crosby, Stills and Nash, the Raspberries, The Turtles, and many other '60s–'70s pop groups. These are disparate acts and, obviously, Rich Young Ruler can't sound like *all* of them. Perhaps it is best just to note what all of the aforementioned artists have in common: to a greater or lesser extent, they all sound like the Beatles. And that's it: *Rich Young Ruler* comes across like some just-discovered Greatest Hits package by a previously unknown Summer of Love combo who should have been filling the AM radio airwaves thirty years earlier with sounds inspired by the greatest pop band of all time. They don't really sound like *any* of the just-named stars any more than those stars sound like each other. *Rich Young Ruler* is an indisputable retro-masterpiece, and it arrived on scene as a timely antidote to GenX's whiny "complaint rock" that might have been able to present itself as rebellious and edgy in 1990 but by 1998 just seemed annoying. As such, *Rich Young Ruler* fit in with such trends in the general market as the rise of Oasis, the rediscovery of Big Star, and the endeavors of indie alternative acts like Pennsylvania's Greenberry Woods. Critical phrases lathered on the band include "at once innocent and world wise," "positive without being pompous," and "refreshingly free from sloganeering." Group member Ron Mukai describes the sound by saying, "We focus on melody and harmony, on texture and layers of sound to achieve a real warmth."

Rich Young Ruler arose out of a music ministry based in a Southern California church where Rob Bender, Mead (who prefers no last name), and Mukai served as a worship team. An early form of the group ended up participating in some evangelistic outreach programs in Japan. *Storytime* catches the group in development. Produced by Scott Silletta of **PlankEye,** who joined the band for the one album only, the record is a competent offering of folk-tinged worship songs. It would invoke Simon and Garfunkel comparisons and be described as having "a peaceful, easy Eagles feeling," but such analogies were hyperbolic—the songs are certainly not catchy enough or performed well enough to satisfy fans of such artists. The high points are probably "Show Yourself" and "Easy Now," which display soaring harmonies and vulnerable lyrics that express a longing for and promise of intimacy with God.

Three years later, it was apparent that something exciting had happened. Part of that "something" is known: **Terry Scott Taylor** saw promise in the group and took them under his wing, producing the eponymous project. Taylor, a member of **Daniel Amos,** the **Lost Dogs, The Swirling Eddies,** and several other groups, has shown himself to be more than adept at translating the basic appeal of Beatlesque '60s pop in ever new ways for ever-changing populations. It is difficult to know how much credit for the success of *Rich Young Ruler* should be attributed to him. He brought in friends like **Michael Knott** and fellow **Lost Dogs** Gene Eugene and **Michael Roe** to kick the music into a very high gear, and he even cowrote a couple of the best tunes ("Wearing Me Out," "Who's Gonna Make You Happy"). But delighted listeners probably didn't care about such matters any more than they cared who really played those instruments on their old Monkees albums. Bottom line: great songs, jangling guitars, sweet vocal harmonies, memorable melodies, catchy hooks . . . virtually every track bounces and sparkles but not a single one strays into that iffy territory called "bubblegum" (at least, not so deeply that it can't find its way back out again). The material also avoids the danger of "sameness" that attaches to many retro-projects. Mead's voice is similar to that of Matthew Sweet and Rob Bender's is reminiscent of Michael Stipe; they trade off singing to give some winsome variety, with Jennifer Bender providing female vocals occasionally for texture. "Who's Gonna Make You Happy" recalls British pop, with a sound like some old Hollies mega-hit. "All These Sorrows" is more of a folk ballad. "Wearing Me Out" comes right out of the California surf-pop tradition. *CCM* pegged "Take It Anywhere" as sounding uncannily like the long-forgotten group Fotomaker, and *True Tunes* rightly identifies "The Ride" and "In Touch" as sounding like George Harrison outtakes (or, better, like Matthew Sweet covering some old Harrison tunes). "She Runs, She Hides" is a jazz-tinged ballad in the same tradition as some of Simon and Garfunkel's prettier songs ("For Emily," "Flowers Never Bend with the Rainfall"). "Every Time I Reach for You" and "Magic Nowheres" are the sprightly near-bubblegum songs that summon images of British bands like Pilot or Edison Lighthouse. Listening to the album, one gets the feeling that all the songs should be familiar—like some old hit you just can't place—but they're not. They're new and fresh, bringing back the joy of hearing such songs for the first time. Lyrically, Rich Young Ruler's songs are seldom religious in a way that obviously stands out. Most of the songs deal with the subjects of romance and relationships as viewed by people of faith. Sometimes, the faith perspective does little more than provide a sense of purity and innocence that seems appropriate to music of this style anyway. On "The Ride," we hear a smitten voice singing, "You don't know what you do to me / You turn me up inside," while also maintaining, "You can't take me home tonight . . . it's gonna take some time." Some songs like "Every Time You Reach for Me" have that ambiguous quality where one isn't sure whether the love song lyrics are directed to a human partner or to the Lord. In any case, "You've Got the Right Words" offers a contemporary coda with a modern acoustic worship song similar to those on the group's first album.

Sue Rinaldi

1996—*Love Eternal* (N'Soul); 1998—*Promise Land* (Survivor).

Sue Rinaldi is a British composer of contemporary worship songs who seems to be a part of the same movement as **Graham Kendrick, Matt Redman,** and Noel Richards (who has released at least three albums of modern worship songs in the United Kingdom: *By Your Side, Thunder in the Skies,* and *Warrior*). All of these singer/songwriters set heartfelt and often biblically-inspired lyrics to a Brit-pop sound that has become most familiar with American audiences through the recordings of **Delirious?.** Rinaldi's first project suffered from poor production and from an overuse of synthesizers that gave everything a dreamy techno-pop common denominator, rendering the songs indistinct (*Shout* would call it "the musical equivalent of wallpaper"). *Promise Land* is much better, with a mix of worship and performance-oriented material. The theme of revival figures prominently in the songs, driving a number like "Redemption Street" with appropriate enthusiasm. "Lay Myself Down" is an atmospheric track, recalling the first record with its keyboard swirls, but in a manner that really works this time. The theme is a simple prayer for purity: "I will follow you to the cross and lay myself down . . . Cleanse me from all this pollution."

Rising Hope

Michael Goldberg; Susan Goldberg; Ross Johnson. 1975—*Farewell to the Shadowlands* (custom); 1979—*Where the Songs Came From.*

Rising Hope was a Cincinnati "creative arts" ministry associated with The Jesus House coffeehouse founded there by **Randy Matthews** and Terry Fisher. They staged multimedia presentations but are best remembered for two albums of acoustic folk songs. *Farewell to the Shadowlands* has a homemade style that *Harmony* magazine would describe as "simple, soft, and penetrating." The songs are presented free of frills and orchestrations, sung in a Peter, Paul, and Mary type of harmony accompanied with guitar, banjo, flute, and a bit of autoharp. *Jesus Music* compares Susan Goldberg's voice to that of **Debby Kerner,** and most of the songs do have a similar sound to Kerner and Rettino projects. "Song of Praise," "Love to Pass the Days," and "Help O Lord" are standouts, and "The Lord Will Be My Snowtires" is a novelty bluegrass number that probably went over better live. The first album was supposedly influenced by **Jim Valley**'s *Family* record. The second project presents more gentle folk tunes with upgraded production. *Jesus Music*'s Ken Scott calls the record one of his "all-time favorites" due to its "overall atmosphere of charm and radiant joy." He also calls the songs "Here's My Family" and "A Wind in the Door" instances of "exuberant, moving pieces of Jesus music." The acoustic ballad "Listen to the Singer" is also beautiful and touching. For custom albums, both of Rising Hope's records sported unusually attractive cover art with hand lettering and designs by Susan Goldberg and other family members.

Rick Riso

1985—*Gotta Have the Real Thing* (Home Sweet Home); 1986—*Shouting at the Walls;* 1987—*The Best of Rick Riso;* 1995—*A Man of His Word* (Integrity).

Rick Riso was front man for the late '70s act **Messenger,** and in the '90s he would record several worship albums, some with his wife Cathy. His '80s solo albums found the Los Angeles-based artist experimenting with an R&B, dance-oriented sound. *Gotta Have the Real Thing* features a title cut that is reminiscent of Earth, Wind, and Fire's silky smooth material. The song "Remember Me" is also a musically strong and emotionally touching power ballad. The title of the album is a play on the Coca-Cola motto of the day, a fact brought out by lettering and graphics in the cover art that parody those of Coke advertisements.

Johnny Rivers

Selected: 1966—*Changes* (Imperial); 1967—*Rewind;* 1968—*Realization;* 1970—*Slim Slo Slider;* 1973—*Homegrown* (United Artists); 1978—*Outside*

Help (Soul City); 1980—*Borrowed Time* (RSO); 1983—*Not a Through Street* (Priority).

www.johnnyrivers.com

Soulful superstar Johnny Rivers is an ironic enigma for the Christian music culture. Always appreciated for his sensitive, provocative, and morally responsible albums, his music seemed to announce a conversion to Christianity during the Jesus movement revival when many of his peers (**Barry McGuire, Noel Paul Stookey, Larry Norman,** and even **Eric Clapton**) were publicly proclaiming such transformations. But Rivers provided no testimony to accompany his songs and, as it turns out, the suspicions of the more skeptical Jesus freaks were pretty much correct. He would later say that he had not been a Christian during the time that he was being touted as one, but—and here is the real irony—a decade after he had been suspected of being a convert by some and accused of false advertising for pretending to be one by others, he suddenly maintained that he really had been born again. He entered the Christian music scene with the gusto everyone had wanted ten years before, but by then, no one cared. The revival was over, Rivers was no longer a big star, and musical tastes had changed. As the years and decades went by, many ex or aging Jesus freaks would continue to treasure their Johnny Rivers albums, but it was the '70s "Jesus records" (when he wasn't a Christian) rather than the '80s projects (when he was) that they wished would somehow become available on CD; in 1999 that dream was fulfilled, via reissues from a British company called BGO.

Rivers was born John Ramistella in New York City in 1942. He grew up in Baton Rouge, Louisiana, and so would come by his cajun-soul sound a bit more naturally than Creedence Clearwater Revival and others who popularized it some time later. He went into music at an early age and enjoyed some minor success as a songwriter when his song "I'll Make Believe" was recorded by Rick Nelson. He met up with DJ Alan Freed, who gave him his new name, but the big break came when he moved out to Los Angeles and began playing regularly at a club called the Whiskey-a-Go-Go on the Sunset Strip. Here, Rivers recorded a series of highly successful live albums that would bring him several Top 40 hits. Most of these were covers of R&B or straight-out blues tunes, like Chuck Berry's "Memphis" (# 2 in 1964) and "Maybelline" (# 12 in 1964), Harold Dorman's "Mountain of Love" (# 9 in 1964), Leadbelly's "Midnight Special" (# 20 in 1965), Willie Dixon's "Seventh Son" (# 7 in 1965), and Stonewall Jackson's "Muddy Water" (# 19 in 1966). He also scored a huge hit with the theme song for a popular TV series called *Secret Agent Man,* a James-Bond rip-off show starring Patrick McGoohan. Then, on the appropriately titled album *Changes,* Rivers' style changed abruptly. He abandoned his raucous, rough-and-tumble guitar-banging songs for a silky smooth soulful style. This is perhaps best illustrated in "Poor Side of Town," a sweet ballad written by Rivers himself (with Lou Adler) that proved to be the biggest hit of his career (# 1 in 1966). The song was something of an anomaly in an era more given to giddy, punchy sounds—it broke through to the Number One spot in between The Monkees' "Last Train to Clarkesville" and "I'm a Believer," contending against other songs like The Vaudeville Band's "Winchester Cathedral" and The Supreme's "You Keep Me Hangin' On." *Changes* is also notable because on that album Rivers introduces the world to a new songwriter named Jimmy Webb, performing a song called "By the Time I Get to Phoenix." Rivers and Webb would remain close partners for years, and Rivers' soulful take on "Phoenix" remains the best recording of the song—much more powerful emotionally than **Glen Campbell**'s hit version a year later. Rivers' next album, *Rewind,* would feature seven of Webb's songs, and though he would continue to score his biggest hits with R&B covers, he now chose soulful ballads like "The Tracks of My Tears" (# 10 in 1967) and "Baby, I Need Your Lovin' " (# 3 in 1967). Around this time, Rivers made another contribution to popular music. He met up with a vocal soul group called the Hi-Fi's, saw potential that was not being fulfilled, and took them under his wing. Eventually, he would reshape the group, get Webb to write them some songs, and present them to the world as The Fifth Dimension (singing Webb's "Up, Up, and Away").

On *Realization,* Rivers emerges as a hippie flower child, dedicated to love and peace, flowers and beads, happiness, and—above all—spirituality. The album is an important artifact of the time and includes at least three of the best songs of the era: "Summer Rain" (# 14 in 1968) and "Look to Your Soul" (# 49 in 1968), written by James Hendricks, and Rivers' own "Going Back to Big Sur," a gorgeous testimony to the beauty of nature. Hendricks was another songwriter "discovered" by Rivers, and he basically took over the role of Webb, who by now was cranking out songs for the more commercially successful Campbell instead. Actually, Hendricks had quite a history in pop music himself—at one point, he was married to Cass Elliott of the Mamas and the Papas, and he was a founding member of The Mugwumps, the group that eventually morphed into the Lovin' Spoonful. His music remained unknown, however, until Rivers picked it up. "Summer Rain" is a near perfect account of the Summer of Love, when "everyone kept on playing *Sgt. Pepper's Lonely Hearts Club Band.*" But it would be "Look to Your Soul" that would touch the hearts (and, indeed, the souls) of a generation in quest of inner peace. Perhaps no other song of the times better expresses that longing: "I nearly lost myself, trying to be someone else / All of my life, I've been playing the game." What is truly remarkable about the song is that it completely repudiates the counter-culture's simplistic equation of "finding oneself" with "doing your own thing," offering instead a far more radical counter-countercultural message that seems to be based on the teaching of Jesus (Mark 8:34–36): "To live, you must nearly die / Give up the need to say 'I' / Look to your soul for the answer." Hip pastors and church youth groups around the country immediately latched on to the song as one of the very few songs in pop music that expressed a Christian ideology. As for the rest of *Realization,* "Brother, Where Are You" (with its embarrassingly hokey "lookin' for a soul brother" chorus) and Rivers' own, much better "The Way We Live" are songs of social concern. "Somethin' Strange" (written by Rivers and Hendricks) and "What's the Difference?" (written by Scott MacKenzie, who sang but did not write John Phillips' "If You're Going to San Francisco") are also songs about the need for inner change and integrity similar in theme to "Look to Your Soul." *Realization* was Rivers' first self-produced project and it was easily his best album to date. The usual covers (Procul Harum's "Whiter Shade of Pale" and **Bob Dylan**'s "Positively 4th Street") are more than competent but, this time, such songs are only minor attractions.

With *Realization,* Rivers made the transition from sensitive soul singer to prophet of inner peace, and thousands of hippie youth began looking to him the way they would to **Bob Dylan** or John Lennon to show them the way. Indeed, by now Dylan and Lennon had both turned out to be angry and unhappy young men whose indignations might be justified but hardly qualified them as role models for finding peace of mind. For that, Rivers, Donovan, or maybe George Harrison seemed the more likely guide. Thus it is of some significance that Side Two of Rivers' next album opens with "Jesus Is a Soul Man," a cover of a minor hit by Lawrence Reynolds (# 28 in 1969). In the two years since *Realization,* the Jesus movement revival had hit, and artists like **Children of the Day, Love Song,** and **Larry Norman** were naming the one through whom the spiritual quest could be satisfied. To their fans and followers, it seemed that fellow quester Johnny Rivers was doing so, too. Granted, "Jesus Is a Soul Man" is a dumb song (though perhaps no dumber than Norman's "The Rock That Doesn't Roll"), but it sure sounded like Rivers had joined the Jesus movement. He had gone from saying, "Look to your soul for the answer" to proclaiming, "Jesus is a soul man . . . I want to tell you he lives in my heart . . . and I'm sure sold on Him." This time, though, Rivers himself did not contribute to the songwriting, and the very best songs on *Slim Slo Slider* are not the overtly spiritual/ religious ones. Rather, they are the covers of John Fogerty's "Wrote a Song for Everyone" and of Tony Joe White's "Rainy Night in Georgia." Gram Parsons' "Brass Buttons" and "Apple Tree" are also treats. Then, Rivers offers two **Van Morrison** songs, "Slim Slo Slider" (from *Astral Weeks*) and the deeply spiritual "Into the Mystic" (from *Moondance*). Other songs have a gospel (i.e., specifically Christian) orientation. Hendricks pro-

vides two such songs: "Muddy River," an allegorical tale of soul cleansing, and "Glory Train," in which Rivers sings, "One day I'll ride that glory train, wait for Jesus to call my name." A song by Rivers' discovery Bob Ray called "Resurrection" offers a description of transformation that also draws on Christian imagery. The Jesus people were hungry for endorsements and many took Rivers' inclusion of such songs as signs that he was one of them. But Rivers didn't play the part—he didn't give the one way sign and try to witness to the audience at his concerts. He didn't give altar calls or say prayers from the stage. Perhaps most significant, he didn't talk about his faith (newfound or otherwise) in interviews and he didn't interact with any of the other Jesus music artists playing festivals and coffeehouses around the country. Still, it seemed to some that to sing such songs without a *disclaimer* constituted a confession. The Jesus people put *Slim Slo Slider* alongside **Marvin Gaye**'s *What's Goin' On?* as a Christian album by a secular artist and waited to see what would happen next.

What happened next seemed to remove all doubt. Rivers released an album as filled with enthusiastic and personal affirmations of faith as Norman's *Only Visiting This Planet. Homegrown* seems to gush with the joy and exuberance of one who has just been born again. "This is the first day of my new life," Rivers sings, and it would be hard for anyone to doubt that he is describing a regeneration in Christ. The album opens with a song about generic religious quests and revival, "Moving to the Country." That track describes a national phenomenon according to which "the chosen people" are rejecting materialism, realizing "you can't take it with you when you go," and setting out on a pilgrimage to find Moses or Jesus or "whoever else is going to show." The revival of such spiritual interests is a good thing, Rivers maintains ("better days are being born") but as the album continues, he narrows things down and gets specific, ending with songs that name the name of Jesus to an almost annoying degree. He covers James Taylor's "Fire and Rain," which already mentions Jesus ("you gotta look down upon me Jesus, you gotta help me make a stand") but appends a long fade-out chorus at the end, singing, "Help me, Je-e-e-sus, you're my friend" over and over and over again. Then the album concludes with "Think His Name," which mostly just repeats the words "Jesus / Jesus / Jesus Christ / Jesus Christ" over and over for four-and-a-half minutes (in response to the invitation, "Sing his name, sing his name, sing it twice"). Unfortunately, as with "Jesus Is A Soul Man," this most explicitly Christian song is easily the weakest track on the album, perhaps its only musical embarrassment. Still, one can hardly fail to notice the sentiment, especially since this time, Rivers chose "Think His Name" as the only song to release as a single (it peaked at # 65). Three songs on *Homegrown* are Rivers' own compositions: "Look at the Sun" is a spiritual ode about "the

Light returning to all the souls of men"; "Song for Michael" is a beautiful song for Rivers' son, in which he says, "I can't teach him that God is love, though I've done my part . . . I want him to see love everywhere, know that he's part of a plan / I want him to see God everywhere, but mostly in his fellow man"; "Permanent Change" is a rollicking country song about personal conversion and social transformation. Rivers also covers **Curtis Mayfield**'s gospel song "People Get Ready," calling on everyone to "trust in the Lord." Notably, Christian music stars **Mike and Kathy Deasy** are all over the *Homegrown* album, offering instrumental and vocal support on practically every track.

Homegrown was a very strong collection of songs—musical highlights also include renditions of Carole King's "So Far Away" and two Jackson Browne songs ("Our Lady of the Well," "Rock Me on the Waters")—yet it was not a commercial success. Most likely, the commercial failure was due in part to the overpowering religious content. It was perceived as a Jesus music album *especially* by non-Jesus people who saw it as propaganda for a cause that they had chosen to reject or ignore. Almost twenty years later, long after Rivers had revealed that he was not a committed Christian when he made the album, liner notes for the BGO re-release would say,

This is a pretty neat album for anyone with an open mind, that is, anyone who is prepared to listen to an album by an artist who has just discovered a new inspiration. Rivers had evidently found religion. . . . There is no denying that this is a 'born again' type album, but it is no throwaway, even if the inevitable fervor of the new convert is evident and the heart is very much on the sleeve. There is nothing more natural than the newly enlightened broadcasting their good news to anyone who'll listen. . . . **Bob Dylan** did the same thing in the '70s with *Slow Train Coming*.

The irony with these near-apologies and caveats is that Rivers was not a new convert and *Homegrown* is in reality nothing like *Slow Train Coming*. It's more like Joan Baez' *David's Album,* another record full of gospel-oriented songs by a non-Christian who nevertheless finds them generically inspiring and meaningful. "I was always very close to Christianity," Rivers would tell *CCM* in 1983. "The only thing I hadn't really done was make that serious commitment to live as a Christian and take the Bible literally." He went on to explain that he "thought the Bible was a book of symbols" like "some maze you had to figure out," and he even looked to the "Eastern teaching" of other religions to help him sort it through.

The Jesus people seemed to sense this—and *Homegrown* didn't sell particularly well with them either. They'd grown more discerning and/or judgmental in the two years since *Slim*

Slo Rider and were less likely to give anyone who didn't say the right words the benefit of the doubt. Rivers *did* say them, but only when he sang. He still didn't testify on stage or try to witness to reporters when he gave interviews. And what's this Guru Ram Das Ashram singers that Rivers had singing the "Jesus" chorus on "Think His Name"? *That* doesn't sound very orthodox. And the graffiti artwork to *Homegrown* had quotes from Native American spiritual leaders mixed in with verses from the Bible and snippets of poetry. Hmmm . . . The bottom line among Christian music fans at the time was that *Homegrown* seemed like a wonderful collection of some great songs, but . . . it just didn't seem *anointed*. Something didn't feel right about it. Such fans did not fail to notice that, about two years later, Rivers suddenly dropped all religious and spiritual songs from his concert repertoire. He quit singing "Think His Name" and "Jesus Is a Soul Man" (which weren't very good anyway) along with such tamer fare as "Fire and Rain," "Into the Mystic," and even "Look to Your Soul." He had a big hit with a remake of Huey "Piano" Smith's '50s hit, "Rockin' Pneumonia—Boogie Woogie Flu" (# 6 in 1972), which took him back to the Whiskey-A-Go-Go style, and then he scored another one with "Swayin' to the Music (Slow Dancin')" (# 10 in 1977), which recalled his romantic *Changes/Rewind* style. He released more albums (*L.A. Reggae,* United Artists, 1972; *Blue Suede Shoes,* 1973; *Road,* Atlantic, 1974; *Outside Help,* Soul City, 1977), but by 1980 it is safe to say he had been completely forgotten by the contemporary Christian music community that had evolved in the meantime. In 1980, if anyone had been paying attention (but they weren't), they might have noticed that *Borrowed Time* exhibited a sudden return to fascination with spiritual things.

Three years later, advertisements appeared in *CCM* and other magazines announcing Johnny Rivers' "first gospel album." That record, *Not a Through Street,* was released on a Christian label (Priority) and, so, was targeted primarily for the contemporary Christian music community—though Rivers insisted that he hoped it would find acceptance in the general market as well. The artist granted a rare interview with *CCM* and revealed that he had made a "serious commitment to Christ" around 1980. He said (a bit ironically, given the BGO note above) that **Bob Dylan**'s *Slow Train Coming* had a serious effect on him. Furthermore, "I had friends who investigated Christianity and started going to church and rededicating themselves. I could see the change in them, and of course that had an influence on me as well." Unfortunately, *Not a Through Street* did not hold up to the quality of Rivers' other albums—it certainly was not as good as *Realization, Slim Slo Slider,* or *Homegrown*. It was by no means a bad record, if compared to the rank and file of Christian music produced that year; it just didn't hold up to what one might expect from an artist of

Rivers' stature. By inevitable comparison, *Slow Train Coming* was a respectable part of Dylan's oeuvre—even those who resented his ideology had to admit that his faith virtually exploded into songs in remarkable and convincing ways. But Rivers sometimes chose to express his faith on *Not a Through Street* in ways that seemed stilted and awkward. First, having had such success with R&B covers in the past, he decided to do the same with songs that have spiritual impact. **Sam Cooke**'s "A Change Is Gonna Come" was a good choice, but Rivers' version of the difficult song comes off a little flat. Ben E. King's "Stand by Me" (which is often not even recognized as a gospel song) was a poorer choice simply because the tune was already so well known; it had recently been a Top 40 hit in a version by Mickey Gilley (# 22 in 1980), and it had been performed in a far better version than Rivers could ever hope to offer by John Lennon in 1975, when it had also gone into the Top 40 (at # 20). Likewise, a cover of **Marvin Gaye**'s "How Sweet It Is (To Be Loved You)" was not really advisable unless he was prepared to offer a superior version to that recently performed by James Taylor (# 3 in 1975), and he wasn't. Then, there was another problem: for some reason, Rivers chose to Christianize some beloved songs by changing lyrics to make them more Jesus- or God-oriented. Thus, the just-mentioned song became, "How sweet it is to be loved by *Jesus*" and a cover of the old Four Tops song, "Reach Out (I'll Be There)" became Reach out, *He'll* be there." This approach never goes over well with Christian music fans. For one thing, it seems to substantiate the old charge that Christian music is just a derivative copy of what the world produces with more creativity—a touchy matter in the Christian music subculture. On a deeper level, many listeners just find such alterations insulting because they seem to imply that there would be something wrong with a Christian singing a nice song about romantic love *unless* its words can be made to impart a spiritual message.

Still, *Not a Through Street* does have its moments apart from such complaints. Rivers himself wrote the lead-off song, "Nowhere Else to Go," which describes the decision to follow Christ that is sometimes made by those who have expended all other options. He says he was inspired to write the song by a line in the motion picture *An Officer and a Gentleman,* though he might just as well have been inspired by John 6:68. The song offers his personal testimony and its lyrics are boldly printed on the back cover of the album jacket: "I used to think I had it all goin' / Everything I touched turned to gold / I had women and money, fine clothes and cars . . . somethin' in my soul was missin' . . . Lord, I'm comin' to you." Perhaps the most intriguing track on the album is "New Meaning," written by Rivers' old cohort James Hendricks (with G. Hendricks—his wife?). The song goes well beyond "Look to Your Soul" to proclaim an explicit Christian faith: "Jesus, you have given me new life /

You have changed it all / Set my feet on the solid rock." Though nothing is known of Hendricks's story, the song would at least inspire hope among those with long-term memories that the man who so framed the questions they were asking back in the days of *Realization* had found the same answer they had discovered, in part at his prompting. Finally, Rivers also sings a new arrangement of the hymn "The Uncloudy Day," which is perhaps the musical high point of the album.

In 1998, Rivers released a new studio album (his first in fifteen years) called *Last Train to Memphis* (Soul City). It offers a few original songs ("Don't Let the Rain Come Down," the title track) along with some old R&B standards ("Blue Suede Shoes," "Then You Can Tell Me Goodbye").

Christian radio hits: "Live It from Day to Day" (# 40 in 1983).

Rivulets and Violets

2000 lineup: Masaki, gtr., violin; Sam Hernandez, bass; Jen Hollingsworth, voc.; Robyn Spitzer, voc.; Mindy Verdecchio, voc. 1994—*Rivulets and Violets* (Eden); 2000—*Promise* (5 Min. Walk).

http://rivuletsandviolets.com

Rivulets and Violets seems to be an on-again-off-again project for Masaki, who has produced albums for **The W's, Five Iron Frenzy, The Echoing Green,** and **Dryve,** as well as serving as guitarist and principal songwriter for the excellent, underrated band **Dime Store Prophets.** While still with the Prophets, Masaki got together with a female vocalist friend and they created an experimental, mostly instrumental, custom album called *Rivulets and Violets*. Described by one critic as sounding like an odd combination of Enya and the Cocteau Twins, the disc obtained quick obscurity and Masaki devoted himself to other pursuits. Then suddenly in 2000 Rivulets and Violets reemerged as an actual group, featuring three female vocalists. One of these, Jen Hollingsworth, also served as Masaki's songwriting partner for the series of songs on *Promise*. Song styles range from semi-classical pieces propelled by cello and Masaki's violin to edgy rock songs ("Touch"). The dominant mood, however, is pastoral (the group also covers Martin Nysom's "Shepherd of My Soul"), leading *CCM* to describe the project as having the feel of "a walk in the English countryside." The vocals especially have invoked comparisons to **Sixpence None the Richer.** "I Hate You" is a disarmingly sweet rant against the devil ("I hate you dearly"); "In the Stars" and "I See with New Eyes" are charming pop songs, expressive of beauty and gratitude. Masaki has said, "The best way that I can describe Rivulets and Violets is, it's kind of like a six-year-old who's been given a piece of paper and some crayons and decides to draw a picture for their mom because they love their mom. . . . This is what we made for God."

The Road Home

John Falcone, bass; Ed McTaggart, drums; Bill Sprouse Jr., voc., kybrd.; John Wytock, gtr. No albums.

The Road Home was one of the best of the early Jesus music bands associated with Calvary Chapel in Costa Mesa, California. They were on a par with other great Maranatha bands like **Love Song, Daniel Amos,** and **The Way.** Unfortunately, the group only recorded two songs. One of these, "Since I Met Jesus" (from the 1974 compilation album *Maranatha Four*), is one of the best contemporary Christian music songs ever recorded by any artist. The other, "Psalm 5" (from the 1976 compilation album *Maranatha Five*), is one of the best contemporary worship songs of the twentieth century, and one that would continue to be sung in congregations two-and-a-half decades later. After recording those songs and while working on an album, The Road Home toured as the opening act for **Chuck Girard** on one of his first solo tours. Then, on September 5, 1975, singer, songwriter, and front man Bill Sprouse Jr. suffered a heart attack while showering in his home and died instantly. Sprouse weighed over 500 pounds and his weight seems to have been an obvious factor in his early death (at the age of twenty-six). **Erick Nelson** wrote and sang the song "Moving On" as a tribute to the artist, and **Sweet Comfort Band** likewise offered "Golden Ages" in his honor. Although little is known of Sprouse's pre-Christian career, he had been a musician all his life and fronted a previous non-Christian version of The Road Home that actually recorded an album on the ABC/Dunhill label. He experienced a conversion to Christ in 1971 and joined with the Jesus people at Calvary Chapel, where the new version of The Road Home was formed. Guitarist John Wytock had previously played with **Danny Lee and the Children of Truth.** Ed McTaggart went on to play with **Daniel Amos.**

Sprouse appears to have had incredible potential as a songwriter, and he probably had the best voice for country rock of any singer in the world at the time. "Since I Met Jesus" is the perfect vehicle for that voice. Propelled by pedal steel guitar, it is country rock in the tradition of Poco or Buffalo Springfield or *Sweethearts*-era Byrds. Musically compelling, the song is as good as Hank Williams (senior) at his best; it almost certainly could have been a hit on either rock or country radio apart from the religious content. Lyrically, it expresses the joy of conversion from a wasted life of sin: "I used to write songs in dark, old honky-tonks / Brother, I was never satisfied / Since, I met Jesus / There's only one thing on my mind / If I can't sing about the Man from Galilee / Brother, then, I'm not satisfied." Such theological naivete and annoyingly single-minded devotion to a newfound, transforming reality was definitive of the Jesus movement—as it may be of any revival. The song is probably the only contribution from the Jesus movement besides Marsha Stevens' "For Those Tears I Died" that deserves to transcend popular music genres and be placed in the canon of great American songs (like Williams' "I Saw the Light" or such spirituals as "Swing Low, Sweet Chariot" and "Will the Circle Be Unbroken"). It is the sort of song that can and should be appreciated by any open-minded lover of American music, regardless of spiritual orientation, and it is difficult to imagine it ever being performed better than by Sprouse and company on the *Maranatha Four* collection. "Psalm 5" is simply a beautiful hymn that would also be recorded by **Love Song** on their *Feel the Love* live album. Sprouse also wrote the song "Shotgun Angel," which is, shall we say, not as good as "Since I Met Jesus" or "Psalm 5." It nevertheless became the title track for **Daniel Amos**'s second album and a favorite of that group's fans; it would be redone by the **Seventy Sevens** as late as 2000.

Roadside Monument

Doug Lorig, gtr., voc.; Jonathon Ford, bass, voc.; Matt Johnson, drums; Michael Dente (− 1997). 1996—*Beside This Brief Hexagonal* (Tooth and Nail); 1997—*Eight Hours Away from Being a Man*; 1998—*I Am the Day of Current Taste.*

Roadside Monument was a Seattle band that set out to be "both original and accomplished," a goal that was especially daunting in a city where strong influences seemed to dictate the sound of the late '90s. But Roadside Monument was definitely not grunge; the label most applied to them was "emo-punk," though they resented that categorization as well and attempted to defy whatever expectations it might carry. The members—especially Doug Lorig and Jonathon Ford—prized precision in their performances to an extent that suggests advanced studies at the Billy Corgan School of Perfectionism. Lyrically, the group did not produce songs that were evangelistic or worship-oriented but dealt with hard subjects (e.g., death and divorce) as considered from a Christian perspective. Before Roadside Monument, bassist Jonathon Ford had played in **Pedro the Lion** (indeed, he continued to play in the two groups concurrently). Drummer Matt Johnson had played in **Don't Know** and **Blenderhead.** After Roadside Monument disbanded, Johnson joined **Ninety Pound Wuss,** then reunited with Lorig in **Raft of Dead Monkeys.** Ford joined the Jesus People U.S.A. community in Chicago (see listing on **Resurrection Band**) and made one self-titled album with the general market band Scientific (Escape, 1999) before forming **Unwed Sailor.** In addition to the projects listed above, Roadside Monument recorded a seven-inch record titled *My Life Is Green* in 1996 and two "split EPs" (projects on which a group presents two or three songs along with songs from another group), one with **Puller** (1996) and another with Frodus (1997).

The debut album, *Beside This Brief Hexagonal,* met with very mixed reviews. *HM* appreciated the experimentation, noting that it reveals what happens "when a group recognizes the studied musicianship of jazz *and* the chaos of modern rock music." *True Tunes,* however, found it all "tedious" and "bland," like "a less interesting version of Sonic Youth, creating arid soundscapes that manage to weave and bob, but never arrive at anyplace specific." At this point, Lorig described the band's music as "a beautiful mess" and *HM* attempted this explanation: "It exhibits an element of creative surprise. For instance, in parts of the tracks 'Seed' and 'Lobbyest,' vocals are sung and then, without warning, the delivery transforms into punk/hardcore projections.... One cannot sit back and expect to soak in the album."

Eight Hours Away from Being a Man shows vast improvement, while remaining true to the artistic vision with which the original group had started. *True Tunes* would say, "*Eight Hours Away From Being a Man* is a moody, emo-punk record shifting violently from delicate, trebly, indy guitar noodling to massive walls of bass and guitar that disappear just as quickly as they materialize." Again, musical variety is the order of the day. "My Hands Are Thermometers" is hard and fast; the title track and "John Wayne Marina" are comparatively mellow. "Kansas City" uses a horn section to introduce some jazz-influenced sounds. The track that caught the most attention, however, was an opening number expressing anger at child abuse, "Sperm Ridden Burden." Numerous Christian music stores refused to stock the album, taking more offense at the title of the song than the track itself. But the group's penchant for quirky titles would only increase on their swan song, *I Am the Day of Current Taste,* which features "Taxi Riding as an Art Form," "Egos the Size of Cathedrals," and "O J Simpson House Auction." The latter track is actually one of the group's prettier pop songs, while "Cops Are My Best Customers" starts off like a whispery **Starflyer 59** number and then explodes into instrumental histrionics at the midpoint.

Sometime after Roadside Monument had broken up, when Jonathon Ford was in **Unwed Sailor,** he remarked that the group's problems with the Christian music industry stemmed from the fact that Roadside Monument was "not really a Christian band." He claimed that he himself had been "searching" and did not fully decide to become a Christian until after the band had broken up. He further said that he had previously exhibited "a prideful attitude" and that the whole "Sperm Ridden Burden" fight with the Christian music industry was "just pretty petty and ridiculous." In 1999, he told *Bandoppler,* "I definitely do not feel jaded toward the Christian music industry. There are other things to think about."

Austin Roberts

1972—*Austin Roberts* (Chelsea); 1973—*Last Things on My Mind;* 1975—*Rocky;* 1976—*Eight Days: A Personal Journey* (NewPax); 1981—*Paint My Life* (MCA Songbird).

Austin Roberts is best known for the Top 10 bubblegum smash "Rocky," which hit the charts in 1975. This was not Roberts's only contribution to popular music, however, and the artist has also been involved in the Christian music scene. Roberts was born in 1945 in Newport News, Virginia. In the early '70s he replaced Eugene Pistilli in a New York musical trio called Cashman, Pistilli, and West, which had also recorded as the Buchanan Brothers. Roberts wasn't with the group for long, and after he left, Cashman and West continued as a duo to score a few minor hits and, then, became the producers of all of Jim Croce's recordings. Roberts, meanwhile, switched coasts to join a Los Angeles trio called Arkade, which also had two very minor hits with songs that were bigger regionally than the national chart numbers indicate: "Sing Out the Love in My Heart" (# 99 in 1970) and "The Morning of Our Lives" (# 60 in 1971). He connected with TV and became involved with the production of the cartoon programs *Scooby Doo* and *Josie and the Pussycats.* He also became a songwriter of some note in country music. As a solo artist, Roberts hit the charts three times: "Somethin's Wrong with Me" (# 12 in 1972), "Keep On Singin' " (# 50 in 1973), and "Rocky" (# 9 in 1975). The same year that "Rocky" hit, Roberts released the debut of a Christian instrumental group he had formed called **The Sonlight Orchestra.** A year later, he unveiled a Christian musical called *Eight Days: A Personal Journey.* The album reveals a progressive rock style quite different from the teenybopper sound of Roberts's previous hits. There is actually a hard rock edge to much of the music, with upfront synthesizers, classic rock organ, and crunchy guitars. *Jesus Music* dares to compare it to **Daniel Amos**'s *Horrendous Disc.* If that is a bit much, the album would remain by far the best of Roberts's career. It was a commercial failure, however, and five years later his second Christian release, *Paint My Life,* found him displaying a country/pop style similar to records associated with **B. J. Thomas** or with his coproducer **Chris Christian.** Roberts has also produced albums by other Christian artists, including **Petra**'s classic *Come and Join Us* and **Randy Matthews**' *Eyes to the Sky.*

Christian radio hits: "In the Garden" (# 20 in 1981).

Patti Roberts

1983—*Winter to Spring* (Word).

Patti Roberts may be best known as "the former wife of Richard Roberts," the son of TV evangelist Oral Roberts. Richard and Patti were often featured on the latter's programs and their divorce in 1979 hit the Roberts' empire hard. Patti subsequently published an autobiography that reflected negatively on the financial extravagances of the materialistic clan, while admitting to her own participation in what has been called "worldly evangelicalism." Patti, who had recorded inspirational records with her husband, released one album of contemporary Christian music in 1983, four years after the divorce. She later married John Thompson, who cowrote the song "El Shaddai" with **Michael Card.** *Winter to Spring* is typical adult contemporary fare, featuring **Russ Taff** on the title track. "The Bride of Christ" was written by Patti and showcases the quality of her voice to best advantage.

Christian radio hits: "The Bride of Christ" (# 25 in 1983).

David Robertson

1994—*Soul Embrace* (StarSong); 1996—*Someone Who Cares.*

Christian pop singer David Robertson was born in Pennsylvania and raised the son of a second-generation minister. He sang in early camp meetings and revivals for his church, then at the age of eighteen left for Los Angeles to become a music star. He reports that he spent five years in "a prodigal life" of drugs and carousing before two friends who had recently converted to Christ brought him to a Bible study led by Millie Andrzejewski, the mother of rock singer Pat Benatar. "She was on fire for God," Robertson told *CCM.* "She hit me with her best shot, so to speak, and the rest is history." Reconnected with his Christian roots, Robertson joined **The Imperials** for a year, contributing songs to their *Love's Still Changing Hearts* album. Then he released two solo records. *Soul Embrace* includes the hit "I Believe in Love" and a duet with **Dottie Rambo,** "One More Time." *Someone Who Cares* moves into **Steven Curtis Chapman** adult contemporary territory with songs directed to those within the church. On "Borrowed Faith," Robertson sings, "I know I should be standing on the rock of solid ground / instead of leaning on tradition that my heritage passed down." Even more poignant is "I'm for Jesus," in which he contrasts the positive affirmation of faith with being known for "all that I'm against."

Christian radio hits: "I Believe in Love" (# 5 in 1994).

Eddie Robinson

1974—*Reflections of the Man Inside* (Myrrh).

Detroit native Eddie Robinson made one album during the days of the Jesus movement that reflected the Motown sound with more integrity than any of the other Jesus music pioneers. Most Jesus music artists were white, perhaps because the genre of traditional gospel offered sufficient similarities to secular soul to make transformation of the style or creation of a distinct field less immediate for African Americans—the Jesus movement revival itself was also, by and large, a white phenomenon. Exceptions such as Soul Liberation and especially **Andraé Crouch and the Disciples** played music with a truly contemporary black sound, but did not draw fundamen-

tally from Motown. Robinson's *Reflections of the Man Inside* features a style similar to a more jazz-inflected, late '60s version of The Temptations. Expressive ballads sung in a cool, laid-back voice are the order of the day. Lyrically, the songs are mostly first-person accounts describing or giving thanks for how God has transformed the artist from within.

Rocketboy

Trey Bailey, voc., gtr.; Kip Bell, gtr., kybrd.; Slade Curtis, bass; Rob Jones, drums (–1997); one more // Tim Watts, drums (+ 1997). 1996—*No Sign of Intelligent Life* (R.E.X.); 1997—*Now That We Have Your Attention.*

Not to be confused with Blaster the Rocketboy (from Indianapolis), the Christian band from Atlanta, Georgia, called simply Rocketboy is a modern rock outfit that draws upon a wide variety of grunge, blues, and even folk influences. Originally called Cain's Pain, the group starts with a Smashing Pumpkins/Nirvana sound and develops it in ways representative of the melting pot of '90s rock and roll. In 1994, Trey Bailey told *Visions of Gray* that the group's philosophy was, "Life sucks, then you die and go to heaven." Rocketboy's first album, *No Sign of Intelligent Life,* established them as a cool garage band with neo-punk attitude, but *Now That We Have Your Attention* demonstrates more sophistication and puts them in the same league as groups like **Bleach,** Bush, and **Grammatrain.** Most of the songs are issue-oriented: "Cool" (with its repetitive refrain, "I'm so cool it hurts") is about alcoholism and denial. "Mother, May I" (with its eerie refrain "Momma wants to kill me"), is about abortion from the perspective of the fetus—a dumb idea when **Phil Keaggy** tried it ("The Survivor") that didn't improve with time (cf. **Sackcloth Fashion, Kathy Troccoli, Value Pac**). One line of the song especially doesn't seem to fit: "This isn't my song so I'm making up a line." As it turns out, the singer just sang that "made up line" because the song hadn't been finished and was missing a line. Such cavalier disregard for lyrics demonstrate the group's slacker ethos, which seems to appeal to its fans. "Disco Ball" has an appropriate '70s sound to it (though not really disco) supporting the lyric, "I'm spinning like a disco ball," which Bailey says is a metaphor for "basking in God's love." "Siren Song" is an uncharacteristic ballad that reflects on a longing for home in language reminiscent of the prodigal son parable. "Silver Love" has lyrics inspired by Proverbs 2:3–4. As a concluding, hidden track, the group performs the modern worship standard "Lord, I Lift Your Name on High."

Rock 'n' Roll Worship Circus

Gabriel Wilson, voc., gtr.; Melanie "Blurr" Wilson, voc., kybrd.; Zorn, drums; Chris, voc. (–2001) // Solo, voc., gtr. (+ 2001). 2000—*Little Star Logistics* (custom); 2001—*Big Star Logistics* (Sovereign).

Rock 'n' Roll Worship Circus was born of a union of several worship bands at a church in Longview, Washington. The group has a basic industrial pop sound that visits prominent classic rock influences (the Beatles, Led Zeppelin, The Rolling Stones, Pink Floyd) as though they were sideshow attractions. Most of the material on their debut album is indeed oriented toward modern worship. The opening track, "Ride," is a straight-out rock anthem encouraging believers with the message that they will be delivered out of this world soon. "Party Song" (about the wedding feast of the Lamb) and "Come On, Get Down" are similarly joyful celebrations. At other moments, the band adopts a more atmospheric sound with homage to Radiohead and **The Violet Burning.** "Space Angel" is appropriately spacey with high soaring guitars and breathy vocals. "I Will Wait" features female vocals by band leader Gabriel Wilson's wife, Blurr.

Woody Rock

2001—*Soul Music* (Gospel Centric).

Woody Rock is the stage name used by James Green, a founding member of the male R&B combo Dru Hill. The vocal group from Baltimore, Maryland, took its name from the local Druid Hill Park. They enjoyed several general market hits in the late '90s, including pop smashes "Tell Me" (# 18 in 1996), "In My Bed" (# 4 in 1997), and "Never Make a Promise" (# 7 in 1997), with far more hits on the R&B charts. They were especially noted for collaborations with other artists including Babyface ("We're Not Making Love No More," # 13 in 1997), Redman ("How Deep Is Your Love," # 3 in 1998), and Will Smith ("Wild, Wild West," # 1 in 1999). In March of 1999, Rock left the group to return to his gospel roots. *Soul Music* features a collaboration with B. B. Jay on the highly effective "Believer" and brings in such guests as **Gospel Gangstaz** and **Mary Mary** on other tracks. The music is similar to that of **Kirk Franklin,** drawing on both church and street influences.

.rodlaver

Chris Butler, bass; Ryan Fariss, gtr.; Rudy Nielsen, voc.; Joe Sidoti, drums (–2000) // Joey Marchiano, drums (+ 2000, –2001); Jason Martin, drums (+ 2001). 1996—*The Essence of the Game* (Screaming Giant); 2000—*Trying Not to Try;* 2001—*In a Perfect World* (BEC).

Rapcore band .rodlaver (pronounced "dot-rod-laver") was almost an overnight success in Christian music, coming up with a style that hit in just the right place at the right time. The group began with a style similar to general market superstars Korn and Limp Bizkit, which put them in the same general league as Christian acts like **P.O.D.** and **Project 86.** Lead singer Rudy Nielsen objects somewhat to such comparisons, indicating that the latter two bands have a harder sound than .rodlaver, who are "more hip-hop oriented and almost more funk-oriented, more dance, kind of groove stuff." He describes the band's sound as "hip-hop-aggro-rock." The band had been together for only three weeks when they recorded *The Essence of the Game,* which Nielsen would later say, "had about five good songs on it." On the song "E.I.," he raps, "To which one of your stereotypes do I fit in? / I bust phat lines, but I got white skin?" The second album was made with producer Steve Russell (who did **P.O.D.**'s *Warrior*) and showed what *HM* called "massive improvement," with a sound that remained hard and streetwise, but was more diverse and technically competent. *In a Perfect World* is the strongest effort to date, with the rapcore innuendoes gaining credence only here or there. "Janet" opens the album with a hard-hitting reminder to "Never forget where the days come from." On "Time Pieces" Nielsen tips his hat cheerfully to **Steve Taylor** and David Bowie while declaring his resistance to all the influences that would make him a clone: "It's a battle of the ages / We gonna fight these ch-ch-ch-changes." The group gets pretty interesting lyrically: "Doctor Zaius" exposes some NRA foolishness in a rant addressed directly to Charlton Heston; "436" is about an insecure woman who can't see her own beauty but thinks "airbrushed perfection is what men want most." The album closes with an acoustic and melodic love song ("To Karats").

The group has a strong commitment to ministry. "We're missionaries," says Nielsen. "The main reason we got together is so that we could go out on the road and preach the gospel." Again, he told *HM* in 2000, "Our mission statement would just be to try and be men of God when we play and when we go on stage . . . to try and show people that to be a Christian you don't have be a certain way, that the most important thing is the decision you make whether or not to have a relationship with Christ." The group's unusual name has no hidden spiritual meaning. The band members noticed early on that they were all wearing Rod Laver shoes (from Adidas), named after the Australian tennis pro, and they decided that if he could have a shoe named after him, why not a band? The "dot" part arose because Nielsen wanted the name spelled in lower case letters and couldn't find any way to make his computer program keep it in lower case except by putting a period in front of it.

Chris Rodriguez

1999—*Beggar's Paradise* (Word).

Nashville session singer Chris Rodriguez spent many years singing background vocals before finally deciding to step into the spotlight to make an album of his own. Rodriguez has sung on projects by **Steven Curtis Chapman, Amy Grant,** Billy Joel, Kenny Loggins, Michael McDonald, **Rich Mullins,**

Michael W. Smith, Shania Twain, **Jaci Velasquez,** Wynonna, and many others. He even won a Nashville Music Award for Best Background Vocalist. As a songwriter, he cowrote **Michael W. Smith**'s Christian radio hit "Help You Find Your Way." *Beggar's Paradise* was produced by **Brent Bourgeois** and is notable for its nonformulaic approach to pop music. *7ball* would say that Rodriguez' two main influences appear to be the Beatles and Jimi Hendrix, though these and other mentors are all filtered through what *CCM* calls his "commitment not to paint by the numbers." The Hendrix reference becomes most clear on the song "Your Love," a powerful testimony to grace that features some fired-up guitar fuzz. "Saved" (an original composition, not the **Bob Dylan** song) is infectious and upbeat, expressing well the joy of salvation. "I'll Stay There" professes love and commitment to a tune that betrays Eastern influence. "Magdalena" offers testimony to the resurrection and "Retreat" is a sensitive, confessional song expressing a desire for reconciliation. In interviews, Rodriguez often gave thanks to God for whatever gifts he may possess and especially thanked God for restoring a marriage that he thought was over: "We really were at each other's necks four years ago— we're best friends now!"

Michael Roe (and **Safe as Milk**)

By Michael Roe: 1995—*Safe as Milk* (Via); 1996—*The Boat Ashore* (Innocent Media); 2000—*It's for You* (Fools of the World). By Michael Roe and Safe as Milk: 1999—*Live at Cornerstone '97.*

Michael Roe is one of the most revered "geniuses" of the Christian music scene. He is best known as the front man for the **Seventy Sevens**—a group that many critics regard as one of the best, if not *the* best, Christian rock band of all time. He has also been a member of the on-again-off-again "supergroup" called the **Lost Dogs,** though his participation in that band has always seemed about as natural as Neil Young's commitment to Crosby, Stills, Nash and Young. Roe never appeared to be invested in the Dogs; while the other three gelled as a group, he always seemed like a celebrity guest, adding some impressive background noise in return for the opportunity to do a couple of his own songs. Still, judging from audience reaction (and shouts of "Mike Roe rules!") when he did those songs, a goodly number of **Lost Dogs** concert-goers were there primarily for him. In addition to his impressive résumé with the other groups, Roe has made two stellar solo albums and released a couple of recordings of his solo tours. Some critics also regard a 1990 project by a group called **7 and 7 Is** as a Michael Roe solo album, but the bulk of its material consists of live tracks and outtakes from the **Seventy Sevens,** so we have listed it with them. Roe has also played on projects by Mercy River, **Dead Artist Syndrome, Love Coma, Riki Michele, Charlie Pea-**

cock, Perry and the Poor Boys, **Steve Scott, Randy Stonehill,** and **The Swirling Eddies.**

Roe's two solo albums are most remarkable in that they sound practically nothing like his work with the **Seventy Sevens** or the **Lost Dogs.** While the former group is most often compared to the Rolling Stones (and Led Zeppelin) and the latter has an Americana country sound like The Band, the closest general market analogy for Roe's solo work would be Paul Simon. The sound is nowhere near as rocking as his other work, but it is eclectic, moody, atmospheric, and most of all, melodic. The songs are soft but not mellow; they are, for the most part, infectious pop masterpieces that defy all formulas, become memorable after just a few listens and increasingly likable with long-term acquaintance. *Safe As Milk* was issued in two different versions due to record company stupidity. Apparently industry honchos thought three of the songs might be offensive to the gnostic-influenced Christians who constitute a generous portion of the contemporary Christian music subculture (though, perhaps, a much smaller portion of those who would be inclined toward buying a Michael Roe album). The first of these, "It's for You," uses some rather crass imagery to describe the life and perspective of the self-obsessed pleasure seeker ("You shot your wad, when you named yourself God / But your nickname is 'Chump'/ Blowin' chunks out your mouth, wisdom out your rump"). "It's for You" isn't a very good song anyway, and its deletion, though the censorship was ridiculous, actually improves *Safe As Milk* musically. The opposite is true of "Sneakers" and "The Stellazine Prophecy," which are among the album's strongest tracks and its only two rockers. It is difficult to figure out what was objectionable in the first of these, except that it seems to be devoted to expressing interest in a person of the opposite sex and uses some cute-but-obscure double entendres (comparing a girl to a car) in a way that satirizes '50s tunes. Notably, the song was actually an outtake from the **Seventy Sevens**' *Drowning with Land in Sight* album, from which it also had been censored. "The Stellazine Prophecy" compares a girl named Stella to a drug (as in Huey Lewis's "I Want a New Drug") and has a muffled line in which Roe mumbles, "she's one hell of a . . . (something inaudible)." For those able to tolerate such infractions, it is a great, innovative rock song that puts a low, growling vocal underneath a hip-hop, yelping beat to create an effect never heard before in popular music (though Roe would use a similar technique for a track called "Earache" on the **Seventy Sevens**' *Tom Tom Blues* also released in 1995). Reveling in his image as a rebel, Roe seemed to tweak the uptight (and oft upturned) noses of the contemporary Christian music industry by asking for censorship on *Safe As Milk* in other ways as well. In between tracks, he can be heard singing **Bob Dylan**'s lustful ode, "Tonight I'll Be Staying Here with You" at one point and, at another, singing some line with bleeped profanity ("when the *beep* hits the fan") and cursing when he discovers his guitar is out of tune. Nevertheless, *Safe As Milk* without "Sneakers" or "The Stellazine Prophecy" is a tame record—one that is still good, but that has been shorn of exciting and brilliant moments (think *Bridge over Troubled Water* without "Cecilia"). Beyond that, the nine-song version of *Safe As Milk* (which Roe took to calling the "uncurdled version") loses the incarnational earthy-yet-spiritual feel of the intended product. With all earthiness removed, its undeniably wonderful spiritual tracks have no feet of clay and tend to just float away as heavenly meditations detached from life in a world where people do curse and lust and fall in love. That is the brilliance of the twelve-song, curdled version of *Safe As Milk*—we hear an artist whose spirit is not only willing but whose flesh is also weak. Recognition of the latter strengthens the impact of the former.

That said, the nine songs available on any edition of *Safe As Milk* can stand on their own as either beautiful hymns or atmospheric pop songs. "I Want Never Gets" and "Smile" fall in the latter category—the former mixing Grateful Dead guitar work with some slow hip-hop stylings, and the latter sounding like a Brian Wilson outtake. "Holy Day" is a very pretty song of devotion, probably to God, aurally reminiscent of Bryan Ferry's work. "Hold Dearly to Me" and the funny-tragic "Go with God But Go" are Dylanesque folk tunes. "I Need God" is a very churchy song that could be performed as an anthem at any Presbyterian church in America (minus, in some congregations, the gospel piano noodling). "You Leave Me Homeless" is almost *too* pretty, a gorgeous ballad sung in the same sort of jazz-lounge singer style that George Michael used for "Kissing a Fool." The song "Till Jesu Comes" is a soft paean of longing for the day when the Lord returns. Roe adds a touch of class to the latter tune by using the Savior's Latin name Jesu (pronounced *yay-sou*): "I cannot wait till Jesu comes / I cannot wait." But Roe saves the best till last and closes the album with "Ache Beautiful," one of his loveliest songs ever. The imagery of the lyric expresses both the pain and pleasure of the longing expressed in "Till Jesu Comes," the longing that marks every day of life in an-already-beautiful but not-yet-perfect world. Roe sings of that longing in a voice as expressive as the song's title, a voice that aches in a strangely beautiful way.

The next solo album was titled *The Boat Ashore* in a clever but terrible pun on the artist's name (Michael Roe *The Boat Ashore*, get it?). Roe seemed to have relaxed or matured beyond the point of messing with establishment minds. The album was also noticeably affected by the break-up of his marriage, which had ended in divorce. Musically, the Paul Simon analogy mentioned above comes into play even more than on *Safe As Milk*, as Roe experiments with a variety of folk- and blues-based styles. Liner notes identify Roe's band as **7 and 7 Is,** but

the makeup of that so-called group is completely different from the band officially responsible for 1990's *More Miserable Than You'll Ever Be*. This time, **7 and 7 Is** includes Roe, plus the **Seventy Sevens**' Mark Harmon and Bruce Spencer on bass and drums. In any case, *The Boat Ashore* offers a collection of especially poignant and introspective songs, mostly reflecting on the difficulties of human relationships. The title track is apparently sung to God with renewed appreciation for divine faithfulness that sustains *that* relationship in spite of human failing: "I do believe that you truly love me," Roe sings, "but how do I reciprocate when there's nothing good in me?" The next track, "Honey Run," is especially Simon-ish, featuring a lilting vocal on a classic Roe melody. "Love Like Gold" is the album's high point, a country-folk song that strongly recalls Gordon Lightfoot and gets to the heart of what seems to be the album's central theme: "I really want to know what it feels like to have and hold / A precious love, a love like gold / I really want to know what it feels like / The real thing, a love like gold." This chorus is sung against verses in which Roe lays bares his disillusionment with the world and disappointment in himself, brought on apparently by the failure of his marriage ("I never should have made you my reason to live / Cause it killed me, baby, when you walked out the door . . . I thought our love was higher than high / Till we crashed and burned . . . we fell so hard"). Other standouts include "Some Kind of a Dream" and "I Buried My Heart at Bended Knee," which reference the styles of such early '70s artists as Crosby, Stills and Nash and the Grateful Dead. As a bonus, a hidden track called "Tall Trees" takes off in a completely different direction than the rest of the album, invoking the **Seventy Sevens**' Stones-inspired sound; it is, by no coincidence, track number seventy-seven.

Roe likes to play with confusing labels and, so, his 1997 live album was recorded with a band called Safe As Milk—although the album itself was mostly live versions of songs from *The Boat Ashore* with "Stellazine Prophecy" and "I Want Never Gets" added at the end along with the **Seventy Sevens**' "Flowers in the Sand." The group Safe As Milk is essentially the same band that Roe called **7 and 7 Is** on *The Boat Ashore* with a few extras (Caroline Avery, perc.; Michael Gregory, gtr.; Scott Reams, kybrd., perc.). More interesting is the two-disc set *It's for You*, which features songs from an all-request concert including songs from his solo work and **Seventy Sevens** career (but nothing from the **Lost Dogs**—he maintained he was "treated so shamefully" by the other Dogs on their tour that he just couldn't do any of those songs). Most intriguing are a motley assortment of covers, including songs by **Johnny Cash, Barry McGuire,** Roger Miller, Charlie Chaplin, and Leadbelly.

Like **Michael Knott** and a few others, Roe remains in the **Larry Norman** tradition of being viewed primarily as a contemporary Christian music artist even though he doesn't often meet the increasingly defined expectations of the subculture for which that music is targeted. Indeed, Roe can be quite critical of the whole Christian music scene, referring to it in one interview as "fat Elvis in Vegas, ready to die." He maintains that he views his own work as "pop music" in the general sense, regretting that it gets labeled "Christian" and gets set aside for the Christian market merely because he is a Christian and allows his faith inevitably to come through. He claims that he does not write or sing for the Christian marketplace, even if that is where his work ends up: "I don't worry about what *CCM* is going to think or what Word Records is going to think, or even what my fans are going to think, because that tends to corrupt the work." Still, he recognizes the pragmatic reality of his situation: "I make my bread and butter off the fringe of Christian music, like an outcast who's sent to live on the perimeter. . . . You end up developing a unique following for your unique situation—you carve out your own path and draw people who like what you do."

Kenny Rogers

Selected: 1996—*The Gift* (Word Nashville); 1997—*Across My Heart*.

www.kennyrogers.net

Country music superstar (and senior heartthrob) Kenny Rogers has never strayed too far from his Christian upbringing, but he did not officially enter the contemporary Christian music scene until the late '90s. Born in Houston, Texas, in 1938, Rogers got an early start in popular music by playing with a high school group called The Scholars, which had some regional hits. While attending the University of Houston, he sang lead for the Bobby Doyle Trio, and after graduating he joined the New Christy Minstrels (cf. **Barry McGuire**) for their last year together as a group. He formed the First Edition with a few other ex-Minstrels and enjoyed a string of Top 40 pop hits beginning with the atypical "Just Dropped In (To See What Condition My Condition Was In)" (# 5 in 1968), a psychedelic drug song about glue sniffing. Six more big hits and a handful of little ones would follow, including the maudlin "Ruby, Don't Take Your Love to Town" (# 6 in 1969), which was written by Mel Tillis, "Something's Burning" (# 11 in 1970), which was written by Mac Davis, and the Kingston Trio cover "Ruben James" (# 26 in 1969). The songs "Tell It All, Brother" (# 17 in 1970) and "Heed the Call" (# 33 in 1970) were "message songs" with semireligious themes (confession is good for the soul; love one another). From 1971 to 1973, The First Edition had a syndicated TV show, *Rollin' on the River,* although their time in the pop charts was clearly over by then.

In 1976, Rogers staged a major comeback by crossing over to country music. He became one of the most successful country western singers in history, selling over eighty million albums, while remaining one of a handful of country stars (cf. Garth Brooks, **Johnny Cash,** John Denver, **Glen Campbell**) to maintain a consistent presence on the pop charts. Between 1976 and 1983, Rogers would have another seventeen Top 40 hits on *Billboard*'s mainstream pop charts, in addition to charting many more songs that were big hits on country stations. Among his most successful pop songs were the adult contemporary ballads "She Believes in Me" (# 5 in 1979), "You Decorated My Life" (# 7 in 1979), "Through the Years" (# 13 in 1981), and an especially memorable version of Lionel Richie's "Lady" (# 1 for 6 weeks in 1980). Rogers would also make several contributions to the vocal duet craze that Neil Diamond and Barbra Streisand had started in 1978 with "You Don't Bring Me Flowers." Rogers first sang "Don't Fall in Love with a Dreamer" (# 4 in 1980) with Kim Carnes. Then he recorded Bob Seger's "We've Got Tonight" (# 6 in 1983) with Sheena Easton and the Bee Gees' "Islands in the Stream" (# 1 for 2 weeks in 1983) with Dolly Parton. Still, his most memorable songs may be some of the dopier, country ballads: "Lucille" (# 5 in 1977) offers a man's pleas to his wayward wife to reconsider her commitment to hearth and home; "The Gambler" (# 16 in 1978) presents a poker player's metaphorical advice for living ("you gotta know when to hold 'em, know when to fold 'em, know when to walk away, and know when to run"); "Coward of the County" (# 3 in 1979) glorifies a mass murderer whose vigilante actions prove he wasn't such a wimp after all. The latter tune would top many people's lists as the most anti-Christian song ever to hit the airwaves, but aside from a few other questionable choices ("We've Got Tonight" is an ode to one-night stands), Rogers was generally viewed as a family-oriented entertainer. While he is not himself a songwriter, he has usually chosen material that emphasizes love, commitment, integrity, and positive values. His songs sometimes reflected positively on religion and he occasionally incorporated gospel material into his performances. The most obvious example of this would be his rendition of the hymn "Love Lifted Me," which became a major hit on country stations and served as the title track for his first solo album (*Love Lifted Me,* United Artists, 1974).

Rogers would fade from the pop scene in the mid '80s, but he continued to have numerous hits on the country charts, including the Number One songs "Crazy," "Real Love" (with Dolly Parton), "Morning Desire," and "Tomb of the Unknown Soldier." By 1990, however, he had become an American institution, having branched out into a number of enterprises. A relatively successful acting career saw him starring in the feature film *Six Pack* (1982) and several made-for-TV movies (including *The Gambler* and *Coward of the County,* based on the hit songs). He hosted over a dozen music-variety TV specials and a dozen more documentaries on the Old West for the Arts and

Entertainment network. He published two books of photography (*Kenny Rogers' America,* 1986; *Kenny Rogers: Your Friends and Mine,* 1987). He also opened a fast-food franchise featuring rotisserie chicken. In addition to such widespread accomplishments, Rogers became rather famously regarded as one of the most handsome men in America, whose looks only seemed to improve with age. Rogers returned to the general market in 1999 with the album *She Rides Wild Horses* and scored a Number One country and western hit with the song "Buy Me a Rose."

Rogers had already made three Christmas albums prior to 1996's *The Gift,* but the latter album was recorded for Word, a prominent Christian music label that guaranteed primary marketing to the contemporary Christian music community. Thus, the record introduced Rogers to that subculture as an officially Christian artist and it was followed quickly by *Across My Heart,* a collection of nonholiday songs also on Word. Rogers did not have the sort of repentance or conversion testimony that sometimes accompanies such crossovers. For him, the move to Christian music seemed to be a natural development. Many fans of contemporary Christian country music had appreciated Rogers' material all along and, so, *Across My Heart* may have seemed to them to be a Christian music "debut" in industry terms only. The main difference was that one could buy it in a Christian bookstore. In terms of content, *Across My Heart* features more family values songs than outright religious tracks, with an emphasis on adult contemporary love songs. Standout songs include John Hiatt's "Have a Little Faith in Me" and Randy Van Warmer's "Write Your Name (Across My Heart)." There are, however, a few songs of explicit spiritual devotion. "Find a Little Grace" tells the tale of a prodigal who realizes his need for help and mercy. "See Me Through" is a proclamation of faith in God similar in theme to **Andraé Crouch**'s "Through It All." **The Katinas** add vocal support on the album, in addition to general market artists Kim Carnes, Michael McDonald, and All-4-One.

For trivia buffs: Rogers served as a presenter at the 1998 Dove Awards ceremony. In one of that show's few genuinely funny and human moments, copresenter **Geoff Moore** stood next to him, beaming, and said into the camera, "Man, my mom is diggin' this right now!"

Grammy Awards: 1977 Best Country Vocal Performance, Male ("Lucille"); 1979 Best Country Vocal Performance, Male ("The Gambler"); 1987 Best Country Vocal Performance, Duet [with Ronnie Milsap] ("Make No Mistake, She's Mine").

Mike and Von Rogers

1981—*Child of the Father* (Covenant); 1983—*Here's Hoping.*

Very little information is available about the husband and wife duo Mike and Von Rogers, who made two albums for the small Covenant label in the early '80s. Mike Rogers was an especially gifted guitarist who would play different instruments to bring diverse textures to the various songs; for instance, on *Here's Hoping* he uses five different acoustic guitars to create a variety of sounds. Von had a powerful alto voice and traded vocal leads with her husband. *CCM* compared their harmonic mellow style to that of country band Alabama.

Scott Roley (and City Limits)

By City Limits: 1981—*City Limits* (Spirit). By Scott Roley: 1984—*Within My Reach* (Refuge); 1986—*Brother to Brother.*

Christian pop singer Scott Roley was a member of the early Jesus music group **Aslan** (the one that recorded for Airborne, not Maranatha) and then formed the duo **Albrecht and Roley,** which turned into **Albrecht, Roley, and Moore.** After those adventures, he made an album with a group of session musicians called City Limits (including John Rosasco on keyboards and **Joe English** on drums) and embarked on an unusual tour under that name. Basically, Roley would assemble a new version of City Limits in every location, recruiting local musicians in advance and arriving ahead of his concert schedule to practice with them and build them into a band. Roley also recorded two more adult contemporary albums of original songs. Musically, his sound was congruent with the light rock style of late '70s artists like England Dan and John Ford Coley or Seals and Crofts. Roley dubbed the sound "suburban pop" and listed the key elements as "sweet tunes, light piano, warm horns, strong beat, and lots of echo."

Christian radio hits: As City Limits: "Sacrificing Love" (# 5 in 1981).

Judy Romero

1975—*Judy! Judy! Judy!* (Lamb and Lion).

Little information is available about Judy Romero, who recorded one album that *Harmony* magazine described as "white disco" music in the latter days of the Jesus movement. Romero was blind and was especially noted for her piano playing, though keyboards skills were featured more prominently in concerts than on her one recording. She also served as lead singer for a group called The Latinos.

Room Full of Walters

Alan Austin, drums; Kurt Starks, bass; Mark Scheltgen, gtr.; Jamie Woodson, voc. Selected: 1997—*Sleepyhead* (Word); 1999—*El Grande.*

www.roomfullofwalters.com

A modern rock band from Wichita, Kansas, Room Full of Walters has an interesting origin. The group did not begin as a Christian band and, by some accounts, none of the members was a Christian (or at least very excited about his faith) in the first five or six years that they played together as a highly successful regional act. The Walters actually recorded three independent albums at this time (1991—*Wonderful;* 1993—*Swivel;* 1995—*Legend of Room Full of Walters*). Then, while the group was on a break, all four members experienced some sort of spiritual transformation (*HM* says "they all got saved"; Woodson simply remarks, "it was a time when we all started growing spiritually"). At any rate, when the group got back together to record their fourth album, they discovered a common commitment that came to expression lyrically in their songs. Woodson says that there was no conscious decision to make "a Christian record"; rather, "something that important is going to start showing up in things that you do and create. . . . when you become a Christian, it starts to invade all parts of your life. . . . I don't think we realized that we had 'a Christian record' until we sat down and heard all the songs." The group signed with Word, and the new album, *Sleepyhead,* was marketed to the Christian market, while the band continued to play bars and clubs in the Wichita area, blending the new songs in with older material and covers of such mainstream hits as Stevie Wonder's "Sir Duke," Cheap Trick's "Surrender," and—a favorite—the theme song from *The Jeffersons* ("Movin' On Up"). They sometimes experienced rejection from old-time fans who did not appreciate the new orientation; at an outdoor concert that they headlined for the local alternative rock station, fans threw mud at them when they performed "religious songs."

Room Full of Walters describes their sound as "very heavy pop music." They have a sound similar in some respects to such '80s acts as Cheap Trick and The Cars, with more up-to-date similarities to quirky '90s acts like Weezer. Numerous reviewers notice what seems to be the strong influence of composer Elvis Costello. *Sleepyhead* attracted widespread attention for one of its standout tracks, "Jeffrey Dahmer Went to Heaven," which merely states the basic Christian doctrine that divine forgiveness is offered all who repent. It uses the hypothetical (possibly, actual) repentance of the famed mass murderer as an example. The song was regarded as "shocking" by some non-Christians and as "offensive" by a handful of Christian bookstore owners who had apparently missed Sunday school the day that doctrine was addressed. The opening song on *Sleepyhead* is "Home," a powerful, catchy tune that expresses the feeling of getting back on track after having taken various detours in life. "Pete's a Rocket Scientist" is about a kid who is viewed as "a geek" or an outsider for his interest in science and fantasies about space travel. The story line of the latter tune is picked up in a sequel on *El Grande* called "Pete's a Rocket Star." The "Jeffrey Dahmer"-like cut on the latter album, however, would be "Amy They Tell Me," a song about a true-life news story in which a convenience store clerk was murdered by a man who—as it turned out—she had recently

added to her "prayer list" at the request of a mutual friend. Musically, the highlight of *El Grande* is "Snowfort," a fun pop song that evokes musical images of Joe Jackson ("On Your Radio") and Queen ("Bicycle Race"). A song called "Visiting Matthew" is about the Gospel by that name, which Scheltgen says he has come to regard as an old friend.

Randy Rose (and Rose)

Steve Kumada, gtr.; Mark Link, bass; Randy Rose, voc., gtr.; Ben Jacobs, gtr. (– 1995); Don Richart, drums (– 1994) // Stan Lessering, drums (+ 1994, – 1995); Danny Rose, voc. (+ 1994, – 1995). By Randy Rose: 1991—*Sacrificium* (Intense). By Rose: 1993—*Healing; Intense Live Series, Vol. 3* [EP]; 1994—*Crazy Little World;* 1995—*Into the Unknown* (R.E.X.).

Randy Rose is best known as the front man for the Christian group **Mad at the World.** At the same time that he participated in that pop-oriented rock band, however, he recorded a number of side projects that he issued under the name Rose. Officially a solo project, *Sacrificium* is an excursion in heavy metal that even *HM* magazine did not find too impressive, dismissing it as "a clone of Danzig." Subsequent albums were issued by "Rose" as a full band. *Healing* displays refinement of style into a screaming extravaganza reminiscent of early Black Sabbath. Now *HM* took note, calling it "a full-on blitzkrieg assault that hard rockin' metalheads will drool over." The title track and "Seeds of Sorrow" are ominous standouts. Unfortunately, the song "Demons" passes on some unscriptural misconceptions about demon possession: "You let me in with your sin / And I will stay 'till you drive me away" (the Bible never links demonic possession to sin, and no demon-possessed person is ever presented as being able—much less willing—to drive the foul spirits away). A live EP released in the Intense series at about the same time as *Healing* includes a cover of the traditional song "You've Got to Move" (also done by the Rolling Stones). For *Crazy Little World,* Rose eschews the metal approach to present an album of psychedelic, Lenny Kravitz-like songs similar to those on **Mad at the World**'s *Dreamland Café.* Beatles influences can be heard throughout, especially on "Life Passes By" (which replicates guitar lines from "While My Guitar Gently Weeps") and "Crying" (which is so similar to "Rain," that *True Tunes* opined, "Paul deserves some royalties"). *Into the Unknown* seems to take Rose back into the metal fold again, but the album had actually been recorded before *Crazy Little World* and held up for release because, as Randy put it, "the big wigs didn't think it was pop enough." He further describes *Into the Unknown* as having "a very heavy '70s acid sound to it . . . the loudest thing I've ever done." The title song is an antisuicide anthem. Randy Rose went on to found a group called Mothership, which also included his brother Danny and developed a space-synth sound similar to the more somber elements of Depeche Mode. Mothership released an independent album called *LP* on Plastiq Musiq in 1998.

Rose Blossom Punch

Nick Barber, bass; Terry Coggins, gtr.; Paul Mumaw, drums; Aaron Sprinkle, voc., gtr. 1997—*Ephemere* (SaraBellum); 1999—*Sorry to Disappoint You* [EP].

Rose Blossom Punch arose out of the ashes of Christian alternative fave band **Poor Old Lu,** of which Aaron Sprinkle and Nick Barber were both members. Guitarist Coggins formerly played with **Soulfood 76.** The group did not actually intend to be a band, but was assembled for an Aaron Sprinkle solo album and came together sufficiently to identify themselves as a group for a short time. Their only album was well-titled *Ephemere,* which is French for "short-lived"; they would follow it with a swan song EP that was billed as an apology to fans who had thought the band might prove to have more staying power than it did. Rose Blossom Punch's sound is similar enough to that of **Poor Old Lu** to please fans of the former group, with the most noticeable difference being Sprinkle's lead vocals. Less gruff than Lu singer Scott Hunter, his voice gives the songs a more melodic, Posie-like quality. The album's opening track, "Cyclone Fence," is one of its strongest cuts, with acoustic guitars strummed on top of waves of electric distortion. "A Step into the Dark" sounds enough like Matthew Sweet to have listeners double-checking the liner notes. Elsewhere, the album samples a variety of alternative styles, from trippy to hypnotic to overpowering. Rose Blossom Punch's songs are filled with captivating hooks, dreamy melodies, and driving rhythms, and the group was unanimously praised as one of Christian music's best alternative acts, following in the tradition of Lu and **PFR.** Sprinkle describes the theme of *Ephemere* as being "how hard it is to be a human being, and how much we need God." Many songs deal with pain and frustration, with an edge that defies the pretty packaging; lyrics are often poetic in a way that renders any intended meaning obscure.

Nedra Ross

1978—*Full Circle* (NewSong).

Nedra Ross (née Talley) was born in 1946 in New York City and at the age of fifteen became one of the founding members of The Ronettes, along with her cousins Veronica Bennett and Estelle Bennett (sisters). The Ronettes became producer Phil Spector's proudest discovery, though he reportedly only signed the entire group because Veronica—with whom he was in love—refused to sign as a soloist. The group developed a classic look, consisting of tight dresses, dark eye makeup, and tall, black beehive hairdos that helped to establish them as a classic mid-'60s "girl group." *The New Rolling Stone Encyclopedia of Rock and Roll* calls them "the first bad girls of rock," not for any particular off-stage behavior, but rather for a deliberately sultry image antithetical to the wholesome Supremes or Shirelles. The group had several minor hits with various Spector compositions and one colossal smash with his "Be My Baby" (# 2 in 1963). Although it was kept out of the Number One spot for three straight weeks by The Angels' "My Boyfriend's Back," the song "Be My Baby" would remain one of the rock era's most recognizable songs nearly four decades later. More successful at selling concert tickets than records, The Ronettes toured incessantly as Spector's top act; indeed, they had the distinction of touring England as the opening act for The Rolling Stones, and America as the opening act for the Beatles. Spector actually replaced Veronica with a look-alike on the latter tour because, still in love with her, he was afraid she might fall for one of the charismatic Liverpudlians. The thought was not entirely paranoid, as Nedra began dating Ringo Starr. By 1966, the Ronettes were spent as a group and began to come apart. Estelle married a well-known producer named Teddy Vann. Veronica finally did marry Spector, only to reemerge years later as a divorced and liberated solo artist named Ronnie Spector; she had a hit duet with Eddie Money in 1986 ("Take Me Home Tonight," for which the chorus is identical to the tune of "Be My Baby") and wrote a tell-all biography, *Be My Baby,* that same year, claiming that her insanely jealous husband had kept her a prisoner for ten years in their Los Angeles mansion.

Nedra, meanwhile, married Scott Ross, who would turn out to be one of the most influential persons in the early development of Jesus music. Scott was an influential DJ in the New York City area and the two of them had known each other since Nedra was sixteen. They had an off-again, on-again relationship for some years, troubled in part by Scott's problems with drugs. In 1966, while visiting relatives, the two of them attended a small country church in Maryland where, according to Nedra, they "committed their lives to Jesus Christ." The Ronettes disbanded about a month later. After Nedra and Scott were wed, they felt led to abandon their lucrative careers and move to rural Maryland, where they could "learn about Jesus from the old country preacher who had led them to him." Scott took a job working at a country radio station. Eventually, he was tapped by Pat Robertson to join the staff of the fledgling Christian Broadcasting Network. With Robertson's support, he pioneered a syndicated radio show (first called The Joyful Noise, then The Scott Ross Show) which was one of the major forums that first put Christian rock music on the air. In 1967, Scott and Nedra helped to establish Love Inn, a Christian community of about 300 participants in upstate New York. **Phil Keaggy** was an early member of this community; Lynn

Nichols (of **Dust, Chagall Guevara,** and **Passafist**) was raised at Love Inn with the Rosses as his legal guardians. In 1976, Scott and Nedra coauthored the book *Scott Free* (Word), providing their autobiographies and Christian testimonies up to that point.

After leaving the Ronettes, Nedra Ross said she felt her calling was "to be a wife and a mother," not an entertainer. She basically retired from professional music, but did contribute vocals to a 1978 album by Ted Sandquist called *The Courts of the Kings* (NewSong). Then in 1978 she recorded *Full Circle,* an album of Sandquist and Keaggy songs, with one contribution from **Keith Green** ("I Don't Want to Fall Away from You"). Keaggy plays on the album, giving it strong guitar underpinnings. The title track is the album's strongest cut, being one of Keaggy's best pop songs, and one that he himself had not yet recorded. Other Keaggy contributions include "Gonna Keep My Mind (Stayed on You)" and the little-known "Sunrise to Sunset" and "Unchangin' Love for You" (written with Bernadette Keaggy).

Christian radio hits: "Full Circle" (# 8 in 1979).

Jamie Rowe

See **Guardian.**

Royal

Oystein Aase, bass; Tommy Åkerholdt, drums; Remi Christiansen, gtr.; Emil Nikolaisen, gtr., voc.; Elvira Nikolaisen, voc. 1998—*My Dear* (Tooth and Nail).

www.soulscape.com/royal

Royal is a Norwegian quintet that, according to front man Emil Nikolaisen, attempts to blend "noise rock" with elements of jazz and bossa nova. This seems to work best when dollops of the latter two seasonings are applied most generously—as on a lovely track called "M Rke Natt" (sung in Norwegian) and on the intriguing "Seven Days." Otherwise Emil's idea of noise rock seems to favor "noise" over "rock," producing some rather inaccessible stuff here and there. Notably, he has also played with the death metal band Extol, and this influence shows on tracks like "Please," which consists of nothing but some loud pounding punctuated by occasional unintelligible screams. Sister Elvira adds pleasant female vocals to most tracks, which serve to hold them together against all tendencies to fall apart. "Treasure" begins with thirty annoying seconds of a loud metronome ticking, then transforms into a classy Bjork-style pop song. In 2000, Emil told *Bandoppler* that the band had changed its name to The Royal Orkhestra and was planning another release. Emil has also played with his brother Ivar Nikolaisen in what they describe as "a pure punk band" called Silver.

Ruby Joe

Joe Baugh, gtr.; Christina Hock, drums; Amber Reeves, bass; Greg Russinger, voc., gtr. 1997—*Sinking the Eight Ball* (SubLime); 1999—*Hot Rod Deluxe.*

Ruby Joe is a Christian "psychobilly" band from Ventura, California, where front man Greg Russinger serves as youth pastor of the Horizon Foursquare Church. The band sports an all-female rhythm section and a hip "Stray Cats" look, though the closest general market references would be the Rev. Horton Heat and Social Distortion. The group combines basic '50s rockabilly with elements of punk and adds hard rock guitars for a sound that *CCM* described as sounding like a "Stray Cats record played a little faster than intended." *Sinking the Eight Ball* filled a niche in Christian music with songs that vary from fun to serious to theological. Representative of the first sort would be the party songs that celebrate Cadillacs, rock and roll, and "my baby." The serious songs include tracks that address such issues as racism ("Skin"), the enduring horror of the Holocaust ("Death Train"), and the continuing persecution of Christians in China ("Underground People"). Finally, Ruby Joe offers some theological commentary with "Spiritual Heroin," a song that likens the quick-fix promises that attend some presentations of Christ to the allure of drugs. "Fat Cat" takes over a favorite rockabilly term and applies it to the devil, the big pussy described in 1 Peter 5:8. **Michael Knott** coproduced *Sinking the Eight Ball* and critics with good memories noticed some similarities to the sound of **LSU**'s *Shaded Pain.* The sophomore project, *Hot Rod Deluxe,* continues in the same vein, with a bit more influence of "swing" à la **The W's.** The standout tracks include a cool, Ventures-like instrumental ("Self-Righteous Stomp") and the awesome "Oh My Soul," which is propelled by Jerry Lee Lewis killer piano. "Loaded Gun" is straight "Stray Cat Strut" fare, and "Little Angel" slows things down for a tender moment that allows Russinger to reflect on the birth of his first daughter. With a few obscure exceptions ("Flames"), the songs on *Hot Rod* feature lyrics with direct and fairly obvious religious intent.

David Ruis

1992—*True Love* (Vineyard); 1993—*Let the Winds Blow*; 1995—*Break Dividing Walls*; 1997—*Sweet Mercies.*

David Ruis is known primarily as a worship leader in a denomination known as the Vineyard. After a brief stint as pastor at Metro Vineyard in Kansas City, Missouri, he became head pastor of the Winnipeg Centre Vineyard church in Manitoba, Canada. This inner-city congregation identifies its particular call as "to be a safe place for the artist, the poor, the youth generation, and the aboriginal people, within the context of the local church." Ruis also serves as Regional Overseer for the

Vineyard in Canada and he travels widely as a speaker and worship leader. His songs have been featured on numerous worship albums published by Vineyard music, in addition to the solo records listed above. Some of his more popular worship songs include "We Will Dance," "Let Your Glory Fall," "Break Dividing Walls," and "Release Me." *True Love* is a recording of a live worship service. *Sweet Mercies* was identified by *CCM* as reaching out beyond the church service setting with broader appeal for Christian music fans in general. On this project, Ruis minimizes harmonies and sings in a solo voice reminiscent of Sting. His songs are driven by moody, electric guitars and offer both pleas and thanksgivings for the mercies of God referenced in the album's title. "Whom Have I But You?" stands alone as a stark worship song in the midst of these more passionate yearnings.

Run-D.M.C.

Darryl McDaniels, voc.; Joseph Simmons, voc. Selected: 1993—*Down with the King* (Profile).

The rap duo Run-D.M.C. has legendary stature in rap music comparable to that of the Beatles in pop or rock and roll. *Rolling Stone* maintains that "Run D.M.C. invented rap as we know it." The group formed in 1981 in Hollis, a middle class suburb of Queens, New York, when Joseph Simmons (b. 1964) and Darryl McDaniels (b. 1964) joined with Jason Mizell (a.k.a. Jam Master Jay), who would provide turntable scratching and programming behind their rap vocals. They were no doubt assisted by the fact that Simmons' brother Russell was already a figure of note in the music business—he was head of Rush Productions and would later cofound the most important of all rap labels, Def Jam, with Rick Rubin. The duo's name was a simple combination of their stage monikers: Simmons was known as "Run" and McDaniels as "D.M.C." In 1983, they released a single, "It's Like That," which is now generally considered to be the first song to establish rap as a commercially viable art form—the *Rolling Stone Album Guide* calls it "the first taste of rap's hardcore to make it to vinyl." Basically the duo took the break-dancing, hip-hop style of street performers and transformed it into a style that had more in common with rock than its predecessor. Their first two albums (*Run-D.M.C.*, Profile, 1984; *King of Rock*, Profile, 1985) produced a string of hit singles in the R&B market, but the huge break came with a 1986 release bearing the rather un-Christian title *Raising Hell*. In what *Rolling Stone* would dub "the cleverest marketing scheme in recent memory," the duo was teamed with Steve Tyler and Joe Perry of Aerosmith for a rock-rap hybrid remake of that group's hit song "Walk This Way." It was this song that allowed rap to cross over to the mainstream charts (# 4 in 1986) and to court an audience among white kids. *Raising Hell* also produced two more Top 40 hits with "My Adidas" (# 5 in

1986) and "You Be Illin'" (# 29 in 1986). The group had an affecting unconventional style—instead of trading off on verses, they would finish each other's lines. They also introduced a whole new fashion look: hats, gold chains, and untied sneakers. The follow-up album (*Tougher Than Leather*, Profile, 1988) would include "Mary, Mary," based on The Monkees' hit, and "Run's House," a hit that would become something of a signature song for the act. By their next album (*Back from Hell*, 1990), however, the culture had shifted—rap was getting meaner and nastier and Run-D.M.C.'s songs (which avoided the near obligatory references to "niggas" and "bitches") were out of vogue. The two were also suffering personal problems: both were in recovery for drug and alcohol abuse, and Simmons was facing a rape charge that was later dropped.

At some point in the early '90s both Simmons and McDaniels experienced what has been described both as a conversion and as simply "getting in touch" with the faith of their childhood. The two had been raised Roman Catholic and claim that they always were devout and sincere in their beliefs. McDaniel had served as an altar boy and Simmons had given serious thought to ordained ministry. Even during the years of their success as Run-D.M.C., they identified themselves as believers and tried (with varying degrees of success) to be faithful to God's expectations as they understood them. "Run and I always prayed on the road," McDaniels would tell *Syndicate* magazine in 1993, "because we knew God gave us the blessings and was in control of our lives." Likewise, both attributed their ultimate decline in popularity not to any paradigm shifts in the music world but to divine judgment: "We had forgotten to recognize and honor God as the one who gave us everything we had. . . . God needed to get our attention, so He let hard times come our way." A number of factors seem to have played a role in their spiritual renewal. McDaniels ended up hospitalized as a result of over-drinking, and his mother brought him a New Testament, which he claims to have read "over and over again." A bodyguard named Bobby Walker invited Simmons to his church, a charismatic group called Zoe Ministries and then, Simmons in turn got McDaniels to start attending. "We started reading the Word and realized what we were really doing and not doing," McDaniels told *Syndicate*. Simmons just said, "I cannot say exactly who brought about my conversion, because the process of becoming fully committed and born again came gradually, but it has happened." In any case, the group came back in 1993 with a much-publicized Christian album called *Down with the King*. In rap slang, of course, to be "down with" something means to be "into" it or "big" on it, hence the pun of the album title. "Run and I are making our statement," McDaniels announced to the press. "It takes boldness to stand up and say, 'I am down with Jesus.' However, we are saying it, and God is proving that He is with us. Make the statement: Run-D.M.C. is down with God."

Musically, the album *Down with the King* is similar in style to Run-D.M.C.'s other works. *The Rough Guide to Rock* describes it as "much improved" over their last outing, maintaining that it "proved they could hold their own with anybody from the new-school rap crews." It is not a gospel or even a contemporary Christian music record per se but a generally clean rap album with a couple of overtly confessional songs. The title track samples the song "Where Do I Go?" from the original cast recording of the rock musical *Hair* and features the lyric "Only G.O.D. can be a king to me / And if the G.O.D. be in me / Then a king I'll be." The song scored the group their first Top 40 hit since 1986, reaching Number Twenty-one on the mainstream pop chart. At the time that it occupied that position—based on consideration of sales *and* airplay—it was actually the Number Seven selling single in America but was only Number Forty-six in radio airplay, an intriguing discrepancy. *Down with the King* also includes a song called "Whose House? God's House!," which updates the theme of their popular "Run's House" hit.

Having made their statement with *Down with the King,* the artists have not continued to record, though they do appear as spokespersons and guest DJs now and then, offering words of testimony while trying not to be "too preachy," as Simmons puts it. In 1996, Simmons officially changed his stage name to Rev. Run and founded a Christian label called Rev. Run Records. He served as a consultant on the Whitney Houston film *The Preacher's Wife,* with some artists from his label being featured on the soundtrack. In 1997, he made his theatrical debut, starring in the gospel musical, *My Grandmother Prayed for Me.* He also wrote the book *It's Like That: The Way to Spiritual Abundance.* By 2000, Simmons was an ordained minister and McDaniels was serving as a church deacon. In 2001, the duo released another general market album *Crown Royal* (Arista), which featured guest appearances by Kid Rock, Fred Durst (of Limp Bizkit), and Sugar Ray.

Jonathan Rundman

1992—*28 Days in the Yellow Room* (custom); 1995—*Wherever* (Salt Lady); 1997—*Recital*; 2000—*Sound Theology*; 2001—*Field Recordings: lo-fi and Live in the Midwest*.

www.saltlady.com

The mantle of **John Ylvisaker** fell in the '90s upon Jonathan Rundman and, by the end of that decade, he would appear to have received a double portion. Like Ylvisaker in the '70s, Rundman would be one of the only Lutherans noticeably connected to popular Christian music (but see also **Lost and Found**). Lutherans may be the most un-hip denomination in America (they're neck and neck with Episcopalians for that distinction) but they do take theology and liturgy a bit more seriously than most. Rundman (like Ylvisaker and the rest) has done his church proud by producing some of the most theologically articulate, liturgically aware, and yet least-known popular Christian music of the modern era. Fresh out of high school, Rundman toured with a church-sponsored music group that played for youth gatherings in the U.S.A. and Germany. He ended up in Eugene, Oregon, where he worked as a semi-professional actor and musician, recording the custom cassette *28 Days in the Yellow Room.* Then around 1994, he moved to Chicago and founded the independent label Salt Lady Records with a friend. Since that time, he has devoted himself to music full time, recording four more solo albums, including the epic *Sound Theology.* Rundman is eclectic musically, but starts with a base of midwestern "roots rock." His pinched nasal voice is sometimes likened to that of Marshall Crenshaw or Dave Pirner (of Soul Asylum), though reviewers' attempts to describe the off-kilter sound stretch far and wide. *Phantom Tollbooth* called his vocals "a dead ringer for **Keith Green** or **Larry Norman**" (which they really aren't). Others have thought he sounds like "Paul Westerberg meets Matthew Sweet" or "Neil Young singing Arlo Guthrie songs."

Like most independent contemporary Christian musicians, Rundman prefers not to be associated with the genre. "My experience with contemporary Christian music is that it's totally the cheesiest, most white-people experience you've ever had," he says. Such a comment implies more association with **Avalon** or **Plus One** than with **Bruce Cockburn** or **P.O.D.,** but then it all comes down to labeling. Rundman's concept of what constitutes "Christian music" is probably closer to the public mindset than that adopted in this book, for many of his reviewers feel it necessary to point out that his albums are "not what one usually associates with Christian rock." What is clear is that Rundman's music lacks the antisocial element that often provides the raison d'etre for the Christian music industry. Like a good Lutheran, he recognizes no clear dichotomy between sacred and secular—God remains as active and present in the world as in the church, and the latter is no less infected with the brokenness of sin and no less susceptible to the liabilities of the human condition. Rundman does not envision his music as some kind of alternative to that which is made by non-Christians, nor does he target a Christian market as his audience. He plays more frequently in clubs than in churches, yet was tapped by the national leadership of his denomination to compose and perform music for its triannual National Youth Gathering in 2000. The *Illinois Entertainer* describes him as "an ambassador of good will who moves with integrity and ease among multiple enemy camps."

Rundman's first three albums exhibit few overtly Christian references and have been largely perceived as general market releases. *28 Days in the Yellow Room* is a decidedly lo-fi debut made available on cassette only. Favorite songs among Rundman fans include "This July," "My Helen," and "When I Get Bored." *Wherever* features fifteen original songs organized loosely around a geography theme, plus a slacker cover of Madonna's "Borderline." *Billboard* magazine indicated that any one of its songs could (and should) "find a home on AAA radio." The track "Three Months with You" did get some airplay in the Midwest, and David Malbuff, host of the California-based "American Roots" radio show, compared its sound favorably to Uncle Tupelo. "Wide Awake" is quite explicit in its expression of faith and would reappear five years later on *Sound Theology.* Rundman himself calls *Wherever* "midwestern rock and roll," and contrasts it with his third album, *Recital,* which he describes as more of a hybrid of "new-wavey rock and rootsy Americana." On that third project, the song "Grace Is Crying Her Eyes Out" has an interesting origin: while working as an actor in Oregon, Rundman played a criminal on one episode of the TV show *Under Suspicion* in which he ended up getting shot and dying in the arms of actor Grace Zabriskie. "Meeting Nixon" touches on a more overtly theological theme. "We'll be meeting Nixon," sings Rundman, "when we all go to that white house in the sky." The point of the song for Rundman, a Democrat, is a bit like **Room Full of Walters'** "Jeffrey Dahmer Went to Heaven," though the former president may be a less extreme example of someone who, in Rundman's words, "we'd never expect to see there." The most direct statement of faith, however, comes with "When Rising from the Bed of Death," an adaptation of a sixteenth century poem by Thomas Tallis, which Rundman transforms into a modern hymn: "When rising from the bed of death / O'erwhelmed with guilt and fear / I see my maker face to face / O how shall I appear?"

Sound Theology is a project of almost overwhelming, epic proportion. Probably the finest Christian album of the year (2000), it was almost ignored in the Christian music media, though *True Tunes* picked up on it and sang its praises to the indie-oriented, alternative crowd. "The music," they would proclaim, "captures all of what makes heartland rock great—blues licks, rolling instrumentals, passionate performances, and just good, sweaty rock and roll." The scope of the album is incredible, especially for what most Christian music fans would consider a debut project by a "new artist": it presents the equivalent of what would have been a four-record or tape set in the years before compact discs, a total of fifty-two tracks crammed onto two beautifully packaged CDs. The number fifty-two is no happenstance, for Rundman intentionally presents one song for every week of the year. In fact, he offers a song for each week of the *liturgical* year, beginning with the

first week of Advent and proceeding through the seasons of Christmas, Epiphany, Lent, Easter, and Pentecost. The idea of a roots rock concept album designed around the liturgical cycle of the church year may sound strange, but it works surprisingly well. Rundman maintains that the connection is more natural than many would expect: "I think pop music is like liturgy . . . there's a structure that works well with verse-chorus-verse-chorus-solo-etc. and there are textual and melodic hooks that make it catchy." Rundman says he was inspired in part by Liz Phair's *Exile to Guysville* and, as with that album (a song-by-song response to the Rolling Stones' *Exile on Main Street*), the relationship of individual songs to the overriding concept is more obvious at times than it is at others. "Let Me Be Yours" was conceived as a baptism song for the first week of Epiphany (when the Baptism of Jesus is observed), and "Ashes" comes the first week of Lent (as in Ash Wednesday), but even those who miss these connections may enjoy the songs on their own merits. Rundman wrote in the album's liner notes, "I figure if someone needed a resource for weekly meditation, or a teacher wanted an easy Sunday school curriculum, this album could be it. Of course, if you'd rather just listen to it in the car like any other CD, you could do that instead."

Reviewers would note that *Sound Theology* also spans the breadth of rock stylistically. Rundman evokes Lou Reed on "The Loneliness of Happiness." He goes disco for one song with "Find Your Way to Prague" and then sings a country duet with Becki Hemingway (cf. **This Train**) on "Ashes." He salutes Timbuk 3 with "A Little More Than Me," rips off Tom Petty for "If I Ever Get There," and tips his hand to traditional gospel with a pair of spirituals, "I Don't Want to Go to Hell" and "I Want Jesus to Walk with Me." Instrumental interludes between songs quote from such classic hymns as "Come Thou Long Expected Jesus," "In Thee Is Gladness," "Ah, Holy Jesus," "Arise My Soul, Arise," and "What Wondrous Love Is This." Lyrics are an obvious strength for Rundman and the songs on *Sound Theology* account for some of his most poignant thoughts and memorable lines. "Church Directory" is about tracing his family's faith back in history. "You Don't Speak for Me" is directed to Pat Robertson and his ilk in the Religious Right, who Rundman says "make Christians look horrible." The song "Xian Bookstore" describes the kitschy paraphernalia that litters the shelves of Christian market shops and concludes, "I think it's safe to say if Jesus hadn't risen he'd be rolling in his grave." Rundman has a gift for creating songs out of everyday experiences or out of reflection on realities that most take for granted. In "The Glasses Song" (a ragged rocker), he meditates on his need for corrective lenses, saying, "It seems so long since I've seen with my eyes." The remarkable "Carol of the Bells" is about a romantic obsession with a girl (named Carol) who rings handbells in church ("she rings G and she rings A . . . they don't trust those notes with anyone else"). And then on the extremely profound "Deadly Life" he meditates on the simple blessing of going to bed at night:

We didn't starve or thirst to death or fall to some disease
We weren't lost or all alone or left outside to freeze
There was no freeway accident or collapse of the sun
We didn't die the victim of some punk kid with a gun
There was no right wing terrorist or killer flash flood
We weren't sent to fight no war, we got no tainted blood
We weren't in the path of some drunk man at the wheel
The day was rough but we got through, so every night we
   kneel
There's a holy miracle every single night
When we lie down in our beds and turn out all the lights
We breathed ourselves another day, we beat all the odds
We survived this deadly life and gave it back to God.

Unlike most contemporary Christian music artists who try to hide their particular denominational affiliations, Rundman identifies himself explicitly with the issues of modern-day Lutheranism. "I think Christianity in general and Lutheranism in particular, are a hard sell to the general population in this country," he muses in the liner notes to a beautiful song called "Forgiveness Waltz." He continues, "It's difficult for Americans to understand the concept of grace. The American Way is to work hard enough and you can get what you deserve." Grace is, not surprisingly, a recurrent theme on *Sound Theology*. Two back-to-back songs ("My Apology," "Tired, Tired, Tired") address the twin temptations of "cheap grace" and "works righteousness" that Lutherans are taught to beware. Rundman owns up to his tendency either to be lax with regard to holiness or to be judgmental in imposing his standards upon others. As is typical, his confessions are tempered by wit: "I'm so tired of teenage smokers / Standing on the corner, goin' nowhere slow / Passin' round a lighter, cussin' and complainin' / I don't wanna hear it, I don't wanna know." Another two of the album's strongest cuts celebrate a historic but possibly endangered strength of the Lutheran tradition. "I Love You with All of My Mind" is a rock track inspired by Deuteronomy 6:5 but asserting that "the heart and soul are overrated" and celebrating cerebral devotion over emotional attachments. "We're Creating Monsters" is a response to contemporary worship trends ("dumb it down, dumb it down") that lead Rundman to wonder whether the current generation of church-going youth are not "as intolerant of tradition as their grandparents are of drums in the sanctuary."

In many ways Rundman seems analogous to Beck. He doesn't have much of a voice, and much of *Sound Theology* sounds as though it were recorded on a four-track in his bedroom (turns out, much of it *was*). But he's no slacker in the songwriting department. One critic says, "Rundman has made a career out of writing about things that no one else thinks about for very long." That is true, but he also writes about what are common experiences for millions of people (e.g., churchgoers) that are often deemed too private or foreign to serve as fodder for barroom ditties. Most Christians, even (perhaps especially) casual churchgoers, have had the experience of visiting congregations that practice "closed Communion" (i.e., allowing only their own members—those known to be true Christians—to participate in the Eucharist). Why hasn't anyone written a song about it before? Rundman does, and it's a song that allows even non-Christians to get a sense of what that must feel like: "So I sat there like a stranger with nothing / It was all I had / Yeah I knew that we were different / But I didn't know it would hurt so bad" ("Closed Out"). He's the anti-Luther, taking church music into pubs instead of the other way around.

Sound Theology bears the cumbersome subtitle, "Perspectives on faith and rock and roll from a Finnish-American Midwestern Generation X Lutheran at the turn of the millennium." It is revealing and personal in a way that has not failed to attract notice by general market reviewers, who tend to appreciate authenticity and creativity in music with less disdain for religious orientation than apologists for the separatist Christian music culture allege. "I was worried about being shunned by the mainstream rock press," Rundman has said of *Sound Theology*, but all my worries have been unfounded." If anything, the album was better received within the general market than within the Christian music subculture.

Bottom line: apart from the requisite voice lessons and production standards that would probably wreck his muse, Rundman has little chance of ever becoming a mainstream star in either the contemporary Christian or general markets. Still, he is one of Christian music's best songwriters, worthy of consideration alongside **Bruce Cockburn, Mark Heard,** and **Victoria Williams.**

Rundman has also recorded two albums with "bands" that were simply collaborations with childhood friends. After writing songs together over the Internet, he got together with Todd Berg and David Casimir for one week in 1997 to record the basic garage album *May* by The Muckrakers. A similar alliance with his cousin Bruce Rundman led to an album called *Seven Summers* by The Chandlers, though in this case the two did not even meet in a studio but recorded their separate parts on a tape sent back and forth through the mail. Rundman's *Field Recordings* is a sort of homemade bootleg production that includes faux-live versions of numerous favorites along with three new songs, some Muckraker tracks, and a few innovative covers (including Annie Lennox's "Little Bird" and the country gospel standard "Will the Circle Be Unbroken?").

Runforyerlife

Paul Bessenbacher, bass, kybrd.; Ben Butler, trump.; Jim Gibbon, trump., voc.; Weert Goldenstein, gtr.; Jason Toth, drums; Chad Whitacre, sax.; Dave Yun, sax.; Kelly Zouhary, voc. 1999—*Runforyerlife* (Jump Up).

Runforyerlife is an eight-piece swing/ska band from the Chicago area composed of seven men and one female lead singer, all of whom are Wheaton college graduates. The group takes an acid-jazz approach to their brand of ska and is exceptionally professional at pulling off tricky time changes and various chord and key modulations that give the music an impressive, seasoned sound. Most of the songs are about relationships, although there is a subdued theistic perspective behind it all.

Ruscha (a.k.a. **The Russians**)

Nikolai Pankratz, gtr., kybrd.; Peter Pankratz, bass; et al. By The Russians: 1981—*The Russians* (custom); 1983—*Love Forever More* (Voice Box). By Ruscha: 1988—*Testimony* (custom); 1989—*Come Alive* (Pan-Trax).

Ruscha was a Christian hard rock band led by two Siberian immigrants. According to their testimony, Nikolai and Peter Pankratz were born and raised in communist-run Siberia, where their family participated in an underground church that was persecuted by the authorities. Their grandfather was arrested by the KGB and subsequently died of exposure in a Soviet prison. The rest of the family was allowed to leave the country in 1974 at the invitation of relatives in Germany. Five years later, the Pankratz brothers obtained student visas and came to Liberty University in Lynchburg, Virginia. They initially formed the band The Russians to play at churches in exchange for offerings toward their tuition. The group changed its name to Ruscha (pronounced "Russia") after its bus (with the name The Russians on the side) was vandalized. Personnel varied over time. Although no official data are available, the band appears to have initially included Danny Moore on vocals, Scott Cameron on drums, and Rex Schnelle on guitar. By 1988, the non-Pankratz members were Andy Denton, Michael Jackson (who later changed his name to Mike Jacobs), and Billy Williams. These three went on to form **Legend;** Denton was also a member of **Identical Strangers.** Ruscha was better known for its testimony than its music. After each concert, Peter would talk for about fifteen minutes about life in Russia with some graphic detail about the sufferings of Christians under communism. Without doubting the terrible anguish of their experiences, one may at least realize in retrospect (as many did even at the time) that the band was used by the Religious Right to fuel the "evil empire" rhetoric that provided a mandate for power in Reagan's America. In his sole appearance in *CCM,* Peter Pankratz decried the "colleges and universities" of America where "humanism and liberalism and the teaching of communism in indirect ways have affected our new generation so much that they don't know the Truth."

Christian radio hits: "Come Home" (# 4 in 1988).

Sackcloth Fashion

Luke Geraty; Steve Trudeau; Tim Trudeau. 1999—*Something for Everyone to Hate* (Syntax).

www.sackcloth.com

Sackcloth Fashion is a Christian hip-hop group from San Diego. They say that they chose their name because sackcloth is a biblical image for humility—a value not usually found in the hip-hop genre: "While rappers usually get their start by outdoing each other, we're trying to be the opposite. . . . we're just guys who have a desire to be true, living in humility and meekness, and making it a fashion in our lives." A number of guest artists (**E-roc,** B-Twice, Ahmad) appear on the project, and a woman named Lisa Kolbo provides lead vocals on two tracks. The sound of Sackcloth Fashion is very much like that of The Beastie Boys, and many of the songs are issue oriented, addressing worldly concerns from a Christian or fundamentalist perspective. Lyrics are not provided and words are not always understandable, but "Family Ties" deals with domestic abuse and "We've Only Just Begun" promotes faithfulness in relationships. "Sibling Rivalry" is not the Limp Bizkit song by that name but an original track that takes the *Look Who's Talking* theme to its illogical conclusion by presenting a dialogue between twin fetuses who are possessed with adult intelligence and plan their lives out in the womb (one of them will be a dancer, the other a writer) before being brutally murdered in an abortion clinic. Emotional in an irresponsible way, it offers no substantive contribution to the antiabortion protest movement but seems intended only to fuel hatred for those protestors' opponents.

Sacrament

Mike DiDonato, gtr.; Paul Graham, drums; Mike Torone, voc. (– 1993); Brian Toy, bass (– 1993) // Eric Ney, bass (+ 1993); Rob Wolfe, voc. (+ 1993). 1989—*Presumed Dead* [EP]; 1990—*Testimony of Apocalypse* (R.E.X.); 1993—*Haunts of Violence.*

Sacrament was a thrash/death metal band from Philadelphia who strove to bring their version of Christianity to sometimes confrontational secular audiences. A 1992 issue of *HM* (issue # 37) describes a gig in Burlington, Vermont, that had a divided audience of thrashers booing and cheering when DiDonato announced between songs, "We're all Christians. We believe in Jesus Christ. He's God, and He died for our sins, and He rose from the dead." *Testimony of Apocalypse* includes the self-explanatory song "Slave to Sin." *Haunts of Violence* features a title track based on Psalm 74:20 and a song called "Destructive Heresies" that attacks the theory of evolution as attributing life to chance rather than to creation. Mike DiDonato and Erik Ney later joined **Fountain of Tears.**

Sacred Fire

Jimmy Bennett, voc., perc.; Rod Call, drums; Dean Harrington, gtr., perc., synth.; Roger Lowe, kybrd.; Richard Price, bass. 1986—*Sacred Fire* (StarSong).

A Christian rock band from Atlanta, Sacred Fire is best remembered as the starting group for Jimmy Bennett, who went on to sing with **Rex Carroll** in the band **King James.** Dean Harrington had formerly played with **Mylon LeFevre**'s band, Broken Heart, and he serves as the primary songwriter for Sacred Fire's one album. Most of the album's songs are about the transforming power of Christ to give meaning to an otherwise wasted life. Songs like "Nowhere to Hide" and "Don't Turn Away" describe the plight of those who need the Lord, while "Heaven's Love" and "Second Chance" confront the listener and invite him or her to discover what God offers: "Receive him, believe him / Surrender to the Lord of the Second Chance." More effective thematically are the personal testimony of "Quest of Faith" and the worship orientation of "You Are."

Sacred Warrior

Rey Parra, voc.; Rick Macias, voc. (– 1989); Bruce Swift, gtr.; Tony Velasquez, drums; Steve Watkins, bass // John Johnson, gtr. (+ 1989). 1988—*Rebellion* (Intense); 1989—*Master's Command;* 1990—*Wicked Generation;* 1991—*Obsessions;* 1993—*Classics.*

Sacred Warrior was a late '80s "hair metal" band from Chicago that possessed enough talent to rise above the literally hundreds of groups like them and achieve more notice than most. All of the '90s Christian metal groups were children of **Stryper,** but Sacred Warrior took that sound in the operatic direction of acts like Queensryche. Their sound was also compared to that of Iron Maiden, especially on the early projects. The nucleus of Sacred Warrior came out of a general market club band called Nomad, when members Ray Parra, Bruce Swift, and Tony Velasquez decided to get more serious about their Christian faith. According to Swift, "I got saved and led the other two to the Lord," but the three made few changes in their rock and roll lifestyle. At one point, a fan came up to them and said, "I want to be just like you guys—you believe in Jesus, but you still know how to *party*!" That encounter, Parra would later say, caused them to realize the extent to which they were role models and led them to reconsider their priorities. The three determined to clean up their act and, then, to form a ministry-oriented Christian band. Rick Macias was originally a bouncer at a club where the band played, but under their influence he was converted both to Christ and to metal music, which he says he had previously disliked.

Rebellion features anthemic songs with straightforward themes like "Stay Away from Evil." The apocalyptic imagery that often undergirds fundamentalist Christianity comes into play on the antidevil track "Master of Lies" and in songs that announce or celebrate an imminent end of the world ("Day of the Lord," "The Heavens Are Calling"). "He Died" is a power ballad reflecting on the crucifixion and atonement. The title

track is not a call to rebellion, but a plea to "Give it up! Your mind of rage! / Rebellion . . . Turn back to Jesus." *Rebellion* would always be remembered as the group's classic, most passionate, and best album, though *Master's Command* displays the band in better form from a technical perspective, with chops well honed from time on the road. While backing away from the power metal of their debut, the album is a strong collection of hard rock songs and includes the accessible tracks "Paradise" and "Beyond the Mountain," which season the heavy sound with catchy hooks and memorable choruses. "The Flood" offers a vocal duet between Parra and Roger Martinez (of **Vengeance**). The album closes with what most consider to be its highlight, a heavy metal version of the traditional hymn "Holy, Holy, Holy." *Wicked Generation* moves back into the full-bore metal sound, to the delight of reviewers like *HM*'s Doug Van Pelt. An ambitious project, *Wicked Generation* is actually a concept album that traces the stories of three main characters struggling to overcome the emotional, physical, and sexual abuse of their past. Verbal testimonies from the persons are interspersed between tracks. Songs like "No Happy Endings" and "Little Secrets" expose the agony that victims of child abuse, incest, and alcoholism bear, and they deal with the issues with both sensitivity and passion. Van Pelt would credit the band with "creating what some thought impossible: intelligent metal," but later admitted the songs "were too poor to stand on their own." Things come together for *Obsessions,* for which the Queensryche analogies would be at an all-time high, if only because the band had gotten better at producing a credible Christian version of that sound. Van Pelt would call it "a consistent performance," praising the album especially for its sonic quality and pitch-perfect harmonies. "Turning Back" is a particularly strong number, with acoustic guitar worked into the mix. "Remember Me" is a slow, heavy song sung from the perspective of the thief on the cross (Luke 23:42). "Temples of Fire" is a thoughtful testimony song; the haunting "Sweet Memories" offers tribute to a departed loved one. The title track reflects meaningfully on the different agendas that drive people's lives: "As the dollar exchanges the hands of many, there lie the poor who dream of having enough for today."

SaGoh 24/7

Stephen Christian, voc.; Sean Hutson, drums; Dean Rexroat, bass; Shane Schoch, gtr. 1999—*sa goh twenty-four seven* (Rescue); 2000—*Then I Corrupt Youth.*

SaGoh is a punk band from Florida that released a debut album *Bandoppler* would call "strangely legitimate and endearing." The project blends old- and new-school punk with some metal and modern rock influences on songs that are explicitly theological or that address issues from a perspective informed by their religious convictions. "Withstand" presents Satan as a weakling, unable to overcome those who resist (James 4:7). "Fifteen" offers hope to those who have erred in the past. "Days of Our Lives" deals with abortion and with the trials of the younger generation. The band's sophomore project introduces a different sound and a more mature lyrical focus. "When the old album came out, we were in a punk band," says Hutson, "we put out what we thought people wanted to hear." Likewise, songwriter Stephen Christian trashed the eponymous album's lyrics: "It was really weak. I used words so they would rhyme, and I wrote songs that had little meaning, so they would entertain people. Now my lyrics have meaning— every line is formulated and means something to me." *HM* likens *Then I Corrupt Youth* to the sound of The Offspring's second release: "urgent pop melodies with an almost classic metal guitar attack." They also second Christian's take on the lyrical direction: "Lyrically, the band shows a lot of thought with songs like 'The Regrettable Paris,' 'Solace,' and 'The Consistency of Mercury'."

Saint

Richard Lynch, bass; Josh Kramer, voc. (– 1999); John Mahan, gtr. (–1988); Gene McClindon, drums (–1986) // Brian Willis, drums (+ 1986, – 1988); Dee Harrington, gtr. (+ 1988); John Perrine, drums (+ 1988, – 1999); Tim Lamberson, drums (+ 1999). 1984—*Warriors of the Son* (Rotton); 1986—*Time's End* (Pure Metal); 1988—*Too Late for Living;* 1999—*The Perfect Life* [EP] (Armor).

Saint was an '80s metal band noted for pounding out what *HM* called "skin-blistering hard music in the heydey of Christian metal." The group's sound was most often likened to that of Iron Maiden and Judas Priest, with shades of Black Sabbath. The group was known—and often criticized—for its negativity. *Time's End* deals rather negatively with the ultimate destruction of the earth, with no obvious Christian content or explicit reference to Christ. Likewise, *HM* called *Too Late for Living* (with tracks like "Live to Die") a "real downer," dwelling almost exclusively on references to hell and evil. In 1997, Richard Lynch started an independent label called Armor Records and released all three Saint albums on a two-disc set. Then, a decade after the group had disbanded, Lynch, Harrington, and Lamberson got together to record a half dozen new songs and released these as *The Perfect Life.*

Salmond and Mulder

1979—*Salmond and Mulder* (Image VII); 1980—*Stumbling Heavenward;* 1981—*Hoping and Coping;* 1983—*Fun Raiser* (River).

Salmond and Mulder were a Canadian folk-rock duo cut from the same cloth as better-known artists like **Malcolm and Alwyn.** The group fashioned songs that offer wry observations on life and lend a worshipful mood to their perfor-

mances, though they also did so with a sensitivity that brought them respect within the general market. In 1981, the *Winnipeg Free Press,* a secular publication, reviewed a Salmond and Mulder concert in that city indicating that the artists' songs examine human relationships and "admonish the preacher in all of us" while offering a "down-to-earth approach to their religion." The group also adopted the post-Smothers Brothers tradition of many folk duos by incorporating a generous amount of humor into their act. Salmond recorded a solo album called *Up* (River, 1985).

Sal Paradise

John Miller; et al. 1996—*Further* (Tooth and Nail); 2001—*For You and Before You* (Velvet Blue).

Sal Paradise is an Australian Euro-pop band with a sound similar to Modern English or Pavement and a lead singer who recalls Morrissey. *Further* features songs about travel ("Road Movie # 57," "Lost Maps," "Celestial Railway"), all of which hint at spiritual searching and discovery. The album languished and five years later Sal Paradise came out with the acoustic *For You and Before You,* which reprises three of *Further's* best songs in slower, quieter versions ("Lost Maps," "Celestial Railway," "Sideways"). Of the new songs, "Inbetween Times" and "Venturesome" are pop standouts, while "Unknown Love" and "Friday" are worship-oriented. The group takes its name from a figure in Jack Kerouac's *On the Road.*

Sonny Salsbury (and the Reflections)

1969—*The Electric Church* (Word, 1969); 1971—*Reflection* (Word); 1972—*Good Morning, Lord;* 1975—*Love Came Down; Backpacker's Suite;* 1983—*Song of Bethlehem* (label unknown). Date unknown—*Breakfast in Galilee* (Word); *Come Back to the Garden.*

Sonny Salsbury wrote contemporary Christian music for use in youth-oriented church services. His contributions, in that sense, may be compared to those made in the late '60s by such pre-Jesus music pioneers as **Ralph Carmichael, John Fischer,** Kurt Kaiser, **Jimmy and Carol Owens,** and **Ray Repp.** His songs tended to have a ready-for-Vacation-Bible-School sound to them that would have seemed hokey to those outside the church but did help to prepare congregations for a more pop-oriented sound than was evident in the traditional hymnals. His best-known work among the Jesus people was probably *Backpacker's Suite,* which offers an album of worship music for campers, with obvious emphasis on appreciation for the glories of nature and the Creator they reveal. Written and produced by Salsbury, the music on the record was actually performed by a choir, accompanied by an orchestra and an assortment of guitars, banjos, and other acoustic instruments. Blue Samuel Flying—a popular '70s reviewer for *Harmony* magazine—described it as "three years late," providing the kind of production that might have satisfied young Christians' thirst for contemporary worship music in the days before the Jesus movement revival drastically increased their options.

Salvador

Art Gonzales, drums; Josh Gonzales, bass, voc.; Nick Gonzales, gtr., voc.; Adrian Lopez, kybrd., voc.; Eliot Torres, perc., voc. 1999—*Live in Austin* (Word); 2000—*Salvador*.

Latin rock band Salvador arose out of a local praise and worship band that the Gonzales brothers Art and Nick (Josh is their cousin) ran in the Pentecostal church that their mother pastors in Austin, Texas. The group has a sound like that of general market fave Santana, with more of an emphasis on dance music (like that of Santana during their "Everybody's Everything" period). *CCM* and *Phantom Tollbooth* would both also describe their sound as "a poppier version of **Burlap to Cashmere.**" The group's first and best album is a collection of praise songs performed live for the famous Austin City Limits program. One of those tracks, "Lord, I Come before You," also opens the self-titled record that would be the band's official debut. It has an infectious sound worthy of the Santana comparisons, as does "David Danced," a traditional praise song made popular by **Fred Hammond.** It is done here in English and Spanish, with an extended fiery guitar solo. "Crucified" and "Cry Holy" (cowritten by Benjy Gaither of **Benjamin**) are impressive adult contemporary ballads that are both theologically sound and competently performed, though they lack any distinctive quality to set them apart from hundreds of songs performed by other artists. "Montaña" and "Alabar al Señor" (cowritten by **Billy Sprague**) are Spanish songs with a traditional (nonrock) Latin sound to them. The group has stated a strong preference for "vertical music" and they seem to be at their best when they fire up the horns, pull out the maracas, and perform such tunes with uninhibited abandon. Such is the case with "Ain't It Good," a spirited celebration propelled by the simple lyric, "I don't care what they may say / We love Jesus anyway." The name Salvador is Spanish for "Savior."

Salvation Air Force

Michael Gossett; Donnie Gossett. 1978—*Stranger in a Strange Land* (Myrrh); 1979—*Prayer Warriors on Parade* (custom).

Salvation Air Force was a Christian pop duo formed in 1973 during the heydey of the Jesus movement. Although they played at Billy Graham crusades and even did a tour in South Vietnam, they did not get around to recording for five years. The group consisted of two brothers who were sons of the evangelist Don Gossett and consequently grew up traveling with his crusades and listening primarily to gospel music. Both were members of a gospel group called The Centurions before developing a more contemporary sound as Salvation Air Force. The 1978 album features assistance from a number of well-known Christian musicians, including **Sandra Crouch, Tom Howard, Larry Norman, Al Perkins,** and **Randy Stonehill.** Of even greater interest to Jesus music fans, however, is the presence of Dana Angle and Bruce Herring, both of **The Way,** who had been MIA for a few years (Alex MacDougall, drummer for **The Way, Daniel Amos,** and **The Richie Furay Band** makes a showing as well). With all this firepower, the album itself comes off a bit muted, probably (in the opinion of *Jesus Music*) because Myrrh Records was in a mellow doldrums at the time fueled by their temporary success with **B. J. Thomas** and **Glad.** So, *Jesus Music* reports, "most of the album is innocuous soft rock with a light jazz touch . . . only 'Complete and Alive' has any real crunch to it." Of historical interest, however, is a complete version of **Larry Norman**'s "If God Is My Father," which had only appeared in a truncated version on Norman's own *In Another Land.* The Gossetts actually took a rough mix of the track that Norman had recorded (but not used) for *So Long Ago the Garden* and dubbed their own voices and instruments over it. The original version (sans Salvation Air Force) was eventually included as a bonus track on the CD of *So Long Ago the Garden,* but for many years, the SAF recording was the only full version of the classic song available to most audiences.

Sanctum

Jan Carleklev; Marika Ljungberg; Halkan Paullson; Lena Roberts. 1996—*Lupus in Fabula* (Cold Meat Industry); 1998—*The Answer to His Riddle* [EP]; 2000—*New York City Bluster.*

Sanctum is an eclectic Swedish band that starts with a synth/industrial core and adds in elements of goth, ambient, opera, and classical styles. The group was formed by two members of **The November Commandment** who decided to augment their industrial sound with female vocalists who, as it turns out, also add cello and other "make nice" touches to the mix. The attraction of the group lies in their variety and unpredictability. Eschewing all formulas, they seem to view each song as a work of art in its own right and to develop a particular mood and, indeed, a distinctive style for that one track. "Dragonfly," for instance, opens *Lupus* with beautifully sung female vocals and classical strings, then adds dark, ambient synths and distorted male vocals. "Juniper Dream" showcases Lena Roberts's operatic style of singing against an off-pitch flute and simple hand drums. "In Two Minds" is much more brutal, relying on mechanical noises and hard bass beats. The only band to which the group is ever compared (besides **The November Commandment**) is **The Revolutionary Army of the Infant Jesus**—and, even then, the primary similarities lie in the European connection and the skill and creativity with electronics. In 1999, Marika Ljungberg and Roberts were not able to make the trip to America for a concert at CBGB's in New York City. As a result, *New York City Bluster* is a live recording of the band without its female singers, dispensing with all ethereal moments in favor of raw industrial sound. Most of Sanctum's songs feature poetic lyrics (in English) that deal rather generically with spirituality and human emotion. "Closing Remark" on *Lupus* says, "Someday we'll find the answer to our prayers / The dreams are part of our reality / Our minds are connected to another world / Once you find the connection / Get a grip and never let go."

Phillip Sandifer

1981—*Never Steal the Show* (PSP); 1984—*On My Way* (Urgent); 1986— *Keeping the Dream Alive*; 1988—*Constant*; 1990—*The Best of Phillip Sandifer*; 1991—*The Other Side of Salvation*; 1994—*Arizona Highway* (Urgent); 2001—*All by Grace* (Urgent).

Phillip Sandifer (b. 1959) is a singer and guitarist who works out of Austin, Texas, and also serves as A&R director of Urgent Records. Raised in Dallas, Sandifer attended Auburn University in Alabama, where he played football but, after several knee injuries, transferred to the University of Texas in Austin where he studied psychology and law and began working with the organization Campus Crusade for Christ. He later joined the staff of Campus Crusade and remained affiliated with the group into the late '80s. His early material sparked comparisons to such general market artists as Dan Fogelberg and Larry Gatlin. *CCM* was a bit dismissive of his debut, calling it "cotton candy pop," while applauding the artist's effort at transcending traditional Christian themes to comment on human relationships (an innovative tack in 1981). In this regard, "Detour" describes a relationship that leads the singer to God, and "Lesson" offers a flip-side meditation on what is to be learned from a relationship's end. *On My Way* demonstrates significant growth musically and theologically. The album is heavy with ballads, though the tempo picks up on the salsa-flavored "Should It Ever Rain Again" and on a quirky, percussive tune called "Don't Shoot the Wounded." The title track begins with an a capella chorus and testifies to the continuing guidance of God's grace through a life of trials until "the holy name of Jesus will echo as our call and will cause the feeble gates of hell to fall." Sandifer's next two records featured mellow material that established the artist as a staple of adult contemporary pop. Two standout songs from *Constant* ("New Life," "Easy Money") display a jazz influence that reveal his multifaceted interests and facility with a variety of styles. In the '90s, Sandifer assumed the position as Worship Leader and Director of Creative Arts at his church. *The Other Side of Salvation* and *Arizona Highway* feature songs that display an easy-

going but upbeat style that targets a multigenerational audience. On *All By Grace* he explores the fact that being a Christian does not make life trouble free, though there is joy in Christ beyond the struggles of life. "The key," he says, "is learning to see things through God's eyes."

As a composer, Sandifer has had songs recorded by **Bob Bennett, Glen Campbell, Rob Frazier,** and **Fernando Ortega.** He also records as one-half of the duo **Santa Fe.**

For trivia buffs: Sandifer was a guest lead vocalist for the Disney movie *A Bug's Life.* He sang the song "Walking Stick."

Christian radio hits: "On My Way" (# 18 in 1985).

Santa Fe

Michael Sandifer; Phillip Sandifer. 1996—*Moon Circles* (Urgent).

Santa Fe is an acoustic duo composed of two brothers who also record as solo artists. **Phillip Sandifer** has numerous albums to his credit and is fairly well known as an adult contemporary male vocalist and songwriter. As a group, Santa Fe recalls '70s acoustic acts like Poco or America, though the music is updated somewhat with a slight alternative '90s edge. The songs on *Moon Circles* decry materialism and self-centered humanism while also reveling in an unashamed love for God. The title track deals with the theme of God defying human expectations. "Wider Sky" comes from the worship-oriented perspective of one humbled by the vastness of the universe. The album also includes the light pop songs "Love Speaks Louder" and "Wanting the Things That You Get."

Sardonyx

Tom Denlinger, voc.; Rob Feltman, gtr.; Jeff King, kybrd.; et al. 1992—*Majestic Serenity* (Lightshine).

Sardonyx was a Christian metal band with a unique approach to ministry. The group formed in 1988 in the Lancaster, Pennsylvania, area and organized what Denlinger called a ministry base known as Lightshine International Ministries. Lightshine also published a magazine *(Lightshine Metal),* ran a weekly radio show *(Thunder Zone),* and promoted concerts in the area. Denlinger, who says he grew up on **Keith Green** and **Resurrection Band,** had strong feelings about long-term, follow-up ministry, which committed Sardonyx to being regional. *Majestic Serenity* was praised by *HM* as offering "heavy metal, played like it should be: powerful and with all-out energy." The song "Puppet of Beauty" offers a Proverbs-inspired conversation between wisdom and the titular temptress. "Corridor of Light" is an eight-minute epic about passing from death to the throne of God. That song and "Holy Avenger" have a Queensryche feel to them. "Voice of the Prodigal" closes the album on an especially strong note as the most aggressive song on the album. According to Jeff King, Sardonyx broke up due to internal conflicts. King later played with **Fountain of Tears.** Some sources list an additional Sardonyx album, *Rebel of Reason,* without specifying date or label.

Satellite Soul

Ryan Green, drums; Tyler Simpson, bass; Tom Suttle, voc., gtr., kybrd.; Rustin Smith, gtr. (−1999). 1997—*Satellite Soul* (ForeFront); 1999—*Great Big Universe*; 2000—*Ardent Worship: Satellite Soul Live* (Ardent).

www.satellitesoul.com

The wheatfield soul band Satellite Soul got its start in 1994 when Tim Suttle (a graduate student in microbiology at Kansas State University) and Rustin Smith (a preseminarian at Manhattan Christian College) hooked up and started playing coffeehouses. A year later, the group turned into a quartet and began to develop their sound. "At first, we thought we'd be the Christian Gin Blossoms," Suttle would later reminisce, "but then we realized there were already 50 of them, so ever since then, we've been trying to be ourselves." The group at least borrows widely. "Fool," from their debut album, seems to derive its basic musical line from **Larry Norman**'s "The Outlaw," its vocals from The Byrds' "Chimes of Freedom," and its instrumental intro from Blues Traveller's "Hook." This melting pot approach gets the group compared to all of the just-named artists, as well as to the Wallflowers, R.E.M., the Counting Crows, and many others. Suttle, however, cites **Rich Mullins** as his major influence: "I was 15 when I heard 'Elijah' for the first time and decided I could do music. . . . I learned to play piano by listening to him. I also learned guitar and hammer dulcimer because he played them."

The self-titled debut was well received by critics who enjoyed trying to recall just which classic rock artist was being quoted where. The album starts off with "Either Way," a catchy tune with the same sort of Allman-Brothers-go-bubblegum sound that bands like Blues Traveller and Barenaked Ladies made popular. Lyrically, it serves up the artist's note-to-self prayer, "You're still God, and I'm still not." Stronger cuts like "Pieces," "Never," and "Wash" take the Neil Young *Comes a Time/Harvest Moon* route demanding (and rewarding) a little more attention from the audience. "Equal to the Fall" is a particularly powerful track, featuring Suttle's most impassioned vocal on lines that promise God's grace is sufficient for all of life's not-quite-happy endings. *Great Big Universe* opens with a surprise—a Matthew Sweet sound-alike song that takes the group in an electric direction all the previous comparisons had not encompassed. That song, the album's title track, seems to reflect upon life on the road with frank lines like "You send me many places I do not want to go" and "Gonna sing and tell you I love you / Though I do not know your name." The switch from alt-country to chiming pop-rock imbues most of the

album, which also features fuller and heavier production. Songs like "Always the Same" have a very full sound, with orchestral strings and harmony background vocals. "Revive Me" succeeds with a less adorned dulcimer track. Likewise, "Single Moment" is a lovely, stripped bare solo on which Suttle's lyrics are allowed to draw the most attention: "There is not a single moment that you don't see / There is not a single moment that you're not here with me." The band also recorded a specialty album for the Ardent Worship Series, featuring five original praise songs and seven worship standards (including Rick Founds' "Lord, I Lift Your Name on High" and **Rich Mullins**' "Step by Step") recorded live at Kansas City's New Earth coffeehouse.

Christian radio hits: "Say I Am" (# 7 in 1998); "Wash" (# 15 in 1999); "Either Way" (# 25 in 1998); "Equal to the Fall" (# 25 in 1999); "Great Big Universe" (# 8 in 1999); "Revive Me" (# 20 in 1999).

Saviour Machine

Eric Clayton, voc.; Jeff Clayton, gtr.; Doug Forsyth, bass (−1997); Sam West, drums (−1993) // Jayson Heart, drums (+ 1994, −2001); Nathan Van Hala, kybrd., prog. (+ 1994); Charles Cooper, bass (+ 1997); Victor Deaton, drums (+ 2001). 1990—*Saviour Machine* (custom); 1993—*Saviour Machine* (Intense); 1994—*Saviour Machine 2*; 1995—*Live in Deutschland* (MCM); 1997—*Legend, Part 1*; 1998—*Legend, Part 2*; 1999—*Behind the Mask* [EP]; 2001—*Legend, Part 3, Disc 1*; announced for 2002—*Legend, Part 3, Disc 2*.

www.saviourmachine.com

Saviour Machine is an experimental rock band that has few competitors and no equals in the world of Christian rock—or even in the general market. Although it would eventually come to be tagged "Christian music's top goth band," the group's sound draws on industrial music, art-rock, metal, classical, and a variety of other progressive influences, while always preserving an essential melodic core. Although it has frequently been labeled "goth" and been filed under that heading by stores diverse enough to include a goth (much less "Christian goth") section, the band does not seem to use that label for itself. Some of the connection comes from the use of masks and makeup in their live performances. Eric Clayton, who admits to being "very familiar with the goth scene," says, "the mask (or makeup) has always been a representative metaphor of the flesh, and how quickly people judge flesh, instead of what's beneath it." Saviour Machine's concerts have been described by *True Tunes* as "a dramatic staging of symbolism that falls somewhere between performance art and rock opera." For example, during a song that addresses what Clayton calls "the horror of AIDS," he would take about twenty condoms, blow them up like balloons, imprint each with a bloody red handprint and then toss them into the audience. Christian observers did not always get the message he wanted to convey (especially when the audience simply proceeded to play with the "balloons" as though they were beach balls). *True Tunes* has said that, in the early '90s, "There was nothing in Christian music quite as scary as Saviour Machine. . . . front man Eric Clayton's deep brooding voice was matched only in impact by his shaved head and white face paint." The group's lyrics have also been characteristically dark, as Clayton claims to sometimes "write from the point of view of someone who is confused, angry, or living in disbelief." The name Savior Machine comes from a song by David Bowie.

Eric Clayton was raised in a Baptist home, but drifted from the faith in adolescence. Shattered by the untimely death of his stepfather, he became involved with drugs and then, hopeless and suicidal, turned to God for help and rededicated his life to Christ. In 1989, he formed Saviour Machine with his brother Jeff. The first Saviour Machine demo has been described as "dramatic metal-edged ambient music" *(True Tunes)* and as the work of "a dark hard rockin' band grappling with tears of pain" *(HM)*. The sound is more raw and less orchestrated than on later projects (Nathan Van Hala was not yet with the band), much more in keeping with '80s metal. Of primary interest to Saviour Machine fans is a twenty-minute track called "The Revelation," which, divided into five distinct parts, serves as a precursor to their later *Legend* project. A song called "When the Cat Came Home" would turn up with slightly different lyrics on their major label debut as "The Mask." The 1990 *Saviour Machine* would be reissued in 1997 by MCM Music. At the time of its first release, it captured the attention of some alert participants in the growing underground club scene, but was generally too heavy and intense for the Christian music subculture. Frontline, however, took a risk and signed the band, releasing two albums on the aptly named Intense imprint.

The 1993 *Saviour Machine* (sometimes called *Saviour Machine 1* to avoid confusion) reprises "Carnival of Souls" from the custom release, but aside from that song and "The Mask," is all new material. Produced by **Terry Taylor,** the album fits well with that artist's theatrical *(Alarma Chronicles)* interests. Reviewers would note influences of Peter Gabriel, Pink Floyd, and David Bowie, but an even more prominent, though less immediately obvious, progenitor may have been Andrew Lloyd Webber's *Phantom of the Opera* musical. A stunning seventy minutes in length, the concept album seems to deal with the state of the world before the coming of Christ. A theme of escalating spiritual warfare is developed throughout with, again, numerous songs inspired by verses and images from Revelation. Musical styles vary from the big melodic orchestration of "Carnival of Souls" to the quiet piano ballad "Son of the Rain" to the hard driving "Killer." *Saviour Machine 2* runs seventy-six minutes and features far more piano/synth-driven ballads for a softer overall sound that allows for enhanced Pink Floyd com-

parisons. Some of the songs seem to deal with Clayton's autobiographical struggles with hypocritical judges within the church, but many focus on social issues: the plight of Third World nations in "The Hunger Cycle"; child abuse in "The Child of Silence"; and political tyranny and turmoil in "American Babylon." The album's centerpiece is a sixteen-minute epic track called "The Stand." The song "Ceremony" speaks of personal preparation for the return of Christ (Clayton's favorite theme), and the album's closing masterpiece, "Love Never Dies," celebrates the eternal reign of God.

Sometime around 1995, Saviour Machine joined with a European management team to form MCM Music, an independent label that allows the band full artistic freedom; in Europe the albums have been distributed by Massacre, a black-metal label often associated with artists enamored of the occult. The first official release on MCM and Massacre was *Live in Deutschland,* a concert album for which a video version was also released. Some controversy was aroused over horror movie-type scenes, such as one in which Clayton drinks fake blood from a chalice.

The band's next project was one of the most ambitious undertakings in the history of Christian music. They announced a trilogy of albums that would provide a musical interpretation of the entire book of Revelation. Originally, the three records were to be released successively on January 31 of 1997, 1998, and 1999. Those deadlines were not met, and the package grew to a four-disc set, but the result was only the more impressive. Die-hard fans awaited each installment of *Legend* with the anticipation that attends a new *Star Wars* movie, and as the discs appeared, there were few disappointments. Musically, *Legend* is an undeniable triumph. *True Tunes* exaggerated its importance as "a gripping, brilliantly orchestrated, deeply disturbing work that could well reshape the face of popular music," but the work does have potential appeal to both Christian and general market audiences. The style, though very heavy at times, betrays strong classical and operatic influences—Clayton's muse seems to have shifted from Webber to Wagner. Samples, spoken word introductions, dark synths, and other effects are employed throughout. The first installment, *Legend 1,* opens with a haunting, symphonic overture. "I AM" is a brief choral interlude featuring nonverbal harmonies from a German choir. "The Eyes of the Storm" is driven by thundering drums to create a warlike, tribal atmosphere. "The Birth Pangs" brings in heavy electric guitars. "The Woman" features piano and soft melodic singing about the covenant between God and Israel. "The Sword of Islam" has a strong Middle Eastern feel. The eight-minute "Gog: Kings of the North" is built on a foundation of black-metal riffing. "World War III—The Final Conflict" uses more heavy guitars to convey the terror of Armageddon; it is followed by a piano ballad, "Ten-Empire," which conveys the emergence of a new Roman empire after the war. *True Tunes* would call *Legend 1* "a death requiem for the '90s," and all reviewers agreed that the piece had to be consumed in its entirety, rather than being scoured for hits or favorite songs.

Legend 2 is a bit heavier than the first installment, with more distorted guitar and less choral singing; it also features notable multilayered production that one reviewer would say "captures the chaos of the apocalypse in an imaginative way." The sound is generally the same, however, combining well-orchestrated symphonic music with electronic programming, ambient synths, piano, and all the staples of hard rock. The opening track, "The Covenant," is a gothic opus in itself with a choir, an electric guitar, and a spoken word background all competing for the listener's attention. The album also features one song that stands out from the rest with hit single potential: the almost industrial "Behold a Pale Horse," driven by a catchy electro beat, would actually be released as a single and generate some airplay. *Legend 2* clocks in at eighty minutes (just two minutes longer than the first installment), and one song actually had to be cut for it all to fit on a single disc; "New World Order" was subsequently put on the "Pale Horse" single. Reviewers agreed that the second installment, in particular, is a dark and complex work that requires repeated close listening. *HM* notes that there is enormous depth of subtlety, including reprises of musical themes from the first project. The album was accompanied by long and detailed liner notes, including a list of passages from the Old and New Testaments that Clayton apparently regards as predictions of still future events.

Legend 3 is heavier (more metal) than its predecessors, in part perhaps because of the theme: *Disc 1* opens with "1260 days," the length of time during which the Antichrist will supposedly terrorize the earth before Christ intervenes and brings salvation to a faithful few. Musically, "The Locusts" offers a guitar-heavy metal march, while songs like "Rivers of Blood" and "Mark of the Beast" provide goth-metal with its raison d'etre. The most chilling moment on *Legend 3:1* comes with the emotional "The Final Holocaust," which has a sound begging for inclusion on a film score. "The End of the Age" closes the album on a sad note that leaves one longing for the resolution promised in the final installment. Clayton told *HM*, "*Legend III:1* is probably a much more song-oriented record than its predecessor, *Legend II*, which was intended to create an atmosphere of chaos and confusion."

Theologically, *Legend* is not so much based on the book of Revelation as it is informed by a perspective that reads the book as a blueprint for predicting current (twenty-first century?) affairs. Rather than considering Revelation as an example of apocalyptic literature or even as a first-century document, as a biblical scholar would have done, Clayton collates its images with those of completely different writings (es-pecially Ezekiel, Zechariah, and Daniel). For instance, the idea of a forthcoming rapture is introduced into the program, in spite of the fact that no such event is ever mentioned in the book of Revelation (or anywhere else in the Bible, for that matter). The same may be said for all allusions to Islam, World War III, and numerous other elements that provide *Legend* with its content. Clayton has repeatedly said that he did not intend "to give an intellectual or dogmatic interpretation of Scripture, but a musical, artistic interpretation." *Legend*'s music, of course, stands on its own, and biblically oriented Christians may be able to receive it for what it is—an impressive, operatic presentation of twentieth-century fundamentalist apocalypticism that also manages to engage the imagery of Revelation in creative and exciting ways. Dante's and Milton's writings have continued to fascinate persons who have little interest in the doctrinal idiosyncrasies of their authors.

Saviour Machine has a large following in Europe, where Clayton estimates that about two-thirds of their fans are probably not Christians. In 1999, the group issued *Behind the Mask,* a sort of greatest hits EP, with five of their best-known songs. The disc itself is actually shaped like the mask that Clayton used in the band's early performances. In 2000, music from the song "The Bride of Christ" (from *Legend 2*) was used in a film called *Seraglio;* wall posters and other Saviour Machine paraphernalia were also displayed throughout the film. *Seraglio* was nominated for the Academy Award for Best Short Film (Live Action).

In terms of a mission statement, Saviour Machine's website declares, "The message of Saviour Machine finds its biblical inspiration in James 1:12. . . . Those without a faith in Christ are forced to search the world for hope and meaning apart from its Creator, but ultimately find themselves empty-handed and empty-hearted." Likewise, Clayton told *HM* in 1998 that his hope is "that all listeners will use his music as a means of escape from this cruel killing Machine called the world, and find peace with the Savior."

Say-So

Kim Thomas, voc., gtr.; Jim Thomas, gtr., kybrd. 1994—*Laugh, Cry, Play* (custom); 1997—*Say-So* (Organic); 1999—*Still Waters.*

http://members.aol.com/saysofans/music.html

Say-So is a Nashville husband and wife duo who play acoustic folk-pop songs with an appeal to college and adult alternative audiences. General market reference points for their sound would include Sheryl Crow and Shawn Colvin. Kim and Jim Thomas first began writing music together when she was fifteen and he was a lifeguard at the camp she attended. They wound up married and living in Philadelphia, where she was a graphics arts designer and he, the manager of a Christian radio station. In 1986, they began to pursue music full time and for more than a decade toured and sang without a label contract. Jim is a student of philosophy and a sought-after conference speaker. Kim Thomas is also an author and a painter. Her book *Simplicity: Finding Peace by Uncluttering Your Life* (Broadman and Holman, 1999) offers time-management insights laced with humor and reflection on spiritual priorities. Her artwork has been displayed in galleries in Chicago and Nashville and used for the album covers of **Sixpence None the Richer**'s *This Beautiful Mess* and Say-So's self-titled project.

Say-So incorporates several remixes of songs from an earlier custom project. The album opens with "Mercy Me," which showcases the big sound the couple is often able to achieve with a minimum of instrumentation. The song has appealing, poetic lyrics ("wash away today and make all our tomorrows new") set to a vibrant melody. The same style is evident in such catchy songs as "Water and Blood" and "Let It Be Love." "Drink the Water from My Hand" and "Better" (a diatribe against cliques and snobs) have a darker edge to them. Kim Thomas adopts a Frente-like little-girl voice for "Mary Be Merry" and gets appropriately fragile on the delicate "Calling My Name." "Wonderful World" was cowritten with **Phil Keaggy,** and the version here features cameo appearances by **Steve Taylor** and **Charlie Peacock** as a makeshift brass section (trombone and cornet, respectively). "Stand by Me" was featured on episodes of the TV series *Dawson's Creek* and *Party of Five. Still Waters* is a continuation of the first project, opening again with a near-perfect pop song, the soaring "Perfect Love." The songs "Souvenirs" and "How Could We Know?" are similarly strong. Otherwise, the album is not as hook-laden and immediately memorable as *Say-So,* though the Lennonesque piano ballad "In Between" is the sort of song that becomes more endearing with repeated listening. "Remains of the Day" laments the transience of life, and "Job's Mile" offers an empathetic prayer to be able to accept life's turmoil as the biblical character did. The album also features two spoken word recitations of poems ("We Believe" and "Comfort").

Christian radio hits: "More" (# 22 in 1997); "Mercy Me" (# 15 in 1997).

Say What?

Mighty White; Tricky Downbeat. 1990—*Fresh Fish* (StarSong); 1992—*Nuclear Fishin'.*

Say What? was a rap-comedy duo whose ultimate rejection of traditional Christian values (tolerance, compassion) guaranteed their products a quick trip to the bargain bin. Both of their albums mixed pop-rap numbers with short skits and silly stream-of-consciousness sampling. The first record won them an audience with dance floor grooves and a dose of cheeky, and often self-deprecating comedy. A falsetto "I Can Sing Higher

Than Patty" and an anti-video-game rant called "VG Veggies" are simply silly. "Back in a Big Way" retells the story of Joseph and his brothers, and "Johnny Fencerider" samples The Doors' "Riders on the Storm" to present a tale of spiritual compromise. The group did get a warning from critics on the latter track regarding the racist implications of a cowboys-and-Indians analogy used to depict positive and negative poles. On their second album, they stuck to what they wrongly assumed to be safe subjects in the Christian market. A cut called "Star-Spangled Sundae" worked, using samples to present hypothetical interviews with Christian music personalities. "Put Out the Fire," by contrast, displays what even *CCM* (no friend of the MCC) would call "virulent homophobia." As it turns out, Christian audiences were not as hip to gay bashing as Say What? and StarSong had assumed and the duo was not heard from again.

Scarecrow and Tinmen

Brad DeRosia, gtr.; Ryan Gingerich, gtr.; Chris Padgett, voc., kybrd.; Darren Yoder, drums. 1999—*No Place Like Home* (Pamplin); 2000—*Superhero* (Organic).

www.scarecrowtinmen.com

Scarecrow and Tinmen is a Christian band with an eclectic pop sound that seems to draw from the palette of such groups as **The Newsboys, Audio Adrenaline,** and **Jars of Clay.** *The Phantom Tollbooth* pegged them, however, as having a youth-group-friendly sound that ultimately comes off as more similar to Hanson than to any of the just-named acts. The group favors solid melodies, big harmonies, and simple lyrics. In 1999 guitarist Ryan Gingerich married eighteen-year-old singer **Nikki Leonti** and a minor scandal ensued when it was revealed that she was pregnant at the time.

Both of the Scarecrow and Tinmen albums were produced by **John** and Dino **Elefante.** Their debut features two songs that pick up on the *Wizard of Oz* imagery behind their name. A signature song titled "Scarecrow and Tinmen" identifies Christians as people who "have a new heart and mind." "No Place Like Home" repeats that theme, with the added notion that, like Dorothy in Oz, Christians always feel as though they are aliens in a world that is not their home (cf. Hebrews 11:13). The sophomore project, *Superhero,* demonstrates musical maturity and has more of an edge to it. Though reviewers would continue to complain about silly lyrics and derivative sounds, the album has an undeniably fun and buoyant quality to it, not unlike the work of **All Star United.** On "Groovy," the group seems to mock its critics with deliberately simplistic verses ("Take a look at all that Jesus did—I think that it's so groovy") set to a retropsychedelic '60s beat. Likewise, "God Is Good" celebrates its affirmation ("God is good / All the time / All the time / God is good") with the sort of bravado **DeGarmo and Key** once demonstrated when they thumbed their noses at poetry-obsessed critics by recording a song called "God Good, Devil Bad." The album has the loops and rock feel of a live performance. Still, as *Tollbooth* would note, "Jesus Is God" takes its guitar line almost note for note from Cream's "Sunshine of Your Love," "Get off My Back" owes more than a little to Stevie Wonder's "Superstition," and "Big Mouth" is a straight rip-off of hip-hop era **DC Talk.** Scarecrow and Tinmen are at their best when they keep things simple ("The Reason" sounds like **The Newsboys** doing a Partridge Family song). The group has had significant success in ministering to high school youth and is known for an "interactive and hyperactive" show that is geared toward "winning the kids over." They have also launched an organization called Be Warm, Be Filled that encourages youth to bring food, clothing, and blankets to the concerts, which are then collected and distributed to local charitable groups.

Christian radio hits: "Gospel Love" (# 19 in 1999); "You Are My Son" (# 10 in 1999); "Jesus Is God" (# 9 in 2000); "Scarecrow and Tinmen" (# 12 in 2000).

Scaterd Few

Allan Aguirre [a.k.a. Ramald Domkus], voc.; Andrew Domkus, kybrd. (–1998); Omar Domkus, bass (- 1998); Samuel West, drums (–1998) // Paul Figueroa, gtr., kybrd. (+ 1991; –1998); Russell Archer, gtr. (+ 1998); Steve Martens, drums (+ 1998); Steven Meigs, bass (+ 1998). 1990—*Sin Disease* (Alarma); 1991—*Out of the Attic*; 1994—*Jawboneofanass* (Sopa); 1998—*Grandmother's Spaceship* (Jackson Rubio).

www.scaterdfew.com

Scaterd Few is an innovative and accomplished Christian band that comes off as a shotgun wedding between complex musicianship and scathing punk-rock. The group has often attracted controversy within the Christian music subculture, not least because it has sometimes contained members who were not professing Christians. In 1994, Allan Aguirre would tell *HM* that the group contained "two non-professing Christians, two professing Christians (he and Omar Domkus) and my brother Drew, who has experienced the Lord, but hasn't walked with him in about a decade." A year later, in an almost offhand remark, he noted in the same journal, "After the tour last fall, Sam [West] got saved, which just leaves Paul [Figueroa] as the only non-believer." In any case, the band's identification with Christian music is primarily due to Aguirre, who has served as its front man, songwriter, and lead singer. Aguirre also fronts the mellow Middle Eastern-sounding band **Spy Glass Blue,** a testament to his eclectic musical stylings. He possesses a unique voice that has been compared to a combination of David Bowie, Ric Ocasek, and Gary Numan. Scaterd Few has managed to retain a following despite the

fact that it keeps breaking up and despite its defiance of the product-a-year convention of the Christian music industry.

The group basically got its start when Aguirre, who was a fan of **Daniel Amos,** sent a demo tape of his own music to that band's **Terry Taylor,** who very much liked what he heard. Sometime around 1983–1984, Taylor recorded some raw demos with the band. The Christian music scene was clearly not ready for them, and the recordings were shelved, later to resurface as *Out of the Attic.* In 1989, Aguirre relaunched the band and Taylor produced their official debut, *Sin Disease.* That album evinces a sound similar to the general market hardcore group Bad Brains, combining spiritual content with what would later be called old-school punk music. *True Tunes* called the album "a brilliant blend of psychedelic, reggae, punk-metal." Scaterd Few played the Christian *Cornerstone* festival in support of the album but also toured with Bad Brains and took part in such pagan events as a New Age festival sponsored by the organization Earth First. Lyrically, *Sin Disease* deals with such topics as a friend's death as a result of gang violence ("Lights Out") and cocaine addiction ("Glass God"). The opening track, "Kill the Sarx," uses violent imagery in its graphic interpretation of a biblical theme (cf. Galatians 5:24; *sarx* is the New Testament Greek word for "flesh"). There was some controversy over the generally dark focus of the program, which had not yet become the order of the day in 1990 (a year before *Nevermind*). The photo of Aguirre for the album cover originally showed him shirtless, sporting "wild" dreadlocks. The locks remained, but the record company actually drew in a shirt over the singer's bare chest to minimize perceived offense. Almost a decade later, *HM* would call *Sin Disease* "the record that decisively ended the '80s" (for Christian music, that is) and "Christian music's best punk album ever." It would be four years before the group could put out a follow-up (*Jawboneofanass*). In the meantime, Taylor appeased fans by releasing the band's '80s demos on a cassette. *Out of the Attic* was described by *True Tunes* as a collection of "14 songs of pure, unadulterated, hardcore bliss" and as "sounding like it was recorded in somebody's basement on a home tape player." The songs were later remastered and re-released on CD with a half dozen live songs added.

Jawboneofanass has an interesting history in that it was actually recorded three times—first in 1991 for a general market label (Vox Vinyl), then for a different label (**Michael Knott**'s Blonde Vinyl) in 1992, and then again as an indie project in 1994. As such a scenario implies, the years following *Sin Disease* were complicated ones for Scaterd Few, with legal complications and personnel changes. Guitarists came and went, and Aguirre told *HM* that in 1991 he himself had to leave the band because, as he put it, "there was sin in my life." He rejoined in 1992, but after the Blonde Vinyl fiasco, the band broke up again, only to have Aguirre reassemble it a year-and-a-half later. *True Tunes* hailed *Jawbone* as "brilliant" in its portrayal of "psychotic, poetic angst" and predicted the lyrics would spark less controversy this time around: Aguirre "represents the sincere yearning of a saved man crying out in the desert" and "peppers his raw 'grit and bear it' message with doses of humor so as not to be too heavy handed." The closing song, "Pinnacle," may be the album's highlight, with jamming guitars and lyrics taken straight from the book of Jude. "Dreams" features the sort of atmospheric leads that its title suggests, but couples these with funky percussion for an overall quirky effect. The album was sold only through the mail and at band concerts, which were few—especially since the West Coast leg of the group's tour got canceled due to "personal problems at home for one of the members." In 1995, Scaterd Few broke up again. Samuel West went on to join **Stavesacre** and Aguirre formed **Spy Glass Blue.** *Jawboneofanass* would later be repackaged with a KMG reissue of *Sin Disease* that put both albums together on a single disc.

Almost four years later, Aguirre would reassemble an entirely new cast of Scaterd Few and record *Grandmother's Spaceship,* which he describes as "hard punk, funk, reggae, and futuristic, with angst, realism, and psychedelia." He also jokingly referred to the record as *Sin Disease 2,* and most reviewers believe it to be a worthy successor to that revered masterpiece. The record evinces a very aggressive, predominantly punk sound with a science fiction "space alien" theme dominating or affecting many of its songs. The theme sometimes seems to serve as a concept for portraying the alienation of believers who live in a world where they are increasingly unwelcome. But in terms of content, the songs come much closer to mainstream Christian music than previous Scaterd Few projects, with fairly obvious religious allusions. The summons to "Wake up, sleeper" in "Lullaby" echoes Ephesians 5:14, and the cry of "Death, where is your sting?" in "Incorruptible" is from 1 Corinthians 15:55. "Win the Fisher" is a one-line song whose only lyric comes almost straight from Mark 1:17. The most up-front line in "Arbitrator" ("You've knit me, fearfully and wonderfully made") is from Psalm 139:14. But a number of songs explore darker, scarier stuff. "As the Story Grows, V. 2" presents voices that berate Christians from a world that has heard it all: "We like the smell of hell / How dare you try to tell us that / He died to set us free." "Space Junk" records questions that assault the believer ("how can you believe in a god that lets small children suffer?") and ends with a desperate cry ("get out of my mind!") that identifies the assailant, this time, as within. "Bobby's Song" (from which the album title comes) tells a bizarre story about a grandmother waiting for a flying saucer to take her away, with shades of the infamous Heaven's Gate cult suicides; the song features the memorable line, "When you wish upon a star, you better know whose stars they are."

Schaliach

Peter Dalbackk, voc., gtr.; Ole Børud, gtr., bass, drums. 1995—*Sonrise* (Petroleum).

Schaliach is a Norwegian doom metal band, or rather, duo, composed of two men who manage to produce a huge sound that has been likened to "a metal symphony." The almost keyboardless approach focuses on Metallica-style guitar leads on music that bears strong classical influences. Piano and strings are brought in for one instrumental track. Lyrically, the songs draw heavily from Scripture and speak openly of Christ and the love of God for all humans. Ole Børud of Schaliach went on to play with **Extol.**

Jeff Scheetz

1988—*Warp Speed* (Edge); 1990—*Woodpecker Stomp* (Re-Flexx); 1992—*Dig!;* 1997—*Pawn Shop* (custom).
www.jeffscheetz.com

Jeff Scheetz is a professional guitarist especially skilled in technique and noted for his precision in playing a variety of music. Trained in classical, rock, and jazz, he spent many years leading guitar workshops sponsored by Yamaha Guitars and writing a column on guitar technique for *HM* magazine called "Licks and Tricks." For a short time, he played with the Christian band Sign of the Times until, he says, "the singer wigged out, stole two of my guitars and sold them at a pawn shop." He has also recorded at least three albums of instrumental guitar music. *Warp Speed* was apparently a demo and is never listed in his official discographies, though it was reissued with a different cover by a company called Svanzada Metalica in 1992. The official debut, *Woodpecker Stomp,* features an up-tempo version of "Amazing Grace" alongside a number of original tunes in styles ranging from funky jazz-fusion ("Get Busy" and the title track) to soft, acoustic work ("Parker Street"). *Dig!* offers more of the same, with its centerpiece being "King's Triumph," a track that depicts the ultimate victory of Christ in a soaring and uplifting way. *Pawn Shop* (named after the Sign of the Times fiasco) strives for the sort of diversity implied by its title, sampling a variety of sounds. Scheetz is noted for working humor into his performances. A track called "Pike" showcases his bass player (Eddie Pruitt) with a musical depiction of a person's struggle to reel in a fish. *Dig!* offers a piece called "Lime Green Leisure Suit Blues." To capture the Native American vibe of a buffalo drum for a tune called "Dakota" on *Pawn Shop,* Scheetz says, "we just took my 125-pound dog, and we miked him up and patted him on his belly." Like most instrumental musicians in the Christian scene, Scheetz has had to justify how he is able to witness to Christ by performing music without words. "People can enjoy what I'm doing and then learn that I'm a Christian by talking with me," he says. "Sometimes that will have a deeper effect on a person than if I were to speak boldly from the stage for a few minutes."

John Schlitt

1995—*Shake* (Word); 1996—*Unfit for Swine.*

www.johnschlitt.com

A native of Mount Pulaski, Illinois, John Schlitt is best known for his role as lead singer of the very popular Christian rock band **Petra,** a role he has filled since 1986. Before that, Schlitt served as lead singer for the mainstream rock band Head East from 1973 to 1980. The latter group was a quintet from St. Louis that made a few arena rock albums in the late '70s but never gained a strong nationwide following. Their biggest hit was "Since You've Been Gone," a tune that only went to Number Forty-six on *Billboard*'s official charts (in 1978). The tune gained a broader hearing on AOR stations, but Head East was destined to be remembered more for the picture of the braless hitchhiker on one of their album covers than for their music. Schlitt lived like a stereotypical rock star, abusing alcohol and drugs, and winding up addicted to cocaine. In the early '80s, he left the music scene completely, became a Christian, and cleaned up his act. He was recruited for **Petra** by that band's leader, Bob Hartman, who also serves as the group's principal songwriter. The solo projects, Schlitt has emphasized, imply no dissatisfaction with the main band, but allow him another venue for expression and an opportunity to record more of his own material. Schlitt's band for the solo albums has included Dann Huff (gtr.) and David Huff (drums), both of **Giant** and other bands, and Mark Heimermann (kybrd.), who also plays with **DC Talk.**

Shake basically sounds like a **Petra** spin-off, with less anthemic choruses and more of a pop feel than '90s **Petra** usually evinced. *True Tunes* would call it "**Petra**-lite." The album opens with its strongest rocker, "Wake the Dead," on which Huff's histrionics provide a steady foundation for the star's wailing vocals. This is the sort of song that Schlitt seems to like best—a Journey/Foreigner/Loverboy arena track that sounds like it blasted right out of the early '80s. Lyrically, the song calls on Christians to shake off complacency and make a difference in their world. The next song, "Don't Look Back," is a power-pop number with the same message. That same theme informs "Let It Show," a funky tune that sounds like a duet between Michael Jackson and Aerosmith. "Show Me the Way" is a more acoustic prayer for continued guidance in life. "Inside of You" is a particularly emotive power ballad about recapturing the dreams of youth by exercising childlike faith. Schlitt pretty

much abandons rock altogether on the closing track, "Road to Calvary," an adult contemporary offering produced by Greg Nelson (known for his work with **Sandi Patty**).

Unfit for Swine goes in another direction, delivering the sort of experimentation that usually attends solo offerings by members of active bands. Only a couple of tracks ("God Is Too Big," "There Is Someone") seem like **Petra** outtakes. The opening song, "Save Me," has a Zeppelin feel to it that sets it apart from anything Schlitt or his band has ever done. "Can't Get Away" finds the singer using a lower register and moving in an alternative, modern rock direction, with electronically distorted vocals, quirky percussion, and fuzzy guitars. On "Take You On" Schlitt goes for the classic Aerosmith (or maybe **Guardian**) sound again and this time manages to make it his own—it is a compelling song with exciting guitars and a major groove that does not depend on simplified hooks. Almost all reviewers, however, agreed that the best song on *Unfit for Swine* is the album's closing track, "Don't Have to Take It." Musically, the song features wicked guitars, tweaked vocals, and strutting rhythms that put it in a class of its own. *True Tunes* said, "imagine Steve Vai jamming with members of The Chili Peppers and old-school Van Halen." Schlitt himself said, "It's a cool, vibey song . . . way out in left field for me, but I'm liking it, because it's so weird, you know." Lyrically, the song offers simple, generic advice, encouraging youth not to let their lives be defined by the expectations of others. On most of *Unfit for Swine,* however, Schlitt delivers the gospel with explicit enthusiasm, offering message songs that address the searching ("Helping Hand") or the complacent ("Need I Remind You") and that provide personal testimonies from his own faith life ("Take You On"). "I Killed a Man" offers his own statement of responsibility for the death of Jesus. "We Worship You" is an acoustic praise song, free of the bombastic sound of some of **Petra**'s praise material.

Christian radio hits: "Let It Show" (# 7 in 1995); "Show Me the Way" (# 1 for 2 weeks in 1995); "Helping Hand" (# 18 on 1996); "God Is Too Big" (# 15 in 1997).

Mark Schultz

2000—*Mark Schultz* (Word); 2001—*Song Cinema* (Word).

Mark Schultz moved from his home on the Kansas plains to Nashville in hopes of pursuing a music career and wound up serving as youth pastor at First Presbyterian Church. While there, he has written numerous songs for the high school students with whom he works, and his self-titled album collects some of these for wider distribution: "Remember Me" offers his words to graduates about to leave for places unknown and "Learn to Let Go" is his advice to parents (and perhaps himself) watching them leave. "Cloud of Witnesses" summarizes a lesson about the global character of the church, as learned by some teenagers on a two-week trip to Jamaica. Schultz cites Billy Joel as an obvious influence, and his album sounds similar to latter-day projects by **Steven Curtis Chapman** *(Dive)* and **Michael W. Smith** *(Live the Life)*. It opens with two upbeat pop songs: "I am the Way" (presenting reassuring promises of Jesus) and "Let's Go" (inviting comfortable Christians to a life of mission work). Later, "When You Give" offers a taste of traditional gospel, complete with a segue into a cover of **Al Green**'s "Take Me to the River." Such moments provide the record with its most radio-ready singles, but Schultz's vocal and compositional talents truly shine on a handful of tender piano ballads. "He's My Son" presents the earnest prayer of a father whose son has been diagnosed with leukemia. "When You Get Home" is a tribute to the artist's mother. Both of these are tearjerkers, but Schultz arouses such emotions honestly, with empathetic lyrics and powerful, heartfelt singing. *Song Cinema* lacks anything to compare with "He's My Son" but is a more consistent project overall, evincing a brighter, more upbeat sound. The opening song, "When Mountains Fall," offers a declaration of God's care in times of tragedy and, so, would seem especially meaningful in the aftermath of the terrorist assault on America on September 11, 2001. "Back in His Arms" is sung to one of Schultz's young people who strayed from the faith while at college. Schultz also sings a duet with **Rachel Lampa** ("Think of Me") and covers **Mr. Mister**'s "Kyrie Eleison."

Christian radio hits: "I Am the Way" (# 7 in 2000).

Connie Scott

1983—*Heartbeat* (Sparrow); 1985—*Spirit Mover;* 1987—*Hold On* (Image 7); 1988—*Christmas in Your Heart;* 1989—*Forever Young;* 1992—*Live to Tell;* 1997—*Renaissance* (label unknown).

Connie Scott (b. 1964) is a Christian pop singer from Vancouver, British Columbia. A classically trained child prodigy, she became a noted performer even before releasing her debut album at the age of nineteen. When she was three, she sang for Gerry Scott's (her father) gospel radio show, and at five, she began performing with the Scott Family Singers. At ten, she appeared on an NBC TV Christmas special and two years later began touring as a duo with her younger sister Sherri. By the time she began recording, her father had become president of Word Records in Canada.

Scott's 1983 album presented a Barbie-doll image she would later seem to resist (at least for a time). The cover was embellished with cutesy valentine hearts and displayed the pretty blonde amidst a sea of pink and white balloons. Songs on *Heartbeat* include contributions from **Chris Eaton** in addition to a standout track ("Just Another Reason") composed by **David Meece.** David Mullins' "You Changed My Life" opens the collection with an upbeat pop feel, but about half of the songs are MOR ballads. Scott's strong soprano glides over all of the arrangements in a way that reveals her years of vocal training, and *Heartbeat* won her nominations for both Dove and Grammy awards. *CCM* raved about the album when it came out, but in reviews of later albums (both *Spirit Mover* and *Hold On)* they would dismiss the debut as "wimpy" and "filled with sugary sweet little ditties." Their point, in both cases, was that the later albums were "a giant leap forward." Scott's voice would take on more of "a gutsy, husky, emotional edge" (comparable to Kim Wilde), and her choice of material would embrace more songs with a contemporary rock style. *Spirit Mover* was produced by Greg Nelson, known for his work with **Sandi Patty.** It opens with a hook-laden synth-pop title track, also written by David Mullins, and then moves on to an appropriately rocking **Dick and Melodie Tunney** composition called "He's the Rock." The song "D.O.A." (about the avarice of the devil) was cowritten by **Steve Camp** and **Rob Frazier.** Two songs on *Spirit Mover* are particularly insightful with regard to issues that many young girls face when navigating the traumas of adolescence: "Come On, Leah" by **Pam Mark Hall** reflects on the pain of being ostracized by a clique; "Is There an Orphan in Your Home?" (written by Mark Gersmehl of **White Heart**) expresses the strong need for parental affection that many girls experience at this time. The next album, *Hold On,* was produced by Roy Salmond (of **Salmond and Mulder**), who again went for the keyboard-driven techno-pop sound, albeit with a rockier Pat Benatar edge. In an interview, Scott maintained that it was "the first true Connie Scott album," that is, the first on which she had done what she really wanted to do. "I didn't have my own style before," she said. "I was your typical imitator. If I sang, 'You Light Up My Life,' I would sound exactly like **Debby Boone.**" *CCM* called *Hold On* "passionate and powerful," singling out the catchy "Run to the Light" and edgy "Don't Curse the Darkness" as standout tracks. The ballad "Love Is All That Matters" was written by Eric Carmen of The Raspberries fame. After a successful Christmas album, Scott recorded **Bob Dylan**'s "Forever Young" as the title track for an album that was primarily mellow. *CCM* selected "Wild Horse Running" (another Mark Gersmehl tune) as "by far" the best track from that project, calling it "a song that speaks truth, encouraging the vision, dreams, and imagination of the human mind in a poignant and poetic way."

After *Forever Young,* Scott took a three-year break from the Christian music scene, during which time she worked as a session singer in various secular pursuits. In a way that seemed almost *too* predictable for those who remembered her first album, she became a musical spokesperson for Mattel's Barbie dolls, recording commercial jingles to promote the products. She also sang backup vocals for Cher's *Love Hurts* album and joined the Canadian leg of a Michael Bolton tour as one of his background vocalists. Scott's 1992 album, *Live to Tell,* carried signs of the latter two artists' influences. It includes covers of **Ashley Cleveland**'s "Walk to the Well" and a gritty rendition of **Mr. Mister**'s "Healing Waters."

Christian radio hits: "You Changed My Life" (# 40 in 1984); "D.O.A." (# 5 in 1985); "Love Is All That Matters" (# 15 in 1987); "You'll Never Know" (# 9 in 1988); "Healing Waters" (# 14 in 1992).

Mike Scott (and The Waterboys)

1995—*Bring 'Em All In* (Chrysalis); 1998—*Still Burning* (Chrysalis). As The Waterboys: 2000—*A Rock in the Weary Land* (RCA).

Mike Scott (b. 1958) was the leader of The Waterboys, a successful British rock group that never quite caught on in the United States. The group evinced a spiritual mysticism that appealed to many Christian music fans, and in the late '90s, Scott's associations with the Christian music scene increased, though it was never really clear that the artist wanted to be known as a Christian, much less as a Christian musician. The Waterboys were formed in London in 1981; they went through several personnel changes in their fifteen years together with Scott as the only constant member. The group also displayed stylistic changes. They began with a horn and keyboard sound that critics dubbed "big music" (*The Waterboys,* 1983; *A Pagan Place,* 1984; *This Is the Sea,* 1985), then developed a more acoustic style (*Fisherman's Blues,* 1988; *Room to Roam,* 1990), and finally closed out their career with a straightforward electric rock album (*Dream Harder,* 1994).

Scott then surprised everyone with a Celtic folk album in 1995 called *Bring 'Em All In.* That album features a great deal of spiritual imagery, which sometimes draws from specifically Christian sources. *Cornerstone* magazine got the artist to sit down for an interview regarding matters of faith. He told the interviewer that C. S. Lewis was his favorite author and discussed a number of the spiritual (Christian) principles that he found engaging in Lewis's writings. But he also spoke in language laced with what that magazine would regard as "New Age terminology" about all persons being "different points of God" and about God being his own "true self." Pressed with regard to whether he understood himself as having a relationship with God through Jesus Christ, he responded, "No. It's not my way. I respect it and honor it, and, as far as someone standing outside it can, I understand it. But I have a different path, I think, or a different angle on it." This wasn't the end of the rumors that Scott was a Christian singer, however, and three years later, his second solo project would only increase such musings. Musically, *Still Burning* returns him to basic rock and roll similar in style to *Dream Harder.* The songs on *Still Burning,* however, go deeper than any of his previous work in terms of exploring themes of personal redemption, transformation, and the quest to find grace and mercy in an unforgiving world. The

Phantom Tollbooth examined the album in some detail, noting for Christian music fans the manner in which songs like "Love Anyway" bespeak an ethic unlike that which informs previous Waterboys' tunes about heartbreak and disappointment in love. Whereas previous songs ("All the Things She Gave Me," "We Will Not Be Lovers") express bitterness and even a desire for vengeance, "Love Anyway" boasts "You made a fool out of me today / I'm breaking the rule / I love you anyway." What sets that song in context, however, is the album's strongest track, "Everlasting Arms," a virtual hymn to God and a prayer for divine comfort: "Lord, hold me in your everlasting arms . . . let striving cease, that I may come to rest / In perfect peace, renewed and truly blessed." The closing verse continues, "Lord, lift me in your everlasting love . . . I'll go where a temple stands upon a hill / In silence I'll wait upon your will / In your everlasting arms." Scott did not offer any media testimonies to the nature of his faith—newfound or otherwise—but he did perform at the *Greenbelt* Christian music festival (the British equivalent to *Cornerstone*) in the summer of 1998.

That same year, a compilation album called *The Whole of the Moon: The Music of Mike Scott and the Waterboys* (EMI) included selections from Scott's solo albums in a retrospective of his former band's career. A two-disc collection of live recordings (*The Live Adventures of The Waterboys,* New Millennium, 1998) also kept interest in the old band alive. Then in 2000 Scott released what most would regard as his third solo album under The Waterboys' name. *A Rock in the Weary Land* does not resolve any questions the curious might have regarding the orthodoxy of Scott's beliefs, but the presence of faith is once more evident. *Phantom Tollbooth* and others would note that, assessed on its own (apart from the doctrinal disclaimers cited above), the album could easily stand alongside any number of works produced within the contemporary Christian market—and, in fact, it was received as such by many Christian music fans. Not all the songs are religious, but spiritual interests are woven throughout. "Dumbing Down the World" draws strongly on Lewis's *Screwtape Letters* to describe the devil's attempts to blunt the sharpness of wonder in the world. "Let It Happen" addresses the question of why bad things happen to good people and concludes with a Jobian acquiescence: "Whatever needs to happen / Let it happen, let it be / Through it all I am protected / Grace is effected over me."

David Scott-Morgan

1998—*Call* (independent); 1999—*Long Way Home;* 2001—*Reel Two.*

www.scottmorgan.co.uk

David Scott-Morgan was guitarist for the rock band ELO (a.k.a. Electric Light Orchestra) from 1981 to 1986. This was not the band's most productive period—their hits pretty much all came in the '70s. Still, Scott-Morgan did tour several times with the group; he played on the band's *Secret Messages* album (1983) and, later, on group leader Jeff Lynne's solo project, *Armchair Theatre* (1990). He also collaborated with Richard Tandy, ELO's keyboard player, on a number of projects, including a concept album called *Earthrise* (1986). Scott-Morgan has had some success as a songwriter, with some early material being recorded by The Move and one song ("Hiroshima") becoming a Number Four hit in Germany by an artist named Sandy. In 1988, Scott-Morgan says, he became "a born-again Christian" as a result of taking his mother to church. He began writing inspirational songs soon after, and in 1998 he began doing programs with his wife, Mandy, in which the two of them would share their evangelistic testimony, interspersed with original songs, some classic rock and roll tunes, and a few ELO hits. In 1999, the two founded a congregation at a small church in south Birmingham, England, called The Church on the Hill. Morgan-Scott also works as a commercial pilot and flight instructor. *Call* features one song ("God's Good Time") that was produced by Jeff Lynne.

Steve Scott

1983—*Love in the Western World* (Exit); 1988—*Lost Horizon* (Alternative); 1990—*Magnificent Obsession;* 1992—*The Butterfly Effect* (Blonde Vinyl); 1994—*Empty Orchestra* (Twitch); 1996—*We Dreamed That We Were Strangers* (Glow); 1997—*More Than a Dream;* 1998—*Crossing the Boundaries.*

An experimental multitalented artist from Britain, Steve Scott (b. 1951) was a part of the Exit records venture launched by Mary Neely, wife of evangelist Louis Neely, who headed Warehouse Christian Ministries (a Sacramento offshoot of Costa Mesa's Calvary Chapel). WCM had been a significant venue for fledgling Christian music artists during the days of the Jesus movement, and in 1983, the Neelys were once again ahead of the game in providing a platform for artists with an alternative vision nearly a decade before the genre of alternative rock would gain any official recognition. The big stars were **Brent Bourgeois, Charlie Peacock, Vector,** and the **Seventy Sevens.** Steve Scott was "the other one," the artist on the label whose vision was so alternative that he would never achieve the kind of legendary status that would accrue to his Exit colleagues. *True Tunes'* editor, John Thompson, calls him "a walking arts seminar" who is "so far out on the cutting edge that he can hardly be seen without binoculars."

Scott was born in London and educated at Loughton Art School and Croydon College of Art in England. As a young man he established a reputation for working in a variety of media—as an experimental filmmaker and as an author whose works of fiction, nonfiction, and poetry were published in a variety of literary journals. At some point he came to America

and made an album for **Larry Norman**'s Solid Rock records (*Moving Pictures,* 1980), but this would never be released. He became a full-time staff member at Warehouse Christian Ministries, and a new project, *Love in the Western World,* would be one of Exit's first releases; it would be reissued on CD by M8 in 2000. The album met with a mixed reception when it first appeared but would ultimately be regarded as a Christian classic. Jon Trott wrote in *Cornerstone* that *"Love in the Western World* is not an album easily accessible lyrically or melodically, yet within its mesmeric music/lyric combinations are finely crafted paintings of our fallen world." *CCM* said it was "lacking in concept," "monotonous," and "full of tiresome songs expressing the sadness and lostness of mankind." But, then, six years later, a more perceptive critic for the same magazine (Brian Quincy Newcomb) would recall the album fondly, noting that its "intelligent poetic metaphors and bold, angular new music were not completely understood." And *eighteen* years later *HM* magazine would dredge the disc up yet again for special Hall of Fame attention in a feature that proclaimed it "easily the most creative album of the year (1983), maybe of the decade." Okay, so it had to grow on you. Musically, Scott's style on *Love* fit into the general scheme of British new-wave with similarities to such artists as Roxy Music, The Police, and David Bowie. There are also notable similarities to the sound of the **Seventy Sevens'** first three projects (with Roe and company playing on the album), and some vocal inflections reminiscent of Lou Reed. The album's title track (borrowed from a book by Dennis De Rougemont) has a slight Human League feel with lyrics that kind of parallel Bowie's "Modern Love." A bit more profound are "Tower of Babel" (dealing with communication breakdowns) and "Safety in Numbers" (presenting scenes of urban despair). "Wall of Tears" uses Middle Eastern sounds and apocalyptic imagery as backdrops for a simple plea to make some kind of connection with human society. A treat for **Seventy Sevens'** fans is Scott's own rendition of his "Different Kind of Light" (covered on the latter band's *Ping Pong across the Abyss* album). It is presented here in a straightforward rock version left over from Scott's unreleased *Moving Pictures* project. Also from those sessions, an original version of "More Than a Dream" (title track to a later album) seems to find the artist engaging in some Neil Young fantasies; the same could be said of "Safety in Numbers," though Scott would admit only to Peter Gabriel obsessions in the liner notes to the M8 reissue. *Love in the Western World* also includes a spoken word recitation of poetry called "This Sad Music" and a ska-flavored number, "Walking on Water Wasn't Built in a Day." The most rocking moment comes with a live performance of "Call of the Wild," with segues into a rather different (non-Human League-ish) take on "Love in the Western World."

After *Love,* Scott made two more records that would not be released: the full-length album *Emotional Tourist* (1986) and an EP, *Rice* (1987). *CCM* had actually previewed the *Emotional Tourist* album in a feature story in which Scott indicated that, while *Love* was a concept album with "the ideas laid out end to end, . . . on *Emotional Tourist* the ideas are superimposed," making it, supposedly, *less* accessible. Musically, he was backed on *Tourist* by friends from Exit (Peacock and members of **Vector** and the **Seventy Sevens**), and the self-described "eclectic and esoteric" sounds of the project ranged from modern electronic music to a Chinese orchestra to American folk music. The album, Scott explained, was "about people who travel across surfaces without ever understanding the nature of the ground they cover." Audiences would eventually get a chance to experience the work (sort of) when songs from *Love in the Western World, Emotional Tourist,* and *Rice* were broken up and placed on two albums issued on the independent Alternative label. To destroy the sequencing of material from concept albums is, of course, bizarre, but *Lost Horizon* and *Magnificent Obsession* at least allow some of the material to survive. Standout songs on *Lost Horizon* include "Ghost Train," "Not a Pretty Picture," and "Ship of Fools" from *Tourist,* and "Something's Got to Change," "Touch," and "What is the Mystery" from *Rice.* A studio version of "Call of the Wild" is also included. *Magnificent Obsession* reprises what were probably Scott's two best-known songs ("Ghost Train" and "Love in the Western World") along with concert versions of songs from *Moving Pictures* ("Farthest Star," "The Love You Need") and *Love in the Western World* ("Tower of Babel," "No Time Like Now").

Scott pretty much retired from pop music after the '80s and devoted his talents to other pursuits. For a time after *Emotional Tourist* he conducted seminars as a spokesperson for Warehouse Christian Ministries. He also toured as a performance artist, traveled widely, and wrote about those travels. Eventually, he became a regular writer for *Radix, True Tunes,* and numerous other magazines, and a featured speaker at the *Cornerstone* festival. He published several books in the '90s, including *Crying for a Vision* (Stride, 1991), *Like a House on Fire* (Cornerstone, 1997), and three volumes in a series he calls *The Boundaries.* A collection of poems called *The St. Petersburg Fragments* (Cornerstone, 1993) collects poems inspired by a ten-day trip to Russia. By the end of the '90s Scott would probably be best known to Christian music fans in these capacities (speaking and writing), but he also continued to record albums of poetry—collections of spoken word pieces set to sampled loops of sound effects that he has recorded throughout his international travels *(The Butterfly Effect, We Dreamed That We Were Strangers, Crossing the Boundaries).* The last of these, *Crossing the Boundaries,* includes reproductions of multimedia paintings done by visual artist Galen Stewart. Scott and Stewart collaborated on the project, such that poetry and imagery are intertwined—the paintings were allowed to stimulate creation of the poems at the same time that they illustrated them. *Empty Orchestra* departs from the spoken word tradition by offering an all-instrumental album, with poems printed on an accompanying insert to be read by the listener while absorbing the ambient sounds ("empty orchestra" is an English translation of the Japanese word *karaoke*). Finally, *More Than a Dream* combines new recordings of a few old songs ("Ghost Train," "The Sound of Waves," and "Come Back Soon") with selections of beat-poetry.

Note: a completely different artist (a jazz guitarist) by the name of Steve Scott released an independent self-titled album of Christian music in 2001.

For trivia buffs: Steve Scott inadvertently provided the name for the **Seventy Sevens'** 2001 album. **Michael Roe** of that band remembers that in 1978, while recording *Moving Pictures,* the visually oriented artist told his guitarist (Jon Linn) to play a chord that sounded "like a golden field of radioactive crows." The phrase stuck in Roe's head for twenty-three years and became an album title.

The Screamin' Rays

T-Ray, voc.; C-Ray, voc.; Sting Ray, gtr.; X-Ray, gtr.; Johnny Ray, bass. 1999—*Attack of the Screamin' Rays.*

The Screamin'. Rays was a one-project rockabilly/swing band that got together to make a fun album around the time the style was enjoying a revival in the general market with groups like Cherry Poppin' Daddies and Squirrel Nut Zippers. C-Ray is actually **Crystal Lewis,** and Sting Ray is Chris Brigandi, who played with Lewis way back in high school in a band called **Wild Blue Yonder** (and before that was in **The Lifters**). Contrary to many rumors, Lewis's musical husband, Brian—whose last name actually *is* Ray—was not a member of the group. Brigandi and crew come by the sound honestly, having played rockabilly for more than a decade before getting Lewis to join them for the Screamin' Rays experiment. Brigandi wrote a number of the tunes, but the group also tackles public domain standards like "Don't Want to Go Down There" (about avoiding hell) and "Glory, Glory Hallelujah," along with a cover of Cab Calloway's "We the Cats (Shall Hep Ya)." The Screamin' Rays display a more guitar-based version of swing music than the aforementioned Daddies or Zippers, making the Brian Setzer Orchestra a more likely general market comparison—though the combination of Lewis's vocals with T-Ray's authentic Calloway-cum-Elvis stylings give them a sound all their own. *Attack of the Screamin' Rays* remains one of Christian music's pretty little secrets: a jazzy, upbeat album of impressive caliber that should have been enjoyed by a much wider audience.

Seasons in the Field

See **Pensive.**

Seawind

Ken Hutchcroft, brass; Bud Nuanez, gtr.; Larry Williams, brass; Ken Wild, bass; Bob Wilson, voc.; Pauline Wilson, voc.; Jerry Hey, brass (– 1980). 1977—*Seawind* (CTI); 1978—*Window of a Child*; 1979—*Light of the Light* (Horizon); 1980—*Seawind* (A&M); 1995—*Remember* (Noteworthy).

Seawind was a progressive jazz-funk band formed in Hawaii by **Bob and Pauline Wilson,** who also recorded as a duo. The band formed in 1974 under the name Ox, then became Seawind in 1977. Their albums were released on general market labels, and they were criticized in some circles for working outside the official Christian music empire. The albums did, however, feature songs with explicitly Christian lyrics, and the Wilsons in particular were very upfront about their faith. The music on the first three albums generally fell into the progressive jazz category, emphasizing horns and keyboards. Two of the group's best songs, "Countin' the Days" and "Hallelujah," are both from *Window of a Child.* Their self-titled debut on A&M (a different album than the eponymous project for CTI) displays a turn toward more jazz-influenced rock. That album also reveals what *CCM* called "de-Christianized" material, owing to the fact that the Wilsons were now releasing their more faith-oriented songs on Myrrh. *Remember* is a retrospective compilation. Bob Wilson and Larry Williams later played in **The Front** and **What If.** Still later (in the early '90s), Wilson and Nuanez would turn up as the core of a band called 40:31 (after Isaiah 40:31), which *CCM* described as having a sound "like early **Koinonia.**"

Christian radio hits: "Countin' the Days" (# 24 in 1978).

2nd Chapter of Acts (and A Band Called David)

Annie Herring, voc.; Matthew Ward, voc.; Nelly Ward Greisen, voc. Personnel for A Band Called David: Gene Gunnels, drums; Herb Melton, bass; Richard Souther, kybrd.; Rick Azim, gtr. (–1977); Paul Offenbacker, gtr. 1974—*With Footnotes* (Myrrh); 1975—*In the Volume of the Book*; 1976—*To the Bride* [with Barry McGuire and A Band Called David]; 1977—*How the West Was One* [with Phil Keaggy and A Band Called David]; 1978—*Mansion Builder* (Sparrow); 1980—*The Roar of Love*; 1981—*Rejoice*; 1981—*Encores*; 1983—*Together Live* [with Michael and Stormie Omartian]; 1983—*Singer Sower*; 1985—*Night Light* (Live Oak); 1986—*Hymns*; 1987—*Far Away Places*; 1988—*Hymns 2*; 1989—*Hymns Instrumental*; 1992—*20* (Sparrow).

www.2ndchapterofacts.com

The sibling vocal trio known as 2nd Chapter of Acts was one of the Jesus movement's greatest treasures—the very rare example of a group with a completely unique sound and the native talent to outshine all secular competitors. If comparisons are necessary, the group could be placed very loosely into the same grouping as mixed-gender vocal bands like The Mamas and the Papas, Spanky and Our Gang, or Fifth Dimension. But 2nd Chapter was better than any of those groups—they had a more consistent songwriter, stronger vocals, and, especially, tighter harmonies. Beyond that—for four or five years at least—they had the Pentecostal spirit that their name suggests, exhibiting almost unprecedented creativity and internal-combustion energy. Dyed-in-the-wool Jesus freaks thought it sad to watch them turn into a churchy group that their parents would have liked. But that is what happened: 2nd Chapter of Acts became the first of the Christian hippie bands to get scrubbed and tamed. As such, they would also become one of the most successful at finding a second career in the unhip '80s. The fire may have gone out, but the quality of the music as such did not decline, and the group continued to grow in popularity as producers of highly competent worship music.

A brief biography of 2nd Chapter of Acts' career is included with the box set called *20,* released in celebration of their twentieth anniversary. Annie, Nelly, and Matthew Ward were three of nine children born to Walter and Elizabeth Ward in rural North Dakota. Annie sang with her older sisters at schools, fairs, and churches in a group called The Ward Sisters. The family was poor (no indoor plumbing) but eventually moved to California where Annie found a boyfriend named Buck Herring. A novice in the music business, Herring's life was transformed when his former drug supplier "got saved" and took him to church where he too became a "born-again Christian." Though Annie had been active in the Catholic church as a child, she had been sent into a spiritual crisis following her mother's death from a misdiagnosed brain tumor, and her boyfriend's new-found faith helped her to attain a personal and vibrant connection to Christ herself. Annie and Buck married a year later, in 1969—and a year after that, her father, Walter, died of leukemia. The Herrings took in the two younger siblings, Nelly (age fourteen) and Matthew (age twelve), and brought them to the same experience of evangelical faith. The trio of siblings began singing in churches, but their big break came when Buck was asked to produce **Barry McGuire**'s first Christian album *(Seeds),* and 2nd Chapter of Acts was invited to back up the star on the record and in concert. McGuire would jokingly tell about meeting the "skinny kids" for the first time at Herring's home where he felt obliged to listen to his host's wife and children sing—a routine that celebrity musicians must sometimes suffer politely. From the first song, he knew that here was something sensational—not just raw talent, but indeed a whole *new sound* such as had never been heard in popular or religious music before. You could hear some traditional (black) gospel in there, some folk rock, even some classical choral liturgy . . . but, all together, no one had ever heard anything like this before. The group's work with McGuire would lead to a spin-off career as an act in its own right. They recorded a song called "Jesus Is" (with lead vocals by Matthew—on his thirteenth birthday), and it came to the attention of **Pat Boone,** who arranged a contract with MGM records. That didn't ultimately work out, and by 1974 they were recording for the Christian label Myrrh. In terms of church affiliation, the group became associated with Jack Hayford's Church on the Way in Van Nuys, California, at a time when that congregation had fewer than a hundred members, and they remained headquartered there throughout the '70s period of their classic recordings. The members of their backing band (A Band Called David) also belonged to that congregation. In 1981, 2nd Chapter relocated to Lindale, Texas, where they bought a ranch next to the one occupied by **Keith Green**'s Last Days Ministries. Green would die in a plane wreck just one year later.

Like many of the earliest Jesus music groups, 2nd Chapter of Acts was devoted to worship and ministry in ways that often conflicted with the more commercial concerns of the music business. The group did not play outdoor festivals, for instance, because they did not find that environment conducive for what they thought should happen at a concert. Buck Herring once explained that the group understood its role as being to serenade "the two lovers—Jesus and the church . . . to encourage the romance." And, he added, "it's tough to be romantic with frisbees whirring by over your heads." Likewise, the group tended to shun publicity that would smack of "self-promotion" and refused to let their press materials describe their products with "superlatives" or other terms that imply comparison with the gifts of others. At one point (1978), they did an entire year of concerts for voluntary offerings only, refusing ticket sales yet guaranteeing to reimburse promoters out of their own pockets if expenses were not met. As late as 1992, Buck Herring reminisced about such policies without apology: "I would much prefer the days of our beginnings to what we have now. There wasn't anybody clamoring to do what we did, or what **Love Song** or any of the other early Jesus music groups did. There were no charts for us to be Number One on. Now, we have so many magazines, music charts, and popularity contests, it all has the potential to put ministries in competition with each other, rather than coming alongside and working together for Jesus."

True to their name, 2nd Chapter of Acts evinced a more charismatic understanding of ministry than most Christian groups—though this was more evident in their behind-the-scenes planning than in their lyrics or stage comments. An article in *Charisma* magazine summarizing the group's career tells of the signs and wonders that accompanied their ministry, including testimonies to miraculous healings that were per-

formed through the songs; Nelly in particular is identified as being given an "in-concert healing ministry" by God through which "people were healed of cancer, arthritis, and other ailments." Similarly, the aforementioned "biography" included in the group's 20 details the frequent times that the group made major career decisions based on "what the Lord told them" through direct revelations or prophetic words delivered by other Christians. For instance, they made the commercially successful *Hymns* albums after three separate persons came up to them at concerts claiming, "I believe God has a word for you—that you should do a hymn album." Likewise, Herring would regularly refer to herself as "a song receiver," indicating that the songs were given to her directly by divine inspiration. As for the group's name, Buck Herring says he heard the phrase "The 2nd Chapter of Acts" loudly in his mind one day while working in the studio and knew it was to be their name. "It's the nearest I've ever come to hearing God speak in an audible voice," he insists. The members themselves were less than thrilled with this divine selection. "It's an awful name," Annie objected. "People will think we're a play," Matthew opined. But it turned out to be appropriate and memorable. The group would record two of the best and three of the most important Christian music albums of all time, in addition to sharing credit for performance on two of the best and most important live albums of the Jesus music era. Nevertheless, they rarely received applause in their concerts, which were regularly characterized as "spiritual experiences" rather than "performances." As Annie Herring puts it, "One of the reasons people didn't applaud was because we weren't singing songs *about* Jesus, we were singing *to* Him. When people recognized that, they sensed His Spirit. They could see Jesus, and they fell in love with Him." 2nd Chapter of Acts disbanded as a group in 1988, believing that the Holy Spirit had directed them to do so, in spite of their continuing success. They embarked on a farewell tour and performed a final concert in Houston, Texas, on August 12, 1988.

With Footnotes will always be best remembered for its standout track "Easter Song." The song explodes out of the stereo speakers like a modern day "Hallelujah Chorus," leaving little doubt that if Handel had been born in the late twentieth century this is the sort of thing he would have written. It *is* a rock and roll song, but it belongs to that strange class of pieces that rise above the rock genre and seem to be something more, something that could conceivably be played hundreds of years hence when popular music and folk songs have lost their cultural appeal. Set to the most joyful, celebrative tune imaginable, the song invokes mild holiday confusion by sampling a line from a favorite Christmas carol and applying it to the resurrection: "Joy to the world! He is risen! Hallelujah! Hallelujah!" When Herring wrote "Easter Song," she initially dismissed it as unacceptable for the group's repertoire. She offered it to friend **Jimmy Owens,** thinking perhaps he could use it in one of his choral church musicals. Owens was stunned the first time he heard the piece. To his credit, he rejected her offer, insisting, "You *don't* want to give this one away. You've got to record it." It was drummer David Kemper who came up with a new take on the tune in the studio, remolding it from the choir anthem Herring heard in her head into a rock anthem with a solid backbeat. **Michael Omartian** added the unforgettable keyboard track and **Michael Been** (later of **The Call**) played bass. In 1998, a *CCM* poll of thirty critics chose the group's version of "Easter Song" as one of "the ten best contemporary Christian songs of all time" and selected *With Footnotes* as "one of the ten best contemporary Christian albums of all time." That album also includes "Love, Peace, Joy," a bouncy bit of pop candy, with the infectious chorus "Stop, think it over, over again / You can have these if you're born again." Better poetry and more complex vocal arrangements could be found in "Which Way the Wind Blows" and "The Son Comes over the Hill." Matthew Ward belts out "The Devil's Lost Again" in a way that renders the lyric convincing while **Mike Deasy**'s guitar screams like a passel of demons in a herd of pigs. The latter song, especially, displays 2nd Chapter with a harder rock sound than their closest companions in Jesus music, **Children of the Day,** would ever attempt. Likewise, a medley called "I Fall in Love/Change" begins sweetly enough but features Herring practically growling the vocals by the time the song reaches its powerful conclusion.

In the Volume of the Book would be the band's second masterpiece. This time **Phil Keaggy** adds guitar licks to most of the tracks, with Omartian still on keyboards, Been on bass, and Buck Herring continuing (as always) to produce. The song "Hey Watcha Say" continues in the poppy "Love, Peace, Joy," tradition, and "Yahweh" does the "Devil Lost Again" bit one better. Writing in *Harmony* magazine, critic Mark Hollingsworth called the latter song "one of the best rockers put out by a Jesus group yet. . . . musically it is similar to late Free or fast-paced Jefferson Starship material [think: 'Jane'] with Keaggy's screaming licks and Matthew Ward's powerful vocals." Classical influences shine through on the baroque "Start Every Day with a Smile" and the nicely orchestrated "Now That I Belong to You." There are more pretty ballads on *In the Volume,* too, with "Last Day of My Life," "Psalm 63" (sung by Ward again), and "Prince Song" standing out as examples of beautiful songwriting. The last of these became the best-known song on the album, picking up on a fairy tale theme of "someday my prince will come" and applying it to the Christian expectation of the parousia, the coming of the Prince of Peace.

After *In the Volume of the Book,* 2nd Chapter of Acts wrote and produced a cantata of songs based on the novel *The Lion,* *the Witch and the Wardrobe* by C. S. Lewis. That book is actually the first in a series of volumes by the British Christian that are collectively called The Chronicles of Narnia. Though the stories were originally intended for children, they became favorites of the Jesus people, who enjoyed the Tolkien-like fantasy and picked up on the allegorical messages: in *The Lion, the Witch and the Wardrobe,* the central character is a lion named Aslan who voluntarily sacrifices his life for others and is then raised from the dead. 2nd Chapter developed fourteen songs reflecting on key themes, events, and characters in the story and wove these together into a seamless presentation that maintains thematic effect as one tune segues into the next. The project was a risky undertaking and did not have wide appeal to the group's fan base, but David Di Sabatino maintains that it represents their "creative peak" and is "probably the closest contemporary Christian music has ever come to sheer perfection." Due to legal hassles (apparently regarding rights to using Lewis's figures in the songs), the album was held up for three years after it was recorded, not seeing release until 1980.

In the meantime, the next studio album, *Mansion Builder,* would symbolize the transition from Spirit-led Jesus music to market-driven "contemporary Christian music," though it does so in a manner that showcases the benefits rather than the deficits of that transition. Rock fans would miss the guitars, not to mention the ragged edges and spontaneity of those wonderful first two albums, but *Mansion Builder* is an undeniable showcase of professionalism. Lushly arranged and orchestrated, it was hailed as a quintessential example of what Christian music could be. The songs are beautiful. The title track is a particularly strong choral offering with lyrics that employ an effective biblical image (1 Peter 2:5) for Christian growth: "Why should I worry? / Why should I fret? / 'Cause I've got a mansion builder / Who ain't through with me yet." "Rod and Staff" and "Well, Haven't You Heard?" are sprightly pop tunes, and "Psalm 93" is an intriguing Scripture suite with Ward navigating the tempo changes admirably. The highlight of the album, however, turns out to be a cover of **Keith Green**'s "Make My Life a Prayer to You" (written by Melody Green, actually). Thus, *Mansion Builder* was greeted as a mature and refined album, as evidence that the kids were growing up and were ready to make contemporary sounding music for adults.

The albums that followed were competent extensions of what the group had accomplished with *Mansion Builder*—but they were no longer rock albums. They sounded like Christian music and, increasingly, like church music. **Kerry Livgren** took over the keyboards from Michael Omartian on *Rejoice,* but he does not infuse any of the tunes with his distinctive art-rock backdrop. The best song on the album is "Bread of Life," a hymn written by Herring and Ward that actually sounds like it might have been composed in the seventeenth century. It is sung to the accompaniment of a church organ, with the group performing as a small choir. Likewise, "Heaven Came to Earth" is a Christmas hymn that one can easily imagine being sung by a boys' choir at that Roman Catholic church where Herring made her confirmation. "Mountaintops" is more similar to the ballads of the first two albums and is one of Herring's most beautiful songs. *Singer Sower* takes some disappointing turns into synth-pop ("Room Noise," "Ocean Liner") that sound silly and expose the futility of the group's trying to be faddish. It is their weakest album, notable only for inclusion of the song "Lift Me Up," which features lyrics written by **Keith Green** shortly before he died. *Night Light* suffers the same inconsistency, scoring with basic choral numbers like the title track but missing the mark on several tracks on which the trio sing simplistic lyrics ("All at once I was in trouble / I need help and on the double") to artificial robot beeps. *Far Away Places* would be the group's swan song, with Matthew now singing lead on an unprecedented six of the ten tracks. In retrospect, the album seems to display the group's fragmentation, as most of the songs come off as solos with background vocals rather than as showcases for those famous killer harmonies.

In between *Night Light* and *Far Away Places,* 2nd Chapter of Acts recorded an album of traditional hymns, which ended up outselling anything else they had ever done. *Hymns 2* followed, and even *Hymns Instrumental,* an odd project for a vocal group. The hymns albums are, of course, nicely executed, but wholly unremarkable. There no longer remains any discernible difference between what was once Christian music's most vibrant and innovative act and the choirs that fill hundreds of sanctuaries throughout the land. True fans were disappointed, but of course the group can do as it wishes. The bottom line assessment must be that 2nd Chapter of Acts earned their place in Christian music history with their first two albums. With that legacy secure, they were under no compulsion to continue making albums of historic significance. Unlikely rock stars, their hearts seemed more in tune with serving the church though worship and edification—and with few missteps they continued to do that respectably for a decade after completing the projects for which they themselves had been (and continue to be) exalted.

The group also made no fewer than three live albums—all in combination with other artists. The best of these is *To the Bride* (see listing for **Barry McGuire**), which includes several songs not found on the studio albums—including a take on Washington Phillips's "Denomination Blues," a track that would also be performed by the **Seventy Sevens.** *How the West Was One* (with **Phil Keaggy**) was issued as an impressive three-record set, easily the most ambitious undertaking in the marketing of Christian music at that time; it remains a work of

stunning significance, transforming the Christian music industry's vision of what a live recording can offer. On both of these two live projects, 2nd Chapter is accompanied by A Band Called David, a cadre of musicians that earned quite a reputation in their own right. In addition to the albums listed above, 2nd Chapter of Acts performed on the musical *Firewind* (Sparrow, 1976) written by **Jamie Owens (Collins), John Michael Talbot,** and **Terry Talbot,** and on *Come Together* (Light, 1972) written by **Jimmy** and **Carol Owens.** Both **Annie Herring** and **Matthew Ward** also recorded a number of solo albums.

The music of 2nd Chapter of Acts has fallen victim to the lack of historical appreciation that typifies the Christian music industry, and most of their albums remain almost insanely out of print. For a brief moment in time, *With Footnotes* and *In the Volume of the Book* were released on a single CD that pretty much sold out overnight; *To the Bride* has never been released on CD. The *20* compilation suffers from poor song selection, including nothing from *To the Bride,* nothing from Herring's out-of-print debut solo project, and only two songs apiece from the band's classic, most sought-after works.

Christian radio hits: "Mansion Builder" (# 2 in 1978); "Rod and Staff" (# 19 in 1978); "I've Heard the Stars Sing Before" (# 14 in 1980); "Rejoice" (# 1 for 5 weeks in 1981); "Takin' the Easy Way" (# 2 in 1983); "Spin Your Light" (# 31 in 1985); "Humble Yourself" (# 1 for 6 weeks in 1987); "Sing over Me" (# 13 in 1988); "Take It to All the World" (# 15 in 1988).

Dove Awards: 1987 Praise and Worship Album (*Hymns*).

Seeds ('70s)

Bruce Daniels, drums; Bill Huffman, gtr.; Jim Morgan, kybrd., voc.; Leon Muller, gtr., voc.; Timmy Payne, bass; Dwight Preslar, gtr. 1976—*This Could Be the Start of Something New* (Jubilation); 1978—*Into the Wind* (Klesis).

Seeds was a Jesus music band from North Carolina that *Harmony* magazine described as having a "powerful rock sound spiced by folk and jazz influences." Their debut album offers a collection of original evangelistic songs with a new rendition of the hymn "What a Friend We Have in Jesus" and a cover of the song "Lovin' Man" by Bryan Jory. *Jesus Music* says, "Seeds covers a number of styles on their debut album and performs them all well." The songs "Hey Hallelujah" and "You Gotta Decide" are typical Jesus music ballads, but "Know What I'm Talkin' About" and the title track have more jazz-funk styling, and "I Love Him" is an electric rocker. The entire second side is devoted to a "Salvation Suite" presented in three parts, including a jazzy instrumental featuring saxophone played by Jim Morgan's father of the same name. *Into the Wind* takes the band into more predictable adult contemporary territory. There is no connection between the '70s band called Seeds and the group listed below that formed in Chicago in the '90s.

Seeds ('90s+)

Shelly Bock, voc.; Tom Crozier, bass; Colleen Davick, flute, perc.; Scott Knies, gtr.; Mike Troxell, gtr., voc. 1997—*Seeds* (Grrr); 2000—*Parables, Prayers, and Songs.*

The Chicago band called Seeds that formed in the '90s is an acoustic folk rock group associated with the Jesus People U.S.A. community that has also been home to such artists as **Ballydowse, Cauzin' Efekt, Crashdog, The Crossing, Headnoise, Glenn Kaiser, Resurrection Band, Sheesh,** and **Unwed Sailor.** All of the members of Seeds have full-time jobs in the community: Shelly Bock works in the kitchen; Tom Crozier teaches school; Colleen Davick books concerts for some of the just-named acts; Scott Knies works with low-income seniors; Mike Troxell coordinates visits from guests and works with new members. Troxell says that the band formed "by accident" as the various members shared together leading worship in the community. Musically, Seeds shows strong influence from the early Jesus music groups—though they are not related to the '70s Jesus music group from North Carolina that used the same name (see above). They play acoustic folk-rock music enhanced with a variety of percussion, some flute, and the occasional ethnic instrument. Everybody sings and contributes to the songwriting. The group resists being labeled "a hippie band," but their sound and album cover graphics definitely evoke the era of flower power. Troxell cites **Love Song, Keith Green,** and **John Michael Talbot** as significant influences. The self-titled first album has the feel of an informal get together. "Man of Peace" is a raucous romp in anticipation of Christ's triumphant return. "Waiting" addresses a similar theme on a quieter note, as an individual believer yearns to be joined with Christ, possibly through death. "Come Back Home" offers God's plea for prodigals to return and "Come to My Rescue" is a penitent's plea for salvation. "Captain of the Sea" sounds very much like Crosby, Stills and Nash, while "His Love Endures" (the closing track) sounds a lot like **Caedmon's Call.** The album highlight may be the group's cover of a neglected **Terry Talbot** song, "The Road," which encourages the listener to help others through life. Seeds' follow-up project moves toward a more mainstream contemporary Christian music sound, with numerous ballads and Eagles-style acoustic rock. This time out, the group covers **Glenn Kaiser**'s "Blue Water."

Selah (Maranatha)

Joy Strange, voc.; Cindy Young, voc. // John Belles, bass; Alex MacDougall, drums; Craig Stevens, gtr., voc.; Frank Tretter, woodwinds, perc. (−1971); Erick Nelson, voc., kybrd. (+ 1971). No albums.

The group Selah was one of the first Jesus music bands. They began operating out of Calvary Chapel in Costa Mesa, California, around the same time as **Love Song** and **Children of the Day.** The original core seems to have been two high school girls named Joy Strange and Cindy Young. Strange would later be a member of **Parable** and would also record briefly as **Joy Cull.** Later, the band included **Erick Nelson** (who would subsequently join **Good News** and have a successful solo career) and Alex MacDougall, also known for his work with **Daniel Amos, The Way,** and **The Richie Furay Band.** According to Erick Nelson, the band traveled around in a VW bus and played a lot of Maranatha concerts, including ones at the Long Island Beach Auditorium. They were sometimes perceived as "too rocky" for churches and had to fall back on acoustic guitar and piano ballads as the occasion warranted.

The early version of the group (featuring the women with unknown backup musicians) performs the song "In Jesus' Name" on *The Everlastin' Living Jesus Music Concert* (Maranatha, 1971). That song is not necessarily one of the album's highlights, but its mere inclusion on what is easily the most important Christian album ever made guarantees the band its place in history. "In Jesus' Name" tells the basic story of Jesus' life and ministry in just over three-and-a half minutes to a tune that draws on Jewish folk music. As such, it represents Maranatha's only real entry into the messianic music genre pursued by **Lamb** and **The Liberated Wailing Wall,** and its inclusion on *The Everlastin' Living Jesus Music Concert* provides an essential remembrance of this subset of early Jesus music. The song opens with a haunting recorder solo, uncharacteristic for early Christian music, and concludes with a lively Yiddish chorus. For some unfathomable reason, the song was actually deleted from a 1999 CD reissue of the *Everlastin' Living Jesus Music Concert* on Asaph—a lapse that prevents that release from attaining the sort of historical stature it might otherwise have enjoyed.

The later, fuller version of Selah contributed a second song, "He Lives," to *Maranatha Two* (Maranatha, 1972). This time, "He Lives" (an Erick Nelson song) *is* one of the album's highlights—an orchestrated opus that begins with ominous chords, followed by Nelson's plaintive voice addressing "Weary pilgrim strangers in this land" (a probable allusion to Hebrews 11:13). The song has an ebb-and-flow feel to it, swelling up toward its inevitable Easter chorus and then backing away again, with lyrical references more poetic ("veil of countless tears") and, indeed, liturgical ("Jesus Christ, the Lamb of God is slain / Sent to free the spirits in the dark domain") than was common for Calvary Chapel Jesus songs. **Karen Lafferty** plays an uncredited oboe on the track.

The California group Selah should not be confused with the Christian rock group in Ohio that was active a short time later. That band recorded two albums: *Selah* (Pinebrook, 1975) and *With Clouds* (Milk and Honey, 1976). In the late '90s, another two, completely different groups called Selah would appear (see below). A fifth group in Indiana also appears to have recorded a self-titled custom album called *Selah,* but nothing is known of that band—save that they are distinct from all the others. The popular name derives from a word that occurs periodically in Psalms; the meaning is unclear, but many scholars think it indicates the place for an interlude to be played when the psalms were used in worship—a time for silent reflection or meditation. Erick Nelson recalls the time that he first heard of the group and asked Marsha Carter (later **Marsha Stevens**) what the name meant. "Stop and think about it," she told him. He did, and then replied, "I still don't get it." "No—stop and think about it," she replied, and after a bit more confusion, finally explained, "the word *selah* means 'pause for reflection'; it *means* 'stop and think about it'."

Selah (Curb)

Allan Hall, kybrd.; Nicol Smith, voc.; Todd Smith, voc. 1999—*Be Still My Soul* (Curb); 2001—*Press On.*

Not to be confused with the '70s Maranatha band listed above, the group called Selah that began recording for Curb in 1999 is a trio composed of two singing siblings and their accompanying pianist. The three worked together as session performers adding their talents to recordings (and sometimes in concerts) by **Margaret Becker, Amy Grant,** Pam Tillis, and Wynonna. *Be Still My Soul* is a collection of traditional and contemporary hymns, including "When I Survey the Wondrous Cross" and **Andraé Crouch**'s "The Blood Will Never Lose Its Power." *Press On* includes "Amazing Grace" and "How Great Thou Art," along with a surprising cover of the Beatles' "In My Life." **Russ Taff** joins the group for "Were You There." Todd and Nichol Smith also composed two original songs for *Press On,* including "Yesu Azali Awa," a tribute to the time they spent in Africa with their missionary parents. The appeal of both albums lies in the light production. On most songs, the singers are accompanied by little more than piano, acoustic guitar, and a little percussion—a stark contrast to the over-produced, ultra-slick sound that is stereotypically associated with adult contemporary music, especially in the Christian market. **Nicol Smith** has also pursued a solo career.

Yet another (unrelated) vocal group known as Selah released an independent self-titled album of Scripture-based worship songs in 1995. The latter band comes from Florida and has a pop style similar to **4 Him.**

Dove Awards: 2000 Inspirational Album *(Selah).*

Selena

1996—*You're All I Need* (Free Rain).

The contemporary Christian musician who recorded under the name Selena should not be confused with the Tejano superstar who was murdered in 1995. Selena was an eighteen-year-old R&B singer who recorded one album of dance tracks and ballads in 1996. *You're All I Need* opens with its powerhouse title track, a funky dance tune that identifies the Lord as the one who provides all things needful. "Mourning into Dancing" has more of a Latin flavor. "Oh Jesus" is a lovely acoustic ballad. The song "True Love" departs from the overtly religious theme to describe the character of love as something more than feelings: "It's time to learn that love is more give than it is take / And that true love is commitment that one chooses to make."

Selfmindead

Marko Hautakoski, drums; Timo Sillankorva, gtr.; Ilkka Viitasalo, voc.; Tapani Hoikkaniemi, bass (− 2000) // Emil Nikolaisen, bass (+ 2000). 1998—*Selfmindead* (Solid State); 2000—*At the Barricades We Fall.*

Selfmindead is a Scandinavian hardcore band. The group was formed by four Finns in Sweden in 1994. They then moved to Norway, where original bassist Hoikkaniemi was replaced with Nikolaisen from the band **Royal.** The group has been successful in their homelands, garnering generous airplay on Swedish radio. They tend to be classed as part of what is called the "straight-edge" (or sXe) scene—a European movement that supports veganism, abstinence from drugs and alcohol, and a morally upright life. Group members, however, identify themselves specifically as a Christian group. Their name is meant to signify the "crucifixion of selfishness, pride, and ego" that Jesus demands of his followers (cf. Mark 8:34). The group's first album was recorded in 1997 (on Soulscape Records) and was subsequently picked up for an American release by Solid State. The group goes for a chaotic, hard and heavy sound sometimes reminiscent of Rage Against the Machine or **Blindside** or **Embodyment.** There are abundant and sudden changes in time signatures and tempo, with recurrent pauses and bursts of feedback. The group skirts at the edge of rapcore but never quite goes that route; they themselves have sometimes described their sound as "emo-core." Lyrically, the album is angry and intense, focusing on the evils of technological society and humanity's need for God. *HM* would describe their second album as a major step beyond the debut: "they have evolved from a tech metal band to a more up and close hardcore band with some definite metal roots." The sound, while less complex, showed less of the emo stylings and more of a straightforward hardcore assault. This did not please *Phantom Tollbooth,* who complained that the band now sounded "like 400 other groups." *At the Barricades We Fall* features "Liar," a rant against the devil, and "Rules to Break/Laws to Change," a call for personal and social renewal. The angry punk sound works better on such numbers than it does on "The Motivation Song," where Viitasalo barks at the listener, calling him or her to "believe yourself"; likewise, a song like "Everything's Gonna Be O.K." doesn't seem quite the vehicle for tortured screeching. But *Bandoppler* loved the whole thing, calling it all "blistering" and "massive" and advising their readers, "If you don't get it, someone who isn't a loser wuss will."

Send the Beggar

Cris Anthony, gtr.; Matt Bentley, voc.; Brett Fitzer, drums; Chris Freeman, gtr.; Matthew Wooten, bass (−1999). 1997—*Send the Beggar* (Rustproof); 1999—*Closer to Complete.*

Send the Beggar is a Christian pop-rock group from Columbus, Ohio. Like many organic bands, they had their origins in their local church's youth group, where they played praise and worship songs for congregational services. Their name is derived from Luke 16:27. The debut album reveals a band with such influences as **Jars of Clay,** Sting, and Toad the Wet Sprocket. Jangly guitars serve primarily to bolster Matt Bentley's liquid vocals on melodic but tame pop songs. The song "Rome Is Sinking" offers a look at the tendency for Christians to put up a front when their faith is strained: "Sunday shortly after dawn / I'm in a room, full of yawns / Am I there to love you / Or to make them think I do?" The closing track, "Prodigal," is based on the famous parable in Luke 15 and features a duet vocal with **Christine Glass.** The group was not happy with the sound of their debut and complained publicly that it had not come out as they intended. The sophomore release has more of a raw, live sound, with guitars more prominent in the mix. The opening, title track is an especially strong almost-instrumental number with driving guitars and pulsing bass. "Presence of God" is a jangly surefire radio hit. "Leaving Jesus" begins with the line, "I wonder, is Columbus so different from Nazareth" and drops a number of local references (High Street, Schiller Park) for residents of that city; the title refers not to abandoning Christ but to making an impression that "leaves Jesus" with people. In general, the album's lyrics—like those on the first project—are honest, forthright, and challenging. "The Touch" laments a loss of virginity, which despite regret can never be regained. "The Funeral Song" explores the same sort of emptiness addressed in "Rome Is Sinking": "My faith feels as fake / As this smile on my face."

Sequoyah

See **Puller.**

Seraiah

Brad Beckey, voc.; Kyle Dietz, drums; Quinton Gibson, gtr.; Tracey Ferrie, bass. 1989—*Carnival World* (Pure Metal); 1992—*Seraiah* (StarSong).

Seraiah was a Christian metal band from Indiana that refashioned their sound after an unsuccessful debut to produce a sophomore record with more of a classic rock, power-pop appeal. Quinton Gibson was already playing in a high school rock band when the bass player invited him to a church function where he was shocked into conversion through the showing of a Hal Lindsey film. Gibson later met Brad Beckey at Indiana Wesleyan University and together they formed Seraiah. Steve Griffith of **Vector** produced the self-titled sophomore outing and cowrote many tracks, including the two that became hits on Christian radio. Most critics selected "New Kind of Voodoo" as the album's outstanding song, a dark, atmospheric tune that attempts to expose Santeria as a non-Christian cult. Most of the other cuts are more melody-driven pop, some with hard, metal edges. "When It Rains" is fairly rocking for a ballad, and "Fever" even includes a rap break. Beckey and Gibson went on to form **Kid Promise.** Both Gibson and Tracey Ferrie would later play in **Whitecross.** Gibson and Kyle Dietz would eventually reunite in the late '90s grunge band **Stir.**

Christian radio hits: "Time for a Change" (# 7 in 1992); "When It Rains" (# 14 in 1993).

Serene and Pearl

See **Considering Lily.**

Servant (Illinois)

Matt Spransy, kybrd., voc.; Doug Pinnick, bass, voc.; et al. No known recordings.

Two influential Christian groups named Servant appeared in the late '70s. The first was based in Joliet, Illinois, founded there by Matt Spransy in 1977. Spransy had been a member of the seminal Jesus music group **The Sheep,** which emerged from the same community that gave birth to **Resurrection Band** and Jesus People U.S.A. (see the listing for the other **Servant** band below). Spransy and **The Sheep** had gone to England in 1971, and while there Spransy had been involved in launching the *Greenbelt* festival, an annual Christian music event that would still be going strong in 2002. Back in the States, Spransy put together a band that included bass player **Doug Pinnick,** who would later become famous as the front man for **King's X.** Servant had a progressive, art-rock sound along the lines of Emerson, Lake, and Palmer or Yes. According to Christian music historian John Thompson, they "developed a considerable following among musicians, both Christian and not, and were widely thought to be the best Christian band of the day in terms of musical skill." The group was together for only three years and then disbanded in 1980. Spransy subsequently joined the other band named Servant, which was operating out of Oregon.

Servant (Oregon)

Owen Brock, gtr.; Sandie Brock, voc.; David Holmes, drums; Rob Martens, bass; Bruce Wright, gtr.; Bob Hardy, voc. (–1985) // Matt Spransy, kybrd., voc. (+ 1981); Eric Odell, voc. (+ 1985). 1979—*Shallow Water* (Tunesmith); 1981—*Rockin' Revival; 1982—Remix* (Horizon); 1983—*World of Sand* (Rooftop); *Caught in the Act of Loving Him;* 1984—*Light Maneuvers* (Myrrh); 1985—*Swimming in a Human Ocean.*

The Oregon Christian band named Servant is best regarded as a separate entity from the Illinois group with that name, even though, coincidentally, keyboardist Matt Spransy was a member of both outfits. The deep origins of both groups go back to the same source, a Christian community in Milwaukee led by Jim and Sue Palosaari. That group split into four smaller groups, not because of feuds or doctrinal disputes, but to maintain smaller cells that could proselytize more effectively. Music seems to have been important to everyone—one of the Milwaukee splinter groups ended up becoming the Jesus People U.S.A. community in Chicago, famous for producing **Resurrection Band** and many other Christian artists (see the **Resurrection Band** listing for more on this group). The Palosaaris themselves headed for Europe with some members of their group forming a band called **The Sheep.** After touring Scandinavia, they settled in London, where they put together the successful multimedia rock opera *Lonesome Stone.* Eventually, the community returned to the States, where the Palosaaris and a handful of others started a new community on the Applegate River in the Rogue Valley of southern Oregon. They called it the Highway Missionary Society and dedicated themselves to "common life in a missionary training environment." Members of the community (which eventually grew to about eighty adults) followed the example of Christians described in Acts 2:44–45 and 4:32–37, pooling all of their material resources. Owen and Sandie Brock, who had been part of the *Lonesome Stone* cast, became part of this society and headed up its musical outreach. This took the form of a Christian rock band that was first called Higher Ground, then adopted the name Servant. Money from the community was used to support Servant, and all profits from Servant's album and ticket sales went back to the community, supporting refugee settlements, hunger relief, world missions, and other causes to which the members committed themselves. Unbeknownst to the Brocks, Matt Spransy (who had been a member of **The Sheep**) had migrated to Chicago, where he had also formed a band named Servant. Sometime after Spransy's group collapsed, the Oregon Servant (faring much better) came through Chicago on tour. Spransy noticed they didn't have a keyboardist and joined up, bringing with him a significant amount of equipment left over from the first Servant's demise.

The Oregon-based Servant began with a classic rock sound featuring the twin lead vocals of Sandie Brock and Bob Hardy

on blues-based songs that sometimes recalled Jefferson Airplane. *Shallow Water* is a hard-edged product in the same tradition as **Barnabas** and **Resurrection Band,** though not as heavy. The song "Jesus Star" allows Bruce Wright to churn out admirable guitar riffs, and "Fly Away" brings the disc to a hand-clappin', foot-stompin' conclusion. Along the way, they also offer "Holy Roller Blues," a heavy cover of the **Dogwood** song "Watergrave," and a version of Sammy Hagar's "Rich Man." Released as the debut product of a Canadian label, the album is rare and copies pressed on red vinyl are potentially valuable. Musically, *Rockin' Revival* takes a giant step forward, with Spransy's synthesizers giving the group a fuller sound. This second album includes "Isolated," a song lamenting the lone-ranger spirit adopted by Christians who see no need for the church, as well as a couple of '60s-ish social protest numbers ("Ad Man," "Look Out, Babylon"). The song "I'm Gonna Live" was cowritten by **Doug Pinnick** (of the Illinois **Servant** and later of **King's X**) and would become a favorite of Christian music fans for years to come. *Remix* is a best-of collection of remixed songs from the two Tunesmith albums.

On June 23, 1981, tragedy struck the Highway Missionary Society. As the liner notes to *World of Sand* put it, "on just an ordinary summer morning while driving to the dump, a fiery head-on collision abruptly extinguished the lives of three members of our community." One of those killed was the Palosaaris's eight-year-old son, Seth. *World of Sand* is dedicated to those departed friends, and the mini-musical "Sudden Death" (clocking in at over eight minutes) is offered as a tribute to them. The most popular song on the album, however, would be "Jungle Music," an apologetic for Christian rock that pokes fun at the oft-heard (racist) argument put forward by fundamentalists that rock and roll must be demonic because it is based on tribal African rhythms. "Come, Jesus, Come" is an earnest plea for the Lord to transform an individual life; the track is actually a refurbished number from the old *Lonesome Stone* musical. For some odd reason, two of *World of Sand*'s best songs were packaged on a seven-inch single included with the album: "Cog in the Wheel" is a strong rock song, and "Treeplanter Stomp" offers a tribute to workers in the community who helped to keep the outreach ministry of Servant financially viable. Shortly after *World of Sand,* the band released a live album *(Caught in the Act of Loving Him)* as part of what they called the "Great American Album Giveaway" campaign. Some 150,000 to 200,000 records were distributed free to anyone who attended one of the group's concerts (alternatively, those who chose to buy the album in a store received a free concert ticket as part of the package). Instead of presenting live versions of songs from previous records, *Caught in the Act* presents a concert of new material, much of which has a Spransy-influenced new-wave feel (notably on such Euro-pop tunes as "Fall Out" and "Gauges"). "Holding On to You" pledges devotion to a God who has proved faithful through thick and thin; "Now Is the Time" summons Christians to take up the call for missionary service. To the disappointment of headbanging rock fans, the new-wave style would take over on the next two albums. *Light Maneuvers,* however, was the group's most accessible and polished production, helmed by Bob Rock, who was famous at the moment for work with Loverboy and would ultimately earn renown as producer for such acts as Mötley Crüe, Skid Row, Bon Jovi, and Metallica. "We Are the Light" was a well-deserved hit.

Around the time *Light Maneuvers* was released (in 1984), the Highway Missionary Society community relocated to Cincinnati (as the Servant community) in quest of a more urban environment for evangelism. The transition did not sit well, however, and in 1987, the community dissolved for good. Before that happened, the group Servant made one last album, their only project without Bob Hardy on lead vocals. *Swimming in a Human Ocean* continues in the new-wave direction but with a musically darker tone. Brian Quincy Newcomb, who was hardly a reliable fan of the group, wrote in *CCM* that it was now "safe to talk about Servant's music without sniggering." On the strength of songs like "I Will" and the joyful "Love Never Fails," the album closed out the band's career with what Newcomb would call "an artistic and commercially viable triumph." After *Swimming,* all members of Servant except the Brocks left the group—several of them were Canadians, and when the community dissolved, they lost their visas and had to return to their homeland. The couple recruited three new members—**Linford Detweiler,** Ric Hordinski, and Brian Kelly—and this version of the band played together for a while but never recorded. After dissolving, the three new recruits joined with Karin Bergquist to form **Over the Rhine.** Meanwhile Bob Hardy had embarked on a solo career, recording an album called *Face the Distance* by Bob Hardy and the Brigade (Regency, 1990). As of 2001, the Brocks were still located in Cincinnati, Owen working as a graphics designer and Sandie as a massage therapist.

According to John Thompson, Servant deserves credit for helping to perfect the "rock concert as evangelism" program invented by **Petra** and **Resurrection Band.** The group's concerts were "full-on rock experiences," complete with elaborate costumes, laser light shows, pyrotechnics, strobes, smoke, and other wild effects. On their 1982 "World Tour" they were actually big enough in the Christian music scene to take **Petra** along as their opening act. *CCM* says, "Servant was one of the groups instrumental in bringing Christian rock into the mainstream. They brought with them a commitment to high tech production and to touring, sometimes performing over 150 concerts a year."

Christian radio hits: "Come, Jesus, Come" (# 18 in 1983); "Holding On to You" (# 11 in 1984); "We Are the Light" (# 16 in 1985); "I Will" (# 5 in 1986); "Look through His Eyes" (# 11 in 1986).

Seth

Kelly Bagley, kybrd., voc.; Jonathan David Brown, kybrd., voc.; Keith Edwards, drums; David Wayne Hines, gtr.; Debbie Newell Scott, voc.; Rhenda Edwards Tull, voc. 1974—*Seth* (Shalom); 1975—*Psalms;* 1980—*Keep the Fire Burning* (StarSong).

Seth was a vocal group responsible for two albums of worship-oriented adult contemporary songs. The group is historically significant for the later careers of its members. Their projects seem to mark the earliest recordings of Maranatha star **Kelly Willard,** who was Kelly Bagley at the time. The group was led by **Jonathan David Brown,** who would later become one of Christian music's top producers, but whose career would come to a scandalous halt when he was sent to prison as a neo-Nazi symphathizer in 1992. Keith Edwards became a drummer for **Amy Grant** and then went on to play for a number of general market country artists. His sister, Rhenda Edwards Tull, later sang on **Parable**'s first album, though not as an official member of the band. Those who remember the group Seth say that Debbie Scott sounded just like Karen Carpenter and that Tull sounded like a young Michael Jackson or a prototype for **Crystal Lewis.** Surprisingly, Kelly Bagley (Willard) was too shy to sing and mostly just played piano. Brown wrote many of the songs on Seth's two albums for Shalom, though the group also covers tunes by Harlan Rogers and **Danniebelle Hall.** They toured with **The Archers.** In 1980, StarSong put out *Keep the Fire Burning,* a compilation album with tracks from both *Seth* and *Psalms,* along with a newly recorded title track. The cover photo for that album shows Brown looking like he might still be a freshman in high school; Kelly missed the shoot because she was sick.

Seven

See **Fono.**

Se7en

Troy Covey, voc., gtr.; Lester Estelle, drums; Jeff Never, bass; James Nieman, sax; Jason Porter, voc.; Matt Shoaf, gtr. 1998—*Se7en* (Infiniti).

The Kansas City group that spelled its name Se7en with a numeral should not be confused with the British band Seven, which later changed their name to **Fono.** Se7en was the musical ministry of evangelist Troy Covey's Revolution Revival, an outreach that was in turn sponsored by Kansas City's Fish Ministries. The multiracial quintet combined modern pop, hip-hop, and rock on ministry-oriented songs featuring praise choruses and evangelical lyrics. *HM* compared the group to **Reality**

Check, noting that they "squeeze out some energetic power pop" despite a "pretty safe and tame" orientation.

Seven Day Jesus

Chris Beaty, gtr.; Brian McSweeney, voc., gtr.; Wes Simpkins, bass (–1997); Matt Sumpter, drums (–1997) // Kevin Adkins, drums (+ 1997); Russ Fox, bass (+ 1997). 1996—*The Hunger* (5 Min. Walk); 1997—*Seven Day Jesus* (ForeFront).

Seven Day Jesus came on the scene in the mid '90s as a young band of guys from West Virginia who could play East Coast alternative rock like they had been doing it all their brief lives. The band's surprising musical maturity impressed critics and made them something of a sensation for Christians enamored of the Seattle sound, replete with mournful melodies, minor key chord changes, and power guitar chords. Brian McSweeney's gripping voice, however, is an attribute that doesn't quite fit the alternative stereotype: "I'm really a singer," he says. "I don't do well at screaming and that sort of thing." But Chris Beaty can make his guitar scream, in true **Ty Tabor** fashion—leading some critics to compare the group to an odd hybrid of **Michael English** (or maybe **Russ Taff**) and **King's X.** Their debut album offers mainly slow, textural pieces, interrupted by the occasional full-on rock assault. Produced by Luis Garcia of **PlankEye** and Masaki of **Dime Store Prophets,** the music often recalls a tougher version of the latter band. The best song is probably "A Time to Heal," a crunchy guitar-driven prayer that opens the album with a plaintive cry for "the one thing that can heal the hurt inside." The title track is also a very strong number with essentially the same theme: "How I need you Lord / Only you can fill / The hunger." "Forgive You" is ugly in sound and lyric, appropriately so for its theme—the need for a rape victim to forgive her attacker (or, autobiographically, for McSweeney to forgive a man who raped a close friend of his). On this one he does scream, spitting out the line "Rape my soul, Rape my soul / Rape me / You rape my soul" repeatedly in a way that inevitably recalls Nirvana's song, "Rape Me."

Back with a new rhythm section, the group released a more pop-oriented project on ForeFront. Sound comparisons switched immediately from Seattle grunge to power-pop groups like the Gin Blossoms or even to the retro sound of The Cars or '70s Kinks. The album's big hit, "Butterfly," is almost bubblegum, as is the sugar-coated, please-play-me-on-the-radio praise track, "You Are the One." Such songs led more serious-minded outfits like *Phantom Tollbooth* to dismiss the album as "Christian teenybopper material for adolescent girls." Others called the new material "crafty, upbeat, modern pop tunes" *(Release)* or "shiny, happy, melodic, memorable pop" *(CCM).* The album's strongest track, again, is its opening song, "Down with the Ship," a song that relates the decline of society that can be revealed through a remote-control, quick-click tour of TV channels. "Always Comes Around" is a fast-paced song with jangly guitars sustaining its joyful affirmation of Romans 8:28. "End of My Rope" and "Who Am I" are fairly heavy electric guitar songs that should have pleased critics of the lightweight stuff. "Sea of Forgetfulness" is a passionate ballad, testifying to the merciful forgiveness of God.

Christian radio hits: "Butterfly" (# 1 in 1998); "Down with the Ship" (# 4 in 1998); "Everybody Needs Love" (# 5 in 1998); "Always Comes Around" (# 10 in 1998).

7–10 Split

Dancore; Fontaine; Jon Ladd. 1999—*Trial by Stone* (Screaming Giant).

7–10 Split is a hybrid band from Atlanta that attempts to mix punk with metal. *The Phantom Tollbooth,* who doesn't like them much, claims "There's no actual mixing: it's mostly lean but muscular speedy punk that charges into hardcore with death vocals on two or three songs, and speed metal with death vocals on one song." In any case, the group addresses a wide variety of topics from a blatantly Christian perspective. "Instruction Manual" opens the album with a fairly poppy song based on Proverbs 3:5–6. "Remi" is a heavy track with an anthemic antifascism theme. "Vicious Onslaught" deals with death and destruction from a biblical perspective. "Missing Piece" is just a relationship-oriented will-you-go-out-with-me? song. Other tracks touch on fundamentalist doctrine (the rapture) and encourage boldness in the face of what the group regards as persecution. The latter theme is an issue close to their hearts. "A lot of kids deny God in school just because other kids make fun of them," says Dancore. "What's going to happen when someone threatens their lives?"

Seventh Angel

Ian Arkley, voc.; Scott Rawson, gtr.; Tank, drums; Simon Bibby, bass (–1991). 1990—*The Torment* (Pure Metal); 1991—*Lament for the Weary.*

Seventh Angel was an early '90s English thrash metal band with a sound similar to that of **Vengeance Rising.** Their debut album offers emotion-packed songs with lyrics that promise eternal suffering to the unrepentant ("Tormented Forever") and decry such social evils as the existence of abortion clinics ("Dr. Hatchet"). "Expletive Deleted" encourages Christians to clean up their language: "One way to see some darkness defeated / Concentrate on getting the expletives deleted." *Lament for the Weary* is generally slower but heavier than the debut record and is actually a concept album telling the story of a man who is sexually abused as a child and must deal with the lifelong pain and depression this brings. The song "No Longer a Child" offers God's words of consolation: "My little child, I see your pain / I cry with you / Every tear you weep—I weep with you." Front man Ian Arkley formed another doom and gloom metal band, Ashen Mortality, who have released two albums *(Sleepless Remorse, Your Caress)* on Forsaken Records.

Seventh Day Slumber

Tim Parady; Joseph Rojas, voc., gtr.; Joshua Schwartz; Adam Witte. 1999—*Matthew 25* (Afinia).

Seventh Day Slumber has an acoustic-electric rock sound similar to that of Hootie and the Blowfish and a heart for singing songs that present God as the ultimate solution to personal and social dilemmas. The song "Mama Won't Give Up" is an apparently autobiographical tune written by Rojas about how his mother prayed for his salvation when he was her prodigal son. "Miracle" celebrates the answer to her prayers and his own deliverance from cocaine addiction: "I was blind, but now I see the light / The life I lived, O Lord, I know it wasn't right / I feel my heart pumpin' up again / And I'm a miracle." The album is dedicated to "lives touched by the recent tragedies plaguing our nation's schools." It concludes with Rojas's spoken word testimony, an altar call invitation, and a prayer.

Seventy Sevens (and 7 and 7 Is and Moments of Meditation)

Michael Roe, voc., gtr. Mark Tootle, kybrd., gtr., voc. (– 1992); Jan Eric Volz, bass (–1992); Mark Proctor, drums (–1984) // Aaron Smith, drums (+ 1984, –1995); David Leonhardt, gtr. (+ 1992, –1995); Mark Harmon, bass (+ 1992); Bruce Spencer, drums (+ 1995); Scott Reams, gtr., kybrd. (+ 2000). 1983—*Ping Pong over the Abyss* (Exit); 1984—*All Fall Down*; 1987—*The Seventy Sevens* (Island); 1990—*Sticks and Stones* (Broken); *More Miserable Than You'll Ever Be* [sometimes listed as by 7 and 7 Is] (Alternative); 1991—*Eighty-Eight* (Brainstorm); 1992—*The Seventy Sevens* [a.k.a. *Pray Naked*]; 1994—*Drowning with Land in Sight* (Myrrh); 1995—*Tom Tom Blues* (Brainstorm); 1996—*Echoes of Faith* [a.k.a. *Played Naked*] (Fools of the World); 1999—*EP* [EP]; 2000—*Eighty-Eight/When Numbers Get Serious; Late; Daydream* [by Moments of Meditation] (Unison); 2001—*A Golden Field of Radioactive Crows* (Fools of the World).

www.77s.com

The Seventy Sevens are typically regarded as one of the two or three best Christian rock bands of all time. Beloved by critics, they have never had a fan base as large as **DC Talk** or even **Audio Adrenaline,** but their hip alternative credentials rival those of **U2.** What fans they have are intensely, even maniacally, loyal. It has never seemed remarkable to the group's followers that someone would drive ten hours one-way to see the band perform, and it is commonplace to hear Seventy Sevens' fans maintain that the band is not simply good but, indeed, the greatest rock and roll band of all time (Christian or otherwise). Such hyperbolic devotion is found not only among the kids but invades the minds and pens of supposedly reserved journalists.

Dwight Ozzard, director of public relations for Evangelicals for Social Action and frequent contributor to *Prism* magazine, wrote in 1994, "The truth is that the Seventy-Sevens might be the best rock and roll band in the world." Around the same time, *True Tunes* would declare, "They are considered by many to be among the best two or three live bands in the world." Even *CCM's* cautious Brian Quincy Newcomb would weigh in by quoting Keith Richards' comment that on any given night, any band anywhere with the right songs, the right audience, and the right spirit could be the best rock and roll band in the world. "On at least three or four nights in the last decade," Newcomb surmises, "Mike Roe and Co. were that band." But, he continues, "it always left a bittersweet aftertaste knowing that outside of a devoted fan base and a few other scattered enclaves of alternative Christian music fans, the Seventy-Sevens remained an unknown and unheard of quantity." Even within the contemporary Christian music subculture, the band has remained on the edge and is often regarded as controversial. This is odd, as they have never really done anything that smacks much of controversy—other than make music that sounds sufficiently worldly as to raise questions regarding just what qualifies a Christian artist as "Christian." Asked once what the role of a Christian artist should be, Roe replied, "I would say that the first role would be to do art, and then, to do it as good as you can with as much attention to quality as possible. . . . When that's happening, then the art will reflect who you are, and if you are a Christian, it will reflect where you are at that moment, the amount of faith you have, and the journey of your life with Christ, in its ups and downs." **Michael Roe** has also had a successful career as a solo artist and has recorded as a member of the **Lost Dogs.**

The meaning of the band's name has never been revealed. A prominent theory is that it derives from the New International Version of Matthew 18:22, as an allusion to the infinite character of divine forgiveness. *CCM* once opined that it comes from the seventy weeks (i.e., seventy sevens) of Daniel 9—which seems more likely. Some think it refers to a year (1977?) that has some special significance musically or spiritually for Roe or someone else. Or it could be nonsense. In any case, the group has displayed no consistency in writing it as a numeral (the 77s) or in spelling it out (the Seventy Sevens). At one point, for one album, they even changed their name to 7 and 7 Is—sort of. Actually the album cover for *More Miserable Than You'll Ever Be* lists the product as being by 7 and 7 Is, while the label on the disc itself says it is by the Seventy Sevens (the group's website lists it as a Michael Roe solo album).

The Seventy Sevens had rather inauspicious origins for a world-class rock and roll band. According to Roe, the group that would become the Seventy Sevens "was formed at a church by a church. . . . the church leaders wanted a rock and roll group made up of church members for the sole purpose of advertising in the community the kind of concerts that the church was having on the weekends, which were evangelistic." This group was called the Scratch Band, "because we were thrown together from scratch." In retrospect, Roe says that the music of this early group "was not art. It had nothing to do with us, or with us doing art. It was strictly pragmatic, an evangelistic tool." The church for which the Scratch Band proselytized was Warehouse Christian Ministries, an independent fellowship in Sacramento, California, that had been started by evangelist Louis Neely. As a young pastor in the '60s, Neely had a vision for an alternative outreach center that could use modern music as a draw for youth. He purchased an old warehouse and converted it into a facility that could be used in this capacity, then offered it for use by churches of all denominations in the Sacramento area. As it turns out, the churches in the community were not keen on using what they regarded as devil music for godly purposes, and Neely's own denomination rewarded his vision by revoking his ordination and dismissing him from its ranks. About this time, according to John Thompson's history of Christian rock *(Raised by Wolves),* a *Life* magazine article on the Jesus movement told about what was happening in Costa Mesa's Calvary Chapel. Neely's wife Mary went on a pilgrimage to visit that fellowship's head pastor, Chuck Smith, who ended up ordaining Louis as a Calvary Chapel pastor and setting up Warehouse Christian Ministries as a church in its own right. In addition to usual congregational functions, WCM sponsored an influential radio show called *Rock and Religion* (later, *Rock Scope*), built a recording studio, and established Exit Records, a label devoted to Christian performers with artistic vision. The Exit stable included **Brent Bourgeois, Charlie Peacock, Steve Scott,** and **Vector.** Amidst such heady company, the Scratch Band may have seemed like little more than an advertising gimmick—but eventually, they would eclipse even those heavyweights and become the group for which Exit is best remembered. Thompson describes the early music of the Scratch Band around the time they turned into the Seventy Sevens: "They blended everything from new-wave to Zeppelin to The Crampz to **U2** into a musical spasm that worked on every level. Mike Roe's performances, which included flailing his skinny body around the stage like Iggy Pop or screaming into the microphone as if he was engaged in some kind of primal therapy were the stuff of legend. The band was tight, and the Seventy Sevens quickly earned respect as one of the most skilled bands ever to play in the Christian market." In 1984, the Seventy Sevens and **Vector** toured with **Resurrection Band** on what would later be remembered as a dream billing. All three groups played at the very first *Cornerstone* festival, which was also held that year.

Ping Pong over the Abyss was produced by **Steven Soles** of **The Alpha Band.** Thompson, who would later found *True Tunes* magazine, has called it "the album that literally changed my life." Nevertheless, sympathetic critic Brian Quincy Newcomb says it "was an album that promised more than it actually delivered." In those days, *CCM* magazine would gush over almost anything, and they treated *Ping Pong* as a new-wave project from a "street-wise Christian band that pulls no punches," comparing the music to The Police and The Steve Miller Band. This all seems rather silly now. Roe's Jagger swagger can be heard on "A Different Kind of Light" (a **Steve Scott** song) and "Someone New," but on "It's So Sad" he comes off as the poor man's **David Edwards** or Steve Taylor (whose far more impressive debut came out the same year). The strongest cuts would be the title track, with its impressive guitar solo, "Renaissance Man," which was later covered by the general market band **The Ocean Blue** (both as a concert favorite and as the B-side of an early single), and a cover of Washington Phillips's "Denomination Blues," known to Jesus music fans in a very different version by **2nd Chapter of Acts.** The lyrics affirm, "You can go to your college, you can go to your school / But if you ain't got Jesus, you just an educated fool," and again, "Pardon me, Sir, you ain't doin' too well / Spend your whole life sinnin' and you're goin' to hell." *CCM* said the album was "on the fiery cutting edge of contemporary Christian music," which unfortunately may have been true, but the album was still a far cry from what the group would prove capable of delivering. Newcomb nailed the problem: "songs that were clearly conceived as rational exercises, witnessing tools, and apologetics . . . as opposed to personal artistic statements." Indeed, songs like "Renaissance Man" seemed anti-intellectual, dismissive, and almost antiartistic. Roe told *HM* in 1995 that he does not consider *Ping Pong over the Abyss* to be a Seventy Sevens album. "I consider it a Scratch Band album," he said. "That album should never have gone out under the name of the Seventy Sevens."

For their next project, the Seventy Sevens borrowed Aaron Smith from **Vector** and obtained what most would regard as their classic lineup (a fine session drummer, Smith had also played behind The Temptations on their hit "Papa Was a Rolling Stone" and with Romeo Void on "Girl in Trouble"). **Charlie Peacock** produced *All Fall Down,* which Thompson would describe as evincing "a heightened sense of texture, lyrical vulnerability, and candor." Thompson considers *All Fall Down* to be one of the most important records of the Christian music genre, an album that would influence an entire generation of other musicians. In part, this is because the band "held out hope that their music would be heard by the world at large, and they created it accordingly." The project was indeed distributed to the general market through A&M and a video for the song "Mercy Mercy" saw some time on MTV, but the band's moment in the secular sun was brief. *All Fall Down* starts with a first side of songs in a similar new-wavey style to the *Ping Pong* album, but with more mature musical stylings and lyrical perspectives ("Someone New" is remade here in a more dance-oriented version). The opening "Caught in an Unguarded Moment" is a brilliant reflection on mortality—relating anecdotes of those for whom death comes suddenly ("he wasn't ready to go / he had no time to say no"), for whom life on earth is fleeting ("her faith was in apropos / she made a brief cameo"). It is this song that gives the album its title, describing the one thing that all humans have in common: "All fall down, like dominoes." "Something's Holding On" is about a struggle with lust, informed by a biblical spirit-is-willing-flesh-is-weak mentality. "Your Pretty Baby" expresses the conflicting thoughts of a woman facing an unwanted pregnancy, addressing the abortion issue with more sensitivity and intelligence than is usually shown by more rhetorically inflammatory Christian artists. Side Two opens with the oddly titled "Ba Ba Ba Ba Ba," a song that exposes the insecurities within people that leave them open to the psychological and spiritual babbling of various therapies and cults. "Mercy Mercy" is truly the album's triumph, moving beyond the new-wave sound for more of the blues-based Stonesy feel. The lyric (basically, "Lawd, have mercy on me") is not terribly cerebral, but it gets the point across. "You Don't Scare Me" continues in this vein. *CCM* would choose *All Fall Down* as one of the Ten Best Albums of 1984—a good year that put it in company with *Stealing Fire* by **Bruce Cockburn,** *Straight Ahead* by **Amy Grant,** *Lie Down in the Grass* by **Charlie Peacock,** *Meltdown* by **Steve Taylor,** and both *The Unforgettable Fire* and *Under a Blood Red Sky* by **U2.**

In 1987, the Seventy Sevens attempted an ill-fated crossover to the rock and roll mainstream, releasing a self-titled "debut" album on Island Records. Exit colleague **Charlie Peacock** joined them in a parallel endeavor, putting out his own self-titled general market release with the same company at about the same time. Both albums earned favorable reviews and deserved to be hits. The most likely reason they tanked, according to John Thompson, is that another Island band named **U2** put out a record called *The Joshua Tree* that same year. Realizing that they had the album of the decade on their hands, Island poured all their resources into supporting that project and let everything else slide. This was a tad ironic, in that it was only because of Island's moderate success with **U2**'s former albums that the company had been willing to sign the two religious acts in the first place. Nevertheless, *The Seventy Sevens* was an artistic masterpiece—probably one of the ten best albums of the year not simply in the Christian market but in rock and roll, period. The group drops all new-wave pretensions and cranks out a full disc of Stones-cum-Springsteen clas-

sic rock, played as well as anyone has ever played it. The record was favorably reviewed in *Rolling Stone,* where critic Margot Mifflin wrote that "the 77s have come up with a sound that suggests not only that they know where they're coming from, but also that they're going places."

The Seventy Sevens opens with "Do It for Love," a song unknown to most mainstream rock fans despite universal agreement from those few who heard it that *this* is great rock and roll. The central guitar riff was copied from Springsteen, but once one gets beyond that, the song can be received as a vibrant anthem that displays the sort of excitement and emotion that rock was born to engender. It is the kind of song that offers hope and legitimation to Christian music fans, that allows them to smile knowingly when their clueless friends equate "Christian music" with **Debby Boone** or even **Stryper.** The song is also a very secular number with a generic (rather than religious) theme. Its failure to chart as a national hit remains a mystery. Years later, Roe would recall that this failure influenced him to despair of ever attaining commercial success and to concentrate exclusively on artistic merit: "I figured, if we can't get on the radio with a song like that, well, it isn't going to happen."

"Do It for Love" may be the obvious hit-that-never-was on *The Seventy Sevens,* but it is not even the best track. The album continues with "I Can't Get over It," a churning blues rocker that expresses the honest struggle of one who tries to forgive, but just can't forget: "You say you're sorry / I can't get over it / I say, I forgive you / But I can't get over it / You say you'll learn from this mistake . . . I should be giving you a break / But . . ."). The next track "What Was in That Letter?" is another audio assault, a charge of energetic riffs with a melodic chorus. After those three very strong rock tracks, the group experiments with other styles. "Pearls before Swine" is an eight-minute Lou Reed-inspired treat with a long instrumental jam—the type of song that generates real excitement among guitar or R&B aficionados who don't need lots of hooks to keep them interested. Then the group moves on to what would become another classic, a very Byrds-like folk rocker with a long and biblical title: "The Lust, the Flesh, the Eyes, and the Pride of Life." The song is like nothing else on *The Seventy Sevens* with its jangly guitar and whiny Michael Stipe vocal, and it is one where the lyrics take center stage as Roe complains about the things that "drain the life" out of him. Chris Hillman (of The Byrds) loved the song and actually played and sang on an original take that was later included on the *Sticks and Stones* collection. "Don't Say Goodbye" gets the listener's blood pumping again with the most poppy tune on the album—a very melodic and catchy tune that sounds a little bit like the Rolling Stones covering a Monkees song. "Bottom Line" previews the sensitive almost-ballad style that Roe would later perfect as a solo artist, particularly on his *Safe As Milk* album. In 1995, Via Records reissued the Seventy Sevens' first three albums on CD, packaging them all together in a box set with some twenty bonus tracks, including a hidden cover of The Velvet Underground's "Jesus" and an early take on the song "Tattoo," written by Roe and Larry Tagg of Bourgeois-Tagg.

It would be five years before another album of new material by the Seventy Sevens would appear—one that would rather stupidly also be called *The Seventy Sevens*. In the meantime, the group pretty much disintegrated, but not before putting together a collection of demos to shop around in search of a new label. This was later released as *Sticks and Stones*, which is often thought to be the Seventy Sevens' best album. It includes alternative versions of four tracks from *The Seventy Sevens* and a number of previously unreleased songs, several of which are comparable to those treasures. The lead-off tune, "MT" (short for "More Than"), is so good that it seems to provide one of the reasons for rock and roll to exist in the first place. It was written by Roe with Bongo Bob Smith for the explicit purpose of scoring a platinum Top 40 hit, but avoids obvious or formulaic commercialism. The song never got finished and it just fades out in the middle of an infectious, call-and-response chorus, but the three and a half minutes leading up to that provide a taste of some of the finest ear candy ever laid to vinyl. "Perfect Blues" also provides one of the band's finest moments. It's pure Stones, with little touches of Aerosmith and Zeppelin and a big dollop of Jerry Lee Lewis piano (Roe admits in the liner notes that it took eight hands and some multitracking to accomplish what "the killer" could have done with two hands and one take). "Don't, This Way" is a beautiful and sensitive ballad about the ending of a relationship, comparable in sound and quality to Stephen Stills' "4 + 20." It is a song of startling simplicity and power: "Don't leave this way, so many words unsaid. . . ." Roe himself has said it is "maybe the saddest song I've ever heard." Complementing these masterworks are two more pop delights of the "Don't Say Goodbye" sort: "You Walked in the Room" and "Nowhere Else," songs by Mark Tootle that testify to the transformative power of romantic attraction in ways that are evocative and contagious: "There is nowhere else I'd rather be / Than in your arms." As all of these songs attest, there was little on *Sticks and Stones* that would readily identify the Seventy Sevens as a Christian band; rather, these were just songs about life and love being performed by talented and perceptive artists who freely identified themselves as Christians—a novel concept at the time. "God Sends Quails" is perhaps the only obviously religious song—a meandering, experimental track that wants to be a big showpiece number based on the wilderness wanderings of Israel but never quite comes together (cf. **Noel Paul Stookey**'s "Then the Quail Came" for a piece on the theme that works and **Keith**

Green's "So You Want to Go Back to Egypt?" for an example of another one that doesn't).

After the Seventy Sevens had essentially broken up, Michael Roe pulled together some tracks and recorded a few new songs for the 7 and 7 Is project which, as indicated above, was sometimes marketed as a Seventy Sevens album. A hodgepodge of stuff from different sources, it is similar in scope (but not in quality) to *Sticks and Stones*. It includes "Jesus" and "Tattoo," plus four more alternate takes of songs from *The Seventy Sevens*, making nonfanatics wonder whether *that* cow had not been milked dry by now. Minus such extravagances, *More Miserable Than You'll Ever Be* can be boiled down to an EP of four new songs that are essentially Mike Roe solo performances. The near-title track, "Miserable," is offered in two versions, the first a grungy rocker that justifies the album's otherwise questionable reason for existence. Likewise, "UUUU" (pronounced You, You, You, You) is a Chuck Berry-styled old time rock and roll number that would become a concert favorite.

During the fragmented years between the two albums titled *The Seventy Sevens*, Brainstorm also released a recording of a 1988 concert as an album called *Eighty Eight*. The recording is good and the band is tight, but only diehard fans would appreciate the *Wheels on Fire*-style extra-long songs: eleven minutes of "Mercy Mercy" and over twelve minutes of both "You Don't Scare Me" and "I Could Laugh." The novelty highlight is a much quicker run-through of The Yardbirds' "Over, Under, Sideways, Down." There are also a few songs not easy to find elsewhere: "Wild Blue" is a sensational *Let It Bleed*-Stones-era track about not having enough time to do what seems important in life; "Mary and the Baby Elvis" and "Where It's At" are quirky rockabilly songs sung in a faux-Elvis accent (cf. the **Lost Dogs**' "Close But No Cigar"); "Closer" is an excellent cajun boogie that sounds a lot like Creedence Clearwater Revival. In 2000, Magdalene would reissue the by-then-classic album with a bonus disc called *When Numbers Get Serious*, compiling live tracks from the years between 1986 and 1999 (mostly mid-to-late '90s), including covers of the Stones' "Paint It Black" and Robin Trower's "Bridge of Sighs."

In 1992, after a five-year hiatus, a new version of the Seventy Sevens emerged with Roe and Smith still intact and former side men David Leonhardt and Mark Harmon elevated to member status (Mark Tootle became music director at The Warehouse in Sacramento, and Jon Eric Volz became, first, a successful producer of artists like **Charlie Peacock** and **Margaret Becker,** and then road manager for magician David Copperfield). Leonhardt and Harmon had formerly played together in a Sacramento garage band called **Strawmen;** their not-intended-for-the-public recordings would later be released on Liquid Disc. The new version of the Seventy Sevens' first album was originally titled *Pray Naked,* a pun on a popular fraternity motto ("play naked") that was interpreted by way of a title song encouraging listeners to be honest (stripped of pretension) with God. Distributors for the album didn't get it or perhaps were just biblically illiterate enough to think that God would disapprove of anything that had a word like *naked* associated with it. In a move that would remove all doubt regarding their perceptive abilities they renamed the album *The Seventy Sevens,* not realizing (or not caring) that there already was a product by that name and that the duplication would cause endless confusion among consumers and marketers. As late as 2001, when a book would name the first *The Seventy Sevens* album as one of "The 100 Greatest Albums in Christian Music," the accompanying photograph showed the cover of the second album by that name.

The second *The Seventy Sevens* (a.k.a. *Pray Naked*) is probably *not* one of the best Christian albums of all time, but it is a solid collection of alternative rock and pop songs, one that can hold its own in the college radio market with little embarrassment. The opening track, "Woody," is a hard rocker showing the new group's move into more Zeppelin-like territory. "Nuts for You," "Look," and the would-be title track have some of that fire too, but most of the album is quite subdued. "Smiley Smile" seems to be a Beach Boys tribute (if not, it's a rip-off), and "Holy Hold" is a happy pop song. Thematically, though, the album touches frequently on the theme of lost love and broken relationships ("Kites without Strings," "Happy Roy," "Look"). None of these approach "Don't, This Way" in vulnerability, but the confession of struggle and disappointment is very much on the sleeve: "Tangled in you / I aimed for the wild blue / And I hit the ground / What a bitter earth I've found." Interspersed with the broken-heart numbers are tentative affirmations of hope. "I still believe in you," Roe sings in "Smiley Smile." Roe himself would describe the record as "an album of extremes—musically and lyrically," expressing the closeness of God to those who are "at the end of the emotional/spiritual tether." He told *CCM* that the theme of the album is "If you're really messed up and nothing's working, God knows, and he's there."

Although it was not released until 1996, *Echoes of Faith* (a.k.a. *Played Naked*) is a live recording of a mostly unplugged concert from 1992. The band for that show consists of Roe, Harmon, and Leonhardt, with **Steve Hindalong** of **The Choir** on drums and percussion. The group performs only three songs from the current album, however, concentrating on material from their earlier oeuvre.

The next project, *Drowning with Land in Sight,* would mark the band's return to glory as the almost undisputed best rock outfit in the Christian genre. It has a darker tone to it and, musically, picks up on the promise of "Woody," the best song from the *Pray Naked* sessions. Lest anyone have to wonder about

their influences, the group actually opens the album with a reverent cover of Led Zeppelin's arrangement of "Nobody's Fault But Mine"—a song that Zep had actually reconfigured from gospel singer Blind Willie Johnson. Roe does the song Zeppelin style but restores its original lyrics with lines like, "I got a Bible in my house / If I don't read it and my soul dies / Well, it's nobody's fault but mine." The song had long been a feature of the band's concerts but now it was allowed to determine the musical direction of an entire album. The next track, "Snowblind" (not the Styx song), continues in the same Zeppelin tradition. Then Roe debuts a brand new style, laying a distinctive growling vocal over the top of heavy blues riffs; it is a sound he would use again, finally perfecting it on "The Stellazine Prophecy" for his *Safe As Milk* album. Here, the song done in that style is "Snake," with lyrics that apparently refer to the biblical tempter (who continues to haunt human lives and relationships). "Indian Winter" is another heavy Zeppelin-esque song, this time incorporating some of that band's fondness for Middle Eastern music. But the Seventy Sevens are much too smart to simply copy a secular act. Although the Zeppelin references throughout *Drowning* are plenteous, the Seventy Sevens put their own distinctive stamp on everything such that the influence is no more controlling than it has been for, say, Heart or Aerosmith. "Cold, Cold Night" is the album's strongest cut, an appropriately chilling hard blues-rock number (drawing from the Stones again) with shouted lyrics: "Why'd you do that to me? / I wouldn't do that to you / 'Cause I believe in love, baby / And I thought that you did too." The band also admitted to listening to a lot of Hendrix and Alice in Chains and even Black Sabbath while they were making *Drowning.* The mood of the music fit with their emotions at the time, and *True Tunes* would claim, "the themes of despair, loneliness, loss, fear, and hope could not be coupled with more appropriate musical fare than this." The heaviness is broken only occasionally by a handful of pop-oriented tracks ("Film at 11," "The Jig Is Up," "Alone Together") before finally concluding with the acoustic "For Crying Out Loud," which invites the listener to "Look up / Cry out / Don't be afraid to scream . . . You've been waiting for this day for a long time now." At least part of the angst that went into *Drowning* was public: Roe's marriage was disintegrating and would soon end in divorce. In addition, guitarist Leonhardt was diagnosed with Hodgkin's disease at the outset of the recording and was undergoing cancer treatments throughout the entire process. The group would maintain that his suffering and struggle with the disease became a paradigm for the Christian's struggle with self, which is what they sought to depict, à la Romans 7. "The record is about being taken to the deepest and darkest parts of ourselves," Roe explained. "It's deep into the theme of abandonment—complete loss of moral foundations and moorings, both emotionally and spiritually." When Christians could not understand the merit of dwelling on such subjects, he elaborated: "I think a lot of people that grow up in church get strong-armed into the whole business of Christ as Saviour. They don't really appreciate what it means to be saved from oneself, from the world, from sin. In fact, until you're a victim of all those things and realize how totally strangulating they are on your freedom and well being, you may always resent the fact that you had to have a Saviour from something you weren't really sure you wanted to be saved from." In any case, the music connected. John Thompson calls *Drowning with Land in Sight* "one of the best records the Christian music industry has ever seen."

A year later, Roe came back with what might be called "the third version" of the band (Bruce Spencer came over from **Vector;** Smith went on to join **A Ragamuffin Band;** Leonhardt continued to struggle with health problems, but joined Roe on one of his solo tours). A power trio now (Roe, Harmon, and Spencer), the group began billing itself as "The Band That Won't Go Away." *Tom Tom Blues* is an eclectic smorgasbord of various styles, all of them performed remarkably well. *HM* magazine would announce with glee, "Once again, the Seventy Sevens have blown us away with yet another great album." No two songs on the album sound anything alike. "Rocks in Your Head," "Outskirts," and "Gravy Train" perhaps come closest to the Stones-inspired blues that the band's old fans crave. "Honesty" is an affectionate Hendrix tribute, with Roe imitating that master's vocal style in addition to his guitar playing. The well-titled "Earache" is likewise hard and heavy, featuring that growling talk-vocal showcased on "Snake" and "Stellazine Prophecy." And then there is "Flowers in the Sand," a taste of '60s psychedelia that sounds a little bit like Tommy James and the Shondells with a much better guitar player. "You Still Love Me" is psychedelic too, with distorted reverb vocals and more Hendrix-style guitar. "Don't Leave Me Long" is the closest the album gets to a pop song, with a catchy, hook-laden melody and vocals that call to mind "Learning to Fly"-era Tom Petty. "Deliverance" closes the disc on an interesting note, starting out like one of those pretty songs on Roe's *Safe As Milk* solo album, but picking up intensity and passion that turns to screaming before it fades out with blistering guitar and pounding percussion. All told, *Tom Tom Blues* is a Christian music masterpiece, with only one ridiculous low point: a Jimmy Durante-meets Mickey Mouse joke song called "Five in the Nave." Rock groups who think they're cool enough to get away with anything (cf. **Breakfast with Amy**) sometimes place intentionally annoying fodder like this on their albums, knowing that no one will want to hear it more than once (if that) and assuming fans will just program their stereos to skip it. That works for those who have the technology, but reveals just a little too

much about the artists' mentality. In any case, the songs on *Tom Tom Blues* generally offer more windows on a tormented soul. As *7ball* put it, "Roe's songs are hard-luck, end-of-your-rope stories that search for more redemption than they offer." But then who would want to listen to "happy blues"?

Rumors of a new Seventy Sevens album dominated 1999 and 2000. Instead, fans were treated to an EP and an extended single. The EP was actually called *EP* and offered five excellent songs that *Bandoppler* would call "a melange of all the extremes and lived-through periods of the group's history." The first of these, "The Years Go Down," is a reflective track with a sound very similar to some of Paul Simon's material. "Sevens" has a sound that would have been right at home on Roe's *The Boat Ashore.* "Unbalanced" showcases the group's Zeppelinesque period, "Blue Sky" has the gritty Stones anthem feel to it, and "The Best I Have" closes the disc with some melancholy modern rock. Thematically, *EP* seems almost to be a concept album, chronicling what *Phantom Tollbooth* calls "The bittersweet rise and fall of a troubled relationship." In 1999, the band also announced a new album called *A Golden Field of Radioactive Crows* with much-hyped release dates repeatedly declared and forfeited. A single featuring two songs from that project was released, which also included a live version of the old song "Tattoo" and a cover of "Shotgun Angel"—a not very good song by Bill Sprouse of **The Road Home** that was made semifamous by **Daniel Amos.** In an interview included on that disc, Roe described the forthcoming record as "a pop album . . . it has a lot of pop songs in a row, sort of summery, jangly fun songs, and then as the album progresses, it gets a little deeper, into the more complex styles we're noted for." But no album appeared and, pressed by fans, the group put out *Late,* a compilation of the two main songs from the single, all five tracks from *EP,* and eight alternate mixes and live versions of songs from various other projects. Also in 2000, Roe and Harmon signed a multialbum deal to produce a series of instrumental ambient projects under the name Moments of Meditation. This enterprise appeared to be inspired by **Phil Keaggy**'s *Music to Paint By.* The first Moments of Meditation release was a collection of jazz-tinged pop instrumentals called *Daydream.* With warm guitar, soft keyboard, and sparse percussion, the project inspired *Phantom Tollbooth* to endorse it as "wonderful background music" that "just might put you to sleep."

Then in 2001, the new album *(A Golden Field of Radioactive Crows)* finally emerged. True to Roe's predictions, the album was hailed by critics as the group's most pop-oriented project ever. "Their unique blend of melodic rock music has always had that classic rock vibe," one reviewer wrote, "but now it has a stronger 'fun to listen to' quality as well." *Phantom Tollbooth* compared it to *Pray Naked* but also noted a strong holdover of '60s and '70s sounds evident on *Tom Tom Blues.* Musically, the album is one of the group's finest works, and in either Christian or general markets it would have to be considered one of the best (and only) pure rock and roll records of 2001. The album opens with four bluesy, gritty, jangly, hook-and-riff-laden rockers before finally slowing down for one brooding number that takes more than a single listen to become infectious ("Rise"). Then they kick in gear again for a fast-paced Jagger-swagger number called "Leaving." There's a little rockabilly ("Mean Green Season"), one love ballad ("There Forever"), and an ironically titled concluding number ("Begin") that revives the grand rock tradition of jamming. Both pleasing and confounding to the group's fans, *Radioactive Crows* offers a powerful combination of contemporary sounds and classic Zeppelin/Stones/Doors influences. The song "Related" is a slightly grungy tune that rides along on an undercurrent of propulsive R&B riffs and beats, modernized by the addition of turntables and samples. It begins with the words, "Every minute angels come / Gonna take away another one I love" and reaches out to other mortals who quest for hope in the midst of their mortality. Such themes of death are prominent on *Radioactive Crows*, apparently as a result of the death of Roe's good friend and partner Gene Eugene (of **Adam Again** and the **Lost Dogs**). Still, the outlook is mainly positive: on "Genuine," Roe draws on Ecclesiastes to urge listeners to live life to the fullest since "overnight, everything can be so undone." Dysfunctional relationships also continue to provide food for thought. "You're the last blast, baby," Roe sings, "in a long line of ones who tried to change me" ("U R Trippin'"), though in that song he acknowledges the foolishness of thinking "you rise above yourself all by yourself." The song "Mr. Magoo" is an upbeat jangly guitar song with lyrical allusions to the nearsighted cartoon character: "I may be Mr. Magoo, but I see through you."

In 1996, *HM* observed that the Seventy Sevens began as a group of enthusiastic kids just out to share the gospel and "evolved into one of the truest musical reflections of how difficult it is to live the Christian life in the modern world." In 1999, *Bandoppler* would call them "the most unique and hard rocking, spiritually-based, rock band that ever existed." They have continued to offer such reflection without pulling any punches and have made some of the finest albums of the rock era. There is probably no other group described in this encyclopedia that would offer a better entry point for open-minded fans of classic rock (Rolling Stones, Led Zeppelin) to discover what the parallel universe of Christian music sometimes has to offer.

SFC (a.k.a. **Soldiers For Christ**)

Chris Cooper [a.k.a. Super C]; et al. 1989—*Listen Up* (Broken); 1990—*A Saved Man (in the Jungle)*; 1992—*Phase III* (Brainstorm); 1994—*Illumination.*

The sanctified hip-hop group known as SFC was fronted by DJ-turned-rapper Chris Cooper of Southern California. Others participated but their names were seldom revealed. Someone called Brother G. raps alongside Cooper (called Super C) on the debut project. Producer D. J. Dove (also of **Gospel Gangstaz**) accompanies him on the second album. SFC had a pioneering role, helping to introduce hip-hop to the Christian scene in the pre-**DC Talk** days when it was not granted much of a hearing. *Listen Up* offers "This Is What He Went Through," a Michael Peace-type tune that relates the story of Jesus' crucifixion. "Plain and Simple" presents details from the book of Revelation. *CCM* would later list the album as historically significant for its use of "reggae rhythms, sampling, and a streetwise aesthetic." *A Saved Man* introduces generous doses of humor, sampling from **Adam Again** and *Saturday Night Live*'s Church Lady (i.e., Dana Carvey). "Can't Wait (to Get to Church)" presents Sunday morning worship as a positive experience. *Phase III* would be a tougher record with more challenging lyrics for the young black males who were presumed to compose the target audience. "Kill the Spirit" challenges the listener not to blame social conditions or attitudes for the effects of one's own sin. On *Illumination,* Cooper begins to incorporate more jazz influences, reminiscent of Digable Planets or Us3. Cooper told *CCM* his mission was to "reach drug sellers, club hoppers, and other people you wouldn't find sitting down and listening to a church choir." After the four SFC albums, he took a break and then returned as **Sup the Chemist.**

Shack of Peasants

Philip Bardowell, voc.; Lanny Cordola, gtr., banjo, mand., bass, voc.; Chris Farmer, voc.; Gary Thomas Griffin, harm., acc., voc.; D. D. Howard, voc.; Carol Huston, voc.; Taso Kotsos, drums, perc.; Crystal Lewis, voc.; Chris Lizotte, voc.; Darrell Mansfield, harm., voc.; Paul McIntyre, fiddle; Allegra Parks, voc.; Fletcher Quigley, voc.; Sandra Stephens, voc.; Chuck Wright, bass. 1993—*Classic Blues, Vol. I* (Metro One); *Gospel Blues, Vol. 2.*

Shack of Peasants was a special project organized by **Lanny Cordola** (cf. **Chaos is the Poetry, Children of Zion, Magdalen, The Panorama Ramblers,** and **Symbiotica**) and Gary Thomas Griffin to pay homage to pioneers of the blues, with special attention to the roots that blues shares with gospel. A large cast of players and singers cooperated on two albums titled *Classic Blues* and *Gospel Blues,* respectively. Despite the name differences, there is no noticeable distinction of content—both records are filled with songs with strong sacred or spiritual themes. Volume One *(Classic Blues)* includes traditional songs like "I Shall Not Be Moved" and "Stand by Me" along with a couple of Rev. Gary Davis tracks and two of Cordola's own compositions (which are, of course, exceptions to the announced repertoire). Christian music fans may delight to discover "Nobody's Fault But Mine" (the Blind Willie

Johnson song that Led Zeppelin performed without its original religious lyrics) and "Denomination Blues" (a Washington Phillips song that **2nd Chapter of Acts** revived on their classic *To the Bride* album). Both of the latter songs have also been performed by the **Seventy Sevens.** Volume Two *(Gospel Blues)* includes **Bob Dylan**'s "Ring Those Bells" and three more Cordola songs along with a batch of traditional numbers like "Swing Low, Sweet Chariot" and "John the Revelator" (cf. **Phil Keaggy**).

Shaded Red

Jamie Roberts, voc., gtr.; Jon Roberts, voc., kybrd., trump.; Bryan Stacks, bass (–1999) // Ben Miller, drums (+ 1999); Dave Villano, bass (+ 1999). 1997—*Shaded Red* (Cadence); 1999—*Red Revolution.*

Shaded Red is a modern electric-pop band founded by Jamie and Jon Roberts, two brothers from Washington state. The Roberts boys grew up in a church environment where contemporary Christian music was a part of their daily lives. Their father, a pastor, was the creator of the popular Jesus Northwest Festival, an annual Christian music event. Shaded Red has an eclectic, melodic sound that would place them in the same general category as bands like **Audio Adrenaline** or **Third Day,** but they also evince enough unconventional "slacker" stylings to sometimes share a fan base with **Switchfoot.** The group's debut album was generally well received, with the opening track, "Caught," garnering the most attention as an appropriately catchy Spin Doctors rip-off about buying into the world's illusions and delusions. "Let It Out" is about being bold for Christ. Several other songs ("Found Someone," "Dreaming," "Fear Not") are midtempo mellow tunes, and the album closes with a **Rich Mullins**-type piano ballad ("Use Me"). The Roberts brothers made clear in interviews and performances that they were dedicated to evangelistic ministry and viewed their music as an avenue for such work. "We're evangelists," Jamie told *7ball.* "We evangelize night in and night out and have seen thousands of kids come to Christ."

In January of 1998, the band was involved in a tragic accident when their tour van hit a patch of black ice and flipped several times, throwing three of the band members from the car. A new drummer, Chris Yoeman, who had played only one show with the group, was killed, and Jon Roberts was left with a crushed pelvis that caused him to endure months of hospitalization and rehabilitative therapy. Accordingly, the second album, *Red Revolution,* conveys themes of thankfulness for life and of therapeutic recognition of grace in the midst of despair. "We had a Job experience, but now we're on the other side," Jon would declare. The centerpiece of the sophomore project is a remake of **Benny Hester**'s classic song "When God Ran" (based on Luke 15:20). Shaded Red recorded the song in Britain with the London Session Orchestra along with "Wait," a lus-

cious ballad that sounds like it was intended for the soundtrack of a romantic film. Otherwise, *Red Revolution* includes a number of songs that feature Jon Roberts's trumpet more prominently. The opening track, "Revolution," is a guitar rock song with a strong Spanish flavor. Lyrically, it provides a defiant anthem of allegiance to Christ: "I will never say I'm sorry / I will never say I'm wrong / Because I know the one that truly frees me / No other love could be this strong."

Christian radio hits: "Revolution" (# 19 in 1999).

Peter Shambrook

1991—*Peter Shambrook* (Frontline); 1993—*Live at the Café Lido; Love Unseen;* 1999—*Life* (Maranatha).

Australian folk-pop singer Pete Shambrook failed to attract much attention in the United States, despite three impressive albums in the early '90s. Almost nothing was ever written about him in the usual media, except a positive review of his album *Love Unseen* in *CCM.* **Rick Elias** produced his debut project, and Shambrook toured America as the opening act for Elias and headliner **Margaret Becker.** *Love Unseen* was produced by Jesus music veteran **Paul Clark.** It opens with what would become Shambrook's best-known song, a straightforward rock number called "I Believe in You." *Love Unseen* also includes a cover of **Van Morrison**'s "Whenever God Shines His Light." Then Shambrook resurfaced with another album on the Maranatha label at the end of the decade. By then, he was serving as college pastor of Vineyard Christian Fellowship in Newport Beach, California. *Life* includes "You've Overcome," a worship tune that attributes ultimate victory to Christ and looks forward to his return. Shambrook has also sung on a number of other Maranatha projects, including those associated with Promise Keepers.

Christian radio hits: "Through the Ages" (# 19 in 1992); "I Believe in You" (# 8 in 1993).

Helen Shapiro

Selected: 1989—*The Pearl* (ICC); 1992—*Kadosh;* 1995—*Nothing But the Best;* 1997—*Enter into His Gates.*

Helen Shapiro (b. 1946) is a Jewish jazz singer from London who in 1987 declared that she had become a committed believer in Jesus Christ. As a self-proclaimed Messianic Christian, she has recorded albums of gospel music and spoken widely throughout the United Kingdom testifying to Christ as the fulfillment of the hopes of Israel. Shapiro had an early career in '60s pop music, recording such songs as "Don't Treat Me Like a Child," "You Don't Know," and "Walkin' Back to Happiness" when she was only fourteen. She was more successful in Britain than in the United States, where she just barely made it to *Billboard*'s Hot 100 chart only once: "Walkin' Back to Happiness" was Number 100 for one week in 1961. As an adult, she would find a second career in jazz, performing throughout Europe before switching to gospel with her 1989 release, *The Pearl*. Shapiro sings a duet with **Cliff Richard** on the song "We Bring Many," cut for inclusion on her compilation album, *Nothing But the Best*. Her best-received project so far has been *Enter into His Gates*, a worship album with a distinctively Hebraic feel.

The Sheep (a.k.a. **Karitsat**)

As Karitsat: 1972—*Jeesus-Rock!* (Finnievy). As The Sheep: 1973—*The Sheep* (Myrrh UK); *Lonesome Stone* (Reflection).

The Sheep were a group of American Jesus freaks with some historical significance for the international Jesus movement of the early '70s. The origins of the band lie with a group that was initially called the Milwaukee Discipleship Training Community in Wisconsin. This community was led by Jim and Sue Palosaari and also included John and Dawn Herrin, their daughter, and her husband-to-be, **Glenn Kaiser**. As the community grew, it decided to split amicably into smaller groups that could witness more effectively in different locations. The segment led by the Herrins and the Kaisers would eventually become the famous Jesus People U.S.A. community in Chicago, a movement noted for its social activism and sponsorship of the arts (see entry on **Resurrection Band** for more on this community). For some reason, the Palosaaris decided to take their part of the community to Europe. Music was a primary part of the group's ministry, and The Sheep formed as a community band playing music to draw a crowd for preaching and, eventually, offering concerts that were evangelistic in their own right. One member of the group was Matt Spransy, who was involved in launching England's annual *Greenbelt* Christian music festival. The group got the opportunity to tour Scandinavia and were instrumental in spreading the Jesus movement revival there. Back in England, they put together a Christian musical called *Lonesome Stone*, a rock opera along the lines of *Tommy* or *Hair*. According to Christian music historian John J. Thompson, "*Lonesome Stone* was a big deal—with slide shows, pyrotechnics, dramatic lighting, and an emphasis on production." It was originally subtitled "How the Jesus People Came to Life" and it told the story of how a young person from the Haight-Ashbury scene in San Francisco came to faith in Christ amidst the events of the turbulent '60s. Most of the songs were written by Mike Damrow and Greg Nancarrow (who also played guitar and sang a lead role in the production). The Sheep performed all of the music for the program, which varied somewhat over time. The community obtained a financial sponsor and was able to schedule regular shows at the famous Rainbow Theatre. There, *Lonesome Stone* drew significant crowds and was favorably reviewed by the media. At one point, a touring member of the cast of *Hair* got "saved" at a

Sheep concert and jumped ship to join the *Lonesome Stone* cast. After a successful run in Britain, *Lonesome Stone* came over to America, but the show did not fare as well as it had in England, and after only two months, production was shut down. The Palosaaris and a handful of others eventually started a new community (the Highway Missionary Society) in southern Oregon, and there, The Sheep would morph into the influential Christian rock band **Servant**. Owen and Sandy Brock, who had both been members of The Sheep, headed up this new outreach and Spransy eventually joined as well.

The album titled *Jeesus-Rock!* is a historical curiosity recorded by The Sheep during their influential Scandinavian tour. The album was made in Finland, which explains the spelling of the title (*Jeesus* is Finnish for Jesus) and the unusual name of the artist (*Karitsat* is Finnish for Sheep). The record features ten songs, the highlights of which are "Oh Happy Day" (the song made popular in America by the **Edwin Hawkins Singers**) and a hard rock version of the Lutheran hymn "A Mighty Fortress Is Our God," both of which are sung in Finnish. The self-titled album, *The Sheep*, is less of a novelty, featuring a number of original progressive rock songs, with generous Hammond organ played (presumably) by Spransy. "Generation of the King" has a Jefferson Airplane vibe similar to that being developed by sister group **Resurrection Band** at the time. "Alpha and Omega" is a standout track. "Harvest" features bluesy harmonica. Finally, the soundtrack album for *Lonesome Stone* would also be released (though not, technically, as a Sheep product). Curiously, it includes the **Randy Stonehill** song "Vegetables," which would also turn up on that artist's *Get Me Out of Hollywood* album.

Sheesh

John David Herrin, drums, gtr.; Chris Witala, bass; Trevor Witala, voc. 1997—*Sheesh* (Grrr).

Sheesh is a three-piece grunge band associated with the Jesus People U.S.A. community in Chicago (the same community responsible for **Ballydowse, Cauzin' Efekt, Crashdog, The Crossing, Headnoise, Glenn Kaiser, Resurrection Band, Seeds,** and **Unwed Sailor**). John David Herrin is the son of **Resurrection Band** drummer John Herrin Jr. (and grandson of community founders Dawn Herrin and John Herrin Sr.). Twins Chris and Trevor Witala were seventeen years old when the first album was recorded. *Sheesh* was well received by critics, with a few complaints that the band's influences still show a bit too strongly in spots. Musically, they fit with the Seattle sound defined by Nirvana, Pearl Jam, and Soundgarden, though one can tell that they have listened to Live and Better Than Ezra as well. Guitars are messy and chunky, vocals are passionate, and there is some creative experimentation with cello and violin. Lyrically, the group focuses on a variety of serious life issues with no shyness regarding their faith. "Milk Carton Children" expresses brutal anger at the evil of childnapping. "Sad" is a mournful ballad reflecting on unrequited love. "Like a Dog" uses biblical imagery (Proverbs 26:11) in its exposé of the human desire to give in to temptation. The Witala brothers also played in **Left Out** and later joined Bryan Gray to form a new version of **The Blamed.**

Shelter

Personnel list unavailable. 1983—*Prophets and Clowns* (Rooftop).

Shelter was a Michigan-based Christian community that sponsored a band of the same name. After playing together for six years, the group recorded a single album, produced by **Terry Scott Taylor.** The band's composer, David Bunker, claimed their influences were broad, "ranging from Barry Manilow to Toto to **Phil Keaggy.**" The songs on *Prophets and Clowns* display a strong pop orientation, with "Super Heroes" dipping into new-wave. Lyrically, the songs all carry explicit Christian messages, often drawing on Scripture ("Walk in the Spirit," "This Is the Day").

Tim Sheppard

1976—*Diary* (Greentree); 1977—*Inside My Room;* 1979—*Songtailor;* 1981—*Forever;* 1989—*I Am Determined* (Diadem).

Singer-songwriter Tim Sheppard was discovered by **Dallas Holm** and evinces a style similar to that inspirational artist. Sheppard comes from Ft. Worth, Texas, and was devoted to athletics until a knee injury sidetracked him into music. "After becoming a Christian," he says, "I started using my music as a natural expression of my experience." In 1975, he won the American Song Festival's Amateur Songwriter Award in Gospel. Holm heard Sheppard sing at a church and connected him with Phil Johnson, who was producing **The Imperials.** The latter group recorded Sheppard's song "Would You Believe in Me?" In time, the artist would also write for **Andrus, Blackwood, and Co., Brush Arbor, Gary McSpadden,** and **Truth.** Sheppard's own albums are light pop songs with messages similar to those associated with southern gospel. He formed an agency called Servant Outreach that allowed much of his royalties to be diverted into supporting missions and education of seminarians. In 1989, Sheppard would join Holm and Johnson on a trio project called *Soldiers Again* (Greentree).

Christian radio hits: "Hey There Stranger" (# 22 in 1979); "I've Got the Feeling" (# 9 in 1979); "Ever Since the Day" (# 22 in 1979); "Fiddler" (# 16 in 1980).

Bonnie Sheridan

See **Bonnie Bramlett.**

Shiloh

Mike Kelley, voc., gtr.; Dennis McIntosh, voc., gtr. 1975—*Before the Lord* (Adriel); 1976—*Where Is the Peace?* (Sonburst); 1977—*Confession* (Lamb and Lion).

Shiloh was a country-folk Jesus music group composed of Mike Kelley and Dennis McIntosh, who are repeatedly referred to as brothers in literature from the time—though that might just mean brothers in the Lord. They gained national attention when Sonburst released their second album, *Where Is the Peace?* along with a simultaneous reissue of the debut independent project. *Harmony* magazine would liken the sound to "being in a small Appalachian church on a warm summer night." The duo harmonize in Everly Brothers fashion on songs that have the same folk-pop appeal as **Arlo Guthrie**'s arrangement of "City of New Orleans." Standout tracks from the first album include the camp worship songs "Hallelujah" and "Song to God." The sophomore project offers "My Lord" and "Power from on High." But *Confession* is the most interesting Shiloh album from a historical perspective. The record was produced by **Terry Talbot,** and musicians in the band include **Al Perkins** on pedal steel guitar and **Keith Green** on piano. Green completists ensured that it would become a collector's item.

In 2002 a chaotic hard rock/metal band named Shiloh would release a self-titled Christian album on Accidental Sirens. The two groups are not related, and confusion could result in customer dissatisfaction.

ShineMK

Loretta Andrews, voc.; Natasha Andrews, voc.; Hanna Petersen, voc.; Nicola Rodgers, voc. 2000—*Do It Right* (Reunion); 2001—*Keep On Moving.*

www.shinemk.co.uk

ShineMK was assembled in the United Kingdom as a Christian version of the Spice Girls. The group is located in Milton Keynes, England, from which they derive the MK on the end of their name. They may also be viewed as a spin-off of **World Wide Message Tribe,** of which Loretta Andrews was a member. Loretta and her identical twin sister, Natasha, joined with one other British woman (Nicola Rodgers) and a Norwegian (Hanna Petersen) to form the vocal group, whose material was written by **World Wide Message Tribe'**s Zarc Porter. Like the latter group, their ministry has focused on performances within public schools. Unlike America, England not only allows but actually invites the sharing of religious testimonies within the public school system. Thus, ShineMK is able to perform at school assemblies and witness to their faith in required religion classes. The group may be compared to **V*enna,** which has a very similar sound and ministry (cf. also **Aurora,**

Whisper Loud, Zoe Girl). Musically, ShineMK possesses undeniable talent (the Andrews sisters have sung backup for Sting and Diana Ross), but they have been savaged by critics on account of the obviously derivative and repetitive character of their sound. The title track has the definitive Spice Girl sound. "Get a Life" sounds enough like Britney Spears' "Crazy" for *Phantom Tollbooth* to accuse the group of plagiarism. "More Than Words Can Say" sounds very much like a Backstreet Boys song. "Do You Believe in Love?" is not a Huey Lewis cover but another mimicry of the Spice Girls (or maybe All Saints) singing to a prefabricated computer-synthesized backdrop. "Higher Love" actually *is* a Steve Winwood cover, rearranged as a bouncy dance song with a rap interlude. Lyrically, ShineMK's songs are appropriately simple and positive, setting spiritual slogans to tunes that could have been used as advertising jingles. The group's bad reviews may owe something to the fact that critics rarely articulate the perspective of ten-year-old girls, who seem to compose ShineMK's target audience.

Christian radio hits: "Do It Right" (# 12 in 2000); "Higher Love" (# 16 in 2001).

King Shon (and the S.S.M.O.B.)

1996—*Papa Didn't Raise No Punkz* (Metro One).

King Shon is a rap artist whose musical style is rooted in the Death Row Records tradition of Dr. Dré and Snoop Doggy Dogg. He performs with a changing crew he calls the S.S.M.O.B. (for Soul Serving Ministers on Board). The artist's debut major label release, *Papa Didn't Raise No Punkz,* created some controversy in Christian circles for its use of an infamous racial epithet that is commonplace in rap but many felt to be out of place on a Christian recording. The album includes "I Wanna Die," an unflinching account of a life lost without Christ, and "Given Luv 2 My People," an ode to racial harmony. A good dose of humor infuses the latter track as well as the autobiographical "Punk of the Year" and a song called "Da Gangstaz Ya Mutha Luvz."

Shorthanded

Andy Wiseman; et al. 2000—*Forever Yours* (Tooth and Nail).

Shorthanded is a pop-punk band fronted by Andy Wiseman, formerly of the band **Crux.** Reviewers for *HM* and *The Phantom Tollbooth* agreed that, while the group sounds like every other pop-punk band in the crowded market (**Craig's Brother, Ghoti Hook, Slick Shoes, MxPx, Sick of Change, Value Pac**), they display unusual strength with their descriptive but often sarcastic lyrics. The chorus to "Evil Has a Name" goes "Evil has a name / And it's not Satan / It's you / And all the stupid things you do." The song "Goddess" is built around the idea that having a girlfriend will make everything right

with the world. "Curls and Curves" addresses issues of feminine self-image, and "Imitation" deals with pornography.

Shout

Chuck King, gtr., voc.; Ken Tamplin, gtr., voc.; Loren Robinson, bass; Dennis Holt, drums (– 1989); Mark Hugonberger, kybrd. (– 1989) // Joseph Galleta, drums (+ 1989). 1988—*It Won't Be Long* (Frontline); 1989—*In Your Face*; 1992—*At the Top of Their Lungs* (Intense); 1999—*Back* (Tamplin).

Shout was a Christian heavy metal band fronted by **Ken Tamplin,** who would also play with **Magdallan** and have a notable solo career. Chuck King was also a member of **Idle Cure.** Shout made two classic albums that KMG would release on a single compact disc in 2000. Like most glam metal bands of the late '80s, Shout played music that featured sweet harmonies, blazing guitar solos, pounding drums, and expressive vocals. The band broke into the scene a few years after **Stryper** but was more competent than that band and commanded almost unprecedented respect within the mainstream metal market. Tamplin and King recorded *It Won't Be Long* with hired session musicians, but soon recruited the rhythm section from Tamplin's former band Joshua (Robinson and Galleta) to join the group full time.

It Won't Be Long features the anthemic signature song "Shout" along with the crowd favorites "Timeless Love" and "Without You." The song "Winners and Losers" expresses what Tamplin declared was the message the group wanted to share with the world at large: "In God's eyes, winners or losers, we're all the same." As is often the case with Christian metal bands, the only song to gain radio airplay was the atypical ballad "Find a Way" (not an **Amy Grant** cover). *In Your Face* has a harder sound than the first album, with absolutely blistering metal assaults on many songs. Every track soars with an incredible energy but the slightly more pop-oriented "Give Me an Answer" and the novelty Beethoven instrumental "Moonlight Sonata (in 32nd Notes)" attracted special attention. Better sounds inhabit the Scorpions-like title track, "Faith, Hope, and Love" (not a **King's X** cover), "Gettin' Ready," and "When the Love Is Gone." The only ballad, "Waiting for You," finds Tamplin pleading, "Now I see the changes come all over me / I pray for your grace and mercy / I never earned the loving that you show / Teach me how to make your presence known."

There is little question that Shout was one of the four or five best bands in the world playing thrash metal at the time and, propelled by five-star reviews in secular magazines like *Kerrang!,* the group was discovered by some fans of the genre who were willing to tolerate the evangelical thrust of the lyrics. *In Your Face* sold some 40,000 copies in the first month of its release. In general, Shout songs were not filled with as much obvious Jesus/God/Bible talk as **Stryper**'s. Tamplin told *CCM* in 1989 that a songwriter who is too blatant risks turning off listeners who may have had bad experiences with Christianity, but "if you're intellectually clever enough, you can draw them a picture and then let the Holy Spirit drive the point home." Likewise, he thought the group could perform a significant mission just by plowing a course contrary to the generally profane character of its peers. "I am disgusted with the things that I see in rock 'n' roll that epitomize the most repulsive promulgation of garbage being spoon-fed to the youth of today," he told *CCM*. "Our mission is to address issues around us. Instead of putting a Band-Aid on the problems of AIDS and abortion by buying condoms, let's admit the real issue is morality."

The 1992 album *At the Top of Their Lungs* is a compilation disc with four new songs. Then in 1999, Tamplin put the group back together for a reunion album. Basically a fan-pleasing souvenir, *Back* offers a potpourri of hard rock styles with several songs that could have been on the earlier Shout albums mixed with others that sound more like Tamplin's solo efforts.

Christian radio hits: "Find a Way" (# 8 in 1988).

Dove Awards: 1990 Hard Rock Song ("In Your Face").

Thom Shumate

1996—*Promise of Love* (Questar); 1999—'*til you believe* (Bricklayer).

Singer-songwriter Thom Shumate says that his roots are in "the old protest songs" of artists like Crosby, Stills and Nash and **Bob Dylan.** "They utilized their talent to push an agenda," he maintains. "Once I realized I could have a personal relationship with the living Son of God, I knew I had a holy agenda." Shumate was born in Marion, Ohio, and eventually became a youth pastor in the central Ohio area. In 1989, he moved to Nashville where he would become a leader of Cottage Cove, an inner-city daycare ministry to children. While in Nashville, he also worked as a staff songwriter for Benson and Warner Alliance, giving him many contacts in the contemporary Christian music environment. His albums have been described by *Phantom Tollbooth* as "progressive folk rock." **Ashley Cleveland** provides duet vocals for "Freedom, Love, and Forgiveness," which opens *Promise of Love*. **Phil Keaggy** plays guitar for one track ("If It Was All up to Me") on that same album. The celebrity tradition continues on his independently produced '*til you believe,* with **Susan Ashton, Aaron Benward, Lisa Bevill,** and **Erin O'Donnell** offering vocals on various tracks.

Sick of Change

Kevin Scott, voc.; Andrew Tremblay, gtr.; Rich Tremblay, drums; Jon Berry, bass (−2001) // Travis Seinturier, bass (+ 2001). 1999—*In Our Time of Need* (Bettie Rocket); 2001—*These Shattered Lives*.

Sick of Change is a four-piece punk band from Southern California who claim to play "extreme music for extreme times." With a sound similar to that of their neighbors **Slick Shoes,** the group spits out fast, aggressive songs with direct, evangelical lyrics. The projects are generally marked by a level of theological awareness striking for a group of teenagers. The first album opens with a reading of 2 Timothy 3:1–5 (describing the difficult times that mark the era between Christ's resurrection and parousia). The song "Constant Struggle" explicates this theme. "Weakness" describes the apparent human inability to please God, and "Senseless Guilt" addresses the human failure to appreciate fully the grace of God that makes up for human weaknesses. "One Day to the Next" describes the ideal relationship with God as an experience of daily communion. The second album, *These Shattered Lives,* would show marked musical improvement. The group attains a tighter sound with crunchy guitar riffs, stratospheric vocals, and impressive harmonies. Songs continue to deal with the maintenance of faith in the face of the hardships of life, though "All You Are" and "Scarlet" are more like worship anthems. Not everyone appreciated the change in Sick of Change's style. *HM* groused that the sophomore album lacks the shouted background vocals and youth-gutter punk undertones that "made the band enjoyable."

Side Walk Slam

Josiah Curtis, bass; Marcuss Hall, voc., gtr.; Matt Jackson, drums. 2001—*Past Remains* (Tooth and Nail).

Side Walk Slam is one more Christian pop-punk band that sounds like **MxPx** and Green Day (cf. **Craig's Brother, Dogwood, Ghoti Hook, Hangnail, Noggin Toboggan, Shorthanded, Sick of Change, Slick Shoes, Twotimer, The Undecided,** and **Value Pac**). The southern Illinois outfit crafted a debut album that emphasizes lifestyle issues appropriate for the converted—the album title refers to those things that believers carry with them into their new life. Sexual temptations (particularly premarital ones) are a recurrent theme. "Yesterday's Actions, Tomorrow's Regrets" encourages preserving virginity until marriage. "Eve" relates a story of a man led astray by a woman's charms. "Holy Matrimony" presents a marriage proposal set to music. "Not Getting Off" offers lead singer Marcuss Hall's pledge to his wife to work through any situation, no matter how difficult. Hall told *HM,* "Even though all of our songs aren't spiritual, we all three love Jesus Christ with all our hearts, and we try to live according to his word daily."

Sierra

Wendy Foy Green, voc.; Jennifer Hendrix, voc.; Deborah Schnelle, voc. (− 2000) // Marianne Tutalo, voc. (+ 2000). 1994—*Sierra* (StarSong); 1996—*Devotion*; 1998—*Story of Life*; 2000—*Change* (Pamplin); 2001—*The Journey.*

www.sierra1.org

Sierra is an all-female adult contemporary trio that was initially billed as "a Christian version of Wilson Phillips." The well-received sound suggested by such an identification would bring them commercial success on four albums that show few digressions from the established style. Wendy Foy Green began as a solo artist in Austin, Texas, where she made one album. In 1991, she invited Jennifer Hendrix and Deborah Schnelle to join her in becoming a Houston trio known as By Design. The group moved to Nashville and changed their name to Sierra after signing with StarSong. Green would continue to be their apparent leader, writing or cowriting most of the songs and taking the lead as spokesperson in interviews. Lyrically, most of Sierra's material reflects a personal piety that focuses on relating to God in the midst of everyday life. The message of their music and ministry is sometimes geared especially toward Christian women, offering inspiration and encouragement.

Sierra would become the best-selling debut in StarSong's history (over 150,000 copies). For many Christian fans, the sound not only recalled Wilson Phillips but also seemed like a Southwestern version of **Point of Grace,** with beautiful harmonies and just a twinge of country. Schnelle cowrote the song "Tearing Down the Temple," which deals with her own struggle with anorexia. "When I Let It Go" is a song about trust and surrender. *Devotion* includes the exuberant track "I've Got the Joy" and a number of tender ballads ("I Know You Know," "That's When I Find You"). *Story of Life* is a somewhat more acoustic, guitar-driven outing, produced by Gordon Kennedy (of **Dogs of Peace**). The title track and "Willing to Walk" are both more progressive and rock-oriented than anything Sierra had recorded previously. *Story of Life* is also notable for two disparate cover songs, Petula Clark's upbeat "Colour My World" and **Julie Miller**'s poignant "Broken Things." The group also sings the intimate worship chorus "When I Consider" (written by Green with **Carolyn Arends**) and a collaboration with Joel Hanson (of **PFR**) called "Without Love." Schnelle retired from singing with Sierra after the third project and took over managing the group's books. Marianne Tutalo took her place, and the fourth album, *Change,* would not depart significantly from the trademark Sierra sound. **John** and Dino **Elefante** produced the record for a new label (Pamplin). Several songs are presented as prayers to God: the title track and "Make Me" both seek sanctification, a prevalent theme in Sierra's material. "Good Times" and "The Proof's in My Heart" are especially melodic and upbeat tunes. "Everything" is a modern worship song. *The Journey* backs off from the slick production sound a bit but generally continues in the same vein. "Carry Me" has more of an Irish flare, and the title track is reminiscent of **Rebecca St. James**' style, while "I Will Exalt the One" and "That's What I Know" continue to evoke the Wilson Phillips comparisons.

Christian radio hits: "No Stone to Throw" (# 13 in 1995).

Silage

Lance Black, gtr., voc.; Shane Black, bass, kybrd.; Damian Horne, voc., gtr., tromb.; Ryan Clark, drums (– 1998). 1997—*Watusi* (SubLime); 1998—*Vegas Car Chasers*.

Silage was a wildly eclectic modern rock band from Grass Valley, California (the Sacramento area). The Black brothers (Lance and Shane) and friend Damian Horne began playing together six years before recording their debut and learned to run through a variety of styles. By the time they signed with SubLime, they had developed what some critics would call a meatgrinder approach of pouring pop, punk, rap, and ska into a mix that would often allow them to change styles drastically from song to song. General market comparisons were often made to such outfits as Weezer and The Presidents of the United States, in part because, like those bands, Silage often incorporated bizarre humorous elements into their presentation. "We like to share the joy we've found in our relationship with Christ," Horne says. "By incorporating humor and having a fun time with our music, I think that comes through." The group disbanded in 1999. Lance Black and Horne went on to form **Parkway.**

Watusi's best-known song would turn out to be "My Car Makes Me Sin," a little ditty about repenting of road rage. "Drop Some Names" lists forgotten celebrities as a reminder of how fleeting fame can be. "I Love the Radio" is a sarcastic song that exposes the foibles of modern radio broadcasting (and music TV). "Jesus Is My Best Friend" is a more straightforward anthem of unabashed personal piety. The album closes with a cover of the Beach Boys' "Be True to Your School." For *Vegas Car Chasers,* the band would drop the ska elements completely and go for a sound akin to what Horne called "the Foo Fighters meet the Beastie Boys"—a hard mix of punk and rap with pop sensibilities. The opening track, "Original," pokes fun at the oft-heard critical suggestion that good music is supposed to be "wholly original"—which, of course, music never is. "Yo Tengo" uses the words "jazz super stereophonic" to describe the ostensibly indescribable quality of Christian joy. "Billboards" is written from the perspective of a non-Christian who is unable to see beyond the judgmental posture with which Christianity advertises itself to the world. Chuck Cummings of **LSU** and many other bands sits in as drummer for *Vegas Car Chasers,* and guest rapper **Knowdaverbs** joins the group on a song called "Verb." "Walls and Strolls" is a peaceful ballad with a sound like that of **Fold Zandura.**

Christian radio hits: "Billboards" (# 6 in 1998); "Verb" (# 7 in 1999).

Siloam

Brian Lutes, drums; et al. 1991—*Sweet Destiny* (Image 7); 1995—*Dying to Live* (Ocean); 1996—*Croak*.

Siloam is a Canadian hard rock band with a musical style and history similar in some respects to **Holy Soldier.** The group is led by its composer and only constant member, Brian Lutes, who tells a dramatic testimony of becoming a drug addict and a teenage prostitute before finding salvation through Christ. The first incarnation of Siloam was a pop-metal band that somehow got on good terms with the Canadian government and played hundreds of concerts at public schools, where they would deliver a positive "Don't do drugs—Stay in school" message. The group also toured internationally and in their homeland with bands like Mötley Crüe, Bon Jovi, and Van Halen and, according to Lutes, they sold some 400,000 units of their first two albums independently while remaining virtually unknown in the official Christian market. *HM* would be the only Christian publication to pay them any mind, giving favorable reviews to all three albums. On *Croak,* the ever-changing group drops the melodic metal template for a hard alternative approach. Lyrically, Lutes's songs all focus on the dark aspects of life—troubled homes, abuse, and the yearning for love and acceptance.

Silverwind

Betsy Hernandez, voc. (– 1986); Georgian Banov, voc. (– 1986); Angie Whatley, voc. (– 1985) // Patty Grambling, voc. (+ 1985, – 1986); Rick Starrett, voc. (+ 1986); Patsy Hilton-Kline, voc. (+ 1986); Laury Peters, voc. (+ 1986). 1981—*Silverwind* (Sparrow); 1982—*A Song in the Night;* 1985—*By His Spirit;* 1986—*Set Apart;* 1999—*The Unforgettable Hits* (Spark).

Silverwind was a pop trio formed by Georgian Banov of **Candle** and **Agape Force** ministries. Banov is a professionally trained musician who studied violin and other instruments from the age of five, eventually graduating from the Pop Music College of Sofia's Conservatory of Music. In 1965, he founded the first officially recognized rock band in his native Bulgaria, but he discovered that the communist government only allowed the group to exist as a symbol of freedom that was far from real; in truth, the group was viewed as an intrusion of Western culture. Chafing under what he considered to be artistic repression, Banov escaped to the West in a taxicab and immigrated to San Francisco in 1973. There, he was frustrated to find that the freedom he had longed for was compromised by a wantonness of drugs and despair. But he also met Christians at a mission to street people and came to have "a one-to-one, personal relationship with the Lord." For ten years, he became the mastermind of **Agape Force** and its related ministries. In addition to making contributions to contemporary worship

(**Candle**) and children's music (**Agape Force**), he became known for his tales of religious persecution and for his efforts to coordinate aid for Christians behind the Iron Curtain. He founded Silverwind in Tacoma, Washington, in 1980 with two other members of the **Candle** group. The trio was often compared to **2nd Chapter of Acts,** though their sound was actually much closer to the slick Euro-pop of Abba. In 1985, Banov quit **Agape Force** to found Celebration International with his wife, Winnie. Since the fall of the Iron Curtain, he has returned to his homeland and has been active in coordinating both evangelistic and humanitarian relief efforts.

The debut Silverwind album is the most memorable. It opens with "Taking the Narrow Street," a pop song that may be inspired by Matthew 7:13 but is not obviously spiritual or religious in its orientation. But the album also includes Betty Hernandez' "Never Had a Reason," which offers explicit testimony to the faithfulness of Christ: "Never had a reason to doubt you, Jesus / You always answer me when I call." The same sentiment is echoed in "Your Love": "I have peace of mind in your love." Another of the group's best-loved tracks from the sterling debut is "I Am in Love," a testimony song that expresses devotion for Jesus with unashamed romantic imagery ("I am in love with Christ / I'll be in love the rest of my life"). Written by Betty Hernandez' husband, Frank, the song opens with a quote from martyred missionary Jim Elliot: "He is no fool who gives what he can't keep to gain what he cannot lose." **Stormie Omartian** wrote the lyrics to "A New Beginning" from the sophomore project, and **Julie Miller** contributes to "I'm Gonna Follow You" and "Breaking Through" on the third album. Otherwise, Banov forged strong songwriting alliances with each of the Hernandezes, who would contribute the bulk of the material—songs that could easily be picked up by church madrigals and worship teams. *By His Spirit* also features "Heaven Is Being with You," which explicates true paradise as being in the presence of Jesus, and a straightforward worship song called "Praise Anthem." The fourth album, *Set Apart,* would be recorded by a whole new lineup, including two former members of the Continental Singers (Rick Starrett, Laury Peters). Songs such as "Set Apart" and "We Will Be Holy" reflect the artists' commitment to encouraging a "believer's lifestyle" noticeably different from that of the world. In 1999, Banov and Hernandez would reunite with another vocalist (Patty Forney) to record two new songs for the two-disc Silverwind retrospective *The Unforgettable Hits.*

Christian radio hits: "Never Had a Reason" (# 8 in 1981); "New Beginning" (# 8 in 1982); "A Song in the Night" (# 25 in 1982); "Heaven Is Being with You" (# 6 in 1985).

Jeff Silvey

1996—*Little Bit of Faith* (Ransom).

Jeff Silvey is a Nashville songwriter who spent eleven years composing songs for other artists before finally recording an album of his own. Born in Alexandria, Indiana, Silvey began working with hometown stars **Bill and Gloria Gaither** at a young age, and his song "I Can't Stop Talking about Him" became a hit for **The Gaither Vocal Band.** He would also write "He Is" for **Aaron Jeoffrey,** "Closer to the Fire" for **Michael James,** "When It's Time to Go" for **4 Him,** and "Runs in the Blood" for **Ken Holloway.** Silvey's *Little Bit of Faith* features the strong ballad "Nice Place to Visit," which he wrote after his father died of a heart attack while on a family fishing trip. "Life is short and we don't have time to have bad relationships," he told *Shout.* "Earth is just a nice place to visit on the way to heaven."

Simple Minds

Charlie Burchill, gtr., kybrd.; Jim Kerr, voc.; Mike McNeil, kybrd. (–1991); Derek Forbes, bass (– 1984); Brian McGee, drums (– 1981) // Mike Ogletree, drums (+ 1981, – 1984); Mel Gaynor, drums (+ 1984); John Giblin, bass (+ 1984); Robin Clark, voc. (+ 1984, – 1991); Sue Hadopoulos, perc. (+ 1984, – 1991); Peter Vitesse, kybrd. (+ 1991, –1995). 1979—*Life in a Day* (Zoom); 1980—*Real to Real Cacophony; Empires and Dance;* 1981—*Sons and Fascination/Sister Feelings Call* (Virgin); 1982—*New Gold Dream (81–82–83–84)* (A&M); *Themes for Great Cities* (Stiff); *Celebration* (Virgin); 1984—*Sparkle in the Rain* (A&M); 1985—*Once upon a Time;* 1987—*Simple Minds Live: In the City of Light;* 1989—*Street Fighting Years;* 1991—*Real Life;* 1993—*Glittering Prize;* 1995—*Good News from the Next World* (Virgin).

http://simpleminds.com

No one has ever been sure whether the Scottish music group Simple Minds ought to be considered a Christian band or not. There have been frequent rumors that chief composer Jim Kerr is a believer who invests the spiritual images of his songs with specific, personal intent, but he has been too smart ever to comment on such imaginings. If they be true, then he has sacrificed whatever added witness (if any) discussion of his personal faith would grant for the privilege of being allowed to continue making albums in the general market without suffering the death knell categorization that being labeled an officially Christian band can bring. At any rate, many self-identified Christian music fans have enjoyed Simple Minds' albums precisely because of the faith explorations they think they find there, and the records have frequently been reviewed in the Christian music media.

Simple Minds began when childhood friends Charlie Burchill and Jim Kerr formed a Glasgow band with the unlikely moniker Johnny and the Self-Abusers. The latter group morphed into the more artsy Simple Minds under the influence of Roxy Music and David Bowie. They spent a few albums experimenting with techno dance styles and finally came to the attention

of American audiences with *New Gold Dreams (81–82–83–84).* The cover of that album features a large gold cross with a heart emblazoned in the middle of it, making it look for all the world like a collection of hymns by some church choir. Songs display such titles as "Promised You a Miracle," "The Glittering Prize," and "Somebody up There Likes You." It could easily have been a southern gospel album, but in fact is a funky collection of artsy techno-rock. Even *Rolling Stone* would note that, apart from the titles and cover art, the album has "a warm musical feel and positive lyrics, involving much religious imagery." The song "Promised You a Miracle" with its vague but religious-sounding lyrics became a hit on many college radio stations.

The group would enjoy its biggest commercial success with the fluke hit "Don't You (Forget about Me)" (# 1 in 1985), a song they did not write, but recorded for the movie soundtrack of *The Breakfast Club.* It did not even appear on any of their own albums, but *Once upon a Time* would score them two more significant hits with "Alive and Kicking" (# 3 in 1985) and "Sanctify Yourself" (# 14 in 1986). The former song has Kerr affecting a Bono vocal on a song of inspiration: "You lift me up . . . You lead me on . . . You take me home." The same theme is echoed in the album's title track: "You lift me up when I know you're around / But God only knows what God only knows." "Sanctify Yourself" has lyrics calling for listeners to open their hearts and discover that "love is all you need." With a gospel choir singing in the background, it sounds as much like Christian rock as many songs on many albums by self-designated Christian groups. "I hope and I pray that maybe some day you'll come back and show me the way," Kerr sings, while musing that only "love sweeping down from above can give hope for making more chances." On future projects, the spirituality of Simple Minds' songs would turn out to be as spotty as the musical quality. *Street Fighting Years* is a mostly political album, but it includes "Belfast Child," a ballad sung from one whose "faith in God and church and the government" appears to have been shaken but not destroyed. *Real Life* offers "See the Lights," which sounds enough like **U2** to confuse a lot of listeners into thinking they had put *The Unforgettable Fire* on the stereo by mistake. It seems to be about mutual support in spiritual quests ("If you can see the lights, shout out where you'll be"). "Stand by Love" is a self-explanatory gospel anthem. *Glittering Prize* offers a greatest hits package that includes most of the just-mentioned songs.

Then in 1995 the all-but-forgotten band suddenly released the best album of their career, *Good News from the Next World.* The opening cut, "She's a River," may be just a romantic ballad, but it is set to a stirring gospel tune, complete with choir again. Or maybe it's not just a romantic ballad: what *are* these words supposed to mean: "Shadow let me go / There's something you should know / I found my new direction and I hope you like the key . . ."? Other songs, like "7 Deadly Sins" and "And the Band Played On" display a moral conscience and a concern for living in a violent world. In the latter song, Kerr sings, "I was born to live / I was born to die / With the queen of soul / With the king of light / All the power in the land / Pull me through to the shadowland / I was driven by some hidden hand." And on "My Life" he sings, "I can feel it in the darkness / Getting closer in the night / Like a sacred song / You linger on / You give me wings of flight / And I love your sense of power." And so it goes. Christian music fans, some of them at least, would receive the album as a powerful, if anonymous, testament to faith. Of course, **Creed** and **Collective Soul** sing songs like this as well, and they both insist that they are *not* Christian bands. But then artists who want to distance themselves from rumors that they are religious don't usually title their albums *Good News from the Next World.*

Christian critic Brian Quincy Newcomb sums up his take on Simple Minds as follows: "Jim Kerr continues to rely rather heavily on the language of Christian spirituality to express a message of defiant hope and hard love in an angry world. As to whether he has accepted and affirms the Apostles' Creed and participates in Christian fellowship, well, only God knows."

Tommy Sims

2000—*Peace and Love* (Universal).

Tommy Sims is a performer with deep roots in Christian music who released one of the best Christian albums of 2000, a record that was inexplicably completely ignored within the Christian music scene. Sims may be best known to Christian music fans for his role as songwriter and bassist for the seminal band **White Heart,** with whom he played from 1987 to 1990. He was also later a member of **The Players.** He has produced albums for many artists, including **D-Boy, Darwin Hobbs,** Michael McDonald, and **Nicol Smith.** He has also made a significant mark in the general market, playing and singing with such artists as Babyface, Garth Brooks, **Eric Clapton, Amy Grant,** Joan Osborne, and Bruce Springsteen. In 1996 Sims won the Grammy award for Song of the Year for "Change the World," a song that he wrote with **Wayne Kirkpatrick** and Gordon Kennedy (of **Dogs of Peace**); the song was recorded by Eric Clapton and featured in the film *Phenomenon.* Sims also composed (with Kirkpatrick and Kennedy) all of the music for Garth Brooks's album *The Life and Times of Chris Gaines.*

On *Peace and Love* the African American artist revisits classic soul, saluting the golden era of black music with original songs crafted in the styles of R&B's greatest performers. "Write One This Way" invokes Stevie Wonder, and "Alone" summons aural images of **Al Green.** "A New Jam" and the title track could easily have been outtakes from **Marvin Gaye**'s *What's*

Goin' On. This is retro not rip-off—the imitations are more flattering than distracting, and Sims is able to invoke his '70s muses without coming off as either a plagiarist or a novelty impersonator. The album opens with its only cover, a soulful take on one of Jim Croce's lesser-known country songs, "Which Way." Then, "100" offers the purest gospel moment with almost seven minutes of testifying, against a funk-choir of background singers. Stevie Wonder himself adds harmonica to "Summer," which retells the story of Adam and Eve. "Comin' Home" and "When You Go" are midtempo dance tracks. "Love's Patience" is an eight-minute epic tribute to the ultimate triumph of life and faith: "Somewhere in time, there's a light that will someday / Be a sign for all mankind."

Sin Dizzy

See **Stryper.**

The Singing Rambos

Buck Rambo, voc.; Dottie Rambo, voc.; Reba Rambo, voc. Selected: 1994—*Masters of Gospel* (Riversong); 2000—*Rambo's Collection; 20 Favorite Gospel Songs* (Budget).

The Singing Rambos were one of the most successful southern gospel trios of the twentieth century. They released more than fifty albums as a group in addition to various solo projects. The core of the group consisted of husband and wife Buck and Dottie Rambo (née Luttrell), and their style has been described as "a harmonic blend of Buck's country-style singing and Dottie's mountain-style black soul music." The two came from poor, large families in rural Kentucky and married young (in 1950), at the age of eighteen and sixteen. They first began recording as The Gospel Echoes (a trio that also included Pattie Carpenter) in 1964, later changing their name to The Rambos and eventually to The Singing Rambos. For the most part, the group recorded only songs written by Dottie, and her compositional skills would provide their most enduring legacy. Often compared to Fanny Crosby, Dottie Rambo would write more than 2500 songs and ultimately be named Songwriter of the Century by the Country Gospel Music Association. Perhaps her best-known composition is the hymn "He Looked beyond My Fault and Saw My Need." The Singing Rambos' greatest contribution to contemporary Christian music would come by way of daughter **Reba Rambo,** who began recording with the group at the age of thirteen. She later embarked on a career as a solo artist and then recorded with her husband **Dony McGuire.** Buck and Dottie Rambo divorced in the mid '90s, but both continue to record as solo artists.

Dove Awards: For Dottie Rambo: 1982 Songwriter of the Year.

Grammy Awards: For Dottie Rambo: 1968 Best Soul Gospel Performance *(The Soul of Me).*

Situation Taboo

Phil Lovelady, voc.; John Rousseau; et al. 1991—*Crucified* (custom); 1992—*All Out* [EP] (Texas T-Bone Jive); 1993—*Protodemo* [EP] (Flying Tart); 1996—*Injecto Logos* [EP] (Scotoma); 1997—*Digitalis* (Flying Tart).

Situation Taboo is an industrial band from San Antonio, Texas, that released a number of custom tapes and independent EPs in the '90s. They began as a synth-pop group reminiscent of Depeche Mode and finished as an industrial rap band one critic described as sounding like "the Beastie Boys in outer space." Magazines like *Visions of Gray, HM,* and *True Tunes* all referred to them as "underappreciated" but did little to remedy this, as no major profiles of the band were ever published. Bandleader Phil Lovelady cited **Keith Green** as an influence on his songwriting, and this shows in lyrical emphases on submission to Christ, dying to self, and pursuit of holiness. *All Out* features a track called "S.A. Texas" that deals with gang violence in their home city, and "Live as Brothers" from the same project issues a (gender exclusive) call for racial reconciliation. The infusion of hip-hop shows on "More Money" from *Injecto Logos*. *Digitalis* would attract the most attention, combining dark ambient pieces like "Fear" with more aggressive, guitar-driven rap ("G.O.L.").

Six Feet Deep

Myk Porter, voc.; Mike Shaffer, gtr.; Tom Wohlfield, drums; Matt Simmons, bass (– 1996) // Bryan Gray, bass (+ 1996). 1994—*Struggle* (R.E.X.); 1996—*The Road Less Traveled.*

Six Feet Deep was a hardcore Christian punk band from Elyria, Ohio. They played music with an extreme intensity and explicit Christian lyrics, yet had some regional secular success playing clubs in the Cleveland area. Myk Porter maintains that when the band first got together, they had no intention of "doing anything for God" but were simply into "playing parties and being idiots and whatever." But, increasingly, they began to have discussions about spiritual things, and Porter and Tom Wohlfield who were nominal Christians found themselves having to justify their beliefs to the others. "One night at practice," he would relate, "we talked about it for a long time and Matt (Simmons) got saved and we just found a whole new direction." The group's debut album was one of the first Christian entries in the hardcore genre, following close on the heels of **Focused**'s *Bow* and barely preceding **The Blamed**'s debut. As such, the record was treated as something both marginal and special. Its production values were not high, but magazines like *True Tunes* and *HM* took note of the orientation and integrity of the project. "Hardcore to us is just honest and realistic," Porter told *HM*. "It's music stripped of all the extras, so that just the message and the feeling is all that is there." The song "Valley of Salt" is based on Psalm 69. On "Homeless," the

band members declare that this world is not their home. *The Road Less Traveled* would be received as a vast improvement musically, with much better production values, more diversity in song structure, and even "hints of melody here and there" (as *7ball* would put it). The song "Slip" declares "what you embrace is what you become" and calls on Christians to help each other in the struggle for holiness: "Iron sharpens iron, so one man sharpens another / Brother to brother, if you lose your grip / And as air is to a fire, so we will be to each other / One to another if I start to slip." The lack of inclusive language in the foregoing lyric is perhaps offset somewhat by a realization that Six Feet Deep's audience was almost entirely male. But, in reference to the foregoing song, Porter would say, "The whole basis of our band was always to say that everyone's a sinner, and we are not afraid to admit that." So also on "Congruent" Porter owns up to his own wickedness in the midst of passing judgment on another: "For all have sinned and fallen shy / Of the grace that's shown in both our lives." The band adopted as its motto the phrase, "More in sorrow than in anger," giving their lyrics a twist on stereotypical punk rage (the phrase is printed on the *Struggle* disc and is actually quoted in the song "More in Sorrow" on *Road Less Traveled*). So on "Meaningless" Porter addresses the band's more worldly fans, saying, "There's nothing you would die for / And that saddens me" ("Meaningless"). Musically, Six Feet Deep was sometimes compared to bands like White Zombie and Biohazard. "I understand that the kind of music we do isn't going to hit huge," Porter said in 1996. "That's okay. This is what we like, and we don't want to change it." Unfortunately, the R.E.X. label went bankrupt and the band was a casualty of ensuing fiascoes. Porter went on to play with **Brandtson,** and Bryan Gray (who also played with **The Blamed**) formed **Left Out.**

Sixpence None the Richer

Leigh Bingham Nash, voc.; Matt Slocum, gtr., cello // Dale Baker, drums (+ 1995); J. J. Plasencio, bass (+ 1995, – 1997); Tess Wiley, gtr., voc. (+ 1995, – 1997). 1993—*The Fatherless and the Widow* (R.E.X.); 1995—*This Beautiful Mess; Tickets for a Prayer Wheel* [EP]; 1997—*Sixpence None the Richer* (Squint); 1999—*A Portrait of Their Best* (Flying Tart).

www.sixpence-ntr.com

Sixpence None the Richer achieved almost unprecedented success as a crossover band when their song "Kiss Me" soared to the top of the general market charts (# 2 in 1998). Although they had been favorites with Christian music fans since forming in 1992, their sudden entry in the general market was greeted as a debut performance by a new artist. With little knowledge of the group's history or inclinations, the mainstream rock world both embraced and abused them as it is wont to do with any new act—or, to be specific, it treated them in a manner deemed appropriate for any new act fronted by a pretty young woman. "If she keeps lookin' like that, she'll get a lot richer soon," Jay Leno quipped when the group appeared on his show. *Spin* magazine went completely pornographic with comments about Nash that were grossly sexist. Such waters may have been difficult to navigate for introspective Episcopalians from New Braunfels, Texas, but navigate them they did. In 1998 and 1999, Sixpence None the Richer toured as part of the Lilith Fair festival, and in 1999, were nominated for a Grammy award. The band's name comes from an illustration used by C. S. Lewis in *Mere Christianity*. Nash drew applause when she explained this to David Letterman on his *Late Show* in 1999. "A little boy asks his father for a sixpence to go and get a gift for his father," she related. "The father gladly accepts the gift but he also realizes that he is not any richer for the transaction because he gave his son the money in the first place." Following her logic, Letterman noted, "He bought his own gift." Then she continued, "Lewis was comparing that to his belief that God has given him—and us—the gifts that we possess; we should serve him humbly, realizing how we got the gifts in the first place." The audience applauded and Letterman, a bit stunned, replied, "Well, that's beautiful. Charming."

The official debut album, *The Fatherless and the Widow,* was something of a side project for Matt Slocum, who at that time was better known in Christian music circles as the main ax man for San Antonio-based **Love Coma.** Slocum convinced a high school friend with an unusually sweet voice to sing some songs that reflected his more sensitive side, and the duo called Sixpence None the Richer was born. Leigh Bingham (later Nash) was only seventeen when *The Fatherless and the Widow* was released, and she had been two years younger than that when an early cassette demo with some of the songs took the Christian indie scene by storm. Reviewers recognized that the duo sounded a lot like 10,000 Maniacs and The Sundays (or, in Christian music, **Innocence Mission** and **Over the Rhine**) but the competence of Slocum's songwriting and Bingham's vocals seemed to make up for any duplication of general style. *Visions of Gray* described the debut as "billowing with beauty and lined with intimacy." *True Tunes* named it the pristine example of alterna-pop, a label that they themselves had coined a year earlier to describe music with alternative values and pop accessibility. *The Fatherless and the Widow's* most-noticed, standout track is the worshipful "Trust," which sets verses from Proverbs 3:5–7 to music, and occurs in two versions: a folk style with just piano and voice and a more lush second take featuring cello. The title track deals with Slocum's loss of his father, as does the song "Soul." The group also touches on such themes as emptiness ("Meaningless"), failure ("Falling Leaves"), remorse ("Apology"), and shyness ("Spotlight").

Sixpence filled out into a five-person group for *This Beautiful Mess,* a project that was recorded after some incessant tour-

ing helped the members to develop a tight and connected sound. The album title reflects the idea that the design of God can sometimes be seen amidst chaos, though many of the songs acknowledge the difficulty humans have in recognizing this. "I'm alone and I'm beating my soul" Bingham sings with cathartic pathos (on "Bleeding"). And again: "When I kneel to pray, it never seems you're there" ("Circle of Error"). Musically, the album is far more adventurous than the first project. Slocum adds walls of distortion to songs like the opener, "Angeltread," producing a much more rock-oriented sound, and Bingham stretches vocally to develop a darker tone on the tracks where this seems most appropriate ("Bleeding," "Angeltread"). "Love, Salvation, and the Fear of Death" and "The Garden" are especially melodic, previewing the trademark Sixpence sound that would propel "Kiss Me" to the top of the charts two years later. But lyrically, both of the just-named songs are far removed from the pubescent yearnings of the hit to come. The chorus of "Love, Salvation, and the Fear of Death" features the lines, "Come and save my soul / Before it's not too late / I'm not afraid to admit / How much I hate myself." And "The Garden" reflects on the plight of a young woman who trades her white wedding dress for a "long black gown" after losing her lover, possibly to death. The big hit from *This Beautiful Mess,* however, would be "Within a Room Somewhere," a soaring adult contemporary ballad addressed to the Messiah, who somehow enables the confused to "escape the pain": "I know you are there / catching, carrying / this beautiful mess." The song concludes with a killer guitar solo that offsets its sweetness and underscores the album's theme. *This Beautiful Mess* was packaged with a booklet that displays original artwork inspired by each of the album's songs, including works by **Jimmy A,** the Rev. Howard Finster, **Chris Taylor,** and Debbie Taylor (cf. **Steve Taylor**). It set a new standard for graphics in the Christian market, which Sixpence would match again when their 1997 self-titled album won a Dove award for "best packaging."

Tickets for a Prayer Wheel was officially issued as an EP, but with ten tracks and a total play time of over forty-five minutes, it is certainly more than just an expanded single. It includes two versions of "Within a Room" and an odd techno rendition of "Love, Salvation, and the Fear of Death," but there are also two notable new tracks ("Healer," "Dresses"). Creative covers (Patsy Cline's "Love Letters in the Sand" and **Leslie Phillips**'s "Carry You") and two instrumentals give the disc a fun ambience that allows it to serve as a "lighten up" companion to the rather intense *Beautiful Mess.*

All three of the first Sixpence projects were produced by Armand John Petri, who had also worked with 10,000 Maniacs (hence the initial similarities) and the Goo Goo Dolls. The next album, the hugely successful *Sixpence None the Richer,* would be produced by a former superstar of Christian rock, **Steve Tay-lor**—but it would be a long time coming. The band became en-tangled in a mass of red tape when its label, R.E.X., went bankrupt but refused to release the band from its contract (hoping, apparently, to sell them off as a final asset). Exiled from the studio, the group spent two years on a forced sabbati-cal. Bingham married Mark Nash of **PFR**. *This Beautiful Mess* won the 1996 Dove award for best Modern Rock album. **J. J. Plasencio** left the group to join **Plumb** (though he would re-turn as a guest on the 1997 album and then record as a solo art-ist). Tess Wiley left for **Phantasmic** and **Velour 100.** It was Taylor who eventually rescued the band, signing them as the debut act for his fledgling multimedia company, Squint Entertainment.

Sixpence None the Richer will forever be known for "Kiss Me," a song that certainly deserves the success it attained but one that is also atypical for the album as a whole. Even on first listen, "Kiss Me" and "Sister, Mother" (which sounds like it is also about wanting to be kissed but is probably some sort of al-legorical ode to wisdom) stand out on the album as whimsical pop islands in a sea of more morose musings. "This is my forty-fifth depressing tune," Nash sings on "Anything." Indeed, the album's first three tracks ("We Have Forgotten," "Anything," "The Waiting Room") all deal with their record label conflicts and come off as both bitter and vulnerable. *CCM* would call this trilogy "the quietest indictment of the music industry ever to be burned into a compact disc." Then "Kiss Me" arrives to lighten things up with what *True Tunes* dubbed "the most ro-mantic song ever composed in the Christian field." The song "Love" also has a radio-friendly sound, being similar in style and theme to **Sam Phillips**'s "I Need Love" (which the group would later cover—alongside "Love"—for the soundtrack of the film *Here on Earth*). "Moving On" offers hope amidst all the yearning and pondering: "I can sing about the night / How my tunnel without light / Led me to the other side / Where the sky is blue." In general, *Sixpence None the Richer* has a more re-strained sound than *This Beautiful Mess,* with cello and violins often replacing guitars and with pristine production that showcases Nash's emotive voice. Numerous session musicians add their talents, including **Tom Howard, Phil Madeira,** John Mark Painter (of **Fleming and John**), and **Al Perkins.** But it is ultimately Nash's voice that shines. "Her skills have matured many times over since her impressive performances of the past," *True Tunes* opined. "Her ability to nail every emo-tion—from coy flirtations to dizzying introspection to dark determination and wilted faith—sets her apart among a sea of female lead singers. . . . Her ability to get inside Slocum's lyrics and make them her own is the key to the believability and im-mediacy of the material." Slocum provides lyrics to all the songs on *Sixpence None the Richer* save three: "Easy to Ignore" is

a rare Nash composition, offering a tender description of heart-break; "Puedo Escribir" provides an excursion into world music with Latin rhythms, African textures, and Spanish lyrics by ex-iled poet Pablo Neruda; "I Won't Stay Long" is a **Samuel Brinsley Ashworth** song. In 2001, a poll of critics sponsored by *CCM* magazine placed *Sixpence None the Richer* at Number Nineteen on their list of "The 100 Greatest Albums in Chris-tian Music."

The success of "Kiss Me" shook the Christian music indus-try in a manner analogous to that which greeted **Amy Grant**'s "Love Will Find a Way" or **Jars of Clay**'s "Flood." Early review-ers unanimously identified the track as one of those songs that could be a mainstream radio hit, indeed, as one that *would* be a mainstream radio hit if only it weren't being released by an act whose unembarrassed profession of faith caused all of their re-cordings to be relegated to an artificially defined "Christian music market." But such songs are plentiful—anyone familiar with what gets called contemporary Christian music could probably list a couple dozen songs a year that would be major hits on secular radio if ideological stereotypes and prejudices within the music industry did not prevent potential fans from hearing them. How did "Kiss Me" break through and succeed where so many good tunes have failed? A lion's share of the credit apparently goes to **Steve Taylor,** who knows the ins and outs of both Christian and secular markets and who, in Jerry Maguire fashion, promoted the band and its song as though they were his raison d'etre. Though he himself was a bigger star than the group he was managing, Taylor neverthe-less returned to basics and accompanied Sixpence on a grueling tour of Christian bookstores and radio stations to help register some early sales figures. Meanwhile, he also finagled a deal for "Kiss Me" to be featured in the motion picture *She's All That* and, more importantly (since not too many people saw the movie), in the ubiquitous TV ads for that film. Millions of Americans heard a snippet of the song in a religion-free con-text, which allowed them to evaluate it on its own intrinsic (and considerable) merits. The country fell in love with the ditty, and "Kiss Me" became *the* summer romance song of 1999, also being played on episodes of such teen-oriented TV shows as *Dawson's Creek* and *Party of Five.* Suddenly Sixpence was all over MTV and VH1. Three different videos of "Kiss Me" were featured (a live take, a version of the song with footage from *She's All That,* and—the best—a video filmed by Taylor in Paris). Live clips of "Sister, Mother" and "The Lines of My Earth" also garnered some airplay. The group opened for Cher and The Wallflowers, did the Lilith Fair, and appeared on all of the usual TV shows like Leno, Lettermen, Conan O'Brien, *Live with Regis and Kathie Lee, Later, The Today Show, The Martin Short Show, The Rosie O'Donnell Show,* and many more. Taylor rushed out a sec-ond edition of *Sixpence None the Richer* with an additional nonmorose track, a catchy cover of the La's' tune "There She Goes." The latter tune was also featured on motion picture soundtracks (both *Girl, Interrupted* and *Snow Day*) and went to Number Thirty-two on *Billboard*'s general market chart. The group also recorded a cover of Abba's "Dancing Queen" for the soundtrack to the Nixon comedy, *Dick.* Eventually, *Sixpence None the Richer* would go platinum with sales in excess of one million, and "Kiss Me" would be named the most-played song of 1999 in ten different countries. It was also featured during the global broadcast of the royal wedding of Britain's Prince Edward to Sophie Ryhs-Jones.

Sixpence None the Richer's success in the general market brought a predictable backlash of criticism from within the Christian music scene. Such animosity seemed inevitable, given the Christian music industry's roots in fundamentalism, which often departs from mainline Christianity in making radical distinctions between what is of God and what is of the world. In this case, the Gospel Music Association endorsed the latter schism by ruling that "Kiss Me" was not a Christian song and so could not be considered eligible for Dove awards. The point was not that there was anything objectionable about the song; rather, the GMA apparently took the modifier "Christian" as applicable only to a compartmentalized (religious) aspect of existence rather than to the whole of life—if a song is not explicitly "religious" then it cannot be "Christian." The anomalous character of such a pronouncement soon became apparent as the GMA issued an official definition of Christian music that ran counter to any traditional or biblical understanding of what constitutes Christianity and especially violated normative theological understandings of the gospel after which the organization supposedly takes its name (see the Introduction to this volume for more on this fiasco of definition). Still, a reviewer named Thom Hazel wrote in *The CCM Update* (the definitive industry newsletter for most self-described Christian radio stations) that "the song 'Kiss Me' doesn't belong on Christian radio," and some thirty percent of stations in the Christian market refused to play the song. In a particularly nasty on-air interview, Nash was reduced to tears when the host and a number of callers continued to berate her for singing a romantic love song that didn't explicitly mention Jesus or quote from the Bible. *True Tunes* took a decidedly different tack: "The whole Buffy/90210/Melrose/Dawson/Scream/Party of Five universe is turning on to one of the most eloquent and talented Christian bands in a generation. In addition to feasting on a romantic song that steers far clear of any sexual innuendo, the new fans that pick up the record will find lyrics that point to hope amongst despair and faith in the midst of challenge. As believers and as fans of great music, this may be our finest hour."

As is often the case, the artists themselves had the most mature perspective. The group had toured with the Smithereens in 1992 and with 10,000 Maniacs in 1994 and, so, had always maintained some contact with what purveyors of Christian music want to designate "the secular scene." Slocum told *Release* in 1998, "We try not to separate our lives into, 'Now we're creating something Christian' and 'Now we're creating something secular'. I think the key is to just let Christianity infiltrate every area of your life and then your songs will naturally portray your Christianity."

In 1999, two indie albums of cover songs by the group were quietly announced: an EP called *A Sixpack of Sixpence* and a collection of country songs called *On Steel Horses We Ride.* The greatest hits package, titled *A Portrait of Their Best,* contains songs from the group's first three records only. In 2001, Leigh Nash provided vocals on the dance hit "Innocente" (which she also wrote) by the general market group Delirium. By the end of the year, the group was experiencing some deja vu as a newly-recorded album sat unreleased due to shake-ups at the Squint label.

Christian radio hits: "Within a Room Somewhere" (# 7 in 1995); "Thought Menagerie" (# 19 in 1995); "Love" (# 16 in 1998); "Brighten My Heart" (# 8 in 1998); "Breathe" (# 6 in 2000).

Dove Awards: 1996 Modern/Alternative Rock Album *(This Beautiful Mess);* 2000 Group of the Year.

Sixteen Horsepower

David Eugene Edwards, voc., gtr., banjo, acc., kybrd.; Jean-Yves Tola, perc.; Kevin Soll, bass (− 1997) // Pascal Humbert, gtr., bass (+ 1996); Jeffrey-Paul Norlander, violin., cello, gtr. (+ 1997, −2000); Steve Taylor, gtr. (+ 2000). 1995—*Sixteen Horsepower* [EP] (A&M); 1996—*Sackcloth 'n' Ashes;* 1997—*Low Estate;* 2000—*Secret South* (Glitterhouse); 2001—*Hoarse* (Checkered Past).

www.16horsepower.com

Sixteen Horsepower is generally viewed as a Christian band, although they operate decidedly outside the Christian marketplace. They are critical favorites of alternative-minded publications like *True Tunes, HM,* and *Phantom Tollbooth,* but receive no attention whatsoever from the mainline Christian media. Their products are not sold in religious stores, they don't play Christian festivals or church-related venues, and indeed, the band seems almost unaware of the burgeoning Christian music scene from which they might logically draw a following. Rather, the group's audience is securely secular, and front man David Eugene Edwards says that most of their fans just regard the overwhelming biblical and religious imagery of the band's songs as "quirky and queer." The David Eugene Edwards who leads Sixteen Horsepower is not the **David Edwards** who released groundbreaking new-wave albums in the Christian market in the early '80s, and the Steve

Taylor who came on board in 1998 is not the **Steve Taylor** who (also) released groundbreaking new-wave albums in the Christian market in the mid '80s.

David Eugene Edwards was born in 1968 and grew up the grandson of a Nazarene preacher. His earliest memories include traveling from one Colorado town to another listening to fire and brimstone sermons. He says that his father was also supposed to be a preacher but "went the other way" and became a biker instead. At some point, the family became Baptist; at the age of seventeen, Edwards married and, amidst assurances of eternal damnation, joined a nondenominational fellowship. Edwards had taught himself to play a wide variety of musical instruments, and in 1988 he formed a band called The Denver Gentlemen with Jeffrey-Paul Norlander. Sixteen Horsepower formed in 1992. The group's sound is broadly described as "country gothic," with perhaps the closest comparison being **Violent Femmes** (particularly their more country songs, like "Country Death Song"). But there are really no analogies. *True Tunes'* John Thompson reports, "The music is a style all its own: part old-school country (complete with fiddle, hurdy gurdy, banjo, and squeeze box) and part gothic rock. The songs drone, wheeze, and burn into a sound that surprisingly works. And then there is Edwards' voice—song after song, he howls, cries, and at times screams with a beauty I have never heard before." Gordon Gano (of **Violent Femmes**) plays fiddle on two tracks on *Sackcloth 'n' Ashes*. "He doesn't really play the fiddle very well," says Edwards, "but we invited him to be on the record and that's what he wanted to do."

Christian music fans discovered the band with *Low Estate*. "All my love, well it is madness / Freely given to you folks with gladness," Edwards sings. "I will not live and die—no, not by the sword / I am weak without the joy of the Lord" ("For Heaven's Sake"). Again, in "My Narrow Mind," he sighs sardonically, "Wish I was a Bible thumpin' fool . . . A mind as narrow as the road I walk / Always upright when I talk / But take my hand and you will see. . . ." Many of the songs *are* just quirky, with religious imagery woven into poetry the ultimate intent of which is not decipherable. "Hang My Teeth on Your Door" describes an innocent sexual romp with enough vividness ("rolling on the floor naked") to keep *Low Estate* out of the Family Christian Bookstores (cf. **Vigilantes of Love**'s "Love Cocoon"). But "For Heaven's Sake" concludes, "Taste and see that the Lord is good / Let's bend our knees like we know we should / We can't see clear—our eyes are made of wood / Taste and see that the Lord is good." And "Coal Black Horses" seems to be a parousia hoedown: "Just as sure as that sun's gonna shine / When he comes, at his table I will dine / Just as sure as that dog's gonna whine / In my heart no longer will I pine / Just as sure as by evil you are torn / The sky will open up an' angel blow his horn." *The Phantom Tollbooth* called the album

"apocalyptic Appalachian hillbilly grunge." Asked about his lyrics, Edwards told *True Tunes,* "I believe in God. I'm a born-again Christian. I just sing about what comes out of my thoughts, of my mind, what I believe in, and how it affects me."

Secret South lacks the surprise and intensity of *Low Estate*. Its two best songs are actually covers: the traditional "Wayfaring Stranger" and **Bob Dylan**'s "Nobody 'Cept You." *Hoarse* is a live album, reprising songs from the previous projects along with three covers: Creedence Clearwater Revival's "Bad Moon Risin'," Gun Club's "Fire Spirit," and Joy Division's "Day of the Lords."

65 dba

See **dba.**

The Skadaddles

Raymond Gurley, trump.; Eric Haas, tromb.; Chris Malpass, trump.; Mike Malpass, gtr., voc.; Skuter Malpass, bass; Wes Moore, drums; Marco Pineda, voc.; Shawn Whaley, voc. 1999—*Scoop It Up* (Eclectica); *Take Your Heart; Thankx for Laughing.*

Johnny-come-latelies to the ska craze, The Skadaddles are a Christian band from Georgia with a sound indistinguishable from that of West Coast acts like **The Supertones, The Insyderz,** and **Five Iron Frenzy.** With a thirteen-year-old bass player, the young band focused their debut album energies on fun songs with adolescent lyrics about "having a good time while glorifying the name of Jesus" (as *Phantom Tollbooth* would put it). Songs exhort the listener to pray more often, to turn from sin, and to worship the Lord, while also incorporating sillier sentiments such as those expressed in "Matt is a Dork" and "Raining Chili." Apparently, the group released three albums in one year, but by *Thankx for Laughing* they were advertising themselves as a "punk/emo band" and were incorporating some elements of those styles into their still basic ska style. *HM* would say, "Whether they came first or not, the fact is they're good at what they do and bring a freshness to an oft-stale genre."

Ricky Skaggs

Selected: 2000—*Soldier of the Cross* (Skaggs Family).

www.skaggsfamilyrecords.com

Country singer Ricky Skaggs recorded his first official gospel album in 2000, presenting it as the culmination of a career-long commitment to faith and values. Skaggs was born in 1954 in Cordell, Kentucky, and he has always considered himself to be a bluegrass player, though he came to be viewed in the vanguard of what was called neotraditionalist country music. In the early '80s, Skaggs worked with Emmylou Harris and as a solo artist, creating music that hearkened back to the sounds of the '50s, ignoring the slick crossover appeal that had typified '70s music by Crystal Gayle, Eddie Rabbit, and everyone associated with the *Urban Cowboy* film soundtrack. He would have eighteen Top 10 country and western songs, ten of them going all the way to Number One. His skill with guitar, banjo, mandolin, dobro, and fiddle became legendary, and in 1982 he was the youngest performer ever to earn a spot on the Grand Ole Opry. In 1983, he was named Entertainer of the Year by the Country Music Association. His hit "Uncle Pen" (# 1 in 1984) was the first bluegrass song to top the country charts in more than twenty years.

Skaggs' mother was a gospel singer, and he never strayed far from those roots. From the start, Skaggs would eschew the "drinkin' and cheatin' songs" that were the staple of country music in favor of what he called "positive love songs." He also spoke frequently and openly of his Christian faith, sometimes to the dismay of interviewers. "I shared my faith when it seemed appropriate and maybe when it didn't seem appropriate," he said in 1999. "Then, I'd get called on the carpet. Some radio station would call back to the label and say, 'Hey, if we had wanted an evangelist, we would have gotten Billy Graham'." Like many country singers, Skaggs would include the occasional gospel song on his albums or in his concerts. His 1986 Epic release, *Love's Gonna Get Ya',* features "Walkin' in Jerusalem," a song he would sing as a duet with **Amy Grant** at the Country Music Association awards show, and "New Star Shining," a Christmas carol sung with James Taylor. The Christian music industry acknowledged Skaggs' faith, and magazines like *CCM* would occasionally review his albums and run brief profiles on the artist as a Christian musician serving God in the world at large.

In 1997, Skaggs finished his contract with a major label and founded his own Skaggs Family Records. He announced that he was leaving country music, as such, and would henceforth just do whatever was on his heart. He released two bluegrass albums *(Bluegrass Rules!* and *Ancient Tones)* and then recorded *Soldier of the Cross.* The album delves into the riches of old gospel standards by Bill Monroe, the Stanley Brothers, and Flatt and Scruggs. He sings Ralph Stanley's "The Darkest Hour" and persuades that gospel pioneer to join him on "Jacob's Vision." As the album title suggests, many of the songs focus on the cross: "Were You There" and "Remember the Cross." But, as with much southern gospel, the dominant focus is on the life beyond: "Gone Home," "Waitin' at the Gate," "Are You Afraid to Die?" and "I'm Ready to Go."

Skaggs told *CCM* in 1999, "The Lord has allowed me to use country music or bluegrass to open the hearts of people. We don't sing songs about having sex and drinking. We go out and do songs that are relational. Then when we present the gospel,

we see a whole lot more results than by trying to drag people into the church. There's a lot of people that will come to our shows that aren't gonna go to church."

Dove Awards: 2001 Bluegrass Song ("Are You Afraid to Die?").

Grammy Awards: 1984 Best Country Instrumental Performance ("Wheel Hoss"); 1986 Best Country Instrumental Performance ("Raisin' the Dickens"); 1991 Best Country Vocal Collaboration [with Steve Wariner and Vince Gill] ("Restless"); 1998 Best Bluegrass Album *(Bluegrass Rules!);* 1999 Best Bluegrass Album *(Ancient Tomes);* 2000 Best Southern, Country, or Bluegrass Gospel Album *(Soldier of the Cross).*

Skillet

John Cooper, voc., bass, kybrd.; Trey McClurkin, drums (– 2000); Ken Steorts, gtr. (– 2000) // Korey Cooper, kybrd., prog. (+ 2000); Lori Peters, drums (+ 2000); Kevin Haaland, gtr. (+ 2000, – 2001); Ben Kasica, gtr. (+ 2001). 1996—Skillet (Ardent); 1998—Hey You, I Love Your Soul; 2000—Invincible; Ardent Worship; 2001—Alien Youth (ForeFront).

www.skillet.org

Skillet seemed to come from out of nowhere to become one of the two most popular alternative rock bands in the Christian music scene (along with **Bleach**) in the late '90s. The group actually had its origins in a praise band that played at Covenant Community Church in Memphis. The pastor of that fellowship encouraged the three founding members to get together, in spite of the fact that they had widely divergent musical backgrounds and tastes. He also gave them their name, likening their developing style to "southern cooking, where you just toss a bunch of different things into a big ol' skillet and see what it turns out like." The band would impress critics with their competence and creativity, drawing also a strong cadre of fans (called Panheads) who would travel hours to see them and would exhibit their loyalty in feverish ways.

The debut displays the sound of a grunge band most similar, perhaps, to Bush or Candlebox, but with distinctive elements (three-part harmonies, atonal jazziness) that defy any close mainstream comparisons. Most of the songs on *Skillet* are hard rock, including the opener, "I Can," and a fan favorite, "Promise Blender," about God's understanding when humans make extravagant promises that they fail to keep. "Gasoline" would gain a lot of notice for its rather extreme lyrics, which describe the goal of attaining purity of heart through a burning away of the flesh in rather graphic language. "You Thought" has a sound reminiscent of Nirvana, but another three tracks break with the dominant mode for a softer sound. "Saturn" likens belief in God to belief in the unseen rings of that planet, but has an intelligent **Jars of Clay** sound that belies the quirky lyric. "Safe with You" has more of a willowy **Starflyer 59** vocal, and "Splinter" closes the album with a ballad bemoaning the lack of unity in the church. In interviews for the album, Cooper would emphasize the band's strong commitment to ministry: "We want to play what God's doing in us and play what we feel is prophetic. Our goal is to always be creative and always be on the edge."

Skillet adopted a very different sound on their second outing, for the most part eschewing the grunge connections for industrial, techno rock reminiscent of Chemical Brothers, Garbage, and Nine Inch Nails, albeit with some of the pop sensibility of acts like INXS. Several Christian reviewers would style the new sound as a harder version of that made popular by **Audio Adrenaline** or **DC Talk.** The standout song on *Hey You, I Love Your Soul* is the title track, which sounds like nothing ever heard before in Christian or general market music. A slice of techno-jazz, it is propelled by an intriguing, start-stop rhythm that accentuates its oddball lyrics, which give voice to the irrational love of Christ for the undeserving. "Locked in a Cage" is a hard rocker with self-destruction lyrics similar to those of "Gasoline" ("I wanna be locked in a cage / I wanna be strapped in a chair . . . I wanna break my legs / In case a thought to escape"). "Whirlwind" describes the moving of God in this world, with an invitation to the listener to be caught up and swept away. "Your Love (Keeps Me Alive)" has more of a power-pop sound, with lyrics drawn from Psalm 63 about thirsting for God. "Coming Down" is a soft song, a beautiful ode to the coming kingdom of God sung in a style similar to that of **The Choir.** Now Cooper would say, "Our goal is to set an example of an uncompromising lifestyle. By clearly preaching the Good News, we hope to see serious renewal and spiritual fire in people."

In 2000, the group would go through massive personnel changes that would leave John Cooper as the only remaining original member. Eventually, the new Skillet became a male-female quartet fronted by the husband-wife team of John and Korey Cooper with Kevin Haaland (male) on guitar and Lori Peters (female) on drums. Nevertheless, *Invincible* (recorded just before the McClurkin-Peters switch) continues in the same electronic, industrial vein as *Hey You* with an even harder attack on certain songs. The opening onslaught, "You Take My Rights Away," continues in the tradition of expressing devotion to God in attention-getting language that seems to extol servitude. The title track expresses the notion that the faith for which Christians stand can never be defeated and that, indeed, those who stand firm in that faith also have eternal security: "You just can't kill a man when he's dead / You know, the spirit survives." Other hard songs include "You're Powerful," "The Fire Breathes," and "You're in My Brain." Once again, the group turns out a few soft and worshipful numbers, notably "I Rest" and "The One." Shortly after recording *Invincible*, Skillet released a collection of ten worship songs recorded live in their hometown of Memphis. They perform five modern worship classics along with five of their own songs. The project is part of a series of albums commissioned by Ardent (cf. **All Together Separate** and **Satellite Soul**).

Skillet has played a number of mainstream venues, including a Memphis festival where they were paired with the Goo Goo Dolls. Their manager, Layla Davey, said in 2000 that a number of secular companies and venues were interested in the band, with their only reservations being the group's upfront approach to ministry. "The Jesus factor is what is keeping Skillet from moving to the mainstream," he said, "but with so many Christian bands already in the pop market, it's just a matter of time." But their next album would appear to take them in the opposite direction. On *Alien Youth* the band combined the electronic influences with the hard rock of their first album to produce a sound that would remind many of a heavy version of **The Newsboys** (or, for the more aware, of the industrial-pop noise churned out by **Massivivid**). The theme of the album is stated baldly in the title track: "worldwide Jesus domination." That song and "Earth Invasion" summon believing youth to seize the world for Christ: "Come on, freaks, let's go" ("Alien Youth"); "Everyday, the kingdom is advancing . . . to rule all life and display his government" ("Earth Invasion"). Such triumphalism is not without problems theologically and, of course, makes the album offensive to non-Christians and fence-sitters—but on *Alien Youth* Skillet eschews dialogue for cheerleading, and the album generally serves the latter purpose well. "Rippin Me Off" offers a we're-not-gonna-take-it response to Marilyn Manson, but the title seems a bit ironic given the strong Manson/Reznor influence on the music. The better songs, lyrically, are those that are off-theme: "Thirst Is Taking Over" and the grunge-metal attack "Eating Me Away" express well the desperate need for God and the concomitant corruption of human nature by sin. The latter song segues effectively into "Kill Me, Heal Me," a cry to experience the ironic benefit of the cross (Mark 8:34; Galatians 2:20). Perhaps the best song musically is the hook-laden "You Are My Hope," on which the group starts out sounding like Third Eye Blind and then slides into a very **Newsboys**-ish chorus of praise: "You are my hope / You are my strength / You are everything I need." Additional highlights include the power ballad/nightime prayer "Will You Be There?" and the seeking song "Come My Way," which includes the great line, "Am I out of touch or out of reach?" Still, the band really needs to learn some basic Christian doctrine if the Christian community is their target audience. Gnosticism raises its head more than once as the group slams the Creator with such lines as "Save me . . . from my humanity" ("Eating Me Away") and "I feel my skin's just a shell / Underneath is my reality" ("Vapor"). The docetic spirit of "Stronger," which has Jesus claim, "My skin is my disguise" needs to be evaluated in light of 1 John 4:2.

For trivia buffs: John Cooper makes all of his own clothes. After enough people asked him where they could obtain similar attire, he began selling outfits over the Internet (at www.invinciblewear.com).

Christian radio hits: "Safe with You" (# 21 in 1997); "Saturn" (# 11 in 1997); "Whirlwind" (# 15 in 1998); "More Faithful" (# 8 in 1998); "Your Love (Keeps Me Alive)" (# 11 in 1999); "Rest" (# 3 in 2000); "You Are My Hope" (# 1 in 2001).

Skypark

Joey Aszterbaum, gtr.; Tony Deerfield, bass; Keith Gove, drums; Tyrone Wells, voc. 1998—*Am I Pretty?* (Word); 2000—*Overbluecity.*

www.skyparkmusic.com

Skypark is a rootsy modern rock band from Orange County, California, that *Phantom Tollbooth* once described as sounding like "a funked up Pearl Jam with bluesy vocals." The band's influences are broad enough for their sound to qualify as original; while individual songs call to mind specific associations from classic and contemporary arenas, the overall impression is never derivative. Tyrone Wells and Joey Aszterbaum attended Pacific Christian College in Fullerton, California, where they met up with Keith Gove at nearby Cal State. Deerfield comes from a Pentecostal background and had played with numerous bands in the Los Angeles area. An early incarnation of Skypark went by the name Sinai. The group is also reputed to have released two early independent albums (*Live in Room 104* in 1995 and *One More Night with the Frogs* in 1996) before their major debut on Word.

Am I Pretty? includes a number of songs that deal with a basic theme of insecurity. The title track presents the words of someone who obviously connects self-worth with appearance. "Emily's Love Song" recounts the travails of a girl who keeps changing boyfriends. Musically, "The Wizard of Id" and "My Mirror" sound a lot like The Black Crowes, while the oddly psychedelic "Here Come the Bugs" references Lenny Kravitz. The most noticed song on the album, however, would be the novelty track "Starbucks Girl," a little ditty about a crush on a café employee set to an odd Hawaiian tune. "This could be love," Wells muses, "or maybe it's just really good coffee." As this might indicate, most of the songs on *Am I Pretty?* are not explicitly religious, but "Christ Can Save You" does recount a witnessing encounter in a way that proclaims the gospel message in a natural and unashamed manner.

Overbluecity shows maturation particularly with regard to the quality of the songs themselves. The band supposedly wrote some fifty songs for the project and then selected only the best of the batch. What is most noticeable on *Overbluecity* is that all of the tracks are hook-laden and pop-oriented, though performed in a variety of styles. The album was pro-

duced by Ed Stasium, known for his work with The Ramones, Living Colour, and The Smithereens, and similarities to the latter band definitely come to the fore on songs like "That Something," an ode to romantic attraction ("Something lit up the room / I think that something was you"). Another standout track is "The Girl in Your Picture," which finds the singer comparing a real life acquaintance with the fantasy image he has constructed of her: "You're much nicer on Kodak paper / You're always smiling at me." Again, a minority of songs deal overtly with spiritual themes. "What God Does" reflects on God's ability to see beauty in the mess of humanness ("That's what God does / Why can't we?"). "Under Your Mercy" is an anthem of praise for grace: I feel the need to thank you / Now that the Holy Ghost is haunting me / I'm a child of light eternally." The title track is sung as a duet with **Máire Brennan.**

Skypark maintains a commitment to ministry while struggling with the ambiguities of identification with the Christian music subculture. "Everybody in the band is a Christian and takes that relationship with Christ seriously," Wells told *HM.* "Every thought filters through this consideration of 'Who am I because of Jesus Christ?' . . . We want people to know our relationship with Christ and we want them to know what we're going through." At the same time, Joey Aszterbaum told *Bandoppler,* "Nothing says, 'I don't want anybody who doesn't agree with me to enjoy my music' like the words *Christian band.* I like Rage Against the Machine, and I'm not a socialist. I like the Beastie Boys, and I'm not a Buddhist. The words *Christian band* should disappear off the face of the earth. We're just a rock band." To that comment, Grove would add, "We believe that God has given us something to share with the world, but we don't always know how best to accomplish that."

Sleepy Ray (and The Mighty Blood)

The Mighty Blood: Bobby McDonald, bass; Kevin Jarvis, drums. As Sleepy Ray: 1995—*Under the Mighty Blood* (New Breed). As Sleepy Ray and The Mighty Blood: 1996—*Where the Highway Turns* (Vineyard).

Sleepy Ray is Ray McDonald, a blues guitarist who got his start in Christian music playing on a couple of **Chris Lizotte**'s early releases. In the mid '90s, he released a solo album and then joined with a rhythm section to form the band he calls The Mighty Blood. McDonald says he learned about the blues from the masters: "I would go out and look for albums with the oldest black guy on the cover—I figured he played the blues the best." McDonald seems to copy the vocal affectations of soul artists like **Al Green** and **Marvin Gaye,** but his guitar work owes a great deal to Stevie Ray Vaughan. *Under the Mighty Blood* opens with a typical train song with metaphorical lyrics exhorting potential passengers to get on board before it's too late ("Station to Station"). The song "Greatest of These" quotes from the Apostle Paul's hymn to love in 1 Corinthians

13, but Romans 7 provides better inspiration for a song in the true blues spirit: on "Lord Rescue Me," Sleepy Ray pleads, "Lord rescue me from the man that I am." *Where the Highway Turns* offers ten originals and a seven-minute concluding take on Kevin Prosch's "God Is So Good." McDonald evokes James Brown on "You've Gone Bitter" and Motown on the melodic "My Answer." The title track is grounded in a legacy of traditional gospel, and the opening "Underneath Your Mighty Blood" rocks like some long lost Cream outtake. Lyrically, the album focuses on songs of praise and thanksgiving, while also encouraging those who do not know God to seek the Lord while the Lord may be found.

Slick Shoes

Jeremiah Brown, bass; Joe Nixon, drums; Ryan Kepke, voc.; Jackson Mould, gtr. (−2000) // Dale Yob, gtr. (+ 1998, −2000); Greg Togawa, gtr. (+ 2000). 1997—*Slick Shoes* [EP] (Tooth and Nail); 1997—*Rusty*; 1998—*Burnout*; 2000—*Wake Up Screaming*.

Slick Shoes is one of Christian music's premier melodic punk bands, second perhaps only to **MxPx.** Like that band and such groups as **Craig's Brother, Ghoti Hook, Sick of Change,** and **Value Pac,** the group takes Green Day as its primary general market reference point and crafts music that features what *HM* would call "Billy Joe Armstrong vocals; tight, fast, and high pitched drums; and the typical chord progressions and anti-solos." The band formed when most members were still in high school and lead singer Ryan Kepke was only fourteen. They took their name from a scene in the movie *The Goonies.* The debut album, *Rusty,* features "Joe's Sick," which is about the health of the group's drummer, and "By What Right?" which questions the morality of a country that aborts its young and performs lab experiments on helpless animals. Such a mixture of serious and flippant material would become a mainstay of the band. Dale Yob of **Ninety Pound Wuss** joined the group for one album, *Burnout,* which despite its title, reveals the group at an energetic peak. "It just sounded cool," Nixon would say, explaining the title of *Burnout.* "We've kind of had this fascination with flames lately." The album is, however, somewhat darker in tone than previous projects, with most of the songs being written in a minor key. *Wake Up Screaming* is much more melodic, though *Phantom Tollbooth* would complain that it offers "the most dead-on impersonation of **MxPx** yet." The title of the album, again, is in no way representative of its mood or content (Kepke, this time, told *HM* "it just sounded cool"). The songs on *Wake Up Screaming* actually offer a positive outlook on life and love. In "Elisha," Kepke sings, "I cannot imagine what it would be like if you were not around / Only by the grace of God, can I enjoy your precious friendship." And on "Angel," he gives thanks for someone ("my angel without wings") who is constantly in his thoughts and prayers. "Constancy" is a straightforward testimony to the certainty of God's unmerited favor, and "Peace of Mind" offers some atypical advice from a punk band: "When you love someone, you've got to trust them . . . You've got to give them the key to everything that's yours / Otherwise, what's the point?"

As for the focus of their ministry, Kepke says, "We're only human. I don't think we'll ever be spiritual enough for everybody." But, then, he adds, "We want to try to be a good band so that kids can listen to us, and not have to listen to bands that are talking about going out and getting drunk and being with all these girls. . . . We want to be a really good influence on the kids, but we struggle, and we sin and we fall. But we want to be a good example."

Jamie Slocum

1997—*Somewhere under Heaven* (Curb); 1999—*Grace Changes Everything* (Freedom); 2001—*Someone Like You.*

http://jamieslocum.com

Christian pop singer Jamie Slocum embraces the appeal of *pop* music unashamedly, turning out mostly upbeat albums with an accent on encouragement. *Release* says, "In a day when songwriters seem to enjoy bewildering us with wandering, philosophical journeys put to music, Jamie's lyrics are straight ahead, avoiding any confusion." Musically, Slocum's style has been compared to Richard Marx, Bryan Adams, and Rick Springfield. **Wes King** also comes to mind. The title song to *Somewhere under Heaven* has him longing "for a love that's true, that won't break my heart in two." On "Headed for the Light," he turns his attention to Christ as a child: "Did they know that way back then / This little boy would change the hearts of men?" The album earned him a Dove nomination for Best New Artist (he lost to **Jaci Velasquez**), but Slocum still took two years to follow up with the superior *Grace Changes Everything.* He intentionally moved to a smaller record label because it reminded him of what he imagined "the Christian music industry was like 15 or 20 years ago, when ministry was the focus, not money." He was about a decade off on those projected memories, but the spirit of *Grace Changes Everything* does indeed hearken back to the time of the Jesus movement (twenty-five to thirty years ago) when artists and audiences were blissfully unconcerned with being perceived as naive. The title track opens the album with an infectious, jazzy bit of ear candy sung in Slocum's sweet tenor. The theme of that song is later echoed in "God of Second Chances." Slocum also covers **Norman Greenbaum**'s chestnut "Spirit in the Sky" (with that heretical "I never sinned" line amended; cf. **DC Talk**) and he offers a tender reading of "One of These Days," a heart-tugging country ballad reflecting penitentially on insensitive treatment of persons in his bygone days of self-obsessed adolescence. "Spirit of the Lord" is a praise song, and "Bob" draws on traditional gospel, recommending that various characters (a car salesman, a waitress, a gambler) "have a little talk with Jesus" about their problems and goals. "Miss You Missin' Me" is a powerful, straightforward love song. *Someone Like You* solidifies his role in the adult contemporary market with more songs that draw on a variety of classic rock influences but remain in the basic pop genre. *CCM* described the album as evincing a "summer camp vibe." Standout songs include the title track, "Stay in Prayer," "Rackin' Your Brain," and a duet with Shadonna called "This Familiar Place."

Smalltown Poets

Miguel DeJesus, bass; Michael Johnston, voc., gtr.; Kevin Breuner, gtr. (–2000); Byron Goggin, drums (–2000); Danny Stephens, kybrd. (–2000). 1997—*Smalltown Poets* (Ardent); 1998—*Listen Closely*; 2000—*Third Verse*.

www.smalltownpoets.org

Smalltown Poets became one of the most successful of the literate acoustic groups in the late '90s Christian scene, with a sound and style similar to that of **Jars of Clay** and their Atlanta colleagues, **The Waiting.** General market comparisons were most often drawn to Gin Blossoms, though Crowded House, Goo Goo Dolls, and Toad the Wet Sprocket would also be obvious reference points. The group got its start when founding members Danny Stephens and Michael Johnston met in a high school creative writing class and discovered their common artistic and spiritual vision. Byron Goggin was a high school friend too (all three attended North Metro First Baptist Church in Duluth, Georgia), and the three of them formed a group called Villanelle that made one album of acoustic folk-pop titled *Pinwheels and Orangepeels* (Anastasia, 1995). Kevin Breuner and Miguel DeJesus were added in 1996, and the trio morphed into Smalltown Poets. The new name bespeaks humility and artistry, two qualities that would endear the band to the hearts of critics. The Smalltown Poets are competent performers, but they have been praised above all for their songs (melodic, catchy, memorable) and for their demeanor (authentic, vulnerable, and evincing a general lack of rock-star pretension). Stephens and Johnston actually thank their high school English teachers (Larry Bussey and Kay Bowen) in the liner notes to their debut album. Bussey taught them, "The best writing is honest writing. If you're being real about who you are and you let that come across, it's going to move people." The group also benefitted from constant touring under the guidance of manager Mark Hollingsworth, himself a veteran Jesus music critic from early days with *Harmony* magazine and the man often credited with **Petra**'s phenomenal success. Hollingsworth got them singing not only in churches but also at myriad secular venues, including Walmart parking lots. Wherever they played, the Poets would mix their own songs with a generous number of covers (Boston's "More Than a Feeling," Creedence Clearwater Revival's "Down on the Corner," Doobie Brothers' "Listen to the Music," ELO's "Don't Bring Me Down," Three Dog Night's "Joy to the World," etc.). This well-chosen strategy kept the band grounded and established them as players who took their role as entertainers seriously without detracting from their commitment to ministry.

Smalltown Poets sold well for a debut in the Christian market, earning critical acclaim and garnering the group a Grammy nomination. It was produced by John Hampton, who first established himself by working with Gin Blossoms but had since done even more impressive work for other Christian artists (**Audio Adrenaline**'s *Bloom* and **Big Tent Revival**'s *Open All Nite*). The radio-friendly pop song "Everything I Hate" sets the frustrations of the Apostle Paul in Romans 7 to an incongruously upbeat tune (Paul's "that which I would not do, I do" becomes "oh, I'm into everything I hate"). Equally poppy is "If You'll Let Me Love You," which offers comfort to a grieving friend. The more subdued "Prophet, Priest, and King" sounds very much like **Jars of Clay** but explores a creative theme, contrasting the abiding presence of Christ with the inaccessibility of political figures and celebrities who insulate themselves from contact with common folk: "I talk to a prophet who tells me the truth / And I dine with a king in my home in Duluth / Better yet I'm in touch with a much needed friend / Who hears my confessions and pardons my sin." Another song that is strong lyrically is "Trust," which draws on eucharistic imagery in a way that is somewhat rare for contemporary Christian music: "Take this bread / Drink this cup / Know this price has pardoned you / From all that's hardened you / But it's going to take some trust." The song "Monkey's Paw" restates the moral of W. W. Jacobs' classic tale of wish fulfillment: "forevermore to understand that dreams-come-true can kill a man." Musically, "Monkey's Paw" is more intense than the rest of the album, and it evolves out of a nontraditional song structure lacking any clear verse/chorus delineation. "I'll Give" is a quiet ballad of spiritual devotion very similar to the sound of Villanelle. "Who You Are" is a worship song with a strong "glory, glory" chorus. *7ball* would declare *Smalltown Poets* to be "one of the best major-label debuts in many years," and *CCM* would describe it as "wonderfully free from confining trendiness, musical predictability, and lyrical clichés."

The sophomore album, *Listen Closely,* might have been titled "Smalltown Poets 2," for it offers more of the same, with no decline in quality. The opening track, "Call Me Christian," is actually a remake of an old Villanelle song (cowritten with Lee Moody of **The Waiting**) and is one of the album's highlights. An anthem of proud identification, the song declares an unabashed desire to be known as one who aspires to be "a little Christ." The next track, "Anything Genuine," is more electric, with searing guitars appropriate to its image of a refiner's fire: "As I melt, look at what I've got / And separate it all from what I need." The same commitment to purity informs the acoustic folk song, "Hold It Up to the Light." Another creative track, "48 States," finds the band recounting various things they have seen on their travels, in contrast to the refrain "Never the righteous man forsaken" (cf. Psalm 37:25; the lack of inclusive language is unfortunate).

After these two albums, Smalltown Poets all but fell apart. Goggin took a job driving for NASCAR, Stephens decided to try a stint at artist management, and Breuner went into photography. The remaining Poets (DeJesus and Johnston) decided to stick it out all the same, hiring other musicians as needed. *Third Verse,* they say, reflects their primary commitment to "knowing and serving God" and reveals the strong influence of **Charlie Peacock**'s book *At the Crossroads* and Os Guiness's book *The Call.* It focuses on themes of renewal and hope, with many of the songs containing images of light and water. "Clean" expresses the basic Christian doctrine of reconciliation; "Firefly" picks up on Jesus' "you are the light of the world" imagery (Matthew 5:14) to present Christians as "little carriers of God's light." The album was produced by Paul Ebersold, known for his work with Sister Hazel and Three Doors Down, and he managed to bring more intensity to the music. Twin highlights of the record include the covers of "Beautiful Scandalous Night" from *At the Foot of the Cross* (cf. **The Choir**) and "The Lust, the Flesh, the Eyes, and the Pride of Life" by the **Seventy Sevens.**

For trivia buffs: Miguel DeJesus attended Greenville College in Illinois where he was friends with **Jars of Clay.** He receives joint writing credit for one of that band's best-known songs, "Liquid."

Christian radio hits: "Everything I Hate" (# 20 in 1997); "Prophet, Priest, and King" (# 3 in 1997); "If You'll Let Me Love You" (# 1 in 1997); "Who You Are" (# 4 in 1998); "I'll Give" (# 4 in 1998); "Anymore" (# 14 in 1998); "Gloria" (# 2 in 1999); "There Is Only You" (# 8 in 1999); "Anything Genuine" (# 12 in 1999); "Every Reason" (# 10 in 2000); "Any Other Love" (# 10 in 2001); "Firefly" (# 13 in 2001).

The Smiley Kids

George Hosni, voc., gtr.; Kevin Wickes, bass; Mike Wygant, drums. 1999—*Don't Get Bored* (SaraBellum).

The Smiley Kids are a skate-rock punk band from Denver, Colorado. Their debut album, *Don't Get Bored,* was produced by Masaki of **Dime Store Prophets** when the members were all in their early twenties. Stylistically, the record mixes old-school and new-school punk with a variety of other styles, making for more diversity than is usually associated with punk. "Fill the Gaps" has distorted guitars and gang vocals reminiscent of **The Blamed** while "Plants are Dying" comes closer to The Ramones. "Frowney Clowney" works in a bit of hornless ska. Lyrically, the songs vary between what *Phantom Tollbooth* calls "fun-loving junior high type of stuff and more serious straight-up calls to dedication and allegiance to Christ." "Alameda Hill" and "Bomb the Hill" are both tributes to skateboarding. "Fill the Gaps" and "Army of Light" have more spiritual content. "Imitation Cross" is a punk rant against religious pretension.

Craig Smith

1979—*The Grand Arrival* (StarSong); 1981—*Maker;* 1983—*Hymns;* 1988—*Worship* (Benson); 1989—*Songs to the Father of Life;* 1991—*Echoes of Innocence* (StarSong); 1992—*Quest for Freedom;* 1996—*Behind the Veil* (Brentwood).

www.craigsmith.org

Craig Smith is best known as a praise and worship leader, though he has also contributed significantly to Christian pop music. A native of Louisville, Kentucky, Smith grew up playing drums in local rock bands. He was led to Christ by the manager of one such band and moved with his wife to Missouri to attend Bible college. Eventually, the couple landed in Fort Smith, Arkansas, where the now-ordained Smith pastored a church. *The Grand Arrival* is a set of pop songs typical of Christian adult contemporary music (cf. **Bob Bennett, Chris Christian**). By *Maker,* however, critics would notice that most of the songs were "verticals," addressed to God in exaltation and praise. That album has more of a light rock sound to it than was typical of most early '80s worship music, but Smith would do a 180 on *Hymns,* delving into the liturgical riches of church history to present classic hymns to the accompaniment of a chamber orchestra. *Hymns* also features a men's chorus, a boys' choir, some classical guitar, and a mighty organ—but no electric guitars, drums, or synthesizers. *Worship* and *Songs to the Father of Life* offer contemporary praise songs with a pop orientation. But *Echoes of Innocence* returns Smith to the sound of his debut album, with inspirational songs in keeping with the adult contemporary style of **Michael W. Smith** or the above-named artists. *Quest for Freedom* was a special evangelism tool, with Smith's ministry distributing some 200,000 copies of the disc and tape. *Behind the Veil* initiates what the artist says will be a series of worship albums "designed to encourage a deeper, more intimate relationship between the believer and the heart of God." In 2001, Smith said, "At this time in my ministry, I feel that I'm to develop music tools for the body of Christ, as opposed to being presented as a Christian artist."

Christian radio hits: "The Grand Arrival" (# 16 in 1980); "Echoes of Innocence" (# 27 in 1991).

Rev. Dan Smith

1971—*Dan J. Smith* (Real); 1974—*God Is Not Dead* (Biograph); 1975—*Now Is the Time*; 1992—*Just Keep Goin' On* (Glasshouse); 1995—*Live at Fox Hollow* (Time and Strike).

The Rev. Dan Smith is an icon of African American gospel blues. At age eighty-two, he was ushered into a studio by **Buddy Miller** to put some tracks on record. Miller approached the project as though preserving an endangered species, producing *Just Keep Goin' On* in a way that allows the scratchy integrity of the star to stand out in its indigenous form, but placing him in a contemporary setting that keeps the album from becoming too much of an anachronistic novelty. Miller himself plays guitar and his wife, **Julie Miller,** sings with Smith on "I Walk by Faith." Other stars sidle in to offer duets or background vocals: **Bryan Duncan** on the opening "God's Radar"; **Mark Heard** and **Victoria Williams** on the country-tinged "When Your Time Comes to Die." Other strong cuts include the self-explanatory "Jesus Knows My Name" and "I've Never Been to Seminary, But I've Been to Calvary." Smith offers his testimony on "Down through the Years." The album sparked enough interest in Smith's music to prompt the release of a live recording of one of his concerts a few years later. Smith died in the mid '90s.

Howard Smith

1985—*Totally Committed* (Light); 1999—*Season's Change* (Ears 2 Hear).

www.howardsmithgospel.com

Velvet-voiced African American singer Howard Smith first came to the attention of Christian music fans singing for middle-period **Andraé Crouch** albums in the early '80s. Smith sings lead on such songs as "Love Medley (There's No Hatred)," "We Are Not Ashamed," "Can't Keep It to Myself," "His Truth Still Marches On," and "No Time to Lose." In 1985, he released a well-received solo album, *Totally Committed,* which won a Stellar Award and was nominated for a Grammy. The album features a number of soulful adult contemporary songs, the best of which are "We Are One," "Wanna Get to Know You," "Perfect Love," and the title track. Almost fifteen years later, Smith would privately release *Season's Change* for sale over the Internet. He says that the album "picks up where *Totally Committed* left off."

Jami Smith

2000—*Jami Smith* (Vertical); 2001—*Home*.

www.jamismith.com

Jami Smith is a worship leader from Oklahoma. She began leading worship while a student at Oklahoma Baptist University and, after graduating in 1993, continued in a full-time ministry directed to churches and youth conferences. She recorded a number of tapes and independent projects (including a musical called *Mysterious Love* and an early 1994 album with a group called **Mercyme**) but did not obtain national notice until her self-titled debut came out on Vertical. As *CCM* notes, the album transcends the usual limitations of praise and worship music, offering a number of songs that are perhaps too complex for congregational singing but, accordingly, have enough substance to merit repeated listening. The album opens with a simple piano-and-voice rendition of "Psalm 63" but then moves into more rootsy rock numbers. Smith sings in a rich alto that is just right for the more bluesy rock tracks that she mixes in with her acoustic ballads. In 2001, Smith released a live album of worship material recorded at her alma mater. Titled *Home,* the sophomore project includes some familiar tunes ("Lord Reign in Me," "Be the Center"), along with several new originals.

Michael W. Smith

1983—*The Michael W. Smith Project* (Reunion); 1984—*Michael W. Smith 2*; 1986—*The Big Picture*; 1987—*The Live Set*; 1988—*i 2 (Eye)*; 1989—*Michael W. Smith Christmas*; 1990—*Go West Young Man*; 1992—*Change Your World*; 1993—*The Wonder Years: 1983–1993; The First Decade*; 1995—*I'll Lead You Home*; 1997—*Live the Life*; 1998—*Christmastime*; 1999—*This Is Your Time*; 2000—*Freedom*; 2001—*Worship*.

www.michaelwsmith.com

Michael W. Smith is generally considered to be the prettiest singer in Christian music—in terms of physical appearance at least and sometimes with regard to musical output as well. Smith has the musical style of Barry Manilow and is beloved and reviled with the same fervor as that quintessentially MOR star. Murphy Brown would not have liked him, but millions do—he is one of the most commercially successful and artistically polished pop singers in the Christian music genre and has even left a fleeting but impressive mark on the mainstream charts with his song "Place in This World" (# 5 in 1990). Being *impossibly* good looking hasn't hurt, though early on it meant he had to deal with the supermodel syndrome by convincing skeptical critics that he had brains and talent as well. He does have both and, in time, came to be respected and admired even by those whose tastes run counter to his output. In 1992, he received an honorary doctorate from Alderson-Broadus College in West Virginia. In 1994 he opened Rocketown Christian dance club in Franklin, Tennessee (an upscale Nashville suburb), and in 1997 he founded Rocketown Records. He has been instrumental in launching the careers of numerous artists who have a sound quite different from his own, including **Ginny Owens, Plaid,** and **Chris Rice.** Over the years, he has performed for two United States Presidents and, in 1995, played for a Papal Mass in Baltimore, Maryland. In 1996, he hosted the annual Dove Awards ceremony. By 2001, Smith had sold over seven million albums. Seven of his records had gone gold, and one *(Change Your World),* platinum.

Smith was born in Kenova, West Virginia, but moved to Nashville as a young adult in 1978 to pursue a career in music. Although he had been a devout Christian from his youth ("I was a Jesus freak," he says of his adolescence), he drifted into a worldly lifestyle that included what he would later call "a lot of partying and drug abuse." Prayer and renewed commitment enabled him to turn his life around, and in 1982, his first big break came when he was invited to play keyboards for **Amy Grant.** Smith would record numerous albums with Grant, cowriting some of her best-known songs. He toured with the singer in 1982, 1983, 1984, and 1988. Having launched a solo career in 1983, he frequently performed as Grant's opening act, which provided him with unusually high visibility in the Christian music scene. He also gained early notoriety for the worship song "How Majestic Is Your Name," performed by **Sandi Patty.**

Smith's first albums are collections of synthesized, keyboard-driven inspirational songs that were almost definitive of contemporary Christian music for the early '80s. Like projects by **Chris Christian** and **David Meece,** Smith's early albums seem geared for teenagers within the church, although musically they probably have more in common with what the *parents* of those teenagers were listening to. *The Michael W. Smith Project* contains "Friends," an ode to the unfailing (and unending) character of Christian friendship. The song succeeds primarily on sentiment, on the strength of its sweet and poetic lyric (written by Smith's wife, Deborah). "Friends" would become a favorite theme song for graduation ceremonies and other occasions that marked impending separation of those who treasured its reassurance that "friends are friends forever, if the Lord is Lord of them." Almost two decades later, it would still be Smith's best-known and most loved song; in 1998, a *CCM* poll of thirty critics chose Smith's version of "Friends" as the single "best contemporary Christian song of all time." Such an exaggerated estimate of its worth ruins the song's legacy, presenting it as something it can never be. It is not *the* exemplar of what Christian music has to offer the world, but it is a nice little ditty about friendship. *The Michael Smith Project* also includes "Great Is the Lord," a praise song along the same lines as "How Majestic Is Your Name." Smith's second album, *Michael W. Smith 2,* would offer a couple more of these ("Hosanna," "Glorious Grace"), along with a Smith-Grant duet on "Restless Heart" and a song called "I Am Sure," which would become a Christian radio hit by **Deniece Williams** in 1991. Dann Huff of **Giant** plays guitar on the album.

A career shift following Smith's second project was instituted by his management team, which he shared with **Amy Grant.** The duo of Mike Blanton and Dan Harrell (Grant's brother-in-law) determined that Smith, like Grant, should be able to cross over into the general market. This vision gathered steam when Grant scored her first mainstream pop hit with the song "Find a Way," which Smith had written with her. Enthused by the success, Blanton and Harrell took charge of Smith's career and helped him to craft a crossover album called *The Big Picture* for release to the general market on A&M. Unfortunately, the label opted not to release the record, which was consequently sent to Christian markets only (on Reunion). Smith was deeply disappointed and gave up his dreams of being a mainstream pop star, but then, after the almost unnoticed *i 2 (Eye)* record, he found ironic success with *Go West* when the song "Place in This World" put him in the limelight. He was chosen Best New Artist of the Year at the American Music Awards. He was invited to serve as a regular host of the *VH-1 Countdown* show on the popular video network. He appeared on such TV programs as *The Tonight Show, Entertainment Tonight, Live with Regis and Kathy Lee, CBS This Morning, Good Morning America,* and *The Arsenio Hall Show.* And he was featured in *People* magazine as one of "The Fifty Most Beautiful People in the World." Still, the worldly success was fleeting, and despite his renown in the Christian market, Smith would go down in pop music history as a one-hit wonder. Actually, he did have a Top 40 follow-up with "I Will Be Here for You" (# 27 in 1992) and placed two other songs in the Top 100: "For You" (# 60 in 1991) and "Somebody Love Me" (# 71 in 1993). Still, he would later report that " 'Place in this World' was a fluke. . . . There was no marketing set up for it. There was just a woman at Geffen (Clare West) who went in there and it just took off." From this he drew the spiritual lesson that such success is something God grants, often to those who are not chasing it.

Smith's albums from the just-discussed period have the contrived sound of an over-managed artist ("We teach them how to walk, talk, eat, and dress," Harrell boasted of his charges in the mid '80s). But to say this is to grant that the material has a passed-by-focus-group sound that by definition guarantees its appeal to a large, common-denominator audience. Indeed, the albums have been credited with helping to introduce a new concept of what has been called "Christian lifestyle" or "Christian orientation" music; they eschew preachy messages and overtly religious proclamation to offer commentary on social issues and life in general as viewed from a Christian perspective. Musically, *Big Picture* moves away from synth-pop into soft rock territory. "In the first 20 seconds of the album's opener ('Lamu')," wrote critic Lucas Hendrickson, "the listener gets buffeted by a pseudo-jet flying across the landscape, followed by a driving drum loop and scorching guitar that proved this record was absolutely nothing like what Smith had created in the past." The album's songs are youth-oriented, dealing with moral development ("Wired for Sound"), sexual purity ("Old Enough to Know"), apathy ("Goin' through the Motions"), hope ("Pursuit of the Dream"), and encouragement ("You're Alright"). It also includes two of Smith's biggest Christian hits: "I Know" and "Rocketown." The latter song presents a modern parable about a Christlike figure visiting a typical city nightclub; it would be covered by **Brave Saint Saturn** in 2000.

The strangely titled *i 2 (Eye)* offers the atypically rocking "All You're Missin' Is a Heartache" (with **Stryper**'s Michael Sweet and Oz Fox on background vocals) and the pop-rock "Secret Ambition," which describes Jesus as a mysterious preacher who no one knew had come to give his life away. "The Throne" is another worship song, this time with a children's chorus, and "Pray for Me" is almost a remake of "Friends," expressing the parting promises ("pray for me and I'll pray for you") of two friends whose ways must part. In addition to "Place in This World," *Go West* includes the wedding song "Cross My Heart" and a buoyant, ethnic track called "Seed to Sow," featuring an African boys' choir. The title track ("Go West Young Man") uses Horace Greeley's famous dictum as a creative metaphor for repentance ("When the evil go East / Go West young man"). "Emily" is a tender ballad of reassurance for a young and insecure woman facing the enormity of life: "There are doubts to fade / Moments to be made / And one of them is yours." Smith also offers one of his finest worship numbers ever with "Agnus Dei," a new adaptation of a traditional liturgical piece.

Change Your World would be described by *CCM* as "a supremely fun album, with layered melodies and harmonies of the highest caliber." Produced by Mark Heimermann, it offers a number of songs that focus on romance. "I Wanna Tell the World" is Smith's spunky valentine to his wife and "Somewhere, Somehow" is a duet with **Amy Grant** about lovers apart (the "Friends" theme again). "Picture Perfect" reassures a partner that "You don't have to be picture perfect to be in my world." As indicated, the song "I Will Be Here for You" (written with Diane Warren) charted as a general market follow-up to "Place in This World." More overtly religious tracks include "Give It Away," which sets a well-known cliché to music ("Love isn't love till you give it away"), and "Cross of Gold," which reflects on the value and meaning of religious jewelry: "Is it decoration or proclamation?" *Change Your World* also includes a new ten-year anniversary recording of "Friends," done in a more orchestrated anthemic style. After *Change Your World*, Smith would release two summaries of his career to that point. *The Wonder Years* was a limited-edition two-disc set with over thirty songs and elaborate packaging. *The First Decade* samples some of the better-known songs and adds two new tracks, the country-tinged "Kentucky Rose" and romantic ballad "Do You Dream of Me?"

I'll Lead You Home opens with "Cry for Love," a bubbly and melodic song that offers a heartfelt prayer for stability amidst chaos: "My life is like a racing car, hurtling towards the wall . . . Hold me and take my fear away." The prayer is answered in "I'll Lead You Home," a song in which Smith offers the promise of Christ to provide guidance and strength. Up to two years later, Smith would announce the latter song in concerts by saying, "If they had asked me to come and do just one song, I would have come, and this would be the song." Other highpoints of *I'll Lead You Home* include "Breathe in Me," which expresses deep spiritual need, and the jazzy "A Little Stronger Every Day." **Susan Ashton** joins Smith on a country song of eschatological hope ("Someday"). "Breakdown" relies on revisionist history to contrast a supposed decline in American morality with a supposed righteousness that marked the founding of the country. Worship tracks include a gospel arrangement of "Crown Him with Many Crowns" featuring **Anointed** and an adaptation of the Lord's Prayer ("As It Is in Heaven"). Smith made *I'll Lead You Home* with producer Pat Leonard, best known for his work with Madonna, Peter Cetera, and Kenny Loggins.

Live the Life is generally regarded as Smith's best work, opening with two of his best songs. The first of these, "Missing Person," is a fully electric modern rock song that speaks of a search to recover lost innocence: "There was a boy who had the faith to move a mountain . . . Without a trace he disappeared into the void / I've been searching for that missing person." The next track, "Love Me Good," has a strong Paul Simon *Graceland* feel to it, with spoken-word verses that offer humorous snippets about the travails of life juxtaposed with a rollicking chorus that calls, "Give me love, give me love, love me good." The perpetually obtuse Gospel Music Association would disqualify the latter song as a contender for Dove awards, apparently because it doesn't mention Jesus or God by name (though a few years before they had chosen the even more secular "Place in This World" as Song of the Year). In general, *Live the Life* manages to avoid the sameness rut of adult contemporary with more challenging and upbeat songs than Smith had allowed on previous albums. *CCM* would say, "anyone who's pigeonholed Smith's stuff as lite and trite is in for a serious surprise: the new record rocks." Smith would admit in interviews that he composed many of the songs on guitar, which might account for the difference. The almost psychedelic title track challenges Christians to follow St. Francis's encouragement to proclaim the gospel without using words. "Never Been Unloved" has a retro Simon and Garfunkel sound to it and an especially strong lyric (by **Wayne Kirkpatrick**): "I have been undesirable / And sometimes I have been unwise . . . but I know that I have never been unloved." British pop star Nik Kershaw joins Smith on a song they wrote together ("Let Me

Show You the Way"). "In My Arms Again" was originally written for the movie *Titanic,* but did not appear on that soundtrack. The album's closing song, "Hello, Goodbye," is a powerful lament in response to the grief of a couple whose child died a few days after its birth. Smith avoids offering naive comforts and opts for simple empathy: "Where's the navigator of your destiny? / Where is the dealer of this hand? / Who can explain life and its brevity? / 'Cause there is nothing here that I can understand." Finally, a hidden worship track ends the whole album on a stirring high church note.

This Is Your Time set a new record upon release for the highest first-week sales for any Christian album in history. It is similar in style and compass to *Live the Life* but does not quite attain the same quality. The album features a couple of modern rock songs ("Reach Out to Me" and "I Still Have a Dream"), some infectious pop tunes ("Hey You, It's Me," "Worth It All"), and more of the by-now-requisite "Friends"-style ballads ("I Will Be Your Friend" and "I Will Carry You"). Still, there is no single song that stands out as either breathtaking or mind-blowing. The title track, a tribute to Columbine shooting victim Cassie Bernall, was apparently supposed to be the missing highlight, but is spoiled by sensationalist lyrics (contributed by **Wes King**). It was actually chosen by the Gospel Music Association to receive the 2001 Dove Award for Song of the Year, a poor choice that necessitates comment. The whole cottage industry built on Bernall's murder (with "She Said Yes" bracelets, T-shirts, and tracts) tends to be exploitative, but of all the well-intentioned tribute songs to the slain teenager (cf. **According to John, Rick Altizer, Clear, Charlie Daniels, The Kry**), Smith's is the most problematic. According to this song, Bernall was put to the test, "faced with the choice to deny God and live." This is not true. It may be that Bernall's killers asked her whether she believed in God before she was shot (though even this is contested), but there is absolutely no indication that they would have spared her had she answered "No," or that she was killed *because* of her faith. The attempt to turn her murder into a noble martyrdom may lessen the horror of the inexplicably random violence that occurred at Columbine, but by so doing it evades the issues which that event thrusts to the fore and, inevitably, undermines the significance of the other fourteen persons who died that day. If there is a lesson from Columbine, it may be that evil can come without discrimination upon the good and the bad alike, without warning and without mercy: it is *not* a test, and there is no chance for escape—that's what makes it so evil.

Many of Smith's albums have featured stirring instrumental pieces: "Sonata in D Major" from *The Michael W. Smith Project;* "Musical Instruments" and "Wings of the Wind" from *Michael W. Smith 2;* "Ashton" from *i 2 (Eye);* "Song for Rich" (a Celtic tribute to **Rich Mullins**) from *Live the Life;* and "Rince

Dé" from *This Is Your Time.* Indeed, the latter album concludes with an instrumental piano rendition of the song "This Is Your Time" that is far superior to the vocal version, revealing what a lovely melody the song actually has. In 2000, Smith would release an entire album of instrumental music, *Freedom.* The album has the feel of a film score, with lots of piano and strings. Then toward the end of 2001 he released a live album of praise and worship music called simply *Worship.* Recorded with the community choir at Carpenter's Home Church in Florida, *Worship* includes Smith's own "Agnus Dei," **Rich Mullins**' "Awesome God," Chris Tomlin's "Forever," and the modern hymn, "Turn Your Eyes upon Jesus." A highlight of the album may be Smith's presentation of "Above All" (written by Lenny LeBlanc and Paul Baloche), a song that he also performed for George W. Bush's Presidential Inaugural Prayer Service in 2001.

In 2001, a poll of critics sponsored by *CCM* magazine put three of Smith's albums on their list of "The 100 Greatest Albums in Christian Music": *The Big Picture* at Number Twenty-one; *The Michael W. Smith Project* at Number Thirty-four; and *Change Your World* at Number Forty-five. Smith has also released two Christmas projects and an early live album. He masterminded the worship album *Exodus* (Rocketown, 1998), which features original songs by a number of artists, including **DC Talk.** He is the author of several books: *Old Enough to Know* (Contempo, 1987); *Friends Are Friends Forever* (Thomas Nelson, 1997); *It's Time to Be Bold* (Word, 1997); *Your Place in This World* [with Mike Nolan] (Thomas Nelson, 1998); *Cooking With Smitty's Mom* [a cookbook] (Thomas Nelson, 1999); *Where's Whitney* [a children's story, with Debbie Smith] (Zondervan, 1999); *I Will Be Your Friend* [with Debbie Smith] (Thomas Nelson, 2001); *This Is Your Time: Make Every Moment Count* [with Gary Thomas] (Thomas Nelson, 2001). In late 1997, he started a church that meets at his farm in Deer Valley, Tennessee.

As a songwriter, Smith has written or cowritten Christian radio hits for **Amy Grant** ("Emmanuel," "Angels," "Thy Word," "Find a Way," "Stay for Awhile," "Love Can Do," "Lead Me On," "Faithless Heart"), **David Meece** ("And You Know It's Right"), **Sandi Patty** ("How Majestic Is Your Name"); **Billy Sprague** ("Jude Doxology"), **Kathy Troccoli** ("Stubborn Love," "Holy, Holy") and **Truth** ("Sing unto Him"). Smith is not typically a lyricist but tends to contribute the musical half to songwriting partnerships. His wife, Debbie, wrote the lyrics to all of the songs on his first album. By the third project, he had established a long-term relationship with **Wayne Kirkpatrick,** with whom he would craft the majority of his subsequent material. He has also written with **Brent Bourgeois, Gary Chapman,** and **Bob Farrell.** For *This Is Your Time,* he branched out to write with a wide number of known artists, including Beth Nielsen Chapman, Dan Haseltine (of **Jars of**

Clay), Nik Kershaw, **Cindy Morgan, Ginny Owens,** and **Chris Rice.**

Christian radio hits: "Great Is the Lord" (# 1 for 8 weeks in 1983); "Could He Be the Messiah" (# 21 in 1983); "Friends" (# 7 in 1984); "Hosanna" (# 2 in 1984); "I Am Sure" (# 8 in 1984); "I Know" (# 1 for 8 weeks in 1986); "Rocketown" (# 1 for 10 weeks in 1986); "Wired for Sound" (# 4 in 1987); "Voices" (# 19 in 1987); "Old Enough to Know" (# 6 in 1987); "Emily" (# 1 for 2 weeks in 1987); "Nothin' But the Blood" (# 5 in 1988); "Friends (Live)" (# 13 in 1988); "Pray for Me" (# 2 in 1988); "Help You Find Your Way" (# 13 in 1988); "Hand of Providence" (# 4 in 1988); "Live and Learn" (# 7 in 1989); "The Throne" (# 1 for 4 weeks in 1989); "On the Other Side" (# 3 in 1989); "I Hear Leesha" (# 5 in 1990); "Go West, Young Man" (# 1 for 6 weeks in 1990); "Place in This World" (# 1 for 4 weeks in 1991); "How Long Will Be Too Long" (# 2 in 1991); "For You" (# 1 for 6 weeks in 1991); "Seed to Sow" (# 2 in 1992); "Love Crusade" (# 4 in 1992); "I Will Be Here for You" (# 1 for 3 weeks in 1992); "Somebody Love Me" (# 4 in 1993); "Give It Away" (# 1 for 2 weeks in 1993); "Picture Perfect" (# 1 for 2 weeks in 1993); "Kentucky Rose" (# 25 in 1993); "Cross of Gold" (# 24 in 1995); "Cry for Love" (# 1 for 2 weeks in 1995); "Breakdown" (# 4 in 1996); "Straight to the Heart" (# 25 in 1996); "I'll Lead You Home" (# 2 in 1996); "I'll Be Around" (# 3 in 1996); "Little Stronger Every Day" (# 5 in 1996); "Someday" (# 3 in 1997); "Jesus Is the Answer" (# 9 in 1997); "Live the Life" (# 3 in 1997); "Love Me Good" (# 5 in 1998); "Never Been Unloved" (# 9 in 1998); "Missing Person" (# 2 in 1999); "Let Me Show You the Way" (# 16 in 1999); "This Is Your Time" (# 6 in 1999); "I Still Have the Dream" (# 7 in 2000); "Worth It All" (# 7 in 2001); "Above All" (# 17 in 2001).

Dove Awards: 1985 Songwriter of the Year; 1987 Pop/Contemporary Album *(The Big Picture);* 1991 Pop/Contemporary Album *(Go West Young Man);* 1996 Songwriter of the Year; 1999 Artist of the Year; 1999 Producer of the Year; 1999 Pop/Contemporary Album *(Live the Life);* 2000 Songwriter of the Year; 2001 Pop/Contemporary Album of the Year *(This Is Your Time).*

Grammy Awards: 1984 Best Gospel Performance, Male *(Michael W. Smith);* 1995 Best Pop/Contemporary Gospel Album *(I'll Lead You Home).*

Nicol Smith

2000—*Different Light* (Curb).

Nicol Smith is one-third of the trio **Selah,** which won a Dove award for Best Inspirational Album with its 1999 release, *Be Still My Soul.* A native of Detroit, she moved with her family at the age of eight to central Africa, where her parents served as missionaries in Zaire. Returning to the States, she earned a degree in political science at Wheaton College, but then moved to Nashville to pursue a career in music. She sang backup on projects by **Bryan Duncan, Amy Grant,** Michael McDonald, **Cindy Morgan,** and Wynonna. Smith has a husky voice that is very similar to that of **Ashley Cleveland.** Her debut solo album features songs produced variously by **Michael Omartian, Chris Rodriguez,** and **Tommy Sims.** The title track is a slinky, soul-inflected jam with a catchy, sing-along chorus. "Big

Car" is a witty tune about the futility of putting too much stock in material possessions. "Vila Beto Ve" is a tribute to the folks Smith knew in Africa, the title being Kituba for "Don't forget us." Smith also includes a number of adult contemporary ballads written by Chris Faulk, David Mullen, **Billy Sprague,** and Diane Warren.

Paul Smith

1978—*Child of the Father* (Eagle Wing); 1980—*Free Man* (custom); 1986—*Live and Learn* (Dayspring); 1987—*No Frills;* 1989—*Back to Who I Am;* 1991—*Human Touch* (StarSong); 1994—*Extra Measure* (Intersound).

Paul Smith replaced **Russ Taff** in **The Imperials** and sang with that group for about five years before embarking on a solo career as an adult contemporary pop singer. Born and raised in Texas, Smith attended Baylor University in Waco where he studied music and appeared in productions of *Godspell, Jesus Christ Superstar,* and other musicals. He says that he met Christ while at school and felt led toward a career in Christian music. He began work as a concert promoter while singing in churches on the side and recorded two independent albums. He joined **The Imperials** in 1981 and is featured prominently on their albums *Stand by the Power, Side by Side, Imperials Sing the Classics,* and *Let the Wind Blow. Side by Side* actually allowed each of the singers in that group to record a full side of what was essentially solo material. Smith's side rather noticeably outshone the others and produced two Christian radio hits, one of which he sang as a duet with **Leslie Phillips** ("Make My Heart Your Home").

Smith's albums tended to follow general Top 40 trends as he sang songs that were arranged and produced in styles similar to Phil Collins, Bryan Adams, or whoever "the flavor of the month" pop stylist might be. He drew on such songwriters as **Bruce Carroll, Chris Eaton,** and **Bob Farrell,** but cowrote most of his hits himself. Smith also cowrote the song "How Excellent Is Thy Name," which was a Christian radio hit for **Larnelle Harris** and was named the Gospel Music Association's Song of the Year for 1987. Lyrically, most of Smith's material was targeted for the church, with encouragement to righteousness being a prominent theme. A 1986 *CCM* profile presented the artist as an apostle to the "frozen chosen," conveying a "message of motivation to believers gone cold." On *Live and Learn,* he sings about "Everlasting Joy," which can inspire those caught in spiritual lethargy. Likewise, on "Never Be Another" he sings affectionately, "You're my first warm breath of spring / When the winter ends / You're my secret hiding place / When the world is rushing in." *No Frills* would score his biggest hit with "The Right Thing." The **Imperials**-like ballad "Faithful" also went over big, though most of the album is in a rockier vein. *Back to Who I Am* was produced in a **Petra** style by that band's frequent producer **Jonathan David Brown.**

Human Touch was widely perceived (by Smith and others) as an uninspired product, with Chris Eaton's "Under a Moonlit Night" providing its finest moment. Smith took a three-year sabbatical to get his stuff together and then returned with what was called his "comeback album," *Extra Measure*. The hit "Talk about Love" has a bit of a Charlie Daniels sound. "Daddy Came Home Last Night" is a sentimental song about a prodigal father's return to his family.

Christian radio hits: "Wait upon the Lord" [with **The Imperials**] (# 2 in 1984); "Make My Heart Your Home" [with **The Imperials** and **Leslie Phillips**] (# 13 in 1984); "Never Be Another" (# 6 in 1986); "Everlasting Joy" (# 13 in 1986); "Let Love Happen to You" (# 14 in 1987); "The Right Thing" (# 1 for 6 weeks in 1987); "Faithful" (# 4 in 1988); "Back to Who I Am" (# 3 in 1989); "It's Alright" (# 2 in 1989); "Bigger Than Life" (# 6 in 1989); "Beat of a Different Heart" (# 11 in 1990); "Under a Moonlit Night" (# 24 in 1991); "I've Got Love" (# 10 in 1991); "Man of God" (# 23 in 1992); "Talk about Love" (# 7 in 1994).

Snax (a.k.a. **Tasty Snax**)

Dave Farrell, bass; Mark Fiore, voc.; Mark Keller, drums; Eric Pfeiffer, gtr. By Tasty Snax: 1999—*Run, Joseph, Run* (Screaming Giant). By Snax: 2000—*The Snax* (Screaming Giant).

Snax is a punk-based rock band from Huntington Beach, California. The four young men who compose the group were best friends in Mission Viejo, California, and they formed the group while in high school, taking their original name from a sign at a gas station. "The Tasty Snax were really just playing around at being a rock band," Keller would later confess. It was something they did for fun, and that slacker attitude showed, positively and negatively, on the debut album *Run, Joseph, Run*. The band's overall approach was compared to "fun bands" like Weezer and The Presidents of the United States, but critics noticed a musical sloppiness that kept them from fulfilling their potential. The album's title track rehearses the somewhat humorous biblical tale from Genesis 39. Three songs draw on ska influences, and this caused the group to be misidentified and marketed as a ska band. After all four members graduated from college, they decided to get serious and changed their name to reflect this attitude. The initial album from Snax displays more musical competence, mature vocals, and vulnerable lyrics. "I write songs more for me than for the people out there," Fiore says. "I like songs that are lyrically honest about where I'm at." On "New Trend" he sings with irony, "I want to be different, just like everybody else." On "Better Off" he tells a girlfriend, "I was wrong about us and wrong about love / I put my trust in you and not in my hope above."

Adrian Snell

1975—*Fireflake* (Kingsway); 1977—*Goodbye October*; 1978—*Listen to the Peace*; 1979—*Something New under the Sun*; 1980—*The Passion*; 1981—*Cut; The Virgin* (Nelson Word); 1982—*Adrian Snell Classics* (Kingsway); 1983—*Midnight Awake* (Nelson Word); 1984—*Feed the Hungry Heart*; 1986—*The Collection 1971–1985* (Kingsway); 1986—*Alpha and Omega*; 1989—*Cream of the Collection* (Kingsway); 1989—*Song of an Exile* (Nelson Word); 1990—*Father*; 1992—*Kiss the Tears; We Want to Live*; 1993—*Beautiful . . . Or What?*; 1994—*Solo*; 1995—*City of Peace, Part 1: Moriah* (Alliance); 1996—*City of Peace, Part 2: My Every Breath; Light of the World* (Serious); 1997—*The Best of Adrian Snell: My Heart Shall Journey* (Nelson Word); 1998—*Intimate Strangers* (Serious); 1999—*The Early Years: 1975–1981* (Serious).

www.musicworks.nl

Adrian Snell is a British keyboardist and guitarist who has worked in contemporary Christian music in his homeland from the days of the Jesus movement revival to the present. His works span two-and-a-half decades, although he is not well known in the United States and has only rarely been reviewed or profiled in the American media. The son of a bishop, Snell began composing music at the age of six. He eventually received classical training at the Leeds College of Music. His early works are described by *Jesus Music* magazine as "very mellow but with an endearing symphonic presence that can be quite uplifting. . . . the early albums have some nice artsy melodic pop/rock and soothing orchestral folk alongside gentle piano ballads." The third of these records *(Listen to the Peace)* was voted Top British Gospel Album of 1978; it would be the only one of Snell's early works to be released in the United States (by Maranatha). Snell's fifth project *(The Passion)* created the greatest sensation in his homeland. It is a major concept work, something of a rock opera, dealing with the events of Holy Week. Snell recorded it with the Royal Philharmonic Orchestra, and it would continue to be performed for many years by various groups around the world. Throughout England and Europe interest in Snell's first five albums would remain strong, and as late as 1999 they were still being repackaged and sold as a three-disc set.

The second album in his oeuvre to be released in America was *Midnight Awake. CCM* describes that record as offering "heavily orchestrated British pop—punchy upbeat rock 'n' roll tunes and tremendously melodic ballads." **Joe English** and his band **Forerunner** back Snell on the project. The title track proclaims, "Lord if you knew me, you wouldn't have me as your friend / Yet you say you do see, and love me as I bend." *Feed the Hungry Heart* is a follow-up to *Midnight Awake* with more of the power-pop **Petra**esque sound. The title track, again, is the album standout. In the mid '80s, Snell's visit to the site of the former Nazi concentration camp Bergen Belsen had a deep effect on him, propelling him to embrace the Jewish roots of his own faith and to delve into the words of biblical prophets who speak to the exiled and persecuted. The result of this personal journey was a trilogy of albums: *Alpha and Omega, Song of an Exile,* and *City of Peace* (a two-disc set later released in separate volumes). *Song of an Exile* concludes with a poem called "Fear" written by twelve-year-old Eva Pickova, imprisoned near Prague. Snell also wrote two books to accompany these albums: *Children of Exile* (Word, 1990) and *City of Peace* (Monarch, 1996).

Overall, Snell's work has displayed a fusion of classical, rock, and (increasingly) world music influences. Between 1984 and 1994, he frequently worked with members of **Iona,** and indeed, that band is said to have grown out of his recording sessions. Lyrically, he has grown increasingly committed to bridging the gap between the Christian subculture and the world at large, writing music from a faith perspective that demonstrates universal concern for the human condition. *Intimate Strangers* is a disarmingly personal album that found distribution in both Christian and general markets.

Marj Snyder

1971—*A Time of Peace* (Discovery); 1972—*Let the Son Shine;* 1973—*My Lifetime Now;* 1974—*Content in You.*

By 2001, not many Christian music fans would remember hippie folksinger Marj Snyder, but thirty years earlier she was in the same camp as **Honeytree** and **Marsha Stevens,** pioneering the field of Jesus music with soft-sung lyrics accompanied by a tranquil guitar. Snyder was only seventeen when she recorded *A Time of Peace,* an album of campfire, youth group songs like Peter Scholes' "They'll Know We Are Christians by Our Love" and **Ray Repp**'s "I Am the Resurrection." By *Let the Son Shine,* she was letting more of herself come through and comparisons were drawn to Janis Ian. *My Lifetime Now* is probably the Snyder zenith with an emotional range of songs stretching from "High on the Love of Jesus" to "I'm Dyin'." She copies Judy Collins by closing the album with an a capella version of "Amazing Grace." The fourth and last project, *Content in You,* was recorded with **Brush Arbor** and finds Snyder developing into a country-tinged adult contemporary singer.

Soapbox

Par Augustin, gtr.; Brannstrom, voc.; Krister Mortsell, bass; Andreas Rejdvik, drums. 2001—*A Divided Man* (Solid State).

Soapbox is a hardcore punk band from Sweden that took its name from the title of a song by the Christian band **Blenderhead.** Their sound is similar to that group, to label mates **Blindside** and **Selfmindead,** and to the general market group Black Flag. The band formed in Ulmea, Sweden, in the mid '90s, but only broke into the American market after the turn of the millennium. *A Divided Man* is actually a re-release of a previous European project. *HM* notes that lyrics to most of the songs are not intelligible, but apparently involve some

forceful ranting about sin and salvation. "Fight the Racism" has an obvious message put forward in an aggressive manner.

Society's Finest

Josh Ashworth, voc.; Joel Bailey, bass; Rob Pruett, gtr.; Chad Wilburn, drums // Kris McCaddon, gtr., voc. (+ 2000). 1999—*Private Conflicts and Suicides* [EP] (Fury One Sixty One); 2000—*The Journey So Far* (Solid State).

Society's Finest is a Christian metal band from Arlington, Texas, with a sound not unlike **Embodyment** or **Zao.** Their EP *Private Conflicts and Suicides* got them noticed primarily for the professional quality of the work from a hitherto unknown artist. The band added former Embodyment vocalist Kris McCaddon to their lineup for the full-length project, solidifying those comparisons completely. Lyrics are not always understandable, and specific Christian content is less that obvious. Standout cuts on *The Journey So Far* include the opening, chaotic "1955" and the slowly building "Knife Fight."

S.O.H.L. 4UR Tribe

Personnel list unavailable. 1993—*2 Tha Basix*

Little is known of the band S.O.H.L. 4UR Tribe, which issued one album of early East Coast Christian rap music and then disappeared. They were never profiled in any Christian magazine, though *True Tunes* did review the album and notice that the group's sound "finds little or no comparison with any other contemporary Christian music group." In general, S.O.H.L. dispense with the stereotypical sloganeering of Christian rap and take more of a storytelling approach to their songs. They also inject a good deal of humor into the offerings, as on the song "Heaven Sent," in which the rapper is looking for a woman of God: "Some ladies I meet ain't ladies at all; in fact, they remind me more of a Christmas song—Ho, Ho, Ho!"

Steven Soles

1980—*The Promise* (Maranatha); 1983—*Walk by Love* (Good News).

Steven Soles was a member of **Bob Dylan**'s Rolling Thunder Revue and later performed with **T Bone Burnett** in **The Alpha Band.** After that group's demise, he made two solo albums and then took to producing albums for artists associated with the Exit label—including the **Seventy Sevens**' classic *Ping Pong over the Abyss.* He later became manager for **Peter Case.** In reviewing *The Promise, CCM* said, "Soles doesn't have the world's best voice, but it works well with the album's other elements." The real strength of the album, they continued, lay in the quality of its songs, especially "Touch the Power," "The Healer," and "I Found a Love." As might be inferred from the Maranatha label, the album was much more overtly Christian and even praise-oriented than Burnett or **Alpha Band** projects. *Walk by Love* is also a strongly devotional album, with songs like "Joy in All" and "Light of Lights" filled with hallelujahs and testimonies to redemption. Several tracks evince a Jamaican beat with definite reggae influence, similar perhaps to Ry Cooder.

Solomon's Wish

Mike Hurst; Scott Roberts; Kevin Tobias. 2000—*A Wise Man's Tragedy* (Pamplin).

Solomon's Wish is an acoustic vocal group composed of three youth pastors with a sound that begs comparison to **Phillips, Craig, and Dean.** The three members came together in Gatlinburg, Tennessee, just north of Nashville. They bring diverse musical interests to the combo, with Hurst citing R.E.M., Roberts naming Spin Doctors, and Tobias listing **King's X** as dominant influences. *A Wise Man's Tragedy* was inspired by the trio's study of the book *Experiencing God* by Henry Blackaby and Claude King. They identify the theme of the record as "following God, even when it makes no sense" and a "belief that God is in control of circumstances, that He loves us more than we can ever imagine, and that He cares about the details of our lives." The album includes "Circle in the Sand," a kinetic track that was one of the first songs the group wrote together. "So Help Me" is based on Mark 9:24, and "Mary's Alabaster Jar" tells a story from Luke 7 (with the anonymous prostitute in the story being misidentified as Mary Magdalene—a common exegetical error). "The Wish" is something of a signature song inspired by Solomon's decision to ask the Lord for wisdom (1 Kings 3:1–15). "Stop Sign" and "Grand Scheme" are driving acoustic numbers, the former with '70s harmonies reminiscent of Crosby, Stills and Nash, and the latter with the '90s folk sound of **Caedmon's Call.**

Christian radio hits: "Grand Scheme" (# 12 in 2000).

Solveig

1986—*In the World* (Dayspring); 1988—*First Step.*

Norwegian singer Solveig Leithaug was named Female Vocalist of the Year in her native land and proceeded to record two albums for the international contemporary Christian music market. Blonde and beautiful, she was inevitably compared to that other Norwegian woman who recorded under her first name: **Evie.** Solveig appeared at the 1985 and 1986 Christian Artists' Seminars in Estes Park, Colorado, and won a large following among peers and industry types. *CCM* would complain, however, that her first album, *In the World,* failed to capture "the joy and vibrancy" that she so easily communicated in concert. This was remedied on *First Step,* an album produced in Nashville by **Wayne Watson** and Paul Mills.

Solveig wrote many of the songs and she sings them in an angelic, crystal-clear voice. Composer **Chris Eaton** contributes "Land of Promise" to the album, and Watson sings it with Solveig.

Sometime Sunday

Mikee Bridges, voc.; Kevin, gtr.; Zip, bass. 1993—*Pain* (Fearless Donkey); 1994—*Stone* (Tooth and Nail); 1995—*Drain.*

Sometime Sunday was a Christian grunge band from Seattle that never quite seemed to get its act together. They advertised for a drummer throughout their entire career, borrowing various temporaries for each album or tour. Band members went by first names only, though leader Mikee's surname eventually came out. The *Pain* demo would be big with a certain segment of Christian music fans, but critics generally thought the sound was much too close to that of Nirvana, Soundgarden, and Pearl Jam. The band's best work would be on *Stone,* a more raw album recorded analog and produced by Andy Prickett of **The Prayer Chain.** As with the debut, however, pain remains the major topic, and hurt and anger, the primary emotions. "Blue" is a particularly intense song dealing with the almost taboo topic of lust. Other songs deal with pride, loneliness, and suicide. Mikee would tell *HM,* "There are probably as many screwed-up people in the Christian church as there are outside of it. I know for a fact that I'm a really screwed-up puppy." Around this time, Mikee got in trouble with some Christian music fans for smoking (he quit) and for using profanity in an interview in an underground magazine (he dismissed this as irrelevant). Prickett also produced *Drain,* which again had a raw, live sound. Standout tracks on this final product are "Eye," "Needle," and "Feel." Mikee later revealed that many kids who bought the album returned it because "one of the guys in the band says the word *ass* which I guess is foul in some parts of the United States." The group broke up and Mikee launched Push Records, a label whose roster would include **Yum Yum Children.** Commenting on the demise of Sometime Sunday, Mikee told *HM,* "Two of the guys were just in it to play music, not for evangelistic purposes. If I do another thing, I'm gonna do it so blatantly Christian that it'll make your stomach turn." Actually, his next project was a group called Twin Sister, in which he was drummer, not singer. They recorded an independent self-titled album on which the lyrics were all taken verbatim from *Star Wars* movies (e.g., "You like me because I'm a scoundrel" and "Do or do not, there is no try"). After that, he formed **Tragedy Ann,** which came a good bit closer to fulfilling the "blatantly Christian" promise.

Sonicflood

Version One: Aaron Blanton, drums; Jeff Deyo, voc., gtr.; Jason Halbert, kybrd.; Dwayne Larring, gtr. // Rick Heil, bass (+ 2001). Version Two:

David Alan, kybrd.; Rick Heil, bass; Tom Michael, bass, voc.; Todd Shay, gtr., voc.; Brett Vargason, drums. Version One: 1998—*Sonicflood* (Gotee); 2001—*Sonicpraise*. Version Two: 2001—*Resonate* (INO).

www.sonicflood.com

The first Sonicflood was a modern rock worship band from Nashville. Jason Halbert had been a member of **DC Talk**'s backing band and recorded as part of **Zilch**. Aaron Blanton and Jeff Deyo were also unofficial members of that group; the trio joined Dwayne Larring to form a band that would host worship events throughout the world, setting songs of praise to a modern rock sound. Rick Heil, who joined after the debut album was recorded, was also a member of **Big Tent Revival**. Many of the group's members had played as session musicians and backing instrumentalists for a number of Christian artists. Musically, Sonicflood favored a melodic blend of "alternative acoustic" sound and dance rhythms. *HM* would describe their sound as "a faster version of **Steven Curtis Chapman** or a slower version of **DC Talk**." Some critics would complain about individual songs copying the sound of general market artists (cf. "I Want to Know You" to Third Eye Blind's "Semi-Charmed Life" or "Something about That Name" to Radiohead's "Subterranean Homesick Alien"). *Sonicflood* includes a few modern worship classics, such as **Delirious?**'s "I Could Sing of Your Love Forever," **Bill Gaither**'s "Something about That Name," and the Vineyard music staples, "I Want to Know You" and "I Have Come to Worship You." The best of the original songs is "My Refuge," a building anthem with a catchy, rocking chorus. "I Could Sing of Your Love Forever" is very nicely done, with guest vocals from Lisa Kimmey of **Out of Eden**. The project closes with **Matt Redman**'s "The Heart of Worship." In concert, the band took an unusual approach to ministry, leading its audience in worship rather than providing an entertainment or evangelism-oriented performance. Deyo said, "We just realize that if we lift Jesus up, he will do the drawing, and he won't be drawing people to us, he'll be drawing them to himself." The group would also spend time with church leaders in the areas they would visit, conducting seminars on worship leadership. Though released in 2001, *Sonicpraise* is a live recording of a worship event held at the Flevo festival in Holland in 1999. Five of the ten songs are live versions of tracks from the debut album, but these are supplemented by new recordings of such classics as **Delirious?**'s "Did You Feel the Mountains Tremble?" and Rick Founds' "Lord, I Lift Your Name on High." After Sonicflood disbanded, a completely different group (with latecomer Heil as the only connecting link) usurped the name and released a new album called *Resonate*. The style and vision of the new band is essentially the same: eclectic worship songs performed in the styles of mainstream rock acts. *Resonate*'s opening track, "Lord of the Dance," is a syncopated techno piece that recalls acts like Human League. "Your Love" and "In Your Hands" are more traditional contemporary worship offerings, performed in the acoustic style of artists like **PFR**. The title track was cowritten by Heil and James Ingram. **Lisa Bevill** provides guest vocals for "I Lift My Eyes Up."

Christian radio hits: "I Want to Know You (In the Secret)" (# 1 for 5 weeks in 1999); "I Have Come to Worship You" (# 7 in 1999); "I Could Sing of Your Love Forever" (# 1 in 2000); "My Refuge" (# 2 in 2000); "Open the Eyes of My Heart" (# 9 in 2001).

Dove Awards: 2000 Praise and Worship Album (*Sonicflood*).

Sonik Boom of Love

Alexander East; Somphavanh Soudaly; Mike Ylvisaker. 1998—*A Love Supreme* (N'Soul); 2000—*Boom Shock*.

Sonik Boom of Love was a house music project put together by Alexander East, a known quantity in the secular dance scene who had released two vinyl mix records and a full-length CD on his own label (Planet East Records). East comes from Minnesota and incorporates some Minneapolis funk (i.e., Prince) into his basic house mix. *A Love Supreme* opens with "Spirit of Love," a song that samples Smokey Robinson's "I Heard It through the Grapevine" and loops the words "Love is chief among them" throughout its catchy groove. "Am What I Am" deals with racism: "If I looked like you / Would you love me better / Bleached my skin a shade or 2?" East changes styles drastically on *Boom Shock,* eschewing Europop disco for more of a techno R&B sound. There is more emphasis on lyrics. The song "Departure of U" allows that faith differences can end relationships: "You've been my love for so long / But my love for Him is so strong / I've tried to keep up the game / Of loving the both of you the same."

Sonlight

Hadley Hockensmith; gtr., bass; Harlan Rogers, kybrd.; Bill Maxwell, drums; Fletch Wiley, flute, trump. 1972—*Sonlight* (Light).

Sonlight was a jazz-pop combo that formed to serve as the instrumental backing band for **Andraé Crouch and the Disciples.** The members all performed (collectively and individually) as studio musicians on albums by many other artists as well. Maxwell became a producer and was responsible for helming all of **Keith Green**'s albums. **Fletch Wiley** recorded a number of solo albums. Eventually a reunited Sonlight morphed into **Koinonia**.

The Sonlight Orchestra

Austin Roberts; Kim Rose. 1975—*Love Song and Other Greats* (Myrrh); 1976—*Sometimes Alleluia*.

Regarded as a kitschy novelty act even at the time, The Sonlight Orchestra would eventually come to be regarded as a truth-is-stranger-than-fiction parody of contemporary Christian music at its corporate worst. **Austin Roberts** was the pop star turned producer responsible for the Top 10 bubblegum hit "Rocky" in 1975. Kim Rose was an arranger and keyboardist with classical training from the Berklee Music Conservatory. Together they formed The Sonlight Orchestra, which performed muzak versions of Jesus music hits on Moog synthesizers. The first such project turns classics by **Love Song** ("Since I Opened up the Door") and **2nd Chapter of Acts** ("Easter Song") into aural wallpaper. The follow-up makes **Honeytree**'s "Searchlight" and **Chuck Girard**'s "Sometimes Alleluia" appropriate for elevators.

Sons of Thunder

Personnel list unavailable. 1968—*Till the Whole World Knows* (Zondervan); 1972—*Day Follows Night* (Bronte); 1973—*Live at Virginia Beach*; date unknown—*Rock Gospel*.

Sons of Thunder was an early Christian music group that is notable primarily for the date of its first recording. According to David Di Sabatino, the group was an outgrowth of Dick Halversen's ministry at Fourth Presbyterian Church in Bethesda, Maryland. The band was befriended by Billy Graham's pianist, Tedd Smith, who convinced Zondervan to issue the record. The group obviously chose its name a decade before anyone had thought about gender-inclusive language, but it still seems singularly inappropriate for the original lineup: a combo fronted by three female singers who also played bass and lead guitar, backed by two men who played additional guitar and drums. *Jesus Music* describes their sound as "a '60s girl group with a twangy electric beat and groovy go-go organ." The Austin Powers feel is somewhat similar to that of the numerous groups Campus Crusade for Christ would sponsor in the early '70s—cf. **Armageddon Experience** or **Danny Lee and the Children of Truth.** Four years separated the Sons of Thunder's first two albums and personnel shifts probably occurred. *Day Follows Night* features a male singer who copies Johnny Matthis on what sound like Latin lounge numbers (e.g., "I Heard the Voice"). "Mighty Hard Road" and "Long, Long Ago" retain the femme-folk sound of the first project, and a cover of **Larry Norman**'s "Sweet Song of Salvation" presages future developments. The group would release two live albums in the early '70s, mixing covers of secular Top 40 and Jesus music: *Live at Virginia Beach* includes **B. J. Thomas**'s "Mighty Clouds of Joy," Roberta Flack's "Killing Me Softly," and the Beatles' "In My Life." *Rock Gospel* features Johnny Nash's "I Can See Clearly Now" and **Andraé Crouch**'s "I'm Gonna Keep on Singin'."

Sorrow of Seven

See **Aleixa.**

Soterios

Jeff Christensen, voc.; John Hudson, drums; Chris Humphrey, gtr.; Rusty Williamson, bass. 2001—*The Blinding Pain of Unspoken Words* (Clenchedfist).

Soterios is a metalcore band that takes its name from the New Testament Greek word for "salvation." *HM* describes their music as having "a full-on intensity and apparent recklessness," while its "mighty guitar blows are in fact calculated and almost surgical in their effectiveness." Vocals encompass the varied styles of screaming, growling, and shrieking. The band is known for its strong antiabortion stance, which is publicly articulated in their shows. Their debut album features the metal worship song "A Time to Embrace."

Soulfood 76

Samuel Ericson, gtr., voc.; Daniel Fairbanks, voc., gtr., drums; Paul Mumaw, drums, voc., gtr. (– 1998); Kevin Stainer, bass (– 1998) // Ian Hardy, bass (+ 1998); Dan Henry, drums (+ 1998). 1996—*Original Soundtrack* (Freedom); 1997—*Velour* (Retrospective); 1998—*8-Track.*

www.soulfood76.com

Soulfood 76 was a late '90s Seattle rock band that went for a scruffy retro sound. Musically, their orientation was actually much more late '60s than the numeral in their name might suggest—the dominant influences appear to be fuzz-tone bands like Cream, Mountain, and the Jimi Hendrix Experience, but there are just enough Ohio Players disco licks integrated into the mix to justify the eponymous anachronism. The love-it-or-leave-it element in Soulfood 76's sound was Daniel Fairbanks's high, vibrato voice, which set some critics on edge while imparting a distinctive element that others would claim "gives the band its interesting charm" *(The Phantom Tollbooth).*

Original Soundtrack would be the band's defining moment. The vibe is tight and consistent, with songs like "Vortex" effectively evoking the Woodstock era. *Original Soundtrack* is a concept album that really might have served as the soundtrack to some Jesus movement era Christian film (cf. *Time to Run*). Like **Resurrection Band**'s *Lament,* it traces the development of a disillusioned young man's journey to faith. In this case, the protagonist appears to be a slacker who starts out saying, "All I want to do is stay home" ("Vortex"), but eventually realizes that life is passing him by and makes a life-changing decision to respond to an inner voice calling him to follow Christ. As a new convert, he tries to share his faith. "Gloria's Gone" relates his frustration when friends don't welcome his enthusiasm ("No one came to the study again"). Still, the album closes with the worshipful realization that "You bring me where there is no shame" ("Purple"). Like some evangelical version of *That '70s Show,* the album manages to touch on questions of faith and spirituality within the broad contexts of loneliness, alienation, and adolescent angst.

Velour Retrospective is a refurbished reissue of a custom album the band had made before *Original Soundtrack.* That album had revealed a band still struggling to develop its style. As one critic would note, the original *Velour* was "more Average White Band than Lenny Kravitz," lacking both the hard rock edge and the consistency in song quality of later albums. The refurbished 1997 version contains some new tracks, but still does not make much of an impression. Lyrically, most of the songs on *Velour Retrospective* are worship oriented. "Time" is a dreamy Zeppelinesque ballad, and "Praise God" closes the project on a funky, acoustic note.

8-Track was recorded in Muscle Shoals, Alabama, and features the famed Muscle Shoals horns on some tracks. The album is more eclectic than *Original Soundtrack,* with Parliament/Funkadelic influences surfacing often and DJ scratching and rap being introduced here and there. The dominant sound, however, is still an early '70s vibe, and many of the songs have the spiritual feel of early Jesus music (**Love Song, Phil Keaggy, Larry Norman**). "Ain't No Fantasy" is a song of dedication, and "Electrolux" (named for a vacuum cleaner) is a hippie ballad about inviting Jesus into a life that is admittedly a mess ("Come into my room / There's laundry everywhere / My electrolux is broken down / Just sit down in my chair"). By the time *8-Track* was released, Soulfood 76 had announced that they would take "an indefinite break" from touring and recording. Fairbanks called an end to the group in 1998, saying that it just "laid a beating on my marriage and my raising a little girl." Fairbanks later formed a country band called Western Starlight. Paul Mumaw formed a general market band called Saline with Blake Westcott of **Bloomsday** and Ken Stringfellow of The Posies. Terry Coggins went on to play with **Rose Blossom Punch.**

Soul-Junk

Glen Galaxy (b. Glen Galloway), voc., gtr., kybrd.; et al. 1993—*1950* (custom); 1994—*1950: Free Shrimp* (Shrimper); 1995—*1951; 1952* (Homestead); 1996—*1953;* 1998—*1955* (Jackson Rubio); 2000—*1956* (5 Min. Walk).

www.souljunk.com

Soul-Junk is an experimental Christian band fronted by Glen Galaxy (née Galloway) who also performs with the general market group Truman's Water. Headquartered in San Diego, Soul-Junk projects also feature any number of Galaxy's friends and relatives; frequent collaborators have included his brother Jon Galaxy on bass and Nathan Page on drums. The band's sound is wildly eclectic, based primarily on a hybrid of hip-hop with indie rock, but with frequent borrowing from '60s psychedelia, new-wave, grunge, folk, funk, or anything else that comes to mind. "The whole point is to make something that people would want to puzzle over," Galaxy claims. Some critics have compared the group to very early Beck, though a better analogy may be found in **Danielson Familie,** with whom they have often toured (brother Jon is married to Rachel Smith). A reviewer for *Cornerstone* would call Soul-Junk "one of the most intriguing music groups I've ever come across." *True Tunes* says, "Soul-Junk is very clearly a love-it-or-hate-it kind of band." *CCM* calls them "too hip for the room," meaning that their music "goes beyond offbeat, beyond eclectic, beyond ninety-nine-and-a-half-percent of all Christian music to defy description." Notably, the group's lyrics often come straight out of Scripture.

The first Soul-Junk project was a custom album somewhat arbitrarily titled *1950* because "it was a good year for music"; subsequent projects have been named in increments with a few exceptions. *1950: Free Shrimp* is an alternative debut, with a joke on the name of the independent company that released it. Shrimper had actually approached Galaxy about distributing *1950,* but instead, he gave them a set of totally different material that had been recorded in the same sessions as those for the self-released custom project. Shrimper would also release *1951,* but another indie label called Homestead would put out *1952* and *1953.* Galaxy recorded an album called *1954,* but instead of releasing it as such decided to include the *entire album* as "a bonus track" on *1953* (which, accordingly, turns out to be over eighty minutes long). At this point, the group still had a small, albeit loyal, following and was much better known in the general market than in Christian circles, despite their obvious faith and Scripture-based lyrics. The magazine *Alternative Press,* for instance, ran a feature on them in 1997, comparing the sound to Captain Beefheart and indicating that, while Galloway (he was not yet going by Galaxy) may not find much acceptance among Christians, "he really does love Jesus." Then Galaxy signed with Jackson Rubio to release a major label debut, *1955,* a work that would bring the group to the attention of the Christian music scene. A two-disc set, *1995* is far from accessible but it did at least introduce Soul-Junk to open-minded Christian music fans, some of whom were drawn to the group precisely because of their quirky never-heard-anything-like-this-before quality.

The album that would establish Soul-Junk as a significant force in contemporary Christian music is *1956.* The latter project was reviewed in virtually all of the usual media outlets for Christian music, and a number of Internet sites *(Bandoppler, True Tunes)* published major features on the band. *1956* is certainly the most developed album of the Soul-Junk repertoire. It retains the underground, low-tech strangeness of previous work, without sacrificing basic sonic fidelity and musical competence. The hip-hop element also seems to be at an all-time high, with generous programming, loops, samples, and rapped vocals. A few reviewers would compare the band to **P.O.D.**, if only because they broke into the Christian market after gaining credibility in the world at large. Styles vary on *1956* from straightforward hip-hop ("ill-m-I") to college radio rock ("Sweet to my Soul"). On the song "3po soul" (apparently named after *Star Wars'* C-3P0), Galaxy acknowledges his marginalized status with knowing humor: "Just got kicked off the lectern at a worship song summit / My hymns all plummet, cuz church ladies can't hum it / But the kingdom of God? Yo, I'm from it." The song "Lordy Child (Say Abba)" is essentially a paraphrase of Romans 8:15: "We haven't received a spirit of fear but of an / Adoption, by which we reach out to God as Papa." A number called "Pumpfake" appears to be addressed to Satan: "We got the ultimate in blasphemy for your satanic majesty / Check this out: God making connection with all humanity." The song "Sarpodyl," on the other hand, is a bit obscure. "I like making up names that could be mythological creatures or that could be in a Dr. Seuss book," Galaxy explains. "And I think not knowing what these words mean is good, too, because it makes you really want to dive into the song."

In addition to the albums listed above, Soul-Junk has issued a number of seven-inch vinyl singles, all of which are titled with descending numbers: *1949, 1948,* etc.

Soul Mission

1994—*Soul Mission* (Myrrh).

Soul Mission was a one-time project put together by producers Darrell Brown and David Batteau, "two white guys" (in their words) responsible for albums by such artists as Chaka Khan, James Ingram, and Smokey Robinson. The idea was to perform gospel songs in the style of classic '60s soul, and to this end they assembled a crack band and a tag team of various vocalists. The instrumentalists included Booker T. Jones on organ and Steve Cropper on guitar—the two legendary stars responsible for founding Stax Records and defining "Memphis soul" (among other things, Jones fronted Booker T. and the M.G.s, and Cropper composed the hits "Sittin' On the Dock of the Bay" and "Midnight Hour"). Former Doobie Brother Michael McDonald played piano for the Soul Mission sessions, and a host of other well-known session musicians joined in as well. A ten-piece choir called The Church was assembled from background singers for Michael Jackson, George Michael, and **Andraé Crouch.** Mavis Staples (of The Staples Singers) and **Ta'ta Vega** (famous for her work on *The Color Purple* soundtrack) sang lead on a few of the songs, but otherwise Batteau

and Brown preferred to go with new, unknown lead vocalists. The project came off well, with a major highlight being Vega's rendition of "Table in the Wilderness," a song known to contemporary Christian music fans in a version by **Russ Taff.** Alfie Silas sings "Give It All to Jesus," Lynn Davis wails on "Tear This House Down," and Grady Harrell cranks out both the title track and "Settled in Heaven."

Sounds of Blackness

1991—*The Evolution of Gospel* (Perspective); 1992—*The Night before Christmas: A Musical Fantasy;* 1994—*Africa to America* (A&M); 1997—*Time for Healing.*

Sounds of Blackness originated as a thirty-voice ensemble backed by ten instrumentalists at Macalester College in St. Paul, Minnesota. Directed by Gary Hines, the group suddenly got famous when Minneapolis funk star Prince culled their talents for one of his projects and then Prince protégé Sheila E. did the same. Eventually, superstar producers Jimmy Jam and Terry Lewis (who began as part of another Prince offshoot band called The Time) approached the choir about recording for their new Perspective label (a subsidiary of A&M). The resulting sound was a sort of gospel/funk hybrid directed to the club scene but with frequent religious overtones. The group has never been accepted within the contemporary Christian music subculture, perhaps because the devotion to ministry is suspect. And then there is the factor of plain old jealousy: it may seem irksome to many in the Christian music universe that a nongospel group singing gospel songs should reap worldly success beyond that accorded those who have toiled in the vineyard for years. It is true that Sounds of Blackness does not perform gospel songs with the same evangelistic purposes intended by many gospel artists; rather, the focus for Sounds of Blackness has always been on preserving the historical legacy of African American musicians, and the incorporation of gospel is a part of that broader agenda. "We've always included every style of African American music—jazz, blues, gospel, spirituals, reggae," Hines would say in 1997. "Each of these is a sound of blackness." The groundbreaking album *The Evolution of Gospel* features a minimalist remake of Sly and the Family Stone's "Stand" alongside choral numbers "What Shall I Call Him?" and "He Holds the Future." In reviewing the album, *CCM* would say that it "pushes gospel into club territory more aggressively than anything since **Tramaine Hawkins**' late '80s output." *Africa to America* offers a cross-cultural chronicle in music with "I Believe," "Everything's Going to Be Alright," and "A Place in My Heart." *Time for Healing* actually represents the group's twenty-fifth anniversary recording, proof that they have been toiling in their own vineyard longer than many had realized. The album includes "A Spiritual Medley" of hymns from the days of slavery and introduces rapper Craig

Mack on the uplifting "Spirit." Salt 'n Pepa also guest on a hip-hop number, "Hold On (Don't Let Go)," and there are more covers: the O'Jay's gospel-like "Love Train" and another Sly-and-Family song, "You Can Make It If You Try."

Soul Shock Remedy

Ben Ashley, gtr.; Brian Buzard, gtr.; Ken Mari, voc., drums, kybrd.; Mark Stratford, bass. 1995—*Fish Eye Lens* (R.E.X.).

Soul Shock Remedy was an apparently one-shot project organized by drummer Ken Mari, who has played with **Magdallan** and with various other **Lanny Cordola** and **Ken Tamplin** projects. For Soul Shock Remedy, Mari also becomes lead vocalist and shows himself to be a fine rock singer. The album *Fish Eye Lens* was first released independently on the Revolution label, but did not attract notice until remixed and re-released on R.E.X. The sound is psychedelic rock and roll that seems to blend equal parts Jellyfish and Cheap Trick. "Kicking Stones" is the energetic opening track that expresses feelings of futility. "Zero Man" tells a melodramatic tale about a man who cracks under pressure, builds a bomb, and takes hostages. Much better is "Rain," which conveys the simple message that, though one cannot prevent bad things from happening—or even understand why they occur—there is beauty to be found in life as well. "Slow Burn" is not a **Glenn Kaiser** cover but a great, original song that expresses the need to "stand one's ground" as the world burns. "Green Tambourine" actually is a cover of The Lemon Pipers song, and its appearance here provides a bright, fun spot that just might be the album's highlight. "The Machine" and "Silent Haze" aim for an over-the-top late '70s stadium-rock sound.

Richard Souther (a.k.a. Douglas Trowbridge?)

By Richard Souther: 1985—*Heirborne* (Meadowlark); 1986—*Innermission*; 1989—*Cross Currents* (Narada); 1990—*Twelve Tribes*; 1993—*Carols, Rhythms, and Grooves* (NortherSouth); 1997—*Illumination*. By Douglas Trowbridge: 1985—*Songs Unspoken* (Meadowlark); 1987—*Second Story* (Capitol).

Richard Souther's tenure with contemporary Christian music has been long and involved, but no official information is available and what can be gathered is a bit mysterious. Souther first came to the attention of Christian music fans as a member of the "Band Called David" that accompanied **2nd Chapter of Acts** on tour and played on some of their classic albums. Souther handled piano and other keyboards for the band, and his talents with those instruments were as impressive as **Phil Keaggy**'s on guitar. It was here that he probably made his greatest mark and it is in this capacity that he may always be best remembered. In the early '80s, reports circulated

that Souther had died, and memorial tributes to him still appear on some Internet sites devoted to Jesus music. The only clue to what really happened is found in a note from his 1998 Sony publicist: "Souther became active in rock bands, working as a session player, but a near-fatal illness in 1980 changed his direction. During his four-year recovery, Souther mastered the synthesizer/sequencer."

Instrumental albums by the supposedly deceased Souther began appearing in the mid '80s, and the artist is also credited with producing albums for such musicians as **Don Francisco** and **Twila Paris.** Souther's solo work fits into the genre of what was called New Age music in the world at large. Christian music stores and companies refused to call it that under the rather silly supposition that the label implied some sort of linguistic association with what was called New Age religion (a syncretistic brew of Native American spirituality, eastern philosophies, meditation, reincarnation, occult spiritualism, and pretty much anything else that seemed exotic). There doesn't appear to have ever been a connection between New Age music and New Age religion beyond the fact that the two phenomena became popular at around the same time and their circles of supporters occasionally overlapped. The great majority of New Age musicians did not endorse New Age religious beliefs. Still, Christian record stores stubbornly claimed that Souther and his ilk did *not* perform New Age music but instrumental, worshipful, prayerful, meditative music that by sheer coincidence sounded exactly like New Age music. Souther himself wisely avoided the controversies by calling his music "cinemagraphic," like that which might be used for a film score. Such an association came naturally to him in that he was raised in Hollywood a few blocks from Universal Studios. Souther's mother is said to be a movie actress who has appeared in some two hundred films, though her name has never been revealed.

Heirborne and *Innermission* were ignored by the Christian media but enjoyed some success as Christian versions of the popular contemplative music being produced by artists like George Winston and Vangelis (a Christian artist, actually). On *Cross Currents,* Souther joins with **Koinonia** players like Alex Acuña, Justo Almario, and Abe Laboriel to deliver a sound that is more driving and aggressive than contemplative. The same crew returns for *Twelve Tribes,* which blends light jazz with world music influences on a concept piece inspired by the scattering of the twelve tribes of Israel. The '90s would take Souther deep into ethnic and world music. *Carols, Rhythms, and Grooves* draws on a legacy of gothic, Celtic, European, and African sounds. On *Illumination,* he recomposes the works of twelfth-century mystic Hildegard von Bingen and performs these with synthesizers, keyboards, uilleann pipes, and Irish vocalists.

An offhand comment in a 1989 issue of *CCM* indicates that Souther also records under the name Douglas Trowbridge. If this is true, then the two instrumental albums by that artist listed above should also be attributed to his oeuvre.

Sozo

Corey Pryor, kybrd.; Danielle Pryor, voc. // Aaron Julison (+ 1997). 1994—*Purity* (N'Soul); 1997—*The Walk*.

Sozo was a Christian dance band composed of former **Newsboy** Corey Pryor and his wife, Danielle, who had also enjoyed some success as a solo performer opening for **Phil Driscoll** and **Reba Rambo.** A third member, Aaron Julison, is pictured on the cover of their sophomore album but is never mentioned in the credits, making it impossible to determine what he did. Sozo's debut, *Purity,* is techno groove all the way with overt lyrics celebrating the Christian life ("I'm So Glad I'm Saved") and encouraging growth in holiness ("Stop Looking Back"). The opening "Be True" is a more generic number dealing with commitment in friendship. *The Walk* opens with a track that could have been on the first album ("Global Culture Sega Child") but then moves away from the techno obsession to incorporate more pop-rock songs. "Actions" is a powerful midtempo rock number with a memorable melody that drives the simple message "actions speak louder than words" into the consciousness. "139" is an especially lovely ballad based on the Psalm of that number. Danielle seems to adopt Alanis Morissette (or possibly **Plumb**) stylings on a number of tracks ("I'm Defenseless," "Sometimes"). "Life" is another uptempo dance song reminiscent of Snap!'s "The Power."

Spark

Jesse Jackson, voc.; Dave Truscott, voc.; et al. 2001—*Tomorrow Is Today* (Rugged).

Spark is a Christian rock band from Dayton, Ohio, sporting twin lead vocalists and a sound often compared to such general market acts as **Creed** or Live. The band specializes in delivering songs with simplistic but straightforward lyrics about their devotion to Christ and to Christianity: "I know he came and died / Shed his blood on a tree / Three days later he arose / And set me free" ("Believe"). "Beyond the Sunset" is a guitar-filled rock tune that got the group some radio airplay. "Change" challenges the listener to live every day like it is the last—the theme of the album's title. "When a lot of people hear the gospel, they say they will get right tomorrow," says Jackson, "but we are not promised tomorrow. If you are going to accept Christ, you need to do it today."

Sparklepop

Tim Brinkman, gtr.; Miranda Richardson, voc.; et al. 2000—*Sparklepop* (Luminosity); 2001—*Sparklepop* (True Tunes).

www.sparklepop.com

Sparklepop is an offshoot of **Everybodyduck,** fronted by that group's Tim Brinkman and Miranda Richardson (who also recorded a solo project as **Miranda**). As Sparklepop, they issued two different versions of a self-titled album on two different independent labels. Some of the songs, including "I'm So Happy," were also featured on **Miranda**'s solo album. That song, along with "Sugarcoated Saviour" and "Happy Birthday, Jesus," displays the bubblegum appeal of the band, while "Happiness in Sin" and "What Happened When Jesus Went to Nashville" demonstrate a tongue-in-cheek capacity for sarcasm and satire. The latter song is an indictment of the Christian music industry, "the Pharisees and Sadducees making money in his name." The True Tunes edition of *Sparklepop* contains a nice ballad, "Sweet Forgiveness," and a bluesy pop song called "Hard Landing."

Greg and Rebecca Sparks (a.k.a. Sparks)

As Sparks: 1989—*Sparks* (Reunion); 1990—*Through Flood and Fire.* As Greg and Rebecca Sparks: 1993—*Field of Your Soul* (Etcetera); date unknown—*Flesh and Blood* (independent).

www.thesparks.com

The husband and wife duo Greg and Rebecca Sparks began their career as members of the famously cheesy pop bands **Found Free** and **Bash-N-The-Code** but went on to obtain indie credentials for what *True Tunes* would call a "relentless pursuit of honesty, compassion, and integrity through their music." Rebecca joined **Found Free** when she was still in high school. She and Greg met each other in that band and spent five years touring the world as friends before finally marrying. In 1987, the couple decided to tour with **Russ Taff**'s band and pursue a quieter career as a duo. Their four albums, however, have seen them develop a progressively rockier edge.

Sparks features melodic songs that range in style from pop anthems like "Rock Your World" to the piano ballad "One Small Voice." The standout track may be "Rest," a rowdier number than its title implies that promises "Rest for the weary / Peace for the confused / Renewal for the heart that has been used." *Through Flood and Fire* is much more of an R&B phenomenon with a horn section adding flair to a number of tracks. The project opens with the campfire favorite "They'll Know We Are Christians by Our Love" (cf. **Carolyn Arends**). "Jesus Rescues Me" is sung as a gospel anthem with **Russ Taff.** "Work for Love" has a tune similar to that of the Beatles' "Hey Jude" and conveys the simple message that things worthwhile are worth waiting for. The couple's masterpiece would be *Field of Your Soul,* on which songs like "Mercy Me," "This Love Is," and "Do Ya Know What I Got" represent a rock assault worthy of the Rolling Stones. Rebecca would joke about Greg turning her into "a rock 'n' roll mama," and indeed her voice soars in a manner worthy of Tina Turner or **Ashley Cleveland.** The latter artist sings backup on a number of tracks on *Field of Your Soul* (as does Taff) and her guitarist, Kenny Greenberg, adds his wizardry to the project. On the tender side, "Fractured Pieces" is a touching tribute to a friend who died of AIDS, and "Carve a Tunnel" samples Martin Luther King Jr. on a song addressing the persistence of racism in modern society. The independently released *Flesh and Blood* is primarily a worship album that, according to *True Tunes,* "blows away most of the factory created worship music flooding the bookstores."

Speaking of Sarah

Diana Blythe, voc.; Murray Blythe; Tim Jarett; Trevor Hodge. 2000—*Silence Never Lies* (Micah).

Speaking of Sarah is an Australian Christian rock band with a sound that fits into the same general category as bands like Garbage or **Plumb.** *The Phantom Tollbooth* would describe them as sounding like "a female-fronted **Delirious?**" or "a hybrid of **Mukala** and **Sixpence None the Richer.**" Such comparisons suggest the group has a certain unique quality to its sound and this is the case: Diana Blythe's ethereal Madonna-like vocals float above thick rhythms and hard near-metal guitars. *Silence Never Lies* was first released in 1999, then picked up for international distribution by Micah Records in 2000. The band's songs seem more artistic than commercial, with lyrics touching on a variety of themes. "Fades Away" describes the transiency of material things, and "Images" exposes the shallow character of cultural standards for beauty. More specifically Christian themes inform "Unchanging," a reflection on the constancy of God, and "Waiting," which describes the status of believers anticipating a better world when Christ returns.

Michael Speaks

2001—*Praise at Your Own Risk* (Epic).

African American song stylist Michael Speaks released his first album of Christian music in 2001. The artist indicated that he had spent the '90s singing in New York City subways while also appearing on some R&B records of that decade. *CCM* would describe him as "a younger, edgier **BeBe Winans.**" His debut album includes the urban track "I Just Wanna (Dance Now)" and a personal testimony of forgiveness, "Born Again."

Speck

Doug Hutchcraft, voc.; Jarrod Ignacio, drums; Jason Manning, gtr.; Roxanne Manning, bass. 1997—*Speck* (BulletProof); 1999—*Gogglebox* (Gray Dot).

Speck is a Christian modern pop band composed of Native Americans who live on reservations in Arizona and New Mexico. The group has a decidedly youth group sound featuring simple, straightforward lyrics and bouncy, memorable tunes. The style is generally similar to that of early **Audio Adrenaline.** Humor is a definite element and several of Speck's songs offer tongue-in-cheek reflections on life as a believer. *Speck* has a slightly grungy appeal. The opening track, "Mercy," is a bit of a Sunday school chant: "Mercy be a grapefruit tree / Mercy be not far from me." "Brilliant" offers self-deprecating examples of how even believers do dumb and embarrassing things. On a more serious note, "Skin" offers a rant against racism, and "My Friend" describes what it's like to have a personal relationship with the Creator. *Gogglebox* takes its name from British slang for TV, and a couple of tracks reflect on the cultural vacuity of that "vast wasteland." One song is actually called "Kill My TV," containing references to such mind drains as *Three's Company* and *The Dukes of Hazzard.* "Do You Think I'm Cool" gives voice to a loser who pretends to like shows that he thinks will score him points with his peers. The song "Fly on a Plane" lists lame things about flying but concludes with a willingness to fly if it aids in the spread of God's word. "I Am Superman" uses the comic book hero as an image for the power that resurrected Christians will enjoy in heaven. Overall, *Gogglebox* is more pop-oriented and less of a rock album than the self-titled debut.

Judson Spence

1988—*Judson Spence* (Atlantic); 1996—*Pain Faith Joy* (Bold).

Judson Spence is a Christian singer/songwriter who tried with minimal success to break into the post-disco dance market with a release in the general market in 1988. Born in Pascagoula, Mississippi, Spence grew up the son of two ministers who pastored a church in what he calls "the poorest part of that town." Spence formed his friendships in a predominately black housing project and hung out at a lot of local black churches, all of which influenced his decision to try his hand at the "play that funky music white boy" game. *Judson Spence* was not religious or even overtly spiritual, but Spence allowed his strong Christian convictions to show forth in what he considered to be morally responsible songs. In "Hot and Sweaty," he sings, "I know this may sound crazy / There's more to love than sex." Likewise, "If You Don't Like It" encourages youth not to cave in to peer pressure if they have personal convictions about the use of drugs or alcohol. Spence also wrote in the album's liner notes, "Jesus—I love you and give you all the glory." A straight-out dance track "Yeah, Yeah, Yeah" reached Number Thirty-two on *Billboard's* Top 40 chart in November of 1988, but the album did not fare well and the singer was all but forgotten. He recorded a second album that was shelved for a while, and **Amy Grant** pulled one song off of the project to record for her *House of Love* album. That song, "The Power," gave Spence some renewed visibility, and he finally released his sophomore project, *Pain Faith Joy,* independently in 1996. The latter record has a rather different sound than the debut, showing that the artist has kept up to date with the trends. In general, the second record is less bouncy and more laid back, with songs that reflect a soulful and passionate groove.

Jeremy Spencer

1972—*Jeremy Spencer and the Children* (Columbia); 1979—*Flee* (Warner Bros.).

http://jeremyspencer.com

Jeremy Spencer's religious albums are certainly not representative of contemporary Christian music in any traditional sense but, like the works of the **All Saved Freak Band,** they do represent an odd, scary trajectory that heirs to the Jesus movement revival sometimes took. Born in 1948 in West Hartlepool, England, Spencer came to be known as the finest slide guitarist in the land and was tapped by blues master **Peter Green** to form the band Fleetwood Mac. The latter group was destined to become one of the most successful rock groups in history, though, ironically, both of its founding members would jump ship for religious reasons before the leftovers Mick Fleetwood and John "Mac" McVie (after whom the band had been named—as a joke) recruited new talent that would take them to unprecedented heights. Originally Fleetwood Mac was a blues band. Spencer and Green led the group for three albums *(Fleetwood Mac, English Rose, Then Play On)* that critics regard as classics, though they lack the pop sensibilities of later work. Green (see entry) left amidst mixed reports that he had either found Jesus or lost his mind (or both). Spencer played on one more classic album *(Kiln House)* and then he departed as well.

Mick Fleetwood describes the departure in his biography of the band *(Fleetwood: My Life and Adventures in Fleetwood Mac,* William Morrow, 1990). The group was touring in California and had come to Los Angeles shortly after the earthquake of 1971. Immediately after checking into their hotel, Spencer said he wanted to check out a bookstore on Hollywood Boulevard and he left saying, "I'll be right back." He never returned. The band canceled their concert for that evening and notified the police. Spencer's picture was shown on TV stations, the F.B.I. got involved, the band hired a psychic to help locate their

friend, and finally after several days, they heard from "some moderate and helpful Christians" that Spencer had gone off to join the Children of God.

That group was an infamous cult—almost the *definitive* religious cult—that recruited troubled youth and street people in the early '70s. They were often associated with the Jesus movement and considered to represent one of its more outlandish manifestations. While most of the Jesus people embraced traditional Christian doctrines and values (despite their countercultural appearances), the Children of God flaunted its extremism. The group was led by David Berg (a.k.a. Moses David) who claimed that his own writings ("Mo letters") took precedence over Scripture. Berg demanded absolute loyalty from his followers, who were encouraged to surrender all of their earthly belongings to the group and to break off all contact with the outside world. Recruitment efforts were suspect and accusations of brainwashing were common, if difficult to substantiate. Berg did encourage his young female disciples to use sexual charms to help snare new members (what he called "flirty fishing"), and there are claims that he sometimes pressed them into prostitution, interpreting the call to be "fishers of men" to mean "hookers for Jesus." A number of religious sociologists, however, maintain that reports of such abuses have been exaggerated by conservative Christians offended by the sect's doctrinal aberrations.

Fleetwood reports that the Children of God initially denied any knowledge of Spencer's whereabouts but, after some time (and pressure from the authorities), produced the man, his head shaven and answering only to the new name of "Jonathan." Spencer talked for three hours with Fleetwood Mac's manager in a controlled setting, with two community members seated on either side of him, rubbing his arms and softly chanting "Jesus loves you" the entire time. Spencer stated repeatedly that he had left the world and no longer wanted anything to do with Fleetwood Mac. He didn't care what happened to the band and he "trusted Jesus" to take care of his wife and children. Reflecting on this encounter, the manager would later maintain, "his identity and personality had been brainwashed away; the old Jeremy Spencer was . . . *gone.*" This was the last time that anyone not associated with the Children of God would ever see Jeremy Spencer, who was reportedly flown to a Children of God ranch in Texas where he was joined by his wife and one of their two children (the youngest being left with its grandmother). Fleetwood says that he has attempted, with minimal success, to keep up with his former friend. He thinks that Spencer spent most of 1972 being further indoctrinated into the group's teaching, and engaging in street work, proselytizing for the cult.

Once the Children of God discovered they had reeled in a reasonably big fish, they tried to capitalize on Spencer's fame by releasing the album *Jeremy Spencer and the Children*. The songs on the album are apocalyptic in tone but, as with **Family of Love,** the album does not deviate much from traditional Christian views. Songs like "Can You Hear the Song?" and "Let's Get on the Ball" are typical of most early '70s Jesus music. Music historian David Di Sabatino says, "Spencer's talents as a premier slide guitarist are in evidence," and *Jesus Music* magazine styles the record as "a very listenable album, with catchy arrangements, melodies and guitar work." Several years later, Spencer would put out another album of disco-rock songs with sexually-laden messages. The song "You've Got the Right" presents the group's teaching that Jesus and Mary Magdalene were sexually intimate with each other: "Mary Maggie was having fun / With the carpenter's son / Oh, what had they done? / What was it the people saw / Were they breakin' the law / By just lovin'?" Di Sabatino thinks the point of this is to justify the practice of flirty fishing mentioned above. The song continues, "In the name of love, you've got the right!"

Whereas the Children of God has usually had rapid turnover, with a majority of its recruits only remaining with the group for a short time, Spencer's conversion appears to have been permanent. Fleetwood received a report that Spencer ended up at the group's base in Sri Lanka where, after a violent Tamil insurrection, they had to flee for their lives. Later he heard that Spencer was "hiding out" on an atoll somewhere in the Indian Ocean. In 1990, he says, "a strange girl approached me on a beach in Malibu and handed me a cassette. . . . it turned out to be Jeremy singing and playing his guitar, but when and where it was recorded I have no idea."

SpinAround

Alan Moore; Jason McKinney. 2001—*Face the Crowd* (Pamplin).

SpinAround is an eclectic duo that aims its evangelical songs directly at young teen audiences. They take a storytelling approach to songwriting and craft material with a Christianized "after school special" feel to it. Thus, *Face the Crowd* relates songs about the popular high school girl whose life is meaningless without God ("Girl She Used to Be") and the lovestruck boy who pines for the Homecoming Queen but finds fulfillment through Christ instead ("Boy Meets Girl"). Musically, SpinAround sticks mainly to power-pop, with forays into hip-hop ("Boy Meets Girl") and rap-metal (the title track), along with a couple of expected Christian radio ballads ("Forgiveness," "Sweet Lullabye").

Spirit and the Bride

Paul Nauman, voc.; Marijana Nenadic, voc.; Will Shanks; et al. 1997—*Spirit and the Bride* (Ear to the Ground).

Spirit and the Bride is a California indie band with a goth-based sound reminiscent of Tears for Fears, Dead Can Dance, or Peter Murphy. The band is led by Will Shanks, who plays a variety of instruments and serves as composer, producer, and arranger. Shanks' wife, Marijana Nenadic, offers female vocals on about half of the songs, and Paul Nauman, male vocals on the other half. Some reports indicate that there are up to eight instrumentalists associated with the group, though it is not known whether these are band members or not. Nenadic is the daughter of Croatian immigrants, and she sings with an ethnic otherworldliness on worshipful non-English songs like "Dodi Duse Sveti" and "Oce Nas." The album would later be re-released on MCM and given wider distribution. The group's name is derived from Revelation 22:17, and their music has a clear Christian focus, though the band does not consider itself to be involved in outreach. "Music is something I love to do," says Shanks. "I don't see it as a vehicle for evangelism or anything. I just do it because I love it."

Spitfire

Matt Beck, gtr., voc.; Chris Raines, drums; Jimmy Reeves, bass // John Spencer, voc. (+ 2001). 1999—*The Dead Next Door* (Solid State); 2001—*The Slideshow Whiplash* [EP] (Goodfellow).

Spitfire is an aggressive hardcore band with a sound similar to **Embodyment.** The trio comes from Virginia Beach, and all members were in their late teens when the debut album on Solid State was recorded. *Phantom Tollbooth* would describe the sound as "raging vocals, scorching guitars, and melodic bridges." *HM* would call it "very mature hardcore with enough growl and pitch to remind the listener of grind and death metal." Lyrics are almost never understandable, but supposedly reflect the group's Christian convictions. "Not every song has God mentioned in it," says *Tollbooth*, "but they scream about life from the view of a believer." Shortly after the album's release, Matt Beck left the band for a time, then came back in a reconstituted version of the group, featuring a new lead singer. "One of the reasons I left," he told *HM,* "was that I got heavily into drug use. . . . it was like, look, I'm not really walking with the Lord right now. And God did a whole new thing in me." The new Spitfire released an EP that *HM* would hail as "showing a lot of growth in their chosen approach to metalcore."

Split Level

Rob Craner, drums, voc.; Gary Preston, bass, voc.; Adrian Thompson, voc., gtr. Selected: 1991—*View of the World* (Pila); 1992—*Boomerang*; 1997—*glo.bal* (Organic); 2000—*Live*.

Split Level has barely been noticed in the American Christian music scene, though they have been a high-profile British act for many years. The Irish group formed in the late '80s as a

Celtic rock band. They took a while to define both personnel and sound but by 1990 emerged as a solid pop band with a style similar to that of Crowded House. *7ball* has described them as a cross between **U2** and **King's X,** though that implies a heavier take than is evident in most of their material. Oasis is also a frequent reference point. In 1993, Split Level's *Boomerang* (never released in the United States) was named Album of the Year by the European Christian Bookseller's Journal, and in 1995, the group was named Best Christian Rock Band by that same publication. Shortly after that high point, however, the British music scene shifted heavily toward worship music (cf. **Delirious?, Matt Redman**) and Split Level found their audiences dwindling. Lyrically, the band has always taken a down-to-earth approach that offers reflections on all of life from a Christian perspective. "We're interested in telling the truth," Thompson says. "Our songs are about faith and doubts, problems, struggles, healing, and wholeness." In 1997, he complained about the group's fickle British fans: "If we called ourselves a worship band, we'd probably be packing out churches, but, because we call ourselves a rock band, the whole thing's gone real flat." Appropriately, then, they signed with Organic and shifted to the American market. Produced by **Rick Elias,** the album *glo.bal* was well received as buoyant British pop with undertones of "roots rock" and a strong spiritual focus. "Twister" addresses those who distort the truth and contort words to their own intent. "Healing" contrasts various forms of New Age spirituality with the power of Christ. *Live* was recorded in 1998 and leans heavily toward the *glo.bal* material with a few older songs and a cover of **Maria McKee**'s "I Found Love."

Spoken

Matt Baird, voc.; Jeff Cunningham, gtr.; Steven Hawk, bass (– 1999); Ronnie Cripper, drums (– 2000); Brady (B.J.) Watson, gtr. (– 2000) // Travis Pierce, bass (+ 1999); Lewis, drums (+ 2000); Roy, gtr. (+ 2000). 1998—*On Your Feet* (Metro One); 1999—*What Remains*; 2000—*Echoes of the Spirit Still Dwell* (Metrovox); 2001—*Greatest Hits* (Metro One).

Spoken began as a Christian version of Rage Against the Machine, just cashing in on the rapcore craze, but by their third album they managed to develop their own sound and establish themselves as a dynamic hip-hop-influenced metal band that had carved out a niche of its own. The group formed in Arkansas under the leadership of front man Matt Baird and went through a few seasons of personnel changes. By the time *On Your Feet* appeared, the band was a quintet with a strong focus on ministry, but rapcore purists complained about the Rage similarities. Nevertheless the album was nominated for a Dove award for Best Hard Music Album and its title track, for a similar award for Best Hard Music Song. *The Phantom Tollbooth* noted that Baird quits rapping and sings now and then on

what turn out to be the album's best songs. *What Remains* would divide the critics. *Phantom Tollbooth* said it "invites even more comparisons to Rage Against the Machine than their debut did," but most other reviewers saw some growth and diversity. Jyro Xhan of **Mortal/Fold Zandura** produced the sophomore project and sings with the band on a remake of the **Crystal Lewis** song, "People Get Ready . . . Jesus Is Coming." Rapper K2S also guests along with Xhan on "Fly with Me" (not the Frank Sinatra song). "Taken for Granted" is a rapcore standout with strong gospel lyrics: "God loved us so much Christ died to set us free." *Echoes of the Spirit Still Dwell* would finally transcend the Rage analogies with a much more melodic and emotional sound. The group had tired of being labeled rapcore and jokingly told *HM* that they wanted to be known as a "trepcore band," with reference to the emotion of trepidation. That emotion and others come through on *Echoes,* especially in some of the slower songs, which build up to driving choruses with chunky guitar riffs. Lyrically, several of the songs move toward praise and worship.

Spoken has a bold attitude when it comes to proclaiming Christ in their songs, and they are unashamed about identifying themselves as a ministry band. "Spoken is all about advocating the love of Jesus in the boldest possible manner," says Baird. "The only reason to be in a band is to tell others how good our God is." Pierce adds, "We're not here to be musicians. We're here to minister. Music is just how we minister."

Spooky Tuesday

Justin "Pepe" Bundschuh, bass; Jessica "Scooter" Treskon, gtr.; Christapherobin, drums (– 1997); Chad Rego, voc., gtr. (– 1997) // Andrew Neuman, voc. (+ 1997); Kevin Penner, drums (+ 1997). 1995—*It'll Never Fly, Orville* (Innocent Media); 1997—*Happy Dissonance*; 1999—*The Trouble We Make* (Jackson Rubio); 2001—*The Good Friday Service* (independent).

www.jesusfreak.com/spookytuesday

Spooky Tuesday is an alternative pop-folk-rock group from Kauai, Hawaii. The group came together when all four of the original members were in high school. Supposedly, they originally formed to enter a high school talent contest, which they lost to an Elvis impersonator. Undeterred, they recorded and released their first album before graduation. The group is noted musically for its trade-off male/female vocals (one critic describes them as a cross between **Sixpence None the Richer** and early **Dakoda Motor Co.**), and lyrically for tackling issues that explore the dark side of human existence.

Lead singer Chad Rego would describe *It'll Never Fly, Orville* as "jingly, jangly guitar picking music, kind of like The Byrds." The group worked with Gene Eugene of **Adam Again** on the project, which no doubt accounts for some of its alternative credentials—the fact that it was released as the first project on a label founded by Joey "Ojo" Taylor of **Undercover** didn't hurt any in that regard either. Most of the songs relate stream-of-consciousness story lines about people in trouble. "I Still Care" relays the ambiguous thoughts of one smarting from broken trust and a failed romance; "Runaway" is about a teenager who flees her alcoholic-led family only to turn to the bottle herself and begin the cycle anew; "Wrong Image" addresses anorexia; and "Homeless" tells the tale of a woman who freezes to death on the streets of a city. God is only referenced here or there; the focus of the album is clearly more on problems than on answers.

With significant personnel changes, a reformulated Spooky Tuesday would release *Happy Dissonance* in 1997. The very title of the sophomore project seems to promise a more positive scenario than that of the first album, and band members would identify the theme as "finding joy in the Lord in the midst of life's struggles." Songs like "Suicide" and "Selfish Love" continue in the pull-no-punches approach to disturbing subjects, and "Hansel and Gretel" gets downright creepy with its trade-off male/female vocals on a song about a daughter resisting her father's unwanted advances. This time out, however, the group does fold in songs that clearly explicate Christian hope. On "Salvation," the singer adopts the voice of Christ to comfort the penitent and the suffering: "Child, I have forgiven you with the thorn in my hand / Child, I went through hell for you, and I would do it again." Still, as *Phantom Tollbooth* would note, the band's lyrical strength lies in its capacity to be "empathetic, first and foremost, and not necessarily preachy." *Happy Dissonance* was produced by Matt Wignall (of **Havalina Rail Co.**), who would be responsible for all of their subsequent products. Musically, it also includes a number of moody ballads ("Aqua," "Free"), songs that blend acoustic and electric styles in a manner reminiscent of **Jars of Clay.**

Although one might never have guessed it from the subdued spirituality of their first two releases, Spooky Tuesday had from the start served as a praise band at their local church in Kauai. More of the worship focus would come to the fore on their next two albums. *The Trouble We Make* mixes worshipful songs indiscriminately with more numbers about the hard knocks of life. "Enough of Me" likens self-absorption to a drug addiction, and "Richest Man" deals with crass materialism, but several other songs are psalms of devotion. "All I Need" describes the simple act of worship as the goal of every spiritual quest, and both "Take Over Me" and "Offered Myself" are "living sacrifice" songs that present a yielded heart to God as an offering of praise. Shortly after releasing *The Trouble We Make,* Spooky Tuesday also came out with what they call their bootleg album, a collection of live worship songs recorded at the Hyatt Hotel in Kauai. *The Good Friday Service* is a liturgically sensitive collection of modern songs appropriate for the Lenten season. About half of the tracks come from Vineyard music re-sources, though the group also includes several of their own original hymns.

In 1999, lead guitarist Jessica Treskon and drummer Kevin Penner were married.

Billy Sprague

1984—*What a Way to Go* (Reunion); 1986—*Serious Fun;* 1988—*La Vie;* 1989—*I Wish;* 1992—*Torn between Two Worlds* (Benson); 1993—*The Wind and the Wave.*

Billy Sprague is a Christian pop singer and guitarist who has been integrally connected with the contemporary Christian music scene since the early '80s. Born in 1952, the Tulsa native moved to the little town of Borger, Texas. His senior year of high school, he spent nine months in a body cast as part of surgical treatment for scoliosis and during that time a) learned to play the guitar, b) read the New Testament, c) grew close to his mother, and d) listened to a lot of James Taylor. Eventually, Sprague attended Texas Christian University, where he played in a band called Jubal. After graduating from TCU in 1979, he went on to graduate studies in English at the University of Texas. In 1981, he became a part of **Amy Grant**'s first backing band, playing guitar and singing. As a songwriter, Sprague would compose songs recorded by **Brown Bannister, Debby Boone, Sandi Patty, Kathy Troccoli,** and **BeBe and CeCe Winans.** In 1986, Patty's version of his song "Via Dolorosa" won a Dove award for Song of the Year. In 1990, he would produce the album *Friends Forever, Part 2,* which won the Dove award for Best Musical Album that year. In 1996, **Gary Chapman**'s version of his song "Man after Your Own Heart" would win the Dove award for Inspirational Song of the Year.

Sprague began his recording career as a solo artist with three Reunion albums that display disparate styles. *What a Way to Go* pairs him with producer **Michael W. Smith** on a fairly high-tech pop outing that seems to reflect Smith's interests as much as Sprague's. Smith's synthesizers combine with Sprague's acoustic guitar on mostly mellow tunes with soothing verses and more upbeat choruses. The clear standout is "Jude Doxology," a song written by Smith that melds classical themes to a rock beat; the lyrics are drawn from Jude 24–25. *Serious Fun* presents the artist as a Christian Kenny Loggins or, simply, as a male *Unguarded* **Amy Grant.** The songs are punchy, upbeat, and—as the album title implies—fun sounding with a serious message. "Rock the Planet" opens the album with an anthem about the power of faith to change the world; the song was cowritten by Sprague with **Chris Rodriguez** and his new producer **Wayne Kirkpatrick.** "Better Days" is a more intimate and vulnerable song in which Sprague relates a tale of his trip back to Borger for a high school reunion, at which he was invited to sing for his old peers and tell them of the life he had found in Christ. "Invisible Hand" is another powerful number, describing Sprague's bout with depression and pointing to Jesus as "the rescuer." The third Reunion album, *La Vie*, recasts Sprague as a heartland rocker in the mold of John Mellencamp, a guise he wears more authentically. Produced by **Gary Chapman,** *La Vie* actually has a gritty **Mark Heard** sound to it. The title track quotes a French proverb that roughly translates as "life is hard, but God is good." But it is much more poetic as Sprague sings it: "O, la vie est dure, that much is sure / Mais Dieu est bon si bon." *I Wish* is a compilation album containing three songs from each of the earlier albums plus the new, title track.

In 1989, Sprague's fiancé Rosalynn Olivares was killed in an automobile accident while on the way to see him in concert. The artist took a three-year break from recording and performing to mourn her loss and deal with his grief. His next album, *Torn between Two Worlds,* would be an unusually strong offering born of his struggle and sorrow. It is, in effect, a concept piece dedicated to Olivares and others whom he calls "Meek Members of the Resurrection"—those who have had an impact on his life but have passed away. The opening track, "Heaven Is a Long Hello," is a brilliant pop song that sets death and earthly grief in the perspective of eternity. Again, on "A Hazardous World," Sprague describes mortality as "an angry dog missing all his teeth." Still, his personal tributes "Dear Rosalynn" and "For the One Who Sleeps" are touching and poignant reminders of the tragedy of death and the fleeting nature of human existence. Similar sentiments would inform but not dominate *The Wind and the Wave* (with a title drawn from Matthew 8:27). That record opens with "Press On," a very catchy and uplifting song that calls on victims of life's tragedies to rise above self-pity: "I pray your memories will not drag you down / Nor be anchors, but treasures of the love that you found." Likewise, "A Way Back" testifies that there *is* a way back from grief and depression to restored life; Christine Denté of **Out of the Grey** sings with Sprague on the meaningful song. The real evidence of Sprague's personal healing, however, comes in a subtle way: most of the songs on *The Wind and The Wave* focus outward, offering social commentary on a world in need of love. The song "Whatever Happened to Love" is a horn-laden romp that declares, "Love is alive in the name Immanuel." Musically, *The Wind and the Wave* is Sprague's most Beatlesque outing. Although those '60s influences had always been evident in his work, he now goes for it as never before, with a set of especially melodic and McCartneyesque tunes.

In 1994, Billy Sprague would marry a woman named Kellie, and the Christian community rejoiced that he had found happiness in recovery from his horrible loss. But he continued to be able to address the phenomenon of grief with an authenticity that those who have not experienced its depth often have trouble understanding. "Perhaps the worst part is the numb-

ness," he told *CCM*'s Jim Long in 1995. "You feel so separated from the rest of the world. Everybody is just perking along and talking about the game this weekend, and you are not so sure you even want to be on the planet. . . . there is a way back. There is a way out of grief. But the planet will never again be the safe place that you once thought it was."

Sprague has also contributed songs to a compilation album featuring prominent writers performing their own material (*Coming from Somewhere Else,* Rocketown, 2000). He offers his own renditions of "Via Dolorosa" and "Man after Your Own Heart." He also joins cowriters Gordon Kennedy, **Wayne Kirkpatrick,** and **Phil Madeira** in performing the anthemic title track.

Christian radio hits: "Jude Doxology" (# 30 in 1985); "Rock the Planet" (# 18 in 1986); "Love Has No Eyes" (# 2 in 1987); "What Goes Around Comes Around" (# 6 in 1988); "Heaven Is a Long Hello" (# 17 in 1992); "Press On" (# 20 in 1994); "Whatever Happened to Love" (# 23 in 1994).

Dove Awards: 1990 Musical Album (*Friends Forever/Part 2*).

Rita Springer

2000—*All I Have* (Floodgate).

Rita Springer is a composer and performer of worship music from Houston, Texas. For a decade prior to her official debut, she worked with Vineyard music and wrote several worship songs for their compilations of modern praise music. She also penned "You Are Still Holy," which **Kim Hill** recorded on her *Arms of Mercy* album. Springer is also said to have released three unidentified, independent albums of worship music. *All I Have,* produced by Andy Piercy of **After the Fire** fame, presents eleven piano-driven songs sung in a rich voice reminiscent of **Kelly Willard** or **Cheri Keaggy.** "You Said" and "Oh How You Love Me" are the most rocking tracks, building with gradual crescendoes into stirring anthems of praise. Springer says that she was brought up in a poor family where faith was a key element; she describes her father as "a true Jesus freak who continually sought after God." As an adult, Springer has often spoken at women's conferences and is concerned that worship music not become a marketing strategy: "Worship is a sacred thing," she says. "If it is plastic worship, then it is going to go nowhere. Worship is about a lifestyle and attitude before the Lord."

Scott Springer

1993—*Hello, Forever* (Pakaderm).

Scott Springer (b. 1959) was lead singer of **Halo** from 1980 to 1992. After his twelve years with that band, he released a solo album on **John** and Dino **Elefante**'s Pakaderm Records. The Elefantes produced *Hello, Forever* and cowrote most of the songs. The move toward adult contemporary went over predictably well with Christian radio and the album spawned three Number One hits. Reaction from critics was (also predictably) halfhearted as the music represented trademark Elefante riffs and sounds that had already been used on countless **Petra, Halo,** and **Mastedon** projects. "Anytime" is a folksy duet featuring **Jon Gibson.** "Behold the Lamb" is **Petra**esque rock with keyboards reminiscent of Phil Collins. Standout songs include the title track, the acoustic "Stand Up," and a majestic number called "The Victory."

Christian radio hits: "Anytime" (# 1 in 1993); "Hello, Forever" (# 1 for 2 weeks in 1993); "Behold the Lamb" (# 1 in 1994); "On My Knees" (# 3 in 1994); "Promises" (# 17 in 1994).

Bobby Springfield

1980—*Do Your Heart a Favor* (NewPax).

Bobby Springfield was a Nashville songwriter who composed hits for Roy Clark and many other country performers of the day. He was well known in the industry for his Christian faith and in 1980 was coaxed into recording an album of faith-oriented songs. *Do Your Heart a Favor* has what *CCM* would call "a very commercial sound with great hooks and simple melodies" (in those days *CCM* always meant the word *commercial* as a high compliment). The songs are less country than they are MOR pop. The title track proclaims, "Do your heart a favor / Listen to the Savior, let him in / Let him fill you up / With Holy Spirit love / and wash away your sin."

Christian radio hits: "Do Your Heart a Favor" (# 8 in 1981).

Aaron Sprinkle

1999—*Moontraveler* (Organic); 2000—*The Kindest Days*; 2001—*Bareface* (Silent Planet).

www.aaronsprinkle.com

Aaron Sprinkle was a founding member of the Christian rock band **Poor Old Lu** and also fronted the post-Lu experiment **Rose Blossom Punch.** As such, he was regarded as one of Christian music's most brilliant poets and performers even before releasing his first stunning solo album at the end of the millennium. All of Sprinkle's projects are songwriter albums, filled with lush and beautiful melodies and brilliantly introspective lyrics. In this regard, they merely fulfill the expectations of critics, who tend to place Sprinkle in the same songwriter's pantheon as **The Choir**'s **Steve Hindalong.** What critics did not know was that Sprinkle would turn out to be such a good singer. As the guitarist for **Poor Old Lu,** his voice was not often featured up front. It is silky smooth with "just a hint of helium," as *Phantom Tollbooth* would say: not gruff enough for convincing rock but perfect for acoustic bal-

lads, which pretty much fill out the solo projects. It is a voice like Thom Yorke of Radiohead, but Sprinkle applies it to songs more like those Neil Young composes when he falls into one of his ambiguous folkie funks. Sprinkle recorded his solo albums as a one-man band, playing virtually all the instruments except for drums.

Moontraveler opens with "Solace," a devotional song with reflective, unsure lyrics: "I can't decide if you're the missing piece buried in my mind . . . it makes me ill, the way you love me still." The next track, "I Wish I Were You," is addressed to his wife, Karina, as what he would elsewhere call "an apologetic love song," basically about "how I don't feel I'll ever be what she really deserves." Less characteristic of the album as a whole is "Antennae's Wife," which features more distortion, some techno influence, and bizarro lyrics that only begin to make sense with the help of external explanations (Sprinkle says the song is based on a story he made up about a spy for the Russians whose code name was Antennae—the spy, apparently, actually did exist, but the story and the song are fiction). The best song on the album—indeed, the best song of Sprinkle's career—is "A Friend I Had," which was mostly written by Karina. It begins with simple acoustic guitar, then Sprinkle sings the opening verse to a haunting melody, and *then,* from out of nowhere, he introduces a beautiful theme built on a series of notes that run counter to the main flow of the music but stand out in a way that is memorable and effective. It is a musical moment similar to the four-note progression with which John Lennon introduced "And I Love Her"—perfect precisely because of its simplicity. Most critics regarded *The Kindest Days* as even better than *Moontraveler,* though it is essentially an extension of that album with no noticeable change in style. "So Discreet" is a tender ballad that borders on emo melancholy. "Genevieve" spins another of his fictitious tales, this one of a complicated woman defined by contradictions. "Signing My Name" is the album's strange or frivolous cut, bringing in an organ for a circus-calliope sound. As indicated, Sprinkle does not often write or sing about the typical "faith matters" some would associate with contemporary Christian music, yet he integrates his faith into his art in ways that it shows through for those with ears to hear. *Bareface* presents more of the artist's minimalist brilliance, with standout tracks being "Running in My Head" and "Let Me In."

Spudgun (and World Against World)

Jason Kelley, voc.; Josh Weaver, gtr.; Ryan Weaver, gtr. By Spudgun: 1997—*Spudgun* (BulletProof). By World Against World: 1998—*Until the Day Breaks and the Shadows Flee Away* (BulletProof).

Spudgun was an old-school punk band from Atlanta, Georgia, with a sound and style like that of the Sex Pistols or the Dead Kennedys. The closest Christian market comparison may have been statemates **Squad Five-O,** though that band has a somewhat more mature (a relative term, to be sure) approach. As one critic would note, Spudgun "likes to play really, really fast and scream inaudible lyrics in a fake English accent." Some of the songs have a political bent ("Broken by the System," "The Rich Man Is the Politician's Best Friend"). Another, called "The Kids at My School Are Going to Riot," just complains about how everyone thinks the singer is weird. Jason Kelley would later admit that he "hates the song" but wrote it one day in class when "everyone was, like staring at me, and I thought it was funny." Defensive self-righteousness is given a more religious shading in "Watch It Burn" and "Too Late." The group complains in their liner notes about being forced to substitute new cover art for an original drawing that showed a house blowing up (the substitute picture portrays a punk pointing a large gun at the audience—or maybe it's a telescope). As many critics would note, this all smacks of childish cynicism and chip-on-the-shoulder pessimism—but that seemed to be part of Spudgun's appeal to their fans.

The group returned in 1998 under a new name, World Against World. Their album released under that moniker was produced by Chris Colbert of **Breakfast with Amy** and **Duraluxe/Fluffy.** Either his production or a year of growing up brought newfound maturity to the band, such that critics noted they now seemed to really care about their music and to play with practiced competence. They are just as noisy, but *HM* would say that World Against World sounds nothing like "the dirty punk-rock of Spudgun," coming closer to the hardcore sounds of **Scaterd Few** and **The Crucified.** The whiny attitude remains, however, with the dualism implied by their name revealing itself primarily as an obsession with human sinfulness. The songs tend to be wordy and to have unwieldy titles: "Our Nation of Thoughtlessness Celebrates Immorality While Seeking Independence from But Nevertheless Finding a Plague of Sorrow"; "We Dance with the Moment on the 2nd Story of Finality, Unaware of the Flames Slowly Spreading up the Stairs."

Spud Puddle

Billy Cooker, bass; Nick Garrisi, gtr., voc.; Javier Hernandez, gtr.; Kevin Pollard, drums. 1996—*Linoleum* (Brainstorm).

Spud Puddle was a band that recorded one album produced by Erik Tokle and **PlankEye**'s Scott Silletta. The sound is something of a cross between the pop punk of **MxPx** and the more groovy, emotional sounds of **Poor Old Lu** and Silletta-led **PlankEye.** Lyrics on *Linoleum* are explicitly Christian. "Sometimes I feel like I'm going down / Cause of all the sin that surrounds me / So the sinful me tries to find joy in other things . . . I know I should rely on you / On you, Jesus Christ / So I only want more of you" ("Sometimes I Feel"). The band re-

ceived virtually no support from the Christian media, with only *HM* noticing them.

Spy Glass Blue

Allan Aguirre, gtr., voc.; Kane Kelly, gtr.; River Tunnell, bass. 1997—*Shadows* (Organic); 2001—*Loud As Feathers* (Accidental Sirens).

Allan Aguirre is best known as the front man for the punk band **Scaterd Few.** He formed Spy Glass Blue as a side project, to serve as his "mellower, artistic outlet" and to function as more of a ministry band. The group became his main focus for a brief interim (1995–1998) during which **Scaterd Few** was defunct. *Shadows* shows strong influence of general market artists like Bauhaus and Peter Murphy and so was immediately identified as a rare example of Christian goth music. Aguirre objects to the categorization but admits that "a lot of goths were into **Scaterd Few**" and that he "welcomes that audience." The opening track, "Thin and Leaner," displays some of the punk style of Aguirre's main band, but the rest of the album consists of dark, haunting, moody tunes that might recall The Cure on a bad day. Aguirre sometimes mimics David Bowie's vocals (e.g., on "In Sultry Places," "On and On"). "Iron Gray" has an unusually pop sound, as though it might have been intended for radio. Thematically, the album seems to deal with the confusion of life without Christ. "Lodging" appears to liken salvation to coming in out of the cold.

Squad Five-O

Jeff Fortson, voc., gtr.; John Fortson, bass; Jason Anderson, drums (– 2000) // Adam Garbinski, gtr. (+ 2000); Justin Garbinski, drums (+ 2000; – 2002); Kris Klein, gtr. (+ 2002); Dave Peterson, drums (+ 2002). 1997—*What I Believe* (BulletProof); 1998—*Fight the System;* 2000—*Bombs over Broadway* (Tooth and Nail); 2002—*Squad Five-O.*

Squad Five-O is a punk-ska hybrid band from Savannah, Georgia. At first a power trio, the band is fronted by twin brothers, Jeff and John Forton. Eventually, the Fortons would be joined by another pair of brothers, Adam and Justin Garbinski, who are said to be former members of **The Huntingtons** (though they are not listed as having played on any of that band's albums). Adam Garbinski also plays with **One 21,** and that band's Kris Klein is sometimes listed as a member of Squad Five-O. The group earned an early reputation for giving energetic, comical live shows, and *HM* magazine did two cover stories on the band in less than two-and-a-half years. The group's innovative sound combines elements of ska (without the horns) with traditional punk. When the group was just starting out, Jeff Fortson would describe their sound as "if **MxPx** and **The Supertones** ran into each other." The style is sometimes dubbed "skacore" and gets jokingly called "skunk." The group's name is also a hybrid, derived from references to two favorite TV shows, *The Mod Squad* and *Hawaii Five-O.*

Squad Five-O's debut, *What I Believe,* is notable primarily for its standout song, "Our State Flag Sucks." The latter anthem tells it like it is regarding the Georgia state flag, which incorporates an image of the Confederacy into its design: "The flag of our state / A banner of hate . . . It's our heritage, heritage of hatred / Our state flag sucks." Incredibly—but unfortunately not surprisingly—the album was banned from many Christian bookstores on account of the latter song's use of "questionable language" (i.e., the word *sucks*). A second highlight of the debut album is "The Youth (We Are)," an energetic song that exalts the important role youth play in church and society. *Fight the System* was produced by **Aaron Sprinkle** and offers twenty-three songs that average about two minutes in length. Sprinkle also provides glam metal guitar leads here and there, including a faux-metal anthem called "The Ballad of Johnny Rocketship." In a more serious vein, "Kids of the World Unite" speaks of finding unity in a common commitment to God's mission, and "Parental Guidance" provides sincere appreciation for supportive parents. The title track and "A Call to Arms" pick up on spiritual warfare themes in potentially extremist ways, but "All in the Name of God" is worshipful, and "Forever Young" states a commitment never to sacrifice ideals for so-called maturity. On *Bombs over Broadway,* the band dispenses with the ska sound to make an album more in the classic hardcore and glam metal tradition. The project was produced by Duane Baron, famous for working with such artists as **Alice Cooper,** Ozzy Osbourne, and Mötley Crüe. "Lost Boys" continues the theme of "The Youth" and "Forever Young," addressing (perhaps) the older generation: "We're smarter than you think / We'll never be like you." The same rebel yell echoes through "Restless Youth" and "They'll Never Take Me Alive." The latter song is an anthem and a summons: "So raise your fist / Rebel resist / Don't give up your dream just yet." A track called "Rockin' at the Apocalypse" styles the end of the world as the ultimate tailgate party. *CCM* styled the album "a sonic guilty pleasure."

By 2000, the group seemed to be becoming increasingly disenchanted with the contemporary Christian music scene. Jeff Fortson complained to *7ball* about the crass commercialism of using Jesus' name as a marketing tool for selling T-shirts and record albums. And he told *HM,* "I think God needs more real people. He doesn't need more pastors and preachers or people running campaigns. . . . And you don't always have to be all bubbly and giddy. You have to be real. Life does suck sometimes. My Bible says that my God died on a cross for something He didn't do. That's not fair." The group's self-titled 2002 release emphasizes generic messages such as taking responsibility for one's own actions, staying away from drugs,

and eschewing materialism. *HM* praised the album as "an exercise in straight-forward, power-chord merriment." *CCM* granted that it serves up some pretty fine rock and roll but complained (predictably) about the lack of "spiritual depth."

Squirt

Jordan Dickerson, drums, voc.; Chris Fewell, gtr.; Matt Smith, bass. 1998—*Huge* (Absolute).

Squirt was a Christian version of Hanson led by twelve-year-old Jordan Dickerson, son of **Dez Dickerson,** the Christian artist who was once guitarist for Prince and who also owns Absolute Records. Jordan's companions, Fewell and Smith, were fourteen when the first album was released. The group took 1 Timothy 4:12 as their theme verse and said their goal was "to tell young people they don't need to be ashamed of their faith, but should be bold and share their faith in Christ with their friends." This message was articulated most clearly in the song "Go!," a spirited encouragement to enact the Great Commission in one's own neighborhood: "Everyone needs a Savior / They need to know / Up and down my street." The album concludes with a rocking version of Martin Luther's "A Mighty Fortress Is Our God."

S.S. Bountyhunter

John Deas; Josh Plemon; et al. 1997—*S.S. Bountyhunter* (independent); forthcoming—*Serpents for Eggs* (Velvet Blue).

S.S. Bountyhunter is a very strange Christian band with theatrical origins and a sound that is truly their own. The band has a constantly changing roster, but the core of the group is John Deas and Josh Plemon. Josh's wife, Becky Plemon, has also been a fairly constant member, but Josh admits, "It's safe to say that S.S. Bountyhunter is me and John, and we get different people to help us out." The group seems to have begun when Deas and Plemon began playing a sound inspired by '60s surf instrumentals and soundtracks to spy movies. This ultimately evolved into an undefinable blend that includes recognizable traces of industrial, ambient/trance, and goth. Some have said that the closest comparison may be **Havalina Rail Co.,** not because the bands sound alike, but because they are similarly unique and unpredictable. S.S. Bountyhunter's first album was a concept piece built around the theme of bountyhunters. It comes with an illustrated booklet displaying pictures of the group members chasing a woman, capturing her, and then killing her execution style. Lyrics to the songs (e.g., "I Hunt It Down," "The Arsenal," "The Unloading") are geared to this tale. Group members dressed in stereotypical hit man uniforms when they performed: white shirts, skinny black ties, black pants, and guns strapped in holsters. When they played the *Cornerstone* festival in 2000, one band member's sole function throughout the performance was to wield nunchucks and threaten audience members with them.

Of course all this is allegorical. Deas indicates that the letters "S.S." in their name stand for "Serum Seed," which is their term for the Holy Spirit (a serum is an antitoxin and a seed is something planted within; when people receive the Holy Spirit, it is like having the seed that will work against all human illness planted within their bodies). Thus, he explains, "A bounty hunter is someone who receives a bounty either by bringing someone into captivity or putting someone to death. The S.S. Bountyhunters are controlled by the Holy Spirit. The serum seed directs them as to what things need to be brought under captivity or put to death. By doing those things, the S.S. Bountyhunters receive a bounty." So what about the poor woman? "The woman looks like she would never have any reason to be hunted down. What that represents are the things that look innocent, things that you would never think have to be put to death."

Aside from the question of whether such an explanation actually makes the Bountyhunters any less disturbing, the music on their self-titled CD is varied and compelling, offering the sort of chills and adrenaline rushes associated with chase scenes in movies. "The Arsenal" is performed with a country twang, and "Thick, Thick Ribcage" has shouted vocals that give it a Mighty Mighty Bosstones feel. The band was signed to Velvet Blue on account of their innovation. The second album, *Serpents for Eggs,* backs off from the surf sound that runs throughout the debut, relying more on jagged electronics and sinister atmospheric sounds. Deas had promised that it would be "even more eerie and dark" than the first project, and the gruesome lyrics of songs like "Break Your Heart" deliver on that promise: "Digits lost, limbs deployed / Only heart was meant destroyed." The overriding theme of the Tarantinoesque imagery running through the album apparently concerns sacrifice of the self to God and of redemption through suffering. "When will you begin your killing spree?" Deas asks, "Let it begin with me" ("Mystery").

Rebecca St. James

1994—*Rebecca St. James* (ForeFront); 1996—*God;* 1997—*Christmas;* 1998—*Pray;* 2000—*Transform;* 2002—*Worship God.*

http://rsjames.com

Rebecca St. James (b. 1977) established herself in the contemporary Christian music scene as one of the most popular youth-oriented soloists of the '90s with strong potential for adult contemporary success in the new millennium. She was born and raised in Sydney, Australia, where her father was a Christian concert promoter. She fronted her first band in 1991 and toured her native land as the opening act for **Carman** at

the age of thirteen. In 1994, her entire family (including six younger siblings) moved to Nashville, where she began a professional career in the Christian pop market, releasing her self-titled debut album at the age of sixteen. For a time at least, her entire family served as her support staff, accompanying her on tour with all the siblings helping to set up for her stage show. She had a banner year in 1997, with readers of *Campus Life, CCM,* and *Release* all voting her their favorite female artist. St. James is also the author of two devotional books, *40 Days with God* (Thomas Nelson, 1996) and *You're the Voice: 40 More Days with God* (Thomas Nelson, 1997).

St. James' 1994 eponymous record is a collection of inspirational songs with an adult contemporary sound. It produced a string of Christian radio hits, but reviewers thought it odd that an album by a youth would contain nothing marketed for teenagers. *God* would move in the opposite direction, presenting St. James as "the Christian version" of Alanis Morissette, who had just conquered mainstream radio with *Jagged Little Pill.* "You're the Voice" is actually a cover of a song that was a minor general market hit (# 82) in 1990 for John Farnham of Little River Band (it had been more successful in LRB's homeland, where St. James grew up). The version here is such a dead-on imitation of Morissette, squeak for squeak and squawk for squawk, that many critics were inclined to dismiss St. James as a derivative poser, but the full body of her work would ultimately convince them otherwise. The Morissette touches are present throughout *God* but are less obvious on many songs than on "You're the Voice." The title track takes the singer into rock and offers what would be her finest performance until *Transform*'s "For the Love of God." It is a passionate paean to theism that exults in attributing what cannot be explained, or seen or heard or touched or felt, to God. The song "Side by Side" deals with the issue of accountability within Christian circles, expressing in St. James' words "how we need each other to stand for God and make a difference in this world." "You Then Me" is a catchy, melodic pop number about unselfishness, written by Bob Halligan Jr. of **Ceili Rain.** "Speak to Me" and "Abba (Father)" are strong worship numbers, the first a typical ballad, the second an instance of thoughtful folk-rock. "Go and Sin No More" is based on John 8:11. *God* would sell a remarkable 350,000 copies, and its only real low point is "Me without You," a song that suggests different metaphors for what a person is without God. *7ball* said the song "has good intentions but the comparisons are a little goofy and haphazard": "like a crime without a victim / like a sleuth without a clue / like an empty gun / like a fatherless son" etc. Notably, St. James cowrote several of the songs on *God* (including the title track but *not* including "Me without You"). The record was produced by Tedd T., who may be the one responsible for the Morissette cloning, as St. James herself claims to have been unfamiliar with that star's work: "I don't listen to secular radio. I don't touch that stuff. I would never in a million years buy an Alanis Morissette album. I've never even heard an Alanis Morissette song, except if I was passing through a room when someone else was listening to it."

St. James followed *God* with a Christmas project that includes new versions of John Lennon's "Happy Christmas" and **David Meece**'s almost forgotten "One Small Child," in addition to traditional carols and one original composition ("A Cradle Prayer"). Then she released *Pray,* which was also produced by Tedd T., but which abandons Morissette pretensions in favor of a more synth-driven pop sound. The opening, title track draws inspiration from 2 Chronicles 7:14 and states the theme of the album. All but two of the songs are prayers addressed to God, and most of the lyrics seem to have arisen out of St. James' own devotional life. "Mirror" expresses a desire to be more like Christ ("Make me an image of you / 'Cause Lord I want to mirror you"). "Omega" features St. James speaking words of benediction, with a full choir coming in on the chorus. "Come Quickly, Lord" yearns for the parousia, and "Love to Love You" is about just being in love with Jesus. One reviewer would describe *Pray* as having the feel of a work by "someone who just came away from an amazing Spirit-filled youth retreat." The album also includes some well-chosen covers: **Rich Mullins**' "Hold Me Jesus" and **Keith Green**'s "Lord, You're Beautiful" are both revved up for performances that differ significantly from the original versions but that instill the songs with new power for a new day. The project closes with the hymn "Be Thou My Vision."

Transform begins with a beautiful orchestral introduction that moves into the sure-fire hit "For the Love of God." The album as a whole is solid Euro-pop, and this song in particular is musical magic. It has an electronic beat, guitars that sound like *The Joshua Tree* **U2,** distorted vocals, and a harmonic chorus—all in support of lyrics paraphrased from 1 Corinthians 13. "Reborn" is another fast-paced song with a techno beat, focusing on the tried-but-true description of Christian conversion as entrance to "a whole new life." The whole dance-pop experiment comes to a head in "Lean On," which St. James cowrote with **Earthsuit.** "One" (by Regie Hamm and Dan Mukala) takes off in a completely different direction, essentially (though not officially) setting lyrics that exalt Christian unity to the tune of Britney Spears' "Oops, I Did It Again." Another high point of *Transform* comes with "Merciful," a complex song that provides a musical setting (rich in strings and intricate sound effects) for the traditional prayer of confession that is said each week in most liturgical churches. The album also features "Wait for Me," a love song to an unknown future husband encouraging him to stay sexually pure.

Sexual purity is a big deal for St. James and she has made its promotion a focal point (sometimes, it seems, *the* focal point) of her ministry. She wears a purity ring, a symbol analogous to a wedding ring that was placed on her finger in a ceremony in which she vowed to remain a virgin till marriage. She testifies regularly to her continued virginity in concerts and addresses the importance of premarital chastity in her writings. It is not, however, her only concern. She has also been an ardent supporter of the charitable organization Compassion International, which combats world hunger. She spent two months in Romania in 1999 with an organization called City of Hope, providing food and clothing to needy children.

In 1996, St. James appeared on a *Christianity Today* list of America's "Top 50 Evangelical Leaders Under the Age of Forty." That same year, she told *Release* that she strongly understands her participation in the music business as a ministry to which she has been called by God. She does not think it is her (primary) job to provide entertainment or to create art, but to communicate a message: "The stage means nothing to me. . . . If it wasn't for God and the message He's given me to share, I wouldn't be doing this. There's no way. I don't care about the art form of music as much as I care about the message." Theologically, she represents a separatist segment of Christianity that tends to circumscribe holiness to a sacred sphere distinct from life in general or the world at large. She attended a Christian school until eighth grade and was home-schooled by her parents thereafter. She does not drink or smoke. She doesn't date because, she says, "I don't really believe in dating and don't feel like I've missed out." She does not own a CD player; she doesn't buy or listen to any secular music. She rarely goes to the movies and if she is watching TV and the characters start engaging in illicit sex or using inappropriate language (i.e., cursing), she turns it off. Nevertheless, in 2001, she would tell *CCM,* "Every now and then, I'm really surprised at what a goody two-shoes everybody thinks I am." St. James was named national spokesperson for the Center for Reclaiming America, which sought to embolden students to "take God back into their schools" in the wake of school shooting tragedies. As part of that campaign, she wrote the song "Yes, I Believe in God" based on the words attributed to Cassie Bernall, shooting victim at Columbine. In 1999, St. James would accompany Josh McDowell on his multicity "Right From Wrong" crusades aimed at "stemming the moral and spiritual decline in American society."

St. James has said that she might not be called to "minister to the lost but to exhort the found." Her altar calls are not necessarily the stereotypical invitations to access salvation used in some American denominations, but broader invitations for "anyone who really wants to get serious about their commitment to Christ" to pledge that they will do so. In the latter regard, she lays out a five-step plan: dig into the Bible, dig into prayer, become accountable to other Christian friends, get rid of the junk in your life, and get involved in a Christian church where you can be fed. She says, "I want to encourage all of us to live a radical Christian life for God, standing strong for Him in all areas of life. I hope my music will encourage everyone to do that."

For trivia buffs: Rebecca St. James surname is almost always mispronounced in America. The proper pronunciation is not *Saint* but *S'nt* (in the British-cum-Australian tradition).

Christian radio hits: "Here I Am" (# 5 in 1994); "Little Bit of Love" (# 12 in 1994); "Everything I Do" (# 3 in 1995); "Side by Side" (# 6 in 1995); "We Don't Need It" (# 15 in 1995); "Sweet, Sweet Song of Salvation" (# 15 in 1996); "God" (# 1 in 1996); "Go and Sin No More" (# 1 in 1996); "Me without You" (# 1 in 1996); "Abba (Father)" (# 2 in 1997); "You're the Voice" (# 10 in 1997); "Sweet Little Jesus Boy" (# 1 in 1997); "Carry Me High" (# 9 in 1998); "Mirror" (# 1 for 3 weeks in 1998); "Omega" (# 15 in 998); "Pray" (# 1 for 5 weeks in 1998); "Peace" (# 3 in 1999); "Yes, I Believe in God" (# 4 in 2000); "Come Quickly, Lord" (# 12 in 2000); "Don't Worry" (# 1 for 6 weeks in 2000); "Reborn" (# 12 in 2001); "Wait for Me" (# 1 for 2 weeks in 2001).

Grammy Awards: 1999 Best Rock Gospel Album *(Pray)*.

Michael Hakanson Stacy

See **Michael Hakanson-Stacy** (under "H").

Denny Stahl

No albums.

Denny Stahl was a solo acoustic artist in the early days of the Jesus movement. Like many artists, he was associated with Calvary Chapel in Costa Mesa, California, and he frequently performed at many of the big concerts sponsored through that ministry. His most popular song, a piece called "Hey, Hey, Brothers and Sisters," was never recorded. Stahl did, however, contribute two songs to other Maranatha projects. The *Maranatha Two* (1972) compilation album includes his "The Son in My Life," a ballad of love and gratitude addressed to Christ. Stahl was also responsible (though uncredited) for the worship song "Cause Me to Come" on *The Praise Album* (Maranatha, 1974). In 2001, Stahl was serving as pastor of a Calvary Chapel church called Deshutes Christian Fellowship in Deshutes, Oregon.

The Stand

Tony Valenziano, gtr., voc. // Dan Holter, drums; Mark Robertson, bass; Paz Vega, gtr. 1991—*Heartbreak Town* (Wonderland); 1993—*In Three Days*.

The Stand was a heartland rock band that went through two different incarnations in the early '90s. Singer/songwriter

Tony Valenziano formed the group with an initial lineup and recorded *Heartbreak Town*. Although The Stand was supposedly a quartet, their album cover displayed only Valenziano, confirming critics' suspicions that the project was really more of a solo outing recorded with some backing players. *CCM* would style *Heartbreak Town* as an album with a '60s British-invasion sound but with an approach to lyrics that is "unquestionably '90s." The songs are introspective in a way that belies their melodic structure. On the title track, Valenziano sings, "See the fragile heart / So lost in what he becomes." Elsewhere, he complains, "Everything's a distant fear / Mercy cries but no one hears" ("Everyday"). The album also features a martial version of "Amazing Grace."

Valenziano relocated from Los Angeles to Chicago and put together a new version of The Stand that included Mark Robertson, the prolific bassist who had played with the **Allies** and **The Altar Boys** and who had been a founding member of **Brighton** and **Generation.** In time, he would become even better known as a member of **A Ragamuffin Band** and as leader of **This Train.** Robertson helped with the songwriting on *In Three Days,* a concept album that seeks to establish a parallel between the confusion of Jesus' first followers during the interim between crucifixion and resurrection and the confusion that attends many young people in the modern world. The basic sound of this second version of The Stand was copped from The Clash, and the album has a punchy, guitar-driven feel to it that *True Tunes* indicated should appeal to fans of Creedence Clearwater Revival and Neil Young. The opening, "Free Love," uses an old hippie expression to describe the availability of God's grace. An album highlight is the surprising cover of Nick Lowe's "(What's So Funny 'Bout) Peace, Love, and Understanding?" (a very Clash-sounding song originally made famous by Elvis Costello). Of The Stand's mission, Valenziano said, "We're not trying to Bible beat anybody—just plant a seed. I believe that Jesus is who he said he was and that his dying for me saved me from eternal damnation. It's the message we're trying to get out."

Mike Stand

1988—*Do I Stand Alone?* (Alarma); 1990—*Simple Expression*.

Mike Stand was the leader of **The Altar Boys,** one of Christian music's most important and authentic exemplars of '80s punk-rock. In the band's declining years, he recorded two vibrant solo albums that presaged the group's demise. In 1995 he would record with a new band **Clash of Symbols.** As of 2000, he was serving as a music instructor at an elementary school in Santa Ana, California, and leading worship (with his brother) for a church youth group on Wednesday and Sunday nights.

The solo records definitely reveal a kinder, gentler Stand than the yelping punk of the early '80s. "I tended to write songs with sing-along slogans that provided simple answers," Stand wrote in an **Altar Boys** retrospective piece for *CCM* in 1989. "You know, I'm into God and God is into me and no matter what, it will be O.K. . . . Those songs were fun to sing, but they definitely lacked depth and reality. Unfortunately, it is not always so cut and dried." Stand's first solo album, he explained, was born out of "disillusionment with the ministry and music business." *Do I Stand Alone?* features songs like "I've Seen Gray," which insists that answers to many important questions cannot be found: "I've tried so hard to understand this life / I want to know what's wrong, I want to know what's right." Yet he affirms, "The hope that lives inside of me gives this gray a little light . . . It's easy to get angry when this world's unfair / The challenge is to know a faithful God is there." Musically, *Do I Stand Alone?* is more of a roots-rock album, dispensing with the punk stylings. The title track sounds like John Mellencamp covering a **Bob Dylan** song. "What's Goin' On" and the opening "I'm Only Human" invoke the spirit of Springsteen. "Simple Truth" closes the project with an atypical acoustic ballad with folk guitar and harmonica. *Simple Expression* was coproduced by **Rick Elias,** and the latter's band (The Confessions) backs Stand with a Merseybeat, jangling sound that would get them compared to **The Alarm.** "All I Want Is to Live" is a hooky anthem with a catchy Springsteen-like chorus: "All I want is to live / So everything must die / Fall into my Maker's hands / Somebody to hold me / Somebody to love me / Somebody to tell me / It's gonna be alright." The album also includes great rockers like "Footsteps of Love" (like *Reckless* Bryan Adams), "Changes" (like *Rubber Soul* Beatles), and "Great Things Happen" (like *Fifth Dimension* Byrds). "Whisper in the Morning" is an atypical piano ballad with **Ric Alba** on the keyboard.

For trivia buffs: Mike Stand's brother is Kevin Lee, who drummed for an early version of **LSU** called **Lifesavors.**

Christian radio hits: "Do I Stand Alone?" (# 9 in 1989).

Pops Staples

1992—*Peace to the Neighborhood* (Pointblank); 1994—*Father, Father.*

Roebuck "Pops" Staples (1915–2000) was the founder of the successful pop-soul group The Staples Singers, which included his daughters Cleotha, Mavis, and Yvonne and, for a time (until 1971) his son Pervis. Mavis Staples was the lead singer and would also perform as a solo artist and, in the '90s, worked with Prince and with **BeBe** and **CeCe Winans.** The Staples Singers actually began as a gospel group in the early '50s, but in the mid '60s they crossed over to the general market and scored several mainstream hits in the early '70s, including "Respect Yourself" (# 12 in 1971), "I'll Take You There" (# 1 in 1971), "If You're Ready (Come Go with Me)" (# 9 in 1973), and "Let's Do It Again" (# 1 in 1975). In the early '90s, Pops decided to return to gospel and recorded two albums that connected him with his blues heritage. Jackson Browne, Ry Cooder, and Bonnie Raitt put in appearances on his *Peace to the Neighborhood* album—along with a reunited Staples Singers on some tracks. The title cut is a cover of a Los Lobos song, but Staples' original "America" encourages individual citizens to turn toward God in a manner that will affect their country's corporate destiny. He also covers Browne's "World in Motion." Solid gospel numbers include "Pray On My Child," "Pray," and "I Shall Not Be Moved." The indisputable highlight, however, is Pops's own version of "The Last Time," a song he wrote that became an early hit for The Rolling Stones (# 9 in 1965). Gospel tunes abound on the *Father, Father* album, which won a Grammy for Best Contemporary Blues album. On the latter record Ry Cooder produced two songs ("Downward Road" and "Jesus Is Going to Make up My Dyin' Bed"), and Mavis Staples produced two others (the title track and "Hope in a Hopeless World"). Pops also sings **Bob Dylan**'s "Gotta Serve Somebody" and **Curtis Mayfield**'s "People Get Ready" (Mayfield also wrote The Staples Singer's biggest hit, the secular "Let's Do It Again").

Grammy Awards: 1994 Contemporary Blues Album *(Father, Father).*

Starflyer 59

Jason Martin, gtr., voc., kybrd., drums; Andrew Larson, bass (−1997); Dan Reid, drums (− 1995) // Wayne Everett, drums (+ 1996, −2001); Eric Campuzano, bass (+ 1996, −1998); Gene Eugene, kybrd. (+ 1997, −2000); Jeff Cloud, bass (+ 1998); J. Dooley (+ 2001); J. Esquibel (+ 2001). 1994—*Starflyer 59* [a.k.a. *Silver*] (Tooth and Nail); *She's the Queen* [EP]; 1995—*Starflyer 59* [a.k.a. *Gold*]; *Le Vainqueur* [EP]; 1996—*Plugged* [EP] (Velvet Blue); 1997—*Americana* [a.k.a. *Red*] (Tooth and Nail); 1998—*The Fashion Focus;* 1999—*Fell in Love at 22* [EP]; *Everybody Makes Mistakes;* 2000—*Easy Come, Easy Go;* 2001—*Leave Here a Stranger.*

Of all the secret treasures Christian rock has kept to itself over the years, none is more tragically secret or more legitimately treasured than Starflyer 59. Virtually unknown to the world at large, Starflyer 59 features one of the world's greatest living guitarists and was one of the best alternative rock band of the '90s, i.e., one of the most original, creative, and accomplished groups to be making music in either the Christian or general markets throughout that decade. Though the Starflyer sound is sometimes described as an acquired taste, those who do acquire it can't seem to get enough. Fans are rabid, and critics simply stand in awe of the band's prolific output, exhausting all the superlatives their thesauruses supply. As with any truly original band, the group's sound is difficult to describe. It has been said that Starflyer 59 answers the musical question,

"What if Eddie Van Halen were to join the Smashing Pumpkins?" but the analogy could be misleading. Front man Jason Martin does seem to have Billy Corgan's sensibilities, and his prowess with the guitar is at least comparable (though probably not equal) to that of Van Halen. Still, the style is completely different (fuzzy and thick, not soaring and quick). One critic suggested the group sounds like "Chris Isaac fronting Black Sabbath"—a scary thought—but the paragons are too weak: Martin outmopes Isaac even on supposedly happy songs and Starflyer's heavier material makes Sabbath sound like Top 40 pop. Isaac fronting My Bloody Valentine would be a closer fit—but again the technical competence and sheer innovation surpasses whatever images such descriptions might conjure.

The band is basically just Jason Martin and friends. He has changed colleagues from time to time, as the personnel list above indicates, and rare concert tours sometimes feature different backing musicians. Martin was raised in Southern California in a strict home that did not allow any "secular music." Given such deprivation, he chose his influences well, soaking up **Daniel Amos** (whose *Alarma Chronicles* he once called "my favorite records of all time") and **LSU** (whose *Shaded Pain* he once called "the best album ever, Christian or secular"). In time, he would join his brother Ronnie Martin in the techno group **Dance House Children,** whose albums he has since come to view as an embarrassment. The two siblings then seemed to go in opposite directions: Ronnie took techno to its logical extremes with **Rainbow Rider** and **Joy Electric.** Jason eschewed the synthesizers and crafted songs built on metal-inspired guitar. But in reality the differences are not that great. Aside from the choice of instrumentation, both brothers have continued to produce songs that are intrinsically strong in terms of melody, chord progression, rhythm, and structure. Jason claims that The Pixies and The Smiths are two of his greatest influences from among general market acts. Otherwise, the band's music falls roughly into two phases: the first three full-length albums (and two EPs) present them as the world's all-time best "noise pop" band; then, the group had the audacity to change its style, not necessarily as growth but simply to remain creative. "I won't call it a progression, because a lot of people like the earlier stuff better," Martin says, "but I wasn't going to just keep doing the same thing."

The first three full-length albums have nondescript, blank covers—no photos or lettering, not even the name of the group. The covers are different colors, however: silver, gold, and red, respectively. The first two of these albums are both officially titled *Starflyer 59* but are popularly known as *Silver* and *Gold.* The third album actually does have a distinctive name (*Americana*), but usually gets called *Red* anyway. The sound of all three projects is essentially the same, though dyed-in-the-wool fans maintain that *Gold* has more of a hushed feel and

Red (Americana), a more pronounced heavy metal vibe. Likewise, the EPs interspersed between the color albums (*She's the Queen* and *Le Vainqueur*) are of a piece with those albums stylistically (and of equivalent quality). Martin seems to have paid great attention to which songs fit into an overall sonic scheme for each of the color albums and, thus, to have released stellar tracks (not filler!) that didn't fit the schemes on the separate EPs instead. *Plugged,* however, is a live collection of six songs performed in early 1996.

The sound of Starflyer 59's color-album period is basically a very heavy version of what is often dismissed as shoegazer music—with just a touch of goth. Martin typically creates a lush landscape of fuzzy, distorted guitars churning out some of the most amazing riffs ever produced in rock and roll. But unlike most hard rock, the songs are slow and moody, like some kind of hybrid of heavy metal and lounge music. And the vocals are not screamed or shouted or even sung in a normal voice. Rather, Martin whispers them in a delicate and ethereal voice that floats on top of his walls of distortion in constant danger of sinking into the mix where they would be lost forever. The fragility of his voice set against the brutality of his guitars creates an effect that is mysterious and mesmerizing. *Visions of Gray* would say, "Starflyer fuses breathy, uncertain vocals with aggressive rhythm and nearly carefree countermelodies." *Cornerstone* describes the sound as "deafening, riff-centered, and repetitively dreamy." The single most used word in early Starflyer 59 reviews would be "hypnotic."

The silver record was produced by Jerome Fontamilla and Jyro Xhan of **Mortal.** The whole project works together as a single tonal poem, but specific standout cuts would include "Blue Collar Love," "Sled," and "Hazelwould." On "Monterey," Martin imitates the plucking of a piano keyboard on his guitar for a sound that is unusual and fetching. The gold album is the best of the three masterpieces. The history of rock music contains very few non-Hendrix songs with guitar parts as dynamic as those that sustain "A Housewife Love Song" and "When You Feel Miserable." The songs "You're Mean" and "One-Shot Juanita" have more radio accessibility and, indeed, the first of these (with a little bit of surf guitar thrown into the mix) was a Number One hit on Christian "progressive rock" stations (which, admittedly, are not too numerous). Thematically, Martin has described the album as being "about a problem I've had since third grade—being bummed out over girls." "Messed Up over You" and "Stop Wasting Your Whole Life" are confessional and advisory ballads of unrequited love that display its effects with intensely emotional guitars. "Dual-Overhead Cam" is a heavy metal dream. *Gold* is, by all accounts, the best shoegazer or noise pop album ever made; still, Martin resists the labels. "The noise pop label is kind of stupid" he told *Shout* in 1996. "We're not even really doing that anymore. I don't even think we're going to have distortion on the next record. It's going to be like a Smiths record." It wasn't. *Americana* is the second-best shoegazer, noise pop album ever made, more of the *Silver* and *Gold* sound, with just enough variety to justify turning the series into what could have been issued as a three-disc set. "The Voyager" is propelled by an acid-rock riff with a groovy organ interrupting the song when it threatens to become a dirge. "Everyone But Me" and "All You Want Are the Things I Need" are more pop-oriented. "You Don't Miss Me" offers a particularly vivid exercise for Martin to show off his guitar skills. "You Think You're Radical" is a slow-motion guitar waltz that features church organ and a touch of Cowboy Junkies-style country. "The Hearttaker" and "Harmony" are also remarkable, the latter previewing the sort of melodic filigrees that would make songs on *Fashion Focus* a delight. Actually, *Americana* was the project of a temporary supergroup, with Eric Campuzano and Wayne Everett of **The Prayer Chain** joining Starflyer 59 and Gene Eugene from **Adam Again** playing keyboards and producing the classic album.

The Fashion Focus introduces a new era for Starflyer 59 with vocals put forward in the mix ("out of the smoke and haze" *True Tunes* would say) and the dominance of distorted guitars greatly reduced. The familiar wall-of-fuzz sound resurfaces on "The Birthright" and for about half of "Too Much Fun" (which then segues into more of a Radiohead/Oasis type of tune). Otherwise, "Sundown" has an unbelievably cool vibe, and "Holiday," a jaunty beat that had one critic wondering whether the sheltered lad had finally gotten to hear a Beatles record. Both of the just-mentioned tunes are unusual but catchy summer songs that surely would have been huge hits on general market radio if they had ever been given the chance. "We're the Ordinary" is built on lazy arpeggios that twine around Martin's sultry vocals like so much ivy on a lampost. Another standout, "I Drive a Lot," was inspired by Martin's day job as a truck driver. The odds-on favorite song from *Fashion Focus,* however, was the suitable-for-proms ballad, "Fell in Love at 22." The autobiographical song might go a long way toward explaining the less mopey, upbeat quality of *Fashion Focus:* apparently he had found relief from the problem of being bummed out over girls at last (around this time, Martin would also record a side project album with his new wife under the name **Bon Voyage**). "Fell in Love at 22" would also be issued on an extended single or EP, which also contains four new songs. One of these, "Traffic Jam," is a fourteen-minute instrumental; another, "E.P. Nights," contains one of the group's only lyrical references to Jesus. *Everybody Makes Mistakes* continues the evolution begun on *Fashion Focus* with more drastic results. The guitar feedback is all but gone, replaced by aesthetic keyboards. "A Dethroned King" is a grinding rock song, but it owes

as much to Weezer as to the Smashing Pumpkins and features a harpsichord. "No New Kinda Story" leans toward techno-disco. Acoustic guitars are used here and there, and a soft piano is the primary instrument for "20 Dollar Bills." An unnamed "bonus track" closes the album with a beautiful instrumental played on piano and saxophone.

Easy Come, Easy Go is a two-disc compilation, amply illustrated with an informative retrospective on Starflyer 59's career (thus far). The first disc is a traditional "greatest hits" collection that samples from all of their major projects (three songs selected almost arbitrarily from each of the five full-length releases). The second disc compiles twelve rarities (including a cover of **Daniel Amos**'s "Shedding the Mortal Coil") and offers an additional eight live versions of previously recorded studio songs.

Leave Here a Stranger was produced by **Terry Scott Taylor** and so marks another new venture for the band (albums from *Gold* on had been produced by the late Gene Eugene of **Adam Again**). Taylor adds lots of his trademark Beatlesque flourishes to the mix and compels Martin to sing in an audible voice on what ends up sounding like his most melodic batch of songs to date. The group has very few fans who don't like their idol better when he's miserable, and *Stranger* has nothing to compete with "Messed Up over You," but as he said, there's little point in repeating the past. Martin had found love (at twenty-two) and his fans would just have to deal with that. On *Stranger* he sounds content. He sings dreamily about "All My Friends Who Play Guitar" and "Night Music" and, of course, "Your Company." Contentment's a long way from happiness, however, and on "Give Up the War" Martin courts an early midlife crisis, contemplating the achievements of godly men like the Apostle Paul and wondering whether all the chords he's played really count for anything. The brooding title track is also an awesome standout. Many reviewers would note sonic similarities between *Leave Here a Stranger* and the Beach Boys' *Pet Sounds*—and Martin has confirmed that this "was the sound we were going for."

Starflyer 59's consignment to the Christian music ghetto seems ironically unnecessary since the group's lyrics rarely focus on anything specifically evangelical. Indeed, apart from comments in interviews and references thanking "our risen Lord Jesus Christ" in the liner notes, fans would never be able to tell from the music itself that the band has any connection to Christianity or to Christian music. Lyrics tend to be stream-of-consciousness meanderings that are often undecipherable except in the vaguest sort of way. The emphasis, *CCM* would note, "is more on mood than message." *True Tunes* says, "Martin writes in an odd sort of code, one you always feel as if you're just on the brink of understanding." As for topics, Martin said of the *Gold* album, "I want to be a Christian band, but I want to write about stuff that's honest and legitimate. . . . I don't know too many other bands that try to relate on a teenager-in-love kind of angle." But then for *Red (Americana),* he would say, "I feel a little convicted about all the 'woe is me' kind of stuff (on previous projects). I felt like as a Christian I should try to encourage people and sing songs about the faith and not just sing about me all the time." Still, the closest that album comes to a faith song is "The Heart Taker," on which he sings rather ambiguously, "Until you go / You know it's hard to know / Or just believe / Because the heart taker makes it easier." Still, Martin has little patience with Christian artists who seem coy or shy about declaring their faith. "I really do view Starflyer 59 as a ministry that God has given me," Martin says, while acknowledging that he does not conduct altar calls or preach to people. "I'd like to be more of an evangelical band, but I just can't do it," he says. "I don't talk good in front of people, and I don't have these incredible stories to tell. But I really would like to consider myself a minister." What he has to share is music: "I just can't bear to think that there's a decent song and that me and my wife, Julie, will be the only ones to hear it." In 2000, he told *Bandoppler,* "It's just entertainment, but I hope we're glorifying God with what we're doing . . . whether I'm playin' rock 'n' roll or just drivin' a truck, I just give glory to God."

As for the group's name, Martin told *7ball* magazine in 1998 that it doesn't mean anything. "I thought it sounded cool for 1992. It sounds really stupid now. I'm sorry I came up with that name."

Keith Staten

See **Commissioned.**

Candi Staton

Selected: 1983—*Make Me an Instrument* (Berecah); 1985—*Anointing;* 1986—*Sing a Song;* 1988—*Love Lifted Me;* 1989—*Stand Up and Be a Witness;* 1991—*Standing on the Promises;* 1995—*Young Hearts Run Free* (Warner Bros.); 1996—*It's Time* (Intersound); 1997—*Cover Me* (CGI).; 2000—*Here's a Blessing for You* (Lightyear); 2001—*Glorify* (Blue Moon); *Stand Up and Be a Witness.*

www.candi-staton.com/go/PGE_Cover.htm

Gospel diva Candi Staton (b. 1943) enjoyed a brief period of success as a secular soul singer in the early '70s, when she placed ten songs on *Billboard*'s mainstream Hot 100 charts. In the '80s, she would return to gospel with several albums that reflect an easy listening, adult contemporary style. Staton wrote an inspirational autobiography of her life titled *This Is My Story* (Pneuma Life, 1995). The latter volume centers on her spiritual conversion, but also details the abuse that she claims to have suffered at the hands of a number of persons (some of them famous).

Staton was born in Hanceville, Alabama, and was brought up a strict Baptist. She tells stories of sneaking cigarettes with Mavis Staples and singing with early gospel groups like the Four Golden Echoes and the Jewell Gospel Trio. As part of the latter group, she toured with Lou Rawls and **Sam Cooke.** She dated Rawls and at one point they were engaged to be married, but she became pregnant by another man who would become the first of four husbands. The two had four children, but Staton describes the relationship as abusive and controlling. After a divorce, she married soul singer Clarence Carter, who got her started in a secular music career, but, she says, she could not abide his constant womanizing and they divorced. For a time, the single Staton became tabloid fodder as she was romantically linked in the press with **Al Green,** Johnnie Taylor, and other celebrities. As it turns out, her third husband would be a man she now calls "a pimp and a hustler." In 1999, she would claim that the third marriage "was the biggest mistake of my life. He was a big cocaine user and he carried a gun. I was often frightened that he would kill me." It was during this time that Staton's growing problem with alcohol abuse took over: "Alcohol became my lover, my comforter, my god. I worshiped alcohol. . . . I couldn't get out of bed without a drink." Eventually, Staton would enter what appeared from the start to be a doomed marriage to John Susswell (drummer for Diana Ross), who was also a cocaine addict. It didn't go well, but the day before the couple was to meet with lawyers to solidify their impending divorce, Susswell met with a pastor at a Birmingham church and emerged from three hours of counseling "a changed man." Staton was skeptical but could not deny the transformation. "I had been in the church all my life and had seen the abuse and was really turned off to religion," she says. "I did not realize that the Lord Jesus Christ was a relationship, not a religion. He is a person who comes and lives inside of you and lives his life through you." Staton tells in her autobiography that she prayed for Christ to come into her heart and that God saved her marriage. She "received the Holy Spirit," became an ordained minister, and took to recording nothing but gospel music.

In terms of her musical career, Staton first signed a three-year contract with Capitol Records in the '60s, followed by another eight years with Warner. She had no big hits but was on the charts several times, most memorably with her first and last songs: "I'd Rather Be an Old Man's Sweetheart Than a Young Man's Fool" (# 46 in 1969) and "Young Hearts Run Free" (# 20 in 1976); the latter tune would be covered by Kym Mazelle in 1997 and included on the soundtrack of the film *William Shakespeare's Romeo and Juliet.* Staton also recorded a version of Tammy Wynette's "Stand by Your Man" (# 24 in

1970) and Mac Davis's "In the Ghetto" (# 48 in 1972). In the '70s, she became a disco star on the club circuit, and in 1991, was thrust back into that mirrorball spotlight when a bootleg remix of a song she had done called "You Got the Love" made its way back onto the dance charts (it hit Number One in Britain). As a result, Staton would record one more secular album of "positive club songs" called *Outside In* (Warner Bros., 1999).

As noted, Staton's gospel albums (listed above) have fallen more into traditional categories than contemporary ones, with an accent on praise and worship. *Young Hearts Run Free* actually mixes genres, placing a rendition of Thomas Dorsey's classic "Precious Lord, Take My Hand" on an album that includes the disco hit that serves as its title track. *Here's a Blessing for You* features the traditional hymns "Come Ye Disconsolate," "My Faith Looks up to Thee," and "Have Thine Own Way." *Cover Me* has versions of **Andraé Crouch**'s "It Won't Be Long" and Paul Simon's "Bridge over Troubled Water."

Stavesacre

Dirk Lemmenes, bass; Mark Salomon, voc.; Jeremy Moffett, drums (– 1997); Jeff Bellew, gtr. (– 1999) // Sam West, drums (+ 1997); Ryan Denney, gtr. (+ 1999); Neil Samoy, gtr. (+ 1999). 1996—*Friction* (Tooth and Nail); 1997—*Absolutes*; 1999—*Speakeasy*; 2001—*Stavesacre/Denison Marrs* [EP] (Velvet Blue); 2002—*Collective* (Tooth & Nail).

www.stavesacre.com

Stavesacre is a hard alternative band from Orange County, California. Their sound is somewhat difficult to classify, especially since it has shifted over the years, but broad general market comparisons may be drawn to groups like **Creed** or Stabbing Westward. Early on, lead singer Mark Salomon would indicate that the sound has elements of lesser-known bands like Quicksand and Bad Brains. Within the Christian scene, Stavesacre was first seen as something of a "super group," since its members all had successful careers in other favorite bands: Salomon and Jeff Bellew were in **The Crucified,** Dirk Lemmenes was in **Focused,** Jeremy Moffett was lead singer for **The Blamed,** and his replacement, Sam West, had drummed for **Saviour Machine.** Prior to reuniting in Stavesacre, Bellew also performed with **Chatterbox,** and Salomon with **Outer Circle** and **Native Son.** Ryan Denney, recruited for the third album, had played in a band called Outnumbered and toured as a member of **PlankEye.** The new group was quick to point out, however, that their sound would not be that of the hardcore bands from which they had sprung. "I'm burnt out on that music," Salomon told *HM.* "You can only go so long playing the same type of music that's been out for ten years." Again, he said at the time of the group's debut, "There's a soft side to it, and there's a hard side. I'm not into screaming and yelling every five seconds and running around. I want to see if there are other emotions that are available." The spelling of

Salomon's name, incidentally, is one of the great mysteries of Christian rock. *HM* magazine alone has printed it as Solomon, Soloman, Solamon, Solaman, and Salomon. It is rendered Saloman in the liner notes to Stavesacre's *Friction* but Salomon at the band's website.

All three Stavesacre albums were produced by Bryan Carlstrom, a Christian producer who has helmed projects for White Zombie and Alice in Chains. *Friction* was a relatively big-budget production for Tooth and Nail and set new standards of quality for that label and for Christian heavy music in general. It opens with what would become one of the band's most recognizable hits, "Threshold," an apparent address to rebellious punks who raise their fists in anger at a world that is not the way they wish it could be. "I fell unto mercy you despised and denied," Salomon sings. "Watching you torture yourself and whoever else you can bring down with you." "Burning Clean" is another standout, expressing similar sentiments from a different point of view: "If you see me on the way down / Would you smile and send me on my way? . . . Is there something more between you and me? . . . If I see you headed down, I'll do what I can to lift you up again." *Friction*'s masterpiece, however, is the more mellow and melodic "At This Moment." By 2001, the song would resound with shades of future **Creed** (*My Own Prison*) and **Collective Soul** (*Disciplined Breakdown*), but in 1996 it was a brilliantly original, perfect sampling of a new sound that had hardly been heard before. *Shout!* magazine said, "*Friction* gets into that rare zone that is heavy yet melodic, moody yet intense."

Absolutes would take the group in a harder direction that had many critics comparing them to Tool. At the outset, Salomon bellows, "I'm crawling out of my skin / I hope I get under yours." Thus, the theme of the album, implicit in its title, seems to be a denial of relativism. Its centerpiece seems to be "Colt .45," which refuses to let matters of ultimate importance be subjected to the politically correct niceties that demand equal respect for all views: "I thought about what you said and I'm not sorry for a thing," says Salomon, "Every breath you breathe is grasping at the wind." Elsewhere (e.g., "Acquiese"), the band adopts a more modest position, acknowledging the struggles of their own flesh. "Wither/Ascend" features vocals by Bellew along with Salomon and an overall sound reminiscent of **The Prayer Chain**'s "Grylliade," broken toward the end by a military drum roll.

After some more personnel changes, the group adopted a defiantly restrained sound for its third album, partly in reaction to complaints that they had become a Tool-clone. "We don't want to be described as baby Tool," Salomon acknowledged. "I just thought, man, if this many people say we sound like that, as much as I'd like to think we don't, maybe we need to work at *not* sounding like that." Reviews of the album fluctuated widely, not simply in assessment but in their very description of the album's sound. *Phantom Tollbooth* insisted in three separate reviews that, despite the band's declared intent, *Speakeasy* continues in the same, by-now-formulaic vein as the first two albums with little to distinguish it. *Bandoppler* hosted a series of reviews by critics and fans who all thought the album was vastly different from its predecessors and wanted to debate the merits of this evolution/insurrection/betrayal. In any case, the band comes off as a mature rock outfit with lots of metal muscle but nothing to prove. The bone-crunching riffs and sledgehammer rhythms are used as necessary, but melody truly dominates. "Minuteman" opens the album with a plodding tempo and a lyrical call to spiritual readiness. "Keep Waiting" is a passionate-but-poppy song that moves in the direction of emo. *CCM* and others picked the atmospheric "Freefall" as *Speakeasy's* standout masterpiece. Musically, that expressive track "builds from a quiet figure into a storm of layered guitars." Lyrically, it offers an anguished but hopeful cry of repentance: "When I fall down / When I fail you / I hope to find you there." The disc also contains a cover of The Cure's "Fascination Street."

Stavesacre clearly does not see itself as "a ministry band" and is, in fact, quite critical of that designation. Salomon draws a clear line between Christians who may be called by God into a ministry where music is simply a tool of expression and Christians who form a band for artistic reasons and who, indeed, pursue a career in music as "a business." He sees some contradiction between those who claim the former calling and then sell T-shirts and work the whole business angle of the rock and roll industry. He is also unusually articulate about defining just what Stavesacre is and is not: "We are a business not a ministry. . . . frankly, I have no business being a spiritual leader over kids I have never met. . . . Stavesacre is a rock and roll band and we try to turn a profit, but it is a rock and roll band made up of individuals who are Christians, who love God, and who believe they are called to serve God by loving other people." He is also somewhat critical of the very existence of a contemporary Christian music scene: "Jesus didn't die on the cross so Christians can have their own little world, ya know what I mean? You've got Christian T-shirts, you've got Christian car dealerships, Christian coffeehouses, Christian schools, Christian this, Christian that, and pretty soon, you don't have to deal with the outside world ever."

In 2000, Stavesacre was without a label. The next year they produced a "split EP" of new material with the band **Denison Marrs.** *Collective* is a greatest hits compilation.

For trivia buffs: Dirk Lemmenes used to babysit Jeff Bellew when the latter was a child.

Shannon Stephens

1999—*How I Got Away* [EP] (independent); 2000—*Shannon Stephens.*

Shannon Stephens is a progressive, alternative folk singer whose independent recordings have garnered praise from *True Tunes, Bandoppler,* and *Cornerstone.* She began as lead singer for a Michigan band called Marzuki, which also included **Sufjan Stevens.** After two albums with that group, Stephens moved to Seattle, where she would release her melancholic, evocative solo projects. Stephens has a warm and intimate voice and she frames it with simple acoustic guitar, understated banjo, and upright bass. Electric guitars and accordion serve mainly as flourishes. Stephens' songs focus on failed relationships and other frustrations of life with matters of faith seeping in around the edges. *Bandoppler* said it best: her image of Christ seems to be that of a Savior who sits placidly beside her "listening to her unload like a perfect husband would." Indeed, when she sings overtly of God, she uses the same sensual language as when she sings of men. Regardless of whether Stephens is familiar with the work of feminist theologian Sallie McFague, her favorite image of God is that of "lover." Stephens does not really see herself as part of the contemporary Christian music scene, which she thinks often takes the form of "a safe subculture" that does not represent what Christ's followers are called to become. "I'm a Christian, and I play music," she says, "but I feel more comfortable outside of the box, where things are more dangerous and often more real. This is where God utilizes my honesty to be a light in the darkness."

Stereo Deluxx

Ed Cutler, drums; Lewis Lux, kybrd.; Stacey Tiernan, voc. 1999—*So Clearly* (Organic).

Stereo Deluxx is a female-fronted trio that performs music with a progressive techno sound similar in certain respects to Garbage, **Plumb,** and **Miss Angie.** The band was founded by songwriter Lewis Lux at Greenville College in Illinois where they won the campus-sponsored Battle of the Bands, and subsequently earned a spot on the 1999 *Cornerstone* festival's New Band Showcase. The main attraction of the group, however, is clearly its lead singer, Stacey Tiernan, whose voice and style often recalls Madonna. The opening track, "Don't Know," offers a simple statement of life's possibilities, with a classic combination of Jesus and Robert Frost that Christian artists have been applying since **Country Faith:** "There are two ways I could go / One is wide the other straight and narrow." The second song, "Hunger," is the album's best, sung in a voice that recalls Madonna's best work *(Bedtime Stories).* Lyrically, it expresses the desire for spiritual yearning that would give an empty life meaning: "No other way to carry on / There's nothing I can do / No other love can save me / Let me hunger for you." The next track, "Love Will Grow," is the album's only downer, sung in a fake little-girl voice that is not very appealing. On certain songs ("Either Way," "Rubbish") Tiernan is a bit too obvious at trying to copy Fleming McWilliams (of **Fleming and John**). Still, the album's title track is a radio-friendly worship song, "Good Intentions" is pleasant techno-pop, and "Trapped" is a nice piano ballad.

Lux says that he prefers a metaphorical approach to songwriting that speaks of grace and faith in ways that require something of the listener. "I started a band back in high school and we were heavily into praise and worship music. Everything was blatantly Jesus, Jesus, Jesus, but there was no thinking to it. I decided I wanted to create a band that would be more thought-provoking but still be very ministry-oriented."

For trivia buffs: The enhanced CD for *So Clearly* also includes a video car-racing game with cartoon vehicles named for the band members.

Christian radio hits: "So Clearly" (# 5 in 2000).

Hope Sterling

1988—*The Way Things Are* (Image 7).

A Canadian singer with a name that seems too good to be true, Hope Sterling recorded one album of synthesizer-heavy, bouncy rock songs. *The Way Things Are* was produced by Ry Salmond, who also wrote most of the songs (with his wife, Gayle). The recurrent theme of the work is the disparity between humanity's faithlessness to God and God's faithfulness to people. "Oh the distance between knowing God and loving him," Sterling sings. "Who do you know? Who do you love?"

Steve

Nathan Evans, drums; Rees, bass, kybrd.; Lee Slater, gtr., voc.; Neil Wilson, voc., gtr. 2001—*Falling Down* (ForeFront).

www.steverock.com

Steve is a guitar-oriented quartet from Bristol, England. The sound is hook-and-riff-laden modern pop on the same order as that offered by general market bands like Matchbox 20 and Third Eye Blind. *Falling Down* opens with "Zealous Core," a declaration of perseverance on behalf of the truth. "My Ever My All" is an electric worship song, as is "Fine." The latter song doesn't seem to have enough words: "You're so fine, fine, fine, fine, fine / Yeah, You're so fine, fine, fine, fine, fine." Every song on the album appears to be addressed directly to Christ or God, directing all of the artists' thoughts and concerns to a capitalized You.

Justin Stevens

See **Dime Store Prophets.**

Marsha Stevens

1991—*Free to Be* [with Ken Caton and LeRoy Dystart] (BALM); *The Best Is Yet to Come*; 1993—*I Still Have a Dream*; 1995—*I Will Not Behave Like Prey*; *For Those Who Know It Best: Inclusive Hymns for the Church*; 1997—*No Matter What Way*; 1998—*The Gift Is on the Inside*; *Christian Music and Meditation # 1: Rest*; *Christian Music and Meditation # 2: Joy*; 1999—*The Waiting's Over*; 2000—*In Retrospect: A Double CD Collection*; 2001—*Is This the Real You?*

www.balmministries.com

If **Larry Norman** is to be called "the father of Christian rock," then Marsha Stevens certainly deserves to be known as "the mother of contemporary Christian music," a title that *Christian Century* and others have bestowed upon her. She was the leader of what is considered to be the world's first contemporary Christian music group, **Children of the Day,** and she has continued as a solo artist to produce albums of worship-oriented and edifying adult contemporary pop. As such, she remains the progenitor of what, by 2002, would become the single most popular genre in the contemporary Christian music market. Such artists as **Carolyn Arends, Susan Ashton, Margaret Becker, Amy Grant, Kim Hill, Jennifer Knapp, Crystal Lewis, Cindy Morgan, Nichole Nordeman, Twila Paris, Sandi Patty, Rebecca St. James, Pam Thum, Kathy Troccoli,** and **Jaci Velasquez** all sing in her shadow. Whether they know it or not, Marsha Stevens went before them to prepare the way—against odds that they can scarcely imagine. A pioneer of pioneers, Stevens would be one of the only artists from the early Jesus movement to be still recording and touring full time at the end of the millennium (cf. **Daniel Amos, Phil Keaggy, Larry Norman,** and **Randy Stonehill**). And yet—she would be virtually unknown to potential fans of her music, ostracized by an industry whose limits of ecumenicity had been tried and found wanting. The story of Marsha Stevens in many ways parallels the story of the Jesus movement itself. That revival began with spontaneous waves of spiritual renewal and impassioned piety; it ended with controlled legalism that replaced spiritual agendas with political ones. Whether the Jesus movement of the '70s morphed into the Religious Right of the '80s or was killed by it is a matter of historical perspective. In any case, and whoever may be to blame, by the end of the '70s, the Spirit had been quenched and the revival was over. Stevens, who had perhaps typified that revival better than anyone else, was caught in the transition and became one of the first victims of the new order. Whatever one may think of the issues involved, the Christian music community's rejection of Marsha Stevens remains an ugly smirch on its legacy, and a prime example of its often unacknowledged sectarian character.

Born Marsha Carter, the talented performer wrote what would become **Children of the Day**'s classic hit, "For Those

Tears I Died," when she was just sixteen. One of the most popular songs of the Jesus movement, "For Those Tears I Died" is a moving testimony to God's saving grace, replete with images of baptism and liberation. "I know you're here now and always will be," Stevens sings. "Your love lost my chains and in you I'm free . . . But, Jesus, why me?" The wonderment turns to praise: "Saviour, you've opened all the right doors / And I thank you and praise you from earth's humble shores . . . Take me, I'm yours." And then there is the triumphant chorus, with its touch of personal sentiment reflective of her own vulnerability: "Jesus said, Come to the waters, stand by my side / I know you are thirsty, you won't be denied / I've felt every teardrop when in darkness you cried / And I strove to remind you that for those tears I died." The song was featured on what was destined to become the most important Christian music album of all time, Maranatha's *The Everlastin' Living Jesus Music Concert,* the record that put the Jesus movement revival into high gear, spreading its influence from Calvary Chapel in Costa Mesa throughout the country and beyond. "For Those Tears I Died" became one of the best-known Christian folk songs of the decade (along with Kurt Kaiser's "Pass It On"). It would be translated into numerous languages, recorded by countless artists and, for a time, could be found in practically every evangelical songbook in the country. No one in 1969 could have predicted it would have such influence in the decade ahead—much less that, for two decades beyond that, Christian congregations would be ripping the song out of their hymnals, systematically binding up the pages, and mailing them off to Stevens as a symbol of the hostility they felt toward one who continued to love Jesus and sing his praises when they thought she was no longer entitled to do so.

Like many children of the Jesus movement, Stevens grew up a troubled youth in a family that was involved in a mainline Christian church. But the formal rituals of religion did not fulfill her spiritual needs, and the facade of the "typical American family" hid an ugliness the world was not supposed to see. She remembers childhood as a time of terror that she prefers not to discuss: "Let's just say, when you grow up with an alcoholic in the house, you learn that night is a time to hide." She hid in her bed, curled up beneath the covers, crying the eponymous tears of her most famous song. Then, after attending a beachside evangelistic rally, she joined the thousands of other "hippie Christians" in Southern California who were inviting Jesus into their lives. Full of the Spirit and bursting with newfound love for her Lord, she wrote "the song" for a school project—and also for her sister, Wendy, "to lead her to the Lord." She would introduce both Wendy and a friend named Peter Jacobs to the possibility of having "a personal relationship with Jesus," and the three of them formed **Children of the Day** with Jacobs' musical partner, Russ Stevens, whom Marsha

later married. **Children of the Day** recorded six albums and toured relentlessly. *Come to the Waters* and *With All Our Love* remain Christian music classics—among the best albums ever made within this genre. Marsha and the rest also contributed significantly to *The Praise Album* (Maranatha, 1974), the record that introduced (for better or worse) the most significant liturgical innovation of the twentieth century—the use of simple praise choruses that seemed to combine Eastern religious mantras with Madison Avenue advertising jingles to produce an either infectious or annoying (depending on perspective) style of congregational singing that would come to dominate informal worship services around the world. But all was not well, and after seven years of marriage, Russ and Marsha divorced. "You need to find someone else," he told her one day, and she replied, "You know, I think it might be a woman."

It was. Stevens became the first (and as of 2002, the only) singer in the contemporary Christian music subculture to identify herself publicly as a lesbian. She was completely unprepared for what happened next. "The Christian community excised me from its life," she says. Some people from her church came over to insist that she take a "Jesus Is Lord" sign off her door. Churches started ripping her songs out of their hymnals. When her partner's daughter died of congenital heart disease, she was told it was divine vengeance and that her own children would be next. "It became a favorite sermon illustration repeated up and down the West Coast," Stevens recalls: "God killed our baby because we loved each other." Her record company even began refusing to pay her royalties, citing a clause in her contract that allowed for such exclusion if she "publicly renounced the Christian faith." But that was just it. Stevens had in no way renounced her faith. If she had, the matter would have been simple; the Christian community had endured its losses and knew how to respond to true backsliders or apostates—i.e., with sympathy not hostility. But Stevens appeared to love the Lord (and the church) as much as ever, to trust in God's grace and power, to believe strongly in the Scriptures, to be committed to witness and worship and service . . . she seemed in every way except one to be the model of what evangelical Christianity was all about. *Christian Century* has said that Stevens became "conservative Christianity's worst nightmare—a Jesus-loving, Bible-believing, God-fearing lesbian Christian." She wandered for a while, trying to find a church home. "The churches didn't want me," she says, "but I just missed Jesus too much to stay away." She would go incognito to various congregations and sit in the back pew until somebody recognized her, and then never return.

The acceptance of committed gay and lesbian relationships is a matter of great controversy within American Christianity. By the turn of the millennium, some American denominations would come to a point of encouraging, allowing, or at least tolerating the formal blessing of such relationships. Still, even by 2002, the *majority* of scholars and Christian laity probably still hold to the traditional view, believing that the Bible presents homosexual activity as immoral. The point of relevance for Marsha Stevens is that *she* did not believe her life was immoral; she saw no contradiction between living in a committed and loving relationship with a woman who she considered to be her "life partner" and embracing a biblical, evangelical, and often very conservative expression of Christianity. By 2002 millions of American Christians and quite a few of the country's top biblical scholars would agree with her. Not many of these, however, occupied positions of prominence in the contemporary Christian music industry.

Ostracized from the Christian music subculture as such, Stevens discovered a new ministry—taking the love of Christ to gay and lesbian people for whom the very word *Christian* is often synonymous with "the enemy." Her message is simple and direct: "The gospel is for you. Jesus Christ is for you. Don't let any church rob you of this treasure." She has had to learn to suffer abuse of a different kind. In one concert at a gay pride event, someone interrupted a gospel song by shouting, "Christians hate us!" She stopped, smiled, and said, "Christians may hate us, but Christ doesn't. Don't miss Christ because of Christians." At first, Stevens may seem to face a conundrum analogous to what is sometimes called "the **Larry Norman** phenomenon." Just as Norman was caught between being "too Christian" for the rock and roll crowd and "too rock and roll" for the church, so Stevens would seem to be "too gay" for the Christian community and "too Christian" for the gay and lesbian subculture. But in reality only the former part has proved true; she has, for the most part, been accepted as a contemporary gospel singer in the gay and lesbian community. The *Gay Music Guide,* a totally secular publication, has twice placed her albums on their Twenty Best of the Year list. Reviewer Will Grega once wrote, "If Marsha Stevens is the house band in heaven, even I'll be good!"

Stevens founded a company she calls Born Again Lesbian Music, which yields the neat acronym, BALM. The very name reflects Stevens' full orientation—though she is a lesbian, she is not the least bit ashamed of association with the born-again variety of Christianity that came to fruition during the Jesus movement. She is in fact uncomfortable with the liberal Protestant tradition that might make her a poster child for surviving homophobia. Theologically, she identifies herself as a conservative evangelical, strongly committed to the authority of Scripture and passionate about having a personal relationship with Jesus. Certified as a lay evangelist by her denomination (the Metropolitan Community Church), her ministry has focused increasingly on the growing number of gays and lesbians who are drawn to Christ but have trouble with Christian-

ity as a whole. "I try to get gays to stop focusing on how a few Scripture passages *don't* apply to them and get them to see how much of Scripture *does* apply to them," she says. She counsels gay and lesbian Christians not to be on the defensive but to show the rest of the church the evidence of the Spirit in their lives. "We need to let the love of Jesus shine through us," she says. "The first Christians had to be convinced that God was calling Gentiles as Gentiles—and they weren't convinced primarily by exegesis. Sow to the Spirit, reap the fruit of love. Then, the church will see that this, too, is of God."

The majority of Stevens' songs are grace-oriented proclamations of the gospel that contain no hint of the controversy that attends her life. She sees herself much less as an advocate for gay rights than for Christian hope. Her concerts are like love-ins for Jesus, to whom she sings songs of joy and praise. Her recordings do not dwell on "the issue" though, of course, she does touch on the matter from time to time, and the songs in which she does that are favorites among her supporters. On a song called "I Still Have a Dream," she updates Martin Luther King Jr.'s vision of an inclusive society: "I dream of a land where all children can be free / To grow and mature into what they're meant to be / To love whom they love, with no fear of penalty." In another, she celebrates the realization of that dream in her own community: "Here we are, such a motley crew / Gay and straight, and loving You / No matter what way this world defines us / Nothing is stronger than this tie that binds us" ("No Matter What Way").

Free to Be would represent Stevens' return to recording after a hiatus of twelve years from the **Children of the Day** projects. It contains a number of songs written during the '80s, in addition to a nice new version of "For Those Tears I Died." Perhaps for budget reasons, the record has light orchestration and lo-fi production that contrasts noticeably (and for many critics appealingly) with the ultra slick "slathered on" sound evinced by many adult contemporary products in the general market. Quite a few of the songs ("Falling Star," "Romans 8," "I Am Whole") have a Jesus music feel to them, recalling the folk-pop stylings of **Children of the Day.** "Perfect Love" even has the bouncy, hook-laden marks of a Peter Jacobs song, though it was written by Stevens with Ken Caton. Here and there, Stevens employs some vocal histrionics that showcase abilities rarely in evidence in the old days—notably on the title track, which declares, "Someone new, not someone else, Jesus made of me." A standout track called "Mommy's Song" is sung sweetly to a simple acoustic guitar that recalls Simon and Garfunkel's original take on "Sounds of Silence" (the one on the *Wednesday Morning 3 A.M.* album). Lyrically, it seeks to supplement popular images of God as Father in light of the lesser-known biblical presentation of God as being like a mother (Luke 13:34; Isaiah 49:15): "God I've known you as a Father for all these many years . . . but now I'm asking something new / Will you be my Mommy, too?" *The Best Is Yet to Come* offers a big step up in terms of technical quality, recorded in Nashville with musicians from the Nashville symphony. The album opens with "Celebrate," an exuberant modern hymn of praise that sounds like it could have been included on one of those popular musicals by **Jimmy and Carol Owens** in the '70s. **Children of the Day** Marsha returns on "All Your Names Are Love" and on the album's title track. Stevens also covers a powerful Isaac Watts hymn ("Communion Song"). The album's highlight comes with a song called "Can't We Find a Way?" which she announces is for "the friends I've left behind, who feel bewildered and betrayed / Who will never understand the agonizing choice I've made." Musically, it is a beautiful and flowing piano ballad. Lyrically, it offers Stevens' olive branch to the Christian music community: "Can't we find a way to make a truce of heart, if not of mind? / Can't we find a place of peace, where we can share the bread and wine? / Can't we find some love to salvage, can't we find some joy to share? / Can't we find my hand still fits in yours to say a prayer?"

The Best Is Yet to Come was well titled, for Stevens' next few projects would bring her to a point of consistent quality on a par with albums by the best adult contemporary singers in mainline Christian music. The title song to *I Still Have a Dream* (cited above) would provide her with a big hit within the gay and lesbian community, becoming something of an anthem that brought her to the attention of thousands of persons who had no previous interest in Christian music or the faith that inspired it. "Eastern Gate" anticipates eternal friendships to be enjoyed in heaven, and "Cup of Joy" counts blessings to be experienced on earth—both are fairly traditional Christian songs that would be right at home on Christian Hit Radio programs. *I Still Have a Dream* also includes a new lavish arrangement of "For Those Tears I Died" with some lyrics in Spanish. Its highlight, however, may be the surprisingly country ballad "I'm Blessed." One of Stevens' finest songs, this simple affirmation that "I don't say I'm lucky anymore, I say I'm blessed" is the sort of thing that one would expect to hear from **Susan Ashton** or **Paul Overstreet**. *I Will Not Behave Like Prey* has more high-energy musical-style productions, including "Sing a New Song" and "All Things Are Possible." The album's title track introduces a rock beat and allows Stevens to unveil a new vocal style, with just a bit of growl to it. Lyrically effective, it avoids the overconfidence of **Carman**'s victory-over-the-devil songs while affirming the biblical mandate to resist evil and trust in "the power within" (James 4:7; 1 John 4:4). The album's centerpiece, however, is a powerful track called "The Body of Christ Has AIDS," which plays on the biblical metaphor of the church as "the body of Christ" to bring home Christ's identification with his followers who suffer from HIV. A song called "A

Pastor's Heart" offers Stevens' tribute to her minister, Nancy Wilson, a major influence on her spiritual and theological development.

With *No Matter What Way,* Stevens moved in a new direction, turning out a first-rate album of songs that are both more vocally challenging and more radio pop-oriented than her previous material. The album opens with "No Matter What Way" (cited above), which can only be described as a synth-pop dance track. Not to disappoint adult contemporary fans, she offers a cover of "Faithful Friend" by **Twila Paris** and **Steven Curtis Chapman** and "I'm in Love," a fairly traditional love song to God. In that same vein, "Healing Still" is a song that certainly would have topped the Christian adult contemporary charts if it had only gotten airplay: "Lord, let me never stand between the hungry child and food / Let me never turn away, deciding to exclude / Make me instead a lighted path, a beacon on a hill / Guiding others to your heart where you are healing still." The same theme inspires "Light of the World," which draws on traditional gospel and R&B influences to proclaim "The Light of the World, it is our occupation / No hiding in the shadows in this new vocation / We are the Light of the World." Stevens whoops and wails on the chorus and snarls out the verses in a voice that none of her fans had ever heard her master before. "Is It I?" is actually a rock track based on the discussion of the disciples reported in Matthew 26:20–22. She manages to pull off the imitation of a rock singer by adopting a lower register and allowing electric guitars to replace the usual synthesizers. "Will We Ever Know?" also has a dark, rock-inflected edge that befits its subject matter—the unfathomable loss that attends untimely deaths of promising persons. This is a long way from sweet Marsha, the teenage princess of Calvary Chapel; she credits Tim Searcy in her liner notes for "making me believe I can sing this way." Searcy adds background vocals to the project as does John Stevens, the grown son of Marsha and Russ. As it turns out, John escaped the divine vengeance that some preachers had said would fall upon him and became an impressive singer in his own right. Here, he sings a duet with his mother on "Hearts Aflame," a paean to the potential and power of love written by friends he met at a church camp (James Johnson and Drew Keriakedes). John himself wrote the aforementioned "Is It I?" which expresses with unusual vulnerability his uncertainties over becoming a public Christian singer: as the son of famous Christian musicians, he wonders if he will be able to live up to expectations or if he will become the one to betray not only Christ but the family legacy. The song is lyrically powerful in the same way as **DC Talk**'s "What If I Stumble?" with the added irony that its author does not even seem to realize that the Christian music subculture as a whole had already pegged his mother, not him, as the traitor.

The new "diva Marsha" revealed on *No Matter What Way* reappears on the opening track of *The Waiting's Over*—a roof-raising rendition of the traditional hymn "Revive Us Again" that she acknowledges owes a bit to **Ashley Cleveland**'s performance of the song. Six of the tracks on this album were written by Marsha and John, who by now were performing together on a fairly regular basis. The highlight is "Wash over Me," one of the most beautiful adult contemporary Christian ballads of all time, a prayer for sanctification that expresses a heartfelt desire to return to a state in which the presence of God was clearly felt. Although it was probably the best Christian adult contemporary song of 1999, "Wash over Me" missed all Dove nominations and the like; more tragic, it was never heard by thousands who would have cherished it and whose hearts would have been deeply touched by its message and sentiment. On a lighter note, *The Waiting's Over* includes "Don't Change Me," in which Stevens enters **Steve Taylor** territory and lampoons the common human perspective on sanctification: "I don't want to be looked at strangely / I want to be the same only better / I want to be free without fetter / So you can fill me God, but don't change me." This is sung in a bluesy voice that stands out from her usual style. And then, in case anyone should ever doubt her credentials as a spokesperson for "born again Christianity," Stevens offers a title track that is probably the best altar call invitation song since **Ralph Carmichael**'s "The Saviour Is Waiting." Without mentioning homosexuality or anything else controversial, she just addresses all those who feel lonely, misunderstood, or distant from God and tells them "The waiting's over / God's been there all along and wants you to decide / The waiting's over, Jesus calls to your heart / Will you ask him to come inside?"

There is one other track on *The Waiting's Over* that requires special mention, an autobiographical reflection on childhood that Stevens finally found the courage to offer. She says that she spent over four years writing the song called "Jesus Wept." On the surface, it offers a simple meditation on the famous shortest verse in the Bible: "It tells me in this fallen world not all goes as God planned." But the lyrics also hint at the things she's told reporters she'd rather not talk about: "Wish I could sing in glowing terms of family that I had / My mother led the choir, the preacher was my Dad / But other people never saw what went on as I slept / And all I know for certain is Jesus wept . . . Wept for Mommies unbelieving and screams the church forgets / But long into the deepest night there was a vigil kept / Jesus saw and Jesus knew and Jesus wept."

Stevens, who is also a registered nurse, has studied a good deal of theology and her songs generally evince a higher level of theological awareness than is found in the world of contemporary Christian music at large. She has recorded an album of what she calls *Inclusive Hymns for the Church,* consisting mostly of old favorites with a few pronouns changed to reflect the undefinable gender of God: "(Your) Eye Is on the Sparrow" and "(You're) Leading Me." *The Gift Is on the Inside* is a Christmas collection with Stevens fronting a choir of singers drawn from churches around the country, many of whom lead local ministries to gay and lesbian communities. In addition, Stevens has recorded some ambient albums for Christian meditation. These consist primarily of instrumental music with readings from Scripture, devotions, and prayers. *In Retrospect* is an impressive set of thirty-three well-chosen songs from her career, including three new ones and a remake of "Eastern Gate."

Somewhat ironically, Stevens has continued to represent "the spirit of the Jesus movement" more faithfully than anyone else from that era. In the spontaneous and seemingly carefree days of the early '70s, Christian bands often traveled the country in vans or buses, playing wherever and whenever they could in exchange for a free-will offering and a chance to give their testimonies. Likewise, Stevens spent the '90s in a Winnebago doing some two hundred concerts a year. "I'm living the hippie dream!" she said, eschewing worldly possessions, fame, fortune, and all the rest for the simple opportunity of telling "the old, old story of Jesus and his love." But the opposition persists—always on account of her sexual orientation. In Layfayette, Louisiana, a scheduled concert aroused such a storm of protest that it had to be moved to another location. Here and there, she's tracked by newspapers and TV stations caught up in the novelty of a born-again lesbian and wanting to milk the controversy for all its worth. In general, though, the contemporary Christian music subculture has adopted a different, more insidious response: it pretends she doesn't exist. One might have thought that Stevens would be a figure of controversy within that subculture, that the Christian media would alert their readers to her anomalous character, facilitate discussion between her detractors and supporters, and allow music fans to decide for themselves whether they want to purchase Christian albums by a born-again lesbian or not. That has never happened. No Christian music publication has ever interviewed her or reviewed any of her products (positively or negatively). No song by Stevens has ever been played on any Christian radio station, no album carried by any Christian music store, no article about her or even *reference* to her work has ever been made in any media supposedly devoted to covering the contemporary Christian music scene. Christian music fans—many of whom belong to churches that encourage (or even require) acceptance of gays and lesbians regardless of whether one approves of their chosen lifestyle—have been factored out of the equation: they have no opinion of Stevens because they don't even know she exists. In fact, the Christian music industry has tended to take this shunning a curious step further, pretending that Stevens, in effect, *never* existed. Her

Children of the Day colleagues thus suffer banishment on her account as that group's legacy is all but expunged from the record. In 1996, Maranatha records celebrated their twenty-fifth anniversary with a major piece in *CCM* that all but ignored the group that was their first, best-selling, and most popular act. In 1998, when *CCM* magazine celebrated their twentieth anniversary, they presented a long list of "Where Are They Now?" pieces on various stars of the era, but never mentioned one of the only ones that was still involved in the music industry full time thirty years later. In 1999, three members of **Children of the Day** were invited to perform without Marsha at a Calvary Chapel Jesus music reunion concert. They refused to do it without her and were cut from the program.

When pressed, those who need to justify the lack of acknowledgment for Stevens' work in the Christian music scene usually do so by claiming that she is living in "unrepentant sin." One obvious problem with that rationale is that, normally, unrepentant sin is something that would cause an artist to be denounced, not ignored—it is the *lack of scandal* regarding Stevens that requires explanation. But the unrepentant sin label doesn't really apply for other reasons. Stevens is not stubbornly persisting in behavior that she herself knows to be immoral, or that the church to which she is accountable identifies as immoral. As indicated above, she has the full support of her denomination—and of many other church bodies as well. The issue, then, is not so much that of unrepentant sin as it is a doctrinal dispute. Some church bodies maintain that it is sinful for believers to drink alcoholic beverages or to use artificial forms of birth control and that anyone who does so is living in unrepentant sin. With regard to such issues, the contemporary Christian music industry has typically acknowledged that there is controversy, but has not penalized believers whose behavior does not meet the standards of every denomination. The exclusion of Marsha Stevens from participation in the contemporary Christian music scene reveals a tacit endorsement of particular dogmas far more specific than anything that is ever officially stated. *CCM* magazine and the Gospel Music Association, for instance, both have statements of faith to govern their policies, and these contain nothing that does not find ringing endorsement in Stevens' music, life, and testimony. Accordingly, her exclusion proves that the contemporary Christian music industry in general and the Gospel Music Association in particular are much more beholden to distinctive denominational perspectives than they have ever been willing to admit.

For her part, Marsha Stevens does not betray a shred of bitterness toward any of those who have opposed her and she does not seem to resent her exclusion from the contemporary Christian music culture. She speaks kindly of her former husband, tenderly of colleagues in **Children of the Day,** and respectfully of the leaders at Calvary Chapel and other churches that have dismissed or denounced her. She understands their perspectives, she goes out of her way not to be a "troublemaker," and she tries to put the best possible construction on everyone's behavior. And she thinks that she has found her calling: "Does the church really need *another* middle-aged female Christian singer? Check out the racks! I make contemporary Christian music for the gay, lesbian, bi, and transgendered Christian community. It may be a narrow field but, hey, it's *wide* open!"

Sufjan Stevens

1999—*A Sun Came* (Asthmatic Kitty); *Enjoy Your Rabbit.*

Sufjan Stevens once played alongside **Shannon Stephens** in the Michigan folk rock combo Marzuki. He has also played on Stephens' solo recordings and she returns the favor with a few guest appearances on his debut independent disc. *A Sun Came* blends '60s psychedelic pop with eastern influences to create an experimental and uniquely alternative sound. Stevens' lyrics typically take the form of mystical poetry with spiritual tones drawn from the Psalms. *A Sun Came* opens with "We Are What You Say" featuring these absurdist lines: "We are a servant / We have a song / The side of a beehive / A tabernacle choir / We are the sound working in wars / The bishop is gone to the acolyte shores." *Enjoy Your Rabbit* is completely different and stranger—an experimental blend of electronica that often comes across like a soundtrack to a video game. Thematically, the songs all focus on themes derived from the Chinese zodiac ("Year of the Ox," "Year of the Rooster," etc.).

B. W. Stevenson

Selected: 1980—*Lifeline* (Songbird).

B. W. Stevenson was a one-hit wonder in the general market who reappeared in the Christian market seven years later. Born Louis Stevenson in 1949 in Dallas, Texas, the singer was called Buck Wheat by his friends and just B.W. for short. His first twinge of success came when his song "Shambala" was recorded by the rock group Three Dog Night and became one of that band's biggest all-time hits (# 3 in 1973). Later that same year, Stevenson hit the charts himself with the folk ballad "My Maria," (# 9 in 1973; # 1 on adult contemporary chart). Stevenson continued recording but would not place another song in the Top 40. Then in 1980 he quietly released an album of contemporary Christian music. *Lifeline* features songs written with and by **Chris Christian.** On "One True Way," Stevenson sings, "How could anyone imagine / There is no life beyond / I feel I am a part of God's heaven / And a part of God's Son." Stevenson did not follow the album with any more Christian releases, and on April 28, 1988, he died following heart surgery at the age of thirty-eight.

Pete Stewart

1999—*Pete Stewart* (ForeFront).

www.petestewart.com

Pete Stewart was the front man for the hard-rocking Christian band **Grammatrain.** The latter band was Christian music's most authentic grunge act, a part of the Seattle music scene from the early days. When the band broke up, Stewart moved to Nashville and released an album that would display a musical shift roughly appropriate to the geographical location. In that sense, it actually continues the move from grunge to hard pop that had already begun on **Grammatrain**'s *Flying* album. Stewart's debut record both anticipates new alternative turnings and draws upon neglected riches of the past. Most critics got lost in the **DC Talk** connections: Stewart had played guitar on Talk's *Supernatural* album, and Michael **Tait** from that band produced his solo album and cowrote most of the songs; **Toby McKeehan** also wrote lyrics for two numbers ("Out of My Mind," "Don't Underestimate"). The **DC Talk** influence is noticeable if one listens for it, but a far more dominant influence, suddenly, is Jesus music pioneer **Larry Norman.** Stewart mimics Norman's phrasings and vocal inflections throughout the album, and yet the cribbed style does not come off as any more derivative than, say, Tom Petty's Dylanesque stylings. It is not an annoying parallel at any rate, if only because the actual quality of Stewart's voice is quite different from that of Norman and the material itself is almost as powerful as that of Christian music's brave forebear. The bottom line is that, grunge diehards to the contrary, *Pete Stewart* is a better album than either of the **Grammatrain** projects. Indeed, it was one of the best Christian rock albums of 1999, and deserves to be listed as one of the best of all time. Stewart would later join his producer as a member of the band **Tait.**

Pete Stewart opens with some deceptively hard guitar riffing that makes the album sound for just a moment like it might be some blast-from-the-past late-'70s proto-metal dinosaur. But then a melody line comes in and tames the beast, turning the opening song ("Out of My Mind") into a Normanesque rocker instead. Even the title is a Norman-worthy pun: "Out of My Mind" is not about being insane, but about being blissfully obsessed with God: "I think about you and I can't get you out of my mind." The next song, "Better Off," is more of a midtempo rocker with a catchy tune carrying the verses—the chorus is cast against type as less hooky, but then the whole song takes a surprising turn and builds into a chorus of anthemic harmony. Such atypical song structures combine with interesting instrumentation to give *Pete Stewart* numerous unpredictable yet thoroughly memorable moments. Lyrically, "Better Off" offers several poetic descriptions of conversion and its consequences. Stewart himself would tell *HM* the song was his favorite on

the album, because "it's got that Wallflowers/Tom Petty-blue-collar rock vibe that I love." The song "Uphill Battle" does sound just like a **DC Talk** song (with duet vocals by **Tait**) but it is an energetic, commercial song worthy of inclusion with that band's better material. Here, it adds diversity and provides a dose of new millennium music to offset the otherwise retro feel of the project. "Worship Song" is a beautiful ballad sung in the pinched style Norman used to use for his prettier tunes ("I Am a Servant," "One Way"). And then, in what may be the highlight of the album, Stewart covers **Love Song**'s "Little Country Church" (written by **Chuck Girard** and **Fred Field**). The funky little ditty about a hippie revival in an open-minded rural parish is one of the best Christian rock songs ever written and yet, by 1999, remained largely unknown to many contemporary Christian music fans. Stewart not only introduces the classic song to a new generation but revs it up and performs it the way Creedence Clearwater Revival might have if *they* had all gotten saved back in 1971. Two more excellent songs ("Spinning" and "The Reason Is You") offer theologically sound, inspiring reflections on God's grace. "Up in the Sky" and "The One" are more guitar-heavy hard rock, the latter a crunchy love song for Stewart's wife who apparently is too special to have her valentines hummed to the predictable tune of those dime-a-dozen ballads most artists use for such occasions. *Pete Stewart* closes with a hymnic worshipful song called "Waiting for the Sun" that recalls Norman's "Deja Vu"; it is a gorgeous, churchy conclusion to an album that is obviously geared toward believers.

Christian radio hits: "Better Off" (# 6 in 1999); "Worship Song" (# 20 in 1999).

Stir

Kyle Dietz, drums; Quinton Gibson, gtr.; Bob Gross, voc.; Jason Foures, bass. 1998—*Broken Tongues* (Kalubone).

Stir is a band of '80s metal musicians who, having kept up with the times, or just realizing their style of music was no longer in vogue, developed a new hard grunge sound à la Stone Temple Pilots. Kyle Dietz once drummed for **Seraiah,** Quinton Gibson played guitars for both **Seraiah** and **Whitecross,** and Bob Gross is said to have sung for **Xalt** (though their listed lead vocalist is consistently Scott Doerffler).

The band's debut album title is intended as an acknowledgment (with a nod to the Tower of Babel) that "human words and deeds will always be incomplete without the restoring power of God." The title track traces the history of fallen nations that thought themselves eternal or invincible. "Temple Tatoo" and "Second Hand Savior" seek to expose the futility of feigned religion. In general, the band's lyrics reveal the mature perspective of those who have struggled in the faith for some years. As *Phantom Tollbooth* puts it, "they sing against being legalistic, judgmental, and hypocritical, while encouraging believers in plain language to continue looking up and moving toward eternity." The song "Little Love" is a dark acoustic ballad with a light message—the reminder that it only takes a little love to make a big difference in another person's life. Most impressive, perhaps, is the use of Scripture, which is often woven into the lyrics in ways that are compelling without being trite: "Water into wine / Fish split a thousand times / A broken bottle of ancient sweet perfume / The moral of these three / Is what you have, you see / Given to the Lord for him to use" ("We're a Nation"). The song "Joe's Son" is based on Matthew 13:55, where the townsfolk of Nazareth dismiss Jesus as being "just some local boy." Two of the album's songs ("Joe's Son," "Higher") are reprised in Spanish versions, possibly contributing to the band's huge success in Central America, where they played secular venues. "They don't separate secular from Christian there," Gross says, "so we got in more places and got to play for people who would not necessarily have come see us if we'd been labeled a Christian band."

Stitchie

2000—*Real Power* (Lion of Judah).

Stitchie is a reggae singer who once enjoyed some general market success in that field when he recorded under the name Lieutenant Stitchie. In fact, he holds the distinction of being the first reggae artist ever signed to a major American record label (Atlantic). In 1997, he was involved in a near-fatal car accident and, in reflection on his mortality, "came to know God and determined to sing only for the Lord." *Real Power,* his debut Christian album, presents a set of reggae tracks in two basic styles: blistering fast and slower ballads. Both show some influence of jazz and urban gospel music. Stitchie avoids the use of programmed rhythms and goes for more of a "live in the studio" sound. Lyrically, *Real Power* is dominated by praise and worship numbers, mixed with a few inspirational message songs.

Tom Stipe

1991—*Never Too Late* (Bluestone).

Tom Stipe has made a few significant appearances in the history of contemporary Christian music, though the attention accorded him has never seemed to match his contributions. Even apart from recording, Stipe was a fixture at Calvary Chapel in Costa Mesa, California, where the Jesus movement revival came to a full boil. He led a Tuesday night Bible study, hosted the popular Saturday night concerts, organized a musicians' fellowship group, and often spoke at big Maranatha events. Stipe was known as a major supporter of Maranatha

groups (including some of the smaller ones like **Aslan** and **Good News**). He also served as a DJ at KYMS radio in Santa Ana and got a lot of the bands' music on the air.

Stipe was a founding member of the pioneering Jesus music group **Country Faith,** which unfortunately never recorded an album but did place three songs on the quintessential compilation albums by Maranatha music. Stipe cowrote the song "Two Roads," one of many highlights on what would ultimately come to be regarded as the most important album of Christian music ever recorded, *The Everlastin' Living Jesus Music Concert* (1971). He also cowrote a tune called "The Cossack Song" for **Love Song**—arguably the band's worst song—but redeemed himself with "Come Quickly Jesus," a **Country Faith** song on *Maranatha Two* (1972). And then Stipe made his first (and for eighteen years, only) solo appearance with "Big City Blues" on *Maranatha Three* (1973). The latter track is a rollicking retelling of the Good Samaritan parable in hippie street-people language: "He was strollin' down first avenue / Who do you think he'd run into? / Some boys lookin' for some fast cash / They knocked Willie in the head / Split with all his hard earned bread / Tossed him in the alley with a crash." Willie gets predictably ignored by the institutional preacher-types, but then "Another brother came along / Truckin', shoutin', singin' songs / A Bible and a grin from each ear." The Jesus freak fixes Willie up and witnesses to him and before long there are two Jesus freaks walking the street with the characteristic Bibles and grins. The song is one of many Jesus music classics to come out of Calvary Chapel in the early '70s: it is creative, humorous and holds up well to repeated listening.

After **Country Faith** and this one solo outing, Stipe replaced **Chuck Girard** in what was essentially a second edition of **Love Song,** a band called **Wing and a Prayer.** The latter group also recorded no albums but did place two remarkable songs on the *Maranatha Four* compilation (1974). Stipe wrote one of these ("Old Grey Ford"). The big break came when that band (sans **Tommy Coomes**) hooked up with the legendary **Richie Furay** and subsequently reconstituted itself as **The Richie Furay Band.** Stipe was a member of that band and cowrote some of their songs with Furay. By 1980, he was off the radar screen, but after a decade of obscurity he suddenly resurfaced as the owner of Bluestone Records, home to such bands as **The Violet Burning.** Then in 1991 he finally released the solo album that his fans had been wanting for twenty years.

Never Too Late is a country record that, despite its indie status and connections to the supposedly limited contemporary Christian field, was one of the finest country albums of the year. At a time when Garth Brooks and Bonnie Raitt were pushing a hybrid "new country" sound to the hilt, Stipe recorded a traditional album of hearth and home. *Never Too Late* is a warm album that arrives like a visit from an old friend. It is even sentimental at times but the emotions stirred are unforced. The subtle heart-tugging owes as much to execution as to content, as much to the *sound* of the words as to the words themselves. Stipe's plaintive voice is a perfect vehicle for his reflections on the everyday lives of everyday folk, and John Macy's weepy pedal steel provides appropriate accompaniment to those tender reflections. The opening title track is the most radio friendly, and pretty obviously could have been a hit on country stations if radio play were more merit based or audience driven. On "Down the Road," the artist reflects wistfully on the way his in-laws once viewed him with suspicion when he was courting their daughter—and on the way he and his wife now view their own daughter's suitors. The chorus contains some precious lines understandable to a lot of country folk: "Momma wants to know if he's washed in the blood or just in the water / Daddy wants to know, does he make enough to take his daughter." The song "You Should Have Stood by Her" is a nonjudgmental but powerful commentary on unnecessary divorces: the artist recounts meeting an old acquaintance who had left his wife and children during a difficult period some years back, and who is still paying for that decision with "something that time hadn't healed." **Kelly Willard** provides a guest vocal on "Would It Turn Out This Way," probably the best song ever written about spousal abuse. Instead of dwelling on the usual terror of physical abuse, the singer finds a way to describe an even greater hurt, namely the trauma of having to leave a damaged man in spite of the great love she continues to feel for him. More specifically Christian convictions are expressed in the gospel-tinged "Sweet Forgiveness" and in the worshipful "Living Sacrifice."

As of 2001, Stipe was serving as pastor of Crossroads Calvary Chapel Church in Denver, Colorado—just down the road from Boulder where the Calvary Chapel congregation is led by his old pal, Furay.

Miranda Stone

1998—*Brave* [EP] (Earthdress); 1999—*I, 2 Trash a Few . . . 99, 100.*

Miranda Stone is an aggressive Canadian folksinger who likes to describe her music as "folk-punk." She has made two independent albums that captured the affections of *True Tunes* and *The Phantom Tollbooth.* The *Brave* EP features five songs including the electric folk-rock number "Nevertheless the Dog." The strangely titled *1, 2 Trash a Few . . . 99, 100* was recorded live in a Toronto bar and, in addition to several songs, includes a good deal of stage chatter, banter with the audience, and even a band member reading a children's story aloud ("Mr. Bad Cold Germ"). Stone's fans consider her poetic lyrics to be incisive and direct, replete with lines like "Sometimes I'm scared I've

let my love turn selfish and unkind" ("Silverwind"). Oblique biblical and religious references surface here and there. On "3 Stories," she sings about "The dying son of man who kept silent for his cause / When everyone he loved scorned everything he was." On "Don't You Cry Out," she references Joseph's dilemma when faced with Mary's pregnancy: "What could you think to calm you? What was sitting on your chest all night?" Although she has played at the *Cornerstone* Christian music festival, Stone prefers not to call herself a Christian artist. Her music, she says, is more "pro-God than Christian," meaning that it is intended for a wider set of people than just those who subscribe to the Christian creed.

Stonefly

Matt Brown, bass; Mike Clayton, drums; Rusty Forgey, voc., gtr. / Reid Smith, gtr. (+ 1999). 1999—*Stonefly* (Rocket Dog).

Stonefly is a modern rock band from Yakima, Washington. They became the first act to be signed to the fledgling Rocket Dog label and recorded a debut album shortly before adding a second guitarist for full-time touring. Their sound reveals a penchant for basic three-chord rock and roll, augmented with occasional jazz or psychedelic doodling. The closest aural comparison is probably early **PlankEye,** though the band really does have a sound of its own. Lyrically, the songs on *Stonefly* vary between numbers that deal with matters provoking teen angst (girls, or whatever) and ones that offer specifically Christian statements about spirituality. "Hypocrite" provides a self-incriminating confession of inadequacy, while "Search" offers the concurrent promise to do better. "Forest Hut" goes a bit overboard with self-loathing as Rusty Forgey wallows in misery over his inability to control lustful thoughts ("My mind gets so dirty baby / Whenever you walk by me"). The album closes with a traditional worship ballad, "Bow Down."

Randy Stonehill (a.k.a. **Stonehill**)

1971—*Born Twice* (One Way); 1973—*Get Me out of Hollywood* (Phonogram); 1976—*Welcome to Paradise* (Solid Rock); 1980—*The Sky Is Falling;* 1981—*Between the Glory and the Flame* (Myrrh); 1983—*Equator;* 1984—*Celebrate This Heartbeat;* 1985—*Love beyond Reason;* 1985—*Stonehill* [EP] (independent); 1986—*The Wild Frontier* (Myrrh); 1988—*Can't Buy a Miracle;* 1989—*Return to Paradise;* 1990—*Until We Have Wings;* 1992—*Wonderama;* 1993—*Stories;* 1994—*The Lazarus Heart* (Street Level); 1996—*Our ReCollections* (Word); 1998—*Thirst;* 1999—*Where the Woodbine Twineth: The Cottage Tapes, Vol. 1* [with Larry Norman] (Solid Rock).

www.randystonehill.com

A pioneer of the Jesus movement, Randy Stonehill will always be best remembered for his classic *Welcome to Paradise* album, though it is certainly not his only product of merit. Stonehill has a pinched nasal voice (critics often say "reedy") and he has typically performed folk-rock-and-blues songs in a style that consists of equal parts Elvis Costello, Randy Newman, James Taylor, and Neil Young. With a repertoire spanning thirty years and fifteen major albums, he has been able to try out a variety of sounds, but much of his material fits into three broad categories. He is perhaps best known for acoustic pop ballads that offer incisive reflection on the human condition, often expressing compassion and empathy for suffering individuals and/or anger and frustration over the causes of such affliction. He has also done quite a few songs with a more heartland rock/rockabilly sound to them, typically putting this energy at the service of a faith anthem. And then there are what fans call the "Uncle Rand songs": wacky, humorous ditties that satirize foibles of popular culture in a way that would also be typical of **Steve Taylor.** By the year 2002, Stonehill would be one of the only early Jesus music stars to be still recording and performing thirty years after they and a handful of others created what would come to be called "contemporary Christian music" (cf. **Daniel Amos, Larry Norman, Phil Keaggy, Marsha Stevens**).

A native of San Jose, California, Stonehill formed his first band at the age of fifteen. In 1970, he performed the lead role in the Christian musical *Show Me!* (Impact, 1971) by **Jimmy Owens,** which included singing the duet "Long Distance Love" with a very young **Jamie Owens (Collins).** He also cowrote (with **Keith Green** and Todd Fishkind) the classic Christian song "Your Love Broke Through," a tune that would become a signature song for **Phil Keaggy.** In 1972, his song "I Love You" was prominently featured in the film *Time to Run,* a movie distributed by the Billy Graham Evangelistic Association that was a favorite with the Jesus people. **Larry Norman** subsequently covered that song on *In Another Land.* As a result, by 1976, Stonehill probably had "hipness credentials" in the Jesus music subculture second only to Norman himself. It was that year that he released what is unanimously regarded as one of the greatest Christian albums of all time.

Stonehill's ultimately feisty relationship with Norman formed a backdrop for the birth and development of early Jesus music. In 1969, Norman had invited the sixteen-year-old Stonehill to come to Los Angeles. The established star, who had already enjoyed a nationwide hit as the lead singer of People and who had just released what is usually considered to be the world's first Christian rock album *(Upon This Rock),* believed he could help the promising youth break into the music business. Stonehill met Norman through the latter's sister, who had been his girlfriend for a time (he would later admit that his feelings for her had more than a little to do with his accepting the invitation). He did lay down one condition: "As long as you promise not to tell me about Jesus—I'm sick of hearing it." All the same, Stonehill was introduced to the vibrant faith of active Christians—in the Norman household and at College House, a youth outreach of Don Williams' Hollywood Presbyterian Church. He also got a bit of a wake-up call when he was arrested on drug charges and hauled off to jail in handcuffs. Many factors came together, but on August 12, 1970, Norman and Stonehill were washing dishes together in the kitchen, and Norman asked Stonehill, "How are you doing?" Stonehill says he felt the simple question reveal a hollowness within him. Norman asked, "Do you want to pray?" and he said, "No." Norman asked a second time, and then a third, and Stonehill relented. Norman gave him words to say: "Lord, I don't know how to pray. I don't even know if I believe in You . . . but if this outrageous love You demonstrated on the cross has anything to do with my life, I want it." When he prayed this prayer, Stonehill says, "a great weight left me—it was a weight I didn't even know I had been carrying—it was a very physical feeling." After this experience, which he would come to regard as his conversion—the moment at which he was "saved" or "born again"—Stonehill joined Norman in playing Christian folk-rock songs at churches, coffeehouses, and college campuses. At the time, he says, "we were completely alone. Nobody was doing Christian rock music." By the same token, their songs and testimonies received a surprising welcome, as the forces that would soon erupt into the Jesus movement revival began to come together. Stonehill reports, "Kids were telling us, 'Look, I love the Lord, but culturally, the church leaves me cold'." In 1999, **Larry Norman** would release a CD of sixteen songs that he and Stonehill recorded during this time called *Where the Woodbine Twineth: The Cottage Tapes, Vol. 1.*

Eventually, Norman and Stonehill would call on **Pat Boone,** the only person in the entertainment industry who they thought might understand what they were about. Stonehill would later recall the incongruous meeting by saying that they sat in the suave performer's parlor with his numerous daughters (the ultimately famous **Boone Girls**) all seated together on another couch. "They sat lined-up according to age, just like a scene out of *The Sound of Music,*" he says. "And they kept looking back and forth at us and their father, as if to say, 'Are they *real* hippies, Daddy? And can we keep them for pets?' " In any case, Boone did understand what they were about and fronted them money to record their first albums.

Stonehill has said that *Born Twice* "was recorded for eight hundred dollars—and sounds like every penny of it!" Fewer than ten thousand copies were pressed, making it a prized (and valuable) collector's item. Side One of the record consists of a half dozen acoustic songs, including the earliest version of "I Love You" and another classic track called "Norman's Kitchen," which refers to the conversion story reported above, albeit with the use of countercultural metaphors ("I got stoned in

Norman's kitchen"). Also included is "I Need You," a song from *Show Me!* Side Two is live tracks recorded with a full electric band at Westmont College in 1971, including such covers as "Put Your Hand in the Hand" and "He's Got the Whole World in His Hand." The album actually exists in multiple versions. One pressing includes "side one" on both sides. Another substitutes a rocking version of Norman's fabulous "Christmastime" (with extra Stonehill-penned lyrics) for the song "He Is a Friend of Mine." In 1972, Stonehill went to England where he would record a "secular album" called *Get Me out of Hollywood,* a collection of mainstream pop songs and ballads, most focusing on romance and some displaying his acerbic wit. A song called "Vegetables" was incorporated into the *Lonesome Stone* rock opera (cf. entry for **The Sheep**), and two songs, "Puppet Strings" and "Jamie's Got the Blues," would later turn up on other Stonehill projects (*Welcome to Paradise* and *The Sky Is Falling,* respectively). The album was not released and most of the copies were apparently destroyed, making it the Holy Grail of Christian record collectors for some time. In 1999, **Larry Norman** finally brought it out on CD on his private Solid Rock label.

Welcome to Paradise is the undisputed masterpiece. Produced by **Larry Norman** for his Solid Rock label, the album opens with what would become Stonehill's signature song: "King of Hearts." The song showcases the artist's melodic pop style and offers a parable of a lost soul searching for life. "The Winner (High Card)" has a country rock feel and exposes the empty confidence of the materialistic in a manner befitting the unusual perceptiveness of '60s youth. That song and "Keep Me Runnin' " are atypical of mid '70s Christian rock in that they describe the emptiness and alienation of lives apart from Christ without tidying everything up with a too-obvious moral or conversion testimony. "Song for Sarah" is a ballad of startling tenderness that, twenty-five years later, would remain one of the most beautiful songs that Stonehill or any other Christian musician would ever write. It begins, "Sarah, can I love you, will you open up the door? / I know you've heard that misused word a lot of times before." The song is apparently directed to the woman who would become his first wife. "Good News" is a raucous party song that celebrates lives transformed by the gospel. "Lung Cancer" offers a humorous look at the posture of those teenagers who think that they're being *counter*cultural when they yield to the pressures of the tobacco industry. Liner notes for the *Welcome to Paradise* album betray the desperation of early Jesus music to establish legitimacy by way of celebrity name-dropping. The notes describe Stonehill as "a professional who has sat in on sessions with Paul McCartney and Todd Rundgren and hummed a few bars with Robert Plant, Ringo Starr, and Rod Stewart." Stonehill would later admit these were half truths and exaggerations—

he had been a visitor at those recording sessions (without playing at them) saying, "I did meet those people at a party once and I did do some singing there, but it was totally casual. . . . Larry is such a romantic that he thought, well this is sort of true, so we'll put it down." In 1988, a *CCM* critics' poll would list *Welcome to Paradise* as the Number Three Christian album of all time; ten years later, a similar poll would still place it at Number Thirteen.

In 1977, Stonehill would guest as a fast-talking DJ on Norman's humorous parody album *Streams of White Light into Darkened Corners.* He would also make one more album for Norman's Solid Rock label, a diverse but inconsistent product called *The Sky Is Falling.* The latter album is strongly devoted to social commentary, as is most evident on "Through the Glass Darkly," which offers a backward glance at the failed agenda of the Kennedy era and the hippie movement ("all our heroes die in motel rooms and motorcades"). "The Great American Cure" overs a sardonic critique of TV, and "Teen King" takes a crack at celebrity rock stars (with specific inspiration provided by The Eagles' Don Henley and Glenn Frey). Otherwise, "Emily" is a tribute to Stonehill's late sister and "Counterfeit King" is a spiritual warfare piece directed against Satan.

The early '80s were a hard time for Stonehill. *The Sky Is Falling* was not well received, and about the time that it was released, the artist divorced. Also around this time, Stonehill and Norman had a falling out and their friendship came to an end. The exact reasons for the fracture may not be relevant (or knowable), but the obvious concern involved objections to what was perceived as Norman's heavy-handed control of the artists connected to Solid Rock (cf. **Daniel Amos**). As historian David Di Sabatino reports, "the Solid Rock Artist Agency crumbled amidst a maelstrom of financial controversy and innuendo." The deterioration of their friendship and prolonged lack of reconciliation would become something of a scandal within the Christian music scene. In 1981, Stonehill told *CCM* that he left Solid Rock, in part, because he "had great concern about many of the ethical practices at the company." In 1990, he referred to a 1989 interview with Norman in that same magazine by saying, "What really troubled me was him trying to smooth it over . . . because for him to associate with me or my friends sounds like we applaud or embrace who he is and what he does, and I just say, no. Understand, the old days had some special stuff, and I love Larry, but I'm completely out of fellowship with him." In 1998, a profile of Stonehill by James Long in *CCM* spoke repeatedly of "a friend" who had figured greatly in the artist's early career, taking such strained care not to mention that friend by name that the whole piece seemed weirdly oblique to those who didn't know what was up and childishly petty to those who did. Similarly, as late as 2001, Stonehill's biography on his official website would make no mention of Norman or of the undeniable influence that the latter artist had on his life and career. Stonehill's fans, if not Stonehill himself, remained bitter over the fact that Norman retained the rights to Stonehill's two out-of-print Solid Rock albums and did not make them available to a clamoring public. But then, suddenly, in the summer of 2001, Stonehill and Norman appeared together in a surprise reunion at the annual *Cornerstone* music festival, indicating that some sort of reconciliation had apparently occurred. And, in 2002, *Welcome to Paradise* finally was released on CD with song-by-song commentary from Stonehill himself.

Between the Glory and the Flame and *Equator,* produced by **Terry Taylor,** feature **Tom Howard** and the boys from **Daniel Amos** in supporting roles. Musically, *Between the Glory and the Flame* juxtaposes electric rock songs ("Giving It Up for Love," "Fifth-Avenue Breakdown") with acoustic folk-rock and a few tributes to the '60s ("Rainbow" is psychedelic, recalling the Beatles' "Strawberry Fields Forever"). "Song for My Family" is a public attempt to evangelize his parents, who Stonehill said in interviews "still aren't saved yet"; this was a common concern among the Jesus people (cf. **Keith Green**'s "Song for My Parents"). "Grandfather's Song" is also a memorable ballad. "Christine" revisits America's obsession with TV (and the consequent blurring of fantasy and reality) by portraying the thoughts of a man who has fallen in love with a newscaster: "My so-called friends they say that I'm a fool / They say that you don't even know I'm there / Oh but they don't see that magic twinkle in your eye / That special one that says how much you care." A song called "Die Young" offers a satirical statement of the sort of nihilism that artists like Neil Young ("It's better to burn out than to fade away") and AC/DC ("I'm on the highway to hell") were expressing as their philosophies of life at the time. "Find Your Way to Me" is a straightforward evangelistic song, a hymn of invitation built on a reassuring promise of Christ. *Equator* continues to parody ridiculous aspects of popular culture with "American Fast Food" ("we're undernourished but overfed") and the self-explanatory "Cosmetic Fixation." The former presages the **Lost Dogs**' "Bad Indigestion," and the latter, Paul Westerberg's "Mannequin Shop." Uncle Rand also puts in an appearance on "Big Ideas (In a Shrinking World)." Such songs display Stonehill's wackiness with such touches as dueling bagpipes, elf voices, operatic singing, '50s sax, and even a well-placed burp. But for many the highlight of *Equator* would come in a more serious moment, the artist's poignant reflection on "Turning Thirty." The song "Even the Best of Friends" offers commentary on the falling out with Norman. "Light of the World" is standard Christian radio fare, and the reggae stand-against-the-devil anthem, "Shut De Do," is cute enough to be a children's song. In keeping with the global theme of the album's title, "China" offers an expression of sympathy for inhabitants of Communist-ruled China.

Stonehill's next two projects were both produced by Barry Kaye and have a more slick sound than anything he had done previously. *Celebrate This Heartbeat* offers a handful of mostly acoustic soft rock, pop songs, with one track clearly standing out from all the rest. "Who Will Save the Children?" (performed here as a duet with **Phil Keaggy**) was written by Stonehill as a result of his work with the charitable hunger relief organization Compassion International. When he first played it for his wife, Sandi, she said, "This may be the best song you will ever write." She could be right. The title song to *Celebrate This Heartbeat* is a flagrantly Beatlesque song, with Stonehill mimicking John Lennon's voice. "Still Small Voice" and "When I Look to the Mountains" are worshipful; "Modern Myth" attacks popular concepts regarding the inherent goodness of humanity. *Love beyond Reason* features "The Gods of Men" and "I Could Never Say Goodbye," two strong cuts. The first takes Stonehill out of his stuck-in-the-'60s mode long enough to deliver a Duran Duran-style '80s rock song that, despite its ridiculously sexist title (for 1985!), successfully deflates the allure of fame, fortune, and other false idols. The latter is a gorgeous love song to God sung as a duet with **Amy Grant.** *Love beyond Reason* also includes Stonehill's own version of the now-classic "Your Love Broke Through," but one of the more widely noticed songs would be the anthemic "Angry Young Men," on which Stonehill counters the meek and mild image of Christianity: "He wants some angry young men / Ones who can't be bought / Ones who will not run from a fight . . . Rest assured when Jesus comes again / He'll be looking for some angry young men." Note, again, the clueless retention of sexist (and ageist) language, a good five years after most churches had purged their hymnals and liturgies of such references. More satisfying to critics are "Bells" (with background vocals by **Richie Furay**) and the simple "Hymn." *Love beyond Reason* was the first Christian album to be released as a long-form video. Around the same time it came out, Stonehill recorded five secular songs that he hoped might be shopped to studios to see if any mainstream artists would want to cover them. The demo tape ended up being released as a self-titled EP by Stonehill in Britain. One of the five songs, "Dangerous Heart," was recorded by Olivia Newton-John, but never released. It was later performed on the NBC TV program *The Midnight Special* by **Debby Boone** with Stonehill in her backing band.

The next two projects would be produced by Dave Perkins (of **Chagall Guevara** and **Passafist**) and have more of a kick-out-the-jams rock feel to them. The title track to *The Wild Frontier* is Stonehill's finest post-*Welcome to Paradise* rock and roll moment. With a sound and theme similar to **Steven Curtis**

Chapman's "The Great Adventure"—but with much more authentic grit—the song owes an obvious debt to Bruce Springsteen. "The Hope of Glory" sounds like a **Lost Dogs** outtake ten years too soon: a country-tinged hymn that has the same Beach Boys/Eagles hybrid sound that **Terry Taylor** would perfect for that seminal group a decade later. The wonderfully titled "Here Come the Big Guitars" is another rock and roll delight, with Peter Noone (i.e., Herman of Herman's Hermits) joining such Christian music notables as **Gary Chapman, Peter Case** and **Tonio K.** on the background vocals. "Dying Breed" and "Defender" express the artist's Christian convictions with strident boldness bordering on militancy (cf. "Angry Young Men"). Overall, *The Wild Frontier* is Stonehill's finest rock album, and it may be his second-best overall project. It also includes one ballad, the heart-rending "Evangeline," and a cover of The Youngbloods' "Get Together." *Can't Buy a Miracle* opens with another full rock blast, "It's Now," a call to repentance. It features "Don't Break Down," with supporting vocals from **Phil Keaggy,** and "Brighter Day" with **Gary Chapman.** A number of songs (notably, "O How the Mighty Have Fallen") reference the televangelist scandals of the late '80s. "Coming Back Soon" is an expression of God's devotion for those on earth for whom Christ may seem absent but for whom he will soon return. In 1988, Stonehill also played with **Phil Keaggy** in the latter's band for *Sunday's Child* and cowrote songs for that album including the hit title song.

Return to Paradise seeks to recapture the magic of Stonehill's masterpiece, with sparse production by **Mark Heard** that allows Stonehill's acoustic guitar a more prominent place in the mix. The song "Christmas at Denny's" is a poignant ballad for the lonely, inspired by his observation that some folk spend the holiday hunched over coffee at an all-night diner because they have no one with whom to share the season. "I wrote the song thinking about what Jesus might say or do if He was sitting with those people," he says. Heard would also produce *Until We Have Wings,* which is a half-live album with one side of new studio songs. Of the new material, "Faithful" represents Stonehill's first full-fledged entry into the adult contemporary genre, while "Didn't It Rain?" has a more bluesy gospel feel. Somewhat shocking, "Can Hell Burn Hot Enough?" is a "Masters of War"-era Dylan rant against the misery that American corporations produce in Third World countries.

On *Wonderama,* Stonehill would work with producer **Terry Taylor** again and return to the amalgamation sound of *Between the Glory and the Flame* and *Equator.* Thus, the album again includes satirical, looney songs, heart-rending ballads, and experimental mood pieces all mixed together with the eclectic eccentricity for which Taylor is famous. The disc opens with a Magical-Mystery-Tour-fantasyland title track, a song that suggests that everything that follows is to be received through the

eyes of a child. "Great Big Stupid World" and "Barbie Nation" poke fun at the foibles of modern society—and the former provides some energetic, catchy pop 'n' roll to boot. "I Will Follow" (not a **U2** cover) is a faith anthem, and "The Lost Parade" is a moody piece with tortured vocals set against Salvation Army Band horns. "Rachel Delevoryas" tells the story of a misfit woman who found music to be an outlet for expression. "Sing in Portuguese" is a testimony to the romantic commitment of Stonehill's grandparents.

Two albums were officially released under the name "Stonehill" (as opposed to Randy Stonehill), which made the artist sound like a group. These were also put out on the semi-independent label (Street Level) that Stonehill founded in 1994. *The Lazarus Heart,* produced by Jimmie Lee Sloas of **The Imperials** and **Dogs of Peace,** was announced as a comeback album, though the artist had never actually gone anywhere. It would, however, prove amenable to Christian radio and bring him to the attention of a new audience. Stonehill plays with an all-star cast of musicians (**Rick Elias, Phil Keaggy, Phil Madeira**) and vocalists (**Bob Carlisle, Gary Chapman, Riki Michele**). More notably, he turns to numerous Christian artists for help with songwriting. "I Turn to You" was written with **Cheri Keaggy** and is sung with Christine Denté of **Out of the Grey.** "In Jesus' Name" (written with Madeira) is performed with **Michael W. Smith.** A song called "That's Why We Don't Love God" is especially perceptive and theologically profound: "We mask the nakedness of our mortality / Cloaked in this poison pride / And the illusion of control / We need the gift of grace more than the air we breathe / But as it draws us near / Still it repels our stubborn souls." *Thirst* (produced by **Rick Elias**) features "Fire," another Beatlesque romp that builds in intensity. "Little Rose" (cowritten with **David Edwards**) is about a girl helped through Compassion International, and "Sleeping" addresses the apathy with which comfortable people ignore the plight of the rest of the world. "Angels' Wings," "Every Heartbeat Is a Prayer," and "Lonely House" deal with the day-to-day struggles of believers trying to live faithfully for God. The latter of these is especially vulnerable, dealing rather intimately with problems in the Stonehill's own marriage as a way of addressing (in his words) "those times when two people who are deeply in love can nevertheless feel estranged from each other." "Hand of God," a testament to divine providence, is sustained musically by the surprising presence of Scottish guitarist Stuart Adamson (from the '80s band Big Country). Again, the lyrics are both orthodox and provocative: "Can you embrace your sadness / Taste the salt of your tears / Start laughing when you cry / 'Cause it means that you're alive / And thank God you're standing here." *True Tunes'* John J. Thompson has said, "Stonehill's recorded output in the '90s was flawless, yet his audience dwindled to die-hard fans." As of

2001, he was said to be working on a children's project with **Terry Taylor.**

Our ReCollections is a compilation of songs from the nine albums spanning *Between the Glory and the Fame* through *Wonderama*. Although it can only offer one or at most two songs per record, the very best songs are all included and the full spate is representative of Stonehill's various styles. *Stories* is also a compilation album.

For trivia buffs: Randy Stonehill had a role in the 1972 monster movie *Son of Blob* [a.k.a. *Beware! The Blob*]. He serenades Cindy Williams (of later *Laverne and Shirley* fame) with a song he has written, and then the Blob eats him.

Christian radio hits: "The Glory and the Flame" (# 3 in 1982); "Turning Thirty" (# 4 in 1983); "When I Look to the Mountains" (# 7 in 1984); "Who Will Save the Children?" [with **Phil Keaggy**] (# 11 in 1984); "I Could Never Say Goodbye" [with **Amy Grant**] (# 4 in 1985); "Your Love Broke Through" (# 6 in 1985); "The Gods of Men" (# 7 in 1986); "The Hope of Glory" (# 12 in 1987); "Coming Back Soon" (# 15 in 1988); "Brighter Day" (# 10 in 1988); "Faithful" (# 9 in 1990); "Born to Love" (# 24 in 1991); "I Turn to You" (# 1 for 2 weeks in 1994); "In Jesus' Name" (# 11 in 1995); "Hand of God" (# 15 in 1998).

Noel Paul Stookey (and **Bodyworks**)

Personnel for Bodyworks: Denny Bouchard, kybrd.; Jimmy Nails, gtr.; Kent Palmer, perc.; Karla Thibodeau, voc. By Noel Paul Stookey: 1971— *Paul And* (Warner Bros.); 1973—*One Night Stand;* 1977—*Real to Reel* (Neworld); 1978—*Something New and Fresh.* By Noel Paul Stookey and Bodyworks: 1979—*Band and Bodyworks;* 1982—*Wait'll You Hear This* (NewPax); 1984—*There Is Love Anthology;* 1985—*State of the Heart;* 1990—*In Love beyond Our Lives* (Gold Castle).

www.noelpaulstookey.com

Noel Paul Stookey (b. 1937) is best known to the world as the Paul in Peter, Paul, and Mary and as the solo performer whose beautiful "Wedding Song" (# 24 in 1971) would become a staple of many marriage celebrations throughout the last three decades of the twentieth century. Ex- or aging Jesus freaks remember him also as the first and most prominent celebrity convert who shared the experiences of the Jesus movement with them and would later help them interpret what happened (to himself, to the nation, and to music) as a **John Fischer**-like elder statesman for the cause. A smaller number of appreciative fans (a set that overlaps with both of the above groups) realized that he had a career in contemporary Christian music throughout the '70s and '80s. Stookey has generally kept a low profile as a solo performer since his 1971 general market debut (the only album listed by the artist in *The New Rolling Stone Encyclopedia of Rock and Roll*) largely because he found nonsuccess to be a life more conducive to his spiritual priorities, i.e., his family and his own peace of mind. Still, as of 2002, he was still performing, both as a solo artist (usually in

churches) and as a part of Peter, Paul, and Mary (often at fundraisers for symphony orchestras, PBS stations, or socially conscious philanthropies).

Originally from Baltimore, Stookey moved to New York City in 1959. He worked there as a stand-up comic before being invited to join folk singer Peter Yarrow and Broadway vocalist Mary Travers in the trio that would become one of the most successful folk acts of all time. The group's self-titled debut album in 1962 went to Number One on the charts and stayed there for seven weeks. Although it would produce only two Top 40 hits ("Lemon Tree," # 35, and "If I Had a Hammer," # 10), the album would remain on *Billboard*'s Top 100 chart for over three and a half years. For a decade, Peter, Paul, and Mary and Simon and Garfunkel were the two folk acts that really mattered in American music. The group's best-known song would turn out to be the children's tune, "Puff (The Magic Dragon)" (# 2 in 1962). An imaginative *Newsweek* article suggested the song might contain veiled references to drugs and, against all odds, the very G-rated, Walt Disney-ish fantasy song became a center of controversy. Marijuana cigarettes came to be called "magic dragons" in hippie slang because of the controversy (they weren't called that before it), producing a cyclical effect according to which later generations assumed the song was *obviously* about drugs because, duh, that's what a *magic dragon* is. The trio also had a knack for discovering unknown songwriters and helping them to become famous or at least historically significant. In 2002, "If I Had a Hammer" would remain one of the general public's only contact points with folk legend Pete Seeger, who wrote thousands of songs but is otherwise remembered only for "Turn! Turn! Turn!" (because The Byrds sang it). Later, Peter, Paul, and Mary would launch the careers of Gordon Lightfoot by recording his "For Lovin' Me" (# 3 in 1965) and "Early Mornin' Rain," and John Denver by taking his "Leaving on a Jet Plane" to Number One in 1969. But even more significantly, in 1962, the group recorded "Blowin' in the Wind" (# 2 in 1962) and brought **Bob Dylan** to the attention of a national audience. Throughout the '60s, Peter, Paul, and Mary would remain (along with The Byrds, again) one of the main interpreters of Dylan's material for the masses; thousands of people who couldn't abide Dylan's singing came to know such songs as "Don't Think Twice, It's Alight" (# 9 in 1962), "The Times They Are a'Changin'," "Too Much of Nothing" (# 35 in 1967), and "I Shall Be Released" only in the versions that Peter, Paul, and Mary delivered. In that regard, PP&M were sometimes dubbed "folk popularizers." *The Rolling Stone Album Guide* would say that their "early gift was teasing a mainstream audience slightly leftward into music more rootsy than AM radio and, indirectly, into politics of an earnest liberal stripe." The latter comment reflects the trio's involvement in a number of humanitarian causes that were considered liberal at the time—the most notable being the civil rights movement. Peter, Paul, and Mary were part of the historic March on Washington and, indeed, they were the opening act for Dr. Martin Luther King Jr.'s "I Had a Dream" speech, singing "If I Had a Hammer" from the Capitol steps.

Like Joan Baez and early Simon and Garfunkel, Peter, Paul, and Mary often recorded and performed religious songs, many of which were traditional spirituals or just gospel folk songs. Their 1964 album *Peter, Paul, and Mary in Concert* features a sterling version of "Jesus Met the Woman at the Well" and a novelty take on the spiritual "Oh, Rock My Soul" (a.k.a. "Bosom of Abraham"). The group would even have a Top 40 hit with its version of the hymn "Go Tell It on the Mountain" (# 33 in 1964). Stookey himself wrote two songs for the group's albums that have explicitly Christian lyrics: "Early in the Morning" and "Very Last Day." But he would later say of this: "Maybe God used me, but I certainly was not a willing servant then. I just went for all the clichés. I didn't know that God was alive."

In the latter half of the '60s, Stookey, like many disillusioned idealists, set out on a spiritual quest. "I felt as if my life were straight out of the amusement park scene in *Pinocchio*," he would later explain. "So alluring. I traveled first class. I had limos waiting for me at every airport. I was protected. But those things break down the human contact that you have under normal conditions. . . . in the long run, that course is detrimental; you lose touch with reality and you only play at being genuine." Stookey's quest had him practicing meditation, smoking pot (to intensify his senses), reading the Tibetan Book of the Dead, and studying the spiritualist teachings of Edgar Cayce. In a 1967 interview with radio personality Scott Ross (cf. entry on **Nedra Ross**) he discussed his emptiness:

> For people who haven't begun "the search" yet or who don't know what I'm talking about when I say 'the search,' it's like the first time it hits you that the bowling league and the TV dinners and the mindlessness of *Gomer Pyle* are not where it's at. Somehow, there's a big hole inside you and you get moments when you fill it up, when just everything seems to make sense: sometimes it's necking with your old lady; sometimes it's when somebody tells you something that's just a mind-blowing event; and then there's all sorts of occasional glimpses . . . like, I was driving along in the car, I guess it was about a year and a half ago, and I said, "Hell . . . I don't know what I'm looking for; I haven't found it yet."

The talk with Ross, who had become a Christian, was one in a series of revelatory events for Stookey. Ross shared his personal faith with the singer, who would later maintain that he didn't

understand much of what was said but recognized that his interviewer knew God in a way that he did not.

Just prior to the Ross interview, Stookey had sought enlightenment from **Bob Dylan.** "Fame, fortune, love, and humanitarianism had been dead ends," he would testify, "and I had just come back to Bob Dylan's albums, and I sort of wanted to figure out what he thought." Stookey went as a disciple to the master's home in Woodstock, New York, and they spent the day. "I explained what I'd gone through," he would later testify, "and I said, 'Bobby, where do you think it's at?' And he shook his head and said, 'Well, where do you think it's at?' " This Carl Rogers routine continued at some length, but, pressed, Dylan finally gave the troubled star two pieces of advice: 1) Next time you do a concert in the Midwest, go for a long walk in the country; and, 2) Read the Scriptures, which he referred to as "the guidebook." Both suggestions proved helpful. As for the latter, it is not clear what the 1967 pre-Christian, ethnically Jewish Dylan would have meant by "the Scriptures," but Stookey delved into the New Testament, much of which he found bizarre and obscure. He later told *Christianity Today* that, initially, the main effect Bible reading had on him was to provide a context for understanding a lot of Dylan's lyrics, which seemed to be referenced everywhere. But he was also struck by the claims that were advanced "about this Man Jesus: I had always thought that he was a good example, but it had never occurred to me that he could really be the Son of God."

A life-changing encounter would come in 1968. "I was backstage during a concert walking along, click clack, click clack," Stookey would relate to *Free Love* (one of numerous Jesus people newspapers in the early '70s), "and in a Navajo jacket there was a cat standing there with curly blonde hair." The fellow was only a teenager and Stookey was almost thirty, accustomed to being looked upon as a role model and mentor for America's troubled youth. "He seemed to need some kind of help," Stookey recalls. "I wanted to be sort of like a father to him. I asked, 'What is it you want to talk to me about?' And he said, 'I want to talk to you about the Lord.' And *whack* I felt like the time had come." The two went off to Stookey's hotel room and on the ride over, Stookey quizzed him on spiritual subjects. "I asked him, 'Do you believe in reincarnation?' and he said, 'There are more important things to talk about.' He was very grim and mysterious. It was the heaviest thing I had ever metaphysicked into and something inside me was just saying, 'he knows more than you do and what he knows you should know.' " The mysterious stranger told Stookey, "Jesus is real." Stookey replied, "Well, I know that he was real." And he replied, "No, he *is* real. He is a Spirit, and you ask him to come in and live your life." When they reached the hotel room, the boy said they should pray. He got down and began thanking God for many things and then said, "Now I believe Paul wants to talk to you." In the 1972 *Free Love* interview, Stookey would describe what happened next: "So, wow, I started to pray with him and I asked Jesus to come in and take over my life. And I started to cry and he started to cry. I was giddy and crazy. . . . And I'm still giddy now because I'm stoned on the Holy Spirit. I mean, I'm very high on just letting Jesus do his work through me—and he wants people to know this, and that's why I'm telling you!" Six years later, he would describe the same experience in more sophisticated language to *Christianity Today:* "I was washed, cleansed, I couldn't believe it. It was like I had this incredible cantilevered balance. Suddenly, when I admitted I was sorry for the life I had lived without God, everything collapsed and I was perfectly balanced. I had been given day one again."

For most people, the first public notice of Stookey's new faith came with the startlingly beautiful and poignant song, "Hymn," which would appear on Peter, Paul, and Mary's album *Late Again.* Generally regarded as one of the trio's two best songs (the other being another nonhit called "The Great Mandala"), "Hymn" does not so much focus on the reality of personal faith as on the emptiness of religion that lacks it. It begins, "Sunday morning very bright / I read your book by colored light / That came in through the pretty picture window." But such peaceful imagery is a whitewash for the trappings of institutional religion that have no power in themselves to save: "I visited your house again on Christmas or Thanksgiving / A balding man said you were dead but the house would go on living / He recited poetry and as he saw me rise to leave / He shook his head and said I'd never find you."

Peter, Paul, and Mary disbanded in 1970 after ten years together, and popular rumor attributed the break-up to Noel's evangelical proselytizing and moralizing. In fact, the split owed more to reexamined priorities according to which Stookey wanted to cut back on the constant touring and spend more time with his family. The artist withdrew from the hubbub of society, moving to a remote location in South Blue Hill, Maine, where he bought a four-story henhouse and converted it into a recording studio. In 1971, however, the humorously titled album *Paul And* was issued as a series of three solo projects by members of the former trio (the others being *Peter* and *Mary*). It was embarrassingly better than the other two and might have provided Stookey with a major springboard into a successful career as a singer/songwriter in the tradition of Gordon Lightfoot or James Taylor. He chose not to spring, opting instead for a quiet life marked by occasional contributions intended, first, for the emerging contemporary Christian music community and, later, for the world at large. Otherwise, he joined the local Congregational church, sang in the choir, delivered meals to the elderly, and produced a children's radio show called *Sandman.*

Paul And opens with a wonderful cover of **Arlo Guthrie**'s "Gabriel's Mother's Hiway Ballad # 16 Blues," a little-known gospel number featuring the chorus, "Come on children, all come home, Jesus gonna make you well." What the pre-Christian Guthrie was thinking when he wrote the song may be anybody's guess, but Stookey infuses it with soulful intent that obviously comes from a heart renewed. Likewise, the album closes with an autobiographical number that begins, "John Henry Bosworth, late in sixty-eight, decided that the time had come to settle his estate." The fictional Bosworth is, of course, Stookey himself, and the song relates an allegory of his quest and its conclusion: "Every piece of Scripture, every prayer he prayed / Had brought him to this moment of this particular day." By the song's end, Bosworth is able to say, "I got everything to give now and nothing left to hide," and, then, the narrator turns abruptly to the audience for one more probing verse: "And I was wondering if *you* had been to the mountain to look at the valley below . . . ?" Another song on *Paul And* humorously recalls the minor hit "Give a Damn" (# 43 in 1968) by Spanky And Our Gang, speculating as to why such an excellent tune with a socially relevant message did not get more airplay: "You remember the song called 'Give a Damn' some group sang last summer / 'Bout people livin' with rats and things the paper couldn't cover . . . The first thing nobody wanted to hear was 'damn' / That was on the label / I mean it's okay if you just read it there / But you don't bring it up at the table." The very best tracks on *Paul And,* however, are "Sebastian" and "Wedding Song." The first contains Stookey's prettiest melody and features one of his most expressive vocal performances on what is, in reality, an ode to his guitar (which he apparently named Sebastian): "Sing, sweet Sebastian, sing the sweetest song / Sing so sweet that while you sleep, the melody lingers on." Stookey wrote "The Wedding Song (There Is Love)" for his friend Peter Yarrow's wedding, at which he served as best man. Although the song was only a minor radio hit at the time, it would go on to become a standard '60s love song played on oldies shows, and by 2002 it would probably be better remembered than any of the non-"Puff" songs from Peter, Paul, and Mary's repertoire. Stookey refused to accept any royalties for the song, insisting that it had come to him through divine inspiration and that he deserved little credit for being a conduit. The lyrics suggest as much: "He is now to be among you, at the calling of your hearts / Rest assured this troubadour is acting on his part / The union of your spirits here has caused him to remain / For wherever two or more of you are gathered in his name / There is love." In addition to the allusion to Matthew 18:20, the song quotes from Genesis 2:24 and even leaves the agnostic groom with a question to consider: "If loving is the answer, then who's the giving for? / Do you believe in something that you've never seen before?"

Stookey followed *Paul And* with a live album called *One Night Stand* that immediately became a favorite among the Jesus people if only because it gave them access to their favorite Stookey song ("Hymn") on a record that included more faith-inspired numbers: "One Note Melody," "Blessed," "Wedding Song," and the title track. Stookey also performs "The House Song," one of his best contributions to Peter, Paul, and Mary's oeuvre, and he covers Jesse Colin Young's "Get Together" and Peter Yarrow's "Weave Me the Sunshine." Otherwise, *One Night Stand* is oddly eclectic. The antidrug song "Funky Monkey" represents an ill-advised experiment with hard rock, and "Edgar" is a quirky tune about the eventual earthquake that will send California sliding into the sea. But the album does conclude with a wonderful rock and roll rendition of the Christmas song "Jingle Bells."

The next two albums, *Real to Reel* and *Something New and Fresh,* were directed to the contemporary Christian music subculture but display dramatic inconsistency that would keep them from finding much acceptance there or elsewhere. Apparently Stookey exercised total creative control and allowed his most experimental instincts to rule the day for both albums. These are qualities that critics usually think make for masterpieces, but, in this case, they become arguments for the value of focus-group-minded producers who are empowered to set limits. The two albums contain some very good songs: Stookey's rendition of "Psalm 23" on *Real to Reel* is perfect, and most of Side Two of that record is equally strong: "Turn It Over," "Miracles," and "The Winner" are classic Stookey originals with explicitly Christian, poignant lyrics. "Isn't this the way God works his miracles?" he sings. "A sign of love for all the world to see / And like those tears of healing, the Spirit is revealing / That Jesus gave his life for you and me." *Something New and Fresh* contains nothing as strong as these songs, but offers some convincing folk-gospel with "You're the Only One" and "Country Song." The problem is that on both albums there is also a good deal of quirky filler: the children's song "I Know an Old Lady Who Swallowed a Fly" on *Real to Reel* and "Take Me Out to the Ballgame" on *Something New and Fresh.* Not many rock (or folk or gospel) fans want to listen to those songs repeatedly. The latter record also features "4-D," which simply repeats the line "Don't do dat dope anymore" over and over, and "Moremo Ontu Ne" (= More Moon Tune), a play-on-words sequel to *Paul And*'s only bad song ("Ju Les Ver Negre En Che Ese" = Jules Verne Green Cheese). One novelty song that almost does work is "Building Block," a catchy Scripture tune from *Real to Reel* that puts Psalm 118:22 to a sing-along beat with silly echo lines reminiscent of "Oh, Rock My Soul." Ultimately, the problem with both albums is a failure to distinguish the different venues of live performance and recorded product (what works well in concert, where it is only heard once, vs. what becomes

annoying when forced on a listener *ad nauseam*). It is instructive to note that the best-selling *Peter, Paul, and Mary in Concert* album from 1964 features a long track called "Paultalk" in which Stookey delivers a monologue from his stand-up comic days. In a rambling style similar to that of early Bill Cosby, the artist relates tales of adolescent foibles, fast-food restaurants, and drag racing to the accompaniment of anatomically produced sound effects. It is (or was) hilarious, but it serves to place the album in the genre of "historical souvenir" as opposed to a work intended for repeated musical enjoyment. So, on *Real to Reel* Stookey describes a mock trial in which Puff the Magic Dragon is interrogated for supposedly introducing kids to drugs—it is the sort of thing that might have spruced up a concert, but that no one would ever want to listen to on a record—at least, not more than once. The compilation album, *There Is Love,* would salvage the best songs from Stookey's first four projects, creating a very strong collection of material that might otherwise have been overlooked.

Short of a heavy-handed producer, what Stookey needed to direct his muse was a band. In the late '70s he would get not one, but two. In 1978, Peter, Paul, and Mary reunited and the trio would continue to record and perform sporadically. Even more important, in 1979, Stookey adopted a local bar band called Star Song to serve as his long-term musical partners. He rechristened the group Bodyworks, reportedly because he had some strange idea about recording an entire album "using nothing but sounds made from body parts—popping, smacking, whistling." The latter idea would probably not have worked (but cf. **AVB**), and it is precisely the sort of thing that Stookey needed friends and accomplices to keep him from doing. In any event, Stookey and Bodyworks gelled and together made some of the best, though much neglected, music of his career. Notably, none of the members of Star Song/Bodyworks were Christians when Stookey joined the group as its new high-profile front man. As *CCM* would report in 1985, Stookey led them, one by one, over time, to the Lord. "Noel is our spiritual father," female vocalist Karla Thibodeau would say, speaking for the quartet as a whole. "He was led by the Holy Spirit to work with us, and the Spirit drew us to God through him."

Band and Bodyworks is a stellar collection of contemporary folk and gospel songs. The opening track, "I Wanna Testify," is actually a cover of a George Clinton tune that had gone to Number Twenty in 1967 by Parliament. The next song, "Then the Quails Came" is a quiet, introspective number written by **Michael Kelly Blanchard.** It reflects poignantly on the mercy of God that interrupts human murmuring; the biblical inspiration for the song is the story of Israel's wanderings and manna-dissatisfactions in Numbers 11. "Love All Around" is an appreciative love song, written by Courtney Scott. "Every Flower" is an adult contemporary ballad that Stookey wrote with Peter Yarrow and Bob Milstein. "Know Jesus" is an unabashed gospel rock song that concludes with shouts of "Get down! Get back Satan! Get down! Alleluia! I think the Spirit's gonna get ya!" Despite its excellence, *Band and Bodyworks* was destined to be best remembered for one more example of the sort of Christian-music-scene stupidity that keeps both the subculture and its music from ever being taken seriously in the world at large. The original album cover for *Band and Bodyworks* displayed a joyous photo of Stookey waltzing with a partner (Thibodeau) at what appears to be a celebration banquet or party. Sharp-eyed executives at Sparrow noticed that there were glasses and bottles on the tables that might contain alcoholic beverages and, assuming the audience for their products to be theologically immature, nixed the cover as "a controversial design that might imply approval of drinking and dancing" (both of which, of course, the Bible approves). The album was issued with a plain white jacket instead; its commercial success was not equal to that of another album with a plain white jacket once issued by a quartet from Britain.

Wait'll You Hear This is yet another live album, but one that keeps the silliness to a minimum and focuses on presentation of stellar songs from different phases of Stookey's career. Eschewing the hits, the band opts to give neglected songs a new hearing, making the album a perfect companion piece to *There Is Love* (there is no duplication in song selection between the two projects). One highlight of *Wait'll You Hear This* is "Be Ye Glad" a **Michael Kelly Blanchard** song that Stookey and Bodyworks introduced to the world shortly before it would become the signature hit for the Christian vocal group **Glad.** *State of the Heart* provides a second helping of more original material, similar in quality to *Band and Bodyworks*. Standout tracks include "Circuit Rider," a moody, atmospheric rock song, and "Heart's Desire," a smokey ballad sung by Thibodeau. The album's centerpiece is a three-part "Come Away Suite" that Stookey would say, "I hope becomes another 'American Pie'." No chance of that, but the song does provide an eight-minute-plus reflection on America's social conscience that is ultimately more radical in its projections than Don McLean's rehearsal of the '60s. The piece opens with a movement called "Global Destiny," which identifies the obstacles to world peace as something more transcendent than tyrants to be deposed. "A Nation in Love" offers a Lennonesque (cf. "Imagine") picture of a country that has no need of weapons. The concluding movement, "Come Away," invites listeners to think outside of the box, to resist avenues to peace that involve compromise with evil, and to trust fully in God to bring about peace as a fruit of the Spirit. The song was widely received as a call to disarmament, but Stookey would tell *CCM,* " 'Come Away,' is not a political statement. It is about the way we're to live our lives,

what we hope for, and how we're supposed to realize that hope." On a very different note, *State of the Heart* also contains a song called "For Christmas," which relates a tearjerker tale of a department store Santa who finds the daughter he abandoned some years previously sitting on his knee. "I want my Daddy back, for Christmas," she tells him. "And no other present will do / Last night I talked to Jesus / And tonight I'm asking you." The song is unabashedly melodramatic and sentimental in a "Butterfly Kisses" kind of way. "I'm a sentimental man," Stookey said, presenting it. "I've seen *It's a Wonderful Life* six times and cried every time. When I finished 'For Christmas,' I cried too."

The political implications of the "Come Away Suite" mentioned above are one symptom of another reason Stookey has never quite been embraced by the contemporary Christian music community. As part of Peter, Paul, and Mary, he worked in support of political campaigns of a number of Democratic candidates (most notably, George McGovern). As a solo artist and as a member of the trio, his social conscience has often led him to work for causes that are not on the short list of approved topics for contemporary Christian singers. Instead of campaigning for school prayer or abortion restrictions, Stookey has opposed apartheid, endorsed ecological programs, and worked for AIDS relief. His song "El Salvador" critiqued United States policy in Central America and became Peter, Paul, and Mary's best-known post-'60s protest song. "We don't fit the fundamentalist format," Stookey would tell *CCM* in 1985. "We're not evangelical in the traditional sense. . . . We will never be anything more than a facet of contemporary Christian music, because we just haven't bought into that world. I'm not going to call what we do 'Christian music,' because it's about the truth and the truth, in the larger sense, blesses everyone—not just Christians."

On *In Love beyond Our Lives,* Stookey and band would continue to tackle heavy themes with characteristic insight and compassion. "Danny's Downs" is about the difficult choices made by parents of a child with Down's syndrome. "All My Life" actually does take up the abortion issue, but supports the choice for life in an artful manner that avoids polemic and untenable condemnations. "Cookie Jar" is another venture into humor, this time offering a lighthearted meditation on the doctrine of original sin. "Healing in the Feeling" is a beautiful song describing the emotional aspect of a Spirit-filled life. The album features two songs (the title track and "Hungry Eyes") that Stookey would jokingly refer to as "techno-folk" due to their orchestration on a midi'd guitar. The other eight tracks were recorded live at Belmont Church in Nashville, with **Michael Card** and **Buddy Greene** putting in guest appearances.

In addition to his public projects, Stookey has released some private material for special causes. In 1988, he took part in a special project called *Friends of the Family,* in which an album of songs for hospitalized or terminally ill children was distributed free through benevolent organizations. A similar follow-up project focused on dysfunctional families and children of alcoholics. In 1999, Peter, Paul, and Mary would issue an album called *Songs of Conscience and Concern* (Warner), which includes "El Salvador" and "Danny's Downs."

For trivia buffs: *The New Rolling Stone Encyclopedia of Rock and Roll* confuses Noel Paul Stookey with Peter Yarrow in its listing for Peter, Paul, and Mary. The latter entry (in both the 1995 and 2001 editions) mistakenly identifies Yarrow as the member of the trio who "formed a group called the Bodyworks Band, with which he records and performs Christian-oriented music."

Christian radio hits: "Building Block" (# 8 in 1978).

Storm

Beth Redman; et al. 1998—*Storm* (Kingsway).

Storm appears to be an offshoot of **World Wide Message Tribe,** set up by an organization called Soul Survivor as one more effective agency for conveying a positive Christian message to students in the British public schools. In the United Kingdom, where there is no strict separation of church and state as in America, Christian artists are allowed to speak openly about their faith at school assemblies—see the entry on WWMT for more information on how this works. Beth Redman (formerly Beth Vickers) of WWMT is one of the lead vocalists for Storm, and her husband, **Matt Redman,** wrote the music for the group's debut. Storm pursues a different style than the mother group, however, eschewing the frantic dance songs for more of an adolescent pop style similar to that of All Saints (or Destiny's Child or the Spice Girls). The songs vary lyrically from Redman's typical worship songs to provide inspirational messages of encouragement and evangelistic invitations.

Stradhoughton Echo

Jesse Ray Grover, metal pots, water, light bulbs, etc.; Benjamin Paul Kennedy, gtr., voc.; Charles Paul Meredith, drums; Colin Lewis Weaver, bass. 1999—*Stradhoughton Echo* [EP] (independent); 2000—*The North American Foxhunter.*

Stradhoughton Echo is a Northwest antiglam, antigrunge band with a sound not too dissimilar from **Pedro the Lion,** but thus far, they have obtained more notice for being weird than anything else. The group's music is based on eccentric simplicity, with restrained vocals. Although most tracks are based on traditional acoustic guitar lines, these are supplemented by atmospheric effects that involve dripping water, breaking light bulbs, and the like. "The Corpse of Thea Foss,"

from their full-length debut, probably qualifies the band for emo status. "Incentive," from the same album, is thirty minutes long, for no apparent reason. The group took its name from a nineteenth-century British fox hunting periodical, and they claim that their mission is to "play music we love, promote our favorite pastime of fox hunting, and express our passionate spiritual views in everything that we do." Lead Echo Benjamin Kennedy told *Bandoppler* that the band "strongly opposes any polarization of Christian music and secular music," insisting that secular audiences "will listen to openly spiritual artists if the music maintains a certain level of quality." He also insists that, while controversial, fox hunting is supported by Song of Songs 2:15.

Straight Company

1993 lineup: Mark Clemmons; George Gee; Essej Murrah; Jeffrey Murrah; Kim Murrah; Tierra Watkins; Yvette Watkins. 1993—*So Excited, Acapella* (Benson); 1996—*Plugged In.*

Straight Company came on the contemporary Christian music scene as a Christian version of Boyz II Men, though to be fair, the group had actually been harmonizing together for many years. Associated with the Church of Christ, and under the auspices of a Kentucky congregation of that denomination, the African American vocal combo traces its roots way back to 1975, when the Boyz were all in diapers. They were first known as the Music Makers, then in 1979 reformed as Holy Smoke, a name that met with sufficient disapproval from church elders to prompt them to become Straight Company. In 1991, the group decided to go at it full time, and no doubt inspired by the breakout success of the aforementioned mainstream group, they issued their first full album of a capella songs in 1993. The group also displays similarities with **Take 6** on their combination of jazz harmonies with more traditional R&B and gospel. As group leader Essej Murrah would note, however, Christian radio was not as open to a capella singing as secular stations, and Straight Company's debut album was not commercially successful. Slimmed down to a quintet, a slightly different version of the combo recorded *Plugged In,* which kept the basic vocal harmony style but added instrumental accompaniment. They include a remake of The Staples Singers' "Respect Yourself" and embrace a doo-wop style for "Restore." The general mood of the album is one of hopeful encouragement, as conveyed in such songs as "Come Together" and "Imagine" (neither of which are John Lennon covers). They also offer one purely a capella song, "Didn't It Rain."

Str8 Young Gangstaz

Personnel list unavailable. 2000—*Tha Movement* (Grapetree).

Str8 Young Gangstaz was one of many rap groups signed to Grapetree Records, though that label did not list the group among its roster of artists or provide any information concerning them at its website (www.grapetreerecords.com). The album cover displays a picture of five African American men whose names are never identified. The anonymous band appears to be from the West Coast, but their sound hearkens back to such early (and eastern) rappers as Grandmaster Flash on the song "U Kanot C Me" and **Run-D.M.C.** on "Move tha Crowd." The most interesting track on *Tha Movement* is "Chain Gang," which uses snippets of **Sam Cooke**'s song by that name as well as bits from Diana Ross's "(Theme from) Mahogany" as a backdrop for a speed rap regarding the desolation of a world without God.

Strawmen

Bill Harmon, voc.; Mark Harmon, bass; David Leonhardt, gtr. 1996—*At Home* (Liquid Disc).

The Strawmen were essentially the **Seventy Sevens** with Mark Harmon's brother Bill (instead of **Michael Roe**) on vocals. Despite their album's release date, Strawmen were pre-**Seventy Sevens.** The sessions were recorded in 1987 when the trio was just a garage band from Sacramento, California. Mark Harmon and David Leonhardt were recruited by Roe to make up a new incarnation of his band for the '90s, a version that is found on the classic *Pray Naked* and *Drowning with Land in Sight* albums (Harmon would stick around for *Tom Tom Blues* and *A Golden Field of Radioactive Crows*). The sessions on *At Home* were never intended for public release, and Liquid Disc put them out in response to historical interest in the band on the part of **Seventy Sevens** fans. Musically, the album turns out to be a lot better than anyone would have expected (the idea of the **Seventy Sevens** without Michael Roe is a bit like The Doors without Jim Morrison). As *Visions of Gray* would note, the album captures "what Roe heard that inspired him to reform the Sevens and have another go." Indeed, a few of the songs ("Deep End," "Phony Eyes," "Holy Hold") sound very much like **Seventy Sevens** tracks, calling into question the prevailing opinion that Roe has a monopoly on determining that band's sound.

The Straw Theory

Jake Bramante, bass, voc.; Josiah Bramante, drums; Tyler Huston, voc., kybrd. 1999—*The Straw Theory* (KMG).

The Straw Theory is a piano-based Christian rock band that released a stunning debut near the end of the millennium that had them being compared to general market groups like Ben Folds Five. Critics with more imagination and/or longer memories could trace the roots of this brazen pop sound all the way back to early Billy Joel or Elton John. In any case, The Straw Theory stands out from among a plethora of guitar bands and head and shoulders above all the keyboard groups who rely on synthesizers to produce music that, of course, sounds synthetic and synthesized. Billy Smiley of **White Heart** and **Terry Taylor** of **Daniel Amos** produced *The Straw Theory* with the addition of guest musicians drawn from the ranks of **Common Children, The Choir,** and **The Prayer Chain.** Leigh Nash of **Sixpence None the Richer** sings on two tracks ("Man on the Moon," "Showers"). The album opens with its best song, "In and Out," a peppy potential hit with lyrics about avoiding a person who has turned out to be a negative influence ("I found in me something I wasn't sure about / I looked inside and saw you"). "Falling Forward" is another energetic, catchy number, reflecting on the ironic capacity for failings to become occasions for spiritual growth. "We Believe" is a more traditional contemporary Christian radio song with an appealing hook-laden melody. Several of the other songs are dreamy and moody, but on a couple of tracks the band also tries out completely different styles that don't work: "In the Future" is a frenetic punk song about not being a morning person; "Running Thin" is a snarling, prophetic challenge that features the lead singer hissing, "Where is Jee-sus in all of thissss?" The band also sounds way too much like **Smalltown Poets** (and, thus, like **Jars of Clay**) on "Man on the Moon," but when they forget the histrionics and just do what they do best, the results are spectacular. Jake Bramante says, "God has really laid on our hearts that the mission of our band is to bring unity to the body of Christ. We want people to set aside a lot of doctrinal issues and believe the fundamental truth that Jesus came down and died on the cross."

Street Called Straight

Jody Moehring Frankfurt, voc.; Scott Frankfurt, kybrd., perc. 1991—*Street Called Straight* (Frontline); 1992—*Heartsong*.

Street Called Straight is a high-tech husband and wife duo who get easily categorized as a Christian version of Captain and Tennille, albeit with a more '90s sound. Scott Frankfurt and Jody Moehring were songwriting partners before they married and before either of them were Christians (Moehring wrote a song called "Danny" that appeared on pop singer Tiffany's debut album). Jody says, "After my marriage [to someone else] fell apart and my career took a downward turn, I fell to my knees." Scott adds, "We were involved in substance abuse and everything else that comes with the rock 'n' roll lifestyle." The two got right with God individually and as a couple. They married and went from composing to performing together. Scott Frankfurt is known primarily as a sound designer, capable of engineering digital recordings on computers. He worked on Michael Jackson's "Black and White" video, as well as on **Twila Paris**'s *Sanctuary*. The debut album by Street Called Straight (who took their name from Acts 9:11) is said to be the first product in the Christian market to be programmed entirely on a computer, being recorded directly to a MacIntosh hard drive with no tape involved. The album features mostly pop-dance songs with lyrics that speak of choices that help or hinder a relationship with God. Jody's voice has a husky quality similar to that of Taylor Dayne. Two ballads ("Mary's Eyes," "What a Wonderful Night") have Christmas themes. *Heartsong* opens with the Phil Collins-inspired "Apple of My Eye" and also includes a duet with **Philip Bailey** written in response to the 1992 riots in Los Angeles ("Pick Up the Pieces"). *CCM* would describe the second album as being filled with "perfect pop" songs parallel to those of a group like ABBA. The close family orientation comes through on the marital love song "Can't Keep Me Away" and on the ode to a newborn daughter "Joanna's Song." *Heartsong* also includes a breathy cover of Pete Seeger's "Turn! Turn! Turn!"

Christian radio hits: "World without End" (# 4 in 1992); "Apple of My Eye" (# 7 in 1993).

Streetlight

Personnel list unavailable. 1983—*Streetlight* (Sparrow).

Streetlight was a mystery trio sponsored by **Agape Force,** the same ministry responsible for **Candle** and **Silverwind.** The group only made one vinyl record with a paltry three songs per side. The cover photo displays two men and a woman, whose names are never revealed. This anonymous character of the group renders the songs impersonal, a facet that is the more annoying with songs that are obviously intended to reflect on aspects of the artists' own lives. "Jesus in Your Eyes" is subtitled "Our Wedding Song" (the latter tune was written by J. Miller and S. Miller, with R. Krueger—a credit that provides the best possible guess at the identities of the singers). Georgian Banov, the leader of **Agape Force,** produced the record and cowrote a couple of songs. Streetlight's sound was contemporary country, and the harmony vocals seem to have been geared to capitalize on the popularity of male-female duets (e.g., **Kenny Rogers** and Dottie West) at the time.

Stretch Arm Strong

John Barry, drums; Scott Dempsey, gtr.; Jeremy Jeffers, bass; Chris McLane, voc.; David Sease, gtr. 1997—*Compassion Fills the Void* (Rise); 1999—*Rituals of Life* (Solid State); 2001—*A Revolution Transmission*.

www.stretcharmstrong.net

Stretch Arm Strong is an innovative hardcore band from Columbia, South Carolina. Like most hardcore bands, their sound is based in punk-rock with ultra-fast songs and shouted lyrics. The innovative factor lies in their incorporation of nonstereotypical elements. The song "For Now" on *Rituals of Life* begins with a piano solo, moves into speedy, screaming hardcore, then slows down and concludes with harmonious background vocals. This "strange dichotomy," as *Phantom Tollbooth* calls it, sets the band apart from its peers in the crowded hardcore scene. It also helps them avoid the Achilles' heel of punk: all of their songs do *not* sound alike. *A Revolution Transmission* pushes the edge of the envelope even further, with strings, more piano, and a lot more actual singing—mixed, still, with fast and furious punk parts.

The band is also distinctive in its approach to lyrics, advocating positive values rather than just screaming about life's frustrations. The song "To a Friend (Lockdown)" expresses a sentiment more reminiscent of Paul Simon's "Bridge over Troubled Water" or Carole King's "You've Got a Friend" than what is typically associated with hardcore: "And when you're in the depths of despair / Know that, I'll be there, I'll be there! / I'll comfort you . . . until the end, my friend." Or again, these lines from "When Sorrow Falls" seem to bring out hardcore's feminine side (which, until now, no one knew it had): "It's O.K. for me to say I love you / And it's O.K. for you to cry / The sorrow that you are feeling, you cannot deny / So why is it so hard trying to express what you feel?" This wholesome quality seems to be related to the Christian faith espoused by at least some of the band members and it accounts for the reception of Stretch Arm Strong among Christian music fans. The band has played the *Cornerstone* Christian music festival and has received generous exposure in *HM* and other Christian music magazines. Their label, Solid State, is a division of Tooth and Nail, a company strongly associated with the Christian music scene. Still, like many bands associated with Christianity, the group resists being labeled "a Christian band," with concern for accuracy as well as the usual fear of commercial detriment. "Stretch Arm Strong, as a whole, is not a Christian band," explains lead singer Chris McLane. "Myself, the drummer, and a couple other members of the band do consider themselves Christian, or actively pursuing a faith in a higher power. There's other members of the band who are sorting things out. They're not exactly sure. But as a band as a whole, I guess a philosophy we all subscribe to is compassion toward other people, all people." Tolerance and inclusivity become dominant virtues in the band's songs. For example, "Take Back Control" from *A Revolution Transmission* makes a strong statement about gender equality (delivered by the band and guest Patti Davis).

Christian music fans have generally understood the situation as explained above and have been willing to accept the group for what it is (and is not). They do not expect Stretch Arm Strong to sing worship songs or to testify outright to their faith in Jesus Christ. Still, Christians who like hardcore punk music are pleased to find a group whose lyrics they can by and large endorse, especially when they know those sentiments are being expressed by honest persons openly struggling with matters of faith.

Strongarm

Chris Carbonell, drums, voc.; Josh Colbert, gtr.; Nick Dominguez, gtr.; Chad Neptune, bass; Jason Beggren, voc. (– 1997) // Steven Klesiath, drums (+ 1997). 1995—*Atonement* (Tooth and Nail); 1997—*The Advent of a Miracle.*

Strongarm is a hardcore punk band from Palm Beach, Florida. The group has had two distinct incarnations with different lead vocalists and front men. The first band leader, Jason Beggren, says he was not raised a Christian but came to faith with the help of one of his friend's parents. The album on which he does vocals, *Atonement,* includes "Count the Cost" and "Gates of Atonement," which he says "reveal the misery and destruction associated with premarital sex and abortion, respectively." Those two issues were obviously close to Beggren's heart. He told *HM* in 1995, "I always make it clear from the stage exactly what we're about. . . . People need to be responsible for their actions. Abortion is not birth control. I always talk about how I believe sex is something very holy and made for marriage. And a child is sacred." After *Atonement* Beggren became a full-time youth pastor, and drummer Chris Carbonell took over as lead vocalist for *The Advent of a Miracle.* The latter record moves away from metal stylings while emphasizing rhythm and unorthodox tempo changes. *HM* found songs like "Supplication" and "Sorrow Is a Sage" to be especially thoughtful: "the band almost lives in a dichotomy, marrying worshipful and meek lyrics with pure, hardcore speed." Band member Chad Neptune would describe part of the group's ministry as being to distinguish between true Christianity and the Straight Edge movement, with which they are often associated. Straight Edge is a quasi-religious movement within the punk scene according to which individuals seek purity by abstaining from drugs, alcohol, and premarital sex (many Straight Edgers also practice vegetarianism or veganism). "Straight Edge is full of good intentions," says Chad. "It's just not Christianity. Straight Edge is about cleaning up the outside of the vessel, while Christianity is about cleaning the inside." In the late '90s, the band changed its name and style, re-forming (minus Carbonell) as **Further Seems Forever.**

Strong Gurus

Dennis Danell, gtr.; Michael Knott, gtr., voc.; et al. No albums.

Michael Knott formed the band Strong Gurus with guitarist Dennis Danell of Social Distortion. A legend in the punk community, Danell died in 2000 while producing albums for the Christian bands **The Calicoes** and **Value Pac.** The group's manager, Dave Jenison, once described the Strong Gurus' sound as "**Bob Dylan** meets the **Violent Femmes** meets the Smashing Pumpkins." Knott described the group as "a general market band" (like his groups **Bomb Bay Babies** and **Aunt Bettys**). "As long as I've been doing music, I have worked at simultaneously having both a Christian band and a general market band," he told *Bandoppler.* Although the Strong Gurus do not appear to have recorded a full album, they did place three songs on Knott's compilation album, *Things I've Done, Things to Come* (Blonde Vinyl, 2000). Andy Prickett of **The Prayer Chain** also played guitar on their limited recordings. The song "Chelsea's Chasin' Dragons" is about heroin addiction.

Stryken

Joey Knight, drums; Dale Streiker, voc., gtr.; Stephen Streiker, voc., gtr., kybrd.; Ezekiel Vale, bass. 1987—*First Strike* (Chrystal).

For those who found **Stryper** appalling, the Christian glam-metal band Stryken remains an enduring reminder that things could have been (and for a moment, were) a whole lot worse. The group was an obvious **Stryper**-copy, composed of four men who did their best to look and sound like the pioneers of Christian metal, while taking that band's extremes over the edge. To be more specific, they exploited the militant Christians-as-hate-group theme that **Petra** had found to be so successful in Reagan's America. "This isn't just rock 'n' roll. This is war!" exclaimed Stephen Streiker, echoing the titular anthem of **Petra**'s career nadir album released the same year as Stryken's *First Strike.* The latter album opens with the song "Crush the Head," which uses graphic, violent imagery to describe what they plan to do to Satan and his friends. The group regularly dressed in armor and combat gear to symbolize the "spiritual armor" that Christians are told to put on in Ephesians 6, and they testified to the ways that God was protecting them from the demonic forces that Satan worshipers had conjured up to attack them. When more temperate Christians complained that the band's stance could be interpreted as promoting violence, Steven Streiken told *CCM,* "That's true, but it's well-directed violence!"

Stryper

Oz Fox (b. Richard Martinez), gtr.; Tim Gaines (b. Tim Hagelganz), bass; Michael Sweet, voc.; Robert Sweet, drums. 1984—*The Yellow and Black Attack* (Enigma); 1985—*Soldiers under Command*; 1986—*To Hell with the Devil*; 1988—*In God We Trust*; 1990—*Against the Law*; 1991—*Can't Stop the Rock: The Stryper Collection, 1984–1991* (Hollywood).

www.stryper.com

Stryper was the ultimate crossover metal band, a Christian hard rock group that got taken seriously (or at least noticed) in the general market. By their own admission, they were not the best Christian metal group on the scene (cf. **Bride, Guardian, Resurrection Band, Tourniquet, Whitecross**) but they were one of the first and certainly the most successful. They presented themselves in ways that practically begged treatment as a novelty act: heavy makeup, big hair, black and yellow spandex (prompting Saturday Night Live-inspired "killer bee" jokes), and silly publicity stunts. They were, of course, a Christian version of Kiss—and the very idea of such an incarnation struck secular journalists as humorous and worthy of media coverage. There was a lot of mean-spirited criticism (mostly from the Christian side), but Stryper rolled with the punches and, by and large, had fun with it. Like **Pat Boone** in a previous generation, they were able to take the jokes and didn't mind providing their mockers with a steady supply of ammunition. If evangelical Christians got stereotyped for trying to "hit people over the head with the Bible," Stryper would come out on stage with boxes of New Testaments and literally hurl them at people in the audience. If Christian rock stars got stereotyped for reducing the gospel to simplistic cheerleading, Stryper would come on stage and belt out a heavy metal anthem called "To Hell with the Devil." It was all in good fun; most people got it and the squawking of those who didn't only added to the amusement of those who did. In short, Stryper was a Christian party band. They were only controversial to those who had never read (or understood) the banquet parables of Jesus or heeded the witness of his life (Matthew 9:10–13, 14–17; 11:19). Like Boone, they demonstrated an enormous capacity for taking abuse in exchange for the hope that, at some level, the serious component of their message would be heard. It definitely was. Studies show that over two-thirds of the millions of Stryper albums sold were bought by non-Christians. Those consumers, fans even, were certainly aware of Stryper's convictions and, all kidding aside, were genuinely impressed by the sincerity and tenacity of the band's faith. In 1993, Stryper would be the only self-described Christian rock group to warrant an entry in the *New Rolling Stone Encyclopedia of Rock and Roll*. In 2001, they were *still* the only self-described Christian rock group to merit an entry in that volume's third edition (no **DC Talk**, no **Jars of Clay**). In late 2001, the band published an authorized biography by Dale Erickson and Jesse Sturdevant (*Stryper: Loud 'n' Clear*, Endgame).

Musically, Stryper had roots in another metal band called Roxx Regime. The Sweet brothers (Michael and Robert) and Oz Fox (who chose his stage name based on an obsession with Ozzy Osbourne) were members of the latter Orange County, California, outfit, which had a strong regional presence, playing alongside bands like Ratt, Mötley Crüe, and Poison. Roxx Regime was in no way a Christian band, though the members would all later identify themselves as backslidden Christians. The Sweet brothers, for instance, had been led to accept Christ through the TV ministry of Jimmy Swaggart, who they always regarded as a personal hero despite the fact that he would later attack the band as agents of the devil. Nevertheless, the years with Roxx Regime were typified by what Michael Sweet would later describe as "Christians who lived like complete heathens . . . out on the Hollywood strip, playing the clubs, scamming on women, drinking alcohol, not really heavily into drugs, but just complete heathens." In 1983, things changed. "Michael and I rededicated our lives back to the Lord," Robert Sweet recalls. "And shortly after, Oz did also." Another Christian, Tim Gaines, was brought into the band, which decided to change its name to Stryper after a passage in Isaiah 53:5 ("by his stripes, we are healed"; the word *stripes* refers to scars or lashings). Sometimes, the group would also say the name was an acronym for "Salvation Through Redemption Yielding Peace, Encouragement, and Righteousness." But initially there was no foregone conclusion that Stryper would sing evangelical songs or identify themselves publicly as a Christian band. That decision came about gradually. Robert Sweet was reportedly distressed by the message at an otherwise impressive Van Halen concert. The Sweets' mother encouraged them to write and perform songs that testified to Christ. Ken Metcalf came to the group with "a word from the Lord" telling them that God had promised him, "If you glorify Jesus in your songs, you will go straight to the top."

Whatever the influences, Stryper slowly began to develop a repertoire of overtly evangelical songs. Nevertheless, when they prepared a demo for presentation to Enigma records (a division of Capitol), they edited the songs, taking out all the explicitly religious lyrics. Then, after they were signed with the general market label, they presented the company with newly recorded versions of the same songs, with explicit Christian messages intact. There is some question as to whether they had to be so sneaky. Wes Hein, the head of Enigma who signed the band, recalls, "Their tape just knocked my socks off. The songs were great and I was so impressed with the tonal quality, the background vocals, and just what it all sounded like. I had no idea that they were a Christian band and they did not volunteer that information." Still, once the discovery was made, Hein says he felt in no way deceived: "It wasn't an issue. I thought about it and decided, 'Who cares?' They're a great rock band. It's not a big deal." But, then, he adds, "Of course, in time, it would seem that everyone else thought it was a much bigger deal than I did." Thus, Stryper was signed originally on the merits of its music alone, but eventually the Christian aspect of the group was treated as something of a marketing ploy—as a distinctive element to set the band apart from the dozens of other groups that all tended to look and sound alike. Only true fans could tell the difference between Ratt and Quiet Riot and Twisted Sister. But eventually everyone would know that Mötley Crüe was "the one whose drummer dated Pamela Anderson" and Stryper was "the one whose members believed in Jesus."

The Yellow and Black Attack, Stryper's debut minialbum, is a Christian classic that would inspire numerous Stryper clones and wannabes. It offers quintessential proof that overtly Christian artists *can* make it in the general market, even in what is supposedly the most godforsaken corner of that market: the genre known as heavy metal. In 1996, **Leaderdogs for the Blind** would open their debut album with a tribute song titled "The Yellow and Black Attack," and in 1998 **Guardian** would cover the entire album on a project called *The Yellow and Black Attack Is Back.* The album itself actually goes fairly light on the Christian imagery, containing only six songs that are most notable for what they are *not* about (sex, drugs, violence, the occult). Still, five of the tracks (beginning with "Loud and Clear") are bone-crunching paradigms of the style headbangers crave. The sound has an authenticity that would prevent Stryper from being easily dismissed as posers, despite the anomalous G-rated wholesomeness of their lyrics. On "Loud and Clear" they declare, "The hair is long and the screams are loud 'n' clear / The clothes are tight, earrings dangle from the ear / No matter how we look, we'll always praise his name / And if you believe, you've got to do the same." Another fairly explicit statement of faith comes to the fore on "You Know What to Do": "We've found a life that keeps us happy / Yes we have, and we'll live eternally / We'll always have a light to see, and so can you." And the anthemic "From Wrong to Right" would become a signature song: "I changed my ways from wrong to right . . . so many bands give the devil all the glory . . . All we say is Jesus is the way!" *Yellow and Black Attack* also features a typical metal ballad, "You Won't Be Lonely," which can be heard either as a promise of faithfulness to a romantic partner or as a spiritual assurance of God's love for humanity. Interestingly, *The Yellow and Black Attack* was picked up by Japan's most important rock critic, Masa Itoh, who subsequently became a huge Stryper fan, promoting the group heavily in that country (apart from any interest in their ideological message). As a result, Stryper found themselves to be the number one hard rock band in Japan, ahead of such artists as Aerosmith, Bon Jovi, and Van Halen.

By *Soldiers under Command,* the secret was out, and the band eschewed subtlety for direct evangelistic appeals. "The Rock That Makes Me Roll" is a pretty obvious anthemic tribute to Jesus, and the album concludes with a thundering version of the "Battle Hymn of the Republic," complete with what sounds like angelic choirs wailing on the famous "Glory, Glory Hallelujahs." The album's strongest track is "Makes Me Wanna Sing," a celebrative song that *CCM* would describe as combining "the pinpoint harmonies of Styx with the focused guitar assault of Scorpion." It features the bold lyric, "Jesus, King of Kings / Jesus makes me wanna sing." Likewise on "Surrender" the group proclaims, "Jesus Christ is the lover of your soul / And he wants to give you all you need / So freely surrender / Open up unto his majesty." Incredibly for an album featuring so many name-the-name Jesus songs, *Soldiers under Command* would spend twenty-three weeks on *Billboard*'s mainstream Top Pop album chart. The very secular *Spin* magazine reviewed the group favorably, calling their album "high-energy, knee-bending, hand-shaking, head-twisting heavy-metal rock with the power and glory of God." The equally worldly *Circus* said, "If you think all L.A. metal bands can do is rant about sex, drugs, and more sex, you're in for a surprise." *Hit Parader* called them "the best heavy metal band around." England's *Kerrang!* griped a little about the proselytizing but then added, "who can knock their approach when the music is as strong as this?" *Soldiers under Command* also includes a couple of power ballads, which at that time provided Christian metal groups with their only hope of ever getting played on Christian radio stations. "Together As One" is a notable wedding song that sounds a lot like something REO Speedwagon might have done.

A year later, the band that *Rolling Stone* had dubbed "heavy metal Bible belters" released what was to become their most popular album. *To Hell with the Devil* rose to Number Thirty-two on *Billboard*'s general market chart and went platinum with sales of over one million copies—a feat virtually unequaled in Christian music at the time. In addition to the too-obvious anthemic title track, the album features the Air Supply-styled ballad "Honestly," which rose to Number Twenty-three on the secular Top 40 charts and became for a time the number one most-requested video on MTV. The words, again, can either be heard as a pledge of faithfulness from an earthly friend or as a pledge of God's unswerving love: "Call on me, and I'll be there for you / I'm a friend who always will be true." In a perceptive *CCM* review, Brian Quincy Newcomb pegged Stryper's sound as less congruent with the Black Sabbath-Metallica scene than their outward appearance would suggest. Actually, Newcomb averred, the group displays broader-based solid rock bearings "more reminiscent of early Styx without the synthesizers." That analogy certainly holds on *To Hell with the Devil,* where only the title track and a handful of other tunes ("The Way," "Rocking the World," "More Than a Man") really possess a hard rock edge, with Sweet's high-pitched yelps taking them into stereotypical metal territory. A number of the other songs ("Sing Along Song," "Calling on You") are much more pop-oriented. "Holding On" borrows directly from The Who's "Won't Get Fooled Again."

In God We Trust would also reach Number Thirty-two on the general market album chart, but the album was dismissed as "a relative disappointment" by *Rolling Stone,* not because of its spiritual content but because they saw it, musically, as "a blatant attempt to court pop audiences." Basically, the trend Newcomb had noticed on *To Hell with the Devil* was continuing, and almost all reviewers now saw the group as abandoning metal for more of a Bon Jovi or Styx-without-synthesizers sound. The album would still produce minor general market hits with the songs "Always There for You" (# 71) and "I Believe in You" (# 88), both of which did much better on the Christian charts. In general, *In God We Trust* comes off as a tour of stadium rock sounds that were hot at the moment. "Keep the Fire Burning" features gangland vocals and a tune reminiscent of **Kansas**-pop. "Always There for You" and "The World of You and I" are midtempo rockers after the fashion of Journey or REO Speedwagon. "I Believe in You" is a building ballad on which Sweet sounds uncannily like Dennis DeYoung (of Styx). The only song on which the band really sounds like Stryper is the anthemic, opening title track, which offers their trademark simple (or simplistic?) lyrics: "In God we trust / In him we must believe / In God we trust / His Son we must receive." In 1996, however, Ted Kirkpatrick of **Tourniquet** would identify Stryper's *In God We Trust* as a quintessential album of Christian rock: "the buzzsaw guitar, the vocal chorus, and that *huge* drum sound . . . they presented the gospel and the *joy* of fellowship with God in such a clear way!"

Against the Law is remembered primarily as the project on which Stryper backed off from all the overt proselytizing to deliver a package of straightforward, almost secular, rock songs. The band made it clear in interviews that they were in no way "renouncing their faith" but merely "reorganizing, trying to get away from the in-your-face religious imagery" to see if perhaps they had anything *else* to say. The group also did away with the silly spandex and dressed more like ordinary, albeit very hairy, guys. Musically, *Against the Law* is tougher than *In God We Trust;* it doesn't move back into '80s metal but it does display more of a blues-based Aerosmith/Van Halen sound. The closest the group gets to "old Stryper" on *Against the Law* comes in the closing track, "Rock the Hell Out of You," in which they declare "We're the thundering sons / We're the undying ones / With the power of good / Evil never has won . . . We will rock the hell out of you." But "Lady" is just a simple love song (with no maybe-it's-addressed-to-God double entendres), and "Two Bodies, One Mind, One Soul" is a testimony to the intrinsic power of marriage to help a couple transcend their differences. "Not That Kind of Guy" has a sound a little too similar to Van Halen's "Hot for Teacher," but features lyrics ad-

dressed to a groupie, with a gender twist on an old cliché: "I don't give my love away for free / Baby don't you throw yourself at me / When I say no way, you ask me why / Can't you see, I'm not that kind of guy." *Against the Law* was generally hailed as the band's most consistent and best album, and, ten years later, Fox and Gaines would both still name it as Stryper's musical highpoint.

As indicated, Stryper met with almost incessant criticism from isolated voices within the Christian camp who thought they knew God's taste in music and clothing well enough to be certain this band did not merit divine approval. Early on, some groups picketed Christian bookstores that carried the products. Canceled subscriptions and angry letters to magazines like *Christianity Today* and *CCM* would invariably follow any feature on the band. Jimmy Swaggart, through whose ministry the Sweets had become Christians, became one of the band's most virulent opponents, such that they could do no right in his eyes (or ears). He even maintained, for instance, that their distribution of New Testaments to unbelievers showed disrespect for the Word of God that amounted to "casting pearls before swine." The big scandal broke, however, in 1990 when an article in *Rolling Stone* reported that Stryper had become disillusioned with the whole Christian music scene, that the members had begun to "openly drink and smoke," and that they had decided not to sing about God on their next album *(Against the Law).* The article was widely cited in Christian media as evidence that the naysayers had been right all along and that Stryper had gone the way of the world. Actually, Robert Sweet would contend that the article grossly misrepresented the band's views. First, they had only expressed dissatisfaction with certain aspects of the Christian music scene. Second, they had only told the reporter that they do not condemn persons who "openly drink or smoke" without implying any endorsement of those activities. And, third, they had specifically indicated that *Against the Law's* broader lyrical base was a positive "branching out," not a retreat from established commitments. It didn't matter. Benson Records, who distributed Stryper's products to Christian markets, refused to carry *Against the Law,* dooming the product to commercial failure. Benson maintained that the decision had nothing to do with the *Rolling Stone* piece but was made only because the new album "does not contain overtly Christian lyrics and so represents a new direction for the group that no longer conforms to Benson's mission statement." This position became harder to maintain when the company stopped distributing all of Stryper's previous albums as well. Robert Sweet opined that the *Rolling Stone* article was "a set up," crafted by reporters for that magazine who hated the band because of its Christianity and thought "they would have a little fun" by destroying the group's credibility with its fan base.

For some time, the name Stryper became synonymous with gossip and rumors. As a *CCM* retrospective would later report, the air was filled with stories about "disagreements with their mother (and one-time manager); shouting matches with other managers, agents, and promoters; an on-again-off-again relationship with Gaines who quit, then rejoined; trouble with producers; trouble with each other; and so forth." Stryper was planning an additional album but then, suddenly, Michael Sweet left the group in early 1992, apparently taking everyone by surprise. He cited musical differences as the primary reason for his sudden departure: "The band wanted to go in a Guns N' Roses direction, while I wanted to go back toward the style of *To Hell with the Devil.*" A premature announcement indicated that Dale Thompson of **Bride** would replace him in the band, but that never took place and some ill will resulted as Thompson and Stryper gave conflicting stories to the press as to just what agreements had been made. **Michael Sweet** would go on to record as a solo artist. Tim Gaines and Oz Fox formed a band called Sin Dizzy who released an independent album called *He's Not Dead* in 1998. **Robert Sweet** and Gaines both played with **Rex Carroll** in **King James,** and Robert worked with a band called Blank and also recorded a solo project; he has indicated that he thinks there is still unfinished business for Stryper to pursue and that he hopes for an eventual reunion. "I feel it's not over," he said in 1996. "Hopefully, soon, something will happen." In 2000 and again in 2001, the band did reunite for a one-day concert at what seemed likely to become an annual fan convention called the Stryper Expo. No long-term plans for recordings or tours were announced.

Stryper would go down in history as the first and only Christian metal band to produce two platinum and four gold records. At the height of their career, bands like Poison and Metallica opened for them. As years passed and the dust settled, all of the individual members of Stryper would talk frankly with *HM* magazine about the band's legacy and shortcomings. Gaines admitted that he had struggled with alcohol abuse from 1988 on and also indicated that, after the break-up, lawsuits and other nasty surprises took all the money he had made from being in the group. "I can't get into another band because of Stryper," he complained. "I think I've been kind of typecast and blackballed from the music industry because of it. . . . And, I'll be owing people for the rest of my life for money that I never even saw." Fox says, "To be honest, Stryper wasn't what we should have been spiritually . . . there was sin in the band, and the reason it was happening was that we didn't know the Lord like we should have. . . . I can't speak for the other guys, but my heart was focused on wanting to be a rock star and a success." Michael Sweet would say, "Looking back, it wasn't a pretty sight. We were living the same lifestyle offstage that we were condemning on stage." Pressed for more detail, he adds

that "there was a lot of drinking and partying," though "no one was doing drugs and no one was cheating on their wives . . . God stepped in and prevented that, but if the whole thing had gone on, it might have degenerated into that." Still, he insists, "It was such a powerful ministry, a lot more powerful than most people realize. And Stryper's focus was right on. We really wanted to reach a generation of people. We just wanted to tell people about Christ." Robert Sweet also tries to preserve that positive part of the memory. "I'm glad that we made a mark and that we stood up for Christ the way that we did," he declares. "We were just four kids who, musically, weren't that talented, and God just took us to this place where we had the opportunity to share with thousands and thousands of people. We were in awe. We were just so blown away. But the thing people need to know about Stryper is—we were just four guys who didn't deserve anything that God gave us. Without Christ, we're just four losers."

In 1996, a number of artists came together to record a tribute album of Stryper songs. The result, *Sweet Family Music* (Flying Tart) is an odd collection with virtually no metal outings (nothing from **Bride** or **Deliverance**). Instead **Grammatrain** performs a grunge version of "More Than a Man," and several artists **(Aleixa, Argyle Park, The Echoing Green)** reinterpret favorite songs as techno or industrial pieces. **Steve Hindalong** sings a strange acoustic version of "To Hell with the Devil," which he later said he did because he wanted to find out "how it felt to sing the worst lyrics ever written." So, it's a joke and a slam and a tribute all in one. Stryper, no doubt, was used to the abuse. Whatever else might be said about them, they have always been able to *get* the joke, even—especially—when it's on them.

For trivia buffs: Stryper made the national news briefly in 1987 when a high school student in South River, New Jersey, was disciplined for wearing a "To Hell with the Devil" Stryper T-shirt to school. Jamie Bollentin, age sixteen, contended that she should be allowed to wear the shirt because other students were permitted to wear clothing that explicitly glorified Satan. The school contended the shirt was obscene (the word *hell*) and suspended her for three days.

Christian radio hits: "Together As One" (# 3 in 1985); "All of Me" (# 9 in 1987); "Honestly" (# 13 in 1987); "Always There for You" (# 4 in 1988); "I Believe in You" (# 6 in 1988).

Dove Awards: 1989 Hard Rock Album *(In God We Trust)*; 1989 Hard Rock Song ("In God We Trust").

Donna Summer

Selected: 1980—*The Wanderer* (Geffen); 1982—*Donna Summer;* 1983— *She Works Hard for the Money* (Mercury); 1984—*Cats without Claws* (Geffen); 1987—*All Systems Go;* 1989—*Another Time, Another Place;* 1991—*Mistaken Identity* (Atlantic); 1994—*Christmas Spirit* (Mercury).

Donna Summer (b. Donna Gaines in 1948) was to disco music what **Aretha Franklin** was to soul. More than any other artist, she helped establish disco as a viable art form while also expanding that genre and ultimately bursting its boundaries to become recognized as a first-rate diva of pop, rock, soul, and gospel. Summer grew up in Boston, Massachusetts, as part of what she later would call "a lower-middle-class black family." Her family was conservative and church-going, such that she would later claim she could never recall a time when she was not a Christian. She sang in Boston churches from an early age but around the age of sixteen went through what she would call her "Janis Joplin period," doing drugs and fronting a rock and roll band. After about two years of recklessness, she got serious about her life and career, quit the drugs for good, and, after a professional debut at Boston's Psychedelic Supermarket, headed for New York City to audition for the Broadway cast of *Hair!*. She was cast for a German production of that play instead, and was sent to Europe for enough years for her later United States debut to seem like a crossover. After the run with *Hair!*, she joined the Vienna Folk Opera, singing in a version of *Porgy and Bess*. It was while in Germany (as Donna Gaines) that she married and later divorced Helmut Sommer, whose surname she would keep in its anglicized form. She also made the acquaintance of Giorgio Moroder and Pete Belotte, co-owners of Oasis records and producers who would play a large role in bringing the disco craze to America.

Summer's first big hit in the pop market was what she herself would call "a fluke." The sexually charged "Love to Love You, Baby" went to Number Two on the pop charts, making it one of the first disco songs to score anywhere outside of the then narrow dance arena. The song would turn out to be a lifetime embarrassment, as it mainly features Summer simulating orgasms for seventeen minutes against a repetitive disco instrumental backdrop. Summer would later relate that she didn't even realize the tracks were being recorded. She had taken a stab at recording an early version of the song, which was only half-written and didn't have enough words: "I was goofing around. I was lying on the floor moaning and we were all hysterical. It was just so funny." But Moroder played the tape for Neil Bogart of Casablanca, who thought the song would be a great late-night novelty hit—and it was! An abbreviated PG-13 version was cut for pop radio and the full seventeen-minute version sent to clubs where it became one of the most celebrated dance tracks of the decade. Critics, of course, wrote off the whole thing as a bad joke and put Summer at the top of their list of sure-to-be-one-hit-wonders. She wasn't quite that, releasing six albums in three years for a dance-crazed public that paid no attention to the critics who told them the products were unworthy of their affection. Minor hits like the synth-pop "I Feel Love" (# 6 in 1977) and a novelty cover of

Jimmy Webb's "MacArthur Park" (# 1 for 3 weeks in 1978) kept her in the public eye, but no reviewer took her seriously until she recorded a song called "Last Dance" (# 3 in 1978) for the soundtrack of the forgettable motion picture *Thank God It's Friday* (starring Jeff Goldblum and Debra Winger). Her first good song, "Last Dance," showed that Summer had real talent; it had the same effect on critics as Madonna's "Crazy for You," transforming a lightweight sex object into a performer whose skills might appeal to the ears and hearts of those whose hormones were not in overdrive. The next year she released the magnificent *Bad Girls*, which soared to well-deserved success on the strength of its one-two punch singles, the rocking "Hot Stuff" (# 1 for 3 weeks in 1979) and "Bad Girls" (# 1 for 5 weeks in 1979). Things kept getting better. Summer ruled the charts in 1979, the year that she also charted "Heaven Knows" (# 4), "Dim All the Lights" (# 2), and an impressive duet with Barbra Streisand, "No More Tears (Enough Is Enough)" (# 1 for 2 weeks). In early 1980, she released a two-disc greatest hits collection and scored another hit with the stirring ballad "On the Radio" (# 5). But all was definitely not well. A profile published in *Penthouse* magazine related that Summer had struggled with mental illness, insomnia, and other health problems throughout her rise to fame: "Traumatized by the frenzy and the new identity imposed on her," the article maintained, "she went through periods of forgetting her name, developed a chronic ulcer, and occasionally checked herself into hospitals for a week at a time." However much of that is true, she did at least file a ten-million-dollar lawsuit against her managers for mismanagement. But by the end of 1980, Summer would emerge a changed, or at least changing, person. She switched record labels, married her boyfriend, Bruce Sudano (lead singer of Brooklyn Dreams, with whom she had performed "Heaven Knows"), and announced that she was a born-again Christian.

Summer's confession of faith was initially greeted with skepticism in the contemporary Christian music scene. She was second only to Madonna on many Christian music fans' list of "artists we love to hate," and the evangelical empire had recently been stung by the highly publicized but apparently temporary conversion of Larry Flynt of *Hustler* magazine. The announcement also came only one year after **Bob Dylan's** *Slow Train Coming,* and the latter artist might have stolen some of her celebrity-conversion thunder. Unlike Dylan, Summer did not seem to be repudiating everything she had ever done. The claim that she had always been a Christian did not sit well with those whose theology attaches salvation to a turning point decision, and unlike Dylan, Summer did not follow her announcement by recording an album full of evangelistic gospel songs. Instead, she released *The Wanderer,* another Moroder-Belotte production in line with all of her previous projects, with a couple of notable exceptions. For the most part, Summer eschewed the sexpot image for the album, singing secular pop songs about love and romance, minus the sensuality that had often marked her work. Further, she included two straightforward gospel songs on the album, "Looking Up" and the self-composed, concluding track called "I Believe in Jesus." The latter song would become the most noticed piece on the album aside from its hit title track (# 3 in 1980) and would win the singer a Grammy award. Although Christian radio stations and the contemporary Christian music subculture in general ignored the song, it was ironically appreciated within the general market. Dave Marsh wrote in *Rolling Stone,* "The song 'I Believe in Jesus' escapes being cloying only by the narrowest of margins—a chorus so perfectly sung that to deny it is practically inconceivable: 'I believe in Jesus / You know I know him oh so well / And I'm going to heaven by and by / 'Cause I already been through hell.' "

Summer soon found herself caught between expectations of her divergent audiences. Christian music fans objected to the fact that she continued to perform her "old material" in concert, including songs like "Bad Girls" (about prostitution) and the sexually charged "Hot Stuff." She talked to *CCM* about this in June of 1981. She said she "coveted the day" when she could "denounce her repertoire of sexy, suggestive songs," but did not think she could do so at present for a couple of reasons. For one thing, she realized that fans who came to her concerts paid money to hear her perform those songs and she did not think it would be fair to deny them. "If I have to perform those songs, it's part of the weight I have to carry because of the wrong I've done. I have to acknowledge that I built this bed and I've gotta lay in it. There will come a time when I won't have to ever do those things again, but you can't clean your house in one day, so I'm doing it methodically." By the same token, Summer said that she was convinced that God wanted her to be a bridge to the unsaved: "If I were to do an about-face and do nothing but spiritual songs, I would lose contact with all those people that would buy my records." These arguments did not go over very well with the contemporary Christian music community, but by 1983, there was evidence that Summer's gradual, methodical house cleaning just might be working. By then, she had mingled several songs with a generically spiritual or specifically Christian focus into her set. Big hits like "Bad Girls" and "Hot Stuff" were still part of the program, but instead of performing "Love to Love You Baby," Summer explained to her audiences why she would "never sing that song again" now that her "marriage and relationship with God had given love a new meaning." Furthermore, at every concert on the 1983 national tour, Summer would conclude the show with a personal testimony: "You may think this is corny, but frankly, I don't care. A couple years ago, I wasn't doing too well, and I turned my life over to God." Rather than boring or

annoying the entire audience of partygoers with her preaching, she simply invited those who were interested in hearing her story to remain after the show when she would tell it in full. Most did, and they got the same thing they would have received at an evangelism crusade: a personal testimony to the life-changing power of Christ, followed by an altar call in which Summer herself led persons in a prayer to accept Jesus into their hearts.

While Summer continued to be regarded with suspicion by church leaders and the Christian music community in general, her new public personna as "the born-again disco diva" alienated a large segment of her traditional audience. What happened next has been widely reported in inaccurate and sensationalist ways. David Kreps wrote in *Pop View,* "Some of her born-again pronouncements alienated gay fans who had been among the first to buy her records." *Blues and Soul* magazine continues, "Her huge gay following turned away from her in droves. Her records were publicly burned. Demonstrations were held opposing the sale of the music and DJs refused to play her records." Noting all of the above, Mark Joseph styles Summer as a brave Christian whose career was all but martyred for the sake of her faith: "The thought police branded her politically incorrect . . . but Summer stood boldly on her principles." None of this is quite right. It is true that Summer had a huge following among the gay community, but there is no evidence that anyone in that community ever turned on her simply because she became known as a born-again Christian or because she sang songs about believing in Jesus or even because she personally believed homosexual behavior to be incompatible with a Christian lifestyle. Rather, a rumor circulated in the early '80s that Summer had said the emerging AIDS epidemic was God's revenge on homosexuals for living in a way that was an abomination to the Lord. Although she would (much) later deny having made such a comment, the quotation was repeated numerous times in the national media and the denials did not come quickly or strongly enough to stem the tide of understandable backlash against her. The quoted remark not only offended gays, but many persons of conscience—including most Christians. Still, Summer found herself in a no-win situation, in which she knew that too strong a disavowal would be interpreted in ways that would only further alienate the conservative Christian audience she was trying to court. She tried to take a middle road, maintaining in a 1983 issue of *CCM,* that "God loves homosexuals but hates their sin." This, however, was not sufficient to calm the opposition that had by then developed within her former fan base.

It is difficult to tell how much these controversies affected the failure of Summer's next project, on which she broke with Moroder and Bellotte for the first time to record the self-titled *Donna Summer* with superstar producer Quincy Jones.

Thematically, the album backs off from obvious gospel influences. It would produce one hit with "Love Is in Control (Finger on the Trigger)" (# 10 in 1982) but is better known for its centerpiece, a song called "State of Independence," written by Jon Anderson (of Yes) and Vangelis (of *Chariots of Fire* fame). The song features an all-star choir composed of James Ingram, Michael Jackson, Kenny Loggins, Lionel Richie, Dionne Warwick, and Stevie Wonder. Still, it tanked just outside the Top 40, a notable failure for a tune with such apparent potential.

Summer would move deeper into contemporary Christian music with two albums produced by the well-known Christian producer **Michael Omartian.** Geffen reportedly had some qualms about allowing the two born-agains to work together. "They thought we'd make a gospel record, like something out of the '30s," Omartian recalls. What they made, instead, was the most successful and acclaimed album of Summer's career. *She Works Hard for the Money* would redefine the artist as a postdisco rock singer with a breadth of talent and style. Yet, according to Omartian, the project is "a Christian album" from start to finish: "The songs on *She Works Hard for the Money* are positively about the Lord," he says. "It's not blatant, but it feels so good that it opens the door for people being open about the Lord." The best-known song on the album, of course, is its title track (# 3 in 1983), a hard rock tribute to a waitress whom Summer also convinced to pose with her for the album's cover photo. "That song is about a woman I met in a restaurant," Summer explains. "My heart filled with compassion for this woman and her position in life." She also indicates that the song was partly inspired by consideration of Hebrews 13:2, which encourages kindness to strangers. The lyric, written by Summer, simply exhorts, "She works hard for the money, so you better treat her right." Other songs on the album have a more obvious spiritual focus. "He's a Rebel" portrays Christ as a mysterious countercultural figure who's "written up in the Lamb's Book of Life" and whose "love's forever." The song "People, People" is practically a prophetic oracle, announcing that "the Father" wants his people to return to him. "Unconditional Love" (# 43 in 1983) paraphrases 1 Corinthians 13 to a reggae beat exalting the quality of "a new kind of love / and we call it agape" (the latter word is derived from the Greek term used in the Bible to describe the love of God). "Love Has a Mind of Its Own" (# 70 in 1984) may just be a secular, though uplifting, tribute to the quality of romantic love, but Summer sings it as a duet with **Matthew Ward** of **2nd Chapter of Acts,** introducing the latter vocalist to a whole new arena of potential fans.

Cats without Claws offers the purely secular delight "There Goes My Baby" (a cover of The Drifters' 1959 hit); it charted at Number Twenty-one in 1984. Otherwise, God often seems to lurk around the edges (and between the lines) of the songs as an unseen (or unnamed) presence. In "Susanna," Summer admonishes a wayward friend to remember that "someone is watching from on high." Rejection of worldly values is the basic theme underlying the jazzy title track and the rather somber "Maybe It's Over." The song "Supernatural Love" (# 75 in 1984) describes a couple's romantic relationship as being grounded in the heavenly source of love that lies beyond themselves. Two songs, finally, are overt gospel tunes: "I'm Free" is a techno-calypso tune celebrating spiritual deliverance, and the closing song, "Forgive Me," is a selection from **Dony McGuire** and **Reba Rambo**'s award-winning musical based on the Lord's Prayer. Musically, however, *Cats without Claws* is not as creative or as inspiring as Summer's previous projects, and critics sensed, rightly, that she had peaked. *All Systems Go* was a total flop. *Another Place and Time* gave her another hit with "This Time I Know It's for Real" (# 7 in 1989). It would be her last Top 40 hit, though she did win a Grammy in 1997 for a song ("Carry On") performed on a VH1 special and was nominated for another Grammy in 2000 for a song called "I Will Go with You." In 2001, Summer was living in Nashville with Sudano, the two of them having written songs performed by Dolly Parton and Reba McEntire.

Although she ceased to be a pop phenomenon in the '90s, Summer maintained her faith and continued to associate herself publicly with Christian events. In 1992, she performed a special benefit concert for the evangelistic organization Youth With a Mission. By 1994, she had basically retired from performing and recording to spend time with her husband and three daughters. She did take time, however, to make a 1994 Christmas album. "It's a ministry record," Summer would say of *Christmas Spirit.* "Christmastime is the best time to minister to people, to love them, and to share what we believe in." The album contains numerous hymns and carols, including a version of **Amy Grant** and **Chris Eaton**'s "Breath of Heaven."

Grammy Awards: 1978 Best R&B Vocal Performance ("Last Dance"); 1983 Best Inspirational Performance ("He's a Rebel"); 1984 Best Inspirational Performance ("Forgive Me"); 1997 Best Dance Recording ("Carry On").

Summer Hymns

See **Joe Christmas.**

Sunday Blue

Jeff Apel, gtr.; Danna Bachman, voc.; Drue Bachman, voc., bass; Scott Bachman, voc., kybrd.; Michael Bouvier, drums. 1994—*Breathe* (Mootown).

Sunday Blue was a Christian alternative rock band from South Carolina whose only album was later re-released on Gray Dot to find a wider audience. The band was led by Drue Bachman who later formed **My Friend Stephanie.** Female vocals were supplied by Drue's wife, Danna; Scott Bachman is Drue's brother. *HM* said *Breathe* has "an R.E.M. meets Aimee Mann" sort of sound, with raw, clanky guitars supporting dry, soft vocals. Chris Colbert of **Breakfast with Amy/Fluffy** fame did some engineering on the album and apparently adds feedback to the title track. Lyrically, the songs on *Breathe* deal with spirituality, expressing a variety of thoughts on the possibilities and realities of humans relating to God.

Sunday Drive

Joel Huggins, gtr., voc.; Paul Lancaster, perc., voc.; Buddy Mullins, gtr., voc.; Marvin Sims, drums, voc.; Mark Willett, kybrd., gtr., voc.; Westley Willett, bass, voc. 1997—*Sunday Drive* (Brentwood); 1999—*Doors Open Wide* (Diadem).

Sunday Drive is a Christian pop band that emphasizes strong vocal harmonies and tight instrumentation on songs with catchy choruses and evangelical lyrics. Group leader Buddy Mullins says that the history of the band goes back at least twenty years to a family group he led called Mullins and Co. As members came and went, Mullins finally solidified a lineup for his group in 1997 and gave them the name Sunday Drive to emphasize "the goal of pressing toward the high calling of Jesus Christ." The group's sound falls into the rockier side of adult contemporary music. On the lighter numbers, they sometimes recall **4 Him**; otherwise, comparisons to vocal pop combos like **PFR** or **NewSong** come to mind. The lyrical approach favors inspirational slogans and straightforward messages for those trying to live a Christian life. The first album features the evangelistic "God Is Believable" and the reassuring "Universal Love." On the song "I Believe," Mullins supplements traditional creedal statements with the affirmation, "I believe God's in love with me." The sophomore *Doors Open Wide* is a bit more contemporary sounding with its jangly guitar-driven title track, which offers an enthusiastic response to Christ's invitation: "Throw the doors open wide / I'm runnin' in / Gonna bow down to my Savior's feet." If "God Is Good" sounds like a junior high camp song, "Soul Revolution" layers a danceable beat with polished, multipart harmonies to great pop effect. The group also covers **Twila Paris**'s "Lamb of God" as a concluding worship anthem.

Christian radio hits: "God Is Believable" (# 1 in 1997); "Say What You Want" (# 25 in 1998).

Sunday's Child

Michael Hawkins, bass, drums, perc.; J. C. Richardson, gtr.; David Vanderpool, voc. 1997—*Now Then* (BulletProof).

Sunday's Child is a light modern rock band from Georgia. Their sound seems to transition between the ethereal stylings of **The Choir** and the organic acoustic rock of **Vigilantes of Love**. *HM* notes a strong similarity between the vocal presence of David Vanderpool in Sunday's Child and Brad Olsen in **The Waiting**. After working with producer Chris Colbert (of **Breakfast with Amy** and **Fluffy**) on several indie projects, the group put together *Now Then* as a mini-rock opera that tells the allegorical tale of a prodigal husband named Victor Silas who leaves his family for Las Vegas on the eve of the nation's bicentennial. After a trio of songs detailing his midlife crisis, the title tune narrates his arrival in the party town. The beautiful (ethereal) "Grace Whispering" reveals that he still hears a small voice calling to him: "Come on home, little angel, come home." The next track, "The Story of Victor Silas So Far," actually summarizes the plot of the entire opus; it stands on its own (and sounds very much like a **Vigilantes of Love** song). Four more songs describe grace's continued presence and the protagonist's eventual response to her plea. The whole enterprise clocks in at under thirty-six minutes, yet critics would note that the story lacks a middle: the songs basically deal with leaving and returning, without offering much commentary (positively or negatively) on the quality of the life apart. There is no pigsty scene (cf. Luke 15:14–16), and the setting in Las Vegas seems incidental. Still, *HM* would grant, "*Now Then* not only has a fascinating tale of prodigality and subsequent remission, but it's got a lot of nice music as well."

Sundry

Chris Coleman, drums; Brian Gauthier, bass; Mark Gibson, voc.; Mike Payne, gtr. 2000—*The Toughest No-Brainer Yet* (True Tunes).

www.sundry.org

Sundry is an earthy heartland-pop band from Atlanta, Georgia. Their sound is compatible with that of hometown peers **Smalltown Poets** and **The Waiting,** with influences from such general market acts as The Wallflowers and **Collective Soul.** The foursome formed with a different guitarist while all of the members were still in high school. They played covers of Christian rock songs, recorded a custom album and CD, and then got picked up for management by former **Smalltown Poet** Michael Johnston. *The Toughest No-Brainer Yet* includes one song ("The Least of These") with guest lead vocals by Mac Powell (of **Third Day**). The song sounds like a **Third Day** song, and its release as the album's first single would cause some confusion with regard to Sundry's actual sound. The rest of the album demonstrates a penchant for complex but catchy modern pop songs with a variety of styles. "God Looks at the Heart" is a party-rock highlight, and "Famous" (rejecting the false idol of fame, while acknowledging its appeal) is delightfully funky. "Enough's Enough" is less successful with a rap approach copped from Red Hot Chili Peppers (or **Reality Check**). "Inside Your Head" has an especially memorable melody, and appropriately so, since it offers a tribute to the power of a song to deliver a message that sticks with people until they need it. "The Drive" sounds a lot like something by Pennsylvania rockers Live and features interesting lyrics relating the thoughts of a prodigal as he draws ever closer to a reunion with someone he hopes will receive him back. Sundry is firmly committed to ministry through music and in their stage shows. "We're dedicated to putting on a high-energy, have-a-good-time, leave-sweaty show," lead singer Mark Gibson says, "but we believe in presenting the gospel. That is the number one priority in our concerts."

Sunny Day Real Estate

Jeremy Enigk, voc., gtr.; William Goldsmith, drums; Dan Hoehner, gtr.; Nate Mendel, bass (−1998). 1994—*Diary* (Sub Pop); 1995—*LP2* [a.k.a. *Sunny Day Real Estate*]; 1998—*How It Feels to Be Something On*; 2000— *Live; The Rising Tide* (Time Bomb).

Sunny Day Real Estate is the definitive emo band, not just in Christian music but in the general market as well. In fact, the group did not begin as a Christian band, and aside from the eventual convictions of its lead singer and songwriter, Jeremy Enigk, it should probably not be labeled as one—depending, of course, on how one defines the terms. The band seemed to court marginalization. They would not do interviews, they would not allow their picture to be taken, and they refused to tour. Sunny Day Real Estate's first album, *Diary,* is generally regarded as the defining masterpiece of the emo genre, even as the record that establishes emo as a recognizable style. Although it was never a big seller commercially, its sound would serve as the prototype for hundreds of imitators. The group also placed a song called "8" on the *Batman Forever* soundtrack (Atlantic, 1995). During the recording of the second album *(LP2),* Enigk became a Christian (or at least reembraced the faith of his upbringing), and his spiritual commitments led to the breakup of the band. Although there was little overt Christianity in the album's lyrics, Enigk posted strong statements of faith on the band's website. In 2001, he would affirm for *HM* that his newfound faith was "the catalyst" in the group's demise: "When you have God on your side, you don't need anything else. So, I had no problem quitting the band because it didn't hold anything of value to me anymore." After the group disbanded, guitarist Dan Hoehner started a tree farm in Washington, while the rhythm section of Nate Mendel and Will Goldsmith joined Dave Grohl in forming The Foo Fighters. Enigk recorded a solo album. As the popularity of emo grew, Sunny Day Real Estate's albums came to be in more demand than when they were first issued. Thus, Sub Pop invited them to reconvene and record a few new songs to fill out a package of previously unreleased material. Against all odds, since the breakup had been bitter, everyone except Mendel agreed to the reunion and, when things went well, they recorded an entire album of new material *(How It Feels to Be Something On)* and then toured together, producing a concert album *(Live)*. In 2000, the group would record again, turning out the hard-edged *The Rising Tide* for a different indie label.

The early SDRE sound involves wild and sudden disparities of tempo, volume, and pitch to create almost melodramatic emotional effects. *Phantom Tollbooth* described it well: "Vocal explosions punctuated [the first two albums] as Enigk would often raise his frail voice an entire octave to obtain an emotional climax. The drums and bass would usually build throughout a song, the guitars would be strummed louder and louder, until critical mass was reached, and then the fireworks would begin. The band could seemingly switch gears instantaneously, leaving the listener to wonder if someone had changed the CD." *How It Feels to Be Something On* takes a more subdued approach, concentrating on sustaining given emotions throughout entire songs, rather than trying to pack everything into every composition. Accordingly, the songs are more diverse than on previous albums. Lyrically, the songs deal with personal experiences and frustrations. "Every Shining Time You Arrive" seems to be just a romantic ode, propelled by an extraordinary melody carried on piano and other keyboards. But on "Pillars," Enigk seems to dialogue with others about spiritual concerns through lines like, "Don't tell me you've gone astray . . . wait for time to turn around your faith." Some Christian fans were disturbed that one song bears the title, "The Shark's Own Private F***," though the asterisks (which are actually part of the title) may be misleading. The song itself contains no profanity, but deals with Mendel's decision not to rejoin the band. *Live* includes songs from the first three albums and so functions as something of a premature greatest hits collection for those who might be just discovering the band. It was promoted as a way for new Christian fans to sample the group's earlier material. *The Rising Tide* opens with a track called "Killed by an Angel," which draws on biblical imagery to paint a bleak picture of life: "Welcome to the lonesome world of Abel / Where every brother's knife is set to slay you / And paranoia keeps you healthy." "Television" has an uncharacteristic pop appeal, and "Snibe" is especially melodic. On other tracks ("Rain Song," "Fool in the Photograph") the band incorporates Middle Eastern accents.

By 2000, it had become commonplace even for mainstream periodicals like *Alternative Press* and *Guitar World* to refer to Enigk as the born-again leader of the general market band, and there can be no doubt that hundreds of Christian music fans picked up on Sunny Day Real Estate precisely because they believed the leader to be "one of them," regardless of whether the songs themselves were understood as particularly inspirational or edifying. *HM* noted that no one had ever bothered to ask

Enigk himself what he thought of this, and so in 2000 they probed a little deeper. Enigk was frank in his response. "It gets really annoying," he said, "because people tend to assume that, because you have become a Christian that you have become like them or become what they think a Christian is." Asked if God is an important part of his life, he replied, "Yeah . . . but I'm not speaking in, like, a religious way, or, like, going to church. I'm not even talking about accepting Jesus Christ as your savior and all that lingo that Christians have kind of created. . . . But as much as God is a part of everybody's life every day, you know, I think God is a part of my life."

Sunny Day Roses

Jonathan Edwards, drums; Jeff Elbel, gtr.; Dave Pinkston, bass; Lewis Richey, gtr.; Suki Chaney, voc. (– 1997) // Janet Lund, voc. (+ 1997). 1996—*Bloomshine* (Marathon).

www.netads.com/netads/music/marathon/sdr/index.html

Sunny Day Roses is a Southern California band formed by Jeff Elbel, formerly of **Farewell to Juliet.** Drummer Jonathan Edwards and rhythm guitarist Lewis Richey grew up together as children of missionaries in Latin America, and at the time Sunny Day Roses released its first album, they were both students at Life Bible College in San Dimas, California. The band describes its eclectic sound as "progressive, alternative pop, with world beat, funk, and jazz influences." Basically, *Bloomshine* continues in the art-rock vein of **Farewell to Juliet,** but the female vocals give the music more accessibility and commercial potential. *True Tunes* would draw comparisons to Peter Gabriel, **Midnight Oil,** and Genesis. Chris Scott of **Precious Death** provides guest vocals for the hard acoustic song, "Dig." "Bean" offers advice to a young child: "Live your life like Jesus would / Forget the talk of being good / Be strong, speak truth, love life, laugh hard / Build up, grow wise, be on your guard."

Since recording *Bloomshine,* Sunny Day Roses has seen a change in female vocalists and, they say, have lessened the jazz and funk influences on their sound while augmenting the emphasis on melody. In 2001, Elbel formed a band called Ping and released an acoustic album (*No Outlet,* Marathon) to benefit Habitat for Humanity and a memorial fund for the late Gene Eugene (of **Adam Again**).

Superchick

Melissa Brock, gtr., voc.; Tricia Brock, voc.; Ben Dally, drums; Matt Dally, bass; Max Hsu, kybrd., gtr.; Andrew, perc.; Dan, lighting; Dave, gtr. 2001—*Karaoke Superstars* (InPop).

Superchick is a female-fronted pop band with a teenybopper style that suggests The Go-Go's in junior high school. The group calls themselves a "pop-punk, hip-hop, disco-funk garage band," but there is little funk and no punk in their sound. Actually, there isn't much hip-hop or disco either. They do, however, relish their "garage band" status, combining basic musical competence with an attitude that exalts amateur status and defies industry expectations. Their official personnel list includes all the persons named above, plus "whoever's in the van when it leaves." Dan, who appears to work sound and lighting at their shows, gets listed because "we make no distinctions between performers and crew." The band members are insistent about going by first names only, but a little detective work reveals their founder to be Max Hsu, formerly of **Church of Rhythm** (with two pairs of siblings accounting for four of the other members). The songs are invariably peppy and memorable, like advertising jingles with inspirational messages. With lyrics like "Barbie's not a role model / She's only make believe" ("TV Land"), the album is obviously directed to the junior high set. The dominant theme is that it's okay to be ordinary and that one's self-worth ought not be determined by such factors as physical appearance or social popularity. The opening track ("Barlowe Girls") has especially strong lyrics, acknowledging the temptation teenage girls face to use sexuality to get attention and reassuring them that there *are* boys who value purity and restraint. The chorus might claim a little too much by insisting that these (Christian) boys think girls "are the bomb" who "remind them of their mom," but the point stands.

Supershine

Bruce Franklin, gtr.; Doug Pinnick, voc., bass. 2000—*Supershine* (Metal Blade).

Supershine was a collaboration between Bruce Franklin of the '80s doom metal band Trouble and the controversial Doug Pinnick of **King's X;** Jeff Olson of Trouble played drums on half the tracks, and Jerry Gaskill of **King's X,** on the other half. According to Franklin, Trouble never was a Christian band, although the group often sang songs with biblical lyrics. Olson, he says, "got saved" and left the band after its first two albums (ironically, he was replaced briefly by Ted Kirkpatrick of **Tourniquet**). Then in 1987 Olson led Franklin to Christ through persistent witnessing and invitations to a Bible study. Unlike Olson, however, Franklin would continue to play with Trouble even after his conversion, saying that it often gave him a chance to witness to people on the road.

Musically, the Supershine album rocks hard, and the songs "Won't Drag Me Down" and "Kingdom Come" have enough of a melodic base to please fans of both **King's X** and Trouble. *HM* liked the sound, which includes "stomping, romping, bold moves, a rumbling low end, and tasteful guitar leads." But Christian music fans were primarily interested in the project for what it might reveal about the next stage of Pinnick's very public faith journey. At last check, the star—who had been involved with Christian music from the early days of the Jesus movement—had admitted to being gay, confirmed theological struggles that might cause some to question his continued identification as a Christian, and recorded an ambiguous album under the name **Poundhound** while behaving in trifling ways (e.g., flaunting obscenities) that struck some as intended to establish a new (possibly non-Christian) persona. To some, the mere fact that Pinnick would record a new album with persons known to be evangelical Christians was a cause for hope. *Supershine* also contains some obvious references to religious attitudes and beliefs. Most notably, "Candy Andy Jane" says "that woman, she loves Jesus too / Said she's gonna go to heaven too." But, as *HM* editor and chief **King's X** watcher Doug Van Pelt pointed out, mere references to Christian subjects do not exactly constitute confessions of faith. The just-cited words and others on the album could easily be interpreted as expressions of either an insider or outsider. The *Supershine* project, furthermore, had actually been started several years earlier, such that the timeliness of the lyrics as a current reflection of Pinnick's mindset should not be pressed. Van Pelt concludes, "I really, really dig this music, but lyrically, to be honest, I can't figure it out."

The Supertones (a.k.a. **The O.C. Supertones**)

Darren Mettler, trump.; Matt Morginsky, voc.; Tony Terusa, bass; Jason Carson, drums (–2002); Kevin Chen, gtr. (–1999); Dave Chevalier, sax. (–1999) // Dan Spencer, tromb. (+ 1997); Brian Johnson, gtr. (+ 1999, – 2000). 1996—*Adventures of the O.C. Supertones* (Tooth and Nail); 1997—*The Supertones Strike Back* (BEC); 1999—*Chase the Sun;* 2000—*Loud and Clear;* 2002—*Live.*

www.supertones.com

The Supertones were the big indie success story for Christian music in 1996 in much the same way that **MxPx** was in 1995. Together, those two groups made Tooth and Nail one of the most significant indie labels in the American music scene. By 2001, The Supertones would unfortunately be linked to a defunct fad, retaining about as much credibility as the Bee Gees held in 1980. But fickle tastes aside, The Supertones have been responsible for some stunning pop music. Their brief tenure as the hottest band in the universe (i.e., the parallel universe of Christian rock) may have been hyperbolic, but their music has consistently displayed a quality that deserves to transcend momentary fashion. The fad that propelled the band to success was ska, or more accurately, the American ska revival, a mid '90s phenomenon that saw a number of bands discovering the style that had rocked Britain over a decade earlier (cf. Madness, The Specials) and infusing it with generous doses of hip-hop and punk (the '80s movement was itself a revival of

a Jamaican '50s style that had prefigured reggae, such that the '90s American form is sometimes called "third wave ska"). The closest, or at least best-known, general market equivalent to The Supertones would be the East Coast's Mighty Mighty Bosstones, though radically different vocal styles would prevent the two groups from ever being confused. The Supertones are as competent as the Bosstones and have generally been more adventurous. They were the first Christian ska band to gain recognition (cf. **The Insyderz, Five Iron Frenzy**) and they broke before the Bosstones had enjoyed widespread success in the general market; thus, for many Christian music fans, their sound was a wholly new phenomenon, something that just seemed to come from out of nowhere.

The Supertones formed in Orange County, California (hence the O.C. that officially precedes their name) in 1995. Though Matt Morginsky is the charismatic front man, Jason Carson has served as the group's unofficial leader, handling interviews with the press and often preaching from the stage. Morginsky and Terusa are the principal songwriters. At one point, Carson was a member of **Unashamed,** but he traces the roots of The Supertones to a group called Saved, which he formed with Morginsky and Terusa while he was still a junior in high school. Saved played regularly for evangelistic meetings, developing a repertoire that included punk, disco, funk, and metal styles. As ska started to catch on, the group decided to recruit a horn section and reform with a style influenced by the Bosstones and by such lesser-known artists as Shankin' Pickle and Operation Ivy. Carson later formed **Any Given Day** as a side project; Chevalier did the same with **The Dingees,** which ended up taking on a life of its own that influenced his decision to leave The Supertones.

The Supertones' first album is their most raw but also remains their most celebrated. It effectively captures that magic moment when the ska wave was surging, about to crest. The first two songs are the standout tracks, though the record is strong from beginning to end. "Who Can Be against Me?" would be the first hit single and would provide most Christian music fans with their first exposure to the new genre. The song is appropriately accessible, with infectious horns, no rapping, and a very moshable beat. It is also exemplary theologically, setting the affirmation of Romans 8:31 against confessions of human weakness ("No matter how hard I try, I always fail / I'll never be like Christ / I know I'll struggle until the day, the very day I die"). "Who Can Be against Me?" was the perfect first single, but "Adonai," which opens *The Adventures of the O.C. Supertones,* is a far better paradigm of the new American ska sound. Indeed, it probably defines that sound as well as any song by any artist in either the Christian or general markets. As such, it was necessarily an acquired taste, especially for all of the rock and rollers who still thought that they hated rap.

"Adonai" starts out with ominous, crushing guitars and thundering drums, as if its going to be some classic rock tune by Led Zeppelin wannabes, but then, all of a sudden there are horns, and *then* the lead singer starts spitting out rapped vocals as if he's wandered into the wrong song. It all works perfectly and would sound completely natural by the year 2000—but in 1996, it was weird and captivating, hooking fans of musical innovation in the same way that **DC Talk**'s "Jesus Freak" had a year earlier. Lyrically, the song simply serves to introduce the band to its audience: "I don't want to be a gangster / I don't want to be the baddest / I ain't no Al Pacino and I ain't no Al Capone / I'm just a rude boy with a new toy / Add two speakers and a microphone." The song title is set against such verses as a repeated one-word chorus, dedicating the song and the album to God (or to "Adonai," which means Lord in Hebrew). Other strong cuts on *The Adventures of the O.C. Supertones* include the dance-or-mosh cheerleading-for-Jesus anthem "He Will Always Be There" and the equally rowdy "Found."

The sophomore release, *The Supertones Strike Back,* was produced by Steve Kravac, known for his work with The Offspring. With a sound quality greatly improved over the debut, it opens with a bombastic title track that declares, "We want this band to be a big love letter / So we play the ska and it makes you feel better." In general, the band seems to have studied the British ska masters in the interim between releases and to have moved their sound more in the direction of those influences; distinctive two-tone blends of organ and bass turn up on numerous tracks. "Resolution" and "Little Man" are pop gems of a first order. The former sounds an awful lot like a Mighty Mighty Bosstones song but is actually better than anything that group ever did and remains The Supertones' sterling masterpiece. Beautifully melodic and hook-laden, the song is about the simple commitment to make a change. Carson would introduce it in concerts by urging, "Every day, make a resolution to live for the Lord." Often, he would offer an altar call-style invitation for everyone in the audience to commit themselves in prayer to something specific (e.g., "let nothing come out of your mouth except encouragement") for one day only. "Little Man" is innovative in that Chevalier and Spencer trade lead vocals with Morginsky. Each singer takes a verse, presenting different superficial estimates of self-worth (based on health, wealth, power, or possessions) against a chorus that proclaims, "Oh, let my pride fall down / I'm a little man." The band's punk roots are more evident on "Unite," which features shouted, angry vocals directed to "cop-outs and fence-sitters." Otherwise, "Tonight" offers a new ska version of an old bedtime prayer ("If I die tonight, I know my soul is with you"), and "Like No One Else" provides another burst of cheerleading affirmations in the same vein as "He Will Always Be There." A Ventures-styled surf-guitar instrumental called "Caught In-

side" supports the overall party sound of the album. The record closes with "So Great a Salvation," a hymn of devotion strummed on an acoustic guitar. The latter two songs effectively previewed the variety that was to mark the band's next project. Meanwhile, in the interim between *Strike Back* and *Chase the Sun,* The Supertones toured with **Audio Adrenaline** and recorded the fiery rock song "Blitz" with that band.

By 1999, the honeymoon period of America's love affair with ska was over and, realizing this, The Supertones devoted an album to musical experimentation, expertly produced by GGGarth Richardson (Rage Against the Machine, Red Hot Chili Peppers). A handful of songs, including the opener "One Voice" and "In Between," reprise the familiar punk-skacore blend, but for much of *Chase the Sun,* expectations are defied right and left. "We're not really a ska band anymore," Carson told *CCM.* "We're just a rock band with horns." The song "Hallelujah" is Caribbean reggae. "Old Friend" and "Refuge" are ballads, the first set to acoustic guitar and the second to a string section. "Away from You" features surprising duet vocals by **Crystal Lewis,** and the almost hardcore "Grounded" opens with a guitar riff lifted straight from Metallica's "Damage, Inc." The song "Sure Shot" is more pop-oriented with a sing-along chorus. "Revolution" is another surf instrumental with a cool '60s guitar-and-organ vibe. Despite these innovations, the band applies a veneer of ska to the various styles they choose to display, which allows *Chase the Sun* to retain at least an illusion of consistency. The real connecting point is thematic: almost every song speaks of some aspect of life in Christ. "I'm wide awake and thinking about the cross," Morginsky sings in "Sure Shot," and such clear-eyed devotion seems to inform all of the group's theological preoccupations. "In Between" speaks of the struggles of Christian growth: "I'm in between who I am and who I want to be."

Loud and Clear continues along the same lines as *Chase the Sun,* infusing ska-flavored rock with heavy punk and rap influences. This time out, the group tried direct analog recording (as opposed to digital) to achieve more of a live-in-studio effect. *The Phantom Tollbooth* declared the fourth outing to be the band's best, and *CCM* described it as "loaded with irresistibly catchy tracks and a relaxed feel." The songs "Wilderness" (about periods of doubt) and "Jury Duty" (about remaining thankful even on dark days) are particularly melodic and memorable. The opening "Escape from Reason" takes its title from a book by the popular philosopher Francis Schaeffer and lambasts complacent churches to a hardcore beat: "Tell me, who will listen to uneducated congregants? / And why should they, when all we have to say is / Bumper sticker theology doctrine and cute catch phrases? / Does this amaze us that no one will take us seriously?" Those lyrics suggest a move away from the band's earlier "cheerleading songs" and accurately reflect a new seriousness. Instead of singing about "jumping for Jesus," on *Loud and Clear* the group sings about "propitiation," "apostasy," and Trinitarian dogma. The booklet accompanying the CD supplies paragraph explanations for the meanings of most of the songs just to make sure listeners get the most important points. "Return of the Revolution" is another hardcore rap tune that calls for the church to recapture the spirit of the Reformation and the Great Awakening through a renewed commitment to holiness and sound doctrine. This newfound maturity and encouragement of theological leaning is impressive—and all too rare in contemporary Christian music—but the group doesn't always get it right. In the song "Pandora's Box," they include "neoorthodoxy" alongside pornography and LSD on a list of evils let loose in the world, and they define neoorthodoxy as a pseudo-Christian, false philosophy, that "differs from true Christianity in significant ways." Actually, neoorthodoxy is a major Protestant tradition (best represented by Karl Barth) that helped to define the agendas of conservative Christianity in the latter half of the twentieth century; even those who fault the tradition would not characterize it as non-Christian.

The Supertones were one of the '90s most blatantly evangelical (and evangelistic) bands in the Christian market, devoting generous concert time to preaching and proselytizing. Still, they managed to earn some respect in the general market on the merit of their music alone. The video for "Supertones Strike Back" got played on MTV despite its over-the-top spiritual histrionics ("I jump for Jesus who frees us / Let's get dumb like Beavis / I don't care who sees us"). The band also played on that network's *Oddville* show and on Comedy Central's *Viva Variety* as well as providing official entertainment for a party honoring Super Bowl XXXIV Most Valuable Player, Kurt Warner. At the same time, they performed at Billy Graham crusades and played for Pope John Paul II on his historic visit to St. Louis in 1999. In late 2000, it was announced that Jason Carson was leaving The Supertones to take a position as a youth minister. The band continued to perform and planned to continue recording.

Christian radio hits: "Resolution" (# 16 in 1997); "Grace Flood" (# 13 in 1998); "Away from You" (# 8 in 1999); "Old Friend" (# 20 in 1999).

Sup the Chemist

2000—*Dust* (BEC).

Sup the Chemist is the second incarnation of Christian rapper Chris Cooper, who previously recorded as Super C in the group **SFC**. He pronounces his new name "Soup," as in short-for-Super. *Dust* has all the attitude and street credibility of general market releases—a problem for some Christian music fans but an asset of the music for others. It was produced by Gene Eugene (of **Adam Again**) and numerous high-profile, nonrap artists play on it. **Michael Roe,** Andy Prickett (of **The Prayer Chain**), and Eugene are all in the house band laying down some tight grooves for the star to rap over. **Jon Gibson** joins him on one cut, and **Project 86** comes in on the hard, apocalyptic song "Is This a Dream?" Sup's style favors humorous, stream of consciousness raps filled with Dennis Miller-like cultural references. He also likes to throw in surprising changes in style and draw upon unpredictable samples. The song "As the Sun Rises" offers a version of **Kansas**'s "Dust in the Wind" playing in the background. It is this ability for mixing diverse sounds and influences (rock, soul, jazz) that earns him the nickname "the Chemist."

Lyrically, Sup's songs cover a wide range of topics including the role of art in the life of a believer ("Language of Imagination") and his own frustrations with the music industry ("My Shot"). "My message is Number One in my music," he says, "but I am not a Christian rapper. I'm a rapper that is a Christian. I'm not into saying the name of Jesus 500 times a song, but I'm willing to praise his name and lift it up while singing about topics people can relate to." Lyrically, the highlight of *Dust* may be "Photograph," in which Sup wanders into a digression about his son and about his own desire to set a godly example for him to follow. Such moments of vulnerability are few and far between. Otherwise, the album is somewhat spoiled by Sup's incessant bragging about his own abilities. Such boasts turn up in at least three-fourths of the tracks and do not become less pretentious with time.

The Surfers

Peter King, voc., gtr., bass, kybrd.; Rob Machado, voc., gtr., kybrd.; Kelly Slater, voc. 1998—*Songs from the Pipe*.

The Surfers are a new modern rock band founded by Peter King of **Dakoda Motor Co.** For some inexplicable reason, the band was completely shut out of the contemporary Christian music scene; not a single magazine or Internet publication profiled the group or reviewed its album—despite the fact that King had been on the cover of *CCM* two years before. *Songs from the Pipe* was produced by mainstay **T Bone Burnett,** who plays on the album along with Dakoda-exes Chuck Cummings and Derek Toy. Burnett's wife, **Sam Phillips,** adds backing vocals. The group's name is deceptive in that their sound is not primarily '60s or '70s surf music, though touches of Hawaiian guitar show up here and there, and a number of songs ("Going," "I'm Not Your Slave," "Hawaii," "Anything from You") start out like Ventures outtakes before morphing into something much more modern. There is at least as much country influence in the band's sound as beach music; indeed, comparisons to the **Lost Dogs** would not be out of order. The album opens with a meditative instrumental called "Australia" and closes with a Smashing Pumpkins *Mellon Collie*ish piano and guitar piece ("Two Together"). The song "Never" reflects on the failure of good intentions (unkept New Year's resolutions) and has the singer concluding, "If you're lost forever / I will be there too." Likewise, "Spill" is a heavy song explicating the biblical realization that "There is none good / No, not one" (Romans 3:10). On "If" (not a Bread cover), King affirms, "I know I have a future / I know there is a key / I know I have a father / And I know that he knows me."

Sweet Comfort Band

Bryan Duncan, voc., kybrd.; Randy Thomas, gtr.; Kevin Thomson, drums; Rick Thomson, bass. 1977—*Sweet Comfort* (Maranatha); 1978—*Breakin' the Ice* (Light); 1979—*Hold On Tight*; 1981—*Hearts of Fire*; 1982—*Cutting Edge*; 1984—*Perfect Timing*; 1985—*Prime Time*; 1995—*The Light Years*.

Sweet Comfort Band is remembered as one of the most musically original and proficient Christian groups to come out of the Jesus movement. The group played for a time as a trio (without Thomas) before officially organizing as Sweet Comfort Band in 1976. They took the name from 1 Thessalonians 4:16–18. Prior to SCB, Randy Thomas played in the early Jesus music groups Sonrise and **Psalm 150.**

Sweet Comfort Band began with a jazz-rock fusion sound and gradually moved toward a more formulaic mixture of straightforward rock and MOR (cf. Chicago). Sweet Comfort Band was probably the most exciting band in Christian music when they were at their peak in the late '70s and continued to be one of the brighter spots for the scene during the doldrums of the early '80s (the nadir of Christian pop and a low point for rock in general). They were sometimes compared to general market acts like Ides of March or Blood, Sweat, and Tears, though they were much more funky and, frankly, much better than either of those groups—largely due to Duncan's expressive and soulful voice, one of the best in rock and roll. Better analogies may be found in The Rascals, the Doobie Brothers, Hall and Oates, and the Little River Band, though the fact that comparisons to *all* those acts can be sustained testifies to the group's originality. They disbanded in 1984. **Bryan Duncan** went on to pursue a highly successful solo career, and Randy Thomas formed the **Allies** with **Bob Carlisle** and later played in **Identical Strangers.** He and Carlisle have continued to be songwriting partners; they cowrote the latter's general market hit, "Butterfly Kisses" and a Number One country song for Dolly Parton called "Why'd You Come in Here Looking Like That?" The Thomson brothers did not continue to be involved with music full time but settled in Riverside, California, where Rick runs a construction company and Kevin is in the insurance business.

The group's first two albums are probably their best. The self-titled debut on Maranatha is the most raw and possesses an endearing garage band charm. "Get Ready" and "It's So Fine" are especially powerful, and "Childish Things" also shines. "His Name Is Whispered" sets the standard for numerous soulful Sweet Comfort ballads to follow. "Golden Ages" is a tribute to the late Bill Sprouse of **The Road Home.** The best-known song from *Sweet Comfort,* however, would be "Somebody Loves You," a jazzy Duncan composition that personalizes the message of the gospel in a straightforward way: "Somebody loves you / Somebody cares." **Bob Wilson** of **Seawind** produced the group's Light debut, *Breakin' the Ice,* adding orchestra and a much more polished sound. It was rightly described by Bruce Brown of *CCM* as "one of the most legitimate white R&B albums ever released." The song "Searchin' for Love" is a rousing anthem with a sound similar to early Doobie Brothers classics like "Long Train Runnin' " or "China Grove." Two Thomas-Thomson tracks, "Good Feelin' " and "Got to Believe," have a heavier jazz influence and are stellar songs—examples of the best that Christian music has ever had to offer. "I Love You with My Life" is a definitive Christian ballad that would later be redone as a solo offering by Duncan (the SCB version is better). Lyrically, the latter song offers a variation on the "love song to Jesus" theme by presenting words that Christ would presumably say to those whom he loves, pledging his eternal devotion and faithfulness to them. "I Need Your Love Again" is quintessential Duncan, defining the sound that would come to be called blue-eyed soul.

With *Hold On Tight,* Sweet Comfort Band moved away from the jazz roots to adopt a more mainstream R&B rock sound. The title track calls on struggling believers to hold fast to the truth of Christ, which alone can sustain them. "Carry Me" is a slowed-down, moody rock song, a bit like Grand Funk Railroad's "Closer to Home," but with more progressive stylings. "Undecided" is highly melodic radio pop—the kind of song that provides the raison d'etre for Top 40 radio stations. Duncan's voice soars and floats over so many memorable hooks that only the most cynical critic could ever doubt that the song would have been a Top Five hit in the general market had artificial distinctions between Christian and secular formats not pigeonholed it for a venue where its charm was enjoyed by a privileged few.

Hearts of Fire represents a creative step down as the group began to adopt the stylings of arena rock bands and to craft songs that would meet the narrow expectations of "Christian Hit Radio." They come off as a better version of **Petra,** still head and shoulders above most Christian rock outfits of the day but nowhere near the potential they had proved they could fulfill on previous outings. The opening track, "Isabel," employs **Kansas**-like keyboard frills on a song dealing with the hard times that new believers can face in defining themselves over against established life patterns and associations. "You

Can Make It Happen" borrows its main riffs from Toto—not the best arena rock group to emulate. "Contender" is the kind of rock song that Foreigner or Bad Company might have done but, in spite of the derivative quality, provides one of *Hearts'* finer moments. The album's best song is "Feel Like Singing," a celebratory song that hearkens back to the glory days of "Good Feelin'." Otherwise, *Hearts* has many quiet moments. "Can You Help Me?" is a worshipful ballad with lyrics by **Bob Bennett.** "You Need a Reason" is a dime-a-dozen MOR ballad that may be sweet and inspirational but is far from distinctive for the MOR-inundated Christian music scene. "Just Like Me" is a romantic proposal (with a rare lead vocal by Thomas). Lyrically, "The Road" offers an honest report of struggle, and "They Just Go On" portrays the futility of life as some know it without attempting to provide an immediate orthodox antidote to such an existence. As *CCM* would note, the band gains in credibility by not feeling they have to "present the ultimate truth of the universe" in every single song.

The same overly-polished sound that infuses *Hearts of Fire* would also take the edge off *Cutting Edge* and *Perfect Timing.* The former features one great song, "Valerie," which is neither a Monkees nor a Steve Winwood cover but a soaring Randy Thomas ode to some girl with that same musical name. The song requires an unusually powerful vocal performance, and Duncan delivers it. As with *Hearts of Fire,* there are no bad songs on *Cutting Edge,* and the ironically titled album would have been very well received if produced by a band with less potential. "Changed Hearts" and "Haven't Seen You" are beautiful, if typical, adult contemporary ballads. "Runnin' to Win" has great rock passion, and "Breakdown Love" exemplifies a Southern California sound with a touch of Eagles country. "Falling in Love with You" has more of the synth-driven Totoesque or **Kansas**-lite sound. For the final album *(Perfect Timing),* Sweet Comfort Band chose to work with Dino Elefante, who has a reputation for turning out over-produced and too-slick products. The results were predictable: Sweet Comfort Band turned into "**DeGarmo and Key** with a better singer." The songs "Never Should Have Left You" and "You Led Me to Believe" are two more dime-a-dozen adult contemporary ballads; the latter at least has an interesting lyrical theme (betrayal by a spiritual mentor). "Sing for the Melody" tries to be a Queen-like anthem, and "Lookin' for the Answer" goes for the **Kansas** sound again. The only really good song is "Envy and Jealousy," which builds into an irresistible hook-filled song that transcends easy categorization.

Thomas attributes the breakup of the band to the fact that he and Duncan were regarded as "the talent," while the Thomson brothers were in charge of all business matters. Initially effective, this division of labor became "an eight-year time bomb" bound to produce competing agendas. After Duncan left the group to pursue his solo career, **Bob Carlisle** filled in as lead singer for a final European tour. This provided something of a transition from the pairing of Thomas and Duncan in Sweet Comfort Band to the even more (commercially) successful pairing of Thomas and Carlisle in the **Allies** and beyond.

The deterioration of Sweet Comfort Band from one of the most dynamic and creative bands in the rock scene (Christian or otherwise) into a competent no-surprises group that imitated the sounds and styles of decidedly lesser artists speaks volumes about the low self-esteem of the Christian music industry, a perennial problem that would in no way have abated by the turn of the millennium. From its inception, the Christian music industry has often prized mediocrity over artistry, rewarding those artists who have the broadest and most immediate appeal to lowest-common-denominator tastes. In 1983, *CCM* magazine actually boasted that Sweet Comfort Band now sounded like a Christian version of Toto, as though overcoming former pretensions about having a sound of their own and being on the cutting edge of musical creativity was a *good* thing. Normally, critics are entrusted with the sometimes unpleasant task of calling artists on the carpet for sacrificing artistic relevance for the sake of easy commercial appeal; when the critics join forces with the sales reps and hand out accolades for what deserves a scolding, the pressures against retaining artistic integrity become almost insurmountable. For SCB, they did prove insurmountable. Nevertheless, the group left an impressive legacy: two of the finest Christian rock albums in history; one more *(Hold on Tight)* that is excellent; and three that, while formulaic and predictable, at least manage to deliver the expected goods more competently than is sometimes the case. *Prime Time* and *The Light Years* are compilation albums.

For trivia buffs: On March 6, 1982, Sweet Comfort Band discovered that thieves had broken into their van in San Antonio, Texas, stolen their belongings, and left the vehicle disabled. In order to get to their concert that evening in Houston, Thomas rode with the equipment truck and the other three took a private plane. The plane ran into rough weather and crashed, bouncing into a marsh. Although the plane itself was totaled, Duncan and the Thomsons were somehow unharmed and made it to the show a few minutes before it started.

Christian radio hits: "Got to Believe" (# 6 in 1979); "Searching for Love" (# 20 in 1979); "I Love You with My Life" (# 14 in 1979); "Undecided" (# 80 in 1980); "You Need a Reason" (# 7 in 1981); "Never Should Have Left You" (# 30 in 1984).

Michael Sweet

1994—*Michael Sweet* (Benson); 1995—*Real;* 1998—*Truth* (custom); 1999—*Unstryped* [EP].

www.michaelsweet.com

As lead singer for the seminal Christian rock band **Stryper,** Michael Sweet (b. 1963) helped to bring Christian rock to the attention of the general market. In 1992, he abruptly left that band, in part due to artistic differences and, in part, as a reaction to a morass of gossip and criticism that was causing the group and its ministry to come apart at the seams. Two years later, Sweet would emerge as a solo artist. His debut for Benson moves away from the heavy metal sound best associated with **Stryper** to embrace a power-pop approach that, in fact, the band had also displayed on some of its more radio-friendly material ("Calling on You," "Sing Along Song"). Still, the album was hailed as a departure and, while possibly disappointing some of **Stryper**'s most committed headbanging fans, was critically received as a necessary and natural development from '80s glam-metal to a more up-to-date sound. "Tomorrow" and "All This and Heaven Too" are rock songs in the tradition of Bryan Adams or Jon Bon Jovi, featuring big background vocals, memorable melodies, and sing-along choruses. "J.E.S.U.S." is an unambiguous cheerleader song, and "Tomorrow, Tonight" is one of Sweet's prettiest power ballads. Lyrically, "Tomorrow, Tonight" offers Sweet's apology to his wife for what he would call years of neglect and misdirection during the **Stryper** years. "Ain't No Safe Way" is an ode to sexual abstinence. A video for the latter song was rejected by MTV, leading Benson to charge the video network with ideological censorship; a spokesperson for MTV insisted that "the video's quality just wasn't up to our programming standards." A second album called *Real* continues in the same vein, albeit with an even stronger acoustic orientation. On *Real,* Sweet delivers a couple of love songs ("Baby Doll," "Why"), an antiracism song ("Color Blind"), and no fewer than five songs in which Sweet adopts the perspective of Christ and sings a personal message from Jesus to the audience. Of these, the highlight is an acoustic remake of the **Stryper** song "Always There for You." After a hiatus, Sweet would return to recording with privately produced albums sold over the Internet. *Truth* is an eclectic collection with sounds ranging from aggro-metal tracks to very introspective and contemplative numbers. *Unstryped* is a limited edition set of five songs, two of which feature **Guardian**'s Tony Palacios on guitar.

Christian radio hits: "All This and Heaven Too" (# 17 in 1994); "Tomorrow, Tonight" (# 14 in 1995); "Forever Yours" (# 19 in 1995); "Always There for You" (# 1 for 2 weeks in 1995); "The River" (# 3 in 1996); "Remember Me" (# 23 in 1996).

Sweet Nectar

Alicia Luma, voc.; Jairemi Gray Rodgers, bass, voc.; Joe Turner, drums; Devon Thompson, gtr., voc. 1995—*Tired Face in Clown Paint* (R.E.X.).

The alternative grunge band Sweet Nectar received virtually no coverage in the Christian music media aside from a review in the always attentive *HM* and a dismissive remark in *7ball.* The latter mag complained that "the guys in Sweet Nectar seem determined to make their record as inaccessible as possible." *HM,* of course, took that anticommercial tendency as a benefit and praised the debut as a "never boring showcase for a talented band that puts its best foot forward and doesn't disappoint the listener." The group started as a band called Four Living Creatures, who released the indie album *Proletariat Poetry,* also in 1995. The latter record was picked up by R.E.X. but, because of personnel changes, the group changed its name. *Tired Face in Clown Paint* is basically *Proletariat Poetry* redux with a couple of song substitutions. The sound is sometimes similar to Pearl Jam by way of Stone Temple Pilots. The group does, however, revel in its lo-fi sound, such that the songs generally sound like they were recorded on a home cassette recorder set up in somebody's basement. "Tangent" and the title track are particularly intense, standout tracks. Lyrics are obscure but contain many religious references. In "Tangent," someone screams, "Long live the sufferer . . . who learned me how to crave . . . my Christ oblivion." A song called "Twenty-Two" mixes lines from that psalm ("My God, my God, why have you forsaken me?") with phrases from the Song of Songs ("Let him kiss me with the kisses of his mouth").

Robert Sweet

2000—*Love Trash* (World Gone Mad).

Robert Sweet (b. 1960) was drummer for the quintessential Christian metal band **Stryper,** which he founded with his brother **Michael Sweet.** After that group broke up, Robert played with a band called Blank for a while and, at the end of the millennium, recorded an independent solo album. Sweet plays all of the instruments (guitar, bass, drums) on *Love Trash,* but Larry Worley of **Fear Not** provides guest vocals on the eight tracks. The overall sound of the album is that of hard grunge rock with nods to both Nirvana and **White Heart.** Sweet wrote all eight of the songs, many of which bear shock-value titles. "The F Word" is a headbanger about forgiveness. "I'm ?@#$%&!" is addressed to God and features the key lyric, "I'm screwed without you."

Sweet Spirit

Morley Halsmith; Ken Oakes; Dan Pawley (−1976); Mary Taylor (−1976); Mark Turner (−1976); Lester Tany (−1976) // Andrew Affleck (+ 1976); Jerry Britton (+ 1976); Mark Selkirk (+ 1976). 1974—*Into His Presence* (Christopher); 1976—*Sweet Spirit II.*

Sweet Spirit was an early Canadian Jesus music group blending jazz with folk-rock in a mixture that augmented the traditional **Children of the Day-**type sound with generous flute, synthesizer, and saxophone. In fact, they already had a sound in 1974 similar to that which **Children of the Day** was developing on their last album in 1979 (though, of course, they did not have songwriters equal to the four composers with Carter, Jacobs, or Stevens surnames). *Harmony* magazine called Sweet Spirit's first release "one of the best Canadian albums." That magazine's toughest critic (a writer who called himself Blue Samuel Flying) complained about sound quality on *Sweet Spirit II* but noted that the group's songs "rarely preach but rather gently persuade as if saying, 'This is what I've found and you need it too'."

The Swirling Eddies

Jerry Chamberlain, gtr., voc.; Tim Chandler, bass; Greg Flesch, gtr.; David Raven, drums; Terry Taylor, gtr., voc.; Rob Watson, kybrd. // Gene Eugene, gtr. (+ 1989); Michael Roe (+ 1996). 1988—*Let's Spin* (Alarma); 1989—*Outdoor Elvis*; 1994—*Zoom Daddy*; 1996—*The Berry Vest of . . .*; *Sacred Cows.*

www.swirlingeddies.com

The Swirling Eddies has been an on-again, off-again side project for **Terry Scott Taylor** that seems to serve primarily as an outlet for material that doesn't fit into any of his numerous other incarnations (solo material, **Daniel Amos**, the **Lost Dogs,** the **Rap'sures,** and **The Farm Beetles**). Somewhat ironically, however, The Swirling Eddies turned out to be more successful than anyone might have guessed (their debut album outsold any of DA's projects) and went on to assume a life of their own. In that regard, they may be The Monkees of Christian music. They do play their own instruments, but their sound is basically grounded in the '60s with wildly eclectic offerings that sometimes evoke a high degree of wackiness but often stumble upon brilliance. Musically, the more accurate comparisons would be the Beatles and the Beach Boys, with dollops of The Eagles tossed into the mix. In short: incredibly creative, always surprising, pure pop genius. The only rule for the Eddies seems to have been to have fun. When their debut album appeared, Taylor told *CCM,* "I tried not to think very hard on this one. If an idea came and it was fun to think about and fun to listen to, we wanted it." Also in 1988, he told the *Harvest Rock Syndicate,* "The fact that a good deal of the Christian industry doesn't like us makes me feel good because I feel that some of the minds in the industry are the most lazy and narrow. We're in touch with the Creator of the universe and we (i.e., Christian rock bands) have to play these same cheesy licks three years after the secular world, and I hate that." At the very least, The Swirling Eddies gave the Christian music scene some moments it will not soon forget, such as **Terry Taylor,** dressed in drag, belting out a heart-rending version of Helen Reddy's "I Am Woman" at the 1990 *Cornerstone* Christian music festival.

The Swirling Eddies started with appropriately silly hype that presented them as "a mystery group." The members all went by phony "Eddie" names (Taylor was Camarillo Eddy), and a contest was held for fans to figure out their true identities. Most of the Eddies were just members or alumni of **Daniel Amos,** so, in fact, the group can almost be viewed as that band performing under a different name. Gene Eugene from **Adam Again** and later, the **Lost Dogs,** joined on the second album. Superstar **Michael Roe** (also of the **Lost Dogs** and of the **Seventy Sevens**) appears on the silly *Sacred Cows* only. In addition to working with the Eddies, Rob Watson and David Raven have played in a '90s incarnation of The Surfaris, along with Jay Truax of **Love Song.**

Let's Spin turned out to be a much better record than anyone was expecting. It is not an album of novelty songs, but a solid pop contribution with a retro-**Daniel Amos** sound of *Shotgun Angel* and *Horrendous Disc.* In the years preceding its release, DA had been obsessed with their Alarma Chronicles, and many nonphilosophy majors among their fan base viewed the Eddies' project as a return to what the group does best. Some of the songs are perhaps a little too similar to the DA repertoire. "I've Got an Idea" is almost a remake of "I Love You # 19," with added bounce, and "Ed Takes a Vacation" (a minor suite) recalls "Near Sighted Girl with Approaching Tidal Wave," with added Brian Wilson imitations. The title track ("Let's Spin") represents one of Taylor's only ventures into near disco funk, with enigmatic lyrics buoyed up by swirling guitars that provide an aural illustration of both the song's and the group's name. "Big Guns" seems to parody the militant imagery of crusades ancient and modern (cf. **Petra**) to establish righteousness or evangelize the heathen at any cost: "We're gonna bring out the big guns tonight / We're gonna right all the wrong that is right / We're gonna spill some blood and shed some light." The song "Rodeo Drive" offers this reflection: "We all need money and we all need love / But when we get all we need / It's never enough." And again: "People come and go so quickly here / What they want is not exactly clear / Judas kisses fallin' on virgin's ear." Likewise, "What a World, What a World" seems to reflect on the superficiality of Hollywood culture with a longing for some other place "where the people are nice and the air is clean." Musically, the latter song displays Taylor's pop sensibilities at their best, offering yet another example of his frequent rumination on the question, "I wonder what the Beach Boys would have sounded like if they'd gone country?" Finally, "Catch That Angel" is another pop gem with lush harmonies and lyrics that focus rather generically on the universal quest for the blessings of life, love, and happiness.

Outdoor Elvis does have its share of novelty songs, starting with the title track. A Dr. Demento entry that isn't very interesting musically, the song "Outdoor Elvis" is at least sufficiently humorous to be enjoyable nine or ten times (but no more). Lyrically, it relates what happens when Elvis and Bigfoot sightings get confused and a *Life-of-Brian*-style messianic cult grows up around the illusive figure of a giant Elvis supposedly stalking the woods: "You can pretty much tell that he's lost weight by the depth of his footprint." By contrast, "Coco the Talking Guitar" and "Arthur Fhardy's Yodeling Party" are just annoyances that go on too long like lame *Saturday Night Live* sketches. Still, these are minor flaws on a record filled with delights. "Driving in England" is a chugging rock and roll song that uses the image of driving the wrong way on a freeway as a metaphor for life "in the wrong lane." It got airplay on alternative Christian rock stations, becoming the Eddies's one and only "hit" (a relative term, to be sure, when describing the subsubgenre of alternative Christian rock). There are a couple of tunes that parody Christian culture: "All the Way to Heaven" lampoons evangelism fads, including spandex-wearing Christian rockers; "Potential" takes on the "theology of glory" evident in teachings that present Christ as the means to a self-affirming end, and "Attack of the Pulpit Masters" lampoons TV preachers who get rich off of such heresies. "Yer Little Gawd" is addressed to those Christians (including numerous fans of contemporary Christian music) who compartmentalize their spirituality as relating only to nonworldly, "religious" matters. A song called "Knee Jerk" seems to describe in advance the likely reactions to another song: "Hide the Beer, the Pastor's Here," a frat-rock romp with tongue-in-cheek lyrics poking fun at the decidedly nonfrat atmosphere of America's Bible colleges—many of which are named in the song. When the group came under predictable attack from the latter schools, Taylor claimed the song was really about "hypocrisy." Meanwhile, it became a hit among students on Bible college campuses everywhere, and (student) representatives from a number of schools complained that their institutions *didn't* get mentioned. In a more serious vein, "Hold Back the Wind, Donna" calls attention to overlooked things that really matter: "It's the little things you do / That you don't think break through / You build a mansion with God's Son / You light a candle / And the kingdom comes." Similarly, the song "Billy Graham" is a short ode to the famous evangelist whose integrity and "no disguise" contrasts with the styles of "those other guys." "Strange Days" is not a Doors cover but a gorgeous Taylor solo that offers his bittersweet longing for maturity. He sings it in a low, plaintive voice set against a simple acoustic guitar, listing things that could happen "in the strange days of our lives." Finally, "Blowing Smoke," for Taylor's wife, is tender, provocative, and lovely.

The first two Eddies albums had been released nine months apart. After that, the group went dormant for five years, long enough to be forgotten, and then suddenly reappeared with the even more experimental *Zoom Daddy*. It was sort of an album made on a dare. The band reportedly went into the studio and recorded a number of instrumental tracks, then came up with titles, challenging Taylor to write lyrics that would fit them. A party spirit must have prevailed, for many of the titles are of the "he'll never come up with anything for *this*" variety. "God Went Bowling" manages to offer some reflection on the dual nature of humans as both physical and spiritual beings. "I Had a Bad Experience with the C.I.A. and Now I'm Going to Show My Feminine Side" is as odd as it sounds. "Disco Love Grapes" has potential hit single written all over it—musically it is almost as compelling as **The Newsboys**' "Love Liberty Disco," and it has eucharistic imagery and John 15 allusions woven all through it to boot. "Pyro Sets a Wildfire" has a sound in keeping with '90s alternative pop, with little chiming guitars in the background and a very melodic tune (cf. The Church or the Lemonheads). "The Golden Girl of the Golden West" is a "Hotel California"-type exposé of "a liposuckin' diva with a saline chest" who proves that beauty can indeed be only skin deep. The song draws on biblical imagery of "the harlot" as a metaphor for temptation, but can't help but come off a bit sexist for the '90s: "One man's blessing and another man's curse / She's an economic engine with her gears thrown in reverse." Perhaps the Eddies intended to throw Taylor a curve by giving a slow and somber tune a title like "The Twist," but he used that tune to support the group's most serious song. With deadly pathos, it uses graphic descriptions of Christ's agony on the cross as a backdrop to upbraid the lukewarm: "Look me in the face / At least what's left of it / Tell me you still love me just a little bit / Nail me down . . . do me in / But don't leave me hangin', dyin', danglin', twistin' in the wind." Lyrically, "The Twist" turns out to be one of Taylor's most majestic moments, combating not only apathy but the gnostic spirituality that causes it: "Here, touch my side / Let doubt be crucified / Nailed with your wounded pride / To love's grim altar / Here, taste my flesh / My bloody humanness / I am no phantom guest / No skinless martyr / So taste and feel / There's nothing to conceal / You always knew the deal was sacrifice."

The Berry Vest of the Swirling Eddies is a compilation album of mostly well-chosen favorites from their three main projects. Three new songs are added, including an acoustic Taylor solo called "With the Tired Eyes of Faith." *Sacred Cows* is a total novelty project on which the group covers ten "contemporary Christian classics" in ridiculous ways. **Audio Adrenaline**'s "Big House" is done as a prison song medley with **Al Denson**'s "Alcatraz" (*the* big house, get it?). **Amy Grant**'s "Baby Baby" is sung falsetto (in a baby voice, get it?). **DC Talk**'s "I Love Rap Music" is done in a very nonrap lounge singer style. **Carman**'s awful "Satan, Bite the Dust" is sung with a lisp. **Kim Boyce**'s "Not for Me" is performed in a faux blues-rock style. **DeGarmo and Key**'s "God Good, Devil Bad" is now a bit of a polka and has new lyrics that lampoon the song's simplistic sentiment: "sun hot, snow cold / knife sharp, spoon dull / socks stink, flowers don't" (of course, the *original* song was a parody of simplistic lyrics and, so, it perhaps doesn't deserve ridicule on that account). In any case, *Sacred Cows* is a collection of inside jokes for the Christian music subculture, good for nothing more (or less) than a few laughs—a Christian version of Weird Al Yankovic. The Swirling Eddies also released a cassette called *Swirling Mellow,* featuring cheesy muzak versions of their songs. Eventually, this was combined with **The Farm Beetles**' *Meat the Farmbeetles* album for re-release on a single CD.

Switchfoot

Chad Butler, drums; Jon Foreman, gtr., voc.; Tim Foreman, bass. 1997— *The Legend of Chin* (re:think); 1999—*New Way to Be Human;* 2000—*Learning to Breathe.*

www.switchfoot.com

Although there have been many groups that would try to seize the title, San Diego's Switchfoot was Christian music's most authentic answer to Weezer—exponents of slacker rock with strong pop influences as varied as XTC, Sugar, and The Police. Then the band grew up, without the disappointing effects that such a development usually brings. All three members of the group are (or at least were) big-time surfers; their name derives from a surfing term (changing orientation on the board), which they sometimes imbued with spiritual, metaphorical significance. The band formed when Chad Butler and Jon Foreman were students at the University of California, San Diego and little brother Jim Foreman was still in high school. A rough demo tape fell into the hands of **Charlie Peacock** who put the group on the fast track to indie success.

The Legend of Chin is most notable for the song "Chem 6A," which actually gained quite a bit of airplay on regional general market stations. Lyrically, it states a basic adolescent ethos: "I don't wanna read the book, I'll watch the movie . . . I think I'd rather play around . . . I'd rather watch TV . . . I'm just like everybody else my age." Such honest and perceptive songwriting would become a Switchfoot trademark, earning the group a mandate to speak, now and then, of more serious matters. "Ode to Chin," a song directed to a friend of the band members, offers the straightforward conclusion, "Life's more than girls / God's more than words / You're more than this." Musically, most of the songs are bouncy and just a little bit chaotic—few follow the traditional verse and chorus song structure—but the band also slows things down for the occasional emotive ballad ("You").

The sophomore project, *New Way to Be Human,* would suddenly reveal a new, nonslacker Switchfoot. Both Foremans were now in college (Butler had graduated), and apparently they had been doing their homework. The songs on *New Way to Be Human* reveal a wide range of intellectual influences that transcend the usual fundamentalist favorites of the contemporary Christian subculture. The most startling of these is Hebrew Bible scholar Walter Brueggemann, one of the most prolific and insightful theologians of the twentieth century, whose views unfortunately have rarely trickled down to affect the masses in ways that the music of Switchfoot might afford. Such influences appear to surface on the title track, which describes redemption as offering more than just atonement for past wrongs. Likewise, "Something More" relates thoughts from Augustine's *Confessions,* and "Sooner or Later" articulates the humble musings of Søren Kierkegaard. Musically, the group develops more of a power-pop sound without compromising its experimental modern rock credentials—similar in some respects to **PFR.** "Company Car" exposes the emptiness of materialism by exposing a successful businessman as every bit as much a slacker in his own right as the protagonist of "Chem 6A."

CCM hailed the third album, *Learning to Breathe,* as "a brilliant record—musically, it's inventive, yet more accessible than previous efforts." The project finds Switchfoot incorporating Radiohead influences and snippets of technological trickery into their expanding milieu of styles. Thematically, it deals with the concept of "movement" and hence, with growth and development. It begins with the stellar "I Dare You to Move," a deceptively quiet, but powerful song that challenges the listener to live "as though today had never happened before." The title track is both ethereal and anthemic, carrying the theme of the first song forward with specifically spiritual application. "You Already Take Me There" is a driving track musically suggestive of Squeeze. "Love Is the Movement" is a grand opus, featuring a gospel choir chorus with background vocals by **Darwin Hobbs.** Jon Foreman says that its lyrics were inspired by the images of frozen statue-like people awaiting redemption in C. S. Lewis's *The Lion, the Witch and the Wardrobe:* "A day in L.A., and millions of faces are looking for movement / And everything's frozen and everyone's broken / And nobody moves and everyone's scared / That the motion will never come." More in keeping with earlier Switchfoot, "Poparazzi" takes a satirical look at pop culture (and pop music) set to the same sort of quirky fun sound that made "Chem 6A" and "Company Car" fan favorites. Throughout the project, Jon Foreman demonstrates strong songwriting skills, crafting his most melodic songs to date with intelligent and provocative lyrics: "In the economy of mercy / I am a poor and begging man / In the currency of grace / Is where my song begins" ("The Economy of Mercy").

For trivia buffs: Although it has never been mentioned in any interview or article regarding Switchfoot, Chad Butler appears to be the son of Jesus music pioneer **Chuck Butler,** famous for his work with such bands as **Country Faith** and **Parable.**

Christian radio hits: "New Way to Be Human" (# 6 in 1999); "I Turn Everything Over" (# 6 in 1999); "Learning to Breathe" (# 3 in 2000); "Love Is the Movement" (# 8 in 2001).

Symbiotica

Ann Brown, voc.; Kai, voc.; Lamya, voc.; Lygia, voc.; Sandra Stephens, voc.; et al. 1997—*Symbiotica* (Graceland).

Symbiotica is one more project from the trio of producers and instrumentalists responsible for albums by **Shack of Peasants.** Los Angeles superstar **Lanny Cordola** joins with Gary Thomas Griffin and Chuck Wright to present a record of musi-cal styles from around the globe. Instrumentation includes not only guitar, oboe, flute, piano, and accordion, but also the exotic sounds of koto, bazuki, duduk, and melodica. Several vocalists are employed, including Sandra Stephens, who has sung on a number of Cordola's projects (notably, **Shack of Peasants**' albums, plus *Shades of Blue;* see listing for Cordola). The result is an album that might be compared to works by Dead Can Dance, Bjork, Peter Gabriel, or **The Revolutionary Army of the Infant Jesus.** The album opens with a tribute to missionaries: "You don't look for numbers / You don't look for fame / You don't look at colors / Or for anyone to blame / You sow the seeds of Utmost High / You sow the seeds of hope / You sow the seeds and hold a dying child / Your compassion helps them cope" ("Missionary"). Other tracks explore Celtic, Arabic, and Indian sounds, usually with biblical or spiritual lyrics. Cordola has also recorded with **Chaos is the Poetry, Children of Zion, Magdalen,** and **The Panorama Ramblers;** Wright and Griffin took part in some of those projects as well.

Tables of Stone

Colin Genereux, voc.; Ken Mahoney, gtr.; et al. 1998—*Engraved* (independent).

The Canadian band Tables of Stone drew quite a bit of critical attention with their independent release *Engraved* in 1998. The band had released an earlier album in French, and one song here ("Fidele") continues that bilingual tradition. Otherwise, the Tables sound like a harder version of **The Kry,** and Genereux's voice bears more than a little similarity to that of compatriot Bryan Adams. Their songs feature melodic arrangements with big, sing-along choruses. Lyrically, every track is strongly evangelical with messages that proclaim God's eternal grace and call upon the listener to follow Christ. "Choose to Live," "Throne of Grace," and "The River" are standout songs.

Ty Tabor (and Platypus)

By Ty Tabor: 1997—*Naomi's Solar Pumpkin* (independent); 1998—*Moonflower Lane* (Metal Blade). By Platypus: 2000—*Platypus* (Ice Cycles).

Ty Tabor is best known as lead guitarist for **King's X.** He recorded a Beatlesque solo album called *Moonflower Lane* while that band was on hiatus. *Naomi's Solar Pumpkin* was basically a first edition of this record, with slightly different versions of six of the songs plus four songs that would ultimately get scrapped. As a solo artist, Tabor expands on the pop side of the **King's X** equation; most of the songs on *Moonflower Lane* sound like **King's X** songs, specifically like the upbeat, sunnier tunes that are in the minority of that group's repertoire. They are most similar to the occasional **King's X** songs on which Tabor sings lead (**Doug Pinnick** is the usual lead vocalist for **King's X**), songs like "It's Love" and "Mississippi Moon." Several members of the **Galactic Cowboys** back Tabor on the album but the sound is not what would be called hard rock. Tabor favors jangling guitars and acoustic strumming, and these are mixed in generously with the expected power riffs. Harmonies abound. "The Truth" features some "lai, lai, lai" chorus singing. Only "Hollow Eyes," a song of social conscience, captures the dark and angular style of Tabor's main band, breaking down into some discordant scratching, which is in turn interrupted by explosive guitars.

Moonflower Lane opens with the happy sounds of Tabor singing "I've got a good life / Yes, I do" to a tune that could have been on *Sgt. Pepper.* The sentiment of that song ("I Do") establishes the lyrical theme: joyful celebration. The good-to-be-alive feeling informs his family life: "Look at the years just fly away / I'm in love with my love another day" ("Walk with My Love"). The strongest, or most explicit, faith statement may come on "The Truth," where Tabor alludes to John 8:32 ("Let the Truth set me free") and reflects on the need to stop and hear the still, small Voice ("I pray that I don't blow it off again"). The last verse of the song contrasts such spirituality with megachurch consumerism and prosperity preaching: "He said, just believe and get anything / A red Lamborghini, a big diamond ring . . . And I wonder what God thinks of him."

Tabor also recorded an almost-solo album with an assemblage of friends under the group name Platypus. The pseudoband included John Myung and Derek Sherinian of Dream Theater plus Roy Morganstein, drummer for a group called Dixie Dregs. That project, released on the independent Ice Cycles label in 2000, offers an honest but difficult look into a human life dealing with pain and sadness. The opening song, "Oh, God," is a desperate plea for relief and comfort, similar lyrically to some biblical psalms of lament. "Better Left Unsaid" expresses regret for hurtful words: "An absent thought becomes a comment / etched in all eternity . . . my tongue can be a two-edged sword / and you can be the enemy." The project closes with a ten-minute instrumental ("Partial to the Bean"). *HM* magazine preferred the Platypus project to Tabor's previous work.

Ty Tabor produced the album *Lament* for **Resurrection Band** and played guitar on that record. He has also played (along with folks like Brian May, Ted Nugent, Slash, and Steve Vai) on a number of instrumental albums recorded by drummers Carmine Appice (once of Vanilla Fudge) and Munetaka Higuchi (of Loudness).

Joni Eareckson Tada

See **Joni Eareckson.**

Russ Taff

1983—*Walls of Glass* (Myrrh); 1985—*Medals*; 1987—*Russ Taff*; 1989—*The Way Home*; 1991—*Under Their Influence*; 1992—*A Christmas Song*; 1994—*We Will Stand*; 1995—*Winds of Change* (Reprise); 1999—*Right Here, Right Now* (Benson).

Russ Taff (b. 1953) has one of the stronger voices in contemporary Christian music in terms of timbre and quality, and he has used it more sparingly than most, foregoing the usual album-a-year route to provide the Christian subculture with records of well-crafted R&B, pop, and adult contemporary songs. Two of his albums, *Russ Taff* and the comeback *Right Here, Right Now,* are especially noteworthy for their content as well.

Taff grew up in what he calls "a holy roller Pentecostal church" in Farmersville, California. In 1995, years after he had become disaffected with many aspects of Pentecostalism, he would still testify to a spiritual experience he had at the age of nine. At a revival in Missouri, he prayed at the altar, "Jesus, fill me with the Holy Ghost," and was immediately knocked unconscious for forty-five minutes. When he woke up he felt "so close to Jesus" and was speaking in tongues. In fact, he was unable to speak English for half an hour. "I cannot explain that experience," he said to *CCM* over thirty years later. "I've never talked about it because it sounds spooky to some folks. But I know that it happened and I know that it was real." Still, many aspects of Taff's religious upbringing were culturally

limiting. He was not allowed to participate in nonchurch social functions, read newspapers or magazines, watch TV, or listen to nongospel music. His father was the preacher, though he also worked full time as a machinist. He was also an alcoholic, as Taff would relate at a 1983 press conference accompanying the release of his first solo album. At that same conference, Taff testified to the reconciliation between father and son that had finally been achieved, but his struggle with the past and the off-and-on-again aspects of that difficult relationship would continue to provide a backdrop for his career.

Taff began singing in church as a young child and was immediately noticed for his gifts. By the age of ten, he says that he was aware of the power he had to affect people when he sang. With puberty he obtained what **Van Morrison** has called "a rare gift of God"—a voice with "a *yearrgh* at the end"—a soulful rasp that is either there or it isn't but can never be taught or duplicated. When he was fifteen, his family moved to Hot Springs, Arkansas, where he met a lifetime musical buddy, James Hollihan Jr. The two of them formed the Christian group Sounds of Joy (different from that which included pre-**Commissioned** members). They did covers of songs by Jesus music artists like **Love Song** and **Larry Norman** and they recorded three albums, including one produced by **Gary Paxton.** Around this time Taff also sang (uncredited) on a Christian musical called *Yahweh,* released on Shalom Records in the mid '70s. Then he joined **The Imperials** and remained lead singer for that group (with Hollihan as guitarist) throughout what was to be their most successful period. Taff is featured prominently on the group's *Sail On, Live* (1978), *Heed the Call, One More Song for You, Christmas with The Imperials,* and *Priority* albums. His voice would become known to thousands of Christian music fans on such classic songs as "Water Grave," "I'm Forgiven," "Praise the Lord," "The Trumpet of Jesus," and the novelty tune "Oh Buddha." He cowrote the hits "Finish What You Started" and "Be Still My Soul." He left **The Imperials** in 1981, in part because he was paid a straight salary for his services, with no percentage for ticket or album sales—a deal that might have made more sense at a time before Taff turned the group (briefly) into the single best-selling contemporary Christian music group in the country. Since that time, Taff has concentrated on his solo career, though he frequently appears as a guest on albums by other artists. He jokes that his record company was going to put out an album of all the duets he has sung with other artists, until they realized it would have to be a double disc (cf. **Glen Campbell, Carman, O'Landa Draper, Tanya Goodman-Sykes, Phil Keaggy, Koinonia, Mylon LeFevre, Sandi Patty,** and **Patti Roberts**).

Walls of Glass features the huge hit "We Will Stand," on which Taff is backed by an all-star choir of other Christian artists including **Laury Boone, Harry Browning,** and **Cynthia**

Clawson. Taff wrote that song with his wife, Tori, who would continue as his songwriting partner throughout his career. He says it was inspired by an incident in which a concert by gospel singer Archie Dennis Jr. was canceled after the pastor learned the singer was an African American. "We Will Stand" offers a classic statement of unity in mission: "You're my brother, you're my sister / So take me by the hand / Together we will work until he comes . . . And as long as there is love, we will stand." *Walls* also features "Tell Them" (not the **Andraé Crouch** song), which encourages prophetic social commentary. A remake of **Michael and Stormie Omartian**'s "Jeremiah" (which has the same theme) has Omartian himself on keyboards in place of the prominent horns on the original version. The title track is directed against the self-reliance of materialism ("Why judge your worth by what you have / Those things will pass / They will shatter like walls of glass"). The first album also includes "Kathryn's Song," a tribute to the then recently-deceased healing evangelist Kathryn Kuhlman, written by **Patti Roberts**. *CCM* described *Walls of Glass* as having a less pop, more "churchy" sound than **The Imperials** (who most people would think sound pretty churchy).

Taff next won the critics over with what a *CCM* reviewer predicted would be picked as their choice for best album of 1985. That prediction was not fulfilled (1985 being the year **U2** released *The Unforgettable Fire*), but *Medals* would come to be regarded as a Christian classic. Produced by Jack Puig (who began his career engineering for **Brown Bannister** on **Amy Grant** albums and went on to work with Diana Ross, Barbra Streisand, and Kenny Loggins—as well as with such rock bands as Supertramp, Tonic, Semisonic, and Jellyfish), the album draws on many of Los Angeles's finest studio musicians for a crack presentation of high-tech, glossy pop similar to that of Hall and Oates. Taff's voice is even better suited to blue-eyed soul than Daryl Hall's, and he shows himself more than able to perform the upbeat songs like "Medals" and "How Much It Hurts" in a convincing rock style. "Rock Solid" offers a confident declaration of stability in Christ, and "Not Gonna Bow" supplies the concomitant rejection of competing interests. Less of a stretch are the trademark adult contemporary ballads (a style that Taff owns and has practically defined): "Silent Love," "Here I Am," and "God Only Knows." The theme of the album's popular title track is that, since Jesus never won any medals for the battles he won, Christians need to let their lives become those badges of honor for him. The song inspired a short-lived fad among some Christians (encouraged by the Myrrh marketing department) of wearing a badge that looked like a military-type medal on their clothing as "a witnessing tool," i.e., to promote conversation with those who might ask what it meant. A 2001 poll of critics sponsored by *CCM* magazine put *Medals* at Number Thirty-six on a list of "The 100

Greatest Albums in Christian Music." The only criticisms of *Medals* were that its sound was a bit *too* derivative of Hall and Oates and its lyrical themes a bit too geared toward "simplistic triumphalism" (as Brian Quincy Newcomb put it) and expressive of a militancy inappropriate for the Christian gospel (cf. **Petra**).

Those complaints would be satisfied on the next outing, simply titled *Russ Taff*. This eponymous offering features the singer declaring, "It's a long, hard road," followed by a rousing version of **The Call**'s anthem to hard faith, "I Still Believe." Taff would testify in magazines that the album had been preceded by a crisis of faith, in which he specifically came to doubt "the whole charismatic movement, that whole way of believing that had always been with me." From there, he says he questioned more generally "if God is real." This appears to have left its mark on his performance, for the posturing of the first two projects is gone. In general, the *blues* component of R&B gets more emphasis on *Russ Taff*, with the artist howling on "Shake," covering **Charlie Peacock**'s lament "Down in the Lowlands," and offering just a taste of acoustic slide blues on the traditional "Steal Away." Other highlights of the album include "(Living on the) Edge of Time" and "Higher" (which is not the **Creed** song, but a tune cowritten by the Taffs with folk-pop singer John Hiatt). Dann Huff (of **White Heart, Giant**) and **Dave Perkins** offer some blazing guitar work here and there. "Walk between the Lines" (written by Perkins) and "Believe in Love" (written by **Chris Eaton**) are more traditional pop with a discernible orientation toward Christian radio. Years later, *Russ Taff* would still be lifted up in the artist's discography for its stark honesty and "dark night of the soul" feel.

Ballads again come to the fore on *The Way Home,* an album with an organic approach that draws also on the singer's roots in gospel and folk music. "Farther On" is a gentle song that finds Taff singing to Jesus, "I hear you have a soft spot for fools and little children / I'm glad, 'cause I've been both of those." The song "I Cry" is dominated by strings, but "Table in the Wilderness" comes off as a folk song. "Go On" draws on traditional gospel. Both "Winds of Change" and **Michael Anderson**'s "I Need You" have the sound of Bruce Springsteen's midtempo rockers. The above-mentioned *CCM* critics' poll of 2001 put *The Way Home* at Number Eleven on a list of "The 100 Greatest Albums in Christian Music."

Under Their Influence is a special project that seeks to mine the roots of Christian rock (and, indeed, of rock in general) by delving into the music of pre-rock and roll gospel blues, the slide-guitar-based genre of music that Taff had referenced with "Steal Away." Hollihan again is his coproducer and chief collaborator on the project, which strives to update some of the standards with some pop sheen without destroying what the artist calls their "soulful legacy." Standout tracks include "Ain't

No Grave" (a snippet of which Taff had used as an interlude on *The Way Home*) and "Were You There?" The songs "God Don't Never Change" and "God's Unchanging Hand" reveal a prevalent theme (namely, constancy). Taff also remakes his own "Just Believe" (originally from *Walls of Glass*) emphasizing its roots in gritty soulful blues. *Under Their Influence* is dedicated to Taff's mother, who sang with a gospel group called The Johnson Sisters.

After a Christmas project and an uneven hits collection that draws from the first four albums only *(We Will Stand),* Taff released a mainstream country album called *Winds of Change* for distribution in the general market by Reprise (a division of Time Warner). *Winds of Change* includes new versions of two songs from Taff's Christian albums ("I Cry," "Winds of Change") in addition to a handful of new cuts. "Bein' Happy" is a good-time shuffle featuring drums, fiddle, and dobro. "Once in a Lifetime" is a weepy, pedal steel song with a touch of bluegrass. "Home to You" closes the album with a typical "I've been too long on the road" love song.

Right Here, Right Now would mark Taff's return to the Christian pop market, his first regular release to that subculture in a decade. Few people remembered him and, for teenagers at least, the album was for all intents and purposes a debut by a "new artist." That said, the album would go a long way toward winning them over. *Right Here* opens with a powerful classic rock song on which Taff affects a Joe Cocker vocal style ("Somebody's Comin' "). The next track, "Back into Grace," is a country ballad. The juxtaposition of these two songs demonstrates the breadth of Taff's canvas, drawing equally on traditional gospel and southern gospel and bringing the two together more effectively than any artist since Elvis. The title track and "Lazarus" (a baptism hymn, surprisingly) also rock with an impressive energy and urgency, and the album closes with a completely unexpected suite of orchestral music and spoken word moments (including recitation of the Nicene Creed) called "The Shadow of the Cross." The centerpiece of the album, however, concerns a trilogy of original songs on which Taff grapples with the recent loss of his father. The gulf between them had widened, and the seventy-nine-year-old man would die in September of 1997 just one day before Taff flew to his side to make one more attempt at a lasting reconciliation. The song "Things Will Be Different" was written by Hollihan and describes the picture of a mother and her children growing up in denial and defense of "Daddy's little problem." Spouse Tori wrote "Cry for Mercy," a prayer by one who is at the end of his or her rope—possibly the prayer of Taff himself or of his long-suffering mother. But it is "Long Hard Road" (written by Russ and Tori) that scores the album's most poignant and memorable moment. This appears to be the song he announced at the beginning of "I Still Believe" way back on

that eponymous disc, delivered at last. "We loved each other so much" Taff sings to his departed father, "but not very well." The song looks for the ultimate closure to the problems of their relationship in the life beyond: "Don't think that this is over / Don't think this is solved . . . In the New Jerusalem, with all our defenses down / You will say the words I long to hear and healing will be found."

Christian radio hits: "We Will Stand" (# 1 for 15 weeks in 1983); "Pure in Heart" (# 35 in 1983); "King of Who I Am" [with Lulu Roman Smith] (# 15 in 1985); "Silent Love" (# 3 in 1985); "Medals" (# 3 in 1985); "Here I Am" (# 7 in 1985); "I'm Not Alone" (# 6 in 1986); "Walk between the Lines" (# 1 for 10 weeks in 1988); "Believe in Love" (# 16 in 1988); "Down in the Lowlands" (# 6 in 1988); "I Still Believe" (# 6 in 1989); "Farther On" (# 1 for 6 weeks in 1989); "I Cry" (# 1 for 4 weeks in 1989); "Winds of Change" (# 19 in 1990); "Table in the Wilderness" (# 7 in 1990); "I Need You" (# 6 in 1990); "Wipe a Tear" [with O'Landa Draper] (# 17 in 1982); "Your Love Broke Through" [with **Phil Keaggy**] (# 22 in 1992).

Dove Awards: 1981 Male Vocalist; 1982 Male Vocalist; 1984 Male Vocalist; 1986 Pop/Contemporary Artist *(Medals)*; 1989 Rock Album *(Russ Taff)*; 1990 Rock Album *(The Way Home)*; 1990 Rock Song ("The River Unbroken").

Grammy Awards: 1983 Best Gospel Performance, Male *(Walls of Glass)*; 1991 Best Rock/Contemporary Gospel Album *(Under Their Influence)*.

Tait

Chad Chapin, drums; Lonnie Chapin, bass; Pete Stewart, gtr.; Michael Tait, voc. 2001—*Empty* (ForeFront).

www.taitband.com

Tait is a Christian rock band organized around Michael Tait, who is best known as one-third of **DC Talk.** The latter group took an eighteen-month sabbatical in 2000–2001 to allow each of the members to record a solo album. Unlike partners **Toby Mac** and **Kevin Max,** Tait decided to lose himself somewhat in another band, one that included such heavyweights as Lonnie Chapin (formerly of **Petra**) and **Pete Stewart** (formerly of **Grammatrain**). Tait had produced Stewart's two solo albums (he also produced an album for **Heather Miller** and cowrote the Christian radio hit "Show Me" for **Out of Eden**). Musically, Tait has a strong retro-pop sound, drawing on the classic sounds of '70s R&B and blue-collar rock. Of the solo projects by the three Talkers, Tait delivers the most Top 40, hook-laden album—and the one that is most in keeping with the main band's most successful music. The album opens with "Alibi," a song that sounds like a goosed-up version of **The Throes'** "Mess with Me" from *12 Before 9.* "Bonded" is a Lenny Kravitz-inspired song with trite lyrics playing on tired analogies between "the Son" and "the sun." Much better is the hook-laden, soulful "All You Got," which expresses the feeling of spiritual deprivation. "Spy" sounds like one of **DC Talk's** hard-edged songs and deals lyrically with the intrusions that Christian music stars must endure from self-appointed gate-keepers prone to doubt their faith or integrity. "Talk about Jesus" is a catchy pop song creatively written from the perspective of a needy person for whom Christian witness would have to be more than verbal: "I don't understand what you're talking about / All I see is pain when I look around." Sampled comments from what might be called "Voices of White People" infect the song "American Tragedy," an antiracism anthem. "Looking for You" is a sweet ballad of missing someone who is "my soul's desire, all I ever needed." The song "Carried Away" is a near-perfect pop hit, as bouncy as anything by Smash Mouth, with a bit more grit. "Unglued" closes the album with a piano ballad on which the artist reflects on the loss of his father, brother, and sister—all in a single year.

For trivia buffs: While still in college, Michael Tait auditioned for a spot in **The Gaither Vocal Band.** He lost to **Mark Lowry.**

Christian radio hits: "All You Got" (# 1 for 3 weeks in 2001).

Take 6

Alvin Chea, voc.; Cedric Dent, voc.; Mark Kibble, voc.; Claude McKnight, voc.; David Thomas, voc.; Mervyn Warren, voc. (– 1991) // Joey Kibble (+ 1991). 1988—*Take 6* (Reunion); 1990—*So Much 2 Say* (Reprise); 1991—*He Is Christmas* (Warner Bros.); 1994—*Join the Band*; 1996—*Brothers*; 1998—*So Cool*; 1999—*Greatest Hits*; *We Wish You a Merry Christmas*; 2000—*Tonight: Live*; announced for 2002—*Beautiful World*.

www.take6.com

Take 6 is a vocal pop-jazz gospel group from Huntsville, Alabama, that has enjoyed both commercial success and critical respect within the general market. Their sound has its roots in the doo-wop sounds of acts like The Hi-Lo's and The Ink Spots and in the almost-forgotten music of such traditional gospel quartets as the Fairfield Four and the Swan Silvertones. The essential ingredients consist of four-part a capella harmony with a lead vocal, rhythmic background, and walking bass line. To these, they add such jazz elements as extended harmonies and anatomical percussion. *The Rolling Stone Album Guide* says, "Take 6 has revolutionized the pop vocal tradition by using it as a vehicle for communicating their deep and abiding faith in God."

The origins of Take 6 lie in a quartet formed by Claude McKnight at Oakwood College, a Seventh-day Adventist school in Huntsville, in 1980. As the story goes, Mark Kibble heard the four freshmen harmonizing in a rest room and helped them develop from the original barbershop style to foster a more jazz-oriented a capella style with voices imitating instruments. Kibble would serve as the group's primary arranger, and he brought in Mervyn Warren to expand the combo to a sextet. The group went by the name Alliance for a time; then, after some personnel changes, they became Take 6 and began recording in 1987. Their first album was a surprise hit, in part because Stevie Wonder noticed it and sent copies of it to all his friends as Christmas presents; according to group member Alvin Chea, Wonder told the fledgling artists that their music "had changed his life." The group would win a flurry of Grammy awards and would be the first self-identified gospel artist ever to win such an award in a nongospel category when their song "Spread Love" won for Best Jazz Vocal Performance. That same year (1988), they were actually nominated for the Grammy for Best New Artist *not* Best New *Gospel* Artist—the first and only time that a gospel artist has ever been considered for such an award. Similarly, the group would be chosen Best Jazz Vocal Group for four years in a row in *Downbeat* magazine's prestigious readers' poll, and Leonard Feather, jazz critic for the *L.A. Times,* would call them "the best vocal group in the country." By 2000, they would be listed as the only music group in history to have performed on six of America's top award shows: the Academy Awards, the Grammy Awards, the Country Music Awards, the Dove Awards, the ESPYs (sports award show), and the Soul Train Music Awards. All of their albums would go gold or platinum in sales.

In 1997, McKnight said, "One of the things we wanted to do over the years was to sing with and to the people within the industry who needed to hear it." In keeping with this mission statement, Take 6 would interact with general market artists and achieve a presence in secular venues almost unprecedented for Christian music artists who are not named **Amy Grant.** In 1990, the group performed a song called "Ridin' the Rails" with k. d. lang for the motion picture *Dick Tracy.* In 1991, Take 6 recorded the theme song for the TV series *Murphy Brown,* which was written by Mervyn Warren. As time went by, they sang with Stevie Wonder on his *Conversation Peace* album, with Don Henley on *The End of the Innocence,* with **Kenny Rogers** on *Timepiece* and *Something Inside So Strong,* with Johnny Matthis on *Better Together,* and with Randy Travis on *High Lonesome.* They also contributed to such motion picture soundtracks as *The Bodyguard, Boyz in the Hood, Do the Right Thing, Glengarry Glen Ross, The Out-of-Towners,* and *The Prince of Egypt.* Warren left the group in 1991 to become a successful producer; he did the soundtrack album for *Sister Act II,* some records by Manhattan Transfer, and an urban contemporary Christian version of Handel's masterpiece called *Handel's Messiah: A Soulful Celebration.* The latter features a stellar version of "O Thou That Tellest Good Tidings to Zion" performed by Take 6 with lead vocals by Stevie Wonder.

The debut *Take 6* is unanimously considered to be the group's best. It includes the hit "Spread Love," an antigossip composition by Kibble, Warren, and McKnight that calls on the talkative to share good news instead of spreading rumors.

Otherwise, the album is heavy with traditional spirituals like "Mary, Don't You Weep," "Milky White Way," "David and Goliath," and "Get Away Jordan"—all soul gospel standards that the group gave new life with their inventive harmonies. The album's finest accomplishment, however, may come by way of introducing millions of new listeners to the music of **Ralph Carmichael** via a beautiful rendition of his Christian youth group classic "A Quiet Place." *So Much 2 Say* features a larger number of original compositions, including the hip-hop influenced, "I L-O-V-E U," which draws its verses from 1 Corinthians 13. They also offer a humorous take on **Carman**'s "Sunday's on the Way" and another Carmichael standard, "The Savior is Waiting." On *Join the Band* and *Brothers,* the group forsook their trademark a capella style to sing with full instrumental accompaniment. *Join the Band* features collaborations with such artists as Ray Charles, Herbie Hancock, Queen Latifah, and Stevie Wonder. "Biggest Part of Me" is a cover of the Top 10 general market hit for Ambrosia (# 3 in 1980), with lyrics revised to present Christ (rather than a romantic partner) as the object of devotion. *Brothers* was a disappointment, presenting the group as yet one more version of Boyz II Men (or **4 Him**), but with more emphasis on solo voices than harmony. In response to negative reviews of the latter album, the group returned to its a capella roots on *So Cool.* The title track to that album expresses the thought that it would be "so cool" if all the world knew Jesus and his love; Cedric Dent's "Fly Away" is an anticipation of heaven (similar lyrically to the hymn "I'll Fly Away") set to an African tune, with shades of reggae. The group has also released two Christmas albums and a *Live* project. The latter album draws primarily from their first two records, supplemented by a number of covers: Charlie Chaplin's "Smile" and a rewritten Christianized version of **Marvin Gaye**'s "How Sweet It Is (To Be Loved by You)" (cf. **Joe English, Johnny Rivers**).

Take 6 has not made nearly the impression in contemporary Christian music that might have been expected for an explicitly Christian group with such a following in the general market. In part this may be because their a capella style is viewed as something of a novelty or because genre confusion places them more into traditional gospel categories. McKnight says, "To the gospel or contemporary Christian listening audience, Take 6 has always kind of been viewed as a mainstream group, and to the mainstream market, we've always been viewed as a gospel or contemporary Christian group."

For trivia buffs: Cedric Dent has a Ph.D. in Music Theory and Composition. The topic of his dissertation was *Harmonic Development of the Black Gospel Quartet Singing Tradition.*

Christian radio hits: "I L-O-V-E U" (# 3 in 1990); "Something within Me" (# 23 in 1991); "Biggest Part of Me" (# 3 in 1994); "Can't Keep Going On and On" (# 21 in 1994).

Dove Awards: 1989 Group of the Year; 1989 New Artist of the Year; 1989 Contemporary Gospel Album (Take 6); 1989 Contemporary Gospel Song ("If We Ever"); 1991 Contemporary Gospel Album (So Much 2 Say); 1991 Contemporary Gospel Song ("I L-O-V-E You"); 1992 Contemporary Gospel Album (He Is Christmas); 1995 Contemporary Gospel Album (Join the Band).

Grammy awards: 1988 Best Jazz Vocal Performance by a Duo or Group ("Spread Love"); 1988 Best Soul Gospel Performance by a Duo, Group, Choir, or Chorus (Take Six); 1989 Best Gospel Vocal Performance by a Duo, Group, Choir, or Chorus ("The Savior Is Waiting"); 1990 Best Contemporary Soul Gospel Album (So Much 2 Say); 1991 Best Jazz Vocal Performance by a Duo or a Group (He Is Christmas); 1994 Best Contemporary Soul Gospel Album (Join the Band); 1997 Best Contemporary Soul Gospel Album (Brothers).

The Talbot Brothers

John Michael Talbot, voc., gtr., banjo; Terry Talbot, gtr., voc. 1974—*The Talbot Brothers* [a.k.a. Reborn] (Warner Bros.); 1980—*The Painter* (Sparrow); 1990—*No Longer Strangers;* 1995—*The Talbot Brothers: A Collection of 35 Favorite Songs.*

The Talbot Brothers is the duo consisting of **John Michael Talbot** and **Terry Talbot,** both of whom have had solo careers in contemporary Christian music. A dwindling number of classic rock fans also remember them as the core of the almost-forgotten country rock band Mason Proffit. Driven by acoustic guitars and vocal harmonies, the latter group had a sound that was more rootsy than The Eagles and more folksy than The Outlaws. The closest comparisons would probably be Buffalo Springfield, Poco, and the also almost-forgotten band Little Feat. Like the latter group, Mason Proffit enjoyed a strong underground following. The group would mix traditional folk songs like "Stewball" in with original compositions by the Talbots. They never had a hit, but they did produce four popular albums for Warner Bros.: *Wanted* (1969); *Movin' toward Happiness* (1970); *Last Night I Had the Strangest Dream* (1971); and *Bareback Rider* (1972). A two-record compilation set, *Come and Gone,* came out in 1973; its title seems ironic or prophetic, since a song called "Come and Gone" (a gospel tune) would actually appear on *The Talbot Brothers* a year later and become one of the group's best-known post-Mason Proffit tracks. In the late '90s an independent company called One Way Records would release *Come and Gone* on CD as a favor to collectors and to fans of the Talbots' later solo work.

In the early '70s, first John and then Terry became Christians and their heightened spirituality caused tension within the band. Thus, the brothers disbanded the group and made an album of subtle Christian material as a duo. On *The Talbot Brothers,* they are backed by a group of legendary Los Angeles session players: Sneaky Pete Kleinow (steel gtr.), Russ Kunkel (drums), David Lindley (gtr.), and Leland Sklar (bass). The album is generally thought to exceed any of Mason Proffit's works in terms of overall quality, though it is sonically of a piece with those albums, and indeed is often listed in discographies as a Mason Proffit album. The project mixes songs that have a clear spiritual message with more traditional country-folk numbers. An obvious standout is their Crosby, Stills and Nash-styled version of Lowell George's "Easy to Slip," a song that would later become Little Feat's best-known semihit. "Trail of Tears" is a beautiful acoustic ballad with Hawaiian guitar by Lindley (famous for his work on Jackson Browne's albums). Lyrically, it offers a sensitive statement of sympathy for the injustices inflicted on Native Americans. "Comin' Home to Jesus" (a somewhat trite description of an old-time church revival) and "Moline Truckin'" (which seems to be about picking up a girl for a one-night stand) are rendered as banjo-pickin' hoedown numbers. "Come and Gone" paints warm pictures and would be *Harmony* magazine's pick for the best spiritual song on the album. "In My Dreams" is a particularly pretty country love song. "And the Time" offers an allegorical description of life's spiritual journey ("every man is a river") with generous applications of pedal steel helping it along. "Over Jordan" is a lively gospel song, and "Hear You Calling" is a short, soft prayer: "Jesus, how I believe in you / Can't keep from cryin' when I think of all the pain you knew for so long / And you know I will always stand beside you . . . and keep your light a growin' in my mind." *The Talbot Brothers* remains a masterpiece of early Christian rock, an exemplar of some of the most authentic and finest country-rock ever produced within the Christian market—though, of course, no Christian market per se existed at the time, which might help to account for the record's noncontrived appeal. Eventually, Sparrow would reissue the album (minus the song "Moline Truckin'") as *Reborn.*

The Talbot Brothers toured briefly as the opening act for The Eagles. Then Terry played with Terry and the Branches (described by John as "a Christian garage band") for a while until, in 1975, he decided to reconstitute Mason Proffit as a Christian group. **Al Perkins, David Diggs,** and other Christian musicians were recruited, and for about a year the band toured playing both old and new songs in bars and honkytonks. "We don't have to go around in robes," John Michael told *Harmony* (with a note of irony, given his later vocation). "We can just be dudes, but we're Christians and it does change our lives." The new incarnation of Mason Proffit never recorded. In 1976, John Michael and Terry Talbot cowrote the Christian musical *Firewind* with **Jamie Owens.** They also performed on the *Firewind* album (Sparrow, 1976) along with **Keith Green, Barry McGuire,** and **2nd Chapter of Acts.**

The brothers went on to pursue their divergent solo careers, with John Michael becoming contemporary Christian music's most famous Roman Catholic singer and liturgical balladeer. The two would reunite two more times on special projects. Songs for *The Painter* originated as part of John Michael's famous *Mass in the Key of D-Major,* a project that also produced his classic *The Lord's Supper* album. He split the Mass into separate projects at the urging of Sparrow, presenting the more liturgical portions as *The Lord's Supper* and allowing the concept songs surrounding the theme of God as artist to develop into *The Painter.* Terry was brought in to add vocal harmonies and provide the album with more pop appeal; still, he remains something of a backing musician on what is clearly his brother's project. John Michael wrote all of the songs save one for *The Painter,* and the record has the sound of a praise and worship album consistent with John Michael's solo work. Terry's contribution, "Create in Me a Clean Heart" was originally written as a rock song but it is refashioned here as an a capella number similar in style to a Gregorian chant; it would become a favorite choir anthem in many churches. *The Painter,* recorded with the London Chamber Orchestra, evinces a higher level of artistic quality than could usually be found in contemporary Christian music at the time. It also has an unusually joyful quality to it; the brothers sing in high, happy harmonies, propelled by often aggressive folk and classical guitar playing. "Behold Now the Kingdom" is an adult contemporary ballad; "The Advent Suite" has a Hebraic sound, sung to the accompaniment of strummed guitar and flute and punctuated by occasional choral vocals. "The Empty Canvas" proclaims, "Jesus is the Master Painter / and the Holy Spirit is the Master's brush / To be dipped within the colors / That portray a Father's love / That the Master's painting might be born in us." *CCM* selected *The Painter* as one of the Ten Best Albums of 1980; twenty years later, the brothers would still remember it as their finest moment together.

No Longer Strangers, recorded a full decade later, was not as happy an experience, and the Talbots would both admit to being frustrated with the album's not turning out as they intended. The opening title track is a country-folk ballad based on 1 Peter 2:9–10 and, just for a moment, it hearkens back to the old Talbot brothers sound that fans wished the duo would replicate. But with the second track, "He Is Risen" (different from the song by that name on John Michael's first solo album), it becomes apparent that the album is to be another praise and worship record with churchy songs sung by alternating soloists backed by a choir. Given that, Terry's "Isaiah 68" is a standout track. John Michael offers an ode to asceticism in "Lady Poverty," and, on "Few Be the Lovers," returns to the challenging prophetic tenor of his first solo album (*John Michael Talbot*) to chasten the lukewarm: "Few will be the lovers of the cross / Yet many here still seek exaltation / And many here still seek to be found first / And many here still seek a consolation / Demanding blessings when deserving the curse."

The Talbot Brothers Collection offers a two-disc career retrospective of the brothers' work together, of Terry's solo material, and of John Michael's less-liturgical projects. Six songs from *The Talbot Brothers* and almost all of the songs from *The Painter* (seven out of nine tracks) are included in the thirty-five-song compilation.

Christian radio hits: "Advent Suite" (# 8 in 1980); "He Is Risen" (# 17 in 1984).

John Michael Talbot

1976—*John Michael Talbot* (Sparrow); 1977—*The New Earth*; 1979—*The Lord's Supper*; 1980—*Beginnings; Come to the Quiet*; 1981—*For the Bride; Troubadour of the Great King*; 1982—*Light Eternal*; 1983—*Songs for Worship, Vol. 1*; 1984—*The God of Life*; 1985—*Songs for Worship, Vol. 2; The Quiet* (Meadowlark); 1986—*Empty Canvas; Be Exalted* (Sparrow); 1987—*Heart of the Shepherd; Quiet Reflections*; 1988—*The Regathering*; 1989—*The Lover and the Beloved; Master Collection*; 1990—*Hiding Place; Come Worship the Lord, Vol. 1; Come Worship the Lord, Vol. 2; The Quiet Side; The Birth of Jesus: A Celebration of Christmas*; 1992—*The Master Musician* (Troubadour for the Lord); 1993—*Meditations in the Spirit*; 1994—*Meditations from Solitude*; 1995—*The John Michael Talbot Collection* (Sparrow); *Chant from the Hermitage* (Troubadour for the Lord); 1996—*Brother to Brother* [with Michael Card] (Word); *Troubadour for the Lord* (Sparrow); *The Early Years; Our Blessing Cup* (Troubadour for the Lord); 1997—*Table of Plenty*; 1998—*Pathways of the Shepherd; Quiet Pathways; Spirit Pathways; Hidden Pathways; Pathways to Solitude; Pathways to Wisdom*; 1999—*Cave of the Heart*; 2000—*Simple Heart*; 2001—*Wisdom*.

www.john-michael-talbot.org

John Michael Talbot has had two incarnations in the field of contemporary Christian music, first as a hippie Jesus freak responsible for a pair of seminal albums that remain among the most highly acclaimed offerings of the Jesus movement revival, then as a devout Roman Catholic whose liturgical offerings would expand the genre by drawing on historic and universal traditions of the faith. Overlapping both incarnations are occasional projects with his brother **Terry Talbot,** as indicated in this book's entry on **The Talbot Brothers.** Talbot is hailed as Catholic music's number one selling recording artist and has been the second Catholic artist in the history of contemporary Christian music to have his songs find wide acceptance among Protestants (the first being **Ray Repp**). With over forty albums made and four million records sold, Talbot would come to be recognized as the twentieth century's most prolific and significant composer of worship songs. Christian music historian Paul Baker describes John Michael Talbot as something of an enigma: he is one of contemporary Christian music's top stars, yet his best-known music is as traditional as can be; he loves people and enjoys being with them, yet has spent most of his adult life as a hermit, living in relative solitude; he is a Roman Catholic but his music is popular among conservative Protestants. The early years of his life and mission are re-

counted in *Troubadour for the Lord: The Story of John Michael Talbot* by Dan O'Neill (Crossroad, 1983) and in *Changes: A Spiritual Journey* by John Michael Talbot (Crossroad, 1984). An updated second edition of the first work is forthcoming; the latter volume contains excerpts from the artist's diaries and journals.

Born in Oklahoma City in 1954, Talbot taught himself to play a number of stringed instruments at a very early age and, when he was eleven, formed a band with his brother Terry called The Quinchords. The group enjoyed some local success, and in 1969 morphed into Mason Proffit, a seminal country folk-rock band with a sound similar to Buffalo Springfield or Little Feat. As songwriter, singer, and guitarist for that group, John Michael attained national prominence as a rock star for a few years. His disillusionment with the emptiness of fame and fortune led him, like many others, to embark on a spiritual quest, ignoring the Christianity of his youth for more exotic paths of Native American spirituality and Eastern religions. Then one night in 1971, in a Holiday Inn hotel room, he had a spiritual experience. He had adopted the custom of praying to "whatever God there might be" and, on this occasion, he lay on his bed and said aloud, "Lord, who are you?" What happened next may be recounted in his own words:

> Light seemed to fill the room, intensifying by degrees as if controlled by an unseen rheostat. Startled, I sat up, blinking my eyes, assessing the situation. There before me, in mind-bending brilliance, was the figure of a man in white robes, arms outstretched, with long hair and a beard. He didn't say anything—he was just there. I felt in him a sense of awesome power, overwhelming strength, yet the capacity to be very, very gentle. I felt he could judge me in my smallness and sinfulness, but I perceived his forgiveness instead. He stood before me, somehow almost *around* me, in infinite greatness yet total humility. I felt compassion. And I felt acceptance. I knew it was Jesus.

As years went by, Talbot would describe this experience without ever attempting to explain it. Queried as to whether the vision might have been some sort of hallucination or dream, he would only maintain the life-changing effect it had on him. He did not claim to have witnessed a miracle or an actual manifestation of the risen Christ, suggesting rather that God is the lord of psychoemotional lives and can work wonders in those realms as well. What he did claim, however, was that "I experienced a changed life for the positive. I felt deep love for others, forgiveness, tenderness—new levels of compassion, as if I had somehow absorbed these qualities from the Christ figure in the vision. I suppose you could say that I became a Christian again. I rediscovered something from my childhood faith. I felt that it completed me as a human being."

Thus, Talbot entered the hippie Jesus freak phase of his career. He continued to record with Mason Proffit, witnessing to the other band members and bringing his brother Terry to faith. The two of them recorded a classic Jesus music album *The Talbot Brothers* (later reissued as *Reborn*). They also collaborated with **Jamie Owens** to produce the early Christian musical *Firewind*. Then in the mid '70s John Michael would deliver the one-two punch of *John Michael Talbot* and *The New Earth*. Those two projects are masterpieces of edgy folk-rock. Vague comparisons might be drawn to Gordon Lightfoot, but few mainstream folk artists have ever invested their material with the same tough passion evident here. **T Bone Burnett** and **Mark Heard** are better touch points. The self-titled album opens with "He Is Risen," an up-tempo masterpiece propelled by energetic acoustic guitar (it is a completely different song from the John Michael Talbot song that is also called "He Is Risen" featured on **The Talbot Brothers**' *No Longer Strangers* album). "Jerusalem" is bluesy, and "How Long" is funky. "Greenwood Suite" is an almost thirteen-minute opus ending in hymnic praise: "Who is the King of Glory? / Who reigns but Jesus the Lord?" A coda, "Hallelu," closes the album with a simple praise song. The two latter tracks preview (in theme if not in style) Talbot's eventual interest in worship, but other songs on *John Michael Talbot* betray a strong antipathy for what many hippie Christians regarded as the cold, dead religion of institutional churches. Hypocrisy is an obvious and easy target. "Would You Crucify Him?" is addressed to the modern Pharisees who use religion to justify their lifestyles: "Would you crucify him? / Talkin' 'bout the sweet Lord Jesus / Would you crucify him / If he walked down here among us once again?" The song "Woman" is likewise addressed to the church, which Talbot now styles as the harlot of Old Testament prophecies (or of Revelation) and calls to repentance with scathing rhetoric: "Will you let go the gavel to hold the nail-scarred hands he bore?" When asked twenty years later about the anti-institutionalism of his youth, Talbot would say with a smile, "It is interesting that I would end up a Catholic, but I tell people I wouldn't have any problem singing those songs today. Neither would the great saints of old."

The New Earth is a happier album with more emphasis on celebration and praise. It opens with another suite (called simply "The Suite"), which begins with an exposition of love as the greatest of all gifts and ends with folk praise to Jesus as "King of Kings." Talbot would later say that he thought this piece represents the high point of his early career. Other tracks like "Dance with Him" and "Let the People Sing Amen" are joyous Appalachian praise tunes with lots of banjo, mandolin, and high vocal harmonies. "Cast Down Your Cares" is a Light-footesque pretty tune that summons listeners to radical cross-bearing discipleship. "The Coming" is a four-minute instru-mental prelude to the album's title track, which in turn announces the central theme that Jesus is returning to create a new earth for his people. "Prepare Ye the Way" recalls the prophetic, angry challenge of some of the first album's songs, and its mood is augmented by Talbot's singing in an eerie disembodied voice; he would later explain that he had a bad cold the day he recorded it. In 2000, **Caedmon's Call** would resurrect the song "Prepare Ye the Way" for their *Long Line of Leavers* album.

Two compilation albums would eventually collect songs from Talbot's first two albums: *Beginnings* and *The Early Years*. A smattering of songs from the projects would also be featured in a two-disc retrospective called *The Talbot Brothers Collection* (Sparrow, 1995). Talbot would come to describe the period as his "fundamentalist phase." Without renouncing the music that he and his brother produced between 1974 and 1976, he would develop a somewhat jaundiced perspective on his own spiritual orientation at that time. Like many of the young converts caught up in the Jesus movement, Talbot embraced what his biographer, O'Neill, would call the "false harbor of safety" accessible through the dogmatic certainty and zeal of fundamentalist Christianity. "I became a walking, talking Jesus freak who had a quote from Scripture for every conceivable problem," Talbot would recall. "I began to push the Bible too legalistically. I would visit old friends and come on like a Bible thumper, condemning their lifestyles and spitting out Scripture verses to make my points. I really entered into what I would call a caricature of Christianity. I believed—as I had been taught at this stage of things—that this particular brand of Christianity represented the whole truth. Everyone else was a little off, except Catholics, who were way off."

Talbot's dogmatism drove a wedge between him and his wife, Nancy, who had also embraced Christianity but was growing toward a less dogmatic version of the faith. The two had married when Talbot was seventeen, and the relationship had been a troubled one. But having already endured so many of the problems associated with rock star marriages, it seemed incredible that matters of faith would bring things to a point beyond reconciliation. Such thinking did not jibe with John Michael's understanding of God or the Bible, and when the relationship ended in divorce, he was thrown into a spiritual crisis. The dissolution was one of the first to involve a major artist in the contemporary Christian music scene, but it was handled quietly and without scandal. With the notable exception of **Keith Green** (who told Talbot he was going to hell), the fairly small community of artists and industry personnel came together to offer the damaged singer pastoral support (he cites **Phil Keaggy, Honeytree, Barry McGuire, Mike Warnke,** and especially Sparrow president, Billy Ray Hearn, as "good Samaritans" in his time of need). But, surprisingly, Talbot found the greatest source of help in the works of a number of Roman Catholics. He became enamored of St. Francis of Assisi and visited the Alverna Franciscan retreat center in Indiana. There he found a mentor in Father Martin Wolter, and eventually became a Roman Catholic. The failed marriage continued to trouble him. For some time, he appears to have held out hope of a reconciliation. Then, according to his published journals, when his former wife remarried, he consigned himself to celibacy as "a life-long penance for the mistakes of my youth." Eventually, he would come to a deeper understanding of grace and would remarry (in 1989).

In 1978, Talbot sold (almost) everything that he owned. He fashioned a monk's habit from old army blankets, which would become his trademark vestment, an outward sign that he is "God's property." Initially, he says, "I planned to live a life of quiet meditation as a hermit, but as I studied the history of the church, I saw that community had always been a part of it." He became a Third Order Franciscan—most Roman Catholic orders (Franciscan, Dominican, Benedictine) have lay associates called "Third Order members" who adhere to the same evangelical counsels as their monastic brothers and sisters (poverty, chastity, and obedience) but follow a less rigorous calling; they may, for instance, marry, live in homes with their families, or work in jobs outside the community. But in 1982, Father Wolter advised Talbot to found his own community and begin a music ministry. As it turns out, the only worldly possession Talbot had been unable to divest was a plot of twenty-five acres in the Ozark mountains that he had bought on a whim while touring with Mason Proffit. "Nobody would buy it," he says. "It seemed God had a special purpose for it." Thus, Talbot became founder and General Minister of a Catholic community called The Brothers and Sisters of Charity, located at the Little Portion Hermitage near Eureka Springs, Arkansas. Composed of about forty permanent residents, it is the only integrated monastic community in the United States (encompassing celibates, singles, and families) to have been granted canonical recognition by the Roman Catholic Church. The community is not officially part of the Franciscan order, though it retains the legacy of Franciscan heritage. John Michael and his wife, Viola, are regarded as the spiritual father and mother of the community, with positions similar to those of a monastic abbot. All proceeds from Talbot's music and books contribute to the funding of the community and its ministry, which includes support of the international humanitarian agency Mercy Corps, the maintenance of a free medical clinic, operation of an agricultural mission in Nicaragua, and the running of a retreat center. Talbot has said that two terms the community lives by are "gentle revolution" and "street-level Christianity": "we must become aware of the needs of our brothers and sisters and do our best to meet their needs as Christ did and as Francis did while they were on earth."

With *The Lord's Supper,* Talbot's style changed drastically, and he would devote the rest of his career to creating church music on the borderline between contemporary and traditional. He did not, for instance, turn out youth group/summer camp songs in the tradition of **Ray Repp,** but crafted music with a contemporary feel that nevertheless fits easily into the historic liturgies of the church. "I can still rock if I want to," he told skeptical *CCM* readers in 1982. "It's still a part of me. If I want to use rock to express something, then I'm gonna use it. But if I want to express something that's awesome and majestic, then I go back to the classics. And if I want to express something in nature, God's creation, I go back and use impressionistic modes." Talbot's most frequent collaborator has been Phil Perkins, who provides orchestration for his songs. In composing his various albums, however, Talbot tries to keep in mind the needs of various churches, turning at times to simple folk melodies because "some high liturgical churches don't have large choirs and orchestras." Yet he has also promoted the development of liturgical dance. The one thing he has never done is try to make anything that would have commercial appeal or be perceived as popular. "Sometimes, I scratch my head and say it's amazing that people who like contemporary, pop Christian music buy my stuff, too!" he says. "That's beautiful, though. It's part of the diversity of the body of Christ." Prompted to reflect more deeply on the reasons for the phenomenal success of his music, he could only conclude, "There are an awful lot of people out there looking for something more than what status-quo Christianity has to offer."

The Lord's Supper represents Talbot's earliest attempt to set significant portions of the historic Christian liturgy to a contemporary, orchestrated, sound. The album began as a project called *Mass in the Key of D-Major,* which was subsequently split into two parts—thematic songs were recorded by **The Talbot Brothers** as *The Painter,* and liturgical selections were recorded as *The Lord's Supper* by John Michael. The album actually presents a live worship experience recorded at the charismatic Body of Christ church in Indianapolis. As Talbot recalls, he brought in a number of people who could sing and gave them few instructions except "to just sing in the Spirit," an approach that gives the album a fascinating liturgical-yet-spontaneous feel. "These are amateurs in the truest sense of the word," Talbot says of the performers. "They love art and they love God, and we just let them worship the Lord. On some of the cuts, they were singing on their knees as we recorded. It was a truly worshipful experience." The folks at Sparrow Records were taken aback by the very strange new product from their big-selling folk-rock star. "We've never heard music like this before," president Hearn said. They put the album out and it sold hundreds of thousands of copies, easily becoming Sparrow's best-selling record and, indeed, one of the best-selling Christian albums of all time. Talbot had intended the record as his swan song, a farewell gift of music to the church before embarking on his quiet life of prayer and devotion. But the surprising reception of the project led him, instead, into a lifelong ministry. *Come to the Quiet* followed, with stark and austere songs based on the *Divine Office, The Liturgy of the Hours* psalter, and the Anglican *Book of Common Prayer.* When it, too, was well received, the Christian humor magazine, *The Wittenburg Door,* ran a parody article noting that the former rock singer's next project was to be an album called *Shut Up, Already!* featuring two sides of total silence.

To the nonspecialist or casual fan, Talbot's albums might seem to blend together, but many of the projects do have a distinctive focus. *For the Bride* is something of a ballet with classical guitar and orchestral treatments intended to accompany performances by liturgical dancers. *Light Eternal* is a grand opus recorded with orchestra and two choirs that was often compared to a modern version of Handel's *Messiah. Troubadour of the Great King* is a lavish two-record set composed as a tribute to St. Francis in celebration of his 800th anniversary. The two *Songs for Worship* albums offer a variety of spiritual songs based on Scripture. *The God of Life* is a celebration of St. Patrick and of the legacy of Celtic Christianity, with about half the songs actually employing distinctive Celtic styles. *The Quiet* and *The Empty Canvas* are meditative instrumental recordings with both new material and reworked versions of songs from previous projects. *Be Exalted* does not contain any original songs, but collects popular worship tunes being used in churches (including three by **Kemper Crabb**) and presents these in arrangements performed by Talbot and friends. *Heart of the Shepherd* is ostensibly a collection of songs for church leaders, though many laity would find it inspiring as well. On *The Lover and the Beloved,* Talbot sets poems by ancient and modern mystics (St. John of the Cross, Sister Mary Anthony, Thomas Merton) to music. *Hiding Place* is a collection of tone poems on which Talbot picks his acoustic guitar and sings multitracked vocals against the backdrop of a chamber orchestra arranged by Perkins. *The Master Musician* offers a musical allegory reminiscent of **Larry Norman**'s *The Tune* but grander in its conception and execution; the story presents individual Christians as musical instruments who are brought together by God to blend their sounds in a beautiful symphony of praise. *Chant from the Hermitage* seems inspired by the successful *Chant* project by the Benedictine monks of Santo Domingo de Silos, offering English versions of psalms, canticles, and Gregorian chants performed to light guitar and piano accompaniment. All six of the *Pathways* albums from 1998 are instrumental albums intended

for different moods of meditation (cf. **Phil Keaggy**'s *Music to Paint By* series).

In 1996, Talbot received extraordinary attention in the contemporary Christian music media for recording an album with **Michael Card** called *Brother to Brother.* Card maintains that Talbot was his inspiration for going into Christian music in the first place, and the two artists had long been appreciative of each other's work. On *Brother to Brother,* Talbot sings six of his favorite Card songs and Card offers his renditions of a half dozen Talbot numbers. **Phil Keaggy** and **Wes King** play guitar on the album, which was hailed as "a giant leap for ecumenism" in the Christian music industry. While that might be an overstatement, the persistence of uninformed anti-Catholic bigotry among American fundamentalists should not be underestimated. *Moody* magazine, which used Michael Card's *Joy in the Journey* album in a subscription promotion drive, has regularly refused to accept advertising for any of Talbot's albums.

Cave of the Heart is a bit of an anomaly in that it returns Talbot to more of the country-folk style of his early pre-Catholic days. **Phil Keaggy, Phil Madeira,** and **Michael Card** all play on the album, and Bonnie Keen of **First Call** is thought to offer uncredited female vocals. Thematically, the album provides something of an apologetic tract for the Christian faith. The first three songs focus on universal truths shared by most religions. Then the next six tracks address specifically Christian matters, with a more traditional, for Talbot, liturgical feel. The album concludes with three numbers ("Common Fire," "Inflame the Flame," and "Walk and Follow Jesus") that hearken back to '70s country folk rock. *True Tunes* hailed the album as a welcome return, with the reviewer indicating, "meditative works are fine, but since I am not a monk there is only so much quiet I can stand."

A number of compilation albums offer selections from the artist's Catholic period: *Quiet Reflections* collects songs from previous albums and represents them with appropriate readings from Scripture and from the church fathers and various Franciscan sources. *The Quiet Side* compiles thirty-four of Talbot's more meditative songs intended to accompany times of solitude. A more representative collection of various styles is offered by the two-disc, thirty-five song set, *The John Michael Talbot Collection.*

"Music is an extension of my life," Talbot told *Shout* magazine in 1996. "When I became a Christian, my music became Christian music. When I became a Catholic, my music became Catholic music." Furthermore, he says, "the music I write isn't gospel or contemporary Christian. It's sacred, which touches those categories but isn't really a part of them." Talbot believes that sacred music is sacramental, capable of "taking the listener on a closer walk with God, actually taking them into the heart of the Lord." In terms of style he likes to call his work "meditative music." He told *Christianity Today* in 2001, "In my music, silence is just as important as the notes. The only other style of music that attempts to go to the deeper place of the silence that is music is new age music." But sacred music "brings out the mysterious and speaks the unspeakable, bringing to light that which is beyond human reason." By the same token, Talbot has been somewhat critical of the contemporary Christian music industry as such. In 1982, he sounded an alert to *CCM* that "American Christians need to break out of the American culture and become more universal, more creative, more expanded in their vision, and more spiritually oriented." He was disturbed, even then, that "the direction of the whole Christian contemporary music thing has gone toward imitating the world—in terms of style, advertising, and promotion." This trend, of course, would not abate in the next decade and, by 1993, Talbot was saying, "I think most Christian music today is anemic in its sense of mission because *the church* is anemic. The church is following the American Christian heresy that promotes consumerism more than Christlike poverty. We live in a world where Americans are six percent of the world's population using over fifty percent of the world's resources, and there is nothing you can call that but sin." In 2001, he said, "American pop culture glorifies independence and individualism and evangelical pop culture often does the same. People are looking for something that's the real deal; if Christianity isn't bringing forth change, it's not the real deal."

Talbot is also a prodigious author of devotional books. His writings include three volumes on the lectionary readings from the Gospels *(Reflections on the Gospels, Vols. 1 and 2* and *A Passion for God)*, a work on the Holy Spirit *(The Fire of God)*, a study on the Beatitudes *(Blessings)*, a book on disciplined living *(Simplicity)*, a volume on his favorite saint *(The Lessons of St. Francis)*, an explication of Franciscan spirituality *(Hermitage)*, and a 1999 theological study that argues for "an integrated understanding of the harmony, balance, and proportion of everything God has made" *(The Music of Creation)*. Several books have also been issued to accompany specific recordings: *The Lover and the Beloved* (1985); *Regathering Power* (1988); *The Master Musician* (1992); *Meditations from Solitude* (1994).

Talbot has sung for Mother Teresa and for Pope John Paul II. Profiles on the artist have appeared in such unlikely places as *The Wall Street Journal* and *People* magazine, and he has appeared on *Good Morning America*. In 1986, he received the President's Merit Award from the National Academy of Recording Arts and Sciences for a song called "Song of the Poor." He is also the founder and president of the Catholic Association of Musicians, an organization dedicated to the support of musicians within the Roman Catholic church. In 1997, he was elected to the editorial board of *New Covenant* magazine, a journal devoted to spiritual renewal within the Catholic church.

Christian radio hits: "Forever Will I Sing" (# 26 in 1983).

Dove Awards: 1982 Worship Album *(Light Eternal)*.

Terry Talbot

By Terry Talbot: 1976—*No Longer Alone* (Sparrow); 1977—*Cradle of Love*; 1978—*A Time to Laugh . . . A Time to Sing*; 1981—*A Song Shall Rise* (Birdwing); 1982—*On Wings of the Wind*; 1984—*Sings the Stories of Jesus* (Sparrow); 1985—*Face to Face: The Teachings of Christ*; 1987—*Wake the Sleeping Giant*; 1988—*Terry Talbot* (Live Oak).

Terry Talbot is a Christian country-folk-rock singer whose career extends back to the pioneering days of the Jesus movement revival. He is the brother of **John Michael Talbot** (renowned for composing and performing worship music), and the two of them have sometimes recorded together as **The Talbot Brothers.** He is married to **Wendy Talbot,** who has recorded as one-half of the duo **Wendy and Mary.**

Talbot was born in Oklahoma City and began playing music with his brother at an early age. In 1962, they formed a band called The Quinchords and got jobs backing such musicians as **Glen Campbell,** Chad Mitchell, and Sonny and Cher. Then in 1969 they formed Mason Proffit, a country-rock outfit that would attain national acclaim as an underground group with a style similar to Buffalo Springfield or Little Feat. It was while touring with Mason Proffit that John Michael became a Christian, and about a year later, Terry was won to the Lord through his brother's example. "When I was with Mason Proffit, I believed that Jesus was who he said he was, but I didn't know him as my Savior and my Lord," he told *Cornerstone* in 1976. "My brother John got saved and by his countenance and the life he lived—not by a word that he spoke—I saw that a real change had taken place in his life that I wanted." Mason Proffit could not endure the inner tensions of two evangelical believers who wanted the group to become a Christian band, so Terry and John recorded what is often considered to be the band's last album as an official side project with session players *(The Talbot Brothers,* later reissued as *Reborn)*. Terry would later put together a new all-Christian lineup and tour as Mason Proffit in 1975–1976, but for the most part his musical future lay in the creation of solo albums and occasional projects with his brother. In 1976, he and John Michael cowrote the Christian musical *Firewind* with **Jamie Owens** and sang on the soundtrack album for that project (Sparrow, 1976) along with **Barry McGuire, 2nd Chapter of Acts,** and **Keith Green.**

Musically, Terry Talbot crafted a style similar to that of general market artist Jackson Browne. *No Longer Alone* was coproduced by **Al Perkins,** who plays his spectacular pedal steel guitar on many of the country-tinged tracks. Musically, the album fits right in with the country-pop style that The Eagles had made so popular at the time. "Down to the Well" offers Talbot's testimony with biblical parallels: "A blind man spoke to the Light / And now his eyes can see / My own blindness / Was worrying me." *Cradle of Love* has slicker production quality with the addition of strings and keyboards. "Mighty Wind" and "Takin' Me Higher" are especially strong tracks. Although both *No Longer Alone* and *Cradle of Love* were issued on Sparrow, they would be ignominiously ignored when that company released a box-set compilation of songs by Terry and John Michael (*The Talbot Brothers Collection*, 1995). Indeed, the liner notes to that project falsely identify *A Time to Laugh . . . A Time to Sing* as Terry's "first solo album." The latter project offers songs in a variety of styles, from Stones-inspired rockers to gentle acoustic folk. The more mellow material proved most endearing to the increasingly rockophobic contemporary Christian music market. The tender and worshipful song "Father" is a standout track with a sound similar to John Denver's ballads.

Talbot would seem to follow in his brother's footsteps with his next two albums. Both *A Song Shall Rise* and *On Wings of the Wind* offer worship songs with less of the country-folk sound and a stronger classical orientation. Some of that sound would also imbue *Sings the Stories of Jesus*, a concept album presenting reflections on events in the life of Christ. The opening track, "I am He," relates the story of Christ's arrest in the Garden of Gethsemane. "I Saw Him" is sung from the perspective of the Roman centurion as a big adult contemporary ballad. "Come Forth" is a powerful retelling of the resurrection of Lazarus. "Rose of Sharon" departs from the thematic concept to present a pretty folk song with lyrics of praise and wonder. *Face to Face* would be the commercial highpoint of Talbot's solo career. The successful album is subtitled *The Teachings of Christ* and so represents something of a companion to *Sings the Stories of Jesus*, offering songs that reflect upon significant words of Scripture. "Narrow Is the Gate" is the most true in actualization of this concept, sampling numerous sayings from the Sermon on the Mount. "Lay Down the Stones" is based on the story in John 8. "I Have Overcome" paraphrases sayings from John's gospel along with messages from New Testament epistles, placing all of these on the lips of the risen Lord, addressed to the modern church. "Mighty Rushing Wind" presents Christ's promise of the Holy Spirit. The title track is a big crowd pleaser with a sound like that of Foreigner's "I Want to Know What Love Is" and lyrics about Christian social concerns and politically conservative causes being justified at the parousia: "And for everyone who called in vain while injustice raised its head / The ones who cried in hunger and yet could not be fed / There shall come a new beginning, they will all be glorified / We'll see every murdered, unborn child standing by His side!"

Terry's final album for Sparrow, *Wake the Sleeping Giant*, is a prophetic album of nine rock ballads. "The Call" exhorts Christians to holy living and the almost title track, "Wake Up, America," reminds Christian activists of the need to work for spiritual as well as political goals: "As we legislate morality / We've only covered up the flaws / While we work to heal the symptoms / We must not forget the cause." After this, he would record another independent pop-rock piece titled simply *Terry Talbot*, and then he began to perform and tour with his wife, **Wendy Talbot**. They made two custom albums together, the live *Concert of Praise* (1989) and the folk-oriented *The Fullness of Time* (1993). The Talbots sometimes hooked up with old friends **Barry McGuire** and **Don Francisco** and, in 1995, Terry and Barry decided to form the folk duo **Talbot-McGuire**. They would continue to record and perform together into the next millennium, sometimes touring with **John Michael Talbot**.

Christian radio hits: "I Am He" (# 12 in 1984).

Talbot-McGuire

1995—*When Dinosaurs Walked the Earth* (custom); 1997—*Ancient Garden*; 1999—*Frost and Fire*; 2000—*Talbot-McGuire Live*.

www.talbotmcguire.com

Talbot-McGuire is a folk duo composed of two aging Jesus freaks, **Terry Talbot** and **Barry McGuire**, pioneers of early Jesus music who between the two of them sang on over sixty albums between 1965 and 1995. Eschewing any realistic hope of commercial success in the grunge/alternative/boyband universe of late-'90s music, the two friends just decided to make custom albums for their own amusement and for the joy of those few who were fortunate enough to discover them. For those who do find the Talbot-McGuire projects (distributed by Broken Records, but sold primarily over the Internet), it is almost as though the '70s, '80s, '90s, and '00s never happened. The sound is that of Peter, Paul, and Mary or early Simon and Garfunkel—the Kingston Trio even—as the two stars get back to their *early* roots. It is safe to say that in the late '90s no one in either Christian or general market music was performing folk music with more integrity or authenticity. In the liner notes to *When Dinosaurs Walked the Earth*, the artists write, "We have been called a couple of 'dinosaurs' in the music industry. We don't take offense at that term. In fact we love it! And we thought it would be fun to put together a collection of songs, both prehistoric and new, that we still love to sing." Fun is an understatement. *Dinosaurs* and the albums that follow are masterpieces of the folk genre, recapturing something essential to popular music that had been lost a long time ago. This is music made by artists who simply enjoy making music; it is uncontrived, delightful music, free of market expectation, music that comes from the heart and from the soul.

The group combines their own songs with traditional folk tunes. *When Dinosaurs Walked the Earth* includes two of Talbot's best songs ("Love Me Like I Am" and "Love One Another") and McGuire's huge hit "Eve of Destruction" along with covers of the Beatles' "Help," **The Call**'s "Let the Day Begin," and **Bob Dylan**'s "When the Ship Comes In." There are also two old Peter, Paul, and Mary/New Christy Minstrel/Kingston Trio hits, "A Soalin'" and "If I Had My Way." *Ancient Garden* offers more of those traditional folk songs with "This Train," "Well Well Well," the title track, and Dylan's "Blowin' in the Wind." This time, however, there is a shift toward more contemporary songs, with covers of John Stewart's "I Remember America," Vince Gill's "Jenny Loves Trains," and Sting's "Fields of Gold." Talbot contributes "Love Finds a Way," a modern folk song that takes its main lyrics from Ecclesiastes 3:1 (as did Pete Seeger's "Turn! Turn! Turn!") but weaves these around an infectious chorus of "lai lai la lai's." The whimsical "Galaxy Song" (written by Monty Python's Eric Idle) comes as a surprise, as does "Drinkin' Gourd," an almost-forgotten slave song. *Frost and Fire* is a Christmas album recorded live on December 24 at Northpointe Community Church in Fresno, California; a number of the tracks show Celtic influence as the duo is backed by a band that includes bagpipes, borun, ewi pipes, and fiddle. *Talbot-McGuire Live* records a more traditional concert with about a dozen songs from the first two projects. As special treats, each of the artists relates his personal story; they also perform McGuire's children's classic, "Bullfrogs and Butterflys," and reach way back for "Firewind," the title track for a Christian musical in which they both sang twenty-five years earlier.

McGuire says, "What we are doing isn't so much ministry. We just want to bring some joy and laughter. There are lots of other good ministers out there. We want to bring wholesome entertainment."

Wendy Talbot

1987—*People of Promise* (Birdwing).

Wendy Talbot (née Hoffheimer) was one-half of the duo **Wendy and Mary.** After she married Jesus music pioneer (and former Mason Proffit front man) **Terry Talbot,** family commitments made touring with Mary (Hopkins) difficult to maintain. Thus, Wendy recorded a solo album. *People of Promise* is an acoustic, guitar-based record that steers clear of late-'80s techno obsessions for a sound that finds its roots in the work of such artists as the Beatles, Loggins and Messina, or Joni Mitchell. Thematically, it relates the stories of people from the Old Testament in a style similar to that adopted by husband Terry on his successful *Face to Face* album. Terry and Wendy would also make two custom albums together: *Concert of Praise* (1989) and the folk-oriented *The Fullness of Time* (1993).

Tamarack

Wayne Brasel, gtr.; John Patitucci, bass; Cathy Spurr, voc.; Dave Spurr, drums; Debbie McNeil, voc.; Rob Watson, kybrd. 1981—*Tamarack* (Parbar).

The one self-titled album by Tamarack is a historical curiosity of Jesus music because the band included John Patitucci, who would go on to make a name for himself in jazz and classical recordings. Patitucci is generally considered to be the finest bass player who has ever lived, with many recordings to his credit (see www.johnpatitucci.com). Joining Patitucci in Tamarack were Rob Watson of **Daniel Amos** and **John Mehler** of **Love Song,** though the latter does not appear to have played on the album. Patitucci also played bass on a couple of **Bob Bennett**'s early albums, and in 1995, he would join **Love Song** for their *Welcome Back* reunion album. Tamarack was a reggae-inflected pop band with female vocals. Their album opens with Debbie McNeil's "Carry My Blues Away" and also includes Watson's "Come Back Jesus," which laments the quality of life before the parousia ("life without you is a lie").

Ken Tamplin

1990—*An Axe to Grind* (Intense); 1991—*Soul Survivor*; 1993—*Tamplin* (Benson); 1995—*In the Witness Box*; 1995—*We the People* (Rugged); 1997—*Liquid Music* (Ceem); *The Colors of Christmas*; 1998—*When Dinosaurs Ruled the World*; *Where Love Is.*

www.kentamplin.com

Ken Tamplin is the pop-metal master who played, sang, and wrote songs for the Christian bands **Shout** and **Magdallan.** While with the latter group, he also began a solo career. A musician's musician (and first cousin to Sammy Hagar), Tamplin is widely known and respected within the general market—especially for his incredible four-to-five-octave voice, arguably one of the best in rock and roll. He is able to count Peter Frampton, John Entwistle (of The Who), Jeff Lynne (of ELO), and Robin Zander (of Cheap Trick) among his fans. An advertisement for 1993's *Tamplin* included testimonials to the artist by members of Boston, Foreigner, Kiss, Mötley Crüe, Ratt, and Toto.

Tamplin was brought up in a Christian home and began playing guitar at the age of six. When he was twelve, he almost died when a homemade rocket exploded in his presence; years later, he would still describe his recovery from this accident as "a medically documented case of miraculous healing through prayer." Nevertheless, he was quick to backslide and spent the next year of young adolescence dealing cocaine and other drugs. Four overdoses on angel dust kept him in touch with mortality and, at fourteen, he says, he finally recommitted his life to Christ and has "been on fire for him ever since."

An Axe to Grind was recorded after the demise of **Shout** and prior to Tamplin's album with **Magdallan.** It is a loose and experimental affair, featuring eclectic outings with diverse session musicians and friends. Five tracks are instrumentals. Most of the tracks are stereotypical hard rock in the mode of Def Leppard, with "Holding On" being one of the most **Shout**-like. There are a couple of **Petra**-ish power ballads ("Never Give Up," "I Hear Cryin' "). "Believin' Is the Hardest Part" offers overtly evangelical lyrics set to a Beatlesque acoustic tune. On *Soul Survivor,* Tamplin would leave most of the guitar playing to his cohort Steve Van Zen and concentrate on vocal histrionics. The sophomore project moves even further toward the more commercial sound of groups like Boston or Journey, mixing hard tracks like "Take It Now (or Nothing)" with more art-rock meanderings like "(I'm Gonna) Live Forever." *Tamplin* is perhaps his career high point as a solo artist, filled with commercial hard rock songs like "Suspicious Eyes" and "Slave Trade" (on the trap of materialism, i.e., being a slave to mammon). "Mystery Train" has a big melodic chorus, and "Testify" incorporates traditional gospel influences. On the song "Don't Let the Sky Fall on Me," the artist somewhat presumptuously offers testimony to his own righteousness as a protection against divine judgment: "I've seen crooked men walk a crooked mile / Yet I've resisted the devil's daughter of desire / So don't let the sky fall on me." *In the Witness Box* finds Tamplin taking on a number of social issues. "Feed Me" deals with media sensationalism in a manner similar to Don Henley's "Dirty Laundry," while "Strange Fascination" puts the shoe on the other foot and examines the public appetites that drive such frenzies. Alcoholism is addressed in "Death by Inches," and racial tension, in "Colorline." The song "Alma Rose" is a tribute to a Jewish violinist who was forced to play at executions inside a concentration camp. Although *Witness Box* is mostly hard rock, Tamplin also performs the classic praise song "Sing Hallelujah" and delivers a bizarre cover of Stevie Wonder's "Signed, Sealed, Delivered," rewritten with new, Christianized lyrics.

On *We the People,* Tamplin would declare that he was "broadening his horizons" and attempting to reach a different audience. Abandoning the hard rock genre altogether, he now works with a twelve-piece string orchestra, horns, and a church choir. The eclectic album includes entrees into a wide variety of styles, including adult contemporary and synth-driven dance tracks. "There's a Way" is a Latin number, and "When Angels Cry" (an antiabortion song) incorporates a bit of disco. The connecting link that holds most of the disparate sounds together seems to be a Motown influence, rarely evident in Tamplin's previous work (except perhaps in the aforementioned Wonder cover). Tamplin also sings in a lower register on the album, almost making the material sound like

that of a different artist. *We the People* would be Tamplin's last project to receive notice in the Christian media, though he continued to record and release independent albums. In 2001, he produced a compilation of worship songs called *Make Me Your Voice* (Benson) as a benefit album for victims of persecution in the Sudan (such artists as **Andraé Crouch** and **Charlie Peacock** contributed to the project). At that time, it was reported that he was serving as music director of the Living Stones Fellowship in California, where his brother Lance was pastor. He had recently written music for the motion pictures *The Perfect Storm* and *Joan of Arc* and for the TV series *The X-Files.*

Dove awards: 1994 Hard Rock Album *(Tamplin).*

Tantrum of the Muse

Personnel list unavailable. 1998—*The Heart Is a Two-Headed Sperm* (Takehold); 2000—*Modern Mu$ic 2000.*

http://tantrumofthemuse.cjb.net

Tantrum of the Muse is a post-hardcore noise rock band that tries to be radical and controversial while maintaining the basic credentials of traditional (even fundamentalist) Christianity. Musically, the band favors chaos and abrupt style changes from song to song, but they stay within hard rock parameters. *HM,* who likes the band, says, "Sometimes the vocals are very whiny and off key [on purpose, of course] and other times the vocals are screechy and intense, like the singer is being burned at the stake." The group says that their debut album, *The Heart Is a Two-Headed Sperm,* is "a document about the confusion of sex and death, and other struggles in American teen life." The controversy, if there is any, comes in the songs' frank exposition of lust and its power over the teenage psyche, but this is all balanced by unabashed calls to personal purity. Other songs vent against racism and "religion" (here defined as something antithetical to a "relationship with Jesus"). The latter assault continues on *Modern Mu$ic 2000* with songs like "$Screw the Christian Industry$" (about materialism) and "Caught with Your Halo around Your Knees" (about hypocrisy). Again, the group tries to be on the edge with songs addressing such supposedly taboo topics as pornography and masturbation. Actually, such topics are staples of fundie rants (as are materialism and hypocrisy), and *Bandoppler's* labeling of *Modern Mu$ic* as "the most Family-Bookstore-unfriendly album of the year" holds only with regard to the group's rhetorical packaging, not its messages.

Tasty Snax

See **Snax.**

Tavani

Linda Tavani, voc.; Stephen Tavani, voc. 1992—*Urban Missionaries* (Broken).

Although few people know her name, Linda Tavani of the contemporary Christian duo Tavani was one of the biggest soul stars of the late '70s and has a voice that would still be recognizable to millions two decades later. In 1977, she was recruited by Herb Fame to become his third partner in the duo Peaches and Herb, and took that group to its greatest heights (the previous Peaches was Francine Barker, with Marlene Mack filling in for two years in 1968–1969). Born Linda Green in Washington, D.C., Tavani was raised the daughter of a church music director, but she says she drifted from the moorings of her faith. She would record five Peaches and Herb albums with Fame, the most significant being *2 Hot* (Polydor, 1978). That album produced the disco smash "Shake Your Groove Thing" (# 5 in 1978) and the romantic ballad "Reunited" (# 1 for 4 weeks in 1979). "Reunited" would sell over nine million copies and become standard fare on late-night love-song radio programs for years to come, remaining one of America's best-known and beloved soul songs. *2 Hot* went platinum and spawned a spate of imitation acts by other groups who sought to duplicate the formula of combining disparate soft and hard moods (romance and disco tunes) on a single album. Peaches and Herb also had minor hits with "We've Got Love" (# 44 in 1979) and "I Pledge My Love" (# 19 in 1980). They continued to perform and record through 1983, when their song "Remember" was a Top 40 hit on R&B charts.

In 1985, Linda met Stephen Tavani, a successful songwriter who had composed "Love Don't Give No Reason" for Smokey Robinson in addition to music for six consecutive *Circus of the Stars* TV specials. The son of a minister, Stephen helped Linda to rediscover the faith of her upbringing. The two married in 1988 and became part of Jack Hayford's Church on the Way in Van Nuys, California. At Hayford's urging, they began a music ministry, traveling with evangelists Nicky Cruz and Mario Murillo. *Urban Missionaries* was produced by Bill Schnee, with **Michael Omartian** offering assistance on arrangements and keyboards. It has a soulful adult contemporary sound and includes the song "Answer the Call," a summons for people to consider work on the mission field.

For trivia buffs: As Peaches, Linda Tavani (then Green) became the first African American female artist ever to perform in mainland China.

Christian radio hits: "Love Me So Right" (# 4 in 1993).

Melissa Tawlks

2001—*Mystery Revealed* (Pamplin).

Melissa Tawlks began singing with **Acquire the Fire** when she was fourteen and became a featured worship leader with that group. At the age of twenty, she recorded her first solo album, *Mystery Revealed*. Tawlks has a calming voice similar to that of Sarah McLachlan and offers inspirational songs of love and praise. "Your Name Is Great" and "Close" exemplify a more upbeat style, while the title track and "The One Thing" are more typically ethereal.

Chris Taylor

1998—*Down Goes the Day* (Rhythm House); 2000—*Worthless Pursuit of the Things on the Earth*.

www.christaylormusic.com

Chris Taylor from San Antonio, Texas, was front man for the band **Love Coma** (which also included Matt Slocum, who left to form **Sixpence None the Richer**). After the bankruptcy of the R.E.X. label did in his band, along with a number of other Christian groups, Taylor took a break and then reentered the Christian market as a solo artist. His solo albums show him moving away from the modern, alternative rock stylings of **Love Coma** in favor of a more straightforward roots rock sound that draws on such myriad influences as **The Alarm, U2,** Jeff Buckley, and Counting Crows. Taylor also adopts a more direct approach to his songwriting with material that deals with explicitly Christian themes. "I decided that I want to tell it like it is and strip away all the metaphors and stuff I had worked so hard to create with **Love Coma,**" he said. "I want it plain and simple. If an album doesn't do anything for your spirit and doesn't have the Holy Spirit moving through it, it's worthless really."

The songs on *Down Goes the Day* often revolve around the theme of seizing the moment and making every moment count. The opening track, "God Only Knows," is an energetic roller coaster of a song, listing a variety of lessons learned: "I never knew I had a purpose and a call / I never knew that I could make such a mess of it all." The very U2-ish "Jesus Is Alive" is essentially a prayer: "Father mercy, teach us how to love / For all the empty ones who feel like giving up / So we'll know, Jesus is alive." A haunting, closing number called "Salt of the Earth" evokes Lou Reed with a rambling yarn set to the slow accompaniment of a vaguely Hendrix guitar. Basically a fifteen-minute poetry jam, the unlisted bonus track is moody magic of the same sort offered by **Bob Dylan** on "Highlands" from his *Time Out of Mind* album. For his second album, however, Taylor says he decided to forego atmospherics and "rock out." *Worthless Pursuit of Things on the Earth* was produced by **Rick Elias** and Mark Robertson (both of **A Ragamuffin Band**) and is more geared toward melodic rock than its predecessor. The Ragamuffins, including also **Jimmy Abegg** on guitar and Aaron Smith on drums, function as his house band for the record. A song called "The Secret of the Universe" features a driving "Let God love you" chorus that *CCM* says is "as memorable as hit songs get." Another such highpoint is the hook-laden "Accidental Charm." Taylor references Bono again on "The River" (not a Bruce Springsteen cover) and is joined by fellow Bono imitator **Kevin Max** on the gospel rave-up "Higher Ground" (not a Stevie Wonder cover). "Bleeding Hearts Club" is a bit more artsy, with a slow blues stomp and a talk-sing vocal similar to that used on "Salt of the Earth."

For trivia buffs: In 1997, Chris Taylor won the grand prize in a Dove soap jingle contest with a song called "Lather Up" that he wrote to the tune of the Rolling Stones' "Start Me Up." The prize included a cash award of $5,000 and a year's supply of suds.

Danny Taylor

1971—*Taylor Made* (Jubal); 1972—*Live at Carnegie Hall* (Tempo); 1976—*A Time for Love*; 1978—*Live/I'm Not a One-Man Show* (NewPax).

Danny Taylor was to early Christian music what Dan Hill (the Toronto singer who scored a Number Three hit with "Sometimes When We Touch" in 1977) was to mainline rock and roll. His *very* mellow acoustic, folk sound seemed a generation removed from what young people supposedly preferred, but there was something disarming about his vulnerability and sincere presence. Taylor made John Denver seem hip, but he became a guilty pleasure for many Jesus people and a blatant, unmodified pleasure for those who had been liberated from worrying about whether what they liked met with the approval of Casey Kasem or *Rolling Stone*. Taylor also became a spokesperson for the Jesus movement in many quarters and wrote a column called "Tuning Up" for *Harmony* magazine that set the tone for **John Fischer**'s "Consider This" column that would later run in *CCM*. Early on, Taylor was part of the Love Inn community (cf. **Phil Keaggy**, Lynn Nichols, **Nedra Ross**), and he worked with Pat Robertson in the early days of his Christian Broadcasting Network. His first album was a custom job that finds its justification primarily with "The Eyes of the Saint" and "Lady of Roses," two songs that depart from the country-folk style for a more haunting, minor key approach. Taylor would also issue two live albums. The first, *Live at Carnegie Hall,* is a collection of simple acoustic ballads, but *I'm Not a One-Man Show* offers the same sort of Jesus music souvenir as **Randy Matthews**' *Now Do You Understand?* Like the latter project, *I'm Not a One-Man Show* is a double album, packed with nineteen songs and a good deal of chatter. Taylor plays in a Kansas City church with a small band that includes his wife, Sandra, on vocals. The mood is fun and upbeat, with tracks like "Snatchin' All the Children from the Pits of Hell," "Boogie Woogie Preacher Man from New Orleans," and "The Jesus Gonna Love Ya Rag." Regardless of how well the songs hold up, the album provides a vital documentary of the Jesus movement (in its late stages), revealing a good-time vibe that didn't always come across in the revived Christians' interactions with outsiders.

But Taylor remains best known for his 1976 masterwork, *A Time for Love*. The latter album is a collection of Christian love songs directed not to God but to a human partner. The concept behind such a record was innovative in 1976, and indeed, the idea of such potentially sensuous material struck many as controversial. An easy listening project designed for candlelight dinners, *A Time for Love* features songs written by Danny and Sandra over the span of a marriage that had already produced four children. The songs are played on guitar with rich orchestral backing. "Praise God, I Love You" breaks the mood with a country-rock, fiddle tune akin to Denver's "Thank God, I'm a Country Boy," but otherwise the album is soft and luxurious. The Taylors sing to each other, "This day before we say good night / We'll pray his will be done / For in the union of our hearts / The Spirit makes us one."

Taylor would also record as part of the **Matthews, Taylor, and Johnson** trio. The trio toured with **Mike Warnke** and yielded to the temptations that the latter's "no accountability" approach to ministry afforded. "I can't say **Mike Warnke** *made* me do anything," Taylor admits. "I made some bad choices and I take responsibility for them." In any case, by the time Warnke's career had ended in disgrace, Taylor would be long gone from the Christian music spotlight. As of 2000, he was managing a music hall in Oberlin, Louisiana, and producing public access TV programs.

Christian radio hits: "Hey Mon" (# 8 in 1978).

Steve Taylor

1982—*I Want to Be a Clone* [EP] (Sparrow); 1984—*Meltdown*; 1985—*On the Fritz*; 1986—*Limelight: Live at Greenbelt*; 1987—*I Predict 1990* (Myrrh); 1988—*The Best That We Could Find + Three That Escaped* (Sparrow); 1993—*Squint* (Warner Alliance); 1994—*Now the Truth Can Be Told* (Sparrow); 1995—*Liver* (Warner Alliance).

Few artists in Christian music have had as great an impact as Steve Taylor. Like **Charlie Peacock,** he has seemed omnipresent, figuring not only as a recording artist in his own right but also as a songwriter and producer for other artists, as a statesman expanding the concept of what contemporary Christian music can be, and ultimately as an executive responsible for discovering and developing new talent. Often regarded as controversial with regard to what amount to nonissues (it has never taken much to be controversial in the Christian music subculture), Taylor first got his bearings as a performer similar to David Bowie, Elvis Costello, and The Clash, but he has progressed to explore a number of different incarnations. In terms of content, the man who *Newsweek* dubbed "evangelical rock's court jester" is almost as well known for his wit as for his music. More than any other artist, he would develop satire and parody as art forms within the Christian music scene. He has often been criticized for this on the grounds that Christians should not engage in a form of rhetoric based on ridicule; he defends his position by pointing to the example of Elijah and the prophets of Baal (1 Kings 18:27) and to numerous sayings of Jesus (e.g., Matthew 23:23–28).

Taylor was born in 1957 in Brawley, California, but the family soon moved to Denver, Colorado, where he grew up. Taylor was raised the son of a Baptist minister and has always been careful to say that his songs exposing foibles and hypocrisies of church leaders do not derive from his own situation: "My church experience was great. My parents were very consistent with what they said and what they did. They were good examples for me." Taylor attended Biola University in Los Angeles (where he failed an audition for the choir) and later graduated with a degree in music from the University of Colorado in Boulder in 1980. He also spent five years serving as a youth pastor at his father's church and became involved with a number of surprisingly traditional music programs. In the summer of 1979, he attended a summer camp hosted by nightclub singer John Davidson featuring such mentors as Tony Orlando and Florence Henderson (for this honor, he had to compete to become one of 100 persons selected from 20,000 for admission). In 1981, he toured as assistant director of Cam Floria's Continental Singers. In 1982, he served as director for Chuck Bolte's Jeremiah People, a Christian group that often performed at Youth for Christ rallies with a variety show consisting of contemporary church songs (not rock) and skits that used satirical bad examples of Christian behavior as foils for driving home evangelical messages. The latter aspect seems to have had a strong influence on Taylor's orientation, but a more important musical influence was the 1979 release of The Clash's *London Calling*. "It saved my life, musically," he would say. "I'd found my mission." He made a demo of original songs that year and, when Sparrow decided to take a chance on him, his debut EP was quickly recorded just before he and Jeremiah People commenced their nine-month tour. By the end of that tour, the somewhat cheesy variety show's director would be one of the most famous Christian musicians in the land, commanding an audience a hundred times that of the troupe he had been managing.

I Want to Be a Clone offers a half dozen songs that, in the words of Paul Baker, lampoon "the sanctimonious comfort of the padded pew as well as the 'alternative lifestyles' of the pseudo-hip." On the title track, Taylor adopts the voice of a young convert who seems to regard his newfound faith as a fashion statement. He describes discipleship in language that most evangelicals would have thought more appropriate for what they called "cults": "I've learned enough to stay afloat / But not so much I'd rock the boat / I'm glad they shoved it down my throat / I want to be a clone." The song features a number of little Taylorisms; he sort of quotes Judy Collins singing "Send in the clones" and mimics **Bob Dylan,** whining, "Everybody must get cloned" (indeed, he would later admit the song was inspired by bathroom graffiti in a science hall rest room, which included those song titles and many more: "Behind Cloned Doors," "A Clone Again, Naturally," and so on). "Steeplechase" mocks the habit of church shopping on the part of Christians who cannot commit to a congregation but keep looking for one that allows them to feel more comfortable. To put the shoe on the other foot, "Whatcha Gonna Do When You're Number's Up?" and "Whatever Happened to Sin?" take on the dismissive attitude that modern liberal philosophies harbor toward notions of revealed or absolute truth. The first of these addresses the materialist and the philosophy student ("you're so open-minded that your brain leaked out"). The latter takes its title from a book by Karl Menninger and portrays the arguments of Christian academics who approve of abortion and homosexual lifestyles as an obvious rejection of biblical morality. As such, the point is stilted and the attack unfair—the disagreements over those issues among Christian ethicists involve how key texts are to be interpreted not whether the texts are authoritative, and in fact, some of the interpretations Taylor thinks are self-evident are almost certainly untenable (the condemnation of gang rape at Sodom and Gomorrah does not clinch the argument that all forms of homosexual behavior are evil)—but satire is by nature often inaccurate and unfair. Given the song's (questionable) premise, it is effective rhetorically and hence revealing of Taylor's typical strength. His songs do not offer reasoned arguments to convince the unpersuaded but, rather, provide prodding for the predisposed.

Meltdown is a full-length CD with nine new songs and three bonus remixes of the title track. That song creatively imagines what would happen if the thermostat at Madame Tussaud's famous wax museum got turned up too high. The resulting chaos is related with great humor and plentiful puns ("the queen is losing face"; "a general's been disarmed"; Howard Hughes' assets "have all been liquefied"). It is, of course, an apocalyptic portrait of judgment day with very visual reminders of the temporal quality of life. Even more memorable is the antiracism anthem "We Don't Need No Colour Code," aimed directly and unapologetically at Bob Jones University, the Christian school in North Carolina that until 2000 had a strict segregationist policy that, for one thing, forbade interracial dating. "Guilty by Association" again takes on the silliness of

Christian culture, this time chiding those who think they should only do business with other Christians ("You'll be keeping all your money in the kingdom now / And you'll only drink milk from a Christian cow"). "Am I in Sync?" exposes the foolishness of desire for celebrity recognition; "Meat the Press" rebuts the notion of media neutrality, especially with regard to religion. A few of the songs on *Meltdown* eschew parody for a more somber and straightforward treatment of serious topics. "Hero" is a sensitive ballad reflecting on the disillusionments that come with maturity as all one's idols and even one's own aspirations turn out to be tainted. "Jenny" describes a young woman who is unable to forgive herself and is driven to suicide. "Sin for a Season" presents three vignettes exposing the consequences of sin (e.g., the long-term psychological effects of marital infidelity). "Baby Doe" is a story ripped from the headlines, the true account of an Indiana baby that was allowed to starve to death in a hospital because it was born with Down's syndrome. "Over My Dead Body," which deals with the violent persecution of Christians in Poland, was subsequently picked up by the Voice of America for broadcast to Eastern bloc countries. In 2001, a critics' poll sponsored by *CCM* magazine put *Meltdown* at Number Eighteen on a list of "The 100 Greatest Albums in Christian Music."

On the Fritz picks up where *Meltdown* left off with no drastic changes in style. The opening track is another energetic dance track describing a church that has gone disco in its efforts to stay relevant, promising to "only play the stuff you want to hear." A song called "I Manipulate" gives Bill Gothard the same sort of treatment Bob Jones so richly deserved on the previous record (Gothard was big in some quarters in the '80s, perpetrating a sort of Christian fascism involving strict power hierarchies intended to keep women, adolescents, and other potentially dangerous subgroups in their place; he also claimed that Christian singers like **Sandi Patty, Michael Card,** and **Bill Gaither** encourage teenagers to live a life of sin). In a similar vein but with less invective, Taylor also takes aim at TV evangelists ("You Don't Owe Me Nothing"), posturing rock stars ("You've Been Bought"), and amoral politicians ("It's a Personal Thing"). The standout tracks, however, are two more serious songs. On "To Forgive," Taylor adopts a sound reminiscent of The Who, in exaltation of a prime virtue; he says the song was inspired by the news photos of Pope John Paul II standing in a prison cell, forgiving the man who tried to assassinate him. "I Just Wanna Know" provides a relatively rare look into the artist's own heart, as he struggles with his intents and aspirations: "I just wanna know, am I pulling people closer? / I just wanna be pulling them to you / I just wanna stay angry at the evil / I just wanna be hungry for the true." But the best-known tracks on the album would turn out to be a couple of novelty songs. "Drive, He Said" relates a conversation that Tay-

lor has with Satan when the devil suddenly appears in the back seat of his car. "Lifeboat" narrates an all-too-realistic "values clarification" exercise in which school children are asked to determine who should live and who should die in a disaster situation. A video for the latter song—which is hilarious despite its seemingly serious subject matter—featured Taylor in drag as the school marm; it was such a hit that he says he found he had consigned himself to putting on a dress for encores at concerts for many years to come.

Taylor found himself without a label after *On the Fritz* (which sold in excess of 100,000), in part because Sparrow had wearied of the controversies concerning him and because they thought (correctly) that Christian music was moving toward more adult contemporary, praise and worship styles. Myrrh picked up *I Predict 1990,* which was Taylor's best album up to that point. It displays a more solid rock base and less of the trendy new-wave stylings. As *CCM* would note, Taylor's vocals are "gruffer and less coy" and the production by **Dave Perkins** is excellent. The album opens with "I Blew Up the Clinic Real Good," a magnificent rock song with generous horns and rock star yelping. Lyrically, the song presents the self-justifying rationale of a loser who has bombed an abortion clinic, in part because he drives an ice cream truck and needs the future youngsters to ensure his job security. Only partly tongue-in-cheek, the song also introduces what may be the album's central theme—a prediction of what the '90s could bring if people continue to believe that "the end justifies the means." The next track, "What Is the Measure of Your Success?" is a modern parable (with a sound that slightly recalls The Moody Blues) about a materialist who discovers what "old men learn all too late . . . you can't buy time or a good name." The sarcastic "Since I Gave Up Hope I Feel a Lot Better" describes the lack of a moral compass that seemed to be evident in the postmodern philosophies of liberal academia *and* in the political conveniences of the Reagan administration (the line "I can't precisely recollect" appears to be an Iran-contra scandal quote from Ollie North or Reagan himself—or even from George Bush for that matter [they all said it]). As a bit of music trivia, Papa John Creach of Jefferson Airplane plays fiddle on the latter track. "Jim Morrison's Grave" is one of Taylor's strongest rock songs and actually gained brief exposure on MTV. "Innocence Lost" is a heart-rending account of an eleventh hour but sincere conversion by a death row inmate on the eve of his execution; the song strongly foreshadows the theme and tone of the motion picture *Dead Man Walking,* which would not be made until eight years later. "A Principled Man" calls on the listeners (or at least *half* of the listeners, given the gender exclusion) to examine themselves and consider whether they are in fact people who stand for something: "Are *you* a principled man?" The song "Harder to Believe Than Not To" (based on a Flannery O'Connor quote) is a ballad set within an unusual musical framework that includes operatic singing and a chamber orchestra; lyrically, it testifies to the difficulty of faith in a way that defies stereotypes of Christianity as a crutch ("Now you know why the chosen are few").

Despite its undeniable brilliance and universal critical acclaim, *I Predict 1990* failed to generate significant commercial sales. This was at least in part because it was branded early on as a controversial record (which in the Christian market tends to *hurt* sales) for what seem to have been ludicrous reasons. First, an evangelist in Texas organized a boycott campaign because he believed the cover of the album, designed by Taylor's wife, Debbie, displayed a picture of the artist on a tarot card and so constituted an endorsement of the occult. Whether the campaign was motivated by sincere stupidity or deliberate dishonesty has never been determined. It is *hypothetically* possible that the evangelist actually was so obtuse as to conclude on the basis of an album cover design that a devout Christian artist was endorsing occult practices in his collection of explicitly evangelical songs. But then, it is also possible that the evangelist knew full well that this was not the case yet saw the tarot card scandal as a way of getting back at Taylor for something, possibly the previous attacks on borderline Christian evangelists and political leaders. (Debbie Taylor also did noncontroversial artwork for *The Best That We Could Find,* as well as for **Sixpence None the Richer**'s *This Beautiful Mess.*) In any case, a second scandal soon erupted concerning the song "I Blew Up the Clinic Real Good." Persons who had heard *of* the song but apparently never *heard* it (or at least listened to the lyrics) decided it was an anthem encouraging people to blow up abortion clinics. Taylor spent numerous hours calling Christian book and music stores throughout the United States one by one to talk to the managers about these matters. Nevertheless, *I Predict 1900* did not sell as expected, and the extent to which the controversies contributed to its failure will never be known.

In 1990, Taylor left the Christian music scene for a time and moved to London. He then formed the general market band **Chagall Guevara,** a group that went over big with critics whose reviews were ignored by consumers. Taylor would say that the band's only album "sold tens of copies." A *Rolling Stone* reviewer compared their sound favorably to that of The Clash in a piece that no doubt pleased Taylor very much. A few years later, Taylor returned to the Christian market with his comeback album *Squint,* an exceptional project equal to *I Predict* in overall quality. Musically, the record belongs solidly to the mid '90s: pogo beats and saxophones are absent, replaced by near-grunge riffs and neoindustrial sounds. He is accompanied by Wade Jaynes (bass) and Mike Mead (drums), the rhythm section for **Chagall Guevara.** Again, Taylor shows dramatic im-

provement as a vocalist. A reviewer for *Visions of Gray* would write, "Whereas in the past, he seemed more of a commentator, now the vocals seem to come from something much larger within, reminding at times of Roger Waters' vacillations between screams and whispers." The album opens with a guitar riff that strongly recalls The Troggs' "Wild Thing" and segues into a boisterous ode to mortality with the unwieldy title "The Lament of Desmond R. G. Underwood-Frederick IV." Taylor shouts, "The news of my impending death came at a really bad time for me!" and then goes on to rag about the inconveniences of being read one's "expiration date." The lyrics throughout are typical of his creative and perceptive spark: "I was starting to track with my inner guide / I was getting in touch with my feminine side . . . When they cancel your breathing policy / Tends to steal a bit of the old *joie de vivre.*" The next song, "Bannerman," is a surprising tribute to the guy (whoever it is) who holds up those "John 3:16" signs at sporting events. One might have thought this person would be a prime target for some caustic ridicule, but no, Taylor views him as an odd sort of hero: "There's something about the motive of a guy like that I don't necessarily get, but I admire. Partly it's because I don't have the nerve to do it myself." This appraisal, as it turns out, is in keeping with *Squint*'s recognition that God often appreciates (indeed, prefers) the misfits and rejects of society. In general, *Squint* is less sardonic and more laced with compassion than any other Taylor project; it is also more revealing of the artist's own vulnerabilities. "Sock Heaven" (drawing on the metaphor of that mythical place where socks that get lost in the wash must surely go) deals with his disappointments with both the contemporary Christian music industry and the failed **Chagall Guevara** experiment. The nearest glimpses of old Taylor come on "Easy Listening" (which applies the label for an unchallenging variety of music to what many persons seem to want from religion—something nonradical and soothing) and "Cash Cow" (a minidrama in three acts that relates the golden calf of the Sinai apostasy to American materialism). "Curses" is a strongly worded biblical proclamation of judgment on fathers who desert their families. "The Moshing Floor" is wild modern rock that offers stream-of-consciousness commentary on a lot of things, including wild modern rock. "Smug" ridicules the fad attitude of Generation X, pointing out some of the unhip forebears (Rush Limbaugh, Barbra Streisand) who mastered the art of smugness long before Kurt Cobain made it cool. Another Taylor classic is found in "The Finish Line," which picks up the storyline of the song "Hero" (from *Meltdown*), relating the often difficult and halting trek of a Christian as viewed from the perspective of eschatological glory. The indisputable highlight of the *Squint* album, however, is a song called "Jesus Is for Losers," a midtempo modern rock number that expresses the biblical concept of grace more eloquently than any song in recent memory. The title alone is a striking double entendre (Jesus is *for* losers, not against them—and he came to call the sinners, not the righteous, cf. Matthew 9:13).

True Tunes has said that Steve Taylor was probably the best live performer in Christian music during the early to mid '80s. At his very first *Cornerstone* appearance, he jumped off the stage early in the show and broke his ankle. He finished the concert, but required surgery and had to cancel a trip to Ireland. *Limelight* presents a 1985 show from the *Greenbelt* festival in England. It includes a greatly improved version of "Colour Code" (done in an ironic African American call-and-response style) and a duet with **Sheila Walsh** on a song ("Not Gonna Fall Away") that had also been featured in a studio version on an album called *Trans-Atlantic Remixes* (Sparrow, 1985). *Liver* is a souvenir from the Squinternational tour (to support the *Squint* album) a decade later.

Taylor has also issued two compilation albums: the single disc *The Best That We Could Find* and the two-disc box set of thirty-four tracks, *Now the Truth Can Be Told*. Both of these contain two standout tracks not found elsewhere: "Bouquet" and "Under the Blood." The first of these is a poignant, sad song about a failed marriage: "Marry two half people and shouldn't one make the other whole?" The second is a full-bore rocker that lambasts the concept of what Dietrich Bonhoeffer called "cheap grace" so prevalent in American Christianity. In 1994, a tribute album featuring Taylor songs performed by various artists was released as a benefit project for the Cornerstone Community Outreach program sponsored by Chicago's Jesus People U.S.A. Community. The album was titled *I Predict A Clone* (R.E.X., 1994), and Taylor would say he was embarrassed, first by the attention, and second by the fact that all the new versions were better than his own. The latter comment may just have been a bit of self-deprecating humility, but is actually true with regard to "Drive, He Said" by **Argyle Park** and "Bouquet" by **Sixpence None the Richer.** Other contributors include **Bride** ("We Don't Need No Colour Code"), **Circle of Dust** ("Am I in Sync?"), **Deliverance** ("On the Fritz"), **Dig Hay Zoose** ("Steeplechase/I Want to Be a Clone"), **Fleming and John** ("Harder to Believe Than Not To"), **Hot Pink Turtle** ("A Principled Man"), **Starflyer 59** ("Sin for a Season"), and **The Wayside** ("To Forgive").

Taylor has rarely, if ever, shown any bitterness toward those who have been his opponents. When he left the Christian music scene for the Chagall experiment, he made it clear that he was not angry or resigning. Likewise, when he returned, he did so not as one who had failed to make it in the world at large, but with the air of one who had been on a sabbatical and was now refreshed and ready to give himself to Christian music with deeper commitment than ever. "I realize

that it may be 'Steve Taylor, Christian artist' for the rest of my life, but if that's how it is, then I'm fine with that." At the same time, Taylor has always considered the distinction between Christian music and secular music to be artificial, as his work in both fields would demonstrate.

As indicated, Taylor's entire career has been marked by moments of sometimes subtle, often wacky, humor. He was on the cover of the Christian humor magazine *The Wittenburg Door* (later, just *The Door*) in November 1984. When *CCM* asked about his marital prospects that same year, he said, "I'm waiting for a girl who's warm, loving, and owns a Greyhound tour bus" (nine months later he would marry Debbie, on the apparent premise that "two out of three ain't bad"). His official résumé lists under graduate studies "listened to French for Tourists, Tape One." When he returned to the Christian music market in 1993, he held a press conference pledging not to try to buy the support of the media, while tossing candy bars and other trinkets into the press corps. He once wrote an article for *The Wittenburg Door* under the pseudonym Martin Wroc, called "Things Americans Should Know about Christianity in England." It contained such revelations as "Scotland is a country near England, where the people are mainly Scottish" and "As a student at Oxford in the 1960's, Bill Clinton never met C. S. Lewis."

As a true pioneer, Taylor has the distinction of many firsts in Christian music. He was the first artist on a small label to have his music come out on compact disc. He was the first Christian music artist to issue remixes of his songs. He was the first to produce a long-form concept video to accompany his album and, according to *True Tunes,* he was the first Christian artist to make a video, period, that "didn't completely suck." In 1988, he emptied his bank account to self-finance a video of "Meltdown at Madame Tussaud's" in the hope of landing it on MTV. He continued to produce videos for most of his projects, including a few ("Lifeboat," "Jim Morrison's Grave") that would achieve classic, cult status in a fledgling field where outlets for exposure were exceptionally few and far between. He would ultimately be responsible for a number of highly rated videos for other artists as well, including **Margaret Becker**'s "Deep Calling Deep" and **Twila Paris**'s "What I Am without You," in addition to an ambitious minimovie with **The Newsboys** called *Down under the Bigtop*. Taylor has also been working for many years on a film called *St. Gimp,* which he intends for major theatrical release.

It is not correct to say that Taylor was shunned or ostracized within the contemporary Christian music industry. Though there were a few tense moments, he was nominated for the Dove award for Artist of the Year in 1994 and for seven Doves in 1995 (he had won the Best Long Form Video Award for *Limelight* in 1987). As Mark Joseph observes in his book *The*

Rock and Roll Rebellion, "Taylor found wide acceptance in the very community he was mocking because he attacked from the social, theological, and cultural right wing. Evangelical Christians have long been open to—and sometimes have even welcomed—attacks upon their style of living from somebody accusing them of not being conservative and Christian enough, as Taylor did." Taylor himself claims that, "I've always gone out of my way not to align myself with either the right or the left," but Joseph's analysis is essentially correct and points up the greatest weakness in the artist's early work. The satires on his pre-Chagall albums are basic extensions of the Jeremiah People-type humor—critiques from within that do not question the basic assumptions that underlie some of the foibles of Americanized Christianity (e.g., a presupposition of gnostic or Platonic dualism, an obsession with private, individualistic piety, and an almost unthinking acceptance of preferred, often uncritical interpretations of Scripture). Joseph perhaps goes too far in likening Taylor's early success to that of Ralph Reed a decade later, but there is something to the analogy: both discovered that "a powerful coalition could be built among modern evangelical Christians who opposed the racism that had infected American Christianity in the past and who loathed the secularist establishment that seemed to have nothing but contempt for the simple faith practiced quietly by millions."

In the '90s, Taylor would retain the commitments that supported such a coalition while also exhibiting greater theological depth and affirming more incisive and transcendent commentary on the intersection of life and faith. But from the start, Taylor described his mission as one of simple communication: "I want people to question things," he said in 1986. "I want the non-Christians to open their minds to the idea that maybe a lot of them have been lied to about what Christianity is all about . . . and for the Christians, I want them to think about what it means to be a Christian in today's society, how that affects everyday life, and what demands that makes on us as believers."

In the '90s, Taylor turned to producing, and crafted albums for **Guardian** and **The Newsboys.** He helped the former group survive the '80s, transforming them from a spandex hair-metal band into a legitimate hard-rocking group that was at least conversant with grunge and alternative (cf. Aerosmith). **The Newsboys** were by their own admission "a lousy band" that had made three embarrassing records when Taylor discovered them and helped turn them into one of the finest pop groups in the history of contemporary music (Christian or otherwise); Taylor himself gives far more credit for their success to head Newsboy, Peter Furler, playing down his own influence on the band. Still, with both **Guardian** and **The Newsboys**, he served not only as producer, but also as co-composer of significant songs. His Christian radio hits for **The**

Newsboys include "I'm Not Ashamed," "Where You Belong," "Upon This Rock," "Dear Shame," "Be Still," "Shine," "Let It Rain," "Spirit Thing," "Real Good Thing," "Truth and Consequences," "Reality," "Take Me to Your Leader," "Let It Go," "Breakfast," and "It's All Who You Know." For **Guardian,** he contributed lyrics to such classic songs as "This Old Man," "Lead the Way," "Lion's Den," "Bottle Rocket," "Coffee Can," and many more. In 1992, Taylor founded Squint Entertainment. The name of the company intentionally presents its aspirations in what are stereotypically secular terms *(entertainment* not *ministry)* in keeping with Taylor's vision that the projects will attempt to bridge the gulf that separates the Christian industry and the general market: "I believe we live in a post-Christian society, and in the entertainment world that means Christians have little or no influence. I'd like to play a part in changing that, but my experience has been than being tagged as a 'Christian' company can keep you out, regardless of the quality of your work. I like working in the Christian market, and I like working in the general market, but I am trying to avoid making it an either-or proposition." The greatest success would come when he managed to get **Sixpence None the Richer**'s song "Kiss Me" included on the soundtrack for the movie *She's All That* and landed the Christian group a place on the very secular Lilith Fair tour. The band, who Taylor had rescued from contractual obligations to a nonsupportive company, wound up with what was probably the biggest summer romance hit of 1998, one of the very few instances in which a Christian artist who is not named **Amy Grant** has gained significant exposure in the mainstream. Squint was also responsible for discovering **Burlap to Cashmere, Chevelle,** and **Waterdeep,** for reuniting **PFR,** and for guiding **The Insyderz** to an unprecedented level of success with their *Skalleluia* album. In 2001, the Squint label was taken over by Word, who replaced Taylor as general manager.

For trivia buffs: Taylor was the first Westerner ever to shoot a music video in Vietnam.

Christian radio hits: "This Disco (Used to Be a Cute Cathedral)" (# 3 in 1985); "I Just Wanna Know" (# 3 in 1986); "Bannerman" (# 5 in 1993).

Terry Scott Taylor

1986—*Knowledge and Innocence* (Shadow); 1987—*A Briefing for the Ascent* (Frontline); 1991—*The Miracle Faith Telethon of Love* [by Dr. Edward Daniel Taylor] (Alarma); 1998—*John Wayne* (KMG); 1999—*Glimpses of Grace: The Best of Terry Scott Taylor;* 2000—*Avocado Faultline* (Silent Planet); *Ruckus at the End of Nowhere* [by Terry Taylor and Friends] (M8).

Although his solo albums have amounted to little more than curious side projects, Terry Scott Taylor is generally regarded as one of Christian music's most significant artists. A prolific songwriter, performer, and producer, Taylor has stuck it out for well over thirty years in an environment where the financial rewards have been meager and the official accolades (chart hits, Dove awards) practically nonexistent. Still, there have been very few significant projects in the history of contemporary Christian music that have not borne his influence, if not his fingerprints. Taylor is best known as the front man for three of Christian music's most popular and critically acclaimed groups: **Daniel Amos**, the **Lost Dogs**, and **The Swirling Eddies**, though he has turned up in a variety of other incarnations as well (the **Rap'sures, The Farm Beetles**). A native of Orange County, California, his most obvious musical influences are the Beatles, The Eagles, and the Beach Boys, any of whose styles he can mimic at will. But Taylor is anything but derivative. One of the most creative forces in popular music of the late twentieth century (Christian or otherwise), Taylor has set new standards for defining such adjectives as eclectic, quirky, and inspired. One critic suggests, "If there is a constant theme in his songs, it may be that Christians are foolish when they think they have God all figured out." Taylor himself states his goal as a Christian artist as being, "To be an artist. That's it. If you're a tailor and you're a Christian, you make great suits. If you're a ditch digger, dig a great ditch. I'm a Christian, and I'm an artist. I want to be a good artist. That's a testimony in and of itself."

By most counts, Taylor has made four legitimate solo albums, each of which served as a concept piece that allowed him to explore matters that were perhaps too personal for any one of his bands. *Knowledge and Innocence* is a deeply introspective project inspired by the death of Taylor's grandfather. Musically, the songs are situated somewhere between *Rubber Soul* (Beatles) and *Pet Sounds* (Beach Boys); lyrically, the closest reference points would be to William Blake, Frederick Buechner, Flannery O'Connor, and C. S. Lewis. With striking poetic imagery, the songs address the paradoxes and ambiguities of faith, with frequent reference to mortality. The most Beatlesque of all is "Ever After," which describes a family too busy to experience the blessings of life all around them. "(Out of) The Wild Wood" sets a poetic description of journeying from this world to the next to a tune that recalls David Bowie. "Song of Innocence" is a children's song, or at least a song about songs for children, offered as a duet with **Randy Stonehill**. "One More Time" is sung directly to Taylor's departed grandfather: "One more time I'd love to see you my friend / One more time I wish I could hold your hand / One more time I'd look into your eyes / And tell you I love you one more time." At the other end of the mortal coil spectrum, "Light Princess" addresses the death of an infant. The song begins with the sound of the baby's heartbeat recorded within the womb, then presents the words of the father who offers his miscarried child back to God. The musical numbers on *Knowledge and Innocence* are interrupted by personal moments, including a recording of a Christmas cele-

bration at the Taylor house. For some reason, there are muzak instrumental reprises of two songs. An extended track called "Old Time Gospel Camp Meeting" presents Taylor singing a medley of his grandfather's favorite hymns in a scratchy version meant to convey the sound of an old radio program.

A year after recording *Knowledge and Innocence,* Taylor wrote a series of songs for his grandmother who would soon follow her husband on the road to glory. The result, *A Briefing for the Ascent,* is a concept piece for the dying; it was written in a two-week period before her death and was actually performed for her on her deathbed. As such, the album is even more personal and reflective than the first project. "I didn't write these songs for an audience," Taylor would say. "I don't expect much in the way of sales. It's more just a musical diary." Even so, many persons who struggle with grief have found Taylor's *Briefing* helpful. The project is organized around the theme of an art gallery with four paintings that inspire the various, successive meditations. The quiet songs are interspersed with instrumentals and spoken word affirmations. It is obviously intended for reception as a whole, but some of the songs stand out apart from their context. "Beyond the Wall of Sleep" articulates the promise of eternal life, and "The Wood Between the Worlds" describes the ambiguous posture of those who remain on this side of the veil ("I'm in a world I don't belong / I've got a home in the world to come").

The next official solo album, *John Wayne,* was recorded some three years before release but got tied up in whatever holding pattern noncommercial projects (even by big stars) sometimes find themselves in. *John Wayne,* however, has the sound of a potentially very commercial project. As *Phantom Tollbooth* would put it, "None of the songs sound the same, and every one of them is catchier than striped bass in a fish breeding pond." The overall theme of the alterna-pop gems concerns life in Orange County—for which the dominant icon remains John Wayne, visibly enshrined in an enormous statue erected at the entrance to John Wayne International Airport. The closest reference point to this stated idea comes in "Hey John Wayne," a mocking tribute to the movie star that manages to lampoon Southern California's cultural values (rhyming "My Sharona" with "carcinoma" in the process). The same theme crops up in "Ten Gallon Hat," a cowboy tune reminiscent of early **Daniel Amos** or late **Lost Dogs**. Otherwise, the songs seem to deal more with Taylor's self-awareness of his own failings. The opening, "Writer's Block," seems to bear an ironic title for a composition by the most prolific composer in Christian music. But Taylor owns up to a disparity between quantity and quality: "Please now consider the source / Count my golden vanities in the fire of remorse / I've made an art of clever demonstrations / But can't exchange it for my occupation / As the fallen cleric, chief of sinners, poor of spirit." The second song, "Mr. Flutter," is a jangly anthem to struggling-but-wavering faith: "I got a friend on high and he feels my pain / But I still got this dust flowin' through my veins / And I want to have faith and I want to know grace / But it's hard to break through when the rent's overdue." A song called "Too Many Angels" criticizes Christian kitsch, particularly the proliferation of "little knick knack cherubs" and the attendant piety that "blocks the heart's connection to the knees" and obscures commitment to "the only One who bleeds." Taylor also delivers the Dylanesque "You Told Them Exactly What I Didn't Say," a possibly humorous/potentially bitter diatribe against journalists who misquote him. But *John Wayne*'s closing track, "You Lay Down," is a hymn of breathtaking beauty, praising Jesus as the one who died on behalf of his abusers. Taylor's makeshift band for *John Wayne* included Derri Daugherty of **The Choir**, Gene Eugene of **Adam Again, Phil Madeira,** Andy Prickett of **The Prayer Chain, Michael Roe,** and various **Daniel Amos** alums.

John Wayne was actually subtitled *Orange Grotesques, Part 1*. *Avocado Faultline* might be Part 2, as a fascination with Los Angeles continues to be the driving theme of the songs. Again, Taylor is backed by an all-star band (**Jimmy A, Steve Hindalong, Riki Michele,** Daugherty, Eugene, Madeira, Roe, and many others). The sound is predominantly country. *Avocado Faultline* comes in a package with a thirteen-page booklet in which Taylor reminisces about growing up in that city, expresses his love/hate relationship with the area and its strange denizens (of which he, admittedly, is certainly not among the least strange), and offers some **Larry Norman**-ish defensive remarks about past criticisms of previous projects. "Cowboys with Engines" seems to be about road-rage freeway shootings. "Startin' Monday" sounds like a Jimmy Buffet song, complete with humorous Buffetesque lyrics that present a laundry list of all the worthwhile things the procrastinating singer intends to take care of soon. "With What I Should Have Said" is similar, this time listing moments when the perfect comeback has occurred to the protagonist sometime after the moment for delivery is long past. "Papa Danced on Olvera Street" offers a Father's Day memory from Taylor's own life, but most of the songs on *Avocado Faultline* are more empathetic than autobiographical. Taylor adopts the personalities of various (fictional?) California residents and presents songs from their perspectives. "Capistrano Beach" offers the wistful reflections of a Hispanic native whose life hasn't turned out as he planned. "Pretend I'm Elvis (for Just One Night)" offers the desperate pleas of a loser barfly trying to pick up women. No stranger to contemporary Christian music culture, Taylor appends a note to the latter song indicating that because "some people out there are a little thick and quick to vent some kind of knee-jerk condemnation and self-righteousness when they

hear such a song," he feels constrained to point out that " 'Pretend' is fiction; I am *not* this person." In a more traditionally spiritual vein, "The Afternoon" offers the reflections of a pious father who has lost a daughter ("Oh how she loved the morning, so God took her in the afternoon"). "Kind Word" closes the album with a simple, hopeful song about the merits of showing kindness in a mean-spirited world: "I know it isn't much but a blade of grass can crack the pavement / And if enough of us would go against the grain / In time we'd be a green field dressed in God's finest raiment / Soakin' up the sunshine and laughing in the rain."

Three other albums are also listed in the discography above. *The Miracle Faith Telethon of Love* is a bizarro compilation album in which Dr. Edward Daniel Taylor (= Terry Scott Taylor) puts on a faux telethon (called "The Prickly Heat Telethon of Love" on the album) by some loony televangelist, with songs interspersed between the craziness. The songs include previously unreleased **Daniel Amos** outtakes ("I'm on Your Team," "Riders in the Sky") and other rarities: an acoustic, beach party version of **The Swirling Eddies**' "Hide the Beer, the Pastor's Here," a muzak instrumental of that group's "The Big Guns," and a parody of heavy metal called "Sprinkler Head" (originally recorded by Christian comedy troupe Isaac Air Freight). Side Two of the project is a bit more sane, with three songs from *Briefing for the Ascent* and remixes of various **Daniel Amos** and **Swirling Eddies** songs. *Glimpses of Grace* is a more authentic retrospective album, with songs from *Knowledge and Innocence, Briefing for the Ascent,* and *John Wayne* and a few other nuggets: "Only One" is a song Taylor wrote for **Wild Blue Yonder** that previously was only available on the obscure *Miracle Faith Telethon* album; "Will Have to Do for Now" is a gorgeous and theologically profound song from the **Browbeats**'s *Unplugged Alternative* album; "Into the Deep" comes from *Surfonics* (discussed below); "Glorious Dregs" and "With the Tired Eyes of Faith" are Taylor solos that were originally included as bonus tracks on **The Swirling Eddies**' greatest hits compilation. Finally, for no reason at all, *Glimpses of Grace* concludes with a rendition of the Boy Scout song, "The Happy Wanderer" (the one that goes, "val-de-ri, val-de-ra . . . with a knapsack on my back!"). *Ruckus at the End of Nowhere* is not really a Terry Scott Taylor solo project at all. It is a live recording of the artist jamming with the usual suspects at the 1997 *Cornerstone* music festival. Most of the songs are either **Daniel Amos** or **Swirling Eddies** tunes, though "John Wayne" and "You Lay Down" are also treated to what may have been their first public performance.

In addition to all of the projects listed above, Taylor has had his fingers in a number of other pots. He has made two albums for children tracing the adventures of a character called Megamouth (*Rap Battle in the Big City,* Frontline, 1987; *The Great*

Skateboard Adventure, Frontline, 1988) and two more involving a detective named Harry Whodunit (*The Mystery of the Nine Samsons,* Frontline, 1986; *The Mystery of the Sea Serpent Swindle,* Frontline, 1989). Other children's albums include *Fruits of the Spirit: The Whole Armour of God* (Frontline, 1990) and *A Mouse Family Christmas* (label and date unknown). For a slightly older crowd, he has developed soundtracks for video games, including *The Neverhood* (IBM, 1996), *Skull Monkeys for Playstation* (Dreamworks, 1998), and *Boombots for Playstation* (Dreamworks, 1999). The Neverhood project apparently generated enough interest for the soundtrack to be released separately on compact disc as *Neverhood Songs* (Dreamworks, 1999). Many of the songs do have vocals, though the lyrics defy any reasonable attempt at conceptualization. A typical track would be "Potatoes, Tomatoes, Gravy, and Peas" for which the lyric goes, "Tomatees and potatees and my peas / I put 'em in my hat / And I eat 'em just like that / I put 'em in my ears and in my shoes / I put 'em in my pants / And I do a little dance / This always seems to take away my blues."

On a more serious note, Taylor also wrote and produced a project called *Surfonic Water Revival* (KMG, 1998), an excellent collection of surf music with Christian themes. Veteran surf guitarist **Paul Johnson** joins Taylor, but the real novelty in the project comes through the involvement of other artists. Rather than performing all of the songs himself (or with one of his typical bands) Taylor doles out the tunes to a wide variety of artists, including **All Star United, The Insyderz, Phil Keaggy, PlankEye, Plumb, Silage, Smalltown Poets, Starflyer 59, Randy Stonehill,** and **The Supertones.** Somehow, Taylor even managed to coax **Chuck Girard** out of retirement. **Rick Altizer** also wrote a few songs for the project, including ones performed by **Skillet** and **Rebecca St. James.** The result is nothing short of stellar. The album has the feel of a collection of hits from some bygone era, and almost every track sounds like it could easily have been a Top 10 smash back in the days when this type of music was big. Thus, the record affords fans of such music the joy of discovering songs that would have been their favorites for years, if only they had heard them before now. *Surfonic Water Revival* was treated as something of a novelty project, but it was easily one of the best pop musical offerings of 1998, showcasing Taylor's songwriting at its best as well as the undeniable talents of some of Christian music's best performers. The "Christian themes" furthermore, are fairly subdued and would hardly offend more secular-minded audiences.

T-Bone

1993—*Redeemed Hoodlum* (Metro One); 1995—*Tha Life of a Hoodlum;* 1997—*Tha Hoodlum's Testimony;* 2001—*The Last Street Preacha* (Flicker); *The Boneyard Box Set* (Metro One).

www.houseofbone.com

San Francisco-based Latino rapper T-Bone (not to be confused with **T Bone Burnett**) has had a pivotal influence on the emergence of urban music within the contemporary Christian music scene. T-Bone was one of the first rap artists other than **DC Talk** to gain acceptance and exposure in Christian music and, unlike the latter group, he came at the style with street credibility that would hold up among ethnic fans from outside the Christian subculture. In 1999, he also gained widespread acceptance within the general market, primarily through exposure on MTV. T-Bone became one of 160 contestants involved in an MTV series called *The Cut.* The program featured four of the contestants each week performing before a panel of judges with one being selected to continue to the next level of competition. T-Bone progressed to the final level where he eventually finished as the Number Four overall performer. His numerous appearances on *The Cut* featured blatant preaching and delivery of explicit Christian testimony that drew widespread notice.

With a father from Nicaragua and a mother from El Salvador, T-Bone grew up speaking Spanish with a keen awareness of ethnic and cultural diversity. His father was also the pastor of a bilingual church in the San Francisco area that held services for the Latino community, so T-Bone grew up in church, playing drums and piano, and directing a choir. At the same time, he began rapping on the streets at the age of eight and by the time he was eighteen would record his first Christian rap album. "I talk to the kids about staying in school, and tell them don't drink, don't drop out," he told *CCM* in an early 1993 interview. "I think it's something kids need to hear from somebody they can relate to. I know when I was in school, the teacher would tell me all that and I didn't even listen. It's different when you come at them with the kind of music that they like." His own favorite artists included LL Cool J, **Run-D.M.C.,** Ice Cube, and Mr. Grimm, a rapper for Snoop Doggy Dogg who went solo and had a hit on the *Higher Learning* film soundtrack. As for T-Bone's self-professed "Redeemed Hoodlum" image, he admits that he personally never strayed too far from the fold, though "when I was around 16, I chose to go my own way for a while. I always knew what was right and what was wrong because I was brought up in the Word, but I chose to reject it for a while." Still, he grew up in the culture and remembers well the day that one of his best friends was killed right next to him in a drive-by shooting. With a bullet through his heart, the pal could only manage to say, "Make sure everyone wears red at my funeral." T-Bone would later reflect on the emptiness of such a thought: "Ralphie didn't say, 'I'm going to miss you guys' or 'Tell Momma I love her.' All he cared about was the (gang) colors his friends would wear at his funeral." The event was a turning point for him and led him to get more serious about the message he wanted to convey through his own raps.

Redeemed Hoodlum was produced by L.A. Posse, responsible for works by LL Cool J. It features smooth production, streetwise delivery, and some impressive, tongue twister, full-on speed rapping. A provocative number called "Lyrical Assassin" would garner the most attention. The title track and "Saved to the Bone" offer the artist's testimony, while other tracks decry racism and gangbanging. The concluding "Hoodlum's Prayer" offers a prayer of salvation for gang members. T-Bone toured relentlessly behind the album, doing some two hundred concerts a year, and became known for performing more shows than anyone else in rap, Christian or mainstream. As the result of his ministry, one of his musical mentors, Mr. Grimm, became a Christian, as did one of his producers, Muffla. Then in 1994 the artist was assaulted and almost killed by a group of four young men who broke into his apartment and beat him severely with pipes. He would never know what prompted the attack, but speculates that it was a gang initiation, according to which the kids were supposed to make a kill to earn their colors. He also thinks that, perhaps, someone had heard he had made a record and assumed (incorrectly) that he must have a lot of money. Not finding anything in the apartment, the attackers tried to drag him out to his car and, once outside, he managed to get away, bloodied and bruised, but thankful to be alive.

Tha Life of a Hoodlum is a slicker and more mature production, with a diversity of styles. "Drunk in the Spirit" features appropriately blissed-out singing, and "Life After Death" offers something of a novelty telephone-grabbing duet between T-Bone and Mr. Grimm. Set against these fun tunes are deadly serious numbers like "Throwin' Out the Wicked" and "187em Demons," which take up spiritual warfare. The latter theme is overdone in Christian rap and is typically fraught with theological problems, but T-Bone generally avoids the naivete and militant extremism of artists like **Cross Movement.** The theme gets picked up again, less successfully, with "Demon Executor" on his third album, *Tha Hoodlum's Testimony,* but he manages to transcend the obsession and provide more orthodox and edifying fare with tracks like "Tomorrow's Not Promised" and "Keep On Praising." As its title implies, *Tha Hoodlum's Testimony* is T-Bone's most personal statement, offering a mini rap opera on the artist's struggles with trying to pursue a godly career in the Bay Area. By the time he released *The Last Street Preacha,* mainstream rap had become a commercial, middle-class phenomenon with little connection to the streets of its origins. T-Bone seems to realize and resist this. A few tracks ("Street Life," "Getcha Hands Up") continue to deal with the drugs and thugs theme that he figured kids in the streets still needed to hear. But T-Bone also seemed to recognize that in 2001 his albums were getting played mainly by church youth groups, so he shifted the focus of his ministry somewhat accordingly. "Up on Game" challenges the Christian music industry to be more accepting of urban music styles while also challenging rappers who are only into providing entertainment not ministry. "Friends" is a funky tribute to homie companions, and "Turn This Up" is just a celebration of hip-hop without any particular spiritual overtones. "Conversion" declares T-Bone's dedication to evangelism ("preach the Word in every alley crack and ghetto curb") and reports on his continuing warfare with demons, which he maintains are trying to kill him. "Nuttin' 2 Somethin' " and "Father Figure" (not the George Michael song) are infectious and joyous. *The Boneyard Box Set* is a three-disc collection of past tracks.

Tempest

Bobby Andrews; Darren Lee; Jamie Rowe, voc.; Mikk Rowe, gtr. 1987—*A Coming Storm* (Pure Metal); 1988—*Eye of the Storm;* 1999—*Lost in the Storm* (M8).

Tempest was a hard rock band from Indiana that is best remembered as the birthing ground for Jamie Rowe, who went on to fame as the lead singer for **Guardian.** Jamie was only fifteen when Tempest recorded their first album. The group was led by his older brother, Mikk Rowe, who was nineteen and played lead guitar. The band pulled off something of a coup in that they managed to gain endorsements from a number of major manufacturers, who gave them free instruments and musical equipment in exchange for a listing on the back cover of the group's second album. They were the first Christian rock group to obtain such favors, and since the band was by no means one of the bigger acts on the Christian scene, jealous promoters wondered just how they pulled this off. A decade later, Mikk Rowe would reveal the secret: "It was just, like, a lot of phone calls. I just called everybody and hounded them, and they said, well, yeah, this is a place we've never been before, so we'll try it." Of the two albums, *Eye of the Storm* is definitely the more mature production. It has a Bon Jovi sound (particularly on the ballad "Goodbye") and *CCM* would call it "fun, mid-western, hard rock with lots of feeling." Other notable Tempest songs include "True Love," "Goin' Nowhere," and "All for One."

In 1997, the two Tempest albums were made available on a single custom CD. For the truly obsessive, M8 productions then released an early Tempest demo as *Lost in the Storm* in 1998. Mikk Rowe reflected on the band's history in a retrospective for *HM* that year: "We were all so young. . . . I had no business being out there in a Christian band trying to tell others about their problems when I had so many problems in my own life. . . . But God did use Tempest, because we've seen a lot of that in our fan mail and just at our concerts."

Temple Yard

Johnny Guerro, bass, sax., voc., kybrd.; Bill Kasper, gtr., voc.; Marky Rage, kybrd., voc.; Eric Sundin, voc., gtr.; Ken Yarnes, drums. 1999—*Temple Yard* (Gotee).

Temple Yard was formed due to a division in the Christian reggae band **Christafari.** The leader of that group, Mark Mohr, kept the band's name and continued to produce albums with a variety of different backing musicians, while most of the other members reconstituted themselves as Temple Yard. The division was supposedly precipitated by disputes over musical direction, and this is evident in Temple Yard's exploration of connections between reggae and pop, soul, and gospel music. Their sound is similar in many respects to that of UB40 and Big Mountain. The group's self-titled debut album opens with one of its grittier tracks, "Lion of Judah," which promises eventual deliverance from current tribulation: "How long shall I have to listen to the cries of the poor / While the angel of death, 'im jus' bust down your door / Children never fear because redemption is sure." The song "Runnin' " incorporates a little bit of swing in its brass sections, while "Tell Me" and "By Your Side" are soulful R&B songs on which the less accessible (to American audiences) elements of reggae are subdued.

Christian radio hits: "Tell Me" (# 30 in 1999).

Tenderfoot

Louis DeFabrizio, bass; Jeff Irazarry, drums; Brett Levsen, voc., gtr.; Adam Vandergriff, gtr. 2000—*The Devil and Rock and Roll* (BulletProof).

Tenderfoot arose out of the ashes of the almost-emo band **Dear Ephesus** in which three of its members had played. They inherited that group's contract with BulletProof and made one album to fulfill the Dear Ephesus obligation before seeking what they hoped would be a career in the general market. As to whether they should be considered a Christian group, lyricist and lead singer Brett Levsen says, "We are Christians and we play in a band, so call it what you will. I don't consider myself an evangelist and I don't preach from the stage." The group has also been critical of the Christian music industry. "It's all image and no depth," DeFabrizio says. "And I dislike it when Christian record companies talk about ministry being their main goal when they are investing money in artists only to make huge returns." *The Devil and Rock and Roll* is straightforward hard rock with only traces of emo here and there. A song called "The Beauty of Iowa" has lyrics that reminded an *HM* reviewer of the Beatles' "Ob-La-Di, Ob-La-Da," though Levsen says it is about his grandmother. A number of tracks ("Hindsight," "Scapegoat," "Paid in Full") seem to be about the band's frustrations with the music industry. Specifically Christian themes regarding sin and Christ come out in "The Lion's Share" and "All the Stars."

Ten Shekel Shirt

Lamont Hiebert, voc., gtr.; Tommy Lee, bass; Austin Morrison, drums. 2001—*Much* (Vertical).

Ten Shekel Shirt is a praise and worship band affiliated with the organization Youth With a Mission. They have a lively acoustic sound reminiscent of Toad the Wet Sprocket and **Caedmon's Call,** with touches of **U2** and **Delirious?.** The group is located in New Haven, Connecticut, and their music seems directed to a college crowd. Lead singer Lamont Hiebert is also the songwriter. The title track takes Luke 7:40–47 to heart with its chorus, "I am the one who's been forgiven much / I am the one who loves much." Hiebert proclaims the worthiness of God in "Unashamed Love" ("Worthy, you are worthy"). In "Dream," he describes his own ambition: "To be great in your eyes is my dream / To be the one who makes you smile is everything."

Christian radio hits: "Ocean" (# 1 for 2 weeks in 2001); "Sweet Embrace" (# 19 in 2001).

Ten to One

Bill; Chad; Chris; Daniel; Nick. 1999—*Never Alone* (BulletProof).

Ten to One was one more Christian group to jump on the ska bandwagon after that style had already been pronounced dead as a doornail by all critical authorities. Of course, fans are notorious for not listening to critics (who also had disco dead and buried sometime around 1984). Composed of five men who lack surnames, the band at least plays the style well, and its songs are both explicitly evangelical and relevant to adolescent themes. As *HM* would note, their obsessions are twofold: God and girls. "Fill the Hole" deals with the first of these, with allusions to Paschal and baptism: "The Holy Spirit will fill the hole / Through water God will cleanse your soul." For the second, see "Past Times": "I miss your smiling face and your sparkling blue eyes."

Teramaze

Dean Wells, gtr.; et al. 1995—*Doxology* (independent); 1997—*Tears to Dust* (Rowe).

Teramaze is an Australian metal band with an interesting testimony tied to another Christian group. The group began as a purely secular act, playing bars and clubs in their homeland. None of the five members professed to be Christian. Guitarist Dean Wells told *HM* what happened: "Most of my life, I was quite rebellious. I got into drugs and the like and I was searching for something but I didn't know what. Then, I got a **Tourniquet** CD from some guy that I'd never met, and never seen since. I gave the CD a listen and thought about the lyrics for a while and when everything came to a crunch, I called out to

God to save me if he was really there, and he was." Wells shared his newfound faith with the rest of the band and, one by one, they all became Christians as well. As a result, he continues, "We felt compelled to preach the gospel through our music." Their first album, *Doxology,* was heavy on praise (as its title suggests) and, Wells would later admit, pretty much just copied **Tourniquet** in style. *Tears to Dust* draws on the glory days of classic metal with some progressive influences. *HM*'s Doug Van Pelt, who is not given to exaggeration, described the band's sound on this album as like "Dream Theater on a good day with Ronnie James Dio in his prime on vocals." Lyrically, the songs reflect on the pain that people feel when they are without God and the hope for release offered in Christ. "The only way to release that pain," Wells says, "is to give it to God and be reduced to tears."

The Pat Terry Group (and Pat Terry [solo])

Randy Bugg, bass; Sonny Lallerstedt, gtr.; Pat Terry, voc., gtr. By The Pat Terry Group: 1974—*Pat Terry* (custom); 1975—*The Pat Terry Group* (Myrrh); 1976—*Songs of the South;* 1978—*Sweet Music;* 1979—*Heaven Ain't All There Is* (Chrism); 1980—*The Best of the Pat Terry Group* (Myrrh); 1981—*Final Vinyl* (NewPax). By Pat Terry (solo): 1982—*Humanity Gangsters* (Myrrh); 1983—*Film at Eleven;* 1984—*The Silence.*

The Pat Terry Group is a legendary Jesus music group that formed in 1973 and became popular during the second phase of the Jesus movement revival as the focus shifted from Southern California (i.e., Costa Mesa's Calvary Chapel) to the Midwest. Pat Terry (b. William Patrick Terry) played in rock bands in high school and in 1970, at the age of nineteen, became a Christian. Though he did not envision a career in contemporary Christian music (hardly a possibility at the time), he did begin to write and play songs that expressed the joy of his newfound faith with a passion that was infectious and, therefore, potentially evangelistic. "I wanted to do music that would introduce people to Jesus," he says. Terry recruited two former members of **Dove** to form an Atlanta-based trio that would develop a melody-oriented acoustic folk sound that bore the influence of groups like The Byrds or Buffalo Springfield and, in retrospect, anticipated the sound of early R.E.M. Terry's voice has a quality similar to that of Cat Stevens. On most of the group's albums, however, the sound is toned down with an MOR sheen that reflects the era's cautious prioritization of pleasant over gritty. For this and other reasons, Terry's solo albums surpass the group's better-known projects in terms of enduring quality, but The Pat Terry Group albums still succeed if only on the strength of the songs themselves. Terry appears to have had a natural gift for songwriting and from the start was able to craft tunes with melodies and structures appropriate to the lyrics. Naively optimistic in a manner that would ultimately

bother the artist, the early songs are more wonderful than he allows. They convey the buoyancy of revived spirits and the enthusiasm of spiritual discovery, serving as religious or spiritual counterparts to romantic songs that describe the feeling of being in love ("Happy Together" by The Turtles may not deal very realistically with the existential struggle of sustaining a relationship, but it's still one of the best pop songs about romantic love ever written).

The group's first album is called simply *Pat Terry,* a title that reveals an initial identity crisis at this emergent stage. A custom affair, it appears to have been recorded on a nonexistent budget and was sold only at concerts. The good songs all appear later on more official albums, but Ken Scott of *Jesus Music* considers *Pat Terry* to be the band's best recording musically, due to the stripped bare, underproduced quality. For most fans, though, *The Pat Terry Group* (identity crisis temporarily resolved) would be the first album to count. An impressive debut, it offers the two songs that would remain the best-known and most beloved songs heard by the group itself (as opposed to "in cover versions"). "I Can't Wait" became a literal anthem of the Jesus movement, a jubilant and jangly canticle of anticipation that avoids the rapture fantasies of most parousia songs of the period (e.g., **Larry Norman**'s "I Wish We'd All Been Ready"). "Tell me how it's gonna be, read it from the Bible again," Terry sings with childlike wonder. "I can't wait to see Jesus, 'cause Jesus is coming again!" The same theme is visited with a touch of humor in "When the Lord Comes Back," where Terry sings "The Lord may come before I sing / The last line of this song." But *The Pat Terry Group*'s second big smash was "That's the Way," a wonderful wedding song that took its place alongside **Paul Clark**'s "Climb the Hill Together" and **Noel Paul Stookey**'s "Wedding Song" as one of the most-used numbers as the Jesus people began to marry each other. The song is subtitled "For Randy and Brenda," and was written for the band's bass player and his wife.

Songs of the South, however, is by all accounts the group's masterpiece. They come together more as a band on the second major label offering, with Sonny Lallerstedt's guitars (mostly acoustic but sometimes electric) being featured much more prominently in the mix. **Al Perkins** produced the album, and **Matthew Ward** adds his powerful voice to a rock song called "What Good's It Gonna Do Ya." One of the album's best songs is the somewhat gritty "You Got Me," but the real prizes are "Home Where I Belong" and "Happy Man," two country-flavored ballads that were subsequently recorded as inspirational hits by **B. J. Thomas.** In fact, the two songs served as the title tracks for Thomas's first two Christian albums and became the best-known offerings from his gospel repertoire. Thomas transformed the songs into beautiful adult contemporary numbers, but the original folk versions have a homey, genuine quality that many find more effective. *Songs of the South* also includes a country tune called "Restored" that appears to be an old **Dove** song; Lallerstedt sings the lead vocal on this song written by **Bob Farrell,** who was also a part of that group.

Sweet Music is often remembered for its album cover—a humorous cartoonish portrait that depicts the band members as scoops of ice cream in a giant banana split. **Al Perkins** again does production, and **2nd Chapter of Acts** adds background vocals. The autobiographical title cut testifies to the blessing and gift of music the artist had experienced throughout his life. "I Feel Free" slams a variety of cults and nutty religious teachings in a manner that isn't very politically correct but is pretty humorous and has a catchy beat. "New New New" and "Ladder of Love" also became fan favorites, and Lallerstedt gets to sing again on "Never Lose a Minute." After the Myrrh records, The Pat Terry Group pretty much vanished from the radar screen. Their next two albums for Chrism and NewPax did not get reviewed (appearing after the demise of *Harmony* and before *CCM* had gotten its act together), and the tastes of Christian music fans were shifting away from Jesus music folk to either adult contemporary, slick pop, or rock and roll. Music historian David Di Sabatino picks the title track and "Written in the Book of Life" as standout tracks from *Heaven Ain't All There Is* and "One More Try" and "Bring Me to the Balance" (the two side openers) from *Final Vinyl.* The latter record also includes "Everyday Man," which was covered by **B. J. Thomas** without repeating the success of the two songs mentioned above.

In 1980, Terry disbanded the group, admitting to frustration and personal dissatisfaction with what had become an industry and a subculture devoted to Christian music. "Evangelicals seemed to think that music was only a tool and had no intrinsic value," Terry recalled in a 1997 retrospective. "I just wasn't there anymore." Basically, Terry had moved spiritually beyond that initial honeymoon-revival phase where most of his thoughts and, quite naturally, most of his songs were about God, Christ, the Bible, and other religious subjects. As an artist, he wanted to write about other matters that were on his mind but felt constrained by a field that now encouraged production of spiritual songs for evangelistic and/or commercial purposes. "After I broke up the band," he remembers, "I sat around for about a year just trying to get a handle on what it means to be a Christian and an artist." His friend **Mark Heard** persuaded him to visit L'Abri, a community and retreat center for Christian artists in Switzerland founded by Francis and Edith Schaeffer. Lallerstedt and Bugg, meanwhile, founded Twelve Oaks Recording Studio in Smyrna, Georgia.

In the early '80s, Terry released three critically acclaimed but commercially unsuccessful solo albums. Musically, the records move away from acoustic folk toward more of a southern rock sound; lyrically they reveal a social consciousness ("The Open Door" on *Humanity Gangsters* and "The World around Us" on *Film at Eleven*) and a broader conception of theology. "The gospel I'm singing about now is a bigger gospel that I sang about in The Pat Terry Group," he said in 1982. "Now it's a gospel of salvation for the whole person, the whole personality, of everything we enter into, the hub of our values and morality and life." *Humanity Gangsters* takes its name from the notion that, in Terry's words, "our humanity is robbed within the institution of the church." The titular "gangsters" in other words are the preachers, teachers, and everyday Christians who expect every believer to become a cliché—a concept quite similar to that which fueled **Steve Taylor**'s *I Want to Be a Clone* released that same year. But Taylor's project had the novelty of new-wave going for it (not to mention the winsome appeal of self-deprecating humor), and, as a brand new artist, he did not have to contend with the alienation of old fans complaining that he had *changed.* Taylor went over big; Terry didn't. "I honestly did not think that what I would do as a soloist would cause controversy," he told *CCM* some years later. "I think I underestimated how opposed some members of the church would be to certain musical forms and lyrical styles. It surprised me to hear that people were saying that I had left the faith or that I had sold out for the money."

Humanity Gangsters features solid rock songs like "Open the Door" and "Too Many Voices" mixed with a couple of more mellow, radio-friendly cuts, "Sounds So Simple" and "Nothing I Say." In "Sounds So Simple" he admits that Christians come off as arrogant when they act as though they have found the meaning of life from which the whole world will benefit if they only proclaim it often (or loud) enough. *Film at Eleven* continues in the same vein of realism with "Change Takes Time," which seems to encourage Christian musicians (and others) to realize the relatively limited impact that they are going to have in a world filled with problems. Likewise, "In My Dream" relates an account of a person dreaming gloriously about life in the world to come only to be awakened suddenly when someone turns on a TV that is blaring news of recent disasters. "Shadows" deals with spiritual deception, but at least a couple of its lines seem to bear an unmistakable connection to the artist's former eschatological obsessions: "I could have sworn I saw the New Jerusalem coming down in all her glory / It was only the way the shadows filled the territory." On *The Silence,* he addresses his fans' consternation directly: "Sometimes they play me on the radio / I know it's nothing like the music of my past / Some people wonder why I let it go / I had to change it or retreat behind a mask" ("Parallel Lines"). "Man of Sorrows" is sung as a duet with **Leslie Phillips.**

Terry went on to become a successful country songwriter. His compositions have been recorded by John Anderson, Foster and Lloyd, Travis Tritt, and Tanya Tucker. "Help Me to Hold

On" actually became Tritt's first Number One song on the country charts; Tucker's rendition of his "It's a Little Too Late" was also a hit.

Christian radio hits: By The Pat Terry Group: "I Feel Free" (# 25 in 1978). By Pat Terry (solo): "The Right Place" (# 3 in 1982).

John Tesh

Selected: 1993—*Monterrey Nights* (GTS); 1995—*Live at Red Rocks* (GTSP); 1997—*Victory: The Sports Collection; Avalon*; 1998—*Grand Passion*; 1999—*One World*; 2000—*The Graceful Music Collection: Pure Hymns; The Graceful Music Collection: Pure Gospel*; 2001—*The John Tesh Project: Pure Orchestra; Classical Music for a Prayerful Mood* (Faith MD Music); announced for 2002—*A Deeper Faith* (Garden City Music).

www.teshmusic.com

John Tesh is well known in several capacities that have nothing to do with contemporary Christian music, but he has also served as something of an ambassador for Christian music to the world at large and he has recorded a number of easy listening albums that fit loosely into the contemporary Christian genre. From 1986 to 1996, Tesh served as cohost of the very popular, if somewhat tabloidish, *Entertainment Tonight* TV program. At the same time, and since, he has maintained a visible presence as an announcer for CBS Sports, covering a variety of events. But despite his success as a media personality, Tesh's strongest background and interest has always been in music. A native of Garden City, New York, he began playing trumpet and piano at the age of six, studied with teachers from the Julliard School of Music, and was named to the New York State Symphonic Orchestra while still in high school. Tesh first began composing musical scores associated with his TV projects, and as early as 1983 he won an Emmy for a theme he wrote for the Pan American Games. He composed music for the animated TV series *Bobby's World* for five years, and he wrote the theme music for NBC's televised NBA games (a little piece called "Roundball Rock"). He continued to provide music for broadcasts of the Olympics, Wimbledon, NFL games, the World Gymnastics Championships, and the Ironman Triathalon. In 1987, he won another Emmy for music contributed to the Tour de France, and in 1991, a third one for NBC's World Track and Field Championships.

In 1992, Tesh founded GTS Records (named for stepson Gib, himself, and actress-wife Connie Selleca; in 1995 it would become GTSP Records when daughter Prima was born). He began to concentrate more seriously on his music, eventually leaving *Entertainment Tonight* to compose and perform full time. Tesh has recorded numerous albums, only a handful of which are listed above. His trademark style (sometimes called teshmusic) is an easy listening variety of New Age that features piano instrumentals, sometimes with orchestra accompaniment. Similar artists include **Jim Brickman** and Yanni. It is

the sort of music associated with bubble baths and massage therapy sessions or, for the less romantically inclined, elevators and dentists' offices. Tesh's music is so definitively bland that, like Lawrence Welk in a previous generation, he often becomes the subject of jokes. He accepts these with good humor. "People who watch PBS are the people who come to my concerts," he says in an interview at his website. "Some of them get dragged there by their wives or girlfriends, but then they'll come backstage and tell me, 'Wow! That was . . . less boring than I thought'." Several of his albums have no obvious connection to Christian music. *Monterrey Nights* is an early set of romantic instrumentals perfect for a candlelit dinner. *Live at Red Rocks* and *Avalon* are popular albums from PBS specials featuring orchestral accompaniment. *Victory* is a collection of favorite pieces for sporting events. *Grand Passion* includes two of his biggest adult contemporary hits: "Give Me Forever (I Do)," with James Ingram on vocals, and "Mother I Miss You" with Dalia. *One World* is perhaps the most remarkable project he has completed so far. As part of a televised PBS special, Tesh travelled to several different countries, performing original music with local musicians and dancers in exotic settings. Thus, he samples Native American music in Arizona, performs with an Italian orchestra in Rome, accompanies two opera singers in Vienna, and joins a village jam session at a neighborhood pub in Ireland. Christian music group **Point of Grace** makes a guest appearance on one track.

In 2000, Tesh released two collections of hymns and gospel songs for sale over the Internet but not in stores; **4 Him** appears on the *Pure Hymns* set. A similar *Pure Orchestra* project was also marketed only over the Internet and included renditions of songs by Brickman, Yanni, and Enya. *Classical Music for a Prayerful Mood* is one of six albums of classical music released in 2001 (the series also includes *Classical Music for an Intimate Mood,* etc.). The compositions are specifically intended for meditation during times of private worship.

Tesh was the son of a Baptist Sunday school minister and credits his family with instilling a lasting faith within him. He indicates, however, that certain crises in his life, including the deaths of each of his parents and the birth of his daughter, were milestone events precipitating growth in faith. Likewise, when he married Selleca, she brought him back to regular church attendance. Sometime around 1992, Tesh attended a Promise Keepers' conference that would have a major effect on his understanding of professional life. As he recalls, speaker Tony Evans said, "It's not okay to be a closet Christian. If you're in the public eye, it's your job to come out of the closet." Tesh continues, "There must have been 80,000 of us there, but I felt like he was looking right at me. Come out of the closet—that's basically what I decided to do." Throughout the '90s, he would become increasingly vocal about spiritual commitments, not only sharing his testimony at Christian events, but openly discussing his faith in Jesus Christ in *Newsday, People,* and *Entertainment Weekly* magazines. The media took special interest in his revelation that he and Selleca had a sex-free courtship, prompting numerous inquiries regarding the convictions that would prompt such an arrangement. As a Christian celebrity, however, he has often been teased about being a goody two-shoes and has had to make choices regarding what sort of associations and actions are appropriate for one known to be a believer (cf. **Pat Boone**). Tesh has done so in ways that most evangelicals would praise as uncompromising, but not always in ways that pass muster with the simply prudish. In 1998, a number of Christian music fans protested when he engaged in some scripted banter with Jay Leno on *The Tonight Show* that involved sexual innuendo. Tesh said, "After cutting about twenty things out of the script, we did stuff that was funny. I thought, maybe there'll be people who see this and think, Gee, Christians aren't all that stodgy."

In 1998 and 1999, Tesh cohosted the annual Dove Awards presentations, calling more attention to that ceremony in the mainstream media. He consistently maintains that all of his music is inspirational and godly. "There is music that can move people apart from lyrics," he told *CCM*. "It might not be a gospel piece, it might be a piano piece with an eighty-piece orchestra, but people get it."

Bili Thedford

See **Andraé Crouch and the Disciples.**

Thee Spivies

Chris, drums; Clark, voc., gtr.; Ivan, gtr., voc.; Rob. 1997—*Ready or Not, Here We Come* (Jackson Rubio).

Thee Spivies is a retro band from Gary, Indiana, whose members go by first names only and all dress in matching suits with white shirts and skinny ties. Their sound incorporates touches of early '60s rock (as in Dave Clark Five), rockabilly, and Ventures-style surf music. Although they are marketed as a Christian band on a Christian label, there is little in their lyrics to suggest any overt religious or spiritual orientation. Most of the tracks are about good times and girls. "Jupiter in My Rear View Mirror" and "Banjo" are surf tunes. "Hey Girl," "So Tell Me," and "You Told Me So" are all about the sort of relationships depicted in old beach party movies. "It's all part of hearkening back to a better time," says Clark.

These Five Down

Nate Bauman, voc.; Rob Brunell, gtr.; Andy Hittle, drums; Justin Pletscher, bass; Brandon Whitlock, gtr. 2000—*These Five Down* (Absolute).

These Five Down are a metal-hardcore band that says their purpose is to "reach kids who may find judgmental attitudes leveled at them from the church." A pastor's son with multiple facial piercings, bandleader Rob Brunell relates his own struggles with keeping the faith to his experiences with being looked upon as an outcast because of his outward appearance. He credits his father with continuing to reach out to him even when he was alienated from religion and involved in the world of drugs. The band has a sound that merges elements of rapcore Korn with old-school Pantera, with Bauman's vocal attack bearing similarities to Godsmack. The self-titled debut album was produced by **Dez Dickerson.** It opens with "Low" (not the Cracker song), a danceable address to those looking for chemical escapes ("How low did you go to get that high?"). "I Am the Media" deals with the adverse influences of modern media, with the clever novelty of some lyrics being sung backwards. Several of the songs seem to be informed by a fundamentalist or Pentecostal doctrine of spiritual warfare ("Hymn," "Get It Back," "Revelation War"). Brunell says, "We go into bars where the devil saturates the place and 'Hymn' is the song we start out with because it's a prayer against all the various spirits of evil that can enslave us and we want to clear all the spirits out of there so God's anointing can come in."

Third Day

Tai Anderson, bass; Brad Avery, gtr.; David Carr, drums; Mark Lee, gtr.; Mac Powell, voc., gtr. 1996—*Third Day* (Reunion); 1997—*Conspiracy No. 5;* 1999—*Time* (Essential); *Southern Tracks* [EP]; 2000—*Offerings: A Worship Album;* 2001—*Come Together.*

www.thirdday.com

Third Day is a southern rock band from Atlanta, Georgia. The group formed in Marietta in 1994 when Mac Powell and Mark Lee, who were playing in an acoustic Christian group, met their future rhythm section (Tai Anderson and David Carr) at a youth event where they performed. A perceptive pastor put the four together and Third Day was off and running, picking up another lead guitarist (Brad Avery) on the way to their debut album. The group (affectionately known as 3D to fans) would become one of Christian music's top draws in the late '90s, though critics were a harder sell and savaged their first two albums as derivative of Hootie and the Blowfish and Pearl Jam, respectively. Powell would object to implications that they had actually fashioned their sound after one group or another: "I really don't mind being compared to other bands, but we don't want people to think that we're *trying* to sound like somebody else. That's what hurts." Most of the comparisons are based more on Powell's vocals than on the sound of the band as an overall unit. His natural voice actually sounds uncannily like that of Cat Stevens—though *that* comparison is seldom noticed. On the first album, however, he does employ phrasings and histrionics like those of Darius Rucker (of Hootie and the Blowfish), and on the second album he adopts the spit-out-as many-syllables-in-one-breath-as-possible approach of Eddie Vedder (Pearl Jam). The similarities are unmistakable for anyone who has heard either of the other groups. Still, Third Day are no mere copycats, and dismissals of the band as such are certainly exaggerated. For one thing, there is more going on than just vocals—instrumentally, they often come closer to recalling The Black Crowes or The Dave Matthews Band. Eventually (by the third album) all but the most grudging critics would chill and recognize that, despite some initial overly obvious influences, Third Day is one of the tightest and most proficient exponents of southern-fried rock making music in either the Christian or general market. They had certainly outlasted Hootie, proving themselves to be far more creative and competent than the band they had supposedly cloned.

Third Day sold over 200,000 copies, a very strong showing for a debut in the Christian market. It was initially released in 1995 on Gray Dot, and Powell would repeatedly point out that it had been recorded *before* Hootie and the Blowfish's *Cracked Rear View*. Thus, the similarities do appear to be more coincidence than imitation—the two bands were working in the same arena at the same time and drawing on the same classic influences (Allman Brothers, Lynyrd Skynyrd, Creedence Clearwater Revival). Nevertheless, the Christian music subculture discovered *Third Day* when Reunion released a spruced-up version of the album, and if the "Christian version of *Cracked Rear View*" label hurt the band critically, it probably helped them commercially—in the Christian music industry, marketing an artist as the Christian version of some secular act tends to be a reliable formula for short-term (usually one album) success. The group also evinces a strong ministry focus on *Third Day,* with practically every song citing Scripture and/or naming the name of Jesus. The opening track, "Nothing at All," is a distortion-soaked rocker about the ambiguous power of human speech to bless or curse; the biblical inspiration is James 3:5–10, though the titular advice ("If you can't say something good, say nothing at all") actually owes to the father of Thumper in the movie *Bambi*. The strongest track on the album—and the clear audience favorite—is "Consuming Fire," an appropriately blazing rocker that derives from Hebrews 12:29 (or Deuteronomy 4:24). "Did You Mean It?" opens with the guitar solo from **U2**'s "Where the Streets Have No Name" and moves into a jangly song that sounds like it should be fun; the lyrics, however, attempt to induce guilt in the hearts of any who have made promises to God that they have failed to keep. The gospel can be heard, however, in songs like "Holy Spirit" and "Take My Life," which testify to grace in the midst of a

typical "I don't deserve this" orientation. **Rich Mullins** plays hammered dulcimer on some of the album's quieter tracks.

On *Conspiracy No. 5,* Third Day remade itself in key ways, coming out as a grungier, hard rocking outfit. Powell would admit in interviews that this was an intentional effort to prove that "we don't sound like Hootie and the Blowfish." The harder sound also appears to have represented some attempt at crossing over into mainstream rock. In 1997, the group gained national exposure through a recording of a jingle for Coca-Cola, and overtly Christian themes are much more subdued on *Conspiracy No. 5* than they were on the debut project. Sam Taylor, producer for ZZ Top, **King's X,** and **Galactic Cowboys,** brings out the tougher sound in tracks like "Have Mercy," a chugging blues-rock song that almost seems inspired by the sound of *Let It Bleed*-era Rolling Stones. "You Make Me Mad" is another smoker, with lyrics that describe the power of music: "You make me dance, you make me cry, you make me laugh / You make me shout, you make me smile, you make me mad." The song "How's Your Head?" is a melodic love song that relates a time when Powell called his wife from the road to ask if she still had a headache. Such songs would broaden the band's appeal even among Christian audiences, who no longer felt they were being assaulted with sermons at every turn. Even the most overtly spiritual songs on the sophomore project reflect more humility and seem to come from a more secure experience of faith as a positive influence on life. The opening cut, "Peace," testifies to the experience of knowing "the grace of God has set me free." The album's peculiar title plays on America's fascination with conspiracy theories, and the album art picks up on this with pictures of the Kennedy assassination and other supposedly unexplained phenomena. The centerpiece song, "Alien," however, is not about Roswell cover-ups but is a prayer to God that draws on Psalm 146:9: "I am just like the alien, the fatherless, and the widow / Keep your watch over me." In short, Third Day exhibits incredible growth artistically and theologically on *Conspiracy No. 5,* and despite the fact that the album did not sell as well as the debut, it was universally recognized by critics as the superior product. The band would eventually reveal the meaning of the "No. 5" part of the title: in at least one dictionary, the word *conspiracy* is given several definitions, and definition number five reads, "when two or more people agree on something" (cf. Matthew 18:19–20).

The third album, *Time,* moves decidedly back toward the southern rock sound of *Third Day,* minus the more obvious Hootie-isms. Having given up on any prospect of general market success, the band once again offers songs with obvious Christian content, albeit with a more enhanced worship focus. More diversity in sound is also obtained, in part through the employment of a female gospel choir and a horn section on key tracks ("Took My Place," "What Good"). The album opens auspiciously, however, with a song that is not a rocker, but an acoustic ballad called "I've Always Loved You." It is sung from the perspective of Christ, offering a strong statement of his unfailing love for every human being. Later, "Your Love Oh Lord," based on Psalm 36, offers the appropriate human response to this statement: wonder, appreciation, and praise. In between those two parts of the divine-human dialogue, the group cranks up the volume for more of its trademark southern rock: "Believe" challenges those who are "always looking for a sign," urging them to just take the leap of faith that is needed. "Never Bow Down" offers a bold statement of no-compromise faith, inspired by the example of Shadrach, Meshach, and Abednego in Daniel 3. In general, though, *Time* has a much more relaxed, looser feel than either of the previous records. Producer Monroe Jones reportedly had the band set up in a circle in the studio and play all of the songs live with a minimum of overdubs. "Don't Say Goodbye" is a midtempo ballad addressed to a friend who has turned way from the faith; the lyrics are sensitive and appropriate to the situation described ("I hate to see you leave without a fight"). "Sky Falls Down" is an upbeat pop song, which the band describes as "a happy little ditty about the end of the world." The closing track, "Give," is an emotional worship song that serves as an effective segue between *Time* and the next project, *Offerings*. Some special editions of *Time* were packaged with an EP called *Southern Tracks* that contains four extra songs.

Offerings is a curious hybrid of an album: half live and half worship. Six songs are simply live recordings of favorites from previous projects, some of which have a worshipful focus; the most notable is "Agnus Dei," a track that otherwise was available only on a collection of worship songs by various artists (*Exodus,* Rocketown, 1998). To these, the group adds three more original praise songs, the best of which is "King of Glory," performed with a full choir. The band also covers "These Thousand Hills," a neglected song originally performed by **Jacob's Trouble.** The clear highlight of the album, however, is neither a live track nor a worship song. Third Day offers a rip-roaring version of **Bob Dylan**'s "Saved"; the song seems completely out of place on *Offerings* (sandwiched between two quiet praise anthems) but nevertheless represents a high point of the group's recording career. Other than that, *Offerings* is the band's weakest album, but it would prove to be their most successful, going gold (with sales over 500,000) within a year of its release. It also probably accounted for the group's receiving the 2001 Dove Award for Artist of the Year—the first time that an actual rock act was so honored.

Come Together is representative of the band's new hippie period, with a flower child theme, Beatlesque title, and psychedelic pop-art graphics. This was all false advertising—stylistically, the record is neo-Hootie, similar to the band's debut or to the less grungy portions of *Conspiracy No. 5.* But as such, it is a collection of strong material, showcasing a tighter band with better songs than those first two albums. The title track is not the Beatles song, but a new exhortation to unity with a catchy sound similar to **Audio Adrenaline** and lyrics that recall The Youngbloods: "We've got to come together / 'Cause in the end we can make it alright / We've got to learn to love." This is followed by "40 Days," a fast-paced rocker with encouraging lyrics for times of trial. Also driving and passionate is "Get On," a rant against gossip and slander that supplements its southern-fried boogie sound with wailing gospel choir background vocals. The album's best song, "Still Listening?" is a bluesy romp vaguely reminiscent of The Rolling Stones' "Honky Tonk Women"; lyrically, it is about waiting to hear God's still, small voice. "My Heart" is a soaring pop song unlike anything the group has done before. "Show Me Your Glory," "Nothing Compares," and the Caribbean "Sing Praises" provide the album with its now-requisite post-*Offerings* worship songs.

Christian radio hits: "Love Song" (# 20 in 1996); "Forever" (# 3 in 1996): "Praise Song" (# 3 in 1996); "Holy Spirit" (# 5 in 1996); "Who I Am" (# 1 for 2 weeks in 1997); "My Hope Is You" (# 2 in 1998); "This Song Was Meant for You" (# 5 in 1998); "Agnus Dei" (# 2 in 1998); "How's Your Head?" (# 23 in 1999); "I've Always Loved You" (# 1 in 1999); "Sky Falls Down" (# 1 for 5 weeks in 2000); "What Good" (# 1 in 2000); "Your Love, Oh Lord" (# 1 for 2 weeks in 2000); "These Thousand Hills" (# 5 in 2001); "Come Together" (# 7 in 2001).

Dove Awards: 1998 Rock Song ("Alien"); 1998 Rock Album *(Conspiracy No. 5)*; 2000 Rock Album *(Time)*; 2001 Group of the Year; 2001 Artist of the Year; 2001 Rock Song ("Sky Falls Down"); 2001 Praise and Worship Album *(Offerings: A Worship Album)*.

3rd Root

Chilli Fields, voc.; Andre Torres, gtr.; et al. 2000—*Spirit of Life* [EP] (Solid State); *A Sign of Things to Come.*

San Diego-based 3rd Root is a Christian band with a sound and history similar to that of **P.O.D.** Lead singer Chilli Fields adds a somewhat unique factor to their style, however, through his love of reggae, which seeps into the overall mix. Fields' voice and vocal mannerisms are sometimes reminiscent of Bob Marley or Peter Tosh, but guitarist Andres Torres is more of a Def Leppard fan, and this also shows. Torres was raised Catholic but ultimately found more satisfaction in the "personal relationship with Jesus" approach to spirituality offered in a nondenominational Protestant church where Marcos Curiel of **P.O.D.** served as worship leader. Unfortunately he has spoken polemically of his heritage in magazines like *HM,* contrasting "Catholic churches" with "Christian ones" and maintaining that he was not raised a Christian. The band's songs (written by Fields) offer a militant and triumphalist portrait of Christian life and destiny. "War is on the rise," Fields declares in the apocalyptic "Prophet's Eye." In "Zion," he exults, "Joy will never be destroyed, 'cause we are the children." In 2000, Fields had surgery to remove polyps from his throat and the future of the band was uncertain.

This Train

Joe Cobra, drums; Jordan Richter, gtr.; Mark Robertson, voc., bass; Becki Hemingway, voc. (−1998). 1996—*You're Soaking in It* (Etcetera); 1998—*Mimes of the Old West* (Organic); 1999—*The Emperor's New Band.*

This Train is a highly original, eclectic Christian band in the tradition of **The Swirling Eddies,** the **Lost Dogs,** or **Jacob's Trouble.** The group is led by Mark Robertson, who has also been a member of **Brighton, Generation, The Stand, Under Midnight,** and **Rich Mullins' A Ragamuffin Band,** in addition to playing bass with the **Allies, The Altar Boys, Mark Pogue,** and numerous other artists. This Train has a base sound that can be described as a hybrid of The Stray Cats and either Barenaked Ladies or They Might Be Giants. They seem to be a rockabilly group that also likes to play punk, country, surf, and power-pop—all these divergent styles come into the mix at one point or another. They display a penchant for quirky and, indeed, funny songs, but sometimes play it serious and occasionally take a middle, ambiguous, and potentially confusing route.

You're Soaking In It opens with a raucous remake of **Amy Grant**'s "Baby, Baby," which might be intended as a joke but works on a straightforward level, revealing the song to be way cooler than most rock and roll fans could ever have imagined. An equally rollicking groove informs "Monstertruck," a blue-collar love song in which the singer tries to woo his potential amour with promises of an exotic life in his double-wide: "You're so sweet and young and nubile / I got plans to make you mobile." The song "Like It or Not" is pretty much straight rockabilly with the possibly reassuring (or intimidating) pledge to someone, "I'm going to love you whether you like it or not." Relationships are the subject of many songs, especially relationships gone south. "Fairweather Friend" and "The Silence" both treat the subject of a broken trust or lost friendship. "That's Ex-Doormat to You" has an **MxPx** pop-punk sound and offers these words to a former girlfriend: "Sorry you don't have no place to wipe your feet no more / No one to manipulate, I know that makes you sore / But I couldn't help but wonder what it would be like / To give my life to someone who knows how to treat me right." Disillusionment is also a favorite theme. "Every Word You Said" is a song about a boy who grew up believing everything he heard on *Mr. Rogers' Neighborhood* only to discover life in the real world to be a bit less friendly. "Mary Alice" (the only song written and sung by Becki Hemingway) describes a child's fear for her parents' marital status after the marriage of a playmate's parents ends in divorce. The album closes with an uncharacteristically plaintive number, "I Don't Mind"; the only number on the album with any recognizably Christian content, it presents a prayer of desperate devotion to God: "Do what you have to / Do what you must / I'll learn to love You / I'll learn to trust."

Mimes of the Old West became the group's runaway hit album, bringing them to the attention of an audience that had for the most part missed the first record. Its title track is indeed about what mimes would have done in the Old West: "They throw imaginary ropes around imaginary cattle / No one was amused / They get themselves all trapped inside invisible boxes / And yet they seem confused." The real point comes in simple reflection on how such simple souls might have been received: "Well, people these days they feel so sorry for themselves / They think they got it hard / Try walking through Dodge City in the 1800s / Dressed in a unitard . . . No one had it harder / These boys passed the test / No one got beat up more often / Than the mimes of the Old West." Catchy and hook-laden, the song is a masterpiece of quirky pop. It is difficult to imagine The Barenaked Ladies or They Might Be Giants *not* covering the song—if they ever heard it. Also on *Mimes,* This Train delivers "We're Getting Nowhere Fast" as a celebration of the band's low-profile garage-group status, similar in theme to Neil Young's "Prisoners of Rock and Roll." Two songs are announced in the album cover's tongue-in-cheek graphics as "Hit Singles!": "The Missing Link" is not about evolution theories as such, but about gaps in one's faith system. (Robertson explains it by saying, "Some things in life don't need to be complicated . . . it's o.k. not to have all the answers.") The other supposed hit, "A Million Years," is an acoustic guitar-driven pop song that Robertson wrote with **Rich Mullins** and **Mitch McVicker.** "Who's Stopping You" is another failed-relationship song with duet vocals by **Ashley Cleveland,** who also sings backup on five other tracks (replacing Hemingway, who departed for a solo career). Richter's guitar gets more of a workout than on the debut, being featured on two surf instrumentals ("Hangar 84," "Seafoam Green") that are kind of like The Ventures with a lot more distortion. The group also covers Hank Williams' "I Saw the Light" and (as a bonus track) a southern gospel song called "The Great Atomic Power." Robertson's struggles with the flesh inform two tracks: "I Don't Want to Know" is a shameful acknowledgment of his temptation to turn a deaf ear to the cries of the "hungry, the homeless, the insane, and the 'least of these'." The closing ballad, "Goodbye," is addressed to his former self (the "old Adam," in biblical language), who keeps showing up despite dismissals. Musically, "The Wailing Wall" is a direct rip-off of Concrete Blonde's "Bloodlettin'," albeit with lyrics about Middle East peace (and the lack thereof).

The Emperor's New Band is a major step down for the group, taking them almost into novelty territory. Ironically, the songs are generally less zany than some of the best-known tracks on the first two records, but for some reason This Train decided to jump on the swing bandwagon and duplicate the retro '20s sounds of numerous secular acts (The Squirrel Nut Zippers, The Cherry Poppin' Daddies). Of course, the same might be said of **The W's,** but This Train were Johnny-Come-Latelies to the style. On their third album, they just come off as **W's** wannabes and pale in comparison to both that band and **The Deluxtone Rockets.** *The Emperor's New Band* opens with "I Wanna Be Your Man," which is not a Beatles' cover but a youth group camp song addressed to God (thus, "I want to be a man of God"). It's not very good. The swing style works much better on "Leave the Light On," "She's a Rocket," and "No, Not One" (a rendition of the traditional hymn), but is still unquestionably derivative. Fortunately, the group drops its pretensions on a few of the songs. "The Way It Sounds" revisits their surf style, and the title track is a country ballad that offers a flip-side perspective to "We're Gettin' Nowhere Fast" (bemoaning the loss of artistic integrity in a mythical band that enjoys too much success too quickly). The album also includes a re-make of "Monstertruck" and a cover of **Rich Mullins'** only bad song, "Screen Door."

This Train moves back and forth between religious and secular material in a way that is natural and exemplary. "I've been criticized by the label and other people for not being overtly spiritual enough in the songs," Robertson told *7ball* in 1999. "I've always *avoided* that, very intentionally. I hate the idea of trivializing Christ for the sake of a hit."

Christian radio hits: "A Million Years Ago" (# 14 in 1998).

Lloyd Thogmartin

1983—*Simple Direction* (Rooftop); 1989—*Still the One.*

Inspirational singer Lloyd Thogmartin recorded two MOR albums of Christian music in the '80s. *Still the One* was completely ignored by the Christian media, but *Cornerstone* called Thogmartin's *Simple Direction* "a pleasant and listenable album," while *CCM* styled it as "comprising a smooth and ever-so-beautiful arresting quality." Lyrically, Thogmartin seems a bit obsessed with apocalyptic themes, with "Armageddon" and "Last Days" representing the album's standout tracks. "Armageddon" sets what the artist understands to be prophetic statements from the book of Revelation to a calypso beat. "My Yahweh" offers a tongue-in-cheek look at comparative religions, while "Victory in Jesus" and "If You Will Ask" communicate a somewhat naive confidence regarding the potential of life in Christ.

B. J. Thomas

Selected: 1977—*Home Where I Belong* (Myrrh); 1978—*Happy Man;* 1979—*You Gave Me Love (When Nobody Gave Me a Prayer);* 1980—*For the Best* (MCA); *The Best of B. J. Thomas; In Concert* (MCA); 1981—*What a Difference You Made in My Life* (Word); 1981—*Amazing Grace* (Myrrh); 1982—*Peace in the Valley; Miracle;* 1983—*The Best of B. J. Thomas, Vol. 2; Love Shines* (Priority); 1995—*Precious Memories* (Warner Bros.); 1997—*I Believe* (Warner Resound).

B. J. Thomas was one of the most successful pop singers of the late '60s and early '70s, racking up a dozen Top 40 hits between 1966 and 1972. He became a born-again Christian in the mid '70s, and the tensions following his crossover into Christian music brought to light serious theological problems in the Christian music subculture's understanding of art and ministry. He encountered problems of a sort that would no doubt dissuade other celebrities from considering such a conversion or crossover, but he also made some memorable music and, arguably, rejuvenated an otherwise flagging career. Thomas has told his story in two different inspirational autobiographies: *Home Where I Belong* by B. J. Thomas with Jerry B. Jenkins (Word, 1978) and *In Tune* by B. J. and Gloria Thomas (Fleming H. Revell, 1983).

Thomas was born in 1942 in Hugo, Oklahoma. His family moved to Pasadena, Texas (near Houston), where he fronted a high school band called The Triumphs and had several regional hits, the biggest of which was "Billy and Sue" in 1964 (the song later went to # 34 on the national charts when it was re-released in 1966). Thomas first gained significant national exposure with the Triumphs' Top 10 rendition of Hank Williams' "I'm So Lonesome I Could Cry" (# 8 in 1969). The latter song has a distinct country feel, but Thomas soon learned to bend his mellifluous voice to more MOR stylings and scored big with a song written by his Houston buddy Mark James called "Hooked on a Feeling" (# 5 in 1968); James would also write "Suspicious Minds" and "Always on My Mind" for **Elvis Presley,** and "Eyes of a New York Woman" (# 28 in 1968) for Thomas. Then the biggest songwriters of the day, Hal David and Burt Bacharach, tapped Thomas to sing their "Raindrops Keep Falling on My Head" for the motion picture *Butch Cassidy and the Sundance Kid.* The song was Number One for four weeks in 1969 and remains Thomas's signature tune, one of the best-remembered and most-beloved songs of the era. He had another minor hit with the quirky Bacharach/David song "Everybody's Out of Town" (# 26 in 1970) and a well-deserved big one with Barry Mann and Cynthia Weil's "I Just Can't Help Believing" (# 9 in 1970). His best song to date, "Most of All" (written by J. R. Cobb and Buddy Buie of the Atlanta Rhythm Section), only went to Number Thirty-eight, while the dumb "No Love at All" (about how it is better to stay in an unhealthy relationship than to risk a lifetime of loneliness) went to Number Sixteen. "Rock and Roll Lullabye" (# 15 in 1972) wasn't very good but remains of interest because it features guitar by '60s star Duane Eddy and backing vocals by The Blossoms. Thomas had a spate of flops but then hit big one last time with

"(Hey, Won't You Play) Another Somebody Done Somebody Wrong Song" (# 1 in 1975).

In his autobiographies, Thomas would reveal that he had been brought up in a dysfunctional family with an alcoholic father. He would eventually speak publicly of being an abused child, a subject addressed in his song "Broken Toys." During the most successful period of his career as a pop star, he developed an addiction to drugs (amphetamines and cocaine) and would attempt suicidal overdoses on a number of occasions. By 1975, he was separated from his wife, Gloria, whom he had married when he was twenty-six and she was seventeen. She called one day to inform him that she and their daughter had both "become born-again Christians." He was unimpressed, but after coming near death from another drug overdose in Hawaii, he agreed to come for a visit. Gloria took him to the same couple (Jim and Micah Reeves) who had facilitated her conversion, and on January 28, 1976, B. J. prayed with Jim Reeves for Christ to come into his life. "It was the first truly sincere thing I'd ever done," he would later relate. "I told God, 'Lord I am undone. I can't handle it. I just want to turn it over to you. I want to accept your Son as my Savior.' Man, I started dancing all over this guy's house. I couldn't stop laughing and he couldn't stop crying. It was a miraculous thing." Thomas quit drugs immediately and would maintain that, miraculously, he experienced no withdrawal symptoms from the addiction.

Thomas did not immediately switch to singing gospel music. Somewhat ironically, he had already had a Top 40 hit with the gospel song "Mighty Clouds of Joy" (# 34 in 1971), and almost all his hits were family-oriented love songs that did not contain anything objectionable from a Christian perspective. Thus, he simply continued performing his family-oriented material at family-oriented concerts. But he did begin to testify to his faith. At one of his first concerts after the life-changing night of prayer, he told the audience, "You know, this is the first time I've ever seen the faces of the audience. For so many years, I've come out on stages like this and I was always stoned. I was so caught up in my drugs, I never saw people. But God made a change in my life, and I'm different now." Before long, word of Thomas's public comments came to the attention of executives at the Christian record company Word and a contract was offered for him to record contemporary Christian music. The artist did not really want to abandon his pop audience for some isolated parallel universe, so he hit upon the scheme of recording for the two markets simultaneously. In 1977, he made *Home Where I Belong* as a Christian album for the Christian market and *B. J. Thomas* (MCA) as a secular pop album for the secular market. In time, many pundits would see the implicit compartmentalized dualism of that marketing decision as symbolic of what is fundamentally wrong with contemporary Christian music, a guild that defines itself over against the world at large and so is, *by definition,* divorced from, out of touch with, and irrelevant to life in the real world. What happened in the years to come would bear this out. But at first, the scheme seemed to work: Thomas's secular album produced another Top 40 hit with his cover of the Beach Boys' chestnut "Don't Worry Baby" (# 17 in 1977) and *Home Where I Belong* went platinum. No one, certainly not Thomas, had thought that the contemporary Christian experiment would prove to be the biggest-selling album of his career. No one, not even the executives at Word, had realized the potential in the Christian market for a top-draw attraction like Thomas. B. J. was only a medium-sized fish in the secular pop ocean, but he was a whale in the Christian pond—a pool that suddenly did not appear as tiny as everyone had always thought.

Home Where I Belong was produced by **Chris Christian,** who also wrote or cowrote half the songs. The Christian/Thomas pairing would appear as a match made in heaven as the two artists had always evinced very similar styles. Thus, the songs on *Home Where I Belong* are of a piece stylistically with those of Thomas's secular music. They *sound* the same, with lyrics being the only identifying feature to mark the one set of songs as Christian. The title track to *Home Where I Belong* is a **Pat Terry** tune equal to the best of Thomas's popular output; there is no legitimate reason why it could not have been a major hit on Top 40 radio stations, despite the lyrical focus on yearning for the promised life that lies beyond this troubled one. Another standout track is the catchy "Without a Doubt," which Thomas himself cowrote with Christian. "I Wanna Be Ready" also focuses on future glory, and "Hallelujah" is a straightforward worship song. The album also introduces songwriter Archie P. Jordan to the contemporary Christian market. Jordan cowrites three of the songs, including "Storybook Realities" (with Gloria Thomas) and "You Were There to Catch Me" (with **Chris Christian**). The latter tune exemplifies what would prove to be Jordan's forté—ambiguous love songs that could be about either God or an earthly paramour, and thus could be appreciated by diverse audiences for completely different reasons.

Home Where I Belong would prove to be Thomas's best-received album of explicitly Christian music. Future projects continued to deliver more of the same, according to a formula that worked with his we-don't-like-surprises audience. Critics, however, grew tired of the trend and feared that Thomas's success with predictable MOR pop was defining the genre of contemporary Christian music in ways that discouraged creativity. *Happy Man* contains another strong **Pat Terry** song as its title track, giving Thomas another well-deserved hit on Christian radio and another should-have-been-a-hit song for the general market. That album also contains Thomas's version of Archie Jordan's definitive composition, "What a Difference

You've Made in My Life." Thomas sings it to the Lord, of course, but country singer Ronnie Milsap picked up the commercial potential of the tune as a straightforward love song and scored a Number One country hit with it (**Amy Grant** also had a Christian hit with the song). *You Gave Me Love (When Nobody Gave Me a Prayer)* is almost exclusively a collection of Archie Jordan songs (eight of ten selections) including the title track and "Using Things and Loving People." Thomas worked with **Chris Christian** again on *For the Best,* singing that artist's "Walkin' on a Cloud" and "Everything Works Out for the Best," along with **Pat Terry**'s "Everyday Man." Various compilations would package and repackage songs from these albums, sometimes combining them with general market hits (*In Concert* is basically a live version of songs from *For the Best* augmented with "Raindrops" and "Mighty Clouds of Joy"). Thomas also released two albums of traditional hymns (*Amazing Grace, Peace in the Valley*). In 1982, he recorded *Miracle,* an album that attempted to mix spiritual and secular songs together: "Satan, You're a Liar" has an uncharacteristic rock edge; "Would They Love Him Down in Shreveport?" challenges judgmental attitudes among Christians. *Love Shines* moves Thomas into more of a country vein, albeit with more songs with an overt gospel focus ("He's Coming Back in a Blaze of Glory").

The real challenge in appealing to both Christian music fans *and* general market audiences came with concert performances. In keeping with his new personna, Thomas mixed a number of his contemporary Christian songs into his usual set of family-oriented material, while cutting from the set anything that might be remotely offensive to Christian fans. Surprisingly, concertgoers drawn from his secular audience did not seem to mind this at all and accepted the faith songs as a facet of who he was. But Thomas and his promoters had underestimated the capacity for offense among the Christians. For some reason, many Christian music fans had assumed that he would or should sing *only* songs about religion and they objected to anything else. Thus, when Thomas sang innocent tunes like "Raindrops Keep Falling on My Head" or odes to fidelity like "Most of All," Christian fans would boo, jeer, or attempt to disrupt the show. Such problems occurred throughout the artist's "Christian" career, but it all came to a head on a 1982 tour, at a point where Thomas had several Christian albums behind him and was arguably the top draw in the contemporary Christian music market. "There are people screaming and hollering, and people coming up to the stage calling me the devil," Thomas complained to *CCM.* "It's got to be some kind of Christian cliché or Bible song, or else they feel like it's their right before God to reject and judge and scoff." The opening act for the 1982 tour was **Andraé Crouch,** a poor choice if only because he sang nothing but faith songs in his portion of the show and

exhorted the crowd to "be one hundred percent for Jesus." Crouch also made disparaging jokes about performers of that "other" music who don't have their priorities straight—some reviewers and a lot of fans actually thought Crouch was alluding to Thomas with such remarks, implying that the concert headliner was only halfhearted in his commitment. Crouch would vigorously deny this and, as the disastrous tour continued, he would stop making the remarks and even plead with the audience to be accepting of his "friend and partner in ministry" who was coming on next. It was to no avail. Thomas encountered what appeared to be organized hecklers in every arena—catcalls and shouted insults (or Scripture verses) interrupting any part of the performance that did not satisfy someone's narrow understanding of Christianity. On more than one occasion, Thomas got in shouting matches with members of the audience. At a show in Norman, Oklahoma, he stalked off stage in the middle of his performance. At times, significant portions of his audience walked out on him. In Denver, Colorado, an organized group of protesters took it upon themselves to chant "Jesus is Lord" loudly, as though to drown out the artist when he sang a song that wasn't on their approved list.

After the 1982 tour, Thomas gave a bitter interview to *CCM* magazine and then left Christian music, apparently for good. The next year, he released an album for the country market and had two Number One hits on *Billboard*'s Country and Western chart ("What Ever Happened to Old Fashioned Love?" "New Looks from an Old Lover"). To their credit, *CCM* magazine—who had supported Thomas with editorials throughout the previous debacles—reviewed his nonreligious country albums in 1983 and 1984, commending them as "wonderful collections of positive love songs that are both commercial and affirmative." But in 1984, the artist was caught at a very bad time in an interview in Zurich, Switzerland. Following a country concert (that had also not gone very well), a Christian DJ talked to him on tape for a radio broadcast, probing him to clarify his position vis-à-vis Christianity and Christian music. Thomas was angry, arrogant, and rude. He used startling profanity and dissed the Christian audience that he had courted a few years before:

"You have recorded some gospel records for church people, right?"

"I don't record for them. They can go to hell as far as I'm concerned. I record my music for everybody, not for a bunch of Christians. I don't believe in organized religion. I think it's just a cop-out. I'm definitely not a gospel singer, either."

"May I ask you, are you a Christian?"

"Well, I'm not a fundamentalist Christian, no. I mean, you know, I'm not a member of those born-again people—those Christians that are going to heaven while other people have to go to hell. I'm not a part of that."

"Are you born again?"

"No. No. No."

"You don't believe in religion?"

"I don't believe in organized religion, no."

"You don't care whether we listen to your music?"

"I don't give a f**k."

"Let me ask you two more questions: What is most important in your life, and to whom do you give credit for your success?"

"The most important thing in my life right now is getting the f**k out of Switzerland, and I credit no one except myself with my success."

Well, that was a bad day, and Thomas did not subsequently stand by his remarks. But it seemed clear that he could be written off as one who had been lost to the contemporary Christian music culture. The artist became mainly associated with oldies shows, but continued to enjoy moments of mainstream success. In 1985, he was tapped to record "America Is," the theme song for the rededication of the Statue of Liberty at the conclusion of an extensive renovation program. He later recorded "As Long As We Got Each Other" as the theme song for the hit TV series *Growing Pains*. Mark Joseph, author of *The Rock and Roll Rebellion,* would later say, "Although many in the contemporary Christian music world were certain that Thomas had lost his faith, he really only lost *their* faith." A decade after leaving Christian music in anger, Thomas returned to make peace of sorts with two more albums of hymns. *Precious Memories* and *I Believe* are collections of Christian standards similar to the earlier *Amazing Grace* and *Peace in the Valley*.

In 1997, Thomas would reflect at length on his experience as the first artist to try (unsuccessfully) to pursue a career in both contemporary Christian music and secular pop: "Somebody had to take the beating and take the judgment and take the condemnation that I took at the time. Somebody had to show that it ain't a sin for somebody like **Amy Grant** to have huge pop records, it's not something that doesn't glorify the heavenly Father, it's not something you need to condemn. Our hearts were really broken over what happened, but I'm as proud of that [i.e., his body of Christian recordings] as anything I've ever done." Further, he would identify a basic misunderstanding, which he now believed had caused things to go so terribly wrong: "There's no such thing as gospel music or pop music. Those are just labels and clichés that we live under. . . . All music is God's music."

For trivia buffs: **Bob Dylan** was originally slated to sing the theme song for the movie *Butch Cassidy and the Sundance Kid*. Hal David and Burt Bacharach wrote "Raindrops Keep Falling on My Head" specifically for him. He passed on it.

Christian radio hits: "Home Where I Belong" (# 21 in 1978); "Happy Man" (# 5 in 1979); "What a Difference You've Made in My Life" (# 6 in 1979); "He's Got It All Under Control" (# 18 in 1978); "From the Start" (# 20 in 1979); "Jesus on My Mind" (# 1 for 4 weeks in 1980); "The Faith of a Little Child" (# 7 in 1979); "Nothing Could Be Better" (# 19 in 1980); "Everything Always Works Out for the Best" (# 10 in 1980); "Satan, You're a Liar" (# 6 in 1982); "Pray for Me" (# 4 in 1983); "Odessa Beggarman" (# 35 in 1984).

Dove Awards: 1976 Album by a Secular Artist (*Home Where I Belong*); 1981 Album by a Secular Artist (*Amazing Grace*).

Grammy Awards: 1977 Best Inspirational Performance (*Home Where I Belong*); 1978 Best Inspirational Performance (*Happy Man*); 1979 Best Inspirational Performance (*You Gave Me Love When Nobody Gave Me A Prayer*); 1981 Best Inspirational Performance (*Amazing Grace*).

Donn Thomas

1980—*Live Wires* (Myrrh); 1981—*You're the One*.

Donn Thomas was an inspirational African American singer from Toledo, Ohio. He performed mainly praise and worship songs in an R&B style that might mark him as a link between '70s **Andraé Crouch** and '90s **Kirk Franklin.** Even before recording his own material, Thomas cowrote the popular praise song "A Shield about Me" with Charles Williams. The track was included on Maranatha's *Praise 5* compilation and became well known in churches open to contemporary music. Thomas relocated from northern Ohio to Southern California before beginning his solo career and became an assistant pastor at a Vineyard Christian Fellowship church. *Live Wires* was produced by **David Diggs** and includes "A Shield about Me" and other original songs written by Thomas and/or Williams. **Bryan Duncan** and Randy Thomas of **Sweet Comfort Band** joined Thomas for his second project, *You're the One.* The title track for that album is based on Jeremiah 29:11 and stresses that God has a particular blessing for every individual.

Christian radio hits: "The Keeper of My Love" (# 15 in 1982).

Dale Thompson

1981—*Lost in His Love* [EP] (custom); 1994—*Speak into the Machine*; 1995—*Dale Thompson and the Religious Overtones* (Rugged); 1998—*Testimony* [By Dale Thompson and the Kentucky Cadillacs] (Organic); 1998—*Acoustic Daylight* (M8).

Dale Thompson is lead singer for the very successful Christian metal band **Bride**. From time to time he has released solo albums that explore his love of the blues. These have been regarded as side projects and marketed in an appropriately low-key manner. Indeed, three of the projects (*Lost in His Love, Speak into the Machine, Acoustic Daylight*) were limited-edition custom releases available only to a select number of obsessive fans or collectors. *Speak into the Machine* is notable for the odd subject matter of its songs. "I've Never Seen War" sounds like a '60s protest song with lyrics commenting on the relative safety

Americans have enjoyed with no war on their own soil for over a century. "One Shot" relates a horror story from the Holocaust in which Jewish victims are lined up so as to be killed with a single bullet. The odd "Shower Scene" features a preacher wailing away while someone takes a shower in the background.

Dale Thompson was announced as the artist's first official solo record. Its songs are divided into two "Acts," the first of which presents eight songs that relate the story of a troubled veteran named Harlan who experiences a dramatic conversion to Christ. In the liner notes, Thompson says, "Every song is factual, taken from true events, and placed together to tell of one man's journey to find the truth and of the many broad roads of destruction that he foolishly traveled before finding Jesus." Act 2 then presents four more personal songs unrelated to the main theme. On the album Thompson calls his band The Religious Overtones, a group that includes **Bride** members as well as Greg Martin of the Kentucky Headhunters. The next official solo album, *Testimony,* would be considerably rockier, with lots of saxophone, trumpets, and Hammond organ added to the mix. This time, the band (composed of Louisville session players) gets titular billing as The Kentucky Cadillacs. Thompson adopts a raspy voice very similar to that of John Fogerty. On this outing, instead of singing traditional songs about first-person heartache, Thompson prefers to issue various warnings ("Better Watch What You Say," "Don't Judge the Preacher"). Musical highlights include the post-psychedelic stomp, "Road Less Traveled," and the traditional blues screamer, "Who'll Bell the Cat?"

Thompson's solo outings often seem strange to fans of his hard rock material who wonder why he leaves that niche to experiment in such a different genre. "I have always loved the blues and felt that the Lord wanted me to do something to minister to a different crowd," he commented on the release of one project. "The blues are about life, and what better way to introduce Jesus to someone as the author and finisher of life than with a blues record?"

Thousand Foot Krutch

Joel Bruyere, bass; Geoff Laforet, drums; Trevor McNevan, voc., gtr.; Dave Smith, gtr. 2000—*Set It Off* (DJD).

Thousand Foot Krutch is a rapcore band with a sound similar to a lighter version of Limp Bizkit, fronted by Trevor McNevan of Petersborough, Ontario. The group was signed to a private label by D. J. Dove of the rap groups **SFC** and **Gospel Gangstaz.** Dove discovered McNevan years before when the latter sent him a tape. "He was doing straight rap, straight hip-hop," Dove says. "This guy was doing all that and he was just 15 years old and he was a white kid from Canada." The group's songs are explicitly Christian in theme and evangelistic

in orientation. "Hopefully, the Christian kids will enjoy it," McNevan says of the band's debut album, *Set It Off,* "but it's not to reach them because those kids basically already know what it's about." *Set It Off* includes a cover of the EMF techno-funk song "Unbelievable" with new evangelical lyrics rapped between the choruses.

Thread

Scott Leger, voc.; Nate Navarro, gtr.; Steve Rude, bass; Curtis Ryker, drums; Eddie Willis, gtr. 1999—*Wide Awake* (True Tunes).

Thread is a Washington state modern rock band with a sound that falls somewhere on the spectrum that stretches from **Jars of Clay** to **Third Day,** with definite shades of **Black-Eyed Sceva.** Their debut, *Wide Awake,* did not attract much attention in the ironically crowded alternative market, but was well received where it was noticed. *Phantom Tollbooth* wrote it off as just one more example of "meaningful, well-played modern rock" that they predicted would get lost in the miasma of similar releases by artists on bigger labels with more backing. *Wide Awake* contains few explicit references to God or Christ, but all the songs betray a Christian perspective on life. The album's strongest cut, "Misfits," applies the titular identification as a compliment to those who resist the pressure of a culture that expects them to dress and act like their peers. "Hey Now" advises a slowed-down approach to life that savors experiences while they are still happening. "Tug of War" deals with the struggle between God and self, a conflict that Scott Leger says, "I don't want to win."

3 Car Pile-up

Paul Asciutto III, drums; Jason Hollis, bass; Joshua Stump, voc., gtr. 1997—*3 Car Pile-up* (Narrowpath).

3 Car Pile-up is a noise pop band that *Phantom Tollbooth* would liken to **Driver Eight** and **Luxury** in overall sound. The group was never profiled in the Christian media and their debut album failed to capture much attention. Everyone who reviewed it agreed that the best song was an atypical number called "Dweeb," which features some tongue-in-cheek lyrics: "When I was in grade school my friends made fun of me / They used to call me stupid names like Jesus boy's a freak / But I knew come Sunday I would be number one / Cause I knew all my verses and I would get some gum." The chorus to the song ("I'm a dweeb for Jesus") appears to pick up on the Apostle Paul's "fool for Christ" motif (1 Corinthians 3:18). The band also uses mild profanity ("Is there anyone who even gives a damn?") on another song about social compassion ("Care"), a step that may have alienated them from their target audience.

Three Crosses

"Keith" Ralph Barrientos, kybrd.; Steve Pasch, voc., gtr.; Ed Nicholson, gtr., voc. (−1998) // Greg Harrington, perc. (+ 1998); Anthony Krizan, gtr. (+ 1998); Antoine Silverman, violin (+ 1998). 1995—*Three Crosses* (Benson); 1996—*Jefferson Street*; 1998—*Skinny Flowers*.

A roots-rock band from New Jersey, Three Crosses has its origins in the general market group NYC, of which Keith Barrientos and Steve Pasch were both members. Pasch's work in the music industry had also included writing songs that were recorded by Poco, Lenny Kravitz, and Contraband. As Christians, however, Pasch and Barrientos became increasingly unhappy with what they felt were compromising situations and tried to steer NYC toward more spiritual goals. Eventually the group even changed its name to New Religion but, still dissatisfied, Barrientos and Pasch left the band altogether to form the Christian group Three Crosses with an old high school chum, guitarist Ed Nicholson. Influenced by such classic rock groups as The Band and The Rolling Stones, the trio fashioned a style similar in some respects to The Subdudes or The Black Crowes.

Three Crosses features the standout cut "This is Not My Home," which sets a repudiation of worldly attachments to the tune of a John Mellencamp-styled rocker. "Just Another Sign of the Times" and "Calvary" also invoke Mellencamp, but "God's House" is more of a country ballad that presents a modern parable about a homeless street preacher. Ballads and midtempo songs predominate, but "Devil Ain't Got No Hold on Me" is a bit rowdy with tinkling barroom piano underscoring its confident lyric. The album was produced by veteran Barry Beckett, responsible for projects by **Bob Dylan,** Dire Straits, **Aretha Franklin,** Lynyrd Skynyrd, and Bob Seger. Andrew Krizan of Spin Doctors adds guest guitar on several tracks and, later, he would join the group outright. *Jefferson Street* backs off from the gritty, original sound of the debut album to embrace the more predictable heard-it-before contemporary Christian sounds of bands like **White Heart** or **Petra.** The lead song, "Michelangelo," could have been a **DeGarmo and Key** track, with lyrics insisting that God is a better artist than Picasso or Michelangelo (or whoever). Most listeners, furthermore, probably did a double take when "The Stone Was Rolled Away" came on the stereo, as it sounds nothing like Three Crosses and everything like **Jars of Clay.** As it turns out, the song was written by Ed Nicholson with two of the Jars boys and he (rather than Pasch) sings lead on it in a voice that imitates Dan Haseltine's vocal stylings perfectly. "Welcome to the Jesus Movement" is clever in that it invokes the image and spirit of the early '70s revival to describe what the band believed to be happening afresh in the mid '90s. "What we saw in this past year is just such a revival," Pasch would declare, referring to "what was going on with Promise Keepers, See You at

the Pole, and True Love Waits." *Jefferson Street* contains several much better songs in the same vein as those on the debut album (the funky "Blind Faith," a quirky rocker called "Getting Ready," and the southern-fried rock song "The House of the Lord"), but, predictably, the less innovative and most derivative songs scored the biggest with radio audiences, tempting the band to abandon quality for pablum (cf. **Big Tent Revival** and "What Would Jesus Do?"). They did not take the bait. *Skinny Flowers* moves decidedly toward a classic rock sound that most modern groups can only hope to invoke. "You Make It Easy" sounds like it could be (though it isn't) a cover of an early Rod Stewart song (from *Every Picture Tells a Story*). Likewise, "I Have Never Seen the Wind" could be a Crosby, Stills and Nash cover. "Blue Motel" and "Maybe Tonight" have an Eagles feel. While some critics would invoke the dreaded D-word ("derivative") to fault the band on these accounts, the influences are in fact so basic as to seem bright and fresh in the late '90s. The group's cover photo and press materials for *Skinny Flowers* indicate that the band had expanded to become a six-piece (sans Nicholson), but a paucity of information in the credits leaves one of the new members unidentified.

Pasch has made two independent worship-oriented albums, *100% Saved* (1999) and *The Power of Worship* (2000), both of which are available at his private website: www.stephenmarkpasch.com. Three Crosses also released a live album in Europe only (*Live at Flevo,* 1999).

Christian radio hits: "Sign of the Times" (# 23 in 1995); "Seven Days" (# 5 in 1995); "God's House" (# 7 in 1996); "Calvary" (# 8 in 1996); "Stone Was Rolled Away" (# 1 for 3 weeks in 1996); "Michelangelo" (# 18 in 1997); "Bring Me to My Knees" (# 8 in 1997); "Maybe Tonight" (# 21 in 1998).

Three Strand

Aimee Joy Weimer, voc.; Kara Williamson, voc.; Scott Williamson, voc. 1999—*Famished* (40).

Three Strand is a trio of siblings who emerged in late 1999 with the apparent intent of becoming a third-millennium **2nd Chapter of Acts,** singing hymns of praise and adoration in a slick and polished pop style. The group has deep roots in Christian music, as the three once sang with a family group, The Williamsons, which included their parents, Dave and Jan, and recorded for StarSong in 1989. Sisters Aimee Joy and Kara have sung backup on a number of projects including **Amy Grant's** successful Christmas tours. Scott Williamson is a session drummer who has performed on albums by **DC Talk, 4 Him, The Katinas,** and **Jaci Velasquez.** He has also produced albums for **Point of Grace** and **FFH.** *Famished* includes original, emotionally potent songs of worship that focus primarily on private devotion: love for God and a personal experience of joy and truth.

The Throes

William Campbell, voc., gtr., kybrd.; Harold Evans, drums (– 1993, + 1996); Joy Gewalt, bass, voc. (– 1993) // David Lash, bass (+ 1993, –1996); Jeff Booth, gtr. (+ 1993, –1995); Matt McCartie, drums (+ 1993, –1995); Robert Yarborough, gtr. (+ 1993, –1995); David Cooper, drums (+ 1995); Drue Bachman, bass (+ 1996); Joan George, voc. (+ 1996); Julie Gruver, bgv. (+ 1996); Robert Malitek, sax. (+ 1996); Shawn Matthews, harmonium, bgv. (+ 1996). 1989—*The Era of Condolence* [EP] (R.E.X.); 1990—*All the Flowers Growing in Your Mother's Eyes*; 1993—*Fall on Your World* (Glasshouse); 1995—*12 Before 9* (Rode Dog); 1996—*Ameroafriasiana* (Brainstorm).

The Throes are one of Christian music's most beloved alternapop bands, a group that plays intelligent, meditative songs with a sweet, melodic sound that draws upon neopsychedelic jinglejangle guitars. Located in the northern Virginia/Washington, D.C., area, the group has never been commercially successful, but remains an underground treasure for those who like commercial-sounding pop music but hope for a bit more substance musically and lyrically than is usually found in the Top 40 hits that make it on Christian radio stations. The Throes' sound might be described as a happier version of **The Choir** or R.E.M. Of course, as the personnel list above indicates, The Throes would turn out to be just Bill Campbell playing with a constantly changing roster of friends.

After a cassette-only demo (*Era of Condolence,* later rereleased along with *12 Before 9* in an elaborate two-disc set), The Throes made themselves known to the Christian music subculture as a whole with *All the Flowers Growing in Your Mother's Eyes*. At this point, the trio seemed to be a genuine band, with Harold Evans writing all of the lyrics and much of the music. Strong comparisons were drawn to R.E.M. as Campbell brought to life catchy, poetic songs that offer an honest look at a variety of phenomena. The title track deals with ecological concerns. "Black Birds" uses the biblical affirmation that God knows every sparrow that falls from the sky (Matthew 10:29) as an image of providential care. "Skin Kings" addresses the warfare of flesh and spirit that seems intrinsic to human nature. The latter song is especially upbeat, borrowing its central riff from **Van Morrison**'s "Gloria."

All the Flowers was well received within the Christian alternative market, but Evans left the group to form **Poole** with his brother—a band that seven years later Campbell would also join, making it a sort of Throes reunion. For almost three years, Campbell road tested various Throes members and then finally recorded *Fall on Your World* with a momentarily stable quintet. The three-guitar assault of this version of the band gave them a deeper, more southern rock sound. Similarities to **The Choir** are even more in evidence, partly because that band's **Steve Hindalong** and Derri Daugherty produced the album with Campbell. "Jordan" is a loving ode to Campbell's infant child,

complete with chiming guitars suggestive of the imaginative journeys he promises they will take together. In a very different vein, "Oh Well" expresses the artist's frustration with the difficulties that plagued his efforts to keep the group afloat. It is a bitter song, aimed at people who behave in ways that he regards as insensitive. Lacking the poetry or the melody that makes a similar song like **Bob Dylan**'s "Positively 4th Street" work in spite of itself, it just comes off as so much adolescent whining. More poignant is "Blow Out the Candle," which expresses the artist's confused and ambiguous reaction to a Christian friend who confides that he is gay. The closing track, "Sounds Like Heaven," is more conventional in its musings about what heaven might be like.

An almost completely different group finally got it together for *12 before 9,* the Throes' masterpiece that would earn Campbell a permanent spot in the mythical Alternative Christian Rock Hall of Fame. The opening track, "So Controversial," is a perky tune that sounds a little bit like The Smiths covering a Monkees song; lyrically it appears to be taking a swipe at those who like to arouse controversy for its own sake. "It Bothers Me" also invokes '60s bubblegum with cutesy "na na na na na" choruses. For some reason, the group starts out playing The Cars' "My Best Friend's Girl" at the beginning of "Mess with Me" before moving into a completely different song about how Campbell's wife likes to keep the frustrated artist guessing ("she doesn't know what she wants from me . . . she won't tell, she'll just mess with me"). The album's three best songs are "Words," "Confidence Man," and "Stunned," all of which are catchy and hook-laden, yet with enough depth to keep them interesting after repeated listening. The lyrics are cryptic, but the first of these three numbers ("Words") appears to be about the need to speak words of love and reassurance in a relationship; it is enhanced by Campbell's all-time best guitar solo. "Confidence Man" is stranger, using the Roman madman Caligula as a symbol for the way charismatic leaders get away with abuses of power. "Stunned" is about the mystical experience of being struck by the incomprehensible power of the Holy Spirit.

All pretense of The Throes being a band was dropped on *Ameroafriasiana*. Pretty much anybody who played anything on any track gets listed as a group member, but it is a Campbell solo album from start to finish. Old buddy Harold Evans returns to coproduce the project with Campbell, but the latter remains the principal songwriter. Overall, the material on *Ameroafriasiana* is less aggressive, and more lush and moody than that on earlier albums. Lyrics remain a bit obscure, but the focus is on relationships. "Slip" addresses someone who tells the artist what he wants to hear but continually lets him down. "Don't" offers a heartfelt plea for someone in a complex or fractured relationship not to give it up and leave. "Satiable" is another love song for Mrs. Campbell and provides the album with a decidedly joyous break from melancholy: "To awake by your side is more pleasurable than any other sensation in this life."

Through the Eyes of Katelyn

See **Zao.**

Pam Thum

1977—*Bless This Day* (Shalom); 1978—*I Love You;* 1993—*Pam Thum* (Benson); 1994—*Faithful;* 1995—*Feel the Healing;* 1997—*Believe;* 2000— *Let There Be . . .* (Ministry).

http://members.aol.com/jbonline2u/pamthum.htm

Adult contemporary pop singer Pam Thum (b. 1966), the only child of traveling Assemblies of God evangelists Bruce and Ruth Thum, grew up singing at their fundamentalist, Pentecostal revival meetings. The Thum ministries were perhaps best known for producing an evangelistic drama called *Heaven's Gates and Hell's Flames.* Before adolescence, Thum recorded two independent albums that no longer receive acknowledgment from her publicists. Her official entry into the contemporary Christian music field came in 1987 when **Trace Balin** recorded her song "We Are an Army" and she signed a contract as a professional songwriter with a Christian label. She also served for several years as cohost of the TV program *100 Huntley Street,* a Canadian copy of *The 700 Club.* Thum began recording solo albums in 1993 and would turn out a series of pop-oriented albums with a sound comparable to that of Kim Carnes or **Amy Grant.** Thum has been especially popular in South Africa, where she was chosen the Favorite International Female Artist in a Christian music poll of 1993.

Thum's first two albums on Benson were produced by the team of Robert White Johnson (Celine Dion's producer) and Bill Cuomo (producer for Barbra Streisand, Steve Perry, and Kim Carnes). The self-titled debut tries to present her in a Melissa Etheridge mode, with a nod perhaps to the early work of **Margaret Becker.** "If Ever There Was Love" is typical of the up-tempo approach, but *CCM* and other reviewers found the rock stylings strained and thought Thum was more convincing on ballads. "One Voice Now" duplicates **Amy Grant**'s sultry style. The album also features an innovative cover of Pete Seeger's "Turn! Turn! Turn!" invested with new harmonies reminiscent of The Mamas and The Papas. *Faithful* continues in the same vein, mixing emotional ballads with hook-laden pop songs. Typical of the latter is "Love Conquers All," a radio-friendly bit of ear candy similar in style to many of Grant's bouncier tunes (ditto for "No Shadows, No Doubts"). More satisfying over the long haul are "Faithful Heart" and "Holding Me," quiet songs that testify to the depths of faith with an in-

timacy unusual in an artist so young. The latter song closes the album with a testimony to God's faithfulness in the midst of trouble. Another of the sophomore album's strong cuts is the invitational "Will You Come to Jesus?"

Faithful would be Thum's first mature album, a project on which the singer's true self seems to come through to a greater extent than previously. By all accounts, 1996 was a rough year for Thum, filled with what *CCM* would judiciously call "difficult changes in relationships personal and professional." The artist admitted to struggling with doubts about her faith and to having something of an identity crisis: "I had tried so hard to be thankful and submissive to the people around me, I guess I got to the point where I didn't know what Pam felt about anything." The songs on *Faithful* have a darker tone to them and reveal a faith shaped in the crucible of struggle. "Life is hard, the world is cold," she sings on a typical track, "We're barely young and then we're old / But every falling tear is understood / Yes, life is hard, but God is good" ("Life is Hard"). *Believe* displays eclectic styles ranging from the urban world-beat flair of "Go Down to the River" (with shades of Sting or Paul Simon) to the ethereal "As the Angels Sing" (featuring abundant strings and a children's chorus). Thum wrote "There's a Future for This World" specifically for her South African fans, and the song is performed with twin choirs from Johannesburg and Atlanta. "It's Okay to Cry" is a piano ballad sung with David Pack (formerly with the general market band Ambrosia). **The Katinas** join Thum on the upbeat "Lazarus Generation," and **Tammy Trent** lends vocal support to "This Is What I Believe." Thum would switch labels for *Let There Be . . . ,* an album critics would describe as "so consistent with her previous two projects as to please fans looking for more of the same." Again, pop worship tunes ("Let There Be Light," "Joy") complement inspirational ballads ("Cry Mercy," "Your Love Changes Me").

Christian radio hits: "If Ever There Was Love" (# 1 in 1993); "One Voice Now" (# 6 in 1994); "No Shadows, No Doubts" (# 8 in 1994); "Love Conquers All" (# 10 in 1995).

Titanic

Ray Kilsdonk, bass; Bill Menchen, gtr.; Tim Palmatier, drums; Simon Tyler, voc. // Robert Sweet, drums (+ 2000). 1995—*Maiden Voyage* (independent); 2000—*Maiden Voyage* (reissue) (M8).

Titanic was a classic metal band styled after such '80s dinosaurs as Ratt, Cinderella, and the great Christian behemoth **Stryper.** The band made one album of no-ballad headbanging anthems for independent release in 1995. Shortly after the record was released, **Robert Sweet,** who was a founding member of **Stryper,** actually joined the band. His tenure with the group was brief, but in 2000 the group's only album was re-released with three new bonus tracks featuring Sweet on drums. The better songs, however, are ones from the original effort:

"Ocean of Blood" and "Gods of War" are hard rockers that exhibit metal's typical fascination with violent imagery. "Freak Show" conveys the simple message that "Everyone is weird to someone."

Chris Tomlin

2001—*The Noise We Make* (Sixsteps).

Chris Tomlin (b. 1972) was a founding member of the **Passion** worship team responsible for the "One Day" series of worship conferences and recordings. Tomlin grew up in East Texas (born in Grand Saline and transplanted to The Woodlands) and plays a variety of acoustic rock that shows strong influence of such artists as **U2** and **Steven Curtis Chapman.** An active worship leader at The Woodlands United Methodist Church in his hometown, Tomlin says he is less concerned with being a performer than with "connecting with people while responding to the Lord." A number of reviewers, however, characterize him as a genuine artist whose debut album holds up to regular listening, apart from any sing-along audience participation. *The Noise We Make* opens with the title track, an upbeat rocker that seems atypical for praise and worship music. Likewise, "America" is more of an inspiring anthem based on 2 Chronicles 7:14. "Forever" and "Kindness" are congregational songs, closer in style to what one usually expects to find on a praise and worship album. Tomlin also covers **Delirious?**'s "The Happy Song" and offers a new adaptation of the hymn "When I Survey the Wondrous Cross." Tomlin described his goal to *CCM:* "When I was in junior high, I heard a guy leading worship at a youth camp. I left that service and knelt down to open myself up to God. I want my listeners to have all of me, and I want them to be touched by God through me just like I was by that leader."

Tonéx

1997—*Pronounced Toe-Nay* (Rescue).

www.yotonex.com

Multi-instrumentalist and singer Tonéx is Christian music's answer to Prince. The San Diego artist has a style similar to that eclectic general market artist, though his voice is more like Stevie Wonder's. Tonéx's parents are the senior pastor and assistant pastor of Truth Apostolic Community Church in Spring Valley, California. He grew up surrounded by urban gospel music and would perform with such artists as **Yolanda Adams, T-Bone,** Boyz II Men, **Shirley Caesar, Andraé Crouch,** Sheila E, **Kirk Franklin,** John P. Kee, and **DeLeon Richards.** Tonéx wrote, performed, produced, and recorded his 1997 album, *Pronounced Toe-Nay,* in his home. The tiny Rescue Records printed 7,000 copies, which sold out immediately;

in a matter of weeks they received orders for 30,000 more, which they could not fill, and the company shut down. An instant collector's item, the album also earned the artist a number of celebrity fans—including Missy Elliot and Prince himself. A master of self-promotion, Tonéx hyped the work as "a classic in its own time." Four years later, *Pronounced Toe-Nay* was re-released on Verity and reached a much wider audience.

The album is divided into six sections that represent different genres of music: 1) Hip-hop/Rap, 2) Retro-Funk, 3) The Future, 4) Jazz, 5) Mellow Grooves, 6) Soul-Gospel. Seventeen legitimate songs and a couple of silly throwaways are presented under these categories. The first section features guest rapper Big J of Unity Klan on "One Good Reason," a funkadelic anthem reminiscent of some of **Marvin Gaye**'s material. The Retro-Funk section offers two winners: "The Good Song" quotes from both The New Seekers' "I'd Like to Teach the World to Sing" and Gaye's "Save the Children" on an ode to world peace. Its hippies-for-the-'90s lyrics include the line, "From the White House to the crack house, we gotta all come together." Next, "Personal Jesus" is a groove-thick cover of a classic **Al Green** song. The section that Tonéx optimistically calls The Future just offers more rap and hip-hop (with an emphasis on those genre's more annoying features, such as incessant turntable scratching). The artist goes for a **Take 6** or Manhattan Transfer sound on the Jazz and Mellow Grooves sections, including a smooth jazz version of the traditional hymn "Pass Me Not." He recovers his best form again on songs in the Soul-Gospel division: "Cry No More" is a ballad similar to some of **Andraé Crouch and the Disciples**' '70s songs (e.g., "Tell Them"), and "Restoration" is actually a cover of a little-known Crouch tune.

Tonéx says that he initially had trouble finding acceptance within the traditional gospel community because of his "look": tatoos, piercings, and spacey clothes that betray a Lenny Kravitz fashion sense. But by 1998, he had founded his own gospel label and predicted that his roster of artists (T. Boy, 5.0, 4th Element, Shelley Gaines, Three-in-One) would "set the precedent for gospel music in the new millennium." He also predicted that by 2002, gospel music would "become the most prominent force in popular music and outsell every other genre."

Tonio K.

See under "K."

Tonjip

Phil Usher, voc.; Joel Hockey, gtr.; et al. 2000—*Tun-jip*

Tonjip is a modern rock band from Australia. Although the band's full lineup has never been publicized, the group is fronted by Phil Usher, who was also the lead singer for **Beanbag.** Tonjip, however, sounds nothing like that rapcore outfit, preferring a layered pop sound that takes after the Beatles and the Beach Boys. The songs are mostly cheerful and many have a distinct worship focus. The opening track, "Beautiful," features rolling percussion, chiming guitars, and ethereal harmonies, all at the service of lyrics that declare humanity to be God's handiwork and, so, beautiful in God's eyes.

Torn

Carter McLaughlin, voc.; et al. 1995—*Solitude* (independent); 2000—*Tree* (Ionic).

Torn is a grunge-influenced modern rock band that critics have compared to general market acts like Tool, Silverchair, and Alice in Chains. In 1995, Canadian songwriter Carter McLaughlin hired some musicians to accompany him on what he called "a collection of songs I wrote during the lowest time in my life." Originally titled *Solitude,* this album would later be remastered and re-released as *Tree* five years later. Having endured a time of homelessness and despair, McLaughlin performs the songs with powerful sorrow-tinged vocals. "Tree" is sung from the perspective of Christ on the cross.

Evie Tornquist

See **Evie.**

Totally Committed

Gregory Collier; Michael Cottrell; Ventwaughn Cvain; Alfonzo McHattan. 1997—*A Silver Lining* (CGI).

Totally Committed is an urban vocal quartet from Milwaukee with a slick sound comparable to that of **Commissioned.** The African American, all-male ensemble harmonizes on modern gospel numbers that generally steer toward the midtempo, adult contemporary stylings popularized by such artists as **BeBe and CeCe Winans.** Their debut album, *A Silver Lining,* comes close to traditional gospel quartet music on "Saved and Sanctified," while "Behind Every Cloud" and "In His Presence" are more reflective of their penchant for ballads.

Touch of Faith

Shavada Adams, voc.; Shawn Adams, voc.; Tondzra Adams, voc. 1997—*Touch of Faith* (Big Doggie).

A trio of sisters, Touch of Faith is a Milwaukee urban vocal group that sounds like a female counterpart to **Totally Committed.** The group offers soulful R&B songs in the tradition of **CeCe Winans.** They mix in small amounts of hip-hop and go for a few up-tempo tracks, but seem to be at their best with inspirational ballads. "Thank You" was written by their mentor

(Winans) and comes off like a Hallmark card to God, expressing gratitude for the varied experiences of life.

Tourniquet

Ted Kirkpatrick, drums; Gary Lenaire, gtr., voc. (−1998); Guy Ritter, voc. (−1994); Mark Lewis, gtr. (−1991) // Victor Macias, bass (+ 1991, −1998); Eric Mendez, gtr. (+ 1991, − 1994); Luke Easter, voc. (+ 1994); Aaron Trotter, gtr. (+ 1994, −1998); Aaron Guerra, gtr. (+ 1995). 1990—*Stop the Bleeding* (Intense); 1991—*Psycho Surgery*; 1993—*Pathogenic Ocular Dissonance*; 1994—*Intense Live Series, Vol. 2*; *Vanishing Lessons*; 1995—*Carry the Wounded* [EP]; 1996—*The Collected Works of Tourniquet*; 1998—*Crawl to China* (Diadem); 1999—*Acoustic Archives* (independent); 2000—*Microscopic View of a Telescopic Realm* (Metal Blade).

http://members.aol.com/~tourniqt

Tourniquet is one of Christian music's premier heavy metal bands. They are probably the paradigm in Christian music for "thinking metal," imbuing the somewhat abused genre with uncharacteristic variety and perceptive depth. The group formed in Los Angeles in 1988 and gained notice at first for playing thrash metal—the sound that the general market band Metallica is sometimes credited with creating and always credited with perfecting. But like Metallica, Tourniquet would not remain tied to a single style. Kirkpatrick would become the band's leader and, eventually, its only charter member. An aficionado of classical music and of allegory, he has often allowed those influences to affect the group's basic hard rock stance. The band also became somewhat famous for its theatrical performances, which included stage demonstrations by a fire-breathing illusionist called Devino.

Writing in *CCM,* Brian Quincy Newcomb would describe *Stop the Bleeding* as blending "classic gothic lyrics based on Scripture with music that allows creative bursts of energy." The group's style had not yet gelled on this record, which was produced by Roger Martinez of **Vengeance,** and the group has a sound representative of standard late '80s metal being played by hundreds of bands. They were also rather unimaginative lyrically at this point. "You Get What You Pray For" takes the **Stryper** approach of persuasion through screaming. Ritter shrieks encouragements to prayer against a backdrop of fire-and-brimstone warnings: "All of a sudden, God's grace will be torn / And billions of hellbound will wish they'd never been born / Let us pray!" Still, *HM* would note one factor that, even at this stage, set Tourniquet apart from their ilk: their technical ability. The album would score big with a song about animal rights called "Ark of Suffering." Composed by Kirkpatrick, who would become the band's principal songwriter, the song deplores the training of beasts for circus acts and the killing of animals "just for sport." The song raises significant ethical issues that are rarely addressed in (conservative) Christian circles. It would also be one of the only Tourniquet songs ever to gain a hearing outside those circles. MTV picked up "Ark of Suffering" for airplay in 1991.

The next two albums were produced by Bill Metoyer and represent what is sometimes called the group's medical period, due to a certain fascination with medical terminology in many of the songs. *Psycho Surgery* demonstrates maturity over the debut and displays a group capable of delivering an entire album that fulfills the potential of the "Ark" song. The title track is the closest thing the group has to a signature song. It opens with the dissonant sounds of an orchestra tuning, then introduces strangely growled vocals beneath a barrage of other sounds. Radical and abrupt time changes, dissonant harmonies, and a melodic vocal chorus all account for the song's initially inaccessible but ultimately mesmerizing appeal. The allegorical lyrics about all sorts of medical practices seem to be about the process of developing a new heart and a new mind. "Viento Borrasco" (i.e., "devastating wind"), an instrumental that arose out of Kirkpatrick's fascination with tornadoes, tries to convey the drama of those phenomena musically. A song called "Spineless" is similarly adventurous musically, combining thrash metal with rapping courtesy of guests **P.I.D.** The themes of child neglect and child abuse, which would surface often in Tourniquet's oeuvre, are addressed in the songs "Vitals Fading" and "Broken Chromosomes." The first of these describes a dying child who, ignored by his calloused family, finds eternal peace at last in the arms of the Lord. The second gives voice to a mentally retarded child who suffers abuse from a father who has rejected him as a disappointing defect: "You stopped playing father as soon as mom conceived / The only time we touched was just before I screamed." A similar theme is played out in "The Skeezix Dilemma" from *Pathogenic Ocular Dissonance,* a song that is set against a circus calliope beat with metaphorical lyrics based on the Uncle Wiggly board game. The unwieldy title track from the latter album uses the condition of "pathogenic ocular dissonance" (a medical term for "color blindness") as a metaphor for human perceptions that might not do justice to the full spectrum of spiritual truth; the song is basically an appeal for humility with regard to religious and doctrinal issues. "Truth *is* absolute," says Kirkpatrick, "but to think we can fathom, discern, and attain all truth here is absolute foolishness." The album also features songs with such titles as "Ruminating Virulence," "Spectrophobic Dementia," and "Gelatinous Tuberles of Purulent Ossification."

Tourniquet became a minor news story in 1992 when their scheduled (and advertised) appearance at the Milwaukee Metalfest rock festival was canceled for no other reason than that the group was Christian. The fracas began when Glenn Benton of the defiantly blasphemous band Deicide (= murder of God) got into an argument with radio host Bob Larson over the musical integrity of Christian rock. Benton told Larson on the show that "all Christian bands are wimps and couldn't compete on the same stage with a real band." Larson said the fans at the upcoming Metalfest in Milwaukee would get a change to decide for themselves whether that was true when Tourniquet and Deicide both played there the next month. Benton was shocked to learn Tourniquet was on the bill and said, "We'll see about that!" As it turns out, Deicide's own manager was the event's organizer, and at Benton's insistence, Tourniquet was dropped from the festival lineup. *USA Today* and a number of other national publications picked up the story as a rather overt instance of religious bigotry—and of cowardice on the part of Benton, who obviously didn't want to have his claims put to the test.

Lead singer Guy Ritter left Tourniquet after the first three albums, and Luke Easter was hired as the new singer—creating a division between Tourniquet sounds analogous to the David Lee Roth/Sammy Hagar divide in Van Halen's repertoire. Curiously, the band recorded a live album during the interim between vocalists. Their entry in the *Intense Live Series* features **Bloodgood** singer Les Carlsen doing Tourniquet hits, in addition to "The Messiah" (a **Bloodgood** song) and an old **Trouble** song, "The Tempter."

The first album with Easter, *Vanishing Lessons,* has what *True Tunes* would call "a decidedly more progressive orientation," moving into the realm of "artistic heavy metal" that would keep groups like Extreme and Queensryche relevant in the '90s. Kirkpatrick's love of classical music shows on the instrumental "K517," which features rock drums against a Scarlatti harpsichord sonata. "Sola Christus" is a progressive jam with screaming guitars. "Silently Vanishing" describes the ephemeral character of all earthly things with some lyrical inspiration from Edgar Allen Poe. "Acidhead" addresses drug abusers and asks them, "Where will you be when you're dead?" The song "Pushing Broom" is a very heavy, plodding number about the adolescent dream to leave behind a dead-end job for the big time. "Pecking Order" is about the superficial standards according to which status is granted or withheld in adolescent (and adult) society. The standout track, "Bearing Gruesome Cargo," verbalizes lame excuses people use to justify not making changes in their dysfunctional and destructive lives ("this is the way that I am . . . if you knew what I'd been through, you'd do the same thing too"). The song also addresses (again) the cycle of child abuse, exposing attempts to excuse inexcusable behavior as the result of baggage inherited from one's own upbringing. "Twilight" has a much more pop sound than is typical for Tourniquet and would score the group its one and only Christian radio hit. With nary a trace of metal, much less thrash, it is a melodic Lenny Kravitz-type song with a simple message about showing respect and concern for the elderly. The song ends with the lines, "Do you know someone who stares at the walls? / I think you know what to do." Another melodic ballad is offered with "My Promise," a rather touching song expressing the desire of a new stepfather to bond with his stepson. All told, Easter comes off as an expressive metal vocalist who can handle the screams, the shouts, the growls, and even the singing (*Phantom Tollbooth* says, "his voice always fits the music and mood of the lyrics, and you can always understand him"). *True Tunes* would say of the new Tourniquet: "they haven't lost their edge, they've just widened their blade."

The band next released an EP called *Carry the Wounded* that provides a showcase for their eclectic range. The title song is the only straightforward metal number, a tune that exhorts Christians to be Good Samaritans and care for those whose "lives have come undone." It also includes an acoustic remake of "My Promise," a love song to Kirkpatrick's new fiancée ("When the Love Is Right") and a striking cover of Fleetwood Mac's "Oh Well." The band's compilation album *Collected Works* also includes two new songs: "Perfect Night for a Hanging" expresses the somewhat regretful thoughts of Judas Iscariot (cf. Matthew 27:5), who did what he did because, "I just gotta be me . . . "; "The Hand Trembler" deals with the questions of doubt that assail a couple whose child dies in spite of their prayers: "There are things in this life we can never explain / On the wicked and the righteous come sunshine and rain."

After *Collected Works,* Tourniquet continued as a trio with Kirkpatrick as the only original member, supported by Easter on vocals and Guerra on guitar. Victor Macias left the group as a result of increased devotion to Russian Orthodoxy; Kirkpatrick indicates that the band had no problem with his beliefs at a personal level but says that everyone came to recognize a disunity in belief systems that was creating problems for the band as an entity. Founding member Gary Lenaire also departed on good terms, albeit with regard to what he would call "leadership issues" between him and Kirkpatrick; the latter says these involved commitments to the band's musical direction. Unlike Lenaire, the trio remained committed to an unabashed heavy sound, defying the whole alternative rebuttal to metal. In 1999, Lenaire joined with original Tourniquet singer Mark Ritter to release an album under the name **Echo Hollow** that seemed more oriented toward alternative rock on at least some of the tracks.

Crawl to China (produced by Metoyer again) preserves the metal focus of classic Tourniquet but continues to experiment with the formulas. *CCM* would call it "an unusual album," one that contains "everything you'd expect of hardcore metal, plus banjo, recorder, jaw harp, all kinds of sound bites, and a wide variety of guitar sounds." Easter and Guerra wrote two songs, including the allegorical "Tell-Tale Heart," based on a Poe story. Kirkpatrick contributes another animal rights anthem, "Going,

Going . . . Gone," which addresses the poaching of endangered species. "Proprioception" presents another scientific big-word allegory by likening a cat's propensity for always landing on its feet to the innate sense of direction that all humans have. "White Knucklin' the Rosary" deals with the very human tendency to call upon God only in emergencies. A variety of sounds are stirred into the metal mix: the title track tries a little rapcore; "Enveloped in Python" signals memories of **Alice Cooper.** "If I Was There" is a six-minute acoustic song reflecting on Christ's ordeal and sacrifice on the cross.

In 1999, the trio released an unplugged album with all-acoustic versions of some of their hits, similar to **Resurrection Band**'s *Ampendectomy.* Then another major label release called *Microscopic View of a Telescopic Realm* would appear on Metal Blade (the general market label that has also carried albums by **Galactic Cowboys** and **King's X**). *The Phantom Tollbooth* chose this record as its "Pick of the Month," heralding it as the band's "return to form," that is, to the thrash metal style of their first three records. Surprises and innovations still abound—a cello suddenly appears on "The Tomb of Gilgamesh"; flute solos and even a bit of whistling pop up here and there. Still, the sound is heavier overall than previous work with Easter had been. The opening track, "Besprinkled in Scarlet Horror," begins like a Bach fugue, moves into a shredding metal anthem, and finally concludes as a praise and worship song complete with lilting flute. The theme seems to be the excessive queasiness that some people have toward grotesque subjects, which in fact figure prominently in the Bible. "Drinking from the Poisoned Well" has Easter growling, sneering, and screaming lyrics about the destructiveness of holding on to anger. The same theme informs "Caixa de Raiva": "Six years and counting, why don't you let go of your rage?" The album concludes with "The Skeezix Dilemma, Part II," which revisits the abused child of the original song with a message of hope: "You can win the battle when you pray without fear . . . And the ones who bring sadness will bow to the crown."

Christian radio hits: "Twilight" (# 19 in 1994).

Tragedy Ann

Mikee Bridges, voc., gtr.; Eric Whittington [a.k.a. Johnny Bronco a.k.a. Lucky Seven], gtr.; Dave Bosley, bass (−1999); Bob Sable, drums (−1999) / / Jon Bruncko [a.k.a. Shorty Valentine], bass (+ 1999); Gabriel "Banjo" Wilson [a.k.a. Chaps McGuire], drums (+ 1999). 1997—*Lesser* (Organic); 1999—*One Nation under God*; 2000—*Viva la Revolución.*

www.tragedyann.com

Tragedy Ann is a Seattle rock band formed by Mikee Bridges of **Sometime Sunday.** The group crafted a less grunge but far-from-mellow sound roughly similar to that of other gritty vocal bands like **Grammatrain** and **Black-Eyed Sceva.**

Classic and southern rock influences are evident, with recent influences seeming to include such modern bands as Cracker, Social Distortion, and the Foo Fighters. Some of the band members apparently revel in changing their names from album to album, making genuine personnel changes difficult to document.

The first Tragedy Ann album, *Lesser,* reveals a group with understandable, explicitly Christian lyrics that describe Bridges' ongoing relationship with God. The first track, "Him," begins "I wish that I could tell you about myself" and continues, "If you don't know Him, well you don't know me." Likewise in "Little One," Bridges celebrates the childlike faith of his daughter, and in "Siren 2," he expresses his inability to offer any help outside of Christ ("Don't look to me / I can't help you / I can only watch Him work inside of you"). "Waste" is a musical treat, with lots of post-grunge hard guitars. *One Nation under God* opens with a song called "Preachin' Lies," which is set to the instantly recognizable guitar riffs of Concrete Blonde's "Bloodlettin'." The song would be dynamic if not for the aural plagiarism; as is, it just seems a rip-off, in spite of powerful lyrics regarding self-esteem. Bridges says the song is about "the people who told me all my life that I wouldn't amount to anything and the youth pastors that pushed me away because I listened to Christian underground music instead of to **Michael W. Smith** and **Petra**." Notably, many of the songs on *One Nation under God* are hard rock praise offerings ("Hey, Hey," "Seek," "Merciful God"). Bridges also offers a song called "Tank" with its repeating refrain, "I want to be your hero," written for a second daughter. *Viva la Revolución* opens with five rockers like those on the first two albums, but then changes gears. "Nothing But the Blood" is a country stomp cover of the traditional Robert Lowry hymn. "Why Can't the World Love?" is an unplugged acoustic pop tune that recalls flower child folk anthems from the '60s. So too does the closing de facto title track ("La Revolución") with its Graham Nash "we can change the world" lyric, children's chorus, and background voices intoning "brothers, love your brothers / sisters, love your sisters." One of the opening rock tracks, "Your Escape," is a rare antiabortion song that avoids mindless rhetoric in favor of a personal expression of instinct that is more honest and effective: "I thought of (my babies) before they were born / I love them so much / Don't tell me it's ok to stop this gentle newborn heart."

Tragedy Ann has identified itself as a ministry band in a way that **Sometime Sunday** never did. "We're not rock stars," Bridges told *HM.* "We're just trying to minister the gospel the only way we know how." This means-to-an-end understanding of his vocation is also expressed in a notable line from the song "Eugene" (from *One Nation under God*): "I don't want to be a rock star / But if I wasn't, could I talk to you about Jesus?"

Training for Utopia

Morley Boyer, drums; Don Clark, gtr.; Ryan Clark, voc., gtr.; Steve Saxby, bass. 1997—*The Falling Cycle* [EP] (Tooth and Nail); 1998—*Plastic Soul Impalement; Split EP* [EP with Zao]; 1999—*Wrench into the American Music Machine.*

Training for Utopia is a hardcore band from Sacramento, California, featuring Ryan Clark (lead guitarist for **Focal Point**) on vocals. The group came together in 1996 and has been the focus of some controversy in the Christian music scene ever since. "We get some flak because we're not blatantly Christian," says guitarist Don Clark. "And then we get flak from some non-Christians for being on Tooth and Nail (a label associated with Christian music)." The group's first full-length album featured a picture of a Ken doll nailed to a board, and was subsequently banned from most Christian bookstores. The group has been profiled in *HM* and elsewhere as one of many "faith-mixed membership" bands. Ryan Clark says, "Training for Utopia is not a Christian band. Some of the members are Christian. I, the lyricist, am a Christian, so it's inevitable that the lyrics will turn out somewhat spiritual." The main point seems to be that the band does not understand itself as involved in any sort of ministry. Don Clark says, "We just got together to have fun. We're not like **The Supertones** where we have some message that we want to get out. We're just kids that are into rock." The group objects in a similar way to being classed as a hardcore band, not so much for musical reasons as ideological ones. They have intentionally sought to distance themselves from the hardcore scene that made up their initial and primary fan base, citing what they regard as the "militancy, close-mindedness, political correctness, and unoriginality" of that subculture.

Musically, Training for Utopia strives for a noisy and chaotic sound, with an eclectic mix of industrial and speed metal influences. The sound tends to be vocal driven in a manner typical of hardcore, and a reviewer for *The Phantom Tollbooth* says, "I like the vocalist's singsong style that moves between talking and screaming, with a sprinkling of yelling thrown in." The group itself describes its sound as encompassing "the better aspects of complete insanity and utter chaos rolled into one. We play music that is not in any certain genre, and we don't want it to be. Heaviness is definitely a factor, but we don't let it control. Complete psychotic chaos is our goal—if we reach that, we're happy."

The Falling Cycle includes six songs that Don Clark says are about "backsliding, about slipping up in life, and about the frustration of doing things you shouldn't do over and over." *Plastic Soul Impalement* was produced by Bryan Carlstrom, known for his work with White Zombie and Alice in Chains (also **Stavesacre**). The song "Single-Handed Attempt at Revolution" seems to refute the popular American piety that advises people to find the truth inside themselves: "All I know is that I don't know / I am a fool, my pride dies with me." *Throwing a Wrench into the American Music Machine* is a much more experimental album—as its title implies. The group tones down the noise factor, while keeping the sound heavy. They incorporate electronics and, in terms of content, move away from the dark and ominous tone of previous material. There is an element of humor in songs like "Burt Reynolds vs. Godzilla" and "New York City Is Overrated." The album was not distributed in Christian outlets and makes no obvious references to matters of faith. It was, however, reviewed by several sources associated with Christian music. An *HM* critic called it "one of the most chaotic, frenetic albums I have ever heard." *Bandoppler* said, "The overall sound cannot be pigeonholed into any scene or existing style." In keeping with the group's fondness for the unexpected, *Throwing a Wrench* includes one tender and beautiful love song called "Everything, Including the Stars, Is Falling (Baby)." *Bandoppler* says it "stands as an accessible oasis amongst the torrent of bratty massacre surrounding it." The group also placed two songs on a split EP that also contains two tracks by **Zao.**

Tramaine

See **Tramaine Hawkins.**

Transformation Crusade

Daryl Fitzgerald, voc.; Andre Sims, voc.; Kathy Sims, voc.; Chris Williamson, voc. 1990—*Transformation Crusade* (Benson); 1991—*Makin' It Happen.*

Transformation Crusade was a rap group organized at Jerry Falwell's Liberty University, where **DC Talk** also got its start. The group was noted for taking a strong stand against the influence of Nation of Islam within African American communities and was rather confrontational in its attacks on secular rap music. The presence of at least four rappers (the debut album has six people in the cover photo) gave Transformation Crusade a somewhat distinctive sound, and the female vocals of Kathy Sims were particularly remarkable at a time when very few women were performing rap. The group's albums were produced by **Fred Hammond** of **Commissioned,** the second being noticeably superior in sound, with more polish and better definition. Lyrically, the first album shies away from gospel messages or spiritual themes to focus more prominently on cultural and moral lifestyle issues. Maintenance of virginity (especially for women) is a prominent concern. "Hold On" advises against "missionary dating" (i.e., dating non-Christians in an effort to convert them) because of the threat it poses to Christian girls' virginity. A similar moral stoicism informs "It Costs to Be Cool" and "To Be Down," which offers an unfortunate and uninformed diss on welfare mothers. *Makin' It Hap-*

pen adopts a somewhat broader vision. "The Statement" tries to mention every book in the Bible with one-line summaries of what is offered therein (cf. **Aaron Jeoffrey**'s "He Is"). "Race Thing" is a rant against both apartheid and Islam. Lifestyle and cultural issues remain dominant themes ("Life-Style," "Street Life"), but "It's Good to Sing Praises" does put the focus on God in a way that transcends fundamentalist legalism.

In 1990, lyricist Chris Williamson told *CCM* that he had been into secular rap before getting straight with God his first year at Liberty. After that, he would not listen to secular music at all, but said, "I let the Lord give me all the ideas for the songs." Both Daryl Fitzgerald and Andre Sims were psychology students. Kathy Sims studied fashion merchandising and said she joined her husband in the group in order "to provide a godly role model for the young ladies, so they can hold on to their virginity."

Travail

Brian, gtr.; Daniel, drums; Duane, bass; Matt, voc. 2001—*Beautiful Loneliness* (Metrovox).

Travail is a hardcore metal band from Texas with a sound sometimes likened to Godsmack or **Embodyment.** The group's *Beautiful Loneliness* was issued in a different form as *Anchor of My Soul* in 1998 and then again with one additional song in 1999. *HM* decided the third time was the charm and praised the remixed Metrovox version of the disc for its "devastating intensity and monster riffage." Lyrically, the band ponders the persistent mercy of God on "When I Fall" and celebrates its victory over Satan in "A Song for My Friend": "We can't fall with the devil / Got to whack him with a shovel." They get almost philosophical in a song called "And So I Was Thinking": "There's a dead cat in a box on the ground beside me / Is it a metaphor of my flesh in this house of ill repute / Or it is just a dead cat in a box on the ground beside me / With no meaning at all in a world that has no meaning."

Tree 63 (a.k.a. Tree)

John Ellis, voc.; Martin Engel, gtr.; Daryl Swart, drums. By Tree: 1997—*Overflow* (independent); 1998—*63* (Kingsway). By Tree 63: 2000—*Tree 63* (InPop).

Tree 63 is a "stadium rock" praise and worship band from Durban, South Africa. The trio of performers came together in 1996 and released two albums under the name Tree. The second of these, on Britain's Kingsway label, was titled *63* in reference to Psalm 63. After signing with InPop for an American release, the group amended its name to include the same biblical reference. Musically, Tree 63 has a sound similar to that of Britain's **Delirious?,** though their styles also draw upon a number of other European influences. The song "Treasure" summons images of Supergrass, and "Can I See Your Face?" recalls the early Police. "Anthem" and "1*0*1" are especially **U2** influenced. Lyrically, the group's songs are God-oriented, offering prayers and thanksgivings with a joyful intensity. *CCM* says, "They manage to sound vulnerable and optimistic without being trite or oblivious to everyday struggles."

Christian radio hits: "Treasure" (# 1 in 2001); "Look What You've Done" (# 1 for 2 weeks in 2001).

Dove Awards: 2001 Rock Album.

Tammy Trent

1995—*Tammy Trent* (R.E.X.); 1997—*You Have My Heart* (Light); 2000— *Set You Free* (Sparrow).

http://tammytrent.gospelcom.net

Dance-pop diva Tammy Trent (née Buffum) was born in Grand Rapids, Michigan, in 1966 and was brought up in an Assemblies of God church. She began performing gospel music early on by traveling with her mother, Judy Buffum, an ordained minister and gospel singer. As a teenager, she excelled at both basketball and singing, eventually earning twin scholarships to Southeastern Bible College. Trent moved to Nashville in 1991 to become a backup singer for best friend **Pam Thum.** She married Trent Lenderink and launched a solo career, adopting a stage name derived from her and her husband's first names. "Lenderink was not a realistic marketing option," she says. Trent's spunky persona conveys a contagious enthusiasm that she tries to channel into a faith imbued with spiritual optimism. "I don't think there's enough laughter in the world," she told *CCM* in 1997. "Even in the church, people don't know how to laugh anymore and to find that peace that God is talking about, and that joy." She is not naive about life's adversities, having been raised in a home where alcoholism ultimately led to divorce. Still, she says, "Some really horrible things happen in life. Deal with it; let God work through you, but then let it go, move on. Jump into the river of life and let him take you down the river."

Trent's debut album is a collection of urban dance songs that present her as what some would call a Christian equivalent of Mariah Carey doing Janet Jackson tunes. The album's best cut, "Your Love Is 4 Always," displays Trent's trademark perky style, while a remake of Carole King's "You've Got a Friend" reveals a different, more shuffling sound. "Emotional" celebrates the feelings of joy and peace that Trent has found in Christ. "Starting to Believe" is a midtempo ballad sung as a duet with **Pam Thum.** *You Have My Heart* is a somewhat more adult-oriented project, although "My Friend" is funky hip-hop, complete with turntable scratching. Still, the album includes a number of ballads ("You Don't Have the Strength," "Run to the Cross," "Say You'll Stay") in addition to an R&B cover of The

Spinners' hit "I'll Be Around." *Set You Free* is again packed with upbeat R&B tracks, including "Everybody Move with It," which includes a funky rap by **DJ Maj** and background vocals by Lisa Kimmey Bragg of **Out of Eden.** Trent would tell *Release* magazine, "I will not change my style. I love that Minneapolis Jimmy Jam/Paula Abdul thing. I don't know why there's not more of it."

In September of 2001, Trent Lenderink (Tammy's husband) was killed in a scuba diving accident while the couple was vacationing off the coast of Jamaica.

Christian radio hits: "Your Love Is 4 Always" (# 1 in 1995); "Starting to Believe" [with **Pam Thum**] (# 6 in 1995); "Love's Not So Far" (# 11 in 1996); "Someone 2 Love" (# 18 in 1996); "Welcome Home" (# 7 in 1997); "It's All about You" (# 11 in 1998); "I'll Be Around" (# 13 in 1998).

Tribe of Dan

Dan Donovan, voc., gtr.; Del Currie, voc., gtr.; et al. // Dan Harris, bass (+ 1998); Matt Middleton, drums (+ 1998). 1991—*Shook Up, Shook Up* (Mister M.); 1998—*The Bootus Red* (Mister M).

Tribe of Dan is singer/songwriter **Dan Donovan**'s on-again, off-again general market band. The group is not readily identifiable as a Christian band but is of interest to fans of Christian music because of Donovan's connections with the Christian music scene. Musically, Tribe of Dan has a raw, garage band sound that Donovan himself calls "swamp rock." The group's debut album did fairly well in native England, with *Melody Maker* calling the group "a band that crunches and grunts in all the right places." Del Currie, who would go on to sing with **Split Level** and **Fono,** was in this initial incarnation of Tribe of Dan. The group broke up so that Donovan could pursue his more meditative and acoustic solo career. Then in 1998 Donovan put together a new Tribe of Dan (he was the only returning member) and recorded *The Bootus Red.* Some Christian listeners detected religious imagery in a song called "The Blood," but the album is not overtly religious or evangelical.

Trin-i-tee 5:7

Chenelle Haynes, voc.; Angel Taylor, voc.; Terri Brown-Britton, voc. (−1999) // Adrian Anderson, voc. (+ 1999). 1998—*Trin-i-tee 5:7* (B-Rite); 1999—*Spiritual Love.*

Trini-i-tee 5:7 is a fashion conscious African American trio assembled by entrepreneur Kenneth Grant in the apparent hope of coming up with another Christian version of En Vogue or Destiny's Child. The group turned out to be better than the acts they were expected to emulate. Unfortunately, they would sometimes be as well known for their image as for their talent—a calculated effort on the part of the women and their handlers that was more successful than it should have been in a subculture that supposedly values spirituality. The women in

Trin-i-tee 5:7 were blatantly promoted as beauty models, dispensing fashion advice and tips for shopping in upscale stores. "It's ridiculous for me to say I'm representing God and not have any clue what's going on in the fashion world," Chanelle Haynes says. "We need to know what's going on with hairstyles and makeup trends *and* know what's going on in the Bible." The women claim that being "image conscious" and "on the cutting edge" assists their ministry. "We want the youth to know that God is a fun God," Angel Taylor insists. "Life doesn't have to be boring because you're saved." Good looks and good taste no doubt helped them to cross over to mainstream venues where, for instance, they performed for the 1999 New York Spring Fashion Show. A short while later, they entered into a lucrative endorsement deal with Revlon. *In Style* magazine listed Trin-i-tee 5:7 as one of the "Top 100 Best Things of 2000."

The group's name derives from 1 John 5:7, which mentions all three persons of the Trinity, but the group delights in quoting numerous other 5:7 verses as well: 1 Peter 5:7 ("cast your cares on him, for he cares for you"); Deuteronomy 5:7 ("Have no other gods before me"); 2 Corinthians 5:7 ("we walk by faith not by sight"). The first Trin-i-tee 5:7 album sold a phenomenal 400,000 copies. Terri Brown-Britton then left to become a full-time mother and was replaced by the group's makeup artist Adrian Anderson.

Musically, Trin-i-tee 5:7 was inevitably compared to **Out of Eden** (another female Christian African American trio), a comparison they justifiably resented. "Our sound is totally different," Angel Taylor said, "Their music is more dance, and ours is more hip-hop." Actually, there is no hip-hop and very little dance music on the group's debut album. The group breaks out of those limited (and limiting) genres to deliver a solid record of what was once called soul music. The album opens with a gorgeous a capella spiritual called "I Won't Turn Back," which more than one reviewer would liken to the sound of a female **Take 6.** Later, they perform "Mary, Don't You Weep," the traditional spiritual that was actually a big hit for **Take 6** on their first album. But unlike that smooth jazz group, Trin-i-tee's normative style does not consist of blending their voices into incredible harmonies; rather they intertwine diverse voices that support each other while also maintaining intriguing contrasts—a female version of The Temptations would perhaps offer the closest analogy. One of the women (probably soprano Taylor, but no credits are provided) is able to adopt Madonna's sweet bedroom voice when she chooses, while another typically sings in a voice like that of Lauryn Hill but is able to effect a credible Macy Gray when the mood suits. Given these propensities, *every song on Trin-i-tee 5:7 shines,* albeit in startlingly different ways. "Sunshine" may provide the best example of the Madonna/Lauryn Hill duet sound, with yet a third voice

wandering around the other two. "God's Grace" (written and produced by R. Kelly) is a silky, soulful testimony to God's goodness that minces no words in testifying to all things that come through Christ Jesus. "God's Blessing" (written and produced by **Kirk Franklin**) makes the same point to a funkier beat. "Holy and Righteous" is a gorgeous worship hymn. "With All My Heart" is another worship song with the Macy Gray impersonator adding spice to the arrangement. "You Can Always Call His Name" is a funky urban number set to a tune very similar to The Gap Band's "Outstanding," but incorporating rapped lyrics that prevent that similarity from becoming too distracting. "Respect Yourself" is a well-chosen cover of the Luther Ingram song that was once a general market hit for The Staples Singers.

Spiritual Love opens with an innovative, infectious song that is almost too good to be true. "Put Your Hands" incorporates snippets from two disparate hits, "Put Your Hand in the Hand" by Ocean (# 2 in 1971) and "(Every Time I Turn Around) Back in Love Again" by L.T.D. (# 4 in 1977). These are blended into a completely new funk mix that also quotes from a veritable medley of other hymns and spiritual songs ("Have a little talk with Jesus," "Take it to the Lord in prayer"). What could have been a mess turns into a brilliant mosaic and provides the group with one of its finest musical moments. After the auspicious beginning, the group opts for more predictable songs with uncomplicated arrangements. Rejecting the style that made the first album work so well, they now try to blend their voices to copy the style of lesser groups like TLC or SWV. That said, "How You Living?" is at least rugged and rocking, with someone singing in a snippy Michael Jackson voice. Otherwise, the sophomore album is less R&B than the debut and more adult contemporary. The song "Highway" features a traditional gospel lead by **Tramaine Hawkins,** "There He Is" (another R. Kelly song) is performed with **Kirk Franklin,** and "I Promise You," with **Crystal Lewis.** Aside from the opening track, however, the second album's obvious best song is the no-guest-star "Gonna Get Myself Together," a soulful ballad that sounds very much like something **Danniebell Hall** would have sung on some '70s album by **Andraé Crouch and the Disciples.** But like that song, "My Body" and the title track are practically solos, and the latter sounds like something Britney Spears would do. "My Body" is somewhat redeemed by strong lyrics, an ode to chastity that comes off like a Christian version of Alanis Morissette's "UnInvited": "My body is the Lord's temple / Don't mess with me, God's property."

For trivia buffs: Most of the Bible verse from which Trin-i-tee 5:7 takes its name (1 John 5:7) does not actually belong in Scripture. The passage was added to the Bible centuries after the original manuscripts were written (possibly as a result of a monk's marginal comment being mistaken by another copyist as part of the text). Bible scholars are unanimous in rejecting the authenticity of the added words, though no one disagrees with the content or sentiment that they express. Responsible Bible translations put the added words in the footnotes or omit them entirely.

Christian radio hits: "Put Your Hands" (# 16 in 2000).

Trip

Andy Hunter; Martin King. 1999—*Cultural Shift* (Alliance).

Trip is a British techno duo sponsored by an organization called New Generation Ministries, responsible also for **dba** and **Hydro.** The two perform a rather specialized form of dance music called "jungle" or "drum and bass," and their album, *Cultural Shift,* has been hailed as the first full-length drum and bass record in the Christian market. Exactly what makes it Christian is ambiguous, as most of the music is instrumental and what vocals are present are not overtly religious. Still, *Cultural Shift* has been marketed as a Christian album on a Christian label. The sound is emphatically rhythmic, featuring fast drums and distorted bass with synthesizers laid over the top. Guest vocalist Tanya Farthing sings in a soothing voice now and then, but the vocals are primarily a sonic effect. *Phantom Tollbooth* would highlight "Dark Storm" as a particularly frenetic standout track.

The band Trip that records on the Alliance label should not be confused with an American bass player who records instrumental albums under the name Trip for the indie Alternative Route label.

Trouble

See **Supershine.**

Kathy Troccoli

1982—*Stubborn Love* (Reunion); 1984—*Heart and Soul;* 1986—*Images;* 1987—*Portfolio;* 1991—*Pure Attraction;* 1994—*Kathy Troccoli;* 1995— *Sounds of Heaven;* 1996—*Best of . . . Just for You;* 1997—*Love and Mercy;* 1998—*Corner of Eden;* 1999—*Together* [with Sandi Patty] (Monarch); *A Sentimental Christmas* (Reunion); 2000—*Love Has a Name.*

www.troccoli.com

Kathy Troccoli (b. 1958) is a Christian pop singer from New York. She has a throaty, powerful voice and a style that is sometimes similar to that of general market artist Cher. Born in Brooklyn, she grew up in the small Long Island town of East Islip. Her father died when she was a teenager, but her widowed mother worked to support her career in music. She attended Berklee College in Boston for a year and then graduated from Suffolk County Community College, where she sang in a jazz band. She continued to pursue a music career by singing in

nightclubs but also worked a day job, where a born-again coworker named Cindy witnessed to her about faith in Christ. Troccoli, who had been raised an Italian Catholic, says that the love and joy she saw in Cindy eventually connected with the faith of her upbringing; she went to church with the girl and there she "met the Lord." Eventually, a pastor invited her to sing some songs of faith at a church meeting where she met the vocal group **Glad.** Ed Nalle of that group was so impressed with her talents that he had her make a demo tape with the band backing her. The tape came to the attention of the Christian music management team of Mike Blanton and Dan Harrell (best known for handling **Amy Grant** and **Michael W. Smith**), and in 1982 she moved to Nashville at their invitation where she lived with the Harrell family and sang backup for Grant on her *Age to Age* album and tour.

Troccoli has had a number of brushes with fame in the general market. She has hosted the *VH1 Countdown* for that video network, as well as a national cable show, *Queens.* In 1987, she moved to Long Island and did session work with Taylor Dayne. She also performed as the opening act for Jay Leno's Las Vegas shows and has toured with such artists as Boyz II Men, Kenny Loggins, Michael Bolton, and the Beach Boys. Troccoli remains best known, however, within the contemporary Christian music world, and most of her products have been geared primarily to that market. For a time she cohosted a popular TV program called *The Mark and Kathy Show* with **Mark Lowry** on the Inspirational cable network. She has also served as a national spokesperson for Teen Life (a Roman Catholic youth organization) and for Chuck Colson's Prison Fellowship. She has been a featured performer at Women of Faith conferences, Time Out for Women Only events, and Heritage Keepers conferences. She is author of the women's devotional book *My Life Is in Your Hands* (Zondervan, 1997). She is also the founder of A Baby's Prayer Foundation, a support organization for prolife causes named, unfortunately, after what is probably her only bad song.

With her breathy alto voice, Troccoli was prone from the start to singing in a more sultry R&B style than was fashionable in the contemporary Christian market. These distinctive features were blunted, however, on her debut album, *Stubborn Love,* where Blanton and Harrell attempted to present her as "the new **Amy Grant.**" The album was released with much hype as the debut project on Word subsidiary Reunion Records, a label that Blanton and Harrell had created just for Troccoli. The ruse worked; *Stubborn Love* became the best selling debut by any female artist in the history of Christian music, besting even Grant's first project. Produced by **Brown Bannister,** the album sports songs by such high-profile composers as Grant, **Gary Chapman, Michael W. Smith, Billy Sprague,** and Bannister himself. The album opens with a

Christianized version of the Ashford and Simpson hit "You're All I Need to Get By." The same all-star songwriter approach informs *Heart and Soul,* but this time Troccoli told producer **Brown Bannister** that she wanted a meaty, soulful sound. She sings **Phil Madeira**'s "Mighty Lord" as though it were a traditional gospel song. **Chris Eaton** and **Pam Mark Hall** also join the bevy of composers mentioned above, contributing "Island of Love" and "Open my Eyes," respectively. With regard to the record, Troccoli said she wanted to make an album that (unlike her first) wouldn't "sound like Christian pop." Apparently she succeeded, for *CCM* warned their readers that "the more conservative might be uncomfortable with the sensual feel of some of the songs." Again, Troccoli had said, "I want to make a Christian album for people who don't usually listen to Christian music," and *CCM* would confirm, *"Heart and Soul* is an album that will minister to those who want a heavy sound and a light message—enough gospel to encourage or pique an interest in the Lord, but with no deep theology." Troccoli's third album, *Images,* was produced by Dann Huff (of **White Heart** and **Giant**) and Phil Naish. She cowrote many of the songs, along with **Wayne Kirkpatrick** and her producers. Musically, the album moves away from the edgy R&B that was so appealing on *Heart and Soul* to more of the teen dance-pop sound that would become associated with **Lisa Bevill,** who sings background vocals on a couple of tracks. But lyrically, *Images* is a stronger album than the previous projects, dispensing with the predictable God-talk clichés to describe realistic scenes from a fragmented life. "If Only" recalls Troccoli's adolescent grief when her father died, and "Talk It Out" describes the silent treatment partners give each other when they shut each other out. "Ready and Willing" and "Love Stays" both try to address the pain of a failed romance from a Christian perspective. *Portfolio* was a critical and commercial disappointment and contributed to the artist's disillusionment with the Christian music industry.

Troccoli took a hiatus from Christian music to pursue some of the mainstream connections mentioned above. *Pure Attraction* was heralded as a comeback and was received enthusiastically within the Christian music media as the artist's most "commercially viable and musically potent" project yet *(CCM).* In publicity for the project, Troccoli would identify it as the first album that truly represented who she was. "I look back at old pictures and old interviews," she said in 1992, "and I don't know who that person is." A principle problem, she said, was discomfort with being marketed as *either* a Christian singer *or* a secular artist: "When I was doing gospel music, I really missed singing the torch songs, but I didn't realize how much I love singing about my faith until I left gospel. I know a lot of people have trouble incorporating both, but for me it's well rounded." *Pure Attraction* evinces the secular sound that Troccoli desires

and generally allows spiritual content to be more inferred than stated outright. Musically, the album mixes ballads with powerhouse dance songs. It was produced by Ric Wake, known for his work with Mariah Carey. The first two tracks ("Everything Changes" and "Can't Get You Out of My Heart") were written by Diane Warren (the composer responsible for Cher's "If I Could Turn Back Time," Michael Bolton's "When I'm Back on My Feet Again," and other Top 40 hits). Troccoli cowrote all the other songs, except for a cover of Stevie Wonder's "You and I." A number of the songs feature ambiguous pronouns that allow them to be heard either as worship songs addressed to God or as love songs for an earthly partner. "Help Myself to You," however, is a fairly obvious paean to the Almighty ("To be at this place is an act of your grace . . . Pour your life into me / Fill me with your glory"). The song "You're Still Here" expresses the return theme with vague reference to the parable of the Prodigal Son (Luke 15:11–32), and some would think the words applied also to Troccoli's own appreciation for Christian fans who had not forgotten her: "It's dark outside / I've been away from home too long / I see a light / You've left it on while I was gone." Troccoli was quick to point out, however, that she was *not* returning to Christian music hanging her head like some sort of penitent who had been wrong to work in the secular arena. Somewhat ironically, Troccoli would only now find the general market success she had sought during her sabbatical when the single "Everything Changes" from *Pure Attraction* crossed over to mainstream radio and eventually charted at Number Fourteen on *Billboard*'s Top 40 chart. It would be Troccoli's only general market hit.

Troccoli would describe her next album, the self-titled *Kathy Troccoli,* as "the most peaceful, exciting, joyous record I've ever done." She worked with five different producers on the project, including Ric Wake and **Michael Omartian.** As with *Pure Attraction,* she viewed the album as a hybrid product straddling the artificial boundary between Christian and secular music. The album includes her remake of The Association's 1967 hit "Never My Love" (also covered by Fifth Dimension in 1971 and by Blue Swede in 1974); Troccoli sings the song in what she calls her "chesty voice" accompanied by saxophone, a treatment the tune deserves—but the effect is spoiled somewhat by little filigree overlays that diminish the torch factor. Troccoli also delivers "Takin' a Chance," written by Whitney Houston and **BeBe Winans.** The strongest faith statement is offered in the self-penned "My Life Is in Your Hands."

On *Sounds of Heaven,* Troccoli abandoned all general market pretensions and fully embraced her identity as a contemporary Christian singer. Troccoli herself would compare the project to her first *(Stubborn Love),* which she now said was her favorite of her albums. The style of *Sounds of Heaven* is Christian adult contemporary, with praise anthems replacing dance tracks and message-oriented ballads standing in for love songs. From the opening "I Will Choose Christ" on, the album offers overtly Christian, inspirational songs. "That's How Much I Love You" is sung from the perspective of Christ, expressing his unfailing love for every individual. The album's best tracks were written by **Chris Rice**: "Go Light Your Own World" encourages Christians to fulfill Jesus' call to carry light into the darkness and make a difference in the world (Matthew 5:14–16); "Hallelujahs" is an elaborately orchestrated worship song; "Missing You" expresses yearning for the parousia. From a critical perspective, the album is something of a disappointment in that it makes Troccoli just one more representative of a style already represented by dozens of other talented artists. There was room, however, in the crowded adult contemporary camp for one more singer willing to sacrifice innovation for comfortable predictability. *Sounds of Heaven* would put five Number One songs on the Christian adult contemporary chart.

Troccoli spoke appealingly at the time *Sounds of Heaven* came out of her intention to record an entire album of '40s torch songs. As of 2001, that had not happened; the transition to commercially accessible Christian adult contemporary appeared permanent. That said, *Love and Mercy* would be a vast improvement over *Sounds of Heaven*. It succeeds on the strength of several ballads sung in Troccoli's wonderful dusky voice: "I Call Him Love," "He Will Never Leave Me," "Faithful to Me," and others are adult contemporary offerings on a par with the very best of the genre (i.e., **Kim Hill**). Unfortunately, the album's two weakest tracks would receive the most attention. "Love One Another" is a grand ecumenical anthem about Christians of all denominations demonstrating a common love for Christ and for each other. A choir of vocalists (including **Carolyn Arends, Audio Adrenaline, Carman, Amy Grant, The Newsboys,** and **Michael W. Smith**) join Troccoli on the song, which was recorded as a benefit for the His Touch ministry to persons with AIDS. It's a nice idea but, musically, has a melodramatic "We Are the World" sound that has been heard too many times before. Worse is "A Baby's Prayer," a mawkish, sentimental ballad that presents the thoughts of a fetus that is supposedly able to hear its mother discussing plans for an abortion, understand her every word, and respond by praying to God for her forgiveness. Of course, this has also been done before (cf. **Phil Keaggy**'s "The Survivor," **Rocketboy**'s "Mother, May I," **Sackcloth Fashion**'s "Sibling Rivalry," or **Value Pac**'s "Final Request"). Troccoli's song is actually better than the other offerings but, as in those cases, the attempt to ascribe adult intelligence and reasoning to an unborn child sensationalizes the rhetoric surrounding the abortion debate in an irresponsible way and makes those who are opposed to abortion look silly.

Corner of Eden is free of anything resembling the just-mentioned embarrassments. Adult contemporary all the way, the album presents the diva backed by an orchestra and choir singing theologically sound songs of inspiration and praise. Troccoli wrote all of the lyrics for *Corner of Eden,* which accordingly offers some of her more personal statements. "When I Look at You" reflects on the loss of her mother to breast cancer. The theme of death and grief also informs the touching "Goodbye for Now" and a lovely new rendition of "Psalm 23." Ballads predominate, but "He Will Make a Way" diverts from that dominant style with an R&B traditional gospel sound and a musical line almost-cribbed from Bill Withers' "Lean on Me." General market rock star Steve Winwood plays guitar on the latter track. *Love Has a Name* finds Troccoli working with a variety of producers again. The album is considerably more upbeat than the previous few projects. The opening, "Parade" (on which she invites God to "rain on my parade"), is more celebrative than anything since *Pure Attraction.* "On My Way to You" features a catchy blues lick, and the salsa-flavored "God Said It" is a happy example of the Scripture-quoting Christian cheerleading genre. These songs are interspersed with more of the familiar MOR ballads that Troccoli does so well. She even includes a cover of Foreigner's "I Want to Know What Love Is." The *Together* project by Troccoli and **Sandi Patty** finds the two artists trading off vocally on Gershwin and Garland classics. This is not the promised torch song album but it does allow both singers to move out of the confines of Christian music long enough to get in touch with some important influences—and, perhaps, to move some of their fans to do the same.

Christian radio hits: "Stubborn Love" (# 2 in 1983); "I Belong to You" (# 3 in 1984); "Holy, Holy" (# 17 in 1985); "Talk It Out" (# 5 in 1986); "All the World Should Know" (# 3 in 1987) [with **Glad**]; "Love Was Never Meant to Die" (# 8 in 1992); "Help Myself to You" (# 1 for 2 weeks in 1992); "Everything Changes" (# 1 for 4 weeks in 1992); "You've Got a Way" (# 8 in 1992); "Love Has Found Me Here" (# 10 in 1992); "My Life Is in Your Hands" (# 24 in 1994); "Mission of Love" (# 2 in 1994); "I'll Be There for You" (# 2 in 1995); "Sounds of Heaven" (# 4 in 1996); "Fill My Heart" (# 11 in 1996); "Love One Another" (# 12 in 1997).

Dove Awards: 1998 Inspirational Song ("A Baby's Prayer"); 1999 Inspirational Album *(Corner of Eden).*

True 4 U

Teddy Ovletrea, voc.; Matt Parramore, voc. 1991—*We R Here* (Myrrh).

True 4 U was a vocal/rap duo that released one album in the early '90s and was never heard from again. *We R Here* was produced by **Tim Miner** and has programmed drums and an ensemble of background vocalists. Teddy Ovletrea sang and Matt Parramore rapped. The track "Mercy Me" is a soulful dance number, but unfortunately the group reaches its poetic peak with the ballad, "Hell Is Not a Place You Want to Dwell." *CCM* said, "one wishes for more substantive lyrics with production this seamless."

True Solace

Loretta Akhpan; et al. 1999—*A New Beginning* (Atlantic).

True Solace is noteworthy primarily for scoring a rare contemporary gospel release on a general market label. The group is an all-female quintet assembled by producer and music industry veteran Errol Henry. The five were all members of the same church choir in the London area when Henry met them through Loretta Akhpan, who had intended to record a solo album. Henry fashioned the combo to be a Christian version of Destiny's Child, but *CCM* said the debut album, *A New Beginning,* comes off as more churchy than streetwise.

True Vibe

Jason Barton, voc.; Nathan Gaddis, voc.; Jonathan Lippmann, voc.; Jordan Roe, voc. 2001—*True Vibe* (Essential).

True Vibe came on the scene a bit late as one more "boy band" with a sound like that of Backstreet Boys, *NSYNC and 98 degrees. Their songs, for the most part, all sound alike, and most of them sound like that one polished, formulaic tune that the just-mentioned groups sent to the top of the charts repeatedly in slightly different forms in 1999 and 2000. *CCM* completely missed the point, however, in criticizing the band for its shallow "spiritually lite lyrics" that espouse little more than "simple positivity." The group's target audience is preteens for whom theological depth is not a realistic or appropriate option. Thus, the opening song "Jump, Jump, Jump" offers a chorus that begs for hand motions to be added when summer camp counselors perform it as a sing-along for fourth-graders: "Can you feel the joy / Don't it make you want to jump, jump, jump / Don't it make you want to move, move, move / Throw your hands to the roof, roof, roof." A piano ballad called "Sweet Jesus" changes the mood temporarily with a more traditional adult contemporary gospel song. The album closes with a Boyz II Men-style a capella song called "I Live for You."

Christian radio hits: "Now and Forever" (# 1 for 3 weeks in 2001); "Jump, Jump, Jump" (# 4 in 2001).

Truth

Personnel list unavailable (see below). 1972—*Truth* (Impact); *Get All Excited*; 1973—*We Want to Love, We Want to Shine*; *Because He Lives*; *There's Something in the Air*; 1974—*You Don't Know What You're Missing*; *That's Worth Everything*; 1975—*Would You Believe?*; 1976—*Songs That Answer Questions*; 1977—*On the Road*; *The Best of Truth*; *Not Just a Coincidence* (Paragon); 1978—*Departure*; *Now This Is Christmas*; 1979—*The Bright Side* (Impact); *Nothin' But* (Paragon); 1980—*Get It from the Source*; *Standing Room Only*; 1981—*Changin' Directions* (Mighty Miracle); 1982—*Miracles*;

Keeper of My Heart (Paragon); 1983—*Celebrate the Glory*; 1984—*Second to None*; *Aerobic Truth*; 1985—*Wind of the Spirit* (Benson); 1986—*Still the Truth*; 1987—*Makin' It Matter*; 1988—*Now and Forever* (Benson); 1989—*The Mission*; *Your Heart Is Where Christmas Is Found*; 1990—*Keep Believing*; *Live!*; 1991—*More Than You'll Ever Imagine*; *How Great Our Joy*; 1992—*A Decade of Truth: So Far, So Good*; *Truth Praise*; 1993—*Something to Hold On*; 1994—*Equation of Love* (Integrity); *You Are Emmanuel*; 1995—*Truth Sings the Word*; *One*; 1997—*25th Anniversary*; 1999—*Never Be the Same* (Pamplin); *Not a Silent Night*; 2000—*It's All about Grace*.

www.truthmusic.org

Truth was an MOR vocal chorale that performed church choir renditions of contemporary Christian music songs with a bit more exotic instrumentation and considerably more polish than the average congregation's ensemble would be able to muster. The group was founded in 1971 by Roger Breland who, at that time, was music minister and director of a choir called the Spring Hill Singers at a church in Mobile, Alabama. The group had a constantly changing membership with singers typically putting in two-year stints; the total size of the choir has ranged from six to eight vocalists in addition to a variety of instrumentalists. Their biggest Christian radio hit was the 1983 song "Jesus Never Fails," which went to Number One on the Christian adult contemporary charts. "Sing unto Him" from *Second to None* was written by **Michael W. Smith,** who played synthesizers on that album.

With a sound that fell somewhere between The Continental Singers and **The Imperials,** Truth took their share of abuse from critics. Their music and presentation was regularly regarded as cheesy in comparison to contemporary rock. Still, the criticisms were generally unfair, based on an assumption that the group should be something (a pop group) other than what it was (a church choir). Thus, *CCM*'s dismissal of *Wind of the Spirit* as "faceless corporate pop" completely misses the point—the music may be faceless, but it isn't pop, much less corporate pop. Of course, the group sometimes brought such reproach upon itself through misguided efforts at making itself relevant to the "now generation": '80s synthesizers on *One* that only served to prove the group was about ten years behind (*Shout* sent this memo: "few people liked such music *then* and it's even worse leftover cold in the '90s"); a silly attempt at rap on *Keep Believing*.

Truth's contributions to contemporary Christian music have been threefold: First, the group was (and remains) a paradigm for literally thousands of other acts around the country. Many Christian congregations and most church colleges sponsor contemporary praise groups with a similar style. Truth brings to the task a high degree of professionalism that others emulate. As *The Phantom Tollbooth* (no friend to MOR music) put it, "After nearly 30 years in existence, Truth is still the model for the inspirational mixed chorale. . . . the stability and consistency of 'the Truth sound' is aspired to by college choirs and mixed ensembles around the country—though none can execute it as well as Truth does."

Second, the group succeeded in bridging a gap between what might be called inspirational music and adult contemporary. Though rock fans may have trouble hearing any distinction between the two (just as MOR fans have trouble distinguishing the various subgenres of metal), the differences are real. Truth is an intermediate step between traditional church music and the music of groups like **Avalon, 4 Him,** and **Point of Grace.** In their early years, Truth introduced many congregations and church musicians to songs by such composers as **Ralph Carmichael, Andraé Crouch,** and **Bill and Gloria Gaither,** helping to legitimize the music of these artists for the church at large. They have continued to do this throughout the years with regard to a wide stable of contemporary songwriters.

Finally, and perhaps most important, Truth has served as a wellspring of talent and as something of a training academy that groomed numerous artists for service within the church and enabled quite a few stars to get their start in contemporary Christian music. The most notable include **Steve Green** (1976–1978), both **Dick and Melodie Tunney** (1978–1980), all four members of **4 Him** (1986–1990); Russ Lee of **NewSong** (1990–1993), two members of **Avalon** (Jody McBrayer and Joanna Potter), **Natalie Grant,** and **Peter Penrose.** Other Truth alumni include Linda Dove, who released a solo EP (*Linda Dove,* Greentree, 1984) and album (*If We Have Love,* Benson, 1986); and John Thom, bassist for **White Heart.** Truth alum Alicia Williamson also later made a mark with two albums of R&B adult contemporary music similar in style to **Larnelle Harris** (*The Rescue,* Integrity, 1996; *Faithful Heart,* Discovery, 1999). Karen Childres and Leigh Cappillino (both in Truth from 1991 to 1994) recorded a self-titled album as KarenLeigh (*Integrity,* 1995). In the thirty years of the group's ministry, over four hundred persons were members of Truth, and according to Breland, one hundred of those would be serving as pastors or in other full-time church positions in the year 2001.

Sometime around 1995, Roger Breland passed the effective leadership of Truth to his sons Jason and Justin Breland. The group moved toward a more contemporary sound, but as *CCM* would put it, the changes were "more of a tune-up than an overhaul." In 2000, Roger Breland and Truth were inducted into the Gospel Music Hall of Fame. In June of 2001, the group embarked on what was announced as a "farewell tour," and called an end to the thirty-year program. Roger Breland told *The CCM Update,* "In the early '70s, to take a group with drums and a guitar into the church was unheard of. The response from young people was great, and I just wanted to use our music as a tool to share the gospel." He contrasted this scenario with the current situation. "The whole music scene has moved to arenas, so we see the trends turning and it's a new generation. It's tough to find people these days who have a missionary spirit and who are willing to make as little money as we do, because there are teenagers signing record contracts for a million dollars."

Christian radio hits: "Jesus Never Fails" (# 9 in 1983); "Sing unto Him" (# 14 in 1984); "Gentle Hands" (# 28 in 1984).

Trytan

Larry Dean, gtr., voc.; Steve Robinson, bass, kybrd.; Scott Blackman, drums (−1990) // Jim Dobbs, drums (+ 1990). 1987—*Celestial Messenger* (R.E.X.); 1990—*Sylentiger.*

Trytan was a Chicago-based trio that played pop hook-infested progressive music with a strong metal edge. They were generally regarded by critics as a "Christian version of Rush." The group first released its classic album, *Celestial Messenger,* in a slightly different form as a demo on North Star records in 1987. The eight-song R.E.X. version would come to be revered as a masterpiece by Christian metal fans. Three years later, *Sylentiger* lacked the surprise (or novelty) of the debut, but featured an even harder sound and generally more solid songs. The group disbanded in 1991, and leader Larry Dean became pastor of a church called Heart Maneuvers Christian Fellowship, affiliated with the Warehouse Church denomination. Demand for the albums remained high and a company would release both of the records illegally on compact disc in 1998. Partly in response to this, the band reissued *Celestial Messenger* on M8 with an extra twenty minutes of music, including songs from the original demo version and from an early (1982–1983) demo EP.

The original *Celestial Messenger* album features songs that call on persons to follow Christ. "Rip Van Winkle" uses the character in the famous Washington Irving story to issue this summons: "Wake up, wipe the sleep from your eyes / Stand up, come and follow me!" Likewise, "Don't Turn Away" and "Nowhere to Run" present life in Christ as the only viable alternative. "Beyond the Night" relates a melodrama in which two persons in a suicide pact discuss whether they should carry out their plan; one wants to back out because he has heard of the life Christ offers. Arminian theology informs *Sylentiger* with songs like "Make Your Move" and "Take Cover" presenting the offer of salvation with a strong emphasis on the need for human decision. The most interesting track is a cover of **Leslie Phillips**'s "By My Spirit."

A decade after Trytan disbanded, Dean told *HM* the highlight of being in the band was "just being able to bring glory to the Lord and lift up Jesus in what we thought was an effective way, using the music as a tool . . . and to see lives changed as people encountered the truth of his cross and his loving word and came out of drugs, suicidal tendencies, and all kinds of garbage we find ourselves in apart from the Lord."

Tuesday's Child

Linda Elias, voc.; Lesley Glassford, voc. 1995—*Tuesday's Child* (Benson); 1997—*The More Things Change.*

Tuesday's Child is a female duo composed of **Linda Elias** and **Lesley Glassford,** both of whom had previously released solo albums. The two did not know each other before Bill Baumgart, A&R director for Benson, brought them together. Baumgart and **Rick Elias** (Linda's husband) produced the debut album, which reveals a sound comparable to that of Wilson Phillips. Musically, the songs are rather syrupy, but filled with catchy hooks. Glassford and Elias trade off on solo vocals and harmonize at climactic points. The piano ballad "Pilgrims" (written by **Rick Elias** and Regie Hamm) portrays the Christian life as a journey, while "Standing by the Cross" offers an anthem to steadfast faith. "Count on Me" is a song of female friendship with a sound reminiscent of Sheryl Crow. *The More Things Change* (produced by Rick) continues in the same vein. Its strongest track, "I'm Alive," has a Go-Go's rock edge. "A Scarlet Thread of Faith" is an adult contemporary ballad about a prodigal runaway with AIDS. The duo's primary audience is adult women, and they have committed themselves to performing songs that address issues of concern to women. "This is where our ministry is," says Linda Elias. "So many women today have to go back to work right after giving birth. They have to face the challenge of all these different things in their lives—it's hard for all of us, and sometimes it helps when you can share that."

Michelle Tumes

1998—*Listen* (Sparrow); 2000—*Center of My Universe;* 2001—*Dreams.*
www.mtumes.com

Michelle Tumes is a classically trained artist from Adelaide, Australia, who creates adult contemporary pop music featuring ethereal vocals sustained by piano-dominated instrumentation. Tumes' songs display haunting melodies, lush harmonies, and intricate orchestration. She has been compared to such artists as Sarah MacLachlan, Tori Amos, and especially Enya, though her music also shows a strong influence of Sting. Tumes grew up within the church in her native land, where she began playing piano at the age of four. She moved to Nashville when she was twenty-two and composed songs for a number of contemporary Christian artists, including **Jaci Velasquez, Point of Grace,** and **Rachel Lampa.**

Tumes' debut, *Listen,* was produced by **Charlie Peacock.** The opening title track sets the mood with its otherworldly sound and imagery of fields and waves. *CCM* would identify her sound as "bordering on the so-called New Age musical category," and *Release* would say that she "calls to mind far off places and long ago times." Other reviewers would use adjectives like "soothing," "delicate," and "fragile." The lyrics to most of the songs are openly devout and worshipful, almost like those of **Twila Paris.** "Heaven Will Be Near Me" is a melodic, loping song that captures well the blend of poetic imagery and sonic intimacy. "Please Come Back" offers a heartfelt plea to a prodigal. On "Christ of Hope" Tumes sounds uncannily like **Amy Grant.** Tumes coproduced her second project, *Center of My Universe,* with David Leonhardt, who has worked with Barenaked Ladies and **Indigo Girls.** The album continues in the same mystical, quiet strains as the debut with a few exceptions. The opening track, "Deep Love," is a more upbeat, exciting praise song, and "Do Ya" is set to a catchy pop-rock tune. A different mood affects "Chant," inspired by Orthodox liturgy, and "Christe Eleison," which takes its cue from the Latin Mass. The second album's title, surprisingly, does not describe God as the center of the artist's universe. Rather, it derives from her song "Lovely," which is sung to humanity from God's point of view: "Oh, you're lovely, lovely / You're the center of my universe." Tumes also contributed a rendition of the Anglican hymn "My Song Is Love Unknown" to a compilation of songs by female Christian artists (*Listen to Our Hearts,* Sparrow, 1998). *Dreams* represents a radical departure from these mature sounds in favor of teen pop fluff. *CCM* reports, "the title cut kicks off with sounds worthier of Britney Spears or Christina Aguilera." A bit more substance can be found on "One and Only," but most of the songs go for light and generic themes set to catchy melodies.

Christian radio hits: "Hold On" (# 13 in 1999); "Heaven's Heart" (# 15 in 2000); "Dream" (# 17 in 2001).

Dick and Melodie Tunney (and Dick Tunney)

By Dick Tunney: 1990—*Come before Him* (label unknown); 1991—*Twila Paris Piano Classics* (StarSong). By Dick and Melodie Tunney: 1991—*Let the Dreamers Dream* (Warner Bros.); 1993—*Left to Write* (Warner Alliance); 1996—*No Dejes de Sonar;* 1998—*Legacy.*

Dick and Melodie Tunney have a long history of connections in contemporary Christian music that involve both performing and songwriting. Dick Tunney (b. 1956) was raised in Dayton, Ohio, and graduated from Cumberland College with awards for outstanding musical merit in 1978. Melodie Tunnie (née Ware, b. 1960) grew up in the Dallas/Ft. Worth area. The two met when they both became members of the vocal chorale **Truth** (1978–1980), though according to Dick they didn't like each other for the first year and a half. That changed, and when Dick received an offer to play keyboards for **The Imperials,** he proposed and the two left Truth as a couple. After a stint with **The Imperials**, Dick Tunney went on to play for **Sandi Patty** and then became her musical director (1986–1989). In 1988 and 1989 he also served as musical director for the Dove Awards TV broadcast. In 1989, he was elected to the Gospel Music Association's Board of Directors. The couple ended up in Nashville, where Melodie became a founding member of the group **First Call.** She would continue with that group until 1989, when the couple decided to record some of the material that they had been writing for other performers. Dick Tunney also recorded two albums of solo piano music. Musically, the Tunneys' albums occupy the inspirational (nonrock to light pop) side of the adult contemporary continuum. The songs are variously worship or message oriented, always with spiritually uplifting and encouraging themes. "I'm Praying for You" (from *Let the Dreamers Dream*) was inspired by a ladies' prayer group at the Tunneys' church where, Melodie says, "when we prayed for each other, in some way, God answered our prayers."

As songwriters, Dick and Melodie Tunney have composed hits for **Sandi Patty** ("O Magnify the Lord," "Let There Be Praise") and have had their songs recorded by many other artists, including **Connie Scott, Steve Green,** and **First Call.** Their song "How Excellent Is Thy Name" (recorded by **Larnelle Harris**) won the Dove award for Song of the Year in 1987. The duo has appeared on *The Tonight Show* and on *Live with Regis and Kathie Lee.*

Christian radio hits: "I'm Praying for You" (# 17 in 1992).

Dove Awards: For Dick and Melodie Tunney: 1987 Songwriter of the Year. For Dick Tunney: 1991—Instrumental Album *(Come before Him).*

Twenty Twenty

Ernie Chaney, kybrd.; Ron Collins, voc.; Greg Herrington, drums; Gary McAnelly, bass; Roscoe Meek, gtr. 1985—*Twenty Twenty* (Benson); 1987—*Altered.*

Twenty Twenty was a synthesizer-led stadium rock band from Louisiana that seemed to emulate such art-rockers as Styx and **Kansas.** The group's debut album was produced by Billy Smiley of **White Heart.** The song "You Are So True" is a martial anthem with its repetitive chorus addressed to Jesus: "You are so true / I said that, You are so true / I know that, You are so true." Another track, "You Can Know Them All," is commercially melodic and invites the listener to get to know the entire Trinity: "Three-in-one are living today / And you can know them all." Twenty Twenty's lead singer, Ron Collins, told *CCM* in 1985 that the group's focus was on ministry to churched youth: "Often at our concerts, we try to reach the young person who goes to church but isn't really there. They only go because they were brought up in the church or their parents made them go."

20/20 Blind

Schon Alkire, bass; Wallace Chase, voc.; Chris Laurents, drums; Mike McNeely, gtr.; Doug Middleton, gtr. 1994—*Never Far* (Intersound).

The Christian group called 20/20 Blind (not to be confused with **Twenty Twenty**) was a hard rock band from Houston. The group played together for some three-and-a-half years before signing with Intersound. Around the same time as their album's release, three members (Alkire, Laurents, and McNeely) were involved in a serious traffic accident, sustaining long-term injuries when their van was hit by a drunk driver. The group told the story of the accident and of their recovery in *HM,* including the opportunity they had to offer forgiveness to the man responsible for the accident when they met him in court. Musically, 20/20 Blind had a sound influenced by groups like **King's X** and Queensryche, with an emphasis on melody and competent musicianship. "Do I?" is a heavy pop song that deals with the issue of sexual temptation. "Only Hope" exemplifies the band's straightforward evangelical approach to lyrics: "When the storm is all around / And you think you're going to drown / You know your only hope is in Jesus."

Two Hearts

Carrie McDowell Hodge, voc.; Michael Hodge, gtr. 1992—*Stand Your Ground* (StarSong); 1993—*Give 'Em the Word.*

Two Hearts is a husband and wife duo with a strong R&B pop sound. Singer Carrie Hodge, born Carrie McDowell in 1965 in Des Moines, Iowa, had an early career as a child star. At the age of nine, she began opening shows for Liberace and appeared on such TV programs as *The Tonight Show with Johnny Carson* and *Rowan and Martin's Laugh-In,* as well as on specials hosted by George Burns and Danny Thomas. As a teenager, she spent three years (1981–1984) in New York City performing in off-Broadway musicals and singing jingles. She formed a jazz fusion band in Iowa in 1984 and then, at the age of twenty-two, was signed to Motown Records and performed as an opening act for Smokey Robinson. In 1987, she recorded a song called "Uh-Uh, No No (Casual Sex)," which aired on VH-1 but failed to chart on *Billboard*'s Hot 100 (the song might have been intended for the 1988 motion picture "Casual Sex?" starring Victoria Jackson—who is also public about her Christian faith—but another song called "No More Casual Sex" by Kid Creole and the Coconuts was used in the film instead). At any rate, McDowell also met Michael Hodge in 1987 and the two married a year later. Michael had grown up in California and, after a stint touring as guitarist for Chaka Khan, became involved in the Christian music industry. He played for **Kim Boyce** and **Margaret Becker** and served as music director for both Boyce and **Benny Hester.** The Hodges met at a church where Michael led a Bible study group, introduced by a mutual friend at a prayer meeting.

The musical focus of Two Hearts is clearly on Carrie's voice, with Michael serving as arranger, guitarist, and principal composer. The vocal delivery is a tad more sassy than traditional for contemporary Christian music, drawing comparisons to singers like **Maria McKee** (in her less country moments). *Stand Your Ground* features the urban rocker "Promise Me Tonight" and a sparkling pop song called "Celebrate New Life." As these titles indicate, the group favors songs of joyful encouragement. "Miracles" is an acoustic ballad describing the ways that the couple experienced God's healing in their marriage. *Give 'Em the Word* led the group to a corporate sponsorship program with Tyndale House Publishers, according to which the duo promoted that company's Life Application Bible on their accompanying tour. The title song for the album encourages regular Bible reading. The highlight of the sophomore project is "Because of You," a Motownesque song with lyrics by Carrie about seeing God's hand in the intricacies of nature.

Christian radio hits: "Holy Fire" (# 2 in 1992); "Hold on Me" (# 1 in 1992); "Celebrate New Life" (# 7 in 1993); "Because of You" (# 6 in 1994); "I Will Be Faithful" (# 9 in 1994); "Give 'Em the Word" (# 9 in 1994).

Two or More

Eddie Aguas; Renatto Aguas; Walter Aguas; Lance Mowdy (– 1998). 1996—*Life in the Diamond Lane* (StarSong); 1998—*Walking on the Water* (Pamplin).

Two or More is an R&B-oriented vocal combo founded by three brothers from Orange County, California. The group first formed in 1987 as a general market act (presumably under a different name) with friend Lance Mowdy as part of the act. Mowdy, however, experienced a spiritual renaissance shortly thereafter and left the band to pursue a church vocation. He continued to witness to his friends in the band, and eventually, Renatto Aguas committed his life to Christ and also left the band. Then, in what the group would later call a "domino effect," the transformation in Renatto's life ultimately led brothers Eddie and Walter to similar decisions. In 1995, the brothers decided to reform their band as a Christian group; Mowdy joined them for the first effort, an album called *Life in the Diamond Lane.* It was produced by **John** and Dino **Elefante,** who cowrote most of the songs. It opens with a bubblegum anthem called "He's There" that features an unforgettable "na-na-na-na" chorus (à la Journey). The Elefantes' trademark stuck-in-the-'80s sound infuses most of the record ("Heaven Is Calling Your Name" recalls Survivor or Night Ranger). The band's own (more authentic) R&B sound comes through more clearly on "If I Could," an offering of thankfulness for all God has done.

The second album, *Walking on the Water,* is another Elefante project, but this time **Billy Batstone** contributes five songs, which are probably the album's best. The title track is a retelling of Matthew 14:28–31 with metaphorical contemporary application. Unfortunately, the group also does an original song called "Forefathers" that contrasts modern culture with a good-old-days picture of a holy past. The contemporary situation is caricatured (school teachers telling children they come from monkeys) and the architects of American democracy are inaccurately portrayed as devout believers when, in fact, most (Jefferson, Franklin, Payne) were non-Christians, or only nominally so for political purposes (Washington). On a brighter side, the group covers the song "Hole Hearted" by **Extreme.**

In interviews, members of Two or More have revealed a theological orientation that defines Christianity as a "personal relationship with Jesus," which they then articulate in contrast to traditional understandings that emphasize incorporation through baptism into a communal entity that is identified as Christ's body. "We've come to find that a lot of those denominations and backgrounds have taken the place of a relationship with Jesus Christ," Eddie Aguas says. "It's important to be plugged into a church," adds Walter, "but it's just as important to realize that you're not going to be saved by your church or denomination. The key is to have a relationship with God."

Christian radio hits: "He's There" (# 5 in 1996); "Heaven Is Calling Your Name" (# 12 in 1996); "What Would You Say?" (# 13 in 1997).

TwoThirtyEight

Jake Brown, bass; Chris Staples, voc.; D. J. Stone, drums (–2000); Kevin Woerner, gtr. // Jason Frasier, drums (+ 2000). 1998—*Missing You Dearly* (Takehold); 1999—*Regulate the Chemicals;* 2000—*Matter Has a Breaking Point.*

www.twothirtyeight.com

TwoThirtyEight is a Christian modern rock band from Florida with a sound that has been compared variously to **PlankEye** and **Sunny Day Real Estate.** The group started out as an emo band but moved progressively to develop more of a mature pop sound. The band takes its name from Acts 2:38, which they say summarizes their understanding of ministry. Front man Chris Staples says, "Our purpose as a band is to portray God's love and mercy as real and honest as we can, and tell everyone we can about Jesus Christ's saving power." The original lineup for TwoThirtyEight included Kevin Glass on bass. When Glass was killed in a 1997 automobile accident, Jake Brown took over playing bass, though he did not officially join the band until two years later. The group has been sidetracked by lesser tragedies as well. Shortly after releasing their debut album, Staples broke his leg in a skateboarding accident, necessitating a six-month hiatus from touring.

Missing You Dearly is dedicated to Glass, to whom the title track is addressed. Staples has said that it was the sadness involving his death that gave the record its somber (emo) quality. *Regulate the Chemicals* moves to a more upbeat style, reminiscent at times of Weezer or The Cure. "Hands of Men" picks up on the titular theme with a noninclusive language protest against behavioral medicine. Staples resents the fact that he was given Ritalin as a child to control his behavior and says that he thinks "people overuse prescription drugs in ways that cover up their personalities." The song "This Town Will Eat You" is about the band's hometown, Niceville, Florida. The group really comes into its own on the brief (eight song) *Matter Has a Breaking Point.* In the title track, Staples offers some poetic lyrics: "Box cars with cheap brakes make for accidents / Improper maintenance has its consequences / A fuse blows, a cord snaps / Matter has a breaking point / Flesh, like these, is a weak beam / Likely to break under the slightest weight of temptation." Again on "Suitcases for Always" he muses that "The world is bitter at both ends / And nothing makes you become it / Quite like running from it." The standout track is also the most overtly Christian: "You Made a Way for Moses" is a gentle prayer to Jesus set against piano and simple orchestration.

Twotimer

Jason Anderson, drums; James Taylor, gtr.; Jeremy Welch, gtr.; Steven Welch, voc., bass. 2000—*See What Happens from Here* (Screaming Giant).

Twotimer is yet another new-school punk band, this time from Colorado. Their sound is of a piece with that of Green Day and Blink 182 (or, in Christian music, **Craig's Brother, MxPx, Slick Shoes,** and **The Undecided**). The group's competence was quickly recognized when their debut album appeared in 2000, with *Bandoppler* summing up what appeared to be a unanimous critical opinion with the description, "a high quality offering of the same old thing." *Phantom Tollbooth* also noted that, as is usually the case with all of the above bands, "the biggest enemy is monotony," as most of the songs sound alike. The band is oriented toward ministry, and describes its songs as conveying "God's disapproval of sin, his mercy that we are given freely every day, and how he longs for us to be more like him." Their name is an oblique reference to being born again (i.e., born twice).

Iva Twydell

See **After the Fire.**

Becky Ugartechea

1976—*House between Two Rivers* (Maranatha); 1979—*Songs of Faith* (Light).

Becky Ugartechea (née Rife) was a smoky-voiced pioneer of Jesus music associated with Calvary Chapel in Costa Mesa, California. Her last name (pronounced u-gar-te-shay-a) means "house between two rivers," providing a title for her first album. Long before it was released, however, Ugartechea would record her best-known song, "God Don't Care Who You Are," for inclusion on the important *Maranatha Three* compilation disc (Maranatha, 1973). Although *Maranatha Three* was not as well received as the two hugely significant collections that it followed, Ugartechea's song was generally recognized as the highlight of the package. Almost thirty years later, producer **Erick Nelson** regarded the overall project with some dissatisfaction while noting, "Funny thing is, Becky Ugartechea was just great and even bad production couldn't wreck her song." That song states a rather straightforward gospel message that was a source of much inspiration to Jesus freaks: "God don't care who you are / He can change your life / God don't care what you were / He just wants to love you." Ugartechea performs it as a rhythmic folk song, with an ultimately wailing vocal set against strummed guitar and off-beat percussion.

Fans of that single song would have to wait three years to get more. By the time *House between Two Rivers* appeared, the simple Jesus music scene had burgeoned into a developing contemporary Christian music industry, and the project was almost overlooked amidst a flurry of similar releases by female vocalists like **Honeytree** and **Janny.** Years later, historian David Di Sabatino would describe the album as "stylistically reminiscent of Olivia Newton-John," but that does not do justice to Ugartechea's darker voice. *Jesus Music* describes the sultry "Take All the Lonely Times" as a song that "makes you swear you were sitting in a dark, smoky nightclub." *House between Two Rivers* opens with a rock track, "Who's the Master?" featuring **Matthew Ward** on background vocals. The other members of **2nd Chapter of Acts** put in appearances also, along with **Paul Clark, Jamie Owens, Terry Talbot,** and many of the Maranatha artists. The album was produced by **Al Perkins,** who also plays pedal steel and gives many of the songs a distinctive country flavor. A song called "Nightingale" was featured on the almost unnoticed *Maranatha Six* compilation (Maranatha, 1977). Another three years passed before Ugartechea's second album, *Songs of Faith.* Given the short memory of the Christian market, the project (also produced by Perkins) was treated as a debut from a new artist who was officially called simply "Becky." Mostly MOR, it slides definitively into adult contemporary; a few tracks with country leanings seem to preview the later work of **Susan Ashton.**

Ultimatum

Robert Gutierrez, gtr.; Steve Trujillo, gtr.; Scott Waters, voc., Mike Lynch, drums (– 1998) // Tom Michaels, bass (+ 1995); Sean Griego, drums (+ 1998). 1994—*Fatal Display* [EP] (custom); 1995—*Symphonic*

Extremities; 1998—*Puppet of Destruction* (Rowe); 2001—*The Mechanics of Perilous Time.*

www.ultimatum.net

Ultimatum is an unabashed Christian metal band with a sound in the same ballpark as '80s groups Iron Maiden or Megadeath. At a time when many former metal groups were developing into grunge or hard alternative acts and when many Christian composers were changing their focus to write songs about life in general, Ultimatum bucked the trends and played metal music that testifies to Christ without subtlety. Lead singer Scott Waters told *HM,* "We love metal, so we play metal, and we love Jesus, so we sing about him." The group was founded by guitarist Robert Gutierrez in 1992. Their first full-length album, *Symphonic Extremities,* was originally a custom project, but it was re-released in 1997 by Juke Box Media with a bonus track ("World of Sin") that became its best-known song. True to their name, Ultimatum has stressed the consequences of moral decisions in all of their material. *Symphonic Extremities* has songs dealing with suicide, abortion, and participation in non-Christian religious cults. *Puppet of Destruction* includes "Never," about selling out one's integrity in order to be fashionable, "Gutterbox," about the degradation of modern TV, and "Repentance," describing the depravity of society as a whole. *The Mechanics of Perilous Time* includes a metal praise song called "The Purging" and a cover of the song "Burn" by **Vengeance Rising.**

Ultrabeat

Erik Augustsson, voc., prog., kybrd. 2000—*Trip to a Planet Called Heaven* (BEC); 2001—*Beyond the Stars.*

Hailing from Sweden, the one-man band called Ultrabeat offers techno praise and worship music programmed by Erik Augustsson, who leads Bible studies at Joshua Christian Church, where his father is pastor. *The Phantom Tollbooth* dissed the debut album *(Trip to a Planet Called Heaven)* as combining the worst elements of two shallow genres: the monotony of techno with the simplistic lyrics of praise and worship. But more generous reviewers would recognize the work's undeniable appeal for Eurodisco dance aficionados. Futuristic synths swirl around most of the tracks while Augustsson sings lyrics like, "The love of God is in this place / We can dance before him because of his grace." There are a couple of instrumentals, and the *X-Files*-inspired song "The Truth Is Out There" consists mainly of that phrase being shouted periodically over a phat beat. A catchy song called "Pure Heart" appears to be an unacknowledged cover of the praise song "Create a Clean Heart" with new lyrics and a slightly different melody. "I Wanna Live 4 Him" is an atypical adult contemporary piano ballad. *Beyond the Stars* is split in two parts, with nine songs with lyrics being

followed by six instrumentals. "Jesusrave" is exactly what it sounds like—a rave dance track with words extolling the Lord: "Jesus Christ is living and alive / Gave his life so you can survive."

Unashamed

Jeff Jacquay, voc.; Danno McManigal, gtr.; Bobby, gtr. (– 1995); Chris, drums (– 1995); Shane, bass (– 1995) // Jason Carson, drums (+ 1995); Mike Hernandez, bass (+ 1995). 1994—*Silence* (Tooth and Nail); 1995—*Reflection.*

Unashamed is a hardcore punk band from Orange County, California, notable for the praise and worship focus of their lyrics. The group has been compared to the seminal Christian punk act **The Crucified** in sound, but whereas the '90s trend in Christian punk was to express anger at a godless world and at the pain of temporal life, Unashamed's chief singer and songwriter, Jeff Jacquay, takes his cue from the book of Psalms and mixes laments with doxologies. Aside from one song about divorce and the anguish of coming from a broken home, Jacquay says, "Most everything I sing is praise to God. Many of the words even come out of the Psalms. . . . The Psalmist always says the words I want to say, but never can." Thus, "Blessed Redeemer," from *Silence,* has words like those of a church hymn, despite the fact that Jacquay growls it to a soundtrack that could have provided the grist for a Judas Priest song. "Sustained" quotes from Psalm 23 in a slow breakdown section. *Reflection* is even harder and faster as a whole, though again, *HM* would note that the opening track, "Meet Us Here," has lyrics one would expect to find on a Hosanna or Vineyard tape. Unashamed's rhythm section for the second album consists of two members of **The Supertones** (Jason Carter and Mike Hernandez).

The Undecided

Steven Dueck, drums; Matthew Fast, voc.; John-Paul Peters, gtr., voc.; Dan Thomas, bass, voc. 2000—*The Undecided* (Tooth and Nail); 2001—*More to See.*

www.theundecided.net

The Undecided arrived on the scene a bit late as one more pop-punk band in the Tooth and Nail stable. With a sound similar to **Craig's Brother, Ghoti Hook, MxPx, Slick Shoes, Twotimer, Value Pac,** and many others, the band would rise above the fray on the strength of its theologically sound and socially conscious lyrics. The group is based in Steinbeck, Manitoba, and represents Tooth and Nail's first Canadian signing. The group formed in 1994 with some personnel differences, and, according to drummer Steve Dueck, "at that time we were out to party, not spread the Word." Guitarist John-Paul Peters suffered a drug overdose in 1997 that caused him to rethink his life and enter a Bible school in Austin, Texas.

The Undecided were initially dismissed by critics: *Phantom Tollbooth* was less harsh than *Bandoppler* in saying, "The Undecided have joined the mass of punk bands that are tight, competent, professional, and totally unnecessary." True punk aficionados, however, do not think that all those bands sound alike and they would recognize Undecided as having a faster, somewhat sugary style reminiscent of NOFX and especially Ten Foot Pole. Then people began to notice the songs themselves. The debut album packs eighteen numbers into thirty-three minutes—most of these deal with the typical subjects of girls, politics, and relationships, but a distinctive Christian perspective is observable in the treatment of such concerns. "I'm Not Strong Enough" and "Forgotten" offer acknowledgment of personal sin and weakness. "Unconditional" is a powerful statement of forgiveness, deriving from what the band says is a true-life story of a person they know who forgives a parent for a long history of wrongs. Elsewhere, front man Matthew Fast sings, "Through everything, remember what's important in your life / You're saved by grace / Never let anything take his place." A year later, the band issued the vastly improved *More to See* on which they develop a tighter sound that often leans in the direction of Cheap Trick. Now more than ever, the quality of their lyrics would get them noticed. "Time for Change" summons Christians to eschew mediocrity and embrace the lifestyle to which they are called. "What Happened to Our Love?" similarly challenges self-righteous and judgmental attitudes. The standout song "Cries for Jubilee" gives expression to a liberation theology rare in contemporary Christian music, decrying "capitalism in the name of Christianity" and voicing the Third World's rejection of "an American Jesus" who does not challenge his followers' proliferation of social injustice. "Lifted" offers encouragement for those struggling with faith, and a little ditty called "Counter Culture" rocks out with a punk vibe sure to please any fan of the genre.

Undercover

Gym Nicholson, gtr., voc.; Joey (Ojo) Taylor, kybrd., bass, voc.; Ric Alba, bass, voc. (−1983); Bill Walden, voc., sax. (−1986) // Gary Olson, drums, voc. (+ 1983, − 1994); Sim Wilson, voc. (+ 1986, − 1994); Chuck Cummings, drums (+ 1994); Rob Gallas, voc. (+ 1994); David Raven, drums (+ 1994). 1982—*Undercover* (Maranatha); 1983—*God Rules*; 1984—*Boys and Girls Renounce the World*; 1986—*Branded* (Blue Collar); 1988—*3-28-87* (Broken); 1990—*Balance of Power*; 1992—*Devotion* (Brainstorm); 1994—*Forum*; 1996—*Undercover Anthology 1* (Innocent Media); 1997—*Undercover Anthology 2*; 2000—*Live at Cornerstone 2000* (M8).

Undercover came out of the Southern California Jesus music scene and, like **Daniel Amos** a decade before them, transcended the confines and expectations of that market to become one of the strongest forces in Christian alternative music. They began with little promise as just one more bouncy band of evangelical teenagers singing simplistic songs about God, but developed into an artistic group willing to forego industry expectations for the sake of intensity and honesty. A common theme runs through all critical assessments of their work: growth. *True Tunes* said in 1992, "Undercover has grown with its audience both musically and spiritually," which seems to explain the intense loyalty of many fans who continue to prize *all* of the band's works. *CCM* once dubbed Undercover, "the band that grew up in public." The heart of the band seems to have been Joey (Ojo) Taylor (who served as chief songwriter) and guitarist Gym Nicholson. Taylor recorded one solo album as **Ojo**. Ric Alba played only on the first Undercover album, then joined **The Altar Boys** and also recorded a solo album. Bill Walden sang lead on the first three Undercover albums and then went on to form a band called The Fourth Watch, which released an album titled *Dare to Be the One*. In 1987 he joined The Mirrors (formerly known as **Malcolm and the Mirrors**).

Undercover got its start as a second-generation Jesus movement band operating out of Calvary Chapel in Costa Mesa, California, at a time when many Christian music fans were surprised to discover that entity still existed. In the early '70s, Calvary Chapel had been ground zero for the Jesus movement, and more than half of the significant artists in the field were associated with their ministries. By 1980, the church's interval of fame was over and the Maranatha music company had turned into a purveyor of inspirational praise and worship choruses. Undercover debuted on a division of Maranatha (MRC) with a collection of pogo-pop punk songs that are basically bubblegum cheers for Jesus: "You'll have to excuse us / But we're in love with Jesus" ("Excuse Us"). While there is nothing on that debut album that could be considered significant musically, critics (most of whom had roots in the early '70s Jesus movement revival) appreciated the unabashed, joyful naivete evident now in a new generation. The group continued in the same style on *God Rules* with songs like "Jesus for Me" and "Jesus Is the Best." The album may be best remembered for its new-wave version of the classic youth group song, "I Am the Resurrection" (by **Ray Repp**). Other standouts include the title track, "New Creation," and "Jesus Girl." Somewhat ironically, *CCM* spent their review of the album delineating the difference between new-wave music (which, they say, is appropriate for Christian artists) and punk (which isn't). The reviewer then defended Undercover as aficionados of the former style not the latter: "the anarchy of punk is a philosophy 180 degrees opposite of these boys." *Boys and Girls Renounce the World* shows the first promising signs of serious talent. The record moves decidedly toward straightforward punk as opposed to what Taylor now dismissed as "the frantic, pogo-bop new-wave style" of their first two projects. The title song addresses high school youth, the band's target audience. "Three Nails" is an anthemic song, summarizing Christ's passion and its effect with the chorus, "Three nails, three days, one way to God." The most remarkable song is another cover—this time a rapid-fire punk rendition of the traditional hymn "Holy, Holy, Holy." *CCM* (different reviewer) now complained that the band wasn't punk enough, that they had the punk look and the punk speed "without the slamming passion and fervor of the punk mentality." It is at least safe to say that artistic expression in and of itself was still not a priority. Taylor told *Cornerstone* that the whole purpose of Undercover was "to see kids get saved." He freely admitted that the band members adopted punk stylings (hair, dress, and music) as a ruse: "If all the kids we're trying to reach were wearing cowboy hats, then we'd be wearing cowboy hats too."

If the band's punk credentials were suspect, they would all but abandon punk and new-wave stylings on their future releases, which evince far more authenticity. *Branded* and *Balance of Power* represent what is usually called Undercover's gothic period. Lyrically, those albums show an evolution light years beyond their previous incarnation as a band of teenagers proclaiming "Loving God makes me a happy boy" and "Jesus rose from the dead / Jesus can fix your head." Taylor himself describes the projects as "dark, epic albums" in which the music was "colored by tragedy." At least part of this ominous mood came from the fact that Taylor went through a devastating divorce in 1985. *True Tunes* has said that *Branded* came "from out of nowhere, a dark, passionate plea for mercy and compassion in a bleak existence." Taylor himself has said, "I tried for ten years as a super-fundamental Christian to make everything I was taught fit into life. After meeting more and more kids and seeing my own failures and realizing that life is tough, I said, 'Hey, I can't make it fit anymore. There has to be more to Christianity than I've been taught.'" Thus, the next two studio albums would exalt the discovery of grace in the midst of disgrace and call for justice and mercy in a world of woe. Pain and broken hearts are constant themes on *Branded,* such that every other song seems to mention "tears." The album opens with the declaration, "I cried last night / I face my fears" ("I'm Just a Man"). Faith comes into the picture through the recognition of God's empathy with human suffering: "Anguish and despair surround me like a flood / And I know you once were there / Sweating tears that turned to blood" ("Darkest Hour"). Nicholson contributes one of the album's ten songs, called "Cry Myself to Sleep": "God in heaven up above / Has compassion and love / His hands wet with my tears / He's been drying them for years." The light at the end of the tunnel comes in the two final songs: "Come Away with Me" offers the Lord's invitation to the brokenhearted, and "If I Had a Dream" expresses the hope of ultimate justice at the end of the world.

After *Branded,* the group took a two-and-a-half-year hiatus, during which time it was widely believed that they had broken up for good. Indeed, the live album *3–28–87* was advertised as the group's swan song. Recorded at Six Flags Magic Mountain, it contains two new songs: Nicholson's "One to One" and Taylor's "You and I," on which he appears to evince some disillusionment with the spiritual trip he had been on ("They promised I would have my fill / And yet I find I'm thirsty still"). Taylor told *CCM* that the band's breakup was due to different musical and spiritual visions: "I was going one way and the band was going the other. They were happy just doing 'God Rules,' and I'm not there anymore. I've experienced a whole new realm of problems, and that has taken precedence over Christian cheerleading." Taylor also allowed, "I'm kind of disillusioned with most of institutional Christianity. . . . I'm not convinced we need multimillion-dollar satellite TV networks and megachurches and all this stuff to share the honest gospel of Christ's love." During what turned out to be a temporary break, Taylor became active as a producer, working on the classic *Shaded Pain* album for **LSU** and on a project for his brother, who recorded as **Pat Nobody** (a.k.a. Nobody Special). He wrote a song for the latter album called "Get Off the Air" related to the Jimmy Swaggart/Jim Bakker televangelist scandals. He would also release his solo album at this time (under the name **Ojo**). Nicholson, meanwhile, played guitar for **Steve Taylor** (on *I Predict 1990*) and for Brian Healy's **Dead Artist Syndrome** (on *Prints of Darkness*); he formed a side project band called Boy's Club with Sim Wilson.

Then, at the beginning of the '90s, Undercover burst back onto the scene with the powerhouse rocker *Balance of Power.* The album has a much harder sound, which many critics likened to that of The Cult. *HM* started calling Undercover "a metal band," though Taylor rejected that label. The album was affected by more tragedies in the band's life: Taylor's mother was diagnosed with cancer, and Nicholson's young bride died suddenly. Taylor would tell *HM,* "It was my intention to bring the band out of the depression of *Branded.* We started writing the album, and then three weeks before we went to record it, Gym's wife passed away, which kind of depressed us all over again. So, the album is definitely darker than we had intended." The album opens with an ominous rocker called "The World Comes Crashing Down" and proceeds to the complaint that "You never told me the end of the story / Along the Via Dolorosa." The latter line comes from a song called "Via Dolorosa," which would become one of the band's best-known numbers. The Latin expression *via dolorosa* is usually translated "way of the cross" and in Christian tradition refers to the events leading up to Jesus' crucifixion. The words literally translate "way of suffering" (via = road; dolor = pain), but for some reason Taylor tells people they translate it "the way of the rose." Apparently, he appreciates the confusion, which is abetted by a mysterious line in the song, "Here's another clue for you all / There are fourteen in all." Fourteen what? He won't say, but in liturgical tradition (e.g., Roman Catholic), observances of the Via Dolorosa in the Lenten scene are marked by fourteen stages on the way to the cross (the arrest, the trial, the whipping, etc.). In any case, *Balance of Power* concludes with the equally powerful "Mea Culpa/Remember Me," a confessional/benediction that begins with the words "I've seen my faults today," and ends with the affirmation, "Live for you, die for you / I'm head and heels in love with you / Remember me." Taylor now described the band's mission as being to "offer people a haven . . . people who are alienated from society, alienated from church, maybe alienated from their parents, or their spouses, or whatever—we offer them a haven. And that haven is the gospel of salvation through Jesus Christ."

Taylor would tell *True Tunes* that the next Undercover project *(Devotion)* was, in many ways, "a rebellion against *Balance of Power*, which is now one of my least favorite records." The album returned somewhat to the aggressive punk sound with a more positive focus. The songs, however, continued to make much of artistic imagery, eschewing blatant exhortations or overt messages. This is illustrated in the aptly titled "Work It Out," which contrasts the experience of life in the fast lane with a simple moment of grace when Taylor saw a school of dolphins swimming toward his fishing pier at five o'clock one morning. "My goal in general has become to be less and less literal," he told *True Tunes*. "You're going to have to find religion, to find God in the dolphins for yourself. Our intent (on *Devotion)* was to create Christian art, not just some message all wrapped up in a nice little package." The title track to *Devotion* is about a troubled teenage girl who cannot find any answers for her questions in life from her parents (who can't relate to her) or from her church (which is just a social club).

Undercover's long-standing lineup fell apart after *Devotion*, but the group would make one more album with a new singer (Rob Gallas, formerly with the band Black and White World) and with two different drummers (Chuck Cummings, who has also played in **Common Bond, Dakoda Motor Co., LSU, Aunt Bettys,** and **Fanmail**) and David Raven of **The Swirling Eddies**). *Shout* said, "*Forum* is brilliant, a richly diverse album of subtle emotional music that is symphonic in range and scope." Other reviewers agreed but found it easier to praise the album than to describe it. Everyone agreed that it didn't sound like Undercover. "Basically, the only thing truly consistent with Undercover here is that it's good," said *True Tunes*. Gallas's vocals are more restrained than Wilson's, helping the band to move from punk to alternative, modern rock.

"Carmenita" has a Spanish sound with dancing violins, and "Whoa, Nellie" is a cowboy song with driving guitars. "The Moon and the Blue Around" has a California '70s sound. "Spill" hearkens back to the harder rock of previous albums. The seven-and-a-half-minute title track has a mellow, trippy sound to it.

Never really appreciated in their time, Undercover would nevertheless enjoy a legacy that continued to emphasize their significance as a paradigm for the development of Christian music. In 1997, *7ball* would say, "Like many bands that get to a certain place first, Undercover was not necessarily the best at what they did. **Daniel Amos** took new-wave to new heights, **The Choir** grafted complex arrangements onto basic chord structures, and **Michael Knott** broke the mold when it came to honest lyrics. But none of those artists would likely have achieved what they did without the contribution of Undercover." In the late '90s all eight of the band's albums were reissued in two deluxe sets with lavish notes (*Anthology 1* includes the first four on two discs and *Anthology 2*, the last four on four discs). A version of the band (with unlisted members) played the *Cornerstone* 2000 festival, a recording of which was released by M8 Productions.

Under Midnight (a.k.a. Zero)

Frankie; db Allen. By Under Midnight: 1992—*Under Midnight* (Wonderland); 1994—*Void* (WAL). By Zero: 1993—*RAVEnous* (Wonderland).

Under Midnight is a Christian industrial band that has had a groundbreaking effect within the alternative market. The semianonymous duo of performers who call themselves Frankie (a.k.a. producer Caesar Kalinowski) and db Allen (a.k.a. Mark Robertson of **This Train** and **A Ragamuffin Band**) mix up a stew that combines dance and techno-pop music with thrash metal in a manner somewhat similar to such general market acts as Ministry, Prong, and Nine Inch Nails. The first self-titled record is something of a concept album, with the tracks relating a cautionary tale of emerging technologies, as two persons search for the truth in a near-future society that has lost its soul. The moral implications of gene-splicing, information overload, and especially virtual reality are all explored. Kurt Bachman of **Believer** plays thrash guitar on the project and numerous samples (e.g., from the film *Blade Runner*) are employed, yet the songs also display enough memorable melodies and sing-along choruses to make it all accessible (cf. **Mortal**). The second release, *Void*, is less linear, but still seems to operate out of an implicit narrative referenced in the liner notes (involving a genetically engineered android who ponders whether he has a soul). Technology, again, is the main antagonist, though now legalistic Christians and antirock purists also seem to be aligned with the forces of darkness (cf. Styx's *Mr. Roboto*). Musically, the album is wildly eclectic and experimental. "Oh

Boy" weds industrial metal to rockabilly and surf music, with almost nonstop samples from rock and roll heroes of the past (Elvis, Duane Eddy, etc.). The title track employs grunge guitars to create an industrialized version of the Seattle sound.

In 1993, Frankie and db Allen recorded one of Christian music's first rave albums under the name Zero. The record *RAVEnous* features beaucoup synthesizers with rapid percussion in the European tradition. Guest diva Donna McAfee wails on a few tracks.

Underoath

Corey Steger, gtr.; Dallas Taylor, voc.; Aaron Gillespie, drums; Octavio, bass; Tim McTague, gtr. 1999—*Acts of Desperation* (Takehold); 2000—*Cries of the Past;* 2002—*The Changing of Times* (Solid State).

Underoath is a Florida band that originally advertised its style as "a mix of hardcore with black metal." The strongest evidence of the latter style on their first album is found in lead singer Dallas Taylor's high-yelp vocals. *Acts of Desperation* offers six songs that take up some fifty-five minutes, with two surpassing the ten-minute mark. The band states in the liner notes to the album that "the sole purpose of this record is to let you know that you are freed by the blood of Jesus Christ." The songs, however, are more issue-oriented than evangelistic. The title track deals with suicide, and "Innocence Stolen" is about the agony caused by rape and child abuse. "Heart of Stone" describes a coldhearted Christian who does not seem to care that others are perishing. "A Love So Pure" is the most positive song, about the joy of living in Jesus. On their follow-up album, *Cries of the Past,* Underoath amplifies the black metal accents with keyboards, double bass, and blistering guitar riffs. *HM* said, "If brutal death/black-metal-influenced hardcore with a touch of '80s metal is right up your alley, then Underoath is the band for you." The third outing, *The Changing of Times,* moves away from the strict metal paradigm to incorporate a good bit more variety. "It's honest," Tim McTague said of *Changing of Times.* "We just played what came out, and if we liked it, we kept it." The songs "Alone in December" and "The Best of Me" address the dysfunctions of human relationships.

Unity Klan

Jasmine Alarcon [a.k.a. Jaz]; Danny Guzman [Danny Boy]; Jarrod Richardson [Big J]. 1997—*Eternal Funk* (custom); 2000—*One Day* (Eternal Funk).

Unity Klan is a rap trio from San Diego, California, whose style seems to favor creating a classic R&B groove and layering energetic, hyperactive raps over it. Lyrics are a bit clichéd but tend to present a militant stance against sin, though both of the group's two albums begin with praise and worship introductions. "Fire" from *One Day* seems to be built on the bass line from Earth, Wind, and Fire's "Let's Groove," while the title

track from that album offers a reinterpretation of the same band's "Fantasy."

Unwed Sailor

Jonathon Ford; et al. 1998—*Firecracker* [EP] (Made in Mexico); 2000—*The Faithful Anchor* (Lovesick).

Unwed Sailor is an instrumental rock band associated with Chicago's Jesus People U.S.A. community, the same socially active, spiritually focused camp responsible for **Ballydowse, Cauzin' Efekt, Crashdog, The Crossing, Headnoise, Glenn Kaiser, Resurrection Band, Seeds,** and **Sheesh.** The group organizes around Jonathon Ford, who was formerly in Seattle's **Roadside Monument.** Ford moved to Chicago after Roadside disbanded, made one album with the general market newwave band Scientific and went to work in the food pantry at the JPUSA community. He would later say that he "decided to become a Christian while at JPUSA." In fact, he told *Bandoppler* that "**Roadside Monument** was not a Christian band. I know for myself, personally, I was searching a lot at that time. I couldn't really talk about Christianity if I wasn't sure what I believed about it." He became "jaded with the Christian music industry," which never quite knew how to react to the band, but would now admit that this attitude was "pretty ridiculous and petty . . . it was a prideful way to think." Unwed Sailor's recordings do not feature lyrics, but Ford says that he regards the music as "very spiritual" and hopes that this will come through. "It is a representation of my belief in Christ as Creator . . . and how he has changed and continually changes my life through experience." In case that message is not clear, he makes a point of testifying to his faith between songs in concerts. Ford was joined by such musicians as Dave Bazan and KC Westcott on the EP *Firecracker* and by former **Roadside Monument** drummer Matt Johnson on *The Faithful Anchor.*

Upside Down Room

Bruce Lund, gtr., voc.; Darryl Mitchell, bass; David Zavala, drums. 1995—*Upside Down Room* [EP] (Tooth and Nail); 1997—*Drag, Baby, Drag.*

Upside Down Room is a Christian old-school punk band composed of three thirty-somethings who define punk with more reference to The Clash than to Green Day. Influences from the '70s (and earlier) abound, such that one critic even told the band their live sound reminded him of "Creedence Clearwater Revival meets The Ramones," to which front man Bruce Lund replied, "Well, those are two of our favorite bands." The band made two albums for Tooth and Nail, of which the first is by far the better for what appears to be one simple reason: it was produced by Jason Martin of **Starflyer 59.** Martin gets the band to revel in their retro sound, with walls of distortion and feedback building up behind the driving, sometimes plodding rhythms. *Upside Down Room* features only seven songs, but none of them sound alike—a near miracle for punk. Lyrically, most of the songs are not obviously religious, but they sometimes lend themselves to Christian interpretation. "You Are a Liar" could be addressed to the devil. The most evangelical tract, "Letter to Amy," recalls a conversation with someone about God and sin and ultimate destiny. *Drag, Baby, Drag* has a more straightforward Ramones/Clash-inspired sound, without the feedback or prepunk influences. The opener, "I Need a Thrill," is a keeper, though the final lines ("I know a God, he talks to me / I know the Truth, he lives in me") come out of nowhere as a rather incongruous conclusion to what is otherwise an ode to hedonism. The closing track, "53 Mercury," is a surf-instrumental that comes as a welcome change after fourteen songs that, this time, do sound a bit too much alike.

Urban Hillbilly Quartet

Erik Brandt, gtr., acc., mand., voc.; Jeremy Szopinski, gtr.; Gary Tippett, bass; Mikey Bales, fiddle (− 2000); Jon Lucca, drums (− 1998) // David Strahan, banjo (+ 1998; − 1999); Sena Thompson, fiddle, voc. (+ 2000). 1997—*Living in the City* (independent); 1998—*St. Paul Town*; 1999—*Beautiful Lazy*; 2000—*Lanky But Macho.*

www.urbanhillbillyquartet.com

The Urban Hillbilly Quartet is a rock, folk, and jazz ensemble from Minnesota. A regional hit in the Twin Cities (i.e., Minneapolis/St. Paul) since 1995, the group credits their appearance at the 2000 *Cornerstone* festival with bringing them to the attention of a national audience. The band's name is somewhat misleading as, despite personnel shifts, they have rarely been a quartet. Rather, the three words in the name are codes for the types of music that they attempt to blend into their eclectic mix: urban = rock; hillbilly = folk; quartet = jazz. To make matters a bit more confusing, they are sometimes classed as a bluegrass group; *St. Paul Town* even won a 1999 Minnesota Music Academy Award for "Best Bluegrass Album." The group's sound betrays the influence of Uncle Tupelo, **Bruce Cockburn,** the Grateful Dead, and **Vigilantes of Love,** all of whom group leader Ed Brandt acknowledges are objects of their affection. Spirituality in the group's songs attracted the attention of alternative Christian media, which connected the group with Christian music venues they had not even known existed. "We don't tout ourselves as a Christian band," says Brandt, who works a day job as a high school teacher. "But I'm the main songwriter and I'm a Christian so a lot of what I write comes out spiritually oriented." The third record, in particular, seems to pick up on faith themes. The title track, "Beautiful Lazy," is about being still long enough to hear the voice of God. *True Tunes* describes the group as a band that "keeps one eye in the gutter with the other in the sky." Brandt acknowledges the

gritty realism: "I just write what I see. I'm an inner-city high school teacher and a lot of times there's just nothing nice about the lives of the kids I teach." Thus, the song "One Day" allows that sometimes real hope can only be found in a world beyond this present one: "One day we will walk above the earth / Laughing till our bellies hurt."

At last report in 2001, Greg Tippett and Sena Thompson were engaged to be married.

Urban Hope

Helena Barrington; Kenneth Barrington; Phaphael Green; Carolyn Johnson; David Johnson; Flynn Johnson; Richard Johnson; Renee Pullam; Donn Thomas; Lonnell Warner. 1992—*The Right Message . . . The Right Time* (Integrity).

Urban Hope was a ten-member African American combo that Integrity music signed in hopes of duplicating in black churches the kind of success they had enjoyed in suburban (largely white) megachurches with their Hosanna worship series. The group produced one album of mostly mellow praise and worship songs that draw on traditions of soul music and, occasionally, African pop ("Standing Together"). The songs are sung in smooth voices with deliberate adult appeal. Lyrics are unambiguously spiritual with frequent reference to Scripture.

Uthanda

Robert Beeson, voc.; Bret Pemelton, gtr.; Bob Wohler, bass; Danny Wood, drums. 1991—*Groove* (Broken); 1992—*Believe* (Essential).

Uthanda was a power-pop band from Southern California that drew most of its audience from the alternative Christian music scene. The band was variously compared to such diverse acts as Cheap Trick, Squeeze, and (on their first album) INXS, as well as to Christian acts like **Jacob's Trouble** and **The Violet Burning.** Blending funk and rock, they crafted songs with catchy melodic hooks but played these with just a little too much of an edge (i.e., unpredictability, lack of polish) for most Christian radio stations. The band was led by Robert Beeson, who was raised as the son of missionaries in South Africa. During his senior year of high school, his parents divorced and the family was recalled and, he says, "treated horribly" by the church they had served so many years. This incident seems to have been formative for the group's take on spirituality, which was always spiced with heavy doses of realism. "I think the biggest thing that Uthanda wants to say is 'Get real!'," Beeson told *CCM* when the group debuted. "The fact that people have found the Lord does not stop the problems that we deal with in life." The band's original drummer was Chuck Cummings, who has played with **LSU, Dakoda Motor Co.,** and the **Aunt Bettys,** but he left before the first album was recorded.

Groove was produced with more commercial polish than its follow-up and granted the band a little initial radio exposure. Most of the songs deal with relationships, with standout cuts being "Sweet Soul Salvation" and the title track. The band also covers "Don't Let Me Be Misunderstood," once made popular by Eric Burdon and the Animals (# 15 in 1965). *Believe* provides a similarly inspired cover of Gary Numan's "Cars" (# 9 in 1980). The album's low point is "Citizen," another Religious Right-inspired complaint about how America isn't as holy/religious as it supposedly used to be. But "My Addiction" moves beyond typical antidrug songs to address the problem of codependency. "Fear" is a strong rock track dealing with the controlling aspect of that experience on people's hearts and minds. "Did You?" is a theologically perceptive ballad encouraging Christians to question their faith in ways that produce growth and tolerance of others, as opposed to just clinging to prescribed beliefs and writing off all opponents. "Shadow Play" is another profound and perceptive song in which Beeson recalls a time in which he did everything he thought was right and it still made no difference in his life. The song concludes, "Weakness is the only strength in me / Your forgiveness is the only way."

U2

Bono (b. Paul Hewson), voc., gtr.; Adam Clayton, bass; The Edge (b. David Evans), gtr., kybrd., voc.; Larry Mullen Jr., drums. 1980—*Boy* (Island); 1981—*October;* 1983—*War; Under a Blood Red Sky* [EP]; 1984—*The Unforgettable Fire;* 1985—*Wide Awake in America* [EP]; 1987—*The Joshua Tree;* 1988—*Rattle and Hum;* 1991—*Achtung Baby;* 1993—*Zooropa;* 1997—*Pop;* 1998—*The Best of 1980–1990; The B-Sides;* 2000—*All That You Can't Leave Behind* (Interscope).

One of the most commercially successful and critically acclaimed rock bands of all time, **U2** is not typically identified as a Christian band, although their fascination and flirtation with Christianity is apparent to even the most superficial fan. For example, "Wake Up, Dead Man" (from *Pop*) is nothing less than a personal and heartfelt prayer—albeit one in which lead singer/songwriter Bono pleads for Jesus to save him from this "f**ked-up world." Change the adjective, and the song could have been on any album by **Audio Adrenaline, Delirious?, Guardian,** or **The Newsboys.** In fact, U2 references Jesus by name more often on *Pop* than did **Michael W. Smith** or **Sixpence None the Richer** on their 1997 releases. The references are undeniably sincere. So, is U2 just a Christian band that talks dirty?

The group came together as an Irish quartet in the late '70s when the members were students at Mount Temple High School, the only nondenominational school in Dublin. First called Feedback, three members of the group (Bono, the Edge, Larry Mullen) were active in an organization called the Shalom Group. This charismatic prayer and Bible study group met twice a week for two hours of worship and discussion of spiritual themes. Bono was baptized in the Irish Sea and became enamored of the writings of Chinese pietist Watchman Nee, whose books (*Sit Walk Stand, The Spiritual Man, The Normal Christian Life*) were also very popular among evangelical and fundamentalist Christians in America at the time. Bono himself had grown up the son of a Catholic father and a Protestant mother. His mother died when he was a child, a tragedy that he says first drew him into deep faith and one that would seemingly leave him with an early and permanent appreciation for the uncertainties of life. Mullen also embraced Christianity following the death of his mother in a motorcycle accident. The Edge came to faith more slowly but, it would seem to many, more reflectively. For years, he would struggle with his vocation, sensing a call to ministry and wondering whether playing in a rock band was the best way to serve God. To these three, the Shalom Group presented itself as a nondenominational "third option" breaching the divide between Protestants and Catholics in war-torn Ireland. It also encouraged its members to integrate their faith into every aspect of their lives and to find ways of articulating this without being preachy. Bono would later say that he and the others left the Shalom Group "at the time structure and hierarchy started to emerge." Still, in the early years of U2, the trio would continue to have Bible studies together on their tour bus and in their hotel rooms. There was tension between the three Christians and Adam Clayton, who did not share their faith and was jokingly referred to as "the token pagan" in the band.

U2's first album, *Boy,* produced only one minor hit ("I Will Follow," a tribute to Bono's mother) but drew the attention of critics who heralded the band's potential. *Rolling Stone* called the album "pop music with brains" but also took notable delight in publishing the nineteen-year-old leader's first words to an American journalist: "I don't mean to sound arrogant, but even at this stage, I do feel that we are meant to be one of the great groups . . . like the Stones, The Who, or the Beatles." Bono, the Edge, and Mullen were also forthright about their faith, identifying themselves as believers with an evangelical enthusiasm. The Christian press took note and wished the group well in its mission to make music for the world rather than the church, but also expressed concern about whether they fully appreciated the "sheep in the midst of wolves" phenomenon (Matthew 10:16). In addition, there was a general hope that the band would record songs that expressed their faith as explicitly as did their comments in interviews.

This hope was fulfilled with *October,* an album that ended up being explicitly marketed as a Christian album, sold in Bible bookstores and reviewed in all the Christian music magazines. *CCM* called it "a constructive and succinct statement about biblical longings in the Kingdom of God"; *Cornerstone* noted that the group "centers its message on Christ" such that "a Christian can easily recognize their faith" in ways that might not be obvious to the uninformed or unbeliever. The lead song, "Gloria" (what *CCM* called "a realist's lament to the Lord"), incorporates elements of the Latin Mass. "Rejoice" invokes a biblical summons to defy this-worldly cynicism, a theme that is picked up again in the song "Scarlet" (where the word "rejoice" is repeated over and over). "Stranger in a Strange Land" seems to invoke **Larry Norman**'s *Only Visiting This Planet* theme as much as it does the titular Robert Heinlein novel (Bono has identified himself as knowledgeable and appreciative of Norman's work). "Fire" is openly apocalyptic, and in "Tomorrow" Bono sings, "Open up to the Lamb of God / To the love of He who made the blind to see / He's coming back . . . Jesus is coming . . . I want to be there . . . I believe it."

If *October* was widely received within the contemporary Christian music subculture as the work of a Christian band, so too was *War*, which finally brought the group widespread commercial success. It reached Number Twelve in the United States (# 1 in Britain) on the strength of such radio hits as "Sunday, Bloody, Sunday," "New Year's Day," and "Two Hearts Beat as One." As the first two of these songs illustrate, the mood of the album is more political than spiritual, but the band's take on social issues is informed by distinctively Christian ideals of justice and mercy. The album opens with a call to "claim the victory Jesus won" ("Sunday Bloody Sunday") and closes with a hymnic meditation on Psalm 40 ("40"). A common refrain from the psalter ("How long shall we sing this song?") becomes its theme, woven antiphonally into both the just-mentioned songs. Along the way, Bono quotes from Isaiah 40:31 in what appears to be an empathetic expression of God's concern for suffering humanity ("Drowning Man"), and he searches within himself for the answer to the world's problems: "Angry words won't stop the fight / Two wrongs won't make it right / A new heart is what I need / Oh, God, make it bleed" ("Like a Song"). *CCM* Magazine chose *War* as their critic's choice for the best contemporary Christian album of the year. They did the same a year later with *The Unforgettable Fire,* and they also placed the band's live recording *Under a Blood Red Sky* on their year's ten best list. But by 1985 such placements were beginning to look odd. The Christian music media was not only touting U2 as "a Christian band" but as the world's *best* Christian band. Yet the group was topping all sorts of lists and polls in the secular media as well, where few seemed to think of the group as crossover artists from some separate Christian field (like **Stryper** or **Amy Grant**). Notably, *The Unforgettable Fire* (produced by Brian Eno and **Daniel Lanois**) scores primarily with two songs reflecting on the message and ministry of Martin Luther King Jr.: "Pride (In the Name of Love)" and "MLK." Such songs had special meaning for Christians, who regard King as a preacher, a prophet, a theologian, and a saint. But, of course, King belongs to the world as well and, like U2, is appreciated by millions without specific reference to his faith.

U2 will always be best remembered for *The Joshua Tree,* produced (again) by **Daniel Lanois** and Brian Eno. Some pundits may have thought it premature for *Rolling Stone* to name U2 "the most important band of the '80s" in 1985, but when this masterpiece arrived two years later, all doubt was suspended. The album features the band's two biggest hits, "With or without You" and "I Still Haven't Found What I'm Looking For" (both # 1 for weeks) in addition to the much-played, radio-friendly "Where the Streets Have No Name" and "In God's Country." Beyond that, it summarizes the conscience of the '80s, portraying a world where a singular assault on TV evangelists ("My God is not short on *cash*") and United States foreign policy in El Salvador makes sense—where, indeed, these are a common foe, to be addressed in a single song ("Bullet the Blue Sky"). As a whole, *The Joshua Tree* is built around the theme of discovering persistent, defiant life in the midst of a desert (thus, the title and the cover photo—depicting a gnarled desert tree named by Mormons for its perseverance in the wilderness). Several of the lesser-known songs address specific issues of human suffering: "Running to Stand Still" is about heroin addiction, and "Exit," about suicide (originally inspired by the story of Gary Gilmore); "Mothers of the Disappeared" concerns the families of political prisoners, and "Red Hill Mining Town," victims of unemployment.

Suddenly, U2 was on the cover of *Time* magazine, and in 1987 the band or its individual members took first place in all the following categories in *Rolling Stone*'s annual Readers' Poll: Artist of the Year, Best Band, Best Album, Best Single, Best Male Singer, Best Songwriter, Best Guitarist, Best Bass Player, Best Drummer, Best Live Performance, Best Video, and Best Album Cover. Bono was also voted Sexiest Man Alive. In the midst of all this, while the band was at the all-time height of its popularity, Bono and his wife Ali disappeared for over a month, traveling in private to Ethiopia where they engaged in famine relief efforts (they wrote songs and plays to help familiarize children with nutritional and other health concerns). *The Joshua Tree,* meanwhile, sold over fifteen million copies, making it one of the best-selling records of all time and channeling a new trend in music toward deeper and more serious themes. Music of the period can almost be divided along pre- and post-*Joshua Tree* lines, even for artists that sound nothing like U2. Madonna's last pre-*Joshua Tree* song was "Causin' a Commotion"; her first post-*Joshua Tree* song was "Like a Prayer." When mainstream rock critics composed their best-albums-of-all-time lists at the end of the millennium, it was difficult to find anyone who did not include U2's *The Joshua Tree* in the Top 10—and quite a few put it at Number One. For a group from the supposedly insignificant Christian music market to have produced a work of such profound quality and undeniable significance seemed incredible—and many within the contemporary Christian music subculture thought that their moment in the sun had come at last. The problem, again, was that by 1987 no one outside of that little parallel universe seemed to think of U2 as a Christian band—and before long, even those within that world would come to have their doubts.

Though Christian music fans may have regarded U2 as one of theirs, the group had never given them permission to do so, nor had they ever been a part of any separatist Christian music subculture. All of their albums had been released on a general market label. Bono did not grant interviews to *CCM* or other Christian music magazines. The group did not normally perform at Christian music festivals or interact with self-acknowledged Christian music stars (they did play England's *Greenbelt* festival once—early on—and Bono has subsequently returned incognito just to watch). They did not view their music as a vehicle for promoting Christianity, but as art with intrinsic (even spiritual) value of its own. Nevertheless, the initial understanding within the Christian music scene was simply that the group had to keep a relatively low profile in order to overcome prejudices against Christianity operative in the mainstream rock world. But after *The Joshua Tree,* when the band had become, hands down, the biggest rock group in the world, the low Christian profile seemed to shrink ever lower, leaving Christian fans dismayed and disappointed with the band for most of the '90s. "I am a Christian, but at times I feel very removed from Christianity," Bono said in 1987. The secular media picked up on this shift. Two years earlier, in 1985, a *Rolling Stone* article had announced, "U2 dares to proclaim its belief in Christianity—at top volume—while grappling with the ramifications of its faith." But by 1987, that same magazine was describing the group much more generically, referring to its music as "postalienationist rock that stresses communion over segregation, compassion over blame, hope over despair."

Musically, the years following *The Joshua Tree* saw U2 struggling with the mantle of classic rock. The band obviously did not want to rest on its laurels, become an oldies act, or be regarded as classic anything. The solution was to mess with the formula that had served them so well (soaring, reverb-laden guitars topped by Bono's piercing, sensuous vocals). They spent the next decade tinkering. Some of the experiments (collaborating with blues master B. B. King on "When Love Comes to Town") paid off; others (the quirky techno music of *Zooropa*) proved commercially unappealing. The group's major success for the '90s came with their European-sounding *Achtung Baby*

album, which scored five sensuous, melodic hits. Of these, "One" is a magnificent anthem to life that would have the whole world singing lines like "One life with each other / Sisters and brothers" and "We're one but we're not the same / We get to carry each other." It was almost as if the '60s had returned, though Bono has indicated that the song actually has a rather dark subtext and is about the relationship between a father and his estranged son who is dying of AIDS. "Have you come here for forgiveness?" the son asks. "Have you come to raise the dead? / Have you come here to play Jesus / To the lepers in your head?" *Achtung Baby* was widely hailed as "the album of the decade" (i.e., the '90s) in a manner analogous to *The Joshua Tree* before it; according to The Edge, the melancholy feel of the record derived from the breakup of his marriage and Bono's empathy with him throughout that ordeal. A year later, Bono sang a hugely successful duet with Frank Sinatra on "I've Got You Under My Skin" that gave the standard an unexpected new life; he had wanted them to record "These Boots Are Made for Walking" but Sinatra's cooler head prevailed. U2 also had considerable success contributing songs to the soundtracks of such motion pictures as *Batman Forever, Until the End of the World, Faraway So Close,* and *The Million Dollar Hotel.*

But is U2 a Christian band? No doubt some of the ambivalence that has attended the group's classification stems from the fact that their ideology is just not in sync with that of the evangelical American mainstream. Theologically, Bono rejects the dualism that infects and often justifies the very existence of much Christian music: "We're always being given this choice," he complains, "to choose between the flesh and the spirit. I don't know anybody who isn't both." He likewise has some sympathy for liberation theology, as evidenced on a trip to Nicaraguan churches, after which he proclaimed, "What is religion, without commitment to the poor? It's a black hole." More to the point, the band's social and political involvements favor causes that have not been priorities for the so-called Religious Right. While other Christian stars champion virginity and campaign at Right to Life rallies, U2 seeks money for HIV research and supports Amnesty International. Indeed, Bono would close out the millennium by meeting with the Pope and appearing before the United Nations, campaigning tirelessly for the reduction of Third World debt. Of course, there are millions of Christians in America who ally themselves with liberal causes—but such Christians do not usually compose the traditional fan base for what gets called "contemporary Christian music."

Lyrics, furthermore, lend themselves to polyvalent interpretation. When "I Still Haven't Found What I'm Looking For" rose to the top of the charts, many Christian fans were aghast. They took the song as a clear signal that Bono had lost his faith. Having previously claimed to have "found Jesus," he was now admitting that this had just been a phase. Others understood the song as a straightforward biblical confession, expressing the Christian view that, whatever pleasures this world may afford, our hearts will not rest until they are joined with God in heaven. "I believe in the kingdom come," Bono sings in the anthemic song. And to whom would these words be addressed, if not to Christ: "You broke the bonds / You loosed the chains / You carried the cross / And my shame / You know I believe it." The Edge has called the song "a gospel hymn," and to underscore that interpretation, the group would re-record it on *Rattle and Hum* with a church choir singing the chorus. On a broader scale, U2 has demonstrated a lyrical preference for talking about faith as a struggle, for expressing what one critic calls a "tug-of-war between lighter and darker instincts" and another describes as "a compelling mix of confession and confusion." On "When Love Comes to Town," Bono sings, "I was there when they crucified my Lord / I held the scabbard when the soldier drew his sword / I threw the dice when they pierced his side / But I've seen love conquer the great divide." Some songs express honest doubt: "God is good, but will he listen?" ("Staring at the Sun"); "God has got his phone off the hook / Would he even pick up if he could?" ("If God Will Send His Angels"); "Jesus, I'm waiting here, boss / I know you're looking out for us / But maybe your hands aren't free" ("Wake Up Dead Man"). Other songs are more startling: "I have cursed thy rod and staff, they no longer comfort me" ("Love Rescue Me," cowritten by Bono and **Bob Dylan**). But coming from a man who on the same album sings "I don't believe in riches—but you should see where I live!" ("God, Part II"), such sentiments seem more self-deprecating than defiant. The latter song continues: "I feel like I'm falling, spinning on a wheel / It always stops beside a name, a presence I can feel." That name, of course, is the name of Jesus Christ, and Bono has never hesitated to say so.

Perhaps the most troubling aspect about U2 to traditional Christian music fans has been the front man's whimsical penchant for deconstructing his supposed "holy stature." For some reason, Bono decided to adopt an alter ego he called The Fly in the '90s, and for a time he would only appear in public as that character. The Fly wore shades and vinyl clothes, answered questions in riddles, and provided interviewers with false information for which Bono felt no need to offer apology. And with rock stardom come rock star antics. Here's Bono in *Entertainment Weekly* French-kissing Liam Gallagher (a man). A *Rolling Stone* cover shows him dressed in black leather hamming it up with a couple of transvestites. The album art for *Achtung Baby* contains a montage of small photos, one showing Bono with a topless woman, another displaying Clayton completely nude (censored in America), and a couple more featuring the band in drag. On the group's '92 "Zoo tour," Bono

performed an encore spouting devil's horns and identifying himself as a demonic character called MacPhisto who claimed that the Pope and the Archbishop of Canterbury were "doing his work." Bono told various interviewers that "organized religion is the enemy of God" and that "living by the Spirit means this is my life and it's between me and God and nobody else." The band issued free condoms at their concerts. There was a U2 song that used "the Playboy mansion" as a metaphor for heaven. Bono wrote a country song with **T Bone Burnett** called "Having a Wonderful Time, Wish You Were Her." Bono told a *Mother Jones* reporter, "It's better to be drunk on the Spirit (cf. Ephesians 5:18), but sometimes a bottle of Jack Daniels is handier!" In London, he stripped naked in a public restaurant during an interview. Even secular artists thank God when they win a Grammy award—in 1993 Bono accepted his with a speech that used the f-word so many times even *Rolling Stone* felt compelled to criticize his limited vocabulary. For those watching the show on national TV, it seemed like every fifth word got bleeped (and even then, they missed a couple). Such moments caused the star to rise to the top of many a prayer list, and probably led many Christian music fans to write him off completely. "Bono himself is a whole contradiction," The Edge told *CCM* Magazine in 1988, a bit embarrassed that the image of the group inevitably gets defined by its most flamboyant member. Indeed, it is sometimes difficult to know how much to take seriously. In late 1999, Bono wrote an introduction to the book of Psalms for a new edition of the King James Bible. Referring to his childhood in Ireland, he claimed that the essential difference between Protestants and Catholics was that the former had all the best tunes while the latter had good theater. Then he owned up to abandoning both faiths, personally, "for a different kind of religion . . . being in a rock and roll band." Still, a poll of Christian music critics conducted by *CCM* magazine in 2001 would put *The Joshua Tree* at Number Six and *October* at Number Forty-one on their list of "The 100 Greatest Albums in Christian Music." Base profanities and liberal pieties were not sufficient to dissuade some folks in the Christian music subculture from *still* thinking of U2 as "a Christian band."

Despite such holdouts, and despite the fact that U2 had sold more "Jesus records" than any artist in history, by the end of the millennium the group's failure to meet normative expectations of the religious establishment had become a prominent part of its identity and image. Sometimes, they seemed to celebrate this fact as part of their rock star rebel status—but not always. Perhaps the most telling of all U2 lyrical quotes comes in the song "Acrobat" from *Achtung Baby*: "I'd join the movement, if there was one I could believe in / I would break the bread and drink the wine if there was a church I could receive in / Because I need it now." *Zooropa* includes "The Wanderer" (sung with

Johnny Cash), which tells of a visit to a church where "they say they want the kingdom, but they don't want God in it." On 1998's *Pop* Bono would claim, "Jesus never let me down you know / Jesus used to show me the score / Then they put Jesus in show business / Now it's hard to get in the door" ("If God Will Send His Angels"). Whatever that means, one senses more alienation from Christendom than from Christ.

At the start of the new millennium, something remarkable happened. No one—not even U2's staunchest supporters—thought the aging group capable of making another album on the same level as *The Joshua Tree,* and when *Rolling Stone* announced that they had done exactly that (a month before the official release), the rock world developed a breathtaking wait-and-see attitude. No one in the Christian music scene expected U2 ever to record an album of nakedly pious songs, and by the time *CCM* acknowledged that they had done just that, the need for waiting was over. *All That You Can't Leave Behind* (once again produced by **Daniel Lanois** and Brian Eno) is certainly U2's most fully realized work musically and spiritually. From beginning to end, it offers stellar pop-rock songs better than anything that any other band was performing at the time, and many of these openly point to a road-tested faith that somehow has endured. Practically every track reflects confident hope and trust in the God of the Bible, leaving even the most secular reviewers to wonder what exactly had happened. The key, it turns out, is *grace,* which Bono extols as though he has only just discovered it.

As with many works of literature or theology, *All That You Can't Leave Behind* must be understood in light of its conclusion, a song that is actually called "Grace." Like John Dunne, St. Theresa of Avila, and the author of the Song of Solomon, Bono personifies this central attribute of God as a woman, but in case his audience should prove too dense to get it, he explains the allegory: "Grace," he sings, "It's the name of a girl . . . it's also a thought that changed the world." And then he proceeds to describe this lover who has entered his life and transformed his world: "She takes the blame . . . she covers the shame . . . she removes the stain . . . she travels outside of karma . . ." It is this influence that explains the most noticeable and otherwise inexplicable quality of the entire album: not spiritual questing, not adolescent insurgency, not cynical challenges or even legitimate protests, but . . . an overwhelming sense of gladness. The disc bursts open with its exuberant hit single, "Beautiful Day," a simple celebration of how good it is to be alive. The song is a bit like The Rascals' "It's a Beautiful Morning" but more grounded in Scripture and in reality. "See the bird with a leaf in her mouth," Bono sings in an obvious reference to Noah. "After the flood, all the colours came out / It was a beautiful day." Verses about traffic jams, bad luck, and other frustrations unravel into an explosive chorus on which

Bono sweeps everything aside with one soaring exhortation: "It's a beautiful day—don't let it get away!" Similarly, "Stuck in a Moment and You Can't Get Out of It" (a Motown-ish hit single if ever there was one) counsels the depressed and disenchanted about the foolishness of worry and encourages some reevaluation of priorities as a hedge against obsession ("you can never get enough of what you don't really need"). Essentially the same point is made in the very different-sounding "In a Little While," on which he seeks to take his own advice with reference to those sad times when he feels lonely and separated from his wife while on the road. On another surefire hit ("Elevation"), Bono sings (apparently to God) about his desire to experience "elevation" not "excavation": "Lift me up out of these blues / Won't you tell me something true / I *believe* in you!" In such company, even a completely nonreligious song like "Wild Honey" suddenly seems spiritual; the Beatlesque tune, many critics have observed, is the happiest song that U2 has ever sung. Commenting on *All That You Can't Leave Behind,* a reviewer for *Phantom Tollbooth* said, "Anger is easy. Sarcasm's a cinch. This time, U2 has discovered something very hard to find in modern rock music: *joy!*"

What made the group lighten up after all these years? Lighten up? No, they didn't exactly lighten up. The profound aspect of the album is that, here, joy is not mere optimism. As many reviewers would note, over half the songs on *All That You Can't Leave Behind* deal with dark themes involving mortality and death—and Bono himself would admit that the suicide of his close friend Michael Hutchence (of INXS) influenced his writing for the album (in addition to another "rather personal crisis" that he prefers not to specify). "If you've had a fright, or someone close to you dies, things come into sharp focus," he told *Rolling Stone.* But on *All That You Can't Leave Behind* the specifics of that focus involve Christian hope. "This is not good-bye" he sings on "Kite" (to Hutchence perhaps) and then says on his own account, "I'm not afraid to die / And I'm not afraid to live / And when I'm flat on my back / I want to say that I did." Most powerful of all perhaps is the song from which the album's title is taken: a gospel hymn complete with choir, "Walk On" views all of life through the "sharp focus" of mortality as the band prompts the listener to consider, as Jesus did his disciples, what it is that they can't do without: "You're packing a suitcase for a place none of us has been / A place that has to be believed to be seen." He provides a list of inappropriate contents ("all that you fashion, all that you make / all that you build, all that you break / all that you measure / all that you fear . . . you can leave it all behind"). The one thing that can't be left behind is "love," which obviously has a sense beyond that of romance. That sense, as with the sense of the entire album, is filled out in the closing song: Love = Grace. As it turns out, *grace* is what brings the colors out after the flood and exalts those naturally inclined toward "excavation." And grace is the only thing that can't be left behind on the journey to that place that has to be believed to be seen.

On two songs on *All That You Can't Leave Behind,* Bono sings directly and explicitly to Jesus. Back to back, the songs are obviously meant to be taken together. The first is the much noticed faux-Christmas song "Peace on Earth." This beautiful carol has antithetical lyrics that bemoan the continuance of war and suffering in Ireland, in Bosnia, and around the world (the song is dedicated to human rights champion Aung San Suu Kyi, imprisoned in Burma). Bono reminds Jesus of the Gloria in Excelsis sung on the night of his birth (Luke 2:14) and says, "Peace on earth / I hear it every Christmastime / But hope and history won't rhyme / So what's it worth?" The honest sentiment is simultaneously irreverent and yet deeply religious in a manner like no other song since John Lennon's "Imagine." And it is followed by "When I Look at the World," in which Bono now attributes his impatience with unredressed suffering to an inability to see the world the way that God sees it: "I try to be like you / Try to feel it like you do / But without you it's no use." On *All That You Can't Leave Behind,* this struggle with theodicy (the inexplicable nature of suffering) is the only remaining damper on Bono's otherwise exuberant (and thoroughly orthodox) faith. And even this, like everything else, gets resolved in the final song: "What left a mark / No longer stings / Because Grace makes beauty / Out of ugly things."

With *All That You Can't Leave Behind,* U2 would sweep the Grammys again—this time without profanity. It was widely said that they had made the album of the year, possibly of the decade (again), probably of their career. The Christian music press sought to reclaim the band, reviewing *All That You Can't Leave Behind* as one of the most spiritually profound and devout albums ever made. Bono—and the rest of U2—kept their distance. They did not give interviews to any overtly Christian publications and they did not perform for any explicitly religious venues. Yet in their global 2001 tour, Bono regularly introduced the other members of the band to the audience with comments about their intellectual leanings, religious beliefs, and the like (he called The Edge "a zen Presbyterian"). A *Rolling Stone* interviewer noted that, as the one doing the introductions, nothing was said about *him.* "Yeah, well, I don't know who I am, mate," he replied, and then added whimsically, "I've sort of made a career out of my personality crisis, you know."

All the same, Bono seemed more upbeat on the 2001 tour than in previous years, and more comfortable with his identification as a person of faith. He introduced "Where the Streets Have No Name" by reading from Psalm 116, and during "Walk On" he offered impromptu exclamations of "Hallelujah!" At many shows, after the final encore, he strode to the center of the stage and addressed the audience, stating simply "Thanks to the Almighty," before leaving.

In late 2001, a new Christian publisher issued a book on U2's travels in the faith written by the chaplain of Queen's University at Belfast: *Walk On: The Spiritual Journey of U2* by Steve Stockman (Relevant). In 2002, the British publication *Q Magazine* published an account by Noel Gallagher (of the band Oasis) that allows a rare glimpse into Bono's style of what might be called "personal witnessing." Gallagher says he asked Bono after a concert what was up with "the whole God thing." He continues: "We had a good three-hour conversation about his religious philosophy, which is basically, 'Go to God, tell him what all your flaws are and say Can you walk with me?' which is completely different from the 'Don't drink, don't screw, don't take drugs, always go to church bullocks.' Two days later, the delivery guy hands me two books. There's a little note, 'I don't know if you were serious the other night, but here's something that might give you a bit more of an understanding.' I tell you, I'm gonna read 'em cover to cover!"

For trivia buffs: The cover photo for U2's *All That You Can't Leave Behind* shows the group in an airport. In one corner of the picture, a sign pointing to gates reads "J 33–3." In the '70s, some members of charismatic prayer groups used those figures as a code for prayer, based on Jeremiah 33:3 ("Call to me and I will answer you"). Confronted with this discovery by a journalist, Bono responded sheepishly, "Yeah. It's, like, God's phone number."

Grammy awards: 1987 Best Rock Performance by a Duo or Group *(The Joshua Tree);* 1987 Album of the Year *(The Joshua Tree);* 1988 Best Rock Performance by a Duo or Group ("Desire"); 1992 Best Rock Performance by a Duo or Group *(Achtung Baby);* 1993 Best Alternative Music Album *(Zooropa);* 2000 Best Rock Performance by a Duo or Group ("Beautiful Day"); 2000 Record of the Year ("Beautiful Day"); 2001 Best Pop Performance by a Duo or Group ("Stuck in a Moment and You Can't Get Out of It"); 2001 Best Rock Performance by a Duo or Group ("Elevation"); 2001 Best Rock Album *(All That You Can't Leave Behind);* 2001 Record of the Year ("Walk On").

Gary V.

1995—*Out of the Dark* (Graceland).

Filipino Gary V. is sometimes called "the Michael Jackson of the Philippines," though in terms of Christian music analogies, **Cliff Richard** might make for a better comparison. Like Richard, Gary V. is a major star in his homeland, where he is publicly known as a person of faith, but he remains almost unknown in the United States—in Christian music venues as well as in the general market. The artist scored his first national hit in 1983 when "Hang On" became the Number One song in the Philippines. He has had numerous gold and platinum albums since and has won dozens of AWIT Awards (basically, a Philippine Grammy). He has also toured Europe and starred in a number of motion pictures. Gary V. says that he and his wife "recommitted their lives to the Lord" in 1985 and that since then he has tried to use his music as a means of conveying life-changing messages and has evinced a desire to reach others for Christ. In 1995, he recorded an album of evangelical songs for release in America's contemporary Christian music market. *Out of the Dark* features a mix of hip-hop dance tracks ("That's Why") and heart-wrenching ballads ("Could You Be the Messiah?").

Jim Valley

1971—*Family* (Light).

One of the early traits of the '70s Jesus movement revival was a near obsession with finding celebrity converts whose endorsement supposedly made it hip or at least socially acceptable among countercultural youth to be into Jesus. Thus, one was constantly reminded that **Larry Norman** had sung with People, **Barry McGuire** was the guy who did "Eve of Destruction," **Phil Keaggy** had played with **Glass Harp, John** and **Terry Talbot** were from Mason Proffit, and of course **Noel Paul Stookey** was the Paul from Peter, Paul, and Mary. The Jesus People may not have realized how silly this seemed to the world at large—especially since none of these celebrities were persons who would have been likely to show up on covers of *Rolling Stone* at any recent point prior to their conversion. Efforts to claim **Eric Clapton** failed, and the Jesus freaks were too suspicious to latch on to **Marvin Gaye** or **Aretha Franklin,** questioning, respectively, their orthodoxy or sincerity. They didn't much care that **Chuck Girard** had been with The Hondells or **Ray Hildebrand** with Paul and Paula, since only their older siblings (or parents) had ever listened to that stuff. The only really big celebrity to be stumping for Jesus in the early days was **Pat Boone,** whose name did not exactly carry much weight with the counterculture. In time, the Jesus freaks would be able to add **Richie Furay** to their list and, *then,* they got **Bob Dylan** (for a little while), but in the early days, they would take whoever they could get.

All of this is background for understanding the hype surrounding Jim Valley, a simple folk singer who, apparently, just wanted to make a simple record about some of the things in life he appreciated: nature, his family, God, and life itself. Valley was touted everywhere as *another* big convert, a former member of the huge '60s band Paul Revere and the Raiders (where he went by the name "Harpo"). Of course, he wasn't Paul Revere, nor was he Mark Lindsay, that band's charismatic lead singer. He was just a quiet guitarist who had played off to the side somewhere. In fact, he had only played his guitar on one album for the band, albeit a pretty good one (*Just Like Us,* 1966). But not a single article noted that. Rather, *Harmony* praised the Lord that yet another "major rock star" had been added to the fold as God continued "to build a veritable army of contemporary musicians, calling the finest performers of the day to be his disciples."

Valley was no major rock star, but he did produce a nice album of Jesus music that unfortunately got lost in all the hoopla. It is unlikely that anyone persuaded to buy *Family* on account of a perceived Paul Revere and the Raiders connection would have liked the album, as its sound is pretty far removed from that band's raucous party rock and funky blues. *Family* is a very laid-back collection of acoustic folk songs. In reality, it is less a solo album than the work of a duo, as Valley sings most of the songs with buddy Steve Schurr. They are backed by a rhythm section consisting of Max Bennett on bass and John Guerrin on drums, known at the time as part of The L.A. Express, a.k.a. Joni Mitchell's backing band. The overall sound is reminiscent of contemporary works by The Youngbloods (i.e., Jesse Colin Young) and John B. Sebastian. Lyrically, the songs express wonder at the beauty of God's creation, with "Savior" moving also to thanksgiving for grace shown in Jesus Christ. The title track, "Family," is actually the conclusion to a short suite of songs that begins with "She Walks in Beauty," a love song for Valley's wife. The whole album concludes with a foot-stomping version of the campground classic "Give Me Oil in My Lamp." Ken Scott of *Jesus Music* reports that Valley's *Family* was a major influence on the group **Rising Hope**'s debut.

Value Pac

Ryan Sheely, gtr., voc.; Ben Cator, drums (−2000); Isaiah Coughran, bass (− 1998) // Sean Humestan, bass (+ 1998, − 2000); Sean Paul, bass (+ 2000). 1996—*Value Pac* (Tooth and Nail); 1998—*Jalapeno* (BEC); 2000—*Incognito* (Four Door).

Value Pac is a Christian punk band from the West Coast that didn't begin with much promise but would develop into a band noted for both integrity and innovation. Lyrically, the group is up front about matters of faith and spiritual vision, while engaging a wide range of issues relevant for adolescent audiences. Their self-titled debut album displays a sound virtually indistinguishable from that of **Craig's Brother, Face Value, MxPx, Slick Shoes,** and **Sick of Change:** fast, melodic punk songs that all possess the same trademark suitable-for-bungee-jumping pogo sound. *Value Pac* opens with "Graduation Day," which expresses the mixed feelings associated with reaching a milestone that marks achievement but also precipitates uncomfortable transitions ("the day we leave our past behind"). "Sunday Christian" deals with the hypocrisy of churchgoing youth who don't live what they supposedly believe. "Happy Star" is a worship song addressed to God, and "Final Request" is another in a long series of not-very-effective Christian antiabortion tracks that try to describe the tragedy from the point of view of the fetus (cf. **Phil Keaggy, Rocketboy, Sackcloth Fashion, Kathy Troccoli**). But then Value Pac developed a sound of their own and made a vastly improved second album. Produced by Peter King of **Dakoda Motor Co.,** *Jalapeno* mixes the *pop*-punk with punk-*rock,* introducing songs more similar to **The Altar Boys** or The Clash than to all the Green Day clones with which the band had previously been classed. The best tracks are the opening "Nothing" and the closing "Big Dream"; both feature urgent rhythms, strong hook-laden melodies, and luscious vocals; the opener even has some "wo-oh-oh" harmonies on the chorus. In between these highlights, "We Are the Ones" is hornless ska (cf. **Squad Five-O**), and "This Boy" is a nonpunk cover of the classic Beatles song; together, these two tracks provide what every punk album desperately needs: variety. Lyrically, the song "Preacher Man" is interesting, describing an easy target for ridicule—a street preacher—as an emblem of radical faithfulness.

After the second, highly acclaimed album, Value Pac broke up amidst a flurry of personal troubles, including different conceptions of ministry. Front man Ryan Sheely would not talk about the problems for a time, but in 2000 decided to own up to his part in the fiascos as a warning to others. He told *Bandoppler* that he had not become a Christian until he was fifteen years old and some friends took him to a church camp. Just two years later, he was a Christian rock star of sorts: "It wasn't a huge amount of success, but not many seventeen-year-olds get to play for a thousand people and sign autographs and stuff. So, it went to my head, and I don't think I knew how to handle it. I was a jerk, and I lost a lot of friends. And there was alcohol . . . so, what do you do?" In 2000, however, Sheely said he had tamed his personal demons and he joined with bass player Sean Paul to form a new version of the band for a third album. The process was beset with tragedy, as first Sheely's mother and then Paul's grandfather died while the two were working on *Incognito.* The album was produced by Dennis Danell (guitarist for the general market band Social Distortion), who also died before the project was completed. "He was definitely a believer," Sheely told *7ball* of the late Danell, a legend in the punk world (cf. **Strong Gurus**). *Incognito* continues to allow the band's original new-school punk sound to be affected by healthy doses of classic rock, such that *Bandoppler* would liken the sound on some tracks (e.g., "Showdown") to that of nonpunk bands like **Tragedy Ann** or even

Aunt Bettys. Lyrically, the songs have a darker edge that reflects their travails. "Dear God" draws upon the book of Job and questions where God is to be found in the midst of suffering. *Bandoppler* would say the latter song "is so soaked with genuine anger, pain, lament, and cries of mercy that it should bring even the hardest tuff guy to an anxious state of mind."

Vonda Kay Van Dyke

1970—*New Kind of Happiness* (Word); 1971—*Day by Day* (Myrrh); 1972—*Here's Vonda Kay* (Word).

Vonda Kay Van Dyke (b. 1942) was Miss America 1965, chosen in 1964 while she was a senior at Arizona State University. She fulfilled three firsts in the pageant history. She was the first Miss America to have used ventriloquism as her talent (singing a duet with a dummy on a song called "Together"). She was the first (and as of 2001, still the only) Miss America also to be chosen Miss Congeniality by her fellow contestants. And she was the first person in pageant history to mention God on national TV. She was asked in the final round of interviews if the Bible she was known to carry was "a good luck charm" and responded, "It is the most important book I own. I believe in God and trust in Him." Van Dyke would eventually marry a minister (David Tyler Scoates) and move to California. She has written several books and recorded a number of albums. The three records listed above are collections of inspirational songs. *Day by Day* came out as the Jesus movement revival was breaking, but the hippie Jesus people weren't really impressed by beauty pageants, and if anything, Van Dyke's credentials probably counted against her. The album has a folk gospel sound to it similar to much of what would be popular in the Jesus music of the early '70s. The title track is a version of the popular *Godspell* song. Van Dyke also covers **Randy Matthews**' "Hallelujah Brother," helping that artist to gain some early (nonhippie) respectability.

Tara VanFlower

1999—*This Womb Like Liquid Honey* (Projekt).

Tara VanFlower is lead singer for an atmospheric goth band called Lycia. At some point, she became a Christian and, without leaving Lycia, released a solo album as a side project. The songs on *This Womb Like Liquid Honey* relate her journey from childhood through a life of abuse into involvement with the occult and finally to an embrace of Christian faith. In interviews, VanFlower would say that she didn't even know that there was a Christian goth scene at the time the record was being made, but was delighted to discover she could be warmly received by such a subculture. She says, "My intentions are never to beat anyone over the head with my opinions, but I definitely think it's evident what my beliefs are on this disc."

The song "Talitha Koum" tells the story of Jesus raising Jairus's daughter from the dead (Mark 5:21–43) from the perspective of the child.

Van Halen

See **Extreme.**

Jeni Varnadeau

1996—*Colors of Truth*; 1998—*No Hesitation* (Pamplin); 2000—*Tracing His Hand.*

www.jenivarnadeau.com

Jeni Varnadeau is a Christian rock singer with a powerful voice that lends itself to a number of pop styles. Born in Albuquerque, New Mexico, she moved to Nashville in 1992 to attend Belmont College. Varnadeau began recording just a couple of years after **Rebecca St. James** and has a style similar to that artist's. Varnadeau's debut is filled with edgy pop songs that showcase her vocal abilities while copping the sounds of a number of general market performers (e.g., "For My Love" sounds like Alanis Morissette) and sampling so many genres as to leave her own style undefined. The two best tracks are the most energetic: "Stronger Than You" and "Why Would You Go Back?" The hit title song has a Celtic feel with junior-high lyrics: "Purple was the sky draped like a robe on a king / Brown were the thorns that proved love evergreen / Red was the blood shed for me, spilled for you / These are the colors of truth." *No Hesitation* offers several rockers in the same vein as the first album's standouts. The opener, "Mercy," is a crisp, power-pop anthem. "I Need You" (written with Jimmie Lee Sloas of **Dogs of Peace**) is propelled by a Hendrix-styled guitar and a vocal that growls on the verses and screams on the chorus. The album was produced by **John** and Dino **Elefante,** who provide the artist with capable songwriters and a stellar band of session players. "Free to Be Free" and "If I Believed" are especially strong lyrically. The former expresses the biblical thought of Galatians 5:1, 13. The latter (while admittedly an adult contemporary ballad) was written with Mark Gersmehl (of **White Heart**) and expresses well the thought underlying the album's title: "If I believed with holy passion / I'd throw hesitation to the wind / If I would love you with abandon / My trust in you would never end." *Tracing His Hand* pretty much abandons guitar-driven rock for slick pop songs, which Varnadeau nevertheless performs with style and verve. The opening track, "Right Here," is an especially radio-friendly bit of ear candy. "It's All Good" and "Captured" belong solidly to an aural repertoire associated with Mariah Carey. "Remind Me" and the almost-title track "Tracing Your Hand" are adult contemporary ballads. "Takin' in the Air" closes the album on a retro disco note. The album's best song, "Adventure with You," is a fairly upbeat pop tribute to marriages that manage to stay together.

Christian radio hits: "Colors of Truth" (# 19 in 1997); "Stronger Than You" (# 8 in 1997); "Mercy" (# 9 in 1999).

Vector

Jimmy Abegg, gtr., voc.; Steve Griffith, voc., bass; Charlie Peacock, kybrd., voc. (– 1985); Aaron Smith, drums (– 1985) // Bruce Spencer, drums (+ 1985, – 1989). 1983—*Mannequin Virtue* (Exit); 1985—*Please Stand By*; 1989—*Simple Experience* (GaGa); 1995—*Temptation* (Liquid Disc); *Time Flies*.

A progressive rock combo from Sacramento, California, Vector would eventually receive near-mythic status in the annals of Christian rock as the band's meager discography came to be more appreciated with age. Indeed, Vector became one of the first Christian groups to be accorded the box-set treatment. The *Time Flies* collection issued in 1995 puts their three classic records on two compact discs, along with a handful of alternative mixes and outtakes. In the liner notes to that collection, Christian music's premier critic, Brian Quincy Newcomb, compared the group's impact on him a decade earlier to that of **U2** and **The Alarm.** That impact, he decides, was due to more than just the lyrics, which were uplifting and exhilarating: "it was the meaning communicated not merely in the words, but suggested in the very sounds themselves."

Vector began as one of the handful of artists associated with Warehouse Fellowship and Exit records, an innovative adventure in ministry and marketing whose tale is recounted more fully in this book's entry on the **Seventy Sevens.** In addition to Vector and the **Seventy Sevens,** the Exit roster included **Brent Bourgeois** and **Steve Scott.** Like some sort of Christian Yardbirds, Vector boasted the lineup of an ex post facto supergroup. **Charlie Peacock** would release a masterpiece solo album *(Lie Down in the Grass)* a year after his work on Vector's debut and would go on to become one of Christian music's most influential performers and producers. Chuck Wild, who replaced Peacock on Vector's second album and also produced it (without ever being formally added to the band roster), was a member of Missing Persons. Both Aaron Smith and Bruce Spencer would end up drumming for the **Seventy Sevens;** Smith had been a member of Romeo Void before joining Vector and would later join **A Ragamuffin Band.** But Vector's core was always the duo of **Jimmy Abegg** and Steve Griffith, two underappreciated stars who never made it huge but whose fingerprints are all over the history of contemporary Christian rock. Abegg has released a pair of highly acclaimed solo albums and has played with numerous outfits, including **Rex Carroll**'s band, the **Charlie Peacock** trio, and **A Ragamuffin Band.** Griffith has also played with a wide assortment of artists but he would become best known for his

work as a producer. He has helmed significant projects for big name artists like **The Altar Boys** and **Bride** while also working with such underdogs as **Crowd of Faces, Curious Fools, Kid Promise, Neale and Webb, Nina,** and **Seraiah.**

Mannequin Virtue displays the same emotional/intelligent sound that was evident in the work of such '80s acts as INXS and The Cure. In the general market the album might have been received as just one among many competent projects, but in the little pond of '80s Christian rock, it was almost without peer. *CCM* dubbed it "the debut of the decade." *Mannequin Virtue* displays a consistent, professional quality on a par with what was being produced in the general market without sounding the least bit derivative. It was an album every bit as good as contemporary offerings by The Fixx, **The Call,** INXS, or The Cure, though it comes no closer to sounding like the work of those artists than they come to sounding like each other. With muted spirituality (God is referred to only obliquely, e.g., as "the light that strikes with power and personality"), the record was obviously intended to appeal to a wider audience than the kids who bought albums in Bible bookstores. The opening title track is a powerful synthesizer-driven rocker about those whose virtue is only skin deep. "Substitute" draws on fundamentalist interpretations of apocalyptic literature to paint the unlikely picture of an earthly paradise that will be established on earth before "a second run Caesar makes a whole lot of trouble in the Holy Place." More theologically sound, "Lost without Love" gives voice to the children of Adam and Eve who have been exiled from the garden and must bear "the mark of Cain." *Mannequin Virtue*'s strongest cuts may be two songs that work together to express the gospel's simultaneous power to repel and attract: "Running from the Light" and "The Hunger and the Thirst." The first of these has lead vocals by Peacock and showcases what would later become a trademark sound for that artist. The latter is an Abegg song that uses a variety of poetic analogies to describe a constant spiritual yearning that unites "the needy and the needed." Griffith's finest contribution to the project is "Desperately," a musically adventurous ode to "lovers and strangers" (i.e., homeless beggars and prostitutes) that sets churning guitar riffs against quirky new-wave synthesizers. As the song nears conclusion, Abegg's guitar goes out of tune and then the tape runs out abruptly—happy accidents that capture the sort of chaos the song intends to convey. The album also includes "All Around the World," a pop-oriented tribute to global consciousness, and "Only to Fail Again," a pop-oriented plea for listeners to learn from history and not let past social injustices be repeated. The whole thing concludes with "I Love Them All," which is sort of an '80s rewrite of Crosby, Stills, Nash and Young's "Everybody I Love You," with Christian aspiration replacing hippie naivete.

Please Stand By is a stronger album than the first project, almost on a song-by-song basis. The opening track, "Hear What I Say," expresses the frustration the artists sometimes felt when speaking of the superficialities of modern culture to those whose values had been so defined by society that they could not see the hollowness of their own lives. "America" features lyrics by **Steve Scott** that issue a call for the country to return to the essential principles of its founding. "Surrender" is a particularly melodic song that Griffith wrote to offer his one word of advice to the anonymous persons he would see on the subway, persons whose pained expressions seemed to betray resistance, a reluctance to do or say what they intrinsically knew was necessary; the song would be a major hit for **Sheila Walsh** when she covered it in 1989. "Dance" makes the same point in a more upbeat fashion, inviting people to let go of their reliance on lesser things and experience true joy: "Dance in the light around you / Hope in the world to come." By contrast, "Running to the Memory of You" is addressed to believers, suggesting that a singular focus on what theologians call "the Christ event" can provide secure historical grounding for contemporary faith. "Fallen Star" (about trusting in the wrong things) is a quirky new-wave tune with spoken word vocals set against a backdrop of almost falsetto singing. "I Can't Help Falling in Love" is a love song Griffith wrote to express the way that the birth of his daughter Chelsea had inspired an almost incomprehensible devotion within him: "My balance lost / There wasn't time / To even count the cost." *Please Stand By* concludes with the apocalyptic art-rock opus "Scottish Coast," on which Griffith imagines he is looking out over Europe in the aftermath of Armageddon.

If critical acclaim for Vector's first two albums was somewhat hyperbolic in the Christian press, their third and supposedly final project truly deserved the praise that was heaped upon it. Here at last was a Christian rock album that was not only exceptional within the limited subculture, but one that could legitimately be regarded as exceptional even in the big world of mainstream rock. *Simple Experience* is on a par with '80s albums by The Cars or The Police. This is the more amazing, as the album was originally an indie endeavor, self-released on cassette only and often available only through the mail. The band chucked some of their overworked synthesizers for a more guitar-dominated project that is less new-wavey and more rock and roll. It opens with a burst of enthusiasm via the energetic "I Want to Know," which almost seems to start midsong. Most Christian music fans assumed the lyric ("I want to know-oh-oh-oh / Why you love me so") was addressed to God, but Griffith actually wrote it to his wife. "Fine Line" deals with temptation, and "Where Are You Now?" addresses one who gave in and, in Griffith's words, "gave up everything that had any value or importance because of one moment of passion." The song succeeds emotionally because it

begins with a picture of the innocents who suffered as a result of this transgression and then moves to address the transgressor directly: "Now that the smoke has cleared the air / Can you see your future? / Does it look as bright as you dreamed? / Does it taste as sweet? / Are you free at last? / Can you forget the past?" "Be Undone" is a lyrically powerful song that deals with the distance modern media establishes between global spectators and the horrific events they regularly view on the evening news: "A man is asked to give more than a man should give / Thrown in jail brutally murdered for the color of his skin / And we sit at home and wonder what's that got to do with me / And where in hell is South Africa anyway." The album's strongest track musically is "I Burn Myself Away," which sets a meditation on 1 Peter 1:7 by the sixteenth-century monk St. John of the Cross to a jam of appropriately scorching guitars. Almost as compelling is "Have Mercy," a driving plea for God's grace in the face of evil. "Sometimes" is an uncharacteristic Vector song—a tender ballad that Griffith says he originally wrote for **Amy Grant** to sing, expressing the insecurities and loneliness experienced by lovers apart.

Vector disappeared after *Simple Experience* proved to be even more of a commercial disappointment than their first two releases, but six years later Abegg and Griffith reunited for one more go. *Temptation* sports fourteen songs, six of which had been released (in weaker versions) on a limited-edition tape in 1993. In general, the duo updates their sound for the '90s with the assistance of **Phil Madeira** on keyboards and Davia Vallesillo of **Dakoda Motor Co.** on supporting vocals. Vallesillo's contributions in particular set the 1995 Vector apart from earlier incarnations, such that *Temptation* hardly seems to have been recorded by the same band. The sound, however, is a far cry from mid '90s grunge or alternative rock. It moves away from progressive rock toward contemporary pop, incorporating some worldbeat influences and elements reminiscent of Peter Gabriel ("My Own Eyes"), Sting ("Temptation"), or Paul Simon ("Let It Slide"). *Temptation* opens with "The Power of Love," which is not a cover of either the Huey Lewis or **T Bone Burnett** song by that name, but a new power-pop tune by Griffith about an experience with the numinous presence of the divine. "Mr. Color Wheel" evokes Beatles psychedelia. The dominant sound on *Temptation,* however, is a plodding soft rock carried by melodic bass lines and subdued hooks that are more often found in the echoes and underpinnings than in upfront riffs. Such a formula is especially effective on "It Comes Down to You" and "All I Need." There is little firepower, however, not even in a song like "Can't Get Enough of You," a tribute to religious passion that practically cries out for some "Burn Myself Away" guitar licks. The specter of Pink Floyd haunts "When It All Stops," a song of building intensity that deals with the acceptance of mortality. The same theme is revisited on a more personal level in the album's closing track, "She Won't Say Goodbye," a soft ballad about an elderly woman (Griffith's grandmother) waiting on death for years following a debilitating stroke. *Temptation* also contains some sterling love songs, the beautiful pop duet (between Griffith and Vallesillo) "Watch Over Me," and Abegg's "10,000 Wishes," written for his wife and children as an expression of empathy at a time of sadness: "Whatever they do to you, they do to me," the artist tells his family before promising, "If I had 10,000 wishes, I think that I would use every one to make you so happy again." Such sentiments fill the album with a sweetness and a melancholy not always felt on previous projects.

For some reason, Vector's two best songs were not included on any of their four albums but were saved for the *Time Flies* collection, where they are each presented in multiple versions. "Who Were You?" is one of the most effective antiabortion songs ever written (cf. **Kendall Payne**'s "It's Not the Time" and **The Wayside**'s "I Cry Myself to Sleep"). Instead of relying on inflammatory baby-killer rhetoric that sounds convincing only to the prepersuaded (no one who believes abortion is murder thinks it should be allowed), Griffith humanizes the agonizing consequences that even those who favor a pro-choice position must admit make the option a tragic one. He places himself in the position of a man whose wife had an abortion years ago and records the lingering thoughts of that couple on what might have been their child's sixteenth birthday: "Would you have been someone who changed my life? . . . How would I have felt when you called my name?" The second masterpiece is very different. "Spontaneous Reaction" provides a long but funky tribute to the vibrant connection that can typify a life empowered by the Spirit of God.

Christian radio hits: "I Can't Help Falling in Love with You" (# 3 in 1986); "Dance" (# 10 in 1986); "Where Are You Now?" (# 10 in 1990).

Ta'ta Vega

Selected: 1999—*Now I See* (Qwest).

www.tatavega.com

Ta'ta Vega (b. 1952) is an African American gospel and R&B singer who only came to the attention of the contemporary Christian community at the end of the twentieth century. She did achieve brief notice in 1985 for her powerful vocal on the song "God Is Trying to Tell You Something" from the motion picture *The Color Purple* (an actor lip-syncs the song in the film, but the actual voice is Vega's). Then she vanished from the consciousness of most Christian music fans. Vega also contributed to the soundtracks of *The Lion King, Forrest Gump,* and *Amistad,* but her own life was filled with as much trauma as any Hollywood film. Her troubles started when she was fifteen years old and went on an outing to the beach with her family. Having wandered off to a secluded spot, she was brutally raped, con-

tacted a sexually transmitted disease, and became pregnant. She bore the child but was so angry that her parents would not let her keep it that she ran away to Hollywood where she tried to make money singing on street corners. Accepting a ride from strangers, she was raped again at gunpoint at the age of sixteen and again became pregnant. This time she sought help from a church, which facilitated an abortion. For the next few years, she says, she became promiscuous and had several more abortions before her twentieth birthday. After a period of living on the streets and doing drugs, she was helped by a Christian musician friend to come to a relationship with Christ. She got her life together for a little while and signed a contract with Motown, for whom she would record several albums, singing also on records by Babyface, Chaka Khan, and Stevie Wonder. After nine years with that company, she says she was told she was "too old and too fat" and was released from her contract. She then met **Andraé Crouch,** who had a strong impact on her life spiritually and professionally—it was Crouch who supervised the soundtracks for *The Color Purple* and *The Lion King;* he also got her spots singing on his own albums and on works by Michael Jackson and Madonna. Around this time, however, she ended up in another bad relationship with a man whom she would marry. He turned out to be a drug dealer, and Vega became a serious cocaine addict, a fact that she sought to hide from Crouch and other Christian friends as she continued to work in gospel music. Eventually, her husband went to prison, she got a divorce, and set about raising a daughter as a single mother.

In 1999, Vega would finally emerge on the other side of a long and troubled life with a testimony of healing and recovery. She told her story to a number of Christian magazines *(Christianity Today, Today's Christian Woman)* and celebrated her new life with an album called *Now I See.* The project was produced by Quincy Jones and features Vega singing in a style that recalls both Patti LaBelle and **Aretha Franklin.** Highlights of the album include the uplifting "Brand New Dance," a joyous romp that seems free of this world's cares and sorrows. "Are You Ready?" and "I Got Shoes" anticipate the glories of heaven. Vega touches on traditional gospel by singing Thomas Whitfield's "Walk with Me" and on contemporary sounds with **Andraé Crouch**'s "Oh, It Is Jesus." She also covers **DeGarmo and Key**'s "I'm Accepted" as an honest expression of her own struggle to affirm self-worth. "What a messed up life I've lived," she said in 2000. "But God's been so good to me. He's the God of second and third and fourth chances."

Christian radio hits: "In Your Light" (# 14 in 1988).

Veil (and Veil of Ashes)

Sean Doty, voc., gtr.; Sterling, bass, voc.; Lance Harris, gtr. (– 1992); Phil Meads, drums (– 1992) // Mike Jackson, drums (+ 1992); Rich Medina, kybrd. (+ 1992); Brendan Merithew, gtr., voc. (+ 1992). By Veil of Ashes:

1987—*Negro* (Reality); 1989—*Pain* (Graceland); 1992—*The Young and Reckless: The Regression of Veil of Ashes* (Blonde Vinyl). By Veil: 1992—*Mr. Sunshine* (Eden).

Veil of Ashes was an alternative Christian band from Oakland, California, that was a favorite in the Bay Area but never found a national audience. Hipness credentials were incredibly high: Gene Eugene of **Adam Again** produced *Pain,* they opened for bands like **The Choir** and the **Seventy Sevens,** and they covered the Rolling Stones' "Play with Fire" in concert. Still, the group only obtained brief notice, and a second incarnation called simply Veil did not fare much better commercially. The group built a cult following sufficient to justify a compilation album on **Michael Knott**'s doomed Blonde Vinyl label. Musically, the band has a sound that sometimes recalls The Doors, though critics would also notice touches of more obscure bands like The Cult and Gene Loves Jezebel.

The *Negro* album was a cassette-only demo, but it came to be in demand among fans. The title is not a reference to a racial classification but a literal rendering of the Spanish word for black. Songs deal with the darkness of life as revealed through the light of faith. The advisability of using the word "negro" with negative connotation is of course questionable. In any case, *Pain* would establish Veil of Ashes as a socially conscious Christian band that was at least sensitive to harsh issues of political injustice even if they weren't tuned into the niceties of political correctness. The album opens with an inspired cover of **Bob Dylan**'s "The Times They Are a-Changin'," and proceeds with songs that address cultural and moral issues, including racism, depression, lust, and suicide. On *Mr. Sunshine,* the new band lightens up a bit, but only a little. "The Hunger" is a melodrama about heroin addiction, but "Queen for a Day" is a humorous, envious ode to the British rock group ("Oh, to be Queen for a day!") that also functions as a memoir to the late Freddy Mercury. "Good Times" appears to be a party song about free-flowing booze and one-night stands, but it is probably intended as a sarcastic put-down of such a lifestyle. Several songs take a litany approach to lyrics. "Marilyn's Right to Twinkle" lists celebrities who died unglamorously in a manner reminiscent of The Jim Carroll Band's "People Who Died." The song "Pimps and Preachers" lists divergent pairs who exemplify stereotypical "winners and losers" to emphasize that none are preferred in God's economy of grace (cf. the **Lost Dogs**' later "Breathe Deep [the Breath of God]"). And "20 Loves (One with Promise)" lists several empty and deceitful expressions of love before concluding with a description of the love displayed on Calvary. Veil also delivers a new version of the Beatles' "Norwegian Wood."

Jaci Velasquez

1996—*Heavenly Place* (Myrrh); 1998—*Jaci Velasquez*; 1999—*Llegar a Ti* (Sony); 2000—*Crystal Clear* (Word); 2001—*Mi Corazon* (Sony).

www.planetjaci.com

Jaci Velasquez (b. 1979) began singing with her parents' Christian music ministry at the age of nine and at sixteen recorded a groundbreaking debut album that established her as one of the most significant adult contemporary Christian artists of the late '90s. Her father, David Velasquez, was a member of The Four Galileans, a southern gospel group that was popular in the '70s. They disbanded before Jaci was born, but some years later he felt called back into the ministry and began touring churches in the southwest with his wife and youngest daughter (Jaci has four older siblings who had already moved on). From fourth grade on, she was home-schooled on the road by her mother. At first she would sing one song at the family concerts (a country tune called "The Master of the Wind"), but by the age of thirteen, she was doing full concerts of her own. Usually, her parents would lead the adults in worship, while the barely teenaged Jaci would sing for the youth and children. In 1992, she sang at the White House. At the age of fourteen, she sang at the First Baptist Church in Houston, Texas, where the booking agent for **Point of Grace** was in attendance. Connections were made and she was offered a recording contract. As a teen star, Velasquez has been tapped as a primary national spokesperson for the True Love Waits campaign, which encourages chastity until marriage. "I have my own ring as a sign of that," she says, referring to a "purity ring" that some Christians wear as a commitment to premarital virginity. "Keeping yourself pure until marriage is a huge thing for me, and I've made that promise." Velasquez keeps a strong focus on ministry in her career. At eighteen, she told *CCM,* "I want to bring hope. No matter what kind of life you lead, no matter where you come from or where you're going, hope is there, waiting for you." In addition to her recordings, Velasquez has often been tapped as a writer for youth-oriented devotional materials. She coauthored a devotional book, *A Heavenly Place: Words of Inspiration to Bring a Little Bit of Peace and Paradise into your Life* (Fireside, 1998) with Thom Granger. She has also served as a columnist and frequent contributor to *Campus Life* magazine.

Velasquez' first album, *A Heavenly Place,* would eventually go gold, selling over half-a-million copies, an impressive showing even for a debut in the general market and an almost unknown phenomenon within the more limited Christian arena. The success was calculated. Having been impressed by Velasquez at a 1995 Gospel Music Association's artist showcase, the teenager was assigned to a top-drawer producer (Mark Heimermann, the man responsible for **Michael W. Smith**'s *Change Your World* and **DC Talk**'s *Free at Last*), and a cast of fine songwriters were assembled to write material for her. **Chris Eaton, Bob Farrell,** Dann Huff (of **White Heart** and **Giant**), **Wayne Kirkpatrick, Nicole Mullen,** and others contributed songs. Thus, the album is a completely industry-driven project without the slightest shadings of authenticity or spirituality that appeals to the alternative crowd. It is, nevertheless, a proficient offering of adult contemporary pop, equivalent in style and in quality to general market products by such singers as Mariah Carey or Gloria Estefan. The effective title track, "Un Lugar Celestial," is sung partly in Spanish and speaks of proleptic experiences of divine paradise that touch on lives in the present. Another ballad, "On My Knees," is a simple tribute to the power and comfort of prayer. "Shelter" is sung as a duet with **Chris Rodriguez.** Velasquez demonstrates a vocal maturity far beyond her years, though at times she seems to be singing (albeit convincingly) about matters that must lie beyond her ken. The depth of emotion invested in Eaton's "Flower in the Rain" seems almost ironic coming from an adolescent: "Here I am again / Willing to be opened up and broken . . . To die and then be raised / To reach beyond the pain." The one personal touch on the album is "I Promise," an ode to virginity cowritten by Velasquez. It is perhaps the only song on the record addressed to her own age group.

The second album, unfortunately, would be a near duplicate of the first, with more big-name songwriters providing more adult not-very-contemporary songs for the now eighteen-year-old to perform. Even *Release* magazine, which had led Jaci mania on the first album, woke up to what was going on: "The powers-that-be asked Jaci to try on all sorts of different costumes, and they're holding their breath until they see which one the general public likes best. Variously, she tries to be Celine Dion, **Twila Paris,** and **Rebecca St. James,** with various levels of discomfort." Still, that magazine's dismissal of the sophomore album as "dull" is unfair. It is anything but dull; it's just ingenuine, like the first (which *Release* loved). Velasquez is less an artist than an instrument being played by Heimermann and company. But she is a Stradivarius-quality instrument and the powers-that-be play her well. Fans of adult contemporary music, almost by definition, prize predictability over innovation and technical competence over authenticity. With that in mind, *Jaci Velasquez* could be received as one of the best adult contemporary albums of the year. "God So Loved" by **Chris Eaton** provides an anthemic opening track, based on the familiar words of John 3:16; the track is reprised as the album closes in a Spanish version translated by David Velasquez. "You," by **Michelle Tumes,** is a smiley, childlike worship song. "Show You Love" by Heimermann is sassy, with a touch of Latin spice. "Child of Mine" is the token rock song with Velasquez' edgy vocals being accompanied by wailing electric guitars. "Made My World" touches, if only for a moment, on the teen style of singers like Christina Aguilera or Jennifer Lopez. *CCM* would offer a kinder analysis of this "different costume" approach than that suggested above:

Velasquez emerges as a song interpreter, able to use "rich, varied, and reflective approaches" to the diversity of material she is given.

Then, Velasquez took a risk. In 1999, she released a Spanish language album, *Llegar a Ti,* on a general market label. Cynics dismissed this as an attempt to cash in on the current Latin pop craze that had brought a number of artists to the top of the charts. Velasquez would admit in interviews that, though she is ethnically one-half Hispanic, her family has lived in America for three generations and she does not have deep roots in the Hispanic community. The album includes six Spanish versions of songs from her two previous albums along with five new tracks that are less overtly spiritual. Still, Velasquez was adamant about being recognized as "a Christian singer" within the mainstream Latin market. "I'm not willing to compromise who I am," she said. "First of all, before anything else, I'm a Christian and then, after that, everything else follows." She devoted a year of her life to doing interviews on Spanish language stations throughout the southwest and in Puerto Rico, the Dominican Republic, and Mexico, with frequent discussion of her faith. "I want to reach people with a message," she would explain. "Especially the teenage girls, who need to hear, 'It's okay to be a virgin till you get married.' They need to know it's okay to dress modestly. They will still be pretty, they will still be talented. But that's not what they're being told by most Latin artists." The title track to *Llegar a Ti* would become the first song by a self-described Christian artist ever to reach Number One on *Billboard*'s "Hot Latin Tracks" chart. The album would be followed by yet another Latin release, *Mi Corazon,* in 2001, which would also produce a Number One Latin single in "Como Se Cura Una Herida."

All ears were attuned to discover what *Crystal Clear* would bring—the first album by the artist as an official twenty-something adult. Heimermann returned as producer, and the exact same all-star approach to song selection was pursued according to what seemed like a no-risk formula for success. By now, however, even *Campus Life* readers had figured out that Velasquez was singing for their parents, not them. Shed of expectations that her music should be youth-oriented, the album was finally evaluated as the others should have been— as a carefully orchestrated, blatantly commercial presentation of inspirational songs performed in the styles of leading adult contemporary divas. A strong Latin influence shows up on two bouncy, Estefanesque tracks: the opener "Eschuchame (Listen to Me)," cowritten by Velasquez with Heimermann, and "You Don't Miss a Thing." Tijuana horns infuse both tracks with a special flair. The ballad "Come As You Are" is sung as a duet with the famous Latin crooner Luis Fonzi. Lyrically, several of the songs reflect an inspirational piety: "He's My Savior" is an appreciative and worshipful declaration; "Center of Your Love" specifies life's goal as being "to be in the center of God's love, able to live and breathe and know Him every day and every second of my life"; the title track paints a portrait of falling in love with Jesus; "Adore" is a straightforward worship song offering child-like praise to the Heavenly Father. The project closes with a Celine Dion-like anthem, "Just a Prayer Away," in which Velasquez' passionate vocal is set against a simple piano and acoustic guitar accompaniment. *The Phantom Tollbooth* would sum up the album thus: "While not striking out into new musical territory, *Crystal Clear* is a carefully calculated fan-pleaser destined for commercial success."

For trivia buffs: In 1970, David Velasquez won the Dove Award for "Best New Artist" as a member of The Four Galileans. Twenty-seven years later, his seventeen-year-old daughter Jaci won the same award.

Christian radio hits: "If This World" (# 4 in 1996); "Flower in the Rain" (# 15 in 1996); "Un Lugar Celestial" (# 7 in 1997); "Baptize Me" (# 6 in 1997); "We Can Make a Difference" (# 7 in 1997); "God So Loved" (# 4 in 1998); "Glory" (# 4 in 1998); "One Silent Night . . . God So Loved" (# 24 in 1998); "Speak for Me" (# 11 in 1999); "Show You Love" (# 1 for 3 weeks in 1999); "Center of Your Love" (# 1 for 3 weeks in 2000); "Every Time I Fall" (# 1 for 2 weeks in 2001); "You're Not There" (# 17 in 2001).

Dove Awards: 1997 New Artist of the Year; 1999 Female Vocalist; 2000 Female Vocalist; 2000 Spanish Language Album *(Llegar a Ti)*.

Velocipede

Dann Gunn, voc., gtr.; Mark Waldron, drums (–1994) // Mike Santrick, drums (+ 1994). 1993—*Wheels, and Gears, and Spinning Things* [EP] (custom); 1994—*Sane* (R.E.X.).

Velocipede is a hard pop band that consists mainly of Dann Gunn, an auto mechanic from Tennessee who writes songs, then finds a drummer to play with him on what gets issued as a Velocipede recording. Raised the son of a Southern Baptist minister, Gunn says he was influenced strongly by the '80s music of **The Altar Boys, Daniel Amos,** and **Undercover.** He played in a Christian band for a time in which he says he wrote and sang songs with "clear Christian content." With Velocipede, he says he tries to just write about what he is feeling and thinking and then balance that with what it means to him as a Christian. "Life makes me angry" he admits. "Life is made up of things that are ridiculous, redundant, and useless—like working jobs that seem to be going nowhere. I think we were built for spiritual depth and closeness and it angers me to live in a way that counteracts this." Such a sentiment is clearly expressed in the song "Why Not Now," from *Sane:* "We're always breaking, but never breaking through / I know we were built for better things, and I'll die believing that it's true." Musically, Velocipede has been classed as "hard pop." Gunn plays near metal guitars with a grunge attitude, but keeps everything in a

distinctively melodic groove with pounding catchy rhythms. Most of the songs, in fact, seem to be driven by throbbing bass lines. Comparisons to both Henry Rollins and David Bowie crop up here and there. Lyrically, the songs are literate and intelligent, expressing the various struggles of faith in ways that invite conversation. Gunn has also released independent solo albums, including *Losing Steam* (1997) and a later EP titled *Floating, Spinning (Upside Down).*

Velour 100

Trey Many, gtr., kybrd., bass, drums; Amon Krist, voc. (–1997) // Jeremy Dybash, drums (+ 1997); Matthew Hudson, gtr. (+ 1997, –1999); Rose Thomas, voc. (+ 1999). 1996—*Fall Sounds* (Tooth and Nail); 1997—*Songs from the Rainwater* [EP]; *Of Colour Bright;* 1999—*For an Open Sky* [EP] (Distant Sound).

Michigan-based Velour 100 is something of a hybrid band that has altered its style from soft alterna-folk to more intense emo-rock. The group is fronted by Trey Many, who has also served as drummer for the general market band His Name Is Alive; despite its Christian-sounding name, His Name Is Alive is not usually connected with the Christian music scene. Many, however, is openly Christian and discusses his faith freely in public interviews. Velour 100 has received very little attention in the Christian media but is better known within the general market, where the group is regularly identified as "a Christian band." For example, Velour 100 was once featured in an article on Christian rock in the secular publication *Alternative Press,* where the group was discussed alongside **MxPx** as an example of one of Christian music's top acts. Many discussed his spiritual commitments with the reporters for that magazine, emphasizing the importance of regular church attendance and of not letting anything "get in the way of your relationship with God."

The first incarnation of Velour 100 appears to have consisted of Many (who played all instruments) and female vocalist Amon Krist, daughter of the acclaimed folk singer **Jan Krist.** Together they created an album of ethereal modern music that critics compared to the sounds of Mazzy Star or to such groups as **Innocence Mission** and **Over the Rhine.** Two more instrumentalists were added for a subsequent EP, which for the most part re-recorded songs from an older demo tape that had been called *Rainwater.* On both of these projects, Velour 100's songs were regarded as imaginative and poetic, but were described in Christian music magazines as more "spiritually reflective" than openly evangelical. Many clarified that he did not understand Velour 100 as "a vehicle to promote Christianity." He said, "I write about things in my life that I am familiar with (feelings, conversations, experiences) and I hope that what I believe comes through in what I write, but I don't ask myself, 'What aspect of my walk with Christ can I write about?' I don't force issues."

Krist left the group before they made *Of Colour Bright,* and on that album the band was temporarily without a singer. Many doled the songs out to different guest female vocalists: Karin Oliver (of His Name is Alive), Sydney Rentz (of **Morella's Forest**) and Tess Wiley (of **Sixpence None the Richer** and **Phantasmic**). The group also added another dimension to its sound, creating what one reviewer would call a Jekyll and Hyde approach: sudden bursts of slashing guitars and techno-industrial chaos that destroyed moments of calm without warning. Comparisons to **Starflyer 59** sometimes seemed appropriate. At the same time, Many would describe the songs on *Of Colour Bright* as his most optimistic. "Clouds" and "Shine," he says, "are more about God's grace and influence in my life rather than being about my personal shortcomings." But he would admit that the Christian content of songs is not always evident: " 'Shine' may sound like a love song, but it's really about wanting to be taught by God how to love him." After *Of Colour Blind,* the group all but disappeared, then issued a custom EP for sale over the Internet. The group responsible for this latter project (called *For an Open Sky*) features yet another female vocalist (Rose Thomas), with Many adding backing vocals to create more depth.

Vengeance Rising (a.k.a. Vengeance)

Roger Martinez, voc.; Larry Farkas, gtr. (−1991); Glen Mancaruso, drums (−1991); Roger Martin, bass (−1991); Doug Thieme, gtr. (−1991) // Jamie Mitchell, gtr. (+ 1992); Johnny Vasquez, drums (+ 1992). As Vengeance: 1988—*Human Sacrifice* (Intense). As Vengeance Rising: 1990—*Once Dead* (Intense); 1991—*Destruction Comes;* 1992—*Released upon the Earth;* 1993—*Anthology.*

Christian grindcore band Vengeance Rising made some groundbreaking albums that remain classics of the genre prized by collectors and fans. The group is even better remembered, however, for the somewhat sad tale of its front man's subsequent apostasy and vehement hostility toward the Christian music scene and, indeed, everything associated with the name of Christ. The group began recording under the name Vengeance but changed to the longer moniker after their first album as a result of confusion with another group (from Holland) by that name.

Human Sacrifice is often hailed as the first Christian thrash metal album—though others would assign that honor to **Bloodgood.** Actually, in terms of genre labels, *Human Sacrifice* is more exemplary of what would come to be called "death metal" (or grindcore), but Vengeance was playing that sound before anyone in the Christian music scene knew that the style existed, and they were classed as "thrash metal" for lack of a better term. Their album was, at any rate, the heaviest sound-

ing record ever to appear in Christian music at the time, surpassing anything by **Bloodgood** or anyone else in frantic aural terror. *CCM* began their review, "This is the most radical Christian album ever released. If **Larry Norman** started Christian rock and **Stryper** revolutionized it, Vengeance has flipped it upside down." Martinez growls the vocals "like a wolfman from a horror movie." The album cover itself displayed a rather shocking, graphic depiction of Christ's nail-pierced hand, and the same fascination with violence informed the band's lyrical presentations of fundamentalist theology ("Beheaded," "Fill This Place with Blood"). "I Love Hating Evil" is a bit scary in its enthusiasm. "White Throne," which would become a Christian metal classic, is a gleeful, fire and brimstone account of the final judgment when those who deserve torment get what is coming to them: "Nowhere to run / Nowhere to hide / Now's the time to die!" The anthem "Burn" is addressed to the devil with the repeated refrain, "Burn, Satan, Burn!" The track called "Fill This Place with Blood" offers an orthodox if pedantic understanding of substitutionary atonement: "You will either stand before God, bearing all your sins / And pay the penalty, or let Christ stand there for you / As he did at Calvary, to give you a gift / Justification, the gift of righteousness." Not much changed on *Once Dead,* which features a song celebrating "Herod's Violent Death" (Acts 12:20–23), and other tracks titled "Cut into Pieces," "Frontal Lobotomy," and "The Wrath to Come." One of the least offensive songs is probably the only nonreligious one, a cover of Deep Purple's "Space Truckin'." But, then, "Can't Get Out" is a fairly straightforward antidrug rant.

Vengeance Rising broke up after the two aforementioned albums, with everyone but Martinez leaving to form the group **Die Happy.** A third, sludgy mistake-of-an-album called *Destruction Comes* lost Martinez the temporary respect of fans and critics, but then in 1992 he recovered to produce *Released upon the Earth* with a new crew. That final album is, if anything, darker than ever, opening with a throbbing opus called "Help Me" and featuring a gothic anthem called "Human Dark Potential." The first of these songs is an account of a lost soul crying out to Christians for assistance. The title track also urges believers to be actively involved in evangelism, and even "Human Dark Potential" suggests that Jeffrey Dahmer's serial killings might have been prevented if only someone had witnessed to the troubled boy while he was working in that candy factory. In short, the album generally displays a maturity that moves beyond describing the fate of the damned toward motivational pieces for the saved. A song titled "Damnation of Judas and Salvation of the Thief" does not contrast damnation and salvation so much as empty religiosity (symbolized by Judas) and passionate seeking (represented by the thief on the cross); the two attitudes are opposed to each other in a manner similar to that of the Pharisee and the tax collector in one of Jesus' more famous parables (Luke 18:9–14). Shortly after the fourth album was released, George Ochoa (formerly of **Deliverance**) replaced Jamie Mitchell as Vengeance Rising's guitarist for what was to be the band's final tour.

Roger Martinez' formative spiritual background appears to have been in the Foursquare Gospel church, a fundamentalist Pentecostal sect. By the time of the first Vengeance album *(Human Sacrifice)*, he was serving as pastor (or church leader) of a Hollywood congregation associated with the neodenomination Sanctuary. By the time the fourth album came out, he had left Sanctuary to concentrate on the band full time and was a member of Calvary Chapel in Glendale, California. Even at that time, however, he still considered himself to be heavily involved in ministry, telling *HM,* "I have students worldwide who I keep in touch with through my teaching tapes." It struck many Christians as odd, therefore, when letters from Martinez began circulating in which he railed about how he had been treated by his record company and by various Christians throughout the Vengeance Rising years. One of these (nicknamed "the f-word letter") made abundant use of profanity. Then in 1997, Martinez gave an interview to *HM* magazine in which he explained that he was now a committed atheist. His reasons for rejecting the faith and adopting that philosophy seemed to be well thought out (not just some emotional reaction), but he also offered extensive rants against what he called "Christianity" that in fact protested a phenomenon that bears little resemblance to global, historic, or biblical understandings of the faith. Rather, the "Christianity" that Martinez renounced and attacked was a fairly narrow caricature of the faith that might represent the teaching of a few fundamentalist Pentecostal groups but that would be rejected by most Christian denominations. The key point involved claims to supernatural healings that he had discovered to be fraudulent; a second was the "bigoted" teaching that Christians are to avoid contact with unbelievers and with "the world." In any case, Martinez announced that he was preparing to issue a new Vengeance Rising album, tentatively titled *Realms of Blasphemy.* He said the musical style would again be "grind/death/black metal" but that the message would now be a promotion of atheism in hopes of reaching "the people who were actually deceived into believing the nonsense that I propagated before." He also indicated that he was preparing a counter tape to correspond to every teaching tape he had issued as a Sanctuary pastor.

Veni Domine

Fredrik Ohlsson, voc.; Magnus Thorman, bass; Tomas Weinesjo, drums; Torbjorn Weinesjo, gtr. 1992—*Fall Babylon Fall* (R.E.X.); 1994—*Material Sanctuary* (Massacre); 1998—*Spiritual Wasteland.*

Veni Domine is an operatic power metal band from Sollentuna, Sweden. The group formed in 1987 as Glorify, changed its name to Seventh Seal, then became Veni Domine when they discovered an American group already went by the name Seventh Seal. The group's sound has been described by *HM* as "a hybrid of Queensryche and Black Sabbath." The group's debut album features apocalyptic songs with most of the lyrics being drawn directly from Scripture. *Material Sanctuary* branches out to include "The Mass," a haunting worship song (with a choir), and "The Meeting," about an old man surveying his life as he prepares to meet God. Judgment themes also pervade "Beyond the Doom" and "Behold the Signs," which continues the first album's fascination with the end times. The title track expresses the futility of accumulating material possessions.

V*enna

Lucy Britten, voc.; Sharnessa Shelton, voc. 2000—*Where I Wanna Be* (Essential).

www.v-enna.com

V*enna came on the twenty-first-century scene as one more teenybopper vocal group put together by evangelicals who had noticed the overwhelming popularity of artists like Britney Spears and Jessica Simpson and realized the potential for using the style as a forum for celebrating something besides shopping sprees and hormone surges. In this case, the evangelical in question was Marc Pennells of **World Wide Message Tribe,** who brought the British Lucy Britten and the American Sharnessa Shelton together to form a sort of international, truncated version of the Spice Girls. The duo's sound actually owes a good bit to such Scandinavian popsters as Ace of Base and ABBA. Preteens probably don't think the group sounds anything like **ShineMK,** but anyone who is not a fan may have trouble distinguishing the two (cf. also **Aurora, Whisper Loud, Zoe Girl**). V*enna has targeted primary school children as the main focus of their ministry, stating, "We want to reach kids for Christ and challenge them to grow in their faith instead of following the crowd." A strong point in the group's favor is that Britten and Shelton are young adult women, beyond adolescence, and as such are not presented to the kids as bubbly girls who speak and act in ways that are just oh-so-cute. And though both women are undeniably attractive, their physical appearance is not exploited in superficial ways that would distract from or contradict the seriousness of their message (cf. **Trin-i-tee 5:7**). The title song from their debut, *Where I Wanna Be,* has the distinctive sound of an *NSYNC hit, with harmony vocals proclaiming a WWJD message addressed to Christ in the second person, "I wanna live the way you live . . . I wanna see the way you see." V*enna also delivers a number of ballads, including "All the Way to Heaven," which was a radio hit in the United Kingdom. "Make That Noize" has '70s disco flair, and the grand finale "Don't Get Left Behind" sounds very much like the Spice Girls' "Goodbye."

Christian radio hits: "All the Way to Heaven" (# 6 in 2000); "Where I Wanna Be" (# 6 in 2000); "Do You Wanna Know?" (# 15 in 2001).

Vessel

Michael Fealko, gtr., voc.; Joshua King, drums; Andrew Labedz, voc.; Steven Roberts, bass. 2000—*Vessel* (Burning Records).

Vessel is a metal hardcore band from Youngstown, Ohio, signed to an independent label out of Philadelphia. Musically, the group goes in for a rap-to-chaos sound, with vocals in the tortured screaming tradition of **Blindside** or **Selfmindead.** Lyrically, they exhibit a penchant for violent images and recycled gangsta rap clichés. In the opening track, Andrew Labedz screams, "I'll hitcha with some 12 gauge of Holy Spirit between your eyes. Boom."

Vigilantes of Love

Bill Mallonee, gtr., voc.; Mark Hall, acc. (−1992) // Travis McNabb, drums (+ 1992, −1995); Billy Holmes, mand.; bass (+ 1992, − 1994, + 1995, −1996); Newton Carter, gtr. (+ 1994, −1995); David LaBruyere, bass (+ 1994, − 1995); Matt Donaldson, drums (+ 1995, − 1996); Chris Donohue, bass, gtr., kybrd. (+ 1995, −1996); John Keane, gtr., perc. (+ 1995, −1996); Chris Bland, bass (+ 1996, −1998); Tom Crea, drums (+ 1996, − 1998); Scott Klopftenstein, drums (+ 1998, − 2000); Jacob Bradley, bass (+ 1998); Kenny Hutson, gtr., mand., dobro, pedal steel (+ 1998, −2000); Kevin Heuer, drums (+ 2000). 1990—*Jugular* (independent); 1991—*Driving the Nails* (Core); 1992—*Killing Floor* (Fingerprint); 1994—*Welcome to Struggleville* (Capricorn); 1995—*Blister Soul*; 1996—*VOL* (Warner Resound); 1997—*Slow Dark Train* (Capricorn); 1998—*To the Roof of the Sky* (Meat Market); *Live at the Forty Watt* (Pastemusic); 1999—'*Cross the Big Pond* [a.k.a. *Free for Good*] (independent); 2000—*Audible Sigh* (True Tunes); 2001—*Electomeo* [EP] (custom); *Summershine*.

www.billandvol.com

The prolific general market band Vigilantes of Love hails from Athens, Georgia. They are fronted by singer/songwriter/guitarist Bill Mallonee, an outspoken and devout Christian whose worldly piety seems to be cut from the same cloth as that of **T Bone Burnett, Bruce Cockburn,** and **Mark Heard.** As with those artists, his primary musical muse seems to be *John Wesley Harding*-era **Bob Dylan.** The Vigilantes of Love are often described as "thinking person's roots rock." They have a distinctive sound, but have been compared to such groups as The Band or Tom Petty and the Heartbreakers on the one hand and to Wilco or Uncle Tupelo on the other. Songwriting is a strong suit, with the material often rising to the same standards of quality set by Heard or even Dylan himself (i.e., light years ahead of the norm for what is called contemporary Christian music). Mallonee also prizes a raw sound that prioritizes

authenticity over precision: "I'm a big Neil Young fan," he once told *7ball*. "I like that teach-the-band-a-song-and-record-it-five-minutes-later approach." A clear critical favorite, Vigilantes of Love has never enjoyed widespread commercial success, though their music is accessible and their songs often display a hook-laden, radio-friendly sound. Mallonee's refusal to conform to expectations of the contemporary Christian music market easily account for the lack of reception within that scene. The underdog status within the general market is less explicable. They have received some attention on college radio (especially around the time of *Welcome to Struggleville* and *Blister Soul*), but remain unknown to most of the consumers who would probably appreciate their work. It seems odd that more critics within the mainstream market have not promoted the band over the years, as they have Burnett, Cockburn, **Van Morrison, Sam Phillips,** and other spiritually charged artists.

With regard to personnel, the list above suggests that the Vigilantes of Love is not really a band but an elaborate solo outfit. With personnel shifts on every project, a case might be made that the albums are really the works of Mallonee, who just hit upon a cool name for the varying cast of backing musicians that he assembles anew for every venture or tour. That would be a bit of an exaggeration, though, and Mallonee himself likes to speak of the constantly changing group as a band. He insists both graciously and persistently that his so-called "backing musicians" be granted full "band member" status. He is also quick to indicate that the frequent departures of members have rarely been the result of conflict, but owe more to the lack of commercial success that renders continued full-time involvement an economic hardship for most. He says he derived the group's cool name from a line in a New Order song, though the Vigilantes' sound is about as far from that of New Order as can be imagined.

Mallonee grew up in a family where his parents were nominal Christians (his father a Roman Catholic and his mother a Southern Baptist), but he has said that he made his real connection with the faith while in high school. There was no big conversion, but he began reading a copy of the *Good News for Modern Man* New Testament that a friend had given him and, he says, he just came over a period of about three months to a point where "I just knew Christ was who he was and I knew that he had died for me." Mallonee went on to earn a history degree at the University of Georgia, where he was active in InterVarsity and other parachurch organizations. After college, he spent some time teaching emotionally disturbed teenagers. He also became a committed member of a small Presbyterian church in Athens that was led by Dr. Dan Warren, whom Mallonee has often identified as his spiritual mentor. In 1989, he started the first incarnation of Vigilantes of Love.

The Vigilantes' debut album, *Jugular,* is a stripped-down, folk-rock affair that *True Tunes* would say "sounds like it was recorded in a cabin." The most notable song, "Love Cocoon," would later be redone for *Slow Dark Train,* where it would become the focus of controversy. Other tracks from *Jugular* include "Who Knows When the Sunrise Will Be?" which quotes from Martin Luther ("except for one instance, no one can die for another") and "America," a song of disillusionment with modern culture. "Losin' It," offering a simple statement of persistent belief with reference to the example of Job, is sung in a style that closely recalls that of Dylan's early folk songs. In 1993, a remixed edition of *Jugular* (with two new tracks) was released on **Mark Heard**'s Fingerprint Records, which brought the album to a broader, post-*Killing Floor* audience.

The second Vigilantes album, *Driving the Nails,* is a bit of an anomaly (not to mention a collector's item). It was recorded in 1991 for an independent label (Core), which folded. Apparently, the owner of that defunct company disappeared with the master tapes. Some time later, after the band's third album had already been released, copies of the lost sophomore project showed up in a distribution warehouse, where they were discovered by alert representatives from *True Tunes* who bought up all the copies. Mallonee himself knew nothing of the discs' existence and was surprised when *True Tunes* informed him of their find. The project was pretty much ignored anyway and remains unknown to all but the most avid fans. *Driving the Nails* has the same folk sound quality as *Jugular,* albeit with a confessional tone that comes through on songs called "Casualty" and "Shadowlands." Its theme is expressed with special poignancy in its title track: "I've been driving the nails firmly in your tree / You've been talkin' to your Father on behalf of me / Nothin' at these check points I care to defend / So why do I raise the hammer and drive the nails again?" "Odious" offers a peek into the mind of an abortion clinic bomber in a manner similar to (but less sarcastic than) **Steve Taylor**'s "I Blew Up the Clinic Real Good."

Killing Floor was the record that first garnered attention. It was produced by **Mark Heard** and by Peter Buck of R.E.M. and displays a fuller sound than the first two projects. It opens with the line, "Hey, look at me now, I've been impaled on the horns of your sacred cow," which establishes a prevalent theme: a failure and/or reticence to conform to the stereotypical mold of the American and/or Christian status quo. The same song ("Real Down Town") continues with what sounds like a jibe at the contemporary Christian music industry, but was actually inspired by the artist's observation of a more generic conflict between commerce and art within the Athens music scene: "The butcher down the street / He's gonna sell you some meat market music / Cut, dried, and cheap." On "Hip Train" the artist admits that he "ain't no saint, ain't no

prophet / ain't no angel—ask my wife about it." He sings about buying a "crap detector" in "Earth Has No Sorrow That Heaven Can't Heal," which borrows its title from an old hymn. Some of the songs are a bit obscure (the album title comes from the song "Undertow," a bouncy, almost rockabilly romp with quirky lyrics that come close to expressing a Unabomber portrait of life as one big anti-me conspiracy). Others are tender and more explicitly devout. "Andersonville" comes closest to invoking Robbie Robertson, as Mallonee gives voice to a Civil War soldier's letter to his wife. "River of Love" is an acoustic ballad on which Mallonee sings with a Dylanesque twang, "I will shed my skin, when I jump right in, to this river of love." Finally, "I Can't Remember" tells the story of a train wreck that leaves the singer lying in a snowbank next to a dying friend: "I saw Jesus brush away the snowflakes and bestow on you a kiss / He gathered you up in his arms / God, you looked so fine / That white dress you were wearin' darlin' like a million stars did shine."

Welcome to Struggleville represents the band's major label debut, recorded by a solid quartet lineup (Mallonee, Carter, LaBruyere, and McNabb) that, at least for a time, really did seem like "a band." The sound is definitely more developed, picking up elements of groups like R.E.M. or The Black Crowes, with some of the southern blues influence of *Exile*-era Rolling Stones. The album was produced by Sting's producer, Jim Scott, and got the Vigilantes noticed by *Rolling Stone* for a moment. The opening title track leaps out of the gate with shimmering Byrds guitars and an infectious rhythm that marks it, musically, as the group's finest contribution up to that point. Lyrically, the song uses the biblical story of the beheading of John the Baptist as a backdrop for images that convey the modern world's obsessions with evil. "Welcome all you suckers to Struggleville," Mallonee announces, making clear that he has discovered life is no picnic (or, if it is, then it is one where the heads of prophets get served on platters). The album continues to develop this theme with songs of social conscience: "Vet" and "Cold Ground" are story songs that deal respectively with the plight of maladjusted Vietnam veterans and with the stubborn perpetuation of racism in America. Mallonee cheerfully mixes metaphors on "Babylon," juxtaposing that biblical image to describe a world gone wrong with the more contemporary analogy of a shipwreck: "This is no pleasure cruise in the South Pacific / I'm bailing ice water up to my neck / Titanic's captain said God couldn't sink her / You might say he learned a healthy respect." The laments and indictments continue on the laid-back "All Messed Up" and frenetic (again, almost rockabilly) "Runaway Train" (not the Soul Asylum song). But, amidst it all, Mallonee proclaims, "From upper rooms and empty tombs / Love's reigning down on me / So you see I do not need your sympathy." *Struggleville* also includes the uncharacteristically pretty song "Between the Glory and the Dream," inspired by Georgian folk artist The Rev. Howard Finster (who, incidentally contributed a painting for the artwork accompanying **Sixpence None the Richer**'s *This Beautiful Mess*). Singer John Mellencamp reportedly called *Struggleville* his "favorite record."

After the *Struggleville* band disintegrated, Mallonee retreated somewhat from the gritty rock of the project to recapture more of the acoustic soloist feel of the first recordings. *Blister Soul* is generally more folk than rock. The exception to that caveat may be the opening title track which, in *Struggleville* fashion, sounds more like The Byrds' covers of early Dylan than the master's less accessible readings of his own work. Even that song is reprised in a more straightforward Dylan-esque style (and with different verses) to provide the album with a fitting antiphonal conclusion. The first edition of the song seems addressed to those who live as best they can in a damaged world; it speaks obliquely of "the thing that's yours for free / is the thing I need the most / stifles every boast, stifles every boast." Then in the Reprise the artist addresses God directly, marveling at Christ's sacrifice: "Why did you give it all / Poured out on little misers / And the returns are so small." Set between these bookends are "Skin," a quiet ballad reflecting on Vincent Van Gogh's misunderstood devotion and gift, and the country-tinged "Different Slant of Life." Slightly more upbeat (musically, if not lyrically) are "Five Miles outside Monroe," a blues-rock number that again takes on the issue of continuing racism, and "Tempest," a rollicking ditty about internal and relational conflicts. *Visions of Gray* would suggest that the thematic focus that holds the disparate songs together is that of the universal search for redemption, a quest that Mallonee claims, even in these relativistic times, has a definitive solution. On "Bethlehem Steel," he sings, "It's one thing to be dead in your trespasses, and then again, it's quite another to remain in them." *Blister Soul* also includes a new version of "Real Down Town," which would get some airplay on AAA radio.

In 1996, some folks at Warner Brothers noticed the obvious disproportion between the quality of the Vigilantes of Love's work and the band's commercial success and decided that, perhaps, the group should be marketed more toward the burgeoning contemporary Christian music audience. Warner Resound thus issued a compilation of some of the group's more spiritual songs called *VOL*. The latter project was not intended as a greatest hits package per se but as a selection of tunes that seemed most likely to appeal to Christian audiences. In addition to twelve previously released tracks, most of which are mentioned above, *VOL* features four new songs recorded by a trio that Mallonee expected to become a stable lineup (it didn't). Of those new songs, "Double Cure" is particularly remarkable (it is, again, found in both full band and solo acoustic

presentations). Imbued with a sentiment that is both sensible and sincere, it offers a heartfelt testimony to authentic faith: "I want to drink out of that fountain on a hill called Double Cure / I want to show you my allegiance, Lord / I want to be a son of yours." It is, perhaps, the Vigilantes' first true gospel song, a tune directed to the Lord, expressive of a private prayer that the audience almost feels they were never intended to hear. And then, at its conclusion, Mallonee seems to glance over his shoulder at his eavesdroppers and offers this quick postscript: "You ask me why I love him? / He gave riches to the poor / Yes, and I will one day see that Face / Over yonder shore."

VOL did indeed succeed at introducing Mallonee and his Vigilantes to the Christian marketplace—the album was widely reviewed in Christian media, and the band was featured in several Christian music magazines, including a cover story for *7ball*. Their next release, although still on the general market label Capricorn, was set up to be shipped through Warner Resound to all the usual Christian markets as an album by "a Christian band." But there was a problem. The completed record *Slow Dark Train* contained a new, electric version of the song "Love Cocoon" from Vigilantes' *Jugular*. That song celebrates conjugal bliss (i.e., marital sex), which Mallonee contrasts with the vain sexuality in the world all around him: "The whole world keeps on banging, they just come and go / It's just a part of their scenery, a part of their show / But I've got this wedding band, wrapped around my finger. . . ." Conservative Christians might find that a bit blunt, but it would be hard to fault the sentiment. But then the song gets a lot more specific, as Mallonee tries to emulate the Song of Solomon with images of shameless passion: "I wanna attack your flesh with glad abandon / I wanna look for your fruits, I wanna put my hands on 'em / I wanna pump up your thermostat beneath your skin / I wanna uncover your swimming hole and dive right in." This was too much for the contemporary Christian music subculture, which is often credited with embracing a gnostic understanding of human sexuality (and other things). Similar brouhahas had occurred over much milder songs by **Charlie Peacock** and **Ashley Cleveland** that also dealt with sexuality in a forthright way. To be more accurate, however, the Christian music subculture never really got a chance to decide whether the Vigilantes' song was too much for them or not. Rather, certain gatekeepers assumed that fans of Christian music would be unable to appreciate the song. The primary culprit was Family Christian Stores, Warner Resounds' single biggest client, which informed the distributor they would not stock *Slow Dark Train* on account of the song. FCS's senior buyer, Bob Elder (the man who made the decision), told *CCM* rather unconvincingly that the action should not be construed as censorship because it was not based on any objection to the song as such but on an assessment of the problems that stocking the album would likely produce for store managers and sales representatives. Mallonee said much more convincingly, "I think this decision was based on the fear of alienating a segment of people who don't want to talk about sex and who probably are not even thinking biblically about the issue." One does wonder where Family Christian Stores thinks that *families* come from.

In addition to "Love Cocoon," *Slow Dark Train* contains a number of evangelically inspired songs that embrace a wider range of styles than any of the Vigilantes' previous projects. Potential songs had been previewed at concerts, and fans were allowed to vote on which were ultimately included. The album opens with three electric rock tracks. "Locust Years" is loud and fast, enough so to get the band noticed in *HM* magazine (which is generally devoted to hard alternative rock or metal). "This album rocks," editor Doug Van Pelt declared to all the readers who he figured "thought they'd never see a Vigilantes review in these pages." The chunky "Tokyo Rose" uses the image of a WWII radio propaganda ploy to address generic betrayals of the truth: "we all need someone to lie to us," Mallonee says, with just a touch of sarcasm. "Black Crow" is a third driving track that teeters on the edge of nihilism in its dark imagery. Mallonee explained in interviews around this time that he had been diagnosed as someone who suffers from periodic bouts of depression, and perhaps that ailment accounts for the overload of negative images in "Black Crow" and some of *Slow Dark Train*'s other songs ("Sitting," "Only a Scratch"). Indeed, it might account for the album's title (apparently a play on Dylan's *Slow Train Coming*), which derives from the album's acoustic closing track ("Judas Skin"): "What is it that I fear? Why is it I don't trust? / When hiding out becomes career, what am I covering up? / On my slow, dark train, how is it that I'm found . . . in my Judas skin, spinning down." But the darkness is not ultimate. The just-mentioned song continues "when I come out of this spin, I see you're still my friend." Likewise, "All the Mercy We Have Found" speaks of God's capacity to meet people in the depths of their despair. Such glimmers and conclusions imbue the project with the strong witness of one whose faith enables him to cope with depression, to live in the world without perhaps always being an overcomer, but at least as one who is not overcome. In 1998, Mallonee would comment on his alleged pessimism in *CCM* saying, "You're going to feel some sense of world weariness, if you're clued in at all. But making a choice for the gospel saves you from bitterness and cynicism."

The commercial failure of *Slow Dark Train* was something of a last straw for the Vigilantes' tenure with Capricorn. Critics had maintained for years that the latter label did nothing to support the band, and it had actually been at the insistence of Capricorn executives (against Mallonee's better judgment and advice) that the song "Love Cocoon" was added to the doomed album, keeping it out of the venues were it might have sold best (they had naively thought the song would be a hit). But wherever the blame may lie, the Vigilantes of Love found themselves out on the street and without a contract. The indie status seemed to agree with them, and Mallonee exulted that now at last he could make the album he had always wanted to make. *To the Roof of the Sky* reveals what *Phantom Tollbooth* would call "a kinder, gentler Vigilantes of Love," with an emphasis on ballads and alt-country stylings. A few electric offerings ("Perishable Things," "Proving Ground") continue in the Wilco tradition, but the addition of multi-instrumentalist Kenny Hutson would allow the band to incorporate more mandolin, dobro, and pedal steel guitar on tracks that hearken back to the group's early (pre-*Struggleville*) days. "Opposite's True" is a bit of a shuffle, and the standout tracks "On the Verge" and "Further up the Road" are built around acoustic guitar. The former is laced with references to one of Mallonee's favorite writers, Flannery O'Connor. In 1998, the Vigilantes also recorded a concert at the 40 Watt Club in Athens, Georgia. *Live at the 40 Watt* includes mostly songs from *Slow Dark Train* and *To the Roof of the Sky,* along with two new numbers. In 1999, the band released another almost-live album, the raw *'Cross the Big Pond,* which they recorded on a whim over a four-day period in England when they happened into some studio time. With eight songs and a running time of around thirty minutes, it is a long EP that offers rough takes on otherwise unavailable material. One of the tracks is a Christmas song called "On to Bethlehem." The whole project has the feel of a lark (not originally intended for public consumption) but it may be the more endearing for that reason. It was also released in the United Kingdom (where the title wouldn't have made much sense) as *Free for All.*

Audible Sigh was coproduced by **Buddy Miller** and features guest vocals both from his wife, **Julie Miller,** and from country superstar Emmylou Harris (in whose band Buddy regularly plays). One highpoint of the record is the ballad "Resplendent," a Dust Bowl historical saga sung with Harris. Equally moody and even more melancholy is the album closer, "Solar System," which invites the listener to "Put all your love where it hurts the most / And expect a little visit from the Holy Ghost." At the other end of the spectrum musically, "She Walks on Roses" is a near frantic folk-blues number about the wrongs people do to each other and the continual struggle for scarred individuals to transcend such past hurts in their current relationships. "They say that pride is the chief of sins," Mallonee sings. "Well, I know all of his deputies." On "Black Cloud over Me," Mallonee acknowledges his morose tendencies with a touch of dark humor and then dispels them on "Could Be a Whole Lot Worse." The sweet "Nothing Like a Train" continues a series of songs the artist has written for his family while on the road: "Here's another song for Brenda / Yeah, another tune for Josh and Joe / Another postcard from the highway / My God, where do these days go?"

CCM's Bruce Brown once said, "It takes a delicate hand to balance social commentary, wry humor, Bible-based faith, and gothic pathos. Mallonee does not use a broadsword where a scalpel will do." Mallonee has always been more adept than most Christian artists at living the noncompartmentalized life, traversing supposedly sacred and secular spheres with equal aplomb.

At the time *Welcome to Struggleville* was recorded, Mallonee freely admitted in interviews that he was "the only believer in the group," but saw no contradiction or problem with that. "I love these guys; they're great friends and great players," he told *CCM.* "I've learned to accept where they're at, and I certainly don't ram my faith in Christ down their throats. I would like for them to come to see their need for Christ, but our first job is to be a good band and play good music." But later on, when the group was a trio of Mallonee, Tim Bland, and Chris Crea, he would say, "The Lord has blessed me with two guys who are Christians," likening their cross-country tour in a cargo van to "a Bible study that rocks in its own wheels."

In 2001, Mallonee made a limited edition of a four-song EP called *Electomeo* available through his website. This was followed by *Summershine,* a similar indie collection of thirteen new songs with the basic Americana sound showing some influence from '60s Brit rock (The Kinks, Paul Revere and the Raiders). That sound especially informs "Stand beside Me" and "Putting Out Fires (with Gasoline)," which borrows its theme from David Bowie. The album opens explosively with "You Know That (Is Nothing New)," a dynamite pop song in the vein of such diverse acts as Dire Straits, Gin Blossoms, and **The Call** that would likely have been one of the year's biggest hits on AAA radio (Adult Album Alternative) if released on a label that is noticed by such stations. "Galaxy" is an odd sort of waltz with a hopeful lilt ("We're both gonna be alright"). Mallonee does his best Tom Petty on the comical "I Could Be Wrong (But I Don't Think I Am)," a song that recalls **Bob Dylan**'s "Feel a Whole Lot Better" (which Petty once covered). In general the album evinces the sunny atmosphere its title seems to promise, albeit with a strong sense of stubbornness, of a conscious decision not to let the weight of the world drag one down: "This stuff you buy in place of the truth / Won't stay strong / Let your worries be gone / Put your dancing shoes on / For your green summer lawn" ("Green Summer Lawn").

Villanelle

See **Smalltown Poets.**

Vincent (a.k.a. **Höglund Band**)

Per Höglund, voc.; Jonas Holmstrom, gtr.; Robert Ivansson, bass; Dan Nylén, drums; Per Nylén, kybrd. As Höglund Band: 1989—*Faces* (Alarma). As Vincent: 1990—*Vincent* (Alarma).

Vincent was a Scandinavian rock band led by Per Höglund, the son of a well-known Swedish evangelist. Per grew up traveling with his father and singing at crusades in a family group. When he formed his band, they were known in the homeland as The Höglund Band to capitalize on the family name, but when they decided to release an album in America, a more pronounceable moniker was chosen. "It doesn't mean anything," Höglund said of the name Vincent, lest someone suspect them of homage to a Dutch artist, "It just sounds good." Musically, the band presents a powerful "white blues" sound reminiscent of Steve Winwood or the Little River Band. *Faces* features upbeat songs that confidently proclaim "Miracles—they still happen!" ("Miracles"). *Vincent* opens with its strongest cut, "Someone Who Never Says Goodbye." The lyrics of that song establish the hope of Christianity as ultimate and transcendent, setting the mood for songs that address both difficulties and joys of life in the present world.

James Vincent

1974—*Culmination* (Columbia); 1976—*Space Traveler* (Caribou); 1978—*Waiting for the Rain;* 1980—*Enter In* (Sparrow).

www.nahenahe.net/jvincent

James Vincent was a general market jazz-fusion artist from Chicago who made two albums reflective of his Christian convictions. Something of a musician's musician, Vincent has commanded great respect within the general market and played with a number of major stars. Early on, he formed a Chicago band called The Exceptions with Peter Cetera, who would later leave to join the Chicago band that was actually *called* Chicago. While Cetera went on to become a superstar of power-pop rock, Vincent played as a session musician with Minnie Ripperton and the Paul Butterfield Blues Band. He then joined the group H.P. Lovecraft and moved to San Francisco. Later, he was a member of Jerry Garcia's band, Hooter Roll, and of a group called Majavishnu Orchestra. He toured as a guitarist with Rufus, Santana, Etta James, Gregg Allman, and others.

In the '70s, Vincent made a few solo albums that have a style similar to that of George Benson (especially to the latter's *Breezin'*). The first two projects, *Culmination* and *Space Traveler,* are purely secular affairs, but while recording *Waiting for the Rain,* Vincent became a Christian. Seeking retreat from the jazz lifestyle and what he called its "chemical trappings," he disappeared from the music scene. Meanwhile, *Waiting for the Rain* started to get radio airplay, especially on San Francisco's prominent KSAN station. A frantic search by his record company found him in Hawaii, working a construction job and taking time out to grow in the faith. Vincent says they insisted that he return and tour to support his album. He continues, "I balked, but realized that part of Christianity is dealing fairly with people." They reached a compromise, according to which he would tour, provided he could share openly about his new life in Christ. He did, turning an interview at a Berkeley radio station into a discussion on the significance of the blood of Christ. Radio support for the album ceased immediately when station programmers realized it was "a Christian record," and Vincent retired unperturbed to enjoy a quiet life with his family in northern California. He was coaxed into making one more album for the Christian label Sparrow, but would describe production of that project *(Enter In)* as exhausting "physically, emotionally, and domestically," and begged off from touring to support that record as well. He did perform some opening sets for **Phil Keaggy** at one point, but for the most part, Vincent's conversion led him to increased withdrawal from the music world and, in retrospect, his two Christian albums were released as part of this exit.

Waiting for the Rain and *Enter In* both evince the '70s style of multitextured arrangements with horns, strings, and backup singers, all as a backdrop for Vincent's acoustic and electric guitars. He creates soundscapes to illustrate aurally the theme of each piece, e.g., religious hypocrisy in "What's Goin' On?" (not the **Marvin Gaye** song). There is a wide diversity of arrangements, from carefully structured compositions to what appear to be free-form improvisations. Lyrically, his songs often draw on Scripture and on themes from the liturgical and hymnic traditions of the church. *Waiting for the Rain* was re-released on Priority in 1982. The exact same song ("How Can I Thank You Enough") was released twice as a single, four years apart, and went to Number Twenty-one on the Christian radio chart both times. *Enter In* features message-oriented songs encouraging respect for Scripture ("Don't Trust Your Feelings") and commitment to Christ ("Take My Life"). "Come Follow Me" is openly evangelistic.

In 1986, Vincent was invited to join the rock band Chicago to replace Peter Cetera, who had gone on to a solo career. Though he did not do so, the invitation did jog his musical interests again, and he made an independent album that he played for Cetera. Reportedly, the latter loved it and tried to get it released on a major label. These efforts proved unsuccessful, and Vincent took the lack of label support as confirmation of his own inclination to leave music alone. In 1989, Vincent was living in Oregon and said, "I know that I am saved and I enjoy spending time with my family that I didn't have before because of music." In 2000, John J. Thompson would report in his book *Raised by Wolves* that Vincent "is still active as a ses-

sion player and has recently released a new instrumental jazz album called *Second Wind.*"

Christian radio hits: "How Can I Thank You Enough" (# 21 in 1978); "How Can I Thank You Enough" (# 21 in 1982).

Tony Vincent

1993—*Love Falling Down* [EP] (independent); 1995—*Tony Vincent* (StarSong); 1997—*One Deed* (StarSong).

http://tonyvincent.com

Tony Vincent (b. Anthony Strascina in 1973) is a Christian synth-pop performer from Albuquerque, New Mexico. His most noticeable quality is an effeminate alto-falsetto voice. Vincent moved to Nashville in 1990 to attend Belmont College. He sent a demo tape of a song he had done called "Love Falling Down" back to a radio station in his hometown, where it went to Number One. This success brought him to the attention of **The Newsboys,** who invited him to open a concert tour, and to the attention of StarSong, who offered him a recording contract.

Prior to his major label releases, Vincent released an independent EP that evinces a much less commercial or poppy sound than that for which he would later be known. *Love Falling Down* has more in common with down-tempo synth groups like Depeche Mode, Spandau Ballet, and The Cure. The song "I Still Believe" is actually a cover of a number from *The Lost Boys* motion picture soundtrack. Big name producers **Brent Bourgeois** and **Charlie Peacock** would take the helm for the official debut album, and reviewers would instantly note that *Tony Vincent* is chock full of potential radio hits. The sound is somewhat similar to **Eric Champion**'s early work, combining jumpy dance tunes with midtempo ballads. "Whole New Spin" has a Todd Rundgren (or, for that matter, **Brent Bourgeois**) feel to it, while "High" seems like a techno version of a Beatles song. "Simple Things" sounds like an annoying advertising jingle, with the trite lyric, "Simple things make me see / Simple things set me free . . . etc." Better numbers include the opening track, "Must Be the Season," and **The Newsboys**-like "Out of My Hands," which testifies to the working of God's grace apart from any human effort. The album also features a rendition of "Holiday," which is not a Bee Gees or Madonna cover, but a song by **Michael Roe** that the latter artist would include with different lyrics on his own *Safe As Milk* album. For his next album, Vincent eschewed the bubblegum and added guitars to the omnipresent keyboards. He also wrote a number of deeper songs with more complex lyrics and performed them in a slightly darker intellectual pop style similar to that of Peter Gabriel or Sting. *One Deed* is a better album than *Tony Vincent* in every way. The best of the best is the closing song, "Closer to Your Dreams." Vincent sets optimistic, hope-filled lyrics to a paradoxically dreary tune in a minor key: "Just beyond this world of sorrow and of pain / Lie the shores of hope where seasons always change / Through the eyes of love, I'll try and help you see / The moment of believing brings you closer to your dreams."

Christian radio hits: "Love Falling Down" (# 25 in 1993); "Simple Things" (# 1 for 4 weeks in 1995); "Out of My Hands" (# 1 for 3 weeks in 1995); "Must Be the Season" (# 6 in 1995); "Whole New Spin" (# 1 for 2 weeks in 1996); "High" (# 3 in 1996); "One Deed" (# 8 in 1996); "Do You Really" (# 8 in 1997); "Can't Have One without the Other" (# 10 in 1997); "Reach Out" (# 6 in 1997).

Violent Femmes

Victor DeLorenzo, perc.; Gordon Gano, gtr., voc.; Brian Ritchie, bass. 1982—*Violent Femmes* (Slash); 1985—*Hallowed Ground*; 1986—*The Blind Leading the Naked*; 1989—*3* (Warner Bros.); 1991—*Why Do Birds Sing?*; 1993—*Add It Up* (Slash); 1994—*New Times* (Elektra); 1995—*Rock* (Mushroom).

www.vfemmes.com

The connections that quirky, alternative rock band Violent Femmes have to contemporary Christian music are even more tenuous than those of a general market band like **U2.** Despite the fact that they sang a couple of songs about Jesus back in the '80s (so did the Doobie Brothers!), the group is probably better known for profane irreverence than for proclamation or even endorsement of the Christian faith. Still, *CCM* would review three of the band's albums in the '80s, and as late as 2000 (long after the band's supposed "Christian period" had passed), *The Rough Guide to Rock* would refer to front man Gordon Gano as "a committed Christian" whose penchant for what they consider to be "an odd righteousness" served to define (negatively, in their view) the group's ongoing spiritual agenda.

Violent Femmes formed in Milwaukee, Wisconsin, in 1981. They established themselves as the primary forebears of a new nerd rock whose music possessed a self-mocking and sarcastic demeanor that would be picked up a decade and a half later by bands like Weezer and Green Day. Their self-titled debut is by all accounts their landmark album, if only because it was so new and fresh. There is nothing even remotely Christian or religious about the record; indeed the boys seem obsessed with the single topic of sexual frustration, singing mostly about how they are too uncool or unlucky to get what they want from girls. The album was one of the first to use explicit language in a way that would definitely require parental advisory stickers a few years later. The big hit "Blister in the Sun" is an ode to masturbation. Still, those familiar with Christian music could not help but notice the unmistakable influence of Christian rock star **Larry Norman** on Gordon Gano's singing and songwriting. As it turned out, the young artist was the son of a Baptist minister—and this revelation did not initially sit well

with Christian music fans. Here, apparently, was a foul-mouthed brat who had grown up listening to the father of Christian rock, practiced Norman's vocal inflections, studied his offbeat sense of humor, and put it all in service of his own apostate musings. In one sense, it was kind of flattering to have the world copping styles (and attitudes) from Christian music for a change. But the really frustrating part was that no one seemed to notice: everyone knew that **DeGarmo and Key** were ripping off Styx and that **Amy Grant** (at that point) was trying to be "a Christian version of Madonna," but when Gano cloned Norman, the ignorant mainstream press applauded his effort as something "never heard before" (aside from the Lou Reed affectations).

Then the second album came out. Titled *Hallowed Ground*, the record features several songs that deal explicitly with Christian themes. Alongside the frightening "Country Death Song" (a look inside the head of a man who murders his daughter), the group sings Sunday school tunes like "It's Gonna Rain" and "Jesus Walking on the Water." The first of these is a wonderfully quirky and energetic account of the Noah story. The latter is a full-fledged gospel song that not only tells the story of Jesus walking on the water, but also reflects on the meaning of the crucifixion and humanity's hope of salvation. Both songs are musical masterpieces and would receive widespread airplay on college radio stations. The title track to *Hallowed Ground* is also a strong testimony to ultimate hope in God, in the face of nuclear threats and other contemporary fears: "Bury your treasure where it can't be found / Bury it deep in hallowed ground" (cf. Matthew 6:19–21). In terms of both critical reception and popular appeal, "Country Death Song" and the three just-mentioned religious songs were unanimously regarded as the album's best tracks. Ironically, *Hallowed Ground* came out at precisely the time when many Christian bands were taking a subtle approach to lyrics, for example singing worship songs with ambiguous pronouns that might be mistaken as simply love songs apart from knowledge of the artist's intent. The Violent Femmes were suddenly on the radio singing about Jesus, the Bible, and other spiritual things without diplomacy. From a simple content perspective, *Hallowed Ground* would have to be regarded as one of the most blatantly, unashamed Christian releases of the year.

So what was up? Suspicious Christians speculated that the artist was just drawing on gospel roots for the musical value he found there or even that he was making fun of Christian subjects by singing the songs tongue-in-cheek (which is how legions of Violent Femmes fans took them). But in 1986, Gano gave an interview to *CCM* and explained a few things. He said that he had written a number of gospel songs early on and would have put them on the first album except that bass player Brian Ritchie was strongly opposed to the material and, in fact, said he would refuse to appear on stage with Gano when he sang about anything to do with Christianity. When they were preparing the follow-up album, however, Ritchie reluctantly reversed his position. "They're your best songs," he told Gano. "So let's do them." Gano also told the *CCM* reporter, "I think it's important to do songs like that and do them sincerely in a context where people would never expect it." He defended his other material as representing personas that might not be autobiographical. Like most songwriters, he claimed, he adopts the point of view of some fictional character and writes about sex or violence or drugs from what he imagines to be that person's perspective. Gano seemed content only to offer this much of an explanation without caring too much whether *CCM* readers would buy it or not. He clearly showed no interest in courting Christian music audiences, for whom his albums were not intended. Indeed, he seemed perplexed and perturbed at the basic questions Christian music fans were asking. "The idea of somebody being surprised by religion and sex placed back-to-back—I have some understanding of that," he said. "But what I don't like is when they get kind of aggressive about it, saying 'How can you claim that you're sincere?' I start to take a little offense at that. You know, 'How can you sing this song and then sing that one?' To me, that just doesn't seem to reflect much thinking ability."

The next Violent Femmes album, *The Blind Leading the Naked,* would score its biggest points with the political rant "Old Mother Reagan" (speculating negatively on the President's eternal destiny) and the inspired cover of T. Rex's "Children of the Revolution." But "Faith" is another prominent gospel song that minces no words: "Got my faith, baby, in the Lord . . . I believe in the Father, I believe in the Son, I believe there is a Spirit for everyone." Elsewhere, "No Killing" is a prayer for peace addressed to God ("We don't want no killing, Lord") and "Love and Me Make Three" rails against empty religiosity ("Christ is crying outside your church door / Don't let him in / He'll get mud on the floor"). After making this album, the Violent Femmes broke up temporarily, in part due to tensions over Gano's increasing "gospel obsessions." Sources close to the band maintain that Ritchie had reversed his opinion again and that well into the '90s he would remain "violently opposed to Christian content" in the band's songs. In any case, Gano formed another group called **The Mercy Seat** and toured for a while performing nothing but Christian material.

When the group came back together, they released the inappropriately titled 3 (their fourth album). The main focus of the album is failed and foiled relationships with the opposite sex, but spiritual themes seep into the songs here and there. "Just Like My Father" addresses the biblical theme of sins being passed from one generation to the next, and the cynicism of "Nothing Worth Living For" is couched in the form of a prayer

to God that this not be true. The clearest moment of devotion comes in "Outside This Palace": "God help me to know I've been in love my whole life / And not to get so confused between the struggle and the strife."

The Violent Femmes' 3 would be their last album to gain any notice in the contemporary Christian music scene. The band would score its biggest hit ever with "American Music" from *Why Do Birds Sing?* and would attract some attention on alternative stations with "Breaking Up" from *New Times.* Spiritual themes and gospel lyrics seemed a thing of the past, however, and whatever connections the band might once have had to Christian music were almost completely forgotten. As indicated above, by 2000 critics in the general market were still referring to Gano as "a Christian singer and songwriter" but no one in the contemporary Christian music industry or subculture ever seemed to give the Violent Femmes a passing thought.

The Violet Burning

Michael J. Pritzl, voc., gtr.; Lonnie Tubbs, drums (– 1998); Kirt Gentry, bass (- 1992, + 1994, –1996) // Scott Tubbs, bass (+ 1992, –1994); Sean Tubbs, gtr. (+ 1992, –1994); Jeff Schroeder, gtr. (+ 1994, –1998); Jason Picksergill, bass (+ 1996, – 1998); Andy Prickett, gtr. (+ 1996, – 1998); Herb Grimaud, bass (+ 1998); Robbie Farr, gtr. (+ 1998, –2000); Mike Kalmar, drums (+ 1998, – 2000). 1990—*Chosen* (New Breed); 1992—*Strength* (Bluestone); 1994—*You Wouldn't Understand Anyways* [EP] (independent); 1995—*Lillian Gish* [EP]; 1996—*Violet Burning* (Domo); 1998—*Demonstrates Plastic and Elastic* (Ruby Electric); 2000—*Faith and Devotions of a Satellite Heart; I Am a Stranger in This Place* (custom).

www.thevioletburning.com

The strained history of the progressive and critically acclaimed rock band The Violet Burning parallels that of groups like **LSU** in certain ways. The band began as a somewhat naive outreach ministry for a local church but came to prize artistic expression over propaganda in ways that put them on the fringe of the Christian music industry. Also like **LSU** (or the very different sounding **Vigilantes of Love**), The Violet Burning has turned out to be less of a band than a musical environment for its only consistent member. Michael J. Pritzl founded the group and it would be his emotive voice and introspective songwriting that would define its evolving sound. *True Tunes* once said, "The Violet Burning is, in effect, Michael Pritzl and whomever he assembles to back him up." Pritzl was born in Long Beach and brought up in Huntington Beach, California. Raised Roman Catholic, he had a dramatic conversion experience to evangelical Christianity as a teenager and joined the Vineyard Fellowship. That church would sponsor the earliest incarnation of Violet Burning, which cheerfully described itself in *CCM* as "an alternative/funk group with a church as its label and PR firm." The group said that its name means "impassioned for Christ," since *burning* is an expression for passion and *violet* is the biblical color representing Jesus (i.e., the color of royalty). Pritzl announced in 1990, "We want to be a band that will change the way the world and Christians alike look at Christian music." That turned out to be the case, though perhaps not quite in the manner that he anticipated.

Brian Quincy Newcomb described *Chosen* as "a highly-crafted and well-produced debut," noting that the group had "accomplished in one album what it takes most bands three or four albums to accomplish." The music on *Chosen* is moody modern rock, with Peter Gabriel and Brian Ferry influences. The songs tend to fall into two types. Those that the band had recorded first ("If You Let Me") have a high-tech passion to them similar to that of general market artist Murphy, whose hit "Cut Me Up" was on the mainstream charts at the time. Indeed, "If You Let Me" features a Sly Stone vibe (as in "I Want to Take You Higher") that seems to cry out for airplay. But while making *Chosen,* the band had moved toward more of an atmospheric rock sound that would ultimately prove definitive. "Rise Like the Lion" evinces this latter texture and would become *Chosen*'s hit single, rising to Number One on Christian rock charts. A particularly wrenching number called "The Killing," about the crucifixion of Jesus, was performed live as a dramatic performance-art piece that *CCM* would report often left the audience in tears.

With minor personnel shifts, the group developed its atmospheric sound more fully on *Strength,* adding Beatlesque elements à la The Cure or **Simple Minds.** They cover the Lennon/McCartney standard "Eleanor Rigby" and include the very melodic "Like the Sun," which recalls the work of Morrissey. The emotive nature of *Strength* would raise some questions regarding the tenacity of the band's faith. In fact, Pritzl explained that the album title was ironic, derived from St. Paul's affirmation that "when I am weak, then I am strong" (2 Corinthians 12:10). "Each song addresses my weakness, and my need for something stronger than me," he told *Visions of Gray.* The cathartic nature of the album owes somewhat to Pritzl's dealing with the deaths of a number of his friends and of empathizing with another who was going through a divorce. But he would also later reveal to *True Tunes* that *"Strength* was written knowing what was going to happen due to the choices that I was going to make, that I was going to lose many things—friendships, jobs, relationships." The group would score another hit on Christian rock stations with "There's No One Like You," one of the album's more accessible tunes and one that is most easily recognizable as a traditional "Christian song." But in general, the songs on *Strength* do not try to offer faith statements but seek to express various feelings and states of mind. In "Through My Tears," Pritzl sings, "I've held the hand of fear in the night—I was shaking—I drank the cup of sorrow, the taste so sweet on my lips." A song about Vincent Van Gogh presents the misunderstood artist (a Christian who had studied for the ministry) as one who was abused by culture that insisted his art should be religious. "We have a myopic view of what ministry is," Pritzl said in reference to that song and to Violet Burning's mission. "Ministry could be just playing a beautiful song." At the same time, he acknowledged that he still thought of his group as *having* a ministry: "We want to impact the life, soul, or spirit instead of just being a band chicks dig."

Strength was supposed to be released on the church-owned New Breed label, but that company had problems with the album's lyrical content, and the group chose to release the album on Bluestone Records, a label owned by Jesus music pioneer **Tom Stipe** and sponsored by a church in Denver, Colorado. Exactly what happened next is hard to determine but a fax was sent to several churches and, thence, widely disseminated within the Christian community alleging that the members of The Violet Burning were "fornicators and drunkards." Band members denied all the charges but the ensuing controversy caused Scott and Sean Tubbs to quit the band and left Pritzl with some lasting resentment for segments of the Christian music subculture. The group floundered for a couple of years, recording a couple of independent EP demos (*You Wouldn't Understand Anyways* includes an inspired cover of Neil Young's "Cinnamon Girl").

The third full-length album, *Violet Burning,* is generally regarded as the band's best. The addition of Andy Prickett, guitarist for **The Prayer Chain,** noticeably affects the sound, bringing the group almost into the territory of that band's *Mercury* era at times. The music is haunting and mystical, alternately spacey and sparkling, while evincing hard rock vibes reminiscent of The Cult. The most noticed aspect in Christian circles, however, would be the lyrics, which no longer contain any direct references to God and often seem to express doubt and a loss of faith ("I can't see the light"). "Underwater," the record's standout, core track, offers the plea of a drowning man who is not sure whether he will be rescued: "The more I live, the less I know / When we walked on water, we were perfect . . . Now, I'm caught in the undertow." Likewise, on "Silver" Pritzl sings, "We were the lovers with silver wings / Wings to fly / Wings that don't fly anymore." Disturbing to some, he allows a burst of guitar feedback to obscure what according to the lyric sheet is a use of the infamous f-gerund on the song "Fever": "I will break their - - - -ing heart." But Pritzl had certainly not abandoned his faith. Rather, he says, the songs on *Violet Burning* express the yearning for attachment and healing similar to those found in Psalms and the book of Lamentations. "I haven't given up the struggle at all," he told *True Tunes.* "For me, being a man who would put his faith in Christ, it's because he was a friend of sinners."

Demonstrates Plastic and Elastic is the work of a wholly new Violet Burning (save for Pritzl). It is an indie band recording of more upbeat songs for private distribution. Michael Misiuk of **Acoustic Shack** and **The Kreepdowns** plays with the band on several tracks (Misiuk is Pritzl's brother-in-law and had actually been an early member of Violet Burning prior to the recording of *Chosen*). The new group's sound often seems to draw on such up-to-date influences as Smashing Pumpkins and Radiohead, layered on top of a still-present Cure moodiness. Pritzl manages to vary his voice so dramatically throughout the project that many reviewers would indicate it sounds like there are at least four different persons singing. For instance, he does a credible Billy Corgan impression on "Oceana" and "I'm No Superman," which contrasts radically with the emotive weeping sound he uses for "Elaste" (which opens the project). While moody ballads predominate, "Moon Radio" and "Berlin Kitty" are hook-laden pop songs that seem perfectly appropriate for airplay on alternative college-rock radio. On the latter song, Pritzl actually sings about "Berlin city," but decided to change the title of the track for the album listing because "it sounded cooler" (Boy George once did the same thing with his Top 40 hit called "It's a Miracle" on which, if one listens closely, he can be heard to be actually singing, "It's America"). In general, though, lyrics are not treated in so cavalier a fashion. *Phantom Tollbooth* and others would note that they contain "no evidence of faith," but that judgment could be dispelled by Pritzl's own commentary on some of the songs. He told *True Tunes,* for instance, that the track called "Seamonster" reflects his imaginative picture of forgiveness: "My sins get thrown into the sea and there's this sea monster, and it just swallows them up and gets rid of them." The song "Elaste" also seems to offer portraits of redemption "Pour your love over me / All my days are with thee / Let your love cover me"). The title of the album, Pritzl explained, contrasts the inner and the outer natures of humanity. Outwardly, people keep up appearances that are "plastic" and artificial, but the soul is "elastic," able to stretch as "God shapes and molds our lives." Many in the Christian community rejected the album out of hand because of a photograph that showed band members smoking.

The common thread for Violet Burning's diverse adventures seems to be Pritzl's unflinching honesty. "I can only write from what God brings me through in life," he told *True Tunes* in 1999. "I write about my experiences and the experiences of those around me." In answer to repeated inquiries about the status of his faith, he declared in 2000, "Jesus Christ is my Savior and my Lord. He is my friend, and the friend of all sinners. He is Creator and Maker of all that is seen and unseen, the Eternal God, the worthy Lamb." That same year, he would release two projects through his website: *Faith and Devotions of a Satellite Heart* and *I Am a Stranger in This Place.* The former offers worship songs sung by Melissa Barnett from behind a veil of tranced-out atmospheric guitars; the latter contains newly arranged versions of previously issued Violet Burning songs.

For trivia buffs: Pritzl intended for his band's best-known album, *Violet Burning,* to be titled *Lipstick and Dynamite Wonder,* but his label at the time (Domo) nixed this, for reasons unknown.

Virtue

Karima Trotter Kibble, voc.; Shavonne Floyd Sampson, voc.; Ebony Trotter, voc.; Negelle Sumter, voc. (−2001). 1997—*Virtue* (Verity); 1999—*Get Ready;* 2001—*Vituosity.*

Virtue is an African American female vocal group similar in style to En Vogue or Destiny's Child. The group came together at Oakwood College in Huntsville, Alabama (from whence **Take 6** also sprang). The women view their career as a ministry and say they are devoted first and foremost to "reaching people for Christ." Musically, they attempt to bridge gaps between adult contemporary and urban gospel sounds. The group's debut album was ignored by the Christian media but produced a radio hit with "Greatest Part of Me" nevertheless. It finished third in the "Favorite Contemporary Gospel Album" category in *CCM* magazine's 1998 Reader's Poll, not bad for a record the magazine had not even deemed worthy of review. *Get Ready* received much more attention. Songs like "My Heart's with You" and "Love Me Like You Do" are straight up adult contemporary tunes similar to works by **Avalon,** while "Super Victorious" and "Put Your War Clothes On" reveal more of the traditional gospel roots. The latter two songs also display some of the same lyrical (theological) weaknesses that have sometimes plagued **Carman,** touting an overly optimistic theology of glory on the one hand and anachronistic militant imagery on the other. "Be Grateful" is better theologically and musically, hearkening back to the sounds of '70s soul. *Virtuosity* reveals a vocal trio with a slick R&B sound comparable to **Trin-i-tee 5:7** or **Out of Eden,** though the group's harmonies and a capella interludes actually hearken all the way back to **2nd Chapter of Acts.** *CCM* described "He's Been Good" as "good time dance-floor funk" and highlighted the Latin acoustic number "Something about That Way" and soulful "You Are My Everything" as standout tracks. As the latter song indicates, the group is often at its best singing worship songs directly to God.

Virus

Stephanie Dorsen; Stefan Nelson; Greg Young. 1995—*Analogue* (N'Soul); 1996—*Odd.*

Very little is known about the ambient techno band Virus, as they have never been profiled in any Christian music publication. Still, the group has been responsible for releasing some groundbreaking music in its field and is often cited as an influence on many other synthesizer-based mostly-instrumental groups (e.g., **Cloud 2 Ground**). Virus is apparently a trio from Missouri. The core of the group is two guys with keyboards and computers, Stefan Nelson and Greg Young, who write songs with classic pop structures (verse-chorus-verse) and record them on synthesizers and drum machines with lots of attendant samples, loops, and machine-generated effects. Real piano is sometimes played over the top, and the most fortunate numbers get poetic lyrics written and sung in an angelic voice by Stephanie Dorsen (who is identified in one source as Stefan Nelson's wife). Virus has released two double-disc sets of music for the Christian market. *Analogue* is considered one of the first trance/ambient recordings to gain notice within the Christian scene—and Virus is sometimes credited with introducing ambient music to the Christian music subculture through the latter album. Likewise, *Odd* is usually considered to represent the first Christian foray into vocal-driven trip-hop, a form of electronic music that has rarely been tried in Christian circles (cf. Paradigm Shift). The latter set includes one disc of all electronic music that recalls **Moby** at times and another disc of music with vocals that brings the group's interest in spirituality to the fore. "Angels" contemplates the nature of celestial beings, and "Absalom" draws on the biblical story of David's wayward son to dream of a time when parents and prodigals are all reunited. On "Sun," Dorsen sings, "I am a creature of the light." Virus has been compared to the general market band Portishead. Nelson and Young also create techno music under the names **Ambient Theology, Bubblebaby,** and Resolution.

Vision

David Jinright, synth.; Leonard Jones, voc., gtr.; Mike Maple, drums; Rocco Marshall, voc., gtr.; Billy Powell, kybrd.; Leon Wilkeson, bass (– 1985); Martin Tomlinson, bass (+ 1985). 1984—*Vision* (Dunamis); 1985—*Vision* (Heartland).

Vision burst on the Christian scene in the mid '80s poised to be another arena rock band in the tradition of **Stryper** and **White Heart.** Somehow, they managed to snag Billy Powell and Leon Wilkeson from Lynyrd Skynyrd to be members of the group. Skynyrd was on indefinite hiatus following the 1977 plane crash that killed front man Ronnie Van Zant. In early concerts involving the band, Powell gave a testimony to the miraculous way in which Wilkeson had survived that holocaust. In fact, he said, "Wilkeson was pronounced dead at the scene but a spirit-filled nurse laid hands on him and raised him from the dead." Wilkeson played on Vision's first album only.

The second project (a completely different collection, though also self-titled) shows improved production and features the anthemic song "Standing on the Rock," which some critics would hail as "one of the absolute best Christian rock songs of the era." The second *Vision* also includes a good-time rockin' song called "You're the One," an appropriately upbeat "The Lord Is My Joy," and a word-for-word rendition of "Psalm 23" from the King James Version (with all the "maketh" and "anointest" language intact). Both Powell and Wilkeson returned to Skynyrd in 1991; Wilkeson died in 2001.

The real leader of Vision was Rocco Marshall, whose life of faith apparently encountered some hard times. **Mark Farner** addresses the song "Rocco" to him on his 1989 *Wake-up* album: "Caught in your emotions, you've gone stumblin' down the road / That leads to only death / But by the grace of God you know there's a better way to live / For your family and for yourself / I don't understand why men fall away. . . ."

A different group called Vision released a self-titled album on Light in 1973. A Christian rap trio also named Vision appeared in 2000 and released a debut record *(Starting from Scratch)* on the independent Marxan label. The latter group is from Sandusky, Ohio.

Viva Voce

Anita Robinson, voc., gtr.; Kevin Robinson, drums, gtr. 1998—*Hooray for Now* (Cadence); 2000—*Weightless* [EP] (Viva).

Viva Voce is a female-fronted alternative Christian band with a sound similar to such general market groups as Belly, The Breeders, and Veruca Salt. The group is actually a husband and wife team that, despite the distinctive Dayton sound, come from Alabama (settling eventually in Nashville). They confess to affection for such bands as **The Prayer Chain, Starflyer 59,** and **The Violet Burning,** but the closest equivalent to their style is found in **Miss Angie** or **Morella's Forest** (with whom they have toured). The group began under the name Nectarine and even recorded a song for a compilation album under that moniker. Viva Voce is Latin for "by word of mouth." *Hooray for Now* offers explicitly Christian songs with themes of worship ("He Touches Stars") and humanity's need for spiritual repair ("Bent"). "Fear of Flying" deals with the tendency of Christians just to coast in their spiritual life without pressing on to greater growth. Anita Robinson says that "Heartstring" is about "the emotion you feel when something you've prayed about comes to fruition." A couple of songs ("June," "Beautiful") are romantic odes growing out of the couple's relationship. Unfortunately, the band's label (Cadence) collapsed and the group found themselves without distribution. In 2000, they released an independent EP that includes a cover of The Cure's "Love Song" and three new original songs. "Free (Like I'm Meant to Be)" is sugary noise pop similar to material on the debut album, but the other two new tracks are slow and meandering numbers that point in a different, experimental direction.

Karen Voegtlin

1979—*Misty Morning* (Greentree); 1981—*Love Explosion*; 1984—*He's My Leader* (Light).

Karen Voegtlin (pronounced vōg-lin) was a Christian singer whose voice and style reminded many people of Olivia Newton-John. After singing as a member of **Andrus, Blackwood, and Co.,** she made three albums of adult contemporary pop songs, working closely with **Sherman Andrus,** who produced *Love Explosion.* Andrus also wrote "Faithfulness" for *He's My Leader,* but Voegtlin penned all of the other songs herself. The title track for that final outing describes her heavenly father as the still-present leader of her band in a way that seems intended to present a deliberate contrast with Dan Fogelberg's song "Leader of the Band" (about his departed earthly father). "Hosanna" is a worship song with more promising lyrics blessing God for the beauties of creation.

Greg Volz

1986—*The River Is Rising* (Myrrh); 1988—*Come Out Fighting*; 1989—*No Room in the Middle* (River); 1991—*The Exodus*; 1999—*Let the Victors In* (independent); *Break Out Praise*; *Ready or Not . . . Here He Comes.*

Best known as lead vocalist for **Petra** during their golden years (1980–1986), Greg Volz was born in 1950 and grew up in Metamora, Illinois. At the age of thirteen, he formed a rock band called The Wombats and later, while attending Illinois State University, formed another group called Gideon's Bible. In 1970, Volz moved to Indianapolis where he founded what was to become a pioneering Jesus music group that bore the curious name **e band.** The group was a power trio like Cream or **Glass Harp,** composed of Volz, Greg Dunteman on bass, and Dave Eden on drums. They never did decide (or reveal) what the "e" stood for—depending on who was asked (and when), it could be said to mean "Emmanuel" or "eternity" or "everything." Apparently, the group was not at first a Christian band but after being invited to a meal provided for them by an older Christian woman, the entire group came to faith in Christ. For three years, the band was one of the heartland's major Jesus music acts, occupying a regional position similar to that of **Liberation Suite** or **Hope of Glory** in that other Jesus movement outpost known as Texas (the great majority of the early '70s Jesus groups were in Southern California). In 1996, Volz would reminisce about the band: "**e band** was the forerunner of all Jesus Rock groups—not Christian rock but 'Jesus Rock'. Everything revolved around Jesus. The band lived all together in one seven-bedroom house. We held all things in common.

We had one bank account. Musically, **e band** was **Petra** ten years earlier. They were the sound that **Petra** became in 1982." Unfortunately, **e band** did not record a full album as such, though they did place some songs on a rock musical called *Because I Am* in 1971. The group broke up in 1973, and Volz moved again, this time to Springfield, Missouri, where he worked with **Phil Keaggy.** Around this time, he also performed the lead role in a stage version of another Christian rock musical, *Ezekiel.* In 1976, he sang on **Petra**'s second album, the now-classic *Come and Join Us.* Following that experience, he was invited to join that band full time, but almost simultaneously was offered the position of lead vocalist in the general market group REO Speedwagon. After weighing the pros and cons of singing in a Christian ministry band or working as lead singer in a high-profile secular group, Volz chose to go with **Petra.** He sang lead on many of the band's most acclaimed albums, including *Never Say Die, More Power to Ya, Not of this World, Beat the System,* and *Captured in Time and Space.* Notably, two of **Petra**'s better-known songs during this period, "The Coloring Song" and "Praise Ye the Lord" were actually remakes of old **e band** songs—the former written by Dave Eden and the latter by Volz. In 1986, Volz left **Petra** because the constant touring was exacting too great a toll on his family life, though personality clashes with Bob Hartman had also been widely reported. For a brief time he formed a band called Pieces of Eight with former Wings drummer **Joe English.** Then he embarked on a solo career.

Volz produced four solo albums between 1986 and 1991, with his longtime friend Mike Schmitz serving as a primary songwriter. *The River Is Rising* was produced by frequent **Petra** producer **Jonathan David Brown,** but departs significantly and deliberately from trademark **Petra** sounds. Perhaps what is most notable about the album is the virtual absence of worship songs, the material for which Volz had been best known while singing with **Petra** (he wrote or cowrote mainly praise songs for that band, including "Let Everything That Hath Breath," "Without Him We Can Do Nothing," and "Praise Ye the Lord"). Now Volz told *CCM* that he was more interested in "relational music—real heartfelt songs about real life, about living in this world." The title track to *The River Is Rising* is an R&B ballad quite unlike anything Volz had done previously. *Come Out Fighting* would be more **Petra**-like, with several Schmitz songs featuring big, hooky choruses. But Volz also covers Aerosmith's "Dream On," bringing out the song's latent spirituality. The album's title track is a song by Bob Halligan Jr. (cf. **Ceili Rain**) that was also recorded by **Geoff Moore and The Distance** on their *A Place to Stand.* After the two albums for Myrrh, Volz founded his own label, River Records. He solicited **Jonathan David Brown** again to helm his first release for the new company, *No Room in the Middle.* The title track and "Walk Toward the Light" were, again, remakes of old **e band** songs, cowritten with Eden. Volz would maintain that he was trying to recapture the revival spirit of those early days on the album and said that "performing the twenty-year-old songs helps me to recapture my first love for the Lord."

Christian radio hits: "Man Like You" (# 9 in 1986); "Hold On to the Fire" (# 5 in 1986); "The River Is Rising" (# 3 in 1987); "Still Waters" (# 3 in 1987); "Take Me to the End" (# 6 in 1988); "Up to the Mountain" (# 10 in 1989); "Walk Towards the Light" (# 2 in 1989); "Waiting on Someday" (# 2 in 1990); "Servant and Witness" (# 3 in 1990); "Love Moves in a Different Circle" (# 16 in 1991).

W

The W's

Bret Barker, trump.; James Carter, sax.; Todd Gruener, bass; Valentine Hellman, sax, clarinet; Brian Morris, drums; Andrew Schar, voc., gtr. 1998—*Fourth from the Last* (Sara Bellum); 1999—*Trouble with X* (5 Minute Walk).

www.thews.org

Just one step removed from the ska craze spearheaded by **Five Iron Frenzy, The Insyderz,** and especially **The Supertones,** the sextet from Corvallis, Oregon, known strangely as **The W's** became the primary incarnation of the swing revival in Christian music. They were, in that sense, the Christian equivalent of The Squirrel Nut Zippers or The Cherry Poppin' Daddies, but they played with an authenticity that seemed anything but derivative. Like Brian Setzer, they infused the sounds of Big Band with generous doses of rockabilly—the '40s never sounded this fun or this funky. Of course, no one in the '90s was seriously tempted to exchange their rock and roll birthright for a pot of Glenn Miller's porridge. Like their more secular compatriots, The W's seemed destined to be viewed as something of a novelty act. Their success at transcending this distinction makes the-little-band-that-could all the more impressive. The group turned out to be far more popular within the Christian scene than the one-hit wonder Zippers or Daddies ever were in the world at large. With a subdued approach to ministry that went light on testifying and heavy on entertaining, they might have been big in the general market as well. As it turns out, the aforementioned groups provided all the swing that the market could apparently bear, but The W's

were one of the best purveyors of the form, and mainstream fans of the genre missed out by not hearing them. As of 2002, however, the group was still alive and well, despite the passing of the fad that had momentarily made them big fish in the little Christian music pond.

The W's formed at Oregon State University, where some of its members were students. They shopped what they now call their "cruddy little demo tape" around for a while before finally getting to play it for a 5 Minute Walk executive at a **Five Iron Frenzy** album release party. Both of their subsequent albums for that label were ably produced by Masaki, once of **Dime Store Prophets.** In 1998–1999, The W's opened for **DC Talk** on that band's *Supernatural* tour. In 1999, they were chosen to play for Pope John Paul II on his historic visit to St. Louis. They recorded "The Rumor Weed" for *Larry Boy and the Rumor Weed,* a popular installment in the Veggie Tales videos. Asked often about the meaning of their name, they only point out that it is the *twenty-third* letter of the alphabet. Actually, Gruener confides, the name has no meaning at all: it was "just the product of very bored college students sitting around scratching themselves and not thinking too hard."

The first record *Fourth from the Last* would score two well-deserved hits in the Christian market. "Moses" refers to the famous lawgiver (along with other biblical characters) but the main focus of the song is on the present: how God can use "an itty bitty man like me." Somehow the swing beat allows the latter phrase to sound cool instead of silly. The same can be said for the "skid-ily-ily-do's" of the band's biggest smash,

"The Devil Is Bad." The song is bouncy, infectious, and humorous in a **Charlie Daniels** way that seems to just cry out for radio airplay. As *Release* would note, The W's resisted the temptation of just doing "twelve copies of one song" on their debut album and instead turned out a collection of tunes that all jump, jive, and wail but also reveal a remarkable diversity of sound within what could be a limiting genre. Other standout songs include the anthemic "King of Polyester" and the tight-and-jazzy "Open Minded." The latter track is addressed to critics and/or fans tempted to dismiss the group's music because of its members' public beliefs ("Spoke a word or two about our God / Then we're not the people we were before / Put your label on us, we suck now / A couple of words have changed our sound"). In a move of superb irony, Lifeway Christian Resources (a.k.a. the Baptist Sunday School Board) pulled the album from its stores as "an objectionable product" because the group uses the word *suck* in this song.

One song on *Trouble with X* tops everything on the debut album. That track is the surprising cover of John Denver's "Take Me Home, Country Roads," a tune that by all accounts shouldn't have worked as a swing standard but for some reason does. The W's' almost unrecognizable version of the song transforms it into a modern masterpiece that juxtaposes the original melody with sprightly horn frills and flourishes. Otherwise, *Trouble with X* displays a tighter, more practiced sound than *Fourth from the Last,* with **Five Iron Frenzy**'s Dennis Culp beefing up the brass a bit. "Rather Be Dead" is a straight-on love song ("Without you, girl, I'd rather be dead"), and sarcastic humor continues to drive some of the message songs ("Stupid," "Used Car Salesman"). This time out, the messages are clearly directed to believers. "Stupid" describes a ludicrous spectacle of Bible bangers and abortion clinic bombers singing "They'll know we are Christians by our love."

Christian radio hits: "The Devil Is Bad" (# 6 in 1998).

Dove Awards: 1999 Alternative/Modern Rock Album *(Fourth from the Last);* 1999 Alternative/Modern Rock Song ("The Devil Is Bad").

Michele Wagner

1989—*Michele Wagner* (Benson); 1991—*A Heart Set Free* (Benson); 1992—*Safe Place;* 1994—*Heart of the Journey.*

Michele Wagner is a singer/songwriter from Lakewood, Ohio (near Cleveland), who first came to the attention of the Christian music scene as a composer of profound and inspirational songs for other artists. Moving to Nashville in 1984, she worked as a songwriter for Meadowgreen music and wrote "Psalm 1" for **Kim Hill** and "Whatever You Ask" for **Steve Camp.** Her own debut, *Michele Wagner,* would include her renditions of both of those songs, in addition to "You're Beautiful," a song that affirms the value of wounded humanity from

God's perspective. Wagner typically would close her concerts with the latter song. She told *CCM,* "I have everyone hold hands and sing it to each other and people cry sometimes. God ministers through the song because there are a lot of hurting hearts out there." Wagner's style consists of mostly adult contemporary ballads delivered with just a twinge of country, and a few midtempo, upbeat songs thrown into the mix—sort of like a female James Taylor. *A Heart Set Free* includes "Jesus Answers" sung as a duet with **Bob Carlisle.** *Safe Place* offers songs that emphasize rest and the discovery of security in harsh surroundings. Wagner drew on her own experience of growing up in a family marred by alcohol abuse in crafting quiet songs like the almost-title-track, "Safe, Safe Place." She also sings "Nothing's Gonna Stop This Love," a marriage song inspired by her own recent nuptials. *Heart of the Journey,* produced by **Phil Madeira,** has a more acoustic flavor than earlier projects. The theme of growing in Christ is emphasized throughout and is expressed with special poignancy in "I'll Give It All." **Billy and Sarah Gaines** sing with the artist on another track, "Come by Here."

Christian radio hits: "Jesus Answers" (# 23 in 1991); "Only One Love" (# 18 in 1992).

The Waiting

Clark Leake, bass; Brad Olsen, voc.; Todd Olsen, gtr.; Brad Thompson, drums. 1994—*Blue Belly Sky* (Anastia); 1997—*The Waiting* (Sparrow); 1998—*Unfazed;* 2001—*Wonderfully Made.*

www.thewaiting.com

The Waiting is an alternative rock band from Atlanta that combines just enough elements of pop with their edgy sound to inspire comparisons with that other Atlanta band, R.E.M. More upbeat neo-jangle groups like Gin Blossoms, Toad the Wet Sprocket, and especially The Connells probably offer even better comparisons. *The Phantom Tollbooth* describes The Waiting as having "a rootsy folk-pop sound with some distorted guitar and the odd mandolin thrown in." Lyrics are poetic and filled with imagery, and Brad Olsen's distinctive half-spoken vocals (with what sounds like a slight British/Irish accent) keep the R.E.M. comparisons from becoming overwhelming. Most of the band's songs are written by the Olsen brothers, but each project also features a few Leake compositions, and the latter songwriter adds spice to the mix with more hooky, Graham Nash-like songs that often have the feel of '70s pop radio. The group took their name from the Tom Petty song "The Waiting (Is the Hardest Part)."

The Waiting is somewhat remarkable in that they have performed songs that are more celebrative and explicitly Christian than most alternative bands. Like **Smalltown Poets,** they have played their share of clubs and secular establishments, without trying to distance themselves from the church youth group circuit. "We're really a ministry, not simply a band," Todd Olsen told *CCM* in 1995. He explicated this for *Release:* "I think people can be brought closer to God if you simply tell them what the Lord is doing in your life." As something of a gimmick, the group dressed in '40s-era clothing like characters out of the film *Casablanca* during their early years, but they dropped this ruse by the time their second album appeared. Olsen has summed up the difficulty of being a Christian songwriter by explaining "A lyric has to come from emotion, but emotion and theology don't always agree."

Blue Belly Sky was produced by Gene Eugene of **Adam Again** and was immediately hailed by *Cornerstone* and others as "one of the best alternative rock records of the year." The opening song, "Look at Me," is cheerful and creative, inspired by biblical assurances that God sees believers as more pure and precious than they ever appear to be through human eyes (e.g., Ephesians 1:4). Lyrically, the song comes off like an updated Song of Solomon: "I love the way you look at me / The way you steer your eyes / To see the bride beneath the harlot's skin / The virtue underneath the skin." In concert, the band would go from this song into a medley of wedding songs, including The Dixie Cups' "Chapel of Love," George Strait's "Forever and Ever, Amen," **Noel Paul Stookey**'s "Wedding Song," and The Georgia Satellites' "Keep Your Hands to Yourself." The second song, "It's Amazing," is equally vibrant, shimmering with wonder at God's famously amazing grace. This upbeat quality carries throughout most of the album. "Mercy Seat" and "Is This the Day?" have a slower, worshipful tone. "Wonderstuff" (one of the Leake compositions) is a sprightly bubblegum surprise that sounds like a Monkees song with quirky They Might Be Giant lyrics (about someone who was born with legs ten feet tall). In spite of receiving rave reviews, *Blue Belly Sky* did not sell well, having been issued on a custom label with no market clout. Sparrow would re-release the album in 1998 (when the band had gained more of a following) with four new tracks, including a cover of The Jackson Five's "I Want You Back."

The Waiting's sophomore album was actually recorded for R.E.X. but the band got caught up in the same fiasco following the corporate takeover of that firm that attended **Sixpence None the Richer.** By the time *The Waiting* came out on Sparrow, the album had become a curious hybrid of indie alternapop and typical Christian radio fare. Once again, the album opens with one of its most shimmery, upbeat tracks, a celebration of God's radiance called "Never Dim." Two bubblegum tracks garnered a lot of attention: Leake's "Number 9," a nursery rhyme about the failure of people to live life in its potential abundance, and "How Do You Do That?" which expresses wonder at God's ability to forget human sin. A somewhat darker tone informs "Put the Blame on Me," an apparently sar-

castic response to the resistant ("Don't blame your doubt, if you hate belief / But if it makes it easy, put the blame on me"). The album's best track, by all accounts, is "Hands in the Air," a musically creative opus that employs different textures and paces. Cowritten with *The Waiting*'s coproducer, **Steve Hindalong,** the lyrics to "Hands in the Air" play on the dual imagery of raised hands as symbolizing worship (in the church) and surrender (in the world at large).

Unfazed was described by *CCM* as "strikingly different from the band's first two outings," but the differences are more of degree than kind. The sound remains essentially the same but the quality of that sound and, especially, the quality of the songs themselves improves exponentially. Vocals take center stage (with greatly improved harmonies) on an album of catchy tunes. This is pop music, but it is intelligent, alternapop, with underlying mature textures and melancholy themes. The too-friendly character of the band's more trite songs is gone, such that the songs on *Unfazed* succeed in being memorable without sounding like advertising jingles. Olsen worked with a number of outside songwriters. The band also engaged three different producers and, for the first time, had the support of a major label that was already convinced of the band's commercial viability. Numerous critics noticed the potential of *Unfazed* for crossover success, as most of its songs (with a more muted spirituality) would be right at home on college rock radio. The opening title track deals with the theme of remaining secure in Christ's calling. "Easy to See" has a strong singalong chorus. "Company to Keep" reverses the usual notion that Christians should avoid keeping bad company with reflection on Jesus' association with the outcasts of his day.

The much-awaited *Wonderfully Made* was released on Christmas Eve 2001. Its title track takes its theme from Psalm 139:14 and celebrates positive self-images grounded in recognition of God's responsibility for creation. "Diamonds to Dust" focuses on materialism and the transient nature of earthly desires. Mac Powell of **Third Day** cowrote four songs on *Wonderfully Made,* and the album evinces a more generically pop-oriented style that is sometimes oddly reminiscent of **Larry Norman** fronting **The Newsboys** (the Norman part deriving from some of Olsen's vocal affectations). Lyrically, the songs are strongly evangelical with "What Else Can I Say," "Every Word," and "A Thousand Years (Is Not Enough)" striding into the praise and worship/love song to Jesus genre.

For trivia buffs: Leake attended Mississippi State University and while there played in a band with **Kim Hill.**

Christian radio hits: "Mercy Seat" (# 10 in 1995); "Staring at a Bird" (# 7 in 1995); "Look at Me" (# 4 in 1995); "Truly Amazing" (# 8 in 1996); "Wonderstuff" (# 15 in 1996); "Never Dim" (# 1 for 2 weeks in 1997); "How Do You Do That?" (# 1 for 2 weeks in 1997); "My Pride" (# 2 in 1997); "Hands in the Air" (# 11 in 1998); "Still So Pretty" (# 6 in 1998);

"Unfazed" (# 1 for 3 weeks in 1999); "Speak" (# 1 for 3 weeks in 1999); "So Much of Me" (# 4 in 1999).

Rick Wakeman

Selected: 1987—*The Gospels* (Stylus); 1990—*In the Beginning* (Asaph); 1993—*Prayers*; 1996—*The New Gospels* (Hope); *The Word and Music; Orisons; Can You Hear Me?*; 2000—*Morning Has Broken.*

www.rwcc.com

Classically trained pianist Rick Wakeman (b. 1949) is generally considered to be one of the two or three best keyboard players in rock history—his most obvious competitor being Keith Emerson of Emerson, Lake, and Palmer. Wakeman is best known to rock fans for his work with the quintessential art-rock group Yes. He has also recorded literally dozens of solo albums (109 listed at his website in mid 2001), some of which he intends as expressions of his abiding Christian faith.

Raised in Middlesex, England, Wakeman first worked as a session musician playing, for instance, the classic piano line on Cat Stevens' hit "Morning Has Broken" and the memorable mellotron part for David Bowie's "Space Oddity." He joined a successful British band called The Strawbs and then, in 1971, hooked up with Jon Anderson in the already-formed Yes. He missed the band's breakthrough record, *The Yes Album* (featuring "I've Seen All Good People") but joined in time for *Fragile* (featuring "Roundabout" and "Long Distance Runaround"). He would play on most of the better-known albums throughout the '70s, though he quit for a period in 1974–1975 because of tensions over spiritual beliefs. Somewhat ironically, *he* was the one who had trouble with the spirituality of the rest of the group; *The New Rolling Stone Encyclopedia of Rock and Roll* reports that "Wakeman was an extroverted, meat-eating beer drinker, while the other players were sober vegetarians." The history of Yes in the '80s and '90s became a complicated mess as each album featured different versions of the group, with all the players including Wakeman coming and going in what appears to have been a sporadic fashion. Notably, Wakeman did not play on the somewhat distinct *90125* album (1983), which would turn out to be the group's biggest seller (with the Number One hit "Owner of a Lonely Heart"). Eventually, there were two different groups composed of sometime Yes members and, incredibly, a court decision gave name rights to the faction that did *not* include Jon Anderson and Rick Wakeman, the two members who had always seemed to be the most important. Thus, the latter two ended up touring and recording with a group called Anderson, Bruford, Wakeman, and Howe. They reunited with the now-official Yes in 1991 for the double platinum *Union* album. Wakeman would also tour and record in the '90s with his grown son Adam (also a keyboardist) under the name Wakeman with Wakeman.

A biography of Wakeman's early life and career called *Rick Wakeman: The Caped Crusader* was written by Dan Wooding (with a Foreword by Elton John) in 1976. Much later, the artist would pen his own autobiography (*Say Yes,* Hodder and Stoughton, 1995). According to Wooding, Wakeman "accepted Christ into his life and was baptized in a Baptist church" when he was a teenager. He remained active in that congregation and at one point was a Sunday school teacher. Still, fame, drugs, and money took their toll, and by the end of the '70s, having survived one heart attack and two failed marriages, he had to come to grips with a serious drinking problem. A romance with British actor and singer Nina Carter led him to an encounter with a British clergyman who refused to marry the couple without counseling them first. As a result of the counseling, Rick ended up rededicating his life to Christ, with Carter also adopting a vibrant faith in Christ. The two married in 1984.

Wakeman had recorded solo projects both while he was with Yes and during the off-times. The best known of the multitudinous works are a trio on A&M: *The Six Wives of Henry VIII* (1973); *Journey to the Center of the Earth* (1974); and *The Myths and Legends of King Arthur and the Knights of the Round Table* (1975). As the titles imply, these works take the form of soundtracks to what could have been stage productions or films. Indeed, the *King Arthur* opus was staged, on ice no less, with a full orchestra and fifty-voice choir. *Journey to the Center of the Earth* was Wakeman's top solo success: recorded with the London Symphony Orchestra, the album was a Top 10 hit, and Wakeman toured, performing it (with orchestras) worldwide. Wakeman also scored a number of films, from Ken Russell's artistic *Lisztomania* to the less-acclaimed *Creepshow 2.* Three years after marrying Carter, Wakeman was encouraged by his old biographer, Dan Wooding, to "get into the Bible and use his musical talents to create a major biblical opus." He did, the result being a two-disc, two-hour work called *The Gospels,* recorded with the Eton College Chapel Choir. *The Gospels* features narration by British actor Robert Powell (who played Jesus in the TV film *Jesus of Nazareth*) and vocals by operatic tenor Ramon Remedios. The work is divided so as to present key scenes from each of the four Gospels, emphasizing key themes from each. In 1988, a performance of the program with the Israel Symphony Orchestra was recorded for Beckman Home Video.

In 1990, Wakeman issued an album called *In the Beginning,* which features his wife, Nina, reading selected Scripture passages while he plays piano softly in the background. It is no doubt intended as an album for quiet meditation, but was not advertised as such. Critics cried foul when deceptive packaging led consumers to believe they were buying a new work of music by Rick Wakeman only to discover they'd purchased a Bible-on-tape package instead. The album was actually recorded as a benefit project with all proceeds going to a charitable organization called ASSIST.

Wakeman never entered the contemporary Christian music scene in any overt way, but throughout the '90s he would continue to pop up in faith-oriented venues now and then while recording a steady stream of secular works for his usual fans. In 1993, he released *Prayers,* a collection of spiritual songs featuring Chrissie Hammond on vocals mixed with some spoken word readings by wife Nina. In 1996, a spate of religious works appeared on the new Hope label. *The New Gospels* is a re-recorded rendition of the 1987 piece, still with Remedios on vocals but with Garfield Morgan replacing Powell as narrator. *The Word and Music* is another collection of biblical readings similar to *In the Beginning,* this time featuring only Old Testament passages and this time clearly labeled "Biblical Narration by Nina Wakeman with music by Rick Wakeman." *Orisons* is a collection of songs and readings like those on *Prayers,* and *Can You Hear Me?* compiles only songs with vocals by Chrissie Hammond and the English Chamber Choir. In 2000, Wakeman released *Morning Has Broken,* an instrumental collection of hymns that concludes with the Anglican classic he had played for Cat Stevens over thirty years ago.

The back cover of Wakeman's *Say Yes* offers his dedication to "four people who have touched my life: Mildren Wakeman who brought me to life; Cyril Wakeman who shaped my life; Nina Wakeman, my partner in life; and Jesus Christ, who gave me life." His testimony of faith runs like a thread throughout the book as he relates his experiences, past, present, and future, from a perspective informed by a transcendent belief in God.

Albertina Walker

Selected: 1993—*He Keeps on Blessing Me* (CGI); 1994—*Songs of the Church* (Verity); 1996—*On the Road to Glory* (Benson); 1997—*Live in Chicago* (Verity); *I'm Still Here*; 2000—*The Divas of Gospel* [with Yolanda Adams] (Uni); 2001—*The Very Best of Albertina Walker* (Verity).

Like **Shirley Caesar,** Albertina Walker is a mainstay of twentieth-century traditional gospel music. Beginning her career as a protégé of Mahalia Jackson, she sang with Caesar and James Cleveland in The Caravans, and eventually went on to record over sixty albums in a career that by 2002 had spanned more than five decades. She won a Grammy award in 1995 for her album *Songs of the Church.* Walker starred alongside Steve Martin in the motion picture *Leap of Faith* (1992), which brought her to the attention of a broader audience. Thus, in the mid '90s, some fans of contemporary Christian music began to discover her work, though the musical style remained consistent with traditional gospel. *CCM* reviewed Walker's *I'm Still Here,* calling it "spine-tingling, emotional music," especially the hand-waving testimonial "I've Got Jesus" and the closing prayer "Close to Thee"; they didn't much like her inclusion of the sappy Broadway song "The Impossible Dream," though. *The Divas of Gospel* is an interesting collection that

pairs songs by Walker with ones by **Yolanda Adams.** *The Very Best of Albertina Walker* is an excellent though brief compilation of songs from Walker's '90s repertoire.

Hezekiah Walker (and the Love Fellowship Tabernacle Choir)

By Hezekiah Walker: 1987—*I'll Make It* (Sweet Rain); 1989—*Oh Lord, We Praise You;* 1991—*Focus on Glory* (Benson); 1992—*Best of Hez* (Sweet Rain); 1993—*Live in Toronto* (Benson); 1994—*Gospel Greats.* By Hezekiah Walker with the Love Fellowship Tabernacle Choir: 1995—*Live in New York by Any Means;* 1997—*Live in London at Wembley* (Verity); 1999—*Family Affair;* 2001—*Love Is Live!*

Hezekiah Walker is pastor of the Love Fellowship Tabernacle in Brooklyn, New York, and leader of that community's choir. Born and raised in the public housing projects of Brooklyn, Walker started the church in 1994 with eight members. The community grew intensely and by 1998 would add another sanctuary in Bensalem, Pennsylvania, to serve commuting members. Peter Jennings from *ABC World News Tonight* did a feature on the church, reporting that the local police precinct credits the ministry's community programs with producing a thirty percent drop in crime in the surrounding neighborhood. Walker is also a gospel singer, who had been making traditional gospel albums since 1987. In 1995, he authorized the formation of a choir at Love Fellowship Tabernacle, under the direction of Joeworn Martin. He has produced a number of live recordings with that group modeled after the successful recordings of **Walter Hawkins.** Though less contemporary in sound than projects by **Kirk Franklin,** Walker and the LFT choir do include songs in R&B and dance-oriented styles. *Live in New York* is the most bland of the choir projects, going heavy on Peabo Bryson-styled songs that tend to sound the same. *Live in London* turns up the heat considerably, with the celebratory "Jesus Is My Help" opening the album. "I'm Waiting" is a dance tune, "To Be Like Jesus" has a slow soulful groove, and "Hold Out" is a funky, keyboard-driven number showcasing the vocal talents of singer Ann McCrary. *Family Affair* mixes live and studio tracks. The latter (including "Let's Dance" and "Give 'Em Your Life") actually come off as club-oriented numbers.

Grammy Awards: 2001 Best Gospel Choir or Chorus Album *(Love Is Live!).*

Rob Walker

See **Wish for Eden.**

Walk on Water

Flord, gtr.; Tot, voc.; Eric Strombold; Magnus Wahl. 1989—*Walk on Water* (Record Station).

Walk on Water was a Swedish synth-pop band with a sound similar to Duran Duran. Lead singer Tot says that none of them were Christians when they signed to make their first album on the general market Record Station label. "I became a Christian and, as we were making the record, the others got saved as well," he explains, also noting that the company was a bit surprised and a little embarrassed by the gospel content of the songs on the final product. The album was a moderate hit in Sweden all the same, with a video for the song "What's the Noise?" winning a national competition. Frontline picked up the album for American distribution and presented it as the inaugural release of their Alarma World Music label, a division set up to import international Christian music to the States. "Time" is the heaviest cut on the record, featuring scorching guitars. Otherwise, the songs tend toward midtempo numbers with layered synthesizers and stacked vocal harmonies. A few acoustic tracks reminded reviewers of Crowded House.

Christian radio hits: "Time" (# 28 in 1991).

Alwyn Wall (and Alwyn Wall Band)
See **Malcolm and Alwyn.**

Sheila Walsh

1982—*Future Eyes* (Sparrow); 1983—*War of Love*; 1984—*Triumph in the Air*; 1985—*Don't Hide Your Heart*; 1986—*Portrait*; *Shadowlands* (Myrrh); 1987—*Say So*; 1989—*Simple Truth*; 1990—*Hymns and Voices* (Word); 1991—*For a Time Like This* (StarSong); 1998—*Hope* (Integrity); 2000—*Blue Waters*; *Peace: A Celtic Christmas*; 2001—*Love Falls Down.*

www.sheilawalsh.com

Scottish music star Sheila Walsh became one of the biggest stars of '80s music in the Christian scene when she broke through to American audiences. She was widely regarded as being at the forefront of the punk and new-wave movements. In fact, she did not perform either style with authenticity but, like Deborah Harry of Blondie, was able to infuse the forms with enough pop sensibilities to transcend their inherent limitations and make them accessible to a much broader audience. But Walsh has been significant in other ways as well. Ultimately she would be less known as a Christian rock star than as a speaker, author, and TV personality. For several years, she was married to Norman Miller, the successful Christian producer responsible for the *Young Messiah* productions of the early '90s (in which she took part).

Walsh was born in Ayr, Scotland, in 1957 and brought up a strict Baptist who could testify to having known the Lord all her life. Her first adventure in popular music appears to have been with a Scottish group called Unity. She received classical training and studied at the London Academy of Operatic Art, which might account for some of the vocal histrionics that she sometimes displayed on her earlier recordings (especially *Future Eyes*). After graduating from London Bible College in 1979, she became an associate evangelist with the organization British Youth for Christ. She sang with a Christian group called The Oasis (not to be confused with Oasis) and then, in 1981, launched a solo career.

Walsh's musical style was defined by what was hot in the United Kingdom, which at that point was several years ahead of the United States. She toured Britain with **Cliff Richard** without incident and, she says, had no idea how radical her music was until she came to the United States to open for **Phil Keaggy** in 1983. "We used lots of special effects, smoke bombs, and fireworks and things," she told *CCM* in a 1996 retrospective. "One woman in Houston was upset that the lights that were shining on me were red and green. These were the devil's favorite colors, she told me. If I had gone for something in mauve, I guess it would have been fine."

Walsh apparently released an early British album called *No One Loves Me Like You,* about which no information is available. *Future Eyes,* regarded as her official debut, was the first album to receive distribution in the United States (a year after its release in a slightly different form on Britain's Chapel Lane). *Future Eyes* was coproduced by husband Miller (who was also president of Chapel Lane Records) and **Larry Norman.** A bulk of the material was written by **Graham Kendrick.** *CCM* named the album one of their Ten Best for the year and gushed over it as representing "electronic, new-wave pop of the first order." They compared Walsh's soaring soprano to that of Barbra Streisand and the bouncy songs to those of Elton John (neither of whom had much to do with new-wave). Lyrically, most of the songs on *Future Eyes* deal with the anonymity and chaos of urban life: "The subway shadows seem to stare at me tonight / Pale fugitive of color hiding in the black and white" ("Mona Lisa"). A year later, *War of Love* would turn up on another *CCM* Ten Best list, and the magazine called it "progressive music disguised as pop." *War of Love,* produced by **Cliff Richard,** opens with a synthesizer-heavy remake of Pete Seeger's "Turn! Turn! Turn!" The song "Mystery" recalls The Pretenders and is probably the standout track. *Cornerstone* magazine claimed, " 'Mystery' is the finest pop tune released this year by a Christian artist, easily comparable to secular chartbusters." *War of Love* also includes "Fooled by a Feelin'," written by **Jamie Owens-Collins.** For her next album, *Triumph in the Air,* Walsh would draw on three songwriters: Kendrick, **Teri DeSario,** and **Chris Eaton.** The latter contributes the ballad "Surrender," an intimate and poignant song that contrasts greatly with the album's explosive title track (by Kendrick). *Don't Hide Your Heart* offers another crystalline ballad, "It's All for You" (by Kendrick), and the radio-friendly "Jesus Call Your Lamb" (by DeSario), an overtly commercial duet with **Cliff Richard.** Also on the latter album, Kendrick's "Not Guilty" retains Walsh's urgent, new-wave approach, while "We're All One" (by **Bryn Haworth**) displays a more straightforward rock sound.

Shadowlands marks a turning point for the artist, and is generally regarded as her finest work. Comparing the project to her Sparrow albums, *CCM* reviewer Devlin Donaldson would say, "Somehow her earlier music now seems to amount to so much acting or posing and not so much a statement of who Sheila is." That perception was accurate, for Walsh would later admit, "In the past, I've tried to be hipper than I really am" and would even allow that the whole new-wave persona (complete with leather jacket and Sheena Easton hair) misrepresented her. In any case, on *Shadowlands* she moves into adult contemporary pop, with enough traces of a Euro-disco sound to keep things interesting. All but one of the songs are products of a songwriting team composed of Rod Trott and Jon Sweet, with whom she would continue to work. "Sand in the Hand" contrasts temporal existence (à la **Kansas**'s "Dust in the Wind") with the eternal love of God. "Keeper of the Key" exalts Jesus (not St. Peter) as the one who holds the key to freedom and life. "Valley of Tears" expresses the theme implied in the album's title (which is taken from the writings of C. S. Lewis): the realization that love and pain are inextricably connected. *Say So* continues in the same musical vein as *Shadowlands* and shows Walsh's first development as a songwriter. She composed the lyrics to "It Could Have Been Me" on a restaurant napkin right after hearing about the sex scandal that would topple Jim and Tammy Bakker's PTL Club ministries. *Say So* produced three hit singles, including a cover of **Vector**'s "Surrender" and two more songs cowritten by Walsh ("Jesus Loves the Church," "Winds of Change"). *Simple Truth* continues the trend toward what *CCM* called "a kinder, gentler Walsh" with a collection of songs produced by Greg Nelson, best known for his work with such MOR singers as **Steve Green, Larnelle Harris,** and **Sandi Patty.** She covers "This Time" by Neil Diamond as a song for her husband and contributes two of her own compositions, "Come into the Kingdom" and "Love Alone."

Walsh's tenure as a Christian pop star was interrupted by what struck many as an anomalous invitation to become cohost of evangelist Pat Robertson's Christian talk show, *The 700 Club.* Her gifts with media were not in question—early on, she had hosted a program called *The Gospel Rock Show* for the BBC. What seemed odd was the very idea of a rock star being paired with someone as terminally unhip as Robertson to host a program that appealed primarily to fundamentalists (Walsh would admit that the first time she saw *The 700 Club* on a trip to America she initially thought it was some kind of *Saturday Night Live* parody of religious TV—and then suddenly realized it wasn't supposed to be funny). But even those who question

Robertson's theology have rarely doubted his savvy. The addition of Walsh was what *The 700 Club* needed to refurbish its staid image and attract a younger audience. Walsh took the gig and played Kathie Lee to Robertson's Regis from 1987 to 1992. At the same time, she hosted another TV program called *Heart to Heart.* In 1992, Walsh was awarded the House of Hope Humanitarian Award and became a national spokesperson for that organization.

Walsh continued to record during her time with *The 700 Club* but drastically changed her style in view of what she has called her "new audience." She not only moved away from punk-rock but away from rock period—even away from pop. "I walked away from doing contemporary music," she explained to *CCM* "to music that was more accessible (to fans of *The 700 Club*)." Thus, *Hymns and Voices* is an a capella collection of traditional hymns and inspirational songs. But in 1991, she would maintain that her "easy listening period" (beginning with *Simple Truth*) was her "least truthful work." She told *CCM,* "I was saying to the public, 'Let me try to make myself acceptable' to you, and I just don't think it worked. There was no heart and no passion in it." Even Robertson complained, furthermore, that she had gotten too mellow and lost her edge. Thus, *For a Time Like This* would return her briefly to a more pop-oriented sound. The album features duets with **Michael English** ("When Love Comes Home") and **Russ Taff** ("A Dove amongst Eagles"). A catchy, standout track is "Heaven Is Holding Us Now," which displays Celtic influence and touches of bagpipes.

In 1992, Walsh was diagnosed as suffering from clinical depression and checked into a psychiatric hospital. She would later recount her struggle for health and healing in a best-selling autobiographical book, *Honestly* (Zondervan, 1996). During the process, her marriage dissolved and she retreated from the public eye. Leaving *The 700 Club,* she went to seminary and earned a master's degree in theology. She became affiliated with the Women of Faith organization, serving as a frequent speaker at their conferences. Walsh did not record again for seven years, but then returned with *Hope* and *Blue Waters.* Both albums display strong Celtic influence. On *Hope* she offers the traditional hymn "I Know That My Redeemer Lives" and recasts her song "Trapeze" from *Say So.* The latter song uses aerial acrobatics as an image for catch-me-or-I'll-die trust; it was originally written after problems with her vocal chords forced a tour cancellation. *Blue Waters* is structured as a concept album chronicling the artist's struggles with mental illness. "Throne of Grace" speaks of the initial decline, while the title track offers a cry for deliverance, and "Saving Grace" describes God's liberating intervention. Walsh also sings "Beautiful, Scandalous Night" (cf. **The Choir**) accompanied by bagpipes, sitar, and flute. A Celtic Christmas album followed in quick succession, and then 2001 brought *Love Falls Down,* a collection of worshipful songs, most of which were written by John Hartley and Gary Sadler. "I'll Be Waiting" and "No One Loves Me Like You" were composed with **Chris Eaton.**

Walsh has been a prolific author of devotional literature. In addition to the aforementioned autobiography, she has written numerous inspirational books: *God Put a Fighter in Me* (Hodder and Stoughton, 1985); *Never Give Up* (Fleming H. Revell, 1986); *Holding On to Heaven with Hell on Your Back* (Thomas Nelson, 1990); *Sparks in the Dark* (Thomas Nelson, 1993); *Gifts for Your Soul* (Zondervan, 1997); *Bring Back the Joy* (Zondervan, 1998); *Life Is Tough But God Is Faithful* (Thomas Nelson, 1999); *Stories from the River of Mercy* (Thomas Nelson, 2000); and *Living Fearlessly* (Zondervan, 2001). She has also written a forthcoming children's book tentatively titled *In Search of the Great White Tiger* and has contributed to numerous other volumes. She is not, however, the author of the numerous romance novels by another author named Sheila Walsh (one of which was made into the motion picture *Runaway Bride*).

Christian radio hits: "Star Song (There Is Born a Child)" (# 21 in 1983); "Mystery" (# 19 in 1983); "Surrendering" (# 21 in 1984); "We're All One" (# 6 in 1985); "Christian" (# 2 in 1986); "What Do You Know (That I Don't)?" (# 4 in 1986); "Angels with Dirty Faces" (# 6 in 1988); "Jesus Loves the Church" (# 3 in 1988); "Wind of Change" (# 7 in 1988); "Surrender" (# 11 in 1989); "Heaven Is Holding Us Now" (# 23 in 1991).

Dove Awards: 1983 International Artist; 1985 International Artist.

The Walter Eugenes

Rick May, kybrd., drums, gtr., bass; Paul Robinette, voc. 1991—*The Walter Eugenes* (Ocean); 1995—*Beautiful* (StarSong); 2000—*Something Sick Inside My Head* (M8).

The Walter Eugenes are an alternative rock duo from the Columbus, Ohio, area that has recorded sporadically, producing three albums in a decade. The band's name is derived from the members' own neglected personal names: Paul Robinette's first name really is Walter, and Rick May's middle name is Eugene. "These are the kinds of names you don't want the other kids to find out about when you're in school," Robinette says. Using the supposedly nerd-names for their band represents a "reverse of peer pressure" that indicates the group's countercultural "be who you are" stance. After playing some bars and clubs, however, the band found their niche to lie far more in church-related venues. Nevertheless, the duo has described their goal as being "to show a more realistic approach to Christianity, rather than just 'love God and everything's gonna be okay'." That said, there is nothing alternative or particularly countercultural about the Walter Eugenes' debut album. Musically, it is straightforward, keyboard-driven '80s rock similar perhaps to the once-big but somewhat forgettable sound of Asia. **John Elefante, Petra,** and **DeGarmo and Key**

would be reference points within the Christian scene. Lyrically, virtually all the songs strive to prompt greater faithfulness to Christian principles. Robinette would later reveal that the album had actually been recorded as a demo, with no expectation of release to the general public. He said in 1995 that "lyrically, it's not quite as honest (as their later work), partially because I didn't have the confidence at that time to really say what I wanted to say."

Beautiful was produced by Dave Perkins and Lynn Nichols of **Chagall Guevara/Passafist,** who encouraged the duo toward an edgier, more guitar-based sound. The most obvious analogy now becomes **U2,** especially on songs like the title track where Robinette offers fairly obvious imitations of Bono's vocal style. Dashes of Sting artistry crop up as well, but the closest sonic equivalent to the *Beautiful* Walter Eugenes would be other **U2**-ish Christian bands like **Dime Store Prophets** and **Seven Day Jesus.** Lyrically, the songs move much more intentionally toward reflecting the classic theological tension between "the already and the not yet" indicated in Robinette's comments above. On the one hand, the songs clearly describe the chaos of modern reality, where "every corner has its prophet" and "the pool of speculation is mighty deep" ("Clear My Head"). On the other hand, they express hope in an ultimate truth that does at times reveal itself, when heaven touches earth and gives reason to believe ("I Need You"). These are songs filled with the disillusionments of personal ambition ("Beautiful"), national pride ("America"), and religious doctrine ("Hands That Feed Us"), yet they are also songs that testify to God's transcendent promises: "I bring you joy / I bring you peace/ And comfort when most will mourn" ("Joy").

After recording *Beautiful,* Rick May got an invitation to play drums for **DC Talk,** which led to other gigs and various pursuits. But five years later, the buddies allowed for the release of a third Walter Eugenes project, the indie *Something Sick Inside My Head.* The album is mostly a collection of preproduction demos from the *Beautiful* sessions. Reviewers were generally impressed with the raw quality of the songs frontloaded on the disc, while acknowledging that the several instrumentals and apparently unfinished songs that make up the latter half of the album get a bit boring. Indeed, the first three tracks easily surpass anything on previous albums, displaying a sound (and an attitude) closer to latter day **Seventy Sevens** than to the more tried-but-true Christian radio sound of the **U2**-ish sophomore outing. "More Than Understanding" opens the album with a bluesy rock and roll celebration of amazing grace and divine wonder. "Great White Lawyer" is a raucous rant about a justice system that often seems to prioritize the system over the justice. "Where Are You?" is the band's funkiest tune, with lyrics that express the desperation of unrequited love in language similar to a biblical psalm of lament.

For trivia buffs: Paul Robinette is also a successful inventor who has earned a number of patents. He was responsible for inventing a "Serious Lock" used on BFI garbage dumpsters.

James Ward

1973—*To the Glory of God* (Peniel); 1974—*Himself* (Dharma); 1979—*Mourning to Dancing* (Music AD); 1981—*Faith Takes a Vision* (Lamb and Lion); 1983—*No Violence* (Music AD); 1986—*Good Advice* (Greentree); 1990—*Blue Believer* (Music AD); 1991—*All over the World*; 1992—*Two Days at Shiloh*.

www.jameswardmusic.com

James Ward is a Christian musician whose basic pop style has often shown strong influences of classical, jazz, and R&B stylings. The son of a Reformed Presbyterian minister, Ward is in fact the descendant of several generations of clergy, and he would credit his religious upbringing with giving him the secure confidence of faith to be a Christian performer. "I don't want to be some guy who does records who is also a Christian," he once said. "I want to be known publicly as a Christian musician." While attending college in Chattanooga, Tennessee, Ward fell in love with traditional gospel music and put together an early '70s outfit called The James Ward Black and Blues Band, copied, he would admit, after the **Edwin Hawkins Singers.** After graduating, he worked for a time with InterVarsity Christian Fellowship, doing solo concerts on college campuses and recording two custom albums *(To the Glory of God* and *Himself)*. Then he put together an avant garde Christian jazz group called Elan, which played together until 1978 doing everything from bebop to progressive jazz. The group was apparently ahead of its time, as Ward would later say "Christian people hated what we were doing." At the same time, however, Ward established himself as a prominent Christian songwriter, penning "Holy Spirit Speak to Me" for **The Imperials** as well as songs for **Pat Boone, Truth,** and other artists.

After Elan's inevitable disbanding, Ward made the album that will always be regarded as his strongest (or at least most commercially accessible) project. *Mourning to Dancing* was initially a custom release like his previous albums, but in 1980 it was re-released on Lamb and Lion with new artwork. Musically, Ward fuses his eclectic styles into a high-energy, R&B flavored pop that *CCM* would compare to Steely Dan. The title track (from Psalm 30:11) and "So His Honor" are overtly evangelical, but a number of songs on the record ("Highway," "Late at Night Again," "Gotta Get Home") represent what Ward would call his "non-confessional Christian songs"; that is, songs that do not contain anything in their lyrical content to identify them as Christian but that nevertheless arise from

his experience of life as a Christian. In March of 1982, Ward would write an editorial for *CCM* defending "high school love songs" and Scripture-based creedal music as different forms of Christian songwriting. Ward thus became one of the first spokespersons for a concept that would eventually come to be taken for granted in the contemporary Christian music subculture. Already in the late '70s he was arguing that "there is no prescribed formula for Christian music" and that Christianity encompasses all of life, not just compartmentalized religious or spiritual aspects. While such a notion is obviously biblical and has always been embraced by historic, orthodox Christianity, the contemporary Christian music industry arose out of American fundamentalism, where such ideas were questioned—indeed where they would *still* be questioned by the fundie-influenced Gospel Music Association twenty years later (cf. entry on **Sixpence None the Richer**).

In any case, Ward's next album, *Faith Takes a Vision,* was produced by Turley Richards and, though it would not be remembered with the same fondness as *Mourning to Dancing,* it was received well at the time. The style again is light rock, with the standout songs being "Take Hold," the title track, and a little treatise in apologetics called "Don't Blame It on My God." After *Faith Takes a Vision,* Ward took another extended hiatus, during which time he wrote "I Belong to You" for **Kathy Troccoli** and issued a number of diverse custom projects, including two cassettes of solo piano music (not listed above, but titled *More Piano Please, Vol. 1* and *Vol. 2*). In 1985, Ward suffered severe back problems that left him bedridden for three months, during which time he composed music for what would be his third (and last) major label release. The album, *Good Advice,* documents his experience in songs like "Growing Pains": "Immobilized on the bed I lay / Nothing to do but pray / Time passed, I began to see / God had something he was saying to me." As the foregoing lyric implies, a fundamental lesson of the forced sabbatical was the value of prayer. Thus, the standout track on *Good Advice,* and no doubt the best-known song of Ward's career, is "Pray, Pray, Pray," a slow gospel workout that features **Kerry Livgren** on guitar, **Joe English** on drums, and Troccoli, **Marty McCall** (of **Fireworks** and **First Call**), and **Greg Volz** on choral vocals. Ward would go back to releasing somewhat obscure indie projects in the '90s and would pretty much vanish from the radar screen of the contemporary Christian music scene. *Blue Believer* is an introspective album that combines low-key solo performances with a handful of R&B shouters performed with Muscle Shoals session musicians. Ward once stated his ambition as being "to dance before God in a way that pleases Him, and to be someone on whose shoulders someone else can stand in later generations."

Christian radio hits: "So His Honor" (# 11 in 1981); "Faith Takes a Vision" (# 5 in 1982); "Pray, Pray, Pray" (# 13 in 1986); "Good Advice" (# 17 in 1986).

Matthew Ward

1979—*Toward Eternity* (Sparrow); 1987—*Armed and Dangerous* (Live Oak); 1988—*Fade to White*; 1990—*Fortress*; 1992—*The Matthew Ward Collection* (Benson); *Point of View*; 1997—*My Redeemer* (Newport); 2000—*Even Now* (Discovery House).

www.matthewward.com

Matthew Ward (b. 1958) is best known as one-third of the successful recording trio of siblings called **2nd Chapter of Acts,** with whom he sang from 1971 to 1979. Like his older sister, **Annie Herring,** however, he has also recorded a number of solo albums. Ward is naturally gifted with a powerful voice and was generally considered to be the best male vocalist in contemporary Christian music throughout the '70s. His piercing, soaring vocals are so distinctive and memorable that by the mid '80s thousands who had heard **2nd Chapter of Acts** ten years previously would be able to identify his voice wailing behind **Donna Summer** on her Number One hit, "She Works Hard for the Money"; he later offered the same vocal support to LeeAnn Rimes on her country albums *Blue* and *Sittin' on Top of the World.* Still, Ward himself would turn down numerous offers to go mainstream over the years, claiming simply, "I don't want to sing dead music." Rather, he maintains, "When all is said and done, I don't want people to remember me for my ability to sing, but that I always turned their eyes to Jesus." Ward has been reluctant to tour in support of his albums, maintaining that "the Lord has not told me to do so."

Ward was raised in a Roman Catholic home, and when both his parents died, he was, at the age of twelve, adopted by his twenty-three-year-old sister Annie and her new husband Buck Herring. Caught up in the charismatic piety of the emerging Jesus movement revival, the Herrings helped him to come to experience the personal relationship with Christ that some Protestants often identify as synonymous with salvation. When he was just thirteen, music producer Buck recorded him singing an upbeat contemporary gospel song, "Jesus Is." That song (now found on **2nd Chapter**'s *20* album) came to the attention of **Pat Boone** and helped the trio of siblings to get their first recording contract.

Ward's debut solo album, *Toward Eternity,* came out while he was still performing with **2nd Chapter of Acts** and, like Herring's *Through the Eyes of a Child,* was regarded as a side project rather than as the launching of a new or distinctive career. The project remains a classic of '70s Jesus music with an all-star cast of performers including **Keith Green, Phil Keaggy, Michael Omartian,** and Abe Laboriel (of **Koinonia** and Weather Report). Ray Parker Jr. (of later "Ghostbusters" fame plays guitar on the song "Your Love Comes over Me"). Jesus music historians and obsessive Greenophiles also treasure the album as containing four obscure Green compositions, the most notable of which may be the ballad "Summer Snow." Another Green song, "Gotta Do Better Than This," is one of that artist's stereotypical piano stomps with lyrics expressing his stereotypical I-know-I-can-achieve-holiness-if-I-just-try-harder lyrics. "Noah's Song" is a Keaggy composition, a pretty and poetic song offering a prayer of thanks such as Noah might have prayed on beholding (at last) those blue skies with heaven's rainbow. The album's most rocking moments come surprisingly on a worship song called "Till the Walls Fall Down," which has a sound reminiscent of Keaggy's "Still the Same" or "Take Me Closer." Most of the other songs were written by sister Annie, some with assistance from Omartian. "Hold On" is a melodic power-pop song that sounds nothing like Ward's work with 2nd Chapter, but rather like something Stevie Wonder might have put on his *Songs in the Key of Life.* "It's All Right" is a paranoid apocalyptic tract sung with an urgency appropriate to the theme. "Angels Everywhere" is a trite embarrassment with lyrics similar to another bad song ("Angels") that **Amy Grant** would do five years later—and, for that matter, to a more circumspect but very good song ("Maybe Angels") that Sheryl Crow would do *twenty* years later. "The Vineyard" closes the album with a beautiful, classically influenced wordless meditation on Mark 12:1–11.

For a long time it appeared that *Toward Eternity* was a one-time fluke. **2nd Chapter of Acts** broke up and Ward was scarcely heard from for eight years. In 1984, he sang on that **Donna Summer** album and he even recorded a duet with the diva called "Love Has a Mind of Its Own" (the song reached Number Seventy on *Billboard*'s mainstream Hot 100 chart). Still, by the time Ward came back with *Armed and Dangerous* in 1986, the Christian music scene had changed and not many of the album's potential new fans could be counted on to remember him. With only eight songs and clocking in at thirty-three minutes, *Armed and Dangerous* is little more than an EP, but it contains some of Ward's rockier offerings. Thematically, it is the artist's low point if only because of the suggestion in the title and title track that Christians are people the world needs to fear. The song "Armed and Dangerous" actually ends with the lines, "No more excuses / No more retreat / Until my enemies lie dead at my feet." Incredibly, two of Christian music's biggest acts (**Petra** and **DeGarmo and Key**) would deign to emulate this bad idea and also record songs called "Armed and Dangerous" in the next decade. Militant imagery continues on Ward's sophomore album with the more biblically sound "Put on the Armour" (cf. Ephesians 6:10–20). Otherwise, the record focuses on inculcating praise ("Glory to God"), trust ("Trust in You"), and other values completely at variance with the implications of the title track. Indeed, it opens with "Red and Yellow, Black and White," a paean to human diversity that builds on a line from a popular children's song. And "Love" is a testimony to the prayers of his mother, imitated now in his prayers for his own children. When Newport Records decided to start releasing Ward's back catalogue on CD in 1999, they compiled the first and third projects together into a single package, skipping over *Armed and Dangerous* as though it never existed. The favored third album, *Fade to White,* is a much more slick production, and Ward has said that he regards it as his most commercial album (which he means as a positive attribution). Ward himself cowrote all of the songs with his producer, John Andrew Schreiner. The best-known track would turn out to be the somewhat atypical "Perfect Union," a wedding song that sounds a lot like that one big adult contemporary ballad that kept coming back in different forms throughout the '80s (Chicago's "You're the Inspiration," Richard Marx's "Right Here Waiting"). "Far Behind" is a funkier, more R&B-influenced number. *Fortress* includes a modern adaptation of Martin Luther's hymn "A Mighty Fortress Is Our God." The thundering opening track is another unfortunately militant but undeniably impressive rock song called "Warrior." A well-titled jazz instrumental called "Psalm 33:3" showcases Ward's band for the album, which includes Dean Castronovo of Bad English. "Faithful and True" and "You" are worship songs, and "Since I Found You" is another suitable-for-weddings love song. *Point of View* is a cohesive and somewhat nostalgic collection that defies all the divergent trends of '90s rock. "Waterfall" sounds like a '70s 2nd Chapter song, and Ward's siblings even come back to join him on "Faces Once More," a memoir to their parents. "Talk About" and "Sin for a Season" (not a **Steve Taylor** cover) are '80s rockers in the tradition of groups like Night Ranger or Survivor. "Forever Stay" is yet another wedding song.

In January of 1994, Matthew Ward was diagnosed at the age of thirty-six as having three different types of cancer. For two-and-a-half frightening and uncertain years he battled the diseases, ultimately experiencing full remission. *My Redeemer* is his emotional testimony to this struggle. Ward would say, *"My Redeemer* is a direct reflection of the power of God to reach into places you think He simply won't. It represents God's heart toward me while I was going through one of the toughest things I've ever had to experience." Eschewing most trappings of rock and roll, Ward delivers ten soft but heartfelt songs designed to foster an atmosphere of praise and thanksgiving. The same spirit informs *Even Now,* which Ward says is intended as a devotional meditation on the cross. He sings Isaac Watts's "When I Survey the Wondrous Cross" and Martin Smith's "Oh, Lead Me" alongside the self-penned hymn "Bring Me to the Cross." Although the album belongs musically to an inspirational praise and worship genre that betrays few indications that it is

the work of a (former?) rock star, it is unquestionably the highpoint of Ward's solo career. He has rarely sung better and the songs are well-chosen anthems to express his sincere and passionate devotion. The best of the best include "There Is One Thing" and "I Will Lift up My Eyes." Both *My Redeemer* and *Even Now* were completely ignored by all media associated with the contemporary Christian music scene, which is notorious for neglecting its own history and quickly forgetting even its most important artists.

For trivia buffs: Matthew Ward's debut, *Toward Eternity,* was supposed to be titled *Matthew 18* as a joke-variation on the **2nd Chapter of Acts** name—the artist was eighteen years old and the biblical chapter Matthew 18 is famous for its teaching on Christian community. The project's release was held up sufficiently for *Toward Eternity* to seem more appropriate.

Christian radio hits: "Hold On" (# 4 in 1980); "It's All Right" (# 13 in 1980); "Love" (# 4 in 1986); "Red and Yellow, Black and White" (# 13 in 1986); "Light of the World" (# 6 in 1987); "Far Behind" (# 7 in 1989); "Perfect Union" (# 9 in 1989); "Racing for the Goal" (# 15 in 1989); "You" (# 22 in 1991); "Since I Found You" (# 15 in 1991).

Sammy Ward

2000—*My Passion* (40).

Sammy Ward is a praise and worship artist on the same order as **Matt Redman** but is distinctive for the southern rock sound that he brings to his material. *My Passion* is mostly a collection of modern worship songs including such well-known songs as "Lord, I Lift Your Name on High" and "I Could Sing of Your Love Forever." Still, Ward performs the songs in surprising arrangements that transform them into almost unfamiliar pop-rock numbers that could just as well be played on college radio stations as in charismatic church services. He also contributes three new songs: the title track, "It's for You," and "Let Your Anointing Fall," which features guest vocals by Michael **Tait** of **DC Talk.**

Warlord

Tim Henderson, drums; Ricky Rodgers, gtr., voc.; Phil Smith, bass. 1998—*Warlord* [EP] (Solid State); 1999—*Rock the Foe Hammer.*

Warlord is a heavy band whose music has been described as doom hardcore with some comparisons of the group to **Zao.** They appear to draw on the basic metal influence of Black Sabbath, to which they add grindcore and death metal tones. The group first hit with a self-titled four-song EP, on which the tracks all appeared to be connected to some sort of medieval fantasy scheme reminiscent of Tolkien's novels (the songs were titled "The Quest," "Where the Road Forks," "The Legend," and "The Gathering"). In fact, the group's front man, Ricky Rodgers, would reveal that they took the lyrics to all the songs from eighteenth- and nineteenth-century hymnals, with slight rewording. Thus, "The Gathering" opens with the following churchy lyrics: "Sing with all the sons of glory / Sing the resurrection song / Death and sorrow, earth's dark story / To the former days belong." Unedited gender-exclusive language aside, such lyrics give the songs a depth and veneer of profundity more akin to **ArkAngel** than the usual heavy metal headbanging anthems. After the EP's release, *HM* magazine reported that Warlord was changing its name to This Fire Within. This did not appear to happen. The full-length Warlord album, *Rock the Foe Hammer,* drops the medieval and hymnic pretensions altogether to present a fairly generic hardcore album that lacks any distinct appeal. Rodgers' vocals are apparently delivered through a processor, in an overdriven shouting style that had critics from *HM* and *Phantom Tollbooth* complaining. Several of the songs are based on specific Scripture passages: "To Die For" draws on Isaiah 53, and "In Vain We Fail," on 1 Corinthians 13. The most interesting song is "Internal Combustion," which sets to music a satirical tract that made the rounds during the '60s, recasting the words of Jesus in Matthew 25:35–36 to address lukewarm mainline churches: "I was hungry and you formed a humanities club to discuss my hunger . . . I was imprisoned and you crept off quietly to your chapel to pray for my release."

Mike Warnke

1976—Mike Warnke Alive! (Myrrh); 1977—Jester in the King's Court; 1978—Hey, Doc!; 1981—Coming Home; 1982—Higher Education [with Rose Warnke]; 1983—Growing Up [with Rose Warnke]; 1985—Stuff Happens (Dayspring); 1986—Good News Tonight; 1988—One in a Million; 1989—Live . . . Totally Weird; 1991—Out of My Mind; 1992—Full Speed Ahead; 2001—Jesus Loves Me (independent).

www.mikewarnke.org

Mike Warnke is not a musician but a Christian minister whose role as a successful Christian comedian had a powerful impact on the contemporary Christian music scene in the '70s and '80s. Warnke was the first Christian comic of the rock and roll era and, as of 2002, would remain without parallel in that admittedly small field. Subsequent performers like **Mark Lowry** have lacked his irreverence and native ability. While Lowry might be a worthy successor to Grady Nutt, he belongs to a different school with ultimate roots in vaudeville—both Lowry and Nutt are Christian companions to Red Skelton, Carl Reiner, and Mel Brooks. Warnke, by contrast, is cut from the same cloth as John Belushi and Sam Kinison. The fact that he worked Christian venues necessitated tamer material (e.g., Warnke is afraid of flying, but a Christian friend assures him, "You're not going to go until it's your time"; he responds, in a voice borrowed from George Carlin, "Yes, but what if it's the *pilot's* time?"). Still, he *performed* that material with the same

hyperactive and unpredictable shock value that marks those artists who look less to vaudeville than to Lenny Bruce for an ultimate muse. Furthermore, Warnke faced challenges that Belushi and Kinison never did. He had to be just as funny while working with tamer material *and* he had to be able to turn a corner in every performance that the secular comics never had to maneuver. He had to get serious at the end of the program, preach a sermon, and deliver an altar call. Could the others have done it? What if someone had told John Belushi in 1978, "Do a performance with no jokes about sex, drugs, or scatology—and no cuss words—but keep everyone howling for an hour-and-a-half and then wind it all up with a deadly serious message that will have them promising to change the way they live." Could he have done it? Viewed in such a light, Warnke's success is nothing short of phenomenal and his skill as a consummate performer can hardly be exaggerated. But unfortunately, the enormous ego that propelled such success would be his undoing. In the '90s, Warnke would no longer be remembered for his skill or for his comedy. Rather, he came to be known as a fraud who had managed to deceive Christian publishers, promoters, and audiences for well over a decade. Despised by those who once adored him, he now served as the Christian music subculture's quintessential example of a "wolf in sheep's clothing."

Warnke first came into the spotlight not as a comedian but as the author of a sensationalist book called *The Satan Seller* (Logos, 1972). In that volume he presented himself as a bornagain convert from satanism. He told in great detail about his former life when he was recruited as a college student to become a servant of the devil and, ultimately, a high priest of satanic worship. The book is filled with outlandish tales of supernatural occurrences as Warnke discovers, for instance, that he and his cohorts can be transported instantly from one place to another. A witch magically appears in his room, gives him a message from her Grand Master, then disappears. Warnke becomes privy to an inner circle of illuminati who in fact control world events. The book is also filled with titillating tales of sex and violence: Warnke and his friends eat severed fingers of sacrifice victims in a mock communion meal; Warnke kidnaps a college coed and supervises a service in which she is gang-raped on a satanic altar; Warnke is rewarded for his service with two female sex slaves, who also seem to have magical powers (one of them is inexplicably replaced when he wishes for someone different). It seems incredible that anyone took the book seriously—legal authorities obviously didn't, since Warnke's confession to felonies did not lead to his arrest—but it became a best-seller among gullible fundamentalists and paranoid Pentecostals who thought its fantastic depiction of a world ruled by spirits and regularly interrupted by miracles offered proof for their literalistic readings of biblical narrative.

Four years after *The Satan Seller,* Warnke emerged in the new, unlikely guise of a Christian comedian. He maintained that the evolution had come about gradually as he began taking speaking engagements on the subject of the occult and added some humor to leaven out what would otherwise make for a very dark presentation. Eventually, he began speaking about other topics as well and, he says, "the comedy began to take on an entity all its own." His first album, *Mike Warnke Alive,* features testimonies about his adventures as a satanic high priest (as well as stories about when he was a pimp and a drug dealer), but allusions to that supposed phase of his life quickly dissipated. By 1982, Warnke told *CCM* in a major profile that "more people think of me as a comedian than as an ex-satanist." In fact, he seemed to shy away from the ex-satanist identification, even when interviewers inevitably brought it up. "The Jester in the King's Court," as he liked to call himself, and the author of *The Satan Seller* seemed like two completely different people.

Warnke was a staple of the concert circuit, regularly performing at festivals and other events featuring Christian musicians. He was a frequent contributor to magazines like *CCM* and during the early '80s wrote a regular column for the magazine called *Rough Cut.* In 1979, he married a woman named Rose who joined him in his comedy routines, adding songs to the sketches. He authored a second book, *Hitchhiking on Hope* (Doubleday, 1979). In terms of content, the first spate of Warnke albums *(Alive!* through *Coming Home)* present the comic primarily as a storyteller, rehashing biblical tales in a hip way alongside accounts of his own pre- and post-Christian experiences. He is adept at making fun of religiosity and of the more ridiculous aspects of evangelicalism. The two albums with Rose *(Higher Education* and *Growing Up)* are of a different order, fueled by her participation but also taking on a more acerbic quality. The Lenny Bruce-to-Sam Kinison trajectory is best seen on the later albums (from 1985 on), as Warnke allows himself to shout and stomp in what might be viewed as a sort of righteous anger. All of his albums sold in numbers consistent with those of Christian music's top performers, making him one of the biggest names in the Christian entertainment media for at least fifteen years running. Mainline Protestants stayed away, remembering *The Satan Seller* excesses, but most of them would not have been inclined toward Warnke's altar-call-oriented brand of ministry anyway. Among revivalistic traditions, he was a guaranteed hit, and thousands of people committed their lives to Christ at comedy shows that turned into crusades. But even after he had become known as a charismatic entertainer and evangelist, the "Satan stuff" never went away. At one point the respected TV newscast *20/20* interviewed him as "an expert on satanism" and he appeared in a similar capacity on *Larry King Live* and *The Oprah Winfrey Show.* In pub-lished newsletters, he solicited money to help "ex-satanists and victims of satanic abuse." As late as 1991, he authored another book titled *Schemes of Satan* (Victory House).

Problems began to arise. Warnke seemed unduly interested in money. He frequently performed for a free-will offering, but then would come out after the show and plead with the audience to give more freely. Buckets would be passed two or three times as Warnke or an associate lamented how much money they were losing on the particular performance and prayed for God to touch enough people that they might just recoup their expenses. As such strategies seemed to become SOP, Warnke got a bad rap in a number of venues. In 1991, Mike and Rose Warnke divorced, but there was no public scandal attached. After they both remarried, they would author a book together called *Recovering from Divorce* (Victory House, 1992).

In June of 1992, about the time the divorce book came out, *Cornerstone* magazine published a devastating, detailed exposé of Warnke's ministry. Most distressing to his fundamentalist followers (but unsurprising to everyone else) was direct evidence that Warnke had fabricated many if not all of the stories reported in his *Satan Seller* book two decades earlier. According to Warnke's own testimony, the events of the book transpired after he entered college and before he joined the navy (where he became a Christian). As it turns out, this was only an eight-month period. During that time frame, a previously clean-cut Warnke supposedly became an alcoholic, then a drug addict, a pusher, and a pimp; he became infected with hepatitis four times, was pistol-whipped five or six times, and shot in the leg once; he got involved in satanism, became the leader of a 1500-member cult, and was elevated to the rank of High Priest; he subsequently met with Charles Manson and Anton LaVey, commanded love slaves, and supervised wild orgies, gang rapes, and ritual sacrifices—all while attending college. He also marched with Martin Luther King Jr. *Cornerstone* reporters Mike Hertenstein and Jon Trott interviewed over fifty persons for their article (eventually one hundred for a subsequent book) who knew Warnke at the time, including his college roommate and the woman who everybody says was his girlfriend for the entire period (neither of whom are ever mentioned in his book). Such witnesses (persons who appear frequently with him in photographs) say that they knew Warnke reasonably well, spent much time with him, and that none of the above incidents ever happened. In fact, they say, Warnke didn't drink or use drugs and, in fact, lived a rather quiet life. In *The Satan Seller,* Warnke describes himself as having waist length white hair and twelve-inch fingernails, painted black; photographs reveal a short-haired, manicured kid who looks a lot more like Anthony Edwards from *Revenge of the Nerds* than Rob Zombie. Faced with such allegations, Warnke joked to the press, "It is an unusual accusation to be charged with not being as bad as you claim." He also maintained that the apparent contradictions could be explained by the fact that the book's editors had manipulated timelines and the like in order to protect the privacy of some of the individuals involved, but that "the events were absolutely as described."

Warnke would eventually admit to "the existence of some exaggeration and embellishment in *The Satan Seller,* which resulted from the dramatic recreation of the incidents in my life." At the same time he adamantly said, "I stand by my testimony of former satanic involvement." This clearly was not enough for the evangelical community, which felt they had been duped. They came to regard Warnke as a bald-faced liar who had made up a dramatic testimony in order to sell books and get speaking gigs. It is possible that the Christian subculture might have been more forgiving if Warnke had been more contrite. If, for instance, he had admitted that his ministry had *started* with a hoax but then turned into something genuine, they just might have gone for it. Indeed, it seems unfortunate that Warnke's fifteen years as a legitimate (and groundbreaking) performer must be trashed on account of an early mistake. More than one analyst has noted that part of the appeal of Warnke's comic routines lay in his ability to exaggerate, embellish, and completely fabricate stories, albeit ones that were presented knowingly as fiction. Hypothetically, then, the evangelical community *might* have come to regard *The Satan Seller* debacle as youthful folly on the part of an overly enthusiastic performer who had not yet found his niche. But that didn't happen, in part because of Warnke's stubborn refusal to own up to what the evidence seemed to indicate, and in part because of other matters.

One of the other matters was the simple revelation by *Cornerstone* that Rose Warnke had been the artist's third wife since beginning his public ministry. He had been a rather flagrant "womanizer," openly living with women before marriage, engaging in adulterous liaisons, and encouraging the Christian musicians who traveled with him to do so as well. Such artists as Mike Johnson, Randy Matthews, and Danny Taylor would eventually testify to Warnke's off-stage decadence (drunkenness, drug abuse), admitting to their own participation as well. Their careers came undone with his, sucked into a vortex of no accountability that he appeared to have instigated.

And then there was the matter of Warnke's finances. Spurred on by the *Cornerstone* piece, the *Lexington Herald-Leader,* a Kentucky newspaper published in the area near Warnke Ministries' headquarters, disclosed that in 1991 Warnke paid himself and Rose Warnke (his former wife, who still served as codirector of the organization) each a salary of $250,000, apart from all royalties on books, albums, and videotapes. Also in 1991, when Mike and Rose divorced, she received a $600,000 home, 350 acres of land valued at well over half a million dollars, a nearby condominium valued at $241,500, another condominium in Florida valued at $340,000, a Cadillac, several horses, and over $100,000 in cash as *her* share of the property division. That same year (1991), Mike Warnke solicited donations in newsletters and mailings to fund a crisis hotline for runaways and abandoned children. In fact, the newspaper reports, the so-called hotline was simply the toll-free number for Warnke Ministries; it consisted of one phone that was answered by the office secretary from eight-to-five Monday through Friday, as it had always been. The Warnkes told the paper that a "shortage of funds" prevented a separate phone line from being installed or the current one from being staffed additional hours—despite the fact that they had just given themselves raises totaling over $130,000.

The crisis resulting from these controversies would never be resolved. As of 2002, Warnke continued to operate a website where he posts extensive documents from his self-appointed Board of Elders (Baptist and Nazarene minsters) attesting to the full investigation into all allegations and to his complete restoration. The website also continues to present him as a former "satanist high priest." In 2001, Warnke and his fourth wife, Susan, celebrated their tenth wedding anniversary. That same year, he released another album, titled *Jesus Loves Me.* Meanwhile, Hertenstein and Trott had continued their research and published an in-depth account as *Selling Satan: The Tragic History of Mike Warnke* (Cornerstone Press, 1993). As the book indicates, the whole debacle had serious implications for the Christian entertainment industry, including the contemporary Christian music culture. Hertenstein and Trott end up pointing their fingers at a morally compromised marketing system that evaluates products in terms of their sales potential rather than their intrinsic worth. Promoting books that offer outlandish testimonies without bothering to secure any substantiation of the content is but one instance of such a market-driven approach. The Warnke incident fueled a disgust with industry that would destroy the myth that Christian record companies were somehow more godly than corporations in the general market. As a result, an increasing number of Christian artists sought either to sign with general market labels or to explore alternative and independent outlets.

War Rocket Ajax

Lance Jones, voc., gtr.; Reuben Martinez, drums; Ben Perez, bass // Joe Curiel, gtr. (+ 2001). 1999—*War Rocket Ajax* (Bettie Rocket); 2001—*I Lost My Mind.*

War Rocket Ajax is a punk-influenced rock band from San Antonio, Texas. Their first album for the Bettie Rocket label features what is sometimes called a "punkabilly" sound (i.e., punk with a distinctive retro-southern accent), while the second moves more toward basic rock and roll with nods to Social

Distortion and The Ramones. *War Rocket Ajax* includes "Bullet Train to Heck," a humorous tune that contrasts two trains, one "not so nice" headed for Paradise and another comfy, luxury one (recliner seats and pretty waitresses) headed for that other place. *I Lost My Mind* offers "Human Torch," a creative adaptation of Christ's admonition to "Let your light shine" (Matthew 5:16).

Washington

1990—*Every Time* (Frontline); 1991—*Serious.*

The urban gospel performer who went by the single name Washington tried to effect a unique sound that must have seemed like a good idea but failed to catch on. Washington practiced a form of melodic talking that was about halfway between rap and singing, the idea being to appeal to those who found straight rap to be insufficiently musical as an art form. Washington alternates between singing, rapping, and melodic talking on his debut album, *Every Time.* The project might have been successful as some sort of transition from R&B to rap in a day before hip-hop gained widespread popularity. But it didn't work. In 1990, most Christian music fans didn't like rap, period, and those who did apparently wanted the real thing. Thus, Washington almost dispenses with rap on his follow-up, *Serious,* singing the R&B songs in a smooth tenor voice. Notably, neither album features strong bass lines, an odd deficit for dance-oriented material. Both records were produced by **Tim Miner** and feature a number of songs cowritten with Miner and/or **Angie Alan.** Lyrically, the songs on both records are explicitly Christian, with the songs containing ministry-oriented messages. The title track for *Every Time* is about God's accessibility through prayer. "You're No Good" from that album samples Linda Ronstadt's hit (# 1 in 1975) in a song addressed to the devil. "Pinocchio" is a more secular, generic song about the hazards of lying. *Serious* offers a pair of songs that anticipate the parousia with a dialogue between humanity ("Wanna Be Ready") and Christ ("If You Wanna Go"). The one hip-hop offering on the album, "Shout It Out," is a radically reworked version of the old Tears for Fears song that was Number One for three weeks in 1985.

Watashi Wa

Lane Beirmann, drums; Mike Newsom, gtr.; Seth Roberts, voc., gtr.; Roger Tomkins, bass. 2000—*Lost a Few Battles . . . Won the War* (Bettie Rocket); 2001—*What's in the Way.*

Watashi Wa is a self-described aggressive pop band from Southern California. Their label markets them as a pop-punk band and even as an emo-pop-punk band, but the group objects to categories. Watashi Wa formed in 1999 and made two albums while all of the members were still in high school. Their sound tends toward that of **MxPx** and Green Day but, as

7ball would insist, "is different enough to be taken seriously." Melodic guitar lines are emphasized over the trademark start/stop tendencies of their mentors. The band's songs focus generally on struggles with families, relationships, and with each other. The sophomore project departs from the punk influences in favor of more straightforward pop hooks. It offers "Cure for a Disease," which Roberts says is what the band is all about—to "give hope." The name Watashi Wa means "I am" in Japanese, and so is a reference to God's own self-identification in the Bible (e.g., Exodus 3:14).

The Waterboys

See **Mike Scott.**

Waterdeep

Don Chaffer, voc., gtr.; Brandon Graves, drums (−2001) // Lori Coscia Chaffer, voc., gtr. (+ 1997); Kenny Carter, bass (1998, −2001); Christena Graves, kybrd. (+ 1998, −2001). 1995—*Chase Away the Birds* (independent); 1997—*Sink or Swim*; 1998—*Everyone's Beautiful* (Squint); 2001—*You Are So Good to Me.*

A college rock neohippie band from Wichita, Kansas, Waterdeep attained a somewhat legendary status as a Midwest indie band before signing with **Steve Taylor**'s Squint label and taking their sound to the masses. The group, whose intensely loyal fans sometimes follow the band from place to place on tour, seem to be unusually adept at fostering community. Taylor says, "They've got a telepathy on stage that's usually only found in jazz." Furthermore, "the songwriting is both deep and *wide*—their songs are profound but still accessible to a broad audience." By the time of their Squint debut, the group developed a sound sometimes compared to the Dave Matthews Band (with female vocals), though Phish and the Grateful Dead would also provide obvious reference points. That sound had evolved out of a Dylanesque singer/songwriter style evident on an early indie solo album that Don Chaffer had made called *You Were at the Time for Love.* As a student at the University of Kansas, Chaffer also played with Brandon Graves and future wife, Lori Coscia, in a band called Hey Ruth, which recorded some projects between 1990 and 1992. Waterdeep initially formed as a folk group in 1995 with Chaffer, Graves, and a few other instrumentalists playing acoustic songs on *Chase Away the Birds.* Things began to heat up when Coscia and Chaffer married and she joined the group, adding ethereal and disarming vocals, in addition to songwriting and guitar skills. The band was not just Hey Ruth redux, however, for *Sink or Swim* revealed the new full-tilt hippie rock that would become their signature sound: an eclectic mix of funk, rock, and folk with distinct textures. By the time they signed with Squint, the lineup had solidified to include bassist Kenny Carter and

Graves' wife, Christena, on keyboards and additional vocals. Dan Chaffer would attempt to describe the group's odd aural mix to *Release* magazine: "First, there's an acoustic singer/songwriter balladry sort of thing that happens, second, a rock and roll/pop thing, and third, an atmospheric side." The band is also known for its improvisational jams and for its incorporation of worship into all of its various styles.

Everything's Beautiful opens with a few acoustic sing-alongs. "He Will Come" juxtaposes images of the glory to be experienced at Christ's parousia ("He'll remove his flashing garment, place it on the lowest harlot") with mundane scenes from daily life ("She spilled her coffee in her Chevy on her way to work at 8:05"). "Sweet River Roll" has a flowing gospel sound with soothing lyrics about comfort in the midst of pain. Funky electric tunes include "Wicked Web" (a more alliterative paraphrase of Shakespeare's "what a tangled web we weave") and the melodramatic "Confessions of a Broken Down Man," with Dan Chaffer on lead vocals. *Everything's Beautiful* also includes an almost calypso cover of **Van Morrison**'s "Whenever God Shines His Light," which doesn't really work any better than it sounds. In general, the album is much more subdued than the band's live shows—the Phish comparisons that are regularly made by concertgoers would probably not occur to anyone whose only experience of the band was *Everything's Beautiful*. But other complimentary analogies commend themselves: *Phantom Tollbooth* would say that on this album the group "could easily be compared to the late **Mark Heard**, pointing out hope to the disenfranchised, while playing some kick-butt folk music at the same time." The title track is not a Ray Stevens' cover but a compassionate account of memories that allows past foolishness and even the sins of youth to be offered to God with mixed measures of penance and thanksgiving. As for atmospherics, "I'm Still Here" is an achingly beautiful ballad in the tradition of some of Don Henley's Eagles' songs, and "Hush" is a gorgeous, building showcase for Lori Chafer's voice. The album closes with a worshipful interpretation ("Psalm 131").

Worship music would dominate the next major phase of Waterdeep's ministry. In late 1999, the group joined with a husband and wife duo known as 100 Portraits to produce an unofficial album not listed above called *Enter the Worship Cycle* for an independent label (Blue Renaissance Music). That disc presents fifteen original acoustic worship songs, many of which draw heavily on Scripture. Then in 2001 the band would announce that, due to financial restraints, the group's official lineup was being cut back to just a duo (Dan and Lori Chaffer). "Essentially, we laid everybody off," Dan said, indicating a hope that the full band would be able to come back together again in the future. In the meantime, the duo released another worship album titled *You Are So Good to Me*. Virtually all of the eleven tracks are sung directly to Jesus as personal expressions of love and praise. *CCM* called the album "a throwback to the Jesus movement," noting that "the simplicity of both the songs and the arrangements conveys a sense of privacy." The title track uses music as a metaphor for divinity ("You are beautiful, my sweet, sweet song"). **Fernando Ortega** offers guest vocals on "You Are Lovely."

Waterdeep is partnered with Wichita Vineyard Christian Fellowship and has an official mission statement: "to be a part of a community that leads people into a deeper relationship with Christ through the arts." Chaffer describes the band's songwriting as a relational exercise in communication: "The biggest thing an artist can do is say something other people feel but haven't been able to put into words."

Water into Wine Band

Pete McMunn; Trevor Sanford; Bill Thorp; Ray Wright. 1974—*Hill Climbing for Beginners* (Myrrh); 1976—*Harvest Time* (custom).

The Water into Wine Band was an early British Jesus music group that obtained a strong cult following in its native land, with some of the obsessive loyalty leaking across the pond to America. Basically a folk group, the band capitalized on vocal harmonies and augmented their sound with classical arrangements and creative use of various woodwinds, interesting percussion, and stringed instruments. Violinist Bill Thorp was later accepted into the London Symphony Orchestra. The group is really only known for one album, *Hill Climbing for Beginners*. That project features an eleven-minute opus titled "Song of the Cross" in addition to crowd favorites "Stronger in the World" and "I Used to Be Blind (But Now I'm Shortsighted)." Unfortunately, when the album was released in America, the suits at Myrrh thought it needed to be spruced up and the whole project was remixed in a supposedly more rock-oriented format that would sound more like what everyone else in Christian music was doing at the time. Critics consider the American issue a travesty, while collectors price the original British edition at £250. The Water into Wine Band also recorded a follow-up project called *Harvest Time*, but only 500 copies were pressed and they were all sold at a single engagement—the third annual *Greenbelt* festival in 1976. The latter rarety opens with a song called "Wedding Song" (not a **Noel Paul Stookey** cover) and contains a beautiful ballad showcasing Thorp's violin ("Waiting for Another Day"). The ambitious title track is an artistic classically-influenced composition that takes up all of Side Two. Copies of *Harvest Time* are priced at £750.

Watermark

Christy Nockles, voc.; Nathan Nockles, gtr., voc. 1998—*Watermark* (Rocketown); 2000—*All Things New*; 2002—*Constant*.

Watermark is a husband and wife duo that leads worship regularly at the First Baptist Church in Houston, Texas, the congregation from whence **Caedmon's Call** also sprang. In 1998, they began releasing albums of worship songs that have strong pop sensibilities and demonstrate concern for artistic integrity. Christy Nockles, who handles most of the lead vocals, says they concentrate on "making worship music connect the human soul to the living God." Nathan Nockles says they view the *music* portion of a song as more than just a backdrop for lyrics: "the music should be expressive of worship in its own right; it should say as much as the lyrics and make a whole picture." The couple's first album, *Watermark,* would inspire obvious comparisons to **Out of the Grey,** though Christy's voice is probably more similar to **Susan Ashton** than to Christine Denté. Ten of the eleven tracks are addressed directly to God, with thanksgiving as the primary sentiment. "Gloria" derives its chorus from the *Gloria in excelsis Deo* of the Latin Mass. "Stranded in Delaware" departs from the narrow praise focus somewhat to present a prayer for God's presence when feeling lost and far from home (the state of Delaware is used as an allegorical reference for "the middle of nowhere," an image that might work better in Houston than in New England). *Watermark* sold quite well for a debut worship project (over 100,000 copies), but the couple's joy over this success was muted by personal tragedy as Christy suffered two miscarriages within a year. One song on their follow-up album, *All Things New,* conveys the grief over these losses ("Glory Baby"), but otherwise the album continues in the melodic, spunky, flowing vein of the first project. Several of the songs are explicitly based on Scripture: "Good for Me" from Psalm 37:4; "Lord, You Are My Stronghold" from Psalm 37; "Where to Find Me" from 2 Chronicles 16:9; and the title track from 2 Corinthians 5:17. The most noticeable shift on the second album, however, is a trend away from the worship paradigm toward more typical Christian adult contemporary message songs. "More Than You'll Ever Know" is a song about human friendships. "Where to Find Me" presents God's words to humanity (rather than human praise to God). Still, the majority of the songs are praise-oriented. "Who Am I" was written by the couple but originally recorded by **Point of Grace;** it is sung here as a medley with "Grace Falls Down," a song written by members of **Passion,** whose *The Road to One Day* Nathan produced.

Wayne Watson

1978—*Canvas for the Sun* (Archive); 1980—*Workin' in the Final Hour* (Milk and Honey); 1982—*New Lives for Old;* 1984—*Man in the Middle;* 1985—*Best of Wayne Watson; Giants in the Land* (Dayspring); 1987—*Watercolor Ponies; Wayne Watson in Concert;* 1988—*The Fine Line;* 1990—*Home Free;* 1991—*The Early Works* (Benson); 1992—*How Time Flies* (Dayspring); 1993—*A Beautiful Place; Signature Songs* (Greentree); 1994—*One Christ-mas Eve* (Word); 1995—*The Very Best; Field of Souls* (Warner); 1998—*The Way Home* (Word); 2000—*Wayne Watson.*

Wayne Watson has been performing Christian MOR pop for over twenty years, rarely generating the sales of a major star like **Steve Camp** or **Steven Curtis Chapman** but constantly producing records of a style and quality similar to those artists' works. With over fifteen albums (not counting compilations) to his credit, Watson's longevity and tenacity in a field noted for burn-out is remarkable. He has remained a staple of Christian radio throughout his career, almost defining the preferred sound of male inspirational singers for adult contemporary stations. Watson was born in Wisner, Louisiana, in 1955 and raised a Southern Baptist, first there and then in Houston, Texas. While attending Louisiana Tech University, he performed with the Continental Singers. After graduating, he began his solo career.

Watson's independent debut features only one original song ("If You Will Trust"), concentrating instead on gospel standards like "Give Them All to Jesus." The three Milk and Honey releases that followed sold about 150,000 copies total—impressive figures for that time—and displayed Watson's talents as songwriter and producer as well as performer. *CCM* actually compared the artist to Jackson Browne in their review of *Workin' in the Final Hour* and to **Keith Green** in a profile of *Man in the Middle.* Neither of those analogies would come up again, as the artist only flirted with rock and seemed much more comfortable in easy listening venues. *Workin' in the Final Hour* features four self-penned songs, but the radio hit would come with Phil McHugh's "One Day." *New Lives for Old* would earn Watson Dove nominations for Male Artist and Inspirational Album of the year. "The Sacrifice" breaks with the dominant inspirational ballad sound to provide a more interesting, mysterious tune that tells the story of the crucifixion to the accompaniment of flute and guitar. *Man in the Middle* is a more personal offering, presenting songs born out of the artist's experiences with his family.

By 1985, Watson had established his own studio (Rivendell Recorders) in Pasadena, Texas, and switched labels to sign with DaySpring, a division of Word. The title track to *Giants in the Land* is more of a power-pop song similar to something that **Petra** or **White Heart** might have performed. The song offers an indictment of the social trend toward blatant paganism: "They're not hiding anymore / They're not ashamed anymore / Evil deeds once done in secret / They're celebrating sin on the streets." The songs "Look Me in the Heart" and "Peace That Passes Understanding" were written out of Watson's struggles with his uncle's suicide. "Somewhere in the World" is a sentimental ode to children growing up in the faith and, specifically, to one such child whom Watson hopes to meet someday: "I don't even know her name / But I'm prayin' for her just the same / That the Lord will write his name upon her heart /

'Cause somewhere in the course of his life / My little boy will need a godly wife." *Watercolor Ponies* also dips into modern rock with its title track, which uses a sweet image for innocent childhood to reflect wistfully on the ambiguous feeling of loss parents feel as their little ones grow up (the titular watercolor ponies are in pictures that decorate a refrigerator door). The best-known track from the album, however, would become "I Still Believe," an inspirational anthem that, unfortunately, defines faith negatively as stubborn anti-intellectualism and as rejection of modern culture rather than in positive terms of trust and hope. A much better song, "That's Not Jesus," would grace *The Fine Line*. A response to the public foibles of televangelists like Jimmy Swaggart and Jim Bakker, the song states the obvious fact that such shenanigans do not reflect on the Lord but only expose the weakness of "some flesh and blood like you and me somehow gone astray." While it is unlikely that anyone (outside of fundamentalism) ever took Swaggart or Bakker seriously as representatives of Christ, the song scores its point to a catchy roots-rock beat augmented by **Bruce Carroll**'s harmonica. "Before My Very Eyes" also sees Watson keeping up with the times, adopting a world-beat rock and roll sound reminiscent of Paul Simon. "Untouched by Human Hands" is a more typical, building inspirational anthem with a powerful message: "I disregard the Lord's command / When I walk through my journey untouched by human hands." *The Fine Line* shows thematic depth on a number of other tracks as well. "Yesterday's News" reflects on how quickly concern for the starving children of Africa passed from the national consciousness. "I Could Live without You" states a realization of adult faith that calls for a new assessment of commitments and priorities: "I could live without you / I know I could get by / Millions of people do / Why can't I?" Above all, the title track deconstructs tidy categories intrinsic to self-righteous religion: "There's a fine line between contentment and greed / Between the things that I want and the things that I need." *The Fine Line* would remain Watson's best and most critically acclaimed work.

As Watson entered the '90s, *CCM* would note that his "music is moving closer to an adult audience," without apparently realizing that this had been his market all along. *Home Free* goes from adult contemporary to adult traditional, with choral praise anthems ("Almighty," "When God's People Praise") and easy listening ballads ("Home Free") like those that one would hear on an Oral Roberts or Lawrence Welk TV special. The title track was inspired by the death of a close friend, a thirty-three-year-old wife and mother who succumbed to leukemia. "Teenager in the House" offers an exception to the album's dominant sound and mood with a more hip and humorous reflection on current adventures (e.g., driving lessons) with the heroes of "Watercolor Ponies" a few years down the road. On *A Beautiful Place,* the artist made a 180-degree

turn, putting together a live band and recording upbeat songs with a **Bryan Duncan** pop/R&B feel to them. The standout cut, "Walk in the Dark," declares, "I'd rather walk in the dark with Jesus / Than to walk in the light on my own."

Watson would finish out the millennium with three albums produced by **Michael Omartian.** His collaboration with the latter maestro produced a consistent mature pop sound similar in some respects to that of general market artist Don Henley. Watson accepts his status as an adult contemporary singer but draws on the legacy of classic rock with a penchant for what seems more timeless than trendy. *Field of Souls* features an anthemic title track that calls on believers to become evangelists, reaping the harvest for the kingdom. It also includes "Class of '95," a song written for his eldest son's high school graduation and packaged as a single for sale with a congratulations greeting card. *The Way Home* continues the ongoing series of songs about parenting and child rearing with "Come Home," a song describing the anxiety of a parent waiting at night for an almost grown child to return. "What Are You Still Doing Here?" is a sentimental song for Watson's wife, and "For Such a Time as This" is an anthem of encouragement inspired by professional athlete Ken Rutgers (of the Green Bay Packers). "Here in This Town" is a song written by Gordon Kennedy (of **Dogs of Peace**) and **Phil Madeira** with profound lyrics about religion in America: "Here in this town / They all say your name / Sunday it's holy / Monday profane." The self-titled *Wayne Watson* features a stripped-bare sound with songs that are especially introspective. Watson says he was inspired to write and record it after seeing James Taylor perform in 1999 and being impressed all over again with the "power of simplicity." He offers a tribute to his departed father on "Turning into Dad" and mourns overlooked victims of the Columbine tragedy on "The Ones Left Standing." All three of Watson's late '90s projects demonstrate theological maturity such as that evident on *The Fine Line:* a grappling with uncertainties of life and with the problem of pain, yet with deep appreciation for the mysteries of grace. "Merciful Heaven" from *Wayne Watson* expresses well the idea that, while life may not be fair, people may at least be thankful that they do not get what they deserve.

Watson's songs have been repackaged on several compilation albums, none of them definitive. *Best of Wayne Watson, The Early Works,* and *Signature Songs* all collect songs from the early Milk and Honey years. *How Time Flies* and the mistitled *The Very Best* concentrate exclusively on the period from *Giants in the Land* on. Watson is also author of the book *The Way Home* (Howard, 1998), which offers devotionals based on twenty-five different songs from his career. An earlier volume, *Watercolor Ponies* (Word, 1992), offers meditations on parenting and child rearing, with (watercolor) illustrations by Sandra Shields.

Christian radio hits: "One Day" (# 9 in 1981); "New Lives for Old" (# 5 in 1982); "The Sacrifice" (# 6 in 1983); "People of God" (# 21 in 1983); "Celebrate" (# 2 in 1984); "Love Found a Way" (# 17 in 1984); "Man in the Middle" (# 10 in 1985); "Peace That Passes Understanding" (# 12 in 1986); "Giants in the Land" (# 10 in 1986); "Somewhere in the World" (# 18 in 1986); "Friend of a Wounded Heart" (# 5 in 1987); "Material Magic" (# 2 in 1987); "Watercolor Ponies" (# 12 in 1988); "I Still Believe" (# 9 in 1988); "That's Not Jesus" (# 2 in 1989); "Long Arm of the Lord" (# 12 in 1989); "Another Time, Another Place" [with **Sandi Patty**] (# 8 in 1991); "Home Free" (# 6 in 1991); "Almighty" (# 12 in 1991); "Freedom" (# 14 in 1991); "It's Time" (# 15 in 1993); "Walk in the Dark" (# 6 in 1993); "More of You" (# 25 in 1994); "Say What You Say" (# 9 in 1994); "Field of Souls" (# 9 in 1995); "Don't You Remember" (# 11 in 1996); "Rock Steady" (# 25 in 1996).

Dove Awards: 1988 Pop/Contemporary Album *(Watercolor Ponies)*; 1989 Male Vocalist; 1992 Pop/Contemporary Song ("Home Free").

The Way

Dana Angle, gtr., voc., bass; Gary Arthur, gtr., kybrd., bass; Bruce Herring, voc.; Ric Latendresse, gtr., voc. (−1973) // John Wickham, gtr., bass (+ 1973); Alex MacDougall, drums, perc. (+ 1975). 1973—*The Way* (Maranatha); 1975—*Can It Be?*

The Way is often referred to as "a better version of America," though they might also be described as "an almost-as-good version of Crosby, Stills and Nash." One of the earliest of the pioneering Jesus music groups to come out of Calvary Chapel in Costa Mesa, California, The Way perfected acoustic country-folk music and played it as well as anyone. Their tenure was brief, but their influence strong. They are best remembered for their first album, which showcases memorable melodies sung in what seem to be impossibly pretty voices to the accompaniment of frill-free acoustic guitar. Simplicity is a forté—there are no extraneous passages, no extra notes, no histrionics, no horns, and absolutely no synthesizers. Lyrics are not a strong point, but the down-home sincerity generally atones for lack of sophistication or poignancy. There is no "Sister Golden Hair" or "Suite: Judy Blue Eyes" in their repertoire, but song-for-song, The Way's debut album is as fine a product as many packages by either of the groups that produced those masterpieces. Their other material is worthy of note as well.

The Way first came to the attention of the Jesus people with a song called "If You Will Believe" on *The Everlastin' Living Jesus Music Concert* (Maranatha, 1971). The latter album was the compilation project from Calvary Chapel that introduced Jesus music to the world; it is now regarded as the most historically significant album of Christian music ever recorded. For that reason, "If You Will Believe" may be The Way's best-known song, though it is far from their best. It has the primitive but affecting quality of a summer camp sing-along, which, indeed, it became. Lyrically, it presents the outcome of faith as a connection with God that is to be experienced emotionally:

"If you will believe, then you will receive and feel / The gift of love, and love from above, is real." Taken to an extreme, this linking of emotion with the assurance of faith would prove theologically problematic, but in the early days of the Jesus movement revival, the emphasis on God's grace as something that could be *felt* (cf. **Love Song**'s "Feel the Love") served as a counterpoint to orthodox religion, which was perceived as staid and emotionally detached.

The Way would place three more songs on Maranatha compilation albums. *Maranatha Two* (1972) includes "Jesus Is the One" and "Jesus Is All That We Need." Both are strong tracks, and the latter is stellar—a classic folk tune that, a decade later, might have been turned into a schmaltzy adult contemporary ballad. Here it is saved from such ignominy and rendered as a simple acoustic song with a direct and unembellished message. Perhaps more than any other song by The Way, it possesses that mysterious quality that the Jesus people would describe as "an anointing." No one ever figured out how to impart such a quality to songs or performances—perhaps because it cannot be imparted. Anointed songs, like this one, are rendered with such sincere devotion as to be inspiring in a way that cannot be feigned, contrived, or reproduced. Notably, the lyric to "Jesus Is All That We Need" again expresses a prominent theme of the Jesus movement, while avoiding the pitfall of individualism to which converts were often susceptible. It would have been easy (and expected) for Gary Arthur to have written a song called "Jesus Is All That *I* Need." As it is, The Way offers a psalm of testimony to the mystery of a corporate relationship with Christ (as opposed to the Jesus people's usual fixation on a personal relationship with Jesus). The *Maranatha Four* compilation (1974) also includes one number by The Way called "Have You Heard?" which appears to be an outtake from the debut album. At some point prior to the recording of that album, founding member Jon Latendresse left the group to become Maranatha's first and longtime accountant. The addition of John Wickham, a phenomenal guitarist, was quite a coup and set the group up for the more rock-oriented electric style of their second outing.

As indicated above, *The Way* presents ten near perfect country folk songs, each of which is distinctive and remarkable on its own terms. "Son Come Out" opens the project with a confident melody and indelible chorus that represents one of the first uses of what would become a very overworked play on words ("sonshine") as Jesus music developed. "You're Caught in a World" is more of a Top 40 pop song built on an infectious hook that belies the seriousness of the lyric. The song promises those whose life is "sometimes hard to take" that "there is only one way to escape." An uncharacteristic electric guitar kicks off "Song of Joy," which also features a piano interlude and an overlay of instruments that builds with some intensity before resolving in a haunting, almost a capella summons: "Listen to Jesus / Listen to his word / Listen to Jesus / And think about what you've heard." The next track is the album's prettiest country ballad, "Come on Down," a song that, apart from its evangelical lyrics, would not have been out of place on Neil Young's *Comes a Time* album. After these four excellent tracks, Side One closes with the album's absolute best: a gorgeous, worshipful song of yearning called "Closer to God," which features what might be the finest guitar harmonics ever put on record.

Side Two of *The Way* opens with the album's darkest tone, another electric song called "New Song." Edgier than the rest of the album, the song once again addresses those who may be searching for peace and love, promising that Jesus "can make you happy" and provide "life abundantly, with no more envy or strife." A very simple and very pretty acoustic guitar line leads out of that song's momentary darkness to introduce "There's a Love," another basic folk song sung almost as a solo with slight percussion kicking in at key moments. "He's the Reason to Go On" is a country ballad reminiscent of Poco. "Harvest Time" also has a country flavor, but works better than the previous song, presenting words of warning based on Jesus' rural parables: "Jesus said, you will reap what you've sown / When judgment comes, what you've done will be made known." Such a theme offsets the predominantly sunny character of *The Way* and provides it with necessary grounding in more melancholy sounds and somber themes. The next track, "Are You Listening?" has a similar gloomy but haunting quality, allowing the listener to feel as well as hear the seriousness of its inquiry and claim: "Are you listening? / Can you hear? / The Holy Spirit is drawing you near / Are you feeling? / Can you feel? / The Son of God will show you it's real."

The Way's second album bears little resemblance to its first, but remains exceptional in its own right. The band added rock and roll to its panoply of styles and came up with a wildly eclectic collection of material that lacks focus but preserves more innovation than had been demonstrated by any other group at the time (this was still a year before **Daniel Amos** released their debut album and two years before *Shotgun Angel*). The album opens with "A Cowboy's Dream," a melodic country-rock song that differs from the country-folk of the debut through employment of broader, electric instrumentation and pedal steel (courtesy of **Al Perkins,** the album's producer). It is basically in the same musical ballpark as Pure Prairie League, minus the twang. "Days of Noah" comes closest to the folk stylings of the first album, though again the arrangements are richer, with layered vocal harmonies, fuller instrumentation, and extended electric guitar solos. Lyrically, "Days of Noah" testifies to the imminent return of Christ with reference to Matthew 24:37. "I've Been Sealed" is a pure country romp with

a hand-clappin', foot-stompin' chorus that declares, "Ain't nobody gonna take my joy away . . . I've been washed in the blood and I know that I'm here to stay"; someone really does go "Yee-ha" halfway through. Likewise, "Sittin' in the Pew" is a hillbilly jug-band indictment of those whose participation in church activities seems to lack any true devotion. Both of the former two songs ("I've Been Sealed," "Sittin' in the Pew") have elements of the Ozark Mountain Daredevils. By contrast, two more songs move toward guitar-dominated art-rock. "Do You Feel The Change?" combines fluid guitars reminiscent of *Tommy*-era Who with Santana-like percussion and almost choral vocals in service of a song that, unfortunately, does not have the lyrical strength that such an opus deserves ("Jesus is why we can sing / Freedom is what he can bring / New life is what you will live / Heaven is what he can give"). The title track is more successful, a spooky, atmospheric meditation on the mysteries of the universe that contains subtle sonic allusions to artists like Pink Floyd or Emerson, Lake, and Palmer. The real surprise of *Can It Be?,* however, is "Living on the Bottle," an almost blistering rock track with raw lyrics about debauchery, appealing to those whose lives need a "change in style" and whose souls need to be "saved from hell." The album also contains a unique, down-tempo ballad called "Bearded Young Man." With strings arranged by **David Diggs,** the latter song develops with unpredictable textures and, again, atmospheric effects. Lyrically, it presents the historical figure of Jesus as a first-century hippie in a manner similar to **Larry Norman**'s "The Outlaw."

Before playing with The Way, Alex MacDougall was a member of **Selah.** He later joined **Daniel Amos** and **The Richie Furay Band.** Gary Arthur and John Wickham became members of **Parable.** Bruce Herring contributed his vocals to many other Maranatha projects, notably the first few praise albums in what became the label's most successful series. **Erick Nelson** recalls, "Bruce was the backbone of the 'group vocal' sound on those projects. He could sound so smooth and almost anonymous. I used to stand next to Bruce, for every record, and try to get into his vibe."

The Way Sect Bloom

Jeff Bruce; et al. 1995—*God* [EP] (independent); 1997—*Effloresce* (Flaming Fish).

The Way Sect Bloom is a guitar-driven industrial band from New York. Spearheaded by Jeff Bruce, the act creates music influenced by Skinny Puppy and **Mortal,** with the most obvious sonic parallels being to **Circle of Dust.** Indeed, Klay Scott of the latter band produced some of the tracks on The Way Sect Bloom's first full-release *Effloresce.* The latter album collects songs that Bruce had been recording since 1993, some of which had appeared on previous compilation albums of industrial or aggressive techno music. There are instrumentals, including the opening "Live," but the selections with lyrics generally reflect Christian themes. Many are written as first-person prayers to God. The title track states, "Inside your word I find my rest / And by your grace I effloresce."

The Wayside

John Thompson, voc., gtr.; Michelle Thompson, voc.; Rob Anstee, bass (–2000); John Mezzano, drums (–2000) // Marc Ludena, bass (+ 2000); Chris Wicklas, drums (+ 2000). 1993—*Play, Dreams and Imitation* (Etcetera); 2000—*Farm* (True Tunes).

www.thewayside.net

Thus far (as of 2002), neither John Styll nor Rick Edwards of *CCM* have fronted rock bands. But as proof of the adage that critics (editors) are frustrated players, Doug Van Pelt of *HM* started **Lust Control** and John J. Thompson of *True Tunes* formed The Wayside (with his wife, Michelle). The band is an on-again, off-again project that seems to have grown out of another, brasher group called Vague that Thompson led in the mid '80s, about which he would later say, "being loud and frenzied can sometimes cover the fact that you're not very good." The Wayside is a credible entity that deserves to be taken seriously in its own right, in spite of the fact that running *True Tunes* has made sufficient demands on Thompson's time to allow only two recordings over the years.

True Tunes began as a print journal devoted to alternative Christian music and transformed into an electronic publication in the late '90s. Related ministries have included a retail store, a mail order catalogue, and even an independent record label. Thompson is also the author of *Raised by Wolves: The Story of Christian Rock and Roll* (ECW, 2000), the single most important resource on the subject of the subtitle ever written. Thus, he is one of contemporary Christian music's most important scholars and critics, an expert whose opinions and values have helped to define the genre or, at least, to pull it closer to realms of good taste and reasonable theology than it would have chosen on its own. A proponent of art over propaganda, Thompson has often been responsible for seeing that nonindustry darlings like **Michael Knott,** the **Seventy Sevens,** and the **Vigilantes of Love** get the respect they deserve.

Not surprisingly, The Wayside has a folk-rock sound not too dissimilar from that of some of Thompson's heroes—**T Bone Burnett, Mark Heard,** and even the Buffalo Springfield, whose "For What It's Worth" the band covers on its debut album. John and Michelle share vocals. He turns out to have a husky voice; she sings in a smooth but powerful tone that *CCM* would liken to Susannah Hoffs of The Bangles, and *Phantom Tollbooth,* to Emmylou Harris. *Play, Dreams and Imitation* has a pop-rock sound that one reviewer would compare to groups like Squeeze and Crowded House. Such comparisons are most noticeable on the upbeat numbers like "Walking through Doors" (featuring John) and "Reach" (featuring Michelle). "One Raindrop" is a bluesy tune, complete with harmonica. The aforementioned "For What It's Worth" is actually sung with Jesus People USA's Grace and Glory choir, which transforms it into a gospel number with a sound Stephen Stills is unlikely ever to have imagined. "I Cry in My Sleep" also deserves special mention as one of the two or three most effective antiabortion songs ever written or performed by a contemporary Christian group (cf. **Kendall Payne**'s "It's Not the Time," **Vector**'s "Who Were You?"). Eschewing polemical rhetoric and untenable perspectives that make Christians look stupid, the song focuses on the undeniably tragic aspect of abortion by expressing a woman's grief and remorse in living with the consequences of her decision. Actually, as *Visions of Gray* would point out, the song never indicates specifically that the woman's pregnancy was terminated deliberately, allowing it also to serve as an empathetic lament for those who have suffered miscarriages.

Six years later, The Wayside's second album, *Farm,* would display a rootsy Americana feel that seemed to pay stylistic homage to a number of Thompson's *Canadian* heroes: The Band, Jackson Browne, and Neil Young. The dominant mood is bluesy alt-country songs ("So Long," "Summer Song") with a few strong rockers ("I'm Not Askin'," "Long Time") thrown in. Lyrically, the record is a loose concept album, with songs connected to an autobiographical portrait of Thompson growing up on a Midwest farm with a dysfunctional, sometimes abusive, and often absentee father. In the opening track ("See You"), the preadolescent Thompson prays, "Bless Momma as much as you can / Keep him outta here." This account of a troubled soul's quest to find peace in God makes for an interesting companion piece to **Resurrection Band**'s *Lament.* The latter album relates a similar tale, but there the obstacles to be overcome are the ultimately empty pleasures of this world; here, it is more the *lack* of pleasure that compels the quest to find something more. The image of the farm itself, with all the rural hardship of bringing in a harvest, serves as an effective, allegorical backdrop. Thompson writes in the album's liner notes: "Life is not a picnic; it's a farm. We work the ground all our days and still are at the mercy of God for a little rain to fall."

Wedding Party

Victor Deaton, drums; Chad Hall, kybrd., perc.; Ken Lemery, kybrd., samp.; Libbey Luckey, choreography; James McCavanaugh, gtr., kybrd.; Justin Savacool, theatrics; Sean Savacool, gtr.; Sheri Luckey Watters, voc.; William James Watters, voc., gtr.; John Williams, bass. 1998—*Anthems* (MCM).

Wedding Party describes themselves as "a Native American euro-goth band," though what is supposed to be Native American about them remains unclear. The troupe was founded in the early '90s by William and Sheri Watters and Libbey Luckey, who perform operatic music in a goth-metal style and record on a German label (MCM). Their overall sound is often compared to that of **Saviour Machine,** and indeed, Eric Clayton from that band produced their debut album. *Anthem* presents twelve somewhat melodramatic songs of adoration, confession, thanksgiving, and supplication, all of which are intended to extol the virtue of living for Christ. William Watters says that "the songs on *Anthems* are for believers in the last days." The opening track, "War Memorial," calls on Christians to be ready to die for Christ if and when it becomes necessary. Sherri Watters, however, sees the band's focus as evangelistic: "We just want people to understand the Father's heart, who the Father is, and about Jesus and the salvation he has to offer as a free gift."

The Wednesdays

Jamie Barrier, gtr.; Jeremy Barrier, drums; Joey Barrier, bass, voc. 1998— *American Midnight* [EP] (Tooth and Nail); 1999—*Midnight Songs in Time of War* (Jackson Rubio); announced for 2002—*Fury* (Arkam).

The Wednesdays are a trio of siblings from Alabama who crafted an original sound that sometimes gets classed as punkabilly or psychobilly for lack of better categorization. The group draws on the influences of artists like Social Distortion and The Rev. Horton Heat but critics agree that they do not really sound like anybody else. *True Tunes* calls it "greasy rock and roll with a cowpunk leaning." The members themselves say they are "a cross between **Johnny Cash** and The Misfits." They also say they were completely unaware of any Christian music scene before the folks from Tooth and Nail and Jackson Rubio contacted them about recording contracts. As the title to their first full-length album indicates, the band's songs tend to focus on the struggles of everyday life. These struggles include dysfunctional families ("Glass Bottle Soda Pop" is about growing up with an alcoholic father) but also the peculiar struggles of faith ("Truth? Lies?" "Barbed Wire"). "Heart Break-A-Go-Go" deals with a common personal problem, but "How the South Was Lost" and "Cowboys in the Graveyard" address social deterioration and the loss of ideals.

Wendy and Mary

Wendy Hofheimer, voc.; Mary Rice Hopkins, voc. 1981—*Out of the Fullness* (Birdwing); 1983—*The Wind Came Singing*; 1985—*Battle of the Heart.*

Wendy and Mary were a folk-pop duo who wrote and sang worship-oriented songs in the early '80s. Their arrangements emphasized acoustic guitars and vocal harmonies. Wendy mar-

ried **Terry Talbot** and released a solo album as **Wendy Talbot** as well as duo projects with her husband. Terry produced Wendy and Mary's sophomore project, *The Wind Came Singing,* which features a previously unheard song by brother **John Michael Talbot** ("Psalm 62"). The title song to that same project (written by Hofheimer) testifies to the work of the Spirit at creation, in the incarnation of Christ, and in the artist's own life. "Lion and Lamb" (written by Hopkins) draws on prophetic imagery to describe the coming era of paradise and peace.

Christian radio hits: "Second Wind" (# 20 in 1982); "Lion and Lamb" (# 12 in 1984); "The Wind Came Singing" (# 26 in 1984).

Scott Wenzel

1993—*Heart Like Thunder* (WAL); 1995—*Film at Eleven* (Word).

Scott Wenzel was lead singer for the Christian hard rock band **Whitecross** and recorded two solo albums as side projects while that group was still active. For *Heart Like Thunder,* Wenzel hired guitarist Billy Heller from the rock band Fighter to give the project a different sound from that obtained with the **Rex Carroll** pairing in his main group. The album moves away from metal stylings to embrace a sound more like that associated with Rod Stewart or Bryan Adams. "His Eyes" narrates the biblical story of the woman caught in adultery (John 8:1–11), focusing on how Christ saw the sinner differently than the religious authorities of his day. On *Film at Eleven* he revamps a ballad from the debut **Whitecross** album ("You're Mine") and gets Jamie Rowe and Tony Palacios from **Guardian** to join him on a standout worship song, "He Is Amazing." Another highlight is the heartland rocker "Inside Out," which offers an ode to revival: "Let's turn this church inside out / Let's show the world what love's about."

What If

See **The Front.**

Lisa Whelchel

1984—*All Because of You* (MCA).

Lisa Whelchel (b. 1963) is best known as the actor who portrayed Blair Warner on the popular TV sitcom *The Facts of Life.* Whelchel grew up in Littlefield, Texas, and got her first break at the age of twelve when she became part of the cast for *The New Mickey Mouse Club. Facts of Life* ran from 1979 to 1983. Whelchel also put in numerous guest appearances on such programs as *Love Boat, The Mary Tyler Moore Show,* and *Diff'rent Strokes.* She appeared in the made-for-TV movies *The Double McGuffin, The Magician of Lublin,* and *Twirl.* Whelchel was introduced to people in the Christian music business by **B. J. Thomas.** She wrote what would become the title track to her only album as an anthem of appreciation to God for all the good things that had come into her life ("Everything I am is all because of you"). The project was produced by John Rosasco and **Kelly Willard** with **Bruce Hibbard** helping with the songwriting. **Steve Taylor** contributed a song called "Good Girl," which Whelchel performs as the album finale.

Christian radio hits: "How High, How Deep, How Wide" (# 42 in 1984).

Whisper Loud

Keri Blumer, voc.; Alana Caris, voc.; Tessa Gaskill, voc. 2000—*Different Kind of Beautiful* (Benson).

Whisper Loud is a teenaged female trio who have a sound that alternates between the energetic rhythmic style of **Raze** and the adult contemporary musings of **Point of Grace.** The former presentation obviously suits them best and comes to the fore on the bouncy "Circle Song" and youthful "Hey, Yeah You" from their debut album. The group may be compared to other Christian new-millennium girl groups like **Aurora, ShineMK, V*enna,** and **Zoe Girl.**

Christian radio hits: "Like a Circle" (# 20 in 2001).

Brian White and Justice

Stephen Dale, drums; Anthony Gonzalez, gtr., voc.; Bill Randall, kybrd., voc.; Brian White, voc.; Scott Wilson, bass, voc. (– 1995) // Sam Mullins, bass (+ 1995). 1993—*Livin' in the Sight of Water* (Broken); 1995—*The Least That I Can Do* (Diadem).

Brian White is a heartland rock singer who fronts the band called Justice. White worked as a youth pastor throughout the '70s, serving at churches in Iowa and Tennessee. In the early '80s, he became a staff songwriter for Benson and wrote major hits for **Michael English** ("Holding Out Hope to You," "There is a Love") and **Larnelle Harris** ("Everything You Are"). He began performing his own material in the early '90s, playing primarily for public school assemblies, where the group was allowed to deliver a generic positive message (Don't do drugs; Stay in school; Don't have sex before marriage; Believe in a higher power) and invite youth to an off-campus evening concert where the gospel could be shared in more specific terms. *Livin' in the Sight of Water* presents the group as a lighter version of Bon Jovi, with an arena rock style. The title track and "You Can Get There from Here" both describe the desperation of those who lack inner peace but can't bring themselves to let go of guilt and accept God's invitation of grace. "Out of the Wilderness" is a more midtempo, melodic pop song narrating the happy ending for those who do make the decision the previous songs urge: "They know God has changed them forever." *The Least That I Can Do* strips back slightly such that the group often comes off as a rootsy acoustic band on the order of Black Crowes, with touches of nonparty-mode Bruce Springsteen.

"Reason to Believe" (not the Tim Hardin song—or the Springsteen one) is a slow, southern blues piece with Hammond organ and impassioned guitar. "I Wanna Go to Heaven (When I Die)" and the title track are gritty garage band rockers, and "To the End of the Age" is a ballad testifying to God's enduring and ultimate faithfulness.

In addition to the songs named above, White has written or cowritten Christian radio hits performed by **Brian Becker** ("Children of the Image"), **Al Denson** ("Say It with Love"), and **Brent Lamb** ("Another One Snatched Away"); as well as songs recorded by **Debby Boone, 4 Him,** and **Michele Wagner.** The Brian White who leads the overtly Christian band Justice is not the same Brian White who recorded several albums of country songs and enjoyed a handful of Number One country hits in the '90s.

Christian radio hits: "You Can Get There from Here" (# 8 in 1994); "Out of the Wilderness" (# 19 in 1994).

Whitecross

Scott Wenzel, voc.; Rex Carroll, gtr., voc. (– 1994); Mark Hedl, drums (–1989); Jon Sproule, bass (–1989) // Michael Feighan, drums (+ 1992); Butch Dillon, bass (+ 1992, –1993); Scott Harper, bass (+ 1993, –1994); Tracy Ferrie, bass (+ 1994, – 1997); Barry Graul, gtr., voc. (+ 1994, –1997); Brent Denny, bass (+ 1997); Quinton Gibson, gtr. (+ 1997); Troy Stone, drums (+ 1997). 1987—*Whitecross* (Pure Metal); 1988—*Love on the Line* [EP]; *Hammer and Nail*; 1989—*Triumphant Return*; 1991—*In the Kingdom* (StarSong); 1992—*High Gear*; 1993—*To the Limit*; 1994—*Unveiled* (R.E.X.); 1995—*By Demand* (StarSong); *Equilibrium* (R.E.X.); 1997—*Flytrap*; 1998—*One More Encore* (CGI).

Whitecross has had two distinct incarnations. The best-known version is that of a quintessential Christian metal band fronted by guitar hero **Rex Carroll** and prime screamer **Scott Wenzel,** both of whom have also recorded solo projects. A decade later, that group would still be remembered as one of Christian metal's Big Five (along with **Bride, Guardian, Resurrection Band,** and **Stryper**). When Carroll was replaced by Barry Graul (formerly of **Halo** and **White Heart**), Whitecross really became a whole new band. Carroll had sensed the death knell of metal at the beginning of the '90s and wanted to explore other musical styles, which he did with **King James** and other outfits. But Wenzel didn't want the band to become some lumbering dinosaur either, so he reshaped post-Carroll Whitecross to have more of a hard alternative sound. In either case, though, the core of Whitecross has been a singer and a guitarist, backed by a rotating rhythm section. Tracy Ferrie and Quinton Gibson had previously played with **Seraiah** and **Kid Promise.** Gibson would later form the late '90s grunge band **Stir.**

The first version of Whitecross formed in Chicago in 1984. Carroll, who has a degree in classical guitar from Northern Illinois University, was actually Wenzel's guitar teacher. Wenzel's voice is very similar to that of Steven Pearcy, who was known at that time for fronting the general market band Ratt. For this reason, Whitecross was immediately pegged as "a Christian Ratt," but both Carroll and Wenzel cite **Glenn Kaiser** and **Resurrection Band** as more dominant influences. From the start, the band eschewed all the spandex, leather, and big hair of many '80s bands. They also dubbed their sound pop-metal, incorporating lots of hooks and melodies into a mix that they hoped (correctly) would make the sound appeal to a broader audience. When they set out on their first tour, Carroll made an appeal in *CCM* for Christians who "think they hate heavy metal" to come out and give them a chance. "We're not a Neanderthal heavy metal band," he said. "We're just a rock and roll band with, like, really loud guitars." It was clearly those guitars that drew the most attention. Carroll quickly became known as the best metal guitarist in Christian music, indeed one of the best in rock music, period. Spurning the histrionics of thrash, he developed an emotive style that often recalled (and rivaled) Eddie Van Halen. In fact, Carroll is well known to guitar aficionados outside the Christian music subculture. He has been written up in magazines like *Musician* and *Guitar Player.* Whitecross's self-titled debut was favorably reviewed in *Kerang!, Powerline,* and *Metal Forces,* none of which would normally show any interest in the Christian music scene. This is the more amazing when one realizes that the band's songs were anything but subtle in their proclamation of evangelical themes. From the start, the group identified itself first and foremost as a ministry. Wenzel told *CCM* in 1989, "We want to entertain people, we want them to enjoy the music, but we also want the message to tear their heart out. We invite people to accept the Lord every night. That's why we do this."

Whitecross made three albums for the Pure Metal label, which, according to music historian John J. Thompson, "also released some of the worst music ever heard." Basically, Thompson alleges, Pure Metal was bankrolled by Whitecross and **Bride,** while also containing a large stable of copycat acts who tried to play the same music but lacked the technical competence to pull it off. Eventually, StarSong bought Pure Metal just to get Whitecross and **Bride** on their roster, and immediately dropped all the other groups. In any case, *Whitecross* was greeted with widespread critical acclaim, even in magazines not usually friendly to the metal genre. *CCM* presented it to their readers as the long-awaited album that has "enough of an edge for the metal heads but also enough melody and pop sensibility for everyone else." *Whitecross* opens with the hard rocking "Who Will You Follow?" which picks up where **Bob Dylan**'s "Gotta Serve Somebody" left off and asks listeners to consider their options: "Who will you follow? / Satan or the Author of Life?" Such no-fence-sitting dualism informs the

whole project, which ultimately concludes with the triumphant "He Is the Rock," an arena anthem in the grand tradition of Bon Jovi. The most noticed and most outstanding track on *Whitecross,* however, is "Nagasaki," a two-minute feedback-laden guitar solo by Carroll that recalls Van Halen's "Eruption." The song "You're Mine" is a softer tune that gave sympathetic programmers an avenue to get the band on the radio. "Enough Is Enough" sums up the album's theme with a pledge of "no more foolin' with compromise . . . one foot in, and one foot out."

Hammer and Nail opens with "Livin' on the Edge," which should not be confused with the 1993 Aerosmith song of that name but which, like that song, derives its crunchy guitar sound from the canon of Jimmy Page and Led Zeppelin. "When the Walls Tumble Down" uses the Jericho reference to describe the persistent love of God as having the effect of a hammer and chisel on the wall of human pride. "Because of Jesus" provides a typical example of Whitecross's frequent cheerleader approach to lyrics: "Because of Jesus / I have peace of mind / Because of Jesus / I'm no longer blind." The standout track, "Take It to the Limit," would become a Whitecross signature song. It is not, of course, an Eagles cover. Doug Van Pelt would say (in *CCM*), "This song has got it all: loud shaking drums, a tight bass line, fast and difficult guitar leads filling every nook and cranny, and vocals that soar with clarity and precision." Other standout tracks include the energetic "Top of the World" (not the Carpenters' song). The requisite power ballad, "Walk with Me," seems artificial and is less impressive but, like "You're Mine," served a commercial function.

For *Triumphant Return,* Whitecross was officially just a duo, but they recruited **Rick Cua** (bass) and Frank Liva (drums) to fill in the vacant spots. Some bios list bassist Rick Armstrong (later of **Lovewar**) and drummer Mark Elliott as joining the group in 1991, though neither appears to have played on any of the albums (Cua and Mike Mead of **Chagall Guevara** would provide the guest rhythm section for *In the Kingdom*). On *Triumphant Return,* the band makes some efforts toward innovation that keep the album from just being "more of the same." Carroll offers a guitar instrumental called "Flashpoint" that seems inspired by Bach. An acoustic number called "Simple Man" also provides a change from the usual pace, but otherwise the album is filled with songs geared for the legion of fans. "Attention Please" has the sound of an electrifying concert opener, proclaiming, "We have a reason to get excited / His name is Jesus / He knows all about you." More inventive musically is the help-for-addicts song "Down," which features a particularly melodic groove and a Whitesnake-inspired bridge. Likewise, "Shakedown" offers a powerful description of the judgment, with reference to the troubling words of Matthew 7:21–23.

The two StarSong albums represent the band's creative nadir, and, already with *In the Kingdom,* anyone who was paying attention could tell that Carroll and Wenzel would not be making music together for that company over the long haul. Around the time that *In the Kingdom* was released, Carroll complained in a *CCM* cover story that the album was a compromise project dictated by commercial interests that ran counter to his own artistic instincts. "I have mixed emotions about the album," he said. "Politics came into play. StarSong wants to push us more mainstream." In this case, *mainstream* would mean **Petra**esque big pop anthems ("Love Is Our Weapon") and an unusual quotient of ballads. "There are a couple of tracks on *In the Kingdom* I'm scared of," Carroll continued in the *CCM* interview, "including one ('In His Hands') that sounds like something by **Michael W. Smith.**" He also allowed that there was division in the band, with Wenzel supporting the changes for the sake of the evangelistic possibilities they might create: "Scott's vision is ministry first, with music just as a vehicle." Carroll, on the other hand, was trying to stick to his guns as an artist and was not persuaded by Wenzel's arguments for greater ministry potential or by StarSong's promise of more widespread commercial success. "We've never had the privilege of traveling in a tour bus," he told *CCM.* "But if I have to sound like **Michael W. Smith** to sell more records, I'd guess I'd rather stick with my trailer and van. Because, rock 'n' roll is a beautiful thing."

Highpoints on *In the Kingdom* include the title track, a bluesy ballad that does work. Written by **Dez Dickerson,** the song contrasts the vision of the world's status and destiny that might be derived from modern news media with that which is revealed in the Bible: contrary to appearances, "God's glory is coming down." The hard-rocking "No Second Chance" (which retells the biblical parable of the Rich Man and Lazarus) continues in classic Whitecross form, and "Good Enough" clones Van Halen's "Hot for Teacher." The most interesting song, however, is the five-minute-plus minimusical "Holy War," which actually starts out as a rap song (with rapping provided by **D.O.C.**) and transforms midway into a metal anthem with choral vocals celebrating God's ultimate victory. The group was falling apart on *High Gear,* which comes off as *In-the-Kingdom-*Part-Two with "contractual obligation" written all over it. "We Know What's Right" is another cheerleader anthem that sounds like a lesser version of many of the band's other songs, while "Dancin' in Heaven" (about a staid Sunday school class that gets disrupted when the Spirit falls on some kids with scandalizing results) could have been something special but ends up sounding kind of silly. "In America" is one of the band's worst ballads, a syrupy "We Are the World" song with trite lyrics and predictable vocal arrangements. The best tracks,

"Gonna Keep On" and "Long Road to Walk," got shuffled to the end of the disc.

Carroll's years with Whitecross have been summed up in two compilation packages: *To the Limit* and *By Demand.* There is no duplication between the projects, but the former has more of the radio hits and the latter, more of the innovative, accomplished, and better songs. *To the Limit* also features two previously released songs: "It's My Life" and "You're My Lord," both of which are strong numbers, representing the group's affection for such bands as Aerosmith and Guns N' Roses.

Wenzel announced in *CCM* that the second edition of Whitecross would be "a band that kids and their parents could enjoy together." The first two albums were produced by Jimmie Lee Sloas of **Dogs of Peace.** *Unveiled* reveals a hard pop band with few traces of the metal sounds of yore. The ballad "Angels' Disguise" (about looking beyond appearances to see people as God sees them) was actually written by **Cindy Morgan,** and a number of other songs employ Beatlesque harmonies that make the new Whitecross sound a little bit like **PFR.** "Salt City" and "Home in Heaven," however, are powerhouse rockers that come the closest to pleasing traditional fans. The album's best song may be "Goodbye Cruel World," a midtempo, Zeppelin-blues song that Wenzel wrote for his recently departed father. *Equilibrium* moves the band into grunge territory with a sound that recalls groups like Alice in Chains in fairly convincing ways but would be greeted by many critics as a bit too calculated. "Faraway Places" is a standout rock song on that album, and both "Rubberneck" (based on descriptions of instability in James 1:5–8) and "Balance" (the de facto title track) are also impressive. "Full Crucifixion" is distinctive for its lead vocals by Graul. Billy Smiley of **White Heart** contributes the song "Windows." As it would turn out, the whole grunge experiment was only a one-record trial. On *Flytrap,* Wenzel and an entirely new band move decidedly back toward the early Whitecross sound with emphasis on a classic rock sound reflective of Led Zeppelin and early Aerosmith. By now, Wenzel had adopted at least three distinct vocal styles. In addition to his metal scream—no longer much in evidence—he could sing in a ferocious, raspy growl or in what he came to call his "church voice," with a cleaner, sweeter tone. On *Flytrap,* the growl is used to great effect on "Get Real," the Metallica-flavored opening cut, and the church voice comes into play for "Say a Prayer," a folk ballad that features harmonica. *Flytrap* was produced by **David Zaffiro.** *One More Encore* is a compilation album that collects songs from the three post-Carroll projects.

Christian radio hits: "You're Mine" (# 4 in 1988); "Walk with Me" (# 7 in 1989); "In His Hands" (# 4 in 1991); "If He Goes before Me" (# 29 in 1991); "In the Kingdom" (# 2 in 1992); "In America" (# 1 in 1993); "Coming Home" (# 14 in 1993); "I Keep Prayin' " (# 11 in 1994); "End of the Line" (# 17 in 1997).

Dove Awards: 1990 Hard Music Album *(Triumphant Return);* 1992 Hard Music Album *(In the Kingdom);* 1995 Hard Music Song ("Come unto the Light").

White Heart

Billy Smiley, kybrd., gtr.; Mark Gersmehl, kybrd., voc.; Gary Lunn, bass (– 1987); David Huff, drums (– 1986); Dann Huff, gtr. (– 1985); Steve Green, voc. (–1984) // Scott Douglas, voc. (+ 1984, –1986); Gordon Kennedy, gtr. (+ 1985, – 1990); Rick Florian, voc. (+ 1986); Chris McHugh, drums (+ 1986, – 1990, + 1992, – 1993); Tommy Sims, bass (+ 1987, –1990); Billy Wooten, gtr. (+ 1990, –1997); Antony Sallee, bass (+ 1990, –1995); Mark Nemer, drums (+ 1990, –1992); Jon Knox, drums (+ 1992, –1997); John Thorn, bass (+ 1995, –1997). 1983—*White Heart* (Myrrh); 1984—*Vital Signs;* 1985—*Hotline* (Home Sweet Home); 1986—*Live at Six Flags; Don't Wait for the Movie* (Sparrow); 1987—*Emergency Broadcast;* 1989—*Freedom;* 1990—*Powerhouse* (StarSong); 1992—*Tales of Wonder;* 1993—*Highlands;* 1994—*Nothing But the Best: Radio Classics* (StarSong); *Nothing But the Best: Rock Classics;* 1995—*Inside* (Curb); 1996—*The Early Years* (Sparrow); 1997—*Redemption* (Curb).

www.whiteheart.com

White Heart was a Christian band that played well-produced, competent power-pop for a decade and a half, finally disbanding in 1998. Their closest market equivalent was **Petra,** though like that band, they varied their style over the years. The group was formed in 1982 by members of the Bill Gaither Band, an instrumental combo that backed **The Bill Gaither Trio** and **The New Gaither Vocal Band.** There have been numerous personnel changes over the years, but the constant members have been Billy Smiley and Mark Gersmehl, with the band achieving four more or less distinct incarnations under their leadership. White Heart has served as a fertile field for developing talent, with many of the group's members having achieved prominence elsewhere. David Huff was leader of **David and the Giants** and played with his brother Dann Huff in **Giant.** The latter had also played with **The Front;** he become legendary as a session guitarist and would take part in a one-time project called **The Players. Steve Green** sang with **The New Gaither Vocal Band** and went on to a sterling solo career. Chris McHugh became one of the most sought-after drummers in Nashville. Gordon Kennedy founded the short-lived **Dogs of Peace** and earned renown as a songwriter penning hits for such mainstream artists as Garth Brooks, Kathy Mattea, Wynonna, and Trisha Yearwood. He won the 1996 Record of the Year Grammy award for "Change the World," performed by **Eric Clapton. Tommy Sims** cowrote that song with Kennedy, in addition to all the material for Garth Brooks's *The Life and Times of Chris Gaines* project. He was also a member of **The Players** and would release a stellar solo project in 2000. All of these musicians have been in demand as session

players: Dann Huff has played guitar for Michael Jackson, and Sims, bass for Bruce Springsteen. Smiley himself is one of Christian music's premier producers and songwriters, having helmed projects and written songs for such artists as **Rhonda Gunn, Human, JAG, Angie Lewis, Heather Miller, The Normals, One, Rachel Rachel,** and **Whitecross.** Gersmehl married Brynn Beltran of **Rachel Rachel.** He is also a prolific songwriter, responsible for some of **Connie Scott**'s finest material ("Wild Horse Running," "Is There an Orphan in Your Home?").

The trademark White Heart sound was once described in *CCM* as featuring "steaming guitar work, strong gutsy vocals, and tight soaring harmonies." Being composed primarily of trained studio musicians, the group had the feel (and sometimes the sound) of a band like Toto: their professionalism surpassed that of most artists in the field, though the music lacked appeal for those who favor more raw or spontaneous work. Critics generally liked the band, but from the start, words like "formulaic" and "homogenized" would turn up in reviews. Indeed, *CCM* might have inadvertently offered a career summary of the group's sound in their review of the band's very first project: "The music could be considered to be formula rock, but it's a formula that works." Some critics also objected to what they considered to be shallow lyrics. At a time when the most acclaimed Christian bands **(The Choir, Daniel Amos, LSU,** the **Seventy Sevens)** were opting for poetic imagery and for writing Christian songs about life in general, White Heart favored the **DeGarmo and Key** or **Petra** approach: simple, direct songs with explicit evangelical messages. Both of the above concerns would be redressed to a great extent as the group moved through its oeuvre, however, and a number of critics have noted that, overall, each new White Heart album tends to be an improvement over the last. Still, the band has always maintained a strong focus on ministry. Their concerts have regularly included an invitation for persons in attendance to meet with spiritual leaders after the show for prayer and guidance on various matters. Such invitations might be evangelistic, but most of the group's material is knowingly addressed to the church. Rick Florian once said, "Our gift from God to our fans is our music. Through our music we have always wanted to say that God does not love us because we are valuable, but that we are valuable because He loves us."

The first three White Heart albums reveal a group in constant transition. *White Heart* is notable for featuring superstar-in-the-making Green. The project opens a tad deceptively with "Hold On," which recalls **The Imperials,** but then moves into a sound more reminiscent of groups like Journey, Survivor, and Asia, who were all major chart attractions at the time. "He Is Returning" is a climactic anthem written by Gersmehl. The debut project sold an impressive 70,000 copies. On *Vital Signs* and *Hotline,* Scott Douglas takes over as principal singer. "Walking in the Light" has the distinctive Toto sound. "Following the King" presents White Heart at its rocking best, while "Quiet Love" and "We Are His Hands" are more MOR ballads. The title track asks the listener to consider, "Are your actions connected with what's inside your head?" *Hotline* was the first project with Kennedy on board (minus the Huff brothers). Its standout track is "Jerusalem," cowritten by Smiley and Gersmehl with **DeGarmo and Key,** which is similar in theme to the **Gentle Faith** song of the same name.

In 1985, shortly after the release of *Hotline,* White Heart suffered a crisis that would have destroyed most bands. Lead singer Scott Douglas (née Scott Mathieson) was arrested and sentenced to thirty years in prison for three counts of sexual assault (the incidents involved sexual relations between the thirty-two-year-old singer and girls aged eleven and thirteen). Nashville news media displayed his picture in handcuffs, and newspaper headlines announced, "Christian Singer Arrested on Sex Charges." Eventually, *CCM* would run a cover story on the crisis, which included a prison interview with the penitent singer, who confessed to suicidal guilt ("My sin is ever before me") and acknowledged some link between his inexcusable behavior and his inability to resolve issues stemming from the sexual abuse he himself had experienced as a child. The issue—similar to that concerning **Raze** that would come up over fifteen years later—was a wake-up call for the Christian music subculture concerning the reality and depth of sin. In the wake of the scandal, Home Sweet Home Records would demonstrate startling poor taste by releasing a live recording of a two-year-old concert by the band featuring Douglas's lead vocals. The group itself did not authorize the release of *Live at Six Flags* (which wasn't very good anyway), and Douglas himself denounced the record company from prison, claiming, "I have lost the right to that microphone."

Former White Heart roadie Rick Florian took Douglas's place as lead singer in the band. As a running joke, Florian's first name would be spelled differently in the liner notes of almost every successive album: Ric, Rick, Rikk, Riq, Ricke, Rhic, and so on. The album *Don't Wait for the Movie* is an understandably fragmented project, recorded under traumatic circumstances, but it would produce a handful of hits and classics all the same—a critics' poll sponsored by *CCM* in 2001 would include it at Number Seventy-four on a list of "The 100 Greatest Albums in Christian Music." The song "Convertibles" is a good-time summer tune with a carefree chorus that betrays nary a hint of stress or strife. But "How Many Times (Seventy Times Seven)" represents Gersmehl's attempt to reflect on the unlimited character of God's forgiveness in light of Douglas's stated fear that he had somehow "found the crack in grace" and

fallen beyond the reach of mercy. A different tragedy would affect the recording of *Emergency Broadcast* when Kennedy's sister-in-law, without any indication of previous despair, suddenly took her own life. "Montana Sky" was intended as a cathartic response to her death. *Emergency Broadcast* also includes "No Taboo," a rocking track with trade-off vocals announcing unrestricted access to abundant life. The band's third album for Sparrow, *Freedom,* would be the final installment in what has since come to be regarded as the group's recovery trilogy. The rockiest album so far, *Freedom* was also hailed as the group's most consistent and best effort to date. It was produced by **Brown Bannister** and recorded by a band with a (temporarily) stabilized lineup. The sound is tight and natural, with Kennedy's crunchy guitar often taking center stage. "Sing Your Freedom" brims with revitalized energy, and "Bye Bye Babylon" has touches of metallic pop. "The River Will Flow" is a stunning ballad with a melody and style similar to that which would later inform Bruce Springsteen's "Secret Garden." In general, the lyrical content on all three of the Sparrow albums show marked growth over the penchant for clichés on the earliest works. By 1990, *CCM* would be describing the typical White Heart song as offering "personal glimpses of the pain experienced in this world and personal revelations of how the loving and knowing hand of God can comfort, deliver, and cleanse."

Myriad personnel shifts again marked the start of the band's StarSong era. Still, *Powerhouse* was greeted as a consistently strong collection of power-pop songs in a slightly tamer vein than those on *Freedom.* The title track and "Independence Day" are punchy rockers, but the clear standout track is "Desert Rose," a soaring ballad that showcases Florian's melodic voice. The song is a tribute to those who seize the opportunity to bring beauty and life into dry and lonely environments. By sheer coincidence, the Desert Storm war with Iran broke out shortly after the song was released, giving it added poignancy for some listeners. *Powerhouse* was produced by Bill Drescher, noted for his work with Rick Springfield and The Bangles. *Tales of Wonder* would be a surprising and glorious success. Delving deep into metaphor, the album delivers a cohesive collection of songs that, in the words of *CCM* reviewer Brian Quincy Newcomb, "exhibit a broader world context and, necessarily, a bigger message of hope to touch the greater human suffering." In an unprecedented move, the band would release all ten of the album's songs as singles, with each one charting in the Top 40 of one or another Christian radio chart. "Say the Word" sets words of encouragement to an adult contemporary pop melody. "Vendetta" and "Who Owns You?" address the struggle to live for God in an unfriendly social environment. "Light a Candle" has an anthemic feel, with words inspired by Jesus' exhortation in Matthew 5:14–16. *Highlands* features the more hard-edged "Nothing But the Best," a Foreigner/Journey-like rocker that eschews mediocrity in faith and service to God. "Once and for All" is a power ballad reflecting poignantly on the significance of Christ's crucifixion. Songs from both the Sparrow and StarSong years would be collected on the well-organized two-volume *Nothing But the Best* compilation. The *Radio Classics* disc collects the more mellow songs, and the *Rock Classics,* the more energetic tunes. Both volumes also include two new songs. A later compilation called *The Early Years* contains a smattering of both hard and soft styles.

White Heart sought to reinvent themselves for the '90s by switching to Curb Records, a general market label that they hoped would be able to promote them successfully outside the Christian subculture. They made *Inside* with superstar producer Ken Scott, who has worked with such artists as Elton John, David Bowie, Supertramp, and Duran Duran, but who, Florian would say, "neither knows nor cares to know anything about 'Christian music'." The album reveals a harder Aerosmith-inspired sound, lacking the trademark (but dated) layered vocals of previous White Heart projects. The opening title track is empathetic, giving voice to the probing struggle of a seeker: "I wanna feel / I wanna dream / I wanna live on the inside." The Aerosmith leanings come to fullest expression on "Dominate," a plea for God to control the heart and mind of the singer. "Living Sacrifice" calls on those nihilistic souls who would emulate Kurt Cobain as a role model to "bury the dead messiah" and "follow the living one home." With an eye to Christian radio, "Even the Hardest Heart" and "It Could Have Been You" are acoustic ballads reminiscent of America and **Extreme,** respectively.

After recording *Inside,* White Heart's rhythm section left, and Mike Mead (drums) and Kevin Mills (bass) were recruited to tour behind the record. 1996 was a rough year. Florian went through a divorce, and Gersmehl and Smiley both confess to being less inspired for the ongoing work of White Heart: "I remember looking out at the people and thinking, 'I don't have the burning for them I used to'," Gersmehl would write in *Release.* The trio considered packing it in, but determined to make one more album "for the healing of it." *Redemption* is the perfect swan song, a cathartic and introspective concept piece that differs from most of the previous work but, Smiley said, was worth it "even if no one ever hears it but us." Musically, the album is laid back and moody, recalling some of the early albums of Pink Floyd. It opens with the confessional "Looking Glass" and moves through a song cycle that traces a discovery of need and of grace, concluding at last with the wonderfully pious "Jesus." The latter song is perhaps the most fitting final song by any major artist since the Beatles released "Let It Be." It brings the long White Heart saga to an end with the words, "One way / One truth / One life / One Lord / Jesus."

For trivia buffs: Like Rick (?) Florian, White Heart has had trouble deciding how to spell their name. Album cover graphics and other official band materials variously render it as White Heart, Whiteheart, and WhiteHeart.

Christian radio hits: "He's Returning" (# 34 in 1983); "Carry On" (# 23 in 1983); "Following the King" (# 29 in 1984); "We Are His Hands" (# 1 for 4 weeks in 1984); "Jerusalem" (# 2 in 1985); "How Many Times?" (# 2 in 1986); "Convertibles" (# 20 in 1986); "Fly, Eagle, Fly" (# 2 in 1987); "Maybe Today" (# 1 for 4 weeks in 1987); "Montana Sky" (# 3 in 1988); "Edge of the Dream" (# 7 in 1988); "The River Will Flow" (# 1 for 4 weeks in 1989); "Eighth Wonder" (# 1 for 2 weeks in 1989); "Over Me" (# 3 in 1990); "Desert Rose" (# 2 in 1991); "A Love Calling" (# 12 in 1991); "Lay It Down" (# 1 for 5 weeks in 1991); "Storyline" (# 10 in 1992); "Say the Word" (# 1 for 2 weeks in 1992); "Unchain" (# 2 in 1992); "Light a Candle" (# 2 in 1993); "Silhouette" (# 1 in 1993); "Where the Thunder Roars" (# 3 in 1993); "Once and for All" (# 1 for 4 weeks in 1994); "The Flame Passes On" (# 1 for 2 weeks in 1994); "Heaven of My Heart" (# 1 in 1994); "My Eyes Have Seen" (# 2 in 1995); "Morningstar" (# 8 in 1995); "Even the Hardest Heart" (# 2 in 1995); "It Could Have Been" (# 5 in 1996); "Come One, Come All" (# 6 in 1996); "Find a Way" (# 20 in 1996); "Jesus" (# 12 in 1997); "Fall on Me" (# 14 in 1998).

Steve Wiggins

1991—*Steve Wiggins* (Sparrow).

Steve Wiggins became famous in Christian music circles as the leader of the Memphis blues-rock band **Big Tent Revival,** but before he formed that group in 1994, he recorded a solo album at the age of twenty-three for Sparrow Records. The self-titled project was produced by Tom Laune, the same man responsible for R.E.M.'s *Green.* The style is more acoustic/folk oriented than that for which BTR would become known, though it is not a far cry from the latter band's debut album. Songs like "Jesus Is Real" display the artist's strong Christian leaning. "All the Darkness" received some airplay on the more progressive Christian radio stations.

David Wilcox

1987—*The Nightshift Watchman* (independent); *Breakfast at the Circus* (A&M); 1991—*Home Again;* 1994—*Big Horizon;* 1996—*East Asheville Hardware* (Koch); 1997—*Turning Point;* 1999—*Underneath* (Vanguard); 2000—*What You Whispered.*

David Wilcox is a Christian folk singer who has recorded only for the general market but who came to the attention of the Christian music subculture toward the end of the millennium. Wilcox, with voice and vocal stylings uncannily similar to those of James Taylor, tends to write songs that have a highly literate, personable storytelling quality to them. For example, a popular number called "Fearless Love" tells of a man who goes to protest a march by a group whose social values he does not approve of. While there, someone else in the crowd of protestors throws a brick and hits one of the marchers. Shocked, the song's protagonist administers first-aid to the victim, then picks up the man's sign and takes his place in the march he had come to protest. Such songs are thought-provoking in a manner that transcends easy analysis and facilitates conversation: did the protagonist of the above song change his mind or compromise his convictions, or was he merely insisting that even his opponents should not be silenced through violence? Some critics have noted similarities with songwriters like **Bruce Cockburn** and **Pierce Pettis** in Wilcox's body of work, and he acknowledges his appreciation for those like-minded contemporaries.

Wilcox's songs sometimes touch on spiritual themes, though as Brian Quincy Newcomb notes, "Faith is portrayed with mystery and longing rather than with the blunt overtures of evangelism." His *Big Horizon* album, in particular, resonates with themes of spiritual seeking. Some notice of his work in Christian music circles came when **Glad** recorded his "Show the Way" and **Smalltown Poets** did "Hold It Up to the Light." A musician's musician, Wilcox has also frequently been cited as an influence by numerous Christian singers (**Matt Auten, Bebo Norman, Jill Phillips, Chris Rice**) even at a time when he was virtually unknown to those singers' own fans. *CCM* broke the silence with a profile of the artist in 1999 and published the first major review of any of his works to appear in a Christian music magazine. They singled out "Spirit Wind" (inspired by Native American music) and "Sex and Music" (which compares the two phenomena as losing quality when performed to "get people to like you") as standout cuts on *Underneath.* Then in 2000 **Jars of Clay** invited Wilcox to open a national tour that also included **Burlap to Cashmere,** introducing the compelling folk artist to a broad new audience. *CCM* also reviewed *What You Whispered,* which features the Jars boys on two songs ("Rule Number One" and the uncharacteristically funky "Start with the Ending").

The North Carolina singer clearly has mixed feelings about being identified with the contemporary Christian music subculture, of which he has never sought to be a part. Although Wilcox will speak freely about his faith in interviews, he rarely if ever does so in concert performances. Furthermore, he says that he has theological problems with Christians seeking to define themselves over against the world at large. "Jesus doesn't talk about protecting yourself, or removing yourself, or claiming that you are a special, secluded and divided people," he says. "I have tears of frustration when I try to listen to what is marketed as 'contemporary Christian music.' It tells people who are not Christians that we are scared, frightened, that we have to hide within these little walls."

Vince Wilcox (and **Wilcox and Pardoe**)

By Vince Wilcox: 1993—*Reconciled* (Benson). By Wilcox and Pardoe: 1995—*. . . Till They Know How Much You Care* (Light).

Vince Wilcox worked at Benson Records for fifteen years, starting out in the warehouse and ending up as vice-president of marketing. Then he decided he wanted a recording career for himself and released the solo album *Reconciled.* Musically, the album has the '70s coffeehouse style of country-flavored singer/songwriter music. Most of the songs concern family themes. "While the very pace of our lifestyles pull families apart," Wilcox told *CCM,* "the central message of the gospel of Christ came to put lives and relationships back together." The album was not a commercial hit, but two years later Wilcox tried again by joining with Don Pardoe, a road manager, backup singer, and keyboardist for various country artists, to form the duo Wilcox and Pardoe, possibly modeled on the mainstream country duo Brooks and Dunn. The two gathered songs from a variety of writers that express positive images of family, friendship, and fidelity. "I Think about You" addresses the male problem of viewing women as sex objects. "To Keep the River Runnin' " is an Eagles-like country rock tune explaining the ultimate benefit of trials in life.

Wild Blue Yonder

Chris Brigandi, gtr.; Crystal Lewis, voc.; Paul Martin, bass; Joey Mitchell, drums. 1986—*Wild Blue Yonder.*

Wild Blue Yonder is best remembered as the training group for later Christian superstar **Crystal Lewis.** She was fifteen at the time the band made its only album. Chris Brigandi formed Wild Blue Yonder as a second edition of his somewhat successful new-wave band **The Lifters.** But Wild Blue Yonder was not new-wave. *CCM* describes them as being "a rockabilly, cow-punk band, with influences ranging from Stray Cats to Lone Justice." Their album, which was produced by **Terry Scott Taylor,** "features boppin', good-feelin', guitar rock." A country shuffle called "Revival Meeting" is clearly an album highlight, but the most treasured and interesting song is "Only One," which was written by Taylor and features duet vocals between the producer (leader of **Daniel Amos, The Swirling Eddies,** and the **Lost Dogs**) and the teenaged Lewis. Another historical souvenir is "Cryin' Eyes," which was cowritten by **Michael Knott.** The album concludes with Lewis singing "Somewhere over the Rainbow" (cf. **Reba Rambo**). Brigandi went on to become a successful producer, responsible for the classic **LSU** album *Shaded Pain.* He and Lewis were briefly reunited in a one-shot band called **The Screamin' Rays.**

Malcolm Wild

See **Malcolm and Alwyn.**

Fletch Wiley

1977—*Ballade* (StarSong); 1979—*Spirit of Elijah*; 1981—*Nightwatch*; 1985—*The Art of Praise*; 1986—*The Art of Praise 2*; 1990—*Repeat the Sounding Joy* (Word); 1992—*Urban Reel* (Visual); 1993—*Lift High the Lord* (Word); 1996—*Almighty God*; 1998—*Hymns*.

www.fletchwiley.com

Fletch Wiley is a significant instrumentalist who deserves the lion's share of credit for introducing instrumental music to the contemporary Christian music genre. Wiley is gifted with flute, trumpet, and flügelhorn. He started out backing **Andraé Crouch and the Disciples** in a band that also recorded on their own as **Sonlight.** That experiment was more historically significant than commercially successful, but in 1977—a year before Keaggy's *The Master and the Musician* and four years before Phil Driscoll's *Ten Years After*—Wiley issued his own solo record, *Ballade.* Musically, the album was considered to be Christian jazz, though it really tended more toward easy listening from a stylistic point of view. All the members of **Sonlight** play with him on the project, as they do on the follow-up *Spirit of Elijah.* Beginning with *Nightwatch,* members of **Koinonia** (Alex Acuña, Abraham Laboriel) would also join him on most of his recordings. Sporadic vocals are provided by the likes of Crouch and other members of the Disciples, and also by The McCrarys on *Nightwatch.* It wasn't until the two *Art of Praise* albums that Wiley really began to play a more progressive jazz style. *Urban Reel* mixes in doses of rock on tracks like "Samba for Kate," "DanceTuit," and a cover of Sly Stone's "Stand."

Especially in his early years, Wiley had to justify how music without words could qualify as Christian music. The most common way for the association to be made was for artists to perform instrumental versions of well-known songs, such that listeners would hear the inspirational unsung lyrics in their minds. This was the philosophy that sustained numerous successful instrumental praise albums released by Maranatha. Wiley did include versions of hymns ("A Mighty Fortress" on *Ballade* and "Amazing Grace" on *Spirit of Elijah*), but from the very start he also did instrumental originals that had never had any words ("Ballade for God" is described as "a meditation on Romans 8:32"). This was actually controversial among many contemporary Christian music fans who would ask, for instance, why a Wiley instrumental was to be considered more Christian than, say, a Chuck Mangione piece. Most Christian theologians would probably stress that all music (Mangione's or Wiley's) can be received as inspirational gifts from Christ (John 1:3; Colossians 1:16). Wiley went beyond this to indicate a belief that, at least potentially, music created by Christians can be intrinsically different from that created by non-Christians. He told *CCM* in 1987, "I trust that there would be a measurable difference. . . . I really believe that the anointing and the spirit and the prayer that go into an album should have a tremendous impact on the listener." At any rate, the controversies regarding instrumental music had all but vanished by the '90s, and Wiley's increasingly competent and innovative works continued to bless all but the most narrow-minded fans of instrumental jazz.

Fletch Wiley has also served as producer for a wide array of Christian artists, helming projects by **Steve and Annie Chapman, Andraé Crouch, Fireworks, Marty McCall,** and **Ken Medema.** He also produced the hugely successful children's musical *The Music Machine* (see **Agape Force**), which sold over 1.5 million copies. Wiley authored a booklet called *Biblical Concepts in Music.*

Stephen Wiley

1985—*Bible Break* (Brentwood); date unknown—*Rappin' for Jesus; Rap it Up; Get Real;* 1990—*Rhythm and Poetry* (StarSong); 1991—*Rhapsody.*

A pioneer in rap music, Stephen Wiley (b. 1958) grew up in Tulsa, Oklahoma, and graduated from the University of Oklahoma. He began performing as a jazz drummer in 1979 and recorded a song called "Basketball" that later became a novelty hit for Kurtis Blow (# 71 in 1985). In 1982, he began performing Christian rap, a year before **Run-D.M.C.** would bring the rap genre to the attention of mainstream audiences. In 1984, Wiley became a chaplain at a juvenile detention center. In 1985, he released a rap album called *Bible Break,* the title song for which he maintains is "the first nationally distributed Christian rap song of any kind." Actually, a Christian rap singer named Pete McSweet had released a twelve-inch single called "Adam and Eve, the Gospel Beat" on Lection as early as 1982, but McSweet never followed this up with a full album. Wiley is probably at least tied with the **Rap'sures** (a not very authentic project) for the honor of releasing the first Christian rap *album.* In 1988, an article in *Spin* magazine actually referred to him as "the Grand Master of Rap." Christian music critics, however, were not kind to Wiley's Brentwood repertoire (four albums). The projects went by and large unreviewed, and *CCM*'s rap critic Jamie Lee Rake would later refer to them as "a string of embarrassments." Wiley moved to Los Angeles and became a youth pastor there at Crenshaw Center. He gained his first real exposure in the contemporary Christian music scene when he released a full-length album on StarSong called *Rhythm and Poetry.* That album offers a reworking of **Mylon LeFevre**'s "Love God, Hate Sin," with **Rex Carroll** providing metal guitar. Wiley also performs a duet with **Reneé García** on the song "Peace." The follow-up album, *Rhapsody,* broadens the spectrum of sounds to provide more appeal to traditional gospel fans. "Real" is carried by soulful harmonies with members of the gospel group **Witness.** "Morning Time" features samples from Martin Luther King Jr. *CCM*'s Rake reviewed both *Rhythm and Poetry* and *Rhapsody,* noting vast improvement over the early works.

Christian radio hits: "Bible Break" (# 14 in 1986); "Peace" (# 13 in 1990); "Attitude" (# 14 in 1991).

Tess Wiley

See **Phantasmic.**

Kelly Willard

1978—*Blame It on the One I Love* (Maranatha); 1981—*Willing Heart;* 1984—*Psalms, Hymns, and Spiritual Songs;* 1986—*Message from a King;* 1991—*The Garden* (Asaph); *Looking Back;* 1997—*Homesick for Heaven* (Coyote).

Kelly Willard (née Bagley, b. 1957) was probably the first truly adult contemporary singer to make an impression on the maturing Jesus freaks who had been involved in the early '70s revival that birthed contemporary Christian music. For the most part, the Jesus freaks had respected **Pat Boone** but they hadn't bought his albums. They did buy everything Maranatha issued, however, and though, in retrospect, albums by **Debby Kerner** and **Karen Lafferty** might seem pretty MOR, these were received as singer/songwriter projects equivalent to the works of secular hippies like Joni Mitchell or Judy Collins. Willard lacked any semblance of hippie credentials, but by 1978 the '60s really were *almost* over and many among Maranatha's former tie-dyed countercultural audience were now obsessed with car pools and PTA meetings. The times had shifted, and when Willard's *Blame It on the One I Love* came out on the Maranatha label (as opposed to Word or Light), astute observers would know that this was the wave of the future.

Willard grew up in Winter Haven, Florida, where she learned to play piano by ear as a child. At the age of sixteen, she traveled to Nashville and found a job as piano player for the southern gospel group The Jake Hess Sound (Jake Hess being the founder of **The Imperials**). At seventeen, she switched to playing for the Oak Ridge Boys and then accepted a short stint with **The Archers** (as Nancy Short's replacement, before Janice Archer joined). Next, she became a founding member of the Oklahoma City Christian rock group **Seth,** which was led by **Jonathan David Brown** (destined to become one of Christian music's top producers, though his career would end ignominiously). At some point, she married Dan Willard, who became a recording engineer at Maranatha. After leaving **Seth,** she joined a band called Harlan Rogers and Friends, led by the keyboard player for **Andraé Crouch and the Disciples.** Up until that point, Willard had always functioned primarily as a piano player, but Rogers was interested in her primarily as a singer—perhaps because keyboards were his own forté or perhaps just because he realized she had the voice of an angel—a powerful (but sweet) angel at that. She had to be coaxed into singing lead vocals, but by the time the players in Harlan Rogers and Friends had moved on to **Koinonia** and other pursuits, Willard was ready for her debut. At the age of twenty-one she had already been working full time in Christian music for five years and seemed to have played, sung, or written songs with just about everyone in the business.

Blame It on the One I Love was produced by **Jonathan David Brown** and actually has more of a contemporary pop feel to it than Willard's later projects. Still, the focus is on inspirational ballads carried by the artist's incredible, soaring vocals. The title track was a huge hit on the very new Christian radio charts, tying up the Number One spot for four weeks the first year that such charts were kept. Lyrically, it sparkles with Jesus movement naiveté: "People stop me and ask why I'm so happy . . . They say I don't seem to have a worry in the world." Willard also sings **Bob Bennett**'s "You're Welcome Here" and her own "A Friend So True," which juxtaposes its affirmation that Jesus "ain't like no other man" with verses similar in theme to the traditional hymn "What a Friend We Have in Jesus." Willard coproduced her subsequent albums with her husband, and they all evince a trademark offering of mellow praise and worship tunes not too dissimilar from those that **Twila Paris** and **Pam Thum** would deliver in the '90s. In other words, there is a discernible difference between the worship music that Willard produced for Maranatha and the popular sing-along choruses that fill the numerous *Praise* albums the company was releasing at the same time. Willard's offerings are more complete songs, often too complex for congregational participation. The melodies are confident and soothing, but the arrangements are sophisticated and innovative, often worked out in collaboration with musicians like Harlan Rogers, **Bruce Hibbard,** Hadley Hockensmith, Abe Laboriel (of **Koinonia** and Weather Report), and other top session players who would regularly join her on the recordings. Perhaps the most accessible of the albums is *Psalms, Hymns, and Spiritual Songs* which offers three different types of songs in keeping with Ephesians 5:19: "Silver and Gold" comes in the psalm category, as a **Billy Batstone** song that paraphrases words from Psalm 119; the medley "Nothing But the Blood of Jesus/Washed in the Blood of Jesus" exemplifies the hymn category with two well-known numbers from churches in the revival tradition; "Our Love" is a modern spiritual song cowritten by **Tommy Coomes** of **Love Song.** Five years after the last Maranatha release, she recorded one more farewell album for the Maranatha offshoot Asaph. On it, she offers renditions of **Julie Miller**'s "Love Will Find You" and **Danniebell Hall**'s "Like a Child."

In 1991, when *Garden* was released, Willard announced her retirement as a regular performer, though she has continued to sing on special occasions. *Looking Back* is a career retrospective compilation. In 1997, Willard told *CCM* she was devoting herself to family full time while trying to stay involved with Christian music (singing background vocals, writing songs) as her schedule allowed. "I hope that I can continue to record albums and release them, although I feel somewhat on the fringe of the Christian music world," she said. "I guess I have learned and am learning to take things one day at a time." The custom project *Homesick for Heaven* was released only in Europe. A *Maranatha Anthology* collection released in 2001 includes her version of "Thy Throne, O God" a gorgeous worship anthem written by Batstone in 1982.

In addition to her solo albums, Willard contributed to two children's albums called *Bless My Little Girl* and *My First Christmas*. She sang backup vocals for a great many different artists.

Christian radio hits: "Blame It on the One I Love" (# 1 in 1979); "A Friend So True" (# 13 in 1979); "Our Love" [with **Roby Duke**] (# 4 in 1984); "Nothing But the Blood" (# 10 in 1984); "Silver and Gold" (# 26 in 1985).

Brett Williams

1996—*Seven Days of Light* (Absolute).

Brett Williams was front man for the Seattle Christian band that called itself The Reach, then **In Reach,** and finally Brett Williams and In Reach on their final outing. Williams' first solo album was produced by **David Zaffiro.** *Seven Days of Light* samples a variety of styles with a strong emphasis on optimistic pop. The opening title track is a catchy song with a literally sunny philosophy: "Into every life a little rain must fall / But it won't be long till the sunshine comes again." Elsewhere, "Blessed Are These" is an infectious bubblegum tune, while "Wings and Wheels" invokes the Beatles, and "Maker of Days," **Bob Dylan.** "All Part of Being a Man" is an Earl Klugh-type jazz ballad. *CCM* appreciated the diversity, while noting that the album requires some breadth of taste.

Brooks Williams

Selected: 1990—*North from Statesboro* (Red Guitar Blue); 1991—*How the Night Time Sings*; 1992—*Back to Mercy* (Green Linnet); 1994—*Inland Sailor*; *Red Guitar Plays Blue: Vintage Recordings 1986–1987* (Red Guitar Blue); 1996—*Knife Edge* (Green Linnet); 1997—*Seven Sisters*; *Ring Some Changes* [with Jim Henry] (Signature); 1999—*Hundred Year Shadow*; 2000—*Little Lion*; *Dead Sea Café* (Silent Planet); 2001—*Skiffle Bop* (Signature).

www.brookswilliams.com

Brooks Williams is a self-professed Christian folksinger from Boston. Born and raised in Statesboro, Georgia, his music shows a definite blues influence. His style and sound are most often compared to early James Taylor, though similarities to **Bruce Cockburn, Mark Heard, Buddy Miller** and **David**

Wilcox can also be detected. Williams has a much greater following in the general market than in the Christian music scene, but he has played at the *Cornerstone* festival and his albums are occasionally reviewed in Christian music magazines. His songs are not usually explicitly religious, but they do convey perspectives informed by faith. This seems to be especially true on *How the Night Time Sings,* where several songs display overt attention to spiritual themes ("Dusty Road," "Streets of Heaven," "When I Reach"). *CCM* reviewed *Back to Mercy,* noting that on a number of songs ("Stormy Weather," "All That Glitters," "Mercy Illinois"), Williams "keeps one eye on the Scriptures and the other on the works of authors such as Frederick Buechner and J. R. R. Tolkien." *Inland Sailor* reflects on the passing of **Mark Heard** and speaks of life as a sometimes difficult journey to a better place ("Through the Darkening Night," "Home by Dawn"). *Little Lion* is a collection of guitar instrumentals. *Dead Sea Café* is a compilation of favorite songs from 1992 to 1997.

Deniece Williams

1976—*This is Niecy* (Columbia); 1977—*Songbird*; 1978—*That's What Friends Are For* [with Johnny Mathis]; 1979—*When Love Comes Calling* (ARC); 1981—*My Melody*; 1982—*Niecy*; 1983—*I'm So Proud* (Columbia); 1984—*Let's Hear It for the Boy*; 1986—*From the Beginning* (Sparrow); *So Glad I Know*; *Hot on the Trail* (Columbia); 1987—*Water under the Bridge*; 1989—*As Good As It Gets* (Columbia); *Special Love*; 1990—*Change the World* (CBS); 1991—*Lullabies to Dreamland* (Word); 1994—*Greatest Gospel Hits* (Sparrow); 1996—*Love Solves It All* (Upstage); *Gonna Take a Miracle: The Best of Deniece Williams* (Legacy); 1998—*This Is My Song* (Harmony); 2000—*Love Songs* (Sony).

Deniece Williams (née Chandler) is a major pop-R&B star who crossed over to make albums for the contemporary Christian music market in the mid '80s. Like **Philip Bailey** and **Donna Summer,** she continued to pursue a simultaneous career in mainstream music. She does not, however, date her involvement in Christian music to the 1986 debut albums for Sparrow but maintains that she had been singing for the Lord all along—and indeed *CCM* and other Christian music media outlets had reviewed her secular albums and profiled her as "a believer in the entertainment industry" long before she crossed the artificial line to become an official Christian music star.

Williams was born in Gary, Indiana, in 1951. She was raised in the Pentecostal Church of God in Christ, singing in the choir and developing both the musical skills that would eventually propel her career and the antigospel legalism that would initially hold her back (she would later describe her upbringing as long on "Thou Shalt Nots" and short on "Thou Cans"). She took a job working in a record store and one day was "discovered" by the owner singing along to an **Aretha Franklin** song when she thought she was alone. He helped her to make an independent recording, which first introduced her to the idea of singing outside of churches in some professional capacity. Williams went off to Morgan State University in Maryland to study nursing but accepted an invitation to audition for Stevie Wonder's backing group, Wonderlove. Offered a coveted spot in the superstar's ensemble, she says she prayed greatly about whether to accept. Convinced it was God's will, she went off on a tour with Wonder and The Rolling Stones but suffered great abuse from her home church, where she was castigated for deserting the Lord to sing for the devil. "I was essentially excommunicated," she reminisced in 1998. "It took me many, many years to understand their anger." In fact, she embarked on the tour under a dark cloud of guilt, and four months into what seemed like the opportunity of a lifetime, she quit and returned home to work for the Indiana phone company. Nevertheless, three years later an understanding Wonder called her in the midst of another tour to ask if she could fill a vacancy for three weeks. She ended up singing with him for three years and can be heard prominently on what are generally regarded as his two best albums: *Talking Book* (1972) and *Songs in the Key of Life* (1976).

Eventually, Williams came to the attention of Maurice White of Earth, Wind, and Fire, and she made her first two albums with his production company. *This Is Niecy* gave her a Top 40 hit with the song "Free" (# 27 in 1977; # 2 on the R&B chart). Then in 1978, she performed a duet with Johnny Mathis on the song "Too Much, Too Little, Too Late," which went to Number One not only on the pop chart but also on the R&B and adult contemporary charts. An entire album with Mathis followed, spawning another R&B hit with a cover of **Marvin Gaye**'s "You're All I Need to Get By" (# 47 in 1978; # 10 on the R&B chart). Another career highpoint came in 1981 when she worked with the wizard of Philly soul, Thom Bell, on *My Melody,* an album that produced the hit "It's Gonna Take a Miracle" (# 10 in 1982; # 1 on the R&B chart). Her biggest moment, however, arrived with the song, "Let's Hear It for the Boy" (# 1 for 2 weeks in 1984; # 1 on the R&B chart) from the *Footloose* motion picture soundtrack. After that triumph Williams would continue to have hits on the R&B charts (e.g., "Never Say Never," # 6 in 1987), but as styles changed, she did not have any more Top 40 hits in the mainstream pop market. She became especially popular in Britain and gave numerous royal performances, including concerts for Prince Charles, Princess Ann, and Lady Sarah Ferguson.

Williams made a decision early in her career to include one gospel song on every album she recorded. She admitted that she was not completely happy with this token approach to proclamation but she also says she received continual resistance over just that much. "For eleven years, they've been telling me it will ruin my career," she said in 1987. In at least one case *(Let's Hear It for the Boy),* the lyrics to the token gospel song were intentionally left out of the liner notes where lyrics to all the other songs were included. To avoid giving offense in her concert performances, Williams took to singing gospel songs as an encore set at the end of the evening, allowing those who had come for purely secular entertainment to excuse themselves if they didn't want to hear them (cf. **Donna Summer**). At least some of the time, the token gospel songs were among her best. "God Is Truly Amazing" from the otherwise flaccid *Songbird* album won two Grammys and probably accounted for most of the record's admittedly limited sales. Other gospel highlights from the one-song-per-album repertoire include "They Say," a duet with **Philip Bailey** on *I'm So Proud,* "Whiter Than Snow" from *Let's Hear It for the Boy,* and "I Believe in You" from *Water under the Bridge* (which would also win a Grammy). Eventually, all of these songs would be compiled for *From the Beginning* released by Sparrow in 1986. That record also includes Williams' rendition of "I Am Sure," the **Michael W. Smith** song that was a Christian radio hit for that artist in 1984, and "We Are Here to Change the World," a song written by Michael Jackson.

Despite the inclusion of gospel songs from the very start, a major turning point in Williams' amalgamation of entertainment and ministry came in 1979 when **Philip Bailey** called her and said, "Deniece, I'd like to do a show where we get a bunch of Christian entertainers together and we just thank God for all that we've been allowed to experience over the years." The program ended up being called *Jesus at the Roxy* and had an enormous impact on everyone involved. Williams (hot off her success with Johnny Mathis) and Bailey headlined the program. **Marilyn McCoo** was in the audience and years later would testify to how her husband Billy Davis Jr. (lead singer for Fifth Dimension) accepted Christ that night. Williams says the experience rejuvenated her own spiritual life and prompted her to get more serious about her ability to witness to the gospel. In preparation for the *Jesus at the Roxy* show, Philip Bailey, Deniece Williams, Syreeta Wright, **Leon Patillo,** and a number of other Christian entertainers began meeting regularly for prayer and Bible study in **Donna Summer**'s studio. At one point, Williams would actually say, "From those services, I got saved. I had always been in the church, but I had never had a personal walk with Christ." At other times she would speak of the meetings as the time when she "became convicted," but whatever evangelical language is used, it was clearly a highpoint in her journey of faith. She says that she became "much more careful" about which songs she would sing. Williams had never done the sort of sexually charged material that Summer had to live down after she "got convicted," but now she headed off any speculation as to what the options might be, stating publicly, "You'll never hear me sing any of that shake-your-booty stuff." She and Bailey also formed an organization together called Living Epistles that focused on the role of Christians in the entertainment industry.

In 1986, Williams formed her own production company, Gateway Music, and married her business partner, Brad Westering (it was her third marriage, and she had already raised two sons as a single mother). That same year, she moved overtly into Christian music and would make two albums of new material for Sparrow, both of which were produced by Westering. *So Glad I Know* opens with a high-energy number called "Just in Time" and then moves into the calypso-flavored "Wings of an Eagle." The song "They Say" gets reprised now as a duet with **Sandi Patty.** "Straight Ahead" is not an **Amy Grant** cover, but an infectious dance track written by Williams with **Richard Souther** about the need to be on the alert for Satan's wiles. Williams also sings the traditional hymn "I Surrender All" and includes a Christianized rewrite of the old Chaka Khan hit "What You Do for Me." *So Glad I Know* sold over 250,000 copies and earned Williams two more Grammy awards. The follow-up, *Special Love,* includes a rapturous version of the hymn "His Eye Is on the Sparrow" and a duet with Natalie Cole, "We Sing Praises." The title track is a dance number *CCM* found similar to Prince's "Sign-o-the-Times," and the song "Healing" is a remake of a tune she originally put on *Hot on the Trail.*

Like **Philip Bailey, Donna Summer, B. J. Thomas,** and other Christian performers who did not renounce their ties to secular music, Williams continued to be criticized by conservative Christians for continuing to record for the general market at the same time that she was making albums for contemporary Christian music fans. "There are people in the church who will tell you to quit driving a city bus and start driving a Sunday School bus," she said at one point, "but our responsibility is to seek God where he has us." Furthermore, she did not attempt to justify her secular work as some sort of means to an end, as is often done. In other words, she did not maintain that the purpose of singing secular songs was to gain an audience among unbelievers whom she could then hit with the gospel. Although she always seemed willing to share her faith with anyone in either setting, the so-called secular songs had an integrity all their own. "There is nothing wrong with singing about the love between a man and a woman," she insisted, bewildered that the point even had to be made. "I really don't think that I'm living in two separate worlds or that my Sparrow and Columbia albums say two different things," she told *CCM* in 1987. And, then, three years later she would add, "I know that there are a lot of Christians that don't understand what I do, or what **Amy Grant** does, but I've got one judge and He doesn't look anything like them."

In 1991, Williams' career in Christian music would come unraveled when her marriage to Westering ended in divorce. "I got Grammy awards and an American Music Award and Stellar Awards, but it all came with sacrifice," she told *CCM*. "Time away from home created a troubled marriage." She left America and moved to London, where she starred in the theatrical production of *Mama I Want to Sing.* "After the divorce, I just wanted to hide," she would admit seven years later. Still, she did not retreat too far. In Britain, she became host of a BBC radio program called *Gospel Train.* The show changed its name to *The Deniece Williams Show* but continued to view its primary purpose as being to promote Christian music in the United Kingdom. Then, after seven years, Williams returned to the contemporary Christian music market with another album of gospel songs. *This Is My Song* offers her collection of classic hymns, including "Blessed Assurance," "Just As I Am," and "It Is Well." The song "I Love Him Above All Things" is a soaring highpoint. "These are the songs that would pop up in my spirit during my difficult times," she told *CCM*. "These songs are life-givers. They need to be exposed and shared."

In 1997, Williams told *Release,* "Reflecting over the past few years, I've learned we have to keep focused on God, not on circumstances or people. I've had to realize I have to find my peace, hope, and security in Christ alone, not in a career, industry, or person, only Jesus. I am in the entertainment business, but I see *life* as a ministry."

Christian radio hits: "So Glad I Know" (# 14 in 1986); "They Say" [with **Sandi Patty**] (# 1 for 2 weeks in 1987); "Wings of an Eagle" (# 6 in 1987); "I Believe in You" (# 5 in 1988); "Healing" (# 3 in 1989); "Every Moment" (# 3 in 1989); "Special Love" (# 4 in 1990); "We Sing Praises" (# 23 in 1990); "Somebody Loves You" (# 8 in 1990); "Fire inside My Soul" (# 9 in 1991); "I Am Sure" (# 7 in 1991).

Grammy Awards: 1986 Best Soul Gospel Performance, Female ("I Surrender All"); 1986 Best Soul Gospel Performance by a Duo or Group, Choir, or Chorus [with **Sandi Patty**] ("They Say"); 1987 Best Gospel Performance, Female ("I Believe in You"); 1998 Best Pop/Contemporary Gospel Album (*This Is My Song*).

Evan Williams

See **Harvest Flight.**

Joy Williams

2001—*Joy Williams* (Reunion).

Joy Williams is another teenage female singer (cf. **Rachel Lampa, Nikki Leonti, Stacie Orrico**) put forward by the Christian music industry in an attempt to capitalize on the success of artists like Britney Spears and Christina Aguilera in the general market. Reunion Records blatantly attempted to market the seventeen-year-old on the basis of her physical appearance, even to the point of distributing sixteen-month calendars that display her in a variety of chaste but attractive poses. As with the above-mentioned artists, however, sexist exploitation could not obscure the raw talent.

Williams moved to California when she was about ten years of age and was raised by evangelical parents who ran a Christian retreat center. She has a powerful voice similar to Jessica Simpson and **Rebecca St. James.** The usual star songwriters (including Regie Hamm, Joel Lindsey, Ty Lacy, and Dan Mukala) provided her with age-appropriate material for her self-titled debut album, on which many of the songs deal with expressions of personal faith and with the exercise of personal responsibility in life. The song "I Believe in You" was featured in the soundtrack to the motion picture *Left Behind.* On "Serious" she proclaims, "I'm serious about the talk I'm talking / The evidence is in the walk I'm walking / Serious about love and purity / I'm serious as I can be."

Kelli Williams

1996—*Kelli Williams* (Word); 1998—*I Get Lifted;* 2000—*In the Myx* (Myrrh).

Kelli Williams came on the contemporary Christian music scene as a teenaged star in traditional gospel, sort of an African American counterpart to **Rachel Lampa.** Just as Lampa forsook the expected Britney and Christina analogies to become a Christian version of Celine Dion, so Williams ignored Brandy and Monica, fashioning herself after Whitney Houston. In both cases, the phenomenon of adolescents performing music targeted for people their parents' age was striking.

Williams had brushes with fame early on when, as a child, she was a three-time winner on *Star Search.* At age sixteen, she recorded her first, self-titled album, obviously modeled on the works of **Tramaine Hawkins** and **CeCe Winans.** On that record, she covers **The Winans'** hit "People Need the Lord" and delivers a lung-busting diva performance on "Counting on You." The song "Never Alone," cowritten with **Angie Winans,** offers reassurance of God's abiding care. Williams then toured with **CeCe Winans,** singing background vocals and performing duet vocals on the song "Count on Me" (which CeCe had recorded with Whitney Houston). Percy Bady would produce her sophomore album, with **Walter Hawkins** coming in to produce three tracks. Reviewers could not help but note that Williams' vocal resemblance to the latter's former wife (Tramaine) is at times uncanny. *I Get Lifted* scores primarily with ballads like "Friend of Mine" and "Love Wouldn't" (a duet with David Hollister of Blackstreet). Surprisingly, on *In the Myx,* the artist, who was now officially an adult (twenty-one) and married, delves into more youth-oriented sounds. The third project was produced by **Tonéx** (and an associate who calls him- or herself 5.0). It features the dance track "Bustin' Loose" and an

industrial-influenced hip-hop number called "Remyx Me" (a creative plea for spiritual renewal).

Christian radio hits: "Serious" (# 6 in 2001).

Victoria Williams

1987—*Happy Come Home* (Geffen); 1990—*Swing the Statue* (Mammoth); 1994—*Loose* (Atlantic); 1995—*This Moment in Toronto;* 1998—*Musings of a Creek Dipper;* 2000—*Water to Drink.*

www.victoriawilliamsonline.com

Victoria Williams (b. 1959) is a Christian singer and songwriter who commands widespread respect in the general market while remaining virtually unknown to Christian music fans—at least to those who limit their listening to music produced within the official Christian music industry. Williams' shrill voice is admittedly an acquired taste, though as many critics have pointed out, it is not unusual for *male* singers with idiosyncratic voices to gain strong followings (David Byrne, **Bob Dylan,** Michael Stipe, Tom Waits). Still, Williams is generally more revered as a songwriter than as a performer, though her fans will insist that her own interpretations of her material outshine all others.

Williams grew up in a Methodist household in Shreveport, Louisiana, and played with a number of bands before marrying **Peter Case** of The Plimsouls. The union was short-lived (1985–1989), but it was during that time that she released her first album, *Happy Come Home.* This debut record would be best remembered for a line from one song that became a slogan for her career: "Everyday is poetry." Otherwise, *Happy Come Home* presents songs about home and family life that one reviewer would describe as "redolent of frontier Americana in all of its *Little House on the Prairie* innocence." The song "Main Road" is about picking wildflowers in the rural countryside. In "Frying Pan," Williams sings that "these are precious times," and in "Merry Go Round" she offers a disarmingly optimistic way of viewing a life that seems to just go in circles: "The key to the merry-go-round is the *merry."* But the centerpiece of *Happy Go Home* is "Opelousas (Sweet Relief)," which juxtaposes narratives of slinking through life with choruses promising where pleasure can be found: "Some find it in a bathtub or a backrub / The clothes they wear or just in the air . . . It's in a handshake or a lucky break / In a bottle of wine or just losing some time."

Williams' second album, *Swing the Statue,* is usually thought to be her masterpiece. It includes her most compelling song, "Summer of Drugs," which reflects on a woman's coming of age as part of a generation that felt they were "too late to be hippies." The title of the song plays cleverly on the media's romanticized portrait of 1967 as the Summer of Love. Williams wistfully characterizes her generation as one that "missed out on the love," though drugs were still around. The poetry of her lyrics, furthermore, is like something out of a Gabriel García Márquez novel: "Sister got bit by a copperhead snake in the woods behind the house / Nobody was home so I grabbed her foot and I sucked that poison out / Sister got better in a month or two when the swellin', it went down / And I started out my teenage years with a poison in my mouth." The tenor of this unforgettable song is balanced with "Holy Spirit," an original gospel revival tune in which she recalls how the Holy Spirit has flowed and moved in her life at different junctures. It is one of the most powerful and explicitly Christian testimonies ever to appear on a general market recording, but it is not the only song with spiritual overtones. "Lights" is basically an exposition of Jesus' words in Matthew 5:14–16, prompting her audience to consider what kind of life they might live if they could choose: "Would you want to make something good that you could look on / To give you pleasure? Yeah you would." But then the song takes an unexpected turn to plumb the nature of grace: "What if this thing you made wasn't perfect? / Would you love it anyway?"

In 1992, as Williams toured as an opening act for Neil Young, she was plagued during her concerts by a numbness in her hands that made it difficult to play guitar. She was subsequently diagnosed as having degenerative multiple sclerosis—and, like many musicians, had no health insurance to cover her medical bills. Shocked, friends within the music community gathered to produce a benefit album on her behalf. An all-star cast of performers recorded favorite Williams songs and packaged them as *Sweet Relief* (Sony, 1993). The album was successful in a number of ways. It raised more than enough money to cover Williams' expenses and enabled her to found the Sweet Relief Fund to help other musicians in need. It also introduced whole new audiences to her songs, as Soul Asylum's version of "Summer of Drugs" and Pearl Jam's take on "Crazy Mary" (a previously unreleased song about a deranged or retarded woman) became major hits on college radio. *Sweet Relief* also unearths another unknown Williams song, "This Moment," performed by Matthew Sweet. **Maria McKee** and **The Waterboys** also participate, alongside Buffalo Tom, Lou Reed, and Evan Dando of The Lemonheads. Michelle Shocked sings "Holy Spirit" with a number of Christian music stars **(Ashley Cleveland,** Bonnie Keen of **First Call, Phil Madeira, Russ Taff)** helping out.

At some point around 1993 or 1994, Williams married Mark Olson, leader of The Jayhawks. Despite her failing health, she has continued to compose songs and record. The album *Loose* came hot on the heels of *Sweet Relief*'s success and was embraced by critics (Jon Pareles of *The New York Times* included it on his list of the ten best albums of the year). Some Christian music magazines also noticed her for the first time. *True Tunes*

(usually a step ahead of the rest) gave it a lengthy, song-by-song accounting. On *Loose,* Williams continues to offer a defiantly positive outlook on life, which comes through even in two songs inspired by the recent death of her father: "Harry Went to Heaven" and "Happy to Have Known Pappy." Explicitly gospel lyrics are heard in the affirming "You R Loved." The song "My Ally" is a rare ode to platonic friendships sung as a duet with Soul Asylum's Dave Pirner. In addition to the original material, Williams offers a twelve-minute jazzy version of Louie Armstrong's "What a Wonderful World." *Loose* also includes Williams' own version of "Crazy Mary" and the song "Love," which would later be covered by **Sarah Masen.** It concludes with "Psalms," a spiritual track with lyrics by Williams that sound like they could have come from Scripture: "Although the Lord be high above / He doth recall the lowly / And deep within thy secret heart / The Lord shall surely know thee."

This Moment in Toronto is a live recording featuring favorite songs and covers of a few standards ("Smoke Gets in Your Eyes," "Imagination"). *CCM* finally discovered Williams with *Musings of a Creek Dipper* and placed the project in the capable hands of their best critic, Brian Quincy Newcomb. He gets to the heart of what makes her so affecting: she takes life for what it is and sees miracles that others miss. The color of the sky one morning ("Periwinkle Sky"), a vision of birds flying up from a cemetery ("Blackbirds Rise"), or a memory from her childhood ("Grandpa in the Cornpatch") is all that is necessary for poetry to happen and for God's presence to be affirmed. *Musings* includes a wedding song called "Let It Be So," which another reviewer would say "carries so much conviction that it's easy to forget about broken homes." Williams sings, "Rejoice in this moment and many hereafter / Sweet and holy because of your laughter / Oh, let it be so!" A song called "Nature Boy" would later be used in the motion picture *Moulin Rouge* where its refrain would become a recurrent theme: "The greatest thing you'll ever learn / Is just to love and be loved in return."

Water to Drink offers more songs of affirmation ("You Can Be") and thankfulness ("The Joy of Love"), along with some covers of smoky songs like João Gilberto's "Agua de Beber" ("Water to Drink") and Billie Holiday's "Until the Real Thing Comes Along." *Rolling Stone* would say, "Both homespun and hymnlike, the songs on *Water to Drink* are the fullest expression yet of Williams' cockeyed genius."

Williams maintains a number of contacts with the contemporary Christian music guild. She has regularly sung on projects by other Christian artists who are on the fringes of that subculture, including **Robert Deeble** and **Buddy** and **Julie Miller.** She sang on **Rev. Dan Smith**'s blues compilation and contributed to the *At the Foot of the Cross* worship project put together by members of **The Choir.** Although Williams' compositions and recordings are universally lauded by critics in the general market, the faith that informs and sustains her work is sometimes viewed as a deficit. *The Rough Guide to Rock* offers a too-typical example of this prejudice in saying that, in spite of Williams' obvious poetic and musical gifts, she "continues to flirt with rather simplistic Christian imagery" that must be regarded "as either charmingly nostalgic or stomach-twistingly naive." If the *Rough Guide*'s reviewer had accompanied her on a tour in 1999, he might have found ample opportunity to be charmed and/or stomach-twisted by what he observed. The artist regularly followed up her concerts with trips to hospital wards to visit patients who suffer from multiple sclerosis and other debilitating conditions. One news account read: "An hour after her concert was over, Victoria Williams could be found sitting on the floor in the entrance of Park West holding a young man as he wept and shared of his struggle with an obviously crippling disability. As the man got up to leave, he asked her what made her keep going despite her illness. She smiled and answered, 'Jesus gives me the strength. He loves me and he loves you. Remember that'."

For trivia buffs: Victoria Williams had a small role in the movie *Even Cowgirls Get the Blues* (1995).

Alicia Williamson

See **Truth.**

Chris Willis

1996—*Chris Willis* (StarSong).

Chris Willis is a contemporary Christian singer who leans toward R&B styles and worked for many years as a background vocalist before finally releasing an album of his own. Willis has sung on albums and tours by artists like **Anointed, Clay Crosse, Twila Paris,** and **Michael W. Smith.** At one point, he recorded a full album for Warner Reprise (produced by his cousin Mervyn Warren of **Take 6**) that the label decided not to release. It would be a few more years before he would try again and come out with the official debut, *Chris Willis,* on StarSong. The album's standout song is "Diamond in Me," a tribute to God's ability to use human trials to bring out the best in people. The record also includes the mellow jazz "Nobody But Jesus" and the syncopated "Cover Me."

Wilshire

Lori Wilshire, voc., gtr.; Micah Wilshire, gtr., voc. 1998—*Wilshire* (Rocketown); 2000—*Second Story.*

Wilshire is a husband and wife duo who specialize in crafting Beatlesque songs with strong melodic hooks and vocal har-

monies. They might be compared to **One Hundred Days,** with female vocals. Shawn Colvin influences are also apparent, and **Out of the Grey** comparisons are inevitable. Micah and Lori Wilshire were both involved in Christian music before they married, singing background vocals and playing as session musicians. They met when Micah was hired as a backup vocalist for what was once intended to be Lori's first solo album. Eventually, the couple was prominently featured on **Michael W. Smith**'s "I'll Lead You Home" tour, performing with the artist and as an opening act. Smith was so impressed with them that he was inspired to create his Rocketown Records label with them as the inaugural act. Wilshire's songs do not focus exclusively or even prominently on religious or spiritual themes. Rather, most Wilshire songs are simply about life and love and happiness (cf. Smith's "Love You Good" hit) and would not be immediately recognizable as Christian songs apart from the context that the group itself imparts to them. The debut self-titled album features the standout songs "Over My Head" (not a Fleetwood Mac cover), "Ms. Innocence," and "Closer Still." *Second Story* offers "Tonight," a love song from the perspective of a woman awaiting the homecoming of her soldier husband who has been off to war. Micah says, "We write love songs because we're married and we love each other." Lori adds, "Being in love in huge to us. How can we not sing about it?"

Christian radio hits: "Closer Still" (# 4 in 1998); "Over My Head" (# 8 in 1998); "Ms. Innocence" (# 24 in 1998).

Bob and Pauline Wilson

1981—*Somebody Loves You* (Myrrh).

Bob and Pauline Wilson were the core members of the mainstream jazz-fusion band **Seawind** (Bob was the primary songwriter and Pauline the lead singer). The group included some songs with Christian lyrics on its albums, but was never perceived as "a Christian band," even though most of its members were Christians. Bob Wilson in particular made a point of distancing himself and the group from the Christian music scene, stating at one point that "We and the whole band were treated worse by our brothers and sisters [than by people in the secular environment], and I just decided I didn't want to have anything to do with them." The remarkable thing about the latter comment is that it was offered in 1980; twenty years later, hundreds of alternative Christian artists would echo similar sentiments, insisting that they were not in a Christian band but were merely "Christians in a band." Still, Wilson maintains that God overcame his resistance: "In prayer time one morning, the Lord, like out of a book, said, 'I want you and Pauline to do an album. I want it to be a Christian album that's going to start a broader platform for your ministry.'" Pauline reportedly didn't like the idea, but the two of them yielded to the explicit divine instructions and recorded *Somebody Loves You* for the contemporary Christian music market. The album is for all intents and purposes a **Seawind** album (the whole band plays on it), and reviewers would note that the sound of the record is indistinguishable from that of **Seawind**'s products. It was released on Myrrh, however, and the company was constrained by A&M from using the name of **Seawind** in conjunction with it. The songs are jubilant and specific in their testimony. "Jesus Is My Lord" is a quiet confession of faith. "You Can't Hide" features hard-hitting horns and a hound-of-heaven theme. The title track offers a straightforward evangelistic proclamation of the gospel message that the Wilsons indicate is the main theme of the album. "Our biggest concern," Bob says in the liner notes, "is for the people on the street who don't realize that Jesus loves them." Bob Wilson later played in **The Front** and **What If,** and in the early '90s he formed a jazz-rock group 40:31 (after Isaiah 40:31).

Christian radio hits: "Joyful Melody" (# 12 in 1981); "Somebody Loves You" (# 14 in 1981).

Wilson-McKinley

Jim Bartlett, bass, voc.; Mike Messer, gtr., voc.; Tom Slipp, drums; Randy Wilcox, gtr., kybrd., voc. 1970—*On Stage* (custom); 1971—*Spirit of Elijah* (Voice of Elijah); 1972—*Heaven's Gonna Be a Blast;* 1974—*Country in the Sky* (custom); *Yesterday/Forever;* 2000—*Message Brought to Us* (Tanignak).

www.tanignak.com

Washington state's Wilson-McKinley was in many ways the quintessential Jesus freak band. They did not enjoy the same success as the numerous Calvary Chapel bands signed to Maranatha in Costa Mesa, California—and their recordings are nowhere near as good—but they actually provide a better witness to what was happening in the Jesus movement revival of the early '70s than those groups with which the movement is usually associated. This may be because their recordings are earlier, or simply because their spiritual leader (Carl Parks) was more gracious than Calvary Chapel's Chuck Smith in allowing the freakier aspects of the Jesus freaks to come through. Those who want a historically accurate glimpse into the Jesus movement (or just an authentic souvenir) do well to begin their research with Wilson-McKinley.

The group was intimately involved with a ministry that seems to have been variously known as the Jesus People Army and as the Voice of Elijah (the one label might have applied to the community itself and the other to its outreach program, which involved recordings and publications). They became best known nationally for publishing a newspaper called *Truth,* which was distributed all over the West Coast and sent in bulk quantities (free of charge, if necessary) to anyone who re-

quested it. Pockets of otherwise marginalized Jesus freaks all over America (and sometimes overseas) subscribed, and *Truth* became a staple witnessing tool for campus prayer groups everywhere. It represented the countercultural side of the Jesus movement, as opposed to the very straight-laced Campus Crusade for Christ. Along with the *Hollywood Free Paper* (published by Duane Pederson), *Truth* was the primary oracle of the Jesus freaks, a national underground 'zine published by and for hippie Christians who never really fit into the whole Navigators, Young Life, Youth for Christ, Young Republicans, pre-Religious Right ethos.

The Jesus People Army/Voice of Elijah community was located in Spokane, Washington, and was led by charismatic evangelist Carl Parks. Composed of converted hippies, the community had all the appearances of what would later be termed a religious cult, but it seems to have escaped the trappings of less fortunate groups that went that route (cf. entries for **All Saved Freak Band, Family of Love, Jeremy Spencer**). Members of the community pooled all their possessions (after the example in Acts 2:44–45; cf. entries for **Resurrection Band, Servant**) and devoted their lives single-mindedly to evangelism and spiritual devotion in expectation of an imminent return of Christ. There is some evidence that they also tended to suspend capacities for critical thinking in favor of receiving the inspired teachings of their leader, but Parks did not take advantage of this. The group's doctrinal idiosyncrasies were no more extreme than those endemic to Pentecostal fundamentalism, and there is no evidence of undue coercion or manipulation of members. Indeed, Parks—very much to his credit—disbanded the community and shut down the Voice of Elijah ministry sometime around the end of 1974, believing that it had served its purpose. As an article by Timothy Smith (available at the website listed above) indicates, "It was impossible to maintain a communal lifestyle, eating, sleeping, and ministering together without a break for years on end. Members of the community felt pressure to get married, start families, hold traditional jobs, go on vacation, do something noncommunal." Parks realized all of this, and has said that the whole ministry was formed out of a revival and served the needs of that revival; it was never intended to become a permanent entity unto itself. As time passed, more effective opportunities for conducting ministry arose that did not require the austere sacrifices that participation in JPA had entailed—and this was viewed as a good thing. Still, the disintegration of the community was devastating to some who had dedicated themselves to it, and twenty-five years later some former members would remain bitter about the experience.

Wilson-McKinley existed as a non-Christian hippie rock band prior to any involvement with the Jesus movement. They enjoyed some regional success in the Pacific Northwest and had a contract to produce a nationally distributed album. Then in June of 1970 the members began attending rallies set up in a local park by Parks and his crew. One by one, three of the four members got saved and determined to join the community. They initially assumed this meant renouncing rock music as part of an old sinful life, but Parks soon suggested that they reassemble the group (with a new bass player) and adopt a means-to-an-end attitude. An unidentified group member told *Truth* in November of 1971, "We learned that we could function as a drawing card. Street people are drawn to rock and it gives the others in the body a chance to witness to people that normally wouldn't come to anything Christian." Thus, the band became the centerpiece of what was called a "full body" approach to proselytizing. A large number of community members called highway missionaries would accompany Wilson-McKinley whenever and wherever the group would play, mingling with the crowd to pass out tracts and witness for Jesus. At first, the band served only to draw a crowd (cf. **All Saved Freak Band**), and for that purpose they might as well have played secular tunes (cf. **The Exkursions**). But in time they discovered that the music could be a ministry in its own right. "Something else I've learned," the unidentified band member told *Truth,* "is that people will receive a message in music that they wouldn't if just being talked to." Thus, the group began singing songs about Christ and testifying to their own relationships with Jesus, allowing the highway missionaries to survey faces in the crowd for signs of receptivity and focus their attention on those who indicated any positive reaction to what was being said (and sung). This turned out to be an effective strategy for evangelism within the cultural context of the day, and thousands of converts were made. Most of these did not join the community (which was never strongly encouraged), but many would remain faithful Christians thirty years later, still active in various churches. Eventually, the group also had a prominent ministry playing at Washington state penitentiaries and reformatories.

Those who heard Wilson-McKinley play live often say the band had a psychedelic blues-rock sound similar to Quicksilver Messenger Service. This comes through only occasionally on their recordings, which reveal more of a country-folk style analogous to The Byrds, Buffalo Springfield, and especially the Grateful Dead. None of the albums were recorded very well, but beginning in 2000 (thirty years to the month after the group's conversion), an independent company called Tanignak began issuing greatly improved, digitally remixed samples of their music on compact disc. The first product, *Message Brought to Us,* is merely an anthology of selected songs from the first four albums (the fifth is best forgotten). Tanignak apparently plans to issue the full albums, in addition to other previously unreleased material (mostly concert recordings).

The first Wilson-McKinley album, *On Stage,* was not really recorded on a personal cassette player placed at the foot of the stage by an audience member, as is often reported (cf. Di Sabatino's *The Jesus People Movement*). It was actually recorded intentionally off of the sound board at a concert in Pender Auditorium in Vancouver, British Columbia. It does, however, sound like some bootlegged product in mono with major balance and fidelity problems. Furthermore, the concert itself appears to have been a big family jam, with enthusiastic nonband members beating on congas and adding guitars in a manner that reveals they are not professional musicians. The members of Wilson-McKinley were reportedly appalled by the project, but it was released all the same and through advertisements in *Truth* went out across the country as what some continue to regard as the world's first Christian rock album (actually, **Azitis** and **Mylon LeFevre** also had albums out in 1970—and **Larry Norman** had them all beat by a full year). With spontaneous shouts of "Hallelujah, Jesus!" intermingling with and sometimes overpowering the music, *On Stage* remains what Timothy Smith would call "one of the most outstanding testimonies to the joy of conversion that one could hope to find." It is probably *the* most authentic representation of what early Jesus music concerts tended to be like. The best songs are those reproduced on the *Message Brought to Us* anthology: "You Gotta Hear about My Friend" is an acoustic Grateful Dead-type tune, featuring the memorable lines, "Word's gettin' out fast / World ain't gonna last"; "The Love of My Saviour" is a more bluesy plea that alternates between testimony and direct appeal to the Lord: "Je-e-e-sus, I'm standing here with tears in my eyes. . . ." Less notable are rewritten Christianized versions of two secular songs—The Byrds' "He Was a Friend of Mine" and **Bob Dylan**'s "You Ain't Goin' Nowhere." In keeping with its homemade nature, *On Stage* was originally issued in cardboard envelopes made from old circus posters, folded and then handstenciled by members of the community.

Spirit of Elijah is universally regarded as the band's best project. Songs like "Tree of Life" give credence to the Quicksilver Messenger Service comparisons, moving from a hand-clapping folk fest into a bluesy electric jam. The title track is also an outstanding psychedelic rock song, unlike anything that anyone other than **Azitis** was doing in Christian music at the time. With a running time of over six minutes, it offers an apocalyptic call to repentance in an opus that transitions from a subdued first movement to a sped-up, frantic conclusion in a fashion that was considered really cool at the time (cf. Led Zeppelin's "Stairway to Heaven"). "Come on Home" is a more conventional Christian song that actually sounds quite a bit like something **Love Song** might have done. Wilson-McKinley also performs a bluesy version of the traditional hymn "His Eye Is on the Sparrow" and a boogie rave-up take on the church youth group favorite, "They'll Know We Are Christians by Our Love" (a.k.a. "We Are One in the Spirit"). Again, they display an annoying penchant for christianizing secular songs, but at least this time they pick some obscure numbers (Moby Grape's "He" and the Moody Blues' "It's up to You") and perform them well. Again, Wilson-McKinley lacked funds to pay for professional mixing, and the *Spirit of Elijah* record ended up being issued with embarrassing production problems—most notably a reverb sound that runs throughout Side Two.

Heaven's Gonna Be a Blast shows a more mature band performing all original songs in a country-blues style that some would liken to the Allman Brothers (without the double lead guitars). "Standin' at the Crossroads" is one of the most Allmanesque numbers and is surely a standout track. "Heaven's Gonna Be a Blast" is also a treat, a strong composition that is performed as another Grateful Dead sound-alike. The testimony song, "Never Cry No More," is not very interesting musically but it does offer a tender and compelling portrait of Christ's Lordship: "He doesn't rule with an iron hand / It takes a servant to be a King." The bouncy and energetic "Then I Fell in Love" feels like something **The Talbot Brothers** might have done on their debut *Reborn* album. A piano ballad called "Warm and Sunny Day" previews the Maranatha sound again, this time suggesting some of **Chuck Girard**'s solo work with its high, Brian Wilson-like vocals. "Almighty God" closes the album with an innovative atmospheric piece that uses soft jazz stylings.

In 1974, the community that sponsored Wilson-McKinley was on its last legs, but the band made two more cassette-only releases that became so rare that some collectors doubted their very existence. Both were spurred on by Parks's direction for the band to expand its audience and neither is very good. *Country in the Sky* has a mellow, MOR sound; the group apparently aims for the sort of sound featured on Eagles ballads but winds up sounding like a dozen other acts that were doing the same thing, often better (cf. **Bethlehem, Daniel Amos**). The horrible *Yesterday/Forever* album almost seems like a joke—a collection of instrumental muzak versions of old hymns like "In the Garden," "Amazing Grace," and "How Great Thou Art." Apparently, Parks had wanted a tape that could be used in work with retirees and older church folk. Smith likens the employment of Wilson-McKinley for the production of such a tape to "using a racehorse to haul hay."

Smith says, "Wilson-McKinley was the first known band to come out of a secular rock and roll background and into the Kingdom of Heaven, name and all, bringing their instruments and rocking style with them." In retrospect, the effectiveness of Wilson-McKinley's ministry lay precisely in their willingness to use rock and related musical genres to convey gospel messages. In the early '70s, this was so novel as to communi-

cate something in and of itself. The group once declared (in an issue of *Truth*) that "showing the street people that Jesus isn't bound to a particular mode of music helps them to understand how much freedom there is in Christ."

In 1999, Mike Messer of Wilson-McKinley released a solo album called *Good Ol' Days* (Tanignak).

For trivia buffs: Early on, the pre-Christian Wilson-McKinley actually recorded one quick album for Alshire Records under the name California Poppy Pickers—a set of cover versions of hot-at-the-moment hits to be marketed in grocery stores to undiscerning consumers who just liked the songs and didn't care if they were performed by the original artists.

The Winans

Carvin Winans Jr., voc.; Marvin Winans, voc.; Michael Winans, voc.; Ronald Winans, voc. 1981—*Introducing the Winans* (Light); 1983—*Long Time Comin'*; 1984—*Tomorrow*; 1985—*Yesterday, Today, and Tomorrow; Let My People Go* (Qwest); 1987—*Decisions*; 1988—*Live at Carnegie Hall*; 1990—*Return*; 1993—*All Out*; 1995—*Heart and Soul; The Light Years* (Light).

The Winans are an R&B gospel quartet composed of four brothers whose additional siblings would also become famous gospel stars. Actually the whole Winans legacy begins with **Mom and Pop Winans** who raised their children in Detroit in a home where participation in the Pentecostal Holiness church constituted one's social life and gospel music reigned supreme. "We never really had any choice," Carvin Winans told *CCM* in 1987. "We were more or less forced to do it, because our parents were singers and they wanted us to be singers. But it sure paid off, because none of us are out there getting into trouble." The Winans family would come to be known as "the first family of gospel music," with analogies to The Jacksons in mainstream music. Nine of Mom and Pop's ten children would become recording artists: **Angie Winans, BeBe Winans, CeCe Winans, Daniel Winans, Debbie Winans,** in addition to Carvin, Marvin, Michael, and Ronald—who make up the quartet that is officially called The Winans. Marvin's spouse, **Vickie Winans,** also records, and children of Carvin, Marvin, and Michael make up yet another group known as **Winans Phase 2.**

The Winans quartet has a smooth harmony sound similar to that of **Commissioned,** who also hail from Detroit. The siblings first formed as a group called The Testimonial Singers in 1975. Michael Winans was not a part of that group, but **Howard Smith,** who would later sing with **Andraé Crouch,** was. The Testimonial Singers recorded two albums (*Love Covers* and *Thy Will Be Done*) on their own Jonah label. Crouch discovered the group through Smith and helped them get their start. The Winans (with Michael) sang with Crouch and toured with **Walter Hawkins** in the late '70s. They began recording in the '80s and would remain one of urban gospel's top vocal combos for fifteen years.

The Winans' first three albums established them as mellow purveyors of soulful tunes with rich harmonies. Crouch produced *Introducing the Winans,* which scored a gospel hit with the song "The Question Is" and was nominated for a Grammy. *Long Time Comin'* features "J.E.S.U.S.," a remake of an old Testimonial Singers song. The title song on *Tomorrow* would give the group its first radio hit on the Christian pop chart (as opposed to the more specific traditional gospel chart). The latter album built noticeably on the '70s foundation of **Andraé Crouch and the Disciples,** being produced by former Disciple Bill Maxwell and featuring instrumentation by the jazz players of **Koinonia** (most of whom were also former Disciples). The style fit into the same groove as the '80s sounds of Earth, Wind, and Fire or nondisco Michael Jackson, and its ten original songs provided The Winans with what many critics consider to be their artistic peak. In 2001, a poll of critics sponsored by *CCM* magazine put *Tomorrow* at Number Forty-eight on a list of "The 100 Greatest Albums in Christian Music" (they also put *The Return* at Number Sixty-one). Thom Granger, one of Christian music's finest critics, regards the title track and "Bring Back the Days of Yea and Nay" as the album's best songs.

After three acclaimed albums, The Winans signed with Quincy Jones' Qwest label in hopes of achieving some success in the general market. Their first album on Qwest, the self-produced *Let My People Go,* displays a more raw R&B sound with songs like "Redeemed" and "Very Real Way" moving into funkier territory than the group had explored previously. The title track uses the biblical imagery of the exodus to address contemporary social situations in South Africa and the Middle East. "Special Lady" is a ballad sung as a memorial tribute to the brothers' grandmother. "Choose Ye" has a Latin/calypso feel and features guest vocals by **Vanessa Bell Armstrong.** The next album, *Decisions,* ups the ante considerably with collaborations with big-name mainstream performers. Jazz great Anita Baker joins the brothers on "Ain't No Need to Worry," and former Doobie Brother Michael McDonald sings on "Love Has No Color." Around this time, The Winans also provided backing vocals for Michael Jackson on the song "Man in the Mirror" on his *Bad* album. The group's transformation into a truly contemporary-sounding act would be complete on *Return,* which opens with what they call "a new jack swing" number, "It's Time." The latter song was produced by Ted Riley (responsible for work by Bobby Brown). It features rap vocals (still rare for Christian music in 1990) and addresses the album's theme of repentance with specific reference to urban violence. "We're tired of seeing young black urban teens being killed, shot, and not really knowing why," Marvin said of the song. It would be their first major crossover success, charting at Number Five on *Billboard'*s mainstream urban chart. "Every-day the Same" from *Return* features vocals and harmonica from Stevie Wonder, and "When You Cry" is a soulful ballad with saxophone by Kenny G. "Don't Leave Me" and "A Friend" are two more beat-happy songs produced by Riley. The album was certified gold with sales of over 500,000.

Return was a breakthrough album for The Winans, one that put them in the same league as **Take 6** and their ultra-successful siblings **BeBe** and **CeCe.** Still, they did receive some flak from conservative followers in the gospel community, an arena strongly influenced by American fundamentalism, which (contrary to traditional Christianity) views the secular world as intrinsically evil and teaches that what is worldly is to be shunned by believers. Thus, the Winans were criticized for using secular musicians and employing worldly sounds (like hip-hop and rap) on their albums. Still, the group found that their mainstream connections opened many doors for them in terms of ministry. In 1992, they were able to host a ninety-minute televised Christmas special featuring numerous secular performers.

All Out would continue in the same vein as *Return,* opening with another hip-hop (new jack swing) track called "Payday," featuring rap breaks by R. Kelly. "Money Motive" is also dance oriented. Country crooner Ricky Van Shelton joins them for the ballad "If He Doesn't Come Tonight," and pop star Kenny Loggins sings on "Love Will Never Die." Then the vocal group made an abrupt shift on *Heart and Soul,* delivering an entire album of adult contemporary ballads with no celebrity duets. Two of the best tracks on that album are "Prone to Wander," which *CCM* likened to Elton John's big Disney songs, and "Smile on Me," which they found reminiscent of Earth, Wind, and Fire.

In the late '80s, Carvin Winans recorded a children's album with *The Facts of Life* TV star Kim Fields titled *The Gospel Buggy* (Selah). Marvin Winans is founder and pastor of The Perfecting Church in Detroit. He has also hosted a six-night-a-week gospel radio show. He began the new millennium by recording an album with his church choir (*Friends* by Marvin Winans and the Perfecting Praise Choir, Diamante, 2001). Michael Winans has also recorded an album with his wife, Regina: *Always Remember* by Michael and Regina Winans (MCG, 2000). As early as 1990, Ronald Winans had formed a choir and would tour and record several albums with them; one such project is *Ron Winans Presents Family and Friends* (Chordant, 1996). In early 1997, Ron Winans checked himself into an Ann Arbor hospital believing he had the flu only to have doctors discover he had suffered a heart attack and torn his aorta. The doctors told his family he had only a two percent chance of surviving the imminent surgery, and one of them reportedly said, "If this man walks out of here, then we're all going to church." The latter comment became occasion for a service of praise at Marvin's

Detroit church in March, when hospital personnel gathered with the Winans clan to give thanks to God for what they all maintain was a miraculous recovery.

For trivia buffs: Although they do not look very much alike, Marvin and Carvin Winans are twins.

Christian radio hits: "Tomorrow" (# 17 in 1985); "Ain't No Need to Worry" [with Anita Baker] (# 9 in 1987); "Love Has No Color" [with Michael McDonald] (# 2 in 1988); "It's Time" (# 1 for 8 weeks in 1990); "Everyday the Same" (# 1 for 2 weeks in 1990); "A Friend" (# 20 in 1990); "Don't Leave Me" (# 13 in 1991); "Together We Stand" (# 25 in 1991); "Payday" (# 8 in 1993); "That Extra Mile" (# 6 in 1993).

Dove Awards: 1986 Contemporary Gospel Album (*Let My People Go*); 1988 Contemporary Gospel Album (*Decisions*); 1990 Rap/Hip Hop Song ("It's Time").

Grammy Awards: 1985 Best Soul Gospel Performance by a Duo, Group, Choir, or Chorus (*Tomorrow*); 1986 Best Soul Gospel Performance by a Duo, Group, Choir, or Chorus (*Let My People Go*); 1987 Best Soul Gospel Performance by a Duo, Group, Choir, or Chorus [with Anita Baker] ("Ain't No Need to Worry"); 1988 Best Soul Gospel Performance by a Duo, Group, Choir, or Chorus (*The Winans at Carnegie Hall*); 1993 Best Contemporary Soul Gospel Album (*All Out*).

Winans Phase 2

Carvin Winans III, voc.; Juan Winans, voc.; Marvin Winans Jr., voc.; Michael Winans Jr., voc. 1999—*We Got Next* (Myrrh).

www.winansphase2.com

Winans Phase 2 is an R&B-flavored gospel group composed of four teenagers, all of whom are children of members of the popular gospel quartet **The Winans.** Carvin III, Marvin Jr., and Michael Jr. are sons of their respective namesakes in the latter group; Juan is also the son of Carvin Winans Jr (and, thus, is Carvin III's brother). As a group, Winans Phase 2 has a slick harmonic sound that blends R&B and hip-hop to create similarities to both Boyz II Men and Dru Hill. The members were aged sixteen to eighteen when they recorded *We Got Next*. The album features silky harmonies on "Just for a Day" and especially smooth vocals on the acoustic "Always for You." The song "Come On Over" has a faster tempo and offers an invitation to the listener to cross whatever chasm needs to be crossed to get in touch with spiritual matters. This dualistic perspective seems to inform the entire album, which Carvin III says is "about letting the young people know who Jesus is, and how they need to come over to this side and give up the ways of the world." *We Got Next* also includes the somewhat edgier "Let Him In" (with the lyric "He's making love to my heart") and a braggadocio rap number "I'm a Winans, Too," in which each member in turn lays claim to the family legacy. There is also a cover of the Bee Gees' "Too Much Heaven."

Angie and Debbie Winans (a.k.a. **Angie and Debbie**) (and **Angie Winans** [solo])

By Angie and Debbie Winans: 1993—*Angie and Debbie* (Capitol); 1997—*Bold* (Against the Flow). By Angie Winans: 2001—*Melodies of My Heart* (Against the Flow).

Angie (b. 1968) and Debbie (b. 1971) Winans are the youngest children of **Mom** and **Pop Winans.** Their older siblings include all four members of **The Winans,** plus BeBe, CeCe, and **Daniel Winans.** The two sisters began singing background vocals on albums and tours by **BeBe** and **CeCe** when they were fifteen and twelve years old and continued to do so for ten years before recording on their own in 1993. They have a sound that combines ingredients of R&B, hip-hop, and gospel in support of strongly evangelical lyrics. Their debut album was produced by brother **BeBe.** Whitney Houston sings with them on the song "Light of Love," and she invited them to tour with her as an opening act. Debbie wrote the song "Simply a Fanatic," which she says is about "who we are and what we're about." Angie contributes "Why Won't You Let Me Love You?" and "He Lives," which tend toward adult contemporary balladry. The upbeat songs "Fact Is, Truth Is" and "What a Place" (about heaven) offer strong and specific testimonies to Christian hope.

The follow-up album was the mistitled *Bold,* which presents a number of songs that rely on tired clichés to support status-quo positions of the Religious Right. On "It's Not Natural," Angie takes on the issue of homosexuality: "I was chilling on my couch one night, looking at my screen TV / There were people celebrating and congratulating the new addition to the gay community / I was vexed in my spirit and I began to write this song . . . It's not natural, no, that's not the way it goes / Just because it's popular doesn't mean it's cool." She would later maintain that the song was inspired by the "coming out" episode of the TV program *Ellen,* in which the TV character admitted to being a lesbian. *Bold* was attacked by gay rights advocates and sympathizers, and the protests took a hyperbolic turn: "Bigots with angel faces" one review of the album read. The sisters ended up in a defensive posture: "We're not trying to bash anybody," they maintained in a press release. "We're bringing the Word to people." Still, the public presentation of Christians as "opponents to gays" rather than as "promoters of Christ" was disturbing even to those Christians who agree with the sisters' stance on the issue.

The hubbub over "It's Not Natural" not only derailed Angie and Debbie's career but also detracted from album tracks that are more evangelical in focus. A few other tunes also make social statements ("Rebuke the Devil," "Never Gonna," "Strange Woman"), but the topics (teenage pregnancy, urban violence, marital infidelity) are ones on which their views are non-controversial. "I Believe" and "Love Will Lead the Way" are spiritually uplifting in ways that should not be overshadowed by the one misstep. "Ryan's Song" is a testimony of unconditional love to Angie's young son. Angie Winans recovered from the *Bold* debacle with a first-class solo album, *Melodies of My Heart.* The latter record displays her love of smooth jazz. She leans toward ballads with "Roses," "He Loves Me," and "The Lord's Prayer," and the album also includes some jazz instrumentals featuring her producer husband, Cedric Caldwell.

Christian radio hits: "Light of Love" (# 3 in 1993); "Simply a Fanatic" (# 24 in 1994).

BeBe and CeCe Winans (and BeBe Winans [solo] and CeCe Winans [solo])

By BeBe and CeCe Winans: 1984—*Lord, Lift Us Up* (PTL); 1987—*BeBe and CeCe Winans* (Sparrow); 1988—*Heaven;* 1991—*Different Lifestyles;* 1992—*First Christmas;* 1994—*Relationships;* 1996—*Greatest Hits.* By BeBe Winans: 1997—*BeBe Winans* (Sparrow); 2000—*Love and Freedom* (Motown) [as BeBe]. By CeCe Winans: 1995—*Alone in His Presence* (Sparrow); 1998—*His Gift; Everlasting Love* (Pioneer); 1999—*Alabaster Box* (Wellspring Gospel); 2001—*CeCe Winans.*

www.bebewinans.com

www.cecewinans.com

BeBe (b. 1962) and CeCe (b. 1964) Winans have become the most famous and successful members of the Winans clan. Although their given names are Benjamin and Priscilla, they would always be known as BeBe and CeCe for reasons no one quite remembers—speculation holds that "BeBe" might be a corruption of "baby" and CeCe of "sissy" (i.e., sister), both names being bestowed by older siblings. BeBe was the seventh child and CeCe the eighth (and first girl) born to **Mom and Pop Winans.** Four of their older brothers would be the first to gain notoriety as members of **The Winans** quartet, a groundbreaking group that was one of the first to blend contemporary urban music into a style replete with conventional traditional gospel harmonies. Brother **Daniel Winans** also formed a group and made a mark in more traditional gospel music. Eventually, brother Marvin's wife **Vickie Winans** and little sisters **Angie and Debbie Winans** would also be making records, as would a collection of nephews known as **Winans Phase 2.** But it was BeBe and CeCe who shattered all expectations regarding what gospel singers can accomplish in the modern musical environment. They would not only become two of the biggest names in contemporary Christian music but would also draw considerable notice and command tremendous respect within the general market. In terms of sound, BeBe Winans is often regarded as Christian music's Luther Vandross, and CeCe, as Christian music's Whitney Houston. Dismissed by cynical critics as purveyors of "black yuppie music," they would perfect a contemporary form of gospel that would

be equally at home in pop, adult contemporary, and R&B formats. It would be hard to find two better voices in the Christian music scene or to find albums more flawlessly produced. Their songs consistently tell of faith, without recognizing any artificial boundary between religious and secular spheres of life.

Raised in Detroit as members of the Pentecostal Holiness church, the two grew up singing together. First, BeBe and CeCe joined brother Daniel (and for a time, Michael) in a group called Winans Part II (not to be confused with Winans Phase 2). Then in 1982, they both became part of The PTL Singers associated with Jim and Tammy Faye Bakker's doomed TV ministry. They made their first album, *Lord, Lift Us Up,* as a part of that group. The track from which the title is taken is "Up Where We Belong," a Christianized version of a song that had been a Number One general market hit for Joe Cocker and Jennifer Warnes a year earlier (in 1982). Nevertheless, the Winans' version ended up being nominated for a Grammy and became the first (and only) song associated with the Bakkers ever to leave a mark on the Christian Hit Radio charts. The album also includes "I'm Gonna Miss You," a touching love song that BeBe wrote for his sister's wedding. This early success allowed the duo to see the possibility of breaking through to mainstream white audiences, something that no traditional gospel singer had really done successfully since **Andraé Crouch.** The Winans also came through the PTL scandals unruffled and with a winsome attitude of grace. "I look into my pocket and I can't even find a pebble to throw," BeBe said after Jim Bakker was humiliated by sex scandals and imprisoned for financial improprieties. "We're talking about two wonderful people that had a big dream and big hearts, who had big mistakes—and there but for the grace of God go I."

The group's next self-titled album (their official "debut" according to most listings) would make them major contemporary Christian music stars. Interestingly, **Billy Sprague** worked with them on the project and cowrote some of the songs, including the love song to God "For Always" and the Christian radio hit "I.O.U. Me," a creative expression of self-denial and commitment to God. The latter song was the duo's first crossover hit, reaching # 25 on *Billboard*'s mainstream adult contemporary chart. "Love Said Not So" is another adult contemporary ballad sung by BeBe in a style very similar to Peabo Bryson. "Change Your Nature" is not specifically directed to homosexuals as some might assume but, according to BeBe (the composer), offers a generic promise to "dope addicts or alcoholics" or anyone else who needs God's help in being transformed—the song conveys the basic gospel promise that (contra Ben Franklin) God helps those who *are unable to* help themselves. For some reason that marketers have never managed to figure out (one theory: appreciation of undeniable talent) the album *BeBe and CeCe Winans* attracted the attention of numerous general market performers, and the gospel duo suddenly could count such persons as Anita Baker, Natalie Cole, Freddie Jackson, and Whitney Houston as numbering among their biggest fans. The next album, *Heaven,* was significant in that the group capitalized on these connections to bridge the gap between churchly and worldly markets. Houston sings with the Winans on the standout track "Hold up the Light" and on "Celebrate New Life," both of which transcend blandness in ways worthy of the titular lyrics. "Trust Him" is a bit funky also, but otherwise ballads rule: the title track to *Heaven* speaks of longing for paradise; "Lost without You" is a love song to Jesus; "Meantime" (a BeBe solo) offers a pledge to keep on loving Christ even when the reality of heaven or paradise seems a distant hope. The album also includes an ethereal cover of Paul Simon's "Bridge over Troubled Water." Perhaps on the basis of the first three songs mentioned above, the album reached the Top 10 on *Billboard*'s general market R&B chart, the first gospel album to do so since 1972 (**Aretha Franklin**'s *Amazing Grace*). Certified gold (with sales over 500,000), it also won Grammys and Doves, in addition to a Soul Train Music Award, an NAACP Image Award, and six Stellar Awards (given for traditional gospel music).

The really big BeBe and CeCe album would arrive next. *Different Lifestyles* is their *Rumours* or *The Joshua Tree*. It would go platinum (over a million copies sold) and win the group another NAACP Image Award (plus more Grammys, Doves, and Stellars). In 2001, a poll of critics sponsored by *CCM* chose the album as Number Ten on their list of "The 100 Greatest Albums in Christian Music" (they also put *Heaven* at Number Thirty-seven and CeCe's *Everlasting Love* at Number Fifty-one). The album itself became the Number One R&B record in the country and scored two Number One hits on *Billboard*'s general market R&B chart. The first of these would be "I'll Take You There," a remake of the old Staples Singers hit featuring Mavis Staples herself on lead vocals. The second was "Addictive Love," a strong track featuring call-and-response vocals between the two stars. Lyrically, "Addictive Love" recycles the theme of Robert Palmer's big general market hit ("Addicted to Love," # 1 in 1986) with spiritual implications similar to **Carman**'s "Addicted to Jesus." It would provide the duo with their biggest hit on Christian radio. In 2001, "Addictive Love" by BeBe and CeCe Winans was included on a list of "the 365 most significant songs of the twentieth century" prepared by the Recording Industry Association of America. When *Different Lifestyles* first appeared, however, the most noted song was "The Blood," primarily because it features a guest rap performance by **M.C. Hammer,** then at the height of his career. The song was also significant because it represented a move away from the by-now formulaic adult contemporary ballads that

had filled previous projects. Likewise, "Searching for Love (It's Real)" features a more gritty, passionate R&B vocal track than BeBe had often allowed himself to deliver. As *CCM*'s Thom Granger would say, "the *Distinctive Lifestyles* album finds BeBe and CeCe replanting their gifts in soil rich with pop, R&B, hip-hop, and jazz," and "the outgrowth is a charmed, magical organism that stretches across genres and racial barriers." In the ballad department, however, *Different Lifestyles* offers one of the best: "It's O.K." is a wrenching, vulnerable plea for marital reconciliation from BeBe, written at a time when he says he thought his marriage might end. "A lot of people think that because they're Christians, they shouldn't have marital problems," he told *CCM*. "Not so. That doesn't eliminate heartaches, troubles, ups and downs. Recording that song was painful; all of us broke down and cried in the studio, but the tears were tears of joy because God had brought us through it."

BeBe and CeCe Winans, Heaven, and *Different Lifestyles* were all produced by Keith Thomas, who also cowrote many of the songs. Thomas also made **Amy Grant** a household name with *Heart in Motion* the same year that *Different Lifestyles* was released. Still, after this string of successes, BeBe and CeCe went Thomasless on their final project, *Relationships,* working with several different producers on various tracks. The album is noticeably more subdued than its predecessor and features no celebrity guests. The standout track is "Count It All Joy," a swingbeat dance number built on James 1:2. "Right Away" is also bouncy, hearkening back to '70s disco. As the album title suggests, however, a running theme concerns relationships, human and divine, and in this regard the adult contemporary ballad "If Anything Ever Happened to You" makes a strong contribution. The song "These Whatabouts" offers another installment on BeBe's public marital problems. He says, "It's about my marriage falling apart . . . Divorce court here I come. . . . So I wrote it, then God put things back together." The duo's *Greatest Hits* collection would offer most of the essential songs (except, inexplicably, "Hold up the Light") plus a new recording of "Up Where We Belong." In 1995, BeBe and CeCe also recorded Carole King's "You've Got a Friend" for a tribute to that artist called *Tapestry Revisited* (Atlantic, 1995).

In 1995, CeCe Winans pursued a solo career that would allow her to maintain many connections with the world at large while still recording faith-based songs. Her first project was to record the duet "Count on Me" with Whitney Houston for the *Waiting to Exhale* soundtrack. The song became a Top 10 hit on general market radio (# 8 in 1996) and she would perform it with Houston during the 1996 Grammy telecast. She hosted a TV program on the Odyssey channel called *CeCe's Place* and became a spokesperson for Revlon cosmetics and Crest toothpaste. She published an autobiography, *On a Positive Note: CeCe Winans—Her Joyous Faith, Her Life in Music, and*

Her Everyday Blessings (Pocket Books, 1999). Notably, the book was written with Renita J. Weems, a theology professor at Vanderbilt University and one of the most highly respected Womanist (i.e., African American feminist) biblical scholars in the world.

CeCe's debut solo album, *Alone In His Presence,* is a worship-oriented record that sticks much closer to traditional gospel than BeBe and CeCe's duo projects. The album was co-produced by Cedric Caldwell (**Angie Winans'** husband) and includes "Every Time" (written by Marvin Winans) and "His Strength Is Perfect" (written by **Steven Curtis Chapman**). CeCe also performs the hymn "Great Is Thy Faithfulness" with her mother, Delores **(Mom Winans)**. Other hymns are also included ("I Surrender All," "Blessed Assurance"). The album was certified gold. *Everlasting Love* returns CeCe to the R&B-flavored adult contemporary style. She worked with several different producers on the album, giving it the feel of a compilation, lacking coherence but exuding diversity. The set opens with a jazzy soul track, "Well, Alright" (produced by Keith Crouch, Andraé's nephew), which encourages people to persevere during hard times. The other standout song is an apocalyptic, hymnic track called "On That Day," written and produced for the artist by Lauryn Hill. "Come On Back" and the bluesy "Slippin' " are addressed to believers who've fallen or turned away from the faith. After a Christmas collection *(His Gift),* CeCe would reprise the praise and worship style of her first solo album on *Alabaster Box,* albeit with everything thrown into a higher gear. **Fred Hammond** produced the album with Chris Harris; the Brooklyn Tabernacle Choir with the Nashville Symphony Orchestra participated on many songs. The album opens with "Fill My Cup," a traditional spiritual that was the first solo CeCe ever sang in church (at age seven). It closes with a heartfelt prayer of communion with Christ called "Blessed, Broken, and Given." In between, **Take 6** joins CeCe on "One and the Same." The next album, simply titled *CeCe Winans,* would be a soulful R&B jamboree, more like a Whitney Houston record than anything CeCe had ever done. It bristles again with diversity, though everything is held together by consistent production from **Brown Bannister** and **Tommy Sims.** Twin high points include the electrifying funk anthem "Anybody Wanna Pray?" which features a rap break courtesy of **Grits,** and the worship chorus "Holy Spirit." The very poppy opening track, "Say a Prayer," is a hook-filled delight, as is the melodic, bouncy "Heavenly Father." One of the requisite adult contemporary ballads, "Bring Back the Days of Yea and Nay," sounds very much like a BeBe and CeCe song, but is actually a duet with her older brother Marvin Winans, who wrote the song (and in fact won a Grammy for his performance of it in 1985). Commenting on her vision for the album, CeCe said, "I

want to reach people I haven't reached before. Then I want to reach the world."

In 1993, even before the *Relationships* album, BeBe Winans produced one song for Whitney Houston ("Jesus Loves Me") on her album *The Bodyguard.* As such, he ended up sharing in Grammy honors for Producer of the Year when that album ran away with practically every award for which it was eligible. This opened doors for him, and after CeCe went solo, BeBe turned increasingly to production, helming album projects for his sisters **Angie and Debbie Winans,** as well as for Bobby Brown, **The Clark Sisters,** and Stephanie Mills. He also costarred with Mills in a New York City production of *Your Arm's Too Short to Box with God* (cf. **Al Green**) and later traveled with a theater production of *The Civil War.* As time went by, BeBe became more outspoken, commenting on matters that troubled him within the music industry, especially racism and ethical treatment of artists. As to the former, he protested *Billboard's* segregation of Christian music into "(black) gospel" and "Inspirational" charts and told *CCM* in 1998 that, in spite of progress, "society has grown and developed a pattern of racism" that infests the Christian music business as well as the general market. As for the latter, he told *CCM* in 2000 that the Christian music business copies the general market in taking advantage of artists, especially younger performers who either don't know how to negotiate a contract or lack the leverage to get what is just. He considers this to be especially distressing in the Christian scene: "It's more difficult to be raped by people who are supposed to be kindred spirits than it is to be taken advantage of financially by people who don't know who Jesus is."

In 1997, BeBe released his own self-titled debut album to critical acclaim. The opening track, "In Harm's Way," was inspired by the devotion he felt for his brother Ron at a time when it seemed the sibling would surely die (see entry on **The Winans**). BeBe would later reflect, "I felt that I was willing to give my own life if only it would save my brother," and this experience led to a musical meditation on the overwhelming power of love to make any sacrifice. Oscar winner Denzel Washington directed a video for the song, which cracked the mainstream pop charts but stalled at Number Eighty-three. "Thank You" sets a heartfelt expression of gratitude to a '70s groove with helping vocals from Luther Vandross. **Eric Clapton** plays guitar on "This Song," an introspective look at a songwriter's feeling of inadequacy at expressing spiritual truth in simple poetry. BeBe also remakes the **Edwin Hawkins Singers'** hit "O Happy Day" with **Walter Hawkins'** Love Fellowship Choir backing him. Three years later, he reappeared on the general market Motown label, refashioned as a tough-looking soul man known only as "BeBe" (no last name). He made it clear, however, that he was not abandoning his faith and, indeed, the songs on *Love and Freedom* continue to convey the same nonspecific spiritual themes as most of his work. "Coming Back Home," for instance, could be about the return of a prodigal husband to his wife or the return of a wayward soul to God.

For trivia buffs: In 1989, CeCe Winans was chosen by *Ebony* magazine as "One of the 10 Most Beautiful Black Women in the World."

Christian Radio Hits: By BeBe and CeCe Winans: "Up Where We Belong" [with The PTL Singers] (# 27 in 1983); "I.O.U. Me" (# 2 in 1987); "Love Said Not So" (# 11 in 1987); "Change Your Nature" (# 8 in 1988); "Heaven" (# 3 in 1989); "Lost without You" (# 1 for 4 weeks in 1989); "Celebrate New Life" (# 4 in 1989); "Meantime" (# 15 in 1990); "You" (# 24 in 1990); "Addictive Love" (# 1 for 8 weeks in 1991); "I'll Take You There" (# 1 for 2 weeks in 1991); "It's O.K." (# 7 in 1992); "Depend on You" (# 2 in 1992); "The Blood" (# 8 in 1992); "Can't Take This Away" (# 13 in 1993); "If Anything Ever Happened to You" (# 16 in 1994); "Count It All Joy" (# 7 in 1995). By BeBe Winans: "It's Only Natural" [with Keith Thomas] (# 10 in 1986). By CeCe Winans: "For Always" (# 12 in 1988).

Dove Awards: BeBe and CeCe Winans: 1988 New Artist of the Year; 1990 Group of the Year; 1990 Contemporary Gospel Song ("With My Whole Heart"); 1990 Pop/Contemporary Album *(Heaven)*; 1990 Pop/Contemporary Song ("Heaven"); 1992 Group of the Year; 1992 Contemporary Gospel Song ("Addictive Love"); 1998 Contemporary Gospel Song ("Up Where I Belong"). CeCe Winans: 1996 Female Vocalist; 1996 Traditional Gospel Song ("Great Is Thy Faithfulness"); 1997 Female Vocalist; 1997 Contemporary Gospel Song ("Take Me Back"); 2001 Contemporary Gospel Song ("Alabaster Box").

Grammy Awards: For BeBe and CeCe Winans: 1991 Best Contemporary Soul Gospel Album *(Different Lifestyles)*. For BeBe Winans: 1988 Best Soul Gospel Performance, Male ("Abundant Life"); 1989 Best Gospel Vocal Performance, Male ("Meantime"). For CeCe Winans: 1987 Best Soul Gospel Performance, Female ("For Always"); 1989 Best Gospel Vocal Performance, Female ("Don't Cry"); 1995 Best Contemporary Soul Gospel Album *(Alone in His Presence)*; 2001 Best Pop/Contemporary Gospel Album *(CeCe Winans)*.

Daniel Winans (and The Second Half)

1987—*Daniel Winans and The Second Half* (Rejoice); 1989—*Brotherly Love*; 1991—*My Point of View* (Tribute); 1994—*Not in My House* (Glorious); 1997—*On the Inside* (Insync).

Daniel Winans is one of **Mom** and **Pop Winans**' numerous singing children who, in contemporary Christian music circles at least, is clearly "the neglected Winans." Daniel's siblings include all four members of **The Winans** as well as **BeBe, CeCe, Angie,** and **Debbie Winans.** He began singing in a group called Winans Part II, which included BeBe and CeCe and brother Michael, and eventually others, including Rita Henry, Marvie Wright and Vickie Bowman (later **Vickie Winans,** married to Marvin). This group eventually morphed into The

Second Half, with whom Daniel would record some of his albums. Those albums tend toward traditional gospel in a way atypical for the more modern urban stylings of his sisters and (especially) brothers. As a result, he has been almost completely ignored by all media devoted to contemporary Christian music. *My Point of View* merited a brief review in *CCM* because they detected some "contemporary overtones." The songs "Hot Rain" and "Out of Love" have a hip-hop orientation, and "Sweet Jesus" recalls the classic soul stylings of **Sam Cooke.**

Grammy Awards: 1989 Best Soul Gospel Vocal Performance by a Duo, Group, Choir, or Chorus ("Let Brotherly Love Continue").

Mom and Pop Winans (and Mom Winans [solo] and Pop Winans [solo])

By Mom and Pop Winans: 1990—*Mom and Pop Winans* (Sparrow). By Mom Winans: 1999—*It's Been an Affair to Remember* (Diamante). By Pop Winans: 1999—*Uncensored* (Diamante).

Mom and Pop Winans are the forebears of what would become known as "the first family of gospel." The two raised ten children, nine of whom would go on to become prominent gospel recording stars: Carvin, Marvin, Matthew, and Michael first formed the quartet with the family name **The Winans.** Later **BeBe, CeCe, Angie, Debbie,** and **Daniel** would also make albums. Marvin's wife, **Vickie Winans,** would also record as a soloist. Eventually, four of the couple's grandchildren would form a group called **Winans Phase 2,** and a fifth (Mario Winans) would become an R&B singer in the general market. Mom and Pop (actually Delores and David) had sung gospel music for years, performing as part of the Lemon Gospel Singers in Detroit and participating in projects by Lou Rawls and **Sam Cooke.** They encouraged the offspring in their respective careers, but did not actually begin recording themselves until after several of the kids had already made it big. Not surprisingly, the parents steer clear of rap and hip-hop on their debut *Mom and Pop Winans,* opting mostly for smooth ballads produced by son Marvin. Terry Henderson also produces three tracks, which are more uptempo and energetic. In 1992, they took part in a major world tour featuring the entire Winans clan. In 1999, they would each record solo albums. Delores (Mom) interprets classic hymns, favoring songs about prayer ("Kum Ba Yah," "Sweet Hour of Prayer," "What a Friend"). David ("Pop") offers a collection of traditional gospel songs, including "This Train" and "Pass Me Not."

The couple also authored a book called *Mom and Pop Winans: Stories from Home* (FMG Books, 1992). Among other nuggets, the "autobiography of a dynasty" reveals that the couple were firm believers and practitioners of corporal punishment, though Pop Winans is a pacifist who thinks Christians should abstain from killing even in time of war. Members of the Pentecostal Holiness church, they did not allow their children to listen to any music other than traditional gospel (though they could play **Andraé Crouch** and **Tramaine Hawkins** albums when Pop wasn't home). The size of the family brood is also explained: the couple received teaching early in their marriage that God does not approve of family planning, though after the tenth child was born Mom decided enough was enough.

For trivia buffs: Mom and Pop's only nonrecording child is the eldest, David Jr.

Vickie Winans

1987—*Be Encouraged* (Light); 1989—*Total Victory* (CGI); 1991—*The Best of All;* 1992—*The Lady* (MCA); 1994—*Vickie Winans* (Intersound); 1997—*Live in Detroit* (CGI); 1999—*Live in Detroit, Vol. 2* (Intersound); *Share the Laughter.*

www.vickiewinans.com

Vickie Winans (née Bowman) grew up in Detroit and attended the same Pentecostal Holiness church where the famous Winans family clan was able to fill twelve seats at each service. She sang in the church's youth choir and eventually joined **Daniel Winans** and **BeBe and CeCe Winans** in a vocal combo called Winans Part II, modeled after the quartet of older siblings that was enjoying some success in gospel music as **The Winans.** Eventually Vickie married Marvin Winans, leader of the latter group, and ended up pursuing a distinctive career as a gospel soloist. Like brother-in-law Daniel, however, Vickie tends toward a more traditional style of gospel that keeps her off the horizon for most fans of contemporary Christian music. She seems to take after **Tramaine Hawkins,** but ultimately belongs to the same line of gospel divas as **Albertina Walker,** Dorothy Norwood, and **Shirley Caesar.** Winans did attempt to follow BeBe and CeCe's lead for a brief juncture in the early '90s, releasing an album called *The Lady* that she said she hoped would "get secular airplay, because that's exactly where the gospel needs to be." That album features an atypical dance track called "Don't Throw Your Life Away." Otherwise, her albums are oriented toward spirituals and standards. *Be Encouraged* features her signature song, "We Shall Behold Him." *Live in Detroit* opens with a medley of the hymn "Great Is Thy Faithfulness" and **Andraé Crouch**'s "My Tribute (To God Be the Glory)." *Share the Laughter* is actually a comedy album, composed of humorous narrations and anecdotes Winans has shared in concerts over the years.

Vickie and Marvin Winans have at least two sons. Marvin Jr. is a member of the urban gospel group **Winans Phase 2.** Mario Winans is a successful R&B singer who has recorded albums of chaste love songs for the general market (*Story of My Heart,* Motown, 1997). Regarding Mario, Vickie Winans would tell *Gospel City,* "Naturally, I want him to come on over here and give God the talent he's given him. I pray that the Lord will put that on his heart to come on back and do gospel only."

Wing and a Prayer

Tommy Coomes, gtr., voc.; John Mehler, drums; Al Perkins, pedal steel; Tom Stipe, kybrd., voc.; Jay Truax, bass. No albums.

Wing and a Prayer is best thought of as a transition group between two of the best Christian rock bands of all time: **Love Song** (which included **Tommy Coomes, John Mehler,** and Jay Truax) and **The Richie Furay Band** (which included **Tom Stipe,** Mehler, and Truax). Basically, Wing and a Prayer was a new incarnation of **Love Song,** without **Chuck Girard,** whose influence had dominated that group's sound. The new members included Stipe (from **Country Faith**) and **Al Perkins,** former member of such eventual obscurities as The Flying Burrito Brothers, The Souther Furay Hillman Band, Manassas, and **Mason Proffit;** Perkins is generally thought to be one of the best pedal steel guitar players who has ever lived. At one point in the group's short history, **Beau MacDougall** was a member (in place of Perkins).

Wing and a Prayer never made an album but they did record two songs for the *Maranatha Four* compilation (Maranatha, 1974)—the best of that company's seven compilation projects. Both songs are sensational, revealing a band with a Buffalo Springfield-like sound and incredible potential. "Old Grey Ford" is one of Tom Stipe's best songs, opening with anthemic chords and moving into a midtempo country rock number that narrates a young man's spiritual and geographical trek through the south. "Jesus Is Standing Here" has a completely different sound—it is an overtly worshipful Coomes song that celebrates the risen presence of Christ among believers.

After Wing and a Prayer, Coomes, Mehler, and Stipe would eventually make solo albums. Coomes became an executive at Maranatha and was a major force behind their successful series of praise albums. Perkins produced numerous albums for Christian artists and continued to play with dozens of different groups, occasionally being listed as an official member (**'Ark**). He also played in the one-time project **Hillman, Leadon, Perkins, and Scheff.**

Wish for Eden

Rob Walker; et al. 1993—*Pet the Fish* (Tooth and Nail).

Wish for Eden was a heavy grunge band that is destined to be remembered as the debut artist on the premier alternative label in Christian music, Tooth and Nail. They helped that fledgling label to gain an early reputation for bringing neglected artists of outstanding quality to the fore—eventually Tooth and Nail would introduce the world to **MxPx, The**

Supertones, Starflyer 59, and countless others. But Wish for Eden also set a precedent for what would sometimes become another Tooth and Nail trademark: they were a band composed of openly Christian musicians who did not feel any compulsion to be blatant about their spiritual beliefs. The songs on *Pet the Fish* do not offer obvious Christian slogans but all represent a perspective informed by faith. The group had a sound similar to bands like Helmet or Tool, with evident influence from the new Seattle artists, Pearl Jam, Nirvana, and Alice in Chains. They played numerous shows at churches and other Christian venues but did not understand their status as a Christian band to involve commitment to proselytizing their audience. "I'm not good at speaking," front man Rob Walker once told *HM,* "and I don't feel it's my calling. There's a big misperception in the Christian industry that you're only in a ministry band if you preach from the stage. There are other ways to minister than just preaching." Thus, Wish for Eden became one of the first groups in Christian music to reject the idea that a Christian artist's work should always serve as propaganda for the faith, as opposed simply to creating art that has intrinsic value. They suffered somewhat as pioneers of what, by 2000, would become a widespread phenomenon. Walker related to *HM* the embarrassment he felt when after doing one concert, a youth pastor invited him back to speak to the kids. Likewise, he says that he was sometimes asked to sign contracts for concerts in which he promised to "talk about God" during the show. As opposition to the band grew in some circles, someone started a rumor that the title of the album *Pet the Fish* was a secret reference to masturbation. In 1995, the group announced that they were moving into the general market and "would not be making another Christian record." In 1996, front man Rob Walker released a raw and aggressive solo album, *Strobe* (Tooth and Nail), that evinces a basic Soundgarden style.

Witness

Original lineup: Lisa Page Brooks, voc.; Diane Campbell, voc. (– 1993); Tina Brooks, voc. (– 1993); Yolanda Harris (– 1993) // later additions: Leah Brooks, voc.; Candice Smith, voc.; Ayanah Thomas, voc. Selected: 1986—*We Can Make a Difference* (Fixit); 1993—*Standard* (CGI); 1994—*He Can Do the Impossible;* 1996—*A Song in the Night;* 1997—*Mean What You Say* (Intersound); 1998—*Love Is an Action Word* (CGI); 1999—*The Best of Witness.*

The traditional gospel quartet Witness was founded in the '80s by Michael Brooks of **Commissioned.** The group has gone through numerous undocumented personnel changes, and no reliable information regarding its history is available. Their later albums contain no personnel information or credits whatsoever, but Lisa Page Brooks (who is married to Michael Brooks) appears to remain as one original member; Leah, her sister, joined in 1988 according to some official accounts, or in 1991 according to others. The group scored a Christian radio hit with the song "Old Landmark" (written by Michael Brooks) from *We Can Make a Difference,* but generally stayed within the traditional gospel market. They took a turn toward more contemporary sounds with *A Song in the Night,* inspired, it seems, by the success of artists like **Anointed.** On songs like "Oh What Love" and "That's What You Mean to Me," Witness emulates the latter group with breathy, jazzy harmonies. **Lisa Page (Brooks)** would also record solo albums.

Christian radio hits: "Old Landmark" (# 14 in 1990).

Amy Wolter

See **Fighter.**

Wondergroove

Charles Norman, gtr., kybrd., bass; Aslak Nygren, voc. 2000—*Hi-Fi Demonstration Record* (Solid Rock).

Wondergroove made one rollicking, good-time album that should be of interest to Christian music fans, although it is largely unknown to them. The group consisted mainly of Charles Norman (brother to **Larry Norman,** the father of Christian rock) and Aslak Nygren, a Norwegian singer who fronted a very popular band in that country called Sister Rain. Although Charles Norman has been involved in some Christian music projects (e.g., playing on some of his brother's records), he also maintains connections within the wild and wooly world of general market rock and roll (as does Larry). In 1992, Norman (i.e., Charles) was touring with Guns N' Roses, writing songs with the band and working on a side project with keyboardist Dizzy Reed (who has also played on some of **Larry Norman**'s albums). While in Oslo, the group hooked up with Sister Rain, and some impromptu jam sessions inspired Norman and Nygren to record together. The album that was supposed to be their collaborative effort was originally recorded in Los Angeles and featured GN'R's Slash on guitar, along with Frank Black (a.k.a. Black Francis) of The Pixies and a few other celebrity guests. The L.A. area earthquake of January 1993, however, disrupted everything and the master tapes were destroyed. Norman and Nygren later re-recorded the record sans luminaries and released it in Norway under the band name Merchants of Venice. In that country, the record came out on Warner Music and was nominated for a Grammy award. For the American release, the group chose the name Wondergroove in deference to another band that had decided to call themselves The Merchants of Venice. The album came out on **Larry Norman**'s private label, Solid Rock, and was available only by mail order or through the Internet (www.larrynorman.com).

The Christian music press, which doesn't like the elder Norman very much, completely ignored Wondergroove and their sole recording. But the music is creative and Nygren has an excellent voice for rock and roll. *Hi-Fi Demonstration Record* is a tribute to the glory of vinyl, with the sound of a turntable stylus in a record's grooves filling the gaps between songs; the record even "skips" toward the end of the opening song. Lyrically, Wondergroove's songs are edgy and literate, free of clichés and simplistic Christian propaganda. Norman and Nygren try for an empathetic approach that expresses spiritual and emotional concerns in a way that may help perceptive listeners to connect a few dots without promising them a full rendering of the big picture. The outstanding "What Am I Looking For?" sounds like it belongs on a Cracker album. Thematically, it communicates a basic sense of spiritual emptiness analogous to **U2**'s similarly titled song, but at a deeper level (stopping to ask "what *am* I looking for?" goes a step beyond complaining that "I still haven't found it"). The song "Postcards from Heaven" presents the thoughts of a blissfully ignorant person who apparently thinks he's in heaven when he's actually spending time in what some would call "the looney bin." Spanish guitars come from out of nowhere to enhance "One Man," and an explosion of near metal thrashing interrupts "The Arms of Morpheus." The song "I Want It All" is a synthy space rock number that, stripped of its effects, would reveal a tune similar to that of "Turn," the opening track from **Larry Norman**'s 2001 *Tourniquet* album. "Morning Glory" is a song that was originally recorded by **Larry Norman** for a never-released *Orphans from Eden* album in 1974. Charles Norman would say of the project in 2001, "it's a nice document of a bunch of friends from diverse backgrounds having fun writing and recording songs together. That's pretty much all it was intended to be from the start." Brother Larry waits courteously till the end and then offers his own lead vocals on remakes of two tracks ("Down to the Water," "I Want It All").

The Wordd

Chris Jones, voc.; Stan Jones, voc. 2000—*How You Gonna Live?* (Myrrh).

The Wordd is composed of a pair of siblings from Detroit. Chris and Stan Jones are two rather large and tough-looking African American men; on the cover photo for their debut album, they look much more like bouncers than youth ministers or gospel singers. The Wordd's debut album was produced by Tony Rich, a childhood friend who was once a member of an early incarnation of the group before he formed his own Tony Rich Project and went on to win Grammys as a performer and producer. Rich also collaborates with songwriting and offers some occasional vocal harmony, but the Jones' gritty vocals carry most of the songs. The group samples a wide variety of styles, from rap to dance to hip-hop to soul. Traditional evangelical themes are expressed in most of the lyrics, with an emphasis on praise and worship.

World Against World

See **Spudgun.**

World Wide Message Tribe

Andy ("Heavyfoot") Hawthorne, voc.; Andy Pennells, voc. (–1998), Zarc Porter, voc. (–1994) // Sani, voc. (+ 1994, –1998); Elaine Hanley, voc. (+ 1994); David Mark Pennells, voc. (+ 1994, –1997); Cameron Danté, voc. (+ 1997); Beth Vickers, voc. (+ 1997, –1998); Deronda Lewis, voc. (+ 1998); Tim Owen, voc. (+ 1998). 1993—*World Wide Message Tribe* (N'Soul); 1994—*Dance Planet;* 1996—*We Don't Get What We Deserve* (Warner Alliance); 1997—*Revived;* 1998—*Heatseeker;* 1999—*Frantik.*

www.thetribeuk.com

World Wide Message Tribe is a ministry-oriented techno-rave group from England that puts on energetic shows featuring gymnastics, high-tech lighting, and a strong evangelistic message. They received permission to perform in the public schools in native Manchester and developed a ministry providing a portion of the religious education component required there by law. Typically, the group will visit a school for a week at a time, meeting with classes and performing at assemblies, all of which leads up to an evangelistic concert complete with altar calls. "We're not allowed to say, 'You must believe this or you will go to hell,' " head rapper Danté explains. "The way we have to do it is say, 'This is what I believe. I'm not forcing my views on you. It's entirely up to you.' " The group has also spearheaded the Eden Project, a campaign by which Christians have intentionally moved into low-income, government housing projects in order to be salt and light for those who live there.

After gaining widespread notice in Britain, World Wide Message Tribe was subsequently introduced to the United States by Scott Blackwell. Musically, they strive for an amalgamated sound that incorporates a wide variety of dance styles apropos to what is hot in the high school market at the time of each release. They sometimes pull it off but occasionally end up sounding like some kind of *Sesame Street* ensemble (as *True Tunes* noted). The group was founded by fashion designer Andy Hawthorne and singer Marc Pennells in 1991. African singer Sani added distinctive female vocals for two projects. Cameron Danté, a DJ who had enjoyed a global hit with the band Bizarre Inc. ("I'm Gonna Get You"), was converted at a 1995 concert and joined the group thereafter, eventually becoming their front man and premier vocalist. Beth Vickers left the group to marry **Matt Redman** but resurfaced in the spin-off band **Storm** in 1998. The comings and goings indicated in the personnel list above are somewhat deceptive in that departing members (e.g., Porter, Pennells) have often maintained connections with the group in nonperforming capacities. On any given project, World Wide Message Tribe also features any number of additional vocalists, instrumentalists, and dancers (Hanley has sung with them from the debut album on, but was not listed as an official member until 1996).

The sometimes large and often changing cast adds to the anonymity of the music, but songs typically feature particular soloists rather than being sung by the whole outfit. Hawthorne himself has a unique, gravel-voiced rap style (*True Tunes* thinks he sounds like Cookie Monster) that is effective on certain tracks ("Revolution"). Danté is a more traditional rapper. Female vocals tend to be soulful and sweet. Doronda Lewis, who came on board in 1997, brings a traditional gospel flair to many tracks.

The group's self-titled debut album opens with a high-voltage number called "Maximum Level," but also includes the more suave, pop-oriented "Make It Happen." *Dance Planet* continues with a collection of songs that *True Tunes* would say are all "basically the same, the major distinctions being who shows up on a given track's vocals, and what bells and whistles are thrown in." The songs "I'm on My Way to Zion" and "Peace" garnered the most attention and radio airplay. *We Don't Get What We Deserve* was the band's breakthrough project. It features "The Real Thing" (their best song) and "Revolution." Both tracks are very high energy, jumping, bouncing, back-flipping-for-Jesus songs that were performed on stage as heavily choreographed, big production numbers. "The Real Thing" crossed over into the general market, reaching Number Twenty-two on *Billboard*'s Dance Chart. Unfortunately, *We Don't Get What We Deserve* also includes "We Talk to the Lord," a dumb Vacation Bible School song with silly B-I-B-L-E lyrics about prayer ("We talk, talk, talk to the Lord"). On stage, the group would perform the song by strutting about with big cardboard hands lifted toward heaven like they were in some kind of amateurish junior high school program. On a better note, "There Is a Green Hill" reinterprets the traditional crucifixion hymn to a shuffling beat with Simon and Garfunkel-style harmonies. "Sweet Salvation" blends soulful voices on an effective techno jam. *Revived* is a premature compilation album with some of the former hits remixed. *Heatseeker* is another strong collection, notable primarily for "Hypocrite," the group's first venture into hardcore—Henry Rollins-style with metal guitars and shouted lyrics. Inspired by the Apostle Paul's acknowledgment of his own "hypocrisies" in Romans 7, the song is appropriately dark and theologically profound. Also remarkable on *Heatseeker* is a house version of **Bob Dylan**'s "Precious Angel." Adding to the variety, "Messiah" recalls the sound of Prodigy or the Chemical Brothers, while "Everything I Need" is '70s disco. *Frantik* backs off from the overall hard char-

acter of *Heatseeker,* going for a pop sound that *Phantom Tollbooth* would describe as "cheesy." The sound, in fact, is closer to WWMT protégées **Raze** than to the group's own previous work. "Eat the Word" is another too simplistic Bible school song not likely to go over with a high-school-and-over crowd.

Christian radio hits: "Make It Happen" (# 12 in 1993); "The Cross" (# 7 in 1994); "I'm on My Way to Zion" (# 1 in 1994); "Where Are You Going?" (# 11 in 1995); "Peace" (# 5 in 1996); "Sweet Salvation" (# 12 in 1996); "There Is a Green Hill" (# 8 in 1996); "Nobody Knows" (# 17 in 1996); "The Real Thing" (# 20 in 1997); "Joy" (# 14 in 1997); "Come All Ye Faithful" (# 15 in 1998); "When the Day Is Over" (# 20 in 1998); "Everything I Need" (# 15 in 1999).

Dove Awards: 1997 International Artist; 1998 Rap, Hip/Hop Song ("Jumpin' in the House of God"); 1998 Rap/Hip Hop Album (*Revived*); 1999 Rap/Hip Hop Album (*Heatseeker*).

Bernard Wright

1990—*Fresh Hymns 1* (Frontline); 1991—*Brand New Gospel Format;* 1992—*Fresh Hymns 2.*

Bernard Wright is a jazz musician who once played keyboards for Miles Davis and was once named Best New Jazz Vocalist by *Billboard* magazine. In the early '90s he issued two albums of hymns recast in jazz arrangements. *Fresh Hymns 1* is largely instrumental and includes new takes on classic hymns like "Amazing Grace," "Have Thine Own Way, Lord," "Great Is Thy Faithfulness," and "There Is Power in the Blood." *Fresh Hymns 2* is decidedly more funk-driven and focuses almost exclusively on recent hymns of the African American tradition, including **Andraé Crouch**'s "Bless His Holy Name." On a couple of tracks ("Give Thanks," "In the Name of Jesus") Wright sounds uncannily like Stevie Wonder. *CCM* would liken *Fresh Hymns 2* to collections by **Sounds of Blackness.** The format is broken primarily by a light jazz Ferrante and Teicher-type reading of "How Great Thou Art," the only instrumental. Another surprising inclusion is the closing track, "Search Me," by (non-African American) **Bob Bennett.** In between the *Hymns* albums, Wright released a collection of his own songs (*Brand New Gospel Format*). The opening cut, "Power and Love," presents him as an R&B singer in the light pop mold of Michael Jackson, but the title track is a modern jazz opus with semirapped vocals.

Christian radio hits: "Trust and Obey" (# 21 in 1990).

Wyrick

Travis Wyrick, gtr., kybrd., bass, prog., voc. 1998—*Mental Floss* (Rugged); date unknown—*Aggressive State.*

www.wyrickmusic.com

Wyrick is a Christian industrial band (officially, an "electronic modern rock" band) composed entirely of Travis Wyrick, who formerly played with the general market group Sage. His music contains the most pervasive and explicit testimonies to Christian faith found in the industrial rock genre. Hard music fans sometimes jokingly refer to Wyrick as "the Christian **Circle of Dust**," referencing the supposedly Christian industrial band whose lyrics are more subtle in terms of faith content. Before becoming a Christian, Wyrick achieved moderate success with Sage, opening for Bad Company and Peter Frampton, but he also had stereotypical rock star problems with drug and alcohol abuse. He credits the Christian bands **Disciple** and **Nailed** with having a profound influence on him before he got saved, as the members persistently witnessed to him in appropriate ways whenever their paths would cross. He would later produce an album for Disciple. The death of his mother inaugurated a spiritual crisis that finally led him to a conversion documented on Wyrick's first album. *Mental Floss* is of a piece with work by artists like Chemlab, Prodigy, Filter, and Pop Will Eat Itself. Critics took some shots at the artist for the opening track, "Supernatural," which seems to copy Filter's song "Hey Man, Nice Shot" musically. The similarities are *so* striking (with the words "A-men" being sung in exactly the same fashion as Filter's "Hey, man") that the artist may have intended the comparison as a satire, not a plagiarism. Lyrically, "Supernatural" presents Wyrick's words to the person he was before his conversion. Likewise, "Can't Be Saved" negates the feeling that any sin is too great for God's forgiveness. "In the Way" brings the evangelistic message home with words addressed to Wyrick's own sister, inviting her to find Jesus. The sophomore project, *Aggressive State,* moves into the darker sounds of Marilyn Manson and Nine Inch Nails, with one song ("Second Coming") introducing elements of rapcore. Wyrick has indicated that whereas the first album was evangelistic ("about getting saved"), the second is directed more to those living within the faith ("about being saved"). "More of You" calls on believers to show Christ in their actions in addition to proclaiming him in their words. Theologically, the messages on *Aggressive State* seem to be informed by a dualism that regards "the world" as the enemy. This produces a few obtuse moments, such as in "Justify Your Sin," when he equates a court ruling against state-sponsored prayers with "taking God out of the schools" (which he further assumes is the ultimate cause of school violence and other social problems). "Inside Out" is more introspective and pleasantly recalls some of the better work of Stabbing Westward.

Xalt

Randy Carlson, bass; Scott Doerffler, voc., Jim Erdman, gtr. 1988—*Dark War* (E&E); 1990—*Under the Ruins* (Pure Metal); 1991—*History*; 1997—*Helium Blue Gazebo* (Kalubone).

http://xalt.hypermart.net.

Xalt was a Christian metal band from Lansing, Michigan, that came to the attention of most critics and fans with the 1991 album *History*. The latter project was not a retrospective compilation (as its title might imply), but was actually their third recording, following a custom demo and a debut for Pure Metal that went ignored. *History* starts out strong with "Standing" and continues to deliver all-out rockers like the title track and "Heart of Stone." More commercially oriented are "Babel Again" and the funky guitar showcase "Walk Away" (not a James Gang cover). The requisite ballad "Unconditional Love" sounds a bit like an **Extreme** song, as does an acoustic worship track, "Lord, Lord." Six years later, long after the group had been forgotten by all but its most ardent fans, Xalt came back with a new sound for a new generation. *Helium Blue Gazebo* draws much more on classic rock influences, and includes a southern rock cover of the **Russ Taff** hit "Winds of Change." Critics hailed "Pizza Driver," a modern rock song about superstitious people, as the album's standout. Bob Gross, who sang with the late '90s grunge band **Stir,** is said to have also sung for Xalt, though Doerffler is always listed as lead vocalist.

Christian radio hits: "Unconditional Love" (# 22 in 1991).

xDISCIPLEx (and xDISCIPLEx A.D.)

Dan Quiggle, voc.; Dave Quiggle, gtr.; Adam, drums; Junior, gtr.; Neil, bass. By xDISCIPLEx: 1995—*Lantern* [EP] (custom); 1996—*Scarab* [EP] (S. A. Mob); 1997—*Imitation of Love* (Goodfellow); 1999—*No Blood, No Altar Now* [EP]. By xDISCIPLEx A.D.: 2000—*Heaven and Hell* (Triple Crown); 2002—*Doxology* [EP] (Facedown).

www.hxc.com/xdisciplex

xDISCIPLEx (as the name is officially spelled) is a hardcore band from Erie, Pennsylvania. The group is fronted by brothers Dan and David Quiggle (other members only get cited by first names). The group adopted its unusual name (the word DISCIPLE in all capitals bookended by x's) because they wanted to be called Disciple but feared they would be confused with another hard rock Christian band that already had that name (cf. **Disciple**). The two groups were often confused anyway, so xDISCIPLEx eventually added the suffix A.D. to their name, in hopes that this would prevent further misidentifications. It didn't.

In spite of explicit Christian content and a group commitment to ministry, all of xDISCIPLEx's recordings have been issued on general market labels. After a homemade seven-inch vinyl EP called *Lantern,* the group really got its start with an EP on S.A. Mob, followed by two discs on Goodfellow. *Scarab* allows for little ambiguity in "Yahweh," a song that pledges their allegiance to the God of the Bible. *Imitation of Love* draws on Psalm 46 to proclaim that this God is the band's "Refuge and Strength." A few other songs bring in social commentary, informed by the group's theology. "Candy Apple" addresses what they view as a tendency for the government to candy-coat the issue of abortion, such that (in Dan Quiggle's words), "a lot of people who are pro-choice don't know the facts and don't see abortion for what it really is." In a similar vein, "Counterfeit" seeks to expose the phony veneer of cultural values that equate self-driven vanity or lust with love. *No Blood, No Altar Now* displays a preoccupation with atonement, as its title suggests. "Death of Death" and "River of Life" explicate the saving effects of Christ's sacrifice. Finally, *Heaven and Hell* offers more overtly evangelical songs like "Christ Shaped Vacuum" and "Revival" played in a style that *HM* calls "unrelenting metal." One track called "Fast Song" allows the punk component of their hardcore sound to triumph over the metal stylings, but otherwise a sound that recalls Iron Maiden or Judas Priest prevails. *Doxology* is a collection of five songs that had previously been issued on various compilation albums. David Quiggle is a graphic arts designer and has been responsible for the album covers of xDISCIPLEx's works, which tend to be suitable-for-framing works of art.

XL

1993—*Sodom and America* (Brainstorm).

Christian rapper XL (he says it "stands for Extra Large 'cause I'm a big boy") is known for producing the first album in the Christian market to merge rap with metal, preceding the explosion of works by groups like **EDL, P.O.D.,** and **Pax 217** toward the end of the millennium. XL performed with a band he called DBD (or Death Before Dishonor), which on *Sodom and America* consisted of Greg Minier (gtr.) and Mark Salomon (voc.) from **Crucified,** and Jimmy Brown (gtr., voc.) and Mike Phillips (gtr.) from **Deliverance.** The project was superficially compared to general market artist Bodycount, which featured rapper Ice-T leading a metal band. XL's style, however, was considerably different than Ice-T's, featuring more genuine rapping than screaming. Closer sonic comparisons might be drawn to some of the funk-rock of Red Hot Chili Peppers. The artist maintains, a bit hyperbolically, that the title track to *Sodom and America* is "about American values and how they have reached an all-time low." The judgment song "Sifting with the Sickle" has lyrics written by Jason Martin (of **Dance House Children** and, later, **Starflyer 59**).

X-Propagation

Byron Payne, samp.; Brent Stackhouse, synth., voc. 1993—*Conflict* (Intense).

X-Propagation was a one-time project of Brent Stackhouse, who was one-half of the duo **Deitiphobia.** Stackhouse wrote and programmed all the music, with Byron Payne adding samples (many of which involved bits of preaching). In terms of overall sound, X-Propagation's *Conflict* is best classified as heavy electronic music, combining elements of industrial,

techno, rave, and metal. Spiritual and internal warfare are principal themes. The opening song, "Hold On," encourages steadfastness in face of Satan's continual assaults on homes and families. The title track presents the Christian life as a continual struggle, but not one devoid of victories. "Peace" combines a conventional benediction ("Go in peace / Go with the grace of God") with a call to prepare for combat ("Fight with the holy armor of the Lord").

X-Sinner

Greg Bishop, gtr.; Michael Buckner, drums; Rob Kniep, bass (– 1991); David Robbins, voc. (– 1991) // Andrew Langsford, bass (+ 1991); Rex Scott, voc. (+ 1991). 1989—*Get It* (Pakaderm); 1991—*Peace Treaty*; 2001—*Loud and Proud* (M8).

X-Sinner came on the Christian scene at the end of the '80s as a blatant Christian version of AC/DC. Whereas many Christian bands resent the implication that they are a sanctified clone of some mainstream act, X-Sinner seems to have reveled in their status and used it to earn some short-term fame. Both of the group's original albums were produced by **John** and Dino **Elefante** and were released on the Elefantes' Pakaderm label; *Loud and Proud* is a postbreakup collection of previously unreleased demos. The song "Living on the Edge" (not to be confused with the later Aerosmith song by that name) from their first album debuted at Number One on the Christian Metal chart the first week that such a chart was ever printed, and within two weeks three other songs from the *Get It* album ("Lift Him Up," "Medicine," and the title track) were also doing well on that chart. Somewhat ironically, "Living on the Edge" is one of the band's only songs that *doesn't* sound like AC/DC, but has a distinctive Def Leppard ring to it. On the strength of *Get It,* readers of *HM* selected X-Sinner as their "Favorite New Band" in a 1989 Readers' Poll.

David Robbins left X-Sinner, and the group found a new lead singer in Rex Scott, who had previously fronted a band called Zion, responsible for the album *Thunder from the Mountains* (Image, 1989). Surprisingly, the AC/DC comparisons did not stop with this personnel change. As Doug Van Pelt of *HM* would note, whereas Robbins had sounded a lot like AC/DC's second vocalist Brian Johnson, Rex Scott sounded a lot like the latter band's original singer Bon Scott (no relation). *Peace Treaty* bases its theme on the biblical concept of covenant. The album scores with a funky rocker called "Peer Pressure" and closes with another Def Leppard clone, "Don't Go" (dedicated to those who have lost a loved one to suicide). The band reportedly changed its name to The Angry Einsteins after recording *Peace Treaty.*

XT

Sonny Larsson, voc.; Bjorn Stigsson, gtr.; Hakan Andersson, bass (–1993); Michael Ulvsgärd, drums (–1993) // Niklas Jonsson, kybrd. (+ 1993); Mike

Nordstrom, drums (+ 1993, –1995); P-O Larsson, bass (+ 1993, –1995); Kjell Andersson, drums (+ 1995); Johan Stark, bass (+ 1995). 1992—*XT* (Viva); 1993—*Taxfree;* 1995—*Extended Empire.*

XT formed in the early '90s as a follow-up to Bjorn Stigsson's band **Leviticus.** He and heavy metal vocalist Sonny Larsson formed the core of the Scandinavian band, fronting a constantly changing rhythm section. The band's sound was not too different from that of **Leviticus,** with influences of Queensryche showing up here and there. Their albums continued in the tradition of offering explicitly evangelical songs, albeit ones that dealt with a wide variety of tough issues. "Standin' for Jesus Christ" from the first record is a bold anthem. *Taxfree* offers two catchy, hook-filled rockers with "The One" and "Face to Face," along with "My First Morning," an acoustic ballad. "The False Prophet" from that same album introduces a theme that may be continued with "Castles in the Sky" (about TV evangelists) on the third outing. *Extended Empire* also includes "Five Minutes to Midnight," a song about the world's violence as reflected in a quick remote-control tour of TV channels.

Y

John Ylvisaker

1964—Don't Cut the Baby in Half (label unknown); 1967—Cool Livin' (Avant Garde); 1968—A Love Song; 1972—Recorded at a Heartwarming for Fritzie (Solar Module); date unknown—Borning Cry: Collected Works, Vol. I (New Generation); Called to Freedom: Collected Works, Vol. 2; We Are Alive: Collected Works, Vol. 3; The Prodigal/Mass for a New Generation: Collected Works, Vol. 4; Living in the Saviour's Love: Collected Works, Vol. 5; Awake My Heart; The Long Journey Home; Amigos de Cristo (The Folk Collection); Rejoice in the Lord (The Rock Collection); Stir Up the Love (The Country Collection); My Song Is Love (The Classic Collection); Always Remember Me (The Pop Collection); Sing for Dreams (The Christmas Collection).

www.ylvisaker.com

John Ylvisaker's greatest impact on contemporary Christian music came in the late '60s when he played a role among Lutherans analogous to that of **John Fischer, Ray Repp,** and **Ralph Carmichael** in other denominations. Lutherans tend to keep to themselves and—though they did use Repp's songs—their youth groups missed out on most of the contemporary folk worship produced in the '60s for no other reason than that it was not written by Lutherans (the Roman Catholic Repp was deemed "close enough to count" by liberals—and pretty much any Lutheran who played a guitar in the '60s was, by definition, a liberal). Born in Moorhead, Minnesota, and a graduate of Concordia College, Ylvisaker was in the forefront of "the guitars in the sanctuary wars." He toured Lutheran congregations, giving evening concerts in which he played Pete Seeger/**Bob Dylan**-type songs with socially-conscious but theologically relevant messages. He even played *electric* guitar

and was often accompanied by his wife, Amanda Ylvisaker, who also sang and played the flute. Eschewing the type of stuff Carmichael or Kurt Kaiser were producing, Ylvisaker drew freely from a repertoire of secular hits, for instance performing Crispian St. Peter's "The Pied Piper" (# 4 in 1966) as a Communion hymn at a National Lutheran Youth Gathering in 1967. An original song called "Moratorium" touched a few nerves with its seeming endorsement of antiwar sentiments. The Civil Rights movement and racial integration of churches were also themes for Ylvisaker to address, but he seemed especially keyed into liturgical reform. He wrote in his liner notes to *Cool Livin'*, "The fact that a word or group of words was meaningful five hundred years ago does not imply that they will speak clearly to this age, an electric age, an age of high speed and high emotion." *A Love Song* contains the song "The Old Is Really Not So Old," which points out the secular sources behind some sacred traditions (including, for instance, the literary dependence of the Bible on other Mesopotamian literature).

When the Jesus movement hit, Ylvisaker was swept away and all but forgotten. The revivalistic spirit of the movement cast the whole contemporary worship phenomenon in a different idiom. Even among Lutherans, guitar-led worship teams sprang up everywhere, often in connection with the organizations Lutheran Youth Alive and Lutheran Youth Encounter, both founded by Dave Anderson. These parachurch groups were radically ecumenical, introducing sheltered Lutheran kids to whole new worlds of music, some of which were created by

Baptists and Pentecostals. Throughout the '70s, LYA and LYE sponsored uncharacteristically lively youth Congresses featuring concerts by the likes of **Dennis Agajanian, Verne Bullock, Andraé Crouch and the Disciples, Liberation Suite,** and **Love Song.** Ylvisaker became part of the establishment, where some would say he made even greater contributions. He continued to compose hymns and entire liturgical settings, many of which would become popular in college contexts, especially after the '70s revival fires died down. By 2001, he would hold copyrights to more than one thousand songs, the best known of which is probably his composition "I Was There to Hear Your Borning Cry." He also served as the producer for SCAN, an award-winning weekly radio program sponsored by the Evangelical Lutheran Church in America. He has composed much of the original music for Lutheran Vespers radio broadcasts and ELCA videos.

Sherri Youngward

1997—*Faces, Memories, Places* (5 Min. Walk); 1998—*No More Goodbyes;* 1999—*Sons and Daughters* (custom); 2002—*Six Inches of Sky* (BEC).

www.sherriyoungward.com

Sherri Youngward is a singer/songwriter from the San Francisco Bay area whose alterna-folk style is often compared with that of Shania Twain or Sarah McLachlan. She was not raised in a religious family and had no connection to the faith until she was eighteen and came under the influence of a Christian family. She says that her attendance at a **Keith Green** concert made a strong impact on her, instilling a lifelong confidence in the ability of music to "communicate the heart of Jesus to people." She subsequently became involved with the music ministries of Youth With a Mission. All three of Youngward's albums have been produced by Aaron Sprinkle of **Poor Old Lu** and **Rose Blossom Punch.** Her songs often tell stories of people she has encountered in life, with lyrics tending to be poetic, but not mysterious. The subdued music has more appeal to fans of indie artists like **Damien Jurado** and **Pedro the Lion** (friends and collaborators of Youngward) than with commercial radio-pop audiences. Thus, Youngward herself would go independent on her third release, distributing it primarily through her website.

The debut album, *Faces, Memories, Places,* features "Restore," a remake of Psalm 23 written for a young Christian who died of AIDS. "Broadway" applies the teaching of Jesus in Matthew 25:31–46 to a street in Seattle where a number of homeless people can be found. "Stories" responds to a friend's revelations of abuse, and "Beyond These Skies" offers a plea to one who is abandoning the faith. *No More Goodbyes* includes "Hole" written with David Bazan (of **Pedro the Lion**), one of many songs in contemporary Christian music inspired by

Pascal's remark that every human life has "a God-shaped hole" (cf. **Extreme**'s "Hole Hearted" and **xDISCIPLEx**'s "Christ Shaped Vacuum" for two very different takes on the same theme). "Jesus Saw Her" describes Youngward's understanding of her own conversion, about which she has said, "Christ came after me when I didn't even care about Him." Thus, she can also prompt her listeners to consider, "What if God up above has a heart full of love . . . meant for you?" ("Meant for You"). "All I Need to Know" maintains that the words of God offered in Romans 8:38–39 are the only biblical promise humanity really needs. *Sons and Daughters* is an especially worshipful project, featuring a Judy Collins-like version of "Amazing Grace" and a lovely rendition of "O Sacred Head Now Wounded." The album also includes "Empty the Ocean," written with **Brett Williams,** and a remake of the song "Peace" from her debut album. Youngward's major label release on BEC *(Six Inches of Sky)* broadens her neo-folk style somewhat with touches of electronica on "First Fire" and dreamy Pink Floyd vibes on "This Dream of Mine." Youngward also offers the traditional hymn "I'll Fly Away" as a Beatlesque pop song.

Youth Choir

See **The Choir.**

Yum Yum Children

Dennis Childers, kybrd.; Jennifer Goodenough, voc.; Leon Goodenough, voc., gtr.; Bob Sable, perc.; Craig Smith, bass. 1994—*Tastythanks* (custom); 1995—*Dufisized* (Boot to Head); 1996—*Used to Would've* (5 Min. Walk).

Yum Yum Children are an oddball band from Vancouver, Oregon, headed by Leon Goodenough, former guitarist for **The Clergy.** All traces of that band's hardcore sound vanish away in Yum Yum Children's decidedly alternative mix. After two very independent releases, the band was marketed as "a Christian version of The Monkees" in an attempt to gain some commercial potential for their major label release *Used to Would've,* but the analogy doesn't fit. More appropriate comparisons could be drawn to Devo, the B-52s, They Might Be Giants, and **Violent Femmes,** as the Yum Yum Children actually employ fairly complex song structures and arrangements in their imaginative and sometimes silly repertoire. "It's kinda weird," a *True Tunes* reviewer would write, "but if you think you're open-minded and progressive, then I dare you to check it out." The song "Refrigerator" is heavy with distortion and offers a not completely decipherable parable about faith—or something like that. "Kind and Loving Man" is a fast and funky pop song that articulates some basic questions of theodicy. "Life without Jesus" offers another parable, this one a soft, spoken word story about a child lost at sea.

David Zaffiro

1989—The Other Side (Alarma); 1990—In Scarlet Storm (Intense); 1992—Surrender Absolute (Frontline); 1994—Yesterday's Left Behind.

David Zaffiro was lead guitarist for the Christian metal band **Bloodgood.** He left that group to pursue a solo career, crafting four albums with a sound that for the most part abandoned the metal stylings for more pop-oriented sounds. *The Other Side* features a couple of arena rock anthems ("Stay," "I See Red") but tends decidedly toward **Petra**esque power-pop tunes. The project closes with "Spirit of the Lord," a somewhat atmospheric midtempo song with haunting piano frills buried in the mix. *In Scarlet Storm* is heavier overall, both in sound and content. Lyrically, the album addresses some personal trials that Zaffiro had experienced, with the title track using the story of Jesus stilling the storm at sea as a metaphor for deliverance through faith. "Blue Ice" is a guitar instrumental, and "I Give This Life to You" is a somewhat syrupy ballad. But there are also more arena anthems: "Holding Fast" picks up again on the theme of persistence through troubles, and "He's Lyin' to Ya" is an appropriately noisy screamer about spiritual deception. The third record provides the most significant departure from the old **Bloodgood** sound, with three instrumentals and a collection of mostly pop songs that the artist had originally written to be recorded by other artists. Also, Zaffiro recruited a vocalist to sing lead on most of the songs (Australian Randall Waller, who had recorded a 1980 album called *Midnight Fire* on the Tunesmith label). He would return to doing his own vocals for the swan song *Yesterday's Left Behind,* a record that he himself would describe as "no metal adult-rock." The album features a particularly interesting instrumental called "Bottle Tap" on which the guitars are made to match the sound of a bottle spinning on a table. Zaffiro does give up the mic on one song, "The Winds of September," featuring **Holy Soldier**'s ex-lead singer Steven Patrick on what sounds very much like the final **Holy Soldier** song he may have wanted to do. Zaffiro would become a much sought after producer, responsible for projects by artists as diverse as **Acquire the Fire, Holy Soldier, In Reach, Whitecross,** and **Brett Williams.** He cowrote the song "Amazing," performed by **Point of Grace.**

Zao

Jesse Smith, drums; Shawn Jonas, voc. (−1998); Roy Goudy, gtr. (−1998); Mike Cox, bass (−1998) // Dan Weyandt, voc. (+ 1998, −1999); Russ Cogdell, gtr. (+ 1998, −2000); Brian Detar, gtr. (+ 1998, −1999); Rob Horner, bass (+ 1999); Scott Melinger, gtr. (+ 2000). 1995—*All Else Failed* (custom); 1997—*The Splinter Shards the Birth of Separation* (Solid State); 1998—*Where Blood and Fire Bring Rest;* 1999—*Liberate Te Ex Inferis;* 2000—*(Self-Titled).*

Zao is a hard rock Christian band with such an insane history of personnel changes as to render the very word *band* seemingly anomalous. There has, however, been a fair consistency of sound with the exception of the change in lead singers that occurred with the 1998 album. Critics usually speak of Zao as two distinct entities: Zao 1 was a hardcore band featuring shouted vocals by Shawn Jonas, with most of the material being written by the de facto band leader Jesse Smith. Zao 2 was a metal group that brought Dan Weyandt to the fore as both lead singer and prifncipal songwriter. As of 2001, no one was sure what Zao 3 (with Corey Darst supposedly replacing Weyandt on vocals) would sound like or whether the labelless outfit would continue to record. Three members of Zao were in **Seasons in the Field** (see also **Pensive**). Brian Detar also formed **The Juliana Theory,** and drummer Jesse Smith plays with **Left Out.** In 1999, Smith would release an experimental solo album under the faux-band name Through the Eyes of Katelyn (*Your Role Model's Dead,* 1999); he provides all instrumentation and vocals on the project, which collates quiet emo songs with noisy metalcore tracks.

Zao was originally formed by four members of a Pentecostal church in Belpre, Ohio, not far from West Virginia—at first, and though another vocalist (Eric Reeder) was the band's singer, Jonas took over for the first recording. At that time, Smith says, they were "just four spirit-filled Christians" seeking to glorify God and win souls for Christ. The latter goals would never vanish, but continued projects did bring the group some crossover success within the general market with a shift at times toward entertainment and art for art's sake. The group's lyrics—though not always understandable—have consistently reflected their interest in matters of faith.

The debut album, *All Else Failed,* was a custom affair that went unnoticed, but M8 Productions would eventually re-release it as a treat for fans. It reveals, as *True Tunes* would indicate, that the group appears to have "burst onto the scene fully formed." The album holds up as a strong debut with driving hardcore rhythms and powerhouse vocals that mark Zao as one of the most competent acts in the hardcore scene. *The Splinter Shards the Birth of Separation* did get noticed, with Christian media quickly drawing comparisons between it and seasoned projects by **Everdown, Focused,** and **Unashamed.** Lyrically, the album favors praise songs, as in "Particle": "I will lift you up / I will praise your awesome name." Comparisons would shift to **Extol** and other Scandinavian bands when the new metal Zao (with Weyandt) unveiled *Where Blood and Fire Bring Rest.* Critics praised them again for technical competence, but also now for musical depth and texture. Though most of the record is very hard and Weyandt's vocals are of the scary "tortured animal" variety, there is also a surprising emotional intensity. *HM* would describe the band's new sound as "black metalcore, transitioning seamlessly between slower, more melodic sections and all-out extreme metal riffage." The album concludes with "Violet," an instrumental piano track reminiscent of Smashing Pumpkins' *Mellon Collie and the Infinite Sadness.* The group's next project was an epic production titled *Liberate Te Ex Inferis* (Latin for "Save Yourself from Hell"). It is organized with reference to the five cycles of hell described in Dante's *Inferno:* "Limbo," "The Lustful," "The Gluttonous,"

"The Hoarders and the Spendthrift," and "The Wrathful." Two songs are offered for each cycle. "If These Scars Could Speak," for instance, belongs to the second cycle and presents the thoughts of a rape victim. While the cantata makes clear that no one can actually save themselves from hell, it never spells out the biblical hope that Christ can save them either. The album called *(Self-Titled)* was announced as the band's final project, though Smith appears to have later reconsidered and hired the new vocalist, Darst. *(Self-Titled)* opens with "5 Year Winter," an exceptionally powerful barnstormer. "Alive Is Dead" moves into grindcore, and "FYL" is a lovely ballad with actual singing.

Zao has occasionally been the focus of mild controversy. The original artwork to *Liberate Te Ex Inferis* was recalled due to complaints that the photo of Smith on the cover reveals him to have tattoos of scantily clad women. "They're just pin-up girls, not pornography" Smith said in defense of his body art. "They're from a time when I liked the '50s. I've got tattoos of Christ, angels, even my mom. It's not like I only have girls on my arms." The band has also been more vocal than most about responding to unkind comments, such as those posted by amateur critics on various Internet bulletin boards. They have lashed out at such "unthinking and hurtful posers" in interviews, and Smith wrote a song called "Trashcan Man" that mentions some of their specific nemeses by their screen names.

The Christian hard rock band Zao should not be confused with a progressive French jazz-fusion group by the same name that released several albums in the '70s. The latter group's records are still in print, and because of name confusion, products by both groups often appear together on a single Zao discography (e.g., at amazon.com).

Zero

See **Under Midnight.**

Zilch

Jason Halbert, kybrd., voc.; Otto "Sugarbear" Price, bass, voc.; Mark Townsend, gtr., voc. 1997—*Platinum* (Gotee).

Zilch is a trio composed of three musicians who serve as the backing band for **DC Talk.** The group put together an album of their own during a seven-day period between programs for that band. *Platinum* has a distinct retro-rock sound with a strong late-'60s/early-'70s vibe.

"Here We Go" and "Christiana" are especially Beatlesque, and "Surfer Psalm" is almost a Beach Boys satire. "Yeah" sounds like an **Audio Adrenaline** outtake (cf. "God Is Not a Secret"). The album has a party spirit with a generous amount of humor: sound effects, false starts, and a cover of the song "My Hero Zero" from Schoolhouse Rock, which is followed by a lengthy disclaimer after the fashion of those that John Cleese once delivered on behalf of Monty Python. The music is very much directed to the church with simple but direct cheerleading lyrics. "Things are better than they seem / There's no ending to the dream," the band sings. "We do happy, pop melodies," Halbert declared. "We're not angry about anything. We missed the X part of Generation X, I guess." The song "In the Sky" is written as a direct response to Joan Osborne's (much more profound) song "One of Us": "My God's not in the sky / He's here with you and I" (actually, according to Jesus, God *is* in the sky—e.g., Matthew 5:34; 23:9). The group's name comes from a nonsense song by The Monkees, the title of which has become a slang term for "nothing" or "meaningless." Halbert has also played with **Sonicflood.**

Christian radio hits: "Everything" (# 8 in 1997).

Zion

See **X-Sinner.**

Zippy Josh and the Rag Tag Band

Brandon Baizian, drums; Tim Duzan, bass; Josh Handley, gtr., voc. 1999— *Stupidville* (Screaming Giant).

Zippy Josh and the Rag Tag Band is the second outfit for Josh Handley of Ventura, California. Handley began his Christian music career as guitarist for the punk band **Officer Negative.** His Rag Tag Band has more of a hard-edged acoustic sound that one critic described as "the Sex Pistols meet **Bob Dylan.**" The style of *Stupidville* is intentionally raw and "underproduced," with vocals upfront. "Salvation Train" has a country blues sound reminiscent of The Meat Puppets. Handley describes the entire album as "worship music to God."

Zoe Girl

Chrissy Conway, voc.; Alisa Girard, voc.; Kristin Swinford, voc. 2000— *Zoe Girl* (Sparrow); 2001—*Life.*

Zoe Girl is a new millennium girl group similar to **Aurora, ShineMK, V*enna,** and **Whisper Loud.** The group's style is basically a female counterpart to the "boy band" fad in general market music—Backstreet Boys, *NSYNC, 98 degrees. For some reason, teenaged *girl* groups became far bigger in Christian music than in the general market, though the basic style was defined by their elders The Spice Girls and then refined by other past-teen general market phenoms like Destiny's Child and All Saints. If Zoe Girl is up-to-the-minute in its sound, however, they also have roots and connections in Jesus music that go back long before they were born. Alisa Girard is the daughter of **Chuck Girard** of **Love Song,** one of the founding fathers of contemporary Christian music, and Zoe Girl's debut

album was produced by Lynn Nichols, who was a member of **Dust** (not to mention **The Phil Keaggy Band, Chagall Guevara,** and **Passafist**). With so much talent around them, the young women are nevertheless strongly independent, writing all the songs on their first album themselves. The opening track, "Believe" (by Girard), is a straightforward testimony to conversion: "There was a day when somebody introduced me to you / And you breathed your life in me, you set me free." The girls sound sultry as they own up to past temptations on "Little Did I Know," but on "Give Me One Reason" they present a strong testimony to the invasive effect of faith on personal relationships. Lyrically, the latter song is similar to Matthew Sweet's "Evangeline" or Billy Joel's "Only the Good Die Young"—only from the pursued Christian woman's point of view: "How can you expect me to walk with Him and give myself to you?" the heroine asks, and then concludes, "Baby, I love you, but I can't stay with you unless you love Him too." The bouncy "Upside Down" (not a Diana Ross cover) is about the shallowness of popular culture, with well-deserved potshots at "the psychic network" and *Who Wants to Be a Millionaire*? Nichols also produced *Life,* which continues in the same vein as the debut. The songs are appropriately encouraging. "With All My Heart" is a worship song of joyful surrender. "Even If" affirms the constancy of God in a dangerous and distressing world, and "Ordinary Day" similarly declares that God can redeem the value of stressful days ("Things are crazy but it's alright . . ."). "Plain" addresses those teenaged girls who may think they are less than beautiful, with a sentiment similar to **Steven Curtis Chapman**'s "Fingerprints of God." Musically, "Nick of Time" has edgy Tina Turner vocals that set it apart from the rest of the happy tunes, and "R U Sure about That?" is enlivened by Spanish guitars and hip-hop flourishes.

Christian radio hits: "Anything Is Possible" (# 8 in 2001); "No You" (# 4 in 2001); "With All of My Heart" (# 11 in 2001).

Zoo Babies

Steve Curtsinger; Jerry McBroom. 2000—*The Fine Art of Self-Destruction* (Ionic).

Zoo Babies formed as a spin-off of the classic Christian metal band **Bride.** After that group called it quits, Steve Curtsinger and Jerry McBroom put together a low-budget grunge project called *The Fine Art of Self-Destruction.* The sound bears some similarities to Stone Temple Pilots; an *HM* reviewer said it reminded him of Alice in Chains covering **Audio Adrenaline** songs. Lyrically, the songs do not contain obvious Christian words or phrases, but fans who know the band's background will recognize most songs as addressed to God, often as prayers for help, expressing a desire to change.

Darlene Zschech

1998—I Believe the Promise (Hillsong); Touching Heaven, Changing Earth; Shout to the Lord; 1999—Shout to the Lord 2000; 2000—For This Cause; You Shine; The Power of Your Love Symphony; 2001—You Are My World; date unknown—Your Side; God Is in the House; Hills Praise; Jesus Christmas: Worship Down Under; Millennium: The Story So Far.

www.hillsong.com

Darlene Zschech (pronounced "check") is not a recording artist per se but a minister of worship at Hills Christian Life Centre in Sydney, Australia. The ten thousand-member congregation has a large televised ministry and often records special worship services, which are then marketed as Darlene Zschech albums. Zschech was a child star of an Australian TV series called *Happy Go 'Round.* She was traumatized at the age of thirteen when her parents divorced and a custody battle ensued. At fourteen, she struggled with bulimia. A year later, she was brought into a serious relationship with Christ through her father and, as a young adult, sang jingles for numerous international companies including McDonalds, KFC, and Diet Coke. In 1993, Zschech would write the modern worship standard "Shout to the Lord," a song that propelled her to international fame. She says that she actually composed the praise anthem (based on Psalm 96) at a time when she was feeling discouraged: "I felt I could either scream and pull my hair out—or praise God." Zschech has penned dozens of other praise and worship songs, which are featured on the numerous albums distributed through Hillsong (Integrity in the United States). *The Power of Your Love Symphony* places the singer in front of a small orchestra conducted by **Ralph Carmichael.** Darlene and her husband, Mark Zschech, are executive directors of the Australian branch of Mercy Ministries, a charitable organization devoted to helping teenage girls struggling with pregnancy, drugs, abuse, and eating disorders.

Glossary

AAA

an acronym for Adult Album Alternative, a radio format that targeted college students and young adults in the '90s. AAA music was stylistically diverse, encompassing both grunge and alternative rock, but tended to feature artists who rarely had hit songs on *Billboard*'s Top 40 charts. Sample artists: Matthew Sweet; the Smashing Pumpkins; **The Prayer Chain; Vigilantes of Love.**

adult contemporary

a formulaic style of pop music that emphasizes technical competence and artistic excellence. Adult contemporary music tends to favor softer songs that draw on the influence of rock but remain tame and predictable. Sample artists: Barry Manilow; Whitney Houston; **Kim Hill; Michael W. Smith.**

alternative

a term that arose in the '90s to describe music that often had pop sensibilities but defied convention in ways that set it apart from mainstream Top 40. Alternative rock tended to be rough-edged and adventurous, prioritizing innovation and artistic integrity; the artists were supposedly making the music they wanted to make as opposed to what they thought would sell. Sample artists: Beck; the Dave Matthews Band; **Bleach; Skillet.**

ambient

an atmospheric variety of techno music that is usually instrumental and sometimes intended to accompany meditation. Sample artists: **Ambient Theology.**

Americana

a loosely defined genre of music that draws upon styles that are uniquely American, especially folk, country, bluegrass, and gospel. Sample artists: The Band; **Lost Dogs.**

AOR

an acronym for Album Oriented Rock, a radio format that broke with typical Top 40 playlists in the early '70s to feature album cuts by artists who did not concentrate on producing hit singles. The term "AOR music" came to be applied more broadly to describe any style of rock that did not present itself as overtly commercial. In time AOR music became virtually synonymous with "classic rock." Sample artists: Led Zeppelin; Rush; **Resurrection Band; Seventy Sevens.**

arena rock

a bombastic style of music associated with the '80s that eschewed intimacy in favor of a powerful sound that could be played effectively in large venues (also called stadium rock). Sample artists: Foreigner; Journey; **Petra; White Heart.**

art-rock

a style of music associated with the '70s and '80s that sought to infuse rock with classical influences and to create pieces that were artistically complex. Sample artists: Emerson, Lake, and Palmer; Yes; **Kerry Livgren.**

black gospel

see traditional gospel.

bubblegum

a style of music associated primarily with the late '60s and early '70s that featured sweet and catchy songs with simple structures, repetitive lyrics, and memorable melodies. Sample artists: The Bay City Rollers; The Monkees; **Everybody-duck; Hokus Pick.**

dancehall

an offshoot of reggae music that became popular in urban nightclubs in the United States in the '90s. Dancehall typically features a DJ manipulating sound system controls and talking over the music in a style called "toasting." Thus, for American audiences, dancehall may seem similar to rap and hip-hop, though it was actually a precursor to those forms.

death metal

a variety of heavy metal that emphasizes morbid themes and often seeks to illustrate these with intentionally grotesque musical stylings. A typical feature of death metal is growled vocals that either supplement or replace the usual screaming associated with the mother genre. Sample artists: Megadeth; **Crimson Thorn; Mortification.**

disco

an extremely dance-oriented genre of music that grew out of R&B funk in the '70s to facilitate communal dancing in nightclub settings. Disco exhibited a characteristic rhythm pattern with a strong thump on each beat, but would lend itself to a diversity of stylistic variations, eventually giving birth to hip-hop, house, and other forms. Sample artists: KC and the Sunshine Band; Chic; **Donna Summer; Disco Saints.**

drum and bass

a type of house/rave music in which the rhythm section is unusually dominant and determinative of song structure. Rather than using the straight 4-4 beat of house and techno music, d&b relies on backbeats that are often sped up to rates of 160 to 180 beats per minute. The label "drum and bass" does not imply that only drums and bass are used, as other instruments, particularly synthesizers, are featured as well. Sample artists: **Faith Massive.**

easy listening

see MOR.

emo

a style of technically precise music that is often characterized by melodramatic shifts in volume and texture. The term *emo* is short for emotion, implying a strong emphasis on emotional expression. Stereotypical emo music consists of breathy vocals that are accompanied by slow and deliberate lead guitar played over ripping rhythm guitars, all leading to sudden organized chaos during the musical bridge or chorus. Sample artists: **Sunny Day Real Estate; Dear Ephesus.**

funk

a highly percussive and syncopated style of music that grew out of R&B and became popular in the '70s. Basically a form of African American dance music, funk was the precursor of disco and, ultimately, of hip-hop. Sample artists: Sly and the Family Stone; Ohio Players.

frat-rock

an ambiguous term used to describe the sort of rock music that would supposedly be popular among beer-drinkers at college fraternity parties. Frat-rock songs are usually basic rock and roll tunes that do not display either artistic pretensions or sentimental lyrics (e.g., The Kingsmen's "Louie Louie").

gangsta rap

a subset of rap music that is characterized by violent themes addressed in an angry, forceful vocal style. Sample artists: Ice-Cube; Snoop Doggy Dogg; **Gospel Gangstaz.**

goth

a dark and brooding style of music that came to the fore in the '80s and was associated with a subculture of musicians and fans who tended to favor black clothing and make-up. Goth music typically explores such themes as alienation, death, and depression with lyrics set to minor-key, mopey melodies. Sample artists: Nick Cave; The Cure; **Eva O; Tara VanFlower.**

grindcore

see death metal.

grunge

a chaotic and defiant style of music that arose primarily in Seattle in the '90s as a cynical rejection of stereotypical hard rock. In many ways grunge was to hard rock and metal what alternative rock was to pop and Top 40, though grunge also tended to be noted for depressing lyrics that complained about the social and human condition. Grunge artists prioritized innovation and artistic integrity while eschewing all expectations of commercialism. Sample artists: Nirvana; Soundgarden; **Grammatrain.**

hardcore

a stylistic variation of punk rock characterized by a louder, faster style and by nihilistic lyrics that are often shouted over a chaotic din of rapidly changing guitar chords. Sample artists: Black Flag; the Dead Kennedys; **Blackhouse; The Crucified.**

heavy metal

a heavily amplified style of rock that emphasizes electric guitar and is characterized by histrionics of speed and volume. Vocals are often screamed and frenzied guitar solos are a staple ingredient. Sample artists: Black Sabbath; Van Halen; **Bride; Stryper.**

hip-hop

a somewhat ambiguous term sometimes used for rap music intended for dancing. In some instances, hip-hop just appears to be disco or funk music with rapped lyrics. In a more pure form, the genre makes abundant use of "found sounds," including samples from other recordings, turntable manipulation, and looped percussive elements or guitar riffs. Sample artists: De La Soul; **Bi-Faith.**

house

a groove-oriented variety of techno music that originated at a Chicago club in the early '80s and first became popular among gay African Americans. House music accentuates the drum and bass beats in speedy disco music. A sub-variety called acid-house incorporates hypnotic, psychedelic effects.

industrial

an extremely mechanical variety of rock that adds such elements as drum machines and voice modulators to heavy metal to obtain a sound intended to suggest factory noise. Sample artists: Skinny Puppy; Nine-Inch Nails; **Circle of Dust; Klank.**

inspirational

a term used in the Christian music market to describe gospel singers with an MOR style.

Jesus music

a specific genre of music that arose out of the Jesus movement revival of the early '70s. Much (but not all) Jesus music was of a light pop, hippie-folk variety, but the defining criteria were more spiritual than stylistic. The focuses of Jesus music were worship, edification, and evangelism— the music lacked commercial intent but eventually morphed into what came to be called contemporary Christian music once its commercial potential was recognized and exploited. Sample artists: **Children of the Day; Love Song; Larry Norman.**

jungle

a variety of reggae music that emphasizes pounding drums and tribal rhythms, with the apparent intent of accompanying communal dance.

metal

in describing musical styles, the term *metal* is usually used as an abbreviation for heavy metal (see listing); there is no metal music that is not heavy, though many metal bands would also record token light rock songs (called power ballads).

MOR

an acronym for Middle of the Road, referring to a tame variety of music that strives to be pleasantly unpredictable. MOR music (also called easy listening) is often regarded as a subset of adult contemporary, with even less overt influences from rock. In Christian music, MOR singers tend to be called "inspirational." Sample artists: Andy Williams; **Steve Green; Sandi Patty.**

new age

instrumental meditative music that draws upon classical impressionism (Debussy), jazz, and indigenous world music to create a mood of reflective calm. New age music is often associated with new age philosophy or spirituality, but the connection is no more intrinsic than that of reggae to Rastafarianism or of R&B to Pentecostalism. Sample artists: Vangelis; George Winston; **John Tesh; Richard Souther.**

new jack swing

a variety of hip-hop developed in the late '80s that uses traditional R&B vocals rather than rap and tends to focus lyrically on fantasy and romance. Sample artists: Keith Sweat; Bobby Brown; **Go rin no sho.**

new wave

an ambiguous term that was applied to some cutting-edge acts in the late '70s who infused pop music with punk influences. Sample artists: The Cars; The Talking Heads; **David Edwards; Steve Taylor.**

pop

music that places a premium on accessibility. What gets classed as pop changes with the times, but in recent decades pop music has tended to feature simple structures, strong melodies, danceable rhythms, and distinctive elements called "hooks" that make a tune instantly recognizable and memorable.

pop-punk

a hybrid of two seemingly disparate styles that represents the opposite development of punk rock than that evidenced by hardcore. In pop-punk, the short, fast style of punk rock is maintained, but an effort is made to create melodies and song structures that potentially distinguish one song from another. Sample artists: Green Day; **MxPx.**

punk

an abrasive and anarchist style of music that originated in London in the mid '70s. Punk rock is defiantly minimalist and aggressively amateurish, striving for a raw, basic sound that avoids all concessions to commercial accessibility. Stereotypical punk songs are short and fast, with a forced sound that allows songs to lose their individuality. By the '90s, punk rock would by and large separate into hardcore and pop-punk. Sample artists: The Sex Pistols; The Ramones; **Crashdog; The Huntingtons.**

R&B

an abbreviation for Rhythm & Blues, the music that arose out of gospel in the late '60s to become a popular secular sound primarily associated with African American artists. R&B is essentially synonymous with "soul music," though eventually the term soul would be applied increasingly to ballads and R&B to more rhythmic dance styles.

rap

a streetwise, intensely rhythmic style of pop music for which the most noticeable characteristic is spoken (as opposed to sung) vocals. Typically, rap vocals are spoken in rhythm and in rhyme. Sample artists: Grandmaster Flash; **Run-D.M.C.; M.C. Hammer.**

rapcore

a hybrid style of rap and metal that became extremely popular in the late '90s. Rapcore artists laid rapped vocals on top of heavy metal instrumentation in a way that rejuvenated the latter form and helped to popularize rap among white audiences. Sample artists: Korn; Limp Bizkit; **EDL; P.O.D.**

rave

see techno.

reggae

a catch-all term for a variety of styles derived from the combination of Afro-Caribbean music with American R&B. Reggae originated primarily in Jamaica in the late '60s and emphasizes dance rhythms. Offshoots of reggae include dancehall, ska, and jungle. Sample artists: Bob Marley; Peter Tosh; **Christafari; Temple Yard.**

rockabilly

a hybrid of R&B and "hillbilly" country music first effected by Elvis Presley in the '50s. Rockabilly served as the immediate predecessor to what would be called rock and roll, and continues to be performed by various nostalgia acts. Sample artists: The Stray Cats; The Rev. Horton Heat; **The Calicoes; The Lifters.**

ska

ska music has had at least three incarnations: a '50s Jamaican style that prefigured reggae; an '80s British revival of that music with contemporary innovations; and a '90s American fad sometimes called "third wave ska." The latter style combines a reggae beat with punk-rock vocals and song structures, while also introducing the conspicuous use of brass instruments. Sample artists: The Mighty Mighty Bosstones; **The Supertones; The Insyderz.**

soul

originally a term for black pop music, soul music grew out of traditional (black) gospel, infusing the sound with secular lyrics. For a time, the labels soul and R&B were synonymous, but eventually R&B would be used more for upbeat music that was intended for dancing, and soul for emotive ballads evocative of romantic or spiritual passions.

southern gospel

a variety of gospel music that developed in lower class white churches alongside black (or traditional) gospel at a time when worship was officially segregated. Southern gospel often emphasized close quartet harmonies and acoustic instrumentation (including banjo and flat-picked guitar). Sample artists: The Blackwood Brothers; **The Bill Gaither Trio.**

southern rock

a distinctive blend of hard rock and blues that came to prominence in the southeastern United States in the '70s; sometimes called southern-fried rock. Sample artists: Lynyrd Skynyrd; ZZ Top; **Charlie Daniels; Third Day.**

speed metal

see thrash metal.

stadium rock

see arena rock.

surf music

a style of music emanating from Southern California in the late '60s that featured high harmonies and bouncy, twanging guitars (with more emphasis on treble than bass). Sample artists: The Beach Boys; The Ventures; **Paul Johnson and the Packards; Terry Scott Taylor.**

swing

a style of music that developed out of jazz in the late '30s and enjoyed a brief revival among rock fans in the late '90s. Swing music often features brass and woodwind instruments, with the players improvising on melodies to create a lively sound suitable for ballroom dancing. Sample artists: Cherry Poppin' Daddies; Squirrel Nut Zippers; **The Deluxtone Rockets; The W's.**

techno

a computer-generated style of dance music that combines disco beats with the rapid intensity of punk. Techno is performed by DJs who create the sound by programming sound systems and by making use of digital samplers, sequencers, and a variety of "found sounds." The music is often mercilessly repetitive, intending to produce a trance-like state in its audience. Techno music is also called rave music, after the name given to the dance parties at which it is played. Sample artists: **Moby; Scott Blackwell.**

trance

a rhythmic but "spaced-out" variety of techno music that favors psychedelic effects intended to have a hypnotic effect on audiences.

thrash metal

a subgenre of metal that emphasizes extremely fast playing; also called speed metal. Sample artists: Metallica; **Believer.**

traditional gospel

the politically correct term adopted by the Gospel Music Association for what most people continue to call black gospel. Traditional gospel music developed out of the worship experiences of African American churches into a recognizable style of music that served as a predecessor to both R&B and rock and roll. Distinctive features include call and response vocals between a soloist and backing choir, bluesy rolling keyboards, and a rhythmic approach that builds songs to revivalistic climaxes. Sample artists: James Cleveland; **Shirley Caesar.**

urban

a politically correct term adopted by many critics in the late '90s to describe music that appeared to be directed primarily toward inner-city African Americans (though in reality the fan base for such music was much more diverse). Urban music became something of a catch-all term for varieties of rap and hip-hop.

world music

a sweeping category that applies to the native music of peoples around the world. When rock and pop musicians seek to draw on the influence of world music they might employ exotic instrumentation or use an alternative musical scale to infuse their music with a distinctive sound.

Entries